経済・金融ビジネス英和大辞典

DICTIONARY OF ECONOMIC AND FINANCIAL BUSINESS TERMINOLOGY

菊地義明 編

日外アソシエーツ

Dictionary of Economic and Financial Business Terminology

Compiled by

©Yoshiaki KIKUCHI

●

Nichigai Associates, Inc.

Printed in Japan, 2012

本書はディジタルデータでご利用いただくことができます。詳細はお問い合わせください。

まえがき

　本書は国内最大級の金融ビジネス専門用語辞典で、証券・銀行・保険の金融3分野の専門用語を柱に据えて、金融と密接な関係にある経済、財政・財務、経営関連の用語も多数盛り込んであります。

　これらは経済・金融ビジネス専門紙誌等を読み解く上で必要不可欠な各専門分野の基本用語と慣用語句で、見出し語や関連語句、文例は、過去10年のデータベースに基づき、また私自身の翻訳者としての視点に立って選定しました。

　本書は、基本的に「見出し語＋語義＋見出し語の関連語句＋文例」で構成されています。これまでの金融用語辞典の見出し語は、主に名詞と形容詞で構成されていますが、実用性を考慮して名詞、形容詞のほかに動詞・動詞句や前置詞、副詞なども見出し語として掲げてあるのが、本書の特徴です。

　このほか、語義は一語一訳方式ではなく、金融専門分野の多様な語義を広範に網羅し、文例の文脈に応じて適切な語義を選択できるように構成してあるのも、本書の特徴です。

　類書に例を見ない文例は、実用性を重視して、可能なかぎり最新性の高いトピックを取り入れてあります。実用性の高い豊富な文例とその的確な訳例をとおして、翻訳表現辞典として利用することもできます。

　なお、必要に応じて見出し語、関連語句の簡単な解説、同義・同意表現や、反意語を示すとともに、参照語句も適宜、表示していますので、これらも大いに活用していただければと思います。

2012年3月

菊地　義明

凡　例

1．本書の内容

　本書は、金融専門分野の多様な語義と関連語句、文例を網羅した金融ビジネス用語の英和辞典です。

2．収録基準

　証券、銀行、保険の3金融分野を柱として、過去10年のデータベースに基づき、経済・金融ビジネスに関する各種公式文書、報告書、アナリスト・レポート、専門紙誌等を読み解く上で必要な各金融分野の基本用語、重要語句、最新用語のほかに適宜、文例が添えてあります。

3．収録語数

　収録語数は、見出し語約10,800語、関連語句約37,000項目で、文例は約17,000件に達しています。

4．構成要素

1）見出し語と副見出し語

　見出し語は、基本的にアルファベット順に配列してあります。ただし、とくに単数形と複数形で意味が異なる名詞や同音異義語については、それぞれ別個に見出しを立ててあります。

　また、見出し語を含む関連語句は、副見出し語としてアルファベット順に配列してあります。

2）品　詞

　品詞の略記は、以下のとおりです。
　　（動）動詞　　　　（接尾）接尾語
　　（名）名詞　　　　（他動）他動詞
　　（前）前置詞　　　（自動）自動詞
　　（形）形容詞　　　（代）代名詞
　　（副）副詞

3）語　義

　見出し語の後に表示してある語義は、基本的に証券・銀行・保険の各専門分野の多様な語義で、文脈に応じて適切な語義を選択できるようできるだけ広範に網羅されています。

4) 参照事項

　見出し語の語義の後に表示してあるカッコ内の語句は、基本的に見出し語の簡単な説明と参照事項です。

　カッコ内のイコール記号（＝）で示される語句は、見出し語の同義・同意表現です。また、矢印（⇒）の後の語句を参照すると、見出し語を含む文例や関連語句が掲げてあります。

> 例）　**business confidence**　景況感，業況感，業況判断，企業マインド，企業心理，ビジネス・コンフィデンス
> （=business mind, business sentiment; ⇒diffusion index of business confidence）

5) 文例と訳例

　見出し語には、その語義と用法の理解に役立てるため、できるかぎり文例とその訳例が添えてあります。訳例中のカッコ（　）内は基本的に説明語で、カギカッコ［　］内は同意語または同意表現として示してあります。

6) 解　説

　重要な見出し語に関しては、解説を見出し語の末尾に付してあります。

A

A$ 豪ドル （=Australian dollar, Aussie dollar; ⇒ Australian dollar）
◆We purchased the firm for A$ 30 million last year. 当社は昨年、同社を3,000万豪ドルで買収した。

A Aの格付け, シングルA （⇒rating symbol）
Aaa　Aaa格, トリプルA
Single A credit　シングルA格
triple-A credit rating　トリプルAの格付け
◆Moody's Investors Service cut Citigroup debt one notch to A3, its fourth-lowest investment grade. 米国の格付け会社ムーディーズ・インベスターズ・サービスは、米金融大手シティグループの債券格付けをA3（下から4番目の投資適格格付け）に1段階引き下げた。◆Moody's Investors Service has downgraded its long-term senior unsecured debt rating for Toyota and its subsidiaries to Aa1 from Aaa. ムーディーズ・インベスターズ・サービスは、トヨタとトヨタの子会社の長期上位無担保債務格付けを、最上位のAaaからAa1に1段階引き下げた。◆Moody's Investors Service Inc. cut its rating on yen-denominated government bonds by two notches to A2 from Aa3. ムーディーズ・インベスターズ・サービスは、円建て国債の格付けをAa3からA2に2段階引き下げた。◆Rating agency Moody's may place a negative outlook on French government's Aaa debt rating as the government's financial strength has weakened. 格付け会社のムーディーズは、フランス国債のAaa（トリプルA）格付けについて、仏政府の財務体質［財務力］が弱まっているため「ネガティブ（弱含み）」の見通しを示す可能性がある。◆The World Bank enjoys a triple-A credit rating. 世界銀行は、トリプルAの格付け［信用格付け］を受けている。

AA ダブルA, ダブルAの格付け （⇒long-term Japanese government bonds, rating symbol）
AA minus　ダブルAマイナス, AAマイナス
AA minus rating　ダブルAマイナスの格付け
AA-plus　ダブルAプラス, AAプラス
◆The AA minus rating by S&P is the fourth highest in terms of credit quality on a scale of 22. 米格付け会社のスタンダード・アンド・プアーズ(S&P)による「ダブルAマイナス」の格付けは、22段階ある信用度中、上から4番目に当たる。◆The S&P cut in the U.S. long-term credit rating by one notch to AA-plus from AAA resulted from concerns about the nation's budget deficits and climbing debt burden. スタンダード・アンド・プアーズ(S&P)が米国の長期国債格付けを最上級のAAA（トリプルA）からAA（ダブルA）に1段階引き下げた理由は、米国の財政赤字と債務負担の増大に対する懸念だ。◆The U.S. rating agency Standard & Poor's downgraded Japan's long-term sovereign credit rating to AA minus from AA. 米格付け会社のスタンダード・アンド・プアーズ(S&P)は、日本の長期国債格付けを現在の「ダブルA」から「ダブルAマイナス」に引き下げた。

AAA トリプルA, トリプルAの格付け
（=triple A; ⇒rating symbol）
AAA company　トリプルAの会社, トリプルAの格付けの会社, 超一流企業
AAA-rated borrower［credits］　トリプルA格の発行体, AAA格の発行体
AAA rating　トリプルAの格付け
assign a rating of AAA　トリプルAの格付けを与える, トリプルAの格付けをする
top-tier AAA credit rating　最上位のトリプルAの格付け, 最上級のAAA［トリプルA］の格付け
◆Fitch Ratings Ltd. will keep its rating on long-term U.S. debt at the highest grade, AAA. 英米系の格付け会社フィッチ・レーティングスは、米国の長期国債格付けを、最上級のAAA（トリプルA）に据え置く方針だ。◆The bonds of six eurozone countries such as Germany and France are rated AAA by S&P's credit ratings on them. 独仏などユーロ圏6か国の国債は、スタンダード・アンド・プアーズ(S&P)の格付け［信用格付け］でトリプルAに格付けされている。◆The company is a AAA company. 同社は、トリプルAの超一流企業だ。◆The United States lost its top-tier AAA credit rating from S&P for the first time. 米国債の格付け［米国の長期国債格付け］が、スタンダード・アンド・プアーズ(S&P)による最上級のAAA（トリプルA）の格付けから史上初めて転落した。

ABA 米国銀行協会 （American Bankers' Associationの略）

abandon （動）廃止する, 解除する, 中断する, 中止する, 断念する, （権利や財産を）放棄する, 廃棄する, 遺棄する, 除却する, （船舶や積み荷を）委付する, 訴訟を取り下げる　（名）気まま, 奔放（ほんぽう）, 羽目を外すこと
in wild［gay］abandon　気ままに
with abandon　思うままに, 奔放に, 羽目を外（はず）して
◆Banks' fund-raising costs have increased, reflecting the rise in market rates after the Bank of Japan abandoned its zero-interest policy. 日銀のゼロ金利政策解除に伴って市場金利が上昇したのを反映して、銀行の資金調達コストが増大した。◆Investors around the world are selling stocks with abandon as a global recession is under way. 世界的な景気後退の進行で、世界中の投資家が株を売りまくっている。◆Shinsei and Aozora banks have abandoned their plan to merge. 新生銀行とあおぞら銀行が、両行の合併計画を断念した。◆The company has to abandon the option of self-rehabilitation. 同社は、自力再建の道［選択肢］を断念しなければならない。◆The minimum regulatory capital requirements were abandoned. （会社設立時の）最低必要資本金制度は、廃止された。

abandonment （名）除却, 放棄, 遺棄, 廃棄, 引渡し, 中断, 中止, 委付, 保険委付, 委付保険, 訴訟の取下げ
abandonment value　廃棄価値
asset abandonment　資産除却
equipment abandonment　設備の廃却
property abandonment　財産放棄
◆These provisions include $110 million for closing facilities, lease terminations and asset abandonments associated with centralizing customer support services. この引当金には、顧客支援サービス部門の集中化に関連した施設閉鎖費、リース解約費と資産除却費用の1億1,000万ドルも含まれています。

abate （動）緩和する, 軽減する, 無効にする, 弱まる, 和らぐ, 衰える, 減少する, 低下する
abated currency inflows　資金流入の減少
abated inflationary pressures　インフレ圧力の低下
◆Global stock market plunges caused by the European fiscal crisis triggered by Greece have shown no signs of abating. ギリシャ発の欧州財政危機による世界同時株安は、止まる気配がない。◆There have been no signs of a rebound in the amount of outstanding loans, which continues on an abated decline. このところ引き続き減少傾向にある銀行の貸出残高に、反転の兆しは見えない。

ABC agreement ABC契約, ABC協定 （ニューヨーク証券取引所(NYSE)の会員資格を取る際、証券会社が自社従業員に融資して会員権を購入させる契約のこと）

aberration （名）脱線, 脱線行為, （常軌の）逸脱, 精神の異常, 異常, 変異, 異状, （レンズの）収差
◆The U.S. FRB's recent decision on further quantitative easing is only an aberration. 米連邦準備制度理事会(FRB)の今回の追加金融緩和の決定は、常軌を逸した行為と言わざるを得ない。

ability （名）能力, 技能, 技術, ～力, アビリティ
ability to access the market　市場での調達能力
ability to borrow overseas　対外借入能力

ability to buy back shares　自社株を買い戻す能力, 自社株買戻し能力, 買戻し能力
ability to finance　資金調達力
ability to finance in markets　市場での資金調達力
ability to generate cash　収益力, キャッシュ・フロー生成能力, キャッシュ・フローを生み出す能力
ability to generate returns　収益生成能力, 収益を生み出す能力
ability to invest　投資力, 投資実行力
ability to meet cash capital requirements　資金需要を賄（まかな）う能力
ability to meet debt payments due　債務の返済能力
ability to pay　支払い能力,（債務）返済能力
ability to pay down debt　債務返済能力
　　（＝ability to meet debt payments due）
ability to raise equity　資本調達力
ability to refinance　借換え能力
ability to repay debt　債務返済能力
ability to repay principal　元本返済能力
ability to service debt obligations　債務返済能力
ability to withstand credit risk　信用リスクに対する耐久力
debt ability　借入能力, 債務能力
debt-paying ability　債務返済能力
　　（＝debt servicing capacity）
earnings ability　収益力
financial [pecuniary] ability　資力, 財力
lending ability　貸出能力
repayment ability of issuers　発行体の債務履行能力
◆An overvalued dollar is seriously crimping U.S. Manufacturer's ability to export. ドル高が, 米国の製造業界の輸出力を大いに妨げている。◆Concerns have been raised over the ability of Internet banking services to verify the identity of new depositors or to guarantee the security of customer transactions. インターネット・バンキングについては、新規預金者の身元確認や対顧客取引の安全保証の点で、その能力に対して懸念が提起されている。◆In the case of an insolvent borrower, it no longer has the ability to pay all its debt even though lenders offer to defer the time of repayment. 返済不能の借り手の場合、貸し手が返済期間の延長を申し出ても、借り手はもはや債務を全額返済できない状況にある。◆Major European banks are to take additional stress tests to examine their ability to withstand a long recession. 景気の長期低迷への耐久力を調べるため、欧州の主要銀行は再度、ストレス・テストを受けることになっている。◆To compete against online trading systems, stock exchanges must improve their ability to process buy and sell orders. 電子取引システムに対抗するには、証券取引所が売買注文の処理能力を高める必要がある。

abolish　（動）撤廃する, 廃止する, 解散する
◆The government plans to abolish the ¥10 million ceiling on the amount of postal bank deposits. 政府は現在、1人当たり1,000万円のゆうちょ銀行預け入れ限度額を撤廃する方針だ。

abort　（動）（計画などを）中止する,（提携などを）解消する, 失敗させる, 流産させる, 中絶する
◆Suzuki Motor Corp. Will abort its alliance with Volkswagen AG. スズキが、独フォルクスワーゲンとの提携を解消することになった。

abortive saving　不妊貯蓄

about-face　（名）方向転換,（態度や政策などの）180度転換［転向、転回］, 急転換, 回れ右　（＝about-turn）
　do an about-face　180度転換する, 回れ右をする, 態度を一変させる
　do an about-face in economic policies　経済政策を180度転換する
◆The bank's serious financial difficulties have forced it to do an about-face. 同行の深刻な経営難で、同行は方針転換を迫られている。

about par　パー近辺で
　trade about par　パー近辺で取引される

above　（前）～を上回る, ～より上の, ～以上の, アバブ（形）上記の, 上述の
　above and below the exchange rate　為替相場の上下の
　above par（value）　額面超過, 額面以上で, 打ち歩（ぶ）で（at a premium）, 額面以上の状態, 割増, 水準以上, オーバー・パーの
　above the market　市価［時価］を上回る, アバブ・ザ・マーケット注文
　above the market strategy　市価以上戦略, 高価格市場戦略
　be above the average　平均を上回る
　be above the expansion/recession dividing line of 50 percent　景気の拡大と後退の分かれ目になる50％を上回る
　be above trend　トレンドを上回る
　buy a close above A　終値でAを上回れば買い
◆A reading of below 50 percent in the coincident index is considered a sign of economic contraction and a figure above that is viewed as a sign of expansion. 一致指数で50％以下の数値は景気収縮［景気後退］を示す指標と見られ、それ以上の数字は景気回復［景気拡大］を示す指標と見なされる。◆Gold extended its rally to a record above $1,900 an ounce amid increased uncertainties over the U.S. and European economic outlook on the Comex in New York. ニューヨーク商品取引所では、米欧景気見通しへの懸念［米欧経済の先行き不透明感］の高まりを受け［懸念の高まりから］、金価格が急騰して、1トロイ・オンス＝1,900ドルを史上初めて突破した。◆If the yen rises above its all-time high of ¥79.75 to the dollar, the company may have to revise its assumed exchange rate once more. 円高が1ドル＝79円75銭の史上最高値を更新したら、同社は再び同社の想定為替レートの修正を迫られかねない。◆In Sumitomo's tender offer for Jupiter Telecommunications Co., about 2.6 million J:COM shares were offered, far above the 875,834 shares it was willing to purchase. 住友商事のジュピターテレコム（JCOM）株の株式公開買付け（TOB）では、約260万株の応募があり、買付け予定株数の87万5,834株を大幅に上回った。◆The European bond market is truly in a knife-edge situation as the yield on 10-year Italian government bonds has surged above 7 percent, the so-called danger zone that may result in a debt crisis. 10年物イタリア国債の流通利回りが、債務危機に陥る「危険水域」とされる7％超に上昇したため、欧州債券市場は予断を許さない状況にある。◆The yen's value still remains high and is likely to reach a postwar record value above the ¥76-to-the-dollar level. 円相場は依然高く、1ドル＝76円台を上回る戦後最高値に達する可能性がある。

above-average　（形）平均以上の, 平均［市場平均］を上回る
　above-average profit　平均以上の利潤
　above-average return　平均以上の収益
　above-average yield　市場平均を上回る利回り

above the line　経常損益計算, 経常損益, 税引き前利益, 経常収支, 経常支出, 範囲内, マスメディア広告, マスコミ媒体を使った広告, アバブ・ザ・ライン（「アバブ・ザ・ライン」は事業の経常的な収益と費用を指し, lineは損益計算書の経常利益または当期純利益を指す）
　be shown above the line　経常損益として表示される
　take A above the line　Aを税引き前利益として処理する

above-the-line [above the line]　（形）経常損益計算の, 総合収支の, 一定の範囲内の, マスメディアの, 広告

代理店を通した
above-the-line category company　マスメディア広告企業
above the line costs　経常損益に区分されるコスト
above the line funds　経常損益上処理される資金
above the line items　通常の損益項目
above-the-line profit　経常利益
above trend　トレンドを上回る
above trend growth　トレンドを上回る成長率, トレンドを上回る伸び率
at an above-trend rate　トレンドを上回るペースで
grow at an above-trend rate　トレンドを上回るペースで拡大［成長］する
rebound to an above-trend growth rate　トレンドを上回る水準に反発する
abrasion of coins　貨幣の摩滅
ABS　資産担保証券, アセットバック証券（asset-backed securitiesの略）
absolute　（形）絶対の, 絶対的な, 安全な, 純粋な, 無条件の, 全面的な
absolute acceptance　単純引受け, 絶対引受け（=clear acceptance）
absolute delivery　無条件引渡し
absolute endorsement　単純裏書き
absolute insolvency　絶対的債務超過
absolute level of credit risk　信用リスクの絶対水準
absolute level of leverage　負債の絶対水準
absolute order to pay　単純支払い指図
absolute profit　純益
absolute title　絶対的権原, 無疵（むきず）の権利
absolute total loss　絶対全損, 絶対海損（=actual total loss）
in absolute terms　金額ベースで, 絶対ベースで, 絶対値で
absolute assignment［conveyment］　無条件譲渡
◆In life insurance, absolute assignment refers to the type of legal transfer of ownership rights that transfers complete ownership of a policy permanently. 生命保険での無条件譲渡とは, 法的所有権移転の一種で, 契約の全所有権を恒久的に移転することを指す。
absorb　（動）吸収する, 吸収合併する, 併合する, 受け入れる,（間接費を）配賦（はいふ）する, 填補（てんぽ）する, カバーする, 消化する, 税金などを負担する, 解消する, 緩和する, 受容する, 理解する
absorb credit costs　信用費用を吸収する
absorb fixed overhead as a cost of product　固定間接費を製品原価の一部として配賦する
absorb one's external exposure　～の対外債務を肩代わりする
absorb the company as wholly owned subsidiary　同社を完全子会社として吸収する, 同社を完全子会社化する
absorb the costs of merger　合併のコストを吸収する, 合併費用を負担する
absorb the excess supply　供給過剰を解消する
absorb the increase　増加分を消化する
absorb the new supply　新発債を吸収する
absorb the withholding tax　源泉課税［源泉税］を負担する
absorb unforeseen risks　不測のリスクを吸収する
be absorbed into　～に吸収される, ～に併合される, ～に吸収合併される
◆All assets of the company being absorbed are taken over by the surviving firm at book value. 吸収される会社（消滅会社）の資産は, すべて存続会社が簿価で引き継ぐ。◆In the case of Japanese government bonds, 95 percent of them are stably absorbed domestically. 日本の国債の場合は, 95%が国内で安定的に消化されている。◆Nippon Oil Corp. absorbed Kyushu Oil Co. on Oct. 1, 2008. 新日本石油は, 2008年10月1日に九州石油を吸収合併した。
absorb a loss　損失を吸収する, 損失をカバーする
absorb credit losses　信用損失を吸収する
absorb unforeseen losses　不測の損失を吸収する
equity to absorb losses　損失を吸収する自己資本
◆Major financial institutions are forced to hold additional capital so that they can better absorb losses during financial crises. 金融危機の際の損失吸収力を高めるため, 大手金融機関は, 資本［自己資本］の積み増しを迫られている。
absorb funds　資金を吸い上げる
◆The Bank of Japan may heighten the effects of monetary easing by not absorbing funds the government funnels into the market as yen-selling intervention. 日銀は, 政府が円売り介入で市場に放出した資金を吸い上げないで, 金融緩和の効果を高めることもできる。
absorbency　（名）吸収力, 吸収性
loss absorbency　損失吸収力
◆A bank's core capital, or Tier 1capital, is deemed to have high loss-absorbency and resilience. 銀行の中核的自己資本は, 損失吸収力と弾力性が高いとされている。
absorption　（名）吸収, 吸収合併, 配賦, 賦課, 填補
absorption of deposits　預金吸収
mergers and absorptions　吸収・合併
overhead absorption　間接費の配賦
tax absorption fee　課税負担手数料
◆All mergers are regarded as absorption in the United States, even if some are effectively on an equal basis. 実際には対等の立場での合併であっても, 米国では合併はすべて吸収合併と見なされる。
abstractions of bank funds　銀行のお金の横領
abundant　（形）豊富な, 豊かな, 潤沢（じゅんたく）な
abundant international credit　資金需給が国際的に緩いこと
abundant supply　潤沢な供給
abundant fund supply　潤沢な資金供給
◆The nation's monetary base in May 2011 increased 16.2 percent from a year earlier as the Bank of Japan continued its abundant fund supply operations following the March 11 disaster. 東日本大震災（2011年3月11日）を受けて日銀が潤沢な資金供給オペを続けたため, 日本の2011年5月のマネタリー・ベースは, 前年同月比で16.2%増加した。
accelerate　（動）加速する, 加速させる, 促進する, 推進する, 拍車をかける　（⇒stock price fall）
accelerated amortization　加速償却, 加速減価償却, 加速なし崩し償却
accelerated disposal of bad loans　不良債権処理の加速（=speeding up the disposal of nonperforming loans）
◆A move to adopt the IFRSs has accelerated worldwide. 国際財務報告基準（IFRSs）を採用する動きは, 世界的に加速している。◆A series of accounting scandals and delays in the recovery of corporate performance are accelerating falls in stock prices on the U.S. markets, along with the weakening of the dollar. 一連の［相次ぐ］企業会計の不祥事と企業業績回復の遅れで, 米国の株安とドル安が加速している。◆As the financial markets' confidence in the U.S. currency has been shaked, stock prices may fall worldwide and the dollar-selling trend may accelerate. 米ドルへの金融市場の信認が揺らいでいるため, 株価が世界的に下落し, ドル売りの流れが加速する可能性もある。◆Export-oriented companies will be hit hard if the yen accelerates its rise. 円高が加速すると, 輸出企業は大きな打撃を受ける。◆Hostile mergers and acquisitions have been increasing rapidly as the dissolution of cross-shareholding ties among companies accelerates. 企

業間の株式持ち合い関係の解消が加速するにつれ、敵対的M&A（企業の合併・買収）の件数は急増している。◆Moves toward a full-scale realignment have been accelerating in the commodity futures trading industry, involving companies from other business fields. 商品先物取引業界では、異業種の企業を巻き込んだ総力を挙げての再編の動きが加速している。◆The rise in the yen's value is accelerating. 円高が加速している。

accelerate financial sector realignment 金融再編を加速する
◆To resolve the financial unrest in EU nations, accelerating financial sector realignment in countries such as Germany must be worked out. EU諸国の金融不安を解決するには、（2,000もの金融機関がひしめく）ドイツなどでの金融再編の加速も課題だ。

accelerate selling pressure on the U.S. stocks and the dollar 米国の株・ドル売りを加速する
◆Concern over the revival of the twin deficits is accelerating selling pressure on the U.S. stocks and the dollar. 双子の赤字の復活懸念が、米国の株・ドル売りを加速している。

accelerate the disposal of bad loans 不良債権処理を加速する
◆FSA audits of the banks' accounts urged them to reclassify 149 of their major corporate borrowers more strictly in terms of their creditworthiness in a bid to accelerate the disposal of bad loans. 金融庁による銀行の財務書類監査で、不良債権処理を加速するため、銀行は大口融資先149社の信用力による債務者区分の見直しを強化するよう強く求められた。◆Overly radical methods for accelerating the disposal of bad loans would panic the banking sector and the financial market, possibly driving banks to shy away from extending new loans and even to call in existing loans. 不良債権処理を加速するための余りにも強硬な手法は、銀行や金融市場をおびえさせ、貸し渋りや貸しはがしにつながることにもなる。

accelerate the influx of foreign funds 海外からの資金流入を加速する
◆Higher interest rates would accelerate the influx of foreign funds. 利上げ［金利の引上げ］は、海外からの資金流入を加速することになる。

accelerated （形）加速した、促進された、拍車がかかった
　accelerated amortization 加速償却、加速減価償却、加速なし崩し償却
　accelerated cost recovery system 加速原価回収制度［回収法］、加速償却制度、加速償却法、エイカーズ、ACRS
　accelerated growth 加速的成長
　accelerated inflation インフレの加速
　accelerated method 加速償却法
　　（=accelerated depreciation method）
　accelerated price decline 価格下落の加速
　accelerated restructuring efforts リストラ策の加速

accelerated depreciation 相場下落の加速、加速償却、加速減価償却、加速償却法
◆The dollar's accelerated depreciation could hurt not only the Japanese economy but also the global economy as a whole. ドル安の加速は、日本経済だけでなく、世界経済全体にとってもマイナスだ。

accelerated disposal of bad loans 不良債権処理の加速　（=speeding up the disposal of nonperforming loans）
◆The accelerated disposal of bad loans will augment deflationary pressures on the economy. 不良債権処理の加速は、経済［景気］のデフレ圧力を強める。

accelerated disposal of nonperforming loans 不良債権処理の加速
◆The economy could sink into a double-dip recession due to the clouds hanging over the U.S. economy and rising deflationary pressures that will accompany the accelerated disposal of nonperforming loans. 米国経済の行方（米国経済への先行き不安）や、不良債権処理の加速に伴うデフレ圧力の高まりなどで、景気が底割れする恐れがある。

accept （動）承諾する、受諾する、受け入れる、受ける、同意する、手形や注文などを引き受ける、認める、容認する
　a time draft drawn on and accepted by a bank 銀行宛に振り出され銀行が引き受けた期限付き手形
　accept a bill 手形を引き受ける
　accept a bill for collection 取立てのため手形を受け入れる
　accept a bill for discount 割引のため手形を受け入れる
　accept a bill of exchange 為替手形を引き受ける
　accept a cargo 船荷を引き受ける
　accept a credit card クレジット・カード［カード］での支払いを認める、カードでの支払いを受ける
　accept a risk 危険を引き受ける、リスクをとる
　accept an offer 申込みを受諾する
　accept such assignment and delegation 当該譲渡と委託を引き受ける
　accepted bill 引受手形
　accepted draft 引受済み手形
　accepted S.P. （第三者による）参加引受け
　accounting principle generally accepted in Canada カナダで一般に認められた［一般に公正妥当と認められた］会計基準

◆Banks will not accept future loan requests if they have to forgive the debt. 金融機関が債権放棄をせざるを得ないとなると、金融機関は今後の融資要請には応じないだろう。◆In the 21-day tender offer, a surprisingly large number of individual shareholders accepted the deal. 21日間の株式公開買付け（TOB）で、当初の予想を上回って多くの個人株主がTOBに応募した。◆Prime Minister Aso has accepted the government's fiscal stimulus measures to turn around the flagging economy. 麻生首相は、低迷する景気を回復させるための［経済対策のための］政府の財政出動を容認した。◆TCI, a British investment fund, asked J-Power to accept two TCI executives as board members. 英投資ファンドのTCIは、JパワーにTCI役員2人の取締役受入れを求めた。◆The consolidated financial statements have been prepared in accordance with accounting principles generally accepted in Canada. 連結財務書類［連結財務諸表］は、カナダで一般に公正妥当と認められた会計基準に従って［会計基準に準拠して］作成されています。◆We will have to accept heavy taxation to foot the bill for the lax fiscal discipline of past governments. われわれは今後、過去の政府の放漫な財政運営のつけを負担するために、重税を受け入れなければならなくなる。

acceptance （名）申込み［オファー］に対する承諾、承認、手形の引受け、引受済み手形、商品の受領、検収
　absolute acceptance 単純引受け
　　（=clean acceptance）
　acceptance advice 手形引受通知書、引受通知（輸出地の銀行から信用状開設銀行へ送付される手形引受の通知）
　acceptance and guarantee 支払い承諾
　acceptance by intervention 手形の参加引受け
　acceptance commission 手形引受手数料
　acceptance credit 引受信用状　（=usance L/C: 信用状に基づいて振り出される手形が、一覧後60日などの期限付きであることを規定した信用状）
　acceptance house 手形引受業者、引受商社、手形引受商社、アクセプタンス・ハウス
　　（=accepting house, merchant banker）
　acceptance of bill 手形引受け
　acceptance of import bill 輸入手形引受け
　acceptance rate 輸入決済相場、一覧払い輸入手形決済

相場
acceptance supra protest [supraprotest]　引受拒絶証書作成後の参加引受け
acceptance syndicate　引受シンジケート団
acceptance up to 90 days　90日までの引受手形
acceptance without security　無担保手形引受け
accommodation acceptance　融通手形引受け
bank acceptance　銀行引受手形, BA
　(=banker's acceptance)
banker's acceptance liabilities　支払い承諾(取引)
clean acceptance　単純引受け
collateral acceptance　担保差し入れ引受手形
conditional acceptance　条件付き引受け
documentary acceptance　荷為替付き引受け
documentary against acceptance　引受渡し
　(=documents against acceptance)
eligible acceptance　適格手形
(fine) trade acceptance　(一流)商業引受手形
General acceptance　単純引受け
ineligible acceptance　不適格手形
London acceptance credit　ロンドン銀行引受信用状
partial acceptance　一部引受け
prime banker's acceptance　一流銀行引受手形
qualified acceptance　手形の条件引受け, 条件[制限]付き引受け, 限定[制限]引受け
refuse acceptance of a bill　手形の引受けを拒絶する
secure acceptance of a bill　手形の引受けを確保する
special acceptance　特殊引受け
◆GM expects to receive about $14 billion from the sale of General Motors Acceptance Corp. GMは、販売金融子会社GMACの売却により、約140億ドルを確保する見通しだ。

accepting bank　引受銀行
accepting house　手形引受業者
　(=acceptance house)
acceptor [accepter]　(名)手形引受人, 手形引受業者, 受領者
accommodation acceptor　融通手形引受人
access　(動)(資金などを)調達する, 接続する, 利用する, データを検索する, 閲覧する, 入手する, 参加する, 参入する, 加入する, 立ち入る, 接近する
access cash　資金を調達する
access external sources of cash　外部から資金調達する
　(=access external sources of funding, access external funding sources)
access information on　～の情報を入手する, ～の情報を閲覧する
access the capital markets　資本市場で資金を調達する, 資本市場で調達する
access the market　起債する, 市場で資金を調達する
access the public markets　公募債市場で資金を調達する
◆Banks are allowed to access part of their legal capital reserves and transfer such funds to retained earnings. 銀行は、法定準備金の一部を取り崩して、その資金を剰余金に振り替えることができる。◆Four credit card holders received bills for accessing subscription Web sites via cell phones even though they had no recollection of doing so. 利用した覚えがないのに、携帯電話の有料サイトの利用代金請求書が、4人のクレジット・カード会員に届いた。◆Personal computers of individuals and corporations were used to illegally access accounts and withdraw money. 口座に不正アクセスして現金を引き出すのに、個人や企業所有のパソコンが使われていた。◆Shareholders can access the company's special Web site and vote on decisions, including the election of board members. 株主は、同社専用のホームページを利用して、取締役選任などの議決に投票することができる。◆The bank does not issue conventional bankbooks for cardholders, but offers electronic bank books that are used via the Internet and accessed through personal computer and cell phones. 同行は、カード会員に従来の銀行通帳は発行せず、パソコンや携帯電話でアクセスしてインターネット上で使用する電子通帳[ウェブ通帳]を提供している。

access　(名)(資金の)調達, 参入, 参入機会, 市場アクセス, 加入, 参加, 利用, 閲覧, (コンピュータ・システムやネットワークへの)接続, アクセス
access to assets　資産の取扱い
　(⇒authorization)
access to funding [financing]　資金調達, 資金源の確保
access to information　情報の入手, 情報の閲覧
access to markets on an unsecured basis　無担保ベースでの資金調達
access to records and books of account　会計記録と会計帳簿の閲覧
access to the market　起債, 市場での資金調達, 市場への参入, 市場への参入機会, 市場進出, 市場アクセス, 市場へのアクセス　(=market access)
gain direct access to the bond market　債券市場から直接資金を調達する
instant access account　(英国の)普通預金
◆Illegal access of Internet banking accounts using account holders' user IDs and passwords was confirmed at 51 financial institutions. 口座名義人のユーザーID[ユーザー名]やパスワードを使ったネット・バンキングの口座への不正アクセスが、51金融機関で確認された。◆In illegal access of Internet bank accounts, nearly all of the money in the illegally accessed account was sent to other accounts. ネット・バンキングの口座への不正アクセスで、不正アクセスされた口座の現金はほぼ全額、他人名義の口座に送金されていた。◆The merits of being listed include access to a wide variety of measures to raise funds. 上場のメリットとしては、資金調達手段の多様性が挙げられる。◆The shareholders' auditors have full access to the audit committee, with and without management being present. 経営者の同席の有無にかかわらず、監査委員会とは会計監査人が密接に連絡を取っています[監査委員会には会計監査人が毎回参加することができます]。

access to capital　資金調達, 資金調達力
limited access to capital　資金調達力の限界
reduced access to capital　資金調達力の低下
◆Our plans, which require significant investments, are at risk because of limited access to capital. 大幅投資が必要な当社の計画は現在、資金調達力にも限界があるため、危機にさらされています。

access to financing　資金調達, 資金源の確保
　(=access to funding)
◆We have easy access to financing when we need it. 資金調達については、当社は必要な時にたやすく資金調達ができます。

access to funding　資金調達, 資金源の確保
　(=access to financing)
◆The downgrade could further hamper GM's access to funding. 今回の格下げで、GMの資金調達はさらに厳しくなる可能性がある。

accident　(名)事故, 災難, 思いがけない出来事, 偶然, アクシデント
accident insurance　障害保険
credit accident and health insurance　信用傷害健康保険
family personal accident insurance　家族傷害保険
individual accident and health　個人傷害・医療保険
industrial accidents　労働災害, 業務災害

personal accident insurance　傷害保険
traffic personal accident insurance　交通事故傷害保険
work accidents　労働災害
workmen's accident compensation　労災補償

accommodate　(動)(金を)融通する,融資する,金を貸す(lend money to),用立てる,便宜を図る,調節する,調停する,～に対処する,～に対応する,収容する
accommodate a person with money　～に金[資金]を融通する
accommodated party　被融通者
◆The bank accommodated the company with a loan of ￥10 million.　同行は、同社に1,000万円を融資した。

accommodating　(形)融通の利(き)く,協力的な,好意的な,調節的[調整的]な,好意的な,景気刺激型の
accommodating fiscal and monetary policies　景気刺激型の財政・金融政策
accommodating monetary policy　追認的金融政策,順応的金融政策(＝accommodative[accommodatory] monetary policy)
accommodating stance　緩めのスタンス
accommodating transaction　調節の取引,調整の取引

accommodation　(名)融通,融資,貸出,融通手形,貸金,借入れ,便宜,供与,適応,和解,調停,収容,収容施設,宿泊施設
accommodation agency　住宅斡旋業者,不動産業者
accommodation bill[acceptance]　融通手形[融手],空(から)手形,書き合い手形 (＝kite, wind-bill)
accommodation bills issued　融通証券発行高
accommodation draft　融通手形,表紙手形
accommodation drawer　融通手形振出人
accommodation endorsement　手形保証,手形裏書き,融通手形裏書き
accommodation endorser　融通手形裏書人
accommodation line　小口火災保険,(保険契約の)営業政策的引受け,特別引受け
accommodation loan　無担保融資
accommodation note　融通約束手形,空手形
accommodation of funds　融資
accommodation paper　融通手形,手形裏書流通証券
accommodation party　融通手形関係人,融通当事者,融通手形の当事者
accommodation payment　馴れ合い支払い
apply for accommodation to a Federal Reserve Bank　米連邦準備銀行に借入れを申し込む
bank accommodation　銀行融資
credit accommodation　信用供与
cross accommodation　交互融通,手形の書き合い
financial accommodation　資金融通
financing by accommodation bill　融手[融通手形]操作 (＝financing of accommodation)
loan accommodation　貸出融通
obtain accommodation from　～から[～の]貸出を受ける
official credit accommodation　公的輸出信用供与
overnight accommodation　一晩だけの融通
sound credit accommodation　信用供与の健全性
temporary accommodation　一時融通

accommodative　(形)協調的な,協力的な,緩和基調の,緩和基調で運営されている,景気刺激型の
accommodative monetary policy　緩和基調の金融政策,緩和基調で運営されている禁輸政策
accommodative stance of monetary policy　緩和姿勢の金融政策,金融政策での緩和姿勢
monetary policy is accommodative　金融政策は緩和基調で運営されている
non-accommodative monetary policy　景気刺激型でない金融政策

accommodator　(名)融通者,融資者,便宜提供者,調停人

accompany　(動)～に同行する,～に同伴する,～に重なる,～に付随して起こる,～と同時に起こる,～に添える[加える],～に付属する
accompanying booklet　添付の解説書
accompanying document[papers]　添付書類,付属書類
be accompanied by　～を伴う,～が添付してある
◆An increase in transactions that brokerages handle has accompanied the brisk stock market business.　証券会社が扱う取引の増加は、そのまま株式相場の盛況と重なる。◆The economy could sink into a double-dip recession due to the clouds hanging over the U.S. economy and rising deflationary pressures that will accompany the accelerated disposal of nonperforming loans.　米国経済の行方[米国経済への先行き不安]や、不良債権処理の加速に伴うデフレ圧力の高まりなどで、景気が底割れする恐れがある。◆The fall in import prices that accompanies a strong yen could further prolong Japan's deflation.　円高に伴う輸入価格の下落で、日本のデフレがさらに長期化する可能性がある。

accomplish　(動)達成する,成し遂げる,完遂(かんすい)する,完了する
accomplish long-term financing　長期資金を調達する
accomplish the goal　目標を達成する
successfully accomplish　～を成功させる
◆One way for a company to accomplish long-term financing is through the issuance of long-term debt instruments in the form of bonds.　会社の長期資金調達方法の一つは、社債の形で長期債務証券を発行して行われる。◆Our long-term financing was accomplished through the issuance of long-term debt instruments.　当社の長期資金調達は、長期債務証券を発行して行われた。

accord　(名)意見の一致,同意,合意,合意書,合意文書,和解,協定
accord and satisfaction　代物弁済,代物弁済契約,同意と満足
Basel Accord of 1988　1988年のバーゼル合意
Plaza Accord of 1985　1985年のプラザ合意 (＝1985 Plaza Accord)
sign an accord with　～と合意文書に調印する
◆Citigroup will buy back the auction-rate securities from investors under separate accords with the Securities and Exchange Commission and state regulators.　米シティグループは、米証券取引委員会(SEC)や州規制当局との個々の合意に基づいて投資家から金利入札証券(ARS)を買い戻す。◆Commercial banks have created special investment vehicles (SIVs) in order to escape the capital adequacy regulation imposed by the Basel accord.　銀行は、バーゼル協定[バーゼル合意]による自己資本比率規制を回避するため、特別投資会社(SIV)を新設している。◆Under the accord, the banking, trust and brokerage units of MTFG will be the surviving companies, respectively.　合意書によると、三菱東京側の銀行、信託、証券会社がそれぞれ存続会社となる。

account　(名)口座,預金,勘定,勘定書,計算,計算書,収支,決算,決算書,会計,取引関係,取引先,説明,報告,理由,考慮,重要性, a/c　(⇒accounts)
account agreement　口座開設約定書
account books　会計帳簿,売掛債権帳,売掛帳,決算書 (＝accounting books, books of account, financial books)
account conversion　口座振替
account day　決済日

account due　未収金
account holder　口座名義人
account information　口座情報, 口座関連情報
　（=account-related information; ⇒account PIN）
account number　口座番号
account payable　買掛金, 未払い金, 支払い勘定, 支払い債務, 買入れ債務, 購入債務, 仕入債務
account receivable　売掛金, 未収金, 未収入金, 受取勘定, 売掛債権, 売上債権, 受取債権
　（=account due, sales credit）
bank account　銀行口座, 銀行預金口座, 銀行勘定, 預金
bank's automatic accounts transfer system　銀行自動引落し制度
branch account　支店勘定
cash account　現金勘定
checking account　小切手勘定, 当座預金
close a bank account　口座を解約する
close an account　口座を閉める
closing accounts for the year　年次決算
corporate account　法人口座
current account　当座預金, 当座勘定
current account balance　経常収支
current account deficit　経常赤字, 経常収支の赤字
current account surplus　経常黒字, 経常収支の黒字
deposit account　普通預金, 預金勘定
error account　エラー・アカウント
fund account　資金勘定
general account　一般会計
head office account　本店勘定
individual retirement account　個人退職預金口座, IRA
midyear accounts　中間決算
My Account　個人用口座, マイ・アカウント
　（=personal account）
non-interest-bearing account for individuals　個人向け無利子の預金
nostro account　当行勘定
off-the-book account　簿外口座
open account　当座預金, 当座勘定, 交互計算
open an account　口座を開設する, 口座を設ける
ordinary account　普通口座
our account [a/c]　当方勘定
personal account　個人口座, 個人用口座, パーソナル・アカウント
professional account　プロフェッショナル用口座
savings account　普通預金, 貯蓄性預金, 貯蓄預金
services account　貿易外収支
settlement account　決済口座
special account　特別会計, 特別取引先
specified account　特定口座
trade account　貿易収支
two sets of account books　二重帳簿
Web account　ウェブ口座, インターネット口座
your account　先方勘定
　（=their account, vostro account）

◆Amid the continued yen's historically high levels, increasing numbers of people are opening foreign currency deposit accounts. 歴史的な円高水準が続くなか, 外貨預金口座を設ける人が増えている。◆An individual investor began depositing money in U.S. dollars using a major bank's Web account. 個人投資家が, 大手銀行のウェブ口座[インターネット口座]を利用して米ドルの外貨預金を始めた。◆Customers will have to open a new account to use the Internet banking services. このネット・バンキングのサービスを利用するにあたって, 顧客は新規に口座を開設しなければならない。◆In illegal access of Internet bank accounts confirmed at financial institutions, money was transferred from a client's account to a second account. 金融機関で確認されたネット・バンキング口座への不正アクセスでは, 顧客の口座から現金が他人名義の口座に振り込まれていた[送信されていた]。◆In illegal access of Internet bank accounts, nearly all of the money in the illegally accessed account was sent to other accounts. ネット・バンキングの口座への不正アクセスで, 不正アクセスされた口座の現金はほぼ全額, 他人名義の口座に送金されていた。◆In the case of this ATM card, even if a cardholder's card or PIN number should be stolen, no one else can withdraw cash from the account. このキャッシュ・カードの場合は, カード会員がたとえカードや暗証番号を盗まれても, 本人以外は口座から預金を引き出せない。◆In the one-time password system, clients' passwords are changed whenever they log into their accounts. ワンタイムパスワード方式だと, 顧客が口座を利用するたびに, 顧客のパスワードは変更される。◆In this type of life insurance products, the rate of return after canceling the insurance contract can be higher than that of a savings account if a policyholder upholds the contract for five to 10 years. この種の生保商品では, 保険契約者が保険契約を5～10年続けると, 解約後の利回り（予定利率）は預金よりも高い利回りが見込める。◆In wrap accounts, a customer sets the overall investment policy, including investment period and profit target. ラップ口座では, 顧客が投資期間や運用益の目標などの大まかな運用方針を決める。◆Pyongyang's accounts with Banco Delta Asia in Macao were frozen under U.S. financial sanctions. マカオの銀行「バンコ・デルタ・アジア」にある北朝鮮の口座が, 米国の金融制裁を受けて凍結された。◆Regional bank accounts were hit hardest by illegal transfers via foreign malware. 海外のマルウエア（コンピュータ・ウイルスの一種）による不正送金の被害は, 地方銀行の口座が最多だった。◆The accounting firm is responsible for auditing the accounts of about 7,000 companies. 同監査法人は, 約7,000社の会計監査[財務書類の監査]を担当している。◆The brokerage firm manages client assets of ￥520 billion in about 150,000 accounts. この証券会社は, 口座数約15万で顧客預り資産は5,200億円に達する。◆The company pioneered a variety of innovative promotions to add new accounts. 同社は, 各種の斬新な販促活動によって, 新口座[新規顧客]を増やした。

account balance　勘定残高, 銀行口座の残高, 口座残高
◆Account balance can be checked on the Internet. 口座の残高は, インターネットでチェックできる。◆The 2009 condensed consolidated balance sheet reflects full consolidation of ABCD's account balances. 2009年度の要約連結貸借対照表は, ABCD社の勘定残高の完全連結を反映しています。

account book　通帳, 銀行通帳
◆These troubles caused by the computer malfunction ranged from dysfunctional ATMs to delayed money transfers, and to deductions from accounts that were recorded in account books although no money was actually transferred. 今回のコンピュータの障害・誤作動で生じたトラブルとしては, ATM（現金自動預け払い機）障害や口座振替の遅れ, さらには現金が実際には未払いなのに[払戻しされていないのに], 通帳に口座からの引落しが記載されたケースなどがあった。

account books　会計帳簿, 決算書　（=accounting books, books of account, financial books）
◆Using the seals and bankbooks of heavily indebted people, the man forged account books and other documents for a fictitious construction firm. 多重債務者の印鑑と銀行通帳を使って, この男は, 架空の建設会社の決算書[会計帳簿]などを偽造した。

account executive　証券会社のセールスマン, 広告代理店などの営業責任者, アカウント・エグゼクティブ, AE
account for　計上する, 処理する, 会計処理する, ～を占

める, 説明する
◆Financial services account for about 60 percent of the company's overall sales. 金融事業は、同社の売上全体の6割を占めている。◆In the past, the finance subsidiaries of the Corporation were accounted for by the equity method. これまで、当社の金融事業を営む子会社は、持ち分法で会計処理していました。◆Intellectual assets account for about 70 percent of the total market value of all corporate assets in the United States. 知的資産は、米国では全企業資産の総時価評価額の約70%を占めている。◆The insurer's revenues from the single-premium whole life insurance products account for about 30 percent of the company's total revenues from insurance premiums. 同保険会社の一時払い終身保険商品の収入保険料は、保険料収入[収入保険料]全体の約3割を占めている。◆The Osaka Securities Exchange accounts for 50 percent of domestic trading in derivatives including stock price index futures. 大証は、株価指数先物などデリバティブ(金融派生商品)の国内取引で5割を占めている。◆Under the book value method, the carrying value of the convertible bonds at the date of the conversion would be used to account for the conversion. 簿価法では、転換時の転換社債の簿価が、転換の会計処理に使われる。

account holder 口座名義人, 口座保有者, 口座を持っている顧客 (⇒account number)
◆Account holders can withdraw money at will from liquid deposits, such as ordinary deposits. 普通預金などの流動性預金から、口座保有者は金を自由に下ろすことができる。◆Illegal access of Internet banking accounts using account holders' user IDs and passwords was confirmed at 51 financial institutions. 口座名義人のユーザーID[ユーザー名]やパスワードを使ったネット・バンキングの口座への不正アクセスが、51金融機関で確認された。◆The account holder could not be contacted as the phone number was bogus. 偽の電話番号なので、口座名義人と連絡が取れなかった。

account number 口座番号
◆Existing account holders can switch their accounts to the settlement-specific deposit without changing their account numbers. すでに口座を持っている顧客は、口座番号を変えないで決済用預金に口座を切り替えることができる。

account officer アカウント・オフィサー
account PIN 口座の暗証番号
(PIN=personal identification number)
◆In phishing, offenders lure victims to fake financial institution Web sites to enter their account PINs and other account information. フィッシングでは、犯罪者が被害者を金融機関の偽ホームページに誘導して、被害者の口座の暗証番号などの口座情報を入力させる。

account settlement 決算
(=settlement of accounts)
account settlement term 決算期
account settlement term ending in March 3月決算期, 3月期
March account settlement 3月期決算
midyear account settlement 中間決算
(=midterm account settlement)
the first-half account settlement 上半期決算, 中間決算
the latest account settlement 今決算
◆In the latest account settlements, not only Resona but other banking groups gave up including sizable deferred tax assets in their equity capital. 今決算では、「りそな」だけでなく他の銀行グループも、巨額の繰延べ税金資産の自己資本への計上を見送った。◆In the latest account settlements, some banking groups gave up including sizable deferred tax assets in their equity capital. 今決算では、一部の銀行グループが、巨額の繰延べ税金資産の自己資本への計上を見送った。◆With the midyear account settlement scheduled in September, concerns over the stability of the nation's financial system inevitably will grow again should stock prices dip further. 9月中間決算を前に、株価がさらに下がれば、再び日本の金融システム不安が当然、台頭してくる。

account settlement term 決算期
◆Stock prices will tumble, if banks try to sell a large amount of banks crossheld shares in the market ahead of the account settlement term at the end of March. 3月末の決算期を控えて、銀行が大量の持ち合い株式を市場に放出すれば、株価は急落する。

account settlement term ending in March 3月決算期, 3月期
◆All business sectors registered year-on-year increases in earnings and profit for the account settlement term ending in March. 3月期は、前年同期比で全業種が増収増益だった。

accountability (名)義務, 責任, 実施義務, 説明責任, 報告責任, 会計責任, 企業責任, アカウンタビリティ
accountability of assets 資産に対する企業責任
accountability to customers 顧客への説明責任
business accountability 独立採算
corporate accountability 企業の説明責任
Government Accountability Office 米政府説明責任局, GAO
management accountability 経営の説明責任, 経営の説明責任能力
operational accountability 経営責任
stewardship accountability 受託責任
◆Corporation's internal controls are designed to adequately safeguard, verify and maintain accountability of assets. 当社の内部統制は、資産に対する企業責任を十分に保証・確認・維持するよう図られています。

accountable (形)～する責任がある
accountable for ～に対して責任がある, ～の責任がある
be held accountable for ～の責任を問われる, ～について責任がある
hold a person accountable for 人に～の責任を持たせる, 人に～の責任を問う, ～の責任は人にある
make shareholders accountable for financial difficulties 経営不振の株主責任を明確にする
◆Executives will be held accountable if the low-rated government bonds they have purchased fail to produce profits. 経営者が購入した格付けの低い国債が利益を生み出さなかったら[経営者が格付けの低い国債への投資で失敗したら]、経営者が(株主から)その責任を問われることになる。◆Kanebo will reduce its capital by 99.7 percent to ¥100 million to make shareholders accountable for its financial difficulties. カネボウは、経営不振の株主責任を明確にするため、99.7%の減資を実施して資本金を1億円とする。◆The bank's investigation committee is compiling a report that holds several former executives accountable for the enormous losses. 同行の調査委員会は、旧経営陣数名に多額の損失の責任を問う内容の報告書をまとめている。◆The company will reduce its capital by 99.7 percent to ¥100 million to make shareholders accountable for its financial difficulties. 経営不振[経営危機]に対する株主責任を明確にするため、同社は1億円に99.7%の減資を実施する[99.7%の減資を実施して資本金を1億円とする]。

accountant (名)会計士, 会計・経理担当者, 会計専門家, 監査人
accountant in charge 担当会計士
accountant's certificate [report] 監査報告書
accountant's legal liability 会計士の法的責任
accountant's opinion 会計士の意見
certified public accountant 公認会計士
chartered accountant 勅許会計士, 公認会計士, C.A
independent accountant 独立会計士, 独立監査人, 独立した会計監査人, 一般に公認会計士という

◆Four certified public accountants at ChuoAoyama PricewaterhouseCoopers were involved in the window dressing. 中央青山監査法人の4人の公認会計士が、粉飾決算に関与していた。◆Independent accountants are retained to examine our financial statements. 独立した会計監査人が、当社の財務書類[財務諸表]を監査しています。◆The Financial Services Agency will give an official warning to Chuo Aoyama Audit Corp. under the Certified Public Accountants Law over negligence in its checking of Ashikaga Bank's accounts. 金融庁は、足利銀行の財務書類の監査内容が不十分であったとして、公認会計士法に基づき中央青山監査法人に対して正式に戒告処分を出す。◆The Tokyo Stock Exchange has no power to directly supervise certified public accountants. 東京証券取引所に、公認会計士を直接監督する権限はない。

accounting （名）会計, 会計処理, 会計処理方法, 会計学, 経理, 計算, 算定
  accounting date 決算日
  accounting malpractice 不正会計
  accounting method 会計処理方法, 会計方法
  accounting scandal 不正経理や粉飾決算などの企業会計疑惑, 会計疑惑, 会計処理疑惑, 会計不祥事, 会計スキャンダル, 不正会計事件
  accounting term ending in September 2012 2012年9月期, 2012年9月中間決算, 2012年9月に終了する会計期間
  accounting year 会計年度 （=accounting period, business year, fiscal year, operating period）
  consolidated accounting 連結決算
  corruption in accounting 不正会計
  current value accounting 現在価値会計, 時価主義会計, CVA （=mark-to-market accounting, market value accounting）
  deceptive accounting 虚偽の会計処理, 不正な会計操作, 不正会計
  distrust in corporate accounting 企業会計不信
  false accounting 不正経理
  mark-to-market accounting 時価会計 （=fair value accounting, market value-based accounting）
  uniform accounting system 統一会計制度
  ◆Even if the banks record their bad loans as losses in their corporate accounting, such loans are not treated as losses in their tax accounting. 銀行が企業会計で不良債権を損失として計上[処理]しても、税務会計ではこれらの不良債権は損金扱いにならない。

accounting documents 経理書類
  ◆The company falsified accounting documents relating to the payment. 同社は、この支出に関する経理書類を改ざんしていた。

accounting error 経理ミス
  （=accounting mistake）
  ◆Toyota failed to report a total of about ￥5 billion including simple accounting errors. トヨタは、単純な経理ミスを含めて総額で約50億円を申告しなかった。

accounting firm 監査法人
  ◆The accounting firm is responsible for auditing the accounts of about 7,000 companies. 同監査法人は、約7,000社の会計監査[財務書類の監査]を担当している。

accounting fraud 会計操作, 不正会計処理, 粉飾決算
  （=accounting manipulation; ⇒punishment）
  ◆A certified public accountant took part in an accounting fraud for the company. 公認会計士が、同社の粉飾決算に加担していた。◆The firm's former president denied the leading role in the company's accounting fraud. 同社の前社長は、同社の会計操作での主導的役割[首謀]を否定した。◆The Securities and Exchange Surveillance Commission launched a full-scale investigation on the company on suspicion of accounting fraud. 証券取引等監視委員会は、粉飾決算の疑いで同社の本格調査に乗り出した。

accounting income 会計上の利益
  ◆The Company provides for income taxes based on accounting income for tax purposes included in the financial statements. 当社は税務上、財務書類に表示する会計上の利益に基づいて法人所得税を算定しています。

accounting irregularities 不正経理, 不正会計
  ◆The accounting irregularities were carried out by all of the firm's seven branch offices. 不正経理は、同社の7支店全店で行われていた。◆The company's alleged accounting irregularities have developed into a case concerning a violation of the Unfair Competition Prevention Act. 同社の不正経理事件は、不正競争防止法違反事件にまで発展した。

accounting malpractice 不正会計

accounting manipulation 会計操作
  （=accounting fraud）
  ◆Such an accounting manipulation can be done simply by doctoring the books. このような会計操作は、帳簿に手を加えるだけで簡単にできる。

accounting mistake 経理ミス
  （=accounting error）
  ◆The amount that the company failed to declare totaled about ￥2 billion if accounting mistakes are included. 同社の申告漏れの額は、経理ミスを含めると総額で約20億円にのぼった。

accounting period 会計期間, 会計年度, 事業年度, 計上時期 （=financial period, financial year, fiscal period, fiscal year: 財務書類（財務諸表）の基本会計期間は1年となっている）
  the accounting period ending March 31 3月31日終了会計年度, 3月期決算
  the latest accounting period 当事業年度, 当期
  ◆Japan Post Service Co. was notified of its mistake in the accounting period regarding postcard and stamp sales. 郵便事業会社は、はがきや切手などの売上について、計上時期の誤りを指摘された。◆Major corporations' percentage of the drop in after-tax gains significantly exceeded that of the fall in recurring profits during the latest accounting period. 当期は、大手企業の税引き後利益の減少率が経常利益の減少率を大きく上回った。◆Most major commercial banks are likely to record losses in the accounting period ending March 31 due to bad loan write-offs. 大手都市銀行（大手銀行）の大半は、3月期決算（3月31日終了の会計年度）では、不良債権処理で赤字になりそうだ。◆The bank recorded losses in the accounting period ending March 31 due to bad loan write-offs. 同行は、不良債権処理のため、3月期決算[3月31日終了の会計年度]で赤字になった。

accounting practices 会計実務, 会計慣行, 会計処理
  （⇒generally accepted accounting principles, mark-to-market accounting practices）

accounting principle 会計原則, 会計基準, 会計処理基準, 会計処理の方法
  （⇒generally accepted accounting principles）
  ◆The financial statements have been prepared in accordance with Canadian generally accepted accounting principles. この財務書類は、カナダの会計基準に準拠して[カナダの一般に認められた会計基準に従って]作成されています。

accounting records 会計記録
  ◆The U.S. Securities and Exchange Commission began taking actions, filing suits against companies for window-dressing their accounting records. 米証券取引委員会（SEC）は、会計記録の粉飾（粉飾決算）で企業を提訴するなどの行動をとり始めた（米証券取引委員会は粉飾決算企業を提訴するなどの行動をとり始めた）。

accounting report 会計報告書, 有価証券報告書, 財務

情報
◆Corporate accounting reports are the most important criterion for investment decisions. 企業の財務情報は、特に重要な投資判断の材料だ。◆Four certified public accountants conspired with the firm's former executives to falsify accounting reports. 公認会計士4人が、同社の旧経営陣と共謀して会計報告書[有価証券報告書]に虚偽の記載をした。

accounting rule 会計規則, 会計基準, 会計ルール
◆There were no specific accounting rules that regulated investment partnership. 投資事業組合(ファンド)を規制する会計ルールは、とくになかった。◆Under the new accounting rules introduced in April 2001, banks are required to deduct 60 percent of appraisal losses on shareholdings from retained earnings. 2001年4月から導入された会計規則(時価会計)で、銀行は保有株の評価損(含み損)の6割を剰余金から差し引かなければならない。

accounting scandal 不正経理や粉飾決算などの企業会計疑惑, 会計疑惑, 会計処理疑惑会計不祥事, 会計スキャンダル, 不正会計事件
◆A series of accounting scandals and delays in the recovery of corporate performance are accelerating falls in stock prices on the U.S. markets, along with the weakening of the dollar. 一連の(相次ぐ)企業会計の不祥事と企業業績回復の遅れで、米国の株安とドル安が加速している。

accounting standards 会計基準, 会計原則
(=accounting criteria)
◆For the business year ending in March 2008, we will post more than ¥3 trillion in consolidated operating profits based on U.S. accounting standards. 2008年3月期連結決算で、米国会計基準に基づく当社の連結営業利益は3兆円を上回る見通しだ。

accounting system 会計制度, 会計基準, 会計組織, 会計システム, 計算制度, 計算体系
◆In financial institutions, an accounting system to evaluate assets based on market values was introduced in April 2004. 金融機関の場合は、時価会計制度(時価に基づいて資産を評価する制度)が、2004年4月から導入された。◆Internal auditors continually review the accounting and control systems. 内部監査人は、継続して当社の会計処理システムと管理システムを検討しています。◆The drastic overhaul of the Japanese accounting system is expected to add a massive administrative burden to companies. 日本の会計基準の抜本的変更は、企業にとって大幅な事務負担の増加を強いられることになる。

accounting treatment 会計処理
accounts (名)財務書類, 財務諸表, 計算書類
(=financial statements)
accounts settlement ending in March 3月期決算
annual accounts 年次財務諸表, 年次財務書類, 年次計算書類
(=annual financial statements, final accounts)
banks' accounts 銀行の財務書類
book of accounts 会計帳簿, 財務帳簿
(=accounts book)
closing of accounts 決算 (=closing of books)
consolidated accounts 連結財務書類, 連結財務諸表
(=group accounts)
external accounts 対外収支
final accounts 決算報告書, 決算, 年次財務書類, 年次財務諸表
group accounts グループ財務書類, 連結財務書類
(=consolidated accounts)
income and expenditure accounts 収支計算書
interim accounts 中間財務諸表, 中間財務書類, 半期財務書類
(=interim financial statements, interim statements)
midyear accounts 中間決算
profit and loss accounts 損益計算書
statement of accounts 決算, 決算報告, 決算報告書
the half-year closing of fiscal 2012 accounts 2012年度中間決算
the last period of settlement of accounts 最終決算期
window-dress accounts 決算を粉飾する
◆Banks are about to settle their midyear accounts. 銀行は、これから中間決算をまとめるところだ。◆FSA audits of the banks' accounts urged them to reclassify 149 of their major corporate borrowers more strictly in terms of their creditworthiness in a bid to accelerate the disposal of bad loans. 金融庁による銀行の財務書類監査で、不良債権処理を加速するため、銀行は大口融資先149社の信用力による債務者区分の見直しを強化するよう強く求められた。◆The company may have window-dressed accounts over three years up to March 2008. 同社は、2008年3月期までの3年間にわたって、決算を粉飾していた疑いがある。◆The consolidated financial statements include the accounts of the corporation and all subsidiary companies. 連結財務書類には、当社と当社の全子会社の財務書類(経営成績と財政状態に関する情報)が含まれています。◆The 1.4 trillion rise in credit costs stems from tougher FSA audits of the banks' accounts. 不良債権処理額が1兆4,000億円増えたのは、金融庁による銀行の財務書類の監査が厳しくなったからだ。◆The total amount of money deposited in individual foreign currency accounts has continued to increase in recent years. 個人向け外貨預金残高は、ここ数年増え続けている。◆Yen can be exchanged for foreign currencies and deposited in foreign currency accounts at most major banks. 円は、大半の大手銀行で外貨と替えて外貨預金口座に預け入れることができる。

accounts payable 未払い金, 買掛金, 支払い債務
accounts receivable 売掛債権, 売掛金
(=sales credits)
◆In the loans to be extended to the company by the Development Bank of Japan, accounts receivable will be taken as security. 日本政策投資銀行の同社への融資では、売掛金が担保に取られる。◆The problem concerning accounts receivable is not a new issue in China. 売掛債権(売掛債権の回収)に関する問題は、中国では今に始まった問題ではない。

accounts settlement ending in March 3月期決算
accredited investor 適格投資家, 信用のある投資家
(米証券取引委員会(SEC)に登録されていない私募債に投資できる投資家で、純資産100万ドル以上または年収20万ドル以上の個人、純資産500万ドル以上の団体などを指す)

accrual (名)(利子や権利などの)発生, 未払い金, 未払い費用, 未払い額見越し, 見越し額, 見越し項目, 引当金, 見積り額, 増加額, 増加部分
accrual of interest 利息の未払い, 発生利息, 発生利息の計上
accrual rate 経過金利

accrue (動)生じる, 発生する, 付加する, 付与する, 増加する, 計上する, 見越し計上する
accrued income taxes 未払い法人税等
accrued pension cost 年金負債
◆The right to exercise options generally accrues over a period of four years of continuous employment. オプションを行使する権利は、原則として勤務期間[在任期間, 勤続年数]が4年を経過した時点で発生します。

accrued interest 発生済み利息, 発生利息, 未払い利息, 未収利息, 経過利息 (=interest accrued)
◆The payoff system guarantees only the refund of a principal of ¥10 million plus accrued interest. ペイオフ制度で保証されるのは、元本1,000万円とその利息の預金払い戻しだけである。◆This amount includes the appropriate accrued interest. この金額には、適切な未収利息が含まれています。

accrued liabilities　未払い負債, 未払い債務, 未払い費用, 見越し負債
◆Interest expense is the interest on short-term and long-term debt and accrued liabilities. 支払い利息は、短期および長期負債と未払い債務に対する利息です。

accrued plan benefits　年金給付債務, 年金給付債務額
◆The actuarial present value of the accrued plan benefits and the net assets available to discharge these benefits at December 31 are as follows: 12月31日現在の年金給付債務額の年金数理原価と年金給付債務に充当可能な年金純資産は、以下のとおりです。

accumulate　（動）集める, 蓄積する, 累積する, 積み上げる, 積み増す, 築く
　accumulate financial assets　金融資産を積み増す
　accumulate the debt　借金を積み上げる, 債務を積み上げる
◆The debt the government has accumulated is the money the people have borrowed through the government itself. 政府が積み上げている借金は、国民が政府自体を通じて借り入れている金である。◆The U.S. lawmakers will decide how much debt the Treasury can accumulate. 米議会議員がこれから決めるのは、財務省がどのていど債務を積み上げることができるかだ。◆There were apparent moves among companies drawing more money from savings to accumulate operating funds. 明らかな動きとして、企業は運転資金を積み増すため、預金から資金を引き出している。

accumulated　（形）蓄積した, 累積した, 積み増した
　accumulated and accrued plan benefits　累積年金給付債務額
　accumulated benefit obligation　累積給付債務
　accumulated capital　蓄積資本
　accumulated deficit　累積赤字, 累積損失, 欠損金（＝accumulative deficit）
　accumulated depreciation（and amortization）　減価償却累計額, 減価償却引当金（＝accrued depreciation, allowance［reserve］for depreciation）
　accumulated earnings　利益剰余金, 留保利益, 累積利益, 積立利益（＝accumulated income, accumulated profit, earned surplus, retained earnings）
　accumulated net profits　累積純益
　accumulated plan benefits　年金未支給額, 年金給付累計額, 累積給付額, 累積給付債務額
　accumulated postretirement benefit obligation　累積退職後給付債務
　accumulated preferred stock　累積的優先株式
　accumulated profit　利益剰余金, 留保利益（＝accumulated income）
　accumulated surplus　積立剰余金
◆Two companies' accumulated know-how in online trading will be useful in the commodity futures market. 商品先物市場では、両社の蓄積しているネット取引のノウハウが役に立つだろう。

　accumulated dividend　累積配当, 累積利益配当, 累積未払い配当,（保険の）積立配当金, 積立配当金残高
◆When the policyholders of single-premium whole life insurances die, beneficiaries receive the designated benefits plus accumulated dividends. 一時払い終身保険の契約者が死亡した場合、保険金の受取人は、特定の（死亡）保険金のほかに積立配当金を受け取れる。

　accumulated fiscal deficit　累積財政赤字, 積もり積もった財政赤字
◆The governments of European countries are being forced to reduce their accumulated fiscal deficits. 欧州各国政府は、積もり積もった財政赤字の削減を迫られている。

　accumulated latent assets　蓄えた含み資産, 含み資産の蓄え
◆Japanese financial institutions have seen their accumulated latent assets almost depleted. 日本の金融機関は、これまでに蓄えた含み資産をほぼ吐き出してしまった。

　accumulated liability　累積債務
◆When we adopted the new standard, we had an accumulated liability related to past service from retirees and active employees. 当社が新基準を採用した時点で、当社には退職者と現従業員の過去勤務に関する累積債務がありました。

　accumulated long-term debts　累積長期債務, 長期債務残高
◆The accumulated long-term debts of the central and local governments exceed ¥800 trillion in total. 国と地方自治体の長期債務残高は、総額で800兆円を超している［国と地方自治体の累積長期債務は、総額で800兆円を超している］。

　accumulated losses　累積損失
◆The amount of the bank's accumulated losses over the period up to the end of its 2008 business year was five times the level of its operating revenue. 同行の2008年度末までの累積損失額は、経常収益の水準の5倍となった。

　accumulated nonperforming loans　累積不良債権, 累積債務
◆The prolonged economic malaise is due to accumulated nonperforming loans held by financial institutions. 長引く景気低迷の要因は、金融機関が抱える累積不良債権にある。

　accumulated postretirement benefit obligation　累積退職後給付債務
◆Increasing the assumed trend rate by 1% in each year would raise our accumulated postretirement benefit obligation at December 31, 2011 by $700 million. 予想傾向値が毎年1％ずつ上昇すると、当社の累積退職後給付債務は、2011年12月31日現在で7億ドル増加します。

　accumulated surplus funds　累積剰余金, 特別会計の積立金
◆Accumulated surplus funds from previous years are referred to as "hidden treasure" by politicians. 過年度の累積剰余金（積立金）を、政治家は「埋蔵金」と呼んでいる。

　accumulated total　累計額
◆The accumulated total of Japanese investment in China exceeds $30 billion. 日本の対中投資（対中直接投資）の累計額は、300億ドルを超えている。

accumulation　（名）蓄積, 増加, 累積, 積立て, 蓄財, 積み増し, 利殖, アキュムレーション
　accumulation fund　蓄積資金, 蓄積基金
　accumulation method　アキュムレーション法
　accumulation plan　積立プラン
　accumulation swap　アキュムレーション・スワップ
　accumulation trust　蓄財信託
　asset accumulation　資産蓄積, 年金保険
　asset accumulation product　年金商品, 貯蓄性商品
　capital accumulation　資本蓄積, 資本主義的蓄積（＝accumulation of capital）
　contractual accumulation　契約積立て
　debt accumulation　累積債務, 債務累積
　employee capital accumulation plan　従業員の資本蓄積プラン
　group asset accumulation　団体年金保険
　individual asset accumulation　個人年金保険
　international reserves accumulation　外貨準備高の増加
　property accumulation savings　財形貯蓄
　savings accumulation　貯蓄の増加
　voluntary accumulation　任意積立て
　voluntary accumulation plan　任意積立プラン

accumulative　（形）累積の, 累積的, 次第に増加する, 利殖を好む, 金を貯めたがる

accumulative deficit　累積赤字
accumulative desire　貯蓄心
accumulative dividend　累積配当, 未払い配当
accumulative investment　累積投資
accumulative rate　累積利率, 累積率
accumulative stock　配当積立額, 累積配当型株式
accumulator　(名)蓄財家
accuse　(動)告発する, 告訴する, 起訴する, 訴える, 非難する, 責める, 指摘する
◆A major credit guarantor company has been accused of concealing taxable income by the Tokyo Regional Taxation Bureau. 大手の信用保証会社が、東京国税局から課税所得隠しを指摘された。◆The former president of the company was accused of making false accounting reports in violation of the former Securities and Exchange Law. 同社元社長は、旧証券取引法に違反して虚偽の有価証券報告書を作成したとして起訴された。
achieve　(動)達成する, 実現する, 完了する, 獲得する, 確保する, もたらす　(=rack up)
achieve currency stabilization　通貨の安定を実現する
achieve high credit ratings　高格付けを達成する
achieve improved results　業績が改善する
achieve one's planned growth　成長目標を達成する
achieve profitability　黒字転換を果たす
achieve results　成果を出す
achieve solid results　堅実な結果を残す
achieve success　成功を収める
achieve the inflation target　インフレ目標を達成する
◆Officials of many leading companies encouraged employees to take action and achieve results. 多くの主要企業の経営者は、実行に移して成果を出すよう社員に求めた。
achieve a surplus　黒字化する
◆The first goal of Japan's fiscal reconstruction is for the central and local governments to achieve a surplus in their primary balances by fiscal 2019. 日本の財政再建の第一目標は、国と地方[地方自治体]の基礎的財政収支を、2019年度までに黒字化することだ。
achieve currency stabilization　通貨の安定を実現する
◆To fulfill its responsibilities as the nation's central bank, the Bank of Japan must achieve currency stabilization by availing itself of a range of measures, including stabilization of the exchange rate. 日本の中央銀行としての責任を果たすには、日本銀行は、為替相場の安定を含めて広範な手段を活用して通貨の安定を実現しなければならない。
achieve economic recovery　景気回復を実現する
◆Priority measures to achieve economic recovery are stopping deflation and mobilizing all possible fiscal measures, financial policies and taxation reforms. 景気回復を実現するための優先課題は、デフレ阻止と、可能な財政政策、金融政策や税制改革を総動員することだ。
achieve higher investment returns　一段と高い投資収益を得る
◆Investors must generally take higher investment risks in order to achieve higher investment returns. 投資家が一段と高い投資収益を得るには、一般に一段と高い投資リスクを取る必要がある。
achieve the targeted reduction　削減目標を達成する
◆Greece will not be able to achieve the targeted reduction in its fiscal deficits by 2012. ギリシャは、2012年まで財政赤字の削減目標を達成できないようだ。
acid test　厳しい検査, 最終的な厳しい考査, 厳しい試験, 酸性試験, 吟味, 厳しい試練, 試金石, 正念場　(=severe test)
◆All major banking groups now face the acid test of whether they can regain profitability this fiscal year. 大手銀行・金融グループは、すべて今期の収益力回復に向けて正念場を迎えている。
acid test ratio　当座比率, 酸性試験比率　(=quick ratio: 企業の短期的な支払い能力を示す財務指標の一つで、流動負債に対する当座資産(現金・預金、受取勘定、市場性有価証券などの合計額)の割合)
◆The acid test ratio refers to the ratio of a firm's liquid assets to current liabilities. 酸性試験比率とは、企業の流動負債に対する当座資産の割合のことを言う。
ACLI　全米保険業協会, アメリカ生命保険協会　(American Council of Life Insuranceの略)
ACMI　アジア金融市場育成イニシアチブ(Asian Capital Markets Initiativeの略)
acquire　(動)取得する, 購入する, 引き受ける, 買収する　(=buy, purchase)
acquire a company via a share swap　株式交換で会社を買収する
acquire the company's shares through a takeover bid　株式公開買付け(TOB)で同社株を取得する
acquired business　買収した事業, 非買収事業
acquired company　被買収会社, 被買収企業
　(=acquiree company, acquired firm)
use shares of the parent to acquire a Japanese company　親会社の株を用いて日本企業を買収する
year acquired　取得年度
◆A targeted company demanded a company trying to acquire its stocks to present a business plan. 買収の標的企業は、買収企業[標的企業の株式を取得しようとしている企業]に事業計画の提出を求めた。◆By the delisting of its stocks, the firm will not be able to repeat stock swaps to acquire other companies. 同社株の上場廃止により、同社は今後、株式交換を繰り返して企業を買収することはできなくなる。◆Following the tender offer, Oji Paper would acquire the remaining Hokuetsu shares through a share swap to turn it into a wholly owned subsidiary. 株式公開買付け(TOB)後に、王子製紙は、株式交換で残りの北越製紙の株を取得して北越製紙を完全子会社化する。◆Fuji Television Network Inc. acquired 36 percent of the outstanding shares in Nippon Broadcasting System Inc. through a takeover bid. フジテレビが、株式公開買付け(TOB)でニッポン放送の発行済み株式の36%を取得した。◆Olympus ostensibly paid about ¥70 billion in commissions to two investment advisers when the company acquired a British medical equipment maker for about ¥210 billion. オリンパスが英国の医療機器メーカーを約2,100億円で買収した際、同社は表向きには仲介手数料として約700億円を投資助言会社2社に支払った。◆Restricting an influx of capital prevents foreigners from acquiring domestic assets. 資本流入[資本輸入]の規制で、外国人は国内資産の購入が難しくなる。◆Ripplewood Holdings will use the fund to acquire Japan Telecom's shares from Japan Telecom Holdings Co., Japan Telecom's holding company. リップルウッド・ホールディングスは、その資金を使って、日本テレコムの持ち株会社「日本テレコム・ホールディングス」から日本テレコムの株式を取得する。◆Sumitomo Heavy Industries Ltd. offered to acquire Axcelis Technologies of U.S. for $544 million. 住友重機械工業は、米国のアクセリス・テクノロジー社を5億4,400万ドルで買収する提案を行った。◆The bank will acquire ¥100 billion in new shares and carry out a ¥50 billion debt-for-equity swap. 同行が、新株1,000億円を引き受けるほか、500億円分の債権(借り手にとっては債務)の株式化を実施する。◆The situation is that it is difficult to acquire more than 50 percent of shares in the firm. 今の状況では、同社株の50%超を取得するのは厳しい。
acquire a firm via a share swap　株式交換で会社を買収する

◆The company acquired six firms via a share swap in 2010. 同社は、2010年に株式交換で六つの会社を買収した。

acquire capital from the market　市場から資金を引き出す
　◆Declines in credit ratings will prevent businesses from acquiring capital from the market or financial institutions. 信用格付けが低下すると、企業は市場や金融機関から資金を引き出せなくなる。

acquire shares [stocks]　株式を取得する
　◆The government may acquire shares of TEPCO to increase its involvement in the firm's management. 東電の経営に対する国の関与を強めるため、国が東電株を取得する可能性もある。◆We acquired shares in the company. 当社は、同社の株式を取得しました。

acquired company　被買収会社, 被買収企業
　（=acquiree company）

acquiree　（名）被買収企業, 被取得企業

acquirer　（名）買収会社, 買収企業, 買収者, 取得者, 取得企業, 購入者, 買取り手
　corporate acquirer　企業買収者, 買収企業
　friendly acquirer　友好的買収者
　potential acquirer　買収者候補
　would-be acquirer　買収希望者, 買収側
　◆A foreign acquirer of a Japanese company is allowed to pay shareholders of the Japanese entity "merger consideration" in the form of cash and the parent company's shares. 日本企業を買収する外国企業は現在、「合併の対価」を、現金や親会社の株式の形で日本企業の株主に支払うことができる。
　◆A "white knight" is a friendly acquirer sought by the target of an unfriendly takeover. 「ホワイト・ナイト」とは、非友好的買収の標的企業が探し求める友好的買収者をいう。◆The would-be acquirer has no intention of taking part in the management of a company it aims to take over. 買収側［買収希望者］に、買収対象企業の経営に参加する意思はない。

acquisition　（名）取得, 購入, 買取り, 買付け, 買収, 企業取得, 企業買収, 事業買収
　acquisition and development　アクイジッション・アンド・ディベロプメント, A&D（買収により新技術や商圏を取り込み、成長戦略の武器にすること）
　acquisition bid　買収
　acquisition-date fair value　取得日の公正価値
　acquisition of business　企業買収, 企業取得, 事業の買収
　　（=business acquisition）
　acquisition offer　買収の申込み, 買収提案
　acquisition strategy　買収戦略
　acquisition talks　買収交渉
　add-on acquisition　アドオン型企業買収（既存事業を拡充するために行う企業買収）
　asset acquisition　資産買収
　bolt-on acquisition　製品ライン拡充のための買収
　business acquisition　企業買収
　cash-and-stock acquisition　現金交付・株式交換併用買収
　finance [fund] an acquisition　買収資金を調達する
　friendly acquisition　友好的買収
　hostile acquisition　敵対的買収
　international acquisition　海外企業買収
　major acquisition　大型買収
　make an acquisition　買収する, 買収を行う
　neutral acquisition　中立的買収
　policy acquisition　保険契約取得
　stock acquisition　株式取得, 株式購入
　　（=share acquisition）
　strategic acquisition　戦略的企業買収

◆MGM has been hunting for ways to grow larger, either through acquisitions or mergers, for the past two years. MGMはこの2年間、買収か合併による規模拡大の方策を模索してきた。◆Nippon Life Insurance Co. plans to raise ￥50 billion for acquisitions and to strengthen its capital base. 日本生命保険は、買収資金として500億円を調達して、同社の資本基盤も強化する方針だ。◆Nonmonetary balance sheet items and corresponding income statement items are translated at rates in effect at the time of acquisition. 貸借対照表の非貨幣性項目とこれに対応する損益計算書項目は、取得日の為替レートで換算されています。◆Olympus wrote off more than 75 percent of about 70 billion spent on the acquisitions of three domestic firms as impairment losses. オリンパスは、国内3社の買収に投じた約700億円の75%以上を、減耗損失として処理していた。◆Since April 30, 2009, in respect of the Corporation's capital stock, there has not been any direct or indirect redemption, purchase, or other acquisition of any such stock. 2009年4月30日以降、本会社の株式に関しては、当該株式の直接・間接の償還、買取りやその他の取得も一切行っていない。◆The murky acquisitions of several companies by the major precision equipment maker were intended to paper over losses on investments the company made. この大手精密機器メーカーによる不透明な企業買収のねらいは、同社が行った投資の損失隠しだった。◆We make an acquisition when that seems the most effective way to take advantage of a particular market opportunity to further our growth goals. 当社が企業を買収するのは、特定の市場機会をとらえて当社の成長目標をさらに推進する上で、それが最も効果的な方法であると思われるときです。

acquisition price　取得価格, 買付け価格, 取得原価, 買収価格, 買収額
　◆Olympus fired its president who had pointed out the integrity of the acquisition prices and commission fees. オリンパスは、買収額や買収手数料の適正性を指摘した社長を解任した。

acquisition proposal　買収提案
　（=acquisition offer）
　◆Panasonic Corp. will make a formal acquisition proposal to its biggest stockholders. パナソニック（旧松下電器産業）は、同社の大株主に正式に買収提案をする予定だ。

across-the-board　（形）一括の, 一律の, 全面的, 総括的, 全業種一律の, 全社的
　across-the-board compliance　法令・規則の全社的順守
　across-the-board cut　一括引下げ
　　（=across-the-board decrease）
　across-the-board cuts in social security spending　社会保障費の一律カット
　across-the-board drop　全面安, 一斉下落
　across-the-board increase　一括引上げ, 一律昇給, 一律賃上げ
　across-the-board selling　売り一色
　across-the-board tax cut　一律減税
　across-the-board wage hike　一律値上げ
　◆The city has ordered an across-the-board 10 percent cut on all items in next fiscal year's budget. 同市は、来年度予算の全項目一律10%カットを指示した。◆The company will push ahead with "across-the-board compliance" as its most urgent task. 同社は、社の最緊急課題として「法令・規則の全社的順守」を推進する。

across the board　（副）全面的に, 全般的に, 軒並み, 一括して, すべてに公平に
　appreciate across the board　全面高となる, 軒並み上昇する
　be down across the board　全面安となる
　fall across the board　全面安となる
　improve across the board　全面高となる

plunge across the board　全面安となる
retreat across the board　全面安となる
　（=fall across the board）
rise across the board　全面高となる, 軒並み上昇する
sell shares across the board　全銘柄にわたって株を売る
soar across the board　全面高となる
　（=go up across the board）
tumble across the board　全面安となる
widen across the board　全面的に拡大する
◆Affected by the New York sentiment, the Tokyo market was down across the board. ニューヨーク市場の地合いを受けて、東京市場は全面安となった。◆Investors sold shares across the board to lock in profits. 利益を確定するため、投資家が全銘柄にわたって株を売り進めた。◆On the Tokyo stock market and other Asian markets, stock prices plunged across the board. 東京株式市場や他のアジア市場などでも、軒並み株安となった。◆Shares of leading banks came under selling pressure across the board. 大手銀行株は、軒並み売られた［売り圧力がかかった］。◆The yields on government bonds of deficit-ridden countries including Greece have been rising across the board in Europe. 欧州では、ギリシャなど財政赤字国の国債利回りが、軒並み上昇している。◆Tokyo stocks appreciated across the board. 東京株[東京株式市場の株価]は、全面高となった。

across the curve　全般に, 全満期にわたって
　buy across the curve　満期を問わず買う
　lower rates across the yield curve　全満期に渡る利回りの低下

act　（動）行動する, 行動を起こす, 活動する, 役割を果たす, 役割をする, 作用する, 演じる, 振る舞う
　act for　～の代理を務める
　act in concert with　～に呼応する
　act on　～に効く, ～に作用する
　act quickly to put the matters right　事態を収拾するために素早く動く[行動する]
◆An improving trade deficit can act to boost the economy. 貿易赤字の改善は、景気浮揚の一因になる可能性がある。◆Europe is urged to act promptly to halt financial crisis. 欧州は、金融危機回避の早急な対策を迫られている。◆If Japan is acting weak in currency intervention, speculators will try to capitalize on that. 日本が為替介入に弱腰なら、投機筋に付け込まれることになる。

act　（名）行為, 行動, 法律, 条令, 制定法
　Act Against Unfair Competition　不正競争防止法
　act of bankruptcy　破産行為
　act of honor　（手形）参加引受
　act of indemnity　免責法
　act of insolvency　（銀行の）支払い不能状態を示す行為（手形の支払い拒絶や預金の払戻し拒否など）
　Bank Holding Company Act　銀行持ち株会社法
　Banking Act of 1993　1933年銀行法
　Bankruptcy Reform Act　連邦改正破産法, 連邦破産法
　Community Reinvestment Act　地域社会再投資法
　Consolidation Act　統合法
　Consumer Credit Protection Act　消費者信用保護法
　Currency and Banknotes Act　通貨および銀行券条例
　Depository Institution Act of 1982　1982年預金金融機関法
　Depository Institutions Deregulation and Monetary Control Act　金融制度改革法
　Electronic Fund Transfer Act　電子資金振替法
　Fair Credit Billing Act　公正信用請求法
　Federal Deposit Insurance Act　連邦預金保険法
　Financial Service Act　金融サービス法
　Investment Advisers Act　投資顧問法
　National Insurance Act　国民保険法
　Pension Reform Act　年金改革法
　Securities Act　証券法
　Securities Exchange Act　証券取引所法
　Securities Investor Protection Act　証券投資者保護法
　trust by act of law　法定信託
　Uniform Bills of Lading Act　統一船荷証券法
　Uniform Sales Act　統一売買法
◆Citigroup Private Bank repeatedly committed acts contrary to the public goods, such as the buying and selling trusts and securities that the division was not permitted to trade. シティバンクのプライベート・バンク部門は、取引が禁止されている信託や証券を売買するなど、公益に反する行為を繰り返していたという。

act as　～を務める, ～として働く, ～として行為する, ～の要因になる
　act as a go-between　仲介者としての役割を果たす
　act as co-manager　副幹事を務める
　act as financiers　資金を提供する
　act as lead manager　主幹事を務める
　act as sole manager　単独主幹事を務める
　act as the chairman of the arbitration panel　仲裁機関の議長を務める
◆A financial intermediary acts as a middleman between cash surplus units in the economy（savers）and deficit spending units（borrowers）. 金融仲介機関は、経済の資金余剰主体（貯蓄者）と資金不足主体（借り手）との間に立つ仲介者として機能している。◆We have received a number of proposals from investment banks who want to act as go-betweens between drug companies for mergers. 投資銀行からは、製薬会社の経営統合の仲介をしたい旨の提案が数多く来ている。

acting in concert　共同投資行為, 共同投資

action　（名）行動, 活動, 実行, 動き, 行政上の処分, 措置, 対応, 決議, 決定, 訴え, 訴訟, 裁判の判決, 行為, 作為, アクション
　additional action　追加措置
　administrative action　行政処分
　class action　集団訴訟, 集団代表訴訟
　concerted actions　協調行動
　countercyclical action　景気対策, 反景気循環的措置
　decisive action　断固たる措置, 断固とした措置
　derivative action　株主代表訴訟, 派生訴訟
　disciplinary actions　懲戒処分
　executive actions　行政措置
　legal action　訴訟, 法的手続き
　legislative [legislation] action　法的措置
　line of action　行動方針
　price action　値動き
　rating action　格付け見直し, 格付け変更
　safeguard action　緊急輸入制限措置
◆As joint actions, major industrial nations have taken such measures as further interest rate reductions, quantitative monetary relaxation to increase the money supply, the injection of public funds and increased public spending. 協調行動として、主要先進諸国は、さらなる金利の引下げ、通貨供給量を増やすための量的金融緩和や公的資金の注入、財政出動[公共支出の拡大]などの措置を取った。◆Europe promised the Group of 20 major economies to take concerted action to contain the financial crisis. 欧州は、結束して金融危機を封じ込めることを主要20か国・地域（G20）に公約した。◆Eurozone countries were so slow to take necessary actions that the sovereign debt crisis expanded. 欧州の必要な対応が後手に回ったために、ソブリン危機[政府債務危機]が拡大した。◆

If Hokuetsu Paper Mills decides to carry out the poison pill, Oji Paper Co. is likely to take legal actions against it. 北越製紙が買収防衛策を実施したら、王子製紙は法的措置を取る可能性が高い。◆Japanese banks failed to take quick actions to dispose of nonperforming loans following the bursting of the bubble economy. 邦銀は、バブル崩壊後の不良債権処理に迅速に対応しなかった。◆Speculators believe the government will not take any specific action to stem the yen's rise for the time being. 政府は当分、とくに円高阻止に動くようなことはない、と投機筋は踏んでいる。◆Speculators capitalized on the Bank of Japan's delay in taking action. 投機筋は、日銀の対応の遅れを突いた。◆The financial markets are calling for additional concerted actions of the G-7 leading economies. 金融市場は、先進7か国の一段の協調行動を求めている。◆The financial watchdog took an additional action of criminal complaint other than administrative punishment as the bank's operations were so malicious. 同行の業務運営の仕方があまりにも悪質なので、金融監視機関の金融庁は、行政処分のほかに刑事告発の追加措置を取った。◆The government could take further decisive actions, including an additional intervention. 政府は、追加介入を含めてさらに断固たる措置を取る可能性がある。◆The government will take decisive actions including intervention, if necessary. 政府は、必要な時には介入も含めて断固たる措置を取る方針だ。◆The rational actions for survival taken by individual companies herald a danger that could lead the Japanese economy into contracted equilibrium. 生き残りをかけて個々の企業が取っている合理的な行動が、日本経済を縮小均衡に導く危険性をはらんでいる。◆Victim firms have entered into talks to file a class action suit for compensation. 被害企業が、損害賠償に向けて集団訴訟のための協議を開始した。

activate (動)活性化する, 活発にする, 促進する, 作動させる, 起動させる, 活動させる, 行動させる, 実行に移す, 行使する, 戦時編成する, 戦闘配備する, 浄化する, 作動する, 始動する
   activate the domestic demand　内需を活性化する
   activate the facility　借入れを実行に移す
   activate the option　オプションを行使する
   ◆The key to activating domestic demand lies in Japan's savings ratio. 内需を活性化するカギは、日本の貯蓄率の活用にある。

activation (名)活性化, 促進, 作動, 始動, 就職活動活性化対策, 浄化, 放射化

active (形)活発な, 活動的な, 活況を呈している, 取引量の多い, 積極的な, 現役の, 現職の, 勤続中の, アクティブ
   active account　活動口座, 活動勘定
   active assets　活動資産, 生産活動資産, 生産資産, 生産資本
   active bad debt account　回収可能性のある不良資産
   active balance　黒字バランス
   active balance of payments　国際収支の黒字
   active bond　花形債券, 利付き公債
   active bond portfolio manager　積極運用を行う債券ポートフォリオ・マネージャー
   active buying　買い進み
   active capital　活動資本
   active circulation　（貨幣の）現在流通高, 銀行券流通高
   active debt　利付き貸付け, 能動的公債
   active deposit　流動預金, 活動預金
   active investor　能動的投資家
   active life fund　在職者基金
   active management　積極的運用［積極運用］, アクティブ運用, 積極的な経営陣
   active market　活発な市況［市場］, 活況市場, 好況市場, 好況市況, 好況
   active money　活動現金, 取引貨幣, 金融活発
   active partner　（合名会社（partnership）の）業務担当社員
   active plan participant　勤続中の［現役の］制度加入者
   active planning　実行計画, 活動計画
   active policy　積極方針
   active reserve　活動積立金
   active securities　花形証券, 人気証券
   active stock　人気株, 花形株
   （=active real share）
   active stock market　活発な株式市場, 株式市場の活況
   active trade balance　貿易収支の黒字
   active trading　活発な取引
   ◆Companies continue to be active in plant and equipment investment. 企業の設備投資が、引き続き活発だ。

activist shareholder　物言う株主
   ◆One who once was called a lucky adventurer among activist shareholders lost his fame due to his involvement in insider trading. かつては「物言う株主」の風雲児と呼ばれた男が、インサイダー取引に関与して名声を失った。

activity (名)活動, 動き, 働き, 活動範囲, 活動度, 操業, 事業, 業務, 業務活動, 取引, 活気, 活況, 景気, 好景気
   acquisition activities　企業買収活動
   activity data　景気指標
   arbitrage activity　裁定取引
   banking activities　銀行業務, 金融業務
   business activities　事業活動, 企業活動, 営業活動, 経営活動, 景気, 商況, 業況
   capital markets activities　資本市場事業
   core activities　中核事業, 主力事業
   （=core business, main activities）
   credit activities　与信業務, 信用事業
   cyclical activities　景気循環型事業
   derivatives activities　派生商品事業, 派生商品取引
   economic activity　経済活動, 景気, 経済動向
   falling activity　景気低迷, 景気減速
   financial activity　資金調達活動, 財務活動
   financial arbitrage activity　財テク
   financing activities　財務活動, 資金調達活動, 金融活動, 資金調達と返済に関する活動
   fund procurement activities　資金調達活動
   global activity　世界の景気
   hedging activities　ヘッジ取引, ヘッジ操作
   illicit activity　違法行為
   indexes of industry's activities　産業活動指数
   individual activity report　個別業務報告［報告書］
   industrial activity　製造業の景気, 産業活動
   international activities　国際事業
   investing activities　投資活動
   investment banking activities　投資銀行業務
   leasing activities　リース事業
   lending activities　貸出業務, 貸付け業務
   loss-making activities　赤字事業
   main activities　主力事業
   manufacturing activity　製造業の景気
   nonbanking activities　非銀行業務
   off-balance sheet activity　オフ・バランス取引
   operating activities　営業活動
   pick-up in activity　景気回復
   primary activity　起債活動
   principal areas of activity　中核事業
   private activity bond　民間事業債

profit or loss from [on] ordinary activities　経常損益
purchasing managers' index on industrial activity　全米購買部協会景気総合指数
rating activity　格付け変動
real estate activity　不動産市場
securities activities　証券業務
securities-related activities　証券関連業務
statement of activity　営業報告書, 活動報告書
statement of financial activity　財務活動計算書
trading activities　業務展開
trends in activity　景気動向
weakness in activity　景気低迷, 景気の減速

◆Companies have restarted fund procurement activities for a recovery in production as the bond market turbulence after the March 11 earthquake and tsunami has subsided. 東日本大震災後の債券市場の混乱が収束したので、企業各社は生産回復に向けて資金調達活動を再開した。◆Domestic megabanks are increasing their financing activities overseas. 国内メガバンクは、海外での融資活動を強化している。◆Due to an increase in the purchase of marketable securities, net cash used for investing activities increased by $5 million from the same period last year. 市場性ある有価証券の購入量が増えたため、投資活動に使用した純キャッシュは、前年同期比で500万ドル増加しました。◆Economic activity strengthened in most of U.S. regions with the exception of St. Louis where plans to close several plants were announced, the U.S. FRB said. 米連邦準備制度理事会(FRB)は、(全12地区連銀のうち)一部の工場閉鎖計画を発表したセントルイスを除く11地区で景気が好転している、と述べた。◆Falling activity in the biggest economies of the eurozone could lead to a technical recession. ユーロ圏最大の経済国(ドイツやフランス、イギリス)の景気低迷[景気減速]は、定義上の景気後退[2四半期連続のマイナス成長]につながる可能性がある。◆Goldman Sachs was subpoenaed over its activities leading up to the financial crisis. ゴールドマン・サックスは、金融危機を招いた[引き起こした]同社の証券業務の件で、召喚された。◆Laws already in place on narcotics and organized crime oblige financial institutions to report to the FSA any deals possibly linked to profits from criminal activities. すでに実施されている麻薬や組織的犯罪に関する法律は、犯罪収益絡みと思われる取引について、金融庁への報告(届出)を金融機関に義務付けている。◆Much of the financing activity shown on our statement of cash flows relates to these refinancing activities. 当社のキャッシュ・フロー計算書に示した資金調達活動の大半は、これら負債の借換え関連です。◆Our business activities and results could be significantly affected by the policies of foreign governments and prevailing social and economic conditions. 当社の事業活動と営業成績は、各国政府の政策や社会経済情勢の影響を強く受ける可能性があります。◆The capital increase is designed to secure financial resources for the expansion of the bank's investment banking activities abroad. 同行の増資の目的は、海外での投資銀行業務拡大の資金確保にある。◆The chairman of the company masterminded the firm's illegal fund-raising activities. 同社の会長が、同社の不正な資金集め活動を主導していた。◆The government plans to translate laws such as the Civil Code and the Commercial Code into English in a bid to facilitate foreign investments and help domestic firms expand their international business activities. 政府は、外国からの投資促進や国内企業の国際ビジネス支援のため、民法や商法などの法律の英訳を行う方針だ。◆The TSE and four other exchanges extended their morning trading sessions by 30 minutes to boost market activity. 東証など5証券取引所が、取引活性化のため午前の取引時間を30分間延長した。◆The U.S. government froze the assets of four individuals and eight entities that were involved in illicit activities such as money laundering, currency counterfeiting and narcotics trafficking. 米政府は、資金洗浄(マネー・ロンダリング)や通貨偽造、麻薬取引などの違法行為に関与している4個人、8団体の資産を凍結した。◆This amount of cash was provided by business activities. この現金額は、営業活動で得られたものだ。

actual　(形)実際の, 実地の, 現実的, 現実の, 実質的, 事実上の, 現行の
actual achievement　実績
actual balance　直物持ち高
actual credit performance　実際の信用成績
actual deposits　実質預金
actual exchange rate　直物レート
actual inflation　実際のインフレ率
actual interest rate　実効金利
actual investment　実際の運用
actual losses　実際の損失額, 実損
actual margin　実効証拠金率
actual market　顕在市場
actual money rate　実際の金利
actual position　現物[直物]為替持ち高
actual rate of interest　実際金利, 実質利子率 (=actual interest rate)
actual return on plan assets　実際年金運用収益

actual demand　実需
◆Service charges or tax on crude oil futures trading should be raised to curb the inflow of speculative money not related to actual demand. 実需に関係ない投機マネーの流入を抑えるため、原油先物取引の手数料の引上げや課税強化をすべきだ。◆The flow of speculative money into the oil market did not reflect actual demand. 投機マネーの原油市場への流入は、実需を反映していなかった[実需に基づくものではなかった]。

actual losses　実際の損失額
◆The taxes banks pay in writing off their nonperforming loans are refunded to banks after the amount of the actual losses is determined. 銀行が不良債権処理の際に納める税金は、実際の損失額が確定した後、銀行に戻ってくる。

actual value　実際の価格, 実価, 実際値, 実質価値, 実績値
◆Under the current earthquake insurance system, insurance payments remain capped at half the actual value of a home and its contents. 現行の地震保険[地震保険制度]では、保険金の支払い額の上限は、住宅や家財の実質価値の半額までとなっている。

actuals　(名)現物商品

actuarial　(形)年金数理計算上の, 年金数理上の, 保険数理上の
actuarial asset value　保険数理による資産価値
actuarial clause　保険数理条項
actuarial cost method　保険数理原価法, 保険数理による原価計算法, 年金数理計算方式
actuarial gains and [or] losses　保険数理上の損益, 年金数理上の誤差, 数理計算上の差異(年金基金の運用時に生じる見積り額と実際額との差額)
actuarial liability　保険数理上の債務
actuarial measurement of pension cost and obligation　年金費用および年金債務額の統計的手法による測定
actuarial method　年金数理法, 保険数理法
actuarial reserve　数理的準備金
actuarial risk　保険数理上のリスク
actuarial valuation　保険数理評価, 保険数理価値
actuarial valuation method　保険数理上の評価方法

actuarial assumption　年金数理計算上の仮定, 保険数理上の仮定, 保険数理上の計算基礎, 年金数理計算上の基礎率

◆Pension cost in 2008 was lower than in 2007 principally due to actuarial assumption changes in the U.S. and several non-U.S. plans. 2008年度の年金費用は、主に米国内制度と一部の米国外制度の年金数理上の仮定の変更により、前年度より減少しました。

actuarial present value　年金数理上の現在価値, 保険数理上の現在価値
 actuarial present value of plan assets　制度資産の保険数理上の現在価値
 actuarial present value of the accrued plan benefits　年金給付債務額の年金数理現価
 assumed rates of return used in determining the actuarial present values　保険数理上の現在価値測定に用いられた仮定割引率
 ◆The actuarial present value of the accrued plan benefits and the net assets available to discharge these benefits at December 31 are as follows: 12月31日現在の年金給付債務額の年金数理現価と年金給付債務に充当可能な年金純資産は、以下のとおりです。

actuarially computed value　保険数理上の計算価値

actuary　（名）保険数理士, 保険計理士, 保険数理専門家, 年金数理人, アクチュアリー
 ◆An actuary applies the theory of probability to the business of insurance and is responsible for the calculation of premiums, policy reserves and other values. 保険数理士は、保険業に確率論を適用して、保険料、保険契約準備金やその他の価値を計算するのが仕事だ。

ACU　アジア通貨単位, アキュ（Asian currency unitの略）

A/D [a/d]　振出日後

ADB　アジア開発銀行（Asian Development Bankの略）
 ◆The ADB lowered its 2011 growth forecast in Asian nations due to growing worries about weak demand from key trading partners including the United States and Europe. アジア開発銀行（ADB）は、主要貿易相手国である欧米での需要減退懸念が高まっていることから、アジアの2011年の成長見通し［GDP成長率見通し］を下方修正した。

add　（動）加える, 追加する, 加算する, 合計する, 付加する, 付け加える, 増す, 強化する, 高める, 押し上げる
 add back to　～に振り戻す
 add in　～を算入する, ～を含める, ～を加える
 add on　付け足す, 加える, 追加する, 建て増す, 増築する
 add synergy　相乗効果を高める
 add to　～を増す, ～を増大させる, ～を高める, ～を強める
 add up　～を考慮する
 add up to　合計して～になる, 結局～になる, 押し上げる
 add value to　～の付加価値を高める
 to add to　～に加えて
 ◆For the computation of the earnings per share, assuming full dilution, dividends on convertible preferred shares have been added back to income. 完全希薄化を仮定した場合の1株当たり利益の算定では、転換可能優先株式［転換優先株］に対する配当は、利益に振り戻してあります。◆In the case of au Insurance's cell phone-based policy sales, policyholders are allowed to pay premiums by adding them to monthly mobile charges. au損害保険の携帯電話での保険販売の場合、保険契約者は、保険料を携帯利用の月額に加算して保険料の支払いをすることができる。◆That eurozone GDP shrank in the second quarter as well would add up to two consecutive quarters of negative growth-a definition of a technical recession. ユーロ圏のGDP（域内総生産）が第2四半期も低下したことで、ユーロ圏は2四半期連続のマイナス成長（定義上、テクニカル・リセッション）となった。◆The company pioneered a variety of innovative promotions to add new accounts. 同社は、各種の斬新な販促活動によって、新口座［新規顧客］を増やした。◆

The drastic overhaul of the Japanese accounting system is expected to add a massive administrative burden to companies. 日本の会計基準の抜本的変更は、企業にとって大幅な事務負担の増加を強いられることになる。◆Weak U.S. jobs data added to speculation that the U.S. Federal Reserve may implement further monetary easing. 米国の雇用統計の悪化で、連邦準備制度理事会（FRB）による追加の金融緩和策実施の観測が高まった［連邦準備制度理事会（FRB）が追加の金融緩和に踏み切るとの観測が強まった］。

addition　（名）追加, 追加投資, 付加, 加算, 増築, 増設, 増加, 拡大
 addition to reserves　積立金繰入れ
 additions and betterments［improvements］reserves　増改築積立金, 増設改良積立金
 additions or alterations　追加・変更
 additions to long-term debt　長期債務の増加
 capital additions　追加資本, 追加投資, 追加設備投資
 ◆We had lower depreciation expense because we reduced plant additions. 工場の増設を手控えたため、減価償却費は低下しました。

additional　（形）追加的な, 付加的な, 特別の
 additional assessment　追徴金
 additional budget　追加予算, 補正予算
 additional capex　設備投資の追加
 additional charge　追加料金, 追加費用, 割増料金
 additional easing　一層の金融緩和, 追加金融緩和（=additional monetary easing）
 additional equity capital　増資（=additional equity）
 additional minimum liability　追加最小負債
 additional monetary easing measure　追加金融緩和策
 additional paid-in capital　株式払込み剰余金, 払込み資本剰余金, 資本剰余金, 払込み剰余金, 付加的払込み資本, 追加払込み資本（=capital surplus）
 additional shares　追加株式, 増資株, 増資, 株式数の増加
 additional tax penalty　追徴税額
 additional taxation　追徴課税
 additional working capital　追加的運転資金
 ◆Major European banks are to take additional stress tests to examine their ability to withstand a long recession. 景気の長期低迷への耐久力を調べるため、欧州の主要銀行は再度、ストレス・テストを受けることになっている。◆The federal government will invest an additional $30 billion into GM. 米政府は、GMに300億ドルの追加融資［追加投資］を行う。

additional action　追加措置
 ◆The financial watchdog took an additional action of criminal complaint other than administrative punishment as the bank's operations were so malicious. 同行の業務運営の仕方があまりにも悪質なので、金融監視機関の金融庁は、行政処分のほかに刑事告発の追加措置を取った。

additional bailout　追加支援
 ◆Greece urgently needed an additional bailout. ギリシャは、早急に追加支援を必要とした。

additional benefits　追加給付金, 追加保障
 additional benefits insured　付加給付金額
 additional benefits under the policy　元受契約追加保障額
 additional death benefits　追加死亡保障

additional capital　追加資本, 増加資本, 資本上積み, 資本の積み増し
 ◆As in the past, the Corporation and its subsidiaries raised additional capital during this year's first half. 従来どおり、当社と子会社は当上半期も追加資本を調達しました。◆Major financial institutions are forced to hold additional capital so that they can better absorb losses during financial crises. 金融危機の際の損失吸収力を高めるため、大手金融機関は、資本

［自己資本］の積み増しを迫られている。◆The three Japanese biggest banks are likely to be required to hold additional capital of 1 percent to 1.5 percent. 日本の3メガ銀行は、1～1.5%の資本［自己資本］上積みを求められる見込みだ。

additional capital injection　追加出資
◆Shinginko Tokyo asked the metropolitan government for an additional capital injection of ¥40 billion. 新銀行東京は、都に400億円の追加出資を要請した。

additional concerted actions　一段の協調行動
◆The financial markets are calling for additional concerted actions of the G-7 leading economies. 金融市場は、先進7か国の一段の協調行動を求めている。

additional contribution　追加拠出
◆The government pledged an additional contribution of ¥7.08 billion to the Japan Fund for Poverty Reduction set up within the Asian Development Bank. 政府は、アジア開発銀行（ADB）内に設立されたADBの「貧困削減日本基金」に対して、70億8,000万円の追加拠出を公約した。

additional credit easing steps　金融緩和の追加措置
◆Behind the improvement in economic sentiment is a series of measures taken to date, including the government's antideflation package and the Bank of Japan's additional credit easing steps. 景況感好転の理由として、政府のデフレ対策や日銀の金融緩和の追加措置など、これまでにとられた一連の措置が挙げられる。

additional easing measures　追加の金融緩和策, 追加緩和策, 一層の［一段の］緩和策
（＝further easing measures）
◆Any additional easing measures would only have a limited impact if they were made at the urging of financial markets. 市場に催促される形で追加緩和を行っても、追加緩和策の効果は限定的に過ぎない。

additional easing steps　追加緩和策, 追加の金融緩和策, 一段の［一層の］緩和策
◆Prime Minister Naoto Kan tacitly demanded the BOJ come up with additional easing steps as early as possible. 菅首相は、早期に追加の緩和策に踏み切るよう日銀に暗に求めた。

additional financial assistance　追加金融支援
◆The additional financial assistance to the Nuclear Damage Liability Facilitation Fund is to be used by the fund to purchase TEPCO's corporate bonds. 原子力損害賠償支援機構に対する追加金融支援は、同機構による東電の社債買取りなどに活用される。

additional financial sanctions　追加金融制裁
◆The U.S. government has imposed additional financial sanctions on North Korea. 米政府は、北朝鮮に対する追加金融制裁を発動した。

additional fund　追加資金
◆MMC had to spend the additional fund collected through the capital increase on debt repayment. 三菱自動車は、増資で集めた追加資金を債務返済に充てざるを得なかった。

additional interest rate cut　追加利下げ
◆The ECB is considering an additional interest rate cut to support the European economy. 欧州中央銀行（ECB）は、欧州景気下支えのため、追加利下げを検討している。

additional intervention　追加介入
◆The government could take further decisive actions, including an additional intervention. 政府は、追加介入を含めてさらに断固たる措置を取る可能性がある。

additional investment　追加投資, 新規投資, 追加出資, 新規出資
◆The company will increase its capital by ¥50 billion with additional investment of ¥10 billion from the IRC and with the debt-for-equity swap. 同社は、産業再生機構による100億円の追加［新規］出資と債務の株式化で、500億円増資する。◆The principal requirement for funds is for capital expenditures and to acquire new and additional investments. 資金需要は、主に資本的支出と新規および追加投資を行うにあたって発生します。

additional loan　追加融資, 新たな融資
seek additional loans　追加融資を受ける
◆Failed companies find it difficult to secure additional loans from commercial banks. 経営破たんした企業は、都市銀行から追加融資を確保するのは難しくなっている。

additional monetary ease　追加の金融緩和, 追加金融緩和
◆The latest additional monetary ease put a downward pressure on interest rates. 今回の追加の金融緩和で、金利は低下した。

additional monetary easing　追加金融緩和, 追加金融緩和策（＝further monetary easing）
◆To alleviate the influence of the U.S. government's additional monetary easing, the Bank of Japan must adopt a more proactive stance toward monetary relaxation. 米政府の追加金融緩和策の影響を和らげるには、日銀も金融緩和の姿勢を強める必要がある。

additional monetary easing measures　追加の金融緩和策, 追加金融緩和策, 一層の金融緩和［金融緩和策］
◆Pressure for additional monetary easing measures will increase if the slowdown of the world economy continues. 世界的な景気減速がこのまま続けば、一層の金融緩和［金融緩和策］を求める圧力が強まるものと思われる。◆The Bank of Japan is considering taking additional monetary easing measures ahead of the next Monetary Policy Meeting. 次回の金融政策決定会合に向けて、日銀は現在、追加金融緩和策の実施を検討している。

additional monetary easing policy　追加の金融緩和策, 追加金融緩和策, 一層の金融緩和
◆By conducting additional monetary easing policy, the Fed attempts to preemptively contain growing deflationary concerns in the United States. 追加金融緩和策を実施して、米連邦準備制度理事会（FRB）は、米国で高まるデフレ懸念に先手を打とうとしている。

additional monetary easing steps　追加の金融緩和策, 追加の金融緩和
◆The BOJ was boxed into a corner by financial markets and the government desperate for additional monetary easing steps. 日銀は、追加の金融緩和策を強く求める金融市場と政府に追い込まれた。◆The BOJ's additional monetary easing steps include an increase in the amount of funds to purchase government bonds and corporate debentures. 日銀の追加金融緩和には、国債や社債などを買い入れる基金の増額が含まれている。◆The BOJ's policy meeting is expected to consider taking additional monetary easing steps. 日銀の政策決定会合では、追加の金融緩和策の実施を検討する見通しだ。

additional monetary relaxation measures　追加の金融緩和策, 追加の金融緩和
◆The BOJ could take additional monetary relaxation measures if there are any changes in the financial situation. 金融面で動きがあるとすれば、日銀が追加の金融緩和策を実施する可能性もある。

additional money easing　追加の金融緩和
◆The U.S. Federal Reserve Board decided to effectively conduct additional money easing after significantly lowering its forecast for the U.S. economy. 米連邦準備制度理事会（FRB）は、米景気判断を大幅に引き下げて［下方修正して］、事実上の追加金融緩和策の実施を決めた。

additional pump-priming measures　追加景気対策
◆Additional pump-priming measures through strengthening cooperation between advanced countries and emerging economies will be a major subject of discussion at the financial summit meeting in Washington. 先進国と新興国の連携強化による追加景気対策の検討が、ワシントンで開かれる金融サミットで検討される主要テーマとなる。

additional quantitative easing measures　新たな量的緩和策, 追加の量的緩和策
◆The Bank of Japan decided to adopt additional quantitative easing measures in October 2010, setting up a fund to purchase government and corporate bonds. 日銀は、2010年10月に新たな量的緩和策の導入を決め、国債や社債を買い入れる基金を新設した。

additional steps　追加措置
◆To alleviate the influence of the U.S. government's additional steps to ease the supply of money, the Bank of Japan must adopt a more proactive stance toward monetary relaxation. 米政府の追加金融緩和策[通貨供給量を増やす米政府の追加措置]の影響を和らげるには、日銀も金融緩和の姿勢を強める必要がある。

additional taxation　追徴課税
◆An additional taxation of about ￥500 million was imposed on the group. 同グループに、約5億円の追徴課税が課された。

additional taxes　追徴税, 加算税, 増税
◆The Tokyo Regional Taxation Bureau did not impose additional taxes because the company fell into the red. 同社が赤字だったため、東京国税局は追徴税を課さなかった。

add-on　(名)追加, 付属品, 付加装置, アタッチメント, (法案などの)追加条項, アドオン
　add-on equipment　追加機器, 付属機器, 付属設備, アタッチメント
　add-on rate　アドオン金利(当初元本に基づいて利息を計算)
　add-on software　アドオン・ソフト (=add-in software: 既存のアプリケーション・ソフトに組み込んで、さらに別の機能を加えることができるユーティリティ・ソフト)
◆These pork-barrel add-ons will further deplete the United States' coffers. 議員の人気取りが目的のこれら法案の追加条項は、米国の財政を一段と疲弊させることになる。

address　(動)取り組む, 取り扱う, 処理する, 対応する, 対処する, 応対する, 調整する, 提出する, 話しかける, 呼びかける, 演説[講演]する, 声明を発表する, ~にあて名を書く, (注意などを)~に向ける[注ぐ], 申し込む, 委託する, 託送する, 請願[嘆願]する, ~の解任請求をする
　address a warning to　~に警告を発する
　address market risk　市場リスクに対応する
　address the conference　会議の出席者に講演を行う
　address the consumption tax issue　消費税問題に取り組む
　address the yen's strength　円高に取り組む
　(⇒demonstrate)
◆Heightened tensions and significant downward risks for the global economy must be addressed decisively. 世界経済の緊張の高まりと重大な下方リスクに、断固として対処しなければならない。◆The Bank of Japan demonstrated its resolve to address the yen's strength. 日銀は、円高に取り組む決意を明確に示した。◆U.S. President Barack Obama addressed reforming Wall Street in his first State of the Union address. オバマ米大統領は、同大統領初の一般教書演説で、ウォール街(金融街)の改革を呼びかけた[打ち出した]。

adequacy　(名)充実, 充実度, 妥当性, 適切性, 適正, 適応性　(⇒capital adequacy ratio)
　adequacy of disclosure　開示の適切性
　BIS capital adequacy standards　BIS(国際決済銀行)の自己資本比率基準
　capital adequacy　資本充実度, 自己資本の充実, 資本要件, 自己資本比率
　loan loss reserve adequacy　貸倒れ準備金の適切性
◆The capital adequacy ratio is used to determine the financial health of financial institutions. 自己資本比率は、金融機関の経営の健全性[財務の健全性]を判断するのに用いられる。

adequate　(形)適切な, 適正な, 十分な, 相当な
　adequate amount　適正量
　adequate cause　十分な理由, 相当な理由
　adequate disclosure　適切な開示, 適正な開示
　adequate gold and foreign exchange reserves　適正外貨準備高
　adequate liquidity　適正流動性
　adequate protection　十分な補償
　submit an adequate financial report　適切な財務報告書を提出する
◆These disciplinary measures include increased penalties on securities fraud and a newly installed penalty on corporate directors in cases of failure to submit adequate financial reports to authorities. これらの懲戒処分には、証券詐欺に対する罰則の強化や、当局に適切な財務報告をしなかった場合の企業取締役に対する罰則の新設などが含まれている。

adjust　(動)修正する, 調整する, 調節する, 是正する, 補正する, 織り込む
　adjust the payout ratio　配当性向を調整する
　adjust to the rise in inflation　インフレ率上昇率を織り込む
　adjust trade balance　貿易不均衡を是正する
　adjusted current earnings　調整後当期利益, ACE
　adjusted debit balance　信用取引融資残高
　adjusted earnings per share　調整後1株当たり利益
　adjusted for inflation and taxes　インフレと税金修正後の
　be adjusted downward　下方修正される
　in seasonally adjusted dollar terms　季節調整済みのドル表示額で
　in seasonally adjusted GDP　季節調整済みGDPの
　not seasonally adjusted　季節調整前の
　risk-adjusted yield [returns]　リスク調整後の利回り
　seasonally adjusted annual rate　季節調整済み年率
　the value of assets adjusted to market　時価に修正した資産価額
◆All references to shares outstanding, dividends and per share amounts have been adjusted on a retroactive basis. 発行済み株式数と配当、1株当たりの金額については、すべて過去に遡及して調整してあります。◆Japan and European countries should keep trying to adjust trade imbalances with the United States. 日欧は、対米貿易不均衡を是正する努力を続ける必要がある。◆Through continuing gains in annual earnings, it will be possible, over time, to adjust the payout ratio while still maintaining our dividend record. 年間利益の増大を続けることによって、当社の配当実績を今後とも維持しながら、時期が来たら配当性向を調整することは可能である。◆We recognized a $80 million benefit from adjusting our deferred tax assets for the new tax rate. 新税率を適用して当社の繰延べ税金資産を調整した結果、8,000万ドルの利益を認識しました。

adjustable　(形)調整可能な, 調節可能な, 伸縮的
　adjustable life insurance　調整生命保険, アジャスタブル保険(契約者のニーズに応じて保険金額や保険料額を変更できる生命保険のこと)
　adjustable peg　調整可能な固定為替相場制度, アジャスタブル・ペッグ
　adjustable rate convertible note　変動利付き転換社債, ARCN
◆In an attempt to get on the bandwagon, many people are shifting their fixed rate mortgages to adjustable rate ones. 時流に乗ろうとして、固定金利型住宅ローンを変動金利型住宅ローンに変更する人が多い。

adjustable rate mortgage　変動金利型抵当貸付け, 変動型金利[変動金利型]の住宅ローン, 変動金利モーゲー

ジ, 変動利付きモーゲージ, ARM
◆If the Bank of Japan's interest rate takes an upward turn, an adjustable rate mortgage would weigh more heavily on borrowers than would the fixed-rate type. 日銀の政策金利が上昇に転じた場合、固定金利型の住宅ローンと比べて変動金利型のほうが、ローン利用者［借り手］の負担が重くなる。◆There has been a sharp increase in the number of people taking out adjustable rate mortgages against the backdrop of the Bank of Japan's ultralow interest rate policy. 日本銀行の超低金利政策を背景に、変動金利型住宅ローンの利用者が急増している。

adjustable-rate mortgage interest rates 変動型金利の住宅ローン金利
◆Adjustable-rate mortgage interest rates are reviewed every six months. 変動型金利の住宅ローンの金利は、半年ごとに見直される。

adjustable types of home loans 変動金利型の住宅ローン, 金利変動型の住宅ローン
◆Adjustable types of home loans will continue to be popular as long as interest rates are expected to remain low. 金利の先安感が強い間は、（金利）変動型の住宅ローンの人気が続くようだ。

adjustment （名）調整, 修正, 照合, 整理, 査定, 精算, 期末整理, 決算整理
 adjustment bond　整理社債
 adjustment for fractional differences　四捨五入による調整
 adjustment for taxable income　税務調整, 申告調整
 adjustment inflation　調整インフレ
 adjustment of financial statements of prior periods　過年度の財務諸表修正
 backlog adjustment　遡及修正
 　（＝catch-up adjustment）
 capital adjustment　資本修正
 closing adjustment　決算整理, 決算整理事項
 　（＝close adjustment）
 currency translation adjustment　外貨換算調整勘定
 downward adjustment　下方修正, 減額修正, 下方調整
 exchange rate adjustment　為替レートの調整
 loss adjustment expense　損害査定費
 prior period adjustment　過年度修正, 過年度損益修正, 前期損益修正
 quarter-point adjustment　0.25％の調整
 seasonal adjustment　季節調整
 structural adjustment　構造調整
 upward adjustment　上方修正, 増額修正
◆A stronger yen will compel the Japanese economy to undergo severe structural adjustment. 円高は、日本経済に厳しい構造調整を求めることになる。◆The latest rate increase marked the 15th consecutive quarter-point adjustment since June 2004. 今回の利上げで、2004年6月から15回連続0.25％の調整となった。

administration （名）経営, 経営管理, 経営陣, 理事会, 執行部, 管理, 運営, 運用, 統括, 監督, 事務, 事務管理, 業務, 執行, 執務, 実行, 実施, 政権, 政府, 行政, 政府部局, 行政当局, 政権運営, 政権担当期間, 任期, 投薬, 投与, 治療
 （⇒credit rater, oversight, positive impact）
 administration process　社内手続き, 事務手続き
 business administration　企業経営, 商工経営, 経営管理, 経営学　（＝business management）
 capital and administration　資本と経営
 financial administration　財務管理, 財政, 金融行政
 personnel administration　人事管理
 policy administration　政策運営
 the Farmers Home Administration　農業住宅局
 the Federal Housing Administration　米連邦住宅局
 wage administration　賃金管理
◆Financial administration should have been handled with prudence. 金融行政は、慎重を期さなければならない。◆Market confidence in the Silvio Berlusconi administration's fiscal rehabilitation measures is virtually nonexistent as the administration is on its last legs. イタリアのベルルスコーニ政権が機能不全に陥っているため、同政権の財政再建策に対する市場の信認は事実上、失墜している。◆Operation Twist was conceived by President John F. Kennedy's administration during 1960s. オペレーション・ツイストを発案したのは、1960年代のジョン・F・ケネディ（第35代米大統領）政権だ。◆The administration of U.S. President Barack Obama proposed the stringent financial regulations. 米オバマ政権は、金融規制の強化を打ち出した。◆The Obama administration failed to cut federal spending. オバマ政権は、連邦支出を削減しなかった。◆The U.S. administration will spend up to $700 billion to buy up soured mortgage-related securities and other devalued assets held by ailing financial institutions. 米政府は、経営不振の金融機関が保有するモーゲージ関連の不良証券などの不良資産を、最大7,000億ドル投入して買い取る方針だ。◆We see no hint of an administration attempt to lift the nation's economy out of its deflationary trend. 日本経済のデフレ脱却へ向けての政権の決意が、まったく見えてこない。

administration of shares　株式事務
◆Since July 1971, all newly listed companies must consign the administration of their shares to third parties, such as trust banks. 1971年7月以降、新規上場企業はすべて株式事務を信託銀行などの第三者に委託しなければならない。

administrative burden　事務負担
◆The drastic overhaul of the Japanese accounting system is expected to add a massive administrative burden to companies. 日本の会計基準の抜本的変更は、企業にとって大幅な事務負担の増加を強いられることになる。

administrative order　行政命令
◆The FSA will require directors at banks that receive the administrative order to increase earnings to step down if they again fail to meet earnings goals. 金融庁は、業務改善（収益改善）の行政命令を受ける銀行が収益目標（収益計画）を達成できない場合には、銀行トップの退陣を求める方針だ。

administrative punishment　行政処分
◆The financial watchdog took an additional action of criminal complaint other than administrative punishment as the bank's operations were so malicious. 同行の業務運営の仕方があまりにも悪質なので、金融監視機関の金融庁は、行政処分のほかに刑事告発の追加措置を取った。

administrator　管財人, 金融整理管財人, 遺産管理人, 管理人
 bankruptcy administrator　破産管財人, 金融整理管財人
 　（＝administrator in bankruptcy）
 plan administrator　年金制度管理者
◆The FSA appointed three administrators to take charge of the failed bank's administration, operations and asset management. 金融庁は、破たんした銀行の経営、業務と資産の管理に当たる金融整理管財人3名を指名した。

adopt　（動）採用する, 採択する, 選出する, 指名する
◆After a two day meeting in Paris, the financial chiefs and central bank governors from the Group of 20 leading economies adopted a communique. パリで開かれた2日間の会議の後、主要20か国・地域（G20）の財務相・中央銀行総裁は共同声明を採択した。◆The Bank of Japan decided to adopt additional quantitative easing measures in October 2010, setting up a fund to purchase government and corporate bonds. 日銀は、2010年10月に新たな量的緩和策の導入を決め、国債や社債を買い入れる基金を新設した。◆The BOJ's total assets at

the end of August 2011 increased to ¥141 trillion from ¥79 trillion as of the end of March 1999 when its zero-interest rate policy was first adopted. 日銀の2011年8月末時点の総資産は、ゼロ金利政策を初めて導入した1999年3月末現在の79兆円から141兆円に増えた。◆The IFRSs are based on mark-to-market accounting and was adopted by the London based International Accounting Standards Board. 国際財務報告基準（IFRSs）は、時価会計をベースとし、ロンドンに本部を置く国際会計基準審議会（IASB）によって採択された。◆The special statement on the world economy adopted by the APEC forum specified a timeline for implementing the measures. アジア太平洋経済協力会議（APEC）で採択された世界経済に関する特別声明は、その対策実施の期限を明記した。◆To alleviate the influence of the U.S. government's additional steps to ease the supply of money, the Bank of Japan must adopt a more proactive stance toward monetary relaxation. 米政府の追加金融緩和策[通貨供給量を増やす米政府の追加措置]の影響を和らげるには、日銀も金融緩和の姿勢を強める必要がある。

ADR 米国預託証券（American depositary [depository] receiptsの略）

ADR 裁判外紛争解決手続き, 事業再生ADR（alternative dispute resolutionの略）
◆ADR has been adopted for the revitalization of Aiful, a consumer loan firm, and Willcom Inc., the nation's largest mobile service provider of personal handy phones. 事業再生ADRはこれまで、消費者金融のアイフルやPHS（簡易型携帯電話）国内最大手のウィルコムなどの企業再生で採用されている。

ADR for the revitalization of a business 事業再生ADR（裁判外紛争解決手続き）
（⇒lending institution）
◆ADR for the revitalization of a business is a private procedure. 事業再生ADR（裁判外紛争解決手続き）は、私的再建手続きである。
解説 事業再生ADRとは：第三者機関が過剰債務を抱える企業と金融機関等との調整を取り持って、債務削減などの再建計画を策定する私的再建手続き。

advance （動）提供する, 前渡しする, 前払いする, 増加する, 上昇する, 向上する, 値上がりする, 進歩する, 発展する, 前進する, 進出する, 進める, 促進する, 提出する, 予定を繰り上げる
advance funds 資金を提供する
advance modestly 小幅増加する, 小幅上昇する
advance strongly 力強く伸びる, 力強く値上がりする, 大幅に伸びる, 大幅な伸びを示す, 力強い伸びを示す
advance thirty percent of the face amount 額面金額の30％を融資する
◆The firm's consolidated sales advanced 13.4 percent to ¥21.04 trillion. 同社の連結売上高は、前期比13.4％増の21兆400億円となった。◆The 225-issue Nikkei Stock Average advanced 217.25 points from the previous day to 9,516.56. 日経平均株価（225種）は、前日比217円25銭高の9,516円56銭だった。

advance （名）前払い, 前渡し, 前貸し, 貸出, 貸付け（米連邦準備銀行の市中銀行に対する手形貸付け）, 融資, 借入れ, 前払い金, 前渡し金, 前貸し金, 前受金, 前金, 仮払い金, 立替え金, 借入金, 増加, 上昇, 騰貴, 向上, 値上がり, 進歩, 発展, 進展, 革新, 前進, 進出
a further advance of the yen 一層の円高
advance accounts 貸付け勘定
advance against collateral [security] 見返り担保貸付け
advance against securities 証券担保貸付け
advance bill [draft] 前貸し手形
advance business 先取引
advance dating 前日付け

advance-decline line 騰落株線 （=A-D line）
advance-decline ratio 騰落比率（値上がりした銘柄と値下がりした銘柄の比率）
advance-deposit ratio 預貸率 （=advances ratio）
advance deposits 前払い保証金, 前払い証拠金
advance deposits requirements for import 輸入保証金制度
advance exchange 取立て為替
advance fee 前払い手数料
advance freight 前払い運賃
advance from customers 顧客からの前受金
advance funding method 事前積立て方式
advance in bond prices 債権相場の上昇
advance in profits 増益
advance interest 前払い利息
advance money 前払い金, 立替え金
advance of funds 資金の提供
advance on imports 輸入前払い, 輸入立替え金
advance on promissory notes 手形貸付け
advance order 予約
advance premium 前払い保険料
advance [advances] received 前受け金 （=advance receipt）
advance refunding 社債の満期日前償還（期中償還と同義）, 借換え債務の事前負担, 期前借換え, 事前借換え, 見なし借換え
advance refundings of tax exempt debt 免税債の見なし借換え
advances on subscription 申込み証拠金
advances payable 借入金, 前受金
advances receivable 貸付け金, 前渡し金
advances to customers 顧客への貸出
an advance (on one's salary) 前借り, 給料前払い （=advance of salary）
an advances ratio 預貸率
bank advance 銀行貸出
cash advance 頭金, 現金前貸し
cash advances facility 前貸し融資枠
export advance bill 輸出前貸し手形
export advance system 輸出前貸し制度
generate a strong advance 業績を大幅に伸ばす
gradual advance じり高
heavy advance 大暴騰
interest advance 前払い利子
make a liquidity advance 資金を提供する, 流動性を供与する
monthly payment in advance 月賭け金
pay in advance 前払いする, 前金で払う, 前納する （⇒refund動詞）
payable in advance 前金制
payment in advance 前払い, 前納, 前金支払い, 前金
post a healthy advance 好調な伸びを示す
premium paid in advance 保険料の前納
receive an advance 前受金を受け取る
revenue received in advance 前受け収益
secured advance 担保貸し, 担保付き貸付け
special advances rate 特別貸出金利
strong advance 力強い伸び, 大幅な伸び
the advance of the dollar ドルの反発, ドルの上昇, ドル高

the yen's sharp advance　急激な円高, 円の急上昇, 円の急騰
unsecured advance　無担保貸付け
wages and means advances　財源貸出金
◆Another strong advance will be seen. 今後は、もう一段の力強い伸び[もう一段の上げ相場]が期待される。◆Deferred tax assets are essentially taxes paid in advance that are expected to be refunded when the bank incurs losses, for instance by writing off bad loans resulting from the bankruptcy of corporate borrowers. 繰延べ税金資産は本質的に前払いした税金で、例えば融資先企業の倒産などで不良債権を処理して、銀行が損失を被った時点で戻ってくる。◆The yen's sharp advance could undermine the slight recovery in the economy, diminishing profits gained by exporting companies. 円急騰は、輸出企業の収益を圧迫して、かすかな景気回復に悪影響を及ぼしかねない。

advance of the yen　円高
◆The talks between Prime Minister Kan and Bank of Japan Gov. Shirakawa led to a further advance of the yen and offloading of stocks as disappointment spread among market players. 菅首相と日銀総裁の会談は、一層の円高と市場筋の失望売りを誘った。

advance payment　前払い, 前納, 前払い金, 前渡し金, 前渡し補償金, 立替金, 前受け金
◆Tokyo Tomin Bank plans to start providing advance payments to part-time workers on behalf of their companies before payday. 東京都民銀行は、パートなどの準社員を対象に、働いた分の給与を支給日前に会社に代わって前払いする「前借りサービス」の提供を開始する方針だ。

advanced　(形)前渡しの, 期限前の, 繰上げの, 進んだ, 進歩・発展した, 先端の, 最新の, 最新鋭の, 高度な, 高等の, 上級レベルの
advanced deposit requirement on import　輸入担保
advanced export receipt　輸出前受け金
advanced funding　(年金の)事前積立て方式
advanced GDP figures　GDP速報値
advanced redemption　繰上げ償還, 期限前償還
　(=early redemption)
◆Nippon Life Insurance Co., the top shareholder in Olympus Corp., will continue supporting Olympus in light of its advanced technology in its core business such as endoscopes. オリンパスの筆頭株主の日本生命は、内視鏡などオリンパスの中核事業の高い技術力を踏まえて、引き続きオリンパスを支えていく方針だ。

advancers　(名)値上がり株　(gainersともいう。値下がり株=decliners, losers)

advantage　(名)有利, 利点, 強み, メリット, 利益, 優勢, 優位, 優位性, 競争力, 優遇措置
competitive advantage　競争力, 競争上の優位
cost advantage　コスト面での競争力
gross advantage　総利益
hold a competitive advantage　競争力を維持する, 競争上の優位を保つ
marginal advantage　利ざや
net advantage　正味利益
take advantage of　〜を利用する, 〜を生[活]かす, 〜に付け込む, (機会を)とらえる[利用する]
tax advantages　税制上の優遇措置, 節税効果
the biggest advantage　最大の利点, 最大のメリット[強み]
◆An urgent task facing each financial group is to improve its financial conditions and profitability on the strength of advantages gained from merger. 合併・統合で得られる相乗効果を生かして、財務内容と収益力を向上させることが、各金融グループの現在の急務だ。◆In today's borderless world, operators spend their every second of the day looking for marginal advantage. 今日の国境なき世界では、株の相場師が一日中、利ざやを求めて動いている。◆It's common to shift huge sums of capital to take advantage of international tax shelters. 巨額の資金を移し替えて、国際的な節税策を講じるのは常識だ。◆Policy-based financing operations which take advantage of government subsidies are adversely affecting the price mechanism in the financial market. 政府の補給金を受けて運営される政策金融は、金融市場の価格メカニズムを歪めている。◆Some borrowers have taken advantage of lax screening of credit guarantee corporations. 信用保証協会の手薄な審査に便乗している借り手もいる。◆Speculators apparently take advantage of the sluggish response of the government and the Bank of Japan to the yen's appreciation. 投機筋は、政府・日銀の円高への対応の鈍さに付け込んでいるようだ。◆The biggest advantage for the bank in entering the venture will be to increase its customer base without having to open expensive new branch offices. 同行にとってこの新規事業への参入の最大の利点は、コストのかかる新店舗を開設するまでもなく、顧客基盤を拡大できることだ。

adventurer　(名)投機家, 相場師, 山師, 策士

adverse　(形)逆の, 反対の, 逆向きの, 不都合な, 不利な, 不利益な, 意に添わない, 不運な, 不幸な, 批判的な, 有害な
adverse balance　国際収支の赤字
　(=adverse balance of payments)
adverse balance of trade　輸入超過
　(=adverse trade balance)
adverse budget　赤字予算
adverse comment　非難, 批判
adverse conditions　悪条件
adverse current　逆流
adverse economic conditions　経済情勢の悪化
adverse environment　厳しい環境
adverse exchange　逆為替, 下げ相場
adverse factor　悪材料
adverse opinion　不利な意見, 批判的な意見, 不適正意見, 反対意見
adverse selection　逆選択(保険事故発生の可能性が高いリスクを保険契約者が進んで生命保険に入りたがる傾向をいう)
adverse situation　困難な状況
adverse times　逆境
be bond-adverse　債券相場に打撃を与える
be under adverse circumstances　逆境にある

adverse effect　逆効果, 不利な影響, 悪影響, マイナス影響, 悪材料　(=adverse impact, negative effect)
◆If crude oil prices exceed $150 per barrel, further adverse effects cannot be avoided. 原油価格が1バレル=150ドルを超えるようなことがあれば、さらなる悪影響は避けられない。◆Mainly due to fears over the adverse effects of Greece's fiscal deficit, selling ballooned on the New York Stock Exchange. 主にギリシャの財政危機がもたらす悪影響に対する懸念から、ニューヨーク市場[ニューヨーク証券取引所]は売りが膨らんだ。◆The possible downgrade of Treasury bonds is raising fears of adverse effects on the world's markets. 想定される米国債の格下げで、世界の市場に及ぼす悪影響への懸念が高まっている。

adversely affect　悪影響を及ぼす, マイナス影響を与える, 〜に逆効果である
◆Fluctuations in stock prices could adversely affect major life insurers' finances. 株価変動は、大手生保各社の財務内容にマイナス影響を与えかねない。◆Policy-based financing operations which take advantage of government subsidies are adversely affecting the price mechanism in the financial

market. 政府の補給金を受けて運営される政策金融は、金融市場の価格メカニズムを歪めている。

adviser [advisor] (名)顧問, 顧問業務, 顧問業, 顧問会社, 諮問, 相談役, 助言者, 米大統領補佐官, アドバイザー
　　advisor to the Financial Services Agency　金融庁顧問
　　commodity trading adviser　商品取引顧問会社, 商品投資顧問会社
　　financial adviser　財務顧問, 資金調達のアドバイザー, フィナンシャル・アドバイザー
　　investment adviser　投資顧問, 投資顧問業, 投資顧問会社
　　security adviser　証券顧問業者, 証券アドバイザー
　　◆Former president of the bank was deeply involved in the nation's financial administration as an advisor to the Financial Services Agency. 同行の前社長は、金融庁の顧問として、国の金融行政に深くかかわった。

advisory (形)顧問の, 諮問の, 助言の, 勧告の, アドバイザリー
　　advisory client account　投資顧問口座
　　advisory fees　投資顧問料
　　advisory income　投資顧問収益
　　advisory service　顧問業務, 投資顧問業, 助言サービス, アドバイザリー業務 (=advisory business)
　　advisory services business　投資助言業務
　　bank advisory committee　銀行諮問委員会
　　corporate finance advisory service　企業金融アドバイザリー業務, 企業金融アドバイザリー・サービス
　　discretionary advisory account　一任投資顧問口座
　　financial advisory service　財務顧問業務, 財務顧問業, 財務顧問サービス
　　investment advisory company　投資顧問会社 (⇒corporate pension assets, financial derivatives)
　　investment advisory service　投資顧問業務, 投資顧問サービス
　　management advisory service　経営助言サービス
　　◆An advisory report by Sumitomo Mitsui Banking Corp. said "both tie-up plans are almost the same." 三井住友銀行の意見書は、「両社の提携案は優劣つけがたい」としていた。
　　◆The Financial System Council is an advisory body to the prime minister. 金融審議会は、首相の諮問機関だ。

advisory business　顧問業務, 顧問業, 投資顧問業 (=advisory service)
　　◆Increasing M&A advisory business helped Nomura grab the No. 1 spot in Japan's M&A league table for the first half of this year. 今年上半期はM&A顧問業務が増加したため、日本のM&A案件の引受実績で野村證券がトップの座を占めた。

affair (名)仕事, 業務, 事務, 事業, 事態, 情勢, 状況, 事柄, 問題, 事件, 出来事, 事項, 関心事, 関係
　　financial affairs　財務内容, 財務状態, 財務状況 (=financial position)
　　get one's affairs straight　財務を整理する
　　on business affairs　商用で, 所用で (=on business)
　　state of affairs　事態, 形勢, 財政状態
　　statement of affairs　状況報告書
　　◆Companies disclose their financial affairs through financial statements. 企業は、財務諸表[財務書類]で企業の財務内容を開示する。

affect (動)影響を及ぼす, 影響を与える, 〜に影響する, 〜を対象とする (adversely affect)
　　affect a stock price　株価に影響を与える
　　affect the market　相場に影響を与える
　　affect the stock market　株式相場に影響を与える
　　be affected adversely　逆風となる, 向かい風となる, 悪影響を受ける, 不利な影響を受ける, (投資家心理など が)冷え込む (=be adversely affected, be negatively affected)
　　be affected by　〜により影響を被る, 〜の影響を受ける, 〜に心を動かされる, 〜を悲しむ, 残念に思う
　　negatively affect　〜に悪影響を及ぼす, 〜にマイナス影響を及ぼす
　　unfavorably affect　不利な影響を与える, マイナス影響を与える, 悪影響を及ぼす
　　◆Affected by the New York sentiment, the Tokyo market was down across the board. ニューヨーク市場の地合いを受けて、東京市場は全面安となった。◆Among other factors that could adversely affect the national economy are possible setbacks in the Chinese and U.S. economies as well as high oil prices. 国内景気に悪影響を及ぼす恐れがある他の要因として、中国や米国の景気後退や原油高がある。◆Countries likely to be affected by the fiscal and financial crisis in Europe will basically be able to obtain the IMF's short-term loans immediately after applying for them. 欧州財政・金融危機が波及しそうな国は、IMF（国際通貨基金）に要請すると、基本的にIMFの短期融資を即時に受けられる。◆Hungary was seriously affected by the global financial crisis. ハンガリーは、世界的金融危機の影響が深刻だった。◆The confusion triggered by Greece's possible debt default could affect Japan and the United States. 予想されるギリシャの債務不履行（デフォルト）による混乱の影響は、日米に及ぶ可能性もある。◆The hollowing-out of the pension system may increase companies' personnel costs so much that it could negatively affect their international competitive edge. 年金の空洞化で人件費が上昇し、国際競争力に悪影響を及ぼす恐れがある。◆The pressures on gross margins and earnings that affected the last half of 2010 will continue through the first half of 2012. 2010年下半期[下期]の業績に影響を及ぼした売上利益率と利益の低下は、2012年上半期[上期]まで続く見通しです。◆This accounting change does not affect cash flows. この会計処理の変更は、キャッシュ・フローには影響しない。

affiliate (動)提携する, 合併する, 傘下入りする, 加入する, 加盟する, 友好関係を結ぶ, 提携させる, 合併させる, 系列・傘下に置く, 支部にする, 加入させる
　　◆Promise decided to affiliate with Sumitomo Mitsui Banking Corp. in June. プロミスは、6月に三井住友銀行の傘下入りを決めた。

affiliate (名)関係会社, 関連会社, 系列会社, 子会社, 外郭団体, 関係者, 提携者, 加入者, 参加者, アフィリエイト (=affiliate firm, affiliated company, associate)
　　consolidated affiliate　連結対象の関連会社, 連結対象の持ち分法適用会社
　　consumer financing affiliate　消費者金融子会社
　　investment in affiliate [affiliated company]　関係会社への投資, 関係会社株式
　　nonbank affiliate　系列ノンバンク（銀行以外の金融機関）
　　noninsurance affiliates　保険以外の関連会社
　　unconsolidated affiliates　非連結関連会社, 連結対象外関連会社
　　◆Business performance of the group's consumer financing affiliate has been in a slump. 同グループの消費者金融子会社の業績は、低迷している。◆The company's affiliate in Japan operates a flagship store in Aoyama, which opened in 1995. 同社の日本子会社が、1995年にオープンした青山の旗艦店を運営している。◆The firm's former president spread false information about corporate purchases with the aim of inflating the stock prices of its affiliate. 同社の前社長は、関連会社の株価をつり上げるため、虚偽の企業買収情報を公表していた。

affiliated (形)系列の, 系列下の, 提携している, 加盟[加入]している, 支部の, 付属の (⇒government-affiliated)

affiliated agency 提携代理店
affiliated card 提携カード, 共用カード
affiliated common stock 関係会社普通株式
affiliated loan 提携ローン, ローン提携
affiliated nonblank 系列ノンバンク
affiliated person 利害関係者
affiliated with 〜の息のかかった, 〜系列の
　(⇒apply for a loan, take control of)
bank-affiliated credit card company 銀行系クレジット・カード会社, 銀行系カード会社
bank-affiliated securities subsidiary 銀行系証券子会社
foreign-affiliated company 外資系企業
government-affiliated financial institution 政府系金融機関
insurance affiliate 保険関連会社
◆A special account is used to finance public investment and loans to government-affiliated financial institutions. 特別会計は, 政府系金融機関に財政投融資の資金を供給するのに用いられる。◆Both companies are affiliated with Mizuho Financial Group. 両社は, みずほフィナンシャルグループの系列会社だ。◆The Japan Credit Card Association is an organization made up of bank-affiliated credit card companies. 日本クレジットカード協会は, 銀行系カード会社で構成されている団体だ。

affiliation　(名)系列, 系列化, 系列関係, 親密, 親善, 親善関係, 関係, 養子縁組, 縁組, 入籍, 父子関係の決定, 提携, 協力, 協力関係, 合併, 併合, 同盟, 入会, 加入, 参加, 加盟
affiliation proceedings 父子鑑定検査
　(=paternity test)
business affiliation 企業の系列, 企業の系列化
capital affiliation 資本提携
corporate affiliations 系列関係
industrial affiliations 企業系列
transaction through affiliation 系列取引
◆The Proxy Statement includes biographies of the Board's nominees for director and their principal affiliations with other companies or organizations, as well as the items of business to be voted on at the Annual Meeting. 議決権代理行使勧誘状には, 定時株主総会で票決される議案のほかに, 取締役会で選出された取締役候補者の略歴や取締役候補者の他の会社・組織との主な協力・兼任関係などが記載されている。◆There is a chance that the technological cooperation will develop into a capital affiliation. 技術協力が資本提携に発展する可能性がある。

affirm　(動)肯定する, 断言する, 断定する, 確認する, 据え置く, 追認する
◆The EU's short-term A-1＋ rating was affirmed. 欧州連合(EU)の短期信用格付け「Aマイナス1プラス(A-1＋)」は, 据え置かれた。

afloat　(形)流通している, (水面・空中に)浮かんでいる, 不安定になっている, 借金しないでいる, 借金[負債]がない　(副)破産しないで, 経営破たん[破たん]しないで, 流通して, 浮動して
　(⇒bailout fund)
help the economy stay afloat 経済危機に対応する
keep afloat 借金[破産, 経営破たん]しないでいる, 借金しないでやっていく
keep the company afloat 同社の破たんを避ける, デフォルトを避ける
stay afloat 経営破たん[破たん]を避ける, 借金しないでやって行く
◆Fannie Mae and its sister company Freddie Mac have needed $148.2 billion in public funds to stay afloat, about $63.1 billion of which is being used by Freddie Mac. 経営破たんを避けるため, ファニー・メイ(米連邦住宅貸付金庫)とその姉妹会社フレディ・マック(米連邦住宅貸付抵当公社)が必要としている公的資金総額は1,482億ドルで, このうち約631億ドルはフレディ・マックに充てられる。◆The American taxpayers are keeping American International Group Inc. afloat. (経営再建中の米保険大手)AIGの経営破たんを防いでいるのは, 米国の納税者だ。◆The ¥1 trillion reserve funds were included in this fiscal year's budget for measures to help the economy stay afloat. 経済危機への対応策として, 1兆円の予備費が今年度予算に盛り込まれた。◆The U.S. government refused to provide public funds to keep Lehman Brothers afloat. 米政府は, リーマン・ブラザーズの破たんを避けるための公的資金の注入[投入]を拒んだ。◆The White House is ready to consider tapping a $700 billion Wall Street bailout fund to help keep the U.S. automakers afloat. 米政府は, 米自動車メーカーの破たんを避けるための支援策として, 7,000億ドルの金融業界救済資金(金融安定化法の公的資金)の活用を検討する用意ができている。

AFRA　2009年米国再生・再投資法(American Recovery and Reinvestment Act of 2009の略)

after　(前)〜差引き後, 〜控除後, 〜を控除した[差し引いた]うえで, 事後の, 事後的, 〜後, 〜以後, 〜以降, 〜の後に, 〜してから, 〜に続いて, 〜の次に, 〜を受けて, 〜の結果として, 〜を求めて, 〜の例にならって, 〜に従って
after bill date 手形振出日後
after date 振出日後
after dividends on preferred shares 優先株式配当額を控除したうえで
after sight 一覧後
after sight bill 一覧後定期払い手形
three days after sight 一覧後3日払い(提示の日を含まないで, 次の日から数えて3日)
within 30 days after the date of the invoice 請求書の日付けの翌日から起算して30日以内に, 請求書の日付け後30日以内に
◆After the government's move of intervention, the yen plunged to the ¥85 level against the dollar. 政府の市場介入の動きを受けて, 円相場は1ドル＝85円台まで急落した。◆After the integration of Monex Inc. and Orix Securities, Orix will become the largest shareholder in Monex Group with a 22.5 percent share. マネックス証券とオリックス証券の合併に伴い, オリックス証券はマネックスグループの株式を22.5%保有して, 同グループの筆頭株主になる。◆Italy's economy is the third largest after [following] those of Germany and France in the eurozone. イタリアの経済規模は, ユーロ圏ではドイツとフランスに次いで3位だ。◆The provisions, after giving effect to taxes and minority interest, reduced 2010 earnings by $200 million. これらの引当金繰入れで, 関連税額と少数株主持ち分利益控除後の2010年度の純利益は, 2億ドル減少しました。

after-hours　(形)定時を過ぎた, 時間外の
after-hours equity trading business 時間外の株式取引業務
after-hours equity trading business for retail investors 個人投資家向けの時間外株式投資業務[時間外株式取引業務]
small-lot after-hours trading 立会い外分売, 時間外分売

after-hours electronic trading 時間外電子取引, 時間外コンピュータ取引
◆Gold futures for December delivery gained to $1,897 an ounce at 4:13 p.m. in after-hours electronic trading on the Comex in New York. ニューヨーク商品取引所の時間外電子取引で, 金先物の12月渡し価格は, 午後4時13分の時点で1トロイ・オンス＝1,897ドルまで上昇した。

after-hours trading 時間外取引
　(⇒off-hours trading)

◆Former head of the Murakami Fund instructed Livedoor to buy up Nippon Broadcasting System Inc.'s shares during after-hours trading. 村上ファンドの元代表が、ライブドアに対して、時間外取引でニッポン放送株を買い占めるよう指南していた。◆The Jasdaq can begin small-lot after-hours trading by its transformation from an over-the-counter stock market to a securities exchange. ジャスダックは、店頭市場から証券取引所への移行により、立会い外分売(取引時間外に大株主などが保有株を小口に分けて売り出すこと)も可能になった。

aftermarket (名)流通市場 (=secondary market: 新規発行株式が取引される発行市場に対して、「流通市場」は証券取引所や店頭市場など、いったん発行された株式が二次的に売買される市場をいう。⇒secondary market)

afternoon trading 午後の取引
◆The Nikkei Stock Average recovered to the ¥9,000 mark in the morning, but trimmed earlier gains in afternoon trading. 日経平均株価は、朝から9,000円台に回復したが、午後の取引で午前の上昇幅が縮小した。

after-tax balance 税引き後利益
◆The two banks' total after-tax balance will move into the red from the previous projection of a ¥125 billion profit. 2行合算ベースの税引き後利益は、1,250億円の黒字予想から赤字に転落する見通しだ。

after-tax loss 税引き後損失, 税引き後赤字
◆All seven major banking groups reported after-tax losses for the second consecutive business year in their fiscal 2002 earnings reports due to the burden of disposing of bad loans and slumping stock markets. 2003年3月期決算で[2002年度の決算報告で]、不良債権処理の負担(不良債権処理損失)や株式市況の低迷で、大手銀行7グループすべてが2期連続の税引き後赤字となったことを発表した。◆Three leading shipbuilding and machinery companies recorded after-tax losses because they failed to absorb increases in the value of the yen against the dollar and rising prices of steel products. 造船・重機大手3社は、円高と鋼材価格の上昇分を吸収できなかったため、税引き後で赤字となった。

after-tax margin 税引き後利益率
◆Worldwide net earnings for the nine months were $3 billion in 2011, with after-tax margins of 7.5 percent. 2011年度1-9月期の世界全体での純利益は30億ドルで、税引き後利益率は7.5%でした。

after-tax profit 税引き後利益, 税引き後黒字 (「税引き後利益」は、決算書上では一般に「当期純利益」と表記され、企業の収益から諸費用や税金を差し引いて残った最終的な利益のこと。企業は、この「税引き後利益」から株主配当をしたり、将来の投資や財務基盤強化のための内部留保に回したりする)
◆The company's after-tax profit returned to the black for the first time in six years. 同社の税引き後利益は、6期ぶりに黒字に転換した。◆The state-funded Japan Post Holdings' after-tax profits are expected to be ¥508 billion in fiscal 2008. 政府出資の持ち株会社、日本郵政グループの2008年度の税引き後利益は、5,080億円が見込まれている。

against (前)〜に対して(versus), 〜と引換えに, 〜を裏付けとして, 〜と比べて, 〜に備えて, 〜を妨げる, 対〜 (⇒versus, weak)
 a hedge against inflation インフレ・ヘッジ
 a plunge of the won against major currencies 主要通貨に対するウォン相場の下落, 主要通貨に対するウォン安
 advance funds against (the) receivables 債権を裏付けとして資金を提供する (=fund against the receivables)
 against a contract 契約と引換えに
 against actuals 現物受け渡し
 against all risks 全危険担保, AAR (=all risks)
 appreciate against the yen 対円で上昇する
 be hedged against dollar losses 対ドルでの為替差損をヘッジする
 cash against documents 書類引換え渡し, 船積み書類引換え現金渡し, CAD
 delivery against B/L 船荷証券引換渡し
 documents against acceptance 手形受渡し, 手形引受書類渡し, 引受渡し
 documents against payment 手形支払い渡し, 手形支払い書類渡し, 支払い渡し
 event insured against 保険事故
 fund against the receivables 債権を裏付けとして資金を提供する
 funding against a l/c L/C付き資金[資金供与]
 long dollar positions against the yen 円売りドル買い
 negotiable against a draft at sight signed by 〜が振り出した一覧払い手形と引換えに買い取られる
 protection against own-injury coverage 自損事故保険
 rebound slightly against the dollar 対ドルで小幅反発する
 the depreciation of major currencies against the yen 円に対する主要通貨安
 the dollar strengthened against the yen ドルが対円で反発した
 the yen gained against all currencies 円が全面高になった
 the yen's depreciation against the dollar 円安ドル高
 the yen's rise [appreciation] against other major currencies 主要通貨に対する円相場の上昇, 主要通貨に対する円高
 the yen's value against the dollar 円の対米ドル相場

◆ABC shall have no recourse against XYZ for any obligations under the original agreement assigned pursuant to this assignment agreement. ABCは、この譲渡契約に従って譲渡された原契約上の債務については、XYZに履行の請求を一切求めないものとする。◆After the government's move of intervention, the yen plunged to the ¥85 level against the dollar. 政府の市場介入の動きを受けて、円相場は1ドル=85円台まで急落した。◆At 5 p.m., the euro was quoted at $1.1712-1715 and ¥126.54-58 against Tuesday's 5 p.m. quotes of $1.1665-1675 and ¥126.30-40 in New York. 午後5時、ニューヨークの外国為替市場では、ユーロ相場が火曜日(前日)午後5時の1ユーロ=1.1665-1675ドルと126.30-40円に対して、1ユーロ=1.1712-1715ドルと126.54-58円の値を付けた。◆If Hokuetsu Paper Mills decides to carry out the poison pill, Oji Paper Co. is likely to take legal action against it. 北越製紙が買収防衛策を実施したら、王子製紙は法的措置を取る可能性が高い。◆In foreign currency deposits, depositors can earn profits by exchanging their foreign currency deposits into yen when the yen's value against major foreign currencies falls. 外貨預金では、主要外貨に対して円相場が下落した時点で預金者が外貨預金を円に戻せば、利益を上げる[儲ける]ことができる。◆Japan's exports will stagnate and corporate performance will suffer if the yen remains in the historically high ¥75-range against the dollar. 円相場が1ドル=75円台の史上最高値が続けば、日本の輸出は低迷し、企業の業績は悪化する。◆Major currencies are rising against the dollar on account of the Fed's monetary easing policy. 米連邦準備制度理事会(FRB)の金融緩和策で、主要通貨はドルに対して上昇している[ドル安・主要通貨高が進んでいる]。◆Prime Minister Kan and Bank of Japan Gov. Shirakawa did not discuss a currency intervention to stem the yen's rise against other major currencies. 菅首相と白川日銀総裁は、主要通貨に対する円相場の上昇を阻止するための為替介入については協議しなかった。◆Record low U.S. borrowing costs are boosting the appeal to bullion as a hedge against inflation. 米国の資金調達コストが過去最低の水準にあるため、インフレ・ヘッジと

しての金[金地金]の人気が高まっている。◆South Korea has seen a plunge of the won against major currencies amid the worldwide financial meltdown. 世界的な金融危機に伴って、韓国では主要通貨に対してウォン相場が下落している[ウォン安となっている]。◆The euro traded $1.5763-5766 against late Friday's quotes of $1.5670-5680 in New York. ユーロは、ニューヨークの外国為替市場では、前週末(午後5時)の相場1ユーロ=1.5670〜5680ドルに対して、1ユーロ=1.5763〜5766ドルで取引された。◆The guard raised against a possible financial meltdown during a financial sector-triggered recession several years ago has been lifted. 数年前の金融不況時に想定された金融崩壊に対する厳戒態勢は、すでに解かれている。◆The SEC filed fraud charges against WorldCom in federal district court in New York. 米証券取引委員会(SEC)は、ワールドコム(米長距離通信会社)を詐欺罪でニューヨーク連邦地裁に提訴した。◆The United States and European nations embrace the depreciation of their currencies against the yen. 欧米諸国は、円に対する自国通貨安を容認している。◆The U.S. dollar has dropped sharply in value not only against the yen, but also against the euro, the South Korean won, the Thai baht and other currencies. 米ドルは、円に対してだけでなく、ユーロや韓国ウォン、タイ・バーツなどに対しても、急落している。◆The U.S. government failed to take drastic countermeasures against its fiscal deterioration. 米政府は、財政悪化に抜本的な対策を取れなかった[大胆なメスを入れられなかった]。◆The U.S. 10 leading banks need a combined capital buffer of 74.6 billion against the risk of a deeper recession and higher unemployment over the next two years. 米主要金融機関の10社は、今後2年の景気悪化リスクと失業増大に備えて、10社合計で746億ドルの資本増強を求められている。◆The yen has been hovering near its record high of ¥76.25 against the U.S. dollar in Tokyo. 東京外国為替市場の円相場は、戦後最高値の1ドル=76円25銭に迫る水準で推移している。◆The yen has been strengthening against the dollar. 円高ドル安が続いている。◆The yen may appreciate further to ¥70 against the U.S. dollar. 円高は、さらに1ドル=75円まで進む可能性がある。◆The yen's exchange rate has appreciated to ¥76 against the dollar, so it is the best time to buy U.S. dollars. 円の為替レートが1ドル=76円に上昇したので、今が米ドルの買い時だ。

against the backdrop of　〜を背景に
◆Standard & Poor's revised upward the outlook on its ratings on six major Japanese insurance companies against the backdrop of their improved financial profiles. スタンダード&プアーズは、日本の大手保険会社6社の財務力見通し改善を背景に、6社の格付け見通しを上方修正した。

age　(名)年数, 年齢, 経過期間, 経過年数, 耐用年数, 時代
　age at entry　(保険の)契約年齢, 保険年齢
　age at issue　加入年齢
　age depreciation　経年減価
　attained age method　到達年齢方式
　entry age cost method　加入年齢方式
　old age pension　老齢年金
　pensionable age　支給開始年齢
　remaining economic age　経済的残存耐用年数
　retirement age incidence　年齢別退職者発生率
　the age of dollar primacy　ドル支配の時代
　the age of the insured　被保険者年齢
　weighted average loan age　加重平均ローン経過期間
◆The age of dollar primacy is said to be coming to an end. ドル支配の時代は終わりに近い、と言われている。◆The compilation of fiscal rehabilitation measures including raising the pension age is imperative for the Italian parliament. 年金受給年齢の引上げなどを含む財政再建策の取りまとめが、イタリア議会の急務となっている。◆The Democratic Party of Japan will postpone a plan to raise the pension eligibility age. 民主党は、年金の支給開始年齢を引き上げる案の実施を見送る方針だ。◆The insurance premiums are determined by the age and other characteristics of policyholders. この保険料は、保険加入者の年齢などの特性に応じて決められる。

agency　(名)行政機関, 代理, 代理権, 代理行為, 代理業, 代理店, 代理関係
　administrative agencies　行政機関
　agency arrangement　取引約定書, コルレス契約
　agency-backed compounder securities　政府機関証券担保ゼロ・クーポン債
　agency bank　系列代理銀行, 代理店銀行
　agency bill　代理手形
　agency bonds　米政府機関債
　agency loan(s)　代理貸付け, 代理貸付け金
　agency notes　(1年物, 2年物の)政府機関証券
　agency operations　代理業務
　agency securities　政府機関債, 政府機関証券
　agency yields　政府機関債の利回り
　authorized agency　公認格付け機関
　banking agencies　金融当局
　bond rating agency　債券格付け機関
　collection agency　債権取立て業者
　commercial [mercantile] agency　興信所, 信用調査機関
　credit agency　信用調査機関　(=credit reporting agency, inquiry agency, mercantile agency)
　credit rating agency　信用格付け機関, 格付け機関, 格付け会社
　export agency　輸出代理店
　export credit agency-supported finance　輸出信用機関保証によるファイナンス
　federal agency securities　連邦政府機関証券
　federally sponsored agency　連邦政府系機関
　funding agency　基金積立て機関
　general insurance agency　損害保険[普通保険]の代理店業務
　government-sponsored agency bonds　政府系機関債, エージェンシー債
　independent (credit) rating agency　独立した格付け機関, 独立格付け機関
　International Organization of Securities Commissions Similar Agencies　証券監督者国際機構
　privately owned agency　民間機関
　rating agency　格付け機関
　recognized (rating) agency　評価の確立した格付け機関
　regulatory agency　規制機関, 規制当局
　U.S. federal housing agencies　米連邦住宅金融機関

agenda　(名)議題, 課題, 協議事項, 案件, 予定, 予定表, 予定案, 政策, 覚書, 備忘録, アジェンダ
　fiscal agenda　財政政策
　lending agenda　融資案件
◆At the G-7 talks, concern over soaring public debts was to top the agenda. G7(先進7か国財務相・中央銀行総裁会議)の協議では, 増大する公的債務問題[公的債務への懸念]が最大の議題[課題]になる予定だった。

agent　(名)代理店, 代理人, 代行業者, 仲介業者, 幹旋業者, 担当者, 保険外交員, セールスマン, エージェント
　agent bank　幹事銀行, 事務幹事銀行, エージェント行　(=lead bank, lead manager)
　agent commission　代理店手数料
　clearing agent　通関代理店, 交換代理銀行
　insurance agent　保険外交員, 保険代理店

listing agent　上場代理人
management agent　運営代理人, 幹事行
paying agent　支払い代理人
process agent　送達受領代理人, 送達受取人
sales agent　保険などの営業職員, 保険外交員
shopping agent　ショッピング・エージェント（オンライン・ショッピングの支援・代行業者）
transfer agent　名義書換え代理人, 証券代行機関
◆The firm excluded fees it received from acting as an agent from its tax return. 同社は、受け取った仲介手数料を税務申告から外していた。◆The Local Autonomy Law authorizes local governments to conduct extraordinary inspections of financial institutions that they have designated as agents. 地方自治体法で、地方自治体は、代理機関に指定した金融機関に対して特別検査を行う権限が与えられている。◆To boost business performance, the company's sales agents obtained contracts by telling would-be policyholders that they did not need to detail health conditions. 業績を伸ばすため、同社の保険外交員は、保険契約希望者に「健康状態の詳細な告知は必要ない」といって契約を獲得していた。

aggravate　(動)悪くする, 悪化させる, 激化させる, 増幅させる, (罪や負担などを)一層重くする, 怒らせる, 悩ませる
◆The eurozone's critical mistake is the eurozone's belittling of the risk of the sovereign debt crisis aggravating the banking crisis and vice versa. ユーロ圏の重大な誤りは、国家の財政危機と銀行の危機[経営危機]が相互に増幅し合う危険性を、ユーロ圏が軽視したことにある。◆The financial crisis is aggravating housing-market correction in several European economies at a time when external demand is fading rapidly. 外需が急速に落ち込んでいるときに、金融危機で、住宅市場の調整が欧州の一部で負担増となっている。

aggregate　(名)総計, 総額, 合計, 総体, 集合体, 集団 (形)総計の, 合計の, 総体の, マクロの, 集計的
aggregate bank credit　銀行貸出総額, 総銀行信用
aggregate basis　一括基準
aggregate borrowing limit　借入限度額
aggregate cost method　総合保険料方式 (=aggregate method)
aggregate exercise prices　総行使価格
aggregate fund in-flow out-flow　総合資金需給表
aggregate funds　総合資金, 総合資金積立金
aggregate guarantee　総合保証
aggregate indebtedness　総負担額
aggregate investment　総投資
aggregate limits　総額規制
aggregate money income　総貨幣所得
aggregate nominal amount　券面総額
aggregate payment　支払い総額
aggregate principal amount　元本総額
aggregate real income　実質総所得
aggregate reserve　総準備
aggregate savings　総貯蓄
aggregate social capital　総社会資本, 社会的総資本
aggregate wage measures　マクロの賃金指標
broad liquidity aggregate　広義流動性
closed aggregate cost method　閉鎖型総合保険料方式
industry aggregates　業界平均
monetary aggregate　金融総量, マネー・サプライ, マネー・サプライ伸び率
monetary aggregate M3　マネー・サプライM3, マネー・サプライM3の伸び率
monetary aggregate targets　マネー・サプライ伸び率目標圏
money [monetary] aggregates　量的金融指標, マネー・サプライ指標, マネー・サプライ指標の伸び率, マネー・サプライ
M2 aggregate　マネー・サプライM2

aggregate market value [price]　時価総額 (=market valuation, total market value; ⇒listed stock)
◆An aggregate market value represents a corporate value in terms of stock price. 時価総額は、株価による企業価値を示す。
◆Japanese steel manufacturers are vulnerable to takeover bids because their aggregate market values are relatively low compared with their foreign counterparts. 日本の鉄鋼メーカーは、海外勢に比べて時価総額が比較的低いため、買収されやすい。

aggressive　(形)積極的な, 意欲的な, 精力的な, やる気のある, 攻撃的な, 好戦的な, 攻めの, 侵略的な, 押しの強い, 強引な, 強気の, 野心的な, 粗россные, 乱暴な, 大幅な, 大量の, 大型の, 破格な, 過剰な, アグレッシブ
aggressive bid　破格の入札条件
aggressive business strategy　攻めの経営戦略, 攻めの事業[企業]戦略
aggressive cost cutting measures　積極的なコスト削減策
aggressive easing (of monetary policy)　積極的な金融緩和, 大幅な金融緩和
aggressive growth fund　攻撃的投資信託
aggressive (interest) rate cuts　大幅な利下げ
aggressive investment　攻撃的投資, 大幅な投資
aggressive mark-up inflation　攻撃的マークアップ・インフレ
aggressive offer　強気のオファー
aggressive portfolio　攻撃的資産運用, 積極運用型資産運用, 短期値上がり期待ポートフォリオ
aggressive pricing　値下げ攻勢, 厳しい金利条件
aggressive pricing strategy　強気の価格戦略, 積極的な価格戦略
aggressive propensity to consume　過剰な消費性向
aggressive RP operation　積極的なレポ
aggressive spread　きつめのスプレッド
aggressive stimulus package　大型の財政出動

aggressive asset management strategy　強気の資産運用戦略
◆Yamato Life Insurance Co., a midsize life insurer, collapsed due to its aggressive asset management strategy. 中堅生命保険会社の大和生命保険は、強気の資産運用戦略で経営破たんした。

aggressive investment strategy　攻撃的な投資戦略
◆Investment banks and other entities have capitalized on such huge money flows to resort to aggressive investment strategies. 投資銀行などは、この膨大な資金の流れを利用して、攻撃的な投資戦略を展開してきた。

aging　(名)高齢化, 加齢, 老化, 老朽, 老朽化, 熟成, 年齢調べ, 年数調べ, 経過期間, エイジング
accounts-receivable aging　売掛金の年齢調べ, 未収金の経過期間 (=aging of accounts receivable)
aging of bad debt　不良債権のエイジング管理
aging of receivables　債権の経過期間, 売掛金の年齢調べ
aging schedule　(売掛債権の)年齢調べ表, 売掛金滞留期間別分類表
aging society and declining birthrate　少子高齢化
rapid aging of the population　急速な高齢化

aging of society　高齢化, 高齢化社会 (=a graying of the population, an aging society, an aging population, the graying of society)
◆The aging of society, coupled with the declining birthrate,

AGM

will affect not only the pension system, but also medical care costs. 年金だけでなく医療費も、少子高齢化の影響を受ける。

AGM 年次株主総会, 定例株主総会, 定時株主総会, 年次社員総会 (=shareholder AGM:annual general meetingの略)

agree (動)同意する, 合意する, 合意に達する, 承認する, 承諾する, 賛成する, 取り決める, 決定する
  agree a price 話し合いで価格を決める
  agree in writing 書面で同意する
  agree on [upon] ～について合意に達する, ～について合意する
  agree to ～することに合意する, ～することに同意する
  agree to disagree [differ] about 意見の違いを認め合う
  agreed framework 枠組み合意
  as agreed 合意に従って
  as previously agreed すでに取り決めたように
  be agreed on ～に関して同意見である
  mutually agree 相互に同意する, 合意する

◆American International Group, one of the largest U.S. insurance companies, agreed to pay a $10 million civil fine to settle the SEC's allegations that it fraudulently helped another company falsify its earnings report and hide losses. 米保険大手のAIG(アメリカン・インターナショナル・グループ)は、同社が他社の業績報告書改ざんと損失隠しに不正に手を貸したとする米証券取引委員会(SEC)の告発を受け、この問題を解決するために民事制裁金1,000万ドルを支払うことに同意した。◆During a regular board meeting, Fuji TV directors agreed to file a claim against Livedoor for losses of more than ¥30 billion incurred from selling off Livedoor shares. 定例取締役会で、フジテレビの役員は、ライブドア株の売却で被った300億円超の損失について、ライブドアに損害賠償を請求することで合意した。◆France and Germany agreed on the need to boost the capital of European banks. フランスとドイツは、欧州銀行の資本増強の必要性で一致した。◆General Motors Corp. and Fuji Heavy Industries Ltd. agreed to terminate their capital and business alliance, which started in 1999. 米ゼネラル・モーターズ(GM)と富士重工業は、1999年から開始した両社の資本・業務提携関係を解消することで合意した。◆Greece has to agree to new austerity measures before it receives any financial aid from the European Union. ギリシャは、欧州連合(EU)の金融支援を受ける前に、追加の財政赤字削減策[緊縮財政策]に同意しなければならない。◆The APEC members agreed to pursue comprehensive economic cooperation. アジア太平洋経済協力会議(APEC)加盟国は、包括的な経済提携を目指す方向で一致した。◆The European Union agreed on comprehensive measures to deal with the current fiscal and financial crisis. 欧州連合(EU)は、現在の財政・金融危機について、包括的な対応策で合意した。◆The 17 eurozone countries agreed to expand the European Financial Stability Facility at a meeting of their finance ministers. ユーロを採用しているユーロ圏17か国は、ユーロ圏財務相会合で、欧州金融安定基金(EFSF)の規模を拡大することで一致した。◆Zenno and Itochu Corp. already have agreed to fund the issuance of new shares of Snow Brand Milk stock to boost the company's capital base. 全農(全国農業協同組合連合会)と伊藤忠は、雪印乳業の資本基盤を強化するため、同社の新株発行(増資)を引き受けることですでに合意している。

agreement (名)契約, 契約書, 合意, 合意書, 合意事項, 同意, 同意書, 協定, 協約, 取決め
  agency agreement コルレス契約, 代理店契約(agency contract) (=correspondent agreement)
  agreement among managers 幹事団契約
  agreement among underwriters シンジケート・ローンの引受契約, 引受会社間協定
  assignment agreement 譲渡契約
  bank credit agreement 銀行融資枠
  Basle Convergence Agreement BIS基準
  change-of-control agreement チェンジ・オブ・コントロール(資本拘束)条項の契約
  clearing agreement 清算協定
  CP dealer agreement CPディーラー契約
  credit agreement 借入契約, 与信契約 (=financing agreement)
  currency swap agreement 通貨スワップ契約
  debt agreement 借入契約, 債務契約 (=financing agreement)
  deferred payment agreement 延べ払い契約
  exchange payment agreement 為替支払い協定
  financial agreement 金融協定
  forward exchange agreement 先渡し為替契約
  forward rate agreement 金利先渡し契約, FRA
  hypothecation agreement 担保契約
  indemnity agreement 損失補償契約
  interest rate swap agreement 金利スワップ契約
  investment protection agreement 投資保証協定
  irrevocable credit agreement 取消し不能与信契約
  lending agreement 融資予約
  letter of agreement 約定書
  listing agreement 上場協定
  loan agreement 借入契約, 融資契約, 貸付け契約
  loan purchase agreement ローン購入契約
  major stockholder agreement 主要株主契約
  margin agreement 証拠金契約
  master resale agreement 包括レポ契約
  monetary agreement 通貨協定
  multilateral netting agreement 多者間ネッティング契約
  net worth agreement 純資産維持契約
  netting agreement ネッティング契約
  open repurchase agreement オープン・レポ
  original agreement 原契約
  provisional agreement 仮契約
  rate cap agreement 金利キャップ契約
  rate collar agreement 金利カラー契約
  rate floor agreement 金利フロア契約
  reinsurance agreement 再保険契約
  repo agreement レポ取引
  repurchase agreement 現先取引, 現先, レポ, 売戻し条件付き買いオペ
  repurchase and resale agreements 買戻し・売戻し条件付き証券売買
  resale agreement 売戻し契約, レポ取引
  reverse repurchase agreement リバース・レポ取引, 逆現先, リバース・レポ
  revolving credit agreement 回転信用契約
  revolving loan agreement 回転融資契約
  sales repurchase agreement レポ取引
  security agreement 担保契約
  stand-by [standby] agreement 借入予約協定, 残額引受契約, スタンドバイ契約
  sub-underwriting agreement 副引受協定
  subordination agreement 劣後契約
  subunderwriting agreement シンジケート・ローンの副引受契約, 副引受協定
  syndicate agreement シンジケート契約
  trust agreement 信託契約

underwriting agreement　引受契約
◆ABC shall have no recourse against XYZ for any obligations under the original agreement assigned pursuant to this assignment agreement. ABCは、この譲渡契約に従って譲渡された原契約上の債務については、XYZに履行の請求を一切求めないものとする。◆GM obtained agreements from a majority of creditors in negotiations to reduce its debts significantly. 米ゼネラル・モーターズ（GM）は、巨額の債務削減交渉で、大半の債権者から合意を取り付けた。◆If such delay shall exceed two months, either party may give written notice of termination of this agreement. このような遅延が2か月を超える場合、いずれの当事者も、書面で本契約を解除する通告を出すことができる。◆The company struck an agreement with its debtholder to win their support for reconstruction. 同社は、会社再建について債権者の支持を得ることで、債権者と合意に達した。◆The Corporation acknowledges the assignment and other terms and provisions included in the assignment agreement. 当社は、この譲渡契約書に定められた譲渡とその他の条件および規定を確認する。◆The firm is currently negotiating with its domestic capital partners to conclude change-of-control agreements. 同社は現在、国内の資本提携先とチェンジ・オブ・コントロール（資本拘束）条項の契約を結ぶ交渉を進めている。◆The 17 eurozone nations must ratify the agreement on bailout measures to arrange a rescue system for Greece. ギリシャへの支援体制を整えるには、ユーロ圏の17か国が、支援策についての合意事項を承認しなければならない。◆The Tokyo Stock Exchange and the Osaka Securities Exchange have reached a final agreement to merge as early as autumn 2012. 東京証券取引所と大阪証券取引所が、早ければ2012年秋に経営統合することで最終的に合意した。◆These interest rate swap agreements involve the exchange of floating rate for fixed rate payments without the exchange of the underlying principal amounts. これらの金利スワップ契約では、元本の交換は行わず、変動金利による支払い利息を固定金利による支払い利息と交換することになっている。◆Under the existing agreement, the IMF cannot buy government bonds through the EFSF as the IMF can only offer loans to countries. 現行協定では、IMF（国際通貨基金）は国にしか融資できないので、欧州金融安定基金（EFSF）を通じて国債を購入することはできない。◆U.S. president Bush turned to former Secretary of State James Baker for the complex task of winning an international agreement on reducing Iraq's foreign debt. ブッシュ米大統領は、イラクの対外債務削減に関する国際合意を取り付ける複雑な仕事の担い手として、ジェームズ・ベーカー元国務長官に白羽の矢を立てた。

aid　（名）援助，支援，応援，救援，救援物資，協力，手助け，補助器具，補助具，助手
　additional aid　追加支援
　aid bond　補成公債
　aid fund　助成金，助成基金，支援資金，援助資金
　aid package　支援策，テコ入れ策
　aid receipts　援助受取額
　aid society　共済組合
　aid-tying　ひも付き援助
　aid volume　援助額，援助量
　financial aid　財政援助，財政支援，金融支援，金融援助
　grant aid　無償援助
　grant in aid　助成金
　scholarship aid　奨学金
　state aid　政府補助，国家補助，国庫補助，国庫補助金
　tied aid　ひも付き援助，タイド援助，タイド・エイド
◆As Greece may default on its debts, the IMF and the EU have worked out a policy of deciding on a second aid tranche of €120 billion in July 2011. ギリシャが債務不履行（デフォルト）に陥る可能性があるため、国際通貨基金（IMF）と欧州連合（EU）は、2011年7月に1,200億ユーロ（約13兆8,000億円）規模の第二次金融支援策を決定する方針を打ち出した。

ailing　（形）経営不振の，業績が悪化している，経営が行き詰まった，不調の，不況の，病める
　ailing company　経営不振の会社，経営不振企業
　ailing construction firm　経営不振の建設会社
◆Four major creditor banks to the ailing supermarket chain operator are considering having the company reduce its capital by canceling a portion of its preferred shares held by the banks. 経営不振の大手スーパーの主力取引銀行4行は現在、4行が保有する同社の優先株（議決権がない代わりに配当が高い株式）の償却による同社の資本金引下げ[減資]を検討している。◆U.S. investment bank Goldman Sachs Group Inc. will invest ¥41 billion in the reconstruction of ailing construction firm Fujita Corp. 米投資銀行のゴールドマン・サックス・グループが、経営不振のフジタ（総合建設会社）の再建に410億円投資する。

ailing business　経営難の事業，経営不振の企業
◆When ailing businesses are revamped, those who invested in them benefit. 経営不振企業を再建すると、出資者が利益を得られる。

ailing economy　病める経済，不況の経済
◆The government should take all possible fiscal and financial means to bring the still ailing economy back on the road to recovery. 政府は、いまだにどん詰まり状態にある景気を回復の軌道に乗せるために、財政と金融の両面からの政策を総動員すべきだ。

ailing financial institution　経営不振の金融機関
◆The U.S. administration will spend up to $700 billion to buy up soured mortgage-related securities and other devalued assets held by ailing financial institutions. 米政府は、経営不振の金融機関が保有するモーゲージ関連の不良証券などの不良資産を、最大7,000億ドル投入して買い取る方針だ。

AIM　代替投資市場（ロンドン証券取引所のベンチャー株式市場。1995年6月創設）

aim　（名）目的，目標
◆The aim of a fund established by the Development Bank of Japan is to infuse money into auto parts makers hit by the March 11 earthquake and tsunami. 日本政策投資銀行が設立するファンドの目的は、東日本大震災で被災した自動車部品メーカーに資金を行き渡らせることにある。◆The bank's aim is to help circulate dormant individual assets in the local economy. 眠れる個人の金融資産を地域経済に循環させるのが、同行の目的だ。

algorithm trading　アルゴリズム取引（コンピュータのアルゴリズム（問題解決のための処理手順）を株式売買の執行に応用したもので、あらかじめ組み込んだプログラムに基づき、株の値動きに応じてコンピュータが自動的に大量の売買注文を実行する）

all　（形）すべての，全体の，全～，～一色　（代）全体，全部，～全部
　all buyers　買い一色
　all in［all-in］insurance　全危険保険，全損害保険
　all-inclusive statement　包括主義損益計算書
　all-moneys debenture　オール・マネー債券
　all or none　一括売買注文，AON
　all rights off　諸権利落ち
　all risk insurance　全危険担保保険
　all risks　全危険担保，全危険負担，オール・リスク担保
　all savers certificate　非課税貯蓄証書
　an against all risks clause　全危険担保約款，オール・リスク約款　（=all risks clause）
　Consumer Price Index for All Urban Consumers　全都市消費者物価指数

all banks　全国銀行，全銀，全銀ベース
　banking accounts of all banks　全国銀行銀行勘定，全銀

勘定
loans outstanding of all banks by kind of collateral　全国銀行担保別貸付け残高

allegation　(名)申立て, 主張, 弁明, 申し開き, 容疑, 疑惑
allegations of illegal donations　違法献金疑惑
◆American International Group agreed to pay a $10 million civil fine to settle the SEC's allegations that it fraudulently helped another company falsify its earnings report and hide losses. 米保険大手のAIG(アメリカン・インターナショナル・グループ)は, 同社が他社の業績報告書改ざんと損失隠しに不正に手を貸したとする米証券取引委員会(SEC)の告発を受け, この問題を解決するために民事制裁金1,000万ドルを支払うことに同意した。◆Financial regulators asked prosecutors to investigate allegations that UFJ Holdings Inc.'s banking unit illegally obstructed recent inspections by reporting misleading information about its nonperforming loans. 金融当局は, UFJ銀行が不良債権に関する虚偽の情報を報告して最近の検査を違法に妨害したとして, 同行を検察当局に刑事告発した。

allege　(動)主張する, 断言する, 断定する, 宣言する, 指摘する, 証言する, 申し立てる, 引合いに出す
◆A real estate investment fund was alleged to have failed to report about ¥18 billion in income from transaction involving land and property taken as collateral for nonperforming loans. 不動産投資ファンドが, 不良債権の担保に取った不動産関連の取引で得た所得約180億円の申告漏れを指摘されていた。

alleged　(形)～とされる, ～したとされている, 取り沙汰されている, 真偽の疑わしい, ～疑惑の, 申し立てられた, ～事件
alleged illegal transactions　仮装売買疑惑
alleged insider trading　インサイダー取引容疑
an alleged pyramid scam　マルチ商法詐欺事件
an alleged reason　申し立て理由
◆A bank employee was arrested for alleged insider trading of shares in four companies. 銀行の行員が, 4社の株でインサイダー取引を行った容疑で逮捕された。◆The company garnered about ¥126 billion from about 37,000 people in the alleged pyramid scam. 同社は, マルチ商法詐欺事件で, 37,000人から1,260億円もの資金を集めた。

allegedly　(副)報道によれば, 伝えられるところでは, 調べによると, 申立てによれば, 申立てによると, ～と言われている, ～したとして, ～容疑で, ～疑惑で
（=according to allegation; ⇒bank account）
◆A former vice president of the Osaka Securities Exchange and a number of his erstwhile subordinates allegedly conducted falsified stock option dealings and manipulated the stock market. 大阪証券取引所の元副理事長とかつての部下らが, 株式オプション取引で偽装売買を行い, 株式相場の操縦をしていたという。◆American International Group Inc. sued Bank of America for allegedly selling it faulty mortgage investments. 米保険大手のAIGが, 欠陥商品のモーゲージ証券を同社に販売したとしてバンク・オブ・アメリカを提訴した。◆The company allegedly amassed about ¥1 billion in off-the-book funds through its Southeast Asian projects. 同社は, 東南アジアでの事業を通じて, 約10億円の裏金を捻出したとされる。◆The former chairman of Daio Paper Corp. allegedly received more than ¥10 billion in loans from the firm's group companies for private purposes. 報道によれば, 大王製紙の前会長が, グループ企業から100億円超の私的融資を受けた。

alleviate　(動)和らげる, 緩和する, 軽減する, 軽くする, 楽にする
alleviate debt burden　債務負担を軽くする[軽減する]
alleviate the bankruptcy shock　破たんショックを和らげる
alleviate the debt burden　債務負担を軽くする, 債務を削減する

alleviate the exchange risk　為替リスクを軽減する
◆The pump-priming measures carried out four times since last year have helped to alleviate the rapid increase of corporate bankruptcy and unemployment. 昨年以降4回実施された景気対策で, 企業倒産や失業が緩和されている。◆To alleviate the influence of the U.S. government's additional steps to ease the supply of money, the Bank of Japan must adopt a more proactive stance toward monetary relaxation. 米政府の追加金融緩和策[通貨供給量を増やす米政府の追加措置]の影響を和らげるには, 日銀も金融緩和の姿勢を強める必要がある。◆U.S. President Barack Obama engineered a softer landing for GM with a set of measures to alleviate the bankruptcy shock as much as possible. オバマ米大統領は, GMの破たんショックを極力緩和するための一連の措置で, 同社の軟着陸に向けた手を打った。

alleviation　(名)軽減, 緩和

allfinanz　(名)総合保険, 銀行兼保険業務, オールファイナンス

alliance　(名)提携, 提携関係, 連携, 統合, 同盟, 同盟関係, 同盟国
（=tie-up; ⇒business alliance, capital alliance）
business alliance　業務提携, 経済団体
capital alliance　資本提携
comprehensive alliance　包括的提携, 包括提携
　　（=broad alliance）
equity alliance　資本提携関係
four-way alliance　4社提携
strategic alliance　戦略提携, 戦略的提携
◆Alliances between securities houses and banks are likely to gain momentum. 証券界と金融界の連携の動きが, 一層加速しそうだ。◆General Motors Corp. and Fuji Heavy Industries Ltd. agreed to terminate their capital and business alliance, which started in 1999. 米ゼネラル・モーターズ(GM)と富士重工業は, 1999年から開始した両社の資本・業務提携関係を解消することで合意した。◆Japan Post is discussing an alliance with Suruga Bank to offer mortgages and other loans to individuals. 日本郵政は現在, 住宅ローンなど個人ローン商品の販売に向けて, スルガ銀行と業務提携協議を進めている。◆Major consumer loan company Promise Co. is considering dissolving its alliance in the consumer loan business with UFJ Bank. 消費者金融大手のプロミスは, UFJ銀行と結んでいる消費者金融業務の提携関係の解消を検討している。◆Suzuki Motor Corp. will abort its alliance with Volkswagen AG. スズキが, 独フォルクスワーゲンとの提携を解消することになった。◆The two companies have formed an alliance in investment banking operations. 両社は, 投資銀行業務で提携関係を結んでいる[提携関係にある]。

alliance partner　提携先, 提携相手
◆GM has sold shares in its alliance partners including Fuji Heavy Industries Ltd., Isuzu Motors Ltd., and Suzuki Motor Corp. to help balance its books. GMは, 富士重工業やいすゞ自動車, スズキなど提携先の保有株式を売却して, 財務体質の改善に取り組んでいる。

alliance strategy　提携戦略
◆The tie-up between MFG and Norinchukin Bank likely will attract attention as a new alliance strategy for the mega-banks, compared with the traditional tie-ups among major commercial banks. みずほフィナンシャルグループと農林中央金庫の提携は, 従来の大手都市銀行間の提携と比べて, 巨大金融グループの新たな提携戦略として注目されそうだ。

all-in　(形)制限なしの, 全部込みの, 全費用込みの, オールインの
all-in cost　総原価　(=total cost)
all-in fee　全費用込みの料金
all-in insurance　全危険保険, 全危険災害保険, 全損害保険

all-in policy　全危険担保保険証券
all-in rates　絶対値
all-in swap rate　絶対値によるスワップ・レート, 出来上がりレート
all-in yield　オールインの利回り, オールイン利回り

allocate　(動)割り当てる, 配分する, 配賦(はいふ)する, 割り振る　(=allot)
allocate investments　投資配分を決める
allocate on a reasonable basis　合理的な基準で配分する
allocate 500 million of the newly issued common shares to　新規発行株式のうち500万株を〜に割り当てる, 新規発行普通株式のうち500万株は〜が引き受ける
allocated insurance arrangements　配分済み保険契約
amounts allocated to income tax liabilities　未払い税金に配分された額
be allocated to the underwriters　引受行が負担する
tax effects allocated to stockholders' equity　資本勘定に配分される税効果額
◆Any related unrealized exchange gains and losses are allocated to currency translation adjustment. これに関連する未実現為替差損益は, すべて為替換算調整勘定に配賦されています。
◆Hokuetsu Paper Mills Ltd. decided to allocate 50 million new shares to trading house Mitsubishi for ¥607 per share and form a business tie-up with the trading house. 北越製紙は, 三菱商事に1株607円で新株5,000株を割り当て, 三菱商事と業務提携することを決めた。◆The new shares of common stock are being allocated to plan participants over ten years as contributions are made to the plan. この普通株式新株は, 制度への資金拠出と並行して, 10年にわたり制度加入者に割り当てられています。◆Under the third-party share allotment scheme, the bank will allocate 116 million new shares to about 8,000 companies and investors with each share priced at ¥130. この第三者株式割当て計画によると, 同行は, 約8,000の企業と個人投資家に1株130円で1億1,600万株の新株を割り当てる。

allocation　(名)割当て, 配分, 配賦(ふ), 割振り, 配当　(=allotment)
allocation change　組入れ率の変更
allocation of capital　資本の投入
allocation of funds　資金の割当て, 資金配分
allocation of interest　利息の配分
allocation of revenue　収益の配分
allocation of shares　株式割当て
(=share allocation)
asset allocation　資産配分, 資金の割当て
credit allocation　信用配分
equity asset allocation　株式運用の資産配分
exchange allocation　為替割当て
exchange rate allocation　外貨割当て
foreign exchange allocation　外貨割当て, 外貨資金割当て
fund allocation　資金配分
liquidity allocation　資金の供給
private allocation　縁故者割当て
scale back [cut back] allocations　各行割当額を削減する, 割当額を削る
share allocation　株式割当て
tax allocation　税金配分, 税金配分の処理, 税金の期間配分
underwriters' allocations　引受行の割当額
◆We intend to rebuild its financial structure by a large-scale allocation of the new shares to the third parties. 当社は, 大規模な第三者割当増資で資本構成を再構築する考えだ。

allocation of new shares [stocks] to a third party
第三者割当て, 第三者割当増資　(=third party allocation, third-party share allotment)
◆The firm intends to rebuild its financial structure by a large-scale allocation of the new shares to the third parties. 同社は, 大規模な第三者割当増資で資本構成を再構築する考えだ。

allocation of newly issued shares to third parties
第三者割当増資
◆The company procured about ¥50 billion through an allocation of newly issued shares to third parties, including the Development Bank of Japan. 同社は, 日本政策投資銀行などを引受先とする第三者割当増資で, 約500億円を調達した。

allocation of shares　株式割当て
(=share allocation)
◆The TSE and the OSE will decide the exact allocation of shares based on a ratio of 1.7 TSE shares to one OSE share. 東証と大証は, 正確には大証の1株に対して東証は1.7株の割合で(新会社の)株式の割当てを決めることになった。◆With a fair and balanced allocation of shares, the company laid the foundation for a stable and long-term shareholder structure. 公正でバランスのとれた株式割当てにより, 同社は安定した長期的株主構成の基盤を据えた。

allot　(動)割り当てる, 分配する　(=allocate)
allot new shares to　〜に新株を割り当てる
allot on a pro rata basis　比例配分する
◆MMC will raise ¥120 billion by allotting ¥50 billion worth of new shares to Mitsubishi Heavy Industries, Ltd. and ¥70 billion to Mitsubishi Corp. 三菱自動車は, 三菱重工に500億円, 三菱商事に700億円の新株割当増資で, 1,200億円を調達する。

allotment　株式の割当て　(=allocation)
allotment of new shares　新株割当て
(=new share allotment)
final allotments　最終割当額
increase share allotments to existing shareholders　既存株主への割当発行をする, 株主割当発行をする
over-allotment option　超過引受オプション
third-party allotment　第三者割当て
(=allotment to third parties)
third-party share allotment scheme　第三者株式割当て
◆The struggling firm will raise ¥4.5 billion via third-party allotment. 経営再建中の同社は, 第三者割当て[第三者割当増資]で45億円を調達する。◆Under the third-party share allotment scheme, the bank will allocate 116 million new shares to about 8,000 companies and investors with each share priced at ¥130. この第三者株式割当計画によると, 同行は, 約8,000の企業と個人投資家に1株130円で1億1,600万株の新株を割り当てる。◆With a fair and balanced allotment of shares, the Corporation laid the foundation for a stable and long-term shareholder securities. 公正でバランスのとれた株式割当てにより, 当社は安定した長期的株主構成の基盤を据えることとなりました。

allow　(動)許す, 認める, 許容する, 容認する
◆Allowing banks to claim a tax refund by carrying a loss back to the previous year has not been allowed since fiscal 1992 in Japan, due chiefly to the fiscal plight of the central government. 銀行が欠損金を前年度に繰り戻して税金還付を請求できるようにする制度(欠損金の繰戻し還付)は, 主に国の財政難を理由に, 日本では1992年度から凍結されてきた。◆Banks are allowed to sell insurance policies to clients. 銀行は, 顧客に保険を販売することができる。◆During the business suspension, the company will not be allowed to extend new loans, solicit new customers or call in loans. 業務停止の期間中, 同社は新規融資や新規顧客の勧誘, 貸出[貸金]の回収業務ができなくなる。◆In December 1998, trust funds became the first financial products offered by securities firms and life insurers that banks were allowed to sell. 1998年12月に, 投資信託は, 証券会社と生命保険会社が提供する金融商品

のうち銀行窓口での販売が認められた最初の商品となった。◆In the case of au Insurance's cell phone-based policy sales, policyholders are allowed to pay premiums by adding them to monthly mobile charges. au損害保険の携帯電話での保険販売の場合、保険契約者は、保険料を携帯利用の月額に加算して保険料の支払いをすることができる。◆In the joint venture with an Indian investment bank, Tokio Marine Holdings Inc. put up about 26%, the maximum a foreign investor is allowed in an Indian company, of the new firm's capital. インドの投資銀行との合弁事業で、東京海上ホールディングスは、新会社の資本金の約26%（外資の持ち分比率の上限）を出資した。◆Since 1976, U.S. tax authorities have twice allowed tax refunds for banks. 1976年以来、米国［米国の税務当局］、は銀行については税金還付を2度承認している。◆U.S. authorities are poised to allow the weak dollar to continue for the foreseeable future. 米当局は、ドル安の進行を当面、容認する構えだ。◆When serious financial difficulties are expected, the Financial Services Agency is allowed to order a company to improve its operations in the early stages without releasing the information to the public. 深刻な財務悪化が予想される場合、金融庁は、非公表で早めに業務改善命令を発動することができる。

allowance （名）引当金、見込み額、値引き、控除、手当て、承認、許可、排出権、排出割当て
  allowance for depreciation　減価償却累計額減、減価償却引当金　（=accrued depreciation, accumulated depreciation, depreciation allowance, reserve for depreciation）
  allowance for investment losses　投資損失引当金
  allowance market　排出権市場、排出割当ての取引市場
  allowances from whatever source are granted　その財源がどんなものであれ補助金が支払われる、財源を問わず補助金が支払われる
  ◆A significant economic boost cannot be expected from the flat-sum allowance and child-rearing allowances. 定額給付金やこども手当てから、大きな景気浮揚は期待できない。

allowance for credit losses　貸倒れ引当金
  （=allowance for bad debts, allowance for doubtful debts, allowance for uncollectible debts）
  ◆We compute present values for impaired loans when we determine our allowances for credit losses. 当社の貸倒れ引当金を決定するにあたって、当社は不良債権の現在価値を計算します。

all-time high　過去最高、過去最高値、市場最高、史上最高値、上場来の高値、市場最高値、過去最多、過去最悪
  ◆Crude oil prices have exceeded $100 a barrel in London and New York, setting all-time highs on these markets. ニューヨークとロンドン市場で原油価格が1バレル＝100ドルを上回って、両市場最高値を記録した。◆If the yen rises above its all-time high of ￥79.75 to the dollar, the company may have to revise its assumed exchange rate once more. 円高が1ドル＝79円75銭の史上最高値を更新したら、同社は再び同社の想定為替レートの修正を迫られかねない。◆The benchmark gold future price surged to all-time high of ￥4,725 per gram in trading on the Tokyo Commodity Exchange. 東京工業品取引所の取引で、金取引の指標となる金先物価格が、過去最高の1グラム＝4,725円まで急騰した。◆The previous all-time high of Japan's forex reserves was $1.07 trillion marked at the end of November 2009. 日本の外貨準備高のこれまでの過去最高は、2009年11月に記録した1兆700億ドルだ。◆The yen's value reached an all-time high in 1995, with the U.S. currency traded in the ￥79 range. 円相場は1995年に史上最高に達し、米ドルは79円台［1ドル＝79円台］で取引された。

all-time low　過去最高値、史上最安値、上場来の安値、過去最低
  ◆Stock prices have dropped to an all-time low since the collapse of the bubble economy. 株価は、バブル崩壊後の最安値まで落ち込んだ。◆Stock prices have set new all-time lows. 株価は、史上最安値を更新した。

ALM　資産負債総合管理、資産負債管理、バランス・シート管理（asset liability management の略）

already-issued bonds　既発債
alternate liquidity　代替流動性
alternate policy　保険副証券
alternative　（形）代わりの、代用の、代替的、選択的（名）代案、代替策、選択肢、代わるべき手段
  alternative accounting principle　代替的会計基準
  alternative borrowing sources　代替的資金調達源
  alternative funds　代替資金
  alternative investment　オルタナティブ（代替）投資（ヘッジ・ファンドがオルタナティブ投資の代表的なもので、投資家から募った資金を複数のベンチャー・キャピタルや企業再生ファンドに投資する商品や、株価指数、為替、原油、農産物など世界の先物市場を対象に分散投資を行う商品もある）
  Alternative Investment Market　代替投資市場（ロンドン証券取引所の小規模成長企業の株式市場）
  alternative investment products　競合する投資商品
  alternative liquidity　代替流動性、代替的流動性
  alternative minimum tax　選択的最低限税
  alternative source of funds　資金調達源、代替流動性源
  alternative source of funds to bank lending　銀行融資に代わる資金調達源
  alternative stability　選択的安定
  alternative trading system　代替的取引システム、ATS
  financing alternative　資金調達手段
  investment alternative　投資手段

amass　（動）集める、ためる、蓄える、蓄積する、捻出する
  amass a fortune　財産を貯め込む
  amass foreign exchange reserves　外貨準備高「外国為替予備金」を蓄える
  amassed loan loss reserves　積み立てられた貸倒れ引当金
  ◆Banks would keep amassing cash by disposing of distressed assets as quickly as possible to avert collapse after having difficulty raising funds. 資金調達が困難になって経営破たんするのを避けるため、金融機関［銀行］は、できるだけ早めに危険資産を処分［売却］して、現金を抱え込もうとする。
  ◆The company allegedly amassed about ￥1 billion in off-the-book funds through its Southeast Asian projects. 同社は、東南アジアでの事業を通じて、約10億円の裏金を捻出したとされる。◆The effective book value is calculated by subtracting amassed loan loss reserves from the original amount of money that was lent. 実質簿価は、債権の元々の額［貸し付けた元々の金額：簿価］から、（銀行が）積み立てた貸倒れ引当金を差し引いて算定する。

American　（形）アメリカの、米国の、アメリカン
  American Bankers Association　米国銀行協会
  American College　アメリカン大学、アメリカン・カレッジ（米生命保険業界の教育機関）
  American Council of Life Insurance　アメリカ生命保険協会
  American depositary shares　米国預託株式
  American Eagle gold coin　アメリカン・イーグル金貨、米イーグル金貨
  American option　アメリカ型オプション、アメリカン・オプション（満期日までいつでも権利を行使できるアメリカン・タイプ（American type）のオプション）
  American Recovery and Reinvestment Act of 2009　2009年米国再生・再投資法
  American Stock Exchange　アメリカン証券取引所（⇒AMEX［Amex］）

American terms 米ドル建て相場
◆The U.S. Mint's sales of American Eagle gold coins have totaled 91,000 ounce so far in August. 米造幣局のアメリカン・イーグル[米イーグル]金貨の販売総量は、9月1日以降現時点で9万1,000オンスに達している。

American depositary [depository] receipts 米国預託証券ADR[ADRs]（外国企業の原株式に代わって米国の証券取引所や店頭で売買される代替証券のこと。この米国預託証券は米国の銀行が発行し、原株式は発行国の銀行に預けておく仕組みになっている）
◆Loss hiding scandal-tainted Olympus Corp. was sued by an investor in its American depositary receipts seeking class-action status. 損失隠しの疑惑をもたれたオリンパスが、同社の米国預託証券（ADR）を保有している投資家に、集団訴訟を求めて訴えられた。

American International Group Inc. アメリカン・インターナショナル・グループ, AIGグループ, AIG
◆American International Group Inc. sued Bank of America for allegedly selling it faulty mortgage investments. 米保険大手のAIGが、欠陥商品のモーゲージ証券を同社に販売したとしてバンク・オブ・アメリカを提訴した。◆Sumitomo Mitsui Banking Corp. has jointly developed with American International Group Inc. a foreign bond investment product targeting retired baby boomers. 三井住友銀行が、団塊の世代の定年退職者をターゲットにした外債の金融商品を、米保険最大手のAIGグループと共同開発した。

AMEX [Amex] アメリカン証券取引所, アメックス（American Stock Exchangeの略）

amid [amidst] （前）～の真ん中に, ～の中に［中で］, ～の真っ最中に(in the course of), ～の状況で, ～を受けて, ～に伴って, ～を背景に
（⇒banking group）
amid emerging signs of ～の兆しが見られる中
amid heavy profit taking 大量の利食い売りに押されて
amid the confusion 混乱の中にあって
amid the depleted state coffers 財政悪化が進む中
◆Amid a widening slump in global auto sales and the yen's sharp appreciation against the U.S. dollar, the firm is expected to report an unconsolidated operating loss in fiscal 2011. 世界の新車販売の落ち込み拡大と急激な円高・ドル安に伴って、同社の2011年度［2010年3月期決算］の営業損益は、単独ベース［単独決算］で赤字が見込まれている。◆Amid the continued yen's historically high levels, increasing numbers of people are opening foreign currency deposit accounts. 歴史的な円高水準が続くなか、外貨預金口座を設ける人が増えている。◆Amid the depleted state coffers, it is difficult to implement a major stimulus package to rectify the rise in the yen's value. 財政悪化が進む中［国の財源が枯渇する中］、円高是正のため大規模な財政出動を行うのは難しい。◆Amid the European fiscal and financial crisis, plunges on the world's stock markets and wild fluctuations in foreign exchange markets may continue. 欧州の財政・金融危機を受けて、世界同時株安と為替市場の乱高下は今後も続く可能性がある。◆Amid the protracted economic slump and the ongoing deflationary trend, the life insurance industry has been hit by a trio of predicaments. 景気の長期低迷とデフレ傾向が進行するなか、生保業界は三重苦に見舞われている。◆Consumer spending waned amid the global financial crisis that followed the Lehman Brothers collapse in autumn 2008. 2008年秋のリーマン・ブラザーズの破たん後に生じた世界的金融危機を受けて、個人消費が低迷した。◆Domestic bank are stepping up oversea project financing due to the lack of growth in lending to domestic borrowers amid protracted deflation at home. 国内銀行各行は、国内ではデフレが続いて［デフレが続く状況で］国内融資先への貸出が伸びていないことから、海外の事業向け融資を強化している。◆Gold extended its rally to a record above $1,900 an ounce amid increased uncertainties over the U.S. and European economic outlook on the Comex in New York. ニューヨーク商品取引所では、米欧景気見通しへの懸念[米欧経済の先行き不透明感]の高まりを受け[懸念の高まりから]、金価格が急騰して、1トロイ・オンス＝1,900ドルを史上初めて突破した。◆South Korea has seen a plunge of the won against major currencies amid the worldwide financial meltdown. 世界的な金融危機に伴って、韓国では主要通貨に対してウォン相場が下落している[ウォン安となっている]。◆The major securities house attributed the poor earnings to sharp drops in brokerage fees and trading profits amid the extended slump in the domestic stock market. この大手証券会社は、減益の要因として、国内株式市場の長期低迷による株売買手数料と売買益の大幅減を挙げた。◆There is a limit to conventional pump-priming measures amid a continued decline in birthrate and a consequent graying and shrinking population. 少子高齢化や人口減少などが進行するなかで、従来の景気刺激策[景気テコ入れ策]では限界がある。

amortization [amortisation] （名）償却, 減価償却, 定額償却, 償却額, 償還, 年賦償還, 割賦償還, 減算
amortization funds 負債償却準備金
amortization of intangibles [intangible assets] 無形資産[無形固定資産]の償却
amortization of past service cost 原始過去勤務原価の償却
amortization of principal 元本の返済
amortization of the bond premium 社債プレミアムの償却
amortization or accumulation period 元本償還期間または元本積立期間
amortization payments 割賦金支払い
amortization period 元利払い期間, 元本償還期間
amortization reserves 償却準備金
amortization schedule （ローンの）元本返済予定, 割賦返済予定
bond discount amortization 社債発行差金償却
bullet maturity amortization 満期一括償還
early amortization risk 期限前償還リスク
goodwill amortization 営業権の償却
negative amortization 負の返済
non-amortization period 金利支払い期間
◆Amortization of the excess of cost over the net assets acquired is to be recorded over sixty months. 取得した純資産に対する取得価額超過額の償却は、60か月にわたって行う予定です。

amortize （動）償却する, 負債などを割賦償還する, 定期的に返済する, 不動産を譲渡する
◆For financial reporting purposes, we amortize investment tax credits as a reduction to the provision for income taxes over the useful lives of property that produced the credits. 財務報告上、投資税額控除については、当社は対象資産の耐用期間にわたって法人税繰入れ額の減少項目として償却しています。

amount （名）金額, ～高, 総額, 総計, 元利合計, 量
a broken amount 半端な金額
a large amount of funds 大量の資金
a round amount 概算額
a sizable amount of government bonds 大量の国債
amount advanced 貸付け金額
amount assigned 担保提供額
amount at risk 保険負担金, 負担保険金[保険金額]
amount brought forward 前期繰越し高, 前期繰越し
amount carried forward 次期繰越し高, 次期繰越し
（=amount carried over）

amount covered　保険金額
amount deducted　控除額
amount deposited　預金高
amount due　未払い金額, 満期支払い高, 満期決済額, 当然支払われるべき金額
amount earned for equity　普通株主持ち分利益
amount financed　貸出額, 融資額, 元金
amount funded　積立額
amount in [on] hand　手元有り高
amount in nominal dollars　名目ドルによる金額
amount of annuity　年金終価
amount of claim　請求額
amount of clearing　手形交換高
amount of indebtedness　負債額
amount of issue　発行額
amount of liabilities　負債金額
amount of settlement　決済代金, 清算代金
amount of the first payment　初回金
amount of the loan　融資金額
amount outstanding　未払い高, 発行残高
amount overbought　（為替手形の）買持ち高
amount oversold　（為替手形の）売持ち高
amount owed　未払い額, 未払い金
amount paid　払込み金額
amount pledged　譲渡済み金額
amount raised　調達額
amount supplied　供給量
amount to be reinsured　再保険金額
amount traded during the day　その日の出来高
amount with interest added　元利合計額
amount written off　償却額
amounts brought to account　計上される金額
amounts cleared　手形交換高
　（=amounts of clearings）
amounts deducted　控除額
Amounts differ　金額相違, 小切手の不渡り事由　（=In the wrong amount, Words and figures do not agree）
amounts in arrears　未払い金額
amounts in figures　数字で示した金額
amounts in words　文字で書いた金額
amounts past due　期限経過金額
amounts payable　支払い金
amounts receivable　受取金
amounts repaid　返済された金額
an enormous amount of negative yields　巨額の逆ざや
assessed amount　査定額
capital amount　資本金額
carrying amount　簿価, 帳簿価額
collected amount　収納金額
contract amount　契約高
debt interest amounts　債券利息金額
debt principal amounts　債券元本金額
delinquency amount　延滞金
dividend equivalent amount　配当相当額
fixed amount　定額, 定量
fund amounts for postretirement benefits　退職後給付額を積み立てる
future amount　複利終価
insurance amount　保険金額
invested amount　投資額
invoice amount　送り状金額, 送り状価額

monetary compensating amount　貨幣的補償額, MCA
nominal amount　名目元本, 額面金額
original amount　当初発行額
original loan amount　借入元金
original mandated amount　調達予定額
outstanding amount　現在高, 残高, 未払い金額, 発行高
principal amount　元本
recoverable amount　回収可能額
tax amount　税額
the amount of a bill [draft]　手形金額
the amount of interest　利払い額
the amounts relating to the pension plan　年金制度に関連する金額
the correct amount of this payment　本件支払いの正当金額
the face amount　額面金額
the outstanding amount of BOJ loans　日銀貸出残高
the same amount　同額, 同量
　（=a matching amount）
total amount of money　総貨幣量, 貨幣総量
total amount of money deposited in individual foreign currency accounts　個人向け外貨預金残高
total amount of money in circulation　流通通貨量
transition amount　取引金額
upfront amount　前払い金額

◆A suprapartisan committee set up within Congress will work out a plan to cut the fiscal deficit by $1.5 trillion while raising the debt limit by a matching amount. 今後は米議会内に設置される超党派委員会が、1.5兆ドルの財政赤字削減策をまとめる一方、債務上限を同額引き上げる。◆All the insurers are now saddled with an enormous amount of negative yields as returns on their investments have plunged due to ultra-low interest rates—a consequence of the bursting of the bubble. 生保各社は現在、バブル崩壊後の超低金利時代で運用利回りが急低下し、巨額の逆ざやを抱えている。◆Greece was bailed out temporarily in May 2010, but it may default on its debts if it fails to secure necessary funds to redeem a sizable amount of government bonds. ギリシャは2010年5月に一時的に救済されたが、大量の国債の償還に必要な資金を確保できない場合、債務不履行（デフォルト）に陥る可能性がある。◆It is the Corporation's practice to fund amounts for postretirement benefits, with an independent trustee, as deemed appropriate from time to time. 随時適切と思われる退職後給付額を、独立した信託機関に積み立てるのが、当社の慣行となっています。◆Participants in the market process information transmitted globaly in real time, manipulate it in some cases and try to win profit by moving large amounts of money in this information war zone. 市場参加者は、リアルタイムでグローバルに伝達される情報を処理し、場合によってはそれを操作しながら、この情報戦争の戦場で巨額な資金を動かして利益を得ようとしている。◆Some of huge amounts in loans extended to JAL by the DBJ have been guaranteed by the government. 日本政策投資銀行が日航に行った巨額融資［貸付け］の一部は、政府が保証している。◆Tab for Fannie Mae and Freddie Mac could soar to as much as $259 billion, nearly twice the amount Fannie and Freddie have received so far. ファニー・メイ（米連邦住宅抵当金庫）とフレディ・マック（米連邦住宅貸付け抵当公社）の追加の公的資金必要額は、両社がこれまでに受け取った額の約2倍の2,590億ドルに急増する可能性がある。◆The amount of net selling of Japanese stocks further increased in September. 9月は、日本株の売り越しの額がさらに増えた。◆The amount of straight corporate bond issuance came to ¥981 billion in July 2011, the highest level in 10 months. 2011年7月の普通社債発行額は、過去10か月で最高水準の9,810億円に達した。◆The Bank of Japan has supplied a large amount of funds to the market by purchasing long-term government bonds and corporate bonds. 日銀は、長期国債や社債の買入れで、大量の資金を市場に提供している。◆The BOJ's additional monetary easing steps include an increase in the amount of funds to purchase government bonds and corporate debentures. 日銀の追加金融緩和には、国債や社債などを買い入れる基金の増額が含まれている。◆The Development Bank of Japan asked the Japan Finance Corporation to pay ¥53.6 billion, the amount guaranteed by the government. 日本政策投資銀行は、政府保証分の536億円の支払いを日本政策金融公庫に請求した。◆The effective book value is calculated by subtracting amassed loan loss reserves from the original amount of money that was lent. 実質簿価は、債権の元々の額(貸し付けた元々の金額：簿価)から、(銀行が)積み立てた貸倒れ引当金を差し引いて算定する。◆The federal government will initially make a spending cut of $900 billion, while it will raise the debt ceiling by the same amount immediately. 米政府はまず0.9兆ドルの歳出削減を行う一方、債務上限を直ちに引き上げる。◆The total amount of loans owed by companies and individuals to private financial institutions stands at ¥2.8 trillion in the three prefectures' coastal areas hit by the March 11 tsunami. 津波被災地の3県(宮城、岩手と福島)沿岸部では、企業や個人の民間企業からの借入金総額が、2.8兆円にのぼっている。◆The total amount of money deposited in individual foreign currency accounts has continued to increase in recent years. 個人向け外貨預金残高は、ここ数年増え続けている。◆Without the government financial support, TEPCO will fall into debt as the utility has to pay the huge amounts in compensation. 政府の金融支援がなければ、東電は巨額の賠償金を支払わなければならないので、債務超過に陥ると思われる。

amount of deposits 預金量, 預金額
◆Financial institutions pay insurance premiums to the Deposit Insurance Corporation according to the amount of deposits they hold. 金融機関は、保有する預金量に応じて預金保険機構に保険料を納付している。

amount of federal government's financial support 米政府の金融支援額
◆The amount of federal government's financial support to GM will reach ¥5 trillion in total. GMに対する米政府の金融支援の総額は、5兆円に達する。

amount of insurance money 保険金額
◆The bank raised the amount of insurance money from the current ¥5 million limit to a maximum of ¥10 million for cash card fraud. 同行は、キャッシュ・カード詐欺の保険金額を、現在の上限500万円から最大1,000万円に引き上げた。

amount of investment 投資額
◆Of the amount of investment, about a half was invested in foreign government bonds with low credit ratings. この投資額のうち約半分は、格付けの低い外国債に充てられていた。

amount of net assets 純資産額
◆Book value per share refers to the amount of net assets of a company represented by one share of common stock. 1株当たり純資産[簿価]とは、普通株式1株当たりの企業の純資産額のことを言う。

amount of outstanding loans 貸出残高, 貸出残高の額, 融資残高
◆There have been no signs of a rebound in the amount of outstanding loans, which continues on an abated decline. このところ引き続き減少傾向にある銀行の貸出残高に、反転の兆しは見えない。

amount of refunding bonds issued 借換え債の発行額
◆The amount of refunding bonds issued to redeem ordinary government bonds is expected to exceed ¥100 trillion. 普通国債償還のための借換え債の発行額が、100兆円を突破する見込みだ。

amount of window-dressing 粉飾額
◆The total amount of window-dressing over the four years since 2005 may be more than $10 billion. 総粉飾額は、2005年以降の4年間で100億ドルを超えると見られる。

amount to (数量、金額が)～に達する,～になる,～にのぼる,～も同然である,～に等しい, つまり[要するに]～ということだ
◆Loan write-off costs at the bank amounted to ¥450 billion for the half-year ended Sept. 30. 同行の9月中間決算の不良債権処理費用は、4,500億円だった。◆Our contributions to the savings plans amounted to $330 million in 2010. 当社の貯蓄制度に対する会社側の拠出額は、2010年度3億3,000万ドルでした。◆The bank's bad loan charges amounted to ¥322.5 billion for the April-June quarter. 同行の4-6月期(第一・四半期)の不良債権額は、3,225億円となった。◆The issuance of government bonds amounts to ¥44 trillion in the fiscal 2011 budget though tax revenues are ¥41 trillion. 2011年度予算では、41兆円の税収に対して国債の発行額は44兆円にのぼる。

ample funds 潤沢(じゅんたく)な資金
◆The Bank of Japan previously adopted a policy of providing ample funds to the financial markets toward the fiscal year-end, setting a target for the outstanding balance of current account deposits held by private financial institutions at the bank of ¥15-20 trillion. これまで日本銀行は、日銀当座預金残高(民間金融機関が日銀に保有している当座預金残高)の目標を15-20兆円程度に設定し、年度末に向けて金融市場に潤沢な資金を供給する方針であった。◆The BOJ previously adopted a policy of providing ample funds to the financial markets toward the fiscal year-end. これまで日本銀行は、年度末に向けて金融市場に潤沢な資金を供給する方針であった。◆The G-7 joint statement made clear the stance of supporting the financial markets by supplying ample funds. G7の共同声明は、潤沢な資金供給によって金融市場を下支えする姿勢を明らかにした。

ample liquidity 高い流動性, 流動性の高さ, 豊富な資金, 大量の資金, 潤沢(じゅんたく)な資金
◆Despite the ample liquidity, bank lending remains stalled. この豊富な資金[高い流動性]にもかかわらず、銀行貸出は依然、落ち込んでいる。◆The Bank of Japan decided to continue providing ample liquidity to financial markets. 日本銀行は、金融市場に大量の資金を続けることを決定した。

ample supply of funds 資金の潤沢な供給 (⇒abundant fund supply)
◆Under the zero-interest rate policy, the Bank of Japan ensures an ample supply of funds to the money market, making it easier for many banks to secure funds there. ゼロ金利政策のもと、日銀が金融市場に資金を潤沢(じゅんたく)に供給して、多くの銀行は金融市場での資金確保が楽になった。

AMRO (ASEANプラス3諸国の)域内マクロ経済リサーチ・オフィス, アムロ (⇒analyze [analyse])
◆The ASEAN plus Three Macroeconomic Research Office, or AMRO, was set up in Singapore in April 2011 to coordinate decision-making for providing emergency liquidity to member states. ASEANプラス3(日中韓)の域内マクロ経済リサーチ・オフィス(AMRO)は、参加国に緊急時の流動性を提供する際の意思決定調整機関として、2011年4にシンガポールに設立された。

解説 **AMRO**とは: the ASEAN＋3 [ASEAN plus Three] Macroeconomic Research Officeの略。2011年4月、アセアン域内各国の経済を監視する機関としてシンガポールに設立。加盟国の金融危機時の資金支援決定に必要な報告書を、意思決定機関である執行委員会に提出する。15人で発足した組織で、初代トップの事務局長に中国の魏本華(ウェイ パンホワ)・前国家外貨管理局副局長が就任。2012年から、日本の根本洋一財務省参事官が2代目を引き継ぐことになっている。

AMU アジア通貨単位 (Asian Monetary Unitの略)

analyse ⇒analyze [analyse]
analysis (名)分析, 解析, アナリシス
  analysis of financial statements　財務諸表分析, 財務書類分析　(=financial statement analysis)
  break-even analysis　損益分岐点分析, 採算点分析
  business analysis　経営分析
  business investment analysis　企業投資分析
  credit analysis　信用分析
  financial analysis　財務分析
  financial market analysis　金融市場分析
  fundamental analysis　ファンダメンタル分析
  funds analysis　資金分析
  mark-to-market analysis　時価分析
  portfolio analysis　ポートフォリオ分析
  securities analysis　証券分析
  stock price analysis　株価分析
  technical analysis　テクニカル分析
  ◆Credit rating is merely an evaluation a private rating firm makes based on its own analysis. 信用格付けは、民間の格付け会社が独自の分析に基づいて行う評価に過ぎない。
analyst (名)分析家, アナリスト
  analysts' earnings estimate　アナリスト収益予想
  analysts' opinions　アナリスト評価
  bond market analyst　債券アナリスト
  credit analyst　信用アナリスト
  current analysts' consensus estimates　最新アナリスト予想
  economic analyst　経済アナリスト, 経済情勢分析家
  equity analyst　証券アナリスト
  Financial Analysts Federation　全米証券アナリスト協会
  fundamental analyst　ファンダメンタル・アナリスト
  industry analyst　業界アナリスト, 産業アナリスト
  investment analyst　投資アナリスト
  political risk analyst　政治的リスク測定の専門家
  securities analyst　証券アナリスト
  Society for Investment Analysts　証券アナリスト協会
  stock analyst　株式アナリスト
  street analyst　証券会社のアナリスト
  technical analyst　テクニカル・アナリスト
  ◆The move to inject liquidity into Dubai's banks by the central bank of the United Arab Emirates was seen by analysts as the bare minimum. ドバイの銀行に資金を供給するアラブ首長国連邦（UAE）の中央銀行の動きを、アナリスト（専門家）は「最低限必要な量にすぎない」と見ている。
analyze [analyse] (動)分析する, 検討する, 審査する
  analyze an issuer's balance sheet　発行体の財務内容［財務、貸借対照表］を分析する
  analyze credit risk　信用リスクを審査する
  analyze return on investment　投下資本収益率を分析する
  analyze the business and insurance risks of the insurer　保険会社の経営内容と保険リスクを分析する
  analyze the credit strength　信用力を分析する
  ◆AMRO, as the surveillance unit of CMIM, plays an important role to monitor and analyze regional economies. AMROは、（参加国が通貨急落といった危機に直面した際に外貨を融通し合う）多国間通貨交換［スワップ］協定（CMIM）の監視機関として、域内経済を監視し分析する重要な役割を担っている。
and Company [and Co., & Co.] (小切手)銀行渡り
and interest　経過利子付き
angel (名)ベンチャー企業への個人投資家, 資金提供者, 新興企業への後援者, エンジェル　(=business angel: 主にベンチャー企業に出資の形で資金を提供し, 経営の助言なども行って株式公開時に大きな利益が得られることを期待するハイリスク・ハイリターン型投資家の個人投資家を「エンジェル」という。ベンチャー企業育成のため、ベンチャー企業に個人投資家が投資をしやすくする税制を「エンジェル税制」という)
  angel-funded start-up　エンジェルが出資したベンチャー企業［新興企業］
  angel investment　エンジェルの投資
  business angel　企業後援者, 企業［新興企業］への資金提供者, 新事業への個人投資家, ベンチャー投資家
announce (動)発表する, 公表する, 表明する, 知らせる, 告げる
  ◆Bank of America, the second-largest U.S. bank, announced it would acquire Merrill Lynch, the third-largest U.S. securities firm. 米銀行2位のバンク・オブ・アメリカが、米証券3位のメリルリンチを買収すると発表した。◆Doubts over the effectiveness of the announced stock price measures have already been expressed among Japanese market players. 今回発表された株価対策の効果については、日本の市場関係者の間ですでに疑問視する声がある。◆Economic activity strengthened in most of U.S. regions with the exception of St. Louis where plans to close several plants were announced, the U.S. FRB said. 米連邦準備制度理事会（FRB）は、（全12地区連銀のうち）一部の工場閉鎖計画を発表したセントルイスを除く11地区で景気が好転している、と述べた。
announcement (名)発表, 公表, 告示, 告知, 声明, 表明, お知らせ
  announcement day [date]　募集開始日, 募集発表日
  announcement of business results　業績発表, 決算発表, 決算短信　(=results announcement)
  auction announcement　入札予定の発表, 入札予定発表
  dividend announcement　配当発表
  earnings announcement　利益発表, 業績発表
  results announcement　業績発表, 決算発表　(=announcement of business results)
  the announcement of underreporting　虚偽記載［過少記載］の発表　(⇒underreport)
annual (形)年間の, 年次の, 通期の, 年1回の, 毎年の, アニュアル
  actuarial annual percentage rate　実質年利
  annual accounting　年次決算　(=annual accounts settlement)
  annual audit　年次監査
  annual basis　年率ベース, 年間計算
  annual consolidated financial statements　年次連結財務書類, 年次連結財務諸表
  annual earnings　年次利益, 年間所得
  annual equivalent　年換算利回り
  annual financial report　年次財務報告
  annual financial statements　年次財務諸表, 年次財務書類, 年次報告書, 年次有価証券報告書　(=annual accounts)
  annual general meeting of shareholders　年次株主総会, 定例［定時］株主総会
  annual growth rate　年成長率, 年間伸び率［成長率］
  annual loss　年間赤字, 通期での赤字
  annual meeting　定時総会, 年次総会, 定時株主総会, 年次株主総会
  annual percentage rate　年利率, 年利, 実質年率, 年間パーセント
  annual premium caps　年間保険料の上限, 保険料の年間の上限
  annual profit and loss　年次損益

annual report to stockholders ［shareholders］　株主向け年次報告書, 年次報告書
annual results　通期決算, 通期業績, 年間業績, 年間成績
annual return　年次報告書, 年次届け出書（英国の会社が会社登記官に届け出る財務報告書）
annual securities report　年次有価証券報告書
annual settlement of accounts　年次決算
annual statement　年次報告書（米国の保険会社が州保険局長官に提出する財務報告書）, 年次営業報告書

annual accounts settlement　年次決算
（＝annual settlement of accounts）
◆A large majority of First Section-listed companies close their books at the end of March for their annual accounts settlement. 東証1部上場企業の大半が、年次決算のため3月末に帳簿を締める。

annual consolidated financial statements　年次連結財務書類
◆The audit committee reviews the corporation's annual consolidated financial statements and recommends their approval to the board of directors. 監査委員会は、当社の年次連結財務書類を閲覧して、取締役会にその承認を求めます。

annual general meeting of shareholders　年次株主総会, 定例株主総会, 定時株主総会, 年次社員総会, AGM
（＝annual general meeting, annual general shareholders meeting, annual shareholders meeting, annual shareholders' meeting）
◆In Japan, annual general meetings of shareholders are generally held in June. 日本では、一般に年次株主総会は6月に開かれる［6月に集中する］。

annual income　年間所得, 年収
◆If a housewife whose annual income is ¥1.3 million or more, or her husband becomes self-employed, the housewife must join the national pension plan and pay premiums. 主婦の年収が130万円以上の場合、または夫が脱サラした場合には、主婦も国民年金に加入して保険料を支払わなければならない。

annual interest　年利, 年間利子, 年間金利
◆The BOJ decided to introduce a new open market operation by supplying ¥10 trillion to private financial institutions in three month loans at an ultralow annual interest of 0.1 percent. 日銀は、民間の金融機関に年1％の超低金利で貸出期間3か月の資金を10兆円供給する新型の公開市場操作（オペ）の導入に踏み切った。

annual interest rate　年間利子率, 年間利率, 年間金利
◆Some financial institutions are offering products with annual interest rates starting at 1 percent or less. 一部の金融機関は、当初の金利［適用金利］が年1％以下の商品を提供している。

annual meeting　定時総会, 年次総会, 定時株主総会, 年次株主総会
annual meeting of policyholders' representatives　総代会
（⇒policyholders' representative meeting）
annual meeting of shareholders ［stockholders］　年次株主総会, 定例株主総会, 定時株主総会
（＝annual shareholders meeting）
annual shareowners ［shareholders, stockholders］ meeting　年次株主総会
◆The annual meeting of the shareholders of this corporation was held on May 15, 2010. 当社の年次株主総会は、2010年5月15日に開催された。

annual report　年次報告書, 年次決算報告書, 年次営業報告書, 有価証券報告書, 年報, アニュアル・レポート
（⇒quarterly report）
annual report and accounts　年次報告書
annual report to stockholders ［shareholders, shareowners］　株主向け年次報告書
annual report to the Securities and Exchange Commission　SEC（米証券取引委員会）向け年次報告書
◆Form 10-K is our annual report to the Securities and Exchange Commission. 様式10-Kは、当社が米証券取引委員会に提出する年次報告書です。

|解説| 年次報告書とは：英国ではannual report and accountsともいわれるが、アメリカの場合はSEC（米証券取引委員会）向け年次報告書と株主向け年次報告書がある。SEC向け年次報告書は、SECに登録している企業が株式、社債などの証券を発行した後、決算期ごとに毎年提出する報告書で、その様式は米国企業がForm 10-K（様式10-K）、外国企業がForm 20-F（様式20-F）となっている。SECへの提出期限は、様式10-K（米国企業）が60日以内、様式20-F（外国企業）は6か月以内となっている。米国企業の提出期限を従来の90日以内から60日以内に変更することにSECが決定したのは2002年8月27日で、これは米エネルギー大手エンロンや長距離通信大手ワールドコムなど、エンロンの経営破たんをきっかけに相次いで発覚した米国企業の経営者による不正な会計操作を時間的に難しくするのが目的だ。また、会計不祥事の再発防止に向けて、年次決算報告書の提出期限の短縮化とともに、企業幹部による自社株取引の報告期限も従来の40日以内から2日以内に大幅に短縮された。これら報告期限の短縮のほか、一連の会計不祥事の再発を防ぐため、米国企業だけでなく米株式市場に上場する外国企業にも、決算報告の正確さを保証する宣誓書の提出が義務付けられた（米国企業の場合、2002年7月に成立した企業改革法（サーベンス・オクスレー法：Sarbanes-Oxley Act）に基づくSECの措置として、2002年8月29日から年次報告書だけでなく四半期報告書についても決算宣誓書の提出が義務付けられている）。SECの会計基準で作成されるこれらのSEC向け年次報告書に対して、「一般に公正妥当と認められた会計原則（会計基準）」（generally accepted accounting principles：GAAP）に従って作成されるのが、株主向け年次報告書である。これは、各企業が毎年1回、定期的に作成して、年次株主総会（the annual meeting of shareholders）の委任状説明書（proxy statement：株主総会の議案内容などを説明した文書）を送る前に、株主その他利害関係者（stakeholders）に送ることになっている。

Annual Report on the Japanese Economy and Public Finances　経済財政白書, 年次経済財政報告（内閣府が年1回作成）
◆The Annual Report on the Japanese Economy and Public Finances for fiscal 2010 urges lower corporate taxes and a high consumption tax rate. 2010年度の経済財政白書は、法人税の引下げと消費税率の引上げを促している。

annual results　通期決算, 通期業績, 年間業績, 年間成績
◆Toyota's consolidated annual results for the business year up to the end of March are predicted to see a huge fall in operating profits. トヨタの3月期連結決算は、本業の儲けを示す営業利益が大幅に減る見通しだ。

annual securities report　年次有価証券報告書
◆The presence of investment funds on the share register is generally unknown until their names are listed in annual securities reports. 株主名簿上の投資ファンドの存在は、一般にそのファンド名が年次有価証券報告書に記載されるまで分からない。

annual stock report　年次株式取引報告書, 年間の株式取引報告書
◆The securities companies will calculate capital gains and losses, compile taxation documents, gather annual stock reports and file tax returns on behalf of investors free of charge. 今後は、証券会社が投資家の代わりに無料で譲渡損益を計算したり、税務書類を作成したり、年間の株式取引報告書を揃えたりして税務申告書（納税申告書）を提出することになる。

annualized ［annualised］　（形）年率換算の, 年換算の,

年率の
annualized growth　年率の伸び, 年率の伸び率
annualized rate　年率
annualized terms　年率換算, 年換算, 年率
　（=annualized basis）
on an annualized basis　年率換算で, 年換算で, 年率で
quarter on quarter annualized rate　前期比年率
seasonally adjusted annualized rate　季節調整済み年率
◆The real growth in annualized terms was 5.6 percent, showing clear signs of an economic recovery. 年率換算での実質成長率は5.6%で, 明らかに景気回復基調を示した。◆The real-term gross domestic product in the fourth quarter grew at an annualized rate of 3 percent over the same period of the previous year. 第4四半期の実質国内総生産（GDP）の成長率は, 前年同期比で年率3%だった。
annualized basis　年率換算, 年換算, 年率
◆The government revised downward the real growth rate in gross domestic product for the July-September quarter to 0.2 percent rise on an annualized basis. 政府は, 7-9月期のGDP（国内総生産）の実質成長率を年率換算で0.2%増に下方修正した。
annualized growth rate　年率換算の成長率
◆The annualized growth rate was significantly lower than 4 percent expected by the market. 年率換算の成長率は, 市場が事前予想した4%を大きく下回った。
annuitant　（名）年金受給者, 年金受給権者, 年金受取人
　（⇒life annuity）
annuity　（名）年金, 年金保険制度, 年金受領権［受給権］, 年間配当金, 年賦金, 出資金, 掛金
　amount of annuity　年金終価　（=final value of annuity, future value of annuity）
　annuity agreement［contract］　年金契約
　annuity bond　年金証書, 年金債券（perpetual bond: 満期の記載や利子の支払い期日がない債券）
　annuity certificate　年金証書
　annuity cost　年金費用
　annuity deposits　年金預り金
　annuity depreciation　年金法, 年金式減価償却法
　　（=annuity method of depreciation）
　annuity due　期首払い年金, 期首払込み金
　　（=annuity in advance）
　annuity factor　年金係数
　annuity for life　終身年金　（=life annuity, perpetual annuity, straight life annuity）
　annuity form　年金形態
　annuity in advance　期首年金, 前払い年金
　annuity in arrears　期末払い年金
　annuity in immediate　即時払い年金
　annuity in reversion　据え置き年金
　annuity loan　年金型ローン
　annuity method（of depreciation）　減価償却の年金法, 年金式減価償却法, 年金法, 年金償還法
　annuity option　年金の選択
　annuity payable in advance　期首払い定額年金
　annuity policy　年金保険証券
　annuity rider　年金特約
　annuity scheme　年金制度
　annuity table　年金生命表
　annuity trust　年金信託
　annuity unit　年金ユニット
　bank annuity　銀行年金
　consolidated annuities　整理公債, コンソル公債

contingent annuity　偶発年金
continued［continuous］annuity　連続年金
deferred annuity　据え置き型年金, 据え置き年金
deposits of funds of national annuities　国民年金預託金
document of annuity　年金証書
endowment annuity　養老年金
equity annuity　普通株年金, 株式年金
exponential annuity　定率上昇年金
farm retirement annuity　離農年金
farmer's annuity　農業者年金
final value of annuity　年金終価
　（=amount of annuity, future value of annuity）
fixed annuity　定額年金
fixed period annuity　期間限定年金
fixed rate annuity product　定額年金商品
flexible premium deferred annuity　変額保険料年金
future value of annuity　年金終価
　（=amount of annuity, final value of annuity）
group annuity　団体年金
guaranteed annuity　保証年金
immediate annuity　即時型年金, 即時払い年金
increasing annuity　増額年金, 漸増（ぜんぞう）年金
individual annuity　個人年金
individual deferred annuity　個人据え置き型年金, 個人据え置き年金
insurance against annuity　年金保険
joint and last survivor annuity　夫婦年金, 共同生存年金
joint annuity　共同年金
level annuity　定額年金
life annuity　終身年金, 生命年金
life annuity insurance　終身年金保険
life annuity with a period certain　期限付き終身年金
limited annuity　有期限年金, 有限年金
long-term annuity　長期年金
market-value-adjusted annuity　市場価額調整年金
national annuity　国民年金　（=national pension）
nonparticipating annuity　非参加配当年金
occupational annuity　企業年金
ordinary annuity　普通年金, 期末払い年金
participating annuity　参加配当年金, 利益配当年金
pay annuities for employees　従業員のために掛金を払う
pension annuity　養老年金
period certain annuity　期間限定年金
　（=fixed period annuity）
perpetual annuity　終身年金
postal［post-office］annuity　郵便年金
present value of annuity　年金現価
present value rate of life annuity　生命年金現価率
private annuity　自家年金
private enterprises［enterprise］annuity　企業年金
purchase a fixed annuity with a single payment　定額年金を一時払いで購入する
purchased life annuity　買入れ終身年金
reduced annuity　利率累減年金
refund annuity　死亡時払戻し金付き年金
retirement annuity　退職年金
reversionary annuity　生き残り年金, 帰属年金
seasoning of the annuity bloc　年金商品の経過期間
straight life annuity　終身年金

survivor's annuity　遺族年金
　　survivor's annuity insurance　遺族年金保険
　　temporary annuity　一時年金, 有限年金
　　term annuity　定期年金
　　terminable annuity　有期年金
　　terminal funding annuity　最終積立型年金
　　Tontine annuity　トンチン年金
　　variable annuity　変額年金, 変動年金
　　variable annuity plan　変額年制度, 可変年金制度
　　variable immediate annuity　変額即時年金
　　whole life annuity　終身年金
　　◆In the corporate type of defined-contribution pension plans, companies pay annuities for employees. 企業型の確定拠出年金制度では、企業が従業員のために掛金を支払う。
annuity certain　確定年金（複数形＝annuities certain）
　　annuity certain and for life　保証期間付き生命年金
　　annuity certain due　期首払い確定年金
　　annuity certain immediate　即時払い確定年金
annuity contracts　年金契約, 年金の保有契約高
　　the life insurers' combined outstanding balance of individual life insurance and annuity contracts　生保合計の個人保険・年金の保有契約高
　　the number of individual annuity contracts　個人年金契約数
　　◆The 10 life insurers' combined outstanding balance of individual life insurance and annuity contracts declined for five consecutive years to ￥1.15 quadrillion. 生保10社合計の個人保険・年金の保有契約高（保険の総額）は1,150兆円で、5年連続（5期連続）で減少した。
annuity insurance　年金保険
　　group annuity insurance　団体年金保険
　　individual life and annuity insurance　個人生命保険と個人年金保険
　　◆AFLAC replaced Nippon Life Insurance Co. as the largest holder of individual life and annuity insurance contracts in Japan. 個人生命保険と個人年金保険の保有契約件数で、アフラック（アメリカンファミリー生命保険）が日本生命に代わってトップに立った。
annuity insurance policy　年金保険証券, 年金保険
　　◆Among products likely to be subject to the eased restrictions on sales of life insurance products at banks are individual annuity insurance policies that offer fixed or variable payments upon maturity. 銀行での生保販売（生保商品販売）解禁の対象となる商品は、満期時に一定額の年金を受け取れる定額と変額の個人年金保険になる見通しだ。
annuity scheme　年金制度
　　◆The defined-contribution annuity scheme is the Japanese version of the 401-k annuity scheme in the United States. 確定拠出年金制度は、米国の企業年金制度「401k」の日本版である。
anomaly　(名)市場の変則性, 価格の歪み, アノマリー（市場価格がなんらかの非合理的な理由で理論上の価格とずれている状態のこと）
anonymous association　匿名（とくめい）組合
　　◆The Dutch companies contributed capital to a firm specializing in purchases of bad loans through an anonymous association. このオランダの企業数社は、匿名組合を通じて不良債権買取り専門会社に出資していた。
　　解説 匿名組合とは：商法で定められた出資契約で、営業者の事業に出資した匿名組合員が、その出資額に応じて事業による利益の分配を受ける。投資リスクが出資額だけに限定されるため、資金が集まりやすい利点がある。事業を行う上で出資者が表に出ないので、匿名性を持つ。(2002年5月29日付讀賣新聞)

anti-bullionism　(名)反地金主義
anti-terror funding law　テロ資金供与処罰法
anticipate　(動)予想する, 見込む, 見越す, 期待する, 予定する, 期限前に支払う, 見越して手を打つ
　　anticipate a fall in interest rates　金利の低下を見越す
　　anticipate a Fed ease　FRBによる利下げを予想する
　　anticipate a payment　期限前に支払う, 支払いを早くする
　　anticipate a rise in interest rates　金利上昇を見越す
　　anticipated acceptance　満期前払い引受手形
　　anticipated income　予想所得, 予想利益
　　anticipated inflation rate　予想インフレ率
　　anticipated loss　見込み損失, 予想損失（＝anticipatory loss）
　　anticipated payment　満期前支払い
　　anticipated profit　見込み利益, 予想利益, 期待利益（＝anticipatory profit）
　　higher-than-anticipated　予想を上回る〜
　　lower-than-anticipated　予想を下回る〜
　　◆The company anticipates a group net loss of ￥34 billion for this current business year. 同社は、今年度は340億円の連結税引き後赤字[連結純損失]になる見通しだ。
anticipation　(名)予想, 予期, 予測, 予見, 想定, 見込み, 見越し, 見通し, 期待, 予定, 先手, 先取り, 予防, 事前行為, (信託財産の)期限前処分, 期限前返済, 予見性, 先行技術
　　anticipation discount　期限前支払い割引
　　anticipation of an advance　先高見通し
　　anticipation of decrease　先細り予想
　　anticipation of life　寿命の想定
　　anticipation of tax　課税見越し, 課税見込み
　　anticipation rate　前払い割引率, 期限前払い値引き
　　bond anticipation note　債券見込み債, 長期債借換え予定証券
　　grant anticipation note　補助金見込み債, 贈与見込み証券
　　long-term equity anticipation securities　長期株式期待証券
　　revenue anticipation note　歳入見込み証券
　　tax anticipation bill　納税準備証券, 租税証券
　　tax anticipation note　税収見込み債, 税収見込み証券
anticipatory　(形)予想の, 予想しての, 見越しての, 予期の, 先行の, 先回りの, 先取りした, 仮の
　　anticipatory breach　期限前契約不履行
　　anticipatory investment　先行投資
　　anticipatory letter of credit　輸出前払い信用状
　　anticipatory payment　手形の満期日前払い
　　anticipatory profit　見込み利益
anticounterfeiting　(名)偽造防止
　　◆New banknotes have been produced with advanced anti-counterfeiting technology, including a hologram. 新札は、ホログラムなど偽造防止の先端技術を駆使して造られている。
antideflation measures　デフレ対策
　　◆Even at this juncture, the government has yet to come up with comprehensive antideflation measures. この期に及んでも、政府の総合デフレ対策は出てこない。
antidilution [anti-dilution]　(名)逆希薄化, 希薄化防止, 濃縮効果
　　antidilution clause　希薄化防止条項
Antimonopoly Law　独占禁止法（⇒business alliance）
　　◆As far as the debt equity swap is concerned, its main banks' holdings of outstanding shares may increase further than the 5 percent limit stipulated by the Antimonopoly Law. 債務の株式化に関するかぎり、主力取引銀行の発行済み株式の持ち株

ANTI

比率が、独占禁止法で定める5%の上限を上回る可能性がある。◆Corporate merger screening is conducted by the Fair Trade Commission of Japan in light of the Antimonopoly Law. 企業の合併審査は、独占禁止法に照らして[基づいて]公正取引委員会が行う。◆The bank was found to have forced corporate borrowers to buy financial products in violation of the Antimonopoly Law. 同行は、独占禁止法に違反して融資先企業に金融商品を無理に購入させていたことが判明した。

antiselection （名）逆選択（=adverse selection: 保険事故発生率が高い危険ほど、保険契約者が保険をかける傾向）

antispeculation （名）投機規制（形）投機規制の

antitakeover measure 買収防衛策、買収への対抗措置
◆More than 100 companies are expected to seek shareholder approval of their antitakeover measures. 100社を超える企業が、買収防衛策の株主承認を求める見通しだ。◆The firm's share prices declined after it announced an antitakeover measure in May. 同社が5月に買収防衛策を発表した後、同社の株価は下落した。

antitakeover method 買収防衛方式、買収防衛策、買収への対抗策
◆The company's poison pill scheme is inappropriate as an antitakeover method before a potential acquirer emerges. 同社のポイズン・ピル防衛策は、買収者候補が現われる前の買収への対抗策[買収への事前の対抗策]としては相当性を欠いている。

antitrust law 独占禁止法、反トラスト法
◆The U.S. Federal Trade Commission concluded there was not enough evidence that a Sony-BMG merger would violate U.S. antitrust laws. 米連邦取引委員会（FTC）は、ソニーとBMG（独複合メディア大手ベルテルスマンの音楽事業部門）の統合が米国の独占禁止法に違反することを示す十分な証拠はない、との結論を下した。

antivirus software ウイルス対策ソフト、ウイルス駆除ソフト（=virus protection software）
◆Users of online banking services had better take security measures by using antivirus software. ネット・バンキングの利用者は、ウイルス対策ソフトを使ってセキュリティ対策を取ったほうが良い。

APEC アジア太平洋経済協力会議、エイペック（Asia-Pacific Economic Cooperationの略）
◆APEC groups 21 economies, including Japan, the United States, China, South Korea, Russia, Southeast Asian countries, Canada and some Latin American nations. APECには、日本、米国、中国、韓国、ロシア、東南アジア諸国、カナダ、中南米諸国など21の国・地域が参加している。◆The envisaged timeline of APEC leaders for overcoming the global financial crisis may result in an empty promise. 世界的な金融危機を克服するためのアジア太平洋経済協力会議（APEC）首脳の目標期限は、空手形に終わる可能性がある。◆The special statement on the world economy adopted by the APEC forum specified a timeline for implementing the measures. アジア太平洋経済協力会議（APEC）で採択された世界経済に関する特別声明は、その対策実施の期限を明記した。

apparent （形）明白な、はっきりした、明示的、外見上の、表見的、見かけの
　apparent adversity （為替の）目先逆調（通貨価値の低下による為替相場の下落傾向）
　apparent authority 表見的権限、表見権限
　apparent easement 明示的地役権
　apparent good order and condition 外観無故障（船会社の積み荷引受条件）
　apparent yield 見かけの利回り

appeal （動）懇願する、懇請する、求める、（資金を）募（つの）る、異議を申し立てる、控訴する、上告する、訴え（る）、抗議する、アピールする

appeal against the verdict　判決を不服として控訴する
appeal for funds　資金を募る
appeal for money to help refugees　難民救済の資金を求める
appeal one's case to a higher court　事件を上級裁判所に控訴する
appeal to the Supreme Court　最高裁判所に上訴する[上告]する
◆Belarus has appealed to the IMF for a $8 billion rescue loan. ベラルーシは、国際通貨基金（IMF）に80億ドルの金融支援融資を要請した。◆The bank appealed last week's court order. 同行は、先週の裁判所命令に異議を申し立てた。◆The company appealed to the Tokyo High Court the same day. 同社は即日、東京高裁に抗告した。

appeal （名）懇願、懇請、要請、要求、訴え、抗議、異議申立て、不服の申立て、高等裁判所への控訴・抗告、最高裁判所への上告・上訴、魅力、人気、アピール
　a court of appeal　控訴裁判所（=appeal court）
　appeal against the verdict　判決を不服として控訴する
　appeal point　訴求点
　be on appeal to the Supreme Court　最高裁に上告中である
　have wide appeal　幅広い人気がある
　hold little appeal for　〜にはほとんど魅力がない
　lodge[enter, file] an appeal with the Tokyo High Court　東京高裁に控訴する
　reject an appeal[appeals]　上告を棄却する
◆If the appeal is rejected, we'll appeal to the Tokyo High Court. 異議申立てが却下されたら、当社は高裁に抗告する。◆Record low U.S. borrowing costs are boosting the appeal to bullion as a hedge against inflation. 米国の資金調達コストが過去最低の水準にあるため、インフレ・ヘッジとしての金[金地金]の人気が高まっている。

appear （動）〜に見える、〜する模様である、〜の感がある、現れる、登場する、出現する、（市場に）出回る、並ぶ、（新聞などに）載る
　appear expensive　割高感がある
　appear inexpensive　割安感がある
　appear on the market　市場に出回る、上場する
　appear to have hit bottom　底入れ感が出る
◆Nippon Life Insurance Co. appears to remain Olympus Corp.'s leading shareholder though the insurer's stake in Olympus has been reduced to 4.9 percent from 8.1 percent. 日本生命のオリンパス株保有比率は8.1%から4.9%に下がったものの、同生保はオリンパスの筆頭株主にとどまるものと見られる。

appetite （名）欲求、欲望、好み、意欲、選好、選好度、需要
　appetite for cash　現金需要、資金需要
　appetite for goods　消費ブーム
　appetite for high yielding assets　高利回り資産選好度
　appetite to pay　ペイ意欲
　investor appetite　投資家の需要、投資家の投資意欲
　risk appetite　リスク選好、リスク選好度[リスク選好の度合い]、リスクを積極的に取る意欲、リスクを取って投資するという意欲、リスク許容度[許容量]
　the appetite of foreign investors　外国人投資家の投資意欲
◆Investors have lost all their risk appetite for the Greek bonds. 投資家に、ギリシャの国債に対して積極的にリスクを取る意欲がまったく見られなくなった[ギリシャの国債に対する投資家のリスク選好が、まったく見られなくなった]。

appetite from customers 顧客需要
◆Employers are chopping costs to cope with dwindling appetite from customers. 企業は、コストを削減して、顧客需要

の減少に対応している。

applicable （形）適用される, 適用できる, 適用可能な, 応用できる, 配賦可能な, 〜に帰属する, 妥当な, 適当な, 適切な, 適格な, 対応する
  amounts applicable to　〜に配分された額
  applicable Federal rate　適格連邦税率
  applicable fees　適用料金
  applicable financial statements　適格財務諸表, 適格財務書類
  applicable government price index　適格政府物価指数
  applicable income taxes　適用所得税, 当該所得税
  applicable installment obligation　適格割賦債権
  applicable interest rate for the loan　ローンに適用される金利
  applicable law　適用される法律, 適用法, 準拠法
  applicable tax rate　適用税率
  applicable usury law　適用される利息制限法
    （⇒delinquent amounts）
  consolidated net income applicable to common shares　普通株式に帰属する連結純利益

applicable interest rate　適用される金利
  ◆The applicable interest rate for the loan will be 53/8 percent p.a. その融資に適用される金利は, 年率で5.375%です。

applicable legal contract rate　適用される法定約定金利
  ◆Any payment not made when due will, in addition to any other right or remedy of Licensor, incur a finance charge at the lesser of three hundred basis points over the 3-month London Inter Bank Offered Rate ("LIBOR＋3") on the date payment was due or the highest applicable legal contract rate. 支払いが支払い期日までに履行されない場合, ライセンサーの他の権利や救済請求権に加えて, 支払い期日時点の3か月物ロンドン銀行間取引金利（LIBOR）プラス3%（LIBOR＋3%）または適用される最高法定約定金利のうち, いずれか低いほうの金利の金融費用が発生する。

applicant　（名）申請人, 応募者, 申告者, 志願者, 依頼人
  applicant for shares　株式申込み人［申込み者, 応募者］
  applicant for the credit　信用状発行依頼人
    （＝letter of credit applicant）
  applicant for the letter of credit　信用状開設依頼人, 信用状発行依頼人
    （＝letter of credit applicant）

application　（名）申込み, 申請, 出願, 申請者, 申込み者, 申請書, 応募書類, 願書, 依頼書, 信用状開設依頼書, 運用, 適用, 応用, 使途, 配賦, 予定配賦, 割賦適用業務, アプリケーション・ソフト, 応用ソフト, 応用システム, 適用業務, アプリケーション
  application account　（株式申込み）証拠金勘定
  application and allotment book　（株式の）申込み・割当帳
  application for court protection under the Civil Rehabilitation Law　民事再生法の適用申請
  application for error correction　（顧客からの委託注文について間違いがあった場合に, 証券会社が証券取引所に対して行う）過誤訂正の申請
  application for export license　輸出願書
  application for import license　輸入承認申請書
  application for insurance　保険申込み書
  application for loan form　借入申込み用紙
  application for new warrant　（税関への）倉荷証券再下付願い
  application for quotation　上場申請
  application for registration　登録申請, 登録申込み
  application for shares　株式の申込み
  application form　申込み書［用紙］, 申請書
    （＝application blank）
  application money（on［for］stock）　株式申込み証拠金, 株式申込み金, 申込み金
  application of automatic account transfer　預金口座振替依頼書
  application slip　保険申込み書, 申込み書
  application taking　申込み受付け
  application to open a current account［a/c］　当座取引申込み書
  application to refinance existing loans　ローン借換えの申込み
  credit ceiling application　貸出限度額の適用
  deny an application　申請を却下する
  drawback application　戻し税申請
    （＝application for drawback）
  economic application　経済的応用
  extraterritorial application　域外適用
  file［lodge, make, send in］an application for　〜の申請書を提出する, 〜の申請を出す
  fill out an application　申込み書［申請書］に記入する
  foreign exchange application　外国為替申込み, 外国為替申告
  foreign investment applications　外国からの投資申請
  grant an application　申請を認める, 承認を与える
  index of applications for home purchases　住宅購入用モーゲージ申込み指数, 住宅ローン申込み指数
  investment applications　投資申請件数, 投資申請
  license application　免許申請
  listing application　上場申請
  loan application　融資申込み, 貸付け申込み, 借入申込み, ローンの申込み
  mortgage application　住宅ローンの申込み, モーゲージ申込み
  mortgage applications　モーゲージ申請件数, モーゲージ申込み件数
  pay-on application　請求払い, P/A
  preliminary application for listing　上場の仮申請
  priority order of application　充当順位
  qualification for the application of a loan　ローン審査
  refinancing applications　借換え申請件数
  screen investment applications　投資申請を審査する
  share application form　株式申込み用紙
  shipping application　船積申込み書
    （＝application for shipment）
  source and application of working capital　運転資金の源泉と使途
  statement of（source and）application of funds　資金運用表
  submit an application　申請書［応募書類］を提出する, 申請を出す
  the amount payable on application　申込み証拠金
  time limit for application　申込み期限
  ◆An insurance agent is a sales person who represents a life insurance company for the purpose of soliciting applications, collecting initial premiums, and servicing insurance contracts. 保険募集人は, 生命保険会社を代表して保険契約の勧誘, 初回保険料の徴収, 保険契約に関する役務を提供する販売員である。◆At the time of its application for court protection under the Civil Rehabilitation Law, the firm had debts amounting to ¥2.2 billion. 民事再生法の適用申請時に, 同社は総額22億円の負債をかかえていた。◆The Group's sales figures have been restated following the retrospective appli-

cation of new International Financial Reporting Standards. 当グループの売上高の数値は、新国際財務報告基準(IFRS)を遡及的に適用して、再表示されています。◆The number of applications for compensation under the workers compensation insurance system made at labor standards inspection offices nationwide increased 19 percent to 819 from 690 cases in the previous year. 全国の労働基準監督署で行われた労災保険制度に基づく給付請求の件数は、前年度の690件に比べて19％増加して819件に達した。

application for self-declared bankruptcy 自己破産の申立て
◆The number of annual applications for individual and corporate self-declared bankruptcy cases surpassed 200,000 for the first time in 2002. 1年間の個人と法人の自己破産申立て件数が、2002年に初めて20万件を突破した。

application of funds 資金運用, 資金の使途, 資金の適用
 application of funds statement　資金運用表
  （=statement of application of funds）
 worksheet for statement of application of funds　資金運用精査表

application of international rules 新国際基準の適用
◆Twenty-eight banks of the world will face capital surcharges of 1 percent to 2.5 percent by the application of international rules to rein in too-big-to-fail lenders. 大きすぎて破たんさせられない銀行［金融機関］を規制する国際基準が適用されると、世界の28行が、1～2.5％の資本［自己資本］上積みの対象となる。

apply （動）適用する, 応用する, 利用する, 当てはめる, 配賦（はいふ）する
 apply a provisionary rating to a shelf registration　一括登録に予備格付けを用いる
 apply an acceptable actuarial method　認められている保険数理法を適用する
 apply for a new mortgage　新規モーゲージを申し込む［申請する］
 apply for approval to issue offshore　外債発行の認可を申請する
 apply restraint　緊縮政策を取る
 apply to refinance existing loans　ローンの借換えを申請する
◆Countries likely to be affected by the fiscal and financial crisis in Europe will basically be able to obtain the IMF's short-term loans immediately after applying for them. 欧州財政・金融危機が波及しそうな国は、IMF（国際通貨基金）に要請すると、基本的にIMFの短期融資を即時に受けられる。

apply for a loan 融資を申し込む, 融資を申請する
 （⇒take control of）
◆The bank recommended a person affiliated with it be appointed as an executive to a company that had applied for a loan. 同行は、同行の息のかかった人物を、融資を申し込んできた会社の役員に選任するよう推奨していた。

apply for bankruptcy protection 会社更生手続き申請する, 会社更生手続きの適用を申請する
◆JAL and its two subsidiaries applied to the Tokyo District Court for bankruptcy protection under the Corporate Rehabilitation Law. 日航とその子会社2社が、会社更生法に基づいて会社更生手続きの適用を東京地裁に申請した。

apply for protection from creditors 会社更生手続きを申請する, 破たん申請する, 資産保全を請求する
 （=file for protection from creditors）
◆The credit union was forced to apply to the Financial Services Agency for protection from creditors. 同信組は、金融庁への破たん申請を迫られた。

apply for protection from creditors under the bankruptcy reform law 民事再生法の適用を申請する　（=file for protection from creditors under the Civil Rehabilitation Law）
◆The firm applied for protection from creditors under the bankruptcy reform law at the Tokyo District Court. 同社が、東京地裁に民事再生法の適用を申請した。

appoint （動）指名する, 任命する, 選任する, 指定する, 定める
 appoint an administrator　管財人を指名する
 appointed account　指定口座
 appointed transfer account　振込み指定口座
◆In the proposal, the investment fund requests nine people be appointed board members. この提案で、同投資ファンドは、9人を取締役に選任するよう求めている。

appraisal （名）評価, 査定, 鑑定, 見積り
 appraisal capital　評価替えによる資本
 appraisal of asset　資産の鑑定
 appraisal of real estate　不動産評価
 appraisal profits and losses　含み損益, 評価損益
  （=latent profits and losses, unrealized profits and losses; ⇒basic profit）
 appraisal report　鑑定報告書
 appraisal right　株式買取り請求権
 appraisal surplus　評価替え剰余金
 appraisal value　評価額, 評価価値, 鑑定評価額, 査定価値
  （=appraised value, assessed value）
 performance appraisal　業績評価

appraisal gain 含み益, 評価益
 （=appraisal profit, latent gain）
◆The increase in seven insurers' core operating profits is due to appraisal gains in their stockholdings. 生保7社の基礎利益（本業のもうけに当たる）の増加は、保有株式の含み益によるものだ。◆The nine insurers booked about ¥5 trillion in combined appraisal gains on their shareholdings. 生保9社の保有株式の含み益は、総額で約5兆円となった。

appraisal loss 含み損, 評価損, 保有株の評価損を損失に計上する減損処理額
 （=latent loss, valuation loss）
◆Appraisal losses on securities holdings dealt a blow to the firm's earnings. 保有証券の含み損［評価損］が、同社の収益に打撃を与えた。◆Banks are regulated to reduce the capital in the event of hefty appraisal losses, as a way of requiring shareholders to share the burden of the losses. 巨額の含み損［評価損］の場合、銀行規制で銀行は、株主にもその損失の負担を引き受けさせるために資本金を削減することになる。◆If the appraisal losses swell excessively, banks failing to meet the regulatory minimum capital adequacy requirements will have to go under. 含み損が余りにも膨らむと、規制当局の最低自己資本比率基準を満たせない銀行は、経営破たんに追い込まれることになる。◆In the event of hefty appraisal losses, banks must avoid a situation in which their creditors, including depositors, will be affected by the impairment of bank-owned assets. 巨額の含み損が出た場合、銀行は、預金者などの債権者が銀行保有資産の評価減の影響を受けるような状況がないようにしなければならない。◆The nine nonlife insurers suffered total appraisal losses on securities of ¥360 billion. 損保9社が、9社合計で3,600億円の有価証券評価損を計上した。◆The top ten life insurers in the nation reported a total of ¥1.46 trillion in appraisal losses on their securities holdings for the business year that ended in March. 国内主要生保10社の保有有価証券の減損処理額は、3月期決算で1兆4,600億円に達した［1兆4,600億円を記録した］。

appraisal loss of stocks 株式の評価損
◆Under the mark-to-market accounting system, if banks suffer appraisal losses of stocks they are holding, they are required to subtract 60 percent of those losses from their sur-

plus funds. 時価会計制度では、金融機関が保有する株式の評価損が出た場合、金融機関は評価損の6割を剰余金から取り除かなければならない。

appraisal profit 含み益, 評価益
（=appraisal gain, latent profit）
◆According to an estimate by Mizuho Securities Corp., reevaluating the 785 tons of gold bullion owned by the Bank of Japan at the current market value would generate about ¥400 billion in appraisal profits. みずほ証券の試算によると、日銀保有の金地金785トンを時価で再評価することによって約4,000億円の評価益を捻出できる。

appraise （動）評価する, 査定する, 鑑定する, 見積もる
◆When the sovereign debt crisis broke out in the peripheral countries in 2010, the eurozone governments did not accurately appraise losses from sovereign debt portfolios on the part of banks. 2010に財政危機が周辺国で発生した際、ユーロ圏の各国政府は、銀行の国債関連資産の損失を正確に評価しなかった。

appreciate （動）上昇する, 騰貴する, 相場が上がる, 高く評価する, 好感する, 正しく認識［理解］する, 鑑賞する, 感謝する （⇒export-oriented business）
appreciate across the board　全面高となる
appreciate against［relative to］the US$　対米ドルで上昇する, 米ドルに対して上昇する, 米ドルと比べて, 米ドルに照らして
appreciating yen　円高
◆If the yen starts to appreciate, this will have a negative effect on the revenues of exporting companies. 円高に転じれば、輸出企業の収益は円高のマイナス影響を受けることになる。◆In the case of foreign currency deposits, losses may balloon if the yen appreciates further and may cause a loss of principal. 外貨預金の場合、円高がさらに進めば損失が膨らみ、元本割れになる恐れもある。◆The dollar appreciated relative to the euro and the yen. ドルが、ユーロや円より上昇した。◆The yen has stopped appreciating against the dollar. 円高ドル安に、一服感が出ている。◆The yen may appreciate further to ¥70 against the U.S. dollar. 円高は、さらに1ドル＝75円まで進む可能性がある。◆The yen's exchange rate has appreciated to ¥76 against the dollar, so it is the best time to buy U.S. dollars. 円の為替レートが1ドル＝76円に上昇したので、今が米ドルの買い時だ。◆Tokyo stocks appreciated across the board. 東京株［東京株式市場の株価］は、全面高となった。

appreciation （名）価格・相場の上昇, 騰貴, 急騰, 増価, 平価切上げ, 正当な評価, 評価増, 評価切上げ, 評価益, 増加額 （「増価」は、資産価値の増加を意味する）
application form　申込み書, 保険申込み書
appreciation bond　増価償還国債
appreciation of foreign currencies　外貨高
appreciation of one's own currency　自国通貨高
appreciation surplus　評価剰余金, 評価替剰余金, 再評価積立金 （=appraisal surplus）
asset appreciation　資産価値の上昇, 資産の値上がり （=appreciation of assets）
benefits of the yen's appreciation　円高差益 （=foreign exchange profits from the yen's appreciation）
capital appreciation　資本増価, 値上がり益, キャピタル・ゲイン
currency appreciation　通貨高, 通貨騰貴, 通貨価値の騰貴
deflation from yen appreciation　円高デフレ
dollar appreciation　ドル高, ドル切上げ
equity appreciation　株価上昇
exchange appreciation　為替の切上げ
exchange gain from yen appreciation　円高差益
exchange rate appreciation　為替レートの切上げ

land appreciation　地価上昇, 土地増価
price appreciation　値上がり
rapid appreciation of the dollar　急激なドル高
　（=rapid dollar appreciation）
sharp yen appreciation　急激な円高, 円の急騰
　（=sharp appreciation of the yen）
small dollar appreciation　小幅なドル高, ドルの小幅上昇
　（=small appreciation of the dollar）
stock［share］price appreciation　株価上昇
strong yen appreciation　大幅な円高, 円の大幅上昇
　（=strong appreciation of the yen）
the appreciation of foreign currencies　外貨高
the appreciation potential of a company's common stock
　企業の普通株式の株価見通し
the pace of appreciation of the renminbi by China　中国の人民元の切上げペース　（⇒monitor）
the yen's appreciation against the dollar　円高・ドル安, ドルに対する円相場の上昇
the yen's excessive appreciation　行き過ぎた円高
the yen's extremely rapid appreciation　超円高
◆Amid a widening slump in global auto sales and the yen's sharp appreciation against the U.S. dollar, the firm is expected to report an unconsolidated operating loss in fiscal 2010. 世界の新車販売の落ち込み拡大と急激な円高・ドル安に伴って、同社の2011年度［2011年3月期決算］の営業利益は、単独ベース［単独決算］で赤字が見込まれている。◆As one option to avoid excessive currency appreciation in emerging countries with inflationary trends, they can restrict an influx of capital. インフレ気味の新興国で行き過ぎた［過度の］通貨高を避けるための手段として、資金流入を規制することができる。◆The yen's extremely rapid appreciation may deliver a bitter blow to the domestic economy. 超円高は、国内経済に大きな打撃を与える可能性がある。

appreciation of currencies　通貨高
（=currency appreciation）
◆Speculative money is causing appreciation of currencies and inflation in emerging economies. 投機マネーが、新興国の通貨高やインフレを招いている。

appreciation of one's own currency　自国通貨高
◆The surest way to arrest the appreciation of one's own currency is to continue to buy dollars against its own currency. 自国通貨高を回避するための最も確実な方法は、自国通貨を売ってドルを買い進めるやり方だ。

appreciation of the U.S. dollar　ドル高
◆The rapid appreciation of the U.S. dollar would impair the current improvement in the Japanese economy. 急激なドル高は、日本の景気回復の腰を折ることになる。

appreciation of the yen　円高, 円の騰貴, 円為替相場の上昇
（=the yen's appreciation, yen appreciation）
a rapid［sharp］appreciation of the yen　急激な円高, 円の急騰　（⇒rapid）
appreciation of the yen against［versus］the U.S. dollar
　円高・ドル安, 円の対ドル相場の上昇, 米ドルに対する円相場の上昇
cope with the appreciation of the yen　円高に対応する
further appreciation of the yen　一層の円高, 円高進行
premature appreciation of the yen　時期尚早の円高
small appreciation of the yen　円の小幅上昇, 円相場の小幅上昇, 小幅な円高
strong appreciation of the yen　円の大幅上昇, 円相場の大幅上昇, 大幅な円高
the current appreciation of the yen　現在の円高
◆It's difficult to offset losses from further appreciation of the

yen with interest as interest rates in many foreign currency deposits are low. 外貨建て預金の多くは金利が低いので、円高進行による損失分を利息で相殺する[取り戻す]のは難しい。◆Japan should find a new source of economic growth to cope with the appreciation of the yen. 日本は、新たな経済成長の源泉を見い出して、円高に対応すべきだ。◆Premature appreciation of the yen is not favorable. 時期尚早の円高は、好ましくない。◆The appreciation of the yen has pushed exports downward, slashing corporate profits. 円高で輸出が低迷し、企業収益も減少している。◆The current appreciation of the yen, if left unabated, would slow the recovery of the economy, causing the stock market to weaken. 現在の円高がこのまま進行すれば、景気回復に水を差し、株安を招くことになる。

appreciation of the yen and the fall of the dollar 円高・ドル安
　◆Dollar-selling pressure has eased and put a temporary brake on the sharp appreciation of the yen and the fall of the dollar. ドル売り圧力が弱まり、急激な円高・ドル安にいったん歯止めがかかった。

appreciation of the yuan 人民元の切上げ
　(=appreciation of the value of the yuan [renminbi])
　◆Appreciation of the yuan would curb inflation in China. 人民元の切上げは、中国のインフレ抑制につながる。◆China's renminbi may attain a reserve-currency status by the steady appreciation of the yuan and the country's enormous capital surpluses. 中国の人民元は、人民元の着実な切上げと中国の膨大な資本剰余金によって、準備通貨の地位を獲得する可能性がある。

appreciation pressure on the yen 円高圧力
　◆In spite of the government and the BOJ's market intervention to stop the yen from surging, appreciation pressure on the yen still remains. 政府・日銀は円急騰に歯止めをかけるため市場介入したが、円高圧力はまだ残っている。

approach （動）～に近づく[接近する]、～を迎える、～に話を持ちかける、～に打診する、接触する、（問題などを）検討する、取り上げる、～に取り組む、～に取りかかる[着手する]
　approach a bottom　底入れが近い、底値圏に近づく
　approach financial institutions banks about　～について金融機関に打診する
　be approached to participate in the syndication　シ団への参加を打診される
　◆Tokyo Electric Power Co. has approached financial institutions about selling its assets to raise funds for the massive amount of compensation it is likely to pay. 東京電力は、同社が支払う予定の巨額の賠償金の資金調達のため、金融機関に同社の資産売却をすでに打診している。

approach （名）主義、方法、方式、手法、取組み、取組み方、姿勢、政策、路線、研究、研究法、解決法、進入、接近、アプローチ
　analytic approach　分析手法、分析的アプローチ
　asset-liability [asset and liability] approach　資産負債法、資産・負債法
　bottom-up approach　ボトム・アップ型アプローチ
　business-oriented approach　企業寄りの政策
　　(=probusiness approach)
　cash balances approach　現金残高接近法
　cost approach　原価法
　flow-of-funds approach　資金循環アプローチ
　full cost approach　全部原価法
　hybrid financing approach　混合金融手法
　income approach　所得分析、所得接近法
　key currency approach　基軸通貨方式
　liquidity approach　流動性アプローチ
　management approach　経営方法、意思決定論的アプローチ
　mark-to-market approach　値洗い方式
　master valuation approach　包括評価法
　monetarist approach　マネタリスト・アプローチ
　monetary approach　貨幣的接近法
　net-of-tax approach　税額控除法
　net profit approach　純利益法
　portfolio approach　ポートフォリオ手法
　prior-savings approach　事前貯蓄アプローチ
　quasi-reorganization approach　準更生手続き
　rating approach　格付け方法
　risk-adjusted approach　リスク調整法
　top-down approach　トップ・ダウン型アプローチ
　◆BHP sweetened its initial approach by 13 percent, offering 3.4 of its shares for every Rio share. 英豪系資源最大手のBHP社は、最初の提示条件を13%引き上げ、リオ1株に対してBHPの株式3.4株の株式交換比率を提示した。◆The eurozone's crisis management approach is always behind the curve. ユーロ圏の危機管理への取組みは、いつも後手に回っている。

appropriate （動）充当する、当てる[充てる]、支出する、予算に計上する、支出を承認する、占有する、私物化する、私用に供する、着服する、横領する、盗用する
　appropriate a common interest　公共の利益を独占する
　appropriate public money for one's own use　公金を横領する
　appropriated retained earnings [income]　処分済み利益剰余金　(=appropriated earned surplus)
　appropriated surplus　処分済み剰余金
　retained earnings appropriated for bond　減債積立金

appropriate （形）適切な、適正な、ふさわしい
　appropriate action　適切な措置
　appropriate credit protections　適切な信用補強
　appropriate example　適例
　appropriate interest rate　適正な利率、適正な金利
　appropriate portfolio diversification　適切な分散投資
　appropriate rating　適切な格付け
　appropriate tax authorities　所轄の税務当局
　appropriate yield-to-maturity　適正な最終利回り

appropriation （名）充当、充用、配分、処分、収用、利益処分、剰余金処分、充当金、支出金、積立金、承認済み予算額、割当予算額、配分額、歳出予算、政府支出金
　additional appropriation　追加予算
　appropriation budget　割当予算
　appropriation for special allowances　特別引当金充当金、特別積立金積立額
　appropriation fund　充当基金
　appropriation of earned surplus　利益剰余金の処分
　appropriation of net income　純利益の処分
　appropriation of surplus　剰余金処分
　appropriation of surplus for reserves　準備金積立て
　appropriations for redemption of bonds　社債償還積立金
　budgetary appropriation　予算の計上
　budgetary appropriations　予算割当額
　capital appropriations　資本処分、資本準備金
　lump sum appropriation　総括予算、一括割当て
　profit appropriation　利益の処分
　surplus appropriation statement　剰余金処分計算書
　◆The basic pension plan has been covered by premiums paid by subscribers and government budgetary appropriations. 基礎年金は、加入者が支払う保険料と政府の予算割当額（国の負

担）で賄（まかな）われている。

approval （名）承認, 承諾, 是認, 賛成, 賛同, 同意, 支持, 認可, 許可
 approval for the issue 発行認可
 conditional approval 条件付き認可
 credit approval 与信承認, 信用供与承認, 与信決裁
 investment approvals 投資承認額, 投資認可額
 loan approval procedures ローン承認手続き
 shareholder approval 株主の承認
 ◆At an emergency shareholders meeting, the company obtained shareholder approval to transfer ¥199 billion from its legal reserves to provide for write-offs of nonperforming loans. 臨時株主総会で同社は、株主から、不良債権処理に備えて法定準備金から1,990億円を取り崩す案の承認を得た。◆More than 100 companies are expected to seek shareholder approval of their antitakeover measures. 100社を超える企業が、買収防衛策の株主承認を求める見通しだ。◆The approval of numerous stockholders must be gained for a retirement of 50 percent of common shares. 普通株式の50%消却については、多くの株主の承認を得なければならない。◆The firm controls its exposure to credit risk through credit approvals, credit limits and monitoring procedures. 同社は、信用供与承認や信用限度、監視手続きを通じて信用リスクを管理している。◆The Tokyo Stock Exchange has canceled its approval for the company's plan to go public on the Mother's market. 東京証券取引所は、同社の東証マザーズへの上場計画承認を取り消した。

approval for a triangular [triangle] merger 三角合併の承認
 ◆Approval for a triangular merger should be based on a special resolution. 三角合併の承認は、特別決議によらなければならない［三角合併には、特別決議による承認が必要だ］

approve （動）承認する, 承諾する, 賛成する, 賛同する, 同意する, 支持する, 認可する, 許可する
 approved acceptance 承認引受手形
 approved carrier rating guide 公認保険業者格付け一覧
 approved methods for the preparation of balance sheet statements 公認貸借対照表作成方法
 approved pension scheme 適格年金制度
 the number of investments approved 投資認可件数
 ◆A federal appeals court in New York approved the sale of Chrysler assets to Fiat. ニューヨークの米連邦控訴裁判所は、クライスラー資産のフィアットへの売却を承認した。◆An initiative to strengthen the functions of the European Financial Stability Facility (EFSF) was approved at the 17 eurozone countries' parliaments. 欧州金融安定基金（EFSF）の機能強化案が、ユーロ圏17か国の議会で承認された。◆In the conventional IMF's scheme, countries were only given a credit line even after the IMF approved loans and they could not withdraw funds unless the fiscal crisis facing them worsened. 従来のIMF（国際通貨基金）の仕組みだと、各国は融資の承認を得ても融資枠を与えられるだけで、財政危機が深刻化しないと資金を引き出すことができなかった。◆JAL hopes the banks will approve the new loans for procuring new equipment by the end of this year. 日航は、新たな機材を調達するための新規融資について、年内に銀行団の同意を得たい考えだ。◆The company's board approved a plan to issue subscription warrants to all shareholders on its shareholders list as of March 31, 2011. 同社の取締役会は、2011年3月31日現在［時点］の株主名簿に記載されている全株主を対象に、新株予約権を発行する計画を承認した。◆Under the firm's rehabilitation plan approved by the district court, financial institutions will waive 87.5 percent of the unsecured loans they extend to the firm. 地方裁判所が認可した同社の更生計画では、金融機関が、同社に行った無担保融資［同社に対する無担保債権］の87.5%を放棄することになっている。

April-December period 4-12月期
 (=the nine months to Dec. 31)

April-June quarter 4-6月期（3月期決算企業の第1四半期、12月期決算企業の第2四半期）
 ◆In the April-June quarter, major high-tech companies suffered losses or profit declines. 4-6月期は、主要ハイテク企業が赤字や減益に苦しんでいる。

April-June revenue 4-6月期の売上高, 4-6月期の収益

April-September fiscal first half 3月期決算企業の上半期, 4-9月期の上半期, 4-9月期の上半期決算, 9月中間決算

April-September period 4-9月期, 9月中間決算, （3月期決算企業の）上半期［上期］
 (=the six months to September 30)
 ◆The combined sales of 813 nonfinancial companies in the April-September period grew 6.3 percent over the previous year. 金融を除く企業813社の上期（4-9月期）の売上高の合計は、前年同期比で6.3%増加した。◆The firm posted a net profit of ¥1.5 billion for the April-September period. 同社は、9月中間決算で15億円の税引き後利益を計上した。

APU アジア決済同盟（Asian Payment Unionの略）

arbiter （名）審判者, 決定者, 決定機関, 判定者, 判定機関, 採決者, 仲裁者, 仲裁人調停者, （ある分野の）権威
 ◆The U.S. business cycle arbiter declared that the U.S. economy slipped into recession in December 2007. 米国の景気循環の判定機関が、米経済は2007年12月から景気後退局面（リセッション）に入ったことを公表した。

arbitrage （名）裁定, 裁定取引, さや取り売買, アービトラージ（裁定取引とは、市場間の価格差や現物と先物との間の価格差を利用する取引のこと）
 arbitrage opportunities 裁定取引の機会, 裁定機会
 generate swap arbitrage opportunities スワップによる裁定機会を生み出す
 interest rate arbitrage 金利裁定
 (=interest arbitrage)
 new issue arbitrage 新発債の裁定取引, 起債裁定
 risk arbitrage リスク裁定取引, リスクを伴った裁定取引, リスク・アービトラージ
 (=takeover arbitrage)
 riskless arbitrage 無リスク裁定
 stock index arbitrage インデックス裁定取引
 structured arbitrage 仕組み裁定取引
 (=structured arbitrage transaction)
 swap arbitrage opportunities スワップによる裁定機会
 (=arbitrage opportunities against swaps)

arbitrate （動）裁定する, 仲裁する
 arbitrated exchange rate 裁定為替［外国為替］相場
 (=arbitrate rate of exchange)
 arbitrated interest rate 裁定金利
 arbitrated rate 裁定相場

area （名）地域, 領域, 部門, 分野, 圏, エリア
 area headquarters 地域本部
 area superintendent 地域担当管理部長
 bonded area 保税地域
 diversify into related areas 関連分野への多角化を進める, 関連分野に多角化する
 geographic area information 地域別情報, 地域セグメント情報
 key areas 主要分野, 中核業務
 leading-edge area 先端分野
 market area 市場地域, 営業地域, 商圏
 trade area 商圏, 商勢圏, 貿易圏
 trade-area size 商圏規模, 商圏の大きさ
 U.S. dollar area 米ドル圏

◆Aeon Co. now owns a number of large stores in suburban areas, such as Jusco. イオンは現在、ジャスコなど郊外で展開する大型店を多く所有している。

ARM 変動金利型抵当貸付け, 変動金利モーゲージ, 変動利付きモーゲージ (adjustable rate mortgageの略)

arm (名)子会社, 部門, 部局, 支店, アーム (⇒unit)
- brokerage arm 証券子会社, 証券会社, 証券部門
- consulting arm コンサルティング部門, コンサルティング会社
- finance arm 金融子会社
- financing arm 金融子会社, 金融部門
- long-arm jurisdiction 域外適用管轄権
- research arm 研究所, 研究部門
- treasury arm 財務部門

◆General Motors Acceptance Corp. (GMAC), GM's finance arm, is giving the boost to the struggling automaker's bottom line. GMの金融子会社GMACが、経営再建に取り組む米自動車メーカーGMの業績の後押しをしている。◆General Motors Corp. has reached an agreement to sell a 51 percent stake in its finance arm. ゼネラル・モーターズ(GM)は、金融子会社(GMAC)の株式の51%を売却することで合意した。

around (前・副)〜前後の, 約[ほぼ, 大体]〜
- account for around 10 percent 約10%を占める, 10%前後を占める
- be traded around ¥76 ほぼ[約]76円で取引される, 76円近辺で取引される
- remain stable at around 10 percent level ほぼ[約]10%の水準で安定している

◆The Bank of Japan kept the key short-term interest rate steady at around zero to 0.1 percent. 日銀は、短期の政策金利をほぼ0〜0.1%に据え置いた。◆The U.S. dollar was traded at around ¥76 on the currency market. 為替市場では、1ドル＝76円をはさんだ取引が続いた。

arrange (動)手配する, 取り決める, 手はずを整える, 取りまとめる, 準備する, 打ち合わせる, 解決する, 同意する, アレンジする
- arrange a term loan facility ターム・ローン(有期貸付け)案件をアレンジする
- arrange an initial public offering 株式公募を取りまとめる
- arrange an insurance facility 保険ファシリティを締結する, 保険の案件をアレンジする
- arrange for 〜の手配をする (=make arrangements for)
- arrange interim financing つなぎ融資をアレンジする
- arrange the financing package 融資パッケージをアレンジする
- arranged total loss 妥協全損 (=agreed total loss)
- arranging bank アレンジ行

◆The firm appointed Deutsche Bank AG and Daiwa Securities SMBC to arrange an initial public offering to raise about ¥100 billion. 同社は、約1,000億円を調達するため、ドイツ銀行と大和証券SMBCを株式公募の取りまとめ役に指名した。◆The 17 eurozone nations must ratify the agreement on bailout measures to arrange a rescue system for Greece. ギリシャへの支援体制を整えるには、ユーロ圏の17か国が、支援策についての合意事項を承認しなければならない。

arrangement (名)手配, 準備, 打合せ, 取決め, 協定, 合意, 契約, 取りまとめ, 調整, 仲介, 債務整理, 和議, 解決, アレンジメント
- agency arrangement 代理店契約, コルレス契約, 取引約定書
- arrangement fee アレンジメント手数料
- bank credit arrangement 銀行貸出枠
- borrowing arrangement 借入協定, 借入れの取決め
- business arrangement 業務協定, 業務契約, 業務提携
- correspondent arrangement コルレス契約
- currency arrangement 通貨協定
- custodial arrangement 保管の取決め
- deed of arrangement 債務整理証書
- financial arrangements ファイナンスの仲介
- formal arrangement 正式取決め
- General Arrangements to Borrow (IMFの)一般借入取決め
- IMF standby arrangement IMFのスタンドバイ契約
- Indemnification arrangement 補償契約
- insurance arrangements 保険契約
- international banking supervisory arrangements 国際銀行監督協定
- listing arrangements 上場取決め
- make arrangements for 〜の手配をする (=arrange for)
- margin offset arrangements 証拠金相殺制度
- monetary arrangement 通貨協定
- netting arrangement ネッティング契約
- phase-in arrangement 段階的実施の措置
- project financing arrangement プロジェクト金融の取決め
- refinancing arrangement 借換え協定
- revolving credit arrangement 回転信用契約
- standby arrangement スタンドバイ協定, スタンドバイ取決め, 借入予約協定
- swap arrangement スワップ協定
- unallocated insurance arrangements 未配分保険契約

◆The two firms have built a relationship during a three-year business arrangement. 両社は、3年前からの業務提携で信頼関係を築いた。

arranger (名)外債発行手続きの仲介をする斡旋人, 主幹事団, アレンジャー

arrears (名)延滞, 遅滞, 延滞金, 滞納金, 未納金, 未払い金, 延滞債務
- arrears on loan repayments 延滞債権
- be in arrears on principal and interest payments 元利の返済に遅れが出ている
- in arrears 延滞している, 遅滞している, 遅れが出ている, 未払いの, 未納の, 後払いで
- interest for arrears 延滞利息
- payable quarterly in arrears 年4回の後払い, 年4回の後払い方式で

◆The bank has about ¥2.6 trillion in loans to firms that are in arrears on principal and interest payments. 同行には、元利の返済に遅れが出ている企業向け融資額[債権]が約2兆6,000億円ある。

ARS 金利入札証券, オークション・レート・セキュリティーズ (⇒auction-rate debt, auction-rate security)

◆The $330 billion ARS market collapsed in February 2008. 3,300億ドル規模の米金利入札証券(ARS)市場は、2008年2月に崩壊した。

articles (名)(会社の)定款(ていかん), (法律などの)条項, 届出書
- articles of agreement 契約[協約]の条項, 契約書, 契約覚書, 社団の規約
- articles of amendment 修正条項
- articles of association 米国の会社の基本定款(articles of incorporation), 英国の会社の通常定款(英国の会社の

基本定款＝memorandum of association), 団体規約
　　articles of consolidation　合併届出書
　　articles of dissolution　解散届出書
　　articles of partnership　組合定款, パートナーシップ定款, パートナーシップ契約
　　initial articles of incorporation　設立時の定款, 設立定款
　　memorandum and articles　定款
　　revised articles of incorporation　変更定款

articles of incorporation　基本定款, 設立定款, 定款
　(=articles of association)
　◆Listed companies revised their articles of incorporation to make stock certificates paperless by holding shareholders meetings. 株券をペーパーレス化するため、公開企業は、株主総会を開いて会社の定款を変更した。◆The articles of incorporation authorize the Directors to issue such shares in one or more series and to fix the number of shares of each series prior to their issue. 定款では、これらの株式をシリーズで1回以上発行する権限と、その発行前に各シリーズの発行株式数を決定する権限は、取締役会に与えられています。◆The company amended its articles of incorporation at the shareholders meeting to allow its management to purchase all of its shares through a buyout. 同社は、株主総会で定款を変更して、株式の(公開)買付けですべての自社株を取得できる[買い取れる]ようにした。

as a percentage of　～に対する比率[割合], ～に占める比率
　as a percentage of GDP　国内総生産(GDP)に対する比率, GDP比で
　as percentages of total revenues　総収益[総売上高]に対する比率[百分率]
　current assets as a percentage of current liabilities　流動負債に対する流動資産の比率, 流動比率
　net income as a percentage of average assets　平均資産に対する純利益の比率, 総資本純利益率
　net income (loss) as a percentage of revenues　収益[売上高]に対する純利益(損失)の比率, 対収益純利益(損失)率, 純利益(損失)率
　operating income (loss) as a percentage of revenues　収益[売上高]に対する営業利益(損失)の比率, 対売上高営業利益(損失)率, 営業利益(損失)率
　total debt as a percentage of total capitalization　資本総額に対する債務総額の比率
　◆The BOJ's total assets as a percentage of GDP stand at nearly 30 percent. 国内総生産(GDP)に対する日銀の総資産の比率[日銀の総資産の国内総生産(GDP)比]は、約3割を占めている。◆The firm's total debt as a percentage of total capitalization was 33 percent at yearend 2011, compared with 27 percent at yearend 2010. 同社の資本総額に対する債務総額の比率は、2010年末時の27%に対して、2011年末では33%に拡大した。◆Total debt as a percentage of total capitalization was 20 percent at yearend 2011. 資本総額に対する債務総額の比率は、2011年末現在で20%だった。

as a response to　～を受けて
　◆The Fed raised the discount rate to 0.75 percent from 0.5 percent as a response to improved financial market conditions. 米連邦準備制度理事会(FRB)は、金融市場の環境改善を受けて、(銀行に貸し出す際の金利である)公定歩合を現行の年0.5%から0.75%に引き上げた。

as of　～現在で, ～の時点で:～現在の, ～の日付けで, ～の日付けに
　◆Life Insurance Policyholders Protection Corp. will provide ¥145 billion to partially cover the life insurer's negative net worth, which was ¥320 billion as of the end of last September. 生命保険契約者保護機構は、昨年9月末現在の同生保の債務超過額3,200億円の一部を支援するため、1,450億円を支出することになっている。◆The bank reported a capital adequacy ratio of 4.54 percent as of the end of fiscal 2011. 同行の2011年度末現在[時点]の自己資本比率は、4.54%だった。◆The BOJ's total assets at the end of August 2011 increased to ¥141 trillion from ¥79 trillion as of the end of March 1999 when its zero-interest rate policy was first adopted. 日銀の2011年8月末時点の総資産は、ゼロ金利政策を初めて導入した1999年3月末現在の79兆円から141兆円に増えた。◆The government holds a 53.4 percent stake in Tokyo Metro Co., which was valued at ¥174.9 billion at book value as of the end of March 2010. 国は東京地下鉄(東京メトロ)の株式の53.4%を保有しており、その簿価での評価額は2010年3月末時点で1,749億円になる。

ASEAN plus Three　東南アジア諸国連合と日本、中国、韓国, ASEANプラス3(日中韓), ASEANプラス3 (=ASEAN＋3;⇒financial turmoil)
　◆As an attempt to expand a free trade area, China has advocated the ASEAN plus Three—Japan, China and South Korea. 自由貿易圏を拡大する試みとして、中国は、東南アジア諸国連合(ASEAN)に日本、中国と韓国を加えた「ASEANプラス3」を提唱してきた。

ASEAN plus Three [ASEAN＋3] finance ministers and central bank governors meeting　ASEANプラス3財務相・中央銀行総裁会議

ASEAN plus Three Macroeconomic Research Office　域内マクロ経済リサーチ・オフィス, AMRO (⇒AMRO)
　◆The ASEAN plus Three Macroeconomic Research Office, or AMRO, was set up in Singapore in April 2011 to coordinate decision-making for providing emergency liquidity to member states. ASEANプラス3(日中韓)の域内マクロ経済リサーチ・オフィス(AMRO)は、参加国に緊急時の流動性を提供する際の意思決定調整機関として、2011年4にシンガポールに設立された。

Asia　(名)アジア
　Asia bond market　アジア起債市場, アジア・ボンド・マーケット　(=Asian bond market)
　Asia fund　アジア・ファンド(アジア株式市場を対象とする外国投資信託)

Asiadollars　(名)アジア・ダラー
　(=Asian dollars)

Asian　(形)アジアの, アジア地域の
　Asian bond market　アジア起債市場
　Asian Bonds Markets Initiative　アジア債券市場育成イニシアチブ, ABMI
　Asian Capital Markets Initiative　アジア金融市場イニシアチブ, ACMI
　Asian Currency Unit　アジア通貨単位, アキュ, ACU (アジア通貨(アセアン10か国と日中韓3か国の通貨)の加重平均値を示す尺度)
　Asian Development Fund　アジア開発基金
　Asian financial crisis　アジア金融危機
　Asian monetary unit　アジアの統一決済通貨単位(アジア決済同盟加入国の統一決済通貨単位)
　Asian Payment Union　アジア決済同盟
　Asian Reserve Bank　アジア準備銀行
　East Asian Insurance Congress　東アジア保険会議

Asian Development Bank　アジア開発銀行, ADB (本部はマニラ。⇒ADB, additional contribution)
　◆The Asian Development Bank trimmed its 2011 forecast for economic growth for 45 developing countries or newly industrializing Asian countries, excluding Japan. アジア開発銀行(ADB)は、日本などを除くアジア太平洋45か国・地域の2011年の国内総生産(GDP)成長率見通しを、下方修正した。◆The Asian Development Bank upgraded its 2010 growth forecast for 14 East Asian countries. アジア開発銀行は、東アジア14か国の2010年の成長率予測を上方修正した。

Asian dollar アジア・ダラー（＝東南アジアの銀行に預けられた米ドル）
　Asian-dollar bond アジア・ダラー債
　Asian-dollar market アジア・ダラー市場, アジア・ドル市場
Asian market アジア市場
　◆By the TSE's extension of the morning trade session to 11:30 a.m., investors will be able to trade Japanese stocks more easily while keeping an eye on economic trends in Asian markets. 東証が午前11時30分まで午前の取引時間を延長したことによって、投資家は今後、アジア市場の経済動向を見ながら日本株の取引をすることが容易になる。◆Major Asian markets such as Shanghai and Hong Kong also show a situation that could be dubbed as a spontaneous global market crash. 上海や香港などアジアの主要市場も、世界同時株安の様相を見せている。◆On the Tokyo stock market and other Asian markets, stock prices plunged across the board. 東京株式市場や他のアジア市場などでも、軒並み株安となった。
ask （動）頼む, 要請する, 求める, 要求する, 請求する, 誘う, 尋ねる
　asked 売り唱え
　asked price 売り呼び値
　be ask only [ask-only] at ～で売り気配となっている
　bid and ask prices 売り・買い呼び値
　bid and asked (price) 呼び値
　bid and asked prices [quotations] 買い呼び値と売り呼び値
　bid-asked price 呼び値
　bid-asked [bid/ask] spreads 呼び値スプレッド
　◆Greece asked other eurozone member states for financial support to help it stem its budget crisis in early 2010. 2010年初めにギリシャは、財政危機を回避するため、他のユーロ圏加盟国に金融支援を求めた。◆The Bank of Japan asked the Federal Reserve Bank of New York to intervene in the New York foreign exchange market on its behalf through yen-selling, dollar-buying operations for the first time in 15 months. 日銀は、1年3か月ぶりにニューヨーク連銀に委託して、ニューヨーク外国為替市場で円売り・ドル買いの介入に踏み切った。◆The Development Bank of Japan asked the Japan Finance Corporation to pay ¥53.6 billion, the amount guaranteed by the government. 日本政策投資銀行は、政府保証分の536億円の支払いを日本政策金融公庫に請求した。◆With a view to stemming the airlines' financial hemorrhaging, the Construction and Transport Ministry in late May asked the Development Bank of Japan to provide emergency loans to the two carriers. 航空会社の損失を阻止するため、5月下旬に国土交通省は、日本政策投資銀行に対して両航空会社への緊急融資を要請した。
asking price 提示価格, 売り呼び値
assertive shareholder モノ言う株主
　◆The pension fund association is an assertive shareholder that makes tough demands on corporate managements. 企業年金連合会は、企業の経営姿勢に厳しい注文をつけるモノ言う株主でもある。
assess （動）評価する, 査定する, 審査する, 算定する, 判断する
　assess the financial status of large borrowers 大口融資先の財務内容を審査する
　assessed value 査定価額, 査定評価額, 査定価値, 課税価額
　assessed value of fixed assets 固定資産税評価額
　◆Banks must assess their assets more rigidly. 銀行は、銀行の資産査定を厳格化しなければならない。◆Managers must continuously assess their resource needs and consider further steps to reduce costs. 経営陣は、つねに資源の必要性を評価して、コスト削減のための一段と進んだ方法を考える必要がある。◆The EU's stress test criteria for assessing the banks' assets were not sufficiently rigorous. 銀行資産を査定するためのEU（欧州連合）のストレス・テスト（特別検査）の基準は、甘かったと言える。
assessment （名）評価, 事前評価, 鑑定, 査定, 審査, 算定, 課税, 賦課, 更正, 判断, 評価額, 鑑定額, 査定額, 賦課金, 追徴金, アセスメント
　assessment at the source 源泉課税
　assessment insurance 賦課式保険
　assessment of bank properties 銀行資産の査定
　assessment of the economy 景気の基調判断, 景気判断（＝assessment on the state of the economy, economic assessment）
　assessment plan （年金の）賦課方式, 賦課式保険
　assessment rate (of collateral) 担保掛け目, 掛け目
　assessments receivable 受取追徴金
　asset assessment 資産査定, 資産評価（＝asset appraisal, asset evaluation）
　asset value assessment 資産評価
　basis [standard] of assessment 課税標準
　capital stock assessment 追出資
　collateral assessment 担保評価
　credit assessment 信用評価, 信用分析
　damage assessment 損害査定
　official assessment method 賦課課税方式
　rating assessment 格付け評価
　risk assessment 利助評価
　self-assessment 申告納税
　tax assessment 課税査定額, 租税の査定
　◆Outstanding nonperforming loans held by banks are increasing due to poor business results of borrowers and the strict asset assessment methods. 金融機関が抱える不良債権残高は、貸出先［融資先］の業績不振や資産の査定方法の厳格化で増加している。◆The Bank of Japan raised its assessments for seven of the nation's nine regional economies as the export-led recovery continues. 輸出主導の回復が続いているため、日本銀行は、全国9地域のうち7地域の景気判断を引き上げた。◆The Financial Services Agency will check the credibility of the banks' debtor companies, including their management efficiency and the accuracy of their collateral assessment. 金融庁は、銀行の融資先の経営効率や担保評価などを含めて、銀行の融資先の信用力を洗い直す。◆The nonlife insurance company will provide the company with know-how on damage assessment and product development. この損害保険会社は、同社に損害査定や商品開発に関するノウハウを提供する。
assessment of bank assets 銀行資産の査定
　◆The Oct. 30, 2002 financial revitalization plan sought stricter assessments of bank assets. 2002年10月30日の「金融再生プログラム」は、銀行資産の一段と厳しい査定を求めた。
assessment of economic conditions 景気判断
　◆The Bank of Japan downgraded its overall assessment of the country's economic conditions for the second consecutive month. 日本銀行は、全般的な日本の景気判断を2か月連続で下方修正した。
assessment of the outlook of U.S. fiscal reconstruction 米国の財政再建見通しの評価
　◆The U.S. credit rating agency Standard & Poor's made a grim assessment of the outlook of U.S. fiscal reconstruction. 米国の信用格付け機関のスタンダード・アンド・プアーズ（S&P）は、米国の財政再建の見通しを厳しく評価した。
assessment value 評価額, 換算額
　◆A weaker dollar against the euro led to a rise in the assessment value of assets denominated in the single European currency. ドル安・ユーロ高で、(保有する)ユーロ建て資産の

ドル換算額が増えた。
asset (名)資産, 財産, アセット （⇒assess）
 actuarial asset value　保険数理による資産価値
 asset acquisition　資産買収, 資産取得
 asset appraisal　資産査定, 資産評価
 asset assessment　資産査定, 資産評価（=asset appraisal, asset evaluation）
 asset-backed securities　資産担保証券, 商業用不動産証券, アセットバック証券, ABS（銀行の貸出債権や企業の売掛債権などを担保に発行される証券）
 asset base　資産基盤, 資産構成
 asset basis　資産基準
 asset coverage　資産担保率
 asset deficiency　債務超過
 asset disposition　資産処分
 asset erosion　資産の目減り, 資産価額の低下
 asset finance　資産金融, アセット・ファイナンス
 asset investment　資産運用
 asset issues　資産株
 asset liability management　資産負債総合管理, 資産負債管理, バランス・シート管理, ALM
 asset market　資産市場, 金融市場
 asset pricing　資産評価
 asset provision　資産評価損引当金, 資産評価損引当金繰入れ額
 asset sales　資産売却
 asset securitization　資産の証券化
 asset swap　資産交換, アセット・スワップ
 asset turnover　資産回転率
 asset under management　運用資産, 取扱い資産, 預かり資産
 asset value　資産価値, 資産価格, 純資産
 assets acquired　取得資産
 assets and liabilities　資産と負債
 bad assets　不良資産
 capital asset　資本資産, 資本的資産, 固定資産（=fixed asset, fixed capital, long-lived asset, permanent asset）
 commercial assets　商業資産
 consol assets　連結資産
 current assets　流動資産（=liquid assets）
 customer assets　預り資産, 顧客からの預り資産
 earning assets　収益性資産
 excess of liabilities over assets　債務超過
 external assets　対外資産
 federal fund assets　連邦政府年金資産
 financial assets　金融資産
 fixed assets　固定資産
 foreclosed asset　担保権実行資産, 抵当権実行資産, 担保権行使で取得した資産
 foreign assets　対外資産, 海外資産
 freezing terrorist-related assets　テロ関連資産の凍結
 hidden assets　含み資産
 high credit quality asset　信用の質の高い資産
 high return asset　利回りの高い資産, 高リターン資産
 high-risk assets　高リスク資産, 損失リスクの高い資産（⇒capital flight）
 high yielding asset　高利回りの資産
 individual asset　個人資産
 intangible assets　無形資産, 無形固定資産
 invested assets　投資資産, 運用資産（=investment assets）
 leased asset　リース資産
 liquid financial assets　短期金融資産
 live assets　収益資産
 low-risk assets　低リスク資産, 損失リスクの低い資産（⇒investment capital）
 monetary asset　金融資産, 貨幣性資産
 net assets available for benefits　給付額に充当可能な純資産
 out-of-book assets　簿外資産（=nonledger assets）
 plan assets　制度資産
 quick assets　当座資産
 real assets　不動産
 reduction in assets　資産の取り崩し
 riskier assets such as exchange-traded funds　上場投資信託などの高リスク資産
 securitized assets　証券化資産, 証券化した資産
 sell off assets　資産を売却する
 sell-off of assets　資産の売却
 tangible assets　有形資産, 有形固定資産
 total assets　総資産
 toxic asset　不良資産
 wasting assets　減耗資産, 消耗資産, 減耗性資産, 涸渇性資産
 weaker asset　不良資産

◆A federal appeals court in New York approved the sale of Chrysler assets to Fiat. ニューヨークの米連邦控訴裁判所は、クライスラー資産のフィアットへの売却を承認した。◆According to sources, Tokyo Electric Power Co. will commission four trust banks to sell its assets. 関係者によると、東京電力は4信託銀行に保有資産の売却業務を委託する。◆Companies are usually considered likely to collapse when their liabilities surpass their assets. 企業は、一般に債務超過になった場合に「破綻懸念先」となる。◆Daiwa Securities has about ¥10 trillion in total assets. 大和証券の総資産は、約10兆円だ。◆Every member of the nation will now be forced to face the risks involved in the management of their own assets. これからは、国民一人ひとりが資産運用リスクに正面から向き合わざるを得なくなる。◆GM's weaker assets will be liquidated through the New York Bankruptcy Court. GMの不良資産は、ニューヨーク破産裁判所を通じて清算される。◆In terms of net asset calculation, a reduction in assets is tantamount to an increase in liabilities. 純資産の計算上、資産の取り崩しと負債の増加は同じことだ。◆Investors have begun switching their funds from bank deposits to assets that entail some risks. 投資家が、銀行預金からリスクを伴う資産へと資金の運用を切り替え始めている。◆Making the creditor banks waive loans to TEPCO will cause the utility to fall into capital deficiency, with liabilities exceeding assets. 取引銀行に東電への債権を放棄させると、東電は資本不足に陥り、債務超過になってしまう。◆Mizuho Financial Group Inc. is the world's second-largest bank by assets. みずほフィナンシャルグループは、資産で世界2位の銀行だ。◆Our business is the management of assets, and in doing so, we must look at both short-term and long-term considerations. 当社の業務は資産管理であり、資産の運用に当たっては、短期的視点と長期的視点に基づく判断が要求されます。◆Public funds should be injected not only to buy up toxic assets, but also to boost the capital bases of enfeebled financial institutions. 公的資金は、不良資産の買取りだけでなく、弱体化した[体力の落ちた]金融機関の資本増強にも注入すべきだ。◆The assets of the various plans include corporate equities, government securities, corporate debt securities and income-producing real estate. 各種制度の年金資産は、株式、政府証券、債券や収益を稼得する不動産でなどで構成されています。◆The Bank of Japan purchased riskier assets such as exchange-traded funds and real estate investment trusts in mid-December 2010. 日銀は、2010年12月半ばから、上場投資信託や不動産投資信託（リート）などの高リスク資産を買い入れた。◆The bank's aim is to help circulate dormant individual assets in the local economy. 眠れる個人の金融資産を地域経済に循環させるのが、同行の目的だ。◆The brokerage firm manages client assets of ￥520 billion in about 150,000 accounts. この証券会社は、口座数約15万で顧客預り資産は5,200億円に達する。◆The company will put all its efforts into increasing its profitability and promptly selling its unnecessary assets. 同社は、利益水準の向上や不要資産の即時売却などに全力を挙げる方針です。◆The company's financial statements are not based on the book value of the assets at time they were obtained. 同社の財務諸表は、取得時の資産の簿価を基準としていない。◆The firm's liabilities exceeded its assets by ￥8 billion in its settlement of accounts at the end of February last year. 同社は、昨年2月期決算で、80億円の債務超過になった。◆The U.S. government froze the assets of four individuals and eight entities that were involved in illicit activities such as money laundering, currency counterfeiting and narcotics trafficking. 米政府は、資金洗浄（マネー・ロンダリング）や通貨偽造、麻薬取引などの違法行為に関与している4個人、8団体の資産を凍結した。◆To raise money for compensation related to the Fukushima No. 1 nuclear power plant crisis, TEPCO will sell off assets through four trust banks. 福島第一原発事故関連の賠償資金を調達するため、東電は、4信託銀行を通じて資産を売却することになった。

asset allocation　資産配分, 資金の割当て, アセット・アロケーション
　asset allocation model　資産配分モデル
　asset allocation of the fund　ファンド（投資資金）の資産配分
　asset allocation policy　資産配分政策
　asset allocation shift　資産配分の変化
　tactical asset allocation　戦術的資産配分

asset appraisal　資産査定, 資産評価
　◆The major commercial banks deserve praise for working toward making their asset appraisal more stringent. 大手各行が資産査定の厳格化に動き出したことは、評価できる。

asset assessment　資産査定, 資産評価
　（=asset evaluation）
　◆Outstanding nonperforming loans held by banks are increasing due to poor business results of borrowers and the strict asset assessment methods. 金融機関が抱える不良債権残高は、貸出先［融資先］の業績不振や資産の査定方法の厳格化で増加している。◆The major banks attributed their increased bad loans to the poor performance of their borrowers due to the prolonged economic slump and Financial Service Agency inspections resulting in a stricter review of their asset assessments. 大手銀行は、不良債権が増えた理由として、長引く景気低迷で貸出先の経営が悪化したことと、金融庁の検査を受けて大手行が資産査定を厳しくしたことを挙げた。

asset at the bank　預け入れ資産
　◆Customers whose assets at the bank total about ￥10 million will receive a maximum of ￥2 million in insurance if their money is withdrawn illicitly by a third party with a bogus card. 同行では、預け入れ資産が1,000万円程度の預金者が、第三者に偽造カードを使って不正に預金が引き出された場合には、最大200万円の保険金が支払われる。

asset-backed　（形）資産を担保にした, 資産担保の, 資産を裏付けにした
　asset-backed bond　資産担保債券
　asset-backed certificate　アセットバック証書, アセットバック証券（ABS）
　asset-backed CP［commercial paper］　アセットバックCP
　asset-backed financing　アセットバック証券による資金調達
　asset-backed FRNs［floating rate notes］　アセットバック変動利付き債
　asset-backed market　アセット・バック証券市場
　asset-backed obligation　アセットバック債務証書
　asset-backed preferred stock　アセットバック優先株
　asset-backed swap　資産交換, アセット・スワップ（=asset swap）

asset-backed commercial paper　資産担保CP, 資産担保コマーシャル・ペーパー, アセットバックCP, ABCP
　◆Asset-backed commercial paper refers to commercial paper whose creditworthiness is guaranteed by sales credit that the corporate issuer has with its debtors. 資産担保CPとは、企業発行体がその債務者に対して保有する売掛金によって信用度が保証されるコマーシャル・ペーパーを指す。

asset-backed securities　資産担保証券, 商業用不動産証券, アセットバック証券, ABS（銀行の貸出債権や企業の売掛債権などを担保に発行される証券）
　◆It is vital to improve the secondary market circulating such asset-backed securities for investors. 投資家向けに、このような資産担保証券の流通市場の整備も不可欠である。◆The Bank of Japan decided to relax the rules under which it buys asset-backed securities. 日銀は、資産担保証券の買入れ基準を緩和することを決めた。◆The Bank of Japan should quickly materialize a new policy of listing asset-backed securities—securities backed by assets such as sales credits—as a possible option for purchase. 日銀は、資産担保証券（企業の売掛債権などの資産を裏付けにした証券）を買入れの対象にする新方針を、早く具体化するべきだ。

解説 アセットバック証券とは：住宅ローン、商業用不動産、自動車ローンなどの資産を担保として発行される証券の総称。1970年に米国で、投資機会の多様化を図るために、住宅ローンを担保にしたMBS（mortgage-backed securities）が発行された。MBSは、米政府系機関が元利払いを保証する証券が多く、米国債同様の信用力がある。このほか、ホテルなどの商業用不動産を担保とするCMBS（commercial mortgage-backed securities）と自動車ローンなどを担保にするABS（asset-backed securities）がある。アセットバック証券は、信用力が高い割に利回りが高いため、比較的好調な運用成績を残している投信が多い。ただし、金利変動により価格が変動する点は、アセットバック証券も他の債券と変わらない。

asset base　資産基盤, 資産構成
　◆A steady annual improvement in earnings of five percent or more is a reasonable goal given the weight of regulated companies in our asset base. 当社の資産構成で規制対象企業が大きな比重を占めていることを考えると、毎年5％以上の利益率増加の安定確保は、妥当な目標と言えるでしょう。◆ABC Inc. management took vigorous steps during 2011 to reinforce the performance of ABC's asset base. ABCの経営陣は、資産運用実績を強化するため、2011年度に思い切った措置をとりました。◆We sold some assets in return for an interest in a larger entity with greater potential for growth and a more diversified asset base. 当社は、大きな潜在成長力と一段と多様化した資産基盤をもつ大規模企業の株式を取得する対価として、一部資産を売却しました。

asset-based　（形）資産を担保にした, 担保付きの
　asset-based financing　資産を担保にした資金調達, 資産担保金融
　asset-based lending　資産担保貸付け
　asset-based loan　担保付き貸出［貸付け］

asset deflation　資産デフレ
　◆In addition to asset deflation in the form of falling stock and land prices, the deepening recession has seen a sharp rise in corporate bankruptcies. 株価や地価の下落という形での資産デフレに加え、不況の深刻化で企業倒産が急増している。

asset erosion 資産の目減り, 資産価額の低下
◆Progress in the disposal of nonperforming loans and receding concerns over further deterioration in regional economies have led to diminished risk of asset erosion. 不良債権処理の進展や地域経済がさらに悪化する懸念の後退などで、資産が目減りする恐れが薄らいでいる。

asset evaluation 資産の査定
（=asset assessment）
◆Outstanding nonperforming loans held by banks are increasing due to poor business results of borrowers and the strict asset evaluation methods. 金融機関が抱える不良債権残高は、貸出先（融資先）の業績不振や資産の査定方法の厳格化で増加している。

asset impairment accounting 減損会計
（=accounting for the impairment of assets）
◆The revision of projected business results stems from slumping sales in overseas markets and the introduction of asset impairment accounting. 業績予想の修正の主因は、海外市場での販売不振と（資産価値を厳格に評価し、簿価と時価の差額を損失計上する）減損会計を導入したためだ。◆The rule of asset impairment accounting requires companies to post valuation losses on fixed assets whose market value has fallen sharply from their book value. 減損会計基準は、固定資産の時価が簿価から大幅に下落した場合の固定資産の評価損の計上を、企業に義務付けている。◆This extraordinary loss of ¥581.06 billion stems partly from the write-offs of appraisal losses in fixed assets under an asset impairment accounting rule. この5,810億6,000万円の特別損失の一因は、減損会計基準に基づく固定資産の減損処理によるものだ。
[解説]減損会計とは：企業が保有する土地やビル、工場、店舗などの固定資産から生じる収益が、投資額に見合うかどうかを判断する会計基準。企業の固定資産価値の下落を企業業績に反映させる減損会計は、米国ではすでに導入され、日本では2005年4月以降の事業年度から義務付けられている。企業財務の透明性を高め、投資家を保護する狙（ねら）いがある。収益実績に基づいて固定資産が将来稼ぎ出す利益などを資産ごとに試算し、投資額の回収が見込めない場合には、簿価と回収可能額の差額を一定の基準で損失計上する。（2004年6月8日付読売新聞）

asset liability management [assets and liability management] 資産負債総合管理, 資産負債管理, バランス・シート管理, ALM

asset management 資産管理, 資産運用, 投資顧問
　asset management account　資産管理口座, 資産運用口座
　asset management division　投資顧問部門
　asset management trust　資産運用信託, アセット・マネジメント・トラスト, AMT
　current asset management　流動資産管理
◆All these events are part of a larger strategy of our asset management. これらの措置は、当社の資産運用戦略の一環としてとられたものです。◆The bank is strong in all retail service fields such as securities and asset management as well as banking. 同行は、銀行業務のほか証券、資産運用などリテール（個人向け取引）業務全般に強みを持つ。◆The man intentionally dodged the tax payments as he transferred the money for asset management to another country. 男は、資産運用の資金を他国に移動させていることから、意図的に納税を免れていた。◆Tosho Academy provides individual investors with information on asset management. 東証アカデミーは、個人投資家に資産運用情報を提供している。

asset management advisory services 資産運用顧問業務, 資産運用アドバイス業務
◆The brokerage's main services for individual customers will be asset management advisory services, focusing on the sale of products such as investment trust funds that invest in foreign equities, and money market funds denominated in foreign currencies. 同証券会社は、株式の主な個人顧客向け（売買仲介）業務として、外国株を組み込んだ投資信託や外貨建てMMF（マネー・マーケット・ファンド）などの商品の販売を中心に、資産運用顧問業務を展開する方針だ。

asset management business 資産運用業務
◆This pretax profit is bolstered mainly by earnings from the asset management business launched last year. この経常利益は、主に昨年から開始した資産運用業務の（手数料）収入によるものです。

asset management company 資産管理会社, 資産運用会社
◆The corporate group's core firm will be split into a business operating firm and an asset management company. 同社グループ企業の中核会社は、事業会社と資産管理会社に分割される。

asset management services 資産運用サービス
◆The new firm will offer asset management services to individual investors whose net worth is ¥100 million or more. 新会社は、純資産が1億円以上の個人投資家に資産運用サービスを提供する。

asset management strategy 資産運用戦略
◆The firm's asset management strategy is geared to seek high returns. 同社の資産運用戦略は、高収益を狙ったものだ。

asset management subsidiary 資産運用子会社
◆Nippon Life Insurance's asset management subsidiary Nissay Asset Management Corp. increased its shareholding in Olympus to 0.21 percent from 0.08 percent. 日本生命の資産運用子会社であるニッセイアッセトマネジメントは、オリンパス株の保有比率を0.08%から0.21%に買い増した。

asset management unit 資産運用会社
◆Sumitomo Trust & Banking Co. is considering buying two asset management units of the UFJ banking group. 住友信託銀行は現在、UFJ銀行グループの資産運用会社2社の買収を検討している。

asset protection 資産保全, 資産保護
◆The financial authorities filed a declaration of bankruptcy and a request for asset protection with the Tokyo District Court for the brokerage firm. 金融当局は、同証券会社の破産宣告と財産保全処分を東京地裁に申し立てた。

asset provision 資産評価損引当金, 資産評価損引当金繰入れ額
◆The company took an investment and asset provision of $72 million. 同社は、7,200万ドルの投資および資産評価損引当金繰入れを実施した。

asset purchase fund 資産買入基金
◆The Bank of Japan maintained the 10 trillion asset purchase fund. 日銀は、10兆円の資産買入基金を維持した。

asset quality 資産の質, 資産内容
　asset quality of loan books　銀行資産の質
　asset quality pressures [problem, weakening]　資産の質の悪化[低下], 資産内容の悪化
　deterioration in asset quality　資産の質の悪化, 資産内容の悪化　（=asset quality deterioration, deteriorating asset quality, weakening asset quality）
　improved [strengthened] asset quality　資産の質の改善, 資産の質の向上
　monitor the asset quality of financial institutions　金融機関の資産の質[資産内容]を監視する
　weakened [weakening] asset quality　資産の質の悪化[低下]

asset value 資産価値, 資産価格, 純資産
◆A certified public accountant evaluated the asset value of the advertising agency. 公認会計士が、この広告会社の資産価値を評価[算定]した。◆Investment funds are circling like vultures over companies that have large asset values but small market values. 投資ファンドは、株式の時価総額に比べ

て資産価値が大きい企業をハゲタカのように狙っている。

assign (動)割り当てる, 任命する, 指定する, 与える, 譲渡する, 委託する
   assign a rating to the issuer　発行体に格付けを与える[付与する]
   assign an AAA long-term rating to　～に対してトリプルAの長期格付けをする
   assigned account　担保勘定(融資を受ける際に担保として銀行に提供した売掛金勘定)
   assigned accounts receivable　割当債権
   assigned capital　持ち込み資本
   assigned in blank　株券などの白地式譲渡
   assigned rating　格付けの付与, 付与された格付け
   assigned risk　割当危険分担, 割当不良物件, アサインド・リスク
   ◆ABC shall have no recourse against XYZ for any obligations under the original agreement assigned pursuant to this assignment agreement. ABCは、この譲渡契約に従って譲渡された原契約上の債務については、XYZに履行の請求を一切求めないものとする。◆Standard & Poor's currently assigns a BBB long-term rating to the bank. スタンダード＆プアーズは現在、同行に対してトリプルBの長期格付けをしている。

assignment (名)譲渡, 譲渡条項, 譲渡証書, 選任, 任命, 派遣, 管財人割当て, 案件, 任務, 割り当てられた仕事 (⇒assign)
   assignment broker　譲渡仲介業者
   assignment brokering　譲渡の仲介
   assignment charge [fee]　譲渡手数料
   assignment of charter hire　用船料債権の譲渡
   assignment of claims　請求権の譲渡
   assignment of contract　契約の譲渡
   assignment of duties　義務の譲渡
   assignment of insurance policy　保険金請求権の譲渡
   assignment of lease　リースの譲渡
   assignment of receivables　債権の譲渡
   assignment valuation　譲渡時の評価
   carry out an assignment　任務を遂行する
   federal Assignment of Claims Act　連邦請求権譲渡法
   irrevocable assignment　確定譲渡
   legal assignment　法的譲渡
   overseas assignment　海外勤務
   partial assignment　一部譲渡
   perfect an assignment　譲渡の対抗要件を整える
   personnel assignment　要員配置
   priority assignment　最優先の仕事
   statutory assignment　制定法上の譲渡
   take on an assignment　仕事を引き受ける
   unaccompanied assignment　単身赴任
   wage assignment　給料控除, 給料からの分割控除
   written assignment　譲渡証

assignment agreement　譲渡契約, 契約譲渡契約
   ◆The Corporation acknowledges the assignment and other terms and provisions included in the assignment agreement. 当社は、この譲渡契約書に定められた譲渡とその他の条件および規定を確認する。

assist (動)支援する, 援助する, 助力する, 協力する, 助成する
   ◆In order to assist auto parts makers hit by the March 11 earthquake and tsunami, the Development Bank of Japan will raise ¥50 billion to establish a fund. 東日本大震災で被災した自動車部品メーカーを支援するため、日本政策投資銀行が、500億円を調達してファンドを設立する。

assistance (名)支援, 援助, 助力, 協力, 助成, 扶助(ふじょ), 助け, 役に立つこと, 利点
   adjustment assistance　調整援助
   capital assistance　資本支援, 資金協力
   financial assistance　金融支援, 財政援助, 資金援助, 資金協力
   financial assistance package　金融支援策
   governmental financial assistance　政府補助金, 政府助成金, 政府金融支援
   monetary assistance　金融援助, 資金援助, 貨幣的援助
   overnight assistance rate　翌日物介入金利
   pecuniary assistance　金銭的援助
   provide financial assistance to　～に金融支援[資金援助]を行う
   ◆After the IMF called for strict implementation of structural reforms as a condition for loans to financially troubled countries, counties became reluctant to request assistance from the IMF. 財政難に陥った国に対する融資の条件としてIMF(国際通貨基金)が厳しい構造改革の実施を求めてから、各国はIMFへの支援要請をためらうようになった。◆The assistance package of the EU and the IMF is being extended on the condition that Greek government implement measures to rebuild its public finances. 欧州連合(EU)と国際通貨基金(IMF)の支援策は、ギリシャ政府がギリシャの財政立直し策を実施することを条件としている。◆The financial market mess in Europe was triggered by the delay of financial assistance to Greece by the European financial authorities. 欧州の金融市場混乱の引き金となったのは、欧州(金融)当局によるギリシャへの金融支援のもたつきだ。◆With the integration of the Japan Bank for International Cooperation's division for handling yen loans, and other bodies in October 2008, JICA became one of the world's largest development assistance agencies. 国際協力機構(JICA)は、2008年10月に国際協力銀行(JBIC)の円借款部門などを統合して、(事業規模で)世界最大級の開発援助機関となった。

association (名)社団, 団体, 協会, 組合, 連合, 連合体, 提携, 連携
   American Bankers Association　米国[アメリカ]銀行協会
   Association of International Bond Dealers　国際債券取引業者協会, 国際債券ディーラーズ協会, AIBD
   benefit association　共済組合
   Bond Underwriters Association　公社債引受協会
   British Bankers' Association　英国[イギリス]銀行家協会
   British Insurance Association　英国[イギリス]保険協会
   building and loan association　建築資金金融組合
   commercial and industrial association　商工組合
   cooperative credit association　協同信用組合
   credit association　信用金庫
   credit cooperative association　信用協同組合
   Federal National Mortgage Association　米連邦住宅抵当金庫, 米連邦抵当金庫(通称＝Fannie Mae)
   Federation of Bankers Association of Japan　全国銀行協会連合会, 全銀協
   fraternal association　共済組合
   friendly association　共済組合, 友愛組合
   Futures industry Association　先物業協会
   horizontal association　水平の連携
   industry association　業界団体
   International Primary Markets Association　国際引受業者協会
   International Securities Markets Association　国際証券市場協会

investment association　投資会社
labor credit association　労働金庫
Life Insurance Association of Japan　生命保険協会
Lloyd's Underwriter's Association　ロイズ保険業者協会
mutual aid association　共済年金
mutual financing association　無尽講
National Association of Government Guaranteed Lenders　全国政府保証貸手協会
National Association of Insurance Commissioners　全米保険監督官協会
National Association of Pension Funds　英国年金基金協会
National Association of Securities Dealers　全米証券業協会
Pension Fund Association　厚生年金基金連合会
Public Securities Association　公共債協会
Regional Banks Association of Japan　全国地方銀行協会
savings and loan association　貯蓄貸付け組合, 貯蓄金融機関, S&L
savings association　貯蓄組合
Securities Association　証券業協会
Student loan Marketing Association　奨学金融資金庫
U.S. National Futures Association　全米先物協会
vertical association　垂直的連携

assuage　(動) 鎮める, 緩和する, 和らげる
◆The Federal Reserve Board is trying to assuage inflation fears. 米連邦準備制度理事会 (FRB) は, インフレ懸念の緩和に努めている。

assume　(動) 任務や義務・債務を引き受ける, 債務などを肩代わりする, 負担する, 就任する, 就く, 責任を負う, 責任をとる, 引き継ぐ, 継承する, 占有する, ～と仮定する, 推定する, 想定する, 予想する, 予定する, 見込む, 考慮する
　assume liquidity risk　流動性リスクを負担する
　assume the credit risk　信用リスクを負う
　assume the exchange rate in the fiscal 2012　2012年度の為替レートを想定する
　assume the obligations of failing private-sector borrowers　破たんした民間融資先の債務を継承する
　assume the risk for losses　損失リスクを負う, 損失リスクを引き受ける
　earnings per common share—assuming full dilution　普通株式1株当たり利益—完全希薄化 [希釈化, 希釈効果] を考慮した場合, 完全希薄化後普通株式1株当たり利益
　prepayments assumed　期限前返済推定額
　risk assumed　引受リスク
◆In making the estimates, the Cabinet Office has assumed that the economy will grow about 1.5 percent a year in real terms on average from fiscal 2011. 試算案を作成するにあたって, 内閣府は2011年度から実質で年平均約1.5%の経済成長率を前提とした。◆We assumed that the growth in the per capita cost of covered health care benefits (the health care cost trend rate) would gradually decline after 2012. 当社は, 計上済み医療給付費用の1人当たりの伸び率 (医療費用の傾向値) は, 2012年度以降はゆるやかに減少するものと予想しています。

assume a scenario　シナリオを描く
◆The government assumes a scenario in which Japan's economic growth will shift into high gear with overseas demand as a driving force. 政府は, 海外需要をテコに日本の経済成長が本格化する, とのシナリオを描いている。

assume management　経営を引き継ぐ, 経営を継承する
◆MGM's management will be assumed by Gary Barber and Roger Birnbaum, who run a film company. 米ハリウッドの映画会社MGMの経営は, 映画製作会社を経営するゲーリー・バーバー氏とロジャー・バーンバウム氏が引き継ぐことになっている。

assume the exchange rate　為替レートを想定する
◆Big companies assume the exchange rate of ¥81.06 to the dollar for the latter half of fiscal 2011. 大企業の2011年度下期の想定為替レートは, 1ドル＝81円6銭となっている。◆The rise of the yen beyond the level of the exchange rate assumed by many exporters has put them on the ropes. 多くの輸出業者が想定した為替レートの水準を上回る円高が輸出業者を窮地に追い込んでいる。

assumed　(形) 予想される, 推定される, 予定の, 仮の, 架空の, 偽りの, 見せかけの
　assumed bond　保証社債, 継承社債, 引継ぎ社債
　assumed interest rate　(保険の) 予定利率
　　(=assumed rate of interest)
　assumed liability　引継ぎ負債, 債務引受未払い金, 契約責任
　assumed liability policy　仮定責任保険証券
　assumed mortality rate　予定死亡率, 推定死亡率
　assumed premium　受再保険料
　assumed rate of expense　予定事業率 (新契約の募集や保険料の集金, 損害調査の人件費など, 保険料に占める必要経費の割合)
　assumed rate of interest　予定利率
　　(=assumed interest rate)
　assumed rate of return　予想収益率, 予想運用利益率, 予定利率
　assumed rates of return on pension funds　予想年金基金運用収益率
　assumed yield　予想利回り
　deposit in an assumed [a fictitious] name　架空名義預金

assumed exchange rate　想定為替レート (企業が決算見通しを策定するにあたって, 事前に予想するドルなどの外国通貨に対する円の為替レートのこと。輸出企業の場合, 想定より円高になれば為替差損が生じ, 想定より円安になれば為替差益が出る)
◆An exporter company will incur losses if the yen rises above the assumed exchange rate, but benefit if the yen declines. 輸出企業では, その想定為替レートより円高になれば為替差損が生じ, (想定為替レートより) 円安になれば為替差益が出る。◆If the yen rises above its all-time high of ¥79.75 to the dollar, the company may have to revise its assumed exchange rate once more. 円高が1ドル＝79円75銭の史上最高値を更新したら, 同社は再び同社の想定為替レートの修正を迫られかねない。◆Toyota will revise its assumed exchange rate for the second half of fiscal 2010 from the current ¥90 against the dollar to ¥80. トヨタは, 2010年度下半期 (2010年10月～2011年3月) の想定為替レートを, 現行の1ドル＝90円から1ドル＝80円に修正する。

assumed loans　債務の肩代わり
◆The credit guarantee system assumes that 50 percent of assumed loans will be recovered. 信用保証制度は, 債務肩代わり分の50%は回収されると見込んでいる。

assumed trend rate　予想傾向値
◆Increasing the assumed trend rate by 1% in each year would raise our accumulated postretirement benefit obligation at December 31, 2011 by $700 million. 予想傾向値が毎年1%ずつ上昇すると, 当社の累積退職後給付債務は, 2011年12月31日現在で7億ドル増加します。

assuming full dilution　完全希薄化 [希釈化, 希釈効果] 後, 完全希薄化を仮定 [考慮] した場合
◆For the computation of the earnings per share, assuming full dilution, dividends on convertible preferred shares have been added back to income. 完全希薄化を仮定した場合の1株当たり利益の算定では, 転換可能優先株式 [転換優先株] に対

する配当は、利益に振り戻してあります。

assumption （名）義務や債務の引受け、債務などの肩代わり、負担、就任、引継ぎ、継承、占有、仮定、前提、公準、想定、予想、考慮
- actuarial assumption　保険数理上の仮定
- assumption of accounting　会計上の仮定
- assumption of debt　債務の引受け
- assumption of going concern　継続企業の前提
- assumption of mortgage　抵当の引受け、モーゲージの肩代わり
- basic assumption　基礎的仮定
- debt assumption　債務引受け、債務引受契約、債務履行引受け、債務の肩代わり、債務引受契約に基づく債務譲渡、デット・アサンプション
- demographic assumption　人口統計学上の仮定
- economic assumptions　経済見通し
- financial assumption　財務上の仮定、財政上の仮定
- going concern assumption　継続企業の公準
- mortality assumptions　予定死亡率
- risk assumption　リスク負担、リスク[危険]の引受け

◆To use the new accounting method, we made assumptions about trends in health care costs, interest rates and average life expectancy. 新会計処理方法を採用するにあたって、当社は医療給付コスト、金利および平均寿命の傾向について仮定を設けました。◆We made the following assumptions in valuing our postretirement benefit obligation at December 31, 2011. 2011年12月31日現在の退職後給付債務の評価にあたって、当社は以下の仮定を行いました。

assurance （名）保証、確約、確信、確実性、自信、言質（げんち）、保険（insurance）
- assurance company　保険会社
- assurance mutual　相互保険
- assurance of bill　手形保証
- assurance of fixed sums　定額保険
- assurance policy　保険証券 （=policy of assurance）
- assurance social　社会保険 （=social insurance）
- firm assurance　確信
- industrial assurance　簡易保険
- life assurance business　生命保険事業
- quality assurance　品質保証

◆Corporation's internal controls are designed to provide reasonable assurance as to the integrity and reliability of the financial statements. 当社の内部統制は、財務書類の完全性と信頼性について十分保証するよう図られています。◆These GAASs require that we plan and perform the audit to obtain reasonable assurance about whether the financial statements are free of material misstatement. これらの一般に認められた監査基準は、連結財務書類に重要な虚偽表示がないかどうかについての合理的な確証を得るため、私どもが監査を計画し実施することを要求しています。

assurer [assuror] （名）保険者、保険業者、保証者

at （前）〜で
- at a discount　割引価格で
- at a fixed date after date　日付け後定期払い
- at a premium　割増し価格で
- at best　成り行きで
- at call　要求払いで
- at end of period　期末
- at limit　指し値で
- at occupation　業務上
- at or better　指し値またはそれよりいい値段で、アト・オア・ベター
- at par　額面価格で
- at sight　一覧払い、一覧払いで
- at sight buying rate　一覧払い手形買い相場
- at the close　引け値で
- at the close order　取引終了直前の売買取引
- at the location of loss or damage　損失発生地
- at the location of property involved　被保険物所在地
- at the market　成り行き価格で
- at the market order　成り行き注文
- at the money　アト・ザ・マネー（オプション取引の市場価格と行使価格が同じ状態をいう）
- at the opening　寄り付き価格で
- at the opening order　アト・ザ・オープニング・オーダー （=opening only order: 市場開始と同時に実行される条件の売買注文）
- at 30 days'（after）sight　一覧後30日払い

ATM　アト・ザ・マネー（at the moneyの略。オプション取引で、時価と行使価格が等しい状態）

ATM　現金自動預け払い機、現金自動預入引出機 （automated teller machineの略で、automatic teller machineともいう。⇒interbank network of ATMs）
- ATM charges　ATM利用手数料 （=ATM fees）
- ATM network　ATMネットワーク
- transfer utility charges through ATMs　公共料金をATMで振り込む
- withdraw deposits via ATM　ATM（現金自動預け払い機）を利用して預金を引き出す

◆In a bid to clamp down on bank-transfer scams, the police asked financial institutions not to allow people whose faces are obscured with sunglasses or masks to use ATMs. 振り込め詐欺を取り締まるため、警察は、サングラスやマスクで顔を隠したままATM（現金自動預け払い機）を使用できないよう金融機関に要請した。◆Under the bank's monthly fixed-charge system, customers are able to make transactions at the bank's ATMs free of individual charges even outside the bank's office hours. 同行の月額固定料金制では、利用者は時間外でもATMの利用手数料が無料になる。◆Under the new system of postal services, the flat ￥30 fee for paying utility charges at post offices or transferring them through ATMs is ￥240 for bills more than ￥30,000. 郵便事業の新制度では、公共料金を郵便局の窓口やATM（現金自動預け払い機）で振り込む場合の手数料は一律30円だったが、3万円以上の場合は240円になった。

ATM card　ATMカード、キャッシュ・カード

◆ATM cards are the banks' primary weapons to lure new clients. キャッシュ・カードは、銀行にとって新規顧客獲得の有力な手段だ。◆Fake ATM cards were used to steal about ￥400 million since December 2006. 偽造ATMカード[キャッシュ・カード]を使って、2006年12月以降、約4億円が盗み取られた。◆In the case of this ATM card, even if a cardholder's card or PIN number should be stolen, no one else can withdraw cash from the account. このキャッシュ・カードの場合は、カード会員がたとえカードや暗証番号を盗まれても、本人以外は口座から預金を引き出せない。◆The bank issues new ATM cards that also function as credit cards and electronic money. 同行は、クレジット・カードと電子マネーの機能を加えた新型キャッシュ・カードを発行している。◆The counterfeit ATM cards used to withdraw cash illegally from banks were made with personal information leaked from companies. 銀行から違法に現金を引き出すために使われた偽造キャッシュ・カードは、企業から流出した個人情報を使って作られた。

ATM cardholders　キャッシュ・カード会員

◆Mizuho Bank offers a service by which ATM cardholders are given mileage points each time they use the new cards as credit cards, purchase financial products at the bank's branches or receive loans from the bank. みずほ銀行が提供しているサービスでは、キャッシュ・カード会員が新型カードをクレジット・カードとして利用したり、みずほ銀で金融商品を購入したり、ローンを利用したりすると、その取引に応じて毎回、マイレージ・ポイントがもらえる。

ATM fraud　ATM詐欺
◆Many cases of ATM fraud were perpetrated using technique called skimming. ATM詐欺事件の多くは、スキミングと呼ばれる手口を使って行われた。

attach　(動)付ける, 結合する, 差し押さえる(seize), 付帯[付属、付随]する
　attach documents to draft　手形に(船積み)書類を添付する
　attach great importance to　～を重要視する
　attach signature to a deed　証書に調印する
　attach unilateral conditions to　～に一方的な条件を入れる[付ける]
　attached account　差し押さえ口座
　attached goods　差し押さえ物件
　bond with warrants attached　新株引受権付き社債
　have one stock warrant attached　1株の新株引受権証券が付いている

attachment　(名)差し押さえ, 配属, 出向, 付属文書, 添付書類
　attachment bond　差し押さえ保証
　attachment of a file to one's e-mail　Eメールへのファイル添付
　attachment of property　財産差し押さえ
　attachment of the risk　危険開始
　execution [service] of attachment　差し押さえ執行
　file a petition for attachment　差し押さえの申立をする
　order of attachment　差し押さえ命令
　preservative attachment　債権保全
　provisional [auxiliary] attachment　仮差し押さえ
　release from attachment　差し押さえ解除
　warrant [order] for attachment　差し押さえ令状

attack　(動)売り込む, 売りを浴びせる, 襲う, 攻撃する, 攻める, 痛烈に批判する
　attack a weak currency　弱い通貨に売りを浴びせる
　attack the dollar　ドルを売り込む

attack　(名)攻撃, 襲撃, 措置, 対策, 批判, 非難, 酷評, アタック
　attacks in the foreign exchange market　為替市場での投機売り[投棄圧力], 為替市場での投機的な動き
　come under speculative attack　投機売りにさらされる, 投機的な売りにさらされる
　speculative attack　投機筋の攻撃, 投機的な売り, 投機売り

attain　(動)達成する, 成し遂げる, ～に到達する, ～に達する
　aggregate and attained aged normal methods　総合保険料方式と正常到達年齢方式
　attain one's investment objective　投資目的を達成する
　attained age　到達年齢, 現在年齢
　attained age method　到達年齢方式
　attained age normal method　正常到達年齢方式
◆China's renminbi may attain a reserve-currency status by the steady appreciation of the yuan and the country's enormous capital surpluses. 中国の人民元は、人民元の着実な切上げと中国の膨大な資本剰余金によって、準備通貨の地位を獲得する可能性がある。

attempt　(動)～を試みる, ～を試行する, ～しようとする
◆By conducting additional monetary easing policy, the Fed attempts to preemptively contain growing deflationary concerns in the United States. 追加金融緩和策を実施して、米連邦準備制度理事会(FRB)は、米国で高まるデフレ懸念に先手を打とうとしている。

attempt　(名)企(くわだ)て, 企画, 計画, 策, 措置, 試み, 努力, 挑戦, 攻撃, 襲撃, 攻勢, 未遂
　a hostile takeover attempt　敵対的な買収攻勢
　a takeover attempt　買収劇, 買収攻勢
　an attempt to prop up a company　企業支援策
　(⇒giant)
◆Companies should obtain shareholder approval when introducing methods to counter hostile takeover attempts. 敵対的買収への対抗策を導入する場合、企業は株主の承認を得なければならない。◆In an attempt to get on the bandwagon, many people are shifting their fixed rate mortgages to adjustable rate ones. 時流に乗ろうとして、固定金利型住宅ローンを変動金利型住宅ローンに変更する人が多い。◆The revaluation of currency in North Korea appears aimed at clamping down on burgeoning free markets in an attempt to reassert the regime's control. 北朝鮮の通貨改定は、政権の統制力を改めて強めるため、急速に広がる自由市場を厳しく取り締まるねらいがあるようだ。

attention　(名)注意, 注目, 興味, 関心, 焦点, 集中力, 好意, 配慮, 気配り
　investment attention　投資先, 投資の関心
　investors' attention　投資家の関心
　regulatory attention　規制当局の注目
◆The firm received a lot of attention from investors as an emerging company. 同社は、新興のベンチャー企業として投資家から大いに注目された。

attitude　(名)態度, 姿勢, 考え方, 通念, 意見, 主張, 判断, 外観, アティテュード
　attitude toward lending　貸出態度, 融資態度
　lending attitude　(金融機関の)貸出態度
　risk averse attitude　リスク回避の態度
　risk neutral attitude　リスク中立の態度
　risk seeking attitude　リスク選好的態度
　wait-and-see attitude　様子見

attract　(動)引きつける, 顧客などを取り込む, 資金などを集める, 興味を持つ[引く]呼び寄せる, 誘引する, 誘致する
　attract companies　企業を誘致する
　attract customers　顧客を引きつける, 顧客を取り込む, 顧客を開拓する
　attract depositors　預金者を引きつける, 預金者を取り込む
　attract deposits with high interest rates　高金利で預金を集める　(⇒promising)
　attract foreign capital　外国資本を誘致する, 外資を誘致する　(=attract foreign investment)
　attract industries　産業を誘致する
　attract investment　投資を促す
　attract new customers　新規顧客を引きつける, 新規顧客を取り込む, 新規顧客を開拓する
　attract new individual investors　新規個人株主を引きつける[開拓する、拡大する]
◆An increasing number of companies are offering gifts to shareholders to attract new individual investors. 新規個人株主の拡大策として、株主優待制度を実施している企業が増えている。◆Reducing corporate tax is not rare as a measure to attract companies. 企業誘致の手段として、法人税を引き下げるのは珍しくない。◆The nonlife insurance company hopes to attract about 3 million to 4 million new policyholders a year for its new types of insurance. 同損保は、同社の新型保険で、年間約300万～400万件の新規契約獲得を目指している。

attract customers 顧客を引きつける, 顧客を集める, 顧客を取り込む, 顧客を開拓する
　◆The branch-free Internet-based bank can attract customers with higher deposit interest rates. 店舗を持たないネット専業銀行だと、預金の金利を高くして、顧客を集めることができる。

attract investment 投資を促す, 投資を誘致する
　◆Bolivian pro-market President-elect Gonzalo Sanchez took office facing the huge tasks of reviving a stagnant economy and attracting investment. ボリビアの大統領に当選した市場経済主義者のゴンザロ・サンチェス氏が、停滞した経済の回復や投資誘致という重大任務を抱えて就任した。

attraction （名）魅力, 呼び物, 引きつけること
　the attraction of financial products　金融商品の魅力
　the attraction of foreign investment　外資誘致
　◆Lowering the yield of Meiji Yasuda's single-premium whole life insurance will reduce the attraction of the insurer's financial products. 明治安田生保の一時払い終身保険の利回り［予定利率］の引下げで、同社の金融商品の魅力は薄れると思われる。

attractive （形）魅力的な, 妙味のある
　attractive earnings profile　明るい収益見通し
　attractive investment　魅力的な投資, 魅力的な投資対象, 魅力的な銘柄
　attractive investment site　魅力的な投資先
　attractive rates　低利
　attractive return for investors　投資家に魅力的な利回り

attributable to 〜に起因する, 〜に帰属する, 〜による
　（=be caused by, be due to, be traceable to, result from）
　AB is primarily attributable to CD　ABは主にCDに起因する, ABの主な要因［主因］はCDである, ABは主にCDによる
　current cost profit attributable to shareholders　株主帰属現在原価利益
　income attributable to ordinary activity　経常損益（正常な営業活動から生じる損益）
　losses attributable to credit defaults　信用デフォルトに起因する損失
　losses attributable to dilution　減額による損失, 減額に起因する損失, 受取債権の減額による損失
　◆These increases in consolidated revenues were primarily attributable to volume growth rather than price increases. この連結売上高の伸びは、価格引き上げによるものではなく、主に販売数量の拡大によるものです。

attribute （動）（結果などを）, 〜にあるとする［考える］, 〜に帰する
　◆The major banks attributed their increased bad loans to the poor performance of their borrowers due to the prolonged economic slump and Financial Service Agency inspections resulting in a stricter review of their asset assessments. 大手銀行は、不良債権が増えた理由として、長引く景気低迷で貸出先の経営が悪化したことと、金融庁の検査を受けて大手行が資産査定を厳しくしたことを挙げた。◆The major securities house attributed the poor earnings to sharp drops in brokerage fees and trading profits amid the extended slump in the domestic stock market. この大手証券会社は、減益の要因として、国内株式市場の長期低迷による株売買手数料と売買益の大幅減を挙げた。

attribute （名）属性, 特性, 特質
　bond attribute　債券の特性［属性］
　product attribute　製品の特性
　security attribute　証券の特性

auction （名）競売, 競り売り, 公売, 入札, 公募入札, オークション
　auction-based　入札方式による
　auction date　入札日
　auction period　入札期間
　auction price　入札価格
　auction rate note　入札金利債
　auction-rate preferred stock　配当率入札方式優先株
　competitive auction　競争入札
　cumulative auction market preferred stock　配当率入札方式累積優先株
　Dutch auction　ダッチ方式の入札, せり下げ売り, 逆せり, ダッチ・オークション
　e-auction　eオークション
　52-weel bill auction　満期52週のTビル入札
　gilt auction　ギルト債の入札
　government bond auction　国債入札
　issue by auction　入札発行
　long-term auctions　長期入札額
　monthly auction　月次入札
　Net auction　ネット・オークション
　　（=Internet auction）
　note auction　中期債入札
　open auction　公開競売
　quarterly auction　四半期入札, 四半期ごとの入札
　reverse auction　逆オークション, リバース・オークション
　ten-year note auction　10年物の入札, 米国債10年物の入札
　30 year auction　30年物入札, 米国債30年物の入札, 30年物Tボンドの入札
　Treasury debt auction　国債入札
　Treasury note auction　国債入札, Tノートの入札
　two-year auction　2年物の入札
　weekly bill auction　毎週のTビル入札
　yield auction　利回り入札, 利回り入札方式
　◆A vacant lot was sold by auction for about ￥128 million, three times higher than the publicly announced roadside land price. 空き地が、競売で、公表されている路線価の3倍の約1億2,800万円で売却された。◆Dealers are allowed to bid for Treasury bonds by a quarterly auction. ディーラーは、四半期ごとの入札［四半期入札］で米財務省証券への入札が認められている。

auction-rate debt　金利入札証券, ARS
　（⇒ARS, auction-rate security）
　◆In the latest settlement with federal and state regulators, Wachovia Corp. agreed to buy back nearly 9 billion in auction-rate debt. 今回の連邦と州の規制当局との和解で、米大手銀行のワコビアは、約90億ドルの金利入札証券（ARS）を買い戻すことで合意した。

auction-rate [auction rate] market　金利入札証券市場, ARS市場　（=ARS market; ⇒ARS）
　◆The $330 billion auction-rate market normally allows issuers to borrow money for the long term at low, short-term rates. 3,300億円規模の金利入札市場では、発行体は通常、低い短期金利で長期の資金調達をすることができる。

auction-rate security　金利入札証券, ARS　（=auction-rate debt: 米国の地方自治体や美術館などの文化施設が資金調達のために発行する満期20年以上の長期債で、定期的に行われる入札で金利が変わるのが特徴。⇒accord）
　◆Auction rate securities resemble regular corporate debts, except the interest rates are reset at regular auctions. 金利入札証券（ARS）は、金利が定期的に行われる入札で更改されることを除けば、通常の社債に似ている。◆Citigroup Inc. and Merrill Lynch & Co. will buy back almost $20 billion of the so-called auction-rate securities. 米シティグループとメリルリンチが、約200億ドル相当のいわゆる金利入札証券

買い戻す方針だ。◆Citigroup will buy back the auction-rate securities from investors under separate accords with the Securities and Exchange Commission and state regulators. 米シティグループは、米証券取引委員会（SEC）や州規制当局との個々の合意に基づいて投資家から金利入札証券（ARS）を買い戻す。

audit （動）監査する，会計検査する
◆The accounting firm is responsible for auditing the accounts of about 7,000 companies. 同監査法人は、約7,000社の会計監査［財務書類の監査］を担当している。◆The auditing firm audited the accounts of failed companies Yamaichi Securities Co. and Yaohan Japan Corp. この監査法人は、経営破たんした山一証券やヤオハンジャパンの財務書類の監査を担当した。◆The company is required by a special provision of the Commercial Code to be audited by an auditing firm or a certified public accountant in addition to internal auditors. 同社は、商法特例法の規定で、内部監査役のほかに監査法人か公認会計士の監査を受けなければならない。

audit （名）監査，会計検査，検査，立入り検査
  accounting audit 会計監査
  audit certificate 監査証明
  audit corporation 監査法人
    (=auditing firm, auditing house, auditor)
  audit evidence 監査証拠
  audit of books 帳簿監査
  audit opinion 監査意見
  audit procedures 監査手続き
  audit report 監査報告書
  book audit 帳簿監査
  cash audit 現金監査
  continuous audit 継続監査
  external [outside] audit 外部監査
  final audit 期末監査
  financial audit 会計監査
  interim audit 期中監査, 中間監査
  internal audit 内部監査
  limited audit 限定監査
  management audit 経営監査, 業務監査
    (=managerial audit)
  operation audit 業務監査 (=operational audit)
  sabotage [obstruct] an audit by the Financial Services Agency 金融庁の立入り検査を妨害する
  site audit 現場監査
  statement of audit 監査報告書
  statutory audit 法定監査
  the Board of Audit 会計検査院
  voluntary audit 任意監査
  yearly audit 年次監査

◆For the obstruction of an audit by the FSA, an executive of the bank is believed to have fraudulently obtained a password needed to delete e-mails from the bank's computer server. 金融庁の立入り検査を妨害するため、同行の役員が、同行のコンピュータ・サーバーから電子メールを削除するのに必要なパスワードを、不正に入手したと見られる。◆FSA audits of the banks' accounts urged them to reclassify 149 of their major corporate borrowers more strictly in terms of their creditworthiness in a bid to accelerate the disposal of bad loans. 金融庁による銀行の財務書類監査で、不良債権処理を加速するため、銀行は大口融資先149社の信用力による債務者区分の見直しを強化するよう強く求められた。◆Small municipalities have a financial difficulty in setting up an independent audit office or conducting external auditing every fiscal year. 小規模市町村の場合、独立した監査事務局を設置したり、外部監査を毎年度実施したりするのは財政的に困難である。

◆The Metropolitan Police Department searched the bank's head office on suspicion the bank had sabotaged an audit by the Financial Services Agency. 警視庁は、金融庁の立入り検査を妨害した疑いで、同行の本店を捜索した。

audit account report 決算検査報告書
◆The Board of Audit intends to include the total taxpayer contribution to JAL in its audit account report compiled in November 2011. 会計検査院は、2011年11月にまとめる決算検査報告書に、日航に対する総国民負担額を盛り込む方針だ。

audit firm 監査法人
  (=audit corporation, auditing firm)
◆The FSA gave an official warning to this audit firm under the Certified Public Accountants Law over negligence in its checking of the bank's accounts. 金融庁は、同行の財務書類の監査内容が不十分であったとして、公認会計士法に基づきこの監査法人に対して正式に戒告処分を出した。

audit report 監査報告書 (=auditing report)
◆Auditors previously have referred to the possibility of corporate failure in their audit reports. 監査人はこれまで、監査報告書に企業倒産［経営破たん］の可能性について言及する例はあった。

audit sabotage 検査妨害
◆The FSA ordered the bank to suspend some operations due to serious law violations, including audit sabotage. 金融庁は、同行に対して、検査妨害などの重大な銀行法違反で、一部業務の停止命令を出した。

auditing （名）監査, 会計監査
  auditing contract 監査契約 (=audit engagement)
  auditing officer 監査役
  auditing report 監査報告書
  auditing services 監査業務
    (=auditing business, auditing work)
  auditing standards 監査基準 (=audit standards)
  auditing technique 監査技術
  external auditing 外部監査

◆Auditing is the practice of checking financial statements, such as balance sheets and income statements, confirming that annual securities reports have been properly written, and proving that those statements and reports are accurate. 監査とは、貸借対照表や損益計算書などの財務書類［財務諸表］をチェックし、年次有価証券報告書が適正に記載されていることを確認して、財務書類や有価証券報告書が正確であることを証明することを言う。◆The company has established permanent committees of the board of directors to permit continuing review of the areas of auditing, management resources and compensation, pension fund policy, and investment. 同社は、監査、役員人事・報酬、年金基金対策と投資の各分野に関する検討を継続的に行うため、常設の取締役会付属委員会を設置している。

auditing company 監査法人 (=auditing firm)
◆Listed companies are perplexed over one of the country's biggest auditing companies being ordered to suspend business. 国内最大手の監査法人の一角が業務停止命令を受けるという事態に、上場企業各社は戸惑っている。

auditing contract 監査契約 (=audit engagement)
◆Once the auditing services are suspended, auditing contracts become void under the Corporate Law. 監査業務がいったん停止されると、会社法の規定で監査契約は無効になる。

auditing firm 監査法人 (=audit corporation, audit firm, auditing house, auditor:「監査法人」は、5人以上の公認会計士が共同で設立する法人。会計基準などに照らして企業決算が適正かどうかを第三者の立場で審査して、監査証明書（監査報告書）を出す。4大監査法人（みずほ（旧中央青山）、あずさ、トーマツ、新日本）が、上場企業の8割を監査している）

◆Certified public accountants and auditing firms are responsible for preventing corporate managers from window-dressing business results. 公認会計士や監査法人には、企業経営者の粉飾決算を止めさせる責任がある。◆The company is required by a special provision of the Commercial Code to be audited by an auditing firm or a certified public accountant in addition to internal auditors. 同社は、商法特例法の規定で、内部監査役のほかに監査法人か公認会計士の監査を受けなければならない。

auditing services 監査業務
(⇒auditing contract)
◆The auditing firm was ordered to suspend legally bound auditing services for its clients required under the Securities and Exchange Law and the new Corporate Law. この監査法人は、証券取引法と新「会社法」で法的に義務付けられている監査先企業に対する法定監査業務の停止命令を受けた。

auditing work 監査業務 (=auditing business)
◆Arthur Andersen's auditing work for WorldCom was in compliance with SEC standards. ワールドコムに対するアーサー・アンダーセンの監査業務は、米証券取引委員会（SEC）の基準に従って行われた。

auditor （名）監査人, 監査役, 監査法人, 会計検査官, 監査機関
　auditor's certificate　監査証明書, 監査報告書
　　(=auditor's report)
　auditor's consideration　監査人の検討
　auditor's independence　監査人の独立性
　auditor's liability [responsibility]　監査人の責任
　auditors' opinion　監査意見　(=audit opinion)
　auditor's remuneration　監査報酬
　auditor's [auditors'] report　監査報告, 監査報告書, 監査人の報告書　(=audit report, auditor's certificate, auditors' report)
　auditor's statement　監査報告
　bank auditor　銀行監査人
　certified internal auditor　公認内部監査人, CIA
　external auditor　外部監査人
　independent auditor　独立監査人
　internal auditor　内部監査人 (⇒auditing firm)
　outside auditor　社外監査人, 社外監査役
　　(=nonexecutive internal auditor)
　predecessor auditor　前任監査人
　primary auditor　持ち株会社の監査人, 親会社の監査人
　shareholders' auditors　会計監査人
　statutory auditor　法定監査人, 常勤監査役, 監査役
　successor auditor　後任監査人
　system auditor　システム監査人
◆An independent auditor found problems with the way Time Warner accounted for a number of transactions. タイム・ワーナーの一部取引の会計処理方法に問題があることに、独立監査人が気づいた。◆Auditors conduct unannounced site inspection after ISO certification each year. ISO（国際標準化機構）の認定後も、監査機関が毎年、予告なしの現場検査を実施します。◆Companies with more than ￥500 million in capital are required to be audited by an auditing firm or a certified public accountant in addition to internal auditors. 資本金5億円以上の会社は、内部監査人（監査役）のほかに、監査法人か公認会計士の監査も受けなければならない。◆Kanebo decided to change its auditor to Deloitte Touche Tohmatsu from Chuo-Aoyama PricewaterhouseCoopers. カネボウは、同社の会計監査人を中央青山監査法人から監査法人デロイト・トゥーシュ・トーマツに変更することを決めた。◆The bank consulted its auditor to determine their results for the first half of the current fiscal year ending Sept. 30. 9月中間決算［9月30日に終了する今年度上半期の決算］を確定するため、同行は監査法人に意見を求めた。

auditor's certification 監査証明
◆Under TSE regulations, the bourse can delist a company's stock if the company files financial statements without an auditor's certification. 東証の規則では、企業が監査法人の監査証明を得ないで財務書類を提出した場合、同証券取引所は同社の株式を上場廃止にすることができる。

auspices 後援, 援助, 支援, 主催, 指導, 明るい見通し, 前兆, 吉兆
◆The company is undergoing management rehabilitation under the auspices of the Industrial Revitalization Corporation of Japan. 同社は現在、産業再生機構の支援を受けて経営再建に取り組んでいる。

austere （形）厳格な, 質素な, 簡素な, 切り詰めた, 耐乏の
　austere budget　緊縮予算
　be austere against　～に対して厳しい態度を取る
　maintain an austere stance　厳しい姿勢を貫く
◆French Finance Minister Christine Lagarde chosen as the new managing director of the IMF is expected to maintain an austere stance of calling on Greece to reform itself. IMFの新専務理事に選ばれたクリスティーヌ・ラガルド仏財務相は、ギリシャに改革を求める厳しい姿勢を貫くものと期待されている。

austere fiscal policy 緊縮財政政策, 緊縮財政
◆The government needs to shift from an austere fiscal policy as soon as possible, in view of its issuance of no-interest-bearing, tax-exempt government bonds. 政府は、無利子非課税国債などの発行を視野に入れて、早急に緊縮財政から転換する必要がある。

austerity （名）緊縮, 引締め, 緊縮財政, 財政緊縮, 耐乏, 耐乏生活（austerity life）, 質素, 倹約, 厳しさ, 厳格さ
　austerities　耐乏生活, 禁欲生活
　austerity budget(s)　緊縮予算
　austerity drive　緊縮政策
　austerity plan　緊縮政策, 緊縮経済計画
　austerity policy　緊縮財政政策［財政策］, 財政赤字削減策, 耐乏政策
　austerity program　緊縮計画, 耐乏生活計画

austerity measures 緊縮政策, 緊縮策, 引締め政策, 引締め策, 財政赤字削減策, 緊縮財政, 緊縮財政
◆Austerity measures such as drastic cuts in spending on public works projects should be avoided. 公共事業［公共事業費］の大幅カットなどの緊縮政策は、避けるべきだ。◆Demonstrations against Italy's austerity measures took place in Rome and Milan. イタリアの緊縮財政に対する抗議デモが、ローマやミラノで行われた。◆Greece has to agree to new austerity measures before it receives any financial aid from the European Union. ギリシャは、欧州連合（EU）の金融支援を受ける前に、追加の財政赤字削減策［緊縮政策］に同意しなければならない。◆Greece is forced to implement painful austerity measures, including cutting the number of government employees and rising taxes. ギリシャは、公務員の削減や増税など痛みを伴う緊縮財政策の実行を迫られている。◆The European economy might slow down and register negative growth if eurozone states introduce austerity measures. ユーロ圏各国が緊縮財政策を導入すると、欧州の景気は減速し、マイナス成長に陥る恐れがある。

Australian dollar 豪ドル
◆In the case of foreign currency deposits, depositors can invest in foreign currencies such as British pound, Swiss franc and Australian dollar as well as the U.S. dollar and euro. 外貨預金の場合、預金者は、米ドルやユーロのほかに英ポンド、スイス・フランや豪ドルなどにも投資することができる。◆The interest rates of the Australian dollar-denominated deposit service are relatively high among major foreign currencies. 主要外貨のうち豪ドル建て預金サービスの金利は、比較的高い。

authentication （名）インターネットの利用者認証, 認

証, オーセンティケーション
authentication number　認証番号
authentication service　認証サービス
entity authentication　個人認証
user authentication system　ユーザー認証システム
◆This bank requires users to provide special authentication numbers to transfer money. この銀行は、振込みの際に専用の認証番号の入力を利用者に義務付けている。

authorities　（名）当局, その筋　（⇒authority）
　authorities' commitment to monetary stability　金融安定に対する当局の姿勢
　authorities concerned　関係当局, 関係官庁, 当該官庁, その筋
　central authorities　中央当局, 政府
　competent authorities　主務官庁, 管轄庁
　customs authorities　税関当局
　financial and monetary authorities　金融・通貨当局
　financial authorities　金融当局
　government [governmental] authorities　政府当局
　legal authorities　法務当局
　local authorities　地方当局, 地方官庁, 地方自治体
　monetary authorities　金融当局, 通貨当局
　municipal authorities　市当局
　port authorities　港湾当局
　proper authorities　関係官庁, 当局
　relevant authorities　関係機関, 関係当局
　tax authorities　税務当局
　territorial authorities　連邦・地方政府
　U.S. authorities　米政府当局, 米当局
◆A large yen-selling intervention by monetary authorities on Sept. 15 failed to reverse the yen's rising trend. 金融当局が9月15日に実施した大量の円売り介入で、円高傾向を反転[逆転]させることはできなかった。◆In order to prevent the chain reaction of even more devastating financial collapses, financial and monetary authorities in the United States and other nations will need to work together. これ以上の衝撃的な金融破たんの連鎖反応を防ぐには、米国と世界各国の金融・通貨当局の協調が必要だ。◆Market players remain wary of a possible yen-selling market intervention by Japanese authorities. 市場関係者は、日本当局（政府・日銀）による新たな円売り市場介入の可能性をまだ警戒している。◆Since 1976, U.S. tax authorities have twice allowed tax refunds for banks. 1976年以来、米国[米国の税務当局]は、銀行については税金還付を2度承認している。◆The Financial Stability Forum comprises financial authorities of major nations. 金融安定化フォーラムは、主要国の金融当局で構成されている。◆The monetary union's authorities have neglected to strengthen the banking system. 通貨統合の当局は、銀行システムの強化[銀行システムへのテコ入れ]を怠った。◆U.S. authorities are poised to allow the weak dollar to continue for the foreseeable future. 米当局は、ドル安の進行を当面、容認する構えだ。

authority　（名）権限, 権能, 代理権, 権力, 権威, 権威者, 専門家, 公共機関, 当局, 根拠, その筋, ～筋, 許可, 先例
　authority and duties of officers　役員の権限と職責
　authority to pay　手形支払い授権書, 支払い授権書
　　（=authorization to pay）
　authority to purchase　手形買取り授権書, 買取り授権書
　　（=authorization to purchase）
　budgetary authority　予算限度額
　Commodity Exchange Authority　商品取引所監督局
　delegation of authority　権限委譲
　Federal Public Housing Authority　連邦公共住宅局
　international authority　国際機関
　issuing authority　発行当局
　lending authority　貸付け権限
　local authority　地方当局, 地方自治体
　local authority bond　地方債
　local authority loans　地方政府債
　maximum issuing authority　発行枠, 発行限度額
　operating authority　営業権限
　public authority　公的機関
　regulatory authority　規制機関
　statutory borrowing authority　国債発行限度額
◆A market intervention is conducted under the authority of the finance minister in Japan. 市場介入は、日本では財務相の権限で行われる。◆The nation's tax authorities have no authority to tax foreign corporations whose core business is not conducted in this country. 主力事業を日本で行っていない外国法人に対しては、日本の税務当局に課税権はない。◆To assist it in carrying out its duties, the Board has delegated certain authority to several committees. 取締役会は、その職務遂行を補佐する機関として、複数の委員会に特定の権限を委譲しています。

authorization [authorisation]　（名）承認, 承諾, 認可, 許可, 公認, 権限, 授権, 検定, 委任, 委任状
　authorization code　承認番号
　authorization for issuance　起債認可
　authorization limits　利用限度額
　authorization to borrow money　借入授権書
　authorization to charge an account　口座引落し授権書
　authorization to hypothecate　担保契約授権書
　authorization to pay　手形支払い授権書
　　（=authority to pay）
　authorization to purchase　手形買取り授権書
　　（=authority to purchase）
　credit authorization　信用照会, 信用確認
　credit authorization network　信用照会ネットワーク
　credit authorization terminal　信用照会端末装置, 加盟店端末機, クレジット専用端末, CAT
　credit card authorization　クレジット・カードの認証
　debit authorization　借記授権書
　governmental authorization　政府の承認, 政府の認可
　interim authorization　仮認可
　letter of authorization　授権書
　prior authorization　事前の許可
◆Access to assets occurs only in accordance with management's authorization. 資産の取扱いは、かならず経営陣の承認に基づいて行われています。

authorize　（動）権限を与える, 許可する, 認可する, 認定, 公認する, 検定する
◆The articles of incorporation authorize the Directors to issue such shares in one or more series and to fix the number of shares of each series prior to their issue. 定款では、これらの株式をシリーズで1回以上発行する権限と、その発行前に各シリーズの発行株式数を決定する権限は、取締役会に与えられています。

authorized　（形）権限を与えられた[授けられた], 許可[認可]された, 公認の, 検定済みの
　authorized agency　公認格付け機関
　authorized bank　公認銀行
　authorized broker　（取引所の）取引員
　authorized capitalization　授権株式総数
　authorized common stock　授権普通株式数
　authorized dealer　認可業者, 公認取扱い業者
　authorized depository　公認保管業者
　authorized foreign exchange bank　外国為替公認銀行, 外

為公認銀行, AFEB
authorized issue （株式の）授権発行数（=authorized capital）
authorized minimum 必要最低資本額
authorized settlement agent 公認決済代理人
authorized share capital 授権資本
bond authorized 授権社債
initial authorized capital 当初授権株式
authorized capital 授権資本, 授権株式, 授権株式数, 公称資本, 株式発行可能枠 （=authorized capital stock, authorized share capital: 株式会社がその基本定款に基づいて株式発行により調達できる資本の限度額。授権資本を広げる場合は、株主総会での定款の変更が必要となる。授権資本を設定することで、新株発行が制限され、既存株主の権利を守ることができる）
◆Many of listed companies are set to adopt measures to counter corporate acquirers, such as increasing their authorized capital or reducing the quorum of directors. 授権資本（株式発行可能枠）の拡大や取締役の定数削減など、買収防衛策を導入する上場企業も多い。
authorized capital stock 授権資本
◆The authorized capital stock of the Company is as listed below, of which the shares listed below are issued and outstanding. 本会社の授権株式は下記のとおりで、このうち下記の株式が発行され、現在存在している［このうち下記の株式が外部発行済みとなっている］。
authorized shares [stock] 授権株式, 授権株式数
◆We have 100 million authorized shares of preferred stock at $1 par value. 当社には、額面1ドルの優先株式1億株の授権株式があります。
auto （名）自動車, オート
auto finance company 自動車ローン会社
auto loan 自動車ローン
auto loan-backed financing 自動車ローン証券の発行
auto loan-backed securities 自動車ローン証券
auto paper 自動車ローン証券
auto stocks 自動車株
◆GM will buy auto financing company AmeriCredit Corp. for $3.5 billion. GMが、自動車ローン会社のアメリクレジットを35億ドルで買収する。
auto- （形）自己の, 自動化した, 自動車の
auto-backed deal 自動車ローン証券
auto-banking 自動化銀行業務
auto-financing 自己金融 （=self-financing）
automate （動）自動化する, 省力化する, コンピュータ化する, オートメ化する, オートメーション化する
automated billing service system 自動料金請求処理システム
automated bond system 自動債券取引システム
automated clearing house 自動手形交換機構, 自動決済機構
automated fund transfer account 自動振替口座
automated screen trading 証券の自動画面取引, 自動スクリーン取引
automated trading and order-matching system 自動取引・注文執行システム
automated trading system 自動取引システム, コンピュータ売買システム, 自動売買システム
automated teller machine 現金自動預け払い機, ATM （=automatic teller machine）
◆Cash withdrawals and deposits are made through automated teller machines. 現金の入出金は、ATM（現金自動預け払い機）で行われている。 ◆The bank had troubles in its automated teller machines. 同銀行のATM（現金自動預け払い機）にトラブルが生じた。

automatic （形）自動的な, 自動の, 自動式の, 自動装置の, 無意識の, 反射的な, オートマチック
automatic accounts transfer system 自動引落し制度
automatic approval system 自動承認制
automatic bank transfer 銀行自動振込み
automatic cash paying machine 現金自動支払い機
automatic cover limits 自動再保険の適用限度
automatic drawing rights （IMFの）自動引出権
automatic fund transfer 口座自動振替, 自動引落し
automatic liquidation 自動決済
automatic operation 自動操作
automatic ordering 自動発注
automatic payment 自動引落し, 自動支払い
automatic premium loan 保険料自動振替貸付け
automatic reinvestment 自動再投資
automatic renewal 自動更新
automatic settlement 自動決済
automatic standard 自動本位制
automatic stay 自動停止
automatic transfer service 自動振替サービス
automatic payment 自動振込み, 自動支払い
◆For the automatic payment of the electric bills, a fee is paid to an electric power-company's account at the same time the fee is debited from a customer's account. 電気料金の自動振込みの場合は、顧客の口座から料金が引き落とされると同時に、電力会社の口座に電気料金が振り込まれる。
automatic teller machine 現金自動預け払い機, 現金自動預入引出機 （=automated teller machine; ⇒ATM）
◆A depositor can withdraw money from any bank by the interbank network of automatic teller machines. 銀行間のATM（現金自動預け払い機）ネットワークにより（銀行のATM相互利用が普及しているため）、預金者はどの銀行からでも預金を引き出すことができる。
automobile insurance 自動車保険
◆The two life insurers plan to tie up to sell automobile insurance. 両生命保険会社は、自動車保険の販売で業務提携する方針だ。
automotive insurance 自動車保険
◆Automotive insurance is the flagship product of nonlife insurers. 自動車保険は、損害保険会社の主力［目玉］商品だ。
automotive insurance market 自動車保険市場
◆Growth in the automotive insurance market is slowing as fewer young people own cars. 若者の車離れを背景に、自動車保険市場は伸び悩んでいる。
avail （動）〜に役に立つ, 用が足りる （名）利益, 効用, 効力, 甲斐（かい）
avail of [avail oneself of] 〜を利用［活用］する
be of no [little] avail to 〜に何の役にも立たない, 〜に全然役に立たない
without avail [all to no avail] 無益に, 甲斐なく
◆To fulfill its responsibilities as the nation's central bank, the Bank of Japan must achieve currency stabilization by availing itself of a range of measures, including stabilization of the exchange rate. 日本の中央銀行としての責任を果たすには、日本銀行は、為替相場の安定を含めて広範な手段を活用して通貨の安定を実現しなければならない。
availability （名）有効性, 効力, 利用可能度, 可用性, 可用度, 使用可能度, 提供可能性, 提供, 確保, 稼働率, アベイラビリティ
availability date （当座）他店券渡り済み日, 渡り日
availability of funds 流動性のアベイラビリティ
availability of loans 融資枠, 貸出枠
availability period （シンジケート・ローンの）資金引出

し可能期間
availability risk　資金調達困難リスク,アベイラビリティ・リスク
capital availability　資本の利用可能性,資本のアベイラビリティ
credit availability　信用の利用可能性,信用のアベイラビリティ,クレジット利用
　（=availability of credit）
job availability　雇用機会
land availability　土地の取得
oil availability　原油確保,原油供給
the availability of recourse　償還請求権

available　（形）有効な,利用可能な,使用可能な,処分可能な,充当可能な,入手可能な,調達可能な,配送可能な,閲覧可能な
available asset　利用可能資産
available balance　ネット預金残高,利用可能残高
available banking facilities　銀行借入枠
available capital　利用可能資本,使用可能資本
available cash　利用可能現金,手元流動性,十分な現預金
available date　現金支払い可能日
available earned surplus　利用可能利益剰余金,処分可能利益剰余金
available for investment　投資に運用可能な
available-for-sale financial asset　売却可能金融資産
available-for-sale securities　売却可能証券
　（=securities available for sale）
available fund　利用可能資金,引出可能資金
available investment capital　投資可能な資本
available profit　処分可能利益
available surplus　利用可能剰余金
balance available for common stock　普通株主に帰属する利益
be available on the internet　インターネット［ネット］で閲覧できる
become available on the stock exchange　証券取引所に上場する
government-guaranteed trade insurance is available　政府保証付き貿易保険が利用できる
　（⇒credit risk）
have no available cash　手元資金がない
immediately available fund　即時現金化可能資金
make available to　～に提供する
net assets available for plan benefits　年金給付債務に充当可能な純資産
net income available for common stock　普通株主に帰属する純利益［当期純利益］
profit available for dividend［distribution］　配当可能利益
publicly available financial data　公表財務データ
surplus available for dividends　配当可能利益
◆The actuarial present value of the accrued plan benefits and the net assets available to discharge these benefits at December 31 are as follows: 12月31日現在の年金給付債務額の年金数理原価と年金給付債務に充当可能な年金純資産は、以下のとおりです。◆The Annual Report on Form 10-K is available from the date of its filing with the Securities and Exchange Commission in the United States. 様式10-Kに基づく当社の年次報告書は、米国の証券取引委員会（SEC）への提出日以降に入手できます。

average　（動）～の平均をとる,～の平均値を出す,平均して～になる,相殺する,合算する
　average down　ナンピン（難平）買いする,（証券などを売買して）平均値を下げる
　average out　売り抜ける,売買して逃げる,利益ありまたは損失なしの結果で終わる
　average out to　～に落ち着く,平均して～になる,横ばいを脱して～になる
　average up　ナンピン売りする,（証券などを売買して）平均値を上げる
◆Corporate profits will average out to positive growth. 企業収益は、横ばいを脱して積極的な増加［プラス成長］に転じるだろう。◆Under the new securities taxation system, gains and losses on stocks and investment trusts will be averaged before being taxed. 新証券税制では、株式の損益［株式譲渡損益］と投信の損益［投資信託の償還・解約に伴う損益］を合算［相殺］して課税する。

average　（名）平均,海損　（形）平均の
arithmetic average［mean］　算術平均
arithmetic weighted average　加重平均
average gain　合算後の利益,相殺後の利益
　（⇒capital gains tax）
average number of listed stocks［shares］　平均上場株式数,上場株式総数の平均（「平均上場株式数」は（期初の上場株式数＋期末の上場株式数）÷2で算出する）
average number of shares outstanding　期中平均発行済み株式数
average policy size in force　平均有効保険金高
average policy size issued　平均発行保険金
average rate of profit　平均利益率
average rate of return　平均資本利益率
average remaining service period of employees　従業員の平均残存勤続［勤務］期間
average return on investment　平均投資収益率,平均投資収益
average shares outstanding　期中平均発行済み株式総数
average weekly claims for unemployment insurance　週平均失業保険申請件数
average workweek of production workers　製造業週平均労働時間
compound yield based on weighted average　加重平均利回り
moving average　移動平均
return on average equity　平均株主資本利益率
stock average　平均株価
　（=stock price average）
stock price average　平均株価
weighted average price　加重平均株価
weighted average share　加重平均株式数
◆The stock average fell below 9,000 again on the Tokyo Stock Exchange. 東京株式市場は、平均株価がふたたび9,000円を割り込んだ。

average common shares outstanding　発行済み普通株式の平均数,発行済み普通株式の平均株式数
◆Earnings per share for the first nine months of 2011 were based on 308.4 million average common shares outstanding. 2011年1-9月期の1株当たり純利益は、発行済み普通株式数3億840万株に基づいて計算されています。

average daily balance　平均残高,1日平均残高
the average daily balance of bank lending　銀行貸出の平均残高,銀行貸出の1日平均残高
the average daily balance of domestic bank lending　国内銀行貸出の平均残高,国内銀行貸出の1日平均残高
the daily average balance of M2 plus certificates of deposit　M2と譲渡性預金（CD）の1日平均残高
◆The average daily balance of M2 came to ￥738.1 trillion in July. 7月のM2の平均残高は、738兆1,000億円だった。

average daily balance of bank lending　銀行貸出の

平均残高
◆In December 2009 alone, the average daily balance of bank lending fell 1.2 percent from a year earlier, the first drop since January 2006. 2009年12月の単月では、銀行貸出の平均残高は、前年同月比1.2%で、2006年1月以来4年ぶりの減少となった。

average daily balance of domestic bank lending 国内銀行の貸出平均残高
◆The average daily balance of domestic bank lending logged a record 2.2 percent rise in 2009 from the previous year. 2009年の国内銀行の貸出平均残高は、前年比2.2%増で最高の伸び率を示した。

average daily balance of the monetary base マネタリー・ベース（貨幣流通高と日銀当座預金との合計）の1日平均残高
◆The average daily balance of the monetary base in May 2011 totaled about 114.42 trillion. 2011年5月のマネタリー・ベースの1日平均残高は、約114兆4,200億円となった。◆The average daily balance of the monetary base—composed of cash in circulation and the balance of current account deposits held by financial institutions at the Bank of Japan- totaled ¥99.19 trillion in November 2010. 2010年11月のマネタリー・ベース（貨幣流通高と金融機関が日銀に保有する［日銀に預けている］当座預金の残高）の1日平均残高は、99兆1,900億円となった。

average invested capital 平均投下資本
◆Average invested capital is defined as stockholder's equity plus long- and short-term debts less short-term investments (includes short-term investments categorized as cash equivalents). 平均投下資本＝資本＋長期・短期金融債務-短期投資（現預金等価物として表示する短期投資を含む）です。

average market price of common stock 普通株式の平均株価
◆The average market price of the company's common stock was $20 per share during 2008. 同社の普通株式の平均株価は、2008年度は1株当たり20ドルであった。

average number of listed stocks [shares] 平均上場株式数, 上場株式総数の平均 （「平均上場株式数」は（期初の上場株式数＋期末の上場株式数）÷2で算出する。⇒turnover ratio）

average number of shares outstanding 期中平均発行済み株式数, 平均発行済み株式数［株式総数］
(=average shares outstanding)
◆For the nine months ended September 30, 2008, the average number of shares outstanding was 582.8 million. 2008年1-9月期の平均発行済み株式総数は、5億8,280万株でした。

average return on capital 平均資本利益率
◆The average return on capital of Britain's businesses rose 26 basis points to 4.95 percent in this year's first quarter. 今年第1四半期の英国企業の平均資本利益率は、(前年同期比) 0.26%増の4.95%だった。

averaging （名）ナンピン(難平), ドル平均法, 平均化（「ナンピン」は、相場上の損失を売買全体のなかで平均化することで、値上がりするつど信用売りして行くことをナンピン売り上がり、値下がりするつど買って行くのをナンピン買い下がりという）
averaging down　ナンピン買い下がり, 買い下がり
averaging method　ナンピン買い法
averaging of market risk　市場リスクの平均化
averaging up　ナンピン売り上がり
dollar cost averaging　ドル平均法
(=dollar average method)

avert （動）避ける, 防ぐ, 回避する, そらす, 背(そむ)ける
◆Banks would keep amassing cash by disposing of distressed assets as quickly as possible to avert collapse after having difficulty raising funds. 資金調達が困難になって経営破たんするのを避けるため、金融機関［銀行］は、できるだけ早めに危険資産を処分［売却］して、現金を抱え込もうとする。◆Greece must avert a crippling debt default by securing billions of dollars in emergency loans from European countries and the IMF. ギリシャは、欧州諸国［ユーロ圏］と国際通貨基金（IMF）による緊急融資で巨額の資金を確保して、壊滅的な債務不履行を回避しなければならない。◆Japan, the United States and European countries will cooperate to avert financial turmoil stemming from the downgrading of the U.S. credit rating. 日米欧が連携して、米国債の格下げによる金融市場の混乱を回避することになった。◆The government finds it difficult to avert economic contraction in the next fiscal year starting in April. 4月から始まる来年度の景気悪化を回避するのは難しい、と政府は見ている。◆The IMF and the EU are strengthening their cooperation to avert a Greek default and prevent a chain reaction of debt crisis among other countries. ギリシャの債務不履行（デフォルト）を回避し他国間の債務危機の連鎖反応を防ぐため、国際通貨基金（IMF）と欧州連合（EU）は、連携を強めている。

avoid （動）避ける, 回避する, 防ぐ, 敬遠する, 逃れる,（契約などを）無効にする
avoid a financial meltdown　金融危機を回避する
avoid a net loss　赤字決算を避ける
avoid bankruptcy　倒産［破産］を逃れる, 経営破たん［破たん］を逃れる
avoid credit loss　信用損失を避ける
avoid currency volatility　為替相場の極端な変動を防ぐ
avoid default on the debt　債券のデフォルトを避ける［回避する］
avoid exchange rate risk　為替リスクを避ける
avoid payments　支払いを避ける
avoid prepayment risk　期限前償還リスクを避ける［回避する］

◆As one option to avoid excessive currency appreciation in emerging countries with inflationary trends, they can restrict an influx of capital. インフレ気味の新興国で行き過ぎた［過度の］通貨高を避けるための手段として、資金流入を規制することができる。◆Both a freefall in stock prices and a surge in the yen's value have been avoided. 株価の暴落も円の急騰も、回避された。◆Financial chiefs from the Group of 20 advanced and major developing countries vowed to avoid a global currency war. 主要20か国・地域（G20）の財務相・中央銀行総裁が、(各国が自国通貨を安くすることで輸出競争力を高め、景気回復をめざす)世界の通貨安競争を避けることを公約した。◆Ford is the only member of the U.S. Big Three auto giants to have avoided bankruptcy in 2009. 米自動車大手3社「ビッグ・スリー」のうち、2009年に経営破たんを逃れたのはフォードだけだ。◆The financial bailout bill's passage into law marks progress in avoiding a financial meltdown. 金融安定化法案［金融救済法案］が法律として成立したことは、金融危機を回避するうえで一歩前進したといえる。◆The government has tried to avoid economic contraction through huge stimulus measures. 政府は、大型の景気刺激策［経済対策］で景気悪化の回避に努めている。◆The U.S. government could avoid the worst-case scenario of default on payments to investors in Treasury bonds. 米政府は、国債の償還資金がなくなる債務不履行という最悪の事態を避けることができた。◆We must avoid hindering the export-led economic recovery, speeding up deflation and increasing bad loans, which can be brought about by falling stock prices and the weakening dollar. 株安とドル安がもたらす可能性がある輸出頼みの景気回復の挫折、デフレ加速、不良債権の拡大を、われわれは避けなければならない。

award （名）判断, 裁定, 仲裁判断, 仲裁裁定, 裁定額, 裁定金, 報奨金, 賞与, 昇給, 賞品, 賞金

award of attorney fess　弁護士報酬裁定額
bonus awards　ボーナス支給額
cash awards　奨励金
contract awards　契約額
damage award　損害賠償裁定金
stock award plan　株式報奨制度

B

B　Bの格付け, シングルB　(⇒rating symbol)
　BB　ダブルBの格付け, ダブルB
　BBB　トリプルBの格付け, トリプルB
　BBB long-term rating　トリプルBの長期格付け
　◆Standard & Poor's currently assigns a BBB long-term rating to the bank. スタンダード＆プアーズは現在、同行に対してトリプルBの長期格付けをしている。

B of E　(英中央銀行の)イングランド銀行 (Bank of Englandの略)

BA　銀行引受手形 (bank acceptance, banker's acceptanceの略)

baby bond　小額債券, ベビー・ボンド (=small bond: 額面価格が1,000ドル未満の債券)

back　(動)支持する, 支援する, 後押しする, 保証する, 裏付ける, 裏書きする, 裏打ちする, 金などを賭ける
　back a bill　手形に裏書きする
　back a check　小切手に裏書きする
　back out of [from]　〜から手を引く, 〜を取り消す, 〜を破棄する
　back up　市況が急反転する, 上昇する, 支持する, 裏付ける
　backed bill　担保付き手形
　backed bond　抵当付き債券
　be backed by　〜を背景にしている, 〜を裏付けとする, 〜で[〜に]裏付けられる
　be backed by government guarantees　政府の保証が付いている
　collateral backing rated issue　格付け証券を裏付けている担保
　pass-throughs backed by balloons [balloon mortgages]　バルーン(満期元本増額支払い型モーゲージ)を裏付けとするパス・スルー証券
　programs backed by trade receivables　売掛債権を裏付けとするプログラム
　stock market rally backed by good corporate earnings　業績相場
　structured financings backed by financial assets　金融資産に裏付けとした仕組み金融
　the collateral backing rated issue　格付け証券を裏付けている担保
　the underlying assets backed by the security　証券の裏付けとなる資産
　◆Fannie Mae and Freddie Mac were battered by losses on housing loans they backed. ファニー・メイ(米連邦住宅抵当金庫)とフレディ・マック(米連邦住宅貸付抵当公社)は、保証した住宅ローンの焦げ付きの影響をもろに受けた。

back　(形)滞(とどこお)った, 延滞の, 未払いの, 未納の
　back and filling　(価格が)行きつ戻りつの
　back bond　損失補償証書, バック・ボンド
　back interest　未払い利息
　back money　延滞金
　back month　期先物
　back office　事務部門, 後方部門, 事務処理, ディーリング管理業務, バック・オフィス業務, バック・オフィス
　back-office operation　バック・オフィス業務
　back-office procedures　事務処理手続き
　back order　未処理注文, 繰越し注文, 受注残
　back pay　未払い給与
　back payment　未払い支出
　back rent　遅延賃借料
　back spread　逆ざや

back-end　(形)後部の, 後追いの, 最終の
　back-end load　(投資信託や年金保険などの)解約手数料 (=deferred sales charge, exit fee, redemption charge: loadは販売手数料のこと)
　back-end right　最終権, バックエンド・ライト(乗っ取りの対象となった企業が、株主の利益を守るために株主に付与する、株式を現金、優先株や債券に転換する権利のこと)

back-in　(名)バックイン(敵対的買収に対する防衛策の一つで、株主に取締役会が定めた価格で持ち株を売り戻す権利を与えるもの)

back tax　追徴課税
　◆Having determined Lone Star fund tried to avoid tax, the Tokyo Regional Taxation Bureau ordered it to pay about ¥13 billion in back taxes, including penalty taxes due to its failure to declare earnings. 投資ファンド「ローンスター」の租税回避行為と認定して、東京国税局は、ローンスターに無申告加算税を含めて約130億円の追徴課税の支払いを命じた。

back to back [back-to-back]　(形)連続の, 続けざまの, 相次ぐ, 背中合わせの, 見返り信用状の
　back-to-back credit　同時発行信用状 (back-to-back letter of credit), 同時開設信用状, バック・ツー・バック信用状, 見返り信用状 (reciprocal credit), 見返り信用貸し, バック・ツー・バック融資
　back-to-back declines in March and April　3月と4月の2か月連続下落
　back-to-back declines in two months　2か月連続の減少[下落]
　back-to-back loan　異通貨相互貸付け, バック・ツー・バック・ローン
　back-to-back transaction　バック・ツー・バック取引
　◆Japan's industrial output climbed for a second straight month in June, the first back-to-back rise in two years. 日本の6月の鉱工業生産高は、2か月連続で増加し、2年ぶりに2か月連続の増加となった。

backdate　(動)(小切手を)前の日付にする, 実際より前の日付を入れる

backdoor [back-door]　(形)裏口の, 秘密の, 内密の, 不正な　(名)裏口, 間接, 不正手段
　backdoor financing　裏口資金調達, 裏口金融
　backdoor listing　裏口上場(非上場企業が上場企業を買収して上場を果たすこと)
　backdoor practice　裏口操作, 不正操作(正規の手続き= front-door practice)
　backdoor trade　裏取引, ヤミ取引

backdrop　(名)背景, 事情, 要因
　against the backdrop of　〜を背景にして, 〜を受けて
　against this backdrop　こうした事情から, このような背景のもとに, これを受けて, こうした中で
　unfold against a backdrop of domestic unrest　内情不安を背景に展開する
　◆Standard & Poor's revised upward the outlook on its ratings on six major Japanese insurance companies against the backdrop of their improved financial profiles. スタンダード＆プアーズは、日本の大手保険会社6社の財務力見通し改善を背景に、6社の格付け見通しを上方修正した。

backed　(形)〜が支持する, 〜が後押し[後援]する, 〜を裏付けとする, 〜を担保とする, 〜の裏書のある, 〜保

証付きの, ～保証の
（⇒asset-backed securities, state-backed）
asset-backed preferred stock　アセットバック優先株
asset-backed securities　資産担保証券
commodity-backed bond　商品担保社債, 商品償還社債
credit card receivables-backed securities　クレジット・カード証券
Eximbank-backed financing　輸銀保証付き融資［融資案件］
government-backed loans　政府保証融資額
government-backed trade insurance　政府保証付き貿易保険　（=government-guaranteed trade insurance; ⇒trade insurance）
loan-backed　ローンを裏付けとする
mortgage-backed bond　モーゲージ担保債券, モーゲージ証券
mortgage-backed securities　モーゲージ担保証券, 抵当証書担保付き証券, モーゲージ証, MBS
residential mortgage-backed securities business　住宅融資証券事業
retail receivables-backed lending　債権担保融資
state-backed mortgage firms Fannie Mae and Freddie Mac　政府系住宅金融会社のファニー・メイ（米連邦住宅抵当公庫）とフレディ・マック（米連邦住宅貸付抵当公社）
US corporate loan-backed CP　米企業向けローンを裏付けとするコマーシャル・ペーパー
with a government-backed guarantee　政府保証付きで
◆GM, Ford, Chrysler and auto-parts makers are seeking $50 billion in government-backed loans to develop and build more fuel-efficient vehicles. GM, フォード, クライスラーと自動車部品メーカー各社は, 低燃費車の開発・生産に500億ドルの政府保証融資額を求めている。◆In June 2009 prior to Japan Airlines' failure, a ￥67 billion public financing package was extended with a government-backed guarantee to JAL. 日本航空破たん前の2009年6月, 日航に対して政府保証付きで670億円の公的融資が行われた［公的融資策が実施された］。◆State-backed mortgage firm Fannie Mae lost $3.1 billion in its second quarter of this fiscal year. 政府系住宅金融会社ファニー・メイは, 今年度第2四半期の決算で31億ドルの損失［赤字］となった。◆The security firm expects to book about ￥73 billion in losses related to its residential mortgage-backed securities business in the July-September quarter. 同証券会社は, 7-9月期に住宅融資証券事業の関連損失として730億円を計上する見通しだ。

backer　（名）後援者, 支持者, 資金援助者, 支援企業, （競馬などで）賭ける人
backer of a bill　手形の裏書人
Wall Street backers　米金融界の支援企業
◆Wall Street backers failed to rescue community development financial institution ShoreBank in Chicago. 米金融界の支援企業は, シカゴの地域開発金融機関「ショアバンク」を救済できなかった。

backing　（名）裏書き, 裏書保証, 保証, 裏付け, 支持, 支援, 後援, バックアップ, 基盤, 支援団体
（⇒financial backing）
collateral backing　担保の裏付け
financial backing　経済援助, 金融支援, 財源の裏付け
have the backing of a state bank　国有銀行の支援［バックアップ］を受ける
provide the backing for　～のバックアップをする, ～をバックアップする
strong asset backing　強力な資産基盤
warrant backing　令状の裏書き

backing away　バッキング・アウェイ（株や債券市場の流通市場で価格形成を行う証券業者（マーケット・メーカー）が, 自己の取り扱う銘柄の最小取引単位のファーム・ビッド（確約買い呼び値）に応じられないことをいう）

backlog　（動）（未処理のまま）保留しておく, （予備として）取っておく, 注文を登録する

backlogged　（形）保留の, 未処理の, 未決済の
backlogged money transfer　未処理の口座振替, 口座振替未処理部分
backlogged transaction　未決済取引
◆The bank is trying to process about 500,000 backlogged money transfers. 同行は, 約50万件の口座振替未処理部分の処理作業を急いでいる。

backsliding　（名）逆戻り
◆The deteriorating employment situation, the risk of backsliding into deflation and a downturn in foreign economies are continuing risks in the economic outlook. 雇用環境の悪化とデフレへの逆戻りリスク, 海外経済の下振れが, 景気の先行きに残っているリスクだ。

backtest　（名）投資手法の有効性テスト, バックテスト

backup［back-up］　（名）代替, 代役, 予備, 控え, 支持, 支援, 後援, 応援, 上昇, 金利上昇, 利回り上昇, プール資金　（形）代替の, 予備の, 控えの, 補助的な, 後援の
backup credit　バックアップ信用, バックアップ・クレジット　（=backup line）
backup facility　バックアップ・ファシリティ（短期証券の発行などで, 借入人の支払い能力に対する保証や借入人に対する必要額の調達を保証する機能）
backup financing　バックアップ信用枠
backup funding　バックアップ資金, 代替流動性
backup in intermediate rates　中期債利回りの上昇
backup in long rates　長期利回りの上昇
backup in U.S. rates　米国金利の上昇
backup in yields　利回りの上昇
backup lender　バックアップ・ラインを提供する銀行
backup line　バックアップ・ライン, 手数料を取って企業に与える信用供与枠
（=backup credit, backup line of credit）
backup liquidity　代替流動性, バックアップ流動性, バックアップ・ライン
backup servicer　代替サービサー, バックアップ・サービサー
backup withholding　予備源泉徴収
slight backup in (interest) rates　金利の小反発
yield backup　利回りの上昇　（=backup in yields）

backwardation　（名）直先（じきさき）逆転現象, 逆ざや市場　（=inverted market: 商品や為替市場取引で直物価格が先物価格を上回っている状態のこと。このほかロンドン証券取引所では, 売り手が株の受渡しを延期するときに支払う違約金（引渡し延期金, 繰延べ料）を意味する。⇒contango, forwardation）

bad　（形）悪い, 不正な, 不良の, 不適切な, 不当な, 不完全の, 欠陥のある, 有害な
bad bargain　割高な買い物
bad business　不利な取引
bad check　不渡り小切手
bad claim　不当な請求
bad coin　悪貨, 偽金
bad corporate debt　不良資産
bad delivery　不完全受渡し
bad faith　不正
bad inventory　不良在庫
bad investment　不良投資

bad money　悪貨
bad news　悪材料
bad paper　不渡り手形
bad property loans　不動産関連の不良債権
bad reserve　貸倒れ準備金
bad risk　保険会社に不利と見られるリスク, 不良危険
bad times　不況時, 不景気
bad trade　貿易不振
get through a bad time　不況を乗り越える
holder in bad faith　悪意の第三者

bad asset　不良資産
◆If the prices of purchased bad assets are set low, the fiscal soundness of bailed-out financial institutions could be compromised. 不良資産の買取り価格が安ければ, 救済する金融機関の財務の健全性が損なわれる可能性がある。◆Setting the price at which bad assets are purchased poses a dilemma. 不良資産の買取り価格をどう決めるかは, むずかしい問題だ。◆The immediate task for U.S. authorities to forestall a full-blown financial crisis is to use public funds to buy up bad assets held by struggling financial firms. 全面的な金融危機を回避するための米政府当局の緊急課題は, 公的資金を活用して, 経営不振の金融機関が保有する不良資産の買取りだ。

bad bank　バッド・バンク（金融危機の際に政府などが設立し, 公的資金を使って金融機関が抱える不良資産を, 帳簿に記載されている評価額で買い取る専門銀行〔資産管理会社〕）
◆A bad bank is used to hold troubled assets and free up bank lending capacity. バッド・バンクは, 不良資産を買い取って, 銀行が自由に貸出できるようにするのに利用される。◆The IMF threw its weight behind the establishment of a bad bank. 国際通貨基金（IMF）は, バッド・バンクの設立を後押しした。

bad debt　不良債権, 不良貸付け, 貸倒れ, 焦げ付き, 貸倒れ損失　(=bad loan, nonperforming loan, uncollectible loan, unrecoverable loan)
allowance for bad debts (account)　貸倒れ引当金
bad debt expense　貸倒れ損失, 貸倒れ償却
bad debt insurance　貸倒れ保険
bad debt loss percentage　回収不能率
bad debt losses　貸倒れ損失
bad debt provision [reserve]　貸倒れ引当金
bad debt ratio　不良債権発生比率
bad debt recovered　償却債権取立益
bad debt recovery　不良債権回収, 償却済み債権取立益
bad debt reduction　不良債権の削減
bad debt risk　貸倒れリスク
bad debts account　貸倒れ損失勘定
bad debts as initial costs　初期原価としての貸倒れ損失
clear up bad debt　不良債権を処理する
ease the burden of bad debts for banks　銀行〔金融機関〕の償却負担を軽減する
estimate bad debts　不良債権を見積もる
estimated loss from bad debt　予想貸倒れ損失
fully provide one's bad debts　貸倒れ引当金で不良債権を完全にカバーする
fully write off one's bad debts　不良債権を完全に償却する
loss on bad debt　貸倒れ損失
reserve for bad debt [debts]　貸倒れ引当金, 貸倒れ準備金　(=provision for bad debts)
◆The bad debts are covered by the trade insurance of NEXI. この不良債権には, 日本貿易保険（NEXI）の貿易保険が適用される。
解説 不良債権とは：銀行などが融資して回収困難となった貸出金のこと。債権回収の困難さに応じて, 破綻先（法的整理などを申請した企業）, 実質破綻先, 破綻懸念先（債務超過などの企業）, 要管理先（元利金の返済が3か月以上滞っているとか, 貸出条件を緩和している融資）に区分されている。

bad debt clean-up charge　不良債権処理額　(=bad debt clean-up cost, loan loss charge)
◆Mizuho had projected a bad debt clean-up charge of ￥2 trillion in November. みずほ（みずほホールディングス）は, 11月には2兆円の不良債権処理額を予想していた。

bad debt reduction　不良債権の削減
◆The major financial and banking groups will have achieved the bad-debt reduction goals six months earlier than initially planned. 大手金融・銀行グループは, 当初の計画より半年早く不良債権削減の目標を達成したことになる。

bad loan　不良債権, 不良貸付け, 不良貸出, 不良融資, 貸倒れ　(=bad debt, nonperforming loan, uncollectible loan)
bad loan costs　不良債権処理費用, 貸倒れ損失, 貸倒れ償却
bad-loan reduction goal　不良債権の削減目標　(=bad-debt reduction target)
bad loan write-off　不良債権処理　(=write-off of bad loans; ⇒accounting period)
purchase prices for bad loans　不良債権の買取り価格
securitization of bad loans　不良債権の証券化
◆An increase in banks' loan loss reserves is a precondition for raising purchase prices for bad loans. 銀行の貸倒れ引当金の強化が, 不良債権の買取り価格引上げの前提条件となる。◆Bad loans should be bought at market value rather than at effective book value. 不良債権は, 実質簿価でなく時価で買い取るべきだ。◆Even if the banks record their bad loans as losses in their corporate accounting, such loans are not treated as losses in their tax accounting. 銀行が企業会計で不良債権を損失として計上（処理）しても, 税務会計ではこれらの不良債権は損金扱いにならない。◆The major banks attributed their increased bad loans to the poor performance of their borrowers due to the prolonged economic slump and Financial Service Agency inspections resulting in a stricter review of their asset assessments. 大手銀行は, 不良債権が増えた理由として, 長引く景気低迷で貸出先の経営が悪化したことと, 金融庁の検査を受けて大手行が資産査定を厳しくしたことを挙げた。◆The RCC used to buy bad loans at market prices. 整理回収機構は, これまで不良債権を時価で買い取っていた。

bad loan charges　不良債権額
◆The bank's bad loan charges amounted to ￥322.5 billion for the April-June quarter. 同行の4-6月期（第一・四半期）の不良債権額は, 3,225億円となった。

bad loan disposal　不良債権処理　(=disposal of bad loans, writing off bad loans; ⇒financial intermediary function, loss projections)
◆All of the seven major banking groups forecast that bad loan disposal at the end of March next year will be smaller than their net operating profits. 大手銀行・金融7グループ各行の業績予想では, 来年3月期の不良債権処理額はいずれも業務純益の範囲内になる見込みだ。◆Bad loan disposal will lead to deflationary pressures. 不良債権処理は, デフレ圧力を強める。◆The two banks' total loss from bad loan disposal likely will increase from ￥813 billion in the April 28 projection to more than ￥1 trillion. 2行の不良債権処理損失の総額は, 4月28日の業績予想時の8,130億円から1兆円超に膨らむ見通しだ。

bad loan problem　不良債権問題　(=bad loan issue: 銀行の不良債権は, 融資先が経営に失敗して, 元金の返済や利息の支払いができなくなって発生したもの。⇒write-off)
◆The bad loan problem has almost passed its critical phase. 不良債権問題は, おおむね峠を越えた。

bad loan ratio 不良債権比率 （貸出金全体に占める不良債権残高の比率。⇒regional financial institution）
◆These financial groups must reduce their bad loan ratios by further efforts to write off their bad loans. これらの金融グループは、不良債権の処理をさらに進めて、不良債権比率を下げなければならない。

bad performance 業績不振, 経営不振, 望ましくない市場成果
◆In the life insurance sector, the practice of luring customers by touting the bad performances of other insurers has been called into question. 生保業界では、他社の経営不振をあおって顧客を勧誘する行為（風評営業）が問題になっている。

baht （名）バーツ（タイの通貨単位）
◆The U.S. dollar has dropped sharply in value not only against the yen, but also against the euro, the South Korean won, the Thai baht and other currencies. 米ドルは、円に対してだけでなく、ユーロや韓国ウォン、タイ・バーツなどに対しても、急落している。

bail out （動）救う, 救済する, 緊急援助する, 緊急の救済措置を取る, 金融支援する, 経営支援する
◆Banks in the United States and some European countries were bailed out with taxpayers' money. 米国と欧州の一部の銀行は、公的資金で救済された。◆Goldman Sachs Group Inc. and the two Japanese banks bailed out Sanyo Electric Co. in February 2006. 米大手証券のゴールドマン・サックス（GS）と邦銀2行が、2006年2月に三洋電機を救済した。◆Greece was bailed out temporarily in May 2010, but it may default on its debts if it fails to secure necessary funds to redeem a sizable amount of government bonds. ギリシャは2010年5月に一時的に救済されたが、大量の国債の償還に必要な資金を確保できない場合、債務不履行（デフォルト）に陥る可能性がある。◆Greece was bailed out temporarily with financial support of €110 billion (about ¥12.7 trillion) from the IMF and the European Union. ギリシャは、IMFと欧州連合（EU）から1,100億ユーロ（約12兆7,000億円）の金融支援を受けて、一時的に救済された。◆Greece's fiscal reconstruction has made little progress since the country was bailed out with financial support from the IMF and the EU in May 2010. ギリシャの財政再建は、2010年5月にIMFと欧州連合（EU）による金融支援を受けて以来、進展してない。◆Ireland and Portugal also have been hit by financial crises and bailed out by the European Union. アイルランドやポルトガルも、財政危機に見舞われ、欧州連合（EU）に救済された［欧州連合に金融支援を仰いだ］。◆Public funds were injected to bail out Resona Bank. りそな銀行を救済するため、公的資金が注入された。◆The Industrial Revitalization Corporation has decided to bail out Mitsui Mining Co. under a fresh restructuring plan worked out by the company. 産業再生機構は、三井鉱山が策定した新再建計画に基づき同社への金融支援を決定した。◆The Industrial Revitalization Corporation will offer ¥366 billion in financial assistance to bail out the company. 産業再生機構は、同社を救済するため、3,660億円の金融支援を行う。

bailout （名）救済, 緊急援助, 緊急財政援助, 金融支援, 債務棚上げ, 救済措置, 非常時の脱出
（⇒public bailout）
  bailout bill 米国の金融機関改革・再建・強制法（1987年に成立したFinancial Institutions Reform, Recovery and Enforcement Actの通称）
  bailout loan 緊急融資, 救済融資
  banking bailout 銀行業界救済
  U.S. federal bailouts 米政府の救済策, 米政府の救済措置
◆American International Group Inc. has fast become the symbol for the ways in which U.S. federal bailouts went awry. 米保険大手のAIGは、あっという間に米政府の救済策［救済措置］がうまく行っていないケースの象徴となった。◆DaimlerChrysler AG announced its decision to withdraw from a bailout of Mitsubishi Motors. 独ダイムラー・クライスラーが、三菱自動車への金融支援打ち切り決定を発表した。◆Greece will miss 2011-12 deficit targets imposed by international lenders as part of the country's bailout. ギリシャは、同国救済措置の一環として国際融資団（欧州連合（EU）や国際通貨基金）が課した2011-12年の赤字削減目標を、達成できないようだ。◆Since May 2010, Greece has been reliant in regular payouts of loans from a €110 billion bailout from other eurozone countries and the IMF. 2010年5月からギリシャは、他のユーロ圏諸国やIMF（国際通貨基金）などからの1,100億ユーロの金融支援による融資の定期支払い金に頼っている。◆Some of the United States' biggest banks are in for a windfall on top of the $700 billion government bailout thanks to a new tax policy. 米大手銀行の一部は、新税制のおかげで、7,000億ドルの政府救済策［政府の救済措置］に加えて思いがけない利益を上げることになる。◆Taxpayers' burden from the JAL bailout was lowered to ¥47 billion as the firm repaid part of its outstanding debt. 日航救済による国民の負担分は、日航が債務残高の一部を返済したため,470億円に減少した。◆The company has received about ¥780 billion in cash and debt waivers from shareholders and investors in two bailouts. 同社は、2度の金融支援で、株主と出資企業から約7,800億円の資金提供と債務免除を受けている。◆The eurozone and the IMF agreed to a bailout for Greece amounting to €110 billion in May 2010. 2010年5月にユーロ圏［ユーロ圏15か国］と国際通貨基金（IMF）が、ギリシャに対して総額で1,100億ユーロ（約13兆円）の金融支援を行うことで合意した。

bailout deal 救済策
◆A referendum on the EU bailout deal for debt-ridden Greece was called by Greek Prime Minister Papandreou. 負債にあえぐギリシャに対する欧州連合（EU）の救済策の是非を問う国民投票の実施を、ギリシャのパパンドレウ首相が求めた。

bailout fund 救済資金, 緊急支援基金, 金融支援基金
  a massive bailout fund 大規模な緊急支援基金
  tap a Wall Street bailout fund 米金融業界救済資金を活用する
◆Eurozone nations have set up a massive bailout fund that could rescue any member country of Europe's currency union from default. ユーロ圏諸国が、デフォルト（債務不履行）から欧州の通貨統合参加国を救済できる大規模な［巨額の］緊急支援基金を創設［設立］した。◆Part of the bailout funds on the $700 billion financial rescue program went to shore up insurance giant American International Group Inc. and the auto industry. 7,000億ドルの金融支援策に基づく救済資金の一部は、米保険大手のAIGと自動車業界（GMとクライスラー）の強化に充てられた。◆The EFSF is the EU bailout fund for countries with fiscal deficits. 欧州金融安定基金（EFSF）は、欧州の財政赤字国を支援する基金だ。◆The G-20 communique urged the eurozone countries to boost the EFSF, the EU bailout fund. G20（主要20か国・地域）の共同声明は、ユーロ圏諸国に欧州の金融支援基金である欧州金融安定基金（EFSF）の拡充を促した。◆The White House is ready to consider tapping a $700 billion Wall Street bailout fund to help keep the U.S. automakers afloat. 米政府は、米自動車メーカーの破たんを避けるための支援策として、7,000億ドルの金融業界救済資金（金融安定化法の公的資金）の活用を検討する用意ができている。

bailout measure 救済措置
◆The financial market may show signs of instability after the bailout measure for the bank is decided. 同行に対する救済措置（公的資金の注入措置）の決定を発端に、金融市場は今後、不安定な動きを示すかもしれない。◆The 17 eurozone nations must ratify the agreement on bailout measures to arrange a rescue system for Greece. ギリシャへの支援体制を整えるには、ユーロ圏の17か国が、支援策についての合意事項を承認しなければならない。

bailout method 支援手法
◆The eurozone countries agreed to strengthen EFSF func-

tions, such as bailout methods, in July 2011. 2011年7月にユーロ圏諸国は、支援手法など欧州金融安定基金（EFSF）の機能を強化することで合意した。

bailout package　緊急援助策, 救済策, 金融支援策
　（=bailout plan）
◆Debt-saddled supermarket chain operator Daiei, Inc. and its three major creditor banks are finalizing a ¥400 billion bailout package involving swapping about ¥300 billion in loans for Daiei shares. 負債を抱えた［経営再建中の］大手スーパー、ダイエーとその主力取引銀行3行は、ダイエー向け債権約3,000億円の株式化を含めて4,000億円の金融支援策の最終協議に入った。

bailout plan　救済策, 支援策　（=bailout package）
banking bailout plan　銀行業界救済策
◆The firm's creditor banks agreed on the bailout plan. 同社の取引銀行は、金融支援策で合意した。◆The leaders of EU countries agreed on a bailout plan which would extend loans up to €200 billion to countries in fiscal crisis through the IMF. EU（欧州連合）各国首脳は、国際通貨基金（IMF）を通じて財政危機国に最大2,000億ユーロ（約21兆円）を貸し出す［融資する］救済策で合意した。

balance　（名）収支, 差額, 残高, 残金, 均衡, バランス
　（⇒after-tax balance, average daily balance, lending balance, lot, M1, monetary base balance, ordinary balance, outstanding balance of contracts）
account balance　勘定残高, 口座残高
balance as restated　訂正後残高
balance brought down　期首繰越残高
balance brought forward　前期からの繰越し残高
balance carried forward　前頁からの繰越し残高, 期首繰越残高
balance due　請求額, 残金
balance for service　サービス収支, サービス収支尻
balance inquiry　残高照会
balance listing　残高一覧表
balance of contract　契約残
balance of international payments　国際収支
bank balance　銀行残高, 銀行預金残高, 預金残高
　（=balance at the bank）
beginning balance　期首残高
　（=balance at beginning of the year）
cash balance　現金残高, キャッシュ・バランス
certificate of bank balance　預金残高証明書
clearing balance　交換尻
clearing house balance　手形交換尻
closing balance　期末残高
　（=balance at end of year）
current account balance　経常収支
financial balance　金融収支, 収支尻
initial balance　期首残高
　（=beginning balance, opening balance）
major shifts in the global economic balances　地球規模の経済バランスの大変化
negative balance　マイナスの残高
outstanding balance of loan　融資残高
positive balance　プラスの残高
the beginning balance　期首残高
the closing balance　期末残高
the global economic balances　地球規模の経済バランス
total balance　総合収支
trade balance　貿易収支
uncollected balance　未収金
◆The company provided copies of account balances for bank deposits to the auditing firm. 同社は、銀行預金口座の残高（残高証明書）の写しを監査法人に提出した。◆The consortium intends to raise funds to cover one-third of its development costs and expects the government will pay the balance. この共同事業体は、開発費の3分の1は独自に資金調達する方針で、残りは政府の支援を見込んでいる。◆The firm redeemed the balance of its outstanding Second Preferred Shares, Series One held by its subsidiary. 同社は、子会社が保有していた第二優先株式シリーズ1の発行済み残高を全額償還した。◆The improvement in the balance reflected slower imports rather than stronger exports. 貿易収支が改善したのは、輸出の増加よりも輸入の減少によるものだ。

balance for the income account　所得収支
　（=income balance）
◆The balance for the income account reflecting financial flows between Japan and other countries saw a ¥992.4 billion surplus. 日本と海外との資金の流れを示す所得収支は、9,924億円の黒字だった。

balance of bank notes in circulation　銀行券流通高
◆The balance of bank notes in circulation rose 2.9 percent in May 2011 to ¥79.48 trillion from a year earlier. 2011年5月の銀行券流通高は、前年同月比2.9%増の79兆4,800億円となった。

balance of Bank of Japan notes in circulation　日銀券流通高, 日銀券発行高, 日銀券発行・流通高
◆The balance of Bank of Japan notes in circulation increased 1.8 percent in November to ¥77.1 trillion from a year earlier. 11月の日銀券流通高は、前年同月比1.8%増の77兆1,000億円となった。

balance of coins in circulation　貨幣流通高
◆The balance of coins in circulation edged up 0.1 percent in May 2011 to ¥4.52 trillion from a year earlier. 2011年5月の貨幣流通高は、前年同月比で0.1%微増の4兆5,200億円となった。

balance of current account deposits　当座預金の残高, 日銀当座預金残高
　（=the current account deposit balance）
◆The average daily balance of the monetary base is composed of cash in circulation and the balance of current account deposits held by financial institutions at the Bank of Japan. マネタリー・ベースは、貨幣流通高と金融機関が日銀に保有する［日銀に預けている］当座預金の残高から成る。

balance of deposits　預金残高
◆As of the end of December, the balance of deposits held at major commercial banks had increased by 4.1 percent from a year earlier. 12月末現在の大手都銀の預金残高は、1年前より4.1%増えた。

balance of payments　国際収支, 支払い差額, 支払い残高, BOP　（=international balance of payments）
balance of payments constraint　外貨不足
balance of payments deficits　国際収支の赤字
balance of payments equilibrium　国際収支均衡
balance of payments statement　国際収支表
balance of payments statistics　国際収支統計
balance of payments surplus　国際収支の黒字
deteriorated balance of payments　国際収支の悪化
improved balance of payments　国際収支の改善
解説 国際収支とは：国際収支は経常収支（balance of current account）と資本収支（balance of capital account）で構成され、この二つを合わせたものを総合収支（overall balance of payments）という。また、経常収支は貿易収支（balance of trade）と貿易外収支（balance of invisible trade）、移転収支（balance of transfer account）から成り、資本収支は長期資本収支（balance of long-term capital account）と短期資本収支（balance of short-term capital account）から成る。なお、総合収支から短期資本収支を除

いたものを基礎収支(basic balance of payments)という。
balance of current account 経常収支
    balance of trade 貿易収支
    balance of invisible trade 貿易外収支
    balance of transfer account 移転収支
balance of capital account 資本収支
    balance of long-term capital account 長期資本収支
    balance of short-term capital account 短期資本収支
basic balance of payments 基礎収支(総合収支-短期資本収支=基礎収支)
overall balance of payments 総合収支(経常収支+資本収支=総合収支)
balance of time and savings deposits 定期性預金の残高, 定期預金残高 (=balance of time deposits)
◆The average daily balance of time and savings deposits in December last year compared with a year earlier decreased by ￥18.7 trillion, a 6.5 percent drop. 昨年12月の定期性預金の1日平均残高は、1年前より18兆7,000億円(6.5%)減った。
balance of trade 貿易収支(製品類の輸出入取引の収支尻)
    adverse balance of trade 貿易赤字
    balance of merchandise trade 貿易収支
    balance of travel trade 旅行収支
    favorable balance of trade 貿易黒字
balance of trade in goods and services モノとサービスの貿易収支
◆Japan's balance of trade in goods and services posted a surplus of ￥180.9 billion in August, against a deficit of ￥257 billion a year earlier. 8月(2009年)の日本のモノとサービスの貿易収支は、前年同月の2,570億円の赤字に対して、1,809億円の黒字となった。◆The balance of trade in goods and services logged a surplus of ￥3.43 trillion in the April-September period. 4〜9月期のモノとサービスの貿易収支は、3兆4,300億円の黒字を記録した。
balance on services サービス収支 (=balance of service trade)
◆The balance on services saw a ￥255.8 billion deficit as the appreciation of the yen deterred tourism to Japan. サービス収支は、円高で日本への観光客が減ったため、2,558億円の赤字となった。
balance sheet 貸借対照表, バランス・シート, 財務基盤, 財務体質, 財務内容, 財務状況, 財務状態, 財務, 資産, BS (=B/S, position statement, statement of financial condition, statement of financial position: 貸借対照表(バランス・シート)は決算日現在の企業の財政状態を示すもので、総資産と負債および株主資本を記載した計算書。⇒credit)
    analysis of balance sheet 財務分析, 貸借対照表分析
    annual balance sheet 年次貸借対照表
    balance sheet adjustment バランス・シート調整(企業が、投資や支出を減らし、借金の返済やリストラを優先して経営を立て直すこと)
    balance sheet growth 資産の増加
    balance sheet management 財務管理, バランス・シート管理
    balance sheet ratio 財務指標
    balance sheet value 貸借対照表価額, バランス・シート上の価額
    branch balance sheet 支店貸借対照表
    classified balance sheet 分類貸借対照表
    closing balance sheet クロージング日現在の貸借対照表
    common size balance sheet 比率表示貸借対照表
    comparative balance sheet 比較貸借対照表
    condensed balance sheet 要約貸借対照表
    consolidated balance sheet 連結貸借対照表
    constant dollar balance sheet 恒常ドル貸借対照表
    credit balance sheet 信用貸借対照表
    estimated balance sheet 見積り貸借対照表
    fund balance sheet 基金貸借対照表
    improve one's balance sheet 財務体質を改善する
    interim balance sheet 中間貸借対照表
    off-balance sheet financing オフ・バランスシート金融
    overstretch the balance sheet 財務状態が厳しくなる
    post-balance sheet date 決算日後
    post-balance sheet event 後発事象
    preparation of balance sheet 貸借対照表の作成
    remove assets from the balance sheet 資産を簿外に移す
    restatement of balance sheet 貸借対照表の再表示
    strong balance sheet 健全な財務内容, 健全な財務状態
    trim the balance sheet 資産を減らす
◆In the annual government balance sheets, Japan used to boast of a considerable amount of net assets. 政府の年次貸借対照表では、日本は、かつてはかなりの資産超過であった。◆Major banks posted about ￥1.5 trillion in losses due to the gap in the prices of their shareholdings on their balance sheets and the market value. 大手銀行は、全体で約1兆5,000億円の株式評価損(銀行保有株式のバランス・シート上の価格と時価との差による損失)を計上した。◆Nonmonetary balance sheet items and corresponding income statement items are translated at rates in effect at the time of acquisition. 貸借対照表の非貨幣性項目とこれに対応する損益計算書項目は、取得日の為替レートで換算されています。◆Only a small portion of such nonperforming loans have been removed from the banks' balance sheets as a result of the problem borrowers either undergoing consolidation or being reorganized. これら不良債権のほんの一部だけが、問題企業[問題融資先]の整理・再編で銀行のバランス・シートから切り離された[バランス・シートから外れた]。◆The bank has a stronger balance sheet than some of its bigger peers. 同行の財務基盤は、一部の大手の同業他行よりも強固だ。◆The Buyer shall prepare the Closing Balance Sheet at the Buyer's expense as promptly as practicable, but in any event within ninety (90) calendar days following the Closing Date. 買い主は、できるだけ速やかに、ただしどんな場合でもクロージング日以降90暦日以内に、買い主の費用負担でクロージング日現在の貸借対照表を作成するものとする。◆We believe there is an opportunity to leverage the strength of the balance sheet to deal with the demands of the business in the future. 財務内容の強みを生かして、将来、事業のニーズに対応する機会はあると思います。
balanced (形)釣り合い[均衡、平均]のとれた, バランスのとれた
    balanced contraction 縮小均衡
    balanced development 均整発展
    balanced expansion 均衡的拡大[発展]
    balanced finance 均衡財政
    balanced finance principle 均衡予算原則
    balanced fund バランス・ファンド (=balance fund)
    balanced growth 均衡成長
    balanced mutual fund 均衡ミューチュアル・ファンド
    balanced stock 均衡在庫
balanced budget 収支均衡予算, 均衡予算, 均衡財政, 財政均衡(赤字公債に依存しない予算)
    balanced budget bill 均衡予算法案
    balanced budget with surplus 超均衡予算, 黒字予算
◆In 2009, the German government had the parliament pass a balanced-budget bill aimed at tightening fiscal discipline. 2009年にドイツ政府は、連邦議会で財政規律を強化するため

の均衡予算法案を成立させた。

balloon （動）膨らむ, かさむ, 増大する, 急増する, 急騰する, 高騰する, 気球で飛行[上昇]する, 値を挙げる, 膨らませる
◆If the prices of purchased bad assets are set high, the public burden will balloon. 不良資産の買取り価格を高くすると、国民負担が膨らむ。 ◆In the case of foreign currency deposits, losses may balloon if the yen appreciates further and may cause a loss of principal. 外貨預金の場合、円高がさらに進めば損失が膨らみ、元本割れになる恐れもある。 ◆Selling ballooned on the New York Stock Exchange on Tuesday. 火曜日のニューヨーク市場は、売りが膨らんだ。 ◆The financial and economic crisis is leading to ballooning budget deficits across Europe. 金融・経済危機は、欧州全土で財政赤字の急増[膨張]を招いている。

balloon （名）バルーン融資, バルーン型返済, 風船, 気球, バルーン
　advertising balloon　アドバルーン
　backed by balloons　満期元本増額支払い型[バルーン型]モーゲージを裏付けとする
　balloon financing　バルーン融資
　balloon loan　バルーン融資 （=balloon financing）
　balloon maturity　元利合計満期払い, バルーン償還
　balloon mortgage　満期元本増額支払い型モーゲージ, バルーン型モーゲージ
　balloon note　風船手形（消費者の毎月の返済額を最終日だけ大きくするローン）
　balloon payment　満期元本増額支払い, 元利合計支払い, バルーン型返済, バルーン・ペイメント

ballooning （名）株価つり上げ（禁止されている株価操作の一種）, 株価膨らまし, 急増, 高騰

ban （動）禁止する, 停止する, 規制する
　ban job discrimination against women　女性に対する仕事上の差別を禁止する
　ban short-selling financial stocks　金融銘柄の空売りを禁止する[規制する]
◆Four European countries of France, Italy, Spain and Belgium banned short selling on financial stocks to restore confidence in markets. フランス、イタリア、スペイン、ベルギーの欧州4か国が、市場の信認を回復するため、金融銘柄の空売りを禁止した。 ◆France banned short selling on 11 financial stocks for 15 days. フランスは、金融11銘柄の空売りを15日間禁止した。 ◆Washington will not ask Japan to ban crude oil imports from Iran. 米政府は、イランからの原油輸入禁止を求めない方針だ。

ban （名）禁止, 停止, 廃絶, 禁止令
　blanket ban　全面禁止, 全面規制
　import ban　輸入禁止, 輸入停止
　　（=ban on imports）
　impose a ban on　〜を禁止する
　impose a ban on short selling　株の空売りを禁止する
　　（空売りは、株式を別の投資家から借りて売り注文を出す取引手法）
　lift the ban on　〜を解禁する, 〜の禁止を解除する
　put a ban on　〜を禁止する
　　（=impose a ban on, place a ban on）
◆European regulators had previously played down the idea of a blanket ban on short selling. 欧州の規制当局は、空売りの全面規制[禁止]という考え方を以前は問題にしていなかった。 ◆With the import ban, there is a danger of triggering a shortage of beef, along with price increases. 輸入停止で、牛肉の品不足や価格上昇を招く恐れがある。

ban imports　輸入を禁止する
◆The Customs Tariff Law bans imports that infringe on patent, design and commercial brand rights. 関税定率法で、特許、意匠権、商標権などの侵害品の輸入は禁止されている。

ban on short selling　空売り禁止, 空売り規制
　（⇒blanket ban on short selling）
◆France, Italy, Spain and Belgium imposed a ban on short-selling financial stocks. フランス、イタリア、スペインとベルギーが、金融銘柄の空売りを禁止した。 ◆French banks on the list of ban on short selling for 15 days include BNP Paribas and Societe Generale. フランスの15日間株（金融銘柄）の空売り禁止リスト指定行には、BNPパリバやソシエテ・ジェネラールなどが含まれている。

bandwagon （名）勝ち馬, 人気のある政党[主義, 主張], 時流に乗った動き, 波, 〜陣営
　get [climb, hop, jump, leap] on the bandwagon　時流[流行]に乗る, 優勢な側につく, 勝ちそうな政党[候補者]の支持に回る, 時の趨勢に従って行動する
◆In an attempt to get on the bandwagon, many people are shifting their fixed rate mortgages to adjustable rate ones. 時流に乗ろうとして、固定金利型住宅ローンを変動金利型住宅ローンに変更する人が多い。

bank （動）預金する, 銀行に預ける, 稼ぐ, 積み上げる
◆The Da Vinci Code banked an estimated $29 million on its first day in theaters. 「ダ・ヴィンチ・コード」は、公開初日に推定で2,900万ドルを稼いだ。

bank （名）銀行, 金融機関, バンク （⇒citizens bank, commercial bank, core bank, main bank, online bank, regional bank, trust bank）
　accepting bank　引受銀行
　　（=acceptance bank, acceptance house）
　advising bank　信用状通知銀行, 通知銀行
　agent bank　幹事銀行
　bank acceptance rate　銀行引受手形金利, 銀行引受手形利率, BAレート
　　（=banker's acceptance rate）
　bank accommodation　銀行融資 （=bank advance, bank credit, bank lending, bank loan, bank loans and discounts）
　bank advance　銀行融資, 銀行貸出, 銀行ローン （=bank accommodation, bank advances and discounts, bank credit, bank lending, bank loan, bank loans and discounts）
　bank annuities　コンソル公債
　bank balance　預金残高, 銀行預金残高, 銀行残高
　bank barrowing　銀行借入金
　bank bill rate　銀行手形金利, 銀行手形利率
　bank book　銀行通帳
　bank box　銀行貸し金庫
　bank burglary and robbery policy　銀行盗難保険
　bank call　銀行財務報告要求
　bank certificate　銀行残高証明書
　bank charge　銀行手数料
　bank check　銀行小切手
　bank checking　銀行照会
　bank-cleanup package　銀行の不良債権処理係
　bank clearing　交換持出し手形, 手形交換総額, BC
　bank clerk　銀行出納係
　bank credit　銀行信用
　bank debits　銀行預金引落し総額
　bank discount　銀行割引き, 銀行割引料（銀行が貸付け金からあらかじめ差し引く利子額のこと）
　bank draft　銀行為替手形
　　（=banker's check, banker's draft）
　bank examiner　銀行検査官
　Bank for International Settlements　国際決済銀行, BIS
　　（⇒BIS）

bank head　銀行首脳
Bank Holding Company Act of 1956　1956年銀行持ち株会社法
bank inspection　銀行検査
Bank Insurance Fund　米国の銀行保険基金
bank line of credit　銀行借入枠, 銀行与信枠（=credit line）
bank of account　取引銀行
bank overdraft　当座貸越し
bank rate　公定歩合, 銀行利率, 金利　(=official discount rate: 中央銀行が定める貸出金の基準金利)
bank reference　銀行信用照会先
bank statement　預金残高証明書
bank stock prices　銀行株価
bank suspension　支払い停止
bank-transfer scam　振り込め詐欺（⇒in a bid to）
city bank　都市銀行, 都銀, 市中銀行
commercial bank　商業銀行, 民間銀行, 都市銀行, 都銀
computer bank　コンピュータ・バンク
confirming bank　確認銀行
core bank　主力取引銀行
correspondent bank　コルレス銀行
custodian bank　保管銀行, カストディ銀行
data bank　データ・バンク
Farm Credit Bank　米農業信用銀行
Federal Financing Bank　米連邦金融銀行
Federal Home Loan Bank Board　米連邦住宅貸付銀行理事会
Federal Home Loan Bank System　米連邦住宅貸付銀行制度
Federal Reserve Bank　米連邦準備銀行
financially healthy bank　健全行
foreign exchange bank　外国為替銀行
funding bank　貸出銀行, 貸出行
intermediary bank　仲介銀行
issue bank　発券銀行, 紙幣発行銀行
issuing bank　信用状の発行銀行, 開設銀行（=establishing bank, opening bank）
job bank　人材銀行
labor bank　労働金庫
leading banks　大手銀行
local bank　地方銀行, 地場銀行, 国内銀行
long-term credit bank　長期信用銀行
main bank　主要取引銀行, 主力取引銀行, 主力銀行, メインバンク
merchant bank　マーチャント・バンク, 引受銀行
money-center [money center] bank　マネーセンター・バンク（資産規模でトップにランクされる米国の銀行）
mortgage bank　住宅金融会社
national bank　米国の国法銀行, 国立銀行, 全国銀行
nonbank　ノンバンク, 銀行以外の金融機関（=nonbank financial institution）
one bank policy　一行取引主義
ordinary bank　普通銀行
paying bank　支払い銀行
prime bank　一流銀行, 有力銀行
regional bank　地方銀行, 地銀, リージョナル・バンク
retail bank　リテール・バンク
savings bank　貯蓄銀行
second-tier bank　第二地銀

shinkin bank　信用金庫
state bank　米国の州法銀行, 国営銀行
super regional bank　スーパー・リージョナル・バンク（本店所在地とそれ以外の複数の地域にまたがって銀行業務を行っている大規模地方銀行）
top banks　上位行, 上位銀行
trust bank　信託銀行
wholesale bank　法人向けの銀行

◆Banks and life insurers have extended about ￥4 trillion in loans to TEPCO. 銀行や生命保険会社は、東電にこれまで約4兆円を融資している。◆Banks are allowed to sell insurance policies to clients. 銀行は、顧客に保険を販売することができる。◆Banks were less reserve pressure than was in March. 銀行の資本繰りは、3月より緩和した。◆Banks will not accept future loan requests if they have to forgive the debt. 金融機関が債権放棄をせざるを得ないとなると、金融機関は今後の融資要請には応じないだろう。◆European countries are urged to facilitate a safety net for emergencies, including the injection of public funds into deteriorating banks to shore up their capital strength. 欧州は、経営が悪化した銀行［金融機関］に公的資金を注入して資本を増強するなど、非常時に備えた安全網の整備が求められている。◆Former chairman of the bank served as an associate of Heizo Takenaka, then state minister in charge of economic and fiscal policy, and strictly pressured banks to rehabilitate themselves. 同行の前会長は、竹中平蔵元金融相のブレーンを務めて、銀行に経営健全化を厳しく迫った。◆FSA's inspectors are to confirm whether the companies' categorization by banks as debtors is relevant or fair. 金融庁の検査官は、銀行側の企業（融資先企業）の債務者区分が適正かどうかなどを検証することになっている。◆In this cofinancing scheme, the bank will extend a total of about ￥8.5 billion over a 20-year loan period. この協調融資事業で、同行は貸出期間20年で計約85億円を融資する。◆Since three banks integrated their operations, executives from the three predecessor banks served on an equal basis as presidents of the Mizuho group, Mizuho Bank and Mizuho Corporate Bank. 3銀行の経営統合以来、旧3行の経営者が、みずほグループ（FG）、みずほ銀行、みずほコーポレート銀行のトップをそれぞれ分け合あった。◆The bank decided to continue extending loans to the company despite its executives knowing the company was on the ropes. この会社の経営が悪化しているのを経営陣が知りながら、同行は同社への融資継続を決めた。◆The bank plans to provide the money by transferring ￥100 billion in subordinated loans, which it has already extended to the insurer, to the insurer's foundation fund. 同行は、すでに供与している劣後ローン1,000億円をこの保険会社の基金に振り替えて、その資金を提供する方針だ。◆The bank projected itself as "the friend of small and mid-size enterprises." 同行は、「中小企業の味方」という看板を掲げていた。◆The bank will carry out this cofinancing scheme as the lead bank with several U.S. and European banks. 同行は、主幹事行として、この協調融資事業を欧米の複数の銀行と連携して実施する。◆The banks are to be refunded their paid taxes when the amount of their losses has been finally determined as a result of the failure of corporate customers to which they have extended loans. 銀行の場合は、銀行の融資先企業の倒産などで銀行の損失額が最終的に確定した時点で、前払いした税金が戻る。◆The biggest advantage for the bank in entering the venture will be to increase its customer base without having to open expensive new branch offices. 同行にとってこの新規事業への参入の最大の利点は、コストのかかる新店舗を開設するまでもなく、顧客基盤を拡大できることだ。◆The Financial Services Agency will check the credibility of the banks' debtor companies, including their management efficiency and the accuracy of their collateral assessment. 金融庁は、銀行の融資先の経営効率や担保評価などを含めて、銀行の融資先の信用力を洗い直す。◆The firm repaid part of its outstanding debt to the bank. 同社は、債務残高[残りの債務]の一部を同行に返済した。◆The Greek-triggered sovereign debt crisis resulted in the breakup of the French-Belgian bank Dexia which held Greek government bonds. ギリシャが引き金になったソブリン危機(政府債務危機)問題で、ギリシャ国債を保有していた仏ベルギー系金融機関のデクシア(Dexia)が、解体に追い込まれた。◆The increased ownership will raise the bank's risk exposure to the company, whose business environment is severe. 持ち株比率の引上げで、企業環境[経営環境]が厳しい同社に対する同行のリスク・エクスポージャーは今後増大するものと思われる。◆The move to inject liquidity into Dubai's banks by the central bank of the United Arab Emirates was seen by analysts as the bare minimum. ドバイの銀行に資金を供給するアラブ首長国連邦(UAE)の中央銀行の動きを、アナリスト(専門家)は「最低限必要な量にすぎない」と見ている。◆The new Internet bank will be equally owned by the two firms with initial capital of ¥20 billion. 新ネット銀行は、当初資本が200億円で、両社が折半出資する。

bank account　銀行口座, 銀行預金口座, 銀行勘定, 預金
(⇒black-market lending, bogus cash card, identification, sale of bank accounts)
close a bank account　銀行口座を解約する, 口座を解約する
have a bank account with the bank　同行に口座がある
open a bank account　銀行口座を開く, 口座を設ける
put money into a bank account　銀行口座に金を振り込む, 口座に金を払い込む
take money out of a bank account　銀行口座から金をおろす, 口座から金を引き出す
◆About ¥20 million was transferred from this self-employed man's savings account to a bank account under someone else's name. この自営業者の普通預金から他人名義の銀行口座に、約2,000万円が振り込まれていた。◆Bank accounts are bought and sold openly on the Internet. 銀行口座が、インターネット上で公然と売買されている。◆Clients can open bank accounts online. 顧客は、インターネット上で銀行口座を開設することができる。◆The firm's shell companies allegedly pooled about ¥1 billion in slush funds by padding bills for the construction projects in their overseas bank accounts. 調べによれば、同社のペーパー・カンパニーは、建設工事代金[建設工事の請求書]を水増しして、約10億円の裏金を海外の複数の銀行口座にプールしていた。◆The secret funds were pooled in the bank accounts of dummy companies. 裏金は、ダミー会社の銀行口座に蓄えられていた。

bank account dealer　口座屋
◆Sales organizations called bank account dealers specialize in trading bankbooks and bankcards. 口座屋と呼ばれる販売組織は、預金通帳やキャッシュ・カードの売買を専門にしている。

bank account holder　銀行口座名義人
◆The law on the identification of bank account holders was put into force in January 2003. 銀行口座名義人の本人確認に関する法律(本人確認法)は、2003年1月に施行された。

bank card　銀行発行のクレジット・カード, バンク・カード (=bankcard: キャッシュ・カードと同義。⇒bankbook)
◆Under the direct debit system, Nissay's sales employees will scan data on new customers' bank cards using portable terminals when they sign insurance policies. この口座引落しシステムでは、顧客が保険契約をする際、日本生命保険の営業職員が決済の携帯端末を使って新規顧客のキャッシュ・カードのデータを読み取る。

bank counter　銀行窓口
◆Meiji Yasuda's single-premium whole life insurance is one of its flagship products which are sold over bank counters. 明治安田生保の一時払い終身保険は、銀行窓口で販売されている同社の主力商品の一つだ。

bank credit　銀行信用, 銀行信用状, 銀行貸出, 銀行融資, 銀行借入れ
(=bank lending, bank loan, banker's credit)
bank credit agreement　銀行融資枠, 銀行貸出枠
(=bank credit arrangement)
bank credit department　銀行の審査部

bank customers　銀行の顧客, 銀行利用者, 銀行預金者
(=bank clients; ⇒customer)
◆It is natural for bank customers to withdraw deposits when they no longer trust financial institutions. 銀行預金者が銀行を信じられなくなったら、預金を引き揚げるのは当然のことだ。

bank debenture　金融債(金融機関が資金調達のために発行する債券)
bank debenture issued　金融発行債
discount bank debenture　割引金融債
interest bearing bank debenture　利付き金融債

bank deposit　銀行預金 (=deposit at bank; ⇒financial instrument, legal action)
bank deposit insurance　銀行預金保険
ordinary bank deposits for individuals　個人の普通預金
◆In April 2005, the government's blanket protection on bank deposits ended. 2005年4月に、政府の銀行預金全額保証の期間が終了した。◆Investors have begun switching their funds from bank deposits to assets that entail some risks. 投資家が、銀行預金からリスクを伴う資産へと資金の運用を切り替え始めている。◆Ordinary bank deposits for individuals and current deposits for businesses were fully guaranteed until March 31, 2003. 個人の普通預金と企業の当座預金は、2003年3月31日まで全額保証された。

bank employee　銀行員, 行員
◆A bank employee was arrested for alleged insider trading of shares in four companies. 銀行の行員が、4社の株でインサイダー取引を行った容疑で逮捕された。◆The Securities and Exchange Surveillance Commission filed a criminal complaint against a former bank employee with the Tokyo District Public Prosecutors Office on suspicion of violating the Financial Instruments and Exchange Law. 証券取引等監視委員会は、元行員を金融商品取引法違反の疑いで東京地検に刑事告発した。

bank failure　銀行破たん (=bank's collapse)
◆A freeze on the payoff system insuring up to ¥10 million per depositor in the event of bank failure is scheduled to be lifted in April. 銀行が破たんした場合、預金者1人当たり1,000万円まで保証するペイオフ制度の凍結は、4月に解除されることになっている。

Bank for International Settlements　国際決済銀行, BIS (⇒BIS)
◆Internationally active banks are required to have capital adequacy ratios of at least 8 percent under rules stipulated by the Bank for International Settlements (BIS). 国際業務を行う銀行(金融機関)の自己資本比率は、国際決済銀行(BIS)が定める規則で8%以上が義務付けられている。

bank-held stocks　銀行保有株
(⇒bond holdings, bullish stock market)
◆I don't oppose the Bank of Japan's direct purchase of bank-held stocks. 日銀による銀行保有株の直接買取りに、私は反対の立場ではない。

bank holiday　銀行休日, 法定休日, 英国の祝祭日
◆Fearing a massive run, a bank holiday was declared for Friday. 大規模な取付け騒ぎを恐れて、金曜日を銀行休日にする宣言がなされた。

bank issues　銀行株 (=bank shares)
◆Bank issues declined as investors remained wary over the banks' massive bad loan problems. 銀行株は、やはり巨額の不良債権問題の処理に対する警戒感から値を下げた。

bank lending　銀行貸出, 銀行融資

◆Bank lending remains at a trickle. 銀行貸出［銀行融資］は、ぽつぽつの状態で推移している［銀行貸出件数は、依然として少ない状況だ］。◆Despite the ample liquidity, bank lending remains stalled. この豊富な資金［高い流動性］にもかかわらず、銀行貸出は依然、落ち込んでいる。◆The average daily balance of bank lending fell 4.7 percent in October from a year earlier. 10月の銀行貸出の平均残高は、前年同月比で4.7%減少した。◆The average daily balance of domestic bank lending fell 4 percent in 2004 from 2003 to ¥389.03 trillion, down for the eighth straight year. 国内銀行（民間銀行）の2004年の貸出平均残高は、前年比4%減の389兆300億円となり、8年連続で減少した。

bank lending capacity［ability］ 銀行の貸出能力
◆A bad bank is used to hold troubled assets and free up bank lending capacity. バッド・バンクは、不良資産を買い取って、銀行が自由に貸出できるようにするのに利用される。

bank lending rate 銀行貸出金利
◆The Fed left a key short-term bank lending rate at a record low of between zero and 0.25 percent. 米連邦準備制度理事会（FRB）は、短期銀行貸出金利の誘導目標を過去最低水準の0～0.25%に据え置いた。

bank lines of credit 銀行借入枠, 銀行与信枠
（⇒credit line）
◆At December 31, 2011, the corporation and certain subsidiary companies had unused bank lines of credit, generally available at the prime bank rate of interest, of approximately $382 million. 2011年12月31日現在、当社と一部の子会社が一般にプライム・レートで利用できる銀行与信枠未使用残高は、約3億8,200万ドルとなっています。

bank loan 銀行貸付け, 銀行融資, 銀行貸付け金, 銀行ローン, 銀行借入れ, 銀行借入金, 銀行間借款, バンク・ローン （=bank lending）
bank loan-centered indirect financing 銀行融資中心の間接金融 （⇒indirect financing）
bank loan-deposit ratio 預貸（よたい）率
bank loan［loans］payable 銀行借入金
bank loans and discounts 銀行融資
term bank loan 有期銀行借入金, 長期銀行融資［貸付け金］
◆The company repaid its $100 million term bank loan which matured on May 1, 2011. 同社は、2011年5月1日に期限が到来した有期の銀行借入金1億ドルを返済した。

bank management 銀行経営
◆An effective macro policy implemented by the government and the Bank of Japan to drive the national economy out of deflation is a prerequisite for the disposal of bad loans and the recovery of sound bank management. 日本経済のデフレ脱出に向けて政府・日銀が効果的なマクロ政策を実施するが、不良債権処理と銀行経営健全化の前提である。

bank note 銀行券 （⇒banknote）
◆The balance of bank notes in circulation rose 2.9 percent to ¥79.48 trillion in May 2011 from a year earlier. 2011年5月の銀行券流通高は、前年同月比で2.9%増の79兆4,800億円となった。

Bank of America バンク・オブ・アメリカ, バンカメ, BA［BOA］（資産規模で米最大の金融機関）
◆American International Group Inc. sued Bank of America for allegedly selling it faulty mortgage investments. 米保険大手のAIGが、欠陥商品のモーゲージ証券を同社に販売したとしてバンク・オブ・アメリカを提訴した。◆General Motors Corp. agreed to sell up to $55 billion in car and truck loans to Bank of America Corp. over five years. ゼネラル・モーターズ（GM）は、バンク・オブ・アメリカに対して、今後5年間で最大550億ドルの自動車ローン債権を売却することで合意した。

Bank of England イングランド銀行, 英中銀, BoE
◆The Bank of England kept its benchmark interest rate at a record low level of 0.5 percent. 英中銀のイングランド銀行は、政策金利を過去最低水準の年0.5%に維持した［据え置いた］。◆The Bank of England lowered its key interest rate to 5.25 percent from 5.5 percent. 英中央銀行のイングランド銀行（BOE）は、政策金利を現行の年5.5%から5.25%に引き下げた。

Bank of Japan 日本銀行, 日銀, BOJ （⇒BOJ）
Bank of Japan credit 日銀信用
Bank of Japan financial network system 日銀ネット
Bank of Japan loans 日銀貸出高
Bank of Japan notes 日本銀行券
Bank of Japan notes issued 日銀券発行高
Bank of Japan's Monetary Policy Meeting 日銀金融政策決定会合
Bank of Japan's［Japan］Policy Board 日銀政策委員会
（=Bank of Japan's policy board; ⇒current account）
◆Due to increasing uncertainty over the U.S. economic outlook and the yen's rise, the Bank of Japan warned of the downside risks to the nation's economy. 米経済の先行きをめぐる不確実性の高まりと円高で、日銀は日本経済の下振れリスクに警戒感を示した。◆Online bank eBank Corp. began operations in 2001. ネット専業銀行のイーバンク銀行は、2001年に開業した。◆Speculation the Bank of Japan will end its quantitative monetary easing policy soon has sparked a rise in mid- and long-term interest rates. 日銀が近く量的緩和策を解除するとの思惑から、（金融市場では）中長期の金利が上昇し始めた。◆Speculators capitalized on the Bank of Japan's delay in taking action. 投機筋は、日銀の対応の遅れを突いた。◆The Bank of Japan asked the Federal Reserve Bank of New York to intervene in the New York foreign exchange market on its behalf through yen-selling, dollar-buying operations for the first time in 15 months. 日銀は、1年3か月ぶりにニューヨーク連銀に委託して、ニューヨーク外国為替市場で円売り・ドル買いの介入に踏み切った。◆The Bank of Japan continued selling yen and buying dollars intermittently. 日銀は、断続的に円売り・ドル買いを継続した。◆The Bank of Japan decided to adopt additional quantitative easing measures in October 2010, setting up a fund to purchase government and corporate bonds. 日銀は、2010年10月に新たな量的緩和策の導入を決め、国債や社債を買い入れる基金を新設した。◆The Bank of Japan decided to extend a special loan to Namihaya Bank after the second-tier regional bank was declared insolvent. 日本銀行は、第二地方銀行の「なみはや銀行」が破たん認定を受けた後、同行に対して特別融資［特融］を実施することを決めた。◆The Bank of Japan decided to take new steps for further quantitative monetary easing at an extraordinary Policy Board meeting. 日銀は、臨時の金融政策決定会合で、追加の量的金融緩和策を新たに実施することを決めた。◆The Bank of Japan envisages the prospects of economic growth and consumer price trends in its "Outlook for Economic Activity and Prices." 日銀は、「経済・物価情勢の展望」（展望リポート）で、経済成長や消費者物価の先行きを示している。◆The Bank of Japan has long been implementing monetary easing measures. 日銀は、金融緩和を長年続けている。◆The Bank of Japan has supplied a large amount of funds to the market by purchasing long-term government bonds and corporate bonds. 日銀は、長期国債や社債の買入れで、大量の資金を市場に提供している。◆The Bank of Japan is considering taking additional monetary easing measures ahead of the next Monetary Policy Meeting. 次回の金融政策決定会合に向けて、日銀は現在、追加金融緩和策の実施を検討している。◆The Bank of Japan may expand the list of government bonds purchased under the fund, to include those that have more than two years left until maturity. 日銀は、基金で買い入れる国債の対象を拡大して、満期までの残存期間が2年以

上（現行1～2年）の国債を含むようにする可能性がある。◆The Bank of Japan purchases government bonds that have one to two years left until maturity. 日銀は、満期までの残存期間が1～2年の国債を買い入れている。◆The Bank of Japan supplied funds beyond the upper limit of ￥27 trillion soon after the Resona problem surfaced. 日銀は、りそな問題発覚後、27兆円の上限を上回る資金を市場に供給した。◆The Bank of Japan will set up a fund to buy long-term government bonds, exchange-traded funds and other financial assets in a bid to prop up the nation's economy. 日本の景気を下支えするため、日銀は基金を新設して、長期国債や上場投資信託（ETF）などの金融商品［金融資産］を買い入れる。◆The government and the Bank of Japan will likely continue to work together in fighting the sharp rise in the yen's value. 政府と日銀は、急激な円高阻止で協調路線を継続することになりそうだ。◆To fulfill its responsibilities as the nation's central bank, the Bank of Japan must achieve currency stabilization by availing itself of a range of measures, including stabilization of the exchange rate. 日本の中央銀行としての責任を果たすには、日本銀行は、為替相場の安定を含めて広範な手段を活用して通貨の安定を実現しなければならない。

Bank of Japan Gov.［Governor］ 日銀総裁
（=governor of the Bank of Japan）
◆The talks between Prime Minister Kan and Bank of Japan Gov. Shirakawa led to a further advance of the yen and offloading of stocks as disappointment spread among market players. 菅首相と日銀総裁の会談は、一層の円高と市場筋の失望売りを誘った。

Bank of Japan's capital adequacy ratio 日銀の自己資本比率
◆The Bank of Japan's capital adequacy ratio sagged to 7.33 percent as of March 31, 2004. 日銀の自己資本比率は、2004年3月31日時点で7.33％に低下した。

Bank of Japan's interest rate 日銀の政策金利
◆If the Bank of Japan's interest rate takes an upward turn, an adjustable rate mortgage would weigh more heavily on borrowers than would the fixed-rate type. 日銀の政策金利が上昇に転じた場合、固定金利型の住宅ローンと比べて変動金利型のほうが、ローン利用者［借り手］の負担が重くなる。

Bank of Japan's quarterly business confidence survey 日銀短観、日銀の企業短期経済観測調査
◆According to the Bank of Japan's quarterly business confidence survey, the diffusion index of business confidence among major manufacturers stood at minus 38. 日銀の企業短期経済観測調査（日銀短観）によると、大手製造業の業況判断指数（DI）はマイナス38を示した。

Bank of Korea 韓国銀行（韓国の中央銀行）
◆According to the Bank of Korea, South Korea's gross domestic product expanded 0.9 percent in the second quarter compared with the previous quarter. 韓国銀行によると、韓国の第2四半期の国内総生産（GDP）は、前四半期比で0.9％拡大した。◆The Bank of Korea is the central bank of South Korea and was established in June 1950. 韓国銀行は韓国の中央銀行で、1950年6月に設立された。

bank run 銀行の取付け騒ぎ, 銀行取付け, 取付け騒ぎ, 取付け （=a run on a bank）
◆In the subprime crisis, something similar to a bank run happened to an investment bank. 今回のサブプライム問題では、一種の銀行の取付け騒ぎが証券会社［投資銀行］に発生した。◆The central bank's emergency loan is an effective remedy for a bank run. 中央銀行の緊急融資は、銀行の取付け騒ぎの特効薬だ。

bank service fee 銀行手数料
◆The mileage points can be used to get preferential interest rates on loans and discounts on various bank service fees. このマイレージ・ポイントは、ローン金利の優遇や各種銀行手数料の割引などに利用することができる。

bank shares 銀行株 （=bank stocks）
◆Speculation that some major banks may find themselves with capital shortfalls and then nationalized is driving investors to dump the banks' shares. 大手行の一部が自己資本不足に陥って国有化されるとの思惑から、投資家は銀行株の売りに出ている。

bank stocks 銀行株
（=bank issues, bank shares, banks' shares）
◆The government's financial revival plan is expected to exacerbate the credit crunch and result in a further sell-off of bank stocks. 政府の金融再生プログラムは、貸し渋りを加速して銀行株の下落に拍車がかかると予想される。

bank tax 銀行税 （東京都の大手金融機関を対象とした外形標準課税。外形標準課税は、従来の法人所得に課税するのではなく、資本金額や売上高など企業の事業規模がわかる「外形」に応じて課税する方式。⇒fiscal management）
◆The bank tax targeting only the banking sector and only banks holding certain amounts of funds violates Article 14 of the Constitution, which guarantees tax equality. 銀行業だけ、しかも一定の資金量を保有する銀行だけを課税の対象とした銀行税は、税の公平性を保証する憲法14条に違反している。◆The new bank tax is levied on the banks' gross operating profits-their earnings minus basic operating expenses such as interest payments to depositors. 新銀行税は、銀行の収入から基礎的な経費（預金者に対する預金金利の支払いなど）を差し引いた業務粗利益に課される。

bank transfer 銀行振替え, 口座振替え, 銀行間振替え, 銀行送金, 銀行決済, 銀行振込み （⇒firm banking, life insurance policyholder, salary payment）
◆Mizuho Financial Group receives a total of 27 million bank transfers orders per year. みずほグループは、年間2,700万件の口座振替えを扱う。◆The bank does not handle bank transfers or other financial settlement services. 同行は、銀行振込みなどの決済業務［金融決済業務］を行っていない。

bank-transfer scam［fraud］ 振り込め詐欺
◆In a bid to clamp down on bank-transfer scams, the police asked financial institutions not to allow people whose faces are obscured with sunglasses or masks to use ATMs. 振り込め詐欺を取り締まるため、警察は、サングラスやマスクで顔を隠したままATM（現金自動預け払い機）を使用できないよう金融機関に要請した。◆Six members of an organized crime group were arrested on suspicion of involvement in bank-transfer fraud. 組織犯罪グループ（暴力団）の組員6人が、振り込め詐欺に関与していた疑いで逮捕された。

banks with weakened financial strength 財務が悪化した銀行
◆Money loaned by private banks declined because banks with weakened financial strength were less willing to lend, besides a lack of businesses seeking expansion through borrowing. 民間銀行の貸出金が減ったのは、お金を借りてまで事業を拡大しようとする企業がなかったほか、財務が悪化した銀行が貸し渋ったからだ。

bankbook （名）預金通帳, 銀行通帳
（=passbook; ⇒cardholder, transfer名詞）
◆Depositors can continue to use their bankbooks and bank cards. 預金者は、銀行通帳やキャッシュ・カードを引き続き利用することができる。

banker （名）銀行家, 銀行経営者, 銀行員, 銀行マン, 銀行, バンカー
（⇒central banker, corporate racketeer）
American Bankers Association　アメリカ銀行協会, ABA
bankers association　銀行協会
banker's bank　銀行の銀行, 中央銀行（central bank）
banker's bill　銀行手形
bankers' blanker policy　金融機関包括補償保険

banker's blanket bond　銀行の身元保証保険
banker's card　バンカーズ・カード　(=check card, cheque card: 銀行口座のある人を対象に、一定の額まで小切手の支払いを保証した銀行発行のカード)
banker's check　銀行小切手
　(=bank check, cashier's check)
banker's clearing house　ロンドン手形交換所
banker's commercial credit　銀行信用状
banker's deposits　銀行預金
banker's discount　銀行割引
banker's draft　銀行手形, 銀行為替手形
　(=bank draft)
banker's duty of secrecy　銀行の秘密保持義務
banker's guarantee　銀行保証状
banker's (letter of) credit　銀行信用状
banker's opinion　(銀行照会に対する)銀行の意見
banker's order　定額自動送金, 自動振替依頼, 自動引落しの依頼
banker's reference　銀行信用照会先
　(=bank reference)
be paid by banker's order　自動引落しで支払われる
branch banker　支店銀行
British Bankers' Association　英国銀行協会
career bankers　金融のプロ
central banker　中央銀行総裁
central bankers and supervisors from major nations [countries]　主要各国[主要国]の金融監督当局
due from bankers　他行へ貸し
due to bankers　他行より借り
eligible banker's bill　適格銀行手形
Federation of Bankers Association of Japan　(日本の)全国銀行協会連合会, 全銀協
investment banker　投資銀行　(=investment bank)
Japanese Bankers Association　(日本の)全国銀行協会
merchant banker　引受銀行, マーチャント・バンク
　(=merchant bank: 証券発行業務などを手がける)
private banker　個人銀行　(=private bank)
◆Central bankers exchanged views at the G-10 meeting. 先進10か国会議で、中央銀行総裁が意見交換をした。◆Writer Go Egami, who has been appointed as the bank's new president, was a banker at the defunct Dai-Ichi Kangyo Bank. 同行の新社長に就任する作家の江上剛氏は、旧勧業銀行の行員だった。

banker's acceptance　銀行引受手形, BA
　(=bank acceptance, banker's acceptance bill)
banker's acceptance bill　銀行引受手形, BA手形
banker's acceptance rate　銀行引受手形金利, 銀行引受手形利率, BAレート
　(=bank acceptance rate)
eligible banker's acceptance　適格銀行手形
yen-denominated banker's acceptance　円建てBA市場

banking　(名)銀行業, 銀行業務, 金融, 預金, バンキング
　(⇒consumer banking, firm banking, Internet banking, retail banking, retail banking operations)
banking activities　銀行業務
banking administration [administration]　銀行行政
banking agencies　金融当局
banking and finance　金融
banking asset　銀行資産
banking capital　銀行資本
banking community [industry, segment]　銀行業界
banking company [corporation]　銀行会社
banking connection　銀行取引関係
banking correspondent　(銀行の)取引先銀行
banking crash　銀行破たん
banking day　銀行営業日
banking facilities　金融機関
banking hours　銀行の営業時間
banking house [establishment]　銀行, 銀行の建物
banking insolvencies　銀行破たん
banking institution　銀行
banking institutions　金融機関
banking machines　銀行会計機
banking office　銀行の営業所
banking online system　バンキング・オンライン・システム
banking policy administration　銀行行政
banking practices　銀行慣行, 銀行業務, 銀行実務
banking principle　銀行主義
banking product　金融商品
banking quarters　銀行の営業場
banking regulators　銀行規制当局
banking secrecy [secret]　銀行秘密
banking section　銀行部門
banking structures　銀行制度
Banking Supervision Division　銀行監督局
banking syndicate　銀行融資団, 融資団
banking unit　銀行, 銀行業務部門
banking world　銀行業界
Basel Committee on Banking Regulation and Supervision　銀行規制監督に関するバーゼル委員会
branch banking system　支店銀行制度
chain banking　チェーン銀行
commercial banking　商業銀行, 商業銀行業務
commercial banking activities [services]　商業銀行業務
community banking　コミュニティ・バンキング
computer banking　コンピュータ・バンキング
consumer banking　消費者金融業務
core banking business　本業の銀行業務
corporate banking　企業向け銀行業務, コーポレート銀行業務
correspondent banking　コルレス銀行
direct banking　ダイレクト・バンキング
electronic banking　エレクトロニック・バンキング
Federal Banking Commission　米連邦銀行委員会
firm banking　ファーム・バンキング
general banking business　一般銀行業務
home banking　ホーム・バンキング
international banking　国際銀行業務
Internet banking　インターネット・バンキング
　(=Net banking)
interstate banking　州際銀行業務, 州際業務
investment banking　投資銀行業務
mortgage banking　不動産担保銀行業務, 不動産担保金融業務, 不動産担保貸付け
mortgage banking services　不動産担保金融業務
Net banking　ネット・バンキング
offshore banking　オフショア金融
online banking　オンライン・バンキング
outside normal [regular] banking hours　通常の営業時間外に
private banking　プライベート・バンキング
remote banking　リモート・バンキング(通信手段を

使った銀行業務）
- retail banking　小売銀行業務, リテール銀行業務, 小口金融, リテール・バンキング
- telephone banking　テレホン・バンキング
- traditional banking activities　通常の銀行業務
- twenty-four-hour banking　24時間銀行業務体制
- unit banking　単一銀行, 単独銀行
- unit banking system　支店を持たない単一銀行制度
- universal banking　ユニバーサル・バンキング
- wholesale banking　卸売銀行業務, ホールセール銀行業務, 大口金融

◆As the first case in the banking and securities industry of this country, the Nikko Cordial Group disclosed the annual salaries of its four top executive officers. 日本の銀行・証券業界で初めてのケースとして、日興コーディアルグループは、代表取締役4人の年間報酬額を開示した。

banking account　銀行口座
- banking accounts of all banks　全国銀行銀行勘定, 全銀勘定
- banking accounts of city banks　都市銀行銀行勘定
- banking accounts of regional banks　地方銀行銀行勘定
- banking accounts of trust banks　信託銀行銀行勘定

Banking Act　銀行法
- Banking Act of 1933　（銀行業と証券業の分離を定めた）1933年銀行法（通称はグラス・スティーガル・アクト）
- Banking Act of 1935　1935年銀行法
- Banking Act of 1979　（英国の）1979年銀行法
- Banking Act 1987　1987年銀行法
- Competitive Equality Banking Act of 1987　1987年公正競争銀行法, 1987年競争的公正銀行法

banking agent system　銀行代理店制度
◆Leading banks may utilize the banking agent system to increase their presence in regional areas. 大手行は、地方行で拠点を増やすため銀行代理店制度を活用する可能性がある。

banking business　銀行業務, 金融業, 金融業務
（＝banking activities, banking operations, banking services; ⇒incorporate）
- core banking business　本業の銀行業務
- corporate trust banking business　企業向け信託銀行業務

◆The losses the banks incurred far outstripped their net operating profits, obtained from core banking business, such as lending and commissions. 銀行の損失額が、貸付けや手数料など本業の銀行業務による業務純益を大きく上回った。◆The UFJ financial group will transfer the corporate trust banking business of UFJ Trust to UFJ Bank by July 2005. UFJ金融グループは、2005年7月までにUFJ信託の企業向け信託業務をUFJ銀行に移管する方針だ。◆The wall separating banking and securities businesses has been lowered through such moves as the liberalization of banks' securities brokering. 銀行と証券業の垣根は、銀行に対する証券仲介業の規制緩和などの動きで、低くなっている。

banking committee　銀行委員会
- Banking, Housing and Urban Affairs Committee　米上院の銀行住宅都市委員会　（＝Banking Committee）
- house banking committee　米下院銀行委員会
- Senate Banking Committee　米上院銀行委員会

banking crisis　金融危機, 銀行の経営危機, 銀行の危機, 銀行業界の危機
◆Declining stock prices will not only lead to a banking crisis, but also to financial anxieties. 株価の下落が、銀行の経営危機にとどまらず、金融不安の連鎖に直結する。◆The eurozone's critical mistake is the eurozone's belittling of the risk of the sovereign debt crisis aggravating the banking crisis and vice versa. ユーロ圏の重大な誤りは、国家の財政危機と銀行の危機［経営危機］が相互に増幅し合う危険性を、ユーロ圏が軽視したことにある。

banking freeze　銀行業務の凍結, 預金凍結
◆The banking freeze limits cash withdrawals from most accounts to 1,500 pesos a month（about $800）. この預金凍結では、大半の口座からの現金引出し額は1か月1,500ペソ（約800ドル）までに制限されている。

banking group　銀行グループ, 金融グループ, 銀行・金融グループ　（⇒combined losses, deficit settlement of accounts, fiscal year, loss projections）
◆Government steps taken to deal with Resona's collapse did not incorporate a reduction in the banking group's capital. りそな銀行の経営破たん処理に取った国の措置には、同金融グループの減資は織り込まれなかった。◆Japan's six major banking groups saw a combined loss of about ¥990 billion in their stock investments in the nine months through December amid the global financial turmoil. 日本の大手銀行6グループは、4-12月期の連結決算で、世界的な金融危機に伴い株式投資の損失［株式評価損］が全社合わせて約9,900億円となった。◆The change in the method of calculating deferred tax assets has driven each of the banking groups into a corner. 繰延べ税金資産の算定方式の変更が、銀行グループ各行を窮地に追い込んでいる。

banking health check　銀行の健全性検査, 銀行の財務の健全性検査
◆The stress test of the European Banking Authority is a banking health check to ensure banks across Europe have sufficient capital to withstand another financial crisis. 欧州銀行監督機構（EBA）のストレス・テストは、欧州全域の銀行が新たな金融危機に耐えられるだけの資本金を十分に確保していることを保証するための銀行の健全性検査だ。

banking industry　銀行業, 銀行業界, 銀行界
（＝banking sector, banking world; ⇒banking）
◆The banking industry thinks that the new law may invite further bloating of postal banking businesses at the expense of the private sector. 新法は民業を圧迫して郵政の銀行業務のさらなる肥大化を招く恐れがある、と金融業界は見ている。◆The proposed merger would mark a final chapter in the realignment of the Japanese banking industry. この経営統合の申し入れは、日本の銀行業界［金融界］再編の最終章となる。◆There is widespread pessimism in the market concerning the banking industry. 銀行業界については、市場では悲観的な見方が広がっている。

Banking Law　銀行法
◆The Financial Services Agent is expected to issue a business improvement order to Mizuho based on the Banking Law. 金融庁は、みずほに対して、銀行法に基づく業務改善命令を出すと見られる。◆The Incubator Bank of Japan's head office and other locations were searched by the Metropolitan Police Department on suspicion of the Banking Law. 銀行法違反の疑いで、日本振興銀行の本店などを警視庁が捜索した。

banking license　銀行免許
◆The new virtual bank will seek to obtain a banking license. この新仮想銀行は、銀行免許を取得する方針だ。

banking operations　銀行業務, 資金運用（fund operations）
- investment banking operations　投資銀行業務
- retail banking operations　小口取引銀行業務
- streamline banking operations　銀行業務を合理化［効率化、スリム化］する

◆The bank has been relatively weak in retail banking operations dealing with individuals and small and medium-sized firms. 同行は、個人や中小企業向けの小口取引銀行業務が比較的弱い。◆The financial groups should write off their bad loans more efficiently and streamline their banking operations. 銀行グループは、もっと効率的な不良債権の処理と銀行業務の合理化を進めなければならない。◆The two companies have formed an alliance in investment banking operations. 両社は、投資銀行業務で提携関係を結んでいる［提携関係にある］。

banking partner 取引銀行
◆Failed Incubator Bank of Japan was the major banking partner of the company. 破たんした日本振興銀行が、同社の主力取引銀行だった。

banking regulations 銀行規制, 銀行に対する規制
◆An offensive and defensive battle among Japan, the United States and European countries over proposed stricter banking regulations is ever more intensifying. 銀行規制強化案をめぐる日米欧の攻防は、ますます激化している。

banking sector 銀行業, 銀行業界, 銀行, 金融部門, 金融界 (=banking industry, banking world; ⇒economies of scale)
◆Mizuho Financial Group reorganized its banking sector in April 2002. みずほフィナンシャルグループは、2002年4月に銀行部門を再編した。◆Overly radical methods for accelerating the disposal of bad loans would panic the banking sector and the financial market, possibly driving banks to shy away from extending new loans and even to call in existing loans. 不良債権処理を加速するための余りにも強硬な手法は、銀行や金融市場をおびえさせ、貸し渋りや貸しはがしにつながることにもなる。◆Stability in the banking sector is indispensable to halt the spread of financial unrest. 金融不安の拡大に歯止めをかけるには、銀行の経営安定が不可欠である。◆The collapse of a bank may result in the systemic breakdown of the whole banking sector. 銀行1行の破たんが、金融界全体のシステム崩壊［連鎖的な崩壊］につながる可能性がある。

banking services 銀行業務, 銀行サービス, 決済サービス (⇒publicly traded company)
cash withdrawal and other banking services 現金引出などの銀行サービス
full range of banking and financial services 総合的な銀行・金融サービス, 銀行・金融業務全般
full range of traditional banking services 通常の銀行業務全般
◆Lawson Inc. and FamilyMart Co. have installed ATMs in their outlets, offering cash withdrawal and other banking services. ローソンやファミリーマートが店舗にATM（現金自動預け払い機）を設置して、現金の引出しなどの銀行サービスを提供している。

banking stocks 銀行株
◆The DJ Stoxx index of European banking stocks has fallen 37 percent from a peak in February. ダウ・ジョーンズ欧州銀行株指数は、2月のピークから37％下落した。

banking system 銀行制度, 銀行システム, 銀行組織, 銀行業界, 銀行業務の分野, 市中銀行, 市中, 銀行, 金融の仕組み, 金融システム (⇒depreciation of the dollar exchange rate)
banking system deregulation 銀行制度全体の規制緩和
branch banking system 支店銀行制度
deregulation of the banking system 銀行業界の規制緩和, 銀行制度全体の規制緩和
drain reserves from the banking system 市中から資金［リザーブ］を吸い上げる
inject dollar funds into banks ドル資金を銀行に供給する
money allocations to the banking system 市中銀行への資金割当て
net foreign credit of the banking system 銀行の対外純貸出
online banking system オンライン・バンキング・システム
provide reserves to the banking system 市中に資金を供給する
sidestep the banking system 銀行システムを経由しない
systematic collapse in the banking system 銀行システムのシステム崩壊
the U.S. banking system 米国の銀行業界, 米国の銀行制度
unit banking system 支店を持たない単一銀行制度
withdraw funds from the banking system 市中銀行［銀行］から預金を引き出す
◆The banking system has become very complex. 金融の仕組みが、複雑になっている。◆The monetary union's authorities have neglected to strengthen the banking system. 通貨統合の当局は、銀行システムの強化［銀行システムへのテコ入れ］を怠った。◆The reassessment of 14 British banks by Moody's is not driven by a deterioration in the financial strength of the banking system. ムーディーズによる英銀14行の格付け見直しは、銀行［市中銀行、銀行業界］の財務の健全性悪化によるものではない。◆The Spanish government is expected to inject more public funds into its banking system. スペイン政府は、国内の金融システムに公的資金を追加投入［注入］すると見られる。◆Through massive purchases of U.S. Treasury bonds from U.S. commercial banks, the Fed pumps the proceeds into the banking system. 米国の銀行から米長期国債を大量に買い進めて、米中央銀行（連邦準備制度理事会）は、その代金を市中銀行に振り込んでいる。

banking test 銀行検査
◆The European banking tests are lax and ineffective as the collapses of two Irish banks and the Franco-Belgian bank Dexia, shortly after the EBA's stress tests, show. 欧州の銀行検査は、欧州銀行監督機構（EBA）のストレス・テストに合格した［ストレス・テストで安全と判定された］直後にアイルランドの銀行2行やフランス・ベルギー共同の銀行「デクシア」が破たんした事実が示すように、手ぬるくて効果がない。

banking titan 金融大手
◆Banking titan Citigroup Inc. repeatedly misled investors about its potential losses from subprime mortgages. 米金融大手のシティグループは、サブプライム・ローン（低所得者向け住宅融資）による予想損失額について、投資家に繰り返し誤った情報を提供していた。

banking unit 銀行, 銀行業務部門
◆Financial regulators asked prosecutors to investigate allegations that UFJ Holdings Inc.'s banking unit illegally obstructed recent inspections by reporting misleading information about its nonperforming loans. 金融当局は、UFJ銀行が不良債権に関する虚偽の情報を報告して最近の検査を違法に妨害したとして、同行を検察当局に刑事告発した。

banknote （名）紙幣, 札（さつ）, 銀行券, 銀行借入手形 (=bank note; ⇒bill, circulation, hologram)
banknote [bank note] circulation 銀行券流通, 銀行券流通高, 銀行券発行高
banknote issue 銀行券発行
banknote to be issued 発行銀行券
banknotes in circulation 銀行券流通高, 銀行券発行高, 銀行券発行・流通高
Currency and Banknotes Act 通貨および銀行券条例
new banknotes 新札
the balance of banknotes in circulation 銀行券流通高 (⇒balance of bank notes in circulation)
◆New banknotes have been produced with advanced anti-counterfeiting technology, including a hologram. 新札は、ホログラムなど偽造防止の先端技術を駆使して造られている。◆Newly designed ¥1,000, ¥5,000 and ¥10,000 banknotes went into circulation. デザインを一新した千円札、5千円札と1万円札が、発行（流通開始）された。

bankroll （名）金融資産, 資金, 札束, 資金供給, 資金援助, 金融支援 （動）資金援助する, 金融支援する, 融資する

◆To bankroll the winding up of the company, its parent company will sell some of its assets. 同社解散の金融支援をするため、親会社がその資産の一部を売却する。

bankrupt （形）破産した, 倒産した, 経営破たんした, 破たんした, 支払い不能の　（名）破産者, 破たん者, 破産宣告を受けた者, 債務支払い不能者　（⇒bill, checking transaction, prospective yield rate）

  bankrupt creditor　破産債権者
  declare bankrupt　破産を宣告する
  go bankrupt　破産する, 倒産する, 経営破たんする, 破たんする
  the meeting of bankrupt creditors　破産債権者集会

◆The shares became worthless after the bank went bankrupt. 銀行破たんで、株は無価値になった。◆This securities company was officially declared bankrupt by the Tokyo District Court. この証券会社に、東京地裁が正式に破産を宣告した。

bankruptcy （名）倒産, 破産, 経営破たん, 破産手続き
（⇒asset deflation, out-of-court settlement, protection）

  act of bankruptcy　破産行為
  adjudication of bankruptcy　破産宣告
  avoid bankruptcy　倒産を逃れる
  bankruptcy court　破産裁判所
  bankruptcy discharge　破産免責
  bankruptcy estate　破産財産, 破産財団
  bankruptcy filing　破産申請
  bankruptcy notice　破産告知
  bankruptcy order　破産命令
  bankruptcy petition　破産申請, 破産申立て, 更生手続き適用の申立て, 破産申立て書
  （＝petition in [of] bankruptcy）
  bankruptcy prediction　破産予測
  Bankruptcy Reform Act of 1978　1978年米連邦改正破産法, 1978年改正破産法
  bankruptcy-remote　親会社の破産の影響が及ばない
  bankruptcy workouts　破産関連業務
  be driven into bankruptcy　破産に追い込まれる
  chain-reaction bankruptcy　連鎖倒産
  claim in bankruptcy　破産債権
  come out of bankruptcy　更生法の適用を脱する
  corporate bankruptcies　企業倒産
  （＝corporate failure）
  creditors' claims in the event of bankruptcy　破産時の債権者の請求権
  enter bankruptcy　破産に陥る
  face bankruptcy　経営破たんの危機に直面する, 倒産寸前の状況にある
  file a petition in bankruptcy　破産申立てをする
  file for bankruptcy　破産を申し立てる, 破産 [破たん] 申請する, 破産手続きの適用を申請する, 破産法を申請する, 再生法を申請する
  （＝file for insolvency）
  fraudulent bankruptcy　偽装倒産
  go into bankruptcy　経営破たんする, 破たんする, 破産する
  personal bankruptcy　個人破産
  petition of [in] bankruptcy　破産申立て
  （＝filing for bankruptcy）
  petition of voluntary bankruptcy　自己破産の申立て
  risk of involuntary bankruptcy　強制破産のリスク
  voluntary bankruptcy　自己破産
  （＝self-declared bankruptcy）

◆Corporate bankruptcies have led to the swelling of nonperforming loans, posing a heavy burden on banks. 企業倒産が不良債権の増大を生み、銀行に重くのしかかっている。◆Global major financial institutions have been forced to hold extra capital since the financial meltdown following the 2008 bankruptcy of Lehman Brothers Holdings Inc. 米国の投資銀行リーマン・ブラザーズが2008年に経営破たんして生じた金融危機以来、世界の主要金融機関は、資本 [自己資本] の上積み [積み増し] を迫られている。◆The bankruptcy of Incubator Bank of Japan gave rise to concern over the company's financial management. 日本振興銀行の破たんで、同社の資金繰りに懸念が生じた。◆The number of annual applications for individual and corporate self-declared bankruptcy cases surpassed 200,000 for the first time in 2002. 1年間の個人と法人の自己破産申立て件数が、2002年に初めて20万件を突破した。◆The situation surrounding the Japanese economy has suddenly grown tense due to the first bankruptcy of a Japanese insurer in seven years. 7年ぶりの日本の生保破たんで、日本経済を取り巻く環境は一気に緊迫感が高まっている。◆The TSE typically only delists companies at risk of bankruptcy. 東証が上場廃止するのは、一般に経営破たん危機にある企業に限られる。

bankruptcy administrator　破産管財人

◆Shinsei Bank reached an out-of-court settlement in a damage lawsuit with a bankruptcy administrator of a borrower company. 新生銀行が、融資先企業の破産管財人との損害賠償訴訟で示談による和解に達した。

Bankruptcy Code　（米連邦）破産法
（⇒Chapter 11）

  debtor under the Bankruptcy Code　連邦破産法に基づく債務者
  insiders as defined the Bankruptcy Code　連邦破産法に定める内部者

◆In the United States, a troubled company is afforded the opportunity to reorganize under Chapter 11 of the federal Bankruptcy Code. 米国では、経営破たんした企業は、米連邦破産法11章に基づいて企業を再建する機会が与えられる。

bankruptcy procedures　破産手続き
（＝bankruptcy proceedings）

  be undergoing bankruptcy procedures　破産手続き中である
  complete bankruptcy procedures　破産手続きを完了する

◆Creditors of Yamaichi Securities Co. held their last meeting to complete bankruptcy procedures for the major brokerage house, which collapsed in 1997. 山一証券の債権者が最後の集会を開き、1997年に破たんしたこの大手証券会社の破産手続きを完了した。◆Major moneylender SFCG is undergoing bankruptcy procedures. 金融大手のSFCGは現在、破産手続き中だ。

bankruptcy proceedings　破産手続き
（＝bankruptcy procedures）

  initiate involuntary bankruptcy proceedings　強制破産手続きを申し立てる
  the commencement of bankruptcy proceedings　破産手続きの開始
  trap funds in the bankruptcy proceedings　破産手続きで資金を凍結する
  undergo bankruptcy proceedings　破産手続きを進める

bankruptcy protection　会社更生手続き

◆JAL and its two subsidiaries applied to the Tokyo District Court for bankruptcy protection under the Corporate Rehabilitation Law. 日航とその子会社2社が、会社更生法に基づいて会社更生手続きの適用を東京地裁に申請した。

bankruptcy shock　破たんショック

◆U.S. President Barack Obama engineered a softer landing for GM with a set of measures to alleviate the bankruptcy shock as much as possible. オバマ米大統領は、GMの破たん

ショックを極力緩和するための一連の措置で、同社の軟着陸に向けた手を打った。

Banks' Shareholding Purchase Corporation 銀行等保有株式取得機構, BSPC (=Banks' Shareholding [Stockholding] Acquisition Corporation; ⇒second-tier regional bank)
◆Most financial sources predict that sales of banks' shareholdings to the Banks' Shareholding Purchase Corporation will amount to between ¥200 billion and ¥300 billion. 銀行等保有株式取得機構への銀行による持ち株の売却額は2,000〜3,000億円にとどまる、と金融筋の大半は見ている。
解説 銀行等保有株式取得機構とは：金融機関と取引先との株式の持ち合い解消が株価に与える影響を避けるため、金融機関が保有する株式を、市場を通さないで直接買い取るもの。大手銀行や信託銀行などが拠出金を出資し、銀行界から選出した役職員が運営に当たる。2006年9月末まで買取りを行い、設立後10年で解散する。全国128の金融機関が会員となっている。

banks' shares 銀行株

bare (動)露出する, 暴露する, さらけだす, 発表する, 公表する
  bare A [lay A bare A] Aを暴露する[公にする, 明らかにする], Aを打ち明ける
  bare one's feelings 感情をさらけだす
  bare restructuring plan [package] リストラ[経営再建, 事業再編, 人員整理]計画を発表する

bare (形)裸の, 裸体の, 赤裸々な, ありのままの, 偽りのない, 公然の, むき出しの, 露骨な, 覆われていない, 木々のない, 緑のない, 空っぽの, 空の, ぎりぎりの, 最低限の, 最も基本的な, 単なる, ほんのわずかな, (賠償用の)保険をかけていない
  a person bare of credit 信用のない人
  be bare of cash 現金がない
  by a bare majority ぎりぎりの過半数で, やっと過半数で
  go bare 賠償責任保険なしで営業する
  lay A bare [lay bare A] Aを暴露する[公にする, 公表する, 発表する, 明らかにする], Aを打ち明ける
  the bare bones 要点, 骨子
  the bare [barest] essentials 最低限必須のもの
  the bare minimum 最低限の量
  the bare necessities 最低限必要なもの
◆The move to inject liquidity into Dubai's banks by the central bank of the United Arab Emirates was seen by analysts as the bare minimum. ドバイの銀行に資金を供給するアラブ首長国連邦(UAE)の中央銀行の動きを, アナリスト(専門家)は「最低限必要な量にすぎない」と見ている。

bargain buying 押し目買い (=buy on decline, buy on dip, buy on reaction: 上げ歩調の相場が一時的に下がった際, その押し目(一時的な下げ)を狙って買うこと)

barometer (名)尺度, 指標, 兆候, 気圧計, 晴雨計, バロメーター
  business barometer 景気指標, 景気種数
  coincidental barometer 景気の一致指標
  economic barometer 経済指標
  leading barometer 先行指標
◆The capital adequacy ratio is considered a barometer of a bank's financial health. 自己資本比率は, 銀行の経営の健全性を示す指標とされている。◆Wage earners' average overtime pay, a barometer of income conditions, rose 0.4 percent in September from the same month last year to ¥18,452. 9月の賃金労働者の平均残業手当て(所得動向の指標)は, 前年同月比で0.4%増の18,452円だった。

barrel (名)バレル(石油の単位：米国では42ガロンで159リットル, 英国では42ガロンで191リットル), 円筒形のもの, 政治資金, 運動資金, 多量

  barrel per day 日量〜バレル, 日産〜バレル, 1日当たり〜バレル, bpd
  in the barrel 無一文で
  make barrels of money しこたま儲(もう)ける
  on the barrel 即金で
  per-barrel price 1バレル当たりの原油価格 (⇒end名詞)
  scrape (the bottom of) the barrel 残りかすを使う, 最後の財源[方便]に頼る
◆Crude futures soared to $135 per barrel on the New York market. ニューヨーク市場の原油先物価格が, 1バレル=135ドルに急騰した[1バレル=135ドルの高値を付けた]。◆French oil giant Total produced an average of 55,000 barrels per day in 2010. フランスの石油大手トタルは, 2010年に1日当たり平均で5万5000バレルの石油を生産した。

base (名)基準, 基本, 基礎, 基盤, 拠点, 基地, ベース (⇒business base, capital base, capital tie-up, monetary base)
  at the parent base 単独ベースで
  base rating 基礎格付け, 基本格付け
  business base 営業基盤, 経営基盤
  capital base 資本基盤
  core deposit base コア預金基盤, 中核となる預金基盤
  customer base 顧客基盤
  earnings base 収益基盤
  equity base 株主資本基盤
  revenue base 収益基盤
  shore up revenue base 収益基盤を強化する
◆Banks must shore up their revenue base so they can repay all their debts. 銀行の債務返済を完了するには, 銀行が収益基盤を強化する必要がある。◆Shinsei and Aozora banks announced a plan to merge in an effort to expand their customer bases and improve earnings. 新生銀行とあおぞら銀行は, 顧客基盤の拡大と収益力の強化を狙って, 合併計画を発表した。◆The core nationwide CPI, which excludes volatile fresh food prices, stood at 99.3 against the base of 100 for 2005. 全国消費者物価指数のコア指数(値動きの大きい生鮮食品を除く総合指数)は, 99.3(2005年=100)となった。

base lending rate 基準貸出金利
◆The base lending rate of the Housing Loan Corporation and the preferential interest rate for companies have risen. 住宅金融公庫の基準貸出金利や企業向け融資の優遇金利が, 上昇した[引き上げられた]。

base money ベースマネー, 基礎貨幣 (=monetary base: ベースマネーは, 通貨供給の量を量るのに用いられる指標で, 現金と金融機関が中央銀行に預けている準備預金の合計)
◆Base money refers to the total of cash and reserves that financial institutions deposit in the central bank. 「ベースマネー」とは, 現金と金融機関の中央銀行預金の合計をいう。

base rate 基準金利, 基準貸出金利, 基準利率, 基本料金
◆Late payment shall incur an interest charge of 2 percent over the base rate current in XYZ Bank at the time the charge is levied from the due date to the date of payment in full. 支払いが遅延した場合, 支払い期日から全額支払い日まで, 支払い利息[遅延利息]を課す時点でXYZ銀行が適用する基準金利より2%高い支払い利息[遅延利息]が付くものとする。

-based 〜を(営業)基盤とする, 〜を基軸とする, 〜基準の, 〜に本部(本社・本店)を置く, 〜駐在の, 〜型の, 〜をベースにした, 〜に基づく, 〜主義の, 〜建ての, 〜密着型の (=based; ⇒Internet-based commerce, market-based, yuan-based bond)
  broad-based stock index 総合株価指数
  broader-based recovery ほとんどの地域での景気回復[景気持ち直し]

broader-based TOPIX index　全体の指数を示す東証株価指数（TOPIX）
cell phone-based policy sales　携帯電話での保険販売
credit-based financial institutions　貸出を基本業務とする金融機関
dollar-based investor　ドル・ベースの投資家
narrow-based stock index　業種別株価指数
performance-based　成果主義の
renminbi-based bond　人民元建ての債券，人民元建て債
risk-based capital　リスク基準の自己資本，リスク・ベースの自己資本
yuan-based bond　人民元建て債
　（=yuan-denominated bond）

◆A U.S. Federal Reserve Board snapshot of economic conditions bolsters the hope of broader-based recovery. 米連邦準備制度理事会（FRB）の景況報告では、ほとんどの地域で景気持ち直しの期待が強まっている。◆In the case of au Insurance's cell phone-based policy sales, policyholders are allowed to pay premiums by adding them to monthly mobile charges. au損害保険の携帯電話での保険販売の場合、保険契約者は、保険料を携帯利用の月額に加算して保険料の支払いをすることができる。◆NTT Docomo Inc. and SoftBank Mobile Corp. have been offering cell phone-based policy sales by teaming up with nonlife insurers respectively. NTTドコモとソフトバンクモバイルは、それぞれ損保会社と提携して、携帯電話での保険販売のサービスを提供している。◆Some currency traders have recently advised the Malaysian government and the Persian Gulf states to buy renminbi-based bonds, rather than the U.S. dollar. 一部の為替トレーダーは最近、米ドルではなく中国の人民元建て債券を買うようマレーシア政府やペルシャ湾岸諸国に助言している。◆The bank installed a total of 1,200 ATMs compatible with the IC-based cards at its 600 branches. 同行は、600支店の店舗にICカード対応の現金自動預け払い機（ATM）を全部で1,200台設置した。◆The two regional banks based in Ibaraki Prefecture agreed to start negotiations toward merging into a single bank by January. 茨城県を営業基盤とする地方銀行2行が、（2006年）1月合併に向けて合併交渉を開始することで合意した。

Basel [Basle]　バーゼル（スイス北西部バーゼル・シュタット準州の州都。国際決済銀行（BIS）の本部がある）
Basel Accord of 1988　1988年のバーゼル合意、1988年のバーゼル協定
Basel Agreement　バーゼル協定、BIS規制、BIS基準
Basel Capital Accord　BIS自己資本比率規制、BIS規制
Basel Committee on Banking Regulation and Supervision　銀行規制監督に関するバーゼル委員会

Basel Accord [accord]　（1988年の）バーゼル合意、バーゼル協定、BIS規制、BIS基準、BIS自己資本比率規制
　（=Basel Agreement, Basel Capital Accord）
◆Commercial banks have created special investment vehicles（SIVs）in order to escape the capital adequacy regulation imposed by the Basel accord. 銀行は、バーゼル協定［バーゼル合意］による自己資本比率規制を回避するため、特別投資会社（SIV）を新設している。

Basel Committee on Banking Supervision　国際決済銀行（BIS）のバーゼル銀行監督委員会、バーゼル委員会
◆The Basel-based Basel Committee on Banking Supervision is comprised of central bankers and supervisors from major nations. スイスのバーゼルに本部を置くバーゼル銀行監督委員会は、主要各国の金融監督当局で構成されている。◆The challenge of the Basel Committee on Banking Supervision is to develop a regulatory framework while fending off a recurrence of financial strife. バーゼル銀行監督委員会の課題は、金融危機再発の防止と規制の枠組みの策定だ。◆The Financial Stability Board is cooperating with the Basel Committee on Banking Supervision, a body that sets rules for international banking. 金融安定化理事会（FSB）は、国際銀行業務の基準を制定する機関のバーゼル銀行監督委員会と連携している。◆The new regulations decided on by the Basel Committee on Banking Supervision require banks to increase the core tier 1 capital, such as common stock and retained earnings, that they must hold in reserve, to at least 4.5 percent of assets from the current 2 percent. バーゼル銀行監督委員会が決めた新規制は、銀行が支払い準備として保有しなければならない普通株や利益剰余金［内部留保］などの中核自己資本（コア・ティア1）を、現行の資産の最低2%から4.5%に引き上げるよう銀行に義務付けている。

Basel 3　バーゼル3　（金融危機再発防止のため、自己資本の質と量の向上を求める新ルールで、国際銀行業務を展開している銀行の健全性を保持するための新しい自己資本規制のことをいう。2010年9月にバーゼル銀行監督委員会が公表。⇒core capital）

baseline　(名)基準、基準線、基準見通し、指導基準（guideline）、基調、起点、（測量の）基線、遠近線、ベースライン
baseline budget　基本予算、基準になる予算、予算の基準見通し
baseline budget deficit　基準になる財政赤字

basic　(形)基本的な、基本の、基礎的な、初歩的な、重要な、簡素な、必要最小限の、ベーシック
basic balance of payments　基礎収支
basic deduction　基礎控除
basic earnings per share　基本的1株当たり利益
basic guarantee　根（ね）保証
　（=initial guarantee）
basic net earnings per common share　基本的普通株式1株当たり純利益
basic pension　基礎年金

basic agreement　基本的合意、基本合意、大筋合意、基本合意書、基本契約、基本契約書
　（⇒transfer of business）
◆Mitsubishi Tokyo and UFJ intend to conclude a basic agreement by the end of this month. 三菱東京とUFJは、今月末までに基本契約を結ぶ方針だ。

basic asset　基本財産
◆The Public Management Ministry prohibits incorporated foundations from investing their basic assets in financial products which may reduce the principal, such as stocks and foreign currency-denominated bonds. 総務省は、財団法人に対して、その基本的な財産を株式や外貨建て債券など元本割れの恐れのある金融商品に投資するのを禁じている。

basic fund　（保険会社の）基金（株式会社の資本金に相当）
◆Daiichi Mutual Life Insurance Co. plans to increase its basic fund, which is equivalent to the capital of a joint-stock company, by ¥80 billion. 第一生命保険は、株式会社の資本金に当たる基金を800億円増額する方針だ。

basic operating expenses　基礎的経費
◆The new bank tax is levied on the banks' gross operating profits—their earnings minus basic operating expenses such as interest payments to depositors. 新銀行税は、銀行の収入から基礎的な経費（預金者に対する預金金利の支払いなど）を差し引いた業務粗利益に課される。

basic pension　基礎年金
　（⇒national pension plan）
◆The basic pension—both national and company employees' pension schemes—is covered by insurance premiums and national tax revenues. 国民年金も厚生年金も、基礎年金の財源は保険料と国税だ。◆The government raised its share of the burden for the basic pension to half from the current one-third from fiscal 2009. 政府は、2009年度から基礎年金の

国庫負担の割合を、現在の3分の1から2分の1に引き上げた。

basic pension fund 基礎年金基金
◆The government covers 50 percent of the basic pension fund from 2009. 国は、2009年度から基礎年金基金全体の2分の1を負担している。◆The government is poised to issue bridging bonds to make up the expected shortfall in state funding for the basic pension fund. 政府は、つなぎ国債を発行して、予想される基礎年金基金の国庫負担の不足分を賄(まかな)う方針だ。

basic pension payments 基礎年金給付
◆From fiscal 2011, ￥2.5 trillion will be needed to pay for the portion of basic pension payments to be covered by the state. 2011年度から、基礎年金給付の政府負担分の支払いに、2.5兆円が必要になる。◆The government's share of contribution to the basic pension payments was raised to 50 percent from one-third in fiscal 2009. 基礎年金の国庫負担割合は、2009年度に3分の1から50％に引き上げられた。

basic pension plan 基礎年金制度,基礎年金
◆The basic pension plan has been covered by premiums paid by subscribers and government budgetary appropriations. 基礎年金は、加入者が支払う保険料と政府の予算割当額(国の負担)で賄(まかな)われている。◆The basic pension plan is also known as the national pension plan. 基礎年金は、国民年金とも呼ばれている。◆The percentage of government funds from the consumption tax and other tax revenues for financing the basic pension plan remains about 36.5 percent. 基礎年金の財源としての消費税収などによる国の負担金の割合は、まだ約36.5％にとどまっている。◆The state share of the basic pension plan will be raised next year. 基礎年金の国庫負担の割合は、来年引き上げられる。◆To help finance the government burden in running the basic pension plan, the Health, Labor and Welfare Ministry calls for ￥10.67 trillion in funds in its budgetary request for fiscal 2012. 基礎年金運営の国庫負担［国の負担］分の費用として、厚生労働省は、2012年度予算の概算要求で10兆6,700億円を要求している。◆To stabilize the pension system, the government raised its burden in the basic pension plan to 50 percent of the total contribution from fiscal 2009. 年金制度の安定化を図るため、政府は、基礎年金の国の負担割合を2009年度から総給付金の50％に引き上げた。

basic profit 基礎利益 (=fundamental profit)
◆The basic profit excludes appraisal profits and losses from liquidation of securities holdings and write-offs of problem loans. 基礎利益には、保有有価証券の売却や不良債権の処理による評価損益は含まれない。

basis (名)方針,基準,根本原理,主義,方式,基礎,根拠,論拠,土台,主成分,ベース
(⇒black, consolidated basis, day trader)
accrual basis 発生基準,発生主義
aggregate basis 一括基準
all-inclusive［all inclusive］basis 包括主義
arm's length basis 商業ベース
asset basis 資産基準
balance on liquidity basis 流動性ベーシスの国際収支
basis period 基準年度
basis risk ベーシス・リスク（各種金利相互間の関係の変化）
basis swap ベーシス・スワップ（同一または異なる通貨間の変動金利を交換する通貨スワップ）
basis trade ベーシス取引
basis trading 利回りトレーディング(yield trading),ベーシス・トレーディング
be syndicated on a club basis クラブ・ベースでシ団組成が行われる
bond equivalent basis 債券換算利回り
buying on a yield basis 採算買い

cash-basis loans 現金主義の貸出金
cash collection basis 現金回収基準
constant dollar basis 実質ベース
contractual currency basis 契約通貨ベース
equity basis 持ち分法
financial budget balance on a national accounts basis 国民経済ベースの財政収支
first-in, first-out basis 先入れ先出し法
fully diluted basis 完全希薄化法
government bond basis trading 国債ベーシス取引
historical cost basis 取得原価法
income basis 利回りベース
individual（item）basis 個別基準
lower of cost or market basis 低価法,低価主義,低価基準
mark-to-market basis 値洗い基準
market price［value］basis 時価主義
money market basis マネー・マーケット・ベース
money market-equivalent basis（365-day/360） マネー・マーケットと同じ日数計算（365日/360日）
net basis 配当金課税後利益法
nil basis 配当金課税前利益法
nominal dollar basis 名目貨幣基準
on a closing basis 終値ベースで
on a consolidated basis 連結ベースで,一括して
on a coordinated basis 協調ベースで,協融ベースで
on a dollar denominated basis ドル表示で
on a domestic currency basis 国内通貨ベースで
on a freight basis 運賃ベースで
on a full year basis 通年で,通期で
on a global basis 世界全体で,世界全体で見て,世界的規模で
on a group basis 連結ベースで(=on a consolidated basis)
on a negotiated basis 相対ベースで
on a net basis ネット・ベースで,ネットで
on a nominal basis 名目で
on a quota share basis 比例配分ベースで
on a regional basis 地域別に
on a spread basis スプレッドでは
on a stand-by basis 引出可能な状態で
on a straight line basis 定額法で
on a temporary basis 一時的に
on a three-month moving average basis 3か月移動平均ベースで
on a two day settlement basis 2日決済ベースで
on an annualized basis 年率換算で,年換算で
on an assumed basis 再保険ベースで
on an economic basis 経済のファンダメンタルズで見て
on the basis of IMF formula IMF方式で
parent-basis earnings outlook 単独ベースの収益見通し
parent-basis valuation 単独ベースの評価
profitable basis 収益基盤
remittance basis 送金主義
settlement date basis 決済日ベース
stand-alone basis 単独ベース
syndicate the deal on a broad basis 同案件の大型シ団組成を行う
T-bond futures, September basis Tボンド先物9月物
valuation basis 評価基準
◆Fuji TV unveiled a plan to make Nippon Broadcasting System a subsidiary by upping its stake from the 12.39 percent

it had as of mid-January on the basis of the takeover bid. フジテレビは、株式公開買付けでニッポン放送株の保有比率を1月中旬現在の12.39%から引き上げて、ニッポン放送を子会社化する計画を発表した。◆Gains and losses on hedges of existing assets or liabilities are marked to market on a monthly basis. 既存の資産または債務のヘッジに関する損益は毎月、評価替えされている。◆Since three banks integrated their operations, executives from the three predecessor banks served on an equal basis as presidents of the Mizuho group, Mizuho Bank and Mizuho Corporate Bank. 3銀行の経営統合以来、旧3行の経営者が、みずほグループ（FG）、みずほ銀行、みずほコーポレート銀行のトップをそれぞれ分け合った。◆The current account balance is entering an upward trend on a year-on-year basis. 経常収支は、前年同月比ベースで上昇基調に入りつつある。

basis for recovery 景気回復の基盤
 ◆The basis for recovery remains weak. 景気回復の基盤は依然、弱いままだ。

basis point ベーシス・ポイント, bp [b.p.] （為替・金利変動の基準単位で、1ベーシス・ポイント＝0.01%、100ベーシス・ポイント＝1%。⇒percentage point）
 at the floating rate of the LIBOR plus 162.5 basis points per annum ロンドン銀行間取引金利（LIBOR）に年1.625%を加算した変動金利で
 build in a 25bp reduction 0.25%の利下げを織り込む
 dip by 10 basis points 10ベーシス・ポイント（0.1%）減少する
 ease at 25 basis points 25ベーシス・ポイント（0.25%）の利下げがある, 0.25%の利下げがある
 margin of AAbp over LIBOR LIBOR＋AAベーシス・ポイント（bp）の変動金利
 raise short rates a further 10 basis points 短期金利をさらに0.1%引き上げる
 reduce the tracking error risk to AA basis points 追跡誤差リスクをAAベーシス・ポイントに抑える［軽減する、低減する、低下させる］
 widen to 600 basis points 600ベーシス・ポイント（6%）に拡大する
 ◆Any payment not made when due will, in addition to any other right or remedy of Licensor, incur a finance charge at the lesser of three hundred basis points over the 3-month London Inter Bank Offered Rate （"LIBOR＋3"） on the date payment was due or the highest applicable legal contract rate. 支払いが支払い期日までに履行されない場合、ライセンサーの他の権利や救済請求権に加えて、支払い期日時点の3か月物ロンドン銀行間取引金利（LIBOR）プラス3%（LIBOR＋3%）または適用される最高法定約定金利のうち、いずれか低いほうの金利の金融費用が発生する。◆Interest rate differentials between Greek and German government bonds widened to 600 basis points, or six percentage points, from January to May 2010. ギリシャ国債とドイツ国債の金利差は、2010年1月から5月の間に600ベーシス・ポイント（6%）も拡大した。◆The spreads of yields on high-risk junk bonds over the benchmark five-year U.S. Treasury bonds had been around 200 basis points, or 2 percentage points. リスクの高いジャンク債と指標となる5年物財務省証券との金利差（スプレッド）は、2%（200ベーシス・ポイント）程度で推移していた。

basket （名）バスケット,（契約や協定などの）包括的条項, 集まり, 組合せ, グループ, かご
 a basket of currencies 通貨バスケット, 主要通貨のバスケット, 複数通貨レートの組合せ
 a basket of short- and long-term rates 短期金利と長期金利のバスケット
 a cash basket of stocks 現物株のバスケット, 株式の現物バスケット
 basket category （関税の）包括品目
 basket currency バスケット通貨
 basket delivery バスケット方式（いろいろな通貨を組み合わせて新しい合成通貨単位や計算単位を作ること）
 basket of S&P 500 shares S&P500種の株式バスケット
 basket product バスケット商品
 basket purchase 一括購入, 一括買取り
  （＝lump-sum purchase）
 basket transaction ［trade］ バスケット取引, 複数の株式銘柄の一括取引
 baskets of N225 stocks 日経平均（225種）採用銘柄のバスケット
 currency basket system 標準バスケット方式, 通貨バスケット制（主要貿易相手国の通貨を貿易量で加重平均したレートと自国通貨を連動させる方式）
 market basket method マーケット・バスケット方式
 maturity basket 満期バスケット
 revalue the market on a basket basis バスケット通貨としての観点から市場を見直す
 stabilize one's currency against a basket of currencies 自国通貨を主要通貨に連動する
 standard basket（system） 標準バスケット方式
 the exchange rate baskets 通貨バスケット
 ◆The latest rise in the yuan's value against the U.S. dollar and a smooth transition to the currency basket will help stabilize China's external relations. 今回の人民元相場の対米ドル切上げと通貨バスケット制への円滑な移行で、中国の対外関係は安定化に向かうだろう。

batter （動）乱打する, たたきのめす, 激しく打つ, 打ち壊す, 直撃する, 壊滅する, 砲撃する, へこませる, 使いつぶす
 be battered by ～を[～の影響を]もろに受ける, 吹き付けられる, たたきつけられる, 定期的に虐待［家庭内暴力］を受ける
 be battered by a prolonged slump 長期低迷の影響をもろに受ける
 be battered by confusion in financial markets 金融市場の混乱の影響をもろに受ける
 ◆Global economies are battered by confusion in financial markets. 世界経済が、金融市場の混乱の影響をもろに受けている。◆The continued fall in U.S. stock prices and the dollar's depreciation has battered the Japanese economy. 米国の株安とドル安の進行が、日本経済を直撃している［激しく揺さぶっている］。◆The housing industry is being battered by a prolonged slump. 住宅産業は、長期低迷の影響をもろに受けている。◆The 225-issue Nikkei Stock Average dropped below the 9,000 mark Wednesday with the yen's surge set to batter the Japanese economy. 水曜日の日経平均株価（225種）は、円高の日本経済への打撃を見越して、9,000円台を割り込んだ。

battle （動）戦う, 闘争する, ～に取り組む
 battle against inflation インフレと戦う
 battle for control of ～の経営権［支配権、経営支配権］獲得競争を展開する
 battle with ～と戦う
 ◆Citigroup, the largest U.S. bank, and Wells Fargo, the fifth-largest U.S. bank, are battling for control of the sixth-largest U.S. bank Wachovia. 米銀行最大手のシティグループと米銀行5位のウェルズ・ファーゴは、同4位のワコビアの経営権獲得競争［買収合戦］を展開している。

battle （名）戦い, 闘争, 戦闘, 競争, 一戦, 口論, 交渉, 戦争, バトル
 a battle against ～との戦い
 a battle for power 権力闘争, 権力争い
 a battle of wills 根くらべ
 a battle of wits 機知くらべ

a constant battle　不断の戦い
fight a fair battle with　～と正々堂々と戦う
fight a losing battle　できそうにないことに挑(いど)む, 奮闘する
lose [give] the battle　戦いに負ける
the battle for deposits　預金獲得競争
win [gain] the battle　戦いに勝つ, 勝利を得る
◆Battles between realtors over small lots of land have become increasingly fierce. 狭い土地をめぐる不動産業者の競争が, 激化している。

battlefield　(名)戦場, 戦闘区域, 対決場, 論争の的, 論争の場, 争い[闘争]の場　(=battleground)
a key battlefield　主戦場
the main battlefield of monetary policy　金融政策の主戦場
◆The main battlefield of monetary policy likely will shift to deflation. 今後は, デフレが金融政策の主戦場となろう。

BBB　トリプルB, トリプルBの格付け
◆Standard & Poor's currently assigns a BBB long-term rating to the bank. スタンダード＆プアーズは現在, 同行に対してトリプルBの長期格付けをしている。

b/e　為替手形　(bill of exchangeの略)

bear　(動)(リスクなどを)負担する[負う], 受け入れる, (利子などを)生む
bear interest　利息が付く
bear the credit risk　信用リスクを負う
bear the responsibility for　～の責任を取る

bear　(名)弱気筋, 売り方, 軟派, ベア　(形)(相場などが)弱気の, 下がり気味の, 下向きの
be still in a bear trend　下降トレンドからまだ脱していない
bear account　弱気筋, (弱気の)思惑売買
bear bond　ベア・ボンド(償還時の債券利回りが最初に決めた水準より高い場合に償還元本が増加する債券)
bear-bull bond　ベア・ブル・ボンド
bear campaign　ベア・キャンペーン
bear closing [covering]　(空売りの)買戻し, 手仕舞い買い
bear floater　ベア型変動利付債, ベア・フローター
bear hug　逃げようのない買収提案[申し込み], ベア・ハッグ(条件のよい株式公開買付けなどの買収提案)
bear market　弱気市場, 弱気相場, 下げ相場, 売り相場　(=bearish market, weak market)
bear phase　弱気局面
bear position　売り持ち, 空売り
bear raid [raiding]　売り崩し(株価の低下が目的の株式の大量安売り)
bear rally　弱気相場のなかの上昇局面, 長期不況のなかの一時的な持ち直し
bear seller　弱気筋
bear share　弱気株
bear speculator　弱気の投機家
bear spread　ベア・スプレッド(値が下がれば利益が得られる組合せのオプション取引)
bear squeeze [panic]　(外国為替)踏み上げ, 踏み上げ相場, (外為)売り方締め付け, 売り方に対する締め上げ
bear trend　弱気トレンド, 下降トレンド
bull-bear position　強気・弱気状態
the bear [short] interests　弱気筋

bear down on　～にどっと押し寄せる, ～をのみ込む, ～を圧迫する, ～に急に迫る, ～に迫ってくる, ～に襲いかかる
◆On Dec. 1, 2009, the Nikkei Stock Average was bearing down on the 9,000 mark due to the so-called Dubai shock. 2009年12月1日の日経平均株価(225種)は, いわゆるドバイ・ショック(中東ドバイの金融不安)で, 9,000円台を割り込む寸前まで追いつめられていた。

Bear Stearns　(米国の大手投資銀行・証券会社の)ベア・スターンズ(2007年にサブプライム・ローン問題で経営が急速に悪化し, ニューヨーク連銀(連邦準備銀行)が緊急融資を行い, 2008年5月30日付けでJPモルガン・チェースに救済買収された)

bear the risk　リスクを負う, リスクを負担する
bear all the risks　リスクをすべて負担する
bear the credit risk　信用リスクを負う
bear the liquidity risk　流動性リスクを負う
bear the risk of credit loss　信用損失のリスクを負う

bearer　(名)所持人, 持参人　(形)持参人払い式の, 無記名式の
bearer bond　無記名[無記名式]債券, 無記名債
bearer certificate　無記名証書
bearer check　持参人払い式小切手, 無記名式小切手
bearer debenture　無記名社債
bearer depository receipt　無記名預託証券
bearer form　無記名式
bearer note　無記名式中期債
bearer security　無記名証券, 無記名債
bearer share [stock]　無記名株
bill bearer　手形所持人
bill payable to the bearer　持参人払い[持参人払い式]手形
check payable to order and bearer　記名式持参人払い小切手
instrument payable to bearer　持参人払い証券
payable to the bearer　持参人払い
risk bearer　危険負担者, リスク負担者
tax bearer　租税負担者

bearing　(名)(危険などの)負担, 関係
risk bearing　危険負担, リスク負担
tax bearing　租税負担
tax bearing ratio　租税負担率

-bearing　(形)～を生む, ～付きの　(⇒interest-bearing)
fixed interest-bearing securities　確定利付き証券
interest-bearing bank debenture　利付き金融債
interest-bearing bond　利付き債
interest-bearing capital　利子生み資本
noninterest-bearing account　無利息口座
noninterest-bearing bond　無利息社債, 無利息公債
noninterest-bearing debt　無利子債券
noninterest-bearing note　無利息手形
permanent interest-bearing shares　永久利付き証券
variable interest-bearing securities　不確定利付き証券

bearish　(形)弱気の, 弱気含みの, 下落気味の, 下がり気味の, (市況が)軟調の, 軟調傾向の, 見通しが暗い, 悲観的な見方の, 全面安の展開, 売り優勢の展開　(⇒bullish, FOMC)
adopt a bearish stance on　～に対して弱気のスタンスを取る
be bearish of the economy　景気の見通しが暗い
be bearish on the economy　景気の先行きを悲観的に見る
be bond-bearish　債券が売られる
bearish factor　弱気材料, 不安材料
bearish forecast [outlook, story]　弱気の見通し, 弱気の見方

bearish market condition　弱気の地(じ)合い
bearish sentiment　弱気の地(じ)合い, 弱気
　(=bearish mood)
bearish tendency　下降傾向, 下がり気味
bearish tone　弱気, 弱含み基調, 弱気ムード
bearish view　弱気の見方
become more bearish　軟弱傾向を強める
remain bearish on the dollar　ドルの先安感が依然として強い, 依然としてドル安の展開だ
turn bearish　弱気に転じる
◆Market players turned bearish. 市場関係者は、弱気に転じた。◆The Fed deems the U.S. economy to be bearish and as a result the yen will gain further against the dollar. 米連邦準備制度理事会(FRB)が米経済について弱気の見方を示しているため、ドルに対して円高はさらに進むと思われる。◆U.S. administration officials should refrain from making any remarks speculators may consider bearish. 米政府当局者は、投機筋の売り材料にされる発言は慎むべきだ。

bearish market　弱気市場, 弱気相場, 下げ相場, 売り相場, 株価低迷の局面　(=bear market)
◆The bearish market reflected investors' worries over the delay in implementing structural reforms. この下げ相場は、構造改革実施の遅れに対する投資家の懸念を反映したものだ。

bearish mood　先行き不安, 全面安の展開, 弱気の地(じ)合い, 弱気ムード
　(=bearish sentiment, bearish tone)
◆A bearish mood enveloped the Tokyo market Tuesday from the start of the day's trading. 火曜日の東京市場[東京株式市場]は、取引開始から全面安の展開となった。

bearish stock market　株価低迷, 株価低迷局面
◆To immediately sell banks' shareholdings through the stock-purchasing organization would result in huge losses due to the bearish stock market. 株式取得機構を通じて銀行の保有株式をすぐ売却すると、今は株価が低迷しているときだけに多額の売却損失が発生することになる。

bearishness　(名)弱気, 弱気ムード, 下降気味, 悲観的な見方, 見通しが暗いこと

beat　(動)打ち負かす, 〜に勝つ, 〜を上回る, 〜をふっ飛ばす
beat a person down　〜に値段を下げさせる
beat about [around] the bush　(核心に触れないで)遠回しにいう, 本題を避ける
beat the competition　競争に勝つ
beat the drum　一般の注意を引くためにあらゆることをする
beat the index　インデックスを上回る
beat the market　市場平均を上回る

bedrock　(名)根底, 基盤, 根本, 基本原則, 根本原理, 基本的原理, 基本的な事実, 岩床, 岩盤　(形)基本的な, 根本的な
bedrock position　基本的立場
bedrock prices　底値
get [come] down to bedrock　本題に入る, 真相を究める

beef up　(動)強化する, 増強する, 補強する, 拡充する, 向上させる, 食肉処理する　(=strengthen)
beef up one's financial base　財務基盤を強化する, 経営基盤を強化する
beef up production capacity　生産能力を強化する, 生産能力を拡充する
beef up the return　投資利回りを向上させる
◆Sendai Bank is considering beefing up its financial base from public funds to support local corporations hit by the March 11 quake and tsunami. 仙台銀行は、3月11日(2011年)の地震と津波で被災した地元企業を支援するため、公的資金の注入による財務基盤の強化を検討している。◆We will beef up overseas production capacity. 当社は、海外での生産能力を強化[拡充]する方針です。◆What is urgently needed as the EU's rescue package is beefing up the functions of the EFSF and recapitalizing banks that own Greek and Italian government bonds. EU(欧州連合)の支援策として緊急に求められているのは、欧州金融安定基金(EFSF)の機能強化や、ギリシャやイタリアの国債を保有する銀行の資本強化などだ。

beef-up　(名)強化, 増強, 補強
◆The beef-up of the early warning system is expected to enable insurers to make decision on the decrease of guaranteed yields before the companies fail. 早期警戒制度の強化で、生保は破たん前に予定利率引下げを決断できるようになる。

behavior [behaviour]　(名)行動, 行為, 活動, 動向, 動き, 変動, 政策
behavior of inflation　インフレ動向
cost behavior　原価変動, 原価の動き
economic behavior　経済行為, 経済行動, 経済活動, 経済動向, 景気動向, 相場の動き　(=behavior of the economy, economy's behavior)
Fed behavior　FRB(米連邦準備制度理事会)の政策
interest rate behavior　金利動向
　(=behavior of the interest rates)
inventory behavior　在庫の動き
market behavior　市場行動, 市場動向, 市場の動き
noneconomic behavior　非経済的行為
optimal investment behavior　最適投資行動
price behavior　価格動向, 物価動向
profit maximizing behavior　利益[利潤]最大化行動, 利益極大化行動
shady behavior　不正行為
speculative behavior　投機の行動
spending behavior　消費行動, 消費パターン
supply behavior　供給行動
underlying behavior of the economy　景気の基調
yield behavior　利回りの動き
◆Suspicions of other shady behavior by the bank have emerged. ほかにも、同行の不正行為の疑惑が浮上している。

behind　(前・副)〜の後ろで[後ろに], 〜よりも劣って, 〜に負けて, 〜にリードされて, 〜より遅れて, 〜を支持して, 〜の背後[背景]に, 〜の陰に, 〜の裏に, 〜の過去のものに
be [get] behind one's plan　〜の計画を支持する, 〜の計画の後押しをする
be behind the times　時代遅れだ
be behind us　〜は終わる, 〜は過ぎる, 〜は過去のものだ
behind-closed-doors session　非公開の会談, 秘密裏の会談
behind-the-scenes concessions　舞台裏の譲歩, 水面下の歩み寄り
behind-the-scenes negotiations [talks]　舞台裏での交渉, 水面下の話し合い
fall behind　〜に後れをとる
get [go] behind　〜の真意を探る
◆Behind these cautious views among large manufacturers are uncertainty over the debt crisis in the eurozone and the slowdown in the U.S. economy. 大企業製造業のこうした警戒感[慎重な見方]の背景には、ユーロ圏の債務危機不安や米景気の減速がある。◆The rise of the yen's value is behind the improvement in travel abroad. 円高が、海外旅行増加の背景にある。

beige book [Beige Book]　ベージュ・ブック, 米地区連銀景況報告書, 地区連銀景況報告, 地区連銀経済報告
　(=tan book: 米国の12の地区連銀(連邦準備銀行)が管轄

する各地区の景気動向を分析して、作成される経済情勢報告書。米連邦公開市場委員会（FOMC）の会議資料として用いられる。⇒Fed districts）
◆The Beige Book is so named for the color of its cover. ベージュ・ブック（地区連銀景況報告）は、その表紙の色でそう呼ばれている。◆The U.S. economy is improving, but concerns remain about the pace of recovery, the U.S. Federal Reserve said in its "beige book" report. 米連邦準備制度理事会（FRB）は、その「地区連銀景況報告」（ベージュ・ブック）で、米経済は改善しているものの、景気回復の足取りがまだ懸念されると指摘した。◆The U.S. Federal Reserve Board said in its Beige Book release that the U.S. economy deteriorated further in almost all corners of the country. 米連邦準備制度理事会（FRB）は、地区連銀景況報告（ベージュ・ブック）を発表し、米国の経済情勢はほぼ全米で一段と悪化していると指摘した。

belittling （名）過小評価、軽視、軽視する行為、小馬鹿にすること　（形）過小評価の、軽視した、小馬鹿にした、けなす［さげすむ］傾向がある
  belittling comments　小馬鹿にした評論、軽視したコメント
  the act of belittling　過小評価する行為、軽視する行為
  ◆The eurozone's critical mistake is the eurozone's belittling of the risk of the sovereign debt crisis aggravating the banking crisis and vice versa. ユーロ圏の重大な誤りは、国家の財政危機と銀行の危機［経営危機］が相互に増幅し合う危険性を、ユーロ圏が軽視したことにある。

bellwether　（名）指標、（市場動向の目安となる）指標銘柄、（金利などの）誘導目標、先導者、主導［指導］者
  bellwether bond　債券指標銘柄、指標銘柄
  bellwether industry　景気主導型産業
  bellwether long bond　30年物指標銘柄（＝30-year bellwether bond）
  bellwether stock　市場先導株
  ◆The Fed cut its bellwether federal funds rate for overnight loans between banks by a quarter of a percentage point to 1 percent. 米連邦準備制度理事会（FRB）は、銀行同士［銀行間］の翌日物のフェデラル・ファンド（FF）金利の誘導目標を0.25引き下げて年1％とした。

below　（前）〜を下回る、〜より以下の
  average 10 basis points below normal　平均して通常の水準を10ベーシス・ポイント（0.1％）下回る
  be below the 50% level　50％台を割り込む、50％の水準を割り込む
  below-average　平均を下回る、業界平均以下の、業界平均を下回る
  below cost　原価以下、コスト割れの
  below cost sales　コスト割れ販売
  below the line　異常損益項目、特別損益、利益処分、境界線以下、国際収支表の金融勘定（公的部門の短期資本収支）、範囲外、販売促進［販促］媒体による広告、マスメディアによらないプロモーション、映画製作の物の製作費、ビロー・ザ・ライン（line＝損益計算書の経常利益）
  below-the-line　異常損益項目の、特別損益の、境界線以下の、範囲外の
  below-the-market　市場以下の
  below-trend growth　トレンド以下の成長率
  close below key support　主要支持線を割り込んで引ける
  come in at or below market expectations　市場の期待の線かそれを下回る水準になる
  come in below market estimates　市場予想を下回る
  drop below the 9,000 mark　9,000円台を割り込む
  fall［drop］below 50 percent　50％を割り込む
  go below some floor level　下限基準を割り込む
  guide the call rate below the current official discount rate level　コール・レートを現在の公定歩合より低い水準に誘導する
  on a close below　終値で〜を割り込んで
  population below the poverty line　貧困線以下の所得しかない人々
  reduce A below 50%　Aを50％以下に引き下げる、Aを50％以下にする
  remain below　〜以下の水準にとどまる
  remain below the bond yield adjusted equilibrium rate　債券利回り調整後の均衡レートを下回っている
  sink below the 1 percent threshold　1％割れの水準まで低下する
  the Nikkei Index below the 10,000 level　1万円台割れの日経平均
  trade below one's fundamental bond adjusted equilibrium　債券利回り調整後の均衡レートを下回って取引される
  ◆A downgrade below investment-grade by even one ratings agency could boost GM's borrowing costs and wreak havoc on the corporate bond market. 格付け会社が1社でも投資適格格付けより低く格付けを引き下げたら［格付け会社が1社でも投機的格付けに格下げしたら］、GMの資金調達コストが急増し、米国の社債［債券］市場にも大きな影響が出る恐れがある。◆A key gauge of the current state of the economy fell below the boom-or-bust threshold of 50 percent in September for the first time in five months. 景気の現状を示す主要基準（景気一致指数）が、9月は5か月ぶりに景気判断の分かれ目となる50％を下回った。◆A reading of below 50 percent in the coincident index is considered a sign of economic contraction and a figure above that is viewed as a sign of expansion. 一致指数で50％以下の数値は景気収縮［景気後退］を示す指標と見られ、それ以上の数字は景気回復［景気拡大］を示す指標と見なされる。◆The stock average fell below 9,000 again on the Tokyo Stock Exchange. 東京株式市場は、平均株価がふたたび9,000円を割り込んだ。◆The 10-year JGB yield sank below the 1 percent threshold. 新発10年物の日本国債の流通利回りが、1％割れの水準まで低下した。◆The 225-issue Nikkei Stock Average dropped below the 9,000 mark Wednesday to close at the year's low of 8,845.39. 水曜日の日経平均株価（225種）は、9,000円台を割り込み、終値は今年最安値の8,845円39銭となった。◆The yield on the benchmark 10-year Japanese government bond closed below the 1 percent threshold. 長期金利の指標となる新発10年物日本国債の流通利回り［利回り］が、年1％の大台を割り込んで取引を終えた。◆The yield on the benchmark 10-year U.S. government bond has been closing below 3 percent recently. 長期金利の指標となる10年物米国債の利回りは最近、3％を割り込んで［3％割れで］取引を終えている。◆Under the EU's Stability and Growth Pact, countries eligible to join the euro system are required to keep budget deficits below 3 percent of GDP. 欧州連合（EU）の財政安定・成長協定によると、ユーロ加盟国は、加盟の条件として財政赤字をGDPの3％以下に抑えなければならない。◆Under the government guidelines, if earnings come in more than 30 percent below targets set in restructuring plans at any major bank that received public funds to recapitalize in 1988 and 1999, the banks management will have to resign. 政府のガイドラインによると、資本再編のために1988年と1999年に公的資金の注入を受けた大手銀行の収益が、再建計画（経営健全化計画）で設定した収益目標を30％以上下回った場合、銀行の経営陣は辞任しなければならない。

below book value　取得価格を下回る、簿価を下回る
  a price below book value　取得価格［簿価］を下回る価格
  be below book value　取得価格を下回る、簿価を下回る
  ◆The stock dropped to a price below book value. 株価が、簿価を下回った。

below investment［below-investment］grade　投機的格付けの、投資不適格格付けの、非投資適格の、投資

適格格付け未満の
  below-investment grade bond　投機的格付け債券
  below-investment grade rating　投機的格付け
  private below investment grade　非投資適格私募債
  securities rated below investment grade　投機的格付け証券, 投資適格格付け未満の証券
  ◆A downgrade below investment-grade by even one ratings agency could boost GM's borrowing costs and wreak havoc on the corporate bond market. 格付け会社が1社でも投資適格格付けより低く格付けを引き下げたら [格付け会社が1社でも投機的格付けに格下げしたら], GMの資金調達コストが急増し, 米国の社債 [債券] 市場にも大きな影響が出る恐れがある。

below-market　(形) 市場以下の, 市場価格以下の
  below-market level　市場以下の水準, 市場以下
  below-market price　市場価格以下の価格
  below-market rate　市場以下金利

below par　額面割れ, 額面以下の, 赤字の, 水準に満たない, アンダーパーの, 額面以下で, 割引で
  (=under par)
  below-par paper　アンダーパーの銘柄
  below-par priced issues　額面以下の債券

below-par company　赤字会社
  ◆The total losses of a corporate group's below-par companies exceeded 6.25 percent of the total surplus made by its companies in the black. ある企業グループの赤字会社の総損失額 (合計赤字額) が, 同グループの黒字会社の合計黒字額の6.25%を超えた。

belt tightening　金融引締め, 財政引締め, 緊縮政策, 耐乏生活
  belt-tightening management　減量経営
  belt-tightening supplementary budget　緊縮補正予算
  competitive belt tightening by major nations　主要国の金融引締め競争 (主要国が相競って金融引締め政策を取ること)

belt-tightening measures　緊縮政策, 支出削減, 経費削減, 財政緊縮策, リストラ策
  ◆The Democratic and Republican parties are preoccupied with belt-tightening measures. 米国の民主党も共和党も, 財政緊縮策に専念している。◆We must create a business environment in which employees who have quit major companies because of belt-tightening measures would be able to find work at newly emerging businesses and play a positive role in ensuring the growth of such corporations. リストラで大企業を離れた社員が, 新興企業に移って, その会社の躍進に積極的な役割を果たせるような企業環境をつくる必要がある。

belt-tightening monetary step　金融引締め
  ◆U.S. Federal Reserve Board announced an imminent federal funds rate increase to 3.25 percent from 3 percent, making it the first belt-tightening step in five years. 米連邦準備制度理事会 (FRB) は, 近くフェデラル・ファンド金利 (FF金利) を現行の3%から3.5%に引き上げると発表して, 5年ぶりの金融引締めに踏み切った。

belt-tightening policy　緊縮政策, 緊縮路線, 財政引締め策, 引締め政策
  ◆Should the government forge ahead with its belt-tightening policy, the budding economic recovery may be reduced to a short-lived upturn. 政府が緊縮路線をひた走れば, 景気回復の芽も, 薄命の景気回復に終わりかねない。◆The belt-tightening policy of the administration of then Prime Minister Ryutaro Hashimoto included hikes in social insurance premiums and in medical fees borne by the insured. 当時 (1996年) の橋本政権の緊縮政策には, 社会保険料や被保険者 (保険契約者) の医療費負担の引上げが含まれていた。◆The risk of an economic slowdown will increase if countries adopt belt-tightening policies all at once. 各国が一斉に緊縮政策 [財政引締め策] に走れば, 景気失速のリスクが高まる。◆What concerns us is the government's inclination to adopt a belt-tightening policy. 懸念されるのは, 政府が緊縮路線への傾斜を強めていることだ。

bench rate　標準金利, 基準金利

benchmark　(名) 基準, 尺度, 基準値, 測定基準, 基準指数, 基準銘柄, 指標, 指標銘柄, 目安, 誘導目標, 節目, ベンチマーク　(⇒New York Mercantile Exchange)
  benchmark bond　債券指標銘柄
  benchmark corporate lending　基準法人貸出金利
  benchmark futures contract　先物中心限月
  benchmark issue　指標銘柄
  benchmark Nikkei Stock Average　日経平均株価
  benchmark reserves　基準準備金
  benchmark revision　基準改定, 基準変更
  benchmark short-term interest rate　短期金利の誘導目標, 短期金利の指標
  benchmark status　指標銘柄
  benchmark stock　指標銘柄
  benchmark used to price the bond　同債の価格設定に使用された指標銘柄
  benchmark yield　指標銘柄利回り, 指標利回り
  benchmark 30-year US Treasury　30年物国債指標銘柄
  evaluate the portfolio against the benchmark　ベンチマークに照らしてポートフォリオを評価する
  exceed the relevant benchmark　所定のベンチマークを上回る
  have the Nikkei 225 as a benchmark　日経平均 [日経225種] をベンチマークとして指定される
  long-term benchmark　長期金利の指標
  spread over a benchmark yield　指標利回りに対するスプレッド
  use Treasuries as a benchmark　米国債をベンチマークとして使用する
  versus [vis-a-vis] the benchmark　ベンチマークに対して

benchmark federal funds rate　短期金利の指標 [誘導目標] であるフェデラル・ファンド金利
  ◆The unanimous decision by the U.S. central bank's policy setting Federal Open Market Committee moved the benchmark federal funds rate to 1.25 percent. 米連邦準備制度理事会の金利政策を決定する米連邦公開市場委員会の全会一致による決定で, 短期金利の指標であるフェデラル・ファンド金利が年1.25%に引き上げられた。

benchmark five-year U.S. Treasury bonds　指標となる5年物財務省証券
  ◆The spreads of yields on high-risk junk bonds over the benchmark five-year U.S. Treasury bonds had been around 200 basis points, or 2 percentage points. リスクの高いジャンク債と指標となる5年物財務省証券との金利差 (スプレッド) は, 2% (200ベーシス・ポイント) 程度で推移していた。

benchmark for long-term interest rates　長期金利の指標
  ◆The yield on the 10-year government bond is the key benchmark for long-term interest rates. 10年物国債の利回り (流通利回り) は, 長期金利の代表的指標である。

benchmark gold future [futures] price　金取引の指標となる金先物価格
  ◆The benchmark gold future price surged to all-time high of ¥4,725 per gram in trading on the Tokyo Commodity Exchange. 東京工業品取引所の取引で, 金取引の指標となる金先物価格が, 過去最高の1グラム=4,725円まで急騰した。◆The benchmark gold future price topped ¥4,700 per gram for the first time on the Tokyo Commodity Exchange. 東京工業品取引所で, 金取引の指標となる金先物価格が, 史上初めて1

グラム＝4,700円を突破した。

benchmark interest rate 基準金利, 指標金利, 政策金利 (=benchmark rate; ⇒ECB)
◆The ECB cut its benchmark interest rate to 1.25 percent for the first time in 2.5 years in early November 2011, immediately after its new President Mario Draghi assumed office. 欧州中央銀行（ECB）は、マリオ・ドラギ新総裁（イタリア出身）が就任した直後の2011年11月初め、2年半ぶりに政策金利を1.25%に引き下げた。

benchmark rate [interest rate] 基準金利, 指標金利, 政策金利
◆The recent interest rate increase of the People's Bank of China was a modest one—the benchmark rate on one-year yuan loans was raised by 0.27 percentage points. 中国人民銀行の今回の利上げは小幅にとどまり、指標となる人民元の期間1年の貸出金利は0.27%引き上げられた。

benchmark short-term interest rate 短期金利の誘導目標, 短期金利の指標
◆The federal funds rate, a benchmark short-term interest rate, was cut to 3.5 percent per annum and the official discount rate to 3 percent per annum. 短期金利の誘導目標であるフェデラル・ファンド（FF）金利は年3.5%、公定歩合は年3%に引き下げられた。

benchmark 10-year Japanese government bond 長期金利の指標となる10年物日本国債
◆The yield on the benchmark 10-year Japanese government bond closed below the 1 percent threshold. 長期金利の指標となる新発10年物日本国債の流通利回り［利回り］が、年1%の大台を割り込んで取引を終えた。

benchmark 10-year U.S. government bond 長期金利の指標となる10年物米国債
◆The yield on the benchmark 10-year U.S. government bond has been closing below 3 percent recently. 長期金利の指標となる10年物米国債の利回りは最近、3%を割り込んで［3%割れで］取引を終えている。

beneficial (形) 役に立つ, 有益な, 有利な, 利益を受ける, 収益を受けるべき, 好材料の, プラスの
　beneficial effects　プラス効果
　beneficial interest　受益者の利益, （信託の）受益権
　beneficial owner　受益者, 実質所有者
　beneficiary ownership　実質的所有者, 受益権
　beneficiary right of trust　信託受益権
　beneficiary right to the trust　信託受益権
　beneficiary securities　受益証券
　beneficiary securities register　受益証券台帳
　beneficiary trust certificate　受益権証券

beneficiary (名) （年金や保険金、為替などの）受取人, （信用状の）受益者, 受給者, 実質的権利者［所有者］
　beneficiary's trust interest　信託受益権
　contingent beneficiary　偶発受益者
　for a/c of beneficiary　送金受取人負担で
　letter of credit beneficiary　信用状の受益者
　pension beneficiary　年金受給者
　pension fund beneficiary　年金基金の受益者
◆It is illegal to impose income tax as well as inheritance tax on the beneficiaries of life insurance money paid with a linked pension. 年金型の生命保険金の受取人に所得税と相続税の両方を課すのは、違法である。◆Japanese megabanks and Toyota were among the beneficiaries of a slew of emergency liquidity-providing facilities devised by the U.S. Federal Reserve Board. 日本のメガバンクやトヨタも、（2008年秋の金融危機に伴って）米連邦準備制度理事会（FRB）の発案で実施された大規模な緊急貸出制度の恩恵を受けた［緊急貸出制度を活用していた］。◆The pension system may collapse before people qualify as beneficiaries. 年金をもらう前に、年金制度が崩壊する可能性がある。◆When the policyholders of single-premium whole life insurances die, beneficiaries receive the designated benefits plus accumulated dividends. 一時払い終身保険の契約者が死亡した場合、保険金の受取人は、特定の（死亡）保険金のほかに積立配当金を受け取れる。

beneficiary certificate 受益証券, 受益権証書
　beneficiary certificates representing interest in a trust holding foreign loan receivables　外国貸付け債権信託受益証券
　beneficiary certificates representing interest in a trust holding loan receivables　貸付け債権信託受益証券

benefit (動) 利益を与える, ～の利益になる, ～のプラスになる, ～に貢献する, 利益を得る, 恩恵を受ける, 利益が発生する, 為替差益が出る
　benefit both companies　両社にメリットがある
　benefit existing shareholders　株主の利益になる
　benefit if the yen decline　円安になれば為替差益が出る
◆An exporter company will incur losses if the yen rises above the assumed exchange rate, but benefit if the yen declines. 輸出企業では、その想定為替レートより円高になれば為替差損が生じ、（想定為替レートより）円安になれば為替差益が出る。◆If agricultural imports become cheaper due to the lowered tariffs, consumers will greatly benefit. 関税の引下げで輸入農産品が安くなれば、消費者の利点も大きい。◆Integrating management will benefit both companies by increasing Internet and TV advertising revenues as well as distributing TBS programs through broadband. 経営統合は、インターネットとテレビの広告収入拡大やTBS番組のブロードバンド配信などで、両社にメリットがある。◆When ailing businesses are revamped, those who invested in them benefit. 経営不振企業を再建すると、出資者が利益を得られる。

benefit (名) 利益, 利得, 便益, 利点, 効果, 給付, 給付金, 給付額, 年金, 手当て, 受益, 受益金, 税減額効果, ベネフィット (⇒insurance benefits, life annuity, life insurance policy)
　basic benefit　基礎年金
　benefit formula　年金支給額の計算式
　benefit payment　年金給付, 年金支払い, 手当ての支払い
　benefits of policyholders　保険契約者の利益
　child benefit　扶養手当て, 児童手当て
　death benefits　死亡給付金, 契約者給付金
　defined benefit plan　確定給付制度, 給付建て制度, 給付建て年金制度
　disability benefit　障害手当て
　earnings-related benefit　報酬比例の年金給付
　employee benefit　福利厚生
　fixed benefit plan　定額給付制度
　fringe benefit　付加給付, 賃金外給付, 追加給付
　health care benefits　健康保険給付
　incremental benefit　加給年金, 特別加算金
　insurance benefits　保険給付金
　non-vested benefit　受益権非確定給付
　noncontributory defined benefit pension plan　非拠出型確定給付制度
　Pension Benefit Guaranty Corporation　年金給付保証会社
　pension benefits　年金給付, 年金給付額
　retirement benefit　退職給付
　right to benefits　受給権
　vested benefit　受益権確定給付
　welfare benefit　福祉手当て
◆Benefits become vested upon the completion of five years of service. 5年間の在職により、年金の受給資格が生じます。◆Nippon Life Insurance Co. sold some of Olympus's shares with a view to protecting the benefits of policyholders. 日

本生命は、保険契約者の利益保護の観点からオリンパス株の一部を売却した。◆Part of the benefits of quantitative easing will take the form of a depreciation of the dollar. 量的緩和の効果の一部は、ドル安の形で現れる。◆The benefits of the U.S. financial bailout package will take time to show up in the U.S. economy. 米国の金融救済策の効果が米国内経済に現れるのに、時間がかかるだろう。◆Under a variable pension system, pension benefits change in accordance with fluctuations in government bond yield. 変額年金制度では、国債利回りの変動で年金給付額が変わる。◆When the policyholders of single-premium whole life insurances die, beneficiaries receive the designated benefits plus accumulated dividends. 一時払い終身保険の契約者が死亡した場合、保険金の受取人は、特定の（死亡）保険金のほかに積立配当金を受け取れる。

benefit from 〜から利益を得る, 〜の恩恵を受ける, 〜のメリットを受ける, 〜が追い風になる
  benefit from a boom in exports　輸出好調の恩恵を受ける
  benefit from a decline［fall］in interest rates　金利低下から利益を得る, 金利低下のメリットを受ける, 金利低下が追い風になる　（=benefit from declining interest rates, benefit from lower interest rates）
  benefit from a tax refunds　税金還付の恩恵を受ける
  benefit from the weaker yen　円安の恩恵を受ける, 円安が追い風になる

◆Everyone connected with the Corporation, or the people we call our "stakeholders" will also benefit from value-oriented management. 当社と係りのある人たち、つまり当社の「ステークホルダー」といわれる人たち全員も、価値重視の経営によって利益を受けることになる。◆Japanese exporting firms have been enjoying positive earnings, benefiting from thriving markets in the United States and the weak yen. 日本の輸出企業は、米国の好調な市場と円安を追い風に、好業績が続いている。◆The bank benefited from a tax refund. 同行は、税金還付の恩恵を受けた。◆The bank repeatedly lied so that it could benefit from the U.S. government program that insured mortgage. 同行は、米政府の住宅ローン保証プログラムから利益を得るために繰り返し虚偽の説明をした。◆U.S. companies are continuing to benefit from a boom in exports due mainly to the decline in the value of the dollar earlier this year. 米企業は、主に年初来のドル安による輸出好調の恩恵を受けている。

benefit obligation　給付債務
  accumulated benefit obligation　累積給付債務
  accumulated postretirement benefit obligation　累積退職後給付債務
  actuarial present value of benefit obligation　給付債務の保険数理に基づく現在価値
  expected postretirement benefit obligation　予想退職後給付債務
  interest cost on projected benefit obligation　予想給付債務にかかる支払い利息
  plan assets in excess of projected benefit obligation　基金資産の見積り給付債務超過額
  projected benefit obligation　予定給付債務, 見積り給付債務
  unfunded accumulated benefit obligation　未拠出累積給付債務

benefits of policyholders　保険契約者の利益
◆The lowering of promised yields on premium investments would surely protect the benefits of policyholders. 生保が保険契約者に約束した保険料投資の運用利回り（予定利率）を引き下げたほうが、確かに保険契約者の利益を保護することになる。

benefits of shareholders　株主の利益
◆Japanese companies tend to attach greater importance to favorable relations with customers than to boosting benefits of shareholders. 日本企業は、株主の利益を高めるより顧客との好ましい関係を重視する傾向がある。

benefits of the yen's sharp climb against the dollar　急激な円高・ドル安による円高差益
◆Aeon and Ito-Yokado started discount sales of foods imported from the United States to pass along to consumers the benefits of the yen's sharp climb against the dollar. イオンとイトーヨーカ堂は、急激な円高・ドル安による円高差益を消費者に還元するため、米国から輸入した食料品の値下げセールを開始した。

benevolent fund　共済基金

benign　(形)温和な, 慈悲深い, 低水準の, 良好な, 良性の, 見通しが明るい, 落ち着いている
  benign inflation　低いインフレ率, 低水準のインフレ, 低インフレ
  benign neglect　善意の無策, 善意の無視政策, ビナイン・ネグレクト（悪意の無視=malign neglect）
  benign neglect policy　善意の無策の策, 善意の無視政策, 優雅な無策, ビナイン・ネグレクト政策　（=policy of benign neglect: 国際収支が赤字でドル安になっても、その対策を諸外国の通貨当局に任せてしまう政策）
  benign rate［interest rate］environment　良好な金利環境, 良好な金利動向
  policy of benign neglect　善意の無策の策, ビナイン・ネグレクト政策

◆The U.S. government's benign neglect apparently reflects its belief in the need to avoid a financial burden due to an easy rescue effort. この米政府の善意の無視政策は、明らかに「安易な救済策による財政負担を避ける必要がある」との政府の考えを反映している。

Benjamins　(名)米国の100ドル紙幣
◆The new Benjamins will be released in February 10, 2011. 米国の新100ドル紙幣は、2011年10日から発行される。

best　(形)最善の, 最良の, 最も有利な条件の, 優良な, 一流の, 最大の, ベスト
  best bid　最も有利な条件のオファー
  best bid and offer quote　気配値段
  best bid price　最高入札価格
  best case　最も楽観的なシナリオ「想定例」, 期待可能な上限, 最高条件, ベスト・ケース
  best-case scenario　最善のシナリオ, ベスト・シナリオ
  best estimate　最善の推定値
  best execution　顧客にとって最高条件［最も有利な条件］での売買, 最良執行
  best execution duty obligation　最良執行義務
  best leading indicator　最も役に立つ先行指標
  best paper　優良手形, 一流手形
  best price　最良価格, 最高価格
  best-selling line　一番の売れ筋, 売れ筋
  second best problem　次善の問題
  the best of the inflation experience　インフレ率の低下傾向
  the best of the rally　上昇局面

best efforts　(名)最善の努力, 最善の努力をする条件［売れ残ることがあるという前提］での発行引受け, 取扱い引受け, 委託募集, ベスト・エフォート

best-efforts［best-effort］　(形)最善の努力をする条件の, 委託販売の
  best efforts［a best effort］basis　ベスト・エフォート・ベーシス［ベース］（最大限売却に努めるが売れ残ることもあるという条件・前提での発行引受け［募集の取扱い］）
  best efforts issue　（最善努力）売出発行
  best-efforts selling　（債券の）委託販売［取扱い］, 最善努

力売出発行
  conduct syndication on a best effort basis　ベスト・エフォート・ベーシス[ベース]でシ団組成を行う
  handle an offering on a best effort basis　ベスト・エフォート・ベース[ベーシス]で売出しを取り扱う
  raise funds on a best efforts basis　ベスト・エフォート・ベースで資金を調達する[資金を集める]

bet　(動)賭(か)ける, 確信する, 断言する, 主張する, 予想する, 期待する　(⇒fiscal stimulus)
  be betting　～を予想している, ～を期待している
  bet on　～を見越す, ～に賭ける, ～に投資する
  (=gamble on)
  bet on foreign stock index　外国株価指数に投資する
  bet one's bottom dollar　あり金全部を賭ける
  ◆Goldman Sachs Group Inc. is said to have marketed risky investments that bet on the housing market's growth just before the mortgage meltdown. ゴールドマン・サックスは、住宅ローン市場の崩壊直前に、住宅市場の成長を見越した[予想した]高リスクの金融商品[投資商品]を販売したとされる。◆This stablemaster (former sekiwake) is alleged to have habitually bet huge amounts of money on professional baseball games. この親方(元関脇)は、プロ野球の試合に常習的に多額の金を賭けていたとされる。

bet　(名)賭け, 掛け金, 賭けの対象, 予想, 見通し, 意見, 選択, 選択した行動, 選択の手段[方法], 確実な人物[こと, 物]
  a fair bet　正しい判断, 正しい選択
  a good bet　賢明な選択[判断、行動], お薦(すす)め[お薦め品], 確実な人[こと, 物], 賭けの対象
  a reasonable bet　妥当な判断, 合理的な選択[判断]
  a safe [sure] bet　安全な選択, 安全な判断[行動], 安全な方法, (～するのが)確実
  make a long-term bet on premiums　プレミアム物に長期投資する, プレミアム物を長期投資用に買う
  the best bet　最善の方法[手段], 確実な方法, 取るべき手段
  ◆The investment bank reaped billions of dollars from its own bets that the housing market would collapse. この投資銀行は、住宅市場が崩壊するとの独自の予想で、数十億ドルの利益を上げていた。

beta　(名)(証券)ベータ係数, ベータ値　(=beta coefficient, beta line: 個別証券の変動と市場全体の変動との相関関係を示す)
  beta distribution　ベータ分布
  beta line　ベータ係数
  beta share [stock, security]　ベータ株
  beta value　ベータ値
  high beta portfolio　ベータ値が高いポートフォリオ
  industry beta　業種ベータ値
  market beta　市場ベータ値
  stock beta　株式ベータ値

better　(形)優れた, ～の改善, ～の回復, ～の拡大
  at or better　指し値
  better asset management　資産管理の改善
  better bank lending figures　好調な銀行貸出残高
  better margins　利ざやの拡大
  better price numbers　インフレ率の低下
  better risk environment　リスク環境の改善
  better securities market　証券市場の回復

beyond　(前)～を超えて～を越える, ～を上回る, ～以上に, ～に勝って
  be well beyond the average　平均をはるかに上回る
  maturities beyond ten years　10年超の満期
  the rise of the yen beyond the level of the assumed exchange rate　想定為替レートを上回る円高
  ◆The Bank of Japan supplied funds beyond the upper limit of ￥27 trillion soon after the Resona problem surfaced. 日銀は、りそな問題発覚後、27兆円の上限を上回る資金を市場に供給した。◆The rise of the yen beyond the level of the exchange rate assumed by many exporters has put them on the ropes. 多くの輸出業者が想定した為替レートの水準を上回る円高が輸出業者を窮地に追い込んでいる。

BHC　銀行持ち株会社　(bank holding companyの略)

bid　(動)値を付ける, 入札する, 指し値する
  bid for　～に入札する, ～の入札をする, ～に値を付ける
  bid on　～に値を付ける, ～の値を入れる, ～の入札をする
  bid up　価格をつり上げる
  ◆Dealers can bid for Treasury bonds at a quarterly auction. ディーラーは、四半期入札[四半期ごとオークション]で米財務省証券に入札することができる。

bid　(名)入札, 申込み, 入札の付け値, 落札価格, 競り, 提案, 買収提案, 買収, 買い注文, 買い呼び値, 買い気配, 買い唱え(証券などの売買で買い手が希望する値段), ビッド　(=bidding, tendering; ⇒takeover bid)
  agreed bid　合意による株式公開買付け
  bid for a company　企業買収, 企業買収案
  bid-rigging　不正入札, 不正工作, 入札談合, 談合
  bid target　買収の標的
  bid winner　落札業者, 受注業者
  biggest bid　最高入札　(=best bid, highest bid)
  forward bid rate　先物買い相場
  high-stakes bid　一か八かの賭け, 大きな賭け
  hostile bid　敵対的買収提案
  lack a bid from　～の買いが入らない
  lose a bid　入札を失う
  make a bid for　～に入札して値を付ける
  (=enter [put in] a bid for)
  make a successful bid　落札する, 受注する
  open bid　公開入札
  public bid　一般入札
  put in the highest bid　最高額の付け値をする
  reverse bid　逆乗っ取り
  send in a bid　入札に応じる
  special bid　特別買付け
  strong bid for　～を買い上がる動き
  strong bids　強気の買い
  submit a bid for　～の入札をする
  (=tender a bid for)
  submit bids　入札に応じる
  successful bid　落札, 受注
  supplementary bid　追加入札
  the highest bid price　落札価格, 落札値
  win the bid　受注する, 落札する
  winning bid　獲得した買収案件
  ◆Oracle, the world's second-largest software group, boosted its bid over the offer of Germany-based SAP. 世界第二位のソフトウエア・グループのオラクルは、同社の買収提示額をSAP(本社ドイツ)の提示額以上に引き上げた。◆The four companies negotiated and agreed in advance the bid winner and the bidding price. 4社は、事前に談合を行って落札予定会社や入札価格を決めた。

bid and asked price　呼び値, 買い呼び値と売り呼び値, 売買仲値, 仲値　(=bid and asked, bid and asked prices, bid and offer, bid and offered price)
  解説 買い呼び値と売り呼び値について:買い呼び値(bid, bid price)は証券などの売買の際に買い手が希望する値段

で、これ以上だと購入に応じない買い手の最高値を意味する。また、売り呼び値（asked price, offer）は売り手が希望する値段で、これ以下の場合は売却に応じない売り手の最安値を意味する。買い呼び値と売り呼び値をあわせて、気配値（quotation, quote）という。

bid-ask spread 呼び値スプレッド （=bid/ask spread, bid-offer spread: 買い呼び値（bid price）と売り呼び値（asked price）の差額）

bid bond 入札保証, 入札保証金

bid price 買い手の指し値, 買い値, 買い呼び値, 入札価格 （=buying price）

bid rate 買いレート, 買い相場, 資金の取り手レート, 資金の取り手金利, 資金の出し手レート （=offered rate）

bid-to-cover ratio 応札倍率（米財務省証券の公募入札の応札総数と落札総数との比率。一般に、発行利回り（yield）が高いときは応札倍率が高くなる）

bidding （名）入札, 競り, 申込み （=bid, tendering）
◆The bidding for these TEPCO's assets is expected to take place from early to mid-October. これらの東電資産の入札は、10月上旬〜中旬に実施する予定だ。◆The Industrial Revitalization Corporation of Japan will choose a company, or a group, as a formal sponsor through biddings early next year. 産業再生機構は、来年はじめに行う入札で、スポンサー企業・グループ（支援企業・グループ）を正式に選定する。

big （形）大きい, 大手の, 大量の, 豊富の, 巨額の, 大型の, 大規模な, 重大な, 主要な, ビッグ
（⇒too big to fail）
　Big Blue IBMの株, ビッグ・ブルー
　Big Board ニューヨーク証券取引所（New York Stock Exchange）の通称, ビッグ・ボード（ニューヨーク証券取引所の大きい株価表示板）
　big bucks 大金
　big business 大企業, 大手企業
　Big Day 上場初日
　big one 1,000ドル
　big shareholder [stockholder] 大株主 （=large shareholder）
　big three brokers 3大証券
　the big U.S. banks 大手米銀, 米銀大手
　too-big-to-fail lenders 大きすぎてつぶせない銀行［金融機関］, 大きすぎて破たんさせられない銀行
◆The bank has a stronger balance sheet than some of its bigger peers. 同行の財務基盤は、一部の大手の同業他行よりも強固だ。◆Twenty-eight banks of the world will face capital surcharges of 1 percent to 2.5 percent by the application of international rules to rein in too-big-to-fail lenders. 大きすぎて破たんさせられない銀行［金融機関］を規制する国際基準が適用されると、世界の28行が、1〜2.5％の資本［自己資本］上積みの対象となる。

Big Bang ビッグバン, 金融大改革, 金融制度の抜本的改革（1986年10月27日、ロンドン証券取引所で実施された一連の金融・証券制度の自由化措置）
◆The 1998 Japanese version of Britain's Big Bang financial markets deregulation was originally designed to drastically reform the nation's securities market. 1998年の日本版ビッグバン（金融市場の自由化）は、もともと日本の証券市場の抜本的改革を狙ったものだ。

big bank 巨大銀行, メガ銀行, 大手行, 大手金融機関
◆Among 17 big banks targeted by the lawsuits filed by the U.S. government were Bank of America, Citigroup, Credit Suisse and Nomura Holding America Inc. 米政府が提訴した訴訟の対象の大手金融機関17社の中には、バンカメのほかにシティグループやクレディ・スイス、野村ホールディング・アメリカなどが含まれている。◆In the lawsuits against big banks over the sales of risky investments, the U.S. government wants to be compensated for lost principal and interest payments. 高リスク証券の販売をめぐっての大手金融機関に対する訴訟で、米政府は、元本と利払い分の損失補償を求めている。◆U.S. regulator sued 17 big banks for selling risky investments. 米規制当局が、高リスクの金融商品［高リスク証券］を販売したとして大手金融機関17社を提訴した。◆We do not hold the idea that big banks are too big to fail. われわれとしては、「巨大銀行が破たんさせるには大き過ぎる」という考え方は取らない。

Big Four 英国の4大銀行（Barclays Bank, Lloyds TSB, HSBCとNat-Westの4大商業銀行）, 米国の4大公認会計士事務所（Deloitte Touche Tohmatsu, Ernst & Young, KPMGとPricewaterhouseCoopers）

biggest bank 最大手行, 大手銀行, 大手行
◆The collapse of the subprime mortgage market and related credit market turmoil have resulted in $45 billion of write-downs at the world's biggest banks and securities firms. サブプライム・ローン市場の悪化や関連金融市場の混乱で、世界の大手銀行と証券会社の評価損計上額は、これまでのところ450億ドルに達している。◆The three Japanese biggest banks are likely to be required to hold additional capital of 1 percent to 1.5 percent. 日本の3大メガ銀行は、1〜1.5％の資本［自己資本］上積みを求められる見込みだ。◆UBS AG, Switzerland's biggest bank, will buy back $18.6 of debt securities. スイスの最大手行UBSが、186億ドル相当の債務証券を買い戻すことになった。

biggest banking [financial] group 最大手の金融グループ, 最大の金融グループ
◆The New York-based Citigroup, once the world's biggest banking group, faced massive losses in the wake of the subprime mortgage crisis. 世界最大の金融グループだったシティグループ（ニューヨーク）は、サブプライム・ローンの焦げ付き問題を受けて、巨額の損失を抱えていた。

biggest shareholder [stockholder] 筆頭株主, 大株主
◆Ford will relinquish its position as the biggest shareholder of Mazda Motor Corp. by selling most of its 11 percent stake in Mazda. 米フォードは、保有するマツダ株11％の大半を売却して、マツダの筆頭株主の座を降りることになった。◆Panasonic Corp. will make a formal acquisition proposal to its biggest stockholders. パナソニック（旧松下電器産業）は、同社の大株主に正式に買収提案をする予定だ。

BII 事業中断保険（business interruption insuranceの略）

bilateral （形）相互の, 双方の, 両者の, 相対の, 相対ベースの, 二者の, 二者間の, 二国間の, 左右相称の, 両性的の, 双務的な, 相互に義務を負う, 当事者双方が義務を負う, 当事者間の
　bilateral advances 相対の貸出
　bilateral agreement 双務協定, 二国間協定, 双方の合意
　bilateral assistance [aid] 二国間援助
　bilateral clearing 双務的の清算, 二国間清算
　bilateral contract 双務契約, 双方の契約 （片務契約＝unilateral contract）
　bilateral credits 二国間信用供与
　bilateral deal 二国間取引
　bilateral deals （石油の）直接取引 （=bilateral oil purchase deals）
　bilateral facility 相対の銀行信用
　bilateral line 相対取引, 相対ベース
　bilateral loan 相対ローン, 相対ベースの融資
　bilateral netting 二者間ネッティング, 双方向相殺決済, 相互ネッティング
　bilateral payment agreement 二国間支払い協定, 双務的支払い協定

bilateral settlement 双務決済
bilateral short-term advances 相対の短期貸出
bilateral tax agreement 租税条約
bilateral transaction 二国間取引, 双務取引, 双方的取引, 直接相対取引
conclude a bilateral loan 相対ローンを完了する
on bilateral lines 相対ベースで, 相対契約で, 相対取引で
bill (名)手形, 証券, 証書, 紙幣, 札(さつ), 料金, 代金, 請求金額, 勘定書, クレジット・カードなどの利用明細書, 明細書, 請求書, 法案
  (⇒access, denomination)
a huge bill is due next week 多額の請求書の期限が到来する
a set of bills 組手形
accept a bill 手形を引き受ける, 手形の支払いを引き受ける
acceptance of bill (of exchange) 手形引受け
  (=acceptance bill)
accommodation bill 融通手形
agency bill 代理手形
back a bill 手形の裏書きをする
  (=endorse a bill)
bank bill 銀行券, 銀行手形, 銀行引受手形
  (=bank note)
banker's acceptance bill 銀行引受手形, BA手形
banker's bill 銀行手形
bill advice 手形満期通知状
bill discount deposit 歩積(ぶづ)み(金融機関が手形を割り引く際, 割引額の一部を強制的に預金させること)
bill discounted 割引手形
bill for collection 取立て手形
bill for term 定期払い手形
bill holder 手形所持人
bill in blank 白地手形 (=blank bill)
bill of adventure 積送品危険証券
bill of credit 支払い証券, 信用状
bill of date 確定日付け手形
bill of debt 約束手形, 債務証書
bill of dishonor 不渡り手形 (=dishonored bill)
bill of exchange 為替手形, B/E
bill of quantities 建築見積り書
bill of sale 売渡し証, 売買証書
bill of sight 仮陸揚げ許可証
bill on demand 要求払い手形 (=demand bill)
bill on presentation 提示[呈示]払い手形, 一覧手形
  (=presentation bill)
bill payable 支払い手形
bill payable to bearer 持参人払い手形
bill receivable 受取手形
blank bill 白紙の請求書
charge a hefty bill 高額の代金を請求する
  (⇒charge動詞)
check a bill 請求書を確認する
clean bill 裸手形
clean bill of health 完全健康証明書
clear a bill 手形を交換する, 手形を清算する
collect a bill 集金する
commercial bill 商業手形
create a bill from a work order 作業発注書から請求書を起こす
customer's bill 顧客の利用明細書
demand bill 要求払い手形

discount a bill 手形を割り引く
dishonor a bill 手形の支払いを拒否する, 手形を不渡りにする
documentary bill 荷為替手形
domestic bill 内国為替 (=home bill, inland bill)
domiciled bill 他所払い手形
double name bill 複名手形 (=double named bill)
draw a bill on ～に手形を振り出す
due bill 借用証書
duplicate bill 副為替手形
exchequer bill 英大蔵省証券
export bill 輸出手形
fail to honor a bill 手形の支払いをしない, 不渡り手形を出す, 不渡りを出す
fictitious bill 空(から)手形
finance bill 融通手形, 米国の金融手形
first class bill 一流手形 (=gilt-edged bill)
fit [fill] the bill 要求[条件]を満たす, 申し分ない, ぴったりだ
foot the bill 勘定をする, 合計する
foot the bill for ～の勘定をする, ～の勘定を払う, ～の費用を負担する, ～の経費を持つ, ～を合計する
foreign bill 外国為替手形
foul bill 故障手形
government bills 短期国債
honor a bill 手形の支払いをする
import settlement bill 輸入決済手形
interest bill 利付き手形
kite a bill 融通手形を振り出す
long bill 長期手形
  (=long sighted bill, long term bill)
make out a bill to ～宛に請求書を出す
negotiable bill 流通手形
negotiate a bill 手形を買い取る
new $100 bill 新100ドル紙幣
original bill 原手形
outstanding bill 未払い請求書
pay a bill 手形を支払う
  (=honor [meet, take up] a bill)
pay one's bills 請求書の支払いをする
pay the bill for ～の勘定を払う, ～の付けを払う
presentation bill 一覧払い手形, 呈示払い手形
receive a bill for ～の請求書を受け取る
renew a bill 手形を書き換える
renewal bill 書換え手形
security bill 証券担保為替手形
short bill 短期手形
  (=short sighted bill, short term bill)
sight bill 一覧払い手形
single name bill 単名手形 (=single named bill)
sola bill 単独手形, 単独為替手形 (=sole bill)
take up a bill 手形を支払う, 手形の支払いを引き受けて支払う, 手形を引き受ける (=honor a bill)
time bill 期限付き手形
trade bill 商業手形
treasury bill 米財務省短期証券, 英大蔵省証券, 政府短期証券, 短期国債, Tビル
two-name bill 複名手形
unpaid bill 不渡り手形, 代金の踏み倒し
usance bill 期限付き手形
value bill 荷為替手形

way-bill　貨物引換証

◆A bill to revise the Law on Special Measures for Strengthening Financial Functions is designed to facilitate compensations of losses of financial institutions with public funds. 金融機能強化法の改正法案は、公的資金で金融機関の損失の穴埋めを容易にするのが狙いだ。◆A financial bailout bill, after twists and turns, has at last been signed into law in the United States. 米国の金融安定化法案（緊急経済安定化法案）が、迷走の末、ようやく成立した。◆Four credit card holders received bills for accessing subscription Web sites via cell phones even though they had no recollection of doing so. 利用した覚えがないのに、携帯電話の有料サイトの利用代金請求書が、4人のクレジット・カード会員に届いた。◆In the aftermath of past major earthquakes, unethical traders charged hefty bills after suggesting the need for checks of earthquake resistance. 過去の大地震の直後には、悪質業者が「耐震診断の必要がある」と持ちかけて、高額の代金を請求していた。◆The bill is intended to promote foreign investment in Japan. 同法案は、外国資本の対日投資を促すのが狙いだ。◆The firm has gone effectively bankrupt after banks suspended transactions with it on its second failure to honor a bill. 同社が2回目の不渡りを出して銀行取引停止となり、事実上倒産した。◆The head office and branches of the Bank of Japan began delivery of the new bills to financial institutions at 6 a.m. 日銀の本店と支店は、午前6時から新札の金融機関への引渡し（発券業務）を開始した。◆The new design for the $100 bill was introduced in Washington. 米国の100ドル紙幣の新デザインが、米ワシントンで公表された。◆Unpaid bills have emerged as a major structural problem in Chinese business. 中国との取引では、代金の踏み倒しが大きな構造的問題として浮上している。◆We are now being forced to pay the bill for the overheating of the economy. われわれは今、経済の昂揚［景気過熱］の付けを払わされている。◆We will have to accept heavy taxation to foot the bill for the lax fiscal discipline of past governments. われわれは今後、過去の政府の放漫な財政運営のつけを負担するために、重税を受け入れなければならなくなる。

bill at sight　一覧払い手形
　bill at maturity　満期手形
　bill at 30 days' sight　一覧後30日払い手形、30日払い手形
　◆We have drawn a bill at 30 days' sight on you through the bank for $1,000. 当社は、同行経由で1,000ドルの一覧後30日払い手形を貴社宛に振り出した。

bill of lading　船荷証券, 積み荷証券, 貨物引換証, 運送証券, 積み荷証, B/L
◆The date of the bill of lading shall be conclusive evidence of the date of the delivery. 船荷証券の日付は、引渡し日の最終的な証拠とする。

解説 船荷証券の種類：

　air B/L　空輸証券（=aircraft B/L）
　charter party B/L　用船契約船荷証券
　claused B/L　条項付き船荷証券
　clean B/L　無故障船荷証券
　custody B/L　保管付き船荷証券
　Customs B/L　税関用船荷証券
　domestic B/L　国内輸送証券
　export B/L　輸出品船荷証券
　foul B/L　故障付き船荷証券
　negotiable B/L　流通性船荷証券　流通船荷証券　譲渡可能船荷証券
　ocean B/L　海洋船荷証券（=marine B/L）
　on board B/L　船積み船荷証券
　on-carriage B/L　貨車輸送証券
　order B/L　指図式船荷証券　指図人式船荷証券
　original B/L　船荷証券原本
　overseas B/L　海外船荷証券
　port B/L　積出港船荷証券
　prepaid B/L　運賃前払い船荷証券
　railroad B/L　鉄道貨物引換証
　received B/L　受取船荷証券
　received-for-shipment B/L　船積み式船荷証券
　red B/L　赤字船荷証券
　shipped B/L　船積み船荷証券
　short form B/L　略式船荷証券
　stale B/L　時期経過船荷証券
　straight B/L　（荷受人）指名直送船荷証券　記名式船荷証券
　sub-B/L　口別船荷証券
　summary B/L　積み荷明細表
　through B/L　通し船荷証券
　transshipment B/L　積替え船荷証券
　truck B/L　自動貨車積送証券

biometric authentication system　生体認証システム
　（=biometric identification system, biometric system）
◆Bank of Tokyo-Mitsubishi's biometric authentication system installed in new ATMs identifies users by the pattern of veins in their palms. 新型ATM（現金自動預け払い機）に導入した東京三菱銀行の生体認証システムは、利用者の手のひらの静脈パターンで利用者を確認（本人確認）する。

解説 生体認証システムとは：個人差のある身体の特徴（手のひらや指の静脈の形状、指紋、瞳の虹彩（こうさい）など）を使って、本人かどうかを確認するシステム。キャッシュ・カードの場合は、暗証番号を盗まれても、本人でないとATMで預金を引き出せない。

biometric identification　生体認証
◆Major banks are introducing new types of ATM cards, some of which feature biometric identification functions and others that can be used as electronic money or credit cards. 大手銀行が、生体認証機能や、電子マネーやクレジット・カードにも使える機能などの特長を備えた新型のキャッシュ・カードを導入している。

biometric integrated circuit card　生体認証機能付きICカード
◆Bank of Tokyo-Mitsubishi offers customers who use biometric integrated circuit cards at a cost of ￥10,500 annually up to ￥100 million in insurance money if they suffer damages from bogus cards. 東京三菱銀行は、年会費10,500円支払って生体認証機能付きICカードを利用する顧客が偽造カードの被害を受けた場合には、最大1億円の保険金を支払う。

BIS　国際決済銀行　（Bank for International Settlements の略。世界の金融監督当局や中央銀行で構成されている。⇒capital adequacy ratio）
　BIS capital adequacy requirement　国際決済銀行規制, BISの自己資本比率規制, BISの自己資本規制, BIS規制（=BIS asset ratios［capital standards, guidelines］）
　BIS ratio　自己資本比率
　BIS standard　BIS基準
　meet the BIS capital adequacy standards　BISの自己資本比率基準を達成する
◆The Bank for International Settlements（BIS）is considering adding operational risk management measures of computer systems to its regulations. 国際決済銀行（BIS）は現在、コンピュータ・システム運営リスクの管理対策を規制項目に追加する方向で検討している。

BIS requirements　BIS基準, BISの自己資本比率基準
　（=BIS equity standards, BIS standard）
◆After the bank decided to transfer the bad loans to dummy companies to meet the BIS requirements, it established a number of dummy companies. BIS基準達成のためにダミー会社への不良債権飛ばしを決定した後、同行はダミー会社を数

多く設立した。◆The bank may see its capital adequacy ratio fall far short of the BIS requirements. 同行の自己資本比率は、BIS基準に到底達しない可能性がある。

black (名)黒字(the black), 利益, ブラック
  (⇒red)
  be back in the black　黒字転換を果たす
  climb into the black　黒字に転じる, 黒字に転換する
  in the black　黒字で, 儲かって
  keep one's balance in the black　黒字を確保する
  operate in the black　黒字経営する
  return to the black　黒字に戻る, 黒字に転換する, 黒字に転じる
  swing back into the black　黒字に転換する
  turn into the black　黒字に転換する
  ◆Five of the seven major banking groups swung back into the black on a consolidated basis in fiscal 2003. 七つの大手銀行・金融グループのうち5グループが、2003年度（2004年3月期）の連結決算で（前期の赤字から）黒字に転換した。◆Mizuho climbed back into the black, with a net profit of ¥149.8 billion, in the April-June period of 2010. みずほフィナンシャルグループの2010年4〜6月決算は、税引き後利益が1,498億円で黒字に転換した。◆The company was in the black for its first-half account settlement in June. 同社は、6月中間決算は黒字だった。◆The firm's net profits jumped to $900 million, climbing into the black for the first time in three years. 同社の純利益は約9億ドルに急増し、3年ぶりに黒字に転換した。

black (形)黒い, 暗い, 悪い, 悲惨な, 汚れた, 不正な, 闇(やみ)の, ヤミ取引の, ヤミ値の, 望みのない, 悲観的な, 腹黒い, ブラック
  black bourse　ヤミ相場
  black credit market　ヤミ信用市場
  black economy　地下経済, ヤミ経済, 隠し所得, ヤミ売買
  black exchange rate　ヤミ為替相場
  black figure　黒字, 余剰
  black information　信用貸しが危険と思われる人に関して金融機関が持つ情報
  black ink　黒字, 貸方
  black market [mart]　ヤミ市, ヤミ取引, ヤミ市場, アングラ市場, ブラック・マーケット
  black market financing　ヤミ金融
  black market price　ヤミ市場価格, ヤミ値, ヤミ物価, ヤミ相場
  Black Monday　ブラック・マンデー（1987年10月19日（月曜日）に記録したニューヨーク株式市場の株価暴落。⇒stock crisis）
  black money　黒い金, ヤミ所得, 不正所得, ブラック・マネー
  black outlook　暗い見通し
  Black Thursday　暗黒の木曜日（1929年10月24日の木曜日。ニューヨークの株式大暴落が発生し、世界大恐慌の幕開けとなった日）

black-market lending　ヤミ金融
  (=black market financing)
  ◆Bank accounts have become indispensable in crimes such as black-market lending and drug trafficking. 銀行口座は、ヤミ金融や薬物取引などの犯罪の温床になっている。

blank check　金額未記入の白紙小切手, 自由行動権
blank endorsement　白地裏書き（保険証券、手形、船荷証券などの裏書きに行われる）
blank receipt　白紙領収書
  ◆Some utilities companies have even started to issue blank receipts to their customers due to the bank's computer troubles. 同行のコンピュータのトラブルで、顧客に白紙の領収書発行を開始した公益企業もある。

blanket (形)一括の, 一律の, 包括的な, 一斉の, 全面的な
  blanket debt relief　一律の債務削減, 一律の借金棒引き
  blanket policy　包括保険証券
blanket action　一斉摘発
  ◆This is the first time for police to take blanket action against people launching multiple attacks against blogs and Web sites, a type of attack known as "flaming." 「炎上」と呼ばれるブログやサイトなどへの集団攻撃をした者を警察が一斉摘発するのは、今回が始めてだ。
blanket ban on short selling　空売りの全面禁止, 空売りの全面規制
  ◆European regulators had previously played down the idea of a blanket ban on short selling. 欧州の規制当局は、空売りの全面規制という考え方を以前は問題にしていなかった。
blanket protection on bank deposits　銀行預金の全額保証, 銀行預金の全額保護
  ◆In April 2005, the government's blanket protection on bank deposits ended. 2005年4月に、政府の銀行預金全額保証の期間が終了した。

bloat (動)膨(ふく)らます, 増やす, 増加させる
  become bloated　膨らむ, 増加する
  bloat one's market capitalization　時価総額を膨らませる
  bloat the dollar value　ドル価値を高める
  ◆The delisting of Livedoor stocks means a complete end to the group's creative financial strategy of seeking explosive growth by bloating its market capitalization. ライブドア株の上場廃止は、時価総額を膨らませて急成長を求めるという同グループの独創的な財務戦略が、完全に崩れたことを意味する。
bloated (形)膨(ふく)れた, 膨れ上がった, 増大した, 肥大した, 巨大で効率が悪い, 過剰な
  be bloated with pride　威張り腐っている
  become bloated　膨らむ, 膨れ上がる, 増大する
    (⇒handout policies)
  bloated defense budget　国防予算の増大, 膨れ上がった国防予算
  bloated profiteer　悪徳商人
bloated budget　予算の増大, 膨れ上がった予算, 放漫財政
  ◆The fiscal 2010 budget was a typical example of a bloated budget. 2010年度予算は、放漫財政の典型例だった。
bloated inventory　増大した在庫, 過剰在庫, 在庫増
  ◆Ford Motor Co. will temporarily halt production at its assembly plants to reduce bloated inventories. 米フォードは、増大した在庫を削減[圧縮]するため、組立工場での生産を一時中止する。
bloating (名)膨れ上がること, 増大, 膨張, 肥大, 肥大化
  ◆The banking industry thinks that the new law may invite further bloating of postal banking businesses at the expense of the private sector. 新法は民業を圧迫して郵政の銀行業務のさらなる肥大化を招く恐れがある、と金融業界は見ている。

bloc (名)地域, 〜圏, 〜群, 団体, 連盟, 連合, 議員連合, 議員団, ブロック
  bloc investor　大口投資家　(=block investor)
  core bloc　コア通貨
  dollar bloc　ドル地域, ドル・ブロック
    (=dollar area)
  economic bloc　経済圏, 経済ブロック
  free trading bloc　自由貿易地域
  gold [golden] bloc　金本位制地域, 金ブロック
  monetary [currency] bloc　通貨圏, 通貨ブロック
  regional economic bloc　地域経済ブロック, 地域経済圏
  sterling bloc　ポンド地域
  the single-currency bloc　単一通貨・ユーロ圏
  yen (currency) bloc　円ブロック

◆In the Great Depression that began in the United States, each country raised tariffs and tried to divide the world economy into blocs, which deepened the crisis. 米国で始まった世界大恐慌では、各国が関税引上げやブロック経済化に走り、それによって危機が深刻化した。◆The fiscal woes of the single-currency bloc could trigger a new severe global financial crisis. 単一通貨・ユーロ圏の財政危機は、新たに重大な世界的金融危機の発生源になる可能性がある。

block (動)閉鎖する、封鎖する、凍結する、遮断(しゃだん)する、止める、〜の流れを止める、阻(はば)む、阻止する、防ぐ、妨げる、妨害する、ブロックする
　　◆U.S. President Barack Obama vowed to block AIG from handing its executives $165 million in bonuses after taking billions in federal aid. オバマ米大統領は、AIG(米政府の管理下で経営再建中の米保険大手)に対して、数十億ドルの連邦支援を受けた後、経営幹部への1億6,500万ドルのボーナス支払い[ボーナス支給]を止めさせることを明言した。

block (名)大量の有価証券、(年金などの)商品、塊、(株券の)取引単位、ブロック　(形)大量の、大口の、一括の
　　a block of shares　1取引単位の株式
　　a block of 10,000 shares　1万株単位
　　annuity block　年金商品
　　block grants　包括補助金、定額交付金、定額助成金、ブロック交付金
　　block house　大口注文を取り扱う証券会社
　　block insurance　包括保険
　　block investor　大口投資家　(=bloc investor)
　　block offer　一括売出し、ブロック・オファー
　　block order　大口注文
　　block policy　一括担保保険契約、一括担保保険証券
　　block purchase　ブロック買い
　　block trade [trading]　(一般に1万株以上の)大口取引、大量取引、ブロック・トレード
　　block trader　ブロック・トレーダー
　　place a block order　大口注文を出す
　　◆A sudden plunge in the market is believed to have been caused by a trader who mistyped an order to sell a large block of shares. 相場急落は、トレーダーによる大量の株式売買の誤発注により生じたと見られる。◆The company's board approved a plan to issue subscription warrants to all shareholders on its shareholders list as of March 31, 2012. 同社の取締役会は、2012年3月31日現在[時点]の株主名簿に記載されている全株主を対象に、新株予約権を発行する計画を承認した。◆Through Tachibana Securities Co., an overseas investment fund acquired a large block of the firm's shares on margin. 立花証券を通じて、海外投資ファンドが信用取引で大量の同社株を取得した。

block sale　大量販売、大量売却、大量売付け、ブロック売り
　　◆The U.S. government's block sale shares netted about $6.2 billion. 米政府の大量売却株での資金調達額は、約62億ドルだった。

blow (名)打撃、衝撃、ショック
　　deal a blow to　〜に打撃を与える、〜に難問を抱えさせる
　　deal a heavy blow to　〜に大きな打撃を与える、〜が大きな打撃を受ける
　　deliver a bitter blow to　〜に大きな打撃を与える
　　strike a blow against　〜のために反対する、〜に反抗する、〜を断罪する
　　strike a blow for　〜のために努力する、〜に加勢する
　　◆Greece's default on the national debts would be a blow to the operation of financial institutions in France and Germany that hold Greek government bonds. ギリシャが国債の債務不履行に陥った場合、ギリシャ国債を保有するフランスやドイツなどの金融機関の経営は、打撃を受けるだろう。◆Overseas economic growth will slow, which could deal a blow to exports. 今後は海外の経済成長率が鈍化して、輸出に打撃を与える可能性がある。◆The yen's extremely rapid appreciation may deliver a bitter blow to the domestic economy. 超円高は、国内経済に大きな打撃を与える可能性がある。

blue chip (名)優良株、優良安定株、一流株、一流花形株、主要銘柄、優良企業、優良事業、優れた物、一流品、値打ちのある物、ブルー・チップ
　　◆The blue chips fell as much as 149 points to near the 7,000 mark in February 2009. 2009年2月の主要銘柄は、149ドル下落して7,000ドルに近い水準にまで達した。

blue-chip [blue chip] (形)優良な、優れた、一流の、優秀な、値打ちのある、好評な、花形の
　　blue chip borrower　優良借り手
　　blue chip exporter　国際優良株
　　blue-chip industrial companies　一流企業
　　blue-chip issues　優良銘柄、優良企業の銘柄　(=blue-chip stocks)
　　blue chip rate　(一流企業への)最優遇貸出金利
　　blue chip share [stock]　花形株、値ガサ株、優良株、優良銘柄
　　blue chip swap　ブルーチップ・スワップ

blue-chip company [corporation, firm]　優良企業
　　◆Even blue-chip companies—the engine of the national economy—have been forced to drastically cut their workforces due to the slowdown in information technology-related business and price-cutting competition driven by deflationary forces. 日本経済を引っ張ってきた優良企業でも、IT(情報技術)不況やデフレによる値下げ競争の影響で、大幅な人員削減を迫られている。◆Six NYSE-listed blue-chip companies agreed to dual-list on Nasdaq and NYSE. ニューヨーク証券取引所に上場している優良企業6社が、ナスダック(米店頭株式市場)とNYSEへの重複上場に合意した。◆The wrongdoing of Olympus Corp., a blue-chip company that holds the largest share of the global endoscope market, has eroded international faith in corporate Japan. 内視鏡の市場シェアで世界トップのオリンパスの不正行為で、日本企業の国際的な信頼は失墜している。

blue-chip subsidiary　優良子会社
　　◆The ministry proposes setting up a special company to take over the operation of blue-chip subsidiaries. 同省は、優良な子会社の経営を引き継ぐ特殊会社の設立案を提示した。

Blue Cross　米健康保険組合、ブルー・クロス保険組合(被雇用者とその家族を対象とした健康保険組合で入院費の支払いを行う)

blue note　当座借証

Blue Shield　医療保険組合、ブルー・シールド保険組合(職場での団体加入を中心とした非営利の健康保険組合。主に治療費、手術費、出産費などの支払いを行う)

blue sky law　不正証券取引禁止法、不正証券取引取締法、青空法、ブルー・スカイ法

board (名)取締役会(the board of directors)、重役会、理事会、審議会、委員会、会議、省・庁・局・部、掲示板、ボード
　　chairman of the board　取締役会会長
　　　(=chairman of board of directors)
　　Chicago Board of Trade　シカゴ商品取引所
　　executive board　重役会、常務会、理事会、執行委員会
　　Federal Home Loan Bank Board　米連邦住宅貸付け銀行理事会
　　Federal Housing Finance Board　米連邦住宅金融理事会
　　Federal Reserve Board　米連邦準備制度理事会、FRB
　　Financial Accounting Standards Board　財務会計基準審議会

go on the board　上場する
independent oversight board　独立監視委員会
management board　取締役会, 重役会
managing board　運営委員会, 運営理事会
Policy Board of the Bank of Japan　日銀政策委員会
Public Works Loan Board　英国の公共事業資金貸付委員会
Reserve Bank's board meeting　米連邦準備銀行理事会
second board companies　二部上場企業
Securities and Investments Board　英国の証券投資委員会
supervisory board　監査役会
U.S.-style board structure　米国型の取締役会制度
◆DaimlerChrysler's decision to end financial support came at an extraordinary meeting of the company's supervisory and management boards. ダイムラー・クライスラーの金融支援打切りの決定は、同社の臨時監査役・取締役会［監査役会と取締役会の臨時総会］で行われた。

board director　取締役　(=board member)
◆Livedoor plans to buy a majority of shares in Nippon Broadcasting System Inc. (NBS) and to change all the board directors at NBS. ライブドアは、ニッポン放送株の過半数を買い占め、ニッポン放送の取締役を一新する計画だ。

board meeting　取締役会会議, 取締役会, 役員会, 評議員会
◆During a regular board meeting, Fuji TV directors agreed to file a claim against Livedoor for losses of more than ¥30 billion incurred from selling off Livedoor shares. 定例取締役会で、フジテレビの役員は、ライブドア株の売却で被った300億円超の損失について、ライブドアに損害賠償を請求することで合意した。

board member　取締役, 理事
(⇒capital management capabilities)
◆A board member of Germany's federal bank was dismissed for repeating racist remarks about Muslim immigrants and Jews. ドイツ連邦銀行の理事が、イスラム教徒移民やユダヤ人に対する人種差別発言を繰り返して、解任された。◆Shareholders can access the company's special Web site and vote on decisions, including the election of board members. 株主は、同社専用のホームページを利用して、取締役選任などの議決に投票することができる。

Board of Audit　会計検査院
◆The Board of Audit has confirmed that the public financing package extended with a government-backed guarantee to JAL prior to its failure cost taxpayers a total of ¥47 billion. 日航の破たん前に政府保証付きで行われた公的融資の総国民負担額は470億円であることを、会計検査院が確定した。◆The Board of Audit intends to include the total taxpayer contribution to JAL in its audit account report compiled in November 2011. 会計検査院は、2011年11月にまとめる決算検査報告書に、日航に対する総国民負担額を盛り込む方針だ。

Board of Banking Supervision　(英国の)銀行監督評議会

board of directors　会社の取締役会, 役員会, 重役会, 財団などの理事会, BOD
extraordinary meeting of the board of directors　臨時取締役会
regular meeting of the board of directors　定例取締役会
◆In order to dominate management of its clients, the bank pressed its clients to have a majority of seats on their board of directors occupied by people the bank recommended. 融資先の経営を支配するため、同行は融資先に対して、同行が推薦する人物を過半数の取締役に就けるよう迫った。◆Regular meetings of the board of directors shall be held quarterly at the office of the new company or at such other place as the board may designate. 取締役会の定例会議は、新会社の事務所または取締役会が指定する他の場所で四半期ごとに開催する。◆Suzuki Motor's board of directors decided to dissolve its partnership and cross-shareholding relationship with Volkswagen AG. スズキの取締役会は、独フォルクスワーゲンとの提携と株式持ち合い関係の解消を決めた。◆The bank tried to dominate the management of its clients by sending a majority of people to their board of directors. 同行は、融資先の取締役会に過半数の取締役を送り込んで、融資先の経営の支配を図った。◆The IMF's new financing scheme is expected to be agreed on at the Group of 20 summit meeting and will be launched after being approved by the IMF's board of directors. 国際通貨基金（IMF）の新融資制度は、主要20か国・地域（G20）サミット（首脳会議）で合意する見込みで、その後IMF理事会の承認を経てスタートする。

解説 取締役会とは：アメリカの会社の場合、取締役会は会社経営の最高意思決定機関で、株主総会で選任された取締役数名で構成される。会社役員（corporate officer）の選任、株式の発行、配当宣言などについての決定権がある。また、社内取締役（inside director）と社外取締役（outside director）を含めて取締役（director）は株主が選任し、役員は取締役が選任することになっている。

board of directors' meeting　取締役会　(=board meeting, board of directors meeting, meeting of the board of directors)
◆The Commercial Code requires companies to hold board of directors' meeting at least once three every months. 会社の取締役会は最低でも3か月に1回開くことが、商法で義務付けられている。

Board of Governors of the Federal Reserve System　連邦準備制度理事会, 連邦準備理事会

boardroom　(名)証券取引所の立会場, 立会所, 役員室, 会議室
◆Acts of terrorism against investors has been committed in corporate boardrooms. 企業の役員室では、投資家に対するテロ行為が行われている。

body　(名)組織, 機構, 法人, 会社, 団体, 協議会, 委員会, 当局
body corporate　法人
corporate turnaround body　企業再生支援機構
federal bodies　連邦機関
governing and oversight body　統制監督制度
government body　政府機関
regulatory body　規制機関, 監督機関, 規制当局
standing body　常設機関
supervisory body　監督機関
◆JAL's stocks may lose market value to zero if the corporate turnaround body cuts the shares 100 percent by delisting JAL from the Tokyo stock market. 企業再生支援機構が東京株式市場から日航の上場を廃止して日航株を100％減資したら、日航株の市場価値はゼロになる可能性がある。

bogus　(形)偽の, 虚偽の, 粉飾の, 模造の, 模倣の, 架空の　(=fake, fraudulent)
bogus business trip　カラ出張
　(=fraudulent business trip)
bogus product　模倣品, 模造品, コピー商品
◆The account holder could not be contacted as the phone number was bogus. 偽の電話番号なので、口座名義人と連絡が取れなかった。

bogus card　偽造カード
(⇒damage名詞, insurance)
◆Customers whose assets at the bank total about ¥10 million will receive a maximum of ¥2 million in insurance if their money is withdrawn illicitly by a third party with a bogus card. 同行では、預け入れ資産が1,000万円程度の預金者が、第三者に偽造カードを使って不正に預金が引き出された場

bogus cash card　偽造キャッシュ・カード, 偽造カード（=bogus card; ⇒biometric integrated circuit card）
◆The total amount withdrawn from bank accounts with bogus cash cards in six months from April was ¥461 million. 偽造キャッシュ・カードを使って銀行口座から引き出された預金の被害総額は、4月から半年間で4億6,100万円にもなる。

bogus company name　架空の会社名義
◆The man earned ¥10 million by having fees remitted to a bank account he had opened under a bogus company name. この男は、架空の会社名義で開設した銀行口座に料金を振り込ませて、1,000万円を得ていた。

bogus earnings　虚偽の収益, 収益の粉飾額, 粉飾額
◆About ¥10 million in bogus earnings were reported in fiscal 2010. 2010年度は、約1,000万円の粉飾額が計上された。

bogus letter　ウソの文書
◆Bogus letters have been sent to pension beneficiaries, demanding they return excess benefit payments. 最近、年金過払い額の返還を求めるウソの文書が、年金受給者に送りつけられている。

BOJ [BoJ]　日本銀行, 日銀（Bank of Japanの略）
◆The BOJ could take additional monetary relaxation measures if there are any changes in the financial situation. 金融面で動きがあるとすれば、日銀が追加の金融緩和策を実施する可能性もある。◆The BOJ decided to ease its monetary grip further by effectively restoring its zero-interest-rate policy. 日銀は、実質的にゼロ金利政策を復活させて、追加の金融緩和を決めた。◆The BOJ decided to further relax its monetary policy by injecting an additional ¥10 trillion into a fund aimed at purchasing government bonds and corporate debentures. 日銀は、国債や社債などを買い入れるための基金に新たに10兆円を注入[投入]して追加の金融緩和に踏み切ることを決めた。◆The BOJ decided to introduce a new open market operation by supplying ¥10 trillion to private financial institutions in three month loans at an ultralow annual interest of 0.1 percent. 日銀は、民間の金融機関に年0.1％の超低金利で貸付期間3か月の資金を10兆円供給する新型の公開市場操作（オペ）の導入に踏み切った。◆The BOJ lifted its zero-interest rate policy on the strength of its optimistic view on the outlook for the economy in the summer of 2000. 日銀は2000年夏、景気の先行きを楽観してゼロ金利政策を解除した。◆The BOJ's policy meeting is expected to consider taking additional monetary easing steps. 日銀の政策決定会合では、追加の金融緩和策の実施を検討する見通しだ。

bold　（形）大胆な, 思い切った, 際立った, 目立つ
◆The government should not hesitate to intervene in the currency market through bold yen-selling and dollar-buying operations. 政府は、為替市場への大胆な円売り・ドル買い介入をためらうべきではない。

bolster　（動）促進する,（売上などを）伸ばす, 地位などを向上させる, 立場を強める, 強化する, 経済を増強する, 景気を浮揚する, ドルなどを支える, 支持する, 補強する, 救済する, 正当性を理由づける
　bolster competitiveness　競争力をつける
　bolster one's financial standing　財務を強化する
　bolster profitability　収益性を高める
　bolster the dollar　ドルを支える
　bolster the economic recovery　景気回復を下支えする
　bolster the economy　景気を浮揚させる, 景気を下支えする
　bolster the long-suffering housing market　長期低迷の住宅市場を活性化させる
　measures to bolster the economy　景気浮揚策, 景気対策
◆A U.S. Federal Reserve Board snapshot of economic conditions bolsters the hope of broader-based recovery. 米連邦準備制度理事会（FRB）の景況報告では、ほとんどの地域で景気持ち直しの期待が強まっている。◆Acting in an emergency conference call, the U.S. Federal Reserve moved to bolster the flagging economy by cutting interest rates by half a point. 緊急電話会議を開いて、連邦準備制度理事会（FRB）は、景気減速に歯止めをかけるため金利を0.5％引き下げることを決めた。◆As part of the plan to bolster its financial standing, the struggling life insurer will seek capital injection of about 100 billion yen from financial institutions. 財務強化策の一環として、経営再建中のこの生命保険会社は、金融機関に1,000億円程度の基金拠出（基金増資）を要請する方針だ。◆European banks should have bolstered their capital bases when the sovereign debt crisis broke out in the peripheral countries in 2010. 2010年に周辺国で財政危機が発生した際、欧州の銀行は資本基盤［自己資本］を強化すべきであった。◆Exports played a leading role in bolstering the economy in the initial phase of its recovery. 景気回復の初期の段階で、輸出が景気浮揚の牽引役を果たした。◆Japanese banks must bolster their core capital ratios. 邦銀は、自己資本比率の充実に取り組む必要がある。

bolt　（動）逃げ出す, 飛び出す, 急増する, 急上昇する, 離党［脱党］する, 脱会する, 脱退する, 欠席する,（主義や主張を）変える, 口走る, うっかりしゃべる
◆The U.S. jobless rate bolted to 7.2 percent in December 2008, the highest level in 16 years. 米国の2008年12月の失業率は、7.2％に急上昇して、16年ぶり（1993年1月の7.3％以来）の高水準に達した。

bond　（名）債券, 社債, 公社債, 債務証書, 借用証書, 保証証書, 支払い保証契約, 保証, 保証金, 保釈金（⇒corporate bond, day trader, government bond, investment portfolio, yuan-based bond）
　accrued bond interest to date of sale　外部発行時までの社債経過利息
　active bond　利付き債券
　blank bond　無記名債券
　bond anticipation note　債券先行証券, BAN
　bond conversion　社債転換, 社債の転換, 転換社債の株式への転換
　bond discounts　社債発行差金, 社債発行割引差金, 社債割引料（社債の発行価額（売買価格）と額面金額（額面価格）との差額）
　bond flotation market　起債市場
　bond house　債券専門の証券会社, ボンド・ハウス［ボンドハウス］
　bond investment trust　公社債投信
　bond issue expenses　社債発行費, 債券発行費（=bond issue costs）
　bond issued at a discount　割引発行された社債（社債の発行価額（売買価格）が額面金額（額面価格）より低い社債）
　bond issued at a premium　プレミアム発行された社債, プレミアム発行された債券, 打ち歩（うちぶ）発行された社債（社債の発行価額（売買価格）が額面金額（額面価格）より高い社債）
　bond market for financial institutions　金融機関債券市場
　bond outstanding　債券発行残高, 発行済み社債, 未償還債券, 流通社債
　bond payable　未償還社債, 社債（=bonds payable）
　bond payable subscribed　引受済み社債
　bond power　債券譲渡証書
　bond premium　社債発行差金, 社債発行割増金, 社債割増金, 社債プレミアム, 打ち歩（うちぶ）料（社債の発行価額（売買価格）が額面金額（額面価格）を上回ったときの差額）
　bond purchase　債券購入, 国債買入れ

(⇒bond buying, loan rate)
bond sinking fund　減債基金（社債償還のために積み立てた資産）
bond subscription receivable　未払込み社債
bond trading　債券取引,債券売買取引,債券トレーディング
bond unissued　未発行社債
bond unit trust　単位型債券投資信託
bond with interest coupon　利付き債券
bond with stock purchase warrant　株式買取り権付き社債,新株引受権付き社債,ワラント債
bond with warrants　新株引受権付き社債,ワラント付き社債,ワラント債
bonds convertible at market prices　時価転換社債
bonds for improving educational and welfare facilities　教育福祉施設等整備事業債
bonds with detachable warrants　分離型新株引受権付き社債
collateral bond　担保付き社債
collateral for bonds　社債の担保
collateral trust bond　担保信託社債
consolidated bond　整理社債
construction bond　建設国債
convertible bond　転換社債
corporate bond　社債
debenture bond　無担保社債
discount bond　割引発行債,割引債
discount on bonds payable　社債発行差金
　（=premium on bonds payable）
Euro bond　ユーロ債
face value of bonds　社債額面
foreign bond　外債,外国債券
general waste disposal bonds　一般廃棄物処理事業債
government bond　国債,政府債
government-guaranteed bond　政府保証債
high yield bond　高利回り債
interest bearing bond　利付き債
issue of bonds　社債発行,社債の発行
　（=issuance of bonds）
local government bond　地方債
long bonds（the）　米国30年債
Metropolitan areas construction bonds　首都圏建設事業債
mortgage bond　担保付き社債
municipal bond　市債,地方債
participating bond　利益参加社債
passive bond　無利子債券
power bond　電力債
premium on bonds payable　社債発行差金
private placement bond　私募債
public bond　公債
public welfare facilities improvement bonds　厚生福祉施設整備事業債
registered bond　登録債
serial bond　連続社債
special tax bond　特定財源債
straight bond　確定利付き社債,普通社債
tax exempt bond　免税債
time bond　定期社債
Treasury bonds　米国債
U.S. longer-term bond　米国の長期国債
zero coupon bond　ゼロクーポン債（割引債の一種）

◆Many of these banks invest a majority of their funds in bonds rather than stocks. これらの銀行の多くは、その資金の大半を株式ではなく債券で運用している。◆On June 10, 2011, individuals holding $50,000 face value of the Corporation's bonds exercised their conversion privilege. 2011年6月10日、当社の社債権者が、額面5万ドル分の転換権を行使した［額面5万ドル分の株式への転換を行った］。◆One way for a company to accomplish long-term financing is through the issuance of long-term debt instruments in the form of bonds. 会社の長期資金調達方法の一つは、社債の形で長期債務証券を発行して行われる。◆S&P may cut the credit rating of bonds issued by the European Financial Stability Facility (EFSF). スタンダード・アンド・プアーズ(S&P)は、欧州金融安定基金（EFSF）が発行する債券の格付け［信用格付け］を引き下げる可能性がある。◆The bonds of six eurozone countries such as Germany and France are rated AAA by S&P's credit ratings on them. 独仏などユーロ圏6か国の国債は、スタンダード・アンド・プアーズ(S&P)の格付け［信用格付け］でトリプルAに格付けされている。◆The 8% convertible bonds are convertible into 40 shares of common stock for each $1,000 bond, and were not considered common stock equivalents at the date of issuance. 8%利付き転換社債は、1,000ドルの社債についてそれぞれ普通株式40株に転換できるが、発行時には準普通株式とは考えられなかった。◆The European Central Bank needs to provide support to Italy by proactively buying Italian bonds. 欧州中央銀行(ECB)は今後、イタリア国債を積極的に買い入れてイタリアを支援する必要がある。◆The Fed's program of buying $600 billion in Treasury bonds to help the economy is to end in June 2011 on schedule. 景気を支えるために6,000億ドルの国債を買い入れる米連邦準備制度理事会(FRB)の量的緩和政策は、予定通り2011年6月に終了する。

bond buying　債券買入れ,債券購入,国債買入れ
　（=bond purchase）

◆The U.S. Fed's $600 billion bond buying to support the economy will end in June 2011 on schedule. 景気を支えるための米連邦準備制度理事会(FRB)の6,000億ドルの国債買入れは、予定通り2011年6月で終了する。

bond holder　社債権者,社債保有者,債券保有者
　（=bondholder; ⇒delisting）

◆Dividend payments to bond holders have been financed by the rent paid by Mycal to the special purpose company (SPC). 社債保有者に支払う配当金の原資は、マイカルが特定目的会社に支払う店舗の家賃だ。

bond holdings　債券保有,債券所有,保有債券

◆Compared with the latent gains in the bank-held stocks, the latent losses involving the banks' bond holdings were far smaller, with the net gains in the latent value of all securities holdings of the banks reaching an estimated ¥1.4 trillion in the September settlement of accounts. 銀行保有株式の含み益に比べて、銀行保有債券の含み損のほうがはるかに小さいため、9月中間決算での銀行が保有する有価証券全体の含み益は1兆4,000億円（推定値）に達する。

bond index　債券指数,債券インデックス
　bond index fund　債券インデックス・ファンド

bond insurer　金融保証専門会社,金融保証会社,米国のモノライン　（債券など金融商品の保証を専門に行う米国の保険会社。⇒monoline）

◆Bond insurers write policies that promise to cover payments to bondholders if the entity that issued the bonds defaults. 金融保証会社［債券保険会社］は、債券発行体がデフォルト（債務不履行）になった場合に、債券保有者への（元本と利息の）支払い補償を約束する保険を引き受けている。◆Standard & Poor's kept its rating on the two bond insurers of MBIA Inc. and Ambac Financial Group Inc. スタンダード＆プアーズは、MBIAとアムバック・ファイナンシャル・グループ(AMBAC)のモノライン（金融保証会社）2社の格付けを、据え置いた。

bond issuance 社債発行, 債券発行, 国債発行［発行額］
（=bond issue）
◆In order to reduce the government's bond issuance, spending must be reined in as much as possible. 政府の国債発行額を減らすには、できるだけ歳出を抑制する必要がある。◆The most pressing task for the government will be to reduce its bond issuance. 政府の最緊急課題は、政府の国債発行額の削減だ。

bond issue 社債発行, 債券発行
（=bond issuance; ⇒roadshow）
◆The bond issue was sold between interest dates at a discount. この社債は、利息支払い日の中途で割引により外部に発行された。◆The supermarket chain managed to raise ¥138.5 billion from the bond issue to finance its restructuring. この大手スーパーは、社債発行で1,385億円を調達して、リストラの資金に充てた。

bond manager 債券運用者, 債券管理者, 債券運用担当者, 債券管理担当者, ボンド・マネージャー
◆The French financial group has Europe's largest team of bond managers. このフランスの金融グループは、ヨーロッパ最大級の債券運用チームを抱えている。

bond market 債券市場, 公社債市場, 債券相場
◆On the bond market, the yield on newly issued 10-year government bonds, an indicator of long-term interest rates, fell, resulting in a rise in bond prices. 債券市場では、長期金利の指標である新発10年物国債の利回り（流通利回り）が下落し、債券相場［債券価格］は上昇した。◆The European bond market is truly in a knife-edge situation as the yield on 10-year Italian government bonds has surged above 7 percent, the so-called danger zone that may result in a debt crisis. 10年物イタリア国債の流通利回りが、債務危機に陥る「危険水域」とされる7％超に上昇したため、欧州債券市場は予断を許さない状況にある。

bond market rally 債券相場の上昇, 債券市場の上げ相場
◆Stock and bond market rallies came to a halt. 株式市場と債券市場の上げ相場は、一服した。

bond market turbulence 債券市場の混乱, 公社債市場の混乱 （⇒fund procurement activities）
◆Corporate debt issues are recovering as bond market turbulence in the aftermath of the March 11 Great East Japan Earthquake has subsided. 2011年3月11日の東日本大震災直後の債券市場の混乱が収束したため、社債の発行額が回復している。

bond price 債券価格, 債券相場
a rise in bond prices 債券相場の上昇, 債券価格の上昇
an increase in bond prices 債券相場の上昇, 債券価格の上昇
the drops in bond prices in the past half a year 過去半年の債券価格の下落
◆An increase in bond prices means lower interest rates. 債券価格の上昇は、金利の低下を意味する。◆French bond prices slipped as French banks possess a large volume of Greek and Italian bonds. フランス銀行がギリシャやイタリアなどの国債を保有しているため、フランス国債が値下がりした。◆On the bond market, the yield on newly issued 10-year government bonds, an indicator of long-term interest rates, fell, resulting in a rise in bond prices. 債券市場では、長期金利の指標である新発10年物国債の利回り（流通利回り）が下落し、債券相場［債券価格］は上昇した。◆The drops in bond prices in the past half a year have dealt these banks a heavy blow. 過去半年の債券価格の下落で、これらの銀行は大打撃を受けている。

bond redemption 社債償還, 発行済み社債の買戻し, 国債（government bond）の償還
（=redemption of bonds）
◆The two airlines plan to use the loans mainly to finance their planned capital investment and bond redemptions. 両航空会社は、主に予定している設備投資や社債償還の資金に充てるため、この借入金を使う予定だ。

bond redemption burden 社債償還の負担, 国債償還の負担
◆The heavier the bond redemption burden, the larger the tax hikes will be. 国債償還の負担が重いほど、増税の幅も大きくなる。

bond sales by firms 企業の債券発行
◆Credit markets are beginning to thaw as bond sales by firms are on the increase. 企業の債券発行が増えているため、発行市場は雪解けムードが見られる。

bond yield 債券利回り, 長期国債利回り, 長期債利回り
bond yield adjusted equilibrium 債券利回り調整後の均衡レート
bond yield in the possession on period 所有期間利回り
bond yield rise 債券利回りの上昇
government bond yield 国債利回り
long-bond yield 長期債利回り
（=long-term bond yield）
nominal bond yield 債券名目利回り
◆The 10-year bond yield of Spain has likewise neared the 7 percent level, the danger zone that may fall into a debt crisis. スペインの10年物国債利回り［国債流通利回り］も、債務危機に陥る恐れがある危険水域の7％台に迫った。◆U.S. long-term bond yields have moved up from 4.2 percent to 5 percent despite the Federal Reserve having cut short-term interest rates 11 times in 2001. 米連邦準備制度理事会（FRB）が2001年に短期金利を11回切り下げたにもかかわらず、米国の長期国債の利回りは4.2％から5％に上昇した。

bondholder 債券保有者
（=bond holder; ⇒limited）
junior bondholder 後順位の社債権者
meeting of bondholders 債権者集会, 社債権者集会
private bondholders 民間の債券保有者, 民間投資家, 民間債権者（private creditors）
senior bondholder 先順位の社債権者
◆Athens is likely to officially launch talks with banks and other private bondholders for the debt write-down. ギリシャ政府は、銀行などの民間債権者［民間投資家、民間の債券保有者］と債務削減のための協議を開始する見込みだ。◆Bond insurers write policies that promise to cover payments to bondholders if the entity that issued the bonds defaults. 金融保証会社［債券保険会社］は、債券発行体がデフォルト（債務不履行）になった場合に、債券保有者への（元本と利息の）支払い補償を約束する保険を引き受けている。◆The €110 billion bailout for Greece by the EU and the IMF will ensure the redemption of Greek government bonds at maturity for private bondholders. 欧州連合（EU）と国際通貨基金（IMF）のギリシャに対する1,100億ユーロの支援で、民間の債券保有者は、満期の来たギリシャ国債の償還を保証されることになった。

bonus （名）手当て, 賞与, 特別配当, 助成金, ボーナス
bonus dividend 特別配当 （=capital dividend）
bonus issue 特別発行, 無償新株発行, 無償増資, 特別配当株の発行
bonus share［stock］ 特別配当株, 無償株式, ボーナス株, 景品株
bonus system 報奨制度
bonus to directors 役員賞与
◆The executive pay of Merrill Lynch & Co., mostly in bonuses, has become a hot-button issue in the recession as banks and companies fail. メリルリンチの経営幹部報酬は、大半がボーナスだが、銀行や企業が経営破たんする不況時の強い関心を呼ぶ問題になっている。◆U.S. President Obama called AIG reckless and greedy during his blistering attack on the bonuses of the firm's executives. オバマ米大統領は、

米保険大手AIGの幹部ボーナスへの痛烈な批判で、同社を「向こう見ずで貪欲(どんよく)な企業」と言った。

bonus return 保険料割戻し

book (動)計上する、会計処理する、帳簿に載せる、記入する、記帳する、記録する (⇒discontinued business, investment environment)
◆In the first half, the firm booked a special profit of about ￥400 billion on debt waivers by its key lenders. 上半期に同社は、主要金融機関の債務免除[債権放棄]で、約4,000億円の特別利益を計上した。◆Mizuho Financial Group Inc. booked a pretax profit of ￥211.6 billion in the April-June period of 2010, a turnaround from a loss of ￥15.2 billion a year earlier. みずほフィナンシャルグループの2010年4～6月期決算は、税引き前利益が2,116億円で、前年同期の152億円の赤字から業績が改善した。◆The company booked as a loss the total face value of the irrevocable loans. 同社は、不良債権の額面総額を、損金として計上した。◆The security firm expects to book about ￥73 billion in losses related to its residential mortgage-backed securities business in the July-September quarter. 同証券会社は、7-9月期に住宅融資証券事業の関連損失として730億円を計上する見通しだ。

book (名)帳面、～帳、従業員などの名簿、帳簿、会計簿 (⇒account book, bankbook, beige book, cardholder)
　blue book ブルー・ブック (米連邦準備理事会(FRB)とニューヨーク連邦準備銀行(Federal Reserve Bank of New York)が作成して、連邦公開市場委員会(FOMC)の会議資料となる金融情勢の判断資料)
　check book 小切手帳
　closing of books 決算 (=closing of accounts)
　deposit book 預金通帳
　green book グリーン・ブック (米連邦準備理事会(FRB)のスタッフが作成して、連邦公開市場委員会(FOMC)の会議資料となる経済見通し)
　keep books 帳簿をつける、簿記をつける
　tan book 米地区連銀経済報告、ベージュ・ブック (=beige book)
　yield book 利回り表

book building 購入予約、購入予約受付け、注文受付け、需要積上げ、需要動向把握、投資家の需要調査、ブックビルディング (=bookbuilding:「ブックビルディング」は、株式や債券などの新規発行や売出しの際、機関投資家などの意見をもとに投資家の需要を見ながら市場動向に見合った発行・売出額や価格を決定する方式。「需要予測方式」とも呼ばれている)
◆Book building for the share sale will start Feb. 27. 株式発行の購入予約受付けは、2月27日にスタートする。

book income 帳簿上の利益
◆The disparity between book income and taxable income is attributable to timing differences. 帳簿上の利益と課税所得との差は、期間差異に起因している。

book of demand 証券購入の仮需要、ブック (ブックビルディングでの投資家の仮需要の高さ。⇒book building)

book runner ブック・ランナー (=bookrunner: シンジケート・ローンなどの国際金融取引で参加銀行の募集事務を行う幹事銀行)
　equity book runner 株式引受幹事会社
　joint book runner 共同ブック・ランナー

book value 簿価、帳簿価額、帳簿上の価格、純資産額、取得価格 (=book price)
　adjusted book value method 修正純資産方式 (バランス・シートの資産と負債を時価に換算して純資産を計算する方法)
　asset book value 資産簿価、資産の簿価
　below book value 取得価格を下回る
　effective book value 実質簿価
　price book-value ratio 株価純資産倍率
◆Bad loans should be bought at market value rather than at effective book value. 不良債権は、実質簿価でなく時価で買い取るべきだ。◆The fund has since invested in nonperforming loans worth about ￥6 trillion in book value. 同ファンドは、これまで不良債権に約6兆円(簿価)投資している。◆The government holds a 53.4 percent stake in Tokyo Metro Co., which was valued at ￥174.9 billion at book value as of the end of March 2010. 国は東京地下鉄(東京メトロ)の株式の53.4%を保有しており、その簿価での評価額は2010年3月末時点で1,749億円になる。◆The rule of asset impairment accounting requires companies to post valuation losses on fixed assets whose market value has fallen sharply from their book value. 減損会計基準は、固定資産の時価が簿価から大幅に下落した場合の固定資産の評価損の計上を、企業に義務付けている。

book value method 簿価法
◆Under the book value method, the carrying value of the convertible bonds at the date of the conversion would be used to account for the conversion. 簿価法では、転換時の転換社債の簿価が、転換の会計処理に使われる。

book value of the assets 資産の簿価
◆The company's financial statements are not based on the book value of the assets at time they were obtained. 同社の財務諸表は、取得時の資産の簿価を基準としていない。

book value per share 1株当たり純資産、1株当たり純資産額、1株当たり簿価、BPS (企業の純資産を発行済み株式数で割った指数。BPSの数値が高いほど、企業の安定性も高いといわれる)
◆Book value per share refers to the amount of net assets of a company represented by one share of common stock. 1株当たり純資産[簿価]とは、普通株式1株当たりの企業の純資産額のことを言う。

booking (名)帳簿記入、記帳、計上、会計処理
◆The major banking groups ended up posting a combined loss of more than ￥3 trillion mainly from the booking of large-margin declines in the value of their equity holdings as appraisal losses due to recent declines in the values of shares. 大手銀行グループは、主に最近の株価下落による保有株の減損処理などで、最終的に合計で3兆円超にのぼる損失を計上した。

boom (動)急に沸く、急に景気づく、好況になる、急騰する、高騰する、急増する、上昇する、大発展する、急速に繁栄する、急速に経済成長する、鳴り響く、～の人気をあおる、～を景気づかせる
　booming economy 好景気
　booming market 好景気市況、ブームに沸く市場
　booming prices 急騰[高騰]している物価、物価急騰[高騰]
　booming stock market 株式市場の活況
　long-booming emerging economies 長いこと好調の新興国
◆Markets in up-and-coming countries with booming economies are growing rapidly. 好景気の新興国市場は、急成長している。

boom (名)急騰、高騰、急成長、急拡大、急増、景気、好景気、好況、急開発、大流行、ブーム (⇒business boom)
　boom and bust 好不況、景気と不景気
　boom-and-bust にわか景気
　boom-bust credit cycle 信用の緩和とひっ迫のサイクル
　boom-bust dividing line 景気不景気分割線、景気判断の分かれ目 (=boom-or-bust line)
　boom caused by a strong yen 円高景気 (=strong yen-caused boom)

boom period [years]　好況期, ブームの時代
boom town　新興都市, 人口急成長の町
borrowed [false] boom　カラ景気
building [construction] boom　建設ブーム
capital spending boom　設備投資ブーム
condominiums boom　マンション・ブーム
consumer boom　消費景気
consumption boom　消費景気, 消費ブーム
　(=spending boom)
credit boom　借入れブーム
economic boom　好景気, 経済的好況, 経済の活況
equity boom　株式ブーム
export boom　輸出の急拡大
housing boom　住宅建設ブーム
inflation boom　インフレ景気
investment boom　投資景気, 投資ブーム
IT stock boom　IT株ブーム
junk boom　ジャンク債ブーム
property boom　不動産ブーム
quantitative boom　数量景気
secular boom　長期的好況
strong yen-caused boom　円高景気
takeover boom　企業買収ブーム, 買収ブーム
technology boom　ハイテク・ブーム
temporary boom　にわか景気, 中間景気
the recent boom on the Tokyo Stock Exchange　最近の株式市場の活況
wartime boom　戦争景気, 軍需景気
worldwide [world] boom　世界的好況, 世界的好景気, 世界的ブーム
◆Japan's exports, which had been supporting the business boom, lost momentum. 景気を支えてきた日本の輸出が、失速した。◆The longest period of postwar economic expansion was known as an economic boom without feeling. 戦後最長の景気回復は、実感なき景気回復と言われた。◆These firms' performance has rapidly improved thanks to the recent boom on the Tokyo Stock Exchange. これら各社の業績は、最近の東京株式市場の活況を背景に急速に回復した。

boom in stock investing　株式投資ブーム
◆A boom in stock investing among working women has led a number of women to create Web sites and publish guides targeted at this growing market. 働く女性たちの間での株式投資ブームで、この成長市場向けサイトを立ち上げたり、指南本を出したりする女性が増えている。

boom-or-bust line　景気判断の分かれ目, 景気の上向き・下向きの分かれ目　(=boom-bust dividing line, boom-bust threshold, boom-or-bust threshold)
◆The coincident indicator topped the boom-or-bust line of 50 percent in March. (国内の景気の現状を示す)一致指数[景気一致指数]が、3月は景気判断の分かれ目となる50%を上回った。

boom-or-bust threshold　景気判断の分かれ目
　(=boom-or-bust line)
fall (stay) below the boom-or-bust threshold [line] of 50 percent　景気判断の分かれ目となる50%を下回る
top the boom-or-bust threshold [line] of 50 percent　景気判断の分かれ目となる50%を上回る
◆A key gauge of the current state of the economy fell below the boom-or-bust threshold of 50 percent in September for the first time in five months. 景気の現状を示す主要基準(景気一致指数)が、9月は5か月ぶりに景気判断の分かれ目となる50%を下回った。

boon　(名)恵み, 恩恵, 利益, 効果
a life-sustaining boon　延命効果
a real [great] boon　大いに役立つもの
◆The latest depreciation of the euro brought about a life-sustaining boon to the currency. 今回のユーロ安が、ユーロの延命効果を招いた。

boost　(動)推進する, 引き上げる, 増加させる, 拡大する, 押し上げる, 積み増す, 高める, 向上させる, 増強する, 強化する, 拡充する, 需要などを喚起する, 活気づかせる, 活性化する, 刺激する
boost business investment　設備投資を拡大する
boost demand　需要を喚起する, 需要を刺激する
boost domestic demand　内需を拡大する, 内需を喚起(かんき)する, 内需を刺激する
boost economic growth　経済成長率を押し上げる[高める], 景気にテコ入れする, 景気を浮揚させる
boost employment　雇用を拡大する
boost financial health　財務の健全性を強化する, 財務状況[財務体質]を強化する
boost growth　経済成長率を高める, 成長力を高める
boost inflation　インフレ率を押し上げる
boost loss reserves　貸倒れ引当金を積み増す, 損失引当金を積み増す
boost operations　事業を拡大する, 業務を拡大する
boost production　生産を拡大する
boost productivity　生産性を高める, 生産性を向上させる
boost profitability　収益力[収益性]を高める, 利益率を高める
boost profits　利益を押し上げる
boost the bond market　債券市場を活性化する
boost the capital of the bank　同行の資本を増強する
boost the economic growth　景気のテコ入れをする, 経済成長率を高める
boost wages　賃金を引き上げる
◆A downgrade below investment-grade by even one ratings agency could boost GM's borrowing costs and wreak havoc on the corporate bond market. 格付け会社が1社でも投資適格付けより低く格付けを引き下げたら[格付け会社が1社でも投機的格付けに格下げしたら]、GMの資金調達コストが急増し、米国の社債(債券)市場にも大きな影響が出る恐れがある。◆Record low U.S. borrowing costs are boosting the appeal to bullion as a hedge against inflation. 米国の資金調達コストが過去最低の水準にあるため、インフレ・ヘッジとしての金[金地金]の人気が高まっている。◆The G-20 communique urged the eurozone countries to boost the EFSF, the EU bailout fund. G20(主要20か国・地域)の共同声明は、ユーロ圏国に欧州の金融支援基金である欧州金融安定基金(EFSF)の拡充を促した。◆The stakes in major U.S. securities firms by SMFG, Mitsubishi UFJ and Nomura will boost the presence of Japanese financial institutions in the global market. 三井住友銀行、三菱UFJと野村が米国の大手証券会社に出資することで、グローバル市場での日本の金融機関の存在感が高まりそうだ。◆Wealth has been boosted by rallies in stock and bond markets. 株式相場と債券相場の急騰[上昇]で、資産が増加している[資産が膨らんでいる]。◆Zenno and Itochu Corp. already have agreed to fund the issuance of new shares of Snow Brand Milk stock to boost the company's capital base. 全農(全国農業協同組合連合会)と伊藤忠は、雪印乳業の資本基盤を強化するため、同社の新株発行(増資)を引き受けることですでに合意している。

boost　(名)押し上げ, 後押し, 増強, 強化, 財務強化, 活気づけ, 景気刺激, 発展, 向上, 増大, 急増, 上昇, 急上昇
　(⇒economic boost)
a boost in sales in the U.S. market　米国市場での販売急増
be given a boost by the potential for lower interest rates　金利低下の可能性で[可能性を材料に]買われる
boost from fiscal policy　財政政策による景気刺激

capital boost 増資
fiscal boost 財政面からの景気刺激策
get a boost 反発する
give a boost to 〜に活気を与える、〜を後押しする
give the government bond a sharp boost 国債を急反発させる
◆General Motors Acceptance Corp. (GMAC), GM's finance arm, is giving the boost to the struggling automaker's bottom line. GMの金融子会社GMACが、経営再建に取り組む米自動車メーカーGMの業績の後押しをしている。◆The U.S. dollar got a boost. 米ドル相場が、反発した。

boost a key interest rate 政策金利を引き上げる、フェデラル・ファンド金利（FF金利）を引き上げる
◆The U.S. Federal Reserve Board boosted a key interest rate to the highest level in five years. 米連邦準備制度理事会（FRB）は、（短期金利の指標となる）FF金利を5年ぶりに最高水準に引き上げた。

boost from public funds 公的資金による財務強化
◆Sendai Bank is considering a boost from public funds in the aftermath of the March 11 massive quake and tsunami. 仙台銀行は、3月11日（2011年）の巨大地震と津波（東日本大震災）を受けて、公的資金［公的資金注入］による財務強化を検討している。

boost in loans 融資の増加、融資件数の増加
◆The project financing market has seen a boost in loans to businesses in renewable energy field such as solar and wind power generation. プロジェクト・ファイナンス市場は最近、太陽光や風力発電など自然エネルギー分野の事業への融資が増えている。

boost in public spending 財政出動［財政支出］の拡大
◆A boost in public spending seems to be merely an excuse for pork-barrel spending. 財政出動［公共支出］の拡大は、単なる「ばらまき」の口実にすぎないようだ。

boost market activity 取引を活性化する
◆The TSE and four other exchanges extended their morning trading sessions by 30 minutes to boost market activity. 東証など5証券取引所が、取引活性化のため午前の取引時間を30分間延長した。

boost one's capital 資本を増やす、増資する、資本を増強する、（保険会社の）基金を増額する
◆Meiji Life Insurance Co. plans to raise ¥60 billion from group financial firms to boost its capital to ¥220 billion. 明治生命保険は、グループの金融機関から600億円調達して、基金（株式会社の資本金に相当）総額を2,200億円に増額する方針だ。

boost one's capital base 資本基盤を強化する、資本を増強する
◆Fukushima Bank said about 8,000 companies and investors have agreed to buy ¥15 billion worth of its new shares in March to help boost its capital base. 福島銀行によると、約8,000の企業と投資家が、同行の資本基盤を強化するため3月に予定している150億円の増資引受け［新株引受け］に同意した。

boost profitability 収益力［収益性］を高める、利益率を高める
◆The company will cut its global workforce by 15 percent in the coming three years to boost its profitability. 同社は、収益力を高めるため、今後3年間で海外を含めた全従業員を15％削減する。

boost profits 利益を押し上げる
◆The depreciation of the yen also has boosted profits for exporting companies. 円安も、輸出企業の利益を押し上げた。

boost sales 売上を伸ばす
◆The company is aiming to boost its sales to ¥6 billion by 2014. 2014年までに売上高を60億円まで引き上げるのが、同社の目標だ。

boost the capital base of 〜の資本基盤を強化する、〜の資本を増強する
◆Public funds should be injected not only to buy up toxic assets, but also to boost the capital bases of enfeebled financial institutions. 公的資金は、不良資産の買取りだけでなく、弱体化した［体力の落ちた］金融機関の資本増強にも注入すべきだ。

boost the capital of European banks 欧州銀行［欧州の金融機関］の資本を増強する
◆France and Germany agreed on the need to boost the capital of European banks. フランスとドイツは、欧州銀行の資本増強の必要性で一致した。

boost the economy 経済を発展させる、経済［景気］を刺激する、景気を押し上げる、景気を浮揚させる
◆An improving trade deficit can act to boost the economy. 貿易赤字の改善は、景気浮揚の一因になる可能性がある。◆In the case of the United States, increased public spending to boost the economy can hardly be expected. 米国の場合、財政出動による景気浮揚は期待しにくい。◆The Bank of Japan stepped up its efforts to boost the flagging economy following the March 11 earthquake and tsunami by introducing a ¥500 billion cheap loan program. 日銀は、5,000億円の低利融資制度を導入して、東日本大震災で揺れる日本経済の刺激策を強化した。◆The government and ruling parties should explain more carefully how they expect the budget to boost the economy. 政府・与党が期待している予算の景気浮揚効果について、政府・与党はもっとていねいに説明すべきだ。

bootstrap （名）二重価格株式公開買付け　（＝two-tier tender offer）

bootstrap acquisition 持ち株漸増自力買収（取得した株式を担保にして調達した資金を株式の追加取得にあてて、時間をかけて会社を買収すること）

bordereaux （名）再保険契約明細書、再保険報告書, ボルドロ

borrow （動）借り入れる、融資を受ける、資金を調達する、借金する　（⇒Moneylending Business Law）
　borrow from a conventional source 通常の借入先から借り入れる
　borrowed capital 他人資本、借入資本
　borrowed money 借入金、借金
　borrowed security 借入有価証券
◆There will be a domino effect if companies can't borrow. 企業が融資を受けられない［資金調達できない］場合には、ドミノ効果が生じる。

borrow from Peter to pay Paul Aから借金してBに支払う、借金返済のために借金する
　（＝rob Peter to pay Paul）
◆The issuance of refunding bonds to redeem ordinary government bonds means borrowing from Peter to pay Paul. 普通国債を償還するための借換え債の発行は、借金返済のための借金を意味する。

borrow massive amounts of money 巨額［多額］の借入れをする、巨額の融資を受ける
　（＝borrow a large amount of money）
◆Both companies had borrowed massive amounts of money, using real estate as collateral and continued to invest. 両社は、不動産を担保に巨額の借入れを行い、投資を続けた。

borrow money 金を借りる、資金を借り入れる、融資を受ける、資金を調達する
　（⇒auction-rate［auction rate］market）
　borrow money from a bank 銀行から資金を借り入れる、銀行から融資を受ける、銀行から資金を調達する
　borrow money from a broker to buy stocks 証券会社から資金を借りて株を買う　（⇒broker名詞）
　borrow money from a consumer loan company 消費者金融業者［金融会社］から資金を借り入れる、消費者金融から金を借りる
　borrow money from depositors 預金者から資金を調達す

る，預金者から金を預かる
◆A bank makes a profit by borrowing money from its depositors and investing that money in securities and loans. 銀行は、預金者から金を預かり、その金を有価証券や融資に投入して（有価証券やローンで運用して）利益を上げる。◆A rating below investment grade makes it harder and more expensive to borrow money. 投資適格以下の格付けだと、資金の調達が難しくなるし、資金調達コストも高くつく。◆Should the interest rate rise, it will become more expensive for companies to borrow money. 金利が上昇すると［金利上昇局面では］、企業の資金調達コストが重くなる。

borrow money from banks 金融機関［銀行］から資金を借り入れる
◆Companies faced difficulties in raising money by issuing corporate bonds in the aftermath of the financial crisis and resorted to borrowing money from banks. 世界の金融危機の影響で企業は、社債を発行して資金を調達するのが困難になったため、金融機関からの資金借入れに動いた。

borrow money from financial institutions 金融機関から資金を借り入れる
◆The additional financial assistance to the Nuclear Damage Liability Facilitation Fund will be used as collateral when TEPCO borrows money from financial institutions. 原子力損害賠償支援機構に対する追加金融支援は、東電が金融機関から資金を借り入れる際の債務保証などに活用される。

borrow shares 株を借りる（=borrow stocks）
◆Through short selling, an investor borrows shares and sells them on the expectations that their price will fall, and can buy back them at a lower price. 空売りによって投資家は、株価が下がると予想して株を借りて売り、値下がりした時点でその株を買い戻すことができる。

borrow stocks 株を借りる（=borrow shares）
◆Short selling is the practice of borrowing stocks from securities and financial companies and other investors to sell them and then buy them back when their prices drop. 空売りは、証券金融会社や他の投資家（機関投資家など）から株を借りて売り、その株が値下がりした時点で買い戻すことをいう。

borrowed stocks 借り株，借り入れた株
◆There were regulations banning investors from selling borrowed stocks and promising to buy them back later at prices lower than the selling price. 投資家が借り入れた株を売却した後、その株を売却価格より安い値段で買い戻すことを約束することを禁止する規制が、以前はあった。

borrower （名）借り手，借り主，資金の借り手，ローンの借り手，ローン利用者，貸付け先，貸出先，融資先，融資先企業，債務者，発行体，ボロワー（⇒bypass loans, corporate borrowers, disposal of nonperforming loans, failed borrower, financial situation, leverage on borrowers）
AAA rated borrower　トリプルA格の発行体
borrower of record　契約上の借入人
borrower's risk　借り主の危険負担
corporate borrowers　融資先，融資先企業，法人借り主
eligible borrower　適格融資先
frequent borrower　頻繁に起債する発行体，常連のボロワー
large-lot corporate borrowers　大口融資先
major borrowers　大口融資先
opportunistic borrower　発行条件が整えば起債するボロワー，条件が合えば発行する発行体
premium borrower　優良発行体
prime-rate borrower　プライム適用取引先，プライム適用先
problematic borrowers　問題融資先
riskier borrowers　リスクの高い融資先
sovereign borrower　ソブリン発行体
subprime borrower　信用力の低い［劣る］借り手，信用力の低い融資先
top corporate borrower　一流法人貸出先，一流企業融資先［貸出先］

◆A financial intermediary acts as a middleman between cash surplus units in the economy（savers）and deficit spending units（borrowers）. 金融仲介機関は、経済の資金余剰主体（貯蓄者）と資金不足主体（借り手）との間に立つ仲介者として機能している。◆About 50 percent of borrowers taking out new mortgages are opting for adjustable rate home loans since the beginning of this year. 新規住宅ローン利用契約者の約50%は、今年に入ってから変動金利型住宅ローンを選んでいる。◆Another tactic many loan sharks use is to circulate slanderous leaflets to the workplace or the school that the borrower's children attend. 多くのヤミ金融業が使うほかの手は、借り手の勤務先や子どもが通う学校への中傷文書のばらまきだ。◆Banks have to set aside loan loss reserves based on projections of future revenues of their borrowers, not based on bankruptcies in the past. 銀行は、過去の倒産実績ではなく、融資先企業［貸出先］の将来の収益予想などを基にして、貸倒れ引当金を積み立てるべきだ。◆Daikyo was a major borrower of UFJ Bank. 大京は、UFJ銀行の大口融資先だった。◆Domestic bank are stepping up oversea project financing due to the lack of growth in lending to domestic borrowers amid protracted deflation at home. 国内銀行各行は、国内ではデフレが続いて［デフレが続く状況で］国内融資先への貸出が伸びていないことから、海外の事業向け融資を強化している。◆If the Bank of Japan's interest rate takes an upward turn, an adjustable rate mortgage would weigh more heavily on borrowers than would the fixed-rate type. 日銀の政策金利が上昇に転じた場合、固定金利型の住宅ローンと比べて変動金利型のほうが、ローン利用者［借り手］の負担が重くなる。◆In most cases in which the credit guarantee system is used, financial institutions introduce borrowers to credit guarantee corporations. 信用保証制度を利用する場合の多くは、金融機関が借り手を信用保証協会に紹介する。◆In the case of a lack of liquidity, either bridge lending or debt deferment can save the borrower as there is no cash on hand. 流動性不足の場合は、手元に現金がないので、つなぎ資金を貸すか［つなぎ融資か］債務返済の延長で借り手は助かる。◆Mizuho's first-half profit fell 17 percent as credit costs increased and on losses related to investments in U.S. home loans to riskier borrowers. みずほの上半期利益は、与信コストの増加とリスクの高い融資先への米国の住宅ローン投資に関連する損失で、17%減少した。◆Other banks are likely forced to revise their earnings projections downward because of the accelerated disposal of bad loans, business deterioration of borrowers due to the lingering recession and further decline in stock prices. 不良債権処理の加速や長引く不況による融資先の業績悪化、株安などの影響で、他行も業績予想の下方修正を迫られている。◆Some borrowers have taken advantage of lax screening of credit guarantee corporations. 信用保証協会の手薄な審査に便乗している借り手もいる。◆The banks have categorized borrowers based on their financial health. 銀行は、経営の健全度に基づいて融資先（債務者）を区分している。◆The Financial Services Agency has instructed the banks to increase loan-loss provisions for nonperforming loans extended mainly to large borrowers. 金融庁は、主に大口融資先の不良債権に対する貸倒れ引当金の積み増しを、これらの銀行に指示した。◆The FSA's special inspection will check the major banks' large-lot corporate borrowers whose stock prices or credit ratings have sharply declined. 金融庁の特別検査は、大手銀行の株価や格付けなどが急落した大口融資先を査定の対象としている。◆The major banks attributed their increased bad loans to the poor performance of their borrowers due to the prolonged economic slump and Financial Service Agency inspections resulting in a stricter review of their asset assessments. 大手

銀行は、不良債権が増えた理由として、長引く景気低迷で貸出先の経営が悪化したことと、金融庁の検査を受けて大手行が資産査定を厳しくしたことを挙げた。◆The rate at which banks lend their top corporate borrowers is called "prime rate." 銀行がその一流企業融資先に貸し出す利率は、プライム・レートと呼ばれている。◆Under the program of a voluntary liquidation for individuals, housing loan borrowers' voluntary bankruptcies can be prevented by having financial institutions waive repayment of their mortgages. 個人向け私的整理の制度だと、金融機関に住宅ローンの返済を免除させることによって、住宅ローンの借り手の自己破産を防ぐことができる。

borrower company 融資先企業
◆Shinsei Bank reached an out-of-court settlement in a damage lawsuit with a bankruptcy administrator of a borrower company. 新生銀行が、融資先企業の破産管財人との損害賠償訴訟で示談による和解に達した。

borrowing (名)借入れ, 資金調達, 借金, 借入金, 負債, 債務 (⇒excessive borrowing)
　bank borrowing　銀行借入れ, 銀行借入金 (=banking borrowing)
　borrowing costs　資金調達コスト
　borrowing facilities　信用枠
　borrowing from private financial institutions　民間金融機関からの借入れ
　borrowing of stocks　株の借入れ
　borrowing power　借入能力
　borrowing rate　借入金利
　corporate borrowing　企業借入れ
　cut borrowings　借入金を減らす
　excessive borrowing　過剰借入れ
　foreign borrowing　対外借入れ
　foreign currency borrowing　外貨建て借入れ
　government borrowings　政府の借入れ, 政府の借金, 政府債務
　have borrowings in excess of one's equity capital　株主資本を上回る借入金がある
　interest rate on borrowings　借入金の金利, 借入金の利率
　long-term borrowing　長期借入れ, 長期債務
　lower the level of borrowing　借入れの水準を引き下げる
　obtain borrowing at a low interest rate　低金利で借入れをする
　ratio of cash and deposits to borrowings　現預金対借入金比率
　repay one's borrowings　借入金を返済する
　secured borrowing　担保付き借入れ
　securitized borrowings　借入れの証券化
　seek borrowing from　借入先を求める, 借入先を探す
　short-term borrowings　短期借入金 (⇒due)
　undertake borrowing　借入れを行う
　unsecured borrowing　無担保借入れ

◆Money loaned by private banks declined because banks with weakened financial strength were less willing to lend, besides a lack of businesses seeking expansion through borrowing. 民間銀行の貸出金が減ったのは、お金を借りてまで事業を拡大しようとする企業がなかったほか、財務が悪化した銀行が貸し渋ったからだ。◆Some smaller companies are more cautious about borrowing for capital expenditures due to economic uncertainty. 一部の中小企業は、景気の不透明感から、設備投資の借入れに一段と慎重になっている。◆The company's net short-term borrowings amounted to $695 million at June 30, 2010, compared with $180 million at December 31, 2009. 同社の短期借入金純額は、2009年12月31日現在の1億8,000万ドルに対し、2010年6月30日の時点で6億9,500万ドルに達している。◆The government must rely on tax revenues to finance the repayment of its borrowings. 政府は、政府債務の返済資金を税収に頼らざるを得ない。◆This nonprofit foundation is facing its financial difficulties as a result of the borrowing of the money to construct a welfare facility. 福祉施設の建設資金借入れに伴って、この公益法人は現在、その運営に行き詰まっている。

borrowing costs 資金調達コスト, 借入コスト, 借入費用
◆A downgrade below investment-grade by even one ratings agency could boost GM's borrowing costs and wreak havoc on the corporate bond market. 格付け会社が1社でも投資適格格付けより低く格付けを引き下げたら[格付け会社が1社でも投機的格付けに格下げしたら]、GMの資金調達コストが急増し、米国の社債[債券]市場にも大きな影響が出る恐れがある。◆A rise in borrowing costs will curb consumer spending as well as production activity in industrial sectors. 借入コストの増大は、産業の生産活動や個人消費を抑えることになる。◆Record low U.S. borrowing costs are boosting the appeal to bullion as a hedge against inflation. 米国の資金調達コストが過去最低の水準にあるため、インフレ・ヘッジとしての金[金地金]の人気が高まっている。

bottom (名)底, 最低, 下限, 底値, 大底, 底入れ, 景気の谷, ボトム (動)底に届く
　be at the bottom of a business cycle　(景気が)景気循環の底にある
　be at the bottom of the list　まったく重要視されていない
　be at the rock bottom　底値を付ける, (士気などが)低下する, どん底に落ち込む (=hit the rock bottom)
　be close to touching bottom　底入れが近い
　bottom of the cycle　底入れ, 景気の谷
　buy at the bottom　底値で買いを入れる
　close at the bottom of the day's trading　安値引けとなる
　double bottom　二番底 (=second bottom)
　first bottom　一番底
　get to the bottom of　～の真相を究明する, ～の真相を明らかにする
　get to the bottom of the spate of scandals　一連の疑惑の全容を解明する
　hit a five-year bottom　5年来の大底に落ち込む
　hit rock-bottom [an all-time low]　最低水準に達する, 底を打つ
　hit (the) bottom　底を打つ, 谷になる, 底固めする
　hunt bargains at bottom　値頃買いをする
　in the bottom of the first inning　(野球)1回の裏に
　major bottom　大底
　move along the bottom　(景気が)底をはう
　reach (the) bottom　底に達する, 底に届く, 底を打つ, 底入れする
　reach the double bottom　二番底に至る
　stand on one's own bottom　独立する, 自立する
　the bottom falls [drops] out of　～が底を割る, ～が底をぬける, ～が大底をつく, ～が暴落する, ～が大きな痛手を受ける[被る], ～が打撃を受ける
　the bottom of a two-year range　過去2年のレンジの最低水準
　the bottom of the Fed's acceptable range　FRBの目標圏の底
　the bottom of the ladder　社会の下層部, 下積み仕事
　the bottom of the trading range　取引圏の底
　touch (the) bottom　底入れする, 底をつく

◆Stock prices seem to have hit bottom. 株価は、底を打ったようだ。◆The bottom dropped out of the stock market. 株式市場[株式相場]が底をぬけた[株式市場の底がぬけた]。◆

The bottom fell out of the market. 株価が暴落した［底抜け相場となった］。◆The latent profits of major banks' stockholdings have hit bottom. 大手銀行の保有株式の含み益も、底をついた。◆The recession appears to have reached the bottom. 不況は、底をついたようだ。◆The Securities and Exchange Surveillance Commission will get to the bottom of the spate of scandals involving Olympus Corp.'s false financial statements. 証券取引等監視委員会は、オリンパスの有価証券報告書虚偽記載に関する一連の疑惑の全容を解明する［真相を究明する］方針だ。

bottom line （損益計算書の最終行の意味から）純損益、純利益、利益、当期利益、純損失収益性、取引の収支、業績、最終損益、総決算、最終結果・成果、結論、最終決定、最重要事項、要点、カギ、問題の核心、ぎりぎりの線、本音（⇒arm, boost名詞）
  bottom line results 純利益
  bottom lines 業績、収益
  company's bottom line 企業［会社］の損益
  contribute to the bottom line 利益［当期利益］に貢献する、利益に寄与する
  corporate［corporations'］bottom lines 企業収益
  enhance the bottom line 利益を押し上げる、利益を増やす
  flow through to the bottom line 利益に直結する
  ◆Our bottom line shows a loss of $2.80 a share. 当社の最終損益は、1株当たり2.80ドルの損失を示しています。◆The bank's high interest rates policy to lure clients weighed down the bottom line. 集客目当ての同行の高金利策が、経営を圧迫した。◆The bottom line is how to pinpoint what consumers are really interested in. 問題のカギは、消費者が本当に関心のあるものにいかに迫れるかだ。◆The bottom line is that the eurozone governments did not want to inject public money into banks. 結局［要するに］、ユーロ圏各国政府は銀行への公的資金注入を嫌った。

bottom out 底をつく、底を打つ、底入れする、底値に達する、下げ止まる、底打ちする、最低レベルに達する、どん底まで下がる （⇒capital investment）
  ◆Interest rates have bottomed out. 金利が底を打った。◆The economy has bottomed out. 景気は、底入れしている。◆The government announced in its monthly economic report for May that the economy had bottomed out. 政府は、5月の月例経済報告で「景気は底入れしている」と発表した。◆U.S. Federal Reserve Board chairman said the U.S. economy would bottom out soon. 米連邦準備制度理事会（FRB）議長は、「米景気は底入れが近い」と語った。

bottoming out [bottoming-out] 底入れ、底打ち、底離れ、下げ止まり
  ◆Signs of bottoming out can be seen in some areas. 一部に、下げ止まりの兆しが見られる。◆The economy is showing signs of bottoming out due to progress in inventory adjustment. 在庫調整が進展したため、景気が底入れする兆しを見せている。

bounce （名）はずみ、はね返り、反発、回復、反騰、増加、上昇、大きな伸び、弾力、反発力、追放、クビ、解雇、放逐
  a significant bounce in (economic) activity 景気の大幅回復
  a small bounce in ～の小幅上昇
  bounce in business confidence 企業景況感の回復
  earnings bounce 収益回復

bounce back 反発する、反転する、すぐに回復する［立ち直る］、はね上がる、巻き返す、形勢を立て直す、気を取り直す、はね返る、影響がはね返ってくる
  bounce back a little too much 上がり過ぎる
  bounce back from ～から立ち直る
  bounce back in (business) confidence 景況感が回復する

  bounce back sharply 急反発する、反騰する
  bounce back significantly 大幅に増加する、大幅に反発する
  bounce back slightly 小幅反発する、若干反発する［回復する］、小幅増加［上昇］する
  wait for the stock market to bounce back 株式市場の反転を待つ
  ◆Because stock prices have tumbled so far, the Koizumi administration can no longer afford to sit idly by and wait for the stock market to bounce back. ここまで株価が暴落したからには、もはや安穏と株式市場の反転を待つ余裕など小泉政権にはないはずだ。◆Tokyo stocks bounced back after the U.S. government's bailout of embattled U.S. insurer American International Group Inc. 経営不振の米保険会社AIGを米政府が救済するのを受けて、東京株式市場は反発した。◆Tokyo stocks bounced back Wednesday after sharp falls Tuesday following Lehman Brothers decision to file for bankruptcy as financial worries eased. 水曜日の東京株式市場は、リーマン・ブラザーズが前日に破たん申請を決めて急落したものの、金融不安が和らいだため反発した。

bounced check 不渡り小切手
bouncer （名）偽（にせ）小切手、偽造小切手
bounty （名）政府の補助金、助成金、報奨金、賞金
bourse 証券取引所、取引所、株式市況、株式相場（=securities exchange）
  Japanese bourse 日本の株式市況、日本の株式相場
  Paris bourse パリ証券取引所
  ◆As a core bourse in Asia, the TSE envisages integration of stock exchanges in the region. アジアの中核取引所［中核市場］として、東証はアジア地域の証券取引所大連合を構想している。◆Izuhakone Railway Co. and Daiwa Motor Transportation Co. are listed on the bourse's Second Section. 伊豆箱根鉄道と大和自動車交通は、同証券取引所の二部（東証二部）に上場されている。◆Tokyo, Osaka and Nagoya bourses placed Nikko Cordial stock on their respective supervision posts for possible delisting. 東京、大阪、名古屋の3証券取引所が、それぞれ日興コーディアルの株式を、上場廃止の可能性があるため監理ポストに割り当てた。◆Under TSE regulations, the bourse can delist a company's stock if the company files financial statements without an auditor's certification. 東証の規則では、企業が監査法人の監査証明を得ないで財務書類を提出した場合、同証券取引所は同社の株式を上場廃止にすることができる。

BPS 1株当たり純資産 （book value per shareの略。⇒book value per share）

bracket （名）階層、層、グループ、区分、等級
  age bracket 年齢層
  five year bracket 5年物
  low income brackets 低所得者層
  tax bracket 税金区分、税率等級
  ◆In 2025, there will be only two people in the working age bracket of 15 to 64 years old per elderly person aged 65 or older though the ratio was 11-to-1 half a century ago. 2025年には、65歳以上の高齢者1人に対して15～64歳の現役世代は、半世紀前の11人に対して、わずか2人に減る見通しだ。◆The Housing Loan Corporation has for decades provided low interest housing loans to home buyers in relatively low income brackets. 住宅金融公庫は、これまでの数十年間、比較的低所得者層の住宅購入者に低金利の住宅ローンを提供してきた。

brake （名）制動装置、歯止め、抑制、牽制、ブレーキ
  act as a brake on［upon］ ～を抑制する働きをする、～にブレーキをかけることになる
  apply brakes to ～に牽制をかける、～にブレーキをかける
  hit［slam on］the brakes ブレーキを踏む

put on a brake [the brake, the brakes] on 　〜にブレーキをかける　（＝apply a brake on）
put the brakes [a brake] on 　〜の進行を抑える，〜に歯止めをかける，〜にブレーキをかける，〜を食い止める（⇒runaway）
slam the brakes on 　〜に急ブレーキをかける
take off the brake 　ブレーキを緩める，ブレーキをはずす
◆A U.S. housing mortgage meltdown shook the United States, Europe and other countries and slammed the brakes on global growth. 米国の住宅ローン市場の崩壊は、米欧その他の諸国を揺さぶり、世界経済の成長に急ブレーキをかけた。◆Dollar-selling pressure has eased and put a temporary brake on the sharp appreciation of the yen and the fall of the dollar. ドル売り圧力が弱まり、急激な円高・ドル安にいったん歯止めがかかった。◆Long-term debts held by central and local governments are expected to further swell unless the government puts the brakes on government bond issuance. 政府が国債発行に歯止めをかけないと、国と地方[地方自治体]が抱える長期債務は、さらに膨らむ見通しだ。◆There seem to be no brakes on the rise of the yen. 円高に、歯止めがかからないようだ。

branch　（動）支店，支社，支部，支局，出張所，分野
　（⇒bill, corporate loans, joint branch, license）
bank branch 　銀行支店
branch account 　支店口座，支店勘定
branch accounting 　支店独自の会計，支店会計
branch banking 　支店銀行，支店銀行制度（branch banking system）
branch business 　支店業務
branch clearing 　本支店間手形交換
branch settlement account 　本支店勘定
　（＝home-branch accounting）
domestic branch network 　国内支店網
foreign bank branches 　外銀支店，外国銀行の支店
foreign branch account 　外国支店勘定，在外支店勘定
joint branch 　共同店舗
overseas branch 　海外支店，在外支店
resident branch 　現地支店
the Bank of Japan's meeting of branch managers 　日銀支店長会議
　（＝the BOJ's branch manager meeting）
◆Bank of Tokyo-Mitsubishi placed ATMs for the new cards in all of its 267 branches nationwide. 東京三菱銀行は、全国の267店すべてに新型カード対応のATMを設置した。◆Mizuho Bank offers a service by which ATM cardholders are given mileage points each time they use the new cards as credit cards, purchase financial products at the bank's branches or receive loans from the bank. みずほ銀行が提供しているサービスでは、キャッシュ・カード会員が新型カードをクレジット・カードとして利用したり、みずほ銀で金融商品を購入したり、ローンを利用したりすると、その取引に応じて毎回、マイレージ・ポイントがもらえる。◆The Japanese branch of Banco do Brazil was involved in illegal transactions by underground banks. ブラジル銀行在日支店が、地下銀行（代理送金業者）による不正取引に関与していた。

branch-free bank　無店舗銀行，店舗を持たない銀行
◆Sony Corp. launched Japan's second Internet-based bank in the hope the branch-free bank can attract customers with higher deposit interest rates and a range of new financial services based on Sony's cutting-edge information technology. 店舗を持たない銀行だと、預金の金利を高くするとともにソニーの先端的な情報技術をベースに広範な金融サービスを新たに提供して顧客を集めることができるという期待のもとに、ソニーは国内で二番目のネット専業銀行を開業した。

branch office　支店，支社，支所，支部，店舗
　（＝branch house, branch shop）
◆The biggest advantage for the bank in entering the venture will be to increase its customer base without having to open expensive new branch offices. 同行にとってこの新規事業への参入の最大の利点は、コストのかかる新店舗を開設するまでもなく、顧客基盤を拡大できることだ。

breach　（名）不履行，違反，違反行為，反則，侵害，疎遠，割れ目，破れ目，絶好，絶好状態，不和，意見の不一致
（a）breach of confidence 　信用失墜行為，信託義務不履行，秘密漏洩（ろうえい）
a breach of promise 　約束違反，約束不履行，婚約不履行，違約
a breach of the rule 　規則違反，ルール違反
a breach of trust 　背任，信託義務違反
be in breach of 　〜に違反する，〜に抵触する
breach of duty 　義務の不履行，職務怠慢
breach of the agreement 　契約違反，協定違反，違約
heal the breach 　仲直りさせる，和解させる
special breach of trust under the Commercial Code 　商法の特別背任
stand in the breach 　攻撃の矢面（やおもて）に立つ，敵の矢面に立つ，難局に当たる
step（throw oneself）into the breach 　自ら危険に身を投じる，〜の代役に回る，穴を埋める，急場をしのぐ，難局に立ち向かう，進んで難局に対処する，難局を乗り切る
sue a person for breach of promise 　人を約束違反で訴える，人を約束不履行で訴える
◆Years of window-dressing by Olympus to hide investment losses represent nothing but a companywide breach of trust. 投資損失隠ぺいのためのオリンパスによる長年の粉飾決算は、会社ぐるみの背信行為にほかならない。

break　（名）優遇措置，公正な機会，チャンス，運，断絶，中絶，中断，中止，休憩，破損，割れ目，裂け目，切れ目　（動）（記録，契約などを）破る，突き抜ける，更新する，（紙幣などを）くずす，（お金を）細かくする，故障させる，こわす，解散する，（銀行などを）破産させる
a series of tax breaks 　一連の減税措置
AA is broken on a closing basis 　終値ベースでAAを割り込む
break a 10,000 yen bill [note] 　1万円札をくずす
break another record 　記録をさらに更新する
break bulk 　バラ荷，かさ高貨物，ブレイクバルク
break bulk fee 　仕分け手数料
break cost 　解約補償料
break into a new market 　新市場に参入する
break key resistance 　主要抵抗線を突き抜ける
break one's word [promise] 　約束を破る
break out of the current tight range 　現在の狭いボックス圏から抜け出す
break out of the established range 　ボックス圏を抜け出す
break strong resistance 　強固な抵抗線を突き抜ける
break the agreement 　契約[協定]を破る
break the current range to test 　ボックス圏を抜け出して〜をうかがう展開となる
break the law 　法律に違反する
break the syndicate 　シンジケート団を解散する
break through 　〜の水準を突き抜ける[突破する]，〜を抜け出す
break through the established range 　ボックス圏を抜け出す
break through the psychological AA% barrier level 　心理的な壁になっていたAA%の水準を突破する，心理的な壁のAA%から抜け出す
break up the transaction 　案件を複数に分ける

coffee break loan　即時金融
tax break for capital gains　キャピタル・ゲイン税減税
◆The income and corporate taxes have substantially decreased due to the prolonged recession and a series of tax breaks. 所得税や法人税は、長期不況や一連の減税措置で大幅に減少している。

break even　(動)(損益が)五分五分になる, 損得なしに終わる, かろうじて採算が取れる, 〜が採算ラインである

break-even [breakeven]　(形)収支とんとんの, 損益なしの, 損益なしの状態の, 損益分岐点の, 損益分岐点となる, 採算ラインの
　break-even point　損益分岐点
　break-even sales [volume]　損益分岐売上高
　break-even yield　損益分岐点利回り
　return to break-even　収支とんとんになる, 赤字解消になる

break-even chart　損益分岐点の分析表, 損益分岐点図表
◆This is the break-even chart of the company's new product. これは、同社の新製品の損益分岐点図表だ。

breakdown　(名)機械の故障, 機能停止, 交渉の決裂, 中断, 崩壊, 倒壊, 内訳, 構成, 分類, 分析, 好機, 見込み
　a breakdown of the statistics　統計の分析
　breakdown by industry group　業種別内訳, 業種別分類
　breakdown of revenue　売上構成, 売上の内訳
　computer system's breakdown　コンピュータ・システムの障害, システム障害
　　(=computer failure, computer malfunction)
　economic breakdown　経済の崩壊
　political breakdown　政治機能の停止
　the systemic breakdown of the whole banking sector　銀行業界 [金融界] 全体のシステム崩壊, 金融界全体の連鎖的な崩壊
◆A breakdown of the DBJ financial rescue package reveals that ¥70 billion has been loaned to JAL and about ¥15 billion to ANA. 日本政策投資銀行が経営支援策として行った融資の内訳は、日本航空システムに約700億円、全日本空輸が約150億円となっている。◆In spite of Japan's triple whammy of the tsunami- nuclear crisis, electricity shortages and political breakdown, the yen has sharply strengthened. 日本は現在、津波・原発災害、電力不足、政治機能停止の三重苦に直面しているにもかかわらず、円は急騰している。◆The collapse of a bank may result in the systemic breakdown of the whole banking sector. 銀行1行の破たんが、金融界全体のシステム崩壊 [連鎖的な崩壊] につながる可能性がある。◆The yen's further depreciation could have resulted in a currency free fall and breakdown of the Japanese economy. これ以上の円安は、円のフリーフォール (歯止めなき下落) と日本経済の崩壊を招く可能性があった。

breakup　(名)崩壊, 分裂, 決裂, 解散, 解体, 解消, 絶縁, 別離, 別れ, 仲たがい
　breakup and privatization　分割民営化
　breakup value　清算価値, 清算価額
　the breakup of the French-Belgian bank Dexia　仏ベルギー系金融機関デクシアの解体
　the breakup of the Soviet Union　(1991年12月21日の) ソ連邦崩壊, ソ連の解体
◆The Greek-triggered sovereign debt crisis resulted in the breakup of the French-Belgian bank Dexia which held Greek government bonds. ギリシャが引き金になったソブリン危機 (政府債務危機) 問題で、ギリシャ国債を保有していた仏ベルギー系金融機関のデクシア (Dexia) が、解体に追い込まれた。◆The JR group companies were created following the breakup and privatization of the former Japanese National Railways. JRグループ各社は、旧国鉄の分割民営化で誕生した。

BRICs　有力新興国, ブリクス (高い経済成長を続ける Brazil (ブラジル)、Russia (ロシア)、India (インド) と China (中国) の頭文字による造語)
◆Financial exchanges between the BRICs group, Indonesia and South Korea will move toward a tri-reserve-currency regime by losing a dependency on the U.S. dollar. BRICs グループ (ブラジル、ロシア、インド、中国) とインドネシア、韓国の新興6か国間の金融取引は今後、米ドルに依存しなくなるため、3準備通貨体制に移行するものと思われる。◆Six emerging economies (the BRICs nations plus Indonesia and South Korea) will become the major drivers of global economic growth. これからは、新興6か国 (ブラジル、ロシア、インド、中国にインドネシアと韓国) が、世界の経済成長の主要な原動力になる。

bridge　(動)つなぐ, 溝や意見の違いなどを埋める, 困難を乗り越える　(名)橋, 橋渡し, 架け橋, ブリッジ
　bridge (over) many difficulties　多くの困難を克服する
　bridge the economic gap [divide, gulf]　経済の溝 [ギャップ] を埋める
◆Differences among the Security Council members can be bridged. (国連) 安全保障理事会理事国の意見の相違は、埋めることができる。◆France and Germany could not bridge their differences, so Europe's efforts to solve its escalating debt crisis plunged into disarray. フランスとドイツが両国の相違を埋められなかったため、深刻化する欧州の債務危機問題解決への欧州の取組みは、混乱に陥った。

bridge bank　つなぎ銀行, 承継銀行, 受け皿銀行, ブリッジバンク (破たんした銀行の受け皿銀行が見つかるまで、破たん銀行の金融業務を引き継ぐための公的機関)
◆Japan should consider introducing its own version of P&A, as well as continuing the state's special control of failed banks and the use of bridge banks. 日本は、破たん銀行の特別公的管理 (一時国有化) の継続とブリッジバンクの活用に加え、日本独自のP&A (資産と負債の継承) 方式の導入を検討すべきだ。

Bridge Bank of Japan　日本承継銀行
◆The Bridge Bank of Japan will temporarily take over the operation of the collapsed bank. 日本承継銀行は、破たん銀行の営業を一時的に引き継ぐことになる。

bridge financing　つなぎ融資
　(=bridging finance)

bridge lending　つなぎ資金の貸出, つなぎ融資
◆In the case of a lack of liquidity, either bridge lending or debt deferment can save the borrower as there is no cash on hand. 流動性不足の場合は、手元に現金がないので、つなぎ資金を貸すか [つなぎ融資か] 債務返済の延長で借り手は助かる。

bridge loan　つなぎ金融, つなぎ融資, つなぎ資金融資, ブリッジ・ローン　(=bridging loan)
◆At the eurozone finance ministers meeting held on October 3, 2011, a decision on bridge loans of about €8 billion to Greece was expected, but none was done. 2011年10月3日に開かれたユーロ圏財務相会合では、ギリシャに対する約80億ユーロのつなぎ融資の決定が見込まれていたが、これは見送られた。

bridging　(形)つなぎの, 橋渡しする
　bridging advance　つなぎ融資
　　(=bridge loan, interim financing)
　bridging finance　つなぎ融資　(=bridge financing, bridge loan, bridging advance, interim financing)
　bridging loan　つなぎ融資　(=bridging advance, bridging finance, interim financing)

bridging bonds　つなぎ国債
◆Bridging bonds issued by the government will be redeemed through a future increase in the consumption tax rate. 政府発行のつなぎ国債の返済 [償還] は、今後の消費税率の引上げで行う。◆The government is poised to issue bridging bonds to

make up the expected shortfall in state funding for the basic pension fund. 政府は、つなぎ国債を発行して、予想される基礎年金基金の国庫負担の不足分を賄(まかな)う方針だ。◆Unless consumption tax rate is raised, the planned issuance of bridging bonds could lead to further deterioration of the debt-saddled government finances. 消費税率を引き上げないと、予定しているつなぎ国債の発行は、借金を背負っている国の財政の悪化をさらに招く可能性がある。

brief (動)簡潔に報告する,経過報告する,(概況・状況を)説明する[報告する] (名)要約,要約書,概要,概要書,要領書,準備書面
◆At the IR sessions, the Finance Ministry's senior officials will brief investors on the state of Japan's economy and explain the methods of investment in JGBs. この投資家説明会では、財務省の幹部が、日本の景気の現状や日本国債への投資方法について投資家に説明する。

briefing (名)説明会,投資家向け説明会,投資家説明会,経過報告,概要報告,概況・状況説明,背景説明,指示説明,戦況要約,要約書,セミナー
  background briefing 背景説明
  deep background briefing （ニュース・ソースを明かさないという条件での）政府当局者の背景説明
  general briefing 状況説明
  off-the-record briefing オフレコ（報道しないという条件での）説明

briefing for foreign investors 海外投資家向け説明会 (⇒fund manager)
◆The Finance Ministry held its first briefing for foreign investors in London to encourage them to invest in Japanese government bonds. 財務省が、日本の国債への投資を呼びかける同省初の海外投資家向け説明会をロンドンで開いた。◆The firm's briefing for foreign investors was held in New York. 同社の海外投資家向け説明会は、ニューヨークで開かれた。

briefing session 説明会
◆The company held briefing sessions to solicit new investors. 同社は説明会を開いて、新規出資者を募っていた。

briefly (副)一時に、一時、簡単に、要するに (⇒Dow Jones industrial average [Industrial Average])
◆After briefly touching ¥110.90 in early trading in London, the dollar rallied in intraday trading, rising to ¥112.15-25 at 5 p.m. ロンドン市場では早朝の取引で一時1ドル＝110円90銭を付けた後、米ドルは取引時間中の取引で反騰して午後5時現在、同112円15-25銭に上昇した。◆The government's currency intervention on Sept. 15, 2010 helped the dollar briefly rebound by about ¥3. 2010年9月15日の政府の為替介入で、ドルは一時、3円ほど値を戻した。◆The Nikkei Stock Average fell briefly to its lowest level this year on the Tokyo Stock Market. 東京株式市場の日経平均株価は一時、今年の最安値を下回った。

bring (動)もたらす,持ってくる,連れてくる
  bring a large floater 変動利付き債で大型起債を行う
  bring added risks リスクを高める
  bring down inflation インフレ率を押し下げる
  bring the budget to balance 財政収支を均衡させる

bring about 引き起こす,もたらす,招く,成し遂げる,〜の進路を変える
◆The Fed's monetary easing policies have brought about inflation in newly emerging economies. FRB（米連邦準備制度理事会）の金融緩和策が、新興国のインフレを招いた。◆The latest depreciation of the euro brought about a life-sustaining boon to the currency. 今回のユーロ安が、ユーロの延命効果を招いた。

bring in （収益や利益を）もたらす,〜を稼ぐ,〜を持ち込む,導入する,(議案などを)提出する,〜を連行する,(陪審員が)評決する
◆The consumption tax brings in about ¥2.5 trillion a year per percentage point. 消費税の税収は、1％当たり年間で約2.5兆円となる。

brisk (形)活発な,好調な,活気のある,活況の,繁盛している,急速に回復する
  brisk business 活発な取引
  brisk credit expansion 活発な信用拡大
  brisk economic recovery 景気の急速な回復
  brisk exports 好調な輸出
  brisk sales 好調な売れ行き,販売好調,売上好調
◆An increasing number of companies want to undertake IPOs while stock markets remain brisk. 株式市場が活況のうちに上場したい[株式を新規公開したい]、という企業が増えている。◆GM's sales were brisk in North America. 北米でのGMの売上[販売]は、好調だった。

brisk business 活発な取引
◆The index of tertiary industry activity rose 2.2 percent in September from August due to brisk business in the leasing sector. 9月の第三次産業活動指数は、リース部門の活発な取引で前月比2.2%の上昇となった。

brisk performance 好業績
◆The firm that best represents the brisk performances of Japanese companies is Toyota Motor Corp. 日本企業の好業績の代表格は、トヨタ自動車だ。

brisk stock market business 活発な株式市場の取引,株式相場の盛況
◆An increase in transactions that brokerages handle has accompanied the brisk stock market business. 証券会社が扱う取引の増加は、そのまま株式相場の盛況と重なる。

British Bankers Association 英国銀行協会,BBA

British pound 英ポンド
◆In the case of foreign currency deposits, depositors can invest in foreign currencies such as British pound, Swiss franc and Australian dollar as well as the U.S. dollar and euro. 外貨預金の場合、預金者は、米ドルやユーロのほかに英ポンド、スイス・フランや豪ドルなどにも投資することができる。

broad (形)広い,広大な,幅の広い,広範な,一般的な,広範囲に及ぶ,広義の,偏見のない,大体の,大ざっぱな,大筋の,明白な
  a broad index 広範囲の指数
  broad-based stock index 総合株価指数
  broad-based upturn 広範の景気回復
  broad-line strategy 多品種供給戦略
  broad liquidity (aggregate) 広義流動性,広義の流動性
  broad market 大商い,大量取引高,好況市場 (active market)
  broad measure of money supply 広義のマネー・サプライ(通貨供給量)指標
  broad measures of inflation 幅広いインフレ指標
  broad tape ブロード・テープ（大型スクリーンに投影される最新株価情報）
  broader-based TOPIX index 全体の指数を示す東証株価指数(TOPIX)
  broader definition of money 通貨の広義の定義
  broader issuance of debt securities 債券発行の増加
  broader market 広域市場
  real broad monetary growth 広義の流動性の実質伸び率
  syndicate the deal on a broad basis 同案件の大型シ団組成を行う

broad money 広義の通貨,広義のマネー,広義の通貨供給量
  broad money (M2＋CDs) 広義のマネー(M2＋CD),広義の通貨(M2＋CD)
  broad money (M3) growth 広義の通貨供給量(M3)の伸び率,広義のマネー・サプライ(M2＋CD)伸び率

broad money supply　広義の通貨供給量, 広義のマネー・サプライ

broad money to GDP ratio　広義の通貨供給量の対GDP比率

demand for broad money　広義の通貨［マネー］に対する需要

broader-based recovery　ほとんどの地域での景気回復, ほぼ全地域での景気持ち直し
◆A U.S. Federal Reserve Board snapshot of economic conditions bolsters the hope of broader-based recovery. 米連邦準備制度理事会（FRB）の況況報告では、ほとんどの地域で景気持ち直しの期待が強まっている。

broader stock indicators　総合株価指数
（=broad-based stock index）
◆Broader stock indicators such as the S&P 500 index and the Nasdaq composite index also dropped in February. 2月は、S&P500株価指数やナスダック総合株価指数などの総合株価指数も、低下［下落］した。

brochure　（名）（案内・広告などの）パンフレット
◆National 26 nonlife insurance companies have mapped out a policy to improve their brochures to enable consumers to easily compare insurance products. 国内の損害保険会社26社は、消費者が保険商品を容易に比較できるようにするため、パンフレットの記載内容を改める方針を固めた。

brockage　（名）不完全鋳造貨

broken　（形）こわれた, 砕（くだ）けた, 半端（はんぱ）の, 破産した, 断続的な
broken amount　（特別価格で売り出される）特別株, 端銭（はせん）
broken date　（為替予約の）特別期日, 確定日渡し
broken family　欠損世帯
broken line　破線
broken lot　端株, 売買単位に達しない株
（=odd lot）
broken money　小銭
broken number　端数
broken period　（為替予約の）特別期間
（=non-standard period）
broken space　あき荷, から荷
broken term　特定期間渡し

broker　（動）仲介する, 取り次ぐ, 交渉する
brokered deposits　ブローカー預金
brokered trade　ブローカーを通じた取引
◆Convenience stores and supermarkets likely will be allowed to start handling bank deposits and brokering housing loans. コンビニエンス・ストアやスーパーで、銀行預金の取扱いや住宅ローンの取次ぎを開始できる見通しとなった。

broker　（名）株式仲買人, 仲介業者, 証券ブローカー, 証券会社, ブローカー　（証券ブローカーは、顧客の委託を受けて株式や債券の売買の仲介を行う業者のこと。⇒ dealer, e-broker）
arbitrage broker　さや取り業者
assignment broker　譲渡仲介業者
bill broker　手形仲買人, 証券仲買業者
bond broker　公社債ブローカー
broker agent　株式取引員
broker call loan　ブローカー・コール・ローン
（=broker's loan）
broker dealer［broker-dealer］　ブローカー・ディーラー, 証券会社
broker fee　ブローカー手数料
（=broker's commission）
broker's cover note　保険仲介人覚書
broker's loan　証券担保貸付け, ブローカーズ・ローン
broker's loan interest　証券担保貸付け金利, ブローカーズ・ローン金利
broker's market　不活発市場
broker's run　ブローカーの気配値
broker's swap rate　ブローカーのスワップ気配値
bullion broker　地金仲買人
business of broker　委託売買業務
commission broker　手数料ブローカー
curb broker　（証券の）場外市場仲買人, 場外取引仲買人, 場外取引ブローカー
curb-stone broker　場外取引ブローカー
（=kerbstone broker）
customhouse broker　通関代理店
（=customs broker）
customs broker　通関業者
designated broker　指定ブローカー
discount broker　割引ブローカー, 手形割引仲買人
exchange broker　為替ブローカー
executing broker　注文執行ブローカー
Financial Intermediaries, Managers and Brokers Regulatory Association　金融仲介業者規制協会
floor broker　立会場ブローカー, 場内仲買人
forward broker　先物ブローカー
full broker　正ブローカー
futures broker　先物ブローカー
government broker　政府公認ブローカー［仲買人］
insurance broker　保険ブローカー, 保険仲立人
introducing broker　取次ぎブローカー
investment broker　投資仲買人
kerb broker　場外取引ブローカー
lease broker　リース仲介人
Lloyd's broker　ロイズ・ブローカー
money broker　金融ブローカー
New York Board of Cotton Brokers　ニューヨーク綿花取引所
note broker　手形ブローカー
offshore broker　域外仲買人
OTC broker　店頭ブローカー
outside broker　非会員ブローカー
over-the-counter broker　非会員ブローカー
policy broker　証券ブローカー
real estate broker　不動産業者
running broker　手形仲買人
securities broker　証券ブローカー, 有価証券仲買人
securities broker and dealer　証券会社
spot broker　現物仲買人
stock［share］broker　株式ブローカー, 株式仲買人
street broker　場外仲買人
two-dollar broker　2ドル口銭株式仲買人, 2ドル・ブローカー
◆A real estate broker created a dummy company to illegally receive a public credit guarantee. 不動産業者が、架空の会社を作って不正に公的信用保証を受けていた。◆Margin trading is buying stocks with money borrowed from the broker. 信用取引では、証券会社から資金を借りて株を買う。

brokerage　（名）証券業, 証券会社, 仲介, 仲介業, 仲買, 仲買業, 証券仲買会社, 仲介手数料, ブローカー　（⇒ deregulation, futures brokerage, futures trading brokerage, low-priced issues, online brokerage, securities brokerage, stock brokerage）
brokerage account　証券取引口座
brokerage allocation budget　（資産運用機関の売買注文の）発注計画

brokerage allowance　委託販売手数料
brokerage business　委託販売業務
brokerage charge　仲介手数料, 仲買手数料
full-service brokerage　フルサービス証券会社
leading commodity futures brokerage　商品先物大手
member brokerages of the Tokyo Stock Exchange　東証の会員証券会社, 東証の取引参加者
securities brokerage business　証券仲介業, 証券仲介業務, 証券仲介ビジネス
stock brokerage　株式委託売買, 証券仲介業
stock brokerage firm　証券会社
◆A former president of a bankrupt securities company acquired the securities company for ￥350 million although he did not have sufficient brokerage experience. 破産した証券会社の元社長は、証券業の十分な経験がないまま同証券会社を3億5,000万円で買収していた。◆An increase in transactions that brokerages handle has accompanied the brisk stock market business. 証券会社が扱う取引の増加は、そのまま株式相場の盛況と重なる。◆The brokerage's main services for individual customers will be asset management advisory services, focusing on the sale of products such as investment trust funds that invest in foreign equities, and money market funds denominated in foreign currencies. 同証券会社は、株式の主な個人顧客向け（売買仲介）業務として、外国株を組み込んだ投資信託や外貨建てMMF（マネー・マーケット・ファンド）などの商品の販売を中心に、資産運用顧問業務を展開する方針だ。◆The company is the largest U.S. full-service brokerage. 同社は、米国最大手のフルサービス証券会社です。

brokerage commission　株式委託売買手数料, 委託売買手数料, 委託手数料, 仲介手数料, ブローカー手数料　（=brokerage fees; ⇒futures brokerage, liberalization）
◆Brokerage commissions on commodity futures trading were completely liberalized in late December. 商品先物取引の委託手数料が昨年（2004年）末、完全自由化された。

brokerage dealer　証券会社のディーラー
◆Individual investors and brokerage dealers continued to take profits from recent surges in comparatively low-prices issues. 個人投資家と証券会社のディーラーは、最近の比較的割安な銘柄の急上昇で引き続き利食いに出た。

brokerage fees　委託手数料, 仲介手数料, 委託売買手数料, 株式買手数料, 株式売買委託手数料, 仲買手数料
（=brokerage commission）
◆The major securities house attributed the poor earnings to sharp drops in brokerage fees and trading profits amid the extended slump in the domestic stock market. この大手証券会社は、減益の要因として、国内株式市場の長期低迷による株売買手数料と売買益の大幅減を挙げた。◆The two major securities companies cut brokerage fees further for major clients. 大手証券会社2社は、大口顧客に対して株式売買手数料をさらに引き下げた。

brokerage firm　証券会社
（=brokerage house, securities company）
◆The brokerage firm inflated its consolidated earnings for its business year through March 2011. 同証券会社は、2011年3月期の連結利益を水増ししていた。◆The brokerage firm manages client assets of ￥520 billion in about 150,000 accounts. この証券会社は、口座数約15万で顧客預り資産が5,200億円に達する。◆The financial authorities filed a declaration of bankruptcy and a request for asset protection with the Tokyo District Court for the brokerage firm. 金融当局は、同証券会社の破産宣告と財産保全処分を東京地裁に申し立てた。

brokerage house　証券会社　（=brokerage firm, securities company; ⇒business alliance, stock loss）
◆In 1996, brokerage houses were found to have funneled profits to sokaiya corporate racketeers. 1996年には、証券会社の総会屋への利益供与事件が相次いで発覚した。

brokering　（名）仲介, 取次ぎ, 交渉
assignment brokering　譲渡の仲介
securities brokering　証券の仲介, 証券仲介業
◆The wall separating banking and securities businesses has been lowered through such moves as the liberalization of banks' securities brokering. 銀行と証券業の垣根は、銀行に対する証券仲介業の規制緩和などの動きで、低くなっている。

broking　（名）証券売買取引, 株式仲買い, 仲買業, 委託取引, ブローキング
broking function　証券業務
broking house　証券会社
cross-broking　証券売買の相互取引
international broking　国際委託取引, 海外委託取引, インターナショナル・ブローキング, IB
stock broking　証券売買仲介
◆The TSE wants to initially limit to about 50 to 100 issues the number of listed companies covered by cross-broking system. 東証は当初、この相互取引制度の上場企業の対象銘柄を50〜100銘柄に限定したい考えだ。

bubble　（名）バブル, 泡沫　（⇒economic bubble, high-tech bubble, stock bubble）
asset bubble　資産のバブル
bubble collapse　バブル崩壊
bubble company　泡沫会社
bubble in IT investments　IT投資バブル, ITバブル
bubble years　バブル期　（=bubble economic era, bubble period, bubble economy period）
bursting of the yen bubble　円のバブルがはじけること（=burst of the yen bubble）
dot-com bubble　ドットコム・バブル
economic bubble burst　バブル崩壊
financial bubble burst　金融バブルの崩壊
high-tech bubble　ハイテク関連株の狂乱バブル, ハイテク・バブル
IT bubble　IT投資バブル, ITバブル
Net bubble　ネット株バブル, ネット・バブル
postbubble closing low　バブル崩壊後の終値での最安値（=post-bubble closing low）
postbubble low　バブル後最安値, バブル経済崩壊後の最安値
postbubble record low　バブル崩壊後の最安値
◆Before the bubble collapsed, many pundits had predicted that the likely downturn of the U.S. economy would have only a limited impact on the rest of the world. バブル経済の崩壊前には、「米経済はいずれ行き詰まるだろうが、他国への影響は限定的である」と専門家の多くは予測していた。◆The IT bubble and the ensuing swelling of the financial market of late have stemmed from technology innovation coupled with the globalization of the economy. (1990年代後半の)ITバブルとそれに続く最近までの金融膨張を引き起こしたのは、経済のグローバル化の動きと連動した技術革新だ。

bubble burst　バブルの崩壊
◆Many pundits in Tokyo have prophesized the possible demise of U.S. primacy since the financial bubble burst. 金融バブルの崩壊以降、日本では、米一極指導の終焉（しゅうえん）を予言する専門家が多い。

bubble economy　バブル経済, バブル景気, バブル期, バブル
collapse［burst, bursting, rapture］of the bubble economy　バブル崩壊, バブル経済の崩壊
during the bubble economy　バブル期に, バブル期の
postbubble［post-bubble］economy　バブル崩壊後の経済
rise of the bubble economy　バブル経済の出現

the collapse of the bubble economy　バブル経済の崩壊, バブル崩壊
◆During the bubble economy, life insurers sold a large number of policies by promising high yields. バブル期に生保各社は、高い予定利率を約束して多くの保険契約を獲得した。◆Japanese banks failed to take quick actions to dispose of nonperforming loans following the bursting of the bubble economy. 邦銀は、バブル崩壊後の不良債権処理に迅速に対応しなかった。◆Since the collapse of the bubble economy in the early 1990s, Japan has experienced several phases of economic revival. 1990年代はじめのバブル崩壊以降、日本は何度か景気回復局面を迎えた。◆Though stock prices remain low, the number of transactions has already outpaced that during the bubble economy. 株価はまだ低いものの、株取引の件数はすでにバブル期を超えている。

budding economic recovery　景気回復の芽
◆Should the government forge ahead with its belt-tightening policy, the budding economic recovery may be reduced to a short-lived upturn. 政府が緊縮路線をひた走れば、景気回復の芽も、薄命の景気回復に終わりかねない。

budge　(動)少し動く, 意見[態度]を変える, 譲歩する
◆China has not budged an inch to shift the current dollar-yuan exchange rate. 中国は、現在の元・ドル・レートを梃子でも動かそうとしていない。

budget　(名)予算, 予算案, 財政　(⇒fiscal year, implement an expansionary budget, supplementary budget)
　additional budget　補正予算
　amended budget　修正予算
　an initial budget　当初予算
　annual budget　年度予算
　appropriation type budget　割当て型予算
　austere [austerity] budget　緊縮予算
　balance the budget　財政均衡を図る, 財政を均衡させる
　balanced budget　均衡予算
　balanced budgets　財政均衡化
　baseline budget　基本予算
　be over budget　赤字である
　belt-tightening budget　緊縮型予算
　bottom-up type budget　積上げ予算
　bring the budget to balance　財政収支の均衡を図る, 財政均衡を図る
　capital budget　資本予算, 投資予算
　cash budget　現金予算
　cash flow budget　キャッシュ・フロー予算
◆Fiscal resources of ¥1.6 trillion cannot be scrounged together simply by recasting the budget and cutting wasteful spending. 1.6兆円の財源は、予算の組替えや無駄の削減だけでは捻出(ねんしゅつ)できない。◆The ¥44 trillion shortfall including tax revenue and nontax revenue in spending in the fiscal 2010 budget must be made up for by issuing government bonds. 2010年度予算の歳出のうち、税収と税外収入を含めて44兆円の不足分は、国債発行で補填しなければならない。
◆The government bond issuance worth about ¥44 trillion for the current fiscal year is the largest ever projected in an initial budget. 今年度の約44兆円の国債発行額は、当初予算としては史上最高だ。◆The government has begun compiling the budget. 政府が、予算編成作業を開始した。

budget　(形)安い, 格安の, 予算の, 予算に合った, 財政の
　budget account　(銀行の)自動支払い口座, 自動引落し口座
　budget airline　格安航空会社
　budget appropriation [expenditure]　予算支出, 予算の割当て, 予算の計上, 予算の承認
　budget audit [auditing]　決算審査

　budget bill　予算案
　budget ceiling　予算シーリング
　budget committee　予算委員会
　budget compilation　予算編成
　　(=budget drafting, budget preparation)
　budget consolidation　財政立て直し, 財政再建
　　(⇒fiscal consolidation)
　budget constraint　予算的制約, 予算の制限
　budget forecast　財政収支見通し
　budget guideline　予算編成方針
　budget implementation　予算の執行
　budget modification [revision]　予算修正
　budget numbers　財政収支の数字
　budget outlays　財政支出
　budget overruns　予算超過
　budget planning period　予算計画期間
　budget policies　予算編成方針
　budget reform　財政改革
　budget revenue reform　歳入改革
　budget surplus　財政黒字
　enact a budget deal　予算交渉をまとめる

budget allocation　予算配分
◆Lower budget allocations for public works projects are apparently affecting the economy. 公共事業の予算削減[予算配分引下げ]が、明らかに景気に影響を及ぼしている。

budget balance　財政収支
◆The primary balance represents the budget balance, excluding proceeds from government bond issues and debt-servicing costs. プライマリー・バランスは、国債発行による収入と国債費(国債の利払いや償還費用)を除いた財政収支である。

budget compilation process　予算編成作業
◆The fiscal 2011 budget compilation process may become a tool to gain popularity. 2011年度予算の編成作業は、人気取りの手段になる可能性もある。

budget crisis　財政危機
◆Greece asked other eurozone member states for financial support to help it stem its budget crisis in early 2010. 2010年初めにギリシャは、財政危機を回避するため、他のユーロ圏加盟国に金融支援を求めた。

budget cut　予算削減
　stringent budget cuts　緊縮予算
◆In the case of Japan, only a limited number of people are adversely affected by budget cuts. 日本の場合、予算の削減で悪影響を受けるのは、限られた人たちだけである。

budget deficit　財政赤字, 予算の赤字, 赤字財政
　(=budget gap; ⇒federal budget deficit)
　a burgeoning budget deficit　膨れ上がる財政赤字
　a primary budget deficit　基礎的財政収支の赤字
　budget deficit reduction　財政赤字削減
　budget deficit spending　赤字財政支出
　chronicle budget deficits　慢性的財政赤字
　eliminate a budget deficit　財政赤字をなくす
　excessive budget deficits　過度の財政赤字
　finance a budget deficit　財政赤字の穴埋めをする
　huge [massive] budget deficits　膨大な財政赤字, 巨額の財政赤字
　out-of-control budget deficits　手に負えない財政赤字
　reduce budget deficits　財政赤字を削減する, 財政赤字を減らす
　structural budget deficit　構造的財政赤字
　target budget deficit　財政赤字の目標額

the U.S. budget deficit　米国の財政赤字
◆Obama projects the U.S. budget deficit soaring to a fresh record in 2010. オバマ米大統領は、2010年度(2009年10月～2010年9月)の財政赤字は急増して過去最悪[過去最悪の更新]になると見込んでいる。◆Spain also faces a huge budget deficit. スペインも、巨額の財政赤字を抱えている。◆The estimates of the Cabinet Office showed that Japan would log a primary budget deficit of about ¥4.9 trillion in fiscal 2015. 内閣府の試算によると、日本の基礎的財政収支の赤字額は、2015年度で4兆9,000億円程度になる。◆The Greek government has set forth measures to decrease the number of government employees and raise taxes to cut its budget deficits. 財政赤字削減のため、ギリシャ政府は公務員削減や増税策を打ち出した。◆The S&P cut in the U.S. long-term credit rating by one notch to AA-plus from AAA resulted from concerns about the nation's budget deficits and climbing debt burden. スタンダード・アンド・プアーズ(S&P)が米国の長期国債格付けを最上級のAAA(トリプルA)からAA(ダブルA)に1段階引き下げた理由は、米国の財政赤字と債務負担の増大に対する懸念だ。◆The U.S. budget deficit for fiscal 2010 narrowed to $1.29 trillion as tax collections recovered slightly and financial bailout spending fell sharply. 米国の2010会計年度(2009年10月～2010年9月)の財政赤字は、税収がいくぶん回復し、金融救済[金融支援]費用が急減したため、1兆2,900億ドルに縮小した。◆Under the EU's Stability and Growth Pact, countries eligible to join the euro system are required to keep budget deficits below 3 percent of GDP. 欧州連合(EU)の財政安定・成長協定によると、ユーロ加盟国は、加盟の条件として財政赤字をGDPの3%以下に抑えなければならない。

budget discipline　財政規律
(=budgetary discipline, fiscal discipline)
◆French President Nicolas Sarkozy and German Chancellor Angela Merkel agreed a master plan for imposing a budget discipline across the eurozone. サルコジ仏大統領とメルケル独首相は、ユーロ圏全域に財政規律を課す基本計画に合意した。

Budget Message　予算教書　(=budget documents, budget plan, spending plan: 一般教書(the State of the Union address)、経済報告(Economic Report of the President)と合わせて三大教書と呼ばれている)

budget request　(各省庁予算の)概算要求
(=budgetary request)
◆Budget requests for fiscal 2011 totaled ¥96.7 trillion. 2011年度予算の概算要求総額は、96.7兆円となった。◆Ministries and other central government bodies have submitted their fiscal 2011 budget requests to the Finance Ministry. 各府省庁が、2011年度予算の概算要求を、財務相に提出した。

budget shortfall　財源不足,財政赤字
◆The special account borrows from the private sector and other sources to make up for local government's budget shortfalls. 特別会計は、民間などの財源からの借入れで地方の財源不足[財政赤字]の穴埋めをしている。

budget year　会計年度　(=budget fiscal year)
◆The U.S. deficit in the first three months of the current budget year includes $247 billion that has been spent on the $700 billion financial rescue program. 今会計年度(2009年度)の当初3か月(10-12月)の米財政赤字には、7,000億ドルの金融支援策に基づいて支出された2,470億ドルも含まれている。◆The U.S. government's 2012 budget year runs through Sept. 30. 米政府の2012会計年度は、(2011年10月から)2012年9月30日までとなっている。

budgetary　(形)予算の,予算上の,予算案の,財政の
　budgetary adjustment　財政調整
　budgetary authority　予算限度額
　budgetary committee　予算委員会
　budgetary control　予算統制,予算管理
　budgetary deficit　財政赤字,赤字予算,予算不足
　budgetary discipline　財政規律
　budgetary discussion　予算審議
　budgetary planning　予算計画
　budgetary policy　財政政策
　budgetary procedure　予算手続き
　budgetary process　予算編成過程
　budgetary red ink　財政赤字
　budgetary surplus　財政黒字,黒字予算
　priority in budgetary discussion　予算先議権
　significant budgetary stimulus　積極的な財政出動
　take budgetary steps[measures]　予算措置を取る[講じる]

budgetary expenditures　財政支出,歳出
◆To resolve the issue of fiscal deficits, it is necessary to trim budgetary expenditures while securing revenue sources. 財政赤字を解決するには、歳出を削減する一方、税収を確保する必要がある。

budgetary request　概算要求,予算要求
(=budget request, budgetary demand)
◆The Council on Economic and Fiscal Policy approved a ceiling on budgetary request by ministries and agencies for fiscal 2005 budget. 経済財政諮問会議が、省庁による2005年度予算の概算要求基準を了承した。◆To help finance the government burden in running the basic pension plan, the Health, Labor and Welfare Ministry calls for ¥10.67 trillion in funds in its budgetary request for fiscal 2012. 基礎年金運営の国庫負担[国の負担]分の費用として、厚生労働省は、2012年度予算の概算要求で10兆6,700億円を要求している。

budgetary request guidelines　概算要求基準
(=ceiling on budgetary request)
◆According to the budgetary request guidelines, the government will trim public works spending by 3 percent compared to fiscal 2004. 概算要求基準によると、政府は公共投資関係費を前年度(2004年度)比3%削減する。

buffer　(名)緩衝材,クッション,緩衝装置,破産防止手段,バッファー
　buffer action　緩衝作用
　buffer against credit losses　信用損失[貸倒れ]に対するクッション,信用損失を和らげるクッション
　buffer fund　緩衝基金
　buffer inventory[stock]　緩衝在庫
　buffer stock financing facility　緩衝在庫融資,緩衝在庫融資制度
　capital buffer　資本バッファー,資本増強
　capital buffer against　～に備えるための資本増強
　capital conservation buffer　資本保全バッファー
　countercyclical capital buffer　景気連動[変動]抑制的な資本バッファー,カウンターシリカル資本バッファー
　foreign exchange buffer　外貨バッファー
　hit[run into]the buffers　失敗に帰す
　provide a buffer　クッションになる
◆The U.S. 10 leading banks need a combined capital buffer of 74.6 billion against the risk of a deeper recession and higher unemployment over the next two years. 米主要金融機関の10社は、今後2年の景気悪化リスクと失業増大に備えて、10社合計で746億ドルの資本増強を求められている。

buffering　(名)銀行カードの変造

buffet　(動)揺さぶる,苦しめる,痛めつける,打ちのめす,衝撃を与える,翻弄する,襲う,(逆境などと)戦う,戦いながら進む
　be buffeted by　～に翻弄される,～に痛めつけられる,～のショックを受ける,～が襲う
　buffet one's way into great waves　荒波を進む

buffet one's way to riches and fame　苦労を重ねて富と名を成す

buffet the currency　通貨の急落をもたらす, 通貨を揺さぶる

◆In Europe, buffeted by the U.S. financial crisis, four major countries have held a summit meeting to discuss countermeasures. 米金融危機の煽（あお）りを受けた欧州では、主要4か国が最近、首脳会議を開いて対策を協議した。◆Japanese small and midsize firms are being buffeted by the superstrong yen and electricity shortages. 日本の中小企業は現在、超円高と電力不足で痛めつけられている［経営環境が悪化している］。

bulge bracket　バルジ・ブラケット（引受シンジケート団のなかで最も引受数量をこなす投資銀行グループのこと）

bulk　（名）積み荷, 散荷（ばらに）, 大量, 大部分, 大半, バルク

　bulk buying [purchase]　大量買付け, 大量仕入れ, 大量購入, 一括購入, 全量買占め

　bulk commercial real estate sales　商業用不動産の一括売却

　bulk discount　一括購入割引

　bulk order　大口注文, 一括注文, 大量発注

　bulk sale　一括販売, 全量販売, バラ売り, 量り売り, バルク販売, 企業財産の包括的譲渡

　bulk shipment　大量船積み

　bulk trading　一括取引

　bulk transfer　包括譲渡

　the bulk of one's debt　～の負債の大部分

　the bulk purchase of the firm's finance receivables　同社金融債権の一括購入

◆The bulk of the money needed for earthquake reconstruction programs could be collected in three years through raising the consumption tax rate by 3 percent. 震災復興計画に必要な資金の大半は、消費税率を3％引き上げて3年間で賄（まかな）うことが可能だ。

bull　（名）強気筋, 強気, 買い方, ブル

　buying bull　思惑買い

　Charging Bull　ニューヨーク証券取引所前に置いてある「突進する雄牛」像

　dollar bulls　ドルに強気な向き

　take the bull by the horns　（困難などに）勇敢に立ち向かう, 難局に立ち向かう, 英断の処置を取る

◆The equity market is all bulls. 株式市場は、買い方一色だ。◆This year will become the Year of the Bull. 今年は、「強気の年」になるだろう。

bull　（形）強気の, 強気筋の, 上向きの, 買い方の

　a bull factor for the stock market　株式市場の強気要因

　bull account　強気筋

　bull-bear bond　強気弱気債, ブル・ベア債（指標が上がれば金利が下がる債券と金利が上がる債券を組み合わせたもの）

　bull-bear position　強気・弱気状態

　bull bond　強気債, ブル債, ブル・ボンド（償還時の金利水準によって償還額の増減が生じるドル債）

　bull buying　強気買い

　bull campaign　ブル・キャンペーン

　bull clique　強気筋

　bull floater　ブル型変動利債, ブル・フローター

　bull interests　強気筋（=long interests）

　bull operation　強気筋の操作

　bull point　強み, 有利な点

　bull position　買い持ち（long position）, 強気状態, 強気姿勢

　bull purchase　強気買い

　bull raid　強気筋の市場攪乱（かくらん）

　bull-run　相場の上昇局面

　bull share　強気株

　bull speculator　強気の投機家

　bull transaction　強気筋取引

bull market　強気市場, 強気相場, 強気市況, 上げ相場, 上昇相場, 買い相場, 買い手市場
（=bullish market, strong market）

　be stable in the bull market　上げ相場で安定している

　make profits in the bull market　上昇相場［上げ相場］で利益を上げる

　the early return of a bull market　上げ相場の早期回復

◆Gold is in the 11th year of a bull market. 金の上げ相場は、11年続いている。◆Personal investors have made profits in the recent bull market. 個人投資家は、最近の上昇相場で利益を上げている。◆The early return of a bull market is unlikely. 上げ相場の早期回復は、期待できない。◆The stock market is stable in the bull market. 株式市場は、上げ相場で安定している。

bull spread　ブル・スプレッド（原証券（underlying security）の値上がりで利益が出るように、コール・オプションの売りと買い、またはプット・オプションの売りと買いを組み合わせる取引）

　call bull spread　コール・ブル・スプレッド（コール・オプションの売りと買いの組合せ）

　put bull spread　プット・ブル・スプレッド（プット・オプションの売りと買いの組合せ）

bulldog（bond）　（名）ブルドッグ・ボンド（国際機関や外国の政府、企業が、英国の債券市場でポンド建てで発行する債券）

bullet　（名）満期一括償還型証券, 利率満期確定債券, 元本満期一括返済, 元本満期一括, 返済融資, 一括返済（形）弾丸の, 銃弾の, 一括の, 満期一括の一括償還型の, 一括返済の

　bullet bond　満期一括償還債

　bullet loan　満期一括返済融資, 一括返済ローン

　bullet maturity　満期一括償還債

　bullet maturity amortization [amortisation]　満期一括償還

　bullet mortgage　満期一括償還型モーゲージ

　bullet payment　一括返済, 満期一括償還

　bullet payment loan　満期一括返済（方式）融資（=bullet loan）

　bullet repayment　一括払い, 一括返済, 一括返済型

　bullet repayment loan　一括返済型ローン

　five-year bullet deal　5年物の満期一括償還債

　straight bullet issue　満期一括償還型普通債

　ten-year bullet deal　10年物の満期一括償還債

　the bullet　解雇通知

bullion　（名）金塊, 銀塊, 地金, 金地金（きんじがね）, 純金［純銀］, インゴット, 延べ棒

　bullion dealer　金銀塊仲買人

　bullion operation　金銀操作

　bullion point　正貨現送点

　bullion quotation　地金相場

　bullion standard　地金本位制

　demand for bullion　金の需要, 地金の需要, 金塊の需要

　gold bullion　金塊, 金地金

　gold bullion standard　金地金本位制, 金塊本位制

　London bullion market　ロンドン金市場

　silver bullion　銀地金, 銀塊

◆Demand for bullion as a protection of wealth has been

spurred by mounting concern that the global economy is faltering. 世界経済低迷への懸念増大から、安全資産［資産保全］としての金の需要が拡大している。◆Record low U.S. borrowing costs are boosting the appeal to bullion as a hedge against inflation. 米国の資金調達コストが過去最低の水準にあるため、インフレ・ヘッジとしての金［金地金］の人気が高まっている。

bullionism （名）重金主義, 硬貨主義

bullish （形）強気の, 強気材料の, 上がり気味の, 見通しが明るい, 楽観的見方の, 積極的な
（⇒bearish, sentiment）
 be bullish of the economy　景気の見通しが明るい
 be bullish on the economy　景気に楽観的な見方をする, 景気見通しで強気になる
 bullish bias　強気の地（じ）合い
 bullish influence　強気材料, 強材料, 好材料
 （=bullish factor, bullish news）
 bullish market　上昇相場, 相場上昇, 上げ相場, 買い相場, 強気市況
 bullish market sentiment　市場の地合いが強いこと, 市場の強気の地合い
 bullish news　好材料, 強材料
 bullish stock market　堅調な株式市場, 株式相場の上昇, 株高
 bullish tone　強気ムード, 強気
 bullish view on　～について強気の見方
 remain bullish on the dollar　ドルの先高感が依然として強い, 依然としてドル高の展開だ, ドルについて強気の見方を変えない
 turn bullish　強気に転じる
◆The domestic economy is bullish. 国内景気は, 見通しが明るい。◆Top firms are bullish on the domestic economy. 大手企業は、国内景気に楽観的な見方をしている（大企業の国内景況感はきわめて強い）。

bullish sentiment　強気の地（じ）合い, 勢い, 強気心理, 買い気, 上げ相場
◆A recent decline in bullish sentiment among foreign investors in the Japanese stock market has caused domestic stock prices to decline. 外国人投資家の間で日本の株式市場の強気の地合いが［日本の株式市場を支えていた外国人投資家の勢いが］ここに来て弱まり, 国内株価が軟調となっている。

bullish stock market　堅調な株式市場, 株式相場の上昇, 株高
◆The bullish stock market in the past six months has led the unrealized value of bank-held stocks to swell by about ￥3 trillion. 株式市場が過去半年間, 堅調に推移したことで, 銀行保有株式の含み損益が約3兆円増加した。

bullishness （名）強気, 上がり気味, 見通しが明るいこと

bulwark （名）防波堤, 防御［防護］壁, 壁, 障壁, 支持者, 擁護者
◆A Japan-U.S. economic partnership agreement could create a bulwark against protectionist forces, thereby sustaining the liberal and open trading platform. 日米経済連携協定（EPA）は, 保護主義勢力への防波堤となり, それによって自由でオープンな貿易体制を堅持することができる。

Bundesbank （名）ドイツ連邦銀行（ドイツの中央銀行。本部はフランクフルト）

buoy （動）活気づかせる, 浮揚させる, 高める, 支える
 be buoyed by　～で活気づく, ～に支えられる
 buoy the economy　景気を浮揚させる
 have a greater impact in buoying the global economy　～で世界の景気浮揚効果は拡大する
◆Global newspaper circulation is rising, buoyed by demand in Asia and South America. 世界の新聞発行部数は、アジアや南米での需要増に支えられて, 伸びている。◆The Bank of Japan's resorting to quantitative easing in concert with the Fed would have a greater impact on in buoying the global economy. 米連邦準備制度理事会（FRB）と歩調を合わせて日銀が量的緩和に踏み切れば, 世界景気の浮揚効果は拡大すると思われる。

buoyant （形）活況の, 好調の, 上昇傾向の, 上がり気味の
 buoyant areas　好調な分野
 buoyant conditions　活況
 buoyant consumer spending　好調な消費支出, 消費支出の好調
 buoyant demand　需要の拡大, 需要の盛り上がり
 buoyant export　好調な輸出
 buoyant investment income　投資収益の増大
 buoyant performance　好業績, 好決算
 （=brisk performance）
◆Buttressed by buoyant exports and the effect of restructuring moves, such as personnel cutbacks, major firms are substantially improving their earnings. 好調な輸出と人員削減などのリストラ策の効果に支えられて, 大手企業の収益は大幅に改善している。◆Wall Street and Main Street might turn out to be buoyant this autumn. 米国の証券市場と国内産業は, 今年の秋には活況を取り戻すかもしれない。

burden （動）～に重荷を負わせる,（義務, 責任を）負わせる, ～を悩ます, ～を苦しめる
 be burdened with　～を背負わされる, ～を負わされる, ～を背負っている, ～を持っている, ～に苦しめられる, ～で苦しむ
 burden a nation [the people] with heavy taxes　国民に重税を背負わせる, 国民に重税を課す
◆A large number of companies are burdened with massive amounts of excessive liabilities in sectors such as construction and wholesale. 建設や卸売りなどの分野では, 巨額の過剰債務を抱えている企業が多い。◆Japanese companies have long been burdened with high labor costs. 日本企業は, 高い労働コストに長いこと苦しめられてきた。◆To help finance the government burden in running the basic pension plan, the Health, Labor and Welfare Ministry calls for ￥10.67 trillion in funds in its budgetary request for fiscal 2012. 基礎年金運営の国庫負担［国の負担］分の費用として, 厚生労働省は, 2012年度予算の概算要求で10兆6,700億円を要求している。◆To stabilize the pension system, the government raised its burden in the basic pension plan to 50 percent of the total contribution from fiscal 2009. 年金制度の安定化を図るため, 政府は, 基礎年金の国の負担割合を2009年度から総給付金の50％に引き上げた。

burden （名）負担, 費用負担, リスク, 重荷, 間接費, 製造間接費, 経費　（⇒financial burden）
 absorbed burden　製造間接費配賦（はいふ）額, 配賦済み製造間接費　（=absorbed overhead, applied burden, applied overhead）
 bank's burden　銀行の負担, 銀行のリスク
 bond redemption burden　社債償還の負担, 国債償還の負担
 burden charge　負担金
 burden of capital requirements　資本負担
 burden of debt service　金利負担
 burden of disposing of bad loans　不良債権処理の負担, 不良債権処理損失
 burden rate　間接費配賦率, 製造間接費配賦率, 配賦率
 burden share　負担, 分担
 credit burden　債務負担
 debt burden　債務, 債務負担, 債務超過
 （=debt payments burden）
 debt payments burden　債務負担
 deposit insurance burden　預金保険負担

depreciation burden　減価償却負担
double debt burden　二重ローンの負担
　（=dual debt burden）
external debt burden　対外債務
factory burden　製造間接費
financial burden　金融負担, 財務面での負担, 財政負担, 経済負担
fiscal burden　財政負担
interest burden　利子負担, 金利負担
interest payment burden　金利負担, 利払いの負担
　（=the burden of interest payment）
international debt burden　対外的な債務負担
overhead burden　経費
public burden　国民負担
ratio of interest burden　利子負担率
　（=interest burden ratio）
repayment burden　返済負担
servicing burden　債務返済の負担
share the burden　共同負担する
social contribution burden　社会保障負担
tax burden　租税負担, 税負担, 租税負担率（tax burden ratio）
the burden of capital requirements　資本負担
the burden of debt service　金利負担
the burden of interest payments　利払いの負担, 金利負担
　（=the burden of interest payments）
the burden of loss to creditors　債権者の負担
wage burden　人件費
◆Banks are regulated to reduce the capital in the event of hefty appraisal losses, as a way of requiring shareholders to share the burden of the losses. 巨額の含み損[評価損]の場合、銀行規制で銀行は、株主にもその損失の負担を引き受けさせるために資本金を削減することになる。◆If the government financial support is not offered to TEPCO, the utility's creditors and shareholders will have to share the burden. 東電に政府の金融支援がない場合は、同社の債権者と株主が共同負担せざるを得ないだろう。◆If the prices of purchased bad assets are set high, the public burden will balloon. 不良資産の買取り価格を高くすると、国民負担が膨らむ。◆In response to the double loan problem due to the March 11 disaster, financial institutions will be forced to share some burdens including the waiver of debts. 東日本大震災による二重ローン問題への対応では、債権の放棄を含めて金融機関もある程度の共同負担を強いられることになろう。◆It is impossible to maintain the social security system without asking the public to shoulder an additional burden. 国民に負担増を求めないで社会保障制度を維持するのは、不可能だ。◆Public institutions or revitalization funds will buy the loans owed by small and midsize companies that have been hit by the March 11 disaster to lighten their repayment burdens. 公的機関や復興ファンドが、東日本大震災で被災した中小企業の借金を買い取って、被災企業の返済負担を軽減するものと思われる。◆Taxpayers' burden from the JAL bailout was lowered to ￥47 billion as the firm repaid part of its outstanding debt. 日航救済による国民の負担分は、日航が債務残高の一部を返済したため、470億円に減少した。◆The drastic overhaul of the Japanese accounting system is expected to add a massive administrative burden to companies. 日本の会計基準の抜本的変更は、企業にとって大幅な事務負担の増加を強いられることになる。

burden of disposing of bad loans　不良債権処理の負担
◆Major banking groups reported after-tax losses for the second consecutive business year due to the burden of disposing of bad loans and slumping stock markets. 不良債権処理の負担（不良債権処理損失）や株式不況の低迷で、大手銀行は2期連続の税引き後赤字となった。

burgeoning　（形）急成長の, 急発展の, 急速に発展する, 新興の, 急増する
　burgeoning foreign interest　活発な動きを見せる外資, 外資の活発な動き
　burgeoning population　急成長の人口
　burgeoning workforces　従業員の急増, 従業員の過剰
　new burgeoning market　急成長の新市場, 急速に拡大する新市場
◆The serious deterioration of operational efficiency is caused by excess output capacity and burgeoning workforces. 極端な経営効率の悪化は、生産設備と従業員の過剰によるものだ。

burgeoning budget deficit　膨れ上がる財政赤字, 財政赤字の膨張, 財政赤字の急増
◆At the time of 2003, the German government was saddled with a burgeoning budget deficit stemming from the rehabilitation of former East Germany following German reunification. 2003年当時、ドイツ政府は、ドイツ再統一後の旧東独の再建で膨れ上がる財政赤字を抱えていた。

burgeoning free markets　急速に広がる自由市場
◆The revaluation of currency in North Korea appears aimed at clamping down on burgeoning free markets in an attempt to reassert the regime's control. 北朝鮮の通貨改定は、政権の統制力を改めて強めるため、急速に広がる自由市場を厳しく取り締まるねらいがあるようだ。

burn rate　資本燃焼率, バーン・レート（新規企業が営業キャッシュ・フローを生み出す前に支払いのため資本を消費する率）

bursting [burst]　（名）崩壊, 爆発, 破裂

bursting of property bubbles　不動産バブルの崩壊
　（=bursting of the bubble in the real estate market）
◆The recent financial crises have stemmed mainly from the bursting of property bubbles as in the case of Japan. 近年の金融危機は、日本の場合のように、主に不動産バブルの崩壊によるものだ。

bursting of the bubble　バブルの崩壊, バブル経済の崩壊（=bubble economy's collapse, bursting of the bubble economy, bursting of the economic bubble, collapse of the bubble economy）
　bursting of the yen bubble　円のバブルがはじけること
　（=burst of the yen bubble）
◆All the insurers are now saddled with an enormous amount of negative yields as returns on their investments have plunged due to ultralow interest rates—a consequence of the bursting of the bubble. 生保各社は現在、バブル崩壊後の超低金利時代で運用利回りが急低下し、巨額の逆ざやを抱えている。

bursting of the bubble economy　バブル経済の崩壊, バブル崩壊
◆Japanese banks failed to take quick actions to dispose of nonperforming loans following the bursting of the bubble economy. 邦銀は、バブル崩壊後の不良債権処理に迅速に対応しなかった。

bursting of the economic bubble　バブル経済の崩壊, バブル崩壊
◆The lost decade refers to the period of economic stagnation since the bursting of the economic bubble in the early 1990s. 「失われた10年」とは、バブルが崩壊した1990年代初めから続いた景気後退[景気停滞]期のことである。

business　（名）事業, 商売, 商業, 取引, 営業, 業務, 業容, 職務, 職業, 実務, 実業, 実業界, 会社, 企業, 経営, 業績, 保険, 保険の契約, ビジネス
　（⇒banking business, discontinued business）
　a line of business　営業種目
　banking business　銀行業, 銀行業務

business ability　企業運営能力
business acquisition　企業買収
business adjustment　景気調整
business barometers　景気指標
business behavior　企業動向
business capacity　取引能力
business check　業務用小切手
business credit　企業金融
business cycle　景気変動, 景気循環, 景気サイクル, 景気
business deal　商取引, 取引, 商談
　　(=business dealing, business transaction)
business deposits　営業預金
business development　事業展開, 事業開発, 事業拡大
business development and customer relations　渉外業務
business enterprise　営利企業
business entertainment　接待, 交際費
business expansion　事業拡大
business finance　企業金融
business fluctuation　景気変動
business forecast forecasting　景気予測, 業績予測
business funds　事業資金
business hours　営業時間
business improvement administrative order　業務改善行政命令, 業務改善命令
　　(=business improvement order)
business index　景気指標
　　(=business indicators)
business insurance　事業保険
business interruption　事業中断, 営業妨害
business interruption insurance　利益保険
business inventories　企業在庫, 営業在庫
business investment　企業投資, 設備投資, 民間設備投資
business leaders　実業界の指導者, 財界の指導者, 財界首脳, 経済界の首脳
business lending　企業向け貸出
business license　営業免許
business line　事業分野
business liquidity　企業の手元流動性
business loans　事業金融, 事業貸付け, 企業向け融資, 商工業ローン, ビジネス・ローン
business merger　経営統合, 企業の合併
　　(=merger of businesses)
business of banking　銀行業務
business of dealers　自己売買業務
business outlook　業績見通し
business paper　商業手形　(=commercial paper)
business premises　営業所
business record　取引記録, 業務状の記録, 社内文書
business risk　営業リスク, 事業リスク
business shutdown　企業倒産
　　(=business failure)
business sources　市場筋
business status　営業状態　(=business standing)
business term ending in March　3月期, 3月決算期
business terms　取引条件
business to be brought before the meeting　付議事項
business trust　事業信託
business valuation　事業評価, 企業価値評価
business worth　企業価値
claims on private business　民間向け信用
commercial banking business　商業銀行業務

conduct business　議事を進める
core business　中核事業, 中核業務, 主力事業, コア・ビジネス
credit business　信用業務, 信用事業, 与信業務
debit business　受信業務
deposit-taking business　預金事業
enhancement business　信用補強業務
exchange business　為替業務, 為替取引
　　(=forex business)
facultative business　任意再保険
failed business　経営破たんした企業
financial business　金融業務, 金融ビジネス
forex business　為替取引
forward business　先物取引
guarantee business　保証業務
investment advisory business　投資顧問業
life and reinsurance business　生保・再保険事業
morning business　前場
mortgage business　住宅ローン事業, 不動産担保金融
new business　新事業, 新規事業, (保険の)新契約
niche business　得意分野
option business　オプション市場
premiums on in-force business　既存契約の保険料
pro-business　景気重視
securities business　証券業務
suspension of business　取引停止, 営業停止
take the business elsewhere　保険契約を打ち切る
the business　景気(the economy), 本保険
transfer of business　営業譲渡
troubled business　経営の行き詰まり, 経営難, 行き詰まった経営, 経営危機の企業, 経営不振企業
trust business　信託事業
volume of business　取引高

◆Another characteristic of the U.S. management style is that businesses give priority to maximizing shareholders' value. 米国式経営スタイルのもうひとつの特色は、企業が株主の資産価値の極大化を第一に考えることだ。◆In the project financing business, lending banks are repaid loans through profits generated by the projects they have financed. プロジェクト・ファイナンス事業では、貸出行が、融資したプロジェクト(事業)から生まれる利益で融資の返済を受ける。◆Many businesses are cautious about their outlook three months ahead despite the improvement in sentiment. 企業の景況感は改善したものの、多くの企業は3か月先の景気見通しに対しては慎重だ。◆Money loaned by private banks declined because banks with weakened financial strength were less willing to lend, besides a lack of businesses seeking expansion through borrowing. 民間銀行の貸出金が減ったのは、お金を借りてまで事業を拡大しようとする企業がなかったほか、財務が悪化した銀行が貸し渋ったからだ。◆Sberbank of Russia will offer a variety of services, such as ruble-denominated loans to Mizuho Corporate Bank's clients when they do business in Russia. ロシア最大手行のズベルバンクは、みずほコーポレート銀行の顧客がロシアで事業を行う際にルーブル建て融資を行うなどの各種サービスを提供することになった。◆The business of the major banks can only be called fully restored after they have fully repaid the public funds. 大手銀行が公的資金を完済してはじめて、大手銀行の業績が回復した(大手行の経営が健全化した)と言える。◆The company will launch an online stock trading business by the end of this year. 同社は、年内に株のインターネット取引業務に参入することになった。◆The project financing market has seen a boost in loans to businesses in renewable energy field such as solar and wind power generation. プロジェクト・ファイナンス市

場は最近、太陽光や風力発電など自然エネルギー分野の事業への融資が増えている。◆The wall separating banking and securities businesses has been lowered through such moves as the liberalization of banks' securities brokering. 銀行と証券業の垣根は、銀行に対する証券仲介業の規制緩和などの動きで、低くなっている。◆Under the trustee's management, the debtor bank's business will be operated and the refunding of deposits will be temporarily suspended. 金融整理管財人の管理下で、破たん銀行の業務は運営され、預金の払戻しは一時停止される。

Business Accounting Council 企業会計審議会
◆Business Accounting Council is an advisory body to the commissioner of the Financial Services Agency. 企業会計審議会は、金融庁長官の諮問機関である。◆In 2009, the Business Accounting Council decided to require all of the nation's listed companies to use the IFRSs for their consolidated financial statements from 2015. 2009年に企業会計審議会は、2015年にも、国内全上場企業の連結財務諸表（連結財務書類）について、国際財務情報基準（IFRSs）の採用を上場企業に義務付ける方針を打ち出した。

business alliance 業務提携（business tie-up）, 経済団体
◆Many banks and brokerage houses have formed business alliances in launching stock brokerage business at the banks. 銀行での証券仲介業務を開始するにあたって、銀行や証券会社の多くは業務提携している。◆Two of the nation's three main business alliances opposed a proposed bill to revise the Antimonopoly Law aimed at open competition. 日本の主要経済3団体のうち2団体が、公開競争をめざした独禁法改正案に反対した。

business base 営業基盤, 事業基盤, 経営基盤
◆Smaller regional banks are generally trying to enhance their business bases before the payoff system is fully introduced in April. 一般に中小の地銀（地域金融機関）は、4月（2005年）のペイオフ制度全面導入を控えて、経営基盤の強化に務めている。

business boom 景気, 好景気, 好況, 景気上昇
◆Japan's exports, which had been supporting the business boom, lost momentum. 景気を支えてきた日本の輸出が、失速した。

business climate 事業環境, 企業環境, 経営風土, 景況, 商況
◆The business climate for home builders has been severe as housing starts have not expanded much in recent years. 新設住宅の着工戸数がここ数年伸び悩んでいるため、住宅メーカーを取り巻く企業環境は厳しい。

business conditions 景気, 商況, 業況, 業況判断（DI）, 業態, 事業環境, 経営の実態, 営業状況
business condition index 景気動向指数
current business conditions 足元の景気
deteriorating business conditions 景気の悪化
◆Business conditions are rapidly deteriorating due to the global financial crisis and the worldwide economic downturn. 世界的な金融危機と世界的な景気後退で、景気は急速に悪化している。◆If business conditions continue to worsen, financial institutions will face more newly emerging non-performing loans than they can ever keep up with. 景気がこのまま悪化し続ければ、金融機関は新たに不良債権が生まれその処理が追いつかなくなる。◆The Bank of Japan's diffusion indexes are calculated by subtracting the percentage of companies reporting deterioration in business conditions from those perceiving improvement. 日銀のこれらの業況判断指数（DI）は、現在の景況感について「改善している」と感じている企業の割合から「悪化している」と回答した企業の割合を差し引いて算出する。◆The business sentiment index represents the percentage of companies reporting favorable business conditions minus the percentage of those reporting unfavorable conditions. 業況判断指数は、景気が良いと答えた企業の割合（％）から景気が悪いと答えた企業の割合（％）を差し引いた指数だ。◆The diffusion index (DI) of business confidence refers to the percentage of companies that feel business conditions to be favorable, minus the ratio of firms that think otherwise. 業況判断指数（DI）は、景気が「良い」と感じている企業の割合（％）から、「悪い」と感じている企業の割合を差し引いた指数だ。

business confidence 景気感, 業況感, 業況判断, 企業マインド, 企業心理, ビジネス・コンフィデンス
（=business mind, business sentiment; ⇒diffusion index of business confidence）
◆Business confidence among major manufacturers significantly improved in December. 大企業製造業（大手製造業）の業況判断は、12月は大幅に改善した。

business cycle 景気循環, 景気
（=trade cycle, arbiter）
◆The economy still remains in a recovery phase in the business cycle. 景気は、まだ回復局面にある［景気の回復基調はまだ続いている］。◆The NBER's business cycle dating committee concluded that the economic expansion that started in November 2001 had ended. 全米経済研究所（NBER）の景気循環判定委員会の委員は、「2001年から始まった米景気の拡大はすでに終わっている」との見解で一致した。

business day 営業日, 就業日, 平日, 銀行営業日
business day convention 休日調整
（⇒following method）
the due date does not fall on a business day 支払い期日［支払い日］は営業日に当たらない［休日である］
the following business day 翌営業日
the next or immediately following business day 翌銀行営業日
the next or immediately preceding business day 直前の銀行営業日
within five business days of the stock sale 株式売買の5営業日以内に
◆The Securities and Exchange Law requires anyone with an equity stake of more than 5 percent in a listed company to report a sale of stake of 1 percent or more to a local finance bureau within five business days of the sale. 現行の証券取引法では、上場企業に対する株式保有比率が5%を超える株保有者は、株式の売買が株式の保有割合を1%超えるごとに、株式売買の5営業日以内に各財務局にその報告書を提出しなければならない。

business deterioration 景気悪化, 業績悪化, 融資先の経営悪化
◆Greece's tax revenues have slackened due to business deterioration. ギリシャの税収は、景気悪化で伸びていない。

business deterioration of borrowers 融資先の業績悪化
◆Other banks are likely forced to revise their earnings projections downward because of the accelerated disposal of bad loans, business deterioration of borrowers due to the lingering recession and further decline in stock prices. 不良債権処理の加速や長引く不況による融資先の業績悪化、株安などの影響で、他行も業績予想の下方修正を迫られている。

business efficiency 事業効率, 事業の効率性, 経営効率
◆Improving stock exchanges' business efficiency is also important. 証券取引所の経営の効率化も、重要だ。

business environment 経営環境, 企業環境, 事業環境, 景気
◆Moody's Investors Service has upgraded its ratings of nine major Japanese banks in view of progress in their disposal of problem loans and a stabilized business environment. 米大手格付け会社のムーディーズ・インベスターズ・サービスは、不良債権処理の進展と経営環境の安定化を考慮して、日本の大手銀行9行の格付けを引き上げた。◆The increased ownership

will raise the bank's risk exposure to the company, whose business environment is severe. 持ち株比率の引上げで、企業環境［経営環境］が厳しい同社に対する同行のリスク・エクスポージャーは今後増大するものと思われる。◆These moves of the two airlines show the extent of the crisis in the current business environment. 両航空会社のこれらの動きは、現在の経営環境の危機的状況の大きさを示している。

business field 業務分野, 事業分野
◆The five business fields in the tie-up agreement are product development, marketing, insurance underwriting, damage assessment and reinsurance. 提携契約の5業務分野は、商品開発、マーケティング、保険引受け、損害査定と再保険である。

business foundation 事業基盤, 経営基盤, 経営体力
◆Regional banks are trying to enhance their business foundations with mergers to survive fierce competition with their rivals. ライバル行との激しい競争に生き残るため、地銀は統合で経営基盤の強化に努めている。

business improvement order 業務改善命令
(=business improvement administrative order)
◆The Financial Services Agency issued business improvement orders to UFJ Holdings and UFJ Bank last month. 金融庁は先月、UFJホールディングスとUFJ銀行に対して業務改善命令を出した。◆The Financial Services Agent is expected to issue a business improvement order to Mizuho based on the Banking Law. 金融庁は、みずほに対して、銀行法に基づく業務改善命令を出すと見られる。

business integration 事業統合, 経営統合
(=integration of business)
◆The business integration and eventual merger of the TSE and the OSE will be implemented in several steps. 東証と大証の事業統合と最終的な経営統合は、段階的に行われる。◆The two presidents basically agreed on the plan of business integration. 両社社長は、基本的に経営統合計画を進めることで合意した。

business management 経営管理
◆The inadequate decision-making and business management processes of the financial group stem from factional strife within the company. 同金融グループの不十分な意思決定プロセスと経営管理体制は、社内の派閥争いに起因する。

business model ビジネス手法, 事業モデル, 事業計画, ビジネス・モデル (⇒cash flow)
◆The bank's business model of concentrating on loans to small and midsize firms was not successful. 中小企業向け融資を専門に手がけるという同行のビジネス・モデルは、うまく行かなかった。◆The Development Bank of Japan and Aozora Bank have joined hands in extending a loan to a Tokyo venture, taking as collateral the firm's patent for an innovative information-technology business model. 日本政策投資銀行とあおぞら銀行は、革新的なIT（情報技術）を活用したビジネス手法特許（ビジネス・モデル特許）を担保として、東京のベンチャー企業に協調融資した。

business model patent ビジネス・モデル特許
(=business method patent, patent for a business model)
◆The loan was the first of its kind to be extended with a business model patent as collateral. 今回の融資は、ビジネス・モデル特許を担保にした融資としては初めてだ。

business operation 業務運営, 企業運営, 営業活動, 業務活動, 営業運転, 経営
(⇒early warning system)
◆Banks that have received public funds are required to take instructions from the government about their lending and other business operations. 公的資金を受けた銀行（公的資金の注入行）は、貸出などの業務活動について国の指示を受けなければならない。◆The merger of the two exchanges will revitalize stock trading and make it easier for companies to procure funds on the market to expand their business operations. 両証券取引所の経営統合で、株式の売買が活性化し、企業にとっては市場で資金を調達して会社の事業を大きくしやすくなる。◆U.S. and European financial institutions are scaling back their business operations before capital adequacy requirements are strengthened in 2013. 欧米金融機関は、2013年から自己資本規制が強化されるのを前に、業務を縮小している。

business opportunity 事業機会, 商機会, 商機, ビジネス・チャンス (=business chance)
◆Young companies consider ownership of a pro baseball team as a new business opportunity. 若い企業は、プロ野球の球団経営を新たなビジネス・チャンスととらえている。

business outlook 景気見通し
◆The business outlook for the next three months has worsened among both large and small manufacturers. 3か月先までの景気見通しは、大企業と中小企業の製造業で悪化している。

business partnership 業務提携, 業務協力協定
(=business alliance, business tie-up)
◆Mizuho Corporate Bank has formed a business partnership with Sberbank of Russia. みずほコーポレート銀行が、ロシアの最大手行ズベルバンク（Sberbank of Russia）と業務協力協定を締結した。◆Sompo Japan Insurance Inc. began selling "SoftBank Kantan Hoken" insurance by forming a business partnership with SoftBank Mobile Corp. 損保保険ジャパンが、ソフトバンクモバイルと業務提携して、「ソフトバンクかんたん保険」の販売を開始した。

business performance 営業成績, 業績, 経営状況, 決算
(=business results)
◆Business performance of the group's consumer financing affiliate has been in a slump. 同グループの消費者金融子会社の業績は、低迷している。◆Excessive appreciation of the yen will harm business performance, especially for exporters. 過度の円高で、輸出企業を中心に業績の悪化が見込まれる。◆Revenues from the single-premium whole life insurance policies support the life insurer's business performance. 一時払い終身保険による収入［一時払い終身保険の収入保険料］が、同生保の業績を支えている。◆The business performance of carmakers, electronic manufacturers and other exporting companies is beginning to improve at long last. 自動車、電気など輸出企業の業績は、ようやく好転し始めた。

business philosophy 経営理念
◆The slipshod management of failed Incubator Bank of Japan widely diverged from its business philosophy. 破たんした日本振興銀行のずさんな経営は、同行の経営理念とはかけ離れていた。

business plan 事業計画, 経営計画, 経営構想
(=business planning)
◆A targeted company demanded a company trying to acquire its stocks to present a business plan. 買収の標的企業は、買収企業［標的企業の株式を取得しようとしている企業］に事業計画の提出を求めた。◆According to JAL's business plan, the airline will have about ￥26 billion in excess assets due to improved business performance at the end of fiscal 2010. 日航の事業計画では、同社は業績の改善で2010年度末の資産超過額が約260億円に達する見通しだ。◆TEPCO is drafting a special business plan as the premise for getting government financial aid. 東電は、政府の金融支援を受ける前提として、特別事業計画を策定している。◆The company plans to cut its unconsolidated interest-bearing debt by 40 percent by the end of March 2012 under a new business plan. 同社は、新経営計画に基づいて2012年3月末までに非連結有利子負債を40%圧縮する計画だ。◆The company revealed a new medium-term business plan for fiscal 2011-2015. 同社は、2011-2015年度の新中期経営構想を発表した。

business practice 商慣習, 商慣行, 企業慣行, 取引慣行, 取引方法, 営業手法, 業務
◆Financial Services Agency has ordered 26 nonlife insur-

ance firms to correct their business practices, after finding they failed to pay due insurance benefits. 損保各社が支払う義務のある保険金を支払わなかったことが判明したため、金融庁は損保26社に対して業務是正命令を出した。◆The Financial Services Agency ordered Sompo Japan Insurance Inc. to suspend part of its operations as punishment for the major insurance company's illegal business practices. 金融庁は、損保大手の損害保険ジャパンに業務で法令違反があったとして、同社に一部業務停止命令を出した。

business profit　企業収益, 企業利益, 業務利益
◆Before the introduction of the bank tax, the major financial institutions' tax liability had been very low, with only the difference between loan losses and business profits deemed taxable. 銀行税の導入前は、貸倒れ損失額と業務利益との差額だけが課税の対象となっていたため、大手金融機関の納税額は低かった。

business report　営業報告書, 事業報告書, ビジネス・レポート
◆Now is the peak period for listed companies to release their business reports for the business year ending in March. 上場企業の3月期決算の発表が、ピークを迎えている。

business results　営業成績, 企業業績, 業績, 決算
（=business performance; ⇒asset assessment）
◆The bank is mulling a further downward revision of its business results for fiscal 2011 that is expected to result in a massive loss. 同行は、巨額の損失が見込まれる2012年3月期決算[2011年度]の業績予想を、さらに下方修正する方向で検討している。◆The nation's three megabank groups expect a sharp increase in profits in their half-year consolidated business results through the end of September. 日本の3メガバンクは、9月連結中間決算で、大幅増益を見込んでいる。

business sentiment　景況感, 企業の景況感, 企業の業況感, 業況判断, 企業マインド, 企業心理 （=business confidence, business mind, diffusion index of business sentiment）
business sentiment among major manufacturers　大企業・製造業の景況感
corporate business sentiment　企業の景況感
◆Business sentiment among major manufacturers leaped 10 points to plus 22, the highest level since it marked plus 25 in August 1991. 大企業・製造業の景況感は、10ポイント上昇のプラス22で、1991年8月のプラス25以来最高の水準となった。◆Business sentiment and the willingness of household to spend may cool and stall the economy unless the sharp appreciation of the yen is checked. 円の急騰を止めないと、企業の心理や家計の消費意欲が冷え込み、景気が腰折れしかねない。◆Corporate business sentiment improved in the three months to September for the sixth consecutive quarter. 7-9月の企業の景況感は、6期連続で改善した。◆The BOJ's Tankan survey shows business sentiment among large manufacturers rebounded in September from the previous survey three months earlier. 9月の日銀短観は、大企業・製造業の景況感が6月の前回調査から改善したことを示している。◆The diffusion index of business sentiment among large manufacturers recovered to positive territory for the first time in two quarters. 大企業・製造業の業況判断指数(DI)は、2四半期(半年)ぶりにプラスに転じた。◆The recovery in business sentiment was largely due to the improvement in the parts supply chain disrupted after the March 11 earthquake and tsunami. 景況感が改善したのは、主に東日本大震災で打撃を受けたサプライ・チェーン（部品供給網）の復旧が進んだためだ。

business sentiment index　業況判断指数, 業況判断DI
（=diffusion index of business sentiment）
◆The business sentiment index represents the percentage of companies reporting favorable business conditions minus the percentage of those reporting unfavorable conditions. 業況判断指数は、景気が良いと答えた企業の割合(%)から景気

が悪いと答えた企業の割合(%)を差し引いた指数だ。

business settlement　取引決済
◆Checking accounts are mainly used by companies for business settlements. 当座預金は、主に企業の取引決済に利用されている。

business slump　景気低迷, 景気沈滞, 不況, 経営不振, 業績不振 （=slump in business）
◆The ongoing business slump raises the specter of a global downturn comparable to the Great Depression that started in 1929. 今回の不況は、1929年に始まった世界大恐慌に匹敵するほどの世界同時不況の懸念が高まっている。

business soundness　経営の健全性
◆Banks' capital adequacy ratio is an index that shows their business soundness. 銀行各行の自己資本比率は、銀行の経営の健全性を示す指標である。◆Major banks are intensifying their efforts to reduce their risk assets by securitizing and selling their credit to prevent their capital adequacy ratio, an index that shows their business soundness, from declining. 大手各行は現在、経営の健全性を示す指標である自己資本比率の低下を防ぐため、貸出債権の証券化や転売などでリスク資産（リスク・アセット）の圧縮策を加速させている。

business spending on inventories　企業の在庫投資
◆The economy, fueled by a pickup in business spending on inventories, is now expanding at a spanking clip. 企業の在庫投資の回復に支えられた経済は現在、顕著なペースで拡大している。

business strategy　経営戦略, 事業戦略, 企業戦略, ビジネス戦略
◆Japan's four megabanks are now rebuilding their global business strategies. 日本の4大金融グループは現在、グローバル戦略の再構築に取り組んでいる。◆The Sumitomo Mitsui group has recently taken a more aggressive business strategy. 三井住友グループは最近、一段と積極的な事業戦略をとっている。

business strength　経営の体力, 事業の強み
◆According to a commodity futures market insider, futures brokerages depending on commissions for revenue will lose their business strength. 商品先物市場関係者によると、収入を手数料に頼っている先物会社の経営体力は、今後弱まりそうだ。

business suspension　業務停止
◆During the business suspension, the company will not be allowed to extend new loans, solicit new customers or call in loans. 業務停止の期間中、同社は新規融資や新規顧客の勧誘、貸出［貸金］の回収業務ができなくなる。

business term　事業期間, 決算期
business term ending in December　12月終了事業年度, 12月期, 12月期決算, 12月決算
business term ending in March　3月期, 3月決算
business term ending in September　9月期, 9月決算, 9月中間決算
business terms [terms and conditions]　取引条件
◆The bank ran a profit for five consecutive business terms starting with the year to March 2005. 同行は、2005年3月期［3月期決算］から5期連続で黒字を出した。

business trends and conditions　景気動向
◆To implement the consumption tax increase, close attention must be paid to business trends and conditions. 消費税の引上げを実施するには、景気動向にも目配りしなければならない。

business year　営業年度, 事業年度, 会計年度, 年度, 会計期間 （=financial year, fiscal year; ⇒business report, deficit, income forecast）
the business year ending in March 2012　2012年3月期, 2012年3月期決算, 2012年3月終了事業年度, 2011年度
the business year term　決算期

(=business term)
the business year that ended in December 2012　2012年12月期決算, 2012年12月終了事業年度, 2012年度
the settlement of accounts for the business year ending in March　3月期決算, 3月終了事業年度の決算
◆Olympus Corp. inflated its net assets by ￥33 billion in the consolidated financial statements for the business year ended March 2011. オリンパスは、2011年3月期決算の連結財務書類［2011年3月期連結決算］で純資産を334億円水増ししていた。◆The bank paid ￥2.2 billion in dividends for the business year ending in March 2011. 同行は、2011年3月期に22億円の配当金を支払った。◆The brokerage firm inflated its consolidated earnings for its business year through March 2011. 同証券会社は、2011年3月期の連結利益を水増ししていた。◆The company revised downward its business projection for the business year ending in August this year. 同社は、本年8月期決算の業績見通しを下方修正した。◆The listed companies are expected to report significant gains for the whole business year. これらの上場企業は、通期で大幅な増益が見込まれている。◆The top 10 life insurers in the nation reported a total of ￥1.46 trillion in valuation losses on their securities holdings for the current business year. 今期決算で、国内生保の上位（主要）10社の保有有価証券［保有株式］の減損処理額は、1兆4,600億円に達した。

bust　(名)破産, 倒産, 価格の暴落, 不況, 不景気, 失業　(形)破産した, 倒産した, 破たんした
◆All deposits were guaranteed by the government if a bank goes bust. 銀行が破たんした場合の預金は、政府が全額保証していた。

buy　(動)買う(purchase), 購入する, 買い取る, 買い入れる, 買収する(acquire), 株などを引き受ける, (保険に)入る［加入する］, 保険をかける　(名)購入, 買い入れ, 買い, 購買, 買い物, 格安品
(⇒capital, cash deal [dealing])
a buy and hold strategy　長期保有戦略, 購入保持戦略
　(=long-term buy and hold strategy)
a buy and write strategy　証券購入と同時にコール・オプションを売って利回りを上げる投資手法
a good buy　お買い得, 掘り出し物
be wary of buying long-term debt　長期債の買いを手控える
buy a call　コールを買い建てる
buy a cap　キャップを買う
buy a put　プットを買い建てる
buy an insurance policy　保険をかける, 保険に入る, 保険に加入する
　(=purchase an insurance policy)
buy and sell　売買する
buy at best　可能なかぎり安い条件で成り行きで買う
buy at the bottom　底値で買い入れる
buy at the low point　押し目で買う, 安値を拾う
buy at the market　成り行き注文をする, 成り行きで注文する, 成り行き価格で買う, 成り行き買い, 成り行き注文（値段を指定しないで出す売買注文を「成り行き注文」という）
buy at the top　高値づかみになる
buy at the top of the market　高値づかみする
buy bonds on a hold　長期保有目的で債券を購入する
buy contract　金融資産購入契約
buy disciplines　買付けルール
buy foreign exchange in the open market　公開市場で外貨を購入する
buy imbalance　買い気配（売り手より買い手の勢力が上回っていること）

buy in　買い込む, 仕入れる
buy-in　買戻し,（売り手の引渡し不履行による）公開市場での買埋め
buy in at the bottom of　～を底値で拾う
buy in bulk　大量に仕入れる
buy insurance　保険に入る, 保険に加入する
　(=purchase insurance)
buy minus (order)　下値買い注文, バイマイナス注文（現在の相場より安い場合に買うという注文）
buy on close　引け値買い注文
buy on credit　クレジットで買う［購入する、買い物をする］
buy on decline　押し目買い
buy on margin　証拠金購入
buy on opening　寄り付き買い注文
buy on speculation　思惑で買う
buy one's own shares　自社株を買う, 自社株買いを行う
buy-sell [buy-and-sell] agreement　株式買取り契約, ビジネス資産買取り契約, 売買契約
buy stop order　逆指し値注文
buy the dip　押し目で買う, 安値を拾う
buy/sell-back　購入/売戻し取引, 売戻し条件付き買付け
continue to buy dollars against the yuan　元［人民元］を売ってドルを買い進める, 元売り・ドル買いを進める
　(⇒appreciation of one's own currency)
economic buy　経済的発注量
lucky buy　幸運買い
on the buy　盛んに買い付けて
◆According to the World Gold Council, central banks have bought 198 metric tons of gold so far this year. 世界金評議会によると、今年は、世界各国の中央銀行がこれまでに（2011年8月22日現在で）198メートルトン（19万8,000キログラム）の金を買い入れた。◆As part of the emergency deal, the ECB started to buy Greek, Portuguese, and Spanish bonds. 緊急対策として、欧州中央銀行（ECB）はギリシャ、ポルトガルとスペインの国債買入れを開始した。◆Bad loans should be bought at market value rather than at effective book value. 不良債権は、実質簿価でなく時価で買い取るべきだ。◆By buying Greek, Portuguese and Spanish bonds, the ECB infused life into the moribund eurozone markets for these soon-to-be-junk status government bonds. ギリシャやポルトガル、スペインの国債を買い入れて、欧州中銀（ECB）は、崩壊寸前のユーロ圏の投資不適格レベルが見込まれるこれらの債券の市場に生気を吹き込んだ。◆In insurance services that can be bought via cell phones, cell phone companies provide nonlife insurers with policyholders' personal information. 携帯電話で加入できる保険サービスでは、携帯電話会社が（保険）加入者の個人情報を損害保険会社に提供している。◆Manulife Financial Corp., Canada's third largest insurer, agreed to buy U.S. life insurer John Hancock Financial Services Inc. for around $10.8 billion. カナダ3位の生命保険会社マニュライフは、米国の生命保険会社ジョン・ハンコックを約108億ドルで買収することに同意した。◆Premiums are collected together with call charges in insurance services that can be bought via mobile phones. 携帯電話で加入できる保険サービスでは、保険料は通話料と一緒に徴収される。◆The Bank of Japan spent ￥7.15 trillion buying dollars during the previous month. 日銀は、前月に7兆1,500億円のドル買い介入を行った。◆The Bank of Japan will set up a fund to buy long-term government bonds, exchange-traded funds and other financial assets in a bid to prop up the nation's economy. 日本の景気を下支えするため、日銀は基金を新設して、長期国債や上場投資信託（ETF）などの金融商品［金融資産］を買い入れる。◆The European Central Bank needs to provide support to Italy by proactively buy-

ing Italian bonds. 欧州中央銀行（ECB）は今後、イタリア国債を積極的に買い入れてイタリアを支援する必要がある。◆The Fed's program of buying $600 billion in Treasury bonds to help the economy is to end in June 2011 on schedule. 景気を支えるために6,000億ドルの国債を買い入れる米連邦準備制度理事会（FRB）の量的緩和政策は、予定通り2011年6月に終了する。◆The Mitsubishi group is likely to buy ￥200 billion in new shares to be issued by Mitsubishi Motors. 三菱グループは、三菱自動車が発行する新株2,000億円を引き受ける見通しだ。◆The repurchasing method, which has customers buy highly negotiable cash vouchers, violates the industry rule. 顧客に換金性の高い金券類を購入させる買取り方式は、業界の規約に違反する。

buy a policy 保険をかける，保険に入る，保険に加入する　（=buy an insurance policy, purchase a policy [insurance policy]）
◆Nonlife insurers are exploring new types of insurance demand and offering convenient and easy means of buying policies. 損保各社は、新たな保険需要を掘り起こして、いつでも、どこでも簡単に保険に加入できるサービスを提供している。

buy and sell orders 売買注文
◆To compete against online trading systems, stock exchanges must improve their ability to process buy and sell orders. 電子取引システムに対抗するには、証券取引所が売買注文の処理能力を高める必要がある。

buy back 買い戻す，買い取る　（=repurchase）
　ability to buy back shares　自社株［株式］を買い戻す能力，自社株［株式］買戻し能力
　buy back loan claims　債権を買い取る
　buy back one's own shares　自社株買いをする
◆Citigroup will buy back the auction-rate securities from investors under separate accords with the Securities and Exchange Commission and state regulators. 米シティグループは、米証券取引委員会（SEC）や州規制当局との個々の合意に基づいて投資家から金利入札証券（ARS）を買い戻す。◆Short selling is the practice of borrowing stocks from securities and financial companies and other investors to sell them and then buy them back when their prices drop. 空売りは、証券金融会社や他の投資家（機関投資家など）から株を借りて売り、その株が値下がりした時点で買い戻すことをいう。◆The bank charged a hefty commission when asking a major moneylender to buy back loan claims. 大手の金融業者に債権の買い取りを求める際、同行は法外な手数料を支払わせていた。◆The company carried out an operation to buy back its own shares. 同社は、自社株買いを実施した。◆The would-be acquirer is trying to greenmail the target company by having it pay a premium to buy back the shares held by the raider. 買収側［買収希望者］は、この買占め屋［会社乗っ取り屋］が保有する株を標的企業に高値で引き取らせて、標的企業から収益を上げようとしている（標的企業に高値で引き取らせることにより、標的企業にグリーンメールを仕掛けようとしている）。

buy bad loans at market value [prices] 時価で不良債権を買い取る
◆The RCC used to buy bad loans at market value. 整理回収機構は、これまで不良債権を時価で買い取っていた。

buy dollars ドルを買う
◆The yen's exchange rate has appreciated to ￥76 against the dollar, so it is the best time to buy U.S. dollars. 円の為替レートが1ドル＝76円に上昇したので、今が米ドルの買い時だ。◆To arrest the appreciation of the yuan, China continues to buy dollars against its own currency. 元高［人民元高］回避策として、中国は元売り・ドル買いを進めている。

buy-down （名）金利買下げ

buy government bonds 国債を買う，国債を買い入れる

◆The European Central Bank decided to buy Italian and Spanish government bonds in tandem with the issuance of the G-7 emergency statement. 欧州中央銀行（ECB）は、G7緊急声明の発表と連動する形で、イタリアとスペインの国債を買い入れる方針を決めた。◆Under the existing agreement, the IMF cannot buy government bonds through the EFSF as the IMF can only offer loans to countries. 現行協定では、IMF（国際通貨基金）は国にしか融資できないので、欧州金融安定基金（EFSF）を通じて国債を購入することはできない。

buy in [buy-in] （名）（証券）処分買い，買い埋め（buying in），（空売りの）買戻し，ショート・カバー（short covering），（競売品の）自己落札，買戻し，買い込み，仕入れ

buy insurance 保険に加入する，保険に入る　（=purchase insurance）
◆Many policyholders of insurance services that can be bought via cell phones bought such insurance just before embarking on physical exercise regiments and trips. 携帯電話で加入できる保険サービス加入者の多くは、運動や旅行の直前にこの種の保険に入っていた。

buy into 〜に投資する（invest in），会社の株を買い込む，（株を買って）〜の株主になる
◆Investors bought into prospects for growth in the M&A market. 投資家は、M&A（企業の合併・買収）市場の成長力に投資した。

buy long-term government bonds 長期国債を買う，長期国債を買い入れる
◆The Bank of Japan will set up a fund to buy long-term government bonds, exchange-traded funds and other financial assets in a bid to prop up the nation's economy. 日本の景気を下支えするため、日銀は基金を新設して、長期国債や上場投資信託（ETF）などの金融商品［金融資産］を買い入れる。

buy mortgage loans and mortgage securities 住宅ローンやモーゲージ証券を購入する［買い取る］
◆The Federal Housing Finance Agency oversees Fannie and Freddie that buy mortgage loans and mortgage securities issued by the lenders. 米連邦住宅金融局（FHFA）は、これらの金融機関が発行する住宅ローンやモーゲージ証券を購入する［買い取る］連邦住宅抵当金庫（ファニー・メイ）や連邦住宅貸付け抵当公社（フレディ・マック）を監督している。

buy new shares 新株を購入する［買う］，新株を引き受ける，増資を引き受ける
◆Fukushima Bank said about 8,000 companies and investors have agreed to buy ￥15 billion worth of its new shares in March to help boost its capital base. 福島銀行によると、約8,000の企業と投資家が、同行の資本基盤を強化するため3月に予定している150億円の増資引受け［新株引受け］に同意した。

buy or sell order 売買注文　（⇒selling order）
◆Nonresident securities houses without TSE membership are obliged to get Financial Services Agency approval for each buy or sell order to be placed in Tokyo. 東証の参加資格がない（東証の会員でない）海外の証券会社が東証に売買注文を出す場合には、個別に金融庁の許可を得なければならない。

buy order 買い注文，買付け注文　（=purchase order）
◆Sell orders outnumbered buy orders in a wide range of sectors. 幅広い業種で、売り注文が買い注文より多かった。

buy out 権利などを買い取る，買い占める，買い上げる，買収する，乗っ取る
◆On Jan. 30, 2004, Kao announced it wanted to buy out Kanebo's cosmetics division. 2004年1月30日に、花王は、カネボウの化粧品事業部門を完全買収する方針を発表した。

buy shares [stocks] 株を買う，株式［株］を購入する，株式を引き受ける
◆Individual investors are now able to buy stocks at the outlets of banks and other financial institutions. 個人投資家は現在、銀行などの金融機関の店舗で株を購入できる。◆The com-

pany granted an investment firm the right to buy shares to be newly issued by the company as a means of foiling a hostile takeover bid. 同社は、敵対的買収への防衛策として、同社が新規に発行する株式の引受権を投資会社に付与した[投資会社に新株予約権を割り当てた]。

buy the loan ローンを買い取る, 債権を買い取る, 借金を買い取る
◆Public institutions or revitalization funds will buy the loans owed by small and midsize companies that have been hit by the March 11 disaster to lighten their repayment burdens. 公的機関や復興ファンドが、東日本大震災で被災した中小企業の借金を買い取って、被災企業の返済負担を軽減するものと思われる。

buy up 買い占める, 買い取る, 買い進める
　buy up loans 債権を買い取る
　buy up long-term U.S. government debt 米国の長期国債を買い進める[買い切る] (⇒long-dated)
　buy up shares 株を買い占める
◆As an effective measure to prevent the yields of government bonds from soaring and to soothe credit uneasiness in the market, the ECB may buy up a large number of bonds from Italy and other countries. 国債利回りの急騰を抑え、市場の信用不安を鎮静化するための有効な措置として、欧州中央銀行(ECB)は、イタリアなどの国債を大量に買い支える可能性がある。◆The bank bought up loans from nonbanks. 同行は、ノンバンクから債権を買い取った。◆The former head of the Murakami Fund instructed Livedoor Co. to buy up the radio broadcaster's shares during after-hours trading. 村上ファンドの元代表が、同ラジオ放送株を時間外取引で買い占めるようライブドア側に指南していた。◆The U.S. administration will spend up to $700 billion to buy up soured mortgage-related securities and other devalued assets held by ailing financial institutions. 米政府は、経営不振の金融機関が保有するモーゲージ関連の不良証券などの不良資産を、最大7,000億ドル投入して買い取る方針だ。

buy up dormant patents 休眠特許を買い取る
◆The sovereign wealth fund will buy up dormant patents owned by companies and universities. 同政府系投資ファンドは、企業や大学が保有する休眠特許を買い取る方針だ。

buy up government bonds 国債を買い切る, 国債を買い進める
◆Governments facing fiscal hardship sometimes force their central banks to buy up government bonds. 財政がひっ迫した政府は、中央銀行に国債を買い切らせることがある。◆The EUB is banned from buying up government bonds as a bailout for a financially troubled member nation. 欧州中銀(ECB)は、財政ひっ迫の加盟国政府の救済策として、国債を買い切ることが禁止されている。

buy up toxic assets 不良資産を買い取る
◆Public funds should be injected not only to buy up toxic assets, but also to boost the capital bases of enfeebled financial institutions. 公的資金は、不良資産の買取りだけでなく、弱体化した[体力の落ちた]金融機関の資本増強にも注入すべきだ。

buyback 買戻し, 買取り, 自社株買戻し, 自社株買い, 自社株取得 (⇒stock buyback)
　announce a buyback 自社株買いを発表する
　buyback agreement 売戻し条件付き買付け
　engage in stock buybacks 自社株買いをする
　equity buyback 株式の買戻し
　share buyback 自社株買戻し, 自社株買い, 株式買戻し (=stock buyback)
◆The share buyback means a reduction in the company's shareholders to whom it has to pay dividends. 自社株買いは、配当を支払わなければならない会社の株主数が減ることを意味する。

buyback limits 自社株の取得枠, 自社株取得枠 (=share buyback limits, stock buyback limits)
◆Stock buyback limits are to be decided at general shareholders meetings. 自社株の取得枠は、株主総会で決められることになっている。

buyer (名)株などの引受先, 買い主, 買い手, 売却先, 購買者, 仕入担当者, 海外の輸入者, バイヤー (⇒bracket, discontinued business, leveraged buyout)
　bond buyer 債券購入者, 債券の買い手
　buyer's [buyer] credit 輸入者向け信用, バイヤーズ・クレジット (輸出国の金融機関が、輸出相手国の輸入業者に直接信用供与するもの)
　buyer's interest 買い手利害
　buyer's option 買い手選択, 買付け選択権, 買付け権, 買い手オプション (外国為替取引の先物取引で、受渡し期間を買い手が決める場合)
　buyer's option to double 追加購入権付き買付け権
　buyer's rate 買い手相場
　buyer's risk 買い手負担
　buyers over 買い手[買い方]過多, 買い長(なが)
　heavy buyer 大口購入者
　institutional buyer 機関投資家
　potential buyer 潜在的購入者
　prospective buyer 見込み客
◆In commodity futures trading, prices are decided when buyers and sellers make deals. So they can execute trades at promised prices even if the value of goods has changed drastically in the meantime. 商品先物取引では、売り手と買い手が取引契約をする時点で価格を決める。そのため、契約期間中に相場が大きく変動しても、売り手と買い手は約束した値段で取引を執行できる。

buying (名)買い, 買入れ, 買付け, 購買, 仕入れ (⇒intervention, selling)
　buying account 買い玉(ぎょく)
　buying agent 仕入れ代理店, 買付け代理店
　buying balance 買い残
　buying bottoms 底値買い, 底値拾い
　buying contract (為替)買い予約, 輸出予約
　buying disposition 買い気
　buying drives 買い出動
　buying exchange 買い為替
　buying forward 先物買入れ, 先物買付け
　buying futures 先物買い, 信用買い
　buying futures and selling cash 先物買い現物売り
　buying hedge つなぎ買い, 買いつなぎ, 買いヘッジ
　buying interest 買い意欲
　buying limit 買い指し値, 指し値買い
　buying long 思惑買い
　buying of a draft 手形の買入れ
　buying offer 買い申込み, 買いオファー
　buying on a decline 押し目買い
　buying on a yield basis 採算買い, 利回り買い, 利回りを基準にして株を買うこと
　buying on balance 買い越し
　buying on close 引け値買い
　buying on dips 押し目買い
　buying on margin 信用買い, 空(から)買い, マージン買付け
　buying on opening 寄り付き買い
　buying on reaction 押し目買い (=buying on decline, buying on dips)
　buying on scale きざみ買い

buying order　買い注文
buying over　買収
buying power　（証拠金勘定の）買付け余力, 購買力, 買い手支配力
buying price　買い値
buying sentiments　買い気
buying sight rate　満期日の買入れレート
buying spree　買い急ぎ
buying support　買い支え
buying the spread　スプレッドの買い
buying up　買取り, 買占め
consumer buying　個人消費支出
foreign investor buying　外国人買い, 外国人の買い（=foreign buy）
forward buying　先物買入れ
home buying　住宅購入
impulse buying　衝動買い
large-lot buying　大量仕入れ
margin buying　空買い
nomination buying　指名買い
selective buying　物色買い
show limited buying interest　買いを手控える
speculative buying　思惑買い
there is a lot of buying in　〜にかなりの買いが入っている
◆The buying force in the Tokyo stock market is overseas institutional investors. 東京株式市場での買いの主役は、海外の機関投資家だ。◆The surge in the yen is partly due to speculative buying. 円高の一因は、思惑買いにある。

buying factor　買い材料
◆Speculators exploited these buying factors, pushing oil prices up further. 投機筋がこれらの買い材料に反応して[投機筋がこれらの買い材料を利用して]、原油価格の高騰[原油高]を増幅している。

buying operation　買い操作, 買いオペ, 買いオペレーション
BOJ rinban bond buying operations　日銀の輪番オペ
bond buying operations　買いオペ, 買いオペレーション
buying operations under repurchase agreement　売戻し条件付き買いオペ[オペレーション]
unconditional buying operations　無条件買いオペレーション

buying opportunity　買い場, 買いチャンス
create a buying opportunity　買い場になる
look for buying opportunities　買い場を探す

buying rate　買い相場, 買い為替相場, 買入れレート
buying rate of exchange　買い為替相場
buying sight rate　満期日の買入れレート
usance bill buying rate　期限付き手形買い相場

buyout　（名）買収, 会社・経営権の買取り, 買切り, 買占め, 乗っ取り　（=buy-out; ⇒dilute, leveraged buyout, stock buyout）
employee buyout　従業員の会社買取り（=worker buyout）
leveraged buyout　レバレッジド・バイアウト, 借入資金による企業買収, LBO
management buyout　マネジメント・バイアウト, MBO, 経営陣による自社株の公開買付け
strategic buyout　戦略的買収（経営戦略に基づいて行われる企業買収）
the ECB buyouts of sovereign debts of eurozone nations　欧州中央銀行（ECB）のユーロ圏国債の買切り
worker buyout　従業員の経営権買取り
◆The ECB buyouts of sovereign debts of eurozone countries with fiscal laxity are the nightmare scenario Germany has been fearing. 欧州中銀（ECB）による放漫財政のユーロ圏諸国の国債買切りは、ドイツが恐れていた最悪のシナリオだ。◆The firm's defense against management buyout is half-baked. 同社の経営陣による企業買収（MBO）防衛策は、中途半端だ。

buyout firm　企業買収専門会社
◆Sony Corp. and two U.S. buyout firms are in talks to buy U.S. film studio Metro-Goldwyn-Mayer Inc. for about $5 billion. ソニーと米国の企業買収専門会社2社が共同で、米国の映画会社MGM（メトロ・ゴールドウィン・メイヤー）を約50億ドルで買収する交渉を進めている。

buyout fund　買収ファンド
◆Ripplewood Holdings will establish a buyout fund by procuring about ¥200 billion from financial institutions at home and abroad. リップルウッド・ホールディングスは、国内外の金融機関から約2,000億円を調達して、買収ファンドを設立する。

bypass loans　迂回（うかい）融資
◆The bank extended bypass loans to a major borrower that was in financial difficulties. 同行は、経営危機にあった大口融資先に迂回融資していた。

C

C　Cの格付け, シングルC
Caa1　Caa1の格付け, Caa1格
CC　CCの格付け, ダブルC
CCC plus　CCCプラスの格付け, CCC（トリプルC）プラス
◆General Motor's long term debt rating was slashed one level to Caa1 by Moody's Investors Service. ゼネラル・モーターズ（GM）の長期債格付けを、米格付け会社のムーディーズ・インベスターズ・サービスが1段階下のCaa1に引き下げた。◆Standard & Poor's cut its corporate credit rating on Ford to "CC" from "CCC＋." スタンダード＆プアーズは、フォードの企業信用格付けを「CCCプラス」から「CC」に引き下げた。

calculate　（動）計算する, 算定する, 算出する, 計上する, 評価する
calculate credit risk　信用リスクを評価する
calculate deferred tax assets　繰延べ税金資産を算定する
calculate the effective book value　実質簿価を算定する
◆The Bank of Japan's diffusion indexes are calculated by subtracting the percentage of companies reporting deterioration in business conditions from those perceiving improvement. 日銀のこれらの業況判断指数（DI）は、現在の景況感について「改善している」と感じている企業の割合から「悪化している」と回答した企業の割合を差し引いて算出する。◆The change in the method of calculating deferred tax assets has driven each of the banking groups into a corner. 繰延べ税資産の算定方式の変更が、銀行グループ各行を窮地に追い込んでいる。◆The effective book value is calculated by subtracting amassed loan loss reserves from the original amount of money that was lent. 実質簿価は、債権の元々の額[貸し付けた元々の金額：簿価]から、（銀行が）積み立てた貸倒れ引当金を差し引いて算定する。◆The securities companies calculate capital gains and losses, compile taxation documents, gather annual stock reports and file tax returns on behalf of investors free of charge. 証券会社は、投資家の代わりに無料で譲渡損益を計算したり、税務書類を作成したり、年間の株式取引報告書を揃えたりして、税務申告書（納税申告書）を提出する。

calendar day　暦日
◆The Buyer shall prepare the Closing Balance Sheet at the

calibration (名)水準調整

California Public Employees' Retirement System
カリフォルニア州公務員退職年金基金, カルパース
(⇒independent director)
◆The California Public Employees' Retirement System is the largest pension fund in the United States. カルパース（カリフォルニア州公務員退職年金基金）は、米国内最大の年金基金だ。

call (動)支払いを要求する, 支払いを請求する, 〜の返済を求める, 債券の繰上げ償還をする, 償還する, 〜を宣言する
　call default　デフォルトを宣言する
　call the bond　債券を償還する
　call the existing bonds　既発債を償還する
　call the loan　貸付け金の返済を請求する, ローンの償還を請求する
　call the notes at par from investors　投資家から保有債券を額面で購入する
　call the preferred stock issue　優先株式を償還する

call (名)支払い要求, 払込み請求, 債券の繰上げ償還, コール資金, 催告, コール（「コール資金」は, 金融機関同士が貸借する非常に短期の資金のこと）
　call account　未払い勘定
　call by sinking fund　減債基金による定時償還
　call date　繰上げ償還日
　call deposit　通知預金　(=deposit at call)
　call letter　払込み請求書
　call of capital　資本の導入
　call on shareholders　株式払込み請求
　call on the market　市場での調達
　call price　繰上げ償還価格, 任意償還価格, 期前償還価格, 買入れ価格, 買戻し価格, コール価格
　call privilege　任意償還, 任意償還権
　call protection　任意償還保護, 繰上げ償還が始まる前の据え置き期間
　call rate　コール・レート（コール取引による短期資金の貸借に適用される金利で, 年利建て（%表示）となっている）
　call redemption price　繰上げ償還価格
　call report　金融当局宛の業務報告書, 米連邦準備制度加盟銀行の報告書
　call spread　コール・スプレッド（異なる限月のオプションを使った取引）
　call turnover　コール出合　(=call transactions)
　call turnover made　コール出合残高
　　(=call transactions made)
　capital call　資本払込みの要請
　cash call　増資, 株主割当て発行増資
　day-to-day and unconditional call money　翌日物と無条件のコール・マネー
　deposit at call　通知預金
　half-day call　半日物
　long call　コールの買い, ロング・コール
　long position in call　コールの買い持ち
　margin call　追加証拠金, 追い証, マージン・コール
　money at call　コール・マネー
　　(=call money, money on call)
　notice of call　払込み通知
　on call　請求次第支払われる　(=at call)
　overnight call　翌日物コール
　put and call　特権付き売買, プット・アンド・コール
　short call　コールの売り, ショート・コール
　short position in call　コールの売り持ち
　term call　期日物
　yield to call　コール利回り, 繰上げ償還利回り

call center　コール・センター
◆Internet securities companies will continue to offer investors an information service through their call centers. インターネット専業証券各社は、今後も引き続きコール・センターを通じてそれぞれ投資家に情報サービスを提供する方針だ。

call for　要求する, 求める, 訴える, 呼びかける, 唱える, 必要とする, 予報する
◆After the IMF called for strict implementation of structural reforms as a condition for loans to financially troubled countries, counties became reluctant to request assistance from the IMF. 財政難に陥った国に対する融資の条件としてIMF（国際通貨基金）が厳しい構造改革の実施を求めてから、各国はIMFへの支援要請をためらうようになった。◆French President Nicolas Sarkozy and German Chancellor Angera Merkel called for greater economic discipline and unity among European countries. サルコジ仏大統領とメルケル独首相は、経済規律の強化と欧州各国間の結束を求めた。◆The committee called for the president to step down. 同委員会は、社長の辞任を要求した。

call in　(貸金[貸付け金、融資])を回収する, (欠陥品などを)回収する, 取り立てる, (助言や助けを)求める　(=call back)
　call in loans with customers　貸出先から貸付け金を回収する, 貸出先から貸出を回収する
　　(=call back loans with customers)
　forcibly call in loans　貸しはがしする
◆Major commercial banks plan to further reduce their assets by calling in and also securitizing loans. 大手行は、融資の回収や債権の証券化などで、資産の圧縮を加速させる構えだ。

call in existing loans　既存の債権を回収する, 融資残高を回収する, 貸しはがしする
◆Overly radical methods for accelerating the disposal of bad loans would panic the banking sector and the financial market, possibly driving banks to shy away from extending new loans and even to call in existing loans. 不良債権処理を加速するための余りにも強硬な手法は、銀行や金融市場をおびえさせ、貸し渋りや貸しはがしにつながることにもなる。

call in loans　貸付け金[債権]を回収する, 貸出[融資、貸金]を回収する　(⇒prospects)
◆Banks may forcibly call in loans and lower loan assets to improve their capital adequacy ratios. 自己資本比率を引き上げるため、銀行は貸しはがしに走って、貸出資産を圧縮する恐れがある。◆During the business suspension, the company will not be allowed to extend new loans, solicit new customers or call in loans. 業務停止の期間中、同社は新規融資や新規顧客の勧誘、貸出[貸金]の回収業務ができなくなる。

call loan　コール貸付け金, 銀行間の当座貸付け金, 銀行間の短期資金貸出, 当座借入金, コール貸付け金, コール・マネー, 短期融資, 短期資金, 短資, コール・ローン
　　(=call money; ⇒call market, call money)
　call loan broker　短資業者
　call loan dealer's bill　短資手形
　call loan market　短期金融市場, 短資市場, 短期資金市場, コール市場
　call loan rate　コール・ローン金利
　call loan transaction　短資取引, 短期資金取引

call market　短期市場, 短期資金市場, コール市場
　　(=call money market)

[解説]コール市場とは：金融機関や証券会社相互間の短期資金の貸借を行う場が「コール市場」で、資金の貸し手から見た場合をコール・ローン、資金の借り手から見た場合をコール・マネーという。コール取引には当日中に資金決済される半日物、翌日決済の無条件物と、翌々日決済の2日物から7日物までの期日物がある。

call money　コール借入金, 銀行相互間の当座借入金, 短期融資, 短資, コール・マネー（=money at call, money on call; ⇒call loan, call market）
　call money and discount markets　短期金融市場, 短資市場, コール・手形割引市場
　call money borrowed　コール借入金, 借入短期資金, コール・マネー
　call money market　短資市場, コール市場（=call market）

call on [upon]　求める, 要求する
　◆French Finance Minister Christine Lagarde chosen as the new managing director of the IMF is expected to maintain an austere stance of calling on Greece to reform itself. IMFの新専務理事に選ばれたクリスティーヌ・ラガルド仏財務相は、ギリシャに改革を求める厳しい姿勢を貫くものと期待されている。

call option　買付け選択権, 買取り特権, 買う権利, 買いオプション, 債券の任意償還, 繰上げ償還, コール・オプション（「コール・オプション」は、金融商品を権利行使期間に権利行使価格で買う権利のこと）
　call option buyer　コール・オプションの買い手
　call option dealing　コール・オプション取引
　call option price　コール・オプション価格
　call option seller　コール・オプションの売り手
　currency call option　通貨コール・オプション
　implicit call option　潜在的コール・オプション

call premium　任意償還プレミアム, 償還プレミアム, 繰上げ償還時に支払われる割増金, コール・オプションを買うときに支払うオプション料, コール・プレミアム
　◆The benefits of refinancing were partly offset by cost of that refinancing such as call premiums. 借換えの効果は、償還プレミアムのような資金再調達関連費用によって、一部相殺されています。

callable　（形）償還できる, 任意償還可能な, 任意償還権付き, 繰上げ返済請求が可能な, 請求次第支払われる, コール・オプション付き,
　callable bond　繰上げ償還条項付き社債, 任意償還条項付き社債, 随時償還債券, 随時償還公債, 償還公社債, コーラブル債
　callable obligation　繰上げ返済請求が可能な債務, 任意償還条項付き債務
　callable preferred stock　期限前償還請求権付き優先株式, 任意償還優先株式
　callable securities　任意償還可能有価証券, 償還条項付き証券
　callable stock　任意償還株式, 償還株式
　callable swap　コーラブル・スワップ（当事者の一方が中途で止める権利を持つスワップ取引）
　callable warrant　コール・オプション付きワラント, コーラブル・ワラント

calling-in　（名）資金の回収

calm down　〜を静める, 穏やかにする, なだめる, 静まる, 落ち着く, 治まる
　◆The market has calmed down. 市場は、落ち着きを取り戻した。

campaign　（名）活動, 動き, 行動, 運動（drive）, 販売促進運動, 販促キャンペーン, 選挙運動, 軍事行動, 作戦, 対策, 計画, キャンペーン
　advertising campaign　広告キャンペーン, 広告・宣伝活動
　information campaign　広報活動
　productivity campaign　生産性向上運動
　promotional campaign　販促キャンペーン
　run a campaign　キャンペーンを実施する
　sales campaign　商戦, 売出し, 販売キャンペーン, セールス・キャンペーン
　◆The bank ran a campaign to increase deposits by introducing a five-year time deposit with a high interest rate of 1.7 percent. 同行は、年1.7％の高金利の5年定期を導入して預金量を増やすキャンペーンを実施した。

campaign finance law　選挙資金規制法
　◆A conservative group asked federal election officials to investigate whether television ads for "Fahrenheit 9/11" violate the campaign finance law. 保守系団体が、「華氏911」（マイケル・ムーア監督のドキュメンタリー映画）のテレビ宣伝が選挙資金規制法に違反しているかどうか調査するよう、連邦選管当局者に求めた。

Canadian dollar　カナダ・ドル
　◆The Bank of Tokyo-Mitsubishi UFJ will work together with foreign banks to extend 117 million Canadian dollars in joint loans to a mega solar power plant construction. 三菱東京UFJ銀行は、外銀数行の主幹事銀行として[外銀数行と連携して]、カナダの大型太陽光発電所（メガソーラー）建設事業に1億1,700万カナダ・ドルを協調融資する。

cancel　（動）株式を消却[償却]する, 取り消す, 解除する, 解約する, 中止する
　◆In this type of life insurance products, the rate of return after canceling the insurance contract can be higher than that of a savings account if a policyholder upholds the contract for five to 10 years. この種の生保商品では、保険契約者が保険契約を5〜10年続けると、解約後の利回り（予定利率）は預金よりも高い利回りが見込める。◆Sanwa Bank and three other major creditor banks to ailing supermarket chain operator Daiei Inc. are considering having Daiei reduce its capital by canceling a portion of its preferred shares held by the banks. 三和銀行と経営不振の大手スーパー、ダイエーの他の主力取引銀行は現在、この4行が保有するダイエーの優先株（議決権がない代わりに配当が高い株式）の消却によるダイエーの資本金引下げ（減資）を検討している。

cancellation　（名）株式の消却, 契約の解除, 解約, 破棄, 抹消（⇒deposit cancellation, early warning system, policy cancellation）
　cancellation before maturity　中途解約
　cancellation money　解約金
　cancellation of indebtedness　負債の免除
　cancellation of insurance　保険の解約
　cancellation of stocks　株式消却（=cancellation of shares, stock cancellation）
　cancellation premium　解約保険料[再保険料]
　debt cancellation　負債の帳消し, 負債の棒引き
　policy cancellation　保険の解約
　◆Contract cancellations have been on the rise as many households cut spending and are growing more distrustful of life insurers. 家計のリストラ（多くの家庭での支出削減）や生保不信の高まりで、解約が増えている。◆The firm repurchased for cancellation its own common shares for an aggregate amount of $300 million. 同社は、消却の目的で、総額3億ドルの自社普通株式を買い戻した。

cancellation of (a) contract　契約の解除, 解約
　◆The Financial Services Agency introduced the early warning system for life insurers to keep an eye on their business operations, including profit performance, safety and cancellation of contracts. 金融庁は、生保向けの早期警戒制度を導入して、収益性や安全性、解約の状況など生命保険会社の経営

を監視している。
cap （動）上限を設ける［設定する、定める］，キャップを設ける，抑制する，抑える，上部を覆（おお）う，覆う，保証する（cover），しのぐ，勝る，仕上げる，完成する，〜を締めくくる
　cap losses　損失を保証する，損失をカバーする
　cap or limit the interest rate expense　金利経費に上限を設ける
　cap the contractual rate associated with a liability　負債の約定金利にキャップを設ける
　cap the new issuance of government bonds　国債の新規発行を抑える
　cap the surge in oil prices　原油価格の上昇を抑制する
　capped expenditure　上限のある支出［歳出］
　capped floater　上限金利付き変動利付き債，キャップ付き変動利付き債
　capped floating rate note（FRN）　上限金利（特約）付き変動利付き債，キャップ付き債［変動利付き債］
　capped loan　上限のあるローン
　capped mortgage　キャップ付き変動金利モーゲージ
　capped rate　キャップ金利
　capped swap　キャップ付きスワップ（キャップとスワップを組み合わせたもの）
　capped warrant　キャップ付きワラント
　delayed capped FRN　先スタート・キャップ付き変動利付き債
　◆Citigroup Inc. received $45 billion of taxpayer money in October and November, as well as a government backstop to cap losses on $300.8 billion of toxic assets. 米金融大手のシティグループは、(2008年) 10〜11月に450億ドルの公的資金注入のほか、3,008億ドルの不良資産から生じた損失の大半を保証する政府支援も受けている。◆If the government adheres to its stance of capping the annual issuance of government bonds at ¥30 trillion, it should study issuing a new bond whose redemption sources are secured. 国債発行枠30兆円の姿勢にこだわるなら、償還財源の裏付けを持つ新型の国債発行を検討するべきだ。◆The government will cap new government bond issuance below ¥44 trillion in the fiscal 2011 budget. 政府は、2011年度予算で、国債新規発行額を44兆円以下に抑える方針だ。◆Under the current earthquake insurance system, insurance payments remain capped at half the actual value of a home and its contents. 現行の地震保険［地震保険制度］では、保険金の支払い額の上限は、住宅や家財の実質価値の半額までとなっている。
cap （名）上限，最高限度，最高，（長期ローンや変動利付き債の）上限金利，キャップ　（⇒refund cap）
　annual premium caps　保険料の年間の上限，料率の年間の上限
　buy a cap　キャップを買う，上限金利を買う
　buyer［purchaser］of the cap　キャップの買い手
　　（=cap buyer, purchaser of the cap）
　cap-and-collar mortgage　金利変動幅固定型住宅ローン，金利変動幅固定型の担保貸付け
　cap rate　キャップ金利
　cap seller　キャップの売り手
　　（=seller of the cap）
　cap system　キャップ制（政策分野別に歳出上限を定める制度）
　interest rate cap　金利キャップ，キャップ
　life-of-loan cap　貸出期間中にわたる上限金利
　long cap　キャップの買い
　market cap　時価総額
　purchase a cap　キャップを買う，上限金利を買う
　　（=buy a cap）
　rate cap　金利キャップ　（=interest rate cap）
　seasonal cap　季節キャップ
　sell a cap　キャップを売る，上限金利を売る
　set a cap on pension premiums　年金保険料の負担に上限を設ける
　short cap　キャップの売り
　short-dated cap　短期物キャップ
　small cap index　小型株指数
　small cap rally　小型株相場
　small cap stock　小型株
　spending cap　歳出上限
　stripped interest rate cap　分離型金利キャップ
　the largest cap stock　時価総額が最大の銘柄
　there is a cap at A%　A%のキャップが設けられている［付けられている］
　volume cap　発行額の上限
　◆Former Health, Labor and Welfare Minister Chikara Sakaguchi proposed setting a cap on pension premiums. 坂口元厚生労働相は、年金保険料負担に上限を設ける案を示した。◆This ¥30 trillion cap has hobbled the government's economic and fiscal policies. この30兆円枠が、政府の経済・財政政策をがんじがらめにしている。
cap of refunding　預金払戻しの上限
　◆Most of the deposits at the bank are below the cap of refunding guaranteed under the payoff system. 同行の預金の大半は、ペイオフ（預金の払い戻し）制度で保証されている預金払い戻しの上限［ペイオフ制度の預金払い戻し保証額の上限］を超えていない。
cap on deposits　貯金の預入限度額
　◆The postal services reform bill obliges Japan Post Bank Co. to double its cap on deposits to ¥20 million. 郵政改革法案は、ゆうちょ銀行に対して、貯金の預入限度額を2,000万円に倍増するよう義務付けている。
cap on the insurance policy's value　保険契約の評価額上限
　◆In the case of earthquake insurance, the cap on the insurance policy's value for an average house in Tokyo is about ¥10 million. 地震保険の場合、都内の平均的な住宅の保険契約の評価額上限は1,000万円程度だ。
capability　（名）能力，潜在能力，力，可能性，将来性，才能，素質，手腕，技術，機能，通信機能
　bond placement capability　債券の販売能力
　bond redemption capability　社債償還能力
　capability to deal with risk　リスクへの対応力
　capital management capabilities　資産運用力
　debt service capability　債務返済能力
　　（=debt servicing capability）
　profit-making capability　収益力
　unit trust capabilities　投資信託会社
　◆A higher capital adequacy ratio means that a bank has a greater capability to deal with risk. 自己資本比率が高いほど、銀行のリスクへの対応力が高くなる。◆Nonlife insurers are offering customers a new way to purchase insurance, using mobile phones with information transmission capabilities. 損害保険各社が、情報通信機能がある携帯電話を使って保険に加入できる新サービスを提供している。
capacity　（名）能力，資本，資金，キャパシティ
　　（⇒capital spending）
　absorptive capacity　（資本の）吸収能力
　bank lending capacity　銀行の貸出能力
　　（=bank lending ability）
　business capacity　営業力
　capacity to pay interest and repay principal　利払いおよび

元本償還の能力
capacity to support additional debt　追加借入能力
capital capacity　資本生産能力
debt capacity　借入余力
debt servicing capacity　債務返済能力, 返済能力
dividend capacity　配当支払い能力
dividend paying capacity　配当支払い能力
earning capacity　収益力, 稼得力
fiduciary capacity　信託保管能力, 受託者の資格
funding capacity　資金調達能力
lending capacity　貸出能力, 融資能力, 融資できる資金規模, 融資可能額
service capacity　サービス能力, 供給能力
◆A bad bank is used to hold troubled assets and free up bank lending capacity. バッド・バンクは、不良資産を買い取って、銀行が自由に貸出できるようにするのに利用される。◆At the latest G-20 meeting, diverging opinions among member courtiers were exposed over expanding the lending capacity of the IMF. 今回のG20（財務相・中央銀行総裁）会議では、国際通貨基金（IMF）が融資できる資金規模の拡大をめぐって、加盟国の間で意見の食い違いが表面化した。◆Bank of Yokohama plans to expand its lending capacity. 横浜銀行は、貸出増強を計画している。◆The European Union will substantially expand the lending capacity of the EFSF to buy up government bonds in case the fiscal and financial crisis spreads countries as Italy. 欧州連合（EU）は、財政・金融危機がイタリアなどに拡大した場合に国債を買い支えるため、欧州金融安定基金（EFSF）の融資能力を大幅に拡大する。◆The serious deterioration of operational efficiency is caused by excess output capacity and burgeoning workforces. 極端な経営効率の悪化は、生産設備と従業員の過剰によるものだ。

capital　（名）資本, 資本金, 資金, 元金, 出資金, 保険会社の基金（株式会社の資本金に相当）, 正味財産, 純資産, キャピタル　（⇒cancel, deficit settlement of accounts, foundation fund, investment）
　authorized capital　授権資本, 公称資本
　bank capital　銀行の自己資本
　bank capital requirements　銀行の自己資本比率規制
　　（=bank capital standards）
　borrowed capital　借入資本, 他人資本, 外部資本
　capital account　資本勘定
　capital accumulation　資本蓄積
　capital contribution　資本拠出, 資本供与
　capital exporting country　資本輸出国, 資金供給国
　capital grants　投資補助金, 資本費補助
　capital needs　資金需要, 資本必要額, 必要資本
　capital stock cut　減資
　　（=capital decrease, capital reduction）
　capital subscription　出資
　　（=subscription to the capital）
　debt capital　借入資本
　development capital　開発資金
　equity capital　株主資本, 自己資本, 株持ち分, 払込み資本, 株式資本
　fresh capital　新規資本, 新たな資金
　initial capital　当初資金
　issued capital　発行済み資本, 発行済み株式
　　（=issued stock）
　issued share capital　発行済み株式資本
　　（=issued capital）
　operating capital　経営資本, 運転資本
　paid-in capital　払込み資本, 払込み資本金
　　（=paid-up capital）
　return on capital employed　資本利益率, 使用資本利益率, ROCE
　risk capital　危険負担資本, 危険投下資本
　　（=venture capital）
　share capital　株式資本, 株式資本金
　shortfall in capital　資本不足
　working capital　運転資本, 運転資金
◆In the joint venture with an Indian investment bank, Tokio Marine Holdings Inc. put up about 26%, the maximum a foreign investor is allowed in an Indian company, of the new firm's capital. インドの投資銀行との合弁事業で、東京海上ホールディングスは、新会社の資本金の約26％（外資の持ち分比率の上限）を出資した。◆Lone Star built a fund of several hundreds of billions yen in Japan with capital it garnered from investors. ローンスターは、投資家から集めた資金で、日本で数千億円規模のファンドを作った。◆Meiji Life Insurance Co. plans to raise ¥60 billion from group financial firms to boost its capital to ¥220 billion. 明治生命保険は、グループの金融機関から600億円調達して、基金（株式会社の資本金に相当）総額を2,200億円に増額する方針だ。◆Regional banks are having difficulty finding investors to buy the additional stocks they are issuing to boost their capital. 地銀の場合は、増資のため追加株式を発行しても、その引受手［それを引き受ける投資家］が容易に見つからない。◆The company will reduce its capital by 99.7 percent to ¥100 million to make shareholders accountable for its financial difficulties. 経営不振（経営危機）に対する株主責任を明確にするため、同社は1億円に99.7％の減資を実施する（99.7％の減資を実施して資本金を1億円とする）。◆UFJ plans to increase its capital with help from Mitsubishi Tokyo Financial Group by the end of September. UFJは、三菱東京フィナンシャル・グループの支援を得て、9月末までに資本増強（増資）を計画している。

capital adequacy　資本充実度, 自己資本の充実, 自己資本比率, 資本要件, 適正資本量
　capital adequacy requirements against market risk　BISマーケット・リスク規制, BIS第二次規制
　capital adequacy rule　自己資本比率規制
◆A bank's capital adequacy is calculated as a percentage by dividing a bank's core, or Tier 1, capital by its noncore capital. 銀行の自己資本比率は、銀行の中核的自己資本（Tier1）を非中核的資本（投資額や融資額など）で割った比率として算定する。

capital adequacy rating　自己資本比率の評価
◆Capital adequacy rating is used to assess a bank's financial stability. 自己資本比率の評価は、銀行の経営の健全性［財務上の健全性］を判断して評価するのに用いられる。

capital adequacy ratio　自己資本比率　（=capital-asset ratio, capital-to-asset ratio, net worth ratio; ⇒BIS requirements, cost, gain名詞, minimum capital adequacy ratio）
　a bank's capital adequacy ratio　銀行の自己資本比率
　minimum capital adequacy ratio　最低自己資本比率
◆A bank's capital adequacy ratio represents the amount of core capital it has to cushion potential losses, as a percentage of loans and other assets. 銀行の自己資本比率は、融資額などの資産に対して、予想損失の処理に充てられる自己資本［中核資本］がどれだけあるかを示す。◆A higher capital adequacy ratio means that a bank has a greater capability to deal with risk. 自己資本比率が高いほど、銀行のリスクへの対応力が高くなる。◆Banks' capital adequacy ratio is an index that shows their business soundness. 銀行各行の自己資本比率は、銀行の経営の健全性を示す指標である。◆Declines in surpluses are likely to reduce a bank's capital adequacy ratio. 剰余金が減ると、銀行の自己資本比率が低下する恐れがある。◆On a consolidated basis, the capital adequacy ratios of the six banking groups ranged from 10.07 percent to 12.5 percent

as of Sept. 30. 連結ベースで、銀行・金融6グループの自己資本比率は、9月30日時点で10.07〜12.5%となっている。◆The Bank of Japan's capital adequacy ratio sagged to 7.33 percent as of March 31, 2004. 日銀の自己資本比率は、2004年3月31日時点で7.33%に低下した。◆The bank reported a capital-adequacy ratio of 4.54 percent as of the end of fiscal 2010. 同行の2010年度末現在［時点］の自己資本比率は、4.54%だった。◆The bank's capital adequacy ratio was 9.01 percent at end-June. 同行の自己資本比率は、6月末時点で9.01%となっている。◆The capital adequacy ratio is considered a barometer of a bank's financial health. 自己資本比率は、銀行の経営の健全性を示す指標とされている。◆The capital adequacy ratio is used to determine the financial health of financial institutions. 自己資本比率は、金融機関の経営の健全性（財務の健全性）を判断するのに用いられる。◆UFJ Holdings Inc. has agreed to sell UFJ Trust Bank Ltd. to Sumitomo Trust & Banking Co., Ltd. for about ¥300 billion to raise its capital adequacy ratio. UFJホールディングスが、自己資本比率を引き上げるため、UFJ信託銀行を約3,000億円で住友信託銀行に売却することで合意した。

解説 自己資本比率とは：銀行の融資残高などの総資産に対する資本金などの比率をいう。国際銀行業務の銀行の自己資本比率はBIS（国際決済銀行）基準で8％以上、国内銀行業務の銀行の自己資本比率は4％以上とされている。（Baselの関連項目参照）

capital adequacy regulation 自己資本比率規制
(=capital adequacy regulation)
◆Commercial banks have created special investment vehicles (SIVs) in order to escape the capital adequacy regulation imposed by the Basel accord. 銀行は、バーゼル協定［バーゼル合意］による自己資本比率規制を回避するため、特別投資会社（SIV）を新設している。

capital adequacy requirements （銀行への）自己資本比率規制, 自己資本規制
◆A working group of the Financial System Council put together a report concerning capital adequacy requirements. 金融審議会の作業部会が、自己資本比率規制に関する報告書をまとめた。◆Capital adequacy requirements are strengthened in 2013. 自己資本規制は、2013年から強化される。◆If the appraisal losses swell excessively, banks failing to meet the regulatory minimum capital adequacy requirements will have to go under. 含み損が余りにも膨らむと、規制当局の最低自己資本比率基準を満たせない銀行は、経営破たんに追い込まれることになる。◆U.S. and European financial institutions are scaling back their business operations before capital adequacy requirements are strengthened in 2013. 欧米金融機関は、2013年から自己資本規制が強化されるのを前に、業務を縮小している。

capital alliance 資本提携
(=capital link, capital tie-up)
◆Myojo Foods asked Nissin Food Products to play the part of a white knight by forming a capital alliance to thwart the U.S. investment fund's hostile takeover bid. 米系投資ファンドの敵対的TOB（株式公開買付け）を阻止するため、明星食品は資本提携によるホワイト・ナイト（白馬の騎士）としての明星の支援を日清食品に要請した。

解説 資本提携とは：企業が提携関係を強化するため、株式を互いに取得したり、交換したりすること。業務関係だけの提携に比べて、一段と強い関係を構築できる。新株を発行して割り当てる第三者割当て増資や、新株予約権の引受けなどの手法も使われる。

capital and business alliance 資本・業務提携, 資本・業務提携関係
◆General Motors Corp. and Fuji Heavy Industries Ltd. agreed to terminate their capital and business alliance, which started in 1999. 米ゼネラル・モーターズ（GM）と富士重工業は、1999年から開始した両社の資本・業務提携関係を解消することで合意した。◆Sumitomo Mitsui Financial Group Inc. is close to reaching an agreement with moneylender Promise Co. to form a capital and business alliance. 三井住友フィナンシャルグループは近く、消費者金融会社のプロミスと資本・業務提携することで合意に達する見込みだ。

capital and business link 資本・業務提携 (=capital and business alliance［partnership, tie-up］)
◆Aeon will have capital and business links not only with Daiei but also with Maruetsu Inc. of the Daiei group. イオンは、ダイエーのほかに、ダイエー・グループのマルエツとも資本・業務提携する方針だ。

capital and business tie-up 資本・業務提携
(=capital and business alliance［links, partnership］)
◆The two steelmakers started capital and business tie-ups in 2002. この鉄鋼メーカー2社は、2002年に資本・業務提携を開始した。

capital asset 資本資産
 capital asset pricing model 資本資産価格モデル, 資本資産評価モデル, CAPM
 capital-asset ratio 自己資本比率 (=capital adequacy ratio, capital-to-asset ratio, net worth ratio)
 capital/asset requirements 自己資本比率規制

capital base 資本基盤, 自己資本, 資本金
(⇒tax system)
◆European banks should have bolstered their capital bases when the sovereign debt crisis broke out in the peripheral countries in 2010. 2010年に周辺国で財政危機が発生した際、欧州の銀行は資本基盤［自己資本］を強化すべきであった。◆Mizuho Financial Group Inc. will float preferred securities to domestic institutional investors to enhance the core portion of its capital base. みずほフィナンシャルグループ（FG）は、自己資本［中核的自己資本］を増強するため、国内機関投資家向けに優先出資証券を発行する。◆Nippon Life Insurance Co. plans to raise ¥50 billion for acquisitions and to strengthen its capital base. 日本生命保険は、買収資金として500億円を調達して、同社の資本基盤も強化する方針だ。◆Public funds should be injected not only to buy up toxic assets, but also to boost the capital bases of enfeebled financial institutions. 公的資金は、不良資産の買取りだけでなく、弱体化した［体力の落ちた］金融機関の資本増強にも注入すべきだ。◆Resona Holdings Inc. was recently forced to seek an injection of public funds due to a sharp drop in its capital base. りそなホールディングスは最近、自己資本の急激な減少で、公的資金の注入に追い込まれた。◆The banks' capital base was significantly strengthened. 同行の資本基盤は、大幅に強化された。◆Zenno and Itochu Corp. already have agreed to fund the issuance of new shares of Snow Brand Milk stock to boost the company's capital base. 全農（全国農業協同組合連合会）と伊藤忠は、雪印乳業の資本基盤を強化するため、同社の新株発行（増資）を引き受けることですでに合意している。

capital buffer 資本バッファー, 資本増強
 capital conservation buffer 資本保全バッファー
 countercyclical capital buffer 景気変動［変動］抑制的な資本バッファー, カウンターシクリカル資本バッファー
◆The U.S. 10 leading banks need a combined capital buffer of 74.6 billion against the risk of a deeper recession and higher unemployment over the next two years. 米主要金融機関の10社は、今後2年の景気悪化リスクと失業増大に備えて、10社合計で746億ドルの資本増強を求められている。

capital charge 資本費用, 資本コスト
 extra capital charge 追加資本費用, 資本［自己資本］の上積み
◆The Financial Stability Board will impose a progressive extra capital charge of 1 percent to 2.5 percent on risk-adjusted assets held by G-SIFIs. G20（主要20か国・地域）の金融当局で構成する金融安定化理事会（FSB）は、国際金融

システムにとって重要な金融機関(G-SIFIs)が保有するリスク調整後資産に、1～2.5%の資本[自己資本]の上積みを段階的に課すことになった。

capital conservation buffer 資本保全バッファー（新国際金融規制で、銀行が損失を吸収するために追加的に必要な資本保全バッファー（普通株で構成）は、2013年1月から2.5%に設定された。そのため銀行は、狭義の中核的自己資本（コアTier1）相当の資本を、現行の3倍以上の7%以上の水準で確保しなければならなくなった。資本保全バッファーは、規制値を割り込むと、報酬や配当が制限される）

capital control 資本規制, 資本取引規制, 資本移動規制, 為替規制
  capital controls 資本取引規制
  elimination [removal] of capital control 資本規制の撤廃
  have tight capital controls 厳しい資本取引規制を行う
  impose capital control 資本規制を行う
  reintroduction of capital control 資本規制の復活, 為替管理の復活

capital decrease 減資
  (=capital reduction, reduction of capital)
  ◆The Corporation's restructuring plan includes a capital decrease of more than 50 percent. 当社の再建案には、50%超の減資も盛り込まれている。

capital deficiency 資本不足
  ◆Making the creditor banks waive loans to TEPCO will cause the utility to fall into capital deficiency, with liabilities exceeding assets. 取引銀行に東電への債権を放棄させると、東電は資本不足に陥り、債務超過になってしまう。

capital deficit 債務超過, 資本不足
  (=net capital deficiency)
  ◆For the year ending this March, the firm expects to post a capital deficit of ¥10.9 billion. 今年3月期決算で、同社は109億円の債務超過に陥る見通しだ。◆The company expects to post a capital deficit of ¥8 billion for the year ending this March. 同社は、今年3月期決算で、80億円の債務超過に陥る見通しだ。

capital demand 資金需要, 資本需要
  ◆There are too many banks in Japan compared with capital demand. 日本では、資金需要に対して銀行の数が多すぎる。

capital efficiency 資本効率
  ◆Issuance of new shares for this purpose may lead to an increase in payouts to shareholders that will result in drops in capital efficiency. このために新株を発行すると、株主配当（株主資本）が増えて資本効率が落ちる可能性がある。

capital expansion 増資, 資本増強
  (=capital increase)
  ◆The capital expansion will boost the combined stake of the three Mitsubishi group companies in MMC to about 34 percent. 資本増強で、三菱グループ3社の三菱自動車への出資比率は3社合計で約34%に高まる。

capital expenditures 設備投資, 設備投資額, 固定資産投資額, 資本支出額, 資本的支出, 資本投資額
  (=capital investment, capital spending)
  ◆Capital expenditure grew by 1.7 percent in January-March from the previous quarter. 1-3月期の設備投資は、前期比で1.7%増加した。

capital flight 資本逃避, 他国への資本の流出, 資本の国外移転 (=flight of capital)
  ◆The decline in long-term interest rates since May is due to continued capital flight from high-risk assets such as stocks triggered by the debt crisis in Europe. 5月以降、長期金利が低下しているのは、欧州の財政危機をきっかけに株式などリスク[損失リスク]の高い資産からの資金逃避が続いたためだ。
  ◆Triggered by political confusion in Chiapas, capital flight spread even among Mexican residents, reducing the country's foreign reserves to $10.5 billion. チアパス州での政治混乱を引き金に、資本逃避はメキシコの居住者にまで及び、メキシコの外貨準備は105億ドルに減少した。

capital flow 資本の流れ, 資本移動
  capital flows 資本移動, 資本流出, 資本流入
  capital flows in 資本流入 (=capital inflows)
  capital flows out 資本流出 (=capital outflows)
  cross-border capital flows 国際的な資本移動, 国際的な資金フロー
  destabilizing capital flows 不安定な資本移動
  disequilibrating capital flows 攪乱（かくらん）的資本移動
  global capital flows 国際資本移動
    (⇒global liquidity)
  international capital flows 国際的な資本移動[資金移動]
  liberalization [liberalized] capital flows 資本移動の自由化
  neutralize by net capital flows 資本流入の純増で穴を埋める
  restrictions on capital flows 資本流入制限, 資本流入規制
  reversal of capital flows 資本の流れの逆転
  swings in capital flows 資本移動の方向の反転
  ◆Asia faces the risk of volatile capital flows as its growth outpaces the rest of the world. アジアの成長が他国を上回っているため、アジアは資本移動の変動リスクに直面している。
  ◆The U.S. monetary policy has a major impact on global liquidity and capital flows. 米国の金融政策は、国際流動性と国際資本移動に大きな影響力を持つ。

capital for a stock company 株式会社の資本金
  ◆Life insurer's foundation fund is equivalent to capital for a stock company. 生命保険会社の基金は、株式会社の資本金に相当する。

capital gain 資本利得, 資産売却益, 資産譲渡益, 株式売買益, 譲渡所得, 値上がり益, キャピタル・ゲイン (⇒go public, security taxation system)
  capital gain on the principal 元本のキャピタル・ゲイン
  capital gains tax format キャピタル・ゲイン課税方式, 株式譲渡益課税方式
  capital gains yield 資本利得率
  lower capital gains 資産売却益の減少
  net capital gain 純額キャピタル・ゲイン
  net realized capital gain 正味実現キャピタル・ゲイン
  realize capital gains キャピタル・ゲインを実現させる
  realize latent capital gains 含み益を実現する
  realized capital gain 実現キャピタル・ゲイン, キャピタル・ゲイン実現益
  short-term capital gain 短期キャピタル・ゲイン
  taxation on capital gain キャピタル・ゲイン課税, キャピタル・ゲイン税 (=capital gain taxation)
  unrealized capital gains on the investment portfolio 投資ポートフォリオの含み益
  ◆In Germany, individual investors' capital gains are not normally taxed. ドイツでは、個人投資家の譲渡益については通常、非課税となっている。◆In Japan, when an individual investor makes a capital gain by selling stocks, it is taxed at a rate of 26 percent if the investor chooses a separate self-assessment taxation on the final income tax return. 日本では、個人投資家が株式売却で利益（譲渡益）を得た場合、確定申告で申告分離課税を選ぶと税率が譲渡益の26%になる。◆Taxes levied on capital gains should be consolidated to promote securities investment. 有価証券投資を促すために、金融資産課税は一元化するべきだ。

capital gains and losses 資本利得および損失, 資産譲渡損益, 株式譲渡損益, 譲渡損益, 株式売買損益

◆The securities companies calculate capital gains and losses, compile taxation documents, gather annual stock reports and file tax returns on behalf of investors free of charge. 証券会社は、投資家の代わりに無料で譲渡益を計算したり、税務書類を作成したり、年間の株式取引報告書を揃えたりして、税務申告書（納税申告書）を提出する。

capital gains from stock sales 株式譲渡益, 株式売却益
◆The tax breaks on capital gains from stock sales and on dividend income will be extended by one year. 株式譲渡益［株式売却益］と受取配当金の税率軽減措置の期間が、1年延長される。

capital gains tax 株式譲渡益課税, 資本利得税
◆The 20 percent capital gains tax will be imposed on the average gain. 合算後の利益には、税率20％の株式譲渡益課税が課される。

capital holdings 保有資本
◆Increasing capital holdings will continue to be an urgent task for European banks. 欧州の銀行にとって、資本増強が今後も引き続き急務と言える。

capital increase 増資, 資本増強, 保険会社の基金の積み増し［増額］, 基金増資　(=capital expansion, capital increment, capital injection; ⇒deficit settlement of accounts)
　capital increase adjustment 増資調整
　capital increase of A for B B対Aの株主割当発行増資
　dubious capital increase 架空増資
　general capital increase 一般増資
　participate in a capital increase plan［package］ 増資計画に参加する
　proceeds from the capital increase 増資で調達した資金
　the dilutive effect of the capital increase 増資による希薄化効果
　the standards of capital increase 増資基準
◆DaimlerChrysler AG will not participate in a capital increase plan to rescue MMC. ダイムラー・クライスラーは、三菱自動車支援のための増資計画に参加しない方針だ。◆Goldman Sachs' capital increase is partly aimed at regaining the confidence in the U.S. financial market, which has been facing a raft of financial problems. ゴールドマン・サックスの増資は、多くの金融問題を抱える米金融市場の信認回復も狙いの一つだ。◆The capital increase is due after a policyholders' representative meeting in June. この基金の積み増し［保険会社の基金増資］は、6月の総代会後に実施される予定だ。◆The capital increase would bring Meiji Life's solvency margin ratio by about 25 percentage points from 504 percent as of last September. この基金の積み増し［基金増資］で、明治生命のソルベンシー・マージン（支払い余力）比率は、昨年9月末時点の504％から25％ほど上昇する。◆The former company president was indicted on fraud charges regarding a dubious capital increase in the firm. この元社長は、架空増資に関する詐欺罪で起訴された。◆The tie-up included a contribution by Mitsubishi Tokyo to the UFJ group's planned capital increase. 統合には、UFJグループが予定していた増資に三菱銀行の出資も含まれていた。

解説 **増資**とは：会社が資本金を増やすことを増資という。これには、払込み金を取って新株を発行する有償増資と、株主から払込み金を取らない増資がある。

capital increase plan 増資計画
◆The firm did not participate in a capital increase plan to rescue MMC. 同社は、三菱自動車支援のための増資計画に参加しなかった。

capital inflow 資本流入, 資金の流入, 資本輸入, 流入資金, 買い越し　(=the inflow of capital; ⇒foreign capital inflows, inflow)
　attract capital inflows 資本流入を誘う, 資本流入の呼び水となる
　capital inflow figures 資本流入額, 資本収支上の流入額
　direct capital inflows 直接資本の流入
　finance the current account deficit with long-term capital inflow 長期資本の流入で経常赤字を補てんする
　restrict capital inflow 資本流入を規制する
◆China restricts capital inflow. 中国は、資本輸入を規制している。◆Such capital inflows have offset U.S. fiscal and trade deficits and boosted stock prices to record highs. これらの流入資金が、米国の財政や貿易の赤字を埋め合わせ、空前の株高を演出した。

capital injection 資本の注入, 資本の増強, 増資, 保険会社への基金拠出, 保険会社の基金増資
　(=capital increase)
◆As part of the plan to bolster its financial standing, the struggling life insurer will seek capital injection of about 100 billion yen from financial institutions. 財務強化策の一環として、経営再建中のこの生命保険会社は、金融機関に1,000億円程度の基金拠出［基金増資］を要請する方針だ。◆The revival plan calls for capital injection from Mitsubishi group companies. 事業再生計画は、三菱のグループ企業による資本増強を求めている。◆This life insurer sought capital injection of 70 billion yen from financial institutions. この生命保険会社は、金融機関に700億円の基金拠出［基金増資］を要請した。

capital investment 設備投資 (investment in plant and other facilities), 資本投資, 資本投下, 出資, 出資金
　(=capital expenditure, capital spending; ⇒bond redemption, corporate earnings, corporate reconstruction fund)
◆A recovery will be export-driven, dependent on U.S. growth and the yen's depreciation, instead of being led by increased domestic consumption and capital investment. 今後の景気回復は、アメリカ経済の好転や円安を背景にした輸出主導型の回復で、国内の個人消費や設備投資の伸びがその牽引役となるわけではない。◆Capital investment and exports, which have supported the economy, have remained firm. 日本経済を支えてきた設備投資と輸出は、引き続き堅調だ。◆Capital investment, which was the engine for the overall economy, has lost much of its momentum. 景気全体を引っ張ってきた設備投資に、一時の勢いがなくなっている。◆Listed companies are still cautious about making capital investments as they strive to cut costs to be globally competitive. 上場企業各社は、グローバル競争を勝ち抜くためにコスト削減に取り組んでいるので、設備投資にはまだ慎重だ。◆Maintaining an easy monetary policy may lead to excessive corporate capital investment and have a negative impact on the sustainable economic recovery. 金融緩和政策を続けると、企業の過剰な設備投資を生み、景気の持続的回復を阻害する恐れがある。◆Public corporations have received a whopping ¥5.3 trillion a year from the government in subsidies or in the name of capital investment. 特殊法人には、助成金や出資金の名目で年間5兆3,000億円もの巨額の国費がつぎ込まれている。◆The decline in capital investment is likely to bottom out in the future. 設備投資の減少も、先行き下げ止まりの気配が見られる。◆The economy is beginning to lose momentum as exports and capital investments are slowing. 輸出と設備投資が息切れを始め、景気に減速傾向が出ている。

capital loss 資本損失, 資産売却損, 資産譲渡損, 譲渡損失, キャピタル・ロス (⇒term)
◆In the United States, a special deduction system has been implemented that allows investors to carry over capital losses from stock transactions in their current tax return to future years. 米国では、税務申告上、株式売買による譲渡損失を翌年以降に繰り越すことができる特別控除制度が実施されている。

capital management capabilities 資産運用力
◆This financial group will send an outside board member to

Daiwa Trust & Banking to boost the unit's capital management capabilities. この金融グループは、大和銀信託銀行に社外取締役を送り込んで、同行の資産運用力を高める方針だ。

capital market 資本市場, 長期金融市場, キャピタル・マーケット
 (⇒money market, securities market)
 be shut out of capital markets 資本市場から締め出される
 international capital market 国際資本市場
 international capital market system 国際資本市場
 volatility and disruptions in capital markets 資本市場の変動性と混乱
 ◆Greek government bonds are currently shut out of capital markets. ギリシャの国債は現在、資本市場から締め出されている［資本市場が受け付けていない］。◆The capital markets around the globe are plagued by counterparty risks in the aftermath of the collapse of U.S. investment bank Lehman Brothers in 2008. 世界全体の資本市場は、2008年の米証券会社［投資銀行］の経営破たんの影響で、カウンターパーティー・リスクに苦しんでいる。◆Volatility and disruptions in the capital markets became even more pronounced in July. 7月は、資本市場の変動性と混乱が一段と鮮明になった。
 解説 資本市場とは：一般的には、株式・債券の発行市場（primary market: 新規発行の株式や債券が、発行者から投資家に売り渡される市場）と流通市場（secondary market: すでに発行された株式や債券が投資家間で売買される市場）を含めた証券市場とほぼ同義。ただし、広い意味では、金融機関の長期貸出資金をも含めた長期金融市場のこと。短期金融市場はmoney marketという。

capital movement 資本移動
 autonomous capital movement 自主的［自発的］資本移動
 induced capital movement 誘発的資本移動
 international capital movement 国際資本移動
 international short-term capital movement 国際短期資本移動
 long-term capital movement 長期資本移動
 negative capital movement 負の資本移動
 positive capital movement 正の資本移動
 short-term capital movement 短期資本移動

capital of a joint-stock company 株式会社の資本金
 ◆An insurer's basic fund is equivalent to the capital of a joint-stock company. 保険会社の基金は、株式会社の資本金に当たる。

capital outflow 資本流出, 対外投融資
 (=the outflow of capital)
 capital outflow figures 資本流出額, 資本収支上の流出額
 capital outflows 資本流出 (=capital flows out)
 enhance capital outflow 資本の流出を促進する
 induce capital outflows 対外投融資を促す
 leakage of capital flows 資本の国外流出
 long-term capital outflows 長期資本流出
 short-term capital outflows 短期資金の流出
 ◆Direct investment and portfolio are included in capital outflow. 資本流出には、直接投資や証券投資が含まれる。

capital ownership 出資比率
 ◆Matsushita Electric Industrial Co. will increase its capital ownership of the firm from 31.8 percent to 51 percent. 松下電器産業は、同社への出資比率を現在の31.8%から51%に引き上げる。

capital participation 資本参加, 出資
 ◆In establishing a low cost carrier under ANA's wing, ANA will invite capital participation from other industries and foreign funds. 全日空傘下の格安航空会社を設立するにあたって、全日空は異業種や海外のファンドからも出資を募る方針だ。◆The Bank of Tokyo-Mitsubishi UFJ (BTMU) has begun negotiations with Bank of China over BTMU's capital participation in the Chinese bank. 三菱東京UFJ銀行が、中国銀行と、中国銀行への資本参加についての交渉に入った。

capital partner 資本提携先
 ◆The firm is currently negotiating with its domestic capital partners to conclude change-of-control agreements. 同社は現在、国内の資本提携先とチェンジ・オブ・コントロール（資本拘束）条項の契約を結ぶ交渉を進めている。

capital plan 資本計画, 資金計画
 ◆The U.S. FRB accepted capital plans from the 10 banks judged in stress tests to need additional capital to guard against a deeper economic downturn. 米連邦準備制度理事会（FRB）は、特別検査（ストレス・テスト）で景気がさらに悪化した場合に備えて資本の増強が必要と判断された米金融機関10社から提出された資本計画［資本増強計画］を、承認した。

capital position 自己資本比率, 資本ポジション
 ◆The proposed bid price does not reflect the bank's strong capital position and the superior credit quality of its assets. 株式公開買付け（TOB）の予定価格は、同行の自己資本比率の大きさや同行の資産の高い信用力を反映していない。

capital provider 資金提供者
 ◆To avoid sinking into a negative net worth, the firm is seeking ¥300 billion in financial aid from capital providers. 債務超過に陥るのを避けるため、同社は資金提供者に3,000億円の金融支援を要請している。

capital reduction 減資 (=capital decrease, reduction of capital: 減資とは、資本金を減らして捻出した資金を企業再建に使う措置のことをいう。⇒capital increase)
 ◆The company will hold a board of directors to approve a 99.7 percent capital reduction from ¥31.3 billion to ¥100 million. 同社は、取締役会を開いて、313億円から1億円への99.7%減資を承認することになっている。

capital reinforcement 資本増強
 ◆Depending on the degree of JAL's financial deterioration, the government will consider a combination of capital reinforcement under the industrial revitalization law and public assistance by the Enterprise Turnaround Initiative Corp. of Japan. 日航の財務の傷み具合によって、政府は、産業再生法に基づく公的資金による資本増強と、企業再生支援機構による公的支援との組合せを検討する方針だ。

capital requirements 資金需要, 資金の必要額, 必要資本金, 自己資本規制, 自己資本比率規制
 ◆Capital requirements due to the growth of our financial services and leasing business will continue to grow in 2012. 当社の金融サービスとリース事業の拡大により、資金需要は2012年度も引き続き伸びるものと思われます。◆The minimum regulatory capital requirements were abandoned. （会社設立時の）最低必要資本金制度は、廃止された。

capital reserve 資本準備金, 資本剰余金 (⇒legal capital reserves, legal reserves, transfer動詞)
 ◆Many of major banks have no choice but to mobilize parts of their legally prescribed capital reserves. 大手銀行の多くは、法定資本準備金にまで手をつけざるを得なくなっている。

capital shortage 資本不足 (=capital shortfall, shortage of funds, shortfall in capital)
 ◆European banks are forced to shore up their potential capital shortages to restore market confidence. 欧州銀行は、市場の信認を回復するため、潜在的資本不足の増強を迫られている。◆Public funds should be injected only into those financial institutions that experience a capital shortage. 公的資金は、自己資本が足りなくなった金融機関にだけ注入するべきだ。

capital shortfall 資本不足, 資金不足
 (=capital shortage)
 ◆Europe's seven banks judged to have capital shortfall by the stress test will work on increasing their capital. ストレ

ス・テスト（特別検査）で資本不足と認定された欧州の7銀行は、これから資本増強に取り組む。◆Speculation that some major banks may find themselves with capital shortfalls and then nationalized is driving investors to dump the banks' shares. 大手行の一部が自己資本不足に陥って国有化されるとの思惑から、投資家は銀行株の売りに出ている。◆The amount of each European bank's potential capital shortfall has been finally disclosed by the stress test of the Committee of European Banking Supervisors. 欧州各行の潜在的資本不足額が、欧州銀行監督委員会のストレス・テスト（特別検査）でようやく開示された。

capital spending　設備投資, 資本的支出
　（=capital investment）
◆Sluggish capital spending and other negative factors have discouraged corporate customers from taking out loans. 設備投資の低迷などのマイナス要因で、法人向け融資は伸び悩んでいる[法人顧客はローンを組むのを抑えている]。◆The firm revised upward its capital spending plans for fiscal 2012 by ¥70 billion to ¥1.6 trillion as part of its policy of expanding production capacity, both at home and abroad. 同社は、国内外の生産設備拡張政策の一環として、2012年度の設備投資計画を700億円上乗せして1兆6,000億円に上方修正した。

capital stock　株式資本, 株式資本金, 資本金, 資本ストック, 総株式数, 株式, 普通株, 外部の人々が所有する株式
◆Capital stock was sold to provide additional working capital. 追加的の運転資金の調達のため、株式を発行しました。◆During 2011, conversions of convertible debentures resulted in the issuance of 200 shares of the Corporation's capital stock. 2011年度は、転換社債の転換により、200株の当社株式を発行した。◆Since May 31, 2010, in respect of the Corporation's capital stock, there has not been any direct or indirect redemption, purchase, or other acquisition of any such stock. 2010年5月31日以降、本会社の株式に関しては、当該株式の直接・間接の償還、買取りやその他の取得も一切行っていない。◆The company has had no transactions in its capital stock since that time. その時以来、同社の資本金の増減はない。

capital strength　資本力
　shore up one's capital strength　資本を増強する
◆European countries are urged to facilitate a safety net for emergencies, including the injection of public funds into deteriorating banks to shore up their capital strength. 欧州は、経営が悪化した銀行[金融機関]に公的資金を注入して資本を増強するなど、非常時に備えた安全網の整備が求められている。

capital structure　資本構成, 資本構造, 財務基盤
　（「資本構成・資本構造」は、総資本に占める自己資本と他人資本（負債）の割合で、バランス・シート上の資本（純資産（net worth）＋優先株式）と長期債務（long term debt）の合計額を指す。⇒financial structure）
◆The Corporation's capital structure at December 31, 2011 was as follows. 当社の2011年12月31日現在の資本構成は、次のとおりです。◆The upgrade reflects Moody's expectation that the company will continue to exhibit an excellent operating performance and outstanding capital structure. この格上げは、同社が引き続き好業績と際立った財務基盤を示すとのムーディーズの期待感を反映している。

capital surcharge　資本の上積み, 自己資本の上積み, 資本の積み増し　（=additional capital）
◆Twenty-eight banks of the world will face capital surcharges of 1 percent to 2.5 percent by the application of international rules to rein in too-big-to-fail lenders. 大きすぎて破たんさせられない銀行[金融機関]を規制する国際基準が適用されると、世界の28行が、1～2.5%の資本[自己資本]上積みの対象となる。

capital surplus　資本剰余金
◆China's renminbi may attain a reserve-currency status by the steady appreciation of the yuan and the country's enormous capital surpluses. 中国の人民元は、人民元の着実な切上げと中国の膨大な資本剰余金によって、準備通貨の地位を獲得する可能性がある。

capital tie-up　資本提携
　（=capital alliance, capital link；⇒deal名詞）
◆NTT DoCoMo Inc. formed a capital tie-up with Internet shopping mall operator Rakuten Inc. in the Internet auction business. NTTドコモが、インターネット・オークション事業で電子商取引大手の楽天[仮想商店街を運営している楽天]と資本提携した。◆With the capital tie-up with Norinchukin Bank, MFG aims to boost its customer base in the securities sector. 農林中央金庫との資本提携で、みずほフィナンシャルグループは、証券分野の顧客基盤の強化を目指している。

capital-to-asset ratio　株主資本比率, 自己資本比率
　（=capital adequacy ratio, capital-asset ratio, net worth ratio）
◆The capital-to-asset ratios at top eight Japanese banks averaged about 10 percent at the end of September 2001, above an 8 percent global standard. 日本の上位8行の自己資本比率は、2001年9月末の時点で平均して約10%で、グローバル・スタンダードの8%を上回った。

capitalization［**capitalisation**］　（名）資本構成, 資本総額, 資本化, 株式資本化, 資本調達, 収益の資本還元, 資本組入れ, 発行済み株式の時価総額, 長期資本, 資産計上, 資産化, 会社・事業などへの投資, 資本基盤
　（⇒market capitalization）
　bank capitalization　銀行の資本構成, 銀行に資本基盤, 銀行資本
　capitalization issue　資本組入れ株式発行, 資本組入れ発行, 無償発行, 無償増資, 株式無償交付
　capitalization rate　資産化率
　capitalization structure　資本構成
　capitalization value　資本金額
　cessation of capitalization　資産化の停止
　improve capitalization　資本基盤を強化する, 資本[資本基盤]を充実させる
　improved capitalization　資本基盤の改善
　　（⇒erosion）
　insurance company's target capitalization　保険会社の自己資本比率目標
　interest capitalization　利息の資産化, 利息の資産計上, 利子費用の資産計上
　large capitalization stock　大型株
　low capitalization　資本基盤が弱いこと, 脆弱（ぜいじゃく）な資本基盤　（=weak capitalization）
　market capitalization　時価総額
　minimum capitalization requirements　最低必要資本金額
　　（=minimum capital requirements）
　overall market capitalization　市場の時価総額, 株式時価総額
　permanent capitalization　恒久的資本組入れ
　small capitalization stock　小型株
　　（⇒Russel 2000 index）
　strengthen capitalization　資本の充実化, 資本を充実させる, 資本基盤を強化する
　target capitalization　自己資本比率の目標
　total capitalization　資本総額
　total market capitalization　株式時価総額
　　（=overall market capitalization）
　weak capitalization　資本基盤が弱いこと, 弱い資本基盤, 資本基盤の弱さ　（=low capitalization）
◆The other bills implemented in 2006 include a measure eliminating the ¥10 million minimum capitalization requirements for joint-stock companies. 2006年度実施の他の法案には、株式会社の設立に必要な1,000万円の最低資本金制

度の撤廃措置も盛り込まれている。◆The United States and Britain demanded tighter regulations on bank capitalization. 米国と英国は、銀行の自己資本規制の強化を求めた。◆Total debt as a percentage of total capitalization was 20 percent at yearend 2011. 資本総額に対する債務総額の比率は、2011年末現在で20%だった。

capitalize [capitalize] (動)資本化する,資産化する,資産に計上する,現価計上する,資本として使用する,資本に組み入れる,資本を投入する,出資する,投資する
  amounts capitalized　資産化金額
  capitalized costs　資産に計上した費用,資産化費用,費用の資産化 (=capitalized expenses)
  capitalized interest　資産化利息,利息資産化
  capitalized leases　資産に計上したリース,資産化リース,資本化リース,リースの資産化
  capitalized surplus　組入れ資本金,資本化された剰余金
  foreign-capitalized companies　外資系企業
  poorly capitalized　資金力の乏しい
  well capitalized　資金力の豊富な,自己資本の充実した
◆Both foreign-capitalized and Japanese companies are forced to relocate their headquarters functions overseas. 外資系企業も日本企業も、本社機能を海外に移さざるを得なくなっている。◆The new company will be capitalized at ¥100 billion. 新会社の資本金は、1,000億円になる見込しだ。

capitalize on　利用する(take advantage of),活用する,生かす,〜に付け込む,〜に便乗する,(需要などを)見越す
  capitalize on a market opportunity　市場機会をとらえる,市場機会を生かす
  capitalize on huge money flows　膨大な資金の流れを利用する
  capitalize on improved quality at production plants　生産拠点での品質向上を活用する
  capitalize on one's market share　市場シェアを生かす,シェアを生かす
  fully capitalize on one's strengths　持ち味を発揮する
◆If Japan is acting weak in currency intervention, speculators will try to capitalize on that. 日本が為替介入に弱腰なら、投機筋に付け込まれることになる。◆Speculators capitalized on the Bank of Japan's delay in taking action. 投機筋は、日銀の対応の遅れを突いた。

CAPM　資本資産価格モデル,資本資産評価モデル (capital asset pricing modelの略)

car and truck loans　自動車ローン,自動車ローン債権
◆General Motors Corp. agreed to sell up to $55 billion in car and truck loans to Bank of America Corp. over five years. ゼネラル・モーターズ(GM)は、バンク・オブ・アメリカに対して、今後5年間で最大550億ドルの自動車ローン債権を売却することで合意した。

car loan　自動車ローン
◆The U.S. financial crisis stopped an ever-increasing number of Americans from getting car loans, leading to a spectacular dive in U.S. car sales. 米国の金融危機で、自動車ローンを組めない米国人が続出し、米国の新車販売が急減した。

carbon money [Carbon Money]　炭素通貨,カーボン・マネー(1国全体で家計部門に許容できる温室効果ガス排出量(カーボン)を決め、それを小口分割して個人にICチップ・カードの形で付与する仕組み)

card (名)カード,クレジット・カード,キャッシュ・カード (⇒bank card, bogus card, cash card)
  access card　アクセス・カード(クレジット・カードのこと)
  affiliated card　提携カード
  all purpose card　汎用カード(利用する加盟店の範囲、種類が限定されていないクレジット・カード)
  ATM card　キャッシュ・カード,ATMカード
  card holder　カード会員 (=card member)
  card issuer　カード会社
  IC card cashless account settlement system　ICカード・キャッシュレス決済システム,キャッシュレス決済システム
  integrated circuit card　IC(集積回路)カード (=IC card)
  noncontact integrated circuit card　非接触型ICカード
  palm-recognizing ATM card　手のひら認証のキャッシュ・カード
  payment by card　カード決済
◆In addition to being ATM cards, the new cards can also be used as credit cards and to receive loans. 新型カードは、キャッシュ・カードであるほか、クレジット・カードとしても使えるし、ローンの利用にも使える。◆Mizuho Bank offers a service by which ATM cardholders are given mileage points each time they use the new cards as credit cards, purchase financial products at the bank's branches or receive loans from the bank. みずほ銀行が提供しているサービスでは、キャッシュ・カード会員が新型カードをクレジット・カードとして利用したり、みずほ銀行で金融商品を購入したり、ローンを利用したりすると、その取引に応じて毎回、マイレージ・ポイントがもらえる。

card fraud　キャッシュ・カード詐欺 (=cash card fraud; ⇒limit名詞)
◆Banks' slow response and refusal to take responsibility increase the damages caused by card fraud. 銀行の対応の遅れ[対策の後回し]と責任回避が、キャッシュ・カード詐欺による被害を助長している。

card issuer　カード会社,クレジット・カード発行会社 (=card issuing company; ⇒compensation)

card service　カード・サービス
◆The annual fee for the new card service is ¥10,500. 新カード・サービスの年会費は、10,500円だ。

card theft and counterfeiting　カードの盗難や偽造

cardholder　(名)カード会員 (=card holder, card member; ⇒mileage point, scanner)
◆In the case of this ATM card, even if a cardholder's card or PIN number should be stolen, no one else can withdraw cash from the account. このキャッシュ・カードの場合は、カード会員がたとえカードや暗証番号を盗まれても、本人以外は口座から預金を引き出せない。◆The bank does not issue conventional bankbooks for cardholders, but offers electronic bank books that are used via the Internet and accessed through personal computer and cell phones. 同行は、カード会員に従来の銀行通帳は発行せず、パソコンや携帯電話でアクセスしてインターネット上で使用する電子通帳(ウェブ通帳)を提供している。

care (名)医療,医療保険,保護,看護,世話,ケア (⇒health-care insurance system)
  health care　医療,医療保険,医療サービス,ヘルス・ケア
  health care benefits　健康保険給付,医療保険給付
  medical care　保険医療,医療,医療費
  universal health care coverage　国民皆医療保険制度

carrier (名)持参人,保険会社,保険業者,保険者,通信事業者,運送業者,キャリア
  carrier's liability insurance　受託貨物責任保険
  common carrier　公衆電気通信事業者,運送業者,一般運送人,コモン・キャリア
  contract carrier　契約運送人
  insurance carrier　保険業者
  mobile carrier　携帯電話会社,携帯電話事業者
  premium carrier　一流航空会社
  private carrier　専属運送業者,契約運送業者
  type I carrier　第一種事業者,第一種電気通信事業者

type II carrier 第二種事業者, 第二種電気通信事業者
◆With a view to stemming the airlines' financial hemorrhaging, the Construction and Transport Ministry in late May asked the Development Bank of Japan to provide emergency loans to the two carriers. 航空会社の損失を阻止するため、5月下旬に国土交通省は、日本政策投資銀行に対して両航空会社への緊急融資を要請した。

carry (動)計上する, 算定する, 帳簿に記載しておく, 記帳する, 転記する, 保険などを付ける, 設定する, 債務を負う
  be carried at cost　取得原価で計上される
  be carried at FIFO cost　先入れ先出し法で算定される
  be carried to　～に転記される
  carried down　前期繰越し, C/D [c/d]
    (=brought down)
  carried forward　次期繰越し, 次頁繰越し, C/F [c/f]
    (=brought forward)
  carry a bank guarantee　銀行保証が付いている
  carry a risk premium　リスク・プレミアムを付ける
  carry additional covenants　付帯条件が付く
  carry back　繰り戻す, 欠損[欠損金]を前期[前年度以前]に繰り戻す
  carry down　次期へ繰り越す
  carry excessive liabilities　過剰債務を抱える, 債務超過になる
  carry the long-term debt　長期債務を負う
◆Foreign currency deposit accounts carry a degree of risk. 外貨預金口座には、ある程度リスクも伴う。◆If TEPCO's creditor banks forgive the debts when the utility is not carrying excessive liabilities, lenders will not be able to recover either the principal or interest owed. 東電が債務超過でない時点で東電の債権保有銀行が債権を放棄すると、金融機関は元本を回収できず、金利収入も得られなくなる。◆Plant, rental machines and other property are carried at cost. 工場設備、賃貸機械、その他の固定資産は、取得原価で計上されています。

carry back (動)繰り戻す, 欠損(欠損金)を前期(前年度以前に)に繰り戻す
◆Allowing banks to claim a tax refund by carrying a loss back to the previous year has not been allowed since fiscal 1992 in Japan, due chiefly to the fiscal plight of the central government. 銀行が欠損金を前年度に繰り戻して税金還付を請求できるようにする制度(欠損金の繰戻し還付)は、主に国の財政難を理由に、日本では1992年度から凍結されてきた。

carry forward (動)繰り越す, 欠損[欠損金]を次期[翌年度以降]に繰り越す　(=carry over)
◆Also advisable is further study of the idea of extending the period for banks to deduct their losses from taxable income by allowing them to carry their losses forward to following years. 銀行の欠損金を翌年度以降に繰り越して、銀行が欠損金を課税所得から控除できる期間を延長する考え方も、さらに検討するとよい。

carry out 実行する, 実施する, 執行する, 遂行する, 成し遂げる
◆Due to delays in ratification of the agreement on bailout measures by some eurozone countries, concrete measures to rescue Greece have yet to be carried out. 支援策の合意事項について一部のユーロ圏加盟国の承認が遅れたため、ギリシャ救済の具体策はまだ実施されていない。◆If Hokuetsu Paper Mills decides to carry out the poison pill, Oji Paper Co. is likely to take legal action against it. 北越製紙が買収防衛策を実施したら、王子製紙は法的措置を取る可能性が高い。◆The bank will carry out this cofinancing scheme as the lead bank with several U.S. and European banks. 同行は、主幹事行として、この協調融資事業を欧米の複数の銀行と連携して実施する。◆The revitalization plan will be carried out chiefly using ¥400 billion in financial assistance to be extended by the firm's creditor banks. 再生計画は、主に同社の取引銀行が行う金融支援総額4,000億円を使って実施される。◆This joint financing scheme carried out with the bank as the lead bank is expected to help make the presence of Japanese banks more strongly felt in global markets. 同行を主幹事銀行として実施されるこの協調融資事業は、国際市場で邦銀の存在感を高めることになりそうだ。

carry over 繰り越す(carry forward), 持ち越す, 引き継ぐ, 延期する
◆In the United States, a special deduction system has been implemented that allows investors to carry over capital losses from stock transactions in their current tax return to future years. 米国では、税務申告上、株式売買による譲渡損失を翌年以降に繰り越すことができる特別控除制度が実施されている。

carry trade キャリー取引, キャリー・トレード
  yen-carry trade 円キャリー取引, 円キャリー・トレード, 円借入れの対外投資
◆In yen-carry trades, hedge funds borrow yen at low interest rates to invest into financial assets of other major currencies at higher interest rates. 円キャリー取引では、ヘッジ・ファンドが低金利で円を借りて、円以外の高金利の外貨建て資産に投資している。

carrying amount 帳簿価額, 簿価
  (=book value, carrying value)
◆The Company's finance subsidiary purchases customer obligations under long-term contracts from the Company at net carrying amount. 当社の金融子会社は、当社との長期契約によって、顧客の債務を当社から帳簿価格で購入しています。

carrying charge 維持費, 保管費, 月賦販売割増金, 前払い経費, キャリー・チャージ

carrying value 帳簿価額, 簿価, 繰越し価額, 未償却残高
  (=book value, carrying amount)
◆Under the book value method, the carrying value of the convertible bonds at the date of the conversion would be used to account for the conversion. 簿価法では、転換時の転換社債の簿価が、転換の会計処理に使われる。◆We reduced the carrying value of this investment by $70 million because of a sustained decline in its market value. 当社は、この投資の市場価格が長期にわたって下落しているため、その帳簿価額を7,000万ドル引き下げました。

carryover (名)繰越し, 欠損金の繰越し
  (=loss carryover)

cartel (名)企業連合, カルテル(価格形成やマーケット・シェア、生産水準など競争を排除するために結ばれる協定や協定に基づく結合)
  cartel offense　カルテル違反事件
  cartel tariff　カルテル関税
  custodial fee cartel　カストディ手数料カルテル
  depression cartel　不況カルテル
    (=anti-recession cartel, depressed cartel)
  form [run] a cartel　カルテルを結ぶ
  insurance cartel　保険企業連合, 保険カルテル
  international cartel　国際カルテル
  price (fixing) cartel　価格カルテル, 価格協定
  profit-sharing cartel　利益配当カルテル
  securities brokerage commissions cartel　証券売買手数料カルテル

carve out 切り出す, 切り取る, 切り分ける, 分割する, 切り開く, 開拓する
  carve out a career for oneself　独力で世に出る
  carve out a career in business　実業界で自分の力で名を上げる

carveout [carve-out] (名)切出し, 分割, 開拓, カーブアウト

[解説]カーブアウトとは：企業が埋もれた技術や事業、人材を新会社に移し、ファンドなど外部の資本や経営資源を積極的に呼び込んでその成長を狙った新しいベンチャーの形態。

case (名)場合, 問題, 事例, 事態, 症例, 状況, 事件, 判例, 論拠, 理由, 主張, 訴え, 訴訟, 事実, 真相, 可能性, 公算, ケース
 bearish case 弱気の見方
 bring a (court) case against 〜に対して提訴する
 bullish case 強気の見方
 case history 病歴
 case mark 荷印, ケース・マーク
 case note 1ドル札
 Case-Shiller Home Price Indices (S&Pの)ケース・シラー住宅価格指数
 commencement of a bankruptcy case 破産手続きの開始
 drop a (court) case 訴訟を取り下げる
 generally or on a case-by-case basis 包括または個別に, 包括または個別ベースで
 the case for further cut in interest rates もう一段の利下げの可能性[公算], もう一段の利下げをする状況
 the worst case 最悪の事態[場合、ケース], ワースト・ケース
 ◆In the case of foreign currency deposits, depositors can invest in foreign currencies such as British pound, Swiss franc and Australian dollar as well as the U.S. dollar and euro. 外貨預金の場合、預金者は、米ドルやユーロのほかに英ポンド、スイス・フランや豪ドルなどにも投資することができる。◆In the case of foreign currency deposits, losses may balloon if the yen appreciates further and may cause a loss of principal. 外貨預金の場合、円高がさらに進めば損失が膨らみ、元本割れになる恐れもある。◆These disciplinary measures include increased penalties on securities fraud and a newly installed penalty on corporate directors in cases of failure to submit adequate financial reports to authorities. これらの懲戒処分には、証券詐欺に対する罰則の強化や、当局に適切な財務報告をしなかった場合の企業取締役に対する罰則の新設などが含まれている。

cash (動)現金に換える, 換金する, 現金化する
 cash in (債券や小切手などを)現金に換える, 換金する, うまく儲ける
 cash in on 〜でたんまり儲ける, 〜を利用する
 cash up [out] 売上高を合計する
 ◆Quasi money refers to savings at banks that cannot be immediately cashed. 準通貨とは、即時に換金できない[現金に換えられない]銀行預金のことをいう。

cash (名)現金, 預金, 現金預金, 現預金, 通貨, 資金, キャッシュ
 cash account 現金勘定
 cash advance 現金前貸し
 cash and cash items 現金と現金に準じるもの
 cash and due from banks 現金と預け金, 現金預け金
 cash and short term investments 現金預金[現金・預金]および短期投資
 cash and similar items 現物
 cash asset 現金資産, 現金性資産, 現物資産
 cash at bank 銀行預金, 当座預金, 要求払い預金
 cash at bank and in hand 要求払い預金と手元現金
 cash basis 現金基準, 現金主義
  (=receipts and payments basis)
 cash call 株主割当発行増資, 増資, 現金支払い請求
 cash capital requirements 資金需要
 cash carrier 金銭転送機
 cash contract 当日決済, 当日取引
  (=cash trade)
 cash contribution 資金協力
 cash control 現金管理
 cash cow 黒字部門, ドル箱商品[部門], 配当の良い優良株, 頼りになる資金源[収入源]
 cash credit 当座貸し, 当座貸越し
 cash crop 換金作物
 cash customer 現金客
 cash desk レジ, 勘定台
 cash discount 現金割引
 cash dispenser 現金自動支払い機, キャッシュ・ディスペンサー, CD (⇒online system)
 cash down 即金で, 即時[即金]払いで
 cash from operations 営業収益
 cash-generating unit 現金生成単位
 cash-in (貯蓄債券などの)償還 (=cash-out)
 cash in hand 手元現金 (=cash on hand)
 cash income 現金収入
 cash letter 取立小切手送達票, 送達取立小切手明細表
 cash machine 現金自動預け払い機
  (=automatic teller machine, cash dispenser)
 cash management account 金融資産総合口座
 cash management service 資金管理サービス
 cash market 現物債市場, 現物市場, 現金取引市場, 現金市場
 cash on delivery sales 現金引換販売, 代金引換販売
 cash on hand and in banks 手元現金および銀行預金, 現金および預金
 cash option 現金一括払いオプション
  (=cash rider)
 cash-out (貯蓄債券などの)償還(cash-in), 現金支払い, 現金収入, チップを現金に換える[換金する]こと
 Cash paid during the year for 当期現金支払い額
 cash payment 現金支払い, 現金払い
 cash refund annuity 即時償還式年金
 cash refund offer 現金割戻し提供
 cash reserve 現金準備
 cash rider 現金一括払いオプション
  (=cash option, cash up)
 cash sale 証券の当日決済取引(cash trade), 当日取引, 現金販売, 現金売り
 cash-settled option 現金決済オプション
 cash-settled share-based payment transaction 現金決済型の株式報酬取引
 cash settlement 現金決済, (先物やデリバティブなどの)差金決済
 cash settlement option 現金決済オプション
 cash surrender value 保険の解約返戻(へんれい)金
  (=cash value, surrender value)
 cash trade 当日[即日]決済取引, 当日取引
 cash transaction 当日取引, 当日決済取引, 現金売り, 現金販売
 cash transfer 現金振込み
 cash up 現金一括払いオプション
  (=cash rider)
 cash value (生命保険の)解約返戻(へんれい)金(cash surrender value), (損害保険の)時価, 実際価額(actual cash value)
 withdraw cash from the account 口座から預金を引き出す
 ◆Banks would keep amassing cash by disposing of distressed assets as quickly as possible to avert collapse after having difficulty raising funds. 資金調達が困難になって経営

破たんするのを避けるため、金融機関［銀行］は、できるだけ早めに危険資産を処分［売却］して、現金を抱え込もうとする。◆In the case of this ATM card, even if a cardholder's card or PIN number should be stolen, no one else can withdraw cash from the account. このキャッシュ・カードの場合は、カード会員がたとえカードや暗証番号を盗まれても、本人以外は口座から預金を引き出せない。◆Some credit firms have implemented measures that refuse to loan cash when withdrawals of more than the card's maximum amount are conducted late at night or early in the morning. クレジット・カード業界の中には、深夜や早朝にカードの最高額以上の引出し（キャッシング）が行われた場合には、現金の支払いを拒否する対策を実施しているところもある。◆The company has received about ¥780 billion in cash and debt waivers from shareholders and investors in two bailouts. 同社は、2度の金融支援で、株主と出資企業から約7,800億円の資金提供と債務免除を受けている。

【解説】**現金とは**：会計上は、銀行預金のほかに小切手、手形、郵便為替なども含むが、流動資産（current assets）に含まれるcashは手元現金と銀行の要求払い預金を指す。

cash and carry 現金払い持ち帰り方式, キャッシュ・アンド・キャリー方式
  cash and carry system 現金払い持ち帰り制［方式］, 現金決済持ち帰り方式
  cash-and-carry wholesaler 現金問屋

cash and cash equivalents 現預金および現金同等物［現金等価物］, 現金預金および現金等価物, 現金および現金同等物（「現預金および現金同等物」とは、短期間に現金化できるような投資資産で、財務省証券やマネー・マーケット・ファンド、他社発行のコマーシャル・ペーパーなど3か月以内に現金化できる短期の有価証券も含まれる）
  cash and cash equivalents at beginning of year 現金預金および現金同等物［現金等価物］期首残高, 期首の現金預金および現金同等物
  cash and cash equivalents at end of year 現金および現金同等物期末残高, 期末の現金預金および現金同等物
  net change in cash and cash equivalents 現金および現金同等物の純増減額
  net increase (decrease) in cash and cash equivalents 現金および現金同等物の純増（減）
◆Cash and cash equivalents consist of cash and temporary investments with maturities of three months or less when purchased. 現金預金および現金等価物は、現金と、購入時点で3か月以内に満期日が到来する短期投資から成っています。

cash and stock 現金と株式, 現金と株式交換
◆IBM will buy the consulting and technology services arm of PricewaterhouseCoopers, the world's largest accounting firm, for $3.5 billion in cash and stock. 米IBMは、世界最大手の会計事務所「プライスウォーターハウス・クーパース」（PwC）のコンサルティング業務と技術サービス部門を、現金と株式交換により35億ドルで買収することになった。

cash-back [cashback] （名）現金割戻し, 現金用立てサービス, キャッシュバック
  a cash-back method キャッシュバック方式, キャッシュバックの手法
  a cash-back scheme キャッシュバックの手法, キャッシュバック商法
◆The number of people seeking advice about a cashing business and a cash-back scheme rapidly increased after the full enactment of the revised Moneylending Business Law. 改正貸金業法の完全施行（2010年6月18日）後、現金化商法やキャッシュバック商法に関してアドバイスを求める人の数が急増した。

cash balance 現金預金残高, 現預金残高, 現金残高
  cash balance approach 現金残高アプローチ
  cash balance equation 現金残高方程式
  cash balance standard 現金残高標準
◆We raised our cash balance in 2011 so that we could act quickly on new opportunities outside the U.S. 当社は2011年度の現預金残高を増やしましたが、これは米国外での新たな事業機会に即応できるようにするためです。

cash card キャッシュ・カード
（⇒bogus cash card, forged cash card）
◆The new cash card is intended to counter the increase in thefts and counterfeiting of ATM cards. この新型キャッシュ・カードは、キャッシュ・カードの盗難や偽造事件の多発に対応したものだ。

cash card fraud キャッシュ・カード詐欺
◆The bank raised the amount of insurance money from the current ¥5 million limit to a maximum of ¥10 million for cash card fraud. 同行は、キャッシュ・カード詐欺の保険金額を、現在の上限500万円から最大1,000万円に引き上げた。◆The victims of cash card fraud will file a damages suit in March with the Tokyo and district courts against eight financial institutions. キャッシュ・カード詐欺の被害者が3月に、8金融機関を相手取って損害賠償請求訴訟を東京、横浜両地裁に起こす。

cash currency 現金通貨 （=cash currency in circulation, cash in circulation）
◆Cash currency rose 0.4 percent to ¥72.2 trillion in July, while demand deposits fell 1 percent to ¥408.5 trillion from a year earlier. 7月の現金通貨は、前年同月比で0.4%増の72兆円2,000億円に対して、要求払い預金は1%減の408兆5,000億円だった。

cash deal [dealing] 現金取引
◆GM will buy the U.S. auto finance company for $3.5 billion in a cash deal. GMは、米国の自動車ローン会社を35億ドルの現金取引で買収する。

cash dividend 現金配当, 配当金
  cash dividends declared 現金配当宣言額, 現金配当金
  cash dividends paid 現金配当支払い額, 現金配当金, 配当金の支払い
  cash dividends per share 1株当たり現金配当, 1株当たり配当金
◆The Corporation declared a cash dividend of $0.07 per common share in the first two quarters of 2009. 2009年第1四半期と第2四半期に、当社はそれぞれ普通株式1株当たり0.07ドルの現金配当を宣言しました。

cash equivalents 現金同等物, 現金等価物, 現金預金同等物, 現金等価物
◆The Corporation considers all highly liquid investments purchased with an original maturity of three months or less to be cash equivalents. 当社は、取得日から満期日までの期間が3か月以内の流動性の高い投資を、すべて現預金等価物としています。◆We consider investments in money market funds to be cash equivalents. 当社は、MMF（マネー・マーケット・ファンド）への投資を現金等価物と見なしています。

cash flow 現金の収入と支出, 現金収支, 資金収支, 資金の流出入, 資金の動き, 資金の運用・調達, 資金繰り, 現金資金, 純収入, キャッシュ・フロー（「キャッシュ・フロー」は現金収入と現金支出の総称で、企業の一定期間の現金などの流れを指す。⇒discount cash flow method, discount cash flow system, repayment of debt）
  annual cash flow 年間資金収入
  cash flow accounting 資金会計, キャッシュ・フロー会計
  current cash flow 手元流動性
  discounted cash flow キャッシュ・フロー割引
  discretionary cash flow 裁量可能キャッシュ・フロー
  excess cash flow 余剰キャッシュ・フロー, 超過キャッシュ・フロー
  exchange a series of cash flows 各種のキャッシュ・フローを交換する
  expected cash flow 期待キャッシュ・フロー
  fixed cash flow 固定金利のキャッシュ・フロー

(=fixed interest cash flow)
　floating cash flow　変動金利のキャッシュ・フロー
　free cash flow　フリー・キャッシュ・フロー（投資家に配分可能な現金資産）
　future cash flows　将来の資金繰り, 将来のキャッシュ・フロー
　generate cash flow　現金収入を得る
　historical cash flow　過去のキャッシュ・フロー
　internal cash flows　内部キャッシュ・フロー
　negative cash flow　負のキャッシュ・フロー
　operating cash flow　営業キャッシュ・フロー
　retained cash flow　手元キャッシュ・フロー, RCF
　tightened cash flow　資金繰りの悪化
　◆The cash flow, which floundered since the bursting of the bubble economy, has been rejuvenated. バブル崩壊以降、停滞していた資金の動きが、活発化してきた。◆Universities are stable business models capable of creating a cash flow. 大学は、キャッシュ・フロー（現金収入）創出力がある安定した事業モデルだ。

cash flow problem　資金難, 資金繰りの問題
　◆Some companies that turned a profit have gone bankrupt because of cash flow problems. 黒字転換した企業の一部は、資金繰り難で倒産している。◆The nonprofit foundation faced cash flow problems, such as repayment of the debt and meeting personnel costs. この公益法人は、借入金の返済や人件費のやりくりなど、資金繰りの問題に行き詰まった。◆Victims of loan sharks include owners of small and medium-sized enterprises with cash flow problems due to the recession. ヤミ金融業者の被害者には、不況で資金難にあえぐ中小零細事業主なども含まれている。

cash flow situation　資金繰りの状況, 資金繰りの環境, 資金繰り
　◆If the group's cash-flow situation deteriorates further, it may see its creditor banks declining to extend loans. 同グループの資金繰りがさらに悪化すれば、取引銀行が融資を拒否する可能性もある。

cash flow statement　資金収支表, 現金収支計算書, 収支計算書, 現金資金計算書, キャッシュ・フロー計算書（=statement of cash flows）
　解説 キャッシュ・フロー計算書とは：財務諸表（financial statements）の一つで、売上や仕入れ、借金などを通じた純粋なお金の増減を計算したもの。企業の現金支払い能力が分かるため、企業の成長力を示す重要な指標となっている。

cash from operations　営業活動により生じたキャッシュ, 営業収益
　◆We used the cash from operations to pay dividends and to invest in R&D. 配当の支払いと研究開発投資には、営業活動により生じたキャッシュを充てました。

cash handout　定額給付金支給
　◆To implement the cash handout and other measures, the related bills of the extra budget will have to be enacted. 定額給付金支給などの措置を実施するには、補正予算の関連法案の成立が必要になる。

cash in circulation　貨幣流通高, 現金通貨
　◆M3 includes cash in circulation, demand and time deposits and certificates of deposit at all depository institutions, including Japan Post Bank Co. マネー・サプライM3には、現金通貨、要求払い預金、定期性預金や全貯蓄銀行（ゆうちょ銀行を含む）の譲渡性預金（CD）などが含まれる。◆The average daily balance of the monetary base—cash in circulation plus current-account deposits held at the central bank by financial institutions and Japan Post—expanded 6.4 percent in April. 4月のマネタリー・ベース—貨幣流通高と日銀当座預金（金融機関と日本郵政公社の中央銀行預け金）との合計—の1日平均残高は、6.4％増加した。

cash index　現物指数
　cash index fund　現物指数ファンド
　cash index stocks　指数採用銘柄の現物
cash-limit　（動）〜に対して現金支出限界を設ける
cash merger　現金合併, キャッシュ・マージャー（企業の買収・合併の手段として、存続会社が、合併で吸収される会社の少数株主に対して存続会社の株式ではなく現金を交付する方法）
cash on hand　手元現金
　◆Illiquidity refers to the lack of cash on hand. 流動性不足とは、手元に現金がないことを言う。◆In the case of a lack of liquidity, either bridge lending or debt deferment can save the borrower as there is no cash on hand. 流動性不足の場合は、手元に現金がないので、つなぎ資金を貸すか[つなぎ融資か]債務返済の延長で借り手は助かる。◆In the case of a lack of liquidity or liquidity crisis, the debt repayment of an indebted borrower is still possible if a grace period is given, but lack of cash on hand makes it impossible to repay its debt in the short term. 流動性不足や流動性危機の場合、債務を抱えた借り手の債務返済は猶予期間を与えればまだ可能であるが、手元に現金がないため短期での債務返済はできない。

cash provided from　〜から生じた資金, 〜に伴う資金の調達
　cash provided from (used for) financing activities　財務活動に伴う資金の調達（使途）, 財務活動から生じた（財務活動に使用した）資金
　cash provided from (used for) investing activities　投資活動に伴う資金の調達（使途）, 投資活動から生じた（投資活動に使用した）資金
　cash provided from (used for) operating activities　営業活動[事業活動]に伴う資金の調達（使途）, 営業活動[事業活動]から生じた（営業活動に使用した）資金

cash register　レジ, 金銭登録器
　◆With the cell phones, shoppers can settle payments instantly by holding the phone over the cash register. この携帯電話を使えば、買い物客は、レジに携帯電話をかざすだけで瞬時に購入代金の決済を済ますことができる。

cash remittance　現金送金, 送金（=cash transfer）
　◆Both countries are set to stop cash remittances to and trade with North Korea if it starts reprocessing spent nuclear fuel rods or makes any other moves to escalate the situation. 北朝鮮が使用済み核燃料棒の再処理開始や状況をエスカレートさせるその他の動きをした場合、両国は送金・貿易停止などに踏み切る方針だ。

cash requirements　必要資金, 現金必要量, 現金必要見込み額
　◆We expect to meet our cash requirements in 2012 from operations, complemented, if necessary, by external financing. 当社は、業務活動によってもたらされる資金で2012年度の必要資金をまかない、必要に応じて外部資金を調達して補う方針です。

cash reserve(s)　現金準備, 支払い準備, 現預金, 手持ちの現金, 手元現金
　cash reserve rate [ratio]　現金準備率, 支払い準備率（=bank reserve ratio）
　cash reserve requirement　現金準備率
　cash reserve requirements　現金準備制度
　◆Lending by private banks has not increased though their investments into government bonds and cash reserves are increasing. 民間銀行の国債への投資や手持ちの現金は増えているが、民間銀行の貸出は増えていない。

cash-rich　（形）豊富な資金を持つ, 流動性豊かな
cash-strapped　（形）十分な資金のない, 資金繰りが苦しい, 資金難の（=money-strapped）
cash surplus units in the economy (savers)　経済

の資金余剰主体(貯蓄者)
◆A financial intermediary acts as a middleman between cash surplus units in the economy (savers) and deficit spending units (borrowers). 金融仲介機関は、経済の資金余剰主体(貯蓄者)と資金不足主体(借り手)との間に立つ仲介者として機能している。

cash tender offer 現金公開買付け, 現金による株式公開買付け, キャッシュ・テンダー・オファー (買収先の会社の株式を現金で公開買付けする方法)
◆Ford's debt restructuring includes conversion of debt to equity and cash tender offers. 米フォードの債務再編には、債務の株式化や現金による株式の公開買付けが含まれている。

cash transfer 送金 (=cash remittance)
◆The new interpretation of the Foreign Exchange and Foreign Trade Law allows the government to suspend cash transfers and exports under an agreement between Tokyo and Washington, dispensing with the need for a U.N. resolution and a multilateral accord. 外国為替・外国貿易法(外為法)の新解釈では、政府は、国連決議や多国間合意がなくても、日米間の合意に基づいて送金や貿易を停止することができる。

cash transport vehicle 現金輸送車 (=cash transport truck)
◆New banknotes in ¥4 billion stacks were transported to major financial institutions in cash transport vehicles. 40億円の大量の新札が、現金輸送車で主要金融機関に搬送された。

cash voucher shop 金券ショップ
◆Fabricated credit cards have been illegally used at electrical appliances discount stores and cash voucher shops in Japan after the security breach was revealed in the United States. 米国で不正侵入が明らかになった後、偽装されたクレジット・カードが日本の家電量販店や金券ショップなどで不正に使用されている。

cash vouchers 金券, 金券類
◆The repurchasing method, which has customers buy highly negotiable cash vouchers, violates the industry rule. 顧客に換金性の高い金券類を購入させる買取り方式は、業界の規約に違反する。

cash withdrawal 現金引出し (⇒banking freeze, banking services)

cash withdrawals and deposits 現金の入出金
◆Cash withdrawals and deposits will be made through automated teller machines. 現金の入出金は、ATM(現金自動預け払い機)で行われる。

cashier (名)(銀行の)支配人, 出納(すいとう)係, (商店などの)会計[レジ]係

cashier's check 自己宛小切手, 預金小切手 (=bank check, official check)

cashing (名)現金化, 換金
a cashing business 現金化商法
cashing services 換金サービス, 換金業務, 現金化サービス (⇒quasi-loan sharking)
◆A cashing business pays people cash in exchange for buying things with credit cards. 現金化商法では、クレジット・カードを使って購入したものと引換えに現金が支払われる。◆If we use the cashing services, it results in high interest payments. 現金化サービスを利用すると、結果的に高金利[支払い利息が高くつくこと]になる。◆The number of people using cashing services is rising partly because no screening is required to get money. 無審査で金を借りられることもあって、キャッシング・サービス(現金化商法)の利用者は増えている。

cashless (形)現金不要の, 現金のない, 現金を用いないで済ます, キャッシュレスの, キャッシュレス
cashless account settlement system キャッシュレス決済システム
cashless payment system キャッシュレス支払いシステム
cashless society 現金不要の社会, キャッシュレス社会

casual (形)略式の, 普段用の, 普段着の, 臨時の, 一時的な, 短期の, 偶然の, 偶発の, 不定の, 思いつきの, 即席の, 用意なしの, カジュアル
casual cost control 原因別原価管理
casual employment 臨時採用, 臨時雇用, 一時雇用
casual expenses 臨時出費, 臨時支出
casual [casualty] insurance 災害保険
casual loss 偶発損失, 臨時損失
casual profit 偶発利益
casual revenue 臨時収入
casual unemployment 臨時工失業, 季節労働者失業率

casualty (名)事故, 災難, 災害, 損害, 偶発事故, 人的損害, 被害者, 犠牲者, 死傷者, 死傷者数, 犠牲者数, 負傷兵, 戦死者
casualty allowance 災害補償
casualty and surety insurance 災害補償保険
casualty fortuity 偶然の事故
casualty loss 災害損失, 偶発損失, 雑損
casualty loss deduction 雑損控除 (=deduction for casualty loss)
casualty profit 偶発利益
casualty report service ロイズの海難報告サービス
commercial property and casualty 商業用損害保険
deduction for casualty loss 雑損控除
fire and casualty insurance company 火災・傷害保険会社
personal property and casualty 個人損害保険
property and casualty 損害保険
property and casualty insurer 損害保険会社, 損保会社
◆The banking sector is a major casualty of the financial crisis stemming from a U.S. housing mortgage meltdown. 銀行業界[金融機関]が、米国の住宅ローン市場の崩壊から始まった金融危機の最大の被害者[犠牲者]だ。

casualty insurance 災害保険, 障害保険, 損害保険
casualty insurance company 損害保険会社, 損保会社, 損保 (=casualty insurer)
casualty insurance policy 災害保険証券
◆au Insurance Co. has started selling casualty insurance online to cell phone users. au損保保険(株)が、携帯電話ユーザー向けに損害保険のネット販売を開始した。

casualty insurer 損害保険会社, 損保 (=casualty insurance company)
◆The casualty insurer initially planned to kick off its online insurance sales in April, but delayed the start due to the March 11 earthquake and tsunami. 同損保は当初、4月から保険のネット販売を開始する方針であったが、3月11日(2011年)の東日本大震災のため、その営業開始を延期した。

CAT (クレジット・カード用の)信用照会端末機, キャット端末 (credit authorization terminalの略)

catapult (動)突然ある状態にする, 勢いよく飛び出す, 突然[一躍]〜になる
be catapulted out of [from] 〜から放り出される, 〜から急に飛び出す
catapult into [to] 突然〜になる, 〜に突入する
◆Combined sales of Panasonic and Sanyo would catapult Panasonic to the No.3 spot in revenue among listed Japanese companies. パナソニック(旧松下電器産業)と三洋電機の連結売上高を合算すると、上場日本企業のなかで、パナソニックは売上高で一躍第3位となる。

catastrophe (名)大災害, 災難, 不幸, 不幸な事態, 不運(misfortune), 大失敗, 大惨事, 災禍(disaster), 異常損害, 巨大損害, 大変動, 悲劇的結末, 大詰め, 大団円, 破局, 破滅, 破たん, カタストロフィ

catastrophe cover　異常損害再保険, 大災害［異常危険］超過損害再保険
catastrophe excess of loss reinsurance　大災害［異常危険］超過損害再保険
catastrophe hazard　異常危険, 大災害危険
catastrophe insurance　巨大損害保険, 巨額損害保険, カタストロフィ保険
catastrophe loss　異常損失
catastrophe policy　巨額損害保険証券
catastrophe reinsurance　異常損害再保険, 大災害［異常危険］超過損害再保険
fiscal catastrophe　財政破たん
major catastrophe　大規模災害
natural catastrophe　自然災害
political catastrophe　政治的混乱
the March 11 catastrophe　2011年3月11日の東日本大震災
◆If the outstanding debts of the central and local governments are not dealt with, Japan is likely to face a fiscal catastrophe. 国と地方［地方自治体］の債務残高を処理しないと［放置すれば］、日本は財政破たんに直面することになる。

catastrophic　（形）破滅的な, 壊滅的な, 致命的な, 大惨事の, 大異変の, 悲惨な
catastrophic claim loss　災害による支払い損失
catastrophic coverage　高額医療費保険
catastrophic deficits　破滅的な赤字, 莫大な赤字
catastrophic loss　莫大な赤字, 巨大損害損失
catastrophic reinsurance　巨大損害再保険
catastrophic tsunami　巨大津波
◆The March 11 disaster was due to a combination of a magnitude-9 earthquake, catastrophic tsunami and an ensuing crisis at a nuclear power plant. 2011年3月11日の東日本大震災は、マグニチュード9の地震、巨大津波とその後の原発事故が重なって起きた。

categorization　（名）分類, 類別, 区分
customer categorization　顧客区分
the companies' categorization by banks　銀行側の企業［融資先企業］の債務者区分
◆FSA's inspectors are to confirm whether the companies' categorization by banks as debtors is relevant or fair. 金融庁の検査官は、銀行側の企業（融資先企業）の債務者区分が適正かどうかなどを検証することになっている。

categorize　（動）分類する, 類別する, 区分する
◆The banks have categorized borrowers based on their financial health. 銀行は、経営の健全度に基づいて融資先［債務者］を区分している。

category　（名）部類, 種類, 部門, 分野, 範疇, 分類, 区分, 項目, カテゴリー
categories of industry　業種, 産業部門, 産業区分
category width　カテゴリーの幅
emerging growth categories　急成長分野
product category　製品分野, 製品カテゴリー
rating category　格付けの分類, 格付けの区分, 格付け
special category company　特別区分会社

CATS　キャッツ
cats and dogs [cat-and-dog stocks]　ひじょうに投機的な株, がらくた株

cause　（動）もたらす, 引き起こす, 〜を招く, 〜の原因となる
◆Finance ministers and central bank governors from the Group of Seven leading countries held an emergency telephone conference to avert financial turmoil caused by the downgrading of the U.S. credit rating. 米国債の格下げによる金融市場の混乱を回避するため、先進7か国（G7）の財務相と中央銀行総裁が、緊急電話会議を開いた。◆Global stock market plunges caused by the European fiscal crisis triggered by Greece have shown no signs of abating. ギリシャ発の欧州財政危機による世界同時株安は、止まる気配がない。◆Greek financial crisis was caused by the country's lax fiscal management. ギリシャの財政危機は、同国の放漫財政［放漫な財政運営］によって生じた。◆In the case of foreign currency deposits, losses may balloon if the yen appreciates further and may cause a loss of principal. 外貨預金の場合、円高がさらに進めば損失が膨らみ、元本割れになる恐れもある。◆It is difficult to deal with the latest unrest in global financial markets because it has been caused by a complex web of factors. 今回の世界的な金融市場混乱への対応が難しいのは、混乱を招いている要因が複雑に絡み合っているからだ。◆The current deflationary trend seems to be a temporary phenomenon caused by the correction in oil prices after they skyrocketed last year. 現在のデフレ傾向は、昨年の原油高の反動による一時的な現象のようだ。◆The Fed's monetary easing is a factor causing disarray in the foreign exchange markets. 米連邦準備制度理事会（FRB）［米中央銀行］の金融緩和が、為替相場混乱［為替乱高下］の原因だ。◆The financial crisis triggered by the rise in defaults of U.S. subprime loans caused havoc in financial markets worldwide. 米国のサブプライム・ローン（低所得者向け住宅ローン）の不払い増加がきっかけで起こった金融危機は、世界の金融市場を大混乱させた。◆The government considers the economic downturn caused by the March 11 Great East Japan Earthquake and subsequent tsunami to be almost over. 2011年3月11日の東日本大震災［3月11日の東日本大地震とその後の津波］による景気悪化はほぼ収束した、と政府は見ている。◆The yen in record strong territory of ¥76 to the dollar causes hardships in the Japanese economy. 1ドル＝76円台の史上最高の円高水準は、日本経済にとって厳しい。

cause　（名）原因, 要因, 理由, 根拠, 動機, 主義, 主張, 大義（principle）, 運動, 団体, 目標, 目的, 訴訟事由［事実］, 訴訟,（議論の）主題
a cause of action　訴因, 訴訟原因
a main [major] cause　主因, 核心
bring one's cause before the court　提訴する
cause-and-effect relationship　因果関係
cause of death　死因
causes for inflationary concerns　インフレの懸念材料
make common cause with　〜と共同戦線を張る, 〜と手を結ぶ, 〜と協力する
plead a [one's] cause　訴訟理由を申し立てる, 言い分を申し立てる
potential causes of instability　不安定要因
show the cause　訴訟理由を提示する
◆The main cause of the prolonged deflation is that consumer demand has been weak due to the current economic slump. デフレ長期化の主因は、現在の不況で消費需要が低迷していることだ。

caution　（名）注意, 警告, 用心, 警戒, 警戒感
caution money　敷金, 身許保証金, 保証金
inflation caution　インフレへの警戒
market's caution　市場の警戒感
◆Caution grew about possible yen-selling intervention by the government. 想定される政府の円売り介入に対する警戒感が、強まった。

cautious　（形）注意深い, 用心深い, 慎重な
be cautious about [of, with]　〜に注意する, 〜について慎重である, 〜に用心している, 〜を警戒する
cautious consumer spending　慎重な個人消費, 消費者の買い控え
take cautious stand against　〜に対して慎重な立場［スタ

ンス]を取る
the cautious mood　警戒ムード, 慎重ムード
◆Behind these cautious views among large manufacturers are uncertainty over the debt crisis in the eurozone and the slowdown in the U.S. economy.　大企業製造業のこうした警戒感[慎重な見方]の背景には, ユーロ圏の債務危機不安や米景気の減速がある。◆Many businesses are cautious about their outlook three months ahead despite the improvement in sentiment.　企業の景況感は改善したものの, 多くの企業は3か月先の景気見通しに対しては慎重だ。◆The Bank of Japan needs to remain cautious about risks to both higher inflation and slower economic growth.　日本銀行は, 引き続き物価上昇リスクと景気停滞リスクを警戒する必要がある。◆The ECB remains cautious about taking steps of supporting Italy and other distressed countries through massive purchases of their government bonds.　欧州銀行(ECB)は, イタリアなど財政危機国の国債を大量に買い支える措置を取ることに, 慎重な姿勢を崩していない。◆The market has become even more cautious about an anticipated business slowdown.　市場では, 予想される景気減速への警戒感が一段と高まっている。
CB　転換社債 (convertible bondの略)
c.b.l　商業船荷証券 (commercial bill of ladingの略)
CBO　社債担保証券 (collateralized bond obligationの略)
CBO　米議会予算局 (Congressional Budget Officeの略)
CBOE　シカゴ・オプション取引所 (Chicago Board Options Exchangeの略)
　arbitrage opportunities between CBOE options and the cash market　CBOEのオプションと現物市場の裁定機会
　CBOE Market Volatility Index　CBOE株価変動率(ボラティリティ)指数, VIX指数, 恐怖指数
　CBOE VIX　CBOEボラティリティ指数, VIX指数 (=CBOE Volatility Index)
CBOE Volatility Index (VIX)　CBOEボラティリティ(株価変動率)指数, VIX指数, (投資家の)恐怖心理指数, 恐怖指数　(シカゴ・オプション取引所がS&P指数のオプション取引価格から算出。投資家の不安の度合い表す指標で, 「恐怖心理指数, 恐怖指数」とも呼ばれている。通常のVIX指数の数値は10〜20程度で推移することが多く, 数値が高いほど先行き不透明感, 先行き不安が大きいとされる)
◆The CBOE Volatility Index VIX is known as Wall Street's fear gauge.　CBOEボラティリティ(株価変動率)指数は, 米証券市場関係者の「恐怖指数」と呼ばれている。
CBOT　シカゴ商品取引所 (Chicago Board of Tradeの略)
CD　現金自動支払い機, キャッシュ・ディスペンサー (cash dispenserの略。⇒online system)
CD　譲渡性預金, 譲渡可能定期預金証書, 定期預金証書 (certificate of depositの略。⇒certificate of deposit)
CDFI　コミュニティ開発金融機関, 地域開発金融機関 (⇒community development financial institutions)
CDO　債務担保証券 (collateralized debt obligationの略。証券化商品で, 社債やローン(貸出債権)などで構成される資産を担保にして発行される資産担保証券(asset-backed securities)の一種)
◆Subprime-related securities are created partly from highly opaque structured products created by mixing subprime with other collateralized debt obligations.　サブプライム関連証券は, サブプライム証券と他の債務担保証券(CDO)を合成して造られた極めて不透明な仕組み債などで生み出されている。
CDS　クレジット・デフォルト・スワップ (credit default swapの略。高度な金融技術を使った金融派生商品の一種で, 国の財政破たんや企業の倒産による損失を回避するための信用リスク取引。国債の保有者がリスク回避の手段として使うことが多く, CDSの売り手に投資家が保証料を支払うと, 国や企業が債務不履行や破産に陥っても, 補償を受けられる仕組みになっている。CDSの保証料率が大きいほど, 投資家は破産のリスクが高いと見ていることを示す。⇒credit default swap)
◆CDS contracts provide protection against the risk of default by borrowers.　CDS契約によって, 発行体の債務不履行リスクが保証される[カバーされる]。
cedant　(名)出再者 (再保険契約の保険契約者), 出再保険者, 元受保険者
cede　(動)譲渡する, 譲歩する, 委ねる, (再保険で元受保険者が引き受けたリスクを再保険者に)転嫁する, 再保険に出す, 出再する　(名)(権利などの)譲渡, 出再保険
　cede back　再再保険, シード・バック
　cede premiums　出再保険料, 再保険料
　ceded insurance　出再保険
　ceded reinsurance　出再保険, 売再保険
　policy ceded under this agreement　本協定により出再される契約
　reinsurance premiums ceded　再保険料
　risks ceded under this agreement　本協定に基づいて出再される危険
ceding　(形)出再の, 再保険の, 元受の　(名)譲渡, 譲歩, 出再, 再保険
　ceding commissions　出再手数料, 再保険料
　ceding commissions paid　支払い再保険料
　ceding commissions received　受取り再保険料
　ceding company　出再保険会社, 元受会社
　ceding insurer　元受保険者, 出再保険者, 被再保険者, 再保険契約者
　ceding office　出再保険者
　ceding reinsurance　売再保険
ceiling　(名)限界, 限度, 上限, 天井, 最高, 予算の概算要求基準, シーリング, 下限　(=floor; ⇒lift動詞)
　be above the legally allowable ceiling　法律で許される上限を超えている
　credit ceiling　貸出限度, 信用供与限度, 貸出限度額, 融資限度額　(=credit line)
　debt ceiling　債務負担限度, 債務限度, 債務の上限, 債務上限額
　impose a ceiling on the amount of deposits to be funded　預金の払戻し額に上限を設ける
　interest rate ceiling　金利の上限
◆In compiling the 2010 fiscal budget, the Hatoyama administration eliminated the ceiling on budgetary requests established by the previous government.　2010年度予算の編成で, 鳩山政権は, 前政権(自公政権)が設定した概算要求基準(シーリング)を撤廃した。◆The bank's commission for transaction of loan claims was actually interest, which was far above the legally allowable ceiling.　同行の貸出債権[債権]の売買手数料は, 事実上の金利にあたり, その金利は法律で許される上限をはるかに超えていた。◆The freeze on imposing a ceiling on the amount of deposits to be refunded in the event of a bank failure was lifted across the board on April 1, 2005.　銀行が破たんした場合に預金の払戻し額に上限を設けるペイオフの凍結措置が, 2005年4月1日から全面的に解除された。◆The government plans to abolish the ¥10 million ceiling on the amount of postal bank deposits.　政府は現在, 1人当たり1,000万円のゆうちょ銀行預け入れ限度額を撤廃する方針だ。◆The Swiss National Bank set a ceiling on the skyrocketing Swiss franc.　スイス国立銀行(中央銀行)が, スイス・フランの急騰に上限[上限目標]を設定した。
cell phone　携帯電話 (=cellular phone, mobile phone)
　cell phone number portability system　携帯電話番号持ち運び制度　(=mobile number portability system, number portability system)

cell phone service provider　携帯電話会社, 携帯電話の加入会社
◆Four credit card holders received bills for accessing subscription Web sites via cell phones even though they had no recollection of doing so. 利用した覚えがないのに、携帯電話の有料サイトの利用代金請求書が、4人のクレジット・カード会員に届いた。◆In insurance services that can be bought via cell phones, cell phone companies provide nonlife insurers with policyholders' personal information. 携帯電話で加入できる保険サービスでは、携帯電話会社が(保険)加入者の個人情報を損害保険会社に提供している。◆Nonlife insurers started insurance services that can be bought more easily via cell phones with information transmission capabilities. 損保各社が、情報通信機能がある携帯電話を使って、これまでより簡単に保険に入れるサービスを開始した。

cell phone-based policy sales　携帯電話での保険販売
◆In the case of au Insurance's cell phone-based policy sales, policyholders are allowed to pay premiums by adding them to monthly mobile charges. au損害保険の携帯電話での保険販売の場合、保険契約者は、保険料を携帯電話利用の月額に加算して保険料の支払いをすることができる。◆NTT Docomo Inc. and SoftBank Mobile Corp. have been offering cell phone-based policy sales by teaming up with nonlife insurers respectively. NTTドコモとソフトバンクモバイルは、それぞれ損保会社と提携して、携帯電話での保険販売のサービスを提供している。

cell phone company　携帯電話会社
◆To offer customers a new way to purchase insurance, nonlife insurance companies have begun cooperating with cell phone companies. 顧客に保険加入のための新サービスを提供するため、損害保険各社は、携帯電話会社との提携に乗り出した。

center [centre]　(名)中心, 中央, 中枢, 中心地, 中心点, 拠点, 本場, 中心人物, 花形, 指導者, 中間派, 穏健派, 重点地区, 商業地区, 繁華街, 都市, 総合施設, 的, 対象, センター
　business center　取引の中心地, ビジネス・センター
　center of excellence　中核の研究センター, 中核の研究機関, 世界の研究拠点, センター・オブ・エクセレンス, COE
　Centre for Claims Resolution　損害賠償請求解決センター
　commercial center　商業中心地, 商業区域, 商品センター
　commodity exchange center　商品取引所センター
　finance center　金融中心地
　financial center　金融センター, 金融中心地
　international financial center　国際金融センター, 国際金融市場
　International Financial Service Centre　国際金融サービス・センター
　Japan Center for International Finance　国際金融情報センター
　money center banks　ニューヨークの大商業銀行, 金融センター銀行
　offshore banking center　オフショア金融センター
　the principal center of banking　銀行業の主要中心地
　trade center　貿易センター, 商業の中心
　venture enterprise center　研究開発型企業育成センター
　world financial center　世界の金融中心地

-centered　(形)〜中心の, 〜を主体とする
　bank loan-centered indirect financing　銀行融資中心の間接金融
　export-centered industry　輸出中心の産業

central　(形)中央の, 中心の, 中心的な, 主要な, 重要な, 基本的な

central clearing system　中央決済制度
central depository system　振替決済制度, 保管振替制度
central exchange　中央証券取引所
Central Gilts Office　中央ギルト・オフィス(英国国債の振替決済機構)
central information file　(銀行の)顧客取引状態ファイル, シフ, CIF
central parity　中心レート
central paying agent　中央支払い代行機関
central rate　中心相場, 中心レート, セントラル・レート(為替相場の基準レートまたは仲値(ミドル・レート)を意味する場合と、固定相場制での米ドルに対する各国通貨の基準交換比率を指す場合がある)
Central Reserve Bank　米中央準備銀行, CRB
central reserve cities　米中央準備市
central reserve city bank　米中央準備市銀行, (ニューヨーク、シカゴ両市にある)連邦準備加盟銀行
central securities depositories　中央証券預託機関
central treasury　中央金庫

central bank　中央銀行(日本の場合は日本銀行(日銀)を指す)
　central bank authorities　中央銀行当局
　central bank certificates　中央銀行証書
　central bank (discount) rate　中央銀行割引歩合, 公定歩合(discount rate)
　central bank governor　中央銀行総裁
　central bank intervention　中央銀行の市場介入, 中央銀行の為替介入, 中央銀行介入, 市場介入
　central bank money　中央銀行通貨, 中央銀行貨幣
　central bank note　中央銀行券
　central bank sales　中央銀行の売り介入
　central bank swap　中央銀行スワップ (=swap arrangement)
　independence of central bank　中央銀行の独立性
　total assets of Japanese, U.S. and European central banks in proportion to GDP　日米欧の中央銀行の総資産(GDP比)

◆According to the World Gold Council, central banks have bought 198 metric tons of gold so far this year. 世界金評議会によると、今年は、世界各国の中央銀行がこれまでに(2011年8月22日現在で)198メートルトン(19万8,000キログラム)の金を買い入れた。◆Governments facing fiscal hardship sometimes force their central banks to buy up government bonds. 財政がひっ迫した政府は、中央銀行に国債を買い切らせることがある。◆In a joint response to the global financial crisis, the U.S. FRB, ECB and central banks in Britain, Canada, Sweden and Switzerland cut interest rates in unison. 世界的な金融危機への協調対応策として、米連邦準備制度理事会(FRB)、欧州中央銀行(ECB)と英国、カナダ、スウェーデン、スイスの中央銀行は、政策金利[政策金利]を同時に引き下げた。◆In cooperation with the U.S. FRB, the Bank of England, the Bank of Japan and the Swiss National Bank, the European Central Bank decided to conduct three U.S. dollar liquidity-providing operations between October and December. 米連邦準備制度理事会(FRB)、英イングランド銀行、日銀、スイス国立銀行と協調して、欧州中央銀行(ECB)が10〜12月に3回、米ドル資金供給オペを実施することを決めた。◆Some dollar funds injected into banks by the U.S. central bank may send U.S. stock prices soaring because banks will invest some of the new dollar funds in domestic assets such as stocks. 米国の中央銀行(FRB)が金融機関[銀行]に供給したドル資金の一部は、銀行がその新たなドル資金の一部を株のような国内資産に投資するため、米国の株価を上げる可能性がある。◆South Korea's central bank said that the country's gross domestic product expanded 0.9 percent in the second quarter compared with the previous quarter. 韓国の中央銀行（韓国銀行）の発表によると、同国の第2四半期の国内総生産（GDP）は、前四半期比で0.9％拡大した。◆The central bank of Japan has deployed various measures to ease monetary policy, including cuts in the discount rate and hikes in the target for current account deposits held by commercial banks at the central bank. 日銀は、公定歩合の引下げや銀行が日銀に持つ当座預金の残高目標の引上げなどを含めて、各種の金融緩和策を実施してきた。◆The central banks of Japan, the United States and European countries are injecting sizable funds into the financial markets. 日米欧の中央銀行は、金融市場に大量の資金を供給している。◆The European Central Bank cut its main interest rate by 0.25 percent following heavy pressure for a rate cut to spur flagging economic growth. 失速気味の経済成長に刺激を与えるため利下げを求める強い圧力を受けて、欧州中央銀行（ECB）はその主要（政策）金利を0.25％引き下げた。◆The Japanese central bank likely will predict the consumer price index will edge up in fiscal 2010. 日銀は、2010年度の消費者物価指数について小幅プラスの予測を示すと見られる。◆The Japanese central bank's move to increase the outstanding current account target is insufficient to soothe market fears. 日銀の当座預金残高目標の引上げは、市場不安を払拭するには物足りない。◆The move to inject liquidity into Dubai's banks by the central bank of the United Arab Emirates was seen by analysts as the bare minimum. ドバイの銀行に資金を供給するアラブ首長国連邦（UAE）の中央銀行の動きを、アナリスト（専門家）は「最低限必要な量にすぎない」と見ている。◆The ownership of indexed government bonds has been limited to foreign governments, central banks and international organizations. 物価連動債の保有は、これまで海外の政府や中央銀行、国際機関に限られていた。◆The People's Bank of China raised interest rates on loans by financial institutions to corporations and individuals. 中国人民銀行が、金融機関の企業や個人に対する貸出金利を引き上げた。◆The six central banks around the world, including the U.S. FRB and the ECB, participated in the latest coordinated rate cuts. 今回の協調利下げには、米連邦準備制度理事会（FRB）や欧州中央銀行（ECB）など、世界の6か国の中央銀行が参加した。◆The unanimous decision by the U.S. central bank's policy setting Federal Open Market Committee moved the benchmark federal funds rate to 1.25 percent. 米連邦準備制度理事会の金利政策を決定する米連邦公開市場委員会の全会一致による決定で、短期金利の指標であるフェデラル・ファンド金利が年1.25％に引き上げられた。◆The U.S. central bank will buy mortgage-backed securities（MBS）guaranteed by the government-controlled home loan giants Fannie Mae, Freddie Mac and Ginnie Mae. 米連邦準備制度理事会（FRB）は、米政府系住宅ローン大手のファニー・メイ（米連邦住宅貸付公社）、フレディ・マック（米連邦住宅抵当金庫）とジニー・メイ（米政府系住宅金融公庫）が保証した住宅ローン担保証券（MBS）を買い取ることになった。◆To deal with the systemic financial crisis, ministry and central bank officials had to take rescue measures, such as an injection of public funds, while at the same time implementing strict guidelines and sanctions. 連鎖的な金融危機に対処するにあたって、当局は公的資金の投入などの救済措置取ると同時に、厳しい指導や制裁を実施しなければならなかった。◆To fulfill its responsibilities as the nation's central bank, the Bank of Japan must achieve currency stabilization by availing itself of a range of measures, including stabilization of the exchange rate. 日本の中央銀行としての責任を果たすには、日本銀行は、為替相場の安定を含めて広範な手段を活用して通貨の安定を実現しなければならない。◆While minimizing possible adverse effects on the stock market, private consumption and corporate performances, the U.S. central bank will ensure the United States' economic recovery. 株式市場や個人消費、企業業績などへの考えられる悪影響を最小限に抑えながら、米連邦準備制度理事会は、景気回復を確実なものにして行く方針だ。

解説 アメリカの中央銀行について：アメリカには単一の中央銀行が存在せず、連邦準備制度（Federal Reserve System）のもと連邦準備区（Federal Reserve district）に設置された全米12の連邦準備銀行（Federal Reserve Bank）が実際の中央銀行業務をしている。ただし、the U.S. central bankといえば米連邦準備制度理事会（FRB）を指す。

世界主要国の中央銀行：
the Bank of Albania　アルバニア銀行
the Bank of Algeria　アルジェリア銀行
the Bank of Canada　カナダ銀行
the Bank of England　イングランド銀行 BE［B of E, BOE, BoE］
the Bank of France　フランス中央銀行（＝Banque de France）
the Bank of Greece　ギリシャ銀行
the Bank of Indonesia　インドネシア銀行
the Bank of Italy　イタリア中央銀行
the Bank of Japan　日本銀行 日銀
the Bank of Korea　韓国銀行
the Bank of Mexico　メキシコ銀行
the Bank of Portugal　ポルトガル国立銀行
the Bank of Spain　スペイン中央銀行
the Bank of Thailand　タイランド銀行
the Bahrain Monetary Agency　バーレーン金融庁
the Bundesbank　ドイツ連邦銀行
the Central Bank of Argentina　アルゼンチン中央銀行
the Central Bank of Armenia　アルメニア中央銀行
the Central Bank of Brazil　ブラジル中央銀行（＝Banco Central do Brazil）
the Central Bank of China　台湾中央銀行
the Central Bank of Cuba　キューバ中央銀行
the Central Bank of Cyprus　キプロス中央銀行
the Central Bank of Egypt　エジプト中央銀行
the Central Bank of Iceland　アイスランド中央銀行
the Central Bank of Iraq　イラク中央銀行
the Central Bank of Malaysia　マレーシア中央銀行（＝Bank Negara Malaysia）
the Central Bank of Norway　ノルウェー中央銀行
the Central Bank of Russia　ロシア中央銀行（＝Central Bank of the Russian Federation（ロシア連邦中央銀行））
the Central Bank of the Islamic Republic of Iran　イラン中央銀行
the Central Bank of the UAE　アラブ首長国連邦中央銀行
the Central Bank of Uruguay　ウルグアイ中央銀行
the Central Bank of Yemen　イエメン中央銀行
the Czech National Bank　チェコ国立銀行
the European Central Bank　欧州中央銀行 ECB
the Monetary Authority of Hong Kong　香港金融管理局（＝Hong Kong Monetary Authority）
the Monetary Authority of Singapore　シンガポール通貨庁
the National Bank of Azerbaijan　アゼルバイジャン国立銀行
the National Bank of Belgium　ベルギー国立銀行
the National Bank of Ukraine　ウクライナ国立銀行
the Netherlands Bank　オランダ銀行
the People's Bank of China　中国人民銀行（⇒Chinese central bank, corporate goods price index）
the Reserve Bank of Australia　オーストラリア準備銀行
the Reserve Bank of Austria　オーストリア準備銀行
the Reserve Bank of India　インド準備銀行 RBI
the Sveriges Riksbank　スウェーデン国立銀行

the Swiss National Bank　スイス国立銀行　（⇒Swiss National Bank）
the U.S. central bank　米中央銀行 米連邦準備制度理事会（＝the Fed, the Federal Reserve Board）

central bank governor　中央銀行総裁
◆After a two day meeting in Paris, the financial chiefs and central bank governors from the Group of 20 leading economies adopted a communique. パリで開かれた2日間の会議の後、主要20か国・地域（G20）の財務相・中央銀行総裁は共同声明を採択した。◆Finance ministers and central bank governors from the Group of Seven leading countries held an emergency telephone conference to avert financial turmoil caused by the downgrading of the U.S. credit rating. 米国債の格下げによる金融市場の混乱を回避するため、先進7か国（G7）の財務相と中央銀行総裁が、緊急電話会議を開いた。

central bank official　中央銀行関係者, 中央銀行当局者
◆Some central bank officials have become skeptical of the effect of quantitative easing measures. 中央銀行関係者には、量的緩和策の効果について疑問視する声も出てきている。

central banker　中央銀行総裁
（＝central bank governor；⇒coordinated policy）
◆At a recent meeting in Dubai of finance ministers and central bankers from the Group of Seven major economies, Japan's yen-selling market intervention and the undervaluation of the Chinese yuan came under a barrage of criticism. 最近ドバイで開かれた先進7か国（G7）財務相・中央銀行総裁会議で、日本の円売り介入と中国の人民元の過小評価が批判にさらされた。

central bankers and supervisors from major nations [countries]　主要国［主要各国］の金融監督当局
◆The Basel Committee on Banking Supervision is comprised of central bankers and supervisors from major nations. バーゼル銀行監督委員会は、主要各国の金融監督当局で構成されている。

central government　中央政府, 政府, 国
◆The tripartite reforms aim to reduce the amount of subsidies provided by the central government to the local governments; cut local tax grants to local governments; and shift revenue sources from the central government to local governments. 「三位一体」改革は、国の地方政府への補助金削減、地方交付税交付金の削減と国から地方政府への財源の移譲をめざしている。

Centrale de Livraison de Valeurs Mobiliere　セデル, CEDEL（ユーロ債の現物保管・集中決済機構で、ルクセンブルクにある）

certificate　（名）証明書, 証書, 券
　allotment certificate　株式割当証
　bond certificate　社債券, 債券
　central certificate service　株式振替決済制度
　debenture certificate　債券
　deposit certificate　預金証書
　money market certificate　市場金利連動型定期預金
　share certificate　株券
　　（＝certificate of share, stock certificate）
　Treasury certificate　財務省証書
　trust certificate　信託受益証書

certificate of deposit　譲渡性預金, 譲渡可能定期預金証書, 定期預金証書, 銀行預金証書, 預金証書, 有価証券預り証, CD
　balance of certificates of deposits　譲渡性預金の残高
　bank certificates of deposit　譲渡性預金
　negotiable certificates of deposit　譲渡可能（定期）預金証書
　◆The average daily balance of M2—cash in circulation, demand deposits and quasi-money—plus certificates of deposit came to ¥671.2 trillion. 現金通貨と要求払い預金に準通貨（定期預金が中心）を加えたM2と譲渡性預金（CD）の1日平均残高は、671兆2,000億円に達した。

certificateless society　株券なき社会

certified　（形）保証された, 証明付きの, 公認の
　American Institute of Certified Public Accountants　米国［アメリカ］公認会計士協会
　certified copy of the commercial register　登記簿謄本
　certified copy of the resolution of the board of directors　重役会決議の認証付き写し
　certified extract　抄本
　certified financial statements　監査証明済み財務諸表［財務書類］
　certified mail　配達証明付き郵便, 配達証明
　certified minutes　認証議事録
　certified public accountant　公認会計士, CPA
　content-certified mail　内容証明郵便
　delivery-certified mail　配達証明郵便

certified check　支払い保証小切手, 銀行支払い保証小切手, 預金手形
◆The purchase price shall be U.S. $50,000 payable in full at the closing by certified check. 買取り価格は5万米ドルとし、クロージング時に全額、銀行支払い保証小切手で支払うものとする。

cession　（名）譲渡, 財産引渡し, 出再, 再保険に出すこと, 出再保険, 再保険金額
　cession number　再保険番号
　cession series　出再シリーズ
　new cessions　新契約出再
　reinsurance assumptions and cessions　再保険の引受けと付保
　reinsurance cession　出再契約
　the cession of a credit　債権譲渡
　the cession of a finance receivable　債権譲渡
　the cession of an obligation　債権譲渡, 債権担保差し入れ

chain reaction　連鎖反応　（＝domino effect）
　a chain reaction of debt crisis　債務危機［財政危機］の連鎖反応
　prevent the chain reaction of financial collapses　金融破たんの連鎖反応を防ぐ
　set off a negative chain reaction　連鎖破たんを引き起こす
　the chain reaction of financial collapses　金融破たんの連鎖反応
◆In the eurozone, Greece's financial collapse is triggering a chain reaction. ユーロ圏では、ギリシャの財政破たんが連鎖反応を起こしている。◆The possibility that the bank's collapse will set off a negative chain reaction is very low. 同行の破たんが連鎖破たんを引き起こす可能性は、かなり低い。

chain-reaction global decline in the stock values　世界的な株安の連鎖, 世界的な株安連鎖
◆A chain-reaction global decline in stock values was temporarily stopped by a barrage of countermeasures. 世界的な株安連鎖は、矢継ぎ早の対策でいったんは歯止めがかかった。

chain reaction of debt crisis　債務危機の連鎖反応
◆The IMF and the EU are strengthening their cooperation to avert a Greek default and prevent a chain reaction of debt crisis among other countries. ギリシャの債務不履行（デフォルト）を回避し他国間の債務危機の連鎖反応を防ぐため、国際通貨基金（IMF）と欧州連合（EU）は、連携を強めている。

chain reaction of financial collapses　金融破たんの連鎖反応
◆In order to prevent the chain reaction of even more devastating financial collapses, financial and monetary authorities

chalk up (動)収益[利益]をあげる, 〜を記録する, 計上する, 獲得する, 達成する
◆Fannie Mae chalked up $2.3 billion loss in second quarter. 米連邦住宅抵当金庫[抵当公庫](ファニー・メイ)の第2四半期[4-6月期]決算は, 23億ドルの赤字になった。◆UFJ chalked up a consolidated net loss of ￥91.58 billion for the April-June quarter. UFJの4-6月期の連結税引き後純利益は, 915億8,000万円の赤字となった。

challenge (名)挑戦, 課題, 難題, 難問, 苦境, 試練, ハードル, 脅威, やりがいのある仕事, 任務, 要求, 要請, 請求, (競技などへの)参加勧誘・参加呼びかけ, (試合などへの)申込み, 挑戦状, 陪審員に対する拒否, 忌避(きひ), 異議, 異議申立て, チャレンジ
a daunting technical challenge 技術的に難しいがやりがいのある仕事
a global challenge 地球規模の課題
a legal challenge 法的手段による抗議
challenge advertising 挑戦広告, チャレンジ広告
face a challenge 難題に立ち向かう, 試練に立ち向かう, 困難な課題に直面する, 試練に直面する
give a challenge 挑戦する
meet [rise to] a challenge 試練に打ち勝つ, 難局にうまく対処する, 苦境を乗り切る
meet [respond to] the challenges 難題に対応する, 難題に応える, 要請に応じる
practical challenges 実践の場での課題
strategic challenge 戦略的な課題
the challenge in monetary policy for countries 各国の金融政策の課題
◆Discussion among advanced countries alone cannot cope with the challenges facing the world economy. 先進国だけの話合いで, 世界経済が直面している課題に対応することはできない状況にある。◆Great changes are taking place in the sharp rise in crude oil prices. 原油価格の急騰に, 大きな変化が生じている。◆Japanese manufacturing industry has the potential to rise to the latest challenge. 日本の製造業には, 今回の苦境を乗り切る底力がある。◆The challenge in monetary policy for countries now is shifting toward finding a way to move away from ultra-loose money policies. 現在, 各国の金融政策の課題は, 超金融緩和政策からいかに転換するかに移りつつある。◆The challenge of the Basel Committee on Banking Supervision is to develop a regulatory framework while fending off a recurrence of financial strife. バーゼル銀行監督委員会の課題は, 金融危機再発の防止と規制の枠組みの策定だ。◆The global economy is facing serious challenges. 世界経済は, 厳しい試練に直面している。

chance (名)機会, 好機, 見込み, 可能性, 勝算, 勝ち目, 冒険, 危険, 賭(か)け, 偶然, 偶然の出来事, 運, チャンス
an even [a fifty-fifty] chance 五分五分の見込み
be in with a chance 勝つ見込みがある
by chance 偶然に, 思いがけなく
leave it to chance 運に任せる
miss one's chance 好機を逃す
stand a chance 〜する見込みがある
stand no chance of 〜の見込みはまったくない
take a chance [chances] 〜を一か八かやってみる, 危険を冒(おか)す, 思い切ってやってみる
take no chances 危険を冒さない, 危ない橋は渡らない
take one's chance [chances] 運に[成り行きに]任せてやってみる, 出たとこ勝負でやる, 機会をつかむ
◆JAL's creditor banks are dubious about JAL's chances of getting back on its feet. 日航の取引銀行団は, 日航再建の可能性については懐疑的だ。

chancellor (名)(ドイツ, オーストリアなどの)首相, (英国の)大蔵大臣[蔵相], 長官, 高官, 閣僚, 大使館一等書記官, (大学の)学長, 総長, (英大学の)名誉学長[総長]
Chancellor of the Exchequer 英財務省, 英蔵相
German chancellor [Chancellor] 独首相
◆In resolving Greece's debt woes, German Chancellor Angera Merkel urged substantial aid from private creditors. ギリシャの債務問題を解決するにあたって, アンゲラ・メルケル独首相は, 民間債権者に大幅支援を求めた。

change (動)変える, 変更する, 変化させる, 改める, 改造する, 替える, 交換する, 交替する, 両替する, くずす (break), 現金に換える (自動)変わる, 変化する, 移行する
change a five-dollar bill 5ドル紙幣を両替する[くずす]
change from a manufacturing economy to a service economy 製造経済からサービス経済に移行する
change the corporate culture 企業の体質[企業風土]を変える, 社風を変える
change yen into dollars 円をドルに両替する
◆In commodity futures trading, prices are decided when buyers and sellers make deals. So they can execute trades at promised prices even if the value of goods has changed drastically in the meantime. 商品先物取引では, 売り手と買い手が取引契約をする時点で価格を決める。そのため, 契約期間中に相場が大きく変動しても, 売り手と買い手は約束した値段で取引を執行できる。◆In the one-time password system, clients' passwords are changed whenever they log into their accounts. ワンタイムパスワード方式だと, 顧客が口座を利用するたびに, 顧客のパスワードは変更される。◆The Fed has been unable to deal with the current economic woes by changing interest rates as it has been maintaining a policy of virtually zero-percent interest rates. 米連邦準備制度知事会(FRB)はこれまで金利ゼロ政策を続けてきたため, 政策金利を上げ下げして現在の経済的苦境に対応することはできなくなっている。◆The U.S. Federal Reserve Board raised U.S. interest rates, leading the worldwide move to change current super-loose monetary policy. 米連邦準備制度理事会(FRB)が米国の金利を引き上げ, 世界的な超金融緩和の政策転換の先陣を切った。◆The U.S. tighter regulations on investment funds helped to change the trend in crude oil prices. 米国の投資ファンド規制強化で, 原油価格の流れが変わった。◆Under a variable pension system, pension benefits change in accordance with fluctuations in government bond yield. 変額年金制度では, 国債利回りの変動で年金給付額が変わる。

change (名)変動, 変化, 変調, 動き, 変更, 変革, 改革, 改正, 増減, 釣銭, 小銭, チェンジ
capital change 資本の変動
change in debt 債務の増減
change in par value 額面変更
changes in shares 株式異動
currency changes 為替相場の変動
cyclical changes 一時的な変化
dividend change 配当変更
economic change 経済的変化
excessive changes in the exchange rate 為替相場の過度な変動
financial change 金融改革
high change 大変動
interest rate change 金利変動, 金利の変更
job change 転職 (=job changing)
management changes 経営陣の刷新, 経営陣の交替
marketplace changes 市場環境の変化

organizational changes　組織改革
percentage change　百分率変化, 変化率
personnel changes　人事刷新
political change　政治改革, 政権交代
price-level change　物価変動
primary change　1次的変化
radical changes in　～の抜本的改革
rating change　格付け変更
seasonal change　季節変動
secular change　長期変動
social changes　社会変動, 社会情勢の変化
structural change　構造的な変化, 構造的変化
◆The BOJ could take additional monetary relaxation measures if there are any changes in the financial situation. 金融面で動きがあるとすれば、日銀が追加の金融緩和策を実施する可能性もある。◆The economies in the U.S. and China that have aided the Japanese companies' recovery have now started to show signs of change. 日本企業の回復を支えてきた米国と中国の経済に、今は変調の兆しが見え始めている。

change hands　所有者[持ち主]が変わる, 人手に渡る, 変わる, 更迭(こうてつ)する, 推移する, 商品が売れる, 政権を交代する
　change hands after the delivery date　受渡し後に持ち主[所有権]が変わる
　change hands at ￥84 range against [to] the dollar　1ドル＝84円台で推移する
　change hands in a fairly stable manner　かなり安定的に推移する
　change hands most frequently at　～の中心値で推移する
◆The yen changed hands at ￥85.81-82 against the dollar at 9:00 a.m. Friday in Tokyo. 東京為替[外国為替]市場の金曜日の円相場は、午前9時の時点で、1ドル＝85円81〜82銭で始まった。◆The yen has been changing hands in a fairly stable manner at about ￥110 to the dollar. 円[円相場]は、1ドル＝110円程度でかなり安定的に推移している。

change of control　資本拘束, 経営権の変更
◆The firm is currently negotiating with its domestic capital partners to conclude change-of-control agreements. 同社は現在、国内の資本提携先とチェンジ・オブ・コントロール(資本拘束)条項の契約を結ぶ交渉を進めている。

change of control clause　資本拘束条項, チェンジ・オブ・コントロール条項 (ライセンス契約や代理店契約を結ぶ際、買収などで一方の会社の支配権が変わった場合には、相手方の会社が契約を破棄できるとする条項)

changes in the exchange rate　為替相場の変動
◆The government will stem any excessive changes in the exchange rate. 政府は、為替相場の過度な変動を抑制する方針だ。

changes in the share prices　株価動向
◆Overseas investors are considered highly volatile to changes in the share price. 外国人株主は、株価動向にかなり左右されやすいとされている。

chaos　(名)大混乱, 無秩序, 無秩序状態, 混沌状態, 変動, カオス
　chaos in foreign exchange markets　外国為替市場の大混乱, 為替相場[為替レート]の変動
　the financial chaos　金融混乱, 金融危機
　the Greek economic chaos　ギリシャの経済混乱
◆The epicenter of the financial chaos is the United States. 今回の金融混乱[金融危機]の震源地は、米国だ。◆The Fed's policy of quantitative easing foments chaos in foreign exchange markets. 米連邦準備制度理事会(FRB)[米国の中央銀行]の量的緩和政策は、為替相場[為替レート]の変動を招いている。◆The Greek economic chaos was triggered as its national bond rating was lowered. ギリシャの経済混乱のきっかけは、ギリシャの国債格付けが引き下げられたことだ。◆The world economy may be thrown into further chaos. 世界経済は、一層混乱する恐れがある。

chaotic situation in the financial market　金融市場の混乱状況
◆The chaotic situation in the financial market will continue for the time being. 金融市場の混乱状況は、まだしばらく続くものと思われる。

Chapter 7 of the National Bankruptcy Act　米連邦破産法第7章, 米破産法第7章(破たんした企業を再生させずに清算する手続きを定めた法律)

Chapter 10 of the National Bankruptcy Act　米連邦破産法第10章, 米破産法第10章

Chapter 11 [XI]　米連邦改正破産法第11章, 米連邦破産法11章, 会社更生手続き, 会社更生手続きに関する改正破産法第11章, チャプター・イレブン (=Chapter 11 bankruptcy, Chapter 11 of the U.S. Bankruptcy Code, Chapter 11 of the U.S. Bankruptcy Reform Act)

Chapter 11 of the Bankruptcy Act　米連邦破産法第11章, 破産法第11章

Chapter 11 of the federal Bankruptcy Code　米連邦破産法11章 (⇒Bankruptcy Code)

　emerge from Chapter 11 protection　米連邦破産法11章による保護から脱する
　file Chapter 11 petitions in a court　裁判所に米連邦破産法11章による会社更生手続きの適用を申請する
　file for Chapter 11　米連邦破産法(の適用)を申請する, 米連邦破産法11章の適用を申請する
　file for Chapter 11 bankruptcy protection　米連邦破産法11章の適用を申請する, 連邦破産法11章による会社更生手続きの適用を申請する
　set into motion a Chapter 11 filing on　～について米連邦破産法の適用[米連邦破産法11章による会社更生手続き]を申請する
　U.S. Chapter 11 protection　米連邦破産法第11章による保護
◆MGM film studio filed for Chapter 11. メトロ・ゴールドウィン・メイヤー(MGM)映画製作会社が、米連邦破産法11章の適用を申請した。
[解説]企業の法的整理の一種で、日本の民事再生法に相当する。裁判所への申請と同時に、債権取立てが禁止され、経営体制を維持して事業を継続しながら経営再建を目指せる。改正破産法(Bankruptcy Reform Act of 1978)第11章に基づく債務者の「会社更生(reorganization)」を"Chapter Eleven"という場合もある)

Chapter 11 bankruptcy　米連邦改正破産法11章による破産, 米連邦破産法第11章, 米連邦破産法
◆Chapter 11 bankruptcy provides for a business to continue operations while formulating a plan to repay its creditors. 米連邦改正破産法第11章の規定では、企業は事業を継続する一方、債権者への債務返済計画を策定することができる。

Chapter 11 bankruptcy protection　米連邦破産法11章の適用　(⇒corporate failure)
◆General Motors Corp. filed for Chapter 11 bankruptcy protection. 米ゼネラル・モーターズ(GM)が、連邦破産法11章の適用を申請した。◆GM's filing for Chapter 11 bankruptcy protection marks the largest manufacturing corporate failure in history. 米ゼネラル・モーターズ(GM)の連邦破産法11章の適用申請は、製造業として史上最大の企業倒産だ。

Chapter 11 of the U.S. [federal] Bankruptcy Code　米連邦破産法11章
◆In the United States, a troubled company is afforded the opportunity to reorganize under Chapter 11 of the federal Bankruptcy Code. 米国では、経営破たんした企業は、米連邦破産法11章に基づいて企業を再建する機会が与えられる。

characteristic （名）特徴, 特性, 特色, 特質, 性格
　characteristics of policyholders　保険加入者［保険契約者］の特性
　characteristics of the market　市場特性
　credit characteristics　信用の性質
　risk characteristics　リスク特性
　◆The insurance premiums are determined by the age and other characteristics of policyholders. この保険料は、保険加入者の年齢などの特性に応じて決められる。

characterize （動）特徴づける,（性格などを）〜と述べる, 描写する
　A is characterized by B　Aの特長［特色］はBである, AはBが特徴である
　characterize A as B　Aの特徴はBであると言う［述べる、見なす］
　◆The former administration was characterized by populist policies such as dole-out measure and the manner of budget screening. 前政権は、バラマキ政策や事業仕分けの手法など大衆迎合的な政策（ポピュリズム）が特徴だった。

charge （動）請求する, 課する, 要求する, 支払わせる, 負担させる, 借方に記入する, 借記する, 計上する, クレジット・カードで買う, 告発する, 摘発する, 提訴する, 充電する　（⇒loan claims, moneylender）
　be charged to income　費用として計上される, 費用計上される　（＝be charged to earnings）
　be charged with　〜の責任を負っている, 〜を担当している, 〜で告発［摘発］される
　charge a hefty bill　高額な代金を請求する
　charge a hefty commission　法外な手数料を請求する［支払わせる］
　charge against　費用として差し引く, 損失とみて差し引く
　◆In the aftermath of past major earthquakes, unethical traders charged hefty bills after suggesting the need for checks of earthquake resistance. 過去の大地震の直後には、悪質業者が「耐震診断の必要がある」と持ちかけて、高額の代金を請求していた。◆In the case of foreign currency deposits by the U.S. dollar, many online banks charge about ￥0.25 in commission per dollar at the time of deposits and withdrawals. 米ドルによる外貨預金の場合、ネット銀行の多くは、預け入れ時と解約時に1ドルに付き25銭程度の手数料を取る。◆The federal funds rate is the interest that banks charge each other on overnight loans. フェデラル・ファンド（FF）金利は、米国の民間銀行が翌日決済で相互に資金を貸し借りするときに適用する金利のことをいう。◆The Securities and Exchange Surveillance Commission is charged with inspecting the compliance of securities firms with the law, market surveillance and the investigation of abuses such as insider trading and stock price manipulation. 証券取引等監視委員会は、証券会社の法律遵守（じゅんしゅ）に関する検査や市場の監視、インサイダー取引や株価操作など不正行為の摘発を行う。◆The U.S. Commodity Futures Trading Commission charged one investment fund with gaining illicit profits by manipulating crude oil and other markets. 米国の商品先物取引委員会は、原油市場などで不正な利益を上げたとして、投資ファンドの一つを摘発した。

charge （名）費用, 料金, 税金, 課税金, 手数料, 代価, 代金, 請求金額, 借方記入, 負債, 借金, 責任, 義務, 任務, 担保, 担保権, 管理, 監督, 保管, 運営, 処理, 告発, 提訴, 陪審に対する裁判官の説示, チャージ　（⇒fraud charges）
　bank charge　銀行手数料
　call charge　通話料
　cash charge　現金費用
　criminal charge　刑事責任
　customers charge　顧客手数料
　deferred charges　繰延べ費用
　finance charge　金融費用, 融資手数料, 金利　（⇒LIBOR）
　fixed charge　金融費用, 固定費用, 固定担保
　floating charge　浮動担保
　fraud charges regarding a dubious capital increase　架空増資に関する詐欺罪
　interest charge　支払い利息
　lifting charge　取扱い手数料
　mobile charge　携帯利用料金
　one-time charge　一時的費用
　surrender charge　解約手数料
　transferring charge　振替手数料
　◆Household electricity charges are due to rise between ￥42 and ￥161 from October. 家庭の電気料金が、10月から月42-161円値上がりする。◆In the case of au Insurance's cell phone-based policy sales, policyholders are allowed to pay premiums by adding them to monthly mobile charges. au損害保険の携帯電話での保険販売の場合、保険契約者は、保険料を携帯利用の月額に加算して保険料の支払いをすることができる。◆Premiums are collected together with call charges in insurance services that can be bought via mobile phones. 携帯電話で加入できる保険サービスでは、保険料は通話料と一緒に徴収される。◆The Financial Services Agency intends to bring criminal charges within the month against UFJ Bank on suspicion of hindering efforts by FSA to inspect the bank. 金融庁は、UFJ銀行を金融庁の銀行検査妨害の疑いで今月中に刑事告発する方針だ。◆The former company president was indicted on fraud charges regarding a dubious capital increase in the firm. この元社長は、架空増資に関する詐欺罪で起訴された。◆The Shares are free and clear of any liens, charges or other encumbrances. 本株式は、先取特権、担保権その他の制限［負担・障害］の対象に一切なっていない。

chart （名）図, 図表, グラフ,（株式の）罫線（けいせん）, チャート
　break-even chart　損益分岐点の分析表, 損益分岐点図表
　budget chart　予算図表, 予算表
　chart of accounts　勘定科目表, 勘定組織表
　high-low chart　高値・安値チャート
　operational flow chart　工程図表
　organizational［organization］chart　組織図, 会社機構図
　process chart　工程図
　production progress chart　生産進度図表
　profit chart　利益図表, 損益分岐図表
　profit-volume chart　損益分岐点図表
　repayment chart　償還予定表

chartered （形）公認の, 特許を受けた
　chartered accountant　（英国の）勅許会計士
　chartered bank　特許銀行
　chartered financial analyst　公認証券アナリスト
　chartered investment counselor　公認投資カウンセラー
　◆The troubled bank's deposits will be taken over by a newly chartered bank. この破たん銀行の預金は、新たに特許を受けた銀行が引き継ぐ。

cheap （形）安い, 安価な, 廉価（れんか）な, 割安の, 割安感がある, 低コストの, 低金利の, 低利の, 購買力が低下した
　a cheap labor policy　低賃金政策
　a cheap money policy　低金利政策
　be cheap relative to the equity market　株式市場との関連からすると割安である
　cheap bond　割安な債券, 割安債

cheap cash funding　低コストの資金調達,資金調達コストが低いこと
cheap credit　低利融資,低利貸出
cheap government　安上がりの政府,安価な政府
cheap money　低利資金
cheap source of finance　低コストの資金調達,低コストの資金調達源
cheap sources of funds　低コストの資金,低コスト資金源
cheap-to-deliver bond　最割安受渡し債券
cheaper euro　ユーロ安
cheaper mortgages　住宅ローン金利の低下
cheaper sources of funding　低コストの資金調達源
cheaper yen　円安
cheep access to funds　低コストの資金調達
the scope of cheap loans　低利融資枠
◆If agricultural imports become cheaper due to the lowered tariffs, consumers will greatly benefit. 関税の引下げで輸入農産品が安くなれば、消費者の利点も大きい。

cheap loan　低利の融資,低利貸出
◆The Bank of Japan widened the scope of cheap loans to support smaller companies with growth potential. 潜在成長力のある中小企業を支援するため、日銀が低利融資枠を拡大した。

cheap loan program　低利融資制度
◆The Bank of Japan stepped up its efforts to boost the flagging economy following the March 11 earthquake and tsunami by introducing a ¥500 billion cheap loan program. 日銀は、5,000億円の低利融資制度を導入して、東日本大震災で揺れる日本経済の刺激策を強化した。

cheap yuan　割安な人民元
◆As for the issue of China's cheap yuan, the leaders of the Group of Seven industrial powers simply reiterated what they said at the previous G-7 meeting. 中国の割安な人民元問題に関しては、先進7か国の財務相・中央銀行総裁は、前回のG7で述べたことを繰り返しただけだった。

check　(動)阻止する、止める、抑制する、制御する、照合する、検査する、点検する
check the credibility of the banks' debtor companies　銀行の融資先の信用力を洗い直す
check the sharp appreciation of the yen　円の急騰を阻止する
◆Business sentiment and the willingness of household to spend may cool and stall the economy unless the sharp appreciation of the yen is checked. 円の急騰を止めないと、企業の心理や家計の消費意欲が冷え込み、景気が腰折れしかねない。◆The Financial Services Agency will check the credibility of the banks' debtor companies, including their management efficiency and the accuracy of their collateral assessment. 金融庁は、銀行の融資先の経営効率や担保評価などを含めて、銀行の融資先の信用力を洗い直す。◆The FSA's special inspection will check the major banks' large-lot corporate borrowers whose stock prices or credit ratings have sharply declined. 金融庁の特別検査は、大手銀行の株価や格付けなどが急落した大口融資先を査定の対象としている。

check　(名)小切手　(=cheque; ⇒current deposit)
alteration of checks　小切手の変造
antedated check　前(まえ)日付け小切手,事前日付け小切手
bank cashier's check　自己宛小切手,預金小切手
bank check　銀行小切手
　（=banker's check, cashier's check）
bearer check　持参人払い小切手,無記名式小切手
　（=a check to (the order of) bearer）
blank check　白地小切手（金額が記入されていな小切手）

bogus check　偽の小切手
bounced check　不渡り小切手
canceled check　支払い済み小切手,取消し済み小切手
cashier's check　自己宛小切手,銀行小切手
check account　当座勘定
check book [checkbook]　小切手帳
check certification　小切手の保証
check clearing　小切手決済
check collection　小切手の取立て
check collection system　隔地決済制度
check crossed generally　一般線引き小切手
check crossed specially　特定線引き小切手
check drawee　小切手名宛人
check drawer　小切手振出人
check form　小切手の様式
check guarantee card　小切手保証カード
check on a bank　銀行宛小切手
check payable to order and bearer　記名式持参人払い小切手
check payable to (the) bearer　持参人払い式小切手
check rate　（小切手買取りの）一覧払い為替相場
check received　受領小切手
check register　小切手記入帳
check trading　小切手取引
checks and bills　小切手・手形
checks and bills clearing　手形交換
checks and bills in process of collection　取立て中の小切手・手形
checks issued by other banks　他店券
checks on other banks　他行宛小切手
checks only for account　名宛人口座入金専用
crossed check　横線小切手,無記名式小切手
customized check　顧客名を刷りこんだ小切手
dishonored check　不渡り小切手
dishonored checks and bills　不渡り手形
dividend check　配当小切手
duplicate check　控えの小切手
exchange check　小切手
general crossed check　一般線引き小切手
gift check　贈答用小切手
honor [pay] a check　小切手を支払う
inland check　内国小切手
issue a check　小切手を振り出す
kiting check　融通小切手
"On Us" check　統治払い小切手
open check　普通小切手
order check　指図人払い小切手
　（=a check to order）
out of date check　失効小切手
out-of-town check　市外小切手
outstanding check　未決済小切手,未提示小切手
over-due [overdue] check　不渡り小切手,期限経過小切手
paid check　決済小切手
past due check　不渡り小切手
payroll [pay] check　給与・賃金支払い小切手
postal check　郵便小切手
postdated [post-dated] check　先日付け小切手,事後日付け小切手
protested check　不渡り小切手
remittance check　送金小切手

returned check 返却小切手
rubber check 不渡り小切手
salary check 給料小切手
self check 自己宛小切手
　（=a check drawn to self）
spoiled check 書き損じの小切手
stale check 遅延小切手, 長期経過小切手, 期限経過小切手
stolen check 盗難小切手
tear out a check from the book 小切手を切る
traveler's check 旅行者小切手
unclaimed check 未請求小切手
uncrossed check 横線なし小切手
unissued check 未発行小切手
unused check 未使用小切手
U.S. treasury stock 米財務省小切手
voucher check 証票式小切手
◆The Liberal Democratic Party faction received a check for ￥100 million from top executives of the Japan Dental Association. 自民党の派閥が、日本歯科医師会の最高幹部から1億円の小切手を受け取っていた。

check （名）照合, 検査, 点検, 阻止, 抑制, 制御, 伝票, 勘定書, チェック
　check list [checklist] 点検表, 照合表, 一覧表, 総合目録, カタログ
　checks and balances 抑制と均衡
　credit checks 信用調査
　desk check 机上チェック
　financial health check 財務の健全性の検査
　format check 書式検査
　internal check 内部牽制
　keep [hold] A in check Aを防ぐ, Aを食い止める, Aを抑制する
　limit check 限度検査
　range check 範囲検査
　test check 試査
◆A dealer at a leading bank said that market players' concern has kept yen-buying moves in check. 市場関係者の警戒感が円買いの動きを食い止めた[抑制した]、と大手銀行のディーラーが語っている。 ◆The Franco-Belgian bank Dexia collapsed in October 2011 despite passing the 2011 EBA's financial health check. フランス・ベルギー共同の銀行「デクシア」が、2011年に実施された欧州銀行監督機構（EBA）の財務の健全性検査を通過したにもかかわらず、2011年10月に破たんした。

checkable deposit 当座性預金
◆No-interest checkable deposits are used for payment services. 無利子の当座性預金は、決済業務に使われる。

checking account 当座預金, 当座預金口座, 小切手勘定
　（=current account; ⇒checking transaction）
◆Checking accounts are mainly used by companies for business settlements. 当座預金は、主に企業の取引決済に利用されている。

checking transaction 小切手取引
　（=check trading）
◆If a financial institution goes under, companies that have checking accounts at that financial institution will become unable to conclude checking transactions or settle bills and will go bankrupt. 金融機関が破たんすれば、そこに当座預金を持つ企業は、小切手取引の決済や手形の決済ができなくなり、倒産してしまうことになる。

Chiang Mai Initiative チェンマイ・イニシアチブ, CMI （ASEANプラス3（日中韓）が金融危機時に通貨安定のため外貨準備（主にドル）を融通し合う通貨交換[スワップ]協定。⇒CMI）

Chiang Mai Initiative Multilateralization チェンマイ・イニシアチブ多角化体制, 多国間通貨交換[スワップ]協定, CMIM （1997年のアジア通貨[金融]危機の直後、ASEANプラス3諸国の金融危機時にドル流動性を支援するために用意された1,200億ドル規模の多国間通貨スワップ[通貨交換]協定。⇒AMRO）

Chicago Board of Trade 米シカゴ商品取引所

chief executive officer 最高業務執行役員, 最高経営責任者, CEO （⇒independent director, window-dressing accounts）
◆The vice president of Mizuho Corporate Bank will take up the post of president and chief executive officer in the newly merged firm. 合併新会社の社長兼最高経営責任者（CEO）には、みずほコーポレート銀行の副頭取が就任する。

chill （動）（景気などを）冷やす, 冷蔵する, ぞっとさせる, 抑える, 水を差す
　chill the economy 景気を冷やす
　chill the enthusiasm 熱意に水を差す
◆Falling prices may chill the economy and increase unemployment. 物価の下落は、景気を冷やし、失業を増やす可能性がある。

chilled market 市場の冷え込み
◆The U.S. economy has been hit by a chilled housing market and shrinking employment. 米経済は、住宅市場の冷え込みと雇用の落ち込みで打撃を受けている。

Chinese central bank 中国の中央銀行, 人民中央銀行, 中国人民銀行 （=People's Bank of China）
◆The Chinese central bank's recent interest rate hikes is an important move to cool the overheating Chinese economy and guide it toward a soft landing. 中国の中央銀行である人民銀行の今回の利上げ（貸出金利の引上げ）は、景気の過熱（中国経済の過熱）を鎮め、中国経済を安定成長に軟着陸させるための重要な動きである。

Chinese currency 中国の通貨, 中国通貨・人民元, 人民元 （=Chinese yuan）
◆The assessment of the Chinese currency is based on uncertain forecasts of China's current account surplus. 中国の通貨・人民元の評価は、中国の経常黒字の不透明な見通しに基づいて行われている。 ◆The IMF's Executive Board is divided over whether the Chinese currency is undervalued. IMF理事会は、人民元相場が過小評価されているかどうかで、意見が分かれている。 ◆Washington is pressing Beijing to revalue the Chinese currency. 米政府は、中国に通貨（人民元）切上げを迫っている。

Chinese Wall チャイニーズ・ウォール, 社内に設けられる情報の隔壁（一般に、証券会社の引受部門と営業部門間の情報の隔壁を指す）

Chinese yuan rate 中国人民元相場, 中国人民元レート, 中国の元レート （中国人民銀行（People's Bank of China）は2008年7月以降、対ドル人民元レートを1ドル=6.83元付近で固定している。⇒fix）

CHIPS （米銀行の）手形交換所加盟銀行決済システム, チップス（主にニューヨークを拠点とする金融機関同士の銀行間決済システム。Clearing House interbank Payments Systemの略）

choice （名）選択, 選定, 判断, 選択肢（せんたくし）, 選択権, 特選品, 逸品
　asset choice 資産の選択 資産選択
　choice article 精選品, 優良品, 特選品, 極上品
　　（=choice goods）
　choice of law 準拠法の選定, 適用法の選定, 法の選択, 法律選択
　consumer's choice 消費者選択
　economic choice 経済的動機
　household's choice 家計の選択

investment choices　投資先,運用先の選択肢
managerial choice　経営判断
optimal choice　最適選択
organizational choice　組織的選択
portfolio choice　資産選択,ポートフォリオ選択
substitution choice　代替選択

choose　(動)選ぶ,選択する,選定する,～することに決める
◆We must pay attention to commission fees when we choose to deposit foreign currencies. 外貨預金を選ぶときは、為替手数料に注意しなければならない。

chronic　(形)慢性的な,慢性の,長引く,長期の,長期にわたる,絶えず起こる,病みつきの,常習的な,常習の,～の慢性化
chronic and massive trade deficit　長期にわたる[長引く]巨額の貿易赤字
chronic balance of payments deficit　国際収支の慢性的赤字,慢性的国際収支の赤字
chronic budget deficit　長期にわたる[長引く]財政赤字,財政の赤字体質
chronic current account surplus　慢性的な経常黒字,経常黒字の慢性化
chronic deflation　慢性的デフレ,長引くインフレ,長期にわたるデフレ
chronic depression　慢性的不況
chronic disequilibrium　慢性的不均衡
chronic inflation　慢性的インフレ,長引くインフレ,長期にわたるインフレ
chronic labor shortage　慢性的な労働力不足,労働力不足の慢性化
chronic payments deficit　国際収支の慢性的赤字,慢性的収支赤字
chronic payments surplus　国際収支の慢性的黒字,慢性的収支黒字
chronic trade surplus　慢性的な貿易黒字,貿易黒字の慢性化
chronic unemployment　慢性的失業
◆Raising the consumption tax rate is essential in order to escape from the nation's chronic budget deficits. 日本の財政の赤字体質から脱却するには、消費税率の引上げが欠かせない。

circuit breakers　取引一時停止措置,サーキット・ブレーカー

circulate　(動)流通させる,循環させる,配布する,広める,回覧する,流通する,出回る,普及する
circulate dormant funds　眠れる資金を循環させる
circulate the notice　通達を回覧する
◆Another tactic many loan sharks use is to circulate slanderous leaflets to the workplace or the school that the borrower's children attend. 多くのヤミ金融業が使うほかの手は、借り手の勤務先や子どもが通う学校への中傷文書のばらまきだ。◆It is vital to improve the secondary market circulating such asset-backed securities for investors. 投資家向けに、このような資産担保証券の流通市場の整備も不可欠である。◆Not enough money is circulating in the economy. 市中に、金が出回らなくなっている。◆The bank's aim is to help circulate dormant individual assets in the local economy. 眠れる個人の金融資産を地域経済に循環させるのが、同行の目的だ。

circulate funds　資金を循環させる
◆Banks function as a heart to circulate funds in the body of the Japanese economy. 銀行は、日本経済の体内に資金を循環させる心臓の役割を果たしている。

circulating　(形)循環する,流通している,流布している,巡回する,循環～,流通～,流動～
circulating assets　流動資産,棚卸し資産
circulating capital　流動資本,流通資本

(=capital of circulation, floating capital)
circulating fund　運転資金,循環資金
circulating medium　流通貨幣,通貨
circulating theory　循環理論

circulation　(名)配布,流通,循環,回覧,通貨,流通手形,発行部数,サーキュレーション
(⇒cash in circulation, M1, prime lending rate)
active circulation　紙幣流通高,銀行券発行高
bank circulation　銀行手形発行総額
bank of circulation [issue]　紙幣発行銀行
Bank of Japan notes in circulation　日本銀行流通高,日銀券流通高,日銀券発行・流通高(現在流通している日銀券で、日銀窓口から持ち出されて全国に流通している総額を示す)
banknote [bank note] circulation　銀行券流通,銀行券流通高,銀行券発行高
banknotes [bank notes] in circulation　銀行券流通高,銀行券発行高,銀行券発行・流通高
capital of circulation　流通資本
cash currency in circulation　現金通貨流通高
cash in circulation　貨幣流通高
circulation capital　流通資本
circulation market　流通市場,売買市場
circulation of capital　資本の流通,資本の循環
circulation of demand deposit　預金通貨の流通
circulation of national income　国民所得循環
circulation test　循環テスト
coins in circulation　貨幣流通高
come into circulation　流通する
currency circulation　通貨流通高
currency in circulation　通貨流通高,流通通貨
dual circulation period　二重流通期間,移行期間
fiduciary circulation　信用流通
financial circulation　金融的流通
general circulation　一般通貨
go into circulation　流通する,流通開始する,発行される
in circulation　流通している,出回っている,使われている,市販されている
monetary circulation　通貨の流通,流通通貨
money circulation　貨幣流通(高),通貨流通高
(=circulation of money)
money in circulation　流通通貨
note in circulation　銀行券発行高,発券高,紙幣流通高
notes and coins in circulation　流通貨幣
out of circulation　流通していない,出回っていない,使われていない
passive circulation　未発行紙幣
putting into circulation　通貨発行
the balance of Bank of Japan notes in circulation　日銀券流通高,日銀券発行高,日銀券発行・流通高(⇒balance of Bank of Japan notes in circulation)
time of circulation of money　通貨[貨幣]の流通期間
total amount of money in circulation　流通通貨量
velocity of circulation of demand deposit　預金通貨の流通速度
velocity of circulation of money　貨幣の流通速度
◆New banknotes went into circulation on Nov. 1, 2004. 新札は、2004年11月1日に発行された。◆The amount of euros in circulation is determined by the monetary policy of the European Central Bank. ユーロの発行量は、欧州中央銀行(ECB)の金融政策が決める。

Citigroup　(名)米シティグループ

◆Citigroup will buy back the auction-rate securities from investors under separate accords with the Securities and Exchange Commission and state regulators. 米シティグループは、米証券取引委員会(SEC)や州規制当局との個々の合意に基づいて投資家から金利入札証券(ARS)を買い戻す。

citizens bank　市民バンク
（⇒socially responsible investing）
◆"Citizens banks" pool funds from investors and lend them to environmental projects and nonprofit organizations. 「市民バンク」は、投資家から出資金を集め、その資金を環境事業や非営利組織などに融資する。

civil fine　民事制裁金
◆American International Group, one of the largest U.S. insurance companies, agreed to pay a $10 million civil fine to settle the SEC's allegations that it fraudulently helped another company falsify its earnings report and hide losses. 米保険大手のAIG(アメリカン・インターナショナル・グループ)は、同社が他社の業績報告書改ざんと損失隠しに不正に手を貸したとする米証券取引委員会(SEC)の告発を受け、この問題を解決するために民事制裁金1,000万ドルを支払うことに同意した。

claim　(動)請求する, 主張する, 要求する, 支払いを請求する, 損害賠償を請求する
　claim a tax refund　税金還付を請求する
　claim compensation from　～に賠償金を請求する
　claim for the damage on one's insurance　損害の保険金を請求する
　claim payment　支払いを請求する
　claim unemployment benefit　失業保険の支払いを請求する
◆Allowing banks to claim a tax refund by carrying a loss back to the previous year has not been allowed since fiscal 1992 in Japan, due chiefly to the fiscal plight of the central government. 銀行が欠損金を前年度に繰り戻して税金還付を請求できるようにする制度(欠損金の繰戻し還付)は、主に国の財政難を理由に、日本では1992年度から凍結されてきた。◆Retail outlets that suffer loss as a result of fraud can also claim compensation from card issuers. 不正使用により損害を被っている小売加盟店側も、カード会社に賠償金を請求できる。

claim　(名)請求, 賠償請求, 請求権, 請求事項, 特許請求の範囲, 信用, 債権, 債権の届出, 保険金, 保険金請求, 保険金支払い請求, 賠償金, 賠償金請求, 権利, 権利の主張, 苦情, 苦情の申立て, クレーム　(⇒housing loan claim, full payment of insurance claims, insurance claims, loan claims, Sept. 11 terrorist attacks)
　a claim for reimbursement　償還請求
　abandon one's claim　～の請求を放棄する
　ability to meet claims on one's life policies　生命保険契約に基づく保険金請求の支払い能力
　amount of claim　請求額
　asset claim　資産請求権
　assign one's claim to a third party　～の債権[請求権]を第三者に譲渡する
　categorization of loan claims　債権区分
　claim adjustment expense　保険金支払い日
　claim agent　保険金支払い代理店, 海難処理代理店, 損害支払い代理店
　claim cost recognition　保険金費用の認識
　claim department　損害査定部
　claim for a refund　還付請求, 還付申請書
　　(=refund claim)
　claim for income tax credit　所得税控除の申請
　claim for priority　特許の優先権主張
　claim note　保険金請求書
　claim on assets　資産に対する請求権
　claim settlement　損害査定
　claims　保険金請求額
　claims adjuster　損害査定人, 損害査定専門家, アジャスター
　claims adjustment　損害査定
　claims for damages　損害賠償請求, 求償権
　claims handling　クレーム処理
　claims in bankruptcy　破産債権
　claims of creditors　債権者の請求権
　claims on multilateral development banks　国際開発銀行向け債権
　claims on private sector　民間向け信用
　claims paid　保険金, 支払い済み保険金
　claims-paying ability　保険金支払い能力
　claims process　保険金支払いプロセス
　claims settling fee　損害査定手数料, 保険支払い手数料
　claims survey　損害調査
　claims surveying agent　損害査定代理店
　collect claims　債権を回収する
　creditors' claims　債権者の請求権
　file a claim against　～に対する債権を届け出る
　housing loan claim　住宅ローンの債権
　information concerning customer claims　顧客からのクレーム情報
　initial unemployment claims　新規失業保険申請件数
　insurance claim　保険金請求, 保険請求権
　insurance claims　保険金, 保険請求, 保険請求権
　junior claim　劣後請求権
　lay claim to　～に対する権利[所有権]を主張する
　make [put in] a claim for damage　損害の請求をする
　make an insurance claim　保険請求をする, 保険金を請求する
　meet claims of senior policyholders　上位保険契約者の請求を履行する
　money claim　金銭債権
　policy claims　保険金請求, 保険金
　priority claim　優先弁済請求
　put in a claim　保険金を請求する
　refund claim　還付申請書
　refuse a claim　請求を拒(こば)む
　reimbursement claim　還付請求, 償還請求, 未収払戻し金
　　(=claim for reimbursement)
　right of claim　請求権
　satisfy all claims for damages　損害に対する一切の賠償請求に応じる
　secured claim　更生担保権, 担保付き請求権
　senior claim　上位請求権
　trade claim　貿易クレーム, 営業上の債権
　transfer of claims　権利の移転
　waive a claim　請求権を放棄する, 債権を放棄する, 権利を放棄する
　warranty claim　保証債務, 品質保証に基づくクレーム
　withdraw one's claim　請求を撤回する
◆Employees of the fund's Japanese unit assessed assets, collected claims and conducted other business. 同ファンドの日本法人の社員が、資産評価や債権回収などの業務を行っていた。◆Nonlife insurance claims connected to Typhoon No. 12 are expected to exceed ￥10 billion. 台風12号関連の損害保険の保険金請求額は、100億円を超える見込みだ。◆The actual claims will probably be smaller than Japanese insurers estimated. 実際の保険金は、恐らく日本の保険会社が予

想したより少ないだろう。◆The government can tap its special account to cover 50 percent to 95 percent of insurance payment claims when total earthquake insurance payouts exceed ¥115 billion. 地震保険の支払い総額が1,150億円を超えると、政府は特別会計を利用して保険金支払い請求額の50〜95%を負担することができる。◆The total amount of insurance claims to be paid out by nonlife insurers as a result of the Sept. 11 terrorist attacks has yet to be finalized. 2001年9月11日の米同時テロにより損害保険会社が支払う保険金の総額は、まだ最終確定していない。

claimant （名）請求者, 申立て人, 主張者, 要求者, 失業手当請求者, 保険金請求者

class （名）種類, 級, 階級, 集団, クラス
 asset class　資産クラス
 asset guideline class　耐用年数別資産種類
 Class A common stock　クラスA普通株式
 class action　集団代表訴訟, 集団訴訟 （=class action, class action lawsuit, representative action）
 class life　法定耐用年数
 class meeting　種類株主総会（株式の種類に応じて招集される株主総会）
 class of shares　株式の種類, 数種の株式
 class voting　種類別議決
 first class paper　一流手形
 first class securities　一流証券
 issue a single class of bonds　単一クラスの債券を発行する
 issue class of shares with different rights　権利の異なる数種の株式を発行する
 non-voting Class A preferred shares　無議決権クラスA優先株式
 obligations in a defined class　特定の種類の債務
 settle a class action lawsuit　集団訴訟を代表訴訟で決着させる
 the rentier class　金利生活者階級
 ◆On June 15, 2010, the company entered into an agreement for a public issue in Canada of $100 million of non-voting Class A preferred shares, at a price of $25 per share. 2010年6月15日に同社は、無議決権クラスA優先株式1億ドル（1株25ドル）をカナダで公募発行する契約を結んだ。

class action status　集団訴訟
 ◆Loss hiding scandal-tainted Olympus Corp. was sued by an investor in its American depositary receipts seeking class-action status. 損失隠しの疑惑をもたれたオリンパスが、同社の米国預託証券（ADR）を保有している投資家に、集団訴訟を求めて訴えられた。

class action suit　集団代表訴訟, 集団訴訟, クラスアクション（=class action, class action lawsuit:「株主代表訴訟」は、取締役が法令や定款に違反して会社に損害を与えた場合、株主が会社に代わって取締役を相手取り会社に損害を賠償するよう求める訴訟）
 file a class action suit for compensation　損害賠償の集団訴訟を起こす
 shareholders file a class action suit against the company, claiming that 〜　〜したとして株主が同社に対して集団訴訟を起こす
 ◆Company executives have admitted responsibility in a class action suit filed on behalf of a firm. 株主代表訴訟で、企業の幹部が責任を認めた。◆Victim firms have entered into talks to file a class action suit for compensation. 被害企業が、損害賠償に向けて集団訴訟のための協議を開始した。

classification of noncurrent assets　非流動資産の分類

classified stock　種類株, 分類株式（種類株には、普通株より優先的に配当が受けられる優先株や、普通株より配当が後回しになる劣後株などがある。株主への配当や議決権行使など株主が得られる権利が、普通株と異なる）
 ◆Classified stocks are different from common stocks in terms of voting power and dividend payments. 種類株は、議決権や配当の支払いなどの点で普通株と異なる。◆TEPCO's classified stocks differ from common stocks owned by current shareholders. 東電の種類株とは、現株主が保有している普通株とは異なる。

classify （動）分類する, 類別する, （情報を）機密扱いする, 機密指定にする
 be classified as capital　資本として扱われる　資本資産として分類される
 be classified as current　流動資産として扱われる［分類される］
 classified balance sheet　分類貸借対照表
 classified information　機密情報
 classified loan　分類貸金　不良貸金
 classified materials　機密事項
 classified rating system　等級別料率制度
 classified statement of profit and loss　区分式損益計算書
 ◆Nonworking spouses of public servants and company employees are classified as Category III insured. 公務員や会社員の仕事を持たない配偶者は、第3号被保険者と呼ばれている。

clause （名）条項, 箇条, 文言, 約款, 規定
 acceleration clause　期限の利益喪失条項
 all risks clause　全危険担保約款
 anti-dilution clause　希薄化防止条項
 assignment clauses　譲渡条項
 average clause　分損担保
 contract clause　契約条項
 currency indemnity clause　通貨補償条項
 escape clause　免責条款, 例外規定
 exchange clause　為替相場文言
 gold value clause　金価値約款
 indemnity clause　損害補償条項
 institute cargo clauses　保険協会貨物約款
 institute clauses　協会約款
 insurance clause　保険約款
 maintenance of ownership clause　出資比率維持条項
 multicurrency clause　多通貨条項
 negligence clause　免責約款
 red clause (letter of) credit　前貸し信用状, レッド・クローズ付き信用状
 value agreement insurance special clauses　価額協定保険

clean （形）公正な, 瑕疵（かし）のない, 無条件の, 担保権が付いていない, 安全な, 清浄な, クリーン
 clean bill　クリーン手形, 信用手形, 健康証明書
 clean bill of draft　信用手形 （=clean draft）
 clean bill of lading　無故障船荷証券 （=clean B/L）
 clean credit　荷落ち為替信用状, 無担保信用状, クリーン信用状
 clean float　中央銀行が介入しない変動相場制, きれいな変動相場制, クリーン・フロート（中央銀行が介入する変動相場制を「dirty float（汚い変動相場制）」という）
 clean loan　無担保借入れ
 clean sweep　（組織の）全面的改革, 全勝
 documentary clean bill　荷落ち為替手形
 documentary clean (letter of) credit　荷落ち為替信用状

clear （動）清算する, 支払う, （借金を）返済する, （税関などの）検査を通る, 通関手続きを済ます, 純益を上げる, 純益として儲（もう）ける, （市場の）需給を均衡させる, 処分する

be cleared through　～を通じて決済される, ～で決済される
clear A through customs　Aを通関させる
clear gains [profits]　純益
clear one's account　完済する, 未払い金を全額支払う
clear one's books　ポジションを整理する
clear out excess inventories　過剰在庫を一掃する
clear out the backlog of　(たまっている) 案件を処理する
clear up financial institutions' bad debts　金融機関の不良債権を処理する
◆The company intends to clear the ¥319 billion in deficits over seven years beginning in 2012. 同社は, 3,190億円の債務［債務超過額］については, 2012年から7年間で返済する計画だ.

clear　(形) 明らかな, 明確な, 確実な, 掛け値なしの, 正味の
a clear title　無きずの権利
clear days　正味日数
clear profits　純益
the clear market clause　市場秩序維持条項, クリア・マーケット条項
three clear days before maturity　満期までに正味3日間
◆No clear prospect has emerged for resolution of the Greek financial crisis. ギリシャの財政危機を打開する明確な見通しは, まだ立っていない.

clearance　(名) 通関手続き, 出港［出国］手続き, 離陸［着陸］許可, (在庫品の) 一掃, 除去, 撤去, 手形交換, 手形交換高, (証券取引所の) 手じまい, すき, 間隔, 空(あ)き, クリアランス
blanket clearance　包括出入港許可
check clearance　小切手決済, 手形交換
clearance agent　通関代理店
clearance from customs　通関 (=customs clearance)
clearance goods　見切り品
clearance inwards　入港手続き
clearance notice　出港通知書
clearance outwards　出港手続き
clearance (papers)　船舶出港［入港］証明書
clearance sale　在庫品一掃大売出し, 蔵払いクリアランス・セール
clearance work　障害物除去作業
exchange clearance　為替交換, 為替の清算
port clearance　出港手続き, 通関手続き, 出港許可

clearing　(名) 清算, 手形交換, 手形交換高 (clearings) 決済, 通関手続き, 出入港認可書, 除去, クリアリング
amount of clearings　手形交換高
bank clearing　手形交換 (bank clearings=手形交換高)
bill clearing　手形交換
central clearing system for money market instruments　短期金融商品の中央決済システム
checks and bills clearing　手形交換
clearing accounts　手形交換勘定
clearing and settlement　交換決済
clearing balance　手形交換尻, 交換尻
clearing bank　決済銀行, ロンドン手形交換所交換加盟銀行
clearing bills　交換手形類
clearing contract　清算取引
clearing for non-members　代理交換
clearing function　決済機能
clearing items　当所払い券, 交換手形類, 交換持出し

clearing loan　当日貸付け (=day loan)
clearing of a debt　債務の完済
clearing of bills　手形交換
clearing of checks and bills　小切手・手形交換
clearing operation　清算業務, 決済業務
clearing price　清算値段
clearing procedure　決済手続き
clearing system　決済機関, 決済機構, 決済方式, 決済制度, 決済システム, 清算制度
clearing work　交換作業
exchange clearing　為替清算
export clearing　輸出通関
incoming clearings　交換持ち帰り手形
international clearing systems　国際決済機構
Japan Securities Clearing Corp　日本証券クリアリング機構 (⇒clearing house)
online clearing　オンライン決済
parallel clearing　相互決済
settlement and clearing facility　決済システム
stock clearing　株式清算

clearing agreement　清算協定, 決済契約
bilateral clearing agreement　双務的清算協定
exchange clearing agreement　為替清算協定
multilateral clearing agreement　多角的清算協定
standard clearing agreement　標準清算約諾契約

clearing corporation　清算会社, 決済機構, 代行会社
clearing corporation balances　貸借取引残高
National Securities Clearing Corporation　米国証券決済機構, NSCC
Option Clearing Corporation　オプション清算会社

clearing house　手形交換所, 先物取引の清算機関, 清算会社, 決済機関, クリアリング・ハウス
automated clearing house　自動手形交換機構, ACH
banker's clearing house　ロンドン手形交換所
clearing house association　交換所協会
Clearing House Automated Payments System　(英銀行の) 手形交換所加盟銀行自動決済システム, チャップス, CHAPS
clearing house balance　手形交換尻
clearing house bank　決済銀行
clearing house checks　交換決済小切手
clearing house funds　交換決済資金
Clearing House Interbank Payments System　(米銀行の) 手形交換所加盟銀行決済システム, チップス, CHIPS
Clearing House rules and practices　交換所規則
London Options Clearing House　ロンドン・オプション清算会社
recognized clearing house　公認清算会社, 公認清算機関
swap clearing house　スワップ清算機関
the TSE's clearing house　東証の株取引決済機関
◆Japan Securities Clearing Corp., the TSE's clearing house, forced Mizuho Securities Co. to pay ¥912,000 per share in cash to buyers of J-Com shares. 東証の株取引決済機関の日本証券クリアリング機構は, ジェイコム株の買い手に1株当たり912,000円を現金で強制的に支払わせた.

clearing member　清算会員
clearing associate member　清算準会員
general clearing member　一般清算会員
individual clearing member　個人清算会員
non-clearing member　非清算会員

client　(名) 顧客, お得意, 得意先, 得意客, 取引先, 依頼人,

依頼者, ユーザー, 相談者, 監査依頼会社, 被監査会社（examinee corporation）, クライアント（=customer）
  attract clients　顧客を引きつける, 顧客を開拓する
  client assets　顧客預り資産
  client company　取引先, 顧客企業
  client control　顧客管理
  client defection　顧客離れ
  client information　顧客情報
  client management　顧客管理, 得意先管理
    （=customer management）
  client money　顧客資金
  client solicitation　顧客の勧誘
    （=solicitation of clients）
  corporate client　法人顧客, 取引先, 顧客企業, 銀行の融資先企業　（=corporate customer）
  individual client　個人顧客
  major client　大口顧客
  new client　新規顧客
  retail client　個人顧客
  solvent client　支払い能力のある顧客

◆ATM cards are the banks' primary weapons to lure new clients. キャッシュ・カードは, 銀行にとって新規顧客獲得の有力な手段だ。◆Banks are allowed to sell insurance policies to clients. 銀行は, 顧客に保険を販売することができる。◆Banks could forcibly sell insurance policies to clients by utilizing their strong position as creditors. 銀行は, 債権者としての強い立場を利用して, 顧客に保険を強制的に販売する可能性もある。◆Citigroup Private Bank's four offices in Japan will have their licenses revoked for violating the law by ignoring suspected money laundering by clients. シティバンクのプライベート・バンク（PB）の在日4拠点（支店・出張所）が, 顧客のマネー・ロンダリング（資金洗浄）の疑いのある取引を放置するなどして法令違反があったとして, 認可を取り消されることになった。◆In the one-time password system, clients' passwords are changed whenever they log into their accounts. ワンタイムパスワード方式だと, 顧客が口座を利用するたびに, 顧客のパスワードは変更される。◆Olympus Corp. has kept deceiving its shareholders and clients by years of window-dressing. オリンパスは, 長年にわたる粉飾で, 株主や取引先を欺き続けてきた。◆Sberbank of Russia will offer a variety of services, such as ruble-denominated loans to Mizuho Corporate Bank's clients when they do business in Russia. ロシア最大手行のズベルバンクは, みずほコーポレート銀行の顧客がロシアで事業を行う際にルーブル建て融資を行うなどの各種サービスを提供することになった。◆The bank tried to dominate the management of its clients by sending a majority of people to their board of directors. 同行は, 融資先の取締役会に過半数の取締役を送り込んで, 融資先の経営の支配を図った。◆The firm offers loans for retail and corporate clients in addition to offering electronic settlement for online shoppers. 同社は, ネット・ショッパー［オンライン・ショッパー］向けの電子決済業務のほかに, 個人と企業向けの融資も手がけている。◆The two major securities companies cut brokerage fees further for major clients. 大手証券会社2社は, 大口顧客に対して株式売買手数料をさらに引き下げた。

client assets　顧客預り資産
◆The brokerage firm manages client assets of ￥520 billion in about 150,000 accounts. この証券会社は, 口座数約15万で顧客預り資産は5,200億円に達する。

client company　取引先, 顧客企業
（⇒crossholding）
◆Investigators will trace the inner workings of a group of the bank's client companies. 捜査当局はこれから, 同行の取引先グループの実態を解明する。

clientele　（名）顧客層, 得意先, 取引先, 客
client's account　顧客の口座
◆In illegal access of Internet bank accounts confirmed at financial institutions, money was transferred from a client's account to a second account. 金融機関で確認されたネット・バンキング口座への不正アクセスでは, 顧客の口座から現金が他人名義の口座に振り込まれていた［送信されていた］。

client's order　顧客の注文
（=order from a client）
◆A Mizuho Securities employee entered a sell order from a client as "sell 610,000 shares at ￥1 each" though the client's actual order was "sell one share at ￥610,000." 顧客の実際の注文は「61万円で1株の売り」であったが, みずほ証券の社員は「1株1円で61万株の売り」と入力して顧客の売り注文を出してしまった。

climate　（名）条件, 環境, 状況, 情勢, 傾向, 風潮
（⇒economic climate）
  business climate　事業環境, 企業環境, 経営風土, 景況, 商況
  climate for acquisition　買収条件
  deflationary climate　デフレ傾向, デフレ環境, デフレ的雰囲気
  economic climate　経済環境, 経済情勢, 景況, 景気
  financial climate　金融環境, 金融情勢
  investment climate　投資環境
  management climate　経営環境
  organizational climate　組織風土, 組織環境, 経営風土
  political climate　政治情勢, 政治状況, 政治環境, 政治的風土
  regulatory climate　規制環境

◆Currently, China's investment climate is stable. 現在, 中国の投資環境は安定している。◆The business climate for home builders has been severe as housing starts have not expanded much in recent years. 新設住宅の着工戸数がここ数年伸び悩んでいるため, 住宅メーカーを取り巻く企業環境は厳しい。

climb　（動）上昇する, 拡大する, 増加する, 昇進する, 出世する, 登る
  climb into the black　黒字に転じる
  climb out of recession　景気後退から抜け出す, 景気後退から脱出する
  climbing debt burden　債務負担の増大, 債務超過の拡大

◆Japan's imports are also climbing because the economic recovery is fueling domestic demand. 景気回復で国内需要が拡大しているため, 日本の輸入も伸びている。◆The S&P cut in the U.S. long-term credit rating by one notch to AA-plus from AAA resulted from concerns about the nation's budget deficits and climbing debt burden. スタンダード・アンド・プアーズ（S&P）が米国の長期国債格付けを最上級のAAA（トリプルA）からAA（ダブルA）に1段階引き下げた理由は, 米国の財政赤字と債務負担の増大に対する懸念だ。◆The unemployment rate in July climbed to a postwar high of 5.7 percent, up 0.3 percentage point from the previous month. 7月（2009年）の完全失業率は, 前月より0.3ポイント悪化して5.7%となり, 戦後最悪を更新した。

climb　（名）上昇, 上昇傾向, 増加, 向上, 昇進
  benefits of the yen's sharp climb against the dollar　急激な円高・ドル安による円高差益
  market's steady climb　市場の堅調
  straight climb　棒上げ
  the yen's sharp climb against the dollar　急激な円高・ドル安

◆Aeon and Ito-Yokado started discount sales of foods imported from the United States to pass along to consumers the benefits of the yen's sharp climb against the dollar. イオンとイトーヨーカ堂は, 急激な円高・ドル安による円高差益

を消費者に還元するため、米国から輸入した食料品の値下げセールを開始した。

climb-down （名）譲歩，撤回
clinch （動）勝ち取る，獲得する，～を決定的・確定的にする，固定する
 clinch a deal 取引・商談をまとめる，取引にかたをつける
 clinch a debt rollover deal 債務返済繰延べ取引をまとめる
 ◆Argentina clinched a debt rollover deal with the IMF after a year of tortuous negotiations. アルゼンチンは、1年にわたる難交渉の末、国際通貨基金（IMF）との債務返済繰延べ取引をまとめた。◆Toyota Motor Corp. clinched the top spot in corporate income declared to tax authorities for the fourth consecutive year. トヨタ自動車が、法人申告所得（ランキング）で、4年連続トップとなった。

clip （名）素早い動作，速い速度，ペース，切り抜き，抜粋，一こま，一場面，一撃，殴打（おうだ），強打，クリップ
 at a clip 一度に，一回で
 at a spanking clip 顕著なペースで
 clip art ホームページ用画像［映像］集
 clip artist 詐欺師
 ◆The economy, fueled by a pickup in business spending on inventories, is now expanding at a spanking clip. 企業の在庫投資の回復に支えられた経済は現在、顕著なペースで拡大している。

close （動）取引を終える，引ける，取り決める，決める，締め切る，閉鎖する，整理する，清算する
 （⇒initial public offering）
 close a bank account 口座を解約する
 close a business 会社を解散する，店をたたむ
 close a business deal 取引をまとめる
 close at ～で引ける，～で取引を終える，終値は～だった
 close below ～を割り込んで取引を終える
 close below 3 percent 3％を割り込んで取引を終える
 close lower 続落したまま取引を終える
 close speculative long dollar positions against the yen 対円でドルの投機的なロング・ポジションを手じまう（手じまい＝信用取引での売り・買いを反対売買で帳消しにすること）
 close the day at ～で取引を終える
 close the day lower 下落して引ける
 close the week at ～で週を引ける，～で越週する
 ◆Concerning its food business, Kanebo will continue production of sweets and snacks, but will either sell or close its cup noodle, beverage and ice cream operations. 食品事業については、カネボウは菓子部門の生産は継続するが、カップ麺（めん）・飲料・氷菓事業は売却または整理・清算する。◆Ford Motor Co. closed its five North American plants as part of its overhaul plan. 米フォード・モーターは、リストラ策の一環として同社の北米5工場を閉鎖した。◆GM shares dropped $1, or 23 percent, to close at $3.36. GM株［GMの株価］の終値は、1ドル安（23％下落）の3.36ドルだった。◆Gold futures for December delivery lost at $1,891.90 an ounce at 2:05 p.m. on the Comex in New York. ニューヨーク商品取引所では、12月渡しの金先物価格が、午後2時5分の時点で1トロイ・オンス（約31グラム）＝1,891.90ドルに達した。◆Stock prices of many major commercial banks closed lower, as they had in previous tradings. 多くの大手銀行の株価は、続落したまま取引を終えた。◆The dollar-yen exchange rate closed at ￥101.2, a gain of nearly ￥25 since the beginning of the year. 円ドル・レートは、終値で1ドル＝101円20銭で、年初からの円の上昇幅は25円近くになった。◆The June 2012 gold futures contract closed at ￥4,694 per gram, down ￥54 from the previous day's close on the Tokyo Commodity Exchange. 東京工業品

取引所では、2012年6月渡しの金先物価格は、前日の終値より54円安の1グラム＝4,694円で取引を終えた。◆The 225-issue Nikkei Stock Average closed at 7,607.88, the lowest level since the economic bubble burst, on April 28, 2003. 2003年4月28日の日経平均株価（225種）の終値は7,607円88銭で、バブル崩壊後の最安値を付けた。◆The 225-issue Nikkei Stock Average dropped below the 9,000 mark Wednesday to close at the year's low of 8,845.39. 水曜日の日経平均株価（225種）は、9,000円台を割り込み、終値は今年最安値の8,845円39銭となった。◆The yield on the benchmark 10-year Japanese government bond closed below the 1 percent threshold. 長期金利の指標となる新発10年物日本国債の流通利回り［利回り］が、年1％の大台を割り込んで取引を終えた。◆The yield on the benchmark 10-year U.S. government bond has been closing below 3 percent recently. 長期金利の指標となる10年物米国債の利回りは最近、3％を割り込んで［3％割れで］取引を終えている。

close （名）終値，引け値，引け，終了
 after the market close 市場取引終了後に
 at market close 終値で
 buy on close 引け値買い注文
 close guarantee trade 引け値保証取引
 close of business 営業終了，営業時間の終了
 market on close 引け注文
 on a close 終値で
 toward the close of trade 取引終了にかけて
 ◆At the close of trading on Wall Street, the Dow Jones industrial average was down 58.26 at 10,910.96. ニューヨーク株式市場のダウ平均株価（工業株30種）の終値は、前日比58.26ドル安の1万910.96ドルだった。◆On Monday, the Dow Jones industrial average plunged more than 500 points from Friday's close. 月曜日のダウ平均株価（工業株30種）は、先週末の終値に比べて500ドル超も値下りした。◆The company's regular quarterly dividend will be payable June 30, 2011 to shareholders of record at the close of business on June 9, 2011. 当社の通常四半期配当は、2011年6月9日営業終了時の登録株主に対して2009年6月30日に支払われる。◆The firm's stock jumped to ￥1,097 at market close next day. 同社の株価は、翌日の終値で1,097円に跳ね上がった。◆The June 2012 gold futures contract closed at ￥4,694 per gram, down ￥54 from the previous day's close on the Tokyo Commodity Exchange. 東京工業品取引所では、2012年6月渡しの金先物価格は、前日の終値より54円安の1グラム＝4,694円で取引を終えた。◆The Tokyo Stock Price Index of all First Section issues tumbled 26.12 points, or 2.81 percent, to 904.24, its lowest close since Dec. 25, 1984, when it ended at 898.99. 東証一部全銘柄の東証株価指数（TOPIX）の終値は、(前日比で) 26.12ポイント（2.81％）下落して904.24と、1984年12月25日の終値898.99以来の低水準だった。◆The 225-issue Nikkei Stock Average on Monday plunged 202.32 points from Friday's close on the Tokyo Stock Exchange. 東京株式市場の月曜日の日経平均株価（225種）は、前週末比で202円32銭下落した。◆Tokyo stocks plunged across the board, sending the key Nikkei index to its lowest close in more than two months. 東京株［東京株式市場の株価］は全面安となり、日経平均株価（225種）の終値は2か月強ぶりの低い水準となった。

close （形）密接な，親しい，精密な，周到な，互角の，接戦の，僅差（きんさ）の，非公開の，かぎられた
 close company 閉鎖会社（基本的に、株主やパートナーなどの構成員が5名以下の会社）
 close cooperation and coordination 密接な協力体制
 close corporation 株式非公開会社，非公開会社，閉鎖会社 （＝closed corporation）
 close money 金づまり，逼迫（ひっぱく）した金融
 close to ［on］ ～に近い，ほとんど～
 in close cooperation with ～と緊密に連携して

◆On Aug. 31, 2011, the yen rose to the ￥76.50 level against the U.S. dollar in the Tokyo foreign exchange market, close to the postwar record of ￥75.95 registered on Aug. 19. 2011年8月31日の東京外国為替市場の円相場は、1ドル＝76円50銭台まで上昇し、8月19日に付けた戦後最高値の75円95銭に近づいた。◆The Bank of Japan will fight the yen's appreciation in close cooperation with the government. 日銀は、政府と緊密に連携して円高に対応する方針だ。

close below 〜を割り込んで引ける、〜を割り込んで取値を終える、終値は〜を割り込む
　◆The Tokyo Stock Exchange closed below 11,000 points. 東京証券取引所は、1万1,000円を割り込んで取引を終えた。◆The yield on the benchmark 10-year U.S. government bond has been closing below 3 percent recently. 長期金利の指標となる10年物米国債の利回りは最近、3％を割り込んで［3％割れで］取引を終えている。

close off 締切り

close one's accounts 決算をする
　（=close one's books）
　◆Regular FSA inspections are conducted after banks close their accounts in March, and focus on whether their loan reserves are adequate. 金融庁の通常検査は3月の銀行の決算後に行われ、主に債権に対する引当金が十分かどうかなどを点検する。

close one's [the] books （決算などのために）帳簿を締める、決算する、株式名義の書換えを停止する、申込みを締め切る
　close the books at year end 期末に決算をする、決算期に決算する
　listed companies that close their books on March 31 3月期決算の上場企業
　◆More than 60 percent of companies listed on the Tokyo Stock Exchange that closed their books on March 31 held general shareholders meetings Tuesday. 東京証券取引所に上場している3月期決算企業の60％超が、火曜日に株主総会を開催した。◆Sixty-four percent of companies listed on the Tokyo Stock Exchange that closed their books on March 31 held their shareholders meeting on the same day. 東京証券取引所に上場している3月期決算企業の64％が、同一日に株主総会を開いた。◆Sumitomo Mitsui Financial Group Inc. is expected to have slashed its nonperforming loans when it closes its books at the end of March. 三井住友フィナンシャルグループは、3月期決算で不良債権の抜本処理を図る見通しだ。◆These companies close their books between April and June. これらの企業は、4〜6月期決算だ［これらは、4〜6月期決算企業だ］。

close out （動）〜を手じまいする、〜を手じまう、〜の反対売買を行う、安値で処分する　（=unwind）
　close out before expiry 満期までに手じまう
　close out the books for the year 決算をする
　close out the position ポジションを手じまう、ポジションの反対売買を行う

close out [close-out] （名）終了、締切り、手じまい
　（「手じまい」は、信用取引での売り、買いを反対売買で帳消しにすること。言い換えると、取引所で空買いしたものを転売し、空売りしたものを買い戻して、取引関係を完了すること。売りの手じまいを「手じまい買い」、買いの反対売買を「手じまい売り」という）
　close out clauses 契約関係終了条項
　close out netting 一括清算、ポジションの手じまいによるネッティング
　close out of swaps スワップの決済

closed （形）株式非公開の、閉鎖した、閉鎖型の、排他的な
　closed account 決算勘定
　closed aggregate cost method 閉鎖型総合保険料方式
　closed company 非公開会社
　closed exclusive license 完全独占ライセンス
　closed institution 閉鎖機関
　closed register 閉鎖登記簿

closed-end （形）（投資信託が）クローズドエンド型の、資本固定の、資本額固定の、閉鎖式の、（担保が）貸付け金額を固定した、多項選択式の
　closed-end credit system 閉鎖信用体系
　closed-end fund 閉鎖式基金
　closed-end investment company 閉鎖式投資会社、クローズエンド型投資会社　（=closed-end management company, investment trust）
　closed-end investment fund クローズドエンド型投信、クローズドエンド型ファンド
　closed-end investment (trust) company 閉鎖式投資会社、閉鎖式投資信託会社、クローズドエンド型投資会社
　closed-end lease クローズドエンド型リース
　closed-end management company クローズエンド型投資会社
　closed-end mortgage 閉鎖式担保、閉鎖担保、閉鎖式抵当、クローズドエンド・モーゲージ　（=closed mortgage）
　closed-end question 多項選択式質問、限定選択肢質問
　closed-end type investment trust クローズドエンド型投資信託

closing （名）正式契約書の調印式、正式契約書の作成・署名、クロージング、不動産売買の最終手続き、株式の譲渡手続きと代金の払込み手続きの同時履行、取引完了、終値、決済、期末、決算、締切り、工場などの閉鎖、休会、結語
　closing procedures 決算手続き
　（=closing process）
　closing quotation 引け値、終値
　closing rate 引け値、決算日レート、クロージング・レート
　interim closing 中間決算
　on a closing basis 終値ベースで
　◆The closing of the sale and purchase of the Shares shall take place at the offices of ABCD Corp. on June 10, 2005. 本株式の売買取引の実行［本株式のクロージング］は、2005年6月10日にABCDコーポレーションの事務所で行う。

closing balance sheet クロージング日現在の貸借対照表　（⇒date）
　◆The Buyer shall prepare the Closing Balance Sheet at the Buyer's expense as promptly as practicable, but in any event within ninety (90) calendar days following the Closing Date. 買い主は、できるだけ速やかに、ただしどんな場合でもクロージング日以降90暦日以内に、買い主の費用負担でクロージング日現在の貸借対照表を作成するものとする。

closing date 払込み日、払込み期日、締切り日、売上締切り日、決算日、証券の引渡し日、クロージング日
　（=closing day）
　◆The closing date shall be the date of execution of this agreement. クロージング日は、本契約の締結日とする。

closing figure 終値
　（=closing market price, closing price）
　◆The closing figure of the 225-issue Nikkei Stock Average in the First Section of the Tokyo Stock Exchange marked the lowest since Sept. 19, 1983, when it finished at 9,141.25. 東証一部の日経平均株価（225種）の終値は、1983年9月19日（9,141円25銭）以来の低水準だった。

closing high 終値での最高値、終値で最高値
　◆The Nikkei stock index surged 2 percent more to a one-month closing high powered by the yen's plunge against the dollar. 日経平均は、円安・ドル高で2％以上急騰して、終値で1か月ぶりの最高値となった。

closing low 終値での最安値、終値で最安値
　◆Tokyo stocks tumbled to a 15-month closing low as uncer-

tainties continued to grow about the outlook for the Japanese and U.S. economies. 東京株[東京株式市場の株価]は、日米経済の先行き不透明感の高まりを受け、終値で1年3か月ぶりの最安値となった。

closing of accounts　決算
(=closing accounts, closing of books)
the closing of fiscal 2012 accounts　2012年度決算
the half year closing of fiscal 2012 accounts　2012年度中間決算
◆The special inspections will be conducted as banks review the positions of their debtors, and will be finalized before the closing of accounts. 特別検査は、銀行が債務者の経営状態を見直す際に行われ、決算までに完了する。

closing price　終値, 引け値, 引け　(=closing quotation, closing rate; ⇒opening price)
◆Based on Friday's closing price, Mixi's market capitalization stands at ￥219 billion, making the second-largest issue on the Mothers market. 金曜日の終値ベースで、ミクシィの時価総額は2,199億円で、新興企業向け市場の東証マザーズ上場銘柄としては第2位となった。◆On the last day of the takeover bid period, the closing price of NBS shares on the market was 11 percent higher than Fuji TV's purchasing price. TOB (株式公開買付け)期間の最終日は、ニッポン放送株の市場の終値が、フジテレビの買取り価格を11％も上回った。◆The closing price on the first day of these IPO stocks' trading has exceeded their opening price. これらの新規株式公開(IPO)銘柄の取引初日の終値[これらIPO銘柄の上場時の初値(終値)]は、公開価格を上回った。

closure　(名)工場や店舗、事業などの閉鎖、封鎖、閉幕、閉会
◆The closure of the money-losing outlets will result in a surplus of about 2,000 employees out of about 22,000 on a consolidated basis. 赤字の店舗閉鎖に伴い、連結ベースで従業員約22,000人のうち約2,000人が余剰になる。

cloud　(名)暗雲, 暗い影, 不安, 災いの兆し, 雲, 大群 (動)曇らせる, 鈍らせる, 暗い影を投じる, ～を汚す
a cloud on the horizon　将来の不安
a dark cloud hanging over　～に立ち込める暗雲
under a cloud　不信の目で見られて, 疑惑のなかで, 疑惑を受けて, 不興をかって
◆The economy could sink into a double-dip recession due to the clouds hanging over the U.S. economy and rising deflationary pressures that will accompany the accelerated disposal of nonperforming loans. 米国経済の行方[米国経済への先行き不安]や、不良債権処理の加速に伴うデフレ圧力の高まりなどで、景気が底割れする恐れがある。

cm. pf.　累積[累積的]優先株　(=cumulative preference, cumulative preferred stock)

CMA　金融資産総合口座　(cash management accountの略)

CMA　(米国の)管理会計士認定証　(Certificate in Management Accountingの略)

CMBS　商業用[商業]不動産ローン担保証券, 商業用不動産担保証券
(⇒commercial mortgage-backed securities)

CMC　通貨信用委員会(Commission on Money and Creditの略。米民間の研究・提言団体)

CMI　チェンマイ・イニシアチブ(Chiang Mai Initiativeの略。2000年5月、タイのチェンマイで開催されたASEANプラス3(日中韓)の財務相会議で合意した通貨交換協定。2010年に多国間通貨交換[スワップ]協定に移行した)

CMIM　チェンマイ・イニシアチブ多角化体制, 多国間通貨交換[スワップ]協定　(Chiang Mai Initiative Multilateralizationの略。⇒emergency liquidity)

CMO　イングランド銀行の短期金融市場証券の電子決済システム(Central Moneymarkets Officeの略)

CMO　不動産抵当証書担保債券, モーゲージ担保債務証書(collateralized mortgage obligationの略)

CMS　資金管理サービス(cash management serviceの略。通信回線による銀行の企業に対する残高通知や金利の情報提供や送金、振替、資金の集中管理などのサービス)

CMT　米国債理論利回り, 1年満期財務省証券利回り (constant maturity Treasuryの略)
CMT floater　CMTフローター

coffers　(名)金庫, 資金, 財源, 資産, 国庫, 財政
city's coffers　市の財源, 市の金庫, 市の財政
deplete the U.S. coffers　米国の財政を疲弊させる
depleted state coffers　疲弊した国家財政, 枯渇した国の財源, 財政悪化
funds from national coffers　国費
government coffers　国庫
inject public funds into troubled banks from the state coffers　問題の銀行に国庫から公的資金を注入する
public coffers　国庫, 国の拠出金
the coffers of crime groups　暴力団の資金
the coffers of the state　国庫, 国の財源, 国家財政
(=the state coffers)
◆Amid the depleted state coffers, it is difficult to implement a major stimulus package to rectify the rise in the yen's value. 財政悪化が進む中[国の財源が枯渇する中]、円高是正のため大規模な財政出動を行うのは難しい。◆Public funds will be injected into troubled banks from the state coffers. 問題のある[経営難の]銀行には今後、国庫から公的資金が注入される。◆The government will stop injecting funds from national coffers into the four road-related public corporations. 政府は、道路関係4公団への国費投入を打ち切る方針だ。◆These pork-barrel add-ons will further deplete the United States' coffers. 議員の人気取りが目的のこれら法案の追加条項は、米国の財政を一段と疲弊させることになる。

COFI　資金調達コスト指数(cost of funds indexの略)

cofinance [co-finance]　(動)協調融資する, 共同融資する　(名)協調融資, 共同融資
◆Structural adjustment loans are often co-financed with multilateral financial institutions. 構造調整借款は、国際金融機関との協調融資の形をとることが多い。

cofinancing [co-financing]　(名)協調融資, 共同融資
(=joint financing)

cofinancing scheme　協調融資事業
(=joint financing scheme)
◆In this cofinancing scheme, the bank will extend a total of about ￥8.5 billion over a 20-year loan period. この協調融資事業で、同行は貸出期間20年で計85億円を融資する。◆The bank will carry out this cofinancing scheme as the lead bank with several U.S. and European banks. 同行は、主幹事行として、この協調融資事業を欧米の複数の銀行と連携して実施する。◆The cofinancing scheme of the Bank of Tokyo-Mitsubishi UFJ will cover the Stardale mega solar power plant construction project carried out by a Canadian corporation. 三菱東京UFJ銀行の協調融資事業の対象は、カナダの企業が実施している大型太陽光発電所建設プロジェクトの「スターデール」だ。

coin　(動)(コインを)鋳造する, 作り出す, 新造する
coined gold　金貨

coin　(名)貨幣, 硬貨, 金銭, 現金, コイン
abrasion of coin　硬貨の磨滅
antique coins　古銭
bulk coin deposits　大量の硬貨入金
clipped coin　損貨
coin and notes daily balance book　金銭有高帳

coin box　小型金庫, 料金受け箱
coin changer　自動両替機
coin circulation　硬貨の流通
coin counter　硬貨計算機
　(＝coin counting machine)
coin return　コイン返却口
coin slot [slit]　コイン投入口
coin sorter　貨幣選別機
coin toss　(事を決めるための)コイン投げ
coin wrapper　硬貨包装機
coins in circulation　貨幣流通高
　(⇒balance of coins in circulation)
coins withdrawn from circulation　引揚げ貨幣
copper coin　銅貨
counterfeit [false, forged] coin　贋造(がんぞう)貨幣, 贋(にせ)金
defaced coins or notes　汚損硬貨または紙幣
freshly-minted coin　新規鋳造貨幣
gold coin　金貨　(＝coined gold)
gold coin and bullion　金貨と金地金(ぢきん)
loose coins　ばら銭
minor coin　小額硬貨
new coins　新硬貨
reserve for coin issued　貨幣回収準備資金
rolled coins　巻いた硬貨
silver coin　銀貨
small coins　小銭
standard coin　本位貨幣
stock of notes and coins in the economy　流通現金
subsidiary coin　補助貨幣
the other side of the coin　(事柄の)別の面, 違った面, 逆の見方, 正反対の面[見方]
the wear and tear on coins　硬貨の損傷
toss [flip] a coin　コインを投げて(いずれかを)決める
two sides of the same coin　表裏一体, 同じことの表と裏[二つの側面]
coinage　(名)貨幣鋳造, 造幣, 貨幣制度, 硬貨(coins), 硬貨鋳造, 貨幣, 通貨
Coinage Act　貨幣鋳造法
coinage prerogative　造幣高権
coinage ratio　金銀鋳造比率
debasement of coinage　通貨の品質低下
decimal coinage　10進法貨幣制度
free coinage　自由鋳造, 自由造幣
limited coinage　制限通貨, 鋳造制限
limited coinage issue　制限通貨発行
standard coinage　本位貨幣制度, 本位貨幣制
token coinage　名目貨幣制度
coincidence indicator　景気一致指標, 一致指数
　(＝coincident index)
◆The coincidence indicator, the nation's key gauge of the state of the economy, topped the boom-or-bust line of 50 percent in March. 国内の景気の現状を示す一致指数[景気一致指数]が, 3月は景気判断の分かれ目となる50%を上回った。
coincident index　景気一致指数, 一致指数
　(＝coincident indicator: 鉱工業生産指数, 百貨店販売額, 所定外労働時間指数など, 現状の景気の動きと同時期に並行して動く経済指標で, 景気の現状を示す)
◆A reading of below 50 percent in the coincident index is considered a sign of economic contraction and a figure above that is viewed as a sign of expansion. 一致指数で50%以下の数値は景気収縮[景気後退]を示す指標と見られ, それ以上の数字は景気回復[景気拡大]を示す指標と見なされる。

coinsurance　(名)共同保険
coinsurance clause　共同保険条項
coinsurance money　共同保険金
coinsurer　(名)共同保険業者, 共同保険者
cold cash　現金, 即金
collapse　(動)経営破たんする(fail), 破たんする, 倒産する, 暴落する, 急減する, 崩壊する
　(⇒take over)
◆Aoki Corp. became the first general contractor with debt waivers to have collapsed. 債権放棄を受けているゼネコンで経営破たんしたのは, 青木建設が初めてだ。◆Ashikaga Bank collapsed and was temporarily placed under state control. 足利銀行は, 経営破たんして一時国有化された。◆Companies are usually considered likely to collapse when their liabilities surpass their assets. 企業は, 一般に債務超過になった場合に「破綻懸念先」となる。◆Lehman Brothers Holdings Inc., a major U.S. investment bank, collapsed in September 2008. 米投資銀行大手のリーマン・ブラザーズは, 2008年9月に破たんした。◆Merrill Lynch was acquired by Bank of America, while Bear Stearns collapsed and sold to JPMorgan. メリルリンチはバンク・オブ・アメリカが買収し, ベア・スターンズは経営破たんしてJPモルガンに売却された。◆The Franco-Belgian bank Dexia collapsed in October 2011 despite passing the 2011 EBA's financial health check. フランス・ベルギー共同の銀行「デクシア」が, 2011年に実施された欧州銀行監督機構(EBA)の財務の健全性検査を通過したにもかかわらず, 2011年10月に破たんした。◆The investment bank reaped billions of dollars from its own bets that the housing market would collapse. この投資銀行は, 住宅市場が崩壊するとの独自の予想で, 数十億ドルの利益を上げていた。◆The pension system may collapse before people qualify as beneficiaries. 年金をもらう前に, 年金制度が崩壊する可能性がある。◆The U.S. government filed lawsuits against 17 financial firms for selling Fannie and Freddie mortgage-backed securities that turned toxic when the housing market collapsed. 米政府は, 住宅市場崩壊時に不良資産化した住宅ローン担保証券(MBS)をファニー・メイ(米連邦住宅抵当公庫)とフレディ・マック(米連邦住宅貸付け抵当公社)に販売したとして, 大手金融機関17社(バンク・オブ・アメリカやシティグループ, JPモルガン・チェース, ゴールドマン・サックス・グループなど)を提訴した。
collapse　(名)経営破たん, 破たん, 倒産, 崩壊, 倒壊, 決壊, 崩落, 暴落, 急落, 下落, 急減, 悪化, (計画などの)挫折(ざせつ), 失敗, 頓挫(とんざ), (神経などの)衰弱, 虚脱, 虚脱状態　(⇒economic collapse)
a chain reaction of collapses　連鎖破たん
bank's collapse　銀行破たん　(＝bank failure)
chain reaction of financial collapses　金融破たんの連鎖反応
collapse in demand　需要の急減, 需要の大幅落込み
collapse in earnings　収益の落込み[急減], 大幅減益
collapse in stock [equity] prices　株価の急落, 株価暴落
collapse of a ministry　内閣の崩壊
collapse of credit　信用失墜, 信用の崩壊
collapse of financial institutions　金融破たん, 金融機関の経営破たん, 金融崩壊
collapse of market quotation　相場の急落, 相場の暴落, 相場の崩落
collapse of the bubble　バブル崩壊
collapse of the dollar　ドルの下落
collapse of the economic bubble　バブル崩壊
collapse of the housing market　住宅市場の崩壊
collapse of the market　市場の崩壊
collapse of the stock market　株式市場の急落, 株式相場の下落, 株式市場の崩壊

（＝stock market collapse）
corporate collapse　企業倒産, 企業の経営破たん
　（＝corporate failure）
credit collapse　信用崩壊
　（＝the collapse of credit）
earnings collapse　業績悪化, 大幅減益, 収益の落ち込み
economic collapse　経済破たん, 経済の崩壊, 景気悪化
housing collapse　住宅市場の崩壊
Lehman's collapse　リーマン・ブラザーズの経営破たん, リーマン・ブラザーズの破たん
price collapse　価格［物価］の大幅下落
stock collapse　株価急落
stock market collapse　株式相場の下落
systemic collapse　システム崩壊

◆Banks would keep amassing cash by disposing of distressed assets as quickly as possible to avert collapse after having difficulty raising funds. 資金調達が困難になって経営破たんするのを避けるため、金融機関［銀行］は、できるだけ早めに危険資産を処分［売却］して、現金を抱え込もうとする。◆Belarus has asked the IMF for a $8 billion rescue loan to manage the country's most severe financial crisis since the Soviet collapse. ベラルーシは、ソ連崩壊後最も深刻な金融危機を乗り切るため、国際通貨基金（IMF）に80億ドルの金融支援融資を要請した。◆Consumer spending waned amid the global financial crisis that followed the Lehman Brothers collapse in autumn 2008. 2008年秋のリーマン・ブラザーズの破たん後に生じた世界的金融危機を受けて、個人消費が低迷した。◆Government steps taken to deal with Resona's collapse did not incorporate a reduction in the banking group's capital. りそな銀行の経営破たん処理に取った国の措置には、同金融グループの減資は織り込まれなかった。◆In order to prevent the chain reaction of even more devastating financial collapses, financial and monetary authorities in the United States and other nations will need to work together. これ以上の衝撃的な金融破たんの連鎖反応を防ぐには、米国と世界各国の金融・通貨当局の協調が必要だ。◆The collapse of Dai-ichi Kaden on April 16 was the result of speculation by foreign investment funds of a dubious nature. 4月16日の第一家電の経営破たんは、実態不明の海外投資ファンドの投機によるものであった［海外ファンドの投機に食い荒らされた末路であった］。◆The European banking tests are lax and ineffective as the collapses of two Irish banks and the Franco-Belgian bank Dexia, shortly after the EBA's stress tests, show. 欧州の銀行検査は、欧州銀行監督機構（EBA）のストレス・テストに合格した［ストレス・テストで安全と判定された］直後にアイルランドの銀行2行やフランス・ベルギー共同の銀行「デクシア」が破たんした事実が示すように、手ぬるくて効果がない。◆The money lent by the U.S. and eurozone private banks remains at about the same level as those prior to Lehman's collapse. 米国とユーロ圏の民間銀行の貸出金は、リーマン・ブラザーズの経営破たん前とほぼ同水準にとどまっている。◆The possibility that the bank's collapse will set off a negative chain reaction is very low. 同行の破たんが連鎖破たんを引き起こす可能性は、かなり低い。

collapse of a bank　銀行の破たん, 銀行破たん
◆The collapse of a bank may result in the systemic breakdown of the whole banking sector. 銀行1行の破たんが、金融全体のシステム崩壊［連鎖的な崩壊］につながる可能性がある。◆The collapse of the bank will lead to repercussions throughout the finance sector. 同行の破たんは、金融業界全体に影響を及ぼすことになろう。

collapse of financial institutions　金融機関の経営破たん, 金融機関の破たん
◆The global financial crisis was triggered by the collapse of some major financial institutions. 世界的な金融危機は、大手金融機関の破たんで始まった。

collapse of Lehman Brothers（Holdings Inc.）
リーマン・ブラザーズの経営破たん, リーマン・ブラザーズの破たん［倒産］
（＝Lehman Brother's collapse）
◆At two financial summit meetings since the collapse of Lehman Brothers, agreements were made on cooperation to implement large-scale economic stimulus measures and to take monetary relaxation policies. リーマン・ブラザーズの倒産［破たん］以来2回開かれた金融サミットでは、連携して大型の財政出動や金融緩和策を実施することで合意が得られた。◆Ford was prompted to trim its Mazda stake by the changed environment in the global auto market following the September 2008 collapse of Lehman Brothers Holdings Inc. 米フォードは、2008年9月にリーマン・ブラザーズが経営破たんした後、世界の自動車市場の環境が変化したことで、マツダへの出資比率を引き下げることになった。◆Japan, the United States and European countries supported their sagging economies by increasing public spending after the collapse of Lehman Brothers in the autumn of 2008. 2008年秋のリーマン・ブラザーズの経営破たん後、日米欧は、財政出動によって低迷する景気の下支えをした。◆Shinsei and Aozora banks suffered huge losses in their overseas investment business in the aftermath of the global financial crisis triggered by the collapse of Lehman Brothers Holdings Inc. in autumn 2008. 新生銀行とあおぞら銀行は、2008年秋のリーマン・ブラザーズの経営破たんで始まった金融危機の影響で、海外投資事業に巨額の損失が発生した。◆The capital markets around the globe are plagued by counterparty risks in the aftermath of the collapse of U.S. investment bank Lehman Brothers in 2008. 世界全体の資本市場は、2008年の米証券会社［投資銀行］の経営破たんの影響で、カウンターパーティー・リスクに苦しんでいる。

collapse of major financial institutions　大手金融機関の破たん
◆The global financial crisis was triggered by the collapse of some major financial institutions. 世界的な金融危機は、大手金融機関の破たんで始まった。

collapse of the bubble economy　バブル経済の崩壊, バブル崩壊, バブル（経済）の破たん
◆Japan's financial system was badly damaged with the collapse of the bubble economy and deflation. 日本の金融システムは、バブル崩壊とデフレで深手を負った。◆Kan's latest policy speech was an expression of his resolve to settle issues put off during the two lost decades after the collapse of the bubble economy. 菅首相の今回の所信表明演説は、バブル崩壊後の「失われた20年」の間に先送りされた問題を解決するという首相の決意表明であった。◆Since the collapse of the bubble economy in the early 1990s, Japan has experienced several phases of economic revival. 1990年代はじめのバブル崩壊以降、日本は何度か景気回復局面を迎えた。◆Stock prices have dropped to an all-time low since the collapse of the bubble economy. 株価は、バブル崩壊後の最安値まで落ち込んだ。

collapse of the subprime mortgage market　サブプライム・ローン（低所得者向け住宅融資）市場の崩壊, サブプライム・ローン市場の悪化
◆AIG teetered on the edge of failure because of stresses caused by the collapse of the subprime mortgage market and the credit crunch that ensued. 米保険最大手のAIGは、サブプライム・ローン（低所得者向け住宅融資）市場の崩壊とその後の金融危機による経営不振［経営難］で、経営破たんの瀬戸際［危機］にあった。◆Banks across the United States have been devastated by the collapse of the subprime mortgage market. 米全域の銀行が、サブプライム・ローン（低所得者向け住宅ローン）市場の崩壊によって、壊滅的な打撃を受けている。◆The collapse of the subprime mortgage market and related credit market turmoil have resulted in $45 billion of write-

downs at the world's biggest banks and securities firms. サブプライム・ローン市場の悪化や関連金融市場の混乱で、世界の大手銀行と証券会社の評価損計上額は、これまでのところ450億ドルに達している。

collapse of U.S.-style financial business models 米国型金融ビジネス・モデルの崩壊
◆The world is being jolted by the collapse of U.S.-style financial business models. 世界は、米国型金融ビジネス・モデルの崩壊でショックを受けている［米国型金融ビジネス・モデルの崩落が、世界を揺るがせている］。

collapsed bank 破たん銀行
（=failed bank; ⇒Bridge Bank of Japan）

collar （名）金利の上限・下限付き組合せオプション取引、カラー（金利のキャップ（cap: 上限契約）と金利のフロア（floor: 下限契約）の組合せ）
  collar swap カラー・スワップ
  create a collar round one's investment 投資にカラーを設定する
  interest rate collar 金利カラー
  prepayment collar 期限前償還率カラー
  rate collar agreement 金利カラー契約
  weighted collar 加重カラー
  zero cost collar ゼロ・コスト・カラー

collared （形）カラー付きの
  collared floater カラー付き変動利付き債
  collared floating rate note カラー付き変動利付き債（=collared FRN）
  collared swap カラー付きスワップ
  fungible collared floater 統合可能カラー付き変動利付き債

collared FRN カラー付き変動利付き債
（=collared floating rate note）
  fungible collared FRNs カラー付き銘柄統合可能債
  senior collared FRNs カラー付き上位債
  step-up collateral FRNs ステップアップ・カラー付き変動利付き債
  subordinated collared FRNs カラー付き劣後債

collateral （名）担保, 担保物件, 担保品, 担保財産, 見返り担保, 見返り物件, 抵当物件, 副抵当, パス・スルー証券（pass-through security）, 担保証券 （=mortgage, security; ⇒borrow massive amounts of money, business model, efficiency, fixed collateral, margin transaction）
  additional collateral 増し担保, 増担保, 追加担保
  assessment rate of collateral 担保掛け目
  banker's collateral 銀行の担保品
  collateral for bank loans 銀行融資の担保
  collateral for REMICs REMICの裏付け
  demand increased collateral 担保の追加を求める
  deposit as collateral 担保預金
  deposit securities as collateral 有価証券を担保として差し入れる
  eligible collateral 適格担保
  evaluation of collateral 担保評価
  excess collateral 超過担保
  fixed collateral 根（ね）抵当, 根抵当権
  foreclose collateral for a loan 貸出金の担保権を行使する［実行する］
  foreclose on posted collateral 設定された［提供された］担保について担保権を行使する
  foreclosed collateral 担保権の実行, 担保権の行使
  hedge the price risk on the collateral 担保の価格リスクをヘッジする
  low［lower］coupon collateral 低クーポンのパス・スルー証券（pass-through security: モーゲージ担保証券の一種）
  marketable collateral 処分可能な担保
  offer ～ as collateral ～を担保として提供する
  pledge ～ as collateral ～を担保として差し出す
  pledge of collateral 担保の差し入れ
  pledged collateral 担保の差し入れ, 担保の裏付け
  post collateral 担保を差し入れる, 担保を設定する, 担保を積む
  posting of collateral 担保供与
  sensitivity collateral 感応性担保
  share collateral 株券担保
  the real estate used as collateral 担保不動産
  the substitution of collateral 担保差し換え
  the value of collateral 担保価格（=collateral value）
  underlying collateral 担保物件, 裏付けとなる担保
  without securing sufficient collateral 十分な担保を取らずに
◆An increasing number of loans turn out to be nonperforming because of a deterioration in the business situation of the borrower or because the value of the real estate used as collateral has fallen. 融資先の経営悪化や担保不動産の目減りなどによって、不良債権化する貸出が増えている。◆The additional financial assistance to the Nuclear Damage Liability Facilitation Fund will be used as collateral when TEPCO borrows money from financial institutions. 原子力損害賠償支援機構に対する追加金融支援は、東電が金融機関から資金を借り入れる際の債務保証などに活用される。◆The bank demanded increased collateral to its client. 同行は、融資先に担保の追加を求めた。◆The credit union loaned ￥1.95 billion to a golf course operator without securing sufficient collateral. 同信組は、十分な担保を取らずにゴルフ場運営会社に19億5,000万円を融資した。◆Under the credit guarantee system, 52 local credit guarantee corporations guarantee loans to small and midsize companies that do not have enough collateral. 信用保証制度では、全国52箇所の各地の信用保証協会が、担保に乏しい中小企業の借入れに対して債務保証する。

collateral （形）付随する, 付帯の, 見返り（担保）の, 担保の, 担保物件の, 抵当の
  collateral agent 担保代理人
  collateral agreement form 担保約定署
  collateral assignment （保険証券の）担保譲渡
  collateral assurance 副保険
  collateral backing 裏付け
  collateral bond 担保付き社債, 付帯証書
  collateral company 傍系会社
  collateral conditions 付帯条件
  collateral contract 副契約, 副契約書
  collateral credit enhancer 信用補強提供者
  collateral custodian 担保証券保管機関
  collateral documents 担保書類
  collateral export goods 見返り輸出品
  collateral formula 担保必要額の計算式
  collateral goods 担保品, 見返り物資
  collateral heir 傍系相続人
  collateral income bond 担保付き収益社債, 見返り収益社債
  collateral maintenance 担保維持
  collateral margin 担保余力
  collateral market パス・スルー証券市場
  collateral monitoring 担保管理
  collateral monitoring services 担保管理業務
  collateral mortgage 副抵当

collateral mortgage bond 証券担保社債
collateral note 見返り手形, 担保手形, 担保付き約束手形
collateral payment due date 担保に支払い日
collateral policy 担保方針
collateral pool 資産プール
collateral posting 担保の差し入れ
collateral risk 担保リスク, 担保物件のリスク
collateral securities 代用証券, 見返り証券
collateral security 担保, 見返り担保, 副担保, 付随担保, 見返り証券, 代用証券, 代用証
collateral security loan 見返り担保貸付け
collateral spread パス・スルー証券のスプレッド
collateral surety 副保証人
collateral trust bond 見返り信託社債, 担保信託社債, 証券担保付き信託社債, 証券担保社債, 担保付き社債, 付随信託証書
collateral trust certificate 信託担保証券付き証書
collateral undertaking 付随的な引受け
collateral value 担保価格, 担保価値
 (=the value of collateral)
collateral value estimates 担保評価額
underlying collateral pool 裏付けとなる資産プール

collateral assessment 担保評価
◆The Financial Services Agency will check the credibility of the banks' debtor companies, including their management efficiency and the accuracy of their collateral assessment. 金融庁は、銀行の融資先の経営効率や担保評価などを含めて、銀行の融資先の信用力を洗い直す。

collateral for nonperforming loans 不良債権の担保
◆A real estate investment fund was alleged to have failed to report about ￥18 billion in income from transaction involving land and property taken as collateral for nonperforming loans. 不動産投資ファンドが、不良債権の担保に取った不動産関連の取引で得た所得約180億円の申告漏れを指摘されていた。

collateral-free loan 無担保融資, 無担保ローン, 無担保貸し
◆The Bank of Japan extended ￥1.2 trillion in emergency collateral-free loans to Yamaichi Securities in a bid to head off a financial crisis. 金融危機を回避するため、日銀は山一証券に無担保で1兆2,000億円を緊急融資した。

collateral loan 担保貸付け, 証券担保貸付け, 動産担保貸付け, 担保付き貸付け, 抵当貸付け, 担保付きローン, 担保ローン, 担保貸し, 担保貸付け金
bond collateral loans 公社債担保金融
stock collateral loan 株式担保金融

collateral value 担保価値
◆The collection of debts has been delayed due to falling collateral value. 担保価値の下落などで、債権の回収は遅れている。

collateralize [collateralise] (動)担保で保証する, 担保として使う
be fully collateralized as to principal ～については十分担保が付いている
collateralize against receivables 受取債権を担保とする

collateralized [collateralised] (形)担保される, 担保で保証される, 担保付きの, 有担保の
cash-collateralized guarantee 現預金[現・預金]担保保証
collateralized bond obligation 債券担保証券, 社債担保証券, CBO
collateralized debt obligation 債務担保証券, CDO (⇒CDO)
collateralized exit bond 担保付き卒業債
collateralized floating rate note 担保付き変動利付き債
collateralized issue 証券化商品
collateralized loan 担保付き貸付け, 有担保ローン, 担保付きローン, 担保貸し (=collateral loan)
collateralized loan obligation ローン担保証券, CLO
collateralized mortgage obligation 住宅抵当証書担保債, 抵当証券担保付き債券, 不動産抵当証書担保債, モーゲージ担保債務証書, CMO (不動産担保付き社債を担保として発行される証券)
collateralized mortgage securities issue モーゲージ証券
collateralized note 担保付き手形
collateralized overnight 有担保翌日物
floating rate collateralized mortgage obligation CMOフローター
items collaterarised by cash 現・預金担保債権

collation (名)照合, 突き合わせ, 照査
collation of balance 残高照合
collation of seals 印章照査, 照合印

collect (動)(債権や代金、資源などを)回収する, (年金や保険料、税金などを)徴収する, (預金などを)獲得する, (情報を)収集する[集める, 入手する] (⇒financially strapped, illegal lending, insurance agent, loan credits)
collect cash from accounts receivable 売掛金から現金預金を回収する
collect funds from ～から資金を集める
collect information about customers 顧客情報を集める[入手する]
collect loans extended to one's major corporate borrowers 大口融資先[融資先企業]に対する債権を回収する
collect money by issuing stocks 株式を発行して資金を集める
collect receivables 売掛債権を回収する
collect savings deposits from households 個人から預金を集める
◆A reserve of money collected by issuing stocks can be used to cover eventual financial losses. 株式を発行して集めた資金準備は、将来の金融損失の穴埋めに使用することができる。◆More than half of the public welfare loans extended to widows and single mothers are not collected. 母子家庭や寡婦に供与されている福祉資金の5割以上が、回収されていない。◆Sellers of multiple-debtor lists, produced by collecting information about consumer finance customers, are contributing to the spread of illegal moneylending. 消費者金融の顧客情報を入手して作った多重債務者リストを売る名簿業者が、ヤミ金融の横行に一役買っている。◆The large amounts of contributions collected nationwide will be used to help quake victims. 全国から寄せられた多額の義援金は、地震被災者の救援に充てられる。◆The special account is expected to collect a large surplus in fiscal 2011 via the repayment of loans. 特別会計は、貸付け金の返済で2011年度は多額の剰余金が生じる見込みだ。

collect claims 債権を回収する
◆Employees of the fund's Japanese unit assessed assets, collected claims and conducted other business. 同ファンドの日本法人の社員が、資産評価や債権回収などの業務を行っていた。

collect loans 債権を回収する
◆The bank's likelihood of collecting loans extended to its major corporate borrowers has worsened. 同行の大口融資先[融資先企業]に対する債権の回収見通しが悪化した。

collect premiums 保険料を徴収する
◆An insurance agent is a sales person who represents a life insurance company for the purpose of soliciting applications, collecting initial premiums, and servicing insurance contracts. 保険募集人は、生命保険会社を代表して保険契約の勧誘、初回保険料の徴収、保険契約に関する役務を提供す

る販売員である。◆Premiums are collected together with call charges in insurance services that can be bought via mobile phones. 携帯電話で加入できる保険サービスでは、保険料は通話料と一緒に徴収される。

collection （名）債権や代金などの回収, 年金や保険料, 税金などの徴収, 預金などの獲得
 collection and delivery system　集配体制
 collection fee　回収費用
 collection of premiums　保険料の徴収
 collection of principal　元本の回収
 collection of receivables　売掛金［売掛債権］の回収
 collections from customers and others　顧客その他からの回収
 debt collection　債権回収, 貸金取立て, 借金取り
 （=collecting the debt, collection of debts）
 loan collection　債権回収
 tax collection　徴税, 税の徴収
 （=collection of taxes）
 transfer of collections　回収金の送金

collection of debts　債権回収　（=debt collection）
◆The collection of debts has been delayed due to falling collateral value. 担保価値の下落などで、債権の回収は遅れている。◆To make RCC's collection of debts more efficient, the government plans to actively recruit financial experts to RCC from the financial industry. 整理回収機構（RCC）の債権回収の効率化をめざして、政府は、金融界から金融専門家をRCCに積極的に受け入れる方針だ。

collection of national pension premiums　国民年金保険料の徴収［徴収事務］
◆The government transferred the collection of national pension premiums, which had been entrusted to municipal governments, to the central government. 政府は、市町村に任せていた国民年金保険料の徴収［徴収事務］を国に移した。

collective　（形）集団［団体］による, 集団［団体］の, 総合的な, 包括的な, 集産主義の
 collective investment scheme　集合投資ファンド, 集合投資計画
 collective investment vehicle　集合投資手段

collision damage waiver　車両保険免責額補償特約, CDW

colossal　（形）巨大な, 膨大な, 莫大（ばくだい）な, 巨額の, 素晴らしい, 見事な, 途方もない, 驚くべき
 colossal amount of deficit　膨大な赤字
 the U.S. colossal deficits　米国の巨額の財政赤字
◆It is said that most of the U.S. government's colossal deficits had been caused by the faulty tax-and-spend policies of Republican governments. 米政府の膨大な財政赤字の大半は、歴代共和党政権の誤った税制・支出政策によるものだと言われる。

colossal amount of the U.S. twin deficits　米国の巨額の双子の赤字
◆It is feared the colossal amount of the U.S. twin deficits could trigger a freefall of the U.S. dollar. アメリカの巨額の双子の赤字は、ドルの暴落を引き起こす懸念がある。

colossal deficits　膨大な赤字, 膨大な財政赤字, 巨額の財政赤字
◆Moody's may downgrade the U.S. government's credit rating if it does not get its colossal deficits in better order. 米政府が膨大な財政赤字問題に目途をつけないと、ムーディーズは米国債の格付けを引き下げる可能性がある。

combat　（動）〜と戦う, 争う, 〜に反対する, 反抗する, 〜を沈静化させる, 〜防止に努力する, 〜に対応する
 combat financial crisis　金融危機を沈静化させる
 combat market barriers　市場障壁に対応する
◆The Bank of Japan has supplied a large amount of funds to the market to combat the financial crisis. 金融危機を沈静化させるため、日銀は大量の資金を市場に供給してきた。

combination　（名）合併, 連結, 企業結合, 企業連合, 相互利益協定, 結合, 組合せ, 関連性
 business combination　企業結合, 企業合同, 合併, 統合, 企業買収　（=combination of business）
 combination deal　組合せ取引
 combination of cap and swap　キャップとスワップの組合せ
 combination of factors　要因の関連性
 combination of shares　株式併合
 combination rate　船車混合運賃
 combination sale　抱き合せ販売
 combination setting　金庫の組合せ数字
 combination system　併用制
 combinations of companies　企業結合, 企業連合, 企業グループ
 deferred taxes in a purchase combination　パーチェス法による合併での繰延べ税金
 industrial combination　企業結合
 optimal combination　最適組合せ
◆A business combination is a significant economic event that results from bargaining between independent parties. 企業結合は、独立した当事者間の取引から生じるひとつの重要な経済事象である。◆Depending on the degree of JAL's financial deterioration, the government will consider a combination of capital reinforcement under the industrial revitalization law and public assistance by the Enterprise Turnaround Initiative Corp. of Japan. 日航の財務の傷み具合によって、政府は、産業再生法に基づく公的資金による資本増強と、企業再生支援機構による公的支援との組合せを検討する方針だ。◆Goodwill is the difference between the purchase price and the fair value of net assets acquired in business combinations treated as purchases. 営業権は、パーチェス法により会計処理した企業買収で取得した純資産の購入価格と公正価格との差異です。◆The March 11 disaster was due to a combination of a magnitude-9 earthquake, catastrophic tsunami and an ensuing crisis at a nuclear power plant. 2011年3月11日の東日本大震災は、マグニチュード9の地震、巨大津波とその後の原発事故が重なって起きた。

combine　（動）統合する, 合併する, 合算する, 連結する, 結合する, 組み合わせる
 combined instrument　結合金融商品
◆Sendai Bank and Tsukuba, regional banks based in areas stricken by the March 11 earthquake and tsunami, will receive a combined ¥65 billion public aid. 仙台銀行と筑波銀行（東日本大震災被災地の地方銀行）が、計650億円の公的支援を受けることになった。◆The financial assistance will be extended by combining a waiver of debt and a debt-for-equity swap. 金融支援は、債権放棄とデット・エクイティ・スワップ（債務の株式化）を組み合わせて行われる。◆The U.S. 10 leading banks need a combined capital buffer of 74.6 billion against the risk of a deeper recession and higher unemployment over the next two years. 米主要金融機関の10社は、今後2年の景気悪化リスクと失業増大に備えて、10社合計で746億ドルの資本増強を求められている。

combined group net profit　連結税引き後利益の合計額, 連結純利益の合計額
◆Combined group net profit at Japan's six top banking groups totaled a record ¥1.74 trillion for the April-September fiscal first half. 9月中間決算［4-9月期の上半期決算］で、日本の大手銀行・金融6グループ合計の連結税引き後利益が、過去最高益の1兆7,400億円となった。

combined losses　赤字合計額
◆The combined losses of the seven major banking groups totaled ¥4.62 trillion as of the end of March. 大手銀行・金融7グループの赤字合計額は、3月末現在で4兆6,200億円に達

combined net loss　純損失の合計, 全社合わせての赤字
◆These listed companies literally achieved a V-shaped recovery after recording a combined net loss in fiscal 2001. これらの上場企業は、2001年度に全社合計で赤字に転落した後、文字どおりV字型回復を達成した。

combined net profit　税引き後利益の合計額, 純利益の合計額
◆The combined net profits of Mitsubishi Tokyo Financial Group Inc. and UFJ Holdings Inc., which merged in October 2005, exceeded Toyota's group net profits. 2005年10月に経営統合した三菱東京フィナンシャル・グループとUFJホールディングスの税引き後利益の合計額は、トヨタの税引き後利益を上回った。

combined outstanding loans　総貸出残高
◆As of June, combined outstanding loans extended by banks nationwide fell year-on-year for 78 months in a row. 6月現在、全国の銀行の総貸出残高は、78か月連続で前年同月を下回った。

combined pretax profit　経常利益合計
◆Companies listed on the TSE's First Section posted a year-on-year increase of 33.2 percent in combined pretax profit in the first half of the current fiscal year. 東証一部上場企業の今年度上期（4-9月期）の経常利益合計は、前年同期比33.2%増となった。

combined profits and losses　損益の合算, 損益の通算
（=combined profits or losses, consolidated tax system）
◆Under this consolidated tax return system, a joint-stock company and its wholly owned subsidiaries pay corporate taxes in proportion to their combined profits and losses. この連結納税制度では、株式会社とその全額出資子会社は、相互の損益を通算（合算）して法人税を納める。

combined sales　売上高の合計, 全社合計の売上高, 全社合わせての売上高
◆Combined sales of Panasonic and Sanyo would catapult Panasonic to the No.3 spot in revenue among listed Japanese companies. パナソニック（旧松下電器産業）と三洋電機の連結売上高を合算すると、上場日本企業のなかで、パナソニックは売上高で一躍第3位となる。◆The combined sales of 813 nonfinancial companies in the April-September period grew 6.3 percent over the previous year. 金融を除く企業813社の上期（4-9月期）の売上高の合計は、前年同期比で6.3%増加した。

combined strength　統合力
◆One of the aims for the three banks to merge into the Mizuho Financial Group was to survive the global competition by exploiting the banks' combined strength. 3行がみずほフィナンシャルグループに合併する目的（狙い）の一つに、3行の統合力を駆使して国際競争に勝ち抜くことがあった。

come up with　～を提出する, 提案する, 打ち出す, 出す, 考え出す, 見つける, 思いつく, ～を用意する, ～に対応する, 発表する, 生産する
（⇒economic measures）
◆Even at this juncture, the government has yet to come up with comprehensive antideflation measures. この期に及んでも、政府の総合デフレ対策は出てこない。◆The Hatoyama Cabinet will come up with new policies on various issues, including midterm fiscal targets, pension system reform and its new growth strategies. 鳩山内閣は、中期財政目標や年金制度改革、新成長戦略など様々な経済問題について、新方針を打ち出す予定だ。◆The merger will prompt other megabanks to come up with new strategies to reinforcing their corporate health. この統合は他のメガバンクを刺激し、メガバンクは企業体質の強化に向けた戦略を新たに打ち出すことになろう。

Comex（in New York）　ニューヨーク商品取引所
（New York Commodity Exchange）
（=Commodity Exchange）
◆Gold extended its rally to a record above $1,900 an ounce amid increased uncertainties over the U.S. and European economic outlook on the Comex in New York. ニューヨーク商品取引所では、米欧景気見通しへの懸念［米欧経済の先行き不透明感］の高まりを受け［懸念の高まりから］、金価格が急騰して、1トロイ・オンス=1,900ドルを史上初めて突破した。◆Gold futures for December delivery closed at $1,891.90 an ounce at 2:05 p.m. on the Comex in New York. ニューヨーク商品取引所では、12月渡しの金先物価格が、午後2時5分の時点で1トロイ・オンス（約31グラム）=1,891.90ドルに達した。
◆Gold futures for December delivery gained to $1,897 an ounce at 4:13 p.m. in after-hours electronic trading on the Comex in New York. ニューヨーク商品取引所の時間外電子取引で、金先物の12月渡し価格は、午後4時13分の時点で1トロイ・オンス=1,897ドルまで上昇した。

comment　（名）意見, 見解, 論評, 批評, 解説, 説明, 解釈, 注釈,（～の）反映, 現われ, 世評, うわさ, コメント
a matter of general comment　一般のうわさの種
add comments or explanations　注釈または説明を加える
closing comments　締めくくりの意見
comment period　意見公開期間
fair comment　もっともな意見
invite［arouse］comment　人にとやかく言われる
letter of comment　質問書
make outspoken comments on　～に対して遠慮なく論評する, ～に対して率直に意見を言う, ～に対して率直な意見を述べる
nice comments　好意的な論評
positive comments　肯定的な論評
suggestive comments　示唆に富んだ解説
◆These comments were made after a series of currency market interventions by the government to prevent the yen's value from getting stronger. これらのコメントは、政府が円高阻止のための為替市場への介入を断続的に行った後に出された。

Commerce Department　米商務省
◆The U.S. Commerce Department reported that construction of new homes and apartments slid to an annual rate of 965,000 units in July 2008, a 17-year low. 米商務省が発表した2008年7月の住宅着工戸数［件数］は、（季節調整後の）年換算で96万5,000戸に減少し、17年ぶりの低水準となった。

commercial　（形）商業の, 商業上の, 商業的な, 商業ベースの, 通商の, 営利の, 民間の, 民放の, 大量生産型の, 量産的な, 市販の, 消費者向けの　（名）宣伝, 広告放送, コマーシャル
commercial agency　信用調査機関, 商業興信所
　（commercial inquiry office）, 代理店
commercial arbitration　商事仲裁
commercial asset　商業資産
commercial bill　商業手形
　（=commercial paper, trade bill）
commercial bill eligible for rediscounting　再割引適格（商業）手形
commercial capital　商業資本
commercial cofinancing　民間協調融資
commercial company　商事会社
commercial complementary loan　商業補完ローン
commercial correspondence　商業通信文
commercial customers　事業法人顧客
commercial deposits　商業預金, 企業預金
commercial document　商業書類
commercial draft　商業手形
commercial failure　倒産
commercial feasibility　商業的実行可能性
commercial finance　商業金融

commercial financing　商工業融資
commercial invoice　商業送り状, 商業インボイス, 仕切り書
commercial law　商事法
commercial lending　商業貸付け, 商業貸出, 民間融資
commercial lending activity　商業貸出業務
commercial letter of credit　商業信用状（=commercial credit）
commercial office space　賃貸用［賃貸］オフィス・ビル
commercial office vacancy rate　賃貸オフィス空室率
commercial orientation of aid　ひも付き型援助
commercial production　商業生産
commercial property and casualty　商業用損害保険
commercial register［registration］　商業登記
commercial risk　商業リスク, 信用危険, 信用リスク, 企業危険［リスク］
commercial securitization　商業用不動産の証券化
commercial set　主要船積み書類（インボイスや船荷証券, 保険証券, 手形為替などの書類）
commercial transaction　商取引, 商行為, 商業活動
commercial year　営業年度, 商業年（1か月30日、1年360日で計算する年）
commercial bank　商業銀行（米国の場合は、連邦法または州法により認可を受けた銀行）, 都市銀行, 都銀, 市中銀行, 市銀, 銀行（商業銀行の主な業務は、融資、預金の受入れと外国為替。⇒additional loan, alliance strategy, computer system, offset provisions, shift名詞）
commercial bank credit　民間銀行融資
commercial bank creditors　民間銀行債権者, 民間銀行債権団
commercial bank debt　民間銀行債務
commercial bank discounts and loans　市中貸出
commercial bank insolvency　商業銀行の破たん
commercial bank lenders　貸出銀行, 貸出をしている銀行
major commercial banks　大手銀行, 大手都銀
regional commercial bank　地方商業銀行
state commercial bank　州立商業銀行
state-owned commercial bank　国営商業銀行
the burden of bad debts carried by commercial banks　商業銀行が抱える不良債権処理の負担
◆Commercial banks have created special investment vehicles (SIVs) in order to escape the capital adequacy regulation imposed by the Basel accord. 銀行は、バーゼル協定［バーゼル合意］による自己資本比率規制を回避するため、特別投資会社（SIV）を新設している。◆In extending loans to startup businesses with high growth potential, the bank set its interest rates than those offered by major commercial banks. 成長性の高い新興企業に融資する際、同行は大手銀行より高い貸付け金利を設定していた。◆In the subprime crisis, the U.S. Federal Reserve Board had to take the extraordinary step of providing an emergency loan not to a commercial bank but to an investment bank. サブプライム問題で、米国の中央銀行の連邦準備制度理事会（FRB）は、緊急融資を銀行［商業銀行］ではなく証券会社［投資銀行］に対して行う異例の措置を取らざるを得なかった。◆Major central banks will cooperate to offer three-month U.S. dollar loans to commercial banks in the wake of Europe's sovereign debt crisis. 欧州の財政危機を受け、主要中央銀行が、協調して銀行［商業銀行］に3か月物ドル資金を供給することになった。◆Major commercial banks are reaching the final stages of their efforts to write off their nonperforming loans. 大手銀行は、不良債権処理への取組みの最終局面を迎えている。◆Most major commercial banks are likely to record losses in the accounting period ending March 31 due to bad loan write-offs. 大手都市銀行［大手銀行］の大半は、3月期決算（3月31日終了の会計年度）では、不良債権処理で赤字になりそうだ。◆Sberbank of Russia is the largest commercial bank in Russia. ロシアのズベルバンクは、ロシア最大の商業銀行である。◆The central bank has deployed various measures to ease monetary policy, including cuts in the discount rate and hikes in the target for current account deposits held by commercial banks at the central bank. 日銀は、公定歩合の引下げや銀行が日銀に持つ当座預金の残高目標の引上げなどを含めて、各種の金融緩和策を実施してきた。◆The major commercial banks deserve praise for working toward making their asset appraisal more stringent. 大手各行が資産査定の厳格化に動き出したことは、評価できる。◆The remaining ￥1.8 billion will be financed by two other commercial banks and trust banks. 残りの18億円は、他の都銀2行と信託各行が出す。◆This is the first time for major commercial banks to form a comprehensive tie-up with a foreign capital financial group. 大手都銀が外資系金融グループと包括提携するのは、今回が初めてだ。
commercial banking　商業銀行, 商業銀行業務
commercial banking activities　商業銀行業務
commercial banking services　商業銀行業務
domestic commercial banking business　国内銀行業務
Commercial Code　商法　（⇒auditing firm）
◆The government plans to translate laws such as the Civil Code and the Commercial Code into English in a bid to facilitate foreign investments and help domestic firms expand their international business activities. 政府は、外国からの投資促進や国内企業の国際ビジネス支援のため、民法や商法などの法律の英訳を行う方針だ。
commercial credit　商業貸出, 民間融資, 商業信用, 企業間信用, 商業金融, 商業信用状（commercial letter of credit［L/C］）
banker's commercial credit　銀行信用状
commercial credit losses　商業貸出金貸倒れ損失
commercial credit recovery　償却商業貸出金回収
commercial loan　商業貸出, 商業用貸出, 商業貸付け, 民間融資, 短期銀行融資, 市中借入れ, 商業貸出金, コマーシャル・ローン
commercial and industrial loans　商工業貸出, 商工業融資, 商工業向け融資, 商工融資
commercial loan demand　商業銀行業務の融資需要, 市中の借入需要
commercial loan investments　商業用貸出投資
commercial mortgage　商業［商業用］不動産抵当貸付け, 商業［商業用］不動産ローン, 商業モーゲージ
commercial mortgage book　商業用モーゲージ残高
commercial mortgage borrowing　商業［商業用］不動産ローンの借入れ
commercial mortgage delinquency rates　抵当貸付け債務不履行率
commercial［income］property mortgage loan　商業抵当貸付け
nonperforming commercial mortgage　契約不履行の商業不動産ローン
commercial mortgage-backed securities　商業用不動産ローン担保証券, 商業用不動産担保証券, CMBS
◆Wider spreads were also seen in the market for commercial mortgage-backed securities. 金利差（スプレッド）の拡大は、商業用不動産担保証券の市場でも見られた。
commercial paper　商業証券, 商業手形, コマーシャル・ペーパー, CP
asset-backed commercial paper　資産担保CP
commercial paper and similar obligations　商業手形他
commercial paper composite index　CP複合指標
commercial paper house　手形業者

commercial paper outstanding　CP発行残高
commercial paper purchased　買入れCO
Euro commercial [Eurocommercial] paper　ユーロCP
Euro yen commercial paper　ユーロ円CP
issuance of commercial paper　CPの発行, コマーシャル・ペーパーの発行
issue commercial paper and other debt instruments　CPなどの債務証券を発行する
pay off maturing commercial paper　満期を迎えたCPを償還する
repayment of commercial paper　コマーシャル・ペーパーの返済
samurai commercial paper　サムライCP
tax-exempt commercial paper　非課税CP, 免税CP
US commercial paper　米国コマーシャル・ペーパー, 米国CP
◆Asset-backed commercial paper refers to commercial paper whose creditworthiness is guaranteed by sales credit that the corporate issuer has with its debtors. 資産担保CPとは、企業発行体がその債務者に対して保有する売掛金によって信用度が保証されるコマーシャル・ペーパーを指す。◆Higher debt maturing within one year chiefly reflects commercial paper we issued to support financial services. 1年以内返済予定の負債の増加は、主に金融サービス部門の支援のため、当社がコマーシャル・ペーパーを発行したことを反映しています。
解説　コマーシャル・ペーパーとは：為替手形 (bill of exchange, draft)、約束手形 (note, promissory note)、小切手 (check) や預金証書 (certificate of deposit) などを指し、流通証券 (negotiable instrument) と同義。米国では、資金調達のために優良企業が発行する通常2日～270日以内の短期約束手形のこと。

commercial real estate　商業用不動産
commercial real estate exposure　商業用不動産融資
commercial real estate lending　商業用不動産融資
commercial real estate loan　商業用不動産融資
commercial real estate market　商業用不動産市場
vacancy rate of commercial real estate　商業用不動産の空室率

commercialization　(名)商品化, 製品化, 商業化, 実用化, 営利化
◆There can be huge financial rewards from the successful commercialization of technology. 技術の商品化に成功すると、巨額の金銭的な報酬が得られる。

commingled equity fund　合同運用株式ファンド
commingled (investment) fund　合同運用型ファンド

commission　(動)権限を与える, (仕事などを)委託する, 委任する, 任命する, (制作や執筆などを)依頼する, (艦船などを)就役させる
chief commissioned bank　主受託銀行
commissioned bank　受託銀行
◆According to sources, Tokyo Electric Power Co. will commission four trust banks to sell its assets. 関係者によると、東京電力は4信託銀行に保有資産の売却業務を委託する。◆The former senior official of a foreign securities sales department commissioned a Singapore bank to conduct his asset management. 外国証券営業部の元部長は、シンガポールの銀行に自己資産の運用を委託していた。

commission　(名)手数料, 株式引受手数料, 報酬, 口銭, 委任, 委任状, 委託, 代理業務, 授与, 授権, 任命, 任命書, 委員会, 責務, 任務, 権限, 職権, 過失, 作為, 犯行, 犯罪などの実行, コミッション
acceptance commission　手形引受手数料
additional commission　追加手数料

agency [agent] commission　代理店手数料
bank [banker's] commission　銀行手数料
brokerage commission　株式委託売買手数料, 委託売買手数料, 委託手数料, 仲介手数料, ブローカー手数料 (=brokerage fee; ⇒commodity futures trading)
ceding commission　出再手数料
ceding commissions paid or received　支払い再保険料ないし受取再保険料
charge a five percent commission for [on]　～に[～について]5%の手数料を取る
charges and commissions　支払い手数料
charges and commissions received　受入れ手数料
commission and expenses on capital shares　株式発行費用
commission based representative　歩合制の外務員, 歩合外務員
commission broker　手数料ブローカー, コミッション・ブローカー
commission charged　請求手数料
commission house　株式仲買店, 委託販売店
commission income and expense　受入れ手数料と支払い手数料
commission income from securities transactions　有価証券売買委託手数料収入
commission on brokered deposits　ブローカー預金の手数料
commission on issue of shares and debentures　株式・社債発行手数料
commission on underwriting　引受手数料
commission rate　手数料率
commission system　手数料制, 歩合給制度, 歩合い制
Commodities Exchange Commission　商品取引所委員会
Commodity Futures Trading Commission　米国の商品先物取引委員会 (⇒charge動詞)
confirmation and payment commission　(信用状)確認・支払い手数料
earn [make] a commission　手数料を得る
Fair Trade Commission　公正取引委員会
Federal Trade Commission　米連邦取引委員会
fixed commission　固定手数料
foreign exchange commission　外国為替手数料
futures commission agent [merchant]　先物取引業者, 先物取引ブローカー
get a commission　手数料をもらう
insurance commissions　保険監督機関
Interamerican Association of Securities Commissions　米州証券監督者協会
Interstate Commerce Commission　米州際通商委員会
maximum commission　最高手数料
minimum commission　最低手数料
negotiation commission　買取り手数料
offer [pay] a commission　手数料を払う
opening commission　発行手数料
placement commission　販売手数料
prepaid commission　前払い手数料
sale on commission　歩合制による販売
sales commission　販売手数料
stock exchange introduction commission　上場紹介手数料, 上場のための紹介手数料
underwriting commission　引受手数料
United States International Trade Commission　合衆国国際貿易委員会
◆According to a commodity futures market insider, futures

brokerages depending on commissions for revenue will lose their business strength. 商品先物市場関係者によると、収入を手数料に頼っている先物会社の経営体力は、今後弱まりそうだ。◆If the securities firms rush to cut these commissions, they may not be able to continue to rely on income from commissions as a major source of profit. これらの証券会社が手数料の値引き競争に走れば、主な収益源として株式の売買委託手数料による収入に今後とも頼ることは難しくなる。◆In the case of foreign currency deposits by the U.S. dollar, many online banks charge about ￥0.25 in commission per dollar at the time of deposits and withdrawals. 米ドルによる外貨預金の場合、ネット銀行の多くは、預け入れ時と解約時に1ドルに付き25銭程度の手数料を取る。◆Olympus ostensibly paid about ￥70 billion in commissions to two investment advisers when the company acquired a British medical equipment maker for about ￥210 billion. オリンパスが英国の医療機器メーカーを約2,100億円で買収した際、同社は表向きには仲介手数料として約700億円を投資助言会社2社に支払った。◆Securities firms can earn commissions and other revenue through helping firms go public. 証券会社は、企業の上場を手伝うことにより、株式引受手数料などの収益を上げることができる。◆The bank collected commissions for purchasing loan claims from financially strapped moneylenders. 同行は、資金繰りに困っている貸金業者から貸出債権を買い取るのに、手数料を徴収していた。

commission fees 手数料、為替手数料
◆In foreign currency deposits, commission fees are needed when the yen is exchanged into a foreign currency and when the foreign currency is exchanged backed in yen. 外貨預金では、円を外貨に替えるときと、外貨を円に戻すときに、為替手数料が必要になる。◆Olympus fired its president who had pointed out the integrity of the acquisition and commission fees. オリンパスは、買収額や買収手数料の適正性を指摘した社長を解任した。◆We must pay attention to commission fees when we choose to deposit foreign currencies. 外貨預金を選ぶときは、為替手数料に注意しなければならない。

commission rate 手数料率、為替手数料の料率
◆Commission rates in foreign currency deposits vary among foreign currencies or among financial institutions. 外貨預金での為替手数料の料率は、外国通貨や金融機関で異なる。◆Some major banks lower their commission rates of foreign currency deposits if depositors make transactions via online accounts. 外貨預金の預金者がネット口座経由で取引をする場合、一部の大手銀行は、外貨預金の手数料[為替手数料]の料率を引き下げている。

commission revenue 手数料収入
◆It is a matter of urgency to ensure that banks make profit margins that can meet investment risks and that they expand commission revenue as well as promote sweeping restructurings. 抜本的なリストラ推進のほか、投資リスクに見合う利ざやの確保と手数料収入の拡大などが銀行の急務だ。

commissioner (名)委員、理事、監督官、長官、コミッショナー
　commissioner of banking 米州銀行局監督官
　　(=superintendent of banking)
　commissioner of insurance （米州の）保険監督官、保険局長
　Commissioner of Internal Revenue 米国税庁長官
　National Association of Insurance Commissioners 全米保険監督官協会
　National Convention of Insurance Commissioners 全国保険協定委員会
　National Debt Commissioner 英国債務局
◆Business Accounting Council is an advisory body to the commissioner of the Financial Services Agency. 企業会計審議会は、金融庁長官の諮問機関である。

commit (動)（罪、違法なことを）行う、する、犯す、約束する、公約する、確約する、取り組む、関わる、専念する、全力を挙げる、尽力する、引き受ける、委託する、委任する、付す、（法案や議案を）委員会に付託する、（刑務所、精神病院などに）送りこむ、収容［収監］する、（～することを）求める、規定する、（時間や資金などを）用いる、支出する、（名声や立場などを）危うくする
　be committed for trial 裁判にかけられる
　be committed to ～する決意である、～すると誓う、～すると言明する、(主義、主張に)献身的である、傾倒する、～に打ち込んでいる、～に尽力する、～に全力を挙げる
　become committed in the matter この問題にはまり込む
　commit a bill 法案を委員会に付託する、法案[議案]を委員会の審議に付す
　commit a small amount of time to ～に時間を少し割く
　commit oneself 明確に意見を述べる、明確に陳述する
　commit oneself on ～について自分[自己]の立場を明らかにする
　commit oneself to ～の立場を鮮明にする、～を明言する、～を引き受ける、（要求などを）飲む、～を公約する、～する方針を定める、～に身を投ずる決意を固める、～に深く関与する[関わり合う]
　commit oneself to a promise 確約する
　refuse to commit oneself on the matter この問題に対する明言を避ける
　repeatedly commit acts contrary to the public goods 公益に反する行為を繰り返して行う
　　(⇒public goods)
◆Advanced economies have committed to at least halve fiscal deficits by 2013. 先進国は、2013年までに財政赤字を少なくとも半減させることを公約した。◆The G-7's financial ministers and central bank governors are committed to taking necessary measures to support financial stability and economic growth. 先進7か国（G7）の財務相と中央銀行総裁は、金融安定化と経済成長を支えるためにあらゆる手段を講じる決意だ。

commitment (名)委任、委託、公約、誓約、確約、約束、立場の明確な表明、協調融資団への参加意思表示、融資参加の意向表明、融資先、姿勢、取組、売買約定、売買契約、取引契約、未履行債務、コミットメント
　ability to meet commitments to debtholders 債務返済能力
　acceptance commitment 引受債務
　aid commitments 援助約束額
　amount of commitment of resources 融資承認額
　bank's largest commitment 銀行の最大の融資先
　capital commitments 資本参加、出資
　commitment clause 融資約定
　commitment fee 約定料、契約手数料、コミットメント・フィー
　commitment to guarantee 保証予約
　commitment to offtake up 買取り保証
　commitments 引受額、参加額、応募額、契約債務
　commitments and contingent liabilities 契約債務と偶発債務
　contractual lending commitment 契約に基づく貸出義務、貸出予約
　equity commitment note 株式転換約定付き社債
　executory commitment 未履行契約
　financial commitment 資金協力、財政的約定
　firm commitment 買取り引受け、全額引受け、確定契約、成約済み取引
　firm commitment underwriting 買取り引受け
　forward commitments to purchase assets 将来の資産購入

契約
irrevocable revolving commitment　取消し不能回転契約
issuer's ability to meet commitments to debtholders［meet debtholder commitments］　発行体の債務返済能力
lease commitments　リース契約, 賃貸借契約, 賃借義務
letter of commitment　支払い引受書, LC
loan commitment　貸出約定, 融資契約, 融資確約
long-term credit commitment　長期与信契約
make substantial commitments to the market　市場に本格的に進出する
meet debt commitments　債務を返済する
mortgage commitments　モーゲージ承認件数
new commitments　新規ローン約定
new lending commitments　新規融資承認額
new loans commitments　新規融資契約, 新規融資承認額
ODA commitments　ODA約束額
outstanding commitments written　貸付け契約未履行残高
suspension of new commitments　新規ローン約定の差し止め
total commitments　総引受額, 応募総額, 融資総額, 貸付け金の総額
underwriting commitment　引受参加申込み, 引受額
unused commitments　未実行貸出残高
unused portions of commitments　貸出枠未実行残高
◆These financial instruments include commitments to extend credit, letters of credit, guarantees of debt, interest rate swaps and cap agreements, and foreign currency exchange contracts.　これらの金融商品には、信用供与契約、信用状、債務保証、金利スワップおよび金利キャップ契約と外国為替予約が含まれています。◆We had commitments of corporate funds totaling $1 million, plus a Foundation grant award of $50,000.　われわれは総額100万ドルの会社資金のほかに、5万ドルの当財団義援金の確約を得ました。

commitment line　融資枠, コミットメント・ライン
解説 コミットメント・ラインとは：銀行から一定の範囲で自由に借入れができる融資枠の設定のこと。コミットメント・ラインを設定すると、金融機関は安定した手数料収入が得られるほか、優良企業との取引拡大を期待できる。また、企業にとっては、手数料を払う代わりに金利ゼロで融資を受けられるメリットがある。緊急の資金需要に備えられるほか、資金効率の改善効果もある。最近は、経営不振の企業が、信用不安を解消するため主力取引銀行とコミットメント・ライン契約を結ぶことが多い。

committed　（形）約束された, 委託された, 契約に基づく, 与信枠を設けている［設定している］
capital committed　受託資本
committed bank facilities　契約に基づく銀行借入枠
committed bank lines of credit　銀行の信用供与枠
committed costs　決定済み費用
committed finance　受託資金
committed lenders　与信枠を設けている銀行
committed savings　積立型貯蓄

Committee of European Banking Supervisors　欧州銀行監督委員会　（欧州連合(EU)27か国の金融当局で構成。⇒capital shortfall）
◆The EU's Committee of European Banking Supervisors announced the results of a stress test of Europe's major 91 banks.　欧州連合(EU)の欧州銀行監査委員会が、域内の主要91銀行のストレス・テスト（財務の健全性を調べる特別検査）を発表した。◆The stress test by the EU's Committee of European Banking Supervisors measured the financial strength of Europe's major banks.　欧州連合(EU)の欧州銀行監督委員会が行ったストレス・テストで、域内主要銀行の財務の健全性を調べた。◆The stress test results announced by the Committee of European Banking Supervisors are not sufficient to dispel Europe's financial unrest.　欧州銀行監督委員会が発表したストレス・テスト（特別検査）の結果だけで、欧州の金融不安を払拭（ふっしょく）するのは難しい。

commodity　（名）商品, 市況商品, 市況品, 日用品, 製品, 産品, 物品, 生産物, 必需品, 財貨, 財
Commodities Exchange Commission　商品取引所委員会, CEC
commodities in general　市況商品
commodities investment trust　商品投資信託
commodity-backed bond　商品担保社債, 商品償還社債
commodity bill　商品手形
commodity capital　商品資本
commodity commission　商品売買手数料
commodity compensation finance　商品補償融資
commodity credit　商品信用, 商品金融
Commodity Credit Corporation　米商品金融公社, CCC
commodity currency　商品通貨
commodity dealing capital　商品取扱い資本
commodity deals　普通債
commodity dividend　財貨配当, 物品配当
commodity dollar　商品ドル
commodity draft　商品代金取立て手形
commodity flow　財貨の流れ, 財貨流通, コモディティ・フロー
commodity fund　商品ファンド
commodity insurance　商品保険
commodity-linked note　商品リンク債
commodity loan　商品貸借形式の金融, 商品借款
commodity monetary standard　商品貨幣本位制
commodity money　商品貨幣, 物品貨幣, 実物貨幣
commodity option　商品オプション
commodity paper　商品手形, 貨物証券
commodity rate　倉庫証券担保手形優遇レート, 商品別［品目別］運賃
commodity rate of interest　財貨利子率, 商品利子率
Commodity Research Bureau Futures Price Index　CRB商品先物指数
Commodity Research Bureau's index of spot market prices　CRB商品現物指数
commodity reserve currency［money］　商品準備通貨, 商品準備貨幣
commodity security　商品証券
commodity speculation　商品投機
commodity trading adviser［advisor］　商品取引投資顧問, 商品投資顧問会社
commodity transaction　商品取引
commodity via bonds　債券による商品
commodity via money　貨幣による商品
composite commodity　合成財
currency commodity　通貨商品, 貨幣商品
depository instruments with commodity-linked components　商品リンク付き預金商品
exchange-sensitive commodity　為替相場［為替レート］の動きに敏感な商品
investment commodity　投資財
listed commodity　上場商品
◆Sharp rises in the price of crude oil and other commodity would push up consumer prices.　原油など市況商品の価格急騰は、消費者物価を押し上げることになろう。◆Speculative investors are shifting from commodities to stocks.　投機資金が、商品から株式に移っている。

commodity exchange　商品取引, 商品取引所
　Commodity Exchange Act of 1936　1936年商品取引所法
　Commodity Exchange Authority　商品取引所監督局
　London Commodity Exchange　ロンドン商品取引所
　Tokyo Commodity Exchange　東京工業品取引所, TOCOM
　US Commodity Exchange Act　米国商品取引法
　◆Recently, a sizable amount of speculative funds have been flowing into New York's commodities exchanges. このところ、ニューヨークの商品取引所には、大量の投機資金が流入している。◆The benchmark gold future price topped ￥4,700 per gram for the first time on the Tokyo Commodity Exchange. 東京工業品取引所で、金取引の指標となる金先物価格が、史上初めて1グラム＝4,700円を突破した。

Commodity Exchange Law　商品取引所法
　（⇒commodity futures market）
　◆The revised Commodity Exchange Law includes a prohibition on futures brokerages from soliciting people aged 75 or older and those whose annual income is under ￥5 million. 改正商品取引所法には、75歳以上の高齢者や年収500万円未満の人への先物会社の勧誘禁止が盛り込まれている[定められている]。

commodity futures brokerage　商品先物会社, 先物会社, 先物商品会社　（⇒financial documents）
　◆The failed commodity futures brokerage was found to have illegally used customer assets as operating capital. この経営破たんした先物商品会社は、顧客からの預り資産を運転資金に流用していたことが分かった。

commodity futures market　商品先物市場
　（⇒futures market, insider）
　◆Online trading will surely proliferate in the commodity futures market. ネット取引は、商品先物市場でも普及するはずだ。◆The revised Commodity Exchange Law was put into force in May 2005 to improve the integrity of the commodity futures market. 商品先物市場の信頼性を高めるため、2005年5月に改正商品取引所法が施行された。◆Two companies' accumulated know-how in online trading will be useful in the commodity futures market. 商品先物市場では、両社の蓄積しているネット取引のノウハウが役に立つだろう。

commodity futures market insider　商品先物市場関係者
　◆According to a commodity futures market insider, futures brokerages depending on commissions for revenue will lose their business strength. 商品先物市場関係者によると、収入を手数料に頼っている先物会社の経営体力は、今後弱まりそうだ。

commodity futures trading　商品先物取引　（金や石油などの商品について、一定の値段で将来売買することを約束して行う取引で、価格は取引契約を結ぶ時点で決める。⇒liberalization, underlying asset）
　◆Brokerage commissions on commodity futures trading were completely liberalized in late 2004. 商品先物取引の委託手数料は、2004年末に完全自由化された。◆In commodity futures trading, precious metals, petroleum products and other goods are traded. 商品先物取引では、貴金属や石油製品などの商品が取引されている。◆In commodity futures trading, prices are decided when buyers and sellers make deals. So they can execute trades at promised prices even if the value of goods has changed drastically in the meantime. 商品先物取引では、売り手と買い手が取引契約をする時点で価格を決める。そのため、契約期間中に相場が大きく変動しても、売り手と買い手は約束した値段で取引を執行できる。

Commodity Futures Trading Commission　米商品先物取引委員会
　◆The U.S. Commodity Futures Trading Commission charged one investment fund with gaining illicit profits by manipulating crude oil and other markets. 米国の商品先物取引委員会は、原油市場などで不正な利益を上げたとして、投資ファンドの一つを摘発した。

commodity futures trading industry　商品先物取引業界
　◆Moves toward a full-scale realignment have been accelerating in the commodity futures trading industry, involving companies from other business fields. 商品先物取引業界では、異業種の企業を巻き込んだ総力を挙げての再編の動きが加速している。◆The commodity futures trading industry has entered an era of white-hot competition in an all-out struggle for survival. 商品先物取引業界は、生き残りをかけた総力戦で大競争の時代に入っている。

commodity index　商品指数
　commodity index futures　商品指数先物
　commodity price index　商品価格指数
　Dow-Jones commodity index　ダウ・ジョーンズ商品［商品相場］指数
　Nikkei Commodity Index（42 items）　日経商品指数（42種）

commodity market　商品市場
　◆The commodity market of crude futures has become increasingly speculative. 原油先物の商品市場は、次第に投機色を強めている。

commodity price　商品価格, 市況商品価格, 物価
　commodity price indication　商品価格指数
　commodity price policy　物価政策
　commodity price swap　商品価格スワップ
　CRB index of commodity prices　CRB商品指数
　Financial Times index of world sensitive commodity prices　フィナンシャル・タイムズ商品相場指数
　fixed-for-floating-commodity-price-swap　固定・変動価格商品スワップ
　index of commodity prices　商品価格指数
　　（＝commodity price index）
　Nikkei commodity price index for 42 commodities　日経商品指数（42種）
　Nikkei Index of Commodity Prices　日経主要商品価格指数
　Nikkei World Commodity Price Index　日経国債商品指数
　real commodity prices　実質ベースの市況商品価格
　Reuter's index of commodity prices　ロイター商品相場指数
　◆Domestic commodity prices have fallen 54 consecutive months. 国内物価は、54か月［4年半］連続して下落している。

common　（形）共通の, 共同の, 普通の
　common benefit fee　共益費
　common coins　国内通貨
　common collateral　共通担保
　common disaster　同時災害
　common disaster clause　同時災害条項
　common dividend　普通配当, 普通株配当金
　common dividend payout　普通株配当性向
　common dollar　共通ドル
　common external tariff　域外共通関税
　common fund　共通基金
　common law mortgage　普通法上の譲渡抵当
　common market　共同市場
　common ownership　共有
　common property　共有財産
　common seal of a company　社印
　common stockholders' equity　普通株主資本
　common stockholders' equity per share　1株当たり普通株

株主持ち分
common tariff　共通関税
common trust fund　共同信託基金
common currency　共通通貨
　◆European countries are deepening and expanding economic union by introducing a common currency and welcoming East European countries into the European Union. 欧州は、共通通貨の導入や東欧諸国のEU（欧州連合）への取り込みなどで、経済統合の深化と拡大を続けている。◆The EU uses a common currency called the euro. 欧州連合（EU）は、ユーロという共通通貨を使っている。
common equity　普通株式
　return on average common equity　平均普通株主資本利益率
　the market value of common equity　普通株式の時価総額
　◆The company raised $68 million of common equity during the first half of 2011, principally by means of the Dividend Reinvestment and Stock Purchase Plan. 同社は2011年上半期に、主に株主配当再投資・株式購入制度により普通株式を発行して、6,800万ドルを調達した。
common euro bond　ユーロ共通債
　◆The leaders of EU countries failed to agree on a common euro bond to be jointly issued by eurozone countries due to Germany's objections. 欧州連合（EU）各国首脳は、ユーロ圏が共同で発行するユーロ共通債について、ドイツの反対で合意できなかった。
common eurozone [euro-area] bonds　ユーロ圏の共通債券, ユーロ圏共通債
　◆German Chancellor Angela Merkel shut the door on the introduction of common eurozone bonds as a means to solve the debt crisis. ドイツのメルケル首相は、欧州債務危機問題の解決手段としてユーロ圏共通債を導入することに強く反対した。
common share　普通株, 普通株式, 普通株資本金, 資本金（=common equity, common stock, ordinary share, ordinary stock: 普通株は、優先株（preferred share, preferred stock）や後配株（deferred share, deferred stock）のように特別の権利内容を持たない一般の株式のこと。⇒common stock, debt load, deferred share, privately place, quarterly dividend）
　be organized with A authorized shares of $B per value common share　普通株式額面Bドルの授権株式数A株で設立される
　income available to common shares　普通株主に帰属する利益
　issue common shares　普通株式を発行する
　primary earnings per common share　単純希薄化による普通株式1株当たり利益
　weighted average number of common shares outstanding　外部発行普通株式の加重平均
　◆Hokuetsu Paper issued 50 million common shares to Mitsubishi Corp. for ￥30.35 billion, or ￥607 per share. 北越製紙は、三菱商事を引受先として303億5,000万円（1株当たり607円）で普通株式5,000万株を発行した。◆Seiyu will issue 20.5 million common shares at a price of ￥222 per share. 西友は、1株当たり222円で［222円の価格で］普通株式2,050万株を発行する。◆The approval of numerous stockholders must be gained for a retirement of 50 percent of common shares. 普通株式の50%消却については、多くの株主の承認を得なければならない。◆The firm owned approximately 19 percent of the common shares of XYZ Inc. as at March 31, 2011. 同社は、2011年3月31日現在、XYZ社の普通株式の約19%を所有している。◆The reconstruction plan includes the retirement of 50 percent of the firm's common shares. 経営再建策には、同社の普通株の5割消却も含まれている。
common shares outstanding　発行済み普通株式, 発行済み社外流通株式, 普通株式発行総数
　◆We acquired 100 percent of the common shares outstanding of the company for a total consideration of $850 million. 当社は、対価総額8億5,000万ドルで、同社の発行済み普通株式を100%取得しました。
common stock　普通株, 普通株式, 普通株資本金, 資本金（=common share, ordinary share, ordinary stock; ⇒ convertible bond, issued and outstanding）
　a single class of common stock　単一クラスの普通株式
　an exchange of common stock　普通株式の交換
　common stock at par　額面普通株資本
　common stock beta　普通株のベータ値
　common stock equity　普通株主持ち分
　common stock fund　普通株ファンド
　common stock in treasury　自己普通株式, 自社株
　common stock issued and outstanding　普通株式発行済み株式数
　common stock market price　株式の市場価格
　common stock ratio　普通株比率
　common stock share equity　普通株式
　cost of common stock　普通株式の資本コスト
　debt payable in common stock　普通株式で返済可能な債券
　earnings per share of common stock　普通株式1株当たり利益
　issuance of common stock　普通株式の発行
　new common stock　新発普通株
　newly issued common stock　新規発行普通株式
　outstanding common stocks　発行済み普通株式, 外部発行済み普通株式, 発行済み普通株式総数（⇒conversion right）
　par value of common stock　普通株の額面
　potable common stock　プット・オプション付き普通株式
　primary earnings per share of common stock　普通株式1株当たり基本的利益
　put options on common stock　普通株式に対するプット・オプション
　sale of common stock in the offerings　公募による普通株式発行
　sell common stock at book value　簿価で普通株式を発行する
　stock dividend on common stock　普通株式に対する株式配当
　unaffiliated common stock　非関連会社普通株
　voting common stock　議決権付き普通株式
　◆At current stock prices, Daiwa Securities could obtain the equivalent of more than 10 percent of Fuji TV's outstanding common stocks if it exercised the conversion right. 現在の株価（株価水準）だと、転換権を行使した場合、大和証券はフジテレビの発行済み株式総数の10%以上の株式を取得できる。◆Book value per share refers to the amount of net assets of a company represented by one share of common stock. 1株当たり純資産［簿価］とは、普通株式1株当たりの企業の純資産額のことを言う。◆The company is to issue ￥220 billion in preferred stocks and ￥10 billion in common stocks. 同社は、優先株を2,200億円、普通株を100億円発行する。◆The new regulations decided on by the Basel Committee on Banking Supervision require banks to increase the core tier 1 capital, such as common stock and retained earnings that they must hold in reserve, to at least 4.5 percent of assets from the current 2 percent. バーゼル銀行監督委員会が決めた新規制は、銀行が支払い準備として保有しなければならない普通株や利益剰余金［内部留保］などの中核的自己資本（コア・ティア1）を、現行の資産の最低2%から4.5%に引き上げるよう銀行に義

務付けている。◆The new shares of common stock are being allocated to plan participants over ten years as contributions are made to the plan. この普通株式新株は、制度への資金拠出と並行して、10年にわたり制度加入者に割り当てられています。

common stock equivalent 準普通株式
◆The 8% convertible bonds are convertible into 40 shares of common stock for each $1,000 bond, and were not considered common stock equivalents at the date of issuance. 8%利付き転換社債は、1,000ドルの社債についてそれぞれ普通株式40株に転換できるが、発行時には準普通株式とは考えられなかった。

communique （名）声明, 公式発表, 公報, 声明書, コミュニケ
  a joint communique released by the G-7 [G7] 先進7か国会議（G7）の共同声明
  adopt a communique 共同声明を採択する
  issue [release] a joint communique 共同声明を発表する, 共同コミュニケを発表する
◆After a two day meeting in Paris, the financial chiefs and central bank governors from the Group of 20 leading economies adopted a communique. パリで開かれた2日間の会議の後、主要20か国・地域（G20）の財務相・中央銀行総裁は共同声明を採択した。◆The G-20 communique urged the eurozone countries to boost the EFSF, the EU bailout fund. G20（主要20か国・地域）の共同声明は、ユーロ圏諸国に欧州の金融支援基金である欧州金融安定基金（EFSF）の拡充を促した。

community （名）地域社会, 共同社会, 社会, 共同体, 団体, 業界, ～界, 共有, 共用, コミュニティ
  business community 経済界, 財界, 産業界, 実業界（=business circles, business world）
  community activities 地域社会活動
  community bank コミュニティ・バンク
  community banking コミュニティ・バンキング（地域社会密着型の銀行の営業活動）
  community-based services 地域密着型のサービス, 地域密着型の営業活動
  community charge 地域社会税
  community chest 共同募金, 共同募金による基金（=community fund）
  community property 夫婦共有財産, 共有財産
  community reinvestment 地域再投資, 地域再開発
  Community Reinvestment Act 地域再投資法, 地域社会還元法, CRA
  community relations 地域社会との関係, 対地域社会関係, 地域社会との良好な関係維持, 地域社会PR, 地域社会関連活動, 地域社会活動, CR
  community service 地域社会サービス
  community trust 地域社会信託
  economic community 経済界, 財界, 経済圏
  financial community 金融界, 金融業界
  investment banking community 投資銀行業界
  investment community 投資業界
  underwriting community 引受業界
  Web-based community ウェブ上のコミュニティ
◆Bank of Yokohama hopes to compete with major financial groups by providing community-based services. 横浜銀行は、地域密着型の営業活動を展開して、大手金融グループに対抗する方針だ。

community development 地域開発, コミュニティ開発
  community development credit union コミュニティ開発クレジット・ユニオン
  community development loan fund コミュニティ開発ローン基金
  community development venture capital fund コミュニティ開発ベンチャー・キャピタル基金

community development bank コミュニティ開発銀行, 地域開発銀行
◆U.S. regulators closed Chicago-based community development bank ShoreBank. 米規制当局が、シカゴを拠点とする地域開発銀行のショアバンクを閉鎖した。

community development financial institutions コミュニティ開発金融機関, 地域開発金融機関, CDFI
◆Wall Street backers failed to rescue community development financial institution ShoreBank in Chicago. 米金融界の支援企業は、シカゴの地域開発金融機関「ショアバンク」を救済できなかった。

company （名）会社, 企業, 社団, カンパニー （⇒holding company, insurance company, joint stock company, special purpose company, stock company）
  acquired company 被買収会社
  affiliated company 関係会社, 関連会社, 系列会社
  business company 事業会社
  comparable company 類似会社, 類似企業
  fifty-percent-owned company 半数所有会社, 50%所有会社
  joint stock company 株式会社
  Limited Liability Company Law 有限会社法
  listed company 上場企業, 上場会社
  majority owned company 過半数所有会社
  open company 公開会社
  parent company 親会社
  private company 非公開会社, 株式非公開会社, 民間企業
  privately held company 非公開会社, 株式非公開会社, 非上場会社
  public company 株式公開会社, 上場会社, 上場企業
  publicly held company 株式公開企業, 株式公開会社, 上場会社
  quoted company 上場企業, 上場会社
  sister company 姉妹会社
  special purpose company 特別目的会社, 特定目的会社
  subsidiary company 子会社
  target company 買収対象会社, ターゲット・カンパニー
  unlisted company 非上場企業, 非上場会社
◆The new companies to be created after privatizing the public corporations will prepare the same financial statements as any other ordinary private companies. 公団民営化後に設立される新会社は、他の一般の民間企業と同様の財務諸表を作成することになる。

company employee 会社員, 社員, 会社の従業員
◆Full-time housewives of company employees and public servants are not required to pay pension premiums. 会社員や公務員の専業主婦は、保険料を払う必要がない。◆Nonworking spouses of public servants and company employees are classified as Category III insured. 公務員や会社員の仕事を持たない配偶者は、第3号被保険者と呼ばれている。

company employees' pension scheme 厚生年金制度, 厚生年金（=company employees' pension system）
◆Under the company employees' pension scheme, subscribing is mandatory for all firms with five or more employees. 厚生年金制度では、従業員5人以上の法人すべてに加入が義務づけられている

compared to [with] ～と比較して, ～と比べて, ～に対して, ～比で
  compared to a year earlier 前年比で, 前期比で, 前年同期比で

compared to the corresponding period last year 前年同期比で
compared with the same month a year ago 前年同月比で
◆The deflator, which indicates the overall trend in prices, dropped 2.5 percent in the April-June period compared to the corresponding period last year. 物価の総合的な動向を示すデフレーターは、4-6月期は前年同期比で2.5%下落した。◆The diffusion index of business sentiment among large manufacturers rose four points to 26, compared with the previous survey for the three months to June. 大企業・製造業の業況判断指数(DI)は、前回の6月調査(4-6月調査)に比べて4ポイント上昇の26となった。

compensate (動)補償する,補てんする,埋め合わせる,補う,相殺する,カバーする
  compensate by balancing losses with ～で穴を埋める
  compensate for a squeeze in margins 利ざやの縮小をカバーする
  compensate for loss of earnings 失われた収入を補償する,収入の損失を補う
◆In the lawsuits against big banks over the sales of risky investments, the U.S. government wants to be compensated for lost principal and interest payments. 高リスク証券の販売をめぐっての大手金融機関に対する訴訟で、米政府は、元本と利払い分の損失補償を求めている。

compensating (形)補償する,埋め合わせる,求償の,補整的な
  compensating balance 見合い預金,歩積み両建て預金,拘束預金,コンペ・バランス
  compensating deal 求償貿易
    (＝compensation trade)
  compensating duties 相殺関税
  compensating interest (預金の)相殺利子
  compensating official financing 補整的金融
  compensating payment 補整的支払い

compensation (名)報酬,対価,給与,報償,手当て,補償,賠償,代償,報償金,補償金,賠償金,慰謝料 (⇒ approach動詞, coverage, executive, seek compensation from, workers compensation insurance system)
  accident[disaster]compensation 災害補償
  as[in]compensation for ～の補償[賠償]として,～の対価として
  commodity compensation finance 商品補償融資
  compensation balance 見合い預金,コンペ・バランス
  compensation bond 交付公債
  compensation by brokerage houses for the stock market losses 証券会社の損失補てん
  compensation for damages[losses] 損害賠償
  compensation insurance 補償保険
  compensation stock 政府補償株
  compensation trade 求償貿易
  dismissal compensation 解雇手当て
  executive compensation 役員報酬
  financial compensation 賠償金,金銭的報酬,金銭的代償
  government compensation bond 交付公債
  incentive compensation plan 奨励報償制度,インセンティブ報酬制度
  income compensation insurance 所得補償保険
  investors' compensation scheme 投資家補償制度
  liability and compensation insurance 責任補償保険
  loss compensation 損失補償
  lump sum compensation 補償一時金
  multilateral compensation 多角相殺
  multilateral monetary compensation 多角的通貨相殺
  national compensation 国家賠償
  pecuniary compensation 金銭的補償
  raise money for compensation 賠償資金を調達する
  seek compensation from ～に補償を求める,～に賠償請求する
  stock compensation plan 株式報償制度,株式報酬プラン
  unemployment compensation 失業給付,失業手当て,失業補償
  worker's compensation insurance 労災保険
  workmen's accident compensation 労災補償,労働者災害補償
◆Banks will not pay compensation when depositors tell other people their PINs. 預金者が他人に暗証番号を知らせた場合、銀行は補償しない。◆Proceeds from exercising stock options are compensation for labor and service rendered and constitute salary income. ストック・オプション(自社株購入権)を行使して得た利益は、職務遂行の対価なので、給与所得に当たる。◆Retail outlets that suffer loss as a result of fraud can also claim compensation from card issuers. 不正使用により損害を被っている小売り加盟店側も、カード会社に賠償金を請求できる。◆The government established an organization to smoothly provide compensation to the victims of the nuclear disaster. 政府は、原発事故被害者への損害賠償を円滑に進めるための新組織(原子力損害賠償支援機構)を設立した。◆To raise money for compensation related to the Fukushima No. 1 nuclear power plant crisis, TEPCO will sell off assets through four trust banks. 福島第一原発事故関連の賠償資金を調達するため、東電は、4信託銀行を通じて資産を売却することになった。◆Toshiba may demand damage compensation from Sony, and others may follow suit. 東芝はソニーに対する損害賠償請求を検討しており、他社もこれに追随する可能性がある。◆Without the government financial support, TEPCO will fall into debt as the utility has to pay the huge amounts in compensation. 政府の金融支援がなければ、東電は巨額の賠償金を支払わなければならないので、債務超過に陥ると思われる。

compensation for losses 損害補償,損害賠償,損害賠償金,損失補てん (＝compensation for damages)
◆Compensation for the losses was made by transferring funds to accounts set up for the hotels' operations. 損失の補てんは、ホテル事業のために設けられた口座に資金を繰り入れて行われた。◆The KEDO agreement requires the consortium and the North Korea to sign a protocol on compensation for losses due to any accidents that occur during the building of the two LWRs. KEDO(朝鮮半島エネルギー開発機構)の北朝鮮への軽水炉供給協定は、軽水炉2基の工事中に起きた事故による損害賠償に関する協定書に署名するようKEDOと北朝鮮に求めている。

compensation of losses 損失の穴埋め,損失補てん
◆A bill to revise the Law on Special Measures for Strengthening Financial Functions is designed to facilitate the compensations of losses of financial institutions with public funds. 金融機能強化法の改正法案は、公的資金による金融機関の損失の穴埋めを容易にするのが狙いだ。

compensation of top executives 役員の報酬,役員報酬
◆UFJ banking group plans to cut the compensation of its top executives by half from July through September to reflect their responsibility for the group's ¥400 billion net loss in fiscal 2003. UFJ銀行グループは、2004年3月期決算で4,000億円の最終赤字に陥った責任を取るため、役員の報酬を7月から9月までの3か月間、5割削減する方針だ。

compensation payments 賠償金の支払い,賠償金の支払い額
◆Compensation payments to people affected by the ongoing nuclear crisis, triggered by the Great East-Japan Earthquake,

are expected to reach as much as ¥10 trillion. 東日本大震災が誘発した今回の原発事故の被害者への賠償金支払い額は、10兆円にも達すると見られる。◆TEPCO asked the government for the financial support in making compensation payments for damage caused by the crisis at its Fukushima No. 1 nuclear power plant. 東電は、福島第一原子力発電所事故による損害の賠償金を支払うにあたって、政府に金融支援を要請した。
compensation plan 賠償計画, 賠償策, 賠償案
◆The government is hammering out an outline for the compensation plan. 政府は、賠償策の概要をまとめている。
compensation to the individual 個人に支払われた退職金
◆The compensation to the individual was taken care of largely out of our pension fund. 個人に支払われた退職金は、主に当社の年金基金から拠出しました。
compensatory （形）補償の, 賠償の, 代償の, 埋め合わせの, 補整的
  compensatory balances 歩積み両建て預金
  compensatory budget 補正予算
  compensatory damages 損害賠償, 補償的損害賠償（金）, 填補損害賠償（金）
  compensatory demand inflation 補整敵需要インフレ
  compensatory deposit 補償預金, 両建て預金, 歩積み（両建て）預金
  compensatory error 相殺誤差
  compensatory expenditure 補整的支出
  compensatory finance 補整的財政, 補償融資
  compensatory financing 補償融資, 補償融資制度
  compensatory financing facility 補償融資, 輸出変動補償融資, 輸出変動補償融資制度
  compensatory fiscal policy 補整的財政政策
  compensatory official financing 政府の調整的取引
  compensatory payment 補償金, 賠償金, 補償支払い
  compensatory principle （税の）受益者負担原則 （=benefit principle）
  compensatory spending policy 補整的支出政策
  compensatory stock option 補整的自社株購入権
  compensatory tariff 相殺関税
  compensatory tax policy 補整的租税政策
compete （動）競争する, 競う, 争う, 張り合う, 渡り合う, 競合する
  compete against ～と競合する, ～と競争する
  compete for market share シェア［市場シェア］を争う, シェアを巡って争う
◆The two companies have been competing with each other in the domestic market. 国内市場では、両社がせめぎ合ってきた。◆To compete against online trading systems, stock exchanges must improve their ability to process buy and sell orders. 電子取引システムに対抗するには、証券取引所が売買注文の処理能力を高める必要がある。◆To compete fiercely with gigantic foreign rivals, Japanese banks must increase their core capital ratios by steadily making profits. 巨大な外資と激しい競争を展開するには、邦銀は着実に利益を上げて、自己資本を増強する必要がある。
competition （名）競争, 競合 （⇒blue-chip company, business alliance, commodity futures trading industry, global competition, industry association, megabank, speculation）
◆As a result of fierce competition in the past, interest rate profit margins were kept too low to cover loans that went sour. 過去の熾烈（しれつ）な競争の結果、金利の利ざやが小さく抑えられた余り、貸倒れ［貸倒れのリスク］をカバーできなかった［過去の熾烈な融資合戦の結果、不良債権リスクをカバーできないほど利ざやは小さく抑えられた］。
competitive （形）競争力のある, 競争的, 競争上の, 他社に負けない, 安い, 低コストの
competitive devaluation of currencies 通貨の競争的な切下げ, 競争的な通貨の切下げ, 通貨安競争
◆Financial chiefs from the Group of 20 advanced and major developing economies vowed to refrain from competitive devaluation of currencies. 世界［主要］20か国・地域（G20）の財務相・中央銀行総裁は、通貨の競争的な切下げを回避することを公約した。
competitive edge 競争力
◆The hollowing-out of the pension system may increase companies' personnel costs so much that it could negatively affect their international competitive edge. 年金の空洞化で企業の人件費が上昇し、国際競争力に悪影響を及ぼす恐れがある。
competitiveness （名）競争力, 競争
  competitiveness effect 競争力効果
  corporate competitiveness 企業競争力
  cost competitiveness コスト競争力, 費用競争力
  economic competitiveness 経済競争力
  export competitiveness 輸出競争力 （=trade competitiveness）
  external competitiveness 対外競争力
  gain competitiveness 競争力を獲得する, 競争力をつける, 競争力を増す
  global competitiveness 国際競争力 （=international competitiveness）
  increase competitiveness 競争力を高める, 競争力を強める （=enhance competitiveness, improve competitiveness）
  industrial competitiveness 産業競争力, 企業の競争力
  lose competitiveness 競争力を失う （=lose competitive edge）
  market competitiveness 市場競争力
  overseas price competitiveness 海外での価格競争力
  price competitiveness 価格競争力 （=competitiveness in prices）
  promote competitiveness 競争力を高める, 競争力を増進する
  reduce competitiveness 競争力を低下させる （=erode competitiveness）
◆Major U.S. and European banks have been strengthening their market competitiveness. 欧米の大手銀行は、市場競争力を強化してきた。
compilation （名）編集, 編纂（へんさん）, 作成, 策定, 取りまとめ
◆The compilation of fiscal rehabilitation measures including raising the pension age is imperative for the Italian parliament. 年金受給年齢の引上げなどを含む財政再建策の取りまとめが、イタリア議会の急務となっている。
compile （動）編集する, 編纂（へんさん）する, 作成する, 策定する, まとめる,（予算などを）編成する, 集計する, 収集する, 機械語に翻訳する, コンパイルする, 得点を重ねる,（リードを）広げる
  compile a basic policy 基本方針［政策］をまとめる
  compile a package of measures to support ～支援策をまとめる
  compile additional economic measures 経済対策をまとめる
◆The Board of Audit intends to include the total taxpayer contribution to JAL in its audit account report compiled in November 2011. 会計検査院は、2011年11月にまとめる決算検査報告書に、日航に対する総国民負担額を盛り込む方針だ。◆

The company compiled documents for financial institutions it has transactions with. 同社は、取引金融機関向けに資料を作成した。◆The government has begun compiling the budget. 政府が、予算編成作業を開始した。

complaint （名）苦情, 苦情の申立て, 不平, 不満, 抗議, クレーム, 告訴
 criminal complaint　刑事告発
 cross-complaint　逆提訴
 file [lodge] a complaint with　～に苦情を申し立てる, ～に告訴する, ～に提訴する, ～に訴えを起こす
  (=make a complaint to)
 file a criminal complaint against A with B　AについてBに告訴状を提出する, AをBに刑事告発する
 lodge [make] a complaint A with B　AをBに告訴する
 ◆Consumer advice centers around the country have been receiving many complaints and questions about this kind of fraudulent business. 各地の消費者センターには、この種の詐欺商法についての苦情や問い合わせが相次いでいる。◆The financial watchdog took an additional action of criminal complaint other than administrative punishment as the bank's operations were so malicious. 同行の業務運営の仕方があまりにも悪質なので、金融監視機関の金融庁は、行政処分のほかに刑事告発の追加措置を取った。

complete （動）完成する, 達成する, 完了する, 仕上げる, （書類などに）書き込む
 complete a public offering　公募発行を完了する, 公募発行する
 complete the consolidated balance sheet of the company　同社の連結貸借対照表を作成する
 complete the contract　本契約を達成する
 ◆During the first nine months of 2011, the company completed public offerings of $125 million of 9.45% Debentures, due 2021 and $125 million of 10.50% Debentures, due 2018. 2011年1-9月期に同社は、2021年満期9.45%社債1億2,500万ドルと2018年満期10.50%社債1億2,500万ドルを公募発行した。

compliance （名）承諾, 受諾, 遵守［順守］, 遵守性, 準拠性, 適合, 服従, コンプライアンス
 affirmative action compliance program　積極的優遇措置遵守プログラム
 compliance of financial statements　財務諸表［財務書類］の準拠性, 財務諸表の会計原則準拠性
 compliance of securities firms　証券会社の法令遵守
 compliance officer　法令・規則遵守担当役員, 業務監査役, コンプライアンス・オフィサー
 compliance program　法遵守プログラム, 規制遵守プログラム
 compliance with rules　規則の遵守
 legal compliance　法令遵守
  (=regulatory compliance)
 ◆The Securities and Exchange Surveillance Commission is charged with inspecting the compliance of securities firms with the law, market surveillance and the investigation of abuses such as insider trading and stock price manipulation. 証券取引等監視委員会は、証券会社の法律遵守（じゅんしゅ）に関する検査や市場の監視、インサイダー取引や株価操作など不正行為の摘発を行う。

component （名）構成要素, 構成指標, 構成銘柄, 採用銘柄, 成分, 要因, 内訳, 部分, 項目, 構成部品, 部品, コンポーネント
 bond component of portfolio　ポートフォリオの債券部分
 component of stockholders' equity　資本の部　(=a component of shareholders' [stockholders'] equity)
 component percentage　構成比率
  (=component proportion ratio)

 component securities　構成銘柄, 採用銘柄
 component stocks of the Nikkei　日経平均構成銘柄, 日経平均採用銘柄
 debt component　負債部分, 債券部分
 deposit component　預金要素（デリバティブとして会計処理されない契約の構成要素）
 Dow components　ダウ平均構成銘柄, ダウ平均採用銘柄
 equity component　資本部分
 financial component approach　財務構成要素アプローチ
 interest component　金利部分, 利息部分
 interest risk component　金利リスクの構成要素
 liability component　負債部分
 M2＋CD component　M2＋CD
 one of the components of the index of leading indicators　景気先行指標総合指数［景気先行指数］の構成指標の一つ
 one of the ten components of the index of leading economic indicators　10ある景気先行指数の構成指標の一つ
 separate component　独立した構成要素
 separate component companies　傘下企業
 third reserve component　第三の通貨
 ◆Capital requirements have an interest risk component. 自己資本規制には、金利リスクの構成要素がある。

composite （形）総合の, 複合の, 混成の, 合成の　（名）複数銘柄を集めた指数, 合成物
 American stock exchange composite　アメリカン証券取引所銘柄平均
 composite appraisal　総合評点
 composite convertibility　合成交換性
 composite currency　複合通貨
 composite economic indicator　総合経済指標
 composite goods [commodity]　複合財, 合成財, 混成品, 複合商品
 composite legal tender system　（金と銀などの）複合通貨制
 composite market　合成財市場
 composite option　複合オプション
 composite prediction　複合予測
 composite rate of tax　（預金利子に課税される）総合税率, CRT
 composite reserve standard　合成本位制
 composite stock price　総合株価
 composite stock price table　総合株価表
 composite supply　複合供給
 Composite Tape of transactions　平均値 コンポジット・テープ・オブ・トランズアクション値
 Composite Tape of transactions on all major exchanges and nonexchange markets in the U.S.　全米主要証券取引所と店頭市場の平均値
 composite transaction　複合取引
 composite (useful) life　総合耐用年数
 Fed composite rate　FRBの加重平均CPレート

composite index　総合指数, 景気総合指数, 景気合成指数, CI
 commercial paper composite index　CP複合指標
 composite index number　総合指数, 総合指標
 composite index of leading indicators　景気先行指数(CI)
 Nasdaq composite index　ナスダック総合(株価)指数
 New York Stock Exchange Composite Stock Index　ニューヨーク証券取引所(NYSE)総合株価指数
 NYSE Composite Index　NYSE総合株価指数
 Value Line Composite Index　バリュー・ライン総合指数

◆Broader stock indicators such as the S&P 500 index and the Nasdaq composite index also dropped in February. 2月は、S&P500株価指数やナスダック総合株価指数などの総合株価指数も、低下［下落］した。
Composite Index of 11 Leading Indicators　（米商務表省が毎月発表する）先行指数, 景気先行指数
　解説 指数を構成する11の経済指標
　average weekly claims for unemployment insurance　週平均失業保険申請件数
　average workweek of production workers　製造業週平均労働時間
　consumer expectations　消費者期待
　materials prices　原材料価格
　money supply:M2　M2マネー・サプライ
　new building permits　新規建築許可件数
　new orders for consumer goods　消費財新規受注
　plant and equipment orders　設備財受注
　slower deliveries　入荷遅延
　stock prices　株価
　unfilled orders　受注残高
composition　（名）構成, 和解, 和議, 示談, (債務・負債の)一部支払い, 一部弁済, 債務免除, 一部返済金, 内済金, 示談金, 債務一部免除契約
　asset composition　資産の構成
　balance sheet composition　貸借対照表の構成
　capital composition ratio　資本構成比率
　commodity composition　商品構成
　composition by creditors　債権者による和議
　composition deed　示談証書
　composition in bankruptcy　破産上の和議
　composition of creditors　和議契約
　composition of finances　財務構成, 財務内容
　composition with creditors　債権者との和議, 債権者との和解
　compulsory composition　強制和議
　make a composition with a creditor　債権者と和解する, 債権者との示談で負債の一部を支払う
　value composition of capital　資本の価値構成
composition of capital　資本構成
　（=capital composition, capital structure）
　organic composition of capital　資本の有機的構成
　technical composition of capital　資本の技術的構成
compound　（動）(借金などの一部金を払って)示談にする, 示談で済ませる, 内済にする, (負債を)一部だけ支払う, (予約金を)一時金で支払う, (勘定を)打ち切る, (利息を)複利で支払う, 複式計算にする, 複利で計算する, 倍加させる　（自動）妥協する, 折り合う
　compound a debt　借金を示談にする
　compound for A with one's creditors　Aで債権者と折り合いをつける, Aで債権者と和解する
　compound interest on an annual basis　年ベースで複利計算をする, 年ベースで利息を元本に組み入れる
　compound interest semiannually　半期［半年］ごとに利息を複利計算する, 半年ごとに利子を複利で支払う
　compound with one's creditors　債権者と話をつける, 一時金を払って債権者と折り合いをつける
　continuously compounded return　連続複利型リターン
　◆The bank compounds interest quarterly. 同行は、四半期ごとに利子を複利で支払っている。
compound　（形）複合の, 混合の, 複式の, 合成の, 複雑な
　compound annual growth rate　年平均成長率, 年平均伸び率, CAGR　（=compound growth rate）

compound annual rate　複合年率, 複利ベースの年率
compound arbitrage　重複裁定
compound duties [tariff]　複合関税
compound financial instruments　複合金融商品
compound growth rate　年平均成長率, CGR　（=compound annual growth）
compound investment　複合投資
compound (journal) entry　複合仕訳
compound option　重複選択権付き売買, 複合オプション, コンパウンド・オプション
compound present value　複利現価
compound price　複合価格
compound rate　複合金利
compound stock price based on weighted average　加重平均株価
compound sum　複利元利合計
compound transaction　複合取引
compound value　複利価値
compound yield　複合利回り, 複利
compound yield based on weighted average　加重平均利回り
compound interest　複利　（=compounded interest: 元金と利子に付けられる利子。単利はsimple interest）
　compound interest annuity　複利年金
　compound interest method　複利計算法(減価償却の)複利償却法　（=method of compound interest）
　compound interest table　複利表
compounded yield　複利利回り
　annually compounded yield　年複利利回り
　semiannually compounded yield　半年複利利回り
compounding　（名）複利計算
　compounding period　複利期間
　continuous compounding　連続複利計算
　continuously compounding rate　連続複利
　semiannual compounding　半年複利
comprehensive　（形）総合的な, 包括的な, 全面的な, 広範な, 幅広い
　comprehensive antideflationary measures　総合デフレ対策
　comprehensive economic package plan　総合経済対策
　Comprehensive Employment and Training Act　包括的雇用・訓練法, CETA
　comprehensive income　包括利益, 包括的利益
　comprehensive monetary easing　包括的金融緩和
　comprehensive package of economic measures　包括的経済対策
　comprehensive plan　包括的計画
　comprehensive quantitative easing measures　全面的な量的緩和策　（⇒quantitative easing measures）
　comprehensive strategy　包括的な戦略
　take a comprehensive view　大局的な判断をする
comprehensive antideflation measures　総合デフレ対策　（=comprehensive antideflationary measures）
　◆Even at this juncture, the government has yet to come up with comprehensive antideflation measures. この期に及んでも、政府の総合デフレ対策は出てこない。
comprehensive business tie-up　包括的業務提携
　◆Upmarket supermarket chain Kinokuniya Co. and Takashimaya Co. have reached a basic agreement on a comprehensive business tie-up to jointly create upscale, new-style stores. 高級スーパーの紀ノ国屋と高島屋は、包括的業務提携をして富裕消費者向けの新店舗を共同開発することで基

本合意に達した。

comprehensive economic cooperation 包括的経済連携
◆The APEC members agreed to pursue comprehensive economic cooperation. アジア太平洋経済協力会議（APEC）加盟国は、包括的経済提携を目指す方向で一致した。

comprehensive financial group 総合金融グループ
◆We will aim at creating a top, comprehensive financial group in the world that can win the global competition. 当社は今後、グローバルな競争を勝ち抜ける世界屈指の総合金融グループの創造を目指す。

comprehensive financial services 総合金融サービス
◆The nation's mega banking groups have been realigning their securities units to offer comprehensive financial services. 国内の大手金融グループは、総合金融サービスを提供するため、グループ各社の証券会社を再統合している。

comprehensive measures 包括的な対応策
◆The European Union agreed on comprehensive measures to deal with the current fiscal and financial crisis. 欧州連合（EU）は、現在の財政・金融危機について、包括的な対応策で合意した。

comprehensive monetary easing 包括的金融緩和, 包括緩和
◆The Bank of Japan will purchase government bonds from financial institutions as part of its comprehensive monetary easing. 日本銀行は、包括的金融緩和の一環として、金融機関から国債を買い入れる。

comprehensive tie-up 包括提携, 包括的提携
◆This is the first time for major commercial banks to form a comprehensive tie-up with a foreign capital financial group. 大手都銀が外資系金融グループと包括提携するのは、今回が初めてだ。

comptroller （名）通貨監督官, 経理部長, コントローラー （⇒controller）
　Comptroller and Auditor General　会計検査院長
　Comptroller of the Currency　米通貨監督官
　deputy comptroller　副通貨監督官
　Office of the Comptroller of the Currency　米通貨監督局［監督庁］
　U.S. Comptroller of the Currency　米連邦通貨監督官

compulsory （形）強制的な, 義務的な, 法定の, 規定の, 必修の　（=mandatory）
　compulsory auction　強制競売
　compulsory audit　強制監査
　compulsory automobile liability insurance　自賠責
　compulsory collateral substitution　強制的担保差し換え
　compulsory deposit　拘束預金
　compulsory deposit as a condition for a loan　歩積み両建て預金
　compulsory insurance　強制保険
　compulsory liquidation［winding up］　強制清算, 強制解散
　compulsory loan　政府借上金
　compulsory national health insurance　強制国民健康保険
　compulsory purchase　（土地などの）強制収用
　compulsory savings system　強制貯蓄制度
　compulsory settlement　強制和解
　compulsory tie-in sales　強制抱き合わせ販売
　compulsory transfer　強制的移転

computation （名）計算, 算定
　amortization computation　償却計算
　computation of fully diluted earnings per common share　完全希薄化による普通株式1株当たり利益の計算
　computation of pension expense reported on the income statement　損益計算書に計上すべき年金費用の計算
　computation of premium deficiencies　保険料欠損額の計算
　computation of proceeds from bond issue　社債発行手取り金の計算
　computation of stockholders［stockholders'］equity accounts　株主持ち分勘定の計算
　computation of the earnings per share　1株当たり利益の算定
◆For the computation of the earnings per share, assuming full dilution, dividends on convertible preferred shares have been added back to income. 完全希薄化を仮定した場合の1株当たり利益の算定では、転換可能優先株式［転換優先株］に対する配当は、利益に振り戻してあります。

compute （動）計算する, 算定する, 算出する
　actuarial computed value　保険数理上の計算価値
　actuarially-computed pension liabilities　年金数理上の年金債務算出額
　actuarially computed value of vested benefits　受給権が発生した年金給付の保険数理上の計算価値
　compute finance charge　金融費用［金利、融資手数料］を計算する
　compute the amounts relating to the pension plan　年金制度関連の金額を計算する
　compute the primary earnings per common share　単純希薄化による1株当たり利益を計算する
　compute the value of a swap　スワップの価値を計算する
　discount method of computing the finance charge　利息天引き方式
◆We compute present values for impaired loans when we determine our allowances for credit losses. 当社の貸倒れ引当金を決定するにあたって、当社は不良債権の現在価値を計算します。

computer （名）電算機, 電子計算機, コンピュータ
◆Personal computers of many Net banking depositors have been infected with viruses that ravaged computers in the United States and European countries. 多くのネット・バンキング預金者のパソコンが、欧米のコンピュータに爆発的被害を生んだウイルスに感染していた。

computer failure コンピュータ・システムの障害
◆A computer failure brought trading at the Tokyo Stock Exchange to a standstill for more than four hours. コンピュータ・システムの障害で、東京証券取引所の取引が4時間以上も停止した。

computer malfunction コンピュータのシステム障害
◆Transactions on all of the 2,520 issues traded at the TSE were stalled from 9 a.m. due to a computer malfunction. 東証で取引されている2,520全銘柄の取引が、コンピュータのシステム障害で午前9時から停止した。

computer problems コンピュータの故障, コンピュータのトラブル　（=computer glitch）
◆The computer problems at MFG present a lesson for all financial institutions in the nation if they plan to merge or update their computer systems. 「みずほ」のコンピュータのトラブルは、日本の金融機関にとって、コンピュータ・システムの統合や更新を行う際の重要な教訓となっている。

computer system コンピュータ・システム
（⇒computer problems, glitch, integration）
◆Influential overseas commercial banks have maintained an advantage with transactions for derivative products by using high-tech computer systems. 海外の有力行は、最先端のコンピュータ・システムを使って、デリバティブ取引で優位を保っている。◆Under the accord, the companies will jointly develop computer systems to process deposits at leading banks and manage personnel, salaries and expenses for other businesses and hospitals. 合意によると、両社は今後、大手銀行の

預金を処理するコンピュータ・システムや、他の企業や病院の人事、給与、経費などを管理するコンピュータ・システムを共同開発する。

computer system failure コンピュータ・システムの障害, システム障害
◆Mizuho Financial Group's plan to merge Mizuho Bank and Mizuho Corporate Bank in 2013 was prompted by a major computer system failure. 大規模なシステム障害を機に、みずほフィナンシャルグループは、2013年にみずほ銀行とみずほコーポレート銀行を統合する方針を固めた。

computer system's breakdown コンピュータ・システムの障害, システム障害 (=computer failure, computer malfunction, computer system failure)
◆The largest factor behind the computer system's breakdown is that the entire process of integrating the computer systems of the three banks was affected by shifts in policy. システム障害の最大の原因は、3行のシステムの統合作業全体が方針転換に振り回されたことにある。

concern (名)関心, 関心事, 関係, 利害関係, 心配, 懸念, 懸念材料, 不安, 不安材料, 警戒感, 配慮, 問題, 会社, 企業, 企業体, 事業, 業務, 責務, 任務, 重要性 (動)〜に関係する, 利害関係がある, 重要である (⇒economic recovery, inflation)

broader concerns such as the global financial crisis 世界的な金融危機といった広域の懸念材料
concern about corporate performance 企業業績への懸念
concern on what the Fed [Federal Reserve] will decide on interest rates FRBの金融政策をめぐる懸念
concern over [regarding] higher interest rates 利上げ懸念
concern over the global economic slowdown 世界的な景気減速に対する懸念
concern over the recent appreciation of the yen 最近の円高傾向についての懸念
concerns about downside risk 高値警戒感
concerns over oil supplies 原油供給不安, 原油供給への懸念
credit concerns 信用不安, 信用リスクに対する懸念, 信用リスク懸念, 信用力への懸念
deflationary concern デフレ懸念
fading concerns 不安の後退, 懸念の後退
going concern 継続企業, 営業している企業, 企業の存続可能性, ゴーイング・コンサーン (=ongoing concern)
have concern in 〜に出資している
inflationary concern インフレ懸念, インフレに対する懸念
long term concerns 長期的な不安材料
market players' concern 市場関係者の警戒感
on concerns that 〜の懸念を受けて
quitting concern 終了企業
risk concerns リスク警戒感
serious concerns 大きな懸念材料
there are growing concerns that 〜との懸念が高まっている

◆A dealer at a leading bank said that market players' concern has kept yen-buying moves in check. 市場関係者の警戒感が円買いの動きを食い止めた[抑制した]、と大手銀行のディーラーが語っている。◆All the four publicly traded firms that went bankrupt in July 2008 were construction and real estate concerns. 2008年7月に倒産した上場企業4社すべてが、建設会社と不動産会社だった。◆By conducting additional monetary easing policy, the Fed attempts to preemptively contain growing deflationary concerns in the United States. 追加金融緩和策を実施して、米連邦準備制度理事会 (FRB) は、米国で高まるデフレ懸念に先手を打とうとしている。◆Concerns have been raised over the ability of Internet banking services to verify the identity of new depositors or to guarantee the security of customer transactions. インターネット・バンキングについては、新規預金者の身元確認や対顧客取引の安全保証の点で、その能力に対して懸念が提起されている。◆Demand for bullion as a protection of wealth has been spurred by mounting concern that the global economy is faltering. 世界経済低迷への懸念増大から、安全資産[資産保全]としての金の需要が拡大している。◆Finance Minister Yoshihiko Noda and some other Cabinet ministers expressed concern over the recent appreciation of the yen. 最近の円高傾向について、野田財務相や他の一部の閣僚が懸念を表明した。◆In emerging economics, economic overheating and inflation are concerns. 新興国では、景気過熱やインフレが懸念される。◆The FRB's new easy credit policy is not without concerns. 米連邦準備制度理事会 (FRB) の追加金融緩和策には、気がかりな点もある。◆The Japanese economy faces a growing downside risk due to concerns about the future of the U.S. and European economies. 日本経済は、欧米経済の先行き懸念から、景気の下振れリスクが高まっている。◆The S&P cut in the U.S. long-term credit rating by one notch to AA-plus from AAA resulted from concerns about the nation's budget deficits and climbing debt burden. スタンダード・アンド・プアーズ (S&P) が米国の長期国債格付けを最上級のAAA (トリプルA) からAA (ダブルA) に1段階引き下げた理由は、米国の財政赤字と債務負担の増大に対する懸念だ。◆There are growing concerns that the yen's extremely rapid appreciation may deliver a bitter blow to the Japan's economy. 超円高は日本経済に大きな打撃を与えるとの懸念が、強まっている。◆There are serious concerns that the strong yen and the weak U.S. dollar could hurt the current economic upturn led by exports. 大きな懸念材料は、円高・ドル安の進行で現在の輸出主導の景気回復が打撃を受けることだ。◆With the midyear account settlement scheduled in September, concerns over the stability of the nation's financial system inevitably will grow again should stock prices dip further. 9月中間決算を前に、株価がさらに下がれば、再び日本の金融システム不安[日本の金融システムの安定に対する不安感]が当然、台頭してくる。◆Worldwide concern over fiscal sustainability in industrialized countries is growing in the wake of Greece's sovereign debt crisis. ギリシャの財政危機を契機として、先進国の財政の持続可能性に対する世界の関心が高まっている。

concern about the financial crisis in Europe 欧州の金融危機への懸念
◆On the foreign exchange market, there has been no halt to selling pressure on the euro due to concern about the financial crisis in Europe. 外国為替市場では、欧州の金融危機を懸念して、ユーロ売り圧力が止まらない展開となっている。

concern about [over] the U.S. economic outlook 米景気の先行きへの懸念, 米経済の先行きに対する懸念
◆Concerns over the U.S. economic outlook tend to induce yen-buying as a safe haven. 米経済の先行きに対する懸念から、安全な投資手段として円が買われる傾向にある。◆The U.S. dollar traded at the lower ¥85 range in Tokyo over concern about the U.S. economic outlook. 東京金融市場[東京外国為替市場]では、米景気の先行きを懸念して、ドル相場は1ドル=85円台前半で取引された。

concern over a sharp economic slowdown 景気急減速の心配, 景気急減速の懸念
◆There was widespread concern over a sharp economic slowdown for the July-September quarter. 7-9月期は、景気急減速の心配が広がった。

concern over soaring public debts 増大する公的債務への懸念, 公的債務増大への懸念
◆At the G-7 talks, concern over soaring public debts was to top the agenda. G7 (先進7か国財務相・中央銀行総裁会議) の

協議では、増大する公的債務問題[公的債務への懸念]が最大の議題[課題]になる予定だった。

concern over the global economic slowdown 世界的な景気減速懸念, 世界経済の減速懸念
◆Concern over the global economic slowdown grows both at home and abroad. 世界的な景気減速懸念は、国内外で高まっている[広まっている]。◆Concern over the global economic slowdown is spreading. 世界経済の減速懸念が、広がっている。

concern over the revival of the twin deficits 双子の赤字の復活懸念
◆Concern over the revival of the twin deficits is accelerating selling pressure on the U.S. stocks and the dollar. 双子の赤字の復活懸念が、米国の株・ドル売りを加速している。

concerns over a financial system crisis 金融システム不安, 金融システム危機に対する懸念
◆The money market is overheated by massive money inflows from banks on fading concerns over a financial system crisis. 金融システム不安[金融システム危機に対する懸念]の後退により、短期金融市場は、銀行からの巨額の資金流入で過熱感が強まっている。

concerns over oil supplies 原油供給不安, 原油供給への懸念
◆Crude oil futures soared in New York due to concerns over oil supplies. ニューヨーク(ニューヨーク・マーカンタイル取引所)の原油先物が、原油供給不安[原油供給への懸念]から急騰した。

concerned (形)心配する, 懸念する, 警戒する, 気づかう, 配慮する, 関係する
◆Investors grow concerned about the fact that French banks possess a large volume of Greek and Italian bonds. 投資家は、フランスの銀行がギリシャやイタリアの国債を大量に保有していることを警戒している。

concert (名)一致, 協力, 協調, 提携, コンサート
  concert parties 株式の協調買占めグループ, 共謀行為者
  in concert with ～と協同で, ～と協力して, ～と提携して, ～と協調して, ～と歩調を合わせて, ～の波に乗って
◆In concert with the improvement in the global economy, the Japanese economy is expected to emerge from its prolonged recession. 世界経済の上昇の波に乗って、日本経済は長引く不況から抜け出す見込みだ。

concerted (形)一致した, 一致協力した, 協調した, 協調的, 協力して行う, 共同による, 申し合わせた, 一斉の, 熱心な, 集中的な
  concerted raid on ～の一斉手入れ, ～に対する一斉捜査
  make a concerted effort 一斉に進める
  take concerted action with ～と協調行動を取る, ～と一致した行動を取る, ～と足並みを揃える

concerted action 協調行動, 共同行為
◆Europe promised the Group of 20 major economies to take concerted action to contain the financial crisis. 欧州は、結束して金融危機を封じ込めることを主要20か国・地域(G20)に公約した。◆Politicians and bureaucrats failed to take concerted action. 政治家と官僚の足並みが、揃わなかった。◆The financial markets are calling for additional concerted actions of the G-7 leading economies. 金融市場は、先進7か国の一段の協調行動を求めている。

concerted intervention 協調介入 (=concerted market intervention, concerted official intervention, orchestrated intervention)
  concerted central bank intervention (各国)中央銀行の協調介入
  conduct a concerted intervention 協調介入を実施する, 協調介入を行う
  participate in a concerted intervention 協調介入に踏み切る
◆The government and the Bank of Japan should conduct a concerted intervention with the United States and European countries to stem the yen's further rise. 政府・日銀は、米欧と協調介入を実施して、円高進行を阻止しなければならない。◆The United States and European monetary authorities were not willing to participate in a concerted intervention. 欧米の通貨当局が、協調介入に進んで踏み切る情勢ではなかった。

concerted market intervention 協調介入, 協調市場介入
◆Japan should prevent the dollar plunging and the yen from rising too sharply through concerted market intervention with the United States and European countries. 日本は、米欧との協調介入によってドル急落と超円高を阻止すべきだ。◆The possibility of stabilizing the exchange market through concerted market intervention has decreased. 協調介入による為替市場安定[為替安定]の可能性は、遠のいた。

concrete (形)具体的な, 明確な, 確実な, 実際の, 現実の
  concrete measures 具体策
  concrete proposal 具体的提案, 具体的な提案
◆A sense of disappointment has prevailed across the world markets as no concrete measures to rescue Greece were unveiled at the eurozone finance ministers meeting. ユーロ圏財務相会合でギリシャ支援の具体策が明らかにされなかったので、世界の市場で失望感が広がった。◆Due to delays in ratification of the agreement on bailout measures by some eurozone countries, concrete measures to rescue Greece have yet to be carried out. 支援策の合意事項について一部のユーロ圏加盟国の承認が遅れたため、ギリシャ救済の具体策はまだ実施されていない。

condition (名)条件, 基準, 状態, 状況, 情勢, 動向, 環境, 構造 (⇒financial condition, fiscal condition(s), market conditions)
  business conditions 景気, 商況, 業況, 徐業環境
  condition of exchange stability 為替安定条件
  conditions for bond issue 債券発行条件
  conditions for delisting 上場廃止基準, 上場停止基準
  conditions for listing 上場基準
  conditions for payment 支払い条件, 決済条件
  conditions of insurance 保険約款
  conditions of warrants ワラント発行要項, ワラントの基本的発行条件
  credit conditions 信用状態, 信用状況, 信用供与状況
  economic conditions 経済状態, 経済情勢, 景気
  financial market conditions 金融市場の環境
  financial terms and conditions 財務条件
  macroeconomic conditions マクロ経済の構造
  monetary conditions 金融情勢, 金融環境, 金融状況, 金融政策
  open interest parity condition 開放金利均衡条件
  overall financial conditions DI 資金繰り判断DI
  policy conditions 保険約款
  qualifying conditions 年金受給資格
  rate cutting conditions 利下げの環境 (=the conditions to cut interest rates)
  supply-demand conditions 需給関係, 需給
  the conditions of the underlying policy 元受保険約款
◆As a condition for loans to financially troubled countries in the late 1990s, the IMF called for strict implementation of structural reforms. 1990年代後半に財政難に陥った国に対する融資の条件として、IMF(国際通貨基金)は、厳しい構造改革の実施を求めた。◆Business conditions are rapidly deteriorating due to the global financial crisis and the worldwide economic downturn. 世界的な金融危機と世界的な景気後退で、景気は急速に悪化している。◆Domestic stock exchange

entries continue to languish, reflecting the tough conditions faced by emerging firms wanting to publicly list their shares. 国内株式市場への新規上場は、株式上場を目指す新興企業が直面している厳しい状況を反映して、低迷が続いている。◆Greece's fiscal reconstruction is set as a condition for supporting the struggling country by the European Union and the International Monetary Fund. 欧州連合(EU)と国際通貨基金(IMF)は、ギリシャの財政再建を、財政危機にある同国支援の条件としている。◆If business conditions continue to worsen, financial institutions will face more newly emerging nonperforming loans than they can ever keep up with. 景気がこのまま悪化し続ければ、金融機関は新たに不良債権が生まれてその処理が追いつかなくなる。◆Investment conditions have worsened due to confusion in global financial markets in the wake of fiscal and financial crises in Europe. 欧州の財政・金融危機を受けた世界的な金融市場の混乱で、運用環境が悪化している。◆Ten of 12 Fed district banks reported weaker conditions or declines in their regional economies. 全米12地区連銀のうち10連銀が、各地域経済の悪化あるいは地域経済活動の低下を報告した。◆The business sentiment index represents the percentage of companies reporting favorable business conditions minus the percentage of those reporting unfavorable conditions. 業況判断指数は、景気が良いと答えた企業の割合(%)から景気が悪いと答えた企業の割合(%)を差し引いた指数だ。◆The company's financial statements did not correctly reflect its financial condition. 同社の財務諸表は、財務状況を適正に表示していなかった。◆The Fed raised the discount rate to 0.75 percent from 0.5 percent as a response to improved financial market conditions. 米連邦準備制度理事会(FRB)は、金融市場の環境改善を受けて、(銀行に貸し出す際の金利である)公定歩合を現行の年0.5%から0.75%に引き上げた。◆The IMF extends to countries with relatively healthier public finances one- to two-year loans of up to 1,000 percent of their contribution to the IMF without strict conditions. IMF(国際通貨基金)は、財政が比較的健全な国に対して、期間1～2年の資金を厳しい条件なしでIMFに出資している額(クォータ)の最大10倍まで融資している。◆The Japanese economy is experiencing difficult conditions. 日本経済は現在、厳しい状況にある。

conduct (動)行う, 進める, 処理する, 遂行する, 経営する, 案内する, 指導する
  conduct a business 事業を行う, 事業を進める, 事業を経営する
  conduct a concerted intervention 協調介入を行う, 協調介入を実施する
  conduct a feasibility study 実行可能性[企業化]調査を実施する
  conduct a market intervention 市場介入を行う, 市場介入を実施する
  conduct a on-the-spot investigation 現場検証を行う
  conduct external auditing 外部監査を実施する
  conduct foreign trade 外国貿易を行う
  conduct monetary easing policy 金融緩和策を実施する
  conduct share splitting 株式分割を行う
  conduct syndication on a best efforts basis ベスト・エフォート・ベースでシ団組成を行う
  conduct three U.S. dollar liquidity-providing operations 米ドル資金供給オペを3回実施する
◆A market intervention is conducted under the authority of the finance minister in Japan. 市場介入は、日本では財務相の権限で行われる。◆By conducting additional monetary easing policy, the Fed attempts to preemptively contain growing deflationary concerns in the United States. 追加金融緩和策を実施して、米連邦準備制度理事会(FRB)は、米国で高まるデフレ懸念に先手を打とうとしている。◆Finance Minister Yoshihiko Noda decided to conduct a yen-selling market intervention on Aug. 4, 2011. 2011年8月4日に野田財務相は、円売り市場介入の実施を決断した。◆In cooperation with the U.S. FRB, the Bank of England, the Bank of Japan and the Swiss National Bank, the European Central Bank decided to conduct three U.S. dollar liquidity-providing operations between October and December. 米連邦準備制度理事会(FRB)、英イングランド銀行、日銀、スイス国立銀行と協調して、欧州中央銀行(ECB)が10～12月に3回、米ドル資金供給オペを実施することを決めた。◆Small municipalities have a financial difficulty in setting up an independent audit office or conducting external auditing every fiscal year. 小規模市町村の場合、独立した監査事務局を設置したり、外部監査を毎年度実施したりするのは財政的に困難だ。◆The firm's former president sharply increased the firm's stock price in a short period by conducting large-scale share splitting. 同社の元社長は、大規模な株式分割を行うことで同社の株価を短期間で急騰させた。◆The government and the Bank of Japan should conduct a concerted intervention with the United States and European countries to stem the yen's further rise. 政府・日銀は、米欧と協調介入を実施して、円高進行を阻止しなければならない。

conductive to ～に役立つ
◆At the Seoul G-20 summit, all the leaders agreed to introduce "indicative guidelines" that would be conductive to reducing current account imbalances. 主要20か国・地域(G20)のソウル・サミット(首脳会議)で、全首脳が、経常収支不均衡の是正に役立つ「参考指針」を導入することで合意した。

confidence (名)信頼, 信用, 信認, 信任, 信頼度, 自信, 消費者マインド, 企業心理, 景況感, 秘密, 内密, 秘密保持 (⇒consumer confidence index)
  confidence game [trick] 信用詐欺, 取り込み詐欺 (=con game)
  confidence interval 信頼度, 信頼区間
  confidence man 信用詐欺師, 取り込み詐欺師, 詐欺師, ペテン師 (=con artist, con man)
  confidence-sensitive funding 信認に敏感な資金
  confidence-sensitive market 信認に敏感な市場
  erode confidence in government bonds 国債の信用が失われる, 国債への信頼を損なう (⇒erode)
  financial markets' confidence in the U.S. currency 金融市場のドル[米ドル]への信認
  improvement in business confidence 業況感の改善
  lender confidence 貸し手の信認
  market confidence 市場の信認
  public confidence in the Japanese financial system 日本の金融システムに対する国民の信頼
  regain consumer confidence 消費者の信頼を回復する
  rise [increase] in confidence 消費者マインドの向上, 消費意欲の向上 (=improvement in consumer confidence)
  weak confidence 消費者マインドの冷え込み (=depressed [lower] consumer confidence)
◆European banks are forced to shore up their potential capital shortage to restore market confidence. 欧州銀行は、市場の信認を回復するため、潜在的資本不足の増強を迫られている。◆Investors are losing confidence in monetary management. 通貨調節への投資家の信認は、失われている。◆The failure to implement fiscal consolidation in countries where it is necessary could undermine confidence and hamper growth. 財政健全化が必要な国で財政健全化を行わないと、信認を損ない、成長を阻害する可能性がある。◆The Fed does not have confidence in the effect of QE2. 米連邦準備制度理事会(FRB)は、量的緩和第二弾(QE2)の効果に自信が持てないでいる。◆The full implementation of the payoff system may cause a loss of public confidence in the nation's financial system. ペイオフ制度の完全実施は、日本の金融システムに対する国民の信頼を失う可能性がある。◆The repercussions of Olym-

pus Corp.'s false financial statements could lead to a loss of confidence in the governance and in the compliance of all Japanese firms. オリンパスの不正経理[有価証券虚偽記載]の影響で、日本企業全体の統治能力や法令遵守への信頼が失墜する可能性がある。

confidence among small and mid-sized companies 中小企業の景況感
◆Confidence among small and mid-sized companies fell to the lowest in six years as higher energy prices eroded profits. 燃料高[燃料費の高騰]による利益の低下で、中小企業の景況感は、過去6年で最低の水準にまで落ち込んだ[悪化した]。

confidence in government bonds 国債の信用
◆Long-term debts held by central and local governments are expected to further swell, thereby eroding confidence in governments bonds. 国と地方自治体が抱える長期債務は、さらに膨張して、国債の信用が失われるものと見られる。

confidence in markets 市場の信認
(=market confidence)
◆Four European countries of France, Italy, Spain and Belgium banned short selling on financial stocks to restore confidence in markets. フランス、イタリア、スペイン、ベルギーの欧州4か国が、市場の信認を回復するため、金融銘柄の空売りを禁止した。

confidence in the governance 統治能力への信頼
◆The repercussions of Olympus Corp.'s false financial statements could lead to a loss of confidence in the governance and in the compliance of all Japanese firms. オリンパスの不正経理[有価証券虚偽記載]の影響で、日本企業全体の統治能力や法令遵守への信頼が失墜する可能性がある。

confidence in the securities market 証券市場への信頼
◆The company's long-running practice of falsifying its financial statements has hurt investors' confidence in the securities market. 同社の長期にわたる有価証券報告書[財務諸表]虚偽記載の慣行は、証券市場への投資家の信頼を損ねた。

confidence in the single currency of the euro 単一通貨・ユーロの信認
◆Confidence in the single currency of the euro may be undermined by the spread of the Greek crisis to Spain and Portugal. ギリシャ危機のスペインやポルトガルへの波及により、単一通貨・ユーロの信認が揺らぎかねない。

confidence in the U.S. currency 米ドルへの信認, ドルへの信認, 米ドルの信認
◆As the financial markets' confidence in the U.S. currency has been shaken, stock prices may fall worldwide and the dollar-selling trend may accelerate. 米ドルへの金融市場の信認が揺らいでいるため、株価が世界的に下落し、ドル売りの流れが加速する可能性もある。◆The financial markets' confidence in the U.S. currency has been shaken further by the S&P's cutting of the U.S. credit rating. スタンダード・アンド・プアーズ(S&P)が米国債の格付けを引き下げたことで、米ドルへの金融市場の信認が一段と揺らいでいる。

confidence in the U.S. financial market 米金融市場の信認
◆Goldman Sachs' capital increase is partly aimed at regaining the confidence in the U.S. financial market, which has been facing a raft of financial problems. ゴールドマン・サックスの増資は、多くの金融問題を抱える米金融市場の信認回復も狙いの一つだ。

confidence index 信頼度指数, 信頼感指数
Barron's confidence index バロンズ信頼度指数
(=Barron's index)
Conference Board's [Board] consumer confidence index コンファレンス・ボード消費者信頼感指数
Consumer confidence index 消費者信頼感指数

confirm (動)確かめる, 確認する, 確証する, 検証する, 確定する, 強める, 固める, 裏付ける, 認める, 承認する, 批准(ひじゅん)する
confirm the reservation 予約を確認する
◆FSA's inspectors are to confirm whether the companies' categorization by banks as debtors is relevant or fair. 金融庁の検査官は、銀行側の企業(融資先企業)の債務者区分が適正かどうかなどを検証することになっている。◆The Board of Audit has confirmed that the public financing package extended with a government-backed guarantee to JAL prior to its failure cost taxpayers a total of ¥47 billion. 日航の破たん前に政府保証付きで行われた公的融資の総国民負担額は470億円であることを、会計検査院が確定した。

confiscate (動)没収する, 押収する
◆About ¥4 billion acquired by a criminal gang through illegal moneylending operations will be confiscated. 暴力団がヤミ金融で得た約40億円が、没収されることになった。

confusion (名)混乱, 混乱状態, 騒動, 当惑, 混同, 取り違え
be thrown into total confusion 大騒ぎになる
confusion in the chain of command 指揮系統の混乱
confusion of debts 債務の混同
confusion of goods 物品の混和(こんわ)
economic confusion 経済的混乱
political confusion 政治的混乱
◆If Japanese government bonds prices enter a tailspin and throw financial markets into confusion, a financial system crisis would likely occur. 日本国債の価格が下落して、金融市場が混乱すれば、金融システム不安が生じる可能性がある。
◆The confusion triggered by Greece's possible debt default could affect Japan and the United States. 予想されるギリシャの債務不履行(デフォルト)による混乱の影響は、日米に及ぶ可能性もある。

confusion in global financial markets 世界の金融市場の混乱, 世界的な金融市場の混乱
◆Investment conditions have worsened due to confusion in global financial markets in the wake of fiscal and financial crises in Europe. 欧州の財政・金融危機を受けた世界的な金融市場の混乱で、運用環境が悪化している。

confusion in (the) financial markets 金融市場の混乱
◆Due to confusion in the financial markets, interest rates have declined significantly and global stock prices have dropped. 金融市場の混乱で、金利が大幅に低下し、世界的に株価も下落している。◆Global economies are battered by confusion in financial markets. 世界経済が、金融市場の混乱の影響をもろに受けている。

conglomerate (名)コングロマリット, 巨大複合企業, 複合企業, 複合企業体, 多角化企業
(=conglomerate company)
◆If the merger takes place, it will create a full-scale financial conglomerate with a major bank, a major securities house and credit card company under its umbrella. 統合すれば、傘下に大手銀行と大手証券、クレジット・カード会社などを持つ本格的な金融コングロマリット(金融複合企業体)が誕生する。
◆The FSA's guideline for supervising financial conglomerates is aimed at urging operators of financial conglomerates to reinforce their corporate governance to prevent irregularities. 金融庁の金融コングロマリット(複合体)監督指針の狙いは、不正防止に向けて、金融コングロマリットの経営者に経営監視の強化を促すことにある。

consecutive (形)連続した(straight), 通しの, 論理の一貫した
for three consecutive fiscal years 3期連続
(=for three straight fiscal years)
the fifth consecutive quarterly growth 5四半期連続のプラス成長
the third consecutive quarter of growth 3四半期連続のプ

ラス
◆Corporate business sentiment improved in the three months to September for the sixth consecutive quarter. 7-9月の企業の景況感は、6期連続で改善した。◆That eurozone GDP shrank in the second quarter as well would add up to two consecutive quarters of negative growth-a definition of a technical recession. ユーロ圏のGDP（域内総生産）が第2四半期も低下したことで、ユーロ圏は2四半期連続のマイナス成長（定義上、テクニカル・リセッション）となった。◆The latest GDP figures marked the fifth consecutive quarterly growth in the domestic economy. GDP速報値によると、国内経済は5四半期連続のプラス成長となった。◆The subsidiary has actually had a negative net worth for three consecutive fiscal years. 子会社は、実際は3期連続債務超過だった。◆The surplus in the current account stood at ¥1.5 trillion in September 2008, marking the seventh consecutive month of year-on-year declines. 2008年9月の経常収支の黒字；額は、1兆5,000億円となり、7か月連続で前年実績を下回った。◆The 10 life insurers' combined outstanding balance of individual life insurance and annuity contracts declined for five consecutive years to ¥1.15 quadrillion. 生保10社合計の個人保険・年金の保有契約高（保険の総額）は1,150兆円で、5年連続（5期連続）で減少した。◆Tokyo stocks retreated for the fourth consecutive day. 東京株（東京株式市場の株価）は、4日連続で下落した。◆Two consecutive quarters of negative growth are defined as a technical recession. 2四半期連続のマイナス成長は、「テクニカル・リセッション」と定義されている。

consider （動）検討する、考慮する、考える、見なす、討議する
◆A reading of below 50 percent in the coincident index is considered a sign of economic contraction and a figure above that is viewed as a sign of expansion. 一致指数で50%以下の数値は景気収縮［景気後退］を示す指標と見られ、それ以上の数字は景気回復［景気拡大］を示す指標と見なされる。◆The BOJ's policy meeting is expected to consider taking additional monetary easing steps. 日銀の政策決定会合では、追加の金融緩和策の実施を検討する見通しだ。◆The 8% convertible bonds are convertible into 40 shares of common stock for each $1,000 bond, and were not considered common stock equivalents at the date of issuance. 8%利付き転換社債は、1,000ドルの社債についてそれぞれ普通株式40株に転換できるが、発行時には準普通株式とは考えられなかった。◆The government and the Bank of Japan are considering joint market intervention with the U.S. and European monetary authorities to produce the greater results of their market intervention. 政府・日銀は、市場介入の効果を高めるため、米欧の通貨当局との協調介入を検討している。◆The high yields of the yen-denominated government bonds were considered considerably higher than minuscule domestic interest rates. この円建て国債は、国内の超低金利に比べて利回りがはるかに大きいと見られた。◆The White House is ready to consider tapping a $700 billion Wall Street bailout fund to help keep the U.S. automakers afloat. 米政府は、米自動車メーカーの破たんを避けるための支援策として、7,000億ドルの金融業界救済資金（金融安定化法の公的資金）の活用を検討する用意ができている。

consideration （名）対価、代金、手付け金、契約の約因、考慮、要因、材料、要件
　a total consideration of $850 million　対価総額8億5,000万ドル　（⇒common shares outstanding）
　cash or other consideration　現金その他の対価
　consideration for the services　サービスの対価
　consideration transferred　引き渡した対価、対価の引渡し
　contingent consideration　条件付き対価、偶発的対価
　credit risk considerations　信用リスク分析
　fundamental considerations　ファンダメンタルズ要因
　in consideration for the license of the trademark　商標の使用許諾の対価として、商標使用許諾の対価として
　in consideration of the payment of　～の支払いを約因として
　negative consideration　懸念材料
　pay the merger consideration　合併の対価を支払う
◆BCE and Bell Canada entered into an agreement providing for the issue of Bell Canada common shares to BCE for an aggregate cash consideration of $150 million. BCEとベル・カナダは、ベル・カナダの普通株式を、総額1億5,000万ドルの対価でBCEに発行する契約を締結した。◆Under the current law, foreign firms are allowed to pay the merger consideration only in the form of shares of the subsidiary. 現行の法律上、外国企業の場合、合併の対価は（日本に設立した）子会社の株式で［株式という形で］しか支払うことができない。

consistent with　～と一致する、～と整合する、～と矛盾しない、～と一貫性がある
◆If we look at the yen's current exchange rate in terms of its real effective exchange rate, it is basically within a range consistent with the mid- and long-term fundamentals of the economy. 今の円相場［円の為替相場］は、実質実効為替レートで見ると、基本的には中長期的な経済のファンダメンタルズ（基礎的条件）と整合的な範囲内ある。

consolidate　（動）整理統合する、統合する、合併する、一元化する、統廃合する、整理する、強化する、連結する
◆Another important task facing major banks is to curtail their operating costs by consolidating branches. 大手行が抱えているもう一つ重要な課題は、店舗の統廃合による営業コストの削減だ。◆Some of the oil corporation's functions, such as supplying venture capital for oil development and conducting research and development, will be consolidated into the Metal Mining Agency of Japan. 石油開発のためのリスク資金供給機能や研究開発機能など、石油公団の機能の一部が、金属鉱業事業団に統合される。◆Taxes levied on capital gains should be consolidated to promote securities investment. 有価証券投資を促すために、金融資産課税は一元化するべきだ。

consolidated　（形）連結対象の、連結した、整理統合した、統合した、一本化した、一元化した
　companies consolidated　連結対象子会社
　consolidated accounting period figures　連結決算（=group accounting period figures）
　consolidated sales　連結売上高、連結ベースの売上高
　consolidated settlement of accounts　連結決算（=consolidated results）

consolidated accounts　連結決算、連結財務書類（=consolidated accounting period figures, consolidated financial statements）
　consolidated accounts for the business year to March 31　3月期の連結決算
　consolidated accounts for the six-month period through March next year　下半期（10月～来年3月）の連結決算
◆The financial statements reflect the consolidated accounts of the Corporation and its subsidiaries. この連結財務書類は、当社と子会社の財務書類を連結したものです。◆The revision of the firm's assumed exchange rate will translate into an additional ¥150 billion loss in its consolidated accounts for the six-month period through March 2011. 同社の想定為替レートの修正に伴って、同社の2000年度下半期（2000年10月～2011年3月）の連結決算では、追加で1,500億円の為替差損が生じることになる。

consolidated affiliate　連結対象の関連会社、連結対象の持ち分法適用会社
◆With its stake of some 15 percent, Mitsubishi Heavy Industries will make Mitsubishi Motors Corp. a consolidated affiliate. 出資比率が約15%となる三菱重工は、三菱自動車を

連結対象の関連会社とする。

consolidated after-tax profit　連結税引き後利益
◆The financial group has revised its forecast of its half-year consolidated after-tax profit to ￥410 billion from its initial forecast of ￥160 billion in May. 同金融グループは、中間決算の連結税引き後利益予想を、5月の当初予想の1,600億円から4,100億円に上方修正した。

consolidated basis　連結ベース
（=group basis；⇒black名詞, deficit）
◆The bank did not give a year-ago comparison on a consolidated basis. 同行は、連結ベース［子銀行合算ベース］での前期（前年）との比較を行わなかった。◆The closure of the money-losing outlets will result in a surplus of about 2,000 employees out of about 22,000 on a consolidated basis. 赤字の店舗閉鎖に伴い、連結ベースで従業員約22,000人のうち約2,000人が余剰になる。

consolidated earnings　連結利益, 連結純利益, 連結当期利益, 連結業績
　consolidated earnings forecasts　連結業績予想
　consolidated earnings report　連結決算報告, 連結決算報告書, 連結業績報告書
◆The brokerage firm inflated its consolidated earnings for its business year through March 2011. 同証券会社は、2011年3月期の連結利益を水増ししていた。

consolidated financial statements　連結財務書類, 連結財務諸表
（=consolidated accounts, group accounts）
◆In 2009, the Business Accounting Council decided to require all of the nation's listed companies to use the IFRSs for their consolidated financial statements from 2015. 2009年に企業会計審議会は、2015年にも、国内全上場企業の連結財務諸表［連結財務書類］について、国際財務情報基準（IFRSs）の採用を上場企業に義務付ける方針を打ち出した。◆Olympus Corp. inflated its net assets by ￥33 billion in the consolidated financial statements for the business year ended March 2011. オリンパスは、2011年3月期決算の連結財務書類［2011年3月期連結決算］で純資産を334億円水増ししていた。
[解説]連結財務書類について：英国では、連結財務書類［連結財務諸表］のことをgroup accountsと呼んでいる。アニュアル・レポートその他で公表される米国企業の財務書類［財務諸表］は、ほぼ連結財務書類である。これは、親会社（他の会社の発行済み株式の50％超を直接・間接に所有している会社）の財務書類と子会社の財務書類を合算して、親会社を中心とした企業グループとしての経営成績と財政状態を表したものである。

consolidated net assets　連結純資産
◆Olympus Corp.'s consolidated net assets at the end of March 2011 will be revised down to ￥133.4 billion from ￥166.8 billion. オリンパスの2011年3月末時点の連結純資産は、1,668億円から1,334億円に下方修正される。

consolidated net loss　連結純損失, 連結税引き後赤字, 連結税引き後損失　（⇒chalk up）
◆Mitsubishi Motors Corp. likely will post a record consolidated net loss of more than ￥400 billion for fiscal 2004. 三菱自動車は、2004年度決算（2005年3月期決算）で、4,000億円を上回る過去最悪の連結税引き後赤字になる見通しだ。

consolidated net profit　連結純利益, 連結税引き後利益　（=consolidated net income, group net profit）
◆The firm reported a consolidated net profit of ￥1.18 billion in the March-August first half of the 2011 business year. 同社は、2011年度上期（3-8月期）は11億8,000万円の連結税引き後利益を計上した［2011年8月期の連結中間決算で、ダイエーの税引き後利益は11億8,000万円だった］。

consolidated operating profit　連結営業利益, 連結業務利益

consolidated pretax profit　連結経常利益, 連結税引き前利益
◆Toyota became the first company in Japan to have posted a consolidated pretax profit in excess of the ￥1 trillion mark. トヨタは、日本国内で初めて連結経常利益が1兆円の大台を上回る企業となった。

consolidated provision for taxes　連結納税引当金
◆The consolidated provision for taxes also includes an amount sufficient to pay additional United States federal income taxes on repatriation of income earned abroad. 連結納税引当金には、海外で得た利益の本国送金に課される米連邦所得税の追加支払いに十分対応できる金額も含まれている。

consolidated recurring profit　連結経常利益, 企業グループの経常利益
◆The group will be able to raise its consolidated recurring profits to more than ￥20 billion from the current ￥4 billion or so through the reorganization. 再編により、同グループは今後、グループ全体で現在の40億円程度の経常利益を200億円以上にすることができる。

consolidated tax system　連結税制, 連結納税制
（=consolidated tax payment system, consolidated tax return system, consolidated taxation system, corporate group tax system；⇒joint stock company）
◆The consolidated tax system calculates taxes based on combined profits or losses. 連結税制は、企業グループの損益を合算（結合）して税額を算定するシステムだ。

consolidation　（名）新設合併, 統合, 整理, 連結, 連結決算, 強化, 地固め　（⇒balance sheet）
　accounting for consolidation　連結決算
　budget consolidation　財政立て直し
　consolidation and closure　統廃合, 統合と閉鎖
　debt consolidation fund　国債整理基金
　economic consolidation　経済調整
　facility consolidation　工場統廃合
　full consolidation　全部連結
　industry consolidation　業界統合, 業界再編
　market consolidation　市場再編, 市場統合
　partial consolidation　部分連結
　principles of consolidation　連結の方針
　stock consolidation　株式併合
　　（=share consolidation）
◆Major banks need to carry out the consolidation and closure of branches and other restructuring measures more thoroughly. 大手銀行は、支店の統廃合などのリストラ策をさらに徹底させる（さらに徹底して実施する）必要がある。
[解説]連結とは：会計用語の連結（consolidation）とは、簡単にいえば、親会社を中心とする企業グループを一つの企業とみなして、親会社（parent company）と子会社（subsidiary）の損益を合算することをいう。しかし、子会社が全部連結の対象になる（連結の範囲に含まれる）わけではない。米国企業の場合は、親会社が保有する子会社の株式保有の割合によって連結の範囲が決まり、連結の対象になった子会社を連結対象子会社・連結子会社（consolidated subsidiary）、連結の対象から外された子会社を非連結子会社（unconsolidated subsidiary）という。連結の範囲の基準としては、基本的に「他社の発行済み議決権株式（outstanding voting stock）の50％超（過半数）を直接間接に所有している場合、その会社を連結の範囲に含める」ことになっている。ここで議決権とは、株主が会社の総会で取締役の選任などの決議に参加する権利のことで、株主の議決権はその持ち株1株について1個与えられる。ただし、会社が持っている自社株や優先株に議決権はない。また、議決権株式の過半数を所有していても、その企業支配の関係が一時的なものや、更生会社や破産会社など過半数所有が実質的な企業支配に当たらない場合には、連結の範囲に含めないことになっている。

consortium (名)国際借款団, 銀行の協調融資団, 債権国会議, 共同事業体, 共同連合体, コンソーシアム
　a consortium of financial interests　金融関係者の借款団
　a consortium of lenders　融資団, 融資グループ
　consortium bank　国際投資銀行, 多国籍銀行, 国際銀行連合（=multinational bank）
　consortium loans　国際借款
　international banking consortia　国際銀行借款団
　investment consortium　投資組合
　loan consortium　借款団
　◆The foreign investment consortium spent about ¥121 billion to purchase the failed Long Term Credit Bank of Japan. この外資系投資組合は、経営破たんした日本長期信用銀行の買収に約1,210億円出資した。

constrain (動)強制する, 束縛する, 圧迫する, 制限する, 抑える, 抑制する, 拘束する, 無理に~させる, 締め付ける
　constrain consumer outlays　消費支出を抑える
　constrain (economic) recovery　景気回復の足を引っ張る
　constrain growth　成長を阻害する, 経済成長を制約[阻害]する
　constrain inflationary pressures　インフレ圧力を抑える
　constraining factor　制約要因
　◆Risk factors, including weaker prospects for global growth, continue to constrain improved economic performance. 世界の景気見通しの悪化などのリスク要因が、引き続き景気回復の足かせとなっている。

constraint (名)強制, 束縛, 圧迫, 制限, 制約, 限界, 天井, 拘束, 抑制, 締め付け, 阻害要因, 制約要因, 気がね, 遠慮
　alleviate the balance of payments constraints　国際収支のひっ迫を和らげる, 国際収支上の制約を緩和する
　balance of payments constraint　国際収支の天井, 国際収支のひっ迫, 国際収支上の制約
　break the balance of payments constraints　国際収支の天井を破る
　budget[budgetary] constraints　予算の制約, 予算の制限
　business constraints　事業上の制約
　capacity constraints　生産能力の限界, 供給能力の限界, 需給のひっ迫
　constraint to economic growth　経済成長に対する制約
　growth constraint　成長の阻害要因（=constraint to economic growth）
　labor constraints　人手不足
　leverage constraints　借入制限, 借入制限条項
　lift the constraint of the balance of payments on economic growth　経済成長に対する国際収支の天井[制約]を取り除く
　skill constraint　技術的制約
　social constraints　社会の束縛, 社会の束縛, 社会的制約
　supply-side[supply] constraints　供給面の制約, 供給のボトルネック
　tight constraints on domestic demand　内需抑制策
　tighter constraints on credit　金融収縮
　◆Deflation is being exacerbated by tighter constraints on credit. 金融収縮で、デフレが悪化している。◆The government should implement policies that will be effective in avoiding deflation being exacerbated by tighter constraints on credit. 政府は、金融収縮によるデフレの悪化を避ける上で有効な政策を実施しなければならない。

construction (名)建設, 建築, 建造, 建設工事, 工事, 構造, 構文, 構成, 組立て, 構築, 建造物, 構築物,（契約や条項の）解釈, 意味（「解釈」の意味の動詞はconstrue）
　advance on construction　建設工事前渡し金
　building construction permits　建設許可件数

College Construction Loan Insurance Association（Connie Lee）　大学建設融資保険協会（カニーリー）
　commercial construction　商業用不動産建設
　construction bond　建設国債
　construction contract awards　建設契約額
　construction investment　建設投資（=investment in construction）
　construction loan　建設工事期間中の貸出, 建設貸出金, 建設融資, 建設借入金, 建設ローン
　interest during construction　建設利息
　interest on construction　建設中の支払い利息
　portfolio construction　ポートフォリオの構築
　real residential construction spending　実質住宅投資
　◆The Bank of Tokyo-Mitsubishi UFJ will work together with foreign banks to extend 117 million Canadian dollars in joint loans to a mega solar power plant construction. 三菱東京UFJ銀行は、外銀数行の主幹事銀行として[外銀数行と連携して]、カナダの大型太陽光発電所（メガソーラー）建設事業に1億1,700万カナダ・ドルを協調融資する。

constructive (形)建設的な, 前向きの, 良い結果をもたらしそうな, 構造上の, 推定の, 推定による, 解釈上の, 擬制の, 準~, 見なし~
　constructive delivery　擬制引渡し, 推定的引渡し
　constructive distribution　見なし分配
　constructive repayment　見なし弁済
　constructive stock ownership　株式の見なし所有（=constructive ownership of stock）
　constructive tone　基調が明るいこと
　constructive total（loss）　解釈全損, 推定全損, 準全損
　constructive trust　擬制信託, 構成信託（当事者間の信託設定の意思表示なしで法律により設定される信託）

consumer (名)消費者, 利用者, 顧客, 個人, コンシューマー
　association of consumers　消費者組合
　consumer acceptance　消費者承認, 需要者承諾
　consumer (advice) center　消費者センター
　Consumer Affairs Agency　消費者庁
　consumer bankruptcy　消費者破産
　consumer boom　消費ブーム（=consumption boom）
　consumer buying　個人消費支出
　consumer characteristics　消費者特性
　consumer debt　消費者向けローン
　consumer deposit　消費者の預金
　consumer industry　消費財産業
　consumer inflation　消費者物価の上昇
　consumer installment credit　消費者信用残高, 消費者信用
　consumer installment loan　消費者割賦貸出金
　consumer insurance　個人向け保険
　consumer market　消費者市場, 消費市場
　consumer price survey　消費者物価調査
　consumer research　消費者需要調査, 消費者調査
　consumer resistance　消費者の購買拒否（=sales resistance）
　consumer's choice　消費者選択
　interest on consumer's debt　消費者負債利子
　loan to consumers　消費者金融
　transfer of consumer receivables　消費者向け債権の譲渡
　U.S. Consumer Financial Protection Bureau　米消費者金融保護局
　◆Aeon and Ito-Yokado started discount sales of foods imported from the United States to pass along to consumers the benefits of the yen's sharp climb against the dollar. イオ

ンとイトーヨーカ堂は、急激な円高・ドル安による円高差益を消費者に還元するため、米国から輸入した食料品の値下げセールを開始した。◆The life insurer's single-premium whole life insurance is popular with consumers as a form of savings or an investment for retirement. 同生保の一時払い終身保険は、一種の貯蓄や退職金の運用先として顧客に人気がある。◆The new Net-debit service will enable consumers to make purchases on the Internet and have the cost deducted automatically from their bank or postal savings accounts. この新ネット決済サービスを利用すると、利用者はインターネット上で買い物をして、その代金を利用者の銀行か郵便貯金の口座から自動的に引き落としてもらうことになる。

consumer banking 消費者金融業務
◆The bank wants to boost fee income and consumer banking to compensate for eight years of lending decline and reduced trading revenue. 同行は、8年にわたる貸出の減少と保有株の売買収入の減少をカバーするため、手数料収入と消費者金融業務の拡大を目指している。

consumer center 消費者センター, 消費生活センター
◆Consumer centers across the country have received many complaints about drop shipping businesses from contractors. 全国各地の消費生活センターには、ドロップ・シッピング(DS)事業について契約者から多数の苦情が寄せられている。

consumer confidence index 消費者信頼感指数, 消費者態度指数
◆Consumer confidence index is an indicator of consumption trends for the next six months. 消費者態度指数は、今後半年間の消費動向(消費意欲)を示す指標だ。

consumer credit 消費者信用(分割払い、つけ、短期ローンなど), 消費者金融, 消費者信用残高
　consumer credit bill 消費者信用残高
　consumer credit control 消費者信用規制
　consumer credit life insurance 消費者信用生命保険
　consumer credit losses 消費者貸出金貸倒れ損失
　consumer credit protection 消費者信用保護
　consumer credit recovery 償却消費者貸出金回収
　consumer credit reporting agency 個人信用情報センター
　consumer credit reserves 消費者貸倒れ引当金
　consumer's credit profile 個人信用情報
　Uniform Consumer Credit Code 統一消費者信用法典
◆Part-time workers tend to use consumer credit services when they run short of cash before payday. パート社員などは、給与の支給日前にお金がなくなると、消費者金融を利用する傾向がある。

Consumer Credit Protection Act of 1968 米国の1968年消費者信用保護法(信用条件の開示、強要的信用取引や信用情報などに関する規定がある)

consumer demand 消費需要
◆The main cause of the prolonged deflation is that consumer demand has been weak due to the current economic slump. デフレ長期化の主因は、現在の不況で消費需要が低迷していることだ。

consumer finance 消費者金融
◆Consumer finance is a lucrative business in Japan. 消費者金融は、日本では儲かる商売だ。

consumer finance company 消費者金融会社
◆Acom Co. is a major consumer finance company. アコムは、消費者金融会社の大手だ。

consumer finance customer 消費者金融の顧客
◆Sellers of multiple-debtor lists, produced by collecting information about consumer finance customers, are contributing to the spread of illegal moneylending. 消費者金融の顧客情報を入手して作った多重債務者リストを売る名簿業者が、ヤミ金融の横行に一役買っている。

consumer financing 消費者金融
　(⇒core business)

◆Business performance of the group's consumer financing affiliate has been in a slump. 同グループの消費者金融子会社の業績は、低迷している。

consumer lending business 消費者ローン事業, 消費者金融業務 (=consumer loan business)
◆Aiful Corp. has acquired a 5.8 percent stake in Higashi-Nippon Bank for about ¥3 billion in a bid to expand its consumer lending business. 消費者金融大手のアイフルは、消費者金融業務を拡大するため、東日本銀行の株式5.8%を約30億円で取得した。

consumer loan 消費者金融, 消費者貸出金, 消費者ローン (=consumer lending; ⇒alliance)
　consumer loan delinquency ratio 消費者貸出金延滞率
　consumer loan write-off 消費者貸倒れ償却
　sales volume of consumer loan 消費者ローン取扱い高
◆A homemaker in her 50s has used consumer loans to pay for nursing care for her mother. 50代のある主婦は、母親の介護費のため、消費者金融を利用してきた。

consumer loan company 消費者金融会社, 消費者金融業者 (=consumer loan firm)
◆Homemakers need their spouses' written agreement to borrow money from consumer loan companies. 専業主婦が消費者金融(業者)から金を借り入れるには、配偶者の同意書が必要だ。◆It became difficult for some homemakers to borrow money from consumer loan companies after the Moneylending Business Law was revised. 貸金業法の改正後、主婦などは消費者金融(業者)から金を借りにくくなった。◆Promise and Sumitomo Mitsui Banking Corp. are planning to jointly establish a new consumer loan company. プロミスと三井住友銀行は、合弁で消費者金融の新会社を設立する計画だ。

consumer loan firm 消費者金融会社, 消費者金融業者 (=consumer finance company)
◆Consumer loan firms have also been encouraged to enter the Japan Business Federation. 消費者金融会社も、日本経団連への加入を勧められている。◆People indebted to multiple consumer loan firms and financially strapped small-business operators have been the main targets of loan sharks. 多重債務者や資金繰りが苦しい零細事業主が、ヤミ金融業者の主な標的になっている。

consumer price index 消費者物価指数, CPI (=the key gauge of consumer prices)
　consumer price index for all urban consumers 全都市消費者物価指数
　core consumer price index 消費者物価指数のコア指数
　push up the consumer price index 消費者物価指数を押し上げる
◆Temporary factors, including a sharp rise in the price of rice, may have pushed up the consumer price index. コメの急激な値上りなどの一時的な要因が、消費者物価指数を押し上げてきた可能性がある。◆The central bank likely will predict the consumer price index will edge up in fiscal 2011. 日銀は、2011年度の消費者物価指数について小幅プラスの予測を示すと見られる。◆The consumer price index will continue to fall. 消費者物価指数の下落は、止まらないだろう。◆The nation's consumer price index in July fell 2.2 percent from a year earlier, marking the first fall in the 2 percent range in the postwar period. (2009年)7月の全国消費者物価指数は、前年同月比で2.2%下がり、戦後初めて2%台の下落率となった。◆The U.S. Labor Department's consumer price index rose 0.3 percent in June. 米労働省が発表した6月の消費者物価指数は、(前月より)0.3%上昇した。

米国の消費者物価指数
Consumer Price Index for All Urban Consumers 全都市消費者物価指数 CPI-U
Consumer Price Index for Urban Wage Earners and Clerical Workers 都市賃金労働者消費者物価指数 CPI-W

consumer price trends　消費者物価動向
◆The Bank of Japan envisages the prospects of economic growth and consumer price trends in its "Outlook for Economic Activity and Prices." 日銀は、「経済・物価情勢の展望」（展望リポート）で、経済成長や消費者物価の先行きを示している。

consumer spending　消費者支出, 個人消費
（=consumer expenditure, consumption expenditure）
◆Consumer spending waned amid the global financial crisis that followed the Lehman Brothers collapse in autumn 2008. 2008年秋のリーマン・ブラザーズの破たん後に生じた世界的金融危機を受けて、個人消費が低迷した。◆The global recession curbed consumer spending, hurting demand for chips that go into electronics such as computers and handsets. 世界同時不況で個人消費が抑えられ、コンピュータや携帯電話などの電子製品に用いられる半導体の需要も減退している［打撃を受けている］。

consumption tax　消費税
◆The last resort to secure a stable revenue source is raising the consumption tax. 安定した財源確保の頼みの綱は、消費税の引上げだ。◆The percentage of government funds from the consumption tax and other tax revenues for financing the basic pension plan remains about 36.5 percent. 基礎年金の財源としての消費税収などによる国の負担金の割合は、まだ約36.5％にとどまっている。

consumption tax hike　消費税の引上げ
◆A consumption tax hike would increase the financial burden shouldered by Joe Blow. 消費税を引き上げると、一般国民の金融負担［一般国民が負担する金融負担］が増すことになる。

consumption tax increase　消費税の引上げ
（=consumption tax hike）
◆Standard & Poor's downgraded Belgium's financial standing from AA+ to AA. スタンダード・アンド・プアーズ（S&P）は、ベルギー国債の格付けをダブルA（AA）プラスからダブルA（AA）に1段階引き下げた。◆To implement the consumption tax increase, close attention must be paid to business trends and conditions. 消費税の引上げを実施するには、景気動向にも目配りしなければならない。

consumption tax rate　消費税率
◆Bridging bonds issued by the government will be redeemed through a future increase in the consumption tax rate. 政府発行のつなぎ国債の返済［償還］は、今後の消費税率の引上げで行う。◆It will be unavoidable to raise the consumption tax rate to boost the social security purposes. 社会保障の充実のために消費税率を引き上げるのは、やむを得ないだろう。◆The consumption tax rate introduced in 1989 at 3 percent was raised to 5 percent in 1997. 1989年に3％で導入された消費税率は、1997年に5％に引き上げられた。◆The issue of hiking consumption tax rate is an indispensable one when discussing problems in the social security system. 消費税率引上げ問題は、社会保障制度の問題を論じる場合に避けて通れない（不可欠な）問題だ。◆Unless consumption tax rate is raised, the planned issuance of bridging bonds could lead to further deterioration of the debt-saddled government finances. 消費税率を引き上げないと、予定しているつなぎ国債の発行は、借金を背負っている国の財政の悪化をさらに招く可能性がある。

contact　（名）接触, 交流, 連絡, つて, コネ, 関係
business contact　取引関係, 仕事上つながりのある相手
contact a person under separate cover　別途連絡する
contact employee　得意先係
contact name　担当者名
contact numbers　連絡先の番号
contact person　窓口, 担当者
contact person responsible for inquiries　お問い合わせの窓口［担当者］
contact visit　接触訪問
contact with oil and other cargo　油、他貨物との接触損害, COOC
get in contact with　〜と連絡を取る
◆Major financial groups do not have regular business contacts with small and medium-sized auto parts makers. 大手金融機関は、中小の自動車部品メーカーと通常の取引関係がない。

contain　（動）抑える, 抑制する, 阻止する, 封じ込める, 歯止めをかける, 削減する, 含む, 〜に等しい
contain costs　経費を削減する
contain the debt crisis　債務危機を封じ込める
contain the financial crisis　金融危機を封じ込める
preemptively contain growing deflationary concerns　高まるデフレ懸念に先手を打つ, デフレ懸念の高まりに先手を打つ
◆By conducting additional monetary easing policy, the Fed attempts to preemptively contain growing deflationary concerns in the United States. 追加金融緩和策を実施して、米連邦準備制度理事会（FRB）は、米国で高まるデフレ懸念に先手を打とうとしている。◆Europe promised the Group of 20 major economies to take concerted action to contain the financial crisis. 欧州は、結束して金融危機を封じ込めることを主要20か国・地域（G20）に公約した。◆Japan, the United States and emerging countries are upping their pressure on Europe to contain the Greek-triggered sovereign debt crisis. 日米と新興国は、欧州に対して、ギリシャに端を発したソブリン危機（政府債務危機）封じ込めの圧力を強めている。◆The European Central Bank is working more closely with France and Germany to contain the financial crisis. 欧州中央銀行は、金融危機を封じ込めるため、フランス、ドイツと連携を強めている。

contango　（名）（ロンドン証券取引所の）株式決済引取り猶予金, 決済引取り猶予金, 引取り猶予金, 株式決済猶予金,（買い手が支払いを遅らせたときに払う）繰越し日歩（ひぶ）, 順日歩, 遅延金利, 先物価格のほうが直物価格よりも高い状態（forwardation）, コンタンゴ
（=forwardation:「コンタンゴ」は、米国の商品や為替市場取引で先物価格が直物価格を上回っている状態のこと。ただし、英国の証券市場では、トレーダーが次の決済期間まで未決済の売り持ちや買い持ちを繰り越せるようにする取決めをいう。⇒backwardation, forwardation）
contango business [dealing]　繰越し取引
contango day　繰越し決算日, 繰越し決算日（一般に決済期間の最終日でaccount day（決済日）とも呼ばれる）
contango rate　株式決済猶予金のレート, コンタンゴ・レート
normal contango　順ざや先物価格
◆The market is in contango. いまは、順ざや相場だ。

content　（名）情報・情報サービスの内容, 情報の中身, 情報, 趣旨, 要旨, 著作物, ラジオやテレビの番組, 番組の内容, 事業, 収入源, 含有量, 容量, 容積, 体積, 面積, 広さ, 産出量, 満足, コンテンツ
content-certified mail　内容証明郵便
content production　コンテンツ作成, コンテンツの制作
（=production of content）
conversion to different form of insurance contents　保険契約の内容変更
export content　輸出含有量
home and its contents　住宅と家財
job content　職務・仕事の内容
loss content　回収不能, 信用損失
loss content of assets　資産減価
operative content　実効性

regulation of illegal and harmful contents　違法有害コンテンツ規制
Web contents　ウェブ上の著作物, ウェブ・コンテンツ
　(=Web content)
◆As investment for digitalization is costly, NBS needs to establish a more profitable management system, including joint investment in digital-related facilities and content with the Fuji TV group. デジタル化の投資負担は軽くないので、ニッポン放送は、フジテレビ・グループとのデジタル関連施設への共同投資やコンテンツ(情報内容)の共有など、収益力の高い経営システムを確立する必要がある。◆Under the earthquake insurance system, homeowners initially could insure their house and its contents up to a maximum of 1.5 million. 地震保険制度で、住宅所有者は当初、住宅と家財の合計で150万円(現在は住宅5,000万円、家財1,000万円)が保険契約額の上限だった。

contingency　(名)偶発, 偶発性, 偶発事象[事項, 事件], 不測の事態, 緊急事態, 非常事態, 不慮の事故, 臨時費用
　contingency fee　(弁護士の)成功報酬
　contingency fund　臨時費, 偶発資金
　　(=contingent fund)
　contingency package　緊急時対策, 緊急支援資金
　contingency plan　非常事態計画, 不慮の事故対策計画
◆The European Financial Stability Facility set up a €750 billion contingency package together with the International Monetary Fund. 欧州金融安定基金(EU)は、国際通貨基金(IMF)の協力を得て7,500億ユーロ(約90兆円)の緊急支援資金を準備した。

contingent　(形)偶発の, 不確定の, 不確かな, 臨時の, 〜を条件とする, 条件付きの, 〜に付随する
　contingent annuity　不確定年金, 臨時払い年金
　contingent assets　偶発資産
　contingent bargain　条件付き取引
　contingent claim　条件付き請求権
　contingent claim security　条件付き証券
　contingent debt　偶発債務
　contingent gain [profit]　偶発利益, 偶発利得
　contingent interest　偶発的金利
　contingent issues　臨時発行証券, 条件付き証券
　contingent liability　偶発債務(現時点では債務は発生していないが、係争事件で賠償義務が生じるとか保証付きで商品を販売する場合など、将来発生する可能性がある未確定の債務のこと)
　contingent loss　偶発損失
　contingent rent　偶発リース料
　contingent reserve　偶発損失引当金, 偶発損失積立金
　　(=contingency reserve, reserve for contingencies, special contingency reserve)
　contingent settlement provision　条件付き決済条項
　contingent share agreement　条件付き株式契約

continue　(動)続ける, 続行する, 継続する, 延期する
　(自動)続く, 存続する
　continue in effect　効力が存続する, 〜の間有効である, 〜まで有効である
　continue operations　事業を継続する
◆Chapter 11 bankruptcy provides for a business to continue operations while formulating a plan to repay its creditors. 米連邦改正破産法11章の破産の規定では、企業は事業を継続する一方、債権者への債務返済計画を策定することができる。◆Global unrest in the financial markets is continuing. 世界的な金融市場の混乱が、続いている。◆In the global financial markets, unrest is continuing as there is no end in sight to fiscal crises to the United States and some European countries. 世界の金融市場では、米国と一部の欧州諸国の財政危機の収束が見通せないため、混乱が続いている。◆Nippon Life Insurance Co., the top shareholder in Olympus Corp., will continue supporting Olympus in light of its advanced technology in its core business such as endoscopes. オリンパスの筆頭株主の日本生命は、内視鏡などオリンパスの中核事業の高い技術力を踏まえて、引き続きオリンパスを支えていく方針だ。◆The Bank of Japan continued selling yen and buying dollars intermittently. 日銀は、断続的に円売り・ドル買いを継続した。◆The economic recovery continues. 景気回復が続いている。◆The rally in the bond market continued. 債券相場の上昇が続いた[債券相場は、続伸した]。◆The yen continues its relentless surge and stock prices keep falling. 円高に歯止めがかからず、株安も続いている。◆The yen's appreciation continues. 円高は続いている。◆There have been no signs of a rebound in the amount of outstanding loans, which continues on an abated decline. このところ引き続き減少傾向にある銀行の貸出残高に、反転の兆しは見えない。

continue to　引き続き〜する, 継続して〜する, 今後とも〜する, 〜を維持する
　continue to advance strongly　力強い伸びを示す
　continue to fall　下がり続ける, 続落する
　continue to moderate　鈍化傾向が続く
　continue to monitor the currency market　今後とも為替市場の動き注視する
　continue to rise　伸び続ける, 続伸する, 増勢が続く
　continue to rise across the board　全面高が続いている
　continue to show weakness　続落する
　continue to strengthen　引き続き好調である
　continue to strengthen over the period　続伸する
◆If business conditions continue to worsen, financial institutions will face more newly emerging nonperforming loans than they can ever keep up with. 景気がこのまま悪化し続ければ、金融機関は新たに不良債権が生まれてその処理が追いつかなくなる。◆If we are to continue to deliver improved financial results, we must continue to enhance our competitiveness. 今後とも業績[財務成績]向上を図るには、当社の競争力を引き続き高める必要がある。◆Lending by regional banks continued to outpace that of larger lenders in July. 地銀の7月の貸出は、前月に続いて大手金融機関[大手行]の貸出を上回った。◆The Bank of Japan must continue to promptly supply funds to prevent the financial contraction that all corporate managers dread. 企業経営者が恐れる金融収縮を防ぐため、日銀は迅速に資金供給を続ける必要がある。◆The global economy continues to recover, albeit in a fragile and uneven way. 世界経済は、脆弱(ぜいじゃく)で一様ではないが、回復を続けている。◆The government and the Bank of Japan will likely continue to work together in fighting the sharp rise in the yen's value. 政府と日銀は、急激な円高阻止で協調路線を継続することになりそうだ。◆The government will continue to monitor the currency market. 政府は、今後も為替市場の動きを注視する方針だ。◆The ongoing global economic downturn continues to hit demand for flights. 今回の世界的な景気後退[世界同時不況]で、航空需要が引き続き減少している[打撃を受けている]。◆The U.S. dollar continues to strengthen against the yen. ドル高円安が続いている。◆The yen continues to rise. 円高が続いている。

continued　(形)継続する, 償還延期の
　continued bond　償還延期社債, 償還延期公債
　continued bond market rally　債券相場の続伸
◆Amid the continued yen's historically high levels, increasing numbers of people are opening foreign currency deposit accounts. 歴史的な円高水準が続くなか、外貨預金口座を設ける人が増えている。◆The yen's continued rise is worrisome for large manufacturers. 大企業・製造業には、円高進行も懸念材料だ。◆There is a limit to conventional pump-priming measures amid a continued decline in birthrate and a conse-

quent graying and shrinking population. 少子高齢化や人口減少などが進行するなかで、従来の景気刺激策［景気テコ入れ策］では限界がある。

continued fall in U.S. stock prices　米国の株安進行
◆The continued fall in U.S. stock prices and the dollar's depreciation has battered the Japanese economy. 米国の株安とドル安の進行が、日本経済を直撃してい［激しく揺さぶっている。］

continuing　（形）継続的な、継続する、長期化する、断続的な、永続的な、永久の、長年にわたる
　continuing asset deflation　長期化する資産デフレ、資産デフレの長期化
　continuing franchise fee　継続フランチャイズ料
　continuing guarantee　継続保証、継続的保証
　continuing operations　継続事業
　continuing security　継続的担保
　continuous intervention　断続的な市場介入
　ensure continuing supplies　安定供給を確保する
◆Through continuing gains in annual earnings, it will be possible, over time, to adjust the payout ratio while still maintaining our dividend record. 年間利益の増大を続けることによって、当社の配当実績を今後とも維持しながら、時期が来たら配当性向を調整することは可能である。

continuous　（形）連続的な、連続した、途切れない、継続的な、終日の、延々と続く
　continuous budget　継続型予算
　continuous compounding　連続複利計算
　continuous session　接続売買
　continuous time　終日取引

contra broker　相手方ブローカー

contract　（動）契約を結ぶ、契約する、請け負う、感染する、短縮する、縮小させる、減少させる　（自動）縮小する、減少する、収縮する、悪化する、マイナス成長となる、景気が悪化する、景気後退する
　contract in　正式に参加の契約をする、契約に加わる
　contract out　正式に不参加を表明する、（協定などを）脱退する、下請に仕事を出す
◆In an illegal building practice called "maru nage," a project contracted by a construction company is farmed out to subcontractors.「丸投げ」という違法な建築慣行では、建設会社が請け負った仕事が、下請業者に委託される。◆The current account surplus contracted by 28.2 percent in January from a year earlier to ¥774.9 billion. 日本の1月の経常黒字（経常収支の黒字額）は、前年同月比で28.2%減少して7,749億円になった。◆The economies of Ireland and Spain will contract in 2011. 2011年のアイルランドやスペインの経済は、マイナス成長になると思われる。◆The infusion of public funds into major banks was originally meant to free banks from their need to contract total lending to maintain capital adequacy ratios. 大手銀行への公的資金注入のそもそもの狙いは、自己資本比率を維持するために貸出総額を縮小せざるをえない事態から銀行を解き放つことにあった。

contract　（名）契約、契約書、規約、協定、協定書、請負、契約商品、契約品、約定品　（⇒financial settlement, foreign currency exchange contract, forward contract, forward exchange contract, group insurance, insurance agent, investment company, underlying asset）
　bank investment contract　銀行投資契約
　buy contract　買い約定、買い契約
　call option contract　コール・オプション契約
　clearing contract　清算取引
　contract high/low　最高値/最安値
　contract in foreign currency　外貨売買契約
　contract money　契約保証金
　contract month　限月（げんげつ）
　contract not fulfilled　契約不履行（不渡りの文言）
　contract note　売買契約書、契約書、取引確認書、予約票、約束手形、注文成立通知状
　contract of indemnity　補償契約、損害填補契約
　contract of insurance　保険契約
　contract sheet　売買契約記録
　contracting of granting credit　信用供与契約
　deferred payment contract　延払い契約
　deposit administration contract　預託管理契約
　dormant contract　上場休止契約
　exchange contract　為替契約、為替予約
　（exchange）contract slip　為替予約締結確認書
　forward contract　先物契約
　forward contract slip［scrip］　先物為替予約票
　front contracts　期近物
　futures contract　先物契約、先物
　group insurance contract　団体保険契約
　health insurance contract　健康保険契約
　insurance contract　保険契約
　　（=contract of insurance）
　limited-term contract　有期契約
　loan contract　融資契約、貸付け契約
　marine insurance contract　海上保険契約
　pension contract　年金契約
　qualified financial contract　適格金融契約
　reinsurance contract　再保険契約
　sell contract　売り契約、売り約定
　sell short the futures contract　先物を空売りする
　selling contract　売り契約
　spot contract　現物契約
　the contract month　（為替予約の）限月（げんげつ）、実行月、（先物取引での）受渡し期限（the delivery month）
◆AFLAC has increased its number of contracts since it launched Japanese operations in 1974. アフラック（アメリカンファミリー生命保険）は、1974年に日本で業務を開始して以来、契約件数を増やしている。◆Domestic nonlife insurance companies usually renew contracts with most of their corporate clients each April. 国内の損保各社は通常、毎年4月に大半の顧客企業と（保険）契約の更新を行っている。◆In the case of single-premium whole life insurance policies, policyholders make one large premium payment up front when they sign the contract. 一時払い終身保険の場合は、保険契約者が契約を結ぶ際に［契約時に］多額の保険料を前もって一括で払い込む。◆In this type of life insurance products, the rate of return after canceling the insurance contract can be higher than that of a savings account if a policyholder upholds the contract for five to 10 years. この種の生保商品では、保険契約者が保険契約を5〜10年続けると、解約後の利回り（予定利率）は預金よりも高い利回りが見込める。◆Nonlife insurance companies used to disperse the risk of large contracts with new corporate clients through reinsurance contracts with other insurance or reinsurance companies. 損保各社は従来、他の保険会社もしくは再保険会社と再保険契約を結んで、新規顧客企業と大型契約を結ぶリスクを分散してきた。◆The firm hedged its long position in stocks by selling short the futures contract. 同社は、先物を空売りして現物株のロング・ポジションをヘッジした。◆The revised Investment Deposit and Interest Rate Control Law annuls contracts for loans whose interest rates exceed 109.5 percent per annum-the maximum interest rate permitted on loans extended and received by individuals. 今回改正された出資法では、金利が個人間の貸し借りの上限である年利109.5%を超える融資契約を無効としている。◆The 10 life insurers' combined outstanding balance of indi-

vidual life insurance and annuity contracts declined for five consecutive years to ¥1.15 quadrillion. 生保10社合計の個人保険・年金の保有契約高(保険の総額)は1,150兆円で、5年連続(5期連続)で減少した。◆The United Auto Workers ratified a four-year contract with Mitsubishi Motor North America. 全米自動車労組は、北米三菱自動車との4年労使協約を承認した。

contract rate 約定金利
◆Any payment not made when due will, in addition to any other right or remedy of Licensor, incur a finance charge at the lesser of three hundred basis points over the 3-month London Inter Bank Offered Rate ("LIBOR+3") on the date payment was due or the highest applicable legal contract rate. 支払いが支払い期日までに履行されない場合、ライセンサーの他の権利や救済請求権に加えて、支払い期日時点の3か月物ロンドン銀行間取引金利(LIBOR)プラス3%(LIBOR+3%)または適用される最高法定約定金利のうち、いずれか低いほうの金利の金融費用が発生する。

contracted (形)短縮した、縮小した、省略した、契約した、協定した
 contracted equilibrium 縮小均衡
 contracted interest 約定利息[利率], 約定金利, 契約金利
 contracted interest rate 約定金利
  (=contracted rate of interest)
 contracted public works orders 公共工事請負金額
 contracted quantity 契約数量
 contracted salvage charges 契約救助料
 contracted specifications 契約仕様
◆The rational actions for survival taken by individual companies herald a danger that could lead the Japanese economy into contracted equilibrium. 生き残りをかけて個々の企業が取っている合理的な行動が、日本経済を縮小均衡に導く危険性をはらんでいる。

contraction (名)縮小, 収縮, 減少, 減退, 後退, 落込み, マイナス成長, マイナス成長幅, 景気[業況]の悪化, 景気縮小, 景気後退, 不況, (負債を)負うこと, 契約を結ぶこと, 短縮語
 balanced contraction 縮小均衡
 be headed for contraction マイナス成長に向かっている
 business contraction 事業縮小, 業務縮小
 contraction coefficient 収縮率
 contraction in demand 需要の減退, 需要の落込み
  (=demand contraction)
 contraction in the monetary aggregates マネー・サプライの減少
 credit contraction 信用収縮, 信用の収縮
 economic contraction 景気の悪化, 景気収縮, 景気縮小, 景気後退, 不況, マイナス成長
  (=contractionary economy)
 employment contraction 雇用の減少
  (=contractionary employment)
 expansion and contraction in the factory sector 製造業の景気拡大と景気後退[景気縮小]
 experience a contraction マイナス成長となる
 fall into contraction マイナス成長に陥る
 financial contraction 金融収縮
 fiscal contraction 財政支出の削減
 money contraction 通貨収縮
 prevent further contraction 景気の一段の悪化を防ぐ
 production contraction 生産の縮小, 生産縮小
 sharp contraction 大幅なマイナス成長, 急減
 trade contraction 貿易の縮小
◆The Bank of Japan must continue to promptly supply funds to prevent the financial contraction that all corporate managers dread. 企業経営者が恐れる金融収縮を防ぐため、日銀は迅速に資金供給を続ける必要がある。◆The economy is in a contraction phase. 景気は、後退局面にある。◆The eurozone economy recorded its first ever contraction in the second quarter of 2008. ユーロ圏の2008年第2四半期(4〜6月期)の経済は、1999年のユーロ発足以来、初めてマイナス成長となった。

contraction in the service sector サービス業の業況悪化
◆The Dow Jones industrials plunged 370 points after an unexpected contraction in the service sector. 予想しなかったサービス業の業況悪化を受けて、ダウ平均株価(工業株30種)は、前日比で370ドル急落した。

contraction of the real economy 実体経済の後退, 実体経済の景気後退
◆The financial crisis is closely interrelated with the contraction of the real economy. 金融危機は、実体経済の景気後退と密接にかかわっている。

contractor (名)契約者, 請負人, 引受人, 建設請負業者
 construction contractor 建設請負業者
 contractor's all risks and public liability insurance 建設工事保険
 contractor's bond 建設請負業者保険
 contractor's compensation policy 建設請負業者保証保険証券
 contractor's contingent liability policy 建設請負業者未必責任保険証券
 contractor's equipment floater policy 建設請負業者機械器具包括保険証券
 contractor's equipment insurance policy 建設請負業者用具保険証券
 contractor's liability insurance policy 建設請負業者責任保険証券
 contractor's protective liability policy 建設請負業者間接責任保険証券
 general contractor ゼネコン
 major contractor 大手建設会社

contractual (形)契約の, 約定の, 契約上の
 contractual (accumulation) plan 継続利益累積型投資信託, 契約積立てプラン
 contractual capacity 契約締結能力
 contractual currency basis 契約通貨ベース
 contractual interbank performance agreement 銀行間業績契約
 contractual interest rate 約定金利
 contractual lending commitment 貸出予約, 契約に基づく貸出義務
 contractual liability 契約責任, 契約上の責任
 contractual liability insurance 契約責任保険
 contractual life 契約期間
 contractual payment 債務の返済
 contractual rate 約定金利
 contractual savings 契約貯蓄
 contractual service payment 契約返済額
 contractual-type funds 契約型投資信託, 契約型投信
 contractual-type investment fund 契約型投資信託, 契約型投信
 contractual value date 売戻し約定日

contribute (動)出資する, 払い込む, 納付する, 拠出する, 寄与する, 貢献する, 協力する, 支援する, 〜に一役買う (⇒funding, gain名詞, pay-as-you-go formula)
 capital contributed in excess of par or stated value 額面超過払込み資本
 capital contributed in excess of par value 株式払込み剰余金

contribute additional funds 出資金［拠出金］を増やす
contribute to the bottom line 利益に貢献する
◆Japan will contribute an additional $500 million to the Global Fund to Fight AIDS, Tuberculosis and Malaria (GFATM). 日本は、「世界エイズ・結核・マラリア対策基金」に5億ドルを追加拠出する。◆Kanebo will contribute ¥14 billion of the capital and the IRC will put up the remaining ¥86 billion. カネボウが資本金（1,000億円）のうち140億円を出資し、産業再生機構（IRC）が残りの860億円を出資する。
◆Sellers of multiple-debtor lists, produced by collecting information about consumer finance customers, are contributing to the spread of illegal moneylending. 消費者金融の顧客情報を入手して作った多重債務者リストを売る名簿業者が、ヤミ金融の横行に一役買っている。

contributed （形）出資した，拠出された，払い込まれた，貢献［寄与］した
 contributed assets 現物出資される財産
 contributed capital 払込み資本，拠出資本，株主が払い込んだ資本 （=paid-in capital）
 contributed surplus 払込み剰余金，資本準備金

contributing factor 貢献要因

contributing interest 分担利益

contribution （名）出資，拠出，寄与，貢献，寄付，協力，支援，貢献額，寄付金，義援金，拠出金，負担金，掛け金，分担金，共同海損分担金，負担部分，求償権，保険料，納付金 （⇒additional contribution, hedge名詞, national pension, national pension program）
 additional contribution 追加拠出
 additional financial contributions 追加拠出金，追加金融支援
 associate contribution 関連会社の利益寄与
 capital contribution 資本拠出，出資
 cash contribution 資金協力
 charitable contribution 慈善寄付金
 contribution clause 損害分担条項
 contribution-defined 確定拠出型の
 contribution for general average 共同海損分担
 contribution-paid period 保険料納付期間，拠出期間
 contribution plan （生保の）剰余配当制
 contribution profit or loss 貢献損益
 contribution surplus 払込み剰余金
 contribution to capital 出資金，資本への拠出額
 contributions and equity 出資と持ち分
 contributions for social insurance 社会保険負担金
 contributions to affiliated company 関係会社出資金
 contributions to guarantee fund 支払い保証基金拠出金
 contributions to retirement funds 退職基金への拠出金
 defined contribution (pension) plan 確定拠出型［確定拠出］年金制度，確定拠出制度，拠出建て年金制度，保険料建て方式 （⇒investment performance）
 employee contributions 従業員の拠出金
 employers' contributions to social security schemes 社会保険雇い主負担
 equity contribution 出資
 excess contributions to a defined pension plan 確定拠出型年金制度に対する超過拠出金
 financial contribution 資金協力，資金面での協力・貢献，金融支援
 government's contribution 国の負担金，国庫負担
 increase [rise] contributions to multilateral financial institutions 国際金融機関への出資比率を引き上げる［高める］
 level contribution 平準拠出
 national contribution ratio 国民負担率（所得に関して個人と企業が支払う税金と社会保険料の割合）
 primary contribution 最大の貢献
 profit contribution 利益貢献度，利益寄与
 social contribution burden 社会保障負担
 social insurance contribution 社会保険料
 social security contribution 社会保障負担
 taxpayer contribution 国民負担金

◆Contributions collected by the Japanese Red Cross Society and mass media companies will be used to support the livelihood of the disaster victims. 日本赤十字社やマスコミ各社に寄せられた義援金は、被災者の生計支援に充てられる。◆Italy's contribution to the IMF totals about $12.6 billion. イタリアのIMF（国際通貨基金）への出資総額は、約126億ドルだ。◆The Board of Audit intends to include the total taxpayer contribution to JAL in its audit account report compiled in November 2011. 会計検査院は、2011年11月にまとめる決算検査報告書に、日航に対する総国民負担額を盛り込む方針だ。◆The IMF extends to countries with relatively healthier public finances one- to two-year loans of up to 1,000 percent of their contribution to the IMF without strict conditions. IMF（国際通貨基金）は、財政が比較的健全な国に対して、期間1～2年の資金を厳しい条件なしでIMFに出資している額（クォータ）の最大10倍まで融資している。◆The new shares of common stock are being allocated to plan participants over ten years as contributions are made to the plan. この普通株式新株は、制度への資金拠出と並行して、10年にわたり制度加入者に割り当てられています。◆The tie-up is expected to include a contribution by Mitsubishi Tokyo to the UFJ group's planned capital increase. 統合には、UFJグループが予定している増資に三菱銀行が出資することも含まれる見込みだ。◆To stabilize the pension system, the government raised its burden in the basic pension plan to 50 percent of the total contribution from fiscal 2009. 年金制度の安定化を図るため、政府は、基礎年金の国の負担割合を2009年度から総給付金の50％に引き上げた。◆Under the new financing scheme, the IMF will extend to financially strapped countries loans of up to 500 percent of their contribution to the IMF. 新融資制度では、財政の資金繰りが苦しく［厳しく］なった国に対して、その国がIMF（国際通貨基金）に出資している額の最大5倍までIMFが融資する。

contribution ratio 出資比率，拠出比率
◆Sooner or later, the contribution ratio of the IMF member countries will be reviewed as the fast-growing emerging economies gain larger presence. いずれ、IMF加盟国の出資比率は、急成長している新興国が存在感を増していることから、見直されることになろう。

contributor （名）出資者［出資国］，拠出者［拠出国］，献金者，貢献者，寄付者，寄贈者，寄稿者［寄稿家］，投稿者，貢献要因，（事故などの）原因となるもの
◆The United States is the largest contributor to the IMF. 米国は、IMFへの最大出資国だ。

control （動）支配する，掌握する，管理する，抑制する，抑える，操作する，コントロールする （⇒stock swap）
 control capital outflows 資本流出を抑える
 control credit losses 貸倒れ損失を管理する
 control excessive volatility 過度の変動を抑制する［抑える］
 control inflation インフレを抑制する
 control more than 50% of the voting stock 議決権株の50％超を掌握する
 control stock index arbitrage 株価指数［インデックス］裁定取引を規制する
 control the board of directors 取締役会を掌握する
 control the credit supply 信用供給量をコントロールする

control the market　市場を支配する
control the money supply　通貨供給量をコントロールする
◆The market intervention was carried out to control excessive volatility in the exchange market. 為替相場の過度の変動を抑制するため、市場介入[為替介入]が実施された。◆The markets are now controlled by the fund managers of pension funds, investment trust funds, hedge funds and various other funds. 市場は、今では年金基金や投資信託基金、ヘッジ・ファンドなどのファンド・マネージャーによって支配されている。◆The voting rights NBS holds in Fuji TV will be restored if Livedoor can control the board of directors and decrease Fuji TV's holdings in NBS to 25 percent or less by allocating new shares to a third party. フジテレビに対してニッポン放送が保有している議決権は、ライブドアが取締役会を掌握して、第三者割当増資でフジテレビのニッポン放送の持ち株比率を25％以下に下げることができれば復活する。◆We control our exposure to credit risk through credit approvals, credit limits and monitoring procedures. 当社は、信用供与承認や信用限度、監視手続きを通じて信用リスクを管理しています。

control　（名）支配, 統制, 管理, 経営支配権, 経営権, 規制, 抑制, 制御, コントロール　（⇒collapse動詞, credit control, debt-ridden, Federal Reserve Board, state control, stockholder, take control of）
accounts control　信用管理
after the fact control　事後管理
banker's control　銀行支配
before the fact control　事前管理
budgetary control　予算管理, 予算統制
capital control　資本規制, 資本取引規制, 資本移動規制, 為替規制
cash control　現金管理
change of control　経営権の変更
client control　顧客管理
common control　共通の支配
consumer credit control　消費者信用規制
control document　外為取引の確認文書
control market　支配市場
control of credit　信用規制, 信用制限, 信用管理, 与信管理　（⇒credit control）
control of demand and supply　需給統制
control of foreign exchange market　外貨市場管理, 外貨市場統制
control of foreign fund　外資管理, 外国資金規制
control of inflation　インフレ抑制
control of investment risk　投資リスクの管理
control of liquidity ratio　流動性比率管理　（=liquidity ratio control）
control of long-term capital　長期資本規制
control of ownership　経営権
control procedure　内部統制手続き
control rate　（為替の）中心レート　（=pivot rate）
control risk　内部統制上のリスク
control-share acquisition　支配株の取得[買収], 経営支配株の取得[買収]
control stock　支配株, 経営支配株　（=controlling interest [stock]）
controls of investment　投資に対する規制
corporate control　企業経営
credit control　信用管理, 与信管理, 信用規制
currency control　通貨管理　（=control of currency）
Depository Institutions Deregulation and Monetary Control Act　金融制度改革法
divorce of ownership and control　所有と支配の分離
dollar control　金額管理
dual control　二重統制
exchange (rate) control　為替管理　（=control of exchange）
financial control　財務管理, 財政統制, 金融統制
financial qualitative control　金融の質的管理
Foreign Exchange and Foreign Trade Control Law　外国為替及び外国貿易管理法, 外為管理法, 外為法
foreign exchange control　外国為替管理, 為替制限
Foreign Exchange Control Law　外国為替及び外国貿易管理法, 外為管理法
fund control　資金管理, 資金統制
Home Country Control　自国銀行監督の原則
home office control　本店勘定
indirect control　間接支配
interest rate control　利率管理, 利子率管理
internal control　内部統制, 社内管理
maintain the current management's control　現経営陣の経営支配権を維持する
majority control　過半数支配, 過半数所有支配, 過半数子会社
management control　経営支配, 経営支配権, 経営管理
market control　市場統制
minority control　少数支配, 少数派支配
monetary control　金融規制, 貨幣的統制
operating control　業務管理
owner control　所有者支配
pass out of control　経営権を手放す
profit control　利益統制, 利潤統制
retain control over　～に対する経営支配権を維持する
risk control　リスク管理
separation of ownership and control　所有と経営の分離
take control of　～の経営権を握る[掌握する], ～の経営権を支配する, ～の主導権を握る
the control of a specific stockholder　特定株主の支配権, 特定株主の経営支配権
◆Citigroup, the largest U.S. bank, and Wells Fargo, the fifth-largest U.S. bank, are battling for control of the sixth-largest U.S. bank Wachovia. 米銀行最大手のシティグループと米銀行5位のウェルズ・ファーゴは、同4位のワコビアの経営権獲得競争[買収合戦]を展開している。◆In order to bring the European crisis under control, the EU, ECB and IMF must work even more closely together. 欧州危機の収束を図るには、欧州連合（EU）、欧州中央銀行（ECB）と国際通貨基金（IMF）の緊密な連携を強化する必要がある。◆The bank is now under state control. 同行は現在、国有化されている[国の管理下にある]。◆The Greece-induced fiscal crisis is still not under control. ギリシャ発の財政危機は、まだ収束していない。◆The purpose of issuing a sizable amount of new shares is to maintain the control of a specific stockholder over the company. 新株の大量発行は、同社に対する特定株主の支配権[経営支配権]確保が目的だ。◆The purpose of issuing share warrants is to maintain the current management's control over the company. 株式予約権の発行は、現経営陣の会社の経営支配権を維持することを目的としている。

controlled　（形）管理された, 統制された, 制御された, 支配された, 被支配の
controlled amortization　管理償還, 定時償還
controlled company [firm]　傘下企業, 子会社, 被支配会社
controlled currency　管理通貨
controlled economy　統制経済

controlled float　管理された変動相場制, 変動相場制の管理
controlled foreign corporation　在外子会社, 被支配外国会社[法人]
controlled inflation　調整インフレ
controlled rate　統制相場
controlled trade　管理貿易
government-controlled home loan giant　米政府系住宅ローン大手
◆The U.S. central bank will buy mortgage-backed securities (MBS) guaranteed by the government-controlled home loan giants Fannie Mae, Freddie Mac and Ginnie Mae. 米連邦準備制度理事会(FRB)は、米政府系住宅ローン大手のファニー・メイ(米連邦住宅貸付公社)、フレディ・マック(米連邦住宅抵当金庫)とジニー・メイ(米政府系住宅金融公庫)が保証した住宅ローン担保証券(MBS)を買い取ることになった。

controller　(名)経理部長, コントローラー
(=comptroller: 米大手企業の「コントローラー(controller)」は、会社の資金調達や運用などの財務部門を統括する役員の「トレジャラー(treasurer)」と違って、会社の経理や会計監査など経理部門の統括者。中小企業の場合は、トレジャラーがコントローラーを兼務することもある)

controlling　(形)支配する, 優先する, 支配している, 支配できる, 支配的な, 管理する
controlling company　支配会社, 親会社
（=parent company）
controlling families　経営者一族
controlling function　管理機能, 統制機能
controlling shareholder　支配株主
controlling stock [share]　支配株, 経営支配株[株式], 経営支配に必要な株式数

controlling interest　支配(的)持ち分, 支配株主持ち分, 経営支配権, 経営支配株 (=controlling stake:「経営支配権」とは、一般には他社を支配できる議決権株式 (voting stock) の過半数(50%超)を所有することをいう。⇒quality)
◆The IT firm is moving fast to buy controlling interest in Nippon Broadcasting Systems Inc. このIT企業は、ニッポン放送の経営支配株の買い集めを進めている。

controlling stake [stock]　経営支配株[株式], 支配株, 支配持ち分, 支配株主持ち分, 経営支配権
(=controlling interest)
acquire a controlling stake in　〜の経営支配権[支配持ち分]を取得する
purchase a controlling stake in　〜の経営支配権を取得する
◆The tender offer to acquire a controlling stake of more than 50 percent in the company will last through December 10. 同社の50%超の経営支配権[支配持ち分]取得をめざした株式公開買付け(TOB)の期限は、12月10日までの予定だ。

convenience　(名)便利, 便利さ, 利便, 利便性, 便宜, 便益, 打算, コンビニエンス
◆The two exchanges hope to enhance convenience for investors by the merger. 両取引所は、経営統合によって投資家の利便性を高めたいとしている。

conventional　(形)従来の, 在来の, 従来型の, これまでの, 通常の, 伝統的な, 慣習的な, 型にはまった, 月並みの, 独創性のない, 核を使わない, 大会の, 会議の, コンベンショナル
buck conventional wisdom　一般常識を覆す
conventional auction　コンベンショナル入札方式
conventional bond　普通債
conventional gilts　固定利付きギルト債
conventional interest　約定利子

conventional loan　通常型ローン
conventional money rate　約定金利
（=conventional interest [interest rate]）
conventional paradigm　従来の枠組み
conventional tariff　協定関税, 協定税率
conventional value　協定価格
conventional wisdom　世間一般の通念, 一般通念, 世間知, 一般常識, 常識, 市場のコンセンサス
◆In the conventional IMF's scheme, countries were only given a credit line even after the IMF approved loans and they could not withdraw funds unless the fiscal crisis facing them worsened. 従来のIMF(国際通貨基金)の仕組みだと、各国は融資の承認を得ても融資枠を与えられるだけで、財政危機が深刻化しないと資金を引き出すことができなかった。◆There has been a prevailing atmosphere of stalemate insofar as conventional job-related measures are concerned. 従来の雇用関連対策に関するかぎり、手詰まり感が深まっている。◆There is a limit to conventional pump-priming measures amid a continued decline in birthrate and a consequent graying and shrinking population. 少子高齢化や人口減少などが進行するなかで、従来の景気刺激策[景気テコ入れ策]では限界がある。

convergence　(名)集合, 集中, 収束, 収斂(しゅうれん), 統一化, 一本化
amount of interest rate convergence　金利収斂の度合い
convergence in measure　測度収束
convergence postulate　収斂性の公準
credit convergence　信用の質の収斂
economic convergence　経済の収斂, 経済格差の縮小
fiscal and monetary convergence　財政・金融の収斂
interest rate convergence　金利収斂, 金利格差の縮小
international convergence of capital measurement　自己資本算定の国際的統一
regulatory convergence　規制の統一化, 規制の一本化
satisfy the convergence criteria　収斂条件[収斂基準]をクリアする, 収斂基準[収斂条件]を達成する
stochastic convergence　確率的収斂, 確率収束
yield convergence　利回り収斂, 利回りの収斂

conversion　(名)転換, 換算, 交換, 公債などの切替え, 借換え, 利子の元金繰り入れ　(⇒convertible bond)
conversion agent　転換代理人
conversion at low interest rate　低利借換え
conversion at par　(株式の)額面転換
conversion at the market　時価転換
（=conversion at market price）
conversion clause　転換約款
conversion factor　転換要素, 転換要因, 変換係数, 交換比率
conversion in cash　換金
conversion into capital stock　資本組入れ
conversion into money [cash]　換価, 現金化
conversion issue　借換え発行
conversion notice　転換請求書
conversion of goods into money　商品の現金化
conversion of loan　借換え
conversion of securities into cash　証券の現金化
conversion of the current price　時価転換
conversion option　転換オプション
conversion parity　転換平価, 転換パリティ(転換証券(convertible security)を普通株式に転換した場合の理論価格)
conversion period　(社債などの)転換請求期間, 転換期間

conversion premium　転換プレミアム（転換証券の時価が転換パリティを上回った超過分をいう）
conversion price　転換価格（転換証券を普通株式に転換する場合の株式1株当たりの価格のこと）
conversion rate　外貨換算率, 交換比率, 転換比率, 顧客転換率
conversion ratio　転換比率（転換証券を普通株式に転換する場合に何株と交換できるかを示す比率）
conversion reserve　兌換（だかん）準備
conversion stock　転換株, 切換え株
conversion table　為替換算表
conversion to different form of insurance contents　保険契約の内容変更
conversion to gold　金兌換
conversion value　転換価格, 転換価値
date of conversion　転換日, 転換時
debt-equity conversion　債務の株式化
effective conversion price　実効転換価格
exchange conversion　為替換算
exchange conversion rate　為替換算表
industrial conversion　産業転換
◆Under the book value method, the carrying value of the convertible bonds at the date of the conversion would be used to account for the conversion. 簿価法では、転換時の転換社債の簿価が、転換の会計処理に使われる。

conversion of (convertible) debentures　転換社債の転換
◆During 2011, conversions of debentures resulted in the issuance of 200 shares of the Corporation's capital stock. 2011年度は、転換社債の転換により、200株の当社株式を発行した。

conversion of debt to equity　債務の株式化
（⇒debt-for-equity swap）
◆Ford's debt restructuring includes conversion of debt to equity and cash tender offers. 米フォードの債務再編には、債務の株式化や現金による株式の公開買付けが含まれている。

conversion privilege　転換権
◆On June 10, 2011, individuals holding $50,000 face value of the Corporation's bonds exercised their conversion privilege. 2011年6月10日、当社の社債権者が、額面5万ドル分の転換権を行使した[額面5万ドル分の株式への転換を行った]。

conversion right　転換権
◆At current stock prices, Daiwa Securities could obtain the equivalent of more than 10 percent of Fuji TV's outstanding common stocks if it exercised the conversion right. 現在の株価（株価水準）だと、転換権を行使した場合、大和証券はフジテレビの発行済み株式総数の10％以上の株式を取得できる。

convert　（動）転換する, 変える, 改造する, 加工する, 流用する, 公債などを切り替える, 振り替える, 換算する, 両替する, 元金に繰り入れる　（自動）変わる, 転換する, 移行する　（⇒maximum limits）
convert bonds into shares　社債を株式に転換する
convert securities into cash　有価証券を現金に換える, 有価証券を現金化する
convert to a market economy　市場経済に移行する
◆In its third attempt to prop up Citigroup Inc. in the past five months, the U.S. government will convert up to $25 billion in the banking giant's preferred shares to common stock. 過去5か月で3度目のシティグループ支援策として、米政府は、（政府が保有する）最大250億ドル相当の金融大手シティの優先株を普通株に転換する。◆Securities were converted into cash. 有価証券は、現金化された。◆The foreign funds converted the convertible bonds into shares of the company. 海外ファンドが、その転換社債を同社の株式に転換した。◆The shares were converted into approximately 18 million shares of our common stock upon consummation of the merger. この株式は、合併完了時に約1,800万株の当社普通株式に転換されました。◆The weak yen has also inflated the firm's profit, which were converted into Japanese currency from dollars. 円安も、ドルから円に換算した同社の利益を押し上げた。

convertibility　（名）交換性, 兌換性
composite convertibility　合成交換性
convertibility of current account　経常勘定交換性
convertibility to gold　金交換性
currency convertibility　通貨の交換性, 通貨の自由交換性
cut [end] convertibility of the dollar into gold　ドルと金との交換を停止する
full convertibility　完全交換性
general convertibility of currency　通貨の全般的交換性
gold convertibility　金兌換性
limited convertibility of currency　通貨の制限付き交換性
monetary convertibility　通貨の自由交換性, 通貨の兌換性
resident convertibility　通貨の居住者交換性

convertible　（名）転換証券（convertible security）, 転換社債（convertible bond）
delayed convertible　先スタート転換証券
discounted convertible　ディスカウント転換社債
equity convertible　転換社債
gold convertible　金転換証券
straightforward convertible　通常の転換社債
subordinated convertible　劣後転換社債
U.S. dollar denominated convertible　米ドル建て転換社債
yen convertible　円建て転換社債
zero-coupon convertible　ゼロ・クーポン転換社債

convertible　（形）転換可能な, 転換できる, 転換性のある, 変換[交換]可能な
（⇒subordinated obligation）
convertible account　（銀行の）特別預金勘定
convertible bank note　兌換銀行券, 兌換銀行紙幣
convertible class A preferred stock　転換権付きクラスA優先株式
convertible contract　中途切換え契約
convertible currency　交換可能通貨, 兌換通貨
convertible debenture issue　転換社債発行
convertible debt　転換社債
convertible FRN [floating-rate note]　転換変動利付き債
convertible gold note　兌換金券
convertible instruments　転換可能金融商品
convertible insurance　可変保険
convertible loan stock　転換社債
convertible money　兌換紙幣
convertible price　転換価格
convertible privilege term assurance　転換条件付き定期保険
convertible rate　転換比率
convertible reserve　兌換（だかん）準備
convertible securities　転換証券（=convertible, CV: 他の種類の証券と交換できる選択権が付いている証券のことで、一般には普通株式と交換できる選択権が付いている債券や優先株のこと）
convertible security　換価担保
convertible stock　転換株式, 転換株, 転換予約権付き株式（=convertible share）
convertible system　兌換制度
convertible term insurance　変更特典付き定期保険
convertible unsecured loan stock　無担保転換社債
convertible yen　交換可能円, 交換円

convertible yen system　交換円制度
currency convertible in fact　事実上の交換可能通貨
debenture convertible at market price　時価転換社債
debenture convertible at par　額面転換社債
debt convertible　転換可能債券
mandatory convertible instrument［securities］　強制転換社債
perpetual subordinated notes convertible into preference　優先株転換可能永久劣後債
private convertible note　私募転換社債
◆All the first preferred shares are convertible into common shares. 第一優先株式は、すべて普通株式への転換が可能です。
◆The 8% convertible bonds are convertible into 40 shares of common stock for each $1,000 bond, and were not considered common stock equivalents at the date of issuance. 8%利付き転換社債は、1,000ドルの社債についてそれぞれ普通株式40株に転換できるが、発行時には準普通株式とは考えられなかった。

convertible bond　転換社債, CB　（=convertible debenture, convertible debt, convertible loan stock;⇒ financial goods）
callable convertible bond　償還条項のある転換社債
convertible bond fund　転換社債ファンド
convertible bond payable　転換社債
convertible bonds with put option　プット・オプション付き転換社債
convertible bonds with warrants　ワラント付き転換社債
dual convertible bond　デュアル転換社債
mandatory convertible bond　強制転換社債
non-callable convertible bond　任意償還条項のない転換社債
special convertible bond account　特別転換社債勘定
stocks and convertible bonds investment trust　株式・転換社債ファンド
subordinated convertible bond　劣後転換社債
zero coupon convertible bond　ゼロ・クーポン転換社債, ゼロ・クーポンCB
◆The 8% convertible bonds are convertible into 40 shares of common stock for each $1,000 bond. 8%利付き転換社債は、1,000ドルの社債についてそれぞれ普通株式40株に転換できる。◆The foreign funds purchased the convertible bonds at prices equivalent to ¥25 per share. 海外ファンドは、1株25円で転換社債を引き受けた。◆The market value method views the convertible bonds as debt whose conversion was a significant economic transaction. 時価法は、転換社債を債務と見なし、転換社債の転換を重要な経済取引であると見ている。
◆These convertible bonds are not considered common stock equivalents. これらの転換社債は、準普通株式とは考えられていません。◆Under the book value method, the carrying value of the convertible bonds at the date of the conversion would be used to account for the conversion. 簿価法では、転換時の転換社債の簿価が、転換の会計処理に使われる。

convertible debenture　転換社債
◆These convertible debentures are redeemable as of December 2011 at a price of 105% of the principal amount. この転換社債は、2011年10月時点で、元本の105%の価格で償還できる。

convertible debt　転換社債, CD
convertible debt issue　転換社債の起債
convertible debt sweeteners　転換社債に係わる転換誘因
convertible debt with a premium put　プット・オプション付き転換社債

convertible note　転換社債, 兌換（だかん）券
◆Ford increased the amount of convertible notes it is offering to $4.5 billion from $3 billion announced previously. フォードは、転換社債の発行規模を当初計画の30億ドルから45億ドルに引き上げた。

convertible paper　流通手形
convertible paper currency　兌換紙幣
convertible paper money　兌換紙幣

convertible preferred share［stock］　転換優先株式, 転換権付き優先株式　（=convertible preference stock;⇒ maximum limits）
◆For the computation of the earnings per share, assuming full dilution, dividends on convertible preferred shares have been added back to income. 完全希薄化を仮定した場合の1株当たり利益の算定では、転換可能優先株式［転換優先株］に対する配当は、利益に振り戻してあります。

convertible subordinated debenture　転換劣後社債, 劣後転換社債, 後順位転換社債
◆The firm completed a $100 million 8% convertible subordinated debenture issue during 2010. 同社は、2010年に利率8%の転換劣後社債1億ドルの発行を完了した。

convexity　（名）凸状, 凸面, コンベクシティ（デュレーションとイールド・カーブの変動関係）
call-adjusted convexity　コール調整後コンベクシティ
negative convexity　凸面効果, ネガティブ・コンベクシティ
positive convexity　ポジティブ・コンベクシティ

cook books　帳簿に手を加える, 帳簿をごまかす, 帳簿を改ざんする
◆Ashikaga Bank is suspected to have cooked books. 足利銀行は、帳簿を改ざんした疑いが持たれている。◆The company cooked books to cover loss. 同社は、帳簿を改ざんして損失［赤字］を補填した。

cool　（動）冷える, 冷え込む, さめる, 落ち着く, 弱まる
◆Business sentiment and the willingness of household to spend may cool and stall the economy unless the sharp appreciation of the yen is checked. 円の急騰を止めないと、企業の心理や家計の消費意欲が冷え込み、景気が腰折れしかねない。

cool money　インターネット取引で動く投資資金, クール・マネー
◆Cool money flew away from low-interest America toward the higher interest euro-zone. ネット取引で動く投資資金は、金利の低いアメリカから金利の高いユーロ圏に流れた。

cooled　（形）冷え込んだ, 冷やされた, 悪化した
◆A real estate investment trust went bankrupt due to the cooled real estate market. 不動産市況の悪化［不動産市場の冷え込み］で、不動産投資信託が倒産［経営破たん］した。

cooling off　冷却期間, クーリング・オフ　（=cooling-off period）
解説　クーリング・オフとは：消費者保護制度の一つで、消費者が商品を購入する契約を結んでも、契約後20日以内なら無条件で解約できる。ただし米国の証券用語では、有価証券の公募の際、登録届出書を証券取引委員会（SEC）に提出してからその効力が発生し証券が売り出されるまでの約20日間の期間をいう。

cooling-off period　クーリング・オフ期間
◆Municipal governments will distribute pamphlets illustrating the legally stipulated cooling-off period. 地方自治体が、法律で定められたクーリング・オフを解説したパンフレットを配布する。◆We can cancel a contract unconditionally within a cooling-off period even if it is signed with an ethical trader. 仮に悪質業者と契約を結んだ場合でも、クーリング・オフ期間内なら、無条件で契約を解除できる。

cooperate　（動）協力する, 協同する, 協調する, 連携する, 提携する
◆Japan, the United States and European countries will cooperate to avert financial turmoil stemming from the downgrading of the U.S. credit rating. 日米欧が連携して、米国債の

格下げによる金融市場の混乱を回避することになった。◆Major central banks will cooperate to offer three-month U.S. dollar loans to commercial banks in the wake of Europe's sovereign debt crisis. 欧州の財政危機を受け、主要中央銀行が、協調して商業銀行に3か月物ドル資金を供給することになった。◆The Financial Stability Board is cooperating with the Basel Committee on Banking Supervision, a body that sets rules for international banking. 金融安定化理事会(FSB)は、国際銀行業務の基準を制定する機関のバーゼル銀行監督委員会と連携している。◆To offer customers a new way to purchase insurance, nonlife insurance companies have begun cooperating with cell phone companies. 顧客に保険加入のための新サービスを提供するため、損害保険各社は、携帯電話会社との提携に乗り出した。

cooperation （名）協力, 協同, 協調, 協業, 提携, 提供, 援助
business cooperation 事業提携, 業務提携
capital cooperation 資本提携
　（=cooperation by holding capital）
cooperation and coordination 協力・協調関係, 協力・協調, 協調
cooperation between firms 企業間協力
cooperation between management and labor 労使協調
credit cooperation 信用組合
economic cooperation 経済協力
enhance [strengthen] cooperation 連携を強化する
government-business cooperation 官民協調
international cooperation 国際協力
intraregional cooperation 域内協力
multi-economic cooperation 多国間経済協力
simple cooperation 単純協業
technical [technological] cooperation 技術提携, 技術提供, 技術協力
trilateral cooperation 三角協力
voluntary cooperation 自発的協力

◆Additional pump-priming measures through strengthening cooperation between advanced countries and emerging economies will be a major subject of discussion at the financial summit meeting in Washington. 先進国と新興国の連携強化による追加景気対策の検討が、ワシントンで開かれる金融サミットで検討される主要テーマとなる。◆At two financial summit meetings since the collapse of Lehman Brothers, agreements were made on cooperation to implement large-scale economic stimulus measures and to take monetary relaxation policies. リーマン・ブラザーズの倒産[破たん]以来2回開かれた金融サミットでは、連携して大型の財政出動や金融緩和策を実施することで合意が得られた。◆In cooperation with the U.S. FRB, the Bank of England, the Bank of Japan and the Swiss National Bank, the European Central Bank decided to conduct three U.S. dollar liquidity-providing operations between October and December. 米連邦準備制度理事会(FRB)、英イングランド銀行、日銀、スイス国立銀行と協調して、欧州中央銀行(ECB)が10〜12月に3回、米ドル資金供給オペを実施することを決めた。◆Regarding TEPCO's damage compensation, creditor financial institutions have already offered cooperation by refinancing existing loans. 東電の損害賠償に関して、取引金融機関は、既存の融資の借換えなどですでに協力している。◆The Bank of Japan will fight the yen's appreciation in close cooperation with the government. 日銀は、政府と緊密に連携して円高に対応する方針だ。◆The IMF and the EU are strengthening their cooperation to avert a Greek default and prevent a chain reaction of debt crisis among other countries. ギリシャの債務不履行(デフォルト)を回避し他国間の債務危機の連鎖反応を防ぐため、国際通貨基金(IMF)と欧州連合(EU)は、連携を強めている。◆There is a chance that the technological cooperation will develop into a capital affiliation. 技術協力が資本提携に発展する可能性がある。

coordinate （動）調整する, 協調する, 一元化する, 調和させる, 連携させる, 連携を取る, 連携する
　（⇒monetary authorities）
be syndicated on a coordinated basis 協議ベースでシ団組成を行う
coordinate interests 利益を調整する
coordinate with the securities 証券界と調整する
coordinated easing move 協調利下げ
coordinated efforts 協調努力
coordinated intervention 協調介入
　（⇒concerted intervention）
coordinated terrorist attacks of Sept. 11, 2001 2001年9月11日の米同時テロ
　（=Sept. 11 terrorist attacks）
in a coordinated manner 協調して, 足並みを揃えて
the latest coordinated rate cuts 今回の協調利下げ
work in a coordinated manner 足並みを揃えて行動する

◆The ASEAN plus Three Macroeconomic Research Office, or AMRO, was set up in Singapore in April 2011 to coordinate decision-making for providing emergency liquidity to member states. ASEANプラス3(日中韓)の域内マクロ経済リサーチ・オフィス(AMRO)は、参加国に緊急時の流動性を提供する際の意思決定調整機関として、2011年4月にシンガポールに設立された。◆The government and the Bank of Japan worked on economic policy in a coordinated manner. 政府と日銀は、経済政策で足並みを揃えて行動した。◆The government and the BOJ worked in a coordinated manner to stop the sharp rise of the yen. 急激な円高に歯止めをかけるため、政府と日銀が協調して動いた。◆The TSE president is required to coordinate with the securities industry and the Financial Services Agency. 東京証券取引所の社長[東証社長]は、証券界や金融庁との調整を図らなければならない。

coordinated interest rate cuts 協調利下げ
　（=coordinated rate cuts）
◆Coordinated interest rate cuts were introduced immediately after the outbreak of the economic crisis. 協調利下げは、経済危機の発生直後に実施された。

coordinated policy 政策協調
　（=policy coordination）
◆In 1985, finance ministers and central bank governors from the Group of Five major nations agreed to adopt a coordinated policy mainly aimed at rectifying the sharp rise in the value of the U.S. dollar at the meeting held at the Plaza Hotel in New York. 1985年にG5(日米英独仏の主要5か国)の蔵相と中央銀行総裁は、ニューヨークのプラザ・ホテルで開かれた会議で、主にドル高是正のための政策協調を採択することで合意した。

coordinated rate cuts 協調利下げ （=coordinated interest rate cuts; ⇒economic crisis）
◆The six central banks around the world, including the U.S. FRB and the ECB, participated in the latest coordinated rate cuts. 今回の協調利下げには、米連邦準備制度理事会(FRB)や欧州中央銀行(ECB)など、世界の6か国の中央銀行が参加した。

coordination （名）調整, 調節, すり合わせ, 一元化, 統一, 協調, 連携, 整合, 足並み, 同等, 対等, 対等関係
coordination among national regulators 各国規制当局の協調
coordination between monetary and fiscal policies 金融と財政の政策協調
coordination between the two groups 両グループ間の調整
international coordination 国際協調

lack of coordination　足並みの乱れ
policy coordination　政策協調
◆Japan, the United States and European countries have failed to eliminate uneasiness in the financial markets for lack of concrete policy coordination. 日米欧は、具体的な政策協調が見られないため、金融市場の不安感を払拭（ふっしょく）できないでいる。◆Policy coordination efforts between Japanese and U.S. currency authorities are genuine. 日米通貨当局の政策協調努力は、本物だ。◆The enhancement of international coordination is important to stabilize the financial markets. 金融市場の安定には、国際協調の強化が重要だ。◆The government tries to trumpet its coordination with the Bank of Japan to boost the effectiveness of the government's additional economic measures. 政府の追加経済対策の効果を高めるため、政府は日銀との連携をアピールしようとしている。

cope with　〜に対応する，〜に対処する，〜に対抗する，〜に立ち向かう，〜と張り合う，〜を（うまく）処理する，〜を切り抜ける，〜を克服する，〜に備える
　　cope with a task　仕事を処理する
　　cope with corporate needs　企業のニーズに応（こた）える，企業のニーズに対応する
　　cope with difficulties　困難を切り抜ける，難局を切り抜ける
　　cope with economic disasters　経済の惨状を克服する，悲惨な経済状況を切り抜ける
　　cope with labor shortages　人手不足をどうにか切り抜ける，人手不足に備える［対処する］
　　cope with the challenges　課題に対応する，課題を克服する
　　cope with the effects of deflation　デフレの影響に対処する
　　cope with the financial crisis and deflationary pressure　金融危機やデフレ圧力［デフレ懸念］に対応する
　　cope with the situation　事態に対処する，この状況を切り抜ける
　　cope with the yen's rise　円高に対応する
◆Discussion among advanced countries alone cannot cope with the challenges facing the world economy. 先進国だけの話合いで、世界経済が直面している課題に対応することはできない状況にある。◆Japanese firms' moves to shift production abroad to cope with the yen's rise will bring about a hollowing-out of domestic industries. 円高対策として日本企業が生産拠点を海外に移すと、国内産業の空洞化を招くことになる。◆Japanese firms must work out better strategies to cope with the excessive rise of the yen. 日本企業は、超円高に対応できる戦略を練る必要がある。◆The Fed has taken quantitative easing measures twice, or QE1 between December 2008 and March 2010, and QE2 between November 2010 and June 2011, to cope with the financial crisis and deflationary pressure. 金融危機やデフレ圧力に対応するため、米連邦準備制度理事会（FRB）は、これまでに量的金融緩和を2回（2008年12月〜2010年3月の量的緩和第一弾（QE1）と2010年11月〜2011年6月の量的緩和第二弾（QE2））実施している。

core　（名）核，中心，核心，芯（しん），中核，中枢，主力，主軸，基本理念，基本モデル，基本設計，原子炉の炉心，コア（形）核となる，軸となる，中心的な，中核的な，核心的な，基本的な，本業の
　　core activities　主力事業，中核事業，主力業務（=core business）
　　core asset focus　中核資産への集中化
　　core capitalization　コア資本
　　core competence　中核的業務，中核能力，企業固有の技術（スキルや技術），企業固有の競争力の核，自社ならではの強み，コア・コンピテンス（noncore competence＝非中核業務，ノンコア業務）
　　core CPI　コア物価指数（=core consumer price index）
　　core holdings　運用資産の中核部分
　　core ideology　基本理念
　　core nonlife operation　主力［中核］の損保事業，損保の主力事業
　　core operation　中核事業，主力事業，基幹事業，本業（=core business）
　　core plus satellite approach　インデックス型プラス銘柄選定型アプローチ
　　core PPI（producer price index）　コアPPI（生産者物価指数のうち動きの激しいエネルギー・食品価格を除外した指数）
　　core producer prices　生産者物価のコア部分の指数，生産者物価指数コア部分
　　core product lines　主要製品
　　core profitability　主力事業の収益性，コア収益性，コア収益
　　core profitable business　収益の柱
　　core retail deposit　核となる小口預金
　　core stock　コア銘柄，主力銘柄（生保、年金など機関投資家の株式ポートフォリオにどうしても組み入れなければならない主力の銘柄）
　　core trust products　信託銀行の中核業務
　　core values　基本的価値観
core bank　主力銀行，主力行
◆Estimated bad loans at the core bank amounted to ￥2.48 trillion. 主力行の不良債権の予想額は、2兆4,800億円になった。
core business　中核事業，中核企業，主力事業，基幹事業，根幹業務，本業，コア・ビジネス（=core activities, core operation; ⇒banking business, post動詞）
◆A group of major banks decided to extend loans of $2 billion for the WorldCom to use as operating funds to enable it to continue its core businesses, such as Internet access services. 大手銀行団は、ワールドコムに対して20億ドルの運転資金を融資して、同社がインターネット接続サービスなどの中核事業を継続できるようにした。◆Nippon Life Insurance Co., the top shareholder in Olympus Corp., will continue supporting Olympus in light of its advanced technology in its core business such as endoscopes. オリンパスの筆頭株主の日本生命は、内視鏡などオリンパスの中核事業の高い技術力を踏まえて、引き続きオリンパスを支えていく方針だ。◆Retail banking including consumer financing, investment banking and corporate financing are the three core businesses of Shinsei Bank. 消費者金融を含むリテール銀行業務、投資銀行業務、企業金融の三つが、新生銀行の中核業務だ。◆The huge number of delays in money transfers and double withdrawals are serious incidents concerning the banks' core businesses. 口座振替の遅れや二重引落しの大量発生は、銀行の根幹業務にかかわる重大な事件だ。
core capital　中核的自己資本，自己資本の基本的項目，基本的資本項目，中核資本，コア資本（⇒capital adequacy, capital adequacy ratio, minimum core capital requirements）
　　constitute core capital　中核資本［中核的自己資本］を構成する
　　increase one's core capital　中核資本を増強する
　　leading banking institutions' core capital　主要金融機関の中核的自己資本
◆A bank's core capital, or Tier 1 capital, is deemed to have high loss-absorbency and resilience. 銀行の中核的自己資本は、損失吸収力と弾力性が高いとされている。◆Japan's three megabanks must increase their core capital as soon as possible, in accordance with the new rules known as Basel 3. 日本の3大メガバンクは、バーゼル3と呼ばれる新規則に従って、早期に中核資本を増強する必要がある。◆These deferred tax

core capital of banks　銀行の中核的自己資本, 銀行の中核資本, 銀行の自己資本
◆At the end of October 2011, the eurozone states decided to expand the EFSF, reduce Greece's debt and strengthen the core capital of banks. 2011年10月末にユーロ圏は、欧州金融安定基金（EFSF）の拡大、ギリシャ債務削減と銀行の自己資本増強を決めた。

assets account, on average, for nearly 60 percent of leading banking institutions' core capital. これらの繰延べ税金資産は、主要金融機関の中核的自己資本の平均60％近くを占めている。

core capital rate [ratio]　中核的自己資本比率, 自己資本比率
　（=Tier 1 capital rate, tier-one capital ratio）
　bolster one's core capital ratio　自己資本比率を増強する, 自己資本比率の充実を図る
　increase one's core capital rate　自己資本を増強する
　　（⇒management strategy）
◆Japanese banks must bolster their core capital ratios. 邦銀は、自己資本比率の充実に取り組む必要がある。◆The bank's core capital rate falls behind those of many major European and U.S. banks. 同行の中核的自己資本比率は、欧米の多くの大手銀行より下回っている。

core consumer price index [core CPI]　コア物価指数, 消費者物価指数のコア指数, コア指数
◆The BOJ maintained its previous projection that the core consumer price index for fiscal 2010 would fall to 0.5 percent from a year earlier. 「2010年度のコア物価指数（生鮮食品を除く総合指数）は前年度比0.5％の下落」とした日銀の前回予想を、日銀は据え置いた。◆The core Consumer Price Index, which strips out volatile food and energy costs, moved up just 0.1 percent in August. 変動の激しい［変動幅の大きい］食品とエネルギー価格を除いたコア物価指数［消費者物価指数のコア指数］は、8月は0.1％の上昇にとどまった。◆The core nationwide consumer price index, which excludes perishables, rose 0.1 percent in October from the year before. 全国の消費者物価指数のコア指数（生鮮食品を除く総合指数）は、10月は前年同月比で0.1％の伸びにとどまった。

core consumer price inflation rate　コア物価指数の上昇率, 消費者物価指数のコア指数
◆The core consumer price inflation rate, excluding volatile fresh food prices, is currently about 2 percent on year due mainly to soaring food and petroleum product prices. 変動の激しい生鮮食品の価格を除いたコア物価指数［消費者物価指数のコア指数］の上昇率は現在、主に食料品と石油製品の価格高騰の影響で、対前年比で2％程度となっている。

core deposit　コア預金
　core deposit base　中核となる預金基盤, コア預金基盤
　core deposit intangibles　コア預金無形資産
　total core deposits　総コア預金

core earnings　中核事業収益, 主力事業の収益, コア収益
◆Group operating profit shows a company's core earnings strength. 連結営業利益は、企業の主力事業の収益力［本業のもうけ］を示す。

core inflation　基礎インフレ率, コア・インフレ率, コア指数　（=core rate of inflation）
　core inflation differential　コア・インフレ率の格差
　core inflation rate　基礎インフレ率
　core inflation rate in Tokyo　東京都区部の消費者物価指数コア指数
　nationwide core inflation　全国のコア指数
　slowdown in core inflation　基礎インフレ率の低下
◆The run-up in the price of energy and other commodities has had only a modest effect on core inflation. コア・インフレ率に対する原油などの価格高騰の影響は、それほど大きくない。

core nationwide CPI　全国消費者物価指数のコア指数
◆The core nationwide CPI, which excludes volatile fresh food prices, stood at 99.3 against the base of 100 for 2005. 全国消費者物価指数のコア指数（値動きの大きい生鮮食品を除く総合指数）は、99.3（2005年＝100）となった。

core operating profit　（生命保険会社の本業のもうけに当たる）基礎利益　（=core profit）
◆The increase in seven insurers' core operating profits is due to appraisal gains in their stockholdings. 生保7社の基礎利益（本業のもうけに当たる）の増加は、保有株式の含み益によるものだ。

core operation　中核事業, 主力事業, 基幹事業　（=core business; ⇒fundamental profit）
◆Some famous foreign brands will be continued as core operations. 知名度の高い一部の海外ブランドは、今後も中核事業として継続する。

core portion of one's capital base　中核的自己資本, 自己資本
◆Mizuho Financial Group Inc. will float preferred securities to domestic institutional investors to enhance the core portion of its capital base. みずほフィナンシャルグループ（FG）は、自己資本［中核的自己資本］を増強するため、国内機関投資家向けに優先出資証券を発行する。

core profit　コア利益, 主力事業の利益, 生命保険会社の基礎利益
◆Core profits increased at major life insurers in the first half of the current fiscal year from a year earlier. 主要生保の今年度上半期（4-9月）の基礎利益（本業のもうけに当たる）は、前年同期比で増加した。

core profitable business　収益の柱
◆The division is the core profitable business for the company. 同社にとって、同事業部門は収益の柱となっている。

core tier [Tier] 1　コア・ティア1, 中核的自己資本, 中核自己資本, 中核資本
　解説 コア・ティア1とは：金融機関の経営の健全性を測る指標の一つで、普通株式（common stock）と利益から生じる内部留保［利益剰余金］（retained earnings）に限定した「狭義の中核的自己資本」。従来は優先株などを含めることができたが、国際銀行業務を行う銀行の健全性を維持するための新自己資本規制（バーゼル3）により、貸出や投資などの資産（リスク資産）に対する中核資本の比率が段階的に引き上げられることになった。貸出金や投資などの資産（リスク資産）に対するコア・ティア1（中核的自己資本）の比率が高いほど、金融取引で生じた損失を穴埋めできる財務面の体力が強いことを示す。なお、中核自己資本（コア・ティア1）の最低比率は、2013年の3.5％、14年の4％、15年の4.5％から最終的に2019年1月には7％以上に引き上げられる。この基準を下回ると、金融監督当局への資本増強計画の提出を求められ、計画を達成するまで銀行の普通株株主への配当や役員賞与の支払いが制限される。また、主要20か国・地域（G20）の金融当局で構成する金融安定化理事会（FSB）が発表した新金融規制案では、国際的な巨大金融機関（G-SIFIs）の28行にさらに1〜2.5％の資本上積みを求めている。この規制は2016年から段階的に導入され、2019年に完全適用される。

core tier 1 capital　中核的自己資本, 中核資本, 狭義の中核自己資本（普通株式と利益剰余金［内部留保］）
◆The new regulations decided on by the Basel Committee on Banking Supervision require banks to increase the core tier 1 capital, such as common stock and retained earnings, that they must hold in reserve, to at least 4.5 percent of assets from the current 2 percent. バーゼル銀行監督委員会が決めた新規制は、銀行が支払い準備として保有しなければならない普通株や利益剰余金［内部留保］などの中核的自己資本（コア・ティア1）を、現行の資産の最低2％から4.5％に引き上げるよう銀行に義務付けている。

core tier 1 capital ratio　中核的自己資本比率, 中核資

本比率
minimum core tier 1 capital ratio　最低中核的自己資本比率, 最低中核資本比率
◆As of the end of June 2010, the core tier 1 capital ratios of the three Japanese megabanks are said to be between 5 and 7 percent. 2010年6月末時点で、日本の3大メガバンクの中核的自己資本比率は5～7%とされる。

corner　(名)角, 地方, 地域, 窮地, 苦境, 窮境, (株式など商品の)買い占め, 口元, 目元, 横目
　be in a tight corner　窮地に陥(おちい)っている
　cut corners　近道をする, (経費を)切り詰める, 節約する, (仕事の)手を抜く, 手抜きする
　drive [box, force] A into a corner　Aを窮地に追い込む
　have a corner on the market　市場を一手に握っている
　(just) around [round] the corner　間近[目前]に迫って, すぐ近くで, もうすぐで
　make [establish] a corner in [on] the company's shares　同社株を買い占める
　paint oneself into a corner　自分で自分の首を絞める
　the (four) corners of the earth　世界の隅々, 世界の津々浦々
　turn the corner　(病気, 危機などが)峠を越す
　◆The change in the method of calculating deferred tax assets has driven each of the banking groups into a corner. 繰延べ税金資産の算定方式の変更が、銀行グループ各行を窮地に追い込んでいる。

corporate　(形)企業の, 会社の, 法人の, 共通の, 共同の, コーポレート
　corporate accountability　企業の説明責任
　corporate and non-operating　本社および非営業部門
　corporate body　企業体
　corporate breakup　企業分割
　corporate capitalism　株式会社資本主義
　corporate citizen　企業市民, 市民としての企業, コーポレート・シティズン
　　(=corporate citizenship)
　corporate competitiveness　企業競争力
　corporate control　企業経営
　corporate credit quality　企業の信用力, 企業の信用の質
　corporate debenture　社債　(=corporate bond)
　corporate defensive measure　企業防衛策
　corporate deposit　企業預金, 法人預金
　corporate divestiture　企業分割
　corporate employees' pension insurance plan　厚生年金保険, 厚生年金保険制度
　　(⇒premium payment)
　corporate enterprise tax　法人事業税, 法人税
　　(=corporate tax)
　corporate failure　企業倒産, 経営破たん
　　(=corporate bankruptcy; ⇒audit report)
　corporate financial health　企業の財務健全性
　corporate financial statements　会社財務諸表
　corporate goods price index　企業商品価格指数
　corporate governance reform bill　企業統治改革法案
　corporate income　法人所得
　corporate investment　企業投資, 企業の設備投資, 民間設備投資
　corporate irregularities　企業不祥事
　corporate loans　法人向け融資, 企業向け融資, 企業向け貸出
　corporate management　企業経営, 会社経営
　　(⇒resolution)
　corporate member　会員企業

　corporate pension　企業年金
　corporate philanthropy　企業の慈善行為, 企業の慈善活動, 企業のフィランソロピー活動, 企業の慈善事業, 企業の文化・社会への貢献, コーポレート・フィランソロピー
　corporate rebuilding plan　企業再建計画, 経営再建計画, 再建計画
　corporate reconstruction　企業再建, 企業再生
　corporate reconstruction fund　企業再生ファンド
　　(=corporate turnaround fund)
　corporate reform　企業改革
　corporate safeguards　企業防衛策
　corporate social responsibility　企業の社会的責任, CSR
　　(⇒CSR)
　corporate strategy　企業戦略, 経営戦略, 営業戦略
　corporate takeover　企業買収

corporate accounting　企業会計, 企業の会計処理, 企業の会計処理方法, 企業の経理　(⇒accounting)
　corporate accounting system　企業会計制度, 企業会計組織, 企業会計システム
　distrust of corporate accounting　企業会計への不信感
　malpractice of corporate accounting　企業会計の不正
　◆Concerned that the malpractice of corporate accounting may be widespread, the U.S. Congress passed a corporate governance reform bill in July 2002, immediately after WorldCom's bankruptcy was exposed. 企業会計の不正が広がっているとの懸念を強めていた米議会は、米通信大手ワールドコムの破綻が明らかになった直後の2002年7月に、企業統治改革法案を成立させた。◆Distrust of corporate accounting, ignited by the collapse of major energy trader Enron, has hindered the recovery of stock prices. 米エネルギー大手エンロンの経営破たんに端を発した企業会計への不信感が、株価回復の足を引っ張っている。

corporate accounting reports　企業の財務情報
　◆Corporate accounting reports are the most important criterion for investment decisions. 企業の財務情報は、特に重要な投資判断の材料だ。

corporate acquisition　企業買収, 企業取得
　(=acquisition of business, business acquisition, corporate buyout)
　◆The company hid investment losses and tried to cover them up with funds related to corporate acquisitions. 同社は、投資損失を隠ぺいし、企業買収関連資金でそのもみ消しを図った。

corporate assets　全社資産, 全社一般資産
　◆Corporate assets primarily include cash, marketable securities, equity investments and the administrative headquarters of the Company. 全社一般資産の主な内訳は、現預金、市場性有価証券、株式投資と当社の管理本部資産です。

corporate banking　企業向け銀行業務, コーポレート銀行業務
　◆Mizuho Financial Group will integrate its retail and corporate banking units in 2013. みずほフィナンシャルグループ(FG)は、傘下のリテール銀行[リテール銀行業務部門]とコーポレート銀行[企業向け銀行業務部門]を2013年にも合併させる方針だ。

corporate bankruptcy　企業倒産
　(=corporate failure)
　◆Corporate bankruptcies have led to the swelling of nonperforming loans, posing a heavy burden on banks. 企業倒産が不良債権の増大を生み、銀行に重くのしかかっている。◆Corporate bankruptcies stemming from the March 11 earthquake and tsunami totaled 330. 東日本大震災による企業倒産の総件数は、330件に達している。◆If the number of corporate bankruptcies and the unemployment rate soar owing to structural reforms, recessionary pressures will further in-

crease. 構造改革で企業倒産件数や失業率が増えると、不況圧力は一層強まるものと思われる。◆The number of corporate bankruptcies in July 2008 jumped 12.92 percent from a year earlier to 1,372. 2008年7月の企業倒産件数は、前年同期比で12.92%急増して1,372件に達した。

corporate bond 社債,事業債 (=corporate debenture, corporate debt; ⇒financial goods, investment-grade securities, supply動詞)
  amounts outstanding of public and corporate bonds　公社債の残存額
  corporate and government bonds　公社債 (=corporate and government securities)
  corporate bond equivalent　社債換算利回り
  corporate bond fund　社債ファンド
  corporate bond insurance　社債の信用保証
  corporate bond issuer　社債発行体
  corporate bond spread　社債スプレッド
  corporate bond targeting individual investors　個人向け社債
  corporate credit quality　企業の信用力
  foreign corporate bond　外国社債
  investment in medium- and long-term corporate bonds　中長期債への投資
  loans on public and corporate bonds　公社債貸付け金
  qualifying corporate bond　適格社債
  raise money by issuing corporate bonds　社債を発行して資金を調達する
  redeem corporate bonds　社債を償還する
  the limit on corporate bond issues　社債発行限度枠
  traditional corporate bond　普通社債
  U.S. corporate bond　米国事業債, 米国社債
◆Companies faced difficulty in raising money by issuing corporate bonds in the aftermath of the financial crisis and resorted to borrowing money from banks. 世界の金融危機の影響で企業は、社債を発行して資金を調達するのが困難になったため、金融機関からの資金借入れに動いた。◆TEPCO will have to raise about ¥750 billion to redeem corporate bonds it has issued and to repay some of its debt. 東電は今後、発行済み社債の償還と債務の一部返済に、7,500億円ほど調達しなければならない。◆The Bank of Japan decided to adopt additional quantitative easing measures in October 2010, setting up a fund to purchase government and corporate bonds. 日銀は、2010年10月に新たな量的緩和策の導入を決め、国債や社債を買い入れる基金を新設した。◆The Bank of Japan has supplied a large amount of funds to the market by purchasing long-term government bonds and corporate bonds. 日銀は、長期国債や社債の買入れで、大量の資金を市場に提供している。◆The sharp decline in investment in medium- and long-term corporate bonds occurred because the prolonged recession curbed new issues necessary for investment in plant and equipment. 中長期社債への投資が大幅に減少したのは、長引く不況で企業の設備投資に必要な中長期債の新規発行が不振だったためである。
[解説]社債とは：企業の資金調達の手段として企業が発行する債券。企業の資金調達の方法としては、銀行などの金融機関から借り入れる間接金融と、株式や社債などを発行して投資家から資金を集める直接金融の二つがある。

corporate bond issuance 社債発行 (=corporate debt issuance)
◆The amount of straight corporate bond issuance came to ¥981 billion in July 2011, the highest level in 10 months. 2011年7月の普通社債発行額は、過去10か月で最高水準の9,810億円に達した。

corporate bond issues 社債発行額 (=corporate debt issues)
◆Corporate bond issues are recovering from the bond market turbulence following the March 11 earthquake and tsunami. 東日本大震災後の債券市場の混乱から、社債の発行額が回復している。

corporate bond market 社債市場, 債券市場
◆A downgrade below investment-grade by even one ratings agency could boost GM's borrowing costs and wreak havoc on the corporate bond market. 格付け会社が1社でも投資適格格付けより低く格付けを引き下げたら[格付け会社が1社でも投機的格付けに格下げしたら]、GMの資金調達コストが急増し、米国の社債[債券]市場にも大きな影響が出る恐れがある。◆If the decision on the framework of TEPCO's compensation payments is put off further, it may trigger credit instability in the firm and bring about ill effects on the stock and corporate bond markets. 東電の(原子力発電所事故による損害の)賠償金支払いの枠組み決定をさらに先送りすれば、東電の信用不安を招き、株式市場や社債市場に悪影響を及ぼす恐れがある。

corporate borrowers 融資先, 融資先企業, 借り手企業, 法人借り主
  major corporate borrowers　主要融資先, 大口融資先
  the business conditions of corporate borrowers　融資先企業の業況
◆FSA audits of the banks' accounts urged them to reclassify 149 of their major corporate borrowers more strictly in terms of their creditworthiness in a bid to accelerate the disposal of bad loans. 金融庁による銀行の財務書類監査で、不良債権処理を加速するため、銀行は大口融資先149社の信用力による債務者区分の見直しを強化するよう強く求められた。◆Japan's economic recovery helped improve the business conditions of corporate borrowers. 日本の景気回復で、融資先企業の業況が改善した。◆The bank's likelihood of collecting loans extended to its major corporate borrowers has worsened. 同行の大口融資先[融資先企業]に対する債権の回収見通しが、悪化した。◆The economic recovery has helped reduce the number of corporate borrowers going bankrupt. 景気回復で、経営破たんする融資先が減っている。◆The FSA's special inspection will check the major banks' large-lot corporate borrowers whose stock prices or credit ratings have sharply declined. 金融庁の特別検査は、大手銀行の株価や格付けなどが急落した大口融資先を査定の対象としている。

corporate business performances 企業業績
◆The employment situation and corporate business performances have been deteriorating rapidly. 雇用状況[雇用環境]や企業業績が、急速に悪化している。

corporate business sentiment 企業の景況感
◆Corporate business sentiment improved in the three months to September for the sixth consecutive quarter. 7-9月の企業の景況感は、6期連続で改善した。

corporate buyout [buy-out] 企業買収 (=corporate acquisition [takeover]; ⇒stock swapping)
◆Margin trading is also used in a corporate buyout case. 企業買収のケースでは、信用取引も使われている。◆There are problems in laws governing margin trading in a corporate buyout including a management buyout. 経営者による自社買収(MBO)を含めた企業買収では、信用取引に関して法律上の問題がある。

corporate buyout tool 企業買収の手段
◆Two potent corporate buyout tools of stock splits and stock swaps were the key to the remarkable growth of the company. 株式分割と株式交換という二つの強力な企業買収の手段が、同社の急成長のカギだった。

corporate capital investment 企業の設備投資
◆Maintaining an easy monetary policy may lead to excessive corporate capital investment and have a negative impact on the sustainable economic recovery. 金融緩和政策を続け

ると、企業の過剰な設備投資を生み、景気の持続的回復を阻害する恐れがある。

corporate charter　会社定款
（=corporation charter）
◆The power of a veto is used to make important management decisions such as mergers or revision of corporate charters at shareholders meetings. 拒否権は、株主総会で合併や会社定款などの重要な経営の意思決定を行う際に行使される。

corporate client　法人顧客, 顧客企業, 銀行の融資先企業　（=corporate customer）
◆Domestic nonlife insurance companies usually renew contracts with most of their corporate clients each April. 国内の損保各社は通常、毎年4月に大半の顧客企業と（保険）契約の更新を行っている。◆Nonlife insurance companies used to disperse the risk of large contracts with new corporate clients through reinsurance contracts with other insurance or reinsurance companies. 損保各社は従来、他の保険会社もしくは再保険会社と再保険契約を結んで、新規顧客企業と大型契約を結ぶリスクを分散してきた。◆The firm offers loans for retail and corporate clients in addition to offering electronic settlement for online shoppers. 同社は、ネット・ショッパー[オンライン・ショッパー]向けの電子決済業務のほかに、個人と企業向けの融資も手がけている。◆The Japanese branch of Banco do Brazil was ordered to suspend operations related to foreign exchange and remittance transactions for new corporate clients. ブラジル銀行在日支店が、新規法人顧客との外国為替・送金取引関連業務の停止命令を受けた。

corporate debenture　社債
◆The BOJ decided to further relax its monetary policy by injecting an additional ¥10 trillion into a fund aimed at purchasing government bonds and corporate debentures. 日銀は、国債や社債などを買い入れるための基金に新たに10兆円を注入[投入]して追加の金融緩和に踏み切ることを決めた。
◆The BOJ's additional monetary easing steps include an increase in the amount of funds to purchase government bonds and corporate debentures. 日銀の追加金融緩和には、国債や社債などを買い入れる基金の増額が含まれている。

corporate debt　企業債務, 社債
　corporate debt market　社債市場
　corporate debt restructuring　企業債務の再編
　credit quality of corporate debt issuers　社債発行体[社債発行企業]の信用の質

corporate debt issues　社債, 社債発行, 社債発行額
（=corporate bond issues）
◆Corporate debt issues are recovering as bond market turbulence in the aftermath of the March 11 Great East Japan Earthquake has subsided. 2011年3月11日の東日本大震災直後の債券市場の混乱が収束したため、社債の発行額が回復している。

corporate debt securities　債券
◆The assets of the various plans include corporate equities, government securities, corporate debt securities and income-producing real estate. 各種制度の年金資産は、株式、政府証券、債券や収益を稼得する不動産などで構成されています。

corporate director　企業取締役
◆These disciplinary measures include increased penalties on securities fraud and a newly installed penalty on corporate directors in cases of failure to submit adequate financial reports to authorities. これらの懲戒処分には、証券詐欺に対する罰則の強化や、当局に適切な財務報告をしなかった場合の企業取締役に対する罰則の新設などが含まれている。

corporate donations　企業献金, 政治献金
◆This lower house member was indicted for underreporting the amount of corporate donations. この衆院議員は、企業[政治]献金の金額を収支報告書から除いたとして起訴された。

corporate earnings　企業収益
◆The latest survey points to a continued improvement in corporate earnings and capital investment. 今回の調査では、企業収益や設備投資の拡大が続いていることが示されている。

corporate employee pension insurance　厚生年金保険
◆The Pension Fund Association restarted operations as a special privately owned corporation based on a law on corporate employee pension insurance in 2005. 企業年金連合会（旧特殊法人「厚生年金基金連合会」）は、厚生年金保険法に基づく特別民間法人として2005年に再スタートした。

corporate employee pension plan　厚生年金制度, 厚生年金
◆The Employees Pension Fund supports the public corporate employee pension plan. 厚生年金基金は、公的な厚生年金制度を支えている。

corporate employee pension system　厚生年金制度, 厚生年金
◆The Social Insurance Agency paid out less in corporate employee and basic pension system benefits to elderly subscribers. 社会保険庁が、高齢加入者に厚生年金や基礎年金(国民年金)の給付金を少なく支給していた。

corporate employees' pension fund　厚生年金基金
◆This former official of the defunct Social Insurance Agency (SIA) became managing director of a corporate employees' pension fund after working at the SIA. この旧社会保険庁OBは、旧社会保険庁を退職後、ある厚生年金基金の常務理事になった。

corporate enterprise tax　法人事業税, 法人税
（=corporate tax）
◆Banks have paid hardly any corporate enterprise tax though they made even larger gross operating profits than they did during the bubble economic era. 銀行は、バブル期より大きな業務粗利益を上げたものの、法人税をほとんど負担して[支払って]いない。

corporate equity　企業持ち分, 株式
◆The assets of the various plans include corporate equities, government securities, corporate debt securities and income-producing real estate. 各種制度の年金資産は、株式、政府証券、債券や収益を稼得する不動産などで構成されています。

corporate ethics　企業倫理
◆The U.S. tried to prevent an erosion of corporate ethics among financial institutions by refusing to provide public funds to Lehman Brothers. リーマン・ブラザーズへの公的資金の投入を拒否することによって、米政府は金融機関のモラル・ハザード（企業倫理の欠如）を回避しようとした。

corporate executives　企業経営者
◆As a side effect of the zero-interest policy, there is the moral hazard concerning corporate executives. ゼロ金利政策の副作用の一つとして、企業経営者のモラル・ハザード（倫理の欠如）がある。

corporate failure　企業倒産, 企業破たん, 経営破たん
（=corporate bankruptcy）
◆Corporate failures in Oct. 2008 jumped 13.4% from a year earlier to 1,429. 2008年10月の企業倒産件数（負債総額1,000万円以上）は、前年同月比13.4%増の1,429件となった。◆GM's filing for Chapter 11 bankruptcy protection marks the largest manufacturing corporate failure in history. 米ゼネラル・モーターズ（GM）の連邦破産法11章の適用申請は、製造業として史上最大の企業倒産だ。

corporate financing　企業金融, 企業財務, 企業の資金調達, コーポレート・ファイナンス
（⇒core business）
◆The purchase of exchange-traded funds and real estate investment trusts by the Bank of Japan could have a favorable impact on corporate financing. 日銀による上場投資信託や不動産投資信託（リート）の買入れ[購入]は、企業金融に好影響

を及ぼす可能性がある。

corporate goods price index　企業商品価格指数, 企業物価指数, CGPI
◆The Bank of Japan's corporate goods price index, designed to gauge wholesale prices, hit 105.6 against a base of 100 for 2005. 企業の卸売り段階での商品価格を示す日銀の企業物価指数（2005年＝100）は、105.6となった。◆The corporate goods price index of the People's Bank of China recorded a year-on-year jump of 9.6 percent in September. 中国人民銀行の9月の企業商品価格指数は、前年同月比で9.6%上昇した。

corporate governance　会社の管理・運営, 会社管理法, 企業統治, 企業支配, 経営監視, コーポレート・ガバナンス
◆The FSA's guideline for supervising financial conglomerates is aimed at urging operators of financial conglomerates to reinforce their corporate governance to prevent irregularities. 金融庁の金融コングロマリット（複合体）監督指針の狙いは、不正防止に向けて、金融コングロマリットの経営者に経営監視の強化を促すことにある。◆The Japan Association of Corporate Directors is a private group of top executives interested in corporate governance. 日本取締役協会は、企業統治に関心をもつ経営者の民間団体だ。

corporate governance framework　コーポレート・ガバナンス体制
◆The firm has developed a corporate governance framework based on a system comprising corporate auditors, directors and outside directors and a system of voluntary committees. 同社は、監査役、取締役と外部取締役を置く制度と任意の委員会制度に基づくコーポレート・ガバナンス体制を構築している。

corporate governance reform bill　企業統治改革法案
◆Concerned that the malpractice of corporate accounting may be widespread, the U.S. Congress passed a corporate governance reform bill in July 2002, immediately after WorldCom's bankruptcy was exposed. 企業会計の不正が広がっているとの懸念を強めていた米議会は、米通信大手ワールドコムの破綻が明らかになった直後の2002年7月に、企業統治改革法案を成立させた。

corporate governance regulations　企業統治法
◆According to a survey conducted by a law firm, more than half of such companies considered U.S. corporate governance regulations too harsh. ある法律事務所が行った調査によると、調査対象企業の半数以上が、米国の企業統治法［企業改革法］は厳しすぎると思っている。

corporate group tax system　連結納税制度
（＝consolidated taxation system, group taxation system; ⇒ consolidated tax system）
◆The corporate group tax system is designed to encourage spin-offs and other corporate restructuring efforts amid protracted recession. 連結納税制度のねらいは、不況の長期化で分社化など企業の事業再構築努力を促すことにある。

corporate health　企業の健全性, 企業体質, 経営体質
◆The merger will prompt other megabanks to come up with new strategies to reinforcing their corporate health. この統合は他のメガバンクを刺激し、メガバンクは企業体質の強化に向けた戦略を新たに打ち出すことになろう。

corporate income　法人所得, 企業収益
◆The recent appreciation of the yen has eroded corporate income from overseas units. 最近の円高で、海外子会社からの企業収益が伸び悩んでいる。◆Under the application of the Industrial Revitalization Law, companies are allowed to deduct the costs of scrapping or removing their excess facilities and equipment as losses from their corporate income for up to seven years, two years longer than the five-year period recognized by the corporate tax. 産業再生法の適用を受けた企業は、過剰設備や施設の廃棄・撤去にかかった費用を、法人税で認められている5年に2年上乗せした最長7年間、法人所得から「損金」として差し引くことが認められている。

corporate issuer　企業発行体
◆Asset-backed commercial paper refers to commercial paper whose creditworthiness is guaranteed by sales credit that the corporate issuer has with its debtors. 資産担保CPとは、企業発行体がその債務者に対して保有する売掛金によって信用度が保証されるコマーシャル・ペーパーを指す。

corporate Japan　日本株式会社, 日本企業
◆The wrongdoing of Olympus Corp., a blue-chip company that holds the largest share of the global endoscope market, has eroded international faith in corporate Japan. 内視鏡の市場シェアで世界トップのオリンパスの不正行為で、日本企業の国際的な信頼は失墜している。

corporate leaders　企業経営者
◆Corporate leaders must recognize that defrauding investors is a serious crime. 投資家を欺く行為は重大な犯罪である、ということを企業経営者は認識しなければならない。

corporate lending　企業向け貸出, 企業向け貸付け, 企業向け融資, 法人向け貸出, 法人向け貸出業務
◆The firm plans to offer not only retail lending, but also corporate lending by utilizing the customer screening know-how of its partner bank. 同社は、共同出資する銀行が持つ顧客審査のノウハウを活用して、個人向け融資のほかに法人向け融資業務も提供する計画だ。

corporate loans　法人向け融資
◆The 10 new Bank of Yokohama branches will offer a range of services including corporate loans. 横浜銀行の新支店10店舗では、法人向け融資などのサービスを提供する。

corporate manager　企業経営者, 経営者, 企業の管理職, 管理職
◆Corporate managers are cautious about wage hikes for fear of the adverse effects on business performances of the recent fall in stock prices and the yen's appreciation. 最近の株安と円高により企業業績に悪影響が出るとの懸念から、経営側は賃上げに警戒感を示している。◆The Bank of Japan must continue to promptly supply funds to prevent the financial contraction that all corporate managers dread. 企業経営者が恐れる金融収縮を防ぐため、日銀は迅速に資金供給を続ける必要がある。

corporate merger　企業合併
◆Corporate merger screening is conducted by the Fair Trade Commission of Japan in light of the Antimonopoly Law. 企業の合併審査は、独占禁止法に照らして［基づいて］公正取引委員会が行う。

corporate merger plan　企業の合併計画
◆A corporate merger plan is subject to legal screening by the Fair Trade Commission of Japan. 企業の合併計画は、公正取引委員会の法定審査を受けなければならない。

corporate pension　企業年金, 厚生年金
corporate pension plan　厚生年金制度, 厚生年金
corporate pension system　企業年金, 厚生年金
◆Currently those who work less than 75 percent of full-time hours are not eligible to subscribe to corporate pension plans. 現在、就業時間が正社員の75%（4分の3）未満の労働者は、厚生年金［厚生年金制度］への加入資格がない。

corporate pension assets　企業の年金資産
◆About ¥200 billion in corporate pension assets managed by AIJ investment advisory company vanished. 投資顧問会社のAIJが運用している企業の年金資産約2,000億円が、消失した。

corporate pension fund　企業年金基金, 企業年金積立金
◆As of the end of March 2011, AIJ Investment Advisors Co. had been entrusted with about ¥210 billion in corporate pension funds. 2011年3月末現在、投資顧問会社のAIJ投資顧問は、約2,100億円の企業年金基金［企業年金積立金］の運

用を受託していた。

corporate performance　企業業績, 会社業績, 決算
（⇒business performance）
◆Deterioration of corporate performance has spread from information technology-related industries to auto and other manufacturing industries and financial services.　企業業績の悪化は、IT（情報技術）関連産業から自動車などの製造業や金融サービスへと広がっている。◆Efforts to streamline the firm and brisk sales at home and abroad contributed to the improved corporate performance.　同社の合理化策と内外での販売好調が、業績［会社業績］改善の要因だ。◆Japan's exports will stagnate and corporate performance will suffer if the yen remains in the historically high ¥75-range against the dollar.　円相場が1ドル＝75円台の史上最高値が続けば、日本の輸出は低迷し、企業の業績は悪化する。

corporate profit　企業収益, 企業利益
◆Corporate profits will average out to positive growth.　企業収益は、横ばいを脱して積極的な増加（プラス成長）に転じるだろう。◆The increase in exports boosted corporate profits substantially.　輸出拡大で、企業収益が大幅に増えた。

corporate profitability　企業収益性, 企業の収益性, 企業収益
◆The economy may be headed toward a turnaround on the back of improved exports and corporate profitability.　輸出と企業収益が改善して、景気が好転する可能性もある。

corporate purchase　企業買収
◆The firm's former president spread false information about corporate purchases with the aim of inflating the stock prices of its affiliate.　同社の前社長は、関連会社の株価をつり上げるため、虚偽の企業買収情報を公表していた。

corporate racketeer　総会屋
（=corporate blackmailer, corporate extortionist）
◆Holding shareholders meetings on the same day is a measure to keep out sokaiya corporate racketeers.　株主総会の集中開催（株主総会の同一日開催）は、総会屋を排除する手段である。◆This banker pressed the bank's management to terminate its ties with sokaiya corporate racketeers.　この銀行マンは、同行に総会屋との関係を断つよう経営陣に迫った。

corporate raider　企業乗っ取り屋, 企業買収家　（敵対的な方法で大量の株を買い集めて、経営支配権をねらう者のこと。⇒greenmail, greenmailer）
◆The bank had shades of a corporate raider.　同行は、企業乗っ取りまがいの行為をしていた。

corporate rebuilding plan　企業再建計画, 再建計画
◆Under the latest corporate rebuilding plan, MMC intends to supply products through original equipment manufacturing arrangements to Nissan Motor Co. and Peugeot Citroen group.　今回の再建計画では、三菱自動車は、OEM（相手先ブランドでの生産）契約により日産自動車やプジョー・シトロエンに製品を供給する方針だ。

corporate reconstruction　企業再建, 企業再生

corporate reconstruction fund　企業再生ファンド
◆Daiei plans to collect capital investment of ¥100 billion from Marubeni Corp., corporate reconstruction fund and outside investors.　ダイエーは、丸紅や企業再生ファンド、外部の出資者（外部企業）から総額1,000億円の出資を募る計画だ。

corporate rehabilitation　企業再建, 経営再建, 事業再生（corporate revival）
corporate rehabilitation plan　経営再建計画, 企業再建計画
◆The bank will extend loans for businesses in growing fields such as corporate rehabilitation and nursing homes.　同行は、事業再生や老人ホームなどの成長分野への融資を進める方針だ。

corporate rehabilitation fund　企業再建ファンド, 事業再生ファンド, 企業再建基金
（=corporate revival fund）
◆Corporate rehabilitation funds are established by creditor banks and other investors to bail out heavily indebted companies.　企業再建ファンドは、巨額の債務を抱えた企業を救うため、取引銀行や投資家などが設立する基金だ。◆The Bank of Tokyo-Mitsubishi UFJ, Sumitomo Mitsui Banking Corp. and the Development Bank of Japan will jointly set up a corporate rehabilitation fund.　三菱東京UFJ銀行、三井住友銀行と日本政策投資銀行の3行が、共同出資で事業再生ファンドを設立する。

Corporate Rehabilitation Law　会社更生法
◆JAL and its two subsidiaries applied to the Tokyo District Court for bankruptcy protection under the Corporate Rehabilitation Law.　日航とその子会社2社が、会社更生法に基づいて会社更生手続きの適用を東京地裁に申請した。◆Shinsei Bank filed an application with the Tokyo District Court for the Corporate Rehabilitation Law to be applied to First Credit Co.　新生銀行は、東京地裁にファーストクレジットに対する会社更生法の適用を申請した。

corporate rehabilitation process　会社更生法の手続き
◆The company and the institutional investors are odds over how to treat the ownership of the stores as the collateral for the bonds under the corporate rehabilitation process.　同社と機関投資家は、社債の担保である同社の店舗所有権の会社更生法上の取扱いを巡って意見が対立している。

corporate reorganization　企業再編, 会社更生
corporate reorganization law　会社更生法, 民事再生法
◆The Financial Services Agency plans to apply the Corporate Reorganization Law in the event a financial institution fails after the current freeze on the so-called payoff system is lifted April 1.　金融庁は、4月1日のいわゆるペイオフ制度の凍結解除後に金融機関が破たんした場合に、民事再生法を適用する方針だ。

corporate restructuring　企業再編成, 企業再編, 企業リストラ, 事業機構の再編, 経営再建, リストラ
（⇒debt reduction）
◆The three banks and Daiei are expected to work out the framework of a corporate restructuring program for the company.　3銀行とダイエーは、ダイエーの会社再建計画の大枠を固める見通しだ。

corporate revitalization　企業再生
◆The government will improve RCC's corporate revitalization functions to collect secondary losses over a long period.　政府は、整理回収機構（RCC）の企業再生機能を強化し、長期間かけて二次損失を回収する方針だ。

corporate sentiment　企業の心理, 企業の景況感, 企業の業況判断
◆The nominal GDP growth rate takes into account price changes and is considered a more accurate reflection of household and corporate sentiment.　名目GDP（国内総生産）成長率は、物価変動を考慮し、家計や企業の景況感をより正確に反映するとされている。

corporate strategy　企業戦略, 経営戦略
◆The move by the largest regional bank in the country may impact the corporate strategies of major financial groups.　この国内最大の地方銀行の動きは、大手金融グループの経営戦略にも影響を与えそうだ。

corporate takeover　企業買収
（=corporate buyout）
◆Margin trading was used in a corporate takeover by exploiting legal shortcomings.　法の不備を利用して、企業買収に信用取引が使われた。

corporate tax　法人税, 法人事業税　（企業の利潤に対して課される国税。⇒combined profits and losses, corporate income, deduct）
◆The Financial Services Agency calls for lifting a freeze on a system that refunds corporate taxes previously paid by

companies if they fall into the red. 金融庁は、企業が赤字に陥った場合、企業が過去に納めた法人税を払い戻す制度（繰戻し還付制度）の凍結解除を求めている。

corporate tax on gross operating profit 外形標準課税, 業務粗利益への法人事業税（法人税）の課税
（⇒pro forma standard tax）
◆Business circles are opposed to the introduction of corporate taxes on gross operating profit. 産業界は、外形標準課税（法人事業税として業務粗利益に課税すること）の導入に反対している。

corporate turnaround body 企業再生支援機構
◆JAL's stocks may lose market value to zero if the corporate turnaround body cuts the shares 100 percent by delisting JAL from the Tokyo stock market. 企業再生支援機構が東京株式市場から日航の上場を廃止して日航株を100%減資したら、日航株の市場価値はゼロになる可能性がある。

corporate value 企業価値
improve [boost] corporate value 企業価値を高める
（⇒merger and acquisition deal）
increase the firm's corporate value 同社の企業価値を向上させる、同社の企業価値を高める
◆Corporate value is defined as "the total of profits one company will earn in future." 企業価値は、「ある会社が将来稼ぐ利益の合計」と定義される。◆In order to forestall hostile takeover bids, companies should raise their corporate value. 敵対的TOB（株式公開買付けによる企業買収）を未然に防ぐには、企業が企業価値を高めなければならない。◆Rakuten Inc.'s management integration proposal will not increase TBS's corporate value. 楽天からの経営統合の提案は、TBSの企業価値の向上にはつながらないだろう。◆The company is to hold a news conference to unveil a set of its programs to improve its corporate value. 同社は、記者会見を開いて、企業価値を高めるための一連のプログラムを発表する。

correct （動）修正する, 訂正する, 是正する, 調整する
corrected documents 訂正文書
corrected financial statement 訂正有価証券報告書, 有価証券報告書の訂正
◆Financial Services Agency has ordered 26 nonlife insurance firms to correct their business practices, after finding they failed to pay due insurance benefits. 損保各社が支払い義務のある保険金を支払わなかったことが判明したため、金融庁は損保26社に対して業務是正命令を出した。◆The corrected financial statement will be submitted to the Finance Ministry. 訂正有価証券報告書は、財務省に提出される。◆To what extent will the bubble in the real estate market and overheated economy be corrected? 不動産バブルと過熱景気［景気の過熱］の調整は、どの程度進むのだろうか。

correction （名）調整, 調整局面, 訂正, 修正（株式相場の「調整・調整局面」とは, 上昇基調の相場の一時的な下落局面をいう）
announce corrections to one's financial report 有価証券報告書の訂正を公表する
correction of error 誤謬の訂正
large correction in the dollar ドル相場の大幅調整
minor correction 小幅調整
ongoing correction 今回の調整, 今回の調整局面
prolonged housing correction 長引く住宅の調整局面, 住宅の調整局面の長期化
technical correction アヤ戻し （=technical rally, technical rebound: 相場が下げ基調のとき, 一時的に高くなる場合のことを「アヤ戻し」という）
temporary correction 自立反発, アヤ戻し
undergo a correction 調整局面に入る
◆In the United States, there is a risk of deeper and more prolonged housing correction. 米国では、住宅の調整局面が深刻化し、長引く恐れもある。◆Kokudo is suspected of selling a large amount of its Seibu Railway stock to client companies before the railway announced corrections to its financial report. コクドは、西武鉄道が有価証券報告書の訂正を公表する前に、取引先に大量の西武鉄道株を売却した疑いが持たれている。◆The correction of financial statements by Olympus is unlikely to result in the company's debts exceeding its assets. オリンパスの財務書類訂正で、同社の債務超過は避けられる見通しだ。◆The current deflationary trend seems to be a temporary phenomenon caused by the correction in oil prices after they skyrocketed last year. 現在のデフレ傾向は、昨年の原油高の反動による一時的な現象のようだ。

corrective market 訂正相場

corresponding （形）~に対応する, 一致する, 相当する, 類似する,（前に述べたことの）結果として起こる
compared with the corresponding month of last year 前年同月比で
the corresponding amounts 前期の比較対応数値, 対応数値
the corresponding period in the previous fiscal year 前年度同期
the corresponding period (of) last year 前年同期
◆Federal spending for the nine months to date totaled $1.62 trillion, a 6.9 percent increase from the corresponding period in the previous fiscal year. 10-6月期の連邦政府支出の総額は1兆6,200億ドルで、前年度同期比で6.9%の増加となった。◆Nonmonetary balance sheet items and corresponding income statement items are translated at rates in effect at the time of acquisition. 貸借対照表の非貨幣性項目とこれに対応する損益計算書項目は、取得日の為替レートで換算されています。◆The deflator, which indicates the overall trend in prices, dropped 2.5 percent in the April-June period compared to the corresponding period last year. 物価の総合的な動向を示すデフレーターは、4-6月期は前年同期比で2.5%下落した。

cost （動）費用などがかかる, 必要とする, 要する, 原価計算をする, 原価を見積もる
◆The Board of Audit has confirmed that the public financing package extended with a government-backed guarantee to JAL prior to its failure cost taxpayers a total of ¥47 billion. 日航の破たん前に政府保証付きで行われた公的融資の総国民負担額は470億円であることを、会計検査院が確定した。

cost （名）原価, 費用, 経費, 原価法, コスト
（⇒credit costs, financing costs）
actuarial cost method 保険数理原価法, 保険数理による原価計算法
bond issue cost 社債発行費
cut costs 費用を削減する, コスト削減する
financial cost 金融費用, 財務費
financing cost 資金調達コスト, 金融費用
funding cost 資金調達コスト
issuer's cost 発行者利回り
lower operating costs 営業コストを引き下げる
pension cost 年金コスト, 年金原価
personnel costs 人件費 （=staff cost）
◆In the temporary nationalization, the government will take possession of all shares from the bank's holding company at no cost. 一時国有化で、政府は同行の持ち株会社から株式をゼロ円で全株取得することになる。◆Record low U.S. borrowing costs are boosting the appeal to bullion as a hedge against inflation. 米国の資金調達コストが過去最低の水準にあるため、インフレ・ヘッジとしての金［金地金］の人気が高まっている。◆The capital adequacy ratio of the bank fell to about 8 percent due to costs related to the disposal of a massive amount of nonperforming loans. 同行の自己資本比率は、巨額の不良債権処理関連コストで、約8%まで低下した。

cost cutting 経費削減, 費用削減, コスト削減
 (=cost cut)
  cost-cutting efforts コスト削減努力, コスト削減策
   (=cost reduction efforts)
  cost cutting exercise 経費削減策, コスト削減策
  cost cutting measures 経費削減策, コスト削減策
   (=cost-cutting efforts, cost reduction measures)
  drastic cost cutting 思い切ったコスト削減, 徹底したコスト削減
Council of Economic Advisers 米大統領経済諮問委員会
Council on Customs Tariffs and Foreign Exchange and Other Transactions 関税・外国為替等審議会
Council on Economic and Fiscal Policy 経済財政諮問会議
counter （動）対抗する, ～に反対する, 逆襲する, 反撃する, 阻止する, 抑制する, 対応する, 反論する, 反証をあげる
  counter inflationary pressure インフレ圧力を抑制する
  counter the increase in thefts of ATM cards キャッシュ・カードの盗難多発に対応する
  introduce methods to counter hostile takeover attempts 敵対的買収への対抗策を導入する
  ◆Companies should obtain shareholder approval when introducing methods to counter hostile takeover attempts. 敵対的買収への対抗策を導入する場合, 企業は株主の承認を得なければならない。◆The new cash card is intended to counter the increase in thefts and counterfeiting of ATM cards. この新型キャッシュ・カードは, キャッシュ・カードの盗難や偽造事件の多発に対応したものだ。◆The United States is under pressure to make some difficult monetary policy decisions to cool down the overheating economy by countering the inflationary pressures stemming from higher import prices due to the weaker dollar. 米国は現在, ドル安での輸入価格の高騰によるインフレ圧力を抑えて過熱気味の景気を鎮めるための難しい金融政策の決断を迫られている。
counter （名）窓口, カウンター
  bank counter 銀行窓口
  deposit counter （預金の）預け入れ窓口
  foreign exchange counter 外国為替窓口
  pay counter 支払い窓口
counter （形）逆の, 反対の, 店頭の, 窓口の （副）逆に, 反対に
  counter business 窓口営業
  counter check 店頭小切手, 相小切手, 払戻し票
  counter cyclical policy 景気安定化政策
   (=countercyclical policy)
  counter deposits 店頭頭金
  counter fund 見返り資金
  counter guarantee 念書, 念証
  counter items （小切手や手形など）カウンターで受け付けた物件
  counter marketing 有害食品の追放運動, カウンター・マーケティング
  counter purchase 見返り輸入
  counter-recession policy 不況対策
  counter remittance 戻し金送金, 戻し金為替
  counter share 店頭株
  counter speculation 対抗投機
  counter staff カウンター係
  counter trade 見返り貿易, バーター貿易
  the counter party 取引相手方当事者
   (=counter parity)
counterbid （名）逆指し値

countercheck （名）再照合
countercyclical （形）反循環的な, 反景気循環的な, 景気連動［変動］抑制的な
  countercyclical capital buffer 景気連動［変動］抑制的な資本バッファー, カウンターシリカル資本バッファー
  countercyclical gadget 反循環装置
  countercyclical measures 景気対策
  countercyclical policy 景気政策, 反景気循環政策
counterfeit （動）偽造する, 模造する
  ◆It is almost impossible to counterfeit the new bills using computers or color copiers. コンピュータやカラー複写機を使って新札を偽造するのは, ほぼ不可能だ。
counterfeit （名）偽造, 偽造通貨, 偽造品, 模造品, 偽物
  ◆Fiscal 2004 saw the issuance of new counterfeit-proof ¥1,000, ¥5,000 and ¥10,000 bills. 2004年度から, 偽造防止の千円札, 5千円札と1万円札の新紙幣が発行された。
counterfeit （形）偽の, 偽造の, 模造の
   (=fake; ⇒ATM card)
  counterfeit bank notes 偽造紙幣
   (=counterfeit banknotes)
  counterfeit ¥500 coin 偽造された500円硬貨, 偽造500円硬貨, 偽500円玉 （=fake ¥500 coin)
  ◆In order to cut off funds to North Korea's nuclear weapons development program, the government will tighten controls on illegal bilateral transactions, including exports of materials for making missiles and smuggling of narcotics and counterfeit bank notes into the country. 北朝鮮の核兵器開発計画の資金源を断つため, 政府はミサイル製造の関連物資の輸出や麻薬・偽造紙幣の密輸など, 日朝間の不正取引の取締りを強化する方針だ。
counterfeit credit card 偽造クレジット・カード
  ◆The police obtained an arrest warrant for a Chinese-Malaysian man in Malaysia suspected to be involved in smuggling the counterfeit credit cards to Japan. 警察は, マレーシア国内で日本への偽造クレジット・カードの密輸にかかわっていた容疑で, 中国系マレーシア人の男の逮捕状を取った。
counterfeiter （名）偽造者, 通貨偽造者
  ◆To deter counterfeiters, a newly designed $100 bill features a blue three-dimensional security ribbon. 通貨偽造者を阻止するため［通貨偽造の対策として］, 米国の新デザインの100ドル紙幣には, 三次元(3D)安全リボンが（紙幣の中央に）描かれている。
counterfeiting 偽造
  counterfeiting of ATM cards ATMカードの偽造, キャッシュ・カードの偽造
  currency counterfeiting 通貨偽造
  ◆The new cash card is intended to counter the increase in thefts and counterfeiting of ATM cards. この新型キャッシュ・カードは, キャッシュ・カードの盗難や偽造事件の多発に対応したものだ。◆The U.S. government froze the assets of four individuals and eight entities that were involved in illicit activities such as money laundering, currency counterfeiting and narcotics trafficking. 米政府は, 資金洗浄（マネー・ロンダリング）や通貨偽造, 麻薬取引などの違法行為に関与している4個人, 8団体の資産を凍結した。
countermeasure （名）対策, 対応策, 対抗処置, 対抗手段, 対応手段, 報復手段
  a barrage of countermeasures 矢継ぎ早の対策
  take countermeasures 対抗措置を取る
  take drastic countermeasures 思い切った［抜本的な］対策を取る, 大胆なメスを入れる
  the preferred countermeasures against the financial crisis 金融危機への優先的な対応策
  ◆A chain-reaction global decline in stock values was temporarily stopped by a barrage of countermeasures. 世界的な株安連鎖は, 矢継ぎ早の対策でいったんは歯止めがかかった。

◆In Europe, buffeted by the U.S. financial crisis, four major countries have held a summit meeting to discuss countermeasures. 米金融危機の煽(あお)りを受けた欧州では、主要4か国が最近、首脳会議を開いて対策を協議した。◆The U.S. government failed to take drastic countermeasures against its fiscal deterioration. 米政府は、財政悪化に抜本的な対策を取れなかった[大胆なメスを入れられなかった]。

counterpart financing 見返り金融
counterpart fund 見返り資金
counterparty (名)相手方当事者, 当事者, 取引相手, 取引相手方, 顧客, 参加機関, カウンターパーティー
  counterparty rating カウンターパーティーの格付け
  highly rated counterparty 高格付けのカウンターパーティー
  market counterparties 市場参加機関
  mutual dealings between counterparties カウンターパーティー間の相互取引
  nondefaulting counterparties デフォルト(債務不履行)を起こしていない顧客
  the agreement of both counterparties 両当事者の合意
  unrated counterparty 格付けのない顧客
  ◆The process of termination requires the agreement of both counterparties. 解約手続きをするには、両当事者の合意が必要である。◆We do not expect any counterparties, which presently have high credit ratings, to fail to meet their obligations. 現在のところ、信用格付けが高い取引相手が債務を履行しないとは、当社は考えていません。
counterparty risk カウンターパーティー・リスク
  ◆Counterparty risks afflicted the global markets in the aftermath of the collapse of U.S. investment bank Lehman Brothers in 2008. 2008年に米証券会社[投資銀行]のリーマン・ブラザーズが破たんした影響で、世界の金融市場はカウンターパーティー・リスクに悩まされた。◆The capital markets around the globe are plagued by counterparty risks in the aftermath of the collapse of U.S. investment bank Lehman Brothers in 2008. 世界全体の資本市場は、2008年の米証券会社[投資銀行]の経営破たんの影響で、カウンターパーティー・リスクに苦しんでいる。
countervailing credit 相殺信用貸し
country (名)国, 本国, 地方, カントリー
  borrower country 借金国, 借り手国
  countries with debt-servicing difficulties 債務返済が困難な国
  country bank 地方銀行
  country collection 地方取立て, 他所取立て手形
  country collection items 地方取立て物件
  country credit risk カントリー・リスク
  country fund カントリー・ファンド(成長が見込まれる国の株式を集めて投資する投資信託)
  country limit 国の借金全体に対して設ける貸出限度, カントリー・リミット
  country note 地方銀行発行紙幣
  country rating 国別格別, ソブリン格付け
  country risk 国別信用度, カントリー・リスク
  creditor countries 債権国
  debt-ridden country 債務国, 債務困窮国
  deficit country 赤字国, 入超国
  done country 被援助国
  donor country 援助国
  high yielding countries' assets 高利回り国の資産
  highly indebted country 高債務国
  indebted country 債務国
  investment grade country 投資適格国
  middle income countries 中所得国
  refinancing country 対外債務再編成国
  surplus country 黒字国, 出超国
coupling (名)(各国金利の)連動性, 連結, 結合, カップリング
coupon (名)債券の利息, 表面利率(利付き債(coupon bond)の支払い利息率), 利率, 利札(りさつ:利付き債の利息の支払い請求権を表象する証券), 商品券, 景品引換え券, クーポン (⇒long coupon, shortの項のshort coupon, zero coupon bond)
  arrear coupon 繰延べ利札
  bank debentures with coupon 利付き金融債 (=coupon bank debenture)
  bond with interest coupon 利付き債券
  coupon and bond paying agent 債券償還代理人
  coupon bank debenture 利付き金融債
  coupon bearing bonds クーポン債
  coupon bearing securities 利付き債
  coupon book クーポン帳
  coupon clipper 利子生活者
  coupon curve 利付き債のイールド・カーブ
  coupon date 利払い日
  coupon equivalent yield 債券相当利回り
  coupon event クーポン・イベント
  coupon for goods 商品券
  coupon frequency 利払い回数
  coupon fund 利付き資金
  coupon hike 表面利率の引上げ
  coupon interest クーポン金利
  coupon interest payment 表面金利支払い
  coupon off 利落ち, 利札落ち (=ex coupon)
  coupon on 利付き, 利札付き (=cum coupon)
  coupon pad クーポン綴り
  coupon pass クーポン・パス, 米国債の買切りオペ(ニューヨーク連邦準備銀行(Federal Reserve Bank of New York)が、市中銀行に持続的な支払い準備(permanent reserves)を供給するため、公開市場で利付き財務省証券を売戻し条件なしで買い入れること)
  coupon policy クーポン付き保険証券
  coupon premium クーポン・プレミアム
  coupon redemption クーポン回収
  coupon rollover date (変動利付き債の)利率更改日
  coupon stripping クーポン・ストリッピング
  coupon supply 利付き国債の供給, 中長期債の供給
  coupon system 景品付き販売法
  coupon washing クーポン・ウォッシュ取引
  coupon yield 表面利回り, 債券利回り
  coupon yield curve 国債のイールド・カーブ, 債券にイールド・カーブ
  coupons issued 発行済みクーポン
  coupons redeemed 回収クーポン
  cum coupon 利付き, 利札付き (=coupon on)
  debenture coupon 社債利札
  discount coupon 割引券
  dividends and coupons paid to policyholders 契約者に支払われる[支払う]配当金と利息
  down-in-coupon moves 低クーポンへの乗換え
  ex coupon 利落ち, 利札落ち (=coupon off)
  exchange coupon 商品券 (=coupon for goods)
  extended coupon 繰延べ利札

first day of coupon accrual　クーポン発生日
generous coupon　甘めの利率,投資家寄りの表面利率
gift coupon　景品引換券
gross issuance on coupon offering sizes　国債総発行額
half-price coupon　半値券,半額券
high coupon　高利回り,表面利率が高い,高クーポン,ハイ・クーポン
high coupon securities　表面利率が高い銘柄,高クーポン銘柄
higher coupon securities　高クーポン物
higher premium coupon　高クーポン物
interest coupon　利札
issue bonds with a coupon of 3.25 percent　利率3.25%の社債を発行する
long coupons　長期債
low coupon　低利回り,表面利率が低い,低クーポン
low coupon collateral　低クーポンのパス・スルー証券
low coupon currency　低金利通貨
low coupon securities　表面利率が低い銘柄
lower coupon collateral　低クーポン物
minimum coupon bonds　ミニマム・クーポンの銘柄
nominal coupon　名目利子率
nominal coupon of interest　表面利率
offer a coupon of A percent　表面利率A%を提示する
offer a coupon premium　クーポン・プレミアムを付ける
premium coupons　プレミアム・クーポン物
quarterly coupon　年4回の利払い
real coupon　実質利子率
reinvestment of coupons　クーポンの再投資
reprice the coupon　表面利率の再設定をする
short coupons　短期債
single digit coupon　10%以下の表面利率
stepup［step-up］coupon loan　ステップアップ・クーポンの貸金
stripped coupon or principal　金利または元本の分離
swap coupon　スワップ・クーポン(スワップの固定金利のこと)
the fair value of the convertible zero coupon notes due 2015　2015年満期の転換ゼロ・クーポン債の公正価格
Treasury coupon auctions　国際入札
unmatured coupon　満期未到来の利札
unredeemed coupons　未回収クーポン
upfront coupon　当初のクーポン
very high coupon premiums　超プレミアム物
weighted average coupon　加重平均クーポン
zero coupon note［bond］　ゼロ・クーポン債
◆At December 31, 2010, the fair value of the convertible zero coupon notes due 2015 was $135 million compared to the carrying value of $55 million. 2010年12月31日現在、2015年満期の転換ゼロ・クーポン債の公正価格は、1億3,500万ドルで、その帳簿価格は5,500万ドルでした。◆The company issued in Europe $300 million of Series 3 Notes at an annual coupon of 10% maturing on May 28, 2015. 同社は欧州で、3億ドルのシリーズ3ノートを、2015年5月28日満期・年利率10%で発行した。

coupon bond　利付き債(券面に利払いのための利札が付いている債券),固定利付き債,クーポン付き社債,(米財務省証券のうち利息が付される)中長期債,クーポン債　(=coupon note)
coupon-bearing bond　クーポン債
deferred coupon bond　金利繰延べ債
full coupon bond　カレント・クーポン債
high coupon bond　高クーポン債,ハイ・クーポン債
low coupon bond　低クーポン債
stepped coupon bond　段階的利付き債
zero coupon bond　ゼロ・クーポン債
　(=zero coupon note)

coupon payment　利払い,クーポン支払い
coupon payment on debt　債券利息
coupon payment period　利払い期間
debt with coupon payments tied to a measure of interest rates　表面利率が金利指標に連動する債券
redemption and coupon payments　元利払い
reinvestment of coupon payments　クーポンの再投資

coupon rate　(債券の)表面利率,表面金利,債券利率,発行利率
carry a lower coupon rate　表面利率が低い
equity warrants sold at extremely low coupon rates　超低利率で発行したワラント債
◆Convertible bonds carry lower coupon rates. 転換社債は、表面利率が低めだ。

coupon swap　クーポン・スワップ(通貨スワップで金利部分だけを交換するもの)
cross-currency coupon swaps　複数通貨間の金利スワップ
currency coupon swap　通貨クーポン・スワップ
dual coupon swap　デュアル・クーポン・スワップ
put on a coupon swap　クーポン・スワップを行う
single-currency coupon swap　単一通貨の金利スワップ
the credit risk on coupon swap　クーポン・スワップの信用リスク
the fixed interest rate in a coupon swap　クーポン・スワップの固定金利　(⇒swap rate)
US dollar coupon swap　米ドル金利スワップ

court　(名)裁判所,法廷,公判,裁判,裁判官,判事,役員会,重役会,委員会,重役幹部,王室,宮殿,宮廷,御前会議,宮中会議,陳列場の一区画,ご機嫌とり,コート
appear in court　出廷する　(=attend court)
bankruptcy court　破産裁判所,破産審査裁判所
be taken to court　裁判にかけられる
bring A before the court　Aを裁判沙汰にする,Aを訴える
civil court　民事法廷
Claims Court　請求裁判所
court actions　裁判
court appearance　出廷　(=to appear in court)
court case　法廷訴訟
court hearing　法廷審理
court of bankruptcy　破産裁判所
court protection from creditors　資産保全
court ruling　裁判所の裁定,裁判所の判決
court trial　裁判
Courts of the United States　合衆国裁判所,連邦裁判所
criminal court　刑事法廷
district court　地方裁判所　(⇒examine)
general court　株主総会
go through the courts　法的処理をする,法的処理を行う　(⇒go through)
go to court　訴訟を起こす,裁判沙汰にする
high court　高等裁判所
hold (a) court　開廷する,裁判を開く,裁判を行う
in court　裁判で,法廷で
law court　裁判所,法廷
local court　地方裁判所

lower court 下級裁判所
maritime court 海事裁判所
out of court 法廷外で, 示談で, 審理なしで
out-of-court negotiations 示談交渉
settle out of court 示談にする, 示談で解決する
settle the case out of court 事件を示談で解決する
◆A federal appeals court in New York approved the sale of Chrysler assets to Fiat. ニューヨークの米連邦控訴裁判所は, クライスラー資産のフィアットへの売却を承認した。◆Under the firm's rehabilitation plan approved by the district court, financial institutions will waive 87.5 percent of the unsecured loans they extend to the firm. 地方裁判所が認可した同社の更生計画では, 金融機関が, 同社に行った無担保融資[同社に対する無担保債権]の87.5%を放棄することになっている。

court protection from creditors 資産保全
◆An increasing number of publishers have sought court protection from creditors under the Civil Rehabilitation Law in the past few years. ここ2、3年, 民事再生法に基づく資産保全[民事再生法の適用]を申請する企業が増えている。

covenant (名)捺印(なついん)契約, 捺印証書, 契約, 協約, 約款, 約定, 誓約, 誓約条項, 財務制限条項, 特約条項, 約束
a pension plan covering all of the employees 全従業員を対象とした年金制度
a sales man covering the district 同地区担当のセールスマン, この地区を受け持つセールスマン
additional covenants 付帯条件
affirmative covenant 確約
be covered against fire and accident (〜は)火災・事故保険をかけている
be covered by insurance (〜には)保険が付けてある, 保険がかけてある, 保険が適用される
be not covered by insurance (〜には)保険が付けられていない, (〜には)保険が適用されない
breach a covenant 約定条項に違反する
carry additional covenants 付帯条件が付く
cash flow covenants キャッシュ・フロー要件
collateral maintenance covenant 担保維持条項
covenant maker 協約締結者
 (=maker of the covenant)
covenant of title 権限担保約款
covenants contained in the indenture of the rated issues 格付け債券の発行契約に記載[明示]された特約条項
cross covenant 共通制限条項
debt covenant 債務担保条項, 債券の約定条項
dividend covenant 配当制限条項
leaseback covenants リースバック禁止条項
mandatory prepayment covenants 強制期限前弁済条項
negative covenants 消極的約定条項
protective covenant 保護条項
rate covenant 料金条項
restrictive covenant 制限条項
restrictive financial covenant 財務制限条項
trip the dividend covenant 配当制限条項を発動する
violation of covenant 契約違反

cover (動)保険をかける[付ける], (費用や金額などを)賄(まかな)う, (損失の)穴埋めをする, (損失などを)補てんする, (出費, 損失などを)相殺する, 差引ゼロにする, 保証する, (担保で)補償する, 担保に入れる, 抵当とする, (空売り決済のために株を)買い戻す, 買い埋める, 問題などを取り扱う, 〜を対象とする, 〜を担当する, 〜の責任を負う, 〜に応じる, 〜の条件を認める, 含む, 報道する, 取材する, カバーする (⇒basic pension, economic value, loan interest rate, take out, uncollectible)

cover an overdraft 当座貸越しを抵当とする
cover bad loans 不良債権をカバーする
cover cost overruns 予算オーバーを補てんする
cover damage caused by an earthquake or tsunami 地震や津波による損害[被害]を補償する
cover exposure ポジションをカバーする
cover in the forward market 先物市場でカバーを取る
cover investments 設備投資を賄う
cover loss 損失を補てんする, 損害を賄う[補償する], 赤字を補てんする, 損失の穴埋めをする
cover oversold [overbought] amounts カバー取引をする
cover positions with cash ポジションを現物でカバーする
cover shorts [short sales] 空売りした株を買い戻す, 思惑売りした株を買い埋める
cover the damage by insurance 保険で損害を賄う[補てん]する
cover the expenses of 〜の費用を賄う
cover the present credit losses 現在の信用損失をカバーする
cover the property loss of a large number of earthquake victims 多くの地震被災者の物的損害を補償する[物的損害の費用を賄う]
insurance covers 〜 保険で〜が補償される, 保険の補償範囲は〜である, 〜に保険が適用される, 〜に保険がきく, 保険が〜をカバーする
marine insurance covering All Rights 全危険担保条件による海上保険
people not covered by the national health insurance program 国民健康保険制度の対象になっていない人々
◆All shipments shall be covered for 110% of invoice value. 積み荷には, すべて送り状金額の10%増し[110%]で保険を付けるものとする。◆As a result of fierce competition in the past, interest rate profit margins were kept too low to cover loans that went sour. 過去の熾烈(しれつ)な競争の結果, 金利の利ざやが小さく抑えられる余り, 貸倒れ[貸倒れのリスク]をカバーできなかった[過去の熾烈な融資合戦の結果, 不良債権リスクをカバーできないほど利ざやは小さく抑えられた]。◆As the lead bank in the construction project, the bank will cover more than a certain percentage of the joint loan to the Canadian corporation. この建設プロジェクトの主幹事銀行として, 同行はカナダ企業への協調融資のうち一定割合以上を融資する。◆Elective health checkups are not covered by insurance. 一般の検診には, 保険が適用されない。◆Financial institutions have capital which can be used to cover eventual financial losses to ensure debt servicing will not be impaired. 金融機関には, 損失が生じた際にその穴埋めをして, 債務の支払いに支障がでないようにする自己資本がある。◆Life Insurance Policyholders Protection Corp. will provide ¥145 billion to partially cover the life insurer's negative net worth, which was ¥320 billion as of the end of last September. 生命保険契約者保護機構は, 昨年9月末現在の同生保の債務超過額3,200億円の一部を支援するため, 1,450億円を支出することになっている。◆Pension premiums of full-time housewives of company employees and public servants are automatically covered by payments made by all subscribers to welfare and mutual pension plans. 会社員や公務員の専業主婦の年金保険料は, 厚生年金や共済年金の加入者全員の支払い金で自動的にカバーすることになっている。◆The auction was covered 3.5 times. 応札倍率は, 3.5倍だった。◆The basic pension plan has been covered by premiums paid by subscribers and government budgetary appropriations. 基礎年金は, 加入者が支払う保険料と政府の予算割当額(国の負担)で賄(まかな)われている。◆The cofinancing scheme of the Bank of Tokyo-

Mitsubishi UFJ will cover the Stardale mega solar power plant construction project carried out by a Canadian corporation. 三菱東京UFJ銀行の協調融資事業の対象は、カナダの企業が実施している大型太陽光発電所建設プロジェクト（計画）の「スターデール」だ。◆The government covers 50 percent of the basic pension fund from 2009. 国は、2009年度から基礎年金基金全体の2分の1を負担している。◆The new inspection will cover borrowers whose stock prices or credit ratings have not recovered since the previous inspection. 今回の金融庁の検査は、前回の検査から株価や格付けが回復していない融資先企業を対象にしている。◆The payoff system covers up to ¥10 million in deposits plus interest. ペイオフ（預金の払い戻し）制度対象の保証額は、預金1,000万円とその利息である。◆The public loan was covered many times over. 公債には、数倍に上る応募者があった。◆The reserves of private non-life insurers and the reserve fund of the government's special account may be sufficient to cover the property losses of the massive earthquake's victims. 民間損保の準備金と政府の特別会計の積立金があれば、今回の大震災被災者の物的損害の費用を十分賄（まかな）えるかもしれない。◆The trade insurance of Nippon Export and Investment Insurance previously only covered direct exports by domestic firms. 独立行政法人・日本貿易保険の貿易保険はこれまで、国内企業の直接輸出だけが対象だった。

cover （名）保証金, 敷金, 為替資金, 担保品, 保険担保, 保険仮引受書, 保険, カバー
   additional cover　追加証拠金
   adequate insurance cover　十分な保険による補償
   asset cover　資産倍率
   bid cover [bid-to-cover] ratio　応札倍率, 応募倍率
   broker's cover note　保険仲介人覚書
   cover cost　カバー・コスト（為替相場の変動リスクを回避するために予約するコスト）
   cover dealing　カバー・ディーリング
   cover for a loan　融資に対する担保
   cover note　保険料領収書, 保険契約覚書, 仮保険証券, 仮証券, 仮契約書, カバー・ノート
      （=covering note）
   dividend cover　配当倍率, 配当カバー
   exchange cover　カバー取引, 為替カバー
   exchange cover rate　（為替の）出合い相場
   exchange fund cover [operation]　為替資金操作
   exchange position cover [operation]　為替持ち高操作, 為替持ち高調整操作
   exchange risk cover [operation]　為替持ち高調整操作
   fixed charge cover　金融費用カバレッジ
   insurance cover　保険担保, 保険の付保
   interest cover　インタレスト・カバレッジ
   net present value cover ratio　純現在価値カバー率
   outright cover　（外国為替の）アウトライト・カバー
   political risk cover　政治リスク保険
   provisional cover　仮保険証券
   underwriting cover　プレミアム・カバレッジ

cover damage　被害[損害]を補償する
   ◆Major nonlife insurance companies saw a rapid increase in the number of people taking out insurance covering damage due to earthquakes, tsunami, volcanic eruptions and other natural disasters. 大手損保各社では、地震や津波、火山の噴火などの天災による損害を補償する保険（地震保険）の加入者が急増した。◆TEPCO eventually hopes to raise about ¥600 billion through the sales of its real estate and stock to cover damages. 損害補償費用として東電は、最終的に保有する不動産と株式の売却で約6,000億円の資金調達を目指している。

cover damage caused by an earthquake or tsunami　地震や津波による被害を補償する
   ◆Fire insurance did not cover damage caused by an earthquake or tsunami before the 1964 Niigata Earthquake. 1964年の新潟地震以前には、火災保険で地震や津波による被害が補償されなかった。◆The earthquake insurance system was launched after the 1964 Niigata Earthquake as a response to the problem of fire insurance not covering damage caused by an earthquake or tsunami. 地震保険[地震保険制度]は、火災保険で地震や津波による被害が補償されない問題への対応策として、1964年の新潟地震後に導入された。

cover losses　損失の穴埋めをする, 赤字を補填する（⇒tax money）
   ◆About ¥1.9 trillion of taxpayers' money was spent over a ten year span until last fiscal year to cover losses from a surging number of uncollectible loans guaranteed by a public credit guarantee scheme for small and midsize companies. 中小企業のための公的信用保証制度により保証される融資の貸倒れ件数が急増し、それによる損失の穴埋めをするために、昨年度までの10年間で約1兆9,000億円の税金が投入された。

cover payments to bondholders　債券保有者への支払いを補償する
   ◆Bond insurers write policies that promise to cover payments to bondholders if the entity that issued the bonds defaults. 金融保証会社[債券保険会社]は、債券発行体がデフォルト（債務不履行）になった場合に、債券保有者への（元本と利息の）支払い補償を約束する保険を引き受けている。

cover rate　（為替の）出合い相場
cover ratio　応札倍率
   low cover ratio　応札倍率の低迷

cover up　（動）もみ消す, 隠ぺいする, 隠匿（いんとく）する, 隠す
   ◆The company hid investment losses and tried to cover them up with funds related to corporate acquisitions. 同社は、投資損失を隠ぺいし、企業買収関連資金でそのまま隠ぺいを図った。◆To cover up its irregularities, the bank deleted e-mails detailing its business transactions from the bank's server. 不正行為を隠すため同行は、業務取引に関する電子メールを、同行のサーバーから削除した。

cover-up　（名）もみ消し, もみ消し工作, 隠ぺい, 隠ぺい工作, 隠し立て, ～隠し　（⇒veep）
   a huge loss cover-up scandal　巨額損失隠し事件
   bad debt cover-up operations　不良債権の隠ぺい工作
   ◆Olympus Corp.'s deception of its shareholders and clients by window-dressing was due to the cover-up of losses on investments the company made in the 1990s. オリンパスが粉飾決算で株主や取引先を欺いたのは、同社が1990年代に行った投資の損失隠しをするためだった。◆The cover-up of investment losses by Olympus was discovered during an investigation by the company's third-party panel. オリンパスによる投資損失処理の偽装工作は、同社の第三者委員会の調査で判明した。◆The former UFJ Bank vice president engineered the cover-up. UFJ銀行の元副頭取が、隠ぺい工作を発案した。

coverage　（名）保険の担保, 担保範囲, 付保範囲, 適用範囲, 範囲, 限度, 負担能力, 正貨準備[準備金], カバレッジ（⇒group insurance, insurance coverage）
   a policy affording comprehensive coverage　総合担保保険証券
   a 45 percent gold coverage for paper money　紙幣に対する45％の正貨準備[金準備]
   asset coverage　資産担保率
   automobile physical damage coverage　車両保険
   benefit coverage　給付内容
   building coverage ratio　建ぺい率
   catastrophic coverage　高額医療費保険

coverage amount range　保証額の範囲
coverage limit　付保限度
coverage ratio　損失負担能力, 長期支払い能力比率
credit-risk coverage ratio　信用リスク・カバレッジ比率
debt coverage　返済余力
earning coverage　収益カバレッジ
extended coverage　拡張担保, 拡張危険担保
fixed charge coverage　金融費用カバレッジ, 固定費カバレッジ
full coverage　全額保証
health insurance coverage　医療保険加入者
income coverage　収益担保率
insurance coverage　保険担保, 保険の付保, 保険の担保範囲
interest coverage　インタレスト・カバレッジ
life insurance coverage　保険金額, 保険契約金額, 生命保険給付
loan loss coverage　債権損失カバレッジ
make a blanket coverage　一括して引き受ける
make a regular coverage call　担当顧客に（電話で）定期連絡をする
mandatory universal coverage　強制的国民皆保険
protection against own-injury coverage　自損事故保険
renew one's coverage　担保範囲を更新する
retail-oriented primary coverage　リテール型1次保険
stop loss coverage　超過損害担保, ストップ・ロス保険
terrorism coverage exemption clauses　テロ免責条項
time insurance coverage　定期保険保障
universal coverage　国民皆保険
universal health care coverage　国民皆医療保険制度
wholesale-oriented pool coverage　ホールセール型プール保険

◆Family insurance policy is a whole life insurance policy that provides term insurance coverage on the insured's spouse and children. 家族保険契約は, 被保険者の配偶者と子どもに定期保険保障を与える終身生命保険だ。◆Major nonlife insurers in Japan have introduced terrorism coverage exemption clauses for new contracts and contract renewals with the aim of not providing full compensation for losses caused by terrorist attacks. 日本の大手損保は, 新規契約と契約の更改分についてテロ被害に対する全額補償を引き受けないための「テロ免責条項」を導入した。◆Our postretirement benefits include health care benefits and life insurance coverage. 当社の退職後給付には, 医療給付と生命保険給付が含まれています。◆Whole life insurance means life insurance under which coverage remains in force during the insured's entire lifetime, provided premiums are paid as specified in the policy. 終身保険は, 保険契約に明記されている保険料が支払われているかぎり, 保障が被保険者の全生涯にわたって有効な生命保険を意味する。

covered　（形）保護された, 補償された,（担保物で）保証された, 保険をかけた, カバード
bond with covered warrant　カバード・ワラント債
covered bear　保護された弱気筋（=protected bear）
covered call　ヘッジされたコール, カバード・コール
covered expenses　保険対象費用
covered interest arbitrage　カバード金利裁定（取引）, 金利裁定, 金利裁定取引 （=interest arbitrage）
covered option　カバード・オプション（オプション取引の裏付けとなる原証券（underlying security）を保有しながらコール・オプションを売ること, またはオプション取引の裏付けとなる原証券を空売り（short sale）しながらプット・オプションを売ること）
covered transaction　カバー取引
covered warrant　カバード・ワラント
covered writer　カバード・ライター（writer=オプションの売り手。オプション取引の裏付けとなる原証券（underlying security）を保有しながら, コール・オプションを売る者）
write a covered option　カバード・オプションを売り建てる

covering　（名）（空売りを決済するための）株式買戻し, 為替間接払い, 補てん　（形）補てんする, 買戻しの, 関連の, 仮の
be bought on short covering　ショート・カバーの買いが入る
covering by shorts　弱気の買戻し
covering contract　買戻し契約, 戻し買い
covering letter　（同封の）説明書, 紹介書, 添え状
covering note　添え状, 証明書, 仮契約書（cover note）（=covering letter）
covering of a deficit　赤字補てん
covering of actual requirements　実需買い
covering price　込みの値段
covering purchase　手当て買い
covering remittance　為替間接送金
covering schedule　送付状
covering short　空売り株の買戻し, 手当て買い, ショート・カバー　（=short covering）
covering transaction　カバー取引
deficit covering bond　歳入補てん国債[公債], 赤字国債
deficit covering finance　赤字金融
short covering [short-covering]　空売りの買い戻し, 買戻し, ショート・カバー, ショート・カバリング
short-covering rally　買戻し主導の相場上昇

◆There was short covering by traders. トレーダーの買戻しがあった[トレーダーが買い戻した]。

CPI　消費者物価指数　（consumer price indexの略。⇒consumer price index, fiscal year, territory）
average CPI inflation　CPIの平均上昇率
general CPI index　総合消費者物価指数
provisional CPI number　消費者物価指数速報値

◆Including perishables, the nationwide CPI shrank 0.2 percent to 98.1 from the previous year, down for the fifth year. 全国の消費者物価指数（生鮮食品を含む）は, 98.1と前年度に比べて0.2%縮小し, 5年連続の下落となった。

crack down on　～を厳しく取り締まる, ～の摘発を強化する, ～に対して断固たる措置をとる, ～を弾圧する
◆Police must crack down on such moneylenders. 警察は, このような金融業者の摘発を強化するべきだ。

crash　（動）衝突する, 落ちる[墜落する], 倒れる, 壊（こわ）れる, 砕（くだ）ける, 崩壊する, 倒壊する, 倒産する,（株が）大暴落する
◆Stock markets in the United States and European countries crashed again as there is no end in sight to fiscal crises in them. 欧米の株式市場は, 欧米の財政危機の収束が見通せないため, ふたたび総崩れとなった。

crash　（名）崩壊, 倒壊, 破滅, 倒産,（商売などの）失敗,（経済の）恐慌,（株の）大暴落, 株価暴落, 急落, 衝撃, ショック
crash course　緊急特訓コース, 集中講座, 速成コース（cram course）
crash in oil prices　原油価格の急落
crash job　急ぎの仕事
crash of the market　市況の突然の崩れ, 市場の暴落

(=market crash)
crash program　突貫計画, 突貫工事計画, 応急作業計画
economic crash　経済恐慌
spontaneous global market crash　世界同時株安
stock market [exchange] crash　株式市場の暴落, 株価大暴落[暴落], 株式恐慌
stock market crash in October 1987　1987年10月19日（月曜日）の株価暴落, 1987年10月のブラック・マンデー
◆Major Asian markets such as Shanghai and Hong Kong also show a situation that could be dubbed as a spontaneous global market crash. 上海や香港などアジアの主要市場も, 世界同時株安の様相を見せている。◆Tokyo and other major Asian markets also plunged, a situation that could be dubbed a spontaneous global market crash. 東京その他アジアの主要市場も下落して, 世界同時株安の様相を見せている。

create　（動）創造する, 創出する, 創作する, 作り出す, 開発する, 生み出す, 引き起こす, 発生させる, 会社などを設立する, 新設する, 設ける, 担保権などを設定する, 構築する, 伸ばす, 高める
create a deal　案件を組成する
create a floating rate asset　変動金利資産を仕組む
create a market　市場を開拓する
create a portfolio of securities　証券ポートフォリオを構築する
create a security interest　担保権を設定する
create a synthetic put　合成プットを構築する
create an idea　アイデアを生み出す
create jobs　雇用を創出する, 職場・仕事を作る
create sales　売上を伸ばす
create value for (one's) shareholders　株主の価値を創出する, 株主の価値を高める, 株主の利益を高める, 株主に対する資産価値を創出する
create value in diverse markets　広範な市場で収益を生み出す
◆A boom in stock investing among working women has led a number of women to create Web sites and publish guides targeted at this growing market. 働く女性たちの間での株式投資ブームで, この成長市場向けサイトを立ち上げたり, 指南本を出したりする女性が増えている。◆A real estate broker created a dummy company to illegally receive a public credit guarantee. 不動産業者が, 架空の会社を作って不正に公的信用保証を受けていた。◆Commercial banks have created special investment vehicles (SIVs) in order to escape the capital adequacy regulation imposed by the Basel accord. 銀行は, バーゼル協定[バーゼル合意]による自己資本比率規制を回避するため, 特別投資会社（SIV）を新設している。◆If the merger takes place, it will create a full-scale financial conglomerate with a major bank, a major securities house and credit card company under its umbrella. 統合すれば, 傘下に大手銀行と大手証券, クレジット・カード会社などを持つ本格的な金融コングロマリット（金融複合企業体）が誕生する。◆M&A deals among start-up firms are likely to create more demand for equity financing from the autumn. ベンチャー企業間のM&A取引で, 秋から株式発行による資金調達の需要が増える見通しだ。◆Measures to expand and create employment are a pressing task. 雇用拡大と雇用創出策は, 急を要する課題だ。◆The European Union hurriedly created an emergency rescue fund, called the European Financial Stability Facility (EFSF). 欧州連合（EU）は, 欧州金融安定基金（EFSF）という緊急支援基金を急設した。◆The merger between the TSE and the OSE will create the world's second-largest exchange group in terms of the total market value of listed shares. 東証と大証の経営統合で, 上場株式の時価総額で世界第2位の株式取引所グループが誕生する。◆The merger will create the world's largest financial group with assets totaling about ¥190 trillion. この経営統合で, 総資産約190兆円の世界最大の金融グループが誕生する。◆The restructuring will allow us to continue to create value for our shareholders. この事業再編によって, 当社は, 当社の株主価値を今後とも高めることができます。◆The two financial groups plan to integrate their banking, trust and securities operations under a holding company created through the merger of their holding companies. 両金融グループは, それぞれ銀行, 信託, 証券業務を経営統合により新設する持ち株会社の傘下に統合する計画だ。◆This ex-vice president is believed to have been deeply involved in creating a slush fund. この元副社長は, 同社の裏金づくりに深く関与していたとされる。◆To prevent the current fiscal and financial crisis in Europe from spreading, the IMF will create a new short-term lending facility. 現在の欧州財政・金融危機の拡大を防ぐ[封じる]ため, 国際通貨基金（IMF）が, 新たな短期の融資制度を創設することになった。◆We will aim at creating a top, comprehensive financial group in the world that can win the global competition. 当社は今後, グローバルな競争を勝ち抜ける世界屈指の総合金融グループの創造を目指す。

creation　（名）創造, 創作, 創出, 創立, 創設, 設立, 組成, 構築, 開発, 整備, 発明, 創造品, 発明品, 創作品
creation of a security interest　担保権の設定
creation of a synthetic put　合成プットの構築
creation of bank credit　預金通貨の創造
creation of claim　債権発生
creation of job opportunities　雇用機会の創出
creation of money　貨幣の創造
credit creation　信用創出, 信用創造
（=creation of credit）
demand creation　需要創造
deposit creation　預金創造, 預金創出
income creation　所得創出
inflationary credit creation　インフレ的信用創造
job [employment] creation　雇用の創出, 雇用創出
liquidity creation　流動性創出
money creation　信用創造
supply creation　供給創出
trade creation　貿易創出

credibility　（名）信頼, 信認, 信用力, 信用度, 信頼性, 信頼度, 信憑（しんぴょう）性, 確実性, 真実性
（=creditworthiness）
anti-inflation credibility　インフレ抑制姿勢に対する信認, インフレ抑制政策の信頼性
credibility gap　言行不一致, 食い違い, 不信感, 信頼性不足
inflation-fighting credibility　インフレ抑制姿勢に対する信認, インフレ抑制政策の信頼性
the credibility of the banks' debtor companies　銀行の融資先の信用力
the credibility of the government bonds　国債の信認
◆FSA inspectors are to check the credibility of the banks' debtor companies, including their management efficiency and the accuracy of their collateral assessment. 金融庁の検査官は, 銀行の融資先の経営効率や担保評価などを含めて, 銀行の融資先の信用力を洗い直す。◆Greece's credibility plunged due to its slipshod fiscal management in the European financial crisis. 欧州の財政・金融危機で, ギリシャの信認は放漫な財政運営で低下した。◆The U.S. central bank runs the risk of losing its inflation-fighting credibility if it delays fighting growing inflation problems. 増大するインフレ問題の抑制策を遅らせれば, 米連邦準備制度理事会（FRB）はそのインフレ抑制姿勢に対する信認を失うリスクを負うことになる。◆To step toward sound public finance by securing a stable revenue source is the only way to restore the credibility of the

Japanese government bonds. 安定財源を確保して財政健全化に踏み出すことが、日本の国債の信認を回復する唯一の道だ。
credit （動）貸方に記入する，計上する，差し引く，控除する　（⇒failed bank）
　credit A against B　AをBから差し引く，AをBに充当する，AとBを相殺する
　credit to　〜に計上する，〜に貸記する，〜に入金する，〜に充当する
　◆Under the offset provisions, depositors at a failed bank can have their deposits credited against outstanding loans, including mortgages. 相殺規定によると、破たんした銀行の預金者は、預金と住宅ローンなどの借入金残高を相殺してもらえる。
credit （名）信用，与信，債権，貸方，貸金，融資，預金，利益，信用状，支払い猶予期間，税額控除，金融，クレジット（「貸方」は、勘定や勘定式貸借対照表、勘定式損益計算書の右側。⇒asset-backed securities, business soundness, commercial paper, commitment, consumer credit, financial derivatives, lender, loan credits, margin transaction, quality）
　a credit to a current account　当座振込み
　additional credit　新規融資，追加融資
　appetite for credit　資金需要，借入需要
　bank credit　銀行信用
　banker's credit　銀行信用状
　　（=bank credit, banker's letter of credit）
　be denied credit　融資を断られる
　business credit　企業金融
　consumer credit　消費者信用
　credit accident and health insurance　信用傷害健康保険
　credit accommodation　信用供与
　　（=credit extension）
　credit activities　与信業務
　credit administration　与信審査
　credit advice　入金通知，入金通知書
　credit agency　信用格付け機関，信用調査機関，格付け会社，興信所　（=credit rating agency, rating agency;⇒credit rating agency）
　credit agreement　融資契約［契約書］，与信契約書
　credit agreement with limited recourse　責任財産限定特約付き融資契約
　credit appraisal　信用度評価，信用格付け（credit rating）
　credit approval　与信承認，与信の決裁
　credit assessment　信用評価
　credit authority　貸出権限
　credit availability　未使用借入枠
　credit bank　信用金庫，信金，貸付け銀行
　　（=shinkin bank;⇒shift名詞, shinkin bank）
　credit bureau　興信所
　credit business　与信業務，信用事業
　credit ceiling　貸出限度，信用供与限度，貸出限度額
　credit characteristic　信用力の内容
　credit charges　貸付け金利
　credit check［checking］　信用調査，信用情報の確認
　credit concerns　信用リスクに対する懸念，信用リスク懸念
　credit condition　信用状態，信用状況，信用供与状況
　credit cooperative　信用組合
　credit creation　信用創出，信用創造
　credit criteria　与信基準
　credit decision　与信判断，融資判断，信用判断，与信決定
　credit decline［deterioration］　信用の質の低下，信用力の低下
　credit department　審査部，信用調査部，審査部門，信用調査部門，与信部門
　credit derivatives　信用派性商品
　credit-enhanced issue　信用補てん付き銘柄
　credit event　信用事由，債権の信用力を低下させる事由
　credit exchange　交換持ち出し手形，持ち出し手形
　credit exposure　信用リスク，与信リスク
　credit（extending）business　与信業務
　credit extending policy　融資方針
　credit extension　信用供与（extension of credit），信用の拡大
　credit history　信用履歴
　credit hold　入金［信用力］確認のための手続き停止
　credit information　信用情報，信用リスク情報
　credit inquiry　信用照会，信用調査（credit analysis, credit investigation）
　credit institution　銀行
　credit investor　債券投資家
　credit letter　入金依頼状
　credit life　信用生命保険
　credit linked notes　クレジット・リンク債
　credit loan　信用貸付け
　credit management　与信管理，債権管理
　credit management company　債権管理会社
　credit manager　与信審査責任者，与信管理部長，与信部長
　credit market　信用市場，金利市場，債券市場，クレジット市場
　credit maximum　与信限度
　credit memo　入金伝票
　credit money　信用通貨，信用貨幣
　credit note　入金通知　（=advice of credit）
　credit opinion　格付け見解
　credit performance　信用実績，信用動向
　credit policy committee　信用リスク管理委員会
　credit quake　急激かつ深刻な信用収縮
　credit rationing　信用割当て
　credit record　信用履歴，信用情報，与信記録
　credit reference　信用照会先
　credit regulation　信用規制
　credit report　信用調書
　credit reporting agency　興信所
　credit research agency　信用調査機関
　credit score　与信スコア
　credit scoring　信用度採点
　credit standards　与信基準
　credit supply　信用供給
　credit support　信用補完，信用補強，信用補てん
　credit terms　支払い条件，融資条件，信用期間
　deny credit　与信を断る
　documentary（letter of）credit　荷為替信用状
　export credit　輸出信用
　extend credit　信用を供与する，融資する
　extended credit　長期貸付け
　foreign tax credit　税額控除
　grant credit　与信を認める，クレジットの利用を認める
　　（=give credit）
　group credit insurance　団体信用生命保険
　have credit　クレジットの残高がある
　intermediate credit　中期信用
　　（=medium term credit）

intermediated credit　金融仲介機関
irrevocable (letter of) credit　取消し不能信用状
Japan Consumer Credit Association　日本クレジット協会
line of credit　信用供与限度　(⇒credit line)
long-term credit　長期貸付け, 長期信用
making credit　信用供与
mixed credit　混合借款
mortgage credit　不動産金融
name credit　優良貸出先
negotiation (letter of) credit　買取り信用状, 外国為替取組み信用状
offer of credit　与信枠の提供
on credit　掛けで, 付けで
open credit　信用貸し
outstanding credits　融資残高
place a credit hold on an account　ある勘定について信用力確認のための手続き停止を行う
provide credit　信用を供与する, 融資する (=extend credit)
raise credit　資金を調達する
relaxation of credit　金融緩和
reserve for credit losses　貸倒れ引当金
secured credit　有担保貸付け
security credit　証券金融
sell goods on credit　掛売りをする
short-term credit　短期信用
the quantitative relaxation of credit　量的金融緩和, 量的金融緩和策
tightening in the credit policy　金融引締め
trade credit　企業間信用, 企業信用, 輸出・輸入延払い
troubled credits　不良債権
unsecured credit　無担保貸付け, 無担保債権
yen credit　円借款

◆A large amount of credit cannot be removed from the balance sheets of banks even though loan-loss reserves have been set aside. 貸倒れ引当金を積んでも、多くの債権は銀行のバランス・シートから切り離せない状況にある（銀行で最終処理できない債権が多い）。◆Credit represents an addition to a liability, net worth or revenue account, or a deduction from an asset or expense account. 貸方（勘定の右側）は、負債・資本・収益勘定の増加または資産・費用勘定の減少を示す。◆Debates on the pros and cons of a proposal to end the quantitative relaxation of credit by the Bank of Japan are gathering momentum. 日銀による量的金融緩和策を解除する案の賛否をめぐる議論が、活発化している。◆The United States' credit has come into question by the possible downgrade of the U.S. government's credit rating. 米国債の格付けが引き下げられる可能性があることから米国の信用が疑われている。

credit and recovery operations　与信・回収業務
　◆The company has systemized its expertise in credit and recovery operations. 同社は、与信・回収業務のノウハウをシステム化している。

credit approval　信用供与承認, 与信承認
　(⇒delinquent balances)
　◆We control our exposure to credit risk through credit approvals, credit limits and monitoring procedures. 当社は、信用供与承認や信用限度、監視手続きを通じて信用リスクを管理しています。

credit association　信用組合, 信用協同組合
　(=credit union)
　◆The FSA's plan is opposed by shinkin (credit union) banks and credit associations having smaller businesses as main clients. この金融庁の案には、主要顧客として中小企業を抱える信用金庫や信用協同組合が反対している。

credit card　クレジット・カード　(顧客にとって利便性が最も高い決済手段で、B to C (B2C: 企業対消費者) の電子商取引では、代引き、銀行振込み、郵便振替に次いで利用されている。⇒affiliate, due, electronic money, online shopper, personal data)
　credit card business　クレジット・カード事業
　credit card receivables-backed securities　クレジット・カード証券
　◆Electronic money can be bought by inputting the number and expiration date of a credit card on the Internet. 電子マネーは、ネット上でクレジット・カードの番号と有効期限を入力して購入することができる。◆Mizuho Bank offers a service by which ATM cardholders are given mileage points each time they use the new cards as credit cards, purchase financial products at the bank's branches or receive loans from the bank. みずほ銀行が提供しているサービスでは、キャッシュ・カード会員が新型カードをクレジット・カードとして利用したり、みずほ銀で金融商品を購入したり、ローンを利用したりすると、その取引に応じて毎回、マイレージ・ポイントがもらえる。◆The bank began issuing new ATM cards that also function as credit cards and electronic money. 同行は、クレジット・カードと電子マネーの機能を加えた新型キャッシュ・カードの発行を開始した。◆The personal information of customers who used credit cards for premium payments might have been leaked. クレジット・カードを使って保険料を支払った顧客の個人情報が、外部に流出した恐れがある。

credit card company　クレジット・カード会社, 信販
　◆If the merger takes place, it will create a full-scale financial conglomerate with a major bank, a major securities house and credit card company under its umbrella. 統合すれば、傘下に大手銀行と大手証券、クレジット・カード会社などを持つ本格的な金融コングロマリット（金融複合企業体）が誕生する。

credit card data　クレジット・カード情報
　◆Credit card data for Alico Japan's customers are suspected of having been leaked and abused. 外資系生命保険アリコジャパンの顧客のクレジット・カード情報が、外部に流出して不正使用されている疑いがもたれている。

credit card holder　クレジット・カード会員　(=card member, credit cardholder; ⇒personal data)
　◆Four credit card holders received bills for accessing subscription Web sites via cell phones even though they had no recollection of doing so. 利用した覚えがないのに、携帯電話の有料サイトの利用代金請求書が、4人のクレジット・カード会員に届いた。

credit card number　クレジット・カード番号
　(⇒personal data)
　◆The Japan Credit Card Association is studying measures including a ban on printing credit card numbers on customers' bills. 日本クレジットカード協会は現在、顧客の利用明細書にカード番号を印字するのを禁止するなどの対策を検討している。

credit card payment　クレジット・カードの支払い
　◆The percentage of credit card payments that were past due fell in the January-to-March quarter. クレジット・カードの支払い遅延率（期限を過ぎたクレジット・カードの返済遅延率）は、1-3月期に急減した。

credit contraction　信用収縮
　◆Credit contraction may spread at a stroke. 信用収縮が一気に広がる可能性がある。

credit control　与信管理, 信用管理, 信用規制, 信用制限, 信用統制, 金融統制, 債権管理
　(=control of credit, credit management)
　consumer credit control　消費者信用規制, 消費者信用統制
　credit control instrument　信用統制手段, 信用調整手段
　elimination of credit risk　信用規制の撤廃

imposed credit control　信用規制の実施
installment credit control　賦払い信用規制
monetary and credit controls　金融調節, 金融・信用規制, 金融統制
qualitative credit control　質的信用規制, 質的金融統制
quantitative credit control　量的信用規制
rigorous credit control　厳しい与信管理
selective credit control　選択的信用規制
◆We will focus on even more rigorous credit control to avoid risks. 当社は、一段と厳しい与信管理を徹底して、リスク回避を図る方針です。

credit costs　与信費用, 与信コスト, 不良債権処理額 (loan loss charge), 債権処理費用　(⇒accounts)
◆Mizuho's first-half profit fell 17 percent as credit costs increased and on losses related to investments in U.S. home loans to riskier borrowers. みずほの上半期利益は、与信コストの増加とリスクの高い融資先への米国の住宅ローン投資に関連する損失で、17%減少した。◆The bank's credit costs increased as it accelerated disposal of bad loans. 不良債権の処理を加速したため、同行の不良債権処理費用が増加した。

credit crisis　信用危機, 金融危機, 金融ひっ迫, 金融恐慌, 信用恐慌　(=credit crunch, credit squeeze)
◆Banks in the United States and some European countries fell on tough times due to the credit crisis and were bailed out with taxpayers' money. 米国と一部の欧州諸国の銀行が金融危機で経営不安に陥り、公的資金で救済された。◆The rapid spread of Italy's credit crisis is due to intensified fears about the nation's fiscal predicament by Italy's huge fiscal deficits. イタリアの信用不安が急速に広がったのは、イタリアの巨額の赤字で同国の財政ひっ迫への警戒感が高まったからだ。◆The United States and Britain have suffered greatly from the credit crisis. 米国と英国は、金融危機の痛手が大きい。

credit crunch　貸し渋り, 信用危機, 金融ひっ迫, 信用不安, 信用規制, 信用収縮, 金融危機, 金融ひっ迫, 金融ピンチ, クレジット・クランチ　(=credit squeeze, credit crisis)
◆At present, Japan has no credit crunch. 現在のところ、日本に貸し渋りはない。◆The government had funneled public funds twice into banks before-¥1.8 trillion in 1998 and ¥7.5 trillion in 1999—to deal with the widespread credit crunch in Japan. 日本の広範な金融危機への対応策として、政府はこれまでに2回、銀行に公的資金 (1998年の1兆8千億円と1999年の7兆5千億円) をすでに注入している。◆The government's financial revival plan is expected to exacerbate the credit crunch and result in a further sell-off of bank stocks. 政府の金融再生プログラムは、貸し渋りを加速して銀行株の下落に拍車がかかると予想される。◆The sudden credit crunch has dealt a blow to the real economy. 急激な信用収縮は、実体経済に打撃を与えている。◆The U.S. housing industry and the government must respond to a severe credit crunch that began in August 2007. 米国の住宅産業界と政府は、2007年8月に始まった深刻な金融危機への対応を迫られている。

credit default swap　クレジット・デフォルト・スワップ, CDS　(国の財政破たんや企業の破産、債務不履行に伴う損失から投資家を守るため、保証料を払えば債務不履行に陥った債券 (国債や社債) の元利を保証する金融派生商品。⇒CDS)
◆Premiums for credit default swaps (CDS) for Japanese government bonds have been gradually rising of late. 日本国債の信用リスクを保証するCDSのプレミアム (保証料) は最近、上昇している。

credit demand　信用需要, 資金需要, 借入需要
credit demand curve　信用需要曲線
credit demand growth　信用需要の伸び
slowdown in credit demand　信用需要の減速, 信用需要の伸び率減速

credit easing measures　金融緩和政策, 金融緩和措置　(=credit easing steps)
◆The Bank of Japan's Policy Board agreed to a set of credit-easing measures, including interest payments on commercial banks' reserves deposited at the central bank. 日銀の政策委員会は、金融機関が日銀に預ける当座預金 (無利子) に金利を付けることを含めて、一連の金融緩和政策を決めた。

credit easing steps　金融緩和措置, 金融緩和策　(=credit easing measures; ⇒undertake)
◆Behind the improvement in economic sentiment is a series of measures taken to date, including the government's antideflation package and the Bank of Japan's additional credit easing steps. 景況感好転の理由として、政府のデフレ対策や日銀の追加の金融緩和策など、これまでにとられた一連の措置が挙げられる。

credit enhancement　信用補強, 信用補てん, 信用補完, 信用増強, 信用補完措置
be supported by credit enhancements　信用補強を裏付けとする
credit enhancement agreement　信用補完契約
(credit) enhancement business　信用補強業務
credit enhancement facility　信用補強ファシリティ
credit enhancement measure　信用補強手段
credit enhancement provider　信用補強提供者
provide credit enhancement　信用補強 [信用補完] を提供する, 信用補強を供与する, 信用リスクをカバーする
seller-level credit enhancement　売り手レベルでの信用補完

credit expansion　信用拡大, 信用の拡張, 貸出の伸び, 金融緩和
brisk domestic credit expansion　活発な国内信用の拡大, 国内の活発な信用拡大
coefficient of credit expansion　信用拡張係数, 信用膨張係数
the present credit expansion　当面の信用拡大

credit facility　信用供与, 信用供与枠, 信用枠, 与信枠, 与信限度枠, 融資枠, 貸付け枠, 融資契約, 信用の便宜供与, 信用供与制度, 金融制度, クレジット・ファシリティ
credit enhancement facility　信用補強ファシリティ
credit facility agreement　融資枠契約
draw from a credit facility　融資枠から資金を引き出す, 融資枠を利用する
provide a credit facility of $10 billion to　～に対して100億ドルの融資枠を設定する
revolving credit facility　回転融資枠, 回転信用ファシリティ
standby letter of credit facility　スタンドバイL/Cファシリティ

credit fears　信用不安　(=credit crisis, credit crunch)
◆The U.S. dollar temporarily dropped to the upper ¥95 level over credit fears. 米ドルは、信用不安で一時、1ドル=95円後半台まで [後半の水準まで] 下落した。

credit freeze　信用凍結, 信用釘付け, 信用規制
◆A credit freeze hits the economy hard because it forces companies to lay off workers as they cannot make payrolls and to cut planned expansions. 信用凍結によって企業は給与支払いができなくなってレイオフを迫られたり、拡張計画の中止を迫られたりするため、信用凍結は経済に大きな影響を及ぼしている。

credit grade　信用格付け, 信用度, 信用評価
◆Even after Greece's debt load is cut, Greece's credit grade is likely to remain low. ギリシャの債務負担を削減しても、ギリシャの信用格付けは、低水準にとどまる見込みだ。

credit guarantee　信用保証, 信用保証制度

a special credit guarantee　特別信用制度
credit guarantee system　信用保証制度
public credit guarantee　公的信用保証
◆A real estate broker created a dummy company to illegally receive a public credit guarantee. 不動産業者が、架空の会社を作って不正に公的信用保証を受けていた。◆The loss rapidly ballooned since the government implemented a special credit guarantee from October 1988 to March 2001 with relaxed screening criteria. 政府が1998年10月から2001年3月まで審査基準を緩和して「特別信用制度」を実施してから、損失（赤字幅）が急速に拡大した。

credit guarantee association　信用保証協会
　（=credit guarantee corporation）
◆Credit guarantee associations guaranteed ¥15 trillion in loans to 1.38 million companies last year. 信用保証協会の昨年の企業への融資保証額は15兆円で、融資件数は138万件に達した。◆Credit guarantee associations were established to make it easier for small and mid-sized companies to receive loans from financial institutions. 信用保証協会は、中小企業が金融機関から容易に融資を受けられるようにするために設置された。

credit guarantee corporation　信用保証協会
　（=credit guarantee association）
◆In most cases in which the credit guarantee system is used, financial institutions introduce borrowers to credit guarantee corporations. 信用保証制度を利用する場合の多くは、金融機関が借り手を信用保証協会に紹介する。◆Some borrowers have taken advantage of lax screening of credit guarantee corporations. 信用保証協会の手薄な審査に便乗している借り手もいる。

credit guarantor company　信用保証会社
◆A major credit guarantor company has been accused of concealing taxable income by the Tokyo Regional Taxation Bureau. 大手の信用保証会社が、東京国税局から課税所得隠しを指摘された。

credit insecurity　信用不安, 金融不安
　（=credit instability, credit uneasiness）
◆The full introduction of the payoff system may worsen the credit insecurity at banks. ペイオフ制度の全面導入［全面解禁］は、銀行の信用不安を助長しかねない。

credit instability　信用不安
　（=credit insecurity, credit uneasiness）
◆If the decision on the framework of TEPCO's compensation payments for damage by the crisis of its nuclear power plant should be put off further, it could trigger credit instability in the firm. 東電の原子力発電所事故による損害の賠償金支払いの枠組み決定をさらに先送りすれば、東電の信用不安を招く可能性がある。

credit insurance　信用保険
consumer credit life insurance　消費者信用生命保険
credit insurance for lease　リース信用保険
credit life insurance　消費者信用生命保険
employees' general loan credit insurance　一般資金貸付け保険
employees' housing loan credit insurance　住宅資金貸付け保険
Foreign Credit Insurance Association　外国信用保険協会
group credit insurance　団体信用生命保険
group credit life insurance　団体信用生命保険
　（=group life insurance for credit）
installment credit insurance　賦払い信用保険
installment sales credit insurance　割賦販売代金保険
machinery credit insurance　機械類信用保険
◆Products permitted for banks' over-the-counter sales have been expanded from credit life insurance for housing loans and long-term fire insurance to individual annuity insurance and others. 銀行の窓口販売が認められる商品は、住宅ローンの消費者信用生命保険や長期火災保険から個人年金保険などに拡大している。

credit limit　信用限度, 与信限度, 信用貸出限度, 貸出限度額（credit limits）, 信用供与限度額, 信用規制
　（⇒credit approval）
a credit limit on one's credit card　クレジット・カードの利用限度額
banks' credit limits　銀行の信用枠
credit limit overruns　与信枠超過
establish credit limits on　～に与信限度額を設ける
have credit limits　信用枠を設定する
qualitative credit limit　金融［信用］の質的規制, 質的信用規制　（=qualitative credit control）
quantitative credit limit　金融［信用］の量的規制, 量的信用規制　（=quantitative credit control）
◆The firm controls its exposure to credit risk through credit approvals, credit limits and monitoring procedures. 同社は、信用供与承認や信用限度、監視手続きを通じて信用リスクを管理している。

credit line　貸出限度（額）, 貸付け限度（額）, 与信限度（額）, 信用限度, 信用保証枠, 信用供与限度, 信用供与枠, 融資枠, 融資限度額, 利用限度額, クレジット・ライン
　（=credit ceiling, credit limit, line of credit; ⇒bank lines of credit, prime bank rate of interest）
check credit lines　与信枠をチェックする
credit line increase　与信限度額の引上げ
cut back on credit lines　信用枠を縮小する
establish revolving credit lines　融資枠を設定する
　（=extend credit lines）
reduce credit lines　貸出限度を引き下げる
swap credit line　スワップ信用枠
unused credit lines　未使用信用供与枠, 未使用与信枠, 未実行貸出残高
unused retail credit lines　リテール向け未実行貸出残高
unused short-term credit lines　短期借入金借入枠中未借入額
◆In the conventional IMF's scheme, countries were only given a credit line even after the IMF approved loans and they could not withdraw funds unless the fiscal crisis facing them worsened. 従来のIMF（国際通貨基金）の仕組みだと、各国は融資の承認を得ても融資枠を与えられるだけで、財政危機が深刻化しないと資金を引き出すことができなかった。◆U.S. and European banks gradually reduced their credit lines to Japanese banks. 欧米の銀行は、邦銀に対するクレジット・ライン（貸出限度）を次第に引き下げた。

credit loss　信用損失, 貸倒れ, 貸倒れ損失
absorb credit losses on the assets　資産の信用損失を吸収する
allowance for credit losses of banks　銀行の貸倒れ引当金, 銀行の貸倒れ損失引当金
consumer credit losses　消費者貸出貸倒れ損失
control credit losses　貸倒れ損失を管理する
cover credit losses on the receivables　受取債権の信用損失をカバーする
credit loss rate　貸倒れ損失率
expected credit loss　信用損失の期待値
net credit losses　正味貸倒れ損失
offset credit losses　信用損失を補う
percentage of credit losses　貸倒れ率
protection against credit loss　信用損失に対する（投資家）保護
provision for (probable) credit losses　貸倒れ引当金［準

備金], 貸倒れ引当金[準備金]繰入れ額
reduce the risk of credit loss　信用損失のリスクを軽減する
reserve for credit losses　貸倒れ引当金
the risk of future credit loss　将来の信用損失のリスク
◆We compute present values for impaired loans when we determine our allowances for credit losses. 当社の貸倒れ引当金を決定するにあたって、当社は不良債権の現在価値を計算します。

credit market　信用市場, 金融市場, 発行市場
◆Credit markets are beginning to thaw after months of a deep freeze. 債券発行市場は、凍結状態がここ数か月続いた後、雪解けが始まっている。◆Credit markets are beginning to thaw as bond sales by firms are on the increase. 企業の債券発行が増えているため、発行市場は雪解けムードが見られる。◆The collapse of the subprime mortgage market and related credit market turmoil have resulted in $45 billion of write-downs at the world's biggest banks and securities firms. サブプライム・ローン市場の悪化や関連金融市場の混乱で、世界の大手銀行と証券会社の評価損計上額は、これまでのところ450億ドルに達している。

credit market turmoil　金融市場の混乱　(=financial turmoil, turmoil in the financial markets)
◆The collapse of the subprime mortgage market and related credit market turmoil have resulted in $45 billion of write-downs at the world's biggest banks and securities firms. サブプライム・ローン市場の悪化や関連金融市場の混乱で、世界の大手銀行と証券会社の評価損計上額は、これまでのところ450億ドルに達している。

credit policy　金融政策, 信用方針
◆The FRB's new easy credit policy is not without concerns. 米連邦準備制度理事会(FRB)の追加金融緩和策には、気がかりな点もある。

credit problem　信用力の低下, 資金繰りの悪化, 信用リスク要因
◆The firm has faced credit and cash flow problems. 同社は、信用力の低下と資金繰りに窮している。

credit quality　信用の質, 信用度, 信用力
a company's credit quality　企業の信用の質
asset credit quality　資産の信用度
average credit quality of portfolio　ポートフォリオの平均格付け
corporate [company] credit quality　企業の信用の質
credit quality concerns　信用懸念
credit quality of corporate debt issuers　社債発行体の信用の質
credit quality of customers　顧客[取引先]の信用力
credit quality of one's assets　資産の信用力
deteriorated [deterioration in] credit quality　信用の質[信用力, 信用度]の低下, 信用度悪化力 (=declining [decline in] credit quality)
loss of credit quality　信用の質の低下
obligor credit quality　債務者の信用度
superior credit quality　高い信用力
the credit quality of market participants　市場参加者の信用の質
◆The AA minus rating by S&P is the fourth highest in terms of credit quality on a scale of 22. 米格付け会社のスタンダード・アンド・プアーズ(S&P)による「ダブルAマイナス」の格付けは、22段階ある信用度中、上から4番目に当たる。◆The proposed bid price does not reflect the bank's strong capital position and the superior credit quality of its assets. 株式公開買付け(TOB)の予定価格は、同行の自己資本比率の大きさや同行の資産の高い信用力を反映していない。

credit rater　格付け機関　(=credit rating agency)
◆President Barack Obama administration sought tighter rules for credit raters. オバマ政権は、格付け機関に対する規制強化を求めた。◆The Obama administration sent the U.S. Congress legislation seeking to tighten government oversight of credit raters. オバマ政権は、格付け機関に対する政府監督の強化を求める法案を議会に提出した。

credit rating　信用格付け, 企業の信用等級[借金返済能力評価], 格付け評価, 格付け, 借入限度額　(=rating; ⇒acquire capital from the market, analysis, debt moratorium, downgrade, falling company, World Bank)
bank letter-of-credit ratings　銀行信用状の格付け
carry a credit rating　格付けを得ている
corporate credit rating　企業の信用格付け, 企業の信用等級
counterparty credit rating　カウンターパーティー格付け（企業の総合的な信用力を評価してランク付けしたもの）
credit rating system　格付け制度, 格付けシステム
cut one's corporate credit rating on the firm　同社の企業信用格付けを
cut the U.S. credit rating　米国債の格付けを引き下げる
downgrade the firm's credit rating　同社の格付けを引き下げる
foreign government bonds with low credit ratings　格付けの低い外国債
have a good credit rating　よい格付けを得ている
independent credit rating system　独立した格付けシステム
Japan's long-term sovereign credit rating　日本の長期国債格付け　(⇒sovereign credit rating)
long-term credit ratings　長期格付け
lower one's credit rating below investment grade　～の格付けを投資不適格[投資適格未満]に引き下げる
obtain a credit rating　格付けを取得する
the downgrading of the U.S. credit rating　米国債の格下げ
the U.S. long-term credit rating　米国の長期国債格付け
top-notch credit rating　最上位の信用格付け, 最上位の格付け
upgrade the firm's credit rating　同社の格付けを引き上げる
◆Companies with good credit ratings and those that had not issued bonds began to issue bonds. 優良格付けの企業やこれまで債券を発行していなかった企業が、債券を発行するようになった。◆Global turmoil in the financial markets results from the downgrading of the U.S. credit rating. 金融市場の世界的な混乱は、米国債の格下げによるものだ。◆Moody's may downgrade the U.S. government's credit rating if it does not get its colossal deficits in better order. 米政府が膨大な財政赤字問題に目途をつけないと、ムーディーズは米国債の格付けを引き下げる可能性がある。◆Moody's will consider cutting the United States' top-notch credit rating if any progress isn't made in talks to raise the U.S. debt limit. 米政府の債務の法定上限引上げについての（米議会との）交渉で進展がなければ、ムーディーズは、米国債の最上位の格付けを引下げる方向で検討する方針だ。◆Of the amount of investment, about a half was invested in foreign government bonds with low credit ratings. この投資額のうち約半分は、格付けの低い外国債に充てていた。◆S&P lowered Belgium's credit rating from AA+ to AA. スタンダード・アンド・プアーズ(S&P)は、ベルギー国債の信用格付け[格付け]を、ダブルA(AA)プラスからダブルA(AA)に1段階引き下げた。◆Standard & Poor's cut its corporate credit rating on Ford to "CC" from "CCC+." スタンダード&プアーズは、フォードの企業信用格付けを「CCCプラス」から「CC」に引き下げた。◆Standard & Poor's cut

the U.S. credit rating for the first time. スタンダード・アンド・プアーズ(S&P)が、米国債の格付けを史上初めて引き下げた。◆Standard & Poor's is considering a possible downgrade on the credit ratings of long-term sovereign bonds issued by 15 eurozone states. 米格付け会社のスタンダード・アンド・プアーズ(S&P)は、ユーロ圏15か国発行の長期国債格付け[信用格付け]を、引下げ方向で検討している。◆The bonds of six eurozone countries such as Germany and France are rated AAA by S&P's credit ratings on them. 独仏などユーロ圏6か国の国債は、スタンダード・アンド・プアーズ(S&P)の格付け[信用格付け]でトリプルAに格付けされている。◆The FSA's special inspection will check the major banks' large-lot corporate borrowers whose stock prices or credit ratings have sharply declined. 金融庁の特別検査は、大手銀行の株価や格付けなどが急落した大口融資先を査定の対象としている。◆The S&P cut in the U.S. long-term credit rating by one notch to AA-plus from AAA resulted from concerns about the nation's budget deficits and climbing debt burden. スタンダード・アンド・プアーズ(S&P)が米国の長期国債格付けを最上級のAAA(トリプルA)からAA(ダブルA)に1段階引き下げた理由は、米国の財政赤字と債務負担の増大に対する懸念だ。◆The United States' credit has come into question by the possible downgrade of the U.S. government's credit rating. 米国債の格付けが引き下げられる可能性があることから、米国の信用が疑われている。◆The United States lost its top-tier AAA credit rating from S&P for the first time. 米国債の格付け[米国の長期国債格付け]が、スタンダード・アンド・プアーズ(S&P)による最上級のAAA(トリプルA)の格付けから史上初めて転落した。◆Two influential rating firms lowered Ford Motor Co.'s credit ratings a notch deeper into junk territory. 大手[有力]格付け機関2社が、米フォードの信用格付けを「投資不適格レベル」にさらに1段階引き下げた。

[解説]格付けとは：民間の格付け会社が、債券を発行する企業や国、公社などの財務を分析して債務返済能力を判定し、A, B, Cなどとランク付けすること。投資家にとっては信用力の目安となる一方、企業にとっては高い格付けを得るほど低利で債券を発行できるといった利点がある。一般的に、格付けが高いほど安全な投資対象と見なされる。

credit rating agency　格付け機関, 信用格付け機関, 格付け会社, 信用調査機関
　(=credit agency, credit rater, rating agency)
　downgrades by credit rating agencies　格付け機関による評価引下げ
　recognized credit rating agency　一般に認められている信用格付け機関
◆If the negotiations between Republicans and Democrats face rough going and the deficit-cutting plan ends up being insufficient, credit rating agencies may downgrade Treasury bonds. 共和党と民主党の協議が難航して赤字削減策が不十分に終わると、(信用)格付け会社が米国債の格下げに踏み切る可能性がある。◆The rating outlook of "negative" by a credit rating agency means that another downgrade is possible in the next 12 to 18 months. 信用格付け機関による「ネガティブ(弱含み)」の格付け見通しは、今後1年～1年半にふたたび格下げされる可能性があることを意味している。◆The stock market decline can trigger downgrades by credit rating agencies. 株安をきっかけとして、格付け機関による評価が引き下げられる可能性がある。◆The U.S. credit rating agency revised upward the outlook to positive from negative on its rating on Sumitomo Life Insurance Co. この米国の信用格付け機関は、住友生命保険の格付け見通しを「ネガティブ」から「ポジティブ」に上方修正した。◆The U.S. credit rating agency Standard & Poor's made a grim assessment of the outlook of U.S. fiscal reconstruction. 米国の信用格付け機関のスタンダード・アンド・プアーズ(S&P)は、米国の財政再建の見通しを厳しく評価した。

代表的格付け機関：
A.M. Best Company　AMベスト社
Duff & Phelps Inc.　ダフ・アンド・フェルプス
Fitch Investors Service, Inc.　フィッチ・インベスターズ・サービス フィッチ
Fitch Ratings Ltd.　フィッチ・レーティングス(英米系)
Moody's Investors Service Inc.　ムーディーズ・インベスターズ・サービス ムーディーズ
Standard & Poor's Corporation　スタンダード＆プアーズ S&P
Weiss Ratings, Inc.　ワイス・レーティングス

credit rating service　信用格付けサービス
◆Xinhua Finance provides financial news and credit rating services to Chinese and other companies. 新華ファイナンスは、中国などの企業に金融関連ニュースと信用格付けサービスを提供している。

credit research agency　信用調査機関, 信用調査会社
◆The number of domestic companies that went under in October 2008 was the highest figure so far this year, a private credit research agency said. 民間信用調査会社の発表によると、国内企業の2008年10月の倒産件数は、1月からの累計で最多[過去最高]となった。

credit risk　信用危険, 信用リスク, 貸倒れリスク
　(⇒credit approval)
　accept credit risk　信用リスクをとる
　address credit risk　信用リスクに対応する, 信用リスクを対象とする
　analyze credit risk　信用リスクを分析する, 信用リスクを審査する
　assess credit risk　信用リスクを評価する, 信用リスクを算定する　(=calculate credit risk)
　be correlated with credit risk　信用リスクと相関する
　be exposed to credit risk　信用リスクを負う
　bear the credit risk　信用リスクを負う
　control one's credit risk　信用リスクを管理する
　credit risk adjusted yield　信用リスク調整後利回り
　credit risk arbitrage　信用リスク裁定
　credit risk considerations　信用リスク分析
　credit risk evaluation　信用リスク評価
　credit risk guidelines　信用リスク基準
　credit risk insurance　信用リスク保険
　credit risk measurement　信用リスクの算定, 信用リスクの評価　(=measurement of credit risk)
　credit risk rating system　信用リスク格付けシステム
　credit risk trading　信用リスクの売買
　credit risk transfer　信用リスク移転, CRT
　credit risk transfer product [instrument]　信用リスク移転商品　(=CRT product)
　evaluate credit risks　信用リスクを審査する
　financial instruments with concentrations of credit risk　信用リスクの集中した金融手段
　off-balance sheet credit risk　オフ・バランスシートの信用リスク
　rating criteria to one's credit risk　与信基準
　relative credit risk　相対的信用リスク
　take on credit risk　信用リスクをとる
◆If government-guaranteed trade insurance is available, it will increase the acceptable scope, in terms of both country and credit risk, for selecting trading partners. 政府保証付き貿易保険を利用できれば、輸出先のカントリー・リスクや信用リスクの面で、取引先選定の許容度が高まる。◆The firm controls its exposure to credit risk through credit approvals, credit limits and monitoring procedures. 同社は、信用供与承認や信用限度、監視手続きを通じて信用リスクを管理して

いる。

credit spread 利回り格差, 信用力格差, 信用スプレッド
（証券発行体の信用力に応じて付加される超過金利部分を意味する場合と、オプションの売却価格と別のオプションの購入価格とのオプション価格差を意味する場合がある）

credit squeeze 信用規制, 金融引締め
（=credit crisis, credit crunch）
◆Tightening regulations on core capital ratios too quickly would cause a credit squeeze and negatively affect the real economy. 急激な自己資本比率規制の強化は、金融収縮を招いて、実体経済に悪影響を与える。

credit standing 信用状態, 信用度, 信用力
（=credit strength, credit worthiness）
a customer of good credit standing 信用度の高い得意先, 信用力のある得意先
deteriorated［deterioration in］credit standing 信用の質の悪化
investigation on one's credit standing ～の信用調査
◆The company is a customer of good credit standing. 同社は、信用度の高い得意先です。

credit strength 信用度, 信用力, 信用の質
analysis of the credit strength 信用力分析
credit strength of borrowers 借り手の信用の質, 借り手の信用力
fundamental credit strength 信用の質［信用力］のファンダメンタルズ
long-term credit strength 長期的信用力
maintain one's credit strength 信用度を維持する, 信用の質を維持する

credit supply 信用供給
control the credit supply 信用供給量を抑える［コントロール］する
credit supply crunch 信用供給の収縮
marginal credit supply 限界信用供給

credit system 信用制度, 信用システム, クレジット・システム
consumer credit system 消費者信用システム
credit ceiling application system 貸出限度額適用制度
credit-risk rating system 信用リスク格付けシステム
credit scoring system 信用評価システム
credit system of third party transaction 専門機関媒介方式
Federal Farm Credit System 米連邦農業信用制度
revolving credit system リボルビング・システム

credit tightening 金融引締め, 貸出の抑制
◆The Fed will end the credit-tightening move. 米連邦準備制度理事会（FRB）は、金融引締め策を終える方針だ。

credit-tightening stance 金融引締めのスタンス
◆The European Central Bank shifted to a credit-tightening stance late last year. 欧州中央銀行は、昨年末から金融引締めのスタンスに転じた。

credit uncertainty 信用不安, 金融不安
（=credit uneasiness）
◆Credit uncertainty in Europe has spilled over to France which is helping Greece, Italy and Spain facing fiscal crises. 欧州の信用不安は、財政危機に直面しているギリシャやイタリア、スペインを支援しているフランスにも拡大している。◆Credit uncertainty is spreading as there is no end in sight to fiscal crises in the United States and some European countries. 米国と一部の欧州の財政危機の収束が見通せないため、信用不安が拡大している。◆In Europe, credit uncertainty has spread from Greece to Italy, Spain and elsewhere due to the excessively tardy response by Europe. 欧州では、欧州の対応が遅すぎるため、信用不安がギリシャからイタリアやスペインなどに拡大している。◆The yields on Greek government bonds have been rising sharply due to the credit uncertainty. ギリシャ国債の利回りは、信用不安で急上昇している。◆There is no end in sight to fiscal crises in the United States and some European countries as credit uncertainty is spreading. 信用不安が拡大しているため、米国と欧州の一部の財政危機の収束が見通せない。

credit uneasiness 信用不安, 金融不安
（=credit instability, credit insecurity）
◆By increasing its involvement in TEPCO's management, the government aims to fend off credit uneasiness in the utility. 東電への経営関与を強めることにより、国は東電の信用不安を防止しようとしている。

credit uneasiness in the market 市場の信用不安
◆As an effective measure to prevent the yields of government bonds from soaring and to soothe credit uneasiness in the market, the ECB may buy up a large number of bonds from Italy and other countries. 国債利回りの急騰を抑え、市場の信用不安を鎮静化するための有効な措置として、欧州中央銀行（ECB）は、イタリアなどの国債を大量に買い支える可能性がある。

credit union 信用組合, 信用金庫
（=credit association）
◆The credit union suffered a loss of about ¥4.2 billion. 同信用組合は、約42億円の損失を被った。◆The credit union was forced to apply to the Financial Services Agency for protection from creditors. 同信組は、金融庁への破綻申請を迫られた。

credited loans 貸出債権 （⇒lending institution）
◆In the case of JAL, it is crucial to win the approval of the more than 20 financial institutions with credited loans to JAL as soon as possible. 日本航空の場合、同社向け貸出債権を保有する20以上の金融機関の承認をできるだけ迅速に得る必要がある。

crediting rates 保証利率

creditor （名）債権者, 債権国, 債権保有者, 資金供与者, 取引銀行, 取引金融機関, 貸主, 貸方, 仕入先, クレジター （⇒bankruptcy procedures, loan forgiveness）
a committee of creditors 債権者委員会
（=creditors' committee）
a main creditor bank 主力取引銀行
ask a creditor to forgive debt 債権者に債務免除を求める
bail out the creditors 債権者を救済する
bank creditors 債権銀行, 銀行債権者
bankruptcy creditor 破産債権者
be pestered by creditors 債権者から矢の催促を受ける［執拗（しつよう）に催促される］
bond creditor 債券金融業者
creditor balance 貸方残高
creditor business 取引信用保険業務, 債権者企業
creditor control 債権者支配
creditor country 債権国, 黒字国
（=creditor nation）
creditor policy 債権者確保契約
creditor position 債権ポジション
creditors 買掛金, 債権者
creditor's bill 債権者証
creditor's capital gain 債権者の資本利得
creditor's capital loss 債権者の資本損失
creditors' claims 債権者の請求権
creditors' committee 債権者委員会
creditors days ratio 買掛債務滞留日数
creditors' equity 債権者持ち分, 負債, 他人資本
creditors' equity to total assets 負債比率

creditors' group insurance 債権者団体保険
creditors'[creditor's] meeting 債権者会議, 債権者集会
creditor's rating of one's credit risk （取引銀行の）与信判断
creditors' voluntary liquidation 和議
debtor and creditor 借方と貸方
debtor-creditor agreement 債務者・債権者間の使途制限信用供約定
execution creditor 執行債権者
first priority creditor 第一順位債権者
general creditor 一般債権者
hide from a creditor 債権者から逃げる
intra-company creditor 企業内債権者
judgment creditor 判決債権者
junior creditor 劣後債権者, 下位債権者, 後順位債権者
large creditor 大口債権者
major creditor 大口債権者
mortgage creditor 抵当権者
multilateral creditors 国際金融機関
negotiate with a creditor 債権者と交渉する
net creditor 純債権者
net creditor position 純債権国
ordinary creditor 普通債権者
pay a creditor 債権者に弁済する
preferential creditor 優先債権者
preferred creditors' right 先取特権
priority [preferred] creditor 優先債権者（=creditor by priority）
priority of creditors 債権者の優先順位
private creditors 民間相債者
receive forgiveness from a creditor 債権者に債権を放棄してもらう
repay one's creditors 債権者に債務を返済する
secured creditor 有担保債権者
senior creditor 上位債権者, 先順位債権者, 優先順位の高い債権者
senior debt creditor 上位債保有者
short-term creditor 短期債権者
subordinated creditor 劣後債権者, 劣後債の投資家
trade creditor 営業債権者, 仕入先, 買掛金
unforeseen creditor 不測の債権者
unsecured creditor 無担保債権者

◆According to JAL's draft rehabilitation plan, 87.5 percent of the airline's loan will be waived by its banks and other creditors. 日航の更生計画案では、同社借金[借入金]の87.5%は、銀行その他の債権者が免除することになる。◆Banks could forcibly sell insurance policies to clients by utilizing their strong position as creditors. 銀行は、債権者としての強い立場を利用して、顧客に保険を強制的に販売する可能性もある。◆Chapter 11 bankruptcy provides for a business to continue operations while formulating a plan to repay its creditors. 米連邦更正破産法11章の破産の規定では、企業は事業を継続する一方、債権者への債務返済計画を策定することができる。◆Even if it is a sovereign state or a bank, heavily indebted borrowers may face a crisis for insolvency or a lack of liquidity. 国家でも銀行でも、巨額の債務を抱えた発行体は、返済不能か流動性不足で危機に陥る可能性がある。◆Ford announced a plan to cut its $25.8 billion in automotive debt by about 40 percent by offering creditors cash and new shares. 米フォードは、債権者（社債の保有者）に現金と新株を提供し、258億ドルの自動車関連債務を約40%削減する計画を発表した。◆GM obtained agreements from a majority of creditors in negotiations to reduce its debts significantly. 米ゼネラル・モーターズ（GM）は、巨額の債務削減交渉で、大半の債権者から合意を取り付けた。◆If the government financial support is not offered to TEPCO, the utility's creditors and shareholders will have to share the burden. 東電に政府の金融支援がない場合は、同社の債権者と株主が共同負担せざるを得ないだろう。◆In resolving Greece's debt woes, German Chancellor Angera Merkel urged substantial aid from private creditors. ギリシャの債務問題を解決するにあたって、アンゲラ・メルケル独首相は、民間債権者に大幅支援を求めた。◆In the event of hefty appraisal losses, banks must avoid a situation in which their creditors, including depositors, will be affected by the impairment of bank-owned assets. 巨額の含み損が出た場合、銀行は、預金者などの債権者が銀行保有資産の評価減の影響を受けるような状況がないようにしなければならない。◆The company increased the amount of debt forgiveness by its creditors to ¥98.9 billion from ¥90.9 billion. 同社は、取引金融機関による債務免除額を909億円から989億円に引き上げた。◆The eurozone's critical mistake is the eurozone's belittling of the risk of the sovereign debt crisis aggravating the banking crisis and vice versa. ユーロ圏の重大な誤りは、国家の財政危機と銀行の危機が相互に増幅し合う危険性を、ユーロ圏が軽視したことにある。◆Tobishima Corp.'s main creditor was Mizuho Corporate Bank, Ltd. 飛島建設の主力取引銀行は、みずほコーポレート銀行だった。

creditor bank 債権保有銀行, 債権者銀行, 融資銀行, 取引銀行, 信用供与銀行, クレディター・バンク（=creditor）

a group of main creditor banks 主な債権者の銀行団, 主力取引銀行団
main creditor banks 主力行, 主力取引銀行
minor creditor banks 非主力行, 非主力取引銀行

◆A group of JAJ's main creditor banks is expected to approve the draft final plan for JAL's rehabilitation. 日航の主要な債権保有銀行団[主力取引銀行団]は、同社の最終更生計画案を承認する見通しだ。◆Companies must be generating operating profits from their main businesses to seek debt waivers from the creditor banks. 取引銀行に債権放棄を求めるには、企業はその主要な事業部門で営業利益を上げていなければならない。◆If TEPCO's creditor banks forgive the debts when the utility is not carrying excessive liabilities, lenders will not be able to recover either the principal or interest owed. 東電が債務超過でない時点で東電の債権保有銀行が債権を放棄すると、金融機関は元本を回収できず、金利収入も得られなくなる。◆If the group's cash-flow situation deteriorates further, it may see its creditor banks declining to extend loans. 同グループの資金繰りがさらに悪化すれば、取引銀行が融資を拒否する可能性もある。◆JAJ has fallen short of creditor banks' expectations. 日航は、取引銀行団の期待を裏切ってきた。◆JAL's creditor banks are dubious about JAL's chances of getting back on its feet. 日航の取引銀行団は、日航再建の可能性については懐疑的だ。◆JAL's efforts to turn around its failed business will depend on the flagship carrier's ability to secure new loans from its creditor banks. 日航の破たん事業再生への取組みは、この日本を代表する航空会社が取引銀行から新規融資を受けることができるかどうかにかかっている。◆Japan Airlines requested that a large sum of its debt be waived by creditor banks. 日本航空は、債権保有銀行に巨額の債務免除を求めた。◆Making the creditor banks waive loans to TEPCO will cause the utility to fall into capital deficiency, with liabilities exceeding assets. 取引銀行に東電への債権を放棄させると、東電は資本不足に陥り、債務超過になってしまう。◆The creditor banks are considering having the company reduce its capital by canceling a portion of its preferred shares held by them. 同社の取引銀行は現在、各行が保有する同社の優先株（議決権がない代わりに配当が高い株式）の償却による同社の資本金引下げ[減資]を検討している。◆The revitalization plan will be carried out chiefly using ¥400 billion in financial assistance to be extended by the firm's creditor banks. 再生計画は、主に同社の取引銀行が行う金融支援総額4,000億円を使って実施される。

creditor financial institution　債権保有の金融機関, 融資している金融機関, 取引金融機関
◆Creditor financial institutions and shareholders will suffer huge losses if TEPCO falls into debt without the government financial aid. 東電が政府の金融支援を受けられずに債務超過に陥れば、融資している金融機関や株主は、巨額の損失を被ることになる。◆Regarding TEPCO's damage compensation, creditor financial institutions have already offered cooperation by refinancing existing loans. 東電の損害賠償に関して、取引金融機関は、既存の融資の借換えなどですでに協力している。

creditorship　（名）債権者の地位

creditwatch [credit watch]　信用格付け見直し中, クレジットウオッチ［クレジット・ウオッチ］（格付け会社が、企業などの信用格付けを、変更する可能性があるとして見直している状態のこと）
◆Deutsche Bank AG and BNP Paribas SA are among European lenders placed on creditwatch negative by S&P. ドイツ銀行や仏MNPパリバなども、スタンダード・アンド・プアーズ（S&P）が引下げの方向で信用格付けの見直しをしている欧州の金融機関の対象となっている。◆S&P has put the EU's AAA long-term rating on creditwatch negative. 米格付け会社のスタンダード・アンド・プアーズ（S&P）は、欧州連合（EU）の最上級「トリプルA」の長期信用格付けを、引き下げる方向で見直している。

creditworthiness [credit worthiness]　（名）信用力, 信用度, 信用の質, 弁済能力
（=credibility, credit standing）
a loan-seeker's creditworthiness　ローン申込み者の信用力
an indicator of creditworthiness　信用力の目安
（⇒indicator）
creditor's judg(e)ment [tests] of creditworthiness　与信判断
determine one's creditworthiness　～の信用力を判定する
evaluate one's creditworthiness　～の信用力を審査する
overall creditworthiness　総合的な信用力
rate one's creditworthiness　～の信用力の格付けをする
the creditworthiness of lenders　金融機関の信用の質
the creditworthiness of the obligator　借り手の信用力［信用度］（=the borrower's creditworthiness）
the creditworthiness of the subject　本人の信用度
◆Asset-backed commercial paper refers to commercial paper whose creditworthiness is guaranteed by sales credit that the corporate issuer has with its debtors. 資産担保CPとは、企業発行体がその債務者に対して保有する売掛金によって信用度が保証されるコマーシャル・ペーパーを指す。◆FSA audits of the banks' accounts urged them to reclassify 149 of their major corporate borrowers more strictly in terms of their creditworthiness in a bid to accelerate the disposal of bad loans. 金融庁による銀行の財務書類監査で、不良債権処理を加速するため、銀行は大口融資先149社の信用力による債務者区分の見直しを強化するよう強く求められた。◆In Europe, the creditworthiness of Italian and Spanish government bonds is a source of uncertainty. 欧州では、イタリアとスペインの国債の信用力が、金融不安の発生源だ。◆The bonds issued by the EFSF are guaranteed with the creditworthiness of the six eurozone states' bonds. 欧州金融安定基金（EFSF）が発行する債券は、（独仏など）ユーロ圏6か国の国債の信用力で保証されている。

creditworthiness screening standard　与信審査基準
◆The creditworthiness screening standard of U.S. subprime loans was dubious. 米国の低所得者向け住宅ローン「サブプライム・ローン」の与信審査基準は、甘かった。

creeping inflation　忍びよるインフレ

creeping tender offer　ひそかな株の買い占め

crime　（名）罪, 犯罪, 犯罪行為, 法律違反, 悪事, 愚行, 人道にはずれた行為, 恥ずべき行為, 残念なこと
computer crime　コンピュータ犯罪
crime prevention　犯罪防止, 防犯
cybercrime　サイバー犯罪, 電脳犯罪
digital crime　デジタル犯罪
high-technology crime　ハイテク犯罪
network crime　ネットワーク犯罪
organized crime　組織犯罪　（⇒criminal activity）
securities crime　証券犯罪　（⇒securities crime）
◆Corporate leaders must recognize that defrauding investors is a serious crime. 投資家を欺く行為は重大な犯罪である、ということを企業経営者は認識しなければならない。

crime syndicate [gang]　暴力団, 組織暴力団
◆Many loan sharks are known for their links to crime syndicates. ヤミ金融業者の多くは、暴力団と関係があるとされる。

criminal activity　犯罪活動
◆Laws already in place on narcotics and organized crime oblige financial institutions to report to the FSA any deals possibly linked to profits from criminal activities. すでに実施されている麻薬や組織的犯罪に関する法律は、犯罪収益絡みと思われる取引について、金融庁への報告（届出）を金融機関に義務付けている。

criminal complaint　刑事告発
（⇒Financial Instruments and Exchange Law）
an additional action of criminal complaint　刑事告発の追加措置
file a criminal complaint against A with B　AについてBに告訴状を提出する, AをBに刑事告発する
◆The financial watchdog took an additional action of criminal complaint other than administrative punishment as the bank's operations were so malicious. 同行の業務運営の仕方があまりにも悪質なので、金融監視機関の金融庁は、行政処分のほかに刑事告発の追加措置を取った。

criminal gang　暴力団
◆About ¥4 billion acquired by a criminal gang through illegal moneylending operations will be confiscated. 暴力団がヤミ金融で得た約40億円が、没収されることになった。

crimp　（動）しわ［ひだ, 折り目］をつける, 型をつける, 邪魔する（hamper, obstruct）, 妨害する, 妨げる, 減らす　（名）ひだ, しわ, 折り目
crimp on　減らす, 削減する
put a crimp in [into]　（計画などを）邪魔する, 妨害する, 妨げる, 狂わす
◆An overvalued dollar is seriously crimping U.S. manufacturers' ability to export. ドル高が、米国の製造業界の輸出力を大いに妨げている。◆Low cost carriers crimp on personnel costs by making cabin crew clean the aircraft. 格安航空会社は、客室乗務員に清掃も担わせて人件費を減らしている。

cripple　（動）動きを取れなくする, 活動を鈍らせる, ～を無力にする, 麻痺（まひ）させる, 能力［機能］を奪う, 損害を与える, 害する, ～を損なう, 駄目にする, 不具にする, 半身不随にする　（名）身体障害者, 手足の不自由な人, 無能力の人, 沼地, 沼沢（しょうたく）地, 低湿地, 足場
be crippled by the loss of funding　資金援助がなくなって動きが取れない
be crippled in a car accident　自動車事故で身体障害を負う, 自動車事故で半身不随になる
become crippled　動きが取れなくなる, 活動不能になる, 麻痺する
◆The financial system became crippled during the financial crisis. 金融危機の際、金融システムは動きが取れなくなった

[麻痺してしまった]．
crippling （形）動きが取れない，活動不能の，壊滅的な，大打撃[大損害]を与える，重大な障害[影響]を与える
◆Greece must avert a crippling debt default by securing billions of dollars in emergency loans from European countries and the IMF. ギリシャは，欧州諸国[ユーロ圏]と国際通貨基金(IMF)による緊急融資で巨額の資金を確保して，壊滅的な債務不履行を回避しなければならない．

crisis （名）危機，経営危機，重大局面，難局，重大な岐路，分かれ目，（重大事態の）山場，峠，暴落，恐慌，不安，不足，問題，リスク （⇒banking crisis, default, economic crisis, financial crisis, global financial crisis, injection of public funds, management crisis, purchaser, stock crisis）
 bank crisis 銀行恐慌（取付け騒ぎで銀行閉鎖を迫られる事態のこと）
 be at crisis 山場にいる
 be in crisis 危機的状況にある
 business crisis 経営危機
 cash flow crisis 資金繰りが苦しくなること，資金繰りがつかないこと
 commercial crisis 不景気，不況，商業恐慌
 credit crisis 信用恐慌，金融恐慌
 crisis management 危機管理
 currency crisis 通貨危機
 debt crisis 債務危機，累積債務危機
 dollar crisis ドル危機
 economic crisis 経済危機
 energy crisis エネルギー危機
 financial crisis 金融危機，金融恐慌，財政上の難局
 fiscal and financial crisis 財政・金融危機
 fiscal crisis 財政危機，財政破たん危機
 Fukushima No. 1 nuclear power plant crisis 福島第一原発事故
 Greece's sovereign debt crisis ギリシャの財政危機
 liquidity crisis 流動性危機，資金繰りの悪化（＝crisis of liquidity）
 monetary crisis 通貨危機
 oil crisis 石油危機，石油ショック
 stock market crisis 株式市場の暴落，株式市場の混乱
 subprime loan crisis サブプライム・ローン問題，サブプライム危機
 subprime mortgage crisis サブプライム・ローン問題（⇒financial turmoil）
 the euro crisis ユーロ危機
 the spread of the Greek crisis to Spain and Portugal ギリシャ危機のスペインやポルトガルへの波及
 thrift crisis 貯蓄金融業界の危機
 world crisis 世界恐慌
 world economic crisis 世界経済恐慌
◆A U.S. financial crisis would undoubtedly trigger a global crisis. 米国の金融危機は，間違いなく地球規模の（同時）危機を誘発するものと思われる．◆As the Greek fiscal crisis grows more serious, there has been no halt to the worldwide decline in stock prices. ギリシャの財政危機が一段と深刻化するにつれ，世界同時株安に歯止めがかからなくなっている．◆Business conditions are rapidly deteriorating due to the global financial crisis and the worldwide economic downturn. 世界的な金融危機と世界的な景気後退で，景気は急速に悪化している．◆Confidence in the single currency of the euro may be undermined by the spread of the Greek crisis to Spain and Portugal. ギリシャ危機のスペインやポルトガルへの波及で，単一通貨・ユーロの信認が揺らぎかねない．◆Credit uncertainty in Europe has spilled over to France which is helping Greece, Italy and Spain facing fiscal crises. 欧州の信用不安は，財政危機に直面しているギリシャやイタリア，スペインを支援しているフランスにも拡大している．◆In the subprime crisis, the U.S. Federal Reserve Board had to take the extraordinary step of providing an emergency loan not to a commercial bank but to an investment bank. サブプライム問題で，米国の中央銀行の連邦準備制度理事会(FRB)は，緊急融資を銀行[商業銀行]ではなく証券会社[投資銀行]に対して行う異例の措置を取らざるを得なかった．◆Investment conditions have worsened due to confusion in global financial markets in the wake of fiscal and financial crises in Europe. 欧州の財政・金融危機を受けた世界的な金融市場の混乱で，運用環境が悪化している．◆Japan, the United States and emerging economies have pressed European countries to promptly resolve the fiscal and financial crisis. 日米両国と新興国は，欧州に財政・金融危機の迅速な解決を迫った．◆The current global fiscal and financial crisis began in European countries. 今回の世界的な財政・金融危機の震源地は，欧州だ．◆The euro crisis is deepening. ユーロ危機が，深刻化している．◆The European fiscal crisis triggered by Greece has spread to Italy, making the severe situation even more distressing. ギリシャ発の欧州財政危機がイタリアに飛び火し，厳しい事態が一段と深刻化している．◆The global economy has been pulled out of its worst crisis. 世界経済は，その最大の危機は脱した．◆The Greek-triggered sovereign debt crisis has been throwing the eurozone into financial uncertainty and multiple crises. ギリシャに端を発した債務危機問題で，ユーロ圏は金融不安と複合的な危機に陥っている．◆The Japanese economy is by no means facing a serious crisis. 日本経済は，重大な危機に瀕しているわけではない．◆The U.S. government and the Federal Reserve Board took swift actions to deal with the subprime loan crisis of 2007. 米政府と米連邦準備制度理事会(FRB)は，2007年のサブプライム危機に迅速に対応した．◆These moves of the two airlines show the extent of the crisis in the current business environment. 両航空会社のこれらの動きは，現在の経営環境の危機的状況の大きさを示している．◆To overcome the current economic crisis, stimulus measures should take precedence over fiscal reconstruction for the time being. 現在の経済危機を克服するためには，当面は，財政再建よりも景気対策を優先しなければならない．◆To prevent another currency crisis, the G-7 statement spelled out various measures to reform the international financial systems. 通貨危機の再発を防ぐため，主要7か国の声明は，国際金融システム改革の施策をいくつか明確にした．◆To raise money for compensation related to the Fukushima No. 1 nuclear power plant crisis, TEPCO will sell off assets through four trust banks. 福島第一原発事故関連の賠償資金を調達するため，東電は，4信託銀行を通じて資産を売却することになった．◆Worldwide concern over fiscal sustainability in industrialized countries is growing in the wake of Greece's sovereign debt crisis. ギリシャの財政危機を契機として，先進国の財政の持続可能性に対する世界の関心が高まっている．

crisis management 危機管理
◆The eurozone's crisis management approach is always behind the curve. ユーロ圏の危機管理への取組みは，いつも後手に回っている．

criterion （名）基準，規準，標準，尺度（複数＝criteria）
 accounting criteria 会計基準
 authorization criteria 承認基準
 compensation criteria 報酬基準
 consolidation criteria 連結基準，連結の範囲
 convergence criteria 収斂（しゅうれん）基準
 credit criteria 与信基準
 criteria for assessment[assessing] 評価基準，認可基準
 criteria for delisting a security 上場廃止基準
 criteria for listing a security 上場基準

criterion for investment decisions　投資判断の基準, 投資判断の材料
double criteria　二重基準
economic convergence criteria　経済収斂(しゅうれん)基準
eligibility criteria　適格基準, 受給資格, 収斂(しゅうれん)基準

C

hedge criteria　ヘッジ基準
investment criteria　投資基準
lending criteria　貸出基準, 融資基準
optimality criteria　最適性基準
rating criteria to one's credit risk　与信基準
screening criteria　審査基準
selection criteria　選択基準, 選別基準, 融資基準
the convergence criteria　収斂(しゅうれん)基準
underwriting criteria　貸出審査基準
valuation criteria　投資尺度
◆At the firm, curbing repayment amounts is regarded as a criterion for in-house personnel evaluation. 同社では、返還額を抑えることが、社内の人事評価基準と見なされている。◆Corporate accounting reports are the most important criterion for investment decisions. 企業の財務情報は、特に重要な投資判断の材料だ。◆Some firms that were willing to list their shares were unable to meet stock exchanges' eligibility criteria due to the economic slump. 株式上場を目指していた企業の一部は、景気悪化で証券取引所の上場基準を満たすことができなかった。◆The emergency employment package contains a plan to relax criteria for receiving employment-adjustment subsidies. 緊急雇用対策には、雇用調整助成金の受領要件の緩和策も含まれている。◆The government tightened the criteria for granting total exemption from paying national pension premiums. 政府は、国民年金保険料の全額免除の基準を厳格にした。

critical　(形)批判的な, 危急の, 危機的な, 決定的な, 深刻な, 重大な, 枢要な, 最大の, 貴重な
be at a critical stage　岐路に立っている
critical asset　貴重な資産
critical factor　決定的な要因[要素, 役割], 重要な要因
critical issue　深刻な問題, 重要な問題, 決定的な問題, 最大の課題
critical mass　最低限の経済規模, 採算の取れる規模, 望ましい成果を十分得るための確固たる基盤, 限界質量, 臨界質量, 限界量, 臨界量, 臨界, クリティカル・マス
critical point　重点項目
critical situation　危機的な状況
critical source of funds　重要な資金源[資金の源泉]
◆The Japanese economy has reached a critical stage at which it could tumble into a deflationary spiral after brief stability, or be brought back to a recovery path. 日本経済は現在、小康状態から再びデフレの悪循環に落ち込むか、回復軌道に戻せるかどうかの瀬戸際にある。◆This country's debt-laden finances are in a critical situation due to the dole-out policies as well as lavish economic stimulus measures. わが国の借金漬けの財政は、バラマキ政策と大盤振る舞いの景気対策で、危機的な状況に陥っている。

critical path　危機経路, 最長時間経路, 問題経路, クリティカル・パス(プロジェクトを進める上で一番時間がかかる部分)
critical path analysis　危機[最長時間]経路分析, クリティカル・パス分析, CPA分析, CPA
critical path method　クリティカル・パス分析法, クリティカル・パス法, CPM

cross　(形)交差する, 横切った, 斜めの, 反対の, 逆の, 相互の, クロス　(名)両建て, クロス売買(cross-trade), 不正行為　(動)(小切手を)線引きにする

a check crossed specially to the A bank　A銀行を指定した特定線引き小切手
a check crosses generally　一般線引き小切手
cross a check　小切手に横線を引く
cross allocation　相互配賦
cross arbitrage　クロス裁定
cross-bill　逆手形(redraft)
cross collateral agreement　クロス担保契約
cross debt　相対債務
cross-default clause　連鎖債務不履行条項, クロス・デフォルト(連鎖不履行)条項(複数債務の一つが不履行になった場合, 他の債務も不履行と見なす旨の条項)
cross drawing　融通手形振出し
cross effect　交差効果
cross entry　転記, 振替記入, 相殺記帳
cross-firing　空手形の振出し
cross hedge　クロス・ヘッジ(債券先物市場に上場されている債券と他の債券をヘッジすること)
cross holding　株式の持ち合い　(⇒crossholding)
cross investment　交互投資, 相互乗入れ
cross-marketing　追い討ち商法(cross-selling), 既存顧客への追加サービスの販売
cross order　両建て注文
cross ownership　交差所有, 株式の持ち合い(=cross-holding, crossholding)
cross penetration　相互浸透
cross rate (of exchange)　第三国為替相場, クロス相場, クロス・レート(=cross exchange)
cross rate table　第三国同士の通貨交換比率
cross reference　相互参照
cross-selling　抱き合わせ販売, 相互販売, 相互売込み, 追い討ち商法(cross-marketing)
cross slip　振替伝票
cross trade　両建て, クロス売買, 反対売買, 空相場, 仲介貿易, 3国間貿易
cross trading　(先物の)相対(あいたい)売買, 三国間輸送
cross transaction　クロス取引(上場企業の創業者やその一族, 役員など古くからの大株主が, 全持ち株を証券会社に売却して翌日に買い戻すこと)
cross transactions for profit recognition　益出しクロス(利益確定のための取引で, 含み益のある保有株をいったん売ってから買い戻すこと)
exchange cross rate　為替クロス・レート
special cross check　記名式横線小切手

cross-access pact　海外証券取引所との相互取引協定, 海外証券取引所との相互利用協定, 取引参加資格の相互開放協定(=cross-exchange access pact, cross-membership agreement)
◆The Tokyo Stock Exchange and the Singapore Exchange Ltd. (SGX) plan to enter into a cross-access pact. 東京証券取引所とシンガポール取引所(SGX)は、相互取引協定(各取引所の取引参加者(証券会社)に参加加資格を相互開放する協定)を結ぶ方針だ。

cross-border　(形)国境を越えた, 越境の, 国際的な
cross-boarder loan loss reserve　対外融資貸倒れ引当金
cross-border capital flows　国際的な資本移動
cross-border capital movements　越境資本移動
cross-border debt　対外借入れ
cross-border equity investment　国際株式投資
cross-border lending　外国向け融資, 対外融資
cross-border loan　対外融資
cross-border offering　国際的募集, 国際募集

cross-border payment system 国際決済システム
cross-border transaction 国際取引
cross-border transfer 国外への送金
cross-border realignment 国境を越えた再編
◆The financial crisis that originated in the United States is developing into a cross-border realignment of the financial industry that involves Japanese financial institutions. 米国発の金融危機は、日本の金融機関をも巻き込む国境を越えた金融再編[金融業界の再編]に発展している。
cross-border reorganization of stock exchanges 国境を越えた証券取引所の再編
◆Cross-border reorganization of stock exchanges is gathering speed in the United States and Europe. 欧米では、国境を越えた証券取引所の再編が加速している。
cross-currency [cross currency] (形)複数通貨間の、異なる通貨間の、クロス・カレンシー
cross-currency and interest rate swaps 通貨・金利スワップ
cross-currency basis swaps 複数通貨間のベーシス・スワップ
cross-currency coupon swaps 複数通貨間の金利スワップ
cross-currency interest rate swap 異種通貨間の金利スワップ(異種通貨による金利支払い交換)
cross-currency swap 通貨スワップ
cross-currency transaction クロス・カレンシー取引
cross-membership system 証券取引所会員の相互取引制度, 証券売買取引の相互乗り入れ制度 (⇒broking, cross-access pact)
◆The Singapore and Australian exchanges have already launched a cross-membership system on an experimental basis through subsidiaries. シンガポール取引所とオーストラリア証券取引所は、子会社を通じてすでに実験的に証券売買取引の相互乗り入れ制度を始めている。
cross shareholding [cross-shareholding] 株式の持ち合い, 持ち合い株 (=crossholding, cross-holding shares, interlocking shareholdings)
byzantine cross shareholdings 入り組んだ株式持ち合い関係
cross-shareholding ties [relationship] 株式の持ち合い関係
defensive cross shareholdings 企業防衛のための株式持ち合い, 企業防衛目的の持ち合い株
hold cross shareholdings 持ち合い株を保有する
limits on banks' cross shareholdings 銀行の持ち合い株保有制限
sell cross-shareholdings 持ち合い株を売却する
the dissolution of cross-shareholding ties [relationship] 株式持ち合い関係の解消
unbundle [unwind] cross shareholdings 株式の持ち合い関係を解消する, 株式の持ち合いを解消する
◆Hostile mergers and acquisitions have been increasing rapidly as the dissolution of cross-shareholding ties among companies accelerates. 企業間の株式持ち合い関係の解消が加速するにつれ、敵対的M&A(企業の合併・買収)の件数は急増している。◆One insurance company's failure will now have a grave impact on banks that are closely linked to the insurer by means of cross-shareholding. 生保の破たんは、株式の密接な持ち合い関係にある銀行に重大な影響を及ぼす。◆Suzuki Motor's board of directors decided to dissolve its partnership and cross-shareholding relationship with Volkswagen AG. スズキの取締役会は、独フォルクスワーゲンとの提携と株式持ち合い関係の解消を決めた。
crossed (形)交差した, 錯綜した, (小切手の)横線(おうせん)を引いた

crossed check [cheque] 線引き小切手, 横線(おうせん)小切手
crossed market 錯綜相場
crossed money order 横線郵便為替
crossheld shares 持ち合い株, 持ち合い株式 (=crossheld shares, crossheld stocks; ⇒speculative trader)
◆Nonperforming loans will be transferred to the revival account, as well as crossheld shares and idle real estate. 不良債権は、持ち合い株式や遊休不動産などと一緒に「再生勘定」に移す。◆Stock prices will tumble, if banks try to sell a large amount of their crossheld shares in the market ahead of the account settlement term at the end of March. 3月末の決算期を控えて、銀行が大量の持ち合い株式を市場に放出すれば、株価は急落する。
crossheld stocks 持ち合い株, 持ち合い株式 (=crossheld shares)
◆The banks have been selling off crossheld stocks to prevent their financial conditions from being further damaged by falling stock prices. 銀行各行は、株価の下落で銀行の財務基盤が一段と傷つくのを避けるため、持ち合い株式を売却してきた。
crossholding (名)株式持ち合い (=cross-holding, interlocking holding)
◆Crossholding is a practice in which financial institutions and their client companies own a large amount of stock in each other. 株式持ち合いは、金融機関とその取引先企業が相互に大量の株式を保有する慣行である。
crossing (名)(小切手の)線引き, 大口対当売買(cross), クロス (形)組み合わせる, 交差する, 横線を入れる, 付け合わせる
crossing for the purpose of finance 金融クロス(クロス商いのひとつで、その目的が株を手放す側の資金繰り、資金調達である場合のことをいう)
crossing order 付け合わせ注文
general crossing 一般線引き
special crossing 特別線引き
crowding-out (名)(民間資金需要の)締め出し, クラウディング・アウト
crowding-out effect 締め出し効果, クラウディング・アウト効果
crown jewel 最優良資産, 王冠の宝石, クラウン・ジュエル (買収される会社のとくに魅力のある重要資産)
crown jewel defense クラウン・ジュエル防衛, 有望資産売却戦略, 重要資産売却作戦 (敵対的M&A(企業の合併・買収)への防衛策として、買収を仕掛けられた企業が、重要な資産や事業を外部に売却して企業価値を低下させ、買収の意義を失わせること。scorched-earth defense(焦土作戦)とほぼ同じ意味で使われることが多い)
crown jewel defense tactic 最優良資産売却作戦
◆Citigroup's retail brokerage, Smith Barney, was once the crown jewel in its wealth management business. シティグループの個人向け証券会社「スミスバーニー」は、以前はシティグループの資産運用業務の最優良資産だった。
CRT 信用リスク移転(credit risk transferの略)
CRT instrument [product] 信用リスク移転商品, CRT商品, CRTプロダクト
crude futures 原油先物 (⇒commodity market)
◆Crude futures soared to $135 per barrel on the New York market. ニューヨーク市場の原油先物価格が、1バレル=135ドルに急騰した[1バレル=135ドルの高値を付けた]。◆Crude futures were launched on the New York Mercantile Exchange in 1983. 原油先物の取引は、1983年からニューヨーク・マーカンタイル取引所で開始された。
crude oil futures 原油先物

◆Crude oil futures soared in New York due to concerns over oil supplies. ニューヨーク（ニューヨーク・マーカンタイル取引所）の原油先物が，原油供給不安［原油供給への懸念］から急騰した。
crude oil futures trading 原油先物取引
　◆Service charges or tax on crude oil futures trading should be raised to curb the inflow of speculative money not related to actual demand. 実需に関係ない投機マネーの流入を抑えるため，原油先物取引の手数料の引上げや課税強化をすべきだ。
crude oil prices 原油価格
　◆Investment funds have driven up crude oil prices. 投資ファンドが，原油価格の高騰を演出してきた。
CSR 企業の社会的責任（corporate social responsibilityの略。消費者や従業員，社会に対する企業の責任で，法令遵守や環境への配慮，積極的な情報開示などを企業活動に取り入れる企業が増えている。投資家が投資先を選ぶ際の判断基準の一つにもなっている）
cum （前）～付きの，～付きで，～兼，直結した
　（=along with, together with, with）
　cum all 諸権利付き，全利得付き
　cum bonus 特別配当権付き
　cum call （株式の）払込み付き
　cum coupon 利札付き，金利付き（で，の）
　cum distribution 次期所得配当付き
　cum dividend 配当付き，配当付きで
　　（配当落ち＝ex dividend）
　cum interest 利付き
　cum new 新株付き，子株付き，権利付き（cum rights）
　cum rights 権利付き，新株引受権付き
　cum warrants ワラント付き，カム・ワラント
　◆The eurozone states forced Greece to agree to an impracticable repayment-cum-fiscal rehabilitation package though Greece was already insolvent. ギリシャはすでに返済不能であったが，ユーロ圏各国は，実行不可能な財政再建の条件付き返済計画をギリシャに押し付けた。
cumulated （形）累積（るいせき）した
　cumulated deficit 累積赤字 （=cumulative deficit）
　cumulated surplus 累積黒字
　　（=cumulative surplus）
cumulative （形）累積（るいせき）的な，漸増（ぜんぞう）的な，累加的な，併存的，追加的
　cumulative cash flow キャッシュ・フロー累計
　cumulative convertible preference share 累積転換優先株式
　cumulative currency translation adjustment 累積外貨換算調整額
　cumulative deficit 累積赤字 （=cumulated deficit）
　cumulative deposit account 積立預金
　cumulative effect 累積効果，累積影響額，影響累計額
　cumulative interest 累加利子
　cumulative interest arrearage 累積延滞利息
　cumulative lending 累積的貸付け
　cumulative loss 累積損失
　cumulative loss ratio 累積損失率
　cumulative mark-on 累積値入れ額
　cumulative preference [preferred] share 累積優先株式，累積利益配当優先株
　cumulative stock returns 累積総合利回り
　cumulative surplus 累積黒字
　cumulative time deposit 積立預金
　cumulative translation adjustment 為替換算調整累計額，為替換算調整勘定
　the cumulative value of direct investment 直接投資の残高

cumulative dividend 累積配当，累積配当額，累加配当，積置き配当
　◆The first preferred shareholders are entitled to cumulative annual dividends per share in the amount set out in the titles of each series. 第一優先株式の株主には，シリーズごとに規定された［各シリーズの証券に記載された］レートで1株当たり年間累積配当を受ける権利が与えられています。
cumulative preferred 累積優先株式，累積優先株
　cumulative perpetual preferred stock 累積配当型永久優先株
　　（=perpetual cumulative preferred stock）
　cumulative preferred stock [share] 累積優先株，累積的優先株
curb （動）抑える，制御する，抑制する，制限する，削減する，食い止める，防止する，束縛する，拘束する
　（=kerb; ⇒uptrend）
　curb credit expansion 信用拡大を抑える［抑制する］
　curb deficits 赤字を削減する
　curb fiscal [government] spending 財政支出を抑える［抑制する］
　curb inflation インフレを抑制する
　curb the inflow of speculative money 投機マネーの流入を抑える
　◆A rise in borrowing costs will curb consumer spending as well as production activity in industrial sectors. 借入コストの増大は，産業の生産活動や個人消費を抑えることになる。◆At the firm, curbing repayment amounts is regarded as a criterion for in-house personnel evaluation. 同社では，返還額を抑えることが，社内の人事評価基準と見なされている。◆Japan must tackle its large fiscal deficit and curb the growth of public debts. 日本は，巨額の財政赤字と取り組んで，財政赤字［公的債務］の増大を抑える必要がある。◆Service charges or tax on crude oil futures trading should be raised to curb the inflow of speculative money not related to actual demand. 実需に関係ない投機マネーの流入を抑えるため，原油先物取引の手数料の引上げや課税強化をすべきだ。◆The global recession curbed consumer spending, hurting demand for chips that go into electronics such as computers and handsets. 世界同時不況で個人消費が抑えられ，コンピュータや携帯電話などの電子製品に用いられる半導体の需要も減退している［打撃を受けている］。◆The government has already established a framework for curbing spending. 政府は，歳出抑制の大枠をすでに設定している。◆The sharp decline in investment in medium- and long-term corporate bonds occurred because the prolonged recession curbed new issues necessary for investment in plant and equipment. 中長期社債への投資が大幅に減少したのは，長引く不況で企業の設備投資に必要な中長期債の新規発行が不振だったためである。
Curb （名）アメリカン証券取引所，カーブ
　（=American Stock Exchange, AMEX）
curb （名）場外市場，街頭株式取引所
　（=curb market）
　curb broker 場外市場仲買人
　Curb Exchange カーブ取引所 （=Curb, New York Curb Exchange: アメリカン証券取引所（AMEX）は，1950年代初頭までNew York Curb Exchangeと呼ばれていた）
　curb finance 場外金融
　curb market 場外取引市場，場外市場
　　（=curbstone market）
currency （名）通貨，為替，為替相場，通貨流通額，流通，流行，カレンシー （⇒against, carry trade, exchange rate movements, float, foreign currency, hard currency, market-based currency regime, mix）
　a slipping currency もろい通貨
　anchor currency 連動通貨

asset currency 資産通貨
basic currency 基準通貨
big currencies 主要通貨
cash currency 現金通貨
common currency 共通通貨
confidence in currency 通貨信任
controlled currency 管理通貨
convertible currency 交換可能通貨
credit currency 信用通貨
cross currency swap 通貨スワップ
currency alignment 通貨調整
currency amount 通貨額
currency band 通貨変動幅
currency basket 通貨バスケット
currency basket system 通貨バスケット方式
currency bill 外貨手形
　　（＝foreign currency bill）
currency bill payable 外貨支払い為替手形
currency bloc［block］ 通貨圏, 通貨ブロック
currency board カレンシー・ボード制
currency bond 発行国通貨払い債券, CB
currency box 手提げ金庫
currency changes 為替相場の変動, 為替変動
　　（＝currency exchange fluctuations, currency movements, currency swings, exchange fluctuations）
currency circulation 通貨発行高, 通貨流通高
　　（＝notes in circulation, notes issued）
currency commodity 通貨商品
currency conversion 通貨の転換, 通貨の換算, カレンシー・コンバージョン
currency conversion bond カレンシー・コンバージョン債
currency convertibility 通貨の交換性, 通貨の自由交換性
currency deflation 通貨収縮
currency demand deposit ratio 通貨・当座預金比率
currency demanded 通貨需要量
currency depreciation 通貨安, 通貨価値下落, 通貨下落, 為替下落
currency disturbance［instability］ 通貨不安, 通貨混乱
currency doctrine［principle］ 通貨主義
currency exposure 為替リスク, 通貨の価格変動によるリスク負担, 通貨エクスポージャー, アンカバー通貨残高（外貨保有による損失可能額）
currency flow 通貨流量
currency fluctuations 通貨変動, 通貨の騰落, 通貨価値の変動　（＝currency changes）
currency futures 通貨先物取引, 外国為替先物, 為替リスクのヘッジなどに使われる
currency in circulation 流通現金通貨, 流通通貨, 通貨流通高
currency indebtedness 通貨貸借, 通貨負債
currency indemnity 通貨補償
currency inflation 通貨膨張, 通貨インフレ
currency management 通貨管理
currency note 英1ポンド（10ペンス）
currency notes 政府通貨
currency of account 勘定通貨
currency of settlement 決済通貨
currency option 通貨オプション
currency or［and］coin shipment 通貨の積送

currency outstanding 通貨の現在高
currency period 流通期間
currency practice 通貨措置
currency rates 外国通貨建て相場, 通貨の換算率
currency realignment 通貨再調整
currency redenomination デノミ, 通貨の呼称変更
currency risk 為替リスク, 通貨リスク
　　（＝exchange risk）
currency snake 共同変動為替相場制
　　（＝the snake）
currency speculation 通貨投機
currency split 通貨分離
currency stabilization loan 通貨安定借款
currency standard index 通貨標準指数
currency standards 通貨本位, 通貨本位制, 通貨標準
currency supplied 通貨供給量, 貨幣供給量
currency surcharge 為替変動による追加料金
currency system 通貨制度, 通貨体系
　　（＝monetary system）
currency transaction［trading］ 通貨取引
currency translation 通貨換算, 外貨換算
currency translation adjustments 為替換算調整, 外貨換算調整, 為替換算調整勘定, 外貨換算調整勘定
currency turmoil 通貨不安, 通貨動揺
　　（＝currency instability, currency unrest）
currency union （欧州の）通貨統合, 通貨同盟
　　（⇒bailout fund）
currency unrest 通貨不安, 通貨動揺
　　（＝currency turmoil）
currency upvaluation 通貨切上げ
deposit currency 預金通貨
depreciated currency 減価通貨
depreciation of major currencies against the yen 円に対する主要通貨安
depreciation of the currency 通貨価値の下落
designated currency 指定通貨
devaluation of the currency 通貨の切下げ
devaluation prone currency 平価切下げ不安通貨
European currency 欧州通貨
functional currency 機能通貨
hard currency 交換可能通貨, 硬貨, 強い通貨, ハード・カレンシー
　　（＝hard money: 米ドルや金と交換できる通貨）
healthy currency 健全な通貨
home currency 自国通貨
international currency 国際通貨
　　（＝international money）
intervention currency 介入通貨
Japanese currency market 円建て市場
key currency 基軸通貨, 国際通貨, キー・カレンシー
　　（＝key money）
legal currency 法貨, 法定通貨　（＝legal tender）
link a currency to the dollar 通貨をドルに連動させる
local currency 現地通貨（建て）, 国内通貨（建て）, 自国通貨（建て）, ローカル・カレンシー
　　（＝local money）
major currencies 主要通貨　（⇒tumble）
metallic currency 硬貨
national currency 国の通貨
parallel currency 並行通貨
rate in foreign currency 外貨建て相場

scarce currency　希少通貨
secure [sound] currency　健全通貨
single currency　単一通貨
single European currency　欧州単一通貨（統一通貨名＝euro）
soft currency　交換不能通貨, 軟貨, ソフト通貨, 弱い通貨, ソフト・カレンシー（米ドルやその他の主要通貨と直接交換できない通貨）
stabilized currency　安定通貨
standard official currency　基準通貨
strong dollar against other currencies　ドル全面高
the Chinese currency　中国の人民元, 人民元, 中国の通貨
the currency adjustment factor　（海上運送）為替変動による追加料金　（＝the currency surcharge）
the currency basket system　（IMF）標準バスケット方式
the currency clause [option]　通貨条項
the Japanese currency　円
the key international currency　国際基軸通貨, 国際通貨
transferable currency　振替可能通貨
undervalued currency　過小評価された通貨, 通貨の過小評価
vehicle currency　取引通貨, 貿易通貨, 媒介通貨
yen currency　円貨

◆As it stands, the yen is the sole major currency whose value has not stopped increasing. 現状では、円は、相場の上昇が止まらない唯一の主要通貨だ。◆Commission rates in foreign currency deposits vary among foreign currencies or among financial institutions. 外貨預金での為替手数料の料率は、外国通貨や金融機関で異なる。◆Deutsche Bank handles 120 currencies, such as Brazil's real and the Indian rupee. ドイツ銀行は、ブラジルのレアルやインドのルピーなど120種類の通貨を取り扱っている。◆No currency can be considered strong if it is propped up by life support such as intervention. 市場介入というような生命維持装置で支えられている通貨は、強い通貨とはいえない。◆Some European nations which are experiencing fiscal crises seem to rely on drops in their currencies' values as a means of underpinning their economies. 財政危機問題を抱えた欧州諸国の一部は、景気下支えの手段として通貨安を頼みにしているようだ。◆The Japanese currency is about ¥5 lower than its initial projection of ¥115 to the dollar. 円は、当初想定した1ドル＝115円より5円程度安く推移している。◆The Japanese currency's value vis-a-vis the U.S. dollar entered the ¥98 range in foreign exchange markets around the world. 円の対米ドル相場は、内外の外国為替市場で1ドル＝98円台をつけた。◆The latest depreciation of the euro brought about a life-sustaining boon to the currency. 今回のユーロ安が、ユーロの延命効果を招いた。◆The U.S. dollar has dropped sharply in value not only against the yen, but also against the euro, the South Korean won, the Thai baht and other currencies. 米ドル［米ドル相場］は、円に対してだけでなく、ユーロや韓国ウォン、タイ・バーツなどに対しても、急落している。◆The U.S. dollar has enjoyed the massive privileges as the key international currency. 米ドルは、国際通貨としての特権を享受してきた。◆The yen lost ground against higher-yielding currencies. 円は、高金利通貨に対して下落した［高金利通貨に対して売られた］。◆Washington is pressing Beijing to revalue the Chinese currency. 米政府は、中国に通貨（人民元）切上げを迫っている。

currency appreciation　通貨高, 通貨騰貴, 通貨価値の騰貴［上昇］, 為替騰貴
◆As one option to avoid excessive currency appreciation in emerging countries with inflationary trends, they can restrict an influx of capital. インフレ気味の新興国で行き過ぎた［過度の］通貨高を避けるための手段として、資金流入を規制することができる。

currency authorities　通貨当局
（＝monetary authorities）
◆Policy coordination efforts between Japanese and U.S. currency authorities are genuine. 日米通貨当局の政策協調努力は、本物だ。

currency basket　通貨バスケット（「通貨バスケット制」は、複数の外国通貨をバスケット（かご）の中に移すように選んで組み合わせた指標に、為替相場を連動させる仕組み。シンガポールなどでは、バスケット内の通貨の種類と構成比は、国別の貿易量などで決めている）
currency basket system　標準バスケット方式
◆The latest rise in the yuan's value against the U.S. dollar and a smooth transition to the currency basket will help stabilize China's external relations. 今回の人民元相場の対米ドル切上げと通貨バスケット制への円滑な移行で、中国の対外関係は安定化に向かうだろう。

currency counterfeiting　通貨偽造
◆The U.S. government froze the assets of four individuals and eight entities that were involved in illicit activities such as money laundering, currency counterfeiting and narcotics trafficking. 米政府は、資金洗浄（マネー・ロンダリング）や通貨偽造、麻薬取引などの違法行為に関与している4個人、8団体の資産を凍結した。

currency crisis　通貨危機　（＝monetary crisis）
◆The currency crisis wracked Asia in 1997. 1997年に、アジアは通貨危機に見舞われた。◆To prevent another currency crisis, the G-7 statement spelled out various measures to reform the international financial systems. 通貨危機の再発を防ぐため、主要7か国の声明は、国際金融システム改革の施策をいくつか明確にした。

currency devaluation　通貨切下げ, 通貨安
◆Currency devaluation can boost the economy significantly. 通貨安で、景気を大いに刺激することができる。

currency devaluation race　通貨切下げ競争, 通貨安競争
◆The G-20 finance ministers and central bank governors agreed to refrain from a global currency devaluation race. 主要［世界］20か国・地域（G20）の財務相・中央銀行総裁（会議）は、世界の通貨切下げ競争［通貨安競争］を回避することで合意した。

currency exchange　通貨交換, 両替, 通貨の売買, 為替相場
currency exchange fluctuations　為替変動
currency exchange system　為替相場制度
engage in currency exchange transactions　為替取引を行う

currency exchange loss　為替差損
◆The firm plans to make up for some of the currency exchange loss by transferring some of its domestic production operations overseas. 同社は、一部の国内生産拠点を海外に移して、為替差損の一部を穴埋めする方針だ。

currency exchange rate　為替相場, 為替レート
（＝exchange rate; ⇒foreign currency exchange contract）
◆The central bank's decision to raise the upper limit of its liquidity target was prompted by its concerns over the recent instability of the currency exchange rate. 日銀当座預金の残高目標（日銀の流動性目標）の上限引上げ決定の理由に、最近の為替相場の不安定な動きへの懸念があった。

currency friction　通貨摩擦
◆Disarray among the countries became evident over concrete measures to prevent currency friction. 通貨摩擦を食い止める具体策では、各国の足並みの乱れが露呈した。◆G-20 leaders must concretize policy coordination to prevent currency friction and achieve sustainable growth. G-20（世界20か国・地域）首脳は、通貨摩擦を食い止める［防ぐ］ための政策協調を具体化して、持続的成長を実現しなければならない。

currency intervention 為替介入 （⇒rate, weak）
◆If Japan is acting weak in currency intervention, speculators will try to capitalize on that. 日本が為替介入に弱腰なら、投機筋に付け込まれることになる。◆Prime Minister Kan and Bank of Japan Gov. Shirakawa did not discuss a currency intervention to stem the yen's rise against other major currencies. 菅首相と白川日銀総裁は、主要通貨に対する円相場の上昇を阻止するための為替介入については協議しなかった。◆The government's currency intervention through yen-selling and dollar-buying operations on Sept. 15, 2010 was the biggest on record for a one-day operation. 2010年9月15日の政府の円売り・ドル買い操作による為替介入額は、1日の円売り・ドル買い介入(操作)としては過去最高を更新した。

currency market 為替市場, 外国為替市場, 通貨市場
（=foreign exchange market）
◆Currency markets have overvalued the yen. 円は、強く評価され過ぎている。◆Joint intervention by Japan and European countries in the currency markets is possible as the dollar rapidly weakens. ドル安が急速に進んでいることから、為替市場への日欧協調介入もあり得る。◆The government and the Bank of Japan stepped into the currency market for the first time in 6 1/2 years. 政府・日銀が、6年半ぶりに為替市場に介入した［市場介入を実施した］。◆The government will continue to monitor the currency market. 政府は、今後も為替市場の動きを注視する方針だ。◆The U.S. dollar was traded at around ￥76 on the currency market. 為替市場では、1ドル＝76円をはさんだ取引が続いた。◆The value of the U.S. dollar has started to decline on currency markets around the world. 世界の外国為替市場では、米ドル相場が下落しはじめた。◆Washington's intervention in the currency market cannot be expected for the time being. 米国の為替市場への介入は当面、期待できない。

currency market intervention 為替市場への介入, 為替市場介入
◆Despite Japan's currency market intervention on Sept. 15, 2010, the yen began to appreciate again within a few days. 日本が2010年9月15日に為替介入に踏み切ったものの、円相場は2,3日して再び上昇し始めた。◆The government conducted a series of currency market interventions to prevent the yen's value from getting stronger. 政府が、円高阻止のための為替市場への介入を断続的に行った。◆The U.S. Treasury Department mentioned Japan's currency market interventions to stem the sharp rise of the yen in the department's currency report. 米財務省は、同省の為替政策報告書で、日本の急激な円高阻止にための為替市場介入について触れた。◆These comments were made after a series of currency market interventions by the government to prevent the yen's value from getting stronger. これらのコメントは、政府が円高阻止のための為替市場への介入を断続的に行った後に出された。

currency movements 為替相場の動き, 為替相場の変動, 為替変動
（=currency changes, exchange fluctuations）
◆The currency movements are too rapid. 為替相場の動きが、あまりにも急激だ。

currency note 銀行券, 政府通貨, 政府紙幣
◆A group of Liberal Democratic Party lawmakers called on the government to consider issuing government-issued currency notes. 自民党議員グループが、政府に政府紙幣の発行検討を求めた。

currency policy 通貨政策, 為替政策
◆China's currency policy effectively subsidizes the country's exports. 中国の通貨政策は事実上、同国の輸出補助金に当たる。◆Former Bank of Japan Gov. Masaru Hayami, who supported the appreciation of the yen, often clashed over currency policies with the government, which wanted to lower the yen's value to sustain the economy. 円高論者の速水優・前日銀総裁は、為替政策をめぐって、景気下支えのた

めの円安進行を期待する政府と衝突することが多かった。

currency report 為替政策報告書
（⇒manipulator）
◆In its currency report, the U.S. Treasury Department did not call China a manipulator of its currency. 米財務省は、為替政策報告書で、中国を為替操作国と認めなかった。

currency stabilization 通貨安定, 通貨安定化
◆To fulfill its responsibilities as the nation's central bank, the Bank of Japan must achieve currency stabilization by availing itself of a range of measures, including stabilization of the exchange rate. 日本の中央銀行としての責任を果たすには、日本銀行は、為替の安定を含めて広範な手段を活用して通貨の安定を実現しなければならない。

currency strategy 通貨戦略
◆The currency strategies of China and the United States also seem to affect the issue of a free trade area. 中国と米国の通貨戦略も、自由貿易圏の問題に影響を及ぼしているようだ。

currency swap 通貨スワップ（異なる通貨間の固定金利と固定金利を交換する取引。通貨スワップは、金利スワップと違って交換する通貨が異なるので、金利だけでなく元本交換をも伴う）

currency swap bond 通貨スワップ債

multilateral currency swap agreement 多国間通貨交換［スワップ］協定

currency swap agreement 通貨スワップ協定, 通貨交換協定, 通貨スワップ契約 （=currency swap arrangement: 通貨スワップ協定は、資金繰りが行き詰まった国に対して、外貨準備などを活用して短期に米ドルなどの外貨を融通しあう取決めのこと）
◆The currency swap agreement agreed on between the U.S. Federal Reserve Board and the European Central Bank should be expanded and reinforced to other countries. 米連邦準備制度理事会(FRB)と欧州中央銀行(ECB)との間で取り決めている通貨交換協定を、他国にも拡大・強化するべきである。

currency swap deal 通貨［外貨］交換取引, 通貨スワップ取引, 通貨スワップ取引枠
◆Japan, China and South Korea decided to expand their currency swap deals. 日本、中国と韓国は、外貨スワップ(交換)取引枠の拡大を決めた。

currency swings 為替変動 （=currency changes, currency fluctuations, currency movements, forex swings）
◆Eurozone finance ministers and the European Central Bank expressed concern over large currency swings. ユーロ圏の財務相と欧州中央銀行(ECB)は、過度の為替変動に懸念を表明した。

currency system 通貨体系, 通貨制度
international managed currency system 国際管理通貨制度
managed currency system 管理通貨制度
multi-currency intervention system 複数通貨介入制度

currency trader 為替トレーダー
◆Currency traders are now turning to the renminbi (yuan) from the U.S. dollar. 為替トレーダーは今や、米ドルから中国の人民元に目を向けている。◆Currency traders worldwide frantically search for a safe haven in volatile times. 世界の為替トレーダーは、変動の激しい時期の安全な投資先を熱狂的に求めている。◆Some currency traders have recently advised the Malaysian government and the Persian Gulf states to buy renminbi-based bonds, rather than the U.S. dollar. 一部の為替トレーダーは最近、米ドルではなく中国の人民元建て債券を買うようマレーシア政府やペルシャ湾岸諸国に助言している。

currency union 通貨統合, 通貨同盟
◆Eurozone nations have set up a massive bailout fund that could rescue any member country of Europe's currency union from default. ユーロ圏諸国が、デフォルト(債務不履行)

から欧州の通貨統合参加国を救済できる大規模な[巨額の]緊急支援基金を創設[設立]した。◆The 17-nation currency union was slow in responding to the request for financial support by Greece. 17か国から成る通貨統合のユーロ圏は、ギリシャの金融支援要請への対応が遅かった。

currency unit 通貨単位 (=monetary unit)

世界主要国の通貨単位:

国・地域	通貨単位	略号	日本語標記
アメリカ	U.S. Dollar	US$	米ドル
イギリス	Pound (Sterling)	£	ポンド
イラン	Iranian	Rial RLs	リアル
インド	Indian	Rupee I.Re	ルピー
インドネシア	Indonesian Rupiah	Rp	ルピア
オーストラリア	Australian Dollar	A$	豪ドル
カナダ	Canadian Dollar	C$	加ドル
韓国	Korean	Won W	ウォン
シンガポール	Singapore Dollar	S$	シンガポール・ドル
スイス	Swiss	Franc S.Fr.	スイス・フラン
スウェーデン	Swedish Krona	SKr	スウェーデン・クローナ
タイ	Thai Baht	B	バーツ
中国	Yuan	RMB	元
デンマーク	Danish Krone	DKr	デンマーク・クローネ
ノルウェー	Norwegian Krone	NKr	ノルウェー・クローネ
ポルトガル	Portuguese Escudo	Esc	エスクード
マレーシア	Ringgit	M$	リンギ
ユーロ圏諸国	euro	€	ユーロ

currency value 通貨価値
◆Some European nations which are experiencing fiscal crises seem to rely on drops in their currencies' values as a means of underpinning their economies. 財政危機問題を抱えた欧州諸国の一部は、景気下支えの手段として通貨安を頼みにしているようだ。◆The Japanese currency's value vis-a-vis the U.S. dollar entered the ¥109 range in foreign exchange markets around the world. 円の対米ドル相場は、内外の外国為替市場で1ドル＝109円台を付けた。◆The steady strengthening of the renminbi's international currency value is not favorable. 中国人民元の国際的な通貨価値の着実な上昇は、好ましくない。

currency war 通貨安競争
(=currency devaluation race)
◆Financial chiefs from the Group of 20 agreed to avoid a global currency war. 主要[世界]20か国・地域(G20)の財務相・中央銀行総裁は、(各国が自国通貨を安くすることで輸出競争力を高め、景気回復をめざす)世界の「通貨安競争」を避けることで合意した。◆G-20 chiefs have agreed to avoid a global currency war. 主要20か国・地域(G20)財務相・中央銀行総裁は、通貨安競争を回避することで合意した。

current (形)現在の, 当座の, 当期の, 短期の, 臨時の, 経常的, 流動的 (名)流動, 流動性, 1年以内返済予定額, 当期分 (⇒base rate)
current balance 当座残高
current bank loan 短期借入金
current bond 30年債指標銘柄
current bond equivalent yield 政府債換算直接利回り
current cash flow 手元流動性
current cycle 今回の景気サイクル
current delivery 当月限
current deposit 当座預金 (=checking account, current account, current account deposit)
current dollars 名目金額
current fund 当座資金
current futures 通貨先物
current income 運用収益, インカムゲイン (債券保有の場合の利息、株式保有の場合の配当金などの定期収入)
current liabilities 流動負債
current loan receivable 短期貸付け金
current market rates 実勢市場金利
current maturities of long-term debt 1年以内返済長期借入金
current maturity 残存期間, 当期支払い額
current net income 当期純利益
　(=current earnings, current income)
current operating basis [concept] 当期業績主義
current operating income 当期営業利益, 当期操業利益
current operating performance theory [basis, concept] 当期業績主義
current operating profit 当期営業利益, 当期操業利益
current policy intent 現在の政策スタンス
current portion of long-term borrowings 1年以内返済予定の長期借入金
current proceeds 当期収入, 当期収益, 当期売上高, 現在現金受領額
current rate 決算日レート, カレント・レート
　(=closing rate)
current revenue 当期収益, 収入, 歳入
current service cost 現在勤務費用
current tax expense 当期税金費用
current term net loss 当期純損失
current term settlement 当期決算
current yield 直接利回り, 直利 (債券の償還時に発生する額面と購入価格との差益・差損を考慮しないで、1年間の利息を購入価格で割り、100を掛けて算出。債券の購入価格に対する年間利息の割合を示す)

current account 当座預金, 経常収支, 経常勘定
(=checking account)
balance of current account 経常収支
　(=current account balance)
convertibility of current account 経常勘定交換性
credit the current account 経常収支上プラス項目となる
current account problems 経常赤字
current account profit 経常利益 (⇒current profit)
current account share of GDP 経常黒字の対GDP比率
debit the current account 経常収支上マイナス項目となる
the elements of current account 経常収支の構成要素
◆The Bank of Japan's policy board decided unanimously to keep its target for the outstanding balance of deposits in current accounts held by private financial institutions at the central bank in the range of ¥30 trillion to ¥35 trillion. 日銀の政策委員会は、日銀当座預金(民間の金融機関が日銀に保有している当座預金)の残高目標を30兆〜35兆円程度に維持することを、全会一致で決めた。

current account balance 経常収支, 当座預金残高
(=balance of current account)
current account balance is in deficit 経常収支は赤字である
current account balance is in surplus 経常収支は黒字である
◆According to an estimate based on data concerning the BOJ's current account balance, the central bank sold from ¥1.7 trillion to 1.8 trillion on Wednesday alone. 日銀の当座預金残高に関するデータに基づく推計によると、日銀の円売り介入の規模は、水曜日だけで1兆7,000億円〜1兆8,000億円だったと見られる。◆In countries that are based on a genuine market economy model, current account balances are just

the results of imports and exports freely carried out by the private sector. 純粋な市場経済モデルに立つ国では、経常収支は、民間が行う自由な輸出・輸入活動の結果に過ぎない。◆The current account balance is entering an upward trend on a year-on-year basis. 経常収支は、前年同月比ベースで上昇基調に入りつつある。

current account deficit 経常赤字, 経常収支の赤字, 経常収支の赤字額 （⇒numerical target）
　growing [rising] current account deficit 経常赤字の拡大, 経常赤字幅の拡大
　narrowing current account deficit 経常赤字の縮小, 経常赤字幅の縮小
　nation [country] with a current account deficit 経常赤字国, 経常赤字の国
　record [post] a current account deficit 経常赤字を計上する
　run a current account deficit 経常収支が赤字だ
　widening current account deficit 経常赤字幅の拡大
　◆The large U.S. current account deficit might result in a marked decline of its international investment positions. 米国の巨額の経常赤字で、海外投資家のドル資産が大幅に減少する可能性がある[海外投資家の著しいドル資産離れを招きかねない]。◆The twin deficits of the United States—fiscal and current account deficits—are threatening to destabilize the world economy. アメリカの双子の赤字（財政赤字と経常支赤字）が、世界経済の不安定要因となっている。◆The U.S. current account deficit for 2004 grew 25 percent to a new high of $665.9 billion. 2004年の米経常収支の赤字額は、前年比25%増の6,659億ドルで、過去最大を更新した。

current account deposit 当座預金
　（=current deposit; ⇒cash in circulation）
　◆The central bank of Japan has deployed various measures to ease monetary policy, including cuts in the official discount rate and hikes in the target for current account deposits held by commercial banks at the central bank. 日銀は、公定歩合の引下げや銀行が日銀に持つ当座預金の残高目標の引上げなどを含めて、各種の金融緩和策を実施してきた。

current account deposit balance 当座預金残高, 日銀当座預金残高
　（=the balance of current account deposit）
　◆The current account deposit balance represents the sum of funds private financial institutions can use freely. 日銀当座預金残高は、民間の金融機関が自由に使える資金の総額を示す。

current account imbalances 経常収支の不均衡
　◆At the Seoul G-20 summit, all the leaders agreed to introduce "indicative guidelines" that would be conducive to reducing current account imbalances. 主要20か国・地域（G20）のソウル・サミット（首脳会議）で、全首脳が、経常収支不均衡の是正に役立つ「参考指針」を導入することで合意した。◆The sudden joint proposal by Washington and Seoul at the G-20 meeting called for fixing current account imbalances. G20（世界20か国・地域）会議での米国と韓国の突然の共同提案で、経常収支不均衡の是正が求められた。

current account levels 経常収支水準
　◆The g-20 nations will draw up a guideline to correct current account levels. 世界「主要」20か国・地域（G20）は、経常収支水準を是正するためのガイドラインを策定する。

current account surplus 経常黒字, 経常収支の黒字, 経常収支の黒字額 （⇒Chinese currency）
　ballooning of the current account surplus 経常黒字の大幅増, 経常黒字の急拡大
　growing [rising] current account surplus 経常黒字の拡大, 経常黒字幅の拡大
　narrowing current account surplus 経常黒字幅の縮小
　record [post] a current account surplus 経常黒字を計上する
　run a current account surplus 経常収支が黒字だ
　widening current account surplus 経常黒字幅の拡大
　◆Current account surplus is the gauge of trade in goods and services. 経常収支の黒字は、モノやサービスの取引を示す指標である。◆For the first six months of 2010, the current account surplus amounted to ¥8.526 trillion, up 47.3 percent from the same period last year. 2010年上半期の経常収支の黒字額は、前年同期比47.3%増の8兆5,262億円となった。◆The growth of China's current account surplus has slowed. 中国の経常黒字額は、このところ伸び悩んでいる。◆The United States tries to press China to reduce its current account surplus and raise the yuan by restricting its current account with a numerical goal. 米国は、経常収支を数値目標で縛って、中国に経常収支の黒字縮小と人民元切上げの圧力をかけようとしている。

current assets 流動資産 （=floating assets, near-cash assets, liquid assets: 比較的流動性が高く、1年以内に現金化される可能性がある資産）
　current assets and current liabilities 流動資産と流動負債
　current assets to current debts 流動比率
　　（=a current ratio）
　current assets turnover 流動資産回転率
　◆Current assets refer to those assets that are relatively liquid and are likely to be turned into cash within the next year. 流動資産は、比較的流動性が高く、次年度以内に現金化される可能性がある資産のことをいう。

current business year 今年度, 今期, 当年度, 当期
　◆The top 10 life insurers in the nation reported a total of ¥1.46 trillion in valuation losses on their securities holdings for the current business year. 今期決算で、国内生保の上位（主要）10社の保有有価証券[保有株式]の減損処理額は、1兆4,600億円に達した。

current coupon カレント・クーポン （=par yield: 流通価格がパー（par）に等しい債券の最終利回り）
　current coupon bond カレント・クーポン債, カレント・クーポン・ボンド（額面（par value）に近い価格で売買されている利付き債のこと）
　current coupon conventional カレント・クーポンのコンベンショナル
　current coupon pass-throughs カレント・クーポンのパス・スルー証券
　current coupon 30-year MBS カレント・クーポンの30年物モーゲージ証券（MBS）

current deposit 当座預金 （=checking account, current account, current account deposit; ⇒bank deposit, floating deposits）
　◆Ordinary bank deposits for individuals and current deposits for businesses were fully guaranteed until March 31, 2003. 個人の普通預金と企業の当座預金は、2003年3月31日まで全額保証された。◆The existing current deposit is mainly used by corporate depositors who withdraw money in the form of drafts or checks. これまでの当座預金は、主に手形や小切手の形で預金を引き出す法人顧客が利用している。

current economic crisis 現在の経済危機
　◆To overcome the current economic crisis, stimulus measures should take precedence over fiscal reconstruction for the time being. 現在の経済危機を克服するためには、当面は、財政再建よりも景気対策を優先しなければならない。

current economic situation 現在の経済情勢
　◆The government held a meeting on the current economic situation. 政府が、現在の経済情勢に関する会合を開いた。

current economic slump 現在の景気後退, 現在の不況
　◆The government expressed its optimistic expectations of the current economic slump. 政府は、現在の景気後退について楽観的な見通しを示した。

current fiscal and financial crisis 現在の財政・金融

危機, 今回の財政・金融危機
◆The current global fiscal and financial crisis began in European countries. 今回の世界的な財政・金融危機の震源地は、欧州だ。

current fiscal year 今年度, 今期
(=current business year, current year)
◆Companies listed on the Tokyo Stock Exchange's First Section posted a year-on-year increase of 33.2 percent in combined pretax profit in the first half of the current fiscal year. 東証一部上場企業の今年度上期(4-9月期)の経常利益合計は、前年同期比33.2%増となった。◆The government bond issuance worth about ¥44 trillion for the current fiscal year is the largest ever projected in an initial budget. 今年度の約44兆円の国債発行額は、当初予算としては史上最高だ。

current management 現経営陣
◆The purpose of issuing share warrants is to maintain the current management's control over the company. 株式予約権の発行は、現経営陣の会社の経営支配権を維持することを目的としている。

current momentum in the yen 現在の円相場の勢い
◆The current momentum in the yen is likely to take hold. 現在の円相場の勢いは、持続しそうだ。

current profit 経常利益 (=current account profit, pretax profit, recurring profit)
◆Toyota posted a current profit of ¥1 trillion for the business year that ended in March 2002. トヨタは、2002年3月期決算で、1兆円の経常利益を計上した。

current ratio 流動比率
◆Current ratio shows the relationship between current assets and current liabilities. 流動比率は、流動資産と流動負債との関係を示します。

current results 当期業績
◆Many investors set aside the cumulative effects of changes in accounting when looking at current results. 当期業績を見る場合、多くの投資家は、会計処理の変更による累積的影響を除外して考えます。

current service cost 現在勤務費用, 当期の勤務費用
◆Current service costs of retirement plans are accrued currently. 退職金制度の当期勤務費用は、当期に処理されています。

current state of the economy 景気の現状
◆A key gauge of the current state of the economy fell below the boom-or-bust threshold of 50 percent in September for the first time in five months. 景気の現状を示す主要基準(景気一致指数)が、9月は5か月ぶりに景気判断の分かれ目となる50%を下回った。

current value accounting 現在価値会計, 時価主義会計, CVA
 current value accounting standard 時価主義会計基準
 current value accounting system 時価会計制度, 時価主義会計制度 (=mark-to-market accounting system, market value accounting system)
◆The Financial Services Agency's Business Accounting Council adopted a U.S.-style current value accounting standard for corporate mergers to increase transparency of accounting rules. 金融庁の企業会計審議会は、会計規則の透明性を高めるため、会社合併については米国式の時価主義会計基準を採用した。

current yield 直接利回り, 直利 (債券の償還時に発生する額面と購入価格との差益・差損を考慮しないで、1年間の利息を購入価格で割り、100を掛けて算出。債券の購入価格に対する年間利息の割合を示す)

curtail (動)短縮する, 縮小する, 削減する, 節減する, 切り詰める, 弱める
◆Another important task facing major banks is to curtail their operating costs by consolidating branches. 大手行が抱えているもう一つ重要な課題は、店舗の統廃合による営業コストの削減だ。◆Curtailing spending is the right choice for individuals, but it prolongs a slump. 節減は個人の正しい選択ではあるが、それで景気停滞は長くなる。

curtailment (名)短縮, 縮小, 削減, 節減, 切り詰め
 production curtailment 生産削減, 減産, 生産調整, 操業短縮 (=curtailment of production)
 self-active curtailment 自主的操業短縮
 settlements, curtailments and termination benefits 清算、削減[縮小]と退職給付
 the curtailment of business outlays 設備投資の削減
 the curtailment of expenditure 経費削減, 経費節減
 the curtailment of operations 操業短縮, 操短 (=operation curtailment)

curve (名)曲線, 利回り曲線, 湾曲, 湾曲部, 曲がり, 曲線美, 曲線グラフ[図表], (売上などの)上昇, カーブ (⇒yield curve)
 across the curve 全般に, 全満期にわたって
 ahead of the curve 先を見越して, 進んでいる
 always behind curve いつも後手に回った, 後手後手の
 backdrop for the long-end of the curve 長期債相場を支える要因
 be behind the curve 後手に回る
 be on a growth curve 上昇中である
 behind the curve 遅れて
 bell-shaped curve 釣鐘状のカーブ
 buy across the curve 満期を問わず買う
 capital demand curve 資本需要曲線
 credit demand curve 信用需要曲線
 curve flattening 利回り曲線の平坦化, 長短利回り格差の縮小 (=flattening of the curve)
 downward curve 下降曲線
 fall behind the curve 後手に回る 後手を取る
 front end of the curve 短期物
 get ahead of the curve 先手を打つ 先回りする
 indifference curve 無差別曲線
 inflationary demand curve インフレ需要曲線
 inflationary supply curve インフレ供給曲線
 investment demand curve 投資需要曲線
 negative yield curve 利回り曲線が右下がりになっていること, 利回り曲線の右下がり
 normal curve 順イールド (=normal yield curve)
 positive yield curve 利回り曲線が右上がりになっていること, 利回り曲線の右上がり
 regression curve 回帰線
 S-curves 成長曲線
 short-dated area of the curve 短期債
 spread curves スプレッド曲線
 trade through the Government curve 国債利回りを割り込む
 upward curve 上昇曲線
 zero-coupon curve ゼロ・クーポン・カーブ
◆The eurozone's crisis management approach is always behind the curve. ユーロ圏の危機管理への取組みは、いつも後手に回っている。◆The Federal Reserve Board was behind the curve in raising rates. 米連邦準備制度理事会(FRB)は、利上げで後手に回った。

cushion (動)衝撃を和らげる, 弱める, 緩和する, 保護する, (ショックを)吸収する
 cushion potential losses 予想損失に備える, 予想損失を処理する
 cushion the economic downturn 景気低迷の影響を緩和

する, 景気低迷の動きを一部吸収する
　cushion the impact　衝撃［インパクト］を和らげる
◆A bank's capital adequacy ratio represents the amount of core capital it has to cushion potential losses, as a percentage of loans and other assets. 銀行の自己資本比率は、融資額などの資産に対して、予想損失の処理に充てられる自己資本［中核資本］がどれだけあるかを示す。

cushion　（名）対策, 緩和策, 衝撃を和らげるもの, 緩衝材, マイナス効果［悪影響］を除くもの, 予備費, 準備金, 貯蓄, 資金援助, クッション
　capital cushion　資金力
　cash cushion　資金力
　cushion against loan loss　貸倒れ損失に対する準備金
　cushion bond　クッション・ボンド, クッション債券, 値下りしにくい高クーポン債
　financial cushion　財政的保護対策, 財務面での余力
◆The bank is building a comfortable capital cushion, reducing risk and pushing ahead with sales of assets including its insurance business as planned. 同行は現在、リスク軽減を図るとともに計画どおり保険事業などの資産売却を進めて、十分な資金力の増強に努めている。

custodial　（形）管理の, 保管の, 保守の, 保管業務の, 保護の, 保護預りの, 養育権を持つ, 拘留の
　custodial account　保管預り勘定, カストディ勘定, 信託口座, 法定代理人管理口座
　custodial cost　証券保管費用
　custodial fee　保管業務手数料, カストディ手数料
　custodial fee cartel　カストディ手数料カルテル
　custodial receipt　有価証券預り証
　custodial services　証券保管業務, 管理業務
　foreign custodial arrangements　外国保管の取決め
　set aside the funds in a custodial account　資金を信託口座に繰り入れる

custodian　（名）証券保管機関, 保管人, 管理人, 米預託証券（ADR）の副受託銀行, カストディアン
　collateral custodian　担保証券の保管機関, 担保証券のカストディ
　Custodian Agreement　副受託契約
　custodian bank　保管銀行, カストディ銀行
　custodian trustee　保管受託者
　securities custodian　証券保管者

custody　（名）保管, 管理, 保護, 保護預り, カストディ
　custody account　保護預り勘定, カストディ勘定
　　（=custodial account）
　custody agreement　保管契約
　custody bill of lading　保管船荷証券
　custody fee　保管料
　custody service　証券代行業務
　dual custody　二重管理
　global custody　グローバル・カストディ
　international custody　国際保護預り
　one's share are held in custody by the trust bank　～の株式［保有株式］は同信託銀行の保護預りとなっている
　safe［safety］custody　保護預り, 保管
　securities in custody　保管有価証券
　the size of assets in one's custody　～の預り資産の規模
◆The size of assets in Mizuho-Nikko alliance's custody will almost match that of Nomura Holdings. みずほ・日興連合の預り資産の規模は、野村ホールディングスの預り資産の規模にほぼ匹敵することになる。

customer　（名）顧客, 得意先, 得意客, 取引先, 需要家, 投資家, 加入者, ユーザー　（⇒carrying amount）
　borrowing customer　借入先
　business customer　法人顧客, 企業取引先, 企業ユーザー
　commercial customer　事業法人顧客
　consumer banking customer　消費者金融部門の顧客
　consumer finance customer　消費者金融の顧客
　corporate banking customer　企業金融部門の顧客
　corporate customer　法人顧客
　　（⇒capital spending）
　customer agreement　顧客契約（margin agreement（信用取引契約）、hypothecation agreement（担保契約）ともいう）
　customer call　取引先訪問
　customer data　顧客情報
　customer interest　投資家の需要
　customer list　顧客リスト
　customer management system　顧客管理システム
　customer-order-driven dealing　顧客注文による取引
　customer profile　顧客構成, 顧客プロフィール
　customer［customer's］rates　（外国為替）対顧客相場
　customer's liabilities for acceptance and guarantee　支払い承諾見返り
　customers' men　得意先係
　customer's personal information　顧客の個人情報
　customers' securities　保管有価証券
　forward exchange transaction with a customer　対顧客先物為替取引
　individual customer　個人顧客
　large customer　大口顧客
　lure customers　顧客を勧誘する
　major customer　主要顧客, 主要得意先, 大口顧客
　retail customer　小口顧客, 個人投資家
　the customer buying rate　顧客買い相場
　the customer selling rate　顧客売り相場
◆Banks seem eager to attract more individual customers by focusing on mortgage products. 銀行各社は、モーゲージ商品に注目して、積極的に個人顧客の取り込みに取り組んでいるようだ。◆Customers whose assets at the bank total about ¥10 million will receive a maximum of ¥2 million in insurance if their money is withdrawn illicitly by a third party with a bogus card. 同行では、預け入れ資産が1,000万円程度の預金者が、第三者に偽造カードを使って不正に預金が引き出された場合には、最大200万円の保険金が支払われる。◆For bank customers, deposits at banks are equivalent to unsecured loans to financial institutions. 銀行預金者［利用者］にとって、銀行預金は金融機関に対する無担保融資にあたる。◆In the life insurance sector, the practice of luring customers by touting the bad performances of other insurers has been called into question. 生保業界では、他社の経営不振をあおって顧客を勧誘する行為（風評営業）が問題になっている。◆In wrap accounts, a customer sets the overall investment policy, including investment period and profit target. ラップ口座では、顧客が投資期間や運用益の目標などの大まかな運用方針を決める。◆Sellers of multiple-debtor lists, produced by collecting information about consumer finance customers, are contributing to the spread of illegal moneylending. 消費者金融の顧客情報を入手して作った多重債務者リストを売る名簿業者が、ヤミ金融の横行に一役買っている。◆The brokerage's main services for individual customers will be asset management advisory services, focusing on the sale of products such as investment trust funds that invest in foreign equities, and money market funds denominated in foreign currencies. 同証券会社は、株式の主な個人顧客向け（売買仲介）業務として、外国株を組み込んだ投資信託や外貨建てMMF（マネー・マーケット・ファンド）などの商品の販売を中心に、資産運用顧問業務を展開する方針だ。◆The personal information of customers who used

credit cards for premium payments might have been leaked. クレジット・カードを使って保険料を支払った顧客の個人情報が、外部に流出した恐れがある。◆The repurchasing method, which has customers buy highly negotiable cash vouchers, violates the industry rule. 顧客に換金性の高い金券類を購入させる買取り方式は、業界の規約に違反する。◆To offer customers a new way to purchase insurance, nonlife insurance companies have begun cooperating with cell phone companies. 顧客に保険加入のための新サービスを提供するため、損害保険各社は、携帯電話会社との提携に乗り出した。

customer account 顧客の口座
◆The bank made 30,000 double withdrawals for transfers from customer accounts. 同行は、顧客の口座振替で3万件の二重引落しをした。

customer assets 預り資産, 顧客からの預り資産（⇒commodity futures brokerage）
◆The customer assets of Nomura Holdings total around ￥63 trillion. 野村ホールディングスの預り資産総額は、約63兆円（2004年9月末現在）に達する。

customer base 顧客基盤, 顧客層
◆Shinsei and Aozora banks announced a plan to merge in an effort to expand their customer bases and improve earnings. 新生銀行とあおぞら銀行は、顧客基盤の拡大と収益力の強化を狙って、合併計画を発表した。◆The biggest advantage for the bank in entering the venture will be to increase its customer base without having to open expensive new branch offices. 同行にとってこの新規事業への参入の最大の利点は、コストのかかる新店舗を開設するまでもなく、顧客基盤を拡大できることだ。◆With the capital tie-up with Norinchukin Bank, MFG aims to boost its customer base in the securities sector. 農林中央金庫との資本提携で、みずほフィナンシャルグループは、証券分野の顧客基盤の強化を目指している。

customer focus 顧客志向, 顧客重視
◆Customer focus is the firm's core strategy for weathering the forces of competition. 顧客重視［志向］が、競争圧力に対応するための同社の基本戦略だ。

customer repurchase agreement 証券の売戻し条件付き買入れ, カスタマー・レポ（=customer repo, customer RP: 市中銀行の支払い準備（bank reserves）を一時的に増加させることを目的として、ニューヨーク連邦準備銀行（Federal Reserve Bank of New York）が公開市場操作（open market operation）の一環として実施する。⇒repurchase agreement, system repurchase agreement）

customer screening 顧客審査
◆The firm plans to offer not only retail lending, but also corporate lending by utilizing the customer screening know-how of its partner bank. 同社は、共同出資する銀行が持つ顧客審査のノウハウを活用して、個人向け融資のほかに法人向け融資業務も提供する計画だ。

customer statement 顧客勘定書

customer transaction 対顧客取引
◆Concerns have been raised over the ability of Internet banking services to verify the identity of new depositors or to guarantee the security of customer transactions. インターネット・バンキングについては、新規預金者の身元確認や対顧客取引の安全保証の点で、その能力に対して懸念が提起されている。

customer's man 株式のセールスマン, 外務員

customer's personal information 顧客の個人情報

cut （動）削減する, 切り詰める, 節減する, 縮小する, 減らす, 削除する, 供給を止める, 引き下げる, 下げる, 無断で欠席する, 切り取る, 編集する, 製作する, 録音する, カットする
cut back on facilities 設備を削減する
cut labor costs 人件費を引き下げる
cut one's earnings estimate 業績予想を引き下げる, 収益予想を下方修正する
cut one's long-term debt rating ～の長期格付けを引き下げる
cut one's nonperforming loans ～の不良債権を削減する
cut operating costs 営業コストを削減する, 営業経費を削減する
cut payrolls 人員を削減する
cut spending 支出を減らす, 支出を削減する
cut the discount rate 公定歩合を引き下げる
◆Even after Greece's debt load is cut, Greece's credit grade is likely to remain low. ギリシャの債務負担を削減しても、ギリシャの信用格付けは、低水準にとどまる見込みだ。◆Fiscal resources of ￥1.6 trillion cannot be scrounged together simply by recasting the budget and cutting wasteful spending. 1.6兆円の財源は、予算の組替えや無駄の削減だけでは捻出（ねんしゅつ）できない。◆If the securities firms rush to cut these commissions, they may not be able to continue to rely on income from commissions as a major source of profit. これらの証券会社が手数料の値引き競争に走れば、主な収益源として株式の売買委託手数料による収入に今後とも頼ることは難しくなる。◆Moody's Investors Service cut General Motors Corp.'s long-term debt rating. ムーディーズ・インベスターズ・サービス（米国の格付け会社）は、ゼネラル・モーターズ（GM）の長期債格付けを引き下げた。◆Moody's Investors Service cut Japan's yen-denominated debt rating by one notch to Aa3 from Aa2 and maintained a negative outlook. 米国の格付け会社ムーディーズは、日本の円建て国債の格付けを「Aa2」から「Aa3」に一段階引き下げ、「ネガティブ（弱含み）」の見通しを据え置いた。◆Moody's will consider cutting the United States' top-notch credit rating if any progress isn't made in talks to raise the U.S. debt limit. 米政府の法定債務上限引上げについての（米議会との）交渉で進展がなければ、ムーディーズは、米国債の最上位の格付けを引下げる方向で検討する方針だ。◆S&P may cut the credit rating of bonds issued by the European Financial Stability Facility（EFSF）. スタンダード・アンド・プアーズ（S&P）は、欧州金融安定基金（EFSF）が発行する債券の格付け［信用格付け］を引き下げる可能性がある。◆Standard & Poor's cut the U.S. credit rating for the first time. スタンダード・アンド・プアーズ（S&P）が、米国債の格付けを史上初めて引き下げた。◆The company plans to cut its interest-bearing debts to about ￥200 billion this business year. 同社は、今年度中に有利子負債を2,000億円台まで削減する方針だ。◆The federal funds rate, a benchmark short-term interest rate, was cut to 3.5 percent per annum and the official discount rate to 3 percent per annum. 短期金利の誘導目標であるフェデラル・ファンド（FF）金利は年3.5％、公定歩合は年3％に引き下げられた。◆The federal government will cut its fiscal deficit by $2.4 trillion over ten years. 米政府は、今後10年間で財政赤字を2.4兆ドル削減する。

cut （名）削減, 節減, 縮小, 値引き, 引下げ, 切下げ, 配給停止, 中断, 停電, （利益の）取り分, 分け前, 傷口, カット
aid cut 援助削減, 援助カット
budget cuts 予算の引下げ
budget deficit cut 財政赤字の削減
cut in headline rate 利下げ
　　（=cut in interest rates, rate cut）
cuts in expenditures 歳出カット, 歳出削減
　　（=cutting government outlays）
cuts in overtime work 残業カット
cuts in spending 支出削減
dividend cut 配当引下げ, 減配
expenditure cut 支出削減, 経費削減
Fed cut 米連邦準備制度理事会（FRB）による利下げ
further rate cut 追加利下げ, 一層の利下げ, もう一段の利下げ

income tax cut　所得税減税
interest rate cut　利下げ, 金利引下げ, 利率引下げ
　（=rate cut）
key rate cut　公定歩合の引下げ
　（=discount rate cut, official discount rate cut）
parity cut　平価切下げ
pay cut　賃下げ, 賃金引下げ, 賃金削減, 賃金カット
　（=wage cut）
price cut　値下げ, 価格引下げ
production cut　減産　（=output cut）
tax cut　減税　（=tax reduction）
wage cut　賃金引下げ, 賃下げ, 賃金の削減, 賃金カット
workforce cut　人員削減
◆Austerity measures such as drastic cuts in spending on public works projects should be avoided. 公共事業［公共事業費, 公共事業支出］の大幅カットなどの緊縮政策は, 避けるべきだ。◆Economic stimulus measures such as tax cuts and additional public works projects work only as temporary remedies. 減税や公共事業の追加などの景気浮揚策は, 一時的なカンフル剤にすぎない。◆JAL is implementing various corporate restructuring measures, including wage and workforce cuts. 日航は現在, 賃金カットや人員削減などの企業リストラ［リストラ］策をいろいろ進めている。◆The federal government will initially make a spending cut of $900 billion, while it will raise the debt ceiling by the same amount immediately. 米政府はまず0.9兆ドルの歳出削減を行う一方, 債務上限を直ちに引き上げる。◆The G-7 leaders merely welcomed Washington's economic stimulus measures in the form of interest rate cuts and tax cuts as "positive." G7首脳は, 利下げや減税などの形での米政府の景気刺激策を「積極的」として歓迎しただけだ。◆The slump in domestic new car sales has accelerated cuts in output and staffing levels. 国内新車販売の低迷で, 減産と人員削減が加速している。◆There is a limit to the effects of interest rate cuts. 金利引下げの効果には, 限界がある。

cut back on　～を削減［縮小］する, ～を減らす, ～を切り詰める, ～を控える
◆The global economic slowdown has forced foreign and domestic companies to cut back on overseas trips. 世界的な景気後退で, 内外の企業が海外出張を控えざるをえなくなっている。

cut brokerage fees　売買手数料を引き下げる
◆The two major securities companies cut brokerage fees further for major clients. 大手証券会社2社は, 大口顧客に対して株式売買手数料をさらに引き下げた。

cut budget deficits　財政赤字を削減する
◆The Greek government has set forth measures to decrease the number of government employees and raise taxes to cut its budget deficits. 財政赤字削減のため, ギリシャ政府は公務員削減や増税策を打ち出した。

cut down on　～を切り詰める, ～を削減する
◆Government spending must be cut down on as much as possible to reduce the government's bond issuance. 政府の国債発行額を減らすには, できるだけ歳出を切り詰める必要がある。

cut federal spending　連邦支出を削減する
◆The Obama administration failed to cut federal spending. オバマ政権は, 連邦支出を削減しなかった。

cut in the U.S. long-term credit rating　米国の長期国債格付けの引下げ
◆The S&P cut in the U.S. long-term credit rating by one notch to AA-plus from AAA resulted from concerns about the nation's budget deficits and climbing debt burden. スタンダード・アンド・プアーズ（S&P）が米国の長期国債格付けを最上級のAAA（トリプルA）からAA（ダブルA）に1段階引き下げた理由は, 米国の財政赤字と債務負担の増大に対する懸念だ。

cut interest rates　金利を引き下げる, 利下げする
◆In a joint response to the global financial crisis, the U.S. FRB, ECB and central banks in Britain, Canada, Sweden and Switzerland cut interest rates in unison. 世界的な金融危機への協調対応策として, 米連邦準備制度理事会（FRB）, 欧州中央銀行（ECB）と英国, カナダ, スウェーデン, スイスの中央銀行は, それぞれ金利［政策金利］を同時に引き下げた。◆Speculation that the Fed would cut interest rates Tuesday heightened. 連邦準備制度理事会（FRB）が火曜日に利下げに踏み切るとの観測も, 浮上している。

cut into　～を減らす, 下げる, ～に割り込む, ～を妨げる
◆The slowdown in exports has also drastically cut into Japan's current account surplus. 輸出の鈍化で, 日本の経常黒字も激減している。

cut nonperforming loans　不良債権を削減する
◆The merger plan will not go ahead unless the bank makes unstinting efforts to cut its nonperforming loans. 同行が不良債権の削減に向けて惜しみない努力をしないかぎり, 統合計画が前に進むことはないだろう。

cut one's main interest rate　政策金利を引き下げる, 主要金利を引き下げる
◆The European Central Bank cut its main interest rate by 0.25 percent following heavy pressure for a rate cut to spur flagging economic growth. 失速気味の経済成長に刺激を与えるため利下げを求める強い圧力を受けて, 欧州中央銀行（ECB）はその主要［政策］金利を0.25%引き下げた。

cut spending　経費を削減する, 支出を削減する, 予算を削減する　（⇒spending cut）
◆The massive figure of tax revenue shortfall is way beyond what local municipalities can do by cutting spending. この巨額の税収不足は, 地方自治体の経費削減で対応できる範囲を大きく超えている。

cut the shares 100 percent　株式を100%減資する
◆JAL's stocks may lose market value to zero if the corporate turnaround body cuts the shares 100 percent by delisting JAL from the Tokyo stock market. 企業再生支援機構が東京株式市場から日航の上場を廃止して日航株を100%減資したら, 日航株の市場価値はゼロになる可能性がある。

cuts in discount rate　公定歩合の引下げ
◆The central bank has deployed various measures to ease monetary policy, including cuts in the discount rate and hikes in the target for current account deposits held by commercial banks at the central bank. 日銀は, 公定歩合の引下げや銀行が日銀に持つ当座預金の残高目標の引上げなどを含めて, 各種の金融緩和策を実施してきた。

cuts in public spending　公共事業費の削減
◆Because of the prolonged recession and cuts in public spending, the volume of construction businesses continues to shrink by the year. 長引く不況や公共事業費の削減などで, 建設の事業量が年々減少している。

cutback　（名）削減, 縮小, 圧縮, 短縮（複数形で使われることが多い）
cutback in expenditure　支出削減
cutback［cutbacks］in jobs　雇用削減
cutback［cutbacks］in output　生産削減, 減産
　（=production cutback）
cutback in work hours　労働時間の短縮
inventory cutback　在庫削減
power cutbacks　電力削減
◆The impact of cutbacks stemming from the shrinking tax income is affecting local residents. 税収の減少による経費削減の衝撃は, 地元住民にも影響を及ぼしている。

cutting　（名）削減, 引下げ, 割引, 利札（cuttings）
cost cutting　コスト［費用］の引下げ, 経費削減, コスト削減
cost-cutting measures［exercise, plan, steps, strategy］　コ

スト削減策
cutting a melon 利益の分配, メロンの切り分け（従業員に対するボーナスの支給を含めて, 現金や株式配当による利益の分配のこと）
cutting edge 最前線, 最先端, 最新式, 最新型, 最新鋭, 先頭, 主導的地位, 鋭利な刃物（=leading edge, sophisticated, state-of-the-art, top of the line）
cutting government outlays 歳出削減
cutting margins 利益率の引下げ
cutting rates 利下げ, 金利引下げ（=cutting interest rates）
cutting staff 人員削減
deficit cutting 赤字削減（=cut in the deficit）
melon cutting 特別配当, 利益の分配
price cutting 値引き, 価格引下げ
◆The financial markets' confidence in the U.S. currency has been shaken further by the S&P's cutting of the U.S. credit rating. スタンダード・アンド・プアーズ（S&P）が米国債の格付けを引き下げたことで, 金融市場の米ドルへの信認が一段と揺らいでいる。◆The focal point from now on will be a deficit-cutting plan to be discussed by the suprapartisan congressional committee. 今後の焦点は, 超党派の議会委員会が協議する赤字削減策だ。

cyber attack サイバー攻撃
◆The government listed such areas as the central and local governments, the financial sector, electricity, gas, information and communications and airlines as those that should be protected from cyber attacks. サイバー攻撃から守るべき分野として, 政府は政府・地方自治体, 金融, 電気, ガス, 情報通信や航空などの分野を挙げた。

cycle （名）周期, 循環, 動向, 景気, サイクル
a favorable cycle of events 好業績
business cycle 景気, 景気循環, 景気サイクル
cash cycle 現金循環
consumption cycle 消費サイクル
credit cycle 信用サイクル
cycle billing 月締め
cycle recovery 景気回復
declining cycle 景気後退
down cycle 景気悪化, サイクルの下降期
economic cycle 経済循環, 景気循環, 景気動向
economic up-cycle 景気回復
equity capital cycle 自己資本サイクル
growth cycle 成長率循環
housing cycle 住宅サイクル
interest rate cycle 金利サイクル
inventory correction [adjustment] cycle 在庫調整サイクル
inventory investment cycle 在庫投資サイクル
investment cycle 投資サイクル
life cycle 生活循環, 製品寿命, 製品ライフサイクル, ライフサイクル
magnitude of the cycle 景気循環の振幅
ordering cycle 発注間隔
output cycle 生産動向
product life cycle 製品サイクル, 商品サイクル
production cycles 生産サイクル
residential investment cycle 住宅投資サイクル
strengthening of the economic cycle 景気が勢いを増すこと
virtuous cycle 好循環
◆A favorable cycle of events has begun to emerge, with strong performances leading to an increase in jobs and higher wage, resulting in boosts in consumption. 好業績が雇用改善や賃金の上昇につながり, その結果消費も上向くなど, 景気動向に好循環が見えてきた。◆The economy still remains in a recovery phase in the business cycle. 景気は, まだ回復局面にある [景気の回復基調がまだ続いている]。◆The virtuous cycle of growth in production, income and spending has been basically maintained. 生産・所得と支出の伸びの好循環 [好循環メカニズム] は, 基本的に維持されている。

cyclical （形）周期的な, 循環的な, 景気循環の, 景気サイクルの, 景気 [景気変動] に敏感な
be historically cyclical 好不況を繰り返す, これまで景気サイクルに左右されてきた
counter-cyclical 景気循環に逆行する, 反循環的, 景気循環の波を抑える
cyclical activities 景気循環型事業
cyclical adjusted 景気循環調整済みの
cyclical downturn 景気低迷, 景気後退
cyclical ecological system 循環的生態系
cyclical economic factors 景気循環的要因
cyclical effects 景気循環要因（=cyclical element, cyclical reason）
cyclical factors 循環的要因
cyclical fluctuation 景気変動, 周期的景気変動, 循環変動（=cyclical variation）
cyclical indication 景気指標
cyclical industry 市況産業
cyclical peak 景気循環のピーク, サイクルのピーク, 景気の頂上
cyclical pickup 景気回復, 景気の上昇局面
cyclical recovery 景気回復
cyclical stock 景気循環株, 循環株, 景気動向に敏感な（景気動向に左右される）株式銘柄（=cyclicals）
cyclical trough 景気の谷, 景気サイクルの底
cyclical upturn 景気回復（=cyclical upturn in the economy）
cyclical weakness 景気低迷, 景気の下降局面
highly cyclical 景気循環の影響が大きい, 景気循環色が強い, 景気変動に敏感な
reach a cyclical trough 景気が底入れする
◆Cyclical economic factors are to blame for Japan's budget deficit to a certain extent. 日本の財政赤字は, ある程度, 景気循環的要因によるものだ。

D

daily average for a month 月中平均
◆Most companies use the daily average for a month of the share prices in gauging the value of latent gains or losses in their stockholdings. 大半の企業は, 保有株式の含み損益を算出する際に株価の月中平均を使っている。

daily average for the Nikkei index 日経平均の月中平均株価
◆The daily average for the Nikkei index in September stood at 10,649, up 30.3 percent from 8,169 in March. 9月の日経平均の月中平均株価は, 3月の8,169円に比べて30.3％増の10,649円となった。

daily limit 値幅制限（株価の乱高下を防ぐため, 証券取引所や日本証券業協会が制限している1日の株価変動幅のこと）

daily turnover 1日当たりの取引高
◆Average daily turnover on the Tokyo Stock Exchange grew 86 percent year-on-year to ￥663 billion during the April-

June quarter. 東京証券取引所の4～6月期の1日当たり平均取引高［売買代金］は、前年同期に比べて86%増の6,630億円に達した。

damage （動）損害を与える，損傷を与える，損なう，傷つける
◆Factories, shops and farms were destroyed or severely damaged due to the March 11 Great East Japan Earthquake. 2011年3月11日の東日本大震災で、工場や店舗、農地が壊滅もしくは大打撃を受けた。◆If the European financial crisis expands, it will damage the recovering global economy. 欧州の金融危機が拡大すれば、回復途上にある世界経済に打撃を与えることになる。◆Japan's financial system was badly damaged with the collapse of the bubble economy and deflation. 日本の金融システムは、バブル崩壊とデフレで深手を負った。◆Protectionist moves could damage the global economy. 保護主義的な動きは、世界経済に打撃を与えかねない。

damage （名）損害，被害 （複数形には「損害賠償金、損害賠償額、損害額」の意味もある。⇒compensation payments, nonlife insurance company）
actual damages　現実的損害賠償（金），実損
claim damages　損害賠償を請求する
cover damage caused by earthquake or tsunami　地震や津波による被害を補償する
cumulative damages　累積損害賠償額，賠償累計額
direct damages　直接損害
incidental damages　付随的損害，付随的損害賠償，偶発的損害
indirect damages　間接的損害
money damages　金銭による損害賠償
passive damages　逸失利益
punitive damages　懲罰的賠償
seek damages　損害賠償を請求する，損害賠償を求める
◆Fire insurance did not cover damage caused by an earthquake or tsunami before the 1964 Niigata Earthquake. 1964年の新潟地震以前は、火災保険で地震や津波による被害が補償されなかった。◆It is difficult for financial institutions to confirm the amounts of damages from illegal withdrawals with bogus cards. 金融機関が、偽造カードを使った不正な預金引出しによる被害額を確認するのは難しい。◆Three major domestic nonlife insurance companies will set a ceiling for fire-insurance payouts for corporate clients in cases of damages caused by terrorist attacks. 国内の大手損害保険3社は、テロ被害の（テロ攻撃による損害を受けた場合の）顧客企業向け火災保険の補償額に上限を設ける方針だ。

damage assessment　損害査定
◆Many people distrust noninsurance firms for their strict damage assessments. 損害保険会社の厳しい損害査定に対する不信感は、根強い。◆The five business fields in the tie-up agreement are product development, marketing, insurance underwriting, damage assessment and reinsurance. 提携契約の5業務分野は、商品開発、マーケティング、保険引受け、損害査定と再保険である。◆The nonlife insurance company will provide the company with know-how on damage assessment and product development. この損害保険会社は、同社に損害査定や商品開発に関するノウハウを提供する。

damage compensation　損害賠償
◆Regarding TEPCO's damage compensation, creditor financial institutions have already offered cooperation by refinancing existing loans. 東電の損害賠償に関して、取引金融機関は、既存の融資の借換えなどですでに協力している。◆Toshiba may demand damage compensation from Sony, and others may follow suit. 東芝はソニーに対する損害賠償請求を検討しており、他社もこれに追随する可能性がある。

damages lawsuit　損害賠償訴訟
◆Shinsei Bank reached an out-of-court settlement in a damage lawsuit with a bankruptcy administrator of a borrower company. 新生銀行が、融資先企業の破産管財人との損害賠償訴訟で示談による和解に達した。

damages suit　損害賠償請求訴訟，損害賠償訴訟
（=damages lawsuit；⇒file a damages suit against）
◆The ruling came after the same district court dismissed a similar damages suit in May. 判決は、同地裁が5月に同様の損害賠償を求めた訴訟の請求を退けた後に出された。◆The victims of cash card fraud will file a damages suit in March with the Tokyo and district courts against eight financial institutions. キャッシュ・カード詐欺の被害者が3月に、8金融機関を相手取って損害賠償請求訴訟を東京、横浜両地裁に起こす。

dampen （動）弱める，抑える，抑制する，鈍らせる，鈍化させる，～を沈静化させる，～に水を差す，冷え込ませる，～の低迷を招く，～の気勢などをそぐ，減退させる，熱意などをくじく
dampen demand　需要を抑制する
dampen household spending　個人消費を抑える，個人消費の低迷を招く
dampen inflation　インフレを弱める
dampen one's enthusiasm for capital spending　設備投資の意欲を冷え込ませる，設備投資の意欲をそぐ
dampen price fluctuations　価格変動を抑える
dampen the world economy　世界経済の低迷を招く，世界経済の足かせとなる
dampening effect　抑制効果
（=dampening influence）
◆High crude oil prices will dampen the world economy. 原油高は、世界経済の低迷を招く。◆The strong yen will eat into the profits of exporters and dampen their enthusiasm for capital spending. 円高は、輸出企業の利益を減らし、輸出企業の設備投資の意欲をそぐことになる。◆The yen's appreciation may dampen recovering investment in plant and equipment. 円高は、回復してきた設備投資に水を差しかねない。

danger （名）危険，危険性，危機，脅威，危険物，可能性，恐れ
be in danger of　～の危険にさらされている，～する危険性［恐れ］がある
be in danger of slipping into a double-dip recession. 景気の二番底に陥る危険にさらされている，景気の二番底に陥る可能性［恐れ］がある
danger money　危険手当て （=danger pay）
herald the danger　危険性をはらむ
out of danger　危険［危機］を脱して
◆The rational actions for survival taken by individual companies herald a danger that could lead the Japanese economy into contracted equilibrium. 生き残りをかけて個々の企業が取っている合理的な行動が、日本経済を縮小均衡に導く危険性をはらんでいる。◆The U.S. economy is in danger of slipping into a double-dip recession. 米経済は、景気の二番底に陥る可能性［恐れ］がある。

danger zone　危険水域
◆The European bond market is truly in a knife-edge situation as the yield on 10-year Italian government bonds has surged above 7 percent, the so-called danger zone that may result in a debt crisis. 10年物イタリア国債の流通利回りが、債務危機に陥る「危険水域」とされる7%超に上昇したため、欧州債券市場は予断を許さない状況にある。◆The 10-year bond yield of Spain has likewise neared the 7 percent level, the danger zone that may fall into a debt crisis. スペインの10年物国債利回り［国債流通利回り］も、債務危機に陥る恐れがある危険水域の7%台に迫った。

data （名）情報，文書，資料，指標，統計，データ
data on transactions　取引データ
data processing method　情報処理方式，データ処理方式

economic data　景気指標, 経済指標, 経済データ
employment data　雇用統計　(=labor market data)
financial data　財務データ, 財務資料
market data　市場統計, 市場データ, 市場資料, 相場の動き
public data on issuer　発行体に関する公表データ
stock price data　株価資料
trade data　貿易統計
◆Each of the three banks has a different data processing method. 3行の情報処理方式は、それぞれ異なる。◆Mizuho Securities Co.'s sell order error was made when its staffer entered data incorrectly. みずほ証券の誤発注[発注ミス]は、同社の担当者がデータを誤って入力した際に生じた。◆The firm is negotiating with the name-list broker to buy back the leaked personal data to prevent it from spreading further. 個人情報の流出拡大を防ぐため、同社はこの名簿業者と流出した個人情報を買い取る交渉をしている。

date　(名)日時, 日付け　(⇒closing date, due date)
accounting date　決算日
acquisition date　取得日
after bill date　手形振出日後
announcement date　募集発行日
appointed date　約束の期日, 指定期日
approximate date　予想日付け
at three months' date　3か月後の日に
balance sheet date　貸借対照表日付け
base date　基準日
bill of date　確定日付け手形
closing date　決算日, 締切日
closing date for applications　募集締切日
consumer expiration date　有効期限
date and time of execution　約定日時
date bill　期限付き手形
date draft　確定日払い手形, 期限付き手形, 期日後払い手形
date ended　終了日
date of a draft　手形の日付け
date of acceptance　引受けの日付け, 引受日, 受諾日
date of declaration　配当宣言日, 配当発表日
date of delivery　受渡し日
date of expiration　満了日(契約期間が円満に終了した場合)
date of issue　発行日, 保険証券発行日, 提出日, 小切手の振出日, 作成日　(=date of issuance)
date of loading　船積み年月日
date of maturity　満期日, 支払い期日, 支払い日
date of order　注文日
date of payment　支払い日, 支払い期日, 期日, 配当支払い日, 配当日　(=due date)
date of record　配当基準日, 配当受領確定日　(各事業年度に配当を受け取る権利のある株主を決める日のこと。株価は、一般に配当基準日を過ぎると配当の分だけ価値が下がって安くなる)
date of repayment　返済期日
date of shipment　船積み日, 船積み日付け, 出荷期日, 出荷日付け, 発送日, 船会社への貨物の引渡し日
date of the bill of lading　船荷証券日
date of the financial statements　財務諸表日
date of validation　発行日
date order　日付け順
date stamp　日付け印
date started　開始日

deal date　取引日
delivery date　納期, 納入日, 引渡し日
deposit date　預託日
effective date　発効日, 施行日, 実施年月日, 取引開始日
eligible value date　適性為替資金受払い日, 適格資金受払い日
exact date of　〜の確定期日
expiration date　行使期限, 有効期限, 満期日
expiry date　失効日, 有効期限
filing date　申請日, 提出日, 出願日
fixed date　確定日付け
futures date　先物期日
interest payment date　利息支払い日
invoice date　請求書の日付け, 請求日
issue date　発行日
maturity date　満期日
odd date　特別期日
offering date　募集取扱い日, 応募期日, 応募日, 申込み期日, 割当日
opening date for applications　募集開始日
out of date　日限切れ
payable after date　(手形の)日付け後払い
probable date　想定日付け, 予想日付け, 予想期日
report date　決算日
settlement date　決済日, 決算日, 受渡し日
shipping date　船積み日, 発送日
stock-in date　入荷日
stock-out date　出荷日
target date　目標期日, 目標日時
trade [transaction] date　取引日, 約定日
valuation date　評価日
value date　(為替取引の)受渡し日, 手形決済日
◆Any payment not made when due will, in addition to any other right or remedy of Licensor, incur a finance charge at the lesser of three hundred basis points over the 3-month London Inter Bank Offered Rate ("LIBOR+3") on the date payment was due or the highest applicable legal contract rate. 支払いが支払い期日までに履行されない場合、ライセンサーの他の権利や救済請求権に加えて、支払い期日時点の3か月物ロンドン銀行間取引金利(LIBOR)プラス3%(LIBOR+3%)または適用される最高法定約定金利のうち、いずれか低いほうの金利の金融費用が発生する。◆The closing balance sheet fairly presents the financial position of the Corporation at the closing date in conformity with United States GAAP. クロージング時現在の貸借対照表は、米国の一般に認められた会計原則[米国の会計基準]に従って、クロージング日の「会社」の財政状態を適正に表示している。

date of issuance　発行日, 発行時　(=date of issue)
◆The 8% convertible bonds are convertible into 40 shares of common stock for each $1,000 bond, and were not considered common stock equivalents at the date of issuance. 8%利付き転換社債は、1,000ドルの社債についてそれぞれ普通株式40株に転換できるが、発行時には準普通株式とは考えられなかった。

date of (the) conversion　転換日, 転換時
◆Under the book value method, the carrying value of the convertible bonds at the date of the conversion would be used to account for the conversion. 簿価法では、転換時の転換社債の簿価が、転換の会計処理に使われる。

dated　(形)日付けのある, 〜日付けの, 時代遅れの, 古めかしい, 古臭い
a dated date　利息発生日, 利息起算日, 発行日
dated ahead　先日付けの

dated debt　期限付き債
dated money　日付け貨幣
dated securities　期日付き証券, 償還期日が決まっている債券
dated type　日付け式
long-dated bill　長期手形
longer dated debt　長期負債
post-dated check　事後日付け小切手
short-dated bill　短期手形
ultra long dated issuance　超長期債
yields on long-dated paper　長期債利回り

dating　(名)日付けの記入
dating ahead [forward]　前日付け, 事前日付け
dating backward　後日付け
dating machine　日付け機, 日付け打抜き機

DAX　ダックス指数　(ドイツの代表的な株価指数で Deutsche Aktienindexの略)

day　(名)日, 1日, 期日, 期限, デイ
a day book [day-book, daybook]　当座帳,(会計)取引日記帳
a day's high　本日の高値
account day　決算日, 勘定日, 株式受渡し日
announcement day　募集開始日
artificial [civil] days　常用日, 暦日
banking day　銀行の営業日
both end days included　(利息計算での)両端(りょうは)入り日数
business day　営業日
closing day　払込み日, 決算日
contango day　繰越決算日
continuation day　(株式取引の)繰越決算日
current (running) days　連続日数
day count　日数計算
day count basis　日割りベース
day job　本業, 正規の仕事
day loan　当日貸付け
　(=clearance [clearing] loan, morning loan)
day of delivery　交付日
day of maturity　満期日
day order　当日注文(当日だけ有効な注文), 当日限り注文
day service　日帰り介護, デイサービス
day trade　デイ・トレード　(=day trading: インターネットでの株や債券などの取引)
day trade software　デイトレード・ソフトウエア(株式取引専用のソフトウエア)
days of grace　支払い猶予期間, 恩恵日
days payable　買掛金回転日数
days to run　割引日数
declaration day　(株式配当などの)宣言日,(株式購入の)通知日
E-day　ユーロの市中流通開始日
exclusive of days of grace　支払い猶予期間を除いて
five clear days　5営業日, まる5日間
last trading day　最終取引日
mail days interest　郵送期間金利
non-business day　休業日
offering day　募集取扱い日
on day one of the contract term　契約期間の初日
one-day settlement　翌日決済

prompt day　支払い期日, 勘定清算日, 受渡し日
running days　延べ日数, 連続日数
same day funds　同日物資金
same day settlement　同日決済
setting day　(株式の)清算日, 決算日
　(=account day)
settlement day　決済日, 勘定日, 決算日, 受渡し日, 期日
skip-day settlement　2日後決済
term day　支払い日
the day of delivery　(株式などの)受渡し日, 交付日
the day of maturity　満期日
the day of reckoning　決算日, 勘定日, 借金清算日
the days of grace　猶予(ゆうよ)期間, 恩恵日(手形支払い猶予期間, 据え置き期間
　(=grace period)
trade day　取引日
transfer day　名義書換え日
vesting day　発効期日
working day　営業日
◆On European and U.S. markets, stock prices fell sharply the previous day. 前日の欧米市場の株価は, 急落した。

day-to-day　(形)毎日の, 日々の, 日常の, 当座の
day-to-day accommodation　当座貸し
day-to-day cash flow position　日々の資金繰り
day-to-day loan　当座貸し, コール資金の翌日物
　(=call loan)
day-to-day money　当日貸し, 当座貸し 当日借り
day-to-day operations　日常の営業活動, 日常業務
day-to-day repos　翌日物現先(げんさき)
on a day-to-day basis　1日1日単位で, 1日1日を基準に

day trader　デイ・トレーダー　(=scalper: 定職を持たないで, パソコンを通じて1日中, 株取引などをするセミプロの個人投資家のこと。⇒equity market)
◆Day traders buy and sell stocks, bonds or other securities on a moment-to-moment basis, usually using computer terminals linked to vast trading networks. While this holds the promise of quick gains, it also makes it easy to lose money. デイ・トレーダーは, 一般に広範な株取引のネットワークに接続したコンピュータの端末(パソコン)を使って, 瞬間瞬間ベースで株式や債券などの有価証券を売買する。これは素早く儲ける見込みがあるものの, 同時にすぐに損することもある。

day trading　インターネットでの株や債券などの取引, ネット取引, デイ・トレーディング(day trade), 日計(ひばか)り商い
◆Day trading certainly isn't a job for everyone as it requires strong nerves, an ability to make snap decisions and sometimes to take huge risks. デイ・トレーディングは, 図太い神経と即座の決断をする能力のほか, 時には大きなリスクをとる能力も要求されるので, 確かに万人向きの仕事とはいえない。

daylight　(名)日中, 昼, 昼間, 白昼
daylight exposure　当日エクスポージャー, 日中アンカバー額
daylight (exposure) limit　日中許容持ち高, 営業時間中の許容持ち高
daylight overdraft　日中過振り
daylight robbery　法外な金額, 法外な代金請求[要求]
daylight trader　日計り商(あきな)い師
daylight trading　日計り商い, 即日手仕舞い売買(証券を買った日に証券を売ってしまうこと)

DB plan　確定給付型年金, 確定給付型年金ファンド　(DB=defined benefit)

DBJ　日本政策投資銀行(Development Bank of Japanの略)

◆Some of huge amounts in loans extended to JAL by the DBJ have been guaranteed by the government. 日本政策投資銀行が日航に行った巨額融資[貸付け]の一部は、政府が保証している。◆The DBJ and private financial institutions extended loans worth a total of ￥100 billion to JAL in June 2009 though JAL was already in dire financial straits. 日本政策投資銀行と民間金融機関は、日航の経営がすでに悪化していたものの、2009年6月に同社に対して総額1,000億円を融資した。◆The government guaranteed up to 80 percent of ￥67 billion in unsecured loans extended to JAL by the DBJ through the Japan Finance Corporation. 日本政策投資銀行が日航に貸し付けた無担保融資670億円の最大8割については、日本政策金融公庫を通じて政府が保証している。

DC plan 確定拠出型年金
　（DC=defined contribution）
DD 送金小切手、要求払い手形（demand draftの略）
de facto 事実上の、実質的な、実際に[事実上]存在する、現存する、ディファクト （=defacto）
　de facto corporation 事実上の会社
　de facto dismissal 事実上の解雇
　de facto independence 事実上の独立
　de facto interest payment 事実上の支払い利息[金利]（⇒repurchasing method）
　de facto merger 事実上の合併
　de facto standard 事実上の標準、事実上の国際基準、事実上の世界標準、デファクト・スタンダード
de facto holder of the shares 株の実質保有者
　◆The firm was found to be the de facto holder of the shares of the 1,200 individuals. 個人1,200人の株の実質保有者は、同社であることが分かった。
de facto zero-interest (rate) policy 実質ゼロ金利政策、事実上のゼロ金利政策
　◆The de facto zero-interest policy will be maintained until the BOJ can foresee stability in prices. 日銀の事実上のゼロ金利政策[実質ゼロ金利政策]は、物価の安定が展望できるまで継続される。
dead （形）不活発な、活気のない、利益を生まない、不毛の、無価値の、非生産的な、不良の、効力のない、寝ている、死んでいる、廃止になった、デッド
　dead account 睡眠口座、取引がなくなった顧客
　dead asset 休止資産、無価値資産
　dead capital 非生産的資本[資金]、寝ている資金
　dead-cat bounce 一時的反騰
　dead check 振出人死亡小切手
　dead cross （株価の上昇相場から下降相場に転じるケースを表す）デッド・クロス
　dead duty 相殺税
　dead hand poison pill デッドハンド型買収防止策
　dead law 廃止された法律
　dead letter 配達不能郵便[郵便物]
　dead loan 焦(こ)げ付き融資、貸倒れ金、延滞貸金
　dead loss （保険）丸損、純損、まったくの損失
　dead money 死に金、非生産的資金
　　（=dead capital）
　dead season 時季はずれ、不況期
　dead security 無価値担保、非生産的担保
　dead stock 不良在庫、売れ残り、売れ残り品、死蔵品
　reserve for dead loans 貸倒れ引当金
　◆The firm's losses of ￥17 billion were caused through dead stocks and uncollected accounts. 同社の170億円の損失は、不良在庫や（取引先からの）未回収金などで生じた。
deadbeat card holder ふだつきの悪質カード使用者
deadline （名）締切り、期限、回答期限、最終期限、原稿締切時間、行動計画
　bid deadline 入札締切り
　deadline of decision 意思決定の期限
　reply [response] deadline 回答期限
　set a deadline for ～の期限[最終期限]を決める
　work to the deadline 締切りに間に合わせる
　◆The EU intends to propose setting a 100-day deadline for the world's leading economies to decide on the preferred countermeasures against the financial crisis. 欧州連合（EU）は、世界の主要国に金融危機への優先的な対応策を進める100日行動計画の策定を提案する方針だ。
deadlock （名）行き詰まり、こう着状態、閉塞（へいそく）状態、デッドロック
　be in [come to, reach] a deadlock 行き詰まりの状態にある[なる]
　break a deadlock 行き詰まりを打開する
　end in deadlock 行き詰まったまま終わる
　fiscal deadlock 財政の行き詰まり、財政政策の行き詰まり
　◆In the wake of the euro crisis in Europe and the fiscal deadlock in the United States, the yen has sharply strengthened. 欧州のユーロ危機と米国の財政政策の行き詰まりの影響で、円が急騰している。
deadweight debt 死重公債（戦費調達のための国債など、生産に直接役立たない分野に支出される公債）
deal （動）配る、分配する、打撃を加える、（悲しみなどを）与える
　deal in ～を売買する、～の取引をする、～を扱う、～に関係する、～で時間を費やす
　deal in loan claims 債権取引をする
　◆Incubator Bank of Japan was charging interest rates higher than legally allowed in the name of fees when it was dealing in loan claims with moneylenders. 金融業者との債権取引の際、日本振興銀行は、手数料の名目で出資法の上限を上回る金利で貸出を行っていた。
deal （名）取引、商売、売買、政策、対策、計画、協定、協約、労使協約、取決め、合意、契約、協議、協議書、密約、不正取引、事件、案件、物、一勝負、取扱い、扱い、待遇、仕打ち、ディール （⇒emergency deal, financial deal, off-the-book deal, stock deal, strike a deal, swap, unit）
　a big deal 大きな取引、一大事、重大事件、大したこと、非常に重要なこと、大物
　agree a deal 取決めをまとめる
　arrange a car loan securitization deal 自動車ローンの証券化案件をアレンジする
　blockbuster deal 大型債
　bullet deal 満期一括償還債
　cash deal 現金取引
　close the deal 取引をまとめる、商談をまとめる
　cold deal 人気のない銘柄
　compensation deal 補償取引
　conclude a secret deal 裏取引を結ぶ
　deal flow 取引量、ディール・フロー（顧客企業から証券の発行、募集、販売などを委任されている投資銀行の案件数）
　deal stock 被買収会社の株式、買収関連銘柄
　debt rollover deal 債務返済繰延べ取引
　do a deal with ～と取引する
　exchange deal 為替取引
　finalize a deal for ～の最終調整をする、～の最終協議をする、最終調整に入る
　financial deal 金融取引
　fund deal 資金取引
　M&A deal M&A案件
　New Deal (the) ニューディール政策

off-the-book deal　簿外取引
outsourcing deal　業務委託契約
package deal　一括取引, 一括購入, パッケージ・ディール
seal a deal　契約を結ぶ, 取引契約に調印する
secret deal　裏取引
stock deal　株取引, 株式の売買
stock swap deal　株式交換取引
strike a deal　取引をする, 売買する
strike a deal with　～と取引する, ～と合意する
structured deal　仕組み取引, 仕組み債
swap deal　スワップ取引
terminate business deals with　～との取引を打ち切る
trust deal　信託契約

◆A referendum on the EU bailout deal for debt-ridden Greece was called by Greek Prime Minister Papandreou. 負債にあえぐギリシャに対する欧州連合（EU）の救済策の是非を問う国民投票の実施を, ギリシャのパパンドレウ首相が求めた。◆Argentina clinched a debt rollover deal with the IMF after a year of tortuous negotiations. アルゼンチンは, 1年にわたる難交渉の末, 国際通貨基金（IMF）との債務返済繰延べ取引をまとめた。◆Citigroup Inc. wholly owned Nikko Cordial Corp. through a stock swap deal in January 2008. シティグループが, 株式交換取引で2008年1月に日興コーディアルグループを完全子会社化した。◆Financial institutions are obliged to report deals suspected to be linked to terrorism to the financial authorities. 金融機関は, テロ行為に絡んだ疑いのある取引については, 金融当局への届出が義務付けられている。◆In commodity futures trading, prices are decided when buyers and sellers make deals. So they can execute trades at promised prices even if the value of goods has changed drastically in the meantime. 商品先物取引では, 売り手と買い手が取引契約をする時点で価格を決める。そのため, 契約期間中に相場が大きく変動しても, 売り手と買い手は約束した値段で取引を執行できる。◆In the 21-day tender offer, a surprisingly large number of individual shareholders accepted the deal. 21日間の株式公開買付け（TOB）で, 当初の予想を上回って多くの個人株主がTOBに応募した。◆J.P. Morgan Chase & Co. is scrapping a $5 billion outsourcing deal with International Business Machines Corp. JPモルガン・チェース（米銀2位）は, IBMとの50億ドルの業務委託契約を打ち切ることになった。◆Laws already in place on narcotics and organized crime oblige financial institutions to report to the FSA any deals possibly linked to profits from criminal activities. すでに実施されている麻薬や組織的犯罪に関する法律は, 犯罪収益絡みと思われる取引について, 金融庁への報告（届出）を金融機関に義務付けている。◆Mizuho Financial Group Inc. is finalizing a deal for a capital tie-up with Norinchukin Bank. みずほフィナンシャルグループは, 農林中央金庫と資本提携する方向で最終調整（最終協議）に入った。◆Shinsei and Aozora banks have dropped their merger deal. 新生銀行とあおぞら銀行が, 両行の合併計画を断念した［合併協議を中止した］。◆Small and midsize companies have been stepping up equity financing to fund capital investments and prepare for M&A deals. 中小企業は, 設備投資の資金調達とM&A取引に備えて, 株式発行による資金調達を急いでいる。◆The firm received the mandate of an IPO deal in writing. 同社は, 書面でIPO取引（新規株式発行の引受業務）のマンデートを受けた［書面でIPO取引を委任された］。

deal a blow (to)　(～に)打撃を与える
　deal a fatal blow to　～に致命的打撃を与える
　deal a heavy [destructive] blow to　～に大打撃を与える

◆Appraisal losses on securities holdings dealt a blow to the firm's earnings. 保有証券の含み損［評価損］が, 同社の収益に打撃を与えた。◆The drops in bond prices in the past half a year have dealt these banks a heavy blow. 過去半年の債券価格の下落で, これらの銀行は大打撃を受けている。◆The rapid surge in the yen's value would impair the current improvement in the Japanese economy and deal a blow to the world economy. 急激な円高は, 日本の現在の景気回復の腰を折り, 世界経済にも大きなマイナスになる。

deal with　～を処理［処置］する, 解決する, 取り扱う, 扱う, ～と取引する, 取引関係にある, 商う, 商売をする, ～と密約を結ぶ, ～と付き合う, ～と会談する, ～と折衝する, ～に対処する, ～に対応する
　（⇒catastrophe）
　deal directly with　～と直接取引する
　deal with a crisis　危機に対処する, 難局に対処する
　deal with risk　リスクに対応する
　deal with the problem　問題に対処する, 問題に対応する, 問題を解決する

◆A higher capital adequacy ratio means that a bank has a greater capability to deal with risk. 自己資本比率が高いほど, 銀行のリスクへの対応力が高くなる。◆Government steps taken to deal with Resona's collapse did not incorporate a reduction in the banking group's capital. りそな銀行の経営破たん処理に取った国の措置には, 同金融グループの減資は織り込まれなかった。◆In dealing with the dual debt problem due to the March 11 disaster, financial institutions will be forced to share certain burdens. 東日本大震災による二重ローン問題への対応では, 金融機関もある程度の共同負担を強いられることになろう。◆It is difficult to deal with the latest unrest in global financial markets because it has been caused by a complex web of factors. 今回の世界的な金融市場混乱への対応が難しいのは, 混乱を招いている要因が複雑に絡み合っているからだ。◆Measures to deal with surplus facilities are regarded as the center pillar of structural reforms to be initiated by the supply side. 過剰設備の処理対策は, 供給サイドが着手する構造改革の柱とされている。◆South Korea, Brazil and India are guiding their currencies lower to deal with an influx of speculative money. 韓国, ブラジルとインドは, 投機マネーの流入に対応するため, 自国通貨安に誘導している。◆The bank has been relatively weak in retail banking operations dealing with individuals and small and medium-sized firms. 同行は, 個人や中小企業向けの小口取引銀行業務が比較的弱い。◆The bank plans to deal with foreign government bonds at all of its outlets. 同行は, 全店舗で外国国債を扱う方針だ。◆The bank sold all its shares in the U.S. investment firm to raise money to deal with its nonperforming loans. 同行は, 不良債権処理の資金を調達するため, 米投資会社の持ち株を全株売却した。◆The European Union agreed on comprehensive measures to deal with the current fiscal and financial crisis. 欧州連合（EU）は, 現在の財政・金融危機について, 包括的な対応策で合意した。◆The Fed has been unable to deal with the current economic woes by changing interest rates as it has been maintaining a policy of virtually zero-percent interest rates. 米連邦準備制度知事会（FRB）はこれまで金利ゼロ政策を続けてきたため, 政策金利を上げ下げして現在の経済的苦境に対応することはできなくなっている。◆The restructuring plan will focus on dealing with the debts owed to other financial institutions. 再建計画では, 他の金融機関の債権取扱いが今後の焦点となる。◆The U.S. government and the Federal Reserve Board took swift actions to deal with the subprime loan crisis of 2007. 米政府と米連邦準備制度理事会（FRB）は, 2007年のサブプライム危機に迅速に対応した。◆To deal with the systemic financial crisis, ministry and central bank officials had to take rescue measures, such as an injection of public funds, while at the same time implementing strict guidelines and sanctions. 連鎖的な金融危機に対処するにあたって, 当局は公的資金の投入などの救済措置を取ると同時に, 厳しい指導や制裁を実施しなければならなかった。◆Urgent steps should be taken to deal with ominous signs in the real economy. 実体経済の険悪なムードに対処するための緊急措置を取るべきだ。

dealer （名）ディーラー（有価証券取引で、自己の勘定とリスク負担で株式や債券の売買を行う業者のこと）．⇒auction, broker, foreign exchange dealer, low-priced issues, monitor）
  bond dealer　債券ディーラー
  broker dealer　証券会社
  CP dealer　CPディーラー
  dealer bank　ディーラー銀行
  dealer financing　ディーラー金融
  dealer loan　証券在庫金融, ディーラー・ローン
  derivatives dealer　派生商品ディーラー
  exchange dealer　為替ディーラー
  financial futures dealer　金融先物ディーラー
  fixed income dealer　債券ディーラー
  futures dealer　先物ディーラー
  National Association of Securities Dealers　全米証券業協会
  primary dealer　プライマリー・ディーラー, 米国の公認政府証券ディーラー, 政府公認ディーラー
  securities dealer　証券ディーラー
  swap dealer　スワップ・ディーラー

◆A dealer at a leading bank said that market players' concern has kept yen-buying moves in check. 市場関係者の警戒感が円買いの動きを食い止めた［抑制した］、と大手銀行のディーラーが語っている。◆Dealers are watching monitors at a foreign exchange trading company. 為替取引の会社では、ディーラーたちがモニターを注視している。◆Individual investors and brokerage dealers continued to take profits from recent surges in comparatively low-prices issues. 個人投資家と証券会社のディーラーは、最近の比較的割安な銘柄の急上昇で引き続き利食いに出た。◆The revised Financial Futures Law will ban dealers from marketing low-margin foreign exchange products either directly or by phone unless investors ask them to do so. 改正金融先物取引法では、ディーラーは、投資家の依頼でないかぎり少ない証拠金での外国為替商品の直接販売または電話での販売が禁止される。

dealing （名）売買取引, 取引, 売買, 自己売買, ディーリング （⇒falsified stock dealing）
  after-hours dealing　時間外取引
  currency option dealing　通貨オプション取引
  foreign exchange dealing　外国為替取引
  forward dealing　先物取引, 先物為替取引
  insider dealing　インサイダー取引
  interbank dealing　銀行間取引
  money dealing　資金ディーリング
  outside dealing　場外取引
  spot dealing　直物取引, 直物為替取引
  spot exchange dealing　直物為替取引
  stock option dealing　株式オプション取引

◆A former vice president of the Osaka Securities Exchange and a number of his erstwhile subordinates allegedly conducted falsified stock option dealings and manipulated the stock market. 大阪証券取引所の元副理事長とかつての部下らが、株式オプション取引で偽装売買を行い、株式相場の操縦をしていたという。

dealing accounts　自己売買勘定
dealing business　自己売買業務
dealing in futures　先物取引, 定期取引
dealing size　取引単位
dealing spread　ディーリング・スプレッド
dear money　高金利資金
dear money policy　高金利政策
death （名）死亡, 死

complete death of buyers　買い手不在の相場
death benefits　死亡給付金, 死亡保険金, 死亡見舞金, 死亡保障
death bond　死亡債（他人の生命保険金を担保にした保険）
death certificate　死亡証明書
death claims　死亡保険請求
death duty [tax]　相続税
death futures　（末期患者の）生命保険証書
death grant　死亡給付金
death margin　死差益
death of drawer　振出人等の死亡
death rate　死亡率
death risk　死亡危険
death-valley curve　デスヴァレー・カーブ（資金枯渇状態が続く創業当初の急激な資金減少期間）

debacle （名）大失敗, 大惨事, 総崩れ, 混乱, （財政などの）破たん, （市場の）暴落, 崩壊, 瓦解（がかい）, 総崩れ, 大敗北, 大敗走, 完敗, 退散
  debacles in the financial system　金融システムの崩壊, 金融システムの混乱
  Greece's financial debacle　ギリシャの財政破たん
  the U.S. subprime debacle　米国のサブプライム・ローン（低所得者向け住宅融資）問題, 米国のサブプライム・ローン市場の崩壊

◆Europe's debt crisis was triggered by Greece's financial debacle. 欧州の債務危機は、ギリシャの財政破たんに端を発した。◆The debacle of the eurozone's sovereign bond prices caused losses to banks possessing peripheral sovereign debts as their assets. ユーロ圏の国債価格の暴落で、周辺国の国債を資産として抱える銀行は、損失を被った。◆The situation that the business performance of Japanese exporting firms is deteriorating fast can now be described as a debacle. 日本の輸出企業の業績が急速に悪化している状況は、今や「総崩れ」とも言える。◆The subprime mortgage debacle in the United States followed a downturn in property prices after a real estate market bubble. 米国のサブプライム・ローン市場の崩壊は、不動産バブル後の不動産価格の下落に端を発している。

debase （動）（品質などを）低下させる, 落とす, （貨幣を）変造する
debased coin　変造貨幣
debasement （名）貨幣価値の引下げ, 貨幣の価値低下, 悪鋳
  debasement of coinage　貨幣価値の低下, 通貨の品質低下
  debasement of currency　通貨の品質低下, 貨幣価値の低下（=debasement of coinage）

debenture （名）社債, アメリカの無担保債券[無担保債], イギリスの不動産担保付き債券（⇒sinking fund payments, subordinated debenture, subordinated obligation）
  backed debenture　抵当付き債券
  bankers' debenture　銀行債
  bearer debenture　無記名債券
  callable debenture　償還条項付き社債
  capital debenture　劣後債
  convertible debenture　転換社債, 転換権付き社債
  convertible debenture issue　転換社債発行
  corporate debenture　社債
  customs debenture　関税払戻し証明書
  debenture account　債券勘定
  debenture audit　発行社債監査
  debenture bond　無担保債券[社債]（=unsecured bond）
  debenture capital　借入資本金, 無担保社債資本

debenture certificate　債券, 社債券
debenture convertible　転換社債
debenture convertible at current price　時価転換社債
debenture convertible at par　時価転換社債, 転換社債
debenture coupon　社債利札
debenture holder　社債権者, 社債券所持人
debenture holdings　社債券保有高
debenture in foreign currency　外貨債券
debenture in pound sterling　英貨債券
debenture income bond　収益払い社債券
debenture income debenture　収益払い社債券
debenture interest　債券利子
debenture interest rate　債券利子率
debenture investment　公社債投信
debenture issue　社債発行
debenture issued at discount　割引債
debenture mortgage bond　土地担保債券
debenture of drawback　戻し税証明書
debenture redemption　社債の償還, 社債償還
debenture share [stock]　社債券
debenture stock　社債, 社債券, 債務株, 確定利付き株式
debenture subscriptions　債務募集金
debenture to bearer　所持人払い社債, 持参人払い社債
debenture transfer　社債券譲渡
debenture trust　社債券信託
debenture with warrant　ワラント債
defaulted debenture　無償還券
discount bank debenture　割引金融債
discount debenture　割引債
financial debenture　金融債券
first mortgage debenture　第一抵当債
fixed debenture　確定債券
fixed-sum debenture　定額債券
floating debenture　流動債券
guaranteed debenture　保証債券
hypothec debenture　勧業債券
income debenture　収益債券
industrial debenture　事業債
irredeemable debenture　無償還債券
mortgage debenture　担保付き債券[社債], 抵当付き債券
naked debenture　無担保社債
perpetual debenture　永久社債, 無期社債
preference debenture　優先公債
premium-bearing debenture　割増金付き債券
profit debenture　収益債
redeemable debenture　随時償還社債, 有期償還社債
registered debenture　登録債券, 登録債
secured debenture　担保付き社債, 担保付き債券
short-term debenture　短期社債
subordinated debenture　劣後債, 劣後債券
unregistered debenture　無記名社債, 無記名社債券
unsecured corporate debenture　無担保社債

◆During the first nine months of 2011, the company completed public offerings of $125 million of 9.45% Debentures, due 2021 and $125 million of 10.50% Debentures, due 2018. 2011年1-9月期に同社は、2021年満期9.45%社債1億2,500万ドルと2018年満期10.50%社債1億2,500万ドルを公募発行した。◆During 2011, conversions of confvertible debentures resulted in the issuance of 200 shares of the Corporation's capital stock. 2011年度は、転換社債の転換により、200株の当社株式を発行した。◆In addition to long-term debt maturing during the year, the company redeemed all of its U.S. $150 million debentures, due 2013, in June 2011. 当年度に満期が到来する長期債務のほか、同社は2013年満期の社債1億5,000万米ドルの全額を、2011年6月に償還した。◆The BOJ decided to further relax its monetary policy by injecting an additional ¥10 trillion into a fund aimed at purchasing government bonds and corporate debentures. 日銀は、国債や社債などを買い入れるための基金に新たに10兆円を注入[投入]して追加の金融緩和に踏み切ることを決めた。

debit　(動)借り方に記入する, (銀行口座から)引き落とす
debit a sum of reimbursement to a debit account　償還額を負債勘定に借記する
debit an account　勘定を借記する, 口座から(勘定を)引き落とす

debit　(名)借り方, 負債, 引落し, デビット
（⇒direct debit, online debit service）
bank debits　銀行借り方記入
be in debit　(口座が)超過引出になっている
book debit　借り方, 帳簿上の借り方
by direct debit　口座引落しで
debit account　借り方勘定, 負債勘定
debit advice　引落し通知書, 借記通知書
debit [debits] and credit [credits]　貸借, 債権, 債務
debit authorization　借記授権書
debit balance　借り方残高, 貸付け残高, 信用残
debit balance of payments　国際収支の赤字
debit business　受信業務
debit card　デビット・カード, 銀行口座即時決済（金融機関が発行するキャッシュ・カードを利用して、買い物などの支払いができる即時決済方法。利用時に、銀行の預金口座から引落しされる）
debit entry　借記, 借り方記入
debit exchange　交換持ち帰り手形, (手形の)受入れ交換物
debit interest　引落し利息
debit memorandum　借り方票, 借り方記入通知書 (=debit note)
debit overdue account　期限経過債権勘定
debit system　(保険の)地区受持ち制
deferred debit　据え置き借り方, 繰延べ費用
direct debit　自動引落し, 直接引落し, 口座引落し, 直接負債
e-debit　電子デビット
foreign debit balance　対外借り方帳尻
Internet debit　インターネット・デビット
Net-debit service　ネット決済サービス, インターネット即時決済サービス
pay bills by automatic direct debit　自動引落しで請求書の支払いをする
the debit column　借り方欄
the debit side　借り方

◆As of Monday, the bank notified TEPCO of 329,000 debits. 月曜日現在、同行から東京電力に32万9千件の引落し通知があった。◆Debit represents an addition to an expense or asset account, or deduction from a liability, net worth or revenue account. 借り方(勘定の左側に記入すること)は、費用・資産勘定の増加または負債・資本・収益勘定の減少を示す。◆The new Net-debit service will enable consumers to make purchases on the Internet and have the cost deducted automatically from their bank or postal savings accounts. この新ネット決済サービスを利用すると、利用者はインターネット上で買い物をして、その代金を利用者の銀行か郵便貯金の口座から自動的に引き落としてもらうことになる。

debit note　借り方票, 借り方伝票, 債務覚書, 代金請求

DEBT

書,請求書,保険料請求書,デビット・ノート (=debit memo, debit slip, debit ticket)
debit note for claim　保険金請求書
debit note for premium　保険料請求書
debt　(名)債務,負債,借金,財政赤字,債権,借入金,借入債務,債務証券,債券,金銭債務,金銭債務訴訟,デット (⇒bad debt, collection of debts, foreign debt, interest bearing debt)
accrue debts　負債を抱え込む
accumulate debts　債務［借入債務］をふくらませる
accumulated debt　累積債務
assume a debt　債務を引き受ける,債務の肩代わりをする,債務を承継する
bank debt　銀行借入れ
be in a person's debt　〜に借金がある,〜に恩義がある (=be in debt to)
be liable for a debt　債務に責任を負う
be out of debt　債務をすべて弁済する
call up a debt　借金の催促をする
carry high rate debt　高金利の融資を受けている
clear debts　借金を返済する,負債の返済に充てる
clear off one's debt　借金をきれいに清算する
collapse with debts　債務を抱えて破たん［倒産］する
collect a bad debt　不良債権を回収する,不良債権を取り立てる
collecting the debts　債権回収,債権の取立て
construction debt　建設国債
contract［incur］debts　負債を生ずる
corporate debt　企業債務
cover debts　赤字を補てんする
debt accumulation　累積債務
debt adjustment　債務整理
debt and credit　貸借,債権債務 (=debts and credits)
debt burden　債務負担,債務超過
debt buyback　債務の買戻し
debt cancellation　負債［債務］の帳消し,負債の棒引き (=write-off)
debt capital　借入資本,他人資本 (=loan capital)
debt collection　債権回収,貸金取立て,借金取り (⇒collection of debts)
debt collection agency　債権回収代行業者,取立て業者
debt collector　不良債権取立て業者,債権回収業者,貸金・借金取立て人,借金取り
debt consolidation loans　負債合併ローン
debt counseling　債務［負債］カウンセリング
debt counselor　債務［負債］カウンセラー
debt deflation　債務デフレ
debt equity ratio　負債比率,負債倍率,負債・資本比率,負債対資本比率,外部負債比率,デット・エクイティ・レシオ,DER
debt factoring　債権買取り
debt-for-bond swap　債務の債券化,デット・ボンド・スワップ (=debt-bond swap)
debt-for-nature swap　自然保護債務スワップ,債務・環境スワップ
debt forgiveness　債務免除,債務の帳消し
debt investment　債券投資
debt investor　債券投資家
debt issue　固定の債務,長期負債
debt limit［ceiling］　公債発行限度,国債発行限度額,債務限度
debt management　公債管理

debt monetization　公債の貨幣化,中央銀行引受発行
debt of honor　信用借り
debt overhang　デット・オーバーハング(過大債務で新規投資ができない状態)
debt raider　デットレイダー
debt redemption　債券償還,負債償還,債務の返済,借金の返済
debt refunding　債務の借換え,債務借換え
debt rescheduling　債務繰延べ,リスケ,リスケジューリング
debt retirement　債務の返済,債務返済
debt sales　債券営業
debt-swap arrangements　債務の株式化
debt to equity［debt-to-equity］ratio　負債比率,負債・自己資本比率
debt workout　債務再編成 (=debt restructuring)
debtnocrat　(IMFなどの)国際融資担当官
debts payable　借入金
default on debt　債務不履行に陥(おちい)る
drown in debt　借金漬けになる,借金で首が回らなくなる
excess of debt　債務超過
external debt　対外債務 (=foreign debt, overseas debt)
fall into debt　債務超過に陥る
financial debt　金融債務
floating debt　流動負債,一時借入金
forgive debt　債務を免除する,債権を放棄する
funded debt　外部負債,長期債務,利付き長期負債,確定公債
get［fall, run］into debt　借金をする,借財をする
get out of debt　借金を返す
government debt　国債,政府債,財政赤字
guarantee a debt　債務を保証する
have a debt　債務を負っている,債務を抱えている
hidden debts　隠れ借金
high-rate debt　高利融資
in debt　赤字の
incur a debt　債務を負担する
interest-bearing debt　利付き債券
keep out of debt　借金をしないで暮らす
large debts　大口債権
liquidate a debt　借入金を完済する
long-term debt　長期債務
long-term U.S. debt　米国の長期国債
massive debt　巨額の借金
national debt　中央政府債務残高,国債
National Debt　英国債
net debt of the government　政府の純債務
new debt　新発債
off-the-book debts　簿外債務
outstanding debt　既発債,借入金残高,借越し金,債務残高
owe a debt　借金をしている
passive debt　無利息債務
pay a debt　借金を払う
pay back［pay off, wipe off］one's debt　債務を返済する,借入金を返済する,借金を清算する
pay down a debt　債務を圧縮する
person with multiple debts　多重債務者 (=multiple debtor)

provision for doubtful debts　貸倒れ引当金
public debt　公債
recover debts　債権を回収する
reduce one's debt　債務を削減する
repay debt　債務を返済する
reschedule the debt　債務の返済[支払い]を繰り延べる, 返済条件を変更する
retire one's debt　債務を返済する
retirement of debt　債務の返済
running away from a debt　借逃げ
secured debt　有担保債券, 担保付き債務
service one's debt　利払いをする
short-term debt　短期債務
sovereign debt　公的債務
total debt as a percentage of total capitalization　資本総額に対する債務総額の比率
trade debt　営業上の債務
troubled debt　不良債権, 問題債権
unconsolidated debt　単独ベースでの借入金, 非連結子会社の負債
underwrite the national debt　国債を引き受ける
unrecoverable debts　不良債権　(=bad debts, nonperforming loans, uncollectible loans)
unsecured debt　無担保債, 無担保債務, 無担保貸付け金
unsubordinated debt　上位債
with debts of　～の負債を抱えて
write off a debt　貸金を償却する
write off bad debts　不良債権を償却する

◆A referendum on the EU bailout deal for debt-ridden Greece was called by Greek Prime Minister Papandreou. 負債にあえぐギリシャに対する欧州連合(EU)の救済策の是非を問う国民投票の実施を, ギリシャのパパンドレウ首相が求めた。◆Fitch Ratings Ltd. will keep its rating on long-term U.S. debt at the highest grade, AAA. 英米系の格付け会社フィッチ・レーティングスは, 米国の長期国債格付けを, 最上級のAAA(トリプルA)に据え置く方針だ。◆Ford announced a plan to cut its $25.8 billion in automotive debt by about 40 percent by offering creditors cash and new shares. 米フォードは, 債権者(社債の保有者)に現金と新株を提供して, 258億ドルの自動車関連債務を約40%削減する計画を発表した。◆Germany, main creditor to Greece, demanded that private-sector-banks accept a certain amount of trimming of their debts. (財政危機の)ギリシャに主に資金を提供しているドイツは, 民間銀行に対して債権の一部放棄を受け入れるよう求めた。◆GM obtained agreements from a majority of creditors in negotiations to reduce its debts significantly. 米ゼネラル・モーターズ(GM)は, 巨額の債務削減交渉で, 大半の債権者から合意を取り付けた。◆If TEPCO's creditor banks forgive the debts when the utility is not carrying excessive liabilities, lenders will not be able to recover either the principal or interest owed. 東電が債務超過でない時点で東電の債権保有銀行が債権を放棄すると, 金融機関は元本を回収できず, 金利収入も得られなくなる。◆In the case of an insolvent borrower, it no longer has the ability to pay all its debt even though lenders offer to defer the time of repayment. 返済不能の借り手の場合, 貸し手が返済期間の延長を申し出ても, 借り手はもはや債務を全額返済できない状況にある。◆In the latest settlement with federal and state regulators, Wachovia Corp. agreed to buy back nearly 9 billion in auction-rate debt. 今回の連邦と州の規制当局との和解で, 米大手銀行のワコビアは, 約90億ドルの金利入札証券(ARS)を買い戻すことで合意した。◆In view of the country's massive debt, it is essential to reduce spending. 国の巨額の借金を考えると, 歳出削減は欠かせない。◆It's irrational if banks don't offer debt waivers regarding TEPCO's debt. 東電の債務について, 銀行が債権放棄をしないのはおかしい。◆Japan must tackle its large fiscal deficit and curb the growth of public debts. 日本は, 巨額の財政赤字と取り組んで, 財政赤字[公的債務]の増大を抑える必要がある。◆Most other major banks also are considering repayment of their debts to the government. 他のほとんどの大手行も, 国への債務返済を検討している。◆The collection of debts has been delayed due to falling collateral value. 担保価値の下落などで, 債権の回収は遅れている。◆The Conservative promised to scythe through Britain's debts. 英保守党は, 財政赤字削減に大ナタを振るうことを約束した。◆The correction of financial statements by Olympus is unlikely to result in the company's debts exceeding its assets. オリンパスの財務書類訂正で, 同社の債務超過は避けられる見通しだ。◆The Federation of National Public Service Personal Mutual Aid Associations spent between ¥1.5 billion and ¥2.1 billion a year in public funds to cover its debts of hotels run by the federation. 国家公務員共済組合連合会は, 経営するホテルの赤字補てんに毎年15～21億円程度の公的資金を充てていた。◆The firm repaid part of its outstanding debt to the bank. 同社は, 債務残高[残りの債務]の一部を同行に返済した。◆The government of Japan today has a debt of nearly ¥1 quadrillion. こんにちの日本政府は, 約1兆円の債務を抱えている。◆The main aim of the reform of the public highway corporations is to ensure the steady repayment of the entities outstanding ¥40 trillion in debt. 道路公団改革の主な目的は, 同公団の40兆円の債務残高を着実に返済することだ。◆This rule would allow unscrupulous borrowers to flee, leaving their debts unpaid. このような規則を設けたら, 不心得な借り手の借り逃げを許すことになる。◆Total debt as a percentage of total capitalization was 20 percent at yearend 2010. 資本総額に対する債務総額の比率は, 2010年末現在で20%だった。◆We must stop state debt from continuing to increase indefinitely. 国の借金が無限に増え続けるのを, われわれは止めなければならない。◆Without the government financial support, TEPCO will fall into debt as the utility has to pay the huge amounts in compensation. 政府の金融支援がなければ, 東電は巨額の賠償金を支払わなければならないので, 債務超過に陥ると思われる。

debt assumption　債務引受け, 債務引受契約, 債務履行引受け, 債務の肩代わり, 債務引受契約に基づく債務譲渡, デット・アサンプション
◆The Japan Small and Medium Enterprise Corporation covers 70 percent to 80 percent of the debt assumption from its insurance fund. 中小企業総合事業団(特殊法人)が, その保険金[保険資金]で債務肩代わりの7-8割を補填している。

debt balance　債務残高
◆The debt balance of the central government has exceeded ¥900 trillion for the first time. 国の債務残高[国の借金]が, 初めて900兆円を突破した。

debt burden　債務負担, 債務超過　(⇒debt load)
◆It is difficult for the company to survive on its own with its heavy debt burden of ¥500 billion. 同社の場合は, 5,000億円の大幅な債務超過のため, 自力での存続は難しい。◆The government will propose measures to reduce the debt burdens of heavily indebted poor countries (HIPC). 政府は, 重債務貧困国の債務負担削減策を提案する。◆The S&P cut in the U.S. long-term credit rating by one notch to AA-plus from AAA resulted from concerns about the nation's budget deficits and climbing debt burden. スタンダード・アンド・プアーズ(S&P)が米国の長期国債格付けを最上級のAAA(トリプルA)からAA(ダブルA)に1段階引き下げた理由は, 米国の財政赤字と債務負担の増大に対する懸念だ。

debt ceiling　債務負担限度, 債務限度, 債務の上限, 債務上限額, 借金枠　(=debt limit)
a federal debt ceiling　連邦政府の債務上限
raise the debt ceiling of the U.S. government　米政府の債務上限を引き上げる

◆If a new federal debt ceiling isn't set by Aug. 2, 2011, the United States will be forced to default on Treasuries securities as it will not be able to issue new bonds to pay back maturing government debts. 2011年8月2日までに連邦政府の債務上限を新たに設けないと、米国は満期を迎える国債を償還するための国債増発ができないので、米国債の不履行（デフォルト）が発生する。◆The federal government will initially make a spending cut of $900 billion, while it will raise the debt ceiling by the same amount immediately. 米政府はまず0.9兆ドルの歳出削減を行う一方、債務上限を直ちに引き上げる。◆The federal government will raise the debt ceiling by about $2.4 trillion in two stages. 米政府は、2.4兆ドルほどの債務上限引上げを2段階で実施する。◆U.S. lawmakers are forced to consider whether to raise the federal debt ceiling beyond $14.3 trillion. 米議会の議員は、連邦政府の債務上限額を14兆3,000億ドル以上に引き上げるかどうかの検討を迫られている。

debt crisis 債務危機, 財政危機
（⇒financial unrest, financial world）
fall into a debt crisis 債務危機［財政危機］に陥る
the debt crisis in Greece ギリシャの財政危機, ギリシャの債務危機
◆Behind these cautious views among large manufacturers are uncertainty over the debt crisis in the eurozone and the slowdown in the U.S. economy. 大企業製造業のこうした警戒感［慎重な見方］の背景には、ユーロ圏の債務危機不安や米景気の減速がある。◆Europe's debt crisis was triggered by Greece's financial debacle. 欧州の債務危機は、ギリシャの財政破たんに端を発した。◆France and Germany could not bridge their differences, so Europe's efforts to solve its escalating debt crisis plunged into disarray. フランスとドイツが両国の相違を埋められなかったため、深刻化する欧州の債務危機問題解決への欧州の取組みは、混乱に陥った。◆German Chancellor Angela Merkel shut the door on the introduction of common eurozone bonds as a means to solve the debt crisis. ドイツのメルケル首相は、欧州債務危機問題の解決手段としてユーロ圏共通債を導入することに強く反対した。◆Greece has fallen into a debt crisis as a result of its lax financial management. ギリシャは、放漫な財政運営の末に財政危機に陥った。◆It became evident that the Greek debt crisis would spill over into Spain. ギリシャの財政危機がスペインに波及することが、確実になった。◆The debt crisis in Greece threatened to spread to Portugal, Ireland and Spain. ギリシャの財政危機は、ポルトガルやアイルランド、スペインなどに波及する恐れがあった。◆The debt crisis in the eurozone began rocking the global economy. ユーロ圏の債務危機で、世界景気が揺らいできた。◆The debt crisis in the eurozone was triggered by huge deficits in Greece. ユーロ圏の財政危機を引き起こしたのは、ギリシャの巨額の財政赤字だ。◆The decline in long-term interest rates since May is due to continued capital flight from high-risk assets such as stocks triggered by the debt crisis in Europe. 5月以降、長期金利が低下しているのは、欧州の財政危機をきっかけに株式などリスク［損失リスク］の高い資産からの資金逃避が続いたためだ。◆The European bond market is truly in a knife-edge situation as the yield on 10-year Italian government bonds has surged above 7 percent, the so-called danger zone that may result in a debt crisis. 10年物イタリア国債の流通利回りが、債務危機に陥る「危険水域」とされる7%超に上昇したため、欧州債券市場は予断を許さない状況にある。◆The global economy is being rocked by Greece's debt crisis. 世界経済は、ギリシャの財政危機で揺れている。◆The Greek-triggered sovereign debt crisis has been throwing the eurozone into financial uncertainty and multiple crises. ギリシャに端を発したソブリン危機（政府債務危機）問題で、ユーロ圏は金融不安と複合的な危機に陥っている。◆The IMF and the EU are strengthening their cooperation to avert a Greek default and prevent a chain reaction of debt crisis among other countries. ギリシャの債務不履行（デフォルト）を回避し他国間の債務危機の連鎖反応を防ぐため、国際通貨基金（IMF）と欧州連合（EU）は、連携を強めている。◆The 10-year bond yield of Spain has likewise neared the 7 percent level, the danger zone that may fall into a debt crisis. スペインの10年物国債利回り［国債流通利回り］も、債務危機に陥る恐れがある危険水域の7%台に迫った。◆Worries over the spreading of the eurozone debt crisis and the U.S.'s slipping into recession have driven the rout in financial markets. ユーロ圏の財政危機の拡大と米国の景気後退入りへの懸念で、金融市場は総崩れになった。

debt default 債務不履行 （=default）
◆Greece must avert a crippling debt default by securing billions of dollars in emergency loans from European countries and the IMF. ギリシャは、欧州諸国［ユーロ圏］と国際通貨基金（IMF）による緊急融資で巨額の資金を確保して、壊滅的な債務不履行を回避しなければならない。◆The confusion triggered by Greece's possible debt default could affect Japan and the United States. 予想されるギリシャの債務不履行（デフォルト）による混乱の影響は、日米に及ぶ可能性もある。

debt deferment 債務返済の延長
（=deferment of debt repayment）
◆In the case of a lack of liquidity, either bridge lending or debt deferment can save the borrower as there is no cash on hand. 流動性不足の場合は、手元に現金がないので、つなぎ資金を貸すか［つなぎ融資か］債務返済の延長で借り手は助かる。

debt dynamics 債務問題, 債務問題処理, 財政運営, 国債価格の値動き
◆The U.S. fiscal consolidation plan falls short of what would be necessary to stabilize the government's medium-term debt dynamics. 米国の財政再建策は、政府の中期的な債務問題処理［財政運営］の安定化には不十分である。

debt equity swap 債務の株式化, 債権の株式化, デット・エクイティ・スワップ, DES
（=debt-for-equity swap; ⇒debt-for-equity swap）
◆As far as the debt equity swap is concerned, its main banks' holdings of outstanding shares may increase further than the 5 percent limit stipulated by the Antimonopoly Law. 債務の株式化に関するかぎり、主力取引銀行の発行済み株式の持ち株比率が、独占禁止法で定める5%の上限を上回る可能性がある。

debt financing [finance] 債券発行による資金調達, 負債［借入れ］による資金調達, 他人資本調達, 借入金融, 負債金融, デット・ファイナンス （社債の発行や約束手形の振出し、短期・長期の借入金などで資金を調達する方法。⇒equity financing）
accomplish long-term debt financing by issuing bonds 債券を発行して長期資金を調達する, 債券発行で長期借入れによる資金調達を行う
get debt financing 借入れで資金を調達する

debt-for-equity swap （貸し手にとっての）債権株式化,（借り手にとっての）債務株式化, デット・エクイティ・スワップ
（=debt equity swap; ⇒debt forgiveness）
◆The bank will acquire ¥100 billion in new shares and carry out a ¥50 billion debt-for-equity swap. 同行が、新株1,000億円を引き受けるほか、500億円分の債権（借り手にとっては債務）の株式化を実施する。◆The company will increase its capital by ¥300 billion through the debt-for-equity swap. 同社は、債務の株式化で300億円増資する。◆The company will increase its capital by ¥50 billion with additional investment of ¥10 billion from the IRC and with the debt-for-equity swap. 同社は、産業再生機構による100億円の追加［新規］出資と債務の株式化で、500億円増資する。◆The financial assistance will be extended by combining a waiver of debt and a debt-for-equity swap. 金融支援は、債権放棄とデット・エクイティ・スワップ（債務の株式化）を組み合わせて行われる。

解説 債務の株式化とは：金融機関に融資（借入金）を出資

に振り替えてもらい、株券を渡して増資すること。つまり、負債を株に変えて増資すること。こうすると、融資を受けた企業はその借入金を返す必要もなく、また利子を払う必要もない。企業にとっては負債が減る分、資本金などの自己資本が増え、金融機関にとっては債権の株式化によって企業が再建を果たせば配当を受けられるし、株価が値上がりすれば株を売却して利益が得られるメリットがある。債務の株式化は、貸し手（金融機関）にとっては債権の株式化を意味する。

debt-for-equity swap scheme 債務の株式化案
◆The main banks will carry out a debt-for-equity swap scheme to help the firm slash its debts. これらの主力取引銀行は、同社の債務削減支援策として、債務の株式化（同社の債務の一部を出資に振り替える）案を実施する。◆The major four banks view the reduction in capital as necessary to help prevent the firm's stock price from plunging if the banks carry out a debt-for-equity swap scheme to help the firm slash its debts. この主力4銀行は、同社の債務削減支援策として銀行が債務の株式化［同社の債務の一部を出資に振り替える］案を実施した場合に、同社の株価急落を防ぐ上で減資が必要と見ている。

debt forgiveness 債権放棄, 債務の免除, 債務救済
（=debt relief, debt waiver, forgiveness of debt, loan forgiveness, loan write-off）
　ask for debt forgiveness　債務免除を求める［要請する］, 債権放棄を求める
　the amount of debt forgiveness　債務免除額, 債権放棄額
◆A financial aid package that includes a debt-for-equity swap and debt forgiveness was considered by the main banks. 債務の株式化（銀行にとっては債権の株式化）や債権放棄などの金融支援策を、主力取引銀行が検討した。◆The secondary market prices of the peripheral countries' government bonds plummeted as it became known that those bonds might be subject to debt forgiveness. 周辺国の国債は債務減免の必要が生じる恐れのあることが判明したので、周辺国国債の流通市場での価格は暴落した。◆The three main banks are mulling a financial aid package that includes a debt-for-equity swap and debt forgiveness. 主力取引銀行3行は現在、債務の株式化（銀行にとっては債権の株式化）や債権放棄などの金融支援策を検討している。

debt guarantee 債務保証
◆The company plans to honor debt guarantee on a total of ￥86.8 billion. 同社は、総額868億円の債務保証を引き受ける方針だ。

debt holding 債券保有, 国債保有
◆China is reviewing its eurozone debt holdings amid the accelerating fiscal crisis in Europe. 中国は現在、欧州での財政危機の加速を受けて、ユーロ圏の国債の保有を見直している。

debt instrument 債務証券, 債務証書, 債券
（=debt, debt security）
　debt instruments such as bonds and commercial paper　債券やコマーシャル・ペーパーなどの債務証券
　deferred-interest debt instrument　利息繰延べ型債券
　long-term debt instrument　長期債務証券
◆One way for a company to accomplish long-term financing is through the issuance of long-term debt instruments in the form of bonds. 会社の長期資金調達方法の一つは、社債の形で長期債務証券を発行して行われる。◆Our long-term financing was accomplished through the issuance of long-term debt instruments. 当社の長期資金調達は、長期債務証券を発行して行われた。

debt issuance 債券発行, 社債発行, 国債発行［発行額］
◆The current situation of debt issuance exceeding tax revenues has continued since fiscal 2010. 国債発行額が税収を上回る現在の事態は、2010年度から続いている。

debt-laden （形）負債［借金］を抱えた, 借金漬けの
　debt-laden balance sheets　過剰負債, 負債の過剰
　debt-laden finances　借金漬けの財政
◆This country's debt-laden finances are in a critical situation due to the dole-out policies as well as lavish economic stimulus measures. わが国の借金漬けの財政は、バラマキ政策と大盤振る舞いの景気対策で、危機的な状況に陥っている。

debt leverage 債務レバレッジ, 債務テコ入れ, デット・レバレッジ（金融機関からの借入れで企業買収資金の一部をまかなうとき、自己資金にもたらされる収益を拡大するために用いられる方法）

debt limit 債務上限, 米連邦政府の総債務残高の法定上限 （=debt ceiling）
　raise the debt limit　債務上限を引き上げる
　reject the increase of debt limit　債務上限の引上げを拒否する
◆A suprapartisan committee set up within Congress will work out a plan to cut the fiscal deficit by $1.5 trillion while raising the debt limit by a matching amount. 今後は米議会内に設置される超党派委員会が、1.5兆ドルの財政赤字削減策をまとめる一方、債務上限を同額引き上げる。◆Moody's will consider cutting the United States' top-notch credit rating if any progress isn't made in talks to raise the U.S. debt limit. 米政府の債務の法定上限引上げについての（米議会との）交渉で進展がなければ、ムーディーズは、米国債の最上位の格付けを引下げる方向で検討する方針だ。◆U.S. House of Representatives rejected the increase of debt limit. 米下院は、債務上限の引上げ（法案）を否決した。

debt load 債務負担, 借入負担, 債務負担額, 借金額, 借金の重荷 （=load of debt）
◆Even after Greece's debt load is cut, Greece's credit grade is likely to remain low. ギリシャの債務負担を削減しても、ギリシャの信用格付けは、低水準にとどまる見込みだ。◆In a move to reduce its debt load, the company issued 20 million common shares in March 2011. 債務負担の軽減策として、同社は2011年3月に普通株式2,000万株を発行した。

debt moratorium 債務返済停止, 債務返済の凍結, 債務返済の猶予, 債務の支払い猶予
◆Thailand does not want to accept the debt moratorium because of fears of affecting its credit rating. タイは、信用低下につながるとして、債務の支払い猶予には応じない方針だ。

debt obligation 債務, 債務負担, 債券, デット証券, 債務証書, 債務契約書
　ability to meet one's short-term debt obligations　短期債務の返済能力
　debts obligations of sovereign governments　国債
　failure to meet debt obligations　債務返済の遅れ
　long-term debt obligations　長期債
　meet one's debt obligations when due　債務を遅滞なく返済する
　meet one's short-term debt obligations　短期債務を返済する
　quasi-debt obligations　準債務
　senior debt obligations　上位債務, 一般債務
　service one's existing debt obligations　既存債務を返済する
　short-term debt obligations　短期債務
◆If Greece refuses to comply with the certain conditions imposed by the eurozone and the IMF, it will have no choice but to default on its debt obligations. ユーロ圏と国際通貨基金（IMF）が設けた一定の条件に応じるのをギリシャが拒否すれば、ギリシャは、債務不履行の道を選ぶしかなくなる。

debt payment 債務支払い, 債務返済
　ability to meet debt payments due　債務返済能力
　ability to meet debt payments over the long term　長期的な債務返済能力

meet future debt payments　将来債務を返済する
meet the obligatory debt payments　債務返済義務を履行する
suspend foreign debt payments　対外債務支払いを一時停止する
◆Argentina's new president suspended foreign debt payments. アルゼンチンの新大統領が、対外債務支払いを一時停止した。

debt pressure　債務圧力
◆If consumer prices rose mildly over the course of a few years, it would result in a decline in interest rates in real terms and reduced debt pressure. 消費者物価が数年にわたって緩やかに上昇したら、実質金利の低下と債務圧力の低減につながるものと思われる。

debt problem　債務問題, 債務危機問題
◆Gold is still becoming the safe haven as people fear recession in the U.S. and the eurozone debt problems. 米国の景気後退やユーロ圏の債務危機問題への懸念から、まだ金が安全な投資先[資金の逃避先]となっている。◆The Naoto Kan's administration lacks a consistent strategy on the debt problem. 菅政権には、債務問題に対する一貫した戦略が欠けている。

debt rating　債券格付け, 社債の格付け, 債務格付け, 債務証書, 債務契約書　(=bond rating)
French government's debt rating　フランス政府の債務格付け, フランス国債の格付け
issuer's debt ratings　発行体の債券格付け
Japan's yen-denominated debt rating　日本の円建て国債の格付け
long-term debt rating　長期債格付け
long-term senior unsecured debt rating　長期上位無担保債格付け
senior debt rating　上位社債格付け
short-term debt rating　短期債格付け
◆General Motor's long term debt rating was slashed one level to Caa1 by Moody's Investors Service. ゼネラル・モーターズ(GM)の長期債格付けを、米格付け会社のムーディーズ・インベスターズ・サービスが1段階下のCaa1に引き下げた。◆Moody's Investors Service cut Japan's yen-denominated debt rating by one notch to Aa3 from Aa2 and maintained a negative outlook. 米国の格付け会社ムーディーズは、日本の円建て国債の格付けを「Aa2」から「Aa3」に一段階引き下げ、「ネガティブ(弱含み)」の見通しを据え置いた。◆Moody's Investors Service has downgraded its long-term senior unsecured debt rating for Toyota and its subsidiaries to Aa1 from Aaa. ムーディーズ・インベスターズ・サービスは、トヨタとトヨタの子会社の長期上位無担保債務格付けを、最上位のAaaからAa1に1段階引き下げた。◆Moody's Investors Services cut General Motors Corp.'s long-term debt rating. ムーディーズ・インベスターズ・サービス(米国の格付け会社)は、ゼネラル・モーターズ(GM)の長期債格付けを引き下げた。◆Rating agency Moody's may place a negative outlook on French government's Aaa debt rating as the government's financial strength has weakened. 格付け会社のムーディーズは、フランス国債のAaa(トリプルA)格付けについて、仏政府の財務体質[財務力]が弱まっているため「ネガティブ(弱含み)」の見通しを示す可能性がある。

debt ratio　負債比率, 債務比率
(⇒government debt ratios)
cash flow to (total) debt ratio　債務合計に対するキャッシュ・フローの比率
cash flow/net debt ratio　キャッシュ・フロー/純負債比率
debt ratio for total assets　借入金依存度
debt/equity ratio　負債比率, 負債/資本比率
deterioration in the company's debt ratio　同社の負債比率の悪化
government debt ratio　政府の債務比率
have a high debt/equity ratio　負債比率が高い
increase in debt ratio　負債比率の上昇
projected debt ratio　予想債務比率
quasi debt to firm value ratio　準負債比率
◆Excluding financial services and leasing operations, the debt ratio declined to 34.1% at December 31, 2010, compared with 49.1% at December 31, 2009. 金融サービスとリース事業を除くと、2010年12月31日時点の負債比率は、2009年12月31日時点の49.1%から34.1%に低下しました。

debt reduction　債務削減, 債務減らし
◆The increase of exports, corporate restructuring, centered on debt reduction, and government-led structural reforms brought about the economic recovery. 輸出拡大、債務減らしを中心とした企業のリストラと政府が進める構造改革が、今回の景気回復をもたらした。◆This economic recovery is mainly due to the increased exports and corporate restructuring efforts centered on debt reduction. 今回の景気回復の主な要因は、輸出拡大と債務減らしを中心とした企業のリストラ努力だ。

debt relief　債務救済, 債務削減, 債務軽減, 債務負担の緩和, (発展途上国への)債務免除
(=debt forgiveness)
debt relief measures　債務救済措置
debt relief package　包括的債務救済措置
dual [double] debt relief　二重ローンの救済
◆The EU ministers will consider debt relief or freezing payments on debt for the Asian tsunami-hit countries. 欧州連合(EU)の閣僚らは、アジアの津波被災国のため債務削減や債務返済の凍結を検討する。

debt relief process　債務救済手続き, 債務削減手続き
◆Delays in the debt relief process may become obstacles to reconstruction efforts. 債務救済[債務削減]手続きの遅れは、復興の支障[障害]となる可能性がある。

debt repayment　債務返済, 借金返済
(⇒additional fund)
◆In the case of a lack of liquidity or liquidity crisis, the debt repayment of an indebted borrower is still possible if a grace period is given, but lack of cash on hand makes it impossible to repay its debt in the short term. 流動性不足や流動性危機の場合、債務を抱えた借り手の債務返済は猶予期間を与えればまだ可能であるが、手元に現金がないため短期での債務返済はできない。◆The company will use the proceeds from selling its nine TV stations for debt repayment. 同社は、テレビ9局を売却して得た資金を、債務返済に充てる予定だ。◆The nonprofit foundation considered dissolution as one way of resolving the issue of debt repayment. 債務返済問題を解決するための手段として、同公益法人は解散も考えた。

debt restructuring　債務再編, 債務再構成
(=debt workout)
◆Ford Motor Co. is making up to $2.2 billion cash available for the debt restructuring. 米フォード・モーターは、債務再編のため、最大22億ドルの現金を用意している。◆Ford's debt restructuring includes conversion of debt to equity and cash tender offers. 米フォードの債務再編には、債務の株式化や現金による株式の公開買付けが含まれている。

debt-ridden　(形)赤字に悩む, 借金に悩む, 負債[債務]に苦しむ, 経営再建中の
◆A recent tragedy involving a debt-ridden elderly couple roused all parties to impose stricter controls on the moneylending business. 最近起こった借金苦の老夫婦の悲劇が、各党を貸金業の規制強化に突き動かした。◆A referendum on the EU bailout deal for debt-ridden Greece was called by Greek Prime Minister Papandreou. 負債にあえぐギリシャに対する欧州連合(EU)の救済策の是非を問う国民投票の実施を、ギリシャのパパンドレウ首相が求めた。◆Chinese President Hu

Jintao did not promise to buy Portuguese bonds which the debt-ridden country had hoped. 中国の湖錦濤国家主席は、債務に苦しむポルトガルが望んでいた同国の国債購入を約束しなかった。

debt-ridden people 債務者
◆A number of debt-ridden people have killed themselves, fled at night or committed crimes. 自殺や夜逃げしたり、犯罪に走ったりする債務者も出ている。

debt rollover 債務返済の繰延べ, 支払い繰延べ, 借換え
（=rollover）
◆Argentina clinched a debt rollover deal with the IMF after a year of tortuous negotiations. アルゼンチンは、1年にわたる難交渉の末、国際通貨基金（IMF）との債務返済繰延べ取引をまとめた。

debt-saddled （形）借金を背負っている, 負債［債務、赤字］を抱えた, 経営再建中の
◆Debt-saddled supermarket chain operator and its three major creditor banks are finalizing a ¥500 billion bailout package. 負債を抱えた［経営再建中の］大手スーパーとその主力取引銀行3行は、5,000億円の金融支援策の最終協議に入った。◆Unless consumption tax rate is raised, the planned issuance of bridging bonds could lead to further deterioration of the debt-saddled government finances. 消費税率を引き上げないと、予定しているつなぎ国債の発行は、借金を背負っている国の財政の悪化をさらに招く可能性がある。

debt security 債務証券, 債券, 債務証書, 債券, 社債
（=debt, debt instrument；「債務証券」は、一般に債券などの有価証券を指す）
　corporate debt securities　一般社債, 社債
　debt securities held to maturity　満期保有債券
　debt securities markets　債券市場
　discount on the debt securities　社債発行差金
　government debt securities　国債, 政府債
　issuance of debt and equity securities to the public　債券と株式の公募発行
　issue debt securities　社債を発行する, 債券を発行する
　marketable debt securities　市場性ある債券
　municipal debt securities　地方債
　public debt securities　国債, 米財務省証券
　relative credit risk of debt securities　債券の相対的な信用リスク
　short-term debt and related securities　短期債務と関連証券
　underwrite debt securities　債務証券を引き受ける
◆Through this shelf registration, the Corporation will be able to offer, from time to time, up to U.S. $300 million of its debt securities and warrants to purchase debt securities. この発行登録［SECの一括登録制度］により、当社は3億米ドルを上限として、債務証券と債務証券の引受権付きワラントを随時、発行することができます。◆UBS AG, Switzerland's largest bank, will buy back $18.6 of debt securities. スイスの最大手行UBSが、186億ドル相当の債務証券を買い戻すことになった。

debt service 債務返済, 元利払い, 元利返済, 元利償還
　cover debt service　元利返済を行う, 元利返済を賄（まかな）う
　debt service fund　債務処理基金, 長期債務返済特別会計
　debt service obligations　元利返済の債務
　debt service ratio　債務返済比率, 対外債務返済比率

debt servicing 債務返済, 債務の支払い, 元利払い, 元利の支払い利息払い
（=debt paying, debt service）
◆Financial institutions have capital which can be used to cover eventual financial losses to ensure debt servicing will not be impaired. 金融機関には、損失が生じた際にその穴埋めをして、債務の支払いに支障がでないようにする自己資本がある。◆Unlike government bonds, currency bears no maturity date and requires no debt servicing. 国債と違って、通貨には満期も元利の支払いもない。

debt servicing capacity [capability] 債務返済能力
（=debt paying ability, debt service capability）
◆The bank was slipshod in examining the debt-servicing capacity of its borrowers. 同行は、融資先の債務返済能力の審査がずさんだった。

debt servicing costs 債務返済費用, 国債費（「国債費」は、国債の償還とその利払いにあてる費用）
◆Debt servicing costs are intended to repay the principal and interest on government bonds. 国債費は、国債の元利払い（利払いや償還）に充てられる。◆Debt servicing costs for fiscal 2010 reached a record ¥20.6 trillion. 2010年度の国債費は、過去最高の20兆6,000億円に達した。◆The primary balance represents the budget balance, excluding proceeds from government bond issues and debt-servicing costs. プライマリー・バランスは、国債発行による収入と国債費（国債の利払いや償還費用）を除いた財政収支である。

debt servicing expenditures 国債費
（=debt servicing costs）
◆Debt servicing expenditures are used to pay interests for previously issued government bonds and to redeem the bonds. 国債費は、過去に発行した国債の利払いや国債の償還に充てられる。

debt-servicing spending 国債費
◆The Finance Ministry earmarked ¥17.57 trillion of debt-servicing spending on the redemption of government bonds and interest payments. 財務省は、国債の償還とその利払いにあてる国債費として、17兆5,700億円の予算を組んだ。

debt waiver 債権放棄, 債務免除
（=waiver of debt；⇒collapse動詞, lending, repay）
　ask for a debt waiver　債権放棄を求める［要請する］, 債務免除を要請する
　debt waiver request　債権放棄の要請, 債務免除の要請
　seek debt waivers from the creditor banks　取引銀行に債権放棄を求める
　the requested debt waiver　債権放棄の要請, 債務免除の要請
◆Because of a debt waiver by the major banks, the company's interest-bearing debt fell to ¥58 billion from ¥600 billion in the previous year. 主要取引銀行の債務免除で、有利子負債は前期の6,000億円から580億円に減少した。◆Companies must be generating operating profits from their main businesses to seek debt waivers from the creditor banks. 取引銀行に債権放棄を求めるには、企業はその主要な事業部門で営業利益を上げていなければならない。◆In the first half, the firm booked a special profit of about ¥400 billion on debt waivers by its key lenders. 上半期に同社は、主要金融機関の債務免除［債権放棄］で、約4,000億円の特別利益を計上した。◆It's irrational if banks don't offer debt waivers regarding TEPCO's debt. 東電の債務について、銀行が債権放棄をしないのはおかしい。◆The company expects to recover by the end of fiscal 2011 on the back of proceeds from the sale of its cosmetic division as well as the requested debt waiver and new share issue. 化粧事業部門の売却益や債権放棄の要請、新株発行などで、同社は2011年度末までに利益を回復するとしている。◆The company has received about ¥780 billion in cash and debt waivers from shareholders and investors in two bailouts. 同社は、2度の金融支援で、株主と出資企業から約7,800億円の資金提供と債務免除を受けている。◆The firm was granted debt waivers totaling ¥640 billion from its main creditor banks. 同社は、主力銀行から6,400億円の債権放棄を受けた。◆The rescue plan consists mainly of a debt waiver and a debt-for-equity swap. 支援計画の大

きな柱は、債権放棄と債務の株式化だ。◆To improve its financial health, Daiei will seek about ¥410 billion worth of debt waivers from about 30 financial institutions to reduce its interest-bearing debts. 財務体質を改善するため、ダイエーは、約30の金融機関に約4,100億円の債権放棄を求めて、有利子負債を削減する。

debt woes 債務問題, 債務危機, 債務危機問題
◆In resolving Greece's debt woes, German Chancellor Angera Merkel urged substantial aid from private creditors. ギリシャの債務問題を解決するにあたって、アンゲラ・メルケル独首相は、民間債権者に大幅支援を求めた。

debt write-down [writedown] 債務削減
◆Athens is likely to officially launch talks with banks and other private bondholders for the debt write-down. ギリシャ政府は、銀行などの民間債権者[民間投資家、民間の債券保有者]と債務削減のための協議を開始する見込みだ。

debtee (名)債権者 (=creditor)

debtholder (名)債権者, 債券保有者
  debtholder protection 債権者保護, 債券保有者の保護
  debtholder recovery 債権者の回収額
  debtholder's seniority of claim 債権者の請求権の順位
  junior-subordinated debtholders 下位劣後債保有者
  maintain debtholder interests 債権者の利益を守る
  senior unsecured debtholders 上位無担保債保有者
  subordinated [junior] debtholders 劣後の債権者, 後順位の債権者
◆MGM filed for Chapter 11 after striking an agreement with one of its largest debtholders to win the debtholder's support for a restructuring. メトロ・ゴールドウィン・メイヤー (MGM)は、会社再建につて債権者の支持を得ることで最高額債権者と合意に達した後、米連邦破産法11章の適用を申請した。◆The company struck an agreement with its debtholder to win their support for reconstruction. 同社は、会社再建について債権者の支持を得ることで、債権者と合意に達した。

debtor (名)債務者, 融資先, 借方, 債務国
  (⇒inspector)
  debtor country [nation] 債務国, 赤字国
    (=indebted country)
  debtor-creditor relationship 債権債務関係
  debtor in possession 管理処分権保持債務者, 占有債務者, 継承破産人 (=DIP)
  debtor in possession finance 事業再生融資, DIPファイナンス (=DIP finance, DIP financing, DIP plan)
◆Asset-backed commercial paper refers to commercial paper whose creditworthiness is guaranteed by sales credit that the corporate issuer has with its debtors. 資産担保CPとは、企業発行体がその債務者に対して保有する売掛金によって信用度が保証されるコマーシャル・ペーパーを指す。◆FSA's inspectors are to confirm whether the companies' categorization by banks as debtors is relevant or fair. 金融庁の検査官は、銀行側の企業(融資先企業)の債務者区分が適正かどうかなどを検証することになっている。◆The special inspections will be conducted as banks review the positions of their debtors, and will be finalized before the closing of accounts. 特別検査は、銀行が債務者の経営状態を見直す際に行われ、決算までに完了する。

debtor bank 債務行, 破たん銀行
◆Under the trustee's management, the debtor bank's business will be operated and the refunding of deposits will be temporarily suspended. 金融整理管財人の管理下で、破たん銀行の業務は運営され、預金の払戻しは一時停止される。

debtor company 融資先企業, 融資先, 債務者
  (=debtor firm)
◆Debtor companies are currently categorized by the banks into five groups, ranging from normal to bankrupt. 債務者は現在、金融機関が正常先から破たん先まで5段階に分類してい

る。(金融機関は現在、融資先を債務の返済に応じて正常先、要注意先、破たん懸念先、実質破たん先、破たん先の5段階に区分している)◆The Financial Services Agency will check the credibility of the banks' debtor companies, including their management efficiency and the accuracy of their collateral assessment. 金融庁は、銀行の融資先の経営効率や担保評価などを含めて、銀行の融資先の信用力を洗い直す。

debtor firm 融資先企業, 融資先, 債務者
  (=debtor company)
◆The state-backed Industrial Revitalization Corporation of Japan buys bad loans from banks and imposes strict turnaround plans on debtor firms. 政府系の産業再生機構は、銀行(金融機関)から不良債権を買い取り、融資先企業には厳しい企業再建計画を強制する。

debut (動)新規上場する, 上場する, 初登場する, デビューする (⇒start-up)
◆Chinese financial information and services company Xinhua Finance Ltd debuted on the Tokyo Stock Exchange's Mothers market. 中国の金融情報サービス会社の新華ファイナンスが、東証マザーズ(新興企業向け市場)に新規上場した。

debut (名)新規上場, 上場, 初登場, デビュー
  (=initial public offering; ⇒e-broker)
◆Shares in chipmaker Elpida Memory Inc. gained 7.14 percent on their Monday debut. 半導体メーカー、エルピーダメモリの株価は、月曜日の上場で7.14%上昇した。

deceive (動)騙(だま)す, 欺(あざむ)く, 騙(だま)して〜させる
◆Olympus Corp. has kept deceiving its shareholders and clients by years of window-dressing. オリンパスは、長年にわたる粉飾で、株主や取引先を欺き続けてきた。

decelerate (動)速度が落ちる, 低下する, 低迷する, 減速する, 鈍る, 鈍化する, 鎮静化する
  a decelerating world economy 減速する世界経済, 世界経済の減速
  decelerate sharply 大幅に低下する, 急激に低下する
  decelerated economy 減速経済
  decelerated inflation インフレの鎮静化
  decelerating monetary growth マネー・サプライ伸び率の低下
  start to decelerate 低下に転じる
◆Concerns grow over the possibility of a decelerating world economy. 世界経済が減速する可能性に対する懸念が、増大している。

deceleration (名)低下, 減速, 鈍化, 鎮静化
◆Overseas economies are moving out of their deceleration phase. 海外経済は、景気減速局面から抜け出している。

deception (名)詐欺(fraud), 詐欺行為, うそ, ごまかし, ぺてん(trick), まやかし, 騙(だま)し, 欺まん, 策略, 手管, ごまかし物, にせ物, 期待はずれ
  a deception method 詐欺の手口
  a gross deception ひどい詐欺
  a piece of deception 詐欺行為
  be under deception 騙されている
  practice deception on [upon] a person 人を騙す, 人を欺(あざむ)く
◆Olympus Corp.'s deception of its shareholders and clients by window-dressing was due to the cover-up of losses on investments the company made in the 1990s. オリンパスが粉飾決算で株主や取引先を欺いたのは、同社が1990年代に行った投資の損失隠しをするためだった。

decide (動)決める, 決定する, 決断する, 方針を固める, 踏み切る, 解決する, 判断する, 決議する, 判定する, 判決する, 判決[審判]を下す, 裁決する
  decide to introduce a new open market operation 新型の公開市場操作(オペ)の導入に踏み切る

the government decided to issue restoration bonds　政府は復興再生債を発行する方針を固めた
◆A firm requires the support of more than two thirds of shareholders to decide on important matters, such as a merger, at shareholders meetings. 企業が株主総会で合併などの重要事項を決議するには、3分の2以上の賛成が必要だ。◆A major company has recently decided to dissolve its health insurance society. 大企業が最近、同社の健康保険組合の解散を決めた。◆As Greece may default on its debts, the IMF and the EU have worked out a policy of deciding on a second aid tranche of €120 billion in July 2011. ギリシャが債務不履行（デフォルト）に陥る可能性があるため、国際通貨基金（IMF）と欧州連合（EU）は、2011年7月に1,200億ユーロ（約13兆8,000億円）規模の第二次金融支援策を決定する方針を打ち出した。◆Finance Minister Yoshihiko Noda decided to conduct a yen-selling market intervention on Aug. 4, 2011. 2011年8月4日に野田財相は、円売り市場介入の実施を決断した。◆In 2009, the Business Accounting Council decided to require all of the nation's listed companies to use the IFRSs for their consolidated financial statements from 2015. 2009年に企業会計審議会は、2015年にも、国内全上場企業の連結財務諸表［連結財務書類］について、国際財務情報基準（IFRSs）の採用を上場企業に義務付ける方針を打ち出した。◆Meiji Yasuda decided to lower the yield rate of its flagship insurance product because the insurer placed priority on long-term stable management over an increase in the number of policyholders. 明治安田生保は、契約者の数を増やすより長期的な経営の安定を優先したため、主力保険商品の予定利率［利回り］を引き下げることにした。◆Stock buyback limits are to be decided at general shareholders meetings. 自社株の取得枠は、株主総会で決められることになっている。◆The bank decided to continue extending loans to the company despite its executives knowing the company was on the ropes. この会社の経営が悪化しているのを経営陣が知りながら、同行は同社への融資継続を決めた。◆The Bank of Japan decided to continue providing ample liquidity to financial markets. 日本銀行は、金融市場に大量の資金供給を続けることを決定した。◆The Bank of Japan decided to extend a special loan to Namihaya Bank after the second-tier regional bank was declared insolvent. 日本銀行は、第二地方銀行の「なみはや銀行」が破たん認定を受けた後、同行に対して特別融資［特融］を実施することを決めた。◆The Bank of Japan decided to maintain its current monetary policy. 日銀は、金融政策の現状維持を決めた。◆The BOJ decided to further relax its monetary policy by injecting an additional ¥10 trillion into a fund aimed at purchasing government bonds and corporate debentures. 日銀は、国債や社債などを買い入れるための基金に新たに10兆円を注入［投入］して追加の金融緩和に踏み切ることを決めた。◆The BOJ decided to introduce a new open market operation by supplying ¥10 trillion to private financial institutions in three month loans at an ultralow annual interest of 0.1 percent. 日銀は、民間の金融機関に年1％の超低金利で貸出期間3か月の資金を10兆円供給する新型の公開市場操作（オペ）の導入に踏み切った。◆The company decided to seek a helping hand from the investment fund. 同社は、この投資ファンドに支援を求めることにした。◆The European Central Bank decided to buy Italian and Spanish government bonds in tandem with the issuance of the G-7 emergency statement. 欧州中央銀行（ECB）は、G7緊急声明の発表と連動する形で、イタリアとスペインの国債を買い入れる方針を決めた。◆The firm decided to simultaneously list its stocks on the New York and London stock exchanges in October. 同社は、10月にニューヨークとロンドンの両証券取引所に株式を同時上場する方針を固めた。◆The government decided to issue restoration and rebirth bonds, avoiding the issuance of deficit-covering bonds. 政府は、赤字国債の発行を避けて、復興再生債を発行する方針を固めた。◆The markets apparently decided that the dialogue between Prime Minister Kan and Bank of Japan Gov. Shirakawa lacked substance. 菅首相と白川日銀総裁の今回の意見交換を、市場は実質的な内容が乏しいと判断したようだ。◆The Tokyo metropolitan government has decided to deposit more than ¥100 billion in public funds in Citibank, a U.S. bank, to diversify risks. 東京都は、1,000億円を上回る公金を米国の銀行「シティバンク」に預けて、リスクを分散する方針を固めた。◆The TSE and the OSE will decide the exact allocation of shares based on a ratio of 1.7 TSE shares to one OSE share. 東証と大証は、正確には大証の1株に対して東証は1.7株の割合で（新会社の）株式の割当てを決めることになった。

decimalization　（名）株価の小数表示（証券取引所の株価表示方式）

decision　（名）決定, 意思決定, 決断, 判断, 決議, 判定, 判決, 裁決
　bond pricing decisions　債券価格の判断
　business decision　経営判断, 企業の意思決定, 事業決定
　business risk decision　業務上のリスク決定
　capital investment decision　設備投資の決定
　credit decision　融資判断, 貸出決定, 与信判断, 信用判断
　decision of a general meeting of stockholders　株主総会決議
　FOMC decision　連邦公開市場委員会（FOMC）の決定
　investment decision　投資決定, 投資判断, 投資意思決定
　monetary decisions　金融政策
　policy decision　政策決定, 政策策定
　rating decision　格付け判断, 格付けの意思決定
　the decision of investors　投資家の意思決定
　the unanimous decision　全会一致の決定
◆At the eurozone finance ministers meeting held on October 3, 2011, a decision on bridge loans of about €8 billion to Greece was expected, but none was done. 2011年10月3日に開かれたユーロ圏財務相会合では、ギリシャに対する約80億ユーロのつなぎ融資の決定が見込まれていたが、これは見送られた。◆Corporate accounting reports are the most important criterion for investment decisions. 企業の財務情報は、特に重要な投資判断の材料だ。◆DaimlerChrysler AG announced its decision to withdraw from a bailout of Mitsubishi Motors. 独ダイムラー・クライスラーが、三菱自動車への金融支援打切り決定を発表した。◆Shareholders can access the company's special Web site and vote on decisions, including the election of board members. 株主は、同社専用のホームページを利用して、取締役選任などの議決に投票することができる。◆The proper disclosure of important information concerning the incident is necessary for investors to make decisions. この事件に関する重要な情報の適正な開示は、投資家が投資判断をするうえで必要である。◆The unanimous decision by the U.S. central bank's policy setting Federal Open Market Committee moved the benchmark federal funds rate to 1.25 percent. 米連邦準備制度理事会の金利政策を決定する米連邦公開市場委員会の全会一致による決定で、短期金利の指標であるフェデラル・ファンド金利が年1.25％に引き上げられた。◆The United States is under pressure to make some difficult monetary policy decisions to cool down the overheating economy by countering the inflationary pressures stemming from higher import prices due to the weaker dollar. 米国は現在、ドル安での輸入価格の高騰によるインフレ圧力を抑えて過熱気味の景気を鎮めるための難しい金融政策の決断を迫られている。◆The U.S. FRB's recent decision on further quantitative easing is only an aberration. 米連邦準備制度理事会（FRB）の今回の追加金融緩和の決定は、常軌を逸した行為と言わざるを得ない。

decision making　意思決定, 政策決定
　corporate decision making　企業経営

decision-making authority　意思決定権, 決定権
decision-making process　意思決定の過程
decision-making skill　意思決定能力
investment decision-making process　投資意思決定過程
one-man decision making style　ワンマン体制
programmed decision making　定型的意思決定
◆The ASEAN plus Three Macroeconomic Research Office, or AMRO, was set up in Singapore in April 2011 to coordinate decision making for providing emergency liquidity to member states. ASEANプラス3（日中韓）の域内マクロ経済リサーチ・オフィス（AMRO）は、参加国に緊急時の流動性を提供する際の意思決定調整機関として、2011年4月にシンガポールに設立された。◆The inadequate decision-making and business management processes of the financial group stem from factional strife within the company. 同金融グループの不十分な意思決定プロセスと経営管理体制は、社内の派閥争いに起因する。◆To enhance management efficiency and the decision-making process, Mizuho Financial Group will integrate its Mizuho Bank and Mizuho Corporate Bank in 2013. 経営の効率化と意思決定の迅速化を図るため、みずほフィナンシャルグループは、傘下のみずほ銀行とみずほコーポレート銀行を2013年に合併させる。

decisive　（形）決定的な, 決め手となる, 決定づける, 断固たる,（性格などが）果断な, 果敢（かかん）な, 決然とした, 決断力のある, 疑いの余地のない, 明白な, はっきりした
　be decisive of　～を決定づける, ～を決する, ～の決め手となる, ～を終局に導く
　decisive action　断固とした行動, 断固とした措置, 断固たる措置
　decisive evidence [proof]　決定的証拠, 確証
　decisive factor　決定的要因
　decisive manager　決断力のある経営者 [管理者, 監督]
　decisive measures　断固たる措置, 断固とした処置
　play a decisive role in　～で決定的な役割を果たす [役割を演じる]
　take decisive action　断固とした行動を取る
◆The G-7's joint statement praised the decisive actions of the United States and European countries in trying to reduce their fiscal deficits. G7の共同声明は、米国と欧州の財政赤字削減策に関して、米欧の断固たる行動を歓迎した。◆The government could take further decisive actions, including an additional intervention. 政府は、追加介入を含めてさらに断固たる措置を取る可能性がある。◆With the United States facing the worst financial crisis in generations, Bush's White House took decisive measures to safeguard the economy. 米国が過去最悪の金融危機に直面して、ブッシュ政権は経済危機を守るために断固たる措置を取った。

declaration date　配当宣言日
◆The market value of the common stock was $10 per share on the declaration date. 普通株式の配当宣言日の時価は、1株当たり10ドルであった。

declaration of bankruptcy　破産宣告
◆The financial authorities filed a declaration of bankruptcy and a request for asset protection with the Tokyo District Court for the brokerage firm. 金融当局は、同証券会社の破産宣告と財産保全処分を東京地裁に申し立てた。

declare　（動）配当支払いなどを宣言する, 申告する, 計上する, 公表する, 発表する
　（⇒accounting mistake, bankrupt）
　be declared bankrupt　破産宣告を受ける
　be declared insolvent　破産［経営破たん, 支払い不能］の宣告を受ける, 支払い不能と判断される［認定される］
　declare a stock split　株式分割を発表する, 株式分割の実施を発表する

declared capital　公示資本, 表示資本
declared dividend　宣言配当金, 公表配当金, 配当宣言
declared income　申告所得, 所得申告
declared profit　計上利益, 公表利益
dividend declared　宣言配当金 [配当額], 配当金, 配当決議
dividends declared per common share　普通株式1株当たり配当
preferred dividends declared　優先株式の配当宣言額
◆About 100 employees of Credit Suisse Securities and the Tokyo branch of Credit Suisse Principal Investments Ltd. have failed to declare a total of ￥2 billion of income related to stock options. クレディ・スイス証券とクレディ・スイス・プリンシパル・インベストメンツ東京支店の社員約100人が、ストック・オプション関連所得の20億円を申告していなかった。◆The Bank of Japan decided to extend a special loan to Namihaya Bank after the second-tier regional bank was declared insolvent. 日本銀行は、第二地方銀行の「なみはや銀行」が破たん認定を受けた後、同行に対して特別融資［特融］を実施することを決めた。◆The company failed to declare about ￥5 billion in income. 同社は、所得約50億円を申告しなかった。◆Yamaichi Securities Co. was declared bankrupt by the Tokyo District Court in June 1996. 山一証券は、1996年6月に東京地裁から破産宣告を受けた。

declare a cash dividend　現金配当を宣言する
◆The company declared a cash dividend of $0.07 per common share in the first two quarters of 2011. 2011年第1四半期と第2四半期に、同社はそれぞれ普通株式1株当たり0.07ドルの現金配当を宣言した。

declare a net deficit　税引き後赤字を計上する
◆The firm declared a net deficit of more than ￥1 trillion in the fiscal year ending December 2009. 同社は、2009年度に［2009年12月期決算で］1兆円超の税引き後赤字を計上した。

declare default on the national debt　国債の債務不履行（デフォルト）を宣言する
◆A day after declaring default on the national debt, Argentina's new president rolled out an ambitious works program. 国債の債務不履行（デフォルト）を宣言した翌日、アルゼンチンの新大統領は、野心的な労働政策を発表した。

decline　（動）拒絶する, 拒否する, 辞退する　（自動）減少する, 低下する, 下落する, 落ち込む, 悪化する, 低迷する, 後退する, 衰退する, 縮小する, マイナスになる
　decline further　一段と悪化する, さらに落ち込む
　decline sharply　急減する, 急激に低下する, 急落する, 大幅に低下する
◆An exporter company will incur losses if the yen rises above the assumed exchange rate, but benefit if the yen declines. 輸出企業では、その想定為替レートより円高になれば為替差損が生じ,（想定為替レートより）円安になれば為替差益が出る。◆Bank issues declined as investors remained wary over the banks' massive bad loan problems. 銀行株は、やはり巨額の不良債権問題の処理に対する投資家の警戒感から値を下げた。◆Due to confusion in the financial markets, interest rates have declined significantly and global stock prices have dropped. 金融市場の混乱で、金利が大幅に低下し、世界的に株価も下落している。◆If the group's cash-flow situation deteriorates further, it may see its creditor banks declining to extend loans. 同グループの資金繰りがさらに悪化すれば、取引銀行が融資を拒否する可能性もある。◆In the six months to September, Japan's current account surplus declined 37 percent year-on-year to ￥7.86 trillion. 今年4～9月期の日本の経常収支黒字額は、前年同期比37%減の7兆8,600億円となった。◆Money loaned by private banks declined because banks with weakened financial strength were less willing to lend, besides a lack of businesses seeking expansion through borrowing. 民間銀行の貸出金が減ったのは、お金を借りてまで事

業を拡大しようとする企業がなかったほか、財務が悪化した銀行が貸し渋ったからだ。◆Money loaned by private banks declined to ¥419 trillion as of the end of July 2011 from ¥472 trillion at the end of March 1999 when the zero-interest rate policy was first adopted. 民間銀行の貸出金は、ゼロ金利政策が初めて導入された1999年3月末の472兆円から、2011年7月末現在では419兆円に減った。◆Prices have dropped more steeply than those at the time when the BOJ was fighting deflation, and the rate of declining is expected to increase. 日銀がデフレと戦っていた時より物価は急激に下がり、下落率は今後さらに拡大する見込みだ。◆Stock prices declined on Asian markets. アジア市場でも、株が値下がりした。◆The FSA's special inspection will check the major banks' large-lot corporate borrowers whose stock prices or credit ratings have sharply declined. 金融庁の特別検査は、大手銀行の株価や格付けなどが急落した大口融資先を査定の対象としている。

decline （名）減少, 低下, 下降, 下落, 悪化, 低迷, 後退, 衰退, 縮小, 落ち込み
  bond yield decline　債券利回りの下落
  business decline　景気後退, 景気下降
  buy［buying］on decline　押し目買い
  credit decline　信用の質の低下, 信用の低下, 信用度の悪化　（=decline in credit quality）
  decline in asset value　資産価値の下落
  decline in birthrate and a consequent graying　少子高齢化
  decline in cost of funds　資金コストの低下
  decline in deficits　赤字削減, 赤字縮小
  decline in economic conditions　景気の悪化
  decline in global activity　世界的な景気減速［悪化］
  decline in interest rates　金利の低下
  decline in losses　赤字縮小
  decline in money loaned by private banks　民間銀行貸出金の減少
  decline in refinancings　借換えの減少
  declines in credit ratings　信用格付けの低下
    （⇒acquire capital from the market）
  dollar's decline　ドル安
  further declines in economic activity　景気の一段の悪化, 景気の一層の落ち込み
  heavy decline　大暴落
  interest rate decline　金利低下
    （=decline in rates）
  market decline　市場低迷, 市場の悪化, 市場の衰退
  modest decline in inflation　インフレ率の小幅低下
  output decline　生産の減少
    （=decline in production, production decline）
  price decline　価格の下落, 価格低下, 物価の下落, インフレ率の低下　（=decline in prices）
  sales decline　販売の低迷, 販売の落ち込み, 売上の減少
  secular decline in the credit quality　信用の質の長期的低下
  share［stock］price decline　株価下落
  summer decline　夏枯れ
  triple decline　トリプル安

◆Any corporation that has improved its business performance could easily suffer a decline if its top management makes misguided business decisions. 業績が好転した企業でも、トップ・マネジメントが経営判断を誤ればすぐ転落する。◆It remains uncertain whether crude oil prices will undergo an interrupted decline. 原油価格が一本調子で下落するかどうかは、不透明だ。◆Just as the number of people qualifying for pensions is on the rise, the working population, which underpins the pension scheme, is on the decline. 年金受給の資格者は増える一方、年金制度を支える現役世代は減っている。◆Ten of 12 Fed district banks reported weaker conditions or declines in their regional economies. 全米12地区連銀のうち10連銀が、各地域経済の悪化あるいは経済活動の低下を報告した。◆The large U.S. current account deficit might result in a marked decline of its international investment positions. 米国の巨額の経常赤字で、海外投資家のドル資産が大幅に減少する可能性がある［海外投資家の著しいドル資産離れを招きかねない］。◆The surplus in the current account stood at ¥1.5 trillion in September 2008, marking the seventh consecutive month of year-on-year declines. 2008年9月の経常収支の黒字額は、1兆5,000億円となり、7か月連続で前年実績を下回った。◆There have been no signs of a rebound in the amount of outstanding loans, which continues on an abated decline. このところ引き続き減少傾向にある銀行の貸出残高に、反転の兆しは見えない。◆There is a limit to conventional pump-priming measures amid a continued decline in birthrate and a consequent graying and shrinking population. 少子高齢化や人口減少などが進行しているなかで、従来の景気刺激策［景気テコ入れ策］では限界がある。

decline in land prices　地価の下落
  ◆The prolonged slump in the real estate market is maintaining the decline in land prices. 不動産取引市場の長期低迷が、引き続き地価の下落を招いている。

decline in long-term interest rates　長期金利の低下
  ◆The decline in long-term interest rates since May is due to continued capital flight from high-risk assets such as stocks triggered by the debt crisis in Europe. 5月以降、長期金利が低下しているのは、欧州の財政危機をきっかけに株式などリスク［損失リスク］の高い資産からの資金逃避が続いたためだ。

decline in stock prices　株価下落, 株価低迷, 株安
  （=decline in stock prices）
  ◆As the Greek fiscal crisis grows more serious, there has been no halt to the worldwide decline in stock prices. ギリシャの財政危機が一段と深刻化するにつれ、世界同時株安に歯止めがかからなくなっている。◆The industry is under a good deal of stress, as evidenced by pressure on profitability and decline in stock prices over the last several months. 業界は、収益性の悪化やここ数か月の株価低迷でも明らかなように、かなり厳しい状況下にあります。

decline in stock values　株価下落, 株安
  （=decline in stock prices）
  ◆A chain-reaction global decline in stock values was temporarily stopped by a barrage of countermeasures. 世界的な株安連鎖は、矢継ぎ早の対策でいったんは歯止めがかかった。

decline in the value of the dollar　ドル安, ドル相場の下落
  ◆U.S. companies are continuing to benefit from a boom in exports due mainly to the decline in the value of the dollar earlier this year. 米企業は、主に年初来のドル安による輸出好調の恩恵を受けている。

decline in the value of the euro　ユーロ安, ユーロ相場の下落
  ◆The decline in the value of the euro is unlikely to stop. ユーロの下落傾向［ユーロ相場の下落］は、止まりそうにない。

decline in yields　利回りの低下, 利回りの引下げ
  ◆The decline in yields on whole life insurance products effectively raises premiums. 終身保険商品の利回り（予定利率）の引下げは、実質的な保険料の値上げになる。

decliner　値下がり株　（loserともいう。値上がり株＝advancer, gainer, winner）
  ◆Decliners were led by the securities, sea transport and fishery and forestry sectors. 値下がり株は、主に証券、海運と水産・林業の各業種だ。

decliners　値下がり株（losersともいう。値上がり株＝advancers, gainers）

declines in surpluses　剰余金の減少
  ◆Declines in surpluses are likely to reduce a bank's capital

adequacy ratio. 剰余金が減ると、銀行の自己資本比率が低下する恐れがある。
declining （形）減少［低下、低迷、悪化、衰退］する、〜の減少［低下、低迷、悪化、縮小］
   declining asset base　資産基盤の縮小
   declining asset quality　資産の質の低下
   declining equity［share, stock］prices　株価下落
      （=decline in stock prices）
   declining financing cost　資金調達コストの低下
   declining loan yields　貸出金利の低下
   declining market rates　市場金利の低下
decoupling　（名）連動しないこと、非連動、非連動性、脱同調化、ディカップリング
   ◆Those in favor of "decoupling" urged the Japanese to reduce their overdependence on the U.S. economy. 「ディカップリング（非連動）論」支持者は、米経済への過度の依存脱却を日本に促した。
decoupling theory　脱同調化理論、非連動論、ディカップリング［デカップリング］論（世界景気は米国の景気と乖離（かいり）して推移する、つまり米国の景気減速は中国やインドなど新興市場国の発展が続くので世界的な景気減速にはつながらない、という考え方）
   ◆The decoupling theory suggests that China and India would not be hurt by a global slowdown. ディカップリング論によると、中国やインドなどは世界的な景気減速の影響を受けないとされる。◆The so-called decoupling theory holds that the effects of a U.S. slowdown can be offset by growth in emerging nations. いわゆるディカップリング論では、米経済の減速は新興国の成長が補う、と考えられている。
decrease　（動）減少させる、引き下げる、低下させる、軽減する　（自動）減少する、目減りする、低下する
   decrease the risk of financial investments　金融投資のリスクを軽減する
   decrease volatility　ボラティリティを引き下げる、リスクを引き下げる
   decreased capital expenditures　設備投資の削減
   decreased dividend　減配、配当引下げ
   decreased margin　利益率の低下
   decreased profitability　収益力の低下、収益性の低下
   ◆If the current downward trend of stock prices continues, banks' financial resources that could be used to dispose of bad loans will decrease drastically. 株価の下落基調がこのまま続くと、金融機関の不良債権処理の原資は激減する。◆In the case of Toyota, if the yen falls by ¥1 in relation to the dollar, its consolidated operating profit will decrease by about ¥30 billion on an annual basis. トヨタの場合、円がドルに対して1円下落すれば［ドルに対して1円円高が進めば］、同社の連結営業利益は年間で約300億円目減りする。◆The company is rolling out investment strategies that decrease volatility. 同社は、リスクを引き下げる運用戦略を展開している。◆The Greek government has set forth measures to decrease the number of government employees and raise taxes to cut its budget deficits. 財政赤字削減のため、ギリシャ政府は公務員削減や増税策を打ち出した。
decrease　（名）減少、縮小、低下、下落
   announce a decrease in dividends　減配を発表する
   capital decrease　減資
      （=capital reduction, reduction of capital）
   decrease in a bond's yield　債券利回りの低下
   decrease in accounts receivable（net）　売掛金の減少（純額）、受取債権の減少（減額）
   decrease in cash and marketable securities　現金預金および有価証券の減少額
   decrease in customer loans　消費者ローンの減少
   decrease in dividends　減配

   decrease in long-term debt　長期負債の減少、長期負債の返済
   （decrease）increase in cash and short-term investments and borrowings　現金・預金、短期投資および短期借入金の増加（減少）
   decrease of capital　減資　（=capital decrease, capital reduction, reduction of capital）
   rating decrease　格下げ
   ◆The size of the financial assets of Japanese households is still worth a massive ¥1.47 quadrillion despite a decrease in the total over recent years. 日本の個人金融資産の規模は、ここ数年で減少したものの、まだ1,470兆円ほどもあって巨大だ。
decrease in pension benefits　年金給付減
   ◆The instability of the pension system has repeatedly experienced increases in pension premiums and decreases in pension benefits. 年金制度が不安定なため、年金保険料の負担増と年金給付減が繰り返されてきた。
decreasing　（形）減少する、低減する、逓減する、下落する、〜の減少、〜の低減［下落］
   decreasing cost　費用低減
   decreasing marginal efficiency of capital　資本の限界効率逓減
   decreasing term（life）insurance　逓減性定期（生命）保険
deduct　（動）差し引く、控除する、引き落とす　（⇒accounting rule, corporate income, local corporate tax, Net-debit service）
   ◆Corporations in these four fields can deduct a percentage of research and development costs from their corporate taxes. これら4分野の企業は、法人税（法人税額）から研究開発費の一定割合を控除することができる。◆This loss came from deducting recourse loans made to our senior management. この損失は、当社の上級経営陣に対して行った遡求請求権付き貸付け金を控除したことで生じました。
deduction　差引、控除、引落し、差引額、控除額、減少額、減額、損金、損金算入
   （⇒account book, capital loss, double deduction）
   automatic deduction　自動引落し　（=direct debit）
   deductions from income　所得控除
   deferred deduction　繰延べ控除　（⇒term）
   depreciation deduction　減価償却控除
   dividends paid deduction　支払い配当金の控除
   housing loan deduction　住宅ローン控除
   insurance deduction　保険料控除
   tax deduction　税額控除、税控除、減税
      （=tax credit）
   ◆The direct debit system will allow customers to make regular premium payments with automatic deductions from their bank accounts by entering their bank card and personal identification numbers. この口座引落しシステムでは、顧客のキャッシュ・カードと個人の暗証番号を入力して、銀行口座からの自動引落しで顧客が定期的に保険料の支払いをするようになる。
deed　（名）行為、行動、実行、事実、実際、功績、書面、証書、捺印（なついん）証書、譲渡証書、不動産権利証書
   deed absolute　無条件譲渡証書
   deed assignment　財産譲渡証書、財産譲渡
   deed of arrangement　債務整理証書
   deed of association　会社定款、有限責任会社設立定款
   deed of conveyance　譲渡証書
   deed of release　権利放棄証書　（=release deed）
   deed of sale　売約証書
   deed of settlement　会社設立証書
   deed of title　不動産権利証書
   deed of transfer　譲渡証書、財産譲渡証書、株式売買［株

式譲渡］証書, 名義書換え証書
（=deed of conveyance, transfer deed）
 deed of trust　（担保のための）信託証書
 （=trust deed）
 escrow deed　条件付き譲渡証書, 条件付き捺印証書, 未完証書
 loan on deeds　証書貸付け
 mortgage deed　抵当証券
 quit claim deed　権利放棄証書
deem　（動）〜と考える［思う、見なす、解釈する、判断する］
 deem lightly of　〜を軽視する
 deemed corporation　見なし法人
 deemed issue　見なし発行
 taxation on deemed dividend　見なし配当課税
 ◆A bank's core capital, or Tier 1capital, is deemed to have high loss-absorbency and resilience. 銀行の中核的自己資本は、損失吸収力と弾力性が高いとされている。
deep　（形）大幅な, 高率の, 大がかりな, 十分な, 深刻な
 be deep in debt　借金で首が回らない
 deep bid　大量取引用価格
 deep discount bond　高率割引債, 大幅割引債, ディープ・ディスカウント債
 deep discounted bond　高率割引債
 （=deep discount bond）
 deep-gain security　ディープ・ゲイン証券
 deep in the money　オプションの行使で大きい利益が出る状態
 deep market　十分な資本市場
 deep out of the money　オプションの行使で大きい損失が出る状態
 deep recession　深刻な景気後退［不況、リセッション］
 deeper recession　景気悪化
 get deeper in debt　借金がかさむ
 get into financial trouble　深刻な経営難に陥る
deep freeze　凍結, 凍結状態, 一時停止, 棚上げ, 急速冷凍, 冷凍冷蔵庫
 ◆Credit markets are beginning to thaw after months of a deep freeze. 債券発行市場は、凍結状態がここ数か月続いた後、氷解が始まっている。
deep recession　深刻なリセッション, 深刻な景気後退期, 深刻な不況　（=severe recession）
 be in a deep recession　景気後退期にある
 deeper recession　景気悪化
 remain in a deep recession　景気後退に陥っている
 ◆Japan's economy is in a deep recession. 日本経済は、深刻な景気後退期にある。◆The U.S. 10 leading banks need a combined capital buffer of 74.6 billion against the risk of a deeper recession and higher unemployment over the next two years. 米主要金融機関の10社は、今後2年の景気悪化リスクと失業増大に備えて、10社合計で746億ドルの資本増強を求められている。
deepen　（動）深める, 深化させる, （悲しみなどを）増す, 深まる, 濃くなる, 悪化する, 深化する, 深刻化する
 deepen the Japan-U.S. alliance　日米同盟を深化させる
 deepen the puzzle　謎を深める
 deepen ties with　〜との関係を深める, 〜との関係を強化する
 deepened recession　不況の深刻化, 景気後退の深刻化
 deepening global economic crisis　世界的な経済危機の深刻化
 deepening recession　景気後退の深刻化
 ◆Public distrust in the pension system must be prevented from deepening. 年金制度への国民の不信感は、これ以上深まらないようにしなければならない。◆The euro crisis is deepening. ユーロ危機が、深刻化している。◆The government will revise downward its GDP growth estimate in light of a deepening recession. 政府は、景気後退の深刻化を受けて、国内総生産（GDP）成長率の予想を下方修正する方針だ。
deeper housing correction　住宅の調整局面の深刻化
 ◆In the United States, there is a risk of deeper and more prolonged housing correction. 米国では、住宅の調整局面が深刻化し、長引く恐れもある。
deeper recession　景気悪化
 ◆The U.S. 10 leading banks need a combined capital buffer of 74.6 billion against the risk of a deeper recession and higher unemployment over the next two years. 米主要金融機関の10社は、今後2年の景気悪化リスクと失業増大に備えて、10社合計で746億ドルの資本増強を求められている。
default　（動）（義務、債務を）履行しない, 実行しない, 履行を怠る, 義務を怠る, 約束を守らない, 支払わない, デフォルトになる, デフォルトに陥る, デフォルトを起こす
 defaulted assets　デフォルトに陥った資産
 defaulted bonds　無償還債券
 defaulted corporate bonds　デフォルト社債
 defaulted receivables　不履行債権, 不履行発生債権, デフォルトに陥った債権
 ◆Bond insurers write policies that promise to cover payments to bondholders if the entity that issued the bonds defaults. 金融保証会社［債券保険会社］は、債券発行体がデフォルト（債務不履行）になった場合に、債券保有者への（元本と利息の）支払い補償を約束する保険を引き受けている。◆If a new federal debt ceiling isn't set by Aug. 2, 2011, the United States will be forced to default on Treasuries securities as it will not be able to issue new bonds to pay back maturing government debts. 2011年8月2日までに連邦政府の債務上限を新たに設けないと、米国は満期を迎える国債を償還するための国債増発ができないので、米国債の不履行（デフォルト）が発生する。◆It will be the other eurozone countries and the IMF that will suffer losses if Greece defaults. ギリシャの不払い［デフォルト］で損失を被るのは、ギリシャ以外のユーロ圏諸国とIMF（国際通貨基金）だ。◆Under the U.S. government program that insured mortgages, the government has had to foot the bill for mortgage loans that defaulted. 米政府の住宅ローン保証プログラムに基づき、米政府はデフォルト（債務不履行）になった住宅ローンのツケの支払いを迫られている。
default　（名）債務不履行, 支払い停止, 滞納, デフォルト（=default of obligations: 債務者の一方的な債務支払いの停止。⇒foreign capital inflows, net capital deficiency, obligation, subprime lender）
 a Greek default　ギリシャの債務不履行（デフォルト）
 be in default　義務［債務、契約］不履行である
 corporate default　社債のデフォルト
 debt default　債務不履行　（=default）
 declare default on national debt　国債の債務不履行を宣言する
 default in payment　支払いの不履行
 default interest　遅延利息
 default judgment　欠席判決
 default of obligation　債務不履行
 default on the national debt　国債の債務不履行（デフォルト）
 default on Treasury securities　米国債の債務不履行, 米国債の不履行（デフォルト）
 default rate　貸倒れ発生率
 default risk　貸倒れリスク, 債務不履行リスク, 債務不履行に陥る危険性
 default swap　デフォルト・スワップ

DEFA

fall into default　債務不履行（デフォルト）に陥る
go into default　債務不履行になる
in default　債務を履行しないで
in the event of default by the lessee　借り手がデフォルトを起こした場合
loan default　債務不履行
property tax default　固定資産税の滞納
resolve the default within A days　A日以内に債務不履行を是正する
Russian default　ロシアのデフォルト
selective default　選択的デフォルト
technical default　技術的デフォルト（政府の資金繰りがつかなくなった状態）
the possible default on yen-denominated Argentine government bonds　予想される円建てアルゼンチン国債のデフォルト
the rise in defaults of U.S. subprime loans　米国のサブプライム・ローン（低所得者向け住宅ローン）の不払い増加
upon event of default　債務不履行の場合は
◆A Greek default may be unavoidable.　ギリシャ国債のデフォルト（債務不履行）は、避けられないかもしれない。◆If the U.S. government falls into default, the markets' faith in the dollar as the world's key currency would plummet. 米政府がデフォルト（債務不履行）に陥ったら、世界の基軸通貨としてのドルの信認は急落する。◆Many home mortgages went into default. 多くの住宅ローンが債務不履行になった。◆Should the U.S. government fall into default, the prices of the Treasury bonds held by major countries and financial institutions around the world would plummet. 米政府がデフォルト（債務不履行）に陥れば、主要国や世界の金融機関が保有する米国債の価格は暴落する。◆Some Japanese institutional investors, such as foundations and regional financial institutions, face a crisis because of the possible default on yen-denominated Argentine government bonds as a result of that country's deepening economic crisis. アルゼンチンの経済危機の深刻化に伴い、円建てアルゼンチン国債のデフォルトも予想されるため、日本の一部の機関投資家（財団法人や地方の金融機関など）は苦境に立たされている。◆The financial crisis was triggered by the rise in defaults of U.S. subprime loans. 今回の金融危機は、米国のサブプライム・ローン（低所得者向け住宅ローン）の不払い増加がきっかけだった。◆The IMF and the EU are strengthening their cooperation to avert a Greek default and prevent a chain reaction of debt crisis among other countries. ギリシャの債務不履行（デフォルト）を回避し他国間の債務危機の連鎖反応を防ぐため、国際通貨基金（IMF）と欧州連合（EU）は、連携を強めている。◆The news of a rise in the subprime defaults rocked the U.S. financial community. サブプライムの不払い増加のニュースに、米金融業界は動揺した。◆The U.S. government could avoid the worst-case scenario of default on payments to investors in Treasury bonds. 米政府は、国債の償還資金がなくなる債務不履行という最悪の事態を避けることができた。◆The U.S. government's default would throw the financial markets around the world into major turmoil. 米政府がデフォルト（債務不履行）に陥ったら、世界の金融市場は大混乱するだろう。

default on　（債務などを）履行しない、支払わない、返済しない、（利払いなどを）実行しない、〜を怠る
default on debt payments　債務返済でデフォルトを起こす、債務返済でデフォルトに陥る、債務返済を実行しない
default on interest payments　利払いでデフォルトを起こす、利払いを実行できない
default on one's borrowings　借入金の返済をしない、債務不履行に陥る
default on one's obligations　〜の義務を履行しない、〜の義務を実行しない
default on the debt　債務を履行しない、債務が不履行になる、債務がデフォルトになる
homeowners defaulted on their mortgages　住宅所有者の住宅ローンがデフォルト（債務不履行）になった（⇒insurance claims）
◆If a new federal debt ceiling isn't set by Aug. 2, 2011, the United States will be forced to default on Treasuries securities as it will not be able to issue new bonds to pay back maturing government debts. 2011年8月2日までに連邦政府の債務上限を新たに設けないと、米国は満期を迎える国債を償還するための国債増発ができないので、米国債の不履行（デフォルト）が発生する。◆The Bank of Japan will propose an increase in the loan loss reserves banks should maintain to cope with borrowers defaulting on bad loans. 日銀は、不良債権の貸倒れに対処するため銀行が設定する引当金の上積みを提案する方針だ。

default on one's debts　債務を履行しない、債務不履行に陥る、債務不履行に踏み切る
◆As Greece may default on its debts, the IMF and the EU have worked out a policy of deciding on a second aid tranche of €120 billion in July 2011. ギリシャが債務不履行（デフォルト）に陥る可能性があるため、国際通貨基金（IMF）と欧州連合（EU）は、2011年7月に1,200億ユーロ（約13兆8,000億円）規模の第二次金融支援策を決定する方針を打ち出した。◆Greece was bailed out temporarily in May 2010, but it may default on its debts if it fails to secure necessary funds to redeem a sizable amount of government bonds. ギリシャは2010年5月に一時的に救済されたが、大量の国債の償還に必要な資金を確保できない場合、債務不履行（デフォルト）に陥る可能性がある。◆Greece will default on its debts and seek debt forgiveness. ギリシャは今後、債務不履行に踏み切り、債務免除［債務減免］を求めることになろう。

default on the Greek government bonds　ギリシャ国債のデフォルト（債務不履行）
◆Fears about default on the Greek government bonds are smoldering as Greece's fiscal reconstruction measures hit the wall. ギリシャの財政再建策が行き詰まっているため、ギリシャ国債のデフォルト（債務不履行）の恐れがくすぶっている。

default on the national debt　国債の債務不履行（デフォルト）
◆A day after declaring default on the national debt, Argentina's new president rolled out an ambitious works program. 国債の債務不履行（デフォルト）を宣言した翌日、アルゼンチンの新大統領は、野心的な労働政策を発表した。◆Greece's default on the national debts would be a blow to the operation of financial institutions in France and Germany that hold Greek government bonds. ギリシャが国債の債務不履行に陥った場合、ギリシャ国債を保有するフランスやドイツなどの金融機関の経営は、打撃を受けるだろう。

default problem　債務返済不能の問題、返済不能の問題
◆To avert the injection of public money into banks, the eurozone governments stuck to their official standpoint that there are no default problems within the single euro currency area. 銀行への公的資金注入を回避するため、ユーロ圏政府は、単一通貨・ユーロ圏に債務返済不能の問題は存在しないという公式立場に固執した。

defaulter　債務不履行者、税金の滞納者
defaulting party　不履行当事者
defeasance　ディフィーザンス、契約書の失効条項、債務の実質的返済
defend　（動）守る、防ぐ、防衛する、防衛策を取る、保護する、擁護する、弁護する
defend against takeover bids　買収防衛策を取る
defend the currency　通貨を防衛する
introduce measures to defend oneself against a possible

takeover bid　株式公開買付けによる買収防衛策を導入する
◆Last year, more than 400 listed companies introduced measures to defend themselves against possible takeover bids. 昨年は、400社を超える上場企業が株式公開買付けによる買収防衛策を導入した。

defense　(名)防衛, 国防, 防備, 防衛策, 防衛力, 防衛手段, 防衛施設, 防御物, 防御, 保護, 擁護, 弁護, 抗弁, 被告側, ディフェンス
（=defence; ⇒poison pill defense [defence]）
a rigorous defense of the currency　厳しい通貨防衛策
crown jewel defense　クラウン・ジュエル防衛, 重要資産売却作戦
defense bond　国防債
defense for [of] the dollar　ドル防衛
defense measure　防衛策　(=defensive measure)
dollar defense　ドル防衛
（=defense of the dollar）
Pac-Man defense　パックマン防衛
poison pill defense　毒薬条項防衛
takeover defense　買収防衛手段, 防衛手段, 乗っ取り防衛手段, 買収防衛策
yen defense　円防衛

defense against a takeover　買収防衛, 買収防衛策
◆It is necessary to place more emphasis on the dividend policy as part of defense against a takeover. 買収防衛策の一環として、配当政策をさらに重視する必要がある。

defense against management buyout　経営陣による企業買収（MBO）防衛策
◆The company's defense against management buyout is half-baked. 同社の経営陣による企業買収（MBO）防衛策は、中途半端だ。

defense line　防衛ライン
◆¥82 range to the dollar is considered to be a defense line by the Bank of Japan to stop the rapid yen's appreciation. 1ドル＝82円台が、急激な円高阻止のために日銀が引いている防衛ライン[介入ライン]と見られている。

defense strategy　防衛策, 防衛戦略
◆The company's defense strategy is designed so that fresh share warrants can be issued to dilute a takeover bidder's stake if its attempt to acquire more than 15 percent of the company's outstanding shares is deemed hostile. 同社の防衛策は、同社の発行済み株式の15％以上を買収しようとする買収者の行為を敵対的とみなした場合には、買収者の持ち株比率[議決権比率]を下げるために新株予約権を発行できる仕組みになっている。

defensive　(形)守りの, 防備の, 防御の, 守勢の, 自衛上の　(名)防衛, 守勢, 弁護
defensive consumer　消費に消極的な消費者
defensive intervention　防衛介入
defensive investment　防衛的投資
defensive merger　防衛的合併　(敵対的買収を防ぐ手段として、独占禁止法などの法律に抵触する恐れのある同業他社や政府規制を受けている業種の会社などとあらかじめ合併してしまうこと)
defensive mood　警戒ムード
defensive purchase　防衛買い
defensive stock　防衛株, ディフェンシブ銘柄（不景気の時にも強い比較的無難な株式の銘柄）
defensive view of the future　先行きについての慎重な見方

defensive measures　防衛策
◆Only 35.8 percent of the leading companies have already adopted defensive measures against a hostile takeover. 敵対的M&Aに対する防衛策を導入しているのは、主要企業の35.8％にすぎない。

defer　(動)延ばす, 引き延ばす, 延期する, 遅らせる, 先送りする, 据え置く, 猶予（ゆうよ）する, 抑える
defer gains and losses on financial futures　金融先物の損益を繰り延べる
defer payment of share dividend　株式配当の支払いを繰り延べる[遅らせる]
defer preferred stock payments　優先株式の配当を遅らせる
defer the taxes　税金を繰り延べる
defer the time of repayment　返済期間を延ばす[延長する]
◆In the case of an insolvent borrower, it no longer has the ability to pay all its debt even though lenders offer to defer the time of repayment. 返済不能の借り手の場合、貸し手が返済期間の延長を申し出ても、借り手はもはや債務を全額返済できない状況にある。

deferment　(名)延期, 支払い猶予（ゆうよ）, 繰延べ
call deferment　任意償還制限期間
debt deferment　債務返済の延長
（=deferment of debt repayment）
◆In the case of a lack of liquidity, either bridge lending or debt deferment can save the borrower as there is no cash on hand. 流動性不足の場合は、手元に現金がないので、つなぎ資金を貸すか[つなぎ融資か]債務返済の延長で借り手は助かる。

deferred　(形)繰延べの, 据え置きの, 据え置き型の, 未払いの, 延期された
deferred asset　繰延べ資産
deferred contract　期先物
deferred credit　延べ払い, 繰延べ収益
deferred interest mortgage　金利[利払い]繰延べモーゲージ
deferred investment credit　繰延べ投資税額控除
deferred liability　繰延べ負債
deferred ordinary share　後配的普通株
deferred rate setting　金利後決め方式, 条件設定遅延方式
deferred start option　先スタート・オプション
deferred swap　先スタート・スワップ

deferred annuity　据え置き型年金, 据え置き年金
deferred fixed annuity　定額据え置き型年金, 定額据え置き年金
flexible premium deferred annuity　変額保険料年金
individual deferred annuity　個人据え置き年金
single premium deferred annuity　一時払い据え置き年金, 一時払い保険料年金

deferred gains and losses　繰延べ利益と損失
◆Deferred gains and losses are recognized when the future sales or purchases are recognized or immediately if the commitment is canceled. 繰延べ利益と損失は、将来の販売もしくは購入を認識した時点で、または契約を解除した場合には即時に認識します。

deferred income taxes　繰延べ法人所得税, 繰延べ税額, 繰延べ税金
◆Deferred income taxes arise from difference in basis for tax and financial-reporting purposes. 繰延べ（法人）所得税は、税務上と財務会計上の認識基準の差異から生じます。

deferred payment　延べ払い, 後払い, 後日払い
deferred payment contract　延べ払い契約
deferred payment credit　延べ払い信用, 後日払い信用状
deferred payment export　延べ払い輸出

deferred share　劣後株, 後配株　(=deferred stock: 配当や残余財産の分配など利益配分への参加順位が普通の株式(common share)より後位にある株式)
◆Under the plan, Kanebo will issue ¥20 billion worth of

deferred shares to the Industrial Revitalization Corporation of Japan. 同計画では、カネボウは産業再生機構を引受先として200億円の劣後債を発行する。
deferred tax 繰延べ税金
（=deferred income tax）
deferred tax accounting 税効果会計
◆Deferred tax accounting allows banks to calculate their net worth by assuming future refunding of excessive tax payments. 税効果会計では、銀行は、払い過ぎた税金の将来の還付を見込んで自己資本を計算することができる。
deferred tax assets 繰延べ税金資産, DTAs
（=potential tax credits; ⇒core capital, inflate, tier-one ［Tier 1］ capital）
◆In the latest account settlements, not only Resona but other banking groups gave up including sizable deferred tax assets in their equity capital. 今決算では、「りそな」だけでなく他の銀行グループも、巨額の繰延べ税金資産の自己資本への計上を見送った。◆The change in the method of calculating deferred tax assets has driven each of the banking groups into a corner. 繰延べ税金資産の算定方式の変更が、銀行グループ各行を窮地に追い込んでいる。◆Using our former accounting method, we held deferred tax assets and liabilities at their original values even when tax rates changed. 当社の従来の会計処理方法では、税率が変更された場合でも、繰延べ税金資産および負債は、当初の価額で計上していました。
解説 繰延べ税金資産とは：不良債権の前倒し処理などで払った税金を、将来戻ってくると見なして計上した資産。融資先企業が倒産するなどして損失が確定した決算期に、十分な課税所得があれば、納税額を減らす形で回収できる。(2003年11月30日付読売新聞)
deferred tax provision 繰延べ税額
◆The principal items making up the deferred tax provision for 2010 included $250 million for sales-type leases and installment sales. 2010年の繰延べ税額を構成する主な項目には、販売型リースと割賦販売の2億5,000万ドルも含まれています。
deficiency （名）不足, 欠損, 債務超過, 不足額, 損失金, 欠如, 欠乏, 欠陥, 欠点, 弱点, 不備
capital deficiency 資本不足
cash deficiency 現金不足, 資金不足, 不足資金
cash deficiency support 不足資金供与
cover the deficiency 不足額を填補する
cure the deficiency 不足分を埋める
deficiency account 不足金勘定
（=deficit account）
deficiency advances 赤字貸出
deficiency appropriation 補充歳出予算
deficiency bill 一時借入手形
deficiency guarantee 不足額保証
deficiency in assets 債務超過
deficiency judgment 不足金判決
deficiency letter 不備通知書
deficiency of net assets 欠損金
deficiency payment 不足額の支払い, 不足払い, 赤字補てん
deficiency payment system 不足払い制度
demand deficiency 需要不足
excess or deficiency 過不足
fiscal deficiency 財政赤字, 欠陥財政
fund deficiency 資金不足
management deficiency 経営のまずさ
money deficiency 通貨不足
premium deficiencies 保険料の欠損額
premium deficiency 保険料の欠損
supply deficiency 供給不足
◆Making the creditor banks waive loans to TEPCO will cause the utility to fall into capital deficiency, with liabilities exceeding assets. 取引銀行に東電への債権を放棄させると、東電は資本不足に陥り、債務超過になってしまう。◆The EU has been unable to work out its inherent policies concerning the fiscal deficiencies of some of its more reckless member countries. 欧州連合(EU)は、一部の無謀な加盟国の欠陥財政について、一貫した政策を打ち出せないでいる。
deficit （名）損失, 欠損金, 損失金, 営業損失, 赤字, 財政赤字, 不足, 不足額, 債務超過, 債務超過額, 債務
（⇒capital deficit, capital inflow, current account deficit, federal deficit, fiscal deficit）
accumulated deficit 累積赤字
（=cumulative deficit）
budget deficit 財政赤字
capital deficit 債務超過
carryover of deficit 欠損金の繰越し
consolidated deficit 連結赤字
current account deficit 経常収支赤字, 経常赤字
cut in the deficit 赤字削減 （=deficit cutting）
deficit balance 赤字
deficit benefit plan 年金額保証制度
deficit bond 赤字公債
deficit budget 赤字予算
deficit country 赤字国, 入超国
deficit covering loan 赤字金融
deficit disposition ［reconciliation］ statement 損失金処理計算書
deficit financing ［finance］ 赤字財政, 赤字国債の発行
deficit financing bond 赤字国債, 特例国債
deficit for the current term 当期損失金
deficit in revenue 歳入不足
deficit issuance 赤字国債
deficit neutral 財政赤字への影響をゼロにすること
deficit of fiscal balance 財政赤字
deficit reduction 赤字削減, 財政赤字削減
deficit spending 超過支出, 赤字支出
deficit statement 欠損金計算書
deficit unit 赤字主体
deficits with China 対中赤字
external deficit 対外債務
federal deficit 米財政赤字
finance the government deficits 財政赤字を補てんする［穴埋めする］
financial deficit 経営赤字
fiscal deficit 財政赤字
foreign trade deficit 貿易赤字
general financial deficit 一般政府財政赤字
general government deficit 一般政府赤字
government deficit 財政赤字
lower deficit 赤字削減, 財政赤字削減
national budget deficit 財政赤字
operate at a deficit 赤字経営をする
post net deficits 最終赤字になる
primary deficit 基礎的赤字
public sector deficits 公共部門の赤字
revenue deficit 歳入欠陥
run a deficit 赤字を抱える
run a primary deficit 財政の基礎的収支が赤字に転落する
run a trade deficit 貿易赤字になる, 貿易赤字を出す

services deficit（in the current account） 貿易外収支の赤字

structural deficit 構造的赤字, 構造的財政赤字

trade deficit 貿易赤字

twin deficits 双子の赤字

◆Greece's deficit is expected to reach 8.5 percent of gross domestic product in 2011. ギリシャの2011年の財政赤字は、GDP（国内総生産）比で8.5％に達する見通しだ。◆Moody's may downgrade the U.S. government's credit rating if it does not get its colossal deficits in better order. 米政府が膨大な財政赤字問題に目途をつけないと、ムーディーズは米国債の格付けを引き下げる可能性がある。◆Most leading banks are projected to post net deficits on a consolidated basis for the business year that ended March 31. 大手銀行の大半は、3月期決算で連結最終赤字になる見通しだ。◆The debt crisis in the eurozone was triggered by huge deficits in Greece. ユーロ圏の財政危機を引き起こしたのは、ギリシャの巨額の財政赤字だ。◆The deficits of the Greek government in 2009 amounted to more than three times that allowed by the Stability and Growth Pact. ギリシャの2009年の財政赤字は、ユーロ圏の財政安定化・成長協定で定められている赤字幅（GDPの3％以下）の3倍以上にも達した。◆The EFSF is the EU bailout fund for countries with fiscal deficits. 欧州金融安定基金（EFSF）は、欧州の財政赤字国を支援する基金だ。◆The ¥319 billion in deficits will remain after loans are waived by banks and the firm sells off its assets. 銀行の債権放棄や同社の資産売却後も、3,190億円の債務［債務超過額］は残る。◆The U.S. trade deficit narrowed to $40.4 billion in November from October's deficit of $56.7 billion. 米国の貿易赤字は、10月の567億ドルから404億ドルに縮小した。◆U.S. deficits hit record $413 billion. 米財政赤字が、過去最悪の4,130億ドルに達している。

deficit-covering bonds 赤字国債, 赤字地方債（＝臨時財源対策費）, 赤字公債
（⇒issuance of deficit-covering bonds）
◆Local governments will issue 30 percent less worth of emergency deficit-covering bonds than this fiscal year. 地方自治体の緊急赤字地方債（財源不足を補う臨時財政対策債）の発行額は、今年度に比べて30％減少する見通しだ。

deficit-covering government bonds 赤字国債, 赤字地方債
◆Social security expenses are funded by deficit-covering government bonds. 社会保障費の資金は、赤字国債で賄われている［社会保障費の財源は、赤字国債に頼っている］。

deficit-cutting measures 赤字削減策
◆Greece must steadily implement deficit-cutting measures. ギリシャは、赤字削減策を着実に実施する必要がある。

deficit-cutting plan 赤字削減策
（＝deficit-cutting measures）
◆The focal point from now on will be a deficit-cutting plan to be discussed by the suprapartisan congressional committee. 今後の焦点は、超党派の議会委員会が協議する赤字削減策だ。

deficit-financing bonds 赤字国債
（＝deficit-covering bonds）
◆Deficit-financing bonds are issued to make up for budget shortfalls. 赤字国債は、予算の不足分を補うために発行する。

deficit-plagued （形）赤字続きの
◆The Japan Post Service proceeded with the integration to speed streamlining of the deficit-plagued Pelican Service. 郵便事業会社は、赤字続きのペリカン便の合理化を急ぐため、事業統合を進めた。

deficit-ridden （形）赤字に悩む, 財政赤字に悩む
◆The deficit-ridden Chiba prefectural government fell into the red in fiscal 2002. 赤字に悩む千葉県は、2002年度に赤字に転落した。◆The yields on government bonds of deficit-ridden countries including Greece have been rising across the board in Europe. 欧州では、ギリシャなど財政赤字国の国債利回りが、軒並み上昇している。

deficit settlement of accounts 赤字決算
◆Though the seven banking groups increased their capital by a total of ¥2 trillion in fiscal 2002, the effects of the capital increase were offset by the deficit settlement of accounts. 銀行・金融グループ7行は、2002年度に総額2兆円規模の資本増強を実施したが、赤字決算でその増資効果が吹き飛んでしまった。

deficit spending units（borrower） 資金不足主体（借り手）
◆A financial intermediary acts as a middleman between cash surplus units in the economy（savers）and deficit spending units（borrowers）. 金融仲介機関は、経済の資金余剰主体（貯蓄者）と資金不足主体（借り手）との間に立つ仲介者として機能している。

deficit target 赤字削減目標
◆Greece will miss 2011-12 deficit targets imposed by international lenders as part of the country's bailout. ギリシャは、同国救済措置の一環として国際融資団（欧州連合（EU）や国際通貨基金）が課した2011-12年の赤字削減目標を、達成できないようだ。

defiled bank note 汚損銀行券

define （動）明らかにする, 明確にする, 限定する, 定義する, 示す, 規定する
◆Corporate value is defined as "the total of profits one company will earn in future." 企業価値は、「ある会社が将来稼ぐ利益の合計」と定義される。◆Yen loans extended now as part of Japan's ODA are untied in principle, with the source of development materials and equipment to be procured not defined. 日本の政府開発援助（ODA）として供与されている円借款は現在、ひも付きでない「アンタイド」援助が原則で、開発物資の調達先を限定していない。

defined （形）明確化した, 確定した, 限定された, 定義された, はっきりとした, 際立った

be parked for a well-defined period 特定の期間運用される

defined compensation plan 適格補償制度

fund intermediation in broadly-defined financial markets 広義の金融市場での資金仲介

obligations in a defined class 特定の種類の債務

single employer defined postretirement benefit plans 単一事業主給付建て退職後給付制度

defined benefit 確定給付, 確定給付制度, 給付建て

defined benefit liability 確定給付負債

defined benefit obligation 確定給付債務

defined benefit pension plan 確定給付年金制度, 確定給付企業年金, 給付建て年金制度
（＝defined benefit plan）

defined benefit scheme 確定給付年金制度, 確定給付制度, 給付建て年金制度, 給付建て制度
（＝defined benefit plan）

non contributory defined benefit pension plan 非拠出型確定給付年金制度［確定給付制度］, 従業員無拠出の給付額規定年金制度

settlements and curtailments of defined benefit pension plans 給付建て年金制度の清算と削減

defined benefit plan 確定給付年金制度, 確定給付制度, 給付建て年金制度, 給付建て制度
（＝defined benefit scheme）

noncontributory defined benefit plan 非拠出型確定給付年金制度, 非拠出型給付金規定方式による年金制度

shift in corporate pensions from defined benefit to defined contribution plans 企業年金の確定給付制度［給付建て制度］から確定拠出制度［掛け金建て制度］への移行

◆BCE and most of its subsidiary companies have noncontributory defined benefit plans which provide for service pensions, based on length of service and rates of pay, for substantially all the employees. BCEとその大多数の子会社は、実質的に全従業員を対象として、勤続年数と給与額に基づいて年金額を決定する非拠出型確定給付年金制度［非拠出型給付金規定方式による年金制度］を設けている。

defined contribution 確定拠出型年金, DC
 defined-contribution annuity scheme 確定拠出年金制度
 defined contribution corporate pension plan 確定拠出型企業年金制度
 defined contribution effort 確定拠出型年金ビジネスの開拓
 defined contribution market 確定拠出型年金市場
 defined contribution plan 定額拠出制度, 掛金建て制度

defined contribution pension 確定拠出型年金（日本版401k）, 確定拠出年金 （=defined contribution annuity: 退職後の年金給付額が、基金に対する掛金の額と基金の投資収益に基づいて算定される退職給付制度。運用の成否で、将来の年金額が増減する）
 defined contribution pension plan 確定拠出型年金制度, 確定拠出年金制度, 確定拠出制度, 拠出建て年金制度 （=DC plan; ⇒investment performance）

defined contribution pension scheme 確定拠出型年金制度, 確定拠出年金制度
◆The number of companies that have introduced the defined-contribution pension scheme now exceeds 7,000. 確定拠出年金（日本版401k）制度を導入している企業は現在、7,000社を超えている。

definite insurance 確定保険
definite policy 確定保険証券
definitive bond 確定債券, 確定社債券,（仮券面に対する）正式本券, 証券証書
definitive money 確定貨幣
definitive warrant 確定ワラント券

deflate （動）しぼませる,（インフレ安定のために通貨を）収縮させる,（物価水準を）引き下げる, デフレ政策を取る［遂行する］, 自信を失わせる, 鼻をへし折る,（タイヤなどの）空気を抜く,（記事などの）間違いを指摘する
 deflate the inflationary pressures インフレ圧力を抑える
 deflated economy デフレ経済
 wages deflated by consumer prices 消費者物価指数を基準とする実質賃金

deflation （名）通貨収, 物価下落, 収縮, 下落, デフレ, デフレーション （⇒asset deflation, backsliding, easy money policy, economic improvement, forecast, task）
 amid a recession accompanied by deflation デフレ不況下で
 amid deflation デフレの中で
 amid deflation fears デフレ懸念の中
 asset market deflation 資産デフレ
 be in deflation デフレに陥っている
 chronic deflation 慢性的デフレ
 counter［prevent, stop］deflation デフレを阻止する
 creeping deflation 忍び寄るデフレ, 緩やかなデフレ （=mild deflation）
 deflation-adjusted デフレ調整後の
 deflation fears デフレ懸念 （=deflationary concerns）
 deflation from the yen's appreciation 円高デフレ
 deflation-led recession デフレ不況 （=deflationary recession）
 deflation of asset values 資産価格の下落, 資産デフレ
 deflation policy デフレ政策, デフレ対策, 収縮政策
 deflation taking hold of the Japanese economy 日本経済を蝕（むしば）んでいるデフレ
 eliminate deflation デフレを脱却する
 government deflation 政府デフレーション
 halting deflation デフレ阻止 （=stop）
 head off［halt］deflation デフレを阻止する
 hyper-deflation 超デフレーション
 monetary deflation 通貨収縮
 profit deflation 利潤収縮
 protracted deflation 長引くデフレ
 stop［prevent］deflation デフレを阻止する, デフレを止める
 suffer from deflation デフレに苦しむ
 the bad escape from deflation 悪いデフレ脱却
 the good escape from deflation 良いデフレ脱却
 the ongoing deflation デフレの進行
 threat of deflation デフレの脅威（きょうい）, デフレ懸念
 winners in the age of deflation デフレ時代の勝ち組
 worsen deflation デフレを悪化させる
◆A strong yen lowers the prices of imported goods and fuels deflation. 円高は輸入品の価格を下げ、デフレに拍車をかける。◆Domestic bank are stepping up oversea project financing due to the lack of growth in lending to domestic borrowers amid protracted deflation at home. 国内銀行各行は、国内ではデフレが続いて［デフレが続く状況で］国内融資先への貸出が伸びていないことから、海外の事業向け融資を強化している。◆Japan's financial system was badly damaged with the collapse of the bubble economy and deflation. 日本の金融システムは、バブル崩壊とデフレで深手を負った。◆Monetary policies play a big role in stopping deflation. デフレを止めるには、金融政策の役割が大きい。◆Priority measures to achieve economic recovery are stopping deflation and mobilizing all possible fiscal measures, financial policies and taxation reforms. 景気回復を実現するための優先課題は、デフレ阻止と、可能な財政政策、金融政策や税制改革を総動員することだ。◆The biggest challenge the Japanese economy faces today is deflation. 日本経済が現在直面している最大の課題は、デフレである。◆The economy has only recently emerged from a prolonged period of deflation. 経済は、長期のデフレから脱したばかりだ。◆The fall in import prices that accompanies a strong yen could further prolong Japan's deflation. 円高に伴う輸入価格の下落で、日本のデフレがさらに長期化する可能性がある。◆The main battlefield of monetary policy likely will shift to deflation. 今後は、デフレが金融政策の主戦場となろう。◆The yen's appreciation will reduce the volume of exports and worsen deflation. 円高で、輸出数量が減少し、デフレが悪化する。◆There is slow progress in economic improvement among nonmanufacturing businesses, largely as a result of sluggish sales at retailers due to the ongoing deflation. デフレの進行で主に小売業の売上が低迷しているため、非製造業は景気回復の足取りが弱い。

deflation-battered economy デフレ不況に沈んだ経済
◆At long last, a few rays of hope have brightened the deflation-battered economy. デフレ不況に沈んでいた日本経済に、ようやく薄日が差してきた。

deflation concerns デフレ懸念
（=deflation fears, deflationary concerns）
◆Long-term lending rates have fallen since the beginning of August 2010 amid deflation concerns. 2010年8月に入って、デフレ懸念を背景に、長期貸出金利が下がっている。

deflation-inducing trap デフレを呼ぶ罠（わな）
◆By sticking to the ¥30 trillion cap, the Cabinet of Prime Minister Junichiro Koizumi would put the Japanese economy into a deflation-inducing trap in the midst of a world

recession.（国債発行）30兆円枠に固執して、小泉内閣は、世界に不況の嵐が吹く中で、日本経済を「デフレを呼ぶ罠」に落とし込もうとしている。

deflation-led recession デフレ不況 （=deflation-led economic slowdown, deflationary doldrums, deflationary recession）

deflationary （形）通貨収縮の, 物価下落の, デフレの
- deflationary bank credit デフレ的銀行信用
- deflationary bias デフレ・バイアス
- deflationary economy デフレ経済（=deflated economy）
- deflationary effect デフレ効果
- deflationary expectation デフレ期待
- deflationary force デフレ圧力, デフレ要因
- deflationary impact of yen appreciation 円高のデフレ効果, 円高のデフレ圧力
- deflationary influence デフレ作用
- deflationary measures デフレ的措置, デフレ対策
- deflationary mechanism デフレ機構
- deflationary period デフレ期間
- deflationary policy デフレ政策, デフレ対策
- deflationary pricing pressure 値下げ圧力
- deflationary process デフレ過程
- fight deflationary forces デフレ圧力と闘う
- the worst of the deflationary process デフレの最悪期

deflationary concerns デフレ懸念
（=deflation fears）
◆By conducting additional monetary easing policy, the Fed attempts to preemptively contain growing deflationary concerns in the United States. 追加金融緩和策を実施して、米連邦準備制度理事会（FRB）は、米国で高まるデフレ懸念に先手を打とうとしている。

deflationary crisis デフレ危機, デフレ不況
◆The ongoing decline in land prices is a major factor contributing to the current deflationary crisis. 歯止めがかからない地価の下落が、現在のデフレ危機の元凶だ。

deflationary doldrums デフレ不況
◆The money supply for January recorded the lowest growth since December 2000, making it difficult for the economy to pull itself out of its deflationary doldrums. 1月のマネー・サプライは2000年12月以来最低の伸びにとどまり、日本経済がデフレ不況から脱却するのが難しくなっている。

deflationary drop in the price level 物価水準の下落傾向, 価格水準が下落してデフレを招くこと
◆What the United States must avoid is any future deflationary drop in the price level. 米国が回避しなければならないのは、将来、価格水準が下落してデフレを招くことだ。

deflationary environment デフレ環境
◆Escaping deflationary environment takes time. デフレ環境からの脱却［デフレ脱却］には、時間がかかる。

deflationary forces デフレ要因, デフレの影響力, デフレ圧力, デフレ
◆Even blue-chip companies have been forced to drastically cut their workforces due to price-cutting competition driven by deflationary forces. 優良企業でも、デフレによる値下げ競争の影響で、大幅な人員削減を迫られている。

deflationary gap デフレ・ギャップ（総供給が総需要を上回っているときのその超過額）
◆When an economy has a deflationary gap of more than ¥30 trillion, it is a general rule to use macroeconomic measures to stimulate demand. 30兆円を上回るデフレ・ギャップがある経済下では、マクロ政策による需要創出が鉄則である。

deflationary period デフレ期
◆The rate of fall in prices was about the same as that in fiscal 2001 during a serious deflationary period. 物価の下落率は、深刻なデフレ期の2001年度とほぼ同じ水準だ。

deflationary phase デフレ局面, デフレ気味
◆Many developed countries are currently in a deflationary phase while many emerging countries are in an inflationary phase. 現在、先進国の多くはデフレ気味なのに対して、新興国の多くはインフレ気味だ。

deflationary pressure(s) デフレ圧力, デフレ不況, デフレ懸念, デフレ
（⇒accelerated disposal of bad loans）
- a vicious cycle of deflationary pressure デフレの悪循環（⇒vicious cycle）
- accelerate deflationary pressure デフレ不況を加速させる, デフレ圧力を高める
- alleviate deflationary pressure デフレ圧力を緩和する
- counter deflationary pressures デフレ圧力に対応する
- experience deflationary pressure デフレ圧力にさらされる
- increase deflationary pressure デフレ圧力を増す, デフレ圧力を強める
- lead to deflationary pressures デフレ圧力を招く
- lead to more deflationary pressure デフレ圧力を強めることにつながる
- offset deflationary pressure デフレ圧力を跳（は）ね返す
- succumb to deflationary pressure デフレ圧力に屈する, 負ける

◆Bad loan disposal will lead to deflationary pressures. 不良債権処理は、デフレ圧力を強める。◆Businesses are cutting back on hiring to counter deflationary pressures induced by an influx of cheap imports from countries such as China. 企業は現在、中国などからの安価な輸入品の流入に伴うデフレ圧力に対応するため、雇用を抑制している。◆Deflationary pressures continue to exist. デフレは、まだまだ続く。◆It is wise to consider the economy is coming under deflationary pressures. 景気はデフレ圧力が強い、と見たほうが良い。◆The cuts in fiscal spending accelerated deflationary pressure. 歳出削減は、デフレ不況を加速させた。◆The economy could sink into a double-dip recession due to the clouds hanging over the U.S. economy and rising deflationary pressures that will accompany the accelerated disposal of nonperforming loans. 米国経済の行方（米国経済への先行き不安）や、不良債権処理の加速に伴うデフレ圧力の高まりなどで、景気が底割れする恐れがある。◆The Fed has taken quantitative easing measures twice, or QE1 between December 2008 and March 2010, and QE2 between November 2010 and June 2011, to cope with the financial crisis and deflationary pressure. 金融危機やデフレ圧力［デフレ懸念］に対応するため、米連邦準備制度理事会（FRB）は、これまでに量的金融緩和を2回（2008年12月〜2010年3月の量的緩和第一弾（QE1）と2010年11月〜2011年6月の量的緩和第二弾（QE2））実施している。

deflationary recession デフレ不況
◆The most immediate goal for Japan is to get out of the deflationary recession. 日本にとって当面の最大目標は、デフレ不況脱却だ。◆The worsening Iraq crisis causes the deflationary recession—accentuated by falling stock prices. イラク危機の緊迫化で、株価急落などデフレ不況が深刻になっている。

deflationary spiral デフレの悪循環, デフレ的悪循環, デフレ・スパイラル （⇒fiscal measures）
- enter the early phase of a deflationary spiral デフレ・スパイラルの初期段階に入る
- fall into a deflationary spiral デフレ・スパイラルに陥る, デフレの悪循環に陥る
- trigger a deflationary spiral デフレ・スパイラルを引き起こす
- tumble into a dreaded deflationary spiral 恐怖のデフレ・スパイラル落ち込む

◆Excessive discounting would add to a deflationary spiral. 値引き[安売り]が行き過ぎると、デフレ・スパイラル(デフレの悪循環)につながることになる。◆Japan, which is on the verge of falling into a deflationary spiral, should carry out such effective measures as monetary relaxation and the compilation of a supplementary budget. デフレ・スパイラルの縁に立つ日本は、金融緩和や補正予算の編成など効果的な対策を実施するべきだ。◆One misstep could lead to deflationary spiral. 一歩誤れば、デフレ・スパイラル(デフレの悪循環)を招く可能性がある。◆The economy may fall into a deflationary spiral again. 経済は、再びデフレの悪循環に陥る可能性がある。◆The Japanese economy has reached a critical stage at which it could tumble into a deflationary spiral after brief stability, or be brought back to a recovery path. 日本経済は現在、小康状態から再びデフレの悪循環に落ち込むか、回復軌道に戻せるかどうかの瀬戸際にある。

deflationary times デフレの時代
◆In these deflationary times, putting the pension payments on hold is tantamount to increasing them. このデフレ時代に、年金支給額の据え置きは、その増額に等しい。

deflationary trap デフレの罠
◆The government's calls for the Bank of Japan to adopt a "numerical target to stabilize prices" to climb out of the deflationary trap are reasonable. 政府がデフレ脱出に向けて日銀に「物価安定数値目標」の導入を促したのは、妥当と言える。

deflationary trend デフレ傾向, 物価下落の傾向, 価格下落の傾向
◆A deflationary trend emerged with the collapse of the bubble economy. デフレ傾向は、バブル崩壊とともに現れた。◆Amid the protracted economic slump and the ongoing deflationary trend, the life insurance industry has been hit by a trio of predicaments. 景気の長期低迷とデフレ傾向が進行するなか、生保業界は三重苦に見舞われている。◆Japan's deflationary trend continues unchecked. 日本のデフレ傾向に依然、歯止めがかかっていない。◆Nonperforming loans will keep cropping up as long as the deflationary trend continues. デフレ傾向が続く限り、不良債権は発生し続ける。◆The current deflationary trend seems to be a temporary phenomenon caused by the correction in oil prices after they skyrocketed last year. 現在のデフレ傾向は、昨年の原油高の反動による一時的な現象のようだ。◆The United States was able to get out of a deflationary trend relatively quickly. 米国は、デフレ傾向から比較的早く抜け出すことができた。◆Unless the government and the Bank of Japan change their macro fiscal and monetary policies and arrest the deflationary trend, the disposal of nonperforming loans will never be completed. 政府と日銀が財政と金融のマクロ政策を転換してデフレ傾向を止めないかぎり、不良債権処理は終わらないだろう。

deflator (名)価格修正因子, デフレーター
◆The deflator indicates the overall trend in prices. デフレーターは、物価の総合的な動向を示す。◆The deflator, which indicates the overall trend in prices, dropped 2.5 percent in the April-June period compared to the corresponding period last year. 物価の総合的な動向を示すデフレーターは、4-6月期は前年同期比で2.5%下落した。

defraud (動)だまし取る, 詐取する, 欺(あざむ)く
◆Corporate leaders must recognize that defrauding investors is a serious crime. 投資家を欺く行為は重大な犯罪である、ということを企業経営者は認識しなければならない。

defray (動)支払う(pay), (経費を)支出する, (費用などを)負担する
defray costs relating to layoffs 解雇関連費用を負担する
defray the estimated costs 見積費用を負担する
◆The estimated costs of ¥600 million will be defrayed by medical device manufacturers and financial institutions. 6億円の見積り費用は、医療機器メーカーと金融機関が負担することになっている。◆To encourage firms' temporary layoffs, the government will ease requirements for receiving a governmental subsidy to defray costs relating to layoffs. 企業の一時解雇[一時帰休]を支援するため、政府は企業が雇用調整助成金(解雇関連費用を負担する政府助成金)を受けるための要件を緩和する。

defrayment [defrayal] (名)支払い, 支出, 負担

defund (動)〜から資金を引き上げる, 〜への出資を止める, 〜への財政支援をストップする

degearing (名)デギアリング(借入れを削減して自己資本比率を高めること)

degree (名)程度, 度合い, 水準, 規模, 段階, 度, 等級, 資格, 学位
degree of accuracy 正確度
degree of concentration 集中度
degree of dependence on loan 借入金依存度
degree of fiscal soundness 財政の健全度
degree of freedom 自由度
degree of inequality 不均等度
degree of probable loss 予想される損失の規模
degree of recovery 回収率
degree of uncertainty 不確実性の程度
the degree of monetary tightening 金融引締めの程度
there remains a degree of uncertainty about 〜にはかなりの不透明感が残る
◆A surplus in the primary balances of the central and local governments indicates a degree of fiscal soundness. 国と地方[地方自治体]の基礎的財政収支の黒字は、財政の健全度を示す。

Del Cred. 支払い保証(del credereの略)

del credere 買い主の支払い保証[支払い能力保証]の(下に)
del credere agent 支払い保証代理人
del credere agreement 支払い保証契約
del credere commission 支払い保証手数料

delay (動)遅らせる, 延ばす, 延期する, 遅れる, 手間取る
delay cutting rates 利下げを遅らせる
delay interest payments 利払いを遅らせる
◆The casualty insurer delayed the start of its online insurance sales due to the March 11 earthquake and tsunami. 2011年3月11日の東日本大震災のため、同損保は保険のネット販売の開業を延期した。◆The collection of debts has been delayed due to falling collateral value. 担保価値の下落などで、債権の回収は遅れている。

delay (名)遅延(ちえん), 遅滞, 遅れ, 延期, 商品の延着, 猶予(ゆうよ)
budget delay 予算審議の遅れ
delay and extension of time 遅延および期日延長
delay in collection 回収の遅れ
delay in economic improvement 景気回復の遅れ (=delay in economic recovery)
delay in [of] payment 支払いの遅れ, 支払い遅延, 代金支払い遅延 (=delayed payment)
delay of financial assistance 金融支援の遅れ, 金融支援のもたつき
delay of performance 履行遅延
delay or omission 遅滞または不作為
permissible delay 引渡し遅延容認期間
without delay 直ちに
◆Due to delays in ratification of the agreement on bailout measures by some eurozone countries, concrete measures to rescue Greece have yet to be carried out. 支援策の合意事項について一部のユーロ圏加盟国の承認が遅れたため、ギリシャ救済の具体策はまだ実施されていない。◆If such delay shall

exceed two months, either party may give written notice of termination of this agreement. このような遅延が2か月を超える場合、いずれの当事者も、書面で本契約を解除する通告を出すことができる。◆The financial market mess in Europe was triggered by the delay of financial assistance to Greece by the European financial authorities. 欧州の金融市場混乱の引き金となったのは、欧州金融当局によるギリシャへの金融支援のもたつきだ。

delay in economic improvement 景気回復の遅れ（=delay in economic recovery）
◆There is a delay in economic improvement among small and medium companies, as well as nonmanufacturing corporations. 中小企業や非製造業に、景気回復の遅れが見られる。

delay in taking action 対応の遅れ
◆Speculators capitalized on the Bank of Japan's delay in taking action. 投機筋は、日銀の対応の遅れを突いた。

delay in the debt relief process 債務救済手続きの遅れ, 債務削減手続きの遅れ
◆Delays in the debt relief process may become obstacles to reconstruction efforts. 債務救済［債務削減］手続きの遅れは、復興の支障［障害］となる可能性がある。

delay in the disposal of bad loans 不良債権処理の遅れ
◆The 225-issue Nikkei Stock Average dived below the key threshold of 10,000 as investors were disappointed with the continuing delay in the disposal of banks' bad loans and an overnight plunge in U.S. stocks. 日経平均株価（225種）は、投資家が銀行等の不良債権処理が引き続き遅れることや前日の米株価の大幅下落に失望して、1万円の大台を割り込んだ。

delay in the recovery of corporate performance 企業業績回復の遅れ
◆A series of accounting scandals and delays in the recovery of corporate performance are accelerating falls in stock prices on the U.S. markets, along with the weakening of the dollar. 一連の［相次ぐ］企業会計の不祥事と企業業績回復の遅れで、米国の株安とドル安が加速している。

delayed （形）遅れた, 遅延した, 延ばした, 延期された, 先スタートの, ディレード
　delayed capped floating rate note　ディレード・キャップ債, 先スタート・キャップ付き変動利付き債（変動利付債とキャップ付き債を組み合わせたもの）
　delayed convertible　先スタート転換証券
　delayed damages　遅延損害金
　delayed disbursement of interest or principal on an insured security　保証した債券の元利返済の遅延, 保証した債券の金利または元本支払いの遅延
　delayed interest　遅延利息, 延滞利息, 遅延金利
　delayed opening　ディレード・オープニング（売り・買いがアンバランスで始まり値が付かない状態）
　delayed rate setting　金利条件設定繰延べ方式, 条件設定遅延方式
　delayed recognition　遅延認識
　delayed settlement　特約日決済
　delayed settlement transaction　着地取引（約定日から1か月以上先の一定期日に、債券を一定条件で売買することを、あらかじめ約束しておく取引）
　delayed shipment　船積み遅延, 積み遅れ
　delayed tranche　遅延トランシュ

delayed LIBOR　ディレードLIBOR, LIBORベースの金利後決め
　delayed LIBOR option　LIBORベースの金利後決めオプション
　delayed LIBOR swap　ディレードLIBORスワップ
　proceeds of the delayed LIBOR facility　金利後決め方式で調達した資金
　use a delayed LIBOR structure　ディレードLIBORの仕組みを取る

delayed payment　支払いの遅延, 支払いの遅れ, 延納
◆Most companies producing materials and parts in China either have been unable to collect bills or have received delayed payments. 中国に進出している部品や素材メーカーの大半は、踏み倒しや支払いの遅延の被害を受けている。

delete　（動）削除する, 抹消する, 消す
◆For the obstruction of an audit by the FSA, an executive of the bank is believed to have fraudulently obtained a password needed to delete e-mails from the bank's computer server. 金融庁の立入り検査を妨害するため、同行の役員が、同行のコンピュータ・サーバーから電子メールを削除するのに必要なパスワードを、不正に入手したと見られる。

deleverage　（動）負債を削減する, 借入を削減する, レバレッジを低める, 負債が削減される, 借入が削減される, レバレッジが低くなる　（名）負債削減

deleveraging　（名）負債削減, 借入削減, 負債比率低下

delinquency　（名）怠慢, 延滞, 支払い［返済］遅延, 不履行, 不履行債務
　consumer delinquencies　消費者の返済遅延
　credit card delinquency　クレジット・カードの支払い遅延・返済遅延
　defaults and delinquencies　デフォルトや支払い遅延
　delinquency amount　延滞金
　delinquency in payment　支払い不履行, 支払い遅延
　delinquency rate　延滞率, 支払い遅延率, 返済遅延率（=rate of delinquency）
　percentage of delinquency　延滞率
　rate of delinquency　返済遅延率
◆The percentage of credit card delinquencies fell sharply in the first quarter of this year. 今年第1四半期［第一・四半期］のクレジット・カードの返済遅延率は、急減した。

delinquent　（形）債務不履行の, 焦げ付いた, 滞納の, 期限が過ぎても未済の
　delinquent account　延滞口座
　delinquent account receivable　支払い遅延債権
　delinquent charge　延滞金, 遅延損害金
　delinquent loan　延滞融資, 延滞債権, 不稼働資産
　delinquent taxes　滞納税金

delinquent amounts　延滞金額, 延滞額, 延滞金
◆Interest shall accrue on any delinquent amounts owed by Distributor for Products at the lesser of 18% per annum, or the maximum rate permitted by applicable usury law. 利息は、「販売店」が負っている［本製品］の延滞金について発生し、年18%の利率と適用される利息制限法で認められる最高利率のうちいずれか低いほうの利率によるものとする。

delinquent balances　不良債権残高, 回収遅延残高
◆Our credit approval and monitoring have kept our percentage of delinquent balances and write-offs below industry norms. 与信承認条件や検査を厳しくしているため、当社の不良債権残高と償却額は業界水準以下を保っています。

delist　（動）上場を廃止する, 上場廃止にする　（⇒dual-list, falsify, financial data, Jasdaq Securities Exchange, list, relist, watch list）
　be delisted from the First Section of the TSE　東証1部から上場廃止になる
　be delisted from the TSE　東証から上場廃止となる
　criteria［conditions］for listing and delisting a security　上場基準と上場廃止基準
　delist a stock　株式を上場廃止にする
　the bourse's special list of shares to be delisted　同証券取引所の整理ポスト
◆JAL was delisted from the Tokyo Stock Exchange in

February 2010. 日航は、2010年2月に東京証券取引所から上場廃止となった。◆JAL's stocks may lose market value to zero if the corporate turnaround body cuts the shares 100 percent by delisting JAL from the Tokyo stock market. 企業再生支援機構が東京株式市場から日航株を廃止して日航株を100%減資したら、日航株の市場価値はゼロになる可能性がある。◆The company is unable to raise funds in the market as its stocks were delisted from the Tokyo Stock Exchange. 東証が同社株の上場を廃止したので、同社は市場から資金調達することができなくなった。◆The TSE typically only delists companies at risk of bankruptcy. 東証が上場廃止するのは、一般に経営破たん危機にある企業に限られる。◆World Co. has delisted itself from the Tokyo Stock Exchange and Osaka Securities Exchange to proceed with its long-term management strategy. アパレル大手のワールドは、長期的な経営戦略を進めるため、自ら東証と大証からの上場を廃止した。

delisting (名)上場廃止
 be subject to delisting procedures　上場廃止手続きの対象になっている
 delisting requirements　上場廃止基準
 notice of the delisting　上場廃止の通告
 ◆A company listed on the Fukuoka bourse is subject to delisting after two straight years of negative net worth. 福岡証券取引所に上場している企業は、2年連続債務超過になると、上場廃止の対象になる。◆It's better to able to manage a company in a more agile way by delisting. 非上場で、会社をもっと機動的に経営できたほうがよい。◆The delisting means that bond holders could demand the company buy back the bonds for cash. 上場廃止は、社債保有者が同社に対して現金で社債の買戻しを要求できることを意味する。◆The delisting of Livedoor stocks means a complete end to the group's creative financial strategy of seeking explosive growth by bloating its market capitalization. ライブドア株の上場廃止は、時価総額を膨らませて急成長を求めるという同グループの独創的な財務戦略が、完全に崩れたことを意味する。◆Tokyo, Osaka and Nagoya bourses placed Nikko Cordial stock on their respective supervision posts for possible delisting. 東京、大阪、名古屋の3証券取引所が、それぞれ日興コーディアルの株式を、上場廃止の可能性があるため監理ポストに割り当てた。

deliver (動)届ける、配達する、引き渡す、渡す、交付する、送達する、送付する、納入する、提供する、達成する、実行する、判定や評決などを行う、判定を下す、原油などを産出する
 bonds in the cheapest-to-deliver five-year sector　受渡し最割安銘柄の5年債
 deliver A against payment　代金の支払いと引換えにAを引き渡す
 deliver a blow to the domestic economy　国内経済に大きな打撃を与える
 deliver against the day's closing futures　同日の先物価格終値で受け渡す
 Deliver documents against payment　書類は支払い渡しのこと
 deliver newly issued stock upon the exercise of any of the options　オプションの行使に対して新規発行株式を充てる
 Deliver the stocks [shares]　株式を交付する、株式を受け渡す
 Deliver to the order of　～の指図に基づき交付のこと
 ◆If we are to continue to deliver improved financial results, we must continue to enhance our competitiveness. 今後とも業績［財務成績］向上を図るには、当社の競争力を引き続き高める必要がある。◆The yen's extremely rapid appreciation may deliver a bitter blow to the domestic economy. 超円高は、国内経済に大きな打撃を与える可能性がある。

deliverable (形)受渡し可能な、受渡し適格の、決済可能な
 be deliverable into the futures contract　先物で受渡し適格になる
 be physically deliverable　実際に受渡しが可能である、現物決済が可能である
 deliverable bond　受渡し適格銘柄

delivered (形)持込み渡しの、～渡し、配達費込みの
 delivered at frontier　国境持込み渡し条件、国境渡し、DAF
 delivered at frontier price　国境渡し値段
 delivered duty paid　仕向地持込み渡し（関税込み）条件、持込み渡し条件、DDP
 delivered duty unpaid　仕向地持込み渡し（関税抜き）条件、DDU
 delivered ex quay　埠頭（ふとう）持込み渡し条件、DEQ
 delivered ex ship　本船持込み渡し条件、DES
 delivered on rail　貨車積込み渡し
 delivered price　引渡し値段、引渡し価格
 delivered to order　指図人渡し
 delivered to the participants　受給者への引渡し
 free delivered　持込み渡し条件

delivery (名)配達、送達、配送、出荷、納品、納入、完納、引渡し、受渡し、交付、決済、意見の発表、陳述
 alongside [shipside] delivery　自家取り
 announce a coupon pass for Friday delivery　金曜日決済で米国債の買切りオペを行うことを発表する
 April delivery　4月渡し、4月限、4月決済、4月物
 buy for future delivery　先渡しで買う
 calendar month delivery　暦月渡し
 cash on delivery sale　代金［現金］引換販売、COD（=COD sale, collect on delivery sale, sale for cash on delivery）
 collect on delivery　代金引換渡し
 constructive delivery　推定交付
 current monthly delivery　当限（とうぎり）、当限月（げんげつ）
 deferred delivery　（株式や債券の）延渡し
 delivery against letter of guarantee　保証状荷渡し
 delivery against payment　支払い渡し
 delivery bill　引渡し証券
 delivery certificate　配達証明
 delivery charge　配送料金
 delivery date　受渡し日、引渡し日、配送日、配達日、決済日
 delivery expense　配達費、配送費
 delivery in bond　保税渡し
 delivery month　（為替予約）受渡し月、限月（げんげつ）（=contract month: 先物取引で決済日が到来する月）
 delivery note　納品書、物品受領書
 delivery of certificates　証券の受渡し
 delivery of shares　株式の受渡し、株式交付
 delivery on a fixed date　確定日渡し
 delivery options for bond futures contracts　債券先物契約の受渡しオプション
 delivery order　荷渡し指図書、荷物引渡し指図書
 delivery settlement price　受渡し決済価格
 delivery share　渡し株
 delivery system　配送システム、配達システム
 delivery time　納期
 delivery versus payment　支払い渡し、証券と資金の同時決済、DVP

delivery with option　オプション渡し
export delivery　輸出出荷
forward [future] delivery　先物為替, 先渡し, 先限
free delivery　任意受渡し, 無料配送
gold deliver bar　金地金
gold futures for December delivery　12月渡しの金先物
government bond futures for June delivery　国債先物6月物
issue the bond with accrued interest from A to delivery　A日から引渡し日までの経過利息付きで同債を発行する
next-month delivery　中限
orders on hand　手持ち受注分
overnight delivery　翌日渡し
pay on delivery　引渡し同時払い, POD
payment after delivery　受渡し後払い
payment on delivery　受渡し払い, 引換え払い
physical delivery　現物受渡し, 現渡し, 現引き
physical delivery of fixed income options　債券オプションの現物受渡し
port of delivery　貨物引渡し港, 荷降ろし港
product delivery　商品の配送
spot delivery　現物(為替)現場渡し, 現場渡し
State Health Insurance Enrollment and Local Delivery program　州健康保険登録・地域医療供給制度
◆At delivery, the balance sheet will be adjusted for the stock split. 株式の交付時に、貸借対照表は株式分割による調整を行います。◆Gold futures for December delivery closed at $1,891.90 an ounce at 2:05 p.m. on the Comex in New York. ニューヨーク商品取引所では、12月渡しの金先物価格が、午後2時5分の時点で1トロイ・オンス(約31グラム)=1,891.90ドルに達した。

delta　デルタ値
delta risk　デルタ・リスク(オプションの価値が、オプションの対象である原資産の価格変動に応じてどの程度動くかを示す指標)
demand　(動)要求する, 請求する, 求める, 要する, 必要とする
◆A targeted company demanded a company trying to acquire its stocks to present a business plan. 買収の標的企業は、買収企業[標的企業の株式を取得しようとしている企業]に事業計画の提出を求めた。◆The former head of the Murakami Fund was often dubbed a shareholder who demands a lot. 村上ファンドの元代表は、「モノ言う株主」とよく呼ばれた。◆The United States and Britain demanded tighter regulations on bank capitalization. 米国と英国は、銀行の自己資本規制の強化を求めた。◆Toshiba may demand damage compensation from Sony, and others may follow suit. 東芝はソニーに対する損害賠償請求を検討しており、他社もこれに追随する可能性がある。

demand　(名)需要, 要求, デマンド　(⇒capital demand, fiscal policy, fiscal stimulus measures, liquidity demand)
capital demand　資本需要, 資金需要 (=demand for capital)
credit demand　信用需要, 資金需要 (=demand for credit)
demand bill　要求払い手形, 一覧払い手形 (=demand draft, demand note)
demand deposit　要求払い預金, 営業性預金, 当座預金 (checking account), 預金通貨
demand draft　一覧払い[要求払い]為替手形, 一覧払い手形, 送金為替手形, 送金小切手(remittance check), D/D
demand for consumption　実需
demand for foreign exchange　外貨需要
demand for investable funds　資金需要
demand for loans　借入需要, 資金需要 (=loan demand)
demand for money　貨幣需要, 資金需要
demand for new credit　新規借入需要
demand loan　当座貸付け, 当座貸し(call loan), 短期融資
demand note　一覧払い約束手形, 要求払い約束手形, 督促状, 催告書
demand rate　(小切手買取りの)一覧払い為替相場 (=check rate)
demand (registration) rights　株式公開実施請求権, 強制公開権
demand-to-hold securities　証券の保有需要
derivative demand　派生需要
fiscal demand　財政需要
institutional demand　機関投資家の需要
investment demand　投資需要, 設備投資需要
investor demand　投資家の需要
loan demand　借入需要 (=demand for loans)
marginal yen buying demand　円買いの限界需要
market demand　市場の需要
money demand　資金需要
on demand　要求あり次第, 一覧払い, 要求払い
on demand guarantee　要求払い保証契約
payable on demand　一覧払い
secured demand note　担保付き一覧払い手形
sluggish demand　需要の低迷, 需要不振
strong demand　強い需要, 旺盛な需要, 底堅い需要
underlying demand for long bonds　長期債に対する基本的な需要
variable-rate demand debt　変動金利の要求払い債
◆Domestic and foreign demands, the two engines powering Japan's economic growth, are out of kilter. 日本の経済成長を引っ張る原動力の内需と外需が、今のところ不調だ。◆In view of increased social demand for investment, we aim to tie up with regional banks and other financial institutions across the nation. 社会の投資需要の増大にかんがみて、当社は地銀など全国の金融機関との業務提携を目指している。◆M&A deals among start-up firms are likely to create more demand for equity financing from the autumn. ベンチャー企業間のM&A取引で、秋から株式発行による資金調達の需要が増える見通しだ。◆Nonlife insurers are exploring new types of insurance demand and offering convenient and easy means of buying policies. 損保各社は、新たな保険需要を掘り起こして、いつでも、どこでも簡単に保険に加入できるサービスを提供している。◆The ongoing global economic downturn continues to hit demand for flights. 今回の世界的な景気後退[世界同時不況]で、航空需要が引き続き減少している[打撃を受けている]。◆The rise of the yen's value pushed up the demand for travel abroad. 円高が、海外旅行の需要を押し上げた。

demand and supply　需要と供給, 需要供給, 需給 (=supply and demand)
demand and supply [supply and demand] of funds　資金需給 (=demand for and supply of funds)
gap between demand and supply　需給ギャップ
supply and demand for swaps　スワップ取引の需給
◆An exchange rate is a kind of price decided by the demand and supply of a currency. 為替相場[為替レート]は、通貨の需給で決まる一種の価格だ。

demand damage compensation　損害賠償を請求する
◆Toshiba may demand damage compensation from Sony, and others may follow suit. 東芝はソニーに対する損害賠

償請求を検討しており、他社もこれに追随する可能性がある。

demand deposit 要求払い預金
（⇒certificate of deposit, M2）
◆The balance of time deposits has been steadily falling, in step with a surge in the balance of demand deposits. 要求払い預金の残高が急増しているのに対して、定期性預金残高の減少が加速している。

demand for bullion 金の需要、金地金の需要、金塊の需要
◆Demand for bullion as a protection of wealth has been spurred by mounting concern that the global economy is faltering. 世界経済低迷への懸念増大から、安全資産［資産保全］としての金の需要が拡大している。

demand for funds 資金需要
◆There has been greater demand for funds to develop mega solar power plant projects in recent years. 最近は、メガソーラー（大型太陽光発電所）事業開発の資金需要が高まっている。

demand for loans 借入需要、資金需要
（＝loan demand；⇒lending, loan demand）
◆The figure points to a drastic contraction in lending by banks as well as a lack of demand for new loans from the private sector. この数字は、民間企業の新規借入需要［資金需要］の低迷と銀行による融資削減のすごさを物語っている。

demandable liabilities 要求払い負債

demanding （形）割高の、（要求などが）厳しい、過酷な要求をする、自己本位の
◆The stock valuations are demanding. 株価評価は、割高である［株価評価で見て、割高である］。

dematerialization of securities 証券の無証券化

demise （名）消滅、終止、終焉、死亡、不動産権の移転、譲位
◆Many pundits in Tokyo have prophesized the possible demise of U.S. primacy since the financial bubble burst. 金融バブルの崩壊以降、日本では、米一極指導の終焉（しゅうえん）を予言する専門家が多い。

demographic （形）人口動態に関する、人口統計学の、人口統計上の
age-specific demographic structure 年齢別人口構成
demographic analysis 人口動態調査、人口動態分析
demographic data 人口統計データ
demographic revolution 人口革命、人口の急激な変化
（＝demographic transition）
demographic shifts 人口構成の変化、人口の年齢構成の変化 （＝demographic change）
demographic statistics 人口動態統計、人口統計
demographic structure 人口構造、人口構成
demographic trend 人口動態
pyramid-shaped demographic structure ピラミッド型の人口構成

demographic change 人口構造の変化
◆The demographic changes show the inevitability of raising pension premiums unless pension benefits are reduced in the future. この人口構造の変化は、年金給付を今後減額しない限り、年金保険料の引上げは必至であることを示している。

demonstrate （動）表示する、表明する、明示する、説明する、証明する、実証する、立証する、実演する、実際にやって見せる、デモを行う、デモに加わる
◆The Bank of Japan demonstrated its resolve to address the yen's strength. 日銀は、円高に取り組む決意を明確に示した。

demutualization （名）非相互会社化
（相互会社＝mutual company）

demutualize （動）非相互会社化する
◆Mitsui Life Insurance Co. demutualized and became a joint stock company in April 2004. 三井生命保険は、2004年4月から非相互会社化して株式会社になった［2004年4月から会社形態を相互会社から株式会社に転換した］。

denominate （動）表示する、（ある通貨）建てとする、指定する、命名する
be denominated in yen 円で表示されている、円建てである、円ベースである
denominated currency 指定された通貨
denominated in dollars ドル表示の、ドル建ての、ドル・ベースの
have one's own denominated currency 独自の通貨を持つ
◆At present, about 61 percent of foreign reserves are denominated in dollars. 現在、外貨準備の61％がドル建てだ。◆The brokerage's main services for individual customers will be asset management advisory services, focusing on the sale of products such as investment trust funds that invest in foreign equities, and money market funds denominated in foreign currencies. 同証券会社は、株式の主な個人顧客向け（売買仲介）業務として、外国株を組み込んだ投資信託や外貨建てMMF（マネー・マーケット・ファンド）などの商品の販売を中心に、資産運用顧問業務を展開する方針だ。

-denominated （形）～建て、～表示の、～ベースの
（⇒fluctuations in foreign exchange rate, foreign currency-denominated bond, yen-denominated assets）
Australian dollar-denominated deposit service 豪ドル建て預金サービス
dollar-denominated amounts ドル・ベースの総額
dollar-denominated assets ドル建て資産
dollar-denominated deposits ドル建て預金
dollar-denominated export ドル表示の輸出
dollar-denominated project financing ドル建てプロジェクト・ファイナンス
dollar-denominated receivables ドル建て債権
euro-denominated assets ユーロ建て資産
foreign currency-denominated bonds 外貨建て債券
foreign currency-denominated securities 外貨建て債
in dollar-denominated terms ドル建てで、ドル表示で、ドル・ベースで
ruble-denominated loan ルーブル建て融資、ルーブル建てローン
sterling-denominated paper ポンド建て債券
yen-denominated assets 円建て資産
yen-denominated government bonds 円建て国債
yen-denominated long-term debt 円建て長期債務
yen-denominated new issuance 円建て起債総額
yen-denominated new issue 円建て債券の起債
yen-denominated syndicated loan 円建てシンジケート・ローン
yuan-denominated bonds 人民元建ての債券
（⇒float動詞）
◆Sberbank of Russia will offer a variety of services, such as ruble-denominated loans to Mizuho Corporate Bank's clients when they do business in Russia. ロシア最大手行のズベルバンクは、みずほコーポレート銀行の顧客がロシアで事業を行う際にルーブル建て融資を行うなどの各種サービスを提供することになった。◆The high yields of the yen-denominated government bonds were considered considerably higher than minuscule domestic interest rates. この円建て国債は、国内の超低金利に比べて利回りがはるかに大きいと見られた。◆The interest rates of the Australian dollar-denominated deposit service are relatively high among major foreign currencies. 主要外貨のうち豪ドル建て預金サービスの金利は、比較的高い。◆Yen-denominated exports accounted for more than 40 percent of total exports by currency in the first half of this year. 今年上半期（1-6月期）の円建て輸出は、通貨別で総輸出の40％超を占めた。◆Yen-

denominated loans to China account for a good portion of Japan's official development assistance to that nation. 対中円借款は、中国向け政府開発援助（ODA）の大半を占める。

denomination （名）種類, 金種, 額面金額, 券面額, 貨幣金額, 金銭や重量などの単位・名称, 表示
 change of denominations of monetary units 貨幣単位の呼称変更, デノミ　（=denomination change, downward redenomination, redenomination, redesignation of denominations, renaming of monetary units）
 currency denomination 通貨単位, 通貨表示, 金種
 currency of denomination 表示通貨
 denomination of share certificate 株券の種類
 denomination reduction デノミ
 　（=downward redenomination）
 denominations of currency 金種
 in all denominations すべての金種で
 in fixed denominations 一定の金種で
 minimum denomination 最低券面単位
 money of small denominations 小銭
 notes of higher denominations 高額券, 高額の紙幣
 small-denomination money market certificates 市場金利連動型定期預金, 小口MMC
 small denomination note 小額紙幣
 ◆The bonds will be issued in denominations of 100 and 1,000 dollars. この公債は、100ドルと1,000ドルの額面（額面金額）で発行される。◆The $100 bill is the most often counterfeited denomination of U.S. currency outside the United States. 米国の100ドル紙幣は、米国外での偽造件数が最も多い米国の金種だ。

depend on [upon]　～次第である, ～を頼りにする, ～を当てにする
 ◆Depending on moves in foreign exchange markets, there is a risk we may lose initial investments in foreign currency deposits. 為替相場の動き次第で、外貨預金では初期投資額を割り込むリスクがある。

dependence （名）依存, 依存状態, 依存度, 依存症, 依存関係, 常用癖, 信頼, 信用, 左右されること
 dependence on imports 輸入依存
 　（=import dependence）
 dependence on specific market segments 特定市場への依存［依存度］
 economic dependence 経済的依存
 external dependence 対外依存
 trade dependence 貿易依存, 貿易への依存度
 　（=dependence on trade）
 ◆Japanese export companies must end their excessive dependence on North America. 日本の輸出企業は、過度の北米依存を止めなければならない。

dependency （名）依存, 依存度, 依存状態, 依存物, 保護領, 属国
 aged dependency ratio 老年人口指数
 dependency on public bonds 公債依存度
 dependency on the U.S. dollar as the currency of last resort 最後の拠りどころとしての米ドルへの依存［依存度］
 ◆Financial exchanges between the BRICs group, Indonesia and South Korea will move toward a tri-reserve-currency regime by losing a dependency on the U.S. dollar. BRICsグループ（ブラジル、ロシア、インド、中国）とインドネシア、韓国の新興6か国間の金融取引は今後、米ドルに依存しなくなるため、3準備通貨体制に移行するものと思われる。

dependent （名）扶養家族, 被扶養者, 扶養親族
 allowances for dependents 扶養控除
 exemption for dependents 扶養控除
 retirees and their dependent 退職者とその親族者

 ◆Employees of the group companies and their dependents are now enrolled in the state health insurance program for employees of small and midsize companies. グループ企業の従業員とその扶養家族は現在、中小企業従業員向けの国の健康保険制度に加入している。

deplete （動）使い果たす, 消耗する, 消耗させる, 枯渇させる, 疲弊させる, 無力にする, 取り尽くす, 掘り尽くす, 空にする, 減らす　（自動）枯渇する, 減少する, 減耗する
 deplete the United States' coffers 米国の財政を疲弊させる
 depleted asset 減耗資産, 涸渇資産
 depleted cost 減耗償却後原価
 ◆These pork-barrel add-ons will further deplete the United States' coffers. 議員の人気取りが目的のこれら法案の追加条項は、米国の財政を一段と疲弊させることになる。

depleted state coffers　疲弊した国家財政, 国家財政の疲弊, 枯渇した財源
 ◆Amid the depleted state coffers, it is difficult to implement a major stimulus package to rectify the rise in the yen's value. 財政悪化が進む中［国の財源が枯渇する中］、円高是正のため大規模な財政出動を行うのは難しい。◆Japan must tackle the task of replenishing the depleted state coffers. 日本は、疲弊した国家財政立て直しの課題［疲弊した国家財政の立て直しという課題］に取り組まなければならない。

depletion （名）消耗, 枯渇, 疲弊, 減少, 低下, 減耗償却
 depletion allowance 減耗控除, 減耗償却累計額
 depletion asset 減耗資産, 涸渇資産
 　（=depleted asset）
 depletion base 減耗償却基準額
 depletion expense 減耗償却費
 depletion in economic value 経済価値の低下
 depletion of assets 資産の減少
 depletion reserve for land 土地減耗引当金

deploy （動）展開する, 配置する, 配備する, 装備する, 導入する, 効果的に活用する, 実施する
 ◆The central bank of Japan has deployed various measures to ease monetary policy, including cuts in the discount rate and hikes in the target for current account deposits held by commercial banks at the central bank. 日銀は、公定歩合の引下げや銀行が日銀に持つ当座預金の残高目標の引上げなどを含めて、各種の金融緩和策を実施してきた。

deployment （名）展開, 配置, 配備, 装備, 効果的利用, 導入

deposit （動）預金する, 金銭などを預ける, 預け入れる, 預託する, 供託する, （手付け金、保証金として）支払う, （自動販売機などにコインを）入れる
 （⇒depositor）
 deposit a coin and push the button コインを入れてボタンを押す
 deposit funds with an investment firm 投資会社にファンドを預託する
 deposit ¥500,000 on a new house 新しい家に手付け金として50万円を支払う
 ◆Currently, investors separately deposit funds for commodity futures trading at each firm or exchange. 現在、投資家はそれぞれ、商品先物取引の資金（証拠金）を先物会社や商品取引所に預けている。◆The Tokyo metropolitan government has decided to deposit more than ¥100 billion in public funds in Citibank, a U.S. bank, to diversify risks. 東京都は、1,000億円を上回る公金を米国の銀行「シティバンク」に預けて、リスクを分散する方針を固めた。◆The total amount of money deposited in individual foreign currency accounts has continued to increase in recent years. 個人向け外貨預金残高は、ここ数年増え続けている。◆We must pay attention to commission fees when we choose to deposit foreign currencies.

外貨預金を選ぶときは、為替手数料に注意しなければならない。
deposit （名）預金, 預金額, 積立金, 保証金, 敷金, 内金, 手付け金, 預託　（⇒bank deposit, current account, current account deposit, current deposit, demand deposit, ordinary deposits, time deposit）
- bank deposit　銀行預金
- business deposit　営業預金
- cash deposits　現金預金
- collection of deposits　預金獲得
- current deposits　当座預金
- demand deposits　要求払い預金
- deposit agreement　預託契約
- deposit and savings　預貯金
- deposit at bank　銀行預金
  （=deposit money in a bank）
- deposit at notice　通知預金
- deposit component　預金要素（デリバティブとして会計処理されない契約の構成要素）
- deposit for bond redemption　社債償還引当預金
- deposit for safekeeping　保護預り
  （=deposit for safe custody）
- deposit for security　担保預り
- deposit from employees　従業員預り金
- deposit guarantee system　預金保証制度
- deposit in current account　当座預金
- deposit in trust　信託預金
- deposit money　預金通貨　（⇒M1, M2）
- deposit obligations　預金債務, 預金残高
- deposit paid on construction work　工事前渡金
- deposit paid to trade creditor　仕入先前払い代金
- deposit payoff system　預金のペイオフ制度
  （⇒moratorium）
- deposit protection　預金保護
- deposit received　預り金, 保証金
  （=deposited money, money in custody）
- deposit refund　預金払戻し　（=deposit payout）
- deposits at notice　通知預金　（=deposits at call）
- deposits from nonmembers　員外預金
- deposits outstanding　預金残高
  （=outstanding deposits）
- derivative deposits　派生的預金
- exodus of deposits　預金の大量流出
- fixed deposit　定期預金, 定期性預金
- floating deposits　流動性預金
- foreign currency deposits　外貨預金
- influx of deposits　預金の流入
- large term deposits　大口定期預金
- liquid deposits　流動性預金, 決済性預金
- nonresidents' deposits　非居住者預金
- ordinary deposits　普通預金
- personal deposits　個人預金
- protection of deposits　預金保護
- quick deposit　当座預金
- savings deposits　普通預金, 貯蓄預金
- security deposit　保証金
- take in deposits　預金を受け入れる
- time and savings deposits　定期性預金, 貯蓄性預金
- time deposits　定期預金, 定期性預金
  （=term deposits）
- withdraw deposits　預金を引き出す, 預金を引き揚げる

◆Clients moved their deposits from small or midsize financial institutions to major banks. 顧客が、中小金融機関から大手銀行へ預金を移し替えた。◆Currently, a large sum of the deposits we keep at banks is used for government bond purchases. 現在、われわれが金融機関に預けている預金のかなりの額が、国債の購入に充てられている。◆Expecting the natural attrition of fixed deposits, the bank will reduce the deposits to ¥197.4 billion by fiscal 2011. 定期預金の自然減を見込んで、同行は預金量を2011年度は1,974億円まで減額する。◆Financial institutions pay insurance premiums to the Deposit Insurance Corporation according to the amount of deposits they hold. 金融機関は、保有する預金量に応じて預金保険機構に保険料を納付している。◆In the case of foreign currency deposits by the U.S. dollar, many online banks charge about ¥0.25 in commission per dollar at the time of deposits and withdrawals. 米ドルによる外貨預金の場合、ネット銀行の多くは、預け入れ時と解約時に1ドルに付き25銭程度の手数料を取る。◆In the case of foreign currency deposits, depositors can invest in foreign currencies such as British pound, Swiss franc and Australian dollar as well as the U.S. dollar and euro. 外貨預金の場合、預金者は、米ドルやユーロのほかに英ポンド、スイス・フランや豪ドルなどにも投資することができる。◆In the case of foreign currency deposits, losses may balloon if the yen appreciates further and may cause a loss of principal. 外貨預金の場合、円高がさらに進めば損失が膨らみ、元本割れになる恐れもある。◆It's difficult to offset losses from further appreciation of the yen with interest as interest rates in many foreign currency deposits are low. 外貨建て預金の多くは金利が低いので、円高進行による損失分を利息で相殺する［取り戻す］のは難しい。◆The Bank of Japan decided to raise the outstanding balance of current account deposits held by private financial institutions at the central bank to ¥27 trillion-¥30 trillion from ¥22 trillion-¥27 trillion. 日銀は、民間の金融機関が日銀に預けている当座預金（日銀当座預金）の残高目標を22-27兆円程度から27-30兆円程度に引き上げることを決めた。◆The company transferred the deposits of two firms it would acquire to window-dress the books. 同社は、買収予定の2社の預金を付け替えて［移し替えて］粉飾決算をしていた。◆The exchange rate was the same at the time of deposit and withdrawal in a foreign currency deposit. 外貨預金で、為替相場は預け入れ時と解約時で同じだった。◆When the freeze on the payoff system was partially lifted, clients shifted their funds from time deposits to savings deposits that will be protected fully. ペイオフ制度凍結の一部解禁が行われた際には、顧客が預金を定期預金から全額保護される普通預金に預け替えた。

deposit account　預金口座, 預金勘定
◆Amid the continued yen's historically high levels, increasing numbers of people are opening foreign currency deposit accounts. 歴史的な円高水準が続くなか、外貨預金口座を設ける人が増えている。

deposit assets　預り資産
◆Daiwa Securities has about ¥40 trillion of deposit assets. 大和証券の預り資産は、約40兆円だ。

deposit cancellation　預金の解約
◆Not only a panic run on banks, but snowballing deposit cancellation could trigger an ominous chain reaction leading to a financial crisis. パニック的な銀行の取付け騒ぎだけでなく、激しい預金解約も、不気味な連鎖反応の引き金となり、金融恐慌をもたらす可能性がある。

deposit insurance　預金保険
◆As long as the payoff system remains frozen, a depositor is assured of the entire refund of deposit in both principal and interest from a failed financial institution, in line with an exceptional measure under the deposit insurance law. ペイオフ制度が凍結されている間、預金者は預金保険法の特例措置として、破たんした金融機関からの預金払戻しが元本と

利息を含めて全額保証されている。

Deposit Insurance Corporation 預金保険機構, DIC
（⇒depositor, oversee）
◆Financial institutions pay insurance premiums to the Deposit Insurance Corporation according to the amount of deposits they hold. 金融機関は、保有する預金量に応じて預金保険機構に保険料を納付している。

解説 預金保険機構とは：1971年に、政府・日銀と民間金融機関の出資で設立された。ペイオフ制度の運営主体で、100％出資子会社として整理回収機構（RCC）があり、不良債権を買い取って回収する業務にもかかわっている。

Deposit Insurance Corporation of Japan 預金保険機構
◆The Financial Services Agency and the Deposit Insurance Corporation of Japan invoked the limited deposit protection system for the first time. 金融庁と預金保険機構は、ペイオフ制度を初めて発動した。

Deposit Insurance Law 預金保険法
（⇒insolvency, taxpayers' money）
◆In the past, injection of public funds was limited to cases that could trigger a financial crisis under the Deposit Insurance Law. 以前は、公的資金の注入は、預金保険法によって金融危機を招く恐れがある場合に限られていた。◆The government finalized a plan to inject public funds totaling ￥1.96 trillion into Resona Holdings Inc. under the Deposit Insurance Law. 政府は、預金保険法に基づき、りそなホールディングスに対して1兆9,600億円の公的資金を注入する案を最終的に決めた。

deposit insurance system 預金保険制度
◆The government intends to restructure the deposit insurance system as a new financial safety net for protecting settlement systems. 政府は、預金保険制度を、決済システム保護のための新しい金融安全網として再構築する方針だ。◆The main purpose of the deposit insurance system has been to protect depositors. 預金保険制度の主な目的は、預金者保護であった。

deposit interest rates 預金の金利
◆The branch-free Internet-based bank can attract customers with higher deposit interest rates. 店舗を持たないネット専業銀行だと、預金の金利を高くして、顧客を集めることができる。

deposit money 金を預ける, 預金する
　deposit money in a bank　銀行に金を預ける
　deposit money in dollars　ドルで預金する, ドルで外貨預金する

deposit payout 預金の払戻し　（=deposit refund）
◆The Financial Services Agency came up with a proposal to raise the guaranteed deposit payout to more than ￥10 million for regional financial institutions planning to merge. 金融庁は、合併する地域金融機関に対して、（ペイオフの）預金払戻し保証額を1,000万円以上に引き上げる案を示した。

deposit refund cap 預金払戻しの上限, 預金払戻し枠, 預金払戻し額の上限設定措置, 預金払戻しの最高限度額, ペイオフ制度, ペイオフ　（=payoff system）
◆The deposit refund cap—known in the Japanese press as the "payoff" system—has applied to time deposits since April 1, 2002. 日本の新聞等で「ペイオフ」制度と呼ばれている（破たんした金融機関からの）預金払戻し保証額に上限を設ける措置は、2002年4月1日から定期預金に適用されている。

deposit reserve ratio 預金準備率（銀行の預金総額のうち、銀行が中央銀行に預け入れる額の比率）
　bank deposit reserve ratio　預金準備率
　　（=deposit reserve rates）
　deposit reserve requirement ratio　預金準備率
　reserve deposit requirement system　法定準備制度
◆The People's Bank of China raised deposit reserve ratio by 0.5 percentage points. 中国人民銀行（中央銀行）は、預金準備率を0.5％引き上げた。

deposit service 預金サービス, 預金の取扱い
◆Internet-based bank Sony Bank started a deposit service for the Brazilian real in May 2011. ネット専業銀行のソニー銀行が、2011年5月からブラジル通貨レアルの預金サービス［預金の取扱い］を開始した。◆The interest rates of the Australian dollar-denominated deposit service are relatively high among major foreign currencies. 主要外貨のうち豪ドル建て預金サービスの金利は、比較的高い。

deposit taking 預金収集

deposit taking business 預金取扱い業務

depositary （名）保管者, 受託者, 預託機関, デポジタリー　（=depository; ⇒depository）
　American depositary receipt　米国預託証券, ADR
　central certificate depositary service　振替決済制度
　central depositary system　保管振替制度
　depositary agreement　事務委託契約, デポジタリー契約
　depositary bank　受託銀行, 預託銀行
　depositary correspondent bank　デポ・コルレス先
　Depositary Institutions Deregulation and Monetary Control Act of 1980　1980年金融制度改革法, 米金融制度改革法
　depositary receipt　預託証券
　depositary trust company　預託信託会社
　securities investment trust depositary company　投資信託受託会社

deposited money 預金
◆Under the offset provisions, depositors can decide how much of their deposited money should be used to pay back outstanding loans. 相殺規定によると、預金者はその預金をどの程度、借入金残高の返済に充てるかを決めることができる。

depositor （名）預金者, 預金機, 現金預け入れ機
　（⇒credit動詞, deposit insurance, deposited money, failed bank, interbank network of ATMs, investment opportunity, lot）
　a major depositor　大口預金者
　amount of deposits by depositor of all banks　全国銀行預金者別預金［預金統計］
　amounts outstanding by depositor　預金者別残高内訳
　automatic depositor　現金自動預け入れ機
　depositors forgery insurance　預金者文書偽造保険
　domestic depositors　国内預金者
　foreign depositors　外国の預金者
　joint depositor　連名預金者
　know the identity of the depositor　本人確認をする
　retail depositor　小口預金者, リテール預金者
　wholesale depositor　大口預金者, ホールセール預金者
◆Banks will not pay compensation when depositors tell other people their PINs. 預金者が他人に暗証番号を知らせた場合、銀行は補償しない。◆Depositors must strictly assess the management of each financial institution. 預金者は、各金融機関の経営状況を厳しく評価する［見極める］必要がある。◆In foreign currency deposits, depositors can earn profits by exchanging their foreign currency deposits into yen when the yen's value against major foreign currencies falls. 外貨預金では、主要外貨に対して円相場が下落した時点で預金者が外貨預金を円に戻せば、利益を上げる［儲ける］ことができる。◆In the case of foreign currency deposits, depositors can invest in foreign currencies such as British pound, Swiss franc and Australian dollar as well as the U.S. dollar and euro. 外貨預金の場合、預金者は、米ドルやユーロのほかに英ポンド、スイス・フランや豪ドルなどにも投資することができる。◆In the event of hefty appraisal losses, banks must avoid a situ-

ation in which their creditors, including depositors, will be affected by the impairment of bank-owned assets. 巨額の含み損が出た場合、銀行は、預金者などの債権者が銀行保有資産の評価減の影響を受けるような状況がないようにしなければならない。◆Personal computers of many Net banking depositors have been infected with viruses that ravaged computers in the United States and European countries. 多くのネット・バンキング預金者のパソコンが、欧米のコンピュータに爆発的被害を生んだウイルスに感染していた。◆Some major banks lower their commission rates of foreign currency deposits if depositors make transactions via online accounts. 外貨預金の預金者がネット口座経由で取引をする場合、一部の大手銀行は、外貨預金の手数料［為替手数料］の料率を引き下げている。◆The new bank tax is levied on the banks' gross operating profits—their earnings minus basic operating expenses such as interest payments to depositors. 新銀行税は、銀行の収入から基礎的な経費（預金者に対する預金金利の支払いなど）を差し引いた業務粗利益に課される。◆The Tokyo metropolitan government is a major depositor with public funds totaling more than ￥1.1 trillion in time deposits and other investments deposited at 17 different financial institutions. 東京都は、17の金融機関に定期預金などで総額1兆1,000億円を超す公金を預けている大口の預金者だ。◆When a financial institution fails, the Deposit Insurance Corporation refunds up to ￥10 million plus interest per depositor under the payoff system. 金融機関が破たんした場合、ペイオフ制度に従って、預金保険機構が預金者1人当たり元本1,000万円を上限に、利息と合わせて払い戻す。

depository （名）金庫、貯蔵所、倉庫、預かり人、保管人 (depositary)、被寄託者、受託者 (depositary, trustee)、デポ先、デポジトリー　(⇒depositary)
　after-hour depository bag　時間後［夜間］バッグ
　authorized depository　公認保管業者
　central depository clearing system for stock certificate　振替決済制度
　central securities depositories　中央証券預託機関
　depository bank　デポジトリー銀行、デポジトリー・コルレス（預金口座を開設してあるコルレス先）
　depository claims　預金請求権
　depository correspondent　デポジトリー・コルレス（=depository bank: 自行名義でコルレス勘定を持つ海外取引先銀行）
　depository facilities　預託機関
　depository trust company［corporation］　預託信託会社
　global depository share　グローバル預託株式
　non-depository correspondent　ノンデポジトリー、ノンデポジトリー・コルレス
　securities depository　有価証券保管会社
　the night depository of a bank　銀行の夜間金庫

depository [depositary] institution　預金金融機関、預金受入れ金融機関、貯蓄銀行（=depository financial institution）
　Depository [Depositary] Institutions Deregulation and Monetary Control Act of 1980　1980年金融制度改革法
　Garn-St. German Depository Institutions Act of 1982　1982年預金取扱い金融機関法
　insured depository institution　被保険預金機関
　◆M3 includes cash in circulation, demand and time deposits and certificates of deposit at all depository institutions, including Japan Post Bank Co. マネー・サプライM3には、現金通貨、要求払い預金、定期性預金や全貯蓄銀行（ゆうちょ銀行を含む）の譲渡性預金 (CD) などが含まれる。

depository [depositary] receipt　預託証券、預かり証、預金証書、DR
　American depositary receipt　米国預託証券、ADR
　bearer depositary receipt　無記名預託証券
　global depository receipt　グローバル預託証券
　Japanese depository receipt　日本預託証券

depreciable　（形）償却可能な、償却対象の
　depreciable amount　償却可能金額、償却対象価額
　depreciable asset　償却可能資産、償却資産、減価償却資産
　depreciable life　耐用年数
　remaining depreciable lives　残存償却年数

depreciate　（動）低下する、下落する、価値が下がる、通貨を切り下げる、減価償却する、償却する、減価する、減価して見積もる　(⇒yen-denominated assets)
　depreciate fixed assets　有形固定資産［固定資産］の減価償却を行う
　depreciate the currency　通貨を切り下げる
　depreciated asset　資産価値の下落
　depreciated money［currency］　通貨の切下げ、通貨の下落、低落した通貨
　depreciating asset　資産の減価
　depreciating U.S. dollar　米ドルの下落
　◆It has been the dollar's turn to depreciate. ドル相場が下落する番になった。◆The yen has depreciated by more than ￥10 from before the previous enormous intervention. 円は、前回の大規模介入の前より10円強の円安になった。

depreciation　（名）価値低下、（価格などの）低下、（通貨の）下落、減価、平価切下げ、減価償却、減価償却費、償却、償却費（米国では一般に有形固定資産 (property, plant and equipment) の減価償却にdepreciationを使い、無形固定資産 (intangible assets) の償却にはamortizationを使っている）
　a moderate depreciation of the dollar　緩やかなドル安
　accelerated depreciation　加速償却、加速度償却、超過償却
　currency depreciation　通貨安、通貨価値下落、通貨下落、為替下落
　depreciation expense　減価償却費（=depreciation cost）
　depreciation-inflation spiral　通貨切下げとインフレの悪循環
　depreciation of the real exchange rare　実質為替レートの下落
　dollar depreciation devaluation　ドル安、ドル切下げ（=depreciation of (the) dollar）
　gradual depreciation　小幅な通貨切下げ
　market value depreciation　市場価格の低下
　real depreciation in currencies　実質ベースでの通貨下落
　reserve for depreciation　減価償却引当金
　sharp depreciation of the dollar　急激なドル安、ドル急落
　the depreciation of major currencies against the yen　円に対する主要通貨の下落、円高・主要通貨安
　the dollar's excessive depreciation　行き過ぎたドル安
　the yen's depreciation　円安、円価値の下落、円の下落（=depreciation of the yen, yen depreciation）
　the yen's depreciation against the dollar　円安・ドル高、ドルに対する円相場の下落
　◆A recovery will be export-driven, dependent on U.S. growth and the yen's depreciation, instead of being led by increased domestic consumption and capital investment. 今後の景気回復は、アメリカ経済の好転や円安を背景にした輸出主導型の回復で、国内の個人消費や設備投資の伸びがその牽引役となるわけではない。◆Depreciation is calculated generally on the straight-line method using rates based on the expected useful lives of the respective assets. 減価償却費は、原則として個々の資産の見積り耐用年数に基づく減価償却率を用いて、

定額法で計算されている。◆The continued fall in U.S. stock prices and the dollar's depreciation has battered the Japanese economy. 米国の株安とドル安の進行が、日本経済を直撃している[激しく揺さぶっている]。◆The yen's depreciation and stabilized crude oil prices have helped corporate profits. 円安や原油価格の落ち着きが、企業収益に寄与している。◆The yen's depreciation can both help Japanese exporters enhance their competitiveness in the global market and stem the current deflation by raising import prices. 円安は、日本の輸出産業の国際競争力アップにつながるとともに、輸入物価を押し上げることによって現在のデフレ進行の歯止めにもなる。

depreciation of currencies 通貨安
（⇒appreciation of currencies）
◆The United States and European countries have virtually allowed the depreciation of their currencies, resulting in a sharp rise in the yen and a fall in the dollar and euro. 米国と欧州が自国通貨安を事実上容認して、急激な円高・ドル安やユーロ安が進んだ。◆The United States and European nations embrace the depreciation of their currencies against the yen. 欧米諸国は、円に対する自国通貨安を容認している。

depreciation of nonperforming loans' economic value 不良債権の経済価値の減価
◆Current loan loss reserves will not be sufficient to cover the depreciation of nonperforming loans' economic value. 現在の貸倒れ引当金では、不良債権の経済価値の減価を十分にカバーしきれないだろう。

depreciation of the dollar ドル安
◆A depreciation of the dollar may stimulate external demand and ignite an export-driven economic upturn. ドル安は、外需を喚起して、輸出主導の景気回復につながる可能性がある。◆A moderate depreciation of the dollar might be necessary to some extent to reduce the twin deficits. 双子の赤字削減に、緩やかなドル安もある程度やむを得ないかもしれない。◆Part of the benefits of quantitative easing will take the form of a depreciation of the dollar. 量的緩和の効果の一部は、ドル安の形で現れる。◆The effects of the recent depreciation of the dollar have not been seen yet. 最近のドル安の影響は、まだ見られない。

depreciation of the dollar exchange rate ドル相場の下落, ドルの為替レートの下落
◆Some of the dollar funds injected into the banking system by the U.S. central bank will be invested in foreign assets, producing a depreciation of the dollar exchange rate. 米中央銀行（FRB）が市中の銀行に供給したドル資金の一部は、海外資産に投資されて、ドル相場の下落を招く。

depreciation of the euro ユーロ安
◆The latest depreciation of the euro brought about a life-sustaining boon to the currency. 今回のユーロ安が、ユーロの延命効果を招いた。

depreciation of the U.S. dollar ドル安
◆Falling stock prices and the depreciation of the U.S. dollar increased uncertainty over the global economy. 米国の株安やドル安で、世界経済の不透明感が強まっている。◆The rapid depreciation of the U.S. dollar would impair the current improvement in the Japanese economy. 急激なドル安は、日本の景気回復の腰を折ることになる。

depreciation of the yen 円安
benefit from the depreciation of the yen 円安が追い風になる
promote the depreciation of the yen 円安を促す
the recent depreciation of the yen 最近の円安
◆Monetary relaxation helps to promote the depreciation of the yen. 金融緩和は、円安を促す効果がある。◆The depreciation of the yen also has boosted profits for exporting companies. 円安も、輸出企業の利益を押し上げた。◆The slowdown of sales has been blamed on the recent depreciation of the yen, along with the mad cow disease outbreak, which has led many consumers to avoid beef. 売上減少の要因は、最近の円安と、狂牛病騒動による多くの消費者の牛肉離れだ。

depress （動）〜の力を弱める、抑制する、低下させる、（価値を）下落させる
depress economic activity 景気を低迷[沈滞させる]、経済活動を沈滞させる
depress economic growth 経済成長を鈍化させる
depress import growth 輸入の伸びを鈍化させる
depress interest rates 金利を引き下げる
depress personal spending 個人支出の低迷を招く, 消費支出の低迷をもたらす, 個人消費の冷え込みをもたらす
depress spending 消費低迷をもたらす
depress the bond market 債券相場を下落させる, 債券相場に冷や水を浴びせる
◆A prolonged recession has depressed tax revenues. 長引く不況で、税収が低迷した[伸びなかった]。

depressed （形）抑圧された、不景気の、不振の、下落した
depressed area[region] 不況地域, 貧困地区
depressed cartel 不況カルテル
（=depression cartel）
depressed consumer confidence 消費者マインドの冷え込み
depressed economy 景気低迷
depressed industry 不況産業, 産業不振
depressed inflation 抑圧されたインフレ, 抑圧性インフレ
depressed market 沈滞市況, 沈滞した市況, 市場低迷, 相場の下落
depressed prices 物価の下落, 価格低迷
depressed sales 販売低下, 売上高の低下, 販売低迷, 販売不振
depressed stock price 株価低迷

depressing effect 抑制効果, 下押し効果
◆The rate of savings among those people in their 30s and 40s is on an upward trend, which is likely to have a depressing effect on domestic demand. 30〜40歳代の貯蓄率が増大傾向にあり、内需を下押ししている可能性がある。

depression （名）不況, 不況期, 不景気, 景気停滞, 大恐慌, 低下, 停滞, 沈下, 減退, 衰弱, 意気消沈, うつ病, 低気圧
business depression 不景気
（=depression of business）
chronic depression 慢性的不況
commercial depression 商業不振, 商業不況
depressed prices 価格の低迷, 物価低迷, 物価安
depression cartel 不況カルテル
（=depressed cartel）
depression process 不況過程
economic depression 不況, 不景気, 経済不況
financial depression 金融不振, 金融不況, 財界不況, 不況
general[widespread] depression 全般的の不振
industrial depression 産業不振, 産業不況, 不況
inflationary depression インフレ的不況
prolonged depression 景気停滞の長期化
structural depression 構造不況, 構造的不況
the (Great) Depression 大恐慌, 世界大恐慌
trade depression 商売不振, 商況不振, 不景気, 不況, 貿易不振 （=depression in trade）
world[global, worldwide] depression 世界的不況
◆The Great Depression began in the United States in 1929. 大恐慌[世界大恐慌]は、1929年に米国で始まった。◆The ongoing business slump raises the specter of a global downturn comparable to the Great Depression that started in 1929. 今

回の不況は、1929年に始まった世界大恐慌に匹敵するほどの世界同時不況の懸念が高まっている。◆The world economy may remain trapped in a prolonged depression. 世界経済は、景気停滞が長期化する可能性がある。

depth (名)厚さ, 奥行き, 度合い
　depth of the market　市場の厚み, 市場の奥行き
　market depth　取引所の板(「板」は、取引参加者の売買注文を記録する板のことで、金融商品の市場での流動性を表す)

derecognition (名)認識の中止(前に認識した金融資産や金融負債を財政状態計算書(financial position statement)から取り除くこと)

deregulate (動)規制を緩和する, 規制を撤廃する, 自由化する, 市場開放する　(⇒insurance product)
　◆Sales of life insurance products at banks have been deregulated in Britain, Germany and France. 銀行での生保商品の販売は、英独仏では自由化されている。

deregulation (名)規制緩和, 規制撤廃, 自由化, 市場開放　(⇒Big Bang, securities market)
　banking system deregulation　銀行制度の規制緩和
　deposit deregulation　預金の規制緩和
　Depository Institutions Deregulation and Monetary Control Act　1980年金融制度改革法
　deregulation and liberalization　規制緩和と自由化
　deregulation of banking agents　銀行代理店の規制緩和
　financial deregulation　金融の規制緩和
　interest rate deregulation　金利の自由化
　◆Deregulation in the industry allows banks to enter the securities brokerage business from December 2004. 業界の規制緩和で、銀行は2004年12月から証券仲介業務に参入できるようになった。

derivative (名)派生商品, 金融派生商品, デリバティブ　(=derivative product)
　commodity derivatives　市況商品の派生商品
　credit derivatives　信用派生商品
　derivative action　派生訴訟, 株主代表訴訟　(=derivative lawsuit)
　derivative contract　デリバティブ契約
　derivative feature　デリバティブ特質
　derivative investment　デリバティブ投資, 金融派生商品取引
　derivative product　派生商品, 金融派生商品, デリバティブ　(=derivative)
　derivative transaction　デリバティブ取引
　domestic trading in derivatives　デリバティブ(金融派生商品)の国内取引
　equity derivatives　株式派生商品
　exchange-traded derivatives　上場派生商品
　financial derivatives　金融派生商品
　fixed income derivatives　債券派生商品
　interest rate derivatives　金利派生商品
　mortgage derivatives　モーゲージ派生商品
　over-the-counter derivatives　店頭派生商品　(=OTC derivatives)
　weather derivatives　天候デリバティブ
　◆Derivatives such as futures and options are securities that derive their value from another financial assets, such as a share. デリバティブ(金融派生商品)は、株など他の金融資産から価値を引き出す有価証券だ。◆The Osaka Securities Exchange accounts for 50 percent of domestic trading in derivatives including stock price index futures. 大証は、株価指数先物などデリバティブ(金融派生商品)の国内取引で5割を占めている。◆While derivatives can allow investors to realize huge profits with a relatively small amount of capital, losses can be colossal if the transactions sour. デリバティブ(金融派生商品)の場合、投資家は比較的少ない手持ち資金で巨額の利益が得られる一方、取引が失敗すると損失も厖大(ぼうだい)になる可能性がある。

[解説]デリバティブとは：通貨や株式などの現物を取引するのではなく、相場の変動を予測して行う先物取引や異なる金利や通貨を交換するスワップ取引、株式や債券を売買する権利を取引するオプション取引など、特殊な取引を組み合わせた金融派生商品。もともとは株価や金利、為替などの変動リスクを回避するためにアメリカで開発された。少ない原資で多額の取引ができるため、投機的に用いると巨額の利益が得られる一方、判断を誤ると多額の損失を被る危険がある。

derivative instrument　派生商品, 金融派生商品
　construct derivative instruments　派性商品を構築する
　the pricing of derivative instruments　派性商品の価格決定
　trade in derivative instruments　派性商品取引を行う

derivative investment　デリバティブ投資, 金融派生商品取引
　◆The Resolution and Collection Corporation filed a lawsuit with the Tokyo District Court against two executives of a defunct credit union in Tokyo, seeking ¥400 million in compensation for losses created by high-risk derivative investments. 整理回収機構(RCC)は、破たんした東京の信用組合の理事長ら二人に対し、リスクの高いデリバティブ(金融派生商品)取引で生じた損失の損害賠償として4億円を求める訴訟を東京地裁に起こした。

derivative [derivatives] market　派生商品市場, 金融派生商品市場
　◆The sweeping overhaul of U.S. financial regulation includes tough new rules for the derivatives market. 米金融規制の抜本的改革には、派生商品市場についての厳しい新ルールも含まれている。

derivative product　派生商品, 金融派生商品, デリバティブ　(=derivative, financial derivative instrument)
　◆Influential overseas commercial banks have maintained an advantage with transactions for derivative products by using high-tech computer systems. 海外の有力行は、最先端のコンピュータ・システムを使って、デリバティブ取引で優位を保っている。◆U.S. and European banks have advanced into diverse fields, including securities business, by polishing up their financial tools for utilizing derivative products. 欧米の銀行は、デリバティブ(金融派生商品)を活用するための金融技術を磨いて、証券業務などさまざまな分野に進出してきた。

derivative transaction　デリバティブ取引　(=derivative trading)
　◆In 1997, the Osaka Securities Exchange launched option trading of individual stocks, a kind of derivative transaction, at the same time as the TSE. 大阪証券取引所(大証)は、デリバティブ取引の一種である個別株オプション取引を、1997年から東証と同時に開始した。◆The credit union was engaged in derivative transactions with Lehman Brothers' branch office in Tokyo. 同信用組合は、米証券大手のリーマン・ブラザーズ証券東京支店とデリバティブ取引を行っていた。

derivatives trading　金融派生商品(デリバティブ)の取引, デリバティブ取引　(=derivative transaction)
　◆Because of the losses accrued through derivatives trading, Yakult chalked up ¥107.7 billion in extraordinary losses in its account settlement for fiscal 1997. デリバティブ取引で生じた損失のため、ヤクルトは1997年度決算(1998年3月期決算)で1,077億円の特別損失を計上した。◆The OSE is strong in derivatives trading. 大証は、金融派生商品(デリバティブ)の取引に強みを持っている。

design (動)設計する, 計画する, 企画する, 整備する, 意匠を作る
　be designed to　～するよう想定している[考えられてい

る]〜するのが目的だ
designed investment　計画投資
◆A bill to revise the Law on Special Measures for Strengthening Financial Functions is designed to facilitate compensations of losses of financial institutions with public funds. 金融機能強化法の改正法案は、公的資金で金融機関の損失の穴埋めを容易にするのが狙いだ。◆A stock split is a measure designed to enable investors, including those with only limited funds, to invest in a company by reducing the share purchase unit. 株式分割は、株式の購入単位を小口化して、少額の資金しかない投資家でも企業に投資できるようにするための手段[資本政策]だ。◆Corporation's internal controls are designed to provide reasonable assurance as to the integrity and reliability of the financial statements. 当社の内部統制は、財務書類の完全性と信頼性について十分保証するよう図られています。◆The current support system for jobseekers from training to job referrals and to employment is not well designed. 訓練から職業紹介と就職にいたるまで就職困難者を支援するための現在の体制は、十分に整備されていない。◆The fund established by the Development of Japan is designed to finance major auto parts makers hit by the March 11 earthquake and tsunami. 日本政策投資銀行が設立するファンドは、東日本大震災（2011年3月11日）で被災した自動車部品メーカーに出資や融資などの資金支援をするのが目的だ。◆To enhance the stimulating effect of the Fed's rate cuts, swift implementation of fiscal and tax stimulus measures, including tax cuts on investment designed to reinvigorate the stock market, is necessary in addition to the large-scale tax cut program that is under way. 米連邦準備制度理事会（FRB）の金利引下げの刺激効果を高めるためには、現在実施中の大型減税プログラムに加え、株式市場を再活性化するための投資減税など、財政・税制面からの景気刺激策の速やかな実施が必要である。

designated　（形）指定した, 指定の, 指名の, 特定の, 〜と見なされる
　designated bidding　指名競争入札
　designated bonded area　指定保税地域
　designated currency　指定通貨
　designated deposits in foreign currency　外貨指定預金
　designated foreign investor　指定外国投資家
　designated fund　指定基金
　designated (insurance) benefits　特定の保険金
　designated investment exchange　指定投資取引所, 指定取引所
　designated money in trust　指定金銭信託
　designated representative　指定代理人
　designated securities　指定証券
　designated trustee　指定した信託会社
　individually operated designated money trust　単独運用指定金銭信託
　investment designated instruments　投資と見なされる商品
　maturity-designated (time) deposit　期日指定定期預金
◆When the policyholders of single-premium whole life insurances die, beneficiaries receive the designated benefits plus accumulated dividends. 一時払い終身保険の契約者が死亡した場合、保険金の受取人は、特定の（死亡）保険金のほかに積立配当金を受け取れる。

desirable　（形）望ましい, 好ましい
◆Further stability in the financial markets is desirable. 金融市場の一層の安定が、望まれる。

desire　（動）強く望む, 強く求める, 欲する, 期待する, 所望する, 願う
　desired cash balance　所望の現金
　desired consumption　所望の消費
　desired effect　初期の効果
　desired investment　所期の投資, 所望の投資
　desired reserves　所望準備
　desired saving　所期の貯蓄, 所望の貯蓄
　minimum-desired rate of return　最低期待収益率

desire　（名）欲求, 欲望, 要望, 強い願望, 性的衝動, 性欲
　absolute desire　絶対的欲望
　desire for profits　利益追求

destabilize　（動）錯乱（さくらん）する, 不安定にする, 弱体化させる, 動揺させる
◆The financial markets would have been further destabilized if the U.S. House of Representatives had rejected the financial bailout bill. 米議会下院が金融安定化法案（金融救済法案）を否決していたら、金融市場はさらに動揺していただろう。◆The twin deficits of the United States—fiscal and current account deficits—are threatening to destabilize the world economy. アメリカの双子の赤字（財政赤字と経常収支赤字）が、世界経済の不安定要因となっている。

destabilizing factor　撹乱（かくらん）要因

destroy　（動）破壊する, 壊す, 打ち砕く, 滅ぼす, 台なしにする, （文書などを）無効にする, （動物などを）処分する, 殺す
◆Factories, shops and farms were destroyed or severely damaged due to the March 11 Great East Japan Earthquake. 2011年3月11日の東日本大震災で、工場や店舗、農地が壊滅もしくは大打撃を受けた。

deteriorate　（動）悪化する, 低下する, 停滞する, 退化する, 老朽化する
　deteriorated earnings　業績の悪化
　deteriorated profitability　収益性の悪化
◆Business conditions are rapidly deteriorating due to the global financial crisis and the worldwide economic downturn. 世界的な金融危機と世界的な景気後退で、景気は急速に悪化している。◆If the group's cash-flow situation deteriorates further, it may see its creditor banks declining to extend loans. 同グループの資金繰りがさらに悪化すれば、取引銀行が融資を拒否する可能性もある。◆The U.S. Federal Reserve Board said in its Beige Book release that the U.S. economy deteriorated further in almost all corners of the country. 米連邦準備制度理事会（FRB）は、地区連銀景況報告（ベージュ・ブック）を発表し、米国の経済情勢はほぼ全米で一段と悪化していると指摘した。

deteriorating　（形）悪化する, 低下する, 深刻化する, 〜の悪化, 〜の低下
　deteriorating asset quality　資産の質の悪化, 資産の質の低下
　deteriorating balance sheet　財務体質の悪化, 財務内容の悪化
　deteriorating credit quality　信用の質の悪化, 信用度の悪化, 信用力の低下
　deteriorating earnings　収益の悪化, 業績悪化
　deteriorating financial condition　財政状態[財政状況、財務状態、財務内容]の悪化
　deteriorating profitability　収益性の悪化

deteriorating bank　経営悪化の銀行
◆European countries are urged to facilitate a safety net for emergencies, including the injection of public funds into deteriorating banks to shore up their capital strength. 欧州は、経営が悪化した銀行[金融機関]に公的資金を注入して資本を増強するなど、非常時に備えた安全網の整備が求められている。

deteriorating business　経営悪化
◆Studio Ghibli established as a subsidiary of Tokuma Shoten became a division of the company after being absorbed in 1997 due to Tokuma Shoten's deteriorating business. 徳間書店の子会社として設立されたスタジオジブリは、同書店の経営悪化に伴って1997年に吸収されてから、徳間書

店の事業部門の一つとなった。
deteriorating financial conditions　財政の悪化, 財政状態［財務状況］の悪化, 財務内容の悪化
◆It is difficult for Japan, the United States and European countries to support their sagging economies by increasing public spending, due to deteriorating financial conditions. 財政の悪化で, 日米欧は, 財政出動による景気の下支えが難しくなっている。
deteriorating performance　業績悪化
◆The bank's president resigned to take responsibility for the bank's deteriorating performance. 同行の社長は, 業績が悪化したため, 引責辞任した。
deteriorating subprime loan market　低所得者向け住宅融資市場, サブプライム・ローン市場
◆Nomura incurred heavy losses due to the deteriorating subprime-loan market. 米サブプライム・ローン（低所得者向け住宅融資）市場の悪化で, 野村［野村ホールディングス］が巨額の損失を被った。
deterioration　（名）悪化, 低下, 減少, 停滞, 品質低下, 退化, 劣化, 老朽化　（⇒downgrade）
business deterioration　景気悪化, 業績悪化
business deterioration of borrowers　融資先の業績悪化
credit deterioration　信用力の低下
deterioration in (business) sentiment　景況感の低下
deterioration in default risk　デフォルト（債務不履行）リスクの増大
deterioration in financial health　財務の健全性の悪化, 財務体質の悪化, 財務内容の悪化
deterioration in inflation expectations　インフレ期待の高まり
deterioration in the business situation　経営悪化, 景況の悪化
deterioration in the trade balance　貿易収支の悪化
earnings deterioration　収益の悪化, 業績の悪化
economic deterioration　景気の悪化, 景気後退, 景気後退局面
fiscal deterioration　財政悪化
profit deterioration　減益, 利益の減少
◆Greece's tax revenues have slackened due to business deterioration. ギリシャの税収は, 景気悪化で伸びていない。◆Other banks are likely forced to revise their earnings projections downward because of the accelerated disposal of bad loans, business deterioration of borrowers due to the lingering recession and further decline in stock prices. 不良債権処理の加速や長引く不況による融資先の業績悪化, 株安などの影響で, 他行も業績の下方修正を迫られている。◆The U.S. government failed to take drastic countermeasures against its fiscal deterioration. 米政府は, 財政悪化に抜本的な対策を取れなかった［大胆なメスを入れられなかった］。
deterioration in business conditions　景気の悪化, 景況感の悪化
◆The Bank of Japan's diffusion indexes are calculated by subtracting the percentage of companies reporting deterioration in business conditions from those perceiving improvement. 日銀のこれらの業況判断指数（DI）は, 現在の景況感について「改善している」と感じている企業の割合から「悪化している」と回答した企業の割合を差し引いて算出する。
deterioration in the financial strength of the banking system　銀行［市中銀行, 銀行業界］の財務の健全性悪化
◆The reassessment of 14 British banks by Moody's is not driven by a deterioration in the financial strength of the banking system. ムーディーズによる英銀14行の格付け見直しは, 銀行［銀行業界］の財務の健全性悪化によるものではない。
deterioration of operational efficiency　経営効率の悪化

◆The serious deterioration of operational efficiency is caused by excess output capacity and burgeoning workforces. 極端な経営効率の悪化は, 生産設備と従業員の過剰によるものだ。◆Unless consumption tax rate is raised, the planned issuance of bridging bonds could lead to further deterioration of the debt-saddled government finances. 消費税率を引き上げないと, 予定しているつなぎ国債の発行は, 借金を背負っている国の財政の悪化をさらに招く可能性がある。
deterioration of the government finances　財政の悪化
Deutche Bank　ドイツ銀行
◆Softbank and Deutche Bank will tie up in online finance. ソフトバンクとドイツ銀行が, オンライン金融で提携する。
Deutsche Boerse [Borse]　ドイツ取引所
◆Deutsche Boerse agreed to buy NYSE Euronext for $10.2 billion. （フランクフルト証券取引所などを運営する）ドイツ取引所は, （ニューヨーク証券取引所を傘下に持つ）NYSEユーロネクストを102億ドルで買収することで合意した。
deutschemark [Deutsche mark, Deutschemark]　（名）ドイツ・マルク, DM
◆Deutschemark was the most stable of European currencies before the introduction of the euro. ドイツ・マルクは, ユーロの導入以前は欧州で最も安定した通貨であった。
devaluation　（名）平価切下げ, 通貨切下げ, 通貨安, 通貨下落, 価値の低下, 評価切下げ, 低評価, 切下げ
（⇒currency devaluation race）
a global currency devaluation race　世界の通貨切下げ競争
asset devaluation　資産の評価切下げ
compensated devaluation　補正的為替切下げ
competitive devaluation of currencies　通貨の競争的な切下げ, 通貨安戦争（currency war）
currency devaluation　通貨切下げ, 通貨安
de jure devaluation　法律上の平価切下げ
defacto [de facto] devaluation　事実上の切下げ, 事実上の平価切下げ
devaluation of exchange rates　為替相場の切下げ, 為替レートの切下げ
devaluation of the official rate　公定レートの切下げ
devaluation-prone currency　平価切下げ不安通貨
devaluation risk　通貨安のリスク, 通貨切下げのリスク
devaluation-speculation cycle　切下げ・投機循環
dollar devaluation　ドル安, ドル切下げ
effective devaluation　実効為替切下げ
exchange devaluation　為替切下げ
formal devaluation　形式的為替切下げ
further devaluation　もう一段の切下げ, 追加切下げ
gradual devaluation of the dollar　ドルのじり安
gross devaluation　総為替切下げ
net devaluation　純為替切下げ, 純切下げ
outright valuation　直接的切下げ
sharp devaluation　大幅な通貨切下げ
undergo a devaluation　通貨価値が下落する
◆Financial chiefs from the Group of 20 advanced and major developing economies vowed to refrain from competitive devaluation of currencies. 世界［主要］20か国・地域（G20）の財務相・中央銀行総裁は, 通貨の競争的な切下げを回避することを公約した。◆The devaluation of our investments in Thailand is certainly a negative consequence. 当社がタイに投資した分の価値が低下したことは, 確かにマイナス要因です。◆The devaluation will enhance our competitiveness as virtually 100 percent of our products are exported. 当社の製品は100％輸出しているので, 通貨下落で当社の競争力は増すと思われます。

devalue （動）為替レートや通貨などを引き下げる, 平価を切り下げる, 価値を減じる, 通貨安になる（=devaluate）
 devalue the currency　通貨を切り下げる
 devalue the dollar　ドルの為替レートを切り下げる, ドルを切り下げる
 devalue the pound　ポンドを切り下げる
 ◆Argentina will ditch the dollar, fully float the devalued peso and partially lift a savings freeze.　アルゼンチンは、ドルを捨て、切り下げたペソを変動相場制に完全移行して、預金凍結の一部解除を行う方針だ。◆Rectifying trade imbalances mainly with China by devaluing the dollar is the top priority in Washington.　ドル安により主に中国との貿易不均衡を是正するのが、米国の最優先課題だ。

devalued asset　不良資産
 ◆The U.S. administration will spend up to $700 billion to buy up soured mortgage-related securities and other devalued assets held by ailing financial institutions.　米政府は、経営不振の金融機関が保有するモーゲージ関連の不良証券などの不良資産を、最大7,000億ドル投入して買い取る方針だ。

devastate　（動）壊滅の打撃を与える, 完全に破壊する, 荒廃させる, 荒らす, 圧倒する, 圧勝する, 負かす, 唖然とさせる
 ◆Banks across the United States have been devastated by the collapse of the subprime mortgage market.　米全域の銀行が、サブプライム・ローン（低所得者向け住宅ローン）市場の崩壊によって、壊滅的打撃を受けている。

devastating　（形）破壊的な, 衝撃的な, 壊滅的な打撃を与える, 痛烈な, 手厳しい
 ◆In order to prevent the chain reaction of even more devastating financial collapses, financial and monetary authorities in the United States and other nations will need to work together.　これ以上の衝撃的な金融破たんの連鎖反応を防ぐには、米国と世界各国の金融・通貨当局の協調が必要だ。

develop　（動）開発する, 整備する, 改善する, 改良する, 発展する, 育成する, 土地などを造成する, 展開する, 策定する, 現像する
 ◆Sumitomo Mitsui Banking Corp. has jointly developed with American International Group Inc. a foreign bond investment product targeting retired baby boomers.　三井住友銀行が、団塊の世代の定年退職者をターゲットにした外債の金融商品を、米保険最大手のAIGグループと共同開発した。◆The challenge of the Basel Committee on Banking Supervision is to develop a regulatory framework while fending off a recurrence of financial strife.　バーゼル銀行監督委員会の課題は、金融危機再発の防止と規制の枠組みの策定だ。◆There has been greater demand for funds to develop mega solar power plant projects in recent years.　最近は、メガソーラー（大型太陽光発電所）事業開発の資金需要が高まっている。

development　（名）開発, 整備, 教育, 育成, 発展, 進歩, 進展, 展開, 推移, 動き, 情勢, 動向, 新事態, 製品
 ◆Development of new products will be the key to the company's revival.　新商品の開発が、同社再建のカギを握っている。◆The current high price of crude oil stems partly from the lack of investment in oil development for a long period.　現在の原油高の一因は、長期にわたる石油開発投資の不足だ。◆The nonlife insurance company will provide the company with know-how on damage assessment and product development.　この損害保険会社は、同社に損害査定や商品開発に関するノウハウを提供する。

development assistance agency　開発援助機関
 ◆With the integration of the Japan Bank for International Cooperation's division for handling yen loans, and other bodies in October 2008, JICA became one of the world's largest development assistance agencies.　国際協力機構（JICA）は、2008年10月に国際協力銀行（JBIC）の円借款部門などを統合して、（事業規模で）世界最大級の開発援助機関となった。

Development Bank of Japan　日本政策投資銀行（⇒financial aid package）
 ◆Major companies, the Japan Bank for International Cooperation and the Development Bank of Japan established a fund to purchase overseas countries' excess quotas for carbon dioxide and other greenhouse gas emissions.　大手企業と国際協力銀行、日本政策投資銀行が、二酸化炭素など温室効果ガス排出量の削減分（温室効果ガスの排出権）を海外から買い取る基金（ファンド）を設立した。◆Six state-run financial institutions were reorganized into three, the Japan Bank for International Cooperation (JBIC), the Development Bank of Japan and the National Life Finance Corporation.　政府系の6つの金融機関が、国際協力銀行、日本政策投資銀行と国民生活金融公庫の3つに統合された。◆The aim of a fund established by the Development Bank of Japan is to infuse money into auto parts makers hit by the March 11 earthquake and tsunami.　日本政策投資銀行が設立するファンドの目的は、東日本大震災で被災した自動車部品メーカーに資金を行き渡らせることにある。◆The company procured about ￥50 billion through an allocation of newly issued shares to third parties, including the Development Bank of Japan.　同社は、日本政策投資銀行などを引受先とする第三者割当増資で、約500億円を調達した。◆The company will secure ￥270 billion in loans from the Development Bank of Japan and other lenders.　同社は、日本政策投資銀行などの金融機関から2,700億円の融資を受ける［2,700億円を借り入れる］。◆The Development Bank of Japan asked the Japan Finance Corporation to pay ￥53.6 billion, the amount guaranteed by the government.　日本政策投資銀行は、政府保証分の536億円の支払いを、日本政策金融公庫に請求した。◆The Development Bank of Japan will raise ￥50 billion to establish a fund to assist auto parts makers hit by the March 11 disaster.　日本政策投資銀行は、(2011年)3月11日の東日本大震災で被災した自動車部品メーカーの復興を支援するため、500億円のファンドを設立する。◆The public loan was extended to JAL in June 2009 by the entirely state-funded Development Bank of Japan.　この公的融資は、国が100％出資している日本政策投資銀行が、2009年6月に行った。◆With a view to stemming the airlines' financial hemorrhaging, the Construction and Transport Ministry in late May asked the Development Bank of Japan to provide emergency loans to the two carriers.　航空会社の損失を阻止するため、5月下旬に国土交通省は、日本政策投資銀行に対して両航空会社への緊急融資を要請した。

development fund　開発基金
 ◆The trust fund will be set up separate from the development fund for Iraq.　信託基金は、イラク開発基金とは別に設けられる。

DI　景気動向指数, 業況判断指数　（diffusion indexの略。一致指数や先行指数、遅行指数などの景気動向指数は、各種経済指標の現状を3か月前の状況と比較したもの。⇒diffusion index, indicator, index）
 business conditions DI　業況判断DI
 coincident DI　一致指数DI
 leading DI　先行指数DI
 manufacturing DI　製造業の業況判断DI
 overall financial conditions DI　資金繰り判断DI
 price DI　価格判断DI
 sentiment DI　業況判断DI
 ◆DI consists of the leading index, coincident index and lagging index.　景気動向指数は、先行指数と一致指数、遅行（ちこう）指数から成る。

DI reading　DIの数値
 ◆The DI reading among small and medium companies as well as nonmanufacturing corporations remains negative.　中小企業と非製造業のDIの数値は依然、マイナスが続いている。

DIC 預金保険機構（Deposit Insurance Corporationの略）

die （動）死ぬ, 死亡する
◆When the policyholders of single-premium whole life insurances die, beneficiaries receive the designated benefits plus accumulated dividends. 一時払い終身保険の契約者が死亡した場合、保険金の受取人は、特定の（死亡）保険金のほかに積立配当金を受け取れる。

difference （名）差, 差異, 違い, 格差, 差額, 不足分, 区別, 意見の違い[食い違い], 意見の不一致, 意見の対立, 不和, 紛争, 重大な変化[影響]
a difference of opinion 意見の不一致, 意見の相違
a difference with one's superior 上役との不和, 上役との意見の違い
difference or dispute 意見の相違または紛争, 見解の相違または紛争
important [striking] differences 大きな違い
key [principal] difference 最大の違い
make a big [all the, great] difference 重大な相違を生じる, 決定的な違いを生じる, 重大な影響を持つ, 大きな関係がある, 大きな問題である, 大変なことになる, 大変重要である
make a difference 差別をつける, 差をつける, 差異を生じる, 影響する, 重要である
make no difference 少しも重要でない, 変わりはない, どうでもいい
make up [settle] one's differences 不和[紛争]を解決する
make up the difference （～で）差額を埋め合わせする, 必要な金額の残りを出す
market difference 市場の開き
meet [pay] the difference 差額を支払う
regional difference index 地域差指数
split the difference 妥協する, 歩み寄る, 折り合う, 残りを均等に分ける[等分する], 差額の半分をとる
the difference between winners and losers 勝ち組と負け組の差
◆Before the introduction of the bank tax, the major financial institutions' tax liability had been very low, with only the difference between loan losses and business profits deemed taxable. 銀行税の導入前は、貸倒れ損失金と業務利益との差額だけが課税の対象となっていたため、大手金融機関の納税額は低かった。◆Even within the same insurance industry, the difference between winners and losers has become more apparent. 同じ保険業界でも、勝ち組と負け組の差が鮮明になっている。◆France and Germany could not bridge their differences, so Europe's efforts to solve its escalating debt crisis plunged into disarray. フランスとドイツが両国の相違を埋められなかったため、深刻化する欧州の債務危機問題解決への欧州の取組みは、混乱に陥った。

differential （名）格差, 差異, 差額, 差, 開き,（取引単位未満の取引をするときに要求される）割増金, 追加手数料
a differential between interest rates at home and abroad 内外金利差
adjustment for the differential in inflation インフレ格差の調整
core inflation differential コア・インフレ率の格差
differential duties [tariffs] 差別関税（discriminating duties）, 品目別関税率
differential profit 差額利益
differential rate behavior 長短金利動向の開き
interest (rate) differential 金利差, 金利格差, 金利スプレッド, 利子率格差
liquidity differential 流動性格差
risk differential リスク格差
the spot-forward differential 直先（じきさき）の差額

yield differential 利回り格差, 金利格差
◆Interest rate differentials between Greek and German government bonds widened to 600 basis points, or six percentage points, from January to May 2010. ギリシャ国債とドイツ国債の金利差は、2010年1月から5月の間に600ベーシス・ポイント（6%）も拡大した。

difficult （形）困難な, 難しい, 厳しい, 扱いにくい, 問題の多い, 苦しい, つらい
difficult business environment [climate] 厳しい事業環境
difficult economic times 不況
difficult market 市場低迷
◆Amid the depleted state coffers, it is difficult to implement a major stimulus package to rectify the rise in the yen's value. 財政悪化が進む中［国の財源が枯渇する中］、円高是正のため大規模な財政出動を行うのは難しい。◆It is difficult for Japan, the United States and European countries to support their sagging economies by increasing public spending, due to deteriorating financial conditions. 財政の悪化で、日米欧は、財政出動による景気の下支えが難しくなっている。◆It is difficult to deal with the latest unrest in global financial markets because it has been caused by a complex web of factors. 今回の世界的な金融市場混乱への対応が難しいのは、混乱を招いている要因が複雑に絡み合っているからだ。◆It's difficult to offset losses from further appreciation of the yen with interest as interest rates in many foreign currency deposits are low. 外貨建て預金の多くは金利が低いので、円高進行による損失分を利息で相殺する［取り戻す］のは難しい。◆The situation is that it is difficult to acquire more than 50 percent of shares in the firm. 今の状況では、同社株の50%超を取得するのは厳しい。◆Without an economic recovery and the resultant recovery of tax revenues, fiscal reconstruction will be made difficult. 景気回復［経済の再生］とそれによる税収の回復がなければ、今後の財政再建もおぼつかない。

difficulties （名）困難, 問題, 苦境, 難局, 危機, 低迷
balance of payments difficulties 国際収支の悪化
be in difficulties 困難な状態に陥る
debt servicing difficulties 債務返済が困難な状態, 債務返済危機
experience financial difficulties 財政難に直面する, 財政問題を抱える
face difficulties raising funds 資金繰りに窮する（⇒healthy）
financial difficulties 財政的困難, 財政上の困難, 経営危機, 資金繰りが困難な状況
get [run] into difficulties 困難な状態に陥る
have financial difficulties 資金繰りに困る
in-house difficulties 社内問題
overcome difficulties 障害を克服する
serious difficulties 深刻な経営難
serious financial difficulties 深刻な財務悪化
◆Companies faced difficulties in raising money by issuing corporate bonds in the aftermath of the financial crisis and resorted to borrowing money from banks. 世界の金融危機の影響で企業は、社債を発行して資金を調達するのが困難になったため、金融機関からの資金借入れに動いた。◆Earnings of the firm were impacted by difficulties in North American real estate markets. 同社の利益は、北米の不動産市場の低迷による影響を受けました。◆When serious financial difficulties are expected, the Financial Services Agency is allowed to order a company to improve its operations in the early stages without releasing the information to the public. 深刻な財務悪化が予想される場合、金融庁は、非公表で早めに業務改善命令を発動することができる。

difficulty （名）困難, 苦難, 難しさ, 難事, 苦労, 難易度
◆Banks would keep amassing cash by disposing of dis-

tressed assets as quickly as possible to avert collapse after having difficulty raising funds. 資金調達が困難になって経営破たんするのを避けるため、金融機関[銀行]は、できるだけ早めに危険資産を処分[売却]して、現金を抱え込もうとする。◆Small municipalities have a financial difficulty in setting up an independent audit office or conducting external auditing every fiscal year. 小規模市町村の場合、独立した監査事務局を設置したり、外部監査を毎年度実施したりするのは財政的に困難だ。◆Stuck in a financial quagmire, Russia is having difficulty in managing its nuclear arsenal. 財政難から、ロシアは現在、保有する核兵器の管理に苦慮している。

diffusion index 景気動向指数, 業況判断指数, DI （業況判断指数は、日本銀行が景気の実態を把握するため3か月ごとに行う企業短期経済観測調査で、企業の景況感を示す指数）
diffusion index measuring corporate perceptions of the lending stance of financial institutions 金融機関の貸出態度判断DI
diffusion index of large companies 大企業の業況判断(DI)
diffusion index of leading indicators 景気先行指数(DI)
◆The Bank of Japan's diffusion indexes are calculated by subtracting the percentage of companies reporting deterioration in business conditions from those perceiving improvement. 日銀のこれらの業況判断指数(DI)は、現在の景況感について「改善している」と感じている企業の割合から「悪化している」と回答した企業の割合を差し引いて算出する。◆The diffusion indexes of the coincident, leading and lagging indicators compare the current levels of various economic indicators with their levels three months earlier. 一致指数や先行指数、遅行指数などの景気動向指数は、各種経済指標の現状を3か月前の状況と比較したものだ。

diffusion index for large manufacturers 大手製造業(大企業)の業況判断指数(DI), 大企業・製造業の業況判断指数(DI)
◆The diffusion index for large manufacturers has posted the five consecutive quarters of improvements. 大手製造業(大企業)の業況判断指数(DI)は、5期(五四半期)連続で改善した。

diffusion index for small and midsize manufacturers 中小企業・製造業の業況判断指数(DI)
◆The diffusion index for small and midsize manufacturers improved five points to plus 2, hitting positive territory for the first time in 13 years. 中小企業・製造業の業況判断指数(DI)が、前回調査より5ポイント改善してプラス2となり、13年ぶりにプラスに転じた。

diffusion index of business confidence 業況判断指数 （=diffusion index of business sentiment）
◆The diffusion index (DI) of business confidence among large manufacturers marked the first positive reading in 33 months. 大手製造業の業況判断指数(DI)は、2年9か月ぶりにプラスに転じた。◆The diffusion index (DI) of business confidence among large manufacturers stood at plus 1, reflecting a growth in exports due to U.S. economic recovery and a recent surge in domestic stock prices. 大企業の製造業の業況判断指数(DI)が、プラス1となり、米経済の回復による輸出の伸びや最近の国内の株価上昇を反映した。◆The diffusion index (DI) of business confidence refers to the percentage of companies that feel business conditions to be favorable, minus the ratio of firms that think otherwise. 業況判断指数(DI)は、景気が「良い」と感じている企業の割合(％)から、「悪い」と感じている企業の割合を差し引いた指数だ。

diffusion index of business sentiment 業況判断指数(DI)
◆The diffusion index of business sentiment among large manufacturers recovered to positive territory for the first time in two quarters. 大企業・製造業の業況判断指数(DI)は、2四半期(半年)ぶりにプラスに転じた。◆The diffusion index of business sentiment among large manufacturers rose four points to 26, compared with the previous survey for the three months to June. 大企業・製造業の業況判断指数(DI)は、前回の6月調査(4-6月調査)に比べて4ポイント上昇の26となった。

diffusion index of retail prices 販売価格判断DI
◆The diffusion index of retail prices represents the percentage of companies that said retail prices had risen minus the percentage of those that said retail prices had dropped. 販売価格判断DIは、販売価格が「上昇した」と答えた企業の割合から「下落した」と答えた企業の割合を示す。

digit （名）アラビア数字(0から9までの各数字), 数字, 桁(けた)
double-digit increase rate 2桁の伸び率, 10%を超える伸び率
hundred-digit number 100桁の数字
significant digit 有効数字
single digit coupon 10%以下の表面利率
single-digit growth 1桁の成長, 1桁の経済成長, 10%を超える成長
sum-of-the years digits method 等差級数法
three digit inflation 3桁のインフレ
◆The consumption tax may be raised to double-digits. 消費税率が2桁に引き上げられる可能性がある。

digitalmoney 電子マネー, デジタル・マネー （=digital currency, electronic money; ⇒electronic money）
◆The new IC ATM cards of the bank will have advanced functions such as digital money and a point system. 同行の新型ICキャッシュ・カードには、デジタル・マネーやポイント制などの先端機能が採用される。

dilute （動）薄める, 弱める, 希薄化する, 希釈化する, 減額する
adopt a method of diluting the effect of a buyout 買占めの効力を薄める手法を採用する
dilute the value of the existing shares 既存の株の価値を損なう
diluted earnings per share 希薄化後1株当たり利益
diluted earnings per share of common stock 希薄化後普通株式1株当たり純利益
fully diluted 完全希薄化, 完全希薄化後
fully diluted earnings per common share 完全希薄化による普通株式1株当たり利益, 完全希薄化後普通株式1株当たり利益, 潜在株式調整後1株当たり利益
on a diluted basis 希薄化ベースで, 希釈化ベースで
primary and fully diluted earnings per share 単純希薄化と完全希薄化による1株当たり利益
◆In the United States, many firms have adopted a method of diluting the effect of a buyout in which existing shareholders are given a preemptive right to purchase shares of a new issue before it is offered to others when more than a certain ratio of shares are targeted. 米国では、一定比率以上の株式の買占めが目標とされている場合、新株を既有の株主以外の者に提供する前に、既有の株主に新株発行の株式を引き受ける新株引受権(新株予約権)を与えて、買占めの効力を薄める手法を採用している企業が多い。◆Market participants pointed out the issuance of new shares would dilute the value of the company's existing shares. 市場関係者は、増資[新株発行]によって同社の既存株式の価値が損なわれる、と指摘している。

dilution （名）(株式などの)希薄化, 希釈化, 実質的価値の低下, 減額, 減少, 落ち込み, 1株当たりの価値が低くなる[薄まる]こと
anti-dilution 希薄化防止, 反希薄化
dilution factor 希薄化率
dilution from new share issues 新株発行による希薄化,

増資による希薄化
　(=dilution from the issue of new shares)
dilution from the conversion of convertible bonds　転換社債の転換による希薄化
dilution interval　減額期間
dilution of earnings per share　1株当たり利益の希薄化
dilution of labor　労働の希薄
dilution of ownership　新株主の割込み
dilution risk　減額リスク
earnings dilution　利益の落ち込み, 減益
full dilution　完全希薄化, 完全希釈化
losses from [attributable to] dilution　減額による損失 (=dilution losses)
profits dilution　利益の落ち込み[押し下げ], 減益
the dilution in earnings per share from new issues　新規発行(増資)による1株当たり利益[純利益]の希薄化
◆For the computation of the earnings per share, assuming full dilution, dividends on convertible preferred shares have been added back to income. 完全希薄化を仮定した場合の1株当たり利益の算定では, 転換可能優先株式[転換優先株]に対する配当は, 利益に振り戻してあります。◆The dilution in earnings per share from these new issuances was not material. これらの新株発行[増資]による1株当たり利益の希薄化は, 重要視するほどではありませんでした。
解説 希薄化(希釈化)とは：時価発行増資や転換社債の転換, ワラント債の権利行使などによる発行済み株式総数の増加で, 1株当たり利益(earnings per share)の減少や資産価値の目減りを招くことをいう。

dilutive　(形)希薄化の, 1株当たりの価値を減らす[薄める], 1株当たりの利益が希薄化する
dilutive common stock equivalents　希薄化準普通株式
dilutive effect of capital increases　増資による希薄化効果
dilutive effect of the offering　株式発行の希薄化効果
dilutive potential ordinary share　希薄化潜在的普通株式

dime　(名)10セント硬貨, 債券の利回りで10ベーシス・ポイント(0.1%)

DIP　継承破産人(debtor in possessionの略)

dip　(動)一時的に下がる, 下落する, 低下する, 下降する, 減少する, 減退する, 下がる, 落ちる, 急降下する, 沈む
dip below　〜を割り込む　(⇒pessimism)
dip down　減少する, 低下する
dip into currency reserves　外貨準備を使う, 外貨準備を取り崩す
dip into one's savings　貯金[貯蓄]を取り崩す, 貯金の一部を使う[利用, 活用]する
dip into outright recession　完全な不況に落ち込む
dip to the lows　安値を付ける
◆Oil futures dipped below the $100 a barrel for the first time in five months. 原油先物が, 5か月ぶりに1バレル=100ドルを割り込んだ。◆The dollar dipped in value. ドルの価値が, 下がった。◆The 225-issue Nikkei Stock Average continued its plunge Thursday, momentarily dipping into 8,100 territory. 日経平均株価(225種)が木曜日(10月10日)も急落し, 一時8,100円台まで下落した。◆The unemployment rate dipped down a notch to 5.5 percent last month, from 5.6 percent in June. 先月(7月)の失業率は, 6月の5.6%から5.5%に1ノッチ(0.1ポイント)減少した。◆The White House will consider dipping into a $700 billion financial bailout fund to aid the teetering U.S. carmakers. 破たん危機にある米自動車メーカー(ビッグ・スリー)を支援するため, 米政府は7,000億ドルの金融救済資金の一部活用を検討する方針だ。◆With the midyear account settlement scheduled in September, concerns over the stability of the nation's financial system inevitably will grow again should stock prices dip further. 9月中間決算を前に, 株価がさらに下がれば, 再び日本の金融システム不安が当然, 台頭してくる。

dip　(名)下落, 低下, 下降, 減少, 減退, 急降下, 沈下, 押し目　(株価が下がることを「押し目, 押し, 下押し」と言い, 下げ幅が大きい場合を「深押し」と言う。⇒ double dip recession)
business dip　景気下降, 景気減退, 景気後退, 不況
buy on dip [reaction]　押し目買い(押し目を狙って買うこと)
dip in profits　減益
dip on oil prices　原油価格の下落
double dip　(一定期間内の)2度の下降[下落], (景気の)二番底, 二重払い, 二重取り, 二重の収入, ダブル・ディップ
sinking into a double-dip recession　景気底割れ
wait for dip [reaction]　押し目待ち
◆The decline in exports exceeded the dip in imports. 輸出の落ち込みが, 輸入減を上回った。◆U.S. President Barack Obama hinted at new steps to avoid a double dip. オバマ米大統領は, 景気の二番底を回避するための追加策を示唆した。

DIP finance　事業再生融資, DIPファイナンス, デッター・イン・ポゼション融資　(=DIP financing, DIP plan: 不動産担保がなくても事業の継続可能性などを考慮して新規融資する仕組み)

DIP finance formula　DIPファイナンス方式
　(=DIP formula)
◆A debtor in possession (DIP) finance formula, introduced by the Development Bank of Japan in April to help failed companies that still have hope for rehabilitation, will be employed in the Hirota rescue. 「洋菓子のヒロタ」の救済には, 経営破たんした企業のうちまだ再建の希望が持てる企業を支援するために日本政策投資銀行が4月から導入したDIPファイナンス方式が採られる。

DIP formula　DIPファイナンス方式
　(=DIP finance formula)
◆The Development Bank of Japan has extended loans using the DIP formula to five failed companies so far, including the supermarket chain Mycal Corp., which went under in September. 日本政策投資銀行はこれまで, 9月に破たんした大手スーパーのマイカルを含めて経営破たんした企業5社に対して, DIPファイナンス方式による融資を行っている。

DIP plan　事業再生融資制度, DIPファイナンス　(=DIP finance, DIP financing: 再建途上の企業向け融資)
◆Under the DIP plan widely used in the United States, a failed company can get new loans for continuing its business even if it cannot afford to put up property as security. アメリカで広く利用されている事業再生融資制度(DIPファイナンス)では, 経営破たんした企業が, 有体財産[不動産]を担保にすることができなくても事業継続のために新規融資を受けることができる。

dire　(形)狭い, 緊急の, 急を要する, 差し迫った, 深刻な, 危機的な, 悲惨な, 恐ろしい, 極度の, 厳しい, 厳格な, ひどい, 質の悪い
　(⇒issuance of government bonds, straits)
be in dire straits　窮乏している
be thrown into dire confusion　ひどい混乱に陥る
dire financial straits　厳しい財政難, 苦しい財政事情, 極度の財政ひっ迫
dire fiscal situation　厳しい[苦しい]財政事情, 深刻な財政難, 財政難
dire predictions about the stock market　株式相場についての厳しい[悲観的]予測
◆Given the dire fiscal situation, the government cannot afford to continue its handout policies. 財政難の折から, 政府はバラマキ政策を続ける余裕はない。◆Japan is also in dire

financial straits. 日本の財政事情も苦しい。◆Japan remains in dire fiscal condition. 日本の財政は、相変わらず火の車だ。◆The DBJ and private financial institutions extended loans worth a total of ￥100 billion to JAL in June 2009 though JAL was already in dire financial straits. 日本政策投資銀行と民間金融機関は、日航の経営がすでに悪化していたものの、2009年6月に同社に対して総額1,000億円を融資した。

direct （形）直接の, 直接的, ダイレクト
 BOJ direct bond purchases　日銀の国債買いオペ
 direct aid　直接支援, 直接支援
 direct appeal to the public　（公社債の）一般発売
 direct arbitrage　直接裁定, 2点間裁定
  （=two point arbitrage）
 direct bank lending　銀行からの直接融資
 direct banking　ダイレクト・バンキング
 direct bills of lading　直接船荷証券
 direct borrowing　直接借入れ
 direct buying　直接購入, 直接買入れ, 直接買付け, 直接仕入れ
 direct capital　直接資本
 direct capital inflows　直接資本の流入
 direct capitalization　直接収益還元法
 direct credit　（外国税額の）直接控除
 direct credit substitute　直接債務肩代わり（契約）
 direct dealing　外為DD取引（direct exchange dealing）, 直接取引, ダイレクト・ディーリング　（銀行同士で直接外国為替の取引をすること）
 direct debit　（銀行からの）直接借方記入
 direct deposit　直接預金　（=primary deposit）
 direct draft　直接為替
 direct equity investment　直接株式投資, 直接投資
 direct finance [financing]　直接金融
 direct financial burdens　直接的債務
 direct foreign investment　対外直接投資
 direct funding　直接融資
 direct government intervention　政府の直接関与
 direct import　直接輸入
 direct insurance　元受保険
 direct insurance contract　元受保険契約
 direct insurer　元受保険者, 元受会社
 direct intervention　直接介入
 direct issue　（証券などの）直接発行
 direct issue paper　直接売りペーパー
 direct lender　直接融資行, 直貸しをする銀行, 直貸しを供与する銀行
 direct lending bank　直接融資行, 直貸しをする銀行
 direct lending power　直接融資権限
 direct letter of credit　直接信用状
  （=direct L/C）
 direct liabilities　直接債務, 確定債務
 direct loss　（火事による）直接損害
 direct measurement approach　直接的測定法
 direct net debt　直接純債務
 direct nonlife　直接損保事業
 direct paper　ダイレクト・ペーパー（direct issue paper: ディーラーを経由しないで投資家に直接発行するコマーシャル・ペーパー）, 直接為替手形
 direct parity　直接平価
 direct pay　直接支払い, ダイレクト・ペイ
 direct-pay L/C [letter of credit]　ダイレクト・ペイ方式の信用状
 direct payment　直接支払い
 direct payroll deduction　給与天引き方式
 direct placement　（株などの）直接募集, 私募, 非公募, 直接販売
 direct premium　元受保険料
 direct quotation　自国通貨建て相場, 自国通貨による為替相場表示, 支払い勘定建て
  （=giving quotation, pence rate）
 direct quotes　直接呼び値
 direct rate　直接為替相場, 直接為替レート, 直接レート, 自国通貨建て相場
 direct ratio [proportion]　正比例
 direct recourse　直接の償還請求権
 direct securities　直接証券
  （=primary securities）
 direct sendings　直接仕向け物件
 direct settlement　（株式売買の）直接決済
 direct standard　直接本位制
 direct trade　直接貿易
 direct transaction　直接取引, 直（じか）取引, 即時取引
 direct transfer　直接移転
 direct, unconditional and unsecured obligation　直接、無条件、無担保の債務
 direct yield　直接利回り
 ratio of direct and indirect taxes　直間比率

direct access to　～から直接（資金を）調達すること, ～を直接調達する, ～への直接アクセス
 direct access to investors　投資家から直接資金を調達すること [調達する手段]
 gain direct access to the bond market　債券市場から直接資金を調達する
 have direct access to funds　資金を直接調達する
 lose one's direct access to funds　直接資金を調達する手段「道」を失う

direct cash loans outstanding　営業貸付け金残高
 （=balance of direct cash loans, outstanding direct cash loans）

direct cost　直接原価, 直接費
 direct cost method　直接原価評価法
 direct cost system　直接原価計算制度
 initial direct cost　初期直接原価
 manufacturing direct cost　製造直接費

direct debit　自動引落し, 直接引落し, 口座引落し, 自動振替　（⇒deduction）
 ◆Nippon Life Insurance Co. will introduce a system that will allow customers to pay their first insurance premiums by direct debit from their bank accounts. 日本生命保険は、顧客の銀行口座からの自動引落しで（契約時の）初回保険料を顧客が支払うことができるシステムを導入する。

direct debit system　自動引落しシステム
 ◆Under the direct debit system, the life insurer's sales employees will scan data on new customers' bank cards using portable terminals when they sign insurance policies. この口座引落しシステムでは、顧客が保険契約をする際、同生保の営業職員が決済の携帯端末を使って新規顧客のキャッシュ・カードのデータを読み取る。

direct disbursement system　直接支払い制
 （=direct payment system）
 ◆In the United States and Europe, direct disbursement systems are a main pillar of agricultural policy and are used to grant sizable amounts of subsidies every year. 欧米では、直接支払い制は農政の柱で、毎年巨額の補助金を出すのに利用されている。

direct exchange　直接為替, 直接交換
 direct exchange arbitrage　直接為替裁定, 直接裁定

direct exchange bill　直接為替手形
direct exchange dealing　外為DD取引
　(=direct dealing)
direct export　直接輸出
◆The trade insurance of Nippon Export and Investment Insurance previously only covered direct exports by domestic firms. 独立行政法人・日本貿易保険の貿易保険はこれまで、国内企業の直接輸出だけが対象だった。
direct financing　直接金融(direct finance: 証券引受業者(underwriter)を通さないで証券を直接投資家に売って資金調達すること)、直接融資
　direct financing lease　直接金融リース、直接金融型リース、金融型リース
　direct financing type lease　直接金融型リース
　net investment in direct financing lease　直接金融リース純投資額
◆The firm's operations in the financial services and leasing industry involve direct financing and finance leasing programs for its products and the products of other companies. 金融サービスとリース業界での同社の事業には、同社製品と他社製品に関する直接融資とファイナンス・リース事業も含まれている。
direct investment　直接投資
　(⇒FDI, foreign direct investment)
　direct credit substitute　直接債務肩代わり
　direct investment abroad　海外への直接投資
　direct investment by foreigners　対内直接投資
　direct investment for building facilities　生産設備建設のための直接投資
　direct inward investment　対内直接投資
　direct overseas investment　海外直接投資
　dollar amount of direct investment　ドル・ベースでの直接投資
　external direct investment　対外直接投資
　foreign direct investment　海外への直接投資、対外直接投資、外国からの直接投資
　horizontal direct investment　水平的直接投資
　inward direct investment　対内直接投資
　massive direct investment from abroad　海外からの巨額の直接投資
　privatization-related direct investment　民営化関連の直接投資
　regulations limiting inward direct investment　対内投資規制
　vertical direct investment　垂直的直接投資
◆Direct investment in foreign countries by Japanese businesses dropped 9.2 percent from the previous year to ¥4.07 trillion. 日本企業による対外直接投資額は、前年度比9.2%減の4兆700億円だった。◆The rise in foreign assets held by Japanese was mainly caused by an increase in direct and securities investment. 日本の政府・企業・個人が保有する対外資産の増加は、主に直接・証券投資の伸びによるものだった。◆U.S. direct investment in Japan fell 41.2 percent to ¥349.2 billion. 米国の対日投資額は、41.2%減の3,492億円だった。◆While soaring high on massive direct investment from abroad, the Chinese economy started showing signs of overheating in the latter half of 2003. 海外からの活発な直接投資に支えられて、中国経済は、2003年後半から景気過熱の様相を見せ始めた。
direct loan　直接借款(しゃっかん)、直貸しローン、ダイレクト・ローン
　sign an agreement for an untied direct loan to　～向けアンタイド直接借款契約を締結する
　untied direct loan　ひも付きでない直接借款、アンタイド直接借款、アンタイド・ダイレクト・ローン

direct purchase　直接買取り、直接購入
◆I don't oppose the Bank of Japan's direct purchase of bank-held stocks. 日銀による銀行保有株の直接買取りに、私は反対の立場ではない。
direction　(名)方向、方向性、方向感、方針、指針、先行き、傾向、動向、流れ、トレンド、方面、範囲、方角、指示、指図(さしず)、説明、説明書、説明書き、指導、指揮、管理、監督、演出
　a clear sense of direction　明確な指針、明確な方向性
　counter-cyclical direction　景気循環に逆行する方向
　direction as to stopping the negotiability of the notes　裏書き禁止文言
　export direction　輸出地域
　interest rate direction　金利の先行き、金利動向
　　(=the direction of interest rates)
　move in directions favorable to　～に有利な方向に動く、～を優遇する方向に動く
　productivity direction　生産力方向
　the direction of prices　物価動向、物価のトレンド
　the direction of rates [interest rates]　金利動向、金利の先行き
　the direction of the exchange rate　為替相場の方向
　the direction of the market　相場の方向
　the directions of trade　貿易の流れ
　under the direction(s) of　～の指導[指揮、管理、監督、演出]の下で
　wait for direction　方向性を探る
directional investment flow　方向性を持った投資
directional risk　金利上昇リスク
directionless　(形)方向感が定まらない
directive　(名)指令、命令、指図　(形)指令的な、命令的な、指示的な、指導的な、支配的な
　Banking Coordination Directive　銀行指令
　budget directive　予算編成方針
　directive economy　指令経済
　EU directive　EU指令
　Investment Services Directive　投資サービス指令
　Own Fund Directive　自己資本指令
　Solvency Ratio Directive　自己資本比率指令
　unbiased directive　中立的な調節姿勢
　vote a directive biased toward firmness　金融政策引締めに傾ける決定を下す
director　(名)取締役、理事、役員、局長
　board director　取締役
　board of directors　取締役会、役員会、重役会、理事会
　company director　会社役員、役員
　executive director　業務執行取締役、執行取締役、専務・常務取締役
　independent director　独立取締役
　inside director　社内取締役、内部取締役、内部重役
　managing director　英国企業の社長、専務理事、MD
　meeting of board of directors　取締役会会議、取締役会
　outside director　社外取締役、外部取締役
　provisional director　一時取締役
　representative director　代表取締役
　senior managing director　専務、専務取締役
　the managing director of the IMF　IMF専務理事(IMFのトップ)
◆During a regular board meeting, Fuji TV directors agreed to file a claim against Livedoor for losses of more than ¥30 billion incurred from selling off Livedoor shares. 定例取締役会で、フジテレビの役員は、ライブドア株の売却で被った300億円超の損失について、ライブドアに損害賠償を請求するこ

とで合意した。◆French Finance Minister Christine Lagarde chosen as the new managing director of the IMF is expected to maintain an austere stance of calling on Greece to reform itself. IMFの新専務理事に選ばれたクリスティーヌ・ラガルド仏財務相は、ギリシャに改革を求める厳しい姿勢を貫くものと期待されている。◆Trust in the IMF was lost by a scandal involving its former managing director. 国際通貨基金(IMF)の信認は、IMF前専務理事の不祥事で失われた。

directory (名)商工人名録

dirty (形)汚れた, 不正な, 卑劣な, 操作された, 介入された, 政府の介入を受けた, 故障のある, 故障付きの, わいせつな, みだらな, 荒れ模様の, ダーティ
 dirty bill of lading 故障船荷証券, 故障付き船荷証券 (=dirty B/L)
 dirty cargo 粗悪貨物
 dirty float 汚い変動相場制, ダーティ・フロート (=dirty floating rate system: 通貨当局が特定の意図で市場に介入して相場操作をすること)
 dirty money 不正資金, 不正な金, 汚い金
 dirty pool 卑劣な行為, 汚いやり方
 dirty tricks 卑劣な行為, 卑劣な企み, 不正活動, 中傷活動

disability contract 就業不能契約
◆Financial settlement refers to a lump sum payment by an insurer to a disabled insured that extinguishes the insurer's responsibility under the disability contract. 金融決済は, 就業不能契約に基づき, 傷害を負った被保険者に保険会社が一時金を支給して, 保険会社の責任を消滅させることを指す。

disability insurance benefit 高度障害保障

disappoint (動)失望させる, がっかりさせる, 期待を裏切る, 実現を妨(さまた)げる
 disappoint market expectations 市場の期待を裏切る
 disappoint market players 市場筋[市場関係者]を失望させる, 市場筋の期待を裏切る
 disappoint the market 市場の失望を呼ぶ, (〜に)市場が失望する
◆The 225-issue Nikkei Stock Average dived below the key threshold of 10,000 as investors were disappointed with the continuing delay in the disposal of banks' bad loans and an overnight plunge in U.S. stocks. 日経平均株価(225種)は, 投資家が銀行等の不良債権処理が引き続き遅れることや前日の米株価の大幅下落に失望して, 1万円の大台を割り込んだ。

disappointing (形)期待外れの, 〜の期待を裏切る, 予想を裏切った
 disappointing GDP growth rate 期待外れのGDP成長率
 disappointing news 悪材料
 disappointing performance 期待外れの業績, 予想を裏切る業績
 disappointing results 期待外れの業績, 期待を裏切る業績, 予想を裏切る業績 (=disappointing performance)
 disappointing third quarter results 期待外れの第3四半期業績

disappointment (名)失望, 期待はずれ
◆A sense of disappointment has prevailed across the world markets as no concrete measures to rescue Greece were unveiled at the eurozone finance ministers meeting. ユーロ圏財務相会合でギリシャ支援の具体策が明らかにされなかったので, 世界の市場で失望感が広がった。◆The talks between Prime Minister Kan and Bank of Japan Gov. Shirakawa led to a further advance of the yen and offloading of stocks as disappointment spread among market players. 菅首相と日銀総裁の会談は, 一層の円高と市場筋の株の失望売りを誘った。

disarray (名)混乱, 無秩序, 乱雑, 乱脈, 乱れ, 足並みの乱れ, 不統一
 be in disarray 混乱している, 混乱状態だ, 乱雑になっている, 乱れている
 be thrown into disarray 波乱の展開となる
 disarray among the member countries 加盟国各国の足並みの乱れ
 disarray in the foreign exchange markets 為替の混乱, 為替相場の混乱, 外為市場の混乱
 economy in disarray 混乱している経済, 経済の混乱
 plunge into disarray 混乱に陥る
◆Disarray among the countries became evident over concrete measures to prevent currency friction. 通貨摩擦を食い止める具体策では, 各国の足並みの乱れが露呈した。◆France and Germany could not bridge their differences, so Europe's efforts to solve its escalating debt crisis plunged into disarray. フランスとドイツが両国の相違を埋められなかったため, 深刻化する欧州の債務危機問題解決への欧州の取組みは, 混乱に陥った。◆The Fed's monetary easing is a factor causing disarray in the foreign exchange markets. 米連邦準備制度理事会(FRB)[米中央銀行]の金融緩和が, 為替相場混乱[為替混乱]の原因だ。◆The financial market is in complete disarray. 金融市場が, 大混乱している。

disaster (名)災害, 災難, 惨事, 事故, 障害(fault), 不幸, 失敗, 大失敗, ディザスター
 aircraft disaster 航空機事故
 development disaster 開発災害
 disaster area 被災地, 災害地, 災害指定地域
 disaster assistance 災害地支援
 disaster damage prevention measures 防災対策
 disaster-hit areas 被災地域, 被災地
 disaster indemnity 災害補償
 disaster loss 損害損失
 disaster plan 危機管理マニュアル, ディザスター・プラン
 disaster prevention 災害防止, 防災
 disaster prevention [reduction] measures 防災対策
 disaster recovery 障害回復, 災害復興
 disaster relief 災害救助, 災害救援, 災害復旧, 災害支援
 disaster relief work 災害復旧工事
 disaster site 災害の現場, 災害地, 被災地, 事故現場
 disaster-stricken area 被災地域
 economic disaster 経済の惨状, 悲惨な経済状況
 environmental disaster 環境災害
 flood disaster 水害
 housing loan for disaster-hit region [area] 災害復興住宅融資
 industrial disaster 産業災害, 工場災害
 insurance covering damage due to natural disasters 天災による損害を補償する保険
 major disaster 大災害, 大失敗
 man-made disaster 人災
 natural disaster 天災, 自然災害
 natural disaster relief loans 天災救済融資, 天災資金
 serious disaster 激甚災害
 the March 11 disaster 2011年3月11日の東日本大震災 (=the March 11 earthquake and tsunami, the March 11 Great East Japan Earthquake; ⇒hit)
 total [complete] disaster 完全な失敗
 transportation disaster 交通災害
◆Major nonlife insurance companies saw a rapid increase in the number of people taking out insurance covering damage due to earthquakes, tsunami, volcanic eruptions and other natural disasters. 大手損保各社では, 地震や津波, 火山の噴火などの天災による損害を補償する保険(地震保険)の加入者が急増した。

disaster reconstruction 震災復興, 災害復興
 (=reconstruction from the disaster)
 ◆A redemption of the special government bonds for disaster reconstruction is scheduled to begin about 10 years from now. 震災復興債の償還期間は、今から10年程度となる予定だ。◆Funds for disaster reconstruction will be procured by issuing special government bonds. 震災復興の資金は、復興債を発行して調達する。

disaster victim 被災者
 ◆Contributions collected by the Japanese Red Cross Society and mass media companies will be used to support the livelihood of the disaster victims. 日本赤十字社やマスコミ各社に寄せられた義援金は、被災者の生計支援に充てられる。

disband (動)解散する, 解体する
 ◆The firm's health insurance society was disbanded earlier this month. 同社の健康保険組合が、今月はじめに解散した。
 ◆The investment fund is to be disbanded shortly. この投資ファンドは、近く解散することになった。

disburse (動)(費用を)支出する, 支払う(pay out), 分配する, 配分する, 実施する, 実行する
 disburse funds 資金を交付する, 貸出を実行する, 融資を実行する
 disburse interest or principal on an insured security 保証した債券の元利を返済する
 disburse the loan 貸出を実行する, 貸出を行う

disbursement (名)支出, 支払い, 立替え, 出資, 資金交付, 立替え金, 支出金, 実施, 実行
 (⇒direct disbursement system)
 aid disbursement 援助実施額
 cash disbursement 現金支出
 cash receipts and disbursements 現金収支
 delayed disbursement 支払い遅延
 direct disbursement system 直接支払い制
 disbursement account 立替え勘定
 disbursement base 中長期の債務残高, ディスバースメント・ベース
 disbursement book 現金支払い帳
 disbursement of funds 資金の交付, 融資[貸出]の実行
 disbursement schedule 支払い一覧表
 disbursement voucher 支払い伝票
 disbursement warranty 船費保険制限約款
 disbursements clause 船費条項
 disbursements insurance 船費保険
 excess disbursement 支払い超過
 extraordinary disbursement 臨時支出, 臨時歳出
 government disbursement 政府支出
 initial disbursement 第一次実行[実行分], 第一次実施額, 第一次出資金
 loan disbursement 貸出の実行
 missed or delayed disbursement of interest or principal 元利の未払いと支払い遅延
 (national) treasury disbursement 国庫支出金
 petty disbursement 少額支出, 小口支出
 quarterly disbursement 四半期支出
 suspension of disbursements to borrower 借入人に対する資金交付の延期
 the ODA disbursements ODA支出額
 ◆The Japan Fund for Poverty Reduction was launched in 2000 by Tokyo's initial disbursement of ¥10 billion. アジア開発銀行の「貧困削減日本基金」は、日本の第一次出資金(設立当初の出資金)100億円で2000年にスタートした。

discharge (動)荷を降ろす, 解放する, 解除する, 免除する, 解雇する, 解任する, (借金を)返済する, (義務や契約を)履行(りこう)する, 遂行(すいこう)する
 discharge a contract 契約を解除する
 discharge responsibilities 責任を果たす
 discharge senior policyholder obligations and claims 保険加入者に対する上位債務と請求を履行する, 保険契約者に対する契約を履行する
 discharge the obligation 債務を履行する, 義務を果たす, 義務を履行[遂行]する
 discharged bankrupt 免責された倒産債務者, 倒産債務者の免責
 discharged bankruptcy 債務消滅破産
 discharged B/L 荷渡し済み船荷証券
 discharged debt 弁済債務, 債務の弁済
 ◆The actuarial present value of the accrued plan benefits and the net assets available to discharge these benefits at December 31 are as follows: 12月31日現在の年金給付債務額の年金数理原価と年金給付債務に充当可能な年金純資産は、以下のとおりです。

discharge (名)荷揚げ, 荷降ろし, 解放, 免責, 解除, 免除, 解雇, (借金の)返済, 弁済, (義務の)遂行(すいこう), 履行(りこう)
 application of discharge 免責の申立て
 discharge allowance 解雇手当て
 discharge by agreement 合意による契約の解除
 discharge in [of] bankruptcy 破産免責, 破産者の債務免除, 破産手続きの終了
 discharge of a bankrupt 破産者の免責
 discharge of an obligation 義務の遂行
 discharge of contract 契約解除
 discharge of debts 債務免除
 discharge of indebtedness 債務免除
 discharge of lien 差し押さえの解除
 discharge of repayment 償還の免除
 discharge rate 解雇率
 port of discharge 陸揚げ港, 荷揚げ港, 陸揚げ地
 (=discharge port)
 wholesale discharge 大量解雇

disciplinary measures 懲戒処分
 ◆These disciplinary measures include increased penalties on securities fraud and a newly installed penalty on corporate directors in cases of failure to submit adequate financial reports to authorities. これらの懲戒処分には、証券詐欺に対する罰則の強化や、当局に適切な財務報告をしなかった場合の企業取締役に対する罰則の新設などが含まれている。

discipline (名)規律, 規範, 節度, 引締め, 訓練, 鍛練, 統制, 抑制, 学問分野, 分野, 懲罰, 懲戒, 制裁(punishment)
 (⇒fiscal discipline)
 balance of payments discipline 国際収支節度
 (=discipline of the balance of payments)
 budgetary discipline 財政規律
 (=budget discipline, fiscal discipline)
 economic discipline 経済規律
 external pressure for discipline 引締めへの外圧
 financial discipline 金融節度
 fiscal discipline 財政規律, 財政節度, 財政原則
 growth discipline 成長株中心の投資方法, グロース・スタイル
 impose fiscal discipline 財務を引き締める
 market discipline 市場原理
 monetary discipline 金融節度
 price discipline 価格支配力
 value discipline 割安株中心の投資方法, バリュー・スタイル

◆French President Nicolas Sarkozy and German Chancellor Angela Merkel agreed a master plan for imposing a budget discipline across the eurozone. サルコジ仏大統領とメルケル独首相は、ユーロ圏全域に財政規律を課す基本計画に合意した。◆French President Nicolas Sarkozy and German Chancellor Angera Merkel called for greater economic discipline and unity among European countries. サルコジ仏大統領とメルケル独首相は、経済規律の強化と欧州各国間の結束を求めた。◆We will have to accept heavy taxation to foot the bill for the lax fiscal discipline of past governments. われわれは今後、過去の政府の放漫な財政運営のつけを負担するために、重税を受け入れなければならなくなる。

disclose (動)開示する, 公開する, 公表する, 発表する, 明示する (⇒banking)
◆Financial terms of the transaction were not disclosed. 取引の条件[財務条件]は、公表されなかった。◆Sony Corp. and Toyota Motor Corp. shareholders submitted proposals to disclose individual executive salaries at their general shareholders meetings. ソニーとトヨタ自動車の株主からは、株主総会で役員報酬の個別開示を求める案が出された。

disclosure (名)企業内容の開示, 企業経営内容の公開, 企業情報の開示, 情報開示, 情報の公開, 事実の開示, 発明の開示, 開示, 公開, 公表, 内容の特定, 告知, ディスクロージャー
　corporate disclosure　企業による情報開示
　disclosure philosophy　開示主義
　entity-wide disclosure　企業全体の開示
　financial disclosure　財務内容の開示
　global standard information disclosure　世界標準の情報開示
　integrated disclosure system　総合開示制度
　risk disclosure　リスク開示
　the disclosure of corporate information　企業情報の開示
　　(⇒downside)
◆Disclosures of executive salaries have attracted a lot of attention at companies' general shareholders meeting this year. 今年の企業の株主総会では、役員報酬の開示が大きな注目を集めた。◆Financial institutions have no time to lose in enhancing their profitability, streamlining and information disclosure. 金融機関の場合、収益力の向上や一層の合理化、情報開示は待ったなしだ。

discontinued business 非継続事業, 中止事業
　(=discontinued operation)
◆DaimlerChrysler will book its 37 percent stake in Mitsubishi Motors Corp. as a discontinued business until it finds a buyer. ダイムラー・クライスラーは、売却先(買い手)が見つかるまで、同社が保有する三菱自動車の株(発行済み株式の37%)を非継続事業として会計処理する[非継続事業の勘定に計上する]方針だ。

discount (動)割り引く, 割引する, 割り引いて売る・買う, 織り込む, 調整する
◆Excessive discounting would add to a deflationary spiral. 値引き[安売り]が行き過ぎると、デフレ・スパイラル(デフレの悪循環)につながることになる。◆The stock price has already discounted recovery prospects. 株価は、すでに業績回復を織り込んでいる。

discount (名)割引, 割引率, 割引額, 割引料
　(⇒bank service fee)
　bank discount　銀行の手形割引, 銀行割引料
　　(=banker's discount: 手形金額×日数×利率)
　be issued at a discount of　～割り引いて発行される
　be sold on a discount basis　割引発行される
　　(=be issued on a discount basis)
　bill discount　手形割引
　bond discount　社債発行差金
　current discount　現行割引率
　line of discount　割引限度
　official discount rate　公定歩合
　　(=discount rate)
　original issue discount　発行差金
　sales discount　売上割引
　　(=sales cash discount)
　settlement discount　現金割引
　trade discount　卸売割引, 仲間割引
◆Subdistributor Discount means the amount below the prices set forth in the price list, at which the Subdistributor may purchase the products from Distributor. 「二次代理店割引」とは、価格表に記載する価格より低い金額のことで、二次代理店はこの金額で代理店から本製品を購入することができる。

discount bond 割引債, ディスカウント債

discount cash flow キャッシュ・フロー割引, 割引現在価値, ディスカウント・キャッシュ・フロー, DCF
　(=discounted cash flow)

discount cash flow method キャッシュ・フロー割引法, 割引現在価値法, ディスカウント・キャッシュ・フロー方式, DCF方式, DCF法(貸倒れ引当金の必要額の算定方法として、融資先企業の将来の予想収益などを考慮して債権の現在価値を割り出す方式)
◆Under the discount cash flow method based on the U.S. model, loan values are calculated based on projections of how profitable a borrower is likely to be in the future. 米国流の割引現在価値方式では、融資先企業の予想収益に基づいて債権の現在価値を算定する。

discount cash flow system 割引現在価値方式, キャッシュ・フロー割引法, DCF方式 (=discount cash flow method, discounted cash flow formula)
◆If this U.S.-style discount cash flow system is adopted, major banks will be forced to drastically increase their loan loss reserves. この米国流の割引現在価値方式が採用されると、大手行は、貸倒れ引当金の大幅積み増しを迫られることになる。

discount market 手形割引市場, 割引市場, 手形市場

discount on bill 手形割引料

discount on bonds payable 社債発行割引料, 社債発行差金

discount on sale of stock 株式の販売時割引

discount rate 公定歩合
◆Discount rate was kept at 1.25 percent. 公定歩合は、1.25%に据え置かれた。◆The central bank of Japan has deployed various measures to ease monetary policy, including cuts in the discount rate and hikes in the target for current account deposits held by commercial banks at the central bank. 日銀は、公定歩合の引下げや銀行が日銀に持つ当座預金の残高目標の引上げなどを含めて、各種の金融緩和策を実施してきた。◆The Fed raised the discount rate to 0.75 percent from 0.5 percent as a response to improved financial market conditions. 米連邦準備制度理事会(FRB)は、金融市場の環境改善を受けて、(銀行に貸し出す際の金利である)公定歩合を現行の年0.5%から0.75%に引き上げた。◆The U.S. Federal Reserve raised the official discount rate and the target rate of federal funds by 0.25 percentage points in a bid to quell inflation and keep the economy from overheating. 米連邦準備制度理事会(FRB)は、インフレを防ぎ景気の過熱を警戒して、公定歩合とフェデラル・ファンド(FF)の誘導目標金利をそれぞれ0.25パーセント引き上げた。

discount ticket shop 金券ショップ

Discount Window 割引窓口(米連邦準備銀行(Federal Reserve Bank)が市中銀行に対して行う貸出のこと。市中銀行が保有する商業手形の再割引(rediscount)と、適格証券を担保に市中銀行が振り出す約束手形に基づく貸付け(advance)の二つの貸出方法がある)

discount yield 割引利回り
discounted cash flow formula [technique] 割引現在価値方式, ディスカウント・キャッシュ・フロー方式, DCF方式 (=discount cash flow method)
discounting bill 手形の割引
discourage (動)落胆させる, がっかりさせる, ~を止めさせる, 思いとどまらせる, 防止する, 抑える, 認めない
  be discouraged by [about, at, with] ~に落胆する
  discourage a person from 人に~を思いとどまらせる
  discourage banks from lending to ~に対する銀行貸出を抑える
  discourage consumption 消費を抑える
  discourage the market from taking rates lower 市場金利の低下を抑える
  ◆One of the intentions of the government to introduce various regulation measures is to discourage "excessive competition." 各種の規制措置を導入する政府のねらいの一つは, 「過当競争」の防止である。
discrepancy (名)相違, 差異, 差, ずれ, 食い違い, 不一致, 矛盾, 不均衡, ミスマッチ, 書類の不備
  cash discrepancies 現金過不足
discretionary 任意の, 随意の, 自由裁量の, 一任された, 一任勘定の
  discretionary account 一任勘定, 売買一任勘定(投資家が自分の株式投資の運用を証券会社に一任すること)
  discretionary contract 随意契約
  discretionary fund management 一任勘定の投資運用
  discretionary hour 自由裁量時間
  discretionary income 裁量所得, 自由裁量所得, 純可処分所得
  discretionary order 売買一任注文
  discretionary participation feature 裁量権のある参加特質
  discretionary spending 随意支出
  discretionary trust 一任信託, 裁量信託
  discretionary work 裁量労働, みなし労働
  interest [interest rate] discrepancy 金利差
  price discrepancies 価格差
  statistical discrepancy 統計上の不一致
disguise (動)変装[偽装]させる, 偽る, ごまかす, 隠す, ~を装う (名)変装, 偽装, 仮装, 見せかけ, ごまかし, 偽り, 口実
  disguise one's identity 正体を偽る
  disguised unemployment 仮装失業
  ◆The bank disguised these transactions as legitimate trades of loan claims. 同行は, これらの取引については適法な債権売買を装っていた。
dishonor (動)手形などの支払いを拒絶する, 不渡りにする
  ◆The firm dishonored a bill for the first time on Aug. 31. 同社は, 8月31日に最初の不渡りを出した。
disintermediation (名)非金融仲介化, 金融機関離れ, 銀行預金からの高額引出し, 中間業者排除, メーカー直接取引 (⇒reintermediation)
disparity (名)格差, 開き, 差, 相違, 差異, 不一致, 不均衡, 不釣り合い, 不平等
  disparities between public and private sector pensions 年金の官民格差
  disparity in technology 技術格差
  economic disparities among workers 労働者間の経済格差
  income disparity 所得格差
  (=income divide, income gap)

  public-private disparities 官民格差
  societal disparity 社会的格差
  wage disparity between permanent employees and part-timers and temporary employees 正社員とパートや派遣社員との賃金格差
  ◆The issue of eliminating disparities between public and private sector pensions hinges on how quickly the gaps should be closed. 官と民の年金格差[年金の官民格差]是正の問題は, いかに早くその溝を埋めるかにかかっている。
disperse (動)分散させる, 解散させる, 拡散させる, 分散配置する, 広める
  disperse the risk リスクを分散する
  dispersed decision making 分散的意思決定
  widely dispersed creditors 幅広く分散した債権者[債権保有者, 資金供与者]
  widely dispersed markets 幅広く分散した市場
  ◆Nonlife insurance companies used to disperse the risk of large contracts with new corporate clients through reinsurance contracts with other insurance or reinsurance companies. 損保各社は従来, 他の保険会社もしくは再保険会社と再保険契約を結んで, 新規顧客企業と大型契約を結ぶリスクを分散してきた。
disposable income 可処分所得
  ◆The consumer tendency of spending more than consumer's disposable income resulted in a worsening of the massive trade deficit of the United States. 支出が消費者の可処分所得を上回る消費者性向が, 結果として膨大な米国の貿易赤字の拡大を生み出していた。
disposal (名)処分, 処理, 売却
  (⇒bad loan disposal, loan disposal costs)
  asset disposal 資産の処分, 資産売却
  bad-loan disposal 不良債権処理
  disposal by auction sale 競売処分
  disposal of a segment 事業部門の処分
  (=disposal of a business segment)
  disposal of fixed assets 固定資産の除去
  disposal of securities 証券の処分
  disposal of shares 株式の売却
  disposal value 処分価額
  disposition by sale 売却処分
  loan disposal costs 債権処理費用, 不良債権処理費用
  writedown and disposal of loans 債権[貸出]の償却と売却
  ◆Banks mustn't ease up on bad-loan disposal. 銀行は, 不良債権処理の詰めを誤ってはならない。
disposal of bad debts 不良債権処理, 不良債権の処理
  ◆Banks have been preoccupied with the disposal of bad debts, a kind of mop-up operations. 銀行はこれまで, 不良債権の処理という一種の掃討作戦に負われてきた。
disposal of bad loans 不良債権処理 (=disposal of nonperforming loans; ⇒accelerated disposal of bad loans, bank management, credit costs)
  ◆If the current downward trend of stock prices continues, banks' financial resources that could be used to dispose of bad loans will decrease drastically. 株価の下落基調がこのまま続くと, 金融機関の不良債権処理の原資は激減する。◆Overly radical methods for accelerating the disposal of bad loans would panic the banking sector and the financial market, possibly driving banks to shy away from extending new loans and even to call in existing loans. 不良債権処理を加速するための余りにも強硬な手法は, 銀行や金融市場をおびえさせ, 貸し渋りや貸しはがしにつながることにもなる。◆Regional and locally based financial institutions are said to lag behind major banks in the disposal of bad loans. 地域金融機関は, 大手銀行に比べて不良債権の処理が遅れていると

いわれる。

disposal of nonperforming loans 不良債権処理
(=disposal of bad loans, disposal of problem loans; ⇒ double dip recession, macro policy)
◆A majority of the major banking groups appear to have reached the final stage in the disposal of their nonperforming loans. 大手銀行・金融グループの大半が、不良債権処理の最終段階を迎えたようだ。◆UFJ's capital adequacy ratio may fall due to the disposal of nonperforming loans to major borrowers. UFJは、大口融資先の不良債権処理によって、自己資本比率が下がる恐れがある。

dispose of 処分する、売却する、整理する、処理する、始末する、～にけり[決着]を付ける
  dispose of one's fixed assets 固定資産を処分する
  dispose of the asset 資産を処分する
  dispose of unprofitable units 不採算部門を整理する
  when and how disposed of 手形の受取日付とその処置

dispose of distressed assets 危険資産を処分する、危険資産を売却する
◆Banks would keep amassing cash by disposing of distressed assets as quickly as possible to avert collapse after having difficulty raising funds. 資金調達が困難になって経営破たんするのを避けるため、金融機関[銀行]は、できるだけ早めに危険資産を処分[売却]して、現金を抱え込もうとする。

dispose of nonperforming loans 不良債権を処理する
◆Japanese banks failed to take quick actions to dispose of nonperforming loans following the bursting of the bubble economy. 邦銀は、バブル崩壊後の不良債権処理に迅速に対応しなかった。

disposition (名)処分、処理、処置、売却、譲渡、取扱い、配置、配列、使途、自由裁量権、傾向
  asset disposition 資産処分、資産譲渡
  buying disposition 買い気
  capital disposition 資本支出
  disposition by suspension of bank credit 銀行取引停止処分
  disposition by suspension of business 銀行取引停止処分、取引停止処分
  disposition for failure to pay 滞納処分
  disposition notification (送信メールの)開封確認
  disposition of net income 純利益の処分
  disposition of one's estate 不動産の譲渡
  disposition of personal income 個人所得の使途
  disposition of public sale 公売
  disposition of shares 株式の処分
  preferred disposition 優先処分
  provisional disposition 仮処分
  source and disposition of funds 資金の源泉と使途、資金運用表

disrupt (動)混乱させる、中断させる、妨げる、崩壊させる
◆The recovery in business sentiment was largely due to the improvement in the parts supply chain disrupted after the March 11 earthquake and tsunami. 景況感が改善したのは、主に東日本大震災で打撃を受けたサプライ・チェーン(部品供給網)の復旧が進んだためだ。

disruption (名)混乱、中断、停止、分裂、崩壊、破壊、遮断、粉砕、途絶、継続[存続]不可能、通信の途絶、通信障害
  be in disruption 破滅の状態にある
  cause disruption 混乱を引き起こす
  disruption in the economy 経済の混乱
  (=economic disruption)
  labor disruptions 労働争議
  market disruption 市場の混乱、市場崩壊
  supply chain disruption サプライ・チェーン(供給網)の途絶 (⇒supply chain)
  systemic disruption システミック・リスク
  temporary disruptions of telecommunications 通信の一時的途絶[障害]、一時的な通信途絶
  volatility and disruptions in the capital markets 資本市場の変動性と混乱
◆Last month, a firm in Osaka caused widespread disruption to phone lines after placing thousands of random calls to cell phone users. 先月、大阪の業者が、携帯電話のユーザーに手当たり次第に大量発信して、広範な電話回線の通信障害を引き起こした。◆Volatility and disruptions in the capital markets became even more pronounced in July. 7月は、資本市場の変動性と混乱が一段と鮮明になった。

dissolution (名)解散、整理、契約の解除、解消、取消し、解体、解党、廃棄
  dissolution and liquidation 解散と清算
  dissolution of corporation 会社の解散
  dissolution of cross-shareholding ties 株式持ち合い関係の解消
  dissolution of the contract 契約の解消[解除]
  dissolution of unprofitable operations 不採算事業の整理
◆Hostile mergers and acquisitions have been increasing rapidly as the dissolution of cross-shareholding ties among companies accelerates. 企業間の株式持ち合い関係の解消が加速するにつれ、敵対的M&A(企業の合併・買収)の件数は急増している。◆The nonprofit foundation considered dissolution as one way of resolving the issue of debt repayment. 債務返済問題を解決するための手段として、同公益法人は解散も考えた。

dissolve (動)解散する、契約を解除する、解消する、取り消す、解体する、廃棄する (⇒investment fund)
◆A major company has recently decided to dissolve its health insurance society. 大企業が最近、同社の健康保険組合の解散を決めた。◆Misuzu Audit Corp. was dissolved after several accounting scandals. 会計不祥事[監査不祥事]を受けて、みすず監査法人(旧中央青山監査法人)が解散した。◆Suzuki Motor's board of directors decided to dissolve its partnership and cross-shareholding relationship with Volkswagen AG. スズキの取締役会は、独フォルクスワーゲンとの提携と株式持ち合い関係の解消を決めた。

distort (動)歪(ゆが)める、歪曲(わいきょく)する、曲げる、誤り伝える
  distort history 歴史を曲解する
  distort share prices 株価を歪める
  distort the economy 経済を歪める
◆Insider trading distorts share prices and undermines the fairness of the securities market. インサイダー取引は、(適正な)株価をゆがめ、証券市場の公正を損なう。

distortion (名)歪(ゆが)み、ねじれ、偏向、偏向度、歪曲(わいきょく)、曲解、こじつけ、後遺症
  distortion index 偏向度指数
  financial distortion 金融上の歪み
  market distortion 市場の歪み
  monopoly distortion 独占による歪み
  price distortion 価格の歪み、価格偏向
  seasonal distortions 季節要因
  statistical distortions 統計の歪み

distress (名)窮地、苦境、困窮、貧困、経営不振、業績悪化、経営難、悩みの種、動産差し押さえ、差し押さえ動産、差し押さえ物件 (形)投げ売りの、出血販売の
  distress sale 投げ売り、狼狽売り
  (=distress selling)
  distress warrant 動産差し押さえ令状

economic distress　経済の不況, 生活難
financial distress　金融不況, 経営難
◆Financial distress is spreading from smaller firms to mid-size companies. 経営難は、小規模企業から中規模企業に拡大している。

distressed　(形)経営不振の, 経営難の, 経営難に陥っている, 業績悪化の, 窮地の, 困窮している, 苦しんでいる
be distressed with debts　借金で苦しむ
distressed area　不況地域, 疲弊地域, 貧民地区, 被災地
distressed assets　危険資産
distressed bank　経営不振の銀行, 経営難に陥っている銀行
distressed company　経営不振企業, 業績悪化企業
distressed loan　貸倒れ, 回収困難な貸し金
distressed selling　狼狽売り
◆Banks would keep amassing cash by disposing of distressed assets as quickly as possible to avert collapse after having difficulty raising funds. 資金調達が困難になって経営破たんするのを避けるため、金融機関[銀行]は、できるだけ早めに危険資産を処分[売却]して、現金を抱え込もうとする。

distressing　(形)苦悩を与える, 悩ます, 悲惨な, 痛ましい
◆The European fiscal crisis triggered by Greece has spread to Italy, making the severe situation even more distressing. ギリシャ発の欧州財政危機がイタリアに飛び火し、厳しい事態が一段と深刻化している。

distribute　(動)分配する, 分売する, 販売する
◆This U.S. real estate investment fund's profits from the investments were distributed to the Dutch companies as dividends. この米国の不動産投資ファンドの投資事業で得られた利益は、分配金としてオランダの企業に分配されていた。

distribution　(名)有価証券の分売, 分配, 配当, 配布, 交付, 分布, 配信, ディストリビューション（⇒secondary distribution）
distribution of profit　利益配当
distribution of residual assets　残湯財産の分配
exchange distribution　取引所分売
free share distribution　株式の無償交付
required distribution　配当必要額
◆Shareholders agree to cause JVCO to distribute to Shareholders not less than fifty percent（50%）of profits available for distribution by way of dividends in respect of each financial year. 株主は、各年度につき、配当として分配可能な利益の50%以上を株主に対して（株主に対する配当として）JVCO（合弁会社）に分配させることに合意する。
distribution of shares　株式分布（=distribution of stocks: 株式を所有者別, 所有単位数別, 地域別に見た株式の分布状況で、産業界全体の株式分布状況を指す）

distrust　(名)不信, 不信感, 疑惑
◆Public distrust in the pension system must be prevented from deepening. 年金制度への国民の不信感は、これ以上深まらないようにしなければならない。◆S&P's consideration of a possible downgrade on the credit ratings of long-term sovereign bonds issued by 15 eurozone countries illustrates its distrust of the reactions by the political sector. スタンダード・アンド・プアーズ（S&P）がユーロ圏15か国発行の長期国債格付けを引下げ方向で検討しているということは、政治の対応への同社の不信感を示している。◆The distrust of the pension system is gradually spreading among young people. 年金不信が、次第に若者に広がっている。

disturbance　(名)混乱, 騒ぎ, 騒動, 騒乱, 暴動, 動揺, 不安, 心配, 不調, 妨害, 障害, 障害物
balance of payments disturbance　国際収支不安
currency disturbance　通貨不安
disturbance model　(方程式の)誤差模型, 誤差モデル

monetary disturbance　金融不安, 金融混乱
secular disturbance　長期的混乱
◆The downfall of the firm could trigger disturbances throughout the financial market. 同社の凋落（ちょうらく）は、金融市場全体の混乱を招く可能性がある。

dive　(動)急落する, 暴落する, 急降下する, 下がる, 飛び込む, ダイビングする, 潜水する, 没頭する
dive below the key threshold of　〜の大台を割り込む
dive into　〜に乗り込む, 突っ込む, 飛び込む, 飛び降りる, 没頭する, 打ち込む, 深入りする
dive into losses　赤字に転落する, 損失に転落する
dive into policies　政策に没頭する
dive toward　〜に向かって急落する
◆The life insurers' status as large shareholders means that when the market dives, their portfolios also take a tumble. 大株主としての生命保険会社の地位は、株価が大きく下がると資産内容も急激に悪化することを意味する。◆The 225-issue Nikkei Stock Average dived below the key threshold of ¥10,000. 日経平均株価（225種）は、1万円の大台を割り込んだ。◆The 225-issue Nikkei Stock Average dived below 9,000 for the first time in 19 years. 日経平均株価（225種）が、19年ぶりに9,000円を割り込んだ。

dive　(名)急落, 暴落, 急降下, 下落, 落ち込み, 飛び込み, ダイビング
make a dive for　〜に向かって突進する
take a dive　（業績などが）落ち込む, 暴落する, 急落する
take a dive on the stock market　株式市場で暴落する
◆The U.S. financial crisis stopped an ever-increasing number of Americans from getting car loans, leading to a spectacular dive in U.S. car sales. 米国の金融危機で、自動車ローンを組めない米国人が続出し、米国の新車販売が急減した。

diverge　(動)分かれる, 分裂する, 異なる, 分岐する, それる, 外(はず)れる, 逸脱する, 脱線する
◆At the latest G-20 meeting, diverging opinions among member countries were exposed over expanding the lending capacity of the IMF. 今回のG20（財務相・中央銀行総裁）会議では、国際通貨基金（IMF）が融資できる資金規模の拡大をめぐって、加盟国の間で意見の食い違いが表面化した。◆The slipshod management of failed Incubator Bank of Japan widely diverged from its business philosophy. 破たんした日本振興銀行のずさんな経営は、同行の経営理念とはかけ離れていた。

diversification　(名)多様化, 多角化, 分散化, 分散投資
asset diversification　資産の分散, 資産分散化
business diversification　事業多角化, 経営多角化
diversification of business lines　事業分野の多角化, 業務の多様化
diversification of portfolio　ポートフォリオの多様化
diversification of shares　株式の多様化
diversification strategy　多角化戦略
horizontal diversification　水平的多角化
international diversification　国際分散投資
portfolio diversification　ポートフォリオの分散投資
product diversification　製品の多角化, 製品多様化
property portfolio　不動産ポートフォリオ
vertical diversification　垂直的多角化

diversify　(動)多様化する, 多角化する, 資産などを分散する, 分散投資する, 拡大する
build diversified portfolios of stocks, bonds and other financial instruments　株式や債券などの金融商品を組み入れた分散型ポートフォリオを構築する
diversified assets　分散化した資産, 分散化された資産, 資産の分散化
diversified investment　分散投資, 分散型投資, 投資の分散化

DIVI

diversified investment trust　分散投資型投資信託
diversified management　多角経営, 経営の多角化
diversified portfolio　分散投資されたポートフォリオ, リスク分散型ポートフォリオ
diversify customer base　顧客基盤を多様化する, 顧客基盤の多様化, 顧客基盤を拡大する
diversify debt profiles　負債を多様化する, 負債の多様化
diversify funding activities　資金調達の多様化を進める
diversify into new areas　新規分野への多角化を推進する
diversify investment risks　投資リスクを分散する
diversify investment sites　投資先を分散する
　(=diversify one's portfolio)
diversify investments　投資先を分散する, 運用先を分散する
diversify one's holdings　分散投資する, 投資を分散する, 〜の資産を分散する
diversify one's positions　分散投資する
diversify risks　リスクを分散する
diversify the sources of financing　資金調達源の多角化を進める
make diversified investments　投資の分散化を図る, 投資を分散化する, 分散投資をする
　◆The Finance Ministry is studying the possibility of diversifying government bonds targeted at individuals. 財務省は、個人向け国債の多様化の可能性を検討している。◆The Tokyo metropolitan government has decided to deposit more than ¥100 billion in public funds in Citibank, a U.S. bank, to diversify risks. 東京都は、1,000億円を上回る公金を米国の銀行「シティバンク」に預けて、リスクを分散する方針を固めた。

diversion　(名)流用, 転用, 転換, 配置転換, (鉄道貨物の)到着地変更, 迂回路, 回り道, 気晴らし, 娯楽, 牽制行動, 牽制作戦, 陽動作戦 (diversionary tactics), 陽動
farmland diversion　農地転用
trade creation and diversion effect　貿易創出・転換効果
trade diversion　貿易転換

divert　(動)流用する, 転用する, 転換する
divide　(動)分割する, 分ける, 切り分ける, 分離する, 分配する
an indicative dividing line between expansion and contraction signals　景気の拡大と後退判断の分かれ目
the expansion/recession dividing line of 50%　景気の拡大と後退の分かれ目になる50%
　◆After the merger, the TSE and OSE will be divided into four operator firms handling spot trading, derivatives, settlement of trading deals and self-imposed regulations respectively. 経営統合後、東証と大証は、それぞれ現物株、デリバティブ(金融派生商品)、取引決済と自主規制を扱う4事業会社に切り分けられることになっている。

dividend　(名)配当, 利益配当, 配当金, 分配金 (米国では、一般に会社が四半期ごとに配当を支払う。⇒business year, buyback, distribute, illegal payment of dividends, legal capital reserves, quarterly dividend, stock dividend)
accrued dividend　未払い配当金, 経過配当
accumulated dividend　累積配当, 累積未払い配当
bond dividend　社債配当
cash dividend　現金配当
cum dividend　配当付き
dividend policy　配当政策, 配当方針
dividend requirements　配当支払い
dividend revenue　受取配当金, 配当収入
dividend right　配当請求権, 利益配当請求権
dividends declared　宣言配当額
dividends from investment trust funds　投資信託の分配金
dividends payable　未払い配当金
dividends receivable　未収配当金
dividends to policyholders　保険契約者配当金
　(=dividend income)
ex dividend　配当落ち
final dividend　期末配当, 決算配当, 最終配当
high dividend　高配当
imputed dividend　見なし配当
increased dividend　増配
interim dividend　中間配当
　(=regular interim dividend)
no dividend　無配
non-dividend-paying stock　無配株
ordinary dividend　普通配当
quarterly dividend　四半期配当
reduced dividend　減配
regular dividend　普通配当, 通常配当, 定時配当
regular year-end dividend　年度末配当
special year-end dividend　特別年度末配当
stock dividend　株式配当
unclaimed dividend　未請求配当金
unusual dividend　特別配当, 異常配当
with dividend　配当付き
without dividend　配当落ち
　◆Companies are more actively increasing dividends they pay to shareholders. 企業が、以前より積極的に株主への増配をするようになった。◆Currently, those who receive dividends of up to ¥100,000 from a single stock do not have to declare them. 現在、1銘柄当たり年間10万円以下の配当を受けた者は、申告が不要となっている。◆For the computation of the earnings per share, assuming full dilution, dividends on convertible preferred shares have been added back to income. 完全希薄化を仮定した場合の1株当たり利益の算定では、転換可能優先株式[転換優先株]に対する配当は、利益に振り戻してあります。◆Nissan will pay an annual dividend of ¥40 in fiscal 2007. 日産は、2007年度の年間配当支払い額を40円にする方針だ。◆One-third of listed companies resumed or raised dividends. 上場会社の3分の1が、配当の再開または増配となった。◆The company will pay a dividend of ¥1,660 for the first half of the current year as scheduled. 同社は、当年度の上半期については予定どおり1,660円の配当金を支払う。

dividend declaration　配当宣言
dividend in arrears　延滞配当金, 累積未払い配当金, 未払い優先配当金
dividend income　配当所得, 配当収入, 受取配当金
　(=dividend revenue; ⇒taxation system)
　◆Currently, investors are required to pay taxes on dividend income according to the amount of the dividend: ¥100,000 or less, between ¥100,000 and ¥500,000, and ¥500,000 or more. 現在、投資家は、(1銘柄当たり年間)10万円以下、10万円超50万円未満、50万円以上の3段階の配当額に従って、配当所得に対する税金を納めなければならない。◆The tax breaks on capital gains from stock sales and on dividend income will be extended by one year. 株式譲渡益[株式売却益]と受取配当金の税率軽減措置の期間が、1年延長される。

dividend paid　支払い配当
dividends paid deduction　支払い配当控除額
dividends paid to stockholders　株主への配当金支払い
dividends to policyholders　保険契約者に対する配当金
dividend payable　未払い配当金
dividend payment　配当支払い, 配当金の支払い, 配当支払い額, 支払い配当金
　(⇒illegal payment of dividends)
　◆Dividend payments to bond holders have been financed

by the rent paid by Mycal to the special purpose company (SPC). 社債保有者に支払う配当金の原資は、マイカルが特定目的会社に支払う店舗の家賃だ。◆The company hopes to resume dividend payments by the end of March 2007. 同社は、2007年3月末には配当支払いを再開したいとしている。

dividend payout 配当性向, 配当支払い, 配当支払い率 (dividend payout ratio)
◆Stock buybacks are commonly aimed at raising profits per share and enhance dividend payouts to shareholders. 株式買戻しの狙いは、一般に1株当たり利益の引上げと株主への配当支払いの増額にある。

dividend per share 1株当たり配当, 1株当たり配当金, 1株当たり配当額, DPS
◆The company increased the projected dividend per share to ￥6 for fiscal 2005 from the ￥5 paid the previous year. 同社は、2005年度の1株当たり予想配当を前年度の5円から6円に引き上げた(増配した)。

dividend preference 配当優先権

dividend record 配当実績
◆Through continuing gains in annual earnings, it will be possible, over time, to adjust the payout ratio while still maintaining our dividend record. 年間利益の増大を続けることによって、当社の配当実績を今後とも維持しながら、時期が来たら配当性向を調整することは可能である。

dividend yield 配当利回り
◆The dividend yield on Nissan's shares is expected to climb to 2.1 percent this business year, based on the current stock price of ￥1,140. 今年度の日産の株式配当利回りは、現在の株価1,140円ベースで、2.1%に増加する見込みだ。

dividends paid 支払い配当金, 配当金支払い額, 配当支払い
　dividends paid deduction 支払い配当控除額
　dividends paid on preferred stock 優先株式に対する配当支払い

division (名)事業部, 事業部門, 部門, 部・課, 分野, 分割, 分配, 不一致, 分裂
　balance of payments division 国際収支課
　corporate finance division 企業金融部門
　division of banking supervision and regulation 銀行監督・規制部
　division of corporate finance 企業財務部
　division of corporation finance 法人財務部
　division of international finance 国際金融部
　division of resolutions 決済部
　division of trading and markets 売買市場部
　division wall 隔壁
　examination division 審査部, 審査課
　foreign exchange division 為替課
　futures and options division 先物・オプション部
　investment management division 投資管理部[部門]
　mortgage division 不動産担保金融部門
　securities division 証券課, 証券部門
　trade and finance division 販売・金融部門
　unprofitable divisions and [or] units 不採算事業部門, 不採算部門
◆The Citigroup's private banking division is in effect being urged to pull out of the Japanese market. シティバンクのプライベート・バンキング部門は事実上、日本市場からの撤退を迫られている。

DJ Stoxx index European banking stocks ダウ・ジョーンズ欧州銀行株指数
◆The DJ Stoxx index of European banking stocks has fallen 37 percent from a peak in February. ダウ・ジョーンズ欧州銀行株指数は、2月のピークから37%下落した。

dlrs (名)ドル (dollarsの略)
◆President George W. Bush is shoring up his brother's war chest for re-election as Florida's governor by raising dlrs 2.5 million for his party. ブッシュ米大統領は、政党(共和党)のために250万ドルを調達して(集めて)、フロリダ州知事として再選を目指す弟の運動資金を支えている。

do business 営業活動を行う, 営業する, 事業を行う[展開する], ビジネス活動をする, 取引する (=operate)
◆Sberbank of Russia will offer a variety of services, such as ruble-denominated loans to Mizuho Corporate Bank's clients when they do business in Russia. ロシア最大手行のズベルバンクは、みずほコーポレート銀行の顧客がロシアで事業を行う際にルーブル建て融資を行うなどの各種サービスを提供することになった。

document (名)書類, 文書, 書式, 説明書, 仕様書, 明細書, 証書, 証拠書類, 帳票, ドキュメント(複数形には「船積み書類」の意味もある)
　a series of document 一件書類
　aircraft documents 空輸明細書類
　combined transport document 複合運送書類
　commercial document 商業書類
　delivery of document 書類の引渡し
　document of title 権原証券, 権利証券
　documents against [for] acceptance 手形引受書類渡し, 引受渡し, D/A
　documents against acceptance draft 船積み書類引受渡し条件手形
　documents against payment 手形支払い書類渡し, 支払い渡し, D/P
　documents against payment draft 船積み書類支払い渡し条件手形
　documents executed 署名済み書類, 調印済み書類
　export document 輸出書類
　financial document 金融書類
　founding documents 設立文書
　internal document 内部文書
　issue of document 書面の交付
　loan document 借入証書
　marine document 船用書類
　maritime document 海事書類
　negotiable document 譲渡可能書類, 流通書類
　nonnegotiable documents 譲渡不能書類, 非流通書類
　notarial document 公正証書
　on a D/A or D/P basis D/AまたはD/P条件で
　operative documents 営業書類
　original document 正本, 原本
　originating document 原始書類
　payment against documents 書類引換え払い
　shipping documents 船積み書類
　title document 権利証書, 権原証書, 権原証券
　transport documents 運送書類
　trust document 信託証書
◆The company compiled documents for financial institutions it has transactions with. 同社は、取引金融機関向けに資料を作成した。◆The securities companies calculate capital gains and losses, compile taxation documents, gather annual stock reports and file tax returns on behalf of investors free of charge. 証券会社は、投資家の代わりに無料で譲渡損益を計算したり、税務書類を作成したり、年間の株式取引報告書を揃えたりして税務申告書(納税申告書)を提出する。

documentary (形)文書の, 書類の, 記録の
　documentary acceptance credit 荷為替引受け
　documentary against acceptance 引受渡し

documentary bill for acceptance　荷為替引受手形
documentary bill (of exchange)　荷為替手形
documentary bills for collection usance　B/Cユーザンス
documentary clean bill　荷落ち為替手形（船積み書類を添えていない裸手形）
documentary clean credit　荷落ち為替信用状
documentary clean L/C [letter of credit]　荷落ち為替信用状
documentary commercial bill　荷為替商業手形
documentary credit　荷為替信用状
documentary draft　荷為替手形
documentary draft under L/C　信用状付き荷為替手形（=documentary bill）
documentary evidence　書証
documentary exchange　荷為替, 荷為替手形（=documentary bill, documentary paper）
documentary export bill　輸出荷為替手形
documentary foreign bill [of exchange]　荷付き外国為替手形
documentary import bill　輸入荷為替手形
documentary L/C [letter of credit]　荷為替信用状
documentary paper　荷為替手形（=documentary bill, documentary exchange）
documentary proof　証拠書類
documentary sight credit　一覧払い荷為替手形信用状
Uniform Customs and Practice for Documentary Credit　荷為替信用状に関する統一規則および慣例, 信用状統一規則

dodge　(動)逃れる, 巧みにそらす, 巧みにごまかす, さっと身をかわす, うまく避ける, 回避する　(名)言い抜け, ごまかし, 妙案, 策略, 身をかわすこと
dodge an investigation　調査をごまかす
dodge one's obligations　義務を回避する
dodge tax payment　納税を逃れる, 納税を免れる, 脱税する
dodge taxes　脱税する
dodge the accusation　非難を回避する
tax dodge　脱税, 税金を逃れるための手段, 税金逃れの手
◆The man intentionally dodged the tax payments as he transferred the money for asset management to another country. 男は, 資産運用の資金を他国に移動させていることから, 意図的に納税を免れていた。

doldrums　(名)沈滞, 低迷, 不振, 不況, 不景気, 冷え込み, 中だるみ
be out of the doldrums　底を脱する
in the doldrums　不景気で, 不振の, 厳しい状況の, 意気消沈して
remain in the doldrums in most areas　ほぼ全域で冷え込みが続いている　(⇒housing)
the doldrums in the manufacturing industry　製造業の不振
the last period of economic doldrums　前回の景気後退期
◆It is difficult to raise the consumption tax at a time when the economy is in the doldrums. 厳しい経済状況下で, 消費税を引き上げるのは難しい。◆Most regional economies still linger in the doldrums. 地方経済も, 大半はまだ停滞から抜け出せないでいる。◆The doldrums in the manufacturing industry will impede the recovery of Japan's economy. 製造業の不振は, 日本経済の回復の足かせにもなる。◆With domestic stock prices in the doldrums, foreign bond open investment trusts that invest in bonds issued by foreign governments, international institutions and major corporations are gaining in popularity as an investment. 日本株の株価が低迷するなかで, 資金の運用先として外国の国債や国際機関債, 大手企業の社債に投資する外債投信に人気が集まっている。

dole-out measures　バラマキ政策
（⇒handout policies）
◆Mainly due to dole-out measures, the Japanese government's finances are on the verge of bankruptcy. 主にバラマキ政策のせいで, 国[日本政府]の財政は破たん寸前だ。◆The former administration was characterized by populist policies such as dole-out measure and the manner of budget screening. 前政権は, バラマキ政策や事業仕分けの手法など大衆迎合的な政策（ポピュリズム）が特徴だった。

dole-out policies　バラマキ政策
◆This country's debt-laden finances are in a critical situation due to the dole-out policies as well as lavish economic stimulus measures. わが国の借金漬けの財政は, バラマキ政策と大盤振る舞いの景気対策で, 危機的な状況に陥っている。

dollar　(名)ドル, ドル相場　(⇒exchange rate, global economy, selling of the dollar, strong dollar, weak dollar)
Asian dollar market　アジア・ドル市場
Aussie dollar　豪ドル　(=Australia's currency)
be priced in dollars　ドル建てである（=be dollar-based）
buy dollars on speculation　思惑でドルを買う
Canadian dollar　カナダ・ドル
climbing dollar　ドル高
constant dollar basis　恒常ドル基準, 実質ベース
constant-dollar-value plan　定額プラン
constant value dollar　恒常価値ドル
continue to buy dollars against one's own currency　ドル買い・自国通貨売りを進める, 自国通貨を売ってドルを買い進める
correction in the dollar　ドル相場の調整
depreciation of the yen against the dollar　円高ドル安, 円高・ドル安
dollar area　ドル地域, ドル圏
dollar balances　ドル残高
dollar bloc　ドル・ブロック
dollar convertible debenture　ドル建て転換社債
dollar-cost averaging　ドル平均法（=dollar average method, dollar averaging: 相場の動きと関係なく一定間隔で一定額を投資する手法）
dollar-defense measures　ドル防衛策
dollar deficit [drain, gap, shortage]　ドル不足
dollar diplomacy　ドル外交, 金力外交
dollar draft　ドル為替手形
dollar drive　ドル貨獲得促進
dollar exchange　ドル為替
dollar exchange standard (system)　ドル為替本位制
dollar floater　ドル建て変動利付き債
dollar glut　ドル過剰
dollar goods　ドル物資
dollar imperialism　ドル帝国主義
dollar overhang　ドル過剰, ドル過剰状態, 過剰ドル
dollar parity　ドル平価
dollar peg system　ドル連動制
dollar preference　ドル選好
dollar reserve　ドル準備
dollar roll　売却/買戻し取引, ダラー・ロール取引
dollar sector　ドル債市場
dollar shift　ドル・シフト
dollar shock　ドル・ショック
dollar sign　ドル記号（dollar mark）, 金を稼ぐチャンス
dollar standard system　ドル本位制
dollar stock　米国証券, 米国株券

dollar stocks　ドル株式（米国やカナダの株式）
dollar supporting measures　ドル支持政策
dollars and cents　金銭
dollar's continued decline　ドル安基調
dollar's decline against the yen　ドル安・円高, 円高・ドル安
dollar's depreciation　ドル安
dollar's foreign exchange value　ドルの為替相場, ドルの為替レート
dollar's worth　ドル価値, 1ドルの価値
exchange rates for the dollar against the yen　円に対する［対円での］ドルの為替レート
faith in the dollar　ドルの信認
fall of the dollar against the Japanese yen and the euro　円やユーロに対するドル安, ドル安・円高, ユーロ高, ドル安・円高とドル安・ユーロ高
firming of the dollar　ドルの強含み
global dollar sector　米ドル建てグローバル債市場
hold the dollar　ドルを保有する
in constant dollar basis　恒常ドル基準で, 実質ベースで
in current dollar terms　名目ベースで
in dollar terms　ドル表示で, ドル・ベースで, ドルで評価した場合　（=in dollar-denominated terms）
intervention to strengthen the dollar　ドル高誘導の介入
long dollar positions against the yen　円売りドル買い
overvalued dollar　ドル高
plunging of the dollar　ドルの急落
rising dollar　ドル高
selling of the dollar　ドル売り
　（=the dollar selling）
¥76-to-the-dollar level　1ドル＝76円台, 1ドル＝76円の水準
sharp fall in the dollar　ドルの急落
strong dollar against other currencies　ドルの全面高, ドル全面高
the almighty dollar　金力
the Australian dollar　豪ドル
the dollar's depreciation　ドル安
the exchange rate for U.S. dollars　ドルの為替レート
the slump in the dollar　ドル安
the U.S. dollar　米ドル, 米ドル相場
the weak dollar　ドル安
weak dollar　ドル安
weaken the dollar　ドル高を抑える
weakening dollar　ドル安
yen's rise against the dollar　円高・ドル安
◆After the government's move of intervention, the yen plunged to the ¥85 level against the dollar. 政府の市場介入の動きを受けて、円相場は1ドル＝85円台まで急落した。◆An overvalued dollar is seriously crimping U.S. manufacturers' ability to export. ドル高が、米国の製造業界の輸出力を大いに妨げている。◆Big companies assume the exchange rate of ¥81.06 to the dollar for the latter half of fiscal 2011. 大企業の2011年度下期の想定為替レートは、1ドル＝81円6銭となっている。◆Greece must avert a crippling debt default by securing billions of dollars in emergency loans from European countries and the IMF. ギリシャは、欧州諸国［ユーロ圏］と国際通貨基金（IMF）による緊急融資で巨額の資金を確保して、壊滅的な債務不履行を回避しなければならない。◆If the U.S. government falls into default, the markets' faith in the dollar as the world's key currency would plummet. 米政府がデフォルト（債務不履行）に陥ったら、世界の基軸通貨としてのドルの信認は急落する。◆In the case of foreign currency deposits by the U.S. dollar, many online banks charge about ¥0.25 in commission per dollar at the time of deposits and withdrawals. 米ドルによる外貨預金の場合、ネット銀行の多くは、預け入れ時と解約時に1ドルに付き25銭程度の手数料を取る。◆Japan must prevent the yen from soaring again to the level of ¥76 to the dollar. 日本は、円相場が再び1ドル＝76円台に急騰する事態を阻止しなければならない。◆Japan should prevent the dollar plunging and the yen from rising too sharply through concerted market intervention with the United States and European countries. 日本は、米欧との協調介入によってドル急落と超円高を阻止すべきだ。◆Japan's exports will stagnate and corporate performance will suffer if the yen remains in the historically high ¥75-range against the dollar. 円相場が1ドル＝75円台の史上最高値が続けば、日本の輸出は低迷し、企業の業績は悪化する。◆The dollar weakened against the euro. ドルが、対ユーロで弱含みとなった［ドルの対ユーロ相場は下落した］。◆The exchange rate in fiscal 2011 had been predicted to be between ¥80 and ¥83 per dollar by many Japanese exporters. 2011年度の為替レートを、多くの日本の輸出業者は1ドル＝80～83円と想定していた。◆The Japanese currency is about ¥5 lower than its initial projection of ¥115 to the dollar. 円は、当初想定した1ドル＝115円より5円程度安く推移している。◆The rate of exchange to U.S. dollars shall be based upon the rate of exchange quoted by the Bank on the day of payment. 米ドルへの為替相場は、支払い日の銀行の為替相場によるものとする。◆The U.S. dollar as the world's only reserve currency may become merely one of three major currencies, along with the euro and the renminbi. 世界で唯一の準備通貨としての米ドルは、ユーロ、人民元とともに、単なる3大通貨の一つになる可能性がある。◆The U.S. dollar has dropped sharply in value not only against the yen, but also against the euro, the South Korean won, the Thai baht and other currencies. 米ドルは、円に対してだけでなく、ユーロや韓国ウォン、タイ・バーツなどに対しても急落している。◆The U.S. dollar has enjoyed the massive privileges as the key international currency. 米ドルは、国際通貨としての特権を享受してきた。◆The U.S. dollar may lose its current status as the world's only reserve currency. 米ドルは、世界唯一の準備通貨としての現在の地位を失う可能性がある。◆The U.S. dollar was traded at around ¥76 on the currency market. 為替市場では、1ドル＝76円をはさんだ取引が続いた。◆The yen could soon even reach a record high in the ¥79 range versus the dollar. 円は、やがて1ドル＝79円台の史上最高値にまで達する可能性がある。◆The yen hovered in a narrow range in the upper ¥85 level to the dollar. 円相場は、1ドル＝85円台後半の小幅な値動きとなった。◆The yen is currently hovering at a level stronger than ¥80 to the dollar. 円相場は現在［足元の円相場は］、1ドル＝80円を上回る水準で推移している。◆The yen may appreciate further to ¥70 against the U.S. dollar. 円高は、さらに1ドル＝75円まで進む可能性がある。◆The yen may once again rise against the dollar and other major currencies. 今後、ドルなどの主要通貨に対して再び円高が進む可能性がある。◆The yen may soar toward ¥80 to the dollar. 円相場は、1ドル＝80円に向けて急騰する可能性がある。◆The yen's exchange rate has appreciated to ¥76 against the dollar, so it is the best time to buy U.S. dollars. 円の為替レートが1ドル＝76円に上昇したので、今が米ドルの買い時だ。◆The yen's value still remains high and is likely to reach a postwar record value above the ¥76-to-the-dollar level. 円相場は依然高く、1ドル＝76円台を上回る戦後最高値に達する可能性がある。◆There are few signs of the yen reaching the ¥90 range to the dollar for the time being. 今のところ、1ドル＝90円台に達する動き［1ドル＝90円台を目指す動き］は見られない。

dollar buying　ドル買い　（=buying of the dollar）
dollar-buying intervention　ドル買い介入
　dollar-buying and yen-selling intervention　ドル買い円売

り介入
◆Dollar-buying intervention has been stopped since spring. ドル買い介入は、春以来停止している。

dollar-buying operation ドル買い操作, ドル買い介入操作, ドル買いオペ
◆The previous one-day record for a dollar-buying operation was marked on Jan. 9, 2004 at ¥1,666.4 billion. ドル買いオペ[円売り・ドル買い介入操作]のこれまでの1日の最高額は、2004年1月9日の1兆6,664億円だった。

dollar-buying, yen-selling intervention ドル買い・円売り介入
◆The government and the Bank of Japan conducted a dollar-buying, yen-selling intervention for the first time in 6 1/2 years on Sept. 15, 2010. 2010年9月15日に政府・日銀は、6年半ぶりにドル買い・円売り介入を実施した[行った]。

dollar-denominated (形)ドル建ての
　dollar-denominated exports　ドル建て輸出
　dollar-denominated new issues　ドル建て債券の起債
　in dollar-denominated basis　ドル表示で

dollar funds ドル資金
(⇒depreciation of the dollar exchange rate)
◆Some dollar funds injected into banks by the U.S. central bank may send U.S. stock prices soaring because banks will invest some of the new dollar funds in domestic assets such as stocks. 米国の中央銀行(FRB)が金融機関[銀行]に供給したドル資金の一部は、銀行がその新たなドル資金の一部を株のような国内資産に投資するため、米国の株価を上げる可能性がある。

dollar liquidity-providing operation (中央銀行の)ドル資金供給オペ
◆In cooperation with the U.S. FRB, the Bank of England, the Bank of Japan and the Swiss National Bank, the European Central Bank decided to conduct three U.S. dollar liquidity-providing operations between October and December. 米連邦準備制度理事会(FRB)、英イングランド銀行、日銀、スイス国立銀行と協調して、欧州中央銀行(ECB)が10〜12月に3回、米ドル資金供給オペを実施することを決めた。

dollar loans (中央銀行の商業銀行に対する)ドル資金供給
◆Major central banks will cooperate to offer three-month U.S. dollar loans to commercial banks in the wake of Europe's sovereign debt crisis. 欧州の財政危機を受け、主要中央銀行が、協調して銀行[商業銀行]に3か月物ドル資金を供給することになった。

dollar primacy ドル支配
◆The age of dollar primacy is said to be coming to an end. ドル支配の時代は終わりに近い、と言われている。

dollar selling ドル売り
◆Speculation that the drop in U.S. interest rates will reduce the gap between Japanese and U.S. interest rates has encouraged dollar selling. 米国の金利低下で日米の金利差が縮小するとの見方から、ドルが売られている。

dollar-selling pressure ドル売り圧力
◆Dollar-selling pressure has eased and put a temporary brake on the sharp appreciation of the yen and the fall of the dollar. ドル売り圧力が弱まり、急激な円高・ドル安にいったん歯止めがかかった。◆Dollar-selling pressure remains strong due to concerns over the outflow of funds from the United States. 米国からの資金流出に対する懸念で、ドル売り圧力は依然として強い。◆Out of a sense of relief, dollar-selling pressure has eased on the foreign currency markets. 安堵(あんど)感から、外国為替市場では、ドル売り圧力が弱まった。

dollar-selling trend ドル売りの流れ
◆As the financial markets' confidence in the U.S. currency has been shaken, stock prices may fall worldwide and the dollar-selling trend may accelerate. 米ドルへの金融市場の信認が揺らいでいるため、株価が世界的に下落し、ドル売りの流れが加速する可能性もある。

dollar-yen exchange rate 円・ドル為替レート[為替相場], 円・ドル・レート
◆Recent rapid movements of the dollar-yen exchange rates in the markets could have undesirable implications for the Japanese economy and the world economy. 日米為替市場での最近の円・ドル為替レートの急激な変動は、日本経済と世界経済に悪影響を及ぼす可能性がある。◆The dollar-yen exchange rate closed at ¥101.2, a gain of nearly ¥25 since the beginning of the year. 円・ドル・レートは、終値で1ドル＝101円20銭で、年初からの円の上昇幅は25円近くになった。

dollar-yuan exchange rate 元・ドル為替レート[為替相場], 元・ドル・レート
◆China has not budged an inch to shift the current dollar-yuan exchange rate. 中国は、現在の元・ドル・レートを梃子でも動かそうとしていない。

dollar's depreciation ドル安
◆The continued fall in U.S. stock prices and the dollar's depreciation has battered the Japanese economy. 米国の株安とドル安の進行が、日本経済を直撃してい[激しく揺さぶっている。]

dollar's fall against the yen 円高ドル安
◆Profit taking, stirred by the U.S. dollar's fall against the yen, sent Tokyo share prices plunging. 円高ドル安の進行を受けて、利益を得る[確定する]ための売りが先行したため、東京株式市場の株価は急落した。

dollar's value ドルの価値, ドル相場
◆The dollar's value temporarily dropped to the ¥85 level in New York. ドル相場は、ニューヨーク市場で一時、85円台まで下落した[値を下げた]。

dollarization (名)ドル化, ドル建て化

domestic (形)国内の, 内国の, 自国の, 国産の
　domestic accounts　国内投資家
　domestic and international equities　国内株と外国株
　domestic asset quality　国内資産の質
　domestic banking　国内銀行業務
　domestic bill　内国為替, 内国手形
　domestic bill of exchange　内国為替手形
　domestic bill of lading　国内輸送証券
　domestic borrowers　国内融資先, 国内の借り手
　domestic capital　国内資本, 国内貯蓄
　domestic corporate bond market　国内社債市場
　domestic credit　国内信用, 国内発行信用状(domestic letter of credit)
　domestic credit expansion　国内の信用拡大, 国内信用の拡大, 国内信用供与額
　domestic currency　国内通貨
　domestic-currency cash flow　自国通貨建て資金
　domestic-currency obligation[bonds]　自国通貨建て債務
　domestic deposit　国内預金
　domestic depositors　国内預金者
　domestic exchange　内国為替
　　(=inland exchange)
　(domestic) exchange settlement　為替決済
　domestic flotation　国内起債分
　domestic government debt market　国債市場
　domestic interest rates　国内金利
　domestic investment　国内投資, 自国投資
　domestic issue　国内債
　domestic lead manager　国内主幹事
　domestic lending　国内貸出, 国内貸付け, 国内融資
　domestic letter of credit　国内信用状, 国内発行信用状

(=domestic credit, domestic L/C)
domestic loan　内国債
domestic loans transferred overseas　国内店名義現地貸し
domestic monetary policy　国内金融政策
domestic monetary system　国内金融制度, 国内通貨制度
domestic money order　国内為替, 内国送金
domestic player　国内投資家
domestic problem loans　国内不良債権
domestic savings rate　国内貯蓄率
domestic speculators　国内投機筋
domestic stock　内需株
domestic trading in derivatives　デリバティブ（金融派生商品）の国内取引　（⇒domestic trading）
on a domestic currency basis　国内通貨ベースで
straight domestic issue　国内普通債

domestic assets　国内資産
◆Restricting an influx of capital prevents foreigners from acquiring domestic assets. 資本流入［資本輸入］の規制で、外国人は国内資産の購入が難しくなる。◆Some dollar funds injected into banks by the U.S. central bank may send U.S. stock prices soaring because banks will invest some of the new dollar funds in domestic assets such as stocks. 米国の中央銀行（FRB）が金融機関［銀行］に供給したドル資金の一部は、銀行がその新たなドル資金の一部を株のような国内資産に投資するため、米国の株価を上げる可能性がある。

domestic bank　国内銀行
domestic bank credit markets　国内銀行信用市場
the Bank of Tokyo-Mitsubishi UFJ and other domestic banks　三菱東京UFJ銀行などの国内銀行
◆Domestic banks are stepping up overseas project financing as greater yields of interests are expected through such lending than loans to domestic borrowers. 国内銀行は、国内の借り手への融資に比べて海外の事業向け融資のほうが大きな金利収入を見込めるので、海外の事業向け融資（プロジェクト・ファイナンス）を強化している。

domestic bond　国内債, 内国債　（⇒inflate）
◆The national debt caused by domestic bond issues will not be a burden on posterity. 内国債の発行によって生じる国の債務は、後世の負担にはならない。

domestic borrowers　国内の借り手, 国内の融資先, 国内融資先企業
◆Domestic bank are stepping up oversea project financing due to the lack of growth in lending to domestic borrowers amid protracted deflation at home. 国内銀行各行は、国内ではデフレが続いて［デフレが続く状況で］国内融資先への貸出が伸びていないことから、海外の事業向け融資を強化している。◆The margin of profits from a project financing scheme overseas is generally higher than that from loans extended to domestic borrowers. 海外のプロジェクト・ファイナンス（事業融資）事業による利ざやは、一般に国内企業向け融資の利ざやより高い。

domestic demand　国内需要, 内需
◆The rate of savings among those people in their 30s and 40s is on an upward trend, which is likely to have a depressing effect on domestic demand. 30〜40歳代の貯蓄率が増大傾向にあり、内需を下押ししている可能性がある。

domestic economy　国内経済
◆The yen's extremely rapid appreciation may deliver a bitter blow to the domestic economy. 超円高は、国内経済に大きな打撃を与える可能性がある。

domestic stock exchange　国内証券取引所, 国内株式取引所, 国内株式市場
◆Domestic stock exchange entries continue to languish, reflecting the tough conditions faced by emerging firms wanting to publicly list their shares. 国内株式市場への新規上場は、株式上場を目指す新興企業が直面している厳しい状況を反映して、低迷が続いている。

domestic stock market　国内株式市場
◆The major securities house attributed the poor earnings to sharp drops in brokerage fees and trading profits amid the extended slump in the domestic stock market. この大手証券会社は、減益の要因として、国内株式市場の長期低迷による株売買手数料と売買益の大幅減を挙げた。

domestic trading　国内取引
◆The Osaka Securities Exchange accounts for 50 percent of domestic trading in derivatives including stock price index futures. 大証は、株価指数先物などデリバティブ（金融派生商品）の国内取引で5割を占めている。

domestic yield　国内利回り
◆Domestic yields are low relative to those in other nations, causing Japanese money to go overseas. 他国の利回りに比べて国内利回りが低いため、日本の資金が外国に流れている。

domicile　（動）手形の支払い地［場所］を指定する　（名）手形の支払い場所, 居住地, 本拠, 本拠地

domiciled　（形）手形の支払い地を定めた, 支払い地指定の, 住所を定めた
domiciled bill　他所払い手形
domiciled check　他所払い小切手
domiciled in　手形支払い地［支払い場所］が〜の

dominant　（形）支配的な, 優勢な, 有力な, 最有力の, 最大の, 圧倒的な, 顕著な, 目立つ, 主要な, 中心的な
dominant company［firm］　支配的企業, 優越企業
dominant driving force　大きな原動力
dominant factor　支配的要因
dominant growth rate　支配的成長率, 際立った伸び率
dominant market share　圧倒的な市場シェア, 圧倒的なシェア
dominant position　支配的な地位
dominant stake　支配持ち分, 支配株, 経営支配株［株式］
◆The current management holds the dominant stake in the firm. 現経営陣が、同社の経営支配株［支配持ち分］を保有している。

dominate　（動）支配する, 制覇する, 威圧する, 優位に立つ, 〜に強い影響力を持つ, 占領する, 占める
dominate the global market　世界市場を制覇する
dominate the market　市場を支配する, 市場を押さえる, 市場で圧倒的な力を持つ, 市場で圧倒的な地位を占める
family-dominated group　創業者一族が支配する企業グループ
◆The bank tried to dominate the management of its clients by sending a majority of people to their board of directors. 同行は、融資先の取締役会に過半数の取締役を送り込んで、融資先の経営の支配を図った。

domino effect　連鎖反応（chain reaction）, ドミノ効果（連鎖反応による累積的効果）, 将棋倒し
◆There will be a domino effect if companies can't borrow. 企業が融資を受けられない［資金調達できない］場合には、ドミノ効果が生じる。

donation　（名）寄付, 寄付金, 献金, 手当て, 贈与, 贈与品, 寄贈, 寄贈品, 提供
a series of fraud cases involving donations　相次ぐ義援金詐欺事件
charitable donation　寄付金, 慈善寄付
donation from an individual　個人献金
donation tax　贈与税
large［handsome］donations　多額の寄付金
make a donation to charity　慈善事業に寄付をする
out-of-work donation　離職手当て
political donation　政治献金

small donations　少額の寄付金
solicit donations　浄財を募る, 献金[寄付金]を募る
tax credits for donations　寄付金控除
under-the-table donation　ヤミ献金
◆In the aftermath of the 1995 Great Hanshin Earthquake and the 2007 Niigata Prefecture Chuetsu Offshore Earthquake, a series of fraud cases involving donations occurred. 1995年の阪神大震災や2007年の新潟県中越沖地震の直後には、義援金詐欺事件が相次いで起きた。◆Many organizations have been soliciting donations to support the livelihood of the disaster victims. 被災者の生活支援のため、団体の多くが浄財を募っている。◆The income tax regime currently allows tax credits for charitable donations to be the annual total of donations minus ¥10,000. 現在の所得税の仕組みでは、寄付金の控除額は年間の寄付金総額から1万円を差し引いた額となっている。

donor　(名)寄付者, 寄贈者, 支援者, 援助などの供与国, 拠出国, 臓器や血液などの提供者, ドナー
◆Iraq urged international donors to speed up funding for reconstruction. イラクは、イラク復興のための資金拠出加速を世界の拠出国に要請した。

donor country [nation]　援助国, 支援国, 拠出国
◆Japan is Vietnam's largest donor country, providing about ¥100 billion in ODA assistance in 2007. 日本はベトナムにとって最大援助国で、2007年度のODA供与額は約1,000億円に上る。

dormant　(形)活動休止中の, 休眠している, 休眠中の, 現在使われていない,(計画などが)実施されていない, 未行使の, 未発動の, 潜在的な, 潜伏中の, 未開発の
dormant account [accounting] system　複会計制度
dormant balance　休止残高, 不活動残高
dormant claim　眠った権利, 長期間請求されていない権利
dormant execution　強制管理
dormant funds　眠れる資金, 眠っている資金
dormant individual assets　眠れる個人資産, 眠れる個人金融資産
dormant judgment　未発動の判決
dormant partner　匿名組合員, 匿名のパートナー, 匿名社員, 弱小社員　(=secret partner, silent partner, sleeping partner)
dormant partnership　匿名組合
dormant patent　休眠特許
dormant right　未行使の権利, 未発動の権利
◆The bank's aim is to help circulate dormant individual assets in the local economy. 眠れる個人の金融資産を地域経済に循環させるのが、同行の目的だ。◆The sovereign wealth fund will buy up dormant patents owned by companies and universities. 同政府系投資ファンドは、企業や大学が保有する休眠特許を買い取る方針だ。

double　(動)2倍になる, 倍増する, 倍加する
◆Gold prices have more than doubled since the end of 2008 amid increased uncertainties over the U.S. and European economic outlook. 欧米景気見通しの不透明感の高まりを受けて、金価格は、2008年末以降、2倍以上になっている。◆Toyota's consolidated sales, which surpassed ¥10 trillion in the business term ending in March 1997, doubled to ¥21 trillion in the following nine years. トヨタの連結売上高は、1997年3月期に10兆円を突破した後、9年間で21兆円に倍増した。

double　(形)二重の, 2桁(けた)の, 2倍の, 複式の
debt-adjusted double leverage total debt　債務調整済み[債務調整後]ダブル・レバレッジ債務合計[総債務]
double auction　二重競売
double-barreled bond　二重財源債
double bottom　二番底
double-digit gain　2桁の伸び
(=double-digit growth, double-digit increase)
double income and no kids　子どものいない共稼ぎ夫婦
double indemnity　倍額補償, 災害倍額支払い
double insurance　重複保険
double leverage [leveraging]　二重レバレッジ, ダブル・レバレッジ
double recovery　二重賠償
double standard　複本位制度
double taxation relief　二重課税の回避
represent a double blow　二重の打撃になる

double debt　二重ローン, 二重債務
(=double loan, dual debt)
◆Delays in double-debt relief process may become obstacles to restoration efforts. 二重ローン救済手続きの遅れは、復興努力の障害になる可能性がある。◆Many survivors of the Great East Japan Earthquake are struggling under the heavy double debt loads. 東日本大震災の被災者の多くは、二重ローンという重荷[重い負担]を背負って苦しんでいる。

double debt problem　二重ローン問題
(=dual debt problem)
◆In response to the double debt problem due to the March 11 disaster, financial institutions will be forced to share some burdens including the waiver of debts. 東日本大震災による二重ローン問題への対応では、債権の放棄を含めて金融機関もある程度の共同負担を強いられることになろう。

double deduction　二重引落し
(=double withdrawal)
◆A system failure on April 1 hit Mizuho's 7,000 ATMs, preventing some customers from executing transactions, halting 2.5 million money transfers and resulting in thousands of double deductions from accounts. 4月11日に発生したシステム障害はみずほ(みずほホールディングス)の7,000台のATM(現金自動預け払い機)を直撃して、顧客の一部が取引を執行できず、250万件の口座振替作業が停止したほか、口座からの二重引落しが数千件に及ぶ結果となった。

double dip recession　景気の二番底, 景気の底割れ
be in danger of slipping into a double-dip recession.　景気の二番底に陥る危険にさらされている
enter into a double dip recession　景気が二重底に突入する
enter into a genuine double dip recession　景気の本格的な二番底に突入する
sink into a double dip recession　景気底割れする
slip into a double dip recession　景気の二番底に陥る
◆Fears of a double dip recession are likely to rise if the rise in the yen continues. 円高がこのまま続けば、「景気二番底」懸念が高まると見られる。◆The economy could sink into a double-dip recession due to the clouds hanging over the U.S. economy and rising deflationary pressures that will accompany the accelerated disposal of nonperforming loans. 米国経済の行方(米国経済への先行き不安)や、不良債権処理の加速に伴うデフレ圧力の高まりなどで、景気が底割れする恐れがある。◆The U.S. economy is in danger of slipping into a double-dip recession. 米経済は、景気の二番底に陥る可能性[恐れ]がある。

double-sold loans　二重譲渡債権, 債権の二重譲渡
◆Incubator Bank of Japan lost a suit in court over double-sold loans by collapsed moneylender SFCG Co. 経営破たんした金融業(商工ローン大手)のSFCGによる債権の二重譲渡問題をめぐる裁判で、日本振興銀行が敗訴した。

double taxation　二重課税
double taxation agreement　租税条約, 二重課税防止条約
double taxation relief　外国税額控除
double taxation treaty　二重課税防止条約
international double taxation　国際二重課税

double transfer 二重振込み, 二重送金
　◆The bank's 5,000 mistaken transfers, including double transfers to the same accounts, have been resolved. 同じ口座に対する二重振込みなどを含めて、同行の5千件の誤送金問題はすでに解決している。

double withdrawal 二重引落し
　(=double deduction; ⇒customer account)
　◆The huge number of delays in money transfers and double withdrawals are serious incidents concerning the banks' core businesses. 口座振替の遅れや二重引落しの大量発生は、銀行の根幹業務にかかわる重大な事件だ。

doubt （名）疑い, 疑惑, 疑念, 懐疑, 迷い
　doubts over the effect [effectiveness] of the stock price measures　株価対策の効果について疑問視する[懸念を表明する]
　substantial doubt　重大な疑義
　◆Doubts over the effectiveness of the announced stock price measures have already been expressed among Japanese market players. 今回発表された株価対策の効果については、日本の市場関係者の間ですでに疑問視する声がある。

doubtful （形）疑わしい, 問題含みの, 不良の, 不確実な, 不確かな, 未決定の, 要注意の
　a doubtful account　信用力不安先
　doubtful accounts　不良債権　(=doubtful debt)
　doubtful bill [note]　不確実手形
　doubtful debt　延滞貸金, 不良貸付け金, 不良債権
　doubtful loan　焦げ付き融資, 問題含みの貸付け[貸出], 要注意貸付け, 回収疑問貸付け

Dow （名）ダウ
　Dow Chemical　ダウ・ケミカル（世界第2位の総合化学会社）
　Dow components　ダウ平均構成銘柄, ダウ平均採用銘柄
　New York Dow　ダウ平均, ニューヨーク・ダウ
　　(=NY Dow)
　Nikkei Dow average　日経平均株価
　the Dow　ダウ平均株価（工業株30種）, ダウ工業株平均
　　(=Dow Jones industrial average, Dow Jones industrials)
　◆The Dow fell 370.03, or 2.93 percent, to 12,265. ダウ平均株価（工業株30種）は、前日比370.03ドル安（2.93％減）の1万2,265ドルに続落した。

Dow Jones　ダウ・ジョーンズ工業株平均, ダウ工業株平均, ダウ・ジョーンズ社, DJ
　Dow Jones Composite　ダウ・ジョーンズ総合65種平均株価
　Dow Jones Index　ダウ・ジョーンズ指数
　◆The Dow Jones plunged 370 points after an economic report that the service sector shrank in January. 1月のサービス業の業況は悪化したとの経済報告を受けて、ダウ工業株平均は370ドル急落した。

Dow Jones average [Average]　ダウ・ジョーンズ平均, ダウ・ジョーンズ平均株価, 株式ダウ価平均, ダウ平均
　◆The Dow Jones average reached a four-month high of 9,374. ダウ・ジョーンズ平均は、9,374ドルで4か月ぶりの高値を付けた。

Dow Jones industrial average [Industrial Average]　ダウ工業株平均, ダウ工業株30種平均, ダウ（工業株30種）平均, ダウ平均, ダウ平均株価, DJIA
　(=Dow Jones industrials; ⇒Wall Street)
　◆Fears over the adverse effects of Greece's fiscal deficit briefly pushed the Dow Jones industrial average below 10,000. ギリシャの財政赤字に対する懸念から、ダウ平均株価は一時、1万ドルの大台を割った。

Dow Jones industrials　ダウ平均株価（工業株30種）
　(=Dow Jones Industrial Average; ⇒Wall Street)
　◆The Dow Jones industrials plunged 370 points after an unexpected contraction in the service sector. 予想しなかったサービス業の業況悪化を受けて、ダウ平均株価（工業株30種）は、前日比で370ドル急落した。

down （動）撃ち落とす, 撃墜する, 負かす, 飲み干す, 飲み込む　（名）下り, 下り坂, 下降, 不運, 不況　（形）下向きの, 下りの, 下落した, 低下した, 現金での, 頭金の, 即金での, 重苦しい, 陰気な　（副）下方へ, 下がって, 減少して, 現金で, 即金で, 頭金として, その場で
　down payment　頭金（initial payment）, 手付け金, 前渡し金, 自己投下資本
　◆The 225-issue Nikkei Stock Average ended down 149.56 points from the previous day, finishing at 8,165.18, the lowest close since ending at 8,109.53 on March 31, 2009. 日経平均株価（225種）の終値は前営業日比149円56銭安の8,165円18銭で、2009年3月31日の終値（8,109円53銭）以来の安値となった。

downbeat （形）重苦しい, 悲観的な, （見通しが）暗い, 暗たんとした, 陰気な, 下降傾向の, 盛り上がりのない
　(⇒upbeat)
　downbeat market sentiment　市場の暗い地合い
　downbeat outlook　暗い見通し, 見通しの暗さ

downdrift （名）（株の）下げ, 下げ足, 下降, 下落, 低下, 減少, 下押し
　be on the downdrift　減退傾向にある, 下降線をたどっている, 下げている, 下げ足だ
　the moderate downdrift of the price level　物価水準の緩やかな低下

downfall （名）没落, 凋落（ちょうらく）, 急落, 転落, 失脚, 破滅の原因, 大降り, どしゃ降り
　◆The downfall of the firm could trigger disturbances throughout the financial market. 同社の凋落（ちょうらく）は、金融市場全体の混乱を招く可能性がある。

downgrade （動）格下げする, 格付けを引き下げる, 下方修正する　(⇒economic assessment)
　◆If the negotiations between Republicans and Democrats face rough going and the deficit-cutting plan ends up being insufficient, credit rating agencies may downgrade Treasury bonds. 共和党と民主党の協議が難航し赤字削減策が不十分に終わると、(信用)格付け会社が米国債の格下げに踏み切る可能性がある。◆Moody's Investors Service Inc. downgraded its credit rating on Japanese government bonds. ムーディーズは、同社の日本国債の信用格付けを引き下げた。◆Moody's may downgrade the U.S. government's credit rating if it does not get its colossal deficits in better order. 米政府が膨大な財政赤字問題に目途をつけないと、ムーディーズは米国債の格付けを引き下げる可能性がある。◆Some credit rating agencies have hinted at the possibility of downgrading Japanese government bonds. 格付け会社のなかには、日本国債の格下げの可能性を示唆したところもある。◆Standard & Poor's downgraded Belgium's financial standing from AA+ to AA. スタンダード・アンド・プアーズ（S&P）は、ベルギー国債の格付けをダブルA（AA）プラスからダブルA（AA）に1段階引き下げた。◆U.S. Treasury bonds were downgraded by Standard & Poor's because the government failed to take drastic countermeasures against its fiscal deterioration. 米政府が財政悪化に大胆な対策を取れなかったため、米国債はスタンダード・アンド・プアーズ（S&P）に格下げされた。

downgrade （名）格下げ, 評価引下げ, 軽視, 下り坂, 悪化, 衰退, 左前　(⇒government debt ratios, upgrade)
　downgrades by credit rating agencies　格付け機関による評価引下げ
　rating downgrade　格下げ
　review for possible downgrade　格下げの方向で検討する
　under review for possible downgrade　格下げの方向で検討中, 格下げの方向で格付けを見直し中
　◆Moody's Investors Service Inc. is reviewing 14 British banks for possible downgrade. ムーディーズ・インベスター

ズ・サービスは現在、英銀14行の格付けを、格下げの方向で検討している。◆S&P's downgrades do not reflect an increase in Ford's risk of bankruptcy. スタンダード＆プアーズの格下げは、米フォードの倒産リスクの増大を反映していない。◆The downgrade reflects Standard and Poor's concern over the company's ability to avoid a further deterioration in its operating performance. この格下げは、同社の一段の業績悪化は避けられないとのスタンダード＆プアーズの懸念を反映している。◆The rating outlook of "negative" by a credit rating agency means that another downgrade is possible in the next 12 to 18 months. 信用格付け機関による「ネガティブ（弱含み）」の格付け見通しは、今後1年～1年半にふたたび格下げされる可能性があることを意味している。◆The United States' credit has come into question by the possible downgrade of the U.S. government's credit rating. 米国債の格付けが引き下げられる可能性があることから米国の信用が疑われている。

downgrade below investment grade 投資適格以下の格付け, 投機的格付けへの格下げ［引下げ］
　◆A downgrade below investment grade by even one ratings agency could boost GM's borrowing costs and wreak havoc on the corporate bond market. 格付け会社が1社でも投資適格格付けより低く格付けを引き下げたら［格付け会社が1社でも投機的格付けに格下げしたら］、GMの資金調達コストが急増し、米国の社債［債券］市場にも大きな影響が出る恐れがある。

downgrade of Treasury bonds 米国債の格下げ
　◆The possible downgrade of Treasury bonds is raising fears of adverse effects on the world's markets. 想定される米国債の格下げで、世界の市場に及ぼす悪影響への懸念が高まっている。

downgrading of the U.S. credit rating 米国債の格下げ
　◆Global turmoil in the financial markets results from the downgrading of the U.S. credit rating. 金融市場の世界的な混乱は、米国債の格下げによるものだ。◆Japan, the United States and European countries have failed to eliminate unease in the financial market after the recent downgrading of the U.S. credit rating. 日米欧は、今回の米国債格下げ後の金融市場の不安感を払拭（ふっしょく）できていない。◆Japan, the United States and European countries will cooperate to avert financial turmoil stemming from the downgrading of the U.S. credit rating. 日米欧が連携して、米国債の格下げによる金融市場の混乱を回避することになった。

downmarket［down-market］ （形）下げ相場の, 低所得消費者の, 低所得者層向けの, 大衆市場向けの, 低級の, 安物の

downside （名）株価などの下降傾向, 下落傾向, 下落, 下降気味, 業績悪化, 現役, 不利, 不利益, 不利な点, デメリット, 悪い面, 否定的な側面　（形）（株価などの）下降［下落］傾向の, 下降気味の, 不利な
　（⇒upside）
　downside potential 　下落する可能性
　downside protection 　下値不安の乏しさ
　downside relative to the market 　市場平均を下回る［アンダーパフォームする］リスク
　downside support line 　下値支持線
　　（=downside support）
　further downside 　一層の下落
　◆The downsides of being listed include obligations such as the disclosure of corporate information. 上場のデメリットとしては、企業情報の開示などの義務が挙げられる。

downside risk 下落する危険性, 価格下落の危険性, 下振れリスク, 下値（したね）リスク, 下値の余地, 業績悪化のリスク, 減益要因, 可能損失額, ダウンサイド・リスク
　（=downturn risk）
　be marked by downside risks 　下振れリスクが高まる
　rising downside risks 　下振れリスクの増大

　the downside risks to Japan's economy 　日本の景気［経済］が悪化するリスク　（⇒slowdown）
　the downside risks to the economy 　景気［経済］の下振れリスク, 景気が悪化するリスク
　◆Due to increasing uncertainty over the U.S. economic outlook and the yen's rise, the Bank of Japan warned of the downside risks to the nation's economy. 米経済の先行きをめぐる不確実性の高まりと円高で、日銀は日本経済の下振れリスクに警戒感を示した。◆Instability in global markets is increasing with rising downside risks. 下振れリスクの増大とともに、グローバル市場の不安定性は高まっている。◆The downside risks to Japan's economy will increase because concerns over a U.S. slowdown are growing. 米国の景気減速に対する懸念が高まっているため、日本の景気［日本経済］が悪化するリスクは増大している。◆The Japanese economy faces a growing downside risk due to concerns about the future of the U.S. and European economies. 日本経済は、欧米経済の先行き懸念から、景気の下振れリスクが高まっている。

downside risk of real estate prices 不動産価格の下落リスク
　◆It is unknown how the EU's stress test that measured the financial strength of Europe's major banks dealt with the downside risk of real estate prices. 欧州の主要銀行の財務内容［財務の健全性］を調べたEU（欧州連合）のストレス・テスト（特別検査）が、不動産価格の下落リスクをどのように扱ったかは不明だ。

downsize （動）規模を縮小する, 削減する, 人員削減する, 人員整理する, 経営を合理化する, リストラする, 小型化する, 軽量化する
　（=miniaturize, scale down）
　downsize drastically 　大幅に縮小する
　downsize the workforce 　人員を削減する
　downsize unprofitable sections 　不採算部門を縮小する
　◆In various industries, companies are not just downsizing, but are taking other measures, such as entering into cooperation agreements with other firms. 各種業界では、企業は経営の合理化だけでなく、他社と提携するなどの措置も取っている。

downsizing （名）小型化, 規模の縮小化, 縮小, 合理化, 人員整理, リストラ, 脱大型コンピュータ現象, ダウンサイジング　（=miniaturization, scaledown）
　downsizing of long-term auctions 　長期債入札額減額
　downsizing target 　合理化計画, 人員削減計画
　waves of downsizing 　リストラの波
　◆Half of the downsizing target planned for the year 2011 has already been met, with no redundancies being required. 人員過剰による解雇に踏み切るまでもなく、2011年までに予定している合理化［人員削減］計画の目標の半分がすでに達成した。◆Waves of downsizing are wearing down not only corporations and administrations, but also economic organizations. リストラの波は、企業や行政だけでなく、経済団体にも及んでいる。

downstream （名）川下部門, 下流部門, 石油精製・販売部門, 親会社から子会社への販売, ダウンストリーム
　downstream market 　川下部門
　downstream transaction 　ダウンストリーム取引
　downstream merger 　逆吸収合併（子会社が親会社を吸収すること）

downtick （名）景気の退潮, 前回の引け値より安い株価が付く相場の動き（minus tick）

downtrend （名）下降傾向, 下降局面, 下降トレンド, 下げ基調, 下向き, 下押し気配, 下げ足　（⇒uptrend）
　be in a downtrend 　下げ基調にある
　the current downtrend in the stock market 　現在の株安

downturn （名）低迷, 悪化, 下落, 下降, 下降局面, 落込

み, 景気の落込み, 冷え込み, 不況, 後退, 景気後退, 衰退, 不振　（⇒upturn）
business downturn　不景気, 景気後退
　（=downturn in business）
cyclical downturn　景気後退, 景気の悪化, 景気低迷
downturn in demand　需要の冷え込み, 需要の落込み
downturn in economic activity　景気減速
downturn in foreign economies　海外経済の下振れ
　（⇒backsliding）
economic downturn　景気後退, 景気の悪化, 景気低迷, 景気沈滞, 景気の下降局面
global downturn　世界不況, 世界同時不況, 世界的な景気後退　（=global economic downturn）
growth downturn　成長下降点
market downturn　市場低迷, 市場の悪化, 市場［相場］の下落, 市場の下げ
mini-downturn　ミニ不況
normal economic downturn　一般的な景気下降局面
prolong a downturn　景気後退を長引かせる
◆Before the bubble collapsed, many pundits had predicted that the likely downturn of the U.S. economy would have only a limited impact on the rest of the world. バブル経済の崩壊前には，「米経済はいずれ行き詰まるだろうが, 他国への影響は限定的である」と専門家の多くは予測していた。◆Business conditions are rapidly deteriorating due to the global financial crisis and the worldwide economic downturn. 世界的な金融危機と世界的な景気後退で, 景気は急速に悪化している。◆The BOJ has decided to take additional monetary easing steps as the nation's economic outlook is facing greater risks of a downturn than earlier expected. 日本の景気見通しは従来の予想より下振れリスクが高まっているため, 日銀は追加の金融緩和策の実施を決めた。◆The downturn in global financial markets has had a negative impact on insurance products such as single-premium pension insurance policies which are popular as a form of savings. 世界の金融市場の低迷が, 貯蓄用［一種の貯蓄］として人気の高い一時払い年金保険などの保険商品に悪影響を及ぼしている。◆The ongoing business slump raises the specter of a global downturn comparable to the Great Depression that started in 1929. 今回の不況は, 1929年に始まった世界大恐慌に匹敵するほどの世界同時不況の懸念が高まっている。◆There are growing signs of a business downturn in Japan. 日本では, 景気後退色が一段と強まっている。

downward　（形）下向きの, 下方への, 減少の, 落ち目の, 下落する, 下降する, 低下する, 低落する, 衰退する
　（副）下向きに, 減少へ, 低下して, 衰退して, 落ち目に, （上から）下まですべてにわたって
　（⇒upward）
be heading downward［downwards］　下降トレンドを描く
be revised downward　下方修正される
display downward bias　景気の弱さを示す
downward adjustment　下方修正
　（=downward revision）
downward drift　売り先行の展開, 減退傾向, 下降, 下落, 低下, 減少　（=downdrift）
downward movement of prices　物価下落［低落］の動き
downward phase　下降局面
downward revaluation　平価切下げ
downward rigidity of prices　価格の下方硬直性
downward rigidity of wages　賃金の下方硬直性
downward sloping demand　右下がりの需要
downward spiral　悪循環, 縮小均衡
downward swing　景気後退
drift slightly downward　下降気味である, 下押し気味である
from the president downward　社長をはじめ全社員
slight［modest］downward revision　小幅な下方修正
◆Other banks are likely forced to revise their earnings projections downward because of the accelerated disposal of bad loans, business deterioration of borrowers due to the lingering recession and further decline in stock prices. 不良債権処理の加速や長引く不況による融資先の業績悪化, 株安などの影響で, 他行も業績予想の下方修正を迫られている。◆The appreciation of the yen has pushed exports downward, slashing corporate profits. 円高で輸出が低迷し, 企業収益も減少している。

downward pressure　低下圧力, 引下げ圧力, 下げ圧力, 下押し圧力
be under downward pressure　下げ圧力［低下圧力］にさらされている, 下押し圧力下にある
downward pressure on the consumer price index　消費者物価指数に対する引下げ圧力
downward pressure on the wholesale price index　卸売り物価指数に対する引下げ圧力
downward share price pressure　株価の下げ圧力
◆Prices are under constant downward pressure. 物価は, 恒常的な下押し圧力下にある。◆The latest additional monetary ease put a downward pressure on interest rates. 今回の追加の金融緩和で, 金利は低下した。

downward revision　下方修正, 下方改定
downward revision of projected earnings　予想収益の下方修正
modest downward revision　小幅下方修正
◆Many expect losses from bad loan disposals to increase drastically, leading to an inevitable downward revision of banks' business performance. 大方の予想では, 不良債権処理に伴う損失額は今後大幅に増え, 銀行の業績の下方修正は避けられない状況だ。◆The downward revision of the fiscal 2011 growth projection was made due to a drastic slowdown in individual consumption and meager price increases. 2011年度の経済成長見通しの下方修正は, 個人消費の大幅な減速と物価上昇率の鈍化が原因だ。

downward risk　下方リスク, 損失リスク 損失リスク
◆Heightened tensions and significant downward risks for the global economy must be addressed decisively. 世界経済の緊張の高まりと重大な下方リスクに, 断固として対処しなければならない。

downward trend　下落傾向, 下落基調, 下降傾向, 下降トレンド, 低下局面
continuing downward trend　長期的下落傾向［下落トレンド］
downward trend of interest rates　金利の低下局面
◆If the current downward trend of stock prices continues, banks' financial resources that could be used to dispose of bad loans will decrease drastically. 株価の下落基調がこのまま続くと, 金融機関の不良債権処理の原資は激減する。

dowries　（名）民営化支度金, （新婦の）持参金
DPS　1株当たり配当金（dividend per shareの略）
draconian［Draconian］　（形）厳しい, 厳格な, 過酷な, 思い切った
draconian cure for the deficit　厳しい［思い切った］赤字削減策
draconian cut in budget outlays　厳しい財政支出の削減
◆The Bank of Japan should take draconian measures to rectify the rise in the yen's value. 日銀は, 厳しい円高是正措置を取るべきだ。

draft　（動）設計する, 起草する, （下図を）書く, 選抜する, 抜擢（ばってき）する, 徴兵［徴募, 召集］する, 移動する,

派遣する
draft a bill　法案を起草する
draft a contract　契約書を作成する
draft a plan　計画を立てる
draft this year's budget　今年[今年度]の予算を編成する
◆TEPCO is drafting a special business plan as the premise for getting government financial aid. 東電は、政府の金融支援を受ける前提として、特別事業計画を策定している。◆The federal government played a leading role in drafting the restructuring plan of GM. 米政府は、ゼネラル・モーターズの再建計画作りで主導的役割を果たした[GMの再建計画作りを主導した]。

draft　(名)為替手形,手形,小切手,支払い指図書,図案,下絵,草稿,草案,通風装置,選抜,徴兵,ドラフト　(⇒current deposit)
accept a draft　手形を引き受ける
bank draft　銀行振出手形,銀行為替手形,銀行手形,送金小切手　(=banker's draft)
buy a draft　手形を買い入れる
cable draft　電報為替　(=telegraphic draft)
clean draft　普通為替
collect a draft　手形を取り立てる
commercial draft　商業手形
date draft　期日後支払い手形
demand draft　要求払い手形,送金小切手,D/D　(=draft on demand)
discount a draft　手形を割り引く
discount draft　割引手形
dishonored draft　不渡り手形　(=unpaid draft)
documentary draft　荷為替手形
dollar draft　ドル建て払い手形
draft acceptance　手形引受
draft at 30 days' date　日付後30日払い手形
draft drawn at 90 days after sight　一覧後90日払い手形
draft endorsed　手形被裏書人
draft endorsement　手形裏書き
draft endorser　手形裏書人
draft extension　手形支払い期限延長
draft for collection　取立手形
draft holder　手形所持人
draft instructions　手形振出指図
draft rehabilitation plan　更生計画案
draft stock attached　株券付き株金募集手形
draft treaty wording　再保険特約書原案
draft with documents attached　荷為替
draft without recourse　無償還請求手形
draw a draft　手形を振り出す
draw a draft on　〜を支払い人とする手形を振り出す
endorse a draft　手形の裏書きをする
import draft　輸入手形
installment draft　賦払い手形
issue a draft on　〜宛に手形を振り出す
long draft　長期手形　(=long-term draft)
make a draft on [upon]　〜から資金を引き出す
negotiable draft　為替手形,流通手形,流通可能手形
negotiation by draft　手形買取り
pay by draft　手形で支払う
protest of a draft　手形の拒絶証書
recourse draft　償還請求権付き手形
reimbursement draft　償還手形
sight draft　一覧払い手形
　(=draft at [on] sight)
30 days' draft　30日後払い手形
Time draft　定期払い手形
unpaid draft　不渡り手形
◆According to JAL's draft rehabilitation plan, 87.5 percent of the airline's loan will be waived by its banks and other creditors. 日航の更生計画案では、同社借金[借入金]の87.5%は、銀行その他の債権者が免除することになる。◆The draft of the government's new growth strategy includes the establishment of a public-private investment fund to support the content industry in its foreign endeavors. 政府の新成長戦略の原案には、コンテンツ(情報の内容)産業の海外展開を支援する官民出資のファンド設立も盛り込まれている。◆We drew a draft for the invoice amount. 送り状金額に対して、当社は手形を振り出した。

drag　(名)景気などの押し下げ効果,押し下げ要因,減速効果,マイナス要因,阻害要因,邪魔物,足かせ
drag from inventory adjustment　在庫調整による景気押し下げ効果
drag on GDP growth　経済成長率を押し下げる要因,成長率を押し下げる要因
drag on the economy　景気押し下げ効果,景気減速要因,成長率の押し下げ要因,経済成長の足を引っ張る要因
fiscal drag　財政面からの景気押し下げ効果

drain　(動)流出させる,排出する,飲み干す,空にする,使い果たす,枯渇させる,消耗させる,吸い上げる
drain liquidity from the market　市場から流動性を吸い上げる
drain one's savings　貯金を食いつぶす
draining liquidity　流動性の吸い上げ
◆Insurance payments for the March 11 earthquake and tsunami will drain the resources of insurance firms and the government's special account. 東日本大震災の保険金支払いで、保険会社と政府の特別会計の原資は大幅に目減りすることになる。

drain　(名)(頭脳などの)流出,(資源などの)枯渇[無駄遣い],減少,漸減,消耗,消失,負担(burden),金食い虫
cash drain　現金流出　(=drain on cash)
dollar drain　金の流出,資金流出,ドル流出
down the drain　経営状態が悪化して,非常に悪化[低下]して,浪費されて,無駄になって
drain of specie from a country　正貨の国外流出
drain on liquidity　流動性の枯渇
economic drain　経済的消耗,経済的負担
enormous drain on the domestic economy　国内経済に対する莫大な負担
internal drain　内部的枯渇
liquidity drain　流動性の流出,流動性の枯渇,流動性の吸い上げ
technology drain　技術流出
◆The yen's appreciation will accelerate the drain of domestic companies from Japan to other countries. 円高で、日本企業の海外流出が加速するものと思われる。

dramatic　(形)劇的な,急激な,大幅な,ダイナミックな,印象的な,めざましい,注目に値する,驚くような,大げさな
dramatic change　劇的な変化,急激な変化
dramatic economic growth　急激な経済成長,経済の急成長,ダイナミックな経済成長
dramatic effect　劇的な効果
dramatic events　劇的な出来事
dramatic increase in interest rates　金利の急激な上昇
◆The dramatic plunge in the profits of Toyota was triggered by the U.S. financial crisis. トヨタの大幅減益の発端は、米国の金融危機だった。

drastic (形)思い切った, 大胆な, 抜本的な, 徹底した, 徹底的な, 大幅な, 急激な, 激烈な, 猛烈な, 大型の, 大規模な
 drastic cost-cutting efforts 徹底したコスト削減努力
 drastic deregulation measures 極端な規制緩和策
 drastic inventory reduction 在庫の大幅削減
 drastic restructuring 大規模なリストラ
 drastic slowdown in individual consumption 個人消費の大幅な鈍化
 drastic strategic measures 大胆な戦略的動き
 drastic tax-reduction measures 大型減税策, 大型減税措置

drastic countermeasures 思い切った対策, 抜本的な対策, 大胆なメス
 ◆The U.S. government failed to take drastic countermeasures against its fiscal deterioration. 米政府は、財政悪化に抜本的な対策を取れなかった[大胆なメスを入れられなかった]。◆U.S. Treasury bonds were downgraded by Standard & Poor's because the government failed to take drastic countermeasures against its fiscal deterioration. 米政府が財政悪化に大胆な対策を取れなかったため、米国債はスタンダード・アンド・プアーズ(S&P)に格下げされた。

drastic cuts in spending 支出の大幅削減, 支出の大幅カット
 ◆Austerity measures such as drastic cuts in spending on public works projects should be avoided. 公共事業[公共事業費]の大幅カットなどの緊縮政策は、避けるべきだ。

drastic overhaul of accounting system 会計制度[基準]の抜本的変更, 会計基準の抜本的見直し
 ◆The drastic overhaul of the Japanese accounting system is expected to add a massive administrative burden to companies. 日本の会計基準の抜本的変更は、企業にとって大幅な事務負担の増加を強いられることになる。

drastic personnel change 大幅な人事刷新
 ◆The bank will conduct a drastic personnel change and replace about 20 senior officials. 同行は、大幅な人事刷新を行い、幹部約20人を更迭する方針だ。

drastic reform 抜本的改革, 抜本改革
 ◆Drastic reform of the tax system is necessary to restore the nation's fiscal health. 日本の財政健全化には、税制の抜本改革が必要だ。

drastic slowdown 大幅な減速, 大幅な鈍化
 ◆The downward revision of the fiscal 2011 growth projection was made due to a drastic slowdown in individual consumption and meager price increases. 2011年度の経済成長見通しの下方修正は、個人消費の大幅な減速と物価上昇率の鈍化が原因だ。◆The nation's three megabank groups will likely see a drastic slowdown in their business performance in the second half of this fiscal year. 日本の三大メガバンクの今年度下半期の業績は、大幅に鈍化する見通しだ。

draw (動)引き出す, 得る, おろす, (利子)を生む, (小切手・手形)を振り出す, 実行する, (文書などを)起草する, 起案する, 立案する
 a draft drawn at 60 days after sight 一覧後60日払い手形
 drafts drawn in sets of two 2通1組で振り出された手形
 draw a check for $50 on the bank 銀行に50ドルの小切手を振り出す
 draw a check on the bank 同行を支払い人とする小切手を振り出す
 draw a draft at 60 d/s under a confirmed credit to be opened in our favor for the corresponding value of an order 注文相当金額に対して当社を受益者とした確認信用状に基づいて一覧後60日払いの為替手形を振り出す
 draw down existing stocks 在庫を取り崩す
 draw (down) funds 資金を引き出す
 draw down the funds immediately 貸出を即時実行する
 draw money from savings 預金から資金を引き出す
 draw on the loan 資金を引き出す
 draw on you our sight draft 一覧払い手形を貴社宛に振り出す
 draw out excessive liquidity 過剰流動性を吸収する
 draw (out) money from the bank account 銀行口座から金を引き出す
 fully draw the loan within 10 days 10日以内に融資を実行する
 ◆There were apparent moves among companies drawing more money from savings to accumulate operating funds. 明らかな動きとして、企業は運転資金を積み増すため、預金から資金を引き出している。◆We have drawn on you our sight draft No. 10 for the invoice amount, $50,000, under your L/C No. B-50 of XYZ Co. 当社は、XYZ株式会社の信用状B-50号により、送り状金額5万ドルに対して当社の一覧払い手形10号を貴社宛に振り出しました。

draw up 作成する, 作る, 立案する
 draw up a blueprint for ～の綿密な計画を立てる[立案する]
 draw up a will 遺言書を作成する
 draw up an agreement [contract] 契約書を作成する
 ◆JAL has yet to draw up a plan for its turnaround that will fly. 日航は、まだ企業再生計画を作成していない。

drawdown (名)削減, 縮小, 低下, 減少, ローンによる資金の調達, 資金引出し, 資金引出し実行, 借用, 貸出の実行, 融資実行手続き
 drawdown date 融資実行日, 貸出実行日
 drawdown period 資金引出し可能期間, 資金引出し期間
 drawdown swap アキュムレーション・スワップ
 （=accumulation swap: 本が徐々に増額する借入れなどに利用される）
 drawdowns of the export credits 輸出信用の資金引出し

drawee (名)手形名宛人
 drawee bank 名宛銀行
 drawee of a bill 手形名宛人

drawer (名)手形振出人, 振出人, 引出し, タンス
 cash drawer 現金引出し
 check drawer 小切手振出人
 Refer to Drawer 振出人に問い合わせのこと（資金不足で不渡り返還する場合の文言）

drawer savings タンス預金
 （⇒sugar-bowl savings）
 ◆The BOJ (Bank of Japan) believes the Japanese possess about ¥30 trillion in drawer savings. 日本人のタンス預金として30兆円程度ある、と日銀は見ている。

drawing (名)金銭の引出し, 手形の振出し, 貸付け実行, くじ引き, 抽選, 抽選会, 図面, 製図, デッサン
 drawing account 引出金勘定
 drawing advice 送金小切手取組み通知書
 drawing bank 振出銀行
 drawing of bill 手形の振出し
 notice of drawing 借入通知書
 private drawing 私的引出し
 redemption by drawing 抽選償還
 Special Drawing Rights 対外決済に用いられるIMF(国際通貨基金)の特別引出権

drawn (形)引き出された, 振り出された
 drawn bill 振出手形
 drawn bond 抽選償還券, 抽選済み債券
 drawn funds 引き出された資金

dress up 粉飾する (=window-dress)
 ◆In WorldCom's accounting fraud, it dressed up fees payable to other telecoms not as expenses, but as capital in-

vestments. 米通信大手ワールドコムの会計操作では、他の通信会社に支払う回線使用料を経費に計上せず、資本投資[設備投資]に計上していた。

drift (動)流れる、ゆっくり動く、緩やかに変動する、移動する、変化する (名)流れ、動き、移動、緩やかな変化、展開、傾向、趨勢
 continue to drift upwards　　続伸する
 drift downwards　　下げる、力なく下げる
 drift in a narrow range　　もみ合う、もみ合いの展開となる
 drift slowly uphill　　緩やかに上向く
 drifting management　　成行き管理
 rating drift　　格付けの趨勢
 wage drift　　協定外賃金
 ◆The stock continued to drift upwards. 株価は、続伸した。

drifting-down (名)下降、下落、減少、低下

drive (動)運転する、牽引する、～の原動力[牽引力]になる、～を動かす、～をもたらす、～を喚起する、駆り立てる、無理に～させる
 be driven by　　～を原動力とする、～が追い風になる、～が大きな意味を持つ
 drive a hard bargain　　一方的に条件を押し付ける
 drive credit demand　　信用需要を喚起する、信用需要の牽引力となる
 drive customer demand　　消費者需要を喚起する
 drive down cash yields　　債券利回りの低下を招く[もたらす]、～で債券利回りが低下する
 drive down interest rates　　金利を下げる、金利を引き下げる
 drive growth　　成長をもたらす、成長の原動力となる
 drive Japan's economic recovery　　日本の景気回復を牽引する　(⇒recovery)
 drive long-dated interest rates lower　　長期金利の引下げを狙う　(⇒long-dated)
 drive the markets　　相場を動かす
 drive the rout　　総崩れを招く、総崩れとなる
 drive yields down　　利回りの低下を招く[もたらす]
 ◆Higher raw material prices are driving demand from blue-chip companies for loans. 原材料高の影響で、優良企業の借入需要が増えている。◆Japan's economic growth is driven by exports, but it will have to vie for export markets with emerging economies. 日本の経済成長の原動力は輸出だが、今後は新興国と輸出市場の争奪戦になろう。◆Overly radical methods for accelerating the disposal of bad loans would panic the banking sector and the financial market, possibly driving banks to shy away from extending new loans and even to call in existing loans. 不良債権処理を加速するための余りにも強硬な手法は、銀行や金融市場をおびえさせ、貸し渋りや貸しはがしにつながることにもなる。◆Speculation that some major banks may find themselves with capital shortfalls and then nationalized is driving investors to dump the banks' shares. 大手行の一部が自己資本不足に陥って国有化されるとの思惑から、投資家は銀行株の売りに出ている。◆Worries over the spreading of the eurozone debt crisis and the U.S.'s slipping into recession have driven the rout in financial markets. ユーロ圏の財政危機の拡大と米国の景気後退入りへの懸念で、金融市場は総崩れになった。

-driven (形)～志向の、～主導の、～主導型、～優先の、～中心の　(= -led, led by)
 export-driven　　輸出主導の、輸出主導型
 futures-driven　　先物取引中心の
 market-driven　　市場原理に基づく　(=market-oriented)
 order-driven　　注文主導型の
 profit-driven　　利益志向の、利益志向の強い (=profit-oriented)
 retail-driven　　個人投資家主導の
 scale-driven　　数量効果が大きい
 swap-driven　　スワップ主導型の
 ◆A depreciation of the dollar may stimulate external demand and ignite an export-driven economic upturn. ドル安は、外需を喚起して、輸出主導の景気回復につながる可能性がある。◆A recovery will be export-driven, dependent on U.S. growth and the yen's depreciation, instead of being led by increased domestic consumption and capital investment. 今後の景気回復は、アメリカ経済の好転や円安を背景にした輸出主導型の回復で、国内の個人消費や設備投資の伸びがその牽引役となるわけではない。

driver (名)原動力、推進力、牽引役、エンジン、主因、ドライバー　(=cause, driving force)
 growth driver　　成長の原動力
 key drivers　　重要な原動力[推進力]、主要な原動力、主因
 main drivers　　主因　(=key drivers)
 ◆Six emerging economies (the BRICs nations plus Indonesia and South Korea) will become the major drivers of global economic growth. これからは、新興6か国(ブラジル、ロシア、インド、中国にインドネシアと韓国)が、世界の経済成長の主要な原動力になる。◆The United States and European markets are the main drivers of foreign demand. 欧米市場は、外需の主要なエンジン(原動力)である。

driving force　　原動力、推進力、牽引役、牽引車、テコ、主因　(=driver)
 ◆Corporate capital investment has been a driving force for the economic upturn. 企業の設備投資が、景気回復の牽引役となっている。◆Housing investment, a driving force for the U.S. economy until recently, has shown signs of a slowdown. 最近まで米景気を牽引してきた住宅投資に、減速感が見られる。◆The government assumes a scenario in which Japan's economic growth will shift into high gear with overseas demand as a driving force. 政府は、海外需要をテコに日本の経済成長が本格化する、とのシナリオを描いている。

drop (動)落とす、落下させる、下げる、引き下げる(cut)、降ろす、(数、量を)減らす、投下する、止める(call off, cancel, scrap)、(計画などを)断念する、中止する、(関係を)断つ、手を切る、(訴訟)取り下げる、口にする、ほのめかす、解雇する、除名する、除外する、排除する、省略する、(物を)返す、返却する、(麻薬などを)飲む　(自動)減少する、低下する、下落する、落ち込む、悪化する　(=decrease, fall; ⇒lowering)
 drop a full point　　1％低下する
 drop below　　～を割り込む
 drop economic sanctions　　経済制裁を止める
 drop money over the transaction　　取引で損をする
 drop out of the deal　　案件から手を引く
 drop sharply　　急減する、急速に減少する、急落する
 drop significantly　　大幅に減少する、大幅に悪化する
 drop to　　～まで落ち込む
 drop to a new low for 2011　　年初来の最低を更新する
 ◆Broader stock indicators such as the S&P 500 index and the Nasdaq composite index also dropped in February. 2月は、S&P500株価指数やナスダック総合株価指数などの総合株価指数も、低下[下落]した。◆Due to confusion in the financial markets, interest rates have declined significantly and global stock prices have dropped. 金融市場の混乱で、金利が大幅に低下し、世界的に株価も下落している。◆GM shares dropped $1, or 23 percent, to close at $3.36. GM株[GMの株価]の終値は、1ドル安(23％下落)の3.36ドルだった。◆Prices have dropped more steeply than those at the time when the BOJ was fighting deflation, and the rate of declining is expected to increase. 日銀がデフレと戦っていた時より物価は急激に下

DROP

がり、下落率は今後さらに拡大する見込みだ。◆Shinsei and Aozora banks have dropped their merger deal. 新生銀行とあおぞら銀行が、両行の合併計画を断念した[合併協議を中止した]。◆Short selling is the practice of borrowing stocks from securities and financial companies and other investors to sell them and then buy them back when their prices drop. 空売りは、証券金融会社や他の投資家(機関投資家など)から株を借りて売り、その株が値下がりした時点で買い戻すことをいう。◆Standard & Poor's dropped the U.S. rating by one notch for the first time. スタンダード・アンド・プアーズ(S&P)が、米国債の格付けを史上初めて1段階引き下げた。◆Stock prices have dropped to an all-time low since the collapse of the bubble economy. 株価は、バブル崩壊後の最安値まで落ち込んだ。◆The deflator, which indicates the overall trend in prices, dropped 2.5 percent in the April-June period compared to the corresponding period last year. 物価の総合的な動向を示すデフレーターは、4-6月期は前年同期比で2.5%下落した。◆The dollar's value temporarily dropped to the ¥85 level in New York. ドル相場は、ニューヨーク市場で一時、85円台まで下落した[値を下げた]。◆The market is dropping. 相場は、下がっている。◆The 225-issue Nikkei Stock Average dropped below the 9,000 mark Wednesday to close at the year's low of 8,845.39. 水曜日の日経平均株価(225種)は、9,000円台を割り込み、終値は今年最安値の8,845円39銭となった。◆The U.S. dollar dropped to a fresh 15-year low in the lower ¥82 level. 米ドル相場は82円台前半まで下落し、15年ぶりに最安値を更新した。◆The U.S. dollar has dropped sharply in value not only against the yen, but also against the euro, the South Korean won, the Thai baht and other currencies. 米ドルは、円に対してだけでなく、ユーロや韓国ウォン、タイ・バーツなどに対しても、急落している。◆The U.S. dollar temporarily dropped to the ¥84 level in Tokyo. 東京市場では、米ドルは一時、1ドル=84円台まで下落した。◆Uncertainty has prevailed as the value of the euro dropped sharply. ユーロの相場が急落したため、不安[動揺]が広がっている。

drop (名)減少, 低下, 下落, 落ち込み, 低迷, 悪化
 drop in asset quality　資産内容の悪化
 drop in demand　需要の減少, 需要の落込み, 需要の減退
 drop in earnings　減益
  (=drop in income, drop in profits)
 drop in machinery orders　機械受注の減少
 drop in oil prices　原油の値下り
 drop in output　生産低下, 生産の落込み
 drop in profits　減益
 drop in U.S. interest rates　米国の金利低下
 ◆A one-yen drop in the exchange rate against the U.S. dollar would lead to the loss of about ¥200 million in annual profits for the company. 対米ドル為替レートで1円の円安が、同社の場合は年間で約2億円の減益となる。◆Some European nations which are experiencing fiscal crises seem to rely on drops in their currencies' values as a means of underpinning their economies. 財政危機問題を抱えた欧州諸国の一部は、景気下支えの手段として通貨安を頼みにしているようだ。◆Speculation that the drop in U.S. interest rates will reduce the gap between Japanese and U.S. interest rates has encouraged dollar selling. 米国の金利低下で日米の金利差が縮小するとの見方から、ドルが売られている。◆The drops in bond prices in the past half a year have dealt these banks a heavy blow. 過去半年の債券価格の下落で、これらの銀行が大打撃を受けている。◆The major securities house attributed the poor earnings to sharp drops in brokerage fees and trading profits amid the extended slump in the domestic stock market. この大手証券会社は、減益の要因として、国内株式市場の長期低迷による株売買手数料と売買益の大幅減を挙げた。

dual (形)二重の, 両用の, 二元的な
 dual bank rate system　二重公定歩合制度
 dual banking (system)　二重銀行制度(米国の国法銀行と州法銀行の併存制度)
 dual budget system　二重予算制度
 dual capacity　(株式仲買と株式自己売買の)2業務兼営, 兼任, 兼務
 dual chartering　二元免許
 dual circulation period　二重流通期間, 移行期間
 dual control　二重管理, 二重統制
 dual corporate tax system　外形標準課税　(=local corporate tax formula based on the size of business)
 dual economy　二重経済
 dual effect of investment　投資の二重効果
 dual exchange market　二重為替市場, 二重為替市場制
 dual exchange rate system　二重為替相場制, 二重レート (=dual rate system)
 dual exchange rates (the official and swap rates)　中国の二重相場制(公定レートと外貨調整センター・レート)
 dual foreign exchange market　二重相場市場
 dual fund　デュアル・ファンド(dual-purpose fund: 値上がり益と利子配当収入を目的とするもののいずれかを選択できる投資信託)
 dual income family　共働きの家庭
 dual interest policy　二重金利政策
 dual monetary unit　通貨の複本位制
 dual nature [character] of investment　投資の二重性, 投資の二面性
 dual price of gold　金の二重価格
 dual pricing　二重価格制, 二重価格表示
 dual-purpose fund　二重目的ファンド (=dual fund)
 dual rate system　二重運賃制, 二重為替相場制(dual exchange rate system)
 dual responsibility　二重責任(財務諸表・財務書類の作成については経営者、監査報告書の作成については監査人がそれぞれ責任を負うこと)
 dual tariff　二重関税, 複関税
 dual tariff system　二重税率制
 dual taxation　二重課税
 dual trading　二重取引, 二者取引, 二重勘定取引, 向かい呑み行為

dual currency　二重通貨, デュアル・カレンシー
 dual currency bond　二重通貨建て債, 複数通貨建て債, 二重通貨債, デュアル・カレンシー債
 dual currency issue　デュアル・カレンシー債
 dual currency liabilities　デュアル・カレンシー債務
 dual currency loan　二重通貨建てローン
 on a dual currency basis　二重通貨建てで, 二重通貨建ての
 reverse dual currency bond [issue]　逆デュアル・カレンシー債

dual debt　二重ローン, 二重債務
 (=double debt, double loan)
 ◆Measures to lessen the problem of dual debts or multiple debts were also studied at the time of the 1995 Great Hanshin Earthquake. 二重ローンや多重債務問題の軽減は、1995年の阪神大震災の際にも検討された。

dual debt problem　二重ローン問題
 (=double debt problem)
 ◆In dealing with the dual debt problem due to the March 11 disaster, financial institutions will be forced to share certain burdens. 東日本大震災による二重ローン問題への対応では、金融機関もある程度の共同負担を強いられることになろう。

dual exchange rate　二重為替相場, 二重相場, 二重相

場制
◆In January 2002, Argentine President Eduardo Duhalde abandoned the peso's decade long one-to-one peg to the U.S. dollar, replacing it with a dual exchange rate. アルゼンチンのドゥアルデ大統領は2002年1月、10年続いた1ドル＝1ペソの固定相場制を廃止して、代わりに二重相場制を導入した。

dual-list （動）重複上場する
（⇒delist, list, publicly list, relist）
◆Six NYSE-listed blue-chip companies agreed to dual-list on Nasdaq and NYSE. ニューヨーク証券取引所に上場している優良企業6社が、ナスダック（米店頭株式市場）とNYSEへの重複上場に合意した。

dub （動）〜と呼ぶ、〜と称する、あだ名を付ける、（他言語に）吹き替える、追加録音する、音響効果を加える、（せりふや音楽を）入れる、（複数の録音を）合成録音する、（録音したものを）複製［再録音］する、ダビングする
◆Major Asian markets such as Shanghai and Hong Kong also show a situation that could be dubbed as a spontaneous global market crash. 上海や香港などアジアの主要市場も、世界同時株安の様相を見せている。◆The former head of the Murakami Fund was often dubbed a shareholder who demands a lot. 村上ファンドの元代表は、「モノ言う株主」とよく呼ばれた。

Dubai shock [debt crisis, crisis] 中東ドバイ発の金融不安、ドバイ信用不安、ドバイ信用問題、ドバイ・ショック（アラブ首長国連邦のドバイ政府が2009年11月25日、政府系持ち株会社ドバイ・ワールドの債務返済繰り延べを要請したのに伴って生じた世界的な相場急落の現象）
◆On Dec. 1, 2009, the Nikkei Stock Average was bearing down on the 9,000 mark due to the so-called Dubai shock. 2009年12月1日の日経平均株価（225種）は、いわゆるドバイ・ショック（中東ドバイの金融不安）で、9,000円台を割り込む寸前まで追いつめられていた。

dubious （形）疑わしい（questionable）、不確かな、はっきりしない、信頼できない、いかがわしい（shady）、うさんくさい（suspicious）
a dubious answer　はっきりしない返事
a dubious capital increase　架空増資
a dubious creditworthiness screening standard　甘い与信審査基準
assets of dubious value　価値が不明確な［はっきりしない］資産
dubious scheme for making money　金儲けの怪しげな計画
◆JAL's creditor banks are dubious about JAL's chances of getting back on its feet. 日航の取引銀行団は、日航再建の可能性については懐疑的だ。◆The collapse of Dai-ichi Kaden on April 16 was the result of speculation by foreign investment funds of a dubious nature. 4月16日の第一家電の経営破たんは、実態不明の海外投資ファンドの投機によるものであった［海外ファンドの投機に食い荒らされた末路であった］。◆The creditworthiness screening standard of U.S. subprime loans was dubious. 米国の低所得者向け住宅ローン「サブプライム・ローン」の与信審査基準は、甘かった。

dubious capital increase 架空増資
◆The former company president was indicted on fraud charges regarding a dubious capital increase in the firm. この元社長は、架空増資に関する詐欺罪で起訴された。

dud （形）役に立たない、価値のない、無能な、偽の
（名）失敗、へま、役に立たないもの、にせもの、不発弾
dud check　空手形、不渡り小切手
dud coin　偽造硬貨

due （名）料金、勘定、組合費、会員費、会費、使用料、賦課金、負担金
a due from account [balance]　他店貸し勘定
a due to account [balance]　他店借り勘定
annual dues　年会費
club dues　クラブ会費
harbor dues　入港税
membership dues　会費、会員負担金
port dues　入港税

due （形）正当な、正式の、適切な、適正な、適法の、合法の、十分な、相当の、合理的な、履行義務のある、支払い義務のある、満期の、支払い期日のきた、満期の過ぎた、当然支払われるべき、予定されている、〜する予定の（⇒policyholders' representative meeting）
account due　未収金
amount due　満期支払い高
amounts due　債務金額
amounts due from subsidiaries　子会社への預け金
be past due　遅延する、支払い期日を経過する
become due　支払い期日のきた、支払わなければならなくなる
collateral payment due date　担保の支払い日
due and deferred premiums　未収保険金
due bill　借用証書、到期手形
due from banks [bankers]　他行貸し勘定
due from correspondents　外国他店貸し、コルレス先預け金
due from foreign banks　外国他店貸し
due to banks [bankers]　他行借り勘定
due to foreign banks　他店借り勘定、外国銀行借り勘定、コルレス先預り金
due within one year　1年以内に満期を迎える
past due loan　延滞ローン
premium due　未払い保険料
the interest due　支払い利息
the payment due　満期の来た支払い
the principal becomes due　元本が満期償還となる
use due care　相当の注意を払う
◆Any payment not made when due will, in addition to any other right or remedy of Licensor, incur a finance charge at the lesser of three hundred basis points over the 3-month London Inter Bank Offered Rate ("LIBOR+3") on the date payment was due or the highest applicable legal contract rate. 支払いが支払い期日までに履行されない場合、ライセンサーの他の権利や救済請求権に加えて、支払い期日時点の3か月物ロンドン銀行間取引金利（LIBOR）プラス3%（LIBOR＋3%）または適用される最高法定約定金利のうち、いずれか低いほうの金利の金融費用が発生する。◆During the first nine months of 2011, the company completed public offerings of $125 million of 9.45% Debentures, due 2021 and $125 million of 10.50% Debentures, due 2018. 2011年1-9月期に同社は、2021年満期9.45%社債1億2,500万ドルと2018年満期10.50%社債1億2,500万ドルを公募発行した。◆In addition to long-term debt maturing during the year, the company redeemed all of its U.S. $150 million debentures, due 2013, in June 2011. 当年度に満期が到来する長期債務のほか、同社は2013年満期の社債1億5,000万米ドルの全額を、2011年6月に償還した。◆In Canada, the firm issued $300 million of 9% Series 7 Notes, due 2012. カナダで同社は、満期2012年・利率9%のシリーズ7ノート3億ドルを発行した。◆On April 25, 2010, the company sold $300 million of 95/8% notes, due 2015, in the European market to refinance short-term borrowings. 2010年4月25日に同社は、短期借入金の借り換えを行うため、欧州で2015年満期・利率9.625%ノート3億ドルを発行した。◆The percentage of credit card payments that were past due fell in the January-March quarter. クレジット・カードの支払い遅延率［期限を過ぎたクレジット・カードの返済遅延率］は、1-3月期に急減した。

due date 支払い期日, 満期日, 履行期日, 期日 (=date of payment)
  due date of bills 手形の満期
  from due date until paid 支払い期日から支払われる日まで
  from the due date to the date of payment in full 支払い期日から全額支払い日まで (⇒base rate)
  ◆Any unpaid amount shall bear interest from due date until paid. 未払い金額については, 支払い期日から支払われる日まで利息が付くものとする。

due diligence 相当の注意, 正当な努力, 監査手続き (契約締結前, 契約交渉中または契約締結後クロージング前に監査法人や法律事務所によって行われる財務面と法的な監査手続き), 財務調査, 事前精査, デュー・ディリジェンス (=due diligence investigation)

due diligence investigation 事業買収前のデュー・ディリジェンス調査, 事前精査 (事業買収希望者が譲渡側の協力を得て行う専門家による買収対象会社の資産, 債務, 財務内容や営業内容, 従業員などに関する調査)

due insurance benefits 支払う義務のある保険金
  ◆Financial Services Agency has ordered 26 nonlife insurance firms to correct their business practices, after finding they failed to pay due insurance benefits. 損保各社が支払う義務のある保険金を支払わなかったことが判明したため, 金融庁は損保26社に対して業務を正命令を出した。

due term 支払い期日, 期日, 期限
  ◆The National Bank of Cuba will not be able to pay for imports into Cuba in due terms as the country is short of settlement funds. キューバ国立銀行は今後, 国全体の決済資金不足で, 期日どおりにキューバへの輸入代金の支払いができなくなる状況にある。

due to 〜のために, 〜の原因で, 〜で
  due to concern about the financial crisis in Europe 欧州の金融危機を懸念して
  due to the credit uncertainty 信用不安のため, 信用不安で
  ◆Domestic bank are stepping up oversea project financing due to the lack of growth in lending to domestic borrowers amid protracted deflation at home. 国内銀行各行は, 国内ではデフレが続いて[デフレが続く状況で]国内融資先への貸出が伸びていないことから, 海外の事業向け融資を強化している。◆Due to delays in ratification of the agreement on bailout measures by some eurozone countries, concrete measures to rescue Greece have yet to be carried out. 支援策の合意事項について一部のユーロ圏加盟国の承認が遅れたため, ギリシャ救済の具体策はまだ実施されていない。◆Due to the growing strength of the yen, even if exporters' sales grow, their profits will not keep pace. 円高進行で, 輸出企業の売上が増えても, 利益は伸び悩むようだ。◆Japan Airlines Corp. is expected to fall short of its planned fund-raising target by about ¥50 billion due to lower stock price. 日本航空では, 株価の下落で, 当初計画の資金調達目標を約500億円下回る見通しだ。◆On the foreign exchange market, there has been no halt to selling pressure on the euro due to concern about the financial crisis in Europe. 外国為替市場では, 欧州の金融危機を懸念して, ユーロ売り圧力が止まらない展開となっている。◆The yields on Greek government bonds have been rising sharply due to the credit uncertainty. ギリシャ国債の利回りは, 信用不安で急上昇している。

dull (形)元気のない, 不活発な, 閑散な, 低迷した, 停滞した, 沈滞した, 不振の, 軟調な, (商売が)振るわない, (商品などが)さばけない, 需要がない, 鈍い, さえない, 切れ味の悪い, 単調な, 面白くない, 飽き飽きする, 退屈な (⇒sluggish)
  dull market 元気のない市場, 軟調な市場, 景気の悪い市場, 不活発な市場, 閑散な市況
  dull sales volume 販売数量の低迷
  dull tone 低迷
  dull trade 商況不振, 不活発な[停滞した]市況, 活気のない商況
  ◆The stock market is dull. 株式市場は, 閑散としている。◆Trade is dull. 商況が不振だ。

dullness (名)沈滞, 低迷, 不振, 不景気, 不活発, さえないこと

dummy (名)模造品, マネキン人形, 人形, 操り人形, 手先, 傀儡(かいらい), ロボット, 替え玉, (ページの)割付け, 束(つか)見本, ダミー (形)模造の, 偽(にせ)の, 架空の, 見せかけだけの, 名義だけの, 名ばかりの
  dummy company トンネル会社, 架空の会社, ダミー会社
  dummy index ダミー指数
  dummy organization ダミー団体, ダミー組織
  dummy variable regression ダミー変数を用いた回帰分析
  ◆The company purchased tickets for political fund-raising parties in the names of dummy organizations. 同社は, 複数のダミー団体名義で政治資金調達パーティー券を購入していた。

dummy company トンネル会社, 架空の会社, ダミー会社
  ◆A real estate broker created a dummy company to illegally receive a public credit guarantee. 不動産業者が, 架空の会社を作って不正に公的信用保証を受けていた。◆The secret funds were pooled in the bank accounts of dummy companies. 裏金は, ダミー会社の銀行口座に蓄えられていた。

dump (動)投げ売りする, 不当廉売する, 乱売する, ダンピングする, 投げ捨てる
  ◆Speculation that some major banks may find themselves with capital shortfalls and then nationalized is driving investors to dump the banks' shares. 大手行の一部が自己資本不足に陥って国有化されるとの思惑から, 投資家は銀行株の売りに出ている。

duration (名)期間(period), 継続, 継続期間, 存続期間, 持続期間, 有効期間, 債券投資資金の回収期間, (債券投資で元本を回収するまでの)平均残存期間, 債券価格の金利変動に対する敏感度, 金利感応度(金利が変動した場合, 債券価格がどの程度変化するかを表す指標。この値が大きいほど, 金利の変動による債券価格の変動が大きい), デュレーション
  dollar duration ダラー・デュレーション
  duration drift デュレーションの変化
  duration of a bond portfolio 債券ポートフォリオのデュレーション
  duration of a credit 信用状の有効期間
  duration of insurance 保険期間
  duration of note 手形の支払い期限
  duration of the put or call プットとコールの有効期間
  duration-weighted trade デュレーション加重入替え
  effective duration 実効デュレーション
  extend duration デュレーションを長くする, デュレーションを延長する
  increase duration デュレーションを長期化させる, デュレーションを増加させる
  increase the duration of a portfolio ポートフォリオのデュレーションを増加させる
  liability duration 負債のデュレーション
  Macaulay [Macaulay's] マコーレー・デュレーション (=duration)
  negative duration asset 負のデュレーションを持つ資産
  positive duration 正のデュレーション

reduce duration　デュレーションを短縮する
short duration bond　デュレーションが短い債券, 短期物
short duration instrument　短期商品
shorten the duration of the portfolio　ポートフォリオのデュレーションを短縮する
the duration of a credit　信用状の有効期間
the duration of a portfolio　ポートフォリオのデュレーション
the duration of insurance　保険期間
use durations to change asset allocations　デュレーションを利用して資産配分を変更する
weighted average of the durations　デュレーションの平均加重
yields on short-duration bonds　短期物の利回り
◆The news pushed up yields on short-duration bonds. これを受けて、短期物の利回りが上昇した。

during　（前）～の間, ～の期間中, ～の時期に, ～の間に
during the bubble economy　バブル期の, バブル期に
during the period　期中, 当期に, 同期に
during the year　当期, 今年度, 今期, 年間の
during the year to date　年初来
◆During the bubble economy, life insurers sold a large number of policies by promising high yields. バブル期に生保各社は、高い予定利率を約束して多くの保険契約を獲得した。◆During the business suspension, the company will not be allowed to extend new loans, solicit new customers or call in loans. 業務停止の期間中、同社は新規融資や新規顧客の勧誘、貸出[貸金]の回収業務ができなくなる。◆During the first nine months of 2011, the company completed public offerings of $125 million of 9.45% Debentures, due 2021 and $125 million of 10.50% Debentures, due 2018. 2011年1-9月期に同社は、2021年満期9.45%社債1億2,500万ドルと2018年満期10.50%社債1億2,500万ドルを公募発行した。◆During 2011, conversions of debentures resulted in the issuance of 200 shares of the Corporation's capital stock. 2011年度は、転換社債の転換により、200株の当社株式を発行した。◆The guard raised against a possible financial meltdown during a financial sector-triggered recession several years ago has been lifted. 数年前の金融不況時に想定された金融崩壊に対する厳戒態勢は、すでに解かれている。◆The policies offered by the two nonlife insurers pay policyholders if they are injured doing sports or during domestic and overseas trips. この損保2社が提供している保険[保険契約]では、保険加入者[保険契約者]がスポーツや国内外の旅行中に傷害事故にあったときに、保険金が支払われる。◆The yen hit 160 to the dollar during the week. 円は今週、1ドル＝160円の高値を付けた。◆Though stock prices remain low, the number of transactions has already outpaced that during the bubble economy. 株価はまだ低いものの、株取引の件数はすでにバブル期を超えている。

duty paid　通関渡し条件
duty paid price　通関渡し値段
duty paid terms　通関渡し条件
ex dock-duty paid　埠頭渡し関税込み

dwarf　（動）～を小さく見せる, 小さくする, 大きく引き離す, 成長を妨げる
be dwarfed by　～と比べるととても小さい, ～に大きく引き離される
◆In terms of the total market value of listed shares, the Tokyo Stock Exchange is dwarfed by the New York Stock Exchange, the world's biggest. 上場株式の時価総額では、東証は世界トップのニューヨーク証券取引所に大きく引き離されている。

dynamics　（名）力学, 相互の力関係, 動力学, 原動力, 動機となる力, 力, 活力, エネルギー, 動態, 動態学, 動学, 動向, ダイナミクス
competitive dynamics　競争環境
debt dynamics　債務問題
dynamics of the industry　業界動向, 業界動態
economic dynamics　経済動学
group dynamics　集団力学, 集団内相互関係
monetary dynamics　貨幣的動学
systems dynamics　システム・ダイナミクス
◆The government led by the Democratic Party of Japan lacks a coherent strategy to address the negative aspects of Japan's debt dynamics. 民主党政権は、日本のマイナス材料の債務問題への取組みに対する一貫した戦略に欠けている。◆The U.S. fiscal consolidation plan falls short of what would be necessary to stabilize the government's medium-term debt dynamics. 米国の財政再建策は、政府の中期的な債務問題処理[財政運営]の安定化には不十分である。

E

e-broker　（名）ネット専業証券会社, ネット証券, オンライン証券
（=online broker, online brokerage）
◆Shares in the nation's fifth-biggest e-broker, kabu.co. Securities Co., soared 86 percent on its stock market debut. カブドットコム証券（国内第5位のネット専業証券）の株価が、株式の新規上場（証券取引所への上場）で86%急騰した。

e-commerce　（名）電子商取引, ネット商取引, ネット取引, Eコマース　（=e-business, E-commerce, EC, electronic commerce, Internet-based commerce）
◆As e-commerce requires little investment in premises or facilities, many company workers, housekeepers and students take part in Internet-based auction. ネット取引は店舗や設備への投資が不要のため、サラリーマンや主婦、学生の多くがネット・オークションなどに参加している。

e-mail　（名）電子メール, Eメール, eメール, メール
（⇒fraudulent invoice, Internet cafe）
◆The bank deleted e-mails while the Financial Services Agency was auditing the bank. 金融庁が同行の立入り検査検査をしている際、同行は電子メールを削除した。

earlier forecast　当初予想, 前回の予想[見通し]
◆The company lowered its operating profit 62 percent to ¥50 billion from the earlier forecast for ¥130 billion. 同社は、営業利益見通しを前回発表の13,00億円から500億円に62%下方修正した。

early　（形）早い時期[時間]の, 早期の, 初期の, 当初の, 即時の, 期前の
early disposal of bad loans　不良債権の早期処理
early extinguishment of debt　負債の早期償却
early forecast [projection]　当初予想
early payment　期前返済, 早期返済
early phase　初期段階, 初期　（=early stages）
early recovery　早期回復, 早期景気回復
early redemption [pay-off]　繰上げ償還
early repayment　期限前償還, 早期完済
early retirement packages　早期退職プラン
early termination　早期終了, 期限前解約
early withdrawal　期限前解約

early corrective measures　早期是正措置
（=prompt corrective action measures）
◆The Financial Services Agency takes the early corrective measures in ordering troubled life insurers to draw up and submit plans for turning business around if solvency margin rates fall below 200 percent. 生命保険会社のソルベンシー・マージン比率が200%未満に低下した場合、経営危機に陥った

生保に経営改善計画の作成と提出を求めるにあたって、金融庁は早期是正措置をとる。

[解説]生保の早期是正措置とは：生命保険会社の支払い余力を示す「ソルベンシー・マージン比率」が200％未満に低下した場合、首相が業務改善命令を発動、経営の健全性を確保するための改善計画の提出を求める。必要と判断した場合は、業務停止命令を出すことができる。保険業法第132条第2項で規定している。(2003年5月24日付『読売新聞』)

early retirement 早期退職, 希望対象, 期限前返済
◆Fewer pilots than expected applied for JAL's early retirement program. 日航パイロットの早期退職への応募者は、会社側の予想を下回った。

early warning system 早期警戒制度, 早期警戒システム (⇒guaranteed yield)
◆By introducing the early warning system for life insurers, the Financial Services Agency plans to keep an eye on their business operations, including profit performance, safety and cancellation of contracts. 金融庁は、生保向けの早期警戒制度を導入して、収益性や安全性、解約の状況など生命保険会社の経営を監視する方針だ。◆The Financial Services Agency introduced the early warning system for life insurers to keep an eye on their business operations, including profit performance, safety and cancellation of contracts. 金融庁は、生保向けの早期警戒制度を導入して、収益性や安全性、解約の状況など生命保険会社の経営を監視している。

earmark (動)予算を組む, (〜の目的に資金などを)充てる, (資金を)投入する, (予算などを)計上する, 指定する, 特定する, 明示する, 〜を区別する
◆Billions of dollars in Iraqi oil revenue and other funds earmarked for the reconstruction of the country has gone missing in opaque bank accounts. イラクの原油収入と他のイラク復興支金のうち数十億ドルが、不明朗な銀行口座に消えてしまっている。◆On Sept 7, 2008, the U.S. government earmarked a huge amount of public funds to help government-affiliated mortgage financiers Freddie Mac and Fannie Mae. 2008年9月7日に米政府は、政府系住宅金融公社のフレディ・マック(連邦住宅抵当貸付公社)とファニー・メイ(連邦住宅抵当金庫[公庫])を救済するため、巨額の公的資金投入を決めた。◆The Financial Services Agency did not comment on whether any Japanese banks had been earmarked for the G-SIFIs list. 金融庁は、邦銀が国際金融システム上重要な金融機関(G-SIFIs)リストの指定行に入っているかどうかについては、コメントしなかった。◆The firm has earmarked a total of ¥37 billion in the two fields in fiscal 2010. 同社は、両事業分野に2010年度は370億円投資した。

earn (動)稼ぐ, 稼得(かとく)する, 利益を上げる, 報酬などを得る, 獲得する, 生む, もたらす
(⇒commission名詞)
earn above-average returns 市場平均を上回る利益を上げる
earn interest 利息が付く
earn no interest 利息が付かない
income earned from interest and dividends 利子・配当収入
pay-as-you-earn 源泉課税
save-as-you-earn 天引き積立て
◆Corporate value is defined as "the total of profits one company will earn in future." 企業価値は、「ある会社が将来稼ぐ利益の合計」と定義される。◆Hewlett-Packard earned $1.55 billion, or 55 cents per share, for the first quarter ended Jan. 31. ヒューレット・パッカードは、第1四半期(1-3月期)に15億5,000万ドル(1株当たり55セント)の利益を上げた。◆If the two-track income taxation system is introduced, taxpayers will be allowed to offset losses from stock investments from income earned from interest and dividends. 二元的所得課税方式を導入すると、納税者は、利子・配当収入から株式投資による損失を相殺することができるようになる。◆Major moneylender SFCG earned an unsavory reputation for its strong-arm loan collection methods. 金融業者大手のSFCG(旧商工ファンド)の評判は、債権の取立てが強引で芳しくなかった。◆The consolidated provision for taxes also includes an amount sufficient to pay additional United States federal income taxes on repatriation of income earned abroad. 連結納税引当金には、海外で得た利益の本国送金に課される米連邦所得税の追加支払いに十分対応できる金額も含まれている。

earn a profit 利益を上げる
◆Day traders are individual investors who buy and sell stocks many times a day to earn a profit on the trading margin. デイ・トレーダーは、1日に何度も株の売買を繰り返して、その利ざやで利益を上げる個人投資家だ。◆In foreign currency deposits, depositors can earn profits by exchanging their foreign currency deposits into yen when the yen's value against major foreign currencies falls. 外貨預金では、主要外貨に対して円相場が下落した時点で預金を円に戻せば、利益を上げる[儲ける]ことができる。◆The company is expected to continue earning a stable profit for the foreseeable future. 同社は、将来的にも安定した利益が見込める。

earn revenue 収益を上げる
◆The firm earns revenue through real estate investment and through resuscitating failed financial institutions. 同社は、不動産投資と経営破綻した金融機関を再生させることで収益を上げている。

earner (名)稼ぎ手, 稼得者, 取得者, 利益を生み出すもの, ドル箱, 儲(もう)かる仕事
(⇒income earner)
a cash earner 現金稼得者
a foreign exchange earner 外国為替取得者
a high earner 多く稼ぐ人
a high wage earner 高給取り
a low earner 少しだけ稼ぐ人
a low income earner 低所得者
a middle income earner 中所得者
a nice little earner 簡単に儲かる仕事
a salary earner 給料生活者
a top earner for the company 同社の稼ぎ頭
an income earner 個人所得者, 俸給生活者, 所得取得者
high-income earners 高所得者層
small income earners 小額所得者
two-earner family 共稼ぎ世帯
upper income earner 高所得者
wage earner 賃金労働者, 勤労者, 給料生活者
wage earners health insurance 勤労者健康保険
◆The number of high-income earners who will pay the higher tax rates will not change even if progressive tax structure may be reinforced. 累進税の構造を強化しても、最高税率を負担する高所得者層の数は変わらない。◆The sale of Toyota's luxury cars, a top earner for the firm, has become sluggish in the global major markets. トヨタの稼ぎ頭の高級車が、世界の主要市場で低迷している。◆There was unexpectedly strong opposition within and outside the company to the plan to sell off the company's main earner. 同社のドル箱である事業の全面売却案には、社内外から予想外の強い反発があった。

earning (名)利益稼得, 収益, 利益 (⇒earnings)
domestic earning 国内事業の利益
earning coverage 収益カバレッジ
earning process 利益稼得過程
earning ratio 収益指標
lower earning 減益

operating earning rate　営業利益率
primary earning per share　基本的1株当たり利益
recurring earning power　経常的な収益力
revenue-earning activity　収益稼得活動

earning assets　収益性資産, 収益資産
◆Both companies contributed to the growth in these revenues by expanding their portfolios of earning assets. 両社は, 保有収益資産の拡大によってこれらの増収に貢献した。

earning capacity　収益力（=earning power）
◆Japan Post Service will boost its earning capacity by integrating Yu-Pack and Perican services. 郵便事業会社は, ゆうパックとペリカン便を統合して, 収益力を高める方針だ。

earning power　収益力（earning capacity）, 収益性（profitability）（⇒unrealized profits）
earning power of banks　銀行の収益力
　（⇒lowered earning power of banks）
extra earning power　超過収益力
　（=excess earnings power）
future earning power　将来の収益力
improve one's earning power　収益力を高める, 収益力を向上させる
issuer's earnings power　発行体の収益力
lowered earning power of banks　収益力の低下
recurring earning power　経常的収益力
strengthen one's earning power　収益力を強化する
◆Major U.S. and European banks are improving their earning power. 欧米の大手銀行は, 収益力を向上させている。◆MFG, the nation's largest financial group, tied up with two major U.S. banks to strengthen its earning power. 国内金融グループ最大手のみずほフィナンシャルグループが, 収益力の強化を図るため, 米銀大手2行と提携した。◆The instability of life insurance firms and the lowered earning power of banks with massive bad loans have become the two major factors rocking the financial system. 生保各社の経営基盤の不安定と, 巨額の不良債権に苦しむ銀行の収益力低下が, 金融システムを揺るがしている二大要因になっている。

earnings　（名）収益, 利益, 純利益, 利潤, 所得, 収入, 投資利益, 業績　（=gains, profits, returns; ⇒administrative order, corporate earnings, Freddie Mac, retained earnings）
adjusted earnings　調整後利益
after-tax earnings　税引き後利益
　（=earnings after tax）
corporate earnings　企業収益
equity earnings　投資損益
equity in earnings of unconsolidated subsidiaries　非連結子会社の持ち分利益
foreign exchange earnings　外貨収入
higher earnings　増益
interim earnings report　中間決算
operating earnings　営業利益
poor earnings　減益, 減収
pretax earnings　税引き前利益
　（=earnings before tax）
price earnings ratio　株価収益率, PER
quarterly earnings　四半期利益
reported earnings　計上利益, 公表利益, 決算報告上の利益
share earnings　1株当たり利益
statement of earnings　損益計算書
statement of retained earnings　利益剰余金計算書
strong earnings　高収益, 高水準の収益
◆A steady annual improvement in earnings of five percent or more is a reasonable goal given the weight of regulated companies in our asset base. 年5％以上の利益増加率の安定確保は, 規制対象企業が当社の資産構成で大きな比重を占めていることから, 妥当な目標と言えるでしょう。◆All of the nation's six major nonlife insurers suffered sharp falls in earnings for the fiscal first half ended Sept. 30. 今年9月中間決算（9月30日に終了した今年度上半期）の国内損害保険会社の主要6社が, 軒並み大幅な減益となった。◆Shinsei and Aozora banks announced a plan to merge in an effort to expand their customer bases and improve earnings. 新生銀行とあおぞら銀行は, 顧客基盤の拡大と収益力の強化を狙って, 合併計画を発表した。◆The major securities house attributed the poor earnings to sharp drops in brokerage fees and trading profits amid the extended slump in the domestic stock market. この大手証券会社は, 減益の要因として, 国内株式市場の長期低迷による株売買手数料と売買益の大幅減を挙げた。◆The new bank tax is levied on the banks' gross operating profits—their earnings minus basic operating expenses such as interest payments to depositors. 新銀行税は, 銀行の収入から基礎的な経費（預金者に対する預金金利の支払いなど）を差し引いた業務粗利益に課される。◆The pressures on gross margins and earnings that affected the last half of 2010 will continue through the first half of 2012. 2010年下半期［下期］の業績に影響を及ぼした売上利益率と利益の低下は, 2012年上半期［上期］まで続く見通しです。◆The provisions, after giving effect to taxes and minority interest, reduced 2010 earnings by $200 million. これらの引当金繰入れで, 関連税額と少数株主持ち分利益控除後の2010年度の純利益は, 2億ドル減少しました。◆The yen's appreciation puts pressure on the earnings of export-oriented companies. 円高は, 輸出企業の収益を圧迫する。◆Through continuing gains in annual earnings, it will be possible, over time, to adjust the payout ratio while still maintaining our dividend record. 年間利益の増大を続けることによって, 当社の配当実績を今後とも維持しながら, 時期が来たら配当性向を調整することは可能である。◆Under the government guidelines, if earnings come in more than 30 percent below targets set in restructuring plans at any major bank that received public funds to recapitalize in 1988 and 1999, the banks management will have to resign. 政府のガイドラインによると, 資本再編のために1988年と1999年に公的資金の注入を受けた大手銀行の収益が, 再建計画（経営健全化計画）で設定した収益目標を30％以上下回った場合, 銀行の経営陣は辞任しなければならない。

earnings estimate　業績予想, 収益予想
　（=earnings forecast, earnings projection）
◆The FSA urged the financial group to revise its earnings estimate. 金融庁は, 同金融グループに対して業績予想の修正を強く迫った。

earnings forecast　業績予想, 業績見通し, 収益予想, 利益予想　（=earnings estimate, earnings projection, profit forecast; ⇒earnings projection, forecast名詞, full-year (earnings) forecast）
◆This year's upturn in IPOs has been mainly driven by improved corporate earnings forecasts and expectations of an economic expansion. 今年に入って株式公開が増加に転じたのは, 企業の業績見通しが好転したことと景気拡大への期待感によるものが大きい。

earnings goal　収益目標, 業績目標
　（⇒administrative order）

earnings manipulation　利益の不正操作
◆Freddie Mac revealed the details of its earnings manipulation in recent years. フレディ・マックは, 過去数年来行っていた利益の不正操作の詳細を明らかにした.

earnings per share　1株当たり利益, 1株当たり純利益, EPS　（普通株式1株当たりの純利益。1株当たり利益＝当期純利益/普通株式数）
◆A stock buyback means a drop in the number of the company's outstanding shares on the market, helping increase its

earnings per share—thus causing the share price to rise. 自社株買いを実施すると、市場で流通しているその会社の発行済み株式数が減り、1株当たり純利益が増えるため、株価上昇をもたらす効果がある。◆For the computation of the earnings per share, assuming full dilution, dividends on convertible preferred shares have been added back to income. 完全希薄化を仮定した場合の1株当たり利益の算定では、転換可能優先株式[転換優先株]に対する配当は、利益に振り戻してあります。◆The firm's earnings per share were affected both by lower revenues and reduced gross margins. 同社の1株当たり利益は、売上高の減少と売上利益率の低下の影響を受けた。

earnings projection 業績予想、収益予想
（⇒earnings forecast）
◆Other banks are likely forced to revise their earnings projections downward because of the accelerated disposal of bad loans, business deterioration of borrowers due to the lingering recession and further decline in stock prices. 不良債権処理の加速や長引く不況による融資先の業績悪化、株安などの影響で、他行も業績予想の下方修正を迫られている。

earnings report 業績報告、業績報告書、決算、決算報告、収益報告、損益計算書、財務計算書
（⇒after-tax loss, loss projections）
consolidated earnings report 連結決算、連結決算報告
interim earnings report 中間決算、中間決算報告
midterm earnings report 中間決算、中間決算報告
quarterly earnings report 四半期報告、四半期報告書
◆American International Group agreed to pay a $10 million civil fine to settle the SEC's allegations that it fraudulently helped another company falsify its earnings report and hide losses. 米保険大手のAIG（アメリカン・インターナショナル・グループ）は、同社が他社の業績報告書改ざんと損失隠しに不正に手を貸したとする米証券取引委員会（SEC）の告発を受け、この問題を解決するために民事制裁金1,000万ドルを支払うことに同意した。◆In its first earnings report, Japan Post posted a pretax profit of ¥24.71 trillion. 公社化後初めての決算で、日本郵政公社は24兆7,100億円の経常収益（民間企業の税引き前利益に相当）を計上した。◆Major banks and banking groups released their earnings reports for the first half of fiscal 2004. 大手銀行と銀行グループが、2004年9月中間決算を発表した。

earnings structure 収益構造
◆Major banks are forced to review their earnings structure. 大手行は、収益構造の見直しを迫られている。

earnings target 業績目標、収益目標、収益計画
◆Insurers may still meet their full-year earnings targets. 保険会社各社は、まだ通期の収益目標[業績目標]を達成する可能性がある。◆The FSA can order banks that have received injections of public funds to improve their earnings if their net profits fall short of their declared earnings targets by 30 percent or more. 公的資金注入行の税引き後利益が公表した収益計画（収益目標）より3割以上下回った場合、金融庁は、注入行に業務改善[収益改善]命令を発動することができる。

earthquake （名）地震
◆In the aftermath of the March 11 massive earthquake and tsunami, the Financial Services Agency will likely postpone the introduction of IFRSs. 東日本大震災（2011年3月11日）の影響で、金融庁は国際財務報告基準（IFRS）の導入を延期する方向だ。

earthquake insurance 地震保険
◆In the case of earthquake insurance, the cap on the insurance policy's value for an average house in Tokyo is about ¥10 million. 地震保険の場合、都内の平均的な住宅の保険契約の評価額上限は1,000万円程度だ。◆Public interest in earthquake insurance has soared in the aftermath of the Great East Japan Earthquake. 東日本大震災の影響で、地震保険への関心が高まっている。◆The number of people taking out earthquake insurance generally increases directly after an earthquake or tsunami. 地震保険の加入者数は、一般に地震や津波の直後に上昇する。

earthquake insurance payments 地震保険の保険金支払い額、地震保険の支払い額
◆Earthquake insurance payments resulting from the Great East Japan Earthquake are expected to reach ¥1.2 trillion. 東日本大震災による地震保険の保険金支払い額は、（業界全体で）1兆2,000億円に達する見込みだ。

earthquake insurance payout 地震保険の支払い
◆The insurance world should disclose to consumers such basic data as the percentage of earthquake insurance payouts made in full after previous temblors. 保険業界は、これまでの地震で地震保険の満額支払いが行われた割合はどれくらいかなどの基本的なデータを、消費者に開示すべきだ。

earthquake insurance subscriber 地震保険加入者
◆The number of earthquake insurance subscribers has grown rapidly since autumn. 昨秋から、地震保険の加入件数が急増している。

earthquake insurance system 地震保険制度、地震保険
◆The earthquake insurance system was launched after the 1964 Niigata Earthquake as a response to the problem of fire insurance not covering damage caused by an earthquake or tsunami. 地震保険[地震保険制度]は、火災保険で地震や津波による被害が補償されない問題への対応策として、1964年の新潟地震後に導入された。◆Under the current earthquake insurance system, insurance payments remain capped at half the actual value of a home and its contents. 現行の地震保険[地震保険制度]では、保険金の支払い額の上限は、住宅や家財の実質価値の半額までとなっている。

EASDAQ 欧州店頭株式市場（European Association of Securities Dealers Automated Quotationsの略）

ease （動）緩和する、和らげる、緩める、軽くする、軽減する、引き下げる、～の金利を下げる、利下げする （自動）緩む、和らぐ、弱まる、低下する、値下がりする、後退する
（⇒monetary stance）
ease credit conditions 金融を緩和する
ease economic sanctions 経済制裁を緩和する
ease foreign exchange risks 為替リスクを軽減する
ease inflationary pressures インフレ圧力を低下させる、インフレ圧力を和らげる
ease liquidity 流動性を高める
ease (monetary) policy 金融政策を緩和する、金融政策を緩める、金融を緩和する
ease monetary policy further 一段の金融緩和を進める、追加緩和策を取る （⇒stall）
ease money supply 通貨供給量を増やす、金融を緩和する
ease pressure on the appreciating yen 円高圧力を和らげる、円高圧力を低下させる
ease restrictions on ～への規制を緩和する、～への規制を緩める
ease slightly 小幅低下する
ease the burden of interest payments 利払いの負担を軽減する、金利負担を軽減する
ease the money supply 通貨供給量を増やす、金融を緩和する
pressure to ease 利下げ圧力
◆Dollar-selling pressure has eased and put a temporary brake on the sharp appreciation of the yen and the fall of the dollar. ドル売り圧力が弱まり、急激な円高・ドル安にいったん歯止めがかかった。◆Out of a sense of relief, dollar-selling pressure has eased on the foreign currency markets. 安堵（あんど）感から、外国為替市場では、ドル売り圧力が弱まっ

た。◆Restrictions on share buybacks were eased in October 2001. 2001年10月に、自社株買戻しに対する規制が緩和された。◆The Bank of Japan needs to further ease its monetary policy. 日銀は、一段の金融緩和を進める必要がある。◆Tokyo stocks bounced back Wednesday after sharp falls Tuesday following Lehman Brothers decision to file for bankruptcy as financial worries eased. 水曜日の東京株式市場は、リーマン・ブラザーズが前日に破たん申請を決めて急落したものの、金融不安が和らいだため反発した。◆What is urgently needed is measures to ease the pain caused by the economic downturn. 緊急に必要なのは、景気悪化の痛みを和らげる措置だ。

ease （名）金融緩和, 金利引下げ, 金利減免, 利下げ, 低金利下, 利下げ
 additional monetary ease　追加の金融緩和, 追加金融緩和
 Fed ease　FRBによる金融緩和, FRBによる利下げ
 further ease　一層の金融緩和, もう一段の金融緩和
 monetary ease　金融緩和
 ◆The latest additional monetary ease put a downward pressure on interest rates. 今回の追加の金融緩和で、金利は低下した。

ease monetary grip further　金融政策を一段と緩和する, 追加の金融緩和を進める
 ◆The BOJ decided to ease its monetary grip further by effectively restoring its zero-interest-rate policy. 日銀は、実質的にゼロ金利政策を復活させて、追加の金融緩和を決めた。

ease monetary policy　金融政策を緩和する, 金融政策を緩める, 金融を緩和する
 （=relax monetary policy）
 ◆An increase in bond prices is unlikely as many countries around the world have eased monetary policies. 世界各国の金融緩和で、債券価格の上昇は見込みにくい。◆Calls for the Bank of Japan to further ease monetary policy are intensifying among market players. 市場関係者の間では、日銀に一層の［一段の］金融緩和を求める声が強まっている。◆Contrary to prevailing market expectations, the central bank decided not to further ease monetary policy. 市場の大方の期待を裏切って［期待に反して］、日銀は追加的な金融緩和策を見送った。◆The government would ask the Bank of Japan to further ease its monetary policy to help stabilize the nation's financial system by helping financial institutions procure funds. 政府は、金融機関の資金繰りを助けて金融システムの安定化を図るため、日銀に追加の［もう一段の］金融緩和を求める方針だ。

ease monetary policy further　一層の金融緩和を進める, 一段の金融緩和を行う
 （=further ease monetary policy）
 ◆The Fed is ready to ease monetary policy further if the budding U.S. economic recovery withers. 米国の景気回復の芽がしぼんだ場合、米連邦準備制度理事会（FRB）は一段の金融緩和を進める用意がある。

ease requirements for　～の要件を緩和する
 ◆To encourage firms' temporary layoffs, the government will ease requirements for receiving a governmental subsidy to defray costs relating to layoffs. 企業の一時解雇［一時帰休］を支援するため、政府は企業が雇用調整助成金（解雇関連費用を負担する政府助成金）を受けるための要件を緩和する。

ease the money supply　通貨供給量を増やす, 金融を緩和する　（=ease the supply of money）
 ◆To stem the yen's appreciation, the Bank of Japan should promptly ease the money supply by holding an extraordinary meeting. 円高阻止に向け、日銀は臨時会合を開いて、金融緩和を急ぐべきである。

ease the supply of money　通貨供給量［マネー・サプライ］を増やす, 金融を緩和する　（=ease the money supply, increase the supply of money）
 ◆The latest appreciation of the yen was triggered by additional steps taken by the U.S. government to ease the supply of money. 今回の円高は、米政府が取った追加金融緩和策がきっかけだった。◆To alleviate the influence of the U.S. government's additional steps to ease the supply of money, the Bank of Japan must adopt a more proactive stance toward monetary relaxation. 米政府の金融緩和策［通貨供給量を増やす米政府の追加措置］の影響を和らげるには、日銀も金融緩和の姿勢を強める必要がある。

easing　（名）緩和, 軽減, 引下げ, 低下,（圧力などが）和らぐこと, 軟調, 金融緩和, 利下げ　（⇒Fed）
 additional easing　一層の緩和, 一層の金融緩和
 additional easing measures　一層の金融緩和策, 追加の金融緩和策, 追加緩和策
 aggressive easing（of monetary policy）　金融政策の積極的［大幅］な緩和, 積極的な金融緩和, 大幅な金融緩和
 be in an easing mode　金融緩和のスタンスを取っている
 be pricing in on an easing　金融緩和を織り込んだ水準になっている
 cautious easing　慎重な金融緩和, 慎重な金融緩和政策
 coordinated easing　協調利下げ
 credit easing　金融緩和　（=easing of credit）
 easing hopes　金利引下げの期待, 利下げの期待, 金融緩和の期待
 easing in capacity　設備稼働率の低下
 easing in inflation　インフレ率の低下
 easing in monetary policy　金融政策の緩和, 金融緩和
 easing in regulations　規制緩和
 easing in U.S. rates　米国の利下げ
 easing of domestic demand pressure　内需圧力の緩和
 easing of monetary policy　金融政策の緩和
 easing of quantitative credit regulation　量的信用緩和
 easing of the money market　金融緩和
 finish easing　金融緩和を打ち止めにする
 further easing in interest rates　一層の利下げ, もう一段の金利引下げ［利下げ］
 monetary easing　金融緩和, 金融政策の緩和, 利下げ
  （=credit easing, easy money, monetary relaxation）
 monetary policy easing　金融政策の緩和, 金融緩和
 quantitative（monetary）easing　金融の量的緩和
 room for further monetary easing　一層の金融緩和の余地, もう一段の金融緩和の余地
 slight easing　若干の低下, 若干の利下げ, 若干の金融緩和
 start easing policy　金融緩和に動き出す
 the next easing　次回の利下げ
 the scope for further easing move　一層の金融緩和の余地
 ◆Any additional easing measures would only have a limited impact if they were made at the urging of financial markets. 市場に催促される形で追加緩和を行っても、追加緩和策の効果は限定的に過ぎない。◆Part of the benefits of quantitative easing will take the form of a depreciation of the dollar. 量的緩和の効果の一部は、ドル安の形で現れる。◆The Bank of Japan's resorting to quantitative easing in concert with the Fed would have a greater impact on in buoying the global economy. 米連邦準備制度理事会（FRB）と歩調を合わせて日銀が量的緩和に踏み切れば、世界景気の浮揚効果は拡大すると思われる。◆The U.S. FRB's recent decision on further quantitative easing is only an aberration. 米連邦準備制度理事会（FRB）の今回の追加金融緩和の決定は、常軌を逸した行為と言わざるを得ない。

easy　（形）容易な, 簡単な, 楽な, 寛大な, 甘い, 緩やかな, 快適な, 快い, 豊かな, 裕福な,（商品供給や相場、市況などが）だぶついた, 景気刺激型の
 easy budget　予算緩和

easy dollars　低利資金
easy life　豊かな生活
easy market　市場のだぶつき，緩慢な市場
easy payment [installment]　分割払い
easy payment plan [system]　分割払い方式
　（=easy purchase system）
easy terms　分割払い，楽な条件，低利借入れ
money conditions are very easy　金融状況はかなりの景気刺激型である
take the easy way out　安易[楽]な方法で難局を切り抜ける

easy credit　金融緩和，信用緩和，信用拡張
◆The FRB's new easy credit policy is not without concerns. 米連邦準備制度理事会（FRB）の追加金融緩和策には、気がかりな点もある。

easy monetary policy　金融緩和政策，金融緩和策，金融緩和　（=easy credit policy, easy money policy, easy money step; ⇒quantitative monetary easing policy, ultra-loose monetary policy）
◆Maintaining an easy monetary policy may lead to excessive corporate capital investment and have a negative impact on the sustainable economic recovery. 金融緩和政策を続けると、企業の過剰な設備投資を生み、景気の持続的回復を阻害する恐れがある。◆The Bank of Japan should maintain its easy monetary policy until there is no doubt that deflation has ended. デフレが確実に終息するまで、日銀は金融緩和政策を続けるべきだ。

easy money　金融緩和，低利の金，不正に儲（もう）けた金，悪銭
additional easy money step　追加金融緩和政策
easy money times　金融緩和期
easy money with surplus budget　金融緩和と黒字予算

easy money policy　金融緩和政策，金融緩和策，金融緩和　（=easy credit policy, easy monetary policy; ⇒gross domestic product, market liquidity, ultra-easy [ultraeasy] money policy）
◆Even if the United States does decide to shift its easy money policy, Japan will not immediately be in a position to follow suit. たとえ米国が金融緩和政策の転換に踏み切っても、日本が直ちに追随する環境にはないようだ。◆Financial institutions have become more hesitant in lending money despite the central bank's easy money policy. 日銀の金融緩和にもかかわらず、金融機関の貸出は前より厳しくなっている。◆The Bank of Japan should maintain its easy money policy until there is no doubt that deflation has ended. デフレが確実に終息するまで、日銀は金融緩和政策を続けるべきだ。◆The Fed will raise interest rates and shift its easy money policy by summer. FRB（米連邦準備制度理事会）は、今年夏までに金利引上げに動いて、金融緩和政策を転換するだろう。

easy money step　金融緩和策
（=easy monetary policy, easy money policy）
◆The Bank of Japan decided to take an additional easy money step. 日銀は、追加金融緩和策に踏み切ることを決めた。

EBA　欧州銀行機構，欧州銀行監督機構　（European Banking Authorityの略。⇒European Banking Authority）
◆The European Banking Authority's stress tests were only cosmetic and two Irish banks went bankrupt shortly after the EBA's 2010 tests though the banks had passed them. 欧州銀行監督機構（EBA）のストレス・テスト（財務の健全性検査）はほんの体裁[上辺]だけのもので、アイルランドの2銀行は、2010年に実施された同機構のテストに通過したものの、テスト直後に経営破たんした。◆The Franco-Belgian bank Dexia collapsed in October 2011 despite passing the 2011 EBA's financial health check. フランス・ベルギー共同の銀行「デクシア」が、2011年に実施された欧州銀行監督機構（EBA）の財務の健全性検査を通過したにもかかわらず、2011年10月に破たんした。

EBRD　欧州復興開発銀行（European Bank for Reconstruction and Developmentの略）

ECB　欧州中央銀行，欧州中銀
（⇒European Central Bank）
◆By buying Greek, Portuguese and Spanish bonds, the ECB infused life into the moribund eurozone markets for these soon-to-be-junk status government bonds. ギリシャやポルトガル、スペインの国債を買い入れて、欧州中銀（ECB）は、崩壊寸前のユーロ圏の投資不適格レベルが見込まれるこれらの債券の市場に生気を吹き込んだ。◆In order to bring the European crisis under control, the EU, ECB and IMF must work even more closely together. 欧州危機の収束を図るには、欧州連合（EU）、欧州中央銀行（ECB）と国際通貨基金（IMF）の緊密な連携を強化する必要がある。◆The ECB cut its benchmark interest rate to 1.25 percent for the first time in 2.5 years in early November 2011, immediate after its new President Mario Draghi assumed office. 欧州中央銀行（ECB）は、マリオ・ドラギ新総裁（イタリア出身）が就任した直後の2011年11月初め、2年半ぶりに政策金利を1.25%に引き下げた。◆The ECB was obliged to maintain price stability when the euro was launch in 1999. 1999年にユーロが導入された際、欧州中銀（ECB）は、物価安定の維持を義務付けられた。◆The European Central Bank (ECB) decided to leave the benchmark interest rate at a record low of 2 percent for the 20th month in a row. 欧州中央銀行（ECB）は、（ユーロ圏12か国の短期金利の目標となる）主要政策金利を、20か月連続で過去最低の2%のまま据え置くことを決めた。◆The European Central Bank (ECB) raised its key interest rate by a quarter of a percentage point to 2.25 percent. 欧州中央銀行（ECB）は、主要政策金利を0.25%引き上げて年2.25%とした。

ECB buyouts of sovereign debts of eurozone countries　欧州中銀（ECB）によるユーロ圏諸国の国債買切り
◆The ECB buyouts of sovereign debts of eurozone countries with fiscal laxity are the nightmare scenario Germany has been fearing. 欧州中銀（ECB）による放漫財政のユーロ圏諸国の国債買切りは、ドイツが恐れていた最悪のシナリオだ。

ECB President　欧州中銀総裁

economic activity　経済活動，経済動向，経済情勢，景気，実態[実体]経済
acceleration in economic activity　景気加速
decline in economic activity　景気の落ち込み
market-defined economic activities　市場経済活動
matrix on commodity input by kind of economic activity　経済活動別財貨・サービス投入表
matrix on commodity output by kind of　経済活動別財貨・サービス産出表
national economic activity　マクロ経済，経済成長率
pace of economic activity　景気の足取り
rebound in economic activity　景気回復，景気が拡大基調に戻ること，景気の勢いが回復してきたこと
regulate economic activities　経済活動を規制する
remain supportive of economic activity　景気を支える要因になっている
robust economic activity　好調な景気，景気の好調
slowdown of economic activity　景気の減速，景気低迷，景気の軟化
softening of economic activity　景気の軟化
squeeze economic activity　経済活動を圧迫する
stimulate economic activity　景気を刺激する
strong economic activity　景気の好調
weakening economic activity　景気の軟化
weaker economic activity　景気の減速

◆Economic activity strengthened in most of U.S. regions with the exception of St. Louis where plans to close several plants were announced, the U.S. FRB said. 米連邦準備制度理事会(FRB)は、(全12地区連銀のうち)一部の工場閉鎖計画を発表したセントルイスを除く11地区で景気が好転している、と述べた。◆Fed five regions described economic activity as "slow," "subdued" or "weak." 米国の5地区連銀は、経済活動の水準を「鈍い」「低迷」「弱い」と述べた。◆The current financial crisis negatively influences real economic activities. 現在の金融危機は、実体経済に悪影響を及ぼしている。

economic agent 経済主体, 経済行為者
◆Advances in information technology enabled all economic agents to share information of the same quality simultaneously. 情報技術の進歩により、すべての経済主体が均質の情報を同時に共有できるようになった。

economic and financial stability 経済と金融の安定, 経済・金融の安定
◆Volatile movements in the currency market have a negative impact on economic and financial stability. 為替市場の過度な変動は、経済・金融の安定に悪影響を及ぼす。

economic and fiscal management 経済財政運営, 経済・財政運営
◆The government is needed to appropriately proceed with economic and fiscal management. 政府は、適切な経済財政運営の進め方が求められている。

economic and fiscal outlook 経済財政展望, 経済財政見通し
◆The government's midterm economic and fiscal outlook defined the coming two years as an economic adjustment period. 日本政府の経済財政中期展望は、今後2年間を経済調整期間とした。

economic and fiscal policies 経済・財政政策
◆This ¥30 trillion cap has hobbled the government's economic and fiscal policies. この30兆円枠が、政府の経済・財政政策をがんじがらめにしている。

Economic and Monetary Union 欧州経済通貨同盟, EU経済通貨統合, EMU

economic assessment 景気判断, 景気の基調判断
(=assessment of the economy)
◆As a basis for its economic assessment, the report referred to increases in exports, progress in inventory adjustment and the bottoming out of industrial production. 景気判断の根拠として、同報告書は輸出が増加し、在庫調整が進展して、鉱工業生産も底を打ったことを挙げている。◆The Bank of Japan did not change its economic assessment. 日銀は、景気判断を変えなかった。◆The Bank of Japan downgraded its economic assessment for the second straight month. 日本銀行は、景気の基調判断を2か月連続で下方修正した。

economic boom 好況, 好景気, 景気回復, 景気回復局面, 経済の好況, 経済の活況
◆The economic boom, which started in February 2002, may have ended. 2002年2月から続いてきた景気回復局面が、幕を閉じた模様だ。◆The longest period of postwar economic expansion was known as an economic boom without feeling. 戦後最長の景気回復は、実感なき景気回復と言われた。

economic boost 景気浮揚, 景気刺激
◆A significant economic boost cannot be expected from the government's handout policies such as the flat-sum allowance and child-rearing allowances. 定額給付金やこども手当など政府のばらまき政策から、大きな景気浮揚は期待できない。

economic bubble 経済のバブル, バブル
(⇒bubble, equity market, Fed)
◆Surplus funds put out by developed economies' monetary easing measures have flowed into emerging economies to inflate economic bubbles. 先進国の金融緩和策で生じた余剰資金が、新興国に流れ込み、バブルを発生させている。◆The lost decade refers to the period of economic stagnation since the bursting of the economic bubble in the early 1990s. 「失われた10年」とは、バブルが崩壊した1990年代初めから続いた景気後退[景気停滞]期のことである。

economic bubble burst 経済のバブル崩壊, バブル崩壊
◆The 225-issue Nikkei Stock Average closed at 7,607.88, the lowest level since the economic bubble burst, on April 28, 2003. 2003年4月28日の日経平均株価(225種)の終値が7,607円88銭で、バブル崩壊後の最安値をつけた。

economic chaos 経済混乱
◆The Greek economic chaos was triggered as its national bond rating was lowered. ギリシャの経済混乱のきっかけは、ギリシャの国債格付けが引き下げられたことだ。

economic climate 経済環境, 経済情勢, 景況, 景気
◆It is vital now to assess the economic climate carefully. 今は、景気を慎重に見極める必要がある。

economic collapse 経済破たん, 経済の崩壊, 景気悪化
◆The presidency of George W. Bush began with the worst terrorist attack on U.S. soil and ended with the worst economic collapse in three generations. ブッシュ大統領の任期は、米国で最悪のテロ攻撃ではじまり、過去3代で最悪の経済破たん[経済崩壊、景気悪化]で終わった。

economic conditions 経済状態, 経済状況, 経済情勢, 景況, 景気 (⇒worsening economic conditions)
adverse economic conditions 経済情勢の悪化
decline in economic conditions 景気の悪化
improved economic conditions 経済状態の改善, 景気回復
poor economic conditions 景気低迷, 景気の悪化
recessionary economic conditions 景気の低迷
sluggish economic conditions 景気低迷
◆A U.S. Federal Reserve Board snapshot of economic conditions bolsters the hope of broader-based recovery. 米連邦準備制度理事会(FRB)の景況報告では、ほとんどの地域で景気持ち直しの期待が強まっている。◆As long as the global recession continues, severe economic conditions will persist in Japan during fiscal 2009. 世界的な景気後退が続くかぎり、厳しい経済状況は今後も続くと思われる。

economic conference 経済会議
◆The G-7 meeting has maintained its position as the most influential international economic conference. 先進7か国会議(G7)は、最も影響力のある国際経済会議としてその地位をこれまで維持してきた。

economic confusion 経済的混乱, 経済の混乱
◆The rating downgrades have fueled economic confusion in Greece and Ireland. ギリシャやアイルランドでは、格下げで経済の混乱に拍車がかかった。◆To avoid economic confusion, the federal government needs to strengthen official support for companies connected to GM. 経済的混乱を回避するには、米政府はGMの関連企業への公的支援を強化する必要がある。

economic contraction 景気の悪化, 景気収縮, 景気縮小, 景気後退, 不況, マイナス成長
(=contractionary economy)
◆A reading of below 50 percent in the coincident index is considered a sign of economic contraction and a figure above that is viewed as a sign of expansion. 一致指数で50%以下の数値は景気収縮[景気後退]を示す指標と見られ、それ以上の数字は景気回復[景気拡大]を示す指標と見なされる。◆The government found it difficult to avert economic contraction in the next fiscal year starting in April. 4月から始まる来年度の景気悪化を回避するのは難しい、と政府は見ている。◆The government has tried to avoid economic contraction through huge stimulus measures. 政府は、大型の景気刺激策[経済対策]で景気悪化の回避に努めている。

economic crisis 経済危機, 経済恐慌, 恐慌

(⇒emerge, out-of-control)
◆A prerequisite to restoring the country's fiscal health is to promptly and boldly take effective pump priming measures and to overcome the economic crisis. 日本の財政健全化への前提条件は、迅速、果敢に効果的な景気浮揚策を実行して、経済危機を克服することだ。◆Coordinated interest rate cuts were introduced immediately after the outbreak of the economic crisis. 協調利下げは、経済危機の発生直後に実施された。◆Taking to heart the bitter lessons learned from previous economic crises, major industrial nations have adopted various steps to ease the current plight. これまでの経済危機から学んだ苦い教訓を踏まえて、主要先進諸国は、現在の深刻な状況のさまざまな軽減策を実施してきた。◆The United States is in the grip of the worst economic crisis in more than 70 years. 米国は、過去70年以上で最悪の経済危機に見舞われている。◆To overcome the current economic crisis, stimulus measures should take precedence over fiscal reconstruction for the time being. 現在の経済危機を克服するためには、当面は、財政再建よりも景気対策を優先しなければならない。

economic cycle 経済循環, 景気循環, 景気動向, 景気変動
 better economic cycle 景気回復, 景気の上向き
 economic up-cycle 景気回復
 strengthening of the economic cycle 景気が勢いを増すこと
 the momentum of economic cycles 景気の勢い
◆The trend to make capitalism cyber-oriented seems to have significantly increased the frequency and amplitude of the economic cycles. 資本主義のサイバー化の傾向は、この景気循環の頻度と振幅を大きく増大しているようだ。

economic deterioration 景気悪化
◆Financial institutions are pressed with the task of dealing with a growing amount of nonperforming loans as the economic deterioration accelerates. 一段の景気悪化で、金融機関は新たに発生する不良債権の処理問題に追われている。

economic development 経済開発, 経済発展, 経済成長, 景気動向, 経済動向, 経済情勢
 economic development program [plan] 経済開発計画
 economic development zone 経済開発区
 full economic development 完全な工業化
 national economic development 国家経済開発, 全国経済開発
 outward-looking economic development 開放路線による経済開発
 robust economic development 目覚しい経済発展
 steady economic development 安定した経済成長
 theory of economic development 経済開発論
 vigorous economic development 活発な経済開発
◆In anticipation of increased crude oil prices due to heightened demand resulting from the economic development of emerging nations, speculative money flooded into the oil market. 新興国の経済発展による原油需要の増大で原油価格が先行き値上りするとの読みで、投機マネーが原油市場に流入した。◆The index of leading economic indicators predicts economic developments about six months ahead. 景気先行指数は、約6か月先の景気動向を示す指標だ。

economic discipline 経済規律
◆French President Nicolas Sarkozy and German Chancellor Angera Merkel called for greater economic discipline and unity among European countries. サルコジ仏大統領とメルケル独首相は、経済規律の強化と欧州各国間の結束を求めた。

economic disparity 経済格差
◆One of the two functions of tax grants is to adjust economic disparities among local governments. 交付税の二つの機能のうち、一つは地方自治体間の経済格差の調整にある。

economic downturn 経済[景気]減速, 景気後退, 景気の悪化, 景気低迷, 景気沈滞, 景気の下降局面, 不況, 不景気 (⇒capital plan, stimulus measures)
 mitigate economic downturns 景気後退を抑える
 normal economic downturn 景気の一般的な下降局面
◆Business conditions are rapidly deteriorating due to the global financial crisis and the worldwide economic downturn. 世界的な金融危機と世界的な景気後退で、景気は急速に悪化している。◆Financial uncertainty cools down the U.S. real economy and causes an economic downturn. 金融不安が米国の実体経済を冷え込ませ、景気後退を招いている。◆Future external demand is uncertain because of the rising yen and fears of economic downturns in other countries. 円高や海外経済の減速懸念で、外需の先行きは不透明である。◆The government considers the economic downturn caused by the March 11 Great East Japan Earthquake and subsequent tsunami to be almost over. 2011年3月11日の東日本大震災[3月11日の東日本大地震とその後の津波]による景気悪化はほぼ収束した、と政府は見ている。◆The ongoing global economic downturn continues to hit demand for flights. 今回の世界的な景気後退[世界同時不況]で、航空需要が引き続き減少している[打撃を受けている]。◆The sense of crisis is felt by those trying to stem a further economic downturn. これ以上の景気後退を食い止めようとしている人たちは、危機感を抱いている。◆The sudden economic downturn since the autumn has forced the government to drastically lower the forecast rate of real GDP in fiscal 2009. 秋以降の急速な景気悪化で、政府は2009年度の実質国内総生産（GDP）成長率見通しを大幅に引き下げざるを得なかった。

economic effect 経済効果
◆The economic effect of the popular South Korean TV drama series "Fuyu no Sonata" is estimated at ¥230 billion for Japan and South Korea, the Dai-ichi Life Research Institute said. 第一生命経済研究所の発表によると、韓国の人気TVドラマ「冬のソナタ」の経済効果は、日韓両国で2,300億円と試算されている。

economic environment 経済環境, 景気
◆The harsh economic environment is forecast to continue in the next business year. 厳しい経済環境は、来期も続くと予想される。

economic event 経済事象, 経済の動き, 経済動向
◆A business combination is a significant economic event that results from bargaining between independent parties. 企業結合は、独立した当事者間の取引から生じるひとつの重要な経済事象である。

economic expansion 景気拡大, 景気回復, 景気上昇, 経済成長, 経済拡張 (=business expansion)
 chalk off economic expansion 経済成長を抑える
 pace of economic expansion 景気拡大ペース, 経済成長率
 sustained economic expansion 経済の持続的な成長
◆Economic expansion is far from being felt by households. 景気回復は、家計の実感にはほど遠い。◆Expecting the economic expansion will continue, corporations are actively investing in plants and equipment. 景気拡大が続くと見た企業は、設備投資に積極的だ。◆The longest period of postwar economic expansion was known as an economic boom without feeling. 戦後最長の景気回復は、実感なき景気回復と言われた。◆The NBER's business cycle dating committee concluded that the economic expansion that started in November 2001 had ended. 全米経済研究所（NBER）の景気循環判定委員会の委員は、「2001年から始まった米景気の拡大はすでに終わっている」との見解で一致した。◆The rate of economic expansion in the current phase of recovery is much smaller than previous expansionary phases. 現在の景気拡大期[景気拡大局面]の経済成長率は、過去の景気拡大期よりかなり低い。

economic forecast　経済予測, 経済見通し, 景気予測, 景気見通し　(=economic outlook)
◆The economic forecast assumed that the economy would see gradual recovery in the latter half of fiscal 2010. 景気は2010年度後半には徐々に回復する, と経済見通しは想定した。

economic fundamentals　経済のファンダメンタルズ, 経済の基礎的条件, 景気のファンダメンタルズ
(=fundamentals of the economy; ⇒psychological factor)
◆Exchange rates should reflect economic fundamentals. 為替レートは, 経済のファンダメンタルズ（経済の基礎的条件）を反映しなければならない。◆Japan's economic fundamentals differ from those of the United States. 日本経済の基礎的条件［日本の経済の実態］は, 米国とは違う。

economic globalization　経済のグローバル化
　an age of economic globalization　経済のグローバル化時代
　progress in economic globalization　経済のグローバル化の進展
◆An age of economic globalization is characterized by intense competition in the pursuit of maximum profit. 経済のグローバル化時代の特徴は, 利益の極大化を求めて繰り広げられる熾烈な競争である。

economic growth　経済成長, 経済発展, 景気浮揚, 景気, 経済成長率　(=growth of the economy)
　commit to economic growth　経済成長に全力を挙げる
　cyclical downturn in economic growth　景気の悪化
　economic growth policy　経済成長政策
　encourage economic growth　景気浮揚を図る
　facilitate economic growth　経済成長を促す
　great tide [wave] of economic growth　経済成長の大きな潮流
　harmful to economic growth　経済成長を妨げる
　lower economic growth　経済成長率の低下
　maintain economic growth　経済成長を維持する
　pullback in economic growth　景気回復の減速
　qualitative economic growth　質的経済成長, 質的成長
　rapid economic growth　急速な経済成長, 高度経済成長
　sharp falloff in economic growth　景気の急激な減速
　slowdown of economic growth　景気の減速, 経済成長の鈍化
　spur flagging economic growth　失速気味の経済成長に刺激を与える
　stable economic growth　経済の安定成長, 安定した経済成長
　strong economic growth　経済の高成長
　sustained economic growth　経済成長の持続
　the prospects for economic growth　経済成長の見通し, 経済成長率予測
　zero economic growth　ゼロ成長
◆A slowdown in economic growth among emerging economies is expected. 新興国の経済成長鈍化が, 予想される。◆Domestic and foreign demands, the two engines powering Japan's economic growth, are out of kilter. 日本の経済成長を引っ張る原動力の内需と外需が, 今のところ不調だ。◆Due to sluggish stock markets, some Japanese companies are considering listing their shares in other Asian countries where economic growth is expected. 株式市場の低迷で, 日本企業の一部は, 経済成長が見込める他のアジア市場への株式上場を検討している。◆European countries put priority on fiscal reconstruction while the United States attaches importance to economic growth. 景気重視の米国に対して, 欧州は財政再建を優先している。◆Japan's economic growth is driven by exports, but it will have to vie for export markets with emerging economies. 日本の経済成長の原動力は輸出だが, 今後は新興国と輸出市場の争奪戦になろう。◆The Asian Development Bank trimmed its 2011 forecast for economic growth for 45 developing countries or newly industrializing Asian countries, excluding Japan. アジア開発銀行（ADB）は, 日本などを除くアジア太平洋45か国・地域の2011年の国内総生産（GDP）成長率見通しを, 下方修正した。◆The Bank of Japan envisages the prospects of economic growth and consumer price trends in its "Outlook for Economic Activity and Prices." 日銀は,「経済・物価情勢の展望」（展望リポート）で, 経済成長や消費者物価の先行きを示している。◆The current rise in the yen's value may obstruct economic growth. 現在の円高は, 経済成長を妨げる可能性がある。◆The economic growth of the newcomers to the EU is higher than the average of the previous membership. EU新加盟国の経済成長は, 旧加盟国の平均より高い。◆The European Central Bank cut its main interest rate by 0.25 percent following heavy pressure for a rate cut to spur flagging economic growth. 失速気味の経済成長に刺激を与えるため利下げを求める強い圧力を受けて, 欧州中央銀行（ECB）はその主要（政策）金利を0.25％引き下げた。◆The G-7's financial ministers and central bank governors are committed to taking necessary measures to support financial stability and economic growth. 先進7か国（G7）の財務相と中央銀行総裁は, 金融安定化と経済成長を支えるためにあらゆる手段を講じる決意だ。◆The government assumes a scenario in which Japan's economic growth will shift into high gear with overseas demand as a driving force. 政府は, 海外需要をテコに日本の経済成長が本格化する, とのシナリオを描いている。

economic growth rate　経済成長率, 経済の伸び率
◆The economic growth rates for Asian countries, except for such major economies as Japan, have been revised upward to an average of 4.8 percent for this year. 日本など先進国を除いたアジアの今年の経済成長率は, 平均4.8％に上方修正された。

economic improvement　景気回復
(=economic recovery)
◆The recent economic improvement shows that the nation will be able to emerge from deflation sooner or later. 最近の景気回復ぶりは, 日本が遅かれ早かれデフレから脱却できることを示している。◆There is slow progress in economic improvement among nonmanufacturing businesses, largely as a result of sluggish sales at retailers due to the ongoing deflation. デフレの進行で主に小売業の売上が低迷しているため, 非製造業は景気回復の足取りが弱い。

economic indicator　景気指標, 経済指標
◆Economic indicators, such as the unemployment rate, the number of corporate bankruptcies and consumer spending, have been declining sharply. 失業率や企業倒産件数, 個人消費などの経済指標が, 急激に悪化している。◆Recent U.S. economic indicators show the fragility of the world largest economy. 最近の米国の経済指標は, 米経済の弱さを示している。◆Some economic indicators in the United States are showing positive signs. 米国の景気指標の一部は現在, 好転の兆しを示している。◆The diffusion indexes of the coincident, leading and lagging indicators compare the current levels of various economic indicators with their levels three months earlier. 一致指数や先行指数, 遅行指数などの景気動向指数は, 各種経済指標の現状を3か月前の状況と比較したものだ。

economic loss　経済損失
◆Abolishing the housing loan tax break would reduce the number of housing starts by 100,000, which translates into an economic loss of ￥4.6 trillion. 住宅ローン減税（住宅減税）を廃止した場合, 住宅着工戸数は10万戸減り, 経済損失は4兆6,000億円に及ぶ。

economic malaise　景気沈滞, 景気低迷, 経済低迷
◆We cannot help but wonder how long the existing economic malaise will linger. 現在の景気低迷がいつまで続く

のか、首をかしげざるを得ない。

economic management　経済運営
◆Prime Minister Naoto Kan's competence in economic management will be put to the test. これから、菅首相の経済運営の手腕が問われることになる。

economic measures　経済対策, 景気対策
◆The government must come up with new policies seamlessly so that the effects of current economic measures can kick in. 現在の景気対策の効果が息切れしないよう、切れ目のない新たな政策対応が必要だ。

economic mismanagement　経済運営の失敗
◆Tax revenue shortages, stemming from the administration's misreading of economic trends and its economic mismanagement, have been occurring since fiscal 2001. (小泉)政権の景気情勢の見誤りと経済運営の失敗による税収不足は、2001年度から起きている。

economic morass　経済の泥沼状態, 泥沼の経済状況, 経済の難局[苦境, 苦況]
◆The United States should pull out of the economic morass. 米国は、泥沼の経済状況から抜け出すはずだ。

economic organization　経済団体
(=business organization)
◆Economic organizations have also proposed a major increase in the consumption tax rate. 経済団体も、消費税率の大幅引上げを提言している。◆Waves of downsizing are wearing down not only corporations and administrations, but also economic organizations. リストラの波は、企業や行政だけでなく、経済団体にも及んでいる。

economic outlook　経済見通し, 景気見通し, 景気[経済]の先行き, 経済展望
◆Concerns over the U.S. economic outlook tend to induce yen-buying as a safe haven. 米経済の先行きに対する懸念から、安全な投資手段として円が買われる傾向にある。◆Fed Chairman Ben Bernanke described the U.S. economic outlook as "unusually uncertain." 米連邦準備制度理事会(FRB)のバーナンキ議長は、米経済の見通しについて「異例なほど不透明だ」と述べた。◆Gold extended its rally to a record above $1,900 an ounce amid increased uncertainties over the U.S. and European economic outlook on the Comex in New York. ニューヨーク商品取引所では、米欧景気見通しへの懸念[米欧経済の先行き不透明感]の高まりを受け[懸念の高まりから]、金価格が急騰して、1トロイ・オンス=1,900ドルを史上初めて突破した。◆The economic outlook is unusually uncertain. 景気の先行きは、異例なほど不透明だ。◆The government has upgraded the economic outlook to "picking up." 政府は、景気見通しを「持ち直し」に上方修正した。◆The U.S. dollar traded at the lower ¥85 range in Tokyo over concern about the U.S. economic outlook. 東京金融市場[東京外国為替市場]では、米景気の先行きを懸念して、ドル相場は1ドル=85円台前半で取引された。◆This is the economic outlook for this fiscal year as seen by the Bank of Japan in its April forecast of prices. これが、日銀の4月の物価展望で日銀が示した今年度の経済見通しだ。

economic overheating　景気過熱
◆In emerging economics, economic overheating and inflation are concerns. 新興国では、景気過熱やインフレが懸念される。

economic package　経済対策
◆The economic package will include financial assistance for industries that have been hit hard by rising fuel costs, such as farming and fishing. 経済対策には、燃料高で打撃を受けている業界(農漁業者など)への金融支援も盛り込まれる。◆The economic package will include measures to help small and midsize companies procure funds. 経済対策には、中小企業の資金繰り支援策も盛り込まれる。◆The government and ruling parties began considering the economic package as they feared falling stock prices could result in a financial crisis. 政府・与党は、株価の下落で金融危機に陥る可能性があることから、経済対策の検討を開始した。

economic partnership　経済連携
economic partnership agreement　経済連携協定, EPA, 人と資本の交流を含む協定
economic partnership talks　経済連携協議, 経済パートナーシップ協議
economic partnership treaty　経済連携協定
◆The number of bilateral or regional economic partnerships has been on the rise since the early 1990s. 90年代の初めから、2国間や地域的な経済連携の数は増えている。

economic performance　景気, 景気動向, 経済実績, 経済活動, 経済成長率
improved economic performance　景気回復
pickup in economic performance　景気拡大, 景気回復
◆Compared to income and corporate taxes, revenue from consumption tax is hardly affected by economic performance. 所得税や法人税に比べて、消費税による税収[財源]は、景気に左右されにくい。◆Reflecting its good economic performance, Mexico's imports increased. 景気上昇を反映して、メキシコの輸入が増加した。

economic pickup　景気回復
◆China's economic pickup in March showed that its economy would be on track for stronger growth in coming months. 中国の3月の景気回復は、中国経済が今後数か月で力強い成長軌道に乗ることを示した。

economic plight　経済苦境
◆Acceleration of the disposal of bad loans has been criticized as causing the current economic plight, with its falling stock prices and financial uncertainty. 不良債権処理の加速は株価低迷と金融不安という現在の経済苦境を招いた、と批判されている。

economic policy　経済政策
◆The government and the Bank of Japan worked on economic policy in a coordinated manner. 政府と日銀は、経済政策で足並みをそろえて行動した。

economic policy management　経済政策運営
◆The G-7 meeting has repeatedly issued communiques concerning exchange rate fluctuations and economic policy management. 先進7か国会議(G7)は、これまで為替変動や経済政策運営に関する声明を再三、発信してきた。

economic power　経済大国(economic giant), 経済力
major economic power　経済大国, 先進国
massive economic power　経済大国
◆China has emerged as the world's second-largest economic power with year-on-year GDP growth rates approaching double digits. 中国は、前年比で(年率で)2桁近いGDP成長率で、世界第2位の経済大国になった。◆The United States places increasing significance on how it should promote ties with such a newly emerging military and economic power as China. 米国にとって、中国のような新興軍事大国、経済大国との関係をどのように推し進めるかがますます要になっている。◆To shore up their economies, major economic powers seem to be relying more on their monetary policies. 景気テコ入れに、先進国は金融政策頼みの様相が強まっている。

economic prospects　経済見通し, 景気見通し
◆The economic prospects look bright as the Nikkei Stock Average has retained the 10,000 level. 日経平均株価が1万円台を回復したので、景気見通しは明るく見える。

economic prosperity　経済的繁栄, 経済の繁栄, 経済的豊かさ, 経済の発展
◆U.S. economic prosperity is based on the stock markets. 米経済の繁栄の基盤は、株式市場だ。

economic pump-priming measures　景気対策
(⇒pump-priming measures)
◆It is necessary to bolster domestic demand through eco-

nomic pump-priming and employment support measures for the time being. 当面は、景気対策と雇用支援策で内需を支える必要がある。

economic recovery 景気回復, 経済の回復 (=business recovery, economic improvement, economic revival)
  a slowing of the economic recovery 景気回復の減速, 景気の減速
  block economic recovery 景気回復を妨げる
  pace of economic recovery 景気回復の足取り
  slow [sluggish] economic recovery 景気回復の足取りが重いこと
  the export-led economic recovery 輸出主導の景気回復, 輸出頼みの景気回復
  the sustainable economic recovery 景気の持続的回復, 持続的景気回復
  worldwide [global] economic recovery 世界的な景気回復
  ◆Concern is growing over a slowing of the economic recovery due to such factors as higher oil prices. 原油高などの要因を背景に、景気の減速懸念が広がっている。◆Economic recovery is the top priority for Japan. 景気回復が、日本の最優先課題だ。◆For an economic recovery to occur, oil prices must fall, and exports to the United States should recover. 今後の景気回復には、原油価格の下落と米国向け輸出の回復が条件だ。◆Goldman Sachs lowered its forecast for U.S. growth in 2011 on signs that the U.S. economic recovery lost momentum. 米金融大手のゴールドマン・サックスは、米景気回復減速の兆しを受けて、2011年の米国の成長見通しを下方修正した。◆In Europe, the sovereign debt crisis is putting pressure on an economic recovery. 欧州では、財政危機が景気回復の重圧になっている。◆Maintaining an easy monetary policy may lead to excessive corporate capital investment and have a negative impact on the sustainable economic recovery. 金融緩和政策を続けると、企業の過剰な設備投資を生み、景気の持続的回復を阻害する恐れがある。◆Priority measures to achieve economic recovery are stopping deflation and mobilizing all possible fiscal measures, financial policies and taxation reforms. 景気回復を実現するための優先課題は、デフレ阻止と、可能な財政政策、金融政策や税制改革を総動員することだ。◆Should the government forge ahead with its belt-tightening policy, the budding economic recovery may be reduced to a short-lived upturn. 政府が緊縮路線をひた走れば、景気回復の芽も、薄命の景気回復に終わりかねない。◆The diffusion index (DI) of business confidence among large manufacturers stood at plus 1, reflecting a growth in exports due to U.S. economic recovery and a recent surge in domestic stock prices. 大企業の製造業の業況判断指数(DI)が、プラス1となり、米経済の回復による輸出の伸びや最近の国内の株価上昇を反映した。◆The economic recovery seems to be picking up momentum. 景気回復に、勢いが出てきたようだ。◆The employment situation has improved in line with the economic recovery. 景気回復に伴って、雇用環境は良くなっている。◆This economic recovery is mainly due to the increased exports and corporate restructuring efforts centered on debt reduction. 今回の景気回復の主な要因は、輸出拡大と債務減らしを中心とした企業のリストラ努力だ。◆We must avoid hindering the export-led economic recovery, speeding up deflation and increasing bad loans, which can be brought about by falling stock prices and the weakening dollar. 株安とドル安がもたらす可能性がある輸出頼みの景気回復の挫折、デフレ加速、不良債権の拡大を、われわれは避けなければならない。◆Without an economic recovery and the resultant recovery of tax revenues, fiscal reconstruction will be made difficult. 景気回復[経済の再生]とそれによる税収の回復がなければ、今後の財政再建もおぼつかない。

economic reinvigoration 経済再活性化
  ◆Economic reinvigoration of Asia-Pacific nations as a whole is indispensable for a full-fledged recovery of the world economy. 世界景気の本格回復には、アジア太平洋全体の経済再活性化が必須だ。

economic report 経済報告, 経済報告書, 経済白書, 経済教書
  Economic Report of the President 経済報告, 米大統領経済報告, 経済教書 (⇒Budget Message)
  economic reports 景気指標 (=economic results)
  monthly economic report 月例経済報告
  ◆In its monthly economic report for August, the government said the economy "remains essentially flat." 8月の月例経済報告で政府は、景気は「おおむね横ばい」であるとした。

economic revival 景気回復
  ◆Since the collapse of the bubble economy in the early 1990s, Japan has experienced several phases of economic revival. 1990年代はじめのバブル崩壊以降、日本は何度か景気回復局面を迎えた。

economic sentiment 景況感
  ◆Behind the improvement in economic sentiment is a series of measures taken to date, including the government's antideflation package and the Bank of Japan's additional credit easing steps. 景況感好転の理由として、政府のデフレ対策や日銀の金融緩和の追加措置など、これまでにとられた一連の措置が挙げられる。

economic situation 景気全般, 景気, 経済情勢
  ◆Prime Minister Naoto Kan and Bank of Japan Governor Masaaki Shirakawa exchanged views on the recent economic situation. 菅首相と白川日銀総裁が、最近の経済情勢について意見交換した。◆The economic situation may drastically deteriorate. 景気は、大幅に[急激に]悪化する可能性がある。◆The economic situation will improve around the April-June period in 2012. 景気全般は、2012年4-6月期頃には持ち直すだろう。◆The government held a meeting on the current economic situation. 政府が、現在の経済情勢に関する会合を開いた。

economic slowdown 景気減速, 景気後退, 景気低迷, 景気鈍化, 景気腰折れ
  a sharp economic slowdown 景気急減速
  concern over the U.S. economic slowdown 米景気の減速懸念
  maintain guard against an economic slowdown 今後とも景気減速を警戒する
  the world economic slowdown 世界同時不況
  ◆Concern over the U.S. economic slowdown has grown since July. 7月以降、米景気の減速懸念が高まっている。◆The effects of an economic slowdown in industrialized countries stemming from the U.S. subprime woes could spread in the emerging economies. 米国のサブプライム(低所得者向け住宅融資)問題に起因する先進国の景気減速の影響は、新興国にも拡大する可能性がある。◆The Fed has to maintain guard against an economic slowdown and inflationary pressure. 米連邦準備制度理事会(FRB)は、今後とも景気減速とインフレ圧力を警戒する必要がある。◆There was widespread concern over a sharp economic slowdown for the July-September quarter. 7-9月期は、景気急減速の心配が広がった。

economic slump 景気低迷, 景気後退, 景気悪化, 不況, 不景気
  the current economic slump 現在の景気後退, 現在の不況
  the prolonged economic slump 長引く景気低迷
  the protracted economic slump 景気の長期低迷
  ◆Amid the protracted economic slump and the ongoing deflationary trend, the life insurance industry has been hit by a trio of predicaments. 景気の長期低迷とデフレ傾向が進行するなか、生保業界は三重苦に見舞われている。◆Emerging companies' profits declined due to the economic slump. 新興企業

の収益の減少は、景気悪化によるものだ。◆Smaller businesses have had difficulties in obtaining loans from banks and other financial institutions amid the prolonged economic slump. 長引く不況で、中小企業は、銀行その他の金融機関から融資を受けられなくなっている。◆The government expressed its optimistic expectations of the current economic slump. 政府は、現在の景気後退について楽観的な見通しを示した。◆The main cause of the prolonged deflation is that consumer demand has been weak due to the current economic slump. デフレ長期化の主因は、現在の不況で消費需要が低迷していることだ。◆The major banks attributed their increased bad loans to the poor performance of their borrowers due to the prolonged economic slump and Financial Service Agency inspections resulting in a stricter review of their asset assessments. 大手銀行は、不良債権が増えた理由として、長引く景気低迷で貸出先の経営が悪化したことと、金融庁の検査を受けて大手行が資産査定を厳しくしたことを挙げた。

economic stagnation　景気低迷, 景気後退, 景気停滞, 不況
　a remedy for economic stagnation　景気低迷への対策
　the period of economic stagnation　景気後退期, 景気停滞期
◆The lost decade refers to the period of economic stagnation since the bursting of the economic bubble in the early 1990s. 「失われた10年」とは、バブルが崩壊した1990年代初めから続いた景気後退[景気停滞]期のことである。◆The overall supply capacity must be increased through structural reforms as a remedy for economic stagnation. 景気低迷への対策として、構造改革により総供給力を引き上げる必要がある。

economic stall　景気の腰折れ, 景気減速[失速], 経済の失速
◆It was when European countries needed growth to help them wriggle out of the chokehold of debt that the economic stall came. 欧州諸国が債務の首かせから脱するために成長を必要としていたときに、景気減速[景気失速]が到来した。

economic stimulus　景気刺激, 経済刺激, 景気対策, 経済対策
◆The joint statement pointed out the necessity for economic stimulus through increased public spending. 共同声明は、財政出動[公共支出の拡大]による景気刺激策の必要性を指摘した。

economic stimulus measures　景気刺激策, 景気刺激対策, 景気対策, 景気浮揚策, 財政出動
　economic stimulus measures implemented so far　これまで実施された景気対策
　economic stimulus measures producing good results　効果を上げている景気刺激策
　lavish economic stimulus measures　大盤振る舞いの景気対策
　take effective economic stimulus measures　有効な景気対策を打ち出す
◆At two financial summit meetings since the collapse of Lehman Brothers, agreements were made on cooperation to implement large-scale economic stimulus measures and to take monetary relaxation policies. リーマン・ブラザーズの倒産[破たん]以来2回開かれた金融サミットでは、連携して大型の財政出動や金融緩和策を実施することで合意が得られた。◆Economic stimulus measures have produced good results. 景気刺激策が、効果を上げている。◆Economic stimulus measures implemented so far include a supplementary budget for job creation. これまで実施された景気対策としては、補正予算による雇用の創出もある。◆Economic stimulus measures should be prioritized in the government's policy management. 政府の政策運営では、景気刺激策[景気対策]を優先するべきだ。◆Economic stimulus measures such as tax cuts and additional public works projects work only as temporary remedies. 減税や公共事業の追加などの景気浮揚策は、一時的なカンフル剤にすぎない。◆The G-7 leaders merely welcomed Washington's economic stimulus measures in the form of interest rate cuts and tax cuts as "positive." G7首脳は、利下げや減税などの形での米政府の景気刺激策を「積極的」として歓迎しただけだ。◆The government will help Indonesia introduce economic stimulus measures through the soft loan. 政府は、この条件のゆるい借款を通じて、インドネシアの景気刺激導入を支援する。◆The Japanese government and the Bank of Japan should take effective economic stimulus measures as soon as possible. 日本政府と日銀は、早急に有効な景気対策を打ち出すべきだ。◆This country's debt-laden finances are in a critical situation due to the dole-out policies as well as lavish economic stimulus measures. わが国の借金漬けの財政は、バラマキ政策と大盤振る舞いの景気対策で、危機的な状況に陥っている。

economic strain　景気の悪化
◆In Spain, a real estate bubble has burst and added to the nation's economic strain. スペインでは、不動産バブルが崩壊して、景気悪化が深刻化している。

economic struggle　経済危機
◆With signs of hope appearing after two years of economic struggle, Southeast Asia is searching for a new path to revival. 2年来の経済危機から明るい兆しが見え始めた東南アジアは、再生への新しい道筋を模索している。

economic transaction　経済取引
◆The market value method views the convertible bonds as debt whose conversion was a significant economic transaction. 時価法は、転換社債を債務と見なし、転換社債の転換を重要な経済取引であると見ている。

economic trends　景気動向, 経済情勢
◆By the TSE's extension of the morning trade session to 11:30 a.m., investors will be able to trade Japanese stocks more easily while keeping an eye on economic trends in Asian markets. 東証が午前11時30分まで午前の取引時間を延長したことによって、投資家は今後、アジア市場の経済動向を見ながら日本株の取引をすることが容易になる。◆The U.S. Federal Reserve Board will change the pace of raising rates, depending on economic trends. 米連邦準備制度理事会（FRB）は、経済情勢次第で利上げのペースを変える方針だ。

economic turmoil　経済の混乱, 経済の混迷, 経済不安, 経済危機
◆Exporting firms are working all out to secure profits under the current economic turmoil. 現在の経済混乱の状況下で、輸出企業各社は収益の確保に躍起となっている。◆The world's economic turmoil will last several years. 世界経済の混迷は、数年間は続くものと思われる。

economic uncertainty　景気の不透明感, 経済の不透明感
◆Some smaller companies are more cautious about borrowing for capital expenditures due to economic uncertainty. 一部の中小企業は、景気の不透明感から、設備投資の借入れに一段と慎重になっている。

economic union　経済統合, 経済同盟
◆European countries are deepening and expanding economic union by introducing a common currency and welcoming East European countries into the European Union. 欧州は、共通通貨の導入や東欧諸国のEU（欧州連合）への取り込みなどで、経済統合の深化と拡大を続けている。

economic upswing　景気回復
◆The export-led economic growth could falter if the U.S. economic upswing slows down or if there is a rapid surge in the value of the yen. 輸出主導の経済成長は、米国の景気回復にブレーキがかかるか、急激な円高が進めば、大きくつまずく可能性がある。

economic upturn　景気回復
（=economic upswing; ⇒driving force, latest）
◆There are serious concerns that the strong yen and the weak

U.S. dollar could hurt the current economic upturn led by exports. 大きな懸念材料は、円高・ドル安の進行で現在の輸出主導の景気回復が打撃を受けることだ。

economic value　経済価値
◆Current loan loss reserves will not be sufficient to cover the depreciation of nonperforming loans' economic value. 現在の引当金（貸倒れ引当金）では、不良債権の経済価値の減価を十分にカバーしきれないだろう。

economic woes　経済的苦悩, 経済的苦境, 経済不振
◆The Fed has been unable to deal with the current economic woes by changing interest rates as it has been maintaining a policy of virtually zero-percent interest rates. 米連邦準備制度知会（FRB）はこれまで実質的に金利ゼロ政策を続けてきたため、政策金利を上げ下げして現在の経済的苦境に対応することはできなくなっている。

economies　(名)経済, 経済性, 経済地域, 経済群, 経済国, 国, 諸国, エコノミー
　agglomeration economies　集積の経済
　ASEAN economies　アセアン諸国, ASEAN諸国
　developing economies　新興国, 発展途上国
　Economies of East Asia　東アジアの国と地域
　economies of network　連結の経済性（複数の企業や組織間で形成されるネットワークから生み出される経済性のこと）
　economies of scope　範囲の経済, 範囲の経済性, 多様化の経済, エコノミー・オブ・スコープ　(=economy of scope: 複数の製品を生産したほうが、単一の製品を生産する場合よりも生産コストが安くなる現象のことで、製品多様化・経営多角化の経済性を指す)
　economies of speed　スピードの経済, スピードの経済性, エコノミー・オブ・スピード　(=economy of speed)
　emerging economies　新興国, 新興経済群, 新興経済地域, 新興経済国
　external economies　外部経済
　growing economies　新興経済地域
　high income economies　高所得国
　internal economies　内部経済
　leading economies　主要国, 主要国・地域
　less developed economies　発展途上国, 新興国
　localization economies　地域特化の経済
　most developed economies　先進諸国
　newly emerging economies　新興国
　non-dollar economies　非ドル通貨圏
　open-market economies　自由市場経済, 市場経済
　regional economies　地域経済
　size of the economies　経済規模
　the Group of 20 major industrial and emerging economies　主要先進国と新興国の20か国・地域（G20）
◆Surplus funds put out by developed economies' monetary easing measures have flowed into emerging economies to inflate economic bubbles. 先進国の金融緩和策で生じた余剰資金が、新興国に流れ込み、バブルを発生させている。◆The eurozone's three biggest economies, Germany, France and Italy, will not grow at all. ユーロ圏主要3か国（独、仏と伊）の経済は、ゼロ成長になる見通しだ。◆The Fed's monetary easing policies have brought about inflation in newly emerging economies. FRB（米連邦準備制度理事会）の金融緩和策が、新興国のインフレを招いた。◆To shore up their economies, major economic powers seem to be relying more on their monetary policies. 景気テコ入れに、先進国は金融政策頼みの様相が強まっている。

economies of scale　規模の経済, 規模の経済性, 規模の拡大, 規模の利益, スケール・メリット, 数量効果, エコノミー・オブ・スケール　(=economy of scale, scale merit: 少品種大量生産の経済効率を意味する)
　economies of scale strategy　数量効果を追求する戦略
　maintain economies of scale　規模の経済を維持する, スケール・メリットを維持する
　pursue economies of scale　規模の経済を追求する, 規模の拡大を追及する
◆Mergers and acquisitions to pursue economies of scale will be carried out worldwide. 規模の経済[規模の拡大]を追求するためのM&A（企業の合併・買収）は今後、国際的規模で実施される見込みだ。◆The Japanese banking sector is entering a phase of realignment in which banks are seeking economies of scale by combining their respective strengths. 日本の銀行業界は、それぞれの力[強み、得意分野]を統合して規模の拡大を目指す再編の段階に入っている。

economist　(名)経済学者, 節約家, 倹約家, エコノミスト
　business economist　経営学者, 経営経済学者, 企業経営専門家, ビジネス・エコノミスト
　company economist　企業内エコノミスト, カンパニー・エコノミスト
　home economist in business　消費者問題担当者, ヒーブ, HEIB
　leading economist　有力エコノミスト
　Street economist　ウォール街のエコノミスト, 市場エコノミスト　(=Wall Street economist)
◆Italy's new government led by economist Mario Monti must face painful financial reforms. 経済専門家マリオ・モンティ氏を首相とするイタリア新政権は、痛みを伴う財政改革が急務だ。◆Many economists predict the economy will recover in the July-September quarter. 7-9月期に景気は回復する、とエコノミストの多くは予想している。◆Some economists point out that the limited effects of the quantitative easing measures. 一部のエコノミストは、量的緩和策の効果の限界を指摘している。◆Some economists point out the side effects of the Fed's quantitative easing policy. エコノミストのなかには、FRB（米連邦準備制度理事会）の量的緩和策の副作用を指摘する声もある。

Economist Intelligence Unit　エコノミスト・インテリジェンス・ユニット, EIU
◆The Economist Intelligence Unit is a research and analysis division of the Economist. エコノミスト・インテリジェンス・ユニット（EIU）は、英誌『エコノミスト』の調査研究・分析事業部門だ。

economy　(名)経済, 経済性, 景気, 節約, 倹約, 効率的使用[利用], 経済機構, 経済組織, 経済国, 社会, 経済成長率, 成長率, エコノミー　(⇒global economy)
　behavior of the economy　景気動向, 景気の先行き
　booming economy　好景気, 過熱気味の景気
　boost the economy　景気を刺激する, 景気を活性化する
　bottoming out of the economy　景気や物価の底入れ
　discourage the economy　景気の足を引っ張る
　drag on the economy　経済成長率を押し下げる要因
　economy's current condition　足元の景気
　economy's underlying tone　景気の基調
　general economy　経済全体
　global economy　世界経済, 地球規模の経済
　heating up of the economy　景気の過熱
　highly developed economies　先進工業国
　industrialized economies　工業国, 工業先進国
　monetary economy　貨幣経済
　moribund economy　景気低迷
　national economy　国内景気, 国内経済
　outlook of the economy　景気見通し
　picture of economy　景気の状況
　poor economy　景気低迷

power the economy　景気の原動力になる
prop up the economy　景気を下支えする
reflate the economy　景気浮揚を図る
reform the economy　経済改革を進める
restore the economy's dynamism　経済の活力を取り戻す
runaway economy　過熱景気
sagging economy　景気低迷
slow the economy　経済成長を鈍化させる
slowdown of the economy　不況
stabilize the economy　経済を安定化させる
strengthening economy　景気の好転
the economy　景気（=the business）
upturn in the economy　景気回復
weak economy　景気低迷

◆Among other factors that could adversely affect the national economy are possible setbacks in the Chinese and U.S. economies as well as high oil prices. 国内景気に悪影響を及ぼす恐れがある他の要因として、中国や米国の景気後退や原油高がある。◆Behind these cautious views among large manufacturers are uncertainty over the debt crisis in the eurozone and the slowdown in the U.S. economy. 大企業製造業のこうした警戒感[慎重な見方]の背景には、ユーロ圏の債務危機不安や米景気の減速がある。◆If the economy is to see a full-fledged recovery, the government should continue taking all feasible policy steps, including propping up the economy by fiscal means. 本格的な景気回復を見るには、財政面でのテコ入れを含めて、政府は引き続き実行可能なあらゆる政策手段を取るべきである。◆If the government relaxes its policy now, the economy will not be able to get on the recovery track. 政府がいまその政策の手を緩めれば、景気は回復軌道に乗れないだろう。◆In the case of the United States, increased public spending to boost the economy can hardly be expected. 米国の場合、財政出動による景気浮揚は期待しにくい。◆It is necessary to fully study what kind of impact the financial regulations could have on the economy. 金融規制が経済にどのような影響を及ぼすか、十分に検討する必要がある。◆Italy is the third-largest economy of the eurozone. イタリアは、ユーロ圏で第三位の経済大国である。◆Italy's economy is the third largest after [following] those of Germany and France in the eurozone. イタリアの経済規模は、ユーロ圏ではドイツとフランスに次いで3位だ。◆Markets in up-and-coming countries with booming economies, is growing rapidly. 好景気の新興市場は、急成長している。◆Rapid recovery following the so-called Lehman shock has ended and the Chinese economy has entered a phase aimed at stable growth. いわゆるリーマン・ショック後の中国の急回復の時期は終わり、中国経済は、安定成長を目指す段階に入っている。◆Ten of 12 Fed district banks reported weaker conditions or declines in their regional economies. 全米12地区連銀のうち10連銀が、各地域経済の悪化あるいは経済活動の低下を報告した。◆The Bank of Japan will set up a fund to buy long-term government bonds, exchange-traded funds and other financial assets in a bid to prop up the nation's economy. 日本の景気を下支えするため、日銀は基金を新設して、長期国債や上場投資信託(ETF)などの金融商品[金融資産]を買い入れる。◆The economy, fueled by a pickup in business spending on inventories, is now expanding at a spanking clip. 企業の在庫投資の回復に支えられた経済は現在、顕著なペースで拡大している。◆The economy is moving toward an incipient recovery. 景気は、持ち直しに向けた動きが見られる。◆The economy may be headed toward a turnaround on the back of improved exports and corporate profitability. 輸出と企業収益が改善して、景気が好転する可能性もある。◆The economy still remains in a recovery phase in the business cycle. 景気は、まだ回復局面にある[景気の回復基調はまだ続いている]。◆The Fed's program of buying $600 billion in Treasury bonds to help the economy is to end in June 2011 on schedule. 景気を支えるために6,000億ドルの国債を買い入れる米連邦準備制度理事会(FRB)の量的緩和政策は、予定通り2011年6月に終了した。◆The Japanese economy faces a growing downside risk due to concerns about the future of the U.S. and European economies. 日本経済は、欧米経済の先行き懸念から、日本経済の下振れリスクが高まっている。◆The rational actions for survival taken by individual companies herald a danger that could lead the Japanese economy into contracted equilibrium. 生き残りをかけて個々の企業が取っている合理的な行動が、日本経済を縮小均衡に導く危険性をはらんでいる。◆The strong yen can hurt the Japanese economy. 円高は、日本経済にダメージを与える可能性がある。◆The U.S. economy has been hit by a chilled housing market and shrinking employment. 米経済は、住宅市場の冷え込みと雇用の落ち込みで打撃を受けている。◆The U.S. economy has gotten back on the recovery track since the latter half of last year. 米国の景気は、昨年後半からまた回復軌道に乗り始めた。◆The U.S. economy is in danger of slipping into a double-dip recession. 米経済は、景気の二番底に陥る可能性[恐れ]がある。◆The U.S. Federal Reserve Board said in its Beige Book release that the U.S. economy deteriorated further in almost all corners of the country. 米連邦準備制度理事会(FRB)は、地区連銀景況報告(ベージュ・ブック)を発表し、米国の経済情勢はほぼ全米で一段と悪化していると指摘した。◆The U.S. Federal Reserve raised the official discount rate and the target rate of federal funds by 0.25 percentage points in a bid to quell inflation and keep the economy from overheating. 米連邦準備制度理事会(FRB)は、インフレを防ぎ景気の過熱を警戒して、公定歩合とフェデラル・ファンド(FF)の誘導目標金利をそれぞれ0.25パーセント引き上げた。◆This is the fourth straight quarter that the economy has shown growth. これで、4四半期連続のプラス成長となった。◆With the United States facing the worst financial crisis in generations, Bush's White House took decisive measures to safeguard the economy. 米国が過去最悪の金融危機に直面して、ブッシュ政権は経済危機を守るために断固たる措置を取った。

economy-boosting measures [packages]　経済刺激策, 経済対策, 景気刺激策, 景気対策
◆A second supplementary budget is needed to finance already announced economy-boosting measures. 第二次補正予算は、すでに発表された景気対策の財源確保に必要とされる。

economy-slowing factor　景気減速要因
◆The negative growth was due to the stagnancy of corporate capital investment as well as sluggish personal spending and other economy-slowing factors. このマイナス成長は、企業の設備投資が頭打ちの状態だったことと、個人消費の伸び悩みや他の景気減速要因によるものだ。

Economy Watchers index　景気ウオッチャー指数
◆The Economy Watchers index, a survey of barbers, taxi drivers and others who deal with consumers, dropped to the lowest level since October 2001. 消費者を相手に商売している理髪店やタクシー運転手などに街の景気を聞く調査結果の景気ウオッチャー指数は、2001年10月以来最低の水準にまで低下した。

edge　(動)ゆっくり移動する, じりじり動く[進む], 少しずつ変動する, 〜を取り巻く, 〜を縁(ふち)どる
edge down　じりじり下がる[低下する], じり安になる, 少しずつ下がる
edge down a little　弱含む, 小幅ながら減少する
edge downwards [downward]　じり安傾向にある
edge higher　じりじりと上昇する, 小幅上昇する, 小幅ながら引き上げられる, 微増となる
edge lower　じりじりと低下する, 小幅低下する, 小幅ながら引き下げられる, 微減となる

edge up　じりじり上がる［増える］, じり高になる, 少しずつ上がる, 小幅上昇する, 強含む
edge up a little　強含む, 小幅ながら増加する, 微増となる
edge up for the first time since June　6月以来初めて上昇に転じる
edge up through　小幅上昇して～を突破する
edge upwards　じり高傾向にある
◆Exports in September edged up only 2.1 percent to ￥7.04 trillion. 9月の輸出額は、わずか2.1％の微増で、7兆400億円にとどまった。◆The balance of coins in circulation edged up 0.1 percent in May 2011 to ￥4.52 trillion from a year earlier. 2011年5月の貨幣流通高は、前年同月比で0.1％微増の4兆5,200億円となった。◆The central bank likely will predict the consumer price index will edge up in fiscal 2011. 日銀は、2011年度の消費者物価指数について小幅プラスの予測を示すと見られる。

edge　（名）先端, 優位, 優位性, 優勢, 強み, 瀬戸際, 限界, 効果, 刃, 稜線, エッジ
competitive edge　競争上の優位(性), 競争力
cutting edge　鋭利な刃, 最前線, 最先端, 先頭, 主導的地位, 最新式　（=leading edge）
decisive edge　決定的優位
gain an edge on　～に対して優位を勝ち取る
have the edge on［over］　～より少し優れている, ～より少し強みがある, ～より優勢である
leading edge　主導的地位, 最先端, 最前部, 最前線, 先頭, 最新式, トップ　（=cutting edge）
take the edge off　弱める, そぐ, 鈍らせる
technological edge　技術的優位, 技術的優位性

Edge Act　エッジ法, エッジ・アクト（米国の商業銀行に一定の条件で州際業務を認める法律）
Edge（Act）Corporation　エッジ法会社［法人］, エッジ・アクト法人, エッジ・アクト・コーポレーション
Edge Act securities　エッジ法証券（米国の州際業務に関連した証券）

EFF　（IMFの）拡大信用供与制度　（Extended Fund Facilityの略）

effect　（動）行う, 実施する, (取引を)執行する, 成し遂げる, 手配する, 保険を付ける
effect a rate cut　利下げを実施する
effect a transaction　取引を執行する
effect a two-for-one stock split　1対2の株式分割を行う
effect an insurance　保険を付ける
effect payment　支払いを行う, 納付する
◆Only brokers are authorized to effect transactions on the Brussels Stock Exchange. ブリュッセル証券取引所では、ブローカーだけに取引執行の資格が認められている。◆The two-for-one stock splits were effected in the form of 100 percent stock dividends. これらの1対2の株式分割は、100％株式配当形式で実施しました。

effect　（名）影響, 影響額, 発効, 効力, 効果, 施行, 趣旨, 意味　（⇒adverse effect, negative effect）
boomerang effect　ブーメラン効果
cumulative effect　累積影響額, 影響累計額, 累積効果
currency effects　為替の影響
dilutive effect　希薄化効果
effect of accounting change　会計処理変更の影響
effect of exchange rate changes on cash　現金預金に対する為替レート変動［為替変動相場］の影響［影響額］, 為替変動による現金への影響
expansionary effect　景気刺激効果
external economy effect　外部経済効果
give effect to　～を実行に移す

halo effect　ハロー効果, 後光効果, 光背効果
knock-on effect　連鎖反応, 連鎖効果, ドミノ効果　（=domino effect）
leverage effect　他人資本効果, テコの効果, 梃率（ていりつ）効果, レバレッジ効果
net of income tax effect　税効果後
seasonal adjustment　季節調整
side effects　副作用
size effect　規模効果
tax effects of timing differences　期間差異の税効果
the effect of the yen-selling market intervention　円売り介入［市場介入］の効果
◆A merger between life insurance companies will have little effect, because there is no synergy effect. 生命保険同士が合併しても、相互補完関係が生まれないため、効果は薄い。◆Some economists point out the side effects of the Fed's quantitative easing policy. エコノミストのなかには、FRB（米連邦準備制度理事会）の量的緩和策の副作用を指摘する声もある。◆The effects of an economic slowdown in industrialized countries stemming from the U.S. subprime woes could spread in the emerging economies. 米国のサブプライム（低所得者向け住宅融資）問題に起因する先進国の景気減速の影響は、新興国にも拡大する可能性がある。◆The provisions, after giving effect to taxes and minority interest, reduced 2010 earnings by $200 million. これらの引当金繰入れで、関連税金と少数株主持ち分利益控除後の2010年度の純利益は、2億ドル減少しました。◆The rate of savings among those people in their 30s and 40s is on an upward trend, which is likely to have a depressing effect on domestic demand. 30～40歳代の貯蓄率が増大傾向にあり、内需を下押ししている可能性がある。

effect of the Fed's rate cuts　FRB（米連邦準備制度理事会）の金利引下げの効果
◆To enhance the stimulating effect of the Fed's rate cuts, swift implementation of fiscal and tax stimulus measures, including tax cuts on investment designed to reinvigorate the stock market, is necessary in addition to the large-scale tax cut program that is under way. 米連邦準備制度理事会（FRB）の金利引下げの刺激効果を高めるためには、現在実施中の大型減税プログラムに加え、株式市場を再活性化するための投資減税など、財政・税制面からの景気刺激策の速やかな実施が必要である。

effect of the market intervention　市場介入の効果, 為替市場介入の効果
◆Some market players feel the effect of the market intervention will not last long. 市場関係者の間では、為替市場介入の効果は長続きしないとの見方もある。

effect of (the) quantitative easing measures　量的緩和策の効果, 金融の量的緩和の効果
◆Some central bank officials have become skeptical of the effect of quantitative easing measures. 中央銀行関係者には、量的緩和［量的緩和策］の効果について疑問視する声も出てきている。◆Some economists point out that the limited effects of the quantitative easing measures. 一部のエコノミストは、量的緩和策の効果の限界を指摘している。

effect of the quantitative easing policy　量的緩和策の効果, 量的緩和の効果
◆There are mixed views as to the effect of the quantitative easing policy even within the Fed. 量的緩和策の効果については、FRB（米連邦準備制度理事会）内でも意見が割れている。

effect of the yen-selling market intervention　円売り市場介入の効果, 円売り介入の効果
◆The effect of the yen-selling market intervention implemented unilaterally by Japan has already weakened. 日本が単独で実施した円売り介入［市場介入］の効果は、すでに薄らいでいる。

effective　（形）有効な, 効果的な, 効率的な, 実効の, 実施

されている, 実施中の, 効力をもつ, 事実上の, 実際の, 実質の, 実動の
  average effective reserve requirement rate　平均実効準備率
 cost-effective　コスト効率がよい, 費用効率がよい, 費用効果が高い
 effective annual rate　実効年利率
 effective annual yield　実効年利回り
 effective buying income　実質購買所得, EBI
 effective date　発効日, 契約日, 取引開始日, 実施年月日, （スワップの）実行日,（保険期間の）始期
 effective debt　実質債務, 有効負債
 effective demand　有効需要
 effective devaluation　実効為替切下げ
 effective duration　実効デュレーション（金利感応度（デュレーション）のうち, 金利変動が期待キャッシュ・フローに影響するという前提で計算されるものをいう）
 effective exchange rate　実効為替相場, 実効為替レート
 effective income　実質所得
 effective interest　実効利息, 実効利率, 実効金利, 実質利率　（=effective interest rate, effective rate of interest）
 effective interest method　実効利率法
 effective life　有効期間
 effective management　効率経営
 effective money [coin]　硬貨
 effective net worth　有効純資産, 有効正味資産
 effective portfolio　効率的なポートフォリオ, 効率のよいポートフォリオ
 effective premium　実効プレミアム
 effective price index　実効物価指数
 effective quantity of money　有効貨幣量
 effective spread　実効スプレッド
 effective tax　実効税額
 effective valuation　実効為替切上げ
 effective volatility　実効ボラティリティ
 real effective exchange rate　実質実効為替レート　（=real effective FX rate）
 ◆Quantitative easing measures are believed to have been proven effective in stabilizing financial markets. 量的緩和政策は金融市場の安定化に効果的だった, とされている。◆The purchase of foreign bonds is considered an effective method to weaken the yen. 外債の購入は, 円安誘導効果を持つとされている。

effective book value　実質簿価（「実質簿価」は, 取得価格である簿価から貸倒れ引当金を差し引いたもので, 時価よりも高いため不良債権処理を加速する効果がある）
 ◆Bad loans should be bought at market value rather than at effective book value. 不良債権は, 実質簿価でなく時価で買い取るべきだ。◆The effective book value is calculated by subtracting amassed loan loss reserves from the original amount of money that was lent. 実質簿価は, 債権の元々の額（貸し付けた元々の金額：簿価）から,（銀行が）積み立てた貸倒れ引当金を差し引いて算定する。

effective interest rate　実効金利（effective rate: 実際に借りた金額[貸した金額]に対する利子の割合）,（証券の）実効利率, 実効利回り（effective rate: 債券の購入価格に対する受取利子の割合。yield to maturity（満期利回り）とほぼ同義）
  （=effective interest, effective rate of interest）
 effective annual interest rate　実効年利率
 effective interest rate method　実効金利法
 effective interest rate or yield rate　実効利率

effective measure　有効な措置
 ◆As an effective measure to prevent the yields of government bonds from soaring and to soothe credit uneasiness in the market, the ECB may buy up a large number of bonds from Italy and other countries. 国債利回りの急騰を抑え, 市場の信用不安を鎮静化するための有効な措置として, 欧州中央銀行（ECB）は, イタリアなどの国債を大量に買い支える可能性がある。

effective rate　実効利率, 実質収益率, 実勢相場, 実効相場, 実効レート
 effective rate of discount　実質割引率
 effective rate of duty　実効税率
 effective rate of interest　実効金利, 実効利率　（=effective interest rate）

effective tax rate　実効税率
 annual effective tax rate　年間実効税率
 effective income tax rate　実効所得税率, 実効税率, 実効法人税率　（=effective tax rate）
 effective tax rate　実効税率
 estimated annual effective tax rate　見積り年間実効税率

effectively　（副）有効に, 効果的に, 有効に, 効率的に, 有機的に, 実際には, 事実上
 ◆As a tacit understanding with EU member states, the European Central Bank has refrained from implementing monetary policy that is effectively a fiscal bailout. 欧州連合（EU）加盟国との暗黙の了解として, 欧州中央銀行（ECB）は, 財政支援に当たる金融政策の実施を控えてきた。◆The BOJ decided to ease its monetary grip further by effectively restoring its zero-interest-rate policy. 日銀は, 実質的にゼロ金利政策を復活させて, 追加の金融緩和を決めた。◆The decline in yields on whole life insurance products effectively raises premiums. 終身保険商品の利回り（予定利率）の引下げは, 実質的な保険料の値上げになる。

effectiveness　（名）有効性, 効率, 効率性, 効果
 cost effectiveness [cost-effectiveness] analysis　費用・効果分析
 leveraged effectiveness　レバレッジ効果
 the effectiveness of the stock price measures　株価対策の効果
 ◆Doubts over the effectiveness of the announced stock price measures have already been expressed among Japanese market players. 今回発表された株価対策の効果については, 日本の市場関係者の間ですでに疑問視する声がある。

efficiency　（名）効率, 効率性, 効率化, 能率, 有効性
  （⇒business efficiency, capital efficiency）
 asset efficiency　資産の効率性
 bond market efficiency　債券市場の効率性
 boost [enhance, increase] efficiency in capital markets　資本市場の効率性を高める[向上させる]
 business efficiency　事業効率, 事業の効率性, 経営効率
 capital efficiency　資本効率
  （=efficiency of capital）
 cost efficiency　コスト効率
 economic efficiency　経済効率, 経済の効率性, 経済性
 efficiencies of scale　規模の効率性
 efficiency bond　性能担保保証金
 efficiency of fund operation　資金運用効率
 foster [promote] efficiency in the debt securities markets　債券市場の効率性を促進する, 債券市場の効率化を促進する
 improve business efficiency　経営効率を改善する, 経営の効率化を図る
 increase competitiveness through efficiency　効率化を通じて競争力を高める
 investment efficiency　投資効率

management efficiency　経営効率, 経営能率, 事業効率（＝efficiency of management）
market efficiency　市場の効率性
operating efficiency　事業効率, 営業効率
the overall efficiency of the capital markets　資本市場の全体的な効率性
◆FSA inspectors are to check the credibility of the banks' debtor companies, including their management efficiency and the accuracy of their collateral assessment. 金融庁の検査官は、銀行の融資先の経営効率や担保評価などを含めて、銀行の融資先の信用力を洗い直す。◆The efficiency of the financial sector has been enhanced. 金融の効率化が進んだ。◆The serious deterioration of operational efficiency is caused by excess output capacity and burgeoning workforces. 極端な経営効率の悪化は、生産設備と従業員の過剰によるものだ。

efficient　（形）効率的な, 効率のよい, 能率的な, 有能な, 有効な
cost-efficient　コスト効率の高い, 低コストの
cost-efficient source of financing　低コストの資金調達源
efficient financial market　効率的金融市場
efficient functioning　効率的な業務遂行
efficient management　効率的な経営, 経営の効率化
efficient new issuance　効率的な新発債発行
efficient portfolio　効率的のポートフォリオ（効率的市場を念頭に置いて組むポートフォリオ）
efficient rate of interest　有効利子率
efficient resource allocation　効率的資源配分（＝efficient allocation of resources）
more efficient running　運営の効率化
◆Higher gasoline prices have led to brisk sales of fuel-efficient cars in North America. ガソリン高騰で、北米での低燃費車の販売は好調だった。

efflux of gold　金の流出

effort　（名）努力, 試み, 尽力, 取組み, 動き, 活動, 作業, 仕事, 運動, キャンペーン, 募集, 対策, 政策, 策, 努力の成果, 労作, 力作, 立派な演説
（⇒in an effort to）
best efforts　最大限の努力, 最大努力, 最善の努力, 委託募集
collective effort　総力
cooperative efforts　協力関係
cost reduction efforts　コスト削減努力, コスト削減策
expense reduction efforts　経費削減努力
gap-closing efforts　赤字削減努力
joint effort　提携関係
reorganization efforts　再編の動き
restructuring efforts　経営再建策
sales effort　販売努力
self-help efforts　自助努力
steady effort　地道な努力
streamlining efforts　リストラ努力, リストラ策, 合理化措置, 合理化への取組み
◆China will ratchet up efforts to quell inflation in 2011. 中国は、2011年からインフレ抑制策を徐々に強化する方針だ。◆Delays in double-debt relief process may become obstacles to restoration efforts. 二重ローン救済手続きの遅れは、復興努力の障害になる可能性がある。◆Domestic banks are increasing their efforts to finance large overseas projects. 国内銀行各行は、海外での大型事業に融資する（プロジェクト・ファイナンスへの）取組みを強化している。◆France and Germany could not bridge their differences, so Europe's efforts to solve its escalating debt crisis plunged into disarray. フランスとドイツが両国の相違を埋められなかったため、深刻化する欧州の債務危機問題解決への欧州の取組みは、混乱に陥った。◆Further efforts are needed to resolve the financial unrest. 金融不安を解消するには、もう一段の努力が必要だ。◆Major commercial banks are reaching the final stages of their efforts to write off their nonperforming loans. 大手銀行は、不良債権処理への取組みの最終局面を迎えている。◆Policy coordination efforts between Japanese and U.S. currency authorities are genuine. 日米通貨当局の政策協調努力は、本物だ。◆The Bank of Japan stepped up its efforts to boost the flagging economy following the March 11 earthquake and tsunami by introducing a ￥500 billion cheap loan program. 日銀は、5,000億円の低利融資制度を導入して、東日本大震災で揺れる日本経済の刺激策を強化した。◆The merger plan will not go ahead unless the bank makes unstinting efforts to cut its nonperforming loans. 同行が不良債権の削減に向けて惜しみない努力をしないかぎり、統合計画が前に進むことはないだろう。◆The private sector has tackled necessary restructuring efforts earnestly. 民間は、必要なリストラ策に懸命に取り組んできた。◆We must expedite efforts to rebuild a safety net to support the financial system. 金融システムを支える安全網の立直し策を急ぐ必要がある。

EFSF　欧州金融安定基金, 欧州金融安定ファシリティ（European Financial Stability Facilityの略）
◆The bonds issued by the EFSF are guaranteed with the creditworthiness of the six eurozone states' bonds. 欧州金融安定基金（EFSF）が発行する債券は、（独仏など）ユーロ圏6か国の国債の信用力で保証されている。◆The EFSF is the EU bailout fund for countries with fiscal deficits. 欧州金融安定基金（EFSF）は、欧州の財政赤字国を支援する基金だ。◆The European Union will substantially expand the lending capacity of the EFSF to buy up government bonds in case the fiscal and financial crisis spreads countries as Italy. 欧州連合（EU）は、財政・金融危機がイタリアなどなどに拡大した場合に国債を買い込むため、欧州金融安定基金（EFSF）の融資能力を大幅に拡大する。◆The eurozone countries agreed to strengthen EFSF functions, such as bailout methods, in July 2011. 2011年7月にユーロ圏諸国は、支援手法など欧州金融安定基金（EFSF）の機能を強化することで合意した。◆The G-20 communique urged the eurozone countries to boost the EFSF, the EU bailout fund. G20（主要20か国・地域）の共同声明は、ユーロ圏諸国に欧州の金融支援基金である欧州金融安定基金（EFSF）の拡充を促した。◆The 17 eurozone countries agreed to expand the European Financial Stability Facility（EFSF）at a meeting of their finance ministers. ユーロを採用しているユーロ圏17か国は、ユーロ圏財務相会合で、欧州金融安定基金（EFSF）の規模を拡大することで一致した。◆Under the existing agreement, the IMF cannot buy government bonds through the EFSF as the IMF can only offer loans to countries. 現行協定では、IMF（国際通貨基金）は国にしか融資できないので、欧州金融安定基金（EFSF）を通じて国債を購入することはできない。◆What is urgently needed as the EU's rescue package is beefing up the functions of the EFSF and recapitalizing banks that own Greek and Italian government bonds. EU（欧州連合）の支援策として緊急に求められているのは、欧州金融安定基金（EFSF）の機能強化や、ギリシャやイタリアの国債を保有する銀行の資本増強などだ。

EFT　電子資金取引, コンピュータ資金振替システム, 電子決済（electronic funds transferの略）

EIB　欧州投資銀行（European Investment Bankの略）

EIOPA　欧州保険年金機構, 欧州保険年金監督機構（European Insurance and Occupational Pensions Authorityの略）

eke out funds　資金をひねり出す, 財源をひねり出す
◆Given the nation's tough fiscal condition, the government must eke out the necessary funds by scaling down low-priority policy projects. 日本の厳しい財政事情に照らせば、政府に求められるのは、優先度の低い政策プロジェクトを縮小して、必要な財源をひねり出すことだ。

electronic （形）電子の, 電子工学の, コンピュータ化された, エレクトロニック
 electronic authentication 電子認証
 electronic banking エレクトロニック・バンキング, オンライン銀行取引, EB
 （=e-banking: 電子化された銀行業務）
 electronic business banking エレクトロニック・ビジネス・バンキング
 electronic cash 電子キャッシュ, 電子マネー
 （=electronic money）
 electronic cash transfer コンピュータ利用による現金振込み　（=electronic money transfer）
 electronic certification 電子認証
 electronic check 電子小切手
 Electronic Communications Network 電子証券取引ネットワーク, ECN（私設取引システム「PTS」の一種）
 electronic credit 電子クレジット
 electronic data processing system 電子データ処理システム, 電子情報処理システム, 電子情報処理方式
 Electronic Disclosure for Investors' NETwork 電子開示システム, EDINET（金融商品取引法に基づく有価証券報告書等の開示書類に関する電子開示システム）
 electronic market 電子市場　（=e-market, electronic marketplace, Internet exchange）
 Electronic Money Act 電子マネー法
 electronic purse 電子財布
 electronic shopping 電子ショッピング
 electronic toll collection system ノンストップ自動車料金支払いシステム, ETC
 electronic trading 電子取引, 電子商取引, 電子売買, コンピュータ取引, 電子トレーディング, システム売買
 （=e-commerce, e-trading）
 electronic transfer of funds 電子資金振替, 電子決済
 （=electronic fund [funds] transfer）
 electronic wallet 電子財布, 電子ウォレット（パソコンに電子ウォレット専用のソフトをインストールして使うインターネット上, 電子上の財布）
electronic bank book [bankbook] 電子通帳, ウェブ通帳　（=electronic passbook）
 ◆The bank does not issue conventional bankbooks for cardholders, but offers electronic bank books that are used via the Internet and accessed through personal computer and cell phones.　同行は, カード会員に従来の銀行通帳は発行せず, パソコンや携帯電話でアクセスしてインターネット上で使用する電子通帳[ウェブ通帳]を提供している.
electronic bank transfer コンピュータ利用[コンピュータ・システム]による銀行振込み
 ◆Electronic bank transfers from shinkin credit unions across the nation to other financial institutions were halted for almost 24 hours.　全国の信用金庫から他の金融機関へのコンピュータ・システムによる銀行振込みが, 約24時間停止した.
electronic brokerage 電子ブローキング
 ◆We resorted to electronic brokerage in which currency is directly purchased online.　われわれは, オンライン（コンピュータ端末）で直接, 通貨買いを注文する電子ブローキングの手段を使った.
electronic fund [funds] transfer 電子資金振替, コンピュータ資金振替, 電子資金取引, 電子決済, EFT
 （=electronic transfer of funds）
 electronic fund transfer at point of sale 販売時電子資金振替, 販売時電子決済
 electronic fund [funds] transfer system 電子[コンピュータ]資金振替システム, 電子決済システム, EFTシステム
electronic money 電子マネー, 電子貨幣, 擬似通貨, eマネー, エレクトロニック・マネー　（=cybermoney, digital cash, digital currency, digital money, e-cash, e-money, electronic cash; ⇒online shopping, point system）
 ◆Electronic money can be bought by inputting the number and expiration date of a credit card on the Internet.　電子マネーは, ネット上でクレジット・カードの番号と有効期限を入力して購入することができる. ◆The bank began issuing new ATM cards that also function as credit cards and electronic money.　同行は, クレジット・カードと電子マネーの機能を加えた新型キャッシュ・カードの発行を開始した.
electronic money business 電子マネー事業
 ◆Aeon Co. and Lawson Inc. are also discussing a possible alliance in the electronic money business.　イオンとローソンは, 電子マネー事業での提携の可能性も検討している.
electronic payment 電子決済
 （=electronic settlement）
 ◆Electronic money has high-growth potential, and the Company is researching a new electronic payment system.　電子マネーの分野は今後さらなる進展が考えられるため, 当社な新たな電子決済システムの研究に取り組んでいます.
【解説】電子決済の四つの手段:
 Net banking ネット・バンキング　（銀行のホームページ画面をとおして自分の口座から振込みを依頼）
 online payment オンライン決済　（クレジット・カード, Eデビット, 電子マネーでの支払い）
 payment by prepaid card プリペイド決済　（プリペイド・カードでの支払い）
 provider payment プロバイダー決済　（インターネット接続プロバイダーがクレジット・カード決済を代行）
electronic settlement ネット・ショッピングなどの電子決済
 ◆The firm offers loans for retail and corporate clients in addition to offering electronic settlement for online shoppers.　同社は, ネット・ショッパー[オンライン・ショッパー]向けの電子決済業務のほかに, 個人と企業向けの融資も手がけている.
electronic trading 電子取引, 電子売買, コンピュータ取引, 電子トレーディング, システム売買
 ◆Gold futures for December delivery gained to $1,897 an ounce at 4:13 p.m. in after-hours electronic trading on the Comex in New York.　ニューヨーク商品取引所の時間外電子取引で, 金先物の12月渡し価格は, 午後4時13分の時点で1トロイ・オンス＝1,897ドルまで上昇した.
electronics （名）電子機器, 電子製品, 電子工学, エレクトロニクス
 consumer electronics products 家電製品
 electronics company 家電メーカー, 電機企業
 electronics components 電子部品
 electronics industry 家電業界, エレクトロニクス産業
 electronics manufacturer 家電メーカー
 electronics products 電子製品
 ◆The global recession curbed consumer spending, hurting demand for chips that go into electronics such as computers and handsets.　世界同時不況で個人消費が抑えられ, コンピュータや携帯電話などの電子製品に用いられる半導体の需要も減退している[打撃を受けている].
element （名）要素, 要因, 因子, 構成要素, 構成部品, 部材, 成分, 項目, 素子, エレメント
 cost elements 原価要素
 earnings momentum element 利益のモメンタム要因
 Finite Element Method 有限要素法
 guaranteed element 保証要素
 nonoperating elements 営業外項目
 ◆Our quality and total cycle-time reduction initiatives remain the key elements in achieving superior financial results.　当社の品質に対する方針と全サイクル・タイム（工程

期間）短縮の方針は、今でも当社の優れた業績を達成するための中核的要素になっています。

eligibility （名）適格, 適格性, 資格, 有資格, 受給資格, 被選挙資格, 適任
 benefit eligibility　受給資格
 eligibility criteria　受給資格
 eligibility for rediscount　再割引適格
 eligibility requirements　（銀行の）割引適格要件
 eligibility standards　適債基準
 full eligibility date　完全受給資格
 stock exchanges' eligibility criteria　証券取引所の上場基準
 ◆Some firms that were willing to list their shares were unable to meet stock exchanges' eligibility criteria due to the economic slump. 株式上場を目指していた企業の一部は、景気悪化で証券取引所の上場基準を満たすことができなかった。◆The Democratic Party of Japan will postpone a plan to raise the pension eligibility age. 民主党は、年金の支給開始年齢を引き上げる案の実施を見送る方針だ。

eligible （形）有資格の, 適格の, 受給資格がある
 eligible bankers' acceptance　適格銀行手形, 有資格銀行引受手形
 eligible bill［paper］　適格手形
 eligible bond　適格社債, 適格公社債
 eligible charges　給付額, 給付対象費用
 eligible collateral　適格担保
 eligible currency　国際送金通貨, 送金通貨, 送金通貨条項
 eligible employee　有資格従業員, 受給資格のある従業員, 年金加入資格のある従業員　（⇒RONA）
 eligible exports　適格輸出債権
 eligible for discount　割引適格, 割引適格の
 eligible institutions　適格機関投資家（=eligible institutional investors）
 eligible investments　適格投資対象
 eligible paper　再割引適格手形（中央銀行が再割引するのに必要な条件を満たす手形のこと）
 eligible receivables　適格債権
 eligible secured loan　適格担保貸出
 eligible security　適格担保
 eligible subscriber　受給資格のある加入者
 eligible to receive a benefit　給付を受ける資格がある
 eligible value date　適性為替資金受払い日, 適格資金受払い日
 face amount of eligible receivables　適格債権の額面
 fully eligible active plan participants　受給資格取得済み在職制度加入者
 ◆About 1.24 million eligible subscribers to corporate pension plans aged 60 and over had not filed payout requests as of the end of fiscal 20006. 2006年度末の時点で、受給資格のある60歳以上の企業年金加入者の約124万人が、年金支払いの請求手続きを取っていない。◆The employees stock purchase plan enables employees who are not participants in a stock option plan to purchase the Corporation's capital stock through payroll deductions of up to 10 % of eligible compensation. 従業員株式購入制度によると、株式購入選択権制度に加入していない従業員は、俸給の10%を超えない範囲で給与を積み立てて、当社株式を購入することができます。◆Under the EU's Stability and Growth Pact, countries eligible to join the euro system are required to keep budget deficits below 3 percent of GDP. 欧州連合（EU）の財政安定・成長協定によると、ユーロ加盟国は、加盟の条件として財政赤字をGDPの3%以下に抑えなければならない。◆Under the IMF's new lending facility, Italy would be eligible to receive short-term loans of up to about $63 billion. IMF（国際通貨基金）の新融資制度で、イタリアは、最大約630億ドルまでの短期融資を受けることができる。

eliminate （動）撤廃する, 廃止する, 排除する, 削減する, 廃棄する, 除去する, 相殺消去する, なくす, 解消する, 敗退させる, 脱落させる, 失格させる, 殺す, 排泄（はいせつ）する
 eliminate credit control　信用規制を撤廃する
 eliminate dividends　無配にする
 eliminate excessive debt　過剰債務を削減する
 eliminate exposure to interest rates　金利変動リスクをなくす
 eliminate jobs　雇用を削減する
 eliminate stock certificate　株券を不要にする
 eliminate tax incentives　税制上の優遇措置を撤廃する
 eliminate the budget deficit　財政赤字をなくす
 eliminate the waste of overproduction　過剰生産の無駄を省く
 eliminate unease in the financial markets　金融市場の不安感を払拭（ふっしょく）する
 ◆HSBC Holdings PLC will shut its subprime mortgage unit and eliminate 750 jobs. 英銀行大手のHSBCホールディングスは、低所得者向け住宅融資「サブプライム・ローン」事業の米国子会社を閉鎖して、従業員750人を解雇する。◆Japan, the United States and European countries have failed to eliminate unease in the financial market after the recent downgrading of the U.S. credit rating. 日米欧は、今回の米国債格下げ後の金融市場の不安感を払拭（ふっしょく）できていない。◆Japan, the United States and European countries have failed to eliminate uneasiness in the financial markets for lack of concrete policy coordination. 日米欧は、具体的な政策協調が見られないため、金融市場の不安感を払拭（ふっしょく）できないでいる。◆Struggling Victor Co. of Japan will eliminate 1,150 jobs to engineer its rehabilitation. 経営不振の日本ビクターは、再建計画を進めるため、1,150人を削減する。◆The key to returning to stable growth is whether the nation can eliminate excesses common to many companies and promote supply-side structural reforms. 安定成長復帰へのカギは、多くの日本企業に共通して見られる過剰体質を排除して、供給サイドの構造改革を進めることができるかどうかである。

elimination （名）撤廃, 廃止, 排除, 削除, 廃棄, 除去, 相殺消去, 解消,（競技などの）予選, 敗退, 脱落
 elimination period　（保険の）除外期間
 the elimination of budget deficit　財政赤字の解消
 the elimination of intercompany transactions　会社間取引の消去
 the elimination of intra-company transactions　連結消去
 the elimination of tariffs　関税撤廃
 the elimination of the investment tax credit　投資税額控除の廃止
 the elimination of unprofitable business　不採算事業［赤字事業］からの撤退
 ◆Prolonged deflation is another factor making the elimination of budget deficit difficult. 長引くデフレも、財政赤字の解消を難しくしている要因だ。

embark on　～に乗り出す, ～に踏み切る
 ◆Financial markets worldwide are focused on whether the U.S. FRB embarks on a third round of its quantitative easing policy, or QE3. 世界の金融市場は、米連邦準備制度理事会（FRB）が量的緩和策の第三弾（QE3）に踏み切るかどうかに注目している。

embattled （形）多くの問題［困難］を抱えた, 苦境に立たされた, 経営不振の, 敵に包囲された, 陣容を整えた, 防備を固めた
 embattled U.S. insurer American International Group Inc.

経営不振の米保険会社AIG
the embattled eurozone　財政危機に陥ったユーロ圏
◆Tokyo stocks bounced back after the U.S. government's bailout of embattled U.S. insurer American International Group Inc.　経営不振の米保険会社AIGを米政府が救済するのを受けて、東京株式市場は反発した。

embedded　(形)固定した,埋め込んだ,組み込んだ[組み込まれた],内包されている,深く根付いている
　embedded derivatives　組込みデリバティブ
　embedded losses　含み損
　embedded option　内包オプション,組み込まれているオプション
　embedded profits　含み益

embellish　(動)潤色する,粉飾する,装飾する
◆Even after the company fell into financial difficulties, it embellished its financial statements to make it appear profitable.　同社の経営が行き詰まった以降も、同社は決算書を粉飾して、経営状況を良く見せかけていた。

embezzlement of production money　製作費着服
embezzlement scandal　横領事件,着服事件
　(=misappropriation)

embrace　(動)受け入れる,容認する,信奉する,採用する,抱きしめる,抱擁(ほうよう)する
◆The United States and European nations embrace the depreciation of their currencies against the yen.　欧米諸国は、円に対する自国通貨安を容認している。

emerge　(動)現われる,出現する,台頭する,浮上する,発生する,生じる,明らかになる,知られる,明白となる,注目されるようになる,抜け出す,脱却する,脱する
◆Goldman Sachs Group Inc. emerged from the global financial meltdown as Wall Street's most influential bank.　ゴールドマン・サックスは、ウォール街最大手の金融機関として世界的な金融危機を乗り切った。◆In the future also, new types of illegal practices that exploit legal loopholes will emerge in securities markets.　今後も、証券市場では、法の抜け穴を狙う不正取引の手法が新たに現れるものと思われる。◆It is difficult to predict if new explosive factors emerge to plunge the financial market into further turmoil.　金融市場をさらに混乱に陥れる新しい火種があるのかどうか、予測するのは難しい。◆No clear prospect has emerged for resolution of the Greek financial crisis.　ギリシャの財政危機を打開する明確な見通しは、まだ立っていない。◆The U.S. economy is just emerging from the worst period of the economic crisis.　米経済は、ようやく経済危機の最悪期を脱しつつある。

emergency　(名)緊急,有事,緊急事態,非常事態,突発事故
　emergency advances　非常貸出
　emergency aid　緊急援助,緊急支援
　　(=emergency assistance)
　emergency amortization　緊急償却,特別償却,加速償却
　Emergency Banking (Relief Act)　米緊急銀行(救済)法
　emergency borrowing rate　緊急貸付け金利
　emergency credit　緊急融資
　emergency currency　緊急貨幣
　emergency duty　緊急関税　(=emergency tariff)
　Emergency Economic Stabilization Act of 2008　2008年緊急救済安定化法
　emergency facility　緊急資金
　emergency financing mechanism　緊急融資メカニズム
　emergency fund　つなぎ資金,緊急資金,非常資金,非常準備金,特別準備基金,偶発損失準備資金
　emergency funding rate　緊急貸出金利
　emergency funds rate　緊急貸出枠金利
　emergency import curbs　緊急輸入制限
　emergency lending rate　緊急貸出金利
　emergency measures　緊急措置,緊急関税制度
　emergency reserve　緊急準備金
　emergency "safeguard" import restriction　緊急輸入制限(セーフガード)
　financial emergency　財政危機
◆European countries are urged to facilitate a safety net for emergencies, including the injection of public funds into deteriorating banks to shore up their capital strength.　欧州は、経営が悪化した銀行[金融機関]に公的資金を注入して資本を増強するなど、非常時に備えた安全網の整備が求められている。

emergency assistance　緊急支援,緊急援助
　(=emergency aid)
◆The government and the Japan International Cooperation Agency will provide emergency assistance to developing countries hit by the financial crisis.　政府と国際協力機構(JICA)は、金融危機で打撃を受けた発展途上国に対して緊急支援を行う方針だ。

emergency deal　緊急対策
　(=emergency package)
◆As part of the emergency deal, the ECB started to buy Greek, Portuguese, and Spanish bonds.　緊急対策として、欧州中央銀行(ECB)はギリシャ、ポルトガルとスペインの国債買入れを開始した。

emergency employment package　緊急雇用対策
◆The emergency employment package contains a plan to relax criteria for receiving employment-adjustment subsidies.　緊急雇用対策には、雇用調整助成金の受領要件の緩和策も含まれている。

emergency liquidity　緊急時の流動性,緊急流動性,緊急貸出
◆AMRO will coordinate decision-making for providing emergency liquidity to member nations under a $120 billion multilateral currency swap agreement known as CMIM.　AMRO(ASEANプラス3諸国の域内マクロ経済リサーチ・オフィス)は、CMIMと呼ばれる1,200億ドルの貸出枠の多国間通貨交換[通貨スワップ]協定に基づき、参加国へ緊急流動性を提供する際の意思決定の調整に当たる。

emergency liquidity-providing facilities　緊急貸出制度
◆Japanese megabanks and Toyota were among the beneficiaries of a slew of emergency liquidity-providing facilities devised by the U.S. Federal Reserve Board.　日本のメガバンクやトヨタも、(2008年秋の金融危機に伴って)米連邦準備制度理事会(FRB)の発案で実施された大規模な緊急貸出制度の恩恵を受けた[緊急貸出制度を活用していた]。

emergency loan　緊急融資,救援融資,つなぎ融資　(⇒ collateral-free loan, financial hemorrhaging [hemorrhage], uncollectible)
◆Greece must avert a crippling debt default by securing billions of dollars in emergency loans from European countries and the IMF.　ギリシャは、欧州諸国[ユーロ圏]と国際通貨基金(IMF)による緊急融資で巨額の資金を確保して、壊滅的な債務不履行を回避しなければならない。◆In the subprime crisis, the U.S. FRB had to take the extraordinary step of providing an emergency loan not to a commercial bank but to an investment bank.　サブプライム問題で、米国の中央銀行の連邦準備制度理事会(FRB)は、緊急融資を銀行[商業銀行]ではなく証券会社[投資銀行]に対して行う異例の措置を取らざるを得なかった。◆The central bank's emergency loan is an effective remedy for a bank run.　中央銀行の緊急融資は、銀行の取付け騒ぎの特効薬だ。◆The IMF and the EU have worked out a policy of extending emergency loans to Greece.　国際通貨基金(IMF)と欧州連合(EU)は、ギリシャに緊急融資を行う方針を打ち出した。◆The U.S. Federal Reserve Board will provide up to $85 billion in an emergency loan to rescue the

huge insurer American International Group Inc. 米連邦準備制度理事会(FRB)は、米保険最大手AIGを救済するためのつなぎ融資として、AIGに最大850億ドルを投入する。◆Two domestic carriers have been given a total of ￥85 billion in emergency loans by the governmental Development Bank of Japan to overcome losses caused by a downturn in airline passengers as a result of the Iraq war and SARS outbreak. イラク戦争や新型肺炎(SARS)による利用客の減少で発生した損失を補填するため、国内航空会社2社が、政府系金融機関の日本政策投資銀行から計850億円の緊急融資を受けた。◆With a view to stemming the airlines' financial hemorrhaging, the Construction and Transport Ministry in late May asked the Development Bank of Japan to provide emergency loans to the two carriers. 航空会社の損失を阻止するため、5月下旬に国土交通省は、日本政策投資銀行に対して両航空会社への緊急融資を要請した。

emergency loan system　緊急融資制度
◆The EU is discussing the establishment of an emergency loan system utilizing EU funds as a final safety net. EU(欧州連合)は現在、最後の安全網としてEUの基金を活用する緊急融資制度の制定を検討している。

emergency measures　緊急措置, 緊急対策, 金融策, 緊急対応
◆Emergency measures to prevent the debt crisis in Europe from spreading any further are what we need now. 欧州の財政危機拡大を防ぐ緊急措置こそ、いま何よりも必要なことだ。

emergency rescue fund　緊急支援基金, 緊急救援基金
◆The European Union hurriedly created an emergency rescue fund, called the European Financial Stability Facility (EFSF). 欧州連合(EU)は、欧州金融安定基金(EFSF)という緊急支援基金を急設した。

emergency shareholders meeting　緊急株主総会, 臨時株主総会
◆At an emergency shareholders meeting, the company obtained shareholder approval to transfer ￥199 billion from its legal reserves to provide for write-offs of nonperforming loans. 臨時株主総会で同社は、株主から、不良債権処理に備えて法定準備金から1,990億円を取り崩す案の承認を得た。

emergency telephone conference　緊急電話会議
◆Finance ministers and central bank governors from the Group of Seven leading countries held an emergency telephone conference to avert financial turmoil caused by the downgrading of the U.S. credit rating. 米国債の格下げによる金融市場の混乱を回避するため、先進7か国(G7)の財務相と中央銀行総裁が、緊急電話会議を開いた。◆The emergency telephone conference by the G-7 financial ministers and central bank governors was held right before the opening of Asian financial markets. 先進7か国(G7)の財務相・中央銀行総裁による緊急電話会議は、アジアの金融市場が開く直前に開かれた。

emerging company　新興企業, 成長企業, 新興のベンチャー企業
◆The firm received a lot of attention from investors as an emerging company. 同社は、新興のベンチャー企業として投資家から大いに注目された。

emerging countries　新興国　(=developing countries, emerging economies, emerging nations)
◆As one option to avoid excessive currency appreciation in emerging countries with inflationary trends, they can restrict an influx of capital. インフレ気味の新興国で行き過ぎた[過度の]通貨高を避けるための手段として、資金流入を規制することができる。◆Emerging countries are anxious about the possibility of inflation caused by a large influx of funds as the U.S. FRB decided to relax its monetary policy. 米連邦準備制度理事会(FRB)が金融緩和を決めたため、新興国は大量の資金流入によるインフレを懸念している。◆Financial exchanges between a half-dozen emerging countries (BRICs, Indonesia and South Korea) will lose a dependency on the U.S. dollar as the currency of last resort. 今後、ブラジル、ロシア、インド、中国、インドネシア、韓国の新興6か国間の金融取引は、最後の拠(よ)りどころとしての米ドルに依存しなくなると思われる。◆Japan, the United States and emerging countries are upping their pressure on Europe to contain the Greek-triggered sovereign debt crisis. 日米と新興国は、欧州に対して、ギリシャに端を発したソブリン危機(政府債務危機)封じ込めの圧力を強めている。◆Many developed countries are currently in a deflationary phase while many emerging countries are in an inflationary phase. 現在、先進国の多くはデフレ気味なのに対して、新興国の多くはインフレ気味だ。

emerging economies　新興経済国, 新興経済地域, 振興経済群, 新興国
(=emerging countries, emerging nations)
◆Japan, the United States and emerging economies have pressed European countries to promptly resolve the fiscal and financial crisis. 日米両国と新興国は、欧州に財政・金融危機の迅速な解決を迫った。◆Japan's economic growth is driven by exports, but it will have to vie for export markets with emerging economies. 日本の経済成長の原動力は輸出だが、今後は新興国と輸出市場の争奪戦になろう。◆Most emerging East Asian economies are assured of a sharp V-shaped recovery this year. 今年は、東アジア新興国の大半が急激にV字回復するのは確実だ。◆Six emerging economies (the BRICs nations plus Indonesia and South Korea) will become the major drivers of global economic growth. これからは、新興6か国(ブラジル、ロシア、インド、中国にインドネシアと韓国)が、世界の経済成長の主要な原動力になる。◆Speculative money is causing appreciation of currencies and inflation in emerging economies. 投機マネーが、新興国の通貨高やインフレを招いている。◆Stock markets in emerging economies as China are growing rapidly. 中国など新興国の証券市場は、急成長している。◆Surplus funds put out by developed economies' monetary easing measures have flowed into emerging economies to inflate economic bubbles. 先進国の金融緩和策で生じた余剰資金が、新興国に流れ込み、バブルを発生させている。◆The effects of an economic slowdown in industrialized countries stemming from the U.S. subprime woes could spread in the emerging economies. 米国のサブプライム(低所得者向け住宅融資)問題に起因する先進国の景気減速の影響は、新興国にも拡大する可能性がある。◆The proposal to expand the lending capacity of the IMF was supported by Brazil and other emerging economies though Japan and the United States rejected it. 国際通貨基金(IMF)が融資できる資金規模を拡大する案は、日本と米国が受け入れなかったものの、ブラジルなどの新興国は支持した。

emerging firm　新興企業
◆Domestic stock exchange entries continue to languish, reflecting the tough conditions faced by emerging firms wanting to publicly list their shares. 国内株式市場への新規上場は、株式上場を目指す新興企業が直面している厳しい状況を反映して、低迷が続いている。

emerging market　新興市場, 急成長市場, 新興成長市場, エマージング・マーケット
borrowers from emerging market　急成長市場の借り手
emerging market bond index　急成長市場の債券指数
emerging market issues　新興市場銘柄

EMF　欧州通貨基金(European Monetary Fundの略)

employee　(名)従業員, 社員, 職員, 雇い人, 使用人
active employees　在籍従業員, 現従業員
(⇒accumulated liability)
employee compensation　従業員報酬, 従業員給与
employee contribution　従業員拠出
employee deposits　社内預金
employee loan funds　従業員貸付け制度
employee ownership scheme　従業員持ち株制度

employee plan issuances 従業員持ち株制度への発行
Employee Retirement Income Security Act 1974年に制定された米国の従業員退職所得保障法, 1974年退職者年金保障法, 企業年金法, エリサ法, ERISA
employee savings plan 従業員貯蓄制度, 従業員貯蓄計画 (=employees' savings plan)
employee separations 従業員の退職
employee welfare fund 従業員福利厚生基金 (=employee benefit fund)
employees' housing loan credit insurance 住宅資金貸付け保険
employee's savings 従業員預金
inactive employee 休職従業員
junior employee 準社員
◆A bank employee was arrested for alleged insider trading of shares in four companies. 銀行の行員が, 4社の株でインサイダー取引を行った容疑で逮捕された。
employee benefit 従業員給付
employee benefit fund 従業員給付基金, 従業員福利厚生基金
employee benefit plan 従業員給付制度, 従業員福利厚生制度, 従業員給付基金
◆It is the company's practice to fund amounts for pensions sufficient to meet the minimum requirements set forth in applicable employee benefit and tax laws. 適用される従業員の給付に関する法令と税法に規定されている最小限の要求を十分に満たす額を, 年金基金に積み立てているのが当社の慣行です。
employee benefit plan 従業員給付制度, 被雇用者給付制, 従業員給付基金
employee pension benefit plan 従業員年金給付制度
employee welfare benefit plan 従業員福祉給付制度
employee pension 従業員年金
employee pension fund 従業員年金基金, 厚生年金基金
employee pension funding 従業員年金基金への拠出
employee pension insurance system 厚生年金
employee pension plan 従業員年金制度
employee pension premium 厚生年金保険料 (⇒premium payment)
employees' pension insurance 厚生年金保険
◆The Employees Pension Fund is one of many corporate pension plans. 厚生年金基金は, 多くの企業年金制度の一つだ。
Employee Retirement Income Security Act 1974年に制定された米国の従業員退職所得保障法, エリサ法, ERISA
employee stock compensation 従業員株式報酬制度
◆If not for expenses to cover employee stock compensation, the firm would have earned $2.62 per share in the third quarter. 従業員株式報酬制度の費用がなければ, 同社の第3四半期の1株当たり利益は2.62ドルでした。
employee stock option 従業員ストック・オプション
◆In Japan, if company employees exercise employee stock options and obtain shares, the shares are considered salaried income, which is taxable. 日本では, 社員が従業員ストック・オプションの権利を行使して株を取得した場合, その株式は給与所得と見なされ, 課税対象になる。
employee stock option plan 従業員株式購入選択権制度, 従業員株式買取り権制度, 従業員ストック・オプション制度, ESOP
◆Under the Company's employee stock option plans, shares of common stock have been made available for grant to key employees. 当社の従業員株式購入選択権制度では, 幹部社員に普通株式を購入する権利を付与しています。
employee stock ownership plan 米国の従業員持ち株制度, 従業員株式保有制度, ESOP (=employee stock ownership trust)
◆The company's employee stock ownership plan will be used to finance part of the buyout deal. この買収取引の一部の資金調達には, 同社の従業員持ち株制度が利用される。
employee stock purchase plan 従業員株式購入制度, 従業員持ち株制度, ESPP (=employees' stock purchase plan)
◆The employees stock purchase plan enables employees who are not participants in a stock option plan to purchase the Corporation's capital stock through payroll deductions of up to 10 % of eligible compensation. 従業員株式購入制度によると, 株式購入選択権制度に加入していない従業員は, 俸給の10%を超えない範囲で給与を積み立てて, 当社株式を購入することができます。◆The proxy form indicates the number of shares to be voted, including any full shares held for participants in the Employee Stock Purchase Plan. 委任状用紙には, 従業員株式購入制度加入者のために保有している株式をすべて含めて, 行使される議決権数が記載されています。
employees on loan 出向社員
◆Resona currently has about 3,500 employees working for its affiliates, including employees on loan and retired employees. りそなホールディングスの関連会社には現在, 出向者やOBを含めて約3,500人が在籍している。
employees' pension insurance 厚生年金保険 (⇒premium payment)
employees' savings plan 従業員社内預金制度
◆We raised $81 million of common equity by means of our Dividend Reinvestment and Stock Purchase Plan and the Employees' Savings Plan. 当社は, 株主配当再投資・株式購入制度と従業員社内預金制度により普通株式を発行して8,100万ドルを調達しました。
employment adjustment subsidies 雇用調整助成金
◆The emergency employment package contains a plan to relax criteria for receiving employment-adjustment subsidies. 緊急雇用対策には, 雇用調整助成金の受領要件の緩和策も含まれている。
employment insurance 雇用保険
Employment Insurance Law 雇用保険法
employment insurance premium 雇用保険料 (⇒premium payment)
employment insurance program 雇用保険制度 (=employment insurance system)
◆The nation's employment insurance program is on the brink of collapse due to the increasing number of jobless people amid the slumping economy. 日本の雇用保険制度は, 不況による失業者の急増で破たん寸前にある。
employment insurance system 雇用保険制度
◆The number of companies subscribing to the employment insurance system has been steadily increasing. 雇用保険制度に加入している事業所数は, 着実に増えている。
employment situation 雇用状況, 雇用環境
◆The employment situation has grown even more serious. 雇用情勢は, 一段と深刻化している。◆The employment situation has improved in line with the economic recovery. 景気回復に伴って, 雇用環境は良くなっている。
EMS 欧州通貨制度 (European Monetary Systemの略)
EMU EU経済通貨統合, 欧州経済通貨同盟 (Economic and Monetary Unionの略)
◆The debt crisis in Europe has uncovered the deficiencies in the construction of EMU. 欧州の債務危機[財政危機]で, 欧州経済通貨統合(EMU)構築の欠陥があらわになった。
enact (動)法律を制定する, 立法化する, (交渉などを)まとめる, 上演する(perform), 演じる, 〜の役を演じる, (出来事や状況が)繰り返して起こる, 〜を行う
be enacted 〜が行われる, 〜が成し遂げられる, 〜が繰り返して起こる

enact a bill 法案を法律化する
　enact a bill into law 法案を成立させる, 法案を法律化する
　enact a budget deal 予算交渉をまとめる
　enact a law 法律を制定する
　enacted tax rate 法定税率
　◆A revised Foreign Exchange and Foreign Trade Control Law has been enacted to enable the swift freezing of funds belonging to terrorist organizations. テロ組織の資金［資産］凍結を迅速に行うための改正外為法は, すでに成立して［制定されて］いる。◆The struggling JAL's next step will be to start negotiations with its creditor banks over new loans to enact its rehabilitation plan. 経営再建に取り組む日航は今後, 同社の再建計画案の実行に必要な新規融資を巡る取引銀行団との交渉に移ることになる。

enactment （名）制定, 立法, 法律, 法令, 上演
　enactment of a bill 法案成立
　enactment of legislation 立法の制定

encourage （動）促進する, 促す, 助長する, 奨励する, 勧める, 誘致する, 誘導する, 励ます, 勇気づける, 激励する, 刺激する
　encourage a depreciation of the currency 通貨安に誘導する
　encourage banks to buy new assets 銀行に新規資産の購入を促す
　encourage economic growth 景気を刺激する, 景気浮揚を図る
　encourage savings 貯蓄を奨励する
　◆In revitalizing the market, it is necessary to encourage individuals, who have financial assets totaling ¥1.4 quadrillion, to invest in the stock market. 市場の活性化を図るには, 1,400兆円にのぼる金融資産を持つ個人の株式市場への投資を促す必要がある。◆Shareholders incentives are designed to encourage shareholders to hold onto their stocks over the long term. 株主優待の狙いは, 株主の株式の長期保有促進にある。◆To encourage firms' temporary layoffs, the government will ease requirements for receiving a governmental subsidy to defray costs relating to layoffs. 企業の一時解雇［一時帰休］を支援するため, 政府は企業が雇用調整助成金（解雇関連費用を負担する政府助成金）を受けるための要件を緩和する。

encourage investment 投資を促す, 投資を誘致する
　◆The practical implementation of trade insurance, including risk judgment, must be enhanced to encourage investment by private companies and accelerate the export of infrastructure technology. 民間企業の投資を促し, インフラ技術の輸出を加速するには, リスク判断も含めて, 貿易保険の実務能力を高める必要がある。

encourage spin-offs 分社化を促す
　◆The corporate group tax system is designed to encourage spin-offs and other corporate restructuring efforts amid protracted recession. 連結納税制度のねらいは, 不況の長期化で分社化など企業の事業再構築努力を促すことにある。

encumbrance （名）抵当権, 担保権, （権利に関する）制限, 制約, 物上負担, （不動産上の）債務, 厄介もの, 邪魔もの
　be subject to encumbrance 担保権の対象になっている, 担保権［抵当権］が設定されている, （権利に関する）制限を受けている
　create an encumbrance on ～に担保権［抵当権］を設定する
　free from all encumbrances 負担（抵当権や債務など）が一切ない
　free of encumbrances 債務［負担］がない
　◆The proprietary information is free and clear of any liens, restriction on use, or encumbrances of any nature whatsoever. この占有情報は, いかなる担保, 使用制限もしくはどんな種類の負担も存在しない［本占有情報は, 担保, 使用制限, 負担の制約が一切ない］。◆The Shares are free and clear of any liens, charges or other encumbrances. 本株式は, 先取特権, 担保権その他の制限［負担・障害］の対象に一切なっていない。

encumbrancer （名）抵当権者, 担保権者, 物上債権者

end （動）終わる, 終了する, 完了する, 済む, 止む, 停止する, ～の結果になる, 終える, 終わりにする, 収束する, 止める, 廃止する, 解除する, ～をしのぐ, ～を凌駕（りょうが）する
　six months ended December 31, 2012 2012年12月31日に終了する［終了した］6か月（間）, 2012年7-12月期, 2012年下半期, 2012年後期
　the three months ended June 4-6月, 4-6月期, 6月終了の3か月
　the year just ended 前期
　year ended December 31, 2012 2012年12月31日終了事業年度
　◆Companies are now moving toward ending the crossholding of shares. 企業は現在, 株式持ち合いの解消に向かっている。◆Debates on the pros and cons of a proposal to end the quantitative relaxation of credit by the Bank of Japan are gathering momentum. 日銀による量的金融緩和策を解除する案の賛否をめぐる議論が, 活発化している。◆If the negotiations between Republicans and Democrats face rough going and the deficit-cutting plan ends up being insufficient, credit rating agencies may downgrade Treasury bonds. 共和党と民主党の協議が難航して赤字削減策が不十分に終わると, （信用）格付け会社が米国債の格下げに踏み切る可能性がある。◆Japan, U.S. and Europe must hasten to end fiscal crisis to stabilize the global financial markets. 世界の金融市場の安定を図るには, 日米欧が財政危機の収束を急がなければならない。◆Net income rose to ¥143 billion, or ¥78 per share, in the three months ended June. 4-6月期は, 純利益［税引き後利益］が1,430億円（1株当たり78円）に増加した。◆Speculation the Bank of Japan will end its quantitative monetary easing policy soon has sparked a rise in mid- and long-term interest rates. 日銀が近く量的緩和策を解除するとの思惑から, （金融市場では）中長期の金利が上昇し始めた。◆The Fed's program of buying $600 billion in Treasury bonds to help the economy is to end in June 2011 on schedule. 景気を支えるために6,000億ドルの国債を買い入れる米連邦準備制度理事会（FRB）の量的緩和政策は, 予定通り2011年6月に終了する。◆The NBER's business cycle dating committee concluded that the economic expansion that started in November 2001 had ended. 全米経済研究所（NBER）の景気循環判定委員会の委員は, 「2001年から始まった米景気の拡大はすでに終わっている」との見解で一致した。

end （名）終わり, 終了, 満了, 終結, 最後, 結末, 末尾, 破滅, 滅亡, 終焉（しゅうえん）, 廃止, 端, 端部, 先端, 末端, つき当たり, 周辺部, 外縁部, はずれ, 郊外, 限界, 限度, 目的, 究極目的, 目標, 成果, 結果, 部門, 部分, 担当部分, 受け持ち部分, 期末, 年度末
　（⇒closed-end, open-end）
　achieve one's end [ends] 目的を達成する
　balance at end of (the) year 期末残高
　by the end of the year 年内に
　cheap low end 低価格品
　closed end 資本額固定, 閉鎖式, 多項選択式, クローズド・エンド
　discount the end of economic recovery 景気腰折れを織り込む
　end investor 最終投資家
　ending balance 期末残高
　　（＝balance at end of the year）
　front end 短期物, 前段階

in the year just ended　前期
long end (of the market)　長期債, 長期物
loose ends　未処理事項
make ends meet　帳尻を合わせる
open end　限度がないこと, 無制限, 自由回答式, オープン・エンド
opposite [other] end　対極
regular year-end dividend　年度末配当
short end　短期債, 短期物
the end of recovery　景気腰折れ
the end of the year　期末
the higher end of　〜の上限, 〜の後半
the lower end of　〜の下限, 〜の前半
the sales end of the company　同社の販売部門
the top end of　〜の上限
the two ends of the market　市場の両極
upper end of the market　高級市場
year ended December 31, 2012　2012年12月31日終了事業年度, 12月期決算企業の2012年度
◆In the global financial markets, unrest is continuing as there is no end in sight to fiscal crises to the United States and some European countries. 世界の金融市場では, 米国と一部の欧州諸国の財政危機の収束が見通せないため, 混乱が続いている。◆Stock markets in the United States and European countries crashed again as there is no end in sight to fiscal crises in them. 欧米の株式市場は, 欧米の財政危機の収束が見通せないため, ふたたび総崩れとなった。◆The company suffered ¥61 billion in consolidated after-tax losses at the end of fiscal 2010. 同社は, 2011年3月期[2010年度]に, 610億円の連結税引き後赤字に陥った。◆The end-of-year account settlements of Japanese companies are generally announced in May or June. 一般に日本企業は, 5,6月に3月期決算の発表を行う。◆The firm's liabilities exceeded its assets by ¥8 billion in its settlement of accounts at the end of February last year. 同社は, 昨年2月期決算で, 80億円の債務超過になった。◆The per-barrel price has been hovering around the lower end of the $110 level in recent weeks. 1バレル当たりの原油価格は, ここ数週間, 110ドル台前半で推移している。◆The Standard & Poor's 500 index is at the top end of its range for the past two months. スタンダード・プアーズ(500種)株価指数は, 過去2か月のボックス圏の上限にある。◆The yen surged to the higher end of the ¥98 level against the dollar in Tokyo markets due to yen-buying pressure fueled by expectations of the country's economic recovery. 東京為替市場は, 日本の景気回復を期待した円買いが強まり, 1ドル=98円台[98円台の上限]まで円が急騰した。

end to end　端末同士, 端末間, ユーザー同士, エンド・ツー・エンド
　end-to-end digital connection　全デジタル回線接続, 端末間のデジタル回線接続
　end-to-end fiber optics transmission　端末相互間の光ファイバー通信
　end-to-end network management　端末間ネットワークの管理
◆This new network has the potential for end-to-end digital connection to meet the demands for advanced services such as automatic credit validation. この新ネットワークは, 端末間をデジタル回線で接続して, クレジット・カードの自動確認などの高度なサービスに対する需要にも応えることができる。

endeavor [endeavour]　(名)努力, 試み, 対応策, 対策, 策
　make the best endeavors　最大限の努力をする
　relief endeavors for peripheral nations [countries, states]　周辺国救援の対応策, 周辺国救援策
◆The eurozone has conventionally responded as if it was dealing with liquidity crisis, in its relief endeavors for the peripheral member states. ユーロ圏はこれまで, その周辺加盟国救援策では, 流動性危機の処理として対応してきた。

endorse　(動)裏書きする, 裏面に記載する, 裏書譲渡する, 保証する, 推薦(すいせん)する
　endorsed bill [note]　裏書手形
　endorsed bond　裏書債券
　endorsed check　裏書小切手
　endorsed note payable account [a/c]　裏書義務勘定
　endorsed paper　裏書手形
　note endorsed (for payment)　回り手形
　note receivable endorsed　受取手形裏書高

endorsee　(名)被裏書人, 裏書譲渡人
　draft endorsee　手形裏書譲渡人

endorsement　(名)裏書き, 裏書条項, 支持, 承認, 是認, 認定, 批准(ひじゅん), 宣伝文句, エンドースメント (=indorsement)
　blank endorsement　白地裏書き, 白地式裏書き
　conditional endorsement　条件付き裏書き
　endorsement by mark　記号裏書き
　endorsement for collection　(銀行への)取立委任裏書き
　endorsement for pledge　質入れ裏書き
　endorsement for transfer　譲渡裏書き
　endorsement in blank　無記名裏書き, 白地裏書き (=blank endorsement)
　endorsement in full　記名裏書き, 記名式裏書き (=full endowment)
　endorsement of a draft　手形の裏書き
　endorsement to order　指図式裏書き
　endorsement to party liable on bill　戻し裏書き
　endorsement without recourse　無担保裏書き, 免責的裏書き
　extended coverage endorsement　拡張担保特約
　liability for endorsement　手形裏書義務
　natural endorsement　順裏書き
　nonnegotiable endorsement　裏書禁止裏書き, 裏書禁止文句
　partial endorsement　一部裏書き
　Prior endorsements guaranteed　先行の裏書きを保証します。
　prohibition of endorsement　禁転裏書き
　qualified endorsement　無担保裏書き
　restrictive endorsement　裏書禁止裏書き, 譲渡禁止裏書き
　special endorsement　指図式裏書き
　successive endorsement　裏書きの連続 (=succession of endorsement)

endorser　(名)裏書人, 裏書譲渡人 (=indorser)
　accommodation endorser　融通裏書人
　bank endorser　銀行裏書人
　draft endorser　手形裏書人
　general endorser　無記名裏書人
　joint endorser　連名裏書人, 連帯裏書人
　last endorser　最終裏書人
　prior endorser　前裏書人
　qualified endorser　条件付き裏書人
　special endorser　記名式裏書人
　subsequent endorser　後の裏書人

endowment　(名)基金, 基本財産, 寄付, 寄贈, 贈与, 分与, 遺贈
　college endowment　大学基金
　endowment annuity　養老年金

endowment assurance　養老保険
endowment fund　寄贈基金, 寄付基金, 基本基金, 基本金
endowment mortgage　養老保険担保融資, 養老保険モーゲージ
endowment policy　養老保険証券
university endowment　大学基金
◆As the public corporation usually does not cover losses by eating away at its endowment, about ￥400 billion of taxpayers' money was spent last fiscal year. 同特殊法人の場合は通常、基金を取り崩しても赤字が埋まらず、前年度は約4,000億円の税金が投入された。

endowment insurance　養老保険（=endowment assurance, endowment life insurance）
group endowment insurance　団体養老保険
pure endowment insurance　生存保険
single premium endowment insurance　一時払い養老保険

enfeeble　（動）弱くする, 弱める, 弱らす, 弱体化する, 衰えさせる, 衰弱させる　（⇒shortage）
◆Public funds should be injected not only to buy up toxic assets, but also to boost the capital bases of enfeebled financial institutions. 公的資金は、不良資産の買取りだけでなく、弱体化した［体力の落ちた］金融機関の資本増強にも注入すべきだ。

enforcement　（名）施行, 実施, 実行, 権利行使, 強制, 強行, 執行, 判決の強制執行
accounting and audit enforcement　会計・監査執行
Budget Enforcement Act of 1990　1990年予算執行法
credit enforcement　信用補強
enforcement of fiscal measures　財政出動
law enforcement　法執行
law enforcement authorities　警察当局
law enforcement officials　司法当局者, 警官
order of enforcement　執行命令
rights of enforcement　強制権
◆A housing investment slump results from the enforcement of the revised Building Standards Law. 住宅投資の落込みは、改正建築基準法の施行によるものだ。

engage　（動）雇用する, 雇う, 頼む, 委託する, 約束する, 予約する
engage A to manage the investor's securities accounts　投資家の証券勘定の運用をAに委託する
engage an investment manager　投資顧問［投資運用会社, 運用機関, 投資マネージャー］に委託する

engage in　～に従事する, ～に携わる, ～を営む, ～に関与する, ～を行う, ～を展開する, ～に参加する, ～に乗り出す
engage in exchange rate speculation　為替投機を行う
engage in financial activity　財務活動を展開する
engage in investment banking activities　投資銀行業務を行う［展開する］
engage in market intervention　市場介入を行う, 市場介入する
SEC registrants engaged in lending activities　貸出業務を営むSEC登録会社
◆The consultant manipulated the company's stock price by engaging in certain prohibited practices including wash sales. コンサルタントは、仮装売買（売り注文と買い注文を同時に出す方法）などの不正行為で株価を操作した。◆The government and the Bank of Japan engaged in market intervention in mid-September 2010 to stop the yen from surging. 政府・日銀は2010年9月中旬、円急騰に歯止めをかけるため市場介入した。

engine　（名）原動力, 牽引力, 検索エンジン（searching engine）, エンジン
engine of growth　成長の原動力
engine of the regional economy　地域経済の牽引力
the engine that boosts personal consumption　個人消費を押し上げる原動力
◆Capital investment, which was the engine for the overall economy, has lost much of its momentum. 景気全体を引っ張ってきた設備投資に、一時の勢いがなくなっている。◆Domestic and foreign demands, the two engines powering Japan's economic growth, are out of kilter. 日本の経済成長を引っ張る原動力の内需と外需が、今のところ不調だ。

engineer　（動）設計［建設］する, 巧みに処理［管理・運営・計画］する, 仕組む, 誘導する
design and engineer a project　プロジェクトを設計する
engineer a bill through Congress　法案の議会通過を計る
engineer a plot　陰謀をめぐらす［たくらむ, 企てる］, 計略をめぐらす
engineer one's rehabilitation　再建計画を進める（⇒rehabilitation）
engineer the cover-up　隠ぺい工作を発案する
engineered capacity　理想的生産能力（=ideal capacity）
engineered security　仕組み証券
◆The former vice president of the bank engineered the cover-up. 同行の元副頭取が、隠ぺい工作を発案した。◆The OPEC engineered the first oil price hike, which slowed growth in the production of automobiles. 石油輸出国機構（OPEC）が最初の原油価格高騰を作り出し、それによって自動車生産の伸びが鈍化した。◆U.S. President Barack Obama engineered a softer landing for GM with a set of measures to alleviate the bankruptcy shock as much as possible. オバマ米大統領は、GMの破たんショックを極力緩和するための一連の措置で、同社の軟着陸に向けた手を打った。

engineering　（名）工学, 工学技術, 技術, 設計, 工事, 開発, 手法, エンジニアリング
financial engineering　財テク, 金融手法, 金融エンジニアリング
fiscal engineering　大型金融操作

engulf　（動）飲み込む, 巻き込む, 包む　（=ingulf）
◆Japan's export industry is engulfed by the global economic downturn. 日本の輸出産業は、世界同時不況に飲み込まれている。

enhance　（動）増す, 増やす, 高める, 強化する, 向上させる, 容易にする, 改善する
credit-enhanced deal　信用補てん付き案件
enhance cash flow significantly　キャッシュ・フローを大幅に改善する
enhance competitiveness　競争力を高める, 競争力を強化する
enhance creditworthiness　信用の質を強化する
enhance earnings　業績を伸ばす, 業績を向上させる, 業績を改善する
enhance financial health　財務の健全性を高める, 財務内容［財務体質］を改善する
enhance investment performance　運用成績を上げる
enhance stock valuations　株価評価を高める［向上させる］
enhance the return on investment　投資収益率［利益率］を改善する, 投資リターンを改善する, 投資収益を向上させる［上げる］
enhance the return on the portfolio　ポートフォリオの運用成績を上げる
enhance the yield　利回りを向上させる
enhanced earnings　業績向上
enhanced returns　利益率の改善, 収益向上

enhanced service サービスの高度化, 高度サービス, サービスの拡張

enhanced structural adjustment facility 拡大構造調整融資制度

◆Enhancing international coordination is indispensable to stabilize the global financial markets. 世界の金融市場の安定には、国際協調の強化が欠かせない。◆If we are to continue to deliver improved financial results, we must continue to enhance our competitiveness. 今後とも業績［財務成績］向上を図るには、当社の競争力を引き続き高める必要がある。◆Mizuho Financial Group Inc. will float preferred securities to domestic institutional investors to enhance the core portion of its capital base. みずほフィナンシャルグループ（FG）は、自己資本［中核的自己資本］を増強するため、国内機関投資家向けに優先出資証券を発行する。◆The practical implementation of trade insurance, including risk judgment, must be enhanced to encourage investment by private companies and accelerate the export of infrastructure technology. 民間企業の投資を促し、インフラ技術の輸出として加速するには、リスク判断も含めて、貿易保険の実務能力を高める必要がある。◆The two exchanges hope to enhance convenience for investors by the merger. 両取引所は、経営統合によって投資家の利便性を高めたいとしている。◆Through the TSE-OSE merger in January 2013, the two exchanges must enhance their strategies to ensure survival as a major stock market in Asia. 東証と大証の2013年1月の経営統合をテコに、両証券取引所は、アジアの主要市場として勝ち残る戦略を強化する必要がある。◆To enhance management efficiency and the decision-making process, Mizuho Financial Group will integrate its Mizuho Bank and Mizuho Corporate Bank in 2013. 経営の効率化と意思決定の迅速化を図るため、みずほフィナンシャルグループは、傘下のみずほ銀行とみずほコーポレート銀行を2013年に合併させる。◆To enhance the stimulating effect of the Fed's rate cuts, swift implementation of fiscal and tax stimulus measures, including tax cuts on investment designed to reinvigorate the stock market, is necessary in addition to the large-scale tax cut program that is under way. 米連邦準備制度理事会（FRB）の金利引下げの刺激効果を高めるためには、現在実施中の大型減税プログラムに加え、株式市場を再活性化するための投資減税など、財政・税制面からの景気刺激策の速やかな実施が必要である。

enhancement （名）増加, 増大, 増進, 向上, 改善, 上昇, 騰貴, 強化, 整備, 補強, 拡張, 改良
credit enhancement　信用補てん, 信用補完, 信用補強, 信用増強
credit enhancement facility　信用補強ファシリティ
margin enhancement　利益率の上昇
portfolio enhancement　ポートフォリオの強化
provide credit enhancement　信用補完を提供する, 信用リスクをカバーする
service enhancement　サービス強化, サービス向上
the enhancement of international coordination　国際協調の強化
the enhancement of the major banks' revenue bases　大手銀行の収益基盤の強化
◆The enhancement of international coordination is important to stabilize the financial markets. 金融市場の安定には、国際協調の強化が重要だ。◆The enhancement of the major banks' revenue bases is essential for the final disposal of bad loans. 不良債権の最終処理には、大手銀行の収益基盤の強化が欠かせない。

enjoy （動）楽しむ, くつろぐ, 与えられている, 持っている, 享受する, 得る, 受ける
enjoy a strong run　高いパフォーマンスを見せる, 大幅なアウトパフォーマンスになる
enjoy a triple-A credit rating　トリプルAの格付けを受ける
enjoy continued strong growth　引き続き力強く成長する
enjoy some profits　そこそこの利益を上げる
enjoy tax benefits　税制上の優遇を受ける
enjoy the support of a bank　銀行の支援を受ける
◆The U.S. dollar has enjoyed the massive privileges as the key international currency. 米ドルは、国際通貨としての特権を享受してきた。◆The World Bank enjoys a triple-A credit rating. 世界銀行は、トリプルAの格付け（信用格付け）を受けている。

enormous （形）巨大な, 莫大（ばくだい）な, 膨大（ぼうだい）な, 大規模な, 巨額の, 大幅な, 豊富な, ものすごい, はなはだしい, 途方もない, 極悪な, 凶悪な, 無法な, 非道な　（⇒amount）
an enormous amount of information　膨大な量の情報
an enormous fortune　莫大な財産
an enormous intervention　大規模介入
an enormous pressure　ものすごい圧力
China's enormous capital surpluses　中国の膨大な資本剰余金
enormous investments in public infrastructure　インフラ整備［社会資本］への巨額の投資
the enormous supply of funds　豊富な資金提供

enormous capital surpluses　膨大な資本剰余金
◆China's renminbi may attain a reserve-currency status by the steady appreciation of the yuan and the country's enormous capital surpluses. 中国の人民元は、人民元の着実な切上げと中国の膨大な資本剰余金によって、準備通貨の地位を獲得する可能性がある。

enormous deficit　巨額の赤字
◆Both banks ran enormous deficits for the business year to March 2011, adding to their financial woes. 両行は、2011年3月期決算で巨額の赤字になって［赤字に転落して］、財務体質が悪化した。

enormous intervention　大規模介入
◆The yen has depreciated by more than ¥10 from before the previous enormous intervention. 円は、前回の大規模介入の前より10円強の円安になった。

enroll （動）入会させる, 登録する, グループの一員にする, 加入する, 入会する, 記入する
be enrolled in　～に加入する, ～に入学する
enroll at［in］　～に入学する, ～に入会する, ～に登録する
◆About 20 percent of new university graduates had neither secured employment nor enrolled for further education as of May 1. 5月1日現在、大学新卒者の約20%が就職も進学もしていない。◆Employees of the group companies and their dependents are now enrolled in the state health insurance program for employees of small and midsize companies. グループ企業の従業員とその扶養家族は現在、中小企業従業員向けの国の健康保険制度に加入している。◆The firm's workers are enrolled in the Social Insurance Agency-managed health insurance scheme. 同社の従業員は、社会保険庁が運営している健康保険制度に加入している。

ensure （動）確保する, 確実にする, 確実に～になるようにする, 確かなものにする, 保証する, 円滑に進める, (危険などから)守る　（⇒minimize）
ensure A against risk［danger］　危険からAを守る
ensure market position　市場での地位を維持する［強化する］
ensure protectionism　保護主義に傾斜する
ensure stable［uninterrupted］supplies of raw materials　原材料の安定供給を確保する
ensure sufficient money　十分な資金を確保する, 資金を十分確保する

ensure the timely payment　期限どおりの支払いを保証する
◆Disclosure of correct financial information by listed companies is indispensable for ensuring stock is traded fairly. 上場企業による正確な財務情報の開示は、株式取引の公正さを維持する上で重要だ。◆It is a matter of urgency to ensure that banks make profit margins that can meet investment risks and that they expand commission revenue as well as promote sweeping restructurings. 抜本的なリストラ推進のほか、投資リスクに見合う利ざやの確保と手数料収入の拡大などが銀行の急務だ。◆The stress test of the European Banking Authority is a banking health check to ensure banks across Europe have sufficient capital to withstand another financial crisis. 欧州銀行監督機構（EBA）のストレス・テストは、欧州全域の銀行が新たな金融危機に耐えられるだけの資本金を十分に確保していることを保証するための銀行の健全性検査だ。◆To ensure fair international commercial trade, the law against unfair competition stipulates that both individuals involved in bribery and the corporations they belong to should be punished. 公正な国際商取引を確保するため、不正競争防止法には、贈賄（外国公務員への贈賄）に関与した個人と法人を罰する規定（両罰規定）がある。

entail　（動）必要とする、（必然的結果として）〜を伴う、招く、もたらす、生じさせる、（責任などを）負わせる、課す、（不動産の）相続を〜に限定する
　entail a great deal of money and labor　多大な資金［金］と［に］労力を必要とする
　entail on［upon］　（人に）課す、負わせる、限定する
　entail risks　リスクを伴う
◆Investors have begun switching their funds from bank deposits to assets that entail some risks. 投資家が、銀行預金からリスクを伴う資産へと資金の運用を切り替え始めている。

enter　（動）市場などに参入する、団体などに加入する、加盟する、入会する、参加する、参加登録する、入る、記入する、記載する、提起する、提出する、申請する、申し出る、申し込む、正式に記録にのせる、（判決などに）正式に登録する、契約を結ぶ、コンピュータにデータなどを入力する、立ち上げる、〜にログインする、土地に立ち入る、占取する
　enter a protest　異議を申し立てる
　enter a recession　景気後退局面入りする
　enter an action against　〜に対する訴状を提出する、〜を告訴する
　enter into a double-dip recession　景気が二番底に突入する
　enter into an agreement［a contract］　契約を結ぶ、契約を締結する
　enter into force　効力を生じる、発効する
　enter new markets abroad　海外の新市場に進出する
　enter one's account PIN　〜の暗証番号を入力する
　enter the bond market　債券を発行する
　enter the debt market　起債する
　enter the market　市場に参入する、市場に進出する、市場に加わる、市場を利用する
◆A Mizuho Securities employee entered a sell order from a client as "sell 610,000 shares at ¥1 each" though the client's actual order was "sell one share at ¥610,000." 顧客の実際の注文は「61万円で1株の売り」であったが、みずほ証券の社員は「1株1円で61万株の売り」と入力して顧客の売り注文を出してしまった。◆In phishing, offenders lure victims to fake financial institution Web sites to enter their account PINs and other account information. フィッシングでは、犯人が被害者を金融機関の偽ホームページに誘導して、被害者に口座の暗証番号などの口座情報を入力させる。◆Japan's economy has entered a recession. 日本経済は、景気後退局面入りした。◆Major trading houses have also shown interest in entering the new business of Internet share transactions. 総合商社も、株式のネット取引の新規事業に参入する意向を示している。◆Mizuho Securities Co.'s sell order error was made when its staffer entered data incorrectly. みずほ証券の誤発注［発注ミス］は、同社の担当者がデータを誤って入力した際に生じた。◆Rapid recovery following the so-called Lehman shock has ended and the Chinese economy has entered a phase aimed at stable growth. いわゆるリーマン・ショック後の中国の急回復の時期は終わり、中国経済は、安定成長を目指す段階に入っている。◆The biggest advantage for the bank in entering the venture will be to increase its customer base without having to open expensive new branch offices. 同行にとってこの新規事業への参入の最大の利点は、コストのかかる新店舗を開設するまでもなく、顧客基盤を拡大できることだ。◆The firm is preparing to enter the mobile phone business in Japan. 同社は、日本での携帯電話事業への新規参入を目指している。◆The government may reject a company's request for a license to enter the fiduciary market if its executive has been dismissed in the past five years due to a violation of Section 2 of Article 102. 信託市場（信託業）に参入するための免許を申請した企業の役員が、第102条第2項の違反により5年以内に解任命令を受けていた場合、政府はその免許申請［免許交付］を拒否することができる。◆The Japanese currency's value vis-a-vis the U.S. dollar entered the ¥109 range in foreign exchange markets around the world. 円の対米ドル相場は、内外の外国為替市場で1ドル＝109円台を付けた。◆Tokio Marine Holdings Inc. will enter the life insurance market in India on July 1, 2011. 東京海上ホールディングスは、2011年7月1日からインドの生命保険市場に参入する。◆Two conditions must be met for the Kyoto Protocol to enter into force. 京都議定書の発効には、二つの条件が満たされなければならない、

Enterprise Turnaround Initiative Corporation（of Japan）　企業再生支援機構
◆Depending on the degree of JAL's financial deterioration, the government will consider a combination of capital reinforcement under the industrial revitalization law and public assistance by the Enterprise Turnaround Initiative Corp. of Japan. 日航の財務の傷み具合によって、政府は、産業再生法に基づく公的資金による資本増強と、企業再生支援機構による公的支援との組合せを検討する方針だ。◆The Enterprise Turnaround Initiative Corporation of Japan is the administrator of the JAL's rehabilitation. 企業再生支援機構は、日本航空再生の管財人となっている。◆The Enterprise Turnaround Initiative Corporation of Japan will inject ¥350 billion into the JAL group, subject to court approval of the rehabilitation plan. 企業再生支援機構は、裁判所の更生計画案承認を条件として、日航グループ（日航と子会社の日本航空インターナショナル、ジャルキャピタル）に3,500億円を出資する。

entire fiscal year　通期、事業年度全体
◆For the entire fiscal year, Mizuho Holdings plans to post ¥1.04 trillion in losses due to the disposal of bad loans, an increase of ¥440 billion from its initial projection. 通期では、みずほホールディングスの不良債権処理損（不良債権処理による損失額）は、当初見込みより4,400億円多い1兆400億円になる見込みだ。

entirely state-funded　国［政府、州］が100％出資する
◆The public loan was extended to JAL in June 2009 by the entirely state-funded Development Bank of Japan. この公的融資は、国が100％出資している日本政策投資銀行が、2009年6月に行った。

entity　（名）事業体、企業体、組織体、統一体、法的存在者、法主体、事業単位、単位　（⇒LLP）
　a Japanese entity　日本企業
　affiliated entities　関係会社、関連会社、系列会社
　autonomous entity　独立企業
　borrowing entity　発行体

business entity　企業体, 事業体, 企業, 企業実体
corporate entity　企業, 企業体, 法人格
economic entity　経済的実体
foreign entity　海外企業体, 在外企業体, 外国企業
government entity　政府機関
legal entity　法人, 法的実体, 法的存在
provide a liquidity facility to the issuing entity　発行体に流動枠を設定する
special purpose entity　特別目的会社
surviving entity　更生会社
unconsolidated entity　非連結事業体
◆Bond insurers write policies that promise to cover payments to bondholders if the entity that issued the bonds defaults. 金融保証会社[債券保険会社]は、債券発行体がデフォルト（債務不履行）になった場合に、債券保有者への（元本と利息の）支払い補償を約束する保険を引き受けている。◆The bill would allow a foreign company planning to acquire a Japanese company to pay shareholders of the Japanese entity "merger consideration" in the form of cash and the parent company's shares. 同法案では、日本企業を買収する外国企業は、「合併の対価」を現金や親会社の株式の形で日本企業の株主に支払うことができる。◆The U.S. government froze the assets of four individuals and eight entities that were involved in illicit activities such as money laundering, currency counterfeiting and narcotics trafficking. 米政府は、資金洗浄（マネー・ロンダリング）や通貨偽造、麻薬取引などの違法行為に関与している4個人、8団体の資産を凍結した。

entrust　（動）委託する, 委任する, 〜の管理をまかせる
◆As of the end of March 2011, AIJ Investment Advisors Co. had been entrusted with about ¥210 billion in corporate pension funds. 2011年3月末現在、投資顧問会社のAIJ投資顧問は、約2,100億円の企業年金基金[企業年金積立金]の運用を受託していた。◆Entrusted or instructed by the South Korean government, private banks jointly extended loans to the company. 韓国政府の委託や指示を受けて、民間銀行が同社に協調融資した。◆The Tokyo metropolitan government entrusted the bids for the construction project to the company. 東京都は、この建設工事の入札業務を同社に委託した。

entrusted research　研究委託, 委託研究
◆Japanese companies invest ¥200 billion a year in universities and public-run research institutes, through such means as entrusted research. 日本企業は、研究委託を通じて、大学や公的研究機関に毎年2,000億円を投資している。

entry　（名）（株式市場への）新規上場, 記入, 記帳, 記録, 登録, 登記, 記載, 記載事項, 参加, 参入, 入会, 入場, 入国, 参加者, 出品物, 土地への立入り, 通関手続き, 通関申告, 入力
a contra entry　相対記入
age at entry　契約年齢, 保険年齢
book-entry securities　振替決済証券
credit entry　貸記
cross entry　振替記入
current entry cost　購入時価
customs entry　通関手続き
data entry　データ入力
debit entry　借記
domestic stock exchange entry　国内株式市場への新規上場
entry（age）cost method　加入年齢方式
entry age normal method　正常加入年齢方式
entry at customs　税関での手続き
government bonds book-entry system　国債振替決済口座
import entry　輸入手続き
make an entry　記入する, 記帳する
market entry　市場参入
order entry　受注, 受注処理, 注文処理
stock exchange entry　証券取引所[株式市場]への新規上場
the port of entry　通関港, 入国港
◆Domestic stock exchange entries continue to languish, reflecting the tough conditions faced by emerging firms wanting to publicly list their shares. 国内株式市場への新規上場は、株式上場を目指す新興企業が直面している厳しい状況を反映して、低迷が続いている。

environment　（名）環境, 情勢, 動向, 局面, 展開　（⇒business environment, exposure, financial performance, investment environment）
bullish environment　強気市場
business environment　事業環境, 経営環境
competitive environment　競争環境
credit environment　信用情勢
deflationary environment　デフレ環境
developing environments　発展途上国, 開発途上国
economic environment　景気, 経済環境
falling interest rate environment　金利低下局面, 金利低下環境
financial environment　金融情勢, 金融環境
global environment　地球環境
interest rate environment　金利情勢, 金利動向, 金利環境
investment environment　投資環境
market environment　市場環境, 相場
nervous environment　神経質な相場展開
operating environment　営業環境, 事業環境
political environment　政局
regulatory environment　規制環境
restrictive financial environment　金融政策の引締め
rising（interest）rate environment　金利上昇局面
swollen monetary environments　金融膨張の市場環境
technical environment　市場の内部環境
volatile interest rate environment　金利の変動が激しい環境, 金利の変動性が高い環境
◆European countries and China have various kinds of bubbles and/or swollen monetary environments. 欧州や中国は、バブルや金融膨張の市場環境を抱えている。◆These moves of the two airlines show the extent of the crisis in the current business environment. 両航空会社のこれらの動きは、現在の経営環境の危機的状況の大きさを示している。

environmental rehabilitation fund　環境再生ファンド, 環境回復基金
environmental stocks　環境関連株
envisage　（動）明確に心に描く, 心に思い浮かべる, 思い描く, 予想する, 想像する, 予測する, 考察する, 見据える, 直視する, 見込む, 見る, 〜に直面する
envisage a plan　計画を立てる
envisage dangers　危険に直面する
envisage exit strategies　出口戦略を見据える
envisage realities　現実を直視する, 現実を見据える
◆G-7 nations should start envisaging exit strategies and the restoration of fiscal health. 先進7か国は、そろそろ出口戦略と財政の健全化も見据えるべきだ。◆The Bank of Japan envisages the prospects of economic growth and consumer price trends in its "Outlook for Economic Activity and Prices." 日銀は、『展望リポート』で、経済成長や消費者物価の先行きを示している。

envisaged（interest）rate　想定金利
◆The envisaged interest rate for long-term government

bonds has been set at 2.4 percent, compared to 2 percent in fiscal 2010. 長期国債の想定金利は、2010年度の2%に対して2.4%と高く設定されている。

envisaged timeline 目標期限
◆The envisaged timeline of APEC leaders for overcoming the global financial crisis may result in an empty promise. 世界的な金融危機を克服するためのアジア太平洋経済協力会議（APEC）首脳の目標期限は、空手形に終わる可能性がある。

envision （動）予想する, 想像する, 考察する, 見据える, 見込む （＝envisage）
◆Under the envisioned lending facility, the IMF will provide funds to countries where government bond yields remain at high levels to help reconstruct their public finances. この融資制度案では、国際通貨基金（IMF）が、国債の利回りが高止まりしている国に資金を提供［融資］して財政再建を支援する。

epicenter （名）震源地, 震央（震源の真上の地点）, 爆心地, 中心点, 元凶
◆Greece is the epicenter of the sovereign debt crisis in Europe. ギリシャが、欧州の財政危機の元凶［震源地］だ。◆The epicenter of the financial chaos is the United States. 今回の金融混乱［金融危機］の震源地は、米国だ。

EPS 1株当たり利益, 1株当たり純利益 （earnings per shareの略。⇒earnings per share）

equal （形）同じ, 等しい, 同等の, 対等の, 平等な, 公平な, 互角の, 公平な, 〜に匹敵する, イコール
（⇒exercise price）
　Equal Credit Opportunity Act　信用機会均等法, 消費者信用機会均等法
　equal employment opportunity　雇用機会均等, 平等雇用機会
　Equal Employment Opportunity Commission　雇用機会均等委員会, 平等雇用機会委員会, EEOC
　equal monthly payments with interest　元利均等返済
　equal opportunity　機会均等
　equal partner　対等提携, イコール・パートナー
　equal value principle　等価交換原則
　have equal share　均等に出資する
　make equal payments　均等払いにする
　on an equal basis　均等に, 対等で
◆Since three banks integrated their operations, executives from the three predecessor banks served on an equal basis as presidents of the Mizuho group, Mizuho Bank and Mizuho Corporate Bank. 3銀行の経営統合以来、旧3行の経営者が、みずほグループ（FG）、みずほ銀行、みずほコーポレート銀行のトップをそれぞれ分け合った。

equally owned by　〜が折半出資している, 〜が共同所有している
◆Elpida Memory Inc. is equally owned by NEC and Hitachi. 半導体メーカーのエルピーダメモリは、NECと日立が折半出資している。

equilibrium　（名）均衡, 均衡状態, 均衡水準, 均衡レート, つり合い, 平衡, 平衡状態, 平等
　balance of payments equilibrium　国際収支均衡, 経常収支の均衡
　consumption equilibrium　消費均衡
　contracted equilibrium　縮小均衡
　equilibrium（economic）growth　均衡経済成長
　equilibrium for bond yields　債券利回りの均衡水準
　equilibrium of industry　産業の均衡
　equilibrium of the firm　企業の均衡
　equilibrium of trade　貿易の均衡
　fundamental equilibrium exchange rate　ファンダメンタルズ均衡為替レート
　fundamental equilibrium level　ファンダメンタルズ面の均衡水準
　general equilibrium model　一般均衡モデル
　market equilibrium　市場均衡
　neutral equilibrium　中立的均衡
　price equilibrium　価格均衡
　underemployment equilibrium　不完全雇用均衡
◆The rational actions for survival taken by individual companies herald a danger that could lead the Japanese economy into contracted equilibrium. 生き残りをかけて個々の企業が取っている合理的な行動が、日本経済を縮小均衡に導く危険性をはらんでいる。

equities swap　株式交換　（⇒equity swap）
◆NTT DoCoMo is making the move to facilitate purchasing an overseas telecommunications firm through an equities swap and capital tie-up. NTTドコモは現在、株式交換方式による海外の通信会社の買収や資本提携を円滑に進める動きを展開している。

equity　（名）株式, 持ち分, 持ち分権, 自己持ち分, 自己資本, 純資産, 純資産価値, 正味価額, 証券, エクイティ
　at equity　実価による, 持ち分価格で
　common equity　普通株
　cross equity holdings　株式の持ち合い
　debt and equity securities　債券と持ち分証券, 債券と株式
　equities businesses　証券部門
　equity base　株主資本総額
　equity buyback　株式の買戻し, 自社株の買戻し
　equity contribution　出資
　equity instrument　持ち分金融商品
　equity investor　株式投資家, 資本投資家
　equity offering　株式公開, 株式発行
　equity participation　資本参加, 出資, 株式投資
　equity securities　持ち分証券, 持ち分有価証券
　equity-settled share-base payment transaction　持ち分決済型の株式報酬取引
　equity share　普通株式
　equity swap deal　株式交換取引
　　（＝stock［share］swap deal; ⇒swap, unit）
　equity transaction　資本取引
　international equity market　国際株式市場
　international equity options　国際株式オプション
　international equity placement　株式海外売出し
　new equity raising　新株発行
　on the equity basis　持ち分法で
　owners' equity　所有者持ち分
　partners' equity　パートナーの持ち分
　proprietor's equity　事業主の持ち分
　return on equity　株主資本利益率, ROE
　　（＝rate of return on equity）
　shareholders' equity　株主持ち分, 株主資本, 資本の部
　　（＝stockholders' equity）
　straight equity　普通株
　total liabilities and equity　負債資本合計
◆Ford's debt restructuring includes conversion of debt to equity and cash tender offers. 米フォードの債務再編には、債務の株式化や現金による株式の公開買付けが含まれている。◆Partnership interests are recorded at equity. パートナーシップ持ち分は、持ち分価格で評価している。◆The brokerage's main services for individual customers will be asset management advisory services, focusing on the sale of products such as investment trust funds that invest in foreign equities, and money market funds denominated in foreign currencies. 同証券会社は、株式の主な個人顧客向け（売買仲介）業務とし

て、外国株を組み込んだ投資信託や外貨建てMMF（マネー・マーケット・ファンド）などの商品の販売を中心に、資産運用顧問業務を展開する方針だ。◆The remaining debt of ¥230 billion will be converted to equity, with ¥220 billion to be swapped into preferred shares and ¥10 billion into common shares. 残りの債権2,300億円は株式に振り替えられ、このうち2,200億円分は優先株に、また100億円分は普通株に振り替えられる。

equity capital　自己資本, 株主資本, 株主の出資資本, 株主持ち分, 払込み資本, 株式資本　（⇒inflate）
　additional equity capital　増資
　　（=the injection of equity）
　equity capital to total assets　株主資本比率
◆Banks have been allowed to count the taxes they pay in writing off their nonperforming loans as part of their equity capital. 銀行はこれまで、不良債権処理の際に納める税金を自己資本の一部と見なすことができた。◆In the latest account settlements, not only Resona but other banking groups gave up including sizable deferred tax assets in their equity capital. 今決算では、「りそな」だけでなく他の銀行グループも、巨額の繰延べ税金資産の自己資本への計上を見送った。◆Major banks are striving to write off some of their tax assets from their equity capital. 大手銀行は現在、自己資本からの税金資産減らしに取り組んでいる。

equity financing　エクイティ・ファイナンス, 新株発行による資金調達, 自己資本金融, 株式金融増資, 自己資本の調達　（=equity finance：社債発行や借入金によって資本を調達する方法をdebt financingという）
　private equity financing　未上場株の交付による資金調達
　step up equity financing　株式発行による資金調達を急ぐ
◆M&A deals among start-up firms are likely to create more demand for equity financing from the autumn. ベンチャー企業間のM&A取引で、秋から株式発行による資金調達の需要が増える見通しだ。◆Small and midsize companies have been stepping up equity financing to fund capital investments and prepare for M&A deals. 中小企業は、設備投資の資金調達とM&A取引に備えて、株式発行による資金調達を急いでいる。

equity financing deal　新株発行による資金調達の取引, エクイティ・ファイナンス取引
◆The firm raised $80 billion through equity financing deals in 2010. 同社は、エクイティ・ファイナンス（新株発行による資金調達）の取引で、2010年度は800億ドルの資金を調達した。

equity fund　株式ファンド, 投資ファンド
◆The equity fund also operates golf courses at about 40 locations around the country. この投資ファンドは、全国約40か所のゴルフ場も運営している。

equity holding　株式保有, 株式所有, 保有株式, 持ち株, 出資比率
　（=shareholding, stock holding, stockholding）
◆The major banks' stock-related losses ballooned 1.9 fold from a year ago because of the booking of declines in the value of their equity holdings as appraised losses and their sale of stocks due to sluggish stock markets. 大手銀行の株式等関連損失は、株式相場の下落による保有株の減損処理や売却損などで前期の1.9倍に膨らんだ。

equity holding losses　株式含み損, 保有株式の含み損
◆Asahi Mutual Life Insurance Co. has unveiled a business rehabilitation plan, featuring a ¥150 billion capital injection from three banks and a ¥500 billion cut in its equity holding losses. 朝日生命保険は、銀行3行による基金（株式会社の資本に当たる）の1,500億円増額と5,000億円の保有株式含み損処理を柱とする会社再建計画（経営刷新計画）を発表した。（原文は2002年2月17日付THE DAILY YOMIURI）

equity index　株価指数, 株式指数, 株式インデックス
　equity index fund　株式インデックス・ファンド
　equity index participation　株式指数参加商品

　equity index product　株価指数商品

equity investment　株式投資, 直接投資, 出資
　（=stock investment；⇒investment portfolio）
◆The challenge faced by the nation's stock market lies in how to attract individual investors to equity investment. 日本の証券市場が直面している課題は、どのようにして個人投資家を株式投資に呼び込むかにある。

equity-linked　（形）株式に連動した, 株式にリンクした
　equity-linked finance　エクイティ・ファイナンス（自己資本調達）
　equity-linked financing　株式リンク債発行
　　（=equity-linked offering）
　equity-linked issue　株式リンク債
　equity-linked life insurance　エクイティ生命保険
　equity-linked note　株式リンク債
　equity-linked offering　株式リンク債発行
　equity-linked security　株式リンク証券
　the outstanding equity-linked bonds　発行済みの株式リンク債

equity market　株式市場
　（=stock market；⇒Moon Trade）
◆The stock market is now luring not only individual investors such as day traders, but also people who abandoned the equity market after the economic bubble burst. 株式市場（株式投資）は現在、デイ・トレーダーなどのようなセミプロの個人投資家だけでなく、バブル崩壊以降、株式市場から遠ざかっていた一般の人たちをも引き付けている。

equity option　株式オプション
◆A former vice president of the Osaka Securities Exchange instructed subordinates to buy and sell similar quantities of equity options. 大阪証券取引所の元副理事長が、株式オプションの取引で、部下に対して「買い」と「売り」が同数になる注文を出すよう指示していた。

equity option trading　株式オプション取引, 個別株オプション取引
◆Equity option trading is the purchase or sale of stocks of individual issues at specified prices after a specified period. 個別株オプション取引は、個別銘柄の株式を一定期間後に特定価格で売買する取引だ。

equity stake　株式持ち分, 持ち分, 株式保有比率, 出資比率
　boost one's equity stake in the company　同社に対する株式保有比率［株式持ち分］を引き上げる
　reduce one's equity stake in the company to less than 10 percent　同社に対する出資比率を10％未満に引き下げる
　take an equity stake of around 15 percent in the company　同社の株式持ち分約15％を取得する
　　（⇒retail services）
◆Ford reduced its 33.4 percent equity stake in Mazda to about 13 percent in late 2008 in the wake of the global financial crisis. 世界の金融危機を受けて、米フォードは2008年末に33.4％のマツダへの出資比率［マツダに対する株式保有比率］を約13％に引き下げた。◆The Securities and Exchange Law requires anyone with an equity stake of more than 5 percent in a listed company to report a sale of stake of 1 percent or more to a local finance bureau within five business days of the sale. 現行の証券取引法では、上場企業に対する株式保有比率が5％を超える株保有者は、株式の売買が株式の保有割合を1％超えるごとに、株式売買の5営業日以内に各財務局にその報告書を提出しなければならない。◆The U.S. government will boost its equity stake in Citigroup Inc. to as much as 36 percent. 米政府は、米金融大手シティグループに対する政府の株式保有比率［株式持ち分］を36％に引き上げる。

equity stake rate　持ち分比率, 出資比率
◆We have not yet discussed a specific equity stake rate. 具

体的な出資比率については、まだ話し合っていない。

equity swap 株式交換 (⇒equities swap)
◆Kadokawa Holdings Inc. will make film distributor Nippon Herald Films Inc. a wholly owned subsidiary through an equity swap in August. 角川ホールディングスは、映画配給会社の日本ヘラルド映画を株式交換で8月から100％子会社にする。

equity tie-up 資本提携
◆Three major steelmakers reached a final agreement to form an equity tie-up. 鉄鋼大手の3社が、資本提携を結ぶことで最終合意した。

equity trading business 株式取引業務
◆The suspension of this foreign investment bank's after-hours equity trading business reflects poor demand in Japan's equity market. この外資系投資銀行の株の時間外取引業務停止は、日本の株式市場の需要低迷を反映している。

equivalent (名)同等物,同価値のもの,等価物,相当するもの,相当額,相当分,換算,換算額,同意語
(⇒cash equivalents)
 annual equivalent 年換算,年換算利回り
 antidilutive common stock equivalents 反希薄化準普通株式
 bond equivalent basis 債券換算利回り
 cash equivalent value 現金等価額
  (=cash equivalent amount)
 certainty equivalent 確実性等価,確実性等価額
 certainty equivalent return 確実性等価収益率
 common stock equivalent 準普通株式,普通株式等価物
 corporate bond equivalent 社債換算利回り
 corporate taxable equivalent 税引き後債券相当利回り
 exchange of equivalents 等価交換
 exchange of non-equivalents 不等価交換
 interest equivalents 利息相当額,利息相当分
 local equivalent 現地通貨換算額
 London equivalent ロンドン相場換算
 money equivalent 現金等価物
 tariff equivalent 関税等価
 the equivalent of fifty million dollars 5,000万ドルと同価値のもの
 the law of the equivalent of international demand 国際需要均等の法則
 yen equivalent 円換算額,円貨額
◆Net earnings in 2008 were $1.56 billion, or $2.65 per fully diluted common and common equivalent shares. 2008年度の純利益は、15億6,000万ドル（完全希薄化後の普通株式および普通株式相当証券1株当たり2.65ドル）でした。

equivalent (形)同等の,同価値の,等価の,均等の,同額の,同量の
 common equivalent shares 普通株式相当証券
 equivalent annual rate 均等年間利率
 equivalent bond yield 債券相当利回り
 equivalent decrease 同額の減少,同値の減少
 equivalent exchange 等価交換
 equivalent index number 等価指数
 equivalent mean investment period 等価平均回収期間
 yield to equivalent life 相当期間利回り

equivalent to ～に相当する,～に当たる,～と同等［同価値・同量］ (⇒outstanding equities)
◆Goldman Sachs Group Inc. and the two Japanese banks hold preferred shares equivalent to 70 percent of Sanyo. 米証券大手のゴールドマン・サックス（GS）と邦銀2行が、三洋電機の約7割の優先株式（普通株式に換算して議決権の約7割）を保有している。◆Life insurer's foundation fund is equivalent to capital for a stock company. 生命保険会社の基金は、株式会社の資本金に相当する。◆The foreign funds purchased the convertible bonds at prices equivalent to ￥25 per share. 海外ファンドは、1株25円で転換社債を引き受けた。

ERISA エリサ法
(⇒Employee Retirement Income Security Act)

ERM 欧州為替相場メカニズム,欧州為替レート・メカニズム,イーアールエム (European (Exchange) Rate Mechanismの略。英国を除くEC加盟国8か国が加盟して1979年3月に発足し、ユーロが導入される1999年1月1日まで機能した)

erode (動)低下させる,減少させる,低下をもたらす,悪化させる,圧迫する,脅かす,浸食する,蝕（むしば）む,破壊する (自動)目減りする,減退する,徐々に蝕（むしば）まれる
(⇒worsening employment situation)
 erode competitiveness 競争力を低下させる
 erode confidence in ～に対する信認を低下させる［信認の低下をもたらす］
 erode financial reserves 財政基盤を脅かす,財政基盤を浸食する
 erode profitability 収益性を圧迫する
 erode sharply [rapidly] 急落する
 erode the (business) franchise of the bank 同行の営業基盤を浸食する［脅かす］
 erode the issuer's ability to make interest distributions 発行体の利払い能力を低下させる
 eroded business confidence 企業の景況感の悪化
 small savings eroded by inflation インフレで蝕まれる少額の貯蓄［預金］
◆Isuzu Motors Ltd. forecasts its first annual loss in six years as vehicle demands drops and a stronger yen erodes overseas earnings. いすゞ自動車は、需要の減退と円高による海外収益の減少で、6期ぶりに赤字になる見通しだ。◆Long-term debts held by central and local governments are expected to further swell, thereby eroding confidence in governments bonds. 国と地方自治体が抱える長期債務は、さらに膨張して、国債の信用が失われるものと見られる。◆The wrongdoing of Olympus Corp., a blue-chip company that holds the largest share of the global endoscope market, has eroded international faith in corporate Japan. 内視鏡の市場シェアで世界トップのオリンパスの不正行為で、日本企業の国際的な信頼は失墜している。

erosion (名)減少,低下,下落,目減り,悪化,圧迫,浸食,浸食作用,腐食,破壊
 asset erosion 資産の目減り,資産価額の低下
 asset value erosion 資産価値の目減り
 erosion in equity prices 株価下落
 erosion in stock prices 株価の下落
 erosion of corporate ethics 企業倫理の低下,企業倫理の欠如
 erosion of financial assets 金融資産の目減り,金融資産の損失［減少］
 erosion of individuals' capital 家計のひっ迫
 erosion of purchasing power 購買力の低下
 margin erosion 利益率の低下,預貸利ざやの縮小,利ざやの縮小
 market share erosion 市場シェア［シェア］の低下,市場占拠率の低下
 price erosion 価格の下落,価格の引下げ
 the erosion of core operations 主力事業の悪化,中核事業［基幹事業］の悪化
 the erosion of financial flexibility 財務の柔軟性の低下
 the erosion of tax bases 課税基準の浸食

the erosion of the risk/return outlook　リスクとリターンの見通しの悪化
◆If a financial system crisis should occur due to sharp fall in Japanese government bond prices, the Japanese people would suffer an erosion of their financial assets. 日本国債価格の急落で金融システム不安が生じれば、日本国民の金融資産は損失を被ることになる。◆Progress in the disposal of nonperforming loans and receding concerns over further deterioration in regional economies have led to diminished risk of asset erosion. 不良債権処理の進展や地方経済がさらに悪化する懸念の後退などで、資産が目減りする恐れが薄らいでいる。◆S&P's upgrades of its outlooks on the long-term ratings on 11 regional banks reflect diminished risks of asset erosion and improved capitalization supported by a recovery in net profits. スタンダード＆プアーズによる地方銀行11行の長期格付け見通しの上方修正は、資産が目減りする恐れが減り、純利益の回復に支えられて資本基盤が改善したことを反映している。

erosion of corporate ethics　企業倫理の低下, 企業倫理の欠如
◆The U.S. tried to prevent an erosion of corporate ethics among financial institutions by refusing to provide public funds to Lehman Brothers. リーマン・ブラザーズへの公的資金の投入を拒否することによって、米政府は金融機関のモラル・ハザード（企業倫理の欠如）を回避しようとした。

erosion of financial assets　金融資産の目減り, 金融資産の損失[減少]
◆If a financial system crisis should occur due to sharp fall in Japanese government bond prices, the Japanese people would suffer an erosion of their financial assets. 日本国債価格の急落で金融システム不安が生じれば、日本国民の金融資産は損失を被ることになる。

errant　（形）誤った, 不貞の, 道を踏み外した, 軌道[コース]からそれた, 遍歴する
a huge errant sell order　大量の誤った売り注文
◆Mizuho Securities Co. placed a huge errant sell order for the newly listed shares of recruitment firm J-Com Co. みずほ証券が、人材サービス業ジェイコムの新規上場株式に対し、誤って大量の売り注文を出してしまった。

erroneous sell order　誤発注, 発注ミス
◆It's not a beautiful story for securities firms to snap up stocks while being aware of the erroneous sell order. 誤発注と認識しながら、証券会社が間隙を縫って株を取得するのは、美しい話ではない。◆Mizuho Securities Co.'s erroneous sell order was made when its staffer entered data incorrectly. みずほ証券の誤発注（発注ミス）は、同社の担当者がデータを誤って入力した際に生じた。

error　（名）間違い, 誤り, 誤謬（ごびゅう）, ミス, 失策, 思い違い, 考え違い, 誤った信念, 過ち, 悪行, 誤差, 誤審, コンピュータのエラー, 故障, 障害, エラー
accounting error　経理ミス, 会計上の誤謬（=accounting mistake）
an error in [of] judgment　判断ミス
calculation error　計算上の誤謬（=error of calculation）
clerical error　事務上の誤り, 事務的な誤り, 記帳上の誤謬
compensating error　相殺誤差
correct errors　間違いを直す, エラーを訂正する
correction of error　誤謬の訂正, エラーの訂正
critical [fatal] error　致命的エラー
error account　エラー・アカウント
error coin　欠陥硬貨, エラー・コイン
error in principle　原則上の誤謬
error notification　エラー通知, 事故連絡書
error of mistake in writing　誤記上の誤謬, 誤記による誤謬
error on posting　転記上の誤謬, 転記上の誤り
error span [range]　誤差範囲
errors and irregularities　誤謬と異常事項
errors and omissions　誤差脱漏, 誤記・脱漏, 過誤脱漏
errors and omissions (liability) insurance　過失怠慢責任保険
offsetting error　相殺上の誤謬
standard error　標準誤差
system error　システム・エラー
◆Errors in computing systems at financial institutions could lead to problems in making international fund transactions. 金融機関のコンピュータ・システムのエラーは、国際的な資金取引上、トラブルが生じる可能性がある。

escalate　（動）段階的に上昇する, 段階的に拡大[増大]する, 漸増する, エスカレーター方式で（価格, 賃金などが）上昇[下降]する, 急上昇する, 深刻化する, エスカレートする
escalate into financial crisis　金融危機に発展する
escalated tariff structure　逓増的関税構造
escalating debt crisis　深刻化する債務危機, 債務危機の深刻化
escalating land prices　地価上昇
escalating stock prices　株価上昇
◆After the takeover bid was announced, the price of shares escalated. 株式公開買い付けの発表後に、株価は急上昇した。
◆France and Germany could not bridge their differences, so Europe's efforts to solve its escalating debt crisis plunged into disarray. フランスとドイツが両国の相違を埋められなかったため、深刻化する欧州の債務危機問題解決への欧州の取組みは、混乱に陥った。

escalation　（名）上昇, 急上昇, 段階的拡大[増大], 漸増, 深刻化, エスカレーション
cost escalation cover　インフレ保険
escalation in land prices　地価の上昇
tariff escalation　傾斜関税

escalator　（名）自動調整条項, 伸縮条項, 出世コース, エスカレーター
escalator bond　自動調整債
escalator clause　（労使間の）伸縮条項, 均等変動条項, インフレ条項, エスカレーター条項（=escalation clause）
escalator scale　賃金漸増制
escalator system　エスカレーター方式

escape　（動）逃げる, 逃れる, 免れる, 脱出する, 回避する, 漏れる
◆Commercial banks have created special investment vehicles (SIVs) in order to escape the capital adequacy regulation imposed by the Basel accord. 銀行は、バーゼル協定[バーゼル合意]による自己資本比率規制を回避するため、特別投資会社(SIV)を新設している。

escape fund　エスケープ・ファンド（50代でリタイヤーした人が、通常の年金をもらえる60歳までの数年間を過ごすために用意する資金）

ESCB　欧州中央銀行制度（European System of Central Banksの略）

escrow　（名）条件付き捺印証書, 第三者委託金, エスクロー
escrow account　エスクロー勘定, エスクロー口座
escrow agent　エスクロー代理人, 条件付き証書受託者
escrow agreement　エスクロー契約
escrow bond　条件付き譲渡証書
escrow fund　エスクロー資金, 預託資金
escrow L/C [credit]　エスクロー信用状, 寄託信用状

money held in escrow 第三者の手で保管されている金
ESM 欧州安定化メカニズム, 欧州安定メカニズム （財政危機に陥ったユーロ圏の国に対する恒久的な財政支援制度。⇒European Stability Mechanism）
ESMA ECの欧州証券市場機構, 欧州証券市場監督機構 （European Securities and Markets Authorityの略。2010年11月1日に新設）
ESOP 従業員株式購入選択権制度（employee stock option planの略）
ESOP 従業員持ち株制度, 従業員株式所有制度 （=employee stock ownership trust: employee stock ownership planの略。米国が、1974年に自社株を中心とした確定拠出型年金制度として導入）
◆We issued 14 million new shares of common stock in connection with the establishment of an ESOP feature for the non-management savings plan. 当社は、非管理職貯蓄制度の一環として従業員持ち株制度（ESOP）を設けたことに関連して、普通株式新株1,400万株を発行しました。
ESOP debt guarantee reduction ESOP基金債務保証額の減少
ESOT 米国の従業員持ち株制度（employee stock ownership trustの略）
establish （動）設立する, 設ける, 設置する, 創設する, 開設する, 創立する, 樹立する, 形成する, 確立する, 確保する, 達成する, 実現する, 制定する, 定める, 制定する, 引当金や担保権を設定する, 認定する, 関係を築く, 制度などを導入する, 立証する
  establish a common currency 統一通貨を実現する
  establish a consumer finance subsidiary 消費者金融子会社を設立する
  establish a performance achievement target 業績達成目標を設定する
  establish a solid presence [position] in the market 市場で安定した地位を確立する
  establish a wholly [100％] owned trust bank subsidiary 100％信託銀行子会社を設立する
  establish capital guidelines 自己資本比率の基準を定める[設ける]
  establish liquidity 流動性を確保する
  establish short positions ショート・ポジションをとる
  have well-established access to financial markets 金融市場へのアクセスが十分確保されている
◆As investment for digitalization is costly, NBS needs to establish a more profitable management system, including joint investment in digital-related facilities and content with the Fuji TV group. デジタル化の投資負担は軽くないので、ニッポン放送は、フジテレビ・グループとのデジタル関連施設への共同投資やコンテンツ（情報内容）の共有など、収益力の高い経営システムを確立する必要がある。◆Before the new corporate law, at least ¥10 million was required to establish stock companies and ¥3 million to create limited liability companies. 新会社法までは、株式会社の設立に最低1,000万円、有限会社の設立に300万円必要だった。◆Credit guarantee associations were established to make it easier for small and mid-sized companies to receive loans from financial institutions. 信用保証協会は、中小企業が金融機関から容易に融資を受けられるようにするために設置された。◆Following the footsteps of Sony Corp. and Softbank Corp., the company established a new firm to sell shares over the Internet. ソニーとソフトバンクの先例にならって、同社も株式をインターネットで売買するネット取引の新会社を設立した。◆Incubator Bank of Japan was established in 2004 by former Bank of Japan official Takeshi Kimura and members of the Tokyo Junior Chamber International. 日本振興銀行は、日銀出身の木村剛氏と東京青年会議所のメンバーらが2004年に開業した。◆Mizuho Financial Group was established in September 2000 after Dai-Ichi Kangyo Bank, Fuji Bank and the Industrial Bank of Japan integrated their operations. みずほフィナンシャルグループは、第一勧業銀行、富士銀行と日本興業銀行の3行が経営統合して、2000年9月に発足した。◆The aim of a fund established by the Development Bank of Japan is to infuse money into auto parts makers hit by the March 11 earthquake and tsunami. 日本政策投資銀行が設立するファンドの目的は、東日本大震災で被災した自動車部品メーカーに資金を行き渡らせることにある。
establish a fund ファンドを設立する, 基金を設ける
◆The Development Bank of Japan will raise ¥50 billion to establish a fund to assist auto parts makers hit by the March 11 disaster. 日本政策投資銀行は、（2011年）3月11日の東日本大震災で被災した自動車部品メーカーの復興を支援するため、500億円のファンドを設立する。◆The Development of Japan will ask major financial groups to invest in the fund established to assist auto parts makers hit by the March 11 earthquake and tsunami. 日本政策投資銀行が、東日本大震災で被災した自動車部品メーカーを支援するために設立するファンドへの出資を、大手金融グループに呼びかけることになった。
establishment （名）設立, 設置, 創設, 創立, 樹立, 形成, 確立, 制定, 規定, 設定, 認定, 導入, 立証, 組織, 施設, 公共施設, 機関, 会社, 商店, 店, 事業所, 既成社会, 制度, 体制, 体制側, 上層部, 支配層, 支配機構, 常置人員, エスタブリッシュメント
  additional establishment 追加設定
  branch establishment 支店
  business establishment 事業所
  commercial establishment 商社, 商会
  establishment of a law 法律の制定
  establishment of a new company 新会社の設立
  establishment of diplomatic relations 外交関係の樹立
  establishment survey 事業所調査
  government establishments abroad 在外公館
  industrial establishment 工場
  initial establishment 当初設定
  manufacturing establishment 生産会社
  old establishment 老舗（しにせ）
  permanent establishment 恒久的施設
  service establishment 加盟店
  the Establishment of the company 会社の上層部
◆The draft of the government's new growth strategy includes the establishment of a public-private investment fund to support the content industry in its foreign endeavors. 政府の新成長戦略の原案には、コンテンツ（情報の内容）産業の海外展開を支援する官民出資のファンド設立も盛り込まれている。◆The IMF threw its weight behind the establishment of a bad bank. 国際通貨基金（IMF）は、バッド・バンクの設立を後押しした。◆The ministry has decided to support the establishment of funds to help failing general contractors rehabilitate themselves as part of efforts to promote the reorganizations of such contractors outside of major cities. 同省は、経営不振の地方ゼネコンの再編を促進するため、ゼネコンの企業再建支援ファンドの設立を支援することを決めた。
estate （名）財産, 不動産, 地所, 私有地
  estate agent [house] 不動産仲介業者, 不動産業者
  estate surveyor 不動産鑑定士
  freehold estate 自由保有権, 自由保有物権
  income-producing real estate 稼動不動産
  leasehold estate 不動産賃借物権
  legal estate 不動産権
  personal estate 動産
  real estate 不動産

trust estate 信託財産

estimate (名)見積り, 予想, 予測, 概算, 試算, 推定値, 推定量, 評価, 判断, 見積り書, 概算書
(⇒appraisal profit, IMF)
◆The FSA urged the financial group to revise its earnings estimate. 金融庁は、同金融グループに対して業績予想の修正を強く迫った。

ETF 上場投資信託, 株価指数連動型上場投資信託
(exchange-traded fundの略。株式と同じように市場で売買する投信。東証株価指数(TOPIX)や日経平均株価指数などの指数に連動して値動きする。⇒exchange-traded fund, fund名詞)
◆ETFs are investment trust funds that incorporate all issues in the Nikkei Stock Average of 225 selected issues and the Tokyo Stock Exchange Stock Price Index. ETF(上場投信)は、日経平均株価(225種)や東証株価指数(TOPIX)などを構成するすべての銘柄を組み込んだ投資信託である。

ethics (名)倫理, 道徳, 倫理体系, 行動の規範
code of ethics 倫理綱領
(=business conduct code, code of conduct)
corporate ethics 企業倫理 (=business ethics)
erosion of corporate ethics 企業倫理の低下, 企業倫理の欠如, モラル・ハザード
ethics charter 企業行動憲章 (=charter of ethics, corporate ethics charter, ethics code)
◆The U.S. tried to prevent an erosion of corporate ethics among financial institutions by refusing to provide public funds to Lehman Brothers. リーマン・ブラザーズへの公的資金の投入を拒否することによって、米政府は金融機関のモラル・ハザード(企業倫理の欠如)を回避しようとした。

EU 欧州連合 (⇒European Union)
◆In order to bring the European crisis under control, the EU, ECB and IMF must work even more closely together. 欧州危機の収束を図るには、欧州連合(EU)、欧州中央銀行(ECB)と国際通貨基金(IMF)の緊密な連携を強化する必要がある。◆The EFSF is the EU bailout fund for countries with fiscal deficits. 欧州金融安定基金(EFSF)は、欧州の財政赤字国を支援する基金だ。◆The EU has been unable to work out its inherent policies concerning the fiscal deficiencies of some of its more reckless member countries. 欧州連合(EU)は、一部の無謀な加盟国の欠陥財政について、一貫した政策を打ち出せないでいる。◆The EU's responses to the European debt crisis have been slow. 欧州債務危機への欧州連合(EU)の対応は、後手に回ってきた。◆The G-20 communique urged the eurozone countries to boost the EFSF, the EU bailout fund. G20(主要20か国・地域)の共同声明は、ユーロ圏諸国に欧州の金融支援基金である欧州金融安定基金(EFSF)の拡充を促した。◆The IMF and the EU are strengthening their cooperation to avert a Greek default and prevent a chain reaction of debt crisis among other countries. ギリシャの債務不履行(デフォルト)を回避し他国間の債務危機の連鎖反応を防ぐため、国際通貨基金(IMF)と欧州連合(EU)は、連携を強めている。◆The IMF and the EU have worked out a policy of extending emergency loans to Greece. 国際通貨基金(IMF)と欧州連合(EU)は、ギリシャに緊急融資を行う方針を打ち出した。

EU bailout deal 欧州連合(EU)の救済策
◆A referendum on the EU bailout deal for debt-ridden Greece was called by Greek Prime Minister Papandreou. 負債にあえぐギリシャに対する欧州連合(EU)の救済策の是非を問う国民投票の実施を、ギリシャのパパンドレウ首相が求めた。

EU member state EU加盟国
(=EU member country [nation])
◆As a tacit understanding with EU member states, the European Central Bank has refrained from implementing monetary policy that is effectively a fiscal bailout. 欧州連合(EU)加盟国との暗黙の了解として、欧州中央銀行(ECB)は、財政支援に当たる金融政策の実施を控えてきた。

EU ministers 欧州連合の閣僚
◆The EU ministers will consider debt relief or freezing payments on debt for the Asian tsunami-hit countries. 欧州連合(EU)の閣僚らは、アジアの津波被災国のため債務削減や債務返済の凍結を検討する。

EU nations EU諸国
◆To resolve the financial unrest in EU nations, accelerating financial sector realignment in countries such as Germany must be worked out. EU諸国の金融不安を解決するには、(2,000もの金融機関がひしめく)ドイツなどでの金融再編の加速も課題だ。

EU treaty EU条約
◆The leaders of EU countries, including the 17 nations that use the euro, agreed to conclude a new EU treaty that will impose stringent fiscal discipline on its members. ユーロを導入している17か国を含む欧州連合(EU)各国首脳は、加盟国に厳しい財政規律を課すEUの新条約を締結することで合意した。

EU's Committee of European Banking Supervisors 欧州連合(EU)の欧州銀行監督委員会
(⇒evaluation of bank losses)
◆The stress test by the EU's Committee of European Banking Supervisors measured the financial strength of Europe's major banks. 欧州連合(EU)の欧州銀行監督委員会が行ったストレス・テストで、域内主要銀行の財務の健全性を調べた。

EU's rescue package EU(欧州連合)の支援策
◆What is urgently needed as the EU's rescue package is beefing up the functions of the EFSF and recapitalizing banks that own Greek and Italian government bonds. EU(欧州連合)の支援策として緊急に求められているのは、欧州金融安定基金(EFSF)の機能強化や、ギリシャやイタリアの国債を保有する銀行の資本増強などだ

EU's Stability and Growth Pact 欧州連合(EU)の財政安定・成長協定
◆Under the EU's Stability and Growth Pact, countries eligible to join the euro system are required to keep budget deficits below 3 percent of GDP. 欧州連合(EU)の財政安定・成長協定によると、ユーロ加盟国は、加盟の条件として財政赤字をGDPの3%以下に抑えなければならない。

Euribor ユーロ銀行間取引金利, ユーロ銀行間貸し手金利, ユーライボー (Euro inter-bank offered rateの略。欧州銀行協会が公表するユーロ建て取引に関するレートのこと。⇒LIBOR)

euro (名)ユーロ (=Euro: 欧州単一通貨。金融機関、大企業の資金調達や決済用に1999年に導入され、この時点でユーロ圏各国の通貨同士の為替変動が消滅した。2002年1月1日からユーロ紙幣と硬貨が市中に流通して、欧州の通貨統合が完成した。⇒highest value, IMF, weaken)
a weaker dollar against the euro ドル安・ユーロ高
euro area ユーロ圏
euro banknote ユーロ紙幣
euro changeover ユーロ移行
Euro-euro bond ユーロ・ユーロ債
Euro-euros ユーロ・ユーロ(通貨使用国以外に預けられたユーロ建て預金)
euro market ユーロ建て市場 (Euromarketと違って、euro marketはユーロ建て市場のこと)
euro symbol ユーロ通貨記号
radical appreciation of the yen against the euro 急激な円高・ユーロ安
stem Swiss franc's rise against the euro ユーロに対するスイス・フラン高[スイス・フランの上昇]を阻止する、スイス・フラン高・ユーロ安を阻止する
◆At 4 p.m., the euro traded at $1.3813-3814 and ¥113.16-

20 in London. 午後4時の時点で、ロンドン外国為替市場のユーロ相場は、1ユーロ＝1.3813〜3814ドルと113円16〜20銭で取引された。◆At 5 p.m., the euro was quoted at $1.1712-1715 and ￥126.54-58 against Tuesday's 5 p.m. quotes of $1.1665-1675 and ￥126.30-40 in New York. 午後5時、ニューヨークの外国為替市場では、ユーロ相場が火曜日（前日）午後5時の1ユーロ＝1.1665-1675ドルと126.30-40円に対して、1ユーロ＝1.1712-1715ドルと126.54-58円の値を付けた。◆Confidence in the single currency of the euro may be undermined by the spread of the Greek crisis to Spain and Portugal. ギリシャ危機のスペインやポルトガルへの波及で、単一通貨ユーロの信認が揺らぎかねない。◆In the case of foreign currency deposits, depositors can invest in foreign currencies such as British pound, Swiss franc and Australian dollar as well as the U.S. dollar and euro. 外貨預金の場合、預金者は、米ドルやユーロのほかに英ポンド、スイス・フランや豪ドルなどにも投資することができる。◆On January 1st 2002, the European countries began using the new Euro. 2002年1月1日から、欧州各国は新ユーロを使い始めた。◆On the foreign exchange market, there has been no halt to selling pressure on the euro due to concern about the financial crisis in Europe. 外国為替市場では、欧州の金融危機を懸念して、ユーロ売り圧力が止まらない展開となっている。◆The dollar appreciated relative to the euro and the yen. ドルが、ユーロや円より上昇した。◆The ECB was obliged to maintain price stability when the euro was launched in 1999. 1999年にユーロが導入された際、欧州中銀（ECB）は、物価安定の維持を義務付けられた。◆The euro plummeted to the ￥100 level on the foreign exchange market, hitting a 10 year low. 外国為替市場では、ユーロが1ユーロ＝100円台まで急落して、10年ぶりの低水準［10年ぶりの円高・ユーロ安水準］となった。◆The euro traded $1.5763-5766 against late Friday's quotes of $1.5670-5680 in New York. ユーロは、ニューヨークの外国為替市場では、前週末（午後5時）の相場1ユーロ＝1.5670〜5680ドルに対して、1ユーロ＝1.5763〜5766ドルで取引された。◆The latest depreciation of the euro brought about a life-sustaining boon to the currency. 今回のユーロ安が、ユーロの延命効果を招いた。◆The U.S. dollar as the world's only reserve currency may become merely one of three major currencies, along with the euro and the renminbi. 世界で唯一の準備通貨としての米ドルは、ユーロ、人民元とともに、単なる3大通貨の一つになる可能性がある。◆The U.S. dollar has dropped sharply in value not only against the yen, but also against the euro, the South Korean won, the Thai baht and other currencies. 米ドルは、円に対してだけでなく、ユーロや韓国ウォン、タイ・バーツなどに対しても、急落している。◆This announcement can be presumed to strengthen the euro and depress the dollar. この発表には、ユーロを上昇させ、ドルを下落させる意図があるものと推定できる。◆Uncertainty has prevailed as the value of the euro dropped sharply. ユーロの相場が急落したため、不安［動揺］が広がっている。

euro coins　ユーロ硬貨（1ユーロ・セント（100分の1ユーロ）から2ユーロまでの8種類。片側のデザインは加盟12か国で異なる）
◆After two weeks, the historic changeover to euro notes and coins is almost complete. ユーロ導入の2週間後に、ユーロ紙幣とユーロ硬貨への歴史的切替えはほぼ完了した。

euro crisis　ユーロ危機
◆In the wake of the euro crisis in Europe and the fiscal deadlock in the United States, the yen has sharply strengthened. 欧州のユーロ危機と米国の財政政策の行き詰まりの影響で、円が急騰している。◆The euro crisis has spread to Spain and Italy with interest rates on their sovereign debts soaring. ユーロ危機はスペインとイタリアに波及し、両国国債の金利が急騰した。◆The euro crisis is deepening. ユーロ危機が、深刻化している。

euro-denominated assets　ユーロ建て資産
◆If U.S. banks acquire euro-denominated assets, the dollar will depreciate vis-a-vis the euro. 米国の銀行がユーロ建て資産を買えば、対ユーロでドル安が進む。

euro notes　ユーロ紙幣（5、10、20、50、100、200、500ユーロの7種類）
◆Euro notes and coins began circulating in the 12 nations of the euro zone on January 1, 2002. ユーロ紙幣と硬貨の流通は、2002年1月1日からユーロ圏の12か国で始まった。

euro stabilization package　ユーロ安定化策、ユーロ安定化対策
◆The massive euro stabilization package appears to have had a limited impact thus far. 大規模な［大がかりな］ユーロ安定化策の影響は、これまでのところ限定的と思われる。

euro system　ユーロ・システム、ユーロシステム（＝Eurosystem；⇒Eurosystem）
◆Under the EU's Stability and Growth Pact, countries eligible to join the euro system are required to keep budget deficits below 3 percent of GDP. 欧州連合（EU）の財政安定・成長協定によると、ユーロ加盟国は、加盟の条件として財政赤字をGDPの3％以下に抑えなければならない。

euro zone　ユーロ圏、欧州圏　（＝euro area, eurozone；⇒cool money, currency swings, IMF, inflation rate）
◆Inflationary pressures are diminishing in the euro zone as oil prices decline. 原油価格の下落に伴って、ユーロ圏のインフレ圧力は軽減している。
解説 ユーロ圏について：
ユーロ圏とは、欧州連合（EU）に加盟してユーロを導入している諸国で形成される経済圏のことを言う。ユーロを法定通貨としているのは、EU加盟国全27か国のうち17か国で、2011年現在、以下の17か国がユーロ圏、ユーロ圏諸国と呼ばれている。ユーロ圏諸国：アイルランド、イタリア、エストニア、オーストリア、オランダ、キプロス、ギリシャ、スペイン、スロバキア、スロベニア、ドイツ、フィンランド、フランス、ベルギー、ポルトガル、マルタとルクセンブルク。

euro zone countries　ユーロ圏諸国、ユーロ圏各国、ユーロ圏　（＝eurozone countries）
◆Not only the United States but also the 12 euro zone countries revised downward their economic growth predictions for this year. 米国もユーロ圏12か国も、今年の経済成長率の見通しを下方修正した。

Eurobank　（名）ユーロ銀行、ユーロバンク

Eurobanker　（名）ユーロ銀行の幹部［経営者］、ユーロ銀行

Eurobonds　（名）ユーロ債、ユーロボンド（ユーロ債のユーロはヨーロッパの意味ではなく、旧ソ連系銀行のテレックス・コード「Eurobank」に由来する）
解説 ユーロ債とは：欧州市場で発行される米ドル建てのユーロ・ドル（ユーロ・ダラー）債（Eurodollar bond）や円建てのユーロ円債（Euroyen）などのように、表示通貨の発行国以外の国の資本市場（ユーロ市場）で発行、販売される債券のこと。

Eurocapital　（形）ヨーロッパ金融の、ヨーロッパ金融市場の

Eurocheque　（名）ユーロチェック（ユーロチェック・カード（Eurocheque Card）の提示を条件に欧州の提携店で通用する小切手）
Eurocheque Card　ユーロチェック・カード

Euroclear　（名）ユーロクリア（Brusselsに本部を置くユーロボンドの預託・取引・決済機関）

Eurocommercial paper　ユーロコマーシャル・ペーパー、ユーロCP

Eurocredit　（名）ユーロクレジット（ユーロ通貨による貸出）

Eurocurrency　（名）ユーロ通貨、欧州通貨、ユーロ・マ

ネー, ユーロカレンシー[ユーロ・カレンシー](ユーロカレンシーは, 通貨の使用国以外で保有される通貨のことで, 通貨使用国以外に預けられた通貨を「ユーロドル」とか「ユーロ円」などという)

Eurocurrency market ユーロカレンシー市場

Eurodeposit (名)ユーロ預金

Eurodollar (名)ユーロ・ドル[ユーロドル], ユーロ・ダラー[ユーロダラー](米国以外の銀行に預けられているドル預金)

Euroequity (名)ユーロエクイティ(発行会社の本社所在国以外で発行される株式)

eurofanatics (名)ユーロ擁護派

Eurofed (名)ユーロフェド(欧州中央銀行(ECB)の俗称)

Eurogiro (名)ユーロジャイロ(少額資金の電子送金ネットワーク)

eurogroup (名)ユーログループ(ユーロ圏の蔵相会合)

euroland ユーロ圏, ユーロランド(ユーロを共通通貨として導入している地域)

Euromarket (名)ユーロ市場(ユーロ・カレンシー(Eurocurrency)の貸借を行う市場)

Euromart (名)ユーロ市場, ユーロマーケット, 欧州共同市場(European Economic Community)

Euromoney (名)ユーロマネー (=Eurocurrency)

Euro-MP (名)欧州議会議員

Euronext (名)ユーロネクスト (⇒NYSE Euronext)

Euronote (名)ユーロノート(ユーロ市場で発行されるユーロ建て, 米ドル建ての短期無担保の約束手形)

Euronote facility ユーロノート・ファシリティ

Europe (名)欧州, ヨーロッパ, 欧州大陸, 欧州連合(EU), 欧州共同市場(European Common Market)
◆Europe is urged to act promptly to halt financial crisis. 欧州は, 金融危機回避の早急な対策を迫られている。◆Europe promised the Group of 20 major economies to take concerted action to contain the financial crisis. 欧州は, 結束して金融危機を封じ込めることを主要20か国・地域(G20)に公約した。◆France and Germany could not bridge their differences, so Europe's efforts to solve its escalating debt crisis plunged into disarray. フランスとドイツが両国の相違を埋められなかったため, 深刻化する欧州の債務危機問題解決への欧州の取組みは, 混乱に陥った。◆In Europe, credit uncertainty has spread from Greece to Italy, Spain and elsewhere due to the excessively tardy response by Europe. 欧州では, 欧州の対応が遅すぎるため, 信用不安がギリシャからイタリアやスペインなどに拡大している。◆Investment conditions have worsened due to confusion in global financial markets in the wake of fiscal and financial crises in Europe. 欧州の財政・金融危機を受けた世界的な金融市場の混乱で, 運用環境が悪化している。◆On the foreign exchange market, there has been no halt to selling pressure on the euro due to concern about the financial crisis in Europe. 外国為替市場では, 欧州の金融危機を懸念して, ユーロ売り圧力が止まらない展開となっている。◆The yields on government bonds of deficit-ridden countries including Greece have been rising across the board in Europe. 欧州では, ギリシャなど財政赤字国の国債利回りが, 軒並み上昇している。

European (形)欧州の, ヨーロッパの
  European Banking Authority 欧州銀行機構, 欧州銀行監督機構, EBA
  European Banking Federation 欧州銀行協会
  European Exchange Rate Mechanism 欧州為替相場メカニズム, ERM(欧州の為替相場の変動抑制と通貨の安定性確保を目的とした為替相場制度で, あらかじめ変動幅を決め, その範囲を超えたら通貨当局が介入する管理変動方式を採用している)
  European Financial Stability Facility 欧州金融安定基金, 欧州金融安定ファシリティ, EFSF
  European Insurance and Occupational Pensions Authority 欧州保険年金機構, 欧州保険年金監督機構, EIOPA
  European Investment Bank 欧州投資銀行, EIB
  European Monetary Institute 欧州通貨機構, EMI
  European Monetary System 欧州通貨制度, EMS(1979〜1999年まで維持された欧州経済共同体加盟国の地域的半固定為替相場制のこと)
  European option 欧州型オプション(満期日にだけ権利を行使できるオプション)
  European Securities and Markets Authority 欧州証券市場機構, 欧州証券市場監督機構, ESMA(ECの証券市場監督機関で, 米国の証券取引委員会(SEC)に相当)
  European Social Fund 欧州社会基金, ESF
  European System of Central Banks 欧州中央銀行制度, ESCB(ユーロ圏の単一通貨・金融政策を決定して実施する制度)

European Banking Authority 欧州銀行機構, 欧州銀行監督機構, EBA(欧州連合(EU)の欧州議会で2010年11月に設立が議決され, 2011年1月に発足。EU加盟各国の銀行監督当局を統括するとともに, 域内の金融機関を直接検査・監督して金融機関や各国当局へ要請や要求を行う)
◆Major Banks across Europe underwent the stress tests of the European Banking Authority in 2010 and 2011. 欧州全域の主要銀行[金融機関]が, 2010年と2011年に欧州銀行監督機構(EBA)のストレス・テスト(財務の健全性検査)を受けた。◆The stress test of the European Banking Authority is a banking health check to ensure banks across Europe have sufficient capital to withstand another financial crisis. 欧州銀行監督機構(EBA)のストレス・テストは, 欧州全域の銀行が新たな金融危機に耐えられるだけの資本金を十分に確保していることを保証するための銀行の健全性検査だ。

European banking stocks 欧州銀行株
◆The DJ Stoxx index of European banking stocks has fallen 37 percent from a peak in February. ダウ・ジョーンズ欧州銀行株指数は, 2月のピークから37%下落した。

European banking test 欧州の銀行検査
◆In the European banking tests, banks' impaired assets were underestimated. 欧州の銀行検査では, 銀行の不良資産が過小評価された。

European banks 欧州の銀行, 欧州の金融機関
◆European banks are forced to shore up their potential capital shortages to restore market confidence. 欧州銀行は, 市場の信認を回復するため, 潜在的資本不足の増強を迫られている。◆Major European banks are to take additional stress tests to examine their ability to withstand a long recession. 景気の長期低迷への耐久力を調べるため, 欧州の主要銀行は再度, ストレス・テストを受けることになっている。

European bond market 欧州の債券市場
◆The European bond market is truly in a knife-edge situation as the yield on 10-year Italian government bonds has surged above 7 percent, the so-called danger zone that may result in a debt crisis. 10年物イタリア国債の流通利回りが, 債務危機に陥る「危険水域」とされる7%超に上昇したため, 欧州債券市場は予断を許さない状況にある。

European Central Bank 欧州中央銀行, 欧州中銀, ECB (ユーロ圏17か国の金融政策を担(にな)う中央銀行で, 本店はドイツのフランクフルト。不文律として, 任期8年の総裁のほか副総裁と理事4人の計6人のうち4人は, フランス, ドイツ, イタリア, スペインの出身者で占めることになっている。⇒ECB)

◆As a tacit understanding with EU member states, the European Central Bank has refrained from implementing monetary policy that is effectively a fiscal bailout. 欧州連合（EU）加盟国との暗黙の了解として、欧州中央銀行（ECB）は、財政支援に当たる金融政策の実施を控えてきた。◆In cooperation with the U.S. FRB, the Bank of England, the Bank of Japan and the Swiss National Bank, the European Central Bank decided to conduct three U.S. dollar liquidity-providing operations between October and December. 米連邦準備制度理事会（FRB）、英イングランド銀行、日銀、スイス国立銀行と協調して、欧州中央銀行（ECB）が10～12月に3回、米ドル資金供給オペを実施することを決めた。◆The European Central Bank cut its main interest rate by 0.25 percent following heavy pressure for a rate cut to spur flagging economic growth. 失速気味の経済成長に刺激を与えるため利下げを求める強い圧力を受けて、欧州中央銀行（ECB）はその主要（政策）金利を0.25％引き下げた。◆The European Central Bank decided to buy Italian and Spanish government bonds in tandem with the issuance of the G-7 emergency statement. 欧州中央銀行（ECB）は、G7緊急声明の発表と連動する形で、イタリアとスペインの国債を買い入れる方針を決めた。◆The European Central Bank has been purchasing Italian government bonds in an effort to support Italy. 欧州中央銀行（ECB）は、イタリア国債を買い入れてイタリアを支えている。◆The European Central Bank needs to provide support to Italy by proactively buying Italian bonds. 欧州中央銀行（ECB）は今後、イタリア国債を積極的に買い入れてイタリアを支援する必要がある。◆The European Central Bank shifted to a credit-tightening stance late last year. 欧州中央銀行は、昨年末から金融引締めのスタンスに転じた。

European countries　欧州諸国, 欧州
◆European countries are forced to prevent the financial crisis from spreading from Europe to other parts of the world. 欧州は、金融危機の世界的波及阻止を迫られている。◆European countries are urged to facilitate a safety net for emergencies, including the injection of public funds into deteriorating banks to shore up their capital strength. 欧州は、経営が悪化した銀行［金融機関］に公的資金を注入して資本を増強するなど、非常時に備えた安全網の整備が求められている。◆Japan, the United States and emerging economies have pressed European countries to promptly resolve the fiscal and financial crisis. 日米両国と新興国は、欧州に財政・金融危機の迅速な解決を迫った。◆The current global fiscal and financial crisis began in European countries. 今回の世界的な財政・金融危機の震源地は、欧州だ。

European crisis　欧州危機, 欧州の財政・金融危機
（=European fiscal and financial crisis）
◆In order to bring the European crisis under control, the EU, ECB and IMF must work even more closely together. 欧州危機の収束を図るには、欧州連合（EU）、欧州中央銀行（ECB）と国際通貨基金（IMF）の緊密な連携を強化する必要がある。

European debt crisis　欧州債務危機, 欧州の財政危機
◆The EU's responses to the European debt crisis have been slow. 欧州債務危機への欧州連合（EU）の対応は、後手に回ってきた。

European economy　欧州経済
◆France is a predominant player in the European economy alongside Germany. フランスは、ドイツとともに欧州経済を支えている。

European financial authorities　欧州の金融当局
◆The financial market mess in Europe was triggered by the delay of financial assistance to Greece by the European financial authorities. 欧州の金融市場混乱の引き金となったのは、欧州金融当局によるギリシャへの金融支援のもたつきだ。

European financial crisis　欧州の金融危機
◆If the European financial crisis expands, it will damage the recovering global economy. 欧州の金融危機が拡大すれば、回復途上にある世界経済に打撃を与えることになる。

European financial institution　欧州の金融機関
◆U.S. and European financial institutions are scaling back their business operations before capital adequacy requirements are strengthened in 2013. 欧米金融機関は、2013年から自己資本規制が強化されるのを前に、業務を縮小している。

European Financial Stability Facility　欧州金融安定基金, 欧州金融安定ファシリティ, EFSF（財政危機のギリシャなどを支援する緊急融資制度）
◆An initiative to strengthen the functions of the European Financial Stability Facility（EFSF）was approved at the 17 eurozone countries' parliaments. 欧州金融安定基金（EFSF）の機能強化案が、ユーロ圏17か国の議会で承認された。◆S&P may cut the credit rating of bonds issued by the European Financial Stability Facility（EFSF）. スタンダード・アンド・プアーズ（S&P）は、欧州金融安定基金（EFSF）が発行する債券の格付け［信用格付け］を引き下げる可能性がある。◆The European Financial Stability Facility set up a €750 billion contingency package together with the International Monetary Fund. 欧州金融安定基金（EU）は、国際通貨基金（IMF）の協力を得て7,500億ユーロ（約90兆円）の緊急支援資金を準備した。◆The European Union hurriedly created an emergency rescue fund, called the European Financial Stability Facility（EFSF）. 欧州連合（EU）は、欧州金融安定基金（EFSF）という緊急支援基金を急設した。◆The 17 eurozone countries agreed to expand the European Financial Stability Facility at a meeting of their finance ministers. ユーロを採用しているユーロ圏17か国は、ユーロ圏財務相会合で、欧州金融安定基金（EFSF）の規模を拡大することで一致した。

[解説]欧州金融安定基金［欧州金融安定化基金］
2010年5月9日、欧州連合（EU）の27加盟国が合意して創設した基金（特別目的事業体）。危機に陥ったユーロ圏加盟国に対する財政支援を提供することで欧州の金融安定を図ることを目的とし、債券を発行して調達した資金を使って、金繰りに陥った欧州諸国を金融支援する。

European fiscal crisis　欧州の財政危機, 欧州財政危機
◆Global stock market plunges caused by the European fiscal crisis triggered by Greece have shown no signs of abating. ギリシャ発の欧州財政危機による世界同時株安は、止まる気配がない。◆The European fiscal crisis triggered by Greece has spread to Italy, making the severe situation even more distressing. ギリシャ発の欧州財政危機がイタリアに飛び火し、厳しい事態が一段と深刻化している。

European lender　欧州の金融機関
◆Deutsche Bank AG and BNP Paribas SA are among European lenders placed on creditwatch negative by S&P. ドイツ銀行や仏MNPパリバなども、スタンダード・アンド・プアーズ（S&P）が引下げの方向で信用格付けの見直しをしている欧州の金融機関の対象となっている。

European Stability Mechanism　（財政難に陥ったユーロ圏の国を支援する）欧州安定化メカニズム, 財政安定メカニズム, ESM　（⇒ESM）
◆France and Germany agreed to put flesh on the bones of the European Stability Mechanism. フランスとドイツは、欧州安定化メカニズムの枠組みを具体化することで合意した。◆The European Stability Mechanism is a bailout fund which will provide fiscally distressed European countries with financial assistance. 欧州安定メカニズム（ESM）は、欧州の財政危機国に金融支援を行う支援基金だ。

European Union　欧州連合, EU　（⇒EU）
◆Greece has to agree to new austerity measures before it receives any financial aid from the European Union. ギリシャは、欧州連合（EU）の金融支援を受ける前に、追加の財政赤字削減策［緊縮財政策］に同意しなければならない。◆Greece was bailed out temporarily with financial support of €110 billion（about ¥12.7 trillion）from the IMF and the European Union in May 2010. ギリシャは、2010年5月にIMFと欧州連

合(EU)から1,100億ユーロ(約12兆7,000億円)の金融支援を受けて、一時的に救済された。◆Greece's fiscal reconstruction is set as a condition for supporting the struggling country by the European Union and the International Monetary Fund. 欧州連合(EU)と国際通貨基金(IMF)は、ギリシャの財政再建を、財政危機にある同国支援の条件としている。◆Ireland and Portugal also have been hit by financial crises and bailed out by the European Union. アイルランドやポルトガルも、財政危機に見舞われ、欧州連合(EU)に救済された。◆Japan's trade surplus with the European Union grew 29.7 percent in July to ¥372.8 billion after a 28.9 percent decrease in July. 7月の日本の対EU(欧州連合)貿易黒字は、前月に28.9%減少したものの、29.7%増の3,728億円となった。◆The European Union agreed on comprehensive measures to deal with the current fiscal and financial crisis. 欧州連合(EU)は、現在の財政・金融危機について、包括的な対応策で合意した。◆The European Union hurriedly created an emergency rescue fund, called the European Financial Stability Facility (EFSF). 欧州連合(EU)は、欧州金融安定基金(EFSF)という緊急支援基金を急設した。◆The European Union will substantially expand the lending capacity of the EFSF to buy up government bonds in case the fiscal and financial crisis spreads countries as Italy. 欧州連合(EU)は、財政・金融危機がイタリアなどなどに拡大した場合に国債を買い支えるため、欧州金融安定基金(EFSF)の融資能力を大幅に拡大する。

euroskeptics (名)ユーロ懐疑派
(=eurosceptics)

Eurostat (名)欧州連合(EU)統計局, ユーロスタット
(=Eurostat data agency)
◆Eurostat is the European Union's statistics office. ユーロスタット(Eurostat)は、欧州連合(EU)の統計局だ。

Eurosterling (名)ユーロスターリング(英国以外の国の銀行に預けられた英ポンド)

Eurosystem (名)ユーロシステム
(欧州中央銀行(ECB)とユーロ参加国の中央銀行で構成される中央銀行制度のこと。⇒euro system)

Euroyen ユーロ円

Euroyen bond ユーロ円債(海外発行の円債)

eurozone (名)ユーロ圏, 欧州圏 (=euro zone; ⇒ contraction, euro zone, technical recession)
eurozone inflation rate ユーロ圏のインフレ率
quit the eurozone ユーロを離脱する, ユーロから離脱する
the debt crisis in the eurozone ユーロ圏の財政危機, ユーロ圏の債務危機
◆Behind these cautious views among large manufacturers are uncertainty over the debt crisis in the eurozone and the slowdown in the U.S. economy. 大企業製造業のこうした警戒感[慎重な見方]の背景には、ユーロ圏の債務危機不安や米景気の減速がある。◆Britain is not a member of the eurozone. 英国は、ユーロに加入していない。◆Currently, the whole eurozone comprises 17 member states. 現在、ユーロ圏は全体で17の加盟国から成る。◆Eurozone June inflation rate rose 2.4 percent from a year earlier. ユーロ圏6月のインフレ率は、前年同月比で2.4%上昇した。◆Greece's finance minister rejected a proposed referendum on staying in the eurozone. ギリシャの財務相は、提起されていたユーロ圏残留の是非を問う国民投票を拒絶した。◆Italy is the third-largest economy of the eurozone. イタリアは、ユーロ圏で第三位の経済大国である。◆Italy's economy is the third largest after [following] those of Germany and France in the eurozone. イタリアの経済規模は、ユーロ圏ではドイツとフランスに次いで3位だ。◆The debt crisis in the eurozone began rocking the global economy. ユーロ圏の債務危機で、世界景気が揺らいできた。◆The debt crisis in the eurozone was triggered by huge deficits in Greece. ユーロ圏の財政危機を引き起こしたのは、ギリシャの巨額の財政赤字だ。◆The economy of the eurozone 15 countries contracted 0.2 percent in the second quarter against the first quarter of 2008. ユーロ圏15か国の2008年第2四半期(4〜6月期)の経済成長率は、前期に比べて0.2%減少した。◆The eurozone and the IMF agreed to a bailout for Greece amounting to €110 billion in May 2010. 2010年5月にユーロ圏[ユーロ圏15か国]と国際通貨基金(IMF)が、ギリシャに対して総額で1,100億ユーロ(約13兆円)の金融支援を行うことで合意した。◆The Greek-triggered sovereign debt crisis has been throwing the eurozone into financial uncertainty and multiple crises. ギリシャに端を発した債務危機問題で、ユーロ圏は金融不安と複合的な危機に陥っている。◆The money lent by the U.S. and eurozone private banks remains at about the same level as those prior to Lehman's collapse. 米国とユーロ圏の民間銀行の貸出金は、リーマン・ブラザーズの経営破たん前とほぼ同水準にとどまっている。

eurozone countries ユーロ圏諸国, ユーロ圏各国, ユーロ圏加盟国, ユーロ圏 (=euro zone countries)
◆An initiative to strengthen the functions of the European Financial Stability Facility (EFSF) was approved at the 17 eurozone countries' parliaments. 欧州金融安定基金(EFSF)の機能強化案が、ユーロ圏17か国の議会で承認された。◆Due to delays in ratification of the agreement on bailout measures by some eurozone countries, concrete measures to rescue Greece have yet to be carried out. 支援策の合意事項について一部のユーロ圏加盟国の承認が遅れたため、ギリシャ救済の具体策はまだ実施されていない。◆Eurozone countries have tried a series of relief measures, but worries have heightened in the world particularly with regard to the eurozone. ユーロ圏諸国は一連の救済策を取ってきたが、世界ではとくにユーロ圏に関して心配[不安]が高まっている。◆Eurozone countries were so slow to take necessary actions that the sovereign debt crisis expanded. 欧州の必要な対応が後手に回ったために、ソブリン危機[政府債務危機]が拡大した。◆Since May 2010, Greece has been reliant in regular payouts of loans from a €110 billion bailout from other eurozone countries and the IMF. 2010年5月からギリシャは、他のユーロ圏諸国やIMF(国際通貨基金)などからの1,100億ユーロの金融支援による融資の定期支払い金に頼っている。◆The ECB buyouts of sovereign debts of eurozone countries with fiscal laxity are the nightmare scenario Germany has been fearing. 欧州中銀(ECB)による放漫財政のユーロ圏諸国の国債買切りは、ドイツが恐れていた最悪のシナリオだ。◆The G-20 communique urged the eurozone countries to boost the EFSF, the EU bailout fund. G20(主要20か国・地域)の共同声明は、ユーロ圏諸国に欧州の金融支援基金である欧州金融安定基金(EFSF)の拡充を促した。◆The 17 eurozone countries agreed to expand the European Financial Stability Facility at a meeting of their finance ministers. ユーロを採用しているユーロ圏17か国は、ユーロ圏財務相会合で、欧州金融安定基金(EFSF)の規模を拡大することで一致した。

eurozone crisis ユーロ危機
◆The eurozone crisis has spread to the heart of Europe from Greece. ユーロ危機は、ギリシャから欧州の心臓部に拡大した。

eurozone debt crisis ユーロ圏の財政危機
◆Worries over the spreading of the eurozone debt crisis and the U.S.'s slipping into recession have driven the rout in financial markets. ユーロ圏の財政危機の拡大と米国の景気後退入りへの懸念で、金融市場は総崩れになった。

eurozone debt problems ユーロ圏の債務問題, ユーロ圏の債務危機問題
◆Gold is still becoming the safe haven as people fear recession in the U.S. and the eurozone debt problems. 米国の景気後退やユーロ圏の債務危機問題への懸念から、まだ金が安全な投資先[資金の逃避先]となっている。

eurozone finance ministers ユーロ圏の財務相
◆Eurozone finance ministers and the European Central Bank

expressed concern over large currency swings. ユーロ圏の財務相と欧州中央銀行(ECB)は、過度の為替変動に懸念を表明した。

eurozone finance ministers meeting ユーロ圏財務相会合
◆A sense of disappointment has prevailed across the world markets as no concrete measures to rescue Greece were unveiled at the eurozone finance ministers meeting. ユーロ圏財務相会合でギリシャ支援の具体策が明らかにされなかったので、世界の市場で失望感が広がった。◆At the eurozone finance ministers meeting held on October 3, 2011, a decision on bridge loans of about €8 billion to Greece was expected, but none was done. 2011年10月3日に開かれたユーロ圏財務相会合では、ギリシャに対する約80億ユーロのつなぎ融資の決定が見込まれていたが、これは見送られた。

eurozone GDP ユーロ圏のGDP
◆That eurozone GDP shrank in the second quarter as well would add up to two consecutive quarters of negative growth-a definition of a technical recession. ユーロ圏の(域内総生産)が第2四半期も低下したことで、ユーロ圏は2四半期連続のマイナス成長(定義上、テクニカル・リセッション)となった。

eurozone governments ユーロ圏政府, ユーロ圏の各国政府
◆The eurozone governments tried to avert the injection of public money into banks which are politically unpopular. ユーロ圏の各国政府は、政治的に人気のない銀行への公的資金注入を避けようとした。

eurozone markets ユーロ圏市場
◆By buying Greek, Portuguese and Spanish bonds, the ECB infused life into the moribund eurozone markets for these soon-to-be-junk status government bonds. ギリシャやポルトガル、スペインの国債を買い入れて、欧州中銀(ECB)は、崩壊寸前のユーロ圏の投資不適格レベルが見込まれるこれらの債券の市場に生気を吹き込んだ。

eurozone member state [nation] ユーロ圏加盟国
◆Greece asked other eurozone member states for financial support to help it stem its budget crisis in early 2010. 2010年初めにギリシャは、財政危機を回避するため、他のユーロ圏加盟国に金融支援を求めた。

eurozone nations ユーロ圏諸国, ユーロ圏各国, ユーロ圏加盟国, ユーロ圏 (=eurozone countries)
◆The 17 eurozone nations must ratify the agreement on bailout measures to arrange a rescue system for Greece. ギリシャへの支援体制を整えるには、ユーロ圏の17か国が、支援策についての合意事項を承認しなければならない。

eurozone states ユーロ圏諸国, ユーロ圏各国, ユーロ圏 (=eurozone countries, eurozone nations)
◆Standard & Poor's is considering a possible downgrade on the credit ratings of long-term sovereign bonds issued by 15 eurozone states. 米格付け会社のスタンダード・アンド・プアーズ(S&P)は、ユーロ圏15か国発行の長期国債格付け[信用格付け]を、引下げ方向で検討している。

evaluate (動)評価する, 判断する, 検討する, 見極める, ～の数値を求める, 値踏みする
 an accounting system to evaluate assets based on market values 時価に基づいて資産を評価する制度, 時価会計制度
 evaluate a loan-seeker's creditworthiness ローン申込み者の信用力を審査する
 evaluate asset values 資産価値を評価する
 evaluate collateral for bank loans 銀行融資の担保を評価する
 evaluate issuer management 発行体の経営能力を評価する
 evaluate the credit performance 信用実績を評価する
 evaluate the credit risk 信用リスク[与信リスク]を評価する, クレジット・リスクを評価する
◆In financial institutions, an accounting system to evaluate assets based on market values was introduced in April 2004. 金融機関の場合は、時価会計制度(時価に基づいて資産を評価する制度)が、2004年4月から導入された。

evaluation (名)評価, 分析, 診断, 判定 (⇒analysis)
 asset evaluation 資産評価
 cost benefit evaluation 費用便益評価
 credit risk evaluation 信用リスク評価, 信用分析
 evaluation of asset values 資産価値の評価
 evaluation of collateral 担保評価
 evaluation of internal control system 内部統制組織の評価
 evaluation of performance 業績評価 (=performance evaluation)
 market evaluation 市場の評価
 stock evaluation losses 株式の評価損
 wage on job evaluation 職能給
◆The firm is suspected of understating its affiliates' stock evaluation losses in its financial paper. 同社は、有価証券報告書で子会社の株式の評価損を過小計上していた疑いがある。

evaluation of bank losses 銀行の損失の評価
◆The stress test by the EU's Committee of European Banking Supervisors offered only a vague evaluation of bank losses stemming from the government bonds of Greece. EU(欧州連合)の欧州銀行監督委員会が行ったストレス・テスト(特別検査)は、ギリシャの国債保有による銀行損失の評価について、あいまいさが残ったに過ぎない。

evaluation system of securitized products 証券化商品の評価方法
◆An interim report of the Financial Stability Forum called for measures such as a review of evaluation system of securitized products. 金融安定化フォーラムの中間報告は、証券化商品の評価方法見直しなどの措置を求めた。

event (名)動き, 動向, 事象, 事態, 出来事, 事件, 成り行き, 結果, 事由, 事柄, 事項, 行事, 催事, イベント
 credit event 信用事由, 債権の信用力を低下させる事由
 economic events 経済の動き, 経済動向, 景気動向, 経済事象
 event after reporting period 後発事象
 event insured against 保険事故
 event of default 債務不履行, 債務不履行事由 (events of default＝期限の利益喪失条項。これは、契約期限までは借入れができるという利益を借り手が失うこと)
 event risk イベント・リスク(企業買収やリストラなど予期しない事態によって企業の信用度が低下し、株価や社債の格付けが下がるリスク)
 event risk protections イベント・リスク保護条項
 extraordinary event 異常事象
 fortuitous event 偶発的な事象
 fund-raising event 資金集めの行事
 future events 将来発生する事態
 infrequent event 突発事象
 liquidation event 清算事由
 subsequent event 後発事象
 termination [trigger] events 解約事由
◆All these events are part of a larger strategy of our asset management. これらの措置は、当社の資産運用戦略の一環としてとられたものです。◆The Buyer shall prepare the Closing Balance Sheet at the Buyer's expense as promptly as practicable, but in any event within ninety (90) calendar days following the Closing Date. 買い主は、できるだけ速やかに、ただしどんな場合でもクロージング日以降90暦日以内に、買

い主の費用負担でクロージング日現在の貸借対照表を作成するものとする。

event-driven fund イベント・ドリブン型ファンド（国際会議や要人の来日などの重要なイベントに合わせて株価変動の予測を立て、株式を売買する手法）
◆So-called event-driven funds buy and sell stocks by producing forecasts about changes in stock prices that could take place in tandem with such important events as international conferences and visits to Japan by important foreign figures. いわゆる「イベント・ドリブン型ファンド」は、国際会議や外国要人の来日に伴って生じる株価変動を予測して、株式の売買を行う。

eventual （形）結局の、結果として起きる、最終的な、いつかはやってくる、起こり得る、偶発的な
　eventual dividend payments　将来配当支払い、将来配当支払い金［支払い額］
　the eventual merger of stock exchanges　株式［証券］取引所の最終的な経営統合
　the eventual outcome　最終結果
　the eventual profits　予測できる利益
　the eventual winner　最終的な勝者
◆The business integration and eventual merger of the TSE and the OSE will be implemented in several steps. 東証と大証の事業統合と最終的な経営統合は、段階的に行われる。

evergreen credit 回転資金融資（revolving credit）、継続的信用供与

evergreen fund 新会社に対する初期融資、エバーグリーン・ファンド

evergreen loan エバーグリーン融資（解約しない限り自動継続される融資）

ex- （前・接頭辞）〜がない、〜落ち（without）、〜渡し（out of）、前の（former）、元の、以前の、元〜、前〜
　ex ante analysis　事前分析
　ex-bond　ポンカス債
　ex contract　契約上の
　ex coupon［ex-coupon］　利落ち、利札落ち（で、の）
　ex-coupon price of bond　債券の裸相場
　ex date　権利落ち日、配当権利落ち日
　ex dividend　配当落ち、配当権利落ち（配当付き＝cum dividend）
　ex-dividend date　配当落ち日、配当支払い日
　ex dock-duty paid　現地渡し、埠頭渡し関税込み
　ex-execs　旧経営陣、元経営陣
　　（＝former executives）
　ex-executive　元役員、元管理職、元経営者
　ex facto　事実に従って、事実上、行為に基づき
　ex-factory［works］　工場渡し
　ex interest　利落ち
　ex-member　前［元］会員
　ex-new　新株落ち
　ex notes　ポンカス債
　ex parte　一方的な、一方当事者の申立てで、一方の利益のために
　ex post　事後
　ex post facto　事後の［事後に］、過去にさかのぼった、遡及的な［遡及的に］、遡及適用される
　　（＝after the fact, by a subsequent act）
　ex-president　前［元］大統領、前［元］社長
　ex rights　権利落ち、新株落ち
　ex rights price　権利落ち株価
　ex ship　着船渡し
　ex-warrant bond　エックス・ワラント債、ポンカス債
　ex-warrants yield　ポンカス部分の利回り

securities on an ex basis　ポンカス債
◆Ex-Nishimatsu vice president was held on suspicion of smuggled cash. （準大手ゼネコンの）西松建設元副社長が、海外からの資金持ち込み容疑で逮捕された。

exacerbate （動）悪化させる、事態の悪化に拍車をかける、激化させる、増大させる、高める、怒らせる
　exacerbate the employment situation　雇用情勢を悪化させる
　exacerbate the risks　リスクを高める
◆Deflation is being exacerbated by tighter constraints on credit. 金融収縮で、デフレが悪化している。◆France is being plagued by rapidly exacerbating troubles at domestic banks. フランスは、国内銀行の急速な経営状態の悪化に悩まされている［苦しんでいる］。◆The economic slump exacerbated the firm's losses. 景気低迷で、同社の損失［赤字］が膨らんだ。◆The government's financial revival plan is expected to exacerbate the credit crunch and result in a further sell-off of bank stocks. 政府の金融再生プログラムは、貸し渋りを加速して銀行株の下落に拍車がかかると予想される。

exaggerate （動）過大評価する、過大計上する、水増しする、実態以上に見せる、過剰反応を示す
◆Olympus Corp. exaggerated the intangible value of its British subsidiary by ￥33.4 billion in the financial statement. オリンパスは、有価証券報告書で英子会社の"のれん代"について334億円を過大に計上していた。

examine （動）調査する、検査する、試験する、検証する、審査する、診断する、診察する
◆Major European banks are to take additional stress tests to examine their ability to withstand a long recession. 景気の長期低迷への耐久力を調べるため、欧州の主要銀行は再度、ストレス・テストを受けることになっている。◆The FSA's inspection team will examine the reconstruction plans of borrowers whose performances have deteriorated since the previous inspection. 金融庁の検査チームは、前回の検査時から業績（経営）が悪化した融資先企業の再建計画の検証を行う予定だ。

exceed （動）越える［超える］、上回る、〜以上である、〜に勝る　（＝surpass）
　exceed BIS requirements　BIS基準を上回る
　exceed consensus forecasts　市場予想を上回る
　exceed one's equity bases　株主資本総額を超える
　liabilities exceed one's assets　債務超過になる、債務超過に陥る
◆Crude oil prices have exceeded $70 a barrel in London and New York, setting all-time highs on these markets. ニューヨークとロンドン市場で原油価格が1バレル＝70ドルを上回って、両市場最高値を記録した。◆If such delay shall exceed two months, either party may give written notice of termination of this agreement. このような遅延が2か月を超える場合、いずれの当事者も、書面で本契約を解除する通告を出すことができる。◆Making the creditor banks waive loans to TEPCO will cause the utility to fall into capital deficiency, with liabilities exceeding assets. 取引銀行に東電への債権を放棄させると、東電は資本不足に陥り、債務超過になってしまう。◆Nonlife insurance claims connected to Typhoon No. 12 are expected to exceed ￥10 billion. 台風12号関連の損害保険の保険金請求額は、100億円を超える見込みだ。◆The amount of refunding bonds issued to redeem ordinary government bonds is expected to exceed ￥100 trillion. 普通国債償還のための借換え債の発行額が、100兆円を突破する見込みだ。◆The central and local governments' combined outstanding debts are expected to exceed ￥800 trillion by the end of fiscal 2009. 国と地方［地方自治体］の債務残高は、2009年度末には合算して800兆円を上回る［超える］見通しだ。◆The correction of financial statements by Olympus is unlikely to result in the company's debts exceeding its assets. オリンパスの財務書類訂正で、同社の債務超過は避けられる見通しだ。

◆The current situation of debt issuance exceeding tax revenues has continued since fiscal 2010. 国債発行額が税収を上回る現在の事態は、2010年度から続いている。◆The firm's liabilities exceeded its assets by ￥8 billion in its settlement of accounts at the end of February last year. 同社は、昨年2月期決算で、80億円の債務超過になった。◆Volume on the First Section of the Tokyo Stock Exchange has exceeded the 1 billion mark for 42 business days in a row as of Monday, the longest period on record. 東京証券取引所第一部の出来高は、月曜日の時点で、42営業日連続で10億株の大台を超え、過去最長記録となった。

excess （名）超過, 超過額, 過剰, 余剰, 過度, 行き過ぎ
  capital in excess of par value 株式払込み剰余金, 払込み剰余金, 資本剰余金, 株式発行差金
  capital in excess of stated value 株式払込み剰余金, 払込み剰余金, 額面超過金
  consolidated [consolidation] excess 連結のれん
  excess and deficiency 過不足
  excess borrowing power 追加的借入れ能力
  excess cash flow 余剰キャッシュ・フロー, 超過キャッシュ・フロー
  excess cash generation 余剰キャッシュ・フロー
  excess collateral 超過担保
  excess competition 過当競争
  excess disbursement 支払い超過
  excess earning power 超過収益力
  excess fare 不足料金
  excess foreign cash 余剰外貨
  excess funds 余剰資金
  excess investment 過剰投資, 超過投資
  excess issue 制限外発行, 限外発行
  excess loans 過剰融資, 超過融資 （=excessive loans）
  excess money balances 超過貨幣残高
  excess money supply 超過通貨供給量, 超過貨幣供給量
  excess of assets over projected benefit obligation 資産の予測給付債務超過額
  excess of cost over book value 簿価に対する原価超過額
  excess of debt 債務超過
  excess or shortage of funds 資金過不足
  excess over estimate 見積り超過額
  excess over par 資本準備金等組入れ額
  excess payment 超過支払い
  excess profit 超過利潤, 超過利得
  excess reinsurance 超過額再保険
  excess reserves 過剰準備, 過準備金
  excess share 超過株式
  excess windfall profit 望外の過剰利得
  monetary excess 過剰流動性
◆Efforts made by the corporate sector to trim three excesses of debt, workforces and facilities are the second factor propelling the economy forward. 企業が債務、人員、設備という三つの過剰の削減に取り組んだことが、景気回復を推進した第二の要因だ。◆The key to returning to stable growth is whether the nation can eliminate excesses common to many companies and promote supply-side structural reforms. 安定成長復帰へのカギは、多くの日本企業に共通して見られる過剰体質を排除して、供給サイドの構造改革を進めることができるかどうかである。

excess assets 資産超過, 資産超過額
◆According to JAL's business plan, the airline will have about ￥26 billion in excess assets due to improved business performance at the end of fiscal 2010. 日航の事業計画では、同社は業績の改善で2010年度末の資産超過額が約260億円に達する見通しだ。

excess consumption 過剰消費
◆The U.S. current account deficit has passed the annual $800 billion mark, reflecting excess consumption. 米国の経常赤字は、過剰消費を反映して、年間8,000億ドルの大台を超えた。

excess debts 債務超過, 債務超過額
（=excess liabilities）
◆Japan Airlines will be able to clear excess debts by the end of this fiscal year due to larger-than-predicted earnings. 業績が予想を上回ったため、日本航空は、今年度末には債務超過を解消できる見込みだ。◆The firm's excess debts will remain at the end of fiscal 2010. 同社の債務超過は、2010年度末も残る見込みだ。

excess liabilities 債務超過, 債務超過額 （=excess of debts, excess of liabilities over assets, excessive liabilities, liabilities in excess of assets）
◆If the creditor banks forgive the debts though TEPCO is not carrying excess liabilities, senior managements of the lenders may be sued in a shareholders' lawsuit over mismanagement. 東電が債務超過ではないのに債権保有銀行が債権を放棄すると、ずさんな経営で、金融機関の上級経営陣は株主代表訴訟で訴えられる可能性がある。◆Phoenix Resort had excess liabilities of ￥133.6 billion. フェニックスリゾート（宮崎市の大型リゾート施設）は、1,336億円の債務超過額を抱えていた[債務超過に陥った]。

excess liquidity 過剰流動性
  draw out excess liquidity 過剰流動性を吸収する
  squeeze excess liquidity 過剰流動性を吸収する

excess of liabilities over assets 債務超過, 債務超過額 （=excess liabilities）
◆The company likely will face an excess of liabilities over assets for fiscal 2011. 同社は、2011年度は債務超過に陥る見通しだ。

excess of loss 超過損害, 超過損害額
  excess of loss ratio reinsurance 超過損害率再保険
  excess of loss reinsurance 超過損害額再保険, 超過損害再保険

excess output capacity 生産設備の過剰
◆The serious deterioration of operational efficiency is caused by excess output capacity and burgeoning workforces. 極端な経営効率の悪化は、生産設備と従業員の過剰によるものだ。

excess return 超過収益率, 超過リターン
  actual excess return 実現超過収益率, 実現超過リターン
  expected excess return 期待[予想]超過リターン, 期待[予想]超過収益率
  forecast excess return 予想超過収益率
  positive excess return プラスの超過収益率

excess volatility in exchange rates 為替相場の過度の変動
◆Excess volatility in exchange rates is undesirable for global economic growth. 為替相場の過度の変動は、世界の経済成長にとって望ましくない。

excessive （形）過度の, 極端な, 法外な, 不当な, 多すぎる, 過多の, 過剰な, 割高な
  excessive charge 超過料金
  excessive competition 過当競争
  excessive currency appreciation 行き過ぎた通貨高, 過度の通貨高 （⇒currency appreciation）
  excessive debt 過剰債務, 過剰負債, 債務過多
  excessive dividends 過剰な配当金
  excessive inventories 過剰在庫
  excessive lending 過剰融資
  excessive liquidity 過剰流動性

excessive monetary expansion　行き過ぎた金融緩和
excessive profit　暴利, 不当利得, 超過利得
excessive service　過剰サービス, サービス過剰
excessive speculation　過当投機
regulation for excessive lending　過剰融資の規制

excessive appreciation of the yen　行き過ぎた円高, 過度の円高, 超円高　(=the yen's excessive appreciation, the excessive rise of the yen)
◆Japan moved to correct the excessive appreciation of the yen. 日本は、行き過ぎた円高の修正に動いた。

excessive borrowing　過剰借入れ
◆To reduce the twin deficits, U.S. officials should keep trying to control excessive borrowing and overconsumption by raising interest rates steadily. 双子の赤字削減に向け、米当局者は、金利引上げを継続して過剰借入れと過剰消費を抑制する努力を重ねなければならない。

excessive changes in the exchange rate　為替相場の過度な変動
◆The government will stem any excessive changes in the exchange rate. 政府は、為替相場の過度の変動を抑制する方針だ。

excessive competition　過当競争
◆One of the intentions of the government to introduce various regulation measures is to discourage "excessive competition." 各種の規制措置を導入する政府のねらいの一つは、「過当競争」の防止である。

excessive corporate capital investment　企業の過剰な設備投資
◆Maintaining an easy monetary policy may lead to excessive corporate capital investment and have a negative impact on the sustainable economic recovery. 金融緩和政策を続けると、企業の過剰な設備投資を生み、景気の持続的回復を阻害する恐れがある。

excessive currency appreciation　行き過ぎた通貨高, 過度の通貨高
◆As one option to avoid excessive currency appreciation in emerging countries with inflationary trends, they can restrict an influx of capital. インフレ気味の新興国で行き過ぎた[過度の]通貨高を避けるための手段として、資金流入を規制することができる。

excessive discounting　値引きの行き過ぎ, 行き過ぎた安売り, 過度の値引き
◆Excessive discounting would add to a deflationary spiral. 値引き[安売り]が行き過ぎると、デフレ・スパイラル(デフレの悪循環)につながることになる。

excessive funding　過剰融資
◆The investigation committee questioned the bank's excessive funding of a golf course developer. 調査委員会は、ゴルフ場経営会社への同行の過剰融資を問題視した。

excessive intervention in management　過剰な経営介入
◆Excessive intervention in management by a large shareholder may invite self-isolation of listed firms. 大株主の過剰な経営介入は、上場企業の引きこもりを招きかねない。

excessive investment　過剰投資
◆Beset by heavy debts combined with problems of their excessive investment in plants and equipment, Japanese corporations are facing stiff competition from Chinese and other Asian companies. 巨額の債務や過剰設備投資の問題に苦しむ日本企業は、中国などアジアの企業から厳しい競争を仕掛けられている。

excessive liabilities　債務超過, 過剰債務, 債務超過額　(=excess liabilities)
◆A large number of companies are burdened with massive amounts of excessive liabilities in sectors such as construction and wholesale. 建設や卸売りなどの分野では、巨額の過剰債務を抱えている企業が多い。◆If TEPCO's creditor banks forgive the debts when the utility is not carrying excessive liabilities, lenders will not be able to recover either the principal or interest owed. 東電が債務超過でない時点で東電の債権保有銀行が債権を放棄すると、金融機関は元本を回収できず、金利収入も得られなくなる。

excessive movements [moves] of foreign exchange rates　行き過ぎた為替相場[為替レート、外国為替相場]の動き
◆Excessive movements of foreign exchange rates are not desirable. 行き過ぎた為替相場の動きは、好ましくない。◆Excessive movements of foreign exchange rates will have a negative impact on the stability of the economy and financial markets. 行き過ぎた外国為替相場の動きは、経済の安定と金融市場に悪影響を及ぼす。

excessive rise of the yen　行き過ぎた円高, 過度の円高, 超円高
(=excessive appreciation of the yen)
◆Japanese firms must work out better strategies to cope with the excessive rise of the yen. 日本企業は、超円高に対応できる戦略を練る必要がある。

excessive use of funds　資金の過剰使用
◆The People's Bank of China aims to restrain an excessive use of funds by businesses and lead the economy in the direction of sustainable economic growth. 中国人民銀行が目指しているのは、企業による資金の過剰使用の抑制と中国経済の持続可能な経済成長への誘導だ。

excessive volatility　過度の変動, 過度な変動
(=excess volatility)
excessive volatility in exchange rates　為替相場の過度な変動
excessive volatility in the exchange market　為替相場の過度の変動
◆By being vigilant against excessive volatility in exchange rates, the G-20 will reduce the risk of speculative money causing appreciation of currencies and inflation in emerging countries. 為替相場の過度な変動を監視して、世界[主要]20か国・地域(G20)は、投機マネーが新興国の通貨高やインフレを招くリスクを軽減する方針だ。◆The market intervention was carried out to control excessive volatility in the exchange market. 為替相場の過度の変動を抑制するため、市場介入[為替介入]が実施された。

exchange　(動)交換する, 取り替える, 両替する, やり取りする, 契約などを取り交わす, 契約書にサインする
exchange a series of cash flows　各種のキャッシュ・フローを交換する
exchange for stock　株式と交換する
exchange yen into the U.S. dollar　円を米ドルに替える
◆In foreign currency deposits, commission fees are needed when the yen is exchanged into a foreign currency and when the foreign currency is exchanged backed in yen. 外貨預金では、円を外貨に替えるときと、外貨を円に戻すときに、為替手数料が必要になる。◆North Koreans rushed en masse to exchange their notes for goods or foreign currency as the government capped the amount of old notes that could be swapped for new ones. 旧通貨の新通貨への交換額に政府が上限を設けたため、北朝鮮の人々は一斉に手もと通貨の外貨やモノとの交換に走った。◆We had a $200 million gain when we exchanged our remaining 70% interest in the company for about 3% ownership of a leading software development company. 当社は、同社の70%残存持ち分を大手のソフトウェア開発会社に対する3%持ち分と交換して、2億ドルの利益を上げました。◆We plan to exchange one share of the firm for our 1.4 shares, making it a whole subsidiary of us. 当社は、同社株1株に自社株1.4株を割り当てる株式交換を実施して、同社を当社の完全子会社化する方針です。◆Yen can be exchanged for foreign currencies and deposited in foreign

currency accounts at most major banks. 円は、大半の大手銀行で外貨と替えて外貨預金口座に預け入れることができる。

exchange （名）交換, 両替, 為替, 為替相場, 証券や商品の取引所, 取引, 交易　（⇒foreign exchange, international exchanges, SEC, securities exchange, stock exchange）

a means of exchange　交換手段
acceptance of bill of exchange　手形引受け
an exchange against us　為替の逆調
an exchange for us　為替の順調
arbitration of exchange　為替裁定取引
be listed on an exchange　取引所に上場される
be traded on an exchange　取引所で取引される
buying exchange　買い為替
central exchange　中央証券取引所
commodity exchange　商品取引所
Commodity Exchange Act　商品取引法
cross exchange　クロス裁定相場
date of exchange　交換日
deal in foreign exchange　外国為替を取引する
demand exchange　要求払い為替
direct exchange　直接為替
dollar exchange　ドル為替
dollar exchange standard system　ドル為替本位制度
domestic exchange　内国為替
exchange agreement　為替取決め
exchange arbitrage　為替の裁定, 為替裁定
exchange bank　為替銀行
exchange bills payable　順為替
exchange bills receivable　逆為替
exchange broker　為替ブローカー, 為替仲買人, 為替仲立ち人
exchange business　為替業務
exchange clearance［clearing］　為替交換
exchange contract　為替予約
　（=forward exchange contract）
（exchange）contract slip　為替予約確認書
exchange control　為替管理
exchange control risk　為替介入リスク
exchange conversion table　為替換算表
exchange cover　為替の出合い, 為替カバー, カバー取引
exchange dealer　為替ディーラー
exchange dealing［transaction］　為替取引
exchange depreciation　為替切下げ
exchange difference　為替相場の開き
exchange differences　為替換算差額
exchange dumping　為替ダンピング
exchange intervention　為替介入
exchange jobber　為替仲買人
exchange marry［marriage］　為替のマリー, 持ち高相殺
exchange nonresident　非居住者
exchange of money　両替え
exchange operation　為替操作, 持ち高操作
exchange parity　為替平価
exchange pegging　為替の釘付け
exchange permit　為替許可
exchange policy　通貨政策
exchange position［holding］　為替の持ち高
exchange premium　為替の打ち歩(ぶ)
exchange quotation　対顧客公示相場, 為替相場表
exchange restriction　為替制限
exchange risk　為替リスク, 為替変動リスク, 為替変動危険　（⇒external bond financing）
exchange risk insurance　為替変動保険
exchange room　交換室
exchange settlement　為替決済取引
exchange sold　売り為替
exchange speculation　為替投機
exchange stabilization fund　為替安定基金
Exchange Stock Portfolio　取引所ポートファリオ, ESP　（=basket: 主にプログラム売買を行う機関投資家向けの株式バスケット商品）
Exchange Surveillance Commission　証券取引等監視委員会
exchange table　換算表
exchange with equivalent　等価交換
financial exchange　金融取引
floating exchange　変動相場
foreign exchange　外国為替
foreign exchange exposures　為替リスク
foreign exchange gain［profit］　為替差益, 為替利益
foreign exchange market　外国為替市場, 外為市場
forward exchange　先物為替
futures exchange contract　先物為替契約
import exchange　輸入為替
long-dated foreign exchange contract　長期外国為替予約
nonmonetary exchange　非貨幣資産の交換
share exchange　株式交換
　（=exchange of shares）
spot exchange　直物為替
stock exchange　証券取引所, 株式取引所
the Osaka Securities Exchange　大阪証券取引所
the rate exchange　為替相場
the yen-dollar exchange　円・ドル相場, 円ドル・レート
World Federation of Exchanges　国際取引所連合, WFE

◆Financial exchanges between the BRICs group, Indonesia and South Korea will move toward a tri-reserve-currency regime by losing a dependency on the U.S. dollar. BRICsグループ（ブラジル、ロシア、インド、中国）とインドネシア、韓国の新興6か国間の金融取引は今後、米ドルに依存しなくなるため、3準備通貨体制に移行するものと思われる。◆The merger of the two exchanges will revitalize stock trading and make it easier for companies to procure funds on the market to expand their business operations. 両証券取引所の経営統合で、株式の売買が活性化し、企業にとっては市場で資金を調達して会社の事業を大きくしやすくなる。◆The new Jasdaq market began trading on 12 October, 2010 as one of Asia's largest exchanges for emerging enterprises. ジャスダック新市場は、2010年10月12日からアジア最大規模の新興企業向け証券取引所として取引を開始した。◆The Tokyo Stock Exchange and four other exchanges extended their morning trading hours by 30 minutes to 11:30 a.m. 東証など5証券取引所が、午前の取引時間を11時半まで30分間延長した。◆The Tokyo Stock Exchange and the Osaka Securities Exchange have officially agreed to merge in January 2013. 東証と大証は、2013年1月に経営統合することで正式に合意した。◆Through the TSE-OSE merger in January 2013, the two exchanges must enhance their strategies to ensure survival as a major stock market in Asia. 東証と大証の2013年1月の経営統合をテコに、両証券取引所は、アジアの主要市場として勝ち残る戦略を強化する必要がある。

exchange bonds　他社株転換債, EB
◆The credit union purchased exchange bonds, a type of

derivative, from Merrill Lynch Japan Securities Co. between April and December 2000. 同信用組合は、2000年4月から12月の間に、メリルリンチ日本証券からデリバティブ（金融派生商品）の一種の他社株転換債を購入していた。

exchange company group 取引所グループ, 株式取引所グループ
（＝exchange group, stock exchange group）
◆The TSE and the OSE plan to establish an exchange company group as a holding firm under which the two exchanges will be placed as subsidiaries. 東証と大証は、両株式取引所を子会社として傘下に収める持ち株会社として、取引所グループの設立を計画している。

exchange equalization 為替平衡
（＝exchange stabilization）
exchange equalization account 為替平衡勘定
exchange equalization fund 為替平衡資金, 為替安定資金（exchange stabilization fund）
exchange equalization operation 為替平衡操作

exchange fluctuation 為替変動, 為替相場の変動, 為替の騰落, 為替の乱高下 （＝exchange rate fluctuation; ⇒exchange rate movements, float動詞, fluctuation）
exchange fluctuation fund 為替変動準備金
◆The yen's stable rate at about ¥130 against the dollar serves as a stabilizing factor for importers, exporters and others doing business susceptible to exchange fluctuations. 円の対ドル為替相場が130円台（前後）で安定していることは、輸出入業者など為替変動に左右されやすい仕事をしている者にとって安定要因となる。

exchange fund 為替資金
exchange fund cover operation 為替資金操作
exchange fund operation 為替資金操作, 資金操作

exchange gain 為替差益
（＝currency exchange gain, exchange profit）
exchange gain from yen appreciation 円高差益
exchange gain or loss 為替差損益（＝exchange gains/losses, exchange gains and losses）

exchange group 取引所グループ, 株式取引所グループ
（＝exchange company group, stock exchange group）
◆The merger between the TSE and the OSE will create the world's second-largest exchange group in terms of the total market value of listed shares. 東証と大証の経営統合で、上場株式の時価総額で世界第2位の株式取引所グループが誕生する。◆The TSE and the OSE will merge into the world's No.2 exchange group. 東証と大証が統合して、世界第2位の株式取引所グループが誕生する。

exchange loss 為替差損
foreign exchange loss 為替差損, 為替損失

exchange market 為替市場, 取引市場
（⇒excessive volatility, intervene, intervention）
◆The Japanese currency's value vis-a-vis the U.S. dollar entered the ¥87 range in foreign exchange markets around the world. 円の対米ドル相場は、内外の外国為替市場で1ドル＝87円台を付けた。

exchange one's foreign currency deposits into yen 外貨預金を円と交換する, 外貨預金を円に替える
◆In foreign currency deposits, depositors can earn profits by exchanging their foreign currency deposits into yen when the yen's value against major foreign currencies falls. 外貨預金では、主要外貨に対して円相場が下落した時点で預金者が外貨預金を円に戻せば［円に替えれば］、利益を上げる［儲ける］ことができる。

exchange rate 為替相場, 外国為替相場, 為替レート, 交換レート, 交換比率, 換算レート （＝currency exchange rate, rate of exchange; ⇒depreciation of the dollar exchange rate, dual exchange rate, economic fundamentals, flexibility, float, floating exchange (rate), fluctuation, volatility in exchange rates）
a steadily rising exchange rate じり高為替相場
actual exchange rate 直物レート
applicable exchange rate 適用される為替レート
assumed exchange rate 想定為替レート
average exchange rates prevailing during the year 期中の実勢平均為替レート
basic exchange rate 基準為替相場
changes in exchange rate 為替相場の変動
control exchange rates 為替相場をコントロールする
countries with high exchange rates 自国通貨高の国々
current exchange rate 現在の為替相場, 実勢為替相場, 現行為替レート
depreciation of the dollar exchange rate ドル相場の下落, ドルの為替レートの下落
effective exchange rate 実効為替相場, 実効為替レート
engage in exchange rate speculation 為替投機を行う
exchange rate allocation 外貨割当て, 外貨割当配分
exchange rate appreciation 為替レートの切上げ
exchange rate at the date of transaction 取引日レート
exchange rate band 為替変動幅
exchange rate control 為替管理
exchange rate depreciation 為替レートの切下げ
exchange rate fluctuations 為替の変動
（＝exchange fluctuations）
exchange rate for the dollar ドルの為替［交換］レート
exchange rate in foreign currency 外貨建て為替相場
exchange rate in home currency 邦貨建て為替相場
exchange rate parity 為替交換比率, 為替平価
（＝exchange parity）
exchange rate realignment 為替相場の再編成
exchange rate rigidity 為替レートの硬直性
exchange rate risk 為替リスク
（＝exchange risk）
exchange rate speculation 為替投機
exchange rate stability 為替の安定
exchange rate swings 為替相場の変動
exchange rate volatility 為替の乱高下
exchange rates for US dollars 米ドルの為替レート
favorable exchange rate 有利な為替レート
fix the yuan-dollar exchange rate 元・ドル為替レート［為替相場］を固定する, 元［人民元］・ドル・レートを固定する
fixed exchange rate 固定為替相場, 固定為替レート, 固定相場制
fixed exchange rate policy 固定為替相場政策
flexible exchange rates 柔軟な為替相場, 柔軟な為替政策, 屈伸為替相場
floating exchange rate 変動為替相場
foreign exchange rate 外国為替相場, 外国為替レート, 外為相場
forward exchange rate 先物為替相場, 先物為替レート, 先物相場, 先物レート
forward foreign exchange rate 先物予約レート
international exchange rate 国際交換比率
nominal exchange rate 名目為替相場, 名目為替レート
prevailing exchange rate 現在の為替相場, 実勢為替相場, 実勢為替レート
push down an exchange rate 為替レートを押し下げる
push up an exchange rate 為替レートを押し上げる

real effective exchange rate　実質実効為替レート
real exchange rate　実質為替レート, 実勢為替相場（=real rate of exchange）
realistic exchange rate　現実的為替レート
stabilize an exchange rate　為替を安定させる
the dollar's exchange rate against the Japanese yen　円に対するドル相場
the yen-dollar exchange rate　円とドルの為替レート, 円・ドルレート, 円の対ドル相場
the yen's current exchange rate　今の円の為替レート, 今の円の為替相場, 今の円相場
the yen's exchange rate against the dollar　ドルに対する円相場, ドル・円相場
the yuan-dollar exchange rate　元とドルの為替レート, 元・ドル・レート, 元の対ドル・レート
unfavorable exchange rate　不利な為替レート
wild fluctuations in exchange rates　為替の乱高下
◆An exporter company will incur losses if the yen rises above the assumed exchange rate, but benefit if the yen declines. 輸出企業では、その想定為替レートより円高になれば為替差損が生じ、(想定為替レートより)円安になれば為替差益が出る。◆China has not budged an inch to shift the current dollar-yuan exchange rate. 中国は、現在の元・ドル・レートを梃子でも動かそうとしていない。◆China intervenes in the foreign exchange markets to fix the yuan-dollar exchange rate. 中国は、外国為替市場に介入して[為替介入して]元・ドル・レートを固定している。◆Flexible exchange rates are necessary to support a strong and balanced global economy. 力強くバランスが取れた世界経済を支えるためには、柔軟な為替相場[為替政策]が必要だ。◆If we look at the yen's current exchange rate in terms of its real effective exchange rate, it is basically within a range consistent with the mid- and long-term fundamentals of the economy. 今の円相場[円の為替相場]は、実質実効為替レートで見ると、基本的には中長期的な経済のファンダメンタルズ(基礎的条件)と整合的な範囲内にある。◆The current yuan exchange rate is said to be undervalued against the U.S. and the euro. 現在の人民元の為替相場は、米ドルやユーロに対して割安[過小評価されている]と言われる。◆The dollar's exchange rate against the Japanese yen has been about ￥85 to the dollar since early summer. 円ドル相場[円・ドル相場]は、今年の初夏から1ドル=85円前後で推移している。◆The exchange rate in fiscal 2011 had been predicted to be between ￥80 and ￥83 per dollar by many Japanese exporters. 2011年度の為替レートを、多くの日本の輸出業者は1ドル=80〜83円と想定していた。◆The exchange rate was the same at the time of deposit and withdrawal in a foreign currency deposit. 外貨預金で、為替相場は預け入れ時と解約時で同じだった。◆The rise of the yen beyond the level of the exchange rate assumed by many exporters has put them on the ropes. 多くの輸出業者が想定した為替レートの水準を上回る円高が輸出業者を窮地に追い込んでいる。◆The yen's exchange rate has appreciated to ￥76 against the dollar, so it is the best time to buy U.S. dollars. 円の為替レートが1ドル=76円に上昇したので、今が米ドルの買い時だ。◆To fulfill its responsibilities as the nation's central bank, the Bank of Japan must achieve currency stabilization by availing itself of a range of measures, including stabilization of the exchange rate. 日本の中央銀行としての責任を果たすには、日本銀行は、為替相場の安定を含めて広範な手段を活用して通貨の安定を実現しなければならない。

exchange rate against the U.S. dollar　対米ドル為替レート
◆A one-yen drop in the exchange rate against the U.S. dollar would lead to the loss of about ￥200 million in annual profits for the company. 対米ドル為替レートで1円の円安が、同社の場合は年間で約2億円の減益となる。

exchange rate flexibility　為替レートの伸縮性, 為替相場[為替レート]の弾力性
enhance the yuan's exchange rate flexibility　人民元の為替レート[為替相場]の弾力性を高める[強化する], 人民元の為替レートの弾力化を進める[弾力化を図る]
greater exchange rate flexibility　為替レートの柔軟性向上　(⇒flexibility)
◆China will further enhance the yuan's exchange rate flexibility. 中国は、人民元の為替レートの柔軟性をさらに強化する[人民元の為替相場の弾力化をさらに進める]方針だ。

exchange rate fluctuations　為替変動
◆The G-7 meeting has repeatedly issued communiques concerning exchange rate fluctuations and economic policy management. 先進7か国会議(G7)は、これまで為替変動や経済政策運営に関する声明を再三、発信してきた。

exchange rate movements　為替変動, 為替レートの変動, 為替動向, 為替相場の動き, 為替相場の推移　(=exchange fluctuations, exchange rate changes, exchange rate fluctuations, exchange rate moves; ⇒fluctuation)
◆Such foreign bonds and foreign bond open investment trusts that are priced in foreign currencies may incur losses due to exchange rate movements. 外貨建てで売買されるこれらの外債や外債投信は、為替変動によって差損を出す可能性がある。

exchange rate policy　為替政策
fixed exchange rate policy　固定相場政策
floating exchange rate policy　変動相場政策
◆In the Report on International Economic and Exchange Rate Policies, the U.S. Treasury Department said that China is not a manipulator of its currency. 国際経済・為替政策報告書で、米財務省は、中国は為替操作国ではないと述べた。

exchange rate system　為替制度, 為替相場制度　(⇒fixed exchange rate system)
fixed exchange rate system　固定為替相場制度, 固定相場制
floating exchange rate system　変動為替相場制, 変動相場制
free exchange rate system　自由為替相場制
free floating exchange rate system　自由変動相場制

exchange-traded　(形)取引所上場の, 上場〜
exchange-traded derivatives　取引所上場の派生商品, 上場派生商品
exchange-traded futures　上場先物
exchange-traded hedging instrument　上場ヘッジ商品

exchange-traded fund　上場投資信託, 株価指数連動型上場投資信託, ETF　(日経平均株価や東証株価指数(TOPIX)などを構成するすべての銘柄を組み込んだ投資信託。⇒ETF, index mutual fund, risky)
◆The AMEX up to now has had a virtual monopoly on ETF (exchange-traded fund) listing. アメリカン証券取引所(AMEX)はこれまで、上場投資信託(ETF)の上場を事実上、独占してきた。◆The Bank of Japan purchased riskier assets such as exchange-traded funds and real estate investment trusts in mid-December 2010. 日銀は、2010年12月半ばから、上場投資信託や不動産投資信託(リート)などの高リスク資産を買い入れた。◆The Bank of Japan will set up a fund to buy long-term government bonds, exchange-traded funds and other financial assets in a bid to prop up the nation's economy. 日本の景気を下支えするため、日銀は基金を新設して、長期国債や上場投資信託(ETF)などの金融商品[金融資産]を買い入れる。◆The exchange-traded funds (ETFs) are investment products similar to index mutual funds but that trade on stock exchanges like stocks. 上場投資信託(ETF)は、インデックス・ミューチュアル・ファンドに似ているが、株式と同じように証券取引所で売買される投資商品である。

Exchange Trading Requirement　取引所取引法
exchangeable　(形)交換可能な, 交換できる
　convertible exchangeable preferred stock［share］　転換交換可能優先株式［優先株］
　exchangeable debt　交換可能債務証券
　exchangeable into　〜と交換可能な
　exchangeable preferred (share)　交換可能優先株式
　exchangeable securities　交換可能証券
　exchangeable value　交換価値
exchangeable bond　交換可能債券, 他社株転換可能債, 交換社債
　exchangeable bond with a knock-in provision　ノックイン型交換社債
　exchangeable bond with a knock-out provision　ノックアウト型交換社債
　registered exchangeable bond　登録交換可能債
ex-dividend　配当落ち(配当基準日を過ぎて株価が安くなる状態のことをいう)
ex-dividend date　配当落ち日(株式が配当落ちになる日のこと)
execute　(動)執行する, 実行する, 実施する, 遂行する, 施行する, 履行する, 達成する, 完成する, (職務や約束を)果たす, 制作する, 製作する, (契約書などを)作成する, 署名する, 調印する, 正式に締結する, 演じる
　execute a stock［share］split　株式分割を実施する
　execute a trade　取引を執行する
　execute an obligation created by the contract　契約で生じた義務を履行する
　◆In commodity futures trading, prices are decided when buyers and sellers make deals. So they can execute trades at promised prices even if the value of goods has changed drastically in the meantime. 商品先物取引では, 売り手と買い手が取引契約をする時点で価格を決める。そのため, 契約期間中に相場が大きく変動しても, 売り手と買い手は約束した値段で取引を執行できる。
execution　(名)執行(証券会社などが取引を実行すること), 実行, 実施, 履行, 施行, 達成, 成立, 業務, 署名, 作成, 調印, 締結
　daily execution　日常業務
　execution date of this agreement　本契約締結日
　execution of loan　ローンの実行
　execution of stock warrants　ワラント(株式ワラント, 新株引受権)の権利行使
　order execution　注文執行, 注文処理
　　(=execution of order)
　skill in trade execution　取引執行力
　term of execution　履行期限
executive　(名)経営者, 管理職, 重役, 会社役員, 役職員, 執行役員, 執行部, 執行機関, エグゼクティブ　(⇒banking, check, chief executive officer, disclose, file a damages suit against, illegal payment of dividends)
　◆As a side effect of the zero-interest policy, there is the moral hazard concerning corporate executives. ゼロ金利政策の副作用の一つとして, 企業経営者のモラル・ハザード(倫理の欠如)がある。◆At the bank, a string of executives resigned one after another due to differences over management policy. 同行では, 経営路線の違いで役員の辞任が相次いだ。◆Company executives have admitted responsibility in a class action suit filed on behalf of a firm. 株主代表訴訟で, 企業の幹部が責任を認めた。◆Since three banks integrated their operations, executives from the three predecessor banks served on an equal basis as presidents of the Mizuho group, Mizuho Bank and Mizuho Corporate Bank. 3銀行の経営統合以来, 旧3行の経営者が, みずほグループ(FG), みずほ銀行, みずほコーポレート銀行のトップをそれぞれ分け合った。◆The bank decided to continue extending loans to the company despite its executives knowing the company was on the ropes. この会社の経営が悪化しているのを経営陣が知りながら, 同行は同社への融資継続を決めた。◆The government may reject a company's request for a license to enter the fiduciary market if its executive has been dismissed in the past five years due to a violation of Section 2 of Article 102. 信託市場(信託業)に参入するための免許を申請した企業の役員が, 第102条第2項の違反により5年以内に解任命令を受けていた場合, 政府はその免許申請[免許交付]を拒否することができる。◆The Resolution and Collection Corporation sued a former chief executive and another executive of Tokyo Chuo Credit Union, seeking about ¥45 million in compensation for a loss due to uncollectible loans. 整理回収機構(RCC)は, 東京中央信用組合の元理事長と理事ら二人に対し, 回収不能の融資による損害の賠償金として約4,500万円を求める訴訟を起こした。

executive pay　経営幹部報酬
　◆The executive pay of Merrill Lynch & Co., mostly in bonuses, has become a hot-button issue in the recession as banks and companies fail. メリルリンチの経営幹部報酬は, 大半がボーナスだが, 銀行や企業が経営破たんする不況時の強い関心を呼ぶ問題になっている。

exempt　(動)免除する　(名)免除されたもの［人, 機関］, 免税者　(形)免除された, 適用除外の, 適用対象とはならない
　exempt company　適用除外会社
　exempt from　〜を免除された, 〜の適用除外になる, 〜の適用対象とはならない
　exempt income　非課税所得
　exempt securities　適用除外証券, 免除証券
　exempt stock exchange　登録免除取引所
　tax-exempt bond　免税債, 非課税債券
　◆The proposed pact will exempt expats from paying into pension and health insurance plans in the country to which they are posted, provided they stay no more than five years. 協定案では, 海外駐在員の滞在期間が5年以内であれば, 駐在する相手国の年金と医療保険制度への加入を免除される。◆Those with incomes less than a certain level will be exempted from paying a full monthly premium to the national pension system. 一定水準以下の所得者は, 国民年金保険料の月納付額を全額免除される。

exemption　(名)控除, 課税控除, 控除額, 義務の免除, 免責, 例外
　basic exemption　基礎控除
　exemption for dependents　扶養控除
　exemption for spouse　配偶者控除
　exemption of debt　債務免除
　export exemption　輸出免税
　tariff［duty］exemption　関税免除
　tax exemption　免税
　total exemption　全額免除
　◆The exemption will apply to buildings and warehouses valued at ¥1 billion or more and factories valued at ¥1.5 billion or more. この免責が適用されるのは, 評価額が10億円以上のビル・倉庫と15億円以上の工場だ。◆The government tightened the criteria for granting total exemption from paying national pension premiums. 政府は, 国民年金保険料の全額免除の基準を厳格にした。

exemption of personal savings　マル優制度　(=preferential savings system)

exercise　(動)(オプション取引などで権利を)行使する, 実行する, 指導力などを発揮する, 影響・圧力などを及ぼす　(⇒conversion right, income)
　exercise an option　オプションを行使する

exercise call option　コール・オプションを行使する
exercise financial power　金の力に物を言わせる
exercise one's voting right　議決権を行使する
exercise put option　プット・オプションを行使する
exercise stock appreciation rights（SARs）　株式評価受益権（SAR）を行使する
exercise stock rights　新株引受権を行使する
exercise the right to offset［set off］　相殺権を行使する
exercise the warrants　ワラントを行使する, 新株引受権を行使する
　◆During 2010, 167,747 stock appreciation rights（SARs）were exercised. 2010年度は, 167,747株分の株式評価受益権（SAR）が行使された。◆On June 10, 2011, individuals holding $50,000 face value of the Corporation's bonds exercised their conversion privilege. 2011年6月10日, 当社の社債権者が, 額面5万ドル分の転換権を行使した［額面5万ドル分の株式への転換を行った］。◆Proceeds from exercising stock options are compensation for labor and service rendered and constitute salary income. ストック・オプション（自社株購入権）を行使して得た利益は, 職務遂行の対価なので, 給与所得に当たる。◆The broker's officials did not attend the publisher's shareholders meeting to exercise their voting rights. 証券会社の役員は, この出版社の株主総会を欠席して議決権の行使を見送った。

exercise　（名）権利の行使, 行使, 実行, 努力, 策
　allotted exercise period　所定の権利行使期間, 所定の行使期間
　cost-cutting exercise　コスト削減策
　diverse exercise of voting right　議決権の不統一行使
　exercise date　（オプションなどの）行使日
　exercise limit　権利行使限度, 行使限度
　exercise notice　権利行使通知書, 権利通知
　exercise of security right　担保権の行使
　exercise of stock rights　新株引受権の行使
　exercise period　権利行使期間, 行使期間
　refinancing exercise　借換え債の発行
　substitutional exercise of voting right　議決権の代理行使
　warrant exercise　新株引受権の行使, ワラントの行使（＝exercise of warrant）

exercise a veto　拒否権を行使する
　◆Golden shares are special shares that can be used to exercise a veto to kill off merger or integration proposals by hostile bidders. 黄金株は, 敵対的買収者による合併・経営統合などの提案を否決するための拒否権行使に使える特殊な株だ。

exercise employee stock options　従業員ストック・オプションの権利を行使する
　◆In Japan, if company employees exercise employee stock options and obtain shares, the shares are considered salaried income, which is taxable. 日本では, 社員が従業員ストック・オプションの権利を行使して株を取得した場合, その株式は給与所得と見なされ, 課税対象になる。

exercise one's voting right　議決権を行使する
　◆The use of e-mail would make it easier for foreign shareholders to exercise their voting rights. eメールを使うと, 外国人株主は議決権を行使しやすくなる。

exercise price　行使価格, 権利行使価格（＝strike price：プット・オプションやコール・オプションを行使するときの価格）
　◆The exercise price of any stock option is equal to or greater than the stock price when the option is granted. ストック・オプションの行使価格は, オプションが付与されたときの株価と同等, またはそれを上回る価格になっている。

exert　（動）（力などを）用いる, 働かせる, 発揮する, 行使する
　exert all one's strength　全力を出す
　exert authority　権威を示す
　exert great pressure on　～への圧力を強める
　exert influence on　～に影響を及ぼす
　exert more downward pressure on　～をさらに押し下げる要因となる
　exert oneself　努力する, 尽力する
　exert strong pressure on　～に強い圧力をかける, ～への圧力を強める
　◆The government may exert great pressure on the Bank of Japan to further relax its monetary policy. 政府は, 日銀への追加の金融緩和圧力を強める可能性がある。

existing　（形）存在する, 現存する, 存続している, 現行の, 既存の, 従来の, 現在の, 今回の, 実績ベースの, 既存店ベースの
　an add-on to an existing issue　既発債の追加発行分
　call the existing bonds　既発債を任意償還する
　existing customer［client］　既存の顧客, 既存顧客, 既顧客
　existing deposits　既存の預金
　existing home sales　中古住宅販売戸数
　existing insured exposures　既存保険契約
　existing issue　既発債
　existing market　既存市場, 現存市場
　existing mortgage　現存抵当
　existing operations　既存の事業
　existing portfolio　保有ポートフォリオ
　existing receivables　既存の債権
　existing share　既存の株式（⇒hostile acquirer）
　existing tax rates　現行税率
　forcibly call in loans　貸しはがしする
　refinance of existing exposure　融資の借換え
　rollover of an existing credit　借換え

existing affiliates　既存の関連会社
　◆The company will drastically trim its existing affiliates. 同社は, 既存の関連会社を抜本的に整理する方針だ。

existing assets　既存資産
　◆Gains and losses on hedges of existing assets or liabilities are marked to market on a monthly basis. 既存の資産または債務のヘッジに関する損益は毎月, 評価替えされている。

existing debt　既存の債務, 既存の借金
　refinance existing debt　既存の債務を借り換える
　roll over existing debt　既存の債務を借り換える
　◆The government may shoulder interest payments on the existing debts of survivors of the March 11 disaster. 東日本大震災被災者の既存の借金［債務］については, 政府がその利払いを肩代わりする可能性がある。

existing loans　融資残高, 既存の債権, 既存の融資, 既存のローン
　call in existing loans　既存債権を回収する, 融資残高を回収する, 貸しはがしする
　refinance existing loans　ローンを借り換える
　◆Overly radical methods for accelerating the disposal of bad loans would panic the banking sector and the financial market, possibly driving banks to shy away from extending new loans and even to call in existing loans. 不良債権処理を加速するための余りにも強硬な手法は, 銀行や金融市場をおびえさせ, 貸し渋りや貸しはがしにつながることにもなる。◆Regarding TEPCO's damage compensation, creditor financial institutions have already offered cooperation by refinancing existing loans. 東電の損害賠償に関して, 取引金融機関は, 既存の融資の借換えなどですでに協力している。

exit （動）去る, 退場する, 退出する, 〜から撤退する, 終了する, 終える
　exit the market　市場から撤退する, 市場から逃避する
　exit the week　週を終える
　◆The dollar exited the week near its seven-month low against the yen and an all-time low against the euro. ドル［ドル相場］は, 対円で約7か月ぶりの安値, 対ユーロでは史上最安値で週を終えた。◆With such moves to rein in investment funds, speculative money started to exit the markets. 投資ファンドを規制するこうした動きで, 投機マネーが市場から逃避し始めた。

exit （名）退場, 退出, 撤退, 出国, 出口, 流出, 売却
　current exit value　売却時価
　exit barrier　撤退障壁
　exit price ［value］　売却価額

exit strategy　出口戦略
　◆G-7 nations should start envisaging exit strategies and the restoration of fiscal health. 先進7か国は, そろそろ出口戦略と財政の健全化も見据えるべきだ。◆The U.S. Federal Reserve Board is preparing an exit strategy for its unprecedented stimulus efforts. 米連邦準備制度理事会（FRB）は現在, 前例のない［未曾有の］景気対策の出口戦略を策定しているところだ。

exodus of funds　資金の流出, 資金の引揚げ
　◆The accounting scandals have been responsible for the loss of confidence in U.S. stock markets and an exodus of funds from the United States. 米国の株式市場に対する信頼喪失と米国からの資金流出の大きな要因は, 一連の不正会計事件だ。

Exon-Florio provision of the 1988 trade law　1988年通商法のエクソン・フロリオ条項（米国の安全保障を損なう企業買収の禁止）
　◆In the United States, the Exon-Florio provision of the 1988 trade law can prevent takeover bids that are deemed a threat to national security. 米国では, 1988年通商法のエクソン・フロリオ条項で, 国家の安全保障上, 脅威と考えられる企業買収を阻止することができる。

exorbitant （形）法外な, 途方も無い, とんでもない, 不当な, 過度の, 過大な
　exorbitant demand　不当な要求, 途方もない要求
　exorbitant price　法外な値段, とんでもない値段, 不当価格
　exorbitant taxes　法外な課税

expand （動）拡大する, 拡張する, 広げる, 拡充する, 増やす, 増設する, 引き上げる, 展開する, 成長する, 発展する, 上昇する, 膨張する, 改善する, 〜の内容を充実させる, 詳述する
　expand business　事業を拡大する
　expand capacity　設備を拡張する, 生産能力を拡大する
　expand economies of scale　スケール・メリットを追求する
　expand infrastructure　インフラを拡張する
　expand one's customer base　顧客基盤を拡大する
　expand one's operating loss projection　〜の営業損失［営業赤字］予想額を引き上げる
　expand production　生産を拡大する
　expanded economy　景気拡大
　expanded lead managers　拡大主幹事
　expanded reproduction　拡大再生産
　◆At the latest G-20 meeting, diverging opinions among member countries were exposed over expanding the lending capacity of the IMF. 今回のG20（財務相・中央銀行総裁）会議では, 国際通貨基金（IMF）が融資できる資金規模の拡大をめぐって, 加盟国の間で意見の食い違いが表面化した。◆Eurozone countries were so slow to take necessary actions that the sovereign debt crisis expanded. 欧州の必要な対応が後手に回ったために, ソブリン危機［政府債務危機］が拡大した。◆If the European financial crisis expands, it will damage the recovering global economy. 欧州の金融危機が拡大すれば, 回復途上にある世界経済に打撃を与えることになる。◆It is a matter of urgency to ensure that banks make profit margins that can meet investment risks and that they expand commission revenue as well as promote sweeping restructurings. 抜本的なリストラ推進のほか, 投資リスクに見合う利ざやの確保と手数料収入の拡大などが銀行の急務だ。◆Measures to expand and create employment are a pressing task. 雇用拡大と雇用創出策は, 急を要する課題だ。◆Shinsei and Aozora banks announced a plan to merge in an effort to expand their customer bases and improve earnings. 新生銀行とあおぞら銀行は, 顧客基盤の拡大と収益力の強化を狙って, 合併計画を発表した。◆The BOJ's policy meeting plans to consider expanding the list of government bonds purchased under the fund. 日銀の政策決定会合では, 基金で買い入れる国債の対象拡大を検討する予定だ。◆The business climate for home builders has been severe as housing starts have not expanded much in recent years. 新設住宅の着工戸数がここ数年伸び悩んでいるため, 住宅メーカーを取り巻く企業環境は厳しい。◆The company expanded its production from the year 2009. 同社は, 2009年から生産を拡大した。◆The economy, fueled by a pickup in business spending on inventories, is now expanding at a spanking clip. 企業の在庫投資の回復に支えられた経済は現在, 顕著なペースで拡大している。◆The economy is expanding slowly but steadily. 景気は, 緩やかだが着実に拡大している。◆The European Union will substantially expand the lending capacity of the EFSF to buy up government bonds in case the fiscal and financial crisis spreads countries as Italy. 欧州連合（EU）は, 財政・金融危機がイタリアなどに拡大した場合に国債を買い支えるため, 欧州金融安定基金（EFSF）の融資能力を大幅に拡大する。◆The merger of the two exchanges will revitalize stock trading and make it easier for companies to procure funds on the market to expand their business operations. 両証券取引所の経営統合で, 株式の売買が活性化し, 企業にとっては市場で資金を調達して会社の事業を大きくしやすくなる。◆The proposal to expand the lending capacity of the IMF was supported by Brazil and other emerging economies though Japan and the United States rejected it. 国際通貨基金（IMF）が融資できる資金規模を拡大する案は, 日本と米国が受け入れなかったものの, ブラジルなどの新興国は支持した。◆The 17 eurozone countries agreed to expand the European Financial Stability Facility at a meeting of their finance ministers. ユーロを採用しているユーロ圏17か国は, ユーロ圏財務相会合で, 欧州金融安定基金（EFSF）の規模を拡大することで一致した。◆Toyota's strategy to expanding its operations to become the top automaker in the world in terms of both production and sales has gone too far. 生産, 販売両面で世界一の自動車メーカーをめざしたトヨタの事業拡大路線は, 行き過ぎだった。

expansion （名）拡大, 拡張, 設備拡張, 景気拡大, 成長, 上昇, 多角化
　business expansion　事業拡大, 事業拡張, 業容拡大
　credit expansion　信用拡大, 信用拡張, 信用膨張, 貸出の伸び, 金融拡大, 金融緩和
　domestic ［home］ demand expansion　内需拡大
　（＝expansion of domestic demand）
　economic expansion　景気回復, 景気拡大, 景気上昇, 経済成長　（⇒expansionary）
　expansion effect　拡張効果, 拡大効果
　expansion investment　拡張投資
　expansion of job opportunities　雇用拡大
　expansion of money ［the currency］　通貨の膨張
　expansion period　景気拡大局面
　expansion strategy　拡大戦略

export expansion　輸出拡大, 輸出拡張
fiscal expansion　財政拡大
horizontal expansion　水平的拡大
market expansion　市場拡大, 市場拡張
monetary expansion　金融拡大, 金融緩和, 通貨拡大［膨張］
numerical expansion　量的拡大
organizational expansion　組織拡大, 企業組織の拡大
production［output］expansion　生産の増加, 生産の伸び, 生産拡大
productivity expansion　生産力拡充
quantitative expansion　量的拡大, 量的拡張
regional expansion policy　地域開発政策
sustained economic expansion　持続的な経済成長, 経済の持続的な成長
trade expansion　通商拡大, 貿易拡大
　（=expansion of trade）
◆A reading of below 50 percent in the coincident index is considered a sign of economic contraction and a figure above that is viewed as a sign of expansion. 一致指数で50％以下の数値は景気収縮［景気後退］を示す指標と見られ、それ以上の数字は景気回復［景気拡大］を示す指標と見なされる。◆Economic expansion is far from being felt by households. 景気回復は、家計の実感にはほど遠い。◆Money loaned by private banks declined because banks with weakened financial strength were less willing to lend, besides a lack of businesses seeking expansion through borrowing. 民間銀行の貸出金が減ったのは、お金を借りてまで事業を拡大しようとする企業がなかったほか、財務が悪化した銀行が貸し渋ったからだ。◆The capital increase is designed to secure financial resources for the expansion of the bank's investment banking activities abroad. 同行の増資の目的は、海外での投資銀行業務拡大の資金確保にある。◆The longest period of postwar economic expansion was known as an economic boom without feeling. 戦後最長の景気回復は、実感なき景気回復と言われた。

expansion in consumption　消費拡大
◆The eco-car subsidies have significantly contributed to an expansion in consumption. エコカー補助金は、消費拡大に高い効果を上げてきた。

expansion of the monetary base　金融の量的緩和
◆An expansion of the monetary base by the Bank of Japan alone would be limited in its effect. 日銀の金融の量的緩和だけでは、その効果に限界がある。

expansionary　（形）拡大の, 拡張の, 膨張性の, 発展性の
adopt［pursue］an expansionary economic policy　経済拡大政策を取る
expansionary economy　拡張経済, 経済拡大
expansionary effect　景気押し上げ効果, 景気刺激効果
expansionary financial policy　拡張的金融政策
expansionary fiscal policy　財政出動による景気刺激策, 財政政策の緩和
expansionary policy　景気刺激型の政策
expansionary production　拡張的生産
expansionary thrust of fiscal and monetary policy　景気刺激型の金融・財政政策
◆The rate of economic expansion in the current phase of recovery is much smaller than previous expansionary phases. 現在の景気拡大期［景気拡大局面］の経済成長率は、過去の景気拡大期よりかなり低い。

expansionary budget　積極型予算, 積極的予算
◆To make the economy's step toward recovery much firmer, the government should implement another expansionary budget. 景気回復の足取りをずっと確かなものにするためにも、政府はさらに積極型の予算を実施すべきだ。

expansionary course　拡大路線
◆The failed bank took an expansionary course through buying up loans from nonbanks and extending big loans in a reckless manner. 破たんしたこの銀行は、ノンバンクからの債権買取りや無理な大口融資などで拡大路線に走った。

expansionary monetary policy　金融政策の緩和, 金融の量的緩和策, 拡張的通貨政策
◆The BOJ may predict both the CPI's return to positive territory and an end to its expansionary monetary policy. 日銀が、消費者物価指数のプラス転換と、金融の量的緩和策の解除を示唆する可能性もある。

expansionary phase　拡大局面, 拡大期
◆The rate of economic expansion in the current phase of recovery is much smaller than previous expansionary phases. 現在の景気拡大期［景気拡大局面］の経済成長率は、過去の景気拡大期よりかなり低い。

expat　（名）海外駐在員, 海外移住者, 国籍離脱者
　（=expatriate）
◆The proposed pact will exempt expats from paying into pension and health insurance plans in the country to which they are posted, provided they stay no more than five years. 協定案では、海外駐在員の滞在期間が5年以内であれば、駐在する相手国の年金と医療保険制度への加入を免除される。

expect　（動）期待する, 見込む, 予想する, 見積もる, 推定する, 要求する, 求める
expected amount of losses　予想される損失額
expected inflation（figures）　期待インフレ率, 予想インフレ率
expected long-term rate of return on plan assets　年金資産［制度資産］の長期期待収益率, 期待長期資産収益率, 制度資産の予想長期収益率
expected loss　予想損失, 損失の予想, 見込まれる損失, 赤字見通し
expected payout ratio　期待配当性向
expected profit　期待利益, 予想利益, 期待利潤
expected profitability　期待利益率, 予想利益率
expected return　期待収益, 予想収益, 期待収益率
expected return on plan assets　年金資産［年金制度資産］の予想運用利益率, 期待運用収益率, 期待収益率
expected value　期待値
expected yield　期待利回り
expected yield to maturity　期待最終利回り
short-term obligations expected to be refinanced　借換えが予想される短期債務
◆At the eurozone finance ministers meeting held on October 3, 2011, a decision on bridge loans of about €8 billion to Greece was expected, but none was done. 2011年10月3日に開かれたユーロ圏財務相会合では、ギリシャに対する約80億ユーロのつなぎ融資の決定が見込まれていたが、これは見送られた。◆By selling JT shares, the government expects to raise ¥500 billion to ¥600 billion to finance reconstruction from the Great East Japan Earthquake. JT（日本たばこ産業）株の売却で政府は、東日本大震災復興の財源に充てるため、5,000億円〜6,000億円の資金調達を見込んでいる。◆Domestic banks are stepping up overseas project financing as greater yields of interests are expected through such lending than loans to domestic borrowers. 国内銀行は、国内の借り手への融資に比べて海外の事業向け融資のほうが大きな金利収入を見込めるので、海外の事業向け融資（プロジェクト・ファイナンス）を強化している。◆Earthquake insurance payments resulting from the Great East Japan Earthquake are expected to reach ¥1.2 trillion. 東日本大震災による地震保険の保険金支払い額は、（業界全体で）1兆2,000億円に達する見込みだ。◆Expecting the economic expansion will continue, corporations are ac-

tively investing in plants and equipment. 景気拡大が続くと見た企業は、設備投資に積極的だ。◆French Finance Minister Christine Lagarde chosen as the new managing director of the IMF is expected to maintain an austere stance of calling on Greece to reform itself. IMFの新専務理事に選ばれたクリスティーヌ・ラガルド仏財務相は、ギリシャに改革を求める厳しい姿勢を貫くものと期待されている。◆In the case of the United States, increased public spending to boost the economy can hardly be expected. 米国の場合、財政出動による景気浮揚は期待しにくい。◆Japan Airlines Corp. is expected to fall short of its planned fund-raising target by about ￥50 billion due to lower stock price. 日本航空では、株価の下落で、当初計画の資金調達目標を約500億円下回る見通しだ。◆Long-term debts held by central and local governments are expected to further swell, thereby eroding confidence in governments bonds. 国と地方自治体が抱える長期債務は、さらに膨張して、国債の信用が失われるものと見られる。◆MUFG is expected to gain up to 20 percent stake in Morgan Stanley. 三菱UFJフィナンシャル・グループは、モルガン・スタンレーに最大20％出資する見込みだ。◆The amount of refunding bonds issued to redeem ordinary government bonds is expected to exceed ￥100 trillion. 普通国債償還のための借換え債の発行額が、100兆円を突破する見込みだ。◆The bank is mulling a further downward revision of its business results for fiscal 2011 that is expected to result in a massive loss. 同行は、巨額の損失が見込まれる2012年3月期決算［2011年度］の業績予想を、さらに下方修正する方向で検討している。◆The BOJ's policy meeting is expected to consider taking additional monetary easing steps. 日銀の政策決定会合では、追加の金融緩和策の実施を検討する見通しだ。◆The company is expected to continue earning a stable profit for the foreseeable future. 同社は、将来的にも安定した利益が見込める。◆The current official discount rate of 0.1 percent per annum is expected to be raised to between 0.35 percent and 0.5 percent. 年0.1％の現行の公定歩合は、0.35～0.5％程度に引き上げられる見通しだ。◆The mergers and acquisitions many major U.S. companies pursued failed to produce the expected synergy effect. 米国の大企業の多くが追求したM&Aは、予想したシナジー（相乗）効果を上げられなかった。◆The nation's three megabank groups expect a sharp increase in profits in their half-year consolidated business results through the end of September. 日本の3メガバンクは、9月連結中間決算で、大幅増益を見込んでいる。◆The security firm expects to book about ￥73 billion in losses related to its residential mortgage-backed securities business in the July-September quarter. 同証券会社は、7-9月期に住宅融資証券事業の関連損失として730億円を計上する見通しだ。◆This joint financing scheme carried out with the bank as the lead bank is expected to help make the presence of Japanese banks more strongly felt in global markets. 同行を主幹事銀行として実施されるこの協調融資事業は、国際市場で邦銀の存在感を高めることになりそうだ。◆To enhance the stimulating effect of the Fed's rate cuts, the Bush administration is expected to swiftly implement fiscal and tax stimulus measures, including tax cuts on investment designed to reinvigorate the stock market, in addition to the large-scale tax cut program that is under way. 米連邦準備制度理事会（FRB）の金利引下げの刺激効果を高めるため、ブッシュ政権には、現在実施中の大型減税プログラムに加え、株式市場を再活性化するための投資減税など、財政・税制面からの景気刺激策の速やかな実施が期待されている。◆When serious financial difficulties are expected, the Financial Services Agency is allowed to order a company to improve its operations in the early stages without releasing the information to the public. 深刻な財務悪化が予想される場合、金融庁は、非公表で早めに業務改善命令を発動することができる。

expectancy （名）期待、見込み、予想、予測数量、期待利益（expectation interest）、履行利益、将来財産権

expectancy table　予想表
expectancy theory of motivation　モチベーションの期待理論
life expectancy　平均寿命、平均余命
　（=expectancy of life, expectation of life）

expectation （名）期待、思惑、予想、予測、見通し、見込み、見積り、推定、期待値
below expectations　予想以下で、期待以下で
beyond expectations　予想以上に、期待以上に
business expectation　景気見通し
come ahead of expectations　予想［期首］を上回る
come below expectations　予想［期待］を下回る
come in at or below expectations　予想の線かそれを下回る水準になる
come on the high side of expectations　予測［市場予測］の平均を上回る
consumer expectations　消費者の期待、消費者信頼感指数
contrary to ［against all］ expectations　予想に反して
contrary to prevailing market expectations　大方の市場の期待を裏切って
default expectations　デフォルト率予測
downgrade the expectations　予想を引き下げる、予想を下方修正する
earnings expectations　収益予測
expectation effect　期待効果（金利の上昇に伴って貸し手が貸出を控える効果）
expectation horizon　期待視野、期待の範囲
expectation of life　見積り耐用年数、期待耐用年数
　（=expected life）
expectations for the year as a whole　通期予想、通期見通し、年間予想
expectations of lower interest rates　利下げの予想、金融緩和期待
fall short of expectations　期待にそむく、期待に添わない
growth expectations　成長率予測
in expectation of　～を予想して、～を見越して
in line with market expectations　市場の予想どおり、市場予測どおり
inflation ［inflationary］ expectations　インフレ期待、インフレ見通し、インフレ率に対する期待
interest rate expectations　金利予想、金利期待、金利見通し、利子率予想
investor expectations　投資家の予想、投資家期待
　（=expectations of investors）
market expectations　市場予想、市場予測
mean expectation of life　平均余命
　（=expectation of life）
meet ［live up to］ one's expectations　～の期待に添う
on expectations for　～への期待で
on the expectations that　～という期待で、～と予想して
optimistic expectations　楽観的な見通し
prevailing market expectations　市場の大方の期待
　（⇒market expectations）
recovery expectations　景気回復への期待、回収予想金額、回収可能金額
rise the expectations　予想を引き上げる、予想を上方修正する
the higher end of most expectations　予想範囲の上限
the lowest end of expectations　予想範囲の下限

◆Contrary to prevailing market expectations, the central bank decided not to further ease monetary policy. 市場の大方の期待を裏切って［期待に反して］、日銀は追加的な金融

緩和策を見送った。◆On expectations for the new financial steps, the Nikkei Stock Average recovered to the ￥9,000 mark. 今回の金融政策への期待で、日経平均株価は9,000円台に回復した。◆The government expressed its optimistic expectations of the current economic slump. 政府は、現在の景気後退について楽観的な見通しを示した。◆The yen surged to the higher end of the ￥98 level against the dollar in Tokyo markets due to yen-buying pressure fueled by expectations of the country's economic recovery. 東京為替市場は、日本の景気回復を期待した円買いが強まり、1ドル＝98円台［98円台の上限］まで円が急騰した。◆Through short selling, an investor borrows shares and sells them on the expectations that their price will fall, and can buy back them at a lower price. 空売りによって投資家は、株価が下がると予想して株を借りて売り、値下がりした時点でその株を買い戻すことができる。

expedite （動）促進する、早める、急ぐ、手早く片付ける、発送する、派遣する　（⇒safety net）
 ◆We must expedite efforts to rebuild a safety net to support the financial system. 金融システムを支える安全網の立直し策を急ぐ必要がある。

expenditure for servicing government bonds　国債費

expense （動）費用処理する、費用に計上する、費用として計上する
 amounts expensed as pension costs　年金原価として費用処理した額
 be expensed as written off　貸倒れ損失として費用処理する
 ◆Previously, we expensed life insurance benefits as plans were funded. これまで当社は、生命保険給付については、制度に拠出がなされたときに費用として計上していました。

expensive （形）割高感のある、割高の、費用のかかる、金のかかる、高価な
 the market remains expensive　相場は高止まりしている
 the stock［share］is too expensive　株価はかなり割高である［割高感が極めて強い］
 ◆A rating below investment grade makes it harder and more expensive to borrow money. 投資適格以下の格付けだと、資金の調達が難しくなるし、資金調達コストも高くつく。◆The biggest advantage for the bank in entering the venture will be to increase its customer base without having to open expensive new branch offices. 同行にとってこの新規事業への参入の最大の利点は、コストのかかる新店舗を開設するまでもなく、顧客基盤を拡大できることだ。

experience （動）経験する、体験する、感じる、味わう、（問題を）抱える
 experience above-average earnings growth rates　収益の伸び率が平均を上回る
 experience an economic downturn　景気悪化に見舞われる
 experience below-average earnings growth rates　収益の伸び率が平均を下回る
 experience fiscal crises　財政危機問題を抱える
 experience payment default　貸倒れになる
 experience profit taking　利食い売りを浴びる
 ◆Since the collapse of the bubble economy in the early 1990s, Japan has experienced several phases of economic revival. 1990年代はじめのバブル崩壊以降、日本は何度か景気回復局面を迎えた。◆Some European nations which are experiencing fiscal crises seem to rely on drops in their currencies' values as a means of underpinning their economies. 財政危機問題を抱えた欧州諸国の一部は、景気下支えの手段として通貨安を頼みにしているようだ。◆The instability of the pension system has repeatedly experienced increases in pension premiums and decreases in pension benefits. 年金制度が不安定なため、年金保険料の負担増と年金給付減が繰り返されてきた。

experience （名）（保険制度上の）経験（被保険者、保険種類などの損害の記録）、実績
 charge-off experience　貸倒償却実績
 claims experience　保険料請求実績
 consumer credit loss experience　消費者貸倒れ損失実績
 default experience　デフォルト実績
 experience adjustment　実績による修正
 experience rate　（保険の）経験的料率、経験料率
 experience rating　経験料率、経験料率方式（merit rating）、実績格付け方式
 experience table　経験表（mortality table）、経験死亡表
 investment experience　投資経験
 loss experience　貸倒れ損失実績
 mortality experience　死亡率
 operational experience　業績実績

expert （名）専門家、熟練者、有識者、玄人（くろうと）、エキスパート
 accounting expert　会計の専門家
 expert in finance　財政専門家
 expert system　専門家システム、エキスパート・システム　（=knowledge-based system）
 expert witness　鑑定人
 financing expert　金融の専門家
 market expert　市場専門家
 ◆In investigations into securities crime, prosecutorial authorities will have to enhance their investigative abilities by hiring financing and accounting experts. 証券犯罪の捜査では、金融や会計の専門家を採用して、検察当局が捜査力を高めていく必要がある。

expertise （名）専門知識、専門技術、専門家の報告書、ノウハウ　（=knowhow）
 advanced expertise　先端的ノウハウ、高度な専門知識［技術］
 expertise in credit and recovery operations　与信・回収業務のノウハウ
 financial expertise　金融ノウハウ
 product expertise　製品のノウハウ、製品知識、番組などの制作のノウハウ
 technical［technological］expertise　技術ノウハウ、技術的専門意見、専門技術、技術ノウハウ
 ◆The company has systemized its expertise in credit and recovery operations. 同社は、与信・回収業務のノウハウをシステム化している。◆The post of the Japanese finance minister has been filled in many cases by politicians who do not have much expertise in financial and fiscal matters. 日本の財務相には、多くの場合、金融や財政問題にあまり精通していない［詳しくない］政治家が就いている。◆The two prospective partners have extensive expertise in mergers and acquisitions, as well as the securitization of bad loans. 提携する予定の両社は、企業の合併・買収（M&A）や不良債権の証券化などに豊富なノウハウを持っている。

expire （動）（期間が）満了する、終了する、満期になる、（期限が）切れる、（時効が）成立する
 ◆The Financial Function Early Strengthening Law expired at the end of March 2008. 金融機能強化法は、2008年3月末に期限が切れた。

expiry date　満期時、満了日、権利行使期限、有効期限
 ◆The firm will extend the period during which its tender offer is valid to March 2 from the initial expiry date of Feb. 21. 同社は、同社の株式公開買付けの有効期限を、当初の有効期限である2月21日から3月2日まで延長する。

exploit （動）開発する、開拓する、利用する、活用する、搾取する、食い物にする　（名）功績、偉業、業績、手柄

exploit assets　資産を注ぎ込む
exploit buying factors　買い材料に反応する, 買い材料に便乗する, 買い材料を利用する
exploit demand　需要を利用する
exploit legal shortcomings　法の不備を利用する
exploit natural resources　天然資源を開発する
exploit overseas markets　海外市場を開拓[開発]する
exploit scale economies　規模の経済を活用する
exploit the high growth　成長の機会をつかむ
◆In the future also, new types of illegal practices that exploit legal loopholes will emerge in securities markets. 今後も, 証券市場では, 法の抜け穴を狙う不正取引の手法が新たに現れるものと思われる。◆Margin trading was used in a corporate takeover by exploiting legal shortcomings. 法の不備を利用して, 企業買収に信用取引が使われた。◆One of the aims for the three banks to merge into the Mizuho Financial Group was to survive the global competition by exploiting the banks' combined strength. 3行がみずほフィナンシャルグループに合併する目的(狙い)の一つに, 3行の統合力を駆使して国際競争に勝ち抜くことがあった。◆Speculators exploited these buying factors, pushing oil prices up further. 投機筋がこれらの買い材料に反応して[投機筋がこれらの買い材料を利用して], 原油価格の高騰[原油高]を増幅している。

explore　(動)開発する, 掘り起こす, 研究する, 調査する, 調べてみる, 探検する, 踏査する, 探査する, 詮索する, 探る
　explore a possibility　可能性を探る
　explore a question[problem]　問題を調査する, 問題を検討する
　jointly explore　共同開発する
　　(＝explore jointly, jointly develop)
　◆Nonlife insurers are exploring new types of insurance demand and offering convenient and easy means of buying policies. 損保各社は, 新たな保険需要を掘り起こして, いつでも, どこでも簡単に保険に加入できるサービスを提供している。

explosive　(形)爆発的な, 爆発性の, 爆発寸前の, 急激な, 一触即発の, 非常に危険な, 論議を呼ぶ, 強大な
　explosive factor　火種, 危険な要因
　explosive growth　急激な発展, 爆発的な成長, 急成長, 爆発的拡大, 急増, 激増
　explosive increase　爆発的な増加, 急増, 激増
　explosive issue　論議を呼ぶ問題, 議論の紛糾する問題
　◆It is difficult to predict if new explosive factors emerge to plunge the financial market into further turmoil. 金融市場をさらに混乱に陥れる新しい火種があるのかどうか, 予測するのは難しい。

export　(名)輸出, 輸出品, 輸出製品, 供給
　approval of export license　輸出承認
　bounty for export　輸出助成金, 輸出補助金, 輸出奨励金
　　(＝export bounty)
　capital export　資本輸出, 資本供給, 資金供給
　capital goods export　資本財の輸出
　debt/export ratio　輸出総額に対する対外債務の比率
　deferred payment export　延べ払い輸出　(＝export by the deferred payment method, export on a deferred payment basis)
　documentary export bill　輸出荷為替
　export cost[proceeds] insurance　輸出代金保険
　export draft　輸出手形
　export duties　輸出関税
　export exchange　輸出為替
　export financing[finance]　輸出金融

　export financing insurance　輸出金融保険
　export incentive　輸出奨励手段, 輸出刺激, 輸出誘因
　export insurance　輸出保険
　export loan　輸出貸付け, 輸出融資
　export of capital　資本輸出
　export prepayment　輸出前受け金
　export proceeds　輸出代金, 輸出収入, 輸出売上高
　export profitability　輸出採算
　export quotation　輸出相場
　export-related stock　輸出関連株
　　(＝export stock)
　export subsidy　輸出補助金, 輸出助成金, 輸出奨励金
　export trade bill　輸出貿易手形
　export usance bill　期限付き輸出手形
　export without(foreign) exchange　無為替輸出
　◆Japan's exports, which had been supporting the business boom, lost momentum. 景気を支えてきた日本の輸出が, 失速した。◆Japan's exports will stagnate and corporate performance will suffer if the yen remains in the historically high ¥75-range against the dollar. 円相場が1ドル＝75円台の史上最高値が続けば, 日本の輸出は低迷し, 企業の業績は悪化する。◆The FRB's decision to pump $600 billion into the U.S. economy was criticized as weakening the dollar at the expense of other countries' exports. 米経済へ6,000億ドルの資金を投入する米連邦準備制度理事会(FRB)の決定は, 他国の輸出を犠牲にしたドル安誘導であると非難された。◆The revaluation of the Chinese currency may reduce Japan's exports to China. 中国の人民元切上げで, 日本の対中輸出が減少する恐れがある。

export advance　輸出資金前貸し, 輸出前貸し金融
　export advance bill　輸出前貸し手形
　export advance system　輸出前貸し制度

export bill　輸出手形
　documentary export bill　輸出荷為替
　export bill insurance　輸出手形保険

export credit　輸出金融(export financing), 輸出信用, 輸出信用状(export letter of credit)
　export credit agency　輸出信用機関
　export credit financing　輸出信用ファイナンス
　export credit guarantee　輸出信用保証
　export credit insurance　輸出信用保険
　Export Credits Guarantee Department　英輸出信用保証庁
　offer export credit facility　輸出信用を供与する
　use export credit　輸出信用を利用する

export drive　輸出ドライブ, 輸出攻勢, 輸出競争力, 輸出拡大圧力, 輸出促進策
　◆The rapid surge in the yen's value could deal a blow to Japan's export drive and export-related businesses. 急激な円高は, 日本の輸出競争力の低下や輸出関連企業の業績悪化をもたらす可能性がある。

export-driven　(形)輸出主導の, 輸出主導型の
　　(＝export-led)
　export-driven economies　輸出主導型経済
　export-driven growth　輸出主導の成長[経済成長], 外需主導の成長
　◆A recovery will be export-driven, dependent on U.S. growth and the yen's depreciation, instead of being led by increased domestic consumption and capital investment. 今後の景気回復は, アメリカ経済の好転や円安を背景にした輸出主導型の回復で, 国内の個人消費や設備投資の伸びがその牽引役となるわけではない。

export-driven economic upturn　輸出主導の景気回復

◆A depreciation of the dollar may stimulate external demand and ignite an export-driven economic upturn. ドル安は、外需を喚起して、輸出主導の景気回復につながる可能性がある。

export growth　輸出の伸び
　　◆Export growth has slowed due to the high value of the yen and the weakness of economies overseas. 円高と海外経済の減速で、輸出の伸びが鈍った。

export-import　（形）輸出入の
　　export-import bank　輸出入銀行, 輸銀
　　export-import bank guaranteed loan　輸銀保証付きローン
　　Export-Import Bank of the United States　合衆国輸出入銀行, アメリカ輸出入銀行, EX-IM［EXIM］（=EXIM Bank［EX-IM Bank, Eximbank］）
　　export-import credit company　輸出入金融会社
　　export-import financing　輸出入金融

export-led　（形）輸出主導の, 輸出主導型の（=export-driven）
　　export-led growth　輸出主導の成長, 輸出主導の景気拡大, 外需主導の経済成長, 輸出主導型［先行型］成長, 輸出リード型成長
　　export-led industrialization　輸出主導工業化

export-led economic recovery　輸出頼みの景気回復, 輸出主導［輸出主導型］の景気回復
　　◆We must avoid hindering the export-led economic recovery, speeding up deflation and increasing bad loans, which can be brought about by falling stock prices and the weakening dollar. 株安とドル安がもたらす可能性がある輸出頼みの景気回復の挫折、デフレ加速、不良債権の拡大を、われわれは避けなければならない。

export-led recovery　輸出主導の景気回復, 輸出主導型の景気［業績］回復
　　◆The yen's appreciation against the dollar hurts the nation's export-led recovery. 円高・ドル安は、日本の輸出主導の景気回復に悪影響を与える。

export market　輸出市場
　　◆Japan's economic growth is driven by exports, but it will have to vie for export markets with emerging economies. 日本の経済成長の原動力は輸出だが、今後は新興国と輸出市場の争奪戦になろう。

export-oriented　（形）輸出志向の, 輸出中心の, 輸出重視の, 輸出主導型の

export-oriented business　輸出指向型企業, 輸出企業
　　◆If the yen's value against the dollar appreciates too rapidly, export-oriented businesses will suffer. 急激な円高・ドル安が進行すると、輸出企業が打撃を受ける。

export-oriented companies　輸出企業, 輸出産業, 輸出指向型企業
　　◆The yen's appreciation puts pressure on the earnings of export-oriented companies. 円高は、輸出企業の収益を圧迫する。

export-oriented firms　輸出志向企業, 輸出型企業, 輸出企業
　　（=export-oriented businesses［companies］）
　　◆The yen has risen to about ￥90 per U.S. dollar, drastically reducing the profits of export-oriented firms. 円高が1ドル=90円台前後まで進み、輸出企業の利益は大幅に減少した。

exporter　（名）輸出業者, 輸出企業
　　◆Due to the growing strength of the yen, even if exporters' sales grow, their profits will not keep pace. 円高進行で、輸出企業の売上が増えても、利益は伸び悩むようだ。

expose　（動）（危険に）さらす, 暴露する, 公然と売り出す, 陳列する, 展示する, 摘発する, すっぱ抜く, 経験させる
　　be exposed to credit risk　信用リスクを負う, 与信リスクを負う, 信用リスクにさらされる

be exposed to interest rate risk　金利リスクにさらされる
be exposed to losses　損失を被る
　　◆At the latest G-20 meeting, diverging opinions among member countries were exposed over expanding the lending capacity of the IMF. 今回のG20（財務相・中央銀行総裁）会議では、国際通貨基金（IMF）が融資できる資金規模の拡大をめぐって、加盟国の間で意見の食い違いが表面化した。◆The company's single-minded profit-driven corporate culture has been exposed. もっぱら利益追求の同社の企業体質が、浮き彫りになった。◆The financial authorities neglected to expose the bank's lax management for a long time. 金融当局は、同行のずさんな経営体制を長いこと放置していた。

exposure　（名）危険などにさらされること, 影響されること, 損失の危機に瀕していること, （商品の）陳列, （テレビや新聞に）取り上げられること, リスク危険度, 投資, 融資, リスク資産総額, 融資総額, 与信残高, 債権, 債権額, 暴露, 摘発, 発覚, 露顕, 露出, エクスポージャー
　　（⇒foreign currency exchange contract, initial margin）
　　control exposure to credit risk　信用リスクを管理する
　　country exposure　カントリー・リスク, 国別債権額
　　credit exposure　与信リスク, 信用リスク
　　credit risk exposure　信用リスク残高
　　currency exposure　為替リスク, 通貨リスク
　　economic exposure　経済リスク
　　Exposure Draft　米財務会計基準審議会（FASB）などの討議資料, 公開草案, ED
　　exposure limit　与信枠
　　exposure management　エクスポージャー管理
　　exposure to currencies　為替リスク
　　exposure to highly leveraged transactions　負債比率の高い取引（HLT）への融資, HLT融資
　　external exposure　対外債権残高
　　financial exposure　資金負担, 金融リスク
　　forward exposure　先物債権額
　　have a large exposure to　～の運用比率が高い, ～リスクが高い
　　hedge the exposure　リスクをヘッジする
　　interest exposure　金利リスク, 金利変動リスク, 金利エクスポージャー
　　investment exposure　投資リスク, 投資
　　net exposure　純債権額, 純持ち高, ネット・エクスポージャー
　　problem exposures　不良債権
　　real estate exposure　不動産投資, 不動産融資
　　reduce exposure to the currency effects　為替リスクを軽減する［減らす］
　　reduce exposure to the risk of loss　損失リスクを減らす, 損失リスクを軽減する
　　reduce the exposure to bonds　債券の組入れ比率を引き下げる
　　risk exposure　リスク, リスク・エクスポージャー
　　the exposure of personal information　個人情報の暴露
　　◆Japanese financial institutions have exposures to the investment bank of more than ￥400 billion. 日本の金融機関が保有する同投資銀行向け債権額は、4,000億円を超えている。◆The increased ownership will raise the bank's risk exposure to the company, whose business environment is severe. 持ち株比率の引上げで、企業環境（経営環境）が厳しい同社に対する同行のリスク・エクスポージャーは今後増大するものと思われる。

exposure to changes in currency exchange rates　為替相場の変動によるリスク
　　◆To manage our exposure to changes in currency exchange rates, we enter into foreign currency exchange contracts. 為

替相場の変動によるリスクを管理するため、当社は外国為替予約を締結しています。

exposure to changes in interest rates　金利変動リスク　（=exposure to interest rates）
◆We enter into interest rate swap agreements to manage our exposure to changes in interest rates. 金利変動リスクに対処するため、当社は金利スワップ契約を結んでいる。

exposure to credit risk　信用リスク
（=credit risk）
◆The firm controls its exposure to credit risk through credit approvals, credit limits and monitoring procedures. 同社は、信用供与承認や信用限度、監視手続きを通じて信用リスクを管理している。

extend　(動) (援助の手を) 差し伸べる、(援助などを) 与える [行う]、(信用やローンなどを) 供与する、提供する、時間を延長する、延期する、延ばす、拡大する、拡張する、広げる、言葉や祝辞などを述べる
　extend a financial assistance　金融支援を行う
　extend a marketing period　販売期間を延長する
　extend credit　信用を供与する
　extend yen loans as part of Japan's ODA　日本の政府開発援助として円借款を供与する
　extended coverage endorsement　拡張担保特約
　extended fund facility　拡大信用供与制度

◆Banks and life insurers have extended about ¥4 trillion in loans to TEPCO. 銀行や生命保険会社は、東電にこれまで約4兆円を融資している。◆Gold extended its rally to a record above $1,900 an ounce amid increased uncertainties over the U.S. and European economic outlook on the Comex in New York. ニューヨーク商品取引所では、米欧景気見通しへの懸念 [米欧経済の先行き不透明感] の高まりを受け [懸念の高まりから]、金価格が急騰して、1トロイ・オンス＝1,900ドルを史上初めて突破した。◆In June 2009 prior to Japan Airlines' failure, a ¥67 billion public financing package was extended with a government-backed guarantee to JAL. 日本航空破たん前の2009年6月、日航に対して政府保証付きで670億円の公的融資が行われた [公的融資策が実施された]。◆In this cofinancing scheme, the bank will extend a total of about ¥8.5 billion over a 20-year loan period. この協調融資事業で、同行は貸出期間20年で計85億円を融資する。◆The Bank of Tokyo-Mitsubishi UFJ will work together with foreign banks to extend 117 million Canadian dollars in joint loans to a mega solar power plant construction. 三菱東京UFJ銀行は、外銀数行の主幹事銀行として、カナダの大型太陽光発電所 (メガソーラー) 建設事業に1億1,700万カナダ・ドルを協調融資する。◆The bank plans to provide the money by transferring ¥100 billion in subordinated loans, which it has already extended to the insurer, to the insurer's foundation fund. 同行は、すでに供与している劣後ローン1,000億円をこの保険会社の基金に振り替えて、その資金を提供する方針だ。◆The bank's likelihood of collecting loans extended to its major corporate borrowers has worsened. 同行の大口融資先 [融資先企業] に対する債権の回収見通しが、悪化した。◆The financial assistance will be extended by combining a waiver of debt and a debt-for-equity swap. 金融支援は、債権放棄とデット・エクイティ・スワップ (債務の株式化) を組み合わせて行われる。◆The government will cease extending new yen loans to China in fiscal 2008. 政府は、2008年度から対中円借款の新規供与を終了する方針だ。◆The revitalization plan will be carried out chiefly using ¥400 billion in financial assistance to be extended by the firm's creditor banks. 再生計画は、主に同社の取引銀行が行う金融支援総額4,000億円を使って実施される。◆The tax breaks on capital gains from stock sales and on dividend income will be extended by one year. 株式譲渡益 [株式売却益] と受取配当金の税率軽減措置の期間が、1年延長される。◆Tokyo stocks extended their winning streak to a third day with the key Nikkei index finishing above the 9,000 line. 東京の株価 [東京株式市場の株価] は、3日連続で値上がりし、日経平均株価 (225種) の終値は9,000円台を上回った。◆Under the firm's rehabilitation plan approved by the district court, financial institutions will waive 87.5 percent of the unsecured loans they extend to the firm. 地方裁判所が認可した同社の更生計画では、金融機関が、同社に行った無担保融資 [同社に対する無担保債権] の87.5％を放棄することになっている。

extend a special loan　特別融資を実施する、特融を実施する
◆The Bank of Japan decided to extend a special loan to Namihaya Bank after the second-tier regional bank was declared insolvent. 日本銀行は、第二地方銀行の「なみはや銀行」が破たん認定を受けた後、同行に対して特別融資 [特融] を実施することを決めた。

extend debt maturities　債務の償還期限を延長する
◆The company took advantage of favorable levels of interest rates to extend debt maturities by refinancing a substantial amount of long-term debt. 同社は、有利な金利水準を利用して、長期負債の相当額を借り換えて債務の償還期限を延長した。

extend emergency loans　緊急融資を行う、緊急に資金を提供する
◆The IMF and the EU have worked out a policy of extending emergency loans to Greece. 国際通貨基金 (IMF) と欧州連合 (EU) は、ギリシャに緊急融資を行う方針を打ち出した。

extend funds　資金を拠出する、資金を提供する
◆For nearly 10 years, Japan has extended funds for programs aimed at making Russia nuclear-free. 10年近く、日本はこれまでロシアの非核化支援事業に資金を拠出してきた。

extend loans　融資する、資金を供与する
（⇒corporate rehabilitation）
　decide to continue extending loans　融資継続を決める
　decline to extend loans　融資を拒否する
　extend loans to one's member firms　会員企業に融資する
　extend welfare loans　福祉資金を供与する
　jointly extend loans　協調融資する

◆Entrusted or instructed by the South Korean government, private banks jointly extended loans to the company. 韓国政府の委託や指示を受けて、民間銀行が同社に協調融資した。◆If the group's cash-flow situation deteriorates further, it may see its creditor banks declining to extend loans. 同グループの資金繰りがさらに悪化すれば、取引銀行が融資を拒否する可能性もある。◆More than half of the public welfare loans extended to widows and single mothers are not collected. 母子家庭や寡婦に供与されている福祉資金の5割以上が、回収されていない。◆Some of huge amounts in loans extended to JAL by the DBJ have been guaranteed by the government. 日本政策投資銀行が日航に行った巨額融資 [貸付け] の一部は、政府が保証している。◆The bank decided to continue extending loans to the company despite its executives knowing the company was on the ropes. この会社の経営が悪化しているのを経営陣が知りながら、同行は同社への融資継続を決めた。◆The bank extended loans to its member firms, which in turn accepted requests to boost the bank's capital. 同行が会員企業に融資する一方、会員企業は同行の増資要請に応じていた。◆The DBJ and private financial institutions extended loans worth a total of ¥100 billion to JAL in June 2009 though JAL was already in dire financial straits. 日本政策投資銀行と民間金融機関は、日航の経営がすでに悪化していたものの、2009年6月に同社に対して総額1,000億円を融資した。◆The government will provide funds and extend loans to TEPCO through a newly established organization to handle the compensation issue due to the nuclear disaster. 今後は、原発事故による損害賠償問題を扱うために新設された組織 (原子力損害賠償支援機構) を通じて、国が東電に出資し

たり融資したりする。◆The IMF extends to countries with relatively healthier public finances one- to two-year loans of up to 1,000 percent of their contribution to the IMF without strict conditions. IMF（国際通貨基金）は、財政が比較的健全な国に対して、期間1〜2年の資金を厳しい条件なしでIMFに出資している額（クォータ）の最大10倍まで融資している。◆The loan was the first of its kind to be extended with a business model patent as collateral. 今回の融資は、ビジネス・モデル特許を担保にした融資としては初めてだ。◆The public loan was extended to JAL in June 2009 by the entirely state-funded Development Bank of Japan. この公的融資は、国が100%出資している日本政策投資銀行が、2009年6月に行った。◆The public welfare loans are extended to widows and single mothers to help them become economically independent by financing spending for education, living costs, housing costs and funds to start small businesses. 福祉資金は、母子家庭や寡婦に対して教育費や生活費、住宅費、小規模事業の開始資金などを貸し付けて、その経済的自立を助けるために供与されている。◆The tasks of safety management specialists in the field of financial services are essentially to whistle-blow and stop extending risky loans. 金融サービス分野での安全管理専門家の仕事は、基本的に高リスク融資に待ったをかけてそれを止めさせることだ。◆Under the new financing scheme, the IMF will extend to financially strapped countries loans of up to 500 percent of their contribution to the IMF. 新融資制度では、財政の資金繰りが苦しく［厳しく］なった国に対して、その国がIMF（国際通貨基金）に出資している額の最大5倍までIMFが融資する。

extend morning trading hours 午前の取引時間を延長する
　◆The Tokyo Stock Exchange and four other exchanges extended their morning trading hours by 30 minutes to 11:30 a.m. 東証など5証券取引所が、午前の取引時間を11時半まで30分間延長した。

extend new loans 新規融資する、新規融資を行う
　◆During the period of business suspension, the company is not allowed to extend new loans, solicit new customers or call in loans. 業務停止期間中、同社は新規の融資や新規顧客の勧誘、貸出の回収などの業務はできない。◆Overly radical methods for accelerating the disposal of bad loans would panic the banking sector and the financial market, possibly driving banks to shy away from extending new loans and even to call in existing loans. 不良債権処理を加速するための余りにも強硬な手法は、銀行や金融市場をおびえさせ、貸し渋りや貸しはがしにつながることにもなる。

extend unsecured loans 無担保融資する、無担保融資を行う
　◆The government guaranteed up to 80 percent of ￥67 billion in unsecured loans extended to JAL by the DBJ through the Japan Finance Corporation. 日本政策投資銀行が日航に貸し付けた無担保融資670億円の最大8割については、日本政策金融公庫を通じて政府が保証している。

extend yen loans 円借款を供与する
　◆Yen loans extended now as part of Japan's ODA are untied in principle, with the source of development materials and equipment to be procured not defined. 日本の政府開発援助（ODA）として供与されている円借款は現在、ひも付きでない「アンタイド」援助が原則で、開発物資の調達先を限定していない。

extendable swap エクステンダブル・スワップ
extended （形）延ばした、延長した、拡張した、拡大した、長期にわたる
　extended arrangement［facility］ （IMFの）拡大信用供与措置
　extended bond 償還延期公債
　extended cover（clause） 延長担保（約款）
　extended credit 長期金融、延長信用状（extended letter of credit）
　extended fund facility 拡大信用供与
　Extended Fund Facility （IMFの）拡大信用供与制度、EFF
　extended insurance 継続保険
　extended medical payment insurance 拡張医療費保険
　extended payment 延べ払い
　extended payment privilege 長期返済の恩恵
　extended policy 延長保険契約
　extended slump in the domestic market 国内株式市場の長期低迷
　extended term 延長期限、期間の延長
　extended term insurance 延長保険、延長定期保険
　◆The major securities house attributed the poor earnings to sharp drops in brokerage fees and trading profits amid the extended slump in the domestic stock market. この大手証券会社は、減益の要因として、国内株式市場の長期低迷による株売買手数料と売買益の大幅減を挙げた。

extended coverage 拡張担保、拡張危険担保、拡張危険
　extended coverage endorsement 拡張担保［拡張危険担保］裏書き、拡張担保［拡張危険担保］約款
　extended coverage insurance 拡張危険保険

extendible maturity 延長可能満期
extension （名）拡大、拡張、延長、機能拡張、拡張工事、期間延長、付属電話機、内線、範囲、程度
　double extension 二重計算
　extension of a draft 手形期日の延期
　extension of business 事業拡張、業務拡張
　extension of coverage 担保範囲の拡張
　extension of credit 信用供与、信用の拡大
　extension of employment 雇用延長
　extension of loan 返済延期
　extension of market 販路拡張
　extension of payment 支払い猶予（ゆうよ）
　extension of the agreement 契約の延長
　extension of time 支払い猶予
　extension risk 期間延長リスク
　reserve for business extension 事業拡張積立金
　◆By the TSE's extension of the morning trade session to 11:30 a.m., investors will be able to trade Japanese stocks more easily while keeping an eye on economic trends in Asian markets. 東証が午前11時30分まで午前の取引時間を延長したことによって、投資家は今後、アジア市場の経済動向を見ながら日本株の取引をすることが容易になる。◆Even a 30-minute extension of morning trading hours will increase the volume of trading by 6 percent. 午前の取引時間を30分延長しただけでも、売買高は6%増える見込みだ。

extensive （形）大量の、豊富な、広範な、広範囲の、広範囲にわたる、大規模な、大がかりな
　extensive branch networks 広範な支店網
　extensive distribution network 広範な流通網、広範な支店網
　extensive expertise 豊富なノウハウ
　extensive investment 拡張投資
　extensive order 大量注文
　for an extensive period 長期間
　lead to extensive leveraging of corporate balance sheets 企業の負債比率を高める
　◆The two prospective partners have extensive expertise in mergers and acquisitions, as well as the securitization of bad loans. 提携する予定の両社は、企業の合併・買収（M&A）や不良債権の証券化などに豊富なノウハウを持っている。◆Those housewives who have failed to switch to the national pension plan and have not paid premiums for an extensive pe-

riod may receive a pittance or nothing at all. 国民年金への切替えをせず、保険料を長期間払っていない主婦は、低年金や無年金になる可能性がある。

extent （名）程度,範囲,規模,広さ,大きさ,限度,限界,差押え礼状
 the extent of contractual relationship　契約関係の限度
 the extent of disclosure　開示の範囲
 the extent of reduction in prices　物価の下げ幅（⇒widen）
 the extent of test　調査範囲
 the extent of the contract　契約の範囲
 the extent of the market　市場範囲
 the nature, extent and terms of financial products　金融商品の性質、範囲と条件
 to a great [large] extent　大いに
 to some extent　ある程度まで
 to the extent of　〜の範囲[限界]まで
 to the extent that　〜するほど、〜という点で
 to the fullest [maximum] extent　最大限に
 ◆The extent of Lehman's massive losses and write-downs due to the subprime mortgage crisis became evident. サブプライム・ローン（米低所得者向け住宅融資）問題に伴うリーマンの巨額の損失と評価損の規模が、明らかになった。◆The slowdown of Toyota indicates the disastrous extent of the worldwide financial crisis. トヨタの減速[失速]は、世界的な金融危機[世界金融危機]の猛威を物語っている。◆These moves of the two airlines show the extent of the crisis in the current business environment. 両航空会社のこれらの動きは、現在の経営環境の危機的状況の大きさを示している。

external （名）外部の,対外的な,国外の
 external accounts　対外収支,非居住者勘定
 external assets　対外資産,対外資産残高
 external audit　外部監査　（=outside audit）
 external balance　対外均衡,国際均衡,対外収支
 external borrowing　対外借入れ
 external capital　外部資本
 external convertibility　対外交換性
 external debt　対外債務,外部負債　（=foreign debt）
 external deficit　国際収支の赤字
 external demand　海外需要,外需,純輸出
 external diseconomies　外部不経済
 external distribution　社外分配
 external economies　外部経済
 external equilibrium　対外均衡
 external failure costs　外部失敗コスト
 external financing　外部調達資金,外部資金の調達,外部金融　（=external funding; ⇒cash requirements）
 external growth　外部的成長,外部的成長率（合併や買収、合弁事業などによる企業の成長）
 external indebtedness　対外債務
 external labor market　外部労働市場
 external liabilities　対外債務,外部負債,社外負債
 external loan　対外債権,外債
 external monetary reserves　外貨準備
 external payment balance　国際収支
 external position　対外短期ポジション,対外ポジション,国の対外支払い能力を示す指標
 external pressure　外圧　（=foreign pressure）
 external reserves　対外準備,外貨準備
 external surplus　国際収支の黒字
 external trade　外国貿易,対外貿易
 external transaction　海外取引

 external value of money　貨幣の対外価値
external bond　外債,外国債　（=foreign bond）
 out-to-in [out to in] external bond　外(そと)-内(うち)外債
 out-to-out [out to out] external bond　外-外外債
external bond financing　外債発行による資金調達
 ◆Japanese companies can hedge exchange risks and improve their business image abroad through external bond financing. 日本企業は、外債発行による資金調達で、為替リスクを回避するとともに海外での企業イメージアップを図ることができる。
external funds　外部資金,外部調達資金
 ◆External funds required to meet the additional cash requirements in 2011 will be obtained by offering debt securities in the market. 2011年度内に発生する追加資金必要額を賄(まかな)うための外部調達資金は、市場で債券を募集発行して調達する予定です。
externalization　（名）取引所取引,取引所経由の株式売買取引
extra　（形）特別の,臨時の,余分の,追加の,割増の,規格外の,特大の
 extra capital　資本の上積み,追加資本
 extra charge　特別料金,割増料金,付帯費用,差額
 extra cost　超過コスト
 extra discount　特別割引
 extra dividend　特別配当
 extra economic factor　経済外的要因
 extra freight　割増運賃
 extra income　追加所得,副収入
 extra-long-terms bond　特別長期社債
 extra pay　臨時給与
 extra premium　割増保険料
 extra size　特大サイズ
 installment with extra payment at bonus time　ボーナス併用払い
 pay extra charges　特別料金を支払う,割増料金を支払う
 provide extra money [cash]　追加のお金を出す
extra capital　追加資本,資本の上積み,資本の積み増し（=additional capital, capital surcharge）
 ◆According to the Financial Stability Board, 28 banks viewed as global systemically important financial institutions（G-SIFIs）will be subject to a new global rule requiring them to hold extra capital to prevent future financial crises. 金融安定化理事会（FSB）によると、金融システム上重要な国際金融機関（G-SIFIs）と考えられる世界の28行が、金融危機の再発を防止するため、資本の上積みを求める新国際基準[新国際金融規制]の対象になる。◆Global major financial institutions have been forced to hold extra capital since the financial meltdown following the 2008 bankruptcy of Lehman Brothers Holdings Inc. 米国の投資銀行リーマン・ブラザーズが2008年に経営破たんして生じた金融危機以来、世界の主要金融機関は、資本[自己資本]の上積み[積み増し]を迫られている。◆The three Japanese top banks will face the FSB's new international rule requiring them to hold extra capital to prevent future financial crises. 日本の3メガ銀行も、金融危機の再発を防ぐため、資本[自己資本]の上積みを求める金融安定化理事会（FSB）の新国際基準の対象になると見られる。
extra capital charge　追加資本費用,資本費用[資本コスト]の追加,資本[自己資本]の上積み[積み増し]
 ◆The Financial Stability Board will impose a progressive extra capital charge of 1 percent to 2.5 percent on risk-adjusted assets held by G-SIFIs. G20（主要20か国・地域）の金融当局で構成する金融安定化理事会（FSB）は、国際金融システムにとって重要な金融機関（G-SIFIs）が保有するリスク調整後資産に、1〜2.5％の資本[自己資本]の上積みを段階的に

課すことになった。
extramarket transaction 市場外取引
extraordinary （形）特別の，臨時の，異常な
  extraordinary board meeting 臨時取締役会
    （=extraordinary meeting of the board of directors）
  extraordinary board of directors 臨時取締役会
  extraordinary budget 特別予算
  extraordinary disbursement 臨時支出，臨時歳出
  extraordinary dividend 特別配当
  extraordinary dividend payments 特別配当支払い
  extraordinary gains or losses 特別損益
  extraordinary profit 特別利益（保有株式の売却やメーカーの工場売却による利益）
  extraordinary reserve 特別準備
  extraordinary resolution 特別決議
  extraordinary revenue 臨時収入，臨時歳入
extraordinary loss 特別損失，異常損失，経常外損失
  （=special loss）
◆The company remained in the red for the fiscal year ended March 31, 2011 due to appraisal losses on its stockholdings and other extraordinary losses stemming from recalls of some products. 資生堂の2002年3月期決算は、保有株式の含み損（評価損）や一部商品の回収による特別損失などで赤字にとどまった。
extraordinary meeting 臨時総会
  （アメリカではspecial meetingという。⇒board）
  extraordinary general meeting 臨時株主総会
    （=extraordinary meeting of shareholders）
  extraordinary shareholders meeting 臨時株主総会
extraordinary meeting of shareholders 臨時株主総会 （=extraordinary general meeting, special meeting of shareholders, special meeting of stockholders: 原則として年1回開く定時株主総会とは別に、定款変更など株主総会決議が必要な重要事項の決定を行うときに開く）
◆At an extraordinary meeting of shareholders, the shareholders of Kanebo Ltd. endorsed a plan to change the company's auditing house. 臨時株主総会で、（繊維メーカーの）カネボウの株主は、同社の監査法人変更案を承認した。
extraordinary Policy Board meeting （日銀の）臨時の金融政策決定会合
◆The Bank of Japan decided to take new steps for further quantitative monetary easing at an extraordinary Policy Board meeting. 日銀は、臨時の金融政策決定会合で、追加の量的金融緩和策を新たに実施することを決めた。
extraordinary step 異例の措置
◆In the subprime crisis, the U.S. Federal Reserve Board had to take the extraordinary step of providing an emergency loan not to a commercial bank but to an investment bank. サブプライム問題で、米国の中央銀行の連邦準備制度理事会（FRB）は、緊急融資を銀行［商業銀行］ではなく証券会社［投資銀行］に対して行う異例の措置を取らざるを得なかった。
eye （動）注目する，着目する，計画する，もくろむ，視野に入れる，検討する，考慮する，見込む，狙う，関心を示す，希望する
  eye a management integration 経営統合を計画する
  eye post as ～の地位を狙う
  eye tie-up with との提携を計画する［もくろむ］
◆Sumitomo Mitsui Financial Group Inc. and Daiwa Securities Group Inc. are eyeing a management integration and full merger in the future. 三井住友フィナンシャルグループと大和証券グループは、両グループの将来の経営統合と完全統合を計画している。◆The company eyes its even larger group operating loss for the year to March 2012. 同社は、2012年3月期の連結決算で営業赤字の一層の拡大を見込んでいる。

eye （名）目，視力，視覚，注視，注目，注意，観察，見解，意見，判断，判断能力，見分ける力，鑑識眼，鑑識力，探偵，中心，中央部
  at［in］the eye of the storm 論争の的になっている，論争の真っただ中にあって
  cast［run］one's eye over ～にざっと目を通す
  catch a person's eye 人の注意［注目］を引く，人の目に留まる，人と視線を合わせる
  do a person in the eye 人からだまし取る，人をだます
  Eyes Only 極秘，極秘の，マル秘
  give an eye to ～に注目する，～の世話をする
  have an eye on［upon］ ～を監視する，注意深く見守る，～を欲しがる，～に目を付ける
  have an eye to ～を目標とする，～を目当てにする，～に目を付けている，～を慎重に考える
  keep［have］an eye on［upon］ ～を見張る，～を監視する，～から目を離さない，～に気を付けている，～を注意深く見守る
  （=keep an eye out［open］for）
  one in the eye for ～にとって大きな痛手［失望］，～にとって大きな打撃
◆Investors have to keep an eye on market trends. 投資家は、市場動向を注意深く見守る必要がある。◆The Financial Services Agency introduced the early warning system for life insurers to keep an eye on their business operations, including profit performance, safety and cancellation of contracts. 金融庁は、生保向けの早期警戒制度を導入して、収益性や安全性、解約の状況など生命保険会社の経営を監視している。

F

fabricate （動）組み立てる，製作する，製造する，生産する，加工する，ねつ造する，偽造する，でっち上げる，改ざんする
  fabricated data 改ざんされたデータ，データの改ざん
  fabricated earnings 架空収益
  fabricated expenses 架空経費
fabricated credit card 偽造されたクレジット・カード，クレジット・カードの偽造
◆Fabricated credit cards have been illegally used at electrical appliances discount stores and cash voucher shops in Japan after the security breach was revealed in the United States. 米国で不正侵入が明らかになった後、偽造されたクレジット・カードが日本の家電量販店や金券ショップなどで不正に使用されている。
fabricated results 粉飾決算，業績改ざん
◆The president of the company ordered fabricated results. 同社の社長が、粉飾決算を指示した。
face （動）～に直面する，～に見舞われる，～を仕掛けられる，～の対象になる，～を抱える，～に向かう，～に立ち向かう，～に耐える，～を直視する
  （⇒credit problem, flat-lined, woes）
  be faced with difficult decisions 難しい判断を迫られる
  be faced with serious financial problems 深刻な金融問題に直面する
  face a cash flow crisis 資金繰りが苦しくなる
  face a loss 損失を抱える
  face a recession 景気後退に直面する
  face a serious crisis 重大な危機に瀕している
  face a sharp drop in corporate results 企業業績が急激に悪化する
  face a tough business environment 厳しい経営環境に直面する
  face competitive threats 競争圧力に直面する，競争圧力にさらされる，競争力で後れをとる

face interest rate risk　金利リスクに直面する
face many challenges　多くの困難な課題に直面する
face massive losses　巨額の損失を抱える
the challenges facing the world economy　世界経済が直面する課題, 世界経済が抱える課題
◆An urgent task facing each financial group is to improve its financial conditions and profitability on the strength of advantages gained from merger. 合併・統合の相乗効果を生かして、財務内容と収益力を向上させることが、各金融グループの現在の急務だ。◆Another important task facing major banks is to curtail their operating costs by consolidating branches. 大手行が抱えているもう一つ重要な課題は、店舗の統廃合による営業コストの削減だ。◆Companies faced difficulties in raising money by issuing corporate bonds in the aftermath of the financial crisis and resorted to borrowing money from banks. 世界の金融危機の影響で企業は、社債を発行して資金を調達するのが困難になったため、金融機関からの資金借入れに動いた。◆Credit uncertainty in Europe has spilled over to France which is helping Greece, Italy and Spain facing fiscal crises. 欧州の信用不安は、財政危機に直面しているギリシャやイタリア、スペインを支援しているフランスにも拡大している。◆Discussion among advanced countries alone cannot cope with the challenges facing the world economy. 先進国だけの話合いで、世界経済が直面している課題に対応することはできない状況にある。◆Domestic stock exchange entries continue to languish, reflecting the tough conditions faced by emerging firms wanting to publicly list their shares. 国内株式市場への新規上場は、株式上場を目指す新興企業が直面している厳しい状況を反映して、低迷が続いている。◆Every member of the nation will now be forced to face the risks involved in the management of their own assets. これからは、国民一人ひとりが資産運用リスクに正面から向き合わざるを得なくなる。◆Goldman Sachs' capital increase is partly aimed at regaining the confidence in the U.S. financial market, which has been facing a raft of financial problems. ゴールドマン・サックスの増資は、多くの金融問題を抱える米金融市場の信認回復も狙いの一つだ。◆Governments facing fiscal hardship sometimes force their central banks to buy up government bonds. 財政がひっ迫した政府は、中央銀行に国債を買い切らせることがある。◆Italy's new government led by economist Mario Monti must face painful financial reforms. 経済専門家マリオ・モンティ氏を首相とするイタリア新政権は、痛みを伴う財政改革が急務だ。◆Spain also faces a huge budget deficit. スペインも、巨額の財政赤字を抱えている。◆The automobile industry faces a tough business environment. 自動車産業は、厳しい経営環境に直面している。◆The global economy is facing serious challenges. 世界経済は、厳しい試練に直面している。◆The Japanese economy faces a growing downside risk due to concerns about the future of the U.S. and European economies. 日本経済は、欧米経済の先行き懸念から、景気の下振れリスクが高まっている。◆The Japanese economy is by no means facing a serious crisis. 日本経済は、重大な危機に瀕しているわけではない。◆The New York-based Citigroup, once the world's biggest banking group, faced massive losses in the wake of the subprime mortgage crisis. 世界最大の金融グループだったシティグループ（ニューヨーク）は、サブプライム・ローンの焦げ付き問題を受けて、巨額の損失を抱えていた。◆The nonprofit foundation faced cash flow problems, such as repayment of the debt and meeting personnel costs. この公益法人は、借入金の返済や人件費のやりくりなど、資金繰りの問題に行き詰まった。◆The three Japanese top banks will face the FSB's new international rule requiring them to hold extra capital to prevent future financial crises. 日本の3メガ銀行も、金融危機の再発を防ぐため、資本［自己資本］の上積みを求める金融安定化理事会（FSB）の新国際基準の対象となると見られる。◆The Tokyo governor will have to tackle the task of overcoming the continued financial difficulties facing the Shinginko Tokyo bank. 東京都知事は、新東京銀行が直面する経営危機の長期化を克服する課題に取り組まなければならない。◆Twenty-eight banks of the world will face capital surcharges of 1 percent to 2.5 percent by the application of international rules to rein in too-big-to-fail lenders. 大きすぎて破たんさせられない銀行［金融機関］を規制する国際基準が適用されると、世界の28行が、1～2.5%の資本［自己資本］上積みの対象となる。◆With the United States facing the worst financial crisis in generations, Bush's White House took decisive measures to safeguard the economy. 米国が過去最悪の金融危機に直面して、ブッシュ政権は経済危機を守るために断固たる措置を取った。

face　（名）顔, 面, 表面, 券面, 額面, 局面, フェース
　current face　現在額面
　face interest rate　（債券などの）額面金利
　face of instrument　証書の文面
　face par　額面価格, 額面価値, 額面どおりの価値
　new face bond　新顔債, ニュー・フェイス債
　original face　当初額面
　◆Investors seem to be shifting their money from investment trusts to more secured time deposits in the face of global financial turmoil. 世界の金融市場の混乱に直面して、投資家は資金を投資信託から安定性の高い定期預金に切り替えているようだ。

face amount　額面, 額面価値, 券面額, 総額
　face amount certificate　券面額証券, 券面金額証券
　face amount certificate company　券面額証券発行会社
　face amount of principal　額面
　face amount of receivables　債権の額面
　face amount of the bill　請求総額
　issue bonds in the face amount of　額面～の社債を発行する
　mean face amount　平均額面額
　total face amount of life policies surrendered and lapsed　解約・失効した生命保険証書の額面総額

face value　額面価格, 額面金額, 額面, 券面額
　（⇒zero coupon note）
　face value of bonds　社債額面
　fall below the face value　額面を下回る
　issue at face value　額面発行
　the original face value　当初の額面, 元々の額面
　total face value of coupons issued　発行済みクーポンの合計額面金額
　◆On June 10, 2011, individuals holding $50,000 face value of the Corporation's bonds exercised their conversion privilege. 2011年6月10日、当社の社債権者が、額面5万ドル分の転換権を行使した［額面5万ドル分の株式への転換を行った］。◆The company booked as a loss the total face value of the irrevocable loans. 同社は、不良債権の額面総額を、損金として計上した。◆The firm sold its 8% bonds that had a face value of $1,000,000. 同社は、額面100万ドルの8%利付き社債を発行した。◆The prices of these companies' stock have declined to fall below the face value. これらの企業の株価は、額面を下回っている。

facilitate　（動）助長する, 促進する, 進める, 円滑に進める, 整備する, 容易にする, 後押しする, 楽にする, ～の手助けをする, ～を手伝う
　facilitate a safety net for emergencies　緊急時に備えた安全網を整備する
　facilitate economic growth　経済成長を促す
　facilitate market entry into　～への参入を促進する
　facilitate secondary market trading　流通市場での売買を促進する
　facilitate the development　発展を促す, 発展を後押しする

◆A bill to revise the Law on Special Measures for Strengthening Financial Functions is designed to facilitate compensations of losses of financial institutions with public funds. 金融機能強化法の改正法案は、公的資金で金融機関の損失の穴埋めを容易にするのが狙いだ。◆European countries are urged to facilitate a safety net for emergencies, including the injection of public funds into deteriorating banks to shore up their capital strength. 欧州は、経営が悪化した銀行［金融機関］に公的資金を注入して資本を増強するなど、非常時に備えた安全網の整備が求められている。◆The government plans to translate laws such as the Civil Code and the Commercial Code into English in a bid to facilitate foreign investments and help domestic firms expand their international business activities. 政府は、外国からの投資促進や国内企業の国際ビジネス支援のため、民法や商法などの法律の英訳を行う方針だ。◆The Proprietary Trading System and other online trading systems facilitate trading of stocks outside stock exchanges. 私設取引システム(PTS)などの電子取引システムは、取引所外で株の売買(注文)を成立させる。◆The stock market is a public mechanism to facilitate the smooth flow of money in the economy by serving as an intermediary between corporations and investors. 証券市場は、企業と投資家間の仲介役をつとめて日本経済に資金を円滑に流す役割を担う公共財だ。
◆This legal amendment is designed to facilitate the financing of small and midsize companies through the injection of public funds into financial institutions. この法改正の狙いは、金融機関への公的資金注入により中小企業の資金調達を容易にすることにある。

facility （名）融資, 貸付け, 借入れ, 信用供与, 融資枠, 信用枠, 融資案件, 案件, 便宜, 設備, 施設, 機関, 制度, ファシリティ （⇒loan facility, upgrade）
　arrange an insurance facility　保険ファシリティを締結する
　bank facilities　銀行の融資枠, 銀行借入枠
　banking facilities　金融機関, 銀行借入枠
　　（=bank facilities）
　borrowing facilities　信用枠, 借入枠
　bridging facility　つなぎ融資
　buffer stock financing facility　緩衝在庫融資制度
　collection facilities　取立機関
　commit to the facility　融資参加の意向を表明する
　compensatory financing facility　補償融資, 輸出変動補償融資
　credit enhancement facility　信用補強ファシリティ
　credit facility　信用供与, 信用供与制度, 金融制度, クレジット・ファシリティ
　debt issuance facility　債券発行ファシリティ
　deposit facility　預金ファシリティ
　emergency facility　緊急融資, 緊急資金
　emergency liquidity-providing facilities　緊急貸出制度
　European Financial Stability Facility　欧州金融安定基金, 欧州金融安定ファシリティ, EFSF
　extended fund facility　拡大信用供与制度
　external support facility　第三者信用補完ファシリティ
　facility fee　与信枠設定費用, ファシリティ・フィー
　facility trip　公費［官費］旅行
　financial facilities　金融機関
　financial facility　金融制度
　Global Environment Facility　地球環境基金
　guarantee facility　債務保証, 保証ファシリティ
　International Banking Facility　国際金融ファシリティ, IBF
　lender-of-last-resort facilities　最終的貸付け機関
　liquidity facility　流動性枠, 信用供与枠, 流動性ファシリティ
　loan facility　貸付け枠, 融資枠, 与信枠, 借入枠
　monetary facilities　金融機関
　new facilities　新規融資
　note issuance facilities　債券発行保証枠
　outstanding credit facilities　貸出残高
　overdraft facility　当座貸越し
　payment facilities　支払い機関
　provide a loan facility to the issuing entity　発行体に流動性枠を設定する
　revolving credit facility　回転信用枠, 回転信用ファシリティ
　revolving underwriting facilities　中長期資金調達方式, RUF
　set up a loan facility　融資枠［与信枠］を設定する
　settlement and clearing facility　清算・決済業務, 決済システム
　supplementary financing facility　補完融資制度, 補足融資
　support facility　信用補完ファシリティ
　swing facilities　つなぎ融資枠
　syndicate a term loan facility　ターム・ローン融資案件
　time facilities　ユーザンス枠
　upgrade one's facilities　設備を高度化する, 設備の高度化を図る
　usance facility　ユーザンス金融
　working capital facility　運転資金案件, 運転資金ファシリティ

◆Japanese megabanks and Toyota were among the beneficiaries of a slew of emergency liquidity-providing facilities devised by the U.S. Federal Reserve Board. 日本のメガバンクやトヨタも、(2008年秋の金融危機に伴って) 米連邦準備制度理事会(FRB)の発案で実施された大規模な緊急貸出制度の恩恵を受けた［緊急貸出制度を活用していた］。◆The company is expected to invest ¥185 billion in its facilities and equipment for semiconductor materials during fiscal 2011. 同社は、2011年度は半導体設備に1,850億円を投資する見通しだ。◆The facility will be upsized. 融資枠は、拡大される見込みだ。
◆This yen loan facility is for general corporate purposes. この円融資枠は、一般事業目的に使用される。◆To prevent the current fiscal and financial crisis in Europe from spreading, the IMF will create a new short-term lending facility. 現在の欧州財政・金融危機の拡大を防ぐ［封じる］ため、国際通貨基金(IMF)が、新たな短期の融資制度を創設することになった。

factor （動）（企業の）債権を買い取る, 売掛債権を買い取る, 要素として（計算に）入る, 代理業を営む
　factor in [into]　要因として含める, 要因として考慮する
　factor out　要因として除外する
factor （名）要素, 要因, 原因, 因子, 材料, 原動力, 金融業者, 金融機関, ファクタリング業者, 債権買取り業者, 債権金融業, 債権金融業者［会社］, 〜率, 係数, 指数, ファクター （⇒exchange fluctuation, integrate）
　bearish factor　弱気材料, 不安材料
　bullish factor　強気材料
　buying factor　買い材料
　dilution factor　希薄化率
　general factors　一般材料
　individual factors　個別材料
　market factor　市場要因, 市場因子, 市場要素
　negative factor　マイナス要因, 悪材料, 売り材料
　　（=unfavorable factor）
　positive factor　プラス要因, 好材料, 買い材料
　　（=favorable factor）
　principal factor　主因
　psychological factor　心理的要因

(⇒foreign exchange fluctuations)
seasonal factor　季節要因
temporary factor　一時的要因
◆A major factor behind the recent market upswing is a marked increase in listed companies' transaction to buy back their outstanding shares. 最近の堅調な株式市場を支える大きな要因として、上場企業各社が発行済み株式を市場から買い戻す「自社株買い」の急増がある。◆Among other factors that could adversely affect the national economy are possible setbacks in the Chinese and U.S. economies as well as high oil prices. 国内景気に悪影響を及ぼす恐れがある他の要因として、中国や米国の景気後退や原油高がある。◆It is difficult to deal with the latest unrest in global financial markets because it has been caused by a complex web of factors. 今回の世界的な金融市場混乱への対応が難しいのは、混乱を招いている要因が複雑に絡み合っているからだ。◆It is difficult to predict if new explosive factors emerge to plunge the financial market into further turmoil. 金融市場をさらに混乱に陥れる新しい火種があるのかどうか、予測するのは難しい。◆Signs that unfavorable factors are receding are apparent, as crude oil prices have fallen. 原油の値下りなど、悪材料に解消の兆しが見られる。◆Speculators exploited these buying factors, pushing oil prices up further. 投機筋がこれらの買い材料に反応して[投機筋がこれらの買い材料を利用して]、原油価格の高騰[原油高]を増幅している。◆The Fed's monetary easing is a factor causing disarray in the foreign exchange markets. 米連邦準備制度理事会（FRB）[米中央銀行]の金融緩和が、為替相場混乱[為替混乱]の原因だ。◆The increasing trade and fiscal deficits of the United States are a factor behind the dollar sell-off. ドル売りの背景にある要因としては[ドル売りの背景には]、米国の貿易赤字と財政赤字の拡大がある。◆The instability of life insurance firms and the lowered earning power of banks with massive bad loans have become the two major factors rocking the financial system. 生保各社の経営基盤の不安定と、巨額の不良債権に苦しむ銀行の収益力低下が、金融システムを揺るがしている二大要因になっている。

factorage　(名)仲買い手数料,取立て代理業,代理業,(口銭)問屋(といや)業
factoring　(名)売掛債権の買取り,売掛債権売却,(売掛債権の)債権買取り業,取立て代理業,ファクタリング
　debt factoring　債権買取り
　factoring charge　ファクタリング手数料
　factoring company　債権買取り会社,ファクタリング会社
　factoring facility　ファクタリング・ファシリティ
　factoring program　手形割引
factorization　(名)債権差押え通告
facultative　(形)任意の,選択的な,特権を与える,許容的
　facultative acceptance　任意受再
　facultative business　任意再保険
　facultative obligatory reinsurance　任意義務再保険,随時義務再保険
　facultative open cover　任意特約再保険,随時特約再保険
　facultative reinsurance　任意再保険,随時再保険,自由再保険
fade　(動)色あせる,薄れる,落ち込む,後退する,衰える,衰退する,減退する,姿を消す,消失する
　fade in　次第にはっきりする
　fade out　次第に消える
　fading concerns　懸念[不安]の後退
　fading demand　需要の減退
◆The money market is overheated by massive money inflows from banks on fading concerns over a financial system crisis. 金融システム不安[金融システム危機に対する懸念]の後退により、短期金融市場は、銀行からの巨額の資金流入で過熱感が強まっている。

fade-out formula　段階的移譲方式,フェイドアウト方式,FO方式
fail　(動)経営破たんする,破たんする,倒産する,破産する,失敗する,動かなくなる,(供給が)止まる,〜を怠る(名)失敗,決済漏れ,受渡し不能,受渡し不履行(=collapse;⇒take over assets)
　fail at key resistance　主要抵抗線を突破できない
　fail in　〜に失敗する,〜で不合格になる,〜を怠る
　fail in one's duty　義務を怠る
　fail in the marketplace　まったく売れなくなる
　fail to deliver　引渡し不能,引渡し不能約定,引渡し不履行
　fail to receive　引取り不能,引取り不能約定
◆After April 2005, if a bank fails, deposits are guaranteed only up to ¥10 million plus interest. 2005年4月以降、銀行が破たんした場合の預金の保証限度額は、元本1,000万円とその利息となっている。◆As the recession continues, more and more small and midsized companies are failing. 不況の長期化に伴って、中小企業の倒産が急増している。◆The executive pay of Merrill Lynch & Co., mostly in bonuses, has become a hot-button issue in the recession as banks and companies fail. メリルリンチの経営幹部報酬は、大半がボーナスだが、銀行や企業が経営破たんする不況時の強い関心を呼ぶ問題になっている。◆Twenty-eight banks of the world will face capital surcharges of 1 percent to 2.5 percent by the application of international rules to rein in too-big-to-fail lenders. 大きすぎて破たんさせられない銀行[金融機関]を規制する国際基準が適用されると、世界の28行が、1〜2.5％の資本[自己資本]上積みの対象となる。

fail to　〜できない,〜しない,〜することを怠る
　fail to acquire a majority stake in the company　同社株の過半数株式を取得できない
　fail to fully retire CP at the maturity　満期日にCPを全額償還できない
　fail to pay local taxes　地方税を滞納する
　fail to pay one's debts　債務不履行を起こす
◆A real estate investment fund was alleged to have failed to report about ¥18 billion in income from transaction involving land and property taken as collateral for nonperforming loans. 不動産投資ファンドが、不良債権の担保に取った不動産関連の取引で得た所得約180億円の申告漏れを指摘されていた。◆Don Quijote Co. has failed to acquire a majority stake in Origin Toshu Co. in its tender offer. ドン・キホーテ（ディスカウント・ストア大手）は、TOB（株式公開買付け）でオリジン東秀（持ち帰り弁当・惣菜店）株の過半数株式を取得できなかった。◆Financial Services Agency has ordered 26 nonlife insurance firms to correct their business practices, after finding they failed to pay due insurance benefits. 損保各社が支払う義務のある保険金を支払わなかったことが判明したため、金融庁は損保26社に対して業務是正命令を出した。◆Greece was bailed out temporarily in May 2010, but it may default on its debts if it fails to secure necessary funds to redeem a sizable amount of government bonds. ギリシャは2010年5月に一時的に救済されたが、大量の国債の償還に必要な資金を確保できない場合、債務不履行（デフォルト）に陥る可能性がある。◆Idemitsu Kosan failed to tell a local fire department about damages to other tanks discovered after a crude oil tank caught fire immediately after powerful earthquakes hit the region on Sept. 26. 出光興産は、9月26日の十勝沖地震直後に起きた原油タンク火災後に他のタンクの損傷を発見しながら、地元消防署への報告を怠っていた。◆Japanese banks failed to take quick actions to dispose of nonperforming loans following the bursting of the bubble economy. 邦銀は、バブル崩壊後の不良債権処理に迅速に対応しなかった。

◆The company has failed to pay about ¥30 million in local taxes over the last three years. 同社は、過去3年間の地方税約3,000万円を滞納している。◆The mergers and acquisitions many major U.S. companies pursued failed to produce the expected synergy effect. 米国の大企業の多くが追求したM&Aは、予想したシナジー（相乗）効果を上げられなかった。◆The Obama administration failed to cut federal spending. オバマ政権は、連邦支出を削減しなかった。◆The U.S. government failed to take drastic countermeasures against its fiscal deterioration. 米政府は、財政悪化に抜本的な対策を取れなかった［大胆なメスを入れられなかった］。◆Those housewives who have failed to switch to the national pension plan and have not paid premiums for an extensive period may receive a pittance or nothing at all. 国民年金への切替えをせず、保険料を長期間払っていない主婦は、低年金や無年金になる可能性がある。◆We failed to acquire a majority stake in the company in our tender offer. 当社は、TOB（株式公開買付け）で同社株の過半数株式を取得できませんでした。

failed （形）経営破たんした，破たんした，倒産した，失敗した
    failed company　経営破たんした企業, 破たん企業
        （⇒additional loan）
    failed institution　経営破たんした金融機関
        （=failed financial institution）
    failed nonlife insurer　破たん損保
    ◆The slipshod management of failed Incubator Bank of Japan widely diverged from its business philosophy. 破たんした日本振興銀行のずさんな経営は、同行の経営理念とはかけ離れていた。

failed bank　経営破たんした銀行, 破たん銀行, 銀行破たん　（⇒bridge bank, credit動詞, take over assets）
    ◆Depositors at a failed bank can have their deposits credited against outstanding loans. 破たんした銀行の預金者は、預金から借入金残高を差し引くことができる。◆The Financial Services Agency has implemented rescue measures with public funds in the past for failed banks. 金融庁はこれまで、銀行の破たんについては、公的資金による救済策を取ってきた。

failed borrower　融資先企業の経営破たん, 経営破たんした融資先
    ◆The amount of bad loans on the banking groups' books were slashed as a result of a decline in failed borrowers. 融資先企業の経営破たんが減少した結果、銀行グループの帳簿上の不良債権処理額も減少した。

failed business　破たん事業, 破たんした事業
    ◆JAL's efforts to turn around its failed business will depend on the flagship carrier's ability to secure new loans from its creditor banks. 日航の破たん事業再生への取組みは、この日本を代表する航空会社が取引銀行から新規融資を受けることができるかどうかにかかっている。

failed financial institution　破たん金融機関, 経営破たんした金融機関, 金融機関の経営破たん
    （=failed institution; ⇒loan credits）
    ◆The bank earns revenue through real estate investment and through resuscitating failed financial institutions. 同行は、不動産投資と経営破たんした金融機関を再生させることで収益を上げている。

failing　（形）破たんしかけた, 破たん寸前の, 業績悪化の, 駄目になりつつある
    failing business [firm, company]　業績悪化企業
    failing circumstances　倒産状態, 破産状態
    failing division　経営不振部門
    ◆Public funds were used to save failing hotels run by the central government workers' mutual aid association. 国家公務員の共済組合が経営する破たん寸前のホテル救済に、公的資金［公費］が充てられていた。

failure　（名）経営破たん, 破たん, 倒産, 破産, 崩壊,（債務などの）不履行, 遅れ, 失敗, ミス,（交渉などの）決裂,（機械などの）機能停止, 故障, 障害　（=collapse; ⇒bank failure, full payment of insurance claims, payoff system）
    bank failure　銀行破たん, 銀行破産
        （=failure of a bank）
    business failure　企業倒産, 経営難
    computer system failure　コンピュータ・システムの障害, システム障害
    coordination failure　（市場の）協働の失敗
    corporate failure　企業倒産, 経営破たん
    economic failure　経済の崩壊, 経済破たん
    failure cost　不良コスト, 仕損じ原価
    failure in demand　需要不足
    failure in supervision　監督不行き届き
    failure in supply　供給不足
    failure of insurance companies　保険会社の破たん
    failure of payment　支払いの不履行
    failure rate　倒産率, 失業率
        （=rate of business failure, rate of failure）
    failure to meet debt obligations　債務返済の遅れ
    failure to pay　不払い, 支払い不履行
    financial failures　金融破たん
    investment failure　投資機会を逃すこと
    market failure　市場の失敗, 市場の不成立
    related enterprises failures　関連企業の倒産
    system failure　システムの故障, システムのトラブル, システム障害　（⇒double deduction）
    thrift failure　貯蓄貸付け機関の破たん

◆In June 2009 prior to Japan Airlines' failure, a ¥67 billion public financing package was extended with a government-backed guarantee to JAL. 日本航空破たん前の2009年6月、日航に対して政府保証付きで670億円の公的融資が行われた［公的融資策が実施された］。◆The Board of Audit has confirmed that the public financing package extended with a government-backed guarantee to JAL prior to its failure cost taxpayers a total of ¥47 billion. 日航の破たん前に政府保証付きで行われた公的融資の総国民負担額は470億円であることを、会計検査院が確定した。◆The failure of Lehman Brothers Holdings Inc. caused stock prices in New York and other markets worldwide to plummet. リーマン・ブラザーズ（米証券4位）の経営破たんで、株価はニューヨークはじめ世界各地の市場で暴落した。◆The failure of WorldCom resulted in a loss of investor confidence in the corporate governance of U.S. companies. ワールドコム（米国の大手通信会社で現MCI）の経営破たんは、米企業のコーポレート・ガバナンス（企業統治）に対する投資家の信頼を損ねた。◆The failure to implement fiscal consolidation in countries where it is necessary could undermine confidence and hamper growth. 財政健全化が必要な国で財政健全化を行わないと、信認を損ない、成長を阻害する可能性がある。◆The financial group's inadequate preparations for the reorganization resulted in a major computer system failure. 同フィナンシャル・グループの再編の準備不足から、大規模なシステム障害が起こった。◆The issue of the inadvertent failure to switch to the national pension program by full-time housewives must be quickly solved. 専業主婦の国民年金への年金資格切替え忘れ問題は、決着を急ぐべきだ。◆The number of surplus workers approached a peak of 3.59 million in the January-March quarter of 1999, following a spate of failures at major financial institutions. 過剰雇用者数は、大手金融機関の破たんが相次いだ後の1999年1-3月期に、359万人のピークに達した。◆These disciplinary measures include increased penalties on securities fraud and a newly installed penalty on corporate directors in cases of failure to submit adequate financial reports to authorities. これらの懲戒処分には、証券詐欺に対する罰則の強化や、当局

に適切な財務報告をしなかった場合の企業取締役に対する罰則の新設などが含まれている。◆With the promotion of the disposal of nonperforming loans, corporate failures and joblessness will increase in the short time. 不良債権処理を促進すれば、短期的には企業倒産と失業が増える。

fair （形）公正な, 公平な, 平等な, 差別をしない, 妥当な, 適正な, 正しい, 美しい, 魅力的な, 汚れのない, フェア
　fair competition　公正競争
　Fair Credit Reporting Act　公正信用報告法, 公正消費者信用報告法
　Fair Employment Practices Committee　米公正雇用慣行委員会, FEPC
　fair presentation　適正表示, 公正表示
　fair price　適正価格
　fair trade　公正取引, 適正取引
　◆FSA's inspectors are to confirm whether the companies' categorization by banks as debtors is relevant or fair. 金融庁の検査官は、銀行側の企業（融資先企業）の債務者区分が適正かどうかなどを検証することになっている。

fair market value　公正市場価格, 適正市場価格, 公正市場価値, 公正市価, 時価
　◆This realty had a fair market value of $500,000 at the date of the grant. この不動産の贈与時の時価は、50万ドルであった。

Fair Trade Commission　日本の公正取引委員会, FTC
　◆Corporate merger screening is conducted by the Fair Trade Commission of Japan in light of the Antimonopoly Law. 企業の合併審査は、独占禁止法に照らして［基づいて］公正取引委員会が行う。◆The Fair Trade Commission approved a local Web-search partnership between Yahoo-Japan Corp. and Google Inc. 公正取引委員会は、ヤフーとグーグルのインターネット検索の国内提携を承認した。

fair value　公正価格［価額］, 適正価格, 理論価格, 公正な評価額, 公正価値, 適正価値, 適正水準, 時価
　an instrument's fair value　商品の公正価格
　be carried at fair value　公正価額で計上される
　changes in fair value　公正価額の変動
　fair value accounting　公正価値会計
　fair value for the Dow　ダウ工業株平均の適正水準
　fair value hedge　公正価値ヘッジ
　fair value less costs to sell　正味売却額
　fair value model　公正価値モデル
　fair value of a call option　コール・オプションの適正価値
　fair value of a loan portfolio　債権ポートフォリオの公正価格
　fair value option　公正価値オプション
　fair values of financial instruments　金融商品［金融手段］の公正価格
　　（=financial instruments' fair values）
　plan assets at fair value　制度資産時価
　◆The fair value of our pension plan assets is greater than our projected pension obligations. 当社の年金制度資産の公正価額は、予想年金債務額を上回っています。◆The fair values of the Company's financial instruments have been determined based on quoted market prices and market interest rates, as of December 31, 2010. 当社の金融手段［金融商品］の公正価格は、2010年12月31日現在の市場の相場と市中金利に基づいて決定されています。

fairness　（名）公正, 公平, 適正性, 妥当性, 公共性
　◆Insider trading distorts share prices and undermines the fairness of the securities market. インサイダー取引は、（適正な）株価をゆがめ、証券市場の公正さを損なう。

faith　（名）信頼, 信用, 信認, 信念, 信義, 誠実, 約束, 誓約
　bad faith　不正
　full faith and credit bond　十分な信頼と信用に基づく債券, 完全な信用保証債

good faith　善意, 誠実, 誠意, 約定
good faith and fair dealing　誠実で公正な取扱い
holder in bad faith　悪意の第三者
in good faith　誠実に, 誠意をもって, 信用して, 善意の
renewed faith　信認の回復
the market's faith in the dollar　ドルに対する市場の信認, ドルに対する信認
◆If the U.S. government falls into default, the markets' faith in the dollar as the world's key currency would plummet. 米政府がデフォルト（債務不履行）に陥ったら、世界の基軸通貨としてのドルの信認は急落する。◆The wrongdoing of Olympus Corp., a blue-chip company that holds the largest share of the global endoscope market, has eroded international faith in corporate Japan. 内視鏡の市場シェアで世界トップのオリンパスの不正行為で、日本企業の国際的な信頼は失墜している。

fake　（形）偽の, 偽造の, 改ざんした, 偽装した, コピーした, 偽物の, いかさまの, 狂言の
　（=bogus, counterfeit, phony［phoney］）
　fake bill　偽札　（=fake money）
　fake certificate　偽証明書
　fake credit card　偽造クレジット・カード
　　（=counterfeit credit card）
　fake transaction　偽装売買, 偽装取引

fake ATM card　偽造キャッシュ・カード, 偽造ATMカード
　◆Fake ATM cards were used to steal about ¥400 million since December 2006. 偽造ATMカード［キャッシュ・カード］を使って、2006年12月以降、約4億円が盗み取られた。

fake Web site　偽ホームページ
　◆In phishing, offenders lure victims to fake financial institution Web sites to enter their account PINs and other account information. フィッシングでは、犯人が被害者を金融機関の偽ホームページに誘導して、被害者の口座の暗証番号などの口座情報を入力させる。

fall　（動）下落する, 低下する, 減少する, 崩壊する, 失墜する, 手形の期限が来る
　fall across the board　全面安となる
　fall worldwide　世界的に下落する, 世界同時安となる
　◆As the financial markets' confidence in the U.S. currency has been shaken, stock prices may fall worldwide and the dollar-selling trend may accelerate. 米ドルへの金融市場の信認が揺らいでいるため、株価が世界的に下落し［世界同時安となり］、ドル売りの流れが加速する可能性もある。◆In foreign currency deposits, depositors can earn profits by exchanging their foreign currency deposits into yen when the yen's value against major foreign currencies falls. 外貨預金では、主要外貨に対して円相場が下落した時点で預金者が外貨預金を円に戻せば、利益を上げる［儲ける］ことができる。◆Lending by financial institutions to small and medium enterprises has been falling since 1994. 金融機関による中小企業向け貸出は、1994年以降減少している。◆Nomura Holdings' net profit fell 80 percent in the first quarter of fiscal 2010 mainly due to a slump in investment banking. 野村ホールディングスの2010年度第1四半期の税引き後利益は、主に投資銀行業務の低迷で80%減少した。◆On the bond market, the yield on newly issued 10-year government bonds, an indicator of long-term interest rates, fell, resulting in a rise in bond prices. 債券市場では、長期金利の指標である新発10年物国債の利回り（流通利回り）が下落し、債券相場［債券価格］は上昇した。◆Signs that unfavorable factors are receding are apparent, as crude oil prices have fallen. 原油の値下りなど、悪材料に解消の兆しが見られる。◆Stock prices in Tokyo fell by more than 600 points as a state of panic gripped investors and selling pressure snowballed. 東京市場の株価は、投資家がパニック状態に陥り、売り圧力が増大［加速］したため、下げ幅が600円を超えた。◆The DJ Stoxx index of European banking stocks

has fallen 37 percent from a peak in February. ダウ・ジョーンズ欧州銀行株指数は、2月のピークから37%下落した。◆The massive losses mean the bank's capital adequacy ratio is estimated to have fallen to about 8 percent. この大幅な赤字で、同行の自己資本比率は、約8%まで低下する見通しだ。◆The Nikkei Stock Average fell briefly to its lowest level this year on the Tokyo Stock Market. 東京株式市場の日経平均株価は一時、今年の最安値を下回った。◆The rule of asset impairment accounting requires companies to post valuation losses on fixed assets whose market value has fallen sharply from their book value. 減損会計基準は、固定資産の時価が簿価から大幅に下落した場合の固定資産の評価損の計上を、企業に義務付けている。◆The S&P 500 index fell 17.74, or 2.4 percent, to 735.09. S&P500株価指数は、735.09ドルで17.74ドル（2.4%）低下[下落]した。◆The yen continues its relentless surge and stock prices keep falling. 円高に歯止めがかからず、株安も続いている。

fall （名）下落, 低下, 減少, 崩壊, 失墜
　fall in rates [interest rates]　金利の低下
　fall in the jobless rate　失業率の低下, 雇用の増加
　fall in the value of the dollar　ドル安, ドル相場の下落
　free fall of the stock market　株式市場の暴落, 株式市場の急落
　the sharp appreciation of the yen and the fall of the dollar　急激な円高・ドル安
　◆The increase in employment was modest compared with the fall in the jobless rate. 雇用[就業者]の増加は、失業率の減少と比べて緩やかな伸びにとどまった。

fall behind　〜に[〜より〜, 〜が]遅れる, 〜に後れを取る, 〜から落伍（らくご）する, 〜に先行される, 〜を滞納する　(=get [lag] behind)
　fall behind in global competitiveness　国際競争に遅れる, 国際競争から落語する
　fall behind in tax payments　納税が遅れる, 税金を滞納する, 税金が支払えない
　fall behind in the development of　〜の開発で後れを取る
　fall behind schedule　予定より遅れる
　fall behind with one's payments　支払いが遅れる, 決済が遅れる
　◆Japan could fall behind in global competitiveness due to an endless struggle between the ruling and opposition parties for leadership. 日本は、与野党が政権争い[政局次元の争い]に明け暮れているため、国際競争に後れを取る可能性がある。

fall below　〜を割り込む, 〜を割る, 〜を下回る
　◆A key gauge of the current state of the economy fell below the boom-or-bust threshold of 50 percent in September for the first time in five months. 景気の現状を示す主要基準（景気一致指数）が、9月は5か月ぶりに景気判断の分かれ目となる50%を下回った。◆The stock average fell below 9,000 again on the Tokyo Stock Exchange. 東京株式市場は、平均株価がふたたび9,000円を割り込んだ。

fall in import prices　輸入価格の下落
　◆The fall in import prices that accompanies a strong yen could further prolong Japan's deflation. 円高に伴う輸入価格の下落で、日本のデフレがさらに長期化する可能性がある。

fall in stock prices　株価下落, 株安
　(=falling stock prices)
　◆A further fall in stock prices could bring the banks to the brink of collapse. 株価下落（株安）が一段と進めば、これらの銀行は破たん寸前まで追い込まれる可能性がある。◆A series of accounting scandals and delays in the recovery of corporate performance are accelerating falls in stock prices on the U.S. markets, along with the weakening of the dollar. 一連の[相次ぐ]企業会計の不祥事と企業業績回復の遅れで、米国の株安とドル安が加速している。

fall in U.S. stock prices　米国の株安
　◆The continued fall in U.S. stock prices and the dollar's depreciation has battered the Japanese economy. 米国の株安とドル安の進行が、日本経済を直撃してい[激しく揺さぶっている。]

fall into a debt crisis　債務危機に陥る, 財政危機に陥る
　◆The 10-year bond yield of Spain has likewise neared the 7 percent level, the danger zone that may fall into a debt crisis. スペインの10年物国債利回り[国債流通利回り]も、債務危機に陥る恐れがある危険水域の7%台に迫った。

fall into capital deficiency　資本不足に陥る
　◆Making the creditor banks waive loans to TEPCO will cause the utility to fall into capital deficiency, with liabilities exceeding assets. 取引銀行に東電への債権を放棄させると、東電は資本不足に陥り、債務超過になってしまう。

fall into debt　債務超過に陥る
　◆Creditor financial institutions and shareholders will suffer huge losses if TEPCO falls into debt without the government financial aid. 東電が政府の金融支援を受けられずに債務超過に陥れば、融資している金融機関や株主は、巨額の損失を被ることになる。◆Without the government financial support, TEPCO will fall into debt as the utility has to pay the huge amounts in compensation. 政府の金融支援がなければ、東電は巨額の賠償金を支払わなければならないので、債務超過に陥ると思われる。

fall of the dollar　ドル安
　◆Dollar selling pressure has eased and put a temporary brake on the sharp appreciation of the yen and the fall of the dollar. ドル売り圧力が弱まり、急激な円高・ドル安にいったん歯止めがかかった。

fall of the euro　ユーロ安
　◆Germany's economy recovered thanks to the fall of the euro. ドイツ経済は、ユーロ安で回復した。

fall on　襲いかかる, 急襲する, 殺到する,（責任, 義務などが）課せられる,（非難, 疑惑などが）〜に向けられる, 〜に降りかかる, 〜の負担となる, 〜で困窮する, 〜をふと思いつく
　fall on hard [tough] times　つらい時期を経験する, つらい目にあう, 不幸な目にあう, 経営不安に陥る, 落ちぶれる
　◆Banks in the United States and some European countries fell on tough times due to the credit crisis and were bailed out with taxpayers' money. 米国と一部の欧州諸国の銀行が金融危機で経営不安に陥り、公的資金で救済された。

fall short of　〜を下回る, 〜に達しない, 〜を割る, 〜が欠乏[不足]する, 〜に不十分である
　(=come short of)
　◆Japan Airlines Corp. is expected to fall short of its planned fund-raising target by about ¥50 billion due to lower stock price. 日本航空では、株価の下落で、当初計画の資金調達目標を約500億円下回る見通しだ。◆The bank may see its capital adequacy ratio fall far short of the BIS requirements. 同行の自己資本比率は、BIS基準に到底達しない可能性がある。

falling　（形）下落する, 低下する, 下向きの, 経営不振の, 〜の下落[低下, 減少]
　falling backlog　受注残高の減少
　falling demand　需要の低下, 需要の減少
　falling interest rates　金利の低下
　falling market　下げ相場, 下向きの市況, 下降市況
　falling sales　販売の減少, 売上の減少
　falling stock market　株価の下落
　　(=fall in stock prices, falling stock prices)

falling collateral value　担保価値の下落
　◆The collection of debts has been delayed due to falling collateral value. 担保価値の下落などで、債権の回収は遅れている。

falling company　経営不振の会社, 経営不振企業
◆The FSA's inspectors are to target falling companies, based on their stock price levels and outside credit ratings. 金融庁の検査官は, (特別立入り検査では)検査株価や格付けなどを基準にして経営不振の企業に的を絞る方針だ。

falling prices　物価の下落
◆Falling prices have the side effects of chilling the economy and increase unemployment. 物価の下落は, 景気を冷やし, 失業を増大させる副作用がある。

falling stock prices　株価の下落, 株安
◆Falling stock prices and the depreciation of the U.S. dollar increased uncertainty over the global economy. 米国の株安やドル安で, 世界経済の不透明感が強まっている。◆Financial institutions are still struggling with falling stock prices. 金融機関は, 相変わらず株安に苦悩している。◆The government and ruling parties began considering the economic package as they feared falling stock prices could result in a financial crisis. 政府・与党は, 株価の下落で金融危機に陥る可能性があることから, 経済対策の検討を開始した。◆We must avoid hindering the export-led economic recovery, speeding up deflation and increasing bad loans, which can be brought about by falling stock prices and the weakening dollar. 株安とドル安がもたらす可能性がある輸出頼みの景気回復の挫折, デフレ加速, 不良債権の拡大を, われわれは避けなければならない。

fallout　(名)落伍[落後], 離脱, 脱落, 脱退, 後退, 撤退, つまずき, 失敗, 解散, 不測の結果[事態], 後遺症, 放射性物質の降下, 放射性降下物, 原子灰, 放射能塵(じん), 死の灰
fallout from the collapse of the stock market　株式市場急落の後遺症, 株式値下りの後遺症
fallout from the global economic downturn　世界的な景気後退[景気減速]による不測の事態
◆Honda's fallout from F1 due to the global economic downturn may ripple over into sporting businesses. 世界的な景気減速[景気後退]によるホンダのF1(フォーミュラ・ワン)からの撤退の影響は, スポーツ関連事業に広がる[波及する]可能性がある。

false financial statements　虚偽記載の有価証券報告書, 有価証券報告書の虚偽記載, 不正経理　(⇒accuse, major shareholders' stakes)
◆The firm's practice of issuing false financial statements about the holdings of major stockholders dates back to 1980 or earlier. 大株主の保有株式に関して虚偽記載の有価証券報告書を発行する同社の慣行は, 1980年以前にさかのぼる。◆The Securities and Exchange Surveillance Commission will get to the bottom of the spate of scandals involving Olympus Corp.'s false financial statements. 証券取引等監視委員会は, オリンパスの有価証券報告書虚偽記載に関する一連の疑惑の全容を解明する[真相を究明する]方針だ。◆The spate of scandals involving Olympus Corp.'s false financial statements has been widely reported overseas. オリンパスの有価証券報告書の虚偽記載に関する一連の疑惑は, 海外で大きく報じられた。

false information　虚偽の情報
◆The firm's former president spread false information about corporate purchases with the aim of inflating the stock prices of its affiliate. 同社の前社長は, 関連会社の株価をつり上げるため, 虚偽の企業買収情報を公表していた。

false securities report　虚偽記載の有価証券報告書
◆According to the Financial Instruments and Exchange Law, penalties for making false securities reports are tightened from up to five years in prison to up to 10 years in prison. 金融取引法によれば, 有価証券報告書の虚偽記載の刑罰は, 懲役5年以下から懲役10年以下に引き上げられている。

falsification　(名)偽造, 偽装, 偽造, 改ざん, ねつ造, 変造, 詐称, 虚偽記載　(⇒payoff)
◆The former chairman of the company was arrested over alleged involvement in the falsification of its financial statements and insider trading. 同社の前会長が, 有価証券報告書の虚偽記載とインサイダー取引に関与した疑いで逮捕された。

falsified stock dealing　株式の偽装売買, 偽装株式取引　(=fake stock transaction)
◆The Financial Services Agency is considering issuing a business improvement administrative order to the Osaka Securities Exchange on suspicion of falsified stock dealings. 金融庁は, 仮装売買疑惑で, 大阪証券取引所に対する業務改善命令の発動を検討している。

falsified stock option dealing　株式オプションの偽装売買, 偽装株式オプション取引

falsified transaction　不正取引, 仮装売買, 偽装売買, 偽装取引　(=fake transaction, falsified trading)
◆The expanded volume was the result of falsified transaction. 取引高の拡大は, 仮装売買によるものだった。

falsify　(動)偽造する, 偽装する, 改ざんする, ねつ造する, 変造する, 詐称する, 虚偽記載する　(⇒accounting documents, accounting report, loan loss reserves)
falsified financial documents　虚偽の財務書類
falsified financial report　有価証券報告書の虚偽記載, 財務報告書の虚偽記載　(⇒financial documents)
falsified stock dealing　株式の偽装売買, 偽装株式取引
falsified stock option dealing　株式オプションの偽装売買, 偽装株式オプション
falsified transaction　不正取引, 仮装売買, 偽装売買, 偽装取引　(=fake transaction, falsified trading)
falsify one's earnings report　業績報告書を改ざんする　(⇒civil fine)
◆American International Group agreed to pay a $10 million civil fine to settle the SEC's allegations that it fraudulently helped another company falsify its earnings report and hide losses. 米保険大手のAIG(アメリカン・インターナショナル・グループ)は, 同社が他社の業績報告書改ざんと損失隠しに不正に手を貸したとする米証券取引委員会(SEC)の告発を受け, この問題を解決するために民事制裁金1,000万ドルを支払うことに同意した。◆The Tokyo Stock Exchange will delist Seibu Railway Co. for falsifying its financial statements. 東京証券取引所は, 有価証券報告書の虚偽記載で西武鉄道株の上場を廃止する。

falter　(動)低下する, 弱まる, 鈍化する, 低迷する, 伸び悩む, 冷え込む, ふらつく, つまずく
faltering capital spending　設備投資の低迷
faltering demand for new credit　新規借入需要の減退, 新規借入需要の落込み[冷え込み]
faltering economic recovery　足踏み状態の景気回復, 景気回復のふらつき
faltering regional economies　地域経済の低迷, 地域経済の冷え込み[伸び悩み]
◆Demand for bullion as a protection of wealth has been spurred by mounting concern that the global economy is faltering. 世界経済低迷への懸念増大から, 安全資産[資産保全]としての金の需要が拡大している。◆Japan's own economy is faltering. 日本の経済自体も, 足踏み状態だ[伸び悩んでいる]。◆There seems to be no hope left for the recovery of faltering stock prices or the stable growth of the Japanese economy. 低迷する株価の回復も日本経済の安定成長も, 望めないようだ。

family　(名)家族, 家庭, ファミリー
family allowance　家族手当て
family automobile policy　自家用自動車保険証券
family company　同族会社
family expense policy　家族傷害保険証券
family history　家族歴
family income insurance　家族収入[所得]保険, 家族年

金保険

family income policy　家族所得保険, 家族年金保険

family maintenance insurance　家族保証保険, 家族扶養保険

family plan　家族保険, ファミリー・プラン

family policy　家族保険

family protection policy　家族保証保険

family insurance policy　家族保険契約
◆Family insurance policy is a whole life insurance policy that provides term insurance coverage on the insured's spouse and children. 家族保険契約は、被保険者の配偶者と子どもに定期保険保障を与える終身生命保険だ。

Fannie　ファニー・メイ
(=Fannie Mae; ⇒Freddie Mac)
◆The Federal Housing Finance Agency oversees Fannie and Freddie that buy mortgage loans and mortgage securities issued by the lenders. 米連邦住宅金融局(FHFA)は、これらの金融機関が発行する住宅ローンやモーゲージ証券を購入する[買い取る]連邦住宅抵当金庫(ファニー・メイ)や連邦住宅貸付け抵当公社(フレディ・マック)を監督している。◆The price tag for the mortgage-backed securities sold to Fannie and Freddie by 17 financial firms totaled $196.1 billion. 大手金融機関17社がファニー・メイとフレディ・マックに販売した住宅ローン担保証券(MBS)の購入額は、総額で1,961億ドルになる。◆The U.S. government filed lawsuits against 17 financial firms for selling Fannie and Freddie mortgage-backed securities that turned toxic when the housing market collapsed. 米政府は、住宅市場崩壊時に不良資産化した住宅ローン担保証券(MBS)をファニー・メイ(米連邦住宅抵当金庫)とフレディ・マック(米連邦住宅貸付け抵当公社)に販売したとして、大手金融機関17社(バンク・オブ・アメリカやシティグループ、JPモルガン・チェース、ゴールドマン・サックス・グループなど)を提訴した。

Fannie [Fanny] Mae　米連邦住宅抵当金庫[抵当公庫], ファニー・メイ　(=Fannie: Federal National Mortgage Associationの通称で、米政府系住宅金融会社。フレディ・マック(米連邦住宅貸付け抵当公社)の姉妹会社(sister company)。⇒Freddie Mac)

Fannie Mae and its sister company Freddie Mac　ファニー・メイ(米連邦住宅抵当公庫)とその姉妹会社フレディ・マック(米連邦住宅貸付抵当公社)

Fannie Mae Guaranteed Multifamily Structures　ファニー・メイ保証集合住宅仕組み債, ファニー・メイ GeMS

state-backed mortgage firm Fannie Mae　政府系住宅金融会社ファニー・メイ

◆Fannie Mae and its sister company Freddie Mac have needed $148.2 billion in public funds to stay afloat, about $63.1 billion of which is being used by Freddie Mac. 経営破たんを避けるため、ファニー・メイ(米連邦住宅抵当公庫)とその姉妹会社フレディ・マック(米連邦住宅貸付け抵当公社)が必要としている公的資金総額は1,482億ドルで、このうち約631億ドルはフレディ・マックに充てられる。◆State-backed mortgage firm Fannie Mae lost $3.1 billion in its second quarter of this fiscal year. 政府系住宅金融会社ファニー・メイは、今年度第2四半期の決算で31億ドルの損失[赤字]となった。◆Tab for Fannie Mae and Freddie Mac could soar to as much as $259 billion, nearly twice the amount Fannie and Freddie have received so far. ファニー・メイ(米連邦住宅抵当金庫)とフレディ・マック(米連邦住宅貸付け抵当公社)の追加の公的資金必要額は、両社がこれまでに受け取った額の約2倍の2,590億ドルに急増する可能性がある。

Farm Credit Administration　農業信用局

fast-track legislation aimed at rehabilitating troubled financial institutions　金融機関更生特例法

FAT　金融活動税　(financial activities taxの略。金融安定貢献税(FSC)とともにIMFが提案している銀行税の一つ。金融機関を対象に、利益と役職員への報酬の総額に課税。⇒FSC)

faulty　(形)欠陥の, 欠陥商品の, 問題のある

faulty mortgage investments　欠陥商品の[問題のある]モーゲージ証券, モーゲージ証券の欠陥

faulty seasonal adjustment　季節調整の欠陥

◆American International Group Inc. sued Bank of America for allegedly selling it faulty mortgage investments. 米保険大手のAIGが、欠陥商品のモーゲージ証券を同社に販売したとして、バンク・オブ・アメリカを提訴した。

favor [favour]　(名)好意, 支持, 賛意, 賛成, 引立て, 便宜, 便宜供与, 利益供与, 記念品

a life insurance policy in his wife's favor for ¥20 million　彼の妻を受取人とする2,000万円の生命保険証券

dollar's favor　ドル高

establish an L/C [a credit] in our favor　当社を受益者として信用状を開設する

favor-taxes for land trade　陸運奨励関税

in favor of　～を支持して, ～に賛成して, ～の利益になるように, ～を受益者として[受益者とする], ～受取の, ～に有利に, ～を(望ましいと)選択して, ～を求めて

in our favor　当社宛に, 当社を受取人として[受取人とする], 当社を受益者として

move in favor of　～に有利に動く

move in the dollar's favor　ドルに有利に動く, ドルに有利な方向に動く

provide favors to　～に便宜を図る

receive favors from　～から利益供与を受ける

◆EU members agreed to argue in favor of a stable or partially reduced quota for bluefin tuna. 欧州連合(EU)加盟国は、クロマグロ(ホンマグロ)の漁獲割当量の現状維持か一部削減を求めて議論することで合意した。◆Please establish an L/C in our favor. 当社を受益者として、信用状を開設してください。◆Those in favor of "decoupling" urged the Japanese to reduce their overdependence on the U.S. economy. 「ディカップリング(非連動)論」支持者は、米経済への過度の依存脱却を日本に促した。◆We have established a credit for $80,000 in your favor with XY Bank. 当社は、御社を受益者とする8万ドルの信用状を、XY銀行で開設しました。

favorable [favourable]　(形)有利な, 好都合な, 好ましい, 良好な, 好調な, 明るい, 追い風になる, 輸出超過の　(⇒appreciation of the yen, currency value, unfavorable)

favorable economic and political environments　良好な政治・経済環境

favorable exports　好調な輸出, 輸出好調

favorable factor　好材料, 上げ材料, 買い材料

favorable inflation outlook　明るいインフレ見通し

favorable investment returns　高い投資利回り

favorable news　好材料, 強材料

favorable rate of exchange　有利な為替相場, 順調な為替相場

favorable tax treatment　優遇税制, 税制上の優遇措置

favorable (tax) treatment for savings　貯蓄優遇措置

favorable technical factors　テクニカル[市場内部]要因の良さ

favorable tendency of the market　市況好調

favorable tone [trend]　好調

favorable turn　好転

give favorable treatment to foreign companies　外資を優遇する

on favorable terms　有利な条件で

policy of giving favorable treatment to foreign companies 外資優遇策 （⇒policy）
◆The business sentiment index represents the percentage of companies reporting favorable business conditions minus the percentage of those reporting unfavorable conditions. 業況判断指数は、景気が良いと答えた企業の割合（％）から景気が悪いと答えた企業の割合（％）を差し引いた指数だ。◆The diffusion index（DI）of business confidence refers to the percentage of companies that feel business conditions to be favorable, minus the ratio of firms that think otherwise. 業況判断指数（DI）は、景気が「良い」と感じている企業の割合（％）から、「悪い」と感じている企業の割合を差し引いた指数だ。◆This increase in recurring profits is largely due to an expansion in domestic demand for steel sheets used to produce automobiles and favorable steel exports to the Chinese market. この経常利益の増加は、主に自動車生産用鋼板の内需拡大と中国向け鉄鋼輸出の好調によるものだ。

favorable balance 黒字, 受取り超過, 出超
  favorable balance of current account 経常収支の黒字
  favorable balance of payments 国際収支の黒字
  favorable balance of trade 貿易黒字, 輸出超過, 順調な貿易尻

favorable exchange 有利な為替, 順調な為替, 順為替, 為替順調
  favorable exchange rate 有利な為替レート, 有利な為替相場, 順調な為替相場
    （=favorable rate of exchange）
  favorable yen exchange rate 円高相場

FB 政府短期証券
  （=financial bill; ⇒financing bill）

FBI 米連邦捜査局（Federal Bureau of Investigationの略）
  ◆The U.S. FBI is looking at potential fraud by four major financial institutions. 米連邦捜査局は、大手金融機関4社（政府系住宅金融ファニー・メイ、フレディ・マックの2社のほか、米保険最大手のAIGとリーマン・ブラザーズ）による詐欺の可能性を検討している。

FDI 外国からの直接投資, 対内直接投資, 対外直接投資
  （foreign direct investmentの略）
  ◆Foreign direct investment（FDI）in Japan fell 3.2 percent from the previous year to ￥2.11 trillion. 外国からの対内直接投資額は、前年度比3.2％減の2兆1,100億円だった。

FDIC 米連邦預金保険公社（Federal Deposit Insurance Corporationの略）
  ◆The list of banks the U.S. FDIC considers to be in trouble shot up nearly 50 percent to 171 during the third quarter of 2008. 米連邦預金保険公社（FDIC）が経営破たんの可能性があると見ている問題銀行は、2008年第3四半期［7-9月期］に約50％急増して171行［直前の4-6月期は117行］に達した。

FDIC-insured institutions FDIC（米連邦預金保険公社）が預金の支払いを保証している金融機関（米商業銀行と貯蓄金融機関）
  ◆The 171 banks on the FDIC's "problem list" encompass only about 2 percent of the nearly 8,500 FDIC-insured institutions. 米連邦預金保険公社の「問題銀行リスト」に挙げられた171行は、同公社が預金の支払いを保証している金融機関（米商業銀行と貯蓄金融機関）約8,500行の2％程度を占めるにすぎない。

FDIC's problem list 米連邦預金保険公社の問題銀行リスト
  ◆The 171 U.S. banks are on the FDIC's "problem list." 米国の171行が、米連邦預金保険公社（FDIC）の「問題銀行リスト」に挙がっている。

fear （動）恐れる, 心配する, 懸念する, 案じる, 気づかう, 不安になる
  ◆Gold is still becoming the safe haven as people fear recession in the U.S. and the eurozone debt problems. 米国の景気後退やユーロ圏の債務危機問題への懸念から、まだ金が安全な投資先［資金の逃避先］となっている。◆It is feared the colossal amount of the U.S. twin deficits could trigger a defall of the U.S. dollar. アメリカの巨額の双子の赤字は、ドルの暴落を引き起こす懸念がある。◆The ECB buyouts of sovereign debts of eurozone countries with fiscal laxity are the nightmare scenario Germany has been fearing. 欧州中銀（ECB）による放漫財政のユーロ圏諸国の国債買切りは、ドイツが恐れていた最悪のシナリオだ。◆The government and ruling parties began considering the economic package as they feared falling stock prices could result in a financial crisis. 政府・与党は、株価の下落で金融危機に陥る可能性があることから、経済対策の検討を開始した。

fear （名）懸念, 不安, 警戒感, 恐れ, 疑惑
  assuage inflation fears インフレ懸念を緩和する
  credit fears 信用不安
    （=credit crisis, credit crunch）
  deflation fears デフレ懸念 （=deflationary concerns, deflationary fears, fears of deflation）
  fear of unemployment 雇用不安
  fears of a double dip recession 景気二番底の懸念
  fears of an economic slowdown 景気減速への懸念
  fears over economic growth 景気の先行きへの懸念
  fears over the adverse effects of Greece's fiscal deficit ギリシャの財政危機の悪影響に対する懸念
  inflation fears インフレ懸念
    （=fear of inflation, inflationary fears）
  investors' fears 投資家の懸念
  prepayment fears 期限前償還に対する懸念, 期限前償還懸念
  recession fears 景気後退の恐れ
  soothe market fears 市場不安を払拭（ふっしょく）する
  ◆Fears about default on the Greek government bonds are smoldering as Greece's fiscal reconstruction measures hit the wall. ギリシャの財政再建策が行き詰まっているため、ギリシャ国債のデフォルト（債務不履行）の恐れがくすぶっている。◆Fears of a double dip recession are likely to rise if the rise in the yen continues. 円高がこのまま続けば、「景気二番底」懸念が高まると見られる。◆The central bank's move to increase the outstanding current account target is insufficient to soothe market fears. 日銀の当座預金残高目標の引上げは、市場不安を払拭するには物足りない。◆The Federal Reserve Board is trying to assuage inflation fears. 米連邦準備制度理事会（FRB）は、インフレ懸念の緩和に努めている。◆The possible downgrade of Treasury bonds is raising fears of adverse effects on the world's markets. 想定される米国債の格下げで、世界の市場に及ぼす悪影響への懸念が高まっている。◆The rapid spread of Italy's credit crisis is due to intensified fears about the nation's fiscal predicament by Italy's huge fiscal deficits. イタリアの信用不安が急速に広がったのは、イタリアの巨額の赤字で同国の財政ひっ迫への警戒感が高まったからだ。◆The U.S. dollar temporarily dropped to the upper ￥95 level over credit fears. 米ドルは、信用不安で一時、1ドル=95円台後半まで［後半の水準まで］下落した。

Fed 米連邦準備制度理事会, FRB （=Federal Reserve:Federal Reserve Boardの略称。米連邦準備銀行（Federal Reserve Bank）や米連邦準備制度（Federal Reserve System）、米連邦公開市場委員会（Federal Open Market Committee）を意味するときもある。⇒Federal Reserve）
  Fed chief 米連邦準備銀行総裁, FRB（米連邦準備銀行）総裁 （=Fed chairman; ⇒Fed Chairman）
  Fed Wire フェド・ワイヤー（米連邦準備制度の電子資金振替システム）
  the Fed's monetary easing 米連邦準備制度理事会［米中央銀行］の金融緩和

the Fed's monetary easing policy　米連邦準備制度理事会（FRB）の金融緩和策

the Fed's rate cuts　FRBの金利引下げ, FRBの利下げ

◆By conducting additional monetary easing policy, the Fed attempts to preemptively contain growing deflationary concerns in the United States.　追加金融緩和策を実施して、米連邦準備制度理事会（FRB）は、米国で高まるデフレ懸念に先手を打とうとしている。◆Major currencies are rising against the dollar on account of the Fed's monetary easing policy.　米連邦準備制度理事会（FRB）の金融緩和策で、主要通貨はドルに対して上昇している［ドル安・主要通貨高が進んでいる］。◆Speculation that the Fed would cut interest rates Tuesday heightened.　連邦準備制度理事会（FRB）が火曜日に利下げに踏み切るとの観測も、浮上している。◆The Fed cut interest rates 11 times last year by a total of 4.75 percentage points to prevent the bursting of the U.S. economic bubble.　米連邦準備制度理事会（FRB）は、米国のバブル崩壊を防ぐため、昨年1年間で11回にわたって合計4.75％もの利下げを行った。◆The Fed has been unable to deal with the current economic woes by changing interest rates as it has been maintaining a policy of virtually zero-percent interest rates.　米連邦準備制度知事会（FRB）はこれまで金利ゼロ政策を続けてきたため、政策金利を上げ下げして現在の経済的苦悩に対応することはできなくなっている。◆The Fed increased the official discount and Federal funds target rates to 4.75 percent and 5.25 percent, respectively, after a meeting of the Federal Open Market Committee.　米連邦準備制度理事会（FRB）は、連邦公開市場委員会（FOMC）を開いた後、公定歩合を4.75％、フェデラル・ファンド（FF）の誘導目標金利を5.25％にそれぞれ引き下げた。◆The Fed raised the discount rate to 0.75 percent from 0.5 percent as a response to improved financial market conditions.　米連邦準備制度理事会（FRB）は、金融市場の環境改善を受けて、（銀行に貸し出す際の金利である）公定歩合を現行の年0.5％から0.75％に引き上げた。◆The Fed will buy government bonds at a rate of about $75 billion a month through the middle of 2011.　米連邦準備制度理事会（FRB）は、2011年6月末までに毎月750億ドル規模で米国債を買い入れる［買い取る、購入する］。◆The Fed's program of buying $600 billion in Treasury bonds to help the economy is to end in June 2011 on schedule.　景気を支えるために6,000億ドルの国債を買い入れる米連邦準備制度理事会（FRB）の量的緩和政策は、予定通り2011年6月に終了する。◆The Fed's total amount of outstanding notes at the end of June 2011 increased by more than 30 percent from the end of March 2008, prior to the Lehman shock.　2011年6月末時点の米連邦準備制度理事会（FRB）の紙幣の総発行残高は、リーマン・ショック前の2008年3月末から30％以上も伸びた。◆There are mixed views as to the effect of the quantitative easing policy even within the Fed.　量的緩和策の効果については、FRB（米連邦準備制度理事会）内でも意見が割れている。

Fed Chairman　米連邦準備制度理事会（FRB）議長 (=Federal Reserve Board Chairman; ⇒Federal Reserve Board Chairman［chairman］)

◆Fed Chairman Alan Greenspan and his Federal Open Market Committee colleagues-the group that sets interest rate policy in the United States-kept the federal funds rate at 1 percent.　米連邦準備制度理事会（FRB）のアラン・グリーンスパン議長と米国の金融政策を決定する連邦公開市場委員会（FOMC）のメンバーは、短期金利の指標となるフェデラル・ファンド（FF）金利を1％に据え置いた。◆Fed Chairman Ben Bernanke told Congress that policymakers expect to keep U.S. interest rates low for a long time.　米議会でバーナンキFRB議長は、米国の低金利政策は長期化すると政策決定者は予想している、と述べた。◆The new Fed chairman's theory is to introduce inflation targets, thus setting numerical targets for stabilizing prices.　米連邦準備制度理事会（FRB）新議長の持論は、インフレ目標を導入して、物価安定の数値目標を示す［設定する］ことだ。

Fed district banks　米地区連銀

◆Ten of 12 Fed district banks reported weaker conditions or declines in their regional economies.　全米12地区連銀のうち10連銀が、各地域経済の悪化あるいは経済活動の低下を報告した。

Fed districts　全米12の連邦準備区, 全12地区連銀の地区　（⇒Federal Reserve Districts［districts］）

◆The Beige Book is an anecdotal collection of reports from all 12 Fed districts.　ベージュ・ブック（地区連銀景況報告）は、全12地区連銀の観察に基づく状況報告を取りまとめたものだ。

Fed funds　フェデラル・ファンド (=Federal funds)

Fed funds rate　フェデラル・ファンド・レート, FF金利（⇒Federal funds rate）

forward Fed funds　先渡しフェデラル・ファンド取引

higher Fed funds target　FF金利の誘導目標引上げ

unchanged Fed funds target　FF金利誘導目標の据え置き

Fed interest rate　米連邦金利

◆At the recent official May Federal Reserve Open Market Committee meeting, no change in the vital short-run Fed interest rate was decided on.　この5月に行われた米連邦準備制度（FRS）の公開市場委員会の公式会合では、最も重要な短期連邦金利の変更は行わないことを決定した。

Fed policy　米連邦準備制度理事会（FRB）の政策, FRBの金融政策

easier Fed policy　FRBによる利下げ

neutral Fed policy　FRBの金融政策が中立の姿勢［スタンス］を取ること

Fed regions　米地区連銀

◆Four Fed regions—New York, Cleveland, Kansas City and San Francisco—pointed to "signs of stabilization."　ニューヨーク、クリーブランド、カンザス、サンフランシスコの4米地区連銀は、「景気安定化の兆し」を指摘した。

Fed's monetary easing　米連邦準備制度理事会（FRB）の金融緩和

◆The Fed's monetary easing is a factor causing disarray in the foreign exchange markets.　米連邦準備制度理事会（FRB）［米中央銀行］の金融緩和が、為替相場混乱［為替混乱］の原因だ。

Fed's policy of quantitative easing　米連邦準備制度理事会（FRB）の量的緩和政策

◆The Fed's policy of quantitative easing foments chaos in foreign exchange markets.　米連邦準備制度理事会（FRB）［米国の中央銀行］の量的緩和政策は、為替相場［為替レート］の変動を招いている。

Fed's quantitative easing policy　FRB（米連邦準備制度理事会）の量的緩和［量的緩和策］

◆Some economists point out the side effects of the Fed's quantitative easing policy.　エコノミストのなかには、FRB（米連邦準備制度理事会）の量的緩和［量的緩和策］の副作用を指摘する声もある。

Fed's rate cuts　米連邦準備制度理事会（FRB）の金利引下げ

◆To enhance the stimulating effect of the Fed's rate cuts, swift implementation of fiscal and tax stimulus measures, including tax cuts on investment designed to reinvigorate the stock market, is necessary in addition to the large-scale tax cut program that is under way.　米連邦準備制度理事会（FRB）の金利引下げの刺激効果を高めるためには、現在実施中の大型減税プログラムに加え、株式市場を再活性化するための投資減税など、財政・税制面からの景気刺激策の速やかな実施が必要である。

federal　（形）連邦の, 連邦政府の, 連邦制の, 連邦組織の, アメリカ合衆国の

federal agency　米連邦政府機関

Federal agency security　政府機関証券
Federal Agricultural Mortgage Corporation　米連邦農業抵当公社, ファーマー・マック（通称）（＝Farmer Mac）
federal bailouts　米政府の救済措置, 米政府の救済策
federal bodies　米連邦機関
federal budget　米連邦政府予算, 米政府予算
federal court　米連邦裁判所
Federal deficit　米政府の赤字
Federal Deposit Insurance Act　米連邦預金保険法
Federal Deposit［Depository］Insurance Corporation　米連邦預金保険公社, FDIC
Federal Deposit Insurance Corporation Improvement Act　米連邦預金保険公社改革法
federal district　連邦区
Federal Employers' Liability Act　連邦雇用者責任法
federal government　連邦政府
Federal Home Loan Mortgage Corporation　米連邦住宅貸付抵当公社, フレディ・マック（通称）, FHLMC（⇒Freddie Mac）
Federal Housing Administration　米連邦住宅局, FHA
Federal Housing Administration insurance　FHA保険制度
Federal Housing Finance Board　米連邦住宅金融委員会, FHFB
federal income tax　連邦所得税, 連邦法人税
Federal Insurance Contribution Act　米連邦保険料法, 米連邦保険拠出金法, FICA
federal investigator　連邦政府調査官, 連邦調査官
Federal National Mortgage Association　米連邦住宅抵当金庫, 米連邦抵当金庫, ファニー・メイ（通称＝Fannie Mae）
federal regulation　米連邦規則
Federal Retirement Thrift Investment Board　米連邦職員退職貯蓄投資委員会
Federal Savings and Loan Insurance Corporation　米連邦貯蓄貸付け保険公社
federal spending　連邦政府支出, 連邦支出, 連邦予算, 国家支出
federal tax　米連邦税
Federal Trade Commission　米連邦取引委員会, FTC（＝U.S. federal antitrust regulators: 米国の独占禁止法施行機関. ⇒antitrust law, FTC）
Federal Truth in Lending Act　貸付けにおける真実法
Federal Unemployment Tax Act　米連邦失業保険税法
federal unemployment taxes payable　米連邦失業保険税未払い金
U.S. federal bailouts　米連邦政府［米政府］の救済措置, 米政府の救済策

federal bankruptcy code　米連邦破産法
◆The firm filed for protection from its creditors in a Delaware court under Chapter 11 of the federal bankruptcy code. 同社は, 米連邦破産法の第11章に基づき, デラウエア州連邦地裁に資産保全を申請した.

federal budget deficit　米財政赤字
（＝federal deficit）
◆The U.S. federal budget deficit surged to a record $413 billion in 2004. 米国の2004会計年度（2003年10月-2004年9月）の財政赤字は, 急増して過去最大の4,130億ドルとなった. ◆The U.S. federal budget deficit surged to a record $455 billion in 2008. 米国の2008会計年度（2007年10月-2008年9月）の財政赤字は, 急増して過去最大の4,550億ドルとなった.

federal debt　米連邦政府の債務, 米政府の債務
◆The U.S. federal debt has reached its current statutory limit of $14.3 trillion（about1.1 quadrillion）. 米政府の債務は, 現在の法定上限の14.3兆ドル（約1,100兆円）に達している.

federal debt ceiling　米連邦政府の債務上限, 米政府の借金枠　（＝federal debt limit）
◆If a new federal debt ceiling isn't set by Aug. 2, 2011, the United States will be forced to default on Treasuries securities as it will not be able to issue new bonds to pay back maturing government debts. 2011年8月2日までに連邦政府の債務上限を新たに設けないと, 米国は満期を迎える国債を償還するための国債増発ができないので, 米国債の不履行（デフォルト）が発生する.

federal deficit　米財政赤字
（＝federal budget deficit）
◆The U.S. federal deficit for the new year will likely exceed $500 billion even with the strengthening economy. 米国の新年度の財政赤字は, 景気が好転しても5,000億ドルを超える見込みだ.

federal district court　米連邦地裁
◆The SEC filed fraud charges against WorldCom in federal district court in New York. 米証券取引委員会（SEC）は, ワールドコム（米長距離通信社）を詐欺罪でニューヨーク連邦地裁に提訴した.

Federal Election Campaign Act　米連邦選挙資金規正法（米国の大統領選や連邦議員選の資金などを規制する法律）
hard money　ハード・マネー（連邦議会選挙の候補者への直接献金のこと）
soft money　ソフト・マネー（政党活動費や意見広告など政党への献金のこと）

Federal［federal］funds　フェデラル・ファンド, 米連邦準備制度の自由準備預金, 政府資金, 即日利用可能預金, FF　（＝Fed funds: アメリカの市中銀行が連邦準備銀行（FRB）に預けている資金）
federal funds market　フェデラル・ファンド市場, ニューヨーク連邦資金市場（＝federal fund market）
federal funds purchased　フェデラル・ファンド取入れ, フェデラル・ファンド借入金
federal funds sold　フェデラル・ファンド放出, フェデラル・ファンドの貸出残高
the target rate of federal funds　フェデラル・ファンド（FF）の誘導目標金利
◆The U.S. Federal Reserve raised the official discount rate and the target rate of federal funds by 0.25 percentage points in a bid to quell inflation and keep the economy from overheating. 米連邦準備制度理事会（FRB）は, インフレを防ぎ景気の過熱を警戒して, 公定歩合とフェデラル・ファンド（FF）の誘導目標金利をそれぞれ0.25パーセント引き上げた.

Federal funds rate　短期金利, FFレート, FF金利, フェデラル・ファンド金利, フェデラル・ファンド適用金利, フェデラル・ファンド・レート　（＝Fed funds rate, federal funds rate: 短期金融市場の状況を最も敏感に反映する指標金利の一つで, 日本のコール・レートに相当. アメリカの市中銀行同士がフェデラル・ファンドを翌日決済で貸し借りするときに適用する金利のこと. ⇒benchmark federal funds rate, Fed Chairman, official discount rate）
◆Policymaking members of the U.S. Federal Open Market Committee voted unanimously to keep its trendsetting federal funds rate for overnight loans between banks at 1.75 percent. 米連邦公開市場委員会の政策決定メンバーは, 銀行同士の翌日物のフェデラル・ファンド（FF）金利の誘導目標を, 現行の1.75%に据え置くことを全会一致で決めた. ◆The federal funds rate, a benchmark short-term interest rate, was cut to 3.5 percent per annum and the official discount rate to 3 percent per annum. 短期金利の誘導目標であるフェデラル・ファンド（FF）金利は年3.5%, 公定歩合は年3%に引き下げられた. ◆The federal funds rate is the interest that banks charge each other on overnight loans. フェデラル・ファンド（FF）金

利は、米国の民間銀行が翌日決済で相互に資金を貸し借りするときに適用する金利のことをいう。◆The Federal funds rate now remains at 3.75 percent. 短期金利（FFレート）は現在、年3.75%にとどまっている。

Federal funds target rate フェデラル・ファンド（FF）の誘導目標金利 (=the target rate of federal funds; ⇒Federal Reserve)
◆The Fed increased the official discount and Federal funds target rates to 4.75 percent and 5.25 percent, respectively, after a meeting of the Federal Open Market Committee. 米連邦準備制度理事会（FRB）は、連邦公開市場委員会（FOMC）を開いた後、公定歩合を4.75%、フェデラル・ファンド（FF）の誘導目標金利を5.25%にそれぞれ引き上げた。

Federal Housing Finance Agency 米連邦住宅金融局, 米住宅金融局, FHFA
◆The Federal Housing Finance Agency oversees Fannie and Freddie that buy mortgage loans and mortgage securities issued by the lenders. 米連邦住宅金融局（FHFA）は、金融機関が発行する住宅ローンやモーゲージ証券を購入する［買い取る］連邦住宅抵当金庫（ファニー・メイ）や連邦住宅貸付け抵当公社（フレディ・マック）を監督している。◆The Federal Housing Finance Agency sued 17 financial firms over risky investments. 米連邦住宅金融局（FHFA）が、高リスク証券を販売したとして大手金融機関17社を提訴した。

federal income taxes 連邦所得税
◆The consolidated provision for taxes also includes an amount sufficient to pay additional United States federal income taxes on repatriation of income earned abroad. 連結納税引当金には、海外で得た利益の本国送金に課される米国所得税の追加支払いに十分対応できる金額も含まれている。

Federal Open Market Committee 米連邦公開市場委員会, FOMC (=Federal Reserve Open Market Committee, U.S. Federal Open Market Committee: 米国の金融政策の最高意思決定機関で、短期金融政策と公開市場操作に関する方針を決定する。連邦準備制度理事会の理事7人（議長を含む）と地区連邦準備銀行の総裁5人で構成。⇒Fed Chairman, Fed interest rate)
◆Policymaking members of the U.S. Federal Open Market Committee voted unanimously to keep its trendsetting federal funds rate for overnight loans between banks at 1.75 percent. 米連邦公開市場委員会の政策決定メンバーは、銀行同士の翌日物のフェデラル・ファンド（FF）金利の誘導目標を、現行の1.75%に据え置くことを全会一致で決めた。◆The Fed increased the official discount and Federal funds target rates to 4.75 percent and 5.25 percent, respectively, after a meeting of the Federal Open Market Committee. 米連邦準備制度理事会（FRB）は、連邦公開市場委員会（FOMC）を開いた後、公定歩合を4.75%、フェデラル・ファンド（FF）の誘導目標金利を5.25%にそれぞれ引き上げた。◆The unanimous decision by the U.S. central bank's policy setting Federal Open Market Committee moved the benchmark federal funds rate to 1.25 percent. 米連邦準備制度理事会の金利政策を決定する米連邦公開市場委員会の全会一致による決定で、短期金利の指標であるフェデラル・ファンド金利が年1.25%に引き上げられた。◆The U.S. central bank's Federal Open Market Committee is composed of seven Fed board members and five regional bank presidents. 米連邦準備制度理事会（FRB）の連邦公開市場委員会（FOMC）は、FRBの理事7人と地区連邦準備銀行の総裁5人とで構成されている。

Federal Reserve 米連邦準備制度理事会（FRB） (=Fed, Federal Reserve Board: 米連邦準備制度（Federal Reserve System）や連邦公開市場委員会（Federal Open Market Committee）、連邦準備銀行（Federal Reserve Bank）を意味することもある。⇒beige book, Fed, Federal Reserve Board, inflation, key rate)
Federal Reserve Act 米連邦準備法
Federal Reserve policy 米連邦準備制度理事会（FRB）の金融政策
Federal Reserve System 米連邦準備制度, FRS, 米国の中央銀行制度
◆The Federal Reserve raised U.S. interest rates for the first time in four years. 米連邦準備制度理事会（FRB）は、金利を4年ぶりに引き上げた。◆The U.S. Federal Reserve raised the official discount rate and the target rate of federal funds by 0.25 percentage points in a bid to quell inflation and keep the economy from overheating. 米連邦準備制度理事会（FRB）は、インフレを防ぎ景気の過熱を警戒して、公定歩合とフェデラル・ファンド（FF）の誘導目標金利をそれぞれ0.25パーセント引き上げた。

Federal Reserve Bank 米連邦準備銀行, FRB （金融政策の執行機関で、地区連銀といわれる。⇒Federal Reserve Districts）
◆U.S. President-elect Barack Obama named New York Federal Reserve Bank President Tim Geithner the next treasury secretary. オバマ次期米大統領は、新政権の財務長官にティモシー・ガイトナー・ニューヨーク連邦準備銀行総裁を指名した。

Federal Reserve Bank of New York ニューヨーク連銀 （=New York Federal Reserve Bank）
◆The Bank of Japan asked the Federal Reserve Bank of New York to intervene in the New York foreign exchange market on its behalf through yen-selling, dollar-buying operations for the first time in 15 months. 日銀は、1年3か月ぶりにニューヨーク連銀に委託して、ニューヨーク外国為替市場で円売り・ドル買いの介入に踏み切った。

Federal Reserve Board 米連邦準備制度理事会, 米連邦準備理事会, 米中央銀行(the Fed, the U.S. central bank), FRB (=Federal Reserve: 米国の連邦準備制度（FRS）の統括機関で、正式名称はBoard of Governors of the Federal Reserve System。理事は7人で上院の承認を経て大統領が任命し、任期は14年。⇒currency swap agreement)
◆A U.S. Federal Reserve Board snapshot of economic conditions bolsters the hope of broader-based recovery. 米連邦準備制度理事会（FRB）の景況報告では、ほとんどの地域で景気持ち直しの期待が強まっている。◆Despite moves by the U.S. Federal Reserve Board to loan more money to financial institutions, banks are still reluctant to lend. 米連邦準備制度理事会（FRB）に金融融資を拡大する動きがあるにもかかわらず、銀行［金融機関］はまだ貸し渋っている。◆In the subprime crisis, the U.S. Federal Reserve Board had to take the extraordinary step of providing an emergency loan not to a commercial bank but to an investment bank. サブプライム問題で、米国の中央銀行の連邦準備制度理事会（FRB）は、緊急融資を銀行［商業銀行］ではなく証券会社［投資銀行］に対して行う異例の措置を取らざるを得なかった。◆The total assets of the Federal Reserve Board have soared to $2.87 trillion at the end of June 2011 from $896.2 billion as of the end of March 2008, prior to the Lehman shock. 米連邦準備制度理事会（FRB）の総資産は、リーマン・ショック前の2008年3月末時点の8,962億ドルから、2011年6月末には2兆8,700億ドルに急増した。◆The U.S. Federal Reserve Board boosted a key interest rate to the highest level in five years. 米連邦準備制度理事会（FRB）は、（短期金利の指標となる）FF金利を5年ぶりに最高水準に引き上げた。◆The U.S. Federal Reserve Board has told Citigroup Inc. to delay big takeover plans until the world's biggest bank tightens internal controls and addresses a slew of regulatory problems at home and abroad. 米連邦準備理事会（FRB）は、世界最大の銀行シティグループが内部統制を強化し、国内外の多くの規制問題に取り組むまで、大型買収計画を延期するようシティグループに伝えた。◆The U.S. Federal Reserve Board raised U.S. interest rates, leading the worldwide move to change current super-loose monetary policy. 米連邦準備制度理事会（FRB）が米国の金利を引き上げ、世界的な超金融緩和の政策転換の先陣を切った。

Federal Reserve Board Chairman [chairman]　米連邦準備制度理事会(FRB)議長, FRB議長　(=Fed Chairman, Federal Reserve Chairman)
◆U.S. Federal Reserve Board Chairman Ben Bernanke took the preemptive action of announcing that the U.S. central bank was ready for further monetary easing steps. 米連邦準備制度理事会(FRB)のバーナンキ議長が、先手を打って、FRBは追加の金融緩和策の用意があると表明した。◆U.S. President George W. Bush renominated Alan Greenspan as U.S. Federal Reserve Board Chairman. ブッシュ米大統領は、アラン・グリーンスパンをFRB議長に再指名した。

Federal Reserve Districts [districts]　全米12の連邦準備区　(=Fed districts: 全米12の連邦準備区に、米国の連邦準備制度(Federal Reserve System)を構成する連邦準備銀行(Federal Reserve Bank)が1行ずつ設置されている)
◆Overall economic activity increased somewhat across all Federal Reserve districts except St. Louis. セントルイスを除く地区連銀の11地区で、経済活動全体がいくぶん増加した。

Federal Reserve Open Market Committee　米連邦準備制度理事会(FRB)の連邦公開市場委員会　(=Federal Open Market Committee)
◆At the recent official May Federal Reserve Open Market Committee meeting, no change in the vital short-run Fed interest rate was decided on. この5月に行われた米連邦準備制度理事会(FRB)の公開市場委員会の公式会合では、最も重要な短期連邦金利の変更は行わないことを決定した。

federal spending　連邦政府支出, 連邦支出
◆Federal spending for the nine months to date totaled $1.62 trillion, a 6.9 percent increase from the corresponding period in the previous fiscal year. 10-6月期の連邦政府支出の総額は1兆6,200億ドルで、前年度同期比で6.9%の増加となった。◆The Obama administration failed to cut federal spending. オバマ政権は、連邦支出を削減しなかった。

fee　(名)料金, 入会金, 納付金, 会費, 手数料, 使用料, 報酬, 謝礼, 実施料, 対価, フィー, 所有権, 相続財産権　(⇒bank service fee, underwriting fee)
　after fee　手数料込みで　(=at full fees)
　brokerage fee　委託手数料, 仲介手数料
　corporate finance fee　企業金融手数料
　fee income　手数料収入　(=commission income)
　fees and commissions　手数料
　incentive fee　成功報酬, 報奨金, インセンティブ・フィー
　listing fees　上場手数料
　loan organization fee　貸出金実行手数料
　management fee　幹事手数料, 運用報酬, 運用手数料, 経営報酬
　medical fees　医療費　(=medical costs)
　redemption fee　解約手数料, 買戻し手数料
　trading and underwriting fees　売買・引受手数料
　transfer fee　振替料
　trust fee　信託手数料
　underwriting fee　引受手数料
　within fees　手数料の範囲内で
◆In foreign currency deposits, commission fees are needed when the yen is exchanged into a foreign currency and when the foreign currency is exchanged backed in yen. 外貨預金では、円を外貨に替えるときと、外貨を円に戻すときに、為替手数料が必要になる。◆Mizuho Financial Group failed to earn sufficient fee income to make up for reduced gains from stock investments. みずほフィナンシャルグループは、株式投資による利益減少分をカバーできるだけの手数料収入が十分得られなかった。

feeder fund　フィーダー・ファンド　(=baby fund: 国内投資家が海外のマスター・ファンド(マザー・ファンド(mother fund)ともいう)に税制上有利に投資できるように設立されるファンドで、ベビー・ファンド(baby fund)ともいう)

fend off　うまくかわす, 払いのける, 防衛する, 防御する, 防ぐ, 防止する, (批判などを)受け流す, そらす, 避ける, 拒(こば)む
　fend off a hostile takeover　敵対的買収をうまくかわす[防衛する、防ぐ]
　fend off a recurrence of financial strife　金融危機の再発を防止する
◆By increasing its involvement in TEPCO's management, the government aims to fend off credit uneasiness in the utility. 東電への経営関与を強めることにより、国は東電の信用不安を防止しようとしている。◆The challenge of the Basel Committee on Banking Supervision is to develop a regulatory framework while fending off a recurrence of financial strife. バーゼル銀行監督委員会の課題は、金融危機再発の防止と規制の枠組みの策定だ。◆The firm's management fended off a hostile takeover by an investment fund. 同社の経営陣が、投資ファンドによる敵対的買収を防いだ。

fetch　(動)～で売れる、～の値を付ける、～の高値を呼ぶ
◆Japan has not intervened in the currency market since March 2004, when the yen fetched about ¥109 per dollar. 日本は、1ドル＝約109円の値を付けた2004年3月以来、為替介入に踏み切っていない。◆The dollar was fetching ¥105.53, near the seven-month low of ¥105.30 reached earlier last week. ドルは一時、1ドル＝105円53銭を付け、先週はじめに達した7か月ぶりの最安値1ドル＝105円30銭に近い水準となった。◆The firm expects the listing to fetch ¥200,000 per share. 同社は、上場で1株当たり20万円の高値を呼ぶと予想している。◆The Mixi stock fetched an initial price of ¥2.95 in the morning on the TSE's Mothers market for emerging companies after its Thursday debut. ミクシィ株は、木曜日の上場後、新興企業向け市場の東証マザーズで、午前に295万円の初値を付けた。

FFRS　米連邦金融規制庁 (Federal Financial Regulatory Serviceの略)

FGI　金融保証保険 (financial guarantee insuranceの略)

FHA insurance　FHA(連邦住宅局)保険制度 (FHAはFederal Housing Administrationの略)

FHFA　米連邦住宅金融局 (Federal Housing Finance Agencyの略)

FHFB　米連邦住宅金融委員会 (Federal Housing Finance Boardの略)

FHLMC　米連邦住宅貸付抵当公社, フレディ・マック (Federal Home Loan Mortgage Corporationの略。⇒Freddie Mac)

FICA　米連邦保険料法, 米連邦保険拠出法 (Federal Insurance Contribution Actの略)

fictitious　(形)架空の, 偽の, 偽りの, うそ の, 虚構の (false), 偽造の, 本物でない (not genuine), 想像上の実体のない, 作り話の, 擬制の
　fictitious account number　架空口座番号
　fictitious annual coupon　見なし利息
　fictitious asset　擬制資産, 架空財産
　fictitious bill [paper]　空手形
　fictitious capital　擬制資本
　fictitious demand [use]　仮需要, 偽りの需要
　fictitious deposits　架空の預金
　fictitious dividend　たこ配当　(=bogus dividend)
　fictitious name　偽名, 架空の名前, 架空名義
　fictitious payee　(手形や小切手の)架空の受取人
　fictitious person　法人　(=artificial person, corporate person)

fictitious price　掛け値
fictitious profit　架空利益
fictitious sales　架空売買, 架空売上
fictitious transaction　架空の取引, 空取引, 擬制取引
fictitious withholding tax　見なし源泉課税
◆A former chairman of an IT-related firm and three others were arrested on suspicion of seeking investments in a fictitious Internet-related business. IT関連企業の元会長ら4人が、実体のないIT関連事業への出資を募った容疑で逮捕された。

fidelity　（名）誠実, 忠実, 誠意, 正確さ, 適合度
　fidelity bond　身元保証, 包括保証, 身元保証保険, 信用保険
　fidelity guarantee insurance　身元保証保険
　fidelity insurance　身元保証保険, 身元信用保険
　fidelity rebate system　運賃割戻し制

fiduciary　（名）受託者, 被信託者　（信託会社（trust company）、破産管財人（trustee in bankruptcy）、遺産管理人（administrator）、遺言執行者（executor）、後見人（guardian）など、財産所有者の委任を受けて特定の第三者の利益のために、委託された財産を管理・保全する者）
　bond fiduciary　債券金融
　named fiduciary　指名受託者

fiduciary　（形）信用の, 信託の, 受託者の, 信用発行の
　elastic fiduciary issue system　屈伸制限制度, 保証準備制度
　fiduciary accounting　信託会計
　fiduciary bond　受託者保証, 受託者保証金
　fiduciary business　信託業務
　fiduciary capacity　信託保管能力, 受託者の資格
　fiduciary circulation　信用流通
　fiduciary contract　信用契約
　fiduciary contribution　信用出資
　fiduciary currency　信用通貨
　fiduciary duty　受託者の義務, 注意義務
　fiduciary estate　信託財産
　fiduciary fund　信託資金
　fiduciary institution　信用機関
　fiduciary issue　信用発行, 保証発行, 無準備発行
　fiduciary law　信託法
　fiduciary loan　信用貸付け, 無担保貸付け, 信用貸付け金
　fiduciary money　信用貨幣, 信託貨幣
　fiduciary note　無準備発行紙幣
　fiduciary paper money　信用紙幣
　fiduciary property　信託財産
　fiduciary reserve　信用準備
　fiduciary responsibility　受託者責任
　fiduciary services　信託業務, 受託業務
　fiduciary work　信託業務
　issue the deal on a fiduciary basis through　～による受託ベースで起債する
　quasi-fiduciary relationship　準信認関係
　securities for fiduciary issue　保証準備

fiduciary market　信託市場
◆The government may reject a company's request for a license to enter the fiduciary market if its executive has been dismissed in the past five years due to a violation of Section 2 of Article 102. 信託市場（信託業）に参入するための免許を申請した企業の役員が、第102条第2項の違反により5年以内に解任命令を受けていた場合、政府はその免許申請（免許交付）を拒否することができる。

field　（名）田, 野原, 領域, 分野, 市場, 実地, 現場, 現地, 出先, （天然資源の）埋蔵地帯, 産出地帯, 競技場, グランド, 運動場, フィールド
　enter a new field　新分野に参入する
　field audit　実地監査, 現場監査, 実物監査
　field marketing staff　第一線の営業員, 外交販売員, 外交員, 巡回営業担当社員　（=field sales force）
　field research　実地調査, 現場調査, 現地調査, フィールド・リサーチ
　field sales force　外務員, 外交販売員
　　（=field salesman, field salesperson）
　field study　実地調査, 現地調査, 実地研究, フィールド・スタディ
　gain the field　市場を獲得する
　growth [growing] field　成長分野
　other business fields　異業種
　playing field　事業環境, 競争条件
　renewable energy field　再生可能エネルギーの分野, 自然エネルギーの分野

◆A project financing scheme is the largest growing field for Japanese banks. プロジェクト・ファイナンス（事業融資）事業は、邦銀にとって最大の成長分野だ。◆Moves toward a full-scale realignment have been accelerating in the commodity futures trading industry, involving companies from other business fields. 商品先物取引業界では、異業種の企業を巻き込んだ総力を挙げての再編の動きが加速している。◆The project financing market has seen a boost in loans to businesses in renewable energy field such as solar and wind power generation. プロジェクト・ファイナンス市場は最近、太陽光や風力発電など自然エネルギー分野の事業への融資が増えている。

fierce　（形）熾烈（しれつ）な, 激しい, 強烈な
　fierce global competition　熾烈な国際競争
　fierce price competition　熾烈な価格競争

fierce competition　熾烈な競争, 激しい競争
　（=cutthroat competition）
◆As a result of fierce competition in the past, interest rate profit margins were kept too low to cover loans that went sour. 過去の熾烈（しれつ）な競争の結果、金利の利ざやが小さく抑えられる余り、貸倒れ［貸倒れのリスク］をカバーできなかった［過去の熾烈な融資合戦の結果、不良債権リスクをカバーできないほど利ざやは小さく抑えられた］。◆GM faces fierce competition with rivals around the world. GMは、世界のライバル各社との激しい競争に直面している。◆To survive fierce competition from foreign rivals, Japan's largest and third-largest steelmakers agreed to merge by October 2012. 海外のライバル企業との激しい競争に勝ち残るため、国内最大手と3位の鉄鋼メーカーが、2012年10月をめどに合併することで合意した。

fight　（動）戦う, 争う, 立ち向かう, 対応する, 抵抗する, 阻止する, 競争する, 努力する, 奮闘する, 口論する, 言い争う
　fight against inflation　インフレと戦う
　fight against terrorism　テロと戦う
　fight back　～に抵抗する, 反撃する, ～をこらえる
◆The Bank of Japan will fight the yen's appreciation in close cooperation with the government. 日銀は、政府と緊密に連携して円高に対応する方針だ。◆The government and the Bank of Japan will likely continue to work together in fighting the sharp rise in the yen's value. 政府と日銀は、急激な円高阻止で協調路線を継続することになりそうだ。

figure　（名）数字, 数値, 値, データ, 統計, 値段, 金額, 総額, 合計, 実績
　advanced GDP figures　GDP速報値
　CPI figure　消費者物価指数
　employment figures　雇用統計
　estimated figure　推定値

first quarter figures　第1四半期の実績, 第1四半期決算
industrial production figures　鉱工業生産統計, 鉱工業生産指数
producer price figure　生産者物価指数
retail price figure　小売物価指数
◆A reading of below 50 percent in the coincident index is considered a sign of economic contraction and a figure above that is viewed as a sign of expansion. 一致指数で50%以下の数値は景気収縮[景気後退]を示す指標と見られ、それ以上の数字は景気回復[景気拡大]を示す指標と見なされる。◆Combined with the amount of government bonds to be issued in fiscal 2005, the figure reaches a horrendous ¥169 trillion. 2005年度の国債発行額と合わせて、国債の発行総額はなんと169兆円に達する。◆Relatively solid retail sales figures inspired another rally on Wall Street. 小売上高が比較的に堅調だったため、ニューヨーク株式市場はまた持ち直した[ニューヨーク株は反発した]。◆The government revised up its economic growth figures for the first three months of the year. 政府は、1-3月期の経済成長率の数値を上方修正した。◆The Group's sales figures have been restated following the retrospective application of new International Financial Reporting Standards. 当グループの売上高の数値は、新国際財務報告基準(IFRS)を遡及的に適用して、再表示されています。

file　(動)提出する, 申請する, 申し込む, 届け出る, 申し立てる, 保管する, 整理保管する
　file a declaration of bankruptcy and a request for asset protection with　～に破産宣告と財産保全の処分を申請する, ～に破産宣告と財産保全の処分を申し立てる
　file a petition with　～に提訴する
　file a preliminary injunction　仮処分を申請する
　　(=apply for an [a provisional] injunction, file a provisional disposition)
　file a request with A for B　Aに対してBを申請する
　file a shelf registration statement with the U.S. Securities and Exchange Commission　米証券取引委員会(SEC)に一括登録[発行登録]届け出書を提出する
　file a suit against A for B　AをBで提訴する, AをBで訴える
　file an indictment against　～を起訴する, 告発する
　file final reports on income for this year　今年度の確定申告書を提出する
　filed documents in a computer　パソコン内の文書ファイル　(⇒virus)
◆The SEC filed fraud charges against WorldCom in federal district court in New York. 米証券取引委員会(SEC)は、ワールドコム(米長距離通信社)を詐欺罪でニューヨーク連邦地裁に提訴した。

file a claim against　～に損害賠償を請求する, ～に対する債権を届け出る
◆During a regular board meeting, Fuji TV directors agreed to file a claim against Livedoor for losses of more than ¥30 billion incurred from selling off Livedoor shares. 定例取締役会で、フジテレビの役員は、ライブドア株の売却で被った300億円超の損失について、ライブドアに損害賠償を請求することで合意した。

file a class action suit　集団訴訟を起こす
◆Victim firms have entered into talks to file a class action suit for compensation. 被害企業が、損害賠償に向けて集団訴訟のための協議を開始した。

file a complaint against　～を告発する
◆The Securities and Exchange Surveillance Commission is discussing whether to file a complaint against the man with the Tokyo District Public Prosecutors Office on suspicion of insider trading. 証券取引等監視委員会は、インサイダー取引の容疑で、この男を東京地検に告発するかどうかを検討している。

file a criminal complaint against　～を刑事告発する
◆The Financial Services Agency filed a criminal complaint against Incubator Bank of Japan. 金融庁が、日本振興銀行を刑事告発した。◆The Securities and Exchange Surveillance Commission filed a criminal complaint against a former bank employee with the Tokyo District Public Prosecutors Office on suspicion of violating the Financial Instruments and Exchange Law. 証券取引等監視委員会は、元行員を金融商品取引法違反の疑いで東京地検に刑事告発した。

file a damages suit against　～を相手取り損害賠償を求める訴訟を起こす　(⇒damages suit)
◆Sumitomo Trust & Banking Co. is considering filing a damages suit against UFJ Holdings and its group executives. 住友信託銀行は現在、UFJホールディングスとUFJグループの経営陣を相手取って損害賠償を求める訴訟を起こすことを検討している。

file a declaration of bankruptcy　破産宣告を申し立てる
◆The financial authorities filed a declaration of bankruptcy and a request for asset protection with the Tokyo District Court for the brokerage firm. 金融当局は、同証券会社の破産宣告と財産保全処分を東京地裁に申し立てた。

file a lawsuit　提訴する, 告訴する, 訴えを起こす, 訴訟を起こす　(=file a suit; ⇒derivative investment)
　file a lawsuit against　～を提訴する
　file a lawsuit with　～に訴えを起こす, ～に提訴する
◆Among 17 big banks targeted by the lawsuits filed by the U.S. government were Bank of America, Citigroup, Credit Suisse and Nomura Holding America Inc. 米政府が提訴した訴訟の対象の大手金融機関17社の中には、バンカメのほかにシティグループやクレディ・スイス、野村ホールディング・アメリカなどが含まれている。◆Sumitomo Trust & Banking Co. has entered the final stages of filing a lawsuit with the Tokyo District Court requesting a freeze on trust merger negotiations between UFJ Holdings Inc. and Mitsubishi Tokyo Financial Group Inc. 住友信託銀行は、UFJホールディングスと三菱東京フィナンシャル・グループによる信託部門の経営統合交渉の差止めを求める訴えを東京地裁に起こす方向で最終調整に入った。◆The U.S. government filed lawsuits against 17 financial firms for selling Fannie and Freddie mortgage-backed securities that turned toxic when the housing market collapsed. 米政府は、住宅市場崩壊時に不良資産化した住宅ローン担保証券(MBS)をファニー・メイ(米連邦住宅抵当公庫)とフレディ・マック(米連邦住宅貸付け抵当公社)に販売したとして、大手金融機関17社(バンク・オブ・アメリカやシティグループ、JPモルガン・チェース、ゴールドマン・サックス・グループなど)を提訴した。

file a provisional disposition　仮処分を申請する
　(=apply for an [a provisional] injunction)
◆Sumitomo Trust & Banking Co. filed a provisional disposition requesting a ban on UFJ discussing the sale of UFJ Trust Bank with MTFG. 住友信託銀行は、UFJ信託銀行の売却に関する三菱東京フィナンシャル・グループとUFJとの交渉差止めを求める仮処分を申請した。

file a suit against A for B　AをBで提訴する, AをBで訴える
◆The U.S. Securities and Exchange Commission began taking actions, filing suits against companies for window-dressing their accounting records. 米証券取引委員会(SEC)は、会計記録の粉飾(粉飾決算)で企業を提訴するなどの行動をとり始めた[米証券取引委員会は粉飾決算企業を提訴するなどの行動をとり始めた]。

file an IPO paperwork with the U.S. SEC　米証券取引委員会(SEC)に株式の新規公開(IPO)書類を提出する
◆General Motors filed an IPO paperwork with the U.S. Securities and Exchange Commission. (米政府の管理下で経

営再建中の）ゼネラル・モーターズ（GM）は、株式の新規公開（IPO）書類を米証券取引委員会に提出した。

file for bankruptcy　破産を申し立てる, 破産［破たん］申請する, 破産法を申請する, 再生法を申請する　（=file for insolvency）

　file for bankruptcy protection　破たん申請する

　file for bankruptcy protection under the Corporate Rehabilitation Law　会社更生法の適用を申請する

　◆The scandal-ridden Incubator Bank of Japan filed for bankruptcy protection. スキャンダルまみれの日本振興銀行が、破たん申請した。◆Tokyo stocks bounced back Wednesday after sharp falls Tuesday following Lehman Brothers decision to file for bankruptcy as financial worries eased. 水曜日の東京株式市場は、リーマン・ブラザーズが前日に破たん申請を決めて急落したものの、金融不安が和らいだため反発した。

file for (court) protection from creditors　資産保全を申請する, 破たん申請する, 会社更生手続きを申請する　（=file for protection from creditors, seek court protection from creditors）

　◆MGM film studio filed for court protection from creditors in November 2010. ハリウッドの映画会社メトロ・ゴールドウィン・メイヤー（MGM）が、2010年11月に、会社更生手続きを申請した。

fill or kill　即時売買注文, 即時執行注文, FOK　（=fill and kill order, fill or kill order）

finance　（動）融資する, 貸し付ける, 出資する, 資金を出す, 資金を供給する, 資金を調達する, 赤字などを埋め合わせる, 補填（ほてん）する, ～の資金に充（あ）てる, 財政を管理する, 財政を切り回す　（⇒bond issue, bond redemption, insurance fund, interest on loans, lion's share, nursing care insurance）

　be financed by debt　借入れで調達する, 負債による資金調達を行う

　be fully financed by　～が100％出資する, ～が全額出資する

　finance a new business　新規事業に融資する

　finance [fund] an acquisition　企業買収の資金を調達する

　finance capital needs　資金需要を賄（まかな）う

　finance earthquake reconstruction programs　震災復興計画の財源を確保する, 震災の復興財源を確保する

　finance government deficits　財政赤字の穴埋めをする, 財政赤字を補填する

　finance mergers or acquisitions　合併や買収の資金調達をする

　finance stock buybacks　自社株買戻しの資金を調達する

　finance the massive earthquake reconstruction programs　（東日本）大震災復興計画の財源を確保する

　finance wisely　うまく財政を処理する

　jointly finance　共同出資する　（=finance jointly）

　reconstruction bonds to finance the second fiscal 2011 supplementary budget　2011年度第二次補正予算案の財源に充（あ）てる震災復興債［復興再生債］　（⇒reconstruction bonds）

　◆A special account is used to finance public investment and loans to government-affiliated financial institutions. 特別会計は、政府系金融機関に財政投融資の資金を供給するのに用いられる。◆By selling JT shares, the government expects to raise ¥500 billion to ¥600 billion to finance reconstruction from the Great East Japan Earthquake. JT（日本たばこ産業）株の売却で政府は、東日本大震災復興の財源に充てるため、5,000億円～6,000億円の資金調達を見込んでいる。◆Dividend payments to bond holders have been financed by the rent paid by Mycal to the special purpose company（SPC）. 社債保有者に支払う配当金の原資は、マイカルが特定目的会社に支払う店舗の家賃だ。◆Domestic banks are increasing their efforts to finance large overseas projects. 国内銀行各行は、海外での大型事業に融資する（プロジェクト・ファイナンスへの）取組みを強化している。◆Greece will be able to finance its public debt without any problem. ギリシャは、問題なくギリシャ国債の資金（国債の償還や金利支払いの資金）を調達できるだろう。◆In the project financing business, lending banks are repaid loans through profits generated by the projects they have financed. プロジェクト・ファイナンス事業では、貸出行が、融資したプロジェクト（事業）から生まれる利益で融資の返済を受ける。◆The child allowance program is being financed by increasing government debt. 子ども手当制度の財源は、政府の借金［政府債務］の上積みで賄われている。◆The firm received a huge capital increase financed by foreign investment funds. 同社は、海外ファンド［投資ファンド］を引受先として巨額の増資を行った。◆The fund established by the Development of Japan is designed to finance major auto parts makers hit by the March 11 earthquake and tsunami. 日本政策投資銀行が設立するファンドは、東日本大震災（2011年3月11日）で被災した自動車部品メーカーに出資や融資などの資金支援をするのが目的だ。◆The government may raise the consumption tax rate to finance the massive earthquake reconstruction programs. 政府は、東日本大震災復興計画の財源を確保するため、消費税率を引き上げる可能性がある。◆The percentage of government funds from the consumption tax and other tax revenues for financing the basic pension plan remains about 36.5 percent. 基礎年金の財源としての消費税収などによる国の負担金の割合は、まだ約36.5％にとどまっている。◆The public welfare loans are extended to widows and single mothers to help them become economically independent by financing spending for education, living costs, housing costs and funds to start small businesses. 福祉資金は、母子家庭や寡婦に対して教育費や生活費、住宅費、小規模事業の開始資金などを貸し付けて、その経済的自立を助けるために供与されている。◆The remaining ¥1.8 billion will be financed by two other commercial banks and trust banks. 残りの18億円は、他の都銀2行と信託各行が出す。◆To help finance the government burden in running the basic pension plan, the Health, Labor and Welfare Ministry calls for ¥10.67 trillion in funds in its budgetary request for fiscal 2012. 基礎年金運営の国庫負担［国の負担］分の費用として、厚生労働省は、2012年度予算の概算要求で10兆6,700億円を要求している。◆To procure funds to finance reconstruction from the Great East Japan Earthquake, the government is planning to sell some of its shares in Japan Tobacco Inc. and Tokyo Metro Co. 東日本大震災の復興費用を賄うための資金［復興費用に充てる資金］を調達するため、政府は日本たばこ産業（JT）と東京地下鉄（東京メトロ）の株式を売却する方針だ。

finance　（名）金融, 財務, 財務内容, 財政, 財力, 財源, 資金, 資金調達, 融資, ファイナンス　（⇒consumer finance, gain名詞, private finance initiative, project finance, sell-off）

　adversely affect one's finance　財務内容にマイナス影響を与える

　asset finance　資産金融, アセット・ファイナンス

　bridging finance　つなぎ融資　（=bridge financing）

　business finance　企業金融

　capital finance　資本調達

　co-finance　共同融資

　commercial finance　商業金融

　consumer finance　消費者金融　（=consumer financing）

　corporate finance　企業金融, 企業財務, 企業の資金調達, 法人金融, コーポレート・ファイナンス

debt finance　負債金融, 負債による資金調達, デット・ファイナンス
debt-laden finances　借金漬けの財政
deficit finance　赤字財政
direct finance　直接金融
equity finance　株式発行による資金調達, エクイティ・ファイナンス
export finance　輸出金融
external finance　外部資金
finance policy　金融政策
government finances　財政 (=state finances)
high finance　大型金融
international finance　国際金融
inventory finance　在庫金融
lease finance　リース金融
local finance　地方財政
long-term finance　長期融資, 長期金融
municipal finance　都市財政
national finance　国家財政
online finance　オンライン金融
political finances　政治資金
provide finance for the project　プロジェクト[事業計画]に資金を供給する
public finance　財政, 政府の資金調達
public finance market　公共債市場, 公募債市場
public finance policy　財政政策
sales finance　販売金融
state finance　国家財政, 財政
structured finance　仕組み金融
surplus finance　黒字財政
trade finance　貿易金融
Treasury finance　財務省の資金調達
unearned finance income　前受け金融収益
U.S. public finance　米国の地方債
◆Disclosure of the university's finances for market evaluation helps to improve the university's reputation. 市場の評価を得るために大学の財務を公開することで、大学の知名度は高められる。◆Mainly due to dole-out measures, the Japanese government's finances are on the verge of bankruptcy. 主にバラマキ政策のせいで、国[日本政府]の財政は破たん寸前だ。◆Softbank and Deutche Bank will tie up in online finance. ソフトバンクとドイツ銀行が、オンライン金融で提携する。◆The economy will not recover and the nation's finances will starve to death if the situation is left as it is. このままだと、景気は回復せず財政も破たんする。◆This country's debt-laden finances are in a critical situation due to the dole-out policies as well as lavish economic stimulus measures. わが国の借金漬けの財政は、バラマキ政策と大盤振る舞いの景気対策で、危機的な状況に陥っている。

finance charge　金融費用, 融資手数料
◆Any payment not made when due will, in addition to any other right or remedy of Licensor, incur a finance charge at the lesser of three hundred basis points over the 3-month London Inter Bank Offered Rate ("LIBOR + 3") on the date payment was due or the highest applicable legal contract rate. 支払いが支払い期日までに履行されない場合、ライセンサーの他の権利や救済請求権に加えて、支払い期日時点の3か月物ロンドン銀行間取引金利(LIBOR)プラス3%(LIBOR＋3%)または適用される最高法定約定金利のうち、いずれか低いほうの金利の金融費用が発生する。

finance company　金融会社 (=finance house)
auto finance company　自動車ローン会社
◆Aiful Corp. is the nation's largest finance company by revenue. アイフルは、収益で国内最大手の金融会社(消費者金融会社)だ。

finance corporation　金融公庫, 公庫, 金融会社
Japan Finance Corporation　日本政策金融公庫
National Life Finance Corporation　国民生活金融公庫
securities finance corporation　証券金融会社

finance minister　財務相, 蔵相
(⇒currency swings, proxy)
a finance ministers' meeting of the Asia-Pacific Economic Cooperation forum　アジア太平洋経済協力会議(APEC)財務相会合
finance ministers of 12 nations in the eurozone　ユーロ圏12か国の財務相
◆A market intervention is conducted under the authority of the finance minister in Japan. 市場介入は、日本では財務相の権限で行われる。◆Finance Minister Yoshihiko Noda decided to conduct a yen-selling market intervention on Aug. 4, 2011. 2011年8月4日に野田財務相は、円売り市場介入の実施を決断した。◆Finance ministers of the ASEAN plus Three hailed the launch of a regional economic research and surveillance body aimed at preventing financial turmoil. ASEANプラス3(日中韓)の財務相が、金融危機予防のための域内経済のリサーチ・監視機関(AMRO)の発足を歓迎した。◆Finance ministers of 12 nations in the eurozone have expressed their intention to stop the dollar's slide. ユーロ圏12か国の財務相は、ドル安阻止の決意を表明している。◆French Finance Minister Christine Lagarde chosen as the new managing director of the IMF is expected to maintain an austere stance of calling on Greece to reform itself. IMFの新専務理事に選ばれたクリスティーヌ・ラガルド仏財務相は、ギリシャに改革を求める厳しい姿勢を貫くものと期待されている。◆Greece's finance minister rejected a proposed referendum on staying in the eurozone. ギリシャの財務相は、提起されていたユーロ圏残留の是非を問う国民投票を拒絶した。◆The 17 eurozone countries agreed to expand the European Financial Stability Facility at a meeting of their finance ministers. ユーロを採用しているユーロ圏17か国は、ユーロ圏財務相会合で、欧州金融安定基金(EFSF)の規模を拡大することで一致した。

finance ministers and central bank governors [chiefs]　財務相[蔵相]と中央銀行総裁, 財務相[蔵相]・中央銀行総裁 (=finance ministers and central bankers, financial chiefs)
◆A meeting of finance ministers and central bank governors from 19 countries and European Union was held in Brazil. 世界19か国と欧州連合(EU)の財務相・中央銀行総裁会議が、ブラジルで開かれた。◆Finance ministers and central bank governors from the Group of Seven leading countries held an emergency telephone conference to avert financial turmoil caused by the downgrading of the U.S. credit rating. 米国債の格下げによる金融市場の混乱を回避するため、先進7か国(G7)の財務相と中央銀行総裁が、緊急電話会議を開いた。

finance ministers [ministers'] meeting　財務相・中央銀行総裁会議, 財務相会合
the eurozone finance ministers meeting　ユーロ圏財務相会合
the Group of 20 finance ministers meeting　世界20か国・地域(G20)財務相・中央銀行総裁会議
◆At the eurozone finance ministers meeting held on October 3, 2011, a decision on bridge loans of about €8 billion to Greece was expected, but none was done. 2011年10月3日に開かれたユーロ圏財務相会合では、ギリシャに対する約80億ユーロのつなぎ融資の決定が見込まれていたが、これは見送られた。◆The mood music at the Group of 20 finance ministers meeting contrasted with the tense summit five months ago. 世界20か国・地域(G20)財務相・中央銀行総裁会議のゆったりした雰囲気は、5か月前の緊迫したG20金融サミット(首脳会議)とは対照的だった。

Finance Ministry　財務省
　（⇒financial instrument, IR campaign）
　◆The Bank of Japan strongly expects the intervention by the Finance Ministry will contribute to exchange rates becoming more stable. 日銀は、財務省の市場介入が為替相場の安定化に寄与することを強く期待している。

finance receivables　金融債権
　◆We are investing in finance receivables, particularly credit card receivables, to increase revenues and earnings from our financial services businesses. 当社は、金融サービス事業による収益と利益を増やすため、金融債権、とくにクレジット・カード債権に投資を行っています。

finance sector　金融業界, 金融セクター, 金融・保険業
　（=financial sector）
　◆The collapse of the bank will lead to repercussions throughout the finance sector. 同行の破たんは、金融業界全体に影響を及ぼすことになろう。

-financed　（形）～出資の, ～系の　（⇒-funded）
　◆The four defendants overcharged the government's Cabinet Office by about ￥141 million in the government-financed chemical weapons disposal project. 被告4人は、政府出資の化学兵器処理事業費として、政府の内閣府に約1億4,100万円を水増し請求した。◆The state-financed Japan Post Bank is expanding on the strength of people's trust in the government. 政府出資のゆうちょ銀行は、国民の政府に対する信用力を後ろ盾として、業容を拡大している。

financial　（形）金融の, 財務の, 財務上の, 金銭的, 金銭面での
　dire financial straits　厳しい財政難, 苦しい財政事情, 極度の財政ひっ迫
　financial ability　財力
　financial accounting　財務会計, 財務報告書（financial statement）を作成するための会計
　financial activity　資金調達活動, 財務活動
　financial adjustment　財政整理
　financial adviser　財務コンサルタント
　financial affairs　財務内容, 財務状態, 財務状況
　　（=financial position）
　financial aid package　金融支援策, 財政援助策
　　（=financial assistance package, financial rescue package）
　financial analysis　財務分析
　　（=financial statement analysis）
　financial assets' deflated prices　資産デフレ, 金融資産の物価下落
　financial capital　金融資本
　financial community　金融業界, 金融界, 金融証券業界
　financial contract　金融契約
　financial contribution　財政支援
　financial control　財務統制
　financial deregulation　金融自由化　（=financial liberalization, the liberalization of the financial industry）
　financial district　金融街
　financial electronic data interchange　電子的財務データ交換システム, FEDI
　financial executive　財務管理者
　financial expense　金融費用, 財務費用（支払い利息や割引料など、資金調達などの財務活動で発生する費用）
　financial expert　財政専門家
　financial flexibility　財務弾力性, 財務上の柔軟性, 不測の事態が生じたときの資金調達能力
　financial flow　資金の流れ, 資金移動
　　（⇒balance for the income account）
　financial foundation　財務基盤, 経営基盤
　　（=financial base, financial footing）

financial hemorrhaging　金融上の損失, 損失
　（=financial loss）
financial incentive　報奨金
financial index［indicator］　財務指標
financial insurance　融資保険
financial intermediary　金融仲介機関
　（⇒middleman）
financial liability　金融負債
financial misconduct　不正会計処理, 粉飾決算
financial news service firm　金融情報サービス会社
financial newspaper　経済紙
Financial Ombudsman　（英国の）金融取引苦情調停委員, 金融オンブズマン
Financial Ombudsman Service　金融オンブズマン・サービス, FOS（英国の金融サービス機構（FSA）の管轄下にあって、金融機関への苦情処理に当たる民間機関。1999年に設立）
financial option　金融オプション
financial performance　財務実績, 財務業績, 財務面での実績, 業績, 財務状態, 財務状況, 財政状況
financial planning　財務計画
financial power　資力
financial product　金融商品
　（=financial goods, financial instrument）
financial profits　金融収益
financial ratio　財務比率
financial rehabilitation　経営再建, 金融再生　（=financial reorganization, financial revitalization, management rehabilitation）
financial reorganization　金融再編
financial requirements　財務負担
financial responsibility law　（米国の州法）賠償資力責任法
financial review　財務概況
financial revitalization　金融の再生, 金融再生
　（=financial reconstruction, financial rehabilitation）
financial revival program　金融再生プログラム
　（=financial revitalization program, financial revival plan）
financial safety net　金融安全網
financial settlement services　金融決済業務, 決済業務
　（⇒handle）
financial shape　財務状態
financial situation　財務状態, 財政状態, 財務状況, 財務体質　（=financial condition, financial position, financial standing）
financial soundness　財務上の健全性, 財政の健全性, 経営の健全性　（=financial health）
financial status　財政状態, 財務状況, 財務内容, 体力
　（=financial position, financial standing）
financial straits　財政難, 財政困難, 財政危機, 財政ひっ迫, 財政的苦境, 困難な資金繰り, 金に困ること, 財務力の低下, 金融機関の体力の低下
　（=financial difficulties; ⇒dire）
financial strategy　財務戦略
financial stress　経営難, 信用ひっ迫
financial stringency　金融ひっ迫
　（=financial pressure, monetary stringency）
financial supermarket　金融コングロマリット, フィナンシャル・スーパーマーケット
financial theory　金融論
financial turmoil　金融不安
financial window-dressing　会計操作

financial world　金融界, 財界
　(=financial circles; ⇒debt crisis)

financial year　会計年度, 事業年度, 営業年度, 会計期間
　(=business year, fiscal year)

financial administration　金融行政, 財務管理, 財政
　◆Financial administration should have been handled with prudence. 金融行政は、慎重を期さなければならない。◆Former president of the bank was deeply involved in the nation's financial administration as an advisor to the Financial Services Agency. 同行の前社長は、金融庁の顧問として、国の金融行政に深くかかわった。

financial aid　金融支援, 財政援助, 奨学金　(=financial assistance, financial backing, financial support)
　◆Greece has to agree to new austerity measures before it receives any financial aid from the European Union. ギリシャは、欧州連合（EU）の金融支援を受ける前に、追加の財政赤字削減策［緊縮財政策］に同意しなければならない。◆If the government financial aid is not offered to TEPCO, the utility's creditors and shareholders will have to share the burden. 東電に政府の金融支援がない場合は、同社の債権者と株主が共同負担せざるを得ないだろう。◆The amount of financial aid needed may change. 必要な金融支援額は今後、変わる可能性がある。

financial aid package　金融支援策
　(=financial rescue package)
　◆A breakdown of the DBJ financial aid package reveals that ¥70 billion has been loaned to JAL and about ¥15 billion to ANA. 日本政策投資銀行が経営支援策として行った融資の内訳は、日本航空システムが約700億円、全日本空輸が約150億円となっている。◆A financial aid package that includes a debt-for-equity swap and debt forgiveness was considered by the main banks. 債務の株式化（銀行にとっては債権の株式化）や債権放棄などの金融支援策を、主力取引銀行が検討した。

financial and monetary authorities　金融・通貨当局
　◆In order to prevent the chain reaction of even more devastating financial collapses, financial and monetary authorities in the United States and other nations will need to work together. これ以上の衝撃的な金融破たんの連鎖反応を防ぐには、米国と世界各国の金融・通貨当局の協調が必要だ。

financial assets　金融資産, 貨幣性資産, 金融商品
　(⇒financial planner, tax-exempt bond)
　financial assets at fair value through profit or loss　公正価格で評価し、変動額を損益計上する金融資産
　financial assets' deflated prices　資産デフレ, 金融資産の物価下落
　individual financial assets　個人金融資産
　personal financial assets　個人金融資産
　　(=financial assets held by individuals)
　virtual financial assets　見かけの金融資産
　◆If a financial system crisis should occur due to sharp fall in Japanese government bond prices, the Japanese people would suffer an erosion of their financial assets. 日本国債価格の急落で金融システム不安が生じれば、日本国民の金融資産は損失を被ることになる。◆In revitalizing the market, it is necessary to encourage individuals, who have financial assets totaling ¥1.4 quadrillion, to invest in the stock market. 市場の活性化を図るには、1,400兆円にのぼる金融資産を持つ個人の株式市場への投資を促す必要がある。◆Japan's individual financial assets amount to nearly ¥1.5 quadrillion. 日本の個人金融資産は、1,500兆円に近い。◆Out of the household financial assets of ¥1.47 quadrillion, about ¥160 trillion can be considered as surplus savings, given the life cycle of the average Japanese individual. 日本人の平均的な個人のライフサイクルから見て、1,470兆円の個人金融資産のうち約160兆円は、余剰貯蓄と考えられる。◆Plummeting stock prices have reduced financial assets held by individuals, thereby dampening consumption. 株安で個人所有の金融資産が目減りして、消費は冷え込んでいる。◆The Bank of Japan will set up a fund to buy long-term government bonds, exchange-traded funds and other financial assets in a bid to prop up the nation's economy. 日本の景気を下支えするため、日銀は基金を新設して、長期国債や上場投資信託（ETF）などの金融商品［金融資産］を買い入れる。◆The size of the financial assets of Japanese households is still worth a massive ¥1.47 quadrillion despite a decrease in the total over recent years. 日本の個人金融資産の規模は、ここ数年で減少したものの、まだ1,470兆円ほどもあって巨大だ。

financial assistance　金融支援, 資金援助　(=financial aid, financial backing, financial support; ⇒heavily indebted poor countries, restructure)
　extend a financial assistance　金融支援を行う, 財政支援を行う
　offer ¥500 billion in financial assistance　5,000億円の財政支援［金融支援］を行う
　◆European countries and the International Monetary Fund have decided to extend financial assistance of up to €110 billion to Greece. 欧州各国と国際通貨基金（IMF）が、ギリシャに最大1,100億ユーロ（約13兆円）の金融支援を行うことを決めた。◆No financial institution would step in to save Lehman Brothers as the U.S. government refused to extend a financial assistance. 米政府が財政支援を拒否したので、リーマン・ブラザーズの救済に乗り出す金融機関は現われなかった。◆The financial assistance will be extended by combining a waiver of debt and a debt-for-equity swap. 金融支援は、債権放棄とデット・エクイティ・スワップ（債務の株式化）を組み合わせて行われる。◆The financial market mess in Europe was triggered by the delay of financial assistance to Greece by the European financial authorities. 欧州の金融市場混乱の引き金となったのは、欧州金融当局によるギリシャへの金融支援のもたつきだ。◆The government will provide financial assistance for the reconstruction of houses damaged by soil liquefaction. 政府は、地表の液状化現象で損傷した家屋の再建に資金の援助を行う方針だ。◆The revitalization plan will be carried out chiefly using ¥400 billion in financial assistance to be extended by the firm's creditor banks. 再生計画は、主に同社の取引銀行が行う金融支援総額4,000億円を使って実施される。

financial authorities　金融当局, 財政当局
　(=monetary authorities)
　◆Financial authorities should stiffen the penalties for illegal transactions to protect the financial system from rumors and speculative investment. 金融当局は違法取引（違法行為）に対する罰則を強化して、金融システムを風評や投機［投機的投資］から守らなければならない。◆Financial institutions are obliged to report deals suspected to be linked to terrorism to the financial authorities. 金融機関は、テロ行為に絡んだ疑いのある取引については、金融当局への届出が義務付けられている。◆The financial authorities filed a declaration of bankruptcy and a request for asset protection with the Tokyo District Court for the brokerage firm. 金融当局は、同証券会社の破産宣告と財産保全処分を東京地裁に申し立てた。◆The financial authorities neglected to expose the bank's lax management for a long time. 金融当局は、同行のずさんな経営体制を長いこと放置していた。◆The financial market mess in Europe was triggered by the delay of financial assistance to Greece by the European financial authorities. 欧州の金融市場混乱の引き金となったのは、欧州金融当局によるギリシャへの金融支援のもたつきだ。◆The Financial Stability Forum comprises financial authorities of major nations. 金融安定化フォーラムは、主要国の金融当局で構成されている。

financial backing　金融支援, 財源の裏付け
　(=financial aid, financial assistance)
　◆The DPJ's handout measures lack financial backing. 民

主党のバラマキ政策は、財源の裏付けがない。◆The restructuring plan includes financial backing of ￥50 billion from Norinchukin Bank and other banks. この再建策には、農林中央金庫（農林中金）などの銀行による500億円の金融支援が盛り込まれている。

financial bailout bill （米国の）緊急経済安定化法案, 金融安定化法
◆A financial bailout bill, after twists and turns, has at last been signed into law in the United States. 米国の金融安定化法案（緊急経済安定化法案）が、迷走の末、ようやく成立した。◆The financial markets would have been further destabilized if the U.S. House of Representatives had rejected the financial bailout bill. 米議会下院が金融安定化法案（金融救済法案）を否決していたら、金融市場はさらに動揺していただろう。◆The rejection of the financial bailout bill by the U.S. House of Representatives roiled the financial markets across the world. 米下院による金融救済法案（金融安定化法案）の否決は、世界の金融市場を大混乱させた。◆The U.S. financial bailout bill has been touted as a trump card to save struggling U.S. financial institutions. 米国の緊急経済安定化（金融安定化）法案は、苦境にあえぐ米国の金融機関を救う切り札と期待されている。◆There was no choice other than to pass the financial bailout bill to forestall a full-blown financial crisis. 全面的な金融危機を回避するには、金融安定化法案を可決せざるを得なかった。

financial bailout package 金融救済策
◆The benefits of the U.S. financial bailout package will take time to show up in the U.S. economy. 米国の金融救済策の効果が米国内経済に現れるのに、時間がかかるだろう。◆The U.S. financial bailout package is not user-friendly. 米国の金融救済策は、使い勝手が悪い。

financial bailout plan 金融救済案
◆The financial bailout plan contains many unclear points that will become apparent when it is actually implemented. この金融救済案は、実際に実施してみないと分からない不透明な点が多い。

financial bailout spending 金融救済費用, 金融支援費用, 金融機関の破たん処理費用
◆The U.S. budget deficit for fiscal 2010 narrowed to $1.29 trillion as tax collections recovered slightly and financial bailout spending fell sharply. 米国の2010会計年度（2009年10月～2010年9月）の財政赤字は、税収がいくぶん回復し、金融救済［金融支援］費用が急減したため、1兆2,900億ドルに縮小した。

financial base 財務基盤, 経営基盤 （=financial footing, financial foundation; ⇒beef up）
◆Consumer loan lender Aiful Corp. will raise ￥120 billion through equity and bond issues to enhance its financial base. 消費者金融のアイフルは、財務基盤［経営基盤］を強化するため、株式と社債の発行で1,200億円を調達する。

financial bill 政府短期証券, FB （=financing bill: 国の一般会計や地区別会計の資金不足を補うために発行される期間60日程度の割引債券。⇒financing bill, intervention to sell yen and buy the dollar）

financial bubble 金融バブル
◆The financial bubble burst in the United States in the autumn of 2008. 米国の金融バブルが、2008年の秋に破裂した。

financial bubble burst 金融バブルの崩壊
◆Many pundits in Tokyo have prophesized the possible demise of U.S. primacy since the financial bubble burst. 金融バブルの崩壊以降、日本では、米一極指導の終焉（しゅうえん）を予言する専門家が多い。

financial burden 金融負担, 財務面での負担, 財務負担, 財政負担, 経済負担
◆A consumption tax hike would increase the financial burden shouldered by Joe Blow. 消費税を引き上げると、一般国民の金融負担［一般国民が負担する金融負担］が増えることになる。◆Financial burdens are expected to sharply rise in the mid-to long-term due to rapid aging of the population and renovation of public facilities. 急速な高齢化や公共施設の更新で、中長期的には、財政負担の急増が見込まれる。◆Financial institutions and TEPCO shareholders should shoulder part of the financial burden in return for government financial support of TEPCO. 政府が東電を支援する見返りとして、金融機関と東電株主も一定の金融負担をするべきだ。◆The launch of a new medical insurance system for the elderly has increased the financial burden on health insurance societies. 新しい高齢者医療制度の導入で、健康保険組合の金融負担［保険料負担］が増えている。◆Those in low-income brackets tend to feel more of a financial burden than high-income earners if the consumption tax rate is raised to 10 percent. 消費税率が10％に引き上げられた場合、所得の多い人より低所得者層のほうが、金融負担感が大きいようだ。

financial business 金融業務
◆Financial business, particularly on an international level, is becoming more like the telecommunications business, in which trading is carried out in the virtual world of cyberspace on the strength of information. 金融業務、とくに国際金融業務は、情報の力でサイバースペース（サイバー空間）と呼ばれる仮想の世界で取引が行われる一種の情報産業化している。

financial business model 金融ビジネス・モデル
◆The world is being jolted by the collapse of U.S.-style financial business models. 世界は、米国型金融ビジネス・モデルの崩壊でショックを受けている［米国型金融ビジネス・モデルの崩落が、世界を揺るがせている］。

financial buyer 金融会社

financial chaos 金融混乱, 金融危機
◆The epicenter of the financial chaos is the United States. 今回の金融混乱［金融危機］の震源地は、米国だ。

financial chiefs 財務相・中央銀行総裁（finance ministers and central bank governors［chiefs］）, 財務相（finance ministers）（⇒finance ministers and central bank governors［chiefs］）
APEC financial chiefs アジア太平洋経済協力会議（APEC）財務相
financial chiefs from the Group of 20 世界20か国・地域（G20）の財務相・中央銀行総裁

financial chiefs and central bank governors from the Group of 20 leading economies 主要20か国・地域（G20）の財務相・中央銀行総裁
◆After a two day meeting in Paris, the financial chiefs and central bank governors from the Group of 20 leading economies adopted a communique. パリで開かれた2日間の会議の後、主要20か国・地域（G20）の財務相・中央銀行総裁は共同声明を採択した。

financial chiefs from the Group of 20 advanced and major developing countries 主要20か国・地域（G20）の財務相・中央銀行総裁
◆Financial chiefs from the Group of 20 advanced and major developing countries vowed to avoid a global currency war. 主要20か国・地域（G20）の財務相・中央銀行総裁が、世界の通貨戦争を避けることを公約した。

financial circles 金融界, 金融業界, 金融筋 （=financial community）
◆The lifting of the freeze on the payoff system will help impress upon international financial circles that Japan's financial sector is now back to a normal state. ペイオフ制度の凍結解除（2005年4月1日）は、日本の金融が現在、平時に戻ったことを国際金融界に印象付けることになる。

financial collapse 金融破たん, 金融機関の経営破たん, 金融崩壊 （=collapse of financial institutions）
◆In order to prevent the chain reaction of even more devastating financial collapses, financial and monetary authorities

in the United States and other nations will need to work together. これ以上の衝撃的な金融破たんの連鎖反応を防ぐには、米国と世界各国の金融・通貨当局の協調が必要だ。◆In the eurozone, Greece's financial collapse is triggering a chain reaction. ユーロ圏では、ギリシャの財政破たんが連鎖反応を起こしている。

financial community　金融界, 金融業界
(=financial circles)
◆The news of a rise in the subprime defaults rocked the U.S. financial community. サブプライムの不払い増加のニュースに、米金融業界は動揺した。

financial company　金融会社
◆Short selling is the practice of borrowing stocks from securities and financial companies and other investors to sell them and then buy them back when their prices drop. 空売りは、証券金融会社や他の投資家（機関投資家など）から株を借りて売り、その株が値下がりした時点で買い戻すことをいう。

financial concerns　金融不安
◆Leaders of European Union countries failed to dispel financial concerns. 欧州連合（EU）各国首脳は、金融不安の払拭（ふっしょく）には至らなかった。

financial condition　財政状態, 財政状況, 財務状態, 財務状況, 財務内容, 財務基盤, 金融情勢　(=financial position, financial state; ⇒crossheld stocks, listing particulars, mark-to-market accounting practices)
corporate financial conditions　企業の財務状況[財政状態]
deteriorating financial conditions　財政状態[財政状況]の悪化, 財務内容の悪化
(=deterioration in [of] financial conditions)
financial conditions of the issuer　発行体の財務状況
management's discussion and analysis of financial condition and results of operations　財政状態と経営成績の経営者による分析・検討
overall financial conditions DI　資金繰り判断DI
uncertainty about [over] financial conditions　財務内容の不透明感, 財務状態についての不透明性
◆An urgent task facing each financial group is to improve its financial conditions and profitability on the strength of advantages gained from merger. 合併・統合で得られる相乗効果を生かして、財務内容と収益力を向上させることが、各金融グループの現在の急務だ。◆It is difficult for Japan, the United States and European countries to support their sagging economies by increasing public spending, due to deteriorating financial conditions. 財政の悪化で、日米欧は、財政出動による景気の下支えが難しくなっている。

financial conglomerate　金融コングロマリット, 金融複合企業体
◆If the merger takes place, it will create a full-scale financial conglomerate with a major bank, a major securities house and credit card company under its umbrella. 統合すれば、傘下に大手銀行と大手証券、クレジット・カード会社などを持つ本格的な金融コングロマリット（複合企業体）が誕生する。◆The FSA's guideline for supervising financial conglomerates is aimed at urging operators of financial conglomerates to reinforce their corporate governance to prevent irregularities. 金融庁の金融コングロマリット（複合体）監督指針の狙いは、不正防止に向けて、金融コングロマリットの経営者に経営監視の強化を促すことにある。

financial contraction　金融収縮
◆The Bank of Japan must continue to promptly supply funds to prevent the financial contraction that all corporate managers dread. 企業経営者が恐れる金融収縮を防ぐため、日銀は迅速に資金供給を続ける必要がある。

financial contribution　資金協力, 資金面での貢献, 財政援助
◆The United States will respond to a UN appeal for emergency relief for North Korean victims with a financial contribution and in-kind donations. 北朝鮮の被災者に対する国連の緊急援助要請に対して、米国は財政支援と現物供与で応じる方針だ。

financial crisis　金融危機, 金融パニック, 金融恐慌, 財政危機, 経営危機, 経営難, 経営破はたん
(=financial difficulties, financial panic)
avoid a financial crisis　金融危機を回避する
full-blown financial crisis　全面的な金融危機
(⇒financial bailout bill)
global financial crisis　世界的な金融危機
systemic financial crisis　連鎖的金融危機
◆According to the Financial Stability Board, 28 banks viewed as global systemically important financial institutions (G-SIFIs) will be subject to a new global rule requiring them to hold extra capital to prevent future financial crises. 金融安定化理事会（FSB）によると、金融システム上重要な国際金融機関（G-SIFIs）と考えられる世界の28行が、金融危機の再発を防止するため、資本の上積みを求める新国際基準［新国際金融規制］の対象になる。◆Business conditions are rapidly deteriorating due to the global financial crisis and the worldwide economic downturn. 世界的な金融危機と世界的な景気後退で、景気は急速に悪化している。◆Europe is urged to act promptly to halt financial crisis. 欧州は、金融危機回避の早急な対策を迫られている。◆Europe promised the Group of 20 major economies to take concerted action to contain the financial crisis. 欧州は、結束して金融危機を封じ込めることを主要20か国・地域（G20）に公約した。◆European countries are forced to prevent the financial crisis from spreading from Europe to other parts of the world. 欧州は、金融危機の世界的波及阻止を迫られている。◆Goldman Sachs was subpoenaed over its activities leading up to the financial crisis. ゴールドマン・サックスは、同社の証券業務が金融危機を招いた［引き起こした］件で、召喚された。◆Greek financial crisis was caused by the country's lax fiscal management. ギリシャの財政危機は、同国の放漫財政［放漫な財政運営］によって生じた。◆If the European financial crisis expands, it will damage the recovering global economy. 欧州の金融危機が拡大すれば、回復途上にある世界経済に打撃を与えることになる。◆Ireland and Portugal also have been hit by financial crises and bailed out by the European Union. アイルランドやポルトガルも、財政危機に見舞われ、欧州連合（EU）に救済された［欧州連合に金融支援を仰いだ］。◆Italy is suffering from the financial crisis that spilled over from Greece. イタリアは、ギリシャから飛び火した財政危機に見舞われている。◆Major financial institutions are forced to hold additional capital so that they can better absorb losses during financial crises. 金融危機の際の損失吸収力を高めるため、大手金融機関は、資本［自己資本］の積み増しを迫られている。◆No clear prospect has emerged for resolution of the Greek financial crisis. ギリシャの財政危機を打開する明確な見通しは、まだ立っていない。◆Preparedness for financial crisis has returned to a normal level from the guard raised during a financial sector-triggered recession. 金融危機への備えは、金融不況時の厳戒態勢から平常レベルに戻っている。◆The European Central Bank is working more closely with France and Germany to contain the financial crisis. 欧州中央銀行は、金融危機を封じ込めるため、フランス、ドイツと連携を強めている。◆The Fed has taken quantitative easing measures twice, or QE1 between December 2008 and March 2010, and QE2 between November 2010 and June 2011, to cope with the financial crisis and deflationary pressure. 金融危機やデフレ圧力に対応するため、米連邦準備制度理事会（FRB）は、これまでに量的金融緩和を2回（2008年12月～2010年3月の量的緩和第一弾（QE1）と2010年11月～2011年6月の量的緩和第二弾（QE2））実施している。◆The financial crisis is closely interrelated with the contraction of the real economy. 金融危機は、実体経済の景気後退と密接にかかわっている。◆

The financial crisis stemmed from a U.S. housing mortgage meltdown. 今回の金融危機は、米国の住宅ローン市場の崩壊から始まった。◆The financial crisis that originated in the United States is developing into a cross-border realignment of the financial industry. 米国発の金融危機は、国境を越えた金融再編［金融業界の再編］に発展している。◆The financial crisis triggered by the rise in defaults of U.S. subprime loans caused havoc in financial markets worldwide. 米国のサブプライム・ローン（低所得者向け住宅ローン）の不払い増加がきっかけで起こった金融危機は、世界の金融市場を大混乱させた。◆The financial system became crippled during the financial crisis. 金融危機の際、金融システムは動きが取れなくなった［麻痺してしまった］。◆The national economy in the new fiscal year remains beleaguered by deflationary pressure and fear of a financial crisis. 新年度入りした日本経済は、依然としてデフレ圧力や金融危機の懸念を抱えている。◆The stress test of the European Banking Authority is a banking health check to ensure banks across Europe have sufficient capital to withstand another financial crisis. 欧州銀行監督機構（EBA）のストレス・テストは、欧州全域の銀行が新たな金融危機に耐えられるだけの資本金を十分に確保していることを保証するための銀行の健全性検査だ。◆The U.S. financial crisis stopped an ever-increasing number of Americans from getting car loans, leading to a spectacular dive in U.S. car sales. 米国の金融危機で、自動車ローンを組めない米国人が続出し、米国の新車販売が急減した。◆The world economy will steer to a growth path again once the financial crisis subsides. 金融危機が沈静化したら、世界経済はまた成長軌道［成長経路］に向かうだろう。◆The worst of the financial crisis is over. 金融危機の最悪期は、脱した。◆To deal with the systemic financial crisis, ministry and central bank officials had to take rescue measures, such as an injection of public funds, while at the same time implementing strict guidelines and sanctions. 連鎖的な金融危機に対処するにあたって、当局は公的資金の投入などの救済措置取ると同時に、厳しい指導や制裁を実施しなければならなかった。◆With the United States facing the worst financial crisis in generations, Bush's White House took decisive measures to safeguard the economy. 米国が過去最悪の金融危機に直面して、ブッシュ政権は経済危機を守るために断固たる措置を取った。

financial crisis in Europe 欧州の金融危機, 欧州金融危機, 欧州の財政・金融危機
◆On the foreign exchange market, there has been no halt to selling pressure on the euro due to concern about the financial crisis in Europe. 外国為替市場では、欧州の金融危機を懸念して、ユーロ売り圧力が止まらない展開となっている。◆Trading is sluggish on stock markets mainly due to the financial crisis in Europe. 株式市場は、主に欧州の財政・金融危機で取引［相場］が低迷している。

financial data 財務データ
◆The Tokyo Stock Exchange delisted the firm on Sept. 4, because it did not consider the firm's financial data reliable. 東京証券取引所は、同社の財務データの信頼性は薄いとの判断から、9月4日に同社の上場を廃止した。

financial deal 金融取引
◆As part of antiterrorism measures, the government has started discussions on obliging legal and accounting experts to inform government bodies and other organizations of suspicious financial deals that may be linked to terrorism or criminal activities. テロ防止対策の一環として政府は、テロや犯罪に絡んだ疑いのある金融取引について、弁護士や会計専門家（公認会計士や弁理士）に政府機関や各種団体への通報を義務付ける方向で検討に入った。

financial debacle 財政破たん
（=financial collapse）
◆Europe's debt crisis was triggered by Greece's financial debacle. 欧州の債務危機は、ギリシャの財政破たんに端を発した。

financial deregulation 金融自由化 （=financial liberalization, the liberalization of the financial industry）

financial derivatives 金融派生商品 （=derivative financial instruments, derivative products, derivatives, financial derivative instruments）
◆Gross foreign assets held by Japanese in the form of direct investment, securities investment, financial derivatives, loans and export credits, deposits, other investments and official foreign reserves came to ¥379.78 trillion at the end of 2001. 直接投資、証券投資、金融派生商品、貸付け金や輸出信用、預金その他の投資および外貨準備高の形で日本の政府や企業、個人が保有する海外資産の総額（対外資産残高）は、2001年末時点で379兆7,800億円に達した。◆Investment advisory company AIJ started investing in financial derivatives through funds based in the Cayman Islands, a tax haven, since 2002. 投資顧問会社のAIJは、2002年から租税回避地の英領ケイマン諸島を営業基盤とするファンドを通じて金融派生商品への投資を始めた。

financial deterioration 財務状況の悪化, 財務の悪化, 財務の傷（いた）み具合
◆Depending on the degree of JAL's financial deterioration, the government will consider a combination of capital reinforcement under the industrial revitalization law and public assistance by the Enterprise Turnaround Initiative Corp. of Japan. 日航の財務の傷み具合によって、政府は、産業再生法に基づく公的資金の増強と、企業再生支援機構による公的支援との組合せを検討する方針だ。

financial developments 金融動向
◆The world will pay a great deal of attention to financial developments in Japan in April and beyond. 世界が、日本の4月以降の金融動向を注視することになる。

financial difficulties 財務悪化, 財政的困難, 財政上の困難, 財政難, 財政ひっ迫, 資金繰りが困難な状況, 経営危機, 経営不振, 経営難, 経営の行き詰まり （=financial disarray, financial distress, financial straits; ⇒accountable, borrowing, capital, public nursing care insurance system）
fall into financial difficulties 経営に行き詰まる
serious financial difficulties 深刻な経営危機, 深刻な経営難［経営不振］, 深刻な財政難［ひっ迫］
suffer further financial difficulties さらに経営難［経営不振］に陥る
◆Bear Sterns, the fifth-largest U.S. securities firm, ran into financial difficulties in March 2008. 米証券第5位のベア・スターンズは、2008年3月に経営危機に陥った。◆Even after the company fell into financial difficulties, it embellished its financial statements to make it appear profitable. 同社の経営が行き詰まった以降も、同社は決算書を粉飾して、経営状況を良く見せかけていた。◆Seven directors will resign from their posts to take responsibility for the financial difficulties. 経営不振に対する責任をとって、取締役7人が引責辞任する。◆The bank's serious financial difficulties have forced it to do an about-face. 同行の深刻な経営難で、同行は方針転換を迫られている。◆When serious financial difficulties are expected, the Financial Services Agency is allowed to order a company to improve its operations in the early stages without releasing the information to the public. 深刻な財務悪化が予想される場合、金融庁は、非公表で早めに業務改善命令を発動することができる。◆Yamaichi decided to stop operations in November 1997 as the company's liabilities of more than ¥260 billion came to light and it then suffered further financial difficulties. 山一は、2,600億円を超える（簿外）債務があることが発覚し、その後さらに経営難に陥ったため、1997年11月に自主廃業を決めた。

financial distress 金融不況, 経営難
◆AIG finds itself in financial distress due to recklessness and greed. 米保険大手のAIGが経営難に陥っているのは、向こう見ずで貪欲だからだ。

financial documents　財務書類
　　（＝financial information）
◆Leading commodity futures brokerage Tokyo General Corp. gave its auditors falsified financial documents concerning its account settlement for the year to March 2002. 商品先物取引大手の東京ゼネラルが、2002年3月期決算の際、同社の監査法人に虚偽の財務書類を提出していた。

financial emergency　財政危機, 金融の非常事態
◆All possible measures, such as injecting funds into markets and lowering rates, need to be taken to ride out this financial emergency. この金融非常事態をうまく切り抜けるには、市場への資金注入［資金供給］や利下げなど、あらゆる可能な措置を取る必要がある。

financial exchange　金融取引
◆Financial exchanges between a half-dozen emerging countries（BRICs, Indonesia and South Korea）will lose a dependency on the U.S. dollar as the currency of last resort. 今後、ブラジル、ロシア、インド、中国、インドネシア、韓国の新興6か国間の金融取引は、最後の拠（よ）りどころとしての米ドルに依存しなくなると思われる。

financial firm　金融機関　（＝financial institution）
◆Meiji Life Insurance Co. plans to raise ￥60 billion from group financial firms to boost its capital to ￥220 billion. 明治生命保険は、グループの金融機関から600億円調達して、基金（株式会社の資本金に相当）総額を2,200億円に増額する方針だ。◆The Federal Housing Finance Agency sued 17 financial firms over risky investments. 米連邦住宅金融局（FHFA）が、高リスク証券を販売したとして大手金融機関17社を提訴した。◆The price tag for the mortgage-backed securities sold to Fannie and Freddie by 17 financial firms totaled $196.1 billion. 大手金融機関17社がファニー・メイとフレディ・マックに販売した住宅ローン担保証券（MBS）の購入額は、総額で1,961億ドルになる。

financial flow　金融の流れ, 資金の流れ, 財務フロー
◆The balance for the income account reflecting financial flows between Japan and other countries saw a ￥992.4 billion surplus. 日本と海外との資金の流れを示す所得収支は、9,924億円の黒字だった。

financial footing　財務基盤, 経営基盤
　　（＝financial base, financial foundation）
◆To establish a solid financial footing, we have been strengthening our shareholders' equity. 磐石な財務基盤（経営基盤）を確立するため、当社は株主資本（自己資本）を強化しています。

financial foundation　財務基盤, 経営基盤
　　（＝financial base, financial footing）
◆Uncertainty about the future of Japan's financial system will persist until the vulnerable financial foundation of life insurance companies is rectified. 生命保険会社の脆弱（ぜいじゃく）な経営基盤を立て直さない限り、日本の金融システムの先行きに対する不安は消えない。

financial function　金融機能
◆A bill to revise the Law on Special Measures for Strengthening Financial Functions is designed to facilitate compensations of losses of financial institutions with public funds. 金融機能強化法の改正法案は、公的資金で金融機関の損失の穴埋めを容易にするのが狙いだ。

Financial Function Early Strengthening Law　金融早期健全化法, 金融機能強化法
◆The Financial Function Early Strengthening Law enables the injection of public funds into small and midsize financial institutions. 金融機能強化法によって、中小金融機関への公的資金の注入［投入］が可能になっている。◆The Financial Function Early Strengthening Law expired at the end of March 2008. 金融機能強化法は、2008年3月末に期限が切れた。

financial function enhancement law　金融機能強化法（公的資金新法）　（地域金融機関の再編や経営基盤の強化を促すため、地域金融機関を主な対象として2008年3月末まで2兆円の公的資金を予防的に注入できるようにした法律）
◆The financial function enhancement law took effect in August 2004 to help strengthen regional banks. この金融機関機能強化法（公的資金新法）は、地銀の強化を支援するため2004年8月に施行された。

financial futures transaction　金融先物取引
　　（⇒dealer）

financial goods　金融商品
　　（＝financial instruments, financial products）
◆There are 10 categories of financial goods listed on the TSE, including convertible bonds, government and corporate bonds, as well as stock index futures and options. 東証の上場金融商品には、転換社債や国債、社債のほか株価指数先物、株価指数オプションなどを含めて全部で10種類ある。

financial group　金融グループ, フィナンシャル・グループ
◆An urgent task facing each financial group is to improve its financial conditions and profitability on the strength of advantages gained from merger. 合併・統合の相乗効果を生かして、財務内容と収益力を向上させることが、各金融グループの現在の急務だ。◆MFG, the nation's largest financial group, tied up with two major U.S. banks to strengthen its earning power. 国内金融グループ最大手のみずほフィナンシャルグループが、収益力の強化を図るため、米銀大手2行と提携した。◆Mitsubishi UFJ Financial Group Inc. is the largest among Japan's six major financial groups. 三菱UFJフィナンシャル・グループは、日本の大手金融6グループで最大だ。◆Mitsubishi UFJ Financial Group Inc., Sumitomo Mitsui Financial Group Inc. and Mizuho Financial Group Inc. are included in the G-SIFIs list of the Financial Stability Board. 主要20か国・地域（G20）の金融当局で構成する金融安定化理事会（FSB）のG-SIFIリスト（国際的な巨大金融機関リスト）には、三菱UFJ、三井住友、みずほの3大金融グループも含まれている。◆The bank became a unit of the financial group through a share swap deal. 同行は、株式交換取引で同金融グループ系の企業になった。◆The Development Bank of Japan will ask major financial groups to invest in the fund established to assist auto parts makers hit by the March 11 disaster. 日本政策投資銀行は、大手金融グループなどに、(2011年) 3月11日の東日本大震災で被災した自動車部品メーカーの復興を支援するために設立するファンドへの出資を呼びかける。◆The financial group's inadequate preparations for the reorganization resulted in a major computer system failure. 同フィナンシャル・グループの再編の準備不足から、大規模なシステム障害が起こった。◆The FSA urged the financial group to revise its earnings estimate. 金融庁は、同金融グループに対して業績予想の修正を強く迫った。◆The merger will create the world's largest financial group with assets totaling about ￥190 trillion. この経営統合で、総資産約190兆円の世界最大の金融グループが誕生する。◆The two financial groups plan to integrate their banking, trust and securities operations under a holding company created through the merger of their holding companies. 両金融グループは、それぞれ銀行、信託、証券業務を経営統合により新設する持ち株会社の傘下に統合する計画だ。

日本の大手銀行5グループ：

Mitsubishi UFJ Financial Group Inc.　三菱UFJフィナンシャル・グループ

Mizuho Financial Group Inc.　みずほフィナンシャルグループ

Resona Bank, Limited　りそな銀行

Sumitomo Mitsui Financial Group　三井住友フィナンシャルグループ

Sumitomo Trust & Banking Co., Ltd.　住友信託銀行

financial guarantee　金融保証, 信用保証
　financial guarantee contract　債務保証契約
　financial guarantee insurance（policy）　金融保証保険
　financial guarantee written　債務保証
financial guarantor　金融保証会社, 信用保証会社
financial guaranty　金融保証
　financial guaranty insurance　金融保証保険
　financial guaranty insurance policy　金融保証保険証券
financial health　財務の健全性, 財務内容, 財務状況, 財務体質, 経営の健全度［健全性］
　（=financial soundness）
　boost financial health　財務体質［財務状況］を強化する, 財務上の健全性を高める
　corporate financial health　企業の財務内容［財務状況］, 企業の財務状態の健全性, 企業の財務体質
　deteriorations in financial health　財務体質の悪化
　◆Concerns have arisen about the financial health of American International Group Inc. 米保険最大手AIGの経営不安説が、流れている。◆Solvency margin is an indicator of an insurance company's financial health. ソルベンシー・マージン（支払い余力）比率は、保険会社の財務の健全性を示す指標の一つである。◆The banks have categorized borrowers based on their financial health. 銀行は、経営の健全度に基づいて融資先（債務者）を区分している。◆The capital adequacy ratio is used to determine the financial health of financial institutions. 自己資本比率は、金融機関の経営の健全性［財務の健全性］を判断するのに用いられる。◆To improve its financial health, Daiei will seek about ¥410 billion worth of debt waivers from about 30 financial institutions to reduce its interest-bearing debts. 財務体質を改善するため、ダイエーは、約30の金融機関に約4,100億円の債権放棄を求めて、有利子負債を削減する。
financial health check　財務の健全性検査
　◆The Franco-Belgian bank Dexia collapsed in October 2011 despite passing the 2011 EBA's financial health check. フランス・ベルギー共同の銀行「デクシア」が、2011年に実施された欧州銀行監督機構（EBA）の財務の健全性検査を通過したにもかかわらず、2011年10月に破たんした。
financial help　金融支援　（=financial aid, financial assistance, financial support）
　◆Struggling supermarket chain operator Daiei Inc. will seek financial help from the Industrial Revitalization Corporation of Japan. 経営再建中の大手スーパー、ダイエーは、産業再生機構に金融支援を求める方針だ。◆The struggling company sought financial help from its main banks. 経営再建中の同社は、主要取引銀行に金融支援を求めた。
financial hemorrhaging［hemorrhage］　金融上の損失, 損失, 資金の流出
　（=financial loss;⇒hemorrhage）
　◆With a view to stemming the airlines' financial hemorrhaging, the Construction and Transport Ministry in late May asked the Development Bank of Japan to provide emergency loans to the two carriers. 航空会社の損失を阻止するため、5月下旬に国土交通省は、日本政策投資銀行に対して両航空会社への緊急融資を要請した。
financial holding company　金融持ち株会社, FHC（銀行・証券・保険会社を子会社に持つ持ち株会社）
　◆Sumitomo Trust will establish a financial holding company in fiscal 2005. 住友信託は、2005年度に金融持ち株会社を設立する方針だ。
financial industry　金融業, 金融産業, 金融業界, 金融界
　（⇒collection of debts, high return）
　◆Against the backdrop of the liberalization of the financial industry, pension funds and investment trust funds grew sharply. 金融自由化を背景に、年金基金や投資信託基金が急成長した。◆The G-20 financial summit meeting will map out concrete measures to strengthen the regulation and governance of the financial industry. 世界20か国・地域（G-20）の金融サミットでは、金融業界に対する規制・監督強化の具体策をまとめることになっている。
financial information　金融情報, 財務情報
　（⇒debut動詞）
　correct financial information　正確な財務情報
　financial information firm　金融情報会社
　financial information system　金融情報システム
　prospective financial information　将来財務情報
　summarized financial information　要約財務情報
　supplementary financial information　補足財務情報
　◆Disclosure of correct financial information by listed companies is indispensable for ensuring stock is traded fairly. 上場企業による正確な財務情報の開示は、株式取引の公正さを維持する上で重要だ。◆Many companies produce financial information more frequently than annually. 企業の多くは、年に何度も財務情報を作成する。
financial inspection　金融検査
　◆Ahead of financial inspections by the Financial Services Agency, the executives of the bank deleted e-mails likely to have been of interest to inspectors. 金融庁の立ち入り検査の前に、同行の首脳陣は、検査官に見られては都合の悪い電子メールを削除していた。
Financial Inspection Manuals　金融検査マニュアル
financial instability　金融不安　（=financial panic, financial uncertainty, financial unrest）
　◆If the value of a huge number of government bonds possessed by financial institutions around the world plummets, financial instability will grow. 世界の金融機関が保有する大量の国債の価格が急落すれば、金融不安が高まることになる。◆There is a possibility that a vicious circle will develop in which the financial crisis undermines the U.S. real economy, producing further financial instability. 金融危機が米国の実体経済を損ない、それがさらに金融不安を引き起こす悪循環が深刻化する可能性がある。
financial institution　金融機関
　agricultural financial institution　農林系金融機関
　banks and other financial institutions　銀行などの金融機関, 銀行・金融機関
　clean sweep of troubled financial institutions　問題のある金融機関の一掃, 経営難の金融機関の一掃, 経営破たんの金融機関の一掃
　early disposal of bad loans held by financial institutions　金融機関の不良債権の早期処理
　failed institutions　破たんした金融機関, 金融機関の破たん
　financial institution obligations　金融機関の債務
　financial institutions' bad debt　金融機関の不良債権
　Financial Institutions Reform, Recovery and Enforcement Act　金融機関改革・再建・強制［施行］法, FIRREA（=bailout bill: 米国の貯蓄貸付け組合（savings and loan associations）などの貯蓄金融機関（thrift institutions）を救済するため、1989年に制定された法律）
　foreign financial institution　外資系金融機関
　full-service financial institution　フルサービスの金融機関
　general financial institution　総合金融機関
　governmental financial institution　政府系金融機関
　　（=government financial institution）
　leading［major］financial institutions　主要金融機関
　loans to financial institutions　金融機関貸付け金
　multilateral financial institutions　国際金融機関
　nonbank financial institution　銀行以外の金融機関
　nonfinancial［non-financial］institution　非金融機関
　private financial institution　民間金融機関

private sector financial institution　民間金融機関
public financial institution　公的金融機関
public sector financial institution　政府系金融機関
realignment of financial institutions　金融機関の再編
regional financial institution　地域金融機関
retail financial institution　リテール金融機関
specialized financial institution　特殊金融機関, 専門金融機関
the asset quality of financial institutions　金融機関の資産内容
the best-capitalized financial institution　資本が最も充実した金融機関
the early disposal of bad loans held by financial institutions　金融機関の不良債権の早期処理
the realignment of financial institutions　金融機関の再編
◆A huge number of government bonds issued by the United States and European countries are possessed by financial institutions around the world. 米国や欧州各国が発行した大量の国債は、世界の金融機関が保有している。◆Commission rates in foreign currency deposits vary among foreign currencies or among financial institutions. 外貨預金での為替手数料の料率は、外国通貨や金融機関で異なる。◆Errors in computing systems at financial institutions could lead to problems in making international fund transactions. 金融機関のコンピュータ・システムのエラーは、国際的な資金取引上、トラブルが生じる可能性がある。◆Financial institutions and TEPCO shareholders should shoulder part of the financial burden in return for government financial support of TEPCO. 政府が東電を支援する見返りとして、金融機関と東電株主も一定の金融負担をするべきだ。◆In most cases in which the credit guarantee system is used, financial institutions introduce borrowers to credit guarantee corporations. 信用保証制度を利用する場合の多くは、金融機関が借り手を信用保証協会に紹介する。◆It is highly likely that the merger between the two financial institutions will be postponed. 両金融機関の統合が延期されるのは必至だ。◆The company compiled documents for financial institutions it has transactions with. 同社は、取引金融機関向けに資料を作成した。◆The DBJ and private financial institutions extended loans worth a total of ￥100 billion to JAL in June 2009 though JAL was already in dire financial straits. 日本政策投資銀行と民間金融機関は、日航の経営がすでに悪化していたものの、2009年6月に同社に対して総額1,000億円を融資した。◆Under the firm's rehabilitation plan approved by the district court, financial institutions will waive 87.5 percent of the unsecured loans they extend to the firm. 地方裁判所が認可した同社の更生計画では、金融機関が、同社に行った無担保融資［同社に対する無担保債権］の87.5％を放棄することになっている。◆U.S. and European financial institutions are hitting roadblocks because of the ongoing global financial turmoil. 欧米金融機関は、世界的な金融市場の混乱で、つまずいている。

financial instrument　金融商品, 金融資産, 金融手段, 金融証書　(=financial goods, financial product; ⇒ commitment)
derivative financial instrument　金融派生商品
financial futures instrument　金融先物商品
financial instruments with credit risk　信用リスクを伴う金融商品
financial instruments with off-balance-sheet risk　オフバランス・シート・リスクを伴う［オフバランス・シート・リスクのある］金融商品
fundamental financial instruments　基礎的金融商品
interest-bearing financial instrument　利息を生む金融商品
long-term financial instrument　長期金融商品

the fair value of financial instruments　金融商品の公正価格
the value of financial instruments　金融商品の価格
unregulated rate financial instrument　自由金利商品
◆The fair values of the Company's financial instruments have been determined based on quoted market prices and market interest rates, as of December 31, 2008. 当社の金融手段の公正価格は、2008年12月31日現在の市場の相場と市中金利に基づいて決定されています。◆The Finance Ministry will use an optional taxpayer ID system to monitor revenues from bank deposits, profits from sales of stocks and dividend, and that gained through other financial instruments. 財務省は、選択制の納税者番号制度を導入して、預金利子、株式売却益、配当などの金融資産で得た所得（金融性所得）を管理する方針だ。

Financial Instruments and Exchange Law　金融商品取引法　(⇒Securities and Exchange Law)
◆A bank employee violated the Financial Instruments and Exchange Law. 銀行行員が、金融商品取引法に違反した。◆Financial Instruments and Exchange Law, with drastic revisions to the former Securities and Exchange Law, came into force in September 2007. 旧証券取引法を抜本改正した金融商品取引法は、2007年9月に施行された。◆The Securities and Exchange Surveillance Commission filed a criminal complaint against a former bank employee with the Tokyo District Public Prosecutors Office on suspicion of violating the Financial Instruments and Exchange Law. 証券取引等監視委員会は、元行員を金融商品取引法違反の疑いで東京地検に刑事告発した。

Financial Intermediaries, Managers, and Brokers Regulatory Association　(英国の)金融仲介業者規制協会, 金融仲介・投資管理・ブローカー規制協会（中小の証券業者、保険ブローカー、投資コンサルタントなどを対象とする自主規制機関）

financial intermediary　金融仲介機関
◆A financial intermediary acts as a middleman between cash surplus units in the economy（savers）and deficit spending units（borrowers）. 金融仲介機関は、経済の資金余剰主体（貯蓄者）と資金不足主体（借り手）との間に立つ仲介者として機能している。

financial intermediary function　金融仲介機能
(=financial intermediating function)
◆The financial intermediary function of the banks—to pour funds into the corporate sector—has yet to be normalized, even though bad loan disposals are well underway. 不良債権処理がかなり進んでも、企業に資金を流す銀行の金融仲介機能はまだ正常化していない。

financial leaders [chiefs] of the Group of Seven　先進7か国（G7）の財務相・中央銀行総裁　(=the Group of Seven financial chiefs [leaders])
◆The meeting of financial leaders of the Group of Seven industrial powers was held in Iqaluit, Canada. 先進7か国財務相・中央銀行総裁会議が、カナダのイカルイトで開かれた。

financial liberalization　金融自由化　(=financial deregulation, the liberalization of the financial industry; ⇒ financial market liberalization)

financial loss　金融上の損失, 金融損失, 損失
(=financial hemorrhage)
◆A reserve of money collected by issuing stocks can be used to cover eventual financial losses. 株式を発行して集めた資金準備は、将来の金融損失の穴埋めに使用することができる。◆Financial institutions have capital which can be used to cover eventual financial losses to ensure debt servicing will not be impaired. 金融機関には、損失が生じた際にその穴埋めをして、債務の支払いに支障がでないようにする自己資本がある。

financial management　財務管理（資金調達やその運用

などの管理），（企業の）資金繰り，金融操作，（政府の）金融管理，財政運営

◆Greece has fallen into a debt crisis as a result of its lax financial management. ギリシャは，放漫な財政運営の末に財政危機に陥った。◆The bankruptcy of Incubator Bank of Japan gave rise to concern over the company's financial management. 日本振興銀行の破たんで，同社の資金繰りに懸念が生じた。◆The International Monetary Fund is urged to monitor Italy's financial management to provide support to Italy. イタリアを支援するため，国際通貨基金（IMF）はイタリアの財政運営の監視を求められている。

financial market　金融市場　（「金融市場」は，資金の供給者である貸し手と資金の需要者である借り手との間で資金取引が行われる場。⇒ample funds, call in, financial system crisis, liquidity demand, money market, official, procure funds, secondary market, supply funds, yuan-based bond）

Asian financial markets　アジアの金融市場
broadly-defined financial market　広義の金融市場
efficient financial market　効率的な金融市場
financial market analysis　金融市場の分析
financial market conditions　金融市場の状況 金融市場の環境 金融市場の動向
financial market deregulation　金融市場の規制緩和
financial market liberalization　金融市場の自由化
international financial market　国際金融市場
New York financial market　ニューヨーク金融市場
overseas financial market　海外金融市場
the price mechanism in the financial market　金融市場の価格メカニズム

◆Any additional easing measures would only have a limited impact if they were made at the urging of financial markets. 市場に催促される形で追加緩和を行っても，追加緩和策の効果は限定的に過ぎない。◆As the financial markets' confidence in the U.S. currency has been shaken, stock prices may fall worldwide and the dollar-selling trend may accelerate. 米ドルへの金融市場の信認が揺らいでいるため，株価が世界的に下落し，ドル売りの流れが加速する可能性もある。◆Excessive movements of foreign exchange rates will have a negative impact on the stability of the economy and financial markets. 行き過ぎた外国為替相場の動きは，経済の安定と金融市場に悪影響を及ぼす。◆Financial markets are still facing uncertainty. 金融市場は，まだ先行きが不透明だ。◆Financial markets worldwide are focused on whether the U.S. FRB embarks on a third round of its quantitative easing policy, or QE3. 世界の金融市場は，米連邦準備制度理事会（FRB）が量的緩和策の第三弾（QE3)に踏み切るかどうかに注目している。◆Further stability in the financial markets is desirable. 金融市場の一層の安定が，望まれる。◆Global financial markets are still shaken by the serious fiscal troubles in Greece. 世界の金融市場は，ギリシャの深刻な財政危機問題で動揺が続いている。◆Global turmoil in the financial markets results from the downgrading of the U.S. credit rating. 金融市場の世界的な混乱は，米国債の格下げによるものだ。◆In the global financial markets, unrest is continuing as there is no end in sight to fiscal crises to the United States and some European countries. 世界の金融市場では，米国と一部の欧州諸国の財政危機の収束が見通せないため，混乱が続いている。◆It is difficult to predict if new explosive factors emerge to plunge the financial market into further turmoil. 金融市場をさらに混乱に陥れる新しい火種があるのかどうか，予測するのは難しい。◆Policy-based financing operations which take advantage of government subsidies are adversely affecting the price mechanism in the financial market. 政府の補給金を受けて運営される政策金融は，金融市場の価格メカニズムを歪めている。◆The Bank of Japan decided to continue providing ample liquidity to financial markets amid concerns over possible negative effects of the U.S.-led war in Iraq on the nation's economy. 日本銀行は，米国主導のイラク戦争が日本経済に及ぼす悪影響への懸念から，金融市場に大量の資金供給を続けることを決定した。◆The emergency telephone conference by the G-7 financial ministers and central bank governors was held right before the opening of Asian financial markets. 先進7か国（G7）の財務相・中央銀行総裁による緊急電話会議は，アジアの金融市場が開く直前に開かれた。◆The financial crisis triggered by the rise in defaults of U.S. subprime loans caused havoc in financial markets worldwide. 米国のサブプライム・ローン（低所得者向け住宅ローン）の不払い増加がきっかけで起こった金融危機は，世界の金融市場を大混乱させた。◆The financial market is in complete disarray. 金融市場が，大混乱している。◆The financial market may show signs of instability after the bailout measure for Resona Holdings Inc. is decided. りそなホールディングスに対する救済措置（公的資金の注入措置）の決定を発端に，金融市場は今後，不安定な動きを示すかもしれない。◆The interest rates a bank pays when procuring funds from the financial market are higher than those paid by other banks. ある銀行が金融市場で資金調達する際に支払う金利が，他行に比べて高くなっている。◆The rejection of the financial bailout bill by the U.S. House of Representatives roiled the financial markets across the world. 米下院による金融救済法案（金融安定化法案）の否決は，世界の金融市場を大混乱させた。◆The U.S. government's default would throw the financial markets around the world into major turmoil. 米政府がデフォルト（債務不履行）に陥ったら，世界の金融市場は大混乱するだろう。◆Turbulence in global financial markets brought the level of liquidity in the country sharply lower. 世界の金融市場の混乱で，国内流動性の水準は大幅に低下した。◆Worries over the spreading of the eurozone debt crisis and the U.S.'s slipping into recession have driven the rout in financial markets. ユーロ圏の財政危機の拡大と米国の景後退入りへの懸念で，金融市場は総崩れになった。

主な金融市場：
bond market　債券市場 ボンド市場
capital market　長期金融市場
foreign exchange market　外国為替市場　(=forex market)
money market　短期金融市場
stock market　株式市場　(=equity market)

financial market bubble　金融バブル
◆The financial market bubble has not brought forth technology innovation or globalization. 金融バブルは，技術革新やグローバル化をもたらしたわけではない。

financial market conditions　金融市場の環境
◆The Fed raised the discount rate to 0.75 percent from 0.5 percent as a response to improved financial market conditions. 米連邦準備制度理事会（FRB）は，金融市場の環境改善を受けて，(銀行に貸し出す際の金利である)公定歩合を現行の年0.5％から0.75％に引き上げた。

financial market instability　金融市場の動揺, 金融市場不安
◆Financial market instability sparked by the U.S. subprime mortgage crisis continues. 米国のサブプライム・ローン（低所得者向け住宅融資）問題に起因する金融市場の動揺は，まだ収まっていない。

financial market liberalization　金融市場の自由化
◆Beijing plans to allow foreign banks to handle the yuan as part of financial market liberalization in December 2006. 2006年12月に中国は，金融市場の自由化の一環として人民元の取扱いを外国銀行に全面解禁する方針だ。

financial market mess　金融市場の混乱
◆The financial market mess in Europe was triggered by the delay of financial assistance to Greece by the European financial authorities. 欧州の金融市場混乱の引き金となったの

は、欧州金融当局によるギリシャへの金融支援のもたつきだ。

financial market turmoil 金融市場の混乱
◆The financial market turmoil is caused by the U.S. subprime loan crisis. 金融市場の混乱は、米国のサブプライム・ローン（低所得者向け住宅融資）問題によるものだ。

financial markets' confidence 金融市場の信認
◆As the financial markets' confidence in the U.S. currency has been shaken, stock prices may fall worldwide and the dollar-selling trend may accelerate. 米ドルへの金融市場の信認が揺らいでいるため、株価が世界的に下落し、ドル売りの流れが加速する可能性もある。

financial measures 金融政策, 金融措置
◆The government will flexibly implement both economic and financial measures to deal with the slowdown in the economy. 政府は、経済対策と金融政策を機動的に実施して、景気減速に対応する方針だ。

financial meltdown 金融崩壊, 金融危機, 金融のメルトダウン（溶解）, 金融市場のメルトダウン, 株価の急暴落 （⇒powerful bank）
emerge from the global financial meltdown 世界的な金融危機を乗り切る
worldwide financial meltdown 世界的な金融危機
◆Global major financial institutions have been forced to hold extra capital since the financial meltdown following the 2008 bankruptcy of Lehman Brothers Holdings Inc. 米国の投資銀行リーマン・ブラザーズが2008年に経営破たんして生じた金融危機以来、世界の主要金融機関は、資本［自己資本］の上積み［積み増し］を迫られている。◆South Korea has seen a plunge of the won against major currencies amid the worldwide financial meltdown. 世界的な金融危機に伴って、韓国では主要通貨に対してウォン相場が下落している［ウォン安となっている］。◆The financial bailout bill's passage into law marks progress in avoiding a financial meltdown. 金融安定化法案［金融救済法案］が法律として成立したことは、金融危機を回避するうえで一歩前進したといえる。◆The guard raised against a possible financial meltdown during a financial sector-triggered recession several years ago has been lifted. 数年前の金融不況時に想定された金融崩壊に対する厳戒態勢は、すでに解かれている。

financial optimism 金融楽観主義
◆An image of the Charging Bull put in front of the New York Stock Exchange is said to be the symbol of financial optimism and prosperity. ニューヨーク証券取引所前に置かれている「突進する雄牛」の像は、金融楽観主義と繁栄の象徴であると言われている。

financial overhaul plan 金融改革案, 金融再編案, 金融監督の改革案
◆U.S. Treasury Secretary Henry Paulson unveiled the 218-page financial overhaul plan. ヘンリー・ポールソン米財務長官は、218ページの金融改革案［金融監督の改革案］を発表した。

financial panic 金融恐慌, 金融不安, 金融パニック （=financial crisis）
◆A rekindling of the life insurance crisis could set off a financial panic. 生保危機が再燃すれば、金融恐慌を引き起こす可能性がある。

financial penalties 制裁金
◆The number of orders to halt corporate activities and financial penalties issued by the SEC in 2002 was up 24 percent compared with the previous year. SEC（米証券取引委員会）が2002年に発動した業務停止命令や制裁金などの件数は、前年比で24％増となった。

financial performance 財務実績, 財務業績, 財務面での実績, 財務状態, 財務状況
◆Our financial performance met growth targets despite the less favorable business and economic environment. 当社の財務面での業績は、事業および経済環境が低調だったにもかかわらず、成長目標を達成しました。

financial planner 個人資産運用コンサルタント, フィナンシャル・プランナー （=financial planning specialist; ⇒Internet securities company）
◆A financial planner plans and manages total financial assets of individuals and corporations. フィナンシャル・プランナーは、個人や法人の資産の総合設計と管理をする。

financial policy 金融政策（monetary policy）, 財務政策, 財務方針（資金調達とその運用に関する方針）, 財政政策 （fiscal policy）
discretionary financial policy 裁量的金融政策
expansionary financial policy 拡張的金融政策
financial policy instrument 金融政策手段
financial policy objective 金融政策目標
◆Priority measures to achieve economic recovery are stopping deflation and mobilizing all possible fiscal measures, financial policies and taxation reforms. 景気回復を実現するための優先課題は、デフレ阻止と、可能な財政政策、金融政策や税制改革を総動員することだ。

financial policymaker 金融政策担当者 （⇒panic selling）

financial position 財政状態, 財務状況, 財務体質, 資金繰り （=financial condition, financial situation, financial standing）
each borrower's particular financial position 各発行体固有の財政状況［財政状態］
improvement in one's financial position 財務体質の改善
statement of changes in financial position 財政状態変動表
statement of financial position ［condition］ 財政状態計算書
year-end financial position 期末財政状態
◆The closing balance sheet fairly presents the financial position of the Corporation at the closing date in conformity with United States GAAP. クロージング時現在の貸借対照表は、米国の一般に認められた会計原則［米国の会計基準］に従って、クロージング日の「会社」の財政状態を適正に表示している。◆UFJ Holdings Inc. is planning to boost its financial position through a merger with MFTG. UFJは、三菱東京FGとの経営統合で財務体質の強化を計画している。

financial pressure 金融ひっ迫, 金融面での圧力, 経営面での圧力, 経済的苦しみ, 財政難 （=financial stringency, monetary stringency）
◆The company's business diversification led to rising debts that placed financial pressure on the company. 同社の事業多角化は、借入金の増大につながり、それが会社の経営を圧迫する結果となった。◆The financial pressure strained the two companies' relationship. 財政難で、両社の関係に亀裂が生じた。

financial problem 金融問題, 財政的問題, 財政問題
◆Goldman Sachs' capital increase is partly aimed at regaining the confidence in the U.S. financial market, which has been facing a raft of financial problems. ゴールドマン・サックスの増資は、多くの金融問題を抱える米金融市場の信認回復も狙いの一つだ。

financial product 金融商品 （=financial goods, financial instrument; ⇒foreign currency-denominated bond, Internet-based commerce, principal guarantee）
◆In December 1998, trust funds became the first financial products offered by securities firms and life insurers that banks were allowed to sell. 1998年12月に、投資信託は、証券会社と生命保険会社が提供する金融商品のうち銀行窓口での販売が認められた最初の商品となった。◆Lowering the yield of Meiji Yasuda's single-premium whole life insurance will reduce the attraction of the insurer's financial products. 明治安

田生保の一時払い終身保険の利回り［予定利率］の引下げで、同社の金融商品の魅力は薄れると思われる。◆Mizuho Bank offers a service by which ATM cardholders are given mileage points each time they use the new cards as credit cards, purchase financial products at the bank's branches or receive loans from the bank. みずほ銀行が提供しているサービスでは、キャッシュ・カード会員が新型カードをクレジット・カードとして利用したり、みずほ銀で金融商品を購入したり、ローンを利用したりすると、その取引に応じて毎回、マイレージ・ポイントがもらえる。◆We want to make a financial product our customers could purchase without any worries or hesitation. 客に迷わず安心して購入してもらえる金融商品を作りたい。

financial profile　財務力見通し
◆Standard & Poor's revised upward the outlook on its ratings on six major Japanese insurance companies against the backdrop of their improved financial profiles. スタンダード＆プアーズは、日本の大手保険会社6社の財務力見通し改善を背景に、6社の格付け見通しを上方修正した。

financial quagmire　財政難
◆Stuck in a financial quagmire, Russia is having difficulty in managing its nuclear arsenal. 財政難から、ロシアは現在、保有する核兵器の管理に苦慮している。

financial reconstruction　金融再生
Financial Reconstruction Commission　金融再生委員会
Financial Reconstruction Law　金融再生法
Financial Reconstruction Law standards　金融再生法基準
◆Financial reconstruction is likely to stagnate under the Italy's new government as it did under the previous one. イタリアの財政再建は、前政権同様、新政権でも難航しそうだ。
◆It is questionable whether the Italian new government will be able to steadily implement measures for financial reconstruction and structural reforms. イタリアの新政権が財政再建策と構造改革を着実に実行できるかどうかは、疑問だ。

financial records　財務記録
◆Financial records are adequate and can be relied upon. 財務記録は、適切で信頼性がある。

financial reform　金融改革, 金融制度改革, 財政改革
◆During the period of structural reform pushed by the Koizumi administration, the former chairman of the bank was lionized as a standard-bearer of financial reforms. 小泉政権が推し進めた構造改革の時代に、同行の前会長は金融改革の旗手ともてはやされた。◆Italy's new government led by economist Mario Monti must face painful financial reforms. 経済専門家マリオ・モンティ氏を首相とするイタリア新政権は、痛みを伴う財政改革が急務だ。

financial regulation(s)　金融規制
an overhaul of financial regulations　金融規制の改革
　（⇒overhaul of financial regulations）
Report on Financial Structure and Regulation　ハント報告
stringent financial regulations　金融規制の強化
tighter［tougher］financial regulations　金融規制の強化
　（⇒World Economic Forum）
◆The administration of U.S. President Barack Obama proposed the stringent financial regulations. 米オバマ政権は、金融規制の強化を打ち出した。◆The G-7 countries agreed to move in the direction of tougher financial regulations. 先進7か国（G7）は、金融規制強化の方向で一致した。◆Various financial regulations have been discussed to prevent another financial crisis. 金融危機の再発防止に向けて、さまざまな金融規制が討議されている。

financial regulators　金融当局
◆Financial regulators asked prosecutors to investigate allegations that UFJ Holdings Inc.'s banking unit illegally obstructed recent inspections by reporting misleading information about its nonperforming loans. 金融当局は、UFJ銀行が不良債権に関する虚偽の情報を報告して最近の検査を違法に妨害したとして、同行を検察当局に刑事告発した。

financial regulatory system　金融監督制度
◆U.S. Treasury Secretary Henry Paulson unveiled the overhaul plan of the U.S. financial regulatory system. ヘンリー・ポールソン米財務長官は、米国の金融監督制度の改革案を発表した。

financial rehabilitation　経営再建, 金融再生
　（=financial reorganization, financial revitalization）
◆The two companies can now seek financial rehabilitation without a management integration. 両社は現在、経営統合によらずとも経営再建を目指せる状況にある。

financial reorganization　金融再編
　（=financial rehabilitation）
◆The latest financial reorganization drama was triggered by UFJ Holdings' corporate plight. 今回の金融再編劇の引き金となったのは、UFJホールディングスの深刻な経営状況だ。

financial report　財務報告, 財務報告書, 業績報告, 有価証券報告書
amended financial report　有価証券報告書の訂正
April-September half-year financial report　4-9月期の中間決算, 中間決算
falsified financial report　有価証券報告書［財務報告書］の虚偽記載
◆Japanese companies listed on the London Stock Exchange will submit financial reports based on the IAS or the U.S. GAAP. ロンドン証券取引所に上場している日本企業は今後、国際会計基準か米国会計基準に基づく［に準拠した］財務報告書を提出することになる。◆Kokudo is suspected of selling a large amount of its Seibu Railway stock to client companies before the railway announced corrections to its financial report. コクドは、西武鉄道が有価証券報告書の訂正を公表する前に、取引先に大量の西武鉄道株を売却した疑いが持たれている。◆The company submitted corrected documents, including an amended financial report, to the Kanto Local Finance Bureau. 同社は、有価証券報告書の訂正など訂正文書を関東財務局に提出した。◆These disciplinary measures include increased penalties on securities fraud and a newly installed penalty on corporate directors in cases of failure to submit adequate financial reports to authorities. これらの懲戒処分には、証券詐欺に対する罰則の強化や、当局に適切な財務報告をしなかった場合の企業取締役に対する罰則の新設などが含まれている。

financial reporting　財務報告, 財務報告書
Financial Reporting Council　（英国の）財務報告評議会, FRC
financial reporting for segments　セグメント別財務報告
financial reporting in hyper inflationary economics　超インフレ経済下の財務報告
Financial Reporting Review Panel　財務報告検討委員会, FRRP
Financial Reporting Standard　財務報告基準, FRS, 英国企業の会計基準
financial reporting to shareholders　株主に対する財務報告
for financial reporting purposes　財務報告上, 財務会計上
fraudulent financial reporting　不正な財務報告, 虚偽の財務報告
general purpose external financial reporting　一般目的外部財務報告
interim financial reporting　中間財務報告
◆The goal of financial reporting is to give investors the information they need to understand how we are doing over time and in comparison with other companies. 財務報告の目標は、当社が現在にいたるまで、また他社との比較でどのような経営をしているかを投資家に理解してもらうために必要な情報を、投資家に提供することにあります。

financial rescue　金融支援, 経営支援
financial rescue package　金融支援策, 経営支援策
　(=financial aid package, financial rescue program)
　◆A breakdown of the DBJ financial rescue package reveals that ¥70 billion has been loaned to JAL and about ¥15 billion to ANA. 日本政策投資銀行が経営支援策として行った融資の内訳は、日本航空システムが約700億円、全日本空輸が約150億円となっている。◆The U.S. deficit in the first three months of the current budget year includes $247 billion that has been spent on the $700 billion financial rescue package. 今会計年度（2009年度）の当初3か月（10-12月）の米財政赤字には、7,000億ドルの金融支援策に基づいて支出された2,470億ドルも含まれている。

financial rescue program　金融支援策, 金融支援プログラム, 経営支援策
　(=financial rescue program; ⇒red ink)
　◆Part of the bailout funds on the $700 billion financial rescue program went to shore up insurance giant American International Group Inc. and the auto industry. 7,000億ドルの金融支援策に基づく救済資金の一部は、米保険大手のAIGと自動車業界（GMとクライスラー）の強化に充てられた。◆The U.S. deficit in the first three months of the current budget year includes $247 billion that has been spent on the $700 billion financial rescue program. 今会計年度（2009年度）の当初3か月（10-12月）の米財政赤字には、7,000億ドルの金融支援策に基づいて支出された2,470億ドルも含まれている。

financial resource　資金, 資本, 資金力, 金融力, 金融資産, 財務資源, 財源, 資金の源泉, 資金源, 原資
　a financial resource for the pension system　年金の財源, 年金制度の財源
　financial resources used to dispose of bad loans　不良債権処理に充てられる資金源, 不良債権処理の原資
　permanent financial resources　恒久的な財源
　◆Financial resources can be secured by stopping the hand-out policies of the Democratic Party of Japan. 民主党のバラマキ政策を止めれば、財源は確保できる。◆If the current downward trend of stock prices continues, banks' financial resources that could be used to dispose of bad loans will decrease drastically. 株価の下落基調がこのまま続くと、金融機関の不良債権処理の原資は激減する。◆Minshuto proposes the introduction of a new consumption tax as a financial resource for the pension system. 年金［年金制度］の財源として、民主党は新消費税（年金目標消費税）の導入を掲げている。◆The capital increase is designed to secure financial resources for the expansion of the bank's investment banking activities abroad. 同行の増資の目的は、海外での投資銀行業務拡大の資金確保にある。

financial results　財務成績, 財務実績, 業績, 金融収支, 決算
　crooked financial results　不正決算, 不正会計
　financial results for the fiscal second-half　下半期［下期］の決算, 下半期の業績
　interim financial results　中間決算
　◆If we are to continue to deliver improved financial results, we must continue to enhance our competitiveness. 今後とも業績［財務成績］向上を図るには、当社の競争力を引き続き高める必要がある。◆Life insurers customarily do not release financial results for the fiscal first-half. 生命保険会社は、慣例として上半期の決算を公表していない。◆Time Warner Inc. will restate its financial results as there were the problems with the way it accounted for a number of transactions. タイム・ワーナーは、一部取引の会計処理方法に問題があったため、同社の財務成績［業績］を修正再表示することになった。

financial revitalization　金融の再生, 金融再生
　(=financial reconstruction, financial rehabilitation)
　◆If the government-set target of halving Japanese mega-banks' ratios of bad loans by the end of fiscal 2004 is achieved, the nation's financial revitalization is sure to be realized. 2004年度末（2005年3月期決算）までに、（2001年度末時点の）日本のメガバンクの不良債権残高比率を半減させる政府目標を達成すれば、日本の金融再生も実現するはずだ。

financial revitalization plan　金融再生プログラム
　(=financial revitalization program, financial revival program)
　◆The Oct. 30, 2002 financial revitalization plan sought stricter assessments of bank assets. 2002年10月30日の「金融再生プログラム」は、銀行資産の一段と厳しい査定を求めた。

financial revival plan　金融再生プログラム
　◆The government's financial revival plan is expected to exacerbate the credit crunch and result in a further sell-off of bank stocks. 政府の金融再生プログラムは、貸し渋りを加速して銀行株の下落に拍車がかかると予想される。

financial rewards　金銭的報酬
　◆There can be huge financial rewards from the successful commercialization of technology. 技術の商品化に成功すると、巨額の金銭的な報酬が得られる。

financial risk　財務リスク, 金融リスク, フィナンシャル・リスク
　解説 財務リスクの種類：
　collection risk　回収リスク
　country risk　カントリー・リスク
　credit risk　信用リスク
　exchange risk　為替リスク（=currency risk）
　failure risk　倒産リスク
　financing risk　資金調達リスク
　hostile acquisition risk　敵対的買収リスク
　investment risk　投資リスク
　market risk　市場リスク マーケット・リスク
　rating risk　格付けリスク

financial safety net　金融安全網
　◆The government intends to restructure the deposit insurance system as a new financial safety net for protecting settlement systems. 政府は、預金保険制度を、決済システム保護のための新しい金融安全網として再構築する方針だ。

financial sanctions　金融制裁
　◆Pyongyang's accounts with Banco Delta Asia in Macao were frozen under U.S. financial sanctions. マカオの銀行「バンコ・デルタ・アジア」にある北朝鮮の口座が、米国の金融制裁を受けて凍結された。◆The U.S. government has imposed additional financial sanctions on North Korea. 米政府は、北朝鮮に対する追加金融制裁を発動した。

financial scandal　金融不祥事, 金融スキャンダル
　◆A financial scandal embroiling Daio Paper Corp.'s former chairman, a member of the firm's founding family, has come to light. 大王製紙の創業家出身の前会長をめぐる金融不祥事が、発覚した。◆The former president of Olympus Corp. reiterated his determination to get to the bottom of one of the domestic biggest financial scandals. オリンパスの元社長は、国内最大級の金融不祥事の真相を究明する決意を改めて語った。

financial sector　金融部門, 金融業界, 金融界, 金融・保険業, 金融セクター
　◆The Fed won't need to continue its relaxed monetary policy if the U.S. housing market and financial sector recover. 米国の住宅市場や金融部門が回復すれば、米連邦準備制度理事会（FRB）は、金融緩和を継続する必要はなくなる。◆The reorganization drama of the financial sector through changes involving leading banks has been put in motion again. 大手銀行の改編による金融再編劇が、再び動き出した。◆The U.S. housing market and financial sector have not recovered yet. 米国の住宅市場や金融部門は、まだ回復していない。

financial sector realignment　金融業界の再編, 金融再編

◆To resolve the financial unrest in EU nations, accelerating financial sector realignment in countries such as Germany must be worked out. EU諸国の金融不安を解決するには、(2,000もの金融機関がひしめく)ドイツなどでの金融再編の加速も課題だ。

financial sector-triggered recession 金融不況
◆Preparedness for financial crisis has returned to a normal level from the guard raised during a financial sector-triggered recession. 金融危機への備えは、金融不況時の厳戒態勢から平常レベルに戻っている。◆The guard raised against a possible financial meltdown during a financial sector-triggered recession several years ago has been lifted. 数年前の金融不況時に想定された金融崩壊に対する厳戒態勢は、すでに解かれている。

financial service(s) 金融事業, 金融サービス, 金融, 投資情報サービス機関 (⇒branch-free bank, capital requirements, corporate performance)
　financial service [services] industry　金融サービス業界
　financial service [services] organization　金融サービス機関
　Financial Services Act of 1986　1986年金融サービス法, FSA
　Financial Services Agency　金融庁, FSA
　Financial Services Agency Commissioner　金融庁長官
　Financial Services and Market Act　金融サービス市場法, FSMA
　Financial Services Authority　(英国の)金融サービス機構, FSA
　Financial Services Committee　金融サービス委員会
　Financial Services Modernization Act　(米国の)金融サービス近代化法 (⇒Gramm-Leach-Bliley Act)
　Financial Services Oversight Council　米金融サービス監督協議会, FSOC
◆Financial services account for about 60 percent of the company's overall sales. 金融事業は、同社の売上全体の6割を占めている。◆Higher debt maturing within one year chiefly reflects commercial paper we issued to support financial services. 1年以内返済予定の負債の増加は、主に金融サービス部門の支援のため、当社がコマーシャル・ペーパーを発行したことを反映しています。◆In the area of financial services, Seven Eleven Japan Co. and Ito-Yokado set up IYBank Co. to provide ATM services at convenience store outlets. 金融サービスの分野では、セブン-イレブン・ジャパンとイトーヨーカ堂がアイワイバンク銀行を設立して、コンビニエンス・ストアの店舗でATM(現金自動預け払い機)サービスを提供している。◆Japan lacks top-notch safety management specialists at least in the field of financial services. 少なくとも金融サービスの分野では、日本に一流の安全管理専門家がいない。◆The firm's operations in the financial services and leasing industry involve direct financing and finance leasing programs for its products and the products of other companies. 金融サービスとリース業界での同社の事業には、同社製品と他社製品に関する直接融資とファイナンス・リース事業も含まれている。

Financial Services Agency　金融庁, FSA (⇒insolvency)
◆The credit union was forced to apply to the Financial Services Agency for protection from creditors. 同信組は、金融庁への破綻申請を迫られた。◆The Financial Services Agency did not comment on whether any Japanese banks had been earmarked for the G-SIFIs list. 金融庁は、邦銀が国際金融システム上重要な金融機関(G-SIFIs)リストの指定行に入っているかどうかについては、コメントしなかった。◆The Financial Services Agency ordered Sompo Japan Insurance Inc. to suspend part of its operations as punishment for the major insurance company's illegal business practices. 金融庁は、損保大手の損害保険ジャパンに業務で法令違反があったとして、同社に一部業務停止命令を出した。◆The major banks attributed their increased bad loans to the poor performance of their borrowers due to the prolonged economic slump and Financial Service Agency inspections resulting in a stricter review of their asset assessments. 大手銀行は、不良債権が増えた理由として、長引く景気低迷で貸出先の経営が悪化したことと、金融庁の検査を受けて大手行が資産査定を厳しくしたことを挙げた。◆The Metropolitan Police Department searched the bank's head office on suspicion the bank had sabotaged an audit by the Financial Services Agency. 警視庁は、金融庁の立入り検査を妨害した疑いで、同行の本店を捜索した。◆When serious financial difficulties are expected, the Financial Services Agency is allowed to order a company to improve its operations in the early stages without releasing the information to the public. 深刻な財務悪化が予想される場合、金融庁は、非公表で早めに業務改善命令を発動することができる。

financial services business　金融サービス業務, 金融サービス事業
◆The company's financial services businesses are growing because it is investing in new assets. 同社の金融サービス業務は、新資産への投資で拡大している。

financial services sector　金融サービス部門, 金融界
◆Japan's financial services sector learned of the importance of safety management through the lost decade. 失われた10年を通じて、日本の金融界は安全管理の重要性を学んだ。

financial settlement　金融決済
◆Financial settlement refers to a lump sum payment by an insurer to a disabled insured that extinguishes the insurer's responsibility under the disability contract. 金融決済は、就業不能契約に基づき、傷害を負った被保険者に保険会社が一時金を支給して、保険会社の責任を消滅させることを指す。

financial settlement services　金融決済業務, 決済業務 (⇒handle)
◆Banks' financial settlement services are closely related to the people's daily lives. 銀行の決済業務は、国民の日常生活と密接に関連している。

financial shape　経営基盤
◆Many of the regional or small and midsize banks are still in poor financial shape. 地方銀行や中小金融機関の多くは、まだ経営基盤がぜい弱だ。

financial situation　財政状態, 財政状況, 財政情勢, 財務状態, 財務状況, 財務体質, 金融情勢, 金融局面, 台所事情 (=financial condition, financial position, financial standing)
◆The BOJ could take additional monetary relaxation measures if there are any changes in the financial situation. 金融面で動きがあるとすれば、日銀が追加の金融緩和策を実施する可能性もある。◆The firm's financial situation has been aggravated by recent poor performance in its main business of developing resorts. リゾート開発の本業がこのところ不振で、同社の財務状況が悪化している。◆The FSA conducted special inspections of UFJ Bank in October to check the financial situations of UFJ's large-scale borrowers. UFJ銀行の大口融資先の財務状況を調べるため、金融庁は10月にUFJの特別検査を行った。

financial socialism　金融社会主義
◆Under a system that can be termed "financial socialism," a government controls the massive amounts of money collected from the private sector. 「金融社会主義」ともいえる制度では、国が民間から集めた巨額の資金を管理する。

financial soundness　財務上の健全性, 財政の健全性, 経営の健全性 (=financial health)
◆The massive negative yields of the life insurance industry threaten the financial soundness of insurers. 生保業界の巨額の逆ざやが、生保各社の財務上の健全性(経営の健全性)を脅(おびや)かしている。

financial sources　金融筋, 財源
（⇒Banks' Shareholding Purchase Corporation）
◆The 10-year bonds were issued in volume in the 1990s to procure financial sources to stimulate the economy. 1990年代に, 10年物国債が景気対策の財源を確保するため大量に発行された。

financial stability　金融システムの安定, 金融の安定, 金融安定化, 財務上の安定性, 経営の安定性[健全性]
◆Capital adequacy rating is used to assess a bank's financial stability. 自己資本比率の評価は, 銀行の経営の健全性[財務上の健全性]を判断して評価するのに用いられる。◆Significant risks remain to economic and financial stability. 経済と金融の安定化には, まだ大きなリスクが存在する。◆The G-7's financial ministers and central bank governors are committed to taking necessary measures to support financial stability and economic growth. 先進7か国（G7）の財務相と中央銀行総裁は, 金融安定化と経済成長を支えるためにあらゆる手段を講じる決意だ。◆Volatile movements in the currency market have a negative impact on economic and financial stability. 為替市場の過度な変動は, 経済・金融の安定に悪影響を及ぼす。

Financial Stability Board　金融安定化理事会, 金融安定理事会, FSB（主要20か国・地域（G20）で構成。金融監督に関する国際基準を制定する機関の金融安定化フォーラム（FSF）に代わる新機関で, スイスに本部を置く）
◆According to the Financial Stability Board, 28 banks viewed as global systemically important financial institutions（G-SIFIs）will be subject to a new global rule requiring them to hold extra capital to prevent future financial crises. 金融安定化理事会（FSB）によると, 金融システム上重要な国際金融機関（G-SIFIs）と考えられる世界の28行が, 金融危機の再発を防止するため, 資本の上積みを求める新国際基準[新国際金融規制]の対象になる。◆Mitsubishi UFJ Financial Group Inc., Sumitomo Mitsui Financial Group Inc. and Mizuho Financial Group Inc. are included in the G-SIFIs list of the Financial Stability Board. 主要20か国・地域（G20）の金融当局で構成する金融安定化理事会（FSB）のG-SIFIリスト（国際的な巨大金融機関リスト）には, 三菱UFJ, 三井住友, みずほの3大金融グループも含まれている。◆The Financial Stability Board is cooperating with the Basel Committee on Banking Supervision, a body that sets rules for international banking. 金融安定化理事会（FSB）は, 国際銀行業務の基準を制定する機関のバーゼル銀行監督委員会と連携している。◆The Financial Stability Board will impose a progressive extra capital charge of 1 percent to 2.5 percent on risk-adjusted assets held by G-SIFIs. G20（主要20か国・地域）の金融当局で構成する金融安定化理事会（FSB）は, 国際金融システムにとって重要な金融機関（G-SIFIs）が保有するリスク調整後資産に, 1〜2.5%の資本[自己資本]の上積みを段階的に課すことになった。

Financial Stability Forum　金融安定化フォーラム, FSF（G-7主要先進国と発展途上国, 国際通貨基金, 世界銀行, 国際証券監督者機構の各代表で構成される。⇒FSB）
◆An interim report of the Financial Stability Forum called for measures such as a review of evaluation system of securitized products. 金融安定化フォーラムの中間報告は, 証券化商品の評価方法見直しなどの措置を求めた。◆The Financial Stability Forum comprises financial authorities of major nations. 金融安定化フォーラムは, 主要国の金融当局で構成されている。

Financial Stability Plan　（米国の）金融安定化プラン

financial stabilization　金融安定化

financial standing　財政状態, 財務状況, 財務体質
（=financial position）
◆As part of the plan to bolster its financial standing, the struggling life insurer will seek capital injection of about 100 billion yen from financial institutions. 財務強化策の一環として, 経営再建中のこの生命保険会社は, 金融機関に1,000億円程度の基金拠出（基金増資）を要請する方針だ。◆Standard & Poor's downgraded Belgium's financial standing from AA＋ to AA. スタンダード・アンド・プアーズ（S&P）は, ベルギー国債の格付けをダブルA（AA）プラスからダブルA（AA）に1段階引き下げた。

financial statement　財務報告書, 財務報告, 有価証券報告書（financial statementは, 以下の関連語句に示すようにfinancial statements（財務書類・財務諸表）の形容詞として使われることもある。⇒falsification, falsify, practice, underreporting）

falsification of financial statements　有価証券報告書の虚偽記載

Financial Statement and Budget Report　（英国の）財政報告予算摘要, FSBR

financial statement date　決算日

financial statement for the year to March 2012　2012年3月期の有価証券報告書, 2011年度の有価証券報告書

financial statement misstatement　財務書類[財務諸表]の虚偽表示

financial statement presentation　財務書類[財務諸表]の表示

for financial statement reporting　財務書類上, 財務諸表上

semiannual financial statement　半期報告書

◆Olympus Corp. exaggerated the intangible value of its British subsidiary by ￥33.4 billion in the financial statement. オリンパスは, 有価証券報告書で英子会社の"のれん代"について334億円を過大に計上していた。◆The company corrected its financial statement for the year to March 2011. 同社は, 2011年3月期[2010年度]の有価証券報告書を訂正した。

financial statements　財務諸表, 財務書類, 企業財務情報, 決算書, 経営分析, 有価証券報告書（⇒company, financial statement, inflate, net capital deficiency）

a complete set of financial statements　完全な一組の財務諸表

annual financial statements　年次報告書

consolidated financial statements　連結財務書類, 連結財務諸表
（=group accounts, group financial statements）

foreign currency financial statements　外貨表示財務諸表, 外貨表示財務書類

integrity and reliability of the financial statements　財務書類の完全性と信頼性（⇒internal control）

interim financial statements　中間財務書類

summarized financial statements　要約財務書類, 財務類要約

unconsolidated financial statements　単独財務書類

◆Even after the company fell into financial difficulties, it embellished its financial statements to make it appear profitable. 同社の経営が行き詰まった以降も, 同社は決算書を粉飾して, 経営状況を良く見せかけていた。◆Independent accountants are retained to examine our financial statements. 独立した会計監査人が, 当社の財務書類[財務諸表]を監査しています。◆The Company provides for income taxes based on accounting income for tax purposes included in the financial statements. 当社は税法上, 財務書類に表示する会計上の利益に基づいて法人所得税を算定しています。◆The company's financial statements are not based on the book value of the assets at time they were obtained. 同社の財務諸表は, 取得時の資産の簿価を基準としていない。◆The figures on the financial statements conflicted with those the company had made public. 財務諸表の数字は, 同社が公表した財務諸表の数字と食い違っていた。◆The financial statements and a score of related documents show that the company has a negative net worth. 財務書類と約20の関連資料は, 同社が債務超過であることを示している。◆The financial statements showing a negative net worth do not exist in any finished form. 債務超過を示す財務諸表は、完成したものとしては存在しない。◆These GAASs require that we plan and perform the audit to obtain reasonable assurance about whether the financial statements are free of material misstatement. これらの一般に認められた監査基準は、連結財務書類に重要な虚偽表示がないかどうかについての合理的な確証を得るため、私どもが監査を計画して実施することを要求しています。

解説 **財務書類について**：通常、財務書類には balance sheet（貸借対照表）、income statement（損益計算書）と cash flow statement（キャッシュ・フロー計算書）のほか、statement of stockholders' equity（株主持ち分計算書）や statement of changes in financial position（財政状態変動表）などが含まれる。米国企業の年次報告書や四半期報告書その他で公表される財務書類は、だいたい連結財務書類で、一般に貸借対照表（balance sheet）、損益および剰余金計算書（statement of income and retained earnings）、財政状態変動表（statement of changes in financial position）、会計処理方針の説明（disclosure of accounting policies）と財務書類注記（notes to financial statements）で構成されている。ただし、会計処理方針の説明は財務書類注記［財務諸表注記］に盛り込まれることもある。このほか、期中に増資（capital increase）や株式の償還（redemption）、自社株取引（treasury stock transaction）などの資本勘定（capital accounts）に変動が生じた場合には、資本勘定計算書（capital statement）が利用される。なお、貸借対照表は財務状態（資産内容）を、また損益および剰余金計算書は経営成績（営業実績）を、また財政状態変動表は資金投下と資金調達（資金繰り）を示す。

完全な一組の財務諸表（a complete set of financial statements）を構成する主な計算書：
  statement of cash flows　キャッシュ・フロー計算書
  statement of changes in equity　持ち分変動計算書
  statement of comprehensive income　包括利益計算書
  statement of financial position　財政状態計算書

financial status　財政状態, 財務内容, 体力
  （=financial position, financial standing）
  ◆The financial status of financial institutions has weakened with the recent plunge in stock prices. 金融機関の体力が、最近の株安で低下している。◆The time vice president of the bank was the head of the department in charge of assessing the financial status of large borrowers. 同行の元副頭取は、大口融資先の財務内容審査部門の最高責任者だった。

financial steps　金融措置, 金融政策
  ◆On expectations for the new financial steps, the Nikkei Stock Average recovered to the ￥9,000 mark. 今回の金融政策への期待で、日経平均株価は9,000円台に回復した。

financial stock　金融銘柄
  ◆France banned short selling on 11 financial stocks for 15 days. フランスは、金融11銘柄の空売りを15日間禁止した。◆France, Italy, Spain and Belgium imposed a ban on short-selling financial stocks. フランス、イタリア、スペインとベルギーが、金融銘柄の空売りを禁止した。

financial straits　財政難, 財政困難, 財政危機, 財政ひっ迫, 財政的苦境, 困難な資金繰り, 金に困ること, 財務力の低下, 金融機関の体力の低下
  （=financial difficulties）
  ◆Russian oil giant Yukos has been in dire financial straits since the administration of Russian President Vladimir Putin hit the firm with a huge tax bill. ロシアの大手石油会社ユコスは、プーチン政権から巨額の追徴課税をかけられ、資金繰りにひどく苦しんでいる。◆The DBJ and private financial institutions extended loans worth a total of ￥100 billion to JAL in June 2009 though JAL was already in dire financial straits. 日本政策投資銀行と民間金融機関は、日航の経営がすでに悪化していたものの、2009年6月に同社に対して総額1,000億円を融資した。

financial strategy　財務戦略
  ◆The delisting of Livedoor stocks means a complete end to the group's creative financial strategy of seeking explosive growth by bloating its market capitalization. ライブドア株の上場廃止は、時価総額を膨らませて急成長を求めるという同グループの独創的な財務戦略が、完全に崩れたことを意味する。

financial strength　資金力, 財務力, 財務体質, 財務面での健全性, 金融機関の体力
  a deterioration in the financial strength of the banking system　銀行［市中銀行、銀行業界］の財務の健全性悪化
  banks with weakened financial strength　財務が悪化した銀行, 財務力が低下した銀行
  financial strength ratings　財務健全度格付け
  insurance financial strength　保険支払い能力
  insurer's financial strength rating　保険会社の保険金支払い能力格付け
  life insurance financial strength rating　生命保険会社の保険金支払い能力
  ◆It is unknown how the EU's stress test that measured the financial strength of Europe's major banks dealt with the downside risk of real estate prices. 欧州の主要銀行の財務内容［財務の健全性］を調べたEU（欧州連合）のストレス・テスト（特別検査）が、不動産価格の下落リスクをどのように扱ったかは不明だ。◆Money loaned by private banks declined because banks with weakened financial strength were less willing to lend, besides a lack of businesses seeking expansion through borrowing. 民間銀行の貸出金が減ったのは、お金を借りてまで事業を拡大しようとする企業がなかったほか、財務が悪化した銀行が貸し渋ったからだ。◆Rating agency Moody's may place a negative outlook on French government's Aaa debt rating as the government's financial strength has weakened. 格付け会社のムーディーズは、フランス国債のAaa（トリプルA）格付けについて、仏政府の財務体質［財力］が弱まっているため「ネガティブ（弱含み）」の見通しを示す可能性がある。◆The company's financial strength has deteriorated since a series of scandals including the mislabeling of beef by its subsidiary. 同社の財務体質は、子会社による牛肉の偽装表示など一連の事件以来、悪化している。◆The reassessment of 14 British banks by Moody's is not driven by a deterioration in the financial strength of the banking system. ムーディーズによる英銀14行の格付け見直しは、銀行［銀行業界］の財務の健全性悪化によるものではない。◆The stress test by the EU's Committee of European Banking Supervisors measured the financial strength of Europe's major banks. 欧州連合（EU）の欧州銀行監督委員会が行ったストレス・テストで、域内主要銀行の財務の健全性を調べた。

financial stress　経営難, 信用ひっ迫

financial stress test　金融の特別検査　（金融機関の財務の健全性を調べる特別検査。⇒Committee of European Banking Supervisors, stress test）

financial strife　金融危機
  ◆The challenge of the Basel Committee on Banking Supervision is to develop a regulatory framework while fending off a recurrence of financial strife. バーゼル銀行監督委員会の課題は、金融危機再発の防止と規制の枠組みの策定だ。

financial stringency　金融ひっ迫
  （=financial pressure, monetary stringency）

financial structural reforms　金融の構造改革
  ◆The lifting of the freeze of the payoff system is a necessary measure to realize financial structural reforms. ペイオフの凍結解除は、金融の構造改革に必要な措置だ。

financial structure　財務構成, 資本構成, 金融組織
  ◆The firm intends to rebuild its financial structure by a large-scale allocation of the new shares to the third parties. 同社

は、大規模な第三者割当増資で資本構成を再構築する考えだ。
解説 財務構成と資本構成について：「財務構成」（資本調達の状態）は資本をどの源泉から調達したかを示すもので、資本構成（capital structure）に短期債務（short term debt）や買掛金（account payable）などを加えたもの。これに対して「資本構成」は、資本総額に占める他人資本（負債）と自己資本の構成割合をいう。

financial summit meeting 金融サミット
◆At the financial summit meeting in Washington, additional pump-priming measures through strengthening cooperation between advanced countries and emerging economies will be a major subject of discussion. ワシントンで開かれる金融サミットでは、先進国と新興国の連携強化による追加景気対策の検討が、主要テーマとなる。◆At two financial summit meetings since the collapse of Lehman Brothers, agreements were made on cooperation to implement large-scale economic stimulus measures and to take monetary relaxation policies. リーマン・ブラザーズの倒産［破たん］以来2回開かれた金融サミットでは、連携して大型の財政出動や金融緩和策を実施することで合意が得られた。

financial support 金融支援, 財政的な援助, 財政支援, 資金面での支援, 資金負担 （=financial aid, financial assistance, financial backing, financial rescue）
financial support from main creditor banks 主力取引銀行による金融支援
government financial support 政府の金融支援
◆DaimlerChrysler AG decided to end its financial support for Mitsubishi Motors Corp. ダイムラー・クライスラーは、三菱自動車への金融支援打ち切りを決めた。◆Financial institutions and TEPCO shareholders should shoulder part of the financial burden in return for government financial support of TEPCO. 政府が東電を支援する見返りとして、金融機関と東電株主も一定の金融負担をするべきだ。◆Financial support is the prerequisite for the two firms' funding of the issuance of new shares. 金融支援は、両社の増資引受けの前提条件となっている。◆Greece asked other eurozone member states for financial support to help it stem its budget crisis in early 2010. 2010年初めにギリシャは、財政危機を回避するため、他のユーロ圏加盟国に金融支援を求めた。◆Greece was bailed out temporarily with financial support of €110 billion（about ¥12.7 trillion）from the IMF and the European Union. ギリシャは、IMFと欧州連合（EU）から1,100億ユーロ（約12兆7,000億円）の金融支援を受けて、一時的に救済された。◆Greece's fiscal reconstruction has made little progress since the country was bailed out with financial support from the IMF and the EU in May 2010. ギリシャの財政再建は、2010年5月にIMFと欧州連合（EU）による金融支援を受けて以来、進展していない。◆The amount of federal government's financial support to GM will reach ¥5 trillion in total. GMに対する米政府の金融支援の総額は、5兆円に達する。◆The restructuring plan includes ¥520 billion in financial support from its three main creditor banks. 再建策には、主力取引銀行3行による5,200億円の金融支援が盛り込まれている。◆The 17-nation currency union was slow in responding to the request for financial support by Greece. 17か国から成る通貨統合のユーロ圏は、ギリシャの金融支援要請への対応が遅かった。◆Without the government financial support, TEPCO will fall into debt as the utility has to pay the huge amounts in compensation. 政府の金融支援がなければ、東電は巨額の賠償金を支払わなければならないので、債務超過に陥ると思われる。

financial system 金融制度, 金融システム
Committee on Financial System Research 金融制度調査会
debackles in the financial system 金融システムの混乱
excessive liquidity in the financial system 金融システムの過剰流動性

financial system balance sheet 金融システムの財務基盤
financial system reform 金融制度の改革
　（=reform of financial system）
financial system stabilization 金融システムの安定化
fragilities in the financial system 金融システムの脆弱（ぜいじゃく）性
global ［world］ financial system 世界の金融システム
international financial systems 国際金融システム
market financial system 市場原理に基づく金融システム
regulated financial system 金融システムの規制, 金融システムに対する規制
remove liquidity from the financial system 金融システムから流動性を吸収する［吸い上げる］
the health of the financial system 金融制度の健全性
◆EU nations must have to further enhance their cooperation to strengthen their financial systems. EU各国は、連携を一段と強めて、金融システムを強化しなければならない。◆Financial authorities should stiffen the penalties for illegal transactions to protect the financial system from rumors and speculative investment. 金融当局は違法取引（違法行為）に対する罰則を強化して、金融システムを風評や投機［投機的投資］から守らなければならない。◆Japan's financial system was badly damaged with the collapse of the bubble economy and deflation. 日本の金融システムは、バブル崩壊とデフレで深手を負った。◆The financial system became crippled during the financial crisis. 金融危機の際、金融システムは動きが取れなくなった［麻痺してしまった］。◆The government would ask the Bank of Japan to further ease its monetary policy to help stabilize the nation's financial system by helping financial institutions procure funds. 政府は、金融機関の資金繰りを助けて金融システムの安定化を図るため、日銀に追加の［もう一段の］金融緩和を求める方針だ。◆The Internet, which can transmit rumors across the country instantaneously, has rocked the financial system. 一瞬のうちにデマを全国に広げることができるインターネットは、金融システムを揺さぶっている。◆The most worrying thing, in terms of future, is the sense of misgiving in the financial system. 今後、最も懸念されるのは、金融不安だ。◆We must expedite efforts to rebuild a safety net to support the financial system. 金融システムを支える安全網の立直し策を急ぐ必要がある。◆With the midyear account settlement scheduled in September, concerns over the stability of the nation's financial system inevitably will grow again should stock prices dip further. 9月中間決算を前に、株価がさらに下がれば、再び日本の金融システム不安が当然、台頭してくる。

Financial System Council 金融審議会
　（⇒settlement）
◆The Financial System Council is an advisory body to the prime minister. 金融審議会は、首相の諮問機関だ。

financial system crisis 金融危機, 金融システム不安
　（⇒injection of public funds）
◆If a financial system crisis should occur due to sharp fall in Japanese government bond prices, the Japanese people would suffer an erosion of their financial assets. 日本国債価格の急落で金融システム不安が生じれば、日本国民の金融資産は損失を被ることになる。◆If Japanese government bonds prices enter a tailspin and throw financial markets into confusion, a financial system crisis would likely occur. 日本国債の価格が下落して、金融市場が混乱すれば、金融システム不安が生じる可能性がある。◆The money market is overheated by massive money inflows from banks on fading concerns over a financial system crisis. 金融システム不安［金融システム危機に対する懸念］の後退により、短期金融市場は、銀行からの巨額の資金流入で過熱感が強まっている。

financial system stability 金融システムの安定
◆The state-run Deposit Insurance Corporation oversees the

nation's financial system stability and public fund injections. 国営の預金保険機構は、日本の金融システムの安定と公的資金の注入を管理している。

financial technology　財テク, 金融技術, 金融テクノロジー

financial terms　財務条件, 金銭的条件, 取引の条件
◆Financial terms of the transaction were not disclosed. 取引の条件[財務条件]は、公表されなかった。

Financial Times　フィナンシャル・タイムズ, FT（英国の経済紙。⇒FT）
　Financial Times index of industrial ordinary shares　フィナンシャル・タイムズ工業株価指数
　Financial Times（Industrial）Ordinary Share Index　フィナンシャル・タイムズ工業株価指数（英国の工業株30銘柄の株価指数）
　Financial Times-Stock Exchange 100 Index　フィナンシャル・タイムズ100種総合株価指数　（=Footsie, FT 100 Share Index, FT-SE index, FTSE 100）

financial tools　金融技術, 金融手法, 金融ツール（=financial technology）
◆U.S. and European banks have advanced into diverse fields, including securities business, by polishing up their financial tools for utilizing derivative products. 欧米の銀行は、デリバティブ（金融派生商品）を活用するための金融技術を磨いて、証券業務などさまざまな分野に進出してきた。

financial transaction　金融取引, 財務取引, 資金取引（⇒identity）
◆Financial institutions remain indifferent to illegal financial transactions. 不正金融取引に対する金融機関の無関心ぶりは、相変わらずだ。

financial transaction tax　金融取引税（株式や債券などの金融商品に対する課税）
◆France and Germany called for the introduction of a common financial transaction tax in a Franco-German letter sent to European Council President Herman Van Rompuy. 仏独両国は、ファン・ロンパイ欧州理事会常任議長（EU大統領）あての共同書簡で、共通の金融取引税の導入を求めた。

financial turbulence　金融危機, 金融不安, 金融[金融市場]の混乱
◆Individual investors have continued to shift their money from investment trusts to more secure time deposits in the face of financial turbulence. 個人投資家は、金融不安を受けて[金融市場の混乱に直面して]、投資信託から安全性の高い[より安全な]定期性預金への資金シフトを続けている。

financial turmoil　金融危機, 金融不安, 金融市場の混乱（⇒banking group, shift動詞, threat）
　avert financial turmoil　金融市場の混乱を回避する
　ongoing global financial turmoil　今回の世界的な金融危機, 今回の世界的な金融市場の混乱
　prevent financial turmoil　金融危機を予防する
　resolve the financial turmoil　金融市場の混乱を収拾する
　the financial turmoil triggered by　～が引き起こした金融危機[金融市場の混乱]
◆Finance ministers of the ASEAN plus Three hailed the launch of a regional economic research and surveillance body aimed at preventing financial turmoil. ASEANプラス3（日中韓）の財務相が、金融危機予防のための域内経済のリサーチ・監視機関（AMRO）の発足を歓迎した。◆Japan, the United States and European countries will cooperate to avert financial turmoil stemming from the downgrading of the U.S. credit rating. 日米欧が連携して、米国債の格下げによる金融市場の混乱を回避することになった。◆Japanese financial institutions have been asked to invest in overseas financial firms amid the financial turmoil triggered by the subprime mortgage crisis. サブプライム・ローン問題が引き起こした金融危機[金融市場の混乱]の影響で、日本の金融機関は、海外金融機関への出資要請を受けている。◆The financial turmoil is caused by the U.S. subprime mortgage mess and soaring oil and materials prices. 金融市場の混乱は、米国のサブプライム・ローン問題と原油・原材料価格の高騰によるものだ。◆The United States and European countries are forced to proceed steadily with fiscal reconstruction and resolve the financial turmoil. 米欧各国は、財政再建を着実に進めて、金融市場の混乱を収拾せざるを得ない状況にある。◆U.S. and European financial institutions are hitting roadblocks because of the ongoing global financial turmoil. 欧米金融機関は、世界的な金融市場の混乱で、つまずいている。

financial uncertainty　金融不安　（=financial instability, financial unrest; ⇒economic downturn, unrest）
◆A vicious cycle, in which financial uncertainty cools down the U.S. real economy and causes an economic downturn, is becoming reality. 金融不安が米国の実体経済を冷え込ませ、景気後退を招く悪循環は、現実になっている。◆Acceleration of the disposal of bad loans has been criticized as causing the current economic plight, with its falling stock prices and financial uncertainty. 不良債権処理の加速は株価低迷と金融不安という現在の経済苦境を招いた、と批判されている。◆The Greek-triggered sovereign debt crisis has been throwing the eurozone into financial uncertainty and multiple crises. ギリシャに端を発した債務危機問題で、ユーロ圏は金融不安と複合的な危機に陥っている。◆Wiping out financial uncertainty will be next to impossible unless U.S. housing prices stop falling. 米国の住宅価格の下落に歯止めがかからないかぎり、金融不安の払拭（ふっしょく）はほとんど不可能だ。

financial unrest　金融不安
（=financial instability, financial uncertainty）
　a source of financial unrest　金融不安の発生源
　EU nations' financial unrest　EU諸国の金融不安
　resolve the financial unrest　金融不安を解消する
◆EU nations' financial unrest originated with the Greek debt crisis. EU諸国の金融不安は、ギリシャの財政危機に端を発した。◆Further efforts are needed to resolve the financial unrest. 金融不安を解消するには、もう一段の努力が必要だ。◆Nonperforming loans are a source of financial unrest. 不良債権が、金融不安の発生源になっている。◆The stress test results announced by the Committee of European Banking Supervisors are not sufficient to dispel Europe's financial unrest. 欧州銀行監督委員会が発表したストレス・テスト（特別検査）の結果だけで、欧州の金融不安を払拭（ふっしょく）するのは難しい。◆To resolve the financial unrest in EU nations, accelerating financial sector realignment in countries such as Germany must be worked out. EU諸国の金融不安を解決するには、（2,000もの金融機関がひしめく）ドイツなどでの金融再編の加速も課題だ。

financial watchdog　金融監視機関
◆Financial ministers of the ASEAN＋3 welcomed the launch of a financial watchdog. ASEANプラス3（東南アジア諸国連合と日本、中国、韓国）の財務相が、金融監視機関の発足を歓迎した。◆The financial watchdog took an additional action of criminal complaint other than administrative punishment as the bank's operations were so malicious. 同行の業務運営の仕方があまりにも悪質なので、金融監視機関の金融庁は、行政処分のほかに刑事告発の追加措置を取った。

financial window-dressing　会計操作
◆Stock option programs are seen as leading to financial window-dressing to manipulate share prices. ストック・オプション制度は、株価操作のための会計操作につながると見られている。

financial woes　財政難, 経営難, 経営危機, 金融危機
（=financial troubles）
◆Both banks ran enormous deficits for the business year to March 2011, adding to their financial woes. 両行は、2011年3月期決算で巨額の赤字になって[赤字に転落して]、財務体質

が悪化した。◆The firm's huge interest-bearing debts exacerbated its financial woes. 同社の多額の有利子負債で、経営危機が悪化した[経営が圧迫された]。◆The government will provide emergency aid to developing countries hit by financial woes through ODA. 政府は、金融危機で打撃を受けた発展途上国に対して、政府開発援助(ODA)による緊急支援を行う方針だ。

financial world 金融界
◆Due to the debt crisis that has engulfed Greece, the financial world is in the turmoil. ギリシャを襲った財政危機[債務危機]で、金融界が揺れている。

financial worries 金融不安
◆Tokyo stocks bounced back Wednesday after sharp falls Tuesday following Lehman Brothers decision to file for bankruptcy as financial worries eased. 水曜日の東京株式市場は、リーマン・ブラザーズが前日に破たん申請を決めて急落したものの、金融不安が和らいだため反発した。

financially (副)財政上,財務上,金融上,金銭上,財政的に,資金面で,金銭的に,金銭面で,カネの面で
be financially difficult　財政難である,財政がひっ迫している,財政難に陥っている,経営不振である
be financially healthy　財務上健全である
be financially solid　財政状態が強固である
be financially sound　財政的に堅実である
be financially strong　財政基盤が強固[健全]である
be financially weak　財政基盤が弱い

financially self-sustaining 資金を自ら賄(まかな)う
◆Raising tens of millions of dollars a year from oil smuggling and other crimes, the Iraq insurgents have become financially self-sustaining. 原油の横流しなどの犯罪行為で年に数百万ドルを調達して、イラクの武装組織は資金を自ら賄えるようになった。

financially strapped 資金繰りに困っている,資金繰りが苦しい,資金繰りが厳しくなった
◆People indebted to multiple consumer loan firms and financially strapped small-business operators have been the main targets of loan sharks. 多重債務者や資金繰りが苦しい零細事業主が、ヤミ金融業者の主な標的になっている。◆The bank purchased loan claims from financially strapped moneylenders by collecting commissions from them. 同行は、資金繰りに困っている貸金業者から、手数料を徴収して貸出債権を買い取っていた。◆Under the new financing scheme, the IMF will extend to financially strapped countries loans of up to 500 percent of their contribution to the IMF. 新融資制度では、財政の資金繰りが苦しく[厳しく]なった国に対して、その国がIMF(国際通貨基金)に出資している額の最大5倍までIMFが融資する。

financially troubled 経営危機に直面している,経営が悪化した,経営不振の,経営難に陥っている,財政がひっ迫した,財政難の,財政難に陥っている
◆As a condition for loans to financially troubled countries in the late 1990s, the IMF called for strict implementation of structural reforms. 1990年代後半に財政難に陥った国に対する融資の条件として、IMF(国際通貨基金)は、厳しい構造改革の実施を求めた。◆Financially troubled General Motors is currently speeding up its efforts to draw up a rehabilitation plan. 経営難に陥っているGMは現在、同社の再建計画づくりを急いでいる。◆Financially troubled Shinginko Tokyo plans to slash its deposits to ¥20 billion by fiscal 2011. 経営難の新銀行東京が、2011年度までに預金量を200億円に圧縮する計画だ。

financially troubled condominium developer 経営不振の分譲マンション開発会社
◆The IRCJ is expected to select major leasing company Orix Corp. to bail out financially troubled condominium developer Daikyo Inc. 産業再生機構は、経営不振の分譲マンション開発会社、大京のスポンサー企業に、リース大手のオリックスを選定する方針だ。

financially troubled customer 経営不振企業
◆Enforcing the Takenaka Plan will further encourage the banks to reduce their loans to financially troubled customers and recover more loans received by such borrowers. 竹中プラン(金融再生プログラム)を強引に進めると、銀行の経営不振企業への貸し渋りや貸しはがしに拍車がかかることになる。

financier (名)金融会社,金融業者,(事業の)資金供給者,投資家,資本家,銀行家,融資家,財務官
act as financiers　資金を提供する
government-affiliated financier　政府系金融会社
government-affiliated mortgage financier　政府系住宅金融会社[金融公社]
◆Freddie Mac and Fannie Mae are the U.S. government-affiliated mortgage financiers. フレディ・マック(連邦住宅抵当貸付公社)とファニー・メイ(連邦住宅抵当金庫[公庫])は、米政府系住宅金融公社[金融会社]だ。◆On Sept 7, 2008, the U.S. government earmarked a huge amount of public funds to help government-affiliated mortgage financiers Freddie Mac and Fannie Mae. 2008年9月7日に米政府は、政府系住宅金融公社のフレディ・マック(連邦住宅抵当貸付公社)とファニー・メイ(連邦住宅抵当金庫[公庫])を救済するため、巨額の公的資金投入を決めた。

financing (名)資金調達,資本調達,金融,融資,借入れ,ローン,財務,資金,ファイナンス (⇒consumer financing, debt financing [finance], debt instrument, equity financing, external bond financing, indirect financing, lease financing, servicing, swap agreement)
arrange interim financing　つなぎ融資を取りまとめる,つなぎ融資のアレンジをする
auto financing　自動車ローン
autonomous financing　自己金融
bank financing　銀行融資,銀行金融
bridge financing　つなぎ融資
cash flows from financing activities　財務活動に伴う現金収支[資金収支]
commercial financing　商工業融資
complementary financing　補完的融資
conditional financing　ひもつき融資,条件付き融資
consumer financing　消費者金融
cooperative financing　協調融資
counterpart financing　見返り金融
credit financing　信用融資
deficit financing　赤字財政,赤字財政策
direct financing via stock markets　株式市場を通じて資金を調達する直接金融
equity financing　持ち分金融,株式発行を伴う資金調達,エクイティ・ファイナンス (=equity finance)
expanded co-financing　拡大協調融資
external financing　外部調達資金,外部金融
Federal Financing Bank　米連邦金融銀行
financing act　出資法
financing agreement　借入契約
financing cost　金融費用,資金調達コスト
financing demand　借入需要,資金需要 (=financing requirements)
financing fees　融資手数料
financing gap　(国の)外貨不足額
financing instruments　金融手段
financing lease　ファイナンス・リース
financing needs　資金ニーズ

financing operations　融資活動, 金融活動, 金融事業, 財務活動, 財務, 市場からの資金調達
financing policy［philosophy］　資金調達方針
financing rate　借入金利
financing standing　財務状態
financing statement　与信公示書
financing technique　金融テクニック
financing transaction　資金調達取引
financing vehicle　金融商品
foreign trade financing　外国貿易金融（輸出入必要資金の融通）
get financing　資金を調達する, 資金を確保する
government financing　政府金融
gross financing needs　総調達額
guarantee the financing for product purchase by customers　顧客が製品購入する際の資金調達を保証する
independent financing　単独融資
inflationary financing　インフレ金融
interim financing　つなぎ資金, つなぎ融資
internal financing　内部調達資金, 内部金融
international financing　国際金融, 国際財務, 海外調達資金
investment financing　投資資金融資
joint financing　協調融資
　（=cooperative financing）
joint financing venture　共同金融事業
lease financing　リース金融
left-hand financing　資産担保資金調達
loan financing　貸付け資金調達
long-term financing　長期資金調達
off-balance-sheet financing　簿外資金調達
outside financing　外部融資
parallel financing　並行融資
pay-as-you-go financing plan　賦課方式
permanent financing　長期資本
private financing　民間資金
product financing arrangements　製品金融の取決め
project financing　プロジェクト金融
provide financing for a project　プロジェクトのファイナンスを引き受ける, プロジェクトに融資する
provide long-term financing　長期融資をする
provide ¥10 billion in financing for the company　同社に100億円を融資する
public financing　公的融資
receivables financing　債権融資
reserve financing plan　積立方式
secure financing　ファイナンス（資金）を確保する
secured financing　担保付き資金調達
security financing　証券金融
self-financing　自己金融
short-term financing　短期資本［資金］の調達
sound financing　堅実融資
sources of financing　資金調達源
stock-pile financing　滞貨金融
straight financing　直接融資
structured financing　仕組み金融, 仕組みファイナンス
surplus financing　黒字財政, 黒字財政策
tax-exempt financing　免税債での資金調達, 免税債
trade financing　貿易金融
up-coming financing　当面の資金調達

◆Our long-term financing was accomplished through the issuance of long-term debt instruments. 当社の長期資金調達は, 長期債務証券を発行して行われた。

financing activities　財務活動, 金融活動, 融資活動, 資金調達活動, 資金調達と返済に関する活動
◆Domestic megabanks are increasing their financing activities overseas. 国内メガバンクは, 海外での融資活動を強化している。

financing bill　政府短期証券, 短期国債, FB
（=financial bill）
◆The BOJ has bought financing bills and other securities from the market to keep money rates low under its ultra-easy money policy. 日銀は, 超低金利政策で低金利を維持するため, 市場から政府短期証券（FB）などの有価証券を買い取ってきた。◆The debt balance of the central government, including government bonds and financing bills, has exceeded ¥900 trillion for the first time. 国債と政府短期証券を含めた国の債務残高［国の借金］が, 初めて900兆円を突破した。◆The yield on the latest three-month financing bills issue has remained at the unusually low level of zero. 最近の政府短期証券3か月物の流通利回りは, 0％と異常に低い水準にとどまっている。
解説 政府短期証券とは：財務省が支出に必要な資金を一時的に調達するため発行する債券。財務省債券（税金が入るまでのつなぎ資金を調達するために発行）や外国為替資金証券（為替介入の円資金を調達するために発行）、石油証券（備蓄石油を買うために発行）などがある。

financing costs　資金調達コスト
◆Certain indirect costs, including financing costs, are capitalized. 特定の間接費は, 資金調達コストを含めて資産計上されている。

financing for smaller companies　中小企業金融
◆Megabanks and other financial institutions are entering the field of financing for smaller companies. メガバンクなどの金融機関が, 中小企業金融の分野に参入している。

financing operations　金融事業, 市場からの資金調達
◆Struggling Mitsubishi Motors Corp. is considering setting up a joint venture with Merrill Lynch & Co. to engage in North American financing operations. 経営再建中の三菱自動車は現在, 米証券大手のメリルリンチと北米で金融事業（販売金融事業）を手がける合弁会社の設立を検討している。

financing operations based on government policies　政策金融

financing scheme　融資制度　（=lending facility）
◆The IMF's new financing scheme is expected to be agreed on at the Group of 20 summit meeting and will be launched after being approved by the IMF's board of directors. 国際通貨基金（IMF）の新融資制度は, 主要20か国・地域（G20）サミット（首脳会議）で合意する見込みで, その後IMF理事会の承認を経てスタートする。◆Under the new financing scheme, the IMF will extend to financially strapped countries loans of up to 500 percent of their contribution to the IMF. 新融資制度では, 財政の資金繰りが苦しく［厳しく］なった国に対して, その国がIMF（国際通貨基金）に出資している額の最大5倍までIMFが融資する。

FINCA　国際地域社会援助協会（Foundation for International Community Assistanceの略）

FinCEN　（米財務省の）金融犯罪取締りネットワーク（Financial Crimes Enforcement Networkの略）

find money　金を工面する, 資金を調達する

finder　（名）（金融案件の）仲介業者, 斡旋（あっせん）業者, 拾得者, 密輸出入品検査係, ファインダー

finder's fee　仲介手数料, 斡旋手数料

fine　（名）罰金, 違約金, 制裁金, 課徴金, 延滞料金, 手数料, 許可料
　a civil fine　民事制裁金
　a fine foe default　過怠金

FINE

an entry fine　登記一時金,登記手数料
fines and penalties　罰金科料,罰金や課徴金
get a fine for　～で罰金を科される,～で罰金をくらう
impose a substantial fine　相当の罰金を課す,重い罰金を課す
in fines　罰金として
large fines or claims　巨額の罰金や損害賠償
pay a heavy［large, substantial］fine　重い罰金を支払う
pay a $10 civil fine　1,000万ドルの民事制裁金を支払う
◆American International Group agreed to pay a $10 million civil fine to settle the SEC's allegations that it fraudulently helped another company falsify its earnings report and hide losses. 米保険大手のAIG（アメリカン・インターナショナル・グループ）は,同社が他社の業績報告書改ざんと損失隠しに不正に手を貸したとする米証券取引委員会（SEC）の告発を受け,この問題を解決するために民事制裁金1,000万ドルを支払うことに同意した。

fine　（形）素晴らしい,見事な,優良な,純良な,優遇の,洗練された,純度が高い,細かい,薄い,難しい
a fine rate　優良手形割引歩合,優良手形割引レート
at the finest rate　最優遇金利で
fine bank acceptance　一流銀行引受手形
fine bank bill　優良銀行手形,一流銀行引受手形
　（=prime bank bill）
fine bill　優良手形　（=fine paper）
fine gold　純金　（=pure gold）
fine judgment　難しい判断
fine（trade）paper　優良手形,優良（商業）手形
fine tuning　微調整

finish　（動）終える,終了する,取引を終える,仕上げる
　（⇒TOPIX）
finish easing　金融緩和を終了する,金融緩和派打ち止めにする
finish the week at　～で1週間の取引を終える,週引けには～になる
finish the week with higher rates　前週末より高い水準で1週間の取引を終える,週引けには前週末より高い水準になる
◆Nasdaq composite index finished at levels not seen since October. ナスダック店頭市場の総合指数は,10月以来の水準で取引を終えた。◆Tokyo stocks extended their winning streak to a third day with the key Nikkei index finishing above the 9,000 line. 東京の株価［東京株式市場の株価］は,3日連続で値上がりし,日経平均株価（225種）の終値は9,000円台を上回った。

fire　（動）首を切る（ax, axe, sack）,首にする,解雇する,発射する,発砲する,（質問などを）浴びせる,あおり立てる,興奮させる　（自動）発砲する,燃えあがる,興奮する,点火する,赤くなる,輝く
◆The Murakami Fund has urged Matsuzakaya Co. to review its business plan by firing all full-time employees and closing some of its stores. 村上ファンドは,正社員の全員解雇と店舗の一部閉鎖による事業計画の見直しを松坂屋に求めた。

fire insurance　火災保険
◆Fire insurance did not cover damage caused by an earthquake or tsunami before the 1964 Niigata Earthquake. 1964年の新潟地震以前は,火災保険で地震や津波による被害が補償されなかった。◆The earthquake insurance system was launched after the 1964 Niigata Earthquake as a response to the problem of fire insurance not covering damage caused by an earthquake or tsunami. 地震保険［地震保険制度］は,火災保険で地震や津波による被害が補償されない問題への対応策として,1964年の新潟地震後に導入された。◆Three major domestic nonlife insurance companies will set a ceiling for fire-insurance payouts for corporate clients in cases of damages caused by terrorist attacks. 国内の大手損害保険3社は,テロ被害の（テロ攻撃による損害を受けた場合の）顧客企業向け火災保険の補償額に上限を設ける方針だ。◆Tokio Marine & Nichido Fire Insurance Co. tied up with NTT Docomo Inc. in April 2011 to offer Docomo One-time Hoken insurance. 東京海上日動火災保険は,2011年4月にNTTドコモと提携して,「ドコモワンタイム保険」を提供している。

firewall［fire wall］　防禦（ぼうぎょ）壁,業務隔壁,情報隔壁,情報漏洩（ろうえい）防止システム,ネット上のセキュリティ・システム,不正侵入防止機能［防止装置］,不正侵入防止ソフト,ファイアウォール（「情報隔壁」は,同グループの銀行と証券会社が顧客情報を共有することを禁止することをいう）
◆The Financial Services Agency mooted a policy of relaxing constraints on a firewall between banking and securities institutions. 金融庁は,銀行と証券会社間のファイアウォール（業務隔壁）規制を緩和する方針を打ち出した。

firm　（動）利上げする,（金利を）引き締める,固める,固まる,安定する,強含む
be firming up　底堅くなっている
firm a little　強含む
firm policy　金融引締めに動く,金融政策の引締めに動く
◆Stock prices around the world firmed after plunging in midweek. 世界の株価は,週半ばに急落した後,小康状態になった。

firm　（形）堅い,堅調な,強固な,安定した,引き締まった,力強い,確定的な,承諾回答期限付きの
firm bid　確定的の買申込み,（取引所での）期限付き指し値買い注文,ファーム・ビッド
firm commitment　確約引受け,買取り引受確約,確定契約（firm contract）,成約済みの取引
firm commitment underwriting　買取り引受け,買取り引受方式　（=firm commitment）
firm loan　（証券会社の）自己勘定取引融資
firm monetary policy　安定した［確固とした］金融政策
firm offer　確定申込み,確定的売申込み,回答期限付き売買申込み,ファーム・オファー
firm order　確定注文,期限指定注文,正式発注
firm price　確定値段,確約値段
firm quote　（値付け業者［マーケット・メーカー］の）確定気配値,確約気配,確約値段
firm rate　（外国為替）ファーム・レート（提示者が変更または取消すまで有効な注文レート）
firm stock　売買確定株
firm underwriting　確定［確約］引受け
firmer market　上げ相場,手堅い市況
firmer tone　堅調な地（じ）合い,強含み
firmer Treasury market　米国債相場の上昇
firmer yen　円高
hold firm　底堅い動きを示す,底堅い値動きを示す
keep money market rates firm　短期市場金利を高めに維持する
maintain a firm bid　買い先行の展開となる
quasi debt to firm value ratio　準負債比率
remain firm　堅調に推移する,順調に推移する
see a firmer bid　～に強気な買いが入る
◆Capital investment and exports, which have supported the economy, have remained firm. 日本経済を支えてきた設備投資と輸出は,引き続き堅調だ。◆The U.S. Treasury bond market has a firm undertone. 米国の長期国債市場の地合いは,堅調［良好］である。◆To make the economy's step toward recovery much firmer, the government should implement another expansionary budget. 景気回復の足取りをずっと確かなものにするためにも,政府はさらに積極型の予算を実施すべきだ。

firm banking　ファーム・バンキング

◆Firm banking is a system that provides information and bank transfers by directly or indirectly connecting bank's computer to company's computer via communication line. ファーム・バンキングは，銀行のコンピュータと企業のコンピュータを，通信回線を介して直接・間接的に接続して，銀行振込み・口座振替や情報を提供するシステムだ。

firming （名）金融引締め，引締め，利上げ
 fear of［concerns about, concerns over］Fed firming 米連邦制度準備理事会（FRB）の金融引締めに対する懸念，FRBの利上げに対する懸念
 Fed firming 米連邦準備制度理事会（FRB）の金融引締め，米中央銀行の金融引締め，FRBの引締め，FRBによる利上げ
 preemptive firming 予防的引締め
 the continuous firming of the short-term money market 短期金融市場の上昇基調
 ◆The U.S. central bank's Federal Open Market Committee emphasized that the extent and timing of any further policy firming would depend on the evolution of the economic outlook. 米連邦準備制度理事会（FRB）の連邦公開市場委員会（FOMC）は，「一層の金融政策引締め［一層の金融引締め］の程度やタイミングは，経済見通しの成り行きによる」と強調した。

first （形）第一の，一番目の，真っ先の，最上の，筆頭の，一流の，主要な，最も重要な，首位の，最高幹部の，ファースト （副）一番目に，最初に，真っ先に，まず
 first aid clause 応急手当条項
 first aid（treatment） 応急手当て
 first audit 初度監査
 first call 第一回払込み，（株式市場の）前場
 first category compensation 第一種相殺
 first cause 第一原因，原動力
 first class bank 一流銀行
 first-class bill［paper］ 一流手形，優良手形（=fine paper）
 first-class securities 一流証券
 first clearing［exchange］ （交換所の）第一交換，午前交換
 first-come-first-served system 先着順制（=first come system）
 first credit tranche 第一クレジット・トランシュ（IMF出資額の100〜125％までの通貨保有のこと）
 first demand bond 要求払い保証金
 first-dollar coverage （団体医療での）無控除担保方式
 first excess 第一超過額
 first excess of loss cover 第一次超過損害再保険特約
 first fruits 初年度収益
 first-line management 第一線の管理職
 first-line reserves （中央銀行の）第一線準備
 first notice day 第一通知日，受渡し開始日
 first party insurance ファースト・パーティー保険（被保険者自身の財産・身体に対する保険）
 first preferred ship mortgage 本船担保，第一順位船舶モーゲージ
 first premium 第一回保険料
 first refusal right 第一先買権，優先権（=right of first refusal）
 first risk policy 第一次危険保険証券
 first six months 上半期，上期 （=first half）
 first stage financing 第一次ファイナンス
 first three months of the fiscal year 第1四半期，第一・四半期
 first-tier stock 一流業績株 （=top-tier stock）
 first time ratings（newly rated issuers） 初回格付け（新規格付け発行体）
 first year commission 初年度手数料
 first year premium 初年次保険料
 fist-time issuer 初めて格付けの対象となる発行体，初回格付け発行体
 take the first opportunity of doing 機会のあり次第〜する
 the amount of the first payment 初回金
 the first board 前場立会い
 the first bottom 一番底
 the first legal charge on the building 建物に対する第一順位の抵当権
 the first of exchange 組手形［1組の為替手形］（bills in a set）の第一券，第一手形
 the first offer （債券の）最初の売出価格
 the first peak 一番天井
 the first preferred share 第一優先株，第一順位優先株式
 the first source of payment of principal and interest 元利返済の一義的責任者
 the first teller 支払いテラー

first half 上半期，上期，前半，1日から15日まで（下半期=latter half, second half）
 first-half account settlement 上半期決算，中間決算（=first-half results）
 first-half earnings forecast 上半期業績予想
 first-half net profit 上半期の税引き後利益［純利益］，上期の税引き後利益［純利益］
 first half of fiscal 2008 2008年上半期，2008年度上期
 first half of the current fiscal year 今年度上半期，今年度上期
 first half of the year 上期 （=first half-year）
 first half-year's results 上期業績，中間決算
 ◆As in the past, the Corporation and its subsidiaries raised additional capital during this year's first half. 従来どおり，当社と子会社は当上半期も追加資本を調達しました。◆Increasing M&A advisory business helped Nomura grab the No. 1 spot in Japan's M&A league table for the first half of this year. 今年上半期はM&A顧問業務が増加したため，日本のM&A案件の引受実績で野村證券がトップの座を占めた。

first-half loss 上半期損失，上期の損失［赤字］
 ◆The firm's first-half loss narrowed 85 percent mainly due to the weaker yen. 同社の上半期損失は，主に円安で85％縮小した。

first half of the current fiscal year ending Sept. 30 9月中間決算，9月30日に終了する今年度上半期（の決算）
 ◆The bank consulted its auditor to determine their results for the first half of the current fiscal year ending Sept. 30. 9月中間決算［9月30日に終了する今年度上半期の決算］を確定するため，同行は会計事務所［監査法人］に意見を求めた。

first half of this year 今年度上半期，今年度上期
 ◆Ford Motor Co. lost $1.4 billion during the first half of this year. フォード・モーターは，今年度上半期に14億ドルの赤字を出した。

first-half profit 上半期利益，上期の利益，1-6月期（3月期決算企業の場合は4-9月期）の利益
 ◆HSBC Holdings PLC's first-half profit declined 29 percent as bad loans rose. 英銀最大手HSBCホールディングスの1-6月期の利益（純利益）は，不良債権の増加で前年同期に比べて29％減少した。◆Mizuho's first-half profit fell 17 percent as credit costs increased and on losses related to investments in U.S. home loans to riskier borrowers. みずほの上半期利益は，与信コストの増加とリスクの高い融資先への米国の住宅ローン投資に関連する損失で，17％減少した。

first loss 最劣後部分（first loss tranche），第一次損害，直接損害，ファースト・ロス

first loss earthquake insurance 一次損害地震保険, 直接損害

first loss insurance（policy） 第一次損害保険, 実損填補保険

first loss letters of credit 一次免責を保証する信用状

first loss mitigation 一次免責の軽減措置

partial first-loss default coverage on individual home mortgages 個々の住宅モーゲージのデフォルトに対する部分的一次免責条項付き保険

first mortgage 第一抵当, 第一順位抵当, 第一順位抵当権

first mortgage collateralized [collateralised] trust bond 第一順位抵当権付き信託債

first mortgage loan 第一担保付き融資, 第一順位担保付き住宅用モーゲージ, 第一順位モーゲージ・ローン
◆The first mortgage bonds of the corporation are secured by a first mortgage and a floating charge on the company. 同社の第一順位抵当権付き社債は、同社の第一順位抵当権と浮動担保権で保証されています。

first mortgage bond 第一順位抵当権付き社債, 第一担保付き債券 （⇒first mortgage）
◆The company elected to redeem, prior to maturity on June 3, 2011, $120 million of first mortgage bonds on May 1, 2011. 同社は、満期が到来する2011年6月3日以前の2011年5月1日に、第一順位抵当権付き社債1億2,000万ドルを償還することを決定した。

First Section of the Tokyo Stock Exchange 東証一部, 東京証券取引所第一部 （=main section of the Tokyo Stock Exchange, Tokyo's first exchange, TSE's First Section）
◆TV Tokyo Corp. listed on the First Section of the Tokyo Stock Exchange on Aug.5, 2004. テレビ東京は、2004年8月5日に東証一部に上場した。◆Volume on the First Section of the Tokyo Stock Exchange has exceeded the 1 billion mark for 42 business days in a row as of Monday, the longest period on record. 東京証券取引所第一部の出来高は、月曜日の時点で、42営業日連続で10億株の大台を超え、過去最長記録となった。

first two quarters 上半期[上期]の第1四半期と第2四半期
◆In the first two quarters of 2011, the Corporation declared a cash dividend of $0.07 per common share. 2011年第1四半期と第2四半期に、当社はそれぞれ普通株式1株当たり0.07ドルの現金配当を宣言しました。

fiscal （形）国庫の, 国庫収入の, 財政の, 財政上の, 会計の, 年度の

deficit of fiscal balance　財政赤字

fiscal accounting year　会計年度, 営業年度

fiscal action　財政措置, 財政出動

fiscal agent　財政[財務]代理人, 財政[財務]代理機関

fiscal and monetary convergence　財政・金融収斂（しゅうれん）

fiscal bankruptcy　財政破たん

fiscal boost　財政政策の景気刺激効果, 財政面からの景気刺激策

fiscal budget　年度予算

fiscal burden（on the nation）　財政負担

fiscal catastrophe　財政破たん　（⇒catastrophe）

fiscal connection　財政連結

fiscal cost　財政コスト

fiscal demand　財政需要

fiscal difficulties　財政難

fiscal dividend　財政配当, 財政の配当金, 財政自然増収

fiscal drag　財政面からの景気押し下げ効果, 財政的障害, 財政的歯止め

fiscal drug　財政の麻薬漬け, フィスカル・ドラッグ

fiscal effect　財政効果
　（=income generating effect）

fiscal expansion　財政拡大

fiscal expenditure　財政支出

fiscal flexibility　財政伸縮性

fiscal foundation　財政基盤

fiscal half year　中間決算

fiscal illusion　財政錯覚

fiscal impulse　財政的刺激

fiscal incentive　財政的誘因

fiscal inflexibility　財政硬直化, 財政の硬直

fiscal instrument　財政手段

fiscal insurance　財政損失保険

fiscal investment　財政投資

fiscal investment and loan　財政投融資

fiscal law　会計法

fiscal-monetary mix　ポリシー・ミックス

fiscal-monetary policy　財政・金融政策

fiscal monopoly　政府の専売, 国の独占, 政府独占
　（=government monopoly）

fiscal operations　財政活動, 財政操作, 会計管理

fiscal package　財政刺激策, 財政面からの景気刺激策［景気刺激対策］, 財政出動

fiscal payment　財政支出

fiscal performance　財政収支

fiscal period　会計期間, 会計年度
　（=accounting period）

fiscal plan [planning]　財政計画

fiscal practice　財政措置

fiscal preference　財政選好

fiscal quarter　会計四半期

fiscal reserves　財政準備金, 財政余剰金

fiscal resources　財源, 原資

fiscal responsibility　財政責任, 財政節度

fiscal restraint　財政引締め, 財政政策の引締め, 財政緊縮, 緊縮財政　（=fiscal tightening）

fiscal restructuring　財政再建

fiscal retrenchment package　財政緊縮策

fiscal revenues　歳入

fiscal revolution　財政改革

fiscal savings package　歳出削減策, 歳出削減案

fiscal science　財政学

fiscal stamp　収入印紙

fiscal statement　会計書類

fiscal stimulation　財政刺激策, 財政出動による景気刺激

fiscal surplus　財政黒字, 財政余剰
◆Big companies assume the exchange rate of ￥81.06 to the dollar for the latter half of fiscal 2011. 大企業の2011年度下期の想定為替レートは、1ドル=81円6銭となっている。

fiscal adjustment 財政政策の調整, 財政再建
◆Synchronized fiscal adjustment across several major economics could adversely impact the economic recovery. 財政の同時調整は、景気回復に悪影響を及ぼす可能性がある。

fiscal and current account deficits 財政赤字と経常収支赤字
◆The twin deficits of the United States—fiscal and current account deficits—are threatening to destabilize the world economy. アメリカの双子の赤字（財政赤字と経常収支赤字）が、世界経済の不安定要因となっている。

fiscal and financial crisis 財政・金融危機
◆Countries likely to be affected by the fiscal and financial

crisis in Europe will basically be able to obtain the IMF's short-term loans immediately after applying for them. 欧州財政・金融危機が波及しそうな国は、IMF（国際通貨基金）に要請すると、基本的にIMFの短期融資を即時に受けられる。◆Investment conditions have worsened due to confusion in global financial markets in the wake of fiscal and financial crises in Europe. 欧州の財政・金融危機を受けた世界的な金融市場の混乱で、運用環境が悪化している。◆Japan, the United States and emerging economies have pressed European countries to promptly resolve the fiscal and financial crisis. 日米両国と新興国は、欧州に財政・金融危機の迅速な解決を迫った。◆The European Union agreed on comprehensive measures to deal with the current fiscal and financial crisis. 欧州連合（EU）は、現在の財政・金融危機について、包括的な対応策で合意した。◆To prevent the current fiscal and financial crisis in Europe from spreading, the IMF will create a new short-term lending facility. 現在の欧州財政・金融危機の拡大を防ぐ［封じる］ため、国際通貨基金（IMF）が、新たな短期の融資制度を創設することになった。

fiscal and monetary [financial] measures　財政・金融上の措置, 財政金融措置, 財政・金融両面からの政策
◆The government and the Bank of Japan should seek to put the economic back on the road to self-sustaining recovery led by growth in domestic demand by implementing additional fiscal and monetary measures. 政府・日銀は、財政・金融両面からの政策の後押しで、内需中心の自律回復をめざすべきだ。

fiscal and tax stimulus measures　財政・税制面からの景気刺激策
◆To enhance the stimulating effect of the Fed's rate cuts, swift implementation of fiscal and tax stimulus measures, including tax cuts on investment designed to reinvigorate the stock market, is necessary in addition to the large-scale tax cut program that is under way. 米連邦準備制度理事会（FRB）の金利引下げの刺激効果を高めるためには、現在実施中の大型減税プログラムに加え、株式市場を再活性化するための投資減税など、財政・税制面からの景気刺激策の速やかな実施が必要である。

fiscal bailout　財政支援
◆As a tacit understanding with EU member states, the European Central Bank has refrained from implementing monetary policy that is effectively a fiscal bailout. 欧州連合（EU）加盟国との暗黙の了解として、欧州中央銀行（ECB）は、財政支援に当たる金融政策の実施を控えてきた。

fiscal balance　財政収支, 財政均衡, 財政バランス
◆The EU countries participating in the new treaty that will impose stringent fiscal discipline will specify the principle of fiscal balance in their respective constitutions. 厳しい財政規律を課す新条約に参加するEU（欧州連合）各国は、財政均衡の原則を参加国の憲法に明記することになる。◆The fiscal balance worsened on increased spending by governments after the collapse of Lehman Brothers. リーマン・ブラザーズの経営破たん以降、各国の財政収支は、財政出動によって悪化した。

fiscal belt-tightening　緊縮財政
◆In light of the critical state of the government's fiscal management, these areas should not be exempted from fiscal belt-tightening anymore. 政府の財政運営の危機的状況を考えると、これらの分野は、これ以上緊縮財政の例外とすべきではない。

fiscal catastrophe　財政破たん
◆If the outstanding debts of the central and local governments are not dealt with, Japan is likely to face a fiscal catastrophe. 国と地方［地方自治体］の債務残高を処理しないと［放置すれば］、日本は財政破たんに直面することになる。

fiscal condition(s)　財政状況, 財政状態, 財政事情, 財政政策
◆Given the nation's tough fiscal condition, the government must eke out the necessary funds by scaling down low-priority policy projects. 日本の厳しい財政事情に照らせば、政府に求められるのは、優先度の低い政策プロジェクトを縮小して、必要な財源をひねり出すことだ。◆Japan's fiscal conditions are tighter than Britain's. 日本の財政状況は、英国より厳しい。◆We must recognize anew the serious fiscal conditions gripping Japan. 日本の［日本をおおう］深刻な財政事情を、われわれは再認識しなければならない。

fiscal consolidation　財政引締め, 財政再建, 財政健全化（⇒growth-friendly fiscal consolidation plan）
◆The failure to implement fiscal consolidation in countries where it is necessary could undermine confidence and hamper growth. 財政健全化が必要な国で財政健全化を行わないと、信認を損ない、成長を阻害する可能性がある。

fiscal consolidation plan　財政再建策
◆The U.S. fiscal consolidation plan falls short of what would be necessary to stabilize the government's medium-term debt dynamics. 米国の財政再建策は、政府の中期的な債務問題処理［財政運営］の安定化には不十分である。

fiscal crisis　財政危機（複数＝fiscal crises）
◆As the Greek fiscal crisis grows more serious, there has been no halt to the worldwide decline in stock prices. ギリシャの財政危機が一段と深刻化するにつれ、世界同時株安に歯止めがかからなくなっている。◆Credit uncertainty in Europe has spilled over to France which is helping Greece, Italy and Spain facing fiscal crises. 欧州の信用不安は、財政危機に直面しているギリシャやイタリア、スペインを支援しているフランスにも拡大している。◆Fiscal crises in Europe have spread to Italy and Spain from Greece. 欧州の財政危機は、ギリシャからイタリアやスペインに飛び火した。◆Greece is struggling with a serious fiscal crisis. ギリシャは、深刻な財政危機にあえいでいる。◆In the conventional IMF's scheme, countries were only given a credit line even after the IMF approved loans and they could not withdraw funds unless the fiscal crisis facing them worsened. 従来のIMF（国際通貨基金）の仕組みだと、各国は融資の承認を得ても融資枠を与えられるだけで、財政危機が深刻化しないと資金を引き出すことができなかった。◆In the global financial markets, unrest is continuing as there is no end in sight to fiscal crises to the United States and some European countries. 世界の金融市場では、米国と一部の欧州諸国の財政危機の収束が見通せないため、混乱が続いている。◆Japan, U.S. and Europe must hasten to end fiscal crisis to stabilize the global financial markets. 世界の金融市場の安定化を図るには、日米欧が財政危機の収束を急がなければならない。◆Most local governments face serious fiscal crises. 地方自治体の大半が、深刻な財政危機に直面している。◆Some European nations which are experiencing fiscal crises seem to rely on drops in their currencies' values as a means of underpinning their economies. 財政危機問題を抱えた欧州諸国の一部は、景気下支えの手段として通貨安を頼みにしているようだ。◆Stock markets in the United States and European countries crashed again as there is no end in sight to fiscal crises in them. 欧米の株式市場は、欧米の財政危機の収束が見通せないため、ふたたび総崩れとなった。◆There is no end in sight to fiscal crises in the United States and some European countries as credit uncertainty is spreading. 信用不安が拡大しているため、米国と欧州の一部の財政危機の収束が見通せない。

fiscal deadlock　財政の行き詰まり, 財政政策の行き詰まり
◆In the wake of the euro crisis in Europe and the fiscal deadlock in the United States, the yen has sharply strengthened. 欧州のユーロ危機と米国の財政政策の行き詰まりの影響で、円が急騰している。

fiscal debt　財政赤字（＝fiscal deficit）
◆Japan's fiscal debts are the worst among advanced

economies. 日本の財政赤字は、先進国で最悪のレベルだ。◆Spain and Portugal hold huge fiscal debts similar to that of Greece. スペインとポルトガルは、ギリシャと同規模の大きい財政赤字を抱えている。

fiscal deficiency　財政赤字, 欠陥財政
　◆The EU has been unable to work out its inherent policies concerning the fiscal deficiencies of some of its more reckless member countries. 欧州連合（EU）は、一部の無謀な加盟国の欠陥財政［財政赤字］について、一貫した政策を打ち出せないでいる。

fiscal deficit　財政赤字, 財政不足, 財政不足額
　（⇒factor）
　◆A suprapartisan committee set up within Congress will work out a plan to cut the fiscal deficit by $1.5 trillion while raising the debt limit by a matching amount. 今後は米議会内に設置される超党派委員会が、1.5兆ドルの財政赤字削減策をまとめる一方、債務上限を同額引き上げる。◆Advanced economies have committed to at least halve fiscal deficits by 2013. 先進国は、2013年までに財政赤字を少なくとも半減させることを公約した。◆Greece will not be able to achieve the targeted reduction in its fiscal deficits by 2012. ギリシャは、2012年まで財政赤字の削減目標を達成できないようだ。◆Japan must tackle its large fiscal deficit and curb the growth of public debts. 日本は、巨額の財政赤字と取り組んで、財政赤字［公的債務］の増大を抑える必要がある。◆The Chinese economy is beset by a rapidly growing jobless rate and snowballing fiscal deficits. 中国経済は、失業者の急増や財政赤字の膨張などが深刻化している。◆The EFSF is the EU bailout fund for countries with fiscal deficits. 欧州金融安定基金（EFSF）は、欧州の財政赤字国を支援する基金だ。◆The federal government will cut its fiscal deficit by $2.4 trillion over ten years. 米政府は、今後10年間で財政赤字を2.4兆ドル削減する。

fiscal deterioration　財政悪化
　◆The U.S. government failed to take drastic countermeasures against its fiscal deterioration. 米政府は、財政悪化に抜本的な対策を取れなかった［大胆なメスを入れられなかった］。◆U.S. Treasury bonds were downgraded by Standard & Poor's because the government failed to take drastic countermeasures against its fiscal deterioration. 米政府が財政悪化に大胆な対策を取れなかったため、米国債はスタンダード・アンド・プアーズ（S&P）に格下げされた。

fiscal discipline　財政節度, 財政規律, 財政運営, 財政原則　（⇒fiscal indiscipline）
　◆Cutting taxes without imposing fiscal discipline would cause investors to lose trust in the government, bringing down the value of government bonds and raising long-term interest rates. 財政節度を無視して減税に走れば、投資家の政府に対する信認が失墜して国債相場が下落し、長期金利は上昇するだろう。◆Fiscal discipline is indispensable for sound economic growth. 健全な経済発展に、財政規律は欠かせない。◆The German government had Bundestag pass a balanced budget bill aimed at tightening fiscal discipline in 2009. ドイツ政府は、2009年に財政規律を強化するための均衡予算法案を連邦議会で成立させた。◆We will have to accept heavy taxation to foot the bill for the lax fiscal discipline of past governments. われわれは今後、過去の政府の放漫な財政運営のつけを負担するために、重税を受け入れなければならなくなる。

fiscal first half ended Sept. 30　今年9月中間決算, 9月30日に終了した今年度上半期
　◆All of the nation's six major nonlife insurers suffered sharp falls in earnings for the fiscal first half ended Sept. 30. 今年9月中間決算（9月30日に終了した今年度上半期）の国内損害保険会社の主要6社が、軒並み大幅な減益となった。

fiscal first half to Sept. 30　9月中間決算, 4-9月期
fiscal framework　財政構造, 財政の枠組み, 財政フレーム
　◆The compilation of guidelines on a medium-term fiscal framework will set a three-year blueprint for budgets starting with fiscal 2011. 中期財政フレームの指針作りは、2011年度から3年間の予算の大枠を決めるものだ。

fiscal hardship　財政ひっ迫
　◆Governments facing fiscal hardship sometimes force their central banks to buy up government bonds. 財政がひっ迫した政府は、中央銀行に国債を買い切らせることがある。

fiscal health　財政の健全性, 財政体質
　improve (the nation's) fiscal health　財政健全化
　restore the nation's fiscal health　財政の健全化
　◆A prerequisite to restoring the country's fiscal health is to promptly and boldly take effective pump priming measures and to overcome the economic crisis. 日本の財政健全化への前提条件は、迅速、果敢に効果的な景気浮揚策を実行して、経済危機を克服することだ。◆At the G-20 summit meeting, Japan made an international pledge to simultaneously achieve economic growth and fiscal health. 世界20か国・地域（G20）首脳会議で、日本は経済成長と財政再建の両立を国際公約した。◆Japan's fiscal health remains the worst among major developed countries. 日本の財政の健全性は、主要先進国のなかでは依然、最悪である。◆The United States' fiscal health has sharply deteriorated. 米国の財政の健全性は、急激に悪化している。

fiscal indiscipline　放漫な財政運営
　（⇒fiscal discipline）
　◆We will have to compensate for the government's fiscal indiscipline. われわれは今後、政府の放漫な財政運営のつけを払わされることになる。

fiscal integration　財政統合
　◆European unity will enter a new phase toward fiscal integration if European countries sign the new EU treaty by March 2012 as scheduled. 欧州各国が予定通り2012年3月までにEU（欧州連合）の新条約に署名すれば、欧州統合は財政統合に向けて新局面に入ることになる。

fiscal investment and loans program　財政投融資計画
fiscal laxity　放漫財政
　◆The ECB buyouts of sovereign debts of eurozone countries with fiscal laxity are the nightmare scenario Germany has been fearing. 欧州中銀（ECB）による放漫財政のユーロ圏諸国の国債買切りは、ドイツが恐れていた最悪のシナリオだ。◆The German government initially hesitated to rescue Greece from a crisis triggered by its own fiscal laxity. ドイツ政府は当初、ギリシャの放漫財政が招いた危機からのギリシャ救済を躊躇（ちゅうちょ）した。

fiscal management　財政運営, 財政管理
　（⇒fiscal belt-tightening）
　◆Greek financial crisis was caused by the country's lax fiscal management. ギリシャの財政危機は、同国の放漫財政［放漫な財政運営］によって生じた。◆The ruling, which described the bank tax as illegal, will affect the fiscal management of the Tokyo metropolitan government. 銀行税の違法判決は、今後の東京都の財政運営に影響を及ぼすと見られる。

fiscal management strategy　財政運営戦略
　◆According to the government's fiscal management strategy, the government aims to halve the ratio of the primary balance deficit to GDP by fiscal 2015. 政府の財政運営戦略によると、政府は2015年度までに国内総生産（GDP）に対するプライマリー・バランスの赤字の半減を目指している。◆At the G-20 meeting, Kan explained Japan's new economic growth and fiscal management strategies, effectively making the two strategies international pledges. G20首脳会議で、菅首相は日本の新経済成長戦略と財政運営戦略を説明し、この二つの戦略が事実上の国際公約になった。

fiscal measures　財政政策, 財政措置

◆Priority measures to achieve economic recovery are stopping deflation and mobilizing all possible fiscal measures, financial policies and taxation reforms. 景気回復を実現するための優先課題は、デフレ阻止と、可能な財政政策、金融政策や税制改革を総動員することだ。◆The series of fiscal measures taken by the government to improve the economy has helped prevent the economy from tumbling into a deflationary spiral. 景気対策として政府がとった一連の財政措置は、日本経済がデフレ・スパイラルに転落するのを防ぐ役割を果たした。

fiscal meltdown 財政破たん
 ◆In the case of fiscal meltdowns, many countries demand that overseas creditors accept partial debt waivers. 財政破たんの場合、海外投資家は借金の一部棒引きを多くの国に求められる。

fiscal period 会計期間, 会計年度 (=accounting period, business year, financial year, fiscal year)
 ◆Olympus will submit by Dec.14 the semiannual consolidated financial statements for the fiscal period ending in September. オリンパスは、12月14日までに9月中間連結決算書を提出する。

fiscal plight 財政難
 ◆Allowing banks to claim a tax refund by carrying a loss back to the previous year has not been allowed since fiscal 1992 in Japan, due chiefly to the fiscal plight of the central government. 銀行が欠損金を前年度に繰り戻して税金還付を請求できるようにする制度(欠損金の繰戻し還付)は、主に国の財政難を理由に、日本では1992年度から凍結されてきた。

fiscal policy 財政政策 (⇒austere fiscal policy)
 alternative fiscal policy 選択的財政政策
 austere fiscal policy 緊縮財政
 boost from fiscal policy 財政政策による景気刺激
 compensatory fiscal policy 補整的財政政策
 coordination between monetary and fiscal policy 金融と財政の政策協調
 discretionary fiscal policy 自由裁量的財政政策, 裁量的財政政策
 ease monetary and fiscal policies 金融・財政政策を緩和する
 exercise expansive [expansionary] fiscal policy initiatives 積極財政を進める
 exercise restrictive fiscal policy initiatives 緊縮財政を進める
 expansionary fiscal policy 積極財政, 財政政策の緩和, 財政出動による景気刺激
 expansive fiscal policy 拡大財政政策
 firm fiscal policy 確固とした財政政策
 fiscal and monetary policy stimulation 財政・金融刺激策
 fiscal and monetary policy stimulus 金融・財政政策による景気対策
 fiscal policy instrument 財政政策手段
 fiscal policy measures 財政政策措置, 財政政策
 fiscal policy objective 財政政策目標
 fiscal policy responses 財政面の対応
 fiscal restraint policy 財政引締政策
 fiscal stabilization policy 財政安定政策
 let fiscal policy loosen 財政政策を緩和する
 loosen fiscal policy through tax cuts and fresh public works 減税と新規公共事業で緊縮財政を緩和する, 減税と新規公共事業による緊縮財政の緩和
 monetary and fiscal policies 金融財政政策
 move to a neutral stance on fiscal policy 財政政策を中立的に戻す
 pro-growth fiscal policy 成長志向型財政政策
 restrictive fiscal policy 緊縮財政政策, 緊縮財政, 緊縮型の財政政策, 財政政策の引締め
 run an expansionary fiscal policy 積極財政を進める
 single fiscal policy 統一財政政策
 stance of fiscal policy 財政スタンス
 stimulative fiscal policy 景気刺激型の財政政策
 tight monetary policy 金融政策の引締め
 tightening fiscal policy 緊縮型の財政政策, 緊縮財政, 財政政策の引締め
 tighter fiscal policy 緊縮財政, 緊縮財政政策, 財政政策の引締め
 turn [shift] to tighter fiscal policy 緊縮財政への転換
 use fiscal policy 財政政策を採用する
 ◆Eurozone countries introduced the single currency, but they have widely different fiscal policies. ユーロ圏は単一通貨(ユーロ)を導入したが、ユーロ各国の財政政策はバラバラだった。◆In 2001, China's economy grew a significant 7.3 percent largely because of the nation's expansionary fiscal policy aimed at increasing domestic demand. 2001年に中国は、主に内需拡大のための積極財政で7.3%の著しい経済成長を達成した。

fiscal policy guideline 財政政策の方針, 財政政策のガイドライン
 ◆The fiscal policy guidelines propose an option of increasing the consumption tax rate by 1 percentage point every year starting from fiscal 2011. 財政政策のガイドラインは、2011年度から毎年1%ずつ消費税率を引き上げる道筋を描いている。

fiscal predicament 財政ひっ迫
 ◆The rapid spread of Italy's credit crisis is due to intensified fears about the nation's fiscal predicament by Italy's huge fiscal deficits. イタリアの信用不安が急速に広がったのは、イタリアの巨額の赤字で同国の財政ひっ迫への警戒感が高まったからだ。

fiscal reconstruction 財政再建, 財政の立て直し 財政健全化 (=fiscal rehabilitation, fiscal restructuring; ⇒ precedence)
 fiscal reconstruction efforts 財政再建策, 財政健全化
 fiscal reconstruction plan 財政再建計画, 財政再建プラン
 fiscal reconstruction policies 財政再建路線
 ◆Fiscal reconstruction cannot be done without economic growth. 経済成長なしに、財政再建は達成できない。◆Greece's fiscal reconstruction has made little progress since the country was bailed out with financial support from the IMF and the EU in May 2010. ギリシャの財政再建は、2010年5月にIMFと欧州連合(EU)による金融支援を受けて以来、進展してない。◆Greece's fiscal reconstruction is set as a condition for supporting the struggling country by the European Union and the International Monetary Fund. 欧州連合(EU)と国際通貨基金(IMF)は、ギリシャの財政再建を、財政危機にある同国支援の条件としている。◆Japan will have to realize fiscal reconstruction that will be recognized by the market. これから日本は、市場に評価される財政再建を実現しなければならない。◆The first goal of Japan's fiscal reconstruction is for the central and local governments to achieve a surplus in their primary balances by fiscal 2019. 日本の財政再建の第一目標は、国と地方[地方自治体]の基礎的財政収支を、2019年度までに黒字化することだ。◆The new prime minister must make growth compatible with fiscal reconstruction. 新首相は、成長と財政再建の両立を図るべきだ。◆The U.S. credit rating agency Standard & Poor's made a grim assessment of the outlook of U.S. fiscal reconstruction. 米国の信用格付け機関のスタンダード・アンド・プアーズ(S&P)は、米国の財政再建の見通しを厳しく評価した。◆To overcome the current economic crisis, stimulus measures should take precedence

over fiscal reconstruction for the time being. 現在の経済危機を克服するためには、当面は、財政再建よりも景気対策を優先しなければならない。◆Without an economic recovery and the resultant recovery of tax revenues, fiscal reconstruction will be made difficult. 景気回復[経済の再生]とそれによる税収の回復がなければ、今後の財政再建もおぼつかない。

fiscal reconstruction measures　財政再建策
◆Fears about default on the Greek government bonds are smoldering as Greece's fiscal reconstruction measures hit the wall. ギリシャの財政再建策が行き詰まっているため、ギリシャ国債のデフォルト(債務不履行)の恐れがくすぶっている。

fiscal reform　財政改革
◆Priority should be given to public spending, to establish a firm foundation for economic recovery and the subsequent job of tackling fiscal reform. 景気を回復し[経済を立て直し]、財政改革に取り組むための強固な基盤を確立するには、公共支出を優先的に考えなければならない。

fiscal rehabilitation　財政再建, 財政の立て直し, 財政健全化　(⇒huge funds, treasury secretary [Treasury Secretary])
◆Japan's fiscal rehabilitation has emerged many times as a key issue for its national policies. 日本の財政健全化は、これまで何度も国政の主要課題になってきた。◆Prime Minister Naoto Kan's government is not sufficiently serious about fiscal rehabilitation. 菅政権は、財政再建への本気度が足りない。

fiscal rehabilitation measures　財政再建策
◆Market confidence in the Silvio Berlusconi administration's fiscal rehabilitation measures is virtually nonexistent as the administration is on its last legs. イタリアのベルルスコーニ政権が機能不全に陥っているため、同政権の財政再建策に対する市場の信認は事実上、失墜している。◆The compilation of fiscal rehabilitation measures including raising the pension age is imperative for the Italian parliament. 年金受給年齢の引上げなどを含む財政再建策のとりまとめが、イタリア議会の急務となっている。

fiscal rehabilitation plan　財政再建計画, 財政健全化計画, 財政健全化策
◆A focus of the summit meeting of European Union members held in Belgium is a fiscal rehabilitation plan to stabilize the euro. ベルギーで開かれる欧州連合(EU)加盟国首脳会議の焦点は、ユーロを安定させる財政健全化策だ。◆Japan's midterm fiscal rehabilitation plan will be compiled in June. 日本の中期財政健全化計画は、6月にまとめられる予定だ。

fiscal resources　財源, 原資
◆Child-rearing support measures require fiscal resources to implement them. 子育て支援策には、それを実施するための財源が必要だ。◆Fiscal resources of ¥1.6 trillion cannot be scrounged together simply by recasting the budget and cutting wasteful spending. 1.6兆円の財源は、予算の組替えや無駄の削減だけでは捻出(ねんしゅつ)できない。

fiscal situation　財政事情, 財政状況
◆Due to Japan's deteriorating fiscal situation, some credit rating agencies have hinted at the possibility of downgrading Japanese government bonds. 日本の財政状況の悪化で、格付け会社のなかには、日本国債の格下げの可能性を示唆したところもある。◆Given the dire fiscal situation, the government cannot afford to continue its handout policies. 財政難の折から、政府はバラマキ政策を続ける余裕はない。◆The domestic fiscal situation is the most critical among the industrialized nations. 国の財政事情は、先進国の中でも最悪だ。

fiscal soundness　財政[財務]の健全性, 財政の健全度
◆A surplus in the primary balances of the central and local governments indicates a degree of fiscal soundness. 国と地方[地方自治体]の基礎的財政収支の黒字は、財政の健全度を示す。◆If the prices of purchased bad assets are set low, the fiscal soundness of bailed-out financial institutions could be compromised. 不良資産の買取り価格が安ければ、救済する金融機関の財務の健全性が損なわれる可能性がある。

fiscal spending　財政支出, 歳出　(=fiscal measures)
additiional fiscal spending　追加の財政支出
fiscal spending cuts　歳出削減
◆It will also become necessary for the government to consider additional fiscal spending in the event of a military attack against Iraq. イラクへの軍事攻撃が行われるときは、政府が追加の財政支出を検討する必要もあろう。◆The cuts in fiscal spending accelerated deflationary pressure. 歳出削減は、デフレ不況を加速させた。

fiscal squeeze　財政のひっ迫
◆Portugal and Spain may face a fiscal squeeze as they now find it difficult to complete government bonds placements. ポルトガルやスペインは現在、国債を消化する[国債の販売を完了する]のが難しいため、財政逼迫(ひっぱく)に見舞われる可能性がある。

fiscal stimulus　財政刺激策, 財政面からの刺激, 財政面からの景気刺激, 財政出動
fiscal stimulus measures　財政刺激策, 財政面からの景気刺激策, 景気刺激策, 財政出動　(=fiscal stimulus package)
fiscal stimulus package　財政面からの景気刺激策, 景気刺激策　(=fiscal stimulus measures)
◆The administration of U.S. President Barack Obama is betting its $787 billion fiscal stimulus will reverse the economy's slide. 米国のオバマ政権は、7,870億ドルの財政刺激策[景気刺激策]で景気の悪化から抜け出せる、と期待している。

fiscal stimulus measures　財政刺激策, 財政面からの景気刺激策, 財政出動　(=fiscal stimulus package)
◆China is seeking to further expand its domestic demand through fiscal stimulus measures. 中国は、財政出動で一層の内需拡大を図る方針だ。◆Prime Minister Aso has accepted the government's fiscal stimulus measures to turn around the flagging economy. 麻生首相は、低迷する景気を回復させるための[経済対策のための]政府の財政出動を容認した。

fiscal straits　財政難, 財政困難, 財政危機, 財政ひっ迫, 財政的苦境, 困難な資金繰り, 金に困ること, 財務力の低下　(=financial difficulties; ⇒financial straits)
◆Japan is in dire fiscal straits as the issuance of government bonds are more than tax revenue. 国債発行額が税収を上回っているため、日本は非常事態の財政下にある[財政ひっ迫の状況にある]。

fiscal structural reform　財政構造改革
◆When the economy was about to recover in 1996, the administration of then Prime Minister Ryutaro Hashimoto launched a fiscal structural reform program. 1996年に景気が回復局面を向かえた際、当時の橋本政権は、財政構造改革プログラムに乗り出した。

fiscal sustainability　財政の持続性, 財政の持続可能性
◆If market players have doubts about Japan's fiscal sustainability, the price of government bonds will decline, causing long-term interest rates to take an upward turn. 市場参加者が日本の財政の持続性に疑念を抱けば、国債相場は下落し、金利は上昇に転じるだろう。◆Worldwide concern over fiscal sustainability in industrialized countries is growing in the wake of Greece's sovereign debt crisis. ギリシャの財政危機を契機として、先進国の財政の持続可能性に対する世界の関心が高まっている。

fiscal target　財政目標
◆The Hatoyama Cabinet will come up with new policies on various issues, including midterm fiscal targets, pension system reform and its new growth strategies. 鳩山内閣は、中期財政目標や年金制度改革、新成長戦略など様々な経済問題について、新方針を打ち出す予定だ。

fiscal troubles 財政危機問題
◆Global financial markets are still shaken by the serious fiscal troubles in Greece. 世界の金融市場は、ギリシャの深刻な財政危機問題で動揺が続いている。

fiscal turbulence 財政的混乱
◆Transition to a tri-reserve-currency (the U.S. dollar plus the euro and the renminbi) regime would not be without fiscal turbulences. 3準備通貨(米ドルとユーロ、人民元)体制への移行には、財政的波乱が伴うだろう。

fiscal turmoil 財政危機
◆The fiscal turmoil in Greece is slowing down a weakened Europe. ギリシャの財政危機で、弱体化した欧州経済はもたついている。

fiscal uncertainty 財政不安
◆Spain faces its own fiscal uncertainty. スペインは、財政不安を抱えている。

fiscal woes 財政危機
◆The fiscal woes of the single-currency bloc could trigger a new severe global financial crisis. 単一通貨・ユーロ圏の財政危機は、新たに重大な世界的金融危機の発生源になる可能性がある。

fiscal year 会計年度, 事業年度, 営業年度, 年度, 会計期間 (=business year, financial year, fiscal period; ⇒deficit-covering bonds, entire fiscal year, general expenditures)
current fiscal year　今年度, 今期
during fiscal year or quarter　年度・期中
first half of the fiscal year　年度前半, 今年度前半, 上半期, 上期
fiscal year end　決算日
new fiscal year　新年度, 新会計年度
next fiscal year　来年度, 来期
preceding fiscal year　前年度, 前期
the first half of fiscal 2012　2012年度前半, 2012年度上半期
the latter half of this fiscal year　今年度後半, 今年度下半期
◆About ¥1.9 trillion of taxpayers' money was spent over a ten year span until last fiscal year to cover losses from a surging number of uncollectible loans guaranteed by a public credit guarantee scheme for small and midsize companies. 中小企業のための公的信用保証制度により保証される融資の貸倒れ件数が急増し、それによる損失の穴埋めをするために、昨年度までの10年間で約1兆9,000億円の税金が投入された。◆All seven major banking groups posted losses for the two previous fiscal years. 過去2年度は[前期まで2期連続]、七つの大手銀行・金融グループが赤字に陥った。◆Gross domestic product will rise 2 percent in inflation-adjusted real terms and 2.2 percent in nominal terms in the current fiscal year from the previous fiscal year. 今年度の国内総生産(GDP)の成長率は、物価変動の影響を除いた実質で前年度比2%、名目で2.2%になる見通しだ。◆The CPI will post a moderate increase of from 0.1 percent to 0.2 percent next fiscal year from the previous year. 来年度の消費者物価指数は、前年度比0.1～0.2%程度の小幅プラスになると見られる。◆The government bond issuance worth about ¥44 trillion for the current fiscal year is the largest ever projected in an initial budget. 今年度の約44兆円の国債発行額は、当初予算としては史上最高だ。◆This is the economic outlook for this fiscal year as seen by the Bank of Japan in its April forecast of prices. これが、日銀の4月の物価展望で日銀が示した今年度の経済見通しだ。

Fitch Investors Service, Inc. フィッチ・インベスターズ・サービス, フィッチ

Fitch Ratings Ltd. フィッチ・レーティングス (英米系の格付け機関)
◆Fitch Ratings Ltd. will keep its rating on long-term U.S. debt at the highest grade, AAA. 英米系の格付け会社フィッチ・レーティングスは、米国の長期国債格付けを、最上級のAAA(トリプルA)に据え置く方針だ。

fix (動)固定する, 設定する, 決める, 特定する, 定める, 取り決める, (問題などを)改善する, 是正する, 立て直す, 解決する, 不正操作する, (賄賂(わいろ)を使って)買収する, 抱き込む, 八百長をする, いかさまをする (名)窮地, 苦境, 苦しい立場, 買収, 八百長, 不正, いかさま, (一時的な)解決策, 理解, プログラムの修正
be in a fix　苦境に陥っている
fix a price　値段を決める, 価格を設定する
fix imbalance　不均衡を是正する
fix the Chinese yuan rate to the U.S. dollar　中国の元相場[人民元元レート]を米ドルに固定する (⇒Chinese yuan rate)
fix the economy　経済を立て直す
fix the exchange rate for the hard core currencies　中核となる通貨のレートを固定する
fix the issue terms　発行条件を確定する
fix the yuan-dollar exchange rate　元・ドル為替レート[為替相場]を固定する
◆China intervenes in the foreign exchange markets to fix the yuan-dollar exchange rate. 中国は、外国為替市場に介入して[為替介入して]元・ドル・レートを固定している。◆The Chinese yuan rate is fixed to the U.S. dollar. 中国の元レートは、米ドルに固定されている。◆The United States and South Korea called for fixing imbalance. 米国と韓国が、不均衡の是正を求めた。

fixed (形)固定した, 固定式の, 固定型, 確定した, 変動しない, 一定の, 安定した
fixed commission　固定手数料
fixed date　確定日, 約定期日, 指定期日
fixed debt　固定借入金
fixed employee stock option plan　固定型従業員ストック・オプション制度
fixed exchange rate　固定為替相場, 固定為替レート, 固定相場
fixed liability　固定負債, 長期負債
fixed loan　固定貸付け金, 長期貸付け金, 長期借入金
fixed rate debt　固定利付き債

fixed asset 固定資産 (会社の営業活動のために長期的に使用される資産。⇒soar)
◆The rule of asset impairment accounting requires companies to post valuation losses on fixed assets whose market value has fallen sharply from their book value. 減損会計基準は、固定資産の時価が簿価から大幅に下落した場合の固定資産の評価損の計上を、企業に義務付けている。

fixed capital formation 固定資本形成 (=fixed capital investment: 設備など固定資本への投資)
◆Public investment or public fixed capital formation fell 5.1 percent as the central and local governments continued cutting expenditure. 公共投資(公的固定資本形成)は、政府や地方自治体による公共事業費などの削減で、5.1%減少した。

fixed-charge system 固定料金制度, 固定料金制
◆Under the bank's monthly fixed-charge system, customers are able to make transactions at the bank's ATMs free of individual charges even outside the bank's office hours. 同行の月額固定料金制では、利用者は時間外でもATMの利用手数料が無料になる。

fixed collateral 根(ね)抵当, 根抵当権
◆The bank had already secured it as fixed collateral. 同行は、それには根抵当権をすでに設定していた。

fixed deposits 定期預金, 定期性預金
◆In April, the government ended measures to guarantee bank customers a total refund of their fixed deposits. 4月

FIXE

に政府は、銀行顧客に定期性預金の全額払戻しを保証する措置を打ち切った。

fixed exchange rate system　固定為替相場制, 固定相場制
◆China and other Asian economies have fixed exchange rate systems. 中国や他のアジア諸国は、固定相場制を採用している。

fixed income　債券, 確定利付き証券, 固定収入, 定額所得
　fixed income asset　確定利付き資産
　fixed income bond　確定利付き[固定付き]債券, 固定金利の債券
　fixed income debt　債券
　fixed income derivative　債券派生商品
　fixed income investment　確定利付き証券, 債券, 債券投資, 確定利付き投資
　fixed income investor　債券投資家, 普通債投資家
　fixed income market　債券市場
　fixed income option　債券オプション
　fixed income paper　債券
　fixed income receiver　定額所得者
　fixed income trading　債券売買
　fixed income warrant　デット・ワラント（=debt warrant）
　international fixed income investor　国際債券投資家

fixed income security　確定利付き証券, 固定金利の証券・債券（=fixed income investment, fixed interest security）
◆The price of fixed income securities falls when interest rates rise. 確定利付き証券の価格は、金利が上昇すると下がる[確定利付き証券は、金利が上がるとその値が下がる]。
解説 確定利付き証券とは：利率や配当率が証券の発行時から償還時まで一定で変わらない証券のこと。これには、社債や国債、地方債など中長期の債券、額面より低い割引価格で発行されるコマーシャル・ペーパーや米財務省短期証券などの短期証券のほかに、一定の配当金支払いがある優先株などが含まれる。

fixed interest　固定金利
　fixed interest bearing securities　固定利付き証券
　fixed interest rate　固定金利
　fixed interest rate loan　固定金利貸付け

fixed-interest postal savings　確定利付きの郵便貯金
◆The tax rate on interest accrued from fixed-interest postal savings and bank deposits whose principals are guaranteed is 20 percent. 元本が保証されている確定利付きの郵便貯金と銀行預金の利子所得の税率は、20%となっている。

fixed pension system　確定給付型年金制度, 確定給付型年金
◆NTT replaced its fixed pension system for retirees with a variable pension formula. NTTは、退職者の確定給付型年金を、変動年金支払い方式に改めた。

fixed rate　固定金利, 定率
　fixed rate bond　固定利付き債
　fixed-rate dollar bond　ドル建て固定利付き債
　fixed-rate funding　固定金利による資金調達
　fixed-rate income tax cut　定率減税（=fixed-rate income tax reduction）
　fixed-rate loan　固定金利ローン, 固定型金利のローン, 固定金利型ローン
　fixed rate market　普通債市場
　fixed-rate tax deductions　定率減税
◆A fixed-rate income tax cut was introduced in 1999 as a measure to stimulate the economy. 定率減税は、景気対策として1999年に導入された。◆There has been a sharp increase in the number of people who shift to adjustable rate mortgages from fixed rate ones. 固定金利型住宅ローンから変動金利型住宅ローンに移行する人が、急増している。

fixed rate mortgage　固定金利型抵当貸付け, 固定金利型住宅ローン
◆Currently, major banks set annual interest rates for 10-year, fixed rate mortgages at about 4 percent. 現在、主要銀行が設定している期間10年の固定金利型住宅ローンの金利は、年4%程度だ。◆In an attempt to get on the bandwagon, many people are shifting their fixed rate mortgages to adjustable rate ones. 時流に乗ろうとして、固定金利型住宅ローンを変動金利型住宅ローンに変更する人が多い。

fixed share exchange　固定株数の交換

flag　(動)低迷する, 活力がなくなる, 衰える, しおれる, 薄れる

flagging　(形)衰えている, 低迷する, 低迷が続く, 下落傾向の, 弱い, 疲れた
　flagging demand　低迷する需要, 需要低迷, 需要の軟調
　flagging yen　円相場の下落, 下落傾向の円

flagging economic growth　失速気味の経済成長, 経済成長の鈍化
◆The European Central Bank cut its main interest rate by 0.25 percent following heavy pressure for a rate cut to spur flagging economic growth. 失速気味の経済成長に刺激を与えるため利下げを求める強い圧力を受けて、欧州中央銀行（ECB）はその主要（政策）金利を0.25%引き下げた。

flagging economy　経済の低迷, 景気低迷, 低迷する経済
◆Acting in an emergency conference call, the U.S. Federal Reserve moved to bolster the flagging economy by cutting interest rates by half a point. 緊急電話会議を開いて、連邦準備制度理事会（FRB）は、景気減速に歯止めをかけるため金利を0.5%引き下げることを決めた。◆Prime Minister Aso has accepted the government's fiscal stimulus measures to turn around the flagging economy. 麻生首相は、低迷する景気を回復させるための[経済対策のための]政府の財政出動を容認した。◆The Bank of Japan stepped up its efforts to boost the flagging economy following the March 11 earthquake and tsunami by introducing a ¥500 billion cheap loan program. 日銀は、5,000億円の低利融資制度を導入して、東日本大震災で揺れる日本経済の刺激策を強化した。

flagging stock prices　急落する株価
◆The measures to boost flagging stock prices focus on encouraging financial institutions to sell off cross-held shares and tightening monitoring of short selling of stocks by international speculative traders. 急落する株価へのテコ入れ策の柱は、金融機関が保有する持ち合い株の売却促進と、海外投機筋による株の空売りへの監視強化である。

flagship　(名)主力商品, 主力製品, 目玉商品, 最重要製品, 目玉, 最も代表的なもの, 最も重要なもの, 旗艦, 最高級船, 最大の船・航空機, 最上位機種, 主力機種
　flagship operation　主力事業
　flagship product　主力製品, 主力商品, 目玉商品
　flagship store　旗艦店, 母店, 主力店, 主力店舗
◆Automotive insurance is the flagship product of nonlife insurers. 自動車保険は、損害保険会社の主力[目玉]商品だ。

flagship insurance product　主力保険商品
◆Meiji Yasuda decided to lower the yield rate of its flagship insurance product because the insurer placed priority on long-term stable management over an increase in the number of policyholders. 明治安田生保は、契約者の数を増やすより長期的な経営の安定を優先したため、主力保険商品の予定利率[利回り]を引き下げることにした。◆Meiji Yasuda Life Insurance Co.'s single-premium whole life insurance is one of its flagship products. 明治安田生保の一時払い終身保険は、同社の主力商品の一つだ。

Flash Crash　一瞬の株価急落[暴落], 閃光のような急落, フラッシュ・クラッシュ（2010年5月6日に発生した株価急落のことで、ニューヨークダウ平均株価が突然、1,000ドル近く下げた。原因は未解明だが、注文処理の

高速化が株価の下落を加速させたといわれる)
flat (形)横ばい, 横ばい状態の, 伸び悩みの, 不振の, 不況の, 変動しない, 一定の, 一律の, 均一の 均等の, 経過利子なしの, 直先(じきさき)フラットの, フラット (名)直先フラット(直物相場と先物相場が等しいこと)
 be essentially [almost, virtually] flat ほぼ横ばい, ほぼ横ばい状態
 be flat on the year 前年同期比で横ばい, 前年同月比で横ばい
 flat activity in the stock market 株価低迷
 flat benefit 均一給付
 flat bond 無利息公債
 flat charge 発行者手数料
 flat [flatter] curve 利回り曲線の平坦化
 flat fee 固定手数料, 定額料金, 定額
 flat grant 均等補助金
 flat-grant-minus system 減額式定額年金制
 flat loan フラット・ローン
 flat market 伸び悩み市場, 軟調の市況
 flat money 名目貨幣
 flat price (証券)裸相場, 均一価格
 flat quotation 裸相場, 裸値段
 flat (rate) tax 均等割り税, 均一税
 flat system フラット制
 flat yield 直接利回り, 均一利回り
 flat yield curve 横ばいイールド・カーブ
 flatter curve 長短利回り格差縮小, 利回り曲線の平坦化
◆Eurozone June consumer prices were flat compared with the previous month. ユーロ圏の6月の消費者物価指数は、前月比で横ばいだった。◆In its monthly economic report for August, the government said the economy "remains essentially flat." 8月の月例経済報告で, 景気は「おおむね横ばい」と政府は言った。◆The nation's industrial output was flat in March. 日本の3月の鉱工業生産高は、横ばいだった。◆The sluggish domestic demand is mainly due to previously robust personal consumption that slumped in the April-June quarter to an almost flat level. 内需低迷の主因は, これまで堅調だった個人消費が, 4〜6月期にはほぼ横ばいまで減速したことにある。

flat-lined (形)低迷する, 伸び悩みの
◆The U.S. Labor Department's report highlighted the hard task President-Barack Obama faces in resuscitating the flat-lined economy. 米労働省の雇用統計は, 低迷する景気の回復でオバマ米大統領が直面している難題を浮き彫りにした。

flat rate 均一料金, 均一運賃, 一律料金, 固定料金, 定額料金, 定額, 固定レート
 flat rate of contribution 均一拠出制
◆Under the new expressway toll plan, the current flat rate of ¥700 for standard cars using the Hanshin and Shuto expressways will be abolished. 今回の高速道路料金案では, 阪神高速と首都高速を利用している普通車で一律700円の現行制度が廃止される。

flat-rate (形)定額料金の, 均一料金の, 一括金利の
 flat-rate formula 定額方式, 均一方式
 flat-rate freight 均一運賃, 均一料金
 flat-rate pricing scheme 定額料金制, 均一料金制
 flat-rate system 定額制, 一律方式
 flat-rate tariff 均一料金表

flat-sum allowance 定額給付金
◆A significant economic boost cannot be expected from the flat-sum allowance and child-rearing allowances. 定額給付金やこども手当から, 大きな景気浮揚は期待できない。

Flat 35 mortgage program フラット35住宅ローン (最長35年の長期固定金利型の住宅ローン)

◆The Flat 35 fixed-rate mortgage program is offered by the Japan Housing Finance Agency in cooperation with private financial institutions. 固定金利型住宅ローンのフラット35は, 住宅金融支援機構(旧住宅金融公庫)が民間金融機関と提携して提供している。

flatten (動)縮小させる, 平らにする, 平準化する, 平坦化する (自動)縮小する, 横ばいになる, 横ばいに転じる, 横ばいで推移する, 安定する
 a flattening yield curve 利回り曲線(イールド・カーブ)の平坦化
 flatten out 横ばいになる, 横ばいに転じる, 平坦化する
 flatten the yield curve 利回り曲線(イールド・カーブ)を縮小させる
 the yield curve flattens from the short end 利回り曲線(イールド・カーブ)が短期物利回りの上昇で平坦化する

flattening (名)縮小, 平坦化, 横ばい
 curve flattening 利回り曲線の平坦化, 長短利回り格差の縮小 (=flattening of the curve, yield curve flattening)
 flattening of capex [capital investment, capital spending] 設備投資の縮小, 横ばい状態の設備投資
 flattening of the yield curve from the short end 短期債利回りの上昇による長短利回り格差の縮小

flaw (名)欠陥, 瑕疵(かし), 欠点, 不備, 弱点, 短所

fleet (名)保有全車両, 全船舶, 全航空機, 船舶隊, 船隊, 航空機隊, 輸送船団, 船団, フリート
 fleet cars 量販車
 fleet policy 自動車一括保険, 多数契約保険証券, フリート保険
 fleet rating フリート料率制度

flex (動)曲げる, 収縮する
 flex one's muscle(s) 力を誇示(こじ)する, 力のあるところを見せつける, 腕を振るう, 影響力を行使する
◆China is trying to flex its muscle with the United States on the strength of its status as the largest holder of U.S. Treasury securities. 中国は, 米財務省証券[米国債]の最大保有国としての地位を背景に, 米国への影響力を行使しようとしている。

flex (形)柔軟性のある, 自由のきく, フレックス
 currency-denominated Flex options 外貨建てフレックス・オプション
 flex benefit フレックス給付(被保険者の必要に応じて契約内容を柔軟に変えられる保険金給付方式)

flexibility (名)柔軟性, 伸縮性, 弾力性, フレクシビリティ (⇒exchange rate flexibility)
 budget flexibility 予算伸縮性
 built-in flexibility 自動伸縮性, 構造的伸縮性
 exchange rate flexibility 為替レート[為替相場]の柔軟性, 為替レートの伸縮性, 為替相場の弾力化
 financial flexibility 財務上の柔軟性
 financing flexibility 資金調達の柔軟性
 fiscal flexibility 財政伸縮性
 flexibility of prices 物価の弾力性, 物価の伸縮性
 funding flexibility 資金調達手段の柔軟性
 have little flexibility to 〜する余地はほとんどない
 managed flexibly (為替の)管理された伸縮性
 money flexibility 貨幣弾力性
 price flexibility 価格伸縮性
 pricing flexibility 価格設定の柔軟性
 the greater flexibility of the Chinese yuan rate 中国人民元相場の弾力化
 upward flexibility 上方伸縮性
◆More flexibility in exchange rates is desirable. 柔軟な為替相場が望ましい。◆The joint declaration of the G-20 leaders

called for greater exchange rate flexibility in some emerging markets. G-20首脳の共同宣言は、一部新興国の為替レートの柔軟性向上を求めた。

flexible (形)柔軟な, 柔軟性のある, 曲げやすい, しなやかな, 屈伸自在の, 機動的な, 弾力性の, 順応性のある, 適応性がある, 適応性に富んだ, 融通のきく, 伸縮的な, 伸縮型の, フレキシブル
 flexible benefits 弾力の付加給付
 flexible budget 弾力性予算, 変動予算
  (=variable budget)
 flexible charge account 伸縮型回転掛売り勘定
  (=all-purpose revolving account)
 flexible exchange policy 柔軟な為替政策
 flexible exchange rate 変動為替相場, 屈伸為替相場
 flexible exchange rate policies 柔軟な為替政策
 flexible money [monetary] policy 伸縮的通貨政策
 flexible mortgage 根(ね)抵当
 flexible tariff 伸縮関税
 flexible trust 管理型投資信託
 introduce flexible rates 変動金利を導入する
 take a flexible response [approach] 柔軟な対応をする, 機動的に対応する

flexible rate 変動金利
 flexible rate mortgage 変動金利抵当貸付け
  (=adjustable rate mortgage)
 flexible rate system 屈伸相場制

flexible stimulus measures 柔軟な刺激策
◆The government should keep taking flexible stimulus measures, both fiscal and financial, to put the economy onto a recovery track. 政府は、財政と金融の両面から今後も継続して柔軟な刺激策を取り、景気を回復軌道に乗せていかなければならない。

flexibly (副)柔軟に, 機動的に, フレキシブルに
◆The government will flexibly implement both economic and financial measures to deal with the slowdown in the economy. 政府は、経済対策と金融政策を機動的に実施して、景気減速に対応する方針だ。

flight (名)逃避, 預金の預け替え, シフト
 absolute flight from cash 現金からの投資
 capital flight 資本逃避, (金融資産の)他国への資本流出 (=flight of capital; ⇒foreign reserves)
 flight capital 逃避資金, 逃避資本
  (=flight money)
 flight from market 市場からの逃避
 flight from (the) currency 通貨からの逃避, 外貨からの逃避
 flight from the dollar ドルからの逃避
 flight of deposits 預金の預け替え
 flight to quality 質への逃避(株価急落などの際に投資資金が信用力の高い国債などの証券市場に流れ込むこと)
 flight to top quality names 超優良銘柄への逃避
◆There are concerns about a massive flight of deposits from less reliable financial institutions to strong ones. 信頼度の低い金融機関から安全な金融機関へ大がかりな預金の預け替えが起きる懸念材料がある。◆This flight from government bonds for liquidity by banks will cause securities investment to dry up, sending stock prices plummeting globally. 金融機関によるこうした資金確保に向けた国債からの逃避が、証券投資の途絶をもたらし、世界的な株安を招いている。

flip (動)フリッピングを行う(新規株式公開で株式を購入後、すぐに売却して利益を得ることを「フリッピング」という)

float (動)株や債券などを発行する, 新規に発行する, 株式公開する, 会社を新規上場する, 会社を設立する, 通貨を変動相場制に移行する, 変動相場制にする, 変動相場制である, 小切手を不渡りにする, 提案する, 提示する
 (⇒devalue)
 float a loan 起債する
 float an issue of stock 株式を発行する
 float Eurobond issues ユーロ債を発行する
 float on the stock exchange 証券取引所に上場する
 float straight bonds 普通社債を発行する
 float the yen 円を変動相場制にする
 freely float the local currency 自国通貨を自由変動相場制にする
 let the currency float 通貨を変動相場制にする, 通貨を変動相場制に移行する
 the yen float 円の変動
◆Argentine government freely floated the local currency for the first time in 11 years. アルゼンチン政府は、11年ぶりに自国通貨ペソを自由変動相場制にした。◆As part of its capital and business tie-ups with Livedoor, Fuji TV paid ¥44 billion for new shares floated by Livedoor under a third-party equity issue. ライブドアとの資本・業務提携の一環として、フジテレビは、第三者割当増資でライブドアが発行した新株を[ライブドアによる第三者割当て増資を]440億円で引き受けた。◆Australia's dollar rose as high as $1.0004 for the first time since the currency was freely floated in December 1983 in New York. ニューヨーク外国為替市場で豪ドル[オーストラリア・ドル]は、1983年12月に自由変動相場制に移行してから初めて、1豪ドル=1.0004米ドルまで上昇した。◆If yuan-denominated bonds are issued, the risk from exchange rate fluctuations will be lessened in the event the Chinese government revalues or floats its currency in the future. 人民元建て債が発行されると、将来、中国政府が人民元を切り上げたり変動相場制に移行したりした場合でも、為替変動リスクが軽減される。◆Mizuho Financial Group Inc. will float preferred securities to domestic institutional investors to enhance the core portion of its capital base. みずほフィナンシャルグループ(FG)は、自己資本[中核的自己資本]を増強するため、国内機関投資家向けに優先出資証券を発行する。◆The bank will discontinue issuing bank debentures to companies next March and float straight bonds instead. 同行は、企業向けの金融債発行を来年3月で停止し、それ以降は普通社債を発行する。

float (名)証券の発行, 株式公開, 新規上場, 通貨の変動, 変動相場制, 流通量, 流動性, 未決済小切手, 取立て中の手形・小切手類, 浮動株数(floating stock, floating supply), 小口現金, 設立, フロート
 added float 追加発行
 cash float 小口現金, 釣銭用の小銭
 clean float きれいなフロート, 自由変動相場制, クリーン・フロート
 closely-policed float 制限付き変動相場制
 controlled float 管理された変動相場制
 dirty float 汚いフロート, 汚い変動相場制, 政府が介入する管理された変動相場制
 free float 自由なフロート, 浮動株, 浮動株式
 joint currency float 共同フロート
 joint float 共同変動相場, 共同フロート
  (=joint floating)
 managed float 制限付き変動相場制, マネージド・フロート
 public float 公開株
 till float 通貨流通量
◆Australia's currency reached parity with the U.S. dollar since its 1983 float. 豪ドルが、1983年に変動相場制に移行して以来初めて、対米ドルで等価水準(1豪ドル=1米ドル)に

達した。◆Sluggish stock markets mean a float is unlikely to raise the desired amount of capital. 株式市場の低迷で、上場しても十分な資金の調達が見込めない。

floatation (名)株式の新規発行, 売出し, 株式公開 (=flotation)

floater (名)証券発行者, 変動金利ローン, 変動利付き債 (floating-rate note), 変動金利商品, 浮動証券, 包括保険証券, フローター
  capped floater　キャップ付き変動利付き債
  collared floater　カラー付き変動利付き債
  dollar floater　ドル建て変動利付き債
  floater policy　包括保険証券
  inverse floater　インバース・フローター
  LIBOR based floater　LIBORベースの変動利付き債
  reversed floater　逆変動利付き債

floating (名)新規株式公開

floating (形)流動的, 流動する, 変動する, 流通する, 浮動的な, 未着の, フローティング
  floating asset　流動資産　(=circulating asset, current asset, near-cash asset)
  floating basis [base]　変動ベース, フローティング・ベース（金融情勢に応じて、金利をあらかじめ決められた基準に従って自動的に変更する方式）
  floating capital　流動資本　(=circulating capital, net current assets, working capital)
  floating cargo　未着貨物
  floating claim　一時債権
  floating currency　変動相場制をとる通貨, 変動通貨
  floating debenture　流動債券
  floating debt　流動負債, 一時借入金 (=current liability, floating liability)
  floating debt finance　一時借入金融
  floating downward　為替相場の下方変動
  floating fund　流動資金
  floating insurance　包括保険
  floating liability　流動負債 (=current liability, floating debt)
  floating Lombard Rate　変動ロンバード金利
  floating money　流動資金, 一時的余裕資金
  floating parity　変動相場制
  floating payment　変動額支払い
  floating policy　予定保険証券, 船名等未詳保険証券, 包括保険証券, フローティング・ポリシー
  floating prime rate　変動型プライム・レート, 変動プライム・レート, FPR
  floating securities　変動証券, 浮動証券
  floating supply　浮動株数 (float) 浮動在庫高, 浮動玉（ぎょく）
  floating system　変動相場制, フロート制
  floating upward　為替相場の情報変動, フロート・アップ
◆The Company's finance subsidiary has outstanding floating to fixed interest rate commercial paper swaps totaling $50 million at December 31, 2010. 当社の金融子会社には、2010年12月31日現在、変動金利を固定金利に変更する総額5,000万ドルの未決済コマーシャル・ペーパー金利スワップ契約があります。

floating charge　浮動担保, 包括担保（社債を発行する場合に設定する担保で、日々変動する会社の資産を包括して担保にするもの）
◆The first mortgage bonds of the corporation are secured by a first mortgage and a floating charge on the company. 同社の第一順位抵当権付き社債は、同社の第一順位抵当権と浮動担保権で保証されています。

floating deposits　流動性預金
◆Floating deposits are ordinary deposits held by individuals and current deposits held by corporations. 流動性預金は、個人保有の普通預金や企業保有の当座預金のことだ。

floating exchange (rate)　変動為替相場, 変動相場 (=flexible exchange rate)
  floating exchange rate policy　変動相場政策
  joint floating exchange rate system　共同変動相場制
◆Many of these East Asian countries have shifted to more flexible currency exchange systems such as floating exchange rates. これらの東アジア諸国の多くは、変動相場制などより柔軟な形の為替相場制度に移行した。

floating exchange rate regime　為替変動相場制, 変動相場制, フロート制 (=flexible exchange rate system)
◆The semiannual currency report of the U.S. Treasury Department said that Japan maintains a floating exchange rate regime. 日本は変動為替相場制［変動相場制］を維持している、と米財務省の為替政策半期報告書は述べている。

floating exchange rate system　変動相場制, 変動為替相場制, フロート制, フロート体制 (=floating exchange rate regime)
◆China should join the floating exchange rate system of Japan, the United States and European countries to realize a fair evaluation of the yuan. 中国は、日本や欧米諸国の変動為替相場制に参加して、人民元の適正な評価が得られるようにする必要がある。

floating interest　変動金利 (=floating interest rate)
  floating interest flows　変動金利キャッシュ・フロー
  floating interest loan　変動金利貸付け
  floating interest mortgages　変動金利の住宅ローン貸出
  floating interest stream　変動金利の流れ, 変動金利のキャッシュ・フロー
  future floating interest　将来の変動金利

floating interest rate　変動金利 (=floating rate)
  floating interest rate loan　変動金利貸付け
  single currency fixed/floating interest rate swap　単一通貨建て固定金利・変動金利の通貨スワップ

floating rate　変動金利, 変動利率 (floating interest rate), 変動相場 (floating exchange rate), 変動レート
  floating rate asset　変動金利資産, 変動金利アセット
  floating rate asset-backed securities　変動利付きアセットバック証券
  floating-rate bank loans　変動金利による銀行借入れ［銀行融資、銀行貸出］
  floating rate bond [debt, issue]　変動利付き債, 変動利付き社債
  floating-rate borrower　変動金利の借り手, 変動金利資金の取り手
  floating rate CD [certificate of deposit]　変動金利CD, 変動利付きCD
  floating rate housing loan　変動金利住宅ローン
  floating rate index　変動金利指標
  floating rate interest　変動金利
  floating rate investments　変動利付き金融商品
  floating rate issue　変動利付き債
  floating rate leg　変動金利部分
  floating rate lender　変動金利資金の出し手
  floating rate lending　変動金利貸出
  floating rate liability　変動金利債務
  floating rate loan　変動金利ローン
  floating rate market　変動利付き債市場

floating rate policy　変動相場政策
floating rate portfolio　変動金利ポートフォリオ
floating rate preferred stock　変動配当率優先株
floating rate repos　変動金利現先
floating rate system　変動為替相場制
floating-rate yen debt　円建て変動利付き債
issue floating rate debt　変動利付き債を発行する
jumbo floating-rate note issue　変動利付き大型債
managed floating rate system　管理フロート
reverse floating rate issue　逆変動利付き債
synthetic floating rate　合成変動金利

floating rate note　変動利付き債, FRN　(=floater)
　bull floating-rate note　逆変動利付き債
　capped floating rate note　キャップ付き変動利付き債
　collared floating-rate note　カラー付き変動利付き債
　collateralized floating-rate note　担保付き変動利付き債
　level pay floating-rate note　定額支払い変動利付き債
　leveraged floating-rate note issues　レバレッジ変動利付き債
　perpetual floating-rate note　永久変動利付き債, 永久FRN
　senior secured floating rate note　有担保変動利付き上位債
　step-down floating-rate note　ステップダウン変動利付き債, ステップダウンFRN

floating rate payments　変動金利の支払い, 変動金利の支払い利率
　◆Floating rate payments are based on rates tied to prime, LIBOR or U.S. Treasury bills. 変動金利の支払い利率は、プライム・レート、ロンドン銀行間取引金利または米財務省短期証券の利回りに基づいて決定されます。

floating shares　浮動株　(=floating stock, floating supply of stocks: 安定株の反対で、市場で転々と流通している株のこと)
　◆Floating shares are vulnerable to a hostile takeover bid. 浮動株は、敵対的TOBに狙われやすい。

flood　(動)氾濫させる, 増水させる, あふれさせる, どっと押し寄せる, 殺到する
　be flooded with calls　電話が殺到する
　be flooded with complaints　苦情が殺到する
　be flooded with inquiries　照会が殺到する
　be flooded with orders for forward exchange contracts　為替予約の注文が殺到する
　be flooded with sellers　大量の売りを浴びせる, 売り一辺倒になる
　◆Just after the start of the market intervention, the banks were flooded with orders for forward exchange contracts. 市場介入の直後、銀行には為替予約の注文が殺到した。

flood the market　売り浴びせる, 売り崩す(売り物を人為的に増やして相場の下落を促進すること), 供給過剰を引き起こす
　◆On the stock market, many are flooding the market and making a killing through illegal short selling. 株式市場では、違法な空売りで売り浴びせて荒稼ぎしている者が多い。

floor　(名)下限, 底, 底値, 最低額, 下限金利, 証券取引所の立会場, 売り場, 店内, 発言権, フロア　(⇒cap)
　be 2 percent below the floor of the narrow band　狭い変動幅の下限を2%下回る
　buy a floor　下限金利を買う, フロアを買う
　buyer [purchaser] of the floor　フロアの買い手
　dip below one's floor　下限を割り込む
　drop through the floor of　〜の下限を突破する
　establish a firm floor　底値が固まる
　fall through the floor of　〜の下限[底]を割り込む, 〜の下限を突破する
　floor broker　場内仲買人, 場立ち, 立会場ブローカー(証券取引所の立会場で売買注文の執行に当たる証券会社の担当者)
　floor buyer　フロアの買い手
　floor finance　在庫金融　(=floor financing)
　floor for money market rates　短期市場金利の下限
　floor loan　最低貸付け, 最低限度の融資, 最小限度貸出額
　floor member　立会場会員
　floor plan　最低額保障型制度, フロア・プラン
　floor-plan financing　在庫金融, 購入資金融資, 即金融
　floor planning　在庫金融
　floor price　(相場の)底値, 最低価格, 下限価格
　floor rate　フロア金利
　floor trader　取引所の場内会員, 登録トレーダー, フロア・トレーダー
　floor trading　立会場取引, 立会い
　　(=trading on the floor)
　go below some floor level　下限基準を割り込む
　interest rate floor　金利フロア, フロア
　long floor　フロアの買い
　price floor　値段の下限
　rate floor　金利フロア
　sell a floor　下限金利を売る, フロアを売る
　seller of the floor　フロアの売り手
　short floor　フロアの売り
　the floor for some time　当面の底
　the floor of one's permitted band of fluctuation　許容変動幅の下限

flooring　(名)在庫金融

flotation　株式公開, 新規発行, 売出し, 起債, 上場
　(=floatation, going public, IPO, listing)
　equity flotation　株式公開
　flotation of a loan　起債, 資金の募集
　flotation of a new company　新会社株式の売出し
　flotation of foreign bonds　外債発行
　◆The flotation of the company is likely to go down in corporate history. 同社の上場は、会社の歴史に残るものと思われる。

flounder　(動)低迷する, 停滞する, 難航する, 苦労する, 問題を抱える, まごつく, 失敗する
　floundering cash flow　資金の動きの停滞
　floundering financial markets　低迷する金融市場
　◆The cash flow, which floundered since the bursting of the bubble economy, has been rejuvenated. バブル崩壊以降、停滞していた資金の動きが、活発化してきた。

flow　(動)流れる, 移転する, 絶え間なく動く, (情報や金が)行き来する, 生じる
　benefits flow from　〜から利益が生まれる
　flow with investment　投資に伴って移転する
　orders flow in on　注文が〜に殺到する

flow　(名)流れ, 流出, 移動, フロー　(⇒cash flow)
　capital flows　資本移動, 資本の流れ, 資本流出, 資本流入
　capital flows in　資本の流入
　capital flows out　資本の流出
　cash flow-through　資金の流れ
　circular flow　循環的流れ, 循環
　circular flow of economy　経済循環
　commodity flow　財貨の流れ, 財貨流通
　consumption flow　消費の流れ
　cross-border capital flows　国際的な資本移動, 国際的な

資金フロー
deal flow　取引量, 取引の案件数
financial flow　金融の流れ, 財務フロー, 資金フロー, 資本移動
flow of goods and money　モノとカネの流れ
international flow of capital　資本の国際移動
money flow　資金循環, マネー・フロー
new coverage flows　新規保険契約の収益
open capital flows　資本移動の自由化
secondary flows　流通市場の取引
the international flow of goods, services and funds　物、サービスと資金の国際的な流れ
trade flows　貿易の流れ, 貿易動向
◆The continuing oil price hikes can be attributed to an uninterrupted flow of speculative funds into the market. 原油の値上がりが続いているのは、投機マネーが絶え間なく[続々と]市場に流れ込んでいるからだ。◆The flow of speculative money into the oil market did not reflect actual demand. 投機マネーの原油市場への流入は、実需を反映していなかった[実需に基づくものではなかった]。

flow into　～に流入する, ～に流れる, ～に流れ込む
◆Investment funds flowed into low-risk Treasury bonds. 投資資金は、リスクの少ない財務省証券市場に流入した。◆Recently, a sizable amount of speculative funds have been flowing into New York's commodities exchanges. このところ、ニューヨークの商品取引所には、大量の投機資金が流入している。◆Surplus funds put out by developed economies' monetary easing measures have flowed into emerging economies to inflate economic bubbles. 先進国の金融緩和策で生じた余剰資金が、新興国に流れ込み、バブルを発生させている。◆The purpose of postal privatization was to do away with the current inefficient system, in which huge funds raised through inflated postal savings and kampo life insurance policies flow into public corporations. 郵政民営化の目的は、肥大した郵便貯金と簡易保険で調達した巨額の資金が特殊法人に流れる現在の非効率的なシステムを、廃止することにあった。

flow of funds　資金の流れ, 資金移動, 資金循環, 資金フロー, マネー・フロー
◆There has been little change in the flow of the funds. この資金の流れは、大きく変わっていない。

flow of goods, services and funds　物[モノ]、サービスと資金の流れ
◆The international flow of goods, services and funds became freer and more globalized. 物、サービスと資金の国際的な流れは、一段と自由になり、また一段とグローバル化した。

flow outward　外へ流出する
◆The funds that so abundantly seek safe haven in New York today can flow outward tomorrow. 安全な投資先を求めて今日ニューヨークにあふれるほど集まった資金も、明日には外へ流出しかねない。

fluctuate　(動)変動する, 上がり下がりする, 乱高下する (⇒JGB)
◆The company's stock price fluctuated sharply afterward. 同社の株価はその後、乱高下した。◆The gain from stock options fluctuates depending on the option holder's investment judgment over the timing of purchase and changes of the stock price. ストック・オプション(自社株購入権)の利益は、購入時期と株価変動に対するオプション保有者(オプションの買い手)の判断[投資判断]によって上下する。◆The interest rate for long-term government bonds fluctuates depending on market developments. 長期国債の金利は、市場の動き次第で大きく変動する。◆With the rating of JGBs being low, internationalizing them may increase the risk that their yield will fluctuate. 日本の国債の格付けが低いので、日本国債の国際化は国債の金利変動リスクを高める可能性がある。

fluctuation　(名)変動, 変化, 上がり下がり, 乱高下, 騰落, 動き　(⇒exchange fluctuation)
business fluctuations　景気変動 (=cyclical fluctuations)
currency fluctuations　為替変動, 為替レートの変動
cyclical fluctuations　景気変動, 周期的の景気変動, 循環変動
dollar fluctuation　ドル価の変動
economic fluctuations　経済変動, 景気変動
exchange fluctuations　為替変動, 為替相場の変動, 為替の騰落, 為替の乱高下 (=foreign exchange fluctuations)
exchange rate fluctuations　為替相場の変動, 為替相場[為替]の動き, 為替変動 (⇒float, watch)
fluctuation band　変動幅
fluctuation in the yen-dollar rate　円・ドル相場の変動
fluctuations in stock prices and credit ratings　株価や信用格付けの動き
foreign exchange fluctuations　為替相場の変動, 為替の変動 (=exchange fluctuations; ⇒psychological factor)
foreign exchange rate fluctuations　為替相場の変動, 外国為替相場の変動
interest rate fluctuations　金利変動
margin of fluctuation　変動幅, 乱高下
market fluctuations　市場変動, 市況の変動
maximum fluctuation　許容範囲
price fluctuation　物価の変動, 価格騰落, 株価の乱高下, 株価変動
seasonal fluctuation　季節変動
trade fluctuation　景気変動
◆Amid the European fiscal and financial crisis, plunges on the world's stock markets and wild fluctuations in foreign exchange markets may continue. 欧州の財政・金融危機を受けて、世界同時株安と為替市場の乱高下は今後も続く可能性がある。◆Investors are swayed by price fluctuations. 投資家は、株価変動に左右される。◆The G-7 meeting has repeatedly issued communiques concerning exchange rate fluctuations and economic policy management. 先進7か国会議(G7)は、これまで為替変動や経済政策運営に関する声明を再三、発信してきた。

fluctuations in exchange rates　為替変動, 為替相場の変動 (=exchange rate fluctuations)
◆Toyota has refrained from releasing consolidated earnings forecasts as its earnings tend to be susceptible to fluctuations in exchange rates. トヨタの業績は為替変動の影響を受けやすいため、トヨタは連結業績予想の発表を控えてきた。

fluctuations in foreign exchange rate　為替相場の変動, 外国為替相場の変動 (=foreign exchange fluctuations, foreign exchange rate fluctuations)
◆Yen-denominated trade frees domestic companies from the risk of fluctuations in foreign exchange rate. 円建て貿易は、国内企業にとって為替変動のリスクがない。

fluctuations in government bond yield　国債利回りの変動
◆Under a variable pension system, pension benefits change in accordance with fluctuations in government bond yield. 変額年金制度では、国債利回りの変動で年金給付額が変わる。

fluctuations of [in] stock prices　株価変動, 株価の乱高下 (⇒adversely affect)
◆Regional small and medium-sized financial institutions are seriously affected by wild fluctuations of stock prices and foreign exchange rates. 地域の中小金融機関は、株価や為替相場の激しい変動[乱高下]によって深刻な影響を受けている。

flying Swiss franc　過度なスイス・フラン高, スイス・フランの高騰
◆The Swiss National Bank put a limit on the flying Swiss

franc. スイス国立銀行（スイスの中央銀行）が、過度なスイス・フラン高に上限を設定した。

FNMA ファニー・メイ、米連邦住宅抵当金庫（Federal National Mortgage Associationの略）

focus （名）焦点、ピント、中心、軸、的、注目の的、集中、集中化、重点、力点、重視、重視の姿勢、志向、傾斜、意図、意義、関心、関心事、課題、震源地、フォーカス
　customer focus　顧客重視、顧客重視の姿勢、顧客志向、顧客の満足度重視、顧客の満足に力を入れる
　focus on service quality　サービスの質の重視
　focus on the bottom line　利益重視、利益を重視する姿勢
　◆A focus of the summit meeting of European Union members held in Belgium is a fiscal rehabilitation plan to stabilize the euro. ベルギーで開かれる欧州連合（EU）加盟国首脳会議の焦点は、ユーロを安定させる財政健全化策だ。

focus on ～に焦点を当てる、～に焦点を合わせる、～に焦点を置く、～に的を絞る、～を重視する、～を強調する、～を中核に据える、～を中核事業にする、～に力を注ぐ、～に注目する、～に執着する、～に結集する、～に専念する
　◆Both lenders will focus on supporting their local corporations in the aftermath of the March 11 quake and tsunami. 3月11日（2011年）の東日本大震災を受けて、両行は地元企業の支援に重点的に取り組む方針だ。◆Financial markets worldwide are focused on whether the U.S. FRB embarks on a third round of its quantitative easing policy, or QE3. 世界の金融市場は、米連邦準備制度理事会（FRB）が量的緩和策の第三弾（QE3）に踏み切るかどうかに注目している。◆The brokerage's main services for individual customers will be asset management advisory services, focusing on the sale of products such as investment trust funds that invest in foreign equities, and money market funds denominated in foreign currencies. 同証券会社は、株式の主な個人顧客向け（売買仲介）業務として、外国株を組み込んだ投資信託や外貨建てMMF（マネー・マーケット・ファンド）などの商品の販売を中心に、資産運用顧問業務を展開する方針だ。◆The firm will focus on its consumer loan services. 同社は今後、消費者ローン業務を中核事業にする。◆The restructuring plan will focus on dealing with the debts owed to other financial institutions. 再建計画では、他の金融機関の債権取扱いが今後の焦点となる。◆The SEC probe was focused on several transactions that had led to higher revenues at AOL Time Warner Inc. 米証券取引委員会（SEC）の調査は、AOLタイム・ワーナーの売上高水増し（疑惑）につながった一部の取引を中心に行われた。

foil （動）計画の裏をかく、くじく、妨害する、失敗させる、負かす、挫折させる
　◆The company granted an investment firm the right to buy shares to be newly issued by the company as a means of foiling a hostile takeover bid. 同社は、敵対的買収への防衛策として、同社が新規に発行する株式の引受権を投資会社に付与した［投資会社に新株予約権を割り当てた］。

-fold （接尾）～倍の、～重の、～倍、～重
　◆The total value of M&A deals involving Japanese firms increased roughly 2.2-fold to $108.85 billion, or about ￥12 trillion in the first half of 2005. 日本企業がかかわった2005年上期のM&A取引金額の総額は、前年同期比約2.2倍増の1,088億5,000万ドル（約12兆円）となった。

fold up 廃業する、商売をやめる、店じまいする、破産する、潰（つぶ）れる、だめになる、中止になる、生産を中止する
　◆The company folded up due to the business depression. 不景気で、同社は潰れた。

follow （動）～の後について行く、～の後に続く、～の後をつける、追跡する、尾行する～と一緒に行く、～に従う、～を真似る、～にならう、理解する、（道を）たどる、～に沿って行く、扱う、～に従事する、～に携わる、続いて起こる

follow on　～から続く、すぐ後から行く
follow out　～を実行する、～に従う
follow the trend　流行を真似る
follow through　～を最後までやり抜く、考え抜く
follow up on　～に基づいて行動する、～をさらに究明する
follow up with　引き続き～を行う
the market that follows the sun　太陽を追う市場、外国為替市場
　（=currency market, foreign exchange market）
　◆Consumer spending waned amid the global financial crisis that followed the Lehman Brothers collapse in autumn 2008. 2008年秋のリーマン・ブラザーズの破たん後に生じた世界的金融危機を受けて、個人消費が低迷した。

follow suit 追随する、先例に従う、前例に倣（なら）う、人のまねをする
　◆Meiji Yasuda will lower the yield of its single-premium whole life insurance and other companies offering the same type of life insurance products could follow suit. 明治安田生命は一時払い終身保険の利回り（予定利率）を引き下げるが、同種の生保商品を販売している他社もこれに追随する可能性がある。◆Toshiba may demand damage compensation from Sony, and others may follow suit. 東芝はソニーに対する損害賠償請求を検討しており、他社もこれに追随する可能性がある。

following （形）次の、後に続く、以下の、下記の、同方向の、順風の　（前）～の後で、～の後に（after）、～に次いで、～の結果、～を受けて
　◆A company's management was reshuffled following a shareholder's proposal. 株主提案を受けて、企業の経営陣が刷新された。◆Corporate bond issues are recovering from the bond market turbulence following the March 11 earthquake and tsunami. 東日本大震災後の債券市場の混乱から、社債の発行額が回復している。◆Following sharp falls on European and U.S. markets, the Nikkei Stock Average fell briefly to its lowest level this year. 欧米市場の株価急落を受けて、日経平均株価は一時、今年の最安値を下回った。◆Following the footsteps of Sony Corp. and Softbank Corp., the company established a new firm to sell shares over the Internet. ソニーとソフトバンクの先例にならって、同社も株式をインターネットで売買するネット取引の新会社を設立した。◆Following the tender offer, Oji Paper would acquire the remaining Hokuetsu shares through a share swap to turn it into a wholly owned subsidiary. 株式公開買付け（TOB）後に、王子製紙は、株式交換で残りの北越製紙の株を取得して北越製紙を完全子会社化する。◆Global major financial institutions have been forced to hold extra capital since the financial meltdown following the 2008 bankruptcy of Lehman Brothers Holdings Inc. 米国の投資銀行リーマン・ブラザーズが2008年に経営破たんして生じた金融危機以来、世界の主要金融機関は、資本［自己資本］の上積み［積み増し］を迫られている。◆Italy's economy is the third largest after ［following］ those of Germany and France in the eurozone. イタリアの経済規模は、ユーロ圏ではドイツとフランスに次いで3位だ。◆Japanese banks failed to take quick actions to dispose of nonperforming loans following the bursting of the bubble economy. 邦銀は、バブル崩壊後の不良債権処理に迅速に対応しなかった。◆Rapid recovery following the so-called Lehman shock has ended and the Chinese economy has entered a phase aimed at stable growth. いわゆるリーマン・ショック後の中国の急回復の時期は終わり、中国経済は、安定成長を目指す段階に入っている。◆The Bank of Japan stepped up its efforts to boost the flagging economy following the March 11 earthquake and tsunami by introducing a ￥500 billion cheap loan program. 日銀は、5,000億円の低利融資制度を導入して、東日本大震災で揺らぐ日本経済の刺激策を強化した。◆The European Central Bank cut its main interest rate by 0.25 percent follow-

ing heavy pressure for a rate cut to spur flagging economic growth. 失速気味の経済成長に刺激を与えるため利下げを求める強い圧力を受けて、欧州中央銀行（ECB）はその主要（政策）金利を0.25％引き下げた。◆The Group's sales figures have been restated following the retrospective application of new International Financial Reporting Standards. 当グループの売上高の数値は、新国際財務報告基準（IFRS）を遡及的に適用して、再表示されています。◆The number of surplus workers approached a peak of 3.59 million in the January-March quarter of 1999, following a spate of failures at major financial institutions. 過剰雇用者数は、大手金融機関の破たんが相次いだ後の1999年1-3月期に、359万人のピークに達した。

following method フォロイング法（国際金融上、支払い期日が休日に当たる場合は、フォロイング法によって翌営業日に先送りされる。ただし、フォロイング法によって翌営業日を支払い期日とすると月が変わってしまう場合は、修正フォロイング法により、当初の支払い期日と同月内の最後の営業日が支払い期日とされる）

FOMC 米連邦公開市場委員会
（⇒Federal Open Market Committee）
 FOMC decision 米連邦公開市場委員会（FOMC）の決定
 FOMC meeting FOMC会議
 FOMC members FOMC（米連邦公開市場委員会）委員
 FOMC minutes 米連邦公開市場委員会（FOMC）の議事要旨
 the Record of Policy Actions of the FOMC 米連邦公開市場委員会（FOMC）の議事録
 ◆The FOMC found the U.S. economy to be bearish. 米連邦公開市場委員会（FOMC）は、米景気について弱気の見方を示した。

foment （動）扇動する、誘発する、〜を招く、助長する、促進する、高める
 foment a civil uprising 民衆の反乱を扇動する
 foment chaos in foreign exchange markets 外国為替市場の大混乱を招く、為替相場［為替レート］の変動を招く
 ◆The Fed's policy of quantitative easing foments chaos in foreign exchange markets. 米連邦準備制度理事会（FRB）［米国の中央銀行］の量的緩和政策は、為替相場［為替レート］の変動を招いている。

foot （動）支払う、負担する、〜の責任を負う、〜を合計する、総計で〜となる
 foot the bill 勘定を支払う、支払いをする、費用を負担する
 foot up an account 勘定書を絞める
 the receipts will foot up to 受け取り金額は絞めて［総計で、総額で］〜となる

foot the bill for 〜の勘定を支払う、〜のツケを支払う、〜の責任を負う
 ◆The U.S. government has had to foot the bill for mortgage loans that defaulted under the government program that insured mortgages. 米政府は、政府の住宅ローン保証プログラムに基づき、デフォルト（債務不履行）になった住宅ローンのツケの支払いを迫られている。◆We will have to accept heavy taxation to foot the bill for the lax fiscal discipline of past governments. われわれは今後、過去の政府の放漫な財政運営のつけを負担するために、重税を受け入れなければならなくなる。

foothold buying 足場作りの買い（会社乗っ取りのためにターゲット会社の株式を少量ずつ買い取って行くこと）

footing （名）合計、合算、突合せ、合計検算、締切り、入会、入会金、立場、足場、足がかり、地歩、地盤、基盤、関係、間柄
 financial footing 資金余力、財務基盤
 on a strong footing 強気の地合いで
 on an equal footing 対等の立場で、対等の関係で

 restore government［state］finances to a sound footing 財政を健全化する　（⇒government finances）
 ◆At the time of debt crisis in Greece, Germany's standing in the EU improved drastically thanks to its strong financial footing. ギリシャの財政危機の際、ドイツのEU域内での地位は、ドイツが持つ豊富な資金余力により大幅に高まった。

Footsie（index） （名）フィナンシャル・タイムズ100種総合株価指数、フッツイー
 （=Financial Times-Stock Exchange 100 index）

footstep （名）足跡、足音、足取り、先例、階段
 follow the footsteps of 〜の足跡をたどる、〜の先例［例］にならう、〜の志を継ぐ
 ◆Following the footsteps of Sony Corp. and Softbank Corp., the company established a new firm to sell shares over the Internet. ソニーとソフトバンクの先例にならって、同社も株式をインターネットで売買するネット取引の新会社を設立した。

for （前）〜のため、〜の目的で、〜上、〜に備えて、〜の代わりに、〜について、〜に関して、〜に賛成して、〜の間
 for a turn 小掬（すく）い（思惑取引の損益を小幅にとどめて素早く決済すること）
 for an initial period 当初期間
 for cash 直（じき）取引
 for cause 正当理由
 for clearing house purposes only 手形交換のためのみ（銀行が手形交換所を通じて小切手を取り立てるのに用いる制限裏書き。制限裏書き＝restrictive indorsement）
 for collection 取立てのために（証券の取立て譲り受け人委託をするときに用いられる制限裏書き）
 for compensation 補償金として
 for deposit 預金のため（証券を銀行に預け入れするときに用いられる制限裏書き）
 for form's sake 形式上
 for one's account 〜の勘定で、〜の負担で
 for one's own account and risk 自己の勘定と危険負担で
 for tax purposes 税務上
 for the account シケ取引（株式取引所の取引）
 for the opening 名義書換え停止後の取引
 for value received 対価受取済み（手形面の文句）、受領した価値あるものを約因として、価値あるものを受領した見返りに、対価を受領したので

for the time being 当分、当分の間、差し当たり、当面、ここしばらくの間、今のところ
 ◆There are few signs of the yen reaching the ￥90 range to the dollar for the time being. 今のところ、1ドル＝90円台に達する動き［1ドル＝90円台を目指す動き］は見られない。

forbearance （名）猶予、（債権者の）支払い猶予（ゆうよ）、債務履行の猶予、催促なし、不作為（ある行為を差し控えること）、（債権者の権利行使の）差し控え、請求の自制、自制、忍耐、寛容
 capital forbearance 不足資本の猶予
 forbearance to sue 訴権の放棄

force （動）強制する、強要する、強いる、押し付ける、押し進める、押し込む、追い込む
 ◆European banks are forced to shore up their potential capital shortages to restore market confidence. 欧州銀行は、市場の信認を回復するため、潜在的資本不足の増強を迫られている。◆European countries are forced to prevent the financial crisis from spreading from Europe to other parts of the world. 欧州は、金融危機の世界的波及阻止を迫られている。◆Every member of the nation will now be forced to face the risks involved in the management of their own assets. これからは、国民一人ひとりが資産運用リスクに正面から向き合わざるを得なくなる。◆Governments facing fiscal hardship sometimes force their central banks to buy up government bonds.

財政がひっ迫した政府は、中央銀行に国債を買い切らせることがある。◆Major financial institutions are forced to hold additional capital so that they can better absorb losses during financial crises. 金融危機の際の損失吸収力を高めるため、大手金融機関は、資本[自己資本]の積み増しを迫られている。◆The credit union was forced to apply to the Financial Services Agency for protection from creditors. 同信組は、金融庁への破綻申請を迫られた。◆The sudden economic downturn since the autumn has forced the government to drastically lower the forecast rate of real GDP in fiscal 2009. 秋以降の急速な景気悪化で、政府は2009年度の実質国内総生産（GDP）成長率見通しを大幅に引き下げざるを得なかった。◆The United States and European countries are forced to proceed steadily with fiscal reconstruction and resolve the financial turmoil. 米欧各国は、財政再建を着実に進めて、金融市場の混乱を収拾せざるを得ない状況にある。

force （名）力, 強さ, 威力, 暴力, 腕力, 猛力, 勢力, 影響力, 支配力, 効果, 効力, 意味, 真意, 有効性, 要因, 実施, 施行, 動き, 法的効力, 拘束力, 兵力, 軍隊, 軍, 部隊, 軍事力, 軍事行動, 風力, フォース
 be in force （法律などが）施行される, 効力を発揮する
 be put into force 実施される, 施行される, 効力を発生する（=come into force）
 bring ~ into force ~を実施する, 施行する
 come [be brought, enter] into force (and effect) 実施される, 施行される, 効力を発生する[生じる], 発効する
 competitive forces 競争原理
 driving force 原動力, 推進力
 economic force 経済力, 経済勢力
 field sales force 外務員, 外交販売員
 force and effect 効力, 有効
 force majeure 不可抗力, 天災
 fundamental force ファンダメンタルズ要因
 guiding force 推進力, 指針
 in force 実施中の, 施行されて, 有効で, 大勢で, 大挙して
 join forces with ~と協力する, ~と力を合わせる, ~と連携する, ~と提携する, ~と一丸となる
 labor force 労働力, 全従業員
 leave the force 退職する
 life insurance in force 生命保険の保有契約高
 market forces 市場の力, 市場諸力, 市場要因, 市場原理, 需給関係
 of no force 効力がない 無効の
 open-market forces 市場原理
 political force 政治力, 政治勢力
 productive force 販売力
 protectionist forces 保護主義勢力 （⇒bulwark）
 put [carry] into force 実施する, 施行する
 sales force 販売員, 販売要員, 販売力
 task force 対策委員会, 対策本部, 専門委員会, 専門調査団, 特殊任務を持つ機動部隊, タスク・フォース
 technical force テクニカル要因
 the force of economic events 経済力
 the force of the law 法律の効力, 法の拘束力
 work force 労働力, 従業員, 労働者, 人員（=workforce）

◆Housing investment, a driving force for the U.S. economy until recently, has shown signs of a slowdown. 最近まで米景気を牽引してきた住宅投資に、減速感が見られる。◆The buying in the Tokyo stock market is overseas institutional investors. 東京株式市場での買いの主役は、海外の機関投資家だ。◆The law on the identification of bank account holders was put into force in January 2003. 銀行口座名義人の本人確認に関する法律（本人確認法）は、2003年1月に施行された。◆Whole life insurance means life insurance under which coverage remains in force during the insured's entire lifetime, provided premiums are paid as specified in the policy. 終身保険は、保険契約に明記されている保険料が支払われているかぎり、保障が被保険者の全生涯にわたって有効な生命保険を意味する。

forced （形）強制的な, 無理な, 不自然な
 forced auction 強制競売
 forced conversion 強制転換
 forced covering 理詰め買い
 forced currency 強制通貨
 forced deposit 強制預金
 forced exchange 強制交換
 forced frugality 強制貯蓄
 forced insurance 強制保険
 forced liquidation 強制破産, 強制清算（=involuntary liquidation）
 forced loan 強制公債
 forced market （株式の）腕力相場, 人為相場
 forced sale [selling] 投げ売り, 強制売買[売却], 株式の強制処分, 競売処分, 公売, 競売
 forced saving program 強制貯蓄制度
 forced savings 強制貯蓄

forecast （動）予測する, 予想する, 見通する
◆All of the seven major banking groups forecast that bad loan disposal at the end of March next year will be smaller than their net operating profits. 大手銀行・金融7グループ各行の業績予想では、来年3月期の不良債権処理額はいずれも業務純益の範囲内になる見込みだ。

forecast （名）予測, 見通し, 予知, 予見, 予想, 予報, 判断（=forecasting; ⇒earnings forecast, full-year (earnings) forecast, growth forecast, income forecast）
 bearish forecast 弱気の見通し
 bond yield forecast 債券利回り予想
 business forecast 景気予測, 景気見通し, 業績見通し, 業績予測, 経営予測
 cash forecast 資金予測, 見積り現金収支（=forecast of cash）
 company forecasts 会社予想
 consensus forecast コンセンサス予想, コンセンサス予測, 市場予想
 demand forecast 需要予測
 earlier forecast 当初予想, 前回の予想[見通し]
 earnings forecast 業績予想, 収益予想, 利益予想
 economic forecast [forecasting] 経済予測, 経済見通し, 景気予測, 景気見通し, 景気判断
 financial forecast 財務予想, 財政予想, 財務見通し, 業績予想[予測], 業績見通し
 forecast budget 予測予算
 forecast excess returns 予想超過収益率
 forecast for the U.S. economy 米景気予測, 米景気判断
 forecast of cash 資金予測, 見積り現金収支（=cash forecast）
 forecast transaction 予定取引
 full-year earnings forecast 通期業績予想
 growth forecast 成長見通し, 伸び率見通し（=growth prospect）
 half-year net profit forecast 半期純利益予想
 initial forecast 当初予想（⇒consolidated after-tax profit）
 operating profit forecast 営業利益予想, 営業利益見通し
 profit forecast 利益予想, 収益見通し, 業績予想

revise one's forecast of one's half-year consolidated after-tax profit　中間決算の連結税引き後利益予想を修正する　(⇒consolidated after-tax profit)
sales forecast　売上高の見通し,売上高予測,予想売上高,販売予測　(=forecast of sales)
◆Goldman Sachs lowered its forecast for U.S. growth in 2011 on signs that the U.S. economic recovery lost momentum. 米金融大手のゴールドマン・サックスは、米景気回復減速の兆しを受けて、2011年の米国の成長見通しを下方修正した。
◆The bank raised its full-year earnings forecast by a third because of fewer bad-loan costs. 同行は、不良債権処理費用(不良債権の処理損失)が予想より少なかったため、通期業績予想を三分の一引き上げた。
◆The company lowered its half-year net profit forecast. 同社は、半期純利益予想を引き下げた。
◆The company lowered its operating profit 62 percent to ¥50 billion from the earlier forecast for ¥130 billion. 同社は、営業利益見通しを前回発表の13,00億円から500億円に62％下方修正した。
◆The U.S. Federal Reserve Board significantly lowered its forecast for the U.S. economy. 米連邦準備制度理事会(FRB)は、米景気判断を大幅に下方修正した。
◆Up until last year, business forecasts were gloomy due to prolonged deflation. 昨年までは、長引くデフレで景気見通しが暗かった。

forecast for economic growth　経済成長見通し,経済成長予測,経済成長率見通し
◆The Asian Development Bank trimmed its 2011 forecast for economic growth for 45 developing countries or newly industrializing Asian countries, excluding Japan. アジア開発銀行(ADB)は、日本などを除くアジア太平洋45か国・地域の2011年の国内総生産(GDP)成長率見通しを、下方修正した。

forecast of prices　物価展望
◆This is the economic outlook for this fiscal year as seen by the Bank of Japan in its April forecast of prices. これが、日銀の4月の物価展望で日銀が示した今年度の経済見通しだ。

forecast rate of real GDP　実質GDP(国内総生産)の成長率見通し
◆The sudden economic downturn since the autumn has forced the government to drastically lower the forecast rate of real GDP in fiscal 2009. 秋以降の急速な景気悪化で、政府は2009年度の実質国内総生産(GDP)成長率見通しを大幅に引き下げざるを得なかった。

foreclose　(動)(抵当物に)担保権[抵当権]を実行する[行使する],担保権を行使する,(抵当物を)抵当流れ処分にする,取立て手続きを取る
foreclose collateral for a loan　貸出金[ローン]の担保権を行使する
foreclose down　後順位抵当権を消滅させる
foreclose (on) a mortgage　抵当物件を処分する
foreclose on posted collateral　提供された担保[抵当]について担保権[抵当権]を実行する
foreclosed asset　担保権[抵当権]実行資産,担保権を行使して取得した資産
foreclosed property　抵当権実行不動産,抵当権を行使して取得した資産,質流れ物件

foreclosure　(名)(住宅などの)差し押さえ,抵当流れ,質流れ,抵当権の請戻し権喪失,担保権[抵当権]の実行,担保権[抵当権]行使,物的担保実行手続き
　(⇒home foreclosure, mortgage foreclosure)
foreclosure of a mortgage　抵当物の差し押さえ
foreclosure of security　担保権[抵当権]の実行
foreclosure proceedings　担保権実行手続き
foreclosure value　抵当物処分価格
home foreclosure　住宅の差し押さえ,住宅ローンの焦げ付き[貸倒れ]
in-substance foreclosure　実質的な担保権行使
mortgage foreclosure　抵当物の差し押さえ,住宅の差し押さえ,抵当流れ
　(=foreclosure of a mortgage)
◆Bankruptcies and mortgage foreclosures are still rising. 破産や住宅ローンの焦げ付き[抵当流れ]は、まだ増え続けている。
◆Mortgage delinquencies and foreclosures are increasing. 住宅ローンの返済遅延や焦げ付きが、増加している[住宅の差し押さえや住宅ローンの延滞件数が、増加している]。

foreign　(形)外国の,海外の,他国の,外国産の,外国行きの,外国人の,対外の,対外的な,対外～,管轄外の,法適用外の,無縁の,無関係の,異質な,有害な
foreign aid　対外援助
foreign bond　外債,外国債券
foreign borrowings　外貨建て債務,対外借入れ
foreign business income　海外事業所得,外国での事業所得
foreign capital　外資,外国資本
foreign cash reserves　外貨準備高,外貨準備　(=foreign currency reserves, foreign reserves)
foreign corporation　外国法人,外国企業
Foreign Corrupt Practices Act　米国の海外不正支払い防止法,海外不正行為防止法
foreign debt　対外債務,外貨債務,外貨建て負債
foreign debt servicing　対外債務の返済,外貨債務の返済
foreign demand　外需,海外需要
foreign entity　在外事業体
foreign financing　対外借入れ
foreign investment fund　海外投資ファンド,海外ファンド
foreign investor　外国投資家,海外投資家,外資
foreign ownership　外国人持ち株比率,外国人保有比率,外国資本の所有
foreign reserve currency　外貨準備のための通貨

foreign assets　海外資産,外国資産,対外資産,在外資産,外貨建て資産(日本の対外資産は、日本の政府、企業、個人が海外に持つ資産。この対外資産の金額から、外国の政府、企業、個人が日本に持つ資産(対外負債)の金額を差し引くと、「対外純資産」となる)
cumulative ownership of foreign assets　対外資産の累計額
gross foreign assets　海外資産の総額,対外資産残高
net acquisition of foreign assets　対外資産の純増
net foreign assets　対外純資産,海外純資産,国外資産
SEC-required disclosure of foreign assets　国外資産に関するSEC(米証券取引委員会)の開示要求
◆Gross foreign assets held by Japanese in the form of direct investment, securities investment, financial derivatives, loans and export credits, deposits, other investments and official foreign reserves came to ¥379.78 trillion. 直接投資、証券投資、金融派生商品、貸付け金や輸出信用、預金その他の投資と政府の外貨準備高の形で日本の政府や企業、個人が保有する海外資産の総額(対外資産残高)は、379兆7,800億円に達した。
◆Japan's foreign assets include investment in companies, securities, loans and savings Japanese made abroad as well as the nation's foreign reserves. 日本の対外資産には日本人(日本の政府・企業・個人)が海外で行った企業や有価証券に対する投資、融資や貯蓄のほか、日本の外貨準備高などが含まれる。
◆Japan's net foreign assets, or the difference between assets and liabilities overseas, rose 16 percent from a year earlier to a record ¥250.2 trillion at the end of 2007. 2007年末の日本の対外純資産(日本の対外資産と対外負債との差額)は、前年末比16％増の250兆2,000億円で過去最高となった。
◆The rise in foreign assets held by Japanese was mainly caused by an increase in direct and securities investment. 日本の政府・企業・個人が保有する対外資産の増加は、主に直

接・証券投資の伸びによるものだった。

foreign bank　外国銀行, 外資系銀行, 外銀, 他店, 他行
◆A sizable number of foreign banks and securities companies short-sold stocks. かなりの数の外銀と外証が、株の空売りを進めた。◆M2 consists of cash in circulation, demand and time deposits, as well as certificates of deposits at domestic banks, including the central bank and Japanese branches of foreign banks. M2は、現金通貨と要求払い預金、定期性預金のほか、国内銀行（日本銀行と外国銀行の日本支店を含む）の譲渡性預金（CD）から成る。◆The Bank of Tokyo-Mitsubishi UFJ will work together with foreign banks to extend 117 million Canadian dollars in joint loans to a mega solar power plant construction. 三菱東京UFJ銀行は、外銀数行の主幹事銀行として[外銀数行と連携して]、カナダの大型太陽光発電所（メガソーラー）建設事業に1億1,700万カナダ・ドルを協調融資する。

foreign bankers　外国の銀行関係者
◆Representatives of China's State Administration of Foreign Exchange met with foreign bankers and discussed the issue of China's review of its eurozone debt holdings. 中国の国家外貨管理局の代表が、外国の複数の銀行関係者と会合を持って、中国によるユーロ圏の国債保有見直し問題を協議した。

foreign bond　外債, 外国債, 外国債券　(⇒exchange rate movements, fund名詞, yen-denominated foreign bond)
◆The central bank should introduce an inflationary target to lift prices to a predetermined level, or weaken the yen by buying foreign bonds. 日銀は、一定の水準まで物価を引き上げるためのインフレ目標の導入や、外債の購入による円安誘導を行うべきである。◆The purchase of foreign bonds is considered an effective method to weaken the yen. 外債の購入は、円安誘導効果を持つとされている。

foreign bond investment product　外債の金融商品
◆The bank has jointly developed with American International Group Inc. a foreign bond investment product targeting retired baby boomers. 同行が、団塊の世代の定年退職者をターゲットにした外債の金融商品を、米保険最大手のAIGグループと共同開発した。

foreign capital　外資, 外国資本

foreign capital financial group　外資系金融グループ
◆This is the first time for major commercial banks to form a comprehensive tie-up with a foreign capital financial group. 大手都銀が外資系金融グループと包括提携するのは、今回が初めてだ。

foreign capital inflows　外資流入, 外国からの資金流入, 外貨の流動性　(=foreign inflows)
◆The shortage of foreign capital inflows saw Mexico on the verge of default and bankruptcy in early 1995. 外貨の流動性不足から、メキシコは1995年の初めには債務不履行と倒産の危機に見舞われた。

foreign currency　外貨, 外国通貨
　accounting for foreign currency transactions　外貨換算会計
　appreciation of foreign currency　外貨高
　bill in foreign currency（money）　外貨手形
　claim in foreign currency　外貨建て債権
　designated deposits in foreign currency　外貨指定預金
　earn foreign currency　外貨を稼ぐ
　exchange rate in foreign currency　外貨建て相場
　foreign currency assets　外貨建て資産
　foreign currency bill　外貨手形
　foreign currency bills receivable　外貨取立て外国為替
　foreign currency bond　外貨債, 外貨建て債
　foreign currency borrowings　外貨建て借入れ, 外貨建て借入金
　foreign currency claims　外貨建て債権
　foreign currency debt　外債, 外貨債務
　foreign currency-denominated securities　外貨建て債
　foreign currency earnings　外貨収益, 外貨建て収益
　foreign currency exposure　為替リスク
　foreign currency fluctuation　為替相場の変動
　foreign currency holdings　外貨保有高, 保有外貨
　foreign currency issue　外貨建て債券
　foreign currency loan　外貨貸し, 外貨建て借入金, 外貨ローン
　foreign currency obligations　外貨建て負債, 外貨建て債務
　foreign currency position　外貨収支, 外貨ポジション
　foreign currency product　為替商品
　foreign currency receivables and payables　外貨建て債権債務
　foreign currency restrictions　外貨規制
　foreign currency risks　為替リスク
　foreign currency swap　外貨スワップ
　foreign currency transaction　外貨建て取引
　shortage of foreign currency　外貨不足
◆An international coalition to monitor the movement of goods, funds and personnel of North Korea has made it difficult for Pyongyang to earn foreign currency by selling weapons and others. 北朝鮮のモノ、カネと人の動きを監視する国際連携で、同国は武器売却などによる外貨稼ぎが困難になっている。◆The brokerage's main services for individual customers will be asset management advisory services, focusing on the sale of products such as investment trust funds that invest in foreign equities, and money market funds denominated in foreign currencies. 同証券会社は、株式の主な個人顧客向け（売買仲介）業務として、外国株を組み込んだ投資信託や外貨建てMMF（マネー・マーケット・ファンド）などの商品の販売を中心に、資産運用顧問業務を展開する方針だ。◆The interest rates of the Australian dollar-denominated deposit service are relatively high among major foreign currencies. 主要外国通貨のうち、豪ドル建て預金サービスの金利は比較的高い。◆We must pay attention to commission fees when we choose to deposit foreign currencies. 外貨預金を選ぶときは、為替手数料に注意しなければならない。

foreign currency account　外貨預金口座
◆Yen can be exchanged for foreign currencies and deposited in foreign currency accounts at most major banks. 円は、大半の大手銀行で外貨と替えて外貨預金口座に預け入れることができる。

foreign currency-denominated bond　外貨建て債券
◆Stocks and foreign currency-denominated bonds are financial products which may reduce the principal. 株式や外貨建て債券は、元本割れの恐れがある金融商品だ。

foreign currency deposit　外貨預金, 外貨預託
　foreign currency deposit system　外貨預託制度
　foreign currency deposits held by individuals in Japanese banks　国内銀行の個人向け外貨預金残高, 国内銀行に個人が保有している外貨預金
　foreign currency wholesale deposits　外貨大口預金
◆Commission rates in foreign currency deposits vary among foreign currencies or among financial institutions. 外貨預金での為替手数料の料率は、外国通貨や金融機関で異なる。◆Depending on moves in foreign exchange markets, there is a risk we may lose initial investments in foreign currency deposits. 為替相場の動き次第で、外貨預金では初期投資額を割り込むリスクがある。◆In foreign currency deposits, commission fees are needed when the yen is exchanged into a foreign currency and when the foreign currency is exchanged backed in yen. 外貨預金では、円を外貨に替えるときと、外貨を円に戻すときに、為替手数料が必要になる。◆In foreign currency deposits, depositors can earn profits by exchanging

their foreign currency deposits into yen when the yen's value against major foreign currencies falls. 外貨預金では、主要外貨に対して円相場が下落した時点で預金者が外貨預金を円に戻せば、利益を上げる[儲ける]ことができる。◆In the case of foreign currency deposits by the U.S. dollar, many online banks charge about ¥0.25 in commission per dollar at the time of deposits and withdrawals. 米ドルによる外貨預金の場合、ネット銀行の多くは、預け入れ時と解約時に1ドルに付き25銭程度の手数料を取る。◆In the case of foreign currency deposits, depositors can invest in foreign currencies such as British pound, Swiss franc and Australian dollar as well as the U.S. dollar and euro. 外貨預金の場合、預金者は、米ドルやユーロのほかに英ポンド、スイス・フランや豪ドルなどにも投資することができる。◆In the case of foreign currency deposits, losses may balloon if the yen appreciates further and may cause a loss of principal. 外貨預金の場合、円高がさらに進めば損失が膨らみ、元本割れになる恐れもある。◆It's difficult to offset losses from further appreciation of the yen with interest as interest rates in many foreign currency deposits are low. 外貨建て預金の多くは金利が低いので、円高進行による損失分を利息で相殺する[取り戻す]のは難しい。◆Some major banks lower their commission rates of foreign currency deposits if depositors make transactions via online accounts. 外貨預金の預金者がネット口座経由で取引をする場合、一部の大手銀行は、外貨預金の手数料[為替手数料]の料率を引き下げている。◆The exchange rate was the same at the time of deposit and withdrawal in a foreign currency deposit. 外貨預金で、為替相場は預け入れ時と解約時で同じだった。

foreign currency deposit account 外貨預金勘定, 外貨預金口座
◆Amid the continued yen's historically high levels, increasing numbers of people are opening foreign currency deposit accounts. 歴史的な円高水準が続くなか、外貨預金口座を設ける人が増えている。◆Foreign currency deposit accounts carry a degree of risk. 外貨預金口座には、ある程度リスクも伴う。◆Increasing numbers of people are opening foreign currency deposit accounts by taking advantage of the yen's historically high levels. 歴史的な円高水準水準を利用して、外貨預金を始める人が増えている。

foreign currency depositor 外貨預金者
◆The foreign currency depositor planned to withdraw the money when the yen's value fell. この外貨預金者は、円安になったら解約するつもりだった。

foreign currency exchange contract 外国為替契約, 外国為替予約
(=foreign exchange contract; ⇒commitment)
◆We enter into foreign currency exchange contracts, including forward, option and swap contracts, to manage our exposure to changes in currency exchange rates, principally Canadian dollars and Japanese yen. 当社は、主にカナダ・ドルと円などの通貨の為替レート変動リスクを管理するため、先物、オプションおよびスワップ契約などの外国為替契約を結んでいます。

foreign currency market 外国為替市場
(=foreign exchange market)
◆Out of a sense of relief, dollar-selling pressure has eased on the foreign currency markets. 安堵（あんど）感から、外国為替市場では、ドル売り圧力が弱まった。

foreign currency reserves 外貨準備, 外貨準備高
(⇒foreign exchange reserves)
◆Thanks to these policy efforts, foreign currency reserves of East Asian countries have increased. これらの政策努力のおかげで、東アジア諸国の外貨準備高が増えた。

foreign currency translation 外貨換算, 外貨換算会計, 外貨換算差額
accumulated foreign currency translation adjustments 外貨換算修正
foreign currency translation adjustment 外貨換算調整, 外貨換算調整勘定
foreign currency translation gains 外貨換算差益
foreign currency translation losses 外貨換算差損

foreign debt 対外債務
foreign debt issue 外債
foreign debt obligations 対外債務
foreign debt position 対外債務状況
foreign debt servicing 外貨債務の返済
◆U.S. president Bush turned to former Secretary of State James Baker for the complex task of winning an international agreement on reducing Iraq's foreign debt. ブッシュ米大統領は、イラクの対外債務削減に関する国際合意を取り付ける複雑な仕事の担い手として、ジェームズ・ベーカー元国務長官に白羽の矢を立てた。

foreign debt repayments 対外債務の返済, 対外債務の返済額
◆The Russian government has demanded cuts in or waivers for its foreign debt repayments. ロシア政府は、対外債務返済の減免を要求している。

foreign direct investment 外国からの直接投資, 対内直接投資, 対外直接投資, FDI (⇒FDI)
◆The strong FDI (foreign direct investment) inflows have helped to swell China's foreign exchange reserves. 海外からの直接投資資金の流入拡大で、中国の外貨準備高が増加した。

foreign equities 外国株
◆The brokerage's main services for individual customers will be asset management advisory services, focusing on the sale of products such as investment trust funds that invest in foreign equities, and money market funds denominated in foreign currencies. 同証券会社は、株式の主な個人顧客向け（売買仲介）業務として、外国株を組み込んだ投資信託や外貨建てMMF（マネー・マーケット・ファンド）などの商品の販売を中心に、資産運用顧問業務を展開する方針だ。

foreign exchange 外国為替, 外国為替取引, 為替差損益, 外貨 (=forex)
foreign exchange account 外国為替勘定
foreign exchange actual balance [position] 外国為替直物持ち高
foreign exchange allocation 外貨資金割当, 外資割当
foreign exchange allocation system 外貨資金割当制度
Foreign Exchange and Foreign Trade Control Law 外国為替及び外国貿易管理法, 外為管理法, 外為法
Foreign exchange application 外国為替申し込み, 外国為替申告
foreign exchange bank 外国為替銀行
foreign exchange bill 外国為替手形
foreign exchange (bill) bought 買入れ外国為替, 買取り外国為替
foreign exchange broker 外国為替ブローカー[仲買い業], 為替仲介人, 為替ブローカー
foreign exchange budget 外国為替予算, 外貨予算
foreign exchange business 外国為替業務
foreign exchange buying 外国為替購入
foreign exchange centralization system 外貨集中制度
foreign exchange concentration clearing system 為替集中決済制度
foreign exchange concentration system 外国為替集中制度
foreign exchange contract 外国為替契約, 外国為替予約
(=foreign currency exchange contract)
foreign exchange control 外国為替管理, 為替制限
(foreign exchange restriction)

Foreign Exchange Control Law　外国為替及び外国貿易管理法, 外為管理法
foreign exchange control system　外国為替管理制度
foreign exchange conversion　外国為替換算
foreign exchange conversion rate　外国為替換算率
foreign exchange department　外国為替部門
foreign exchange difficulties　外国為替難
foreign exchange draft　外国為替手形
（=foreign draft of exchange）
foreign exchange earner　外国為替取得者
foreign exchange earnings　外国為替収入, 外貨収入
foreign exchange financing　外貨金融
foreign exchange fund　外国為替資金
foreign exchange gain　為替差益
foreign exchange holding restriction system　外貨集中制度
foreign exchange operation　外国為替操作, 為替業務
foreign exchange position　外国為替持ち高, 外為ポジション
foreign exchange profit　為替差損
foreign exchange quotations　為替相場表
foreign exchange receipts　外国為替収入, 外国為替受取り高
foreign exchange restriction [control]　為替制限
Foreign Exchange Sale [Purchase] Ticket　外国為替取引メモ
Foreign Exchange Section　外国課
foreign exchange settlement　外貨決済, 為替決済
foreign exchange settlement system　為替決済システム
foreign exchange sold　売渡し外国為替
foreign exchange trader　外国為替トレーダー
foreign exchange trading [dealing]　外国為替取引
foreign exchange transaction　為替取引
◆A portion of the increase in R&D spending was also due to the unfavorable impact of foreign exchange on R&D expenditures most of which are incurred in Canada. 研究開発費の大半はカナダで発生しているため、米ドル為替相場の下落による影響も研究開発費拡大の一因であった。◆Ahead of the current vigorous stock market, there are still some hurdles such as increasing tension in Iraq and foreign exchange issues. 活発な株式市場の先行きには、まだイラク情勢の緊迫化や為替問題などのハードルがある。

Foreign Exchange and Foreign Trade Law　外国為替及び外国貿易法, 外為法　（⇒cash transfer）
◆The revised Foreign Exchange and Foreign Trade Law allows Japan to suspend or limit remittances and trade with North Korea. 改正外国為替及び外国貿易法によると、北朝鮮に関して日本は送金や貿易を停止・制限することができる。

foreign exchange dealer　為替ディーラー, 為替担当者
◆The telephone of a foreign exchange dealer at a bank did not stop ringing with demands from exporters for forward exchange contracts. ある銀行の為替担当者の電話は、輸出企業からの為替予約注文で鳴り止まなかった。

foreign exchange fluctuations　為替相場の変動
◆Foreign exchange fluctuations are affected not only by economic fundamentals, but also by psychological factors. 為替相場の変動は、経済のファンダメンタルズだけでなく、心理的な要因による影響をも受ける。

foreign exchange loss　為替差損
（⇒forward contract）
◆Japanese automakers are considering hiking prices for their new models to be released in the U.S. market in and after September to compensate for potential foreign exchange losses. 日本の自動車メーカー各社は、将来の為替差損を穴埋めするため、9月以降に米国市場に投入する新型車の値上げを検討している。

foreign exchange market　外国為替市場, 為替相場
（=currency market; ⇒reflationary policy）
disarray in the foreign exchange market　為替相場の混乱
intervene in the foreign exchange markets　外国為替市場に介入する
the New York foreign exchange market　ニューヨーク外国為替市場
the Tokyo foreign exchange market　東京外国為替市場
◆Amid the European fiscal and financial crisis, plunges on the world's stock markets and wild fluctuations in foreign exchange markets may continue. 欧州の財政・金融危機を受けて、世界同時株安と為替市場の乱高下は今後も続く可能性がある。◆China intervenes in the foreign exchange markets to fix the yuan-dollar exchange rate. 中国は、外国為替市場に介入して[為替介入して]元・ドル・レートを固定している。◆Depending on moves in foreign exchange markets, there is a risk we may lose initial investments in foreign currency deposits. 為替相場の動き次第で、外貨預金では初期投資額を割り込むリスクがある。◆On Aug. 31, 2011, the yen rose to the ¥76.50 level against the U.S. dollar in the Tokyo foreign exchange market, close to the postwar record of ¥75.95 registered on Aug. 19. 2011年8月31日の東京外国為替市場の円相場は、1ドル＝76円50銭台まで上昇し、8月19日に付けた戦後最高値の75円95銭に近づいた。◆On the foreign exchange market, there has been no halt to selling pressure on the euro due to concern about the financial crisis in Europe. 外国為替市場では、欧州の金融危機を懸念して、ユーロ売り圧力が止まらない展開となっている。◆The Bank of Japan asked the Federal Reserve Bank of New York to intervene in the New York foreign exchange market on its behalf through yen-selling, dollar-buying operations for the first time in 15 months. 日銀は、1年3か月ぶりにニューヨーク連銀に委託して、ニューヨーク外国為替市場で円売り・ドル買いの介入に踏み切った。◆The euro plummeted to the ¥100 level on the foreign exchange market, hitting a 10 year low. 外国為替市場では、ユーロが1ユーロ＝100円台まで急落して、10年ぶりの低水準[10年ぶりの円高・ユーロ安水準]となった。◆The Fed's monetary easing is a factor causing disarray in the foreign exchange markets. 米連邦準備制度理事会（FRB）[米中央銀行]の金融緩和が、為替相場混乱[為替混乱]の原因だ。◆The Fed's policy of quantitative easing foments chaos in foreign exchange markets. 米連邦準備制度理事会（FRB）[米国の中央銀行]の量的緩和政策は、為替相場[為替レート]の変動を招いている。◆The Japanese currency's value vis-a-vis the U.S. dollar entered the ¥82 range in foreign exchange markets around the world. 円の対米ドル相場は、内外の外国為替市場で1ドル＝82円台をつけた。

foreign exchange rate　外国為替レート, 外国為替相場, 為替相場, 為替レート
forward foreign exchange rate　先物予約レート
the forecast of foreign exchange rates　為替相場予測
the problems of foreign exchange rates　為替相場をめぐる問題
the realignment of foreign exchange rates　為替レートの調整
the unification of foreign exchange rates　為替レートの一本化
◆An excessive trade deficit should be corrected through the realignment of foreign exchange rates. 過度の貿易赤字は、為替レートの調整によって是正しなければならない。◆The global economic imbalance lies behind the problems of foreign exchange rates. 為替相場をめぐる問題の背景には、世界経済の不均衡問題がある。

foreign exchange reserves　外貨準備高, 外貨準備
(=foreign currency reserves, foreign reserves, forex reserves; ⇒foreign direct investment, foreign reserves, forex reserves, mix)
◆Japan's foreign exchange reserves consist mainly of securities and deposits denominated in foreign currencies, gold, IMF reserve positions and special drawing rights. 日本の外貨準備高の主な内訳は、外貨建て債、外貨預金、金のほか、IMF（国際通貨基金）の準備ポジションと特別引出し権である。◆The nation's foreign exchange reserves climbed to a record $840.09 billion at the end of November. 日本の11月末時点の外貨準備高は、過去最高の8,400億9,000万ドルに増加した。

foreign exchange risk　外国為替リスク, 為替リスク
diversify against foreign exchange risk　為替リスクを分散する
ease foreign exchange risks　為替リスクを軽減する

foreign exchange trading company　為替取引の会社
◆Dealers are watching monitors at a foreign exchange trading company. 為替取引の会社では、ディーラーたちがモニターを注視している。

foreign financial group　海外金融グループ

foreign fund　外国投信, 外国ファンド, 海外ファンド, 他人資本, 外国債
◆The foreign funds purchased the convertible bonds at prices equivalent to ¥25 per share. 海外ファンドは、1株25円で転換社債を引き受けた。

foreign funds　海外資金, 外国資金, 外資（foreign capital）
foreign funds control　外国資金統制
influx of foreign funds　海外資金の流入, 海外からの資金流入
◆Higher interest rates would accelerate the influx of foreign funds. 利上げ［金利の引上げ］は、海外からの資金流入を加速することになる。

foreign government bond　外国国債, 外国債
◆Of the amount of investment, about a half was invested in foreign government bonds with low credit ratings. この投資額のうち約半分は、格付けの低い外国債に充てていた。◆The bank plans to deal with foreign government bonds at all of its outlets. 同行は、全店舗で外国国債を扱う方針だ。

foreign investment　外国・海外からの投資, 外国資本の投資, 対内投資, 対外投資
◆Bush emphasized he would keep the dollar strong in order to attract foreign investment to the United States. ブッシュ大統領は、外国資本の対米投資を促すため強いドル政策の堅持を強調した。◆Some restrictions must be imposed on foreign investment in major domestic airport operations. 国内空港の運営に対する外国からの投資には、ある程度、制限を設ける必要がある。◆The bill is intended to promote foreign investment in Japan. 同法案は、外国資本の対日投資を促すのが狙いだ。◆The government plans to translate laws such as the Civil Code and the Commercial Code into English in a bid to facilitate foreign investments and help domestic firms expand their international business activities. 政府は、外国からの投資促進や国内企業の国際ビジネス支援のため、民法や商法などの法律の英訳を行う方針だ。

foreign investment and loan program　海外投融資プログラム, 海外融資投資
◆A plan to end the current freeze on investment and loan programs sponsored by the JICA is included in the government's new growth strategy. 政府の新成長戦略には、現在凍結されている国際協力機構（JICA）による海外投融資プログラムを再開する計画が盛り込まれている。

foreign investment fund　海外投資ファンド, 海外ファンド　（⇒finance動詞）
◆Different from high-profile hedge funds, the founders and investment conditions of these foreign investment funds are not clear. 著名なヘッジ・ファンドと異なって、これらの海外投資ファンドの設立者や資金の運用実態は、はっきりしない。◆The collapse of Dai-ichi Kaden on April 16 was the result of speculation by foreign investment funds of a dubious nature. 4月16日の第一家電の経営破たんは、実態不明の海外投資ファンドの投機によるものであった［海外ファンドの投機に食い荒らされた末路であった］。

foreign investor　外国投資家, 海外投資家, 外資
◆A recent decline in bullish sentiment among foreign investors in the Japanese stock market has caused domestic stock prices to decline. 外国人投資家の間で日本の株式市場の強気の地合いが［日本の株式市場を支えていた外国人投資家の勢いが］ここに来て弱まり、国内株価が軟調となっている。◆After the briefing for foreign investors, a fund manager showed interest in investing in Japanese government bonds. 海外投資家向け説明会の後、あるファンド・マネージャーが日本国債への投資に関心を示した。◆Foreign investors have pulled their money out and the entire domestic market has shrunk. 海外の投資家が資金を引き揚げ、国内市場全体が縮小した。◆Foreign investors stepped up their purchase of Japanese stocks. 外国人投資家の日本株買いが活発化した。◆In the joint venture with an Indian investment bank, Tokio Marine Holdings Inc. put up about 26%, the maximum a foreign investor is allowed in an Indian company, of the new firm's capital. インドの投資銀行との合弁事業で、東京海上ホールディングスは、新会社の資本金の約26%（外資の持ち分比率の上限）を出資した。

foreign liabilities　対外負債
◆Japan's foreign liabilities, or the investment foreigners made in Japan, grew 5 percent to a record ¥360.3 trillion in 2007. 2007年の日本の対外負債（外国人が日本で行った投資）は、前年比5%増の360兆3,000億円で過去最高となった。

foreign market　海外市場
◆The yen is surging, hitting a 15 year high in the ¥83 range against the U.S. dollar on foreign markets. 海外市場で15年ぶりに1ドル＝83円台を付けるなど、円が急上昇している。

Foreign Non-Life Insurance Association of Japan　外国損害保険協会

foreign-owned company　外資系企業
◆In 1997, Beijing abolished laws that restricted imports and exports by foreign-owned companies in China. 1997年に中国政府は、中国国内の外資系企業の輸出入業務を制限する法律（貿易権制度）を廃止した。

foreign reserves　外貨準備高, 外貨準備　（=foreign currency reserves, foreign exchange reserves, forex reserves; ⇒financial derivatives, foreign exchange reserves）
◆At present, about 61 percent of foreign reserves are denominated in dollars. 現在、外貨準備の61%がドル建てとなっている。◆Japan's foreign assets include investment in companies, securities, loans and savings Japanese made abroad as well as the nation's foreign reserves. 日本の対外資産には日本人（日本の政府・企業・個人）が海外で行った企業や有価証券に対する投資、融資や貯蓄のほか、日本の外貨準備高などが含まれる。◆South Korean foreign reserves slipped to $305 billion in May 2011 from the record $307 billion logged in April. 韓国の2011年5月の外貨準備高は、4月に記録した過去最高の3,070億ドルから3,050億ドルに減少した。◆Triggered by political confusion in Chiapas, capital flight spread even among Mexican residents, reducing the country's foreign reserves to $10.5 billion. チアパス州での政治混乱を引き金に、資本逃避はメキシコの居住者にまで及び、メキシコの外貨準備は105億ドルに減少した。

Foreign Section of the Tokyo Stock Exchange　東京証券取引所外国部, 東証外国部　（=TSE's Foreign Section）

◆Aktiebolaget Volvo was delisted from the Foreign Section of the Tokyo Stock Exchange following the Swedish automaker's request. スウェーデンの自動車メーカー、アクティエボラゲート・ボルボの要請により、東京証券取引所は同社の外国部上場を廃止した。

foreign trade insurance service 貿易保険事業, 貿易保険業務
◆Nippon Export and Investment Insurance (NEXI) was established in 2001 to provide foreign trade and investment insurance services. 独立行政法人の日本貿易保険は、貿易保険事業と対外投資保険事業を提供するため、2001年に設立された。

forestall (動)～を回避する,～を予防する,～を阻止する,～を未然に防ぐ,～の機先を制する,～を出し抜く,(計画の)裏をかく,(商品を)買い占める
◆In order to forestall hostile takeover bids, companies should raise their corporate value. 敵対的TOB（株式公開買付けによる企業買収）を未然に防ぐには、企業が企業価値を高めなければならない。◆There was no choice other than to pass the financial bailout bill to forestall a full-blown financial crisis. 全面的な金融危機を回避するには、金融安定化法案を可決せざるを得なかった。

forex (名)為替, 外国為替, 為替相場 (forex rate), フォレックス, FX (⇒foreign exchange)
　average forex rate 平均為替レート
　forex business 為替取引
　　(=foreign exchange transaction, forex trading)
　forex gains 為替差益
　forex intervention 為替介入
　forex interventions 為替介入額
　forex-linked bond [note] 為替リンク債
　forex losses 為替差損
　forex rate 為替相場, 為替レート
　forex risk 為替リスク
　the Forex Club フォーレックス・クラブ（外国為替ディーラーの親睦機関）
　the recent forex moves 最近の為替相場の動き

forex moves 為替相場の動き
◆The recent forex moves have been somewhat one-sided. 最近の為替相場の動きは、一部に片寄った方向をたどっている。

forex reserves 外貨準備高, 外貨準備 (=foreign currency reserves, foreign exchange reserves, foreign reserves; ⇒all-time high)
◆Japan's forex reserves stood at $1.11 trillion at the end of September 2010, hitting a record high. 日本の2010年9月末の外貨準備高は、1兆1,100億ドルで、過去最高となった。

forfeited pledge 質流れ

forfeited share [stock] 失権株, 没収株
　(=unclaimed share)

forfeiting (名)買取り金融的割引, 輸出長期延べ払い手形の償還請求権なし割引, 買取り, 買取り金融, フォーフェイティング

forfeiture (名)(財産, 権利などの)喪失, 没収, 剥奪（はくだつ）, 失権, (契約などの)失効, (特許の)消滅, 罰金, 科料
　forfeiture provisions 失権条項
　nonforfeiture clause 不可没収条項

forged (形)偽の, 変造した, 偽造（ぎぞう）した, ねつ造された
　forged bill [note] 偽札
　forged cash card 偽造キャッシュ・カード, 変造キャッシュ・カード
　forged information 偽情報

forged cash card 偽造キャッシュ・カード
◆According to the Japanese Bankers Association, a total of ¥461 million was stolen in 122 cases using forged cash cards between April and September last year. 全国銀行協会によると、昨年度上半期(4-9月)の偽造キャッシュ・カードによる預金引出し事件は122件で、被害総額は4億6,100万円にのぼった。

forgivable loan 返済免除条件付き融資

forgive (動)許す, 容赦する, 大目に見る, 債権などを放棄する, 債務を免除する
　forgive the entire debt 債務[借金]をすべて免除する
　forgive the entire loan 債権[貸付け]をすべて免除する
◆JAL hopes to repay all of its about ¥319 billion in debt by way of having banks forgive some debts and extend new loans. 日航は、銀行団から債権の一部放棄と新規融資を受けて、債務約3,190億円を全額返済[一括返済]する意向だ。◆The firm's main creditor banks forgave ¥150 billion of the ¥300 billion in loans outstanding to the firm. 同社の主力取引銀行は、同社に対する債権[融資残高]3,000億円のうち1,500億円を放棄した。◆The three main creditor banks will forgive ¥170 billion of the ¥400 billion in loans outstanding to the company. 主力取引銀行3行は、同社に対する債権（融資残高）4,000億円のうち1,700億円を放棄する方針だ。◆To help an insolvent borrower, money must be granted for free, or at least a part of the outstanding debt must be forgiven. 返済不能の借り手を助けるには、ただで資金を与えるか、少なくとも債務残高の一部の減免が必要だ。

forgive a part of the outstanding debt 債務残高の一部を減免する
◆To help an insolvent borrower, money must be granted for free, or at least a part of the outstanding debt must be forgiven. 返済不能の借り手を助けるには、ただで資金を与えるか、少なくとも債務残高の一部の減免が必要だ。

forgive the debt 債務を免除する, 債権を放棄する
◆Banks will not accept future loan requests if they have to forgive the debt. 金融機関が債権放棄をせざるを得ないとなると、金融機関は今後の融資要請には応じないだろう。◆If TEPCO's creditor banks forgive the debts when the utility is not carrying excessive liabilities, lenders will not be able to recover either the principal or interest owed. 東電が債務超過でない時点で東電の債権保有銀行が債権を放棄すると、金融機関は元本を回収できず、金利収入も得られなくなる。

forgiveness (名)（債務などの）免除, （債権などの）放棄, 容赦
　debt forgiveness 債権放棄, 債務の免除, 債務救済
　　(=debt relief, debt waiver, forgiveness of debt, loan forgiveness, loan write-off)
　forgiveness of debt 債務免除, 債権放棄
　forgiveness of liabilities 債務免除
　loan forgiveness 債権放棄, 債務免除
◆The company increased the amount of debt forgiveness by its creditors to ¥98.9 billion from ¥90.9 billion. 同社は、取引金融機関による債務免除額を909億円から989億円に引き上げた。◆The request for loan forgiveness totaling ¥405 billion was made during a meeting convened by Daiei and the IRCJ to explain Daiei's reconstruction plan to creditors. 総額4,050億円の債権放棄の要請は、ダイエーの再建計画を取引銀行に説明するため、ダイエーと産業再生機構が開いた会議で行われた。

forgo [forego] (動)控える, 差し控える, 遠慮する, 止める, 見送る, 断念する, 放棄する
◆The Bank of Japan forwent an increase in its key short-term interest rate. 日本銀行は、短期金利（無担保コール翌日物）の誘導目標引上げを見送った。

form (動)設立する, 組織する, 組成する, 結成する, 作り出す, 築く, 構築する, 形成する, 設定する
　form a new firm [company] 新会社を設立する
　form a portfolio ポートフォリオを構築する
　form a tie-up with ～と提携する, ～と提携に踏み切る

form an underwriting group　引受団を組成する
◆Sanwa Bank and Tokai Bank have merged to form UFJ Bank. 三和銀行と東海銀行が合併して、UFJ銀行が誕生した。

form　(名)書式, 様式, 形, 形式, 形態, 形状, 外形, 外観, 種類, 用紙, 申込み書, 決まり文句, 慣用文, フォーム
application form　申込み用紙, 申込み書式, 出願書式
as a matter of form　形式上　(=in form)
blue form return　青色申告
catalog request form　カタログ請求書
fill in the form　書式に記入する
in due form　正式に, 型どおりに
Lloyd's form　ロイド[ロイズ]書式
long form audit report　長文式監査報告書
proxy form　委任状用紙
request form　請求書
short form bill of lading　略式船荷証券
take form　具体化する, 現れる
take the form of　～の形を取る, ～の形で表される, ～の形で現れる, ～の姿をする～に化ける, ～のようになる
true to form　予想どおり, 例のごとく
◆One way for a company to accomplish long-term financing is through the issuance of long-term debt instruments in the form of bonds. 会社の長期資金調達方法の一つは、社債の形で長期債務証券を発行して行われる。◆Part of the benefits of quantitative easing will take the form of a depreciation of the dollar. 量的緩和の効果の一部は、ドル安の形で現れる。◆Softbank will raise ¥1.28 trillion in the form of syndicated loans from seven financial institutions in Japan, Europe and the United States. ソフトバンクは、国内外の7金融機関から協調融資の形で1兆2,800億円を調達する方針だ。◆The downturn in global financial markets has had a negative impact on insurance products such as single-premium pension insurance policies which are popular as a form of savings. 世界の金融市場の低迷が、貯蓄用[一種の貯蓄]として人気の高い一時払い年金保険などの保険商品に悪影響を及ぼしている。◆The proxy form indicates the number of shares to be voted, including any full shares held for participants in the Employee Stock Purchase Plan. 委任状用紙には、従業員株式購入制度加入者のために保有している株式をすべて含めて、行使される議決権数が記載されています。◆These proposals failed to take form. これらの案は、具体化しなかった。

form a business partnership　業務提携する, 業務提携関係を結ぶ, 業務協力協定を締結する
◆Mizuho Corporate Bank has formed a business partnership with Sberbank of Russia. みずほコーポレート銀行が、ロシアの最大手行ズベルバンク(Sberbank of Russia)と業務協力協定を締結した。◆Sompo Japan Insurance Inc. began selling "SoftBank Kantan Hoken" insurance by forming a business partnership with SoftBank Mobile Corp. 損保保険ジャパンが、ソフトバンクモバイルと業務提携して、「ソフトバンクかんたん保険」の販売を開始した。

form a capital alliance　資本提携する
◆Myojo Foods asked Nissin Food Products to play the part of a white knight by forming a capital alliance to thwart the U.S. investment fund's hostile takeover bid. 米系投資ファンドの敵対的TOB(株式公開買付け)を阻止するため、明星食品は資本提携によるホワイト・ナイト(白馬の騎士)としての明星の支援を日清食品に要請した。

form a capital tie-up　資本提携する
◆NTT DoCoMo Inc. formed a capital tie-up with Internet shopping mall operator Rakuten Inc. in the Internet auction business. NTTドコモが、インターネット・オークション事業で電子商取引大手の楽天[仮想商店街を運営している楽天]と資本提携した

form a comprehensive tie up　包括提携する
◆This is the first time for major commercial banks to form a comprehensive tie-up with a foreign capital financial group. 大手都銀が外資系金融グループと包括提携するのは、今回が初めてだ。

form a joint venture　合弁会社を設立する
◆To increase our presence outside the U.S., we are hiring employees, building plants and forming joint ventures. 米国外での当社の事業基盤を強化するため、当社は従業員の雇用、工場建設や合弁会社の設立に取り組んでいます。

form an alliance　提携関係を結ぶ, 提携関係にある, 提携する
◆The two companies have formed an alliance in investment banking operations. 両社は、投資銀行業務で提携関係を結んでいる[提携関係にある]。

Form 10-K,　様式10-K, フォーム10-K(米国の有価証券報告書の一種)
解説 フォーム(様式)10-Kとは：米国の公開会社(証券取引所上場企業や店頭公開企業など)がSEC(米国証券取引委員会)に提出する財務報告書の様式で、株主向け年次報告書と同じく会計監査済み(audited)のものでなければならない。

Form 10-Q　様式10-Q フォーム10-Q(米国の有価証券報告書の一種で、上場会社がSEC(米国証券取引委員会)に提出する四半期ごとの決算報告書の様式。ただし、この四半期報告書は未監査(unaudited)のものでもよい)

formula　(名)方式, 公式, 書式, 算式, 路線, 処理方法, 解決方法, 解決策, 打開策, 案, 食品の製法, 調理法, フォーミュラ
book building formula　需要予測方式, ブック・ビルディング方式
cost compensation formula　コスト上乗せ方式
development-and-import formula　開発輸入方式
earnings-related formula　給与比例方式
flat rate formula　定額方式
formula investment [investing]　フォーミュラ投資(一定の投資計画に基づく証券・株式の投資)
formula plan　フォーミュラ・プラン(フォーミュラ投資を行う場合の一定の投資計画)
◆By following his predecessor's inflation-fighting formula, the new Fed chairman Ben Bernanke has reassured the market. 米連邦制度理事会(FRB)前議長のインフレ抑制路線を継承して、ベン・バーナンキ新議長は、市場に安心感を与えた。

formulate　(動)策定する, 形成する, 立案する, 案出する, まとめる, 体系化する, 公式化[定式化]する, (製法に基づいて)製造する
formulate a plan　計画を策定する, 計画を立案する
formulate a policy　政策を策定する, 政策[方針]を打ち出す
formulate a strategy　戦略を形成する, 戦略を策定する, 戦略をまとめる
◆Chapter 11 bankruptcy provides for a business to continue operations while formulating a plan to repay its creditors. 米連邦改正破産法11章の破産の規定では、企業は事業を継続する一方、債権者への債務返済計画を策定することができる。

formulation　(名)策定, 形成, 立案, 案出, まとめ, 体系化, 公式化, 表現の仕方, (薬などの)調合, 成分, 薬剤, 化粧品

forum　(名)会議, 公開討論会, 討論の機会, 討論の場, 交流の場, 交流広場, 広場, 裁判所, 法廷, 批判, 裁断, フォーラム
ASEAN Regional Forum　ASEAN(東南アジア諸国連合)地域フォーラム
in an open forum　公開の場で
Major Economies Forum　主要経済国フォーラム
open forum　公開討論会

regional economic forum　地域経済会議
South Pacific Forum　南太平洋諸国会議
the forum of public opinion　世論の批判
the six-party forum　6か国協議
◆The Asia-Pacific Economic Cooperation forum was held in Lima just a week after the financial summit meeting of the leaders of the Group of 20 industrialized and developing economies. アジア太平洋経済協力会議（APEC）は、G20（世界の主要20先進国と地域）の首脳による金融サミットの1週間後に、ペルーのリマで開かれた。◆These annual general meetings are the key decision-making forums for joint-stock companies. これらの年次株主総会は、株式会社にとって最も重要な意思決定の場である。

forward　(名)先物, 予約取引, 先渡し取引, 先渡し契約, 繰延べ, フォワード　(形)先物の, 先渡しの, 先を見越しての, 前方への
　　(⇒foreign currency exchange contract)
amount brought forward　前期繰越し
amount carried forward　次期繰越し
balance carried [brought] forward　残高次期繰越し
balance forward　繰越し残高
buy forward　先物を買う
exchange forward contract　為替予約
foreign currency forward　為替先物予約
foreign exchange forward balance [position]　外国為替先物持ち高
forward against forward swap　先物同士のスワップ
forward agreement　先々契約, 先渡し・先渡し契約, フォワード・フォワード契約
forward bargain　先渡し取引, 先物取引, 先物売買
forward bid rate　先物買い相場
forward business　先物取引, 先物金融取引
forward buying　先物の買い, 先物買付け, 先物仕入れ
forward cover　先物カバー, 先物為替資産
forward dealing　先物取引, 先物為替取引
forward delivery　先渡し, 先限(さきぎり)
forward foreign exchange agreement [contract]　為替予約
forward foreign exchange rate　先物予約レート
forward forex market　為替先物市場
forward interest rate　先渡し金利
forward margin　直先相場[直物相場と先物相場]の開き, 直先差, フォワード・マージン
forward market　先物市場, 先渡し市場
　　(=forward exchange market)
forward offer rate　先物売り相場
forward operation　アウトライト操作, 先物取引
　　(=forward transaction)
forward order　先物注文
forward position　先物持ち高, 先物為替持ち高, 先物ポジション
forward premium　先物プレミアム(直物為替相場より先物為替相場が高いこと)
forward purchase　アウトライト先買い
forward quotation　先物相場, 先渡し相場
forward rate　先物レート, 先物相場, 先渡し金利, フォワード・レート
forward sales　アウトライト先売り
forward spread　先物持ち高, 直物相場と先物相場の開き（forward margin), フォワード・スプレッド
forward supply contract　先物注文契約
forward swap　フォワード・スワップ
forward swap start　後からスタートするスワップ

forward transaction　為替予約, 先物取引, 先物為替予約取引, 先・先スワップ　(=forward contract, forward dealing, forward operation)
one year forward rate　1年物先渡し金利
option forward　オプション・フォワード
outright forward delivery　順月渡し
purchase spot and sell forward　現物を買って先物を売る
settle the forward　先渡し取引の決済をする, 先渡し決済をする
spot and forward currency rates　為替の直物と先物
spot-forward spread　直・先スプレッド
the forward date of a swap　スワップの期日

forward contract　先渡し契約, 先渡し取引, 予約契約, 先物為替予約, 為替先物予約, フォワード契約
buying forward contract　買い為替予約, 買い予約
enter into a forward contract to purchase currency　為替の売り予約をする
enter into a forward contract to sell currency　為替の買い予約をする
forward contracts on OTC indices　有価証券店頭指数等先渡し取引
forward contracts on securities　有価証券先渡し取引
forward currency contract　先物先物, 為替予約
have a long position in a forward contract　先渡し取引でロング・ポジションを取る, 買い持ちとなる
have a short position in a forward contract　先渡し取引でショート・ポジションを取る, 売り持ちとなる
◆Management believes that these forward contracts should not subject the Company to undue risk to foreign exchange movements. これらの先物取引契約で当社が過大な為替相場の変動リスクを負うことはない、と経営陣は考えております。
◆The exporting companies are attempting to avoid further foreign exchange losses arising from the yen's appreciation by buying forward contracts. 輸出企業は、買い為替予約[買い予約]で円高による為替差損を避けようとしている。

forward exchange　先物為替
forward exchange agreement　先物為替契約[予約], 先渡し為替契約, 為替予約
forward exchange dealing　先物為替取引
forward exchange dealing rate　先物為替取引相場
forward exchange market　先物為替市場
　　(=market for forward exchange)
forward exchange operation　先物為替操作
forward exchange policy　先物為替政策
forward exchange position　先物為替持ち高
forward exchange rate　先物為替相場, 先物相場
　　(=forward rate of exchange)
forward exchange transaction　先物為替取引

forward exchange contract　先物為替予約, 為替先物予約, 為替予約
　　(⇒foreign exchange dealer, spot rate)
forward exchange contract for speculation　投機を目的とした先物為替予約
forward exchange contract to hedge on　～をヘッジするための先物為替予約
◆Just after the start of the market intervention, the banks were flooded with orders for forward exchange contracts. 市場介入の直後、銀行には為替予約の注文が殺到した。◆Orders for $30 million and $50 million forward exchange contracts have poured in at a much greater rate than usual. 3,000万ドルや5,000万ドルの為替予約が、通常取引の何倍にものぼる勢いで殺到した。

forward looking　先読み, 先行きについての見通し, 未

来志向, フォワード・ルッキング
forward-looking information　先行きについての情報, 将来情報

forwardation　(名)フォワデーション　(=contango: 商品や為替市場取引で先物価格が直物価格を上回っている状態のこと。⇒backwardation, contango)

foundation　(名)基盤, 基礎, 土台, 根拠, 建設, 設立, 創立, 創業, 基金, 維持基金, 奨学基金, 基本金, 財団, 事業団, 基礎化粧品, ファンデーション
(⇒dissolution)
　business foundation　事業基盤, 経営基盤, 経営の根幹, 経営体力
　establish a firm foundation for　～の強固な基盤を確立する
　financial foundation　財務基盤, 経営基盤
　(=financial base, financial footing)
　foundation of management　経営基盤
　strengthen the foundation of existing businesses　既存事業の基盤を強化する
　◆Priority should be given to public spending, to establish a firm foundation for economic recovery and the subsequent job of tackling fiscal reform. 景気を回復し[経済を立て直し], 財政改革に取り組むための強固な基盤を確立するには, 公共支出を優先的に考えなければならない。◆The survey found about 68 percent of M&As were aimed at strengthening the foundations of existing businesses. 調査の結果, M&A(企業の合併・買収)の目的は約68％が既存事業の基盤強化であった。

foundation fund　保険会社の基金　(株式会社の資本金に相当, 基本積立金。⇒capital)
　◆The bank plans to provide the money by transferring ￥100 billion in subordinated loans, which it has already extended to the insurer, to the insurer's foundation fund. 同行は, すでに供与している劣後ローン1,000億円をこの保険会社の基金に振り替えて, その資金を提供する方針だ。◆The bank will likely provide up to ￥100 billion in funds to boost the struggling life insurer's foundation fund, equivalent to capital for a stock company. 同行は, この経営再建中の生命保険会社の基金(株式会社の資本金に相当)を引き上げるため, 最高で1,000億円の資金を供与する見込みだ。

founding family　創業家
　◆A financial scandal embroiling Daio Paper Corp.'s former chairman, a member of the firm's founding family, has come to light. 大王製紙の創業家出身の前会長をめぐる金融不祥事が, 発覚した。◆MUFG will promote talks with Acom's founding family for the share purchases. 三菱UFJフィナンシャル・グループは, 消費者金融大手アコムの創業家と株式取得[株式買取り]の交渉を進める。

fourth market　第四市場, 機関投資家間の直取引市場

FRA　金利先渡し契約, 先渡し金利契約 (forward rate agreementの略)
　buy an FRA　FRAを買う
　conclude an FRA　FRA取引をする
　fix the contract rate at the start of the FRA　FRAの約定時点で約定金利を固定する
　FRA interest period　FRA金利期間
　FRA play　FRAに絡(からんだ)動き
　have a long position (net buyer) in FRA　FRAでロング(買い持ち)ポジションを取る
　have a short position (net seller) in FRA　FRAでショート(売り持ち)ポジションを取る
　make a profit with the FRA　FRAで利益[収益]を上げる
　take out an FRA　FRAをアレンジする

fraction of a share　1株の端数株式
　◆It is hereby declared that in these Articles the expression "share" shall include a fraction of a share. 本定款で「株式」という場合は, 1株の端数株式も含むことをここに宣言する。

fragile　(形)壊れやすい, 傷つきやすい, もろい, 弱い, ひ弱な, 虚弱な, 脆(ぜい)弱な, 不十分な, はかない, 不安定な, 永続しない
　fragile consumer confidence　弱い消費意欲
　fragile economy　脆弱な経済, 弱い経済
　fragile evidence　不十分な証拠
　fragile excuse　見えすいた言い訳
　fragile goods　こわれ物, 易損品
　fragile recovery　弱い足取りの景気回復
　◆The global economy continues to recover, albeit in a fragile and uneven way. 世界経済は, 脆弱(ぜいじゃく)で一様ではないが, 回復を続けている。◆When you have a fragile recovery, it wouldn't seem to me like an opportune time to raise taxes. 景気回復の足取りが弱いときは, 税金引上げの好機とは言えないように思える。

fragility　(名)壊れやすさ, 傷つきやすさ, もろさ, 弱さ, ひ弱さ, 虚弱性, 脆(ぜい)弱性, はかなさ
　fragility of profit structures　収益構造のもろさ
　fragility of the financial markets　金融市場の脆弱性
　fragility of the world largest economy　米経済の弱さ
　◆Drastic changes in the business climate have exposed the fragility of export companies' profit structures. 経営環境の激変で, 輸出企業の収益構造のもろさをさらけ出した。◆Recent U.S. economic indicators show the fragility of the world largest economy. 最近の米国の経済指標は, 米経済の弱さを示している。

framework　(名)枠組み, 骨組み, 基本, 基本構造, 大枠, 体制, 構図, 関係, 体系, 制度, 仕組み, 環境, 場, フレームワーク
　agreed framework on new trade rules　新貿易ルールの枠組み合意
　(=framework agreement on new trade rules)
　economic framework　経済関係
　international supervisory framework for financial institutions　金融業界[金融機関]の国際的監視体制
　(⇒joint statement)
　new budgetary framework　新予算制度
　regulatory framework　規制の枠組み, 規制上の枠組み, 規制体系, 規制環境
　the framework for tackling unemployment　失業対策の骨格
　the framework of compensation payments for damage　損害の賠償金支払いの枠組み
　◆If the decision on the framework of TEPCO's compensation payments for damage by the crisis of its nuclear power plant should be put off further, it could trigger credit instability in the firm. 東電の原子力発電所事故による損害の賠償金支払いの枠組み決定をさらに先送りすれば, 東電の信用不安を招く可能性がある。◆The framework under which external demand compensated for weak domestic demand has collapsed. 低迷する内需を外需がカバーするという構図が, 崩れてしまった。◆The new budgetary framework, which was introduced from fiscal 2004, allows part of a budget to be carried over to successive fiscal years. 2004年度から導入された新予算制度では, 予算の一部を翌年度以降に繰り越すことができる。

fraud　(名)詐欺, 不正, 操作　(=scam; ⇒bank-transfer scam[fraud], card fraud, securities fraud)
　a series of fraud cases involving donations　相次ぐ[一連の]義援金詐欺事件　(⇒donation)
　accounting fraud　会計操作
　bank-transfer fraud　振り込め詐欺
　cash card fraud　キャッシュ・カード詐欺
　(=card fraud)

computer fraud　コンピュータ不正, コンピュータ使用詐欺

corporate fraud　企業詐欺, 企業の不正行為

fraud sales　かたり商法, 詐欺商法

insurance fraud　保険詐欺

'It's me' fraud　おれおれ詐欺

mislabeling fraud　偽装工作

mortgage fraud　住宅ローン詐欺
（⇒mortgage fraud）

online fraud　オンライン詐欺, ネット詐欺
◆Concerning online fraud, the police can't investigate the case unless a bank files a damage report to police. オンライン詐欺については, 銀行が被害届を出さないかぎり警察は捜査できない。 ◆In the aftermath of the 1995 Great Hanshin Earthquake and the 2007 Niigata Prefecture Chuetsu Offshore Earthquake, a series of fraud cases involving donations occurred. 1995年の阪神大震災や2007年の新潟県中越沖地震の直後には, 義援金詐欺事件が相次いで起きた。 ◆The U.S. FBI is looking at potential fraud by four major financial institutions. 米連邦捜査局は, 大手金融機関4社 (政府系住宅金融ファニー・メイ, フレディ・マックの2社のほか, 米保険最大手のAIGとリーマン・ブラザーズ) による詐欺の可能性を検討している。 ◆Wall Street reeled from more revelations out of the U.S. government fraud case against Goldman Sachs. 米政府がゴールドマン・サックスを証券詐欺容疑で提訴して驚くべき多くの新事実が発覚したのを受けて, 米金融街が動揺した。

fraud charges　詐欺罪
◆The former company president was indicted on fraud charges regarding a dubious capital increase in the firm. この元社長は, 架空増資に関する詐欺罪で起訴された。 ◆The SEC filed fraud charges against WorldCom in federal district court in New York. 米証券取引委員会 (SEC) は, ワールドコム (米長距離通信会社) を詐欺罪でニューヨーク連邦地裁に提訴した。

fraudulent bill-sender　架空請求メールの発信者
（⇒Internet cafe）
◆Most fraudulent bill-senders send their e-mail via several servers, including overseas servers, and illegally change their addresses. 架空請求メールの発信者の大半は, 海外のサーバーを含めて複数のサーバーを経由してEメールを送ったり, アドレスを不正に書き換えたりしている。

fraudulent bookkeeping　不正な経理処理, 経理操作

fraudulent invoice　架空請求書
（=fraudulent bill）
◆Most people received e-mails via computers or cell phones containing fraudulent invoices for services they had not used. 大半は, パソコンや携帯電話で, 利用したことのないサービスの架空請求メールが届いた。

fraudulent transaction　不正取引
◆This online auctioneer has been asking sellers for pertinent information, including credit card numbers to reduce fraudulent transactions. 不正取引を防ぐため, このオンライン・オークション業者は, クレジット・カード番号などの関連情報を売り手に求めてきた。

fraudulently　（副）不正に, 詐欺で
◆American International Group agreed to pay a $10 million civil fine to settle the SEC's allegations that it fraudulently helped another company falsify its earnings report and hide losses. 米保険大手のAIG (アメリカン・インターナショナル・グループ) は, 同社が他社の業績報告書改ざんと損失隠しに不正に手を貸したとする米証券取引委員会 (SEC) の告発を受け, この問題を解決するために民事制裁金1,000万ドルを支払うことに同意した。

FRB　米連邦準備銀行（Federal Reserve Bankの略）

FRB　米連邦準備制度理事会（Federal Reserve Boardの略）

◆Economic activity strengthened in most of U.S. regions with the exception of St. Louis where plans to close several plants were announced, the U.S. FRB said. 米連邦準備制度理事会 (FRB) は, （全12地区連銀のうち）一部の工場閉鎖計画を発表したセントルイスを除く11地区で景気が好転している, と述べた。 ◆Emerging countries are anxious about the possibility of inflation caused by a large influx of funds as the U.S. FRB decided to relax its monetary policy. 米連邦準備制度理事会 (FRB) が金融緩和を決めたため, 新興国は大量の資金流入によるインフレを懸念している。

Freddie　フレディ・マック　（=Freddie Mac）
◆The Federal Housing Finance Agency oversees Fannie and Freddie that buy mortgage loans and mortgage securities issued by the lenders. 米連邦住宅金融局 (FHFA) は, これらの金融機関が発行する住宅ローンやモーゲージ証券を購入する［買い取る］連邦住宅抵当金庫 (ファニー・メイ) や連邦住宅貸付け抵当公社 (フレディ・マック) を監督している。 ◆The price tag for the mortgage-backed securities sold to Fannie and Freddie by 17 financial firms totaled $196.1 billion. 大手金融機関17社がファニー・メイとフレディ・マックに販売した住宅ローン担保証券 (MBS) の購入額は, 総額で1,961億ドルになる。 ◆The U.S. government filed lawsuits against 17 financial firms for selling Fannie and Freddie mortgage-backed securities that turned toxic when the housing market collapsed. 米政府は, 住宅市場崩壊時に不良資産化した住宅ローン担保証券 (MBS) をファニー・メイ (米連邦住宅抵当公庫) とフレディ・マック (米連邦住宅貸付け抵当公社) に販売したとして, 大手金融機関17社 (バンク・オブ・アメリカやシティグループ, JPモルガン・チェース, ゴールドマン・サックス・グループなど) を提訴した。

Freddie Mac　米連邦住宅貸付け抵当公社, フレディ・マック　（=Freddie:Federal Home Loan Mortgage Corporation (米連邦住宅貸付抵当公社) の通称。; ⇒earnings manipulation）
◆Freddie Mac revealed its misstatement of earnings. フレディ・マック (米連邦住宅貸付け抵当公社) が, 利益の不実表示をしていたことを明らかにした。 ◆Government-controlled Freddie Mac has asked for $1.8 billion in additional federal aid due to its larger loss in the second quarter. 米政府管理下のフレディ・マック (米連邦住宅貸付け抵当公社) は, 第2四半期（4～6月期）決算で赤字が拡大したため, 18億ドルの政府追加支援を要請した。 ◆Tab for Fannie Mae and Freddie Mac could soar to as much as $259 billion, nearly twice the amount Fannie and Freddie have received so far. ファニー・メイ (米連邦住宅抵当金庫) とフレディ・マック (米連邦住宅貸付け抵当公社) の追加の公的資金必要額は, 両社がこれまでに受け取った額の約2倍の2,590億ドルに急増する可能性がある。

-free　（形）～のない, ～を含まない, ～を受けない, ～に影響されない

branch-free bank　店舗［営業店］を持たない銀行

duty-free　免税の

interest-free　無利息の

risk-free asset　安全資産, 無リスク資産

risk-free rate　無リスク金利

tax-free income　非課税収入, 免税所得

trouble-free　面倒のない, 故障のない

◆The branch-free Internet-based bank can attract customers with higher deposit interest rates. 店舗を持たないネット専業銀行だと, 預金の金利を高くして, 顧客を集めることができる。

free distribution　無償増資

free-fall　（動）売り一色の展開になる, 暴落する, 急落する　（⇒freefall）
◆An international economic recession could begin if the dollar keeps free-falling under such conditions. このような状況でドル急落が続けば, 世界の景気後退が始まる可能性がある。

free fall of the dollar　ドルの暴落
（=freefall of the dollar）
◆A free fall of the dollar would jeopardize the entire economy of the world significantly. ドルが暴落すれば、世界経済全体に大きなダメージを与えることになる。

free financing　ゼロ金利ローン
（=zero financing, zero-percent financing）

free float　浮動株, 浮動株式, 自由なフロート
（=floating stock, floating supply of stocks:「安定株」の反対で、市場で転々と流通している株のこと。一般に、発行済み株式数の多い大型株は浮動株が多く、小型の品薄株は浮動株が少ない。⇒rare stock）

free-floating currencies　通貨の自由な変動, 自由変動通貨
◆Free-floating currencies are essential to global economic activity. 世界の経済活動には、通貨の自由な変動が欠かせない。

free floating exchange rate system　自由変動相場制

free up　～を使えるようにする,（市場や経済、体制などを）解放する, 取り除く
◆A bad bank is used to hold troubled assets and free up bank lending capacity. バッド・バンクは、不良資産を買い取って、銀行が自由に貸出できるようにするのに利用される。

freefall　（名）売り一色の展開, 暴落　（=free fall）
go into freefall　売り一色の展開になる, 棒下げとなる, 買いの手が止まる
send the market into freefall　～で市場が売り一色の展開となる

freefall in stock prices　株価の暴落
◆Both a freefall in stock prices and a surge in the yen's value have been avoided. 株価の暴落も円の急騰も、回避された。◆Prospects remain murky though a freefall in stock prices has been averted for now. 株価暴落はひとまず回避されたが、先行きはまだ不透明である。

freefall of the dollar　ドルの暴落
（=free fall of the dollar）
◆It is feared the colossal amount of the U.S. twin deficits could trigger a freefall of the U.S. dollar. アメリカの巨額の双子の赤字は、ドルの暴落を引き起こす懸念がある。

freeze　（動）凍結する, 据え置く
freeze legal procedures　法的手続きを凍結する
freeze Pyongyang's accounts　北朝鮮の口座を凍結する
freeze some assets owned by Iranian financial institutions　イランの金融機関が保有する資産を一部凍結する
◆Pyongyang's accounts with Banco Delta Asia in Macao were frozen under U.S. financial sanctions. マカオの銀行「バンコ・デルタ・アジア」にある北朝鮮の口座が、米国の金融制裁を受けて凍結された。◆The U.S. government froze the assets of four individuals and eight entities that were involved in illicit activities such as money laundering, currency counterfeiting and narcotics trafficking. 米政府は、資金洗浄（マネー・ロンダリング）や通貨偽造、麻薬取引などの違法行為に関与している4個人、8団体の資産を凍結した。

freeze　（名）凍結, 据え置き　（⇒credit freeze）
a freeze on some assets owned by Iranian financial institutions　イランの金融機関が保有する資産の一部凍結
asset freeze　資産の凍結
credit freeze　信用凍結, 信用釘付け
deep freeze　凍結, 凍結状態, 一時停止, 棚上げ
freeze-in effect　凍結効果　（=lock-in effect）
freeze on the implementation of the payoff system　ペイオフ制度実施の凍結, ペイオフ制度の凍結, ペイオフ凍結
lift a freeze on　～の凍結を解除する
pay freeze　賃金凍結, 給与凍結
price freeze　価格凍結, 物価凍結
（=freeze on prices）
wage freeze　賃金凍結
◆Credit markets are beginning to thaw after months of a deep freeze. 債券発行市場は、凍結状態がここ数か月続いた後、氷解が始まっている。◆The Financial Services Agency calls for lifting a freeze on a system that refunds corporate taxes previously paid by companies if they fall into the red. 金融庁は、企業が赤字に陥った場合、企業が過去に納めた法人税を払い戻す制度（繰戻し還付制度）の凍結解除を求めている。

freeze on some assets　一部資産の凍結, 資産の一部の凍結
◆The EU sanctions include a freeze on some assets owned by Iranian financial institutions. 欧州連合（EU）の独自制裁には、イランの金融機関が保有する資産の一部凍結も含まれている。

freeze on the payoff system　ペイオフ制度の凍結, ペイオフの凍結　（=freeze on the payoff scheme, the freeze on the introduction of the payoff system; ⇒financial circles, lifting of the freeze on the payoff system）
a total end to the freeze on the payoff system　ペイオフの全面凍結解除
the total lift of the freeze on the payoff system　ペイオフの全面凍結解除
◆In April 2002, the freeze on the payoff system was partially lifted. 2002年4月に、ペイオフ制度凍結の一部解禁が行われた。◆When the freeze on the payoff system was partially lifted, clients shifted their funds from time deposits to savings deposits that will be protected fully. ペイオフ制度凍結の一部解禁が行われた際には、顧客が預金を定期預金から全額保護される普通預金に預け替えた。

freeze payments on debt　債務返済を凍結する
◆The EU ministers will consider debt relief or freezing payments on debt for the Asian tsunami-hit countries. 欧州連合（EU）の閣僚らは、アジアの津波被災国のため債務削減や債務返済の凍結を検討する。

freezing of funds　資金の凍結, 資産凍結
◆A revised Foreign Exchange and Foreign Trade Control Law has been enacted to enable the swift freezing of funds belonging to terrorist organizations. テロ組織の資金［資産］凍結を迅速に行うための改正外為法は、すでに成立して［制定されて］いる。

freight/carriage and insurance paid to　輸送費・保険料済み条件, CIP

freight/carriage paid to　輸送費済み条件

freight/carriage paid to price　輸送費支払い済み値段

frequently　（副）しばしば, たびたび, 頻繁に
change hands most frequently at　～の中心値で推移する
trade most frequently at　取引の中心値は～
◆Online banking users can prevent illegal transfers of their deposits by frequently changing their passwords. オンライン・バンキング利用者は、パスワードをこまめに変更して、預金の不正送金を防ぐことができる。◆The yen moved between ¥81.80 and ¥82.38 to the dollar, trading most frequently at ¥81.94. 円相場の値幅は1ドル＝81円80銭～82円38銭で、取引の中心値は81円94銭だった。

fresh　（形）新たな, 新規の, 追加の, 生の, 新鮮な, 生鮮の, 最新の
break fresh ground　新天地を開拓する, 新分野を開拓する, 新事実を発見する
fresh approach　新たな取組み
fresh attempt　新たな試み
fresh data　生のデータ
fresh food prices fluctuations　生鮮食品価格の変動
fresh money　追加資本, 追加資金

fresh signs　景気指標
fresh signs of economic recovery　景気回復を示す景気指標
fresh supply　新規供給, 新規発行
make a fresh start　再出発する, 新規まき直しを図る
raise fresh equity　自己資本を新規調達する, 新たに自己資本を調達する
take a fresh look at the plan　計画を見直す
◆The U.S. dollar dropped to a fresh 15-year low in the lower ¥82 level. 米ドル相場は82円台前半まで下落し、15年ぶりに最安値を更新した。

fresh capital　新規資本, 追加資本, 新たな資金, 増資
◆Japanese companies actively tapped the stock market to raise fresh capital. 日本の企業が、新規資本を調達するため株式市場で積極的に起債した。

fresh reconstruction plan　新たな再建策, 新たな経営再建策
◆Crisis-stricken giant supermarket chain operator announced a fresh reconstruction plan. 経営危機に陥っている巨大スーパーが、新たな経営再建策を発表した。

freshness　（名）新しさ, 目新しさ, 新鮮味
◆The government's additional economic stimulus lacked freshness. 政府の追加経済対策は、目新しさに欠けていた。

friction　（名）対立, 不和, 不一致, 摩擦, あつれき, 抵抗
currency friction　通貨摩擦
financial friction　金融摩擦
investment friction　投資摩擦
tax friction　税制摩擦
trade friction　貿易摩擦, 通商摩擦
◆Disarray among the countries became evident over concrete measures to prevent currency friction. 通貨摩擦を食い止める［防ぐ］具体策では、各国の足並みの乱れが露呈した。

friend　（名）友人, 知人, 友だち同士, 支持者, 支援者, 後援者, 擁護者, 味方, 同盟国, 同志, 仲間, 同人, 同国人
a list of friends of　～後援者［支援者］名簿
be no friend of [to]　～を支持［支援］しない
have friends in high places　有力なコネがある
the friend of small and midsize companies　中小企業の味方
◆The bank projected itself as "the friend of small and midsize enterprises." 同行は、「中小企業の味方」という看板を掲げていた。

friendly　（形）友好的な, 好意的な, 親しい, 親善的な, 交戦状態にない, 敵対関係にない
（⇒growth-friendly fiscal consolidation plan）
be on friendly relation with　～と友好関係にある
friendly acquisition　友好的買収
（=friendly takeover）
friendly press coverage　好意的なマスコミ報道
friendly society　共済組合, 互助組合
（=benefit society）
friendly stock price　高めの株価, 高めの株価水準
friendly takeover bid　友好的株式公開買付け, 友好的TOB, 株式公開買付けによる友好的買収, 友好的買収
friendly wind　順風, 追い風

friendly offer　友好的買収
◆White knight is a company that saves another firm threatened by a hostile takeover by making a friendly offer. ホワイト・ナイトは、友好的な買収により、敵対的買収の脅威にさらされている他企業を救済する企業のことだ。

friendly takeover　友好的買収
（=friendly acquisition）
◆It is difficult to materialize a triangular merger scheme unless it is a friendly takeover. 友好的な買収でないと、三角合併［三角合併案］を実現するのは難しい。

friendly takeover bid　友好的株式公開買付け, 友好的TOB, 株式公開買付けによる友好的買収, 友好的買収
◆Nisshin Food Products has obtained 86.32 percent of Myojo Food's outstanding shares in a friendly takeover bid for about ¥32 billion. 日清食品は、友好的TOB（株式公開買付け）で明星食品の発行済み株式の86.32%を買い取ったが、買取り価格は約320億円だった。

friendly tender offer　友好的株式公開買付け, 友好的TOB　（=friendly takeover bid）
◆Kirin Brewery Co. will launch a friendly tender offer for Mercian shares in a capital and business alliance. キリンビールは、資本・業務提携としてメルシャン株式の友好的TOB（株式公開買付け）を実施する。

front end　債券の短期物, 期近物
front end of the bond markets　債券相場の短期物
front end of the curve　短期物
front end of the Treasury market　米国債短期物
front end of the yield curve　イールド・カーブの短期部分

front-load　（動）前倒しする
◆The Resona plans to front-load by up to two years its current restructuring plan to reduce the group's about 19,000 employees to 16,000 by the end of March 2007. りそなホールディングスは、約19,000人いる同グループの人員を2007年3月末までに16,000人まで削減するとしている現行のリストラ計画を、最大2年前倒しする方針だ。

front money　前金, 前払い金

front month　直近の月, 期近物（front monthは一番手前の月、直近の月、つまり翌月を指す。期近物は、石油先物取引では翌月から9か月の先物商品を指す）
◆The U.S. light crude front month contract rose a further 36 cents a barrel in after-hours electronic trading to top $50. 米国の軽質原油の翌月渡し価格は、時間外の電子取引で1バレル当たり36セント上伸して、1バレル＝50ドルを突破した。

front-runner　（名）最有力候補, 先頭走者, フロント・ランナー　（=frontrunner）
◆Time Warner had been seen as the front-runner for MGM, but Sony raised its offer. タイム・ワーナーがMGM買収の最有力候補とみられていたが、ソニーが提示額を引き上げた。

front running　先回り買い, フロント・ランニング

FRS　米連邦準備制度（Federal Reserve Systemの略）

FRTIB　米連邦職員退職貯蓄投資委員会（Federal Retirement Thrift Investment Boardの略）

FSA　（日本の）金融庁（Financial Services Agencyの略）
FSA Commissioner　金融庁長官
FSA's special inspection　金融庁の特別検査
◆FSA's inspectors are to confirm whether the companies' categorization by banks as debtors is relevant or fair. 金融庁の検査官は、銀行側の企業（融資先企業）の債務者区分が適正かどうかなどを検証することになっている。◆Laws already in place on narcotics and organized crime oblige financial institutions to report to the FSA any deals possibly linked to profits from criminal activities. すでに実施されている麻薬や組織的犯罪に関する法律は、犯罪収益絡みと思われる取引について、金融庁への報告（届出）を金融機関に義務付けている。◆The FSA urged the financial group to revise its earnings estimate. 金融庁は、同金融グループに対して業績予想の修正を強く迫った。◆The FSA's guideline for supervising financial conglomerates is aimed at urging operators of financial conglomerates to reinforce their corporate governance to prevent irregularities. 金融庁の金融コングロマリット（複合体）監督指針の狙いは、不正防止に向けて、金融コングロマリットの経営者に経営監視の強化を促すことにある。◆The FSA's special inspection will check the major banks' large-lot corporate borrowers whose stock prices or credit ratings have sharply declined. 金融庁の特別検査は、大手銀行の株価

や格付けなどが急落した大口融資先を査定の対象としている。

FSA (英国の)金融サービス機構(Financial Services Authorityの略)

FSB 金融安定化理事会, 金融安定理事会
(⇒Financial Stability Board)
◆The Financial Stability Board (FSB) is cooperating with the Basel Committee on Banking Supervision, a body that sets rules for international banking. 金融安定化理事会(FSB)は、国際銀行業務の基準を制定する機関のバーゼル銀行監督委員会と連携している。◆The three Japanese top banks will face the FSB's new international rule requiring them to hold extra capital to prevent future financial crises. 日本の3メガ銀行も、金融危機の再発を防ぐため、資本[自己資本]の上積みを求める金融安定化理事会(FSB)の新国際基準の対象になると見られる。

FSC 金融安定貢献税, 金融安定分担金[負担金]
(financial stability contributionの略。金融活動税(FAT)とともにIMFが提案している銀行税の一つ。金融機関の負債に課税。将来の銀行破たんの際の救済資金を、事前に基金に積み立てておく狙いがある。⇒FAT)

FSF 金融安定化フォーラム
(⇒Financial Stability Forum)

FSOC (米国の)金融サービス監督協議会(Financial Services Oversight Councilの略)

FT フィナンシャル・タイムズ(英国の経済専門日刊紙 Financial Timesの略)
FT-SE index　FT100種株価指数
FT-Stock Exchange 100 index　FT100種指数
FT 100 Share Index　フィナンシャル・タイムズ100種総合株価指数

FTC 日本の公正取引委員会(Fair Trade Commissionの略)

FTC 米連邦取引委員会(Federal Trade Commissionの略)　(⇒antitrust law)
◆The U.S. Federal Trade Commission (FTC) exercises jurisdiction over matters including consumer protection issues in the United States. 米連邦取引委員会(FTC)は、米国消費者保護などの問題を管轄している。

FTSE フィナンシャル・タイムズとロンドン証券取引所(LSE)の合弁会社(Financial Times Stock Exchangeの略)
FTSE [FT-SE] 100　FT100種, FTSE100種 (=FT-SE index)
FTSE-100 futures　FT100種先物, FTSE100種先物
FTSE-100 index　FT100種指数, FTSE100種総合株価指数 (=Footsie: ロンドン証券取引所の時価総額上位100社株価を、1984年1月3日を1,000として指数化したもの)

FTT 金融取引税(financial transaction taxの略。株式や債券、外国為替などに課税)

fuel (動)給油する, 燃料を補給[供給]する, 活気づかせる, 勢いづかせる, 激化させる, 加速する, 拍車をかける, 悪化させる, あおる, あおり立てる, 刺激する, 支持する, ～を支える要因となる
be fueled by　～で動く, ～で勢いづく[拍車がかかる, 高まる, 激化する, 加速する], ～が原動力となる, ～に支えられる
fuel domestic demand　国内需要を拡大する, 国内需要を喚起する[刺激する]
fuel inflation　インフレを加速させる, インフレ再燃をもたらす
fuel inflationary sentiment　インフレ心理をあおる
fuel the yen's rise　円高に拍車をかける
◆A strong yen lowers the prices of imported goods and fuels deflation. 円高は輸入品の価格を下げ、デフレに拍車をか

ける。◆Japan's imports are also climbing because the economic recovery is fueling domestic demand. 景気回復で国内需要が拡大しているため、日本の輸入も伸びている。◆The economy, fueled by a pickup in business spending on inventories, is now expanding at a spanking clip. 企業の在庫投資の回復に支えられた経済は現在、顕著なペースで拡大している。◆The firm cruised to a record profit last business year fueled by a weak yen and robust U.S. sales. 同社の昨年度の利益は、円安効果と好調な米国内販売に支えられて、過去最高に達した。◆The rating downgrades have fueled economic confusion in Greece and Ireland. ギリシャやアイルランドでは、格下げで経済の混乱に拍車がかかった。◆The yen surged to the higher end of the ¥98 level against the dollar in Tokyo markets due to yen-buying pressure fueled by expectations of the country's economic recovery. 東京為替市場は、日本の景気回復を期待した円買いが強まり、1ドル=98円台[98円台の上限]まで円が急騰した。

Fukushima No. 1 nuclear power plant crisis 福島第一原発事故
◆To raise money for compensation related to the Fukushima No. 1 nuclear power plant crisis, TEPCO will sell off assets through four trust banks. 福島第一原発事故関連の賠償資金を調達するため、東電は、4信託銀行を通じて資産を売却することになった。

fulfill [fulfil] (動)(義務や約束などを)果たす, 実現する, 達成する, (可能性を)最大限に実現する, (目的などに)かなう, (命令や指示に)従う
fulfill one's obligations　義務を果たす
fulfill one's potential　可能性を最大限に実現する
fulfill one's responsibilities　責任を果たす
fulfill one's role　役割を果たす
fulfill oneself　自分の力をフルに発揮する, 満足する
◆To fulfill its responsibilities as the nation's central bank, the Bank of Japan must achieve currency stabilization by availing itself of a range of measures, including stabilization of the exchange rate. 日本の中央銀行としての責任を果たすには、日本銀行は、為替相場の安定を含めて広範な手段を活用して通貨の安定を実現しなければならない。

fulfillment (名)(義務などの)遂行, 実践, 成就, 達成, 実現

full (形)完全な, 全部の, 十分な, 全面的, 正式の, 正規の, 詳しい, 充実した, 総額の
full actuarial liability　年金数理上の負債総額
full amount　全額, 総額
full deposit guarantee　預金の全額保証, 預金の全額保護 (=full guarantee of deposits)
full deposit refund cap　預金全額払戻しの上限, 預金全額払戻しの上限設定, ペイオフ制
full dilution　完全希薄化, 完全希釈化, 完全希釈効果
full disclosure　完全開示, 完全表示, 十分な開示, 完全公開性
full eligibility　完全受給権取得, 完全受給資格取得, 完全適格者
full elimination　全額消去
full fair value method　全面時価評価法
full-paid and nonassessable　全額払込み済みで催告を受けない
full pension　完全年金
full provision basis　完全税効果会計, 所得税の完全期間配分 (=comprehensive tax allocation)
full service bank　総合サービス銀行
full service broker　総合金融・証券サービス会社
full stock　額面100ドルの株式, フル・ストック
full value insurance　全額保険

full-blown (形)全面的な, 本格的な, 完全に発達した,

成熟し切った, 満開の
full-blown financial crisis 全面的な金融危機
full-blown monetary crisis 全面的な金融危機
◆There was no choice other than to pass the financial bailout bill to forestall a full-blown financial crisis. 全面的な金融危機を回避するには、金融安定化法案を可決せざるを得なかった。

full faith and credit 十分な信頼と信用
  full faith and credit bond 十分な信頼と信用に基づく債券 (=general obligation bond)
  full faith and credit of the government of the United States 米連邦政府の十分な信頼と保証

full-fledged (形) 本格的な, 本腰を入れた, 一人前の, ひとかどの, れっきとした, 立派な, 十分に訓練を積んだ, 資力十分の, 十分に発達・進展した, 羽毛が生え揃った
  full-fledged multilateral trade system 本格的な多角的自由貿易体制
  full-fledged work on compiling the budget 本格的な予算編成作業

full-fledged recovery 本格的な回復
  full-fledged recovery in corporate investment in plant and equipment 企業の設備投資の本格回復
  full-fledged recovery track 本格回復の軌道
  make a full-fledged recovery 本格的に回復する
  ◆If the economy is to see a full-fledged recovery, the government should continue taking all feasible policy steps, including propping up the economy by fiscal means. 本格的な景気回復を見るには、財政面でのテコ入れを含めて、政府は引き続き実行可能なあらゆる政策手段を取るべきである。◆Under the severe income and employment situations, personal consumption has yet to show indications of a full-fledged recovery. 厳しい所得・雇用環境の下で、個人消費に本格的な復調の気配がまだ見えない。

full-fledged recovery in the real economy 実体経済の本格的な回復
  ◆Capital investment in the private sector is still sluggish and this will delay a full-edged recovery in the real economy. 民間設備投資の動きがまだ鈍いので、実体経済の本格的な回復は遅れる。

full-fledged recovery of the world economy 世界景気の本格回復
  ◆Economic reinvigoration of Asia-Pacific nations as a whole is indispensable for a full-fledged recovery of the world economy. 世界景気の本格回復には、アジア太平洋食全体の経済再活性化が必須だ。

full guarantee 全額保証, 全面保証
  ◆A full guarantee on the repayment of deposits allows financial institutions to be lenient with their management. 預金払戻しの全額保証は、金融機関に経営の甘えを許す結果になっている。

full merger 完全統合
  ◆Sumitomo Mitsui Financial Group Inc. and Daiwa Securities Group Inc. are eyeing a management integration and full merger in the future. 三井住友フィナンシャルグループと大和証券グループは、両グループの将来の経営統合と完全統合を計画している。

full payment of insurance claims 保険金の全額支払い
  ◆It is appropriate to guarantee full payment of insurance claims for a certain period even after the failure of the non-life insurer. 損保の破たん後一定期間は、保険金の全額支払いを保証するのが妥当だ。

full pay-out lease 完全払込みリース
full privatization of three postal services 郵政三事業の完全民営化
full protection for term deposits 定期性預金の全額保護 (⇒term deposits)

full protection of deposits 預金の全額保護
  ◆If the full protection of deposits in savings accounts and checking accounts is lifted in April, shifts of deposits into large banks will accelerate. 4月から普通預金や当座預金などの預金(決済性預金)の全額保護がなくなれば、大手銀行への預金の移動が加速する。

full reconstruction 本格的な再建
  ◆U.S. auto giant General Motors Co. is still on the bumpy road to full reconstruction. 米自動車大手ゼネラル・モーターズ(GM)の本格的な再建の道は、まだ厳しい。

full recovery 本格回復, 全面回復 (=full-scale recovery)
  ◆To put the economy back on the road to full recovery, further progress in the yen's appreciation and the dollar's depreciation must be contained. 景気を本格回復の軌道に乗せるためには、円高・ドル安の進行を抑える必要がある。

full refund 全額払い戻し
  ◆Even with the enforcement of the payoff system, only 3 percent of the failed bank's depositors will face getting less than full refunds on their accounts. ペイオフ[ペイオフ制度]を発動しても、預金の全額払い戻しを受けられないのは、破たんした同行預金者の3%に過ぎない。

full refund cap 全額払い戻しの上限, 全額払い戻し枠, 全額払い戻しの上限設定, ペイオフ制度

full-refund guarantee 全額払い戻し保証
  ◆The balance of quasi-money—most of it time deposits—saw a record drop in the wake of the April 1 abolition of the government's full-refund guarantee on time deposits. 定期預金が中心の準通貨の残高は、4月1日から定期預金に対する政府の全額払戻し保証が廃止されたため、過去最大の減少となった。

full-scale financial conglomerate 本格的な金融コングロマリット
  ◆If the merger takes place, it will create a full-scale financial conglomerate with a major bank, a major securities house and credit card company under its umbrella. 統合すれば、傘下に大手銀行と大手証券、クレジット・カード会社などを持つ本格的な金融コングロマリット(金融複合企業体)が誕生する。

full-scale investigation 本格調査
  ◆The Securities and Exchange Surveillance Commission launched a full-scale investigation on the company on suspicion of accounting fraud. 証券取引等監視委員会は、粉飾決算の疑いで同社の本格調査に乗り出した。

full-scale recovery 本格回復, 本格的な回復, 全面回復, 全面的な回復
  ◆Capital investment posted a 1 percent growth, a far cry from a full-scale recovery. 設備投資は1%の伸びを示したが、本格回復にはほど遠い。

full-service brokerage フルサービス証券会社
  ◆The company is the largest U.S. full-service brokerage. 同社は、米国最大手のフルサービス証券会社です。

full subsidiary 完全子会社
  ◆Major beer maker Sapporo Holdings Ltd. will make major soft drinks maker Pokka Corp. its full subsidiary. ビール大手のサッポロホールディングスが、清涼飲料大手のポッカコーポレーションを完全子会社化することになった。

full-time housewife 専業主婦
  ◆Full-time housewives of company employees and public servants are not required to pay pension premiums. 会社員や公務員の専業主婦は、保険料を払う必要がない。◆The issue of the inadvertent failure to switch to the national pension program by full-time housewives must be quickly solved. 専業主婦の国民年金への年金資格切替え忘れ問題は、決着を急ぐべきだ。◆There are about 420,000 full-time housewives whose unpaid premium periods are long. 保険料の未納期間が長い専業主婦は、約42万人いる。

full-year after-tax profit 通期の税引き後利益

◆The financial group's full-year after-tax profit as of the end of March 2011 will be around ¥550 billion. 同金融グループの2011年3月期決算の通期税引き後利益は、5,500億円程度になる見通し。

full-year (earnings) forecast 通期の業績予想, 通期の業績見通し, 通期の収益予想 （⇒forecast）
◆The securities group does not give a full-year earnings forecast. 同証券グループは、通期の業績見通しは行っていない。

fully diluted earnings per share 完全希薄化1株当たり利益（普通株式に転換可能な全発行済み証券を普通株式に転換したものとして計算される1株当たり利益）

fully fund 全額出資する, 十分積み立てる
◆The government now fully funds Japan Post Group. 政府は現在、日本郵政グループに全額出資している。◆The Industrial Revitalization Corporation of Japan does not intend to fund Daikyo. 産業再生機構は、大京に対して出資しない方針だ。

fully funded affiliate 全額出資子会社

fully integrate 完全統合する
◆It likely will take a few years to fully integrate the markets of the TSE and the OSE. 東証と大証の市場の完全統合は、数年後になる見通し。

fully paid securities 全額払込み済み証券

fully paid share 全額払込み済み株式, 全額払込み済み株式, 払込み済み株式

function （動）機能する, 作動する, 動く, 働く, 職務［機能、役目］を果たす
◆The bank began issuing new ATM cards that also function as credit cards and electronic money. 同行は、クレジット・カードと電子マネーの機能を加えた新型キャッシュ・カードの発行を開始した。◆The U.S. dollar can no longer function as the sole key currency of the world. 米ドルは、もはや世界の単独の基軸通貨としては機能できなくなっている。◆Today's companies do not function without such stakeholders as management, employees, clients and customers that support them. 今日の企業は、企業を支える経営者、従業員、取引先や顧客といったステークホルダーがいなければ成り立たない。

function （名）機能, 職能, 職務, 任務, 業務, 役目, 役割, 働き, 部門, 公式の行事, 関数
　administrative function　経営管理機能
　advanced function　最先端機能
　broking function　証券業務
　consumption function　消費関数
　controlling function　管理機能
　finance function　財務職能
　function of credit card　クレジット・カードの機能
　function of interest rates　金利機能, 金利の関数
　function of regulation　規制の役割
　head office functions such as planning and personnel management　企画や人事管理などの本部機能
　intermediary function　仲介機能
　internal audit function　内部監査機能
　investment function　投資業務, 投資関数
　liquidity preference function　流動性選好関数
　market risk management function　市場リスク管理部門
　marketing function　マーケティング機能
　money demand function　貨幣需要関数
　money function　貨幣の機能 （=function of money）
　money supply function　貨幣供給関数
　pay［wages］according to function　職務給
　R&D functions　研究開発部門
　savings function　貯蓄関数
　synergy and closer coordination between the functions　部門間の相乗効果と緊密な協調関係
　the functions of private banks　民間銀行の業務
◆An initiative to strengthen the functions of the European Financial Stability Facility (EFSF) was approved at the 17 eurozone countries' parliaments. 欧州金融安定基金（EFSF）の機能強化案が、ユーロ圏17か国の議会で承認された。◆In the shareholder vote, there was substantial focus on whether the chair and CEO functions at the company should be split. 株主投票では、とくに同社の会長職とCEO（最高経営責任者）の職を分離すべきかどうかが大きな関心事だった。◆The eurozone countries agreed to strengthen EFSF functions, such as bailout methods, in July 2011. 2011年7月にユーロ圏諸国は、支援手法など欧州金融安定基金（EFSF）の機能を強化することで合意した。◆What is urgently needed as the EU's rescue package is beefing up the functions of the EFSF and recapitalizing banks that own Greek and Italian government bonds. EU（欧州連合）の支援策として緊急に求められているのは、欧州金融安定基金（EFSF）の機能強化や、ギリシャやイタリアの国債を保有する銀行の資本増強などだ。

functional currency 機能通貨
◆Local currencies are generally considered the functional currencies outside the United States. 米国外では、一般に現地通貨を機能通貨と見なしています。

fund （動）資金を調達する, 積み立てる, 資金を賄（まか）う, 〜の資金に充てる, 資金を提供する, 金［資金］を出す, 拠出する, 出資する, 赤字などを補填（ほてん）する, （一時借入金を）長期負債に借り換える, 長期公債に切り替える
　be fully funded　十分積み立てられている
　be funded by the government　政府の助成を受けている, 政府が出資する
　be funded equally by　〜が折半出資する
　be funded out of working capital　運転資金［運転資本］から支払われる
　fund against the receivables　債権を裏付けとして資金を提供する
　fund an acquisition　企業買収の資金を調達する, 買収資金を調達する
　fund floating-interest mortgages　変動金利の住宅ローンの資金を調達する
　fund large public expenditures　巨額の財政赤字を賄う
　fund pension cost as accrued　年金費用を発生時に積み立てる
　fund the bank's lending business　同行の融資業務に充てる
　fund the down payment of　〜の頭金［前渡し金］に充てる
　fund (the government's) budget deficits　（政府の）財政赤字を補填する
　fund through debt issuance　債券発行で資金を調達する
　fund through issuance of debt　債券の発行で資金を調達する
　fund through the private and public markets　私募・公募の資本市場で資金を調達する
　fund via commercial paper program　CP発行で資金を賄（まか）う
◆A petrochemical plant funded equally by BASF and Chinese government-owned China Petroleum & Chemical Corporation started full operation in the suburbs of Nanjing. ドイツの大手化学メーカーBASFと中国国有の中国石油化工集団（SINOPEC）が折半出資した石油化学プラントが、南京市郊外で本格稼動した。◆It is the Corporation's practice to fund amounts for postretirement benefits, with an independent trustee, as deemed appropriate from time to time. 随時適切と思われる退職後給付額を、独立した信託機関に積み立てる

のが、当社の慣行となっています。◆Life insurance for retired employees is largely funded during their working lives. 退職者の生命保険は、勤続期間中にその大部分が積み立てられている。◆Previously, we expensed life insurance benefits as plans were funded. これまで当社は、生命保険給付については、制度に拠出がなされたときに費用として計上していました。◆Sony Bank is an Internet bank funded by Sony Corp. ソニー銀行は、ソニーが出資したネット専業銀行だ。◆The firm will borrow ¥56 billion to fund the introduction of new models. 同社は、新型車導入の資金を調達するため、560億円の融資を受ける。◆The government plans to sell some of its 100 percent stake in Japan Post Holdings Co. to fund reconstruction from the Great East Japan Earthquake. 政府は、東日本大震災の復興財源に充てるため、100％保有する日本郵政の株式の一部も売却する方針だ。

fund　(名)資金,基金,積立金,金,蓄え,蓄積,ファンド (⇒buyout fund, development fund, event-driven fund, foundation fund, hedge fund, investment fund, raise funds)
 automated fund transfer account　自動振替口座
 balanced fund　バランス型ファンド
 be short of funds　資金が足りない,金がない
 bond fund　債券投資信託,債券ファンド
 build a fund　ファンドを作る
 buyout fund　買収ファンド
 classified fund　機密費
 collecting and providing of funds for terrorists　テロ資金の収集・提供
 college fund　大学基金
 commodity fund　商品ファンド
 contribute funds　資金を出す,出資する
 corporate bond fund　社債ファンド
 corporate turnaround fund　企業再生ファンド
 demand for funds　資金需要
 dollar funds　ドル資金
 effective use of funds　資金の効果的な活用,資金の有効利用
 eke out funds　資金をひねり出す,財源をひねり出す
 employee's pension fund　従業員年金基金,厚生年金基金
 establish a fund　ファンドを設立する,基金を設ける (⇒establish a fund)
 exodus of funds　資金の流出,資金の引揚げ
 expanded fund facility　拡大信用供与,拡大融資,拡大信用供与制度
 external fund　外部資金
 foreign fund　海外ファンド (=foreign investment fund)
 fund procurement　資金調達
 fund raising　資金調達,資金集め
 fund-raising event　資金集めのイベント[行事]
 fund to support reform　改革支援基金
 funds provided from net earnings, depreciation, and amortization　純利益と減価償却[減価償却および償却]で得た資金 (⇒investment outflow)
 general fund　一般財源,一般基金,一般資金
 growth fund　成長株ファンド
 hedge fund　ヘッジ・ファンド
 in funds　必要な金[資金]が手元にある
 industry fund　業界基金 (⇒insurance claims)
 internal fund　内部資金
 invest in a mutual fund　投資信託に投資する
 invest in a pension fund　年金基金に投資する
 invest in the fund　ファンドに出資する
 invested fund　投下資本,投資資金
 investment fund　投資資金,投資信託
 macro fund　マクロ投資ファンド
 mutual fund　ミューチュアル・ファンド
 net inflows of funds into the United States　米国への純資金流入額
 out of funds　必要な金[資金]が手元にない
 pension fund　年金基金,年金資金,年金積立金
 plant expansion fund　工場拡張基金
 public funds　公的資金
 public-private investment fund　官民出資のファンド
 raise funds for　～の資金を調達する
 real estate investment fund　不動産投資ファンド
 redemption fund　償還基金
 revolving fund　回転資金
 scholarship fund　奨学資金
 secret funds　裏金
 shift of funds　資金の移動
 sinking fund　減債基金,償却基金,償却積立金
 slush fund　不正資金,賄賂(わいろ)資金,贈賄(ぞうわい)資金
 source and application of funds　資金の源泉と使途
 source and disposition of funds　資金の源泉と使途
 source of funds　資金の源泉
 suspicious fund deals　疑わしい資金取引
 urgent fund　緊急資金
 use of funds　資金の使用

◆Funds for disaster reconstruction will be procured by issuing special government bonds. 震災復興の資金は、復興債を発行して調達する。◆In order to assist auto parts makers hit by the March 11 earthquake and tsunami, the Development Bank of Japan will raise ¥50 billion to establish a fund. 東日本大震災で被災した自動車部品メーカーを支援するため、日本政策投資銀行が、500億円を調達してファンドを設立する。◆Investors have begun switching their funds from bank deposits to assets that entail some risks. 投資家が、銀行預金からリスクを伴う資産へと資金の運用を切り替え始めている。◆Large amounts of funds recently have been flowing into foreign bonds. 最近は、大量の資金が外国債券に流れ込んでいる。◆Other financial institutions will contribute funds to boost the total over ¥10 billion. 拠出金総額を100億円に超に引き上げるため、他の金融機関も出資する[資金を出す]。◆The aim of a fund established by the Development Bank of Japan is to infuse money into auto parts makers hit by the March 11 earthquake and tsunami. 日本政策投資銀行が設立するファンドの目的は、東日本大震災で被災した自動車部品メーカーに資金を行き渡らせることにある。◆The Bank of Japan decided to adopt additional quantitative easing measures in October 2010, setting up a fund to purchase government and corporate bonds. 日銀は、2010年10月に新たな量的緩和策の導入を決め、国債や社債を買い入れる基金を新設した。◆The Bank of Japan will set up a fund to buy long-term government bonds, exchange-traded funds and other financial assets in a bid to prop up the nation's economy. 日本の景気を下支えするため、日銀は基金を新設して、長期国債や上場投資信託(ETF)などの金融商品[金融資産]を買い入れる。◆The BOJ decided to further relax its monetary policy by injecting an additional ¥10 trillion into a fund aimed at purchasing government bonds and corporate debentures. 日銀は、国債や社債などを買い入れるための基金に新たに10兆円を注入[投入]して追加の金融緩和に踏み切ることを決めた。◆The BOJ's additional monetary easing steps include an increase in the amount of funds to purchase government bonds and corporate debentures. 日銀の追加金融緩和には、国債や社債などを買い入れる基金の増額が含まれている。◆The BOJ's policy meeting plans to consider expanding the list of government bonds purchased under the fund. 日銀の政策決定会合では、基金で買い入れる国債の対象拡大を検討する予定だ。◆The Development of Japan will ask major financial groups to invest in the fund established to assist auto parts makers hit by the March 11 earthquake and tsunami. 日本政策投資銀行が、東日本大震災で被災した自動車部品メーカーを支援するために設立するファンドへの出資を、大手金融グループに呼びかけることになった。◆The draft of the government's new growth strategy includes the establishment of a public-private investment fund to support the content industry in its foreign endeavors. 政府の新成長戦略の原案には、コンテンツ（情報の内容）産業の海外展開を支援する官民出資のファンド設立も盛り込まれている。◆The economic policy of the current administration continues to dole out huge funds. 現政権の経済政策は、巨額の金のバラマキを続けている。◆The EFSF is the EU bailout fund for countries with fiscal deficits. 欧州金融安定基金（EFSF）は、欧州の財政赤字国を支援する基金だ。◆The foreign funds purchased the convertible bonds at prices equivalent to ¥25 per share. 海外ファンドは、1株25円で転換社債を引き受けた。◆The funds that so abundantly seek safe haven in New York today can flow outward tomorrow. 安全な投資先を求めて今日ニューヨークにあふれるほど集まった資金も、明日には外へ流出しかねない。◆The higher the level of stock prices, the more funds firms can raise from IPOs. 株価の水準が上がれば、それだけ新規株式公開（上場時の新株発行）による資金調達額も増える。◆The introduction of a payoff system that will cap the guaranteed refund of savings deposits could trigger funds to flow out from relatively less credible banks. 普通預金（貯蓄性預金）の払戻し保証額に上限を設けるペイオフ制度の導入で、信用が比較的低い銀行から資金が流出する恐れがある。◆The percentage of government funds from the consumption tax and other tax revenues for financing the basic pension plan remains about 36.5 percent. 基礎年金の財源としての消費税収などによる国の負担金の割合は、まだ約36.5％にとどまっている。◆The trust fund will be set up separately from the development fund for Iraq. 信託基金は、イラク開発基金とは別に設けられる。◆The two exchanges also aim to lure funds from investors both at home and abroad by the merger. 経営統合によって、両株式取引所は国内外の投資資金を呼び込む狙いもある。◆To help finance the government burden in running the basic pension plan, the Health, Labor and Welfare Ministry calls for ¥10.67 trillion in funds in its budgetary request for fiscal 2012. 基礎年金運営の国庫負担［国の負担］分の費用として、厚生労働省は、2012年予算の概算要求で10兆6,700億円を要求している。

fund capital investments 設備投資の資金調達をする，設備投資の資金を調達する
◆Small and midsize companies have been stepping up equity financing to fund capital investments and prepare for M&A deals. 中小企業は、設備投資の資金調達とM&A取引に備えて、株式発行による資金調達を急いでいる。

fund collecting system 集金システム
◆The company created various fund collecting systems, including one called Akari Kakaku, which pulled in ¥20.7 billion in seven years. 同社は、7年で207億円を集めたシステム「あかり価格」などを含めて、各種の集金システムを考え出した。

fund deal 資金取引
◆The government plans to revise the law against organized crime to add the collection and provision of funds for terrorism to the article defining "suspicious fund deals" in the law. 政府は、組織的犯罪処罰法を改正し、テロ行為のための資金収集・提供を、同法で定める「疑わしい資金取引」の対象に加える方針だ。

fund management 資金運用，資金管理，資金運用管理，投資運用，投資管理，投資顧問
◆The bank handles only time deposits for the purpose of fund management. 同行は、資金運用目的の定期預金だけを扱っている。

fund manager 資金運用者，資金管理者，資金運用担当者，資金管理担当者，金融資産運用者，ファンド・マネージャー　（⇒portfolio weighting）
◆After the briefing for foreign investors, a fund manager showed interest in investing in Japanese government bonds. 海外投資家向け説明会の後、あるファンド・マネージャーが日本国債への投資に関心を示した。◆The markets are now controlled by the fund managers of pension funds, investment trust funds, hedge funds and various other funds. 市場は、今では年金基金や投資信託基金、ヘッジ・ファンドなどのファンド・マネージャーによって支配されている。

fund misappropriation 資金の不正流用
◆The firm's financial statements did not properly disclose important information concerning the fund misappropriation incident by its former chief executive officer. 同社の財務書類は、前最高経営責任者（CEO）による資金の不正流用（事件）に関する重大な情報を適正に開示していない。

fund-of-funds ファンド・オブ・ファンズ（投資信託に投資する投資信託（「投信の投信」）で、投資家から集めた資金の運用を、別の複数の投資信託に最委託する仕組み）
domestic investment in a type of investment fund known as fund-of-funds ファンド・オブ・ファンドと呼ばれる一種の投資信託への国内投資
fund-of-funds product ファンド・オブ・ファンズ商品
◆Domestic investment in a type of investment fund known as fund-of-funds has exceeded ¥1 trillion. ファンド・オブ・ファンズと呼ばれる一種の投資信託への国内投資が、1兆円を突破した。◆Fund-of-funds do not invest capital directly in stocks and bonds, but reinvest it in other investment trusts as a way to minimize risk. ファンド・オブ・ファンズは、（投資家から集めた）資金を株式や債券に直接投資せず、リスクを最小限に抑える手段として他の複数の投資信託に再投資する。

fund-of-funds investment ファンド・オブ・ファンズ投資
◆The benefit of fund-of-funds investment is that it allows investment risks to be minimized. 投資リスクを最小限に抑えるのが、ファンド・オブ・ファンズ投資の利点である。

fund on [in] hand 手元資金，手持ち資金
◆The U.S. private banks' funds on hand grew about three times from March 2008 prior to the Lehman's collapse. 米国の民間銀行の手持ち資金は、リーマン・ブラザーズの経営破たん前の2008年3月から約3倍増えた。

fund procurement activities 資金調達活動
◆Companies have restarted fund procurement activities for a recovery in production as the bond market turbulence after the March 11 earthquake and tsunami has subsided. 東日本大震災後の債券市場の混乱が収束したので、企業各社は生産回復に向けて資金調達活動を再開した。

fund raising 資金調達，資本調達

fund-raising activities 資金調達活動
◆The chairman of the company masterminded the firm's illegal fund-raising activities. 同社の会長が、同社の不正な資金集め活動を主導していた。

fund raising costs 資金調達コスト
◆Banks' fund-raising costs have increased, reflecting the rise in market rates after the Bank of Japan abandoned its zero-interest policy. 日銀のゼロ金利政策解除に伴って市場金利が上昇したのを反映して、銀行の資金調達コストが増大した。

fund-raising target 資金調達目標
◆Japan Airlines Corp. is expected to fall short of its planned fund-raising target by about ¥50 billion due to lower stock price. 日本航空では、株価の下落で、当初計画の資金調達目標を約500億円下回る見通しだ。

fund supply　資金供給
◆The nation's monetary base in May 2011 increased 16.2 percent from a year earlier as the Bank of Japan continued its abundant fund supply operations following the March 11 disaster. 東日本大震災(2011年3月11)を受けて日銀が潤沢な資金供給を続けたため、日本の2011年5月のマネタリー・ベースは、前年同月比で16.2%増加した。

fund the issuance of new shares　新株発行を引き受ける、増資を引き受ける
(⇒funding of the issuance of new shares)
◆Zenno and Itochu Corp. already have agreed to fund the issuance of new shares of Snow Brand Milk stock to boost the company's capital base. 全農(全国農業協同組合連合会)と伊藤忠は、雪印乳業の資本基盤を強化するため、同社の新株発行[増資]を引き受けることですでに合意している。

fund transaction　資金取引、資金のやりとり
◆Errors in computing systems at financial institutions could lead to problems in making international fund transactions. 金融機関のコンピュータ・システムのエラーは、国際的な資金取引上、トラブルが生じる可能性がある。◆The bank has few fund transactions with other financial institutions. 同行は、他の金融機関との資金のやりとりはほとんど行っていない。

fund transfer　資金移動、資金のシフト、口座振替、送金
(=the movement of funds)
◆Such an exceptional measure is unavoidable in order to stop making fund transfers from regional banks. 地方銀行[地域金融機関]からの資金移動に歯止めをかけるには、こうした特例もやむを得ない。◆Such fund transfers are not limited to local governments. このような資金移動が起こるのは、自治体だけではない。

fundamental profit　基礎利益　(=basic profit)
◆The fundamental profit represents earnings from core insurance operations like policy sales. 基礎利益とは、保険の販売など、本業の保険業務による収益(利益)を意味する。

fundamentalism　(名)市場原理主義
　market fundamentalism　市場原理主義
◆U.S.-style financial business models have symbolized neo-liberalism and market fundamentalism. これまでは、米国型の金融ビジネス・モデルが新自由主義と市場原理主義の象徴だった。

fundamentals　(名)基本、原理、基礎、基礎的条件、基本的指標(国の成長率、インフレ率、財政収支、金融情勢、為替レート、経常・貿易収支の六つ)、ファンダメンタルズ　(⇒economic fundamentals)
　company fundamentals　企業のファンダメンタルズ
　economic fundamentals　経済の基礎の条件、経済のファンダメンタルズ
　(⇒foreign exchange fluctuations)
　financial fundamentals　財務面のファンダメンタルズ、財務体質
　friendly fundamentals　ファンダメンタルズ面の強気材料
　long-term credit fundamentals　長期的な信用のファンダメンタルズ
　strong fundamentals　堅調なファンダメンタルズ
　supply fundamentals　供給のファンダメンタルズ
　the mid- and long-term fundamentals of the economy　中長期的な経済のファンダメンタルズ(基礎的条件)
　U.S. fundamentals　米国経済のファンダメンタルズ
◆If we look at the yen's current exchange rate in terms of its real effective exchange rate, it is basically within a range consistent with the mid- and long-term fundamentals of the economy. 今の円相場[円の為替相場]は、実質実効為替レートで見ると、基本的には中長期的な経済のファンダメンタルズ(基礎的条件)と整合的な範囲内ある。◆The single currency should trade in line with economic fundamentals in the medium and long term. 単一通貨(欧州単一通貨のユー

ロ)は、中長期的な経済のファンダメンタルズ(基礎的条件)に沿って、取引されるべきだ。

funded　(形)資金を調達した、積み立てられる[積み立てられた]、資金を提供された、金[資金]を出した、拠出された、出資した[出資された]、助成を受けている、基金に繰り入れられた、赤字などを補填(ほてん)した、(一時借入金を)長期債に借り換えた、長期公債に切り替えた、公債に投資された、〜系の
　amounts funded　積立額
　be fully funded　十分積み立てられている、十分助成を受けている
　be funded out of working capital　運転資金[運転資本]から支払われる
　funded debt　長期債務、長期負債、長期債、外部負債、公債発行借入金、社債発行借入金、英国の有期国債確定公債、確定公債、固定債務　(=bonded debt)
　funded loan　長期公債
　funded pension　積立年金、年金基金
　funded pension plan　積立年金制度、積立型年金制度、年金基金制度、年金基金制
　funded plan　積立プラン
　funded property　財源資産
　funded reserve　投資積立金
　funded status　拠出状態、積立状況、積立過不足額、基金の状態、拠出状態
　funded stock　長期公債
　government funded　政府出資の(state funded)、政府の資金による、政府系の
　jointly funded organization　共同出資の組織
　liability for pension expense not funded　未積立年金費用債務
　net funded debt　純借入債務
　past service cost funded　原始過去勤務原価積立て
　pro forma [pro-forma, proforma] net funded debt　予想純借入れ債務
　publicly funded　公的資金を使った
　state funded　政府出資の(government funded)、州が融資[出資]する、政府系の

-funded　(形)〜が出資した、〜出資の、〜系の
　foreign-funded company　外資企業、外資系企業
　government-funded investment company　政府系投資会社、政府出資の投資会社
　privately-funded starts　民間資金による住宅着工戸数
　publicly-funded　公的資金を使った、公的資金による、公共資金による
　publicly-funded starts　公共資金による着工戸数
　state-funded　国から資金を得た、政府出資の、政府系の
　state-funded Development Bank of Japan　政府系日本政策投資銀行
　state-funded financial institution　政府系金融機関
◆Former PCI president and executives swindled the government out of about ¥300 million by overcharging for a state-funded project to dispose of chemical weapons. PCI元社長と元取締役らは、国をだまして政府出資の化学兵器処理事業の事業費を水増し請求し、約3億円をだまし取った。◆JAL will ask for funds from the state-funded Development Bank of Japan. 日本航空は、政府系日本政策投資銀行からの資金援助を求める方針だ。

funding　(名)資金調達、調達、調達手段、積立て、資金化、資金源、長期債化、長期国債の借換え、基金設立、融資、拠出、資金供与、資金提供、出資、投資、事業費、財政援助
　advance funding method　事前積立方式
　contribute funding to　〜に資金を拠出する
　cost of floating rate funding　変動金利による資金調達コ

スト
cut funding for Pyongyang's development of missiles　北朝鮮のミサイル開発の資金源を絶つ
direct funding　直接融資
employee pension funding　従業員年金基金への拠出
external funding　外部資金調達, 資金調達能力（=external financing, funding capacity）
funding contributions　年金積立額
funding cost　資金調達コスト（=cost of funding）
funding for redemption of corporate bonds　社債の償還資金
funding requirements　資金需要（=funding needs）
funding source　資金調達源, 資金源
funding vehicle　資金調達手段
investment funding　投資金融
long-term funding　長期資金の調達
main funding requirements　必要とする主な資金
minimum funding requirements　最低積立要件
research and development funding　研究開発費
terminal funding　年金現価積立方式
terminal funding method　年金現価充足方式
the bank's excessive funding　同行の過剰融資
◆Financial support is the prerequisite for the two firms' funding of the issuance of new shares. 金融支援は、両社の増資引受けの前提条件となっている。◆It is important to cut funding for Pyongyang's development of missiles and nuclear weapons. 北朝鮮のミサイルや核兵器開発の資金源を断つことが重要だ。◆The introduction of an environmental tax would make it difficult to secure funding for the development of new technology. 環境税を導入したら、新技術開発への投資が困難になる。◆The investigation committee questioned the bank's excessive funding of a golf course developer. 調査委員会は、ゴルフ場経営会社への同行の過剰融資を問題にした。◆The ministries and agencies will request the necessary funding in the fiscal 2012 budget. 各省庁は、2012年度予算で必要な事業費を要求することになる。◆Vodafone also will contribute funding to Ripplewood to maintain business ties with the firm. ボーダフォンも、リップルウッドに資金を拠出して、ビジネス関係を継続する方針だ。

funding for reconstruction　復興のための資金拠出, 再建の資金拠出
◆Iraq urged international donors to speed up funding for reconstruction. イラクは、イラク復興のための資金拠出加速を世界の拠出国に要請した。

funding of the issuance of new shares　新株発行引受け, 増資引受け
（⇒fund the issuance of new shares）
◆Financial support is the prerequisite for the two firms' funding of the issuance of new shares. 金融支援は、両社の増資引受けの前提条件となっている。

funnel　（動）送り込む, つぎ込む, 注ぐ, 放出する,（資金や情報などを）流す, 集中する,（1箇所に）集める, 重点配分する
funnel funds into the market　資金を市場に放出する
funnel special budget to growth fields　特別予算枠を成長分野に重点配分する
illegally funnel　不正につぎ込む
◆The government funneled funds into the market as yen-selling intervention. 政府は、円売り介入で資金を市場に放出した。

further　（動）促進する, 推進する, 助長する, 増進する, 助成する, 助ける
◆We make an acquisition when that seems the most effective way to take advantage of a particular market opportunity to further our growth goals. 当社が企業を買収するのは、特定の市場機会をとらえて当社の成長目標をさらに推進する上で、それが最も効果的な方法であると思われるときです。

further　（形）一層の, 一段の, もう一段の, 追加の, 再度の, 今後の　（副）さらに, もっと, 一段と
further cost cutting　一層のコスト削減
further debt issuance　債券の追加発行, 今後の債券発行
further devaluation　もう一段の切下げ
further earnings decline　業績の一段の悪化, 引き続き減益となること
further ease　一層の金融緩和
further easing in interest rates　一層の金利引下げ, 一層の利下げ, 追加利下げ, もう一段の利下げ（=further interest rate cut）
further easing in monetary policy　金融政策の一層の緩和
further (interest) rate hike　一層の金利引上げ, 一層の利上げ, 追加利上げ, もう一段の利上げ
further payment　追加支払い
further policy firming　一層の金融引締め, 一層の金融政策引締め
further rate cut [cuts]　もう一段の利下げ
further reduction interest rates　一層の[もう一段の]利下げ, 追加利下げ
see further declines　さらに下落する
show further robust growth　さらに大幅に伸びる, 引き続き大幅の伸びを示す
the yen's further appreciation [rise]　円高進行
◆If the group's cash-flow situation deteriorates further, it may see its creditor banks declining to extend loans. 同グループの資金繰りがさらに悪化すれば、取引銀行が融資を拒否する可能性もある。◆If the number of corporate bankruptcies and the unemployment rate soar owing to structural reforms, recessionary pressures will further increase. 構造改革で企業倒産件数や失業率が増えると、不況圧力は一層強まるものと思われる。◆In the case of foreign currency deposits, losses may balloon if the yen appreciates further and may cause a loss of principal. 外貨預金の場合、円高がさらに進めば損失が膨らみ、元本割れになる恐れもある。◆Long-term debts held by central and local governments are expected to further swell unless the government puts the brakes on government bond issuance. 政府が国債発行に歯止めをかけないと、国と地方[地方自治体]が抱える長期債務は、さらに膨らむ見通しだ。◆Speculators exploited these buying factors, pushing oil prices up further. 投機筋がこれらの買い材料に反応して[投機筋がこれらの買い材料を利用して]、原油価格の高騰[原油高]を増幅している。◆The amount of net selling of Japanese stocks further increased in September. 9月は、日本株の売り越しの額がさらに増えた。◆The BOJ decided to ease its monetary grip further by effectively restoring its zero-interest-rate policy. 日銀は、実質的にゼロ金利政策を復活させて、追加の金融緩和を決めた。◆The BOJ decided to further relax its monetary policy by injecting an additional ¥10 trillion into a fund aimed at purchasing government bonds and corporate debentures. 日銀は、国債や社債などを買い入れるための基金に新たに10兆円を注入[投入]して追加の金融緩和に踏み切ることを決めた。◆The BOJ is prepared to hold its policy meeting ahead of schedule if the yen's value further soars before the next meeting. 次回の政策決定会合までに円高が一段と進めば、日銀は会合を前倒しして会合を開く構えだ。◆The government and the Bank of Japan should conduct a concerted intervention with the United States and European countries to stem the yen's further rise. 政府・日銀は、米欧と協調介入を実施して、円高進行を阻止しなければならない。◆The government may exert great pressure on the Bank of Japan to further relax its monetary policy. 政

◆The U.S. central bank's Federal Open Market Committee emphasized that the extent and timing of any further policy firming would depend on the evolution of the economic outlook. 米連邦準備制度理事会（FRB）の連邦公開市場委員会（FOMC）は、「一層の金融政策引き締め［一層の金融引き締め］の程度やタイミングは、経済見通しの成り行きによる」と強調した。◆The U.S. Federal Reserve Board said in its Beige Book release that the U.S. economy deteriorated further in almost all corners of the country. 米連邦準備制度理事会（FRB）は、地区連銀景況報告（ベージュ・ブック）を発表し、米国の経済情勢はほぼ全米で一段と悪化していると指摘した。◆The yen may appreciate further to ¥70 against the U.S. dollar. 円高は、さらに1ドル＝75円まで進む可能性がある。

further advance of the yen 一層の円高
◆The talks between Prime Minister Kan and Bank of Japan Gov. Shirakawa led to a further advance of the yen and offloading of stocks as disappointment spread among market players. 菅首相と日銀総裁の会談は、一層の円高と市場筋の株の失望売りを誘った。

further appreciation of the yen 一層の円高，円高進行
◆It's difficult to offset losses from further appreciation of the yen with interest as interest rates in many foreign currency deposits are low. 外貨建て預金の多くは金利が低いので、円高進行による損失分を利息で相殺する［取り戻す］のは難しい。

further chaos 一層の混乱
◆The world economy may be thrown into further chaos. 世界経済は、一層混乱する恐れがある。

further efforts もう一段の努力，もう一層の努力，今後の努力
◆Further efforts are needed to resolve the financial unrest. 金融不安を解消するには、もう一段の努力が必要だ。

further interest rate reduction 一層の金利引下げ，再度の金利引下げ，さらなる金利引下げ，一層の利下げ，追加利下げ，再度の利下げ，再利下げ
◆As joint actions, major industrial nations have taken such measures as further interest rate reductions, quantitative monetary relaxation to increase the money supply, the injection of public funds and increased public spending. 協調行動として、主要先進諸国は、さらなる金利の引下げ、通貨供給量を増やすための量的金融緩和や公的資金の注入、財政出動［公共支出の拡大］などの措置を取った。

further monetary easing 追加の金融緩和，一段［もう一段］の金融緩和［緩和策］
(=additional monetary easing; ⇒speculation)
◆The Bank of Japan is considering holding an extraordinary policy meeting to discuss further monetary easing. 日本銀行は、臨時の政策決定会合を開いて、追加の金融緩和［量的金融緩和］について協議することを検討している。◆The Bank of Japan seems to have unwillingly implemented measures piecemeal for further monetary easing under pressure from the government and the market. 日銀は、政府や市場にせっつかれて追加の金融緩和策を小出しにした［小出しに実施した］ようだ。

further quantitative easing 追加の量的緩和，追加の量的金融緩和，追加量的緩和
◆The U.S. FRB's recent decision on further quantitative easing is only an aberration. 米連邦準備制度理事会（FRB）の今回の追加金融緩和の決定は、常軌を逸した行為と言わざるを得ない。

further quantitative monetary easing 一段の量的金融緩和，追加の量的金融緩和 (=additional quantitative monetary easing; ⇒Policy Board meeting)
◆The Bank of Japan decided to take new steps for further quantitative monetary easing at an extraordinary Policy Board meeting. 日銀は、臨時の金融政策決定会合で、追加の量的金融緩和策を新たに実施することを決めた。◆The Bank of Japan should introduce further quantitative monetary easing. 日銀は、一段の量的金融緩和に踏み切るべきだ。

further rise in the yen 一段の円高
◆If the numerical goal of G-20 nations' current account surpluses or deficits is introduced, Japan could be pressed to allow a further rise in the yen. G20（世界20か国・地域）の経常収支の黒字または赤字の数値目標が導入されれば、（経常黒字国の）日本は一段の円高を迫られる可能性がある。

further stability in the financial markets 金融市場の一層の安定
◆Further stability in the financial markets is desirable. 金融市場の一層の安定が、望まれる。

future （名）未来，将来，行く末，先行き，前途，今後，これから先，見込み，可能性，将来性，未来時制 （形）未来の，将来の，今後の
the foreseeable future　近い将来
the future of external demand　外需の先行き
the future of the global economy　世界経済の先行き
◆If life insurers continue to offer insurance policies with guaranteed high return rates, the future financial burden in terms of interest payments will increase. 生保が高い利回りを保証した保険の販売を今後とも続けると、将来の利払いの金融負担が増えることになる。◆The company is expected to continue earning a stable profit for the foreseeable future. 同社は、将来的にも安定した利益が見込める。◆The future of external demand is uncertain because of the rising yen and fears of economic downturns in other countries. 円高や海外経済の減速懸念で、外需の先行きは不透明である。◆The future of the global economy is still uncertain. 世界経済の先行きは、まだ不透明だ。

futures （名）先物，先物取引，先物契約，先物為替
(⇒crude futures, spot transaction of stocks)
bond futures　債券先物，債券先物取引
commodity futures　商品先物
currency futures　通貨先物，通貨先物取引
financial futures　金融先物，金融先物取引
financial futures market　金融先物市場
foreign currency futures　通貨先物
gold futures　金先物
index futures　指数先物
interest rate futures　金利先物，金利先物取引
option on futures　先物オプション
stock futures　株式先物
stock index futures　株価指数先物
synthetic futures　合成先物
◆Gold futures for December delivery closed at $1,891.90 an ounce at 2:05 p.m. on the Comex in New York. ニューヨーク商品取引所では、12月渡しの金先物価格が、午後2時5分の時点で1トロイ・オンス（約31グラム）＝1,891.90ドルに達した。◆U.S. light crude hit $42.45 a barrel, the highest since futures were launched in New York in 1983. 米国の軽質原油は1バレル＝42.45ドルで、1983年にニューヨークで先物取引を開始して以来の最高値となった。

futures brokerage 先物会社
(⇒Commodity Exchange Law, insider)
◆According to a commodity futures market insider, futures brokerages depending on commissions for revenue will lose their business strength. 商品先物市場関係者によると、収入を手数料に頼っている先物会社の経営体力は、今後弱まりそうだ。◆Some futures brokerages affiliated with trading houses lowered brokerage commissions on over-the-counter deals early this month. 商社系先物会社の一部は、今月はじめに店頭取引の手数料を引き下げた。

futures contract 先物契約，先物

(⇒initial margin)
◆The firm hedged its long position in stocks by selling short the futures contract. 同社は、先物を空売りして現物株のロング・ポジションをヘッジした。◆The June 2012 gold futures contract closed at ￥4,694 per gram, down ￥54 from the previous day's close on the Tokyo Commodity Exchange. 東京工業品取引所では、2012年6月渡しの金先物価格は、前日の終値より54円安の1グラム＝4,694円で取引を終えた。

futures market　先物市場　(⇒insider)
◆The revised Commodity Exchange Law was put into force in May 2005 to improve the integrity of the commodity futures market. 商品先物市場の信頼性を高めるため、2005年5月に改正商品取引所法が施行された。

futures trader　先物取引業者
◆Futures traders expect a vigorous U.S. recovery. 先物取引業者は、米景気の力強い回復を期待している。

futures trading　先物取引
(＝futures transaction)
◆Bills to tighten controls on futures trading have been submitted to Congress. 先物取引の規制を強化する法案が、米議会に提出された。

futures trading brokerage　商品先物会社
◆About ￥1.6 billion in suspense payments remitted to a former vice president of a futures trading brokerage are unaccounted for. 商品先物会社の元副社長に送金された仮払い金約160億円が現在、会計処理されていない[使途不明になっている]。

futures trading of the 225-issue Nikkei Stock Average　日経平均株価(225種)の先物取引
◆In order to overcome disadvantages in such spot transactions of stocks and to take the lead in futures and derivatives, the Osaka Securities Exchange in 1988 launched futures trading of the 225-issue Nikkei Stock Average. この現物株取引での劣勢を挽回し、先物やデリバティブ(金融派生商品)に活路を開くため、大阪証券取引所は1988年に日経平均株価(225種)の先物取引を始めた。

FX　(名)外国為替　(＝foreign exchange, forex)
FX business　外国為替取引
FX margin trading　外国為替証拠金取引, FX取引 (FX取引では、一定額の現金を証拠金として差し入れ、それを担保にインターネットなどで外貨を売買できる)
◆In FX margin trading, investors can expect high returns from a relatively small amount of capital. 外国為替証拠金取引では、投資家は、比較的わずかな資金でハイリターンを期待できる。

G

G7[G-7]　先進7か国財務相・中央銀行総裁会議, 先進7か国会議, 7か国蔵相会議, G7　(＝Group of Seven: 日・米・英・独・仏・伊・加の7か国が参加。2003年からロシアが参加して、G8(Group of Eight)となる)
◆The G7 has reached a major turn of events in that the latest meeting held in Canada did not release a joint communique for the first time in 12.5 years. カナダで開かれた今回のG7 (先進国7か国財務相・中央銀行総裁会議)が、12年半ぶりに共同声明の採択を見送ったことで、G7は大きな転換点を迎えている。

G-7 financial meeting　先進7か国財務相・中央銀行総裁会議, 先進7か国会議
(＝G-7 meeting, G-7 talks)

G-7[G-7's] financial ministers and central bank governors　先進7か国(G7)の財務相・中央銀行総裁
◆The emergency telephone conference by the G-7 financial ministers and central bank governors was held right before the opening of Asian financial markets. 先進7か国(G7)の財務相・中央銀行総裁による緊急電話会議は、アジアの金融市場が開く直前に開かれた。◆The G-7's financial ministers and central bank governors are committed to taking necessary measures to support financial stability and economic growth. 先進7か国(G7)の財務相と中央銀行総裁は、金融安定化と経済成長を支えるためにあらゆる手段を講じる決意だ。

G-7 joint statement　G-7の共同声明
◆The G-7 joint statement made clear the stance of supporting the financial markets by supplying ample funds. G7の共同声明は、潤沢な資金供給によって金融市場を下支えする姿勢を明らかにした。

G-7 leaders　G7首脳
(＝G7 leaders, Leaders of the Group of Seven)
◆The G-7 leaders merely welcomed Washington's economic stimulus measures in the form of interest rate cuts and tax cuts as "positive." G7首脳は、利下げや減税などの形での米政府の景気刺激策を「積極的」として歓迎しただけだ。

G-7 meeting　先進7か国会議(G7)
(＝G-7 financial meeting, G-7 talks; ⇒influential)
◆The G-7 meeting has repeatedly issued communiques concerning exchange rate fluctuations and economic policy management. 先進7か国会議(G7)は、これまで為替変動や経済政策運営に関する声明を再三、発信してきた。

G-7 meeting of finance ministers and central bank governors　先進7か国財務相・中央銀行総裁会議(G7)　(＝Group of Seven)
◆China is cementing its position as an associate member of the G-7 meeting of finance ministers and central bank governors. 中国は現在、先進7か国財務相・中央銀行総裁会議(G7)の準メンバーとしての地位を固めている。

G-7 talks　G7(先進7か国財務相・中央銀行総裁会議)の協議
◆At the G-7 talks, concern over soaring public debts was to top the agenda. G7(先進7か国財務相・中央銀行総裁会議)の協議では、増大する公的債務問題[公的債務への懸念]が最大の議題[課題]になる予定だった。◆The issue of soaring public debts was pigeonholed at the G-7 talks. 増大する公的債務の問題は、G7(先進7か国財務相・銀行総裁会議)の協議では棚上げされてしまった。

G-20[G20]　世界20か国・地域(G20), G20
(＝the Group of 20, the Group of 20 advanced and major developing countries:G7(日米欧先進7か国)、新興国(中国、インド、南アフリカ、サウジアラビアなど)12か国と欧州連合(EU)の財務相・中央銀行総裁による国際会議)
◆At the latest G-20 meeting, diverging opinions among member countries were exposed over expanding the lending capacity of the IMF. 今回のG20(財務相・中央銀行総裁)会議では、国際通貨基金(IMF)が融資できる資金規模の拡大をめぐって、加盟国の間で意見の食い違いが表面化した。◆The G-20 sought the comprehensive reforms of the IMF and the World Bank in a joint statement. 世界20か国・地域(G-20)の財務相・中央銀行総裁は、共同声明でIMF(国際通貨基金)と世界銀行の包括的改革を求めた。

G-20 communique　G20共同声明
◆The G-20 communique urged the eurozone countries to boost the EFSF, the EU bailout fund. G20(主要20か国・地域)の共同声明は、ユーロ圏諸国に欧州の金融支援基金である欧州金融安定基金(EFSF)の拡充を促した。

G-20 (financial) chiefs　世界[主要]20か国・地域(G20)の財務相・中央銀行総裁
(＝financial chiefs from the Group of 20)
◆G-20 chiefs have agreed to avoid a global currency war. 主要20か国・地域(G20)財務相・中央銀行総裁は、通貨安競争を回避することで合意した。

G-20 summit　G20(主要20か国・地域)首脳会議, G-20サミット(首脳会議)

◆At the Seoul G-20 summit, all the leaders agreed to introduce "indicative guidelines" that would be conductive to reducing current account imbalances. 主要20か国・地域(G20)のソウル・サミット(首脳会議)で、全首脳が、経常収支不均衡の是正に役立つ「参考指針」を導入することで合意した。

G-SIFIs 金融システム上重要な国際金融機関、国際金融システムにとって重要な金融機関、国際的な巨大金融機関、世界経済に大きな影響を及ぼす金融機関(global systemically important financial institutionsの略)
◆The final list of G-SIFIs will be released in January 2014. G-SIFIsの最終リストは、2014年1月に発表される。◆The Financial Stability Board will impose a progressive extra capital charge of 1 percent to 2.5 percent on risk-adjusted assets held by G-SIFIs. G20(主要20か国・地域)の金融当局で構成する金融安定化理事会(FSB)は、国際金融システムにとって重要な金融機関(G-SIFIs)が保有するリスク調整後資産に、1～2.5%の資本[自己資本]の上積みを段階的に課すことになった。

G-SIFIs [G-SIFI] list 国際的な巨大金融機関リスト、G-SIFIリスト (=the list of G-SIFIs)
◆Mitsubishi UFJ Financial Group Inc., Sumitomo Mitsui Financial Group Inc. and Mizuho Financial Group Inc. are included in the G-SIFIs list of the Financial Stability Board. 主要20か国・地域(G20)の金融当局で構成する金融安定化理事会(FSB)のG-SIFIリスト(国際的な巨大金融機関リスト)には、三菱UFJ、三井住友、みずほの3大金融グループも含まれている。◆The Financial Services Agency did not comment on whether any Japanese banks had been earmarked for the G-SIFIs list. 金融庁は、邦銀が国際金融システム上重要な金融機関(G-SIFIs)リストの指定行に入っているかどうかについては、コメントしなかった。

GAAP 一般に認められた会計原則[会計基準]、一般に公正妥当と認められた会計原則、一般会計原則[会計基準]、会計基準、ジー・エイ・エイ・ピー、ギャップ (⇒generally accepted accounting principles)
◆The closing balance sheet fairly presents the financial position of the Corporation at the closing date in conformity with United States GAAP. クロージング時現在の貸借対照表は、米国の一般に認められた会計原則[米国の会計基準]に従って、クロージング日の「会社」の財政状態を適正に表示している。◆The consolidated financial statements have been prepared in accordance with German GAAP. この連結財務書類[財務諸表]は、ドイツの一般に公正妥当と認められた会計基準[ドイツの会計基準]に従って作成されています。

GAAS 一般に認められた監査基準、一般に公正妥当と認められた監査基準 (generally accepted auditing standardsの略)
◆These GAASs require that we plan and perform the audit to obtain reasonable assurance about whether the financial statements are free of material misstatement. これらの一般に認められた監査基準は、連結財務書類に重要な虚偽表示がないかどうかについての合理的な確証を得るため、私どもが監査を計画して実施することを要求しています。

gain (動)得る、獲得する、入手する、達成する、技術などを身につける、経験などを積む、増加する、増大する、増進する、増す、向上する、上がる、上昇する
　gain (by) about 10 basis points 10ベーシス・ポイント(0.1%)上昇[増加]する
　gain control [dominance] 支配権を得る、経営権を得る[握る]、主導権を得る
　gain from the currency turbulence 通貨危機[為替市場の波瀾]から買われる
　gain ground 確実に力をつける、人気が上がる、成功する、徐々に広く知られるようになる
　gain market share シェア[市場シェア]を獲得する、シェアを拡大する、シェアを伸ばす、シェアを奪う
　gain market share from ～からシェアを奪う
　gain substantial value 価値が大幅に上昇する
　gain time 時間稼ぎをする
　gain up to 10 percent stake in the company 同社に最大10%出資する、同社株を最大10%取得する
　the yen gained against all currencies 円は全面高になった
　the yen gains further against the dollar ドルに対して[対ドルで]さらに円高が進む、円高・ドル安がさらに進む
◆An urgent task facing each financial group is to improve its financial conditions and profitability on the strength of advantages gained from merger. 合併・統合の相乗効果を生かして、財務内容と収益力を向上させることが、各金融グループの現在の急務だ。◆For the April-September period, operating profit gained 12 percent from the year before. 4-9月期(3月期決算企業の上半期)の営業利益は、前年同期比で12%増加した。◆Gold futures for December delivery gained to $1,897 an ounce at 4:13 p.m. in after-hours electronic trading on the Comex in New York. ニューヨーク商品取引所の時間外電子取引で、金先物の12月渡し価格は、午後4時13分の時点で1トロイ・オンス=1,897ドルまで上昇した。◆MFG would gain several hundred billion yen in capital gains if the brokerage goes public. みずほフィナンシャルグループは、みずほ証券が上場した場合には数千億円の上場益[株式譲渡益]を見込んでいる。◆MUFG is expected to gain up to 20 percent stake in Morgan Stanley. 三菱UFJフィナンシャル・グループは、モルガン・スタンレーに最大20%出資する見込みだ。◆Shares in chipmaker Elpida Memory Inc. gained 7.14 percent on their Monday debut. 半導体メーカー、エルピーダメモリの株価は、月曜日の上場で7.14%上昇した。◆The Fed deems the U.S. economy to be bearish and as a result the yen will gain further against the dollar. 米連邦準備制度理事会(FRB)が米経済について弱気の見方を示しているため、ドルに対して円高はさらに進むと思われる。

gain (名)利益、利潤、増加、増大、増進、伸び、拡大、上昇、向上、ゲイン (⇒capital gain, day trader, high-tech stock, latent gain, option holder, self-assessment, stockholding gains)
　actuarial gains and [or] losses 保険数理上の損益
　capital gain 資本利得、譲渡所得、値上がり益
　currency gains 為替差益
　earnings gain 収益の伸び
　economic gain 経済拡大
　efficiency gain 生産性の伸び、生産性向上 (=productivity gain)
　employment gain 雇用の伸び、雇用の増加
　exchange gain 為替差益 (=currency gain, foreign exchange gain, forex gain)
　export gain 輸出の伸び
　financial gain 利益の追求
　foreign exchange gain 為替差益、為替差損益 (=exchange gain)
　fraudulent gain 不正利得
　gain from decline in the value of money 貨幣価値利益
　gain from forgiveness of debt 債務免除益
　gain from operations 営業利益
　gain from redemption 償還差益
　gain from reduction of capital stock 減資差益
　gain of insurance claim 保険差益
　gain on conversion of stock 株式転換益
　gain on disposal (資産の)売却益
　gain on sale of bonds 社債売却益
　gains and losses 損益
　gains from trade 貿易利益
　gains in interest income 利子収入の伸び

gains in prices　物価の上昇, インフレ
　　(=price gains)
gains on reacquisition of debt　債務の再取得による利益
holding gain　保有利得
income gain　所得の伸び
job gains　雇用の増加
make market share gains　シェアを拡大する, シェアを伸ばす, シェアを奪う
market share gains　マーケット・シェアの拡大, 市場シェアの拡大
paper gain　含み益
portfolio gains　資産売却益
post net gains　黒字を計上する
price gains　物価上昇, インフレ, インフレ率の上昇
　　(=gains in prices)
realize gains from stock holdings　株式含み益を実現する
redemption gain　償還差益
sales and earnings gains　増収増益
sales gains　売上の伸び
small gain　小幅な[わずかな]伸び, 小幅利益
translation gain　為替差益
unrealized [unrealised] gain　未実現利益, 含み益
◆Gains and losses on hedges of existing assets or liabilities are marked to market on a monthly basis. 既存の資産または債務のヘッジに関する損益は毎月, 評価替えされている。◆Stock-related gains as a result of rising share prices also have contributed to an improvement in the capital-adequacy ratios of the major banks. 株価上昇による株式関連売却益も, 大手銀行の(経営の健全性を示す)自己資本比率の改善に貢献した。◆The dollar-yen exchange rate closed at ¥101.2, a gain of nearly ¥25 since the beginning of the year. 円ドル・レートは, 終値で1ドル＝101円20銭で, 年初からの円の上昇幅は25円近くになった。◆The listed companies are expected to report significant gains for the whole business year. これらの上場企業は, 通期で大幅な増益が見込まれている。◆The next step in the quest for higher gains is to inflate the returns by leverage. 高利益追求の第二の手段は, 借金による利益の膨(ふく)らましだ。◆Through continuing gains in annual earnings, it will be possible, over time, to adjust the payout ratio while still maintaining our dividend record. 年間利益の増大を続けることによって, 当社の配当実績を今後とも維持しながら, 時期が来たら配当性向を調整することは可能である。◆Unrealized gains in stockholdings of major companies and banks will push up their finances by a wide margin thanks to the buoyant stock market. 株式市場の活況で(株価が高くなったことで), 大手企業と銀行の保有株式の含み益により, 財務が大幅に改善する見通しだ。

gain from stock options　ストック・オプション(自社株購入権)の利益
◆Gain from stock options is a reward for dedicated work by an employee. ストック・オプション(自社株購入権)の利益は, 従業員が熱心に勤務したことへの対価である。◆The gain from stock options fluctuates depending on the option holder's investment judgment over the timing of purchase and changes of the stock price. ストック・オプション(自社株購入権)の利益は, 購入時期と株式変動に対するオプション保有者(オプションの買い手)の判断[投資判断]によって上下する。

gainer　(名)値上がり株　(advancer, winnerともいう。値下がり株＝decliner, loser)
◆The lone gainer was the air transport sector. 唯一の値上がり株は, 航空輸送業だった。◆There were 60 winners [gainers] while losers numbered 250 losers. 値下がり株の250銘柄に対して, 値上がり株は60銘柄あった。

gap　(名)格差, 隔たり, 開き, 差, 不均衡, 不一致, 相違点, 落差, 空白, ギャップ　(⇒public sector debt)

asset gap　資産格差
asset/liability gap　資産・負債ギャップ
credibility gap　信頼性の不足
demand supply gap　需給ギャップ
　　(=gap between demand and supply)
dollar gap　ドル不足
foreign exchange gap　外国為替ギャップ
gap analysis　ギャップ分析
gap closing efforts　赤字削減努力
gap financing　つなぎ融資, ギャップ金融
　　(=bridge loan)
gap loan　残額融資
gap management　ギャップ管理(ギャップ分析を使ったリスク管理)
gap opening　放れ寄り付き, 夜放れ, ギャップ・オープニング(前日の終値よりかなり高く[安く]寄り付くこと)
income gap　所得格差
liquidity gap　流動性ギャップ
price gap　価格の開き, 放れ(株価が前日の値動きの範囲と重ならないで変動するときの開き)
rate sensitive gap　金利感応ギャップ
rating gap　信用リスクの格差
the gap in the market　市場参入の好機, 新製品開発の好機
trade gap　貿易赤字, 貿易欠損, 貿易の不均衡
wage gap　賃金格差
yield gap　金利差
◆The drop in U.S. interest rates will reduce the gap between Japanese and U.S. interest rates. 米国の金利低下で, 日米の金利差[金利ギャップ]は縮小すると思われる。◆The issue of eliminating disparities between public and private sector pensions hinges on how quickly the gaps should be closed. 官と民の年金格差[年金の官民格差]是正の問題は, いかに早くその溝を埋めるかにかかっている。

garbatrage　(名)ガーベトラージ(garbageとarbitrageの合成語。大型企業買収の影響で, 関係のない銘柄の株価も上昇すること)

garner　(動)(票などを)獲得する, (注目や支持を)集める(collect, gather), (情報などを)得る(acquire, get), 蓄える(store up), 蓄積する, 貯蔵する, 保管する, (利益を)上げる, (評判などを)取る
garner [have] a sustained reputation as a financial analyst　証券アナリストとして定評がある
garner capital from investors　投資家から資金を集める
garner 50 percent of the vote　50％の票を獲得する
◆Lone Star built a fund of several hundred of billions yen in Japan with capital it garnered from investors. ローンスターは, 投資家から集めた資金で, 日本で数千億円規模のファンドを作った。◆The alleged pyramid scheme scam garnered about ¥126 billion from about 37,000 investors. このマルチ商法詐欺事件で, 約3万7,000人の出資者から約1,260億円を集めた。◆Through the sales of shares of JR companies and NTT it owned, the central government garnered ¥3 trillion and ¥13 trillion of profits, respectively. 国が保有するJR各社とNTTの株式の売却で, 国はそれぞれ3兆円と13兆円の利益を上げた。

Garnet-St. Germain Depository Institutions Act of 1982　1982年ガーネット＝セント・ジャーメイン預金金融機関法, 1982年預金取扱い金融機関法, 1982年ガーン・セントジャーメイン預金金融機関法
　　(=Garn-St. Germain Institutions Act of 1982)

garnishee　(名)第三債務者
garnishee order　弁済禁止命令, 債権差押え命令

garnishee proceedings 債権差押え手続き
garnisher (名)差押え債権者
garnishment (名)債権差押え, 債権仮差押え
  garnishment action 債権差押え令状
  writ [Writ] of garnishment 債権差押え令状
gather momentum 勢いを増す, 拡大する, 活発化する, 本格化する
  ◆Debates on the pros and cons of a proposal to end the quantitative relaxation of credit by the Bank of Japan are gathering momentum. 日銀による量的金融緩和策を解除する案の賛否をめぐる議論が, 活発化している。◆The market is gathering momentum. 市場は上向きだ。
gauge [gage] (動)判断する, 評価する, 測定する, 計測する, 算定する, 算出する
  a key indicator gauging life insurers' ability to pay policyholders 保険契約者への生命保険会社の支払い能力を判断する主要指標
  gauge the value of latent gains or losses in one's stockholdings 保有株式の含み損益を算出する
    (⇒latent gains or losses)
  ◆Most companies use the daily average for a month of the share prices in gauging the value of latent gains or losses in their stockholdings. 大半の企業は, 保有株式の含み損益を算出する際に株価の月中平均を使っている。◆Solvency margin ratio is a key indicator gauging life insurers' ability to pay policyholders. ソルベンシー・マージン (支払い余力)比率は, 保険契約者への生命保険会社の支払い能力を判断する主要指標である。
gauge (名)基準, 尺度, 指標
  (=gage; ⇒insurance company, key gauge)
  gauge of inflation インフレ(物価上昇率)の規準
  gauge of money supply マネー・サプライの指標
  ◆The nation's most closely watched gauge of money supply grew 2 percent in December from a year earlier. 日本の代表的なマネー・サプライの指標[日本のとくに注目されるマネー・サプライの指標M2]が, 12月は前年同月比で2%増加した。◆The U.S. Labor Department's Consumer Price Index is the most widely used gauge of inflation. 米労働省が発表する消費者物価指数は, 最も広く使用されているインフレ(物価上昇率)の基準だ。
GBP 英ポンド (Great Britain Poundの略)
GDP 国内総生産 (⇒gross domestic product)
  advanced GDP figures GDP速報値
  GDP revisions GDP改定値
  nominal GDP 名目GDP
  per capita GDP 人口1人当たりのGDP
  real GDP growth 実質GDP成長率
  ◆Germany's current account surplus is far larger than 4 percent of its GDP. ドイツの経常収支黒字は, 対国内総生産比4%を大幅に超えている。◆The BOJ's total assets as a percentage of GDP stand at nearly 30 percent. 国内総生産(GDP)に対する日銀の総資産の比率[日銀の総資産の国内総生産(GDP)比]は, 約3割を占めている。◆The primary balance deficits of Greece currently stand at 10 percent of GDP. ギリシャの財政赤字は現在、GDP(国内総生産)の10%に当たる。◆The ratio of the country's fiscal deficit to GDP is far higher than that of any other industrialized country. 国内総生産(GDP)に対する日本の財政赤字の比率は, 先進国では群を抜いている。◆Under the EU's Stability and Growth Pact, countries eligible to join the euro system are required to keep budget deficits below 3 percent of GDP. 欧州連合(EU)の財政安定・成長協定によると, ユーロ加盟国は, 加盟の条件として財政赤字をGDPの3%以下に抑えなければならない。
GDP deflator GDPデフレーター
  ◆The GDP deflator, a major inflation barometer, fell 2.7 percent in the July-September period. 7〜9月期のGDPデフレーター(物価動向の主要指数)は, 前年同期比で2.7%下落した。
  解説 GDPデフレーターとは：消費者物価指数が店頭価格の動向を示すのに対して, GDPデフレーターは, 消費のほか投資なども含めた経済全体の物価動向を示す。物価変動を反映する名目GDPを, 物価変動の影響を除く実質GDPで割って産出する。
gear (動)照準を合わせる, (〜を〜に)適合させる[合わせる], 適応させる(adapt), 調整する(adjust), 連動させる, (〜を〜に)切り換える, 振り向ける, 用意する(prepare), 提供する(supply) (自動)かみ合う, 連動する, 資金を借りる
  a highly geared company 借入率の高い会社
  be geared 負債比率を高める, ギアリングを高める
  be geared to [for] 〜向けだ, 〜に照準が合わせてある, 〜するようにしてある, 〜するようになっている
  be geared up for [to] 〜の準備ができている, 〜に順応する
  be highly geared 負債比率が高い, ギアリングが高い
  be low geared 負債比率が低い, ギアリングが低い
  gear up 促進する, 速度を速める, 高速ギアにする
  gear up to 〜しようと準備する, 〜しようと備える
  gear with 〜とかみ合う, 〜と適合する, 〜と連動する, 〜と調和する
  ◆The firm's asset management strategy is geared to seek high returns. 同社の資産運用戦略は, 高収益を狙ったものだ。
gear (名)伝動装置, 機械装置, 装置, 装備, 道具, 用具, 設備一式, 家庭用品, 個人の所有物, 身の回り品, 段階, ギア
  be in low gear 低調だ, 低い
  be out of gear 調子が狂っている, ギアがかみ合わない
  be thrown out of gear 計画からはずれている
  come into gear 連動する
  enter high gear 本格化する
  get into gear 順調に動き出す, 軌道に乗る
  go into full gear 本格化する
  in [into] high gear 全速力で, 全力で
  move into high gear 急ピッチで進む, 全力で進む, 本格化する
  move into the second gear 第二段階に入る
  move into top [full] gear 最高潮に達する
  shift gear ギアを変える, 方向を変える, 方法を変える
  shift into high gear 本格化する
  ◆The government assumes a scenario in which Japan's economic growth will shift into high gear with overseas demand as a driving force. 政府は, 海外需要をテコに日本の経済成長が本格化する, とのシナリオを描いている。
gearing (名)負債, 負債比率, 純負債比率, ギアリング
  (=financial leverage, leverage, trading on the equity)
  acceptable gearing 許容範囲の負債比率
  financial gearing 財務レバレッジ, ギアリング, 借入比率, 負債比率, 資金調達力比率, 企業の資本構成に占める負債の額
  gearing adjustments ギアリング調整[修正], 負債調整額, ギアリング調整額
  gearing effect レバレッジ効果
  gearing proportion 負債調整率, ギアリング調整率
  gearing ratio 株主資本負債比率, 優先資本比率, ギアリング比率, ギアリング・レシオ
    (=the ratio of net debt to equity)
  group gearing 連結純負債比率
  high gearing 大きな負債
  increase [boost, improve] gearing 負債比率[借入比率]を引き上げる

negative net gearing　純負債比率
net gearing　純負債比率　(=net gearing level)
reduce gearing　負債比率を引き下げる
◆We reduced the ratio of net debt to equity (gearing ratio) to 15 percent in 2008. 2008年度は、株主資本純負債比率(ギアリング・レシオ)を15%に引き下げました。

general　(形)一般の、一般的な、全般的な、総合的、多岐にわたる、概略的な、概略の、通常の、総～
　general acceptance　(為替手形の)一般引受、普通引受
　general administrative expense　一般管理費、総務費、本社費　(=general administration cost, general and administrative expense)
　General Agreement on Tariffs and Trade (GATT)　関税および貿易に関する一般協定、ガット
　General Agreement [Arrangements] to Borrow　国際通貨基金(IMF)の一般借入取決め、GAB
　general bond　総括輸入宣誓書
　general broker　保険ブローカー、ゼネラル・ブローカー
　general budget　(政府の)総予算
　general cash account　総合預金口座
　general circulation　一般通貨
　general claim agent　海損処理総代理店、一般請求代理人
　general clearing　一般交換
　general closing　通常決算
　general conditions　普通約款
　general contingency reserve　一般偶発損失準備金
　general convertibility of currency　通貨の全般的交換性
　general corporate bond　一般事業債
　general cover　一括保険
　general credit [L/C]　買取銀行不指定信用状、無条件信用状、オープン・クレジット　(=negotiation credit, open credit)
　general credit contract　無担保取引信用契約、オープン・クレジット契約
　general creditor　一般債権者　(=ordinary creditor, unsecured creditor)
　general crossed check [cheque]　普通横線小切手、一般線引小切手
　general crossing　(小切手や証券の)一般線引き
　general damages　一般的損害賠償金
　general deposit　普通預金、共同海損供託金
　general distributor　元引受人
　general endorsement　(手形の)無記名式裏書
　general exchequer contribution　一般国庫交付金
　general export insurance　普通輸出保険
　general gift　一般贈与
　general grant　一般交付金　(=rate support grants)
　general letter of hypothecation　外国向荷為替手形約定書、荷為替手形副書
　general liability insurance　一般賠償責任保険、賠償責任保険
　general lien　一般担保権、一般的留置権、包括的[一般的]リーエン
　general management trust　一般管理投資信託　(=flexible trust)
　general means of payment　一般的支払い手段
　general mortgage　総括抵当、一般担保、全財産抵当、包括モーゲージ　(=blanket mortgage)
　general mortgage bond　一般担保付き社債、一般モーゲージ付き社債
　general obligation bond　一般財源債、一般財源保証債、一般保証債、GO債　(=GO bond: 米州政府や地方自治体が発行する地方債。full faith and credit bondともいう)
　general policy conditions　普通保険約款
　general (population) mortality table　国民死亡生存表、国民表
　general price index　一般物価指数
　general public investments　一般財投
　general public works　一般公共事業
　general rate (of duty)　一般税率
　general reinsurance　一般再保険
　general reserve　別途積立金
　general revenue sharing　一般交付金
　general risk　普通危険物件、普通物件
　general securities firm [company]　総合証券会社
　general statutory tariff　(一般)固定税率
　general syndication　一般シ団の組成
　general tariff　一般税率
　general tax　国税 (national tax)、普通税
　general warrant　共通預り証券
general account　一括勘定、一般会計
　◆The Great East Japan Earthquake reconstruction fund will be used to redeem the restoration bonds and will be separately managed from the government's general account. 東日本大震災の復興基金は、復興再生債の償還に充(あ)てられ、政府の一般会計から切り離して管理される。
general average　共同海損
　general average adjustment　共同海損清算
　general average balance　共同海損清算尻
　general average bond　共同海損契約書[盟約書]
　general average clause　共同海損条項、共同海損約款
　general average contribution　共同海損分担額
　general average deposit　共同海損供託金
　general average disbursements insurance　共同海損費用保険
　general average expenditure　共同海損費用
　general average guarantee　共同海損保証状
　general average loss　共同海損
　general average sacrifice　共同海損犠牲
　general average settlement　共同海損決済
general equilibrium　一般均衡
　general equilibrium model　一般均衡モデル
　general equilibrium of capitalization　資本化の一般均衡
　general equilibrium of exchange　交換の一般均衡
general expenditures　一般歳出
　◆General expenditures are expected to climb to ¥48.2 trillion in fiscal 2005 from ¥47.6 trillion in the current fiscal year. 一般歳出は、今年度の47兆6,000億円から2005年度は48兆2,000億円に膨らむ見通しだ。
general government　一般政府
　general government account　一般政府勘定
　general government debt　一般政府負債
　general government deficit　一般政府赤字
　general government fiscal balance　一般政府財政収支
　general government sector [section]　一般政府部門
general insurance　損害保険、普通保険
　general insurance agency　損害保険の代理店業務
　general insurance clauses [conditions]　損害保険約款、普通保険約款
general liquidity　一般流動性、一般的流動性
　general liquidity effect　一般流動性効果
　general liquidity position　一般流動性状態

general market 市場全般, 市場平均
 general market conditions 市場全般の状況, 市場の状況一般
 general market fund 市場ファンド
 general- market stock fund 株式市場全体で構成するファンド

general meeting 総会, 株主総会
 (⇒annual meeting)
 annual general meeting 年次株主総会
 extraordinary general meeting 臨時株主総会
 first general meeting 創立総会
 general meeting of members 社員総会
 general meeting of persons effecting insurance 保険契約者総会
 general meeting of stockholders [shareholders] 株主総会
 general meeting of substitutional members 社員総代会
 regular general meeting 定例総会, 定例株主総会
 (=ordinary general meeting)

general shareholders meeting 株主総会 (=general meeting, general meeting of shareholders, general shareholders' meeting, shareholders' general meeting, stockholders' meeting)
 ◆Stock buyback limits are to be decided at general shareholders meetings. 自社株の取得枠は、株主総会で決められることになっている。◆The company began its general shareholders meeting at its head office in Shinagawa at 10 a.m. 同社の株主総会は、品川の本社で午前10時から始まった。

generally accepted accounting principles 一般に認められた会計原則, 一般に認められた会計基準, GAAP (=generally accepted accounting practices)
 ◆This treatment was in accord with generally accepted accounting principles. この処理は、一般に認められた会計原則に従ったものだ。

generate (動)生み出す, 生む, 創造する, 生成する, 引き起こす, 発生させる, 誘発する, 獲得する, 〜を占める, 計上する, 発生する
 ability to generate cash 収益力, キャッシュ・フローを生み出す能力, キャッシュ・フロー生成能力
 ability to generate returns 収益を生み出す能力
 generate arbitrage opportunities 裁定機会を生み出す
 generate capital requirements internally 資金の必要額[必要資金]を内部で生みだす
 generate cash 収益を上げる[生む], 現金を生み出す, キャッシュ・フローを生み出す[生成する]
 generate cash flow 現金収入を得る, キャッシュ・フローを生み出す[生成する]
 generate cash to pay debt 債務返済のキャッシュ・フローを生み出す
 generate foreign currency receipts 外貨収益を生み出す
 generate foreign exchange 外貨を得る, 外貨を獲得する
 generate operating margin 営業収益を計上する
 generate operating profits 営業利益を上げる
 generate profits 利益を生み出す, 利益を生む
 generate returns 収益を生み出す
 internally generated funds 内部調達資金
 ◆Cash requirements in 2012 will be met by internally generated funds. 2012年度の資金必要額は、内部調達資金で賄(まかな)う予定です。◆Companies must be generating operating profits from their main businesses to seek debt waivers from the creditor banks. 取引銀行に債権放棄を求めるには、企業はその主要な事業部門で営業利益を上げていなければならない。◆In the project financing business, lending banks are repaid loans through profits generated by the projects they have financed. プロジェクト・ファイナンス事業では、貸出行が、融資したプロジェクト(事業)から生まれる利益で融資の返済を受ける。◆Profit generated through selling shares of an owned company could result in changes in its capital. 自社株の売却益は、資本の増減にかかわる。◆To generate about ￥7.5 trillion raised through the three percentage point increase in the consumption tax rate, income tax rates would have to be hiked dramatically. 消費税率の3％引上げで調達する予定の7.5兆円相当分を確保するには、所得税率の大幅な引上げが必要になる。

generation (名)発生, 生成, 形成, 創出, 産出, 生産, 発電, 世代, ジェネレーション
 capital generation 資本形成, 資本創出
 cash generation キャッシュ・フローの生成, キャッシュ生成能力(ability to generate cash), キャッシュ・フロー
 employment generation 雇用創出, 雇用産出
 internal capital generation rate 内部資本形成率
 internal cash generation 内部キャッシュ・フロー, 内部キャッシュ生成能力
 meet cash capital requirements through internal cash generation 内部キャッシュ・フローで資金需要を賄(まかな)う
 revenue generation 収益確保
 ◆With the United States facing the worst financial crisis in generations, Bush's White House took decisive measures to safeguard the economy. 米国が過去最悪の金融危機に直面して、ブッシュ政権は経済危機を守るために断固たる措置を取った。

generic rating 包括的格付け

gensaki (名)現先, 現先市場

Germany's 10-year government bonds ドイツの10年物国債
 ◆Germany's 10-year government bonds are regarded as one of the most safest assets in the eurozone. ドイツの10年物国債は、ユーロ圏で最も安全な資産とされている。

get (動)買う, 手に入れる, 入手する, 調達する, 集める, 得る, 獲得する, 受ける, 稼ぐ, 儲(もう)ける
 get away an issue 起債する
 get on top of the current account deficit 経常赤字削減に本腰を入れる
 get out of the positions ポジションを手じまう
 get profit 利益を得る, 利益を上げる
 get through a bad time 不況を乗り越える

get money 金を手に入れる, 金を調達する, 金を稼ぐ, 金を儲ける, 金を借りる
 get more money もっと金を稼ぐ[儲ける], 多額の利益を得る
 get unsecured money 無担保資金を調達する
 ◆The number of people using cashing services is rising partly because no screening is required to get money. 無審査で金を借りられることもあって、キャッシング・サービス(現金化商法)の利用者は増えている。

giant (名)巨大企業, 大手, 大国
 banking giant 金融大手
 economic giant 経済大国
 (=economic power, economic superpower)
 insurance giant 保険大手
 international giant 国際的巨大企業, 国際大手企業
 (=international giant firm, international giant corporation)
 ◆In its third attempt to prop up Citigroup Inc. in the past five months, the U.S. government will convert up to $25 billion in the banking giant's preferred shares to common stock. 過去5か月で3度目のシティグループ支援策として、米政府は、(政

府が保有する）最大250億ドル相当の金融大手シティの優先株を普通株に転換する。◆Part of the bailout funds on the $700 billion financial rescue program went to shore up insurance giant American International Group Inc. and the auto industry. 7,000億ドルの金融支援策に基づく救済資金の一部は、米保険大手のAIGと自動車業界（GMとクライスラー）の強化に充てられた。

gifts （名）株主優待制度 （=shareholders incentives: 企業が配当金以外に株主に商品やサービスなどを提供する制度。配当金は株主総会での議決が必要なのに対して、株主優待制度の実施とその内容は企業が自由に決めることができる。⇒incentive）
◆About 20 percent of listed companies are offering gifts to their shareholders. 上場企業の約20%が、株主優待制度を実施している。◆Some companies use the gifts to maintain contact with shareholders. 株主との接点を維持するため、この株主優待制度を活用している企業もある。

gilt （名）英国政府発行の有価証券, ギルト債, 米国の優良証券

gilt-edged security 米国の優良証券, 優良社債, 一流証券, ギルト債

Ginnie Mae ジニー・メイ（Government National Mortgage Association（米政府住宅抵当金庫）の通称）

glamour stock 花形優良株

Glass-Steagall Act グラス・スティーガル法 （証券と銀行の兼業を禁じた米国の法律で、1933年に制定された。⇒Gramm-Leach-Bliley Act）

glitch （名）突然の故障, 障害, 異常, 誤作動, 突発事故, 欠陥, トラブル （⇒on-the-spot inspection）
  computer glitch コンピュータの誤作動, コンピュータ障害
  software glitch ソフトの欠陥
  system glitch システム障害 （=system failure）
◆The Financial Services Agency carried out an emergency inspection of the Mizuho Financial Group to determine what had triggered a disastrous glitch in its computer system. 金融庁は、みずほフィナンシャルグループに対して、惨さんたるシステム障害の発生原因を解明するため、同グループの緊急検査を実施した。

global （形）全世界の, 世界の, 全世界的, 国際的な, 世界的規模の, 地球規模の, 地球全体の, グローバルな, 広範囲の, 全体的な, 全面的な, 包括的, 総合的な, グローバル
  global activity 世界の景気
  global asset allocation 多通貨分散投資
  global banking system 世界の銀行システム, 世界の銀行制度
  global bearer bond 無記名式仮社債券
  global bearer certificate グローバル無記名預託証券
  global bearer warrant 無記名式仮ワラント債
  global capital markets 国際資本市場
  global certificate グローバル証書
    （=global note）
  global consumer banking 世界的規模の消費者金融
  global CP [commercial paper] outstanding 世界のCP発行残高
  global credit markets グローバル金融市場
  global currency options 国際通貨オプション
  global custodian グローバル・カストディアン
  global custody グローバル・カストディ（国内外の市場にまたがって決済、保管や為替取引、税務などを行う保管サービス）
  global depository [depositary] receipt グローバル預託証券, GDR
  global depository share グローバル預託株式
  global dollar sector 米ドル建てグローバル債市場, 米ドル建てグローバル債セクター
  global economic balances 地球規模の経済バランス
  Global Environment Facility 地球環境基金
  global equity index グローバル株価指数
  global equity offering グローバルな株式発行
  global financial panic triggered by Japan 日本発の世界金融恐慌
  global foreign exchange market 外国為替市場
  global format グローバル債の仕組み
  global fund グローバル・ファンド（米市場で販売されるミューチュアル・ファンド。自国証券のほか、資金の25%以上が外国証券に投資される）
  global growth 世界の景気, 世界の経済成長率
  global note 大券, グローバル・ノート
    （=global certificate）
  global offer 国際募集
  global offering グローバル株式売出し
  global registered exchangeable bond グローバルに売買可能な登録交換可能債
  global reserve currency 世界各国の準備通貨
  global sales 世界全体での売上
  global steering policy 一般的操縦政策（財政金融政策や為替レートの変更など、産業一般に影響することを目的とする産業経過政策の一つ）
  global unhedged benchmark ヘッジしない世界指数
  global yen sector 円建てグローバル債市場, 円建てグローバル債セクター

global bond グローバル債（世界各地で同時に発行される債券）, 仮証券［大券］（本証券が発行されるまで一時的に発行される証券）
  global bond markets グローバル債市場, 世界の債券相場
  global long bond 長期グローバル債
  U.S. dollar global bond 米ドル建てグローバル債
  yen-denominated global bond 円建てグローバル債

global business strategy 企業の世界戦略, グローバル経営戦略, グローバル戦略
  （=international business strategy）
◆Japan's four megabanks are now rebuilding their global business strategies. 日本の4大金融グループは現在、グローバル戦略の再構築に取り組んでいる。◆Toyota's figures are the fruit of its global business strategy of meticulously tailoring its models to satisfy the various needs of customers around the world, coupled with its cost-cutting efforts. トヨタの業績は、合理化努力［コスト削減努力］と、世界各地のユーザーのさまざまなニーズを満たすためにきめ細かな車作りを目指すトヨタのグローバル経営戦略の成果である。

global capital flows 国際資本移動
◆The U.S. monetary policy has a major impact on global liquidity and capital flows. 米国の金融政策は、国際流動性と国際資本移動に大きな影響力を持つ。

global competition 国際競争, グローバルな競争
◆One of the aims for the three banks to merge into the Mizuho Financial Group was to survive the global competition by exploiting the banks' combined strength. 3行がみずほフィナンシャルグループに合併する目的（狙い）の一つに、3行の統合力を駆使して国際競争に勝ち抜くことがあった。◆We will aim at creating a top, comprehensive financial group in the world that can win the global competition. 当社は今後、グローバルな競争を勝ち抜ける世界屈指の総合金融グループの創造を目指す。

global competitiveness 国際競争力
  （=international competitiveness）
◆The goal of the restructuring is to reinforce our global com-

petitiveness. この事業再構築は、当社の国際競争力の強化を目的としている。

global crisis 地球規模の危機, 地球規模の同時危機, 世界恐慌
◆A U.S. financial crisis would undoubtedly trigger a global crisis. 米国の金融危機は、間違いなく地球規模の（同時）危機を誘発するものと思われる。

global currency war 世界の通貨安戦争
◆Financial chiefs from the Group of 20 advanced and major developing countries vowed to avoid a global currency war. 主要20か国・地域（G20）の財務相・中央銀行総裁は、（各国が自国通貨を安くすることで輸出競争力を高め、景気回復をめざす）世界の通貨安競争を避けることを公約した。

global decline in stock values 世界的な株安
◆A chain-reaction global decline in stock values was temporarily stopped by a barrage of countermeasures. 世界的な株安連鎖は、矢継ぎ早の対策でいったんは歯止めがかかった。

global downturn 世界同時不況
（=global economic downturn）
◆The ongoing business slump raises the specter of a global downturn comparable to the Great Depression that started in 1929. 今回の不況は、1929年に始まった世界大恐慌に匹敵するほどの世界同時不況の懸念が高まっている。

global economic downturn 世界同時不況, 世界的な景気後退, 世界的な景気減速
（=the world economic downturn）
◆Concern over the global economic slowdown grows both at home and abroad. 世界的な景気減速懸念は、国内外で高まっている[広まっている]。◆Japan's export industry is engulfed by the global economic downturn. 日本の輸出産業は、世界同時不況に飲み込まれている。◆The ongoing global economic downturn continues to hit demand for flights. 今回の世界的な景気後退[世界同時不況]で、航空需要が引き続き減少している[打撃を受けている]。

global economic growth 世界の経済成長
◆Excess volatility in exchange rates is undesirable for global economic growth. 為替相場の過度の変動は、世界の経済成長にとって望ましくない。◆Six emerging economies（the BRICs nations plus Indonesia and South Korea）will become the major drivers of global economic growth. これからは、新興6か国（ブラジル、ロシア、インド、中国にインドネシアと韓国）が、世界の経済成長の主要な原動力になる。

global economic slowdown 世界的な景気後退
◆Concern over the global economic slowdown is spreading. 世界経済の減速懸念が、広がっている。◆The global economic slowdown has forced foreign and domestic companies to cut back on overseas trips. 世界的な景気後退で、内外の企業が海外出張を控えざるをえなくなっている。

global economic trends グローバル経済の潮流
◆The Fair Trade Commission of Japan is required to consider global economic trends when it screens corporate merger requests in light of the Antimonopoly Law. 公正取引委員会は、独占禁止法に照らして企業合併の申請を審査するにあたって、グローバル経済の潮流も検討する必要がある。

global economy 世界経済, 世界の景気, 地球規模の経済 （=world economy）
◆Demand for bullion as a protection of wealth has been spurred by mounting concern that the global economy is faltering. 深まる世界経済低迷への懸念から、安全資産[資産保全]としての金の需要が拡大している。◆Falling stock prices and the depreciation of the U.S. dollar increased uncertainty over the global economy. 米国の株安やドル安で、世界経済の不透明感が強まっている。◆Global economies are battered by confusion in financial markets. 世界経済が、金融市場の混乱の影響をもろに受けている。◆Heightened tensions and significant downward risks for the global economy must be addressed decisively. 世界経済の緊張の高まりと重大な下方リスクに、断固として対処しなければならない。◆If the European financial crisis expands, it will damage the recovering global economy. 欧州の金融危機が拡大すれば、回復途上にある世界経済に打撃を与えることになる。◆Near-term uncertainty surrounding the global economy continues to grow. 世界経済を取り巻く短期的な先行き不安は、増大傾向が続いている。◆Protectionist moves could damage the global economy. 保護主義的な動きは、世界経済に打撃を与えかねない。◆The Bank of Japan's resorting to quantitative easing in concert with the Fed would have a greater impact on in buoying the global economy. 米連邦準備制度理事会（FRB）と歩調を合わせて日銀が量的緩和に踏み切れば、世界景気の浮揚効果は拡大すると思われる。◆The debt crisis in the eurozone began rocking the global economy. ユーロ圏の債務危機で、世界景気が揺らいできた。◆The dollar's accelerated depreciation could hurt not only the Japanese economy, but the global economy as a whole. ドル安の加速は、日本経済だけでなく、世界経済全体にとってもマイナスだ。◆The global economy continues to recover, albeit in a fragile and uneven way. 世界経済は、脆弱（ぜいじゃく）で一様ではないが、回復を続けている。◆The global economy has been pulled out of its worst crisis. 世界経済は、その最大の危機を脱した。◆The global economy is facing serious challenges. 世界経済は、厳しい試練に直面している。◆The global economy was hit hard by the financial crisis. 世界経済は、金融危機で大打撃を受けた。

global equities 世界の株価, 世界の株式相場, 世界の株式市場
◆Global equities rebounded on Friday. 金曜日の世界の株価[株式市場]は、反発した。

global financial crisis 世界的な金融危機, 世界の金融危機, 世界金融危機
（=international financial crisis）
◆Business conditions are rapidly deteriorating due to the global financial crisis and the worldwide economic downturn. 世界的な金融危機と世界的な景気後退で、景気は急速に悪化している。◆Consumer spending waned amid the global financial crisis that followed the Lehman Brothers collapse in autumn 2008. 2008年秋のリーマン・ブラザーズの破たん後に生じた世界の金融危機を受けて、個人消費が低迷した。◆Hungary was seriously affected by the global financial crisis. ハンガリーは、世界的金融危機の影響が深刻だった。◆Shinsei and Aozora banks suffered huge losses in their overseas investment business in the aftermath of the global financial crisis triggered by the collapse of Lehman Brothers Holdings Inc. in autumn 2008. 新生銀行とあおぞら銀行は、2008年秋のリーマン・ブラザーズの経営破たんで始まった世界的な金融危機の影響で、海外投資事業に巨額の損失が発生した。◆Some observers predicted that the global financial crisis would hurt Japan the least. 日本は世界金融危機による傷が世界で最も浅い、と見る向きもあった。◆The fiscal woes of the single-currency bloc could trigger a new severe global financial crisis. 単一通貨・ユーロ圏の財政危機は、新たに重大な世界的金融危機の発生源になる可能性がある。◆The global financial crisis began in September 2008. 世界の金融危機は、2008年9月に始まった。◆The global financial crisis was triggered by the collapse of some major financial institutions. 世界的な金融危機は、大手金融機関の破たんで始まった。◆World's central banks cut interest rates in unison in a joint response to the global financial crisis. 世界の中央銀行は、世界の金融危機への協調対応策として金利[政策金利]を同時に引き下げた。

global financial markets 世界の金融市場
◆Enhancing international coordination is indispensable to stabilize the global financial markets. 世界の金融市場の安定には、国際協調の強化が欠かせない。◆Global financial markets are still shaken by the serious fiscal troubles in Greece. 世界の金融市場は、ギリシャの深刻な財政危機問題で動揺が続

いている。◆In the global financial markets, unrest is continuing as there is no end in sight to fiscal crises to the United States and some European countries. 世界の金融市場では、米国と一部の欧州諸国の財政危機の収束が見通せないため、混乱が続いている。◆Investment conditions have worsened due to confusion in global financial markets in the wake of fiscal and financial crises in Europe. 欧州の財政・金融危機を受けた世界的な金融市場の混乱で、運用環境が悪化している。◆It is difficult to deal with the latest unrest in global financial markets because it has been caused by a complex web of factors. 今回の世界的な金融市場混乱への対応が難しいのは、混乱を招いている要因が複雑に絡み合っているからだ。◆Japan, U.S. and Europe must hasten to end fiscal crisis to stabilize the global financial markets. 世界の金融市場の安定化を図るには、日米欧が財政危機の収束を急がなければならない。◆The downturn in global financial markets has had a negative impact on insurance products such as single-premium pension insurance policies which are popular as a form of savings. 世界の金融市場の低迷は、貯蓄用［一種の貯蓄］として人気の高い一時払い年金保険などの保険商品に悪影響を及ぼしている。◆Turbulence in global financial markets brought the level of liquidity in the country sharply lower. 世界の金融市場の混乱で、国内流動性の水準は大幅に低下した。

global financial meltdown　世界的な金融危機
（=the worldwide financial meltdown）
◆Goldman Sachs Group Inc. emerged from the global financial meltdown as Wall Street's most influential bank. ゴールドマン・サックスは、ウォール街最大手の金融機関として世界的な金融危機を乗り切った。

global financial turmoil　世界的な金融不安, 国際金融不安, 世界的な金融市場の混乱
（=international financial turmoil）
◆Investors seem to be shifting their money from investment trusts to more secured time deposits in the face of global financial turmoil. 世界の金融市場の混乱に直面して、投資家は資金を投資信託から安定性の高い定期預金に切り替えているようだ。◆U.S. and European financial institutions are hitting roadblocks because of the ongoing global financial turmoil. 欧米金融機関は、世界的な金融市場の混乱で、つまずいている。

global fiscal and financial crisis　世界的な財政・金融危機
◆The current global fiscal and financial crisis began in European countries. 今回の世界的な財政・金融危機の震源地は、欧州だ。

global growth　世界の経済成長, 世界経済の成長
◆A U.S. housing mortgage meltdown shook the United States, Europe and other countries and slammed the brakes on global growth. 米国の住宅ローン市場の崩壊は、米欧その他の諸国を揺さぶり、世界経済の成長に急ブレーキをかけた。

global growth forecast　世界の経済成長率見通し, 世界経済見通し, 世界全体の経済成長率の予測
◆On the back of robust growth in Asia and renewed U.S. private demand, the IMF upgraded its 2010 global growth forecast. アジアの堅調な経済成長と米国の民間需要の回復を受けて、IMF（国際通貨基金）が世界の経済成長率見通しを上方修正した。

global liquidity　国際流動性
◆The U.S. monetary policy has a major impact on global liquidity and capital flows. 米国の金融政策は、国際流動性と国際資本移動に大きな影響力を持つ。

global market　グローバル市場, 世界市場, 国際市場, グローバル・マーケット
（=global marketplace, international market）
◆Instability in global markets is increasing with rising downside risks. 下振れリスクの増大とともに、グローバル市場の不安定性は高まっている。◆The stakes in major U.S. securities firms by SMFG, Mitsubishi UFJ and Nomura will boost the presence of Japanese financial institutions in the global market. 三井住友銀行、三菱UFJと野村が米国の大手証券会社に出資することで、グローバル市場での日本の金融機関の存在感が高まりそうだ。◆This joint financing scheme carried out with the bank as the lead bank is expected to help make the presence of Japanese banks more strongly felt in global markets. 同行を主幹事銀行として実施されるこの協調融資事業は、グローバル市場で邦銀の存在感を高めることになりそうだ。

global project financing loans　世界のプロジェクト・ファイナンスの融資額
◆Global project financing loans totaled about $96.1 billion from January until the end of June 2011. 2011年1〜6月の世界のプロジェクト・ファイナンスの総融資額は、約961億ドルに達した。

global recession　世界的な景気後退, 世界不況, 世界同時不況
◆Investors around the world are selling stocks with abandon as a global recession is under way. 世界的な景気後退の進行で世界中の投資家が株を売りまくっている。◆The financial crisis and the global recession have dealt a fatal blow to the ailing company. 今回の金融危機と世界不況が、この経営不振企業に致命的な打撃を与えた。◆The global recession curbed consumer spending, hurting demand for chips that go into electronics such as computers and handsets. 世界同時不況で個人消費が抑えられ、コンピュータや携帯電話などの電子製品に用いられる半導体の需要も減退している［打撃を受けている］。

global reorganization　国際的な再編
◆The global reorganization of industries has not extended to home appliance manufacturers, as electrical products have different specifications in different countries. 電器製品は国によって製品仕様が異なるため、家電メーカーについてはこれまで国際的な業界再編は進んでいない。

global slowdown　世界的な景気低迷, 世界的な景気減速
（=global economic slowdown）
◆Import growth far outpaced export growth in the face of a global slowdown. 世界的な景気低迷で［世界的な景気減速に直面して］、輸入の伸びが輸出の伸びを大幅に上回った。◆The decoupling theory suggests that China and India would not be hurt by a global slowdown. ディカップリング論によると、中国やインドなどは世界的な景気減速の影響を受けないとされる。

global standard　世界標準, グローバル・スタンダード
◆The International Financial Reporting Standards (IFRSs) have become the global standard in more than 100 countries, especially in Europe. 国際財務報告基準（IFRSs）は、欧州を中心に100か国以上でグローバル・スタンダードになっている。

global stock market plunges　世界の株式市場の低迷, 世界同時株安
◆Global stock market plunges caused by the European fiscal crisis triggered by Greece have shown no signs of abating. ギリシャ発の欧州財政危機による世界同時株安は、止まる気配がない。

global stock prices　世界の株価
◆Due to confusion in the financial markets, interest rates have declined significantly and global stock prices have dropped. 金融市場の混乱で、金利が大幅に低下し、世界的に株価も下落している。

global systemically important financial institutions　国際的な巨大金融機関, 金融システム上重要な国際金融機関, システム上国際的に重要な金融機関, G-SIFIs［GSIFIs］
◆According to the Financial Stability Board, 28 banks viewed as global systemically important financial institutions (G-SIFIs) will be subject to a new global rule requiring them to hold extra capital to prevent future financial

crises. 金融安定化理事会（FSB）によると、金融システム上重要な国際金融機関（G-SIFIs）と考えられる世界の28行が、金融危機の再発を防止するため、資本の上積みを求める新国際基準[新国際金融規制]の対象になる。

global trade 世界の貿易
◆The dollar's role as the major reserve currency is important to global trade. 主要準備通貨としてのドルの役割は、世界の貿易には重要である。

global turmoil in the financial markets 世界の金融市場の混乱, 金融市場の世界的な混乱
◆Global turmoil in the financial markets results from the downgrading of the U.S. credit rating. 金融市場の世界的な混乱は、米国債の格下げによるものだ。

global unrest in the financial markets 世界の金融市場の混乱, 世界的な金融市場の混乱[動揺]
◆Global unrest in the financial markets is continuing. 世界的な金融市場の混乱が、続いている。

globalization （名）世界化, 国際化, 地球的規模化, 全世界一体化, グローバル化, グローバリゼーション
 economic globalization　経済のグローバル化, 経済の国際化
 globalization of society　国際化
 globalization of the world economy　世界経済のグローバル化
 increasing globalization and a worldwide opening of markets　グローバリゼーションの進展と世界的な市場開放
 market globalization　市場のグローバル化
 （=globalization of markets）
◆The financial market bubble has not brought forth technology innovation or globalization. 金融バブルは、技術革新やグローバル化をもたらしたわけではない。◆The IT bubble and the ensuing swelling of the financial market of late have stemmed from technology innovation coupled with the globalization of the economy. （1990年代後半の）ITバブルとそれに続く最近までの金融膨張を引き起こしたのは、経済のグローバル化の動きと連動した技術革新だ。

globalize （動）世界化する, 国際化する, 地球的規模にする, グローバル化する
◆The international flow of goods, services and funds became freer and more globalized. 物、サービスと資金の国際的な流れは、一段と自由になり、また一段とグローバル化した。◆The strengthening of the yen would force Japanese export-oriented manufacturers to globalize themselves further. 円高で、日本の輸出企業はさらなるグローバル化を強いられることになろう。

GNMA　ジニー・メイ, 米政府住宅抵当金庫
（Government National Mortgage Associationの略。⇒ Ginnie Mae）

go bankrupt　破産する, 倒産する, 破たんする, 事業に失敗する　（=go bust, go under）
◆Four exchange-listed companies went bankrupt in July 2008. 上場企業4社が、2008年7月に倒産した。◆The European Banking Authority's stress tests were only cosmetic and two Irish banks went bankrupt shortly after the EBA's 2010 tests though the banks had passed them. 欧州銀行監督機構（EBA）のストレス・テスト（財務の健全性検査）はほんの体裁[上辺]だけのもので、アイルランドの2銀行は、2010年に実施された同機構のテストに通過したものの、テスト直後に経営破たんした。
◆The government and the BOJ sat on the sidelines when Yamaichi Securities Co. and Hokkaido Takushoku Bank went bankrupt in 1997. 1997年に山一証券と北海道拓殖銀行が破たんした際、政府と日銀は座視した。

go belly-up　倒産する, 破たんする, 経営破たんする
　（=go bankrupt, go bust）
◆One year has passed since General Motors Co. went belly-up. ゼネラル・モーターズ（GM）が経営破たんしてから、1年が経過した。◆Yamato Life Insurance Co., a midsize life insurer, went belly-up on October 10, 2008. 中堅生命保険会社の大和生命保険が、2008年10月10日に経営破たんした。

go-between　（名）仲ás者, 仲介人
◆We have received a number of proposals from investment banks who want to act as go-betweens between drug companies for mergers. 投資銀行からは、製薬会社の経営統合の仲介をしたい旨の提案が数多く来ている。

GO bond　米州政府や地方自治体が発行する地方債
　（GO=general obligation）

go-go conglomerate　ゴーゴー・コングロマリット（ベンチャー企業や成長分野の企業を買収して急成長するコングロマリット）

go-go fund　ゴーゴー・ファンド（格付けや知名度に関係なく値上がりしそうな株を取り入れて資産の増大を狙う投資信託）

go into default　債務不履行になる
◆Many home mortgages went into default. 多くの住宅ローンが債務不履行になった。

go private　株式を非公開化する, 非公開会社にする
◆The Zachary Bank of Louisiana took the decision to go private. 米ルイジアナ州のザカリ銀行は、株式を非公開にすることを決めた。

go public　株式公開する, 株式を上場する, 秘密情報を公開する　（⇒IT bubble, lucrative）
◆Companies should not go public to prevent hostile takeover bids. 敵対的買収を防ぐには、企業は株式を上場すべきでない。◆MFG would gain several hundred billion yen in capital gains if the brokerage goes public. みずほフィナンシャルグループは、みずほ証券が上場した場合には数千億円の上場益（株式譲渡益）を見込んでいる。

go sour　計画などが失敗する, 不調に終わる, だめになる, こじれる, 酸っぱくなる
◆As a result of fierce competition in the past, interest rate profit margins were kept too low to cover loans that went sour. 過去の熾烈（しれつ）な競争の結果、金利の利ざやが小さく抑えられた余り、貸倒れ[貸倒れのリスク]をカバーできなかった[過去の熾烈な融資合戦の結果、不良債権リスクをカバーできないほど利ざやは小さく抑えられた]。◆North Korea apparently bilked Saddam's Iraq out of $10 million in a missile deal gone sour. 北朝鮮は、こじれたミサイル取引で、サダム元大統領のイラクから1,000万ドルの借金を踏み倒したようだ。

go through　検討する, 念入りに調べる, 経験する, 味わう, ～に直面する, 切り抜ける, やり通す, 通過する, 承認される, （取引などが）成立する, （手続きなどを）取る
◆GM will go through the court process in 60 to 90 days. GMは、60～90日間で法的整理を終える予定だ。

go under　破産する, 倒産する, 破たんする, 事業に失敗する　（=go bankrupt, go belly-up）
◆If the appraisal losses swell excessively, banks failing to meet the regulatory minimum capital adequacy requirements will have to go under. 含み損が余りにも膨らむと、規制当局の最低自己資本比率基準を満たせない銀行は、経営破たんに追い込まれることになる。◆In January 2010, Japan Airlines went under owing $26 billion in one of the nation's biggest-ever corporate failures. 2010年1月に日本航空は、日本史上最大の企業倒産として260億ドルの負債を抱えて経営破たんした。◆Rumors were swirling among market players that Merrill Lynch would be the next to go under. 市場関係者の間では、「次に破たんするのはメリルリンチ」という噂が渦巻いていた。

goal　（名）目標, 目的, 目的地, ゴール
 achieve one's investment goals　運用目標を達成する
 budget goal　予算目標

company goal　企業目標, 会社目標
　（=corporate goal）
earnings goal　収益目標, 業績目標
　（=earnings target）
economic goal　経済目標
financial goal　財務目標
fiscal reconstruction goal　財政再建目標
　（⇒leave動詞）
goal of price setting　価格設定目標
goal of restructuring　事業再構築の目的
goal-seeking　目標追求, 目標探索
goal setting　目標設定
interim goal　中間目標
long-term goal　長期目標, 長期的目標
marketing goal　マーケティング目標
organization［organizational］goal　組織目標, 企業目標
policy goal　政策目標
profit goal　利益目標
set a goal　目標を掲げる
◆A steady annual improvement in earnings of five percent or more is a reasonable goal given the weight of regulated companies in our asset base. 年5％以上の利益増加率の安定確保は、規制対象企業が当社の資産構成で大きな比重を占めていることから、妥当な目標と言えるでしょう。◆The bank failed to achieve its investment goals. 同行は、運用目標を達成できなかった。◆The firm's goal is to expand its overseas sales to ￥50 billion within three years through mergers and acquisitions. 同社は、M&A（企業の合併・買収）を通じて3年以内に海外の売上高を500億円に拡大する目標を掲げている。◆The first goal of Japan's fiscal reconstruction is for the central and local governments to achieve a surplus in their primary balances by fiscal 2019. 日本の財政再建の第一目標は、国と地方［地方自治体］の基礎的財政収支を、2019年度までに黒字化することだ。◆The goal of the restructuring is to reinforce our global competitiveness. この事業再構築は、当社の国際競争力の強化を目的としている。

going　（形）現在の, 現行の, 一般に行われている, 現存する, うまく行っている, 順調な, 手に入る（available）, 入手できる, 運転中［稼動中］の, 営業中の, 儲（もう）かっている　（名）状態, 状況, 進み具合, 進行, 出勤, 退職, 死去
be in going order　使用できる状態にある
face rough going　難航する
going business　継続企業, 持続的企業, 現に事業活動をしている企業, 順調な経営, 順調な事業, 順調な商売, 儲かっている商売, 営業中の会社［商売］
going interest rate　現行利率
going long　思惑買い, 見込み買い, ロングにする（投資や投機を目的として有価証券を買うこと）
going price　現行価格, 時価
going private　株式の非公開化, 株式を非公開にすること, 非公開会社化（一般に、上場会社が外部発行済み株式を買い戻して自社を非公開会社にすること）
going public　株式の新規公開, 株式公開　（=flotation, IPO, listing: 機密情報の公開, 証券取引所や店頭市場に株式を新規公開して、上場会社になること）
going rate　（市場の）実勢レート, 実勢金利, 現行レート, 現行の利率, 相場, （利息の）現行歩合, 現行料金, 現行運賃
going rate of interest　実勢金利
going rate pricing　実勢価格
going short　思惑売り, 見込み売り, ショートにする（空売り（short sale）と同義で、思惑で有価証券を売ること）
going to a wrong account　口座相違, 口座相違になること
going value　経営価値
going wages　現行賃金
going yield　流通利回り
while the going is good　形勢が有利なうちに
◆If the negotiations between Republicans and Democrats face rough going and the deficit-cutting plan ends up being insufficient, credit rating agencies may downgrade Treasury bonds. 共和党と民主党の協議が難航して赤字削減策が不十分に終わると、（信用）格付け会社が米国債の格下げに踏み切る可能性がある。

going concern　継続企業, 営業中の会社, 企業の存続可能性, ゴーイング・コンサーン
　（=ongoing concern）
going concern rules　企業の継続能力規定, ゴーイング・コンサーン規定　（⇒net capital deficiency）
going concern value　継続企業としての価値
◆The FSA is scheduled to put "going concern" rules in place, starting in the accounting period that ends in March next year. 金融庁は、今年度［来年3月に終了する事業年度］から「ゴーイング・コンサーン」規定を導入する予定だ。

gold　（名）金, 金貨, ゴールド　（形）金の, 金製の
adequate gold and foreign exchange［currency］reserves　適正準備金・外国為替準備, 適正外貨準備［外貨準備高］
bar gold　棒金
conversion to gold　金兌換（だかん）
convertibility of the dollar into gold　ドルと金の交換
convertibility to gold　金交換性, 金兌換性
fine［pure, sterling］gold　純金
gold and foreign exchange［currency］reserves　金・外国為替準備, 外貨準備, 外貨準備高
gold bar　金の延べ棒, 棒金（=gold in bar）
gold basis　金本位基準, 金本位制
gold bloc　金本位制地域, 金ブロック
gold bond　金貨債券, 金貨支払い［払い］債券
gold brick　棒金, まやかし品
gold buying　金購入
gold buying policy　金購入政策
gold card　ゴールド・カード（信用保証付きクレジット・カード）
gold center　金の自由市場
gold certificate　金証券, 金貨証券
gold clause　金約款
gold collateral loan　金担保借款
Gold Commission　米金委員会
gold concentration policy　金集中政策
gold contract　金先物, 5年物先物（Gold contract）
Gold Control Law　金管理法
gold convertibility　金兌換（だかん）性, 金交換性
gold cover　金準備
gold crisis　金危機, 金恐慌
gold currency　金貨
gold currency standard　金貨本位制, 金本位制
gold delivery bar　金地金
gold dollar reserves　金ドル準備
gold drain　金流出
gold dust　金粉, 砂金
gold earmark　金のイヤマーク
gold embargo［ban］　金輸出禁止
gold exclusion　金排除
gold exclusion policy　金排除政策

GOLD

gold export point　金現送点, 金輸出点, 金流出点
gold fiduciary reserve　金保証準備, 通貨発行準備
gold field　金鉱地, 採金地
gold fixing　金の値決め, 金価格設定, 金価格決定, 金の建値決定
gold foil [leaf]　金箔
gold for monetary use　貨幣用金（=monetary gold）
gold fund　金貨支払い社債, 金貨払い社債, 金鉱株ファンド
gold gain　金価値上昇
gold handcuffs　特別優遇措置, 転職防止優遇措置, 優遇条件　（⇒golden handcuffs）
gold holder　金保有者, 金保有国
gold holding　金保有
gold holdings　金保有高, 金準備
gold import point　金輸入点
gold-indexed investment　金価格スライド投資
gold industry　金産業
gold inflow　金の流入
gold ingot　金塊
gold investment account　金投資口座
gold kernel standard　金核本位制（金地金本位制と金為替本位制の総称）
gold-linked note　金リンク債
gold loan　金貸借款
gold market　金市場
gold mine　金鉱, 金山, 宝の山, ドル箱
gold miner　採金者, 金鉱労働者
gold mining company　金鉱開発会社
gold monetization　金の貨幣化
gold movement　金移動, 金流出入
gold mutual fund　ゴールド・ミューチュアル・ファンド
gold note　金貨兌換紙幣, ゴールド・ノート
gold nugget　金塊
gold option　ゴールド・オプション
gold outflow　金流出
gold ownership　金所有
gold par (value)　金平価（=gold parity）
gold parity　金平価
gold passbook account　金預金口座
gold point　金現送点, 金輸出点
gold policy　金政策
gold pool　金プール, 金プール制度
gold preference　金選好（=preference for gold）
gold premium policy　金打歩政策
gold producing country　金産国
gold regulation　金管理規定
gold revaluation　金再評価
gold rush　ゴールド・ラッシュ
gold savings account　純金積立口座
gold selling　金売却
gold sterilization policy　金不胎化政策
gold stock　金保有高, 金手持ち高
gold tranche　ゴールド・トランシュ
gold transaction　金取引
gold value　金価値
gold value clause　金価値約款
gold warrant　金ワラント

London Gold Futures Market　ロンドン金先物取引所
monetary gold　貨幣用金（=gold for monetary use）
paper gold　ペーパー・ゴールド（IMFの特別引出し権（special drawing rights）の通称。⇒special drawing rights）
repeal [lifting] of gold embargo　金解禁, 金輸出解禁
World Gold Council　世界金評議会, ワールド・ゴールド・カウンシル, WGC
◆According to the World Gold Council, central banks have bought 198 metric tons of gold so far this year. 世界金評議会によると、今年は、世界各国の中央銀行がこれまでに（2011年8月22日現在で）198メートルトン（19万8,000キログラム）の金を買い入れた。◆Gold extended its rally to a record above $1,900 an ounce amid increased uncertainties over the U.S. and European economic outlook on the Comex in New York. ニューヨーク商品取引所では、米欧景気見通しへの懸念［米欧経済の先行き不透明感］の高まりを受け［懸念の高まりから］、金価格が急騰して、1トロイ・オンス＝1,900ドルを史上初めて突破した。◆Gold is in the 11th year of a bull market. 金の上げ相場は、11年続いている。◆Gold is still becoming the safe haven as people fear recession in the U.S. and the eurozone debt problems. 米国の景気後退やユーロ圏の債務危機問題への懸念から、まだ金が安全な投資先［資金の逃避先］となっている。

gold and silver　金と銀, 金銀［金・銀］
　gold and silver bimetallism　金銀複本位制度
　legal ratio between gold and silver　金と銀の法定比価, 金銀法定比価
　market ratio between gold and silver　金と銀の市場比価, 金銀市場比価
　ratio between gold and silver　金銀比価
gold bullion　金の地金, 金地金, 金の延べ棒, 金塊（⇒appraisal profit）
　gold bullion market　金地金市場, 金塊市場
　gold bullion quotation　金地金相場, 金塊相場
　gold bullion standard (system)　金地金本位制［制度］, 金塊本位制
gold coin　金貨, 金鋳貨
　American Eagle gold coins　アメリカン・イーグル金貨, 米イーグル金貨
　gold coin clause　金貨約款
　gold coin standard (system)　金貨本位制
　gold collateral loan　金担保借款
◆The U.S. Mint's sales of American Eagle gold coins have totaled 91,000 ounce so far in August. 米造幣局のアメリカン・イーグル［米イーグル］金貨の販売総量は、9月1日以降現時点で9万1,000オンスに達している。
gold exchange　金為替
　gold exchange reserve　金為替準備
　gold exchange standard (system)　金為替本位制（=gold standard system）
gold future [futures] price　金先物の価格, 金先物価格
◆The benchmark gold future price surged to all-time high of ¥4,725 per gram in trading on the Tokyo Commodity Exchange. 東京工業品取引所の取引で、金取引の指標となる金先物価格が、過去最高の1グラム＝4,725円まで急騰した。◆The benchmark gold future price topped ¥4,700 per gram for the first time on the Tokyo Commodity Exchange. 東京工業品取引所で、金取引の指標となる金先物価格が、史上初めて1グラム＝4,700円を突破した。
gold futures　金先物
　benchmark gold futures price　金取引の指標となる金先物価格

gold futures for December delivery　12渡しの金先物, 12月渡しの金先物価格
◆Gold futures for December delivery closed at $1,891.90 an ounce at 2:05 p.m. on the Comex in New York. ニューヨーク商品取引所では、12月渡しの金先物価格が、午後2時5分の時点で1トロイ・オンス（約31グラム）＝1,891.90ドルに達した。◆Gold futures for December delivery topped $1,900 an ounce for the first time on the Comex in New York. ニューヨーク商品取引所で、12月渡しの金先物価格が、史上初めて1トロイ・オンス＝1,900ドルを突破した。

gold futures contract　金先物契約, 金先物
◆The June 2012 gold futures contract closed at ￥4,694 per gram, down ￥54 from the previous day's close on the Tokyo Commodity Exchange. 東京工業品取引所では、2012年6月渡しの金先物価格は、前日の終値より54円安の1グラム＝4,694円で取引を終えた。

gold price　金価格, 金物価
　gold and commodity prices　金などの市況商品価格
　official gold price　公定金価格
　the surge in gold price　金価格の上昇
　two-tier gold price system　金の二重価格制
◆Gold prices have more than doubled since the end of 2008 amid increased uncertainties over the U.S. and European economic outlook. 欧米景気見通しの不透明感の高まりを受けて、金価格は、2008年末以降、2倍以上になっている。

gold reserve　金準備, 正貨準備
　Gold Reserve Act　米金準備法
　gold reserve ratio　金準備率, 正貨準備率
　gold reserves　金準備

gold settlement　金決済
　gold settlement fund　金決済資金
　gold settlement system　金決済制度

gold standard (system)　金本位制, 金本位制度
　gold specie standard　金貨本位制
　international gold standard　国際金本位制度
　managed gold standard　管理された金本位制
　pure gold standard　純真金本位制度

golden　（形）金の, 金色の, 黄金色の, 貴重な, 重要な
　golden ager　老人, 65歳以上の定年退職者
　golden hello　移籍料, ゴールデン・ハロー
　golden opportunity　格好の機会

golden handcuffs　転職防止のための社員に対する特別優遇措置, 転職防止優遇措置, 優遇条件, ゴールデン・ハンドカフ　（＝gold handcuffs: ストック・オプション（自社株購入権）がゴールデン・ハンドカフの手段として使われることもある）

golden handshake　会社重役の高額の退職手当て［退職金、退職金契約］, 重役［幹部］退職金, 退職勧奨金, 定年前の肩たたき, ゴールデン・ハンドシェイク　（＝golden parachute: 敵対的買収を防ぐ手段の一つ）

golden parachute　黄金の落下傘, 会社重役の高額の退職手当て［退職金契約］, 幹部退職金, 特別報酬, 割増退職金, 退職補償金, ゴールデン・パラシュート　（＝golden handshake:parachuteは「退職金」という意味）

golden pension　ゴールデン・ペンション（企業買収交渉で、買収先の会社の役員に対する報酬として、買収する会社が年金の支払いを長期的に保証すること）

golden share　黄金株, 特権株　（「黄金株」は、株主総会での合併などの提案に拒否権を発動できる「拒否権付き株式（種類株式）」のこと。⇒hostile takeover bidder）
◆A company is allowed to set restrictions on the transfer of golden shares. 企業は、黄金株（拒否権付き種類株式）に譲渡制限を付けることができる［黄金株の譲渡に制限を設けることができる］。◆Companies usually issue only one golden share, which can be sold like ordinary shares. 企業は通常、普通株と同じく譲渡できる黄金株を1株だけ発行する。◆Golden shares are special shares that can be used to exercise the veto right to kill merger proposals by hostile takeover bidders. 黄金株は、敵対的買収者の合併提案などを否決するための拒否権行使に使える特殊な株だ。◆Golden shares could fall into the hands of a hostile takeover bidder. 黄金株は、敵対的買収者の手に渡る場合もある。◆Golden shares violate the principle of shareholder equality. 黄金株は、「株主平等の原則」に反する。

Goldman Sachs　（米金融大手の）ゴールドマン・サックス
◆Goldman Sachs lowered its forecast for U.S. growth in 2011 on signs that the U.S. economic recovery lost momentum. 米国の景気回復減速の兆しを受けて、ゴールドマン・サックスは、米国の成長見通しを引き下げた。◆Goldman Sachs was charged with fraud by the U.S. SEC over its marketing of a subprime mortgage product. 米証券取引委員会（SEC）が、低所得者向け住宅融資「サブプライム・ローン」関連の金融商品の販売に関して、詐欺容疑で米金融大手のゴールドマン・サックスを提訴した。

Goldman Sachs Group Inc.　ゴールドマン・サックス・グループ, ゴールドマン・サックス（米国の銀行持ち株会社。M&Aなどを扱う専門投資銀行や証券業務のほか、トレーディング、プリンシパル・インベストメント（自己資金による不動産などへの投資）、資産管理、証券サービスなど世界的に提供している）
◆Goldman Sachs Group Inc. and the two Japanese banks hold preferred shares equivalent to 70 percent of Sanyo. 米証券大手のゴールドマン・サックス（GS）と邦銀2行が、三洋電機の約7割の優先株式（普通株式に換算して議決権の約7割）を保有している。◆Goldman Sachs Group Inc. is said to have marketed risky investments that bet on the housing market's growth just before the mortgage meltdown. ゴールドマン・サックスは、住宅ローン市場の崩壊直前に、住宅市場の成長を見越した［予想した］高リスクの金融商品［投資商品］を販売したとされる。

good　（形）好決算な, 堅調な, 優良の, 優秀な, 良好な, 好材料の, 強気の, 十分な, かなりの, 高い, 大幅な, 一流の, 親切な
　good debt　優良貸付け, 優良債権, 優良貸金, 回収確実な貸金, 簡潔
　good funds　決済完了性を備えた支払い手段, グッド・ファンズ
　good growth　大幅な伸び, 高い伸び率, 高成長
　good liquidity　流動性が良好なこと, 流動性が高いこと
　good news　よい知らせ, 明るい材料, 好材料
　good paper　一流商業手形
　good people　優秀な人材, 優秀な社員
　good results　好業績, 好決算, 業績好調
　good years　業績好調時
◆While these short-term financial results are disappointing, demand for our products and services continues to be good worldwide. 短期の財務成績［業績］は満足が得られるものではありませんが、当社の製品とサービスに対する需要は、引き続き世界各地で好調です。

good credit rating　優良格付け
◆Companies with good credit ratings and those that had not issued bonds began to issue bonds. 優良格付けの企業やこれまで債券を発行していなかった企業が、債券を発行するようになった。

good performance　業績好調, 好業績　（＝good business performance, good results, strong performance）
◆Though the global economy continues to be uncertain, we are cautiously optimistic that 2009 will continue to be another year of good performance. 世界経済はいぜんとして不

確実な状況が続いていますが、慎重に見て、当社は2009年度も引き続き好業績を達成できるものと、楽観的な見通しを持っています。

good-this-month order グッド・ジス・マンス注文, GTM（顧客の出す注文の有効期限を、その月の終わりまでとする注文のこと）

good-this-week order グッド・ジス・ウイーク注文, GTW（顧客の出す注文の有効期限を、その週の終わりまでとする注文のこと）

good-till-canceled order グッド・ティル・キャンセルド注文, GTC（顧客の出す注文の有効期限を、注文が執行されるまでとする注文のこと）

goodwill (名)営業権, のれん, 得意先, 信用, 信頼, 善意, 好意, 親善, 快諾
◆Goodwill is amortized on a straight line method over the periods estimated to be benefited, currently not exceeding five years. 営業権は、その効果が及ぶと見込まれる期間にわたって（現在は5年を超えない期間にわたって）、定額法で償却されています。◆The new trade initiative, announced by Bush in a commencement address at the University of South Carolina, will foster goodwill in the Middle East. ブッシュ大統領がサウスカロライナ大の卒業式で発表した新貿易構想は、中東での信頼醸成につながる。

解説 営業権[のれん]とは：企業の超過収益力（同業種の企業の平均を上回る利益を上げることができる能力）をもたらす無形固定資産で、具体的には企業の有能な人間資産（経営者、従業員）、優れた技術やノウハウ、優良なブランド・イメージ、店舗の立地条件、有利な仕入れ先や得意先との関係などをいう。営業権は企業の財産であるが、これを貸借対照表に資産として計上できるのは、有償で譲り受けた場合か、合併で有償取得した場合に限られる。

goodwill value のれん代　(=intangible value)
◆Olympus Corp.inflated the goodwill value of its British subsidiary by 33.4 billion in the consolidated financial statements. オリンパスは、英子会社の「のれん代」を連結決算で334億円水増ししていた。

Gov. ⇒governor

governance (名)統治, 支配, 管理, 管理法, 経営法, 統治能力, ガバナンス
corporate governance reform bill　企業統治改革法案
information governance　情報ガバナンス, 情報統治
information technology governance　ITガバナンス（IT全般の統治能力のこと）
strengthen the governance of the financial industry　金融業界に対する監督を強化する
◆The G-20 financial summit meeting will map out concrete measures to strengthen the regulation and governance of the financial industry. 世界20か国・地域（G-20）の金融サミットでは、金融業界に対する規制・監督強化の具体策をまとめることになっている。◆The repercussions of Olympus Corp's false financial statements could lead to a loss of confidence in the governance and in the compliance of all Japanese firms. オリンパスの不正経理[有価証券虚偽記載]の影響で、日本企業全体の統治能力や法令遵守への信頼が失墜する可能性がある。◆The United States still seems to be reluctant to bring in the strict regulation and governance of financial institutions. 米国は、厳しい金融業界の規制・監督の実施にはまだ消極的のようだ。◆U.S. corporate governance regulations are too harsh. 米国の企業統治法[企業改革法]は、厳しすぎる。

government (名)政府, 政治, 政権, 行政
claims on local governments　地方公共団体向け信用
debt securities issued by foreign governments　外国政府証券
domestic government (bond) markets　国債市場

external government borrowing　政府の対外借入れ
Government Accountability Office　米政府説明責任局, GAO
government accounting　政府会計
government affairs　対政府活動
government agency obligation　政府機関債
government-aided financing　政策金融
government and corporate bond market　公社債市場
government as fiscal agent　財務代理人としての政府
government bank　政府銀行, 政府系金融機関
government bill　国債, 公債
government borrowing　政府借入れ, 政府借款
government borrowing policy　政府借入政策
government bounty　政府補助金, 政府助成金
government broker　英政府指定の株式仲買人
government capital　政府資本
government check　政府小切手
government-commissioned financial institution　政府系金融機関 (=government financial institution, governmental financial institution)
government compensation bond　政府公債, 交付国債
government control　政府支配, 政府統制, 政府管理
government credit　政府借款
government current expenditure　政府経常支出
government debt-sinking fund　国債償還財源, 国債の減債基金
government deflation　（政府の貨幣縮小などで生じる）政府デフレ
government depository　政府預金受託銀行
government deposits　政府預金
government earnings　政府収入
government enterprise　国営企業
government expenditure　政府支出, 財政支出, 歳出
government financial agency　政府金融機関
government financial institution [organ]　政府系金融機関
government financing　政府金融, 財政融資
government fractional paper money　小額紙幣
government grant　政府補助金
government grant for paying a fixed rate of interest　利子補給
government guaranteed bond [issue]　政府保証債
government-guaranteed, tax-exempt bond　政府保証付き非課税債
government-held shares　政府保有株 (=government's shareholdings)
government housing bank　政府住宅銀行
government indemnity　政府損失補償金
government inflation　（政府の貨幣量増加などで生じる）政府インフレ
government intervention　政府介入
government investment　政府投資, 公共投資, 政府出資
government lending　政府貸出
government market　国債市場
government money [fiat]　政府発行法貨
Government National Mortgage Association　米政府住宅抵当金庫, GNMA　(⇒Ginnie Mae)
government note　政府発行紙幣, 政府紙幣, 政府証券
government obligations　米国債, 米連邦政府証券 (=governments)
government paper　政府発行有価証券, 国債証書

government payment　政府支払い
government pension funds　政府年金基金
government property disposal　国有財産払い下げ
government rate　対当局取引相場, 集中相場
government regulation　政府規制, 公的規制
government revenue　政府収入
government-run nursing care insurance system　介護保険制度
government sponsored enterprise　政府系住宅金融機関, 政府支援企業, 政府援助法人, 政府系機関, 政府関連機関, GSE
government stock　英政府発行証券, 政府国債
government-subsidized　政府補助の, 政府助成の
government subvention　政府助成金
government to government open account agreement　オープン勘定協定
government transfer expenditure　政府移転支出, 政府振替支出
government treasury bills　短期国債
government treasury charge　国庫負担金
government trust fund　政府信託基金
government's share sale　政府保有株の放出, 政府保有株の売却
ordinary government paper　普通国債
US government obligation　米国国債, 米国債
yield on the on-the-run (most liquid) government bond　流動性が最も高い国債指標銘柄の利回り
◆If the government relaxes its policy now, the economy will not be able to get on the recovery track. 政府がいまその政策の手を緩めれば、景気は回復軌道に乗れないだろう。◆It is said that most of the U.S. government's colossal deficits had been caused by the faulty tax-and-spend policies of Republican governments. 米政府の膨大な財政赤字の大半は、歴代共和党政権の誤った税制・支出政策によるものだと言われる。◆Italy's new government led by economist Mario Monti must face painful financial reforms. 経済専門家マリオ・モンティ氏を首相とするイタリア新政権は、痛みを伴う財政改革が急務だ。◆The Development Bank of Japan asked the Japan Finance Corporation to pay ¥53.6 billion, the amount guaranteed by the government. 日本政策投資銀行は、政府保証分の536億円の支払いを日本政策金融公庫に請求した。◆The government and the Bank of Japan will likely continue to work together in fighting the sharp rise in the yen's value. 政府と日銀は、急激な円高阻止で協調路線を継続することになりそうだ。◆The government guaranteed up to 80 percent of ¥67 billion in unsecured loans extended to JAL by the DBJ through the Japan Finance Corporation. 日本政策投資銀行が日航に貸し付けた無担保融資670億円の最大8割については、日本政策金融公庫を通じて政府が保証している。◆The government may exert great pressure on the Bank of Japan to further relax its monetary policy. 政府は、日銀への追加の金融緩和圧力を強める可能性がある。◆The government plans to sell some of its 100 percent stake in Japan Post Holdings Co. to fund reconstruction from the Great East Japan Earthquake. 政府は、東日本大震災の復興財源に充てるため、100%保有する日本郵政の株式の一部も売却する方針だ。◆The sell-off of Tokyo Metro shares planned by the government will likely be opposed by the Tokyo metropolitan government which is the second-largest shareholder. 政府が計画している東京メトロ株の売却には、国に次ぐ大株主の東京都が抵抗すると見られる。◆The tripartite reforms aim to reduce the amount of subsidies provided by the central government to the local governments; cut local tax grants to local governments; and shift revenue sources from the central government to local governments. 「三位一体」改革は、国の地方政府への補助金削減、地方交付税交付金の削減と国から地方政府への財源の移譲をめざしている。◆The United States' credit has come into question by the possible downgrade of the U.S. government's credit rating. 米国債の格付けが引き下げられる可能性があることから米国の信用が疑われている。

government-affiliated　(形)政府系の
(=state-backed; ⇒financier)
government-affiliated agencies [organizations]　政府関係機関
government-affiliated banking institution　政府系金融機関
◆Backed by the South Korean government-affiliated Korea Export Insurance Corporation, private banks extended loans to Hynix. 韓国政府系金融機関の韓国輸出保険公社の支援を受けて、民間銀行がハイニックス社に融資した。

government-affiliated financial institution　政府系金融機関
◆A special account is used to finance public investment and loans to government-affiliated financial institutions. 特別会計は、政府系金融機関に財政投融資の資金を供給するのに用いられる。

government-affiliated mortgage financier　政府系住宅金融公社
◆On Sept 7, 2008, the U.S. government earmarked a huge amount of public funds to help government-affiliated mortgage financiers Freddie Mac and Fannie Mae. 2008年9月7日に米政府は、政府系住宅金融公社のフレディ・マック（連邦住宅抵当貸付公社）とファニー・メイ（連邦住宅抵当金庫［公庫］）を救済するため、巨額の公的資金投入を決めた。

government-backed financing operations　政策金融
(=government-aided financing)
◆Japan must reduce its government-backed financing operations at least to levels comparable to those of Germany and France. 日本は、少なくともドイツ、フランスの水準並みに政策金融を縮小しなければならない。

government-backed guarantee　政府保証
◆The Board of Audit has confirmed that the public financing package extended with a government-backed guarantee to JAL prior to its failure cost taxpayers a total of ¥47 billion. 日航の破たん前に政府保証付きで行われた公的融資の総国民負担額は470億円であることを、会計検査院が確定した。

government-backed loans　政府保証融資, 政府保証融資額
◆GM, Ford, Chrysler and auto-parts makers are seeking $50 billion in government-backed loans to develop and build more fuel-efficient vehicles. GM、フォード、クライスラーと自動車部品メーカー各社は、低燃費車の開発・生産に500億ドルの政府保証融資額を求めている。

government-backed trade insurance　政府保証付き貿易保険　(=government-guaranteed trade insurance; ⇒trade insurance)
◆Government-backed trade insurance previously only covered losses incurred due to unforeseen circumstances such as war, terrorism and default by a foreign government. 政府保証付き貿易保険の対象はこれまで、戦争やテロ、政府の債務不履行など不測の事態により生じた損失に限定されていた。

government bond　国債, 制負債, 政府債券, 行政公債
(=national bond; ⇒indexed government bond, interest burden, long-term interest rate, outright purchase operation, purchaser, yield)
auction of government bonds　国債入札
cash government bonds　現物の米国債
foreign government bonds　外国国債
government bond auction　国債入札
government bond basis trading　国債ベーシス取引
government bond certificate　国債証券

government bond for tax deduction　減税国債
government bond for the purpose of public works　建設国債
government bond futures　国債先物
government bond in foreign currency　外貨国債
government bond issue　国債発行　国債発行高
government bond standard　政府証券本位
government bond yield　国債利回り
government bonds book-entry system　国債振替決済口座
government bonds registration system　国債移転登録制度
Greek government bonds　ギリシャ国債
interest-bearing government bonds　利付き国債
issue new government bonds　新規国債を発行する
Japanese government bonds　日本国債
local government bonds　地方債
long-term government bonds　長期国債
medium-term government bond　中期国債
monetization of government bonds　国債の貨幣化
nonregistered government bonds　証券発行国債
redeem a sizable amount of government bonds　大量の国債を償還する
registered government bonds　登録国債
secondary government bond market　国債流通市場
soon-to-be-junk status government bonds　投資不適格レベルが見込まれる国債
the current value of government bonds　国債の現在の価格
the spread over the government bond yield　国債利回りに対するスプレッド
the ¥30 trillion cap [ceiling] on the issuance of government bonds [national bonds]　国債30兆円枠　国債発行30兆円枠
traditional government bonds　公共目的債（=public purpose bond）
ultra long-term government bonds　超長期国債
US government bonds　米国国債　米国債

◆A huge number of government bonds issued by the United States and European countries are possessed by financial institutions around the world. 米国や欧州各国が発行した大量の国債は、世界の金融機関が保有している。◆A rise in long-term interest rates will increase interest payments the government must make on government bonds. 長期金利が上昇すると、政府の国債利払い費が膨らむ。◆By buying Greek, Portuguese and Spanish bonds, the ECB infused life into the moribund eurozone markets for these soon-to-be-junk status government bonds. ギリシャやポルトガル、スペインの国債を買い入れて、欧州中銀（ECB）は、崩壊寸前のユーロ圏の投資不適格レベルが見込まれるこれらの債券の市場に生気を吹き込んだ。◆During the current fiscal year, the government plans to issue nearly ¥37 trillion of government bonds. 今年度、政府は37兆円近い国債を発行する予定だ。◆Funds for disaster reconstruction will be procured by issuing special government bonds. 震災復興の資金は、復興債を発行して調達する。◆Goldman Sachs Group Inc. agreed to pay $9.3 million to settle charges related to a former economist accused of using inside information to make the bank millions of dollars trading in U.S. government bonds. 米証券大手のゴールドマン・サックス・グループは、内部情報を使って数百万ドルの米国債取引をさせた罪で起訴された元エコノミスト関連の制裁金を清算するため、930万ドルを支払うことで（米証券取引委員会と）合意した。◆Governments facing fiscal hardship sometimes force their central banks to buy up government bonds. 財政がひっ迫した政府は、中央銀行に国債を買い切らせることがある。◆Greece was bailed out temporarily in May 2010, but it may default on its debts if it fails to secure necessary funds to redeem a sizable amount of government bonds. ギリシャは2010年5月に一時的に救済されたが、大量の国債の償還に必要な資金を確保できない場合、債務不履行（デフォルト）に陥る可能性がある。◆Greece's default on the national debts would be a blow to the operation of financial institutions in France and Germany that hold Greek government bonds. ギリシャが国債の債務不履行に陥った場合、ギリシャ国債を保有するフランスやドイツなどの金融機関の経営は、打撃を受けるだろう。◆If the value of a huge number of government bonds possessed by financial institutions around the world plummets, financial instability will grow. 世界の金融機関が保有する大量の国債の価格が急落すれば、金融不安が高まることになる。◆In Europe, the creditworthiness of Italian and Spanish government bonds is a source of uncertainty. 欧州では、イタリアとスペインの国債の信用力が、金融不安の発生源だ。◆Interest rate differentials between Greek and German government bonds widened to 600 basis points, or six percentage points, from January to May 2010. ギリシャ国債とドイツ国債の金利差は、2010年1月から5月の間に600ベーシス・ポイント（6%）も拡大した。◆It is too unconventional for the Bank of Japan to directly underwrite government bonds. 日銀の国債の直接引受けは、禁じ手だ。◆Lending by private banks has not increased though their investments into government bonds and cash reserves are increasing. 民間銀行の国債への投資や手持ちの現金は増えているが、民間銀行の貸出は増えていない。◆Long-term debts held by central and local governments are expected to further swell, thereby eroding confidence in governments bonds. 国と地方自治体が抱える長期債務は、さらに膨張して、国債の信用が失われるものと見られる。◆On the bond market, the yield on newly issued 10-year government bonds, an indicator of long-term interest rates, fell, resulting in a rise in bond prices. 債券市場では、長期金利の指標である新発10年物国債の利回り（流通利回り）が下落し、債券相場［債券価格］は上昇した。◆The amount of refunding bonds issued to redeem ordinary government bonds is expected to exceed ¥100 trillion. 普通国債償還のための借換え債の発行額が、100兆円を突破する見込みだ。◆The Bank of Japan will set up a fund to buy long-term government bonds, exchange-traded funds and other financial assets in a bid to prop up the nation's economy. 日本の景気を下支えするため、日銀は基金を新設して、長期国債や上場投資信託（ETF）などの金融商品［金融資産］を買い入れる。◆The BOJ's policy meeting plans to consider expanding the list of government bonds purchased under the fund. 日銀の政策決定会合では、基金で買い入れる国債の対象拡大を検討する予定だ。◆The European bond market is truly in a knife-edge situation as the yield on 10-year Italian government bonds has surged above 7 percent, the so-called danger zone that may result in a debt crisis. 10年物イタリア国債の流通利回りが、債務危機に陥る「危険水域」とされる7%超に上昇したため、欧州債券市場は予断を許さない状況にある。◆The European Central Bank decided to buy Italian and Spanish government bonds in tandem with the issuance of the G-7 emergency statement. 欧州中央銀行（ECB）は、G7緊急声明の発表と連動する形で、イタリアとスペインの国債を買い入れる方針を決めた。◆The European Central Bank has been purchasing Italian government bonds in an effort to support Italy. 欧州中央銀行（ECB）は、イタリア国債を買い入れてイタリアを支えている。◆The Greek-triggered sovereign debt crisis resulted in the breakup of the French-Belgian bank Dexia which held Greek government bonds. ギリシャが引き金になったソブリン危機（政府債務危機）問題で、ギリシャ国債を保有していた仏ベルギー系金融機関のデクシア（Dexia）が、解体に追い込まれた。◆The high yields of the yen-denominated government bonds were considered considerably higher than minuscule domestic interest rates. この円建て国債は、国内の超低金利に

比べて利回りがはるかに大きいと見られた。◆The yield on the benchmark 10-year U.S. government bond has been closing below 3 percent recently. 長期金利の指標となる10年物米国債の利回りは最近、3％を割り込んで[3％割れで]取引を終えている。◆The yields on government bonds of deficit-ridden countries including Greece have been rising across the board in Europe. 欧州では、ギリシャなど財政赤字国の国債利回りが、軒並み上昇している。◆The yields on Greek government bonds have been rising sharply due to the credit uncertainty. ギリシャ国債の利回りは、信用不安で急上昇している。◆Under the existing agreement, the IMF cannot buy government bonds through the EFSF as the IMF can only offer loans to countries. 現行協定では、IMF（国際通貨基金）は国にしか融資できないので、欧州金融安定基金（EFSF）を通じて国債を購入することはできない。

主要国債：
 Bunds ドイツ国債 ブンズ
 Gilts 英国債 ギルツ
 JGBs 日本国債 ジェー・ジー・ビー（=Japanese Government Bonds）
 US Treasuries 米国債

government bond holdings　国債保有高, 国債保有残高
◆Japanese private banks' government bond holdings soared to ¥154 trillion as of the end of June 2011 from ¥32 trillion as of the end of March 1999. 日本の民間銀行の国債保有残高は、（ゼロ金利政策が初めて）導入された1999年3月末時点の32兆円から、2011年6月末現在で154兆円に膨らんだ。

government bond issuance　国債発行, 国債発行額
◆Long-term debts held by central and local governments are expected to further swell unless the government puts the brakes on government bond issuance. 政府が国債発行に歯止めをかけないと、国と地方［地方自治体］が抱える長期債務は、さらに膨らむ見通しだ。◆The government bond issuance worth about ¥44 trillion for the current fiscal year is the largest ever projected in an initial budget. 今年度の約44兆円の国債発行額は、当初予算としては史上最高だ。◆The new government bond issuance has swollen to ¥44 trillion in fiscal 2010. 2010年度の新規国債発行額は、44兆円に膨らんだ。

government bond issue　国債発行
◆The primary balance represents the budget balance, excluding proceeds from government bond issues and debt-servicing costs. プライマリー・バランスは、国債発行による収入と国債費（国債の利払いや償還費用）を除いた財政収支である。

government bond market　国債市場, 国債相場
◆Long-term interest rates have soared almost fourfold in the past three months as a result of plunges in the government bond market. 国債相場の急落で、長期金利はこの3か月で4倍近くに急騰している。

government bond prices　国債価格
◆If a financial system crisis should occur due to sharp fall in Japanese government bond prices, the Japanese people would suffer an erosion of their financial assets. 日本国債価格の急落で金融システム不安が生じれば、日本国民の金融資産は損失を被ることになる。

government bond yield　国債利回り
◆Under a variable pension system, pension benefits change in accordance with fluctuations in government bond yield. 変額年金制度では、国債利回りの変動で年金給付額が変わる。
◆Under the envisioned lending facility, the IMF will provide funds to countries where government bond yields remain at high levels to help reconstruct their public finances. この融資制度案では、国際通貨基金（IMF）が、国債の利回りが高止まりしている国に資金を提供［融資］して財政再建を支援する。

government bonds outstanding　国債残高, 未償還政府債券
◆Japan has vast sums of government bonds outstanding. 日本は、厖大な国債残高を抱えている。

government budget　政府予算
 government budget cut　政府予算削減［カット］
 government budget restraint　政府予算制約
 government budget restriction　政府予算抑制
 government budget savings　政府経常余剰

government-controlled home loan giant　米政府系住宅ローン大手
◆The U.S. central bank will buy mortgage-backed securities (MBS) guaranteed by the government-controlled home loan giants Fannie Mae, Freddie Mac and Ginnie Mae. 米連邦準備制度理事会（FRB）は、米政府系住宅ローン大手のファニー・メイ（米連邦住宅貸付公社）、フレディ・マック（米連邦住宅抵当金庫）とジニー・メイ（米政府系住宅金融公庫）が保証した住宅ローン担保証券（MBS）を買い取ることになった。

government debt　国債, 公債, 政府の債務, 政府の借金, 国の借金, 政府の財政赤字
 (=national debt; ⇒redeem)
 domestic government debt and stock index contracts　国債・株価指数先物
 domestic government debt markets　国債市場
 government debt expenses　国債費
 government debt interest　国債利子
 government-related debt　政府機関債
 interest payments on the government debt　国債利子払い
 maturing government debts　満期を迎える国債
 outstanding government debt　政府債務残高
 payment of principal and interest of government debt　国債の元利払い
◆If a new federal debt ceiling isn't set by Aug. 2, 2011, the United States will be forced to default on Treasuries securities as it will not be able to issue new bonds to pay back maturing government debts. 2011年8月2日までに連邦政府の債務上限を新たに設けないと、米国は満期を迎える国債を償還するための国債増発ができないので、米国債の不履行（デフォルト）が発生する。◆Italy's government debt is about 120 percent of its gross domestic product. イタリアの政府債務残高は、国内総生産（GDP）比で約120％に達している。◆Our future generation will be heavily burdened with government debt. われわれの将来世代は、政府債務という大きな負担を背負うことになる。◆The child allowance program is being financed by increasing government debt. 子ども手当制度の財源は、政府の借金［政府債務］の上積みで賄（まかな）われている。◆The greater the government debt, the heavier the tax burden to redeem it will be. 政府の借金が大きくなるほど、それを返済するための税の負担は重くなる。

government debt ratios　政府の債務比率, 政府債務比率
◆The downgrade of Japan's long-term sovereign credit rating reflects S&P's appraisal that Japan's government debt ratios will rise further. 日本の長期国債の格下げは、日本の政府債務比率がさらに悪化する、とのスタンダード・アンド・プアーズ（S&P）の見方を反映している。

government debt-to-GDP ratio　政府債務の対国内総生産（GDP）比
◆Advanced economies will at least halve deficits by 2013 and stabilize or reduce government debt-to-GDP ratios by 2016. 先進国は、2013年までに少なくとも財政赤字を半減させ、2016年までに政府債務の対国内総生産（GDP）比を安定化または低下させる方針だ。

government deficit　政府赤字, 公共部門の赤字, 財政赤字
 finance large government deficits　巨額の財政赤字を埋め

合わせる
local government deficits 地方財政の赤字
sustained reduction of government deficits 財政赤字の大幅削減

government-financed 政府出資の
◆The four defendants overcharged the government's Cabinet Office by about ¥141 million in the government-financed chemical weapons disposal project. 被告4人は、政府出資の化学兵器処理事業費として、政府の内閣府に約1億4,100万円を水増し請求した。

government finances 財政, 政府財政, 国家財政, 国の財政 （=state finances）
◆Japan lags badly behind other advanced countries in restoring its government finances to a sound footing. 日本は、財政健全化の点で、他の先進国よりかなり遅れている。◆Unless consumption tax rate is raised, the planned issuance of bridging bonds could lead to further deterioration of the debt-saddled government finances. 消費税率を引き上げないと、予定しているつなぎ国債の発行は、借金を背負っている国の財政の悪化をさらに招く可能性がある。

government financial aid [assistance] 政府の金融支援
◆Creditor financial institutions and shareholders will suffer huge losses if TEPCO falls into debt without the government financial aid. 東電が政府の金融支援を受けられずに債務超過に陥れば、融資している金融機関や株主は、巨額の損失を被ることになる。◆TEPCO is drafting a special business plan as the premise for getting government financial aid. 東電は、政府の金融支援を受ける前提として、特別事業計画を策定している。

government financial support 政府の金融支援
◆Without the government financial support, TEPCO will fall into debt as the utility has to pay the huge amounts in compensation. 政府の金融支援がなければ、東電は巨額の賠償金を支払わなければならないので、債務超過に陥ると思われる。

government fund 政府資金, 公金
government fund transactions 国庫収支
government fund transactions with the Bank of Japan 国庫対日銀収支
government fund transactions with the public 国庫対民間収支

government guarantee 政府保証
◆Japan Post bank and Japan Post Insurance have an implicit government guarantee. ゆうちょ銀行とかんぽ生命保険には、暗黙の政府保証がある。

government-guaranteed financial assistance 政府保証の金融支援, 金融支援の政府保証
◆The limit on government-guaranteed financial assistance to the Nuclear Damage Liability Facilitation Fund was expanded as the increased costs for decommissioning the crippled Fukushima No.1 nuclear power plant would strain TEPCO's corporate management. 機能不全の福島第一原子力発電所の廃炉費用の増加で、東電の経営が圧迫されるので、原子力損害賠償支援機構に対する金融支援の政府保証枠が拡大された。

government loan 国債, 公債, 公的融資, 公的資金, 借款
◆General Motors Co. will start repaying billions of dollars in government loans that helped keep it alive. ゼネラル・モーターズは、同社の存続に充てられた数十億ドルの公的資金の返済を開始する。

government-managed health insurance plan 政府管掌健康保険（制度）
◆Workers at small and medium-sized firms, who belong to a government-managed health insurance plan, will have to pay higher premiums. 中小企業の従業員が加入している政府管掌健康保険の保険料も、アップされる。

government money 政府資金, 公的資金
◆American companies are competing on the basis of their ability to tap government money. 米企業は、公的資金を引き出せるかどうかで競争している。

government revenue 政府収入, 国の税収
◆The income and corporate taxes are an important source of government revenues. 所得税や法人税は、国の重要な税収源である。

government securities 政府発行有価証券, 政府証券, 国債, 公債
government securities dealer 政府証券取扱い業者, プライマリー・ディーラー
government securities market 国債市場, 公債市場
medium-term government securities fund 中期国債ファンド
monetary operation by buying government securities 国債買いオペ
short-term government securities 政府短期証券
◆The assets of the various plans include corporate equities, government securities, corporate debt securities and income-producing real estate. 各種制度の年金資産は、株式、政府証券、債券や収益を稼得する不動産などで構成されています。

government-set target 政府設定の目標, 政府目標
◆Japan's mega-banks are required to achieve by the end of fiscal 2004 the government-set target of halving their respective ratios of bad loans from those posted at the end of fiscal 2001. 日本のメガバンクはそれぞれ、2004年度末（2005年3月期）までに、2001年度末（2002年3月期）時点の不良債権残高比率を半減させる政府目標の達成を義務付けられている。

government spending 歳出, 政府支出, 財政支出 （⇒cut down on）
additional government spending 財政の追加支出
curb [rein in] government spending 財政支出を抑える, 財政支出を抑制する
cut down on government spending 歳出を削減する, 歳出を切り詰める
government spending clampdown 歳出削減, 財政支出の削減
government spending multiplier 財政支出乗数
government spending policy 政府の支出政策
local government spending 地方自治体の支出
massive increase in government spending 大型の財政出動
reduced government spending 財政支出の削減
softness in government spending 政府支出の縮小
wasteful government spending 国費の無駄, 国費の無駄遣い
◆The Government Revitalization Unit kicked off its second round of efforts to trim wasteful government spending. 政府の行政刷新会議が、国費の無駄遣いを削減するための2回目の作業を開始した。

government subsidies 政府補助金, 国庫補助金, 政府助成金
◆Personal consumption surged as a result of robust car sales ahead of the end of government subsidies for eco-friendly cars. 政府のエコカー補助金の期限切れを控えて自動車販売が好調だったため、個人消費が急増した。◆Policy-based financing operations which take advantage of government subsidies are adversely affecting the price mechanism in the financial market. 政府の補給金を受けて運営される政策金融は、金融市場の価格メカニズムを歪めている。

governmental （形）政府［政治、国家統治］の, 政府系の, 国営の, 政府出資の
governmental agencies 政府諸官庁, 政府機関 （governmental organizations）

governmental authorities　政府当局
governmental bodies　政府関係機関, 政府系機関
governmental charge　課徴金, 賦課金, 納付金
governmental Development Bank of Japan　日本政策投資銀行
governmental loan　借款
governmental subsidy　政府補助金, 国庫補助金
Inter Governmental［Inter-Governmental］Conference　各国政府間会議
local governmental units　地方自治体
quasi-governmental mortgage insurer　政府系住宅モーゲージ保証会社
quasi-governmental organization　政府系機関
◆Two domestic carriers have been given a total of ¥85 billion in emergency loans by the governmental Development Bank of Japan to overcome losses caused by a downturn in airline passengers. 利用客の減少で発生した損失を補填するため、国内航空会社2社が、政府系金融機関の日本政策投資銀行から計850億円の緊急融資を受けた。

governments　米連邦政府証券, 米国債, 米政府機関証券（=government obligations）

governor　（名）（銀行の）総裁, 頭取, 理事長, 理事, 知事,（米国の）州知事, 長官, Gov
Bank of Japan Deputy Gov.　日銀副総裁
Bank of Japan Governor［Gov.］　日銀総裁
Board of Governors of the Federal Reserve Board　米連邦準備制度理事会（FRBの正式名称）
central bank governors　中央銀行総裁　（⇒finance ministers and central bank governors［chiefs］）
Governor of the Bank of England　イングランド銀行総裁
the governors of the Stock Exchange　証券取引所理事
◆Prime Minister Naoto Kan and Bank of Japan Gov. Masaaki Shirakawa exchanged views on the recent currency exchange rates. 菅首相と白川日銀総裁が、最近の為替相場について意見交換した。

grab　（動）つかむ, 勝ち取る, 得る, 獲得する, 奪う, ものにする, 利用する, 〜の興味を引く, 注意をひきつける, 心をつかむ, 〜に強い印象を与える, ひったくる, 横領する, 乗っ取る, 強奪する
◆Increasing M&A advisory business helped Nomura grab the No. 1 spot in Japan's M&A league table for the first half of this year. 今年上半期はM&A顧問業務が増加したため、日本のM&A案件の引受実績で野村證券がトップの座を占めた。

grace period　猶予（ゆうよ）期間
◆In the case of a lack of liquidity or liquidity crisis, the debt repayment of an indebted borrower is still possible if a grace period is given, but lack of cash on hand makes it impossible to repay its debt in the short term. 流動性不足や流動性危機の場合、債務を抱えた借り手の債務返済は猶予期間を与えればまだ可能であるが、手元に現金がないため短期での債務返済はできない。

grade　（名）格付け, 等級, 階級, 段階, 程度, 評価, 評点, グレード　（⇒investment-grade securities）
high-grade bond　高格付けの債券
high-grade stock　優良株
investment grade　投資適格格付け（=investment-grade, investment-grade rating）
noninvestment grade　投機的格付け（=speculative grade）
noninvestment grade bond　投機的格付け債, 投資不適格格付け, 高利回り債
speculative grade　投機的格付け
speculative-grade bond　投機的格付け債券
speculative-grade issuer　投機的格付けの発行体
the highest grade　最上級
◆A downgrade below investment-grade by even one ratings agency could boost GM's borrowing costs and wreak havoc on the corporate bond market. 格付け会社が1社でも投資適格格付けより低く格付けを引き下げたら（格付け会社が1社でも投機的格付けに格下げしたら）、GMの資金調達コストが急増し、米国の社債（債券）市場にも大きな影響が出る恐れがある。
◆Even after Greece's debt load is cut, Greece's credit grade is likely to remain low. ギリシャの債務負担を削減しても、ギリシャの信用格付けは、低水準にとどまる見込みだ。◆Fitch Ratings Ltd. will keep its rating on long-term U.S. debt at the highest grade, AAA. 英米系の格付け会社フィッチ・レーティングスは、米国の長期国債格付けを、最上級のAAA（トリプルA）に据え置く方針だ。

graduated　（形）段階的な, 累進的な, 漸増の, 漸増型の
graduated-payment mortgage（loan）　元利返済漸増型モーゲージ
graduated pension　累進年金
graduated tax　累進税
graduated taxation　累進課税

Grameen Bank　グラミン銀行（バングラデシュにある銀行で、貧困層を対象に無担保で金を貸して仕事の手助けをしている。1983年にムハマド・ユヌス総裁が創立。その功績を認められて、同氏はノーベル平和賞を受賞した）

Gramm-Leach-Bliley Act　グラム・リーチ・ブライリー法, GLBA　（=Financial Services Modernization Act（金融サービス近代化法）：銀行と証券の兼業を禁じたグラス・スティーガル法（Glass-Steagall Act）の規制を撤廃して、銀行・証券・保険の相互参入に関する法的枠組みを規定したもの。3人の下院議員の共同提案で1999年に成立）

Gramm-Rudman（Hollings）Act　グラム・ラドマン法, グラム・ラドマン（・ホリングス）法（米国の財政赤字を1990年10月1日までにゼロにすることを義務付けたもので、1985年12月に成立）

Gramm-Rudman-Hollings Deficit Reduction Act of 1985　グラム・ラドマン法, グラム・ラドマン・ホリングス法　（=Gramm-Rudman Hollings Act：3人の米上院議員が共同提案して1985年12月に成立した財政均衡法。「財政均衡法」の正式名称はBalanced Budget and Emergency Deficit Control Act of 1985）

grant　（動）与える, 付与する, 許諾する, 許可する, 承認する, 認める, 譲渡する, 移転する
be granted debt waivers　債権放棄を受ける, 債務免除を認められる　（⇒forgive a part of the outstanding debt, grant of an option）
grant a charge　担保を設定する, 担保として差し出す
grant a license　実施権を許諾する, 実施権を付与する, 使用権を与える使用許諾を与える
grant permission　許可を与える
◆Licensee shall not be permitted to sublicense the license granted hereunder to others. ライセンシー（実施権者）は、本契約に従って許諾された実施権を他者にサブライセンスすることはできない。◆The company granted an investment firm the right to buy shares to be newly issued by the company as a means of foiling a hostile takeover bid. 同社は、敵対的買収への防衛策として、同社が新規に発行する株式の引受権を投資会社に付与した［投資会社に新株予約権を割り当てた］。◆The exercise price of any stock option is equal to or greater than the stock price when the option is granted. ストック・オプションの行使価格は、オプションが付与された時の株価と同等、またはそれを上回る価格になっています。◆The firm was granted debt waivers totaling ¥640 billion from its main creditor banks. 同社は、主力銀行から6,400億円の債

権放棄を受けた。◆The government tightened the criteria for granting total exemption from paying national pension premiums. 政府は、国民年金保険料の全額免除の基準を厳格にした。

grant （名）権利の付与, 授与, 財産の移転, 譲渡, 譲与, 贈与, 実施許諾, 政府の補助金, 助成金, 交付金, 無償資金, 無償給付, 研究助成金, 奨学金
- block grant　包括補助金, ブロック交付金
- capital grant　資本補助金
- categorical grants　使途別補助金
- death grant　死亡補助金
- equalization grant　平衡交付金
- federal grants　政府補助金
- Federal grants to States　連邦から州への交付金
- flat grant　均等補助金
- flat grant minus system　減額式定額年金制
- general grant　一般交付金
- government grant　政府補助金
- grant bonds　交付国債
- grant commitment　助成の約束
- grant deed　不動産譲渡証書
- grant economy　補助金経済
- grant element　（政府借款中の）贈与比率
- grant of license　実施権の許諾, 実施権の付与, 使用許諾, 商標使用許諾
- grant of patent license　特許実施権の許諾[付与], 特許ライセンスの付与
- grant share　贈与比率
- industrial grant　業務災害一時金
- investment grant　投資補助金
- labor grant　労働贈与
- land grant　土地使用権, 無償土地払い下げ
- loan grants　借款
- operation grant　運営費補助
- patent grant　特許許可
- percentage grant　定率補助金
- rate support grants　レート援助交付金
- research grant　研究助成金
- training grant　訓練助成金

◆Chinese President Hu Jintao pledged nearly $100 million in grants and soft loans to Cameroon. 中国の胡錦濤国家主席は、カメルーンに対して約1億ドルの資金援助と長期低利貸付けを約束した。◆The Japanese government provided $1.5 billion in grants to help rebuilding Iraq. 日本政府は、イラク復興支援のため、無償資金で15億ドルを拠出した。◆The tripartite reforms aim to reduce the amount of subsidies provided by the central government to the local governments; cut local tax grants to local governments; and shift revenue sources from the central government to local governments. 「三位一体」改革は、国の地方政府への補助金削減、地方交付税交付金の削減と国から地方政府への財源の移譲をめざしている。

grant aid　無償資金協力
◆The Japanese government will provide grant aid totaling about $1 billion for African nations for primary education, health care and other basic needs over a five-year period from this fiscal year. 初等教育、保健医療などの基礎生活分野を対象に、日本政府はアフリカ諸国に対して今年度から5年間で総額約10億ドルの無償資金協力を実施する。◆This realty had a fair market value of $500,000 at the date of the grant. この不動産の贈与時の時価は、50万ドルであった。

grant award　義援金
◆We had commitments of corporate funds totaling $1 million, plus a Foundation grant award of $50,000. われわれは総額100万ドルの会社資金のほかに、5万ドルの当財団義援金の確約を得ました。

grant element　（政府借款中の）贈与比率, 贈与要素, 援助条件緩和指数, グラント・エレメント
◆Since July 1975, OECF has been in charge of ODA loans with a grant element equal to or exceeding 25 percent. 1975年7月以来、グラント・エレメントが25％以上の円借款業務は、OECF（海外経済協力基金）の業務となっている。

grant-in-aid　無償援助, 補助金, 助成金, 交付金
◆The government should end its yen loans and grant-in-aid to China. 政府は、対中円借款と無償援助を取り止めるべきだ。

grant of an option　オプションの付与
◆Simultaneously with the grant of an option, the employee may also be granted the right to a special compensation payment. オプションの付与と同時に、従業員に対しては、特別報酬の支払いを受ける権利を付与することもあります。

grantee　（名）信用状依頼人, 被譲与者, 被許可者, 被許諾者, 譲受人

granting of credit　信用供与

grantor　（名）譲渡人, 譲与人, 許諾者, ライセンス許諾者, 特許権など知的財産権の使用許諾者, 不動産権設定者

grantor-grantee index　譲渡人・譲受人総覧

gratis　（形）無料の, 無償の, 任意の　（副）無料で, 無償で
- gratis dictum　任意的陳述
- gratis issue　株式分割
- gratis retirement of stocks　株式の無償償却

gray [grey]　（形）灰色の, あいまいな, どっちつかずの, 高齢者の
- gray information　入手困難な科学技術情報, 灰色情報
- gray knight　灰色の騎士（株式公開買付け（TOB）で動向が分からない参加者）
- gray market　発行前取引, 闇類似市場, グレー・マーケット

graying　（名）高齢化　（=ageing, aging: 高齢化社会は aging society, graying society）
◆There is a limit to conventional pump-priming measures amid a continued decline in birthrate and a consequent graying and shrinking population. 少子高齢化や人口減少などが進行するなかで、従来の景気刺激策[景気テコ入れ策]では限界がある。

great　（形）素晴らしい, 大きな, 巨大な, 強大な, 大型の, 偉大な, 卓越した, 多大な, 重要な, 重大な
- great authority　強大な権限
- great company　優良企業
- greater business risks　事業リスクの増大, 事業リスクの高まり
- greater competition　競争激化
- greater dependence on purchased funds　市場資金への依存度の高まり
- greater regulatory controls　規制強化
- the greater likelihood of default loss　デフォルト（債務不履行）損失の可能性の高まり
- the greatest negative force　最大の懸念材料

◆There has been greater demand for funds to develop mega solar power plant projects in recent years. 最近は、メガソーラー（大型太陽光発電所）事業の開発資金の需要が高まっている。

Great Depression　大恐慌, 世界大恐慌, 世界恐慌（=Depression）
◆The Great Depression began in the United States in 1929. 大恐慌[世界大恐慌]は、1929年に米国で始まった。◆The ongoing business slump raises the specter of a global downturn comparable to the Great Depression that started in 1929. 今回の不況は、1929年に始まった世界大恐慌に匹敵するほどの

世界同時不況の懸念が高まっている。

Great East Japan Earthquake　（2011年3月11日の）東日本大震災
◆Earthquake insurance payments resulting from the Great East Japan Earthquake are expected to reach ¥1.2 trillion. 東日本大震災による地震保険の保険金支払い額は、（業界全体で）1兆2,000億円に達する見込みだ。◆The government plans to sell some of its 100 percent stake in Japan Post Holdings Co. to fund reconstruction from the Great East Japan Earthquake. 政府は、東日本大震災の復興財源に充てるため、100％保有する日本郵政の株式の一部も売却する方針だ。◆To procure funds to finance reconstruction from the Great East Japan Earthquake, the government is planning to sell some of its shares in Japan Tobacco Inc. and Tokyo Metro Co. 東日本大震災の復興費用を賄うための資金を調達するため、政府は日本たばこ産業（JT）と東京地下鉄（東京メトロ）の株式を売却する方針だ。

Greece's debt woes　ギリシャの債務問題
◆In resolving Greece's debt woes, German Chancellor Angera Merkel urged substantial aid from private creditors. ギリシャの債務問題を解決するにあたって、アンゲラ・メルケル独首相は、民間債権者に大幅支援を求めた。

Greece's financial debacle　ギリシャの財政破たん
（=Greece's financial collapse）
◆Europe's debt crisis was triggered by Greece's financial debacle. 欧州の債務危機は、ギリシャの財政破たんに端を発した。

Greece's fiscal reconstruction　ギリシャの財政再建
◆Greece's fiscal reconstruction is set as a condition for supporting the struggling country by the European Union and the International Monetary Fund. 欧州連合（EU）と国際通貨基金（IMF）は、ギリシャの財政再建を、財政危機にある同国支援の条件としている。

Greek crisis　ギリシャ危機
◆Confidence in the single currency of the euro may be undermined by the spread of the Greek crisis to Spain and Portugal. ギリシャ危機のスペインやポルトガルへの波及で、単一通貨・ユーロの信認が揺らぎかねない。

Greek default　ギリシャの債務不履行，ギリシャ国債のデフォルト（債務不履行）
◆A Greek default may be unavoidable. ギリシャ国債のデフォルト（債務不履行）は、避けられないかもしれない。

Greek financial crisis　ギリシャの財政危機
◆Greek financial crisis was caused by the country's lax fiscal management. ギリシャの財政危機は、同国の放漫財政［放漫な財政運営］によって生じた。◆No clear prospect has emerged for resolution of the Greek financial crisis. ギリシャの財政危機を打開する明確な見通しは、まだ立っていない。

Greek fiscal crisis　ギリシャの財政危機
◆As the Greek fiscal crisis grows more serious, there has been no halt to the worldwide decline in stock prices. ギリシャの財政危機が一段と深刻化するにつれ、世界同時株安に歯止めがかからなくなっている。

Greek government bonds　ギリシャ国債
◆Fears about default on the Greek government bonds are smoldering as Greece's fiscal reconstruction measures hit the wall. ギリシャの財政再建策が行き詰まっているため、ギリシャ国債のデフォルト（債務不履行）の恐れがくすぶっている。◆The Greek-triggered sovereign debt crisis resulted in the breakup of the French-Belgian bank Dexia which held Greek government bonds. ギリシャが引き金になったソブリン危機（政府債務危機）問題で、ギリシャ国債を保有していた仏ベルギー系金融機関のデクシア（Dexia）が、解体に追い込まれた。

Greek-induced fiscal crisis　ギリシャ発の財政危機
◆The Greece-induced fiscal crisis is still not under control. ギリシャ発の財政危機は、まだ収束していない。

Greek-triggered sovereign debt crisis　ギリシャに端を発したソブリン危機（政府債務危機），ギリシャに端を発した債務危機問題
（⇒Greek government bonds）
◆European leaders reached an agreement to prevent the Greece-triggered sovereign debt crisis from spreading to the rest of the world from Europe. 欧州各国首脳は、ギリシャに端を発した債務危機の欧州から世界各国への拡大を食い止めることで合意した。◆Japan, the United States and emerging countries are upping their pressure on Europe to contain the Greek-triggered sovereign debt crisis. 日米と新興国は、欧州に対して、ギリシャに端を発したソブリン危機（政府債務危機）封じ込めの圧力を強めている。◆The Greek-triggered sovereign debt crisis has been throwing the eurozone into financial uncertainty and multiple crises. ギリシャに端を発した債務危機問題で、ユーロ圏は金融不安と複合的な危機に陥っている。

green　（形）環境の，環境保護の，環境にやさしい，環境に配慮した，許可された，準備完了の，予定通りに進んだ，グリーン
green audit　環境監査
green business　環境事業，環境ビジネス
green card　米国での労働許可証，外国人永住許可証，英国での国際自動車保険証
green consumer　緑の消費者，グリーン・コンシューマー
green effect　温室効果
green goods　にせ札
green labeling［labelling］　緑の表示，エコ表示
green light　正式許可，認可，ゴーサイン
green power　金，金力，財力

green investment scheme　グリーン投資スキーム，GIS
◆The green investment scheme (GIS) obliges Russia to spend profits from the emission quota trade on environmental protection measures. （京都議定書が定める）グリーン投資スキーム（GIS）で、ロシアは排出量取引の売却益を環境対策に使うことが義務付けられている。

greenback　（名）米ドル，米ドル紙幣　（米ドル紙幣の裏面がすべてグリーンなのでこう呼ばれている。⇒short covering）
the appreciation of the greenback　ドル高
the depreciation of the greenback　ドル安
◆If the renminbi rises, the greenback will weaken further. 人民元が切り上がれば［人民元の価値［相場］が上昇すれば］、米ドルはさらに弱体化する。◆The depreciation of the greenback will result in exchange losses on assets held in dollars. ドル安が進むと、保有するドル建て資産に為替差損が生じる。◆The greenback may not be able to maintain its impregnable position as the world's only reserve currency. 米ドルは、世界で唯一の準備通貨としての揺るぎない地位を、維持できないかもしれない。

greenlining　（名）融資の地域差別に対する反対運動

greenmail　（名）買収や高値での引取りを目的にした株式の大量買取り，法外な価格での株の買戻し，グリーンメール　（greenbackとblackmailとの合成語。以下は、greenmailが動詞として使われた文例。⇒corporate raider, raider）
◆The would-be acquirer is trying to greenmail the target company by having it pay a premium to buy back the shares held by the raider. 買収側［買収希望者］は、この買占め屋［会社乗っ取り屋］が保有する株を標的企業に高値で引き取らせて、標的企業から収益を上げようとしている（標的企業に高値で引き取らせることにより、標的企業にグリーンメールを仕掛けようとしている）。

greenmailer　（名）グリーンメールで金儲けをする人，買収などの目的で大量に買い取った株式を高値で売る投資

家, グリーンメーラー
greenshoe （名）追加発行, グリーンシュー条項, グリーンシュー
　greenshoe clause　グリーンシュー条項
　greenshoe option　グリーンシュー・オプション
gridlock （名）交通渋滞, 大混雑, マヒ状態, 行き詰まり, 八方ふさがり状態, 閉塞状態, 停滞
　◆Political gridlock in Washington is part of the reason behind the S&P cut in the U.S. long-term credit rating. 米国の政府・議会の政治的行き詰まりが, スタンダード・アンド・プアーズ（S&P）の米長期国債格下げの一因である。
grim （形）厳しい, 怖い, ぞっとするような, 容赦のない, 冷酷な, 嫌な, 気の進まない
　◆The U.S. credit rating agency Standard & Poor's made a grim assessment of the outlook of U.S. fiscal reconstruction. 米国の信用格付け機関のスタンダード・アンド・プアーズ（S&P）は, 米国の財政再建の見通しを厳しく評価した。
grip （動）しっかりつかむ, 理解する, 把握する, 深い影響を与える, 影響力［支配力］を持つ,（注意, 興味を）引きつける, 心を奪う,（病気が）襲う
　be gripped by　～に心を奪われる, ～に引きつけられる, ～の影響を受ける, ～で動けなくなる
　fiscal crises gripping some European countries　一部の欧州諸国の財政危機
　grip one's attention　～の注意を引く
　grip the point　要点をつかむ
　recession gripping the world　世界をおおう不景気
　◆Stock prices in Tokyo fell by more than 600 points as a state of panic gripped investors and selling pressure snowballed. 東京市場の株価は, 投資家がパニック状態に陥り, 売り圧力が増大［加速］したため, 下げ幅が600円を超えた。◆We must recognize anew the serious fiscal conditions gripping Japan. 日本の［日本をおおう］深刻な財政事情を, われわれは再認識しなければならない。
grip （名）支配, 影響, 支配力, 影響力, 牽引力, 引きつける力, 理解力, 把握力, 処理能力, やる気, 撮影班の裏方, グリップ
　be in［get into］the grip of　～にとらえられる, ～に見舞われている, ～から深刻な影響を受けている, ～にはまる
　come［get］to grips with　～に真剣に取り組む, ～を理解［把握］する, ～とけんかする
　decide to ease monetary grip further　追加の金融緩和を決める
　◆The BOJ decided to ease its monetary grip further by effectively restoring its zero-interest-rate policy. 日銀は, 実質的にゼロ金利政策を復活させて, 追加の金融緩和を決めた。◆The United States is in the grip of the worst economic crisis in more than 70 years. 米国は, 過去70年以上で最悪の経済危機に見舞われている。
gross domestic product　国内総生産, GDP（GNPから海外からの純所得を差し引いたもの）
　◆Gross domestic product will rise 2 percent in inflation-adjusted real terms and 2.2 percent in nominal terms in the current fiscal year from the previous fiscal year. 今年度の国内総生産（GDP）の成長率は, 物価変動の影響を除いた実質で前年度比2%, 名目で2.2%になる見通しだ。◆Italy's government debt is about 120 percent of its gross domestic product. イタリアの政府債務残高は, 国内総生産（GDP）比で約120％に達している。◆To achieve at least 2 percent nominal growth in gross domestic product in fiscal 2006, the government must take stimulus measures, including a cut in corporate income tax, in tandem with the Bank of Japan's easy money policy. 2006年度に2%超の名目GDP成長率を実現するには, 日銀の金融緩和政策と並んで, 政府は法人税減税などの景気刺激策を取らなければならない。◆Total long-term debts of the central and local governments are more than 1.8 times the gross domestic product. 国と地方自治体の長期債務［長期債務残高］の総額は, 国内総生産（GDP）の1.8倍を超えている。◆Washington and Seoul jointly proposed to cap the G-20 nations' current account surpluses or deficits at 4 percent of gross domestic product by 2015. 米国と韓国は, G20（世界20か国・地域）の経常収支の黒字または赤字を2015年までにGDP（国内総生産）比で4%以内に制限するよう共同提案した。
gross margin　売上総利益, 売上利益, 粗利益, 粗利, 売上利益率, 粗利益率
　（=gross margin percentage, gross margin ratio）
　gross margin on sales　売上総利益
　gross margin percentage　売上総利益率, 粗利益率
　　（=gross profit percentage）
　gross margin ratio　売上総利益率, 粗利益率
　　（=gross margin percentage）
　gross profit margin　（売上高）総利益率, 粗利益率
　◆The firm's earnings per share were affected both by lower revenues and reduced gross margins. 同社の1株当たり利益は, 売上高の減少と売上利益率の低下の影響を受けた。◆The pressures on gross margins and earnings that affected the last half of 2010 will continue through the first half of 2012. 2010年下半期［下期］の業績に影響を及ぼした売上利益率と利益の低下は, 2012年上半期［上期］まで続く見通しです。
gross national product　国民総生産, GNP（1年間の総生産額から中間生産物を差し引いたもの）
gross operating profit　業務粗利益　（⇒corporate enterprise tax, corporate tax on gross operating profit, local corporate tax）
　◆It is illegal for the Tokyo metropolitan government to impose corporate taxes on the gross operating profits of major banks in Tokyo. 東京都が東京の大手銀行の業務粗利益に法人税を課すのは, 違法である。◆The new bank tax is levied on the banks' gross operating profits—their earnings minus basic operating expenses such as interest payments to depositors. 新銀行税は, 銀行の収入から基礎的な経費（預金者に対する預金金利の支払いなど）を差し引いた業務粗利益に課される。
gross premium　総保険料, 表定保険料, 営業保険料（営業保険料（gross premium）は, 純保険料（net premium）+付加保険料（loading）で算出される）
　◆Gross premium refers to the amount that policyowners actually pay for their insurance. 総保険料とは, 契約者が実際に支払う保険契約料の額のことをいう。
ground （名）地歩, 立場, 根拠, 理由
　gain ground　前進する, 成功する, 回復する, 影響力を増す, 一般化する
　go to ground　様子見を決め込む
　lose a good deal of ground　反落する
　lose further ground　続落する
　lose ground　地歩を失う, 後退する, 衰退する, 失敗する, 下落する, 値崩れを起こす, 影響力を失う
　lose ground against　～に対して下落する
　　（⇒high-yielding［higher-yielding］currency）
　lost ground　下げ幅
group （動）～をグループとしてまとめる, 傘下に～がある
　◆SMFG groups Sumitomo Mitsui Banking Corp., Sumitomo Mitsui Card Co. and SMBC Friend Securities Co., among other affiliates. 三井住友FGは, 傘下に三井住友銀行のほか, 三井住友カードやSMBCフレンド証券などの関連会社がある。
group （名）集団, 企業集団, 団体, 連結, グループ
　（⇒banking group, financial group）
　corporate group　企業グループ, 企業集団

financial group　金融グループ, 融資団
industry group　業界団体, 経済団体
interest group　利益団体, 利益集団, 圧力団体
investment group　投資グループ
management group　幹事団
manager group　幹事団, 幹事グループ, 幹事銀行団
on a group basis　連結ベースで, 連結ベースの
underwriting group　引受団
◆SMFG's securities division is seen as inferior to those other megabank groups. 三井住友フィナンシャルグループの証券部門は, 巨大銀行グループと比べて見劣りがする。

group accounts　連結財務書類, 連結財務諸表, グループ財務書類, 企業集団財務諸表　(=consolidated accounts, consolidated financial statements)

group annuity　団体年金

group banking　持ち株支配銀行制

group insurance　団体保険, グループ保険
group annuity insurance　団体年金保険
group credit insurance　団体信用保険
group insurance contract　団体保険契約
group life and health insurance　団体生命・健康保険
group pensions insurance　団体年金保険
group term life insurance　団体定期保険
◆Group insurance refers to insurance that provides coverage for a number of people under one contract, called a master contract. 団体(グループ)保険とは, 基本保険契約と呼ばれる単一の契約で複数の人が保障される保険のことをいう。

group net loss　連結純損失, 当期連結純損失, 連結税引き後赤字　(=consolidated net loss: 企業グループ全体の税引き後損失。⇒incur)

group net profit　連結純利益, 当期連結純利益, 連結税引き後利益　(=consolidated net profit: 企業グループ全体の税引き後利益。⇒group sales)
◆Sumitomo Mitsui Financial Group expects a group net profit of ￥180 billion for the year to March 31, 2005. 三井住友フィナンシャルグループは, 2005年3月期決算で1,800億円の連結税引き後利益を見込んでいる。

Group of Five major industrialized countries　先進5か国(G5), 先進5か国財務相[蔵相]・中央銀行総裁会議　(英米独仏日5か国のマクロ経済調整の場。⇒coordinated policy)
◆On Sept. 22, 1985, the finance ministers of the Group of Five major industrialized countries met at the Plaza Hotel in New York. 1985年9月22日に, ニューヨークのプラザ・ホテルで先進5か国(G5)蔵相会議が開かれた。

Group of Seven industrial powers　先進7か国(G7)
◆As for the issue of China's cheap yuan, the leaders of the Group of Seven industrial powers simply reiterated what they said at the previous G-7 meeting. 中国の割安な人民元問題に関しては, 先進7か国の財務相・中央銀行総裁は, 前回のG7で述べたことを繰り返しただけだった。

Group of Seven leading (industrialized) nations　先進7か国, 先進7か国(G7)首脳会議, 先進7か国財務相[蔵相]・中央銀行総裁会議　(G7=G5+カナダ, イタリア。⇒central banker, heavily indebted poor countries)
◆Finance ministers and central bank governors from the Group of Seven leading nations held an emergency telephone conference to avert financial turmoil caused by the downgrading of the U.S. credit rating. 米国債の格下げによる金融市場の混乱を回避するため, 先進7か国(G7)の財務相と中央銀行総裁が, 緊急電話会議を開いた。

Group of Seven meeting of finance ministers and central bank governors　先進7か国財務相・中央銀行総裁会議(G7)　(⇒central banker, G-7 meeting of finance ministers and central bank governors)

Group of 20 finance ministers meeting　世界20か国・地域(G20)財務相・中央銀行総裁会議
◆The mood music at the Group of 20 finance ministers meeting contrasted with the tense summit five months ago. 世界20か国・地域(G20)財務相・中央銀行総裁会議のゆったりした雰囲気は, 5か月前の緊迫したG20金融サミット(首脳会議)とは対照的だった。

Group of 20 major economies　主要20か国・地域, G20
◆Europe promised the Group of 20 major economies to take concerted action to contain the financial crisis. 欧州は, 結束して金融危機を封じ込めることを主要20か国・地域(G20)に公約した。

Group of 20 meeting of finance ministers and central bank governors　世界20か国・地域財務相・中央銀行総裁会議, G20
◆The Group of 20 meeting of finance ministers and central bank governors held in the United States did not probe deeply into the Greek fiscal problem. 米国で開かれた世界20か国・地域財務相・中央銀行総裁会議(G20)は, ギリシャの財政問題にさほど踏み込まなかった。

Group of 20 summit meeting　主要20か国・地域(G20)サミット(首脳会議)
◆The IMF's new financing scheme is expected to be agreed on at the Group of 20 summit meeting and will be launched after being approved by the IMF's board of directors. 国際通貨基金(IMF)の新融資制度は, 主要20か国・地域(G20)サミット(首脳会議)で合意する見込みで, その後IMF理事会の承認を経てスタートする。

group operating loss　連結営業損失, 連結営業赤字　(=consolidated operating loss)

group operating profit　連結営業利益, 連結営業利益　(=consolidated operating profit)

group pension　団体年金

group pretax loss　連結税引き前損失　(=consolidated pretax loss)

group pretax profit　連結税引き前利益, 連結経常利益　(=consolidated pretax profit)
◆The company's group pretax profit was ￥16.63 billion, up 32.9 percent, on a 5.8 percent decline in sales to ￥935.03 billion. 同社の連結経常利益は前年同期比32.9％増の166億3,000万円で, 売上高は同5.8％減の9,350億3,000万円だった。

group sales　連結売上高　(=consolidated revenues, consolidated sales)
◆Toyota Motor Corp. announced record group sales and net profit for the half year to Sept. 30. トヨタ自動車は, 9月中間決算として過去最高の連結売上高と税引き後利益[純利益]を発表した。

group taxation system　連結納税制　(=consolidated return system, consolidated tax payment system, consolidated taxation system, corporate group tax system)

grow　(動)増やす, 伸ばす, 高める, 栽培する　(自動)増加する, 増大する, 拡大する, 高まる, 伸びる, 成長する, 発展する, 向上する
economy grows　景気が拡大する
explosively growing credit markets　信用市場の急速な拡大
grow earnings　利益を増やす, 利益を伸ばす
grow more serious　一段と深刻化する
grow one's book　貸出残高を膨(ふく)らませる
grow quickly　急速に成長する
grow steadily　順調に伸びる
London Home Grown Grain Futures Markets　ロンドン国内産穀物先物市場

◆As the Greek fiscal crisis grows more serious, there has been no halt to the worldwide decline in stock prices. ギリシャの財政危機が一段と深刻化するにつれ、世界同時株安に歯止めがかからなくなっている。◆Caution grew about possible yen-selling intervention by the government. 想定される政府の円売り介入に対する警戒感が、強まった。◆Concern over the global economic slowdown grows both at home and abroad. 世界的な景気減速懸念は、国内外で高まっている［広まっている］。◆Due to the growing strength of the yen, even if exporters' sales grow, their profits will not keep pace. 円高進行で、輸出企業の売上が増えても、利益は伸び悩むようだ。◆If the value of a huge number of government bonds possessed by financial institutions around the world plummets, financial instability will grow. 世界の金融機関が保有する大量の国債の価格が急落すれば、金融不安が高まることになる。◆Markets in up-and-coming countries with booming economies, is growing rapidly. 好景気の新興国市場は、急成長している。◆Near-term uncertainty surrounding the global economy continues to grow. 世界経済を取り巻く短期的な先行き不安は、増大傾向が続いている。◆Stock markets in China and other emerging economies are growing rapidly. 中国など新興国の株式市場［証券市場］は、急成長している。◆The combined sales of 813 nonfinancial companies in the April-September period grew 6.3 percent over the previous year. 金融を除く企業813社の上期(4-9月期)の売上高の合計は、前年同期比で6.3％増加した。◆The U.S. private banks' funds on hand grew about three times from March 2008 prior to the Lehman's collapse. 米国の民間銀行の手持ち資金は、リーマン・ブラザーズの経営破たん前の2008年3月から約3倍増えた。◆The U.S. private banks' outstanding Treasury bond holdings grew by about 50 percent from March 2008, prior to the Lehman shock. 米国の民間銀行の米国債保有残高は、リーマン・ショック前の2008年3月から約5割増えた。◆Worldwide concern over fiscal sustainability in industrialized countries is growing in the wake of Greece's sovereign debt crisis. ギリシャの財政危機を契機として、先進国の財政の持続可能性に対する世界の関心が高まっている。

growing （形）成長する，高まる，激化する，拡大する，増加する，増大する，～の成長［高まり，拡大，増加，増大，激化］

growing cash flow キャッシュ・フローの伸び
growing competition 競争の高まり，競争の激化
growing debt securities markets 債券市場の成長，債券市場の拡大
growing deflationary concerns 高まるデフレ懸念，デフレ懸念の高まり
growing financial assets 金融資産の増加
growing investor interest 投資家の関心の高まり
growing outward investment 対外投資の増加，対外投資の拡大

growing concerns 高まる懸念，強まる懸念，懸念の高まり
◆There are growing concerns that the yen's extremely rapid appreciation may deliver a bitter blow to the Japan's economy. 超円高は日本経済に大きな打撃を与えるとの懸念が、強まっている。

growing deflationary concerns 高まるデフレ懸念，デフレ懸念の高まり
◆By conducting additional monetary easing policy, the Fed attempts to preemptively contain growing deflationary concerns in the United States. 追加金融緩和策を実施して、米連邦準備制度理事会(FRB)は、米国で高まるデフレ懸念に先手を打とうとしている。

growing downside risk 高まる下振れリスク，下振れリスクの高まり，下落リスクの増大
◆The Japanese economy faces a growing downside risk due to concerns about the future of the U.S. and European economies. 日本経済は、欧米経済の先行き懸念から、景気の下振れリスクが高まっている。

growing field 成長分野
◆A project financing scheme is the largest growing field for Japanese banks. プロジェクト・ファイナンス(事業融資)事業は、邦銀にとって最大の成長分野だ。

growing market 成長市場
◆A boom in stock investing among working women has led a number of women to create Web sites and publish guides targeted at this growing market. 働く女性たちの間での株式投資ブームで、この成長市場向けサイトを立ち上げたり、指南本を出したりする女性が増えている。

growing strength of the yen 円高進行
◆Due to the growing strength of the yen, even if exporters' sales grow, their profits will not keep pace. 円高進行で、輸出企業の売上が増えても、利益は伸び悩むようだ。

growing worries 高まる懸念，強まる懸念，懸念の高まり
◆The ADB lowered its 2011 growth forecast in Asian nations due to growing worries about weak demand from key trading partners including the United States and Europe. アジア開発銀行(ADB)は、主要貿易相手国である欧米で需要減退［需要低迷］懸念が高まっていることから、アジアの2011年の成長見通し［GDP成長率見通し］を下方修正した。

growth （名）成長，成長率，経済成長，伸び，伸び率，増加，増大 （⇒capital requirements）

growth area 成長分野
growth discipline 成長株中心の投資方法，グロース・スタイル
growth fund グロース・ファンド（成長企業の株式を中心に運用する投資信託のこと）
growth investing 成長株投資（急成長している業種や企業の株式に対する投資）
growth investing style 成長株投資，グロース株投資，グロース・スタイルの運用
growth stock 成長株，グロース株（収益の伸び率が高い成長企業の株式）
use a growth investing style 成長株投資［グロース・スタイル］の運用を行う

◆A U.S. housing mortgage meltdown shook the United States, Europe and other countries and slammed the brakes on global growth. 米国の住宅ローン市場の崩壊は、米欧その他の諸国を揺さぶり、世界経済の成長に急ブレーキをかけた。◆Growth in the automotive insurance market is slowing as fewer young people own cars. 若者の車離れを背景に、自動車保険市場は伸び悩んでいる。◆Import growth far outpaced export growth in the face of a global slowdown. 世界的な景気低迷で［世界的な景気減速に直面して］、輸入の伸びが輸出の伸びを大幅に上回った。◆Stock option programs have supported the rapid growth of U.S. corporations in recent years. ストック・オプション制度は、米企業のこれまでの急成長を支えてきた。◆The so-called decoupling theory holds that the effects of a U.S. slowdown can be offset by growth in emerging nations. いわゆるディカップリング論では、米経済の減速は新興国の成長が補う、と考えられている。◆This is the fourth straight quarter that the economy has shown growth. これで、4四半期連続のプラス成長となった。◆Two potent corporate buyout tools of stock splits and stock swaps were the key to the remarkable growth of the company. 株式分割と株式交換という二つの強力な企業買収の手段が、同社の急成長のカギだった。

growth forecast 成長見通し，伸び率見通し，成長率予測 （=growth prospect）
◆GDP growth forecasts released by major securities houses and think tanks have varied from 1 percent to minus 1.2

percent. 主な証券会社やシンクタンクが発表した国内総生産（GDP）伸び率の見通しは、1％からマイナス1.2％までばらつきがあった。◆The ADB lowered its 2011 growth forecast in Asian nations due to growing worries about weak demand from key trading partners including the United States and Europe. アジア開発銀行（ADB）は、主要貿易相手国である欧米で需要減退［需要低迷］懸念が高まっていることから、アジアの2011年の成長見通し［GDP成長率見通し］を下方修正した。◆The Asian Development Bank upgraded its 2010 growth forecast for 14 East Asian countries. アジア開発銀行は、東アジア14か国の2010年の成長率予測を上方修正した。

growth-friendly fiscal consolidation plan 成長に配慮した財政健全化計画
◆The key phrase for the G-20 summit meeting was "growth-friendly fiscal consolidation plans." G-20サミット（世界20か国・地域首脳会議）のキーワードは、「成長に配慮した財政健全化計画」であった。

growth in exports 輸出の伸び
◆The diffusion index（DI）of business confidence among large manufacturers stood at plus 1, reflecting a growth in exports due to U.S. economic recovery and a recent surge in domestic stock prices. 大企業の製造業の業況判断指数（DI）が、プラス1となり、米経済の回復による輸出の伸びや最近の国内の株価上昇を反映した。

growth in lending 貸出の伸び
◆Domestic bank are stepping up oversea project financing due to the lack of growth in lending to domestic borrowers amid protracted deflation at home. 国内銀行各行は、国内ではデフレが続いて［デフレが続く状況で］国内融資先への貸出が伸びていないことから、海外の事業向け融資を強化している。

growth of public debts 公的債務の増大, 財政赤字の増大
◆Japan must tackle its large fiscal deficit and curb the growth of public debts. 日本は、巨額の財政赤字と取り組んで、財政赤字［公的債務］の増大を抑える必要がある。

growth path （名）成長経路, 成長軌道, 成長路線（⇒subside）
　balanced growth path 均衡成長経路, 均斉成長経路
　be back on the growth path 成長軌道に戻る［復帰する］
　economic growth path 経済成長経路, 経済成長軌道
　efficient growth path 有効成長経路
　equilibrium growth path 均衡成長経路
　full-capacity growth path 完全能力成長経路
　full-employment growth path 完全雇用成長経路
　get A back on a growth path Aを成長軌道に戻す
　lift A onto a growth path Aを成長軌道に乗せる
　low growth path 低成長軌道
　moderate economic growth path 穏やかな成長軌道
　optimal［optimum］growth path 最適成長経路
　planned growth path 計画的成長経路
　potential growth path 潜在的成長経路
　put A back on the growth path Aを成長軌道に戻す
　remain on a growth path 成長軌道を維持する
　required growth path 必要成長経路
　return onto［to］a moderate growth path 穏やかな成長軌道に戻る
　self-sustained［self-sustaining］growth path 持続的成長経路, 自立的成長経路
　slower economic growth path 低成長時代
　stable growth path 安定成長経路, 安定成長軌道, 安定成長路線
　steady growth path 恒常的成長経路, 安定成長経路
　steer to a growth path 成長軌道に向かう, 成長経路に向かう

　sustainable growth path 持続的成長経路, 持続性のある成長軌道
　unbalanced growth path 不均斉成長経路
　von Neumann balanced growth path ノイマン均斉成長経路
◆The economy is expected to return gradually onto a moderate growth path. 景気は、徐々に穏やかな成長軌道に戻ると予想される。◆The world economy will steer to a growth path again once the financial crisis subsides. 金融危機が沈静化したら、世界経済はまた成長軌道［成長経路］に向かうだろう。

growth potential 成長潜在力, 潜在成長力, 成長余地, 成長能力, 成長ポテンシャル
◆The Bank of Japan widened the scope of cheap loans to support smaller companies with growth potential. 潜在成長力のある中小企業を支援するため、日銀が低利融資枠を拡大した。

growth projection 成長見通し
◆The downward revision of the fiscal 2011 growth projection was made due to a drastic slowdown in individual consumption and meager price increases. 2011年度の経済成長見通しの下方修正は、個人消費の大幅な減速と物価上昇率の鈍化が原因だ。

growth rate 成長率, 経済成長率, 伸び率, 増加率
　annual growth rate 年成長率, 年間伸び率
　dividend growth rate 配当伸び率
　earnings growth rate 収益の伸び率
　growth rate of GNP 経済成長率, 国内総生産の伸び率
　growth rate of total assets 総資本成長率
　inventory growth rate 在庫伸び率
　potential growth rate 潜在成長率
　real growth rate 実質成長率
　sustainable growth rate 持続可能な経済成長率
◆The growth rate of Japan's huge pool of individual financial assets has been slowing. 日本の巨額の個人金融資産の伸び率は、鈍化している。◆The target range for the inflation rate could be set at the same level as the potential growth rate, for example. 物価上昇率の目標値としては、例えば潜在成長率と同水準に設定することもできよう。

growth strategy 成長戦略（＝growth plan）
◆The draft of the government's new growth strategy includes the establishment of a public-private investment fund to support the content industry in its foreign endeavors. 政府の新成長戦略の原案には、コンテンツ（情報の内容）産業の海外展開を支援する官民出資のファンド設立も盛り込まれている。

GSE 政府系住宅金融機関, 政府支援企業, 政府援助法人（government sponsored enterpriseの略）

guarantee （動）保証する, 請け合う, 確約する
　be fully guaranteed 全額保証される
　be guaranteed by a U.S. federal agency 米連邦機関の保証が付いている
　fully guarantee the payment of the receivables by the underlying obligors 原債務者の債務返済を全額保証する
　guarantee corporate debt securities on an assumed basis 再保険ベースで一般社債の保証を行う, 一般社債の保証を再保険ベースで
　guarantee the borrowing 借入金を保証する
　guarantee the loan ローンを保証する, ローンの保証を行う
　guarantee the principal 元本を保証する
◆About ¥1.9 trillion of taxpayers' money was spent over a ten year span until last fiscal year to cover losses from a

surging number of uncollectible loans guaranteed by a public credit guarantee scheme for small and midsize companies. 中小企業のための公的信用保証制度により保証される融資の貸倒れ件数が急増し、それによる損失の穴埋めをするために、昨年度までの10年間で約1兆9,000億円の税金が投入された。◆Asset-backed commercial paper refers to commercial paper whose creditworthiness is guaranteed by sales credit that the corporate issuer has with its debtors. 資産担保CPとは、企業発行体がその債務者に対して保有する売掛金によって信用度が保証されるコマーシャル・ペーパーを指す。◆Concerns have been raised over the ability of Internet banking services to verify the identity of new depositors or to guarantee the security of customer transactions. インターネット・バンキングについては、新規預金者の身元確認や対顧客取引の安全保証の点で、その能力に対して懸念が提起されている。◆Ordinary bank deposits for individuals and current deposits for businesses were fully guaranteed until March 31, 2003. 個人の普通預金と企業の当座預金は、2003年3月31日まで全額保証された。◆Some of huge amounts in loans extended to JAL by the DBJ have been guaranteed by the government. 日本政策投資銀行が日航に行った巨額融資［貸付け］の一部は、政府が保証している。◆The citizens banks do not guarantee the principal, and as a result investing in them is risky. 市民バンクは、元本保証がないため、出資リスクも小さくない。◆The Development Bank of Japan asked the Japan Finance Corporation to pay ￥53.6 billion, the amount guaranteed by the government. 日本政策投資銀行は、政府保証分の536億円の支払いを日本政策金融公庫に請求した。◆The government guaranteed up to 80 percent of ￥67 billion in unsecured loans extended to JAL by the DBJ through the Japan Finance Corporation. 日本政策投資銀行が日航に貸し付けた無担保融資670億円の最大8割については、日本政策金融公庫を通じて政府が保証している。

guarantee （名）保証、保証人、引受人、保証額、保証契約、保証書、保証状、担保、抵当、担保物　（⇒commitment, credit guarantee association, debt guarantee, principal guarantee）
　advancing guarantee　融資保証
　bank guarantee cost　銀行保証料
　basic guarantee　根（ね）保証
　　（=initial guarantee）
　debt guarantee　債務保証　（=guarantee of debt）
　deposit guarantee　預金保証
　　（=guarantee on deposits）
　export credit guarantee　輸出信用保証
　financial guarantee　金融保証、信用保証
　financial guarantee insurance（policy）　金融保証保険
　fulfill the guarantee obligations　保証債務を履行する
　guarantee liabilities　保証債務、支払い保証
　　（=liabilities for guarantee）
　guarantee money　保証金、差入れ保証金
　guarantee of collection　証券取立ての保証
　guarantee of principal　元本保証
　guarantees of indebtedness of others　第三者の債務に対する支払い保証
　loan guarantee　融資保証、貸出保証、信用保証
　maturity guarantee　満期保証
　minimum guarantee　最低保証金
　performance guarantee insurance　履行保証保険、契約履行保証保険
　subordinated guarantee　劣後保証
◆A real estate broker created a dummy company to illegally receive a public credit guarantee. 不動産業者が、架空の会社を作って不正に公的信用保証を受けていた。◆In June 2009 prior to Japan Airlines' failure, a ￥67 billion public financing package was extended with a government-backed guarantee to JAL. 日本航空破たん前の2009年6月、日航に対して政府保証付きで670億円の公的融資が行われた［公的融資策が実施された］。◆Under the credit guarantee system, credit guarantee associations across the nation jointly guarantee financial institutions against risks associated with loans for small and midsize companies. 信用保証制度では、金融機関の中小企業向け融資リスク（融資に伴うリスク）に対して、全国各地の信用保証協会が連帯保証する。

guaranteed （形）保証された、保証付きの、約束された、確定した、～の保証
　federally guaranteed loan　連邦政府保証付きローン
　government-guaranteed bond　政府保証債、政府債
　guaranteed amount　保証額
　guaranteed annuity　保証年金
　guaranteed benefits　保証給付
　guaranteed bill　保証手形　（=backed bill）
　guaranteed bond　保証債、保証付き債券、保証付き社債、保証社債
　guaranteed capital　保証資本
　guaranteed debenture　保証債
　guaranteed dividend　保証配当、確定配当、配当保証
　guaranteed element　保証要素（裁量権のある参加特質を持つ契約に含まれる支払い保証義務）
　guaranteed issue　元利保証証券
　guaranteed lending　保証付き融資
　guaranteed loan　保証付きローン
　guaranteed mortgages　保証担保
　guaranteed obligation　保証債務
　guaranteed rates　保証利率
　guaranteed securities　保証証券
　guaranteed share［stock］　保証株

guaranteed deposit payments　預金払戻し保証額、預金払戻し金の保証
◆The payoff system refers to the limit on guaranteed deposit payments from failed financial institutions of up to 10 million in principal and accrued interest. ペイオフ制度とは、破はたん金融機関からの預金払戻し保証額を元本1,000万円とその経過利息（発生利息）に限る措置のことをいう。

guaranteed yield　予定利率　（=promised yield: 生命保険会社が保険契約者に約束した運用利回りのこと）
◆The beef-up of the early warning system enabled insurers to make decision on the decrease of guaranteed yields before the companies fail. 早期警戒制度の強化で、生保は破たん前に予定利率引下げを決断できるようになった。

guarantor （名）保証人、信用保証会社、信用保証協会
　financial guarantor　信用保証会社、金融保証会社
　principal guarantor　元本保証人
　simple guarantor　単純保証人
◆Many unrecoverable loans were made because guarantors were not screening companies effectively. 多くの焦げ付きが発生したのは、信用保証協会が事実上、企業審査をしていなかったからだ。

guard （名）防護、防衛、防御、警備、警戒、監視、警戒心、用心、不信感、安全装置、保護装置、守衛、警備員、監視員、護衛、守護隊、警備隊、護衛隊、ガード
　be off (one's) guard against　～に油断している
　be on (one's) guard against　～に警戒している
　remain on guard against　～に対する警戒を怠らない
◆The Fed has to maintain guard against an economic slowdown and inflationary pressure. 米連邦準備制度理事会（FRB）は、今後とも景気減速とインフレ圧力を警戒する必要がある。◆The guard raised against a possible financial meltdown during a financial sector-triggered recession several years ago

has been lifted. 数年前の金融不況時に想定された金融崩壊に対する厳戒態勢は、すでに解かれている。

guidance （名）誘導, 指導, 案内, 手引き, 指示, ガイダンス
    administrative guidance on investment　投資への行政指導
    guidance policy finance　政策金融
    window guidance　窓口規制, 窓口指導

guide （動）誘導する, 動かす, 案内する, 導く, 指導する, 説明する, 手引きする, 支配する
    guide a key interest rate to　政策金利を～に誘導する
    guide short-term interest rates down　短期金利を低い水準に［低めに］誘導する
    guide the dollar exchange rate lower　ドル安に誘導する
    ◆South Korea, Brazil and India are guiding their currencies lower to deal with an influx of speculative money. 韓国、ブラジルとインドは、投機マネーの流入に対応するため、自国通貨安に誘導している。◆The BOJ will guide its key interest rate to between zero and 0.1 percent. 日銀は、政策金利の誘導目標を、（現在の年0.1％前後から）0～0.1％程度に引き下げる方針だ。

guide （名）指針, 指導方針, 判断基準, 目安, 指導書, 手引き書, 入門書, ガイドブック, 指導者, 助言者, アドバイザー
    action guide　行動指針
    audit and accounting guide　監査・会計指針

guideline （名）基準, 指導基準, 運用基準, 指導, 指針, 指標, 上限, ガイドライン
    administrative guideline　行政指導
    budgetary request guidelines　概算要求基準
    （＝ceiling on budgetary request）
    capital guideline　自己資本比率の基準
    Cooke Committee guidelines　BIS規制
    credit risk guideline　信用リスク基準
    guideline for supervising financial conglomerates　金融コングロマリット（複合体）の監督指針
    Guidelines for International Investment　国際投資憲章
    guidelines for lending money　貸出基準
    indicative guideline　参考指針
    investment guideline　投資ガイドライン
    issuance guidelines　適債基準
    meet BIS guidelines　BIS規制をクリアする
    risk guidelines　リスク基準
    Tier 1 capital guideline　基本的項目基準
    ◆At the Seoul G-20 summit, all the leaders agreed to introduce "indicative guidelines" that would be conductive to reducing current account imbalances. 主要20か国・地域（G20）のソウル・サミット（首脳会議）で、全首脳が、経常収支不均衡の是正に役立つ「参考指針」を導入することで合意した。◆Savings plans for the majority of our employees allow employees to contribute a portion of their pretax and/or after-tax income in accordance with specified guidelines. 大多数の当社従業員のための貯蓄制度では、従業員は従業員の税引き前所得または税引き後所得（あるいはその両方）の一部を、特定の基準に従って拠出することができます。◆The FSA's guideline for supervising financial conglomerates is aimed at urging operators of financial conglomerates to reinforce their corporate governance to prevent irregularities. 金融庁の金融コングロマリット（複合体）監督指針の狙いは、不正防止に向けて、金融コングロマリットの経営者に経営監視の強化を促すことにある。◆To deal with the systemic financial crisis, ministry and central bank officials had to take rescue measures, such as an injection of public funds, while at the same time implementing strict guidelines and sanctions. 連鎖的な金融危機に処するにあたって、当局は公的資金の投入などの救済措置取ると同時に、厳しい指導や制裁を実施しなければならなかった。◆Under the government guidelines, if earnings come in more than 30 percent below targets set in restructuring plans at any major bank that received public funds to recapitalize in 1988 and 1999, the banks management will have to resign. 政府のガイドラインによると、資本再編のために1988年と1999年に公的資金の注入を受けた大手銀行の収益が、再建計画（経営健全化計画）で設定した収益目標を30％以上下回った場合、銀行の経営陣は辞任しなければならない。

gunslinger （名）思惑, 大型相場師, リスクの大きい大型投資, ガンスリンガー

H

haircut （名）（有価証券担保貸付けの）掛け目, 担保掛け目, （証券会社の純資本算定に用いられる）掛け目, 超過担保, 買戻し条件付き証券売却（レポ取引）の証券時価と売却価格との差額, レポ取引で貸し手が取るマージン, ヘアカット（証券会社の純資本算定に用いられる掛け目（ヘアカット）は、保有証券の時価にかける評価削減率で、一般に国債は0％、株式は30％となっている）

haircut finance　有価証券担保貸付け

half （名）中間, 半期, 半分, 5割
    （⇒first half, second half）
    half-fiscal year account　中間決算
    the first half of the fiscal year　上半期, 上期
    （＝the first half）
    the first half of the January to December business year　1-6月中間期決算, 今年度中間決算, 今年度上半期
    the first half of the year　上半期, 上期, 今年度上半期［上期］, 今年度前半, 今年前半
    （＝the first half, the former half of the year）
    the first half of this business year　今年度上半期［上期］, 中間決算
    the latest fiscal first half　今年度上半期
    （⇒latest fiscal first half）
    the latter half of last year　昨年後半
    the lower half of the target range　目標圏の下半分
    the second half of the fiscal year　下半期
    （＝the latter half）
    the second half of the year［fiscal year］　下半期, 下期, 今年度下半期［下期］, 今年度後半, 今年後半
    （＝the latter half of the year, the second half）
    ◆Big companies assume the exchange rate of ￥81.06 to the dollar for the latter half of fiscal 2011. 大企業の2011年度下期の想定為替レートは、1ドル＝81円6銭となっている。◆More than half of the public welfare loans extended to widows and single mothers are not collected. 母子家庭や寡婦に供与されている福祉資金の5割以上が、回収されていない。◆Of the amount of investment, about a half was invested in foreign government bonds with low credit ratings. この投資額のうち約半分は、格付けの低い外国債に充てていた。◆Resona's 1st-half net profit plunged 74％ from a year earlier to ￥120 billion. りそなの上半期の連結税引き後利益は、前年同期比74％減の1,200億円となった。◆The firm returned to the black in the first-half of this business year. 同社は、今年度上半期に［上期に、中間決算で］黒字に転換した。◆The pressures on gross margins and earnings that affected the last half of 2010 will continue through the first half of 2012. 2010年下半期［下期］の業績に影響を及ぼした売上利益率と利益の低下は、2012年上半期［上期］まで続く見通しです。◆The U.S. economy has gotten back on the recovery track since the latter half of last year. 米国の景気は、昨年後半からまた回復軌道に乗り始めた。

half a point　0.5パーセント, 0.5％
    ◆Acting in an emergency conference call, the U.S. Federal

Reserve moved to bolster the flagging economy by cutting interest rates by half a point. 緊急電話会議を開いて、連邦準備制度理事会(FRB)は、景気減速に歯止めをかけるため金利を0.5%引き下げることを決めた。

half-baked (形)不十分な、不完全な、中途半端な、生半可な、未熟な、常識のない、愚かな、常軌を逸した
a half-baked scheme 不十分な計画 不完全な計画
half-baked measures 不十分な対策 中途半端な対策
◆The firm's defense against management buyout is half-baked. 同社の経営陣による企業買収(MBO)防衛策は、中途半端だ。◆The summit meeting of European Union members, including 17 eurozones countries such as Germany and France, came out with half-baked measures to deal with the debt crisis. 独仏などユーロ圏17国を含む欧州連合(EU)加盟国首脳会議は、十分とは言えない欧州財政危機の収束策を発表した。

half year 半期、中間
a half-year earnings report for the fiscal period up to September 9月中間決算、上半期(4-9月期)業績、上半期決算
a half-year report 半期報告書、中間事業報告書、中間営業報告書
a halt-year earnings report 半期業績報告、中間決算報告、中間決算 (=interim earnings report)
half-year financial statements 中間財務書類、中間企業財務情報
half-year trading figures 中間決算
the first half of this fiscal year 今年度上半期、今年度上期 (⇒drastic slowdown)
the half year ended Sept. 30 9月中間決算、3月期決算企業の4-9月期 (=the half year to Sept. 30)
the half year to Sept. 30 4-9月期、3月期決算企業の上半期[上期]、9月中間決算
the latter half of this fiscal year 今年度下半期、今年度下期
the second half of this fiscal year 今年度下半期、今年度下期

half-year consolidated business results through the end of September 9月連結中間決算
◆The nation's three megabank groups expect a sharp increase in profits in their half-year consolidated business results through the end of September. 日本の3メガバンクは、9月連結中間決算で、大幅増益を見込んでいる。

half-year earnings report for the fiscal period up to September 9月中間決算、上半期(4-9月期)業績、上半期決算
◆The majority of listed companies have released their half-year earnings reports for the fiscal period up to September. 上場企業の大半が、上半期(4-9月期)の業績を発表した(上場企業の9月中間決算が、ほぼ出そろった)。

half-year net profit forecast 半期純利益予想
◆The company lowered its half-year net profit forecast. 同社は、半期純利益予想を引き下げた。

halt (動)中止[停止、休止]させる、止めさせる、終わらせる、(進行を)食い止める、防ぐ、中止する、中断する、止める (名)停止、中止、休止、停戦、中断、停車場、停留所
bring ~ to a halt ~を止める、~を中止[停止]させる、~を中断させる
call a halt to ~に停止を命じる、~に停止命令を出す、~を止める
come to [make] a halt 停止する、止まる、ストップする、一服する
halt talks 交渉[対話]を中断する
halt the outflow of funds 資金の流出を防ぐ
the halt in yen appreciation 円高の進行が止まること
◆As the Greek fiscal crisis grows more serious, there has been no halt to the worldwide decline in stock prices. ギリシャの財政危機が一段と深刻化するにつれ、世界同時株安に歯止めがかからなくなっている。◆Chrysler's five weeks of breakneck-speed bankruptcy proceedings came to a screeching halt. クライスラーの5週間にわたる猛スピードの破たん手続きに、急ブレーキがかかった。◆Europe is urged to act promptly to halt financial crisis. 欧州は、金融危機回避の早急な対策を迫られている。◆It will be no easy task to halt the economy fully out of deflation. デフレからの完全脱却は、決して容易なことではない。◆Mitsui Sumitomo Insurance Co. was ordered to halt sales of medical insurance products for an indefinite period from July 10. 三井住友海上火災保険が、7月10日から医療保険商品販売の無期限停止命令を受けた。◆On the foreign exchange market, there has been no halt to selling pressure on the euro due to concern about the financial crisis in Europe. 外国為替市場では、欧州の金融危機を懸念して、ユーロ売り圧力が止まらない展開となっている。◆The stock market rally came to a halt. 株式市場の上げ相場は、一服している。◆The yen slide came to a halt. 円が、下げ止まった。

halve (動)半減させる、50%削減する、半分に引き下げる、半分に減らす、二等分する、半額にする
◆With this financial support, along with property sales, the company plans to halve its approximately ¥540 billion consolidated interest-bearing debts. この金融支援と資産売却を組み合わせて、同社は約5,400億円の連結有利子負債を半減させる方針だ。

hammer out 打ち出す、まとめる、(徹底的に検討して)考え出す、案出する、(計画を)立てる[練る]、(議論して)合意を打ち出す[解決する]、(曲)を弾く
hammer out a growth strategy 成長戦略をまとめる
hammer out an emergency economic stimulus package 緊急景気対策をまとめる
hammer out urgent proposals to stimulate the economy 景気刺激策として緊急提言をまとめる
◆APEC hammered out a growth strategy that includes measures to rectify imbalances and address environmental problems. アジア太平洋経済協力会議(APEC)が、不均衡是正策や環境問題への対応策などを盛り込んだ成長戦略をまとめた。◆The U.S. government hammered out an emergency economic stimulus package. 米政府が、緊急景気対策をまとめた。

hamper (動)妨げる、妨害する、阻止する、邪魔する、阻(はば)む
hamper growth 成長を阻害する
hamper reforms 改革を阻む
hamper the board's functions 取締役会の機能を妨げる
◆General Electric Co. has asked two of its outside directors to leave as of the end of December due to their close association with former Chairman Jack Welch, which they consider may hamper the board's functions. ゼネラル・エレクトリック(GE)は、ジャック・ウェルチ前会長との交友関係が取締役会の機能を妨げかねないとの判断から、12月末日付けで社外取締役2名の退任を求めた。◆The failure to implement fiscal consolidation in countries where it is necessary could undermine confidence and hamper growth. 財政健全化が必要な国で財政健全化を行わないと、信認を損ない、成長を阻害する可能性がある。

hand (名)手元、手持ち、所有、管理、支配、技量、職工、職人、人手、担当記者、署名、参加、関与
cash in hand 手元現金 (=cash on hand)
change hands 所有者[持ち主]が変わる、株主が変わる、持ち主を変える、人手に渡る、商品が売れる、政権を交替する、更迭する
funds on hand 手元資金 (=funds in hand)
get [become] out of hand 手に負えなくなる、収拾がつかなくなる

goods on hand　在庫品
helping hand　救いの手, 支援の手, 援助の手, 手助け
join hands with　〜と提携する, 〜と手を組む
keep one's hands off　〜に手を出さない, 〜に干渉しない
make money hand over fist　お金をどんどん儲（もう）ける
orders on hand　受注残高
play one's own hand　私利をはかる
set one's hand to　〜に署名する（put one's hand to）, 〜に取りかかる［着手］する（turn one's hand to）
stock on hand　手持ち在庫
strike hands with　〜と契約を交わす, 〜と契約する, 〜と協力を約束する, 〜と手を握り合う
◆Golden shares could fall into the hands of a hostile takeover bidder. 黄金株は、敵対的買収者の手に渡る場合もある。◆The company decided to seek a helping hand from the investment fund. 同社は、この投資ファンドに支援を求めることにした。◆The IMF currently has about $400 billion in resources on hand. IMF（国際通貨基金）は現在、手元に約4,000億ドル分の財源を残している。

handle　（動）取り扱う, 扱う, さばく, 処理する, 操作する
handle an offering on a best effort basis　ベスト・エフォート・ベース［ベーシス］で売出しを取り扱う
handle bank transfers　銀行振込みを取り扱う
handle claims　保険金支払いの処理をする
handle financial settlement services　金融決済業務を扱う, 金融決済業務を行う
handle only time deposits　定期預金だけを扱う
handle orders from　〜からの注文を扱う, 〜からの注文を処理する
handle spot trading　現物取引を扱う
handle the swap　スワップをアレンジする, スワップを引き受ける
◆After the merger, the TSE and OSE will be divided into four operator firms handling spot trading, derivatives, settlement of trading deals and self-imposed regulations respectively. 経営統合後、東証と大証は、それぞれ現物株、デリバティブ（金融派生商品）、取引決済と自主規制を扱う4事業会社に切り分けられることになっている。◆An increase in transactions that brokerages handle has accompanied the brisk stock market business. 証券会社が扱う取引の増加は、そのまま株式相場の盛況と重なる。◆Deutsche Bank handles 120 currencies, such as Brazil's real and the Indian rupee. ドイツ銀行は、ブラジルのレアルやインドのルピーなど120種類の通貨を取り扱っている。◆Edelweiss Tokyo Life Insurance Co. is the first Japanese insurer handling both life and nonlife policies in India. エーデルワイス・トウキョウ・ライフ・インシュランス（本店所在地：インドのマハラシュトラ州ムンバイ市）は、インドで生保と損保を取り扱う日本初の保険会社だ。◆Lehman Brothers' case offered a lesson to be learned on what policies should be taken to handle similar cases in the future. リーマン・ブラザーズの事例は、類似のケースが今後発生した場合の政策対応に学ぶべき教訓を残した。◆Stock trading is handled electronically now. 株取引は現在、電子化されている。◆The bank does not handle bank transfers or other financial settlement services. 同行は、銀行振込みなどの決済業務［金融決済業務］を行っていない。◆The bank handles only time deposits for the purpose of fund management. 同行は、資金運用目的の定期預金だけを扱っている。◆The bank handles transactions for individuals and small and midsize companies. 同行は、中小企業・個人向けの取引を扱っている。◆The government will provide funds and extend loans to TEPCO through a newly established organization to handle the compensation issue due to the nuclear disaster. 今後は、原発事故による損害賠償問題を扱うために新設された組織（原子力損害賠償支援機構）を通じて、国が東電に出資したり融資したりする。◆With the integration of the Japan Bank for International Cooperation's division for handling yen loans, and other bodies in October 2008, JICA became one of the world's largest development assistance agencies. 国際協力機構（JICA）は、2008年10月に国際協力銀行（JBIC）の円借款部門などを統合して、（事業規模で）世界最大級の開発援助機関となった。

handling　（名）取扱い, 操作, 操縦, 処理, 対応, 運用, 運営, 手法, 荷役, 運搬,（商品の）出荷, 盗品の取引, ハンドリング
careful h handling　慎重な扱い［操作、対応］
handling charge　出荷手数料, 取扱い手数料（handling fee）
handling fee［expenses］　取扱い手数料
handling in　倉入れ
handling of individual claims　個々の保険金支払いの処理
handling out　倉出し
poor handling of the situation　状況に対する対応のまずさ

handout　（名）配布, 分配, 譲渡, 声明, 声明文, 情報, 発表文書, 新聞発表（press［news］release）, 配布資料, 宣伝用ビラ［パンフレット］, 広告, ちらし, 試供品, 無料サンプル, 補助金, 給付金, 予算, ハンドアウト
flat-sum（cash）handouts　定額給付金
government handouts　政府予算, 政府補助金, 政府給付金
handout programs［measures］　バラマキ政策
lavish government handouts　政府によるバラマキ
◆In the village, about 80 percent of residents are eligible to receive the flat-sum handouts. 同村では、住民の約8割が定額給付金を受け取る資格がある［定額給付金の給付対象者だ］。

handout policies　補助金政策, バラマキ政策
◆Given the dire fiscal situation, the government cannot afford to continue its handout policies. 財政難の折から、政府はバラマキ政策を続ける余裕はない。◆Handout policies have only slight economic effect. バラマキ政策は、経済効果が薄い。◆The fiscal 2010 budget became bloated due to handout policies pledged in the DPJ's manifesto. 2010年度予算は、民主党のマニフェストで公約した補助金政策で膨らんだ。

hard　（形）強い, 強気の, 高値安定の, 外国貨幣に交換可能な, 硬貨の, 現金の, 困難な, 厳しい, 厳格な
hard cash［money］　硬貨, 現金
hard dollars　ドルの現金払い, サービス代金直接払い方式, ハードドル［ハード・ダラー］
hard-hitting anti-inflation policy　積極的なインフレ対策
hard loan　硬貨借款, ハード・ローン（ドル返済が条件など、返済条件が厳しい国際融資）
hard loan window　ハード・ローン・ウインドウ（国際金融機関などから通常の貸付け条件で融資されるもの）
hard money　硬貨, コイン, 現金, 現ナマ, 兌換（だかん）貨幣（tight money）, 額面通りの価値のある通貨
hard-pressed　（財政的に）苦しんでいる, 苦境にある,（金や時間に）追われている

hard currency　強い通貨, 為替レートが安定しているか上昇基調の通貨, 硬貨, 交換可能通貨, 国際通貨, ハード・カレンシー　（=hard money: 米ドルや金と交換できる通貨。⇒softの項のsoft currency）
hard currency tills　ハード・カレンシーの現金引出し業務
look for hard currency　外貨獲得を狙う
◆Banks reopened their hard currency tills after a night of violence and protests over a draconian banking freeze that limited access to deposits. 預金の利用を制限した厳しい預金凍結措置に対する暴動や抗議行動の一夜が明けてから、銀行

HARD

はハード・カレンシーの現金引出し業務を再開した。

hard landing 景気拡大期に続く急激な下降, ハード・ランディング
 hard-landing economic policy 強行着陸（ハード・ランディング）の経済路線
 hard-landing policy 強硬路線
 ◆The government is likely to maintain the hard-landing economic policy. 政府は、強行着陸（ハードランディング）の経済路線を維持する見込みだ。

harden （動）強化する, 硬化する, 堅調になる, 上昇する

hardening of loan terms 融資条件を厳しくすること, 融資条件の厳しい制限, 貸出条件の厳格化

hardening of the yen 円相場の上昇

hardship （名）困難, 苦難, 苦境, 辛苦
 economic hardship 経済的困窮
 financial hardships 経済的苦難
 fiscal hardship 財政ひっ迫, 財政難
 ◆Governments facing fiscal hardship sometimes force their central banks to buy up government bonds. 財政がひっ迫した政府が、中央銀行に国債を買い切らせることがある。

harm （動）害する, 傷つける, 痛める, 損なう, 危害を加える
 ◆The yen's appreciation will not only reduce the volume of exports but also harm a wide variety of other areas. 円高は輸出の減少だけでなく、その弊害は広範に及ぶ。

haunt （動）苦しめる, 悩ませる, ～の脳裏を去らない, 絶えずつきまとう, よく訪れる, 足繁く通う, よく出入りする
 ◆The twin deficits—fiscal and trade—that haunted the United States in the 1980s have returned. 1980年代のアメリカを苦しめた「双子の赤字」（財政と貿易の二つの赤字）が、再燃している。

have （動）所有する, 持っている, 備えている, ～から成っている, ～を含んでいる, 受け取る, 手に入れる
 have a presence in China 中国に進出している
 have an exposure to the currency market 為替リスクにさらされる
 have commitments of corporate funds 会社資金の確約を得る
 have credit limits 与信枠を設定する
 have no net debt 無借金経営をする
 have one's thumb in a pie 事業に参加する
 have several pension plans 各種の年金制度がある, 各種の年金制度を設けている
 have strong financial position 財務力が強い
 have the best liquidity in the market 市場で最も流動性が高い
 have the bottom drop out of the market 市況が底割れする
 have underwriting obligation 引受義務を負う
 ◆We had commitments of corporate funds totaling $1 million, plus a Foundation grant award of $50,000. われわれは総額100万ドルの会社資金のほかに、5万ドルの当財団義援金の確約を得ました。

have yet to まだ～していない, ～をまだ果たしていない, まだ～でいる
 ◆The company has yet to receive approval for the action at its shareholders meeting. 同社は、同社の株主総会でこの措置の承認はまだ得ていない。

haven （名）回避地, 逃避地, 避難国, ヘイブン
 (=shelter; ⇒tax haven)
 investment haven 安全な投資先
 safe haven 安全な避難所, 安全な投資先, 安全な投資手段, 資金逃避先
 safe-haven quality 質への逃避先, 安全な投資先
 seek safe haven in New York ニューヨークに安全な投資先を求める
 tax haven 租税回避地, 租税逃避地, 租税避難国, 税金天国, タックス・ヘイブン
 ◆Concerns over the U.S. economic outlook tend to induce yen-buying as a safe haven. 米経済の先行きに対する懸念から、安全な投資手段として円が買われる傾向にある。◆Gold is still becoming the safe haven as people fear recession in the U.S. and the eurozone debt problems. 米国の景気後退やユーロ圏の債務危機問題への懸念から、まだ金が安全な投資先［資金の逃避先］となっている。

havoc （名）大混乱, 大損害, 大破壊, 大きな影響, 無秩序, 荒廃 （⇒wreak）
 cause havoc in financial markets worldwide 世界の金融市場を第混乱させる
 cause widespread economic havoc 広範囲にわたって大きな経済損失をもたらす
 wreak havoc on the corporate bond market 社債［債券］市場に大きな影響を与える
 ◆A downgrade below investment-grade by even one ratings agency could boost GM's borrowing costs and wreak havoc on the corporate bond market. 格付け会社が1社でも投資適格格付けより低く格付けを引き下げたら［格付け会社が1社でも投機的格付けに格下げしたら］、GMの資金調達コストが急増し、米国の社債［債券］市場にも大きな影響が出る恐れがある。◆An error in risk management may cause widespread economic havoc. リスク管理のミスは、広範で大きな経済損失につながる可能性がある。◆The financial crisis triggered by the rise in defaults of U.S. subprime loans caused havoc in financial markets worldwide. 米国のサブプライム・ローン（低所得者向け住宅ローン）の不払い増加がきっかけで起こった金融危機は、世界の金融市場を大混乱させた。

hawala （名）ハワラ（海外で働く労働者の国外送金を金融機関を通さないで行う非合法組織）

head （動）進む, ～に向かう, ～を率いる, ～を統括［指揮］する, 主導する, ～の先頭に立つ, 会社を経営する
 be heading downwards 下降トレンドを描く
 head along 前進する
 head down 下げ相場になる
 head for bankruptcy 破産に向かう, 破産に傾く
 head into ～に向かう
 head off ～を防ぐ［防止する］, ～を遮（さえぎ）る, ～を回避する, ～を食い止める, ～させないようにする
 head off to ～に向かう
 ◆Kirin President Kazuyasu Kato and his counterpart at Suntory, Nobutada Saji, have headed merger negotiations. キリンの加藤社長とサントリーの佐治社長が、統合交渉を主導した。◆The company's business management and planning headquarters is headed by its representative director. 同社の経営企画管理本部は、代表取締役が統括している。

head （名）責任者, 最高責任者, 指導者, 経営者, 社長, 党首
 be over head and ears （借金などで）首が回らない, 夢中になっている
 department head 部門責任者, 部門担当責任者
 group head グループ代表
 head count 人口調査, 世論調査, 頭数, 雇用人数
 head hunter [headhunter] 人材スカウト会社, 人材スカウト業, 人材スカウト係, 雇用担当者
 head office 本社, 本店, 本部, 本拠
 (=headquarters, home office)
 official head 社長
 per head 1人当たり
 section head 部門責任者

◆The time vice president of the bank was the head of the department in charge of assessing the financial status of large borrowers. 同行の元副頭取は、大口融資先の財務内容審査部門の最高責任者だった。

head and shoulders 三尊 （株式などのテクニカル分析で使われるチャートの一つ。上昇相場の末期によく現われるパターンで、相場が天井圏に達したことを示す。⇒reverseの項のreverse head and shoulders）

head office 本部, 本店, 本社, 本拠
◆The Incubator Bank of Japan's head office and other locations were searched by the Metropolitan Police Department on suspicion of the Banking Law. 銀行法違反の疑いで、日本振興銀行の本店などを警視庁が捜索した。

health （名）健康, 健全性, 保健, 医療, ヘルス
（⇒financial health）
corporate health　企業の健全性, 企業体質, 経営体質
credit health　信用の健全性, 信用の質
financial health　財務の健全性, 財務上の健全性, 財務体質, 財務状況
individual accident and health　個人傷害・医療保険
National Health Service　国民医療制度
retiree health benefits　退職者健康保険
the health of the financial system　金融システムの健全性
◆The merger will prompt other megabanks to come up with new strategies to reinforcing their corporate health. この統合は他のメガバンクを刺激し、メガバンクは企業体質の強化に向けた戦略を新たに打ち出すことになろう。

health care 健康医療, 健康管理, 医療, 医療保険, ヘルスケア

health care benefits 健康保険給付

health care insurance program 医療保険制度, 医療制度
◆A review of the health care insurance program for people aged 75 or older is called for. 後期高齢者医療保険制度の見直しが、求められている。

health-care insurance system 健康保険制度
◆The health-care insurance system is on the brink of collapse due to sharp increases in medical expenses. 医療費の急増で、医療保険制度は破たん寸前だ。

health care system 医療制度
◆Under the health care system for those aged 75 and over, the health Insurance Society for Temporary Workers will contribute ￥16.1 billion more to cover medical costs this fiscal year from a year earlier. 後期高齢者医療制度に基づいて人材派遣健康保険組合が今年度に拠出する医療費の負担金は、前年度に比べて161億円の増加となる。

health insurance 健康保険, 医療保険
health insurance association　健康保険組合
health insurance card　保険証
health insurance contract　健康保険契約
health insurance coverage　医療保険加入者
health insurance fees　健康保険料
health insurance industry　健康保険業界
Health Insurance Pool Index　健康保険プール指数
health insurance provider　健康保険提供者
indemnity health insurance　実費給付保証型医療保険
national health insurance　国民健康保険
voluntary health insurance　任意健康保険
◆Makeshift measures to reform the three systems of pension, nursing care insurance and health insurance separately will only increase uncertainty in the future. 年金、介護保険、医療保険の三つの制度をバラバラに改革するという場当たり的な対応は、将来不安を増すだけだ。

health insurance plan 健康保険制度, 健康保険
◆The proposed pact will exempt expats from paying into pension and health insurance plans in the country to which they are posted, provided they stay no more than five years. 協定案では、海外駐在員の滞在期間が5年以内であれば、駐在する相手国の年金と医療保険制度への加入を免除される。◆Workers at small and medium-sized firms, who belong to a government-managed health insurance plan, will have to pay higher premiums. 中小企業の従業員が加入している政府管掌健康保険の保険料も、アップされる。

health insurance program 健康保険制度
◆Employees of the group companies and their dependents are now enrolled in the state health insurance program for employees of small and midsize companies. グループ企業の従業員とその扶養家族は現在、中小企業従業員向けの国の健康保険制度に加入している。

health insurance scheme 健康保険制度
◆The firm's workers are enrolled in the Social Insurance Agency-managed health insurance scheme. 同社の従業員は、社会保険庁が運営している健康保険制度に加入している。

health insurance society 健康保険組合
（=health insurance association）
◆A major company has recently decided to dissolve its health insurance society. 大企業が最近、同社の健康保険組合の解散を決めた。

health insurance system 健康保険制度, 医療保険制度　（=health insurance plan）
◆Following pension system and nursing care insurance system reforms, health insurance system reform is planned for fiscal 2006. 年金改革（年金制度の改革）と介護保険改革（介護保険制度の改革）に続いて、2006年度は医療保険改革（医療保険制度の改革）が予定されている。

health insurance union 健康保険組合　（=health insurance association, health insurance society）
◆Due to ballooning medical costs for the elderly, about 90 percent of health insurance unions have recorded deficits. 膨張する高齢者医療費のため、健康保険組合の約90％はすでに赤字だ。

healthier loans 正常債権
◆The bank announced a plan to introduce revival accounts to manage its ￥2.3 trillion nonperforming loans separately from the healthier loans. 同行は、2兆3,000億円の不良債権を正常債権とは別個に管理する「再生勘定」を導入する方針を発表した。

healthy （形）健康的な, 健全な, 好調な, 順調な, 堅調な, 活況の, 活力のある, 有益な, 相当な, かなりの, ヘルシー
healthy balance sheet　健全な財務体質
healthy earnings　好業績
healthy foreign demand　海外からの活発な引き合い, 堅調な外需
healthy growth　健全な成長, 順調な伸び
healthy increase　好調な伸び, 順調な伸び, 堅調な伸び
　（=healthy advance, healthy gain, healthy growth）
healthy profit　かなりの利益, 大きな利益
healthy sales　好調な販売
post a healthy gain [advance, growth, increase]　順調な伸びを示す, 好調な伸びを示す
rise by a healthy margin　大幅に増加する

healthy bank 健全行
◆A healthy bank would not take away proceeds from a loan shark facing difficulties raising funds. 健全行なら、資金繰りに窮した高利貸しの上前をはねるようなことはない。

healthy public finance 健全な財政
◆The IMF extends to countries with relatively healthier public finances one- to two-year loans of up to 1,000 percent of their contribution to the IMF without strict conditions. IMF（国際通貨基金）は、財政が比較的健全な国に対して、期間1〜2年の資金を厳しい条件なしでIMFに出資している額（クォー

タ)の最大10倍まで融資している。

heavily (副)大幅に, 大いに, 大きく
 be heavily dependent on 〜に大きく依存する, 〜に大きく左右される, 〜への依存度が高い
 bet heavily on 〜に大きくかける
 hit A heavily Aに大きな打撃を与える
 invest heavily in 〜に多額の投資をする, 〜に巨額を投資する, 〜に大型投資する
 lend heavily 多額の融資をする
 reserve heavily against 〜に対して多額[巨額]の引当金を積む

heavily indebted borrower 多額[巨額]の債務を抱えた発行体
 ◆Even if it is a sovereign state or a bank, heavily indebted borrowers may face a crisis for insolvency or a lack of liquidity. 国家でも銀行でも, 巨額の債務を抱えた発行体は, 返済不能か流動性不足で危機に陥る可能性がある。

heavily indebted people 多重債務者 (⇒indebted)
 ◆The real estate broker lured heavily indebted people with a false newspaper advertisement that said their debts could be restructured into single loans. この不動産業者は,「借金を一本化する」とウソの新聞広告を出して多重債務者を集めていた。

heavily indebted poor countries 重債務貧困国, HIPCs
 ◆Leaders of the Group of Seven industrialized nations announced in a statement that they would waive a total of $70 billion in financial assistance to heavily indebted poor countries. G7(先進7か国)首脳は, 重債務貧困国に対する資金援助の総額700億ドルを放棄することを声明で発表した。◆The government will propose measures to reduce the debt burdens of heavily indebted poor countries (HIPC). 政府は, 重債務貧困国の債務負担削減策を提案する。

heavy (形)重い, 重質の, 大量の, 大規模な, 大型の, 多額の, 巨額の, 重大な, 活発な
 a heavy decline [fall] 大暴落
 a heavy rise [advance] 大暴騰
 give government bonds a heavy underweight status 国債を大幅にアンダーウェートにする
 heavy additional tax 重加算税
 heavy borrower 大口融資先, 大口の借り手, 主要発行体
 heavy capital investment 大型設備投資, 多額[巨額]の設備投資 (=heavy capex)
 heavy currency intervention 大規模な市場介入
 heavy investment 巨額の投資
 heavy losses 巨額の損失, 大損
 heavy market 下落相場, 軟調相場, 軟弱市況, 鈍調市況
 heavy order 大量注文
 heavy oversubscription 大幅な応募超過
 heavy payment 巨額の支払い, 巨額の支出
 heavy penalty tax 重加算税
 heavy [bouts of] profit taking 大量の利食い売り
 heavy sales 大量売り
 heavy share 根がさ株
 heavy speculative buying 投機的な買いの膨らみ
 remain heavy 高止まりする

heavy double debt load 重い二重ローンの負担, 二重ローンという重い負担
 ◆Many survivors of the Great East Japan Earthquake are struggling under the heavy double debt loads. 東日本大震災の被災者の多くは, 二重ローンという重い負担を背負って苦しんでいる。

heavy pressure 強い圧力
 ◆The European Central Bank cut its main interest rate by 0.25 percent following heavy pressure for a rate cut to spur flagging economic growth. 失速気味の経済成長に刺激を与えるため利下げを求める強い圧力を受けて, 欧州中央銀行(ECB)はその主要(政策)金利を0.25%引き下げた。

heavy taxation 重税
 ◆We will have to accept heavy taxation to foot the bill for the lax fiscal discipline of past governments. われわれは今後, 過去の政府の放漫な財政運営のつけを負担するために, 重税を受け入れなければならなくなる。

heavy trading 大商い, 活発な取引
 ◆The Tokyo stock market has recently been roaring, with record heavy trading seen. 東京株式市場が, 記録的な大商いを続けて, 活況を呈している。

heckle (動)やじり倒す, やじり飛ばす, やじ[質問, 悪口]で妨害する
 heckle a stockholders' meeting 株主総会をやじで妨害する

hedge (動)損失予防策をとる, 売り(買い)つなぎして損失を防ぐ, 分散投資して損失リスクを少なくする, 掛けつなぎする, 掛けつなぐ, リスクを回避する
 cash flow hedge キャッシュ・フロー・ヘッジ
 fair value hedge 公正価値ヘッジ
 hedge against currency risk 為替リスクに対してヘッジする, 為替リスクをヘッジする
 hedge against inflation インフレに対してヘッジする
 hedge against market and currency risk 市場リスクと為替変動リスクをヘッジする
 hedge exchange risk 為替リスクをヘッジ[回避]する (⇒external bond financing)
 hedge foreign currency risks with purchased options 通貨オプションの購入で為替リスクをヘッジする
 hedge interest rate risk 金利リスクをヘッジする
 hedge one's bets 損失の危険を減らす, 損失リスクを回避する
 hedge one's bond portfolio 債券ポートフォリオをヘッジする
 hedge one's long position in stocks 現物株のロング・ポジションをヘッジする
 hedge one's position 残高を掛けつなぐ, ポジションをヘッジする
 hedge the exposure リスクをヘッジする
 hedge the price risk of a stock 株式の価格リスクをヘッジする
 hedge the swap スワップをヘッジする
 ◆A derivative contract is also used to hedge an investor's position. デリバティブ契約は, 投資家のポジションをヘッジするために使われることもある。◆The company has hedged this transaction. 同社は, この取引に対してすでに為替のリスク・ヘッジを行っている。◆The firm hedged its long position in stocks by selling short the futures contract. 同社は, 先物を空売りして現物株のロング・ポジションをヘッジした。◆The trader used a standard option to hedge the price risk of a stock. このトレーダーは, 株式の価格リスクをヘッジするために標準的なオプションを使った。◆We can hedge exchange risk through forward markets. 為替予約で, 為替リスクをヘッジすることができる。

hedge (名)備え, 損失予防手段, 防護策, 掛けつなぎ売買, 保険つなぎ, 為替リスクの防止・軽減, ヘッジ (=hedging)
 as a hedge against 〜に備えて, 〜に対する防壁として, 〜に対するつなぎとして
 as a hedge against drops in stock prices 株価下落リスクに備えて, 株価下落のヘッジとして
 as a hedge against inflation インフレ・ヘッジとして
 as a hedge against losses 損失に対するつなぎとして

asset hedge　資産ヘッジ
futures hedge　先物ヘッジ
hedge-buying　買いつなぎ　(=buying hedge)
hedge-lifting　つなぎ外(はず)し
hedge operation　ヘッジ操作,為替ヘッジ取引
hedge-selling　売りつなぎ　(=selling hedge)
hedged asset　ヘッジ対象資産,ヘッジする資産
hedged bond　ヘッジ債,ヘッジ・ボンド・スワップ債,ヘッジされた債券
hedged position　ヘッジ・ポジション
hedged property　ヘッジ対象資産,ヘッジする資産
hedges of net investment in foreign operations　海外営業活動への純投資のヘッジ
imperfect hedge　不完全ヘッジ
inflationary hedge　インフレ・ヘッジ
　(=inflation hedge)
lift a hedge　ヘッジを外(はず)す
long hedge　買いヘッジ
perfect hedge　完全ヘッジ
portfolio hedge　ポートフォリオ・ヘッジ
rebalance the hedge　ヘッジを見直す
reverse hedge　逆ヘッジ
risk hedge　リスク・ヘッジ
short hedge　売りヘッジ
◆A financial institution will have to offer 8 percent of the value purchased by the stock-purchasing body as an additional financial contribution to the body as a hedge against drops in stock prices. 金融機関は、株価下落リスクに備えて、株式取得機構の買取り価格の8%を追加拠出金として同機構に納付しなければならない。

hedge against inflation　インフレ・ヘッジ
◆Record low U.S. borrowing costs are boosting the appeal to bullion as a hedge against inflation. 米国の資金調達コストが過去最低の水準にあるため、インフレ・ヘッジとしての金[金地金]の人気が高まっている。

hedge fund　ヘッジ・ファンド,短期投資資金　(「ヘッジ・ファンド」は、株式や債券、通貨、原油など幅広い市場で、先物取引やオプションなどの金融派生商品を駆使して収益を追求する一種の投資信託。⇒high-profile, speculative hedge fund)
◆Hedge funds are institutional investors that conduct highly speculative transactions with huge sums of money. ヘッジ・ファンドは、巨額の資金を運用して投機性の高い取引を行う機関投資家である。◆The markets are now controlled by the fund managers of pension funds, investment trust funds, hedge funds and various other funds. 市場は、今では年金基金や投資信託基金、ヘッジ・ファンドなどのファンド・マネージャーによって支配されている。

hedges of existing assets or liabilities　既存の資産または債務のヘッジ
◆Gains and losses on hedges of existing assets or liabilities are marked to market on a monthly basis. 既存の資産または債務のヘッジに関する損益は毎月、評価替えされている。

hedging　(名)つなぎ売買,掛けつなぎ取引,つなぎ,ヘッジ,ヘッジ取引,ヘッジング　(=hedge: 現物の価格変動リスクを先物の価格変動により相殺する取引のこと)
dynamic hedging strategy　ダイナミック・ヘッジ戦略
effect a hedging transaction　掛けつなぎ取引を実行する,ヘッジ取引を実行する
engage in hedging activities　ヘッジをする,ヘッジ操作をする
equity portfolio hedging strategy　株式ポートフォリオのヘッジ戦略
hedging activities　ヘッジ操作,ヘッジ

hedging activities of bookrunners　主幹事のヘッジ操作
hedging contract　ヘッジ契約,掛けつなぎ契約
hedging cost　ヘッジ・コスト,ヘッジに要する費用
hedging foreign currency risks with purchased (currency) options　通貨オプションの購入による為替リスクのヘッジ
hedging fund　ヘッジ・ファンド
hedging gains and losses　ヘッジ損益
hedging in forward exchange　先物為替のつなぎ
hedging instrument　ヘッジ商品,ヘッジ手段
　(=hedge instrument)
hedging margin　ヘッジ証拠金
hedging of new supply　新発債のためのヘッジ売り
hedging operation　ヘッジ操作,掛けつなぎ操作
hedging structure for currency exposure　為替リスクについてのヘッジ手法,為替リスクのヘッジ手法
hedging vehicle　ヘッジ手段
hedging with coupon swaps　クーポン・スワップによるヘッジ
improve hedging precision　ヘッジの精度を高める
liability hedging　負債ヘッジ
long hedging　買いつなぎ
macro hedging　マクロ・ヘッジ
micro hedging　ミクロ・ヘッジ
one-sided hedging　片道ヘッジング
post-hedging return　ヘッジ後の収益率
short hedging　売りつなぎ

heft　(名)重み,重量,重要性,影響力
◆The more the U.S. dollar weakens, the more America's international heft diminishes. ドルが弱まれば弱まるほど、米国の国際的な影響力[重み]は減少する。

hefty　(形)相当な,大幅な,大がかりな,法外な,スケールが大きい,たくましい,がっしりした,大きくて重い,力強い
a hefty bill　高額の代金
a hefty commission　高い手数料,法外な手数料
a hefty fine　高い罰金
charge a hefty bill　高額な代金を請求する
charge a hefty commission　法外な手数料を請求する[支払わせる]
◆Banks are regulated to reduce the capital in the event of hefty appraisal losses, as a way of requiring shareholders to share the burden of the losses. 巨額の含み損[評価損]の場合、銀行規制で銀行は、株主にもその損失の負担を引き受けさせるために資本金を削減することになる。◆In the aftermath of past major earthquakes, unethical traders charged hefty bills after suggesting the need for checks of earthquake resistance. 過去の大地震の直後には、悪質業者が「耐震診断の必要がある」と持ちかけて、高額の代金を請求していた。◆In the event of hefty appraisal losses, banks must avoid a situation in which their creditors, including depositors, will be affected by the impairment of bank-owned assets. 巨額の含み損が出た場合、銀行は、預金者などの債権者が銀行保有資産の評価減の影響を受けるような状況がないようにしなければならない。◆The bank charged a hefty commission when asking a major moneylender to buy back loan claims. 大手の金融業者に債権の買い取りを求める際、同行は法外な手数料を支払わせていた。

heighten　(他動)強める,増す,高める,激しくする　(自動)強まる,増す,高まる,激化する
heightened competition　競争の激化
heightened demand resulting from the economic development of emerging nations　新興国の経済発展に

よる需要の増大
heightened efficiency　効率向上
heightened risk　リスクの増大
heightened tensions　緊張の高まり
◆Eurozone countries have tried a series of relief measures, but worries have heightened in the world particularly with regard to the eurozone. ユーロ圏諸国は一連の救済策を取ってきたが、世界ではとくにユーロ圏に関して心配[不安]が高まっている。◆Heightened tensions and significant downward risks for the global economy must be addressed decisively. 世界経済の緊張の高まりと重大な下方リスクに、断固として対処しなければならない。◆Speculation that the Fed would cut interest rates Tuesday heightened. 連邦準備制度理事会(FRB)が火曜日に利下げに踏み切るとの観測も、浮上している。

help　(動)支援する、援助する、後押しする、助ける、支える、助長する、促進する、改善する、活性化する、～の要因[一因]となる、～に貢献する、～に寄与する、追い風になる、(病気などを)治す、和らげる
fraudulently help　不正に手を貸す
help one's ruin　破滅を早める
help the flood victims　洪水被害者を救済する
help the stock market　株式市場を活性化する
help to raise production　増産を促進する
help to support the stock　株価を支える要因[一因]になる
◆American International Group agreed to pay a $10 million civil fine to settle the SEC's allegations that it fraudulently helped another company falsify its earnings report and hide losses. 米保険大手のAIG(アメリカン・インターナショナル・グループ)は、同社が他社の業績報告書改ざんと損失隠しに不正に手を貸したとする米証券取引委員会(SEC)の告発を受け、この問題を解決するために民事制裁金1,000万ドルを支払うことに同意した。◆Credit uncertainty in Europe has spilled over to France which is helping Greece, Italy and Spain facing fiscal crises. 欧州の信用不安は、財政危機に直面しているギリシャやイタリア、スペインを支援しているフランスにも拡大している。◆Greece asked other eurozone member states for financial support to help it stem its budget crisis in early 2010. 2010年初めにギリシャは、財政危機を回避するため、他のユーロ圏加盟国に金融支援を求めた。◆Increasing M&A advisory business helped Nomura grab the No. 1 spot in Japan's M&A league table for the first half of this year. 今年上半期はM&A顧問業務が増加したため、日本のM&A案件の引受実績で野村證券がトップの座を占めた。◆Solid performances by automakers have helped material suppliers and parts makers boost their business performances. 自動車メーカーの好業績[堅調な業績]が、素材メーカーや部品メーカーの業績向上を後押ししている。◆The bank's aim is to help circulate dormant individual assets in the local economy. 眠れる個人の金融資産を地域経済に循環させるのが、同行の目的だ。◆The economic package will include measures to help small and midsize companies procure funds. 経済対策には、中小企業の資金繰り支援策も盛り込まれる。◆The government will help Indonesia introduce economic stimulus measures through the soft loan. 政府は、この条件のゆるい借款を通じて、インドネシアの景気刺激策導入を支援する。◆The government would ask the Bank of Japan to further ease its monetary policy to help stabilize the nation's financial system by helping financial institutions procure funds. 政府は、金融機関の資金繰りを助けて金融システムの安定化を図るため、日銀に追加の[もう一段の]金融緩和を求める方針だ。◆The public welfare loans are extended to widows and single mothers to help them become economically independent by financing spending for education, living costs, housing costs and funds to start small businesses. 福祉資金は、母子家庭や寡婦に対して教育費や生活費、住宅費、小規模事業の開始資金などを貸し付けて、その経済的自立を

助けるために供与されている。◆The U.S. tighter regulations on investment funds helped to change the trend in crude oil prices. 米国の投資ファンド規制強化で、原油価格の流れが変わった。◆The White House is ready to consider tapping a $700 billion Wall Street bailout fund to help keep the U.S. automakers afloat. 米政府は、米自動車メーカーの破たんを避けるための支援策として、7,000億ドルの金融業界救済資金(金融安定化法の公的資金)の活用を検討する用意ができている。◆To help an insolvent borrower, money must be granted for free, or at least a part of the outstanding debt must be forgiven. 返済不能の借り手を助けるには、ただで資金を与えるか、少なくとも債務残高の一部の減免が必要だ。◆Under the envisioned lending facility, the IMF will provide funds to countries where government bond yields remain at high levels to help reconstruct their public finances. この融資制度案では、国際通貨基金(IMF)が、国債の利回りが高止まりしている国に資金を提供[融資]して財政再建を支援する。

help government-affiliated mortgage financiers　政府系住宅金融公社を救済する
◆On Sept 7, 2008, the U.S. government earmarked a huge amount of public funds to help government-affiliated mortgage financiers Freddie Mac and Fannie Mae. 2008年9月7日に米政府は、政府系住宅金融公社のフレディ・マック(連邦住宅抵当貸付公社)とファニー・メイ(連邦住宅抵当金庫[公庫])を救済するため、巨額の公的資金投入を決めた。

help the economy　景気を支える
◆The Fed's program of buying $600 billion in Treasury bonds to help the economy is to end in June 2011 on schedule. 景気を支えるために6,000億ドルの国債を買い入れる米連邦準備制度理事会(FRB)の量的緩和政策は、予定通り2011年6月に終了する。

helping hand　救いの手、支援の手、援助の手、手助け
◆The company decided to seek a helping hand from the investment fund. 同社は、この投資ファンドに支援を求めることにした。

hemorrhage [hemorrhaging]　(名)流出、損失、出血、大量流出、激減
(⇒financial hemorrhaging [hemorrhage])
asset hemorrhage　資産の流出
financial hemorrhage　資金の流出、金融上の損失、損失
◆U.S. newspaper publishers are hoping they can stop financial hemorrhage by changing the way they do business online. ウェブ・サイトの運営方法を変えることで、資金の流出を食い止めることができる、と米国の新聞発行業者[新聞社の経営者]は考えている。

herald　(動)予告する(foretell)、告げる(announce)、告知する、布告する(proclaim)、案内する、先触れ[前触れ]する
be heralded as　～と公的に告知される、～と発表される、～と報道される
much-heralded　大々的に発表された
◆The rational actions for survival taken by individual companies herald a danger that could lead the Japanese economy into contracted equilibrium. 生き残りをかけて個々の企業が取っている合理的な行動が、日本経済を縮小均衡に導く危険性をはらんでいる。

hesitate　(動)ためらう、躊躇(ちゅうちょ)する、遠慮する
◆The government should not hesitate to intervene in the currency market through bold yen-selling and dollar-buying operations. 政府は、為替市場への大胆な円売り・ドル買い介入をためらうべきではない。

hidden　(形)隠された、隠れた、簿外の、目に見えない
hidden assets　含み資産　(=hidden property)
hidden assets stock　含み資産株
　(=stock with hidden assets)

hidden capital　含み資産
hidden cost　目に見えないコスト
hidden gains　含み益
hidden gains in the stockholdings　株式含み益, 保有株式の含み益
hidden guarantee of obligation　簿外債務保証
hidden inflation　隠れたインフレーション
hidden money　へそくり
hidden property　含み資産
hidden reserves　秘密積立金, 隠匿 (いんとく) 資産, 含み資産　(=secret reserve)
hidden unemployment　隠れた失業, 偽装失業
hidden valuation　含み資産
hidden treasure　埋蔵金, 霞が関埋蔵金 (財務相が管理する特別会計のなかにある積立金のこと)
◆Accumulated surplus funds from previous years are referred to as "hidden treasure" by politicians. 過年度の累積剰余金 (特別会計の積立金) を, 政治家は「埋蔵金」と呼んでいる。◆In the fiscal 2010 budget, the government used the hidden treasure of a special account to augment the revenue side of its general account budget. 2010年度予算では, 特別会計の埋蔵金を使って [取り崩して], 一般会計予算の歳入に充てた。
hide　(動) 隠す, 覆 (おお) い隠す, 隠匿 (いんとく) する, 伏せて置く
　hide investment losses　投資損失を隠ぺいする [隠す]
　hide losses　損失を隠す
◆American International Group agreed to pay a $10 million civil fine to settle the SEC's allegations that it fraudulently helped another company falsify its earnings report and hide losses. 米保険大手のAIG (アメリカン・インターナショナル・グループ) は, 同社が他社の業績報告書改ざんと損失隠しに不正に手を貸したとする米証券取引委員会 (SEC) の告発を受け, この問題を解決するために民事制裁金1,000万ドルを支払うことに同意した。◆The company hid investment losses and tried to cover them up with funds related to corporate acquisitions. 同社は, 投資損失を隠ぺいし, 企業買収関連資金でそのもみ消しを図った。◆Years of window-dressing by Olympus to hide investment losses represent nothing but a company-wide breach of trust. 投資損失隠ぺいのためのオリンパスによる長年の粉飾決算は, 会社ぐるみの背信行為にほかならない。
high　(名) 高値, 最高, 最高値, 最高記録, 新記録
　(⇒capital inflow, hit, intervention, intraday)
　a day's high　本日の高値
　all time highs　過去最高の水準
　an all time high　過去最高, 史上最高値, 上場来の高値, 過去最多, 過去最悪　(=a record high)
　close high　高値で引ける
　52-week high　52週間最高値
　highs and lows on the stock exchange　株式市場の高値と安値
　historical high　過去最高, 過去最高の水準, 史上最高値　(=historic high)
　hit a high for the year　年初来の高値を付ける
　hit a new high　新高値を付ける, 過去最高値を付ける, 最高値を更新する
　hit a record [an all-time] high　過去最高を記録する, 上場来の高値を付ける　(⇒forex reserves)
　hit the week's high　この [その] 週の最安値を付ける
　hit the year's high　この年 [今年] の最安値を付ける, 年初来の高値を付ける, 年間最高値を付ける
　intraday high　日中取引での最高値, 取引時間中の高値, ざら場の高値
　make a high of　〜の高値を付ける
　open high　高値で寄り付く
　rally through the old highs　最高値を更新する
　reach a new historical high　過去最高を更新する
　rebound to record highs　過去最高の水準に反騰する
　recent highs　最近の高値
　record high　過去最高, 過去最高の水準, 史上最高, 史上最高値
　recovery high　戻り高値
　rise higher for the year　年初来の高値を付ける
　session high　前場 (または後場) での最高値
　set a new high　新記録を樹立する, 過去最高を更新する, 過去最高となる
　strike new highs above　〜を上回る過去最高値を付ける
　the day's high　その日の高値, この日の高値
　the week's high　週の高値, この [その] 週の高値
　the year's high　年間最高値, その年 [この年] の高値, 年初来の高値
　touch a high　高値を付ける
◆Interest rates will soon rebound to record highs. 金利は, もうすぐ過去最高の水準に反騰するだろう。◆The unemployment rate in July climbed to a postwar high of 5.7 percent, up 0.3 percentage point from the previous month. 7月 (2009年) の完全失業率は, 前月より0.3ポイント悪化して5.7%となり, 戦後最悪を更新した。◆U.S. oil prices struck new highs above $42 a barrel. 米国の原油価格が, 1バレル=42ドルを上回る過去最高値を付けた。
high　(形) 高い, 高度な, 高水準の, 高級な, 強い, 大きな, 最重要な, 活発な　(副) 高く, 高価に, 高値で, 大量に
　close high　高値で引ける
　high coupon　高利回り
　high credit standing　高い信用力, 高い信用度
　　(=good credit standing)
　high finance　大口融資, 大量融資
　high flyer　高値株
　high-grade corporate bonds　優良社債
　high price stock　値がさ株
　High Street bank　大手銀行
　higher dollar　ドル高
　higher earnings　増益, 高収益
　higher interest rates application system　日銀の高率適用制度
　higher profitability　高収益
　higher profits　増益, 高収益
　higher turnover　売上高の増加, 取引の活発化
　higher yen　円高
　highest-in first-out method　最高価格払出し法, 最高価格先出し法, 最高原価先出し法, 高入先出し法, HIFO
　the highest applicable legal contract rate　最高法定約定金利　(⇒LIBOR)
◆Amid the continued yen's historically high levels, increasing numbers of people are opening foreign currency deposit accounts. 歴史的な円高水準が続くなか, 外貨預金口座を設ける人が増えている。◆If the prices of purchased bad assets are set high, the public burden will balloon. 不良資産の買取り価格を高くすると, 国民負担が膨らむ。◆Investors must generally take higher investment risks in order to achieve higher investment returns. 投資家が一段と高い投資収益を得るには, 一般に一段と高い投資リスクを取る必要がある。◆The AA minus rating by S&P is the fourth highest in terms of credit quality on a scale of 22. 米格付け会社のスタンダード・アンド・プアーズ (S&P) による「ダブルAマイナス」の格付けは, 22段階ある信用度中, 上から4番目に当たる。◆The annual yield of the Italian government bond is currently at a high 6 per-

cent. 伊国債の流通利回りは現在、年6%の高い水準にある。◆The government and the Bank of Japan are seen as poised to stop the yen from rising as high as ￥82 against the dollar. 政府・日銀は1ドル＝82円突入を阻止する構えだ、と見られている。◆The high yields of the yen-denominated government bonds were considered considerably higher than minuscule domestic interest rates. この円建て国債は、国内の超低金利に比べて利回りがはるかに大きいと見られた。◆The higher the level of stock prices, the more funds firms can raise from IPOs. 株価の水準が上がれば、それだけ新規株式公開（上場時の新株発行）による資金調達額も増える。◆The interest rates a bank pays when procuring funds from the financial market are higher than those paid by other banks. ある銀行が金融市場で資金調達する際に支払う金利が、他行に比べて高くなっている。◆The interest rates of the Australian dollar-denominated deposit service are relatively high among major foreign currencies. 主要外貨のうち豪ドル建て預金サービスの金利は、比較的高い。◆The number of high-income earners who will pay the higher tax rates will not change even if progressive tax structure may be reinforced. 累進税の構造を強化しても、最高税率を負担する高所得者層の数は変わらない。◆The SEC probe was focused on several transactions that had led to higher revenues at AOL Time Warner Inc. 米証券取引委員会（SEC）の調査は、AOLタイム・ワーナーの売上高水増し（疑惑）につながった一部の取引を中心に行われた。◆The yen's value still remains high and is likely to reach a postwar record value above the ￥76-to-the-dollar level. 円相場は依然高く、1ドル＝76円台を上回る戦後最高値に達する可能性がある。

high-flying （形）値上がり確実の，値上がりが確実視された
◆CSFB was accused by the SEC and the NASD of charging big customers extraordinarily high trading commissions in exchange for shares of high-flying initial public offerings. クレディ・スイス・ファースト・ボストン（CSFB）は、値上がりが確実視された新規公開株の見返りに法外な取引手数料を優良顧客に請求していたとして、米証券取引委員会（SEC）と全米証券業協会（NASD）に告発された。

high-income earners 高所得者層
◆The number of high-income earners who will pay the higher tax rates will not change even if progressive tax structure may be reinforced. 累進税の構造を強化しても、最高税率を負担する高所得者層の数は変わらない。

high interest 高金利，高利，高利金融
　high interest bearing securities　高利付き証券
　high interest credit　高金利資金
　high interest money　高利金資金
　high interest policy　高金利政策
◆Debtors do not have to pay any interest on their loans if their lenders demand unlawfully high interests. 貸金業者が法外な高金利を要求した場合、債務者は借入金の利息をすべて支払う必要はない。◆If we use the cashing services, it results in high interest payments. 現金化サービスを利用すると、結果的に高金利［支払い利息が高くつくこと］になる。

high oil prices 原油高
◆Among other factors that could adversely affect the national economy are possible setbacks in the Chinese and U.S. economies as well as high oil prices. 国内景気に悪影響を及ぼす恐れがある他の要因として、中国や米国の景気後退や原油高がある。

high-powered money (base) マネタリー・ベース，強力貨幣，強権貨幣，基礎通貨　（＝base money, monetary base: 日本銀行券、貨幣流通高と日銀当座預金（民間金融機関の中央銀行預け金）の合計。⇒monetary base）

high price of crude oil 原油高
◆The current high price of crude oil stems partly from the lack of investment in oil development for a long period. 現在の原油高の一因は、長期にわたる石油開発投資の不足だ。

high-profile （形）脚光を浴びる，世間の注目を集める，人目を引く，目立つ，注目の，著名な，明確な，鮮明な，大型の
　high-profile issues　注目の銘柄，注目を集めている銘柄
　high-profile project　大型プロジェクト
◆Different from high-profile hedge funds, the founders and investment conditions of these foreign investment funds are not clear. 著名なヘッジ・ファンドと異なって、これらの海外投資ファンドの設立者や資金の運用実態は、はっきりしない。◆Livedoor waged a high-profile battle with Fuji Television Network Inc. for control of Nippon Broadcasting System Inc. ライブドアは、ニッポン放送の経営支配権をめぐってフジテレビと、世間の注目を浴びた買収合戦を演じた。

high return 高利益，高収益［高水準の収益］，高い収益率，高い運用益，高利回り，高配当，高いリターン，高リターン，ハイリターン　（⇒FX, return）
　high-risk high return　ハイリスク・ハイリターン（危険性の高い金融資産ほどその高い運用益が期待できること）
　higher return asset　利回りの高い資産
　provide high return　利回りが高い
◆A woman illegally collected money from individuals to invest in stocks, guaranteeing the principal and promising high returns. 主婦が、元本を保証し、高配当［高利回り］を約束して、株式投資への資金を個人から集めていた。◆The conventional method of investing in stocks and bonds could not yield high returns. 株や債券などへの伝統的な投資の手法では、高いリターン（運用益）は得られなかった。◆The factor that engendered this transformation in the U.S. financial industry was harsh competition in search of high returns. 米国金融業界の変貌をもたらした要因は、高利益を求める厳しい競争だ。◆The firm's asset management strategy is geared to seek high returns. 同社の資産運用戦略は、高収益を狙ったものだ。◆These days, nobody invests in a financial institution that cannot realize high returns. 最近は、高利益を上げることができない金融機関に、投資家は資金を出さなくなっている。

high risk 高リスク，リスクが大きいこと，ハイ・リスク
◆The government bonds were considered high risk, rated "speculative" at the time of issuance. この国債は、発行時点で「投機的」格付けで、リスクが大きいと見なされた。

high-risk asset リスクの高い資産，高リスク資産
◆The decline in long-term interest rates since May is due to continued capital flight from high-risk assets such as stocks triggered by the debt crisis in Europe. 5月以降、長期金利が低下しているのは、欧州の財政危機をきっかけに株式などリスク［損失リスク］の高い資産からの資金逃避が続いたためだ。

high-risk junk bonds リスクの高いジャンク債
◆The spreads of yields on high-risk junk bonds over the benchmark five-year U.S. Treasury bonds had been around 200 basis points, or 2 percentage points. リスクの高いジャンク債と指標となる5年物財務省証券との金利差（スプレッド）は、2%（200ベーシス・ポイント）程度で推移していた。

high-tech bubble ハイテク関連株の狂乱バブル，ハイテク・バブル
◆Wall Street stock prices have plunged recently following the 1995-2000 high-tech bubble. ウォール・ストリートの株価は最近、1995年から2000年までのハイテク・バブルの後を受けて、下落している。

high-tech company ハイテク企業
◆Shares of leading banks, in addition to those of high-tech companies whose business performances are deteriorating sharply, came under selling pressure across the board. 業績が急激に悪化しているハイテク関連企業株に加えて、大手銀行株も、軒並み売られた。

high-tech issues ハイテク銘柄

high-tech stock ハイテク株
◆The drop in share prices of high-tech and banking stocks, which have been driving recent gains, was remarkable. 最近の株高を牽引してきたハイテク株と銀行株の株価下落が、とくに目立った。

high value of the yen 円高
◆Export growth has slowed due to the high value of the yen and the weakness of economies overseas. 円高と海外経済の減速で、輸出の伸びが鈍った。

high yield 高利回り, 大きい利回り, 利回りが大きいこと, (保険の)高い予定利率
  bonds with high yields　高利回り債, 高利回り債券
  high yield investor　高利回り債の投資家
  high yield issue　高利回り債
  high-yield savings instrument　高利回りの貯蓄商品
  high yield securities　高利回り債
  promise a high yield　高い予定利率を約束する
  public high yield issuance　高利回り債の公募発行
  the high yields of the yen-denominated government bonds　高利回りの円建て国債
◆During the bubble economy, life insurers sold a large number of policies by promising high yields. バブル期に生保各社は、高い予定利率を約束して多くの保険契約を獲得した。
◆Many of incorporated foundations have invested in bonds with high yields. 財団法人の多くは、高利回り債に投資した。
◆The high yields of the yen-denominated government bonds were considered considerably higher than minuscule domestic interest rates. この円建て国債は、国内の超低金利に比べて利回りがはるかに大きいと見られた。

high yield bond 高利回り債
◆These institutional investors invest in high yield bonds because interest rates are almost zero. これらの機関投資家は、金利がゼロに近いため、高利回り債に投資している。

high yielding 高利回りの, 高金利の
  high yielding assets　高利回り資産
  high yielding markets　高利回り市場
  leave the high yielding bond market　高利回りの債券市場から資金を引き揚げる
  the high yielding bond market　高利回りの債券市場

high-yielding [higher-yielding] currency 高利回り通貨, 高金利通貨
◆The yen lost ground against higher-yielding currencies. 円は、高金利通貨に対して下落した[高金利通貨に対して売られた]。

higher debt 負債の増加, 債務の増加
◆Higher debt maturing within one year chiefly reflects commercial paper we issued to support financial services. 1年以内返済予定の負債の増加は、主に金融サービス部門の支援のため、当社がコマーシャル・ペーパーを発行したことを反映しています。

higher end of ～の後半, ～の上限
◆The yen surged to the higher end of the ￥98 level against the dollar in Tokyo markets due to yen-buying pressure fueled by expectations of the country's economic recovery. 東京為替市場は、日本の景気回復を期待した円買いが強まり、1ドル＝98円台の後半[98円台の上限]まで円が急騰した。

higher gains 高利益
◆The next step in the quest for higher gains is to inflate the returns by leverage. 高利益追求の第二の手段は、借金による利益の膨(ふく)らましだ。

higher interest rates 金利の上昇, 金利の引き上げ, 利上げ, 高金利　(⇒-free)
◆A lowered rating means higher interest rates. 格付けの低下は、金利の上昇を意味する。◆Higher interest rates would accelerate the influx of foreign funds. 利上げ[金利の引上げ]は、海外からの資金流入を加速することになる。

higher investment risks 一段と高い投資リスク
◆Investors must generally take higher investment risks in order to achieve higher investment returns. 投資家が一段と高い投資収益を得るには、一般に一段と高い投資リスクを取る必要がある。

higher return 高収益, 高利益
◆Investors purchased more overseas bonds and stocks to seek higher returns. 投資家は、高利益を求めて外国の債券や株式への投資が拡大した。

higher unemployment 失業増大
◆The U.S. 10 leading banks need a combined capital buffer of 74.6 billion against the risk of a deeper recession and higher unemployment over the next two years. 米主要金融機関の10社は、今後2年の景気悪化リスクと失業増大に備えて、10社合計で746億ドルの資本増強を求められている。

highest grade 最上級
◆Fitch Ratings Ltd. will keep its rating on long-term U.S. debt at the highest grade, AAA. 英米系の格付け会社フィッチ・レーティングスは、米国の長期国債格付けを、最上級のAAA(トリプルA)に据え置く方針だ。

highest value 最高値
◆The euro recorded its highest value against the dollar since its introduction in January 1999. ユーロは、ドルに対して1999年1月導入以来の最高値を付けた。

highly (副)高度に, 極度に, 強く, かなり, ～が高い
  be highly correlated with　～との関連性[相関性]が高い, ～と強く相関している
  highly-indebted countries　多重債務国, かなり負債を抱えた国
  highly rated bank　格付けの高い銀行, 高格付けの銀行
  highly rated insurer　格付けの高い保険会社, 高格付けの保険会社
  highly risk averse investor　リスク回避度の高い投資家
  highly sophisticated public securities markets　成熟度を増した公募証券市場

highly leveraged 負債比率が高い, 財務レバレッジが高い
  highly leveraged company　負債比率が高い企業, ハイ・レバレッジ企業
  highly leveraged issuer　負債比率が高い発行体
  highly leveraged transaction　負債比率が高い取引, ハイ・レバレッジ取引, HLT

highly liquid investment 流動性の高い投資
◆The Corporation considers all highly liquid investments purchased with an original maturity of three months or less to be cash equivalents. 当社は、取得日から満期日までの期間が3か月以内の流動性の高い投資を、すべて現預金等価物としています。

highwater mark 最高水準

hike (動)引き上げる, 上げる, 積みます
  hike interest rates　金利を引き上げる, 利上げする
  hike loan loss provisions　貸倒れ引当金を積みます
  hike the consumption tax　消費税を引き上げる
  hike the debt rating　社債格付けを引き上げる
◆Moody's Investors Service has hiked the debt rating of Nissan Motor Co. and three of its subsidiaries. 格付け会社のムーディーズは、日産と日産の子会社3社の社債格付けを引き上げた。◆The United States hiked interest rates 12 times since June last year. 米国は、昨年6月から12回、利上げした。

hike (名)引上げ, 値上げ, 値上がり, 上昇
  discount rate hike　公定歩合の引上げ
  further [another] rate hike　もう一段の利上げ
  hike in intervention rates　市場介入金利の引上げ

hike in official rates　政策金利の引上げ
hikes in mortgage rates　住宅ローン金利の引上げ
interest rate hike　金利の引上げ, 利上げ
price hike　値上げ, 価格引上げ, 物価上昇
rate hike　利上げ, 金利の引上げ
　　(=interest rate hike)
wage hike　賃上げ, 賃金引上げ
◆A consumption tax hike would increase the financial burden shouldered by Joe Blow. 消費税を引き上げると, 一般国民の金融負担[一般国民が負担する金融負担]が増すことになる。◆Hikes in gasoline prices are accelerating. ガソリン価格の上昇は, 急ピッチだ[加速している]。

hike in the consumption tax rate　消費税率の引上げ
◆In order to secure a sable revenue source, a hike in the consumption tax rate is necessary. 安定財源を確保するには, 消費税率の引上げが必要である。

hikes in raw material prices　原材料価格の上昇
◆Some firms managed to pass hikes in raw material prices on to buyers. 一部の企業では, 原材料価格の上昇分の価格転嫁[製品価格への転嫁]が進んだ。

hikes in the target for current account deposits　当座預金の残高目標の引上げ
◆The central bank has deployed various measures to ease monetary policy, including cuts in the discount rate and hikes in the target for current account deposits held by commercial banks at the central bank. 日銀は, 公定歩合の引下げや銀行が日銀に持つ当座預金の残高目標の引上げなどを含めて, 各種の金融緩和策を実施してきた。

hinder　(動)邪魔する, 妨害する, 足を引っ張る, 妨げる, 阻害する, 遅らせる
◆As the yen's rise puts pressure on the earnings of export-oriented companies, it hinders Japan's economic recovery. 円高は輸出企業を圧迫するので, 日本の景気回復の足を引っ張ることになる。◆We must avoid hindering the export-led economic recovery, speeding up deflation and increasing bad loans, which can be brought about by falling stock prices and the weakening dollar. 株安とドル安がもたらす可能性がある輸出頼みの景気回復の挫折, デフレ加速, 不良債権の拡大を, われわれは避けなければならない。

hindrance　(名)邪魔, 妨害, 阻害, 妨げ, 障害, 邪魔物[者], 妨害行為

hint at　示唆(しさ)する, ほのめかす, それとなく言う
◆Some credit rating agencies have hinted at the possibility of downgrading Japanese government bonds. 格付け会社のなかには, 日本国債の格下げの可能性を示唆したところもある。

HIPCs　重債務貧困国 (heavily indebted poor countriesの略)
◆The government will propose measures to reduce the debt burdens of heavily indebted poor countries (HIPC). 政府は, 重債務貧困国の債務負担削減策を提案する。

historic　(形)過去の, 歴史的な, 歴史上の, 歴史上重要な
a historic interest rate level　過去の金利水準
be at historic low level　過去最低の水準にある
be close to historic lows　過去最低に近い
historic behavior　実績
historic high　史上最高値, 過去最高の水準
historic low　史上最安値, 過去最低の水準
historic standards　過去の平均(historical averages), 過去の水準

historical　(形)過去の, 歴史の, 歴史的な, 歴史に関する
be close to the range of　過去のレンジの底に近い
be low by historical standards　過去最低水準に近い
historical cash flow　過去のキャッシュ・フロー
historical collection rate　過去の回収率, 回収率の実績
historical cost　取得原価

historical data　過去のデータ, 実績データ, 実績値
historical default figures　デフォルト実績
historical high　過去最高, 過去最高の水準, 史上最高値
historical loss experience　過去の損失実績
historical market relative　長期的相対PER(株価収益率), 市場平均に対する相対PERの長期平均
historical net asset value　前期基準の1株当たり純資産
historical peak　史上最高値
historical performance　過去の運用実績, 過去の業績, 過去の実績, 過去の経営数値
historical premium to the market　長期的にPER(株価収益率)が市場平均を上回っていること
historical prices　過去の値動き
historical rate　発生時レート
historical rate rollover　為替予約の延長, HRR
historical return　リターンの実績, 過去のリターン
historical summary　過去の推移, 推移

historically　(副)歴史的に, 過去から見て, これまで, 従来に比べて, 従来
be historically cyclical　過去の例から見て景気に左右される
historically high　過去最高の, 歴史的に高い, 歴史的高値の, 従来に比べて高い, 過去最高値の
historically high earnings　過去最高の収益
historically low level　過去最低の水準, 従来に比べて低い水準
yen's historically high levels　歴史的な円高水準
◆Amid the continued yen's historically high levels, increasing numbers of people are opening foreign currency deposit accounts. 歴史的な円高水準が続くなか, 外貨預金口座を設ける人が増えている。◆The yen remains in the historically high ¥75-range against the dollar. 円相場は, 1ドル=75円台の歴史的高値が続いている。

hit　(動)打撃を与える, ～に達する, 記録する, 打つ
be hard hit　ひどい目にあう, 大きな打撃を受ける
hit a high for the year　年初来の高値を付ける
hit a new high　新高値を付ける, 最高値を更新する, 過去最高値を記録する, 過去最高値となる
hit a new low　新安値を付ける, 最安値を更新する, 過去最安値を記録する, 過去最安値となる
hit a new 15-year low　15年ぶりに最安値を更新する
hit a snag　思わぬ障害にぶつかる
hit a year-to-date high　年初来の高値を付ける
hit an all-time high　過去最高に達する, 史上最高値を記録する, 最高記録に達する
hit an all-time low　過去最低に達する, 史上最安値を記録する, 最低記録に達する
hit an all-time record high　史上最高値を付ける, 上場来の高値を付ける
hit rock-bottom [an all-time low]　最低水準に達する, 底を打つ
hit the day's high　この[その]日の最高値を付ける
hit the market　市場に登場する, 発売される
　　(=go on sale)
hit the wall　行き詰まる, 限界に達する
hit the year's high　年初来の高値を付ける
hit the year's low　年間最安値を付ける, 今年の最安値を付ける, 年初来の安値を付ける
◆Amid the protracted economic slump and the ongoing deflationary trend, the life insurance industry has been hit by a trio of predicaments. 景気の長期低迷とデフレ傾向が進行するなか, 生保業界は三重苦に見舞われている。◆Export-oriented companies will be hit hard if the yen accelerates its rise. 円高

が加速すると、輸出企業は大きな打撃を受ける。◆Fears about default on the Greek government bonds are smoldering as Greece's fiscal reconstruction measures hit the wall. ギリシャの財政再建策が行き詰まっているため、ギリシャ国債のデフォルト（債務不履行）の恐れがくすぶっている。◆If oil prices remain above $45 per barrel for long, the world economy will be hard hit. 1バレル＝45ドルを超える原油の高値が長期化すれば、世界経済は大打撃を受ける。◆Ireland and Portugal also have been hit by financial crises and bailed out by the European Union. アイルランドやポルトガルも、財政危機に見舞われ、欧州連合（EU）に救済された［欧州連合に金融支援を仰いだ］。◆Public institutions or revitalization funds will buy the loans owed by small and midsize companies that have been hit by the March 11 disaster to lighten their repayment burdens. 公的機関や復興ファンドが、東日本大震災で被災した中小企業の借金を買い取って、被災企業の返済負担を軽減するものと思われる。◆Regional bank accounts were hit hardest by illegal transfers via foreign malware. 海外のマルウエア（コンピュータ・ウイルスの一種）による不正送金の被害は、地方銀行の口座が最多だった。◆The euro plummeted to the ￥100 level on the foreign exchange market, hitting a 10 year low. 外国為替市場では、ユーロが1ユーロ＝100円台まで急落して、10年ぶりの低水準［10年ぶりの円高・ユーロ安水準］となった。◆The ongoing global economic downturn continues to hit demand for flights. 今回の世界的な景気後退［世界同時不況］で、航空需要が引き続き減少している［打撃を受けている］。◆The total amount of loans owed by companies and individuals to private financial institutions stands at ￥2.8 trillion in the three prefectures' coastal areas hit by the March 11 tsunami. 津波被災地の3県（宮城、岩手と福島）沿岸部では、企業や個人の民間企業からの借入金総額が、2.8兆円にのぼっている。◆The U.S. currency hit a new 15-year low in the upper ￥82 zone. 米ドル相場は、1ドル＝82円台後半で15年ぶりに最安値を更新した。◆The U.S. economy has been hit by a chilled housing market and shrinking employment. 米経済は、住宅市場の冷え込みと雇用の落ち込みで打撃を受けている。◆The yen hit a 15-year high in the ￥83 range against the U.S. dollar on foreign markets. 海外市場で、円が15年ぶりに1ドル＝83円台を付けた。◆The yen hit ￥160 to the dollar during the week. 円は今週、1ドル＝160円の高値を付けた。◆U.S. and European financial institutions are hitting roadblocks because of the ongoing global financial turmoil. 欧米金融機関は、世界的な金融市場の混乱で、つまずいている。◆U.S. deficits hit record $413 billion. 米財政赤字が、過去最悪の4,130億ドルに達している。

hit bottom 底を打つ, 底をつく, 底入れする
  (=bottom out)
  ◆Stock prices of the New York Stock Exchange finally hit bottom. ニューヨーク証券取引所の株価は、やっと底を打った。◆The latent profits of major banks' stockholdings have hit bottom. 大手銀行の保有株の含み益も、底をついた。

hoard （動）貯蔵する, 秘蔵［退蔵, 保蔵］する, 蓄える, ためる, 買いだめする
  hoard cash for investment in　〜への投資資金を蓄える, 〜への投資に資金をつぎ込む
  hoard cash instead of lending it　貸出をしないで手元資金の確保に動く
  hoard goods　品物を買いだめする
  hoarded cash　退蔵現金
  hoarded currency［money］　保蔵通貨, 退蔵貨幣
  hoarded goods　退蔵品, 退蔵物資
  propensity to hoard　保蔵性向

hoarded stock　タンス株（個人などが株券の形で保有し、証券保管振替機構に預託していない株式のこと）
  ◆The number of hoarded stocks totals 75.6 billion as of March 2007. タンス株は、2007年3月時点で756億株に上っている。

hobble （動）邪魔する, 妨害する, 動けなくする, がんじがらめにする （自動）よろよろする
  ◆This ￥30 trillion cap has hobbled the government's economic and fiscal policies. この30兆円枠が、政府の経済・財政政策をがんじがらめにしている。

hold （動）保有する, 所有する, 保持する, 維持する, 続ける, 保管する, 支える, 支持する, 買い取る, 開催する, 開く
  closely held company　閉鎖会社, 非公開会社, 少数株主支配会社
  cooperation by holding capital　資本提携
  debt securities held to maturity　満期保有債券
  demand-to-hold securities　証券の保有需要
  foreign securities held for securities investment trusts　証券投資信託外国投資
  held-to-maturity securities　満期保有証券, 償還期限まで保有する証券
  hold a majority position［share］　株式の過半数を保有する［握る］
  hold a shareholders［shareholders'］meeting　株主総会を開く
  hold back buying　買いを控える
  hold back selling　売りを控える
  hold bonds to maturity［term］　満期まで債券を保有する
  hold equity positions in the company　同社の株式に投資する
  hold harmless agreement　免責特約, 損失肩代わり契約
  hold monetary policy steady［on hold］　金融政策を据え置く
  hold new issues to maturity［term］　新発債を満期まで保有する
  hold off investment［investing］in　〜への投資を控える
  hold off the market　取引を手控える
  hold［leave, keep, maintain］one's key interest rate unchanged　政策金利を据え置く
  hold one's own　足場を固める
  hold policy steady　金融政策を据え置く
  hold the market　買い占めて市場を左右する
  hold to maturity　満期まで保有する
  hold up　下げ渋る
  hold 30% interest in　〜に30％出資している, 〜の30％の株式を保有している
  securities held in a trading account　商品有価証券
  securities held in an investment　投資有価証券
  share price is held up by　株価が〜で下支えられる
  stocks held by investment trust　投資信託［投信］組入れ株
  totally［wholly］held subsidiary　完全所有子会社, 全額［100％］出資子会社
  widely held company　株主の多い会社
  ◆A bad bank is used to hold troubled assets and free up bank lending capacity. バッド・バンクは、不良資産を買い取って、銀行が自由に貸出できるようにするのに利用される。◆At the eurozone finance ministers meeting held on October 3, 2011, a decision on bridge loans of about €8 billion to Greece was expected, but none was done. 2011年10月3日に開かれたユーロ圏財務相会合では、ギリシャに対する約80億ユーロのつなぎ融資の決定が見込まれていたが、これは見送られた。◆Currently, the government is obliged to hold at least a 50 percent stake in JT. 現在、政府はJT（日本たばこ産業）株の50％以上保有を義務付けられている。◆European banks hold massive volumes of the eurozone's sovereign bonds. 欧州の銀行は、ユーロ圏の国債を大量に抱えている。◆Financial institutions pay insurance premiums to the Deposit Insurance

Corporation according to the amount of deposits they hold. 金融機関は、保有する預金量に応じて預金保険機構に保険料を納付している。◆Goldman Sachs Group Inc. and the two Japanese banks hold preferred shares equivalent to 70 percent of Sanyo. 米証券大手のゴールドマン・サックス（GS）と邦銀2行が、三洋電機の約7割の優先株式（普通株式に換算して議決権の約7割）を保有している。◆Greece's default on the national debts would be a blow to the operation of financial institutions in France and Germany that hold Greek government bonds. ギリシャが国債の債務不履行に陥った場合、ギリシャ国債を保有するフランスやドイツなどの金融機関の経営は、打撃を受けるだろう。◆Listed companies revised their articles of incorporation to make stock certificates paperless by holding shareholders meetings. 株券をペーパーレス化するため、公開企業は、株主総会を開いて会社の定款を変更した。◆Long-term debts held by central and local governments are expected to further swell unless the government puts the brakes on government bond issuance. 政府が国債発行に歯止めをかけないと、国と地方［地方自治体］が抱える長期債務は、さらに膨らむ見通しだ。◆Major financial institutions are forced to hold additional capital so that they can better absorb losses during financial crises. 金融危機の際の損失吸収力を高めるため、大手金融機関は、資本［自己資本］の積み増しを迫られている。◆On June 10, 2011, individuals holding $50,000 face value of the Corporation's bonds exercised their conversion privilege. 2011年6月10日、当社の社債権者が、額面5万ドル分の転換権を行使した［額面5万ドル分の株式への転換を行った］。◆The BOJ is prepared to hold its policy meeting ahead of schedule if the yen's value further soars before the next meeting. 次回の政策決定会合までに円高が一段と進めば、日銀は会合を前倒しして会合を開く構えだ。◆The emergency telephone conference by the G-7 financial ministers and central bank governors was held right before the opening of Asian financial markets. 先進7か国（G7）の財務相・中央銀行総裁による緊急電話会議は、アジアの金融市場が開く直前に開かれた。◆The European Central Bank held its key interest rates unchanged at 1 percent. 欧州中央銀行（ECB）は、（ユーロ圏16か国の短期金利の誘導目標となる）主要政策金利を年1%のまま据え置いた。◆The Financial Stability Board will impose a progressive extra capital charge of 1 percent to 2.5 percent on risk-adjusted assets held by G-SIFIs. G20（主要20か国・地域）の金融当局で構成する金融安定化理事会（FSB）は、国際金融システムにとって重要な金融機関（G-SIFIs）が保有するリスク調整後資産に、1～2.5%の資本［自己資本］の上積みを段階的に課すことになった。◆The government held a meeting on the current economic situation. 政府が、現在の経済情勢に関する会合を開いた。◆The government holds a 53.4 percent stake in Tokyo Metro Co., which was valued at ¥174.9 billion at book value as of the end of March 2010. 国は東京地下鉄（東京メトロ）の株式の53.4%を保有しており、その簿価での評価額は2010年3月末時点で1,749億円になる。◆The Greek-triggered sovereign debt crisis resulted in the breakup of the French-Belgian bank Dexia which held Greek government bonds. ギリシャが引き金になったソブリン危機（政府債務危機）問題で、ギリシャ国債を保有していた仏ベルギー系金融機関のデクシア（Dexia）が、解体に追い込まれた。◆The number of individual investors holding shares in companies listed on the Jasdaq Securities Exchange increased for the 10th straight year. ジャスダック証券取引所に上場している企業（931社）の個人株主数は、10年連続で増加した。◆The proxy form indicates the number of shares to be voted, including any full shares held for participants in the Employee Stock Purchase Plan. 委任状用紙には、従業員株式購入制度加入者のために保有している株式をすべて含めて、行使される議決権数が記載されています。◆The rise in foreign assets held by Japanese was mainly caused by an increase in direct and securities investment. 日本の政府・企業・個人が保有する対外資産の増加は、主に直接・証券投資の伸びによるものだった。◆The so-called decoupling theory holds that the effects of a U.S. slowdown can be offset by growth in emerging nations. いわゆるディカップリング論では、米経済の減速は新興国の成長が補う、と考えられている。◆The U.S. administration will spend up to $700 billion to buy up soured mortgage-related securities and other devalued assets held by ailing financial institutions. 米政府は、経営不振の金融機関が保有するモーゲージ関連の不良証券などの不良資産を、最大7,000億ドル投入して買い取る方針だ。◆The yen held its own against the U.S. dollar. 米ドルに対して、円は持ちこたえた。◆We do not hold the idea that big banks are too big to fail. われわれとしては、「巨大銀行が破たんさせるには大き過ぎる」という考え方は取らない。

hold （名）長期保有, 継続保有, 把持, 把握, 掌握, 勢力, 支配力, 影響力, 威力, 預金口座の払出し停止, 一時的停止［遅れ］, 中止, 延長

be likely to take hold　持続する模様だ, 持続する見込みだ, 持続しそうだ

buy bonds on a hold　長期保有目的で債券を買う

hold monetary policy on hold［steady］　金融政策を据え置く

keep ～ on hold　～を据え置く
　（⇒unsecured overnight call money）

monetary policy is on hold　金融政策は据え置かれている, 金融政策は変更が見送られている, 金利は据え置かれている

put ～ on hold　～を一時中止する, 一時棚上げにする, ～を据え置く

put (monetary) policy on hold　金融政策を据え置く

◆The Bank of Japan kept its key interest rates on hold. 日銀は、政策金利を据え置いた。◆The current momentum in the yen is likely to take hold. 現在の円相場の勢いは、持続しそうだ。◆The Organization of Petroleum Exporting Countries decided to keep oil output limits on hold. 石油輸出国機構（OPEC）は、現行の原油生産枠を据え置くことを決めた。

hold down　（金利などを）低く抑える,（物価などを）抑える, 抑制する, 減らす, 低迷させる, 抑圧する（仕事を）持ち続ける［やり続ける］

hold down long-term interest rates　長期金利を低く抑える

hold down prices　価格を抑える, 物価を抑える

◆Long-term interest rates have so far been held down due to an influx of money from abroad. 長期金利はこれまで、海外マネーの流入で低く抑えられていた。

holder　（名）所有者, 保有者, 保持者, 所持人, 株主, 契約者, 会員, ホールダー　（=owner; ⇒account holder, bond holder, cardholder, option holder, policyholder, shareholder）

bank account holder　銀行口座の名義人

bill holder　手形所持人

bond holder　社債保有者, 債券保有者
　（=debenture holder）

card holder［cardholder］　カード会員
　（⇒cardholder）

check holder　小切手振出人

de facto holder　実質保有者

de facto holder of the shares　株の実質保有者

debenture［bond］holder　社債保持者, 債券保有者

debt holder　債券保有者

draft［bill］holder　手形所持人

equity holder　持ち分証券保有者

fund holder　年金制度の受託者,（英国の）公債所有者, 公債投資家

holder in due course　善意の第三者, 正当所持人

holder of record　株主名簿上の株主, 登録保有者, 登録株主
job holder　定職者, 定職に就いている人, 公務員
land holder　土地所有者
loan holder　債権者
option holder　オプションの買い手
policy holder　保険契約者　(=policyholder)
portfolio holder　金融資産保有者, ポートフォリオ保有者
real estate holder　不動産所有者
savings account holder　普通預金口座所有者, 銀行預金者
security holder　証券保有者, 証券所有者
share holder　株式保有者, 株主
the largest holder of U.S. Treasury securities　米財務省証券の最大保有国, 米国債の最大保有国
total stock holders' equity　株主持ち分合計
wealth holder　資産保有者[所有者]
◆China is the holder of the world's largest foreign exchange reserves. 中国の外貨準備高は、世界一だ。◆China is the largest holder of U.S. Treasury securities. 中国は、米国債[米財務省証券]の最大の保有国だ。◆Kokudo Corp. was found to be the de facto holder of the shares of the 1,200 individuals. 個人1,200人の株の実質保有者は、コクドであることが分かった。◆The law on the identification of bank account holders was put into force in January 2003. 銀行口座名義人の本人確認に関する法律(本人確認法)は、2003年1月に施行された。◆The Life Insurance Policyholders Protection Corporation of Japan helps holders of life insurance policies sold by bankrupt companies to protect their assets. 生命保険契約者保護機構は、破たんした生命保険会社が販売した生命保険証券の保有者[破たんした生保の保険契約者]の財産保護にかかわっている。

holder of U.S. Treasury securities　米財務省証券の保有国, 米国債の保有国, 米国債保有者
◆China is trying to flex its muscle with the United States on the strength of its status as the largest holder of U.S. Treasury securities. 中国は、米財務省証券[米国債]の最大保有国としての地位を背景に、米国への影響力を行使しようとしている。

holders of credit cards　クレジット・カードの会員
◆Personal data, including the names, addresses and credit card numbers of 99,789 holders of credit cards issued by Nippon Shinpan Co., may have been leaked. 日本信販が発行したクレジット・カードの会員99,789人分の名前や住所、カード番号などの個人情報が、流出した可能性がある。

holding　(名)所有, 保有, 保持, 占有, 所有持ち分, 保有株, 持ち株比率, 子会社, 所有財産, 保有財産　(⇒Antimonopoly Law, cross shareholding[cross-shareholding], crossholding, equity holding, holdings, stock holding)
asset holding　資産保有
bank holding issue　銀行持ち株会社債
bond cross holding　債券持ち合い
cash holding　現金保有
cross-holding　株式持ち合い
　(=crossholding, interlocking(share) holding)
debt holding　債券保有
equity holding　株式保有, 合弁
have equity holding　出資する
holding back　売り控え
holding gain and [or] loss　保有損益
holding in the market　防戦買い
holding-off buying　買い控え
holding period　所有期間, 保有期間, 投資期間
holding period return　保有期間利回り

holding times　持続期間
holding trust　持ち株トラスト
lower one's holding in the company　同社の持ち株比率を引き下げる
mutual currency holding　相互通貨保有
mutual holding of stocks　株式持ち合い
portfolio holding　金融資産保有, ポートフォリオ保有
proportionate holding of the share capital of the new company　新会社の所有持ち分比率, 新会社の株主が所有する株式の割合
security holding　証券保有, 証券所有
speculative holding　投機的保有
stock [share] holding　株式保有
wealth holding　資産保有
◆Seibu Railway and Kokudo have already agreed to lower Kokudo's holding in Seibu Railway. 西武鉄道とコクドは、コクドが西武鉄道の持ち株比率を下げることですでに合意している。◆The firm's practice of issuing false financial statements about the holdings of major stockholders dates back to 1957 or earlier. 大株主の保有株式に関して虚偽記載の有価証券報告書を発行する同社の慣行は、1957年以前にさかのぼる。◆Vodafone tried to sell its holding in Japan Telecom to Tokyo Electric Power Co. (TEPCO). But negotiations fell through when Vodafone turned down TEPCO's offer, which was in the region of ¥150 billion. ボーダフォンは、東京電力(東電)に日本テレコム株を売却しようとした。しかし、1,500億円程度の東電側の提示額をボーダフォンが拒否して、交渉は決裂した。

holding company　持ち株会社　(=holding corporation; ⇒financial holding company, operation, stock brokering)
bank holding company　銀行持ち株会社
financial holding company　金融持ち株会社
industrial holding company　製造業持ち株会社
insurance holding company　保険持ち株会社
intermediate holding company　中間持ち株会社
investment holding company　投資持ち株会社
management holding company　経営持ち株会社
multi-bank holding company　複数銀行持ち株会社
one-bank holding company　単一銀行持ち株会社
personal holding company　同族持ち株法人
private industrial holding company　民間持ち株会社
public utility holding company　公益事業持ち株会社
pure holding company　純粋持ち株会社
state-owned holding company　国営持ち株会社
ultimate holding company　最終的な持ち株会社
◆In the temporary nationalization, the government will take possession of all shares from the bank's holding company at no cost. 一時国有化で、政府は同行の持ち株会社から株式をゼロ円で全株取得することになる。◆Seven & I Holdings Co. was formed on Sept. 1, 2005 as the holding company of Ito-Yokado, Seven-Eleven Japan and Denny's Japan Co. セブン&アイ・ホールディングスは、イトーヨーカ堂、セブン-イレブン・ジャパンとデニーズ・ジャパンの持ち株会社として、2005年9月1日に設立された。◆The four planned corporations will be operated under a holding company. 同案での4社は、持ち株会社の下に[持ち株会社の傘下で]運営される。◆The two financial groups plan to integrate their banking, trust and securities operations under a holding company created through the merger of their holding companies. 両金融グループは、それぞれ銀行、信託、証券業務を経営統合により新設する持ち株会社の傘下に統合する計画だ。◆UFJ Holdings, Inc. and Mitsubishi Tokyo Financial Group, Inc. are discussing the merger of their holding companies and banking divisions. UFJホールディングスと三菱東京フィナンシャル・グループは、

持ち株会社と銀行分野の統合を検討している。

解説 持ち株会社とは：他の会社の株式を、投資目的でなく事業活動支配のために保有する会社のこと。傘下のグループ企業を統括し、グループ全体の戦略策定に当たり、投資・資金計画やトップ人事などを支配する。グループ企業は、独立会社として持ち株会社の計画・方針に基づいて独自の計画を立て、事業活動を行い、人事権を持つとされる。(「現代用語の基礎知識」参照)

holding firm 持ち株会社 (=holding company)
◆The TSE and the OSE plan to establish an exchange company group as a holding firm under which the two exchanges will be placed as subsidiaries. 東証と大証は、両株式取引所を子会社として傘下に収める持ち株会社として、取引所グループの設立を計画している。

holdings (名)持ち株,保有株,保有高,持ち株比率,持ち株会社,資産 (⇒bond holdings, control動詞, holding, investment fund, securities holdings)
bond holdings 債券保有高[保有量]
cash holdings 現金保有高,現金保有
company's holdings 会社の資産
diversify holdings 資産を分散する,投資を分散する
dollar holdings ドル保有高
draft holdings 手形保有高
gold holdings 金保有高,金準備
government's shareholdings 政府保有株
　(=government-held shares)
gross money holdings 総貨幣保有高
holdings in associated companies 関連会社株式
latent losses on holdings of stocks 保有株式の含み損
liquidate one's holdings 持ち株[保有債券]を売却する
long-term equity holdings 長期保有株式
national holdings 国家資産
nominal bond holdings 名目的債券保有高[保有量]
outstanding Treasury bond holdings 米国債の保有残高
portfolio holdings 金融資産保有高,ポートフォリオ保有高
private banks' government bond holdings 民間銀行の国債保有高[保有残高]
real estate holdings 保有不動産
sell holdings 保有株を売却する
stock holdings 保有株式,持ち株,出資比率
the market value of real estate holdings 保有不動産の時価
◆Based on Friday's Mazda stock closing price of ¥214 per share, Ford's holdings of about 195 million shares were worth ¥42 billion. 金曜日のマツダ株の終値(1株当たり214円)ベースで、フォードが保有するマツダ株約1億9,500万株の時価総額は420億円となる。◆Dallas-based investment fund Lone Star will offer 30.2 percent of its holdings, or 211,405 shares, ahead of the Tokyo Star Bank's listing on the Tokyo Stock Exchange. 東京スター銀行(旧東京相和銀行)の東証上場前に、ダラスに本部を置く投資ファンドのローンスターが、保有する株式の30.2%(211,405株)を売り出す。◆Japanese private banks' government bond holdings soared to ¥154 trillion as of the end of June 2011 from ¥32 trillion as of the end of March 1999. 日本の民間銀行の国債保有残高は、(ゼロ金利政策が初めて導入された)1999年3月末時点の32兆円から、2011年6月末現在で154兆円に膨らんだ。◆The U.S. private banks' outstanding Treasury bond holdings grew by about 50 percent from March 2008, prior to the Lehman shock. 米国の民間銀行の米国債保有残高は、リーマン・ショック前の2008年3月から約5割増えた。◆Thirteen major banks are swamped by ¥1.4 trillion in latent losses on holdings of stocks and other securities. 大手13行は、1兆4,000億円もの保有株式その他の有価証券の含み損で窮地に陥っている。◆Vodafone is to sell its holdings in Japan Telecom Co. to Ripplewood Holdings, a U.S.-based investment fund, for about ¥260 billion. ボーダフォン(イギリスの携帯電話大手)が、日本テレコムの持ち株[日本テレコム株]を、米投資ファンドのリップルウッド・ホールディングスに約2,600億円で売却する方針を固めた。

holdover items 保留項目

hollow out (動)〜に穴を開ける,〜に空洞をつくる,〜をくり抜く,空洞化する
◆There is a fear that Japanese stock markets will be hollowed out as more Japanese companies are looking to list their shares in other Asian countries. 日本企業が他のアジア市場での株式上場を狙っていることから、日本の株式市場は今後、空洞化する恐れもある。

hollowing-out (名)空洞化
　(=hollowing, hollowing out, hollowization)
a hollowing-out of domestic industries 国内産業の空洞化
the hollowing-out of tax revenue 税の空洞化
the hollowing-out of the national pension system 国民年金の空洞化
◆Japanese firms' moves to shift production abroad to cope with the yen's rise will bring about a hollowing-out of domestic industries. 円高対策として日本企業が生産拠点を海外に移すと、国内産業の空洞化を招くことになる。◆The hollowing-out of the pension system may increase companies' personnel costs so much that it could negatively affect their international competitive edge. 年金の空洞化で人件費が上昇し、国際競争力に悪影響を及ぼす恐れがある。◆This hollowing-out of premium payments threatens to undermine the national pension system. この保険料納付[保険料負担]の空洞化現象が、国民年金システムの土台を揺るがしている。

hologram ホログラム,レーザー写真
◆The hologram of the new banknotes is designed to make the banknotes' color and design appear to change if seen from different angles. 新札のホログラムは、見る角度を変えると新札の色や模様が違って見えるようにデザインされている。

home foreclosure 住宅の差し押さえ,住宅ローンの焦げ付き[貸倒れ]
◆Home foreclosures and late payments on home mortgages are likely to rise for a while longer. 住宅の差し押さえや住宅ローン延滞件数の増加は、しばらく続く見通しだ。

home loan 住宅ローン
　(=home mortgage, housing loan, mortgage loan)
home loan giant 住宅ローン大手
take out home loans 住宅ローンを組む
◆Adjustable types of home loans will continue to be popular as long as interest rates are expected to remain low. 金利の先安感が強い間は、(金利)変動型の住宅ローンの人気が続くようだ。◆Financial institutions and housing developers are working together to introduce products that enable customers to take out home loans with annual interest rates at 1 percent or less. 金融機関と住宅開発販売業者が提携して、顧客が年1%以下の金利の住宅ローンを組める[利用できる]商品を導入している。◆Mizuho's first-half profit fell 17 percent as credit costs increased and on losses related to investments in U.S. home loans to riskier borrowers. みずほの上半期利益は、与信コストの増加とリスクの高い融資先への米国の住宅ローン投資に関連する損失で、17%減少した。◆The U.S. central bank will buy mortgage-backed securities (MBS) guaranteed by the government-controlled home loan giants Fannie Mae, Freddie Mac and Ginnie Mae. 米連邦準備制度理事会(FRB)は、米政府系住宅ローン大手のファニー・メイ(米連邦住宅貸付公社)、フレディ・マック(米連邦住宅抵当金庫)とジニー・メイ(米政府系住宅金融公庫)が保証した住宅ローン担保証券(MBS)を買い取ることになった。

home mortgage 住宅ローン (=home mortgage loan,

housing loan; ⇒home foreclosure)
◆Many home mortgages went into default. 多くの住宅ローンが債務不履行になった。
home mortgage loan 住宅ローン
◆Subprime-related securities are created mainly from home mortgage loans without checking a customer's income. サブプライム関連証券は、顧客の所得審査なしで貸し出される住宅ローンで造られている。
home ownership rate 持ち家率
Homeland Investment Act 本国投資法（米企業が海外子会社の利益や配当金などを米本社に送金し、米国内で再投資すれば税制を優遇するという措置。ブッシュ政権が2005年に1年の期間限定で施行した法律）
Hong Kong Exchanges and Clearing Limited 香港証券取引所, HKEx
Hong Kong market 香港市場
◆By the 30-minute extension of morning trading sessions, investors will be able to trade for a full hour in Japan as they monitor stock price movements on the Hong Kong market. 午前の取引時間の30分延長で、投資家は、香港市場の値動きを見ながら日本市場で丸1時間売買できるようになった。
honor （動）小切手や手形などを引き受ける, 期日に支払う, 債務を返済する, 債務を履行する
（⇒bill, debt guarantee, dishonor）
　honor a contract　契約金額を期日に支払う
　honor a draft　手形を引き受ける
　honor foreign currency obligations　外貨建てローンを返済する
　honor one's checks　〜の振り出した小切手を引き受ける, 〜の振り出した小切手の支払いをする
　honor the claims　債務を返済する, 債務を履行する
◆The solvency margin ratio indicates the ability of insurers to honor insurance claims and other payments. ソルベンシー・マージン比率は、保険会社の保険金その他の支払い金の支払い能力を示す。
hope （動）希望する, 望む, 願う, 期待する
◆The nonlife insurance company hopes to attract about 3 million to 4 million new policyholders a year for its new types of insurance. 同損保は、同社の新型保険で、年間約300万〜400万件の新規契約獲得を目指している。
horizon （名）水平線, 地平線, 視界, 視野, 限界, 範囲, 前途, 目標, 行く手, 対象, 期間, 所有期間, 投資計画期間, ホライズン　（⇒time horizon）
　horizon analysis　投資計画期間分析, 所有期間利回り分析
　horizon return　所有期間利回り
　　（=holding period return）
　investment horizon　所有期間, 運用期間, 投資対象
◆Economic recovery is on the horizon, but the employment situation remains severe. 景気回復の兆しは見えるが、雇用情勢はまだ厳しい。
horizontal （形）水平的, 同業異種間の, 横割りの, 横の, ホリゾンタル　（⇒vertical）
　horizontal acquisition　水平的買収
　horizontal amalgamation　水平的合併
　horizontal combination　水平的企業結合, 同業種間の企業結合
　horizontal competition　水平的競争
　horizontal consolidation　水平的合併, 水平的新設合併, 同業種間の合併［新設合併］
　horizontal diversification　水平的多角化
　horizontal influence　水平的影響
　horizontal integration　水平的統合
　horizontal international specialization　水平的国際分業, 水平的分業

　horizontal market　水平的市場
　horizontal marketing system　水平的マーケティング・システム
　horizontal merger　水平的合併
　horizontal organization　水平的組織
　horizontal price agreement　水平的価格協定
　horizontal publication　総合業界紙
　horizontal specialization　水平的分業, 水平的国際分業
　　（=horizontal international specialization）
　horizontal spread　ホリゾンタル・スプレッド（オプション取引で、行使日だけが違う二つのオプションについて、売りと買いを同時に出すこと）
　horizontal trade　水平貿易
hostile （形）敵対する, 敵対的な
　hostile acquisition　敵対的買収
　hostile fire　（保険）敵対火, 仇火（きゅうか）
　hostile tender offer　敵対的TOB（株式の公開買付け）, 敵対的な株式公開買付け
hostile acquirer 敵対的買収者
　（=hostile bidder, hostile takeover bidder）
◆These subscription warrants could be converted into shares at a ratio of two new shares to one existing share if hostile acquirer obtains a stake of 20 percent or more. この新株予約権は、敵対的買収者が株式を20％以上取得した場合に、既存の株式1株に対して新株2株の割合で株式に転換できる。
hostile bid 敵対的株式公開買付け, 敵対的TOB（株式公開買付け）, 敵対的買収, 敵対的買収提案
　（=hostile takeover bid）
◆We launched the hostile bid for the firm's shares. 当社は、同社株の敵対的公開買付け（TOB）を実施しました。
hostile investment fund 敵対する投資ファンド
◆The firm's management countered with a takeover bid of its own against a hostile overseas investment fund. 敵対する海外投資ファンドに対して、同社の経営陣は自社株の公開買付け（TOB）で対抗した。
hostile mergers and acquisitions 敵対的M&A（企業の合併・買収）, 敵対的M&A
◆Hostile mergers and acquisitions have been increasing rapidly as the dissolution of cross-shareholding ties among companies accelerates. 企業間の株式持ち合い関係の解消が加速するにつれ、敵対的M&A（企業の合併・買収）の件数は急増している。◆In hostile mergers and acquisitions, a company's stock is acquired despite the opposition of the management. 敵対的M&Aでは、経営者が反対するにもかかわらず、企業の株式が買い集められる［取得される］。
hostile takeover 敵対的買収, 敵対的M&A　（=hostile acquisition, unsolicited takeover; ⇒warrant）
　adopt defensive measures against a hostile takeover　敵対的M&Aに対する防衛策を導入する
　fend off a hostile takeover by　〜による敵対的買収を防ぐ
◆More than 70 percent of leading companies are worried about becoming the target of a hostile takeover. 主要企業の70％以上が、敵対的買収の対象になる［敵対的買収を仕掛けられる］のを懸念している。◆Only 35.8 percent of the leading companies have already adopted defensive measures against a hostile takeover. 敵対的M&Aに対する防衛策を導入しているのは、主要企業の35.8％にすぎない。◆The firm's management fended off a hostile takeover by an investment fund. 同社の経営陣が、投資ファンドによる敵対的買収を防いだ。◆White knight is a company that saves another firm threatened by a hostile takeover by making a friendly offer. ホワイト・ナイトは、友好的な買収により、敵対的買収の脅威にさらされている他企業を救済する企業のことだ。
hostile takeover bid 敵対的株式公開買付け, 敵対的TOB, 株式公開買付けによる敵対的買収, 敵対的買収

(=hostile bid; ⇒floating shares, veto right)
counter a hostile takeover bid　敵対的買収に対抗する
forestall hostile takeover bids　敵対的TOBを未然に防ぐ
protective measures against hostile takeover bids　敵対的買収に対する防衛策
thwart a hostile takeover bid　敵対的TOB（株式公開買付け）を阻止する
ward off a hostile takeover　敵対的買収を撃退する
◆Companies should not go public to prevent hostile takeover bids. 敵対的買収を防ぐには、企業は株式を上場すべきでない。◆In order to forestall hostile takeover bids, companies should raise their corporate value. 敵対的TOB（株式公開買付けによる企業買収）を未然に防ぐには、企業が企業価値を高めなければならない。◆Myojo Foods asked Nissin Food Products to play the part of a white knight by forming a capital alliance to thwart the U.S. investment fund's hostile takeover bid. 米系投資ファンドの敵対的TOB（株式公開買付け）を阻止するため、明星食品は資本提携によるホワイト・ナイト（白馬の騎士）としての明星の支援を日清食品に要請した。◆NBS's move is designed to counter Livedoor's hostile takeover bid. ニッポン放送の措置は、ライブドアによる敵対的買収［敵対的TOB］への対抗が目的だ。◆The company granted an investment firm the right to buy shares to be newly issued by the company as a means of foiling a hostile takeover bid. 同社は、敵対的買収への防衛策として、同社が新規に発行する株式の引受権を投資会社に付与した［投資会社に新株予約権を割り当てた］。◆The Tokyo Stock Exchange has called on listed companies to refrain from taking excessively protective measures against hostile takeover bids. 東京証券取引所は、敵対的買収に対する過剰な防衛策の自粛を上場企業に求めている。

hostile takeover bidder　敵対的買収者　(=hostile acquirer, hostile bidder; ⇒golden share)
◆Since golden shares could fall into the hands of a hostile takeover bidder, few listed companies have issued such shares. 黄金株は敵対的買収者の手に渡る場合もあるので、上場企業はこれまでのところ黄金株を発行していない。

hot check　不良小切手, 不渡り小切手, 不正小切手, にせ小切手
hot issue　人気銘柄, 超人気銘柄
◆The stock is a hot issue. この株は、超人気銘柄だ。
hot money　（国際金融市場間を金利差に応じて流れ動く投機的な）短期資金, 国際短期資金, 投機資金, ホット・マネー
hot tip　信頼できる情報
house　（名）商社, 会社, 業者, 取引所, 住宅, ハウス　(⇒brokerage house, securities house)
bond house　証券会社
brokerage house　証券会社
clearing house　決済機関, 手形交換所, 清算機関, クリアリング・ハウス
discount house　手形割引業者, 割引業者, 割引商社
exchange house　為替取引所, 両替所
finance house　金融会社
foreign currency house　両替所
House of Councilors Financial Affairs Committee　参院財政金融委員会
House of Representatives Committee on Financial Affairs　衆院財務金融委員会
House of Representatives Financial Services Committee　米下院金融サービス委員会
issuing house　証券発行会社
securities house　証券会社
swap clearing house　スワップ清算機関
trading house　証券会社, 商社

◆Argentina's peso strengthened slightly against the U.S. dollar as banks and exchange houses reopened. 銀行と両替所の営業再開に伴って、アルゼンチンの通貨ペソの対ドル・レートが若干上昇した。

household　（名）家庭, 世帯, 所帯, 家計
household assets　家計金融資産, 個人の金融資産
household consumption　家計消費, 家計消費支出
household deposit　個人預金高
household income　家計所得
household outlays　1世帯当たり消費支出, 家計支出, 個人消費　(=household spending)
household purchasing power　家計の購買力
household savings　家計の貯蓄, 家計貯蓄
household sector　消費者, 家計部門
household survey　家計調査
households with an annual income less than ¥4 million　年収400万円未満の世帯
low income households　低所得者層
non-salaried household　一般世帯
non-workers household　非勤労者世帯
wage-earning [workers] households　サラリーマン世帯, 勤労者世帯
◆Business sentiment and the willingness of household to spend may cool and stall the economy unless the sharp appreciation of the yen is checked. 円の急騰を止めないと、企業の心理や家計の消費意欲が冷え込み、景気が腰折れしかねない。◆Economic expansion is far from being felt by households. 景気回復は、家計の実感にはほど遠い。◆The nominal GDP growth rate takes into account price changes and is considered a more accurate reflection of household and corporate sentiment. 名目GDP（国内総生産）成長率は、物価変動を考慮し、家計や企業の景況感をより正確に反映するとされている。◆The size of the financial assets of Japanese households is still worth a massive ¥1.47 quadrillion despite a decrease in the total over recent years. 日本の個人金融資産の規模は、ここ数年で減少したものの、まだ1,470兆円ほどもあって巨大だ。◆Wage-earning households account for about 60 percent of total household spending. サラリーマン世帯が、世帯全体の消費支出の約60%を占めている。

household financial assets　個人金融資産
◆Out of the household financial assets of ¥1.47 quadrillion, about ¥160 trillion can be considered as surplus savings, given the life cycle of the average Japanese individual. 日本人の平均的な個人のラフサイクルから見て、1,470兆円の個人金融資産のうち約160兆円は、余剰貯蓄と考えられる。

household savings　家計の貯蓄, 家計貯蓄
◆The level of household savings used to be the highest among industrial nations. （日本の）家計貯蓄の水準は、以前はいちばん高かった。

housewife　（名）主婦　(⇒full-time housewife)
a full-time housewife　専業主婦
housewives of working age　現役世代の主婦
◆If a housewife whose annual income is ¥1.3 million or more, or her husband becomes self-employed, the housewife must join the national pension plan and pay premiums. 主婦の年収が130万円以上の場合、または夫が脱サラした場合には、主婦も国民年金に加入して保険料を支払わなければならない。◆There are about 420,000 full-time housewives whose unpaid premium periods are long as they have failed to switch to the national pension plan. 国民年金への切替えが済んでなくて保険料の未納期間が長い専業主婦は、約42万人いる。

housing　（名）住宅
Housing and Economic Recovery Act of 2008　（米国の）2008年住宅経済回復法
housing bond　住宅債

housing credit　住宅信用
housing data　住宅統計
housing demand　住宅需要
housing development finance　住宅開発金融
housing stocks　住宅関連株
new housing units authorized　新規住宅許可件数
new housing units started　新規住宅着工件数
U.S. federal housing agencies　米連邦住宅金融機関
vacancy rates in rental housing　賃貸住宅の空室率

housing collapse　住宅市場の崩壊
◆The United States is battling a housing collapse and the worst financial crisis since the 1930s. 米国は現在、住宅市場の崩壊や1930年代以来最悪の金融危機と戦っている。

housing correction　住宅の調整局面
◆In the United States, there is a risk of deeper and more prolonged housing correction. 米国では、住宅の調整局面が深刻化し、長引く恐れもある。

housing developer　住宅開発業者, 住宅開発販売業者
◆Housing developers recommend to customers that they take out adjustable rate mortgages to promote home sales. 住宅開発販売業者は、住宅販売を促進するため、変動金利型の住宅ローンを客に勧めている。

housing industry　住宅産業
（⇒mortgage foreclosure）
◆The housing industry is being battered by a prolonged slump. 住宅産業は、長期低迷の影響をもろに受けている。◆The U.S. housing industry and the government must respond to a severe credit crunch that began in August 2007. 米国の住宅産業界と政府は、2007年8月に始まった深刻な金融危機への対応を迫られている。

housing investment　住宅投資　（⇒housing loan）
◆A housing investment slump results from the enforcement of the revised Building Standards Law. 住宅投資の落ち込みは、改正建築基準法の施行によるものだ。◆Housing investment, a driving force for the U.S. economy until recently, has shown signs of a slowdown. 最近まで米景気を牽引してきた住宅投資に、減速感が見られる。

housing loan　住宅金融, 住宅ローン
　housing loan company　住宅金融専門会社, 住専
　Housing Loan Corporation　住宅金融公庫（2007年4月1日に独立行政法人の住宅金融支援機構（Japan Housing Finance Agency）に改称。⇒bracket, housing starts for custom-made houses）
　housing loan for disaster-hit region　災害復興住宅融資
　housing loan guarantee　住宅ローンの保証, 住宅ローン保証保険
　housing loan insurance　住宅融資保険, 住宅ローン保険
　housing loans for individuals　個人向け住宅ローン
◆The preferential tax system for housing loans has taken root as a way of promoting housing investment and sustaining economy. 住宅ローン減税制度は、住宅投資を促し、景気を支える手段として定着している。

housing loan claim　住宅ローンの債権
　housing loan claim trust　住宅ローン債権信託
　securitize housing loan claims　住宅ローン債権を証券化する
◆The Japan Housing Finance Agency plans to securitize housing loan claims bought from financial institutions. 住宅金融支援機構（独立行政法人で、旧住宅金融公庫が2007年4月1日に改称）は、金融機関から買い取った住宅ローンの債権を証券化する方針だ。

housing loan tax break　住宅ローン減税, 住宅減税
（=preferential tax system for housing loans）
◆Abolishing the housing loan tax break would reduce the number of housing starts by 100,000, which translates into an economic loss of ￥4.6 trillion. 住宅ローン減税［住宅減税］を廃止した場合、住宅着工戸数は10万戸減り、経済損失は4兆6,000億円に及ぶ。

housing market　住宅市場
◆Goldman Sachs Group Inc. is said to have marketed risky investments that bet on the housing market's growth just before the mortgage meltdown. ゴールドマン・サックスは、住宅ローン市場の崩壊直前に、住宅市場の成長を見越した［予想した］高リスクの金融商品［投資商品］を販売したとされる。◆If the U.S. housing market and financial sector recover, we won't need to worry about the outflow of funds to emerging countries. 米国の住宅市場や金融部門が回復すれば、新興国への資金の流出を気にしなくて済む。◆The investment bank reaped billions of dollars from its own bets that the housing market would collapse. この投資銀行は、住宅市場が崩壊するとの独自の予想で、数十億ドルの利益を上げていた。◆The U.S. economy has been hit by a chilled housing market and shrinking employment. 米経済は、住宅市場の冷え込みと雇用の落ち込みで打撃を受けている。◆The U.S. government filed lawsuits against 17 financial firms for selling Fannie and Freddie mortgage-backed securities that turned toxic when the housing market collapsed. 米政府は、住宅市場崩壊時に不良資産化した住宅ローン担保証券（MBS）をファニー・メイ（米連邦住宅抵当公庫）とフレディ・マック（米連邦住宅貸付け抵当公社）に販売したとして、大手金融機関17社（バンク・オブ・アメリカやシティグループ、JPモルガン・チェース、ゴールドマン・サックス・グループなど）を提訴した。

housing mortgage meltdown　住宅ローン市場の崩壊
◆A U.S. housing mortgage meltdown shook the United States, Europe and other countries and slammed the brakes on global growth. 米国の住宅ローン市場の崩壊は、米欧その他の諸国を揺さぶり、世界経済の成長に急ブレーキをかけた。◆The financial crisis stemmed from a U.S. housing mortgage meltdown. 今回の金融危機は、米国の住宅ローン市場の崩壊から始まった。

housing starts　住宅着工, 住宅着工戸数, 住宅着工件数, 新設住宅着工戸数
◆Housing starts and public investment also remained sluggish. 住宅着工戸数［住宅投資］や公共投資も、停滞したままだ。◆The business climate for home builders has been severe as housing starts have not expanded much in recent years. 新設住宅の着工戸数がここ数年伸び悩んでいるため、住宅メーカーを取り巻く企業環境は厳しい。

housing starts for custom-made houses　持ち家の住宅着工戸数
◆Among housing starts for custom-made houses, those funded by loans from the state-run Housing Loan Corporation plunged 40.2 percent to 126,105 units. 持ち家の住宅着工戸数のうち、国営の住宅金融公庫（2007年4月1日に独立行政法人の住宅金融支援機構に改称）の住宅ローン利用戸数は、40.2%減の12万6,105戸にとどまった。

hover　(動)推移する,（ある水準に）とどまる, 低迷する, 張り付く, 付きまとう
　hover around 10 percent level　10%前後で推移する, 10%の水準で推移する
　hover at around　〜のあたりを低迷する, 〜前後［近辺］で推移する, 〜あたりだ
　hover in a narrow range　小幅な値動きとなる
◆The firm's stock has been hovering around several hundred yen. 同社の株価は、数百円台で推移している。◆The Nikkei Stock Average has been hovering around the ￥10,000 line. 日経平均株価は、1万円台に張り付いた状態が続いている。◆The per-barrel price has been hovering around the lower end of the $110 level in recent weeks. 1バレル当たりの原油価格は、ここ数週間、110ドル台前半で推移している。◆The ratio of college students graduating next spring who have re-

ceived unofficial job offers hovered at around just 60 percent as of October. 来春の大卒予定者の就職内定率は、10月現在で約60%に低迷している。◆The ten-year Italian bond yield is hovering around 7 percent, which is said to be a dangerous zone that may result in a debt crisis. 10年物イタリア国債の利回り［流通利回り］は、債務危機に陥るとされる危険水域の7%近辺で高止まりしている。◆The 225-issue Nikkei Stock Average has been hovering around its highest level in 50 months. 日経平均株価（225種）は、4年2か月ぶりの高水準で推移している。◆The yen has been hovering near its record high of ￥76.25 against the U.S. dollar in Tokyo. 東京外国為替市場の円相場は、戦後最高値の1ドル＝76円25銭に迫る水準で推移している。◆The yen hovered in a narrow range in the upper ￥85 level to the dollar. 円相場は、1ドル＝85円台後半の小幅な値動きとなった。◆The yen is currently hovering at a level stronger than ￥80 to the dollar. 円相場は現在［足元の円相場は］、1ドル＝80円を上回る水準で推移している。

huge （形）大きな, 巨大な, 多大な, 莫大な（enormous）, 大規模の, 大型の, 大幅な, 巨額の, 超有名な, ビッグな
 a huge amount of public funds 巨額の公的資金
 huge amounts of debt 巨額の負債
 huge current account deficits 巨額の経常赤字
 huge facilities 大規模施設, 大規模な生産拠点
 huge growth in demand 需要の大幅な伸び
 huge stimulus measures 大型の景気刺激策, 大型の経済対策
 ◆A huge number of government bonds issued by the United States and European countries are possessed by financial institutions around the world. 米国や欧州各国が発行した大量の国債は、世界の金融機関が保有している。◆If the value of a huge number of government bonds possessed by financial institutions around the world plummets, financial instability will grow. 世界の金融機関が保有する大量の国債の価格が急落すれば、金融不安が高まることになる。◆On Sept 7, 2008, the U.S. government earmarked a huge amount of public funds to help government-affiliated mortgage financiers Freddie Mac and Fannie Mae. 2008年9月7日に米政府は、政府系住宅金融公社のフレディ・マック（連邦住宅抵当貸付公社）とファニー・メイ（連邦住宅抵当金庫［公庫］）を救済するため、巨額の公的資金投入を決めた。◆Some of huge amounts in loans extended to JAL by the DBJ have been guaranteed by the government. 日本政策投資銀行が日航に行った巨額融資［貸付け］の一部は、政府が保証している。◆Without the government financial support, TEPCO will fall into debt as the utility has to pay the huge amounts in compensation. 政府の金融支援がなければ、東電は巨額の賠償金を支払わなければならないので、債務超過に陥ると思われる。

huge fiscal debts 巨額の財政赤字
 ◆Spain and Portugal hold huge fiscal debts similar to that of Greece. スペインとポルトガルは、ギリシャと並んで巨額の財政赤字を抱えている。

huge fiscal deficits 巨額の財政赤字
 ◆The rapid spread of Italy's credit crisis is due to intensified fears about the nation's fiscal predicament by Italy's huge fiscal deficits. イタリアの信用不安が急速に広がったのは、イタリアの巨額の赤字で同国の財政ひっ迫への警戒感が高まったからだ。

huge funds 巨額の資金
 ◆The administration of Prime Minister Yukio Hatoyama doled out huge funds without showing a clear road map for fiscal rehabilitation. 鳩山政権は、財政再建の道筋を示さないで、巨額の金をバラまいた。◆The purpose of postal privatization was to do away with the current inefficient system, in which huge funds raised through inflated postal savings and kampo life insurance policies flow into public corporations. 郵政民営化の目的は、肥大した郵便貯金と簡易保険で調達した巨額の資金が特殊法人に流れる現在の非効率的なシステムを、廃止することにあった。

huge losses 巨額の損失
 ◆Shinsei and Aozora banks suffered huge losses in their overseas investment business in the aftermath of the global financial crisis triggered by the collapse of Lehman Brothers Holdings Inc. in autumn 2008. 新生銀行とあおぞら銀行は、2008年秋のリーマン・ブラザーズの経営破たんで始まった世界的な金融危機の影響で、海外投資事業に巨額の損失が発生した。

huge sell order 大量の売り注文
 ◆Mizuho Securities Co. placed a huge errant sell order for the newly listed shares of recruitment firm J-Com Co. みずほ証券が、人材サービス業ジェイコムの新規上場株式に対し、誤って大量の売り注文を出してしまった。

huge stimulus measures 大型の景気刺激策, 大型の経済対策
 ◆The government has tried to avoid economic contraction through huge stimulus measures. 政府は、大型の景気刺激策［経済対策］で景気悪化の回避に努めている。

hundreds of billions of yen 数千億円
 ◆Publicly listing Tokyo Metro and selling shares in it could net the government hundreds of billions of yen. 東京地下鉄（東京メトロ）の株式を上場して保有株式を売却すれば、国は数千億円の収入を見込める。

hurt （動）損害を与える, 損なう, 阻害する, 打撃を与える, 悪影響を与える, 妨害する, ダメージを与える（⇒import名詞）
 be hurt by ～で損害を受ける, ～により打撃を受ける
 hurt competition 競争を阻害する
 hurt consumer prices 消費者物価が上昇する
 hurt exports 輸出が打撃を受ける
 hurt one's reputation ～の評判を損なう
 hurt the economy 経済に打撃を与える, 景気に悪影響を与える
 hurt the yen 円が下落する, 円安となる, 円が売られる
 ◆Rising energy and raw material costs as well as weak exports have increasingly hurt the economy. 燃料費や原材料コストの高騰と輸出低迷によって、経済は一段と打撃を受けている。◆Some observers predicted that the global financial crisis would hurt Japan the least. 日本は世界金融危機による傷が世界で最も浅い、と見る向きもあった。◆The decoupling theory suggests that China and India would not be hurt by a global slowdown. ディカップリング論によると、中国やインドなどは世界的な景気減速の影響を受けないとされる。◆The strong yen can hurt the Japanese economy. 円高は、日本経済にダメージを与える可能性がある。◆The yen's appreciation against the dollar hurts the nation's export-led recovery. 円高・ドル安は、日本の輸出主導の景気回復に悪影響を与える。◆There are serious concerns that the strong yen and the weak U.S. dollar could hurt the current economic upturn led by exports. 大きな懸念材料は、円高・ドル安の進行で現在の輸出主導の景気回復が打撃を受けることだ。

hush money 口止め料
 ◆The company paid ￥63 million hush money to a construction firm. 同社は、建築会社に6,300万円の口止め料を支払っていた。

hypothecation agreement 担保契約

I

IAIS 保険監督者国際機構（International Association of Insurance Supervisorsの略）

IAS 国際会計基準, 国際会計基準書（International Accounting Standardsの略。国際会計基準委員会（IASC）

が設定した会計基準書）
◆Japanese companies listed on the London Stock Exchange will submit financial reports based on the IAS or the U.S. GAAP. ロンドン証券取引所に上場している日本企業は今後、国際会計基準か米国会計基準に基づく［に準拠した］財務報告書を提出することになる。

IASB 国際会計基準審議会（International Accounting Standards Boardの略）

IASC 国際会計基準委員会 IBRD（International Accounting Standards Committeeの略。IASBの前身）

IBRD 国際復興開発銀行, 第一世銀, 世界銀行（International Bank for Reconstruction and Developmentの略。国連専門機関の一つで、1946年に設立。ワシントンに本部を置き、日本は1952年に加盟）

IC ATM card ICキャッシュ・カード
◆The new IC ATM cards of the bank will have advanced functions such as digital money and a point system. 同行の新型ICキャッシュ・カードには、デジタル・マネーやポイント制などの先端機能が採用される。

ID 発信者番号, 識別符号, 識別番号（identificationの略）
ID card　身分証明書, IDカード　（=identity card）
user ID　ユーザーID, ユーザー名
（=log-in ID, username）
◆Illegal access of Internet banking accounts using account holders' user IDs and passwords was confirmed at 51 financial institutions. 口座名義人のユーザーID［ユーザー名］やパスワードを使ったネット・バンキングの口座への不正アクセスが、51金融機関で確認された。

ID number ID番号, 識別番号, 納税者番号, 取引先番号（⇒identification number）
◆In the United States and Scandinavian countries, tax administration is based on social security ID numbers or resident ID numbers that are assigned to all members of the populace. 米国や北欧諸国では、納税事務は、全国民に付けられる社会保障番号や住民登録番号に基づいて行われている。

IDA 国際開発協会, 第二世界銀行（International Development Associationの略。発展途上国のうち特に所得の低い貧困国を対象に、主に無利子融資による支援を行う世界銀行グループの国際機関。1960年発足、現在は162か国が加盟しており、現在の資本金は1,093億ドルとなっている）

IDB 米州開発銀行（Inter-American Development Bankの略）

idea （名）考え, 構想, 意見, 見解, 思いつき, 着想, 考え方, 概念, 観念, 思想, 目的, 意図, 計画, 狙（ねら）い, 見当, 感じ, 予感, 印象, 漠然とした知識, アイデア
exchange ideas with　～と意見交換する
fixed idea　固定観念
foolish idea　愚策（ぐさく）
fresh idea　斬新なアイデア
general ideas　一般観念
good idea　名案
idea advertising　意見広告
idea generation　アイデア創造, アイデア発想
new idea　新しいアイデア, 新構想, 新しい思想
original idea　独創的なアイデア
outdated idea　時代遅れの考え方［思想］
product idea　商品［製品］アイデア
task idea　課業アイデア
◆European regulators had previously played down the idea of a blanket ban on short selling. 欧州の規制当局は、空売りの全面規制［禁止］という考え方を以前は問題にしていなかった。
◆The government, labor unions and business leaders have had many discussions about the employment situation and have proposed various ideas. 雇用情勢については、政府、労

組、経済界のトップがこれまでに多くの議論を展開して、さまざまなアイデアを出してきた。◆We do not hold the idea that big banks are too big to fail. われわれとしては、「巨大銀行が破たんさせるには大き過ぎる」という考え方は取らない。

identification （名）本人確認, 身元確認, 照合, 識別番号, 発信者番号, ID
identification papers　身分証明書類
personal identification number　銀行カードの個人暗証番号, PIN
◆The law on the identification of bank account holders was put into force in January 2003. 銀行口座名義人の本人確認に関する法律（本人確認法）は、2003年1月に施行された。

identification number ID番号, 識別番号, 納税者番号, 取引先番号　（=ID number, identifier number; ⇒stock dividend）
◆Viruses used in illegal transfers via online banking services collect Internet banking account-related information such as personal identification numbers and transmit them to remote parties. ネット・バンキングでの不正送金に使われたウイルスは、個人の暗証番号などネット・バンキングの口座関連情報を収集して、外部に送信する。◆We must change our personal identification number first to prevent the recurrence of online fraud. オンライン詐欺の再発を防ぐには、まずパスワードを変えなければならない。

identity 身元, 正体, 身分証明, 本人, アイデンティティ（⇒Internet cafe, scanner）
corporate identity　コーポレート・アイデンティティ, 企業イメージ統合戦略
identity card　IDカード　（=identification card）
verify the identity of new depositors　新規預金者の身元を確認する
◆Concerns have been raised over the ability of Internet banking services to verify the identity of new depositors or to guarantee the security of customer transactions. インターネット・バンキングについては、新規預金者の身元確認や対顧客取引の安全保証の点で、その能力に対して懸念が提起されている。◆One of the three relevant laws requires financial institutions to confirm the identity of people opening accounts and those making financial transactions of more than ￥2 million. 関連3法の一つは、金融機関に対して、口座開設時や200万円を超える資金取引時の顧客の身元確認を義務付けている。

idle real estate 遊休不動産
◆Nonperforming loans will be transferred to the revival account, as well as crossheld shares and idle real estate. 不良債権は、持ち合い株式や遊休不動産などと一緒に「再生勘定」に移す。

IFC 国際金融公社, 第三世銀
（⇒International Finance Corporation）

IFRIC 国際財務報告解釈委員会（International Financial Reporting Interpretations Committeeの略）

IFRS 国際財務報告基準書, 国際財務報告規準（International Financial Reporting Standardの略。国際会計基準審議会（International Financial Reporting Standard）が作成。2004年まで「国際会計基準（IAS）」と呼ばれていた。⇒International Accounting Standards）
the first IFRS financial statements　企業最初のIFRS財務諸表
the first IFRS reporting period　企業最初のIFRS報告期間
◆The Financial Services Agency gave up its initial goal to make the introduction of the IFRS mandatory in around 2015. 金融庁は、2015年にもIFRS（国際財務報告規準）の導入を義務化するという当初の目標を断念した。

IFRSs 国際財務報告基準, イファース［アイファース、アイエフアールエス］（International Financial Reporting Standardsの略。IAS（国際会計基準書）、IFRS（国際財務

報告基準書）と、IFRIC（国際財務報告委員会）解釈指針、SIC（解釈指針委員会）解釈指針等から成る会計基準の総称）
  the date of transition to IFRSs　IFRSsへの移行日
  the first-time adopter of IFRSs　IFRSs初度適用企業
  ◆In the aftermath of the March 11 massive earthquake and tsunami, the Financial Services Agency will likely postpone the introduction of IFRSs. 東日本大震災（2011年3月11日）の影響で、金融庁は国際財務報告基準（IFRS）の導入を延期する方向だ。◆It will take about five to seven years to shift to the IFRSs if they become mandatory. 国際財務報告基準（IFRSs）が強制適用となると、IFRSsに移行するのに5〜7年程度はかかる。◆The consolidated financial statements conform in all material respects with International Financial Reporting Standards (IFRSs). 連結財務書類［連結財務諸表］の重要事項は、すべて国際財務報告基準に適合している。◆The IFRSs are based on mark-to-market accounting and was adopted by the London based International Accounting Standards Board. 国際財務報告基準（IFRSs）は、時価会計をベースとし、ロンドンに本部を置く国際会計基準審議会（IASB）によって採択された。

ignite　（動）〜に点火する、火をつける、発火させる、引き起こす、燃やす、燃え上がらせる、焼く、燃焼させる、〜を引き起こす発端になる、〜に火がつく、〜に燃え移る
  ignite an export-driven economic upturn　輸出主導の景気回復につながる
  ignite fears of inflation　インフレ懸念を呼ぶ
  ◆A depreciation of the dollar may stimulate external demand and ignite an export-driven economic upturn. ドル安は、外需を喚起して、輸出主導の景気回復につながる可能性がある。◆The surge in prices of natural resources could ignite fears of inflation, causing countries around the world to implement tight monetary policies. 天然資源の価格急騰がインフレ懸念を呼び、世界各国が金融引締め政策を実施する可能性がある。

ignore　（動）無視する、耳を傾けない、ないがしろにする、放置する、（重要点を）見落とす、（起訴状を証拠不十分として）却下する (reject)
  ◆Citigroup Private Bank's four offices in Japan will have their licenses revoked for violating the law by ignoring suspected money laundering by clients. シティバンクのプライベート・バンク（PB）の在日4拠点（支店・出張所）が、顧客のマネー・ロンダリング（資金洗浄）の疑いのある取引を放置するなどして法令違反があったとして、認可を取り消されることになった。

illegal　（形）違法な、非合法な、不法な
  illegal access　不正アクセス
  illegal copy　違法コピー
  illegal donations　ヤミ献金、違法献金
  illegal moneylender　違法金融業者、ヤミ金融業者 (=illicit moneylenders)
  illegal moneylending operations　違法金融、ヤミ金融 (⇒confiscate)
  illegal operation　不法操作
  illegal trade　不正取引 (=illegal transaction)
  illegal trafficking　不法売買
  ◆The Financial Services Agency ordered Sompo Japan Insurance Inc. to suspend part of its operations as punishment for the major insurance company's illegal business practices. 金融庁は、損保大手の損害保険ジャパンに業務で法令違反があったとして、同社に一部業務停止命令を出した。

illegal access　不正アクセス
  ◆Illegal access of Internet banking accounts using account holders' user IDs and passwords was confirmed at 51 financial institutions. 口座名義人のユーザーID［ユーザー名］やパスワードを使ったネット・バンキングの口座への不正アクセスが、51金融機関で確認された。◆In illegal access of Internet bank accounts confirmed at financial institutions, money was transferred from a client's account to a second account. 金融機関で確認されたネット・バンキング口座への不正アクセスでは、顧客の口座から現金が他人名義の口座に振り込まれていた［送信されていた］。

illegal activities　違法行為
  ◆The FSA inspections exposed the bank's illegal activities. 金融庁の検査で、同行の違法行為が暴かれた。

illegal lending　違法貸付け、ヤミ金融 (=illegal moneylending)
  ◆In most illegal lending cases, operators were arrested for allegedly collecting interest on loans beyond the legal upper limit of 29.2% a year. ヤミ金融事件の大半は、業者が年29.2％の法定上限金利を上回る高金利の取立てで逮捕されている。

illegal moneylending　違法貸付け、ヤミ金融
  ◆Sellers of multiple-debtor lists, produced by collecting information about consumer finance customers, are contributing to the spread of illegal moneylending. 消費者金融の顧客情報を入手して作った多重債務者リストを売る名簿業者が、ヤミ金融の横行に一役買っている。

illegal moneylending operations　ヤミ金融
  ◆About ¥4 billion acquired by a criminal gang through illegal moneylending operations will be confiscated. 暴力団がヤミ金融で得た約40億円が、没収されることになった。

illegal payment of dividends　違法配当、配当金の違法支払い
  ◆The wrongdoings of former executives, including the illegal payment of dividends, caused enormous losses for the bank. 旧経営陣の違法配当などの不法行為で、同銀行に多額の損失が出た。

illegal practices　不正取引の手法、不正取引慣行
  ◆In the future also, new types of illegal practices that exploit legal loopholes will emerge in securities markets. 今後も、証券市場では、法の抜け穴を狙う不正取引の手法が新たに現れるものと思われる。

illegal short selling　違法な空売り
  ◆On the stock market, many are flooding the market and making a killing through illegal short selling. 株式市場では、違法な空売りで売り浴びせて荒稼ぎしている者が多い。

illegal trades of stock　株の不正取引
  ◆A former Aozora Bank employee arrested for alleged insider trading is now suspected of having conducted additional illegal trades of stock in two more companies. インサイダー取引容疑で逮捕されたあおぞら銀行元行員が、さらに2社の株でも不正取引を行っていた疑いがある。

illegal transaction　仮装売買、不正取引、不正取引の売買業務、違法取引 (=illegal trade)
  ◆Financial authorities should stiffen the penalties for illegal transactions to protect the financial system from rumors and speculative investment. 金融当局は違法取引（違法行為）に対する罰則を強化して、金融システムを風評や投機［投機的投資］から守らなければならない。◆Prosecutors searched the premises of the Osaka Securities Exchange Co. in an investigation into alleged illegal transactions. 検察当局は、仮装売買疑惑の捜査で大阪証券取引所（大証）の社屋を捜索した。

illegal transfer　不正送金
  ◆Illegal transfers of deposits via foreign malware have been jumping. 海外のマルウェア（コンピュータ・ウイルスの一種）による預金の不正送金が急増している。◆In illegal transfers via online banking services, viruses such as Spy Eye and Zbot have been used. ネット・バンキングでの不正送金では、スパイアイやゼットボットなどと呼ばれるウイルスが使われている。◆Online banking users can prevent illegal transfers of their deposits by frequently changing their passwords. オンライン・バンキング利用者は、パスワードをこまめに変更して、預金の不正送金を防ぐことができる。◆Regional bank accounts

were hit hardest by illegal transfers via foreign malware. 海外のマルウエア（コンピュータ・ウイルスの一種）による不正送金の被害は、地方銀行の口座が最多だった。◆The total amount of damage by illegal transfers through Internet banking services came to about ￥265 million in 91 cases since April. インターネット・バンキングでの不正送金による被害総額は、4月から91件で約2億6,500万円に上った。◆Viruses used in illegal transfers via online banking services collect Internet banking account-related information such as personal identification numbers and transmit them to remote parties. ネット・バンキングでの不正送金に使われたウイルスは、個人の暗証番号などネット・バンキングの口座関連情報を収集して、外部に送信する。

illegally obstruct　違法に妨害する
　◆Financial regulators asked prosecutors to investigate allegations that UFJ Holdings Inc.'s banking unit illegally obstructed recent inspections by reporting misleading information about its nonperforming loans. 金融当局は、UFJ銀行が不良債権に関する虚偽の情報を報告して最近の検査を違法に妨害したとして、同行を検察当局に刑事告発した。

illicit activities　違法行為
　◆The U.S. government froze the assets of four individuals and eight entities that were involved in illicit activities such as money laundering, currency counterfeiting and narcotics trafficking. 米政府は、資金洗浄（マネー・ロンダリング）や通貨偽造、麻薬取引などの違法行為に関与している4個人、8団体の資産を凍結した。

illicit loan operator　違法貸金業者, ヤミ金融業者
　（=illegal loan operator）

illicit moneylender　ヤミ金融業者
　（=illegal moneylender）

illiquid　（形）流動性のない, 流動性の低い, 流動性に乏しい, 非流動的な, 現金化できない, 換金しにくい
　illiquid asset　非流動資産, 流動性に乏しい資産, 流動性のない資産
　illiquid core assets　流動性のないコア資産
　illiquid fund　非流動資金
　illiquid funds　非流動資産
　illiquid issues　流動性の低い銘柄
　illiquid market　流動性の低い市場, 流動性を欠く市場

illiquidity　（名）非流動性, 流動性不足, 流動性の欠如
　illiquidity asset　非流動性資産
　illiquidity of the balance sheet　バランス・シートの流動性欠如
　illiquidity problem　流動性不足問題
　illiquidity risk　非流動性リスク
　market illiquidity　市場の流動性低下, 市場の流動性が低いこと, 市場のひっ迫
　◆Illiquidity refers to the lack of cash on hand. 流動性不足とは、手元に現金がないことを言う。◆In the case of liquidity crisis, it is impossible for a borrower to repay its debt in the short term due to illiquidity. 流動性危機の場合は、流動性不足のため［手元に現金がないため］、借り手が短期間で債務を返済することはできない。

imbalance　（名）不均衡, 差, アンバランス
　balance of payments imbalance　国際収支の不均衡
　　（=payment imbalance）
　fix imbalance　不均衡を是正する　（⇒fix）
　global imbalance　世界的な国際収支の不均衡, グローバル・インバランス
　growing global imbalance　世界的な不均衡の拡大
　supply and demand imbalances　需要と供給の不均衡, 需給不均衡
　　（=imbalances between supply and demand）
　trade imbalance　貿易の不均衡, 貿易不均衡

　（⇒import growth）
　◆At the Seoul G-20 summit, all the leaders agreed to introduce "indicative guidelines" that would be conductive to reducing current account imbalances. 主要20か国・地域（G20）のソウル・サミット（首脳会議）で、全首脳が、経常収支不均衡の是正に役立つ「参考指針」を導入することで合意した。◆The undervalued yuan has kept China's international competitiveness, adding to its trade imbalances with the United States and other nations. 人民元の過小評価が、中国の国際競争力を不当に高め、米国などとの貿易不均衡を拡大している。

imbalance of the world economy　世界経済の不均衡
　◆The focus of discussions has shifted from exchange rates themselves to the imbalance of the world economy. 議論の焦点が、為替相場［為替レート］そのものから世界経済の不均衡問題に移っている。

IMF　国際通貨基金
　（⇒International Monetary Fund）
　an IMF statement　IMFの意見書
　deputy managing director of the IMF　IMF副専務理事
　IMF annual consultation　IMF年次協議, IMF年次会議
　IMF Board of Directors　IMF理事会
　IMF Board of Governors　IMF総務会
　IMF credit　IMF借款
　IMF drawing［purchase］　IMF引出し
　IMF executive directors　IMF理事会
　IMF foreign exchange rate system　IMF為替相場制
　IMF general account　IMF一般勘定
　IMF gross fund position　IMFグロス・ファンド・ポジション（（各国出資額×2）- IMFの各国通貨保有額＋一般借入額）
　IMF interim committee　IMF暫定委員会
　IMF managing director　IMF専務理事
　IMF mission　IMF代表団
　IMF par value　IMF平価
　IMF position　IMFポジション
　IMF quota　IMF割当額, IMFクォータ（IMFが加盟国に割り当てている拠出金［IMFの加盟国への出資割当額］）
　IMF repayment　IMF返済
　IMF repurchase　IMF買戻し
　IMF reserve position　IMF準備ポジション（IMF加盟国からの借入金総額で、IMFがいつでも返済することになっている。⇒foreign exchange reserves）
　IMF reserve tranche　IMFリザーブ・トランシュ（IMFから無条件で融資される部分で、IMF割当額とIMF自国保有額との差額）
　IMF special drawing account　IMF特別引出し勘定
　IMF special drawing rights　IMF特別引出し権, SDR［SDRs］　（⇒foreign exchange reserves）
　IMF standby agreement　IMF借入予約協定, IMFスタンドバイ取決め［契約］
　IMF subscription　IMF出資
　limit of financial assistance　金融支援枠 財政支援枠
　managing director of the IMF　IMF専務理事
　request assistance from the IMF　IMFに支援を要請する
　　（⇒reluctant）
　the IMF's Executive Board　IMF理事会
　　（=the IMF's executive body）
　Trust Fund of IMF　IMF信託基金
　◆According to an estimate of the International Monetary Fund（IMF）, should U.S. stocks fall by 20 percent and the dollar fall by the same margin against the yen and euro, the U.S. economic growth rate would fall by 1.4 percent, and that of Japan and euro-zone countries by 1.1 percent, re-

spectively. 国際通貨基金(IMF)の試算によると、米国の株価が20%下落してドルの対円、対ユーロ相場が20%下落すると、米国の経済成長率は1.4%低下し、日本とユーロ圏の経済成長率はそれぞれ1.1%低下する。◆Argentina clinched a debt rollover deal with the IMF after a year of tortuous negotiations. アルゼンチンは、1年にわたる難交渉の末、国際通貨基金(IMF)との債務返済繰延べ取引をまとめた。◆As a condition for loans to financially troubled countries in the late 1990s, the IMF called for strict implementation of structural reforms. 1990年代後半に財政難に陥った国に対する融資の条件として、IMF(国際通貨基金)は、厳しい構造改革の実施を求めた。◆At the latest G-20 meeting, diverging opinions among member countries were exposed over expanding the lending capacity of the IMF. 今回のG20(財務相・中央銀行総裁)会議では、国際通貨基金(IMF)が融資できる資金規模の拡大をめぐって、加盟国の間で意見の食い違いが表面化した。◆French Finance Minister Christine Lagarde was chosen as the new managing director of the IMF. IMFの新専務理事に、クリスティーヌ・ラガルド仏財務相が選ばれた。◆Greece must avert a crippling debt default by securing billions of dollars in emergency loans from European countries and the IMF. ギリシャは、欧州諸国[ユーロ圏]と国際通貨基金(IMF)による緊急融資で巨額の資金を確保して、壊滅的な債務不履行を回避しなければならない。◆Greece was bailed out temporarily with financial support of €110 billion (about ¥12.7 trillion) from the IMF and the European Union. ギリシャは、IMFと欧州連合(EU)から1,100億ユーロ(約12兆7,000億円)の金融支援を受けて、一時的に救済された。◆In order to bring the European crisis under control, the EU, ECB and IMF must work even more closely together. 欧州危機の収束を図るには、欧州連合(EU)、欧州中央銀行(ECB)と国際通貨基金(IMF)の緊密な連携を強化する必要がある。◆In the conventional IMF's scheme, countries were only given a credit line even after the IMF approved loans and they could not withdraw funds unless the fiscal crisis facing them worsened. 従来のIMF(国際通貨基金)の仕組みだと、各国は融資の承認を得ても融資枠を与えられるだけで、財政危機が深刻化しないと資金を引き出すことができなかった。◆Italy's contribution to the IMF totals about $12.6 billion. イタリアのIMF(国際通貨基金)への出資総額は、約126億ドルだ。◆Several nations of the IMF's 24-member Executive Board agreed that the yuan was undervalued. 24か国で構成されているIMF理事会の一部の国は、人民元相場が過小評価されているとの認識で一致した。◆Since May 2010, Greece has been reliant in regular payouts from a €110 billion bailout from other eurozone countries and the IMF. 2010年5月からギリシャは、他のユーロ圏諸国やIMF(国際通貨基金)などからの1,100億ユーロの金融支援による融資の定期支払い金に頼っている。◆The government plans to raise the limit of its financial assistance to the Nuclear Damage Liability Facilitation Fund from ¥2 trillion to ¥5 trillion. 政府は、原子力損害賠償支援機構への金融支援枠を、現在の2兆円から5兆円に拡大する方針だ。◆The IMF and the EU are strengthening their cooperation to avert a Greek default and prevent a chain reaction of debt crisis among other countries. ギリシャの債務不履行(デフォルト)を回避し他国間の債務危機の連鎖反応を防ぐため、国際通貨基金(IMF)と欧州連合(EU)は、連携を強めている。◆The IMF and the EU have worked out a policy of extending emergency loans to Greece. 国際通貨基金(IMF)と欧州連合(EU)は、ギリシャに緊急融資を行う方針を打ち出した。◆The IMF currently has about $400 billion in resources on hand. IMF(国際通貨基金)は現在、手元に約4,000億ドル分の財源を残している。◆The IMF extends to countries with relatively healthier public finances one- to two-year loans of up to 1,000 percent of their contribution to the IMF without strict conditions. IMF(国際通貨基金)は、財政が比較的健全な国に対して、期間1～2年の資金を厳しい条件なしでIMFに出資している額(クォータ)の最大10倍まで融資している。◆The IMF threw its weight behind the establishment of a bad bank. 国際通貨基金(IMF)は、バッド・バンクの設立を後押しした。◆The IMF's Executive Board is divided over whether the Chinese currency is undervalued. IMF理事会は、人民元相場が過小評価されているかどうかで、意見が分かれている。◆The IMF's new financing scheme is expected to be agreed on at the Group of 20 summit meeting and will be launched after being approved by the IMF's board of directors. 国際通貨基金(IMF)の新融資制度は、主要20か国・地域(G20)サミット(首脳会議)で合意する見込みで、その後IMF理事会の承認を経てスタートする。◆The leaders of EU countries agreed on a bailout plan which would extend loans up to €200 billion to countries in fiscal crisis through the IMF. EU(欧州連合)各国首脳は、国際通貨基金(IMF)を通じて財政危機国に最大2,000億ユーロ(約21兆円)を貸し出す[融資する]救済策で合意した。◆The proposal to expand the lending capacity of the IMF was supported by Brazil and other emerging economies though Japan and the United States rejected it. 国際通貨基金(IMF)が融資できる資金規模を拡大する案は、日本と米国が受け入れなかったものの、ブラジルなどの新興国は支持した。◆To prevent the current fiscal and financial crisis in Europe from spreading, the IMF will create a new short-term lending facility. 現在の欧州財政・金融危機の拡大を防ぐ[封じる]ため、国際通貨基金(IMF)が、新たな短期の融資制度を創設することになった。◆Trust in the IMF was lost by a scandal involving its former managing director. 国際通貨基金(IMF)の信認は、IMF前専務理事の不祥事で失われた。◆Under the existing agreement, the IMF cannot buy government bonds through the EFSF as the IMF can only offer loans to countries. 現行協定では、IMF(国際通貨基金)は国にしか融資できないので、欧州金融安定基金(EFSF)を通じて国債を購入することはできない。◆Under the new financing scheme, the IMF will extend to financially strapped countries loans of up to 500 percent of their contribution to the IMF. 新融資制度では、財政の資金繰りが苦しく[厳しく]なった国に対して、その国がIMF(国際通貨基金)に出資している額の最大5倍までIMFが融資する。

解説 IMFについて:1946年、自由貿易の発展に向けて、通貨システムを安定させる組織として設立された。加盟国は現在187か国で、加盟各国の経済政策を監視し、通貨危機に陥った国に対する「外貨の最後の貸し手」としての役割を担っている。出資額は米国が最大で、次いで日本となっている。

IMFC 国際通貨金融委員会, IMF国際通貨金融委員会 (International Monetary and Financial Committeeの略。国際通貨基金(IMF)の諮問機関で、IMFの政策の方向性と優先順位を決める。24人の委員で構成され、年2回開催される)

impact (動)影響を与える, 衝撃を与える
◆Earnings of the firm were impacted by difficulties in North American real estate markets. 同社の利益は、北米の不動産市場の低迷による影響を受けた。

impact (名)影響, 影響力, 効果, 打撃, 衝撃, 衝撃力, ショック, 衝突, 刺激, 強い印象, インパクト
(⇒global liquidity)
adverse impact　悪影響, 悪材料
deflationary impact　デフレ効果
disinflationary impact　インフレ抑制効果
economic impact　経済的衝撃
financial impact　財務上の影響, 財務的影響
forex impact　為替による影響, 為替の影響
 (=foreign exchange impact)
impact aid　米政府の財政的援助, 政府補助金(政府機関の公務員の子弟が通う学区に支払われる)
impact day [date]　発表日, インパクト・デー(株式や

社債の新規発行条件の公表日）
impact effect　即時的効果, 衝撃効果
impact from currency fluctuation　為替変動による影響, 為替変動の影響
impact loan　外貨借款, インパクト・ローン（使途を限定しない外貨貸付け［外貨貸付け, 外貨借入れ］）
impact of currency swings　為替相場の影響
impact of the declining cycle　景気後退の影響
impact on competitive position［moves］　競争力に与える影響, 競争力への影響
inflationary impact　インフレ圧力
lasting impact　長期的影響, 長期的効果, 長期効果
negative impact　マイナスの影響, マイナス効果, 悪影響
overall impact　全体への影響
positive impact　好影響, 好材料
reflationary impact　景気刺激効果
side impact　副次的効果［結果］
social impact　社会的影響
tax impact　租税公課
◆A portion of the increase in R&D spending was due to the unfavorable impact of foreign exchange on R&D expenditures. 研究開発費（R&D）増加の一部は、研究開発費に対する為替相場の不利な影響額によるものだ。◆Any additional easing measures would only have a limited impact if they were made at the urging of financial markets. 市場に催促される形で追加緩和を行っても、追加緩和策の効果は限定的に過ぎない。◆Before the bubble collapsed, many pundits had predicted that the likely downturn of the U.S. economy would have only a limited impact on the rest of the world. バブル経済の崩壊前には、「米経済はいずれ行き詰まるだろうが、他国への影響は限定的である」と専門家の多くは予測していた。◆Maintaining an easy monetary policy may lead to excessive corporate capital investment and have a negative impact on the sustainable economic recovery. 金融緩和政策を続けると、企業の過剰な設備投資を生み、景気の持続的回復を阻害する恐れがある。◆The Bank of Japan's resorting to quantitative easing in concert with the Fed would have a greater impact on in buoying the global economy. 米連邦準備制度理事会（FRB）と歩調を合わせて日銀が量的緩和に踏み切れば、世界景気の浮揚効果は拡大すると思われる。◆The impact of cutbacks stemming from the shrinking tax income is affecting local residents. 税収の減少による経費削減の衝撃は、地元住民にも影響を及ぼしている。

impair　（動）損なう, 弱める, 減じる, 劣化する, 制約する
　impaired capital　資本の欠損, 資本金の欠損
　impaired risks　信用リスク
　writing down impaired assets　不良債権［不良資産］の評価減
◆The rapid surge in the yen's value would impair the current improvement in the Japanese economy and deal a blow to the world economy. 急激な円高は、日本の現在の景気回復の腰を折り、世界経済にも大きなマイナスになる。

impaired asset　不良債権, 不良資産
◆Charges included in other accounts were primarily for expenses related to writing down impaired assets and merger-related expenses. その他の勘定科目に計上した費用は、主に不良資産の評価減と合併関連の費用です。◆In the European banking tests, banks' impaired assets were underestimated. 欧州の銀行検査では、銀行の不良資産が過小評価された。

impaired loans　不良債権, 劣化した貸出金, 貸出金の劣化
◆We compute present values for impaired loans when we determine our allowances for credit losses. 当社の貸倒れ引当金を決定するにあたって、当社は不良債権の現在価値を計算します。

impairment　（名）減損, 資本金の欠損, 損耗, 減価, 価値の下落, 劣化, 評価減
　accumulated impairment losses　減損損失累計
　assessment of impairment　価値の下落の評価
　impairment loss　減耗損失, 減損処理による損失
　impairment of loans　貸出金の劣化, 貸付け金の破損, 不良債権, 貸付け金の評価損
　impairment of value　資産価値の損耗
　indication of an asset's impairment　減損の兆候
　permanent impairment in value　回復不能減価, 条件などを設ける, 売りつける, 押し付ける, 強いる

impairment loss　減耗損失, 減損処理による損失
◆Olympus wrote off more than 75 percent of about 70 billion spent on the acquisitions of three domestic firms as impairment losses. オリンパスは、国内3社の買収に投じた約700億円の75％以上を、減耗損失として処理していた。

impairment of bank-owned assets　銀行保有資産の評価減
◆In the event of hefty appraisal losses, banks must avoid a situation in which their creditors, including depositors, will be affected by the impairment of bank-owned assets. 巨額の含み損が出た場合、銀行は、預金者などの債権者が銀行保有資産の評価減の影響を受けるような状況がないようにしなければならない。

impede　（動）妨げる, 邪魔する, 阻害する, 妨害する, ～の足かせになる
◆The doldrums in the manufacturing industry will impede the recovery of Japan's economy. 製造業の不振は、日本経済の回復の足かせにもなる。

imperative　（形）緊急の, 肝要な, 絶対必要な, 回避できない, 断固とした, 命令的な　（名）命令, 責務, 義務, 規範
◆The compilation of fiscal rehabilitation measures including raising the pension age is imperative for the Italian parliament. 年金受給年齢の引上げなどを含む財政再建策のとりまとめが、イタリア議会の急務となっている。◆The recent surges in the yen's strength have made it imperative for Japanese carmakers to substantially bring down their parts procurement costs by overseas sourcing. 最近の円高で、日本の自動車メーカー各社は、海外調達による部品調達コストの大幅引下げが緊急課題となっている。

implement　（動）実施する, 実行する, 遂行する, 施行する, 適用する
　implement an expansionary budget　積極型予算を実施する
　implement economic stimulus measures　景気対策を実施する
　implement painful austerity measures　痛みを伴う緊縮財政策を実行する
　implement the financial bailout plan　金融救済案を実施する
　implement the guidelines and sanctions　指導と制裁を実施する
◆Amid the depleted state coffers, it is difficult to implement a major stimulus package to rectify the rise in the yen's value. 財政悪化が進む中［国の財源が枯渇する中］、円高是正のため大規模な財政出動を行うのは難しい。◆Economic stimulus measures implemented so far include a supplementary budget for job creation. これまで実施された景気対策としては、補正予算による雇用の創出もある。◆The factory will implement its first renovation before April. 同工場では、4月までにまず最新設備の導入を実施する。◆The failure to implement fiscal consolidation in countries where it is necessary could undermine confidence and hamper growth. 財政健全化が必要な国で財政健全化を行わないと、信認を損ない、成長を阻害する可能性がある。◆The financial bailout plan contains many unclear points that will become apparent when

it is actually implemented. この金融救済案は、実際に実施してみないと分からない不透明な点が多い。◆The government will flexibly implement both economic and financial measures to deal with the slowdown in the economy. 政府は、経済対策と金融政策を機動的に実施して、景気減速に対応する方針だ。◆To deal with the systemic financial crisis, ministry and central bank officials had to take rescue measures, such as an injection of public funds, while at the same time implementing strict guidelines and sanctions. 連鎖的な金融危機に対処するにあたって、当局は公的資金の投入などの救済措置取ると同時に、厳しい指導や制裁を実施しなければならなかった。

implement an expansionary budget　積極型の予算を実施する
◆To make the economy's step toward recovery much firmer, the government should implement another expansionary budget. 景気回復の足取りをずっと確かなものにするためにも、政府はさらに積極型の予算を実施すべきだ。

implement austerity measures　緊縮財政策を実行［実施］する
◆Greece is forced to implement painful austerity measures, including cutting the number of government employees and raising taxes. ギリシャは、公務員の削減や増税など痛みを伴う緊縮財政策の実行を迫られている。

implement economic stimulus measures　景気対策を実施する
◆The government will implement economic stimulus measures worth ¥75 trillion through two supplementary budgets and the fiscal 2009 budget. 政府は、2回の補正予算と2009年度予算で、75兆円規模の景気対策を実施する。

implement fiscal and tax stimulus measures　財政・税制面からの景気刺激策を実施する
◆To enhance the stimulating effect of the Fed's rate cuts, the Bush administration is expected to swiftly implement fiscal and tax stimulus measures, including tax cuts on investment designed to reinvigorate the stock market, in addition to the large-scale tax cut program that is under way. 米連邦準備制度理事会（FRB）の金利引下げの刺激効果を高めるため、ブッシュ政権には、現在実施中の大型減税プログラムに加え、株式市場を再活性化するための投資減税など、財政・税制面からの景気刺激策の速やかな実施が期待されている。

implement monetary easing measures　金融緩和策を実施する、金融緩和を行う
◆The Bank of Japan has long been implementing monetary easing measures. 日銀は、金融緩和を長年続けている。

implement the initial public offering　株式の新規公募を実施する、株式を上場する
◆The management will aim to implement the initial public offering of the company in the autumn of 2011. 経営陣は、2011年秋の同社株式の上場を目指している。

implement the yen-selling market intervention　円売り介入［円売り市場介入］を実施する
◆Japan implemented the yen-selling market intervention unilaterally. 日本は、単独で円売り介入を実施した。

implementation　（名）実施、実行、遂行、履行、施行、運用、適用、開発、構築、実現、実装、インプリメンテーション
　aid implementation　援助実施
　implementation deadline　発効期限
　implementation guide　適用指針
　implementation of lease　リース履行
　implementation of monetary policy　金融政策の実施
　implementation of SFAS No. 60, Accounting and Reporting by Insurance Enterprises　SFAS第60号「保険会社が行う会計処理と報告」の適用
　implementation stage　実施段階
　policy implementation　政策の実施

　standards implementation group　基準適用グループ
◆As a condition for loans to financially troubled countries in the late 1990s, the IMF called for strict implementation of structural reforms. 1990年代後半に財政難に陥った国に対する融資の条件として、IMF（国際通貨基金）は、厳しい構造改革の実施を求めた。◆To enhance the stimulating effect of the Fed's rate cuts, swift implementation of fiscal and tax stimulus measures, including tax cuts on investment designed to reinvigorate the stock market, is necessary in addition to the large-scale tax cut program that is under way. 米連邦準備制度理事会（FRB）の金利引下げの刺激効果を高めるためには、現在実施中の大型減税プログラムに加え、株式市場を再活性化するための投資減税など、財政・税制面からの景気刺激策の速やかな実施が必要である。

implication　（名）影響、結果、かかわり合い、密接な関係、連座、巻き添えにすること、意味、裏の意味、意味合い、要因、材料、含み、含蓄、暗示、黙示、黙示的表示、もつれ合い、紛糾
　credit implications　格付けへの影響
　financial implications　財務上の影響
　have positive credit implications　信用力を高める要因になる、格付けの上でプラス要因である
　　（=have positive implications for credit）
　implications of the scandal　スキャンダルの影響
　inflationary implications　インフレへの影響
　negative implications　マイナス要因、悪材料
　political implication　政治的含み
　positive implications　プラス要因、好材料
　tax implications　税務上の取扱い
　the implications of the recession　不況の影響
◆The implications of the recession are becoming ever more serious. 不況の影響は、一段と深刻化している。

import　（動）輸入する、導入する、データなどを転送する、移動する、取り込む、持ち込む、発生させる
◆Aeon and Ito-Yokado started discount sales of foods imported from the United States to pass along to consumers the benefits of the yen's sharp climb against the dollar. イオンとイトーヨーカ堂は、急激な円高・ドル安による円高差益を消費者に還元するため、米国から輸入した食料品の値下げセールを開始した。

import　（名）輸入、輸入品、輸入製品、輸入額、導入 重要性、意味、インポート
　application for import license　輸入承認申請書
　capital import　資本輸入、資本導入
　　（=import of capital）
　declaration of import　輸入申告
　dollar-denominated import growth　ドル表示の輸入の伸び率
　export and import（price）index　輸出入物価指数
　export-import bank　輸出入銀行
　exports and imports by principal country（customs clearance basis）　主要国別輸出入通関高
　exports and imports of goods & services　財貨・サービスの輸出入
　foreign exchange rationing for imports　輸入のための外貨割当制度
　gold import point　金輸入点　（=import gold point）
　import and export price inflation　輸入・輸出物価上昇率
　import bounty　輸入補助金、輸入奨励金
　import by deferred payment　延べ払い輸入
　import charges［commission］　輸入手数料
　import clearance［clearing］　輸入通関
　import collateral　輸入担保

import cost　輸入物価, 輸入コスト
import deficit　輸入超過赤字
import deposit　輸入担保
　（=import guarantee, import license bond）
import deposit rate　輸入担保率
　（=import license bond rate）
import entry　輸入手続き
　（=import formalities, import procedure）
import exchange　輸入為替
import finance　輸入金融　（=import financing）
import gold point　正貨輸入点
　（=gold import point）
import inflation　輸入インフレ
　（=imported inflation）
import invoice　輸入仕入れ書
import letter of credit [L/C]　輸入信用状
import levy　輸入課税, 輸入課徴金
import mortgage　輸入担保
import of foreign capital　外資導入
　（=importation of foreign capital）
import paper　輸入手形
import payment　輸入代金支払い, 輸入支払い
import payments　輸入総額
import point　正貨輸入点　（=gold import point）
import premium　輸入割増金
import quota system　輸入割当制度
　（=import quota contingent system）
import requirements　輸入必要額, 輸入必要量
import settlement　輸入決済
import special payment　特殊輸入決済方法
import speculation　投機目的の輸入
import subsidy　輸入補助金, 輸入奨励金
import surcharge　輸入課徴金　（=import surtax）
import surplus　輸入超過, 貿易収支赤字
import tariff　輸入関税
import usance　輸入代金の延べ払い, 輸入ユーザンス
import usance facilities　輸入ユーザンス
import value　輸入額
import without (foreign) exchange　無為替輸入
　（=no-draft import）
import WPI [series]　輸入物価指数
invisible export and import　貿易外収支
invisible import　無形輸入
merchandise imports　財の輸入額
nominal import　輸入額
product import　製品輸入　（=manufactured import）
real import　実質輸入額
rise in imports　輸入の伸び [増加]
the dollar value of imports　ドル建ての輸入額
visible import　有形輸入
◆If agricultural imports become cheaper due to the lowered tariffs, consumers will greatly benefit. 関税の引下げで輸入農産物が安くなれば、消費者の利点も大きい。◆Imports were down 25.2 percent to ¥53.78 trillion in fiscal 2009. 2009年度の輸入額は、25.2％減の53兆7,800億円だった。◆In the six months to September, imports posted a stronger 17.8 percent increase to ¥39.4 trillion from a year earlier. 4—9月期の輸入額は、前年同期比17.8％の大幅増で、39兆4,000億円となった。◆While a strong dollar hurts exports, it helps to keep inflation down by making imports cheaper. ドル高で輸出被害を被っているものの、輸入品が安くなるためドル高はインフレ抑制に役立っている。

import bill　輸入手形, 輸入為替手形
　（=import draft）
　acceptance of import bill　輸入手形の引受け, 輸入手形 [輸入為替手形] 引受け
　arrival notice of import bill　輸入為替到着案内
　import bill for collection　輸入取立て手形, 輸入B/C
　import bill of exchange　輸入為替手形
　import bill of lading [B/L]　輸入品船荷証券
　import bills settlement account, Dr.　輸入手形決済資金貸し
　import freight bill　輸入運賃手形
　import settlement bill　輸入決済手形
　import trade bill　輸入貿易手形
　import usance bill　期限付き輸入手形, 輸入ユーザンス手形
import duties　輸入関税
　◆Japanese agricultural products such as rice have been protected by high import duties. 日本のコメなどの農産物は、高い輸入関税で保護されている。
import growth　輸入の伸び, 輸入の増加
　◆Import growth outpaced export growth, thus producing the trade imbalance. 輸入の伸びが輸出の伸びを上回ったため、貿易の不均衡が生じた。
import guarantee　輸入担保, 輸入保証金
　（=import deposit）
　import guarantee money　輸入保証金
　import guarantee rate　輸入担保率
import license [licence]　輸入承認
　import license bond rate　輸入担保率
　　（=import deposit rate）
　import license statistics　輸入承認統計
import price　輸入価格, 輸入物価
　fall in import prices　輸入価格の下落, 輸入物価の下落
　import price index　輸入物価指数
　import price inflation　輸入物価指数上昇率
　rise in import prices　輸入物価の上昇, 輸入価格の上昇
　◆The fall in import prices that accompanies a strong yen could further prolong Japan's deflation. 円高に伴う輸入価格の下落で、日本のデフレがさらに長期化する可能性がある。
import restrictions [restraints]　輸入規制, 輸入制限
　◆Due to concern about radioactive contamination, a number of Japanese agricultural and industrial products have been subject to import restrictions. 放射能汚染への懸念から、日本の農業・工業品の多くは輸入規制の対象となっている。
imported　（形）輸入される, 輸入した, 〜の輸入
　imported capital　資本の導入
　imported goods　輸入品
　imported inflation　輸入インフレ
　　（=import inflation）
　imported input　輸入投入財
　imported item　輸入品目
　imported items in local currency terms　自国通貨建て輸入材
　◆One good point of the rise in the yen is that we can buy imported goods at low prices. 円高のメリットの一つは、輸入品を安く買えることだ。
impose　（動）課税をする, 税金などを課する, 義務などを負わせる, 危険などを与える, 条件などを設ける, 売りつける, 押し付ける, 強いる
　impose a tax on　〜に課税する, 〜に税をかける
　impose additional [more] financial sanctions　追加金融制裁を発動する

impose conditions on　〜に条件を付ける，〜に条件を設ける
impose economic austerity　緊縮政策を遂行する
impose economic sanctions　経済制裁に踏み切る，経済制裁を科する
impose high tariffs on　〜に高率の関税をかける
impose restrictions on　〜を規制する，〜を制限する
the obligations imposed by this agreement　本契約により課される義務

◆An additional taxation of about ¥500 million was imposed on the group. 同グループに、約5億円の追徴課税が課された。◆Commercial banks have created special investment vehicles (SIVs) in order to escape the capital adequacy regulation imposed by the Basel accord. 銀行は、バーゼル協定［バーゼル合意］による自己資本比率規制を回避するため、特別投資会社(SIV)を新設している。◆France, Italy, Spain and Belgium imposed a ban on short-selling financial stocks. フランス、イタリア、スペインとベルギーが、金融銘柄の空売りを禁止した。◆Greece will miss 2011-12 deficit targets imposed by international lenders as part of the country's bailout. ギリシャは、同国救済措置の一環として国際融資団(欧州連合(EU)や国際通貨基金)が課した2011-12年の赤字削減目標を、達成できないようだ。◆No penalty taxes were imposed as the company was in the red. 同社は赤字だったので、追徴課税はされなかった。◆The Financial Stability Board will impose a progressive extra capital charge of 1 percent to 2.5 percent on risk-adjusted assets held by G-SIFIs. G20(主要20か国・地域)の金融当局で構成する金融安定化理事会(FSB)は、国際金融システムにとって重要な金融機関(G-SIFIs)が保有するリスク調整後資産に、1〜2.5%の資本［自己資本］の上積みを段階的に課すことになった。◆The U.S. government has imposed additional financial sanctions on North Korea. 米政府は、北朝鮮に対する追加金融制裁を発動した。

improve　(動)改良する，改善する，整備する，促進する，推進する，強化する，向上させる，高める，上げる，充実させる，拡大する，上昇する，好転する，良くなる
continue to improve a bit　じり高が続く
improve capital adequacy　自己資本比率を高める
improve competitiveness [competitive position]　競争力を高める，競争力を強化する
improve market share　シェア［市場シェア］を拡大する
improve one's balance sheet　財務体質を改善する，財務基盤を改善する
improve one's corporate value　企業価値を高める
improve one's earning power　収益力を向上させる
improve one's finance position　財務ポジションの改善を図る
improve one's financial conditions and profitability　財務内容と収益力を向上させる
improve one's financial health　財務体質を改善する
improve productivity　生産性を高める，生産性を向上させる
improve spreads　スプレッドを拡大する
improve the capital accounts [position]　自己資本比率を高める
improve the financial position　財務体質を改善する
improve the foreign exchange position　外貨収支を改善する
improve the profit margins　利ざやを拡大する

◆An urgent task facing each financial group is to improve its financial conditions and profitability on the strength of advantages gained from merger. 合併・統合の相乗効果を生かして、財務内容と収益力を向上させることが、各金融グループの現在の急務だ。◆Business performance has improved since the latter half of last year. 昨年後半から、業績は向上している。◆Corporate business sentiment improved in the three months to September for the sixth consecutive quarter. 7-9月の企業の景況感は、6期連続で改善した。◆It is vital to improve the secondary market circulating such asset-backed securities for investors. 投資家向けに、このような資産担保証券の流通市場の整備も不可欠である。◆Major U.S. and European banks are improving their earning power. 欧米の大手銀行は、収益力を向上させている。◆Shinsei and Aozora banks announced a plan to merge in an effort to expand their customer bases and improve earnings. 新生銀行とあおぞら銀行は、顧客基盤の拡大と収益力の強化を狙って、合併計画を発表した。◆The company is to hold a news conference to unveil a set of its programs to improve its corporate value. 同社は、記者会見を開いて、企業価値を高めるための一連のプログラムを発表する。◆The company will reduce its interest-bearing debts to improve its financial health. 財務体質を改善するため、同社は有利子負債を削減する。◆The employment situation has improved in line with the economic recovery. 景気回復に伴って、雇用環境は良くなっている。◆The stock market improved across the board. 株式相場［株式市場］は、全面高になった［全面値上がりした］。◆The stock market will improve slightly. 株式市場は、小幅反発が予想される。◆The Tankan index for 10 of the 16 industries in the manufacturing sector improved in September from three months earlier. 製造業16業種中10業種の日銀9月短観の業況判断指数(DI)は、(前回調査の)6月から改善した。◆These firms' performance has rapidly improved thanks to the recent boom on the Tokyo Stock Exchange. これら各社の業績は、最近の東京株式市場の活況を背景に急速に回復した。◆To improve its financial health, Daiei will seek about ¥410 billion worth of debt waivers from about 30 financial institutions to reduce its interest-bearing debts. 財務体質を改善するため、ダイエーは、約30の金融機関に約4,100億円の債権放棄を求めて、有利子負債を削減する。◆When serious financial difficulties are expected, the Financial Services Agency is allowed to order a company to improve its operations in the early stages without releasing the information to the public. 深刻な財務悪化が予想される場合、金融庁は、非公表で早めに業務改善命令を発動することができる。

improved　(形)改善された，改良された，改善した，向上した，好転した，回復した，〜の改善［改良，向上，好転、回復，拡大，増加，伸び］
improved consumer confidence　消費者マインドの向上
improved creditworthiness　信用力の改善
improved economic conditions　経済状態の改善
improved economic outlook　景気見通しの改善，景気見通しの好転
improved economy [economic performance]　景気の回復
improved export volumes　輸出数量の伸び
improved loan trust margins　貸付け信託の利ざや改善
improved market conditions　市場環境の好転
improved price picture　インフレ率の低下
improved productivity　生産性の向上
improved profitability　収益力の改善
improved profits　利益の増加，増益
improved results　業績向上
improved tone of the market　市場の地（じ）合いの好転，地合いの好転

◆The economy may be headed toward a turnaround on the back of improved exports and corporate profitability. 輸出と企業収益が改善して、景気が好転する可能性もある。

improved business performance　業績改善
◆The company's improved business performance should be reflected in our pay. 会社の業績改善を、われわれ社員の賃金に反映させるべきだ。

improved financial market conditions 金融市場の環境改善
◆The Fed raised the discount rate to 0.75 percent from 0.5 percent as a response to improved financial market conditions. 米連邦準備制度理事会（FRB）は、金融市場の環境改善を受けて、（銀行に貸し出す際の金利である）公定歩合を現行の年0.5%から0.75%に引き上げた。

improved financial profile 財務力見通しの改善
◆Standard & Poor's revised upward the outlook on its ratings on six major Japanese insurance companies against the backdrop of their improved financial profiles. スタンダード＆プアーズは、日本の大手保険会社6社の財務力見通し改善を背景に、6社の格付け見直しを上方修正した。

improvement （名）改良, 改善, 促進, 推進, 向上, 増加, 伸び, 上昇, 拡大, 景気などの回復, 好転, 改修工事, 整備
business [operational] improvement order 業務改善命令
cost improvements コスト削減
economic improvement 景気回復, 経済の回復
（=improvement in the economy）
home improvement loan 増改築ローン
improvement in business confidence 企業マインドの向上
improvement in inflation インフレの改善
improvement in loan demand ローン需要の回復, ローン需要の伸び
improvement in one's financial position 財務体質の改善
improvement in profitability 収益性の改善, 収益力の改善
improvement in the financial results 金融収支の改善
improvement in the foreign exchange position 外貨収支の改善
improvement in the sentiment 景況感の改善
improvement in the trade account 貿易収支の改善
improvement of the market 地（じ）合いの好転
market improvement 上げ相場
modest improvement in financial margins 利ざやの小幅拡大[改善]
operating improvements 業績向上
productivity improvement 生産性向上
trade (balance) improvement 貿易収支の改善
（=improvement in the trade account）
yield improvement 利回りの向上, 利回りの改善
◆A steady annual improvement in earnings of five percent or more is a reasonable goal given the weight of regulated companies in our asset base. 年5%以上の利益増加率の安定確保は、規制対象企業が当社の資産構成で大きな比重を占めていることから、妥当な目標と言えるでしょう。◆The Bank of Japan's diffusion indexes are calculated by subtracting the percentage of companies reporting deterioration in business conditions from those perceiving improvement. 日銀のこれらの業況判断指数（DI）は、現在の景況感について「改善している」と感じている企業の割合から「悪化している」と回答した企業の割合を差し引いて算出する。◆The rapid depreciation of the U.S. dollar would impair the current improvement in the Japanese economy. 急激なドル安は、日本の景気回復の腰を折ることになる。◆The recovery in business sentiment was largely due to the improvement in the parts supply chain disrupted after the March 11 earthquake and tsunami. 景況感が改善したのは、主に東日本大震災で打撃を受けたサプライ・チェーン（部品供給網）の復旧が進んだためだ。◆The rise of the yen's value is behind the improvement in travel abroad. 円高が、海外旅行増加の背景にある。◆There is slow progress in economic improvement among nonmanufacturing businesses, largely as a result of sluggish sales at retailers due to the ongoing deflation. デフレの進行で主に小売業の売上が低迷しているため、非製造業は景気回復の足取りが弱い。

improvement in earnings 収益改善, 業績改善, 収益の伸び, 増益
◆Mitsubishi UFJ Financial Group Inc. and Mizuho Financial Group Inc. reported sharp improvements in earnings in the April-June period of 2010. 三菱UFJフィナンシャル・グループとみずほフィナンシャルグループの2010年4～6月期決算は、大幅な業績改善となった。

improvement in sentiment 景況感の改善
◆Many businesses are cautious about their outlook three months ahead despite the improvement in sentiment. 企業の景況感は改善したものの、多くの企業は3か月先の景気見通しに対しては慎重だ。

improvement in the economy 景気回復
◆The rapid surge in the yen's value would impair the current improvement in the Japanese economy and deal a blow to the world economy. 急激な円高は、日本の現在の景気回復の腰を折り、世界経済にも大きなマイナスになる。

improvement in the (trade) balance 貿易収支の改善
◆The improvement in the balance reflected slower imports rather than stronger exports. 貿易収支が改善したのは、輸出の増加よりも輸入の減少によるものだ。

imputation （名）（価値の）帰属, （配当の）付加計算, インピュテーション
imputation method 法人税株主帰属方式, 法人税加算調整方式
imputation of dividends 配当の付加計算
imputation system 帰属方式, インピュテーション方式
imputation transaction 帰属取引

imputed （形）帰属した, 帰属する, 計算上の, 一定の金額の価値があると評価された
imputed cost 付加原価, 帰属原価, 計算原価
imputed delivery 代理交付
imputed dividends 見なし法人
imputed income 帰属収入, 帰属所得
imputed negligence 転嫁過失
imputed price 帰属価格
imputed principal amount 見なし元本の金額
imputed rent 帰属家賃
imputed service 帰属サービス
imputed tax 税額の前払い
imputed value 帰属価値, 計算上の価値
unfunded employee welfare contributions imputed 無基金雇用者福祉帰属負担

imputed interest 計算利子[利息], 実質金利, 適用利息, 付加利子, 帰属利子[利息], 自己資本利子
（=implicit interest）
imputed interest on equity capital 株主持ち分費用, 自己資本利子
imputed interest on stockholder's equity 自己資本に対する計算利息
◆The net present value of such payments on capital leases was $150 million after deducting estimated executory costs and imputed interest. これらのャピタル・リース支払い額の純現在価値は、見積り管理費用と帰属利子の控除後で1億5,000万ドルでした。

IMRO 投資管理規制機関（Investment Management Regulatory Organizationの略）

in a bid to ～するために, ～をめざして, ～しようと試みて, ～しようとして （⇒facilitate）
◆FSA audits of the banks' accounts urged them to reclassify 149 of their major corporate borrowers more strictly in terms of their creditworthiness in a bid to accelerate the dis-

posal of bad loans. 金融庁による銀行の財務書類監査で、不良債権処理を加速するため、銀行は大口融資先149社の信用力による債務者区分の見直しを強化するよう強く求められた。◆In a bid to clamp down on bank-transfer scams, the police asked financial institutions not to allow people whose faces are obscured with sunglasses or masks to use ATMs. 振り込め詐欺を取り締まるため、警察は、サングラスやマスクで顔を隠したままATM（現金自動預け払い機）を使用できないよう金融機関に要請した。◆The Bank of Japan will set up a fund to buy long-term government bonds, exchange-traded funds and other financial assets in a bid to prop up the nation's economy. 日本の景気を下支えするため、日銀は基金を新設して、長期国債や上場投資信託（ETF）などの金融商品［金融資産］を買い入れる。◆The U.S. Federal Reserve raised the official discount rate and the target rate of federal funds by 0.25 percentage points in a bid to quell inflation and keep the economy from overheating. 米連邦準備制度理事会（FRB）は、インフレを防ぎ景気の過熱を警戒して、公定歩合とフェデラル・ファンド（FF）の誘導目標金利をそれぞれ0.25パーセント引き上げた。

in an attempt to 〜しようとして，〜するため
◆The revaluation of currency in North Korea appears aimed at clamping down on burgeoning free markets in an attempt to reassert the regime's control. 北朝鮮の通貨改定は、政権の統制力を改めて強めるため、急速に広がる自由市場を厳しく取り締まるねらいがあるようだ。

in an effort to 〜しようとして，〜しようと努力して，〜するため，〜を目指して，〜を狙って
◆Shinsei and Aozora banks announced a plan to merge in an effort to expand their customer bases and improve earnings. 新生銀行とあおぞら銀行は、顧客基盤の拡大と収益力の強化を狙って、合併計画を発表した。

in concert with 〜と協同で，〜と協力して，〜と提携［連携］して，〜と協調して，〜と歩調を合わせて，〜の波に乗って
◆The Bank of Japan's resorting to quantitative easing in concert with the Fed would have a greater impact on in buoying the global economy. 米連邦準備制度理事会（FRB）と歩調を合わせて日銀が量的緩和に踏み切れば、世界景気の浮揚効果は拡大すると思われる。

in cooperation with 〜と協力して，〜と連携して，〜と協同して
◆In cooperation with the U.S. FRB, the Bank of England, the Bank of Japan and the Swiss National Bank, the European Central Bank decided to conduct three U.S. dollar liquidity-providing operations between October and December. 米連邦準備制度理事会（FRB）、英イングランド銀行、日銀、スイス国立銀行と協調して、欧州中央銀行（ECB）が10〜12月に3回、米ドル資金供給オペを実施することを決めた。◆The Bank of Japan will fight the yen's appreciation in close cooperation with the government. 日銀は、政府と緊密に連携して円高に対応する方針だ。

in excess of 〜を超過して，〜を超えて，〜より多く
　capital contributed in excess of par or stated value　額面超過払込み資本
　capital in excess of par value　株式払込み剰余金, 払込み剰余金, 資本剰余金, 株式発行差金
　capital (paid) in excess of stated value　株式払込み剰余金, 払込み剰余金, 額面超過金
　current assets in excess of current liabilities　流動資産の流動負債超過額
　paid-in capital in excess of par (value)　資本剰余金, 払込み剰余金
　plan assets in excess of projected benefit obligation　制度資産［基金資産］の見積り給付債務超過額

in-house investigation　社内調査, 内部調査
◆As the result of an in-house investigation, it is highly likely that the leaked personal information has been taken from the firm directly. 内部調査の結果、流出した個人情報は社内から直接持ち出された可能性が高い。

in-line　（名）市場平均
in-line buyer　インライン・バイヤー（現在の市場価格で大量の株式を売買したい買い手のこと）

in line with　〜に沿って，〜と一致［調和］して，〜に連動［同調］して，〜に合わせて，〜に従って，〜に伴って，〜に応じて，〜を背景に，〜を追いかける形で
◆The employment situation has improved in line with the economic recovery. 景気回復に伴って、雇用環境は良くなっている。

in return for　〜の見返りとして，〜のお返し［返礼、返報］として，〜の代わりに
◆Financial institutions and TEPCO shareholders should shoulder part of the financial burden in return for government financial support of TEPCO. 政府が東電を支援する見返りとして［前提として］、金融機関と東電株主も一定の金融負担をするべきだ。

in tandem with　〜と並んで，〜と協力して，〜と提携して，〜と連動する形で
◆The European Central Bank decided to buy Italian and Spanish government bonds in tandem with the issuance of the G-7 emergency statement. 欧州中央銀行（ECB）は、G7緊急声明の発表と連動する形で、イタリアとスペインの国債を買い入れる方針を決めた。◆To achieve at least 2 percent nominal growth in gross domestic product, the government must take stimulus measures, including a cut in corporate income tax, in tandem with the Bank of Japan's easy money policy. 2%超の名目GDP成長率を実現するには、日銀の金融緩和政策と並んで、政府は法人税減税などの景気刺激策を取らなければならない。

in terms of　〜では，〜の点で，〜に関して，〜について，〜の見地から
　in terms of market value　時価総額では
　in terms of voting rights　議決権では
◆FSA audits of the banks' accounts urged them to reclassify 149 of their major corporate borrowers more strictly in terms of their creditworthiness in a bid to accelerate the disposal of bad loans. 金融庁による銀行の財務書類監査で、不良債権処理を加速するため、銀行は大口融資先149社の信用力による債務者区分の見直しを強化するよう強く求められた。◆If life insurers continue to offer insurance policies with guaranteed high return rates, the future financial burden in terms of interest payments will increase. 生保が高い利回りを保証した保険の販売を今後とも続けると、将来の利払いの金融負担が増えることになる。◆In terms of market value, the relation between Ito-Yokado and Seven-Eleven is a contradiction. 時価総額（株価による企業価値を示す）では、イトーヨーカ堂（親会社）とセブン-イレブン（子会社）との関係が逆転している。◆In terms of the total market value of listed shares, the Tokyo Stock Exchange is dwarfed by the New York Stock Exchange, the world's biggest. 上場株式の時価総額では、東証は世界トップのニューヨーク証券取引所に大きく引き離されている。◆The AA minus rating by S&P is the fourth highest in terms of credit quality on a scale of 22. 米格付け会社のスタンダード・アンド・プアーズ（S&P）による「ダブルAマイナス」の格付けは、22段階ある信用度中、上から4番目に当たる。◆The hostile investment fund obtained a stake of more than 35 percent in the publisher in terms of voting rights. 敵対するこの投資ファンドが取得した株は、議決権で同出版社株の35%を超えた。◆The merger between the TSE and the OSE will create the world's second-largest exchange group in terms of the total market value of listed shares. 東証と大証の経営統合で、上場株式の時価総額で世界第2位の株式取引所グループが誕生する。◆The Tokyo Stock Exchange was outstripped [outpaced] by the Shanghai Stock Exchange in terms of trading volume. 東証

は、取引規模［売買規模］で上海証券取引所に抜かれた。

in the aftermath of ～の影響で，～の直後，～に続いて，～を受けて，～のさめやらぬ頃
（⇒earthquake insurance）
◆Both lenders will focus on supporting their local corporations in the aftermath of the March 11 quake and tsunami. 3月11日（2011年）の東日本大震災を受けて、両行は地元企業の支援に重点的に取り組む方針だ。◆Companies faced difficulty in raising money by issuing corporate bonds in the aftermath of the financial crisis and resorted to borrowing money from banks. 世界の金融危機の影響で企業は、社債を発行して資金を調達するのが困難になったため、金融機関からの資金借入れに動いた。◆Corporate debt issues are recovering as bond market turbulence in the aftermath of the March 11 Great East Japan Earthquake has subsided. 2011年3月11日の東日本大震災直後の債券市場の混乱が収束したため、社債の発行額が回復している。◆In the aftermath of the March 11 massive earthquake and tsunami, the Financial Services Agency will likely postpone the introduction of IFRSs. 東日本大震災（2011年3月11日）の影響で、金融庁は国際財務報告基準（IFRS）の導入を延期する方向だ。◆In the aftermath of the 1995 Great Hanshin Earthquake and the 2007 Niigata Prefecture Chuetsu Offshore Earthquake, a series of fraud cases involving donations occurred. 1995年の阪神大震災や2007年の新潟県中越沖地震の直後には、義援金詐欺事件が相次いで起きた。◆Shinsei and Aozora banks suffered huge losses in their overseas investment business in the aftermath of the global financial crisis triggered by the collapse of Lehman Brothers Holdings Inc. in autumn 2008. 新生銀行とあおぞら銀行は、2008年秋のリーマン・ブラザーズの経営破たんで始まった世界的な金融危機の影響で、海外投資事業に巨額の損失が発生した。◆The capital markets around the globe are plagued by counterparty risks in the aftermath of the collapse of U.S. investment bank Lehman Brothers in 2008. 世界全体の資本市場は、2008年の米証券会社［投資銀行］の経営破たんの影響で、カウンターパーティー・リスクに苦しんでいる。

in (the) light of ～に照らして，～を考慮して，～を踏まえて，～に鑑（かん）みて，～の見地から
◆Nippon Life Insurance Co., the top shareholder in Olympus Corp., will continue supporting Olympus in light of its advanced technology in its core business such as endoscopes. オリンパスの筆頭株主の日本生命は、内視鏡などオリンパスの中核事業の高い技術力を踏まえて、引き続きオリンパスを支えていく方針だ。◆The Fair Trade Commission of Japan is required to consider global economic trends when it screens corporate merger requests in light of the Antimonopoly Law. 公正取引委員会は、独占禁止法に照らして企業合併の申請を審査するにあたって、グローバル経済の潮流も検討する必要がある。

in the money イン・ザ・マネー （オプションを行使したら利益が出る状態のことで、コール・オプションの場合は行使価格が市場価格より低い状態、プット・オプションの場合は行使価格が市場価格より高い状態をいう。⇒atの項のat the money, out of the money）

in-the-money option イン・ザ・マネー・オプション

in the wake of ～に引き続いて，～に続いて，～の後，～のすぐ後で，～を受けて，～の結果（として），～に従って，～に倣（なら）って，～を契機として，～をきっかけに，～として，～によって
（=in one's wake）
◆In the wake of the euro crisis in Europe and the fiscal deadlock in the United States, the yen has sharply strengthened. 欧州のユーロ危機と米国の財政政策の行き詰まりの影響で、円が急騰している。◆In the wake of the Livedoor case, the Financial Instruments and Exchange Law which drastically revised the former Securities and Exchange Law came into force in September 2007. ライブドア事件を受けて、2007年9月に、旧証券取引法を抜本改正した金融商品取引法が施行された。◆Investment conditions have worsened due to confusion in global financial markets in the wake of fiscal and financial crises in Europe. 欧州の財政・金融危機を受けた世界的な金融市場の混乱で、運用環境が悪化している。◆Major central banks will cooperate to offer three-month U.S. dollar loans to commercial banks in the wake of Europe's sovereign debt crisis. 欧州の財政危機を受け、主要中央銀行が、協調して商業銀行に3か月物ドル資金を供給することになった。◆The New York-based Citigroup, once the world's biggest banking group, faced massive losses in the wake of the subprime mortgage crisis. 世界最大の金融グループだったシティグループ（ニューヨーク）は、サブプライム・ローンの焦げ付き問題を受けて、巨額の損失を抱えていた。◆Worldwide concern over fiscal sustainability in industrialized countries is growing in the wake of Greece's sovereign debt crisis. ギリシャの財政危機を契機として、先進国の財政の持続可能性に対する世界の関心が高まっている。

inactive （形）不活発な，不活動の，不人気の，遊休の，休眠の
　inactive account　睡眠口座，不活発口座，不動口座
　inactive bond　不人気社債，不活発債券
　inactive capital　非活動資本
　inactive corporation　休眠会社
　inactive deposit　不動口預金
　inactive gold　不活動金
　inactive market　閑散市況，閑散とした市場，閉鎖市況
　inactive money　遊休資金　（=idle money）
　inactive money balance　不活動貨幣残高
　inactive stock　不人気株，不活発株式

inadequate （形）不十分な，十分でない，足りない，不備な，適当でない，不適格な，無力な，力不足の，無能な
　inadequate information disclosure　不十分な情報開示
　inadequate management［control］　管理体制の不備
　inadequate preparation for the reorganization　再編の準備不足
◆The financial group's inadequate preparations for the reorganization resulted in a major computer system failure. 同フィナンシャル・グループの再編の準備不足から、大規模なシステム障害が起こった。

inadvertent （形）故意でない，不注意な，不注意から起こった，軽率な，偶然の，不慮の，怠慢な
　inadvertent action　不注意な行為，軽率な行為
　inadvertent joke　つい口をすべらした冗談
　inadvertent remarks　うっかり発言，不注意なことば
◆The issue of the inadvertent failure to switch to the national pension program by full-time housewives must be quickly solved. 専業主婦の国民年金への年金資格切替え忘れ問題は、決着を急ぐべきだ。

inaugurate （動）就任させる，落成式を行う，開会式を行う，開幕させる，（船などを）就航させる，（仕事・事業を）開始する，発足する，始める
◆The Industrial Revitalization Corporation was inaugurated with the aim of revitalizing troubled banks and industries. 産業再生機構は、経営不振の銀行と産業の再生を目指して発足した。

incentive （名）刺激，誘因，動機，励み，奨励，促進策，振興，報奨，報奨金，出来高払い，インセンティブ
　incentive stock option　奨励株式オプション
　　（⇒stock option plan）
　incentive wage　能率給，報奨金
　interest incentive effect　利子刺激効果
　sales incentives　販売奨励金，販売促進策
　　（⇒zero financing）
　savings incentive plan　貯蓄奨励プラン

shareholders incentives　株主優待, 株主優待制度
◆Shareholders incentives are designed to encourage shareholders to hold onto their stocks over the long term. 株主優待の狙いは、株主の株式の長期保有促進にある。

inception　（名）開始, 初め, 当初, 設立当初, 創設, 導入
　　fund inception　ファンドの創設
　　inception of a swap agreement　スワップ契約の締結
　　inception of hedge　ヘッジの開始, ヘッジ当初
　　inception of the lease　リース開始
　　inception of the pension plan　年金制度の導入, 年金制度の採用, 年金制度採用年度

incipient recovery　景気回復の局面, 景気持ち直しの局面, 回復局面
◆The economy is moving toward an incipient recovery. 景気は、持ち直しに向けた動きが見られる。

include　（動）含む, 包含する, 算入する, 組み入れる, 計上する, 処理する, 記載する, 盛り込む, 表示する, 掲載する, 収録する, 定める
　　be included in income　利益として計上される, 損益として計上される
　　Shipping Included　送料込み
◆Economic stimulus measures implemented so far include a supplementary budget for job creation. これまで実施された景気対策としては、補正予算による雇用の創出もある。◆In the latest account settlements, banking groups gave up including sizable deferred tax assets in their equity capital. 今決算で、銀行グループは、巨額の繰延べ税金資産の自己資本への計上を見送った。◆Management is responsible for the integrity and objectivity of the financial information included in this report. 経営者は、本報告書に記載されている財務情報の完全性と客観性について責任を負っています。◆Mitsubishi UFJ Financial Group Inc., Sumitomo Mitsui Financial Group Inc. and Mizuho Financial Group Inc. are included in the G-SIFIs list of the Financial Stability Board. 主要20か国・地域（G20）の金融当局で構成する金融安定化理事会（FSB）のG-SIFIリスト（国際的な巨大金融機関リスト）には、三菱UFJ、三井住友、みずほの3大金融グループも含まれている。◆The Bank of Japan may expand the list of government bonds purchased under the fund, to include those that have more than two years left until maturity. 日銀は、基金で買い入れる国債の対象を拡大して、満期までの残存期間が2年以上（現行1〜2年）の国債を含むようにする可能性がある。◆The Board of Audit intends to include the total taxpayer contribution to JAL in its audit account report compiled in November 2011. 会計検査院は、2011年11月にまとめる決算検査報告書に、日航に対する総国民負担額を盛り込む方針だ。◆The Company provides for income taxes based on accounting income for tax purposes included in the financial statements. 当社は税務上、財務書類に表示する会計上の利益に基づいて法人所得税を算定しています。◆The economic package will include measures to help small and midsize companies procure funds. 経済対策には、中小企業の資金繰り支援策も盛り込まれる。◆To enhance the stimulating effect of the Fed's rate cuts, swift implementation of fiscal and tax stimulus measures, including tax cuts on investment designed to reinvigorate the stock market, is necessary in addition to the large-scale tax cut program that is under way. 米連邦準備制度理事会（FRB）の金利引下げの刺激効果を高めるためには、現在実施中の大型減税プログラムに加え、株式市場を再活性化するための投資減税など、財政・税制面からの景気刺激策の速やかな実施が必要である。

income　（名）利益, 収益, 所得　（⇒corporate income, fee, investment income, kickbacks, net income, security taxation system）
　　after-tax income　税引き後利益
　　business income　企業利益, 企業収益, 事業所得
　　consolidated net income　連結当期純利益
　　corporate income　法人所得
　　fixed income securities　確定利付き証券, 債務証券, 債券
　　income account　所得収支, 損益勘定, 損益計算書
　　income account surplus　所得収支の黒字, 所得黒字
　　income after tax　税引き後利益
　　　（=after-tax income）
　　income benefit　年金支払い
　　income bond　収益社債, 収益債券, 利益参加型社債, インカム・ボンド
　　income fund　収益配当型投資信託, インカム・ファンド
　　income gain　金利・配当収入, インカム・ゲイン, 所得の伸び
　　income insurance　所得保険
　　income policy　年金式支払い保険
　　income settlement　保険金年金払い方式
　　interest income　受取利息
　　investment income　投資収益
　　net income　純利益, 当期純利益
　　nonoperating income　営業外損益, 営業外収益
　　ordinary income　経常損益
　　premium income　収入保険料
　　stock option income　ストック・オプション利益
　　taxable income　課税所得, 申告所得
◆A softening in the value of the yen inflated the yen value of income earned abroad. 円安で、海外収益の円評価額が上昇した。◆About 100 employees of Credit Suisse Securities and the Tokyo branch of Credit Suisse Principal Investments Ltd. have failed to declare a total of ¥2 billion of income related to stock options. クレディ・スイス証券とクレディ・スイス・プリンシパル・インベストメンツ東京支店の社員約100人が、ストック・オプション関連所得の20億円を申告していなかった。◆For the computation of the earnings per share, assuming full dilution, dividends on convertible preferred shares have been added back to income. 完全希薄化を仮定した場合の1株当たり利益の算定では、転換可能優先株式［転換優先株］に対する配当は、利益に振り戻してあります。◆If a housewife whose annual income is ¥1.3 million or more, or her husband becomes self-employed, the housewife must join the national pension plan and pay premiums. 主婦の年収が130万円以上の場合、または夫が脱サラした場合には、主婦も国民年金に加入して保険料を支払わなければならない。◆Proceeds from exercising stock options are regarded as part of a salary and thus subject to a higher tax rate than for one-time income. ストック・オプションを行使して得た利益（ストック・オプション利益）は、給与の一部と見なされるため、一時所得より高い税率（約2倍）が課される。◆The company hid ¥1.8 billion of income in the five years to March 2003. 同社は、2003年3月までの5年間に18億円の所得を隠していた。◆The consolidated provision for taxes also includes an amount sufficient to pay additional United States federal income taxes on repatriation of income earned abroad. 連結納税引当金には、海外で得た利益の本国送金に課される米連邦所得税の追加支払いに十分対応できる金額も含まれている。

income before extraordinary items　経常利益
◆During the fiscal year ended March 31, 2005, income before extraordinary items posted approximately 230.2 billion yen. 2005年3月決算で、経常利益は約2,302億円となった。

income earned from interest and dividends　利子・配当収入
◆If the two-track income taxation system is introduced, taxpayers will be allowed to offset losses from stock investments from income earned from interest and dividends. 二元的所得課税方式を導入すると、納税者は、利子・配当収入から株式投資による損失を相殺することができるようになる。

income earner　個人所得者, 所得者, 俸給生活者, 所得稼

得者
high [upper] income earner　高所得者
high income earners　高所得者層, 高所得層
low income earner　低所得者
low income earners　低所得者層
middle income earner　中所得者
small income earner　小額所得者
◆It seems low income earners and the self-employed have shifted to the cashing services. 低所得者や自営業者が、現金化商法［現金化サービス］に流れているようだ。

income forecast　収益見通し, 収益予想
（＝earnings forecast, profit forecast）
◆Unlike most other listed Japanese companies, the company does not offer income forecasts for the current business year. 日本の他の大半の上場企業と違って、同社は今期の収益予想を出していない。

income from commissions　手数料収入, 株式の売買委託手数料による収入
◆If the securities firms rush to cut these commissions, they may not be able to continue to rely on income from commissions as a major source of profit. これらの証券会社が手数料の値引き競争に走れば、主な収益源として株式の売買委託手数料による収入に今後とも頼ることは難しくなる。

income related to stock options　ストック・オプション関連所得
◆About 100 employees of Credit Suisse Securities and the Tokyo branch of Credit Suisse Principal Investments Ltd. have failed to declare a total of ￥2 billion of income related to stock options. クレディ・スイス証券とクレディ・スイス・プリンシパル・インベストメンツ東京支店の社員約100人が、ストック・オプション関連所得の20億円を申告していなかった。

income tax　所得税, 法人税, 法人所得税
income tax reductions　所得税減税
income tax return　所得税申告　（⇒capital gain）
◆The aim of the investors was to avoid income tax. 投資家［出資者］の目的は、所得税の節税効果だった。◆The Company provides for income taxes based on accounting income for tax purposes included in the financial statements. 当社は税務上、財務書類に表示する会計上の利益に基づいて法人所得税を算定しています。◆The income and corporate taxes have substantially decreased due to the prolonged recession and a series of tax breaks. 所得税や法人税は、長期不況や一連の減税措置で大幅に減少している。

incorporate　（動）設立する, 会社［法人］組織にする, 法人化する, 組み込む, 組み入れる, 盛り込む, 取り入れる, 織り込む, 受け入れる, 合併する, 契約の一部とする, 具体化する
be incorporated (as) a member of a group　グループの一員になる
be incorporated into　～に編入される, ～に組み込まれる
incorporate a ban on　～の禁止を盛り込む
incorporate A into　Aを～に組み込む, Aを～に編入する
incorporate adjustments　調整を加える
incorporate expected changes　予想される変動を織り込む［盛り込む］
incorporate negative factors　マイナス材料［悪材料］を織り込む
incorporate one's suggestions into the report　～の提案を報告書に組入れる
incorporate the newest information　最新情報を取り入れる
incorporated administrative accountant　英国の管理会計士
incorporated business [enterprise]　法人企業
incorporated city　合併でできた市

incorporated company [corporation]　有限責任会社, 有限会社
incorporated institution　法人組織
locally incorporated subsidiary　現地法人の子会社
◆Government steps taken to deal with Resona's collapse did not incorporate a reduction in the banking group's capital. りそな銀行の経営破たん処理に取った国の措置には、同金融グループの減資は織り込まれなかった。◆The manifesto of the Democratic Party of Japan incorporates a ban on political donations from companies and other organizations. 民主党の政権公約には、企業その他の団体からの政治献金の禁止が盛り込まれている。◆The purpose of the corporation is to engage in any lawful act or activity for which a corporation may be organized under the Laws of the State of California other than the banking business, the trust company business, or the practice of a profession permitted to be incorporated. 当会社は、銀行業務、信託会社の業務、知的職業法人（法人化を許された専門職）の業務以外の、カリフォルニア州法に基づいて企業が行うことができる一切の適法行為、合法的な活動に従事することを目的とする。

incorporation　（名）会社の設立, 法人格の付与, 法人組織, 会社, 合併, 編入, 組み込み
capital incorporation　資本の組入れ
country of incorporation　居住国名
incorporation procedure　会社設立手続き
◆Shares taken by the outside subscribers at the time of incorporation of the new company shall be limited to one share each. 新会社の設立時に外部の引受人が引き受ける株式は、それぞれ1株に限るものとする。

Incoterms　インコタームズ　（International Commercial Termsの略。国際商業会議所が1936年に制定した「貿易条件の解釈に関する国際規則（International Rules for the Interpretation of Trade Terms）」の通称で、改訂された2000年版インコタームズではCIF（運賃保険料込み条件）やFOB（本船渡し条件）などを含めて13種類の貿易条件が定義されている。⇒trade terms）
◆Unless otherwise expressly provided for in this agreement, the price and trade term "C.I.F." shall be interpreted in accordance with Incoterms 2000. 本契約に特に明示の規定がないかぎり（本契約で別段に明確に規定しないかぎり）、価格と貿易条件のCIFは、2000年版インコタームズに従って解釈する。

increase　（動）増やす, 上昇させる, 引き上げる, 押し上げる, 拡大する, 高める, 伸ばす, 強化する, 増大する, 増加する, 増える, 伸びる, 激化する
increase ability to meet debt payments　債務の返済能力を高める
increase capital ratios　自己資本比率を引き上げる
increase capital strength　資本基盤を強化する
increase competitiveness　競争力を高める
increase dollar weighting in one's portfolio　ドル資産の組入れ比率を引き上げる［高める］
increase duration　デュレーションを長期化させる
increase exposure to credit　与信リスクを高める
increase gross markups　粗値入れ率を引き上げる
increase interest rates　金利の上昇をもたらす
increase liquidity　流動性を増やす, 流動性を高める［向上させる］
increase margin requirements　証拠金を引き上げる
increase one's customer base　顧客基盤を拡大する
increase one's equity ownership　持ち株比率を引き上げる
increase one's market share　シェア［市場シェア、市場占有率］を拡大する, シェアを高める
increase one's shelf filing　一括登録枠を引き上げる
increase per share earnings　1株当たり利益を高める［押

し上げる、拡大する］
increase provisions [reserves]　引当金を積み増す
increase shareholders value　株主価値を高める, 株主の利益を高める
increase spreads　スプレッドを拡大する
increase the amount of the credit　信用を拡大する
increase the cost of borrowing　借入コストを上昇させる
increase the cost of money　資金コストを引き上げる[上昇させる]
increase the debt service burden　金利負担をさらに重くする（=increase the burden of debt service）
increase the level of indebtedness　負債水準を引き上げる
increase the revaluation reserves　再評価準備金を積み増す
increase the value of ratings　格付けの価値を高める
increase turnover　売上を伸ばす
increase weightings　組入れ比率を引き上げる[高める]
◆A consumption tax hike would increase the financial burden shouldered by Joe Blow. 消費税を引き上げると、一般国民の金融負担[一般国民が負担する金融負担]が増すことになる。◆As it stands, the yen is the sole major currency whose value has not stopped increasing. 現状では、円は上昇が止まらない唯一の主要通貨だ。◆Banks' fund-raising costs have increased, reflecting the rise in market rates after the Bank of Japan abandoned its zero-interest policy. 日銀のゼロ金利政策解除に伴って市場金利が上昇したのを反映して、銀行の資金調達コストが増大した。◆Domestic banks are increasing their efforts to finance large overseas projects. 国内銀行各行は、海外での大型事業に融資する（プロジェクト・ファイナンスへの）取組みを強化している。◆Domestic megabanks are increasing their financing activities overseas. 国内メガバンクは、海外での融資活動を強化している。◆Falling stock prices and the depreciation of the U.S. dollar increased uncertainty over the global economy. 米国の株安やドル安で、世界経済の不透明感が強まっている。◆If the number of corporate bankruptcies and the unemployment rate soar owing to structural reforms, recessionary pressures will further increase. 構造改革で企業倒産件数や失業率が増えると、不況圧力は一層強まるものと思われる。◆In the first half of the year, Honda increased U.S. market share to 8.9 percent from 8.1 percent. 今年度の上半期に、ホンダは米国でのシェア（市場占有率）を8.1％から8.9％に伸ばした。◆Instability in global markets is increasing with rising downside risks. 下振れリスクの増大とともに、グローバル市場の不安定性は高まっている。◆Lending by private banks has not increased though their investments into government bonds and cash reserves are increasing. 民間銀行の国債への投資や手持ちの現金は増えているが、民間銀行の貸出は増えていない。◆Our overall objective is to increase value for our shareholders. 当社は、株主の皆さまの価値[利益]を高めることを、全社的目標としています。◆Pressure for additional monetary easing measures will increase if the slowdown of the world economy continues. 世界的な景気減速がこのまま続けば、一層の金融緩和[金融緩和策]を求める圧力が強まるものと思われる。◆The amount of net selling of Japanese stocks further increased in September. 9月には、日本株の売り越しの額がさらに増えた。◆The biggest advantage for the bank in entering the venture will be to increase its customer base without having to open expensive new branch offices. 同行にとってこの新規事業への参入の最大の利点は、コストのかかる新店舗を開設するまでもなく、顧客基盤を拡大できることだ。◆The central bank's move to increase the outstanding current account target is insufficient to soothe market fears. 日銀の当座預金残高目標の引上げは、市場不安を払拭するには物足りない。◆The hollowing-out of the pension system may increase companies' personnel costs so much that it could negatively affect their international competitive edge. 年金

の空洞化で企業の人件費が上昇し、国際競争力に悪影響を及ぼす恐れがある。◆The number of people taking out earthquake insurance generally increases directly after an earthquake or tsunami. 地震保険の加入者数は、一般に地震や津波の直後に上昇する。◆To increase our presence outside the U.S., we are hiring employees, building plants and forming joint ventures. 米国外での当社の事業基盤を強化するため、当社は従業員の雇用、工場建設や合弁会社の設立に取り組んでいます。◆With the rating of JGBs being low, internationalizing them may increase the risk that their yield will fluctuate. 日本の国債の格付けが低いので、日本国債の国際化は国債の金利変動リスクを高める可能性がある。

increase　（名）増加, 増大, 伸び, 上昇, 引上げ, 拡大, 高まり　(⇒capital increase)
　base rate increase　基準金利の引上げ　(=increase in base rates)
　capital increase adjustment　増資調整
　credit line increase　与信限度額の引上げ
　discount rate increase　公定歩合の引上げ　(=increase in the discount rate)
　dividend increase　増配, 配当引上げ　(=increase in dividends)
　general capital increase　一般増資
　increase in average cost of funds　資金調達の平均コスト
　increase in financial profits　金融収益の増加
　increase in market interest rates　市場金利の上昇
　increase in monetary capital formation　金融資本形成の拡大
　increase in public spending　公共支出の伸び
　increase in rates　金利の上昇
　increase in revenues and profits　増収増益, 収益と利益の増加
　increase in savings rates　貯蓄率の上昇
　increase in stock prices　株価上昇
　increase in volatility　相場変動性の上昇
　increase in weightings　組入れ比率の引上げ
　increase of capital stock　増資　(=increase in capital stock, increase of capital)
　inventory increase　在庫の増加
　mortgage rate increase　住宅ローン金利の引上げ
　net increase in loans　貸出金の正味増加, 貸出金の純増
　paid-in capital increase　有償増資
　post a healthy increase　好調な伸びを示す
　price increase　価格上昇, 価格の高騰, 値上がり, 値上がり率, インフレ率
　productivity increase　生産性の伸び
　rate increase　利上げ, 料金引上げ
　rating increase　格上げ
　sharp increase in the exchange value of the yen　急激な円高　(=sharp [sudden] increase in yen exchange rates)
　tax increase　増税
　yield increase　利回りの上昇
◆Meiji Yasuda decided to lower the yield rate of its flagship insurance product because the insurer placed priority on long-term stable management over an increase in the number of policyholders. 明治安田生保は、契約者の数を増やすより長期的な経営の安定を優先したため、主力保険商品の予定利率[利回り]を引き下げることにした。

increase capital　増資する, 増資を実施する, 資本金を増やす, 資本を増強する
◆By a mechanism the EU has developed, each EU country can inject taxpayer money into banks unable to increase capital on their own. EU（欧州連合）が整備した仕組みで、EU各

国は、自力で資本増強を図れない銀行に対して公的資金を注入できるようになった。◆Europe's seven banks judged to have capital shortfall by the stress test will work on increasing their capital. ストレス・テスト（特別検査）で資本不足と認定された欧州の7銀行は、これから資本増強に取り組む。◆Many regional banks cannot get support from regional companies even if the banks plan to increase their capital. 地銀が増資を計画しても、地域の企業から協力を得られないことが多い。◆The company will increase its capital by ¥50 billion with additional investment of ¥10 billion from the IRC and with the debt-for-equity swap. 同社は、産業再生機構による100億円の追加［新規］出資と債務の株式化で、500億円増資する。

increase in direct and securities investment 直接・証券投資の伸び
◆The rise in foreign assets held by Japanese was mainly caused by an increase in direct and securities investment. 日本人（日本の政府・企業・個人）が保有する対外資産の増加は、主に直接・証券投資の伸びによるものだった。

increase in pension premiums 年金保険料の負担増
◆The instability of the pension system has repeatedly experienced increases in pension premiums and decreases in pension benefits. 年金制度が不安定なため、年金保険料の負担増と年金給付減が繰り返されてきた。

increase in prices 価格の上昇, 価格の高騰, 物価上昇, 値上げ
◆The sharp rise in crude oil prices has caused increases in prices of other fuels and grains, triggering inflation in many parts of the world. 原油価格の高騰は、他の燃料価格や穀物価格の上昇を招き、国際的なインフレを引き起こしている。

increase in risk of bankruptcy 倒産リスクの増大
◆S&P's downgrades do not reflect an increase in Ford's risk of bankruptcy. スタンダード＆プアーズの格下げは、米フォードの倒産リスクの増大を反映していない。

increase in the amount of funds 基金の増額
◆The BOJ's additional monetary easing steps include an increase in the amount of funds to purchase government bonds and corporate debentures. 日銀の追加金融緩和には、国債や社債などを買い入れる基金の増額が含まれている。

increase in transactions 取引の増加
◆An increase in transactions that brokerages handle has accompanied the brisk stock market business. 証券会社が扱う取引の増加は、そのまま株式相場の盛況と重なる。

increase loan-loss provisions 貸倒れ引当金を積み増す
◆The Financial Services Agency has instructed the banks to increase loan-loss provisions for nonperforming loans extended mainly to large borrowers. 金融庁は、主に大口融資先の不良債権に対する貸倒れ引当金の積み増しを、これらの銀行に指示した。

increase of debt limit 債務上限の引上げ
◆U.S. House of Representatives rejected the increase of debt limit. 米下院は、債務上限の引上げ（法案）を否決した。

increase public spending 公共支出を増やす［拡大する］, 財政出動する
◆It is difficult for Japan, the United States and European countries to support their sagging economies by increasing public spending, due to deteriorating financial conditions. 財政の悪化で、日米欧は、財政出動による景気の下支えが難しくなっている。◆Japan, the United States and European countries supported their sagging economies by increasing public spending after the collapse of Lehman Brothers in the autumn of 2008. 2008年秋のリーマン・ブラザーズの経営破たん後、日米欧は、財政出動によって低迷する景気の下支えをした。

increase the money supply 通貨供給量を増やす, マネー・サプライを増やす, マネー・サプライ（通貨供給量）を増やす （⇒money supply）

increased （形）増加した, 引き上げられた, 激化した, 濃縮化した, ～の増加［上昇, 拡大, 伸び, 向上, 高まり, 激化］, ～の引上げ, ～の強化
increased base rates 基準金利の引上げ
increased bond issuance 公債増発
increased bond yield 債券利回りの上昇
increased borrowing 借入れの増加
increased capital demand 資金需要の増加, 資本需要の増加 （=increased demand for capital）
increased competition 競争の激化
increased debt leverage 債務比率の上昇
increased dividends received 受取配当金の増加
increased domestic consumption 国内個人消費の伸び
increased earnings per share 濃縮化1株当たり利益
increased financial assets 金融資産の増加
increased inflationary expectations 期待インフレ率の上昇
increased investment 投資の拡大
increased liquidity preference 流動性選好の高まり
increased productivity 生産性の向上, 生産性の伸び
increased public works spending 公共投資の拡大
increased quarterly dividend 四半期増配, 四半期配当の引上げ
increased risk リスクの増大
increased sales 販売の増加, 販売の伸び, 売上［売上高］の伸び
increased value insurance 増し値保険

increased bad loans 不良債権の増加
◆The major banks attributed their increased bad loans to the poor performance of their borrowers due to the prolonged economic slump and Financial Service Agency inspections resulting in a stricter review of their asset assessments. 大手銀行は、不良債権が増えた理由として、長引く景気低迷で貸出先の経営が悪化したこと、金融庁の検査を受けて大手行が資産査定を厳しくしたことを挙げた。

increased capital investment 設備投資の拡大, 設備投資の伸び
◆A recovery will be export-driven, dependent on U.S. growth and the yen's depreciation, instead of being led by increased domestic consumption and capital investment. 今後の景気回復は、アメリカ経済の好転や円安を背景にした輸出主導型の回復で、国内の個人消費や設備投資の伸びがその牽引役となるわけではない。

increased ownership 持ち株比率の引上げ
◆The increased ownership will raise the bank's risk exposure to the company, whose business environment is severe. 持ち株比率の引上げで、企業環境［経営環境］が厳しい同社に対する同行のリスク・エクスポージャーは今後増大するものと思われる。

increased public spending 財政出動, 公共支出の拡大
◆As joint actions, major industrial nations have taken such measures as further interest rate reductions, quantitative monetary relaxation to increase the money supply, the injection of public funds and increased public spending. 協調行動として、主要先進国は、さらなる金利の引下げ、通貨供給量を増やすための量的金融緩和や公的資金の注入、財政出動［公共支出の拡大］などの措置を取った。◆In the case of the United States, increased public spending to boost the economy can hardly be expected. 米国の場合、財政出動による景気浮揚は期待しにくい。

increased purchases of long-term government bonds 長期国債の買入れ増額
◆If the deflationary trend gets stronger, the Bank of Japan should consider taking additional measures, such as increased purchases of long-term government bonds and the

introduction of a quantitative easing policy. 日銀は、長期国債の買入れ増額や量的金融緩和策の導入などの追加策を検討すべきだ。
increased uncertainties 不透明感の強まり[高まり],不安[懸念]の増大
◆Gold extended its rally to a record above $1,900 an ounce amid increased uncertainties over the U.S. and European economic outlook on the Comex in New York. ニューヨーク商品取引所では、米欧景気見通しへの懸念[米欧経済の先行き不透明感]の高まりを受け[懸念の高まりから]、金価格が急騰して、1トロイ・オンス＝1,900ドルを史上初めて突破した。
increasing (形)増えている, 拡大[増加、伸び、上昇、激化]している, 〜の高まり[増加、増大、上昇、拡大、向上]
　increasing annuity　年金の増額, 逓増(ていぞう)年金
　increasing capital needs　必要資本の増大
　increasing capital outflow　資本流出の増加
　increasing financial requirements　財務負担の増大
　increasing foreign interest rates　海外金利の上昇
　increasing government outlays　財政支出の増加
　increasing interest-bearing debt　利付き負債の増加
　increasing (interest) rates　金利の上昇
　increasing provisions　貸倒れ引当金の増加
　increasing rate　増加率, 上昇率, 逓増率
　increasing rate debt　金利上昇債券
　increasing rate preferred stock　配当率逓増優先株式
◆Amid the continued yen's historically high levels, increasing numbers of people are opening foreign currency deposit accounts. 歴史的な円高水準が続くなか、外貨預金口座を設ける人が増えている。
increasing bad loans　不良債権の拡大
◆We must avoid hindering the export-led economic recovery, speeding up deflation and increasing bad loans, which can be brought about by falling stock prices and the weakening dollar. 株安とドル安がもたらす可能性がある輸出頼みの景気回復の挫折、デフレ加速、不良債権の拡大を、われわれは避けなければならない。
increasing demands for capital　資金需要の増大
◆Increasing demands for capital and tight-money policies adopted by industrial powers pressed many investors to review their investment exposure in emerging economies. 先進国での資金需要の増大と金融引締め策は、多くの投資家に新興経済国[新興市場国]への投資の見直しを迫ることになった。
increasing M&A advisory business　M&A顧問業務の増加
◆Increasing M&A advisory business helped Nomura grab the No. 1 spot in Japan's M&A league table for the first half of this year. 今年上半期はM&A顧問業務が増加したため、日本のM&A案件の引受実績で野村證券がトップの座を占めた。
increasing uncertainty　不確実性の高まり, 不透明感の強まり[高まり], 懸念[不安]の増大
◆Due to increasing uncertainty over the U.S. economic outlook and the yen's rise, the Bank of Japan warned of the downside risks to the nation's economy. 米経済の先行きをめぐる不確実性の高まりと円高で、日銀は日本経済の下振れリスクに警戒感を示した。
increment　(名)(価値などの)増加, 増大, 増強, 増収, 増分, 増価, 増額, 昇給額, 増加評価額, 増大量, 利益, 利得
　annual increment　年次増加
　capital increment　資本増価[増価額], 増資, 増資額
　increment value duty　土地増価税
　investment increment　投資増加, 投資増加分
　periodical increment　定期的増加
　stock dividend of appraisal increment　評価益の株式配当

unearned increment　(土地などの)自然増価, 不労増価
incremental　(形)増加の, 増大する, 増価[増収、増分]の, 漸進的, 利益の, 利潤の
　expected incremental cash outflow and inflow　推定[予想される]増分現金流出入額
　incremental borrowing rate　限界借入金利
　incremental capital output ratio　限界資本・産出高比率
　incremental cash flow　増分キャッシュ・フロー
　incremental change　(データなどの)差分
　incremental cost of capital　限界資本コスト(=marginal cost of capital)
　incremental innovation　漸進的技術革新
　incremental profit　増分利益, 差額利益
　incremental return　増分リターン
　incremental revenue　増分収益
　incremental transaction rate　限界取引レート
　priority incremental budget　優先順位付き積み増し[積み上げ]予算
incrementalism　(名)漸進主義, 段階的な金利調整, 増分主義
◆U.S. Fed Chairman Ben Bernanke has chosen incrementalism over radical change in his first meeting. 米連邦準備制度理事会(FRB)のベン・バーナンキ議長は、最初の連邦公開市場委員会(FOMC)で、急進的な変化よりも漸進主義[段階的な金利調整]を選んだ。
Incubator Bank of Japan　日本振興銀行
◆Incubator Bank of Japan established in 2004 as a protector of small firms specializes in providing loans to small and midsize companies. 中小企業の味方として2004年に設立された日本振興銀行は、中小企業向け融資を専門に手がけている。
◆Incubator Bank of Japan which was scandal-ridden for its lax lending practices and arrests of its executives has finally collapsed. 乱脈融資や経営陣の逮捕など不祥事続きの日本振興銀行が、ついに破たんした。
incur　(動)引き起こす, 発生させる, 招く, 損失や損害を被(こうむ)る[受ける], 負う, 負担する, 引き受ける, 負債に陥(おちい)る, 怒りを買う
　immense bad loans incurred by banks　銀行が抱える莫大な不良債権
　incur a group net loss　連結純損失を被る, 連結税引き後赤字に陥る
　incur a loss　損失を被る
　incur a significant loss　大きい損失を被る
　incur debts　負債を負う, 借金を背負い込む
　incur further damages　さらに損害を受ける
　incur losses　損失を被る, 損失が生じる
　incur losses if the yen rises above the assumed exchange rate　想定為替レートより円高になれば為替差損が生じる
　incur responsibility　責任を負う
　incur the borrowing costs　借入[資金調達]コストを負担する
　incur unseen liabilities　不測の債務を負う, 不測の債務が発生する
　incurred cost　発生原価, 賦課原価(=cost incurred, incurred expense)
　incurred expense　発生費用 (=incurred cost)
　losses incurred by writing off nonperforming loans　不良債権処理で生じた損失額
　losses incurred from selling off shares　株式の売却で被った損失
　losses incurred from the disposal of bad loans　不良債権処理に伴う損失額
　previously incurred liabilities　過去に発生した負債

◆An exporter company will incur losses if the yen rises above the assumed exchange rate, but benefit if the yen declines. 輸出企業では、その想定為替レートより円高になれば為替差損が生じ、(想定為替レートより)円安になれば為替差益が出る。◆Any payment not made when due will, in addition to any other right or remedy of Licensor, incur a finance charge at the lesser of three hundred basis points over the 3-month London Inter Bank Offered Rate ("LIBOR＋3") on the date payment was due or the highest applicable legal contract rate. 支払いが支払期日までに履行されない場合、ライセンサーの他の権利や救済請求権に加えて、支払い期日時点の3か月物ロンドン銀行間取引金利(LIBOR)プラス3%(LIBOR＋3%)または適用される最高法定約定金利のうち、いずれか低いほうの金利の金融費用が発生する。◆During a regular board meeting, Fuji TV directors agreed to file a claim against Livedoor for losses of more than ¥30 billion incurred from selling off Livedoor shares. 定例取締役会で、フジテレビの役員は、ライブドア株の売却で被った300億円超の損失について、ライブドアに損害賠償を請求することで合意した。◆Losses incurred by writing off nonperforming loans are not generally taxable in the United States. 不良債権処理で生じた損失額は、米国では一般に課税の対象とはならない。◆Major banks' losses incurred from the disposal of bad loans totaled more than ¥7.7 trillion and net losses exceeded ¥4 trillion. 大手銀行の不良債権処理に伴う損失額は、総計で7兆7,000億円を上回り、純損失額(最終赤字)は4兆円を超えた。◆The company incurred losses in its stock dealings with other group firms. 同社は、他のグループ企業各社との株取引で損失を被った。◆UFJ Holdings remained in the red, incurring a group net loss of more than ¥400 billion. UFJホールディングスは、4,000億円を超える連結純損失[連結税引き後赤字]となって、赤字を続けた。

indebted (形)負債がある, 借金がある, 債務を抱えた (⇒heavily indebted people)
 be indebted to A for a large amount　Aに多額の金を借りている
 heavily indebted company　巨額の債務を抱えた企業 (⇒corporate rehabilitation fund)
 heavily indebted people　多重債務者
 indebted country　債務国 (=debtor country)
 indebted eurozone governments　債務を抱えたユーロ圏政府
 indebted person　債務者
 people indebted to multiple consumer loan companies [firms]　多重債務者
 ◆People indebted to multiple consumer loan firms and financially strapped small-business operators have been the main targets of loan sharks. 多重債務者や資金繰りが苦しい零細事業主が、ヤミ金融業者の主な標的になっている。

indebted borrower　債務を抱えた借り手, 債務を抱えた発行体 (⇒heavily indebted borrower)
 ◆In the case of a lack of liquidity or liquidity crisis, the debt repayment of an indebted borrower is still possible if a grace period is given, but lack of cash on hand makes it impossible to repay its debt in the short term. 流動性不足や流動性危機の場合、債務を抱えた借り手の債務返済は猶予期間を与えればまだ可能であるが、手元に現金がないため短期での債務返済はできない。

indebted company　赤字会社, 債務を抱えた企業 (⇒corporate rehabilitation fund)
 ◆The company purchased indebted Japanese companies. 同社は、赤字の日本企業を買収した。

indebtedness (名)債務, 負債, 負債額, 貸借, 借入れ, 借入金, 貸付け金
 average indebtedness percentage　平均借入比率[割合]
 balance of international indebtedness　国際貸借
 certificate of indebtedness　米政府短期債券, 債務証書
 currency indebtedness　通貨貸借, 通貨負債
 discharge of indebtedness　債務免除
 excessive indebtedness　負債超過
 floating indebtedness　浮動[流動]貸借
 general obligation indebtedness　一般財源保証債務
 guarantee [guaranty] of indebtedness　債務保証
 indebtedness due on demand　期限の定めのない債務
 indebtedness of affiliates　関係会社貸付け金, 関係会社債権
 indebtedness ratio　国債依存度
 indebtedness to affiliates　関係会社借入金
 international indebtedness　国際貸借
 mortgage indebtedness　モーゲージ債務
 net indebtedness　正味負債, 純負債額, 純借入れ, 純借入比率 (⇒inflow of funds)
 over-indebtedness　債務過多
 portfolio indebtedness　投資用借入れ
 public external indebtedness　公的対外債務 (⇒interest and principal payments)
 public indebtedness　公的債務
 real indebtedness effect　実質負債効果
 the applicable grace period specified in the agreement relating to such indebtedness　本契約に定める当該債務に関する適用猶予期間, 当該債務に関して本契約に定める適用猶予期間
 the level of indebtedness　負債水準
 total hard currency indebtedness　硬貨の総負債額
 treasury certificate of indebtedness　米政府債務証書
 ◆The entire indebtedness evidenced by this Note shall be immediately due and payable on September 30, 2011 (the Maturity Date). 本手形に表示する債務額は、2011年9月30日(支払い期日)に直ちに全額支払うものとする。

indemnity (名)補償, 損失補償, 損害填補, 損失補償契約, 補償金, 賠償, 賠償金
 disaster indemnity　災害補償
 income indemnity　所得補償
 indemnity against a loss　損失に対する補償, 損失補償
 indemnity agreement　補償契約
 indemnity bond　補償契約書, 賠償契約書 (=bond of indemnity)
 indemnity bond for a lost passbook　紛失通帳に対する補償念書
 indemnity for arrears　遅延賠償金
 indemnity in reinsurance　再保険の損害填補
 indemnity insurance　傷害保険
 indemnity on account　保険金内払い
 letter of indemnity　補償状
 letter of indemnity on guarantee　保証念書
 right of indemnity　求償権
 severance indemnity　退職給与
 ◆This is the first time a nonlife insurer has used its right of indemnity concerning the series of faults in MMC-made vehicles. 一連の三菱製自動車の欠陥問題に関して、損保会社が求償権を行使したのは、これが初めてだ。

indenture (名)信託契約書, 信託証書, 債務証書, 契約書
 bond indenture　債券信託証書, 社債信託契約, 社債契約, 社債信託約定書
 debt security's indenture　債務証券の信託証書
 indenture trustee　信託証書受託者
 security's indenture　証券の信託証書
 Trust Indenture Act　信託証書法

independence （名）独立, 独立性, 自立, 自主性
 auditor's independence 監査人の独立性
 independence and integrity 独立性と信頼性
 independence of central bank 中央銀行の独立性
 independence of management 経営の自主性
 the goal independence of central bank 中央銀行の目標の独立性
 the instrument independence of central bank 中央銀行の手段の独立性
 ◆The Tokyo Stock Exchange and the Osaka Stock Exchange are too concerned about maintaining their independence. 東証も大証も、独立性の維持に強い懸念を抱いている。

independent （形）独立した, 自立した, 独立系の, 第三者の, 個別の, 独自の, 自主的な, 単独の
 independent accountant 独立会計士, 独立監査人, 独立した会計監査人（一般に公認会計士という）
 independent administrative institution 独立行政法人
 independent advisory body 独立諮問機関, 第三者による諮問機関
 independent audit office 独立した監査事務局
 independent auditor 独立監査人, 独立した会計監査人, 外部監査人
 independent auditor's report 独立監査人の報告書
 independent consulting firm 独立系コンサルティング会社
 independent contractor 独立業務請負人, インディペンデント・コントラクター, IC（個人が企業と契約して、専門性の高いプロジェクトを請け負う人）
 independent credit rating system 独立した格付けシステム
 independent factory price 公正な工場渡し価格
 independent financial adviser［advisor］ 社外財務コンサルタント, 社外ファイナンシャル・アドバイザー
 independent investment 独立投資
 independent oversight board 独立監視委員会
 independent rating agency 独立格付け機関
 independent regulator 独立規制当局
 independent store 独立店, 独立店舗
 independent valuation 第三者による評価
 ◆Small municipalities have a financial difficulty in setting up an independent audit office or conducting external auditing every fiscal year. 小規模市町村の場合、独立した監査事務局を設置したり、外部監査を毎年度実施したりするのは財政的に困難だ。◆The public welfare loans are extended to widows and single mothers to help them become economically independent by financing spending for education, living costs, housing costs and funds to start small businesses. 福祉資金は、母子家庭や寡婦に対して教育費や生活費、住宅費、小規模事業の開始資金などを貸し付けて、その経済的自立を助けるために供与されている。

independent director 社外取締役, 独立取締役
 ◆The California Public Employees' Retirement System has asked Xerox Corp. to appoint three independent directors and split the position of chairman and chief executive officer, as a way of restoring investor confidence and improving corporate governance. 投資家の信頼回復と企業統治推進のため、カリフォルニア州公務員退職年金基金（カルパース）は、ゼロックスに対して、独立取締役3名の増員や会長と最高経営責任者（最高業務執行役員・CEO）の職務分離を要求した。

independent trustee 独立した信託機関
 ◆It is the Corporation's practice to fund amounts for postretirement benefits, with an independent trustee, as deemed appropriate from time to time. 随時適切と思われる退職後給付額を、独立した信託機関に積み立てるのが、当社の慣行となっています。

independent yen-selling intervention 単独の円売り介入
 ◆The Japanese government and the Bank of Japan conducted an independent yen-selling intervention. 日本政府・日銀は、単独で円売り介入を行った。

index （動）消費者物価指数にスライド［連動］させる, スライド［指数化］方式にする
 a system of indexing benefits to consumer price movements 公的年金給付額を消費者物価の変動にスライドさせる制度［物価スライド制］
 indexed bond インデックス債
 ◆The finance and health ministries will study areas for budget cuts, including the application for the second consecutive year of a system of indexing benefits to consumer price movements. 財務、厚生労働両省は、公的年金の給付額を消費者物価の変動にスライドさせる「物価スライド制度」の2年連続適用などを含めて、予算削減の対象を検討する方針だ。

index （名）指数, 指標, 指針, 索引, インデックス（⇒consumer confidence index, consumer price index, DI, diffusion index, industrial production index, leading index）
 coincident index 一致指数
 commodity index 商品指数
 composite index 景気総合指数, CI
 consumer price index 消費者物価指数, CPI
 cost of living index 生計費指数
 DI index 業況判断指数, 景気動向指数, DI指数（DI=diffusion index）
 diffusion index 景気動向指数
 Dow-Jones index ダウ平均株価指数
 general index 総合指数
 lagging index 遅行（ちこう）指数
 leading index 先行指数
 Nikkei Index 日経平均
 NYSE Composite Index NYSE総合株価指数
 retail price index 小売物価指数, RPI
 S&P 500 index S&P500株価指数
 stock index 株価指数（=stock price index）
 stock price index 株価指数
 Tankan index 日銀短観の業況判断指数（DI）
 ◆Banks' capital adequacy ratio is an index that shows their business soundness. 銀行各行の自己資本比率は、銀行の経営の健全性を示す指標である。◆The DI index has improved considerably among carmakers, machine manufacturers and other export-related businesses. 業況判断指数は、自動車や一般機械などの輸出関連業種が大幅に改善している。◆The DJ Stoxx index of European banking stocks has fallen 37 percent from a peak in February. ダウ・ジョーンズ欧州銀行株指数は、2月のピークから37％下落した。◆The index of leading economic indicators predicts economic developments about six months ahead. 景気先行指数は、約6か月先の景気動向を示す指標だ。◆The S&P 500 index fell 17.74, or 2.4 percent, to 735.09. S&P500株価指数は、735.09ドルで17.74ドル（2.4％）低下［下落］した。◆The Standard & Poor's 500 index is at the top end of its range for the past two months. スタンダード・プアーズ（500種）株価指数は、過去2か月のボックス圏の上限にある。◆The Tankan index for large manufacturers rose to plus 2 in September from the minus 9 registered in June. 9月短観の大企業・製造業の業況判断指数（DI）は、6月調査のマイナス9からプラス2に11ポイント改善した。

index arbitrage 指数裁定, 指数裁定取引, インデックス・アービトラージ（ある株式の現物と株価指数先物との同時売買）

index bond インデックス債, インデックス・ボンド（=indexed bond: 元本や利払い額がインフレ率に連動す

る債券）

index fund　指数ファンド, インデックス型ファンド, インデックス投信, インデックス・ファンド　(=indexed-fund: 株価指数と連動するように設計された株式ポートフォリオを運用の対象とする投資信託で、米国のミューチュアル・ファンドの一種)
- cash index fund　現物指数ファンド
- equity index fund　株価指数ファンド, 株式インデックス・ファンド
- synthetic index fund　合成指数ファンド

index-link　(動)物価[物価指数]に連動させる, 物価[物価指数]にスライドさせる

index-linked [index linked]　(形)物価スライド制の, スライド制の, 指数連動型の, 指数リンクの, インデックス・リンクの
- index-linked bond　インデックス・リンク債
- index-linked gilts　インデックス・リンク・ギルト債
- index-linked minimum wage　物価スライド制最低賃金
- index-linked product　指数リンク商品[金融商品], 指数連動型商品, インデックス・リンク商品　(=index-link product)
- index-linked securities　指数リンク証券
- index-linked structure　指数連動型商品
- index-linked trading　インデックス取引
- index-linked warrant　指数連動型ワラント
- Nikkei 225 Index-linked bonds　日経平均リンク債

index mutual fund　インデックス・ミューチュアル・ファンド　(=index fund: 株価指数と連動するように設計された株式ポートフォリオを運用対象とする投資信託)
◆The exchange-traded funds (ETFs) are investment products similar to index mutual funds but that trade on stock exchanges like stocks. 上場投資信託(ETF)は、インデックス・ミューチュアル・ファンドに似ているが、株式と同じように証券取引所で売買される投資商品である。

index of business conditions　景況判断指数, 業況判断指数
◆The index of business conditions is calculated by subtracting the percentage of companies reporting deteriorating business conditions from that of firms reporting improving conditions. 景況判断指数は、業況が改善していると報告した企業の割合から、業況が悪化していると報告した企業の割合を差し引いて算定する。

index of business confidence　景況判断指数
◆The index of business confidence among large companies is projected to read plus 4.8 for the July-September quarter. 7-9月期の大企業(製造業)の景況判断指数は、プラス4.8の改善が見込まれている。

index of industrial output　鉱工業生産指数, 工業生産指数　(=index of industrial production; ⇒industrial production index)

index of lagging indicators　遅行指数
◆The index of lagging indicators is designed to measure economic performance in the recent past. 遅行指数は、直近の過去の景気動向を示す指標だ。

index of leading economic indicators　景気先行指標総合指数, 景気先行指数, 先行指数(景気先行指数は、景気の現状より約6か月先の景気の動きを示す指標)
◆The index of leading economic indicators, a measure of economic moves about six months ahead, came to 80 percent in March. 景気の現状より6か月先の景気の動きを示す指標である景気先行指数が、3月には80％になった。

index of output at mines and factories　鉱工業生産指数
◆The index of output at mines and factories registered 100.1 in July against the base of 100 for 2000. 7月の鉱工業生産指数は、100.1(2000年=100)となった。

index option　株価指数オプション, 指数オプション(日経平均株価オプションやS&P500オプションなど、株価指数を対象とするオプション取引)

indexation [indexing]　(名)(賃金、年金などの)物価スライド制, 物価スライド方式, 指数化方式, 指数連係, インデックス運用, インデクセーション　(=index-linking)
- automatic indexation to the rise in the cost of living　生活費上昇に対する自動的物価スライド制

indexed　(形)物価スライド制[スライド方式]の, 物価指数スライド制の, 生計費指数に連動した, インデックス運用型の, インデックス型の
- indexed approach　インデックス型アプローチ(市場平均を代表する指数(インデックス)並みであれば十分とする資産運用の手法)
- indexed bond　インデックス債　(=index bond)
- indexed currency option note　為替オプション付き債, ICON
- indexed debt instruments　インデックス債
- indexed fund　インデックス・ファンド　(=index fund)
- indexed gilts　物価指数スライド制優良証券
- indexed portfolio　インデックス型ポートフォリオ(市場平均を上回る運用成績の追求はしないで、市場平均並みの運用成績を確保できれば十分として、一定の指数に連動するようにしたポートフォリオで、パッシブ運用(passive management)の典型例)
- indexed product　インデックス運用型金融商品, インデックス運用型商品
- indexed to inflation　物価スライド制
- inflationary indexed bond　インフレ連動証券

indexed government bond　物価連動債
◆Foreign private companies are allowed to buy indexed government bonds from fiscal 2005. 外国の民間企業は、2005年度から物価連動債の購入を認められている。◆The ownership of indexed government bonds has been limited to foreign governments, central banks and international organizations. 物価連動債の保有は、これまで海外の政府や中央銀行、国際機関に限られていた。

indexing　(名)インデックス運用, インフレ調整条項

indicate　(動)示す, 表示する, 記載する, 表す, 指摘する, 〜をほのめかす, それとなく示す, 参考として示す
- at the tight end of the indicated range of　〜の予想レンジのきつめのところで
- fix the conversion premium above the indicated range　転換プレミアムを仮条件より高く設定する
- indicate a pickup in manufacturing activity　製造業の景気回復[景気持ち直し]を示す
- indicate concerns in the future　今後の懸念材料になる
- indicate investor interest　投資家の関心を示す
- indicate the momentum of economic cycles　景気の勢いを示す
- indicated pricing　仮条件
◆The deflator, which indicates the overall trend in prices, dropped 2.5 percent in the April-June period compared to the corresponding period last year. 物価の総合的な動向を示すデフレーターは、4-6月期は前年同期比で2.5％下落した。◆The proxy form indicates the number of shares to be voted, including any full shares held for participants in the Employee Stock Purchase Plan. 委任状用紙には、従業員株式購入制度加入者のために保有している株式をすべて含めて、行使される議決権数が記載されています。

indication　(名)表示, 兆し, 動き, 気配(けはい), 気配値, 実勢相場, 動向, 指標, 条件の提示, インディケーション

advance indications　事前予想
cyclical indication　景気指標
grey market indication　グレー・マーケットの気配値
indication method　インディケーション方式（外債発行条件の仮の決定方式）
indication of improvement　改善の兆し
indication of interest　インディケーション・オブ・インタレスト,販売希望額,インディケーション（仮募集の期間中に販売団員が引受主幹事に随時申告する販売希望額で,新規発行証券に対する投資家の関心の高さを示す）
indication rate　取引前の段階で提示する為替レート,参考提示為替レート
indications of a full-fledged recovery　本格的な復調の気配
indications only　「できず」（売りと買いの水準に隔たりがあって売買不成立の状態のこと）
objective indications of intent　意図の客観的表示,意図を客観的に示すもの
preliminary indications　仮条件
receive indications from　～から条件の提示を受ける
submit an indication　条件提示を行う,条件を提示する
◆Under the severe income and employment situations, personal consumption has yet to show indications of a full-fledged recovery. 厳しい所得・雇用環境の下で,個人消費に本格的な復調の気配がまだ見えない。

indicative　（形）～を示す,表す,暗示する,～の兆候がある,指示的
indicative dividing line between expansion and contraction signals　景気拡大と景気後退の判断の分かれ目
indicative economic planning　指示的経済計画
indicative price　気配値（=indicative interest quotations）
indicative rating　予想格付け,事前格付け
indicative rating opinions　事前格付け見解
indicative terms　非公式に示された条件
the current indicative market quote　時価

indicator　（名）指数,指標,指針,目安,インディケーター（⇒bond market, consumer confidence index）
coincident indicator　一致指数
DI of the coincident indicators　景気一致指数（DI）
DI of the lagging indicators　景気遅行（ちこう）指数（DI）
DI of the leading indicators　景気先行指数（DI）
economic indicator　経済指標,景気指標
financial indicator　財務指標
inflation indicator　インフレ指標
key economic indicators　主要経済指標
labor market indicators　労働統計
lagging indicator　遅行（ちこう）指数
leading indicator　先行指数
monetary indicators　金融指標
numerical indicator　数値目標
performance indicator　業績指数,業績指標
profitability indicator　収益性指標
◆Solvency margin is an indicator of an insurance company's financial health. ソルベンシー・マージン（支払い余力）比率は,保険会社の財務の健全性を示す指標の一つである。◆The coincident indicator, the nation's key gauge of the state of the economy, topped the boom-or-bust line of 50 percent in March. 国内の景気の現状を示す一致指数［景気一致指数］が,3月に景気判断の分かれ目となる50%を上回った。◆The diffusion indexes of the coincident, leading and lagging indicators compare the current levels of various economic indicators with their levels three months earlier. 一致指数や先行指数,遅行指数などの景気動向指数は,各種経済指標の現状を3か月前の状況と比較したものだ。◆The rating of government bonds is considered an indicator of its creditworthiness. 国債の格付けは,国債の信用力の目安とされている。

indicator of long-term interest rates　長期金利の指標
◆On the bond market, the yield on newly issued 10-year government bonds, an indicator of long-term interest rates, fell, resulting in a rise in bond prices. 債券市場では,長期金利の指標である新発10年物国債の利回り（流通利回り）が下落し,債券相場［債券価格］は上昇した。

indices　（名）指数（indexの複数）
American stock indices　アメリカン株価指数
constituents and weightings of within the indices　指標の構成銘柄と組入れ比率
currency-denominated Flex options American stock indices　アメリカン株価指数の外貨建てフレックス・オプション
derivatives on the FTSE indices　100種指数は制商品
home-purchase mortgage indices　モーゲージ申請指数
indices of urban land prices　全国市街地価格指数
the FTSE indices　FT100種指数
the Major Market indices　メジャー・マーケット・株価指数

indict　（動）起訴する,告発する
◆A former Osaka Security Exchange Company senior executive vice president was indicted without arrest for market manipulation. 大阪証券取引所（大証）の元副理事長が,株価操作の罪で在宅起訴された。◆A House of Representatives member was indicted for accepting bribes in an influence peddling scheme and violating the political Funds Control Law. 衆院議員が,斡旋収賄罪と政治資金規正法違反で起訴された。◆The former company president was indicted on fraud charges regarding a dubious capital increase in the firm. この元社長は,架空増資に関する詐欺罪で起訴された。

indictment　（名）起訴,告発,起訴状
be under indictment for　～の罪で起訴されている,～の廉（かど）で起訴されている
file a summary indictment against　～を略式起訴する
mandatory indictment　強制起訴
merit indictment　起訴相当
written indictment　起訴状
◆The Fukuoka Local Public Prosecutors Office filed a summary indictment against two former executives of Kyudenko's subsidiary in the Philippines who had provided sets of golf clubs to two high-ranking government officials. 福岡区検は,フィリピンの政府高官2人にゴルフ・セットを贈った九電工の現地子会社の元幹部2人を,略式起訴した。◆The special investigation squad of the Tokyo Public Prosecutors Office filed a fresh indictment against the company and its former executives. 東京地検特捜部は,同社と同社の元役員らを追起訴した。

indirect　（形）間接の,間接的な
indirect arbitrage　間接裁定,3点間裁定（=three point arbitrage）
indirect bill　間接為替手形
indirect borrowing　間接借入れ,間接的借入れ
indirect contract　（為替などの）間接予約
indirect credit　間接控除
indirect damages　間接損害,間接的損害賠償金
indirect debt　間接負債
indirect exchange　間接為替,間接的交換
indirect exchange arbitrage　間接為替裁定

indirect exchange bill　間接為替手形
indirect finance　間接金融
indirect financial assets　間接金融資産
indirect foreign investment　対外間接投資
indirect foreign tax credit　外国税額の間接控除
indirect infringement　間接侵害
indirect investment　間接投資
indirect inward investment　対内間接投資
indirect issue　間接発行
indirect liability　間接債務
indirect loan　間接融資
indirect loss　間接損害
indirect ownership　間接所有権
indirect paper　間接為替手形
indirect parity　間接平価
indirect placement　有価証券の間接募集
indirect quotation　外貨建て相場, 受取勘定建て相場
indirect quotes　間接呼び値
indirect rate　間接レート
indirect securities　間接証券
indirect standard　間接本位制
indirect tax　間接税
indirect transfer　間接移転
indirect yield　間接利回り
monetary indirect security　貨幣的間接証券

indirect financing　間接金融
◆Germany's financial sector used to rely on bank loan-centered indirect financing. ドイツの金融業界は、以前は銀行融資中心の間接金融に頼っていた。

individual　（形）個人の, 個々の, 個別の　（名）個人, 個体, 単一体
individual accident insurance　個人障害保険
individual account　個人口座
individual asset accumulation　個人年金保険
individual bank［banker］　個人銀行（=private banker）
individual banking　（銀行の）個人部門業務
individual bill　個人手形
individual bond　個人保証
individual clearing member　個人清算会員
individual consumption　個人消費
individual deferred annuity　個人据え置き年金
individual deposit　個人預金
individual disability　個人就業不能保険
individual disability income　個人所得補償保険
individual equity option　個別銘柄株式オプション
individual estimate　個人評価法, 個別計算法
individual excess of loss cover　個別危険超過損害再保険
individual financial assets　個人金融資産
individual gain　個人的利益
individual insurance　普通保険, 個別保険
individual level premium（method）　個人水準保険料方式
individual life and health　個人生命保険・医療保険
individual meeting　個別訪問（=face-to-face meeting:IR活動の一つで、機関投資家や証券会社に出向いて直接会社の業務内容などを説明）
individual monthly premium　本人保険料個人負担月額
individual proprietor　自営業者, 個人事業主
individual savings　個人貯蓄
individual security　個人保障

individual selection　個別選択
individual stock　個別銘柄
individual stock option　個別株オプション
individual system　個人能率給制
individual trader　個人ディーラー
Individual Training Accounts　個人訓練口座, ITA
individual trust　個人信託
individual underwriter　個人保険業者
individuals' purchase of government bonds　国債の個人消化
◆In revitalizing the market, it is necessary to encourage individuals, who have financial assets totaling ¥1.4 quadrillion, to invest in the stock market. 市場の活性化を図るには、1,400兆円にのぼる金融資産を持つ個人の株式市場への投資を促す必要がある。◆Japan Post is discussing an alliance with Suruga Bank to offer mortgages and other loans to individuals. 日本郵政は現在、住宅ローンなど個人ローン商品の販売に向けて、スルガ銀行と業務提携協議を進めている。◆Ordinary bank deposits for individuals and current deposits for businesses were fully guaranteed until March 31, 2003. 個人の普通預金と企業の当座預金は、2003年3月31日まで全額保証された。◆The bank handles transactions for individuals and small and midsize companies. 同行は、中小企業・個人向けの取引を扱っている。◆The bank has been relatively weak in retail banking operations dealing with individuals and small and medium-sized firms. 同行は、個人や中小企業向けの小口取引銀行業務が比較的弱い。◆The People's Bank of China raised interest rates on loans by financial institutions to corporations and individuals. 中国人民銀行が、金融機関の企業や個人に対する貸出金利を引き上げた。◆The total amount of money deposited in individual foreign currency accounts has continued to increase in recent years. 個人向け外貨預金残高は、ここ数年増え続けている。◆The U.S. government froze the assets of four individuals and eight entities that were involved in illicit activities such as money laundering, currency counterfeiting and narcotics trafficking. 米政府は、資金洗浄（マネー・ロンダリング）や通貨偽造、麻薬取引などの違法行為に関与している4個人、8団体の資産を凍結した。

individual annuity　個人年金
individual annuity contract　個人年金契約
individual annuity insurance policy　個人年金保険証券, 個人年金保険
individual annuity policy plan　個別年金契約方式
◆In the United States, banks are allowed to offer individual annuity insurance policies. 米国では、銀行が個人年金保険の取扱いを認められている。

individual asset　個人資産
◆The bank's aim is to help circulate dormant individual assets in the local economy. 眠れる個人の金融資産を地域経済に循環させるのが、同行の目的だ。

individual consumption　個人消費
◆The downward revision of the fiscal 2011 growth projection was made due to a drastic slowdown in individual consumption and meager price increases. 2011年度の経済成長見通しの下方修正は、個人消費の大幅な減速と物価上昇率の鈍化が原因だ。

individual customer　個人顧客
◆The brokerage's main services for individual customers will be asset management advisory services, focusing on the sale of products such as investment trust funds that invest in foreign equities, and money market funds denominated in foreign currencies. 同証券会社は、株の主な個人顧客向け（売買仲介）業務として、外国株を組み込んだ投資信託や外貨建てMMF（マネー・マーケット・ファンド）などの商品の販売を中心に、資産運用顧問業務を展開する方針だ。

individual investor　個人投資家　（⇒equity market,

Internet trading, investment opportunity, lease financing)
◆An individual investor began depositing money in U.S. dollars using a major bank's Web account. 個人投資家が、大手銀行のウェブ口座[インターネット口座]を利用して米ドルの外貨預金を始めた。◆Day traders are individual investors who buy and sell stocks many times a day to earn a profit on the trading margin. デイ・トレーダーは、1日に何度も株の売買を繰り返して、その利ざやで利益を上げる個人投資家だ。◆In Germany, individual investors' capital gains are not normally taxed. ドイツでは、個人投資家の譲渡益については通常、非課税となっている。◆Individual investors and brokerage dealers continued to take profits from recent surges in comparatively low-prices issues. 個人投資家と証券会社のディーラーは、最近の比較的割安な銘柄の急上昇で引き続き利食いに出た。◆Individual investors are now able to buy stocks at the outlets of banks and other financial institutions. 個人投資家は現在、銀行などの金融機関の店舗で株を購入できる。◆Investment trust funds are popular among individual investors. 投資信託は、個人投資家に人気がある。◆The number of individual investors holding shares in companies listed on the Jasdaq Securities Exchange increased for the 10th straight year. ジャスダック証券取引所に上場している企業(931社)の個人株主数は、10年連続で増加した。

individual life insurance　個人生命保険, 個人保険
◆Nippon Life Insurance Co. lost its position in the individual life insurance market for the first time in postwar Japan. 日本生命保険が、個人生保市場で、戦後日本で初めて首位の座を失った。

individual life insurance and annuity contracts　個人保険と年金の契約
◆The nine insurers had a combined outstanding balance of individual life insurance and annuity contracts of ¥1.04 quadrillion as of March 31, 2004. 生保9社の個人保険・年金の保有契約高は、2004年3月31日現在、9社合計で1,040兆円だった。◆The 10 life insurers' combined outstanding balance of individual life insurance and annuity contracts declined for five consecutive years to ¥1.15 quadrillion. 生保10社合計の個人保険・年金の保有契約高(保険の総額)は、1,150兆円で、5年連続(5期連続)で減少した。

individual retirement　個人退職
individual retirement account　個人年金退職金勘定, 個人退職所得勘定, 個人退職金口座制度, IRA
individual retirement savings plan　個人退職貯蓄制度

individual shareholder [stockholder]　個人株主
◆The company has about 136,000 shareholders, both individual and institutional shareholders. 同社の株主は、個人、法人合わせて約136,000人にのぼる。

induce　(動)引き起こす, 誘導する, 誘発する, 誘って～させる, 促進する, 帰納する
induce a downward bias　低めの結果が出る
induce capital outflows　対外投融資を促す
induce change　変化を引き起こす
induce consumption　消費を誘発する, 消費を促す
induce yen-buying as a safe haven　安全な投資手段として円を買わせる, 安全な投資手段としての円買いを促す
◆Concerns over the U.S. economic outlook tend to induce yen-buying as a safe haven. 米経済の先行きに対する懸念から、安全な投資手段として円が買われる傾向にある。

induced　(形)誘発された, 誘導された, 誘発的, ～発の
-induced　～による, ～発の　(=-triggered)
induced capital movements　誘発的資本移動
induced conversions of convertible debt　転換社債の転換誘導, 転換社債の誘因による転換
induced demand inflation　誘発的需要インフレ
induced export　誘発的輸出

induced inflation　調整インフレ　(=adjustment inflation)

induced investment　誘発投資(所得などの変化に誘発される投資)
induced invisible trade balance　貿易付帯収支
induced price increase　誘発的価格上昇
◆The Greece-induced fiscal crisis is still not under control. ギリシャ発の財政危機は、まだ収束していない。

inducement　(名)誘因, 刺激, 動機, 勧誘, 奨励
foreign capital inducement　外資導入
inducement coefficient　生産誘発係数
inducement to change insurer　(保険の)乗換え契約勧誘
inducement to invest [investment]　投資誘因

industrial　(形)産業の, 工業の, 鉱工業の, 工業の発達した, 工業生産の, 産業[工業]用の, インダストリアル　(名)産業株(industrials), 工業株, 産業社債, 工業社債, 産業[工業]会社, 一般事業会社(industrials)
commercial and industrial loans　商工業融資
financial and industrial holdings　金融・製造業子会社
financial and industrial investments　金融・産業投資
industrial accidents　労働災害, 労務災害, 業務災害　(=industrial injuries)
industrial affiliations　企業系列
industrial average　工業株平均
industrial bank　勤労者銀行, 消費者銀行, 中小の割賦金融会社
industrial bill　工業手形
industrial bond　事業債, 工業債, 産業債, 企業債(事業会社が発行する債券で、一般には社債と呼ばれる。事業債は、電力会社が発行する電力債と、それ以外の一般事業債に区分される)
industrial boom　産業好景気, 好景気, 好況
industrial development bond　産業振興債, 産業開発債, 産業誘致債, IDB　(=industrial revenue bond)
industrial disaster　産業災害
industrial disease　職業病, 産業病　(=occupational disease)
industrial finance corporation　産業金融公社
industrial fund　産業資金
industrial holding company　製造業持ち株会社
industrial insurance　簡易保険, 労働者保険, 簡易生命保険(industrial life insurance)
industrial investment　産業投資, 事業投資
industrial issuer　一般企業の発行体
industrial life　簡易生命保険
industrial life insurance　簡易生命保険　(=debit (life) insurance, home service assurance, home service (industrial) insurance)
industrial loan company　産業融資会社, ILC
industrial portfolio　産業界への投資
industrial revenue bond　産業歳入債, 産業歳入担保債, 免税歳入債, 産業振興債, IRB債, IRB　(=industrial development bond)
industrial savings　勤労者貯蓄, 労務者貯蓄
industrial share [stock]　工業株
NAPM's [National Association of Purchasing Management's] index of industrial activity　全米購買部協会景気総合指数
rating on an industrial bond　事業債の格付け
regional survey of industrial conditions　景況感調査

industrial output　工業生産, 工業生産高, 鉱工業生産高　(=industrial production; ⇒flat)
◆The nation's industrial output rose a seasonally adjusted

0.5 percent in May from the previous month. 日本の5月の鉱工業生産高は、前年同月比で0.5%(季節調整値)増加した。

industrial production index 鉱工業生産指数, 工業生産指数 (=index of industrial output, index of industrial production, industrial output data, industrial output index)
◆The industrial production index improved in May, the first month-on-month rise in three months. 鉱工業生産指数は5月に回復し、3か月ぶりに前月比でプラスに転じた。

Industrial Revitalization Corporation 産業再生機構, IRC (=Industrial Revitalization Corporation of Japan; ⇒auspices, IRC)
◆The Industrial Revitalization Corporation was inaugurated with the aim of revitalizing troubled banks and industries. 産業再生機構は、経営不振の銀行と産業の再生を目指して発足した。

Industrial Revitalization Law [industrial revitalization law] 産業再生法 (⇒corporate income)
◆Depending on the degree of JAL's financial deterioration, the government will consider a combination of capital reinforcement under the industrial revitalization law and public assistance by the Enterprise Turnaround Initiative Corp. of Japan. 日航の財務の傷み具合によって、政府は、産業再生法に基づく公的資金による資本増強と、企業再生支援機構による公的支援との組合せを検討する方針だ。◆The company plans to call for the application of the Industrial Revitalization Law shortly. 同社は、近く産業再生法の適用を要請する方針だ。

industry (名)産業, 工業, 産業界, 工業会, 業界, 〜業, 業種, メーカー
banking industry　銀行業界
building and construction industry　建設業界
Council for the Securities Industry　証券業協議会
credit card industry　クレジット・カード業界
derivatives industry　派生商品業界
financial industry　金融業界, 金融界, 金融産業 (⇒collection of debts)
financial service [services] industry　金融サービス業界, 金融サービス業
Financial Services Industry Association　金融サービス業協会
Financial Times index industry ordinary shares　フィナンシャル・タイムズ工業株価指数
funds industry　ファンド業界
futures industry　先物業界
Futures Industry Association　先物業協会
health industry　健康産業
health insurance industry　健康保険業界
housing industry　住宅産業
industry aggregates　業界平均
industry analyst　業界アナリスト
industry association　業界団体
industry classification　業種分類
industry-government alliance　官民協力, 官民共同
industry group　業界団体, 経済団体, 業種
industry outlook　業界予測
industry sources　業界筋
industry standard　産業基準, 業界標準, 業界規格, 統一基準
leading industries　主力産業
life insurance industry　生命保険業界
loans and discounts by industry　業種別貸出統計
loss-making industries　赤字業界
medical industry　医療産業
regulated industry　規制を受ける業界
service industry　サービス産業 (=service-oriented industry)
◆The firm's operations in the financial services and leasing industry involve direct financing and finance leasing programs for its products and the products of other companies. 金融サービスとリース業界での同社の事業には、同社製品と他社製品に関する直接融資とファイナンス・リース事業も含まれている。◆The move to lower the yields of insurance products is likely to spread through the industry as tough investment conditions persist. 厳しい運用環境が続いているので、保険商品の利回りを引き下げる動きは、業界全体に広がりそうだ。◆The Tankan index for 10 of the 16 industries in the manufacturing sector improved in September from three months earlier. 製造業16業種中10業種の日銀9月短観の業況判断指数(DI)は、(前回調査の)6月から改善した。

industry association 業界団体, 工業団体 (=industry group)
◆Ten U.S., European and Canadian industry associations pressed Japan to remove the threat of unfair competition in the planned privatization of kampo insurance. 欧米とカナダの10業界団体が、予定されている簡易保険民営化での不正競争の脅威を取り除くよう日本に強く求めた。

industry insiders 業界関係者
◆Industry insiders said the refusal to pay insurance benefits over a long period was partly because of former Meiji managers' unreasonable policies. 業界関係者によると、長期間にわたる保険金不払いの一因は、旧明治生命保険の経営者の無理な経営方針だ。

industry realignment 業界再編
◆Many industry observers expect few benefits from industry realignment such as mergers. 多くの業界筋は、合併などの業界再編による効果は薄いと見ている。

industry rule 業界規約, 業界ルール
◆The repurchasing method, which has customers buy highly negotiable cash vouchers, violates the industry rule. 顧客に換金性の高い金券類を購入させる買取り方式は、業界の規約に違反する。

ineffective (形)効果がない, 効力がない, 無益な, 役に立たない, 無能な, 役立たずの
◆The European banking tests are lax and ineffective as the collapses of two Irish banks and the Franco-Belgian bank Dexia, shortly after the EBA's stress tests, show. 欧州の銀行検査は、欧州銀行監督機構(EBA)のストレス・テストに合格した[ストレス・テストで安全と判定された]直後にアイルランドの銀行2行やフランス・ベルギー共同の銀行「デクシア」が破たんした事実が示すように、手ぬるくて効果がない。

inefficiency (名)非効率, 非効率性
◆The inefficiency of the Financial group's two-bank structure has been pointed out as many of operations overlap. 同フィナンシャル・グループの2行体制の非効率は、重複部門が多いため、以前から指摘されてきた。

ineligible (形)資格がない, 不適格の, 不適当な, 不適任な
ineligible bill　不適格手形
ineligible receivables　不適格債権
ineligible securities　不適格証券

inflate (動)膨(ふく)らませる, かさ上げする, 水増しする, 上乗せする, (価格などを)つり上げる, 上昇させる, 押し上げる, 誇張する
inflate bills　請求書を水増しする
inflate sales figures　架空売上げを計上する, 売上を膨らます
◆In the case of Japan, government debt inflates with additional domestic bond issuances. 日本の場合、内国債の追加発行で、政府の借金[政府債務]が積み上がっている。◆The

banks' equity capital is inflated by so-called "deferred tax assets." 銀行の自己資本は、いわゆる「繰延べ税金資産」でかさ上げされている。◆The former executives of Kanebo allegedly ordered section heads to inflate sales figures and reduce expenditures in financial statements. カネボウの旧経営陣は、財務諸表への架空売上の計上や経費の過少計上を各部門の責任者に指示していたといわれる。◆The president of a building inspection company registered falsely inflated capital for the company. 建築確認検査会社の社長が、同社の資本金を不正に多く登記していた。

inflate economic bubbles バブルを発生させる
◆Surplus funds put out by developed economies' monetary easing measures have flowed into emerging economies to inflate economic bubbles. 先進国の金融緩和策で生じた余剰資金が、新興国に流れ込み、バブルを発生させている。

inflate one's consolidated earnings 連結利益を水増しする
◆The brokerage firm inflated its consolidated earnings for its business year through March 2011. 同証券会社は、2011年3月期の連結利益を水増ししていた。

inflate one's net assets 純資産を水増しする
◆Olympus Corp. inflated its net assets by ¥33 billion in the consolidated financial statements for the business year ended March 2011. オリンパスは、2011年3月期決算の連結財務書類［2011年3月期連結決算］で純資産を334億円水増ししていた。

inflate the returns by leverage 借金で利益を膨らませる
◆The next step in the quest for higher gains is to inflate the returns by leverage. 高利益追求の第二の手段は、借金による利益の膨（ふく）らましだ。

inflate the stock prices of one's affiliate 関連会社の株価をつり上げる
◆The firm's former president spread false information about corporate purchases with the aim of inflating the stock prices of its affiliate. 同社の前社長は、関連会社の株価をつり上げるため、虚偽の企業買収情報を公表していた。

inflated （形）膨張した, 膨（ふく）らんだ, 肥大した, つり上げられた, 価格がひどく高い, 物価が暴騰した, インフレの, 大げさな, 仰々（ぎょうぎょう）しい
　inflated balance sheet 膨らんだバランス・シート
　inflated economy インフレ経済
　inflated effect on the market prices 相場の過剰反応
　inflated government debts 膨張した政府の借金, 政府債務の膨張
　inflated postal savings and kammpo life insurance policies 肥大した郵便貯金と簡易保険
　inflated prices 価格のつり上げ, つり上げられた価格
◆The purpose of postal privatization was to do away with the current inefficient system, in which huge funds raised through inflated postal savings and kampo life insurance policies flow into public corporations. 郵政民営化の目的は、肥大した郵便貯金と簡易保険で調達した巨額の資金が特殊法人に流れる現在の非効率的なシステムを、廃止することにあった。

inflation （名）物価上昇, 物価上昇率, 物価高騰, 通貨膨張, インフレ, インフレ率, インフレーション（⇒gauge, peg）
　accelerating inflation 加速するインフレ, インフレ加速
　adjustments to restate costs for the effect of general inflation 一般物価水準変動の影響による修正表示
　aggravate inflation インフレを悪化させる
　asset inflation 資産インフレ
　boost inflation by A percent インフレ率をA％押し上げる
　cause inflation インフレを起こす
　compensate for inflation 物価上昇分を埋め合わせる, 物価上昇分を補てんする
　concerns［fears］over inflation インフレ懸念
　consumer inflation 消費者物価の上昇
　consumer（price）inflation 消費者物価の上昇, 消費者物価上昇率
　contain inflation インフレを封じ込める, インフレを抑制［抑止］する, インフレを抑える
　control［curb］inflation インフレを抑制する, インフレを抑える
　core inflation 基礎インフレ率, コア・インフレ率
　cost-push inflation 生産費の上昇によるインフレ, コスト・プッシュ型インフレ, コストプッシュ・インフレ
　CPI inflation 消費者物価指数（CPI）で見たインフレ率
　creeping inflation 忍び寄るインフレ, 緩やかなインフレ（＝mild inflation: 物価上昇率が2～4％で持続する状態）
　curb inflation インフレを抑える, インフレを抑止する
　cyclical inflation 景気循環に伴うインフレ, 景気循環要因に基づくインフレ
　decelerating inflation 減速するインフレ, インフレ減速
　demand-pull inflation 需要インフレ, デマンド・プル型インフレ, デマンドプル・インフレ（総需要に生産量が追いつかないで起こるインフレ）
　double-digit inflation 2桁インフレ
　enjoy low inflation 低インフレを享受する, インフレ率が低い
　expected inflation 期待インフレ率, 予想インフレ率
　falling inflation インフレの低下
　fears over inflation インフレ懸念
　forestall a potential uptick in inflation インフレ加速の可能性に先手を打つ
　galloping inflation 急激なインフレ
　general inflation 一般物価上昇, 一般物価水準の上昇
　generate greater inflation インフレ悪化を招く
　headline inflation 消費者物価, 消費者物価指数
　high inflation 高インフレ
　higher inflation インフレ率上昇, 高インフレ（＝rising inflation）
　hyper-inflation［hyperinflation］ 超インフレ
　imported inflation resulting from the weaker yen 円安による輸入インフレ
　indexed to inflation 物価スライド制
　inflation breaks out インフレが始まる, インフレが再燃する
　inflation gains and/or losses インフレ損益, インフレ利得および／または損失
　inflation is running at A％ インフレはA％で推移している
　inflation picking up インフレ再燃
　inflation psychology インフレ心理
　inflation risk インフレ・リスク
　inflation statistics インフレ指標
　inflation threat インフレの脅威
　inflation worries インフレ懸念
　inflation's performance インフレ動向
　keep inflation at bay インフレを予防する
　keep inflation down インフレを抑えておく
　land price inflation 地価急騰
　lead to inflation インフレにつながる, インフレを招く
　low inflation 低インフレ
　moderate inflation 穏やかなインフレ, 緩やかなインフレ
　outlook for inflation インフレ見通し（＝inflation outlook）

outlook for the economy and inflation　経済・物価情勢の展望
overall measures of price inflation　物価全般のインフレ指標
PPI inflation rate　生産者物価指数（PPI）の上昇率
producer price inflation　生産者物価上昇率
protect savings against inflation　インフレから貯蓄を守る
push up headline inflation　消費者物価を押し上げる
quell inflation　インフレを抑える［抑制する］，インフレを防ぐ
raging inflation　狂乱物価，狂乱インフレ
reacceleration［re-acceleration］of inflation　インフレの再燃，インフレの再加速
real return net of inflation　インフレ調整後の実質利回り
receding inflation worries　インフレ懸念の後退
reduced inflation　低インフレ
resurging inflation　インフレ再燃
　（=resurgence in inflation, revival of inflation）
retail price inflation　小売物価上昇率
revival of inflation　インフレ再燃
rising inflation　インフレ加速，インフレ［インフレ率］の上昇
risk of inflation picking up　インフレ再燃リスク，インフレ再燃の危険
service inflation　サービス価格上昇率
sign of inflation　インフレの兆し
stable growth without inflation　インフレなき安定成長
stock price inflation　株価急騰
surging inflation　急加速するインフレ，インフレの急加速，インフレの大幅上昇
the risk of rising inflation　インフレが台頭する危険性
true inflation　真性インフレ
underlying inflation　潜在的インフレ，基調としてのインフレ率
uptick in inflation　インフレ加速
vicious inflation　悪性インフレ
　（=malignant inflation）
wage inflation　賃金インフレ
ward off inflation　インフレが生じないようにする
◆China will ratchet up efforts to quell inflation in 2011. 中国は、2011年からインフレ抑制策を徐々に強化する方針だ。◆Concerns about inflation have emerged in some sectors of the U.S. economy, as seen in rising retail prices of gasoline and in soaring prices of houses in urban areas. ガソリン小売価格の高騰や都市部の住宅価格の上昇などに見られるように、米経済の一部にはインフレ懸念も出始めている。◆Emerging countries are anxious about the possibility of inflation caused by a large influx of funds as the U.S. FRB decided to relax its monetary policy. 米連邦準備制度理事会（FRB）が金融緩和を決めたため、新興国は大量の資金流入によるインフレを懸念している。◆Europe believes a weak dollar will help control inflation. ドル安はインフレ抑制にプラス、と欧州は判断している。◆In emerging economics, economic overheating and inflation are concerns. 新興国では、景気過熱やインフレが懸念される。◆Record low U.S. borrowing costs are boosting the appeal to bullion as a hedge against inflation. 米国の資金調達コストが過去最低の水準にあるため、インフレ・ヘッジとしての金［金地金］の人気が高まっている。◆Speculative money is causing appreciation of currencies and inflation in emerging economies. 投機マネーが、新興国の通貨高やインフレを招いている。◆The Federal Reserve raised U.S. interest rates to keep inflation at bay. 米連邦準備制度理事会は、インフレを予防するため、金利を引き上げた。◆

The Fed's monetary easing policies have brought about inflation in newly emerging economies. FRB（米連邦準備制度理事会）の金融緩和策が、新興国のインフレを招いた。◆The sharp rise in crude oil prices has caused increases in prices of other fuels and grains, triggering inflation in many parts of the world. 原油価格の高騰は、他の燃料価格や穀物価格の上昇を招き、国際的なインフレを引き起こしている。◆The U.S. Federal Reserve raised the official discount rate and the target rate of federal funds by 0.25 percentage points in a bid to quell inflation and keep the economy from overheating. 米連邦準備制度理事会は、インフレを防ぎ景気の過熱を警戒して、公定歩合とフェデラル・ファンド（FF）の誘導目標金利をそれぞれ0.25パーセント引き上げた。

inflation-adjusted　（形）インフレ調整後［調整済み］の，実質の
　in inflation-adjusted terms　実質ベースで，物価調整後の数字で見て
　inflation-adjusted long-term rates　インフレ調整後の長期金利
　inflation-adjusted rate of economic growth　実質経済成長率
　inflation-adjusted retail sales　実質小売売上高
　inflation-adjusted yield　実質利回り
inflation-adjusted real terms　インフレ調整後の実質，物価変動の影響を除いた実質
　◆Gross domestic product will rise 2 percent in inflation-adjusted real terms and 2.2 percent in nominal terms in the current fiscal year from the previous fiscal year. 今年度の国内総生産（GDP）の成長率は、物価変動の影響を除いた実質で前年度比2％、名目で2.2％になる見通しだ。
inflation expectations　インフレ予想，インフレ期待，インフレ見通し，予想インフレ率
　assuage inflation fears　インフレ懸念を緩和する
　be dragged down by inflation fears　インフレ懸念で押し下げられる
　ease［calm］inflation fears　インフレ懸念を和らげる
　fuel inflation fears　インフレ懸念を強める，インフレ懸念に拍車をかける
　higher［increased］inflation fears　インフレ懸念の高まり，一段と強まるインフレ懸念
　inflation fears［concerns, worries］　インフレ懸念
　　（=concerns about［over］inflation, fears of inflation, inflation jitters; ⇒ignite）
　offset inflation fears　インフレ懸念を打ち消す
　on inflation fears　インフレ懸念を受けて
　raise inflation expectations　予想インフレ率を押し上げる
　rising inflation expectations　予想インフレ率の上昇
　subsiding inflation fears　インフレ懸念の後退
　◆The Federal Reserve Board is trying to assuage inflation fears. 米連邦準備制度理事会（FRB）は、インフレ懸念の緩和に努めている。
inflation-fighting credibility　インフレ抑制姿勢に対する信認
　◆The U.S. central bank runs the risk of losing its inflation-fighting credibility if it delays fighting growing inflation problems. 増大するインフレ問題の抑制策を遅らせれば、米連邦準備制度理事会（FRB）はそのインフレ抑制姿勢に対する信認を失うリスクを負うことになる。
inflation pressure　インフレ圧力
　（=inflationary pressure）
　◆The Fed is caught between a recession and rising inflation pressure. 米連邦準備制度理事会（FRB）は、リセッション（景気後退）とインフレ圧力の増大との間で板挟みになっている。
inflation rate　物価上昇率，インフレ率

(=rate of inflation)
consumer price inflation rate　消費者物価指数上昇率
core inflation rate　コア・インフレ率, 基礎インフレ率, 消費者物価指数コア指数の上昇率, コア指数
eurozone inflation rate　ユーロ圏のインフレ率
higher inflation rate　インフレ率の上昇
PPI inflation rate　生産者物価指数(PPI)の上昇率
reduced inflation rate　インフレ率の低下
underlying inflation rate　基礎インフレ率
◆Eurozone June inflation rate rose 2.4 percent from a year earlier. ユーロ圏の6月のインフレ率は、前年同月比で2.4%上昇した。◆The core consumer price inflation rate, excluding volatile fresh food prices, is currently about 2 percent on year due mainly to soaring food and petroleum product prices. 変動の激しい生鮮食品の価格を除いたコア物価指数[消費者物価指数のコア指数]の上昇率は現在、主に食料品と石油製品の価格高騰の影響で、対前年比で2%程度となっている。◆The target range for the inflation rate could be set at the same level as the potential growth rate, for example. 物価上昇率の目標値としては、例えば潜在成長率と同水準に設定することもできよう。

inflation target　インフレ目標, インフレ・ターゲット
(=inflation targeting, inflationary target, target inflation rate; ⇒monetary relaxation policy)
achieve the inflation target　インフレ目標を達成する
declare one's inflation target　インフレ目標を宣言する
settle down to a regime of inflation target [targeting]　インフレ・ターゲットの枠組みに移行する
◆The Bank of Japan should clearly declare its inflation target, guiding an increase in consumer prices of between 2 percent and 3 percent, and then continue to increase money supply in the market. 日銀は、消費者物価を2～3パーセント程度上昇させるというインフレ・ターゲットをはっきり宣言して、市場に一段の資金供給を続けるべきだ。◆The new Fed chairman's theory is to introduce inflation targets, thus setting numerical targets for stabilizing prices. 米連邦準備制度理事会(FRB)新議長の持論は、インフレ目標を導入して、物価安定の数値目標を示す[設定する]ことだ。

inflation target policy　インフレ目標政策
◆Many countries have been successful in controlling inflation with inflation target policies. これまでに多くの国が、インフレ目標政策を導入してインフレのコントロールに成功している。

inflationary　(形)インフレの, インフレを誘発する, インフレを引き起こす
anti-inflationary measures　インフレ抑制策
inflationary economy　インフレ経済
(=inflated economy)
inflationary expansion　価格景気
inflationary expectations　インフレ期待, インフレ動向の予想
inflationary gap　インフレ・ギャップ(完全雇用の達成に必要な有効需要を上回る需要があること)
inflationary hedge　インフレ・ヘッジ(株・金・土地などへの投資など、インフレによる通貨価値の下落に伴う損失を防ぐために取る手段)
inflationary jitters　インフレ不安, インフレ懸念, インフレ心理
inflationary pressure　インフレ圧力, インフレ誘発の圧力
inflationary sentiment　インフレ心理, インフレ・マインド
inflationary sign　インフレの兆し
inflationary spiral　悪性インフレ, インフレの悪循環, インフレ・スパイラル
inflationary target　インフレ目標

(=inflation target)
inflationary expectations　インフレ期待, 予想インフレ率
◆Inflationary expectations could be raised by too much reserve expansion. 行き過ぎた金融の量的緩和で、予想インフレ率が上昇する[インフレ期待が高まる]可能性がある。

inflationary phase　インフレ局面, インフレ気味
◆Many developed countries are currently in a deflationary phase while many emerging countries are in an inflationary phase. 現在、先進国の多くはデフレ気味なのに対して、新興国の多くはインフレ気味だ。

inflationary pressures　物価上昇圧力, 上昇圧力, インフレ圧力, インフレ誘発の圧力, インフレ懸念
(=inflationary impacts; ⇒mount)
abated inflationary pressures　インフレ圧力の低下
constrain [deflate] inflationary pressures　インフレ圧力を抑える
contain inflationary pressures　インフレ圧力を抑える
counter [relieve] inflationary pressures　インフレ圧力を抑制する
decline in inflationary pressures　インフレ圧力の緩和
ease inflationary pressures　インフレ圧力を抑制[軽減]する, インフレ圧力を低下させる
offset inflationary pressures　インフレ圧力を相殺する
pickup in inflationary pressures　インフレ圧力の再上昇
reduce inflationary pressures　インフレ圧力を低下させる, インフレ圧力を低減する
releasing of inflationary pressures　インフレの再燃
rise in inflationary pressures　インフレ圧力の高まり, インフレ圧力の上昇
(=rising inflation pressures)
signal inflationary pressures　インフレ圧力を物語る
subdued inflationary pressures　インフレ圧力の鎮静化
wage inflationary pressures　賃金インフレ圧力
weakness of inflationary pressures　インフレ圧力の低下
◆Global inflationary pressures remain high. 物価上昇圧力は、高水準で推移している。◆Inflationary pressures are diminishing in the euro zone as oil prices decline. 原油価格の下落に伴って、ユーロ圏のインフレ圧力は軽減している。◆The Fed has to maintain guard against an economic slowdown and inflationary pressures. 米連邦準備制度理事会(FRB)は、今後とも景気減速とインフレ圧力を警戒する必要がある。◆The United States is under pressure to make some difficult monetary policy decisions to cool down the overheating economy by countering the inflationary pressures stemming from higher import prices due to the weaker dollar. 米国は現在、ドル安での輸入価格の高騰によるインフレ圧力を抑えて過熱気味の景気を鎮めるための難しい金融政策の決断を迫られている。

inflationary target policy　インフレ目標政策
◆Many countries have been successful in controlling inflation with inflationary target policy. これまでに多くの国が、インフレ目標政策を導入してインフレのコントロールに成功している。

inflationary trend　インフレ傾向, インフレ動向, インフレ気味
◆As one option to avoid excessive currency appreciation in emerging countries with inflationary trends, they can restrict an influx of capital. インフレ気味の新興国で行き過ぎた[過度の]通貨高を避けるための手段として、資金流入を規制することができる。

inflow　(名)流入, 流入額, インフロー　(⇒capital inflow, foreign capital inflows, net inflows of funds, outflow)
asset inflow　資産流入額
capital inflow　資本流入, 資金の流入, 流入資金, 買い

越し
combined inflows (outflows)　合算資金収入（支出）
debt inflows　債務の取入れ
deposit inflow　貯蓄の流入
foreign capital inflows　外資流入, 外国からの資金流入, 外貨の流動性
foreign inflows　外資流入, 外貨流入
　（=foreign capital inflows）
import inflow　輸入拡大
massive inflows of risk-aversive funds from abroad　海外からのリスクを嫌う大量の資金流入
money inflow　資金流入
net cash inflow　純資金収入額
net inflow　入超, 流入超
◆Social unrest caused by the assassination of presidential candidate suddenly reduced capital inflows from abroad. 大統領候補の暗殺による社会不安で、海外からの資本流入が突然減少した。◆The money market is overheated by massive money inflows from banks on fading concerns over a financial system crisis. 金融システム不安［金融システム危機に対する懸念］の後退により、短期金融市場は、銀行からの巨額の資金流入で過熱感が強まっている。

inflow of funds　資金の流入
◆Thanks to the inflow of funds from the successful share issue, net indebtedness has been markedly reduced. 成功を収めた（新規）株式発行による資金の流入により、正味負債は大幅に縮小しました。

inflow of speculative money　投機マネーの流入
◆Service charges or tax on crude oil futures trading should be raised to curb the inflow of speculative money not related to actual demand. 実需に関係ない投機マネーの流入を抑えるため、原油先物取引の手数料の引上げや課税強化をすべきだ。

influence　(名)影響, 波及, 影響力, 支配力, 勢力, 威光, 威信, 感化, 感化力, 作用, 効果, 要因
dampening influence　抑制効果
exert enormous influence over　～に大きな影響を与える, ～に大きな影響を及ぼす, ～に強大な影響力を行使する
horizontal influence　水平的影響
inflationary influence　インフレ作用, インフレの影響
influence buying　買収, 買収工作, 影響力を金で買うこと
influence effect　勢力効果
neutral influence　中立的作用, 中立的影響
seasonal influence　季節的影響, 季節的要因
under the influence of　～の影響を受けて, ～に支配されて, ～に左右されて, ～に酔って
vertical influence　垂直的影響
◆People close to the heads of local governments exert their influence in bid-rigging cases on behalf of their leaders. 地方自治体首長の周辺人物が、トップの代わりに入札談合を仕切っている［入札談合で影響力を行使している］。◆Rapidly increasing prices of primary commodities have had a positive influence on corporate performance with the yen's appreciation against the dollar. 円高・ドル安で、これまでのところ一次産品（原油や石炭など）の急騰が、企業の業績に好影響をもたらしている。◆To alleviate the influence of the U.S. government's additional steps to ease the supply of money, the Bank of Japan must adopt a more proactive stance toward monetary relaxation. 米政府の追加金融緩和策［通貨供給量を増やす米政府の追加措置］の影響を和らげるには、日銀も金融緩和の姿勢を強める必要がある。

influential　(形)影響力の強い, 影響力［支配力］の大きい, 有力な, 大手の, 顔がきく
influential overseas commercial banks　海外の有力行
Wall Street's most influential bank　ウォール街最大手の金融機関
◆Goldman Sachs Group Inc. emerged from the global financial meltdown as Wall Street's most influential bank. ゴールドマン・サックスは、ウォール街最大手の金融機関として世界的な金融危機を乗り切った。◆Influential overseas commercial banks have maintained an advantage with transactions for derivative products by using high-tech computer systems. 海外の有力行は、最先端のコンピュータ・システムを使って、デリバティブ取引で優位を保っている。◆The G-7 meeting has maintained its position as the most influential international economic conference. 先進7か国会議（G7）は、最も影響力のある国際経済会議としてその地位をこれまで維持してきた。◆Two influential rating firms lowered Ford Motor Co.'s credit ratings a notch deeper into junk territory. 大手［有力な］格付け機関2社が、米フォードの信用格付けを「投資不適格レベル」にさらに1段階引き下げた。

influx　(名)流入, 参入, 殺到, 流れ込み, 導入
a large influx of funds　大量の資金流入
an influx of complaints　苦情の殺到
an influx of foreign capital　外資導入, 外資の流入
　（=foreign capital influx）
an influx of gold　金の流入　（=gold influx）
an influx of orders　注文殺到

influx of capital　資本の流入, 資金流入, 資本輸入
　（=capital influx; ⇒strengthening）
◆As one option to avoid excessive currency appreciation in emerging countries with inflationary trends, they can restrict an influx of capital. インフレ気味の新興国で行き過ぎた［過度の］通貨高を避けるための手段として、資金流入を規制することができる。◆Restricting an influx of capital prevents foreigners from acquiring domestic assets. 資本流入［資本輸入］の規制で、外国人は国内資産の購入が難しくなる。

influx of foreign funds　海外・国外資金の流入, 海外・国外からの資金流入
◆Higher interest rates would accelerate the influx of foreign funds. 利上げ［金利の引上げ］は、海外からの資金流入を加速することになる。

influx of foreign supermarket operators　外資系スーパーの参入
◆There has been a lively influx of foreign supermarket operators into the Japanese market. 最近は、外資系スーパーの日本市場への参入が活発だ。

influx of funds　資金の流入, 資金流入
◆Emerging countries are anxious about the possibility of inflation caused by a large influx of funds as the U.S. FRB decided to relax its monetary policy. 米連邦準備制度理事会（FRB）が金融緩和を決めたため、新興国は大量の資金流入によるインフレを懸念している。

influx of money from abroad　海外マネーの流入, 海外からの資金流入
◆Long-term interest rates have so far been held down due to an influx of money from abroad. 長期金利はこれまで、海外マネーの流入で低く抑えられていた。

influx of speculative money　投機マネーの流入
◆South Korea, Brazil and India are guiding their currencies lower to deal with an influx of speculative money. 韓国、ブラジルとインドは、投機マネーの流入に対応するため、自国通貨安に誘導している。

information　(名)情報, 消息, 知識, ニュース, インフォメーション　（⇒call center, personal information）
accounting information　会計情報
confidentiality of personal information　個人情報の秘密遵守
financial information　財務情報, 金融情報
incorrect information　誤った情報
information disclosure　情報開示, 情報公開

(⇒disclosure)
information meeting 企業説明会, 会社説明会, インフォメーション・ミーティング（証券アナリストやファンド・マネージャーなどに対して経営方針や経営理念, 業務内容などを定期的に紹介する企業説明会。⇒investor relations）
information memorandum 条件概要書, インフォメモ
personal information 個人情報
trading information 取引情報
◆Kokudo Corp. has provided shareholders with incorrect information for a long time. コクドは長期間, 株主に誤った情報を提供してきた。◆Viruses used in illegal transfers via online banking services collect Internet banking account-related information such as personal identification numbers and transmit them to remote parties. ネット・バンキングでの不正送金に使われたウイルスは, 暗証番号などネット・バンキングの口座関連情報を収集して, 外部に送信する。

information system 情報システム, 情報処理法
◆Both insurance companies do not plan to integrate their information systems for the time being. 両保険会社は当面, 情報システムの統合を行う計画はない。

information technology 情報技術, 情報通信技術, 情報処理技術, 情報工学, 情報科学, インフォメーション・テクノロジー, IT （=Info technology, info-technology, infotech; ⇒branch-free bank, business model, corporate performance, infrastructure, IT bubble）
◆Microsoft Corp. has used a stock option program to attract talented information technology professionals. マイクロソフトは, 有能なIT（情報技術）専門家を確保するためにストック・オプション制度を使っている。

information technology bubble IT（情報技術）バブル, ネット株バブル （=IT bubble, Net bubble）
◆The economy deteriorated partly due to the burst of the information technology bubble. IT（情報技術）バブルの崩壊もあって, 景気が失速した。

information transmission capability 情報通信機能
◆Nonlife insurers are offering customers a new way to purchase insurance, using mobile phones with information transmission capabilities. 損害保険各社が, 情報通信機能がある携帯電話を使って保険に加入できる新サービスを提供している。

infrastructure （名）インフラストラクチャー, インフラ, 経済・社会・産業の基盤, 社会的生産基盤, 基本施設・設備, 社会資本, 企業・組織の下部組織, 下部構造, インフラ整備
◆A system utilizing information technology (IT) is part of the basic infrastructure for banks. IT（情報技術）を駆使したシステムは, 銀行にとって基本的インフラの一部だ。

infuse （動）注ぐ, 注入する, 投入する, 投下する, 行き渡らせる
infuse banks with public funds 銀行［金融機関に］公的資金を注入する
infuse money into ～ ～に資金を注入する［投入する］, ～に資金を行き渡らせる
◆The aim of a fund established by the Development Bank of Japan is to infuse money into auto parts makers hit by the March 11 earthquake and tsunami. 日本政策投資銀行が設立するファンドの目的は, 東日本大震災で被災した自動車部品メーカーに資金を行き渡らせることにある。◆The government will have to infuse any banks with public funds if they have become undercapitalized. 銀行が資本不足に陥ったら, 政府は銀行に公的資金を注入せざるを得ないだろう。

infusion （名）注入, 投入, 投下 （=injection）
capital infusion 資本投下
equity infusion 資本の注入, 資本投下, 資本参加
infusion of public funds 公的資金の注入, 公的資金の投入 （=injection of public funds）
◆The infusion of public funds into major banks was originally meant to free banks from their need to contract total lending to maintain capital adequacy ratios. 大手銀行への公的資金注入のそもそもの狙いは, 自己資本比率を維持するために貸出総額を縮小せざるをえない事態から銀行を解き放つことにあった。

inherent vice （保険）固有の瑕疵（かし）（外力がかからなくても自然変質や自然損傷をもたらす貨物・財産の性質）

initial （形）最初の, 初めの, 初期の, 期首の, 当初の, 設立時の
initial balance 期首残高 （=beginning balance）
initial costs 初期費用
initial filing 初回申請
initial investment 初期投資, 初期投資額, 原始投資, 原初投資 （⇒shoulder）
initial numbers 速報値
initial order 初注文, 当初注文
initial placement 募集業務
initial premium 初回保険料 （⇒insurance agent）
initial projection 当初予想, 当初の見通し （⇒low形容詞）
initial stock 期首在庫, 期首在庫量［在庫高］
initial stock price 初値（はつね）（=initial price, initial share price）

initial budget 当初予算
◆The government bond issuance worth about ¥44 trillion for the current fiscal year is the largest ever projected in an initial budget. 今年度の約44兆円の国債発行額は, 当初予算としては史上最高だ。

initial capital 当初資本, 期首資本, 保険会社の基金（株式会社の資本金に相当）, 開業資金
◆The new Internet bank will be equally owned by the two firms with initial capital of ¥20 billion. 新ネット銀行は, 当初資本が200億円で, 両社が折半出資する。

initial investment 初期投資, 初期投資額, 原始投資, 原初投資
◆Depending on moves in foreign exchange markets, there is a risk we may lose initial investments in foreign currency deposits. 為替相場の動き次第で, 外貨預金では初期投資額を割り込むリスクがある。◆The bank shouldered ¥35 billion as an initial investment for a computer system development for the toto soccer lottery. サッカーくじ「toto」のコンピュータ・システム整備のための初期投資として, 同行は350億円を負担した。◆The initial investment is expected to be several tens of billions of yen. 当初の投資額は, 数百億円になると見られる。

initial margin 当初証拠金
◆Investors can gain a huge exposure based on a small initial margin on a futures contract. 先物（先物契約）の少ない当初証拠金で, 投資家は大幅な投資を行うことができる。

initial ownership 当初の出資比率
◆The firm will have an initial ownership of forty percent of the voting shares of the joint venture company. 同社の当初の出資比率は, 合弁会社の議決権付き株式の40%とする方針だ。

initial payment 頭金, 契約締結時支払い額
◆Under the new installment system of the company, purchasers are not required to pay initial payments. 同社の新割賦制度では, 購入者は頭金を支払う必要がない。

initial premium 初回保険料
◆An insurance agent is a sales person who represents a life insurance company for the purpose of soliciting applications, collecting initial premiums, and servicing insurance contracts. 保険募集人は, 生命保険会社を代表して保険契約の

勧誘、初回保険料の徴収、保険契約に関する役務を提供する販売員である。

initial price 初値（はつね）, 初回価格 （=initial share price, initial stock price; ⇒opening price）
◆Shares in McDonald's Co.（Japan）, a leader in the nation's fast-food industry, fetched an initial price of ￥4,700. ファーストフード業界最大手の日本マクドナルドの株は、1株当たり4,700円の初値を付けた。◆The firm's stock fetched an initial price of ￥2.95 million in the morning on the TSE's Mothers market for emerging companies after its Thursday debut. 同社株は、木曜日の上場後、新興企業向け市場の東証マザーズで、午前中に295万円の初値を付けた。

initial projection 当初予想, 当初の想定, 当初見通し
◆The Japanese currency is about ￥5 lower than its initial projection of ￥115 to the dollar. 円は、当初想定した1ドル＝115円より5円程度安く推移している。

initial public offering 株式公開, 新規株式公開, 新規株式公募, 新規公募, 上場直前の公募, 第1回株式公募, 株式の公開公募, 上場, IPO （=debut, initial public offer; ⇒IPO, public offering）
arrange an initial public offering 株式公募を取りまとめる （⇒arrange）
initial public offering price 公募価格, 売出価格, 公募売出価格
shares of high-flying initial public offerings 値上がりが確実視される新規公開株 （⇒high-flying）
undertake an initial public offering 株式を新規公開する
◆PricewaterhouseCoopers filed to sell its consulting arm through an initial public offering （IPO） to help ease concerns over potential conflicts of interest between its auditing and consulting businesses. 監査業務とコンサルティング業務の潜在的利害の対立に対する懸念を払拭（ふっしょく）するため、プライスウォーターハウス・クーパー（世界最大の会計事務所）は、公開公募によるコンサルティング部門の売却を（SECに）申請した。◆The number of companies undertaking initial public offerings has risen sharply this year. 株式を新規公開する企業が、今年は急増している。◆The shares in chipmaker Elpida Memory Inc. closed at ￥3,750 after the $1 billion initial public offering. 半導体メーカー、エルピーダメモリの株価は、10億ドルの新規公募後、3,750円で取引を終えた。
[解説]IPO（公開公募・新規公募）とは：証券取引所に株式を新規公開するなどして、企業が一般投資家に株式を初めて売り出すこと。一般には、引受業務を担当する投資銀行が、発行会社から株式をまとめて買い取って一般の投資家に売り出す。すでに株式を公開している企業が一般投資家に新規発行株式を売り出す場合を、公募（public offering）あるいは募集（primary offering）という。

initial response 初期対応, 初動対応
◆Initial response to the Fukushima nuclear power plant disaster trailed behind events. 福島原子力発電所事故での初期対応は、後手に回った。

initiate （動）始める, 起こす, 創始する, 設立する, ～に着手する, ～に乗り出す, 創案する, 加入［入会, 入社］させる, 授ける, 伝える, 手ほどきをする, 初歩［コツ］を教える, （議案を）提出する, 提案する, 発議する
initiate a downturn 景気後退をもたらす
initiate a new method 新方法を創案する
initiate a reform 改革に着手する
initiate bankruptcy proceedings against ～に対して破たん処理［破産処理］手続きを開始する
initiate cost-cutting measures コスト削減策に乗り出す
investor-initiated ratings 投資家の依頼による格付け
◆Measures to deal with surplus facilities are regarded as the center pillar of structural reforms to be initiated by the supply side. 過剰設備の処理対策は、供給サイドが着手する構造改革の柱とされている。

initiative （名）独創力, 独自性, 自主性, 率先, 主導権, 議案提出権, 発議, 発案, 提案, ～案, 政策, 構想, 方針, イニシアチブ （⇒PFI, private finance initiative）
◆An initiative to strengthen the functions of the European Financial Stability Facility （EFSF） was approved at the 17 eurozone countries' parliaments. 欧州金融安定基金（EFSF）の機能強化案が、ユーロ圏17か国の議会で承認された。◆The firm tries to restructure itself under the initiative of its banks. 同社は、取引銀行主導のもとに再建を目指している。◆The new trade initiative, announced by Bush in a commencement address at the University of South Carolina, will foster goodwill in the Middle East. ブッシュ大統領がサウスカロライナ大の卒業式で発表した新貿易構想は、中東での信頼醸成につながる。

inject （動）注入する, 投入する, 供給する, 投資する, 出資する, 導入する （=provide; ⇒public money）
dollar funds injected into banks 銀行［金融機関］に供給されたドル資金
inject funds into markets 市場に資金を供給する
inject liquidity into the system 市中に流動性を供給する
inject public funds 公的資金を注入する, 公的資金を投入する
inject $300 billion into banks 金融機関に3,000億ドル供給する
◆Public funds were injected to bail out Resona Bank. りそな銀行を救済するため、公的資金が注入された。◆Some dollar funds injected into banks by the U.S. central bank may send U.S. stock prices soaring because banks will invest some of the new dollar funds in domestic assets such as stocks. 米国の中央銀行（FRB）が金融機関［銀行］に供給したドル資金の一部は、銀行がその新たなドル資金の一部を株のような国内資産に投資するため、米国の株価を上げる可能性がある。◆The BOJ decided to further relax its monetary policy by injecting an additional ￥10 trillion into a fund aimed at purchasing government bonds and corporate debentures. 日銀は、国債や社債などを買い入れるための基金に新たに10兆円を注入［投入］して追加の金融緩和に踏み切ることを決めた。◆The mutual aid association injected ￥1.5 billion into 24 deficit-ridden hotels run by the association. 同共済組合は、経営する赤字の24ホテルに15億円を注入［補填］した。◆The U.S. central bank will inject $200 billion into banks. 米国の中央銀行［連邦準備制度理事会（FRB）］が、金融機関に2,000億ドル供給する。◆The U.S. government injected a total of $45 billion into Citigroup at the depths of financial crisis. 深刻な金融危機の際、米政府はシティグループに総額で450億ドルを注入した。

inject funds into the market 市場に資金を注入する, 市場に資金を供給する
◆All possible measures, such as injecting funds into markets and lowering rates, need to be taken to ride out this financial emergency. この金融非常事態をうまく切り抜けるには、市場への資金注入［資金供給］や利下げなど、あらゆる可能な措置を取る必要がある。

inject liquidity 資金を供給する, 流動性を供給する
◆The central bank of United Arab Emirates injected liquidity into Dubai's banks. アラブ首長国連邦（UAE）の中央銀行が、ドバイの銀行に資金を供給した。

inject public funds 公的資金を投入する, 公的資金を注入する （⇒Deposit Insurance Law）
◆If financial institutions become short of funds in the process of the FSA's special inspections, the government must immediately inject public funds. 金融庁の特別検査で金融機関が資本不足に陥る場合には、政府は直ちに公的資金を注入しなければならない。◆Public funds should be injected not only to buy up toxic assets, but also to boost the capital bases of enfeebled financial institutions. 公的資金は、不良資産の

買取りだけでなく、弱体化した[体力の落ちた]金融機関の資本増強にも注入すべきだ。◆The U.S. and Canadian governments have injected a massive amount of public funds into GM since its collapse on June 1, 2009. GMが2009年6月1日に経営破たんしてから、米国とカナダの政府は、同社に巨額の公的資金を注入している。◆The U.S. government should not have hesitated to inject public funds. 米政府は、公的資金の投入[注入]をためらうべきではなかった。

inject sizable funds into the financial markets 金融市場に大量の資金を供給する
◆The central banks of Japan, the United States and European countries are injecting sizable funds into the financial markets. 日米欧の中央銀行は、金融市場に大量の資金を供給している。

inject taxpayer money 公的資金を注入する
◆By a mechanism the EU has developed, each EU country can inject taxpayer money into banks unable to increase capital on their own. EU(欧州連合)が整備した仕組みで、EU各国は、自力で資本増強を図れない銀行に対して公的資金を注入できるようになった。

injection (名)注入, 投入, 供給
　additional capital injection 追加出資
　capital injection 資本の注入, 資本の増強, 増資, 保険会社への基金拠出, 保険会社の基金増資 (=capital increase)
　injection of equity 増資
　investment injection 投資注入
　liquidity injection 流動性の供給
◆Shinginko Tokyo asked the metropolitan government for an additional capital injection of ¥40 billion. 新銀行東京は、都に400億円の追加出資を要請した。◆This life insurer sought capital injection of 70 billion yen from financial institutions. この生命保険会社は、金融機関に700億円の基金拠出[基金増資]を要請した。

injection of public funds 公的資金の注入, 公的資金の投入 (=public fund injection; ⇒financial system stability)
　compulsory injection of public funds into banks 銀行への公的資金の強制注入
　mandatory injection of public funds 公的資金の強制注入
　preventive injection of public funds 公的資金の予防注入
◆A senior official of the Economy, Trade and Industry Ministry was questioned on insider trading over an injection of public funds to a semiconductor company. 経済産業省の幹部が、半導体企業[半導体メーカー]への公的資金注入をめぐるインサイダー取引の疑いで、事情聴取を受けた。◆As joint actions, major industrial nations have taken such measures as further interest rate reductions, quantitative monetary relaxation to increase the money supply, the injection of public funds and increased public spending. 協調行動として、主要先進国は、さらなる金利の引下げ、通貨供給量を増やすための量的金融緩和や公的資金の注入、財政出動[公共支出の拡大]などの措置を取った。◆Before the new law's enactment, an injection of public funds into a single financial institution was allowed only when there were fears of a financial system crisis. 新法の制定前は、金融危機の恐れがある場合に限って、個別の金融機関に公的資金を注入することができた。◆European countries are urged to facilitate a safety net for emergencies, including the injection of public funds into deteriorating banks to shore up their capital strength. 欧州は、経営が悪化した銀行[金融機関]に公的資金を注入して資本を増強するなど、非常時に備えた安全網の整備が求められている。◆To deal with the systemic financial crisis, ministry and central bank officials had to take rescue measures, such as an injection of public funds, while at the same time implementing strict guidelines and sanctions. 連鎖的な金融危機に対処するにあたって、当局は公的資金の投入などの救済措置取ると同時に、厳しい指導や制裁を実施しなければならなかった。

injection of public money into banks 銀行への公的資金注入
◆The eurozone governments tried to avert the injection of public money into banks which are politically unpopular. ユーロ圏の各国政府は、政治的に人気のない銀行への公的資金注入を避けようとした。

injunction (名)差止命令, 差止請求, 仮処分
◆Sumitomo Trust & Banking Corp. filed a preliminary injunction to halt merger talks between UFJ Holdings Inc. and Mitsubishi Tokyo Financial Group Inc. at the Tokyo District Court. 住友信託銀行は、UFJホールディングスと三菱東京フィナンシャル・グループとの経営統合に関する交渉の差止めを求める仮処分を、東京地裁に申請した。◆The Tokyo District Court granted an injunction to stop NBS from issuing share warrants to Fuji TV. 東京地裁は、フジテレビを引受先とするニッポン放送の新株予約権発行の差止めを命じた。

innovation (名)革新, 革新性, 刷新, 斬新, 改革, 変革, 開発, 新制度, 新制度などの導入, 画期的な新製品, 新機軸, 新工夫, 新手法, 新発明, 技術革新, 経営革新, イノベーション
　business innovation 経営革新
　economic innovation 経済革新, 経済的革新
　export-biased innovation 輸出偏向型技術革新
　innovations in the distribution industry 流通業界の革新
　process innovation 生産工程の刷新・革新, 生産工程の技術革新, プロセス・イノベーション
　product innovation 製品開発, 商品開発, 画期的な新製品, 製品イノベーション
　technical innovation 技術革新 (=technological innovation, technology innovation)
◆The financial market bubble has not brought forth technology innovation or globalization. 金融バブルは、技術革新やグローバル化をもたらしたわけではない。◆The IT bubble and the ensuing swelling of the financial market of late have stemmed from technology innovation coupled with the globalization of the economy. (1990年代後半の)ITバブルとそれに続く最近までの金融膨張を引き起こしたのは、経済のグローバル化の動きと連動した技術革新だ。

innovative (形)革新的な, 斬新な, 新機軸の, 画期的な, 新しい, 最新の (=innovatory)
◆The company pioneered a variety of innovative promotions to add new accounts. 同社は、各種の斬新な販促活動によって、新口座[新規顧客]を増やした。

inside information 内部情報, インサイダー情報, 未公開の重要情報, インサイド情報 (=insider information, nonpublic information; ⇒government bond)
◆The former bank employee obtained inside information on two companies from a colleague. この元銀行行員は、2社の内部情報を同僚から得ていた。

insider (名)インサイダー, 内部者, 関係者 (「インサイダー」は、証券の投資判断に影響を及ぼす未公開の重要情報を知ることができる立場にいる公開会社の役員や取締役、主要株主などをいう)
　a commodity futures market insider 商品先物市場関係者
　industry insiders 業界関係者
　insider dealing インサイダー取引
　insider information インサイダー情報 (=inside information)
　insider lending 内部貸付け
　insider stock trading インサイダー取引 (=insider trading)
◆According to a commodity futures market insider, futures

brokerages depending on commissions for revenue will lose their business strength. 商品先物市場関係者によると、収入を手数料に頼っている先物会社の経営体力は、今後弱まりそうだ。◆Industry insiders said the refusal to pay insurance benefits over a long period was partly because of former Meiji managers' unreasonable policies. 業界関係者によると、長期間にわたる保険金不払いの一因は、旧明治生命保険の経営者の無理な経営方針だ。

insider trading　インサイダー取引, 内部者取引
　（=insider dealing, insider stock trading: 内部情報（insider information）を利用して証券取引を行うこと。⇒falsification, illegal trades of stock, stock price manipulation）
　◆A bank employee was arrested for alleged insider trading of shares in four companies. 銀行の行員が、4社の株でインサイダー取引を行った容疑で逮捕された。◆A former senior economist with Goldman Sachs Inc. who was charged by prosecutors with insider trading was released on an $800,000 bond. 検察当局にインサイダー取引で起訴されたゴールドマン・サックスの元上級エコノミストは、80万ドルの保釈金で釈放された。◆A senior official of the Economy, Trade and Industry Ministry was questioned on insider trading over an injection of public funds to a semiconductor company. 経済産業省の幹部が、半導体企業［半導体メーカー］への公的資金注入をめぐるインサイダー取引の疑いで、事情聴取を受けた。◆Insider trading distorts share prices and undermines the fairness of the securities market. インサイダー取引は、（適正な）株価をゆがめ、証券市場の公正さを損なう。◆Insider trading is prohibited under the Securities and Exchange Law. インサイダー取引は、証券取引法で禁じられている。◆The former head of the Murakami Fund has been arrested on suspicion of insider trading involving Nippon Broadcasting System Inc. shares. 村上ファンドの元代表が、ニッポン放送株を巡るインサイダー取引容疑で逮捕された。◆The Securities and Exchange Surveillance Commission is discussing whether to file a complaint against the man with the Tokyo District Public Prosecutors Office on suspicion of insider trading. 証券取引等監視委員会は、インサイダー取引の容疑で、この男を東京地検に告発するかどうかを検討している。◆The TSE is continuing its investigation into whether there was insider trading of Seibu Railway shares. 西武鉄道株についてインサイダー取引があったかどうか、東証が現在調査を進めている。

insolvency　（名）支払い不能, 返済不能, 債務超過, 倒産, 破たん　（=bankruptcy, business failure）
　absolute insolvency　絶対的債務超過
　an issuer in insolvency　支払い不能に陥った発行体
　banking insolvency　銀行業務の破たん, 銀行破たん
　be heading for insolvency　債務超過に陥るのが近い, 破たんが近い
　be protected against insolvency　支払い不能に対して保護される
　be rescued from insolvency　破たんを救われる, 支払い不能に陥るところを救われる
　commence voluntary insolvency proceedings　自己破産手続きを取る
　economic insolvency　経済支払い不能
　face insolvency　債務超過に直面する, 支払い不能に直面する
　file for insolvency proceedings with　～に破たん処理手続きを申請する
　financial insolvency　金融的支払い不能
　go into insolvency　支払い不能［債務超過］に陥る, 破たんする　（=become insolvent）
　Insolvency Act 1986　英国の支払い不能者法
　insolvency law　破産法

insolvency practitioner　破産管財人, 破産手続き実務者
insolvency problem　資産不良問題
insolvency proceedings　破産手続き, 破たん処理手続き
insolvency statute　（米州法の）支払い不能法
involuntary insolvency　強制的支払い不能
obligor insolvency　債務者の支払い不能
practical insolvency　実質的破産
temporary insolvency　一時的支払い不能
thrift insolvency　貯蓄貸付け機関の破たん
voluntary insolvency　任意支払い不能, 自己破産
◆As the gap between the eurozone-imposed repayment program and the track record began clearly yawning, the Greece's insolvency became apparent. ユーロ圏が押し付けたギリシャの返済計画と実績とのズレが目立つようになるにつれ、ギリシャの返済不能が明らかになった。◆Even if it is a sovereign state or a bank, heavily indebted borrowers may face a crisis for insolvency or a lack of liquidity. 国家でも銀行でも、巨額の債務を抱えた発行体は、返済不能か流動性不足で危機に陥る可能性がある。◆Ishikawa Bank filed for insolvency proceedings with the Financial Services Agency under the Deposit Insurance Law. 石川銀行は、預金保険法に基づき金融庁に対して破綻処理手続きを申請した。

insolvent　（形）支払い不能の, 返済不能の, 債務超過の, 倒産した, 破たんした　（名）支払い不能者, 破産者
　be declared insolvent　破産［経営破たん, 支払い不能］の宣告を受ける, 支払い不能と判断される［認定される］
　be［become］insolvent　支払い不能［債務超過］に陥る, 支払い不能になる, 破たんする
　creditor of an insolvent party　破産債権者
　insolvent debtor　破産者
　insolvent liquidation　支払い不能による清算
　◆Some of the peripheral member nations of the eurozone were already insolvent. ユーロ圏の周辺加盟国の一部は、すでに債務返済不能の状態だった。◆The Bank of Japan decided to extend a special loan to Namihaya Bank after the second-tier regional bank was declared insolvent. 日本銀行は、第二地方銀行の「なみはや銀行」が破たん認定を受けた後、同行に対して特別融資［特融］を実施することを決めた。◆The Corporation took over millions of yen in personal and corporate debts of the insolvent company. 当社は、債務超過の同社の個人債務や法人債務数百万円の肩代わりをした。◆This regional bank became insolvent in the first half of the current fiscal year. この地方銀行（地銀）は、今年度上半期に［今年度の9月中間決算で］債務超過に陥った。

insolvent borrower　支払い［返済］不能の借り手, 債務返済不能の発行体
　◆In the case of an insolvent borrower, it no longer has the ability to pay all its debt even though lenders offer to defer the time of repayment. 返済不能の借り手の場合、貸し手が返済期間の延長を申し出ても、借り手はもはや債務を全額返済できない状況にある。◆To help an insolvent borrower, money must be granted for free, or at least a part of the outstanding debt must be forgiven. 返済不能の借り手を助けるには、ただで資金を与えるか、少なくとも債務残高の一部の減免が必要だ。

inspection　（名）検査, 帳簿の閲覧, 査察, 視察, 点検, 実査, 査閲（さえつ）, 監査　（=investigation; ⇒debtor, examine, financial situation, glitch, inject public funds, regular inspection）
　on-the-spot inspections　立ち入り検査
　physical inspection　実査
　powers to conduct inspections　査察権限
　random inspections　抜き打ち査察
　sampling inspection　抜き取り検査

site inspection 現場検査
surprise inspections 抜き打ち検査
the obstruction of a special inspection 特別検査妨害
the regular inspections of financial institutions 金融機関の通常検査
the special inspections of financial institutions 金融機関の特別検査
◆Before the FSA inspection, the bank secreted away the card boxes containing documents on the financial health of its borrowers. 金融庁の検査前に、同行は融資先の財務内容に関する資料が入った段ボール箱を隠した。◆Financial regulators asked prosecutors to investigate allegations that UFJ Holdings Inc.'s banking unit illegally obstructed recent inspections by reporting misleading information about its nonperforming loans. 金融当局は、UFJ銀行が不良債権に関する虚偽の情報を報告して最近の検査を違法に妨害したとして、同行を検察当局に刑事告発した。◆Regular FSA inspections are conducted after banks close their accounts in March, and focus on whether their loan reserves are adequate. 金融庁の通常検査は3月の銀行の決算後に行われ、主に債権に対する引当金が十分かどうかなどを点検する。◆The major banks attributed their increased bad loans to the poor performance of their borrowers due to the prolonged economic slump and Financial Service Agency inspections resulting in a stricter review of their asset assessments. 大手銀行は、不良債権が増えた理由として、長引く景気低迷で貸出先の経営が悪化したことと、金融庁の検査を受けて大手行が資産査定を厳しくしたことを挙げた。

inspector （名）検査官,監督官,視察官
◆FSA inspectors are to check the credibility of the banks' debtor companies, including their management efficiency and the accuracy of their collateral assessment. 金融庁の検査官は、銀行の融資先の経営効率や担保評価などを含めて、銀行の融資先の信用力を洗い直す。◆FSA's inspectors are to confirm whether the companies' categorization by banks as debtors is relevant or fair. 金融庁の検査官は、銀行側の企業（融資先企業）の債務者区分が適正かどうかなどを検証することになっている。

inspire （動）鼓舞する,励ます,勇気づける,奮起させて〜させる,〜する気にさせる,(考えや感情を)吹き込む,喚起(かんき)する,与える,呼び起こす,抱かせる,示唆する,(うわさなどを)言わせる[書かせる]
be inspired by 〜に触発される,〜がもとになっている
inspire a person with suspicion 人に疑念を抱かせる[起こさせる]
inspire confidence 自信を与える
◆Relatively solid sales figures inspired another rally on Wall Street. 小売売上高が比較的、堅調だったため、ニューヨーク株式市場はまた持ち直した[ニューヨーク株は反発した]。

instability （名）不安,動揺,不安定,不安定な動き,不安定要因,不安定性,優柔不断
（⇒global market, stability）
credit instability 信用不安 （⇒credit instability）
currency instability 通貨不安
economic instability 経済的不安,経済的不安定
export instability 輸出不安定性
financial market instability 金融市場の動揺,金融市場不安,財政的不安定
instability of economic growth 経済成長の不安定性
instability of the currency exchange rate 為替相場の不安定な動き
monetary instability 通貨不安
political instability 政治的不安定,政治不安,政情不安
potential causes of instability 不安定要因
the instability of life insurance firms 生保各社の経営基盤の不安定
the instability of the money market 金融市場の不安, 短期金融市場の不安
the recent instability in the foreign exchange and stock markets 最近の為替相場や株価の不安定な動き
the recent instability of the currency exchange rate 最近の為替相場の不安定な動き
the source of (the) instability 不安定要因,安定を脅かす要因 （=the potential causes of instability）
◆Financial market instability sparked by the U.S. subprime mortgage crisis continues. 米国のサブプライム・ローン（低所得者向け住宅融資）問題に起因する金融市場の動揺は、まだ収まっていない。◆The financial market may show signs of instability after the bailout measure for the bank is decided. 同行に対する救済措置（公的資金の注入措置）の決定を発端に、金融市場は今後、不安定な動きを示すかもしれない。◆The instability of life insurance firms and the lowered earning power of banks with massive bad loans have become the two major factors rocking the financial system. 生保各社の経営基盤の不安定と、巨額の不良債権に苦しむ銀行の収益力低下が、金融システムを揺るがしている二大要因になっている。

instability in foreign exchange and stock markets 為替相場や株価の不安定な動き
◆Due to the recent instability in the foreign exchange and stock markets, the downside risks to the economy warrant attention. 最近の為替相場や株価の不安定な動きの下で、経済の下振れリスク十分注意する必要がある。

instability in global markets グローバル市場の不安定性
◆Instability in global markets is increasing with rising downside risks. 下振れリスクの増大とともに、グローバル市場の不安定性は高まっている。

instability of the currency exchange rate 為替相場の不安定な動き
◆The central bank's decision to raise the upper limit of its liquidity target was prompted by its concerns over the recent instability of the currency exchange rate. 日銀当座預金の残高目標（日銀の流動性目標）の上限引上げ決定の理由に、最近の為替相場の不安定な動きへの懸念があった。

instability of the pension system 年金制度の不安定,不安定な年金制度
◆The instability of the pension system has repeatedly experienced increases in pension premiums and decreases in pension benefits. 年金制度が不安定なため、年金保険料の負担増と年金給付減が繰り返されてきた。

instability of U.S. stock prices 米国の株価不安定
◆The instability of U.S. stock prices results from problems related to massive number of unrecoverable subprime mortgage loans extended to low-income earners in the United States. 米国の株価不安定は、米国の低所得者向け住宅ローン「サブプライム・ローン」の焦げ付き急増関連問題に起因している。

install [instal] （動）（設備を）取り付ける,据え付ける,設置する,インストールする,組み込む,セットアップする,初期化する,ソフトをフロッピー・ディスクやハード・ディスクにコピーする
◆These disciplinary measures include increased penalties on securities fraud and a newly installed penalty on corporate directors in cases of failure to submit adequate financial reports to authorities. これらの懲戒処分には、証券詐欺に対する罰則の強化や、当局に適切な財務報告をしなかった場合の企業取締役に対する罰則の新設などが含まれている。

installment [instalment] （名）分割払い,割賦払い,月賦払い,割賦金
annual installment 年賦,年賦払い
applicable installment obligation 適格割賦債権
daily installment 日掛け

daily installment savings 日掛け貯金
easy installment 分割払い
full installment 全額払い
installment (account) payable 割賦未払い金
installment (account) receivable 割賦売掛金, 割賦未収金, 割賦債権
installment basis 割賦基準
installment bond 連続償還債, 割賦払い債券, 賦払い公債 (=basis of installment)
installment buying 割賦買い, 分割購入, 月賦購入
installment contract 賦払い契約
installment debt 割賦負債, 消費者信用, 消費者ローン残高
installment delivery 分割引渡し
installment finance 割賦金融
installment in full (個人引受株の)全額払込み
installment insurance 賦払い保険, 保険の年賦(ねんぷ), 月賦保険
installment merchandise floater 月賦商品包括保険
installment note 賦払い手形, 賦払い約束手形
installment purchase 割賦購入, 割賦払い購入
installment savings 積立貯金, 定期積金
installment selling 割賦販売
installment settlement 分割払い
installment shipment 分割積み
installment time deposit 積立定期預金, 積立定期
make payments in installments 割賦返済する
money market installment savings 市場金利連動型定期積金
monthly installment sales 月賦販売, 月賦
owing installments 未払い分割払い金
part installment 一部賦払い
payment by installment 割賦払い
payment in installment 割賦返済, 割賦払い, 賦払い
quarterly installment 四半期賦払い
redemption by installment payment 割賦償還
redemption by yearly installment 年賦償還
repayment installment 分割返済
yearly installment 年賦, 年賦払い
◆This payment may be made in five installments. この支払いは、5回の分割払いで行うことができる。

installment credit 割賦信用, 賦払い信用, 割賦債権, 消費者信用残高
consumer installment credit 消費者信用残高, 消費者信用
installment credit as a percentage of after-tax earnings 可処分所得に対する消費者信用残高の比率
installment credit card 割賦カード
installment credit control 賦払い信用規制

installment loan 分割払い貸付け[融資], 割賦貸出金, 割賦債権
consumer installment loan 消費者割賦貸出金

installment method 割賦基準, 賦払い方式
fixed installment method 定額法
installment method of accounting 割賦基準による会計
reducing installment method 逓減(ていげん)賦払い方式

installment payment 分割払い, 割賦返済 (=payment in installment)
installment payment export 延べ払い輸出
installment payment of tax 分割納付

installment plan 割賦制度, 分割払い方式, 割賦方式
◆The newly introduced installment plan allows purchasers to pay no initial payments. 新たに導入された割賦制度では、購入者は頭金[契約金]の支払いが不要となっている。

installment receivables 割賦債権
◆The non-U.S. finance subsidiaries finance installment receivables in some cases. 米国外の金融子会社は、割賦債権に対する金融を行う場合もあります。

installment sales 割賦販売, 割賦販売売上 (⇒deferred tax provision)
installment sales credit 割賦販売
installment sales floater 月賦販売包括保険
installment sales floater insurance 割賦販売代金保険
installment sales floater policy 分割払い販売物包括保険証券
Installment Sales Law 割賦販売法
monthly installment sales 月賦販売, 月賦

institute (名)協会, 研究所, 機関, 原理
Bank Administration Institute 銀行管理協会
Financial Executives Institute 財務担当経営者協会
financial institute 金融機関
institute cargo clauses 保険協会貨物約款
Institute Cargo Clauses 協会貨物約款
Institute of Chartered Financial Analysts 全米公認証券アナリスト
Institute of Credit Management 与信管理協会
Institute of Financial Executives 財務管理者協会
Institute of International Finance 国際金融協会, IIF
Institute of Life Insurance 生命保険協会
Institute of London Underwriters ロンドン保険業者協会
Institute of Marine Underwriters 海上保険業者協会
International Institute of Finance 国際金融協会
Research Institute of Life Insurance Management 生命保険文化研究所

Institute for Supply Management 全米供給管理協会, ISM (毎月発表する「サービス業景況感指数」は、景気の変わり目を知るための代表的な先行指標で、指数は50が好不況を判断する分かれ目となる。⇒ISM)

institution (名)機関, 金融機関, 組織, 法人, 企業, 会社, 施設 (⇒financial institution)
agricultural institution 農林系金融機関
banking institution 金融機関(financial institution), 銀行
check clearing institution 手形交換所
credit institution 信用機関, 銀行, 金融機関
deposit taking institution 預金受託機関
depository institution 預金機関, 預金受入金融機関
fiduciary institution 信用機関
finance institution 金融機関, 金融制度
financing institution 融資機関
foreign financial institution 外資系金融機関
government-affiliated institution 政府関係機関
government financial institution 政府金融機関, 政府系金融機関
government-related lending institution 政府系金融機関
institution buying 法人買い, 機関筋の買い (=institutional buying)
institution selling 法人売り, 機関筋の売り
insured institution 預金保険加盟の金融機関
lending institution 貸出機関, 金融機関
market institution 市場機構, 市場組織
monetary institution 金融機関
moneyed institution 貨幣取扱い機関
non-saving institution 非貯蓄機関
parent institution 親会社

(=patronizing institution)
premier institution　優良企業, 卓越した企業
public institution　公共機関
saving institution　貯蓄機関
successor institution　後継会社
supporting institution　信用補完機関
thrift institution　貯蓄金融機関
weaker institution　弱小金融機関
◆Financial institutions, concerned about MMC's future prospects, began calling in the company's loans. 金融機関は、三菱自動車の先行きを懸念して、同社への融資回収に動いた。

institutional　（形）団体向けの, 法人向けの, 機関の, 機関投資家の, 組織の, 組織的な, 公共機関の, 施設の, 制度[制度上]の, 慣習[慣習上]の, 画一的な, 地味な, 企業イメージを高めるための
institutional assets　制度的資産
institutional bank　機関銀行
institutional banking　法人向け銀行業務, 法人部門銀行業務, 法人部門業務
institutional broker　機関投資家専門ブローカー
institutional buyer　機関投資家, 機関購買者
institutional buying　機関筋の買い, 機関筋の買い物
institutional demand　機関投資家の需要
institutional implement　制度的手段
institutional investment　機関投資
institutional lender　（機関などの）機関融資者[融資家]（商業銀行、貯蓄貸付け組合、生命保険や年金基金など）
institutional money manager　機関投資家の資産運用担当者
institutional ownership　機関所有
institutional selling　機関筋の売り, 機関筋の売り物
institutional stockholder　法人株主, 機関株主
institutional support　政府の支援
large institutional customers　大口法人顧客

institutional investor　機関投資家　（=institutional lender: 資産運用を専門とする銀行や保険会社、年金、投資顧問、各種団体・組合などの投資家の総称）
◆Mizuho Financial Group Inc. will float preferred securities to domestic institutional investors to enhance the core portion of its capital base. みずほフィナンシャルグループ（FG）は、自己資本[中核的自己資本]を増強するため、国内機関投資家向けに優先出資証券を発行する。◆Resona Holdings Inc. will raise about ¥250 billion by issuing subordinate bonds to U.S., European and Asian institutional investors this month. りそなホールディングスは、欧米やアジアの機関投資家向けに劣後債を発行して、約2,500億円を調達する。◆The bonds were purchased by a number of institutional investors, including major commercial banks and regional banks. 同社債は、都銀や地銀などの機関投資家が購入した。

institutionalization　（名）法人化, 機関化, 機関化現象
the institutionalization of security holdings　証券保有の機関化現象
the institutionalization of shareholders [stockholders]　株主の法人化
the institutionalization of the financial market　金融市場の機関化

institutionalized savings　制度的貯蓄

instruction　（名）指示, 指図, 通達, 指示書, 指図書, 依頼書
failing instructions to the contrary　これと逆の指示がない場合には
forwarding instruction(s)　運送指図書

insurance instructions　付保指図書
issue instructions　指示を出す, 達を出す
letter of instruction　（手形買取り）指図書
shipping instructions　船積み依頼書, 積出し指図
standing instructions　継続指示

instrument　（名）証書, 証券, 有価証券, 手形, 法律文書, 手段, 支払い手段, 商品, 機関
（⇒financial instrument）
bank instrument　銀行の支払い手段
bond instrument　公債
borrowing instrument　借入証書
capital market instrument　キャピタル・マーケット商品
capital raising instrument　資金調達手段
cash instrument　現物商品, 原金融取引
commercial instrument　商業証券
credit instrument　（手形、小切手などの）信用証券
（=instrument of credit）
credit instruments　信用手段
debt instrument　債務証書, 債務証券, 債券
deposit instrument　預金証書
depository instrument　預金商品
derivative instrument　派生商品, 金融派生商品
economic policy instrument　経済政策手段
equity instrument　資本証券, 持ち分証券, エクイティ証券, 持ち分金融商品
exchange-traded instrument　上場商品, 取引所で取引される商品
financial futures instrument　金融先物商品
financial instruments　金融手段, 金融商品
financial policy instrument　金融政策手段
financing instruments　金融手段
fiscal instruments　財政手段
fiscal policy instrument　財政政策手段
（=instrument of fiscal policy）
foreign payment instrument　対外支払い手段
funding instrument　積立手段
futures instrument　先物商品
government policy instrument　政府の政策手段
hedge [hedging] instrument　ヘッジ商品, ヘッジ手段
high-yield savings instrument　高利回りの貯蓄商品
hybrid instrument　ハイブリッド商品
inchoate instrument　不完全証券
instrument of conveyance　権利移転証書
instrument of credit　信用証券
instrument of guarantee　保証契約証書
instrument of monetary policy　金融政策手段
instrument of pledge　質入れ証書
instrument payable to bearer　持参人払い証券
instruments of corporate finance　企業の資金調達の手段
insurance instrument　保険商品
（=insurance product）
interest-rate sensitive instrument　金利感応型商品
international policy instrument　国債政策手段
investment designated instrument　投資と見なされる商品
investment instrument　運用手段
lending instrument　貸出証券
long-run policy instrument　長期政策手段
monetary instrument　金融手段, 貨幣調節手段
monetary policy instrument　金融政策手段, 貨幣の政策手段　（=instrument of monetary policy）
money market instruments　短期金融商品, マネー・マー

ケット商品
negotiable instrument （手形や船積み書類などの）流通証券, 流通性のある証書
nonmonetary policy instrument 非金融政策手段, 非貨幣的政策手段
nonnegotiable instrument 譲渡不能証書
off-balance-sheet instrument 簿外取引, オフバランス・シート取引
policy instrument 政策手段
portfolio instrument ポートフォリオ商品
reacquired instrument 買戻し証券
registered instrument 登録証券
savings instrument 貯蓄商品
short-term instrument 短期証券　(=short-dated instrument, short duration instrument)
sophisticated instrument 複雑な商品
synthetic instrument 仕組み商品
transferable loan instrument 譲渡性証書
travel instruments 旅行小切手、旅行信用状等
treasury instruments 米財務省証券
Uniform Negotiable Instruments Law 統一流通証券法
◆One way for a company to accomplish long-term financing is through the issuance of long-term debt instruments in the form of bonds. 会社の長期資金調達方法の一つは、社債の形で長期債務証券を発行して行われる。

instrument of transfer 譲渡証書, 株式譲渡証書, 株式売買証書
◆The instrument of transfer of any share shall be executed by or on behalf of the Transferor. 株式の譲渡証書には、譲渡人またはその代理人が署名するものとする。

instrumental (形)重要である, 要である, 道具[手段]となる, 役立つ, 助けになる, 楽器の, 器楽の, 器械の
be instrumental in ～の担(にな)い手である, ～に尽力する
instrumental capital 手段的資本 (=capital goods, producers' goods)
instrumental errors 証券面の違算
instrumental goods 生産財, 手段財
instrumental industry 生産手段産業
instrumental rationality 手段的合理性
instrumental target 操作目標
instrumental variable 手段変数, 操作変数
instrumental variable estimator 操作変数[手段変数]推定量
instrumental variable method 手段変数[操作変数]推定法

insufficient (形)不十分な, 不足な, 不適切な, 不満足な, 不完全な
insufficient domestic demand 内需不足
insufficient funds 資金不足, 残高不足
insufficient liquidity 流動性不足, 過小流動性
◆The Japanese central bank's move to increase the outstanding current account target is insufficient to soothe market fears. 日銀の当座預金残高目標の引上げは、市場不安を払拭するには物足りない。

insurable (形)保険をかけることができる, 保険が付けられる, 付保可能な, 保険に適する
insurable contingency 保険事故
insurable expense 保険料
insurable hazards 付保可能な危険
insurable interest 被保険利益, 保険契約の目的, 保険の目的
insurable interest of life insurance 生命保険の被保険利益
insurable property 付保可能な財産[資産], 被保険物件
insurable risk 保険体, 付保[保険]可能リスク, 保険の対象となるリスク, 保険事故
insurable title (不動産の)保険可能権利証書
insurable value 保険価額, 法定保険価額
insurable years 加入可能年数

insurance (名)保険, 保険契約, 保険証券[証書], 保険金額, 保険の掛け金, 保険金, 保険料, 保険条件, 予防措置, 備え (⇒belt-tightening policy, earthquake insurance, fire insurance, group insurance, health insurance, life insurance, nonlife insurance company, reinsurance, social security insurance premium, take out)
accident insurance 災害保険
agricultural insurance 農業保険
an insurance against the risk [possibility] of terrorism テロの可能性[テロ・リスク]に対する備え
automobile insurance 自動車保険
be paid for insurance 保険金がおりる
bid guarantee insurance 入札保証保険
bond insurance premiums 社債の信用保険料
burglary insurance 盗難保険
business insurance 事業保険
business interruption insurance 利益保険
buy insurance 保険に入る, 保険に加入する (=purchase insurance)
cancel insurance 保険を解約する
cancer insurance がん保険
cargo insurance 貨物保険
carry insurance 保険に加入している
claim for ～ on one's insurance ～について保険金支払いを求める, ～の保険金を請求する
co-insurance 共同保険
comprehensive general liability insurance 包括賠償責任保険
comprehensive insurance 総合保険
compulsory automobile liability insurance 自賠責保険
compulsory insurance 強制保険, 強制加入保険
consumer insurance 個人向け保険
contingency insurance 未必利益保険
cooperative insurance 共済事業
corporate employees' pension insurance plan 厚生年金保険
corporate insurance 企業保険
cover the loss with insurance 保険で損失をカバーする, 保険で損失の穴埋めをする
definite insurance 確定保険
deposit insurance 預金保険
direct insurance 元受け保険
earthquake insurance 地震保険
endowment insurance 養老保険
export credit insurance 輸出信用保険
export insurance 輸出保険
federal deposit insurance 米連邦預金保険
fidelity insurance 身元信用保険
fire insurance 火災保険
fixed return insurance 定額保険
general insurance 損害保険
General Insurance Association of Japan 日本損害保険協会
government-run nursing care insurance system 介護保険制度

group insurance	団体保険
group pensions insurance	団体年金保険
group term insurance	団体定期保険
health insurance	健康保険
health insurance society	健康保険組合
insurance accounting	保険会計
insurance adjuster	保険精算人 (=loss adjuster)
insurance adviser	保険顧問, 保険アドバイザー
insurance against annuity	年金保険
insurance against death	死亡保険
insurance against loss	損害保険
insurance against nonperformance	契約不履行保険
insurance against theft	盗難保険
insurance against wave	潮害保険
insurance agency	保険代理店, 保険媒介代理業
insurance amount	保険金額
insurance application	保険申込み書
insurance appraiser	保険査定人, 保険被害査定人
insurance assets	保険資産(保険契約に基づく保険者の正味の契約上の権利)
insurance binder	保険仮契約書
insurance broker	保険外交員, 保険ブローカー, 保険仲立人
insurance broker's lien	保険仲立人の留置権
insurance business	保険事業
insurance canvasser	保険勧誘員
insurance carrier	保険会社, 保険業者 (=insurance company [firm], insurer)
insurance cartel	保険企業連合, 保険カルテル
insurance certificate	保険引受証, 保険契約証, 保険証明書, 団体保険被保険者票
insurance clause	保険条項
insurance clauses	保険約款
insurance commissioner	保険監督官
insurance cost	保険費用
insurance counselor [counsellor]	保険顧問
insurance cover	保険担保
insurance covers	保険で～が補償される, ～を保険でカバーする
insurance dividend	保険剰余配当
insurance enterprise	保険企業
insurance exhibit	(保険条件明細の)保険一覧表
insurance expense	支払い保険料, 保険料, 保険事業費
insurance for account of whom it may concern	不特定の他人のためにする保険
insurance for impaired lives	弱体保険
insurance for mortgagee's interest	抵当保険
insurance function	保険機能
insurance in-force	保有契約高
insurance industry	保険事業, 保険産業, 保険業界 (=insurance sector; ⇒insure)
insurance information	保険情報, 保険に関する情報
Insurance Information Institute	米国保険情報協会
insurance institution	保険制度
insurance instrument	保険商品 (=insurance product)
insurance is available	保険に入れる
insurance liability	保険負債(保険契約に基づく保険者の正味の契約上の義務)
insurance man	保険勧誘員
insurance mathematics	保険数学
insurance needs	保険需要 (=insurance demand)
insurance of charter hire	用船料保険
insurance of impaired risks	標準下体保険
insurance of profit on charter	用船利益保険
insurance of substandard lives	標準下体保険
insurance of substandard risks	標準下体保険
insurance on contents other than stock or machinery	動産保険
insurance on freight	運賃保険
insurance on goods	貨物海上保険
insurance on imaginable profit	希望利益保険
insurance on import duty	輸入税保険
insurance papers	保険の必要書類
insurance proposal	保険申込み書
insurance rate	保険料率
insurance recoveries	保険回収物
Insurance Regulatory Information System	保険取締り情報通知制度
insurance reimbursement	支払い保険金, 保険金
insurance reserve fund	保険準備金
insurance risk	保険リスク
insurance salesperson	保険会社の営業社員
insurance salvage	救助被保険物
insurance scam	保険詐欺 (=insurance fraud)
insurance slip	保険申込み書
insurance stamp	(英国)毎週支払いの国民保険 (National Insurance)支払い証明印
insurance stock	保険銘柄
insurance surveyor	保険検査人, 被害検査人
insurance underwriter	保険会社
insurance with annuity policy	満期後年金支払い保険
insurance with index clause	生計費指数保険
insurance with medical examination	有診査保険
insurance with return of premium	保険料返還付き保険
insurance without medical examination	無診査保険
insurance year	保険年度
insurrection insurance	騒じょう保険, 反乱保険
insurrection insurance policy	騒じょう保険証券
interest-sensitive policies	変額保険
loan insurance	融資保険
malpractice insurance	業務過誤保険
marine insurance	海上保険
medical insurance	医療保険
medical insurance premiums	医療保険被
municipal bond insurance	地方債保険
mutual insurance	相互保険
National Association of Insurance Commissioners	全米保険監督官協会
National Credit Union Share Insurance Fund	全米信用組合出資金保険基金
national health insurance	国民健康保険
nonlife insurance	損害保険
Old Age and Survivors Insurance	(米国)老齢・遺族年金保険, OASI
original insurance	元受け保険
over insurance	超過保険
overseas investment insurance	海外投資保険
pension insurance	年金保険
postal life insurance	簡易保険
prepaid insurance	前払い保険料

professional liability insurance　職業賠償責任保険
profit insurance　利益保険
purchase insurance　保険に入る, 保険に加入する
　　（＝buy insurance）
self-insurance　自家保険
sell insurance　保険に入れる
sickness insurance　疾病保険
social insurance　社会保険
social insurance contribution　社会保険料
take out (an) insurance on　〜に保険をかける
take out insurance　保険に入る, 保険に加入する, 保険をかける　（⇒take out）
term of insurance　保険期間
title insurance　権原保険
transport insurance　運送保険
travel insurance　旅行保険
under-insurance　一部保険
unemployment insurance　失業保険
voluntary insurance　任意保険
worker's compensation insurance　労災保険

◆Customers whose assets at the bank total about ¥10 million will receive a maximum of ¥2 million in insurance if their money is withdrawn illicitly by a third party with a bogus card. 同行では, 預け入れ資産が1,000万円程度の預金者が, 第三者に偽造カードを使って不正に預金が引き出された場合には, 最大200万円の保険金が支払われる。◆Elective health checkups are not covered by insurance. 一般の検診には, 保険が適用されない。◆Sompo Japan Insurance Inc. began selling SoftBank Kantan Hoken insurance by forming a business partnership with SoftBank Mobile Corp. 損保保険ジャパンが, ソフトバンクモバイルと業務提携して, ソフトバンクかんたん保険の販売を開始した。◆The nonlife insurance company hopes to attract about 3 million to 4 million new policyholders a year for its new types of insurance. 同損保は, 同社の新型保険で, 年間約300万〜400万件の新規契約獲得を目指している。◆The number of people taking out earthquake insurance generally increases directly after an earthquake or tsunami. 地震保険の加入者数は, 一般に地震や津波の直後に上昇する。◆To offer customers a new way to purchase insurance, nonlife insurance companies have begun cooperating with cell phone companies. 顧客に保険加入のための新サービスを提供するため, 損害保険各社は, 携帯電話会社との提携に乗り出した。◆Tokio Marine & Nichido Fire Insurance Co. tied up with NTT Docomo Inc. in April 2011 to offer Docomo One-time Hoken insurance. 東京海上日動火災保険は, 2011年4月にNTTドコモと提携して,「ドコモワンタイム保険」を提供している。

insurance agent　保険募集人, 保険代理店, 保険代理人　（保険募集人をfield underwriter, life underwriterともいう）
◆An insurance agent is a sales person who represents a life insurance company for the purpose of soliciting applications, collecting initial premiums, and servicing insurance contracts. 保険募集人は, 生命保険会社を代表して保険契約の勧誘, 初回保険料の徴収, 保険契約に関する役務を提供する販売員である。

insurance benefits　保険給付金, 保険金
◆Financial Services Agency has ordered 26 nonlife insurance firms to correct their business practices, after finding they failed to pay due insurance benefits. 損保各社が支払う義務のある保険金を支払わなかったことが判明したため, 金融庁は損保26社に対して業務是正命令を出した。◆Industry insiders said the refusal to pay insurance benefits over a long period was partly because of former Meiji managers' unreasonable policies. 業界関係者によると, 長期間にわたる保険金不払いの一因は, 旧明治生命保険の経営者の無理な経営方針だ。◆The insurer aimed to improve profitability by being reluctant to pay insurance benefits. この保険会社は, 保険金の支払いを渋って収益の向上を目指した。◆When private life insurers go bankrupt, insurance benefits are reduced. 民間の生命保険会社が破たんすれば, 保険金が減額される。◆When yields on whole life insurance products decline, policyholders must pay higher premiums to secure the same amount of total insurance benefits. 終身保険商品の利回りが下がった場合, 加入者[保険契約者]がそれ以前と同額の総保険料を受け取るには, より高い保険料を払わなければならない。

Insurance Business Law　保険業法　（⇒prospective yield rate）
◆The Insurance Business Law prohibits life insurers from lowering their promised yield rates on existing insurance contracts prior to their collapse. 保険業法は, 生命保険会社が破たん前に既契約分の保険契約の予定利率を引き下げることを禁止している。

insurance claims　保険請求権, 損害保険の請求額, 未収保険金, 保険金, 保証金　（⇒claim名詞, full payment of insurance claims, honor）
insurance claims-paying rating　保険金支払能力格付け
insurance claims unsettled　未決済保険金
◆The proposed pool insurance system for terrorism would be jointly run by nonlife insurers to allow insurance claims to be paid from an industry fund. 現在提案されているテロ・プール制度は, 業界基金から（テロ被害の）保険金を支払えるようにするため, 損保各社の共同運営になる。◆The U.S. government has to pay insurance claims when homeowners default on their mortgages, under the government program that insures mortgages. 米政府の住宅ローン保証プログラムに基づき, 米政府は, 住宅所有者の住宅ローンがデフォルト（債務不履行）になったら, 保証金を支払わなければならない。

insurance company　保険会社　（＝insurance firm, insurance underwriter, insurer）
captive insurance company　自家保険会社
casualty insurance company　損害保険会社
financial and insurance companies　金融・保険会社, 金融保険業
fire and casualty insurance companies　火災・障害保険会社
general insurance company　損害保険会社
Insurance Companies Act　英国保険会社法
insurance companies blanket bond　保険会社包括保証
insurance company financial strength ratings　保険格付け
insurance company rating　保険会社の格付け
insurance company senior policyholder　保険会社の一般契約者
monocline insurance company　専門保険会社
municipal bond insurance company　地方債保証保険会社
◆Solvency margin ratios are the most closely watched gauges in assessing the financial health of an insurance company. ソルベンシー・マージン比率は, 保険会社の経営[財務]の健全性を評価する際に特に注目される指標である。

insurance company's financial health　保険会社の財務の健全性
◆Solvency margin is an indicator of an insurance company's financial health. ソルベンシー・マージン（支払い余力）比率は, 保険会社の財務の健全性を示す指標の一つである。

insurance contract　保険契約, 保険契約者　（⇒insurance agent, Insurance Business Law）
insurance contract for account of another person or third parties　他人[他人・第三者]のためにする保険契約
insurance contract notice　保険契約通知書
insurance contract on the life of another　他人の生命の保

険契約
◆In this type of life insurance products, the rate of return after canceling the insurance contract can be higher than that of a savings account if a policyholder upholds the contract for five to 10 years. この種の生保商品では、保険契約者が保険契約を5〜10年続けると、解約後の利回り（予定利率）は預金よりも高い利回りが見込める。◆Meiji Yasuda Life Insurance Co. failed to pay insurance claims and was ordered to suspend signing insurance contracts by the Financial Services Agency. 明治安田生命は、保険金の不払い問題で、金融庁から新規保険契約業務の停止処分を受けた。

insurance coverage　保険担保, 保険の補償範囲, 保険填補（てんぽ）範囲, 付保危険
◆Any additional premium for insurance coverage in excess of the value mentioned above, if so required by ABC, shall be borne by ABC. ABCの要請により、上記価額を超えて付保する場合の追加保険料は、ABCが負担するものとする。

insurance covering damage　損害を補償する保険, 損害補償保険
◆Major nonlife insurance companies saw a rapid increase in the number of people taking out insurance covering damage due to earthquakes, tsunami, volcanic eruptions and other natural disasters. 大手損保各社では、地震や津波、火山の噴火などの天災による損害を補償する保険（地震保険）の加入者が急増した。

insurance demand　保険需要
（=insurance needs）
◆Nonlife insurers are exploring new types of insurance demand and offering convenient and easy means of buying policies. 損保各社は、新たな保険需要を掘り起こして、いつでも、どこでも簡単に保険に加入できるサービスを提供している。

insurance division　保険部門
◆The largest U.S. financial group, Citigroup, is considering spinning off its insurance division, which it took over from Travelers Inc. in a 1998 merger. 米最大手の金融グループ、シティグループは現在、1998年の合併でトラベラーズから引き継いだ保険部門の分社化を検討している。

insurance firm　保険会社
（=insurance company, insurer）
◆Insurance payments for the March 11 earthquake and tsunami will drain the resources of insurance firms and the government's special account. 東日本大震災の保険金支払いで、保険会社と政府の特別会計の原資は大幅に目減りすることになる。◆The instability of life insurance firms and the lowered earning power of banks burdened with massive bad loans have become the two major factors rocking the financial system. 生保各社の経営基盤の不安定さと、巨額の不良債権に苦しむ銀行の収益力低下が、金融システムを揺るがしている二大要因になっている。

insurance fund　保険資金, 保険基金, 保険金, 保険預り金　（⇒debt assumption）
◆The insurance fund is financed with premiums from the local credit guarantee corporations and money to be recovered from the debts that have been taken over. 信用保証制度の保険金[保険資金]は、全国各地の信用保証協会からの保険料と、肩代わりした債権を回収した金で賄（まかな）われている。

insurance market　保険市場
（⇒third-sector insurance market）
◆The so-called "third-sector insurance market" refers to insurance offered other than traditional life and nonlife insurance plans, such as for cancer and other illness-related insurance. いわゆる「第三分野の保険市場」とは、がん保険やその他の病気関連保険など従来の生命保険と損害保険制度以外に提供される保険のことをいう。
保険市場の主要3分野：
First sector（第一分野）
　　term insurance　　定期保険
　　whole life insurance　　終身保険
Second sector（第二分野）
　　automobile insurance　　自動車保険
　　fire insurance　　火災保険
Third sector（第三分野）
　　cancer insurance　　がん保険
　　medical expenses insurance　　医療費用保険
　　medical insurance　　医療保険
　　nursing-care expenses insurance　　介護費用保険
　　nursing-care insurance　　介護保険

insurance money　保険金
（⇒biometric integrated circuit card）
◆Aioi Insurance Co. has called on Mitsubishi Motors Corp. to pay it about ¥30 million, the full amount of insurance money the nonlife insurer paid to a victim of a traffic accident. あいおい損害保険は、同社が交通事故の被害者に支払った保険金の全額約3,000万円の支払いを、三菱自動車に請求した。◆The bank raised the amount of insurance money from the current ¥5 million limit to a maximum of ¥10 million for cash card fraud. 同行は、キャッシュ・カード詐欺の保険金額を、現在の上限500万円から最大1,000万円に引き上げた。

insurance payment　保険金の支払い
◆Earthquake insurance payments resulting from the Great East Japan Earthquake are expected to reach ¥1.2 trillion. 東日本大震災による地震保険の保険金支払い額は、（業界全体で）1兆2,000億円に達する見込みだ。◆Insurance payments for the March 11 earthquake and tsunami will drain the resources of insurance firms and the government's special account. 東日本大震災の保険金支払いで、保険会社と政府の特別会計の原資は大幅に目減りすることになる。◆Insurance payments increased following the Sept. 11 terrorist attacks on the United States. 2001年9月11日の米同時テロの影響で、保険料の支払いが増えた。◆Under the current earthquake insurance system, insurance payments remain capped at half the actual value of a home and its contents. 現行の地震保険[地震保険制度]では、保険金の支払い額の上限は、住宅や家財の実質価値の半額までとなっている。

insurance payment claims　保険金支払い請求額
（⇒insurance claims）
◆The government can tap its special account to cover 50 percent to 95 percent of insurance payment claims when total earthquake insurance payouts exceed ¥115 billion. 地震保険の支払い総額が1,150億円を超えると、政府は特別会計を利用して保険金支払い請求額の50〜95％を負担することができる。

insurance payouts　保険金の支払い額, 保険金の支払い
◆Insurance payouts for the March 11 disaster will reach ¥970 billion. 東日本大震災の保険金支払い額は、9,700億円に達する見込みだ。◆Insurance payouts for the March 11 earthquake and tsunami reached ¥670 billion as of May 12, 2011. 東日本大震災の保険金の支払い額は、2011年5月12日時点で6,700億円に達している。

insurance policy　保険証券, 保険証書, 保険契約, 保険
（⇒annuity insurance policy, bank card, interest insured）
　buy an insurance policy　　保険をかける, 保険に入る, 保険に加入する
　　（=purchase an insurance policy）
　casualty insurance policy　　災害保険証券
　family insurance policy　　家族保険契約, 家族保険
　insurance policy cancellation　　保険の解約, 保険契約の解除
　purchase an insurance policy　　保険をかける, 保険に入る［加入する］　（=buy an insurance policy）
　renew the insurance policy　　保険契約を更新する, 保険の継続手続きをする

sales of automobile insurance policies　自動車保険の販売
sell insurance policies　保険を販売する
the obligations pursuant to the insurance policies　保険契約に基づく債務を履行する
whole life insurance policy　終身生命保険
◆Banks are allowed to sell insurance policies to clients. 銀行は、顧客に保険を販売することができる。◆Banks could forcibly sell insurance policies to clients by utilizing their strong position as creditors. 銀行は、債権者としての強い立場を利用して、顧客に保険を強制的に販売する可能性もある。◆Family insurance policy is a whole life insurance policy that provides term insurance coverage on the insured's spouse and children. 家族保険契約は、被保険者の配偶者と子どもに定期保険保障を与える終身保険だ。◆If life insurers continue to offer insurance policies with guaranteed high return rates, the future financial burden in terms of interest payments will increase. 生保が高い利回りを保証した保険の販売を今後とも続けると、将来の利払いの金融負担が増えることになる。◆In insurance policies that can be purchased via mobile phone, would-be policyholders do not need to input personal data and payments are easier. 携帯電話で加入できる保険では、加入希望者は個人情報を入力する必要がなく、支払いも簡単だ。◆In insurance services that can be bought via cell phones, premiums include an insurance policy that pays ¥300,000 if a policyholder scores a hole in one in golf. 携帯電話で加入できる保険サービスでは、保険料に保険契約者がゴルフでホールインワンした場合に30万円支払われる保険契約［保険］もある。◆In the case of single-premium whole life insurance policies, policyholders make one large premium payment up front when they sign the contract. 一時払い終身保険の場合は、保険契約者が契約を結ぶ際に［契約時に］多額の保険料を前もって一括で払い込む。◆Revenues from the single-premium whole life insurance policies support the life insurer's business performance. 一時払い終身保険による収入［一時払い終身保険の収入保険料］が、同生保の業績を支えている。◆The downturn in global financial markets has had a negative impact on insurance products such as single-premium pension insurance policies which are popular as a form of savings. 世界の金融市場の低迷が、貯蓄用［一種の貯蓄］として人気の高い一時払い年金保険などの保険商品に悪影響を及ぼしている。◆The Financial Services Agency ordered Nichido Fire to partially suspend unapproved sales of automobile insurance policies. 金融庁は、日動火災に対して、認可外の自動車保険の販売業務を一時停止する命令を出した。

insurance policyholder　保険契約者
（⇒policyholder）
insurance policyholder premium　保険契約者の保険の掛け金［保険料］
Insurance Policyholders Protection Corporation　保険契約者保護機構
◆The amount of the negative spread—the margin of loss that occurs when yields from investments made with insurance-policyholder premiums are lower than yields insurers promised their policyholders—totals an annual of ¥1.5 trillion. 逆ざやの総額、つまり保険契約者の保険の掛金［保険料］で行った投資の利回り［運用利回り］が、契約者に保険会社が約束した利回り（予定利率）より低い場合に生じる損失額は、年間1兆5千億円にのぼる。◆There is a negative spread between the yield guaranteed to insurance policyholders and their investment returns. 今は、保険契約者に保証した利回り［予定利率］と運用利回りが逆ざや状態（運用利回りが保険契約者に保証した利回りを下回る状態）にある。

insurance policy's value　保険契約の評価額
◆In the case of earthquake insurance, the cap on the insurance policy's value for an average house in Tokyo is about ¥10 million. 地震保険の場合、都内の平均的な住宅の保険契約の評価額上限は1,000万円程度だ。

insurance premium　保険料, 掛け金　（=insurable expense, insurance expense; ⇒basic pension, direct debit, life insurance premium）
direct premiums　元受正味保険料
insurance premiums for the corporate koseinenkin pension program　厚生年金の保険料
pay insurance premiums　保険料を支払う, 保険料を納付する
premium income　収入保険料
◆Financial institutions pay insurance premiums to the Deposit Insurance Corporation according to the amount of deposits they hold. 金融機関は、保有する預金量に応じて預金保険機構に保険料を納付している。◆Insurance premiums for the corporate koseinenkin pension program may increase from autumn. 厚生年金の保険料が、今秋から引き上げられる可能性がある。◆The insurance premiums are determined by the age and other characteristics of policyholders. この保険料は、保険加入者の年齢などの特性に応じて決められる。◆Under the current Japanese pension system for company employees, employees and employers each pay half of the insurance premiums worth 17.35 percent of the employee's monthly salary, or 13.58 percent of their annual income. 日本の現在の厚生年金保険制度では、従業員と企業がそれぞれ月収の17.35%（年収ベースで13.58%）の保険料を半分ずつ負担している。

insurance premium payment　保険料の支払い
◆Insurance premium payments increased following the Sept. 11 terrorist attacks on the United States. 2001年9月11日の米同時テロの影響で、保険料の支払いが増えた。

insurance product　保険商品
（=insurance instrument; ⇒brochure）
related insurance products　保険関連商品
sales of insurance products　保険商品の販売
◆Bank sales of some insurance products were deregulated in April 2001. 一部の保険商品の銀行窓口での販売は、2001年4月に自由化された。◆Instances of nonpayment involving third-sector insurance products totaled 1,140 for Mitsui Sumitomo Insurance Co. 第三分野（医療保険やがん保険など）の保険金不払い件数は、三井住友海上火災保険が計1,140件もあった。◆The downturn in global financial markets has had a negative impact on insurance products such as single-premium pension insurance policies which are popular as a form of savings. 世界の金融市場の低迷が、貯蓄用［一種の貯蓄］として人気の高い一時払い年金保険などの保険商品に悪影響を及ぼしている。◆The move to lower the yields of insurance products is likely to spread through the industry as tough investment conditions persist. 厳しい運用環境が続いているので、保険商品の利回りを引き下げる動きは、業界全体に広がりそうだ。◆When yields on whole life insurance products decline, policyholders must pay higher premiums to secure the same amount of total insurance benefits. 終身保険商品の利回りが下がった場合、加入者［保険契約者］がそれ以前と同額の総保険料を受け取るには、より高い保険料を払わなければならない。

insurance sales　保険の販売
◆The casualty insurer delayed the start of its online insurance sales due to the March 11 earthquake and tsunami. 2011年3月11日の東日本大震災のため、同損保は保険のネット販売の開業を延期した。

insurance sector　保険部門, 保険分野, 保険業界
（=insurance industry）
◆Investment in plants and equipment by all industries except the financial and insurance sectors expanded for the first time in 3 1/2 years in July-September period. 7-9月期の金融・保険業を除く全産業の設備投資額は、3年半ぶりに増加した。

insurance service 保険サービス, 保険サービス業, 保険業務, 保険事業
◆In insurance services that can be bought via cell phones, cell phone companies provide nonlife insurers with policyholders' personal information. 携帯電話で加入できる保険サービスでは、携帯電話会社が(保険)加入者の個人情報を損害保険会社に提供している。◆In insurance services that can be bought via cell phones, premiums include an insurance policy that pays ¥300,000 if a policyholder scores a hole in one in golf. 携帯電話で加入できる保険サービスでは、保険料に保険契約者がゴルフでホールインワンした場合に30万円支払われる保険契約[保険]もある。◆Nippon Export and Investment Insurance (NEXI) was established in 2001 to provide foreign trade and investment insurance services. 独立行政法人の日本貿易保険は、貿易保険事業と対外投資保険事業を提供するため、2001年に設立された。◆Nonlife insurers started insurance services that can be bought more easily via cell phones with information transmission capabilities. 損保各社が、情報通信機能がある携帯電話を使って、これまでより簡単に保険に入れるサービスを開始した。

insurance underwriting 保険引受け
◆The five business fields in the tie-up agreement are product development, marketing, insurance underwriting, damage assessment and reinsurance. 提携契約の5業務分野は、商品開発、マーケティング、保険引受け、損害査定と再保険である。

insurance world 保険業界
◆The insurance world should disclose to consumers such basic data as the percentage of earthquake insurance payouts made in full after previous temblors. 保険業界は、これまでの地震で地震保険の満額支払いが行われた割合はどれくらいかなどの基本的なデータを、消費者に開示すべ木田。

insurant (名)保険契約者, 被保険者

insure (動)(加入者が~に)保険をかける, (~を)保険に入れる, 保険を付ける, 付保する, (保険業者が~について)保険契約を結ぶ, 保険契約する, 保険を引き受ける, 保険証券を発行する, 保証する, 保障する, 補償する, 請合う, 確保する, 補償する, 請合う, 確保する (⇒large-lot savings, life insurance)
 be insured 保険に入っている, 保険がかかっている
 be insured against theft 盗難保険をかける
 be insured for ~をカバーする保険をかける
 insure a person against death ~(人)に生命保険をかける
 insure against all risks オールリスク保険をかける, 全危険担保の条件で保険契約を結ぶ, 全危険担保で付保する (=insure A.A.R.)
 insure financially against international loss 海外での損失に保険をかける, 課外損失保険をかける, 海外での損失を保険でカバーする
 insure for A against fire on something ある物の火災保険をAのためにかける
 insure mortgage 住宅ローンを保証する
 insure one's life for $300,000 30万ドルの生命保険に入る
 insure one's life with the company 同社と生命保険契約を結ぶ
 insure one's property against fire ~の財産に火災保険をかける
 insure one's property for $500,000 ~の財産に50万ドルの保険をかける
 insure something at invoice value plus 10% ある物に送り状金額の1割増で付保する
 party insuring 保険契約者
 sum insured 保険金額
◆Premiums for insuring a wooden house for ¥10 million are more than ¥30,000 annually in earthquake-prone areas. 木造住宅に1,000万円の(地震)保険をかける場合の保険料は、地震発生リスクが高い地域で年30,000万円を超える。◆The bank distributes palm-recognizing ATM cards that are insured for up to ¥100 million in case they are stolen or damaged. 同行では手のひら認証のキャッシュ・カードを発行しており、このキャッシュ・カードの盗難や(偽造による)預金の被害にあった場合の補償額は、最高で1億円となっている。◆The bank repeatedly lied so that it could benefit from the U.S. government program that insured mortgage. 同行は、米政府の住宅ローン保証プログラムから利益を得るために繰り返し虚偽の説明をした。◆The nonlife insurance industry wants all kinds of buildings and other properties not insured for terrorist attacks. 損害保険業界は、すべての物件をテロ免責にしたいと考えている。◆Under the U.S. government program that insured mortgages, the government has had to foot the bill for mortgage loans that defaulted. 米政府の住宅ローン保証プログラムに基づき、米政府はデフォルト(債務不履行)になった住宅ローンのツケの支払いを迫られている。

insured (形)保険がかかっている, ~に対して保険がかけられている, ~に対して保険がきく[保険に入っている], 保険付きの, 付保された, 被保険~ (名)被保険者, 保険契約者
 federally insured deposits 米連邦預金保険付保預金
 insured account 付保勘定, 保険付き勘定, (預金保険)保険口座
 insured amount 保険金額, 保険契約金額 (=life insurance coverage)
 insured article 被保険物
 insured assets 保険年金資産
 insured bank 被保険銀行, 預金保険加入銀行, 米連邦預金保険制度に加入している銀行
 insured B/L 保険付き船荷証券
 insured cargo 付保貨物, 保険付き貨物
 insured cause 保険事故
 insured commercial bank 被保険商業銀行
 insured credit exposure 付保された信用リスク
 insured debt 保証している債券, 債券の保証
 insured depository institution 被保険預金機関
 insured deposits (預金保険)被保険預金
 insured event 保険事故, 保険事象
 insured firm 被保険企業(保険をかけている企業)
 insured invoice ノン・ポリ(輸出者が保険会社と包括保険契約を結んでいる場合、商業送り状(commercial invoice)の空欄に「当該貨物は付保済みである」旨の文言を記入したものをいう)
 insured ledger 信用状発行元帳
 insured loan 保険付きローン
 insured loss index 保険損失指数
 insured mail 保険付き郵便, 保険郵便
 insured object 被保険物
 insured par 付保総額
 insured pension plan 保険型年金, 保険会社利用方式企業年金
 insured period 加入期間
 insured person 被保険者
 insured plan 保険付き制度
 insured portfolio 保険付きポートフォリオ
 insured principal or debt services 付保対象社債の元本または付保金額
 insured property 被保険物
 insured savings 保険貯蓄
 insured unemployment 保険受給失業者

insured unemployment rate　被保険失業率
insured value　保険価額
insured value of vessel　船舶保険価額
perils insured against　担保危険
the insured　被保険者, 保険契約者
　　(⇒belt-tightening policy, life insurance)
the sum insured　保険金額
　◆Financial settlement refers to a lump sum payment by an insurer to a disabled insured that extinguishes the insurer's responsibility under the disability contract. 金融決済は、就業不能契約に基づき、傷害を負った被保険者に保険会社が一時金を支給して、保険会社の責任を消滅させることを指す。◆Non-working spouses of public servants and company employees are classified as Category III insured. 公務員や会社員の仕事を持たない配偶者は、第3号被保険者と呼ばれている。◆Whole life insurance means life insurance under which coverage remains in force during the insured's entire lifetime, provided premiums are paid as specified in the policy. 終身保険は、保険契約に明記されている保険料が支払われているかぎり、保障が被保険者の全生涯にわたって有効な生命保険を意味する。

insured institution　預金保険加盟の金融機関
FDIC-insured institutions　米連邦預金保険公社 (FDIC) が預金の支払いを保証している金融機関 (米商業銀行と貯蓄金融機関)
　◆The 171 banks on the FDIC's "problem list" encompass only about 2 percent of the nearly 8,500 FDIC-insured institutions. 米連邦預金保険公社 (FDIC) の「問題銀行リスト」に挙げられた171行は、同公社が預金の支払いを保証している金融機関 (米商業銀行と貯蓄金融機関) 約8,500行の2%程度を占めるにすぎない。

insurer　(名)保険会社, 保険業者, 保険者, 保証人
　(=insurance company, insurance enterprise, insurance firm; ⇒financial settlement, life insurer, nonlife insurer, reinsurance)
bond insurer　債券保険会社
casualty insurer　損害保険会社
direct insurer　元受保険者, 元受会社
financial guaranty bond insurer　専業信用保証保険会社
life insurer　生命保険会社
monocline insurer　専門保証会社
mortgage insurer　モーゲージ保証会社
municipal bond insurer　地方債保証 (保険) 会社
mutual life insurer　生命保険相互会社
nonlife insurer　損害保険会社　(⇒claim名詞)
private insurer　民間保険会社
property and casualty insurer　損害保険会社, 損保会社
quasi-governmental mortgage insurer　政府系モーゲージ保証会社
　◆Edelweiss Tokyo Life Insurance Co. is the first Japanese insurer handling both life and nonlife policies in India. エーデルワイス・トウキョウ・ライフ・インシュランス (本店所在地: インドのマハラシュトラ州ムンバイ市) は、インドで生保と損保を取り扱う日本初の保険会社だ。◆Financial settlement refers to a lump sum payment by an insurer to a disabled insured that extinguishes the insurer's responsibility under the disability contract. 金融決済は、就業不能契約に基づき、傷害を負った被保険者に保険会社が一時金を支給して、保険会社の責任を消滅させることを指す。◆In December 2011, the insurer will lower the yield rate to 1.1 percent from 1.5 percent for those who newly purchase the company's single-premium whole life insurance. 2011年12月から同生保は、一時払い終身保険の新規加入者 [新規契約者] を対象に、利回りを1.5%から1.1%に引き下げる。◆In insurance services that can be bought via cell phones, cell phone companies provide nonlife insurers with policyholders' personal information. 携帯電話で加入できる保険サービスでは、携帯電話会社が (保険) 加入者の個人情報を損害保険会社に提供している。◆In the life insurance sector, the practice of luring customers by touting the bad performances of other insurers has been called into question. 生保業界では、他社の経営不振をあおって顧客を勧誘する行為 (風評営業) が問題になっている。◆Insurers set aside provisions for disasters. 保険会社は、災害準備金 [異常危険準備金] を積み立てている。◆Lowering the yield of Meiji Yasuda's single-premium whole life insurance will reduce the attraction of the insurer's financial products. 明治安田生保の一時払い終身保険の利回り [予定利率] の引下げで、同社の金融商品の魅力は薄れると思われる。◆Manulife Financial Corp., Canada's third largest insurer, agreed to buy U.S. life insurer John Hancock Financial Services Inc. for around $10.8 billion. カナダ3位の生命保険会社マニュライフは、米国の生命保険会社ジョン・ハンコックを約108億ドルで買収することに同意した。◆Meiji Yasuda decided to lower the yield rate of its flagship insurance product because the insurer placed priority on long-term stable management over an increase in the number of policyholders. 明治安田生保は、契約者の数を増やすより長期的な経営の安定を優先したため、主力保険商品の予定利率 [利回り] を引き下げることにした。◆The bank plans to provide the money by transferring ¥100 billion in subordinated loans, which it has already extended to the insurer, to the insurer's foundation fund. 同行は、すでに供与している劣後ローン1,000億円をこの保険会社の基金に振り替えて、その資金を提供する方針だ。◆The casualty insurer delayed the start of its online insurance sales due to the March 11 earthquake and tsunami. 2011年3月11日の東日本大震災のため、同損保は保険のネット販売の開業を延期した。◆The increase in seven insurers' core operating profits is due to appraisal gains in their stockholdings. 生保7社の基礎利益 (本業のもうけに当たる) の増加は、保有株式の含み益によるものだ。◆The insurer failed to pay about ¥115 million in dividends to its policyholders in about 47,000 cases between fiscal 1984 and fiscal 2005. 同保険会社は、1984年度から2005年度の間に約47,000件の配当金、約1億1,500万円を支払っていなかった。◆The massive negative yields of the life insurance industry threaten the financial soundness of insurers. 生保業界の巨額の逆ざやが、生保各社の財務上の健全性 [経営の健全性] を脅 (おびや) かしている。◆The situation surrounding the Japanese economy has suddenly grown tense due to the first bankruptcy of a Japanese insurer in seven years. 7年ぶりの日本の生保破たんで、日本経済を取り巻く環境は一気に緊迫感が高まっている。

insuring　(形)保険を付ける, 保証する
insuring agent　保険代理店
insuring agreement　保険引受契約, 保険引受協定
insuring clause　保険引受約款, 保険条項
insuring contract　保険引受契約
insuring office　保険引受事務所
party insuring　保険契約者

intangible　(形)無形の, 無体の, 実体のない
intangible asset　無形資産, 無体資産, 無形固定資産, のれん　(=intangible property, intangibles: 営業権, 知的所有権 (特許権・商標権・著作権・ノウハウ), 借地権, 鉱業権など無形の事実上の資産)
intangible benefit　無形の利益
intangible capital　無形資本
intangible factor　非金銭的要素
intangible property　無形財産, 無体財産権
　(=intangible asset, intangibles: 株式, 債権など)
intangible reward　無形の報酬
intangible value　無形価値, のれん代 (goodwill value)
intangible worth　無形資産
　◆Olympus Corp. exaggerated the intangible value of its

British subsidiary by ￥33.4 billion in the financial statement. オリンパスは、有価証券報告書で英子会社の"のれん代"について334億円を過大に計上していた。

integrate（動）統合する, 一本化する, 系列化する
（⇒information system）
◆Mizuho Financial Group will integrate its retail and corporate banking units in 2013. みずほフィナンシャルグループ（FG）は、傘下のリテール銀行［リテール銀行業務部門］とコーポレート銀行［企業向け銀行業務部門］を2013年にも合併させる方針だ。◆The largest factor behind the computer system's breakdown is that the entire process of integrating the computer systems of the three banks was affected by shifts in policy over which system should be chosen for the new bank. システム障害の最大の原因は、新銀行にどこのコンピュータ・システムを使うのか、方針が二転、三転して、3行のシステムの統合作業全体が方針転換に振り回されたことにある。◆The two financial groups plan to integrate their banking, trust and securities operations under a holding company created through the merger of their holding companies. 両金融グループは、それぞれ銀行、信託、証券業務を経営統合により新設する持ち株会社の傘下に統合する計画だ。

integrate management 経営統合する
◆UFJ Holdings integrated its management with Mitsubishi Tokyo Financial Group. UFJホールディングスは、三菱東京フィナンシャル・グループと経営統合した。

integrate (one's) operations 経営統合する
（=integrate businesses;⇒integrate, stock transfer）
◆Mizuho Financial Group was established in September 2000 after Dai-Ichi Kangyo Bank, Fuji Bank and the Industrial Bank of Japan integrated their operations. みずほフィナンシャルグループは、第一勧業銀行、富士銀行と日本興業銀行の3行が経営統合して、2000年9月に発足した。◆Since three banks integrated their operations, executives from the three predecessor banks served on an equal basis as presidents of the Mizuho group, Mizuho Bank and Mizuho Corporate Bank. 3銀行の経営統合以来、旧3行の経営者が、みずほグループ（FG）、みずほ銀行、みずほコーポレート銀行のトップをそれぞれ分け合った。◆Sumitomo Trust & Banking will complete the purchase by Sept.30 and will integrate operations to form the nation's largest trust bank in fiscal 2005. 住友信託銀行は、9月30日までに買収を完了し、2005年度中に経営統合して国内最大の信託銀行を発足させる。

integration（名）統合, 一元化, 統一, 企業の系列化, 集約化（⇒bourse, business integration, management integration）
business integration 経営統合, 事業統合
currency integration 通貨統合
financial integration 金融統合
horizontal integration 水平統合
integration efficiency 統合効果
integration of affiliates 関連会社の統合
management integration 経営統合（=operational integration;⇒financial rehabilitation）
operational integration 経営統合（=business integration, management integration;⇒option）
system integration システム統合, システム統合化
vertical integration 垂直統合
◆After the integration of Monex Inc. and Orix Securities, Orix will become the largest shareholder in Monex Group with a 22.5 percent share. マネックス証券とオリックス証券の合併に伴い、オリックス証券はマネックスグループの株式を22.5％保有して、同グループの筆頭株主になる。◆With the integration of the Japan Bank for International Cooperation's division for handling yen loans, and other bodies in October 2008, JICA became one of the world's largest development assistance agencies. 国際協力機構（JICA）は、2008年10月に国際協力銀行（JBIC）の円借款部門などを統合して、(事業規模で）世界最大級の開発援助機関となった。

integration of banking computer systems コンピュータ・システムの統合
◆The integration of banking computer systems is enormously complex and tedious, but no errors should be allowed. 銀行のコンピュータ・システムの統合は非常に複雑で大変な作業であるが、ミスは許されない。

integration of businesses 経営統合
◆Kiyo Bank and Wakayama Bank have started negotiations on the integration of their businesses, a possible merger. 紀陽銀行と和歌山銀行は、合併の可能性も含めて、経営統合に向けた協議を開始した。

integration of management 経営統合
（=management integration, operational integration）
◆Japan's two major stock exchanges will start talks shortly on a possible integration of their management. 日本の2大証券取引所が、経営統合に向けて近く協議に入ることになった。

integrity（名）保全, 領土保全, 完全, 無欠, 無傷の状態, 完全性, 一体性, 統一性, 整合性, 一致していること, 誠実, 清廉, 潔白, 信頼, 信認
business integrity 商業道徳
credibility and integrity 信頼と信認
market integrity 市場の整合性
operational and financial integrity of results 営業成績と財務成績の適正性
standards of integrity 倫理基準
the integrity and reliability of the financial statements 財務書類の完全性と信頼性
（⇒internal control）
the integrity of the borrower 借入れ人の誠実さ
◆All companies in the group pride themselves on maintaining the highest standards of integrity in carrying out business activities. 同グループ企業はすべて、事業活動を実施するにあたって最高の倫理基準を維持することを誇りとしている。◆Management is responsible for maintaining a system of internal controls as a fundamental requirement for the operational and financial integrity of results. 経営者は、営業成績および財務成績の適正性を保つ基本的条件として、内部統制組織を維持する責任を負っています。

integrity and objectivity of the financial information 財務情報の完全性と客観性
◆Management is responsible for the integrity and objectivity of the financial information included in this report. 経営者は、本報告書に記載されている財務情報の完全性と客観性について責任を負っています。

integrity of the acquisition prices and commission fees 買収の価格と手数料の適正性, 買収額と買収手数料の適正性
◆Olympus fired its president who had pointed out the integrity of the acquisition prices and commission fees. オリンパスは、買収額や買収手数料の適正性を指摘した社長を解任した。

intend to ～する方針である, ～するつもりである, ～しようと思う
◆The Board of Audit intends to include the total taxpayer contribution to JAL in its audit account report compiled in November 2011. 会計検査院は、2011年11月にまとめる決算検査報告書に、日航に対する総国民負担額を盛り込む方針だ。◆The murky acquisitions of several companies by the major precision equipment maker were intended to paper over losses on investments the company made. この大手精密機器メーカーによる不透明な企業買収のねらいは、同社が行った投資の損失隠しだった。

intensified fears 不安の高まり, 懸念の高まり, 警戒感

の高まり
◆The rapid spread of Italy's credit crisis is due to intensified fears about the nation's fiscal predicament by Italy's huge fiscal deficits. イタリアの信用不安が急速に広がったのは、イタリアの巨額の赤字で同国の財政ひっ迫への警戒感が高まったからだ。

intensified global competition 熾烈（しれつ）な国際競争
◆There were speculations that only three or four Japanese banks could survive intensified global competition. 熾烈な国際競争に生き残れる邦銀は3～4行だけ、と見る向きもあった。

intensify （動）強める, 高める, 強化する, 増強する, 激化する, 強くなる, 深刻化する, 高まる, 活発になる
  intensified global competition　グローバル競争の激化
  intensified price competition　価格競争の激化
◆Competition will further intensify in fast-growing emerging markets. 急成長している新興国市場は、これから競争が一段と激しくなると思われる。◆Major banks are intensifying their efforts to reduce their risk assets by securitizing and selling their credit to prevent their capital adequacy ratio, an index that shows their business soundness, from declining. 大手各行は現在、経営の健全性を示す指標である自己資本比率の低下を防ぐため、貸出債権の証券化や転売などでリスク資産（リスク・アセット）の圧縮策を加速させている。◆The global financial crisis would have intensified if the U.S. House of Representatives had rejected the financial bailout bill. 米下院が金融安定化法案（金融救済法案）を否決していたら、世界の金融危機は深刻化しただろう。

intention （名）意向, 意思, 意欲, 構想
  buying intention　購入意図, 購買意向, 購買意欲
  foreign investment intentions　外国からの投資申請件数
  intention of easing monetary policy　金融政策を緩和する意図
  purchase intention　購入意図
◆One of the intentions of the government to introduce various regulation measures is to discourage "excessive competition." 各種の規制措置を導入する政府のねらいの一つは、「過当競争」の防止である。◆The would-be acquirer has no intention of taking part in the management of a company it aims to take over. 買収側［買収希望者］に、買収対象企業の経営に参加する意思はない。

Inter-American Development Bank　米州開発銀行

interbank　（形）銀行間の, 銀行間で同意された［準備された］, 金融機関相互の
  daily interbank transaction　毎日［日常の］銀行間取引
  interbank lending　銀行間貸出
  interbank market　銀行間市場, インターバンク市場, インターバンク・マーケット（手形売買、外国為替、ドル・コール市場など金融機関だけが参加できる金融市場で、金融機関が相互に短期資金の貸借を行う）
  interbank transaction　銀行間取引, インターバンク取引

interbank network of ATMs　銀行のATM相互利用, ATMの銀行間ネットワーク
◆A depositor can withdraw money from any bank by the interbank network of automatic teller machines（ATMs）. 銀行のATM相互利用が普及しているため、預金者はどの銀行からでも預金を引き出すことができる。

interbank rate　銀行間金利, 銀行間相場（銀行間の取引相場）, インターバンク相場, 市場相場, インターバンク・レート
◆In Japan, interbank rates are close to zero. 日本では、銀行間金利はゼロに近い。

interest　（名）利息, 利子, 金利, 株, 持ち分, 利益, 権益, 利権, 利害関係, 関係者, 同業者, 業界, 企業, ～側
  （⇒accrued interest, bracket, checkable deposit）
  actual interest　実効金利

（=actual interest rate）
any interest in such Stock　当該株式の権利
arrear of interest　遅延利子, 遅延利息
  （=delayed interest）
back interest　未払い利息
bear interest　利息を負担する, 利息を支払う, 利息が生じる, 利息が付く
bond interest　社債利息, 債券利息
compounded interest　複利
  （=compound interest, interest upon interest）
create a security interest　担保権を設定する
debenture interest　社債利息
delayed interest　延滞利息
earn interest　利息が付く
earn no interest　利息が付かない
equity interest　証券持ち分
ex interest　利落ち
have［own］an interest in the firm　同社に持ち株がある, 同社に出資している
interest calculation day　利息起算日
interest-free loan　無利子ローン
interest on borrowings　借入金利息
interest only　利子部分, IO
interest option　金利選択権
interest payable on balances　差引残高の支払い利息
interest-service ratio　金利支払い比率
interest skimming　利息債権の分離, インタレスト・スキミング
interests　海運業界, 海運業者
  （=the shipping interests）
interests in joint ventures　ジョイント・ベンチャーに対する持ち分
loan interest　貸付け利子
majority interest　過半数持ち分, 過半数株式
  （=controlling interest）
market interest　市場実勢金利
minority interest　少数株主持ち分, 過半数以下の出資
negative interest　マイナスの金利, 逆金利
nominal interest　表面利率, 名目金利
overdue interest　延滞金利, 遅延利息
paid interest　返済利息
pay interest　利息を支払う, 利払いがある
receive interest on　～の利息を受け取る
remaining interest　残余権　（=residual interest）
security interest　有価証券利息, 担保権
simple interest　単利
stockholder's interest　株主持ち分
system of interest　金利体系
the banking interests　財界
the shipping interests　海運業界, 海運業者
vested interest　既得権, 既得権益, 確定権利
yields of interests　金利収入
◆After the briefing for foreign investors, a fund manager showed interest in investing in Japanese government bonds. 海外投資家向け説明会の後、あるファンド・マネージャーが日本国債への投資に関心を示した。◆At this level of interest rates, a deposit of ¥1 million will produce an annual interest of only ¥10. この金利水準では、100万円預金しても、1年にたった10円の利息しか付かない。◆Domestic banks are stepping up overseas project financing as greater yields of interests are expected through such lending than loans to domestic borrowers. 国内銀行は、国内の借り手への融資に比べて海外

の事業向け融資のほうが大きな金利収入を見込めるので、海外の事業向け融資（プロジェクト・ファイナンス）を強化している。◆If TEPCO's creditor banks forgive the debts when the utility is not carrying excessive liabilities, lenders will not be able to recover either the principal or interest owed. 東電が債務超過でない時点で東電の債権保有銀行が債権を放棄すると、金融機関は元本を回収できず、金利収入も得られなくなる。◆It's difficult to offset losses from further appreciation of the yen with interest as interest rates in many foreign currency deposits are low. 外貨建て預金の多くは金利が低いので、円高進行による損失分を利息で相殺する［取り戻す］のは難しい。◆Major trading houses have also shown interest in entering the new business of Internet share transactions. 総合商社も、株式のネット取引の新規事業に参入する意向を示している。◆We should not overlook the ultra easy money policy's negative effects, such as on elderly people who count on the interest earned on their savings and bank deposits. 超低金利政策には、とくに預貯金に付く利息を頼りにして生活しているお年寄りなどに対するマイナス効果があることを無視してはならない。

interest and principal payments 元利支払い
　◆Argentina will be deferring interest and principal payments due on its public external indebtedness. アルゼンチンは、公的対外債務の支払い期日の元利支払いを繰り延べる方針だ。

interest-bearing （形）利付きの, 利息がつく, 有利子の, 利息条件付きの, 利息を生む
　fixed interest-bearing securities　固定利付き証券
　interest-bearing asset　利付き資産
　interest-bearing balances with banks　銀行への利付き預金
　interest-bearing bank debenture　利付き金融債
　interest-bearing bond　利付き債, 利付き債券
　interest-bearing capital　利子生み資本
　interest-bearing deposits with banks　利付き他行預け金
　interest-bearing financial instrument　利息を生む金融資産
　interest bearing funds　利付きファンド
　interest-bearing note　利付き手形
　interest-bearing obligation　利付き債券
　interest-bearing receivable　利付き債権
　interest-bearing security　利付き証券
　variable interest-bearing securities　不確定利付き証券

interest-bearing bank deposits 利付き銀行預金
　◆Other securities consist of marketable securities and interest-bearing bank deposits with varied maturity dates. 「その他の有価証券」の内訳は、市場性ある有価証券と満期日が異なる利付き銀行預金です。

interest bearing debt 有利子負債, 利付き債券
　（＝interest-bearing liability; ⇒business plan, financial woes）
　◆Because of a debt waiver by the major banks, the company's interest-bearing debt fell to ¥58 billion from ¥600 billion in the previous year. 主要取引銀行の債務免除で、有利子負債は前期の6,000億円から580億円に減少した。◆Olympus plans to reduce its interest-bearing debts of ¥648.8 billion to ¥408.7 billion in the business year ending March 2015 through restructuring and other measures. オリンパスは、同社の有利子負債6,488億円を、リストラ策などを進めて2015年3月期までに4,087億円に圧縮する計画だ。◆The firm is planning to reduce its interest bearing debts to ¥460 billion by the end of fiscal 2011. 同社は、同社の有利子負債を2011年度末までに4,600億円まで削減する計画だ。◆To improve its financial health, Daiei will seek about ¥410 billion worth of debt waivers from about 30 financial institutions to reduce its interest-bearing debts. 財務体質を改善するため、ダイエーは、約30の金融機関に約4,100億円の債権放棄を求めて、有利子負債を削減する。◆With this financial support, along with property sales, the company plans to halve its approximately ¥540 billion consolidated interest-bearing debts by 2005. この金融支援と資産売却を組み合わせて、同社は約5,400億円の連結有利子負債を2005年までに半減させる方針だ。
　［解説］有利子負債とは：金利を付けて返済しなければならない債務のこと。銀行などから借りた借入金のほか、社債の発行などで市場から調達した資金の償還額なども有利子負債に加えられる。有利子負債の残高は、企業の財務内容の健全性を測る指標の一つになっている。

interest-bearing government bond 利付き国債
　interest-bearing long-term government bond　長期利付き国債
　interest-bearing medium-term government bond　中期利付き国債

interest bearing liability 有利子負債, 利付き債務
　（＝interest bearing debt）
　◆The company will reduce the interest-bearing liabilities to a maximum ¥900 billion from ¥1.57 trillion in the same time frame. 同社は、上記期間に有利子負債を1兆5,700億円から最高9,000億円に削減する方針だ。

interest-bearing savings account 利息が付く普通預金
　◆Though they are both liquid deposits, interest-bearing savings accounts and non-interest-bearing checking accounts should be considered separately. 普通預金も当座預金も流動性預金ではあるが、利息の付く普通預金と無利息の当座預金は区別して考えるべきだ。

interest burden 金利負担
　◆To reduce the interest burden as much as possible, it is crucial to try to curtail the issuance of more government bonds. この金利負担を極力軽減するためには、国債発行額を減らす努力が重要だ。

interest charge 支払い利息
　◆Late payment shall incur an interest charge of 2 percent over the base rate current in XYZ Bank at the time the charge is levied from the due date to the date of payment in full. 支払いが遅延した場合、支払い期日から全額支払い日まで、支払い利息［遅延利息］を課す時点でXYZ銀行が適用する基準金利より2％高い支払い利息［遅延利息］が付くものとする。

interest charged on the loan 返済金利
　◆Mizuho and UFJ borrowed taxpayers' money in 1998, based on contracts that stipulate that interest charged on the loan was to be raised in the sixth year. みずほとUFJは、6年目以降に返済金利の引上げが定めてある契約に基づいて、1998年に公的資金を借り入れた。

interest insured 被保険利益
　◆All insurance policies possessed or owned by the Company together with brief statements of the interest insured are complete and accurate. 「本会社」が所有または保有しているすべての保険証券とその被保険利益についての簡単な説明は、完全で正確である。

interest margin 預貸金利ざや
　interest rate margin　預貸利ざや, 金利マージン
　net interest margin　純預貸金利ざや, 預貸金利ざや, 預貸利ざや, 利ざや

interest on loans 借入金の金利, 借入金利息, 貸付け利子, 貸出金利
　（＝interest rate on loans; ⇒illegal lending）
　◆The company has been in debt since 1996 as a result of having to pay interest on loans acquired to finance the construction of more golf courses. 同社は、ゴルフ・コース増設資金の借入金に伴う金利負担で、1996年以降、赤字経営に陥っている。

interest payment 利払い, 金利の支払い, 利子支払い,

支払い利息
　（⇒principal and interest, repurchasing method）
　a rise in long-term interest rates　長期金利の上昇
　increases in interest payments on deposits　預金の利払い増加　（⇒outweigh）
　interest payment burden　金利負担
　　（=the burden of interest payment）
　interest payment date　利息支払い日
　interest payment moratorium　支払い停止
　◆If life insurers continue to offer insurance policies with guaranteed high return rates, the future financial burden in terms of interest payments will increase. 生保が高い利回りを保証した保険の販売を今後とも続けると、将来の利払いの金融負担が増えることになる。◆If we use the cashing services, it results in high interest payments. 現金化サービスを利用すると、結果的に高金利［支払い利息が高くつくこと］になる。◆In the lawsuits against big banks over the sales of risky investments, the U.S. government wants to be compensated for lost principal and interest payments. 高リスク証券の販売をめぐっての大手金融機関に対する訴訟で、米政府は、元本と利払い分の損失補償を求めている。◆Interest payments would balloon if the interest rate rises. これの金利が上昇すると、利払い費が膨らむ。

interest payment on the existing debt　既存の借金の利払い
　◆The government may shoulder interest payments on the existing debts of survivors of the March 11 disaster. 東日本大震災被災者の既存の借金については、政府がその利払いを肩代わりする可能性がある。

interest payment on the government bonds　国債の利払い
　◆If the interest payment on the government bonds is delayed, the negative impact on Japanese investors may increase. この国債の利払いが遅れた場合、日本の投資家への悪影響が拡大する可能性がある。

interest payments to depositors　預金者に対する預金金利の支払い, 預金者に対する利払い
　◆The new bank tax is levied on the banks' gross operating profits-their earnings minus basic operating expenses such as interest payments to depositors. 新銀行税は、銀行の収入から基礎的な経費（預金者に対する預金金利の支払いなど）を差し引いた業務粗利益に課される。

interest rate　金利, 利息, 利子率, 利率
　actual interest rate　実効金利
　　（=effective interest rate）
　annual interest rate　年間金利, 年間利率, 年間利子率
　appropriate interest rate　適正利率
　average interest rate　平均金利
　benchmark interest rate　基準金利
　bottom of the interest rate cycle　金利の底入れ
　compound interest rate　複利（預金などに適用される金利で、元本と利息に金利が付く）
　contracted interest rate　約定金利
　　（=engaged rate of interest）
　cut interest rates　金利を引き下げる, 利下げする
　deposit interest rate ceiling　預金金利の上限
　deregulation of interest rates　金利の自由化
　downward trend of interest rate　金利の低下局面
　effective annual interest rate　実効年利率
　effective interest rate　実効金利（effective rate: 実際に借りた金額［貸した金額］に対する利子の割合）,（証券の）実効利率, 実効利回り（effective rate: 債券の購入価格に対する受取利子の割合。満期利回り（yield to maturity）とほぼ同義）
　fixed interest rate loan　固定金利貸付け
　　（=fixed-rate interest loan）
　floating interest rate　変動金利
　　（=floating-rate interest）
　forward-forward interest rate　先々金利
　guaranteed minimum interest rate　保証最低利回り
　headline interest rates　政策金利
　high interest rates　高い金利, 高金利
　higher interest rates　金利の上昇, 利上げ, 高金利
　hold interest rates steady　金利を据え置く
　impact interest rates　金利に影響する
　imputed interest rate　帰属利息, 帰属利子, 帰属利率
　increase interest rates　金利を引き上げる, 利上げする
　　（=raise interest rates）
　interbank interest rate　銀行間金利
　interest rate abroad　海外金利
　interest rate adjustment　金利調整
　interest rate arbitrage　金利裁定
　interest rate behavior［environment］　金利動向
　interest rate ceiling　利子上限
　interest rate change　金利変動, 金利の変更
　interest rate characteristics　金利特性
　interest rate developments　金利動向
　interest rate differential［spread］　金利差, 金利格差
　interest rate effect　金利効果, 利子率効果
　interest rate expectation　金利予想, 金利期待
　interest rate futures　金利先物, 金利先物取引
　interest rate index　金利指標
　interest rate level　金利水準
　　（=level of interest rates）
　interest rate move［movement］　金利変動, 金利動向
　interest rate on deposits and debentures　預金債券等利回り
　interest rate option　金利オプション
　interest rate outlook　金利見通し
　interest rate risk　金利リスク, 金利変動リスク
　interest rate sensitive instrument　金利感応商品
　interest rate sensitivity　金利感応性
　interest rate setter　金利設定者
　interest rate setting　金利設定
　interest rate spread　利ざや, 金利差（interest rate differential）, 金利スプレッド
　interest rate stabilization　金利の安定
　interest rate structure　金利構造, 利回り曲線
　interest rate subsidy　利子補給
　interest rate swap involving an upfront payment　アップフロント支払い付きの金利スワップ
　interest rate taker　金利受容者
　interest rate tightening　利上げ
　interest rate uncertainty　金利の先行き不透明感
　interest rate volatility　金利変動率, 金利ボラティリティ
　interest rates for loans　ローンの金利, ローン金利　（⇒market interest rate）
　keep on cutting interest rates　利下げを続ける
　loan interest rate　貸出金利, 融資日歩
　long-term interest rate　長期金利
　low interest rates　低い金利, 低金利
　lower interest rates　金利低下, 利下げ, 低金利
　market interest rate　市場金利, 市中金利
　　（=open market rate; ⇒market interest rate）
　minuscule interest rates　超低金利
　negative real interest rates　マイナスの実質金利

nominal interest rate　名目金利, 表面利率
official interest rate　政策金利
preferential interest rate for companies　企業向け融資の優遇金利
prevailing market interest rates　実勢金利
real interest rate　実質金利, 実効金利（実質金利＝名目金利-インフレ予想率）
reduce interest rate risk［risk of interest rate］　金利リスク［金利変動リスク］を軽減する
reduce interest rates　金融を緩和する
rising interest rates　金利上昇
simple interest rate　単利（単利＝元本×利率）
slash interest rates　金利を大幅に引き下げる, 大幅［大幅な］下げをする
target for overnight interest rates　短期金利の誘導目標
ultralow interest rates　超低金利
upper limit of interest rates　金利の上限, 上限金利
zero-interest rate policy　ゼロ金利政策
　（＝policy of zero interest rates）

◆A lowered rating means higher interest rates. 格付けの低下は、金利の上昇を意味する。◆Due to confusion in the financial markets, interest rates have declined significantly and global stock prices have dropped. 金融市場の混乱で、金利が大幅に低下し、世界的に株価も下落している。◆It's difficult to offset losses from further appreciation of the yen with interest as interest rates in many foreign currency deposits are low. 外貨建て預金の多くは金利が低いので、円高進行による損失分を利息で相殺する［取り戻す］のは難しい。◆Long-term interest rates have soared almost fourfold in the past three months after the rates hit a record low in mid-June. 長期金利は、6月中旬に史上最低を記録した後、この3か月で4倍近くに急騰した。◆Short-term interest rates are generally lower than long-term interest rates. 短期金利は、一般に長期金利より低い。◆Slightly raising the upper limit of interest rates will not get rid of unauthorized moneylenders. 多少の上限金利の変更で、ヤミ金融業者がなくなるわけではない。◆Some financial institutions are offering products with annual interest rates starting at 1 percent or less. 一部の金融機関は、当初の金利［適用金利］が年1%以下の商品を提供している。◆Speculation the Bank of Japan will end its quantitative monetary easing policy soon has sparked a rise in mid- and long-term interest rates. 日銀が近く量的緩和策を解除するとの思惑から、（金融市場では）中長期の金利が上昇し始めた。◆The euro crisis has spread to Spain and Italy with interest rates on their sovereign debts soaring. ユーロ危機はスペインとイタリアに波及し、両国国債の金利が急騰した。◆The Fed has been unable to deal with the current economic woes by changing interest rates as it has been maintaining a policy of virtually zero-percent interest rates. 米連邦準備制度知事会（FRB）はこれまで金利ゼロ政策を続けてきたため、政策金利を上げて現在の経済的苦境に対応することはできなくなっている。◆The high yields of the yen-denominated government bonds were considered considerably higher than minuscule domestic interest rates. この円建て国債は、国内の超低金利に比べて利回りがはるかに大きいと見られた。◆The interest rates a bank pays when procuring funds from the financial market are higher than those paid by other banks. ある銀行が金融市場で資金調達する際に支払う金利が、他行に比べて高くなっている。◆The interest rates of the Australian dollar-denominated deposit service are relatively high among major foreign currencies. 主要外貨のうち、豪ドル建て預金サービスの金利は比較的高い。◆The latest additional monetary ease put a downward pressure on interest rates. 今回の追加の金融緩和で、金利は低下した。◆The U.S. Federal Reserve Board has been maintaining a policy of virtually zero-percent interest rates. 米連邦準備制度理事会（FRB）は、事実上ゼロ金利の政策を維持してきた。◆The U.S. Federal Reserve Board has decided to leave interest rates unchanged. 米連邦準備制度理事会（FRB）は、金利を据え置くことを決めた。◆The U.S. Federal Reserve Board pledged to keep interest rates near zero until mid-2013. 米連邦準備制度理事会（FRB）は、2013年半ばまでゼロ金利政策を維持することを誓った。◆The yield on the 10-year government bond is the key benchmark for long-term interest rates. 10年物国債の利回り［流通利回り］は、長期金利の代表的指標である。

interest rate cut　金利の引下げ, 利下げ
　（＝interest rate reduction）
　aggressive interest rate cuts　大幅利下げ
　further interest rate cuts　一層の利下げ, 追加利下げ, 再度の利下げ, 再利下げ
　more interest rate cuts　追加利下げ, 再利下げ
◆The FRB's policymakers waged war against economic weakness last year with 11 interest rate cuts. （FRBの）政策決定者は、昨年は11回利下げを行って景気低迷と戦った。◆The G-7 leaders merely welcomed Washington's economic stimulus measures in the form of interest rate cuts and tax cuts as "positive." G7首脳は、利下げや減税などの形での米政府の景気刺激策を「積極的」として歓迎しただけだ。◆There is a limit to the effects of interest rate cuts. 金利引下げの効果には、限界がある。

interest rate differentials　金利差
◆Interest rate differentials between Greek and German government bonds widened to 600 basis points, or six percentage points, from January to May 2010. ギリシャ国債とドイツ国債の金利差は、2010年1月から5月の間に600ベーシス・ポイント（6%）も拡大した。

interest rate fluctuations　金利変動
◆To make up for losses and for other purposes, seven life insurers used a total of ¥529.2 billion in reserves, which are set aside in preparation for interest rate fluctuations and natural disasters. 損失の穴埋めなどのため、金利変動や自然災害に備えて積み立てている準備金を、生保7社が5,292億円も取り崩した。

interest rate hike　金利上昇, 利上げ, 金利引上げ
　（＝interest rate increase）
◆China implemented the interest rate hike to hold down soaring prices in real estate and consumer goods. 中国は、不動産価格や消費財価格の高騰を抑えるため、利上げを実施した。

interest rate increase　金利の上昇, 利上げ, 金利の引上げ　（＝interest rate hike）
◆The recent interest rate increase of the People's Bank of China was a modest one-the benchmark rate on one-year yuan loans was raised by 0.27 percentage point. 中国人民銀行の今回の利上げは小幅にとどまり、指標となる人民元の期間1年の貸出金利は0.27%引き上げられた。

interest rate on　～の金利
　interest rate on deposits and debentures　預金債券等利回り
　interest rate on fixed rate mortgage　固定金利モーゲージの金利
　interest rate on overnight borrowing among banks　翌日物銀行間金利
　interest rates on loans by financial institutions　金融機関の貸出金利

interest rate on loans　貸出金利
　（＝interest on loans, loan interest rate）
◆Interest rates on loans at such a high level inevitably pose a considerable burden on the small and midsize firms that we do business with. このような高水準の貸出金利では、取引先の中小企業に当然、相当の負担をかけることになる。◆The People's Bank of China raised interest rates on loans by financial institutions to corporations and individuals. 中国人

民銀行が、金融機関の企業や個人に対する貸出金利を引き上げた。

interest rate on sovereign debts 国債の金利
◆The euro crisis has spread to Spain and Italy with interest rates on their sovereign debts soaring. ユーロ危機はスペインとイタリアに波及し、両国国債の金利が急騰した。

interest rate policy 金利政策 （⇒Fed Chairman）
◆The zero interest rate policy, which is almost unprecedented in the history of the world, has been given high marks both at home and abroad. 世界史上、例を見ないゼロ金利政策が、内外から高い評価を受けている。

interest rate profit margins 金利の利ざや
◆As a result of fierce competition in the past, interest rate profit margins were kept too low to cover loans that went sour. 過去の熾烈（しれつ）な競争の結果、金利の利ざやが小さく抑えられる余り、貸倒れ［貸倒れのリスク］をカバーできなかった［過去の熾烈な融資合戦の結果、不良債権リスクをカバーできないほど利ざやは小さく抑えられた］。

interest rate reduction 金利引下げ, 利下げ
（=interest rate cut）
◆As joint actions, major industrial nations have taken such measures as further interest rate reductions, quantitative monetary relaxation to increase the money supply, the injection of public funds and increased public spending. 協調行動として、主要先進諸国は、さらなる金利の引下げ、通貨供給量を増やすための量的金融緩和や公的資金の注入、財政出動［公共支出の拡大］などの措置を取った。

interest rate sensitive 金利に敏感な, 金利感応型の
（⇒interest-sensitive）
　interest rate-sensitive note 金利感応債, 金利連動債, 金利リンク債
　interest rate-sensitive sector 金利敏感セクター, 金利感応銘柄
　interest rate-sensitive stock 金利敏感株

interest rate swap 金利スワップ （同一通貨間で固定金利と変動金利の債権または債務を交換する取引。⇒agreement, commitment）
◆We enter into interest rate swap agreements to manage our exposure to changes in interest rates. 金利変動リスクに対処するため、当社は金利スワップ契約を結んでいます。

interest rates for adjustable rate mortgages 変動金利型住宅ローンの金利
◆Interest rates for adjustable rate mortgages would not rise in the immediate future as the Bank of Japan is likely to keep its key rates at an ultralow level. 変動金利型住宅ローンの金利は、日銀の超低金利政策が続く見通しなので、当面は上がらないだろう。

interest-sensitive （形）金利に敏感な, 金利感応型の, 金利敏感型の （=interest rate sensitive; ⇒interest rate sensitive）
　interest-sensitive assets （銀行の）金利感応資産, 金利感応資産
　interest-sensitive debt 金利敏感債務
　interest-sensitive instrument 金利感応商品 （=interest rate-sensitive instrument）
　interest-sensitive item 金利感応項目
　interest-sensitive liabilities 金利感応負債
　interest-sensitive measurements 金利敏感度
　interest-sensitive policy 金利感応型保険証券
　interest-sensitive whole life insurance 金利敏感型終身保険

interested in ～に関心がある, ～に興味がある
◆The market is now becoming more and more interested in what steps the Bank of Japan will take next. 市場の関心は、もはや日銀の次の一手に向き始めている。

interim （形）中間の, 半期の, 期中の, 中間会計期間の, 暫定的な, 一時的な, 仮の
　interim aid 暫定援助, 中間援助
　interim audit 期中監査, 中間監査
　interim bonus 臨時ボーナス
　interim closing 中間決算 （=interim results）
　interim committee 暫定委員会
　interim dividend 中間配当, 仮配当
　interim earnings report 中間決算, 中間決算報告, 中間利益報告書 （=interim financial results, interim results, midterm earnings report）
　interim financial report 中間財務報告, 中間財務報告書 （=interim report, interim financial information）
　interim financing つなぎ融資, つなぎ資金
　interim goal 中間目標
　interim net profit 中間期の純利益, 半期の純利益, 中間期の税引き後利益
　interim receipt 仮領収書
　interim stage 中間段階
　issue [deliver] an interim report 中間報告を発表する
　on an interim basis 一時的に, 暫定的に
　pass an interim budget 暫定予算を可決する

interim settlement of accounts 中間決算
◆Neither of Mitsui Trust Holdings, Inc. and another major financial group has yet released reports on its interim settlement of accounts. 三井トラスト・ホールディングスなど2大金融グループは、まだ中間決算報告を発表していない。

interlocked shareholdings 株式の持ち合い

intermediary （形）中間の, 仲介の, 中継の （名）仲介業者, 仲介機関
（⇒financial intermediary）
　financial intermediary 金融仲介機関, 金融仲介業者, 金融機関
　independent intermediary 独立仲介機関
　intermediaries 金融仲介機関, 仲介業者
　intermediary fee 仲介手数料
　international financial intermediary 国際金融仲介機関, 国際金融機関, 国際的な金融仲介機能
　local financial intermediaries 国内金融機関
　market intermediary 証券会社
　Regional Settlement Intermediary 域内決済機関, RMI
　risk intermediary リスク仲介機関
◆The stock market is a public mechanism to facilitate the smooth flow of money in the economy by serving as an intermediary between corporations and investors. 証券市場は、企業と投資家間の仲介役をつとめて日本経済に資金を円滑に流す役割を担う公共財だ。

intermediary bank 仲介銀行, 受け皿銀行, 取立銀行
◆The remaining trust bank operations and retail operations will be sold to an intermediary bank. 他の信託銀行の業務と個人向け業務は、受け皿銀行に営業譲渡される。

intermediary services 仲介業務, 仲介サービス
◆The bank will improve profits through its operations such as intermediary services in corporate mergers and acquisitions and the marketing of financial products. 同行は、企業の合併・買収（M&A）の仲介サービスや金融商品の販売などで、収益基盤を強化する方針だ。

intermediate （動）仲介する, 仲に立つ, 仲裁する
◆A stock brokerage firm intermediated the deal. 証券会社が、この案件の仲介をした。

intermediate （形）中間の, 中間に位置する, 中級の, 中級レベルの, 中期の （名）仲介者, 中期物
　intermediate market 中期市場, 中期物
　intermediate rates 中期債利回り
　intermediate securities 中期債

intermediate target　中間目標
intermediate term loan　中期ローン
West Texas Intermediate　テキサス産軽質油, WTI
　（⇒WTI）
intermediation　（名）金融仲介, 仲介化, 金融仲介機関利用
　finance intermediation　金融仲介
　financial intermediation　金融仲介, 金融仲介活動, 金融仲介業務
　fund intermediation　資金仲介
　intermediation fee　仲介手数料
　intermediation risk　仲介リスク
　maturity intermediation　満期仲介
intermittently　（副）断続的に, 途切れ途切れに
　◆The Bank of Japan continued selling yen and buying dollars intermittently. 日銀は、断続的に円売り・ドル買いを継続した。
internal　（形）内部の, 社内の, 国内の
　internal bonds　内国債
　internal capital generation　内部資本形成, 留保利益
　internal capital growth　内部資本形成率
　internal credit enhancement　内部信用補てん
　internal credit support　内部信用補てん
　internal debt　内部負債, 内債
　internal drain　内部的枯渇（物価上昇で銀行の準備金が減少すること）
　internal exchange　内国為替
　internal factor　内部要因
　internal finance　内部資金, 内部金融
　internal financial management　内部財務管理
　internal financing　内部金融, 自己金融
　internal funds　内部資金, 自己資金
　internal information　内部情報, 社内情報
　internal items　行内伝票
　internal liability　内部負債, 社内負債
　internal loan　内国債, 内債
　internal loss adjustment　内部支払い査定費用
　internal profit　内部利益
　internal purchasing power of money　貨幣の対内購買力
　internal rate of interest　内部利子率
　internal rate of return　内部利益率, 内部収益率, IRR
　internal replacement transaction　転換取引
　internal reserves　内部留保, 社内留保
　internal revenue　内国税収入
　internal revenue fund　内部留保金
　internal source of capital　自己金融
　internal sources　内部資金
　　（=internal resources）
　internal sources of cash［liquidity］　内部流動性
　internal tax　内国税
　internal transaction　内部取引
　internal transfer　内部振替, 振替
　internal transfer profit　内部振替利益, 本支店振替利益
　internal user　内部情報利用者
internal cash　内部資金, 内部キャッシュ
　internal cash flows　内部キャッシュ・フロー
　internal cash generated　内部キャッシュ
　internal cash generated per share　1株当たり内部キャッシュ
　internal cash generation　内部キャッシュ・フロー
　meet cash capital requirements through internal cash generation　資金需要を内部キャッシュ・フローで賄（まかな）う
　net internal cash　内部ネット・キャッシュ
　use internal cash as quasi-equity　内部資金を準資本金として扱う
internal control　内部統制, 社内管理, 内部チェック（内部チェック体制、「内部統制」は、粉飾決算や経営者の不正・ごまかしなど、企業の不祥事を防ぐため、社内の管理・点検体制を整え、絶えずチェックすることをいう。日本の上場企業は、2008年度から内部統制に関する報告が義務付けられている）
　◆Corporation's internal controls are designed to provide reasonable assurance as to the integrity and reliability of the financial statements. 当社の内部統制は、財務書類の完全性と信頼性について十分保証するよう図られています。
　◆Management is responsible for maintaining a system of internal controls as a fundamental requirement for the operational and financial integrity of results. 経営者は、営業成績および財務成績の適正性を保つ基本的条件として、内部統制組織を維持する責任を負っています。
internal resources　内部資金（internal sources）, 手元資金
　finance through internal resources　内部資金で資金を調達する
　make initial investments from internal resources　内部資金で当初投資を行う, 内部資金を当初投資額に充てる
　◆The company plans to make initial investments of about ¥200 billion from internal resources. 同社では、当初の約2,000億円の投資額は内部資金［手元資金］を充てる計画だ。
internalization of international transaction　国際取引の内部化
internally generated funds　内部調達資金, 内部資金
　（⇒generate）
international　（形）国際的, 国際間の, 国際上の, インターナショナル
　international account　国際勘定
　international accounts　国際投資家, 国際収支
　international agency bond　国際機関債券
　international asset and debit positions　対外資産負債残高
　international asset management　国際資産運用
　International Association of Financial Engineers　国際金融エンジニア協会
　International Association of Insurance Supervisors　保険監督者国際機構, IAIS
　International Auditing and Assurance Standards Board　国際監査・保証基準審議会, IAASB
　International banker　国際銀行家
　international bidding　国際入札
　international bimetallism movement　国際複本位運動
　international borrowing　対外借入れ
　international broking　海外仲介業務, 海外委任取引, IB
　international business activities　国際事業活動, 国際ビジネス
　international business finance　国際的企業財務
　international cash management service　国際資金管理サービス, 国際CMS
　International Center for Settlement of Investment Disputes　投資紛争解決国際センター, ICSID
　international character of reinsurance　再保険の国際性
　international check　国際小切手
　international clearing systems　国際決済機構
　International Clearing Union　国際清算同盟
　international commercial banks　国際業務を行う銀行
　International Commodity Clearing House　国際商品取引所

International Congress of Actuaries　国際アクチュアリー会議

international consortium　国際共同事業体, 国際借款団, 国際融資団, 国際引受団

International Convention for the Suppression of the Financing of Terrorism　テロ資金供与防止条約

International Convention for the Unification of Certain Rules Relating to Bill of Lading　船荷証券統一条約

international depository [depositary] receipt　国際預託証券, IDR

international deposits　国際預金

International Development Association　国際開発協会, (通称)第二世界銀行, IDA

international diversification　国際分散投資, 海外分散投資 (＝international diversified investment)

international double taxation　国際二重課税 (＝international double tax)

international equilibrium　国際均衡, 国際収支の均衡 (＝external equilibrium)

International Federation of Risk & Insurance Management Association　国際リスク・保険管理連盟

International Federation of Stock Exchanges　国際証券取引所連合 (2002年にWorld Federation of Exchanges (国際取引所連合) に改称)

International Fiscal Association　国際財政協会

international gold standard　国際金本位制

international group insurance system　国際団体保険制度

international indebtedness　国際債務, 国際貸借

International Institute of Finance　国際金融協会

international interest rate　国際金利

international investor　国際投資家

International Investor Relations Federation　国際IR連盟, IIRF

international issue　外債, 海外売出し

international issuers　国際的な発行体

international lead manager　国際主幹事

international lease　国際リース

international lender　国際的な資金の出し手

international lender of last resort　国際的最終貸し手

international managed currency system　国際管理通貨制度

international monetarism　国際的マネタリズム

international movements of funds　国際資金移動

international mutual fund　国際ミューチュアル・ファンド

international offerings　国際公募

international official price of gold　金の国際公定価格

international oil plays　国際的石油株

International Organization of Securities Commissions　証券監督者国際機構, イオスコ, IOSCO [Iosco]

international payment　国際送金

International Petroleum Exchange　国際石油取引所, IPE (2001年にインターコンチネンタル取引所 (ICE) の子会社になる。現在は、ICE Futuresと呼ばれている)

international policy instrument　国際政策手段

international portfolio diversification　国際分散投資

international portfolio investment　国際証券投資 (＝overseas portfolio investment)

International Primary Market [Markets] Association　国際引受業者協会

International reserves　外貨準備 [準備高], 対外準備, 国際準備 (＝foreign exchange reserves)

International Rules for the Interpretation of Trade Terms 貿易条件の解釈に関する国際規則, インコタームズ (Incoterms)

international seigniorage　国際通貨発行特権

international shares　国際株

international sourcing　国際調達, 海外調達

international spread of risk　国際的危険分散

international stabilization fund　国際安定化基金

International Swap Derivative Association　国際スワップ・デリバティブ協会, ISDA

international syndicate　国際協調融資団, 国際シンジケート

international syndicate loan　国際シンジケート・ローン

international tax convention [treaty]　国際租税条約

international transfer　国際送金

International Union of Aviation Insurers　国際航空保険者連合, IUAI

International Union of Credit and Investment Insurers　国際輸出信用投資保険連合 (Berne Union (ベルン・ユニオン) の正式名称)

International Union of Marine Insurance　国際海上保険連合, IUMI

International Accounting Standards　国際会計基準, IAS
(⇒International Financial Reporting Standards)

International Accounting Standards Board　国際会計基準審議会 [理事会], IASB

International Accounting Standards Committee　国際会計基準委員会, IASC

◆The IFRSs are based on mark-to-market accounting and was adopted by the London based International Accounting Standards Board. 国際財務報告基準 (IFRSs) は、時価会計をベースとし、ロンドンに本部を置く国際会計基準審議会 (IASB) によって採択された。◆The SEC proposed a plan to allow public companies to using international accounting standards for reporting financial results. 米証券取引委員会 (SEC) は、株式公開企業 [上場企業] に対して (2014年をめどに) 決算報告に国際会計基準の導入 [採用] を認める計画を提案した。

|解説| 国際会計基準について：米国の企業会計基準と並ぶ世界の2大会計基準。国際会計基準は、欧州が主導する国際会計基準審議会 (IASB) が作成している。欧州各国のほかに、ロシア、オーストラリア、中南米諸国など約100か国が採用を決めている。欧州連合 (EU) は、2005年から域内の上場企業に国際会計基準の決算開示を義務付け、2007年からは域内上場の外国企業にもEUの国際基準と同レベルの開示を求めている。日本の会計基準は、1999年度に連結会計とキャッシュ・フロー計算書、税効果会計、2000年度に退職給付会計や金融商品の時価会計、2005年度から減損会計が導入された。その結果、日本の会計基準は現在、国際基準と基本的に同等であるとの評価が得られるようなった。なお、国際会計基準審議会 (IASB) が設定する国際会計基準のIASは、2005年1月1日から新しい呼び名として「国際財務報告基準 (International Financial Reporting Standards) に改められた。

international balance of payments　国際収支
(＝balance of payments, balance of international payments)

国際収支関連用語：

basic balance　基礎収支

capital balance　資本収支

current account balance　経常収支 (＝current balance)

foreign reserves　外貨準備

goods & services balance　貿易・サービス収支

income balance　所得収支

  investment balance 投資収支
  invisible balance 貿易外収支
  long-term capital balance 長期資本収支
  overall balance 総合収支
  services balance サービス収支
  short-term capital balance 短期資本収支
  trade balance 貿易収支
  transfer balance 移転収支
international bank 国際銀行
  international bank deposit markets 国際銀行預金市場
  international bank for investment 国際投資銀行
  International Bank for Reconstruction and Development 国際復興開発銀行, (通称)世界銀行, IBRD
  international bank transfer 国際送金
   (=international payment, international transfer)
  International fuel Bank 国際核燃料銀行
  International Resources Bank 国際資源銀行
  International Bank 世界銀行, 世銀, 国際復興開発銀行
   (=International Bank for Reconstruction and Development)
international banking 国際銀行, 国際銀行業務, 国際銀行業, 国際金融
  International Banking Act of 1978 1978年国際銀行法
  international banking activity 国際的な銀行業務
  international banking day 外国為替/国際金融業務取扱い日, 海外送金取扱い日
  international banking facilities 国際金融機関, 国際銀行業務
  international banking facilities account IBF(国際銀行業務)勘定
  International Banking Facility 国際銀行業務, 国際金融ファシリティ, 国際金融勘定, 国際金融業務制度, (俗)ヤンキー・ダラー市場(Yankee dollar market), IBF(米銀行に認められた特別勘定で, 連邦準備制度の預金準備率や金利規制の適用を受けないオフショア市場)
  international banking supervisory arrangements 国際銀行監督協定
  international banking system 国際銀行制度, 国際銀行体制
  ◆The Financial Stability Board is cooperating with the Basel Committee on Banking Supervision, a body that sets rules for international banking. 金融安定化理事会(FSB)は, 国際銀行業務の基準を制定する機関のバーゼル銀行監督委員会と連携している.
international bond 国際債券(国際市場で公募発行した債券)
  international bond fund 国際債券ファンド
  international bond issue [issuance] 国際的債券発行, 国際市場での債券発行
  international bond market 国際債券市場
  international bond trading 国際債券トレーディング
international capital 国際資本
  international capital flows 国際的な資金移動, 国際資本移動, 国際的な資本取引
  international capital market 国際資本市場
  international capital movement 国際資本移動, 国際間の資本移動
  international capital rules for securities firms [companies] 証券会社の国際的自己資本規制
  international capital transaction 国際資本取引
international competitive edge 国際競争力
  ◆The hollowing-out of the pension system may increase companies' personnel costs so much that it could negatively affect their international competitive edge. 年金の空洞化で人件費が上昇し, 国際競争力に悪影響を及ぼす恐れがある.
international competitiveness 国際競争力
  decline in international competitiveness 国際競争力の低下
  enhance international competitiveness 国際競争力を高める
  erode international competitiveness 国際競争力を低下させる
  increase [improve] international competitiveness 国際競争力を高める
  lose international competitiveness 国際競争力を失う, 国際競争力が落ちる
  maintain [retain] international competitiveness 国際競争力を維持する
  ◆A stronger dollar may lead to objections from U.S. businesses that fear their international competitiveness. ドル高がさらに進行すると, 国際競争力を懸念する米国の産業界から反発が強まる可能性がある. ◆If the integration of Japan's two major stock exchanges is realized, it is expected to enhance the international competitiveness of the stock market. 日本の2大証券取引所の統合が実現すれば, 証券市場の国際競争力が高まると期待される.
international coordination 国際協調
  ◆Enhancing international coordination is indispensable to stabilize the global financial markets. 世界の金融市場の安定には, 国際協調の強化が欠かせない.
international currency 国際通貨
  (=international money, key currency)
  international basic currency 国際基準通貨
  international credit currency 国際信用通貨(国際通貨のなかでとくに金と兌換(だかん)可能な通貨)
  international currency disturbance [uncertainty] 国際通貨不安
  international currency markets 国際通貨市場
  international currency reserve 国際通貨準備
  international reserve currency 国際準備通貨
  international settlement currency 国際決済通貨
  international transaction currency 国際取引通貨
  ◆It will be a long time before the yuan is accepted as an international currency. 人民元が国際通貨と認められるのは, まだずっと先のことだ.
international currency system 国際通貨体制
  ◆China's President Hu Jintao called the current international currency system "a product of the past." 中国の胡錦濤国家主席は, (米ドルを基軸とする)現在の国際通貨体制を「過去の産物」と述べた.
international exchange 国際為替, 外国為替, 国際交換
  international exchange market 国際為替市場
  international exchange of commodities 国際商品交換
  international exchange rate 国際交換比率
  international foreign exchange dealers association 国際外国為替ディーラー協会
international exchanges 国際為替市場, 国際取引所
  ◆If a country's currency gets stronger and stronger in international exchanges, the country's exports get more expensive. 国際為替市場である国の通貨がどんどん強くなると, その国の輸出品は高価になる. ◆The value of the dollar is sinking on international exchanges. 国際為替市場で, ドル価値が下落している. ◆The value of the renminbi (yuan) is rising on international exchanges. 国際為替市場で, 中国の人民元の価値が上昇している.
international finance 国際金融(international financing [lending]), 国際金融取引, 国際財務, 海外からの資金
  international business finance 国際的企業財務
  international finance agreement 国際金融協定

international finance and security　国際金融取引と担保
Japan Center for International Finance　国際金融情報センター
◆The heads of Japan, China and ROK signed statements on the tripartite partnership, international finance and the economy, and disaster management cooperation. 日中韓首脳は、3国間パートナーシップ、国際金融・経済と防災対策での連携に関する声明に署名した。

International Finance Corporation　国際金融公社, IFC（世界銀行グループ（World Bank Group）の一つで発展途上国のための金融機関）
◆The World Bank will issue the yuan-based bonds through the International Finance Corporation. 世界銀行は、国際金融公社を通じて人民元建て債を発行する。

international financial　国際金融の
　international financial center　国際金融センター, 国際金融市場
　international financial community　国際金融業界
　international financial machinery　国際金融機構
　international financial markets　国際金融市場
　international financial reporting　国際財務報告
　International Financial Statistics　国際金融統計
　international financial system　国際金融制度, 国際金融体制, 国際金融システム
　international financial transaction　国際金融取引
　international financial trend　国際金融動向, 国際的金融動向
　international financial turmoil　国際金融不安

international financial crisis　国際金融危機, 世界的な金融危機（=global financial crisis）
◆The new rules on banks' corer capital ratios are meant to compel banks to ensure sounder management, to prevent any repeat of the international financial crisis. 銀行の自己資本比率に関する新規則は、国際金融危機の再発防止のため、銀行に経営の健全性向上を求めるのが狙いだ。

international financial futures　国際金融先物, 国際金融先物取引
　London international Financial Futures and Options Exchange　ロンドン国際金融先物オプション取引所
　London International Financial Futures Exchange　ロンドン国際金融先物取引所

International Financial Reporting Standards　国際財務報告基準, IFRS［IFRSs］（国際財務報告規準（IFRS）は、国際会計基準審議会（IASB）が設定するIAS（国際会計基準）の新しい呼び名で、2005年1月1日に採択された。⇒International Accounting Standards）
◆International Financial Reporting Standards (IFRSs) were adopted as from 1 January 2005. 国際財務報告基準（IFRSs）は、2005年1月1日に採択された。◆The government will postpone the introduction of the International Financial Reporting Standards in the wake of the Great East Japan Earthquake. 政府は、東日本大震災を受けて、国際財務報告基準［国際会計基準］の導入を延期する方針だ。◆The Group's sales figures have been restated following the retrospective application of new International Financial Reporting Standards. 当グループの売上高の数値は、新国際財務報告基準（IFRS）を遡及的に適用して、再表示されています。◆The International Financial Reporting Standards (IFRSs) have become the global standard in more than 100 countries, especially in Europe. 国際財務報告基準（IFRSs）は、欧州を中心に100か国以上でグローバル・スタンダードになっている。

international financial systems　国際金融システム
◆To prevent another currency crisis, the G-7 statement spelled out various measures to reform the international financial systems. 通貨危機の再発を防ぐため、主要7か国の声明は、国際金融システム改革の施策をいくつか明確にした。

international financing　国際金融（international finance［lending］）, 国際財務, 国際的資金調達
◆The influence of Cuba's financial situation on the global economy will be limited as its economy has been cut off from international financing. 世界経済に対するキューバの財政状態の影響は、同国経済が国際金融から切り離されているため、限定的と見られる。

international flow of funds　国際的資金の流れ
◆The two oil crises in the 1970s increased international trade imbalances worldwide and stepped up the international flow of funds. 1970年代の2度の石油危機で、世界的な貿易不均衡が激化し、国際的資金の流れが拡大した。

international fund　国際ファンド, インターナショナル・ファンド（米国外の取引所で取引される証券にだけ投資するファンド）
　international fund flows　海外［国外］からの資金流入
　International Fund for Agricultural Development　国際農業開発基金, IFAD

international fund transaction　国際資金取引
◆Errors in computing systems at financial institutions could lead to problems in making international fund transactions. 金融機関のコンピュータ・システムのエラーは、国際的な資金取引上、トラブルが生じる可能性がある。

international investment　国際投資
（=foreign investment, overseas investment）
　international investment bank　国際投資銀行
　international investment division　国際投資分業
　international investment fund　国際投資信託
　international investment trust　国際投資信託
◆The large U.S. current account deficit might result in a marked decline of its international investment positions. 米国の巨額の経常赤字で、海外投資家のドル資産が大幅に減少する可能性がある［海外投資家の著しいドル資産離れを招きかねない］。

international lenders　国際金融機関, 国際融資団
◆Greece will miss 2011-12 deficit targets imposed by international lenders as part of the country's bailout. ギリシャは、同国救済措置の一環として国際融資団（欧州連合（EU）や国際通貨基金）が課した2011-12年の赤字削減目標を、達成できないようだ。

international lending　国際融資, 対外融資, 国際貸出
　international lending agency　国際貸出機関, 国際貸付け機関
　international lending interest rate　国際貸出金利, 国際貸付け金利
　International Lending Supervision Act of 1983　1983年国際貸出監督法

international liquidity　国際流動性
　international liquidity deficit　国際流動性不足
　international liquidity problem　国際流動性問題
　international liquidity reserve　国際流動性準備
　international liquidity surplus　国際流動性余剰

international loan　国際貸付け, 国際貸出
　international loan market　国際貸付け市場, 国際金融市場
　international loan outflows　対外融資
　international loan portfolio　国際ローン・ポートフォリオ
　international monetary　国際通貨の, 国際金融の
　International Monetary and Financial Committee　国際通貨金融委員会, IMFC, IMF総務会の諮問機関
　international monetary collaboration　国際金融協力
　International Monetary Conference　国際通貨会議, IMC
　international monetary cooperation　国際通貨協力, 国際金融協力
　international monetary crisis　国際通貨危機

international monetary institution　国際通貨機関
International Monetary Market　国際通貨市場, IMM
international monetary order　国際通貨秩序
international monetary reform　国際通貨改革
international monetary reserves　国際通貨準備
international monetary strain　国際通貨上の緊張
international monetary system　国際通貨制度, 国際通貨体制
international monetary uncertainty　国際通貨不安, 国際金融不安
new international loans extended　対外融資純増額
Singapore International Monetary Exchange　シンガポール国際金融取引所, SIMEX

International Monetary Fund　国際通貨基金, IMF
(⇒financial assistance, IMF)
◆Cuba is not a member of the International Monetary Fund. キューバは現在、国際通貨基金 (IMF) には加盟していない。◆Greece's fiscal reconstruction is set as a condition for supporting the struggling country by the European Union and the International Monetary Fund. 欧州連合 (EU) と国際通貨基金 (IMF) は、ギリシャの財政再建を、財政危機にある同国支援の条件としている。◆The European Financial Stability Facility set up a €750 billion contingency package together with the International Monetary Fund. 欧州金融安定基金 (EU) は、国際通貨基金 (IMF) の協力を得て7,500億ユーロ (約90兆円) の緊急支援資金を準備した。◆The International Monetary Fund is urged to monitor Italy's financial management to provide support to Italy. イタリアを支援するため、国際通貨基金 (IMF) はイタリアの財政運営の監視を求められている。◆The International Monetary Fund noted the current state of the Japanese economy has led to grave anxiety over deflation and capital investment. 日本経済の現状は、デフレと設備投資について重大な懸念が生じている、と国際通貨基金 (IMF) が指摘した。

international money　国際金融, 国際的貨幣, 国際通貨 (international currency)
international money management　国際的金融管理
international money market　国際金融市場, 国際短期金融市場
international money order　国際送金為替 (銀行や郵便局が扱う少額の外国送金の手段)
international money supply　国際的貨幣供給, 国際的貨幣供給量

international money transfer　国際送金
(⇒money transfer, settlement account)
◆Domestic regional banks are poised to make partnerships with Deutsche Bank to conduct international money transfers. 国内の地方銀行数行が、国際送金の分野でドイツ銀行と提携する見込みだ。◆Many regional banks often find international money transfers to be unprofitable as they are inexperienced in conducting business with foreign banks. 地方銀行の多くは、海外銀行との取引機会が少ないため、国際送金業務は採算が合わないと思っているようだ。◆U.S. authorities are poised to allow the weak dollar to continue for the foreseeable future. 米当局は、ドル安の進行を当面、容認する構えだ。

international organization　国際組織
◆The ownership of indexed government bonds has been limited to foreign governments, central banks and international organizations. 物価連動債の保有は、これまで海外の政府や中央銀行、国際機関に限られていた。

international payment　国際支払い, 国際決済
international payment currency　国際決済通貨
international payments　国際収支
international payments balance　国際収支, 国際収支尻
international payments mechanism　国際決済機構
international payments position　国際収支

international pledge　国際公約
◆At the G-20 meeting, Kan explained Japan's new economic growth and fiscal management strategies, effectively making the two strategies international pledges. G20首脳会議で、菅首相は日本の新経済成長戦略と財政運営戦略を説明し、この二つの戦略が事実上の国際公約になった。

international rule　国際基準
◆The three Japanese top banks will face the FSB's new international rule requiring them to hold extra capital to prevent future financial crises. 日本の3メガ銀行も、金融危機の再発を防ぐため、資本 [自己資本] の上積みを求める金融安定化理事会 (FSB) の新国際基準の対象になると見られる。

international securities　国際証券
international securities market　国際証券市場
International Securities Market Association　国際証券市場協会, ISMA

international settlement　国際決済
international settlement bank　国際決済銀行
international settlement currency　国際決済通貨

international standard　国際標準, 国際規格, 国際本位
international standard index　国際標準指数, 国際基準指数
international standard of value　国際的価値本位

international stock　国際株式
International Stock Exchange　国際証券取引所
International Stock Exchange of Great Britain [the United Kingdom] and Ireland　国際証券取引所

internationalization　(名) 国際化, 国際管理化
internationalization of banking　金融の国際化
internationalization of capital markets　資本市場の国際化
internationalization of the yen　円の国際化

internationalize　(動) 国際化する, 国際管理下に置く
◆With the rating of JGBs being low, internationalizing them may increase the risk that their yield will fluctuate. 日本の国債の格付けが低いので、日本国債の国際化は国債の金利変動リスクを高める可能性がある。

internationally managed currency system　国際管理通貨体制

Internet　(名) インターネット, ネット
(=internet, INET, Net:internetworkの略)
create an Internet-based bank　ネット専業銀行を設立する
have access to Internet services　インターネットにアクセスする
Internet deal　ネット取引
Internet debit　インターネット・デビット (デビット・カードのインターネット判。利用するには登録が必要で、登録後はID (カード番号) とパスワード (暗証番号) で管理する)
Internet-debit service　インターネット・デビット・サービス
Internet firm　ネット企業
(=Internet company, Internet corporation)
Internet investor　インターネット投資家, ネット投資会社, ネット投資機関
internet only bank　ネット銀行, ネット専業銀行, インターネット銀行
Internet-related company　ネット関連会社
Internet securities firm　インターネット証券, ネット証券会社 (インターネットを通じた証券売買の仲介を専門とする証券会社)
◆Following the footsteps of Sony Corp. and Softbank Corp., the company established a new firm to sell shares over the

Internet. ソニーとソフトバンクの先例にならって、同社も株式をインターネットで売買するネット取引の新会社を設立した。
◆The Internet, which can transmit rumors across the country instantaneously, has rocked the financial system. 一瞬のうちにデマを全国に広げることができるインターネットは、金融システムを揺さぶっている。◆The new Net-debit service will enable consumers to make purchases on the Internet and have the cost deducted automatically from their bank or postal savings accounts. この新ネット決済サービスを利用すると、利用者はインターネット上で買い物をして、その代金を利用者の銀行か郵便貯金の口座から自動的に引き落としてもらうことになる。

Internet bank ネット銀行, インターネット専業銀行, ネット専業銀行, インターネット・バンク （=e-banking, Internet-based bank, Internet only bank, Net bank, Net-only bank）
◆Sony Bank is an Internet bank funded by Sony Corp. ソニー銀行は、ソニーが出資したネット専業銀行だ。◆The new Internet bank will be equally owned by the two firms with initial capital of ￥20 billion. 新ネット銀行は、当初資本が200億円で、両社が折半出資する。
[解説]ネット銀行について：店舗・営業店を持たず、インターネットを利用してパソコンなどの画面上で、口座の開設や投資信託の購入、振込みなどのサービスを行う。人件費や店舗の開設・維持費用が圧縮でき、預金金利などを高く設定できるのが強み。預金などの資産の運用益と投資信託手数料、ローンの金利収入などのほかに、ネット銀行の収益源の一つは、預金残高が一定金額を下回った場合に利用者が徴収される口座維持手数料である。

Internet bank account ネット銀行口座, ネット・バンキングの口座
◆In illegal access of Internet bank accounts confirmed at financial institutions, money was transferred from a client's account to a second account. 金融機関で確認されたネット・バンキング口座への不正アクセスでは、顧客の口座から現金が他人名義の口座に振り込まれていた［送信されていた］。

Internet banking インターネット・バンキング, ネット・バンキング （=Net banking, Internet banking service：パソコンからインターネットを通じて振込みや残高証明、口座の開設などができるサービス。IDとパスワードを事前に登録して利用する）

Internet banking account ネット・バンキングの口座 （=Internet bank account）
◆Illegal access of Internet banking accounts using account holders' user IDs and passwords was confirmed at 51 financial institutions. 口座名義人のユーザーID［ユーザー名］やパスワードを使ったネット・バンキングの口座への不正アクセスが、51金融機関で確認された。◆Viruses used in illegal transfers via online banking services collect Internet banking account-related information such as personal identification numbers and transmit them to remote parties. ネット・バンキングでの不正送金に使われたウイルスは、個人の暗証番号などネット・バンキングの口座関連情報を収集して、外部に送信する。

Internet banking service インターネット・バンキング, インターネット・バンキング業務, インターネット・バンキングのサービス, インターネット・バンキング・サービス （=Internet banking, Net banking service）
◆Concerns have been raised over the ability of Internet banking services to verify the identity of new depositors or to guarantee the security of customer transactions. インターネット・バンキングについては、新規預金者の身元確認や対顧客取引の安全保証の点で、その能力に対して懸念が提起されている。◆Customers will have to open a new account to use the Internet banking services. このインターネット・バンキングのサービスを利用するにあたって、顧客は新規に口座を開設しなければならない。◆The total amount of damage by illegal transfers through Internet banking services came to about ￥265 million in 91 cases since April. インターネット・バンキングでの不正送金による被害総額は、4月から91件で約2億6,500万円に上った。

Internet-based bank ネット専業銀行 （=Internet bank, Internet-specialized bank, Net bank, Net-only bank, online bank）
◆Internet-based bank Sony Bank started a deposit service for the Brazilian real in May 2011. ネット専業銀行のソニー銀行が、2011年5月からブラジル通貨レアルの預金サービスを開始した。◆Internet shopping mall Rakuten Inc. and Tokyo Tomin Bank are planning to found a joint Internet-based bank. ネット・ショッピング・モールの楽天と東京都民銀行が、共同出資によるネット専業銀行の設立を計画している。◆The branch-free Internet-based bank can attract customers with higher deposit interest rates. 店舗を持たないネット専業銀行だと、預金の金利を高くして、顧客を集めることができる。

Internet-based banking venture ネット専業銀行業務
◆An Internet-based banking venture between the firms will handle deposits, foreign exchange, small business and personal loans and sales of securities and other investment products. 両社のネット専業銀行業務では、預金や外国為替、中小企業や個人向け融資のほかに、有価証券その他の投資商品の販売も取り扱う。

Internet-based commerce ネット商取引, ネット取引 （=e-business, e-commerce, electronic commerce）
◆Internet-based commerce has been rapidly expanding both in terms of B2B and B2C transactions, covering a wide variety of merchandise, including books, compact discs and financial products. ネット取引は、書籍やCD、金融商品など広範な商品を対象に、企業対企業の取引や企業対消費者の取引で急激に拡大している。

Internet cafe インターネット・カフェ （有料でパソコンを自由に使える店で、架空請求メールなどを送るために使われることもある）
◆To hide his identity, the man sent out 2.35 million e-mails containing fraudulent bills over a four-month period from Internet cafes. 身元を隠すため、男はインターネット・カフェから（インターネット・カフェのパソコンを使って）4か月間に235万通の架空請求メールを送信した。

Internet securities company インターネット専業証券会社, ネット証券会社 （⇒call center）
◆Internet securities companies, such as Nikko Beans, DLJ direct SFG Securities, Inc. and kabu.com, also have sponsored seminars on the new taxation law, in addition to liaising with certified tax accountants and independent financial planning specialists. 日興ビーンズ証券やDLJディレクトSFG証券、カブドットコム証券などのインターネット専業証券会社も、新税法に関するセミナーを開催するほか、公認税理士や外部のフィナンシャル・プランナーなどと提携している。

Internet service firm インターネット・サービス会社
◆He was the mastermind behind a string of violations of the Securities and Exchange Law by the Internet service firm. 同氏は、このインターネット・サービス会社による一連の証券取引法違反行為を主導していた。

Internet share transactions 株式のインターネット取引, 株式のネット取引, インターネットでの株式取引
◆Major trading houses have also shown interest in entering the new business of Internet share transactions. 総合商社も、株式のネット取引の新規事業に参入する意向を示している。

Internet shopping ネット通販, インターネット・ショッピング （=electronic commerce, Net shopping, online shopping, virtual shopping）
use the Internet banking services　ネット・バンキングの

サービスを利用する

Internet trading インターネット取引, ネット取引, インターネット販売, ネット・トレーディング, インターネットによる売買, ネット販売 (=home trade, Net trading, online trade, online trading)
◆Internet trading by individual investors increased. 個人投資家のネット取引が、増加した。

interrelated (形)相互に関係のある
◆The financial crisis is closely interrelated with the contraction of the real economy. 金融危機は、実体経済の景気後退と密接にかかわっている。

interrupt (動)妨げる, 邪魔をする, さえぎる, 中断する
interrupt the economic recovery 景気回復の腰を折る
undergo an interrupted decline 一本調子で下落する
◆It remains uncertain whether crude oil prices will undergo an interrupted decline. 原油価格が一本調子で下落するかどうかは、不透明だ。◆Should the Fed misjudge the timing or level of its next rate hike, it may interrupt the economic recovery and even bring about rapid inflation. 米連邦準備制度理事会(FRB)が追加利上げの幅やタイミングを誤ると、景気回復の腰を折り、急激なインフレを招く可能性もある。

intervene (動)介入する, 干渉する (⇒fetch)
intervene above the obligatory levels 市場介入義務の水準に達する前から介入する
intervene in defense of the dollar ドル防衛のために介入する
intervene in financial markets 金融市場に干渉する
intervene in the New York foreign exchange market ニューヨーク外国為替市場に介入する
intervene to avoid currency volatility 為替相場の乱高下[極端な変動]を防ぐために介入する
intervene to strengthen the dollar ドル高誘導の介入を行う[実施する]
jointly intervene in the market 協調介入する, 為替市場に協調介入する
◆The Bank of Japan asked the Federal Reserve Bank of New York to intervene in the New York foreign exchange market on its behalf through yen-selling, dollar-buying operations for the first time in 15 months. 日銀は、1年3か月ぶりにニューヨーク連銀に委託して、ニューヨーク外国為替市場で円売り・ドル買いの介入に踏み切った。◆The Finance Ministry asked the Bank of Japan to intervene in the market at 10:30 a.m. 財務省は、午前10時30分に、日銀に介入を要請した。◆The government and the Bank of Japan should urge the United States and European countries to jointly intervene in the market. 政府・日銀は、米欧に協調介入を強く働きかけるべきだ。◆The government and the BOJ intervened in Tokyo market for the first time in 6.5 years to stem the yen's sharp appreciation to the dollar. 急激な円高を阻止するため、政府・日銀は6年半ぶりに東京外国為替市場に介入した。

intervene in foreign exchange 為替介入する
◆The government must stress its willingness to intervene in foreign exchange to prevent the yen's further appreciation. 一層の円高阻止に向けて、政府は為替介入も辞さない姿勢を見せるべきだ。

intervene in long-term rates 長期金利に介入する
◆The Bank of Japan has taken the stance that it would not intervene in long-term rates in principle, except for the implementation of outright purchase operation of long-term government bonds worth about ¥5 trillion a year. 日銀はこれまで、年間5兆円程度の長期国債の買切りオペを実施する以外は、原則として長期金利には介入しない姿勢[立場]をとってきた。

intervene in the currency market 為替市場に介入する, 外国為替市場に介入する
◆The government should discuss the possibility of going it alone in intervening in the currency market. 政府は、為替市場への単独介入の可能性を検討すべきだ。◆The government should not hesitate to intervene in the currency market through bold yen-selling and dollar-buying operations. 政府は、為替市場への大胆な円売り・ドル買い介入をためらうべきではない。

intervene in the exchange market 為替市場に介入する, 為替介入する
◆The government and the BOJ should not hesitate to intervene in the exchange market to stem the rapid rise in the yen's value. 政府・日銀は、急激な円高阻止の為替介入[為替市場への介入]をためらうべきでない。

intervene in the foreign exchange markets 外国為替市場[為替市場]に介入する, 為替介入する
◆China intervenes in the foreign exchange markets to fix the yuan-dollar exchange rate. 中国は、外国為替市場に介入して[為替介入して]元・ドル・レートを固定している。

intervene in the market 市場に介入する, 市場介入する
intervene in the market to avoid currency volatility 為替相場の乱高下[極端な変動]を防ぐために市場介入する
intervene in the market to stem the yen's rise 円高を阻止するため[円高阻止に向けて]市場介入する
◆The Bank of Japan intervened in the market Tuesday morning in New York. 日銀は火曜日午前、ニューヨーク外国為替市場に介入した。◆The government and the BOJ intervened in the market for the first time in 61/2 years in September 2010 to stem the yen's rise. 政府・日銀は、円高を阻止する[食い止める]ため、2010年9月に6年半ぶりに(円売り・ドル買いの)市場介入をした。

intervene to buy the dollar ドル買い介入を行う[実施する]
◆The Finance Ministry intervened to buy the dollar on Sept. 15, 2010 for the first time in six years and a half. 財務省は、6年半ぶりとなった2010年9月15日に、(円売り)ドル買い介入を行った。

intervention (名)介入, 市場介入, 協調介入, 仲裁, 調停, 干渉 (⇒currency intervention, currency market intervention, joint intervention, market intervention, unilateral intervention, yen-selling intervention)
a large yen-selling intervention 大量の円売り介入
additional intervention 追加介入
an intervention to sell yen and buy the dollar to stop appreciation of the yen 円高を食い止める[阻止する]ための円売り・ドル買い介入
bank intervention 銀行介入
concerted [coordinated] intervention 協調介入 (⇒joint intervention)
conduct independent yen-selling intervention 単独円売り介入を実施する, 単独で円売り介入を行う
conduct yen-selling intervention 円売り介入を実施する[行う]
continuous intervention 断続的な市場介入
currency intervention 為替介入
currency market intervention 為替市場への介入, 為替市場介入 (=foreign exchange intervention, forex intervention)
defensive intervention 防衛介入
direct intervention 直接介入
dollar-buying intervention ドル買い介入
enormous intervention 大規模介入
foreign exchange intervention 為替介入 (=forex intervention)
intervention band 変動幅
intervention by central banks 中央銀行による協調介入

［介入］
    intervention currency　介入通貨
    intervention operation　介入操作
    intervention point　介入点　(=support point)
    intervention price　介入価格
    intervention rate　市場介入金利
        (=market rate of intervention)
    joint intervention　協調介入, 協調市場介入
        (=coordinated intervention)
    market intervention　市場介入
        (=intervention in [on] the market; ⇒selling)
    market rate of intervention　市場介入金利
    multi-currency [multicurrency] intervention　複数通貨介入
    non-sterilizing intervention　非不胎化介入, 非不胎化的介入　(=unsterilized intervention)
    preemptive intervention　早めの介入
    preemptive regulatory intervention　規制当局による早めの介入
    regulatory intervention　監督当局による介入
    sizeable intervention　大規模な介入, 大規模介入
    sterilized foreign exchange intervention　不胎化為替介入, 不胎化介入, 不胎化された為替介入［介入］
    sterilizing [sterilized] intervention　不胎化介入, 介入の不胎化
    the intervention by the Finance Ministry　財務省の介入
        (⇒stable exchange rates)
    the option of yen-selling intervention in the exchange market　円売りの為替市場介入［市場介入］の選択肢
    three-way [3-way] intervention　三極の市場介入
    unilateral intervention　単独介入
    unsterilized intervention　不胎化を伴わない介入, 非不胎化介入, 介入の非不胎化
    yen-selling, dollar-buying intervention　円売り・ドル買い介入
    yen-selling intervention　円売り介入, 円売りの為替市場介入
    yen-selling intervention in the exchange market　円売りの為替市場介入
    ◆A large yen-selling intervention by monetary authorities on Sept. 15 failed to reverse the yen's rising trend. 金融当局が9月15日に実施した大量の円売り介入で, 円高傾向を反転［逆転］させることはできなかった。◆After their government's move of intervention, the yen plunged to the ￥85 level against the dollar. 政府の市場介入の動きを受けて, 円相場は1ドル＝85円台まで急落した。◆Dollar-buying intervention has been stopped since spring. ドル買い介入は, 春以来停止している。◆Interventions for last year hit a record high of ￥20.43 trillion. 昨年の介入総額は, 過去最高の20兆4,300億円に達した。◆The government and the Bank of Japan conducted a dollar-buying, yen-selling intervention for the first time in 6 1/2 years on Sept. 15, 2010. 2010年9月15日に政府・日銀は, 6年半ぶりにドル買い・円売り介入を実施した［行った］。◆The government and the BOJ are considering the option of yen-selling intervention in the exchange market. 政府・日銀は, 円売りの為替市場介入の選択肢を検討している。◆The government may take further decisive actions, including an additional intervention. 政府は, 追加介入を含めてさらに断固たる措置を取る可能性がある。◆The Japanese government and the Bank of Japan conducted an independent yen-selling intervention. 日本政府・日銀は, 単独で円売り介入を行った。◆The yen has depreciated by more than ￥10 from before the previous enormous intervention. 円は, 前回の大規模介入の前より10円強の円安になった。
intervention to sell yen and buy the dollar　円売り・ドル買い介入
    ◆In an intervention to sell yen and buy the dollar to stop appreciation of the yen, the government issues short-term financing bills to procure yen and then purchases dollars from private banks. 円高を食い止める［阻止する］ための円売り・ドル買い介入では, 政府が政府短期証券（FB）を発行して円を調達し, 調達した円で民間銀行からドルを買い入れる。

intraday　(形)取引時間中の, ざら場の
    intraday high　取引時間中の高値, ざら場の高値
    intraday low　取引時間中の安値, ざら場の安値
    on an intraday basis　取引時間中として
    ◆The stock of Xinhua Finance reached an intraday high shortly before 10:30 a.m. 新華ファイナンスの銘柄は, 午前10時30分直前, 取引時間中の高値に達した。

intraday trading　取引時間中の取引, ざら場の取引
    ◆After briefly touching ￥110.90 in early trading in London, the dollar rallied in intraday trading, rising to ￥112.15-25 at 5 p.m. ロンドン市場では早朝の取引で一時1ドル＝110円90銭を付けた後, 米ドルは取引時間中の取引で反騰して午後5時現在, 同112円15-25銭に上昇した。

introduce　(動)導入する, 発売する, 売り出す, 公開する　(⇒bridge bank, business base, large-lot savings, mezzanine)
    introduce a new product　新商品［製品］を販売する
    introduce a 401(k)-style pension scheme　確定拠出型年金制度（日本版401k）導入する
    introduce economic stimulus measures　景気刺激策を導入する
    ◆Aioi Insurance Co. will introduce a new product named Live Lead on April 2. あいおい損害保険が, 4月2日に新商品の「リブリード」を発売する。◆In most cases in which the credit guarantee system is used, financial institutions introduce borrowers to credit guarantee corporations. 信用保証制度を利用する場合の多くは, 金融機関が借り手を信用保証協会に紹介する。◆Nippon Life Insurance Co. introduced a 401(k)-style pension scheme for about 10,000 office workers in April 2005. 日本生命保険が, 2005年4月から, 約1万人の内勤職員を対象に確定拠出型年金制度（日本版401k）を導入した。◆One of the intentions of the government to introduce various regulation measures is to discourage "excessive competition." 各種の規制措置を導入する政府のねらいの一つは,「過当競争」の防止である。◆The Bank of Japan stepped up its efforts to boost the flagging economy following the March 11 earthquake and tsunami by introducing a ￥500 billion cheap loan program. 日銀は, 5,000億円の低利融資制度を導入して, 東日本大震災で揺れる日本経済の刺激策を強化した。◆The BOJ decided to introduce a new open market operation by supplying ￥10 trillion to private financial institutions in three month loans at an ultralow annual interest of 0.1 percent. 日銀は, 民間の金融機関に年1％の超低金利で貸出期間3か月の資金を10兆円供給する新型の公開市場操作（オペ）の導入に踏み切った。◆The government will help Indonesia introduce economic stimulus measures through the soft loan. 政府は, この条件のゆるい借款を通じて, インドネシアの景気刺激策導入を支援する。◆The new Fed chairman's theory is to introduce inflation targets, thus setting numerical targets for stabilizing prices. 米連邦準備制度理事会（FRB）新議長の持論は, インフレ目標を導入して, 物価安定の数値目標を示す［設定する］ことだ。

introduction　(名)導入, 実施, 発売, 公開, 持ち込み, 紹介　(⇒investment credit, loan interest rate, stock dividend)
    the introduction of a new product　新製品の発売, 新製品の導入
    the introduction of mandatory real-name transaction system　金融実名制の実施

the introduction of stock　株式公開
the introduction of the euro　ユーロの導入
introduction of common eurozone [euro-area] bonds　ユーロ圏共通債の導入
◆German Chancellor Angela Merkel shut the door on the introduction of common eurozone bonds as a means to solve the debt crisis. ドイツのメルケル首相は、欧州債務危機問題の解決手段としてユーロ圏共通債を導入することに強く反対した。
introduction of the IFRSs　国際財務報告基準（IFRS）の導入
◆The Financial Services Agency gave up its initial goal to make the introduction of the IFRSs mandatory in around 2015. 金融庁は、2015年にもIFRS（国際財務報告規準）の導入を義務化するという当初の目標を断念した。
inverse　（形）逆の、反対の　（名）逆、反対、インバース
　inverse coefficient　逆係数
　inverse demand function　逆需要関数
　inverse floater　逆流動証券、インバース・フローター（債）（=reverse floater）
　inverse matrix　逆行列
　inverse proportion　反比例
inversion　（名）逆転、転換、反転
　the curve inversion　利回り曲線の右下がりの傾斜
　yield curve inversion　逆イールド（=the inversion of the yield curve）
　yield inversion　逆イールド
inverted　（形）逆の、反転した、逆転した、逆型の
　inverted demand curve　逆需要曲線
　inverted economic series　逆型経済系列
　inverted head and shoulder formation　逆三尊
　inverted market　直先逆転現象、逆先物市場、逆ヤサ（=backwardation: 商品や為替市場取引で直物価格が先物価格を上回っている状態のこと。⇒backwardation, forwardation）
　inverted scale　逆転スケール
　inverted yield curve　逆利回り曲線、長短金利の逆転［逆転状況］、逆イールド、逆イールド・カーブ（=negative yield curve）
　the yield curve becomes inverted　利回り曲線が右下がりになる［逆イールドになる］
　the yield curve becomes less inverted　逆イールドが緩（ゆる）くなる
invest　（動）投資する、投下する、投入する、運用する（⇒bond, issue 名詞）
　ability to invest　投資実行力
　invest cash［money］in the business　事業に現預金を投資する
　invest heavily　巨額の資金を投入する［提供する］、大金を投入する、巨額の投資をする、巨額を投資する、大型投資をする
　invest overseas　海外投資をする、海外に投資する
　private propensity to invest　民間投資性向
　propensity to invest　投資性向
　willingness to invest　投資意欲
◆General Motors Corp., the world largest automaker, will invest $3 billion in China in the next three years. 世界最大手の米自動車メーカーGMが、今後3年間で中国に30億ドル投資する。◆Some dollar funds injected into banks by the U.S. central bank may send U.S. stock prices soaring because banks will invest some of the new dollar funds in domestic assets such as stocks. 米国の中央銀行（FRB）が金融機関［銀行］に供給したドル資金の一部は、銀行がその新たなドル資金の一部を株のような国内資産に投資するため、米国の株価を上げる可能性がある。

invest in　〜に投資する、出資する、投じる（⇒briefing for foreign investors, investment trust）
　invest in blue chip securities　優良証券に投資する
　invest in common stocks　普通株式に投資する
　invest in financial assets　金融資産に投資する
　invest in land　土地に投資する
　invest in marketable securities　市場性証券に投資する
　invest in R&D　研究開発（R&D）に投資する
　invest in real assets　実物資産に投資する
　invest in real estate　不動産に投資する
◆Nippon Steel Corp. plans to join with Usiminas to invest in a planned steelworks in Brazil. 新日本製鉄は、ブラジルの鉄鋼大手ウジミナスに協力して、同国で予定されている製鉄所に投資する計画だ。◆Of the amount of investment, about a half was invested in foreign government bonds with low credit ratings. この投資額のうち約半分は、格付けの低い外国債に充てられていた。◆The brokerage's main services for individual customers will be asset management advisory services, focusing on the sale of products such as investment trust funds that invest in foreign equities, and money market funds denominated in foreign currencies. 同証券会社は、株式の主な個人顧客向け（売買仲介）業務として、外国株を組み込んだ投資信託や外貨建てMMF（マネー・マーケット・ファンド）などの商品の販売を中心に、資産運用顧問業務を展開する方針だ。◆When ailing businesses are revamped, those who invested in them benefit. 経営不振企業を再建すると、出資者が利益を得られる。
invest in and extend loans to　〜に投融資する
◆Shinsei Bank unveiled a plan to set up a subsidiary that invests in and extends loans to companies having financial difficulties. 新生銀行は、経営難の企業に投融資する子会社を設立する方針を明らかにした。
invest in bonds with high yields　高利回り債に投資する
◆Many of incorporated foundations have invested in bonds with high yields. 財団法人の多くは、高利回り債に投資した。
invest in foreign currencies　外貨に投資する
◆In the case of foreign currency deposits, depositors can invest in foreign currencies such as British pound, Swiss franc and Australian dollar as well as the U.S. dollar and euro. 外貨預金の場合、預金者は、米ドルやユーロのほかに英ポンド、スイス・フランや豪ドルなどにも投資することができる。
invest in Japanese government bonds　日本国債に投資する
◆After the briefing for foreign investors, a fund manager showed interest in investing in Japanese government bonds. 海外投資家向け説明会の後、あるファンド・マネージャーが日本国債への投資に関心を示した。
invest in plants and equipment　設備投資する
◆Expecting the economic expansion will continue, corporations are actively investing in plants and equipment. 景気拡大が続くと見た企業は、設備投資に積極的だ。
invest in properties　不動産に投資する
◆Daikyo fell into financial difficulties by investing in properties after the bubble economy burst in the early 1990s. 大京は、1990年代はじめのバブル経済崩壊後の不動産投資で、経営危機に陥った。
invest in stocks　株式に投資する
◆A woman illegally collected money from individuals to invest in stocks, guaranteeing the principal and promising high returns. 主婦が、元本を保証し、高配当［高利回り］を約束して、株式投資への資金を個人から集めていた。
invest in the fund　ファンドに出資する
◆The Development of Japan will ask major financial groups to invest in the fund established to assist auto parts makers hit by the March 11 earthquake and tsunami. 日本政策投資

銀行が、東日本大震災で被災した自動車部品メーカーを支援するために設立するファンドへの出資を、大手金融グループに呼びかけることになった。

invest in the stock market 株式市場に投資する
◆In revitalizing the market, it is necessary to encourage individuals, who have financial assets totaling ¥1.4 quadrillion, to invest in the stock market. 市場の活性化を図るには、1,400兆円にのぼる金融資産を持つ個人の株式市場への投資を促す必要がある。◆With the economic recovery gaining momentum, U.S. companies have begun investing in the Japanese stock market again, giving a lift to stock prices. 景気回復が力強さを増していることから、米国企業が日本の株式市場に再び投資するようになり、株価を押し上げている。

investable (形)投資可能な, 投資の対象となる (名)よい投資対象
　investable fund　投資可能資金
　investable money　投資資金

invested (形)投資される[投資された], 投入される, 投下される, 運用される
　invested amount　投資額
　invested assets　投資資産, 運用資産
　invested capital　投資資本, 投下資本, 拠出資本, 株主資本 (contributed capital, paid-in capital), 長期資本[証券資本] (会社の正味資産[純資産]と長期債務[負債]の合計額)
　invested fund　投資資金, 運用資金, 投下資本, 資金の運用

investee (名)投資先, 被投資会社, 被投資先
　equity method investee　持ち分法適用会社
　investee company　被投資会社
　investee's profit　被投資会社利益

investible (形)投資可能な
　investible fund　投資資金
　investible surplus　投資可能余剰
　supply of investible funds　資金供給

investigate (動)調査する, 究明する, 研究する, 取り調べる, 捜査する
◆Federal and state regulators have been investigating marketing of the auction rate securities by a number of big banks. 米連邦と州の規制当局は、一部の大手金融機関による金利入札証券(ARS)の販売方法について調査している。◆Financial regulators asked prosecutors to investigate allegations that UFJ Holdings Inc.'s banking unit illegally obstructed recent inspections by reporting misleading information about its nonperforming loans. 金融当局は、UFJ銀行が不良債権に関する虚偽の情報を報告して最近の検査を違法に妨害したとして、同行を検察当局に刑事告発した。

investigation (名)調査, 検査, 審査, 監査, 査察, 研究, 究明, 取調べ, 捜査, 調査[研究]報告, 調書, 調査書, 研究論文
　credit investigation　信用調査
　forcible investigation　強制調査
　internal investigation　内部調査, 社内調査 (=in-house investigation)
　investigation committee　調査委員会
　investigation on fiscal operations　財政監査
　preliminary investigation　予備調査
　the FSA investigation　金融庁の検査
◆Securities and Exchange Surveillance Commission is set to launch an investigation into the company. 証券取引等委員会は、同社の調査に乗り出す見通しだ。◆The cover-up of investment losses by Olympus was discovered during an investigation by the company's third-party panel. オリンパスによる投資損失処理の偽装工作は、同社の第三者委員会の調査で判明した。◆The investigation committee questioned the bank's excessive funding of a golf course developer. 調査委員会は、ゴルフ場経営会社への同行の過剰融資を問題視した。◆The Securities and Exchange Surveillance Commission launched a full-scale investigation on the company on suspicion of accounting fraud. 証券取引等監視委員会は、粉飾決算の疑いで同社の本格調査に乗り出した。◆The TSE is continuing its investigation into whether there was insider trading of the firm's shares. 同社株についてインサイダー取引があったかどうか、東証が現在、調査を進めている。

investing (名)投資, 資金投下 (=investment; ⇒socially responsible investing, stock investing, stock investing club)
　formula investing　フォーミュラ・プラン投資 (あらかじめ設定した投資計画に基づいて行う証券投資のこと)
　growth investing　成長株投資
　investing assets　投資資産
　investing in marketable securities　市場性証券への投資
　value investing　バリュー株投資, 割安株投資

investing activities 投資活動
　cash flows from investing activities　投資活動から生じた[投資活動に伴う]現金収支
　net cash provided by (used in) investing activities　投資活動に伴う正味現金収支
　noncash investing activities　非現金投資活動
◆Due to an increase in the purchase of marketable securities, net cash used for investing activities increased by $5 million from the same period last year. 市場性ある有価証券の購入量が増えたため、投資活動に使用した純キャッシュは、前年同期比で500万ドル増加しました。

investing in equipment 設備投資
◆The financial burden of investing in equipment will be lightened by integrating the trading systems of the TSE and the OSE. 東証と大証の売買システムを一本化することで、設備投資の金融負担が軽減される。

investment (名)投資, 出資, 資金投下, 運用, 運用資産, 投資資産, 投資勘定, 投下資本, 投資資金, 投資額, 投資の対象, 投資先, 運用先, 投資物, 投資商品, 有価証券, 証券, インベストメント (=investing; ⇒brief, capital investment, Commercial Code, direct investment, failed financial institution, FDI, financial derivatives, fixed capital formation, premium investment)
　a good investment　有利な投資
　a profitable investment　有利な投資先, 有利な運用先
　actual investment　実際の運用
　advance investment　先行投資
　attract investment　投資を誘致する, 投資を呼び込む
　attractive investment　魅力的な投資対象, 魅力ある投資対象
　blue-chip investment　優良な投資
　bond investment　投資社債, 債券投資
　business investment　設備投資
　capital investment　資本投資, 設備投資, 公共投資
　corporate capital investment　企業の設備投資
　direct overseas investment　海外直接投資
　diversified investment　分散投資
　equipment investment　設備投資
　equity investment　株式投資
　excessive investment　過剰投資
　financial investment　金融投資
　fixed asset investment　固定資産投資
　forward looking investment　先行投資
　housing investment　住宅投資
　induced investment　誘発投資
　industrial investment　産業投資
　intercompany investment　内部投資

international investments 国際投資
investment adviser [advisor] 投資顧問, 投資顧問業
Investment Advisers Act 投資顧問法
investment advisory company 投資顧問会社
investment advisory service 投資顧問業務
investment alternative 投資手段
investment analyst 投資アナリスト, 証券アナリスト, 証券分析家, インベストメント・アナリスト
investment approvals 投資承認額, 投資認可額
investment asset 投資資産
investment attention 投資先, 投資の関心
investment banker 投資銀行, 投資銀行家, インベストメント・バンカー
investment bond 投資証券
investment business 投資業務, 投資事業, 投資業
investment center 投資センター, 投資中心点
investment certificate 投資証書
investment climate 投資環境 (=investment environment)
investment club 投資クラブ (=stock investing club: 仲間同士でお金を出し合って株を売買するもの。⇒stock investing club)
investment commodity 投資財
investment community 投資業界
Investment Company Act of 1940 1940年投資会社法
investment constraint 運用上の制約[制約事項]
investment consultant firm 投資顧問会社
investment counsel 投資相談
investment counselor [counsel] 投資顧問, 投資相談業者 (=investment adviser [advisor])
investment credit 投資金融, 投資控除
investment currency 投資通貨
investment discipline 売買ルール
investment discretion 一任契約に基づく投資
investment for labor-saving 省力投資
investment funding 投資金融
investment gain 投資収益
investment grant 投資補助金
investment holding period 投資期間
investment horizon 所有期間, 運用期間, 投資対象
investment income account (国際収支での)投資収支
investment information 投資情報
investment instrument 運用手段
Investment Law 投資法 (⇒legal ceiling on interest rates)
investment ledger 有価証券元帳
investment letter 投資目的確約書, インベストメント・レター
investment letter stock 私募株式, 非登録株式, レター・ストック (=investment letter stock, lettered stock, unregistered stock: SECに登録届け出をしないで私募発行された株式)
investment manager 資産運用担当者, 運用機関, 投資顧問, 投資マネージャー, 投資管理人, 投資運用会社, 運用会社, ファンド・マネージャー
investment manager structure 担当運用機関の構成
investment margin 利差損益 (顧客に約束した生保の運用利回りと実際の資産運用益との差額)
investment market 発行市場
investment media 投資対象
investment method 投資方法
investment mix 投資ミックス

investment needs 投資ニーズ
investment objective 投資目標, 運用目標
Investment Ombudsman 投資オンブズマン
investment outlook 投資見通し, 投資環境[運用環境]の見通し
investment oversight 資産運用業務の監督
investment philosophy 投資理念
investment potential 投資収益力
investment process 投資プロセス, 運用プロセス
investment product 運用商品, 投資商品
investment program 投資プログラム, 運用プログラム
investment property 投資不動産, 投資資産
investment property company 不動産投資会社
investment results 運用成績, 運用実績, 運用成果, 投資の成果
investment schedule 投資表
investment securities 投資証券, 投資有価証券
Investment Services Directive EUの投資サービス指令
investment site 投資先
investment spending 投資支出, 公共投資
investment strategy 投資戦略, 運用戦略
investment to foreign securities 対外証券投資
investment turnover 投資回転率 (売上高÷(純資産+長期負債)=投資回転率)
investment value 投資価値
investment yield 投資利回り
investments [securities purchases] by foreign investors 外人投資
labor saving investment 省力化投資
less investment in plant and equipment 設備投資の抑制
liquidate an investment 運用中の資金を現金化する
lose one's investment 投資資金を失う
new investment 新規投資
overseas investment 海外投資, 対外投資
portfolio investment 証券投資, 株式・債券投資, ポートフォリオ投資
public investment 公共投資
quoted investment 上場証券
real estate investment fund 不動産投資ファンド
residential investment 住宅投資
return on investment 投資利益率, 投資収益率, 投資利回り, ROI
risky investment 高リスク投資
risky investments 高リスク[リスクの高い]投資, リスクの高い投資商品[金融商品], 高リスク証券, リスクの高い有価証券
security investment 証券投資
stock investments 株式投資, 保有株

◆Goldman Sachs Group Inc. is said to have marketed risky investments that bet on the housing market's growth just before the mortgage meltdown. ゴールドマン・サックスは、住宅ローン市場の崩壊直前に、住宅市場の成長を見越した[予想した]高リスクの金融商品[投資商品]を販売したとされる。◆If the two-track income taxation system is introduced, taxpayers will be allowed to offset losses from stock investments from income earned from interest and dividends. 二元的所得課税方式を導入すると、納税者は、利子・配当収入から株式投資による損失を相殺することができるようになる。◆In the case of JAL, the DBJ's ultimate total losses came to ¥95.6 billion in loans and ¥20 billion in investments. 日航の場合、日本政策投資銀行の最終的な損失総額は、融資分の956億円と出資分の200億円となっている。◆The company will increase its capital by ¥50 billion with additional investment of ¥10 billion from the IRC and with the debt-for-equity swap. 同社は、産業再生機構による100億円の追加（新規）出資と債務の株式化で、500億円増資する。◆The Federal Housing Finance Agency sued 17 financial firms over risky investments. 米連邦住宅金融局（FHFA）が、高リスク証券を販売したとして大手金融機関17社を提訴した。◆The life insurer's single-premium whole life insurance is popular with consumers as a form of savings or an investment for retirement. 同生保の一時払い終身保険は、一種の貯蓄や退職金の運用先として顧客に人気がある。◆These surplus funds are moving into crude oil and grain markets in search of profitable investments. これらの余剰資金が、有利な運用先を求めて原油や穀物市場に向かっている。

investment adviser [advisor] 投資顧問, 投資顧問業, 投資助言会社
◆Olympus ostensibly paid about ￥70 billion in commissions to two investment advisers when the company acquired a British medical equipment maker for about ￥210 billion. オリンパスが英国の医療機器メーカーを約2,100億円で買収した際、同社は表向きには仲介手数料として約700億円を投資助言会社2社に支払った。

investment advisory unit 投資顧問会社, 投資顧問業
◆The investment fund has disbanded its investment advisory unit in Japan and moved its fund operation functions to Singapore. 同投資ファンドは、日本での投資顧問業を廃業して、そのファンド運用機能をシンガポールに移した。

investment bank 投資銀行, 証券会社 （=investment banker:「投資銀行」の主な業務は、証券引受け（underwriting）、新規株式公開（IPO）とM&A（企業合併・買収）の仲介。⇒equity trading business）
◆In the joint venture with an Indian investment bank, Tokio Marine Holdings Inc. put up about 26%, the maximum a foreign investor is allowed in an Indian company, of the new firm's capital. インドの投資銀行との合弁事業で、東京海上ホールディングスは、新会社の資本金の約26％（外資の持ち分比率の上限）を出資した。◆In the subprime crisis, the U.S. Federal Reserve Board had to take the extraordinary step of providing an emergency loan not to a commercial bank but to an investment bank. サブプライム問題で、米国の中央銀行の連邦準備制度理事会（FRB）は、緊急融資を銀行［商業銀行］ではなく証券会社［投資銀行］に対して行う異例の措置を取らざるを得なかった。◆It has become an international trend of late for investment banks to seek an alliance with retail banks, as in the case of Deutsche Bank's acquisition of Bankers Trust, an investment bank. 最近は、ドイツ銀行が米投資銀行のバンカーズ・トラストを買収したように、リテール銀行との統合が投資銀行の世界的な流れになっている。◆Lehman Brothers Holdings Inc., a major U.S. investment bank, collapsed in September 2008. 米投資銀行大手のリーマン・ブラザーズは、2008年9月に破たんした。◆The capital markets around the globe are plagued by counterparty risks in the aftermath of the collapse of U.S. investment bank Lehman Brothers in 2008. 世界全体の資本市場は、2008年の米証券会社［投資銀行］の経営破たんの影響で、カウンターパーティー・リスクに苦しんでいる。◆The investment bank reaped billions of dollars from its own bets that the housing market would collapse. この投資銀行は、住宅市場が崩壊するとの独自の予想で、数十億ドルの利益を上げていた。◆We have received a number of proposals from investment banks who want to act as go-betweens between drug companies for mergers. 投資銀行からは、製薬会社の経営統合の仲介をしたい旨の提案が数多く来ている。

investment banking 投資銀行業務
　a slump in investment banking　投資銀行業務［業務部門］の低迷
　investment banking community　投資銀行業界
　investment banking group　引受団
（=underwriting syndicate）
◆Nomura Holdings' net profit fell 80 percent in the first quarter of fiscal 2010 mainly due to a slump in investment banking. 野村ホールディングスの2010年度第1四半期の税引き後利益は、主に投資銀行業務部門の低迷で80％減少した。

investment banking activities 投資銀行業務
◆The capital increase is designed to secure financial resources for the expansion of the bank's investment banking activities abroad. 同行の増資の目的は、海外での投資銀行業務拡大の資金確保にある。

investment banking business 投資銀行業務, 投資銀行事業
◆The bank posted strong third-quarter profits as investment banking business surged, stocks rose and interest rates stayed low. 投資銀行業務の急増と株価上昇のほか、金利が低水準を維持したため、同行の第3四半期利益は大幅に増加した。

investment banking operations 投資銀行業務
（=investment banking business）
◆Sumitomo Mitsui Financial Group Inc. and Goldman Sachs have formed an alliance in investment banking operations. 三井住友フィナンシャルグループは、投資銀行業務でゴールドマン・サックスと提携関係にある。◆The two companies have formed an alliance in investment banking operations. 両社は、投資銀行業務で提携関係を結んでいる［提携関係にある］。

investment business 投資事業
◆Shinsei and Aozora banks suffered huge losses in their overseas investment business in the aftermath of the global financial crisis triggered by the collapse of Lehman Brothers Holdings Inc. in autumn 2008. 新生銀行とあおぞら銀行は、2008年秋のリーマン・ブラザーズの経営破たんで始まった世界的な金融危機の影響で、海外投資事業に巨額の損失が発生した。

investment capital 投資資本, 投資マネー（投資に充当する資金）, 設備資金
◆Global investment capital has increasingly been flowing to low-risk assets. 世界の投資マネーは、傾向として損失リスクの低い資産に流れている。◆The funds gained from the sale of shares will permit the firm to undertake capital expenditures without calling on further investment capital from its parent company. 株式売却で調達した資金によって、同社は親会社に追加投資資本［資本投資］を求めることなく、設備投資ができる状況にある。

investment climate 投資環境
◆Currently, China's investment climate is stable. 現在、中国の投資環境は安定している。

investment company 投資会社, 投資信託会社
（=investment firm, investment trust, management company: 一般から広く資金を集めて証券類に投資する投資信託業務を行う会社）
◆An investment company purchased the failed English conversation school chain Geos. 投資会社が、経営破たんした英会話学校「ジオス」を買い取った。◆Daiei will sign a contract with a U.S. investment company to sell its hotel in Fukuoka and the Fukuoka Dome. ダイエーは、福岡市で展開しているホテルと福岡ドーム（球場）を売却する契約を、米国の投資会社と結ぶ。

investment conditions 投資環境（investment environment）, 投資状況, 運用実態, 運用環境
◆Different from high-profile hedge funds, the founders and investment conditions of these foreign investment funds are not clear. 著名なヘッジ・ファンドと異なって、これらの海外投資ファンドの設立者や資金の運用実態は、はっきりしない。◆Foreign players also are expected to enter the commodity futures market in line with the improvement in investment conditions. 投資の環境改善で、外資［海外企業］の商品先物市場への参入も見込まれる。◆Investment conditions have wors-

ened due to confusion in global financial markets in the wake of fiscal and financial crises in Europe. 欧州の財政・金融危機を受けた世界的な金融市場の混乱で、運用環境が悪化している。

investment consortium　投資組合
◆After nationalization in 1998, the Long-Term Credit Bank of Japan was sold to an investment consortium led by Ripplewood Holdings LLC. 1998年に国有化された後、日本長期信用銀行は、リップルウッド・ホールディングスを中心とする投資組合に売却された。◆Because the investment consortium is based outside of the country, the government cannot levy taxes on profits from stock sales. この投資組合は国外に本拠地を置いているため、政府は株式売却益に課税できない。

investment costs　投資コスト
◆Huge investment costs, such as those for developing environment-friendly technology, have made it difficult for an automaker to survive competition on its own. 環境にやさしい技術の開発費など、巨額の投資コストが見込まれるため、自動車メーカー1社が独力で競争に生き残るのは難しくなっている。

investment credit　投資税額控除, 投資減税
(=investment tax credit)
◆Heizo Takenaka, state minister in charge of economic and fiscal policy, would like to see the introduction of investment credits to stimulate the economy. 竹中経済財政相は、景気を刺激するために投資減税の導入を求めている。

investment decision　投資判断, 投資の意思決定, 投資決定
◆Corporate accounting reports are the most important criterion for investment decisions. 企業の財務情報は、特に重要な投資判断の材料だ。

Investment Deposit and Interest Rate Control Law　出資法 (出資の受入れ、預り金や金利等の取締りに関する法律。⇒contract, Moneylending Control Law)
◆A man who operated an illegal moneylending firm was arrested on suspicion of violating the Investment Deposit and Interest Rate Control Law. 違法な金融業の経営者［ヤミ金融の経営者］が、出資法違反容疑で逮捕された。◆Within the moneylending business sector, there are calls for raising the upper limit of the interest rate stipulated in the Investment Deposit and Interest Rate Control Law. 貸金業界には、出資法で定められている上限金利の引上げを求める声がある。

investment environment　投資環境
(=investment climate, investment conditions)
◆In the postal savings business, Japan Post booked ¥2.27 trillion in profit due to improvement of the investment environment during that year. 郵便貯金事業で、日本郵政公社は投資環境の改善で2兆2,700億円の当期利益を計上した。

investment exposure　投資リスク, 投資
◆Increasing demands for capital and tight-money policies adopted by industrial powers pressed many investors to review their investment exposure in emerging economies. 先進国での資金需要の増大と金融引締め策は、多くの投資家に新興経済国［新興市場国］への投資の見直しを迫ることになった。

investment firm　投資会社, 証券会社
◆The company granted an investment firm the right to buy shares to be newly issued by the company as a means of foiling a hostile takeover bid. 同社は、敵対的買収への防衛策として、同社が新規に発行する株式の引受権を投資会社に付与した［投資会社に新株予約権を割り当てた］。

investment for digitalization　デジタル化投資
◆As investment for digitalization is costly, NBS needs to establish a more profitable management system, including joint investment in digital-related facilities and content with the Fuji TV group. デジタル化の投資負担は軽くないので、ニッポン放送は、フジテレビ・グループとのデジタル関連施設への共同投資やコンテンツ（情報内容）の共有など、収益力の高い経営システムを確立する必要がある。

investment fund　投資ファンド, 投資信託（機関投資家などから資金を集めて、不良債権の売買や企業買収などを行う組織）, 投資資金, 運用資金　(⇒asset value, fund-of-funds, hostile investment fund, hostile takeover, subscribe)
an investment fund's hostile takeover bid　投資ファンドの敵対的TOB（株式公開買付け）
closed-end investment fund　クローズド・エンド型投資信託［投信］
investment fund rating company　投信評価会社
open-end investment fund　オープン［オープン・エンド］型投資信託
public-private investment fund　官民出資のファンド
real estate investment fund　不動産投資ファンド
seek a helping hand from the investment fund　同投資ファンドに支援を求める
stock investment fund　株式投資信託
tighter regulations on investment funds　投資ファンドの規制強化
◆A real estate investment fund was alleged to have failed to report about ¥18 billion in income from transaction involving land and property taken as collateral for nonperforming loans. 不動産投資ファンドが、不良債権の担保に取った不動産関連の取引で得た所得約180億円の申告漏れを指摘されていた。◆Investment funds do not hesitate to dissolve a company and strip its assets after acquiring the management rights of the company. 投資ファンドは、会社の経営権を取得した後、会社を解散してその資産を売り払うこともいとわない。◆Investment funds flowed into low-risk Treasury bonds. 投資資金は、リスクの少ない財務省証券市場に流入した。◆Investment funds have driven up crude oil prices. 投資ファンドが、原油価格の高騰を演出してきた。◆Leading British mobile phone operator Vodafone is to sell its holdings in Japan Telecom Co. to Ripplewood Holdings, a U.S.-based investment fund, for about ¥260 billion. イギリスの携帯電話大手のボーダフォンが、日本テレコムの持ち株（日本テレコム株）を、米投資ファンドのリップルウッド・ホールディングスに約2,600億円で売却する方針を固めた。◆Myojo Foods asked Nissin Food Products to play the part of a white knight by forming a capital alliance to thwart the U.S. investment fund's hostile takeover bid. 米系投資ファンドの敵対的TOB（株式公開買付け）を阻止するため、明星食品は資本提携によるホワイト・ナイト（白馬の騎士）としての明星の支援を日清食品に要請した。◆The company decided to seek a helping hand from the investment fund. 同社は、この投資ファンドに支援を求めることにした。◆The draft of the government's new growth strategy includes the establishment of a public-private investment fund to support the content industry in its foreign endeavors. 政府の新成長戦略の原案には、コンテンツ（情報の内容）産業の海外展開を支援する官民出資のファンド設立も盛り込まれている。◆The presence of investment funds on the share register is generally unknown until their names are listed in annual securities reports. 株主名簿上の投資ファンドの存在は、一般にそのファンド名が年次有価証券報告書に記載されるまで分からない。◆The Securities and Exchange Law requires investment funds to register and report the names of their representatives and their locations. 証券取引法は、投資ファンドに対して、投資ファンドの代表者名や所在地などの登録・届け出を義務付けている。◆The U.S. tighter regulations on investment funds helped to change the trend in crude oil prices. 米国の投資ファンド規制強化で、原油価格の流れが変わった。◆With such moves to rein in investment funds, speculative money started to exit the markets. 投資ファンドを規制するこうした動きで、投機マネーが市場から逃避し始めた。

investment fund's investors　投資ファンドの出資者

◆The investment fund's investors and investments have yet to be determined. この投資ファンドの出資者と資産の運用内容[運用先]は、まだ不明だ。

investment grade　投資適格格付け, 投資適格（=investment-grade, investment-grade rating）
- a downgrade below investment grade　投機的格付けへの格下げ, 投資適格以下への格下げ
- a rating below investment grade　投資適格以下の格付け, 投機的格付け
- investment grade bond　投資適格債券, 投資適格債
- investment grade companies　投資適格企業, 投資適格格付けの企業
- investment grade countries　投資適格国
- investment grade credit　投資適格格付け, 投資適格格付けの融資対象
- investment grade quality　投資適格
- investment grade rate [ranks]　投資適格格格付け

◆A downgrade below investment grade by even one ratings agency could boost GM's borrowing costs and wreak havoc on the corporate bond market. 格付け会社が1社でも投資適格格付けより低く格付けを引き下げたら[格付け会社が1社でも投機的格付けに格下げしたら]、GMの資金調達コストが急増し、米国の社債[債券]市場にも大きな影響が出る恐れがある。◆A rating below investment grade makes it harder and more expensive to borrow money. 投資適格以下の格付けだと、資金の調達が難しくなるし、資金調達コストも高くつく。◆Moody's Investors Service cut Citigroup debt one notch to A3, its fourth-lowest investment grade. 米国の格付け会社ムーディーズ・インベスターズ・サービスは、米金融大手シティグループの債券格付けをA3（下から4番目の投資適格格付け）に1段階引き下げた。

investment-grade securities　投資適格債
◆The risk of corporate bonds is low if you stick to investment-grade securities. 投資適格債にあくまでも限定すれば、社債のリスクは低い。

investment in　～への投資, ～への出資, ～投資
- ask investment in the fund　ファンドへの出資を要請する[呼びかける]
- finance investment in the United States　米国内投資の資金を調達する
- investment in affiliated company [concern]　関係会社投資, 関連会社投資勘定
- investment in bonds　債券投資
- investment in common stock　普通株式投資, 普通株式, 投資勘定
- investment in fixed assets　固定資産投資
- investment in foreign countries　対外投資
- investment in foreign securities　外国証券投資
- investment in housing　住宅投資
- investment in information technology　IT（情報技術）投資
- investment in related companies　資本参加
- investment in securities　有価証券投資
- investments in associates　関連会社に対する投資, 関連会社投資
- make an investment in　～に投資する, ～に出資する

◆Japan's foreign assets include investment in companies, securities, loans and savings Japanese made abroad as well as the nation's foreign reserves. 日本の対外資産には日本人（日本の政府・企業・個人）が海外で行った企業や有価証券に対する投資、融資や貯蓄のほか、日本の外貨準備高などが含まれる。◆Mitsubishi UFJ Financial Group Inc. and Nomura Holdings Inc. announced investments in major U.S. securities firms. 三菱UFJフィナンシャル・グループと野村ホールディングスが、米証券大手への出資を発表した。

investment in home building　住宅建設投資

◆Investment in home building in the fourth quarter was slashed by 19.1 percent on an annualized basis. 第4四半期の住宅建設投資は、年率換算で19.1％減少した。

investment in home loans　住宅ローン投資
◆Mizuho's first-half profit fell 17 percent as credit costs increased and on losses related to investments in U.S. home loans to riskier borrowers. みずほの上半期利益は、与信コストの増加とリスクの高い融資先への米国の住宅ローン投資に関連する損失で、17％減少した。

investment in infrastructure　インフラ投資, インフラ投資額
◆Investment in infrastructure around the world is estimated to total $41 trillion by 2030. 世界のインフラ投資額は、2030年までに41兆ドルに達すると推定されている。◆The current high price of crude oil stems partly from the lack of investment in oil development for a long period. 現在の原油高の一因は、長期にわたる石油開発投資の不足だ。

investment in oil development　石油開発投資

investment in plant and equipment　設備投資（⇒excessive investment）
◆The yen's appreciation may dampen recovering investment in plant and equipment. 円高は、回復してきた設備投資に水を差しかねない。

investment income　投資利益, 投資収益, 投資所得, 投資収入, 資産所得
◆Investment income recorded a surplus of ￥2.62 trillion larger than the previous year. 投資収益は、前年より黒字が2兆6,200億円拡大した。

investment insurance services　投資保険事業
◆Nippon Export and Investment Insurance (NEXI) was established in 2001 to provide foreign trade and investment insurance services. 独立行政法人の日本貿易保険は、貿易保険事業と対外投資保険事業を提供するため、2001年に設立された。

investment into government bonds　国債への投資
◆Lending by private banks has not increased though their investments into government bonds and cash reserves are increasing. 民間銀行の国債への投資や手持ちの現金は増えているが、民間銀行の貸出は増えていない。

investment judgment　投資判断
◆The gain from stock options fluctuates depending on the option holder's investment judgment over the timing of purchase and changes of the stock price. ストック・オプション（自社株購入権）の利益は、購入時期と株価変動に対するオプション保有者（オプションの買い手）の判断[投資判断]によって上下する。

investment loss　投資損失
◆Olympus Corp. has admitted hiding past investment losses. オリンパスが、過去の投資損失隠しを認めた。◆The company hid investment losses and tried to cover them up with funds related to corporate acquisitions. 同社は、投資損失を隠ぺいし、企業買収関連資金でそのもみ消しを図った。◆The cover-up of investment losses by Olympus was discovered during an investigation by the company's third-party panel. オリンパスによる投資損失処理の偽装工作は、同社の第三者委員会の調査で判明した。◆Years of window-dressing by Olympus to hide investment losses represent nothing but a companywide breach of trust. 投資損失隠ぺいのためのオリンパスによる長年の粉飾決算は、会社ぐるみの背信行為にほかならない。

investment management　投資運用, 資産運用, 運用, 投資管理, 投資顧問
- investment management company　運用委託会社
- investment management division　投資管理部
- Investment Management Regulatory Organization　投資管理規制機関, IMRO
- investment management responsibility　資産運用の任務
- investment management services　資産運用業務

investment money 投資資金, 投資金, 出資金
◆Investment money from abroad is being withdrawn. 外国の投資マネーが、引き揚げられている。◆The partnerships used the investment money to buy ships, which were then leased to major shipping companies for 10 years. 同組合は、出資金で船舶を購入し、購入した船舶を大手船舶会社に10年間リースした。

investment money from abroad 外国の投資マネー
◆Investment money from abroad is being withdrawn. 外国の投資マネーが、引き揚げられている。

investment opportunity 投資機会, 投資チャンス, 投資対象, 運用先, 収益機会
look for better investment opportunities 高利回りの運用先を探す
offer [provide] an attractive investment opportunity 妙味ある投資機会[投資チャンス]を提供する
represent an investment opportunity 投資機会となる
◆Many bank depositors and individual investors are looking for better investment opportunities amid ultralow interest rates. 超低金利が続くなか、銀行預金者や個人投資家の多くは高利回りの運用先を探している。

investment outflow 投資支出額
◆Funds provided from net earnings, depreciation, and amortization were offset primarily by investment outflow and increased working capital requirements. 純利益と減価償却[減価償却および償却]で得た資金は、主に投資支出額と必要運転資本の増加額で相殺されました。

investment partnership 投資事業組合[ファンド]
◆The company abused investment partnership and reported profits from the selling of its shares as "sales" instead of "capital" in accounting books. 同社は、投資組合を悪用して、会計帳簿に自社株の売却益を(本来計上すべき)[資本]ではなく「売上」に計上していた。

investment performance 運用実績, 運用成績, 投資実績, 投資成績
◆The pension benefits of the defined-contribution plan hinge on investment performance. この確定拠出型年金制度の年金給付は、運用実績次第によって決まる。

investment period 投資期間
◆In wrap accounts, a customer sets the overall investment policy, including investment period and profit target. ラップ口座では、顧客が投資期間や運用益の目標などの大まかな運用方針を決める。

investment policy 投資方針, 投資政策, 運用方針, 基本運用方針
implement the investment policies 運用方針を実行[実践]する
investment policy decision 運用方針の決定
Investment Policy Governing Tax Qualified Pension Asset Management 適格年金資産運用基本方針
investment policy statement 投資方針記述書, 運用政策記述書
set the overall investment policy 大まかな運用方針を決める
◆In wrap accounts, a customer sets the overall investment policy, including investment period and profit target. ラップ口座では、顧客が投資期間や運用益の目標などの大まかな運用方針を決める。

investment portfolio 投資ポートフォリオ, 投資資産, 投資資本構成, 投資の内容, 資産運用ポートフォリオ, 投資目録, 投資リスト
◆As of December 31, 2010, the investment portfolio was predominantly long-term-bonds and equity investments. 2010年12月31日現在、投資ポートフォリオは主に長期債券と株式投資です。

investment product 投資商品
◆The exchange-traded funds (ETFs) are investment products similar to index mutual funds but that trade on stock exchanges like stocks. 上場投資信託(ETF)は、インデックス・ミューチュアル・ファンドに似ているが、株式と同じように証券取引所で売買される投資商品である。

investment profit 投資収益, 運用益
◆In wrap accounts, a customer sets the overall investment policy, including investment period and profit target. ラップ口座では、顧客が投資期間や運用益の目標などの大まかな運用方針を決める。

investment profitability 投資収益性
◆We will adhere to our proactive management policies that place the utmost emphasis on investment profitability. 当社は、今後も投資収益性を重視した攻めの経営姿勢を貫く方針です。

investment ratio 出資比率
◆These five companies are working on the investment ratios and formation of management of the new company. この5社は現在、新会社の出資比率や役員構成などの詰の作業を進めている。

investment return 投資収益, 投資利回り, 運用利回り, 運用収益, 投資リターン
◆Investors must generally take higher investment risks in order to achieve higher investment returns. 投資家が一段と高い投資収益を得るには、一般に一段と高い投資リスクを取る必要がある。

investment risk 投資リスク
(⇒investment return)
◆It is a matter of urgency to ensure that banks make profit margins that can meet investment risks and that they expand commission revenue as well as promote sweeping restructurings. 抜本的なリストラ推進のほか、投資リスクに見合う利ざやの確保と手数料収入の拡大などが銀行の急務だ。◆The benefit of fund-of-funds investment is that it allows investment risks to be minimized. 投資リスクを最小限に抑えるのが、ファンド・オブ・ファンズ投資の利点である。

investment scheme 投資形態, 投資ファンド, 投資計画, 投資システム
◆The firm is suspected to have illegally accumulated the vast sum from about 20,000 members of an investment scheme nationwide. 同社は、全国約2万人の投資会員から巨額の資金を無許可で[無登録で]集めていた疑いがある。◆The Japanese taxation system in recent years has found itself ill-equipped to deal with international investment schemes. 日本の近年の税制は、国際的な投資形態に対応できていない。

investment seminar 投資セミナー
◆Investment seminars targeting women are becoming increasingly popular. 女性対象の投資セミナーの人気が高まっている。

investment strategy 投資戦略, 運用戦略
◆The company is rolling out investment strategies that decrease volatility. 同社は、リスクを引き下げる運用戦略を展開している。

investment superpower 投資大国
◆Japan is shifting from being an export giant to an investment superpower. 日本は、輸出大国から投資大国に変わりつつある。

investment target 投資対象, 投資目標
◆As demand for electricity is expected to keep growing in the United States, the company sees the U.S. electric power industry as a promising investment target. 米国は電力需要の伸びが期待されることから、同社は米国の電力事業を有望な投資対象と見ている。

investment tax credits 投資減税, 投資税額控除
◆Heizo Takenaka, former state minister in charge of economic and fiscal policy, sought the introduction of investment tax credits to stimulate the economy. 竹中元経済財政

相は、景気を刺激するために投資減税の導入を求めた。
investment trust　投資信託, 投信（一般投資家から資金を集め、集めた金を専門家が株や債券などに投資して、その運用益を投資家に還元する金融商品）
 foreign bond open investment trust　外債投信
 investment management fund investment instructions　投資信託財産運用指図書
 investment trust assets　投資信託財産
 investment trust certificate　投資信託証券
 investment trust management company　投信委託会社
 investment trust securities　投資信託証券
 ◆Fund-of-funds do not invest capital directly in stocks and bonds, but reinvest it in other investment trusts as a way to minimize risks. ファンド・オブ・ファンズは、(投資家から集めた)資金を株式や債券に直接投資せず、リスクを最小限に抑える手段として他の複数の投資信託に再投資する。◆Investors seem to be shifting their money from investment trusts to more secured time deposits in the face of global financial turmoil. 世界の金融市場の混乱に直面して、投資家は資金を投資信託から安定性の高い定期預金に切り替えているようだ。◆With domestic stock prices in the doldrums, foreign bond open investment trusts that invest in bonds issued by foreign governments, international institutions and major corporations are gaining in popularity as an investment. 日本株の株価が低迷するなかで、資金の運用先として外国の国債や国際機関債、大手企業の社債に投資する外債投信に人気が集まっている。

investment trust fund　投資信託, 投資信託基金
（⇒fund manager）
 dividends from investment trust funds　投資信託の分配金
 over-the-counter sales of investment trust funds　投資信託の窓口販売
 ◆Against the backdrop of the liberalization of the financial industry, pension funds and investment trust funds grew sharply. 金融自由化を背景に、年金基金や投資信託基金が急成長した。◆Dividends from investment trust funds are taxed at a 20 percent rate, as is the case with interest accruing from deposits and savings. 投資信託の分配金には、預貯金の利子所得の場合と同じように、20％の税率がかかっている。◆Investment trust funds are popular among individual investors. 投資信託は、個人投資家に人気がある。◆The bank plans to start over-the-counter sales of investment trust funds. 同行は、投資信託の窓口販売を計画している。◆The brokerage's main services for individual customers will be asset management advisory services, focusing on the sale of products such as investment trust funds that invest in foreign equities, and money market funds denominated in foreign currencies. 同証券会社は、株式の主な個人顧客向け(売買仲介)業務として、外国株を組み込んだ投資信託や外貨建てMMF(マネー・マーケット・ファンド)などの商品の販売を中心に、資産運用顧問業務を展開する方針だ。

investment trust sales　投資信託の販売
 ◆The two companies agreed to tie up in asset management and investment trust sales. 両社は、資産運用と投資信託の販売面でも連携することで合意した。

investor　(名)投資家, 投資者, 投資会社, 出資者, 出資企業, 資本主, 投資側, 投資国, 権利などの授与者, インベスター　（⇒foreign investor, individual investor, institutional investor）
 accounting for investors　投資家のための会計
 accredited investor　適格投資家, 有資格投資家
 bloc investor　大口投資家
 bond investor　債券投資家
 bottom-line-oriented investor　（運用先の)最終損益を重視する投資家
 debt investor　債券投資家, 債券保有者
 defraud investors　投資家を欺く
 equity investor　株式投資家
 fixed income investor　債券投資家, 確定利付き証券への投資家
 foreign investors　外国人投資家, 海外投資家, 外資
 （=overseas investors）
 fuel investor unease　投資家の不安をあおる
 individual investor　個人投資家
 institutional investor　機関投資家
 （=institutional lender）
 international investor　国際投資家
 investor appetite　投資家需要, 投資家のニーズ
 （=investor demand）
 investor expectations　投資家の期待
 investor-marketing　投資家勧誘
 investors sentiment　投資家の意識
 long-term investor　長期投資家
 major investor　大手の投資家
 overseas investor　外国人投資家, 海外投資家, 外国人株主
 private investor　個人投資家, 民間投資家
 professional investor　機関投資家
 （=institutional investor, wholesale investor）
 retail investor　小口投資家, 個人投資家, 最終投資家
 （=small investor）
 risk-averse investor　リスク回避的な投資家
 risk-neutral investor　リスク中立型の投資家
 risk-seeking investor　リスク選好型の投資家
 short-term investor　短期投資家
 small investor　個人投資家, 小口投資家
 ultimate investor　最終投資家
 upper-level investor　上級出資者
 wholesale investor　機関投資家
 yield-hungry investor　利回り志向の投資家
 （=total return investor）
 ◆By the TSE's extension of the morning trade session to 11:30 a.m., investors will be able to trade Japanese stocks more easily while keeping an eye on economic trends in Asian markets. 東証が午前11時30分まで午前の取引時間を延長したことによって、投資家は今後、アジア市場の経済動向を見ながら日本株の取引をすることが容易になる。◆Corporate leaders must recognize that defrauding investors is a serious crime. 投資家を欺く行為は重大な犯罪である、ということを企業経営者は認識しなければならない。◆Domestic and overseas investors are rushing to the market. 内外の投資家が、相場にあわただしく参入している。◆Foreign investors stepped up their purchase of Japanese stocks. 外国人投資家の日本株買いが活発化した。◆In L&G K.K.'s pyramid scheme, dozens of upper-level investors were deeply involved in the company's business operation under the instruction of the firm's chairman. L&Gのマルチ商法では、幹部会員[上級出資者]数十人が、同社会長の指示に従って同社の業務運営に深く関与していた。◆Investors are losing confidence in monetary management. 通貨調節への投資家の信認は、失われている。◆Investors are swayed by price fluctuations. 投資家は、株価変動に左右される。◆Investors around the world are selling stocks with abandon as a global recession is under way. 世界的な景気後退の進行で、世界中の投資家が株を売りまくっている。◆Investors have begun switching their funds from bank deposits to assets that entail some risks. 投資家が、銀行預金からリスクを伴う資産へと資金の運用を切り替え始めている。◆Investors purchased more overseas bonds and stocks to seek higher returns. 投資家は、高利益を求めて外国の債券や株式への投資が拡大した。◆Investors seem to be shifting their money from investment trusts to more secured time deposits in the face of global financial turmoil. 世界の金融市場の混乱

に直面して、投資家は資金を投資信託から安定性の高い定期預金に切り替えているようだ。◆Investors sold shares across the board to lock in profits. 利益を確定するため、投資家が全銘柄にわたって株を売り進めた。◆Investors who purchased the leasing rights became members in four voluntary partnerships. 持ち分権（リース権）を購入した出資者は、四つの任意組合のメンバーになった。◆It is vital to improve the secondary market circulating such asset-backed securities for investors. 投資家向けに、このような資産担保証券の流通市場の整備も不可欠である。◆Loss hiding scandal-tainted Olympus Corp was sued by an investor in its American depositary receipts seeking class-action status. 損失隠しの疑惑をもたれたオリンパスが、同社の米国預託証券（ADR）を保有している投資家に、集団訴訟を求めて訴えられた。◆More investors are pulling money from stock markets and shifting it into safer time deposits. 株式市場から資金を引き揚げ、引き揚げた資金を安定性の高い定期性預金に移し替える投資家が増えている。◆Overseas investors are considered highly volatile to changes in the share price. 外国人株主は、株価動向にかなり左右されやすいとされている。◆Short selling is the practice of borrowing stocks from securities and financial companies and other investors to sell them and then buy them back when their prices drop. 空売りは、証券金融会社や他の投資家（機関投資家など）から株を借りて売り、その株が値下がりした時点で買い戻すことをいう。◆The aim of the investors was to avoid income tax. 投資家［出資者］の目的は、所得税の節税効果だった。◆The firm received a lot of attention from investors as an emerging company. 同社は、新興のベンチャー企業として投資家から大いに注目された。◆The main investors in eBank are Yahoo Japan, telecommunications giant Japan Telecom Co., and trading house Itochu Corp. イーバンク銀行には、ヤフーや通信大手の日本テレコム、商社の伊藤忠商事などが出資している。◆The moves by Citigroup Inc. and General Electric Co. both unsettled investors. 米金融大手シティグループとGEの今回の動きで、投資家は動揺した。◆The number of institutional and foreign individual investors has increased. 機関投資家や海外の個人投資家（外国人投資家）が増えている。◆The two exchanges also aim to lure funds from investors both at home and abroad by the merger. 経営統合によって、両株式取引所は国内外の投資資金を呼び込む狙いもある。◆The 225-issue Nikkei Stock Average dived below the key threshold of 10,000 as investors were disappointed with the continuing delay in the disposal of banks' bad loans and an overnight plunge in U.S. stocks. 日経平均株価（225種）は、投資家が銀行等の不良債権処理が引き続き遅れることや前日の米株価の大幅下落に失望して、1万円の大台を割り込んだ。◆The U.S. government could avoid the worst-case scenario of default on payments to investors in Treasury bonds. 米政府は、国債の償還資金がなくなる債務不履行という最悪の事態を避けることができた。

investor confidence 投資家の信頼
◆The failure of WorldCom resulted in a loss of investor confidence in the corporate governance of U.S. companies. ワールドコム（米国の大手通信会社で現MCI）の経営破綻は、米企業のコーポレート・ガバナンス（企業統治）に対する投資家の信頼を損ねた。

investor relations 投資家向け広報、投資家向け広報活動、投資家向け情報公開、財務広報、証券広報、戦略的財務広報、対投資家関係、IR活動、インベスター・リレーションズ、IR （⇒IR）
[解説] Investor Relations (IR)とは：株主や投資家に対して投資判断に必要な情報を提供することがインベスター・リレーションズで、一般にIR（アイアール）と呼ばれている。全米IR協会（NIRI）の定義では、IRは「企業の財務機能とコミュニケーション機能を結合して行われる戦略的・全社的なマーケティング活動で、投資家に対して企業の業績と将来性に関して正確な姿を提供するもの

である（同友館発行『戦略的IR』参照）。各企業が実践しているIR活動のツールとしては、アニュアル・レポート（年次報告書）や事業報告書、ファクト・ブック、ニューズレターなどの出版物のほかに、インフォメーション・ミーティング（証券アナリストやファンド・マネージャーなどに対して経営方針や経営理念、業務内容などを定期的に紹介する企業説明会）、決算説明会に加えて、個別訪問（機関投資家や証券会社に出向いて直接会社の業務内容などを説明）などがある。会社や工場見学などを、IR活動の一つにしているところもある。また、ここ数年前からの傾向として注目されるのは、インターネットのホームページ上での情報開示である。このホームページには、一般に会社概要や事業内容、商品情報、採用情報などが掲載されている。そのメリットとしては、情報伝達の即時性、適時性のほかに個人投資家や潜在投資家を含めてすべての投資家に公正に情報を提供できることや、印刷物や郵便物より安価に情報を発信できること、ウェブ・サイト上でアンケート調査もできること、メールを併用すると投資家の質問や意見を得やすいことなどが挙げられている。

investor securities 投資家の有価証券
◆A former president of a securities company removed investor securities worth about ￥3.2 billion from a safe at the company's Tokyo branch, and went missing. 証券会社の元社長は、投資家の有価証券（顧客から預かっていた有価証券）約32億円分を同社東京支店の金庫から持ち出し、行方不明になっていた。

investor [investors] sentiment 投資マインド、投資家心理、投資家の意識
◆A rash of scandals involving such corporate giants as Tokyo Electric Power Co., Mitsui & Co. and Nippon Meat Packers, Inc. are believed to have chilled investor sentiment. 東京電力や三井物産、日本ハムなど業界トップ企業の相次ぐ不祥事が、投資家心理を冷やしていると見られる。

invite （動）招待する、招く、依頼する、要請する
◆Excessive intervention in management by a large shareholder may invite self-isolation of listed firms. 大株主の過剰な経営介入は、上場企業の引きこもりを招きかねない。

invoice （名）送り状、仕入書、請求書、積み荷明細書、インボイス
  commercial invoice 商業送り状、商業インボイス（輸出者が輸入者にあてて作成する積み荷の明細書で、請求書と納品書の性格を持つ。輸出入通関手続きの際、申告書類の一部として税関に提出される）
  customer invoice 顧客［得意先］への請求書
  customs invoice 税関送り状（輸出者が輸入地の税関用に作成し、税関が輸入貨物に対する課税価格を決定する際の資料となる）
  invoice discounting 債権の売却
  invoice price 送り状価格、仕切り状価格、仕切り価格、インボイス価格、請求書価格、直接原価、本体価格、先物契約などの決済価格
  invoice quantity 送り状数量
  invoice value 送り状金額、送り状価格［価額］
  last invoice cost method 最終取得原価法
  official invoice 公用送り状（税関送り状と領事送り状を指し、輸入通関のとき課税価格の決定やダンピング防止などのために使用される）
  paid invoice 支払済み請求書
  proforma [pro forma] invoice 見積り送り状、仮送り状、試算用送り状
  purchase invoice 仕入請求書
  sales invoice 売買送り状、売買送り状（積み荷の明細書で、計算書・請求書の性格をもつ。一般に「送り状（commercial invoice）」というときは、この売買送り状を指す）

shipping invoice　船積みインボイス（契約商品の船積み後に輸出者が作成する商業送り状）
invoice amount　送り状価格, 請求金額
◆We drew a draft for the invoice amount. 送り状金額に対して、当社は手形を振り出した。
invoice value　送り状金額
◆All shipments shall be covered for 110% of invoice value. 積み荷には、すべて送り状金額の10％増し［110％］で保険を付けるものとする。
invoke　（動）（助け、保護などを）求める,（力や法に）訴える, 実施する, 発動する, 行使する, 〜を連想させる
invoke a poison pill scheme　ポイズン・ピル防衛策を実施する
invoke the payoff system [limited deposit protection system]　ペイオフ制度を発動する, ペイオフを発動する　（⇒Deposit Insurance Corporation of Japan）
◆Invoking the payoff system is unlikely to affect Japan's financial system. ペイオフを発動しても、日本の金融システムに影響を与えることはなさそうだ。◆Nireco Corp. has scrapped its plan to invoke the nation's first poison pill scheme to ward off hostile takeover bids. ニレコは、敵対的TOB（株式公開買付けによる企業買収）を防ぐための日本で最初のポイズン・ピル防衛策の実施計画を白紙撤回した。
involve　（動）参加させる, 参入させる, 関与させる, 関わらせる, 巻き込む, 巻き添えにする, 含む, 包含する, 包む, 伴う, 必要とする, 意味する, もたらす, 熱中させる, 夢中にさせる, 没頭させる, 〜に影響を与える, 〜に関わる, 難局に追い込む, 困難な立場に立たせる
be involved in　〜に参加する, 〜に参入する, 〜を行う, 〜を手がける, 〜に関与する, 〜に関わる, 〜に巻き込まれる, 〜に依存している, 〜に協力する, 〜に夢中になる, 〜に熱中している
be involved with　〜に関連している, 〜に関わる, 〜と絡（から）み合っている
◆A real estate investment fund was alleged to have failed to report about ¥18 billion in income from transaction involving land and property taken as collateral for nonperforming loans. 不動産投資ファンドが、不良債権の担保に取った不動産関連の取引で得た所得約180億円の申告漏れを指摘されていた。◆Every member of the nation will now be forced to face the risks involved in the management of their own assets. これからは、国民一人ひとりが資産運用リスクに正面から向き合わざるを得なくなる。◆Former president of the bank was deeply involved in the nation's financial administration as an advisor to the Financial Services Agency. 同行の前社長は、金融庁の顧問として、国の金融行政に深くかかわった。◆In the aftermath of the 1995 Great Hanshin Earthquake and the 2007 Niigata Prefecture Chuetsu Offshore Earthquake, a series of fraud cases involving donations occurred. 1995年の阪神大震災や2007年の新潟県中越沖地震の直後には、義援金詐欺事件が相次いで起きた。◆JAL's reconstruction will have to involve decreasing the amount of its debts. 日本航空の再建には、負債の圧縮［減額］が不可避だ。◆TEPCO is also involved in real estate and hotel management in addition to facilities and land used for its power-generating business. 東京電力は、発電事業に使用している施設や土地以外に、不動産事業やホテル運営も手掛けている。◆The U.S. government froze the assets of four individuals and eight entities that were involved in illicit activities such as money laundering, currency counterfeiting and narcotics trafficking. 米政府は、資金洗浄（マネー・ロンダリング）や通貨偽造、麻薬取引などの違法行為に関与している4個人、8団体の資産を凍結した。◆This ex-vice president is believed to have been deeply involved in creating a slush fund. この元副社長は、同社の裏金づくりに深く関与していたとされる。
involvement　（名）参加, 参入, 関与, 関わり, 関わり合い, 掛かり合い, 介入, 財政困難, 包含

direct involvement　直接関与
involvement in management　経営への関与
involvement in the scandal　不祥事への関与
market involvement　市場への参入, 市場参入の度合い
◆By increasing its involvement in TEPCO's management, the government aims to fend off credit uneasiness in the utility. 東電への経営関与を強めることにより、国は東電の信用不安を防止しようとしている。
IO　利子部分, アイ・オー（interest onlyの略。債券投資から生まれるキャッシュ・フローの利子部分）
IOSCO [Iosco]　証券監督者国際機構, イオスコ（International Organization of Securities Commissionsの略）
IOU [I.O.U., i.o.u.]　借用証書, 借入証書（I owe youの略）
government IOUs　政府の借用証書, 国債
◆Government bonds are government IOUs. 国債は、政府の借用証書である。
IPO　株式公開, 新規株式公開, 新規株式公募, 公開公募, 新規公募, 上場　（initial public offeringの略。会社が一般投資家に株式を初めて売り出すこと。⇒earnings forecast, initial public offering, opening price）
◆An increasing number of companies want to undertake IPOs while stock markets remain brisk. 株式市場が活況のうちに上場したい［株式を新規公開したい］、という企業が増えている。◆Compared with the 121 IPOs in 2003, the number of such offerings this year on the Tokyo Stock Exchange, four other regional stock exchanges and the Jasdaq market for start-up firms is expected to be much higher. 東京証券取引所など全国5か所の取引所と新興企業向け市場「ジャスダック」に上場する［株式を新規公開する］企業数は、2003年の121社に対して、今年はそれをはるかに上回る見通しだ。◆GM's IPO could come as early as October 2010. GMの新規株式公開は、早ければ2010年10月になる可能性がある。◆The higher the level of stock prices, the more funds firms can raise from IPOs. 株価の水準が上がれば、それだけ新規株式公開（上場時の新株発行）による資金調達額も増える。
IPO business　株式公開業務
IPO deal　IPO取引, IPO案件
◆The firm received an IPO deal in writing. 同社は、書面でIPO取引（新規株式発行の引受業務）のマンデートを受けた［書面でIPO取引を委任された］。
IPO paperwork　新規株式公開の書類, 株式の新規公開の書類
◆General Motors filed an IPO paperwork with the U.S. Securities and Exchange Commission. （米政府の管理下で経営再建中の）ゼネラル・モーターズ（GM）は、株式の新規公開（IPO）書類を米証券取引委員会に提出した。
IPO price　公開価格, 公募価格
◆Shares in kabu.com first traded at ¥655,000, up 82 percent from its IPO price of ¥360,000. カブドットコム証券株は、公募価格の36万円を82％上回る65万5,000円の初値を付けた。
IPO shares　新規公開株
◆Salomon Smith Barney allocated IPO shares to former top WorldCom Inc. executives. ソロモン・スミス・バーニー（米金融大手シティグループの証券部門）が、経営破たんした米長距離通信大手のワールドコムの元最高経営者らに（値上がりが確実とされた）新規公開株を配分していた。
IPO stocks' trading　新規株式公開（IPO）銘柄の取引
◆The closing price on the first day of these IPO stocks' trading has exceeded their opening price. これらの新規株式公開（IPO）銘柄の取引初日の終値［これらIPO銘柄の上場時の初値（終値）］は、公開価格を上回った。
IR　投資家向け広報, 投資家向け広報活動, 財務広報, インベスター・リレーションズ

(investor relationsの略。⇒investor relations)
IR operations　IR業務, IR部門
IR representative　IR担当者
[解説]IRとは：株主や投資家に対して投資判断に必要な情報を提供すること。有価証券報告書や決算短信だけでなく、決算説明会や工場見学会などの自主的な開示も含む。最近はインターネットを利用した活動が盛ん。

IR activities　IR活動
◆We conducted a variety of IR activities in Japan 163 times during the ten-month period starting in April. 日本国内では、当社は4月から10か月間に163件の各種IR活動を展開しました。

IR campaign　IRキャンペーン, IR活動, 投資家説明会
◆To promote the sales of Japanese government bonds, the Finance Ministry will launch its first overseas investor relation (IR) campaign in London and New York. 日本の国債の販売を促進するため、財務省はロンドンとニューヨークで同省初のIRキャンペーンを展開する[同省初の投資家説明会を開く]。

IR meeting　投資家説明会, IR説明会, 会社説明会, IRミーティング
◆To enhance the transparency of our financial affairs, and to procure funds from global sources, we held three IR meetings overseas last year. 財務内容の透明性を高めるため、またグローバルな資金調達を行うため、昨年度は海外で3回IR説明会を開きました。

IR session　投資家説明会, IRセッション
(⇒brief)
◆More than 200 institutional investors from financial institutions are expected to attend the IR sessions. この投資家説明会には、金融機関などの機関投資家が200人以上参加する。

IRC　産業再生機構　(=Industrial Revitalization Corporation of Japan:Industrial Revitalization Corporationの略。⇒Industrial Revitalization Corporation)
◆The company will increase its capital by ¥50 billion with additional investment of ¥10 billion from the IRC and with the debt-for-equity swap. 同社は、産業再生機構による100億円の追加[新規]出資と債務の株式化で、500億円増資する。

ironclad finances　鉄壁の財政
IRR　金利リスク(interest rate risk), 内部収益率(internal rate of return)

irrecoverable　(形)回収不能の, 回収できない, 焦げ付いている, 取戻し不能の
irrecoverable cost　回収不能原価
(=irrelevant cost, sunk cost)
irrecoverable debt　回収不能貸金
irrecoverable loan　焦げ付き債権
◆About ¥5.5 billion of the total loans proved irrecoverable. この融資総額のうち約55億円が焦げ付いていることが、判明した。

irredeemable　(形)買戻しのできない, 償還されない, 兌換(だかん)できない, 不換の
irredeemable bank note　不換紙幣
irredeemable bond [stock]　無償還公債, 不償還債
irredeemable debenture　償還不能社債, 無償還社債
irredeemable money　不換通貨
irredeemable share [stock]　無償還株
(=annuity bond, perpetual bond)

irregular　(形)不正規の, 不定期の, 不規則な, 変則な, 破格の, 不正な, 不法の, 乱れた, 不道徳な, 無効の
irregular accounting practices　不正経理業務
irregular deposit　不定期預金
irregular economy　変則経済, 正規外経済
irregular endorsement [indorsement]　変則裏書き, 不規則裏書き
irregular fluctuation　不規則変動

irregular gain and loss　比経常損益
irregular install payment　不均等払い
irregular market　変調市況, 跛行(はこう)相場
irregular practices　不正行為

irregularity　(名)不正行為, 不法行為, 乱脈経営, 乱脈融資, 不祥事, 不品行, 不規則性, 変則, 誤記
accounting irregularities　不正経理
irregularities such as influence-wielding, bid-rigging and subcontracting entire public works contracts　口利きや談合、公共事業の丸投げなどの不正行為
trading irregularities　不正取引
◆Accounting irregularities have been found at 17 labor bureaus of the Health, Labor and Welfare Ministry. 厚生労働省の17の労働局で、不正経理が行われていたことが分かった。◆The bank is suspected to have covered up a series of irregularities. 同行は、一連の不正行為の隠ぺい工作をしていた疑いがある。◆The FSA's guideline for supervising financial conglomerates is aimed at urging operators of financial conglomerates to reinforce their corporate governance to prevent irregularities. 金融庁の金融コングロマリット(複合体)監督指針の狙いは、不正防止に向けて、金融コングロマリットの経営者に経営監視の強化を促すことにある。

irrevocable　(形)取消し不能の, 撤回不能の, 回収不能の, 回収できない, 焦げ付いている
irrevocable and unconditional guarantee　取消し不能の無条件保証
irrevocable assignment　確定譲渡変調市況
irrevocable documentary acceptance credit　取消し不能荷為替引受信用状
irrevocable L/C [letter of credit]　取消し不能信用状
(=irrevocable credit)
irrevocable power of attorney　(債券や株券の)確定委任状
irrevocable power of proxy　確定取引
irrevocable proxy　撤回不能委任状
irrevocable revolving commitment　取消し不能回転契約
irrevocable revolving credit agreement　取消し不能回転信用契約
irrevocable trust　撤回不能信託, 取消し不能信託
uncollateralized irrevocable L/C　担保が付かない取消し不能信用状
◆About ¥110 billion was irrecoverable, making it necessary for that portion to be covered by taxpayers' money. 約1,100億円が焦げついたため、この分を国民負担としなければならなかった[この分を公的資金で補填する必要があった]。

irrevocable loan　不良債権, 焦げ付き債権
◆The company booked as a loss the total face value of the irrevocable loans. 同社は、不良債権の額面総額を、損金として計上した。

irrigation investment　灌漑(かんがい)投資

Islamic　(形)イスラムの, イスラム教の, イスラム教徒の, ムスリムの
Islamic bank　イスラム銀行
Islamic banking　イスラム銀行, イスラム銀行業務(高利を禁止するイスラム教原理に基づく銀行業務), イスラム金融
Islamic bonds　イスラム債　(⇒sukuk)
Islamic Development Bank　イスラム開発銀行, IDB
Islamic finance　イスラム金融(産油国で誕生した独自の金融システムで、シャリーアと呼ばれるイスラム法に従う。イスラム教徒は利子の取引や豚肉、カジノ、アルコール飲料などへの投資を禁じられているため、イスラム金融商品はシャリーアの規則に適合した物に限られる)

ISM 米供給管理協会（Institute for Supply Managementの略。2001年5月に、National Association of Purchasing Management（NAPM）が名称を変更した）
◆The ISM's index of service sector activity dropped below 50, a level that indicates contraction. 全米供給管理協会（ISM）のサービス業景況感指数は、50を割り込んで不況［景気後退期］を示す水準となった。

ISM index ISM指数, ISM景気指数, ISMの景況感指数

issuance （名）発行, 支給, 配給, 発表, 発布, 公布 （⇒borrow from Peter to pay Paul, interest burden, national bond, yuan-based bond）
additional issuance of government bonds　国債の追加発行, 国債増発
CP issuance　CP発行
debt issuance　社債発行, 債券発行
deficit issuance　赤字国債
issuance of capital　株式の発行
issuance of refunding bonds　借換え債の発行
new bond issuance　起債
new issuance　新規発行
◆During 2011, conversions of convertible debentures resulted in the issuance of 968 shares of the Corporation's capital stock. 2011年度は、転換社債の転換により、968株の当社株式が発行された。◆The 8% convertible bonds are convertible into 40 shares of common stock for each $1,000 bond, and were not considered common stock equivalents at the date of issuance. 8％利付き転換社債は、1,000ドルの社債についてそれぞれ普通株式40株に転換できるが、発行時には準普通株式とは考えられなかった。◆The European Central Bank promptly decided to buy Italian and Spanish government bonds in tandem with the issuance of the G-7 emergency statement. 欧州中央銀行（ECB）は、G7緊急声明の発表と連動する形で、イタリアとスペインの国債を買い入れる方針を決めた。◆The government bond issuance worth about ¥44 trillion for the current fiscal year is the largest ever projected in an initial budget. 今年度の約44兆円の国債発行額は、当初予算としては史上最高だ。

issuance of bridging bonds　つなぎ国債の発行
◆Unless consumption tax rate is raised, the planned issuance of bridging bonds could lead to further deterioration of the debt-saddled government finances. 消費税率を引き上げないと、予定しているつなぎ国債の発行は、借金を背負っている国の財政の悪化をさらに招く可能性がある。

issuance of deficit-covering bonds　赤字国債の発行
◆The government decided to issue restoration bonds, avoiding the issuance of deficit-covering bonds. 政府は、赤字国債の発行を避けて、復興再生債を発行する方針を固めた。

issuance of government bonds　国債発行, 国債発行額 （=government bond issuance; ⇒interest burden）
◆In the case of Japan, the issuance of government bonds exceeds tax revenue. 日本の場合、国債発行額が税収を上回っている。◆Japan is in dire fiscal straits as the issuance of government bonds are more than tax revenue. 国債発行額が税収を上回っているため、日本は非常事態の財政下にある［財政ひっ迫の状況にある］。◆The issuance of government bonds amounts to ¥44 trillion in the fiscal 2011 budget though tax revenues are ¥41 trillion. 2011年度予算では、41兆円の税収に対して国債の発行額は44兆円にのぼる。◆The issuance of Japanese government bonds will continue to increase. 日本の国債の発行は、今後も増え続ける。

issuance of long-term debt instruments　長期債務証券の発行
◆One way for a company to accomplish long-term financing is through the issuance of long-term debt instruments in the form of bonds. 会社の長期資金調達方法の一つは、社債の形で長期債務証券を発行して行われる。

issuance of new shares　新株発行, 増資 （⇒capital efficiency, financial support, new share issue）
◆Financial support is the prerequisite for the two firms' funding of the issuance of new shares. 金融支援は、両社の増資引受けの前提条件となっている。◆Zenno and Itochu Corp. already have agreed to fund the issuance of new shares of Snow Brand Milk stock to boost the company's capital base. 全農（全国農業協同組合連合会）と伊藤忠は、雪印乳業の資本基盤を強化するため、同社の新株発行（増資）を引き受けることですでに合意している。

issue （動）証券などを発行する, 売り出す, 起債する, 手形を振り出す, 配当を行う, 発表する, 公表する
average policy size issued　平均発行保険金
average premium issued　平均発行保険料
be issued at face amount　額面で発行される
be issued on a discount basis　割引発行される
be issued to shareholders［stockholders］　株主に発行される
debt issued with stock purchase warrant　新株引受権付き社債
if, as and when issued　発行日取引
issue a five percent stock dividend　5％の株式配当を行う
issue a fixed income bond　固定利付き債券を発行する
issue a margin call　追証を請求する
issue a stock dividend to shareholders of record on　～日現在の株主名簿上の株主に対して株式配当を行う
issue commercial paper　コマーシャル・ペーパー（CP）を発行する
issue common shares［stocks］　普通株式を発行する
issue earnings reports quarterly　四半期ごとに業績報告書を発表する
issue floating rate debt　変動利付き債を発行する
issue in the one and five year range　1～5年の償還期限で発行する
issue mortgage on some of one's property　資産の一部を担保に資金を借り入れる
issue reconstruction bonds　復興債［復興再生債］を発行する （⇒reconstruction bonds）
issue the policy　元受証券を発行する
◆A huge number of government bonds issued by the United States and European countries are possessed by financial institutions around the world. 米国や欧州各国が発行した大量の国債は、世界の金融機関が保有している。◆Bond insurers write policies that promise to cover payments to bondholders if the entity that issued the bonds defaults. 金融保証会社［債券保険会社］は、債券発行体がデフォルト（債務不履行）になった場合に、債券保有者への（元本と利息の）支払い補償を約束する保険を引き受けている。◆Fuji TV issued the moving strike convertible bonds（MSCBs）early this year for subscription by Daiwa Securities SMBC Co. to raise ¥80 billion for its NBS takeover bid. フジテレビは今春、ニッポン放送株の公開買付け（TOB）資金800億円を調達するため、大和証券SMBCを引受先として転換社債型新株予約権付き社債（MSCB）を発行した。◆Funds for disaster reconstruction will be procured by issuing special government bonds. 震災復興の資金は、復興債を発行して調達する。◆Higher debt maturing within one year chiefly reflects commercial paper we issued to support financial services. 1年以内返済予定の負債の増加は、主に金融サービス部門の支援のため、当社がコマーシャル・ペーパーを発行したことを反映しています。◆In Canada, the Corporation issued $300 million of 9% Series 7 Notes, due 2012. カナダで当社は、満期2012年・利率9％のシリーズ7ノート3億ドルを発行しました。◆S&P may cut the credit rating of bonds issued by the European Financial Stability Facility（EFSF）. スタンダード・アンド・プアーズ

（S&P）は、欧州金融安定基金（EFSF）が発行する債券の格付け［信用格付け］を引き下げる可能性がある。◆The bank does not issue conventional bankbooks for cardholders, but offers electronic bank books that are used via the Internet and accessed through personal computer and cell phones. 同行は、カード会員に従来の銀行通帳は発行せず、パソコンや携帯電話でアクセスしてインターネット上で使用する電子通帳［ウェブ通帳］を提供している。◆The company is to issue ￥220 billion in preferred stocks and ￥10 billion in common stocks. 同社は、優先株を2,200億円、普通株を100億円発行する。◆The Federal Housing Finance Agency oversees Fannie and Freddie that buy mortgage loans and mortgage securities issued by the lenders. 米連邦住宅金融局（FHFA）は、これらの金融機関が発行する住宅ローンやモーゲージ証券を購入する［買い取る］連邦住宅抵当金庫（ファニー・メイ）や連邦住宅貸付け抵当公社（フレディ・マック）を監督している。◆The firm intentionally issued false financial statements about the ratio of major shareholders' stakes. 同社は、大株主の持ち株比率について意図的に虚偽記載した有価証券報告書（財務書類）を公表した。◆The firm will issue 20.5 million common shares at a price of ￥222 per share. 同社は、1株当たり222円で［222円の価格で］普通株式2,050万株を発行する。◆The G-7 meeting has repeatedly issued communiques concerning exchange rate fluctuations and economic policy management. 先進7か国会議（G7）は、これまで為替変動や経済政策運営に関する声明を再三、発信してきた。◆The government decided to issue restoration bonds. 政府は、復興再生債の発行を決めた。◆Under the revival plan, the firm intends to issue ￥30 billion worth of preferred shares to the bank. この再生計画では、同社は同行を引受先として300億円の優先株式を発行する方針だ。

issue（名）証券, 株, 銘柄, 発行, 発行債, 発行部数, 交付, 手形の振出し, 問題, 問題点, 争点, 論点 （⇒bank issues, bond issue, broking, hot issue, mainstay issues, new share issue, share issue, subordinated debenture, TOPIX）
amount of bond issues　債券発行量, 国債発行量
amount of public bond issues　公債発行額
asset issue　資産株
authorized issues　授権発行数
bank note issue　銀行券発行
banks and electronics issues　銀行株や電機株
bond issue　社債発行, 債券発行, 公債発行 （=debenture issue）
bonus issue　無償増資, 無償新株, 株式の無償交付, 特別配当株
capital issue　新株発行, 株式発行, 資本発行
capitalization issue　資本金組入れ発行, 資本組入れ株式発行
convertible debenture issue　転換社債発行
corporate debt issues　社債, 社債発行, 社債発行額
corporate issue　事業債
date of issue　（手形の）振出日, 発行日
direct issue　直接発行
discount issue　割引発行
equity issue　出資証券
excess issue　超過発行
fiat issue　不換発行
fiduciary issue　信用発行, 保証発行
foreign issue　外国債
free issue　無償交付
government bond issue　国債発行
government guaranteed issue　政府保証債
inaugural issue　初回発行, デビュー発行 （=debut issue）
issue at face value　額面発行

issue at (the) market price　時価発行
issue bank　発券銀行, 紙幣発行銀行
issue bond at discount　割引発行
issue bought for short-term trade　ディーリング銘柄（短期売買で値上がり益を確保するために買われる銘柄）
issue by tender　入札発行 （=tender offer）
issue costs　発行費用
issue house　発行会社
issue limit　発行限度
issue market　発行市場
issue of bond at discount　債券割引発行, 割引発行
issue of bonds　社債発行
issue of right shares　新株引受権の付与
issue of the policy　保険証券の発行
issue par　発行価格, 売出価格
issues, redemption and amounts outstanding of　〜の発行・償還および残高, 〜の発行・償還および現存額, 〜の発行・償還および現在高
IT issues　IT関連銘柄, IT株 （=information technology issues, IT-related shares）
junior issue　下位証券
junk issue　ジャンク債
letters of credit of your issue　貴行発行の信用状
limited coinage issue　性原通貨発行
low-priced issues　割安な銘柄
make an issue of　〜を発行する
margin trading issues　信用取引銘柄
names of stock issues　個別銘柄
new issue　新規発行, 新規発行株式, 新規発行債, 新発債
new issue market　発行市場, 新株発行市場
new issue volume　起債総額
note issue　紙幣発行, 発券, 銀行券発行
off-the-run issue　周辺銘柄
on-the-run issue　指標銘柄
outstanding issue　既発債, 未済債券発行高, 未払い債券発行高
over issue　超過発行
par issue　額面発行
preferred stock issue　優先株式
premium issue　プレミアム発行, 特別配当株
prospectus issue　目論見書発行
public issue　公募, 公募債
public issue bond　公募債
rated issue　格付け債券
restricted issue of shares　株式の制限付き発行
rights issue　株主割当発行, 株主割当発行増資, 引受権発行
scrip issue　株式配当, 特別配当株
seasoned issues　既発銘柄, 安定証券, 確実証券
senior issue　上位証券
serial issue　連続番号
share and debenture issue expense　株式・社債発行費
share issue expense　新株発行費
stock issue　株式発行, 新株発行, 株式銘柄
stock issue cost　新株発行費
suspension of issue　発行停止
tender issue　英大蔵省証券発行
warrant issue　新株引受権証券発行, ワラント債発行
◆Corporate debt issues are recovering as bond market turbulence in the aftermath of the March 11 Great East Japan Earthquake has subsided. 2011年3月11日の東日本大震災直後の債券市場の混乱が収束したため、社債の発行額が回復し

ている。◆I invested a total of ￥1.5 million in five issues and I'm profiting. 5銘柄に150万円投資して、今のところ黒字だ。◆Individual investors and brokerage dealers continued to take profits from recent surges in comparatively low-prices issues. 個人投資家と証券会社のディーラーは、最近の比較的割安な銘柄の急上昇で引き続き利食いに出た。◆The articles of incorporation authorize the Directors to issue such shares in one or more series and to fix the number of shares of each series prior to their issue. 定款では、これらの株式をシリーズで1回以上発行する権限と、その発行前に各シリーズの発行株式数を決定する権限は、取締役会に与えられています。◆The government will provide funds and extend loans to TEPCO through a newly established organization to handle the compensation issue due to the nuclear disaster. 今後は、原発事故による損害賠償問題を扱うために新設された組織（原子力損害賠償支援機構）を通じて、国が東電に出資したり融資したりする。◆The issue will list on the TSE. 株式は、東証に上場される。◆The primary balance represents the budget balance, excluding proceeds from government bond issues and debt-servicing costs. プライマリー・バランスは、国債発行による収入と国債費（国債の利払いや償還費用）を除いた財政支出である。◆The 225-issue Nikkei Stock Average on Monday plunged 202.32 points from Friday's close on the Tokyo Stock Exchange. 東京株式市場の月曜日の日経平均株価（225種）は、前週末比で202円32銭下落した。◆Transactions on all of the 2,520 issues traded at the TSE were stalled from 9 a.m. due to a computer malfunction. 東証で取引されている2,520全銘柄の取引が、コンピュータのシステム障害で午前9時から停止した。

issue a bond 債権を発行する
◆Companies with good credit ratings and those that had not issued bonds began to issue bonds. 優良格付けの企業やこれまで債券を発行していなかった企業が、債券を発行するようになった。

issue a new bond 新型国債を発行する, 国債を増発する
◆If a new federal debt ceiling isn't set by Aug. 2, 2011, the United States will be forced to default on Treasuries securities as it will not be able to issue new bonds to pay back maturing government debts. 2011年8月2日までに連邦政府の債務上限を新たに設けないと、米国は満期を迎える国債を償還するための国債増発ができないので、米国債の不履行（デフォルト）が発生する。◆If the government adheres to its stance of capping the annual issuance of government bonds at ￥30 trillion, it should study issuing a new bond whose redemption sources are secured. 国債発行枠30兆円の姿勢にこだわるなら、償還財源の裏付けを持つ新型の国債発行を検討するべきだ。

issue at par 額面発行する, 額面[券面額]で発行する, 額面発行, パー発行 (=issue at face value)
◆These 100 million Swiss Francs of 5.125% Notes, Series 5, due 2016 were issued at par. この2016年満期・利率5.125のシリーズ5ノート1億5,000万スイス・フランは、額面で発行された。

issue corporate bonds 社債を発行する
◆Companies faced difficult in raising money by issuing corporate bonds in the aftermath of the financial crisis and resorted to borrowing money from banks. 世界の金融危機の影響で企業は、社債を発行して資金を調達するのが困難になったため、金融機関からの資金借入れに動いた。

issue false financial statements 虚偽記載の有価証券報告書を発行する
◆The firm's practice of issuing false financial statements about the holdings of major stockholders dates back to 1980 or earlier. 大株主の保有株式に関して虚偽記載の有価証券報告書を発行する同社の慣行は、1980年以前にさかのぼる。

issue government bonds 国債を発行する

◆The ￥44 trillion shortfall including tax revenue and non-tax revenue in spending in the fiscal 2010 budget must be made up for by issuing government bonds. 2010年度予算の歳出のうち、税収と税外収入を含めて44兆円の不足分は、国債発行で補填しなければならない。

issue new shares 新株を発行する, 増資する
◆Companies can resort to corporate defense schemes, including a poison pill plan to issue new shares, to fight hostile takeover bids. 敵対的買収への対抗策として、企業は新株発行（増資）のポイズン・ピル（毒薬）方式などの企業防衛策をとることができる。◆The government's new institution established to deal with the compensation payments would underwrite TEPCO's new shares to be issued in the form of preferred stock. 賠償金の支払い対応策として設立される国の新機構は、東電の増資を優先株の形で引き受けることになる。

issue of soaring public debts 増大する公的債務の問題
◆The issue of soaring public debts was pigeonholed at the G-7 talks. 増大する公的債務の問題は、G7（先進7か国財務相・銀行総裁会議）の協議では棚上げされてしまった。

issue preferred stock 優先株式を発行する, 優先株を発行する
◆The bank plans to issue preferred stock to procure about ￥1 trillion over the next few years to repay its debt to the government. 同行は、公的資金の返済に向けて、優先株を発行し、今後数年間で約1兆円を調達する計画だ。

issue share warrants 株式予約権を発行する, 株式引受権[新株予約権]を発行する
◆The purpose of issuing share warrants is to maintain the current management's control over the company. 株式予約権の発行は、現経営陣の会社の経営支配権を維持することを目的としている。

issue subscription warrants 新株予約権を発行する
◆The company's board approved a plan to issue subscription warrants to all shareholders on its shareholders list as of March 31, 2011. 同社の取締役会は、2011年3月31日現在［時点］の株主名簿に記載されている全株主を対象に、新株予約権を発行する計画を承認した。

issued （形）発行される, 発行された, 発行済みの
issued business　発行業務
issued capital　払込み資本金, 発行済み資本金, 発行済み株式資本金
issued capital stock　発行済み株式資本金, 発行株式
issued price　発行価格, 売出価格
issued share capital　発行済み株式資本
net equity issued　純株式発行額
newly issued bond　新発債
newly issued stock　新規発行株式
newly issued 10-year government bonds　新発10年物国債
previously issued bond　既発債
publicly issued bond　公募債
shares issued upon exercise of options　オプションの行使で発行される株式
shares issued upon exercise of warrants　ワラントの行使で発行される株式
stock issued to employees　従業員に発行した株式
total issued capital　発行済み資本
when issued　発行日取引, 発行日決済取引
（=when-issued trading）
◆On the bond market, the yield on newly issued 10-year government bonds, an indicator of long-term interest rates, fell, resulting in a rise in bond prices. 債券市場では、長期金利の指標である新発10年物国債の利回り（流通利回り）が下落し、債券相場［債券価格］は上昇した。◆The amount of refunding bonds issued to redeem ordinary government bonds

is expected to exceed ￥100 trillion. 普通国債償還のための借換え債の発行額が、100兆円を突破する見込みだ。

issued and outstanding 外部発行済み，発行済み，発行済み株式
◆The authorized capital stock of the Company consists of 5,000 shares of common stock of which 2,000 shares were issued and outstanding on the date of this agreement. 「本会社」の授権資本は普通株式5,000株から成り、このうち2,000株は本契約締結日現在、外部発行済みである。

issued outstanding government bonds 国債発行残高
◆By the end of next fiscal year, the value of issued outstanding government bonds will reach ￥538 trillion. 来年度（2005年度）末には、国債の発行残高は538兆円に達する。

issued shares [stocks] 発行済み株式，発行済み株式数，総発行株式（会社の授権株式（会社が発行できる株式の上限数）のうち、すでに発行された株式の総数）
◆Shareholders must send a report online to the FSA when their stake in a listed company exceeds 5 percent of issued shares. 上場企業に対する株式の保有比率が発行済み株式の5％を超えた場合、株主は金融庁にインターネットで報告書を提出しなければならない。

issuer （名）（株式などの）発行体（issuing corporation），発行者，発行会社，（手形などの）振出人
　bond issuer　債券発行体
　card issuer　カード会社
　corporate debt issuer　社債発行体，社債発行会社［企業］
　CP issuer　CP発行体
　credit risks of the issuer　発行体の信用リスク
　debt issuer　債券発行体，発行体
　　（=issuer of debt）
　debt load of the issuer　発行体の債務負担
　default prone issuer　債務不履行（デフォルト）を起こしやすい発行体，デフォルトの可能性が高い発行体
　defaulting issuer　デフォルト（債務不履行）を起こした発行体
　financial conditions of the issuer　発行体の財務状況
　first-time issuer　初めて格付けの対象となる発行体
　fixed-rate issuer　普通債の発行体
　foreign issuer　外国の発行体
　highly-leveraged issuer　負債比率が高い発行体
　industrial issuer　一般企業の発行体
　issuer management　発行体の経営陣
　issuer of uncertain credit risk　信用リスクの不確かな発行体
　issuer registration　発行者登録
　issuer's ability to meet commitments to debtholders　発行体の債務返済能力
　issuer's base rating　発行体の基礎格付け，発行体の基本格付け
　issuer's cost　発行者利回り
　issuer's debt load　発行体の債務負担
　issuer's deleveraging　発行体の負債比率低下，発行体の借入削減，発行体の負債削減
　issuer's exposure to the short-term markets　発行体の短期市場からの調達額
　issuer's financial data　発行体の財務データ
　issuer's financial statistics　発行体の財務数値
　issuer's most senior debt　発行体の最も優先順位が高い債券
　issuer's reimbursement fee　発行者手数料
　issuer's repayment ability　発行体の債務履行能力
　junk issuer　ジャンク債発行体
　less-known issuer　知名度の低い発行体
　long-term public debt issuer　長期公募債発行体
　lower-quality issuer　信用力の低い発行体
　newly rated issuer　新規発行体，初回格付け発行体
　nonresident issuer　非居住者発行体
　put the security back to the issuer　発行体に償還請求する
　rated issuer　格付け取得済み発行体，すでに格付けされている発行体
　short-term-debt issuer　短期債務の発行体
　sovereign issuer　ソブリン発行体
　speculative-grade issuer　投機的格付けの発行体
　top quality issuer　超優良発行体
　upper-speculative-grade issuer　投機的格付け上位の発行体
◆If the worth of the issuer rises, the value of the stock also will rise. 発行体の資産価値が上昇すれば、株式の価値も上がる。◆Retail outlets that suffer loss as a result of fraud can also claim compensation from card issuers. 不正使用により損害を被っている小売り加盟店側も、カード会社に賠償金を請求できる。

issuing （名）発行，起債，（手形などの）振出し，流出，出版（形）発行する，起債する，（手形などを）振出す，流出する
　bond issuing business　債券発行業務
　bond issuing expenses　社債発行費
　issuing authority　発行当局
　issuing bank　（信用状の）発行銀行，信用状発行銀行
　issuing broker　証券発行仲買人
　issuing entity　発行体
　issuing environment　起債環境
　issuing house　証券引受業者，証券発行商社，発行受託会社
　issuing process　起債手続き
　issuing share　発行株式
　L/C issuing bank　信用状発行銀行

IT bubble ITバブル，IT投資バブル
◆A raft of information technology firms went public during the IT bubble in 2000. 2000年のITバブル期には、多くのIT企業が上場［株式を公開］した。

IT-related stocks IT関連株
　（=IT-related shares）

Italian bond イタリア国債
◆The European Central Bank needs to provide support to Italy by proactively buying Italian bonds. 欧州中央銀行（ECB）は今後、イタリア国債を積極的に買い入れてイタリアを支援する必要がある。

Italian bond yield イタリア国債の利回り，イタリア国債の流通利回り
◆The ten-year Italian bond yield is hovering around 7 percent, which is said to be a dangerous zone that may result in a debt crisis. 10年物イタリア国債の利回り［流通利回り］は、債務危機に陥るとされる危険水域の7％近辺で高止まりしている。

Italian government bond イタリア国債，伊国債
◆The annual yield of the Italian government bond is currently at a high 6 percent. 伊国債の流通利回りは現在、年6％の高い水準にある。◆The European Central Bank has been purchasing Italian government bonds in an effort to support Italy. 欧州中央銀行（ECB）は、イタリア国債を買い入れてイタリアを支えている。

Italy （名）イタリア
◆Italy is the third-largest economy of the eurozone. イタリアは、ユーロ圏で第三位の経済大国である。

Italy's economy イタリアの経済
◆Italy's economy is the third largest after［following］those

of Germany and France in the eurozone. イタリアの経済規模は、ユーロ圏ではドイツとフランスに次いで3位だ。

Italy's financial management イタリアの財政運営
◆The International Monetary Fund is urged to monitor Italy's financial management to provide support to Italy. イタリアを支援するため、国際通貨基金（IMF）はイタリアの財政運営の監視を求められている。

Italy's sovereign debt crisis イタリアの財政危機
◆Italy's sovereign debt crisis may spill over to other European countries. イタリアの財政危機は、他の欧州諸国に波及しかねない。

item （名）項目, 品目, 種目, 細目, 事項, 商品, 用品, 品物, アイテム
abnormal item　異常項目
adjustment item　修正項目, 調整項目
balance sheet item　貸借対照表項目
base item　基本項目
basic item　定番商品, ベーシック商品
big item　目玉商品
big-ticket item　高額商品, 高価な商品
brand-named item　銘柄品, メーカー品
corporate items　本社事項
income statement items　損益計算書項目
infrequent item　突発事項
line item　勘定科目
nonmonetary balance sheet items　貸借対照表の非貨幣性項目
operating item　営業項目, 営業品目
popular item　売れ筋商品, 売れ筋, 人気商品（=hot item）
prior period item　前期修正項目
sensitive item　輸入要注意品目
unusual item　特別損益項目
◆Nonmonetary balance sheet items and corresponding income statement items are translated at rates in effect at the time of acquisition. 貸借対照表の非貨幣性項目とこれに対応する損益計算書項目は、取得日の為替レートで換算されています。

items of business　議案, 議事
◆The Proxy Statement describes the items of business to be voted on at the Annual Meeting. 議決権代理行使勧誘状には、定時株主総会で票決される議案についての説明がなされている。

J

Japan Bank for International Cooperation　国際協力銀行, JBIC　（⇒JBIC）

Japan Exchange Group Inc.　日本取引所グループ
◆The TSE and the OSE will merge into a single company by forming a holding company called Japan Exchange Group, Inc. 東証と大証は、持ち株会社「日本取引所グループ」を設立して、経営統合する。

Japan Finance Corporation　日本政策金融公庫
◆The Development Bank of Japan asked the Japan Finance Corporation to pay the amount guaranteed by the government. 日本政策投資銀行は、政府保証分の支払いを日本政策金融公庫に請求した。◆The government guaranteed up to 80 percent of ￥67 billion in unsecured loans extended to JAL by the DBJ through the Japan Finance Corporation. 日本政策投資銀行が日航に貸し付けた無担保融資670億円の最大8割については、日本政策金融公庫を通じて政府が保証している。

Japan Housing Finance Agency　住宅金融支援機構
◆The Japan Housing Finance Agency plans to securitize housing loan claims bought from financial institutions. 住宅金融支援機構（独立行政法人で、旧住宅金融公庫が2007年4月1日に改称）は、金融機関から買い取った住宅ローンの債権を証券化する方針だ。

Japan money　ジャパン・マネー（日本企業の海外投資資金・資本）

Japan Pension Service　日本年金機構

Japan Post　日本郵政グループ（正式名称は日本郵政株式会社）
　Japan Post Bank Co.　ゆうちょ銀行, 株式会社ゆうちょ銀行
　Japan Post Insurance Co.　かんぽ生命保険, 株式会社かんぽ生命保険
　Japan Post Network Co.　郵便局, 郵便局株式会社
　Japan Post Service Co.　日本郵便, 郵便事業株式会社
◆Japan Post will be reorganized in October 2011 to a three-company structure, with Japan Post Co. and Japan Post Insurance Co. under a parent company that will handle mail services. 日本郵政グループは2011年10月、郵便事業を行う親会社の下にゆうちょ銀行とかんぽ生命保険が入る3社体制に再編成される。

Japan Post Bank　ゆうちょ銀行
◆Japan Post Bank does not have much experience compared with private banks. ゆうちょ銀行は、民間銀行と比べて融資経験に乏しい。◆M3 includes cash in circulation, demand and time deposits and certificates of deposit at all depository institutions, including Japan Post Bank Co. マネー・サプライM3には、現金通貨、要求払い預金、定期性預金や全貯蓄銀行（ゆうちょ銀行を含む）の譲渡性預金（CD）などが含まれる。

Japan premium　ジャパン・プレミアム（国際市場での邦銀向け上乗せ金利）
◆In late November 1997, Japan premiums, extra interest rates for Japanese banks, reached 1 percent and Japanese banks faced difficulties in procuring funds in international markets. 1997年11月末に、邦銀向けの上乗せ金利であるジャパン・プレミアムが1%に達し、邦銀の国際市場での資金調達が困難になった。

Japan Securities Dealers Association　日本証券業協会

Japanese Bankers Association　全国銀行協会
◆The Japanese Bankers Association released a preliminary savings and loans report that shows depositors' movements prior to April 1. 全国銀行協会は、4月1日（ペイオフ凍結解除日）前の預金者の動きを示す預金・貸出金速報を発表した。

Japanese banks　邦銀, 日本の銀行, 日本の金融機関
◆A project financing scheme is the largest growing field for Japanese banks. プロジェクト・ファイナンス（事業融資）事業は、邦銀にとって最大の成長分野だ。◆This joint financing scheme carried out with the bank as the lead bank is expected to help make the presence of Japanese banks more strongly felt in global markets. 同行を主幹事銀行として実施されるこの協調融資事業は、グローバル市場で邦銀の存在感を高めることになりそうだ。

Japanese currency　日本の通貨, 円
◆The Japanese currency's value vis-a-vis the U.S. dollar entered the ￥98 range in foreign exchange markets around the world. 円の対米ドル相場は、内外の外国為替市場で1ドル＝98円台をつけた。

Japanese economy　日本経済, 日本の景気
◆The Japanese economy faces a growing downside risk due to concerns about the future of the U.S. and European economies. 日本経済は、欧米経済の先行き懸念から、景気の下振れリスクが高まっている。◆The rational actions for survival taken by individual companies herald a danger that could lead the Japanese economy into contracted equilibrium. 生き残りをかけて個々の企業が取っている合理的な行動が、日本経済を縮小均衡に導く危険性をはらんでいる。◆The strong

yen can hurt the Japanese economy. 円高は、日本経済にダメージを与える可能性がある。

Japanese government bonds 日本国債
◆After the briefing for foreign investors, a fund manager showed interest in investing in Japanese government bonds. 海外投資家向け説明会の後、あるファンド・マネージャーが日本国債への投資に関心を示した。

Japanese stocks 日本株
◆By the TSE's extension of the morning trade session to 11:30 a.m., investors will be able to trade Japanese stocks more easily while keeping an eye on economic trends in Asian markets. 東証が午前11時30分まで午前の取引時間を延長したことによって、投資家は今後、アジア市場の経済動向を見ながら日本株の取引をすることが容易になる。◆Foreign investors stepped up their purchase of Japanese stocks. 外国人投資家の日本株買いが活発化した。◆The amount of net selling of Japanese stocks further increased in September. 9月は、日本株の売り越しの額がさらに増えた。

Japanification (名)日本化, 日本の二の舞

Japanization (名)日本化,(デフレ、超低金利、財政赤字の)日本化現象, ジャパナイゼーション

Jasdaq ジャスダック (Japan Securities Dealer's Association Quotationの略。日本の新興企業向け株式店頭市場。2004年12月13日、店頭市場から証券取引所(Jasdaq Securities Exchange)に移行して取引を開始。その後、ジャスダックとヘラクレスが統合して、2010年10月12日から新ジャスダックとしてスタートした。⇒exchange)
◆It will be difficult for the company to list its stock on the Jasdaq by the end of next March. 来年3月までに同社がジャスダックに株式を上場するのは、難しいようだ。◆The Jasdaq can begin small-lot after-hours trading by its transformation from an over-the-counter stock market to a securities exchange. ジャスダックは、店頭市場から証券取引所への移行により、立会い外分売(取引時間外に大株主などが保有株を小口に分けて売り出すこと)も可能になった。◆The new Jasdaq market was formed by merging the Hercules and old Jasdaq markets at the Osaka Securities Exchange. 新興企業向け新市場のジャスダックは、大阪証券取引所のヘラクレス(市場)と旧ジャスダック(市場)が統合して設立された。◆With 942 listed companies, the Jasdaq overtook the Nagoya Stock Exchange as the third-largest stock market in Japan, after the Tokyo Stock and Osaka Securities exchanges. 上場会社数が942社のジャスダックは、名古屋証券取引所を抜き、東京、大阪両証券取引所に次ぐ国内3番目の株式市場になった。
[解説]新ジャスダックとは:大阪証券取引所が運営するジャスダック、ヘラクレス両市場が統合して、2010年10月12日に発足。アジア最大規模の新興企業向け新市場で、上場企業数は1,000社を超える。実績重視の「スタンダード」と、成長銘柄を集めた「グロース」の2種類の区分が設けてある。上場条件の維持が厳しく、株価が3か月以内に1株10円以上に戻らなかった企業は、上場廃止になる。

Jasdaq Securities Exchange ジャスダック証券取引所, JASDAQ[JQ] (運営法人は大阪証券取引所)
◆Gentosha will be delisted from the Jasdaq Securities Exchange on March 16, 2011. 幻冬舎は、2011年3月16日にジャスダック証券取引所から上場廃止となる。◆The Jasdaq Securities Exchange commenced operation as the nation's sixth securities exchange, transforming from an over-the-counter stock market. ジャスダック証券取引所は、国内6番目の証券取引所として取引を開始して、株式店頭市場から証券取引所に移行した。◆The number of individual investors holding shares in companies listed on the Jasdaq Securities Exchange increased for the 10th straight year. ジャスダック証券取引所に上場している企業(931社)の個人株主数は、10年連続で増加した。

JBIC 国際協力銀行 (Japan Bank for International Cooperationの略)
◆Six state-run financial institutions were reorganized into three, the Japan Bank for International Cooperation (JBIC), the Development Bank of Japan and the National Life Finance Corporation. 政府系の6つの金融機関が、国際協力銀行、日本政策投資銀行と国民生活金融公庫の3つに統合された。

JBRI 日本公社債研究所 (Japan Bond Research Instituteの略)

JCIF 国際金融情報センター (Japan Center for International Financeの略)

JCR 日本格付研究所 (Japan Credit Rating Agencyの略)

jeopardize (動)危険にさらす, 危険[危機]に陥れる, 危うくする, 損なう, ダメージを与える
◆A free fall of the dollar would jeopardize the entire economy of the world significantly. ドルが暴落すれば、世界経済全体に大きなダメージを与えることになる。

JGB 日本国債, 日本の国債
(Japanese government bondの略。⇒brief)
◆The 10-year JGB yield sank below the 1 percent threshold. 新発10年物の日本国債の流通利回りが、1%割れの水準まで低下した。◆With the rating of JGBs being low, internationalizing them may increase the risk that their yield will fluctuate. 日本の国債の格付けが低いので、日本国債の国際化は国債の金利変動リスクを高める可能性がある。

JICA 国際協力機構 (Japan International Cooperation Agencyの略)
◆With the integration of the Japan Bank for International Cooperation's division for handling yen loans, and other bodies in October 2008, JICA became one of the world's largest development assistance agencies. 国際協力機構(JICA)は、2008年10月に国際協力銀行(JBIC)の円借款部門などを統合して、(事業規模で)世界最大級の開発援助機関となった。

job creation 雇用創出
◆Economic stimulus measures implemented so far include a supplementary budget for job creation. これまで実施された景気対策としては、補正予算による雇用の創出もある。

Joe (名)男の名
Joe Bloggs 普通の人, 凡人, 一般大衆
  (=Joe Blow, Joe Public)
Joe Blow 平均的アメリカ人, 一般国民, 一般人, 普通の人[市民]
Joe College 典型的な大学生, (典型的な)男子大学生
Joe Doakes 平均的な男, 普通の人, 一般市民, 平民
  (=Joe Blow)
Joe Public 一般大衆, 聴衆
  (=Joe Bloggs, Joe Blow, Joe Soap)
Joe Six-pack 普通の米国人男性(労働者), 普通の米国人
Not for Joe! まっぴらだ, 嫌だね, 断じて〜ない
◆A consumption tax hike would increase the financial burden shouldered by Joe Blow. 消費税を引き上げると、一般国民の金融負担[一般国民が負担する金融負担]が増すことになる。

join (動)参加する, 資本参加する, 加わる, 入る, 協力する, 協同する, 提携する, 入会する, 入社する, 〜に入る, 加盟する, 合流する, 始める
join a company 入社する
join a syndication シ団に参加する
join forces [hands] 連携する, 提携する, 力を合わせる, 協力する, 手を組む, 手を結ぶ, 勢力を結集する, 統一会派を組む
join the deal 案件に参加する, 同案件に参加する

join the syndicate　シ団に加わる, シ団に参加する
join with [up]　～に協力する, ～と提携する
　◆Nippon Steel Corp. plans to join with Usiminas to invest in a planned steelworks in Brazil. 新日本製鉄は、ブラジルの鉄鋼大手ウジミナスに協力して、同国で予定されている製鉄所に投資する計画だ。◆Under the EU's Stability and Growth Pact, countries eligible to join the euro system are required to keep budget deficits below 3 percent of GDP. 欧州連合（EU）の財政安定・成長協定によると、ユーロ加盟国は、加盟の条件として財政赤字をGDPの3%以下に抑えなければならない。

join hands　連携する, 提携する, 手を結ぶ, 手を組む, 協力する, 力を合わせる, 勢力を結集する, 支援する
　(=join forces)
　◆Mitsubishi Paper Mills Ltd., a member of the Mitsubishi group, also may seek to join hands with Hokuetsu Paper. 三菱のグループ企業の三菱製紙も、北越製紙との提携を求める可能性がある。◆Shinsei Bank may join hands with other banks despite the cancellation of a merger plan with Aozora Bank in May 2010. 新生銀行は、2010年5月にあおぞら銀行との合併計画が撤回された[破談になった]が、他行と連携する可能性がある。

join the board　取締役会に加わる, 取締役に就任する, 取締役に選任される
　◆Four new directors joined the board at last year's annual meeting. 昨年度の定時株主総会で、新取締役4名が取締役会に加わりました[新たに4名が取締役に選任されました]。

join the national pension plan　国民年金保険に加入する
　◆If a housewife whose annual income is ¥1.3 million or more, or her husband becomes self-employed, the housewife must join the national pension plan and pay premiums. 主婦の年収が130万円以上の場合、または夫が脱サラした場合には、主婦も国民年金に加入して保険料を支払わなければならない。

joint　（形）共同の, 合同の, 連帯の, 連合の, 合弁の, 共有の, 共通の, ジョイント
　joint account　（主に夫婦名義の）共同預金口座, 共同勘定
　joint ballot　連記投票
　joint branch　共同店舗
　Joint Committee on the Economic Report　米合同経済委員会, 米経済合同委員会
　joint communique [statement]　共同声明
　joint consultation　労使協議
　joint convention　米両院合同会議
　joint custody　連帯親権, 連帯保護義務
　joint debt　連帯債務
　joint decision　共同決定, 共同決定事項
　joint efforts　一致した努力, 協力
　joint fare　共同運賃
　joint float　共同変動相場制, 変動相場制への共同移行
　joint inquiry　共同調査, 合同調査
　joint investigation team　合同捜査チーム, 合同捜査班
　joint management　共同経営（joint operation）, 共同管理
　joint news [press] conference　共同記者会見
　joint owners　共有者, 共同所有者
　joint press conference　共同会見
　joint product development　製品[商品]の共同開発
　joint project [enterprise]　共同[合同]事業, 共同プロジェクト
　joint property　共有財産
　joint public-private company　第三セクター
　joint purchase　共同購入, 共同仕入れ
　joint responsibility [liability]　共同責任, 連帯責任, 連座制
　joint signature　連署
　joint sponsorship　共同主催, 共催
　joint stake　共同出資, 共同出資比率

joint action　協調行動, 共同行為
　◆As joint actions, major industrial nations have taken such measures as further interest rate reductions, quantitative monetary relaxation to increase the money supply, the injection of public funds and increased public spending. 協調行動として、主要先進諸国は、さらなる金利の引下げ、通貨供給量を増やすための量的金融緩和や公的資金の注入、財政出動[公共支出の拡大]などの措置を取った。

joint branch　共同店舗
　◆Mizuho Bank and Mizuho Investors Securities Co. opened their first joint branch operations in Tokyo. みずほ銀行とみずほインベスターズ証券が、東京で国内初の共同店舗での営業を開始した。

joint company　共同運営会社, 合弁会社
　◆Kanebo will spin off its textile business and transfer it to a joint company to be established by Kanebo and dyeing and finishing company Seiren Co. カネボウは、繊維事業を切り離して、カネボウと染色加工会社のセーレンが設立する共同運営会社に移すことになった。

joint financing scheme　協調融資事業, 共同融資事業
　(=cofinancing scheme)
　◆This joint financing scheme carried out with the bank as the lead bank is expected to help make the presence of Japanese banks more strongly felt in global markets. 同行を主幹事銀行として実施されるこの協調融資事業は、国際市場で邦銀の存在感を高めることになりそうだ。

joint holding company　共同持ち株会社
　(=joint holding firm; ⇒share swap)
　◆Rakuten has proposed integrating the firms' management under a joint holding company. 楽天は、共同持ち株会社の設立による[共同持ち株会社方式での]両社の経営統合を提案した。

joint intervention　協調介入　(=concerted intervention, joint market intervention; ⇒selling yen and buying dollars)
　◆Joint intervention by Japan and European countries in the currency markets is possible as the dollar rapidly weakens. ドル安が急速に進んでいることから、為替市場への日欧協調介入もあり得る。
　解説 協調介入とは：複数の国の通貨当局が、協力して特定の通貨を売買し、為替相場水準の修正を図ること。1か国が単独で行う介入（単独介入）より、効果はずっと大きいとされる。1995年に円相場が1ドル＝79円75銭の史上最高値を付けた際、日銀は約5兆円の介入資金で米欧の通貨当局と円売り・ドル買いの協調介入を行って、円高を是正した。

joint investment　共同投資
　◆As investment for digitalization is costly, NBS needs to establish a more profitable management system, including joint investment in digital-related facilities and content with the Fuji TV group. デジタル化の投資負担は軽くないので、ニッポン放送は、フジテレビ・グループとのデジタル関連施設への共同投資やコンテンツ（情報内容）の共有など、収益力の高い経営システムを確立する必要がある。

joint loan　協調融資
　◆As the lead bank in the construction project, the bank will cover more than a certain percentage of the joint loan to the Canadian corporation. この建設プロジェクトの主幹事銀行として、同行はカナダ企業への協調融資のうち一定割合以上を融資する。◆The Bank of Tokyo-Mitsubishi UFJ will work together with foreign banks to extend 117 million Canadian

dollars in joint loans to a mega solar power plant construction. 三菱東京UFJ銀行は、外銀数行の主幹事銀行として［外銀数行と連携して］、カナダの太陽光発電所建設事業に1億1,700万カナダ・ドルを協調融資する。

joint market intervention　協調介入, 協調市場介入
　（=joint intervention）
　◆The government and the Bank of Japan are considering joint market intervention with the U.S. and European monetary authorities to produce the greater results of their market intervention. 政府・日銀は、市場介入の効果を高めるため、米欧の通貨当局との協調介入を検討している。

joint production venture　共同生産事業
　◆The two firms launched projects together, including a joint production venture in Canada. 両社は、カナダでの共同生産事業などの共同事業を開始した。

joint response to the global financial crisis　世界的な金融危機への協調対応［協調対応策］
　◆In a joint response to the global financial crisis, the U.S. FRB, ECB and central banks in Britain, Canada, Sweden and Switzerland cut interest rates in unison. 世界的な金融危機への協調対応策として、米連邦準備制度理事会（FRB）、欧州中央銀行（ECB）と英国、カナダ、スウェーデン、スイスの中央銀行は、それぞれ金利［政策金利］を同時に引き下げた。

joint stake　共同出資, 共同出資比率
　◆The two companies aim to maintain their joint stake in Elpida at 51 percent or more. 両社は、両社合わせた出資比率は51％以上を維持する方針だ。

joint statement　共同声明, 共同文書
　（=joint communique）
　◆A joint statement adopted in the meeting of G-20 financial chiefs called for strengthening the international supervisory framework for financial institutions. 世界20か国・地域（G20）の財務相・中央銀行総裁会議で採択された共同声明は、金融機関［金融業界］への国際的な監視体制の強化を求めた。

joint stock company　株式会社　（=joint stock corporation; ⇒capitalization, LLP, minimum capital requirements, stock company）
　◆It became possible for an agricultural producers cooperative corporation to turn into a joint stock company. 農業生産法人の株式会社化が、可能になった。◆Mitsui Life Insurance Co. demutualized and became a joint stock company in April 2004. 三井生命保険は、2004年4月から非相互会社化して株式会社になった［2004年4月から会社形態を相互会社から株式会社に転換した］。◆Under this consolidated tax return system, a joint-stock company and its wholly owned subsidiaries pay corporate taxes in proportion to their combined profits and losses. この連結納税制度では、株式会社とその全額出資子会社は、相互の損益を通算（合算）して法人税を納める。

joint venture　合弁会社, 合弁事業, 合弁, 共同企業, 共同企業体, 共同事業, 共同事業体, 共同出資会社, ジョイント・ベンチャー, JV　（⇒servicing）
　◆au Insurance Co. is a joint venture between KDDI Corp. and Aioi Nissay Dowa Insurance Co. au損害保険会社は、KDDI株式会社とあいおいニッセイ同和損害保険会社が共同出資した損害保険会社だ。◆In the joint venture with an Indian investment bank, Tokio Marine Holdings Inc. put up about 26%, the maximum a foreign investor is allowed in an Indian company, of the new firm's capital. インドの投資銀行との合弁事業で、東京海上ホールディングスは、新会社の資本金の約26%（外資の持ち分比率の上限）を出資した。◆NEC Corp. and Hitachi Ltd. have started negotiations with Intel Corp. of the United States, requesting that the world's largest semiconductor chip maker take a stake in their joint venture. NECと日立製作所が、世界最大の半導体メーカーの米インテル社に両者の合弁会社への出資を要請して、同社との協議に入った。

joint venture tender　合弁株式公開買付け（2社以上の会社が資本を持ち寄って他社を乗っ取ること）

jointly　（副）共同で, 合同で, 連帯で, 協調して
　be sponsored jointly by　～の共同主催である, ～が共同主催する
　jointly manufacture　共同生産する
　jointly set up a new company　共同出資で新会社を設立する
　◆The two manufacturers will sign a basic agreement to jointly manufacture refrigerators, washing machines, vacuum cleaners and other appliances. 両社は、冷蔵庫や洗濯機、掃除機などの共同生産の基本契約を結ぶことになっている。

jointly develop　共同開発する
　（=work together to develop［invent］）
　◆The bank has jointly developed with American International Group Inc. a foreign bond investment product targeting retired baby boomers. 同行が、団塊の世代の定年退職者をターゲットにした外債の金融商品を、米保険最大手のAIGグループと共同開発した。

jointly extend loans　協調融資する
　◆Entrusted or instructed by the South Korean government, private banks jointly extended loans to the company. 韓国政府の委託や指示を受けて、民間銀行が同社に協調融資した。

jointly intervene in the market　市場に協調介入する, 協調介入する
　◆The government and the Bank of Japan should urge the United States and European countries to jointly intervene in the market. 政府・日銀は、米欧に協調介入を強く働きかけるべきだ。

jointly own　共同所有する, 共同出資する
　（=equally own）
　◆GM and Toyota are each set to invest tens of billions of yen in a plant they jointly own in California. GMとトヨタはそれぞれ、両社が共同出資する米カリフォルニア州の工場に数百億円を（追加）投資する方針だ。

jolt　（動）揺り動かす, 震動させる, 衝撃［ショック］を与える, ～に動揺を与える, ～を驚かせる, ～に干渉する
　◆The world is being jolted by the collapse of U.S.-style financial business models. 世界は、米国型金融ビジネス・モデルの崩壊でショックを受けている［米国型金融ビジネス・モデルの崩壊が、世界を揺るがせている］。

judge　（動）判断する, 考える, 評価する, 批評する, 非難する, 批判する, 推定する, 見積もる, 裁判する, 審理する, 裁く, 判決を下す
　◆Europe's seven banks judged to have capital shortfall by the stress test will work on increasing their capital. ストレス・テスト（特別検査）で資本不足と認定された欧州の7銀行は、これから資本増強に取り組む。

juice loan　高利貸しの貸付け金

juice man　高利貸し, 取立て人

July-September quarter　7-9月期（3月期決算企業の第2四半期）
　◆The security firm expects to book about ¥73 billion in losses related to its residential mortgage-backed securities business in the July-September quarter. 同証券会社は、7-9月期に住宅融資証券事業の関連損失として730億円を計上する見通しだ。

jumbo　（形）巨大な, 大型の, 特大の, 超特大の, 大口の, ジャンボ・サイズの, ジャンボ　（名）ジャンボ債
　jumbo certificate of deposit　大口定期預金証書, ジャンボ（定期）預金証書, ジャンボCD
　jumbo issue　大型発行, ジャンボ債
　jumbo time deposits　大口定期預金
　U.S. jumbo home mortgage indexes　米国大型住宅モーゲージ指数

jump （動）跳ね上がる, 急増する, 急上昇する, 上昇する, 大幅に上がる, 飛ぶ, 飛躍する,（異例の）昇進をする, 出世する
◆Illegal transfers of deposits via foreign malware have been jumping. 海外のマルウェア（コンピュータ・ウイルスの一種）による預金の不正送金が急増している。◆Jobless rates in the United States and European countries have jumped to nearly 10 percent. 米欧では、失業率が10％近くまで急上昇している。◆The firm's stock jumped to ￥1,097 at market close next day. 同社の株価は、翌日の終値で1,097円に跳ね上がった。

jump （名）急騰, 暴騰, 跳ね上がり, 急増, 急上昇, 急転, 飛躍, 急激な進歩, 画面の飛び, 省略, ジャンプ
 jump in land prices 地価高騰
 jump in prices 価格の上昇, 物価高騰
 sharp jump in exports 輸出急増
◆Wholesale prices rose 1.3 percent from the previous year, reflecting a jump in prices of steel and oil products. 企業物価（日本の旧卸売り物価）指数は、鉄鋼や石油製品の価格の上昇を反映して、前年比で1.3％上昇した。

jumping juvenile（policy） 自動増額子供保険

junior （形）下級の, 下位の, 後順位の, 劣後の, 小規模の, ジュニア
 Junior Chamber of Commerce 青年会議所, JCC
 junior claim 劣後請求権
 junior common stock 劣後普通株式
 junior creditor 下位債権者, 後順位債権者, 劣後債権者
 junior debt 劣後債務
 junior department store 小規模デパート, ジュニア・デパート
 junior partner 少数株主
 junior security 下位証券, 劣後証券（発行会社が破産や清算をしたとき, 債務弁済の順位が他の証券よりも下位にある証券のこと。⇒senior security）
 junior security interest 後順位担保権, 劣後担保権

junk （名）投資不適格, ジャンク債, ジャンク
 junk issue ジャンク債, くず債券, 格付けの低い債券, 高利回り債（=junk bond）
 junk issuer ジャンク債発行体
 junk mail ジャンク・メール（インターネット経由などで送られてくる商品の宣伝に, 不要なＥメール）
 junk status［territory］ 投資不適格のレベル, 投機的レベル
◆Standard & Poor's cut its ratings on General Motors Corp. deeper into junk status. 米格付け会社のスタンダード・アンド・プアーズは、ゼネラル・モーターズ（GM）の格付け（長期債務格付け）を、投資不適格のレベルに（投資不適格レベルのダブルBからダブルBマイナスに）さらに1段階引き下げた。

junk bond ジャンク債, くず債券, 格付けの低い［投資不適格の, 信用度の低い］債券, 投機的格付けの債券, 高利回り債, 不良債券, ジャンク・ボンド
◆High-risk junk bond and asset-backed securities markets virtually collapsed in the United States. リスクの大きいジャンク・ボンドや商業用不動産証券などの市場は、米国では事実上、崩壊した。◆The spreads of yields on high-risk junk bonds over the benchmark five-year U.S. Treasury bonds had been around 200 basis points, or 2 percentage points. リスクの高いジャンク債と指標となる5年物財務省証券との金利差（スプレッド）は、2％（200ベーシス・ポイント）程度で推移していた。

junk status 投資不適格のレベル, 投機的レベル
◆By buying Greek, Portuguese and Spanish bonds, the ECB infused life into the moribund eurozone markets for these soon-to-be-junk status government bonds. ギリシャやポルトガル、スペインの国債を買い入れて、欧州中銀（ECB）は、崩壊寸前のユーロ圏の投資不適格レベルが見込まれるこれらの債券の市場に生気を吹き込んだ。◆Standard & Poor's cut its ratings on General Motors Corp. deeper into junk status. 米格付け会社のスタンダード・アンド・プアーズは、ゼネラル・モーターズ（GM）の格付け（長期債務格付け）を、投資不適格のレベルに（投資不適格レベルのダブルBからダブルBマイナスに）さらに1段階引き下げた。

junk territory 投資不適格レベル（=junk status）
◆Two influential rating firms lowered Ford Motor Co.'s credit ratings a notch deeper into junk territory. 大手［有力な］格付け機関2社が、米フォードの信用格付けを「投資不適格レベル」にさらに1段階引き下げた。

K

keep （動）維持する, 保持する, 据え置く, 続ける, 保存する, 保管する, 管理する, 経営する, 在庫として持つ, 常備する, 書き記す, 記入する, 規則などを守る
 keep hold of market share シェア［市場シェア］を維持する
 keep interest rates near zero ゼロ金利政策を維持する
 keep money rates low 低金利を維持する
 keep one's outlook negative ネガティブ（弱含み）の見通しを据え置く
 keep short rates on hold 短期金利を据え置く, 短期金利を低水準で維持する
 keep the book 帳簿に記入する, 帳簿をつける
 keep the company alive 会社を存続させる, 生き残りをかける
 keep the Federal funds rate unchanged フェデラル・ファンド金利を据え置く
◆Discount rate was kept at 1.25 percent. 公定歩合は、1.25％に据え置かれた。◆Due to the growing strength of the yen, even if exporters' sales grow, their profits will not keep pace. 円高進行で、輸出企業の売上が増えても、利益は伸び悩むようだ。◆Fitch Ratings Ltd. will keep its rating on long-term U.S. debt at the highest grade, AAA. 英米系の格付け会社フィッチ・レーティングスは、米国の長期国債格付けを、最上級のAAA（トリプルA）に据え置く方針だ。◆S&P cut ratings on Japanese banks and kept their outlook negative. スタンダード＆プアーズは、日本の大手行の格付けを引下げ、「ネガティブ（弱含み）」の見通しを据え置いた。◆The BOJ has bought financing bills and other securities from the market to keep money rates low under its ultra-easy money policy. 日銀は、超低金利政策で低金利を維持するため、市場から政府短期証券（FB）などの有価証券を買い取ってきた。◆The U.S. Federal Reserve Board pledged to keep interest rates near zero until mid-2013. 米連邦準備制度理事会（FRB）は、2013年半ばまでゼロ金利政策を維持することを誓った。◆The U.S. Federal Reserve raised the official discount rate and the target rate of federal funds by 0.25 percentage points in a bid to quell inflation and keep the economy from overheating. 米連邦準備制度理事会（FRB）は、インフレを防ぎ景気の過熱を警戒して、公定歩合とフェデラル・ファンド（FF）の誘導目標金利をそれぞれ0.25パーセント引き上げた。◆The White House is ready to consider tapping a $700 billion Wall Street bailout fund to help keep the U.S. automakers afloat. 米政府は、米自動車メーカーの破たんを避けるための支援策として、7,000億ドルの金融業界救済資金（金融安定化法の公的資金）の活用を検討する用意ができている。◆The yen continues its relentless surge and stock prices keep falling. 円高に歯止めがかからず、株安も続いている。◆Under the EU's Stability and Growth Pact, countries eligible to join the euro system are required to keep budget deficits below 3 percent of GDP. 欧州連合（EU）の財政安定・成長協定によると、ユーロ加盟国は、加盟の条件として財政赤字をGDPの3％以下に抑えなければならない。

keepwell agreement 念書
Keogh （名）自営業者退職年金制度, 個人年金積立奨励制度, キオ・プラン［ケオ・プラン］ （＝individual retirement account, qualified pension plan, Keogh plan）
　Keogh account　キオ口座
　Keogh plan　キオ・プラン
key （名）鍵, 要（かなめ）, 要石, 手がかり, 重要地点, 要所, 重要人物, （試験の）問題解答集, 解答, 凡例（はんれい）音程, 調子, 基調, キー
　be the key to　〜の要である, 〜にとって重要である
　hold the key to　〜の鍵を握る
　the key to revitalizing the economy　景気浮揚への鍵
　the key to success　成功の秘訣［鍵］, 成功にとって重要なこと
　◆The key to returning to stable growth is whether the nation can eliminate excesses common to many companies and promote supply-side structural reforms. 安定成長復帰へのカギは, 多くの日本企業に共通して見られる過剰体質を排除して, 供給サイドの構造改革を進めることができるかどうかである。
　◆Two potent corporate buyout tools of stock splits and stock swaps were the key to the remarkable growth of the company. 株式分割と株式交換という二つの強力な企業買収の手段が, 同社の急成長のカギだった。
key （形）重要な, 主要な, 枢要な, 最大の, 基幹の, 中心の, 中核の, 基軸の, キー
　break through key resistance（level）　主要な抵抗線を突き抜ける［突破する］
　close below key support　主要な支持線を割り込んで引ける
　key account　主要得意先, 主要顧客, 上得意先, 重要取引先
　key account management　主要顧客管理
　key areas　中核業務, 主要部門, 主要セクター
　key aspect　重要な局面
　key BOJ interest rate（overnight call rate target）　日銀の政策金利（翌日物コールレート誘導目標）
　key determinant　最大の要因, 主要要因
　key economic data　主要景気指標, 主要経済指標（＝key economic indicators, key economic series）
　key industry　基幹産業, 主要産業
　key issue［question］　重要問題, 最大の問題
　key item　主要品目, 主要商品
　key money　基軸通貨（key currency）, 保証金, 手付け金, 頭金, 礼金, 権利金
　key Nikkei Index　日経平均株価（225種）
　key official［officer］　幹部
　key resistance　主要な抵抗線
　key statistics　主要経済指標
　key tenant　核テナント, 核店舗, キー・テナント
　play a key role　重要な役割を果たす
key benchmark for　〜の代表的指標
　◆The yield on the 10-year government bond is the key benchmark for long-term interest rates. 10年物国債の利回り（流通利回り）は, 長期金利の代表的指標である。
key currency　基軸通貨, 国際通貨, キー・カレンシー（＝international currency, key money, reserve currency）
　◆If the U.S. government falls into default, the markets' faith in the dollar as the world's key currency would plummet. 米政府がデフォルト（債務不履行）に陥ったら, 世界の基軸通貨としてのドルの信認は急落する。◆The U.S. dollar can no longer function as the sole key currency of the world. 米ドルは, もはや世界の単独の基軸通貨としては機能できなくなっている。
key factor　重要な要因, 主要要因, 主な要因, 重要なカギ
　◆A key factor in dealing with the rising yen is the action the Bank of Japan will take. 円高対応の重要なカギは, 今後の日銀の動きだ。◆Consumption is a key factor in an increase in demand. 消費は, 需要拡大の重要な要因だ。
key gauge　指数, 指標, 重要［主要］な基準・尺度
　a key gauge of the current state of the economy　景気の現状を示す主要基準（景気一致指数）
　the key gauge of consumer prices　消費者物価指数
　◆A key gauge of the current state of the economy fell below the boom-or-bust threshold of 50 percent in September for the first time in five months. 景気の現状を示す主要基準（景気一致指数）が, 9月は5か月ぶりに景気判断の分かれ目となる50％を下回った。◆The coincident indicator, the nation's key gauge of the state of the economy, topped the boom-or-bust line of 50 percent in March. 国内の景気の現状を示す一致指数［景気一致指数］が, 3月は景気判断の分かれ目となる50％を上回った。◆The key gauge of consumer prices dropped 0.2 percent from a year earlier. 消費者物価指数は, 前年度に比べて0.2％下落した。◆The key gauge of the nation's money supply rose 2.1 percent in July 2008 from a year earlier as quasi money such as time deposits increased, the Bank of Japan said. 日本銀行の発表によると, 2008年7月のマネー・サプライ（通貨供給量）の指標は, 定期性預金などの「準通貨」の増加に伴い前年同月比で2.1％増加した。
key indicator　主要指標, 指標
　◆Core private machinery orders are widely regarded as a key indicator of corporate capital spending about six months ahead. 船舶と電力を除く民間需要の機械受注は, 一般に企業の約6か月先の設備投資を示す指標とされている。◆The yield on the 10-year Japanese government bond is a key indicator of long-term interest rates. 新発10年物日本国債の流通利回りは, 長期金利の代表的な指標となっている。
key interest rate　（日銀、イングランド銀行、ECBの）政策金利, 主要政策金利, 基準金利, 指標金利, 金利の誘導目標,（米FRBの）FF金利
　（＝benchmark rate, key rate; ⇒key rate）
　boost［raise］a key interest rate to the highest level　政策金利［フェデラル・ファンド金利］を最高水準まで引き上げる
　cut a key interest rate to a razor-thin 0.1 percent　政策金利を超低金利の0.1％に引き下げる
　key short-term interest rates　短期指標金利
　leave［hold, keep, maintain］one's key interest rate unchanged　政策金利を据え置く
　long-term interest rates　長期金利
　raise one's key interest rate by a quarter of a percentage point　政策金利を0.25％引き上げる
　reduce key interest rates　政策金利［基準金利］を引き下げる
　slash［cut, reduce］one's key interest rate by three-quarters of a pointy　政策金利を0.75％引き下げる
　the Bank of England's key interest rate　イングランド銀行（英中央銀行）の政策金利
　the Bank of Japan's key interest rate　日銀の政策金利
　the European Central Bank's key interest rate　欧州中央銀行（ECB）の主要政策金利
　the U.S. Federal Reserve Board's key interest rate　米連邦準備制度理事会（FRB）のフェデラル・ファンド金利［FF金利］
　◆The Bank of Japan decided to keep its key interest rate at 0.1 percent. 日本銀行は, 政策金利を年0.1％に維持する［据え置く］ことを決めた。◆The Bank of Japan lowered its key interest rate by 0.2 percentage points to 0.1 percent. 日銀は, 政策金利を0.2ポイント下げて0.1％とした。◆The European Central Bank left its key interest rates unchanged at 1 percent. 欧州中央銀行（ECB）は,（ユーロ圏16か国の短期金

利の誘導目標となる）主要政策金利を年1%のまま据え置いた。
◆The European Central Bank raised its key interest rate by a quarter of a percentage point to 2.25 percent. 欧州中央銀行（ECB）は、主要政策金利を0.25%引き上げて年2.25%とした。◆The U.S. Federal Reserve Board boosted a key interest rate to the highest level in five years. 米連邦準備制度理事会（FRB）は、（短期金利の指標となる）FF金利を5年ぶりに最高水準に引き上げた。

key international currency 国際基軸通貨, 国際通貨
◆The U.S. dollar has enjoyed the massive privileges as the key international currency. 米ドルは、国際通貨としての特権を享受してきた。

key lender 主要金融機関
◆In the first half, the firm booked a special profit of about ¥400 billion on debt waivers by its key lenders. 上半期に同社は、主要金融機関の債務免除［債権放棄］で、約4,000億円の特別利益を計上した。

key money supply gauge マネー・サプライ（通貨供給量）の指標
◆Japan's key money supply gauge rose a weaker-than-expected 1.8 percent in October 2008 from a year earlier. 10月の日本のマネー・サプライ（通貨供給量）の指標は、予想を下回って前年同月比で1.8%上昇した。

key Nikkei index 日経平均株価（225種）
◆Tokyo stocks extended their winning streak to a third day with the key Nikkei index finishing above the 9,000 line. 東京の株価［東京株式市場の株価］は、3日連続で値上がりし、日経平均株価（225種）の終値が9,000円台を上回った。◆Tokyo stocks snapped a three-day losing streak Wednesday, with the key Nikkei index rebounding strongly from Tuesday. 東京の株価［東京株式市場の株価］は水曜日、日経平均株価（225種）が前日から大幅反発［回復］して、3日連続の値下がりに歯止めがかかった。

key rate 政策金利, 基準金利, 指標金利 (=key interest rate: 米国の場合、key ratesといえば、公定歩合とフェデラル・ファンド金利（FF金利）の誘導目標の二つを指す。⇒key interest rate)
key rate cut 公定歩合引下げ
reduce key rates 基準金利の引下げ, 金利引下げ
◆The Federal Reserve reduced key rates for the seventh time this year. 米連邦準備制度理事会（FRB）は、今年7回目の金利引下げ［基準金利の引下げ］を実施した。

key short-term interest rate 短期金利（無担保コール翌日物）の誘導目標
◆The Bank of Japan forwent an increase in its key short-term interest rate. 日本銀行は、短期金利（無担保コール翌日物）の誘導目標引上げを見送った。

key stock index 主要株価指数
◆The key stock index closed below ¥11,000 for the first time in nearly two years. 主要株価指数の終値は、約2年ぶりに11,000円を割り込んだ。

key target rate in the short-term money market 短期金融市場の誘導目標
◆The Bank of Japan uses the unsecured overnight call rate as the key target rate in the short-term money market. 日銀は、無担保コール翌日物の金利を短期金融市場の誘導目標にしている。

key threshold of ～の大台
◆The 225-issue Nikkei Stock Average dived below the key threshold of 10,000 as investors were disappointed with the continuing delay in the disposal of banks' bad loans and an overnight plunge in U.S. stocks. 日経平均株価（225種）は、投資家が銀行等の不良債権処理が引き続き遅れることや前日の米株価の大幅下落に失望して、1万円の大台を割り込んだ。

key trading partner 主要貿易相手国
◆The ADB lowered its 2011 growth forecast in Asian nations due to growing worries about weak demand from key trading partners including the United States and Europe. アジア開発銀行（ADB）は、主要貿易相手国である欧米で需要減退［需要低迷］懸念が高まっていることから、アジアの2011年の成長見通し［GDP成長率見通し］を下方修正した。

keyhole investment キーホール・インベストメント（市場に新規参入するにあたってその市場内の企業の株式を少量取得すること）

keyman insurance 経営者保険

kick off 始める, 開始する, 始まる, 開幕する, スタートする（=launch, start）
◆The casualty insurer initially planned to kick off its on-line insurance sales in April, but delayed the start due to the March 11 earthquake and tsunami. 同損保は当初、4月から保険のネット販売を開始する方針であったが、3月11日（2011年）の東日本大震災のため、その営業開始を延期した。

kickbacks （名）リベート, 割戻し金, 賄賂（わいろ）, 裏金, キックバック
◆The company failed to declare about ¥1.3 billion in income, including about ¥300 million in kickbacks from a subcontractor. 同社は、下請業者からの裏金約3億円を含めて、所得約13億円を申告しなかった。

kicker キッカー, 甘味料 （⇒sweetener）

kill （動）キャンセルする
kill the bid 買いをキャンセル
kill the offer 売りをキャンセル

killer bees 殺し屋ミツバチ, 兵隊バチ, キラー・ビーズ（敵対的買収に備えて企業が常時雇っている弁護士、委任状勧誘者、信用供与銀行やPR会社などの専門家集団）

killing （名）ぼろ儲（もう）け, 大儲け, 荒稼ぎ, 大当たり
make a killing in the stock market 株でぼろ儲けをする, 株でがっぽり稼ぐ
make a killing through illegal short selling 違法な空売りで荒稼ぎする
◆On the stock market, many are flooding the market and making a killing through illegal short selling. 株式市場では、違法な空売りで売り浴びせて荒稼ぎしている者が多い。

kilter （名）調子, 状態, 好調, 整った状態
out of [off] kilter 不調で
◆Domestic and foreign demands, the two engines powering Japan's economic growth, are out of kilter. 日本の経済成長を引っ張る原動力の内需と外需が、今のところ不調だ。

kit （名）道具一式, 用具ひと揃い, セット, 組立部品一式, キット
campaign kit キャンペーン・キット
demonstration kit デモンストレーション・キット
promotional kit プロモーション用具
selling kit 販売用セット
starter kit ユーロ・スターター・キット （=starter pack: ユーロ導入前に配付された硬貨のお試しセット）
trial kit 試供品セット

kite （動）高騰する, 融通手形を振り出す, 融通手形で金を得る

kite （名）空手形, 融通手形
fly a kite 融通手形を振り出す, 空手形を振り出す, 世論の反応を見る
kite bill 融通手形
kite check 空小切手, 融通小切手（=rubber check）
kite flying 融通手形の振出し, 空手形［小切手］の振出し, 世論を探ること

kite-flier （名）融通手形振出人

kiting （名）株価のつり上げ（相場操縦などで株価をつり上げること）, 空手形［空小切手］の振出し, カイティング
kiting check 空小切手の振出し

kiting stocks　株価のつり上げ操作
knight　(名)騎士, ナイト
　black knight　暗黒の騎士, 敵対的買収者, 企業乗っ取り屋, ブラック・ナイト
　white knight　白馬の騎士, 友好的買収者, ホワイト・ナイト
　◆Myojo Foods asked Nissin Food Products to play the part of a white knight by forming a capital alliance to thwart the U.S. investment fund's hostile takeover bid. 米系投資ファンドの敵対的TOB(株式公開買付け)を阻止するため, 明星食品は資本提携によるホワイト・ナイト(白馬の騎士)としての明星の支援を日清食品に要請した。

knowhow [know-how]　(名)ノウハウ, 技術情報, 技術知識, 専門知識, 専門技術, 製造技術, 技術秘密, 技術秘訣, 手法, 秘伝, 奥義, 秘訣, コツ　(=expertise)
　business knowhow　経営手法, 商売の秘訣, 商売のコツ
　confidential knowhow　秘密ノウハウ
　conveyance of knowhow　ノウハウの供与
　knowhow fee　ノウハウ料
　knowhow license agreement　ノウハウ・ライセンス契約
　knowhow licensing agreement　ノウハウ使用許諾契約
　knowhow transfer　ノウハウ譲渡, ノウハウの移転
　management knowhow　経営のノウハウ, 経営の専門知識
　production knowhow　生産技術のノウハウ
　technical knowhow　技術専門知識, 技術的専門知識, 技術ノウハウ
　transfer of knowhow and technical assistance　ノウハウの移転と技術援助
　◆The firm plans to offer not only retail lending, but also corporate lending by utilizing the customer screening knowhow of its partner bank. 同社は, 共同出資する銀行が持つ顧客審査のノウハウを活用して, 個人向け融資のほかに法人向け融資業務も提供する計画だ。◆The nonlife insurance company will provide the company with know-how on damage assessment and product development. この損害保険会社は, 同社に損害査定や商品開発に関するノウハウを提供する。◆Two companies' accumulated know-how in online trading will be useful in the commodity futures market. 商品先物市場では, 両社の蓄積しているネット取引のノウハウが役に立つだろう。

L

lack　(動)~が欠けている, ~が不足[欠乏、欠如]している
　lack competitiveness　競争力を欠く, 競争力がない
　lack effective monetary instruments　効果的な金融調整の手段を欠く
　lack for funds　資金が不足している
　lack substance　内容が乏(とぼ)しい
　the FRB's lack of action　米連邦準備制度理事会(FRB)の金利据え置き
　◆The government led by the Democratic Party of Japan lacks a coherent strategy to address the negative aspects of Japan's debt dynamics. 民主党政権は, 日本のマイナス材料の債務問題への取組みに対する一貫した戦略に欠けている。◆The markets apparently decided that the dialogue between Prime Minister Kan and Bank of Japan Gov. Shirakawa lacked substance. 菅首相と白川日銀総裁の今回の意見交換を, 市場は実質的な内容が乏しいと判断したようだ。

lack　(名)不足, 欠乏, 欠如, 不備
　for lack of　~がないために, ~不足で
　lack of capital　資本不足
　lack of coordination　足並みの乱れ
　lack of investment　投資不足
　lack of public confidence　国民の信認の欠如
　lack of retail buying　個人投資家の買い控え
　◆Domestic bank are stepping up oversea project financing due to the lack of growth in lending to domestic borrowers amid protracted deflation at home. 国内銀行各行は, 国内ではデフレが続いて[デフレが続く状況で]国内融資先への貸出が伸びていないことから, 海外の事業向け融資を強化している。◆Japan, the United States and European countries have failed to eliminate uneasiness in the financial markets for lack of concrete policy coordination. 日米欧は, 具体的な政策協調が見られないため, 金融市場の不安感を払拭(ふっしょく)できないでいる。◆The current high price of crude oil stems partly from the lack of investment in oil development for a long period. 現在の原油高の一因は, 長期にわたる石油開発投資の不足だ。

lack of liquidity　流動性の不足, 流動性不足
　(⇒liquidity crisis)
　◆Even if it is a sovereign state or a bank, heavily indebted borrowers may face a crisis for insolvency or a lack of liquidity. 国家でも銀行でも, 巨額の債務を抱えた発行体は, 返済不能か流動性不足で危機に陥る可能性がある。◆In the case of a lack of liquidity, either bridge lending or debt deferment can save the borrower as there is no cash on hand. 流動性不足の場合は, 手元に現金がないので, つなぎ資金を貸すか[つなぎ融資か]債務返済の延長で借り手は助かる。

lackluster [lacklustre]　(形)精彩がない, 活気がない[乏しい], 不活発な, 生気がない, 輝きのない, ぱっとしない, さえない, あまり目立たない, つまらない, 不振の, 低迷している, 停滞している, 動きが鈍い, 足取りが鈍い, 伸び悩みの　(=sluggish)
　lackluster consumption　消費の低迷
　lackluster growth　伸び悩み, 伸びの低迷
　lackluster market condition　活気がない市場, さえない市場
　lackluster sales　販売不振, 販売低迷
　lackluster trading　薄商い

lackluster economy　景気停滞, 経済の低迷, 景気低迷
　◆There are signs of life in the lackluster economy. 景気停滞に, 景気の好調を示す兆候がある。

lackluster performance　さえない成績, ぱっとしない業績[成績], 業績低迷[不振]
　◆The company has been dealt a blow by the lackluster performance of its semiconductor business. 同社は, 半導体事業の業績不振で大きな打撃を受けている。◆The TSE and the OSE will merge into a single company by forming a holding company called Japan Exchange Group, Inc. 東証と大証は, 持ち株会社「日本取引所グループ」を設立して, 経営統合する。

-laden　(形)~を積んだ, ~を乗せた, ~を抱えた, ~に満ちた, ~満載の, ~をいっぱい抱えた
　debt-laden　負債[借金]を抱えた, 借金漬けの
　debt-laden balance sheets　負債の過剰
　debt-laden finances　借金漬けの財政
　◆This country's debt-laden finances are in a critical situation due to the dole-out policies as well as lavish economic stimulus measures. わが国の借金漬けの財政は, バラマキ政策と大盤振る舞いの景気対策で, 危機的な状況に陥っている。

lagging indicator　遅行(ちこう)指標　(lagging index: 現状の景気の動きに遅れて動く, (景気の動きに半年から1年遅れる)経済指標)
　◆The diffusion indexes of the coincident, leading and lagging indicators compare the current levels of various economic indicators with their levels three months earlier. 一致指数や先行指数, 遅行指数などの景気動向指数は, 各種経済指標の現状を3か月前の状況と比較したものだ。◆The index of lagging indicators is designed to measure economic perfor-

mance in the recent past. 遅行指数は、直近の過去の景気動向を示す指標だ。

land price 土地価格, 地価
　falling land prices　地価の下落
　the average land price for commercial areas　商業地の全国平均の地価
　the average land price for residential areas　住宅地の全国平均の地価
　◆In many cases, the complicated property tax system results in increased taxes despite decreasing land prices. 多くの場合、固定資産税の仕組みが複雑で、地価が下落しても税額が増える結果になっている。◆The prolonged slump in the real estate market is maintaining the decline in land prices. 不動産取引市場の長期低迷が、引き続き地価の下落を招いている。

land taxation [tax] system　土地税制
　(=land-related tax)
　◆Drastic revision of the land taxation system is unavoidable. 土地税制の抜本的見直しは、避けられない。

languish　(動)低迷する, 停滞する, 活力を失う, 元気がなくなる, 減退する, 弱る, (次第に)衰える
　◆Domestic stock exchange entries continue to languish, reflecting the tough conditions faced by emerging firms wanting to publicly list their shares. 国内株式市場への新規上場は、株式上場を目指す新興企業が直面している厳しい状況を反映して、低迷が続いている。◆The recession has been spreading globally and the Japanese economy has been languishing since last year. 昨年来、世界同時不況が進行し、日本経済は低迷が続いている。

large　(形)大規模な, 巨大な, 巨額の, 多額の, 大型の, 大量の, 大口の, 大手の, 広範囲の, 主要な, 重要な, 大幅な, 全般的な
　a large investor base　広範な投資家層
　declines in large interest rates　金利の大幅下落
　large account　期間投資家, 大口投資家
　large acquisition　大型買収
　large advances　多額の前受金
　large and liquid secondary markets　大規模で流動性の高い流通市場
　large banks　大手銀行, 大手行, 大手各行
　large bill　大口手形
　large borrowers　大口融資先　(⇒financial status)
　large cap　大型株(優良株とほぼ同義)
　large capital [capitalization] stock　大型株
　large cash flows　潤沢(じゅんたく)なキャッシュ・フロー
　large cash position　手元流動性が十分であること
　large cash transaction　大口現金取引
　large credit　高額債権
　large customers　大口顧客
　large debt servicing　巨額の債務返済
　large debtholder　高額債権者
　large equity holder　大株主
　　(=large shareholder)
　large industrial portfolio　産業界への大規模投資
　large inputs of capital　巨額の資本投入
　large investment portfolio　大規模な企業投資
　large item　大口取引
　large losses　多額の損失, 巨額の損失
　large merger　大型合併　(=large-scale merger)
　large shareholder　大株主, 大口株主
　　(=large stockholder, major shareholder)
　large time deposit　大口定期預金
　large trade surplus　巨額の貿易黒字

　maintain a large profit　高水準の利益を維持する
　pay out a large percentage of earnings　配当性向を高める
　report on large stockholders [shareholders]　大量保有報告書　(=large-shareholding report)
　the largest cap stock　時価総額が最大の銘柄
　the largest growing field　最大の成長分野
　the largest net creditor in the world　世界最大の債権国
　the largest world investors　最大級の国際投資家
　◆A project financing scheme is the largest growing field for Japanese banks. プロジェクト・ファイナンス(事業融資)事業は、邦銀にとって最大の成長分野だ。◆All these events are part of a larger strategy of our asset management. これらの措置は、当社の資産運営戦略の一環としてとられたものです。◆Banks made larger gross operating profits than they did during the bubble economic era. 銀行は、バブル期よりも大きな業務粗利益を上げた。◆Domestic banks are increasing their efforts to finance large overseas projects. 国内銀行各行は、海外での大型事業に融資する(プロジェクト・ファイナンスへの)取組みを強化している。◆In the case of single-premium whole life insurance policies, policyholders make one large premium payment up front when they sign the contract. 一時払い終身保険の場合は、保険契約者が契約を結ぶ際に[契約時に]多額の保険料を前もって一括で払い込む。◆Italy is the third-largest economy of the eurozone. イタリアは、ユーロ圏で第3位の経済大国である。◆Italy's economy is the third largest after [following] those of Germany and France in the eurozone. イタリアの経済規模は、ユーロ圏ではドイツとフランスに次いで3位だ。◆Recent U.S. economic indicators show the fragility of the world largest economy. 最近の米国の経済指標は、米経済の弱さを示している。◆The government bond issuance worth about ¥44 trillion for the current fiscal year is the largest ever projected in an initial budget. 今年度の約44兆円の国債発行額は、当初予算としては史上最高だ。◆The merger between the TSE and the OSE will create the world's second-largest exchange group in terms of the total market value of listed shares. 東証と大証の経営統合で、上場株式の時価総額で世界第2位の株式取引所グループが誕生する。

large amount of　大量の, 巨額の
　a large amount of banks crossheld shares　大量の銀行の持ち合い株式
　a large amount of funds　大量の資金
　move large amounts of money　巨額な資金を動かす
　◆Participants in the market process information transmitted globally in real time, manipulate it in some cases and try to win profit by moving large amounts of money in this information war zone. 市場参加者は、リアルタイムでグローバルに伝達される情報を処理し、場合によってはそれを操作しながら、この情報戦争の戦場で巨額な資金を動かして利益を得ようとしている。◆Stock prices will tumble, if banks try to sell a large amount of banks crossheld shares in the market ahead of the account settlement term at the end of March. 3月末の決算期を控えて、銀行が大量の持ち合い株式を市場に放出すれば、株価は急落する。◆The Bank of Japan has supplied a large amount of funds to the market by purchasing long-term government bonds and corporate bonds. 日銀は、長期国債や社債の買入れで、大量の資金を市場に提供している。

large contract　大型契約
　◆Nonlife insurance companies used to disperse the risk of large contracts with new corporate clients through reinsurance contracts with other insurance or reinsurance companies. 損保各社は従来、他の保険会社もしくは再保険会社と再保険契約を結んで、新規顧客企業と大型契約を結ぶリスクを分散してきた。

large deficit　巨額の赤字, 大幅赤字
　large fiscal deficit　巨額の財政赤字

large public deficit　巨額の財政赤字, 魁人
large public sector deficits　公共部門の大幅赤字
◆Japan must tackle its large fiscal deficit and curb the growth of public debts. 日本は、巨額の財政赤字と取り組んで、財政赤字[公的債務]の増大を抑える必要がある。

large influx of funds　大量の資金流入
◆Emerging countries are anxious about the possibility of inflation caused by a large influx of funds as the U.S. FRB decided to relax its monetary policy. 米連邦準備制度理事会（FRB）が金融緩和を決めたため、新興国は大量の資金流入によるインフレを懸念している。

large-lot　（形）大口の, 大量の
　large-lot buying　大量購入, 大量買付け, 大量仕入れ
　large-lot lending　大口貸出
　large-lot loans　大口融資
　large-lot nonperforming loans　大口不良債権
　large-lot saving　大口預金

large-lot corporate borrowers　大口融資先
◆The FSA's special inspection will check the major banks' large-lot corporate borrowers whose stock prices or credit ratings have sharply declined. 金融庁の特別検査は、大手銀行の株価や格付けなどが急落した大口融資先を査定の対象としている。

large-lot savings　大口預金
　（＝large deposits, large-lot deposits）
◆After the new system is introduced, most large-lot savings will not be insured by the government. 新制度の実施後は、大口預金の大半が政府保証の枠外となる。

large manufacturers　大企業製造業, 大企業・製造業
◆Behind these cautious views among large manufacturers are uncertainty over the debt crisis in the eurozone and the slowdown in the U.S. economy. 大企業製造業のこうした警戒感[慎重な見方]の背景には、ユーロ圏の債務危機不安や米景気の減速がある。◆The diffusion index of business sentiment among large manufacturers recovered to positive territory for the first time in two quarters. 大企業・製造業の業況判断指数（DI）は、2四半期（半年）ぶりにプラスに転じた。◆The Tankan index for large manufacturers rose to plus 2 in September from the minus 9 registered in June. 9月短観の大企業・製造業の業況判断指数（DI）は、6月調査のマイナス9からプラス2に11ポイント改善した。◆The yen's continued rise is worrisome for large manufacturers. 大企業・製造業には、円高進行も懸念材料だ。

large-scale　（形）大規模の, 大手の, 大型の, 大量の
　large-scale borrowers　大口融資先
　large-scale capital inflows　資本の大量流入
　large-scale capital outflows　資本の大量流出
　large-scale development　大規模開発
　large-scale shareholder [stockholder]　大口株主, 大株主
　　（＝large shareholder [stockholder]）
　large-scale takeover　大型買収, 大型の[大規模な]企業買収

large-scale economic stimulus measures　大型の財政出動
◆At two financial summit meetings since the collapse of Lehman Brothers, agreements were made on cooperation to implement large-scale economic stimulus measures and to take monetary relaxation policies. リーマン・ブラザーズの倒産[破たん]以来2回開かれた金融サミットでは、連携して大型の財政出動や金融緩和策を実施することで合意が得られた。

large-scale merger　大型合併, 大規模な再編
◆The planned merger of Nippon Steel and Sumitomo Metal may have also an encouraging effect on large-scale merger plans in other industrial sectors. 新日本製鉄と住友金属工業の合併計画は、他業界の大規模な再編計画を促す効果がある

とも言える。

large-scale tax cut program　大型減税プログラム
◆To enhance the stimulating effect of the Fed's rate cuts, swift implementation of fiscal and tax stimulus measures, including tax cuts on investment designed to reinvigorate the stock market, is necessary in addition to the large-scale tax cut program that is under way. 米連邦準備制度理事会（FRB）の金利引下げの刺激効果を高めるためには、現在実施中の大型減税プログラムに加え、株式市場を再活性化するための投資減税など、財政・税制面からの景気刺激策の速やかな実施が必要である。

large shareholder [stockholder]　大株主
◆The life insurers' status as large shareholders means that when the market dives, their portfolios also take a tumble. 大株主としての生命保険会社の地位は、株価が大きく下がると資産内容も急激に悪化することを意味する。

large surplus　多額の剰余金
◆The special account is expected to collect a large surplus in fiscal 2011 via the repayment of loans. 特別会計は、貸付け金の返済で2011年度は多額の剰余金が生じる見込みだ。

large yen-selling intervention　大量の円売り介入, 大規模な円売り介入
◆A large yen-selling intervention by monetary authorities on Sept. 15 failed to reverse the yen's rising trend. 金融当局が9月15日に実施した大量の円売り介入で、円高傾向を反転[逆転]させることはできなかった。

larger lenders　大手金融機関, 大手行
◆Lending by regional banks continued to outpace that of larger lenders in July. 地銀の7月の貸出は、前月に続いて大手金融機関[大手行]の貸出を上回った。

largest financial group　最大手の金融グループ, 金融グループ最大手
◆MFG, the nation's largest financial group, tied up with two major U.S. banks to strengthen its earning power. 国内金融グループ最大手のみずほフィナンシャルグループが、収益力の強化を図るため、米銀大手2行と提携した。

largest holder of U.S. Treasury securities　米財務省証券の最大保有国, 米国債の最大保有国
◆China is trying to flex its muscle with the United States on the strength of its status as the largest holder of U.S. Treasury securities. 中国は、米財務省証券[米国債]の最大保有国としての地位を背景に、米国への影響力を行使しようとしている。

largest shareholder　筆頭株主, 大株主
◆After the integration of Monex Inc. and Orix Securities, Orix will become the largest shareholder in Monex Group with a 22.5 percent share. マネックス証券とオリックス証券の合併に伴い、オリックス証券はマネックスグループの株式を22.5％保有し、同グループの筆頭株主になる。◆The sell-off of Tokyo Metro shares planned by the government will likely be opposed by the Tokyo metropolitan government which is the second-largest shareholder. 政府が計画している東京メトロ株の売却には、国に次ぐ大株主の東京都が抵抗すると見られる。◆With the TBS's completion of the new share issuance and the sale of outstanding shares, Mainichi Broadcasting is expected to become TBS's fifth-largest shareholder. TBSの新株発行と発行済み株式の売却が完了すると、毎日放送がTBSの5番目の大株主[TBSの第5位の株主]になると見られる。

largest U.S. full-service brokerage　米国最大手のフルサービス証券会社
◆The company is the largest U.S. full-service brokerage. 同社は、米国最大手のフルサービス証券会社です。

last　（形）最後の, 最終の, 前回の, 過去の
　a [the] last endorser　最終裏書人
　a last half year　下半期, 下期, 後期
　the last interest date　前回の利息支払い日

the last price　終値
the last quotation　引け
the last recession　前回の景気後退
the last term　前期
the last three years　過去3年
the last trading day　最終取引日

last resort　最後の手段, 最後の頼みの綱, 最後の拠 (よ) りどころ
the last resort to secure a stable revenue source　安定した財源確保の (最後の) 頼みの綱
the lender of lastly resort　最後の貸し手 (=central bank)
the U.S. dollar as the currency of last resort　最後の頼みの通貨としての米ドル, 最後の拠りどころの通貨としての米ドル
◆Financial exchanges between a half dozen emerging countries (BRICs, Indonesia and South Korea) will lose a dependency on the U.S. dollar as the currency of last resort. 今後、ブラジル、ロシア、インド、中国、インドネシア、韓国の新興6か国間の金融取引は、最後の拠 (よ) りどころとしての米ドルに依存しなくなると思われる。◆The last resort to secure a stable revenue source is raising the consumption tax. 安定した財源確保の頼みの綱は、消費税の引上げだ。

latent　(形) 潜在的な, 表面に出ない, 隠れた, 含みを持つ (企業保有資産の現在価値 [市場価値] が帳簿上の価格を上回っている場合に「含みを持つ」という)
latent debts　隠れ借金
latent demand　潜在需要
latent gains or losses　含み損益, 評価損益 (=latent profits or losses)
latent profits and losses　含み損益 (=appraisal profits and losses, latent gains and losses, unrealized profits and losses)
latent property　含み資産
latent stock gains　株式含み益, 株の含み益, 株式評価益 (=latent profits in stocks)
latent stock price losses　株式含み損 (⇒make up for)
latent value　含み益 (=latent gain, latent profit)

latent asset　含み資産 (企業保有資産の現在価値 [市場価値] が、帳簿上の表示価格より大きい場合の差額)
◆Japanese financial institutions have seen their accumulated latent assets almost depleted. 日本の金融機関は、これまでに蓄えた含み資産をほぼ吐き出してしまった。

latent gain　含み益, 評価益 (=appraisal gain, latent profit, unrealized gain; ⇒bond holdings, latent profit)
◆The seven major banking groups' midterm settlement of accounts is expected to record an estimated ¥1.95 trillion in latent gains. 大手7行・金融グループの (9月の) 中間決算では、推定で1兆9,500億円の含み益が出る見通しだ。

latent gains in assets　資産の含み益
◆Latent gains in real estate, stocks or other assets are posted after assessing the assets at market value. 不動産や株などの資産の含み益は、時価で資産を評価した後計上される。

latent gains or losses　含み損益, 評価損益 (=latent profits or losses)
◆In the term-end settlement of accounts at the end of September, most companies use the daily average for a month of the share prices in gauging the value of latent gains or losses in their stockholdings. 9月末の期末決算で [9月中間決算で]、大半の企業は、保有株式の含み損益を算出する際に株価の月中平均を使っている。

latent loss　含み損, 評価損 (=appraisal loss, unrealized loss: 保有する株式や債券などの有価証券や不動産の取得原価 (購入価格) を時価評価額で差し引いて出た損失のこと。⇒bond holdings, holdings, level, portfolio, stock investment)
◆The latent losses in the stockholdings of leading banks are estimated to be in excess of ¥5 trillion. 大手銀行の保有株式含み損は、5兆円を超えたと思われる。◆We must charge off latent losses on our real estate holdings. 当社は、保有不動産の含み損の処理に迫られています。

latent profit　含み益, 評価益 (=appraisal profit, latent gain, unrealized profit, valuation profit: 保有する株式や債券などの有価証券や不動産の取得原価 (購入価格) を時価評価額で差し引いて出た利益のこと)
◆Sluggish stock prices drastically reduced latent profits of seven major life insurers. 株価低迷で、大手生保7社の株式含み益は大幅に減少した。◆The latent profits of major banks' stockholdings have hit bottom. 大手銀行の保有株式の含み益も、底をついた。

latent profits and losses　含み損益 (=appraisal profits and losses, latent gains and losses, unrealized profits and losses)

latent profits in stocks　株の含み益, 株式の含み益
◆We should increase the allowance we set aside for doubtful debts to dispose of bad loans by using latent profits in stocks we hold. 持ち株の含み益を使って、不良債権を処理するための貸倒れ引当金の積み増しを図るべきである。

latent value　含み益 (⇒bond holdings)
◆The massive gains in stockholdings' latent value will raise the banks' net worth ratios markedly. 保有株式の含み益の大幅増加で、銀行の自己資本比率も大きく向上する見込みだ。

latest　(形) 最新の, 最先端の, 今回の, 今年度の, 最終の
the latest change in tone of the economic upturn　今回の景気回復の変調
the latest claims figures　新規失業保険申請者数の最新データ
the latest discount rate cut　今回の公定歩合引下げ
the latest information　最新情報
the latest market unrest　今回の市場の混乱
the latest unrest in global financial markets　今回の世界的な金融市場の混乱
◆At the latest G-20 meeting, diverging opinions among member countries were exposed over expanding the lending capacity of the IMF. 今回のG20 (財務相・中央銀行総裁) 会議では、国際通貨基金 (IMF) が融資できる資金規模の拡大をめぐって、加盟国の間で意見の食い違いが表面化した。◆It is difficult to deal with the latest unrest in global financial markets because it has been caused by a complex web of factors. 今回の世界的な金融市場混乱への対応が難しいのは、混乱を招いている要因が複雑に絡み合っているからだ。◆The latest change in tone of the economic upturn is a temporary phenomenon. 今回の景気回復の変調は、一時的な現象である。

latest account settlement　今決算
◆In the latest account settlements, banking groups gave up including sizable deferred tax assets in their equity capital. 今決算で、銀行グループは、巨額の繰延べ税金資産の自己資本への計上を見送った。

latest coordinated rate cuts　今回の協調利下げ
◆The six central banks around the world, including the U.S. FRB and the ECB, participated in the latest coordinated rate cuts. 今回の協調利下げには、米連邦準備制度理事会 (FRB) や欧州中央銀行 (ECB) など、世界の6か国の中央銀行が参加した。

latest depreciation of the euro　今回のユーロ安
◆The latest depreciation of the euro brought about a life-sustaining boon to the currency. 今回のユーロ安が、ユーロの延命効果を招いた。

latest financial crisis　今回の金融危機
◆The overheating of the real economy has triggered the lat-

est financial crisis. 今回の金融危機の引き金を引いたのは、過熱した実体経済だ。

latest fiscal first half 今年度上半期, 今年度上期, 今年度中間決算
◆In the latest fiscal first half, the six top banking groups booked as extraordinary profits part of their loan-loss provisions set aside in the past. 今年度中間決算で、大手銀行・金融6グループは、過去に積み立てた貸倒れ引当金の一部を「特別利益」として計上した。

latter half 下半期, 下期, 後半
  the latter half of fiscal 2012　2012年度下半期, 2012年度下期
  the latter half of the last year　昨年後半
◆Big companies assume the exchange rate of ￥81.06 to the dollar for the latter half of fiscal 2011. 大企業の2011年度下期の想定為替レートは、1ドル＝81円6銭となっている。

latter term 下半期, 下期, 後期　(=the latter half)

launch (動)開始する, 着手する, 発売する, 売り出す, 市場に出す, ローンチする(有価証券の起債(発行・募集)を市場で発表する), 導入する, 投入する, 上場する, コンピュータ・プログラムを立ち上げる・起動する　(⇒asset management business, branch-free bank, futures, IR campaign)
  launch a publicly traded company　公開企業を設立する
  launch a tender offer　株式公開買付け(TOB)を実施する
  launch ATMs running on a 24-hour basis　24時間稼働の現金自動預け払い機(ATM)を導入する
  launch crude futures　原油先物取引を開始する
  launch funds　ファンドを設定する
  launch futures on stocks　株式先物を上場する
  launch one's first outlet　1号店を開店する
  launch one's takeover bid for the firm's shares　同社株の株式公開買付け(TOB)を実施する
  launch the deal into syndication　案件のシ組成を開始する
  launch the hostile bid for　～に対して敵対的株式公開買付け(TOB)[敵対的買収]を実施する, ～に対して敵対的な買収を仕掛ける　(⇒hostile bid)
◆Crude futures were launched on the New York Mercantile Exchange in 1983. 原油先物の取引は、1983年からニューヨーク・マーカンタイル取引所で開始された。◆Hankyu launched its takeover bid for Hanshin shares. 阪急が、阪神株の株式公開買付け(TOB)を実施した。◆Securities and Exchange Surveillance Commission is set to launch an investigation into the company. 証券取引等委員会は、同社の調査に乗り出す見通しだ。◆The company will launch an online stock trading business by the end of this year. 同社は、年内に株のインターネット取引業務に参入することになった。◆The earthquake insurance system was launched after the 1964 Niigata Earthquake as a response to the problem of fire insurance not covering damage caused by an earthquake or tsunami. 地震保険[地震保険制度]は、火災保険で地震や津波による被害が補償されない問題への対応策として、1964年の新潟地震後に導入された。◆The ECB was obliged to maintain price stability when the euro was launched in 1999. 1999年にユーロが導入された際、欧州中銀(ECB)は、物価安定の維持を義務付けられた。◆The new leadership will be officially launched after a general shareholders meeting in June. 新体制は、6月の株主総会後に正式に発足する。◆UFJ Bank launched automated teller machines (ATMs) running on a 24-hour basis at 308 locations across the nation. UFJ銀行は、全国308か所に24時間稼働の現金自動預け払い機を導入した。

launch (名)起債発表, 発表, 開始, 着手, 新製品の発売, 上市, 導入, 実施, ローンチ　(=launching)
  launch date　発売日, 開始日, 新製品発表の日, ローンチ日, ローンチ当日
  launch of the pathfinder prospectus　募集目論見書の発表
◆With expectations of an economic recovery, U.S. stock prices are about 20 percent higher than they were just prior to the launch of the Iraq war. 景気回復期待を背景に、米国の株価も、イラク戦争開始前に比べて約2割高の水準だ。

laundered funds 洗浄資金, 洗浄された資金, 資金の洗浄
◆Stock transactions were made through the trading accounts at securities firms and laundered funds were channeled back to the crime organization. 株取引は証券会社の取引口座を通じて行われ、ここで洗浄された資金が犯罪組織(暴力団)に還流された。

laundering (名)不正資金の洗浄, 不正資金の出所偽装工作, 犯罪資金の洗濯, マネー・ロンダリング　(=money laundering; ⇒legal ceiling on interest rates, money laundering)
  crime organization's money-laundering operations　犯罪組織[暴力団]のマネー・ロンダリング活動
  money laundering　不正資金の洗浄, 資金洗浄, マネー・ロンダリング
  name laundering　名前ロンダリング
  the laundering of illegally earned profits　違法収益の洗浄, 違法収益の出所偽装工作
◆Financial institutions have effectively cooperated with crime organizations' money-laundering operations and helped them amass wealth. 金融機関はこれまで、犯罪組織(暴力団)のマネー・ロンダリング活動と蓄財にうまく協力してきた。◆Former Taiwan President Chen Shui-bian was held in a laundering probe. 台湾の陳水扁・前総統が、マネー・ロンダリング(総統府機密費の不正流用)調査で逮捕された。◆The U.S. government froze the assets of four individuals and eight entities that were involved in illicit activities such as money laundering, currency counterfeiting and narcotics trafficking. 米政府は、資金洗浄(マネー・ロンダリング)や通貨偽造、麻薬取引などの違法行為に関与している4個人、8団体の資産を凍結した。

lavish (形)気前のよい, 金を惜しみなく使う, 大盤振る舞いの, 派手な, 豊富な, 贅沢(ぜいたく)な, 豪華な
  a lavish spender　浪費家
  lavish economic stimulus measures　大盤振る舞いの景気対策
  lavish spending　無駄遣い
  spend money with almost lavish freedom　金をほとんど湯水のように使う
◆This country's debt-laden finances are in a critical situation due to the dole-out policies as well as lavish economic stimulus measures. わが国の借金漬けの財政は、バラマキ政策と大盤振る舞いの景気対策で、危機的な状況に陥っている。

law (名)法律, 法令, 法規則, 法, 法則, 手法, 規則(rule), 規定, 慣習, 戒律, 法的手段, 訴訟
  Amended Usury Law　改正出資法
  antitrust law　独占禁止法
  applicable law　適用法, 準拠法
    (=governing law, law applicable)
  attorney at law　弁護士, 事務弁護士
  Bank Law　銀行法
  be at law　訴訟中である
  blue sky law　不正証券取引禁止法
  choice of law　準拠法[適用法]の指定
  commercial law　商法
  Commodity Exchange Law　商品取引所法
  company [corporate] law　会社法
  control-share acquisition laws　支配株買収規制法
  Deposit Law　供託法

federal bourse law　連邦証券取引所法
financial futures trading laws　金融先物取引法
Financial Instruments and Exchange Law　金融商品取引法
financial law　金融法
financial services law　金融サービス法
Foreign Exchange and Foreign Trade Control Law　外為法
foreign exchange control law　外為法
governing law　準拠法
insolvency law　破産法
insurance business law　保険業法
investment law　投資法
Law concerning Foreign Investment　外資法
Law concerning the Control of Insurance Soliciting　募集取締り法
Law concerning the Regulation of Interest　利息制限法
law of property　財産法
Law on Special Measures for Strengthening Financial Functions　金融機能強化法
model investment law　モデル投資法
public-law bank　公法銀行
Securities and Exchange Law　証券取引法
Small Loan Law [small loan law]　サラ金法, 小口金融法
trust by act of law　法定信託
usury law　利息制限法, 高利限法
◆A financial bailout bill, after twists and turns, has at last been signed into law in the United States. 米国の金融安定化法案（緊急経済安定化法案）が, 迷走の末, ようやく成立した。◆A revised Foreign Exchange and Foreign Trade Control Law has been enacted to enable the swift freezing of funds belonging to terrorist organizations. テロ組織の資金［資産］凍結を迅速に行うための改正外為法は, すでに成立して［制定されて］いる。◆Before the new corporate law, at least ￥10 million was required to establish stock companies and ￥3 million to create limited liability companies. 新会社法までは, 株式会社の設立に最低1,000万円, 有限会社の設立に300万円必要だった。◆In the United States, the Exon-Florio provision of the 1988 trade law can prevent takeover bids that are deemed a threat to national security. 米国では, 1988年通商法のエクソン・フロリオ条項で, 国家の安全保障上, 脅威と考えられる企業買収を阻止することができる。◆In the wake of the Livedoor case, the Financial Instruments and Exchange Law which drastically revised the former Securities and Exchange Law came into force in September 2007. ライブドア事件を受けて, 2007年9月に, 旧証券取引法を抜本改正した金融商品取引法が施行された。

Law on Special Measures for Strengthening Financial Functions　金融機能強化法
◆A bill to revise the Law on Special Measures for Strengthening Financial Functions is designed to facilitate compensations of losses of financial institutions with public funds. 金融機能強化法の改正法案は, 公的資金による金融機関の損失の穴埋めを容易にするのが狙いだ。

lawsuit　(名)訴訟, 民事訴訟　(=suit; ⇒spur)
civil lawsuit [suit]　民事訴訟
class action lawsuit　集団代表訴訟
derivative lawsuit　株主代表訴訟
enter [bring in] a lawsuit against　〜に対して訴訟を起こす
file a lawsuit with　〜に提訴する
formal [plenary] lawsuit　本訴
lawsuit claims　訴訟による請求権
pending lawsuit　係争中の訴訟
pollution-related lawsuit　公害訴訟
settle a lawsuit　訴訟で和解する
withdraw a lawsuit against　〜に対する訴訟を取り下げる
◆Among 17 big banks targeted by the lawsuits filed by the U.S. government were Bank of America, Citigroup, Credit Suisse and Nomura Holding America Inc. 米政府が提訴した訴訟の対象の大手金融機関17社の中には, バンカメのほかにシティグループやクレディ・スイス, 野村ホールディング・アメリカなどが含まれている。◆In the lawsuits against big banks over the sales of risky investments, the U.S. government wants to be compensated for lost principal and interest payments. 高リスク証券の販売をめぐっての大手金融機関に対する訴訟で, 米政府は, 元本と利払い分の損失補償を求めている。◆Sumitomo Trust & Banking Co. has entered the final stages of filing a lawsuit with the Tokyo District Court requesting a freeze on trust merger negotiations between UFJ Holdings Inc. and Mitsubishi Tokyo Financial Group Inc. 住友信託銀行は, UFJホールディングスと三菱東京フィナンシャル・グループによる信託部門の経営統合交渉の差止めを求める訴えを東京地裁に起こす方向で最終調整に入った。◆The U.S. government filed lawsuits against 17 financial firms for selling Fannie and Freddie mortgage-backed securities that turned toxic when the housing market collapsed. 米政府は, 住宅市場崩壊時に不良資産化した住宅ローン担保証券（MBS）をファニー・メイ（米連邦住宅抵当公庫）とフレディ・マック（米連邦住宅貸付け抵当公社）に販売したとして, 大手金融機関17社（バンク・オブ・アメリカやシティグループ, JPモルガン・チェース, ゴールドマン・サックス・グループなど）を提訴した。

lax　(形)手ぬるい, 甘い, 手を抜いた, 締まりがない, だらしない, 緩(ゆる)んだ
lax financial management　放漫な財政運営
　(=lax fiscal management)
lax fiscal policy　財政政策の緩和
lax underwriting standards　緩い貸出審査基準
◆Greece has fallen into a debt crisis as a result of its lax financial management. ギリシャは, 放漫な財政運営の末に財政危機に陥った。◆The European banking tests are lax and ineffective as the collapses of two Irish banks and the Franco-Belgian bank Dexia, shortly after the EBA's stress tests, show. 欧州の銀行検査は, 欧州銀行監督機構（EBA）のストレス・テストに合格した［ストレス・テストで安全と判定された］直後にアイルランドの銀行2行やフランス・ベルギー共同の銀行「デクシア」が破たんした事実が示すように, 手ぬるくて効果がない。

lax fiscal discipline　放漫な財政運営
◆We will have to accept heavy taxation to foot the bill for the lax fiscal discipline of past governments. われわれは今後, 過去の政府の放漫な財政運営のつけを負担するために, 重税を受け入れなければならなくなる。

lax fiscal management　放漫な財政運営
　(=lax financial management)
◆Greek financial crisis was caused by the country's lax fiscal management. ギリシャの財政危機は, 同国の放漫財政［放漫な財政運営］によって生じた。

lax lending practices　乱脈融資
◆Incubator Bank of Japan which was scandal-ridden for its lax lending practices and arrests of its executives has finally collapsed. 乱脈融資や経営陣の逮捕など不祥手続きの日本振興銀行が, ついに破たんした。

lax management　放漫経営, ずさんな経営
◆The financial authorities neglected to expose the bank's lax management for a long time. 金融当局は, 同行のずさんな経営体制を長いこと放置していた。◆The Incubator Bank of Japan's failure is attributed to its lax management. 日本振興銀行の破たんの原因は, 同行の放漫経営だ。

lax screening　手薄な審査

◆Some borrowers have taken advantage of lax screening of credit guarantee corporations. 信用保証協会の手薄な審査に便乗している借り手もいる。

laxity (名)放漫,ずさん,だらしなさ,手ぬるさ,締まりのなさ,ゆるみ,甘さ,怠慢
　fiscal laxity 放漫財政
　◆The ECB buyouts of sovereign debts of eurozone countries with fiscal laxity are the nightmare scenario Germany has been fearing. 欧州中銀(ECB)による放漫財政のユーロ圏諸国の国債買切りは,ドイツが恐れていた最悪のシナリオだ。

LBO 借入資金による企業買収 (leveraged buyout [buy-out]の略。⇒leveraged buyout)
　◆New York-based Citigroup has advised on about one-third of the about $61 billion of leveraged buyouts (LBO) worldwide this year. シティグループ(ニューヨーク)は,今年の世界のLBO取引約610億ドルの約3分の1について専門的助言を行った。

L/C [**l/c**] 信用状 (letter of creditの略。複数形はL/C's, L/Cs: 銀行が取引先の依頼に応じて,その信用を補強するために発行する証書。⇒letter of credit)
　amend the L/C 信用状を修正する
　an extension of the L/C 信用状の延長
　anticipational L/C 輸出前払い信用状
　back-to-back L/C 同時発行信用状
　bankers'[bank] L/C 銀行信用状
　blank L/C 白地式信用状
　cash L/C キャッシュ・クレジット
　circular L/C 巡回信用状
　clean L/C 無担保信用状
　commercial clean L/C 商業クリーン信用状,無担保信用状
　commercial L/C 商業信用状
　confirmed L/C 確認信用状
　direct L/C 直接信用状
　documentary clean L/C ドキュメンタリー・クリーン信用状
　documentary L/C 荷為替信用状
　doing business on an L/C basis 信用状取引
　domestic L/C 国内信用状
　escrow L/C エスクロウ信用状
　escrow L/C barter trade エスクロウ・バーター貿易
　establish an irrevocable L/C for $5,000 in your favor with XYZ Bank 御社宛に5,000ドルの取消不能信用状をXYZ銀行で開設する
　export L/C 輸出信用状
　fixed L/C 定額信用状
　funding against a L/C facility L/Cファシリティを裏付けとする資金供与
　general [open] L/C 手形買取り銀行無指定信用状,ジェネラル信用状
　　(=circular negotiation L/C, open L/C)
　import L/C 輸入信用状
　impound L/C インパウンド信用状
　irrevocable L/C 取消不能信用状
　L/C advising [notifying, transmitting] bank 信用状通知銀行,信用状取次銀行
　L/C applicant 信用状発行依頼人
　　(=L/C opener)
　L/C basis L/Cベース
　L/C beneficiary 信用状受益者
　L/C confirming bank 信用状確認銀行
　L/C confirming charge 信用状確認手数料
　L/C establishing bank 信用状発行銀行,信用状開設銀行
　　(=L/C issuing bank, L/C opening bank)
　L/C issued account 信用状発行勘定
　L/C issuing [opening] bank 信用状発行銀行,信用状開設銀行,一般に買い主の取引銀行
　L/C margin money 信用状開設保証金
　l/c [letter of credit] opener 信用状発行依頼人
　　(=L/C applicant)
　L/C opening charge 信用状発行手数料
　L/C parties L/C当事者
　L/C received register 信用状通知受入帳
　L/C with guarantee 保証状付き信用状
　local L/C 国内信用状,ローカル・クレジット,ローカルL/C
　negotiation L/C 買取り信用状,ネゴシエイション信用状
　packing L/C 前貸付き信用状
　　(=red clause L/C)
　payment on receipt L/C 受領証払い信用状
　reciprocal L/C 同時開設信用状
　red clause L/C レッド・クローズ付き信用状
　restricted L/C 買取り銀行指定信用状
　revocable L/C 取消可能信用状
　revolving L/C 循環信用状,回転信用状
　sight L/C 一覧払い信用状,サイト・クレジット
　special L/C スペシャル・クレジット
　straight L/C 特定人割引信用状,ストレート信用状
　the L/C is available valid until 信用状は～まで有効である
　transferable L/C 譲渡可能信用状
　traveler's [travellers'] L/C 旅行者信用状,旅行信用状
　unconfirmed L/C 無確認信用状
　usance L/C 引受条件付き信用状
　Within two weeks after receipt of L/C 受領後2週間以内
　without recourse L/C 償還請求権を伴わない信用状
　◆Shipment shall be within two weeks after receipt of L/C. 船積みは,L/Cを受領後2週間以内とする。◆We opened an L/C for $50,000 in your favor with XY bank. 貴社を受益者として,5万ドルの信用状をXY銀行で発行しました。◆We shall be responsible for any consequences arising out of your opening L/C. 当社(L/Cの開設依頼人)は,貴行(L/Cの開設銀行)がL/Cを開設することによって生じるいかなる事態にも責任を負うものとする。

lead (動)先導する,誘導する,指導する,主導する,主導的な位置を占める,主導権を握る,指揮をとる,率いる,主幹事を務める,～に先行する,リードする
　demand-led recovery 需要主導型の業績回復
　export-led recovery 輸出主導型の景気回復
　lead A to the international markets Aの国際市場での起債で主幹事を務める
　lead the economic rebound 景気回復を主導する
　lead the economy down 景気の冷え込みを主導する
　◆A recovery will be export-driven, dependent on U.S. growth and the yen's depreciation, instead of being led by increased domestic consumption and capital investment. 今後の景気回復は,アメリカ経済の好転や円安を背景にした輸出主導型の回復で,国内の個人消費や設備投資の伸びがその牽引役となるわけではない。◆Italy's new government led by economist Mario Monti must face painful financial reforms. 経済専門家マリオ・モンティ氏を首相とするイタリア新政権は,痛みを伴う財政改革が急務だ。◆The rational actions for survival taken by individual companies herald a danger that could lead the Japanese economy into contracted equilibrium. 生き残りをかけて個々の企業が取っている合理的な行動が,日本経済を縮小均衡に導く危険性をはらんでいる。◆

The U.S. Federal Reserve Board raised U.S. interest rates, leading the worldwide move to change current super-loose monetary policy. 米連邦準備制度理事会（FRB）が米国の金利を引き上げ、世界的な超金融緩和の政策転換の先陣を切った。

lead （名）首位，先頭，トップ，優位，優勢，主導権，イニシアチブ，主役，指導，先導，指導的地位，手本，見本，例，手がかり，情報　（形）主要な，中心の，最も重要な，先頭の，首位に立つ，幹事の
　accept the lead's invitation　主幹事の招請を受け入れる
　follow the lead of　～の例にならう
　lead analyst　主任アナリスト
　lead contract　中心限月
　lead lender　原貸主
　lead underwriter　引受主幹事
　take over the lead of　～の主導権を握る

lead bank　幹事銀行，主幹事銀行，主幹事行，主要銀行
◆As the lead bank in the construction project, the bank will cover more than a certain percentage of the joint loan to the Canadian corporation. この建設プロジェクトの主幹事銀行として、同行はカナダ企業への協調融資のうち一定割合以上を融資する。◆The bank will carry out this cofinancing scheme as the lead bank with several U.S. and European banks. 同行は、主幹事銀行として、この協調融資事業を欧米の複数の銀行と連携して実施する。◆This joint financing scheme carried out with the bank as the lead bank is expected to help make the presence of Japanese banks more strongly felt in global markets. 同行を主幹事銀行として実施されるこの協調融資事業は、グローバル市場で邦銀の存在感を高めることになりそうだ。

lead-manage　（動）主幹事を務める
◆In July, Nomura and UBS of Switzerland lead-managed the Japanese government's sales of $4.27 billion of shares in the company. 7月に、野村證券とスイスのUBSが、日本政府による42億7,000万ドルの同社株売却で主幹事を務めた。

lead manager　主幹事，引受幹事，引受主幹事，幹事銀行，幹事行
　act as lead manager　主幹事を務める
　co-lead manager　共同主幹事
　　（=joint lead manager）
　domestic lead manager　国内主幹事
　expanded lead managers　拡大主幹事
　international lead manager　国際主幹事
　lead manager's takes　主幹事の参加額

lead to　～を引き起こす，～をもたらす，～を招く，～のきっかけになる，（結果として）～になる，～に発展する，～に達する，～に通じる，～につながる，～に注ぎ込む
　lead to default on one's debt payments　債務返済でデフォルトを起こす
　lead to deflationary pressures　デフレ圧力を強める
◆Bad loan disposal will lead to deflationary pressures. 不良債権処理は、デフレ圧力を強める。◆Daiei's business diversification led to rising debts that placed financial pressure on the company. ダイエーの事業多角化は、借入金の増大につながり、それが会社の経営を圧迫する結果となった。◆Errors in computing systems at financial institutions could lead to problems in making international fund transactions. 金融機関のコンピュータ・システムのエラーは、国際的な資金取引上、トラブルが生じる可能性がある。◆Maintaining an easy monetary policy may lead to excessive corporate capital investment and have a negative impact on the sustainable economic recovery. 金融緩和政策を続けると、企業の過剰な設備投資を生み、景気の持続的回復を阻害する恐れがある。◆The collapse of the bank will lead to repercussions throughout the finance sector. 同行の破たんは、金融業界全体に影響を及ぼすことになろう。◆The financial and economic crisis is leading to ballooning budget deficits across Europe. 金融・経済危機は、欧州全土で財政赤字の急増［膨張］を招いている。
◆The talks between Prime Minister Kan and Bank of Japan Gov. Shirakawa led to a further advance of the yen and off-loading of stocks as disappointment spread among market players. 菅首相と日銀総裁の会談は、一層の円高と市場筋の株の失望売りを誘った。◆Unless consumption tax rate is raised, the planned issuance of bridging bonds could lead to further deterioration of the debt-saddled government finances. 消費税率を引き上げないと、予定しているつなぎ国債の発行は、借金を背負っている国の財政の悪化をさらに招く可能性がある。

lead up to　～を引き起こす，～を招く，～へ通じる，～につながる，～の糸口となる，結局～となる，～に話を向ける
◆Goldman Sachs was subpoenaed over its activities leading up to the financial crisis. ゴールドマン・サックスは、同社の証券業務が金融危機を招いた［引き起こした］件で、召喚された。

leader　（名）主力株，一流株，指導者，首脳，最大手，おとり商品，目玉商品，リーダー
　business leaders　経済界首脳，財界首脳
　industry leader　業界リーダー
　leaders　主力株
　market leader　主導株，先導株，マーケット・リーダー
◆Corporate leaders must recognize that defrauding investors is a serious crime. 投資家を欺く行為は重大な犯罪である、ということを企業経営者は認識しなければならない。◆The Asia-Pacific Economic Cooperation forum was held in Lima just a week after the financial summit meeting of the leaders of the Group of 20 industrialized and developing economies. アジア太平洋経済協力会議（APEC）は、G20（世界の主要20先進国と地域）の首脳による金融サミットの1週間後に、ペルーのリマで開かれた。

leading　（形）主要な，最重要な，一流の，大手の，有力な，主力の，首位の，主導的
　leading commodity　主力商品
　leading currency　主要通貨
　leading edge　主導的地位，最先端，最前部，最前線，先頭，最新式，最新型，最新鋭，トップ　（=cutting edge, sophisticated, state-of-the-art, top of the line）
　leading-edge area　最先端分野
　leading industries　主力産業
　leading maker［manufacturer］　大手メーカー，有力メーカー
　leading nations［countries］　主要国，先進国
　leading position　主導的地位
　leading stocks　花形株，人気株
　three leading brokerage firms　3大証券
◆After a two day meeting in Paris, the financial chiefs and central bank governors from the Group of 20 leading economies adopted a communique. パリで開かれた2日間の会議の後、主要20か国・地域（G20）の財務相・中央銀行総裁は共同声明を採択した。

leading bank　大手銀行，大手行，主要金融機関
◆A dealer at a leading bank said that market players' concern has kept yen-buying moves in check. 市場関係者の警戒感が円買いの動きを食い止めた［抑制した］、と大手銀行のディーラーが語っている。◆The U.S. 10 leading banks need a combined capital buffer of 74.6 billion against the risk of a deeper recession and higher unemployment over the next two years. 米主要金融機関の10社は、今後2年の景気悪化リスクと失業増大に備えて、10社合計で746億ドルの資本増強を求められている。

leading company　主要企業，大手企業，先導企業，有力企業　（=leading firm）

◆More than 70 percent of leading companies are worried about becoming the target of a hostile takeover. 主要企業の70％以上が, 敵対的買収の対象になる［敵対的買収を仕掛けられる］のを懸念している。

leading economic indicators 景気先行指数, 景気先行指標総合指数
◆The index of leading economic indicators predicts economic developments about six months ahead. 景気先行指数は, 約6か月先の景気動向を示す指標だ。

leading index 先行指数, 景気先行指数, 景気先行指標総合指数 (=leading indicator, the index of leading economic indicators)
◆The leading index comprises such indicators as job offers, new orders for machinery and housing starts, which are considered indicative of how the economy will perform for the next three to six months. 先行指数は, 3か月から6か月先の景気の動きを示すものと考えられる有効求人数や新規機械受注, 新規住宅着工件数などの指標から成る。

leading indicator 先行指標, 先行指数 (=leading index: 鉱工業生産財在庫率指数, 耐久消費財出荷指数など, 現状の景気の動きに先立って動く経済指標)
  DI of the leading indicators 景気先行指数 (DI)
  diffusion index of leading indicators 景気先行指数
  the index of leading indicators 景気先行指標総合指数
◆The diffusion indexes of the coincident, leading and lagging indicators compare the current levels of various economic indicators with their levels three months earlier. 一致指数や先行指数, 遅行指数などの景気動向指数は, 各種経済指標の現状を3か月前の状況と比較したものだ。

leading shareholder 筆頭株主
(=top shareholder)
◆Nippon Life Insurance Co. appears to remain Olympus Corp.'s leading shareholder though the insurer's stake in Olympus has been reduced to 4.9 percent from 8.1 percent. 日本生命のオリンパス株保有比率は8.1％から4.9％に下がったものの, 同生保はオリンパスの筆頭株主にとどまるものと見られる。

leads and lags リーズ・アンド・ラグズ (=leading and lagging of payments: 為替相場や金利の変動によって, 対外支払いや受取りを意識的に早めたり遅らせたりすること)

league table リーグ・テーブル(証券引受業者の引受実績を示すランキング表), 成績表, 実績一覧表, 実績
◆Increasing M&A advisory business helped Nomura grab the No. 1 spot in Japan's M&A league table for the first half of this year. 今年上半期はM&A顧問業務が増加したため, 日本のM&A案件の引受実績で野村證券がトップの座を占めた。

leak (動)漏らす, 流出させる, リークする, 暴露する, 漏れる, 流出する (名)漏れ, 漏洩(ろうえい), 漏れ口, 漏電
  be leaked on the Internet インターネット上に暴露される
  leak the personal information of customers 顧客の個人情報を(外部に)流出させる
  leak the video 映像を流出させる
◆Osaka-based travel agency's customer data were leaked. 旅行会社(本社・大阪市)の顧客情報が, 外部に流出した。 ◆Personal data, including the names, addresses and credit card numbers of 99,789 holders of credit cards issued by Nippon Shinpan Co., may have been leaked. 日本信販が発行したクレジット・カードの会員99,789人分の名前や住所, カード番号などの個人情報が, 流出した可能性がある。 ◆The personal information of customers who used credit cards for premium payments might have been leaked. クレジット・カードを使って保険料を支払った顧客の個人情報が, 外部に流出した恐れがある。

leakage (名)漏れ, 漏洩(ろうえい), 流出
  leakage of capital outflows 資本の国外流出
  leakage of client information 顧客情報の漏洩, 顧客情報の流出
◆Leakage of client information by businesses has gone unabated. 企業による顧客情報の漏洩は, 依然として相次いでいる[一向に減らない]。

leaked personal information 流出した個人情報, 個人情報の流出
◆As the result of an in-house investigation, it is highly likely that the leaked personal information has been taken from the firm directly. 内部調査の結果, 流出した個人情報は社内から直接持ち出された可能性が高い。

lease (動)賃貸しする, 賃借りする, 貸し出す, 借り上げる, リースする
  estimated economic life of leased property リース資産の経済的見積り耐用年数
  estimated residual value of leased property リース資産の見積り残存価値[残存価格]
  lease under sales-type leases 販売画型リースでリースする
  leased asset リース資産, 賃貸資産 (=leased property)
  leased equipment リース資産 (=lease equipment)
  leased equipment under capital leases リース資産, キャピタル・リース設備
  leased facility 専用設備
  leased goods リース物件, 賃貸借物件, 賃借物件, 貸与物件 (=leased object)
  leased machine リース機械
  leased property リース資産, 賃貸物件, リース物件
  leased property and commitments リース資産と約定債務
  leased property under capital leases 賃借資産, キャピタル・リース資産
  the residual value of leased property リース資産の残存価格
◆Nippon Broadcasting System Inc.'s 13.88 percent stake in Fuji TV was leased to Softbank Investment Corp. ニッポン放送が保有する13.88％分のフジテレビ株が, ソフトバンク・インベストメントに貸し出された。 ◆The partnerships used the investment money to buy ships, which were then leased to major shipping companies for 10 years. 同組合は, 出資金で船舶を購入し, 購入した船舶を大手船舶会社に10年間リースした。 ◆We lease our products to customers under sales-type leases. 当社は, 自社製品を販売型リースで顧客にリースしています。

lease (名)賃貸借, 賃貸借契約(書), 借地・借家契約, 鉱物資源の開発契約, リース契約, リース
(⇒leveraged lease)
  capital lease キャピタル・リース, 資産型リース, 資本リース
  equipment held for lease リース用資産
  finance lease ファイナンス・リース, 金融性リース (=financial lease)
  international lease 国際リース, 国際間の賃貸借
  land and building leases 土地と建物のリース
  lease expense リース費用
  lease finance income リース金融収入
  lease interest 不動産貸借権
  lease liability リース債務 (=lease obligation)
  lease obligation リース債務
  lease obligation bond (debt) リース財源債
  lease payments リース料支払い

lease receivable　リース債権
lease revenue　受取リース料
lease term [period]　リース期間
lease terms　リース条件, 賃貸借条件, リース期間
leveraged lease　レバレッジド・リース
maintenance lease　メンテナンス・リース
minimum lease payments receivable　最低リース料債権
net lease　ネット・リース, ネット・リターン保証型リース (物件の所有者に対して物件に投資した分のネット・リターン (net return) を保証するリース契約で、賃借料のほかに税金や維持費などを借り手が負担する)
net minimum lease payments　正味最低リース料
net-net-lease　ネット・ネット・リース (物件の賃借料のほかに物件上の担保債務も借り手が負担するリース)
operating lease　営業型リース, 賃貸性リース, オペレーティング・リース
real estate lease　不動産リース
renewal or extension of lease　リースの更新または延長
rental expense on operating leases　オペレーティング・リースの賃借料
reserve for lease losses　リース損失引当金
sales-type lease　販売型リース, 販売金融リース
sublease　転貸借
◆Certain land and building leases have renewal options for periods ranging from three to five years. 特定の土地と建物のリースには、3〜5年の期間の更新選択権がついている。

lease financing　リース金融
◆The lease-financing project targeted individual investors such as company operators and other affluent people. このリース金融事業の対象は、会社経営者や資産家などの個人投資家だった。

leasing　(名) リース (lease), リース事業, リース業務
equipment leasing　設備リース
finance leasing　ファイナンス・リース
leasing activities　リース事業
leasing agent　管理代理機関
leasing and renting　リース・レンタル
leasing commitment　リース契約債務
leasing company　リース会社
leasing industry　リース産業, リース業界, リース業
leasing real property　不動産のリース業務
leasing receivable　リース債権
leasing receivable securitization　リース債権の証券化
leasing transaction　リース取引
◆The firm's operations in the financial services and leasing industry involve direct financing and finance leasing programs for its products and the products of other companies. 金融サービスとリース業界での同社の事業には、同社製品と他社製品に関する直接融資とファイナンス・リース事業も含まれている。

leasing right　リース権, 持ち分権
◆Investors who purchased the leasing rights became members in four voluntary partnerships. 持ち分権[リース権]を購入した出資者は、四つの任意組合のメンバーになった。

leave　(動) 据え置く, 放っておく, 後回しにする, 残す, 託す, 委ねる, 退職する, 脱退する
be being left behind　過去のものになっている
be left unchanged　据え置かれる, 据え置きになる
leave [hold, keep, maintain] a key interest rate unchanged at 0.5 percent　政策金利を0.5%に据え置く
leave (monetary) policy on hold　金融政策を据え置く
leave monetary [credit] policy unchanged　金融政策を据え置く, 金融政策を維持する
leave one's books flat　ポジションを手じまう
leave one's main interest rate unchanged at 1 percent　政策金利を1%に据え置く
leave the market with good technicals　市場のテクニカル要因が好調だ
leave upside potential　値上がりの[上昇する]余地がある, 値上がりする[上昇する]可能性がある
◆The Bank of Japan may expand the list of government bonds purchased under the fund, to include those that have more than two years left until maturity. 日銀は、基金で買い入れる国債の対象を拡大して、満期までの残存期間が2年以上 (現行1〜2年) の国債を含むようにする可能性がある。 ◆The Bank of Japan purchases government bonds that have one to two years left until maturity. 日銀は、満期までの残存期間が1〜2年の国債を買い入れている。 ◆The European Central Bank left its main interest rate unchanged at 1 percent despite a rise in inflation. 物価上昇にもかかわらず、欧州中央銀行 (ECB) は政策金利を1%に据え置いた。 ◆The Federal Reserve Board left interest rates unchanged. 米連邦準備制度理事会 (FRB) は、金利を据え置いた[現行水準で据え置いた]。

left-hand financing　資産担保資金調達

leg　(名) 期間, 傾向, 段階, 局面, 部分, 取引の一部, 相場分析で用いるチャートの値動きを示す棒状グラフ, レッグ
down-leg　減速局面
fixed-rate leg of the swap　スワップの固定金利部分
floating-rate leg　変動金利部分
floating-rate of the swap　スワップの変動金利部分
lifting a leg　リフティング・ア・レッグ (=ヘッジ取引でどちらか一方の取引を外 (はず) すこと)
long leg　ロング・レッグ (オプション取引 (options trading) 用語。オプション・スプレッドで買いの側を構成するオプションのこと)
short leg　ショート・レッグ (オプション取引 (options trading) 用語。オプション・スプレッドで売りの側を構成するオプションのこと)
up-leg　上昇局面
◆Market confidence in the Silvio Berlusconi administration's fiscal rehabilitation measures is virtually nonexistent as the administration is on its last legs. イタリアのベルルスコーニ政権が機能不全に陥っているため、同政権の財政再建策に対する市場の信認は事実上、失墜している

legal　(形) 法律の, 法律上の, 法定の, 法的な, 合法的な, 適法の, 司法の場での, リーガル
legal assignment　法的譲渡, コモン・ロー上の譲渡
legal capital　法定資本, 法定資本金
legal claim　法的請求権
legal consultation　訴訟協議
legal date　支払い期日, 満期
legal detriment　法的不利益
legal duty of payment　法的支払い義務
legal ethics　弁護士の倫理, 法曹倫理
legal expense　法定費用, 訴訟費用
legal fee　弁護士費用, 法定手数料
legal holiday　祝祭日, 法定休日, 国民休日, 公休日
legal instrument　法定投資
legal interest (rate)　法定金利, 法定利率, 法定利息 (=legal rate of interest)
legal investment　適法投資
legal lending limit　法定貸出限度枠
legal list　法定投資銘柄 (リスト), 法定銘柄 (リスト) (=legal investments)
legal list rule　法定銘柄原則
legal mortgage　法定抵当, 普通法上の譲渡抵当

legal reserve ratio 法定準備率

legal reserve requirements 法定支払い準備率, 法定準備預金額

legal risk 法的リスク

legal stock 法定資本

legal tender 法定貨幣, 法貨, 本位貨幣
◆These loans and capital increases were not legal. これらの融資と増資は、適法ではなかった。

legal action 法的措置, 法的手続き, 訴訟
◆If Hokuetsu Paper Mills decides to carry out the poison pill, Oji Paper Co. is likely to take legal action against it. 北越製紙が買収防衛策を実施したら、王子製紙は法的措置を取る可能性が高い。◆Legal action should be taken against those who refuse to pay national pension premiums, such as seizure of postal savings and bank deposits. 国民年金保険料の納付拒絶者に対しては、預貯金の差押えなどの法的措置をとるべきだ。

legal capital reserves 法定資本準備金, 法定準備金
(=legal reserves, legally prescribed capital reserves, legally required reserves; ⇒capital reserve, legal reserves)
◆Banks are allowed to access part of their legal capital reserves and transfer such funds to retained earnings. 銀行は、法定準備金の一部を取り崩して、その資金を剰余金に振り替えることができる。◆Major financial group UFJ Holdings, Inc. will use ¥1 trillion of its legal capital reserves as a surplus to pay dividends. 大手金融グループのUFJホールディングスは、配当支払いのための剰余金として法定準備金を1兆円取り崩す方針だ。

legal ceiling 法定金利の上限
(=legal cap, legal interest rate ceiling)
◆Borrowers need not pay interest rates exceeding the legal ceiling. 金を借りても、法定金利の上限を超える利息は払う必要がない。

legal ceiling on interest rates 法定金利の上限
(=legal cap on interest rates, legal interest rate cap, legal interest rate ceiling)
◆Investment Law sets legal ceilings on interest rates and prohibits the laundering of illegally earned profits. 投資法は、金利に上限を設けて、違法収益の洗浄(出所偽装工作)を禁止している。

legal contract rate 法定約定金利
◆Any payment not made when due will, in addition to any other right or remedy of Licensor, incur a finance charge at the lesser of three hundred basis points over the 3-month London Inter Bank Offered Rate ("LIBOR+3") on the date payment was due or the highest applicable legal contract rate. 支払いが支払い期日までに履行されない場合、ライセンサーの他の権利や救済請求権に加えて、支払い期日時点の3か月物ロンドン銀行間取引金利(LIBOR)プラス3%(LIBOR+3%)または適用される最高法定約定金利のうち、いずれか低いほうの金利の金融費用が発生する。

legal reserves 法定準備金, 支払い準備, 利益準備金
(=legal capital reserves, legally required reserves; ⇒legal capital reserves, make up for)
◆At an emergency shareholders meeting, the company obtained shareholder approval to transfer ¥199 billion from its legal reserves to provide for write-offs of nonperforming loans. 臨時株主総会で同社は、株主から、不良債権処理に備えて法定準備金から1,990億円を取り崩す案の承認を得た。◆The use of ¥1 trillion from its legal reserves comes at a time when the bank expects to see a ¥2 trillion loss stemming from the disposal of bad loans for the current accounting year ending in March. 1兆円の法定準備金の取り崩しは、同行の今年3月期の不良債権処理による損失が2兆円に達する見通しを踏まえてのことだ。

legal screening 法定審査
◆A corporate merger plan is subject to legal screening by the Fair Trade Commission of Japan. 企業の合併計画は、公正取引委員会の法定審査を受けなければならない。

legal shortcomings 法の不備
◆Margin trading was used in a corporate takeover by exploiting legal shortcomings. 法の不備を利用して、企業買収に信用取引が使われた。

legal upper limit 法定上限金利
◆In most illegal lending cases, operators were arrested for allegedly collecting interest on loans beyond the legal upper limit of 29.2% a year. ヤミ金融事件の大半は、業者が年29.2%の法定上限金利を上回る高金利の取立てで逮捕されている。

legally required reserves 法定準備金
(=legal capital reserves, legal reserves)
◆Many of the banking groups will have to use a portion of their legally required reserves to pay their shareholders' dividends. 銀行グループの多くは今後、株主配当の原資に充てるため、法定準備金の一部の取り崩しを迫られることになる。

Lehman Brothers (米国の大手投資銀行・証券会社の)リーマン・ブラザーズ(2008年9月15日に経営破たんし、これが世界的な金融危機の引き金となった)
◆Consumer spending waned amid the global financial crisis that followed the Lehman Brothers collapse in autumn 2008. 2008年秋のリーマン・ブラザーズの破たん後に生じた世界的金融危機を受けて、個人消費が低迷した。◆No financial institution would step in to save Lehman Brothers as the U.S. government refused to extend a financial assistance. 米政府が財政支援を拒否したので、リーマン・ブラザーズの救済に乗り出す金融機関は現われなかった。◆The U.S. tried to prevent an erosion of corporate ethics among financial institutions by refusing to provide public funds to Lehman Brothers. リーマン・ブラザーズへの公的資金の投入を拒否することによって、米政府は金融機関のモラル・ハザード(企業倫理の欠如)を回避しようとした。◆The worldwide recession began with the financial crisis sparked by the collapse of U.S. investment bank Lehman Brothers. 世界同時不況は、米国の投資銀行リーマン・ブラザーズの経営破たんが誘発した金融危機から始まった。

Lehman Brothers Holdings Inc. リーマン・ブラザーズ, リーマン・ブラザーズ・ホールディングズ・インク
◆Global major financial institutions have been forced to hold extra capital since the financial meltdown following the 2008 bankruptcy of Lehman Brothers Holdings Inc. 米国の投資銀行リーマン・ブラザーズが2008年に経営破たんして生じた金融危機以来、世界の主要金融機関は、資本[自己資本]の上積み[積み増し]を迫られている。◆Lehman Brothers Holdings Inc., a major U.S. investment bank, collapsed in September 2008. 米投資銀行大手のリーマン・ブラザーズは、2008年9月に破たんした。◆Shinsei and Aozora banks suffered huge losses in their overseas investment business in the aftermath of the global financial crisis triggered by the collapse of Lehman Brothers Holdings Inc. in autumn 2008. 新生銀行とあおぞら銀行は、2008年秋のリーマン・ブラザーズの経営破たんで始まった世界的な金融危機の影響で、海外投資事業に巨額の損失が発生した。

Lehman shock [Shock] リーマン・ブラザーズ破たんの衝撃, リーマン・ショック(リーマン・ブラザーズの経営破たんを契機に起こった世界的な株式暴落、金融危機のこと)
◆Rapid recovery following the so-called Lehman shock has ended and the Chinese economy has entered a phase aimed at stable growth. いわゆるリーマン・ショック後の中国の急回復の時期は終わり、中国経済は、安定成長を目指す段階に入っている。◆The Lehman shock cannot be brushed off as a "a fire on the other side of the river." リーマン・ショック

（リーマン・ブラザーズ破たんのショック）は、「対岸の火事」として片付ける訳にはいかない。◆The total assets of the Federal Reserve Board have soared to $2.87 trillion at the end of June 2011 from $896.2 billion as of the end of March 2008, prior to the Lehman shock. 米連邦準備制度理事会（FRB）の総資産は、リーマン・ショック前の2008年3月末時点の8,962億ドルから、2011年6月末には2兆8,700億ドルに急増した。◆The U.S. private banks' outstanding Treasury bond holdings grew by about 50 percent from March 2008, prior to the Lehman shock. 米国の民間銀行の米国債保有残高は、リーマン・ショック前の2008年3月から約5割増えた。

Lehman's collapse リーマン・ブラザーズの経営破たん, リーマン・ブラザーズの破たん
◆The money lent by the U.S. and eurozone private banks remains at about the same level as those prior to Lehman's collapse. 米国とユーロ圏の民間銀行の貸出金は、リーマン・ブラザーズの経営破たん前とほぼ同水準にとどまっている。◆The U.S. private banks' funds on hand grew about three times from March 2008 prior to the Lehman's collapse. 米国の民間銀行の手持ち資金は、リーマン・ブラザーズの経営破たん前の2008年3月から約3倍増えた。

lend （動）貸す, 貸し出す, 貸し付ける, 融資する（⇒citizens bank）
  be less willing to lend　貸し渋る
  be reluctant to lend　貸し渋る
  lend funds to　資金を〜に融資する
  lend money to businesses　企業に金を貸す, 企業の資金を貸し出す［融資する］
  lend to high-leverage credits　負債比率の高い企業に融資する
◆Despite moves by the U.S. Federal Reserve Board to loan more money to financial institutions, banks are still reluctant to lend. 米連邦準備制度理事会（FRB）に金融機関への資金融資を拡大する動きがあるにもかかわらず、銀行［金融機関］はまだ貸し渋っている。◆Few financial institutions would lend money to businesses that have negative net worth. 債務超過の企業に金を貸す金融機関は、まずない。◆Money loaned by private banks declined because banks with weakened financial strength were less willing to lend, besides a lack of businesses seeking expansion through borrowing. 民間銀行の貸出金が減ったのは、お金を借りてまで事業を拡大しようとする企業がなかったほか、財務が悪化した銀行が貸し渋ったからだ。◆The banks are reluctant to lend to small and midsize businesses to protect their capital adequacy and net worth ratios. 銀行は、自己資本比率を守るため（自己資本不足に陥らないための自衛として）、中小企業貸出（中小企業への貸出）に慎重になっている。◆The effective book value is calculated by subtracting amassed loan loss reserves from the original amount of money that was lent. 実質簿価は、債権の元々の額（貸し付けた元々の金額：簿価）から、（銀行が）積み立てた貸倒れ引当金を差し引いて算定する。◆The money lent by the U.S. and eurozone private banks remains at about the same level as those prior to Lehman's collapse. 米国とユーロ圏の民間銀行の貸出金は、リーマン・ブラザーズの経営破たん前とほぼ同水準にとどまっている。◆The rate at which banks lend their top corporate borrowers is called "prime rate." 銀行がその一流企業融資先に貸し出す利率は、プライム・レートと呼ばれている。

lender （名）貸し手, 貸主, 金融機関, 銀行, 融資行, 融資者, 資金の出し手, 貸金業者　（⇒loan facility）
  bank lender　融資銀行
  commercial lender　営利的貸し手
  higher tier lender　上位融資行
  international lenders　国際金融機関, 国際融資団
  larger lenders　大手金融機関, 大手行
  lender bank　貸出銀行, 貸出行

  lender of last resort　最後の貸し手, 最終貸し手, 中央銀行
  lender-of-last resort facilities　最終的貸付け機関
  lender's claim　貸し手の請求権
  lender's interest　貸し手の物権, 貸し手の権益
  lender's policy　貸主用証券
  lender's preference　貸し手の選好
  lender's risk　貸し手のリスク, 貸し手の危険
  money lender　金貸し, 高利貸し
  potential lender　潜在的貸し手
  primary lender　本源的貸し手
  private lender　民間金融機関
  regional lender　地方銀行, 地銀
  sole lender　単独融資行
  too-big-to-fail lenders　大きすぎてつぶせない［破たんさせられない］銀行, 大きすぎてつぶせない金融機関
  ultimate lender　究極的貸し手
◆Both lenders will focus on supporting their local corporations in the aftermath of the March 11 quake and tsunami. 3月11日（2011年）の東日本大震災を受けて、両行は地元企業の支援に重点的に取り組む方針だ。◆Greece will miss 2011-12 deficit targets imposed by international lenders as part of the country's bailout. ギリシャは、同国救済措置の一環として国際融資団（欧州連合（EU）や国際通貨基金）が課した2011-12年の赤字削減目標を、達成できないようだ。◆If TEPCO's creditor banks forgive the debts when the utility is not carrying excessive liabilities, lenders will not be able to recover either the principal or interest owed. 東電が債務超過でない時点で東電の債権保有銀行が債権を放棄すると、金融機関は元本を回収できず、金利収入も得られなくなる。◆In the case of an insolvent borrower, it no longer has the ability to pay all its debt even though lenders offer to defer the time of repayment. 返済不能の借り手の場合、貸し手が返済期間の延長を申し出ても、借り手はもはや債務を全額返済できない状況にある。◆In the first half, the firm booked a special profit of about ¥400 billion on debt waivers by its key lenders. 上半期に同社は、主要金融機関の債務免除［債権放棄］で、約4,000億円の特別利益を計上した。◆Lending by regional banks continued to outpace that of larger lenders in July. 地銀の7月の貸出は、前月に続いて大手金融機関［大手行］の貸出を上回った。◆Mitsubishi Motors Corp. will secure ¥270 billion in loans from the Development Bank of Japan and other lenders. 三菱自動車は、日本政策投資銀行などの金融機関から2,700億円の融資を受ける（2,700億円を借り入れる）。◆The company has been refused additional credit by its lenders. 同社は、融資行［銀行］から新規融資を拒否された。◆The company will secure ¥270 billion in loans from the Development Bank of Japan and other lenders. 同社は、日本政策投資銀行などの金融機関から2,700億円の融資を受ける［2,700億円を借り入れる］。◆The Federal Housing Finance Agency oversees Fannie and Freddie that buy mortgage loans and mortgage securities issued by the lenders. 米連邦住宅金融局（FHFA）は、これらの金融機関が発行する住宅ローンやモーゲージ証券を購入する［買い取る］連邦住宅抵当金庫（ファニー・メイ）や連邦住宅貸付け抵当公社（フレディ・マック）を監督している。◆Twenty-eight banks of the world will face capital surcharges of 1 percent to 2.5 percent by the application of international rules to rein in too-big-to-fail lenders. 大きすぎて破たんさせられない銀行［金融機関］を規制する国際基準が適用されると、世界の28行が、1〜2.5%の資本［自己資本］上積みの対象となる。

lending （名）貸出, 貸付け, 融資, 貸借　（⇒black-market lending, business operation, consumer lending business, demand for loans, illegal lending, unsecured loan）
  bank lending　銀行貸付け, 銀行貸出, 銀行融資
  commercial lending　商業貸出, 商業貸付け, 民間融資
  concerted lending　協調融資

consumer lending　消費者ローン, 消費者金融
corporate lending　企業向け貸出, 企業向け貸付け, 企業向け融資
cumulative lending　累積の貸付け
domestic lending　国内貸付け, 国内融資
excessive lending　過剰融資
foreign lending　対外貸付け, 対外融資
government lending　政府貸出
international lending　国際融資, 国際貸付け, 国際貸出
lending ability［capacity］　貸出能力, 融資能力, 融資力, 融資できる資金規模
lending activity　貸付け業務, 融資活動
lending agency　貸出機関, 貸付け機関
lending attitude［posture, stance］　貸出態度
lending body　貸出機関, 融資機関
lending business　貸出業務, 融資業務（=lending operation）
lending charge　貸出費用
lending criteria　貸出基準
lending directive　（中央銀行の）貸付け指令
lending fee　貸出手数料
lending group　貸出行グループ
lending in small lots　小口貸出
lending institution　貸出機関, 金融機関
lending instrument　貸出証券
lending interest rate　貸出金利　(=lending rate)
lending loss　貸倒れ
lending of money　融資, 資金の貸付け
lending operation　融資業務, 貸出業務, 融資活動, 貸付け操作
lending outlet　貸付け先, 融資先
lending period　貸出期間
lending portfolio　貸付けポートフォリオ
lending power　貸出権限
lending practice　融資慣行
lending race　貸出競争
lending stance of financial institutions　金融機関の貸出態度
lending standard　貸出基準, 与信基準, 融資基準
lending stock　貸株
lending street name　名義貸し
lending under a credit report approved by the head office　稟議（りんぎ）貸し
less lending　融資抑制
Lombard lending　ロンバード貸出
lombard lending　債券担保融資業務
money lending　資金融資, 金貸し
mortgage lending　抵当貸付け, 抵当貸し, 不動産担保貸付け, モーゲージ貸付け
name lending　名義貸し
new lending　新規貸出, 新規融資
off-record lending　浮貸し
overseas lending　海外融資, 海外貸付け
planned lending　計画的融資, 計画的貸出
policy lending　政策融資
preferred lending　優先的貸付け
private lending　民間貸付け
real estate lending　不動産融資
restricted lending　貸し渋り
restrictive lending policy　貸出抑制政策

retail lending　個人向け融資
retail unsecured lending　消費者向け無担保貸付け
seasonal lending　季節的貸出
selective lending　選別融資
sovereign lending　ソブリン融資
state lending　国家貸付け
stock lending　証券貸借
student lending law　奨学金法
the lending limit　貸出限度, （大口）融資規制
unsecured lending　無担保融資, 無担保貸付け

◆Domestic banks are stepping up overseas project financing as greater yields of interests are expected through such lending than loans to domestic borrowers. 国内銀行は、国内の借り手への融資に比べて海外の事業向け融資のほうが大きな金利収入を見込めるので、海外の事業向け融資（プロジェクト・ファイナンス）を強化している。◆Domestic three megabanks are moving to step up their overseas lending. 国内の3メガバンクは、海外融資を強化する方針だ。◆Major banks were ordered to cut their bad loan ratios to less than 5 percent of total lending by next March. 大手銀行は、来年3月までに不良債権比率を融資全体の5%以下に下げるよう行政命令を受けた。◆Most banks blame the decline in lending on weak private-sector demand for loans due to the sluggish economy. 貸出の減少について銀行の大半は、景気低迷で企業の資金需要［借入需要］が弱いため、としている。◆The firm plans to offer not only retail lending, but also corporate lending by utilizing the customer screening know-how of its partner bank. 同社は、共同出資する銀行が持つ顧客審査のノウハウを活用して、個人向け融資のほかに法人向け融資業務も提供するする計画だ。◆The recent decline in lending results from a series of debt waivers offered since April to major borrowers in the construction and distribution industries. 最近の貸出（銀行貸出）の減少は、4月以降、建設や流通業界の大手取引先に実行した一連の債権放棄によるものだ。

lending balance　貸出残高
◆The average daily lending balance by banks in October 2002 dropped 5.2 percent from a year earlier to reach ¥416.61 trillion, the lowest figure recorded since the Bank of Japan began compiling its survey in July 1991. 2002年10月の銀行の貸出残高（月中平均）は、前年同月比5.2%減の416兆6,100億円と、日銀が1991年7月に統計を開始して以降、過去最低に落ち込んだ。

lending bank　貸出銀行, 貸出行, 貸出機関, 融資銀行, 融資行, 金融機関
◆In the project financing business, lending banks are repaid loans through profits generated by the projects they have financed. プロジェクト・ファイナンス事業では、貸出行が、融資したプロジェクト（事業）から生まれる利益で融資の返済を受ける。

lending by financial institutions　金融機関による貸出
◆Lending by financial institutions has been sluggish in Japan. 金融機関の貸出は、日本では伸び悩んでいる。◆Lending by financial institutions to small and medium enterprises has been falling since 1994. 金融機関による中小企業向け貸出は、1994年以降減少している。

lending by private banks　民間銀行の貸出
◆Lending by private banks has not increased though their investments into government bonds and cash reserves are increasing. 民間銀行の国債への投資や手持ちの現金は増えているが、民間銀行の貸出は増えていない。

lending by regional banks　地銀の貸出
◆Lending by regional banks continued to outpace that of larger lenders in July. 地銀の7月の貸出は、前月に続いて大手金融機関［大手行］の貸出を上回った。

lending capacity　貸出能力, 融資能力, 融資できる資金規模, 融資可能額
◆At the latest G-20 meeting, diverging opinions among member countries were exposed over expanding the lending capacity of the IMF. 今回のG20（財務相・中央銀行総裁）会議では、国際通貨基金（IMF）が融資できる資金規模の拡大をめぐって、加盟国の間で意見の食い違いが表面化した。◆The European Union will substantially expand the lending capacity of the EFSF to buy up government bonds in case the fiscal and financial crisis spreads countries as Italy. 欧州連合（EU）は、財政・金融危機がイタリアなどに拡大した場合に国債を買い支えるため、欧州金融安定基金（EFSF）の融資能力を大幅に拡大する。◆The proposal to expand the lending capacity of the IMF was supported by Brazil and other emerging economies though Japan and the United States rejected it. 国際通貨基金（IMF）が融資できる資金規模を拡大する案は、日本と米国が受け入れなかったものの、ブラジルなどの新興国は支持した。

lending facility　融資制度
◆To prevent the current fiscal and financial crisis in Europe from spreading, the IMF will create a new short-term lending facility. 現在の欧州財政・金融危機の拡大を防ぐ［封じる］ため、国際通貨基金（IMF）が、新たな短期の融資制度を創設することになった。◆Under the IMF's new lending facility, Italy would be eligible to receive short-term loans of up to about $63 billion. IMF（国際通貨基金）の新融資制度で、イタリアは、最大約630億ドルまでの短期融資を受けることができる。

lending institution　貸出機関, 金融機関
◆The plan of using ADR for the revitalization of a business is designed to reduce JAL's interest payments by eliminating part of its credited loans from lending institutions and conducting debt-for-equity swaps. この事業再生ADR（裁判外紛争解決手続き）の活用案は、金融機関の貸出債権の一部カットと債権の株式化などで、日航の利払い負担を軽減するのが狙いだ。

lending market　貸付け市場, 貸出市場
（=loan market）
◆In the corporate lending market, loan demand remains weak in the corporate lending market, reflecting the stagnant situation of the economy. 企業向け貸出市場では、経済停滞を反映して、資金需要は依然弱い。

lending policy　貸出政策, 融資方針
◆Some financial institutions are turning their lending policy from fixed-rate type housing loans to adjustable-rate mortgages. 金融機関の一部は、固定金利型［固定型金利］の住宅ローンから変動金利型［変動型金利］の住宅ローンに融資方針を転換している。

lending rate　貸出金利, 貸付け金利, 貸出利率
（=lending rate of interest, loan interest rate; ⇒base lending rate, loan interest rate）
　basic lending rate　基本貸出金利, 貸出基本利率
　emergency lending rate　緊急貸出金利
　general lending rate　一般貸出金利
　official banking lending rate　公定銀行貸出金利
　prime lending rate　一流企業向け最優遇貸出金利, 一流企業に対する短期貸付け金利プライム・レート
　（=prime rate）
　the minimum lending rate　最低貸出金利
◆Long-term lending rates have fallen since the beginning of August 2010 amid deflation concerns. 2010年8月に入って、デフレ懸念を背景に、長期貸出金利が下がっている。

lending to domestic borrowers　国内の借り手への貸出, 国内融資先への貸出
◆Domestic bank are stepping up oversea project financing due to the lack of growth in lending to domestic borrowers amid protracted deflation at home. 国内銀行各行は、国内ではデフレが続いて［デフレが続く状況で］国内融資先への貸出が伸びていないことから、海外の事業向け融資を強化している。

lending to the market　（中央銀行の）資金供給, 資金供給量
◆The Bank of Japan will increase lending to the market by ¥10 trillion, to a total of ¥30 trillion, at extremely low interest rate of 0.1 percent a year. 日銀は、年0.1％の超低金利［低利］での資金供給を10兆円拡大し、総額で30兆円とする。

lessee　（名）賃借人, 借主, 借り手, 借地人, 借家人, レッシー
　leased asset purchased by lessee　賃借人が購入したリース資産
　lessee owner of facility　賃借人たる建造物所有者, 賃借人建造物所有者
　Lessee to comply with laws　賃借人の法律遵守
　lessee's incremental borrowing rate　賃借人の追加借入利率
　purchase of the machine by the lessee　賃借人による機械の買取り
　renewal of the lease of the machine by the lessee　賃借人による機械リースの更新
　sublessee　転貸人
　the lessee of the property　資産の借り手

lessen　（動）軽減する, 緩和する, 減らす, 縮小させる, 起こりにくくする,（速度を）落とす
◆Measures to lessen the problem of dual debts or multiple debts were also studied at the time of the 1995 Great Hanshin Earthquake. 二重ローンや多重債務問題の軽減策は、1995年の阪神大震災の際にも検討された。

lesser grade stocks　低位株

lesser of two evils　次善の策
◆Since shares could become wastepaper after a bankruptcy, the reconstruction program may be seen as the lesser of two evils. 経営破綻後は株式が紙くずになる可能性があるので、再建計画は次善の策かもしれない。

lessor　（名）賃貸人, 貸主, 貸し手, 地主, 家主, リース業者, レッサー
　accounting for leases by lessees and lessors　賃借人と賃貸人によるリースの会計処理
　existing assets of the lessor　賃貸人の既存資産
　lessor's implicit interest rate　賃貸人の包括利率
　maintenance, taxes and insurance paid by the lessor　賃貸人が支払う維持費、税金と保険料
　nonsubstantive lessor　経済的実体を欠く賃貸人
　rights of lessor　賃貸人の権利

letter of credit　信用状, L/C　（⇒L/C）
　acceptance letter of credit　引受信用状
　bank letter of credit　銀行信用状
　commercial letter of credit　商業送り状
　documentary letter of credit　荷為替信用状
　export letter of credit　輸出信用状
　irrevocable letter of credit　取消不能信用状
　negotiation letter of credit　買取り銀行［手形買取り銀行］無指定信用状　（=general L/C, open L/C）
　revolving letter of credit　回転信用状
　usance letter of credit　期限付き信用状, ユーザンス信用状
◆Letters of credit are purchased guarantees that ensure our performance or payment to third parties in accordance with specified terms and conditions. 信用状は、特定の条件に従って当社の第三者に対する義務の履行または支払いを確実なものにするために買い取った保証です。◆The letter of credit set forth above shall be negotiable against a draft at sight signed

by the seller upon the presentation of the following documents. 上記の信用状は、次の船積み書類の提示がある場合には、売り主が振り出した一覧払い手形と引換えに買い取られるものとする。◆This letter of credit shall be opened not less than 30 calendar days before the first anticipated or scheduled shipping date for each order. この信用状は、各注文の最初の出荷予定日から30暦日以上前に開設するものとする。

[解説]信用状について：信用状は銀行が取引先（貿易取引の場合は輸入者）の依頼に応じてその信用を補強するために発行する証書で、主に売買商品の代金決済に用いられる。貿易取引の商品代金の決済に用いられる信用状を商業信用状（commercial letter of credit）という。一般に、発行銀行が手形の引受け、支払いを保証・確約する取消し不能信用状（irrevocable L/C）となっている。)

level　(名)水準, 標準, 幅, 台, 程度, 参考値, レベル　(⇒ business sentiment, interest, stock market level)
　around current levels　当面の水準[現行水準]の周辺
　base rating level　基本格付け水準, 基本格付けレベル
　benchmark［landmark］level of　節目の～台, 節目ともいえる～
　borrowing level　資金調達コストの水準
　debt level　負債水準
　delinquency level　延滞率の水準
　drop to the upper ￥95 level over credit fears　95円台後半まで下落する
　interest rate level　金利水準
　　(=level of money rate, level of interest rates)
　level of cash and deposits　手元現預金水準
　level of credit enhancement　信用補完の水準
　level of employment　雇用水準, 失業率
　level of home ownership　持ち家比率
　level of income　所得水準
　level of inflation　物価上昇率, インフレ率
　level of investment　投資率
　level of next rate hike　追加利上げの幅
　level of price　物価水準
　level of short-term debt　短期債務の水準
　net level　当期利益ベース, 当期利益
　pension level　年金水準
　refinancing level　借換えの水準
　savings level　貯蓄率
　share price level　株価水準
　shoot up to the mid-85 level　85円台半ばまで急騰する［跳ね上がる］
　target level　誘導目標
　the upper ￥76 level to the dollar　1ドル＝76円台後半

◆A market player put the level of short selling in the stock market at between 5 percent to 10 percent of total trading volume. ある市場筋によると、株の空売りは取引全体の5-10％程度といわれる。◆About 40 percent of manufacturing companies will move their factories and R&D centers from Japan to other countries if the yen stays at its current level of ￥85 to the dollar. 円相場が現在の1ドル＝85円の水準で定着すると、製造業の約4割は工場や研究開発拠点を海外に移転すると見られる。◆After the government's move of intervention, the yen plunged to the ￥85 level against the dollar. 政府の市場介入の動きを受けて、円相場は1ドル＝85円台まで急落した。◆Amid the continued yen's historically high levels, increasing numbers of people are opening foreign currency deposit accounts. 歴史的な円高水準が続くなか、外貨預金口座を設ける人が増えている。◆Earnings for 2010 were lower than we had originally anticipated and did not reach 2009 levels. 2010年度の利益[当期利益]は、当初の予想を下回り、前年度[前期]の水準に達しなかった。◆Japan must prevent the yen from soaring again to the level of ￥76 to the dollar. 日本は、円相場が再び1ドル＝76円台に急騰する事態を阻止しなければならない。◆On Aug. 31, 2011, the yen rose to the ￥76.50 level against the U.S. dollar in the Tokyo foreign exchange market, close to the postwar record of ￥75.95 registered on Aug. 19. 2011年8月31日の東京外国為替市場の円相場は、1ドル＝76円50銭台まで上昇し、8月19日に付けた戦後最高値の75円95銭に近づいた。◆Preparedness for financial crisis has returned to a normal level from the guard raised during a financial sector-triggered recession. 金融危機への備えは、金融不況時の厳戒態勢から平常レベルに戻っている。◆Should the Fed misjudge the timing or level of its next rate hike, it may interrupt the economic recovery and even bring about rapid inflation. 米連邦準備制度理事会（FRB）が追加利上げの幅やタイミングを誤ると、景気回復の腰を折り、急激なインフレを招く可能性もある。◆The amount of straight corporate bond issuance came to ￥981 billion in July 2011, the highest level in 10 months. 2011年7月の普通社債発行額は、過去10か月で最高水準の9,810億円に達した。◆The diffusion indexes of the coincident, leading and lagging indicators compare the current levels of various economic indicators with their levels three months earlier. 一致指数や先行指数、遅行指数などの景気動向指数は、各種経済指標の現状を3か月前の状況と比較したものだ。◆The dollar's value temporarily dropped to the ￥85 level in New York. ドル相場は、ニューヨーク市場で一時、85円台まで下落した[値を下げた]。◆The euro plummeted to the ￥100 level on the foreign exchange market, hitting a 10 year low. 外国為替市場では、ユーロが1ユーロ＝100円台まで急落して、10年ぶりの低水準[10年ぶりの円高・ユーロ安水準]となった。◆The money lent by the U.S. and eurozone private banks remains at about the same level as those prior to Lehman's collapse. 米国とユーロ圏の民間銀行の貸出金は、リーマン・ブラザーズの経営破たん前とほぼ同水準にとどまっている。◆The Nikkei Stock Average fell briefly to its lowest level this year on the Tokyo Stock Market. 東京株式市場の日経平均株価は一時、今年の最安値を下回った。◆The rise of the yen beyond the level of the exchange rate assumed by many exporters has put them on the ropes. 多くの輸出業者が想定した為替レートの水準を上回る円高が輸出業者を窮地に追い込んでいる。◆The target range for the inflation rate could be set at the same level as the potential growth rate, for example. 物価上昇率の目標値としては、例えば潜在成長率と同水準に設定することもできよう。◆The 12 major banks probably will have latent losses exceeding ￥3 trillion if the 225-issue Nikkei Stock Average stays at the 10,000 level. 日経平均株価（225種）が1万円台まで下落すると、大手銀行12行が抱える含み損は3兆円強に達する。◆The 225-issue Nikkei Stock Average closed at 7,607.88, the lowest level since the economic bubble burst, on April 28, 2003. 2003年4月28日の日経平均株価（225種）の終値は7,607円88銭で、バブル崩壊後の最安値を付けた。◆The U.S. dollar temporarily dropped to the upper ￥95 level over credit fears. 米ドルは、信用不安で一時、1ドル＝95円台後半まで[後半の水準まで]下落した。◆The U.S. dollar temporarily dropped to the ￥84 level in Tokyo. 東京市場では、米ドルは一時、1ドル＝84円台まで下落した。◆The U.S. Federal Reserve Board boosted a key interest rate to the highest level in five years. 米連邦準備制度理事会（FRB）は、(短期金利の指標となる)FF金利を5年ぶりに最高水準に引き上げた。◆The yen hovered in a narrow range in the upper ￥85 level to the dollar. 円相場は、1ドル＝85円台後半の小幅な値動きとなった。◆The yen is currently hovering at a level stronger than ￥80 to the dollar. 円相場は現在[足元の円相場は]、1ドル＝80円を上回る水準で推移している。◆The yen's value still remains high and is likely to reach a postwar record value above the ￥76-to-the-dollar level. 円相場は依然高く、1ドル＝76円台を上回る戦後最高値に達する可能性がある。◆Under the envisioned lending facility, the IMF will provide funds to countries where government bond yields remain at high levels to help reconstruct their public finances. この融資制度案では、国際通貨基金（IMF）が、国債の利回りが高止まりしている国に資金を提供［融資］して財政再建を支援する。

level （形）平らな，平坦な，水平の，共通の，〜と同等［同位，同程度］の，冷静な，落ち着いた，バランスのとれた，一様な，変化のない
be level with 〜と同じ高さである，〜と同水準にある
level annual premium method 平準積立方式
level annuity 定額年金
level contribution 平準拠出
level pay floating rate note 定額支払い変動利付き債
level payment plan 元利均等返済方式
level pegging with 〜と力が互角の，〜と平等の，〜と同点の，〜と実力伯仲の
level playing field 共通の土俵，同じ土俵，平等の競争条件，平等な立場
level premium 平準保険料
level race 互角の競走［レース］
level yield amortization 一定利回り償却

level of liquidity 流動性の水準
◆Turbulence in global financial markets brought the level of liquidity in the country sharply lower. 世界の金融市場の混乱で、国内流動性の水準は大幅に低下した。

level of stock prices 株価水準，株価の水準
◆The higher the level of stock prices, the more funds firms can raise from IPOs. 株価の水準が上がれば、それだけ新規株式公開（上場時の新株発行）による資金調達額も増える。

level of the exchange rate 為替レートの水準
◆The rise of the yen beyond the level of the exchange rate assumed by many exporters has put them on the ropes. 多くの輸出業者が想定した為替レートの水準を上回る円高が輸出業者を窮地に追い込んでいる。

level off （動）横ばい状態になる，成長が止まる，伸び悩む，水平になる，水平飛行をする，平均化する
（=level out）
◆Corporate profits have remained high although they are leveling off. 企業収益は、伸び悩んでいるものの、高い水準で推移している。◆Negative sentiment among major companies has leveled off chiefly because of a slowdown in the decline of exports and progress in inventory adjustment. 大企業の景況感悪化が横ばい状態になった［大企業の景況感悪化に歯止めがかかった］主な要因として、輸出の減少が鈍ったことと在庫調整が進んだことが挙げられる。

level out 横ばい状態になる，成長が止まる，伸び悩む，水平になる，水平飛行をする，平均化する
（=level off）
◆Commodity prices level out. 市況商品価格は、横ばい状態。

leveling-off [leveling off] （名）横ばい，横ばい状態，踊り場 （=leveling out）
◆A slowdown in personal consumption and the leveling-off of private investment are behind the decline in the real GDP growth rate. 個人消費の伸びの鈍化と民間設備投資の横ばいが、実質GDP成長率が減少した要因だ。◆The economic recovery is increasingly robust following months of leveling off. 景気回復には、ここ数か月続いた踊り場を脱出して力強さが出てきた。

leverage （動）借入金で投機をする，〜を利用する，生かす，借入金で企業などを買い取る
◆Rakuten Inc. demanded a business tie-up with TBS, leveraging a massive number of TBS shares it had acquired. 楽天が取得した大量のTBS株を利用して、楽天はTBSとの事業提携を要求した。◆We believe there is an opportunity to leverage the strength of the balance sheet to deal with the demands of the business in the future. 財務内容の強みを生かして、将来、事業のニーズに対応する機会はあると思います。

leverage （名）借入れ，借入比率，借入余力，負債，負債比率，借入資本，財務レバレッジ，テコ，テコの作用，手段，影響力，力，有利な立場，レバレッジ （「レバレッジ」は投資額に対する借入金の割合で、「財務レバレッジ」は資本金に対する負債の割合（debt-to-equity ratio: 負債自己資本比率、外部負債比率）の高さを示す。⇒debt leverage）
additional leverage 負債比率の上昇
asset leverage index 資産レバレッジ・インデックス
bargaining leverage 交渉力
capital leverage 財務レバレッジ
companies' financial leverage 企業の借入比率
company's [companies'] leverage 企業の負債比率, 企業の借入比率
debt-adjusted double leverage total debt 債務調整済み［債務調整後］ダブル・レバレッジ総債務
debt leverage 債務比率，債務レバレッジ，デット・レバレッジ
economic leverage 経済的影響力
financial leverage 借入比率，負債比率，外部負債，財務レバレッジ
high-leverage acquisition [corporate takeover] 多額の借入れを伴う企業買収，多額の借入れに依存した企業買収
high-leverage transaction レバレッジの高い取引
increase leverage レバレッジを引き上げる
insurance leverage 保険レバレッジ
lending to high leverage credits 負債比率の高い企業に対する融資
leverage effect 梃棹（ていりつ）効果, テコの効果
leverage finance レバレッジ金融
leverage position 財務状況
leverage rules 負債制限
leverage test 債務比率
management's philosophy toward leverage 借入れについての経営陣の考え方
nominal leverage 名目ベースの負債比率
operating leverage 営業レバレッジ
reinsurance leverage 再保険レバレッジ
risk-adjusted leverage リスク調整後の負債比率
use significant amounts of financial leverage 巨額の外部負債を取り入れる，巨額の借入資本を利用する
◆Leverage was increased through a line of credit. 与信限度枠を使って、レバレッジを引き上げた。◆The next step in the quest for higher gains is to inflate the returns by leverage. 高利益追求の第二の手段は、借金による利益の膨（ふく）らましだ。

leverage on borrowers 融資先への有利な立場
◆Banks could use their leverage on borrowers to engage in unfair life insurance sales practices. 銀行が融資先への有利な立場を利用して、不公正な生保販売を行う可能性もある。

leverage ratio 負債比率，レバレッジ・レシオ，レバレッジ比率 （=leverage test）
financial leverage ratio 負債比率

leveraged （形）借入金による，借入金を利用した，借入資金による
conservative-leveraged company 負債比率が低い企業
exposure to highly leveraged transactions HLT融資
financially leveraged company 負債比率の高い企業
high-leveraged acquisition 多額の借入れによる企業買収
highly leveraged company 負債比率が高い企業，ハイ・

レバレッジ企業
highly leveraged issuer 負債比率が高い発行体
highly leveraged transaction 負債比率が高い取引, ハイ・レバレッジ取引, HLT
large leveraged deal 大型LBO案件
leveraged company てこ入れ会社（他人資本の割合が高い会社）
leveraged effectiveness レバレッジ効果, 他人資本効果（＝leverage effect）
leveraged finance レバレッジ金融
leveraged floating-rate note issues レバレッジド変動利付き債
leveraged marketing レバレッジド・マーケティング
leveraged recapitalization [recap] 借入資本利用の資本再構成
leveraged transaction レバリッジ取引
minimum leveraged ratio 最低レバレッジ率

leveraged buyout 借入資金による企業買収, 企業担保借入買取り, レバレッジド・バイアウト, LBO（＝leveraged buy-out: 為替相場や金利の変動によって, 対外支払いや受取りを意識的に早めたり遅らせたりすること。⇒LBO）
◆A leveraged buyout（LBO）is similar to using a mortgage to buy a house: a buyer puts some money down and borrows the rest, using the purchased asset as security. レバレッジド・バイアウト（LBO）は家を買うために住宅ローンを利用するのと同じで, 買い手が購入資金の一部（頭金）を支払い, 残金は購入した資産を担保にして借り入れる仕組みになっている。

leveraged lease レバレッジド・リース
◆We lease airplanes, energy-producing facilities and transportation equipment under leveraged leases. 当社は, 航空機, エネルギー生産設備と輸送機器をレバレッジド・リースでリースしている。

leveraging （名）レバレッジング
（＝gearing; ⇒gearing）
double leveraging ダブル・レバレッジ, 二重レバレッジ（＝double leverage）
leveraging opportunities レバレッジングの機会
leveraging up of balance sheets 負債比率の上昇

levered company [firm] 負債のある企業

levy （動）徴収する, 課する, 課税する, 賦課する, 割り当てる, 取り立てる, 差し押さえる, 押収する, 召集する
levy one's property 〜の財産を差し押さえる
levy taxes on 〜に課税する, 〜に税を課する
levy the tax on accrued interest 経過利息に課税する
◆Because the investment consortium is based outside of the country, the government cannot levy taxes on profits from stock sales. この投資組合は国外に本拠地を置いているため, 政府は株式売却益に課税できない。 ◆Taxes levied on capital gains should be consolidated to promote securities investment. 有価証券投資を促すために, 金融資産課税は一元化するべきだ。 ◆The new bank tax is levied on the banks' gross operating profits-their earnings minus basic operating expenses such as interest payments to depositors. 新銀行税は, 銀行の収入から基礎的な経費（預金者に対する預金利の支払いなど）を差し引いた業務粗利益に課される。 ◆The two companies are expected to be levied about ¥9.2 billion in back taxes, including penalty, corporate and local taxes. 両社は, 加算税や法人税, 地方税を含めて追徴課税として約92億円を課される［徴収される］見通しだ。

liabilities （名）債務, 負債, 借金, 賠償責任
（⇒financial difficulties, liability）
amount of liabilities 負債金額
contingent liabilities 偶発債務
current liabilities 流動負債
external liabilities 対外債務 外部負債
net liabilities 正味負債 債務超過額
noncurrent liabilities 非流動負債
off-the-book liabilities 簿外債務
（＝off-the-book debts, liquidation）
◆Companies are usually considered likely to collapse when their liabilities surpass their assets. 企業は, 一般に債務超過になった場合に「破綻懸念先」となる。 ◆Japan increasingly looks like to have liabilities exceed assets as of the end of fiscal 2010. 日本は, 2010年度末には負債超過になる可能性が高くなっている。 ◆Making the creditor banks waive loans to TEPCO will cause the utility to fall into capital deficiency, with liabilities exceeding assets. 取引銀行に東電への債権を放棄させると, 東電は資本不足に陥り, 債務超過になってしまう。 ◆The firm's liabilities exceeded its assets by ¥8 billion in its settlement of accounts at the end of February last year. 同社は, 昨年2月期決算で, 80億円の債務超過になった。
一般的に負債に含まれるもの：
accounts payable 買掛金
loans payable 借入金
notes payable 支払い手形
other liabilities その他の負債

liabilities and net worth 負債と資産[負債・資本], 負債と資本
assets or liabilities and net worth 資産・負債と資本
operating profit ratio of liabilities and net worth 総資本営業利益率
ratio of current profit to total liabilities and net worth 総資本経常利益率
ratio of net profit to total liabilities and net worth 総資本利益率
total liabilities and net worth 総資本
turnover（ratio）of total liabilities and net worth 総資本回転率

liabilities in excess of assets 債務超過 （＝excess liabilities, excess of liabilities over assets）
◆The company is in danger of accruing liabilities in excess of its assets sometime in the next business year or afterward. 同社は来期以降, 債務超過に陥る危険にさらされている。

liability （名）責任, 義務, 負担, 負担額, 債務, 負債, 借金, 賠償責任, 賠償金 （⇒liabilities, limited liability company, pool insurance system）
asset liability management 資産負債総合管理, 資産負債管理, バランス・シート管理, ALM
（＝assets and liability management）
differentiate a financial liability from an equity instrument 持ち分金融商品と金融負債を区別する
general liability insurance 賠償責任保険
hidden liability 簿外債務
income tax liability 未払い所得税, 未払い法人税
joint and several liability 連帯責任
liability adequacy test 負債適合性テスト
pay liability 賠償金を支払う, 負担金を支払う
prior service liability 過去勤務債務
product liability 製造物責任, PL
property and liability insurance 損害保険
◆Gains and losses on hedges of existing assets or liabilities are marked to market on a monthly basis. 既存の資産または債務のヘッジに関する損益は毎月, 評価替えされている。 ◆In the policies offered by the Sompo Japan and Tokio Marine & Nichido Fire Insurance, the companies also pay liability if policyholders injure or kill someone. 損保ジャパンと東京海上日動火災が提供している保険では, 保険契約者［保険加入

者]が人をけがや死亡させたりした場合に、その相手に支払う賠償金も支払われる。◆The combined liabilities of JAL and its two subsidiaries were ¥2.32 trillion. 日航と子会社2社の負債総額は、合計で2兆3,200億円に上った。

liability insurance　責任保険, 賠償責任保険, 損害賠償責任保険
 automobile bodily injury liability insurance　対人賠償保険
 automobile property damage liability insurance　対物賠償保険
 bailee's liability insurance　受託者賠償責任保険
 compulsory automobile liability insurance　自動車損害賠償責任保険
 contractors' liability insurance　請負業者賠償責任保険
 premises and operations liability insurance　私設所有者賠償責任保険
 product liability insurance　製造物責任保険, 生産物賠償責任保険
 professional liability insurance　専門職業人賠償責任保険, 職業賠償責任保険
 property and liability insurance　損害保険
 sports liability insurance　スポーツ賠償責任保険
 umbrella liability insurance　企業包括賠償責任保険
 ◆Under the Atomic Energy Damage Compensation Law, if the liability insurance falls short in covering damage costs, the remainder will be taken care of by the government. 原子力損害賠償法では、損害賠償責任保険で損害費用をまかないきれない場合、その残りは政府(国)が保障することになっている。

liable　(形)〜に法的責任がある, 〜する義務がある, (税や罰金などを)かけられるべき
 be liable for tax　税金がかかる
 be liable to a fine　罰金に処せられる, 罰金を科される
 be liable to pay the debts　負債を払う責任がある, 借金を払う義務がある
 liable for the damages　損害賠償の責任がある
 liable for the debts　負債[借金]を払う責任がある, 債務を返済する責任がある
 liable to the law　法の適用を受ける
 ◆Who is actually liable for the government's accumulating debt？ 政府が積み上げている借金は実際、誰にその借金を払う責任があるのか。

liberalization　(名)自由化, 規制緩和, 開放, 国際化
 capital liberalization　資本自由化
  (=liberalization of capital transactions)
 exchange liberalization　為替自由化
 financial liberalization　金融自由化, 金融の規制緩和
 full liberalization　全面開放, 完全自由化
 liberalization of exchange control　為替自由化
  (=exchange liberalization, liberalization of foreign exchange)
 liberalization of interest rates　金利の自由化
 liberalization of the financial industry　金融自由化
  (=financial deregulation, financial liberalization)
 liberalization of the Yen　円の国際化
 market liberalization　市場の自由化, 市場開放, 市場の規制緩和
 partial liberalization　部分開放
 total liberalization of brokerage commissions　委託手数料の完全自由化
 ◆The liberalization of brokerage commissions on commodity futures trading has paved the way to potentially dramatic realignment of the industry. 商品先物取引の委託手数料の自由化で、業界が劇的に再編される可能性が出てきた。◆The wall separating banking and securities businesses has been lowered through such moves as the liberalization of banks' securities brokering. 銀行と証券業の垣根は、銀行に対する証券仲介業の規制緩和などの動きで、低くなっている。

liberalize　(動)自由化する, 規制緩和する, 開放する, 解禁する
 liberalize brokerage commissions on commodity futures　商品先物取引の委託手数料を自由化する
 liberalize trade and investment　貿易や投資を自由化する
 liberalize trust business　信託業の規制を緩和する
 ◆Brokerage commissions on commodity futures trading were completely liberalized in late 2004. 商品先物取引の委託手数料は、2004年末に完全自由化された。◆Government plans to liberalize trust business. 政府は、信託業の規制緩和を行う方針だ。

LIBOR　ロンドンの銀行間取引金利, ロンドン銀行間出し手金利, ロンドン銀行間貸し手金利, ロンドン銀行間オファーレート, ライボー　(=Libor:London inter-bank offered rateの略。⇒Euribor, floating rate payments)
 BBA LIBOR　英国銀行協会(BBA)が公表するロンドン銀行間取引金利
 delayed LIBOR swap　ディレードLIBORスワップ
 margin of AAbp over LIBOR　LIBOR＋AAベーシス・ポイント(bp)の変動金利
 the euro BBA LIBOR rate　ユーロ建てBBA LIBORレート(英国銀行協会(BBA)が公表するユーロ建て銀行間取引金利のレート)
 tied to LIBOR　LIBORに連動した, LIBORベースの
 ◆Any payment not made when due will, in addition to any other right or remedy of Licensor, incur a finance charge at the lesser of three hundred basis points over the 3-month London Inter Bank Offered Rate ("LIBOR＋3") on the date payment was due or the highest applicable legal contract rate. 支払いが支払い期日までに履行されない場合、ライセンサーの他の権利や救済請求権に加えて、支払い期日時点の3か月物ロンドン銀行間取引金利(LIBOR)プラス3%(LIBOR＋3%)または適用される最高法定約定金利のうち、いずれか低いほうの金利の金融費用が発生する。
 解説 **LIBORとは**：ロンドンのユーロ市場で資金を貸し出す銀行側が提示するレートで、金融機関が資金調達するときの基準金利。国際金融取引の指標として利用されているが、一般にユーロ建て取引はEuriborベース、米ドルなどユーロ以外の取引はLIBORベースを使用するケースが多い。

license [licence]　(名)許可, 認可, 免許, 特許, 許諾, 実施許諾, 商標やソフトウエアなどの使用許諾, 実施権, 使用権, 鉱業権, 不動産の立入り権, 許可書, 免許状, ライセンス
 banking license　銀行免許
 business license　営業免許
 export license　輸出承認
 general license bank　普通銀行
 import license　輸入承認
 offshore banking license　オフショア支店免許
 ◆Citigroup Private Bank's four offices in Japan will have their licenses revoked for violating the law by ignoring suspected money laundering by clients. シティグループのプライベート・バンク(PB)の在日4拠点(支店・出張所)が、顧客のマネー・ロンダリング(資金洗浄)の疑いのある取引を放置するなどして法令違反があったとして、認可を取り消されることになった。◆The government may reject a company's request for a license to enter the fiduciary market if its executive has been dismissed in the past five years due to a violation of Section 2 of Article 102. 信託市場[信託業]に参入するための免許を申請した企業の役員が、第102条第2項の違反により5年以内に

解任命令を受けていた場合、政府はその免許申請（免許交付）を拒否することができる。◆The new virtual bank will seek to obtain a banking license. この新仮想銀行は、銀行免許を取得する方針だ。◆The Tokyo branch of Credit Suisse Financial Products had its license revoked in 1999. クレディ・スイス・ファイナンシャル・プロダクツ銀行の東京支店が、1999年に免許を取り消されている。

lien （名）先取特権，留置権，物的担保，担保権，リーエン
 equitable lien 先取特権，優先弁済権
 junior lien bond 後順位先取特権付き社債
 lien creditor リーエン債権者
 liens on assets 資産に対する担保権，資産に対する先取特権
 possessory lien 留置権，占有リーエン，コモン・ロー上のリーエン（=common law lien）
 ◆The proprietary information is free and clear of any liens, restriction on use, or encumbrances of any nature whatsoever. この占有情報は、いかなる担保、使用制限もしくはどんな種類の負担も存在しない［本占有情報は、担保、使用制限、負担の制約が一切ない］。◆The Shares are free and clear of any liens, charges or other encumbrances. 本株式は、先取特権、担保権その他の制限［負担・障害］の対象に一切なっていない。

life （名）期間，存続期間，償還期間，行使期間，耐用年数，生命，生命保険，生活，暮らし，活気，好調，ライフ
 asset life 資産の耐用年数
 average life 平均期間，平均償還期間
 composite (useful) life 総合耐用年数
 contractual life 契約期間
 credit life 信用生命保険
 economic life of leased property リース資産の経済耐用年数
 equivalent life 相当期間
 exchange risk insurance 為替変動保険
 expected [estimated] life 見積り耐用年数
 life assured 生命保険契約者
 life bond 年金契約証書
 life expectancy [expectation] 平均余命，平均寿命
 life fund 生命保険基金
 life income （生命保険の）終身所得，終身年金の受取り額
 life income policy 終身年金保険
 life insured 生命保険契約者
 life interest 生涯不動産権，終身権益
 life-kind property 同額資産
 life of the swap スワップ期間
 life office 生命保険会社
 life rate 生命保険料率
 life reinsurance 生命保険再保険
 life table 生命表，死亡表（=mortality table）
 life to call 据え置き期間
 life to put [life-to-put] 残存プット行使制限期間
 life underwriter 生命保険募集人
 limited-life preferred equity 期限付き優先株
 mean expectation life 平均余命
 mutual life company 相互保険会社
 one life 被保険者1名
 option life オプション行使期間
 ordinary life 普通生命保険，簡易生命保険
 property insurance 財産保険，損害保険，物保険
 provisional insurance 予定保険
 remaining life 残存期間，残存年数
 remaining life of the issue 社債の残存期間
 remaining useful life 残存耐用年数
 retired life fund 退職終身基金
 the same life 同一被保険者
 useful life 耐用年数
 useful life of a depreciable asset 減価償却資産の耐用年数
 weighted average life 加重平均償還期間
 yield to average life 平均残存期間利回り，平均償還期間利回り
 ◆There are signs of life in the lackluster economy. 景気停滞に、景気の好調を示す兆候がある。

life annuity 終身年金，生命年金
 （=perpetual annuity）
 immediate life annuity 即時払い終身年金，即時終身年金
 life annuity insurance 終身年金保険
 life annuity insurance policy 終身年金保険証券
 life annuity with a period certain 期限付き終身年金
 present value rate of life annuity 生命年金現価率
 purchased life annuity 買入れ終身年金
 straight life annuity 終身年金
 temporary life annuity 定期終身年金，定期年金
 whole life annuity with guaranteed installment 保証期間付き終身年金
 ◆Life annuity is an annuity that provides periodic benefit payments for at least the lifetime of a named individual, called the annuitant. 終身年金は、年金受取人と呼ばれる特定個人に少なくとも一生涯の給付支払いを定期的に行う年金である。

life assurance 生命保険
 Life Assurance and Unit Trust Regulatory Organization 生命保険・投資信託規制機関
 life assurance business 生命保険事業
 life assurance company 生命保険会社
 life assurance premium relief 生命保険料控除

life insurance 生命保険（⇒individual life insurance）
 cash-value life insurance 貯蓄型生命保険
 consumer credit life insurance 消費者信用生命保険
 credit life insurance 消費者信用生命保険，信用生命保険
 endowment life insurance 養老保険
 equity-linked life insurance エクイティ生命保険
 group credit life insurance 団体信用生命保険
 individual life insurance 個人生命保険
 joint life insurance 連生保険
 life employment 終身雇用
 （=lifelong employment, lifetime employment）
 life insurance agent 生命保険の外務員
 life insurance applicant 生命保険申込み者［申請者］
 Life Insurance Association of Japan 生命保険協会
 life insurance business 生命保険事業
 life insurance contract 生命保険契約
 life insurance deduction 生命保険料控除
 life insurance firm 生命保険会社
 （=life insurance company, life insurer）
 life insurance in force 生命保険の保有契約高
 life insurance medicine 生命保険医学
 life insurance product 生命保険商品，生保商品
 （⇒annuity insurance policy, deregulate）
 life insurance provision 生命保険準備金
 life insurance rate 生命保険料率
 life insurance relief 生命保険料控除
 life insurance sector 生命保険業界，生保業界

(=life insurance industry; ⇒lure)
life insurance trust 生命保険信託
life reinsurance premium 生命保険再保険料
non-life insurance company 損害保険会社
overseas travel life insurance 海外旅行生命保険
participating whole life insurance 配当付き終身保険
permanent life insurance 終身生命保険
postal life insurance 簡易生命保険
single pay life insurance 一時払い生命保険
term life insurance 定期生命保険, 定期保険
universal life insurance ユニバーサル保険
variable life insurance 変額生命保険, 変額保険
whole life insurance 終身保険
◆Life insurance refers to insurance that provides protection against the economic loss caused by the death of the person insured. 生命保険とは、被保険者の死亡により発生する経済的損失を保護する保険のことだ。◆Whole life insurance means life insurance under which coverage remains in force during the insured's entire lifetime, provided premiums are paid as specified in the policy. 終身保険は、保険契約に明記されている保険料が支払われているかぎり、保障が被保険者の全生涯にわたって有効な生命保険を意味する。

life insurance benefits 生命保険給付
◆Previously, we expensed life insurance benefits as plans were funded. これまで当社は、生命保険給付については、制度に拠出がなされたときに費用として計上していました。

life insurance company 生命保険会社, 生保 (=life insurance firm, life insurer; ⇒insurance agent)
fire and casualty insurance company 火災・障害保険会社
life insurance company purchase 生保買い
stock life insurance company 生命保険株式会社
the liquidation of an insurance company 保険会社の清算
◆Because seven life insurers have collapsed in the past five years, policyholders have become distrustful of life insurance companies. この5年間で生保7社が経営破綻したため、契約者は「生保不信」になっている。◆Financial institutions and life insurance companies have extended about ¥4 trillion in loans to TEPCO. 金融機関と生命保険会社は、東電に4兆円ほど融資している。

life insurance coverage 保険金額, 保険契約金額, 生命保険給付 (=insured amount)
◆Our postretirement benefits include health care benefits and life insurance coverage. 当社の退職後給付には、医療給付と生命保険給付が含まれています。

life insurance industry 生命保険業界, 生保業界
(=life insurance sector; ⇒financial soundness)
◆Amid the protracted economic slump and the ongoing deflationary trend, the life insurance industry has been hit by a trio of predicaments. 景気の長期低迷とデフレ傾向が進行するなか、生保業界は三重苦に見舞われている。◆Razor-thin interest rates and slumping share prices have weighed heavily on the life insurance industry. 超低金利と株価低迷が、生保業界の大きな重荷になっている。◆The massive negative yields of the life insurance industry threaten the financial soundness of insurers. 生保業界の巨額の逆ざやが、生保各社の財務上の健全性[経営の健全性]を脅(おびや)かしている。

life insurance market 生命保険市場, 生保市場
◆Tokio Marine Holdings Inc. will enter the life insurance market in India on July 1, 2011. 東京海上ホールディングスは、2011年7月1日からインドの生命保険市場に参入する。

life insurance money 保険金
◆It is illegal to impose income tax as well as inheritance tax on the beneficiaries of life insurance money paid with a linked pension. 年金型の生命保険金の受取人に所得税と相続税の両方を課すのは、違法である。

life insurance policy 生命保険証券
(⇒postal privatization)
a holder of a life insurance policy with a pension contract 年金特約付き生命保険契約者
◆Life insurance policy is a policy under which the insurance company promises to pay a benefit upon the death of the person who is insured. 生命保険証券は、保険会社が被保険者に対して死亡時に給付を確約する証券である。

life insurance policyholder 生命保険契約者
◆Traditionally, life insurance policyholders have been required to pay their first premiums directly to sales agents in cash or by bank transfer. これまで生命保険の契約者は、初回保険料を現金で直接、営業職員に支払うか銀行振込みで支払う必要があった。

Life Insurance Policyholders Protection Corp. 生命保険契約者保護機構
◆Life Insurance Policyholders Protection Corp. will provide ¥145 billion to partially cover the life insurer's negative net worth, which was ¥320 billion as of the end of last September. 生命保険契約者保護機構は、昨年9月末現在の同生保の債務超過額3,200億円の一部を支援するため、1,450億円を支出することになっている。◆The government has to deal with the issue of replenishing the resources of the Life Insurance Policyholders Protection Corp. 政府は、生保契約者保護機構の財源確保問題を処理しなければならない。

Life Insurance Policyholders Protection Corporation of Japan 生命保険契約者保護機構
◆The Life Insurance Policyholders Protection Corporation of Japan helps holders of life insurance policies sold by bankrupt companies to protect their assets. 生命保険契約者保護機構は、破たんした生命保険会社が販売した生命保険証券の保有者[破たんした生保の保険契約者]の財産保護にかかわっている。◆The use of taxpayers' money by the Life Insurance Policyholders Protection Corporation of Japan terminated at the end of March 2009. 生命保険契約者保護機構による公的資金の活用は、2009年3月末で期限が切れた。

life insurance premium 生命保険料
◆A total of ¥340 trillion collected through postal savings and kampo life insurance premiums has been infused into government-affiliated public corporations to sustain inefficient enterprises. 郵便貯金や簡易保険料を通じて集めた総額340兆円の資金は、特殊法人に注入(投入)され、非効率的な事業を支えてきた。

life insurance product 生命保険商品, 生保商品
◆In this type of life insurance products, the rate of return after canceling the insurance contract can be higher than that of a savings account if a policyholder upholds the contract for five to 10 years. この種の生保商品では、保険契約者が保険契約を5～10年続けると、解約後の利回り(予定利率)は預金よりも高い利回りが見込める。◆Meiji Yasuda will lower the yield of its single-premium whole life insurance and other companies offering the same type of life insurance products could follow suit. 明治安田生命は一時払い終身保険の利回り(予定利率)を引き下げるが、同種の生保商品を販売している他社もこれに追随する可能性がある。

life insurance sales 生保販売
◆Banks could use their leverage on borrowers to engage in unfair life insurance sales practices. 銀行が融資先への有利な立場を利用して、不公正な生保販売を行う可能性もある。

life insurance sector 生保業界
◆In the life insurance sector, the practice of luring customers by touting the bad performances of other insurers has been called into question. 生保業界では、他社の経営不振をあおって顧客を勧誘する行為(風評営業)が問題になっている。

life insurer 生命保険会社 (=life insurance company, life insurance firm; ⇒capital injection, foundation fund, insurance benefits, life insurance company)

◆Banks and life insurers have extended about ¥4 trillion in loans to TEPCO. 銀行や生命保険会社は、東電にこれまで約4兆円を融資している。◆During the bubble economy, life insurers sold a large number of policies by promising high yields. バブル期に生保各社は、高い予定利率を約束して多くの保険契約を獲得した。◆Life insurer's foundation fund is equivalent to capital for a stock company. 生命保険会社の基金は、株式会社の資本金に相当する。◆Life insurers have been offering relatively high yield rates to their policyholders. 生保各社は、保険契約者に比較的高い利回り[予定利率]を提示してきた。◆Premium revenues slipped at seven of the nine major life insurers. 保険料収入は、主要生命保険9社のうち7社が減少した。◆Revenues from the single-premium whole life insurance policies support the life insurer's business performance. 一時払い終身保険による収入[一時払い終身保険の収入保険料]が、同生保の業績を支えている。◆The life insurer currently promises its policyholders an annual yield of 1.5 percent for the single-premium whole life insurance. 同生保は現在、一時払い終身保険については年1.5%の利回り(予定利率)を契約者に約束している。◆The life insurer's single-premium whole life insurance is popular with consumers as a form of savings or an investment for retirement. 同生保の一時払い終身保険は、一種の貯蓄や退職金の運用先として顧客に人気がある。◆The merger may help dispel policyholders' distrust in life insurers. 今回の合併で、契約者の生保不信をある程度一掃できるかもしれない。◆To make up for losses and for other purposes, seven life insurers sold a total of ¥529.2 billion in reserves, which are set aside in preparation for interest rate fluctuations and natural disasters. 損失の穴埋めなどのため、金利変動や自然災害に備えて積み立てていた準備金を、生保7社が5,292億円も取り崩した。

life policy　生命保険証券, 生命保険契約, 生命保険, 生保
　life and nonlife policies　生保と損保
　life policy reserves　生命保険契約準備金
　total face amount of ordinary life policies surrendered and lapsed　解約・失効した簡易生命保険証書額面総額
　yield on life policy　保険利回り, 生保利回り
　◆Edelweiss Tokyo Life Insurance Co. is the first Japanese insurer handling both life and nonlife policies in India. エーデルワイス・トウキョウ・ライフ・インシュランス(本店所在地：インドのマハラシュトラ州ムンバイ市)は、インドで生保と損保を取り扱う日本初の保険会社だ。◆Meiji Yasuda Life Insurance Co. will lower the yield on life policy from December 2011. 明治安田生命保険が、2011年12月から保険利回りを引き下げる。

life settlement　ライフ・セトルメント(生命保険の解約を考えている主に60代以上の人を対象に、通常の解約返戻金以上の金額で保険を買い取り、保険の支払いを肩代わりする代わりに死亡保険金の受取人となる契約)
life-sustaining　(形)生命維持の, 延命の
　life-sustaining boon　延命効果
　life-sustaining treatment　生命維持治療, 延命治療
　◆The latest depreciation of the euro brought about a life-sustaining boon to the currency. 今回のユーロ安が、ユーロの延命効果を招いた。
lifeboat　(名)救済資金, 救済基金, 救命ボート, 救命艇, 減刑, 恩赦
lifeboat operation　英中央銀行による銀行救済策
lifeline banking　ライフライン・バンキング
lifetime　(名)終身, 終生, 生涯　(形)終身の, 生涯の
　lifetime income　生涯所得
　lifetime policy　終身保険証券
　lifetime underwriter　生命保険業者
　◆Whole life insurance means life insurance under which coverage remains in force during the insured's entire lifetime, provided premiums are paid as specified in the policy. 終身保険は、保険契約に明記されている保険料が支払われているかぎり、保障が被保険者の全生涯にわたって有効な生命保険を意味する。

LIFFE　ロンドン金融先物取引所(London International Financial Futures Exchangeの略。2002年にEuronextに買収されて、Euronext.liffeとなる)
lift　(動)持ち上げる, 上げる, 高める, 引き上げる, 増やす, 移動する, 輸送する, 空輸する, 解禁する, (制限や禁止などを)解く, 解除する, 廃止する, 盗む, 万引きする, 掘る, 掘り上げる
　lift a hedge　ヘッジを外す
　lift oil prices　原油価格を引き上げる
　lift output　増産する
　lift restrictions [regulations] on　〜に対する制限[規制]を撤廃する
　lift spending　消費を押し上げる, 消費を拡大する
　lift the dollar against the yen　円に対してドルを押し上げる
　lift the economy　景気拡大の要因となる
　lift the government's full-deposit guarantee　政府の預金全額保護(ペイオフ)の凍結を解除する
　lift the import ban　輸入禁止を解く
　lift the offers　オファーを押し上げる
　lift the zero-interest rate policy　ゼロ金利政策を解除する (⇒zero-interest rate policy)
　◆The BOJ lifted its zero-interest rate policy on the strength of its optimistic view on the outlook for the economy in the summer of 2000. 日銀は2000年夏、景気の先行きを楽観してゼロ金利政策を解除した。◆The freeze on the payoff system will be lifted this April. ペイオフ凍結の解除は、今年4月になる。◆The government is making final arrangements to lift the ceiling on postal bank deposits three years from now. 政府は、ゆうちょ銀行の預け入れ限度額を3年後に撤廃する方向で、最終調整に入った。◆The guard raised against a possible financial meltdown during a financial sector-triggered recession several years ago has been lifted. 数年前の金融不況時に想定された金融崩壊に対する厳戒態勢は、すでに解かれている。◆While lifting the zero-interest rate policy will not immediately result in better business performance, there is concern that it may have a bad effect if the timing of the move is wrong. ゼロ金利政策の解除は、企業の業績改善に直ちにつながらないのに対して、その時期を誤れば悪影響を及ぼす心配がある。

lift　(名)持ち上げること, 押し上げること, (価格の)上昇, 昇進, 昇級, 手助け, やる気, 自信
　a lift in prices　物価上昇
　give A a lift　Aを景気付ける, Aを刺激する
　give a lift to stock prices　株価を押し上げる
　give the economy a lift　景気を刺激する
　give the market a lift　相場を反発させる
　◆With the economic recovery gaining momentum, U.S. companies have begun investing in the Japanese stock market again, giving a lift to stock prices. 景気回復が力強さを増していることから、米国企業が日本の株式市場に再び投資するようになり、株価を押し上げている。

lift check　会社宛小切手, 弁済小切手
lifting　(名)持ち上げること, 引上げ, 増大, 解禁, 撤廃, 解除
　lifting a leg　リフティング・ア・レッグ (=taking off a leg：ヘッジングで片方の取引を手じまい、もう一方の取引を残しておくこと)
　lifting charge　(円為替)取扱い手数料, 再割引手数料
　lifting of a ban on treasury stock　金庫株解禁

lifting of the gold embargo　金解禁
lifting of the limit on corporate bond issues　社債発行限度枠の撤廃
lifting of the freeze on the payoff system　ペイオフ凍結解除, ペイオフ制度凍結解除
　◆The lifting of the freeze on the payoff system may trigger a financial crisis. ペイオフ凍結解除は, 金融恐慌の引き金になる可能性がある.
lighten　(動)軽減する, 緩和する, 和らげる, 軽くする, 減らす, 引き下げる, 元気づける
　lighten exposure　組入れ比率を引き下げる
　lighten one's repayment burden　返済負担を軽減する
　◆Public institutions or revitalization funds will buy the loans owed by small and midsize companies that have been hit by the March 11 disaster to lighten their repayment burdens. 公的機関や復興ファンドが, 東日本大震災で被災した中小企業の借金を買い取って, 被災企業の返済負担を軽減するものと思われる.
likelihood　(名)可能性, 見込み, 見通し, 確率, ありそうなこと
　likelihood of collecting loans　債権回収の見込み, 債権回収の見通し
　likelihood of default　デフォルトの可能性, デフォルトの確率
　likelihood of event risks　イベント・リスクの可能性
　◆The bank's likelihood of collecting loans extended to its major corporate borrowers has worsened. 同行の大口融資先[融資先企業]に対する債権の回収見通しが, 悪化した.
likely　(形)有望な, 見込みのある, 有力とされる, 予想される, 見込まれる, 必死である　(副)たぶん, おそらく
　be highly likely　公算が大きい, 可能性が高い
　be likely to　～する見通しだ, ～する見込みだ, ～する模様だ, ～しそうだ, ～の可能性が大きい[高い], ～する公算が大きい
　likely debt burden　予想される債務負担額
　the most likely explanation　最も納得の行く説明
　the most likely scenario　特に可能性が高いシナリオ, 標準的シナリオ
　◆A reduction of the government's stake in Japan Tobacco Inc. is likely to be opposed by tobacco farmers. 政府の日本たばこ産業(JT)への出資比率引下げには, 葉タバコ農家の反発が予想される. ◆Companies are usually considered likely to collapse when their liabilities surpass their assets. 企業は, 一般に債務超過になった場合に「破綻懸念先」となる. ◆Countries likely to be affected by the fiscal and financial crisis in Europe will basically be able to obtain the IMF's short-term loans immediately after applying for them. 欧州財政・金融危機が波及しそうな国は, IMF(国際通貨基金)に要請すると, 基本的にIMFの短期融資を即時に受けられる. ◆Financial reconstruction is likely to stagnate under the Italy's new government as it did under the previous one. イタリアの財政再建は, 前政権同様, 新政権でも難航しそうだ. ◆If Hokuetsu Paper Mills decides to carry out the poison pill, Oji Paper Co. is likely to take legal action against it. 北越製紙が買収防衛策を実施したら, 王子製紙は法的措置を取る可能性が高い. ◆It is highly likely that the merger between the two financial institutions will be postponed. 両金融機関の統合が延期されるのは必至だ. ◆It is highly likely the firm will be delisted. 同社は, 上場廃止になる公算が大きい. ◆M&A deals among start-up firms are likely to create more demand for equity financing from the autumn. ベンチャー企業間のM&A取引で, 秋から株式発行による資金調達の需要が増える見通しだ. ◆The current momentum in the yen is likely to take hold. 現在の円相場の勢いは, 持続しそうだ. ◆The government and the Bank of Japan will likely continue to work together in fighting the sharp rise in the yen's value. 政府と日銀は, 急激な円高阻止で協調路線を継続することになりそうだ. ◆The rate of savings among those people in their 30s and 40s is on an upward trend, which is likely to have a depressing effect on domestic demand. 30～40歳代の貯蓄率が増大傾向にあり, 内需を下押ししている可能性がある. ◆The sell-off of Tokyo Metro shares planned by the government will likely be opposed by the Tokyo metropolitan government which is the second-largest shareholder. 政府が計画している東京メトロ株の売却には, 国に次ぐ大株主の東京都が抵抗すると見られる. ◆The three Japanese biggest banks are likely to be required to hold additional capital of 1 percent to 1.5 percent. 日本の3メガ銀行は, 1～1.5％の資本[自己資本]上積みを求められる見込みだ. ◆The yen's value still remains high and is likely to reach a postwar record value above the ￥76-to-the-dollar level. 円相場は依然高く, 1ドル＝76円台を上回る戦後最高値に達する可能性がある.
limit　(動)制限する, 制限[限度]を設ける, 限定する, 制約する, 抑える
　◆Koizumi adhered to his official pledge of limiting the new issuance of government bonds to ￥30 trillion. 小泉首相は, 国債の新規発行額を30兆円以下に抑える公約にこだわった. ◆Shares taken by the outside subscribers at the time of incorporation of the new company shall be limited to one share each. 新会社の設立時に外部の引受人が引き受ける株式は, それぞれ1株に限るものとする. ◆The ownership of indexed government bonds has been limited to foreign governments, central banks and international organizations. 物価連動債の保有は, これまで海外の政府や中央銀行, 国際機関に限られていた.
limit　(名)限度, 極度, 限界, 制限, 限度額, 規制値, 基準値, リミット
　borrower limit　与信限度
　borrowing limit　借入限度, 借入限度額
　credit limit　信用限度, 与信限度, 信用貸出限度, 借入限度額, 利用限度額
　daily limit　値幅制限
　daily price limit　値幅制限　(＝price limit)
　debt limit　債務上限　(＝debt ceiling)
　export limit　輸出制限
　lending limit　貸出限度
　limit down [low]　ストップ安
　limit move　値幅制限
　limit on banks' cross shareholdings　銀行の持ち合い株保有制限
　limit order　指し値注文(顧客が証券会社に特定の値段を指定して注文すること)
　limit price　指し値
　limit up　ストップ高
　lower limit　値幅制限の下限, 下限　(⇒open動詞)
　manager's discretionary limit　支店長の専決限度
　maximum limit of overdraft　貸越し極度額
　oil output limits　原油生産枠　(⇒hold名詞)
　order without limit　成り行き注文
　policyholder limits　保険契約者に対する与信限度
　price limit　値幅制限, ストップ値段
　risk limits　リスクの上限
　stock buyback limits　自社株の取得枠
　stock-buying limit　株式買入れ枠
　stop limit　ストップ・リミット
　stop limit order　指し値注文
　trading limit　取引制限
　upper limit　上限
　upper limit money rate　上限金利　(＝the upper limit of the interest rate)

◆As a provisional measure until the ¥10 million limit on postal bank deposits is removed, the government intends to raise the ceiling to ¥30 million. ゆうちょ銀行の1人当たり1,000万円の預け入れ限度額を撤廃するまでの暫定措置として、政府は限度額[上限]を3,000万円に引き上げる方針だ。◆Slightly raising the upper limit of interest rates will not get rid of unauthorized moneylenders. 多少の上限金利の変更で、ヤミ金融業者がなくなるわけではない。◆Stock buyback limits are to be decided at general shareholders meetings. 自社株の取得枠は、株主総会で決められることになっている。◆The bank imposed an illegally high interest rate of about 46 percent a year, far above the upper limit stipulated in the Investment Deposit and Interest Rate law. 同行は、出資法で定められている金利の上限をはるかに上回る年約46%の暴利で融資していた。◆The bank raised the amount of insurance money from the current ¥5 million limit to a maximum of ¥10 million for cash card fraud. 同行は、キャッシュ・カード詐欺の保険金額を、現在の上限500万円から1,000万円に引き上げた。◆The Swiss National Bank put a limit on the flying Swiss franc. スイス国立銀行(スイスの中央銀行)が、過度なスイス・フラン高に上限を設定した。◆There is a limit to conventional pump-priming measures amid a continued decline in birthrate and a consequent graying and shrinking population. 少子高齢化や人口減少などが進行するなかで、従来の景気刺激策[景気テコ入れ策]では限界がある。◆U.S. House of Representatives rejected the increase of debt limit. 米下院は、債務上限の引上げ(法案)を否決した。

limit of financial assistance 金融支援枠, 財政支援枠
◆The government plans to raise the limit of its financial assistance to the Nuclear Damage Liability Facilitation Fund from ¥2 trillion to ¥5 trillion. 政府は、原子力損害賠償支援機構への金融支援枠を、現在の2兆円から5兆円に拡大する方針だ。

limited (形)限られた, 限定的, 有限の, 制限付きの, 有限責任の, 有期限の, 狭い, 乏しい, わずかの, 少ない, 不十分な, 特別の
limited annuity 有期限年金, 有限年金
limited assurance 限定的保証
limited check 限度額付き小切手, 制限付き小切手
limited coinage issue 制限通貨発行
limited convertibility (通貨の)制限付き交換性
limited deposit protection 制限付き預金保護, 預金限定保護
limited deposit windows 積立金引出し制限
limited dividend corporation 配当制限会社[企業]
limited guarantee 有限保証
limited legal tender 制限的法貨, 制限法貨
limited-life preferred equity[stock] 期限付き優先株
limited market 薄商い
limited means 小資本, 小資本金
limited offering 限定募集
limited opinion 限定意見
limited order 指し値注文
limited payment insurance (一定期間内に保険料の払込みが完了する)有限払込み保険
limited policy 有限保険, 制限付き保険証券
limited premium 有限保険料, 有限料金
limited price ストップ値段
limited recourse loan 制限償還請求権付きローン
limited upside potential 乏しい上値の余地, 小さい上値の余地
limited voting stock 制限議決権株
show limited buying interest 買いを手控える
◆As 95 percent of bondholders are stable domestic investors, the downside risk for Japanese bonds is limited. 債券保有者の95%は安定した国内投資家なので、日本の国債の価格下落リスクは小さい。

limited access to capital 限られた資金調達, 限られた資金調達先, 資金調達力の限界
◆Our plans, which require significant investments, are at risk because of limited access to capital. 大幅投資が必要な当社の計画は現在、資金調達力にも限界があるため、危機にさらされています。

limited deposit protection system ペイオフ(預金の払い戻し)制度, 制限付き預金保護制度([ペイオフ制度]は、預金の払い戻し保証額を制限する制度)
◆The Financial Services Agency and the Deposit Insurance Corporation of Japan invoked the limited deposit protection system for the first time. 金融庁と預金保険機構は、ペイオフ制度を初めて発動した。

limited effects of the quantitative easing measures 量的緩和策の効果の限界
◆Some economists point out that the limited effects of the quantitative easing measures. 一部のエコノミストは、量的緩和策の効果の限界を指摘している。

limited liability company 有限会社
◆Before the new corporate law, at least ¥10 million was required to establish stock companies and ¥3 million to create limited liability companies. 新会社法までは、株式会社の設立に最低1,000万円、有限会社の設立に300万円必要だった。

line (名)線, 限度, 枠, 信用枠, (保険の)種類[種目, 引受額], 損益計算書の経常利益または当期純利益, 〜台(mark, range), 路線, 方針, 商品の種類, 機種, 事業部門, 組立工程, ライン (⇒bottom line, monoline)
above the line 経常収支, 経常支出, 範囲内
above the line profit 経常利益
advance-decline line 騰落株線
bank line 銀行与信枠
be in line with the market 市場実勢を反映している
below the line 異常損益項目, 範囲外
bottom line results 純利益
budget line 予算線
business line 業務分野
capital market line 資本市場線
commercial lines 企業保険
credit line 信用枠, 与信枠, 信用限度, 貸出限度[限度額]
draw two lines across (a check) 横線引きにする
go on line 稼働し始める
in line 通り相場で, 適正規模に, 適正範囲内に
in the banking line 銀行家として
indicative dividing line between expansion and contraction signals 景気拡大と景気後退の判断の分かれ目
lay [place, put] it on the line 即金で払う, 金を支払う, 皆済(かいさい)する
line guide (保険の)引受限度表, ライン・ガイド (=line sheet)
line item 勘定科目, 項目, 細目
line of discount 割引限度
line sheet (保険の)引受限度表, ライン・シート (=line guide)
move too far out of line 平均から大きく外れる
multiple line policy 総合保険
on economical lines 経済的手段で
on the line 直ちに, 即金で
pay on the line 即金で払う
personal lines 家計保険
restructure one's lines 信用枠を再編する
security market line 証券市場線

straight line depreciation 定額償却, 定額法
swing line つなぎ信用枠
top line 売上高
trend line (株価の)傾向線, 趨勢線, トレンド・ライン
◆Extraordinary losses have also battered the company's bottom line. 特別損失も, 同社の業績を直撃した。◆The coincident indicator, the nation's key gauge of the state of the economy, topped the boom-or-bust line of 50 percent in March. 国内の景気の現状を示す一致指数[景気一致指数]が, 3月は景気判断の分かれ目となる50％を上回った。◆The Nikkei Stock Average has been hovering around the ¥10,000 line. 日経平均株価は, 1万円台に張り付いた状態が続いている。◆The yen, which had been flirting with ¥84 line against the U.S. dollar, fell to the ¥93 range in a month. 1ドル＝84円台まで進んでいた円相場が, 1か月で93円台まで円安方向に動いた。

line of credit 信用限度, 信用供与限度, 信用供与枠, 与信限度額, 融資限度, 貸出限度額, 借入限度額, 借入枠, 借入枠中未借入額, クレジット・ライン
（＝credit line）
◆Leverage was increased through a line of credit. 与信限度枠を使って, レバレッジを引き上げた。

linger (動)長引く, 遅々として進まない, いつまでも残る, なかなか消えない
◆Most regional economies still linger in the doldrums. 地方経済も, 大半はまだ停滞から抜け出せないでいる。

lingering (形)長引く, 遅々として進まない, ぐずつく, なかなか消えない, なかなかすたれない, はかどらない
lingering arbitration 遅々として進まない調停, 長引く調停
lingering effects 後遺症
lingering negotiations 長引く交渉, 遅々として進まない交渉
◆There are lingering concerns that Japan's economy could worsen further still. 日本の景気がさらに底割れする心配も, まだ消えていない。
lingering recession 長引く不況
◆Other banks are likely forced to revise their earnings projections downward because of the accelerated disposal of bad loans, business deterioration of borrowers due to the lingering recession and further decline in stock prices. 不良債権処理の加速や長引く不況による融資先の業績悪化, 株安などの影響で, 他行も業績の下方修正を迫られているようだ。◆The size of employment pie has shrunk amid the lingering recession. 長引く不況のなかで, 雇用全体の規模が縮小した。

link (動)つなぐ, 結びつける, 連結する, 関係[関連]づける, 連動させる, リンクさせる (自動)結びつく, 結合する, 一体化する, 接続する, 提携する, 連合する, リンクする
be closely linked to ～に密接に連動している, ～に密接に関連している
bond linked to stock price index 株価指数連動債
link a currency to the dollar 通貨をドルに連動させる, 通貨をドルにリンクさせる
linked bond リンク債
linked industry 関連産業
warrant linked to cash baskets of stocks 現物株式のバスケットにリンクするワラント
◆Most currencies are linked to the dollar. ほとんどの通貨は, ドルに密接に連動している。◆Public works projects should be narrowed to areas linked to public safety and improving the quality of Japan's infrastructure. 公共工事は, 国民の安全や社会資本の質の向上につながる分野に絞るべきだ。◆The TSE average tends to be linked to those in U.S. markets on the previous day. 東証の平均株価は, 前日の米国市場の株価に連動する傾向がある。

link (名)結びつき, 結合, つながり, 関係, 関連, 連関, 連動, 因果関係, 提携, 連結, (鎖の)輪環, 輪, リンク
compensation link 補償リンク制
exchange link 外国為替のリンク
export-import link system 輸出入リンク制
link-chain index 連鎖指数
link index 連環指数
link structure 連環構造
link system 輸出入リンク制, リンク貿易制
（＝linkage system, linking system）
personal link-up 人的結合
synergistic links 相互補完の関係
trade and capital links 貿易・投資関係
◆Many loan sharks are known for their links to crime syndicates. ヤミ金融業者の多くは, 暴力団と関係があることが知られている。

-linked (形)～に連動した, ～にリンクした
bond-linked to stock price index 株価指数連動債
commodity-linked note 商品リンク債
currency-linked bond 為替リンク債
equity and index-linked notes 株式・指数リンク債
equity-linked issue 株式リンク債
forex-linked bond 為替リンク債
Nikkei-linked bond 日経平均リンク債
oil-linked note 石油リンク債
unit-linked loans 投信リンク型ローン
unit-linked policy ユニット・トラスト（オープンエンド型投資信託）リンク生命保険契約
yen-linked bond 円リンク債

lion's share 最大の比率, 最大のシェア, 最大の部分, 大きい取り分, 大部分, 一番おいしいところ
◆The lion's share of the huge amount of funds collected through postal savings and kampo life insurance services has been loaned to public corporations to finance inefficient projects. 郵便貯金や簡易保険を通じて集めた巨額の資金の大部分は, 特殊法人に貸し付けて（流して）非効率的な事業の資金に充ててきた。

liquid (形)流動性がある, 流動性の高い, 換金性のある, 現金に換えやすい, 当座の, 短期の
liquid capital 流動資本
liquid cash balance 流動的現金残高
liquid cash market 流動性の高い現物市場
liquid financial assets 短期金融資産
liquid fund 流動資金, 当座資金
liquid instrument 流動性金融商品
liquid liabilities 流動負債
liquid property 流動資産
liquid ratio 流動比率
liquid reserve 流動準備金
liquid secondary markets 流動性の高い流通市場
liquid share［stock］ 流動性の高い銘柄
liquid wealth 流動資産
maintain liquid capital 流動資本を維持する
short-term liquid investments 流動性のある短期投資
◆Sovereign bonds are considered in general to be risk-free and highly liquid. 国債は, 一般に安全で現金化しやすいと考えられている。◆Temporary cash investments are highly liquid and have original maturities generally of three months or less. 短期投資は, 非常に流動性が高く, 原則として3か月以内に当初の期限が到来するものです。

liquid asset 流動資産, 流動性の高い資産, 当座資産
liquid asset balance 流動資産残高

liquid asset cycle　当座資産サイクル
liquid asset ratio　当座資産比率, 流動資産比率, 当座資産構成比率
liquid assets to liabilities ratio　流動資産負債比率
net liquid asset　純流動資産
short-term liquid assets　短期の流動資産
liquid deposits　流動性預金, 決済性預金　(=floating deposits; ⇒interest-bearing savings account, no-interest bearing, refund cap)
◆Account holders can withdraw money at will from liquid deposits, such as ordinary deposits. 普通預金などの流動性預金から、口座保有者は金を自由に下ろすことができる。◆The government intends to redefine liquid deposits as deposits to be used for no-interest bearing settlements. 政府は、決済性預金を「金利ゼロで決済のために利用する預金」と定義し直す方針だ。
liquidate　(動)(借金や負債を)弁済する[返済する、支払う]、決済する、清算する、処分する、処理する、(証券や資産などを)売却[現金化、換価処分]する、在庫を削減する、会社などを整理する、解散する、破産する、債務金額を確定する　(⇒weaker asset)
liquidate a claim　請求額を支払う
liquidate a company　会社を清算する[整理する、解散する]
liquidate a debtor's property　債務者の財産を換価処分する
liquidate an investment　運用中の資金を現金化する
liquidate inventories　在庫を減らす[削減する、取り崩す、整理する、調整する]
liquidate legal reserves　法定準備金を取り崩す
liquidate nonperforming loans　不良債権を処理する　(⇒prospects)
liquidate one's holdings　持ち株[保有債券]を売却する
liquidate positions　資金を引き揚げる
liquidate securities　証券を売却する
liquidate the swap　スワップを手じまう
sell or liquidate a plant　工場を売却または清算する
◆Citigroup agreed to make best efforts to liquidate by the end of next year all of the about $12 billion of auction rate securities it sold to institutional investors. 米シティグループは、機関投資家に販売した約120億ドル相当の金利入札証券(ARS)すべての買戻し問題については、来年末までの決着に向けて最大限の努力をすることで合意した。◆GM's weaker assets will be liquidated through the New York Bankruptcy Court. GMの不良資産は、ニューヨーク破産裁判所を通じて清算される。◆Plants in foreign countries will be sold or liquidated. 海外の生産拠点[工場]は、売却または清算する。◆Some banks have been forced to liquidate their legal reserves due to the need to dispose of huge amounts of bad loans and make up for latent stock price losses. 巨額の不良債権の処理と株式含み損の補填に迫られ、一部の銀行は法定準備金の取崩しに追い込まれている。◆The textile plants will be sold or liquidated. 繊維工場は、売却または清算する。
liquidated　(形)清算した、確定された、確定済みの、現金化される
liquidated account　確定済み勘定, 確定勘定
liquidated company　清算会社
liquidated corporation　清算した法人
liquidated damages　確定損害賠償額, 損害賠償額の約定, 定額損害賠償
liquidated debt　確定された債務, 債務の確定
liquidated demand　確定金額の債務支払い請求
liquidating　(形)弁済する、清算する、売却する
liquidating dividend　清算配当, 清算分配金

(=liquidation dividend)
liquidating partner　清算人
liquidating trust　清算信託
liquidating value　清算価値
liquidation　(名)流動性, 流動化, 決済, 清算, 処分, 処理, 整理, 解散, 破産, 売却, 現金化, 換金　(「流動化」は、保有資産の支配権を第三者に移転して資金調達すること。⇒basic profit)
asset liquidation　資産売却
　(=liquidation of the asset)
automatic liquidation　自動決済
compulsory liquidation　強制清算
corporate liquidation　会社整理
creditors' voluntary liquidation　和議
forced liquidation　強制破産
go into liquidation　破産する, 清算を開始する, 清算に入る, 清算する, 解散する
income at liquidation　清算所得
　(=liquidation income)
initiate liquidation proceedings　清算手続きを開始する
insolvent liquidation　支払い不能による清算
inventory liquidation　在庫削減, 在庫整理, 在庫取り崩し
involuntary liquidation　強制破産, 強制整理
　(=compulsory liquidation, forced liquidation)
legal liquidation　法的整理
liquidation affairs　清算事務
liquidation bond　清算保証
liquidation dividend　清算配当
liquidation of bad debts　不良債権の処理
liquidation of claims　債務弁済
liquidation of duties　関税査定
liquidation of government bonds　国債の流動化
liquidation of securities holdings　保有有価証券の売却
liquidation of speculative accounts　玉整理
liquidation partner　清算社員
liquidation preference　残余財産分配優先[優先権]
liquidation proceedings　清算手続き
liquidation profit and loss　清算損益
liquidation right　残余財産分配請求権
liquidation risk　流動性リスク
liquidation value　清算価格, 清算価値
TSE's liquidation post　東証の整理ポスト
voluntary liquidation　任意清算, 任意整理, 私的整理, 自主解散
voluntary liquidation for individuals　個人向け私的整理
◆In November 1997, Yamaichi Securities Co. opted for voluntary liquidation after huge off-the-book liabilities surfaced. 1997年11月に山一証券は、多額の簿外債務が表面化したのを受けて、任意清算を選択した。
liquidation of assets　残余財産の分配, 資産の売却
◆Preferred stocks usually do not carry voting rights but have preference over common stocks in the payment of dividends and liquidation of assets. 優先株には通常、議決権は与えられないが、配当の支払いや清算時の残余財産の分配を普通株より優先して受けられる権利がある。
liquidation post　整理ポスト
◆Investors can trade the Seibu Railway shares for a month after their transfer to the TSE's liquidation post from the monitoring post. 西武鉄道株が東証の監視ポストから整理ポストに移った後1か月間、投資家は西武鉄道株を売買できる。◆The Tokyo Stock Exchange (TSE) will move the company's stock to TSE's liquidation post from the monitoring

post. 東京証券取引所(東証)は、同社株を監理ポストから整理ポストに移す。
liquidator (名)清算人,破産管財人(receiver)
liquidity (名)流動性,(流動資産の)換金性,流動資産の換金能力,流動性の高さ,資金繰り,資金,(企業の)支払い能力 (⇒ample liquidity, market liquidity)
 additional liquidity 追加流動性
 adequate liquidity 適正流動性
 aggressive liquidity injection into money markets 市中への大量の流動性供給
 alternate [alternative] liquidity 代替流動性,代替的流動性
 ample liquidity 高い流動性,流動性の高さ,豊富な資金,大量の資金
 backup liquidity バックアップ流動性,代替流動性,外部流動性
 balance on liquidity basis 流動性ベースの国際収支
 bank liquidity 銀行の流動性,銀行流動性
  (=liquidity of banks)
 be short of short-term liquidity 手元流動性が不足している
 broad liquidity (aggregate) 広義流動性
 business liquidity 企業の手元流動性
 conditional liquidity 条件付き流動性
 corporate [business] liquidity 企業の手元流動性
 deplete one's liquidity 流動性を使い果たす
 dollar liquidity-providing operation ドル資金供給オペ
 drain liquidity 流動性を吸い上げる
 drain on liquidity 流動性の枯渇
 draining liquidity 流動性の吸い上げ
 ease liquidity 流動性を高める
 emergency liquidity-providing facilities 緊急貸出制度(⇒facility)
 establish liquidity 流動性を確保する
 excess liquidity 過剰流動性,余剰資金
 excessive liquidity in the financial system 金融システムの過剰流動性
 external liquidity 外部流動性
 general liquidity 一般流動性
 good [excellent, high] liquidity 流動性が高いこと,流動性の高さ
 increase liquidity 流動性を増やす[高める]
 increase liquidity in the monetary system 市中に流動性を供給する
 inject additional liquidity into the financial system 金融システムに流動性を追加供給する
 inject liquidity 流動性を供給する
 inject liquidity into the (banking) system 市中に流動性を供給する
 insufficient liquidity 流動性不足,過小流動性
 internal liquidity 国内流動性
 internal sources of liquidity 内部流動性
 international liquidity 国際流動性
 issuer's liquidity 発行体の流動性
 liquidities 当座資産,現金
 liquidity advance 資金提供
 liquidity allocation 資金供給
 liquidity analysis 流動性分析
 liquidity approach 流動性アプローチ
 liquidity assets 流動性資産
 liquidity at hand 手元流動性
 liquidity basis 流動性ベース
 liquidity constraint 流動性制約
 liquidity creation 流動性創出
 liquidity crisis 流動性危機,資金繰りの悪さ[悪化]
  (=crisis of liquidity)
 liquidity crunch 信用ひっ迫,流動性ひっ迫
 liquidity decision 流動性決意
 liquidity deficit 流動性不足
 liquidity differential 流動性格差
 liquidity dilemma 流動性ジレンマ
 liquidity drain 流動性の流出,流動性の枯渇
  (=drain on liquidity)
 liquidity effect 流動性効果
 liquidity enhancement 流動性補強
 liquidity equation 流動性方程式
 liquidity function 流動性関数
 liquidity gap 流動性ギャップ
 liquidity in general 流動性一般
 liquidity injection 流動性の供給
 liquidity level 流動性水準
 liquidity management 流動性管理
 liquidity measure 流動性指標
 liquidity needs 流動性需要
 liquidity of a loan or other financial assets ローンなどの金融資産の流動性
 liquidity of banks 銀行流動性
 liquidity of money 貨幣の流動性
 liquidity of secondary market 流通市場の流動性
 liquidity of the banking system 銀行システムの流動性,市中流動性
 liquidity policy 流動性政策
 liquidity premium 流動性打歩,流動性プレミアム
 liquidity pressure effect 流動性圧力効果
 liquidity problem 資金繰り難,流動性問題
 liquidity property 流動性資産
 liquidity provider 流動性提供者,流動性供給者
 liquidity requirements 流動性の基準
 liquidity scarcity [shortage] 流動性不足
 liquidity service 流動性用役
 liquidity sources 資金源
 liquidity structure 流動性構造
 liquidity support 代替流動性
 liquidity surplus 流動性過剰[余剰]
 manage liquidity 流動性を管理する,流動性を抑える
 market liquidity 市場流動性,市場の流動性
 mop up liquidity 流動性を吸収する
 net liquidity balance 純流動性収支
 outside liquidity 外部流動性
  (=outside sources of liquidity)
 private liquidity deficit 民間流動性不足
 private liquidity surplus 民間流動性余剰
 provide liquidity 流動性を提供する,流動性を供給する
 provide liquidity protection 流動性リスクをカバーする
 pump liquidity in the system 市中に流動性を供給する
 ready liquidity 手元流動性
 reduced [thin] liquidity 流動性の乏しさ
 remove liquidity from the financial system 金融システムから流動性を吸い上げる
 secondary market liquidity 流通市場の流動性
  (=liquidity of secondary market)

short-term liquidity 手元流動性
sluggish liquidity 流動性の低さ
sources of liquidity 流動性の供給源, 流動性源, 外部流動性
tightened [tighter] liquidity 資金繰りの悪化, 流動性のひっ迫
total liquidity 総流動性
unconditional liquidity 無条件流動性
withdraw [squeeze out] liquidity from the money markets 短期金融市場から資金を吸い上げる
◆In cooperation with the U.S. FRB, the Bank of England, the Bank of Japan and the Swiss National Bank, the European Central Bank decided to conduct three U.S. dollar liquidity-providing operations between October and December. 米連邦準備制度理事会 (FRB)、英イングランド銀行、日銀、スイス国立銀行と協調して、欧州中央銀行 (ECB) が10〜12月に3回、米ドル資金供給オペを実施することを決めた。◆In the case of a lack of liquidity, either bridge lending or debt deferment can save the borrower as there is no cash on hand. 流動性不足の場合は、手元に現金がないので、つなぎ資金を貸すか [つなぎ融資か] 債務返済の延長で借り手は助かる。◆The Bank of Japan decided to continue providing ample liquidity to financial markets. 日本銀行は、金融市場に大量の資金供給を続けることを決定した。◆The Bank of Japan will inject more liquidity into the banking system by raising the outstanding balance in current accounts held at the bank by commercial financial institutions to ¥10 trillion to ¥15 trillion from the current "more than" ¥6 trillion. 日本銀行は、日銀当座預金 (商業金融機関が日銀に保有している当座預金) の残高 [残高目標] を現在の「6兆円を上回る」から10兆〜15兆円程度」に引き上げて、市中に一段と流動性を提供する方針だ。

解説 流動性とは: 流動性は、一般に株式や債券などの流通性のことで、marketability (市場性: 市場で容易に売買できること) とほぼ同じ意味を持つ。このほかに、現金その他の貨幣性資産の所有状況や自己資産を現金化する能力を意味する場合もある。

liquidity crisis 流動性危機, 資金繰りの悪さ [悪化]
◆In the case of a lack of liquidity or liquidity crisis, the debt repayment of an indebted borrower is still possible if a grace period is given, but lack of cash on hand makes it impossible to repay its debt in the short term. 流動性不足や流動性危機の場合、債務を抱えた借り手の債務返済は猶予期間を与えればまだ可能であるが、手元に現金がないため短期での債務返済はできない。

liquidity demand 流動性需要, 資金需要
◆There is a possibility that liquidity demand will increase further depending on financial market developments. 金融市場の今後の展開次第では、資金需要が拡大する可能性もある。

liquidity facility 信用供与枠, 流動性枠, 流動性ファシリティ
general liquidity facility 使途を特定しない流動性ファシリティ
liquidity facility provider 流動性ファシリティの提供者 [供与者]
liquidity facility sponsoring bank 流動性ファシリティの供与者
multiple provider liquidity facility 複数の提供者による流動性ファシリティ
National Credit Union Administration Central Liquidity Facility 全米信用組合管理機構中央流動性基金

liquidity of the U.S. dollar 米ドルの流動性
◆The liquidity of the U.S. dollar should be kept at a reasonable and stable level. 米ドルの流動性は、妥当な安定水準に維持すべきだ。

liquidity position [picture] 資金ポジション, 流動性ポジション, 流動性状態, 流動性の状況, 流動性水準
general liquidity position 一般的流動性状態
liquidity position guidance 資金ポジション指導
whole liquidity position 総流動性ポジション
world liquidity position 国際流動性状態, 世界流動性状態

liquidity preference 流動性選好
increased liquidity preference 流動性選好の高まり
liquidity preference function 流動性選好関数
liquidity preference proper 本来の流動性選好
marginal rate of liquidity preference 限界流動性選好率
schedule of liquidity preference 流動性選好表 (=liquidity preference schedule)

liquidity ratio 流動性比率 (銀行の総預金残高に占める流動性資産の比率), 当座比率 (acid test ratio), (経営) 流動性比率 (当座比率 (acid test ratio, liquid ratio) や流動比率 (current ratio)、棚卸し資産 [在庫] 回転率 (inventory turnover) など、企業の債務支払い能力を示す各種の財務比率)
liquidity ratio control 流動性比率管理 (=control of liquidity ratio)
liquidity ratio policy 流動性比率政策
maximum liquidity ratio 最高流動性比率
minimum liquidity ratio 最低流動性比率
statutory liquidity ratio 法定流動性比率

liquidity reserve 流動性準備
fixed liquidity reserve requirements 固定的流動性比率制度
international liquidity reserve 国際流動性準備
liquidity reserve requirements 流動性比率制度
variable liquidity reserve requirements 可変的流動性比率制度

liquidity risk 流動性リスク
address liquidity risk 流動性リスクを対象とする
bear the liquidity risk 流動性リスクを負う
market liquidity risk 市場流動性リスク
security's liquidity risk 証券の流動性リスク
◆Citigroup Inc. marketed auction-rate securities as safe despite liquidity risks. 流動性リスクがあるにもかかわらず、米シティグループは、金利入札証券を安全な商品として販売していた。

liquidity target 流動性の目標
◆The Bank of Japan decided to boost the upper limit of its liquidity target. 日銀が、量的緩和の目標 (流動性の目標の上限 [日銀当座預金の残高目標の上限]) を引き上げる決定をした。◆The central bank's decision to raise the upper limit of its liquidity target was prompted by its concerns over the recent instability of the currency exchange rate. 日銀当座預金の残高目標 (日銀の流動性目標) の上限引上げ決定の理由に、最近の為替相場の不安定な動きへの懸念があった。

liquidity trap 流動性のワナ, 流動性の落とし穴
◆Japan's economy has fallen into a so-called liquidity trap, from which further easing of monetary policy cannot rescue it. 日本経済は、追加の金融緩和をしても成長が見込めないいわゆる「流動性のワナ」に陥っている。

list (動) 上場する, 上場される, 上場名簿に載せる, 表示する, 表記する, 記載する, 掲載する, 記録する, 計上する, 登録する, 名を挙げる, 指定する
(⇒delist, dual-list, publicly list, relist)
a company [firm] listed on the First Section of the Tokyo Stock Exchange 東証一部上場企業
be dually listed 二重上場されている
be listed on the TSE 東証に上場される, 東証に上場する

companies listed on the TSE　東証上場会社, 東証上場企業
exclusive rights to list　独占上場権
government bonds listed on the TSE（ten-year benchmark）yield　東証上場国債（10年物指標銘柄）利回り
list on the OTC market　店頭登録する
list on the TSE　東京証券取引所に上場する（⇒issue名詞）
list one's shares　株式を上場する
publicly list　株式を上場する, 上場する
stay listed　上場を維持する

◆A sizable number of companies postponed plans to list shares due to sluggish markets. 株式市場の低迷で, かなり多くの企業が株式上場の計画を見送った。◆Domestic stock exchange entries continue to languish, reflecting the tough conditions faced by emerging firms wanting to publicly list their shares. 国内株式市場への新規上場を目指す新興企業が直面している厳しい状況を反映して, 低迷が続いている。◆GM must secure stable profits by releasing promising models to successfully list its shares again. GMが再上場を果たすには, 売れる車を投入して安定した収益を確保しなければならない。◆If the new companies list themselves on the stock market in the future, the central government, as a major shareholder, will benefit. これらの新設会社の株式が将来, 上場されれば, 大株主である国の懐も潤（うるお）う。◆In the revised financial statement, Kokudo was listed as Seibu Railway's parent company and not an affiliated company. 修正済み有価証券報告書では, コクドは西武鉄道の親会社であり, 関連会社ではないと表示された。◆Japanese companies listed on the London Stock Exchange will submit financial reports based on the IAS or the U.S. GAAP. ロンドン証券取引所に上場している日本企業は今後, 国際会計基準か米国会計基準に基づく［に準拠した］財務報告書を提出することになる。◆Publicly listing Tokyo Metro and selling shares in it could net the government hundreds of billions of yen. 東京地下鉄（東京メトロ）の株式を上場して保有株式を売却すれば, 国は数千億円の収入を見込める。◆Staying listed is very expensive. 上場の維持には, 費用もかさむ。◆The collapse of companies listed on stock exchanges totaled eight in October, of which seven were in the real estate and construction sectors. 証券取引所に上場されている企業の10月の倒産件数は計8件で, このうち7件は不動産と建設関連の倒産だった。◆The company listed its shares on the New York Stock Exchange in fiscal 2007 to expedite fund procurement in the U.S. markets. 米市場で機動的に資本調達するため, 同社は2007年度に米ニューヨーク証券取引所に株式を上場した。◆The company plans to list its stock again at the end of this year or next year. 同社は, 今年末か来年, 株式を再上場する計画だ。◆The firm decided to simultaneously list its stocks on the New York and London stock exchanges in October. 同社は, 10月にニューヨークとロンドンの両証券取引所に株式を同時上場する方針を固めた。◆The number of foreign companies listed on the TSE has plummeted to only 12 from 127 in 1991. 東証に上場している外国企業は, 1991年の127社からわずか12社に減っている。◆The number of individual investors holding shares in companies listed on the Jasdaq Securities Exchange increased for the 10th straight year. ジャスダック証券取引所に上場している企業（931社）の個人株主数は, 10年連続で増加した。

list　（名）表, 名簿, 一覧表, 目録, 明細書, 対象, リスト
　a list of current prices　相場表
　a list of distribution　配分表
　a list of property　財産目録, 棚卸し表
　a list of quotations　相場表
　a list of regular clients　得意先名簿
　a list of weight and measurement　重量・容積証明書
　a white list　優良人物表, ホワイト・リスト
　black list［blacklist］　要注意人物名簿, ブラック・リスト
　close the list　募集を締め切る
　foreign buyers list　海外商社名簿
　free list　免税品目録, 免税品リスト
　G-SIFI list　金融システム上国際的に重要な金融機関リスト, 国際的に重要な金融機関リスト, 国際的な巨大金融機関リスト, G-SIFIリスト
　list company　上場会社
　list supplier　リスト業者
　Lloyd's List　ロイズ海報, ロイズ日報
　Lloyd's Loading List　ロイズ週報
　make a list of　～を表に作る, ～の表を作成する
　multiple debtor list　多重債務者リスト
　negative list　残存輸入制限品目リスト, ネガティブ・リスト
　packing list　包装明細書, 荷造り明細書, パッキング・リスト
　positive list　ポジティブ・リスト
　shipping list　船積み明細書, 輸出品明細書
　shopping list　購入リスト
　stock［share］list　株式相場表
　subscription list　株式申込み一覧表, 株式申込み者リスト
　the FDIC's problem list　米連邦預金保険公社（FDIC）の問題銀行リスト
　the list of authorized signatures　（コルレス銀行が交換する）署名鑑
　the list of partial redemption prices　一部解約価額帳
　the list of sales　見込み客リスト
　the list of stockholders［shareholders］　株主名簿（=stockholder［shareholder］list）
　the list of the largest global companies　世界企業番付け
　the Official List　株式相場表, 公定相場表

◆French banks on the list of ban on short selling for 15 days include BNP Paribas and Societe Generale. フランスの15日間株（金融銘柄）の空売り禁止リストの指定行には, BNPパリバやソシエテ・ジェネラールなどが含まれている。◆Sellers of multiple-debtor lists, produced by collecting information about consumer finance customers, are contributing to the spread of illegal moneylending. 消費者金融の顧客情報を入手して作った多重債務者リストを売る名簿業者が, ヤミ金融の横行に一役買っている。◆The BOJ's policy meeting plans to consider expanding the list of government bonds purchased under the fund. 日銀の政策決定会合では, 基金で買い入れる国債の対象拡大を検討する予定だ。◆The Financial Services Agency did not comment on whether any Japanese banks had been earmarked for the G-SIFIs list. 金融庁は, 邦銀が国際金融システム上重要な金融機関（G-SIFIs）リストの指定行に入っているかどうかについては, コメントしなかった。◆The list of banks the U.S. FDIC considers to be in trouble shot up nearly 50 percent to 171 during the third quarter of 2008. 米連邦預金保険公社（FDIC）が経営破たんの可能性があると見ている問題銀行は, 2008年第3四半期［7-9月期］に約50%急増して171行（直前の4-6月期は117行）に達した。◆The 171 U.S. banks are on the FDIC's "problem list." 米国の171行が, 米連邦預金保険公社（FDIC）の「問題銀行リスト」に挙がっている。◆Wal-Mart remained at the top of the list of the largest global companies for the fourth straight year. 米ウォルマート・ストアーズが, 4年連続, 世界企業番付けのトップにとどまった。

listed　（形）リスト［表］に記載された, 上場された, 公示の　（⇒quoted, unlisted）
　companies listed on stock exchanges　証券取引所に上場されている企業

initial funding with listed securities　上場証券による当初資金の調達
listed and unlisted stocks　上場・非上場株
listed associate　上場関連会社
listed bonds　上場債券
listed brand［commodity］　上場商品
listed derivatives　上場派生商品
listed equity option　上場株式オプション
listed futures　上場先物
listed investment　上場証券に対する投資
listed option on common shares［stocks］　普通株式の上場オプション
listed price　表示価格, 定価, カタログ記載値段　（=list price）
listed property　対象資産
listed securities　上場有価証券, 上場証券, 上場株式, 上場銘柄
transaction of listed stocks　上場株式の取引, 上場株式取引状況
transactions of listed stocks［shares］　上場株式売買高
listed company　上場会社, 上場企業, 公開会社, 公開企業　（=listed firm; ⇒business day, business year, issued shares［stocks］, SGX, stock company）
first-section listed company　1部上場企業
hold equity positions in listed companies　上場企業の株式に投資する
second-section listed company　2部上場企業
◆Combined sales of Panasonic and Sanyo would catapult Panasonic to the No.3 spot in revenue among listed Japanese companies.　パナソニック（旧松下電器産業）と三洋電機の連結売上高を合算すると、上場日本企業のなかで、パナソニックは売上高で一躍第3位となる。◆In 2009, the Business Accounting Council decided to require all of the nation's listed companies to use the IFRSs for their consolidated financial statements from 2015.　2009年に企業会計審議会は、2015年にも、国内全上場企業の連結財務諸表［連結財務書類］について、国際財務情報基準（IFRSs）の採用を上場企業に義務付ける方針を打ち出した。◆Listed companies have to place importance on shareholders' interests.　上場会社は、株主利益を重視しなければならない。◆Listed companies revised their articles of incorporation to make stock certificates paperless by holding shareholders meetings.　株券をペーパーレス化するため、公開企業は、株主総会を開いて会社の定款を変更した。◆Many listed companies may be unable to complete the transition to the IFRSs by 2015.　多くの上場企業は、2015年までに国際財務報告基準（IFRSs）に移行できない可能性がある。◆The Justice Ministry already has decided to allow listed companies not to issue printed stock certificates by 2009.　法務省は、公開会社の株券を2009年までにペーパーレス化することをすでに決定している。◆The majority of listed companies have released their half-year earnings reports for the fiscal period up to September.　上場企業の大半が、上半期（4-9月期）の業績を発表した（上場企業の9月中間決算が、ほぼ出そろった）。◆The Tokyo Stock Exchange has called on listed companies to refrain from taking excessively protective measures against hostile takeover bids.　東京証券取引所は、敵対的買収に対する過剰な防衛策の自粛を上場企業に求めている。◆With 942 listed companies, the Jasdaq overtook the Nagoya Stock Exchange as the third-largest stock market in Japan, after the Tokyo Stock and Osaka Securities exchanges.　上場会社数が942社のジャスダックは、名古屋証券取引所を抜き、東京、大阪両証券取引所に次ぐ国内3番目の株式市場になった。
listed land prices　公示地価　（=listed prices of land, posted prices of land）
◆The listed land prices are used as a benchmark for public and private land transactions, and for government assessment of inheritance and property taxes.　公示地価は、公共用地の取引や民間の土地取引の目安のほか、相続税や固定資産税の国の評価基準に用いられる。
listed share　上場株式, 上場株　（=listed stock）
◆A turnover ratio of 100% means that each of the listed shares was traded once during the year.　売買回転率100％とは、上場株式がそれぞれその年に（平均して）1回売買されたことを意味する。
listed stock　上場株式, 上場株　（=listed share）
◆The aggregate market value of the TSE's listed stocks is the third-highest in the world.　東証の上場株の時価総額は、世界第三位の規模だ。
listing　（名）上場, 不動産仲介, 不動産仲介契約, 名簿, 表, 表の作成　（⇒start-up company）
Admission of Securities to Listing　有価証券上場認可規定
backdoor listing　裏口上場（非上場企業が上場企業を買収して上場を果たすこと）
be granted admission of one's securities to the TSE　東証への株式上場を認められる
eligibility criteria for listing　上場基準
exchange listing procedures　証券取引所上場手続き
exclusive listing arrangements　独占上場取決め
listing agent　上場代理人
listing agreement　上場協定
listing application　上場申請
listing criteria　上場基準
listing fee　上場手数料
listing of beneficiary securities organized according to relevant investment trust price　受益証券基準価額表
listing of portfolio holding　保有有価証券明細
listing on the TSE　東証上場
listing prospectus　上場目論見書
listing requirements　上場基準, 上場要件, 上場審査基準
listing will be［take place］on the TSE　東証に上場される
multiple listing　同時上場
new listing　新規上場
obtain a stock exchange listing　株式の上場を果たす, 株式を上場する
official listing　公的相場表
overseas listing　海外での上場
preliminary application for listing　上場の仮申請
public listing　上場
SEC listing　株式の米国上場
seek a listing　上場を求める, 上場を望む
stock exchange listing　上場証券取引所, 証券取引所への上場, 株式の上場
stock listings　株式上場証券取引所
stockholder［shareholder］listing　株主一覧表
US listing for the stocks［shares］　株式の米国上場
◆Daiei wants the five supermarket chains under Daiei's umbrella to maintain their separate listings on the stock market.　ダイエーは、傘下の食品スーパー5社の上場を維持する考えだ。◆Mitsui Life Insurance Co. intends to postpone its planned TSE listing.　三井生命保険は、計画していた東証（東京証券取引所）への上場を延期する予定だ。◆The firm has postponed the listing of its stock on the New York Stock Exchange and the London Stock Exchange.　同社は、ニューヨーク証券取引所とロンドン証券取引所への株式上場を延期した。◆To maintain its listing, it was necessary for the company to increase the number of shareholders.　上場を維持するため、同社は株

主数を増やす必要があった。

listing particulars 上場目論見書, 上場明細書, 上場開示項目 (⇒prospectus)
◆Listing particulars are a formal statement of the company's business and financial conditions, similar to a US registration statement Form S-1. 上場目論見書は, 米国の登録届出書(登録目論見書)「様式S-1」と同じく, 申請企業の業務と財務内容に関する正式の書面です。

listing requirement(s) 上場基準, 上場審査基準, 上場要件 (=initial listing requirements, listing rule, listing standards)
◆A listing requirement prohibits major shareholders from owning more than an 80 percent stake in a company. 上場基準で, 大株主は80%を超える会社株式の所有は禁じられている。◆The company has failed to meet listing requirements. 同社は, これまで上場基準をクリアしていなかった。

live account (取引の)活発な口座
live assets 収益資産
living standard 生活水準
living trust 生前信託
Lloyd's ロイズ[ロイド]保険者協会, ロイド船級協会, ロイズ[ロイド]
　(=the Corporation of Lloyd's)
　Lloyd's agent ロイズ代理店
　Lloyd's bond 債務承認証書
　Lloyd's broker ロイズ・ブローカー
　Lloyd's form ロイズ・フォーム(ロイズの海上保険証券)
　Lloyd's of London ロイズ保険組合
　　(=the Corporation of Lloyd's)
　Lloyd's Register ロイズ船級協会(the Lloyd's Register of Shipping), ロイズ船舶統計, ロイズ船舶登録簿
　Lloyd's Rooms ロイズ・ルーム(ロイズの別称)
　Lloyd's TSB ロイズTSB(英国の大手商業銀行。1995年にロイズ銀行(Lloyd's Bank)とTSB Group plcが合併して誕生)
　Lloyd's underwriter ロイズ保険者, ロイズ保険業者
　Lloyd's Underwriters' Association ロイド保険者協会
LLP 有限責任パートナーシップ, 有限責任事業組合
　(limited liability partnershipの略)
◆Limited liability partnership (LLP) is a new form of business entity that is not a joint stock company or business union. 有限責任事業組合(LLP)は, 株式会社でもなく, 事業組合でもない新しい事業体だ。

load (名)荷, 積み荷, 重荷, 負担, 積載量, 販売手数料(loading charge), 付加保険料, 割増保険料, (配達料、出張料などの)付加料, ロード
　back-end load (年金保険や投資信託などの)解約手数料
　break-even load factor 損益分岐点
　debt load 債務負担, 債務負担額, 借金の重荷
　　(=load of debt)
　double debt load 二重ローンの負担
　front-end load (年金保険や投資信託などの)当初販売手数料
　load fund ロード・ファンド(購入する際に販売手数料(load)が徴収されるオープンエンド型投資信託)
　no-load fund 無手数料の投資信託
◆Many survivors of the Great East Japan Earthquake are struggling under the heavy double debt loads. 東日本大震災の被災者の多くは, 二重ローンという重い負担を背負って苦しんでいる。

loading charge (証券の)販売手数料(load, load charge), 積み込み費用

loan (動)融資する, 貸し出す, 貸し付ける, 出向させる
　(⇒cash名詞, collateral名詞, financial aid package, lion's share)
◆A breakdown of the DBJ financial rescue package reveals that ￥70 billion has been loaned to JAL and about ￥15 billion to ANA. 日本政策投資銀行が経営[金融]支援策として行った融資の内訳は, 日本航空システムが700億円, 全日本空輸が約150億円となっている。◆About ￥70 billion has been loaned to the company. 約700億円が, 同社に融資された。◆As a condition for loans to financially troubled countries in the late 1990s, the IMF called for strict implementation of structural reforms. 1990年代後半に財政難に陥った国に対する融資の条件として, IMF(国際通貨基金)は, 厳しい構造改革の実施を求めた。◆Despite moves by the U.S. Federal Reserve Board to loan more money to financial institutions, banks are still reluctant to lend. 米連邦準備制度理事会(FRB)に金融機関への資金融資を拡大する動きがあるにもかかわらず, 銀行[金融機関]はまだ貸し渋っている。◆Money loaned by private banks declined to ￥419 trillion as of the end of July 2011 from ￥472 trillion at the end of March 1999 when the zero-interest rate policy was first adopted. 民間銀行の貸出金は, ゼロ金利政策が初めて導入された1999年3月末の472兆円から, 2011年7月末現在では419兆円に減った。◆The bank increased revenues by loaning more money. 同行は, 融資拡大路線で収益を上げた。

loan (名)貸付け, 貸出, 融資, 借入れ, 債権, 貸出債権, 債務, 借款, 債券発行, 貸付け金, 借入金, ローン
　accelerate the loan maturity [the maturity of the loan] 融資の期限の利益を喪失させる
　apply for a loan 融資を申し込む
　approach A for a loan Aに融資が受けられるか打診する
　arrange for a loan 融資を取り付ける
　ask for the loan of 〜を貸してくれと頼む
　bank loan 銀行融資, 銀行貸付け, 銀行貸付け金, 銀行借入れ, 銀行借入金, 銀行間借款, バンク・ローン
　bridge loan つなぎ融資, ブリッジ・ローン
　　(=bridging loan)
　bullet loan 一括返済ローン
　business loan 企業向け融資, 事業融資, ビジネス・ローン
　buy the loan 債権を買い取る, ローンを買い取る
　call in the loan 貸金を請求する, ローンの返済を求める
　close on a loan 融資案件を取りまとめる, 融資契約を結ぶ
　commercial and industrial loans 商工業貸出, 商工業貸出金, 商工業向け融資
　commercial loan 商業貸出, 商業貸出金, 民間融資, 市中借入れ
　consumer loan 消費者金融, 消費者ローン, 消費者貸出金
　cover loans that went sour 不良債権リスクをカバーする
　current loans 融資残高
　domestic and foreign loans 内国債と外国債
　education loan 教育ローン (⇒retail lending)
　extend loans to 〜に融資する, 〜に融資を行う
　extend unsecured loans to 〜に無担保融資する, 〜に無担保融資を行う
　forgive the loan 債権を放棄する, 債務を免除する
　general loan 一般貸付け, 一般融資
　get the loan (of money) from 〜から金を借りる
　give a loan 融資する
　give a person the loan of 人に〜を貸す
　government loans 借款, 国債, 公債
　grant a loan 融資の申し入れを受諾する
　have the loan of 〜を借用する

healthy loan 健全な債権
hold a loan 債権［貸付け債権］を保有する
housing loan rate 住宅ローン金利
interest-free loan 無利子［無利息］の貸付け金
issue a loan 公債を募集する
　(=raise a public loan)
jointly extend ¥100 million in loans 1億円を協調融資する
loan amount 貸付け金額, 融資金額, 融資額
loan approval 貸付け承認, 融資承認
loan approval procedures ローンの承認手続き
loan buyback provision 瑕疵(かし)担保条項（金融機関が買い取った債権の価値が一定限度を超えて下落した場合、その債権の買取りを預金保険機構に要求できる権利を定めた条項）
loan capital 借入資本, 貸付け資本
loan categorization 債務者区分
loan commitment 融資確約, 融資契約
loan consortium 借款団
loan contract [agreement] 融資契約, 貸付け契約, 借入契約
loan default 債務不履行
loan-deposit ratio 預貸率
loan facilitation 融資斡旋(あっせん)
loan finance 融資
loan floatation [flotation] 起債, 募債
loan funds 貸付け資金, 借款
loan guarantee 債務保証, 融資補償, 融資の信用保証, 貸出保証
loan guarantee program 融資の信用保証制度
loan making process 融資手続き
loan package 円借款, 融資策
loan portfolio 貸出残高, 貸出金ポートフォリオ, ローン・ポートフォリオ
loan-purchase body 債権買取り機関
loan seeker ローン申込み者
loan servicing 利払いなどの融資処理
loan sharking 高利貸し業, ヤミ金融, ヤミ金融業
　(=loan shark operation; ⇒quasi-loan sharking)
loan stock 転換社債
loan to consumers 消費者金融
　(=consumer credit)
loan trust 貸付け信託
loan values 債権の現在価値
loans actually made 貸出実行額
loans secured on land 不動産担保ローン
loans to questionable borrowers 問題債権
　(=problem loans)
low cost loan 低金利ローン
　(=low interest loan)
low interest loans 低利融資
make a loan 融資する, 貸し出す, 融資［貸出］を実行する, 貸し付ける, 貸金する
make a loan on a pledge 抵当で金を借りる
make secured loans 担保付き融資を行う
negotiate a loan 融資が受けられるよう交渉する
no-interest loans ゼロ金利ローン
on loan 貸付けて, 借りて, 借り受けて
outstanding bank loans 銀行の融資残高, 銀行の貸付け残高
pay off the loan 融資［ローン］を返済［完済］する, 借金を返す

raise a public loan 公債を募集する
　(=issue a loan, raise a loan)
receive loans from financial institutions 金融機関から融資を受ける
recourse loan 非遡求型ローン, 遡求請求権付き貸付け金
reject a loan 融資を断る
reject the request to forgive the loan 債務免除［債権放棄］の要請を断る
reluctance to extend loans 貸し渋り
repay the loan 融資を返済する, ローンを返済する, 借入金を返済する
savings and loan association 貯蓄金融機関, 貯蓄貸付け組合, S&L
secured loan 担保貸し, 担保付き融資, 担保付き貸付け金, 担保付き借入金
securitizing of loans 債券の証券化, 融資の証券化
security loans 証券金融
service and repay the loan ローンの元利を返済する
small loan 小口金融, サラ金
stock loan 貸し株
syndicated loan 協調融資, シンジケート・ローン
take a loan 借り出す, 借り受ける, 融資を受ける, 借りる
take out a floating rate loan 変動金利のローンを組む
take out a loan 融資を受ける, ローンを組む
unsecured loan 無担保融資, 無担保貸付け
waive the loan 債権を放棄する, 債務を免除する, 借金［借入金］を免除する, 融資の返済を免除する
yen loan 円借款 (=yen denominated loan)

◆According to JAL's draft rehabilitation plan, 87.5 percent of the airline's loan will be waived by its banks and other creditors. 日航の更生計画案では、同社借金［借入金］の87.5%は、銀行その他の債権者が免除することになる。◆As a result of fierce competition in the past, interest rate profit margins were kept too low to cover loans that went sour. 過去の熾烈(しれつ)な競争の結果、金利の利ざやが小さく抑えられる余り、貸倒れ［貸倒れのリスク］をカバーできなかった［過去の熾烈な融資合戦の結果、不良債権リスクをカバーできないほど利ざやは小さく抑えられた］。◆Banks and life insurers have extended about ¥4 trillion in loans to TEPCO. 銀行や生命保険会社は、東電にこれまで約4兆円を融資している。◆Credit guarantee associations were established to make it easier for small and mid-sized companies to receive loans from financial institutions. 信用保証協会は、中小企業が金融機関から容易に融資を受けられるようにするために設置された。◆Domestic banks are stepping up overseas project financing as greater yields of interests are expected through such lending than loans to domestic borrowers. 国内銀行は、国内の借り手への融資に比べて海外の事業向け融資のほうが大きな金利収入を見込めるので、海外の事業向け融資（プロジェクト・ファイナンス）を強化している。◆Entrusted or instructed by the South Korean government, private banks jointly extended loans to the company. 韓国政府の委託や指示を受けて、民間銀行が同社に協調融資した。◆General Motors Corp. agreed to sell up to $55 billion in car and truck loans to Bank of America Corp. over five years. ゼネラル・モーターズ（GM）は、バンク・オブ・アメリカに対して、今後5年間で最大550億ドルの自動車ローン債権を売却することで合意した。◆In the case of JAL, the DBJ's ultimate total losses came to ¥95.6 billion in loans and ¥20 billion in investments. 日航の場合、日本政策投資銀行の最終的な損失総額は、融資分の956億円と出資分の200億円となっている。◆In the project financing business, lending banks are repaid loans through profits generated by the projects they have financed. プロジェクト・ファイナンス事業では、貸出行が、融資したプロジェクト（事業）から生まれる利益で融資の返済を受け

◆Making the creditor banks waive loans to TEPCO will cause the utility to fall into capital deficiency, with liabilities exceeding assets. 取引銀行に東電への債権を放棄させると、東電は資本不足に陥り、債務超過になってしまう。◆Mizuho Bank offers a service by which ATM cardholders are given mileage points each time they use the new cards as credit cards, purchase financial products at the bank's branches or receive loans from the bank. みずほ銀行が提供しているサービスでは、キャッシュ・カード会員が新型カードをクレジット・カードとして利用したり、みずほ銀で金融商品を購入したり、ローンを利用したりすると、その取引に応じて毎回、マイレージ・ポイントがもらえる。◆More than half of the public welfare loans extended to widows and single mothers are not collected. 母子家庭や寡婦に供与されている福祉資金の5割以上が、回収されていない。◆Since May 2010, Greece has been reliant in regular payouts of loans from a €110 billion bailout from other eurozone countries and the IMF. 2010年5月からギリシャは、他のユーロ圏諸国やIMF（国際通貨基金）などからの1,100億ユーロの金融支援による融資の定期支払い金に頼っている。◆The bank decided to continue extending loans to a company despite its executives knowing the firm was on the ropes. この会社の経営が悪化しているのを経営陣が知りながら、同行は同社への融資継続を決めた。◆The company will secure ¥270 billion in loans from the Development Bank of Japan and other lenders. 同社は、日本政策投資銀行などの金融機関から、2,700億円の融資を受ける［2,700億円を借り入れる］。◆The firm offers loans for retail and corporate clients in addition to offering electronic settlement for online shoppers. 同社は、ネット・ショッパー［オンライン・ショッパー］向けの電子決済業務のほかに、個人と企業向けの融資も手がけている。◆The former chairman of Daio Paper Corp allegedly received more than ¥10 billion in loans from the firm's group companies for private purposes. 報道によれば、大王製紙の前会長が、グループ企業から100億円超の私的融資を受けた。◆The government guaranteed up to 80 percent of ¥67 billion in unsecured loans extended to JAL by the DBJ through the Japan Finance Corporation. 日本政策投資銀行が日航に貸し付けた無担保融資670億円の最大8割については、日本政策金融公庫を通じて政府が保証している。◆The project financing market has seen a boost in loans to businesses in renewable energy field such as solar and wind power generation. プロジェクト・ファイナンス市場は最近、太陽光や風力発電など自然エネルギー分野の事業への融資が増えている。◆The public loan was extended to JAL in June 2009 by the entirely state-funded Development Bank of Japan. この公的融資は、国が100%出資している日本政策投資銀行が、2009年6月に行った。◆The total amount of loans owed by companies and individuals to private financial institutions stands at ¥2.8 trillion in the three prefectures' coastal areas hit by the March 11 tsunami. 津波被災地の3県（宮城、岩手と福島）沿岸部では、企業や個人の民間企業からの借入金総額が、2.8兆円にのぼっている。◆This loss came from deducting recourse loans made to our senior management. この損失は、当社の上級経営陣に対して行った遡求請求権付き貸付け金を控除したことで生じました。

loan agreement 貸付け契約, 融資契約, ローン契約, 金銭消費貸借契約, 融資契約書
◆The loan agreement shall be entered into between ABC and the new company immediately after the incorporation of the new company. 融資契約は、新会社の設立直後にABCと新会社の間で締結する。

loan application ローンの申込み
◆Loan applications will be mainly handled over the Internet. ローンの申込みは、主にインターネットで扱う。

loan assets 貸出資産　（⇒call in loans）
◆A U.S.-style formula for calculating loan-loss reserves assesses loan assets more strictly. 貸出資産の評価については、米国流の貸倒れ引当金の算定方式のほうが厳しい。

loan claims 債権, 貸出債権
buy back loan claims 債権を買い取る
commission for transaction of loan claims 債権［貸出債権］の売買手数料
deal in loan claims with moneylenders 金融業者と債権の取引をする
sell off loan claims 債権を売却する
◆Incubator Bank of Japan was charging interest rates higher than legally allowed in the name of fees when it was dealing in loan claims with moneylenders. 金融業者との債権取引の際、日本振興銀行は、手数料の名目で出資法の上限を上回る金利で貸出を行っていた。◆The bank disguised these transactions as legitimate trades of loan claims. 同行は、これらの取引については適法な債権売買を装っていた。◆The bank purchased loan claims from financially strapped moneylenders by collecting commissions from them. 同行は、資金繰りに困っている貸金業者から、手数料を徴収して貸出債権を買い取っていた。◆The bank's commission for transaction of loan claims was actually interest, which was far above the legally allowable ceiling. 同行の貸出債権［債権］の売買手数料は、事実上の金利にあたり、その金利は法律で許される上限をはるかに超えていた。◆The major banks were forced to increase loan-loss reserves and to sell off loan claims. 大手銀行各行は、貸倒れ引当金の積み増しや債権の売却などを迫られた。

loan collection 債権回収, 債権取立て
strong-arm loan collection 強引な債権の取立て
temporarily halt loan collection 債権回収を一時停止する
◆Major moneylender SFCG earned an unsavory reputation for its strong-arm loan collection methods. 金融業者大手のSFCG（旧商工ファンド）の評判は、債権の取立て手法が強引で芳しくなかった。

loan credits 債権
◆The RCC's main function has been purchasing of loan credits from failed financial institutions and then collecting the money. 整理回収機構（RCC）のこれまでの主な業務は、破綻金融機関からの債権買取りとその金（債権）の回収である。

loan demand 借入需要, 資金需要
（=demand for loans; ⇒lending market）
◆Corporate loan demand should pick up once the economy begins recovering. 景気が回復していけば、企業の資金需要［借入需要］も増大するはずだ。◆Profits have been squeezed as interest rates remain near zero percent and loan demands stalls. 金利はまだゼロに近いし、借入需要も停滞したままなので、利益は減少している。

loan disposal costs 債権処理費用, 不良債権処理費用
（=credit costs; ⇒credit costs）
◆Loan disposal costs are likely to result in massive losses. 債権処理費用で、大幅な赤字に陥る見通しだ。

loan facility 融資枠, 融資金　（=credit facility）
◆The lender agrees to make available to the borrower, on and subject to the terms and conditions of this agreement, a loan facility in Japanese Yen in an aggregate amount not exceeding ¥500,000,000 or its equivalents. 貸主は、本契約の条件に従って、借主に対して日本円で合計額が5億円またはその相当額を超えない融資枠を設定することに同意する。◆This yen loan facility is for general corporate purposes. この円融資枠は、一般事業目的に使用される。

loan forgiveness 債権放棄, 債務免除
（=debt waiver, loan waiver, loan write-off）
◆The request for loan forgiveness totaling ¥405 billion was made during a meeting convened by Daiei and the IRCJ to explain Daiei's reconstruction plan to creditors. 総額4,050億円の債権放棄の要請は、ダイエーの再建計画を取引銀行に説明するため、ダイエーと産業再生機構が開いた会議で行われた。

loan funds　融資資金
　◆Leading moneylending businesses make huge profits by securing loan funds from financial institutions at annual average rates of less than 2 percent. 大手の貸金業者は、金融機関から平均年2％以下の金利で融資資金を調達して、高い収益を上げている。

loan interest rate　貸出金利
　(=interest rate on loans, lending rate)
　◆The key to ensuring higher profit margins is the introduction of higher loan interest rates capable of covering risk. 大きい利ざやや確保のカギを握るのは、リスクに見合った高い貸出金利の設定だ。

loan loss　貸倒れ, 貸倒れ損失, 不良債権, 不良貸付け, 融資の焦げ付き, 貸付け金の回収不能
　loan loss allowance　貸倒れ引当金
　loan loss charge　貸倒れ損失額, 貸倒れ引当金, 不良債権額, 不良債権処理額, 不良債権処理損
　　(=bad debt clean-up charge, loan loss cost)
　loan loss reserve ratio　貸倒れ引当金の引当率
　loan losses　貸倒れ損失額　(⇒business profit)

loan loss provisions　貸倒れ引当金, 貸倒れ準備金
　(=loan loss reserves)
　additions to loan loss provisions　貸倒れ引当金繰入額の積み増し
　loan loss provisions for nonperforming loans　不良債権に対する貸倒れ引当金
　◆A massive shortage in the bank's loan loss provisions for nonperforming loans was pointed out through the special investigation by the Financial Services Agency. 金融庁の特別検査で、不良債権に対する同行の多額の貸倒れ引当金不足が指摘された。

loan loss reserves　貸倒れ引当金, 貸倒れ準備金
　(=reserves for bad loans, reserves for loan losses, reserves for possible loan losses; ⇒credit, default on, discount cash flow system, economic value, loan assets, loan claims, loan recipient)
　amassed loan loss reserves　(銀行が)積み立てた貸倒れ引当金
　cover by loan loss reserves　貸倒れ引当金で賄(まかな)う
　increase loan loss reserves　貸倒れ引当金を積み増す, 貸倒れ引当金を強化する
　reduce the loan loss reserves　貸倒れ引当金を減らす
　set aside loan loss reserves　貸倒れ引当金を積み立てる, 貸倒れ引当金を積む
　◆An increase in banks' loan loss reserves is a precondition for raising purchase prices for bad loans. 銀行の貸倒れ引当金の強化が、不良債権の買取り価格引上げの前提条件となる。
　◆Banks have to set aside loan loss reserves based on projections of future revenues of their borrowers, not based on bankruptcies in the past. 銀行は、過去の倒産実績ではなく、融資先企業［貸出先］の将来の収益予想などを基にして、貸倒れ引当金を積み立てるべきだ。◆The effective book value is calculated by subtracting amassed loan loss reserves from the original amount of money that was lent. 実質簿価は、債権の元々の額(貸し付けた元々の金額：簿価)から、(銀行が)積み立てた貸倒れ引当金を差し引いて算定する。◆The former executives reduced the loan loss reserves by falsifying the assessment of the bank's bad loans. 旧経営陣は、同行の不良債権の査定を甘くして、貸倒れ引当金を減らしていた。

loan period　貸出期間
　◆In this cofinancing scheme, the bank will extend a total of about ¥8.5 billion over a 20-year loan period. この協調融資事業で、同行は貸出期間20年で計約85億円を融資する。

loan production office　貸付け事務所

loan rate　貸出金利
　◆The bond purchases by the U.S. Fed was intended to lower loan rates and boost stock prices. 米連邦準備制度理事会(FRB)の国債買入れの狙いは、貸出金利の引下げと株価押し上げにあった。

loan recipient　融資先, 融資先企業
　◆Currently, loan loss reserves are calculated on the basis of the probability of loan recipients going bankrupt. 現在、貸倒れ引当金は融資先企業の(過去の)倒産確率に基づいて算定している。

loan repayment　債務返済, 融資の返済, 借入金の返済, ローンの返済
　◆The company recovered a profit in loan repayment. 同社は、融資の返済として収益を回収していた。

loan request　融資要請
　◆Banks will not accept future loan requests if they have to forgive the debt. 金融機関が債権放棄をせざるを得ないとなると、金融機関は今後の融資要請には応じないだろう。

loan reserves　融資の引当金, 金融機関の債権に対する引当金, 債務引当金
　◆Regular FSA inspections are conducted after banks close their accounts in March, and focus on whether their loan reserves are adequate. 金融庁の通常検査は3月の銀行の決算後に行われ、主に債権に対する引当金が十分かどうかなどを点検する。

loan shark　高利貸し, サラ金, サラ金業者, ヤミ金融業者
　(⇒cash flow problem, crime syndicate, mobile phone number)
　◆Another tactic many loan sharks use is to circulate slanderous leaflets to the workplace or the school that the borrower's children attend. 多くのヤミ金融業者が使うほかの手は、借り手の勤務先や子どもが通う学校への中傷文書のばらまきだ。◆People indebted to multiple consumer loan firms and financially strapped small-business operators have been the main targets of loan sharks. 多重債務者や資金繰りが苦しい零細事業主が、ヤミ金融業者の主な標的になっている。

loan volume　融資高
　◆The company was once the second-largest provider of subprime mortgages in the United States on loan volume. 同社は、かつてはサブプライム・ローンの融資高で米国第2位の住宅ローン会社だった。

loan waiver　債権放棄, 債務免除　(=debt forgiveness, debt waiver, loan forgiveness, loan write-off)
　◆The revival plan calls for Kanebo to obtain 99.5 billion in loan waivers from creditor banks. この事業再生計画は、カネボウに対して取引銀行から995億円の債権放棄を受けるよう求めている。

loan write-off　債権放棄, 債務免除　(=debt forgiveness, loan forgiveness, loan waiver)
　◆Daiei Inc. asked for 81 percent loan write-offs from its creditor banks. ダイエーは、取引銀行に81％の債権放棄を要請した。

loan write-off costs　債権処理費用, 不良債権処理費用
　◆Loan write-off costs at the bank amounted to ¥450 billion for the half-year ended Sept. 30. 同行の9月中間決算の不良債権処理費用は、4,500億円だった。

loanable fund　貸付け資金, 融資資金

loans outstanding　融資残高, 貸出残高, 貸付け残高, 借入金残高
　◆The firm's main creditor banks forgave ¥150 billion of the ¥300 billion in loans outstanding to the firm. 同社の主力取引銀行は、同社に対する債権［融資残高］3,000億円のうち1,500億円を放棄した。

loans to individuals　個人向けローン, 個人ローン, 個人ローン商品
　◆Japan Post is discussing an alliance with Suruga Bank to offer mortgages and other loans to individuals. 日本郵政は現在、住宅ローンなど個人ローン商品の販売に向けて、スルガ

銀行と業務提携協議を進めている。
local （形）地元の, 土地の, 現地の, 地方の, 市内の, 同一区内の, ローカル
 claims outstanding on local governments　地方自治体に対する[地方自治体向け]与信残高
 loans to local authorities　地方自治体向け融資
 local authority　地方自治体, 地方公共団体, 地方官庁, 地方当局
 local authority bond [debt]　地方債
 local bank　地方銀行
 local B/L [bill of lading]　区間船荷証券, ローカルB/L
 local bond　地方債 （=municipal bond）
 local bonds by private subscription　縁故地方債, 縁故募集による地方債
 local borrowings　現地借入れ, 現地借入額
 local businesses [companies]　地元企業, 地場産業, 国内企業, 国内業界
 local check　地方銀行小切手, 地域内小切手
 local clearing　地方[市外]手形交換
 local clearing [item]　当所払い券
 local community　地域社会, 地方社会
 local corporate tax　法人事業税（企業活動に対して課される地方税）
 local cost　現地コスト
 local credit　内地向け信用状（=domestic L/C, local guarantee）
 local economic zone　局地経済圏
 local equity　現地株主所有権
 local equivalent　現地通貨換算額
 local exports　地場輸出
 local finance　地方財政（local public [government] finance）, 現地金融（local financing）
 local financing　現地金融
 local improvements　地域的公共事業, 地域改良
 local interest rates　国内金利
 local interests　地元企業
 local investment　現地投資
 local letter of credit [L/C]　国内信用状, 国内発行信用状, ローカルL/C, ローカル・クレジット
 local loans　地方債
 local manufacture　現地生産
 local markets　現地市場, 地元市場
 local maximum　極大
 local minimum　極小
 local municipalities　地方自治体
 local partner　現地パートナー
 local portion　現地資金負担分, 現地通貨資金部分
 local savings　地方貯蓄
 local sources of finance　現地資金源
 local (stock) exchange　地方証券取引所
 local taxes　地方税
 local usance　現地金融
Local Autonomy Law　地方自治体法
 ◆The Local Autonomy Law authorizes local governments to conduct extraordinary inspections of financial institutions that they have designated as agents. 地方自治体法で, 地方自治体は, 代理機関に指定された金融機関に対して特別検査を行う権限が与えられている。
local company　現地企業, 地元企業
 （=local corporation）
 ◆Sendai Bank is considering receiving public funds in order to meet the pressing needs of local companies in the aftermath of the March 11 earthquake and tsunami. 3月11日（2011年）の東日本大震災の影響でひっ迫している地元企業の資金需要に対応するため, 仙台銀行は, 公的資金の受入れを検討している。
local corporate tax　法人事業税（企業活動に対して課される地方税）
 ◆In April 2000, the Tokyo metropolitan government implemented the ordinance imposing a 3 percent local corporate tax on major banks' gross operating profits—profits before deducting losses due to nonperforming loans—instead of on corporate incomes. 2000年4月から東京都は, 大手銀行の法人所得税の代わりに業務粗利益（不良債権による損失控除前利益）に3％の法人事業税を課す条例を実施した。
local corporate tax formula based on business size　外形標準課税
 ◆The Tokyo metropolitan government proposed negotiations on reaching a settlement in a lawsuit filed by 17 banks seeking to abolish a local corporate tax formula based on business size. 東京都は, 外形標準課税（銀行税）の取消しを求めて銀行17行が起こした訴訟で, 和解交渉を申し入れた。
local corporation　地元企業, 現地企業
 ◆Both lenders will focus on supporting their local corporations in the aftermath of the March 11 quake and tsunami. 3月11日（2011年）の東日本大震災を受けて, 両行は地元企業の支援に重点的に取り組む方針だ。
local currency　現地通貨, 国内通貨, 自国通貨, 現地[国内]通貨建て, ローカル・カレンシー
 local currency obligation　国内通貨建て債務
 non-local currencies　非現地通貨
 subsidiaries operating in a local currency environment　現地通貨を用いる経済環境で営業活動をしている子会社
 ◆Local currencies are generally considered the functional currencies outside the United States. 米国外では, 一般に現地通貨を機能通貨と見なしています。◆Non-U.S. subsidiaries which operate in a local currency environment account for approximately 90% of the Company's non-U.S. revenue. 現地通貨を用いる経済環境で営業活動を営む米国外子会社は, 当社の米国外収益の約90％を占めています[約90％を稼得しています]。
local economy　地域経済, 国内経済, 地元の経済
 ◆The bank's aim is to help circulate dormant individual assets in the local economy. 眠れる個人の金融資産を地域経済に循環させるのが, 同行の目的だ。
local government　地方政府, 地方行政, 地方自治体, 地方公共団体, 地方自治制
 local government bond　地方債
 local government finance　地方財政
  （=local finance）
 local government finance revenue and expenditure　地方財政歳入歳出
 ◆Local governments have stymied the central government's efforts to improve its primary balance. 地方自治体が, 国のプライマリー・バランス改善の足を引っ張っている。◆The special account borrows from the private sector and other sources to make up for local government's budget shortfalls. 特別会計は, 民間などの財源からの借入れで地方の財源不足[財政赤字]の穴埋めをしている。
lock in　利益や価格を確定する, コストを固定する, 確保する
 lock in a purchase price　購入価格を確定する
 lock in an exchange rate　為替レートをあらかじめ確定する
 lock in cheap funds　低コストの資金を確保する
 lock in funding rates　調達コストを確定する
 lock in paper profits　含み益を確定する
 lock in profits　利益を確定する

(=lock profits in)
◆Investors sold shares across the board to lock in profits. 利益を確定するため、投資家が全銘柄にわたって株を売り進めた。

lockup (名)約束手形、債務などの期限延長、塩漬け、塩漬け株、資本の固定、損益の確定、転売禁止、ロックアップ (=lock-up)
  a six-month lockup　6か月のロックアップ期間（新規公開企業の株主は転売禁止で持ち株を処分できない）
  lockup agreement　ロックアップ契約
  lockup CDs　固定預金証書、固定CD
  lockup option　ロックアップ・オプション（敵対的買収に対して、友好的買収者に最良資産を取得する権利を与えること）
  lockup period　転売禁止期間、据え置き期間、ロックアップ期間

[解説]ロックアップ：
企業買収交渉で、買収成立から一切の処理が済むまでのあいだ第三者による買収の脅威をなくすため、買収する会社と被買収会社が取り交わす取決めのことをロックアップという。また、株式公開時の株価暴落を防ぐため、大株主に対して一定期間売買を控えてもらう株式市場での約束事のこともロックアップという。

lodging slip　銀行預入れ票

log (動)（文書に）記録する、記入する、航行する、飛行する、（材木などを）切り出す
  log in　接続する、アクセスする、利用する
    (=access, log on)
  log onto [into, on to]　～に接続する、～にアクセスする、～を利用する
    ◆Japan Post Service Co. logged ¥3.53 billion to pay for taxes. 郵便事業会社は、納税資金として35億3,000万円を計上した。◆Japan's current account balance logged a record ¥173 billion deficit in January 2009. 日本の2009年1月の経常収支は、過去最高の1,730億円の赤字になった。◆South Korean foreign reserves slipped to $305 billion in May 2011 from the record $307 billion logged in April. 韓国の2011年5月の外貨準備高は、4月に記録した過去最高の3,070億ドルから3,050億ドルに減少した。◆The balance of trade in goods and services logged a surplus of ¥3.43 trillion in the April-September period. 4～9月期のモノとサービスの貿易収支は、3兆4,300億円の黒字を記録した。
  log into [onto]　～に接続する、～にアクセスする、～を利用する　(=access, log in, log on, log on to)
    ◆In the one-time password system, clients' passwords are changed whenever they log into their accounts. ワンタイムパスワード方式だと、顧客が口座を利用するたびに、顧客のパスワードは変更される。

Lombard lending　ロンバード貸出、ロンバード型貸出（一時的に資金繰りに困った金融機関の要請に応じて日銀が融資するもの）

Lombard rate　ロンバード・レート（ドイツ連邦銀行が市中銀行に対して債券担保貸付けを行う際に適用する金利）

Lombard Street　ロンバード街、英国の金融市場、英国の金融界（ロンドンのザ・シティにある金融の中心街）

Lombard-type lending system　ロンバード型貸出制度

London (名)ロンドン、ロンドン外国為替市場、ロンドン株式市場
  ◆At 4 p.m., the euro traded at $1.3813-3814 and ¥113.16-20 in London. 午後4時の時点で、ロンドン外国為替市場のユーロ相場は、1ユーロ＝1.3813～3814ドルと113円16～20銭で取引された。

London Inter Bank Offered Rate　ロンドンの銀行間取引金利、ロンドン銀行間貸し手金利、LIBOR

◆Any payment not made when due will, in addition to any other right or remedy of Licensor, incur a finance charge at the lesser of three hundred basis points over the 3-month London Inter Bank Offered Rate ("LIBOR+3") on the date payment was due or the highest applicable legal contract rate. 支払いが支払い期日までに履行されない場合、ライセンサーの他の権利や救済請求権に加えて、支払い期日時点の3か月物ロンドン銀行間取引金利(LIBOR)プラス3%(LIBOR＋3%)または適用される最高法定約定金利のうち、いずれか低いほうの金利の金融費用が発生する。

London Stock Exchange　ロンドン証券取引所
  ◆Japanese companies listed on the London Stock Exchange will submit financial reports based on the IAS or the U.S. GAAP. ロンドン証券取引所に上場している日本企業は今後、国際会計基準か米国会計基準に基づく[に準拠した]財務報告書を提出することになる。◆The firm has postponed the listing of its stock on the New York Stock Exchange and the London Stock Exchange. 同社は、ニューヨーク証券取引所とロンドン証券取引所への株式上場を延期した。

long (名)長期間、買い持ち(long position)、長期債券、強気筋、ロング
  covered long　カバード・ロング
  long of exchange　外国為替の買い越し
  longs　強気筋(long accounts, long interests)、長期債券

long (形)長い、買い持ち(long position)の（「買い持ち」は、値上がり後の売却益を期待して株式などを保有している状態）、(将来の値上がりを期待している)強気の、ロング　(副)強気に
  a bill at the long run　長期手形
  at sight or a longer tenor　一覧払いまたは長期の支払い期間
  buying long　思惑買い
  go long　強気に出る、買いに出る
  long account　借方[買い方]勘定（信用取引の得意先勘定)、買い方顧客勘定、買い建て証券、買い建て商品、買い[買い建て]玉(ぎょく)
  long bill　長期手形
  long call　コールの買い、ロング・コール（オプション取引で、コール・オプション(call option)を購入して保有している状態のこと）
  long cap　キャップの買い
  long credit　長期信用状、長期信用貸し
  long date　長期の支払い期日、長期の償還期日
  long date forward　長期先物為替契約
  long draft　長期手形、長期支払い手形
  long exchange　長期為替
  long exchange rate　長期為替相場
  long figure　高値、多額
  long gilt　長期ギルト債
  long green　ドル札、ドル紙幣、現ナマ、大金
  long hedge [hedging]　買いヘッジ、長期掛けつなぎ
  long leg　ロング・レッグ（オプション・スプレッドで買いの側を構成するオプションのこと）
  long-lived assets　固定資産、長期性資産
  long market　強気市況
  long note [bill]　長期手形
  long on the basis　買いつなぎ済みの
  long pull　(株式の)長期抱え込み
  long put　プットの買い（プット・オプション(put option)を購入して保有している状態）
  long rate　長期料率、長期金利[利率]、期限付き為替相場
  long sale　掛けつなぎ売り、実株売り
  long-standing customer　長年の得意先

long structured paper　長期物の仕組み商品
long-tail business　（保険の）尾を引く問題, ロングテイル・ビジネス
long yield　長期債利回り
take a long chance　危険を承知でやってみる, 一か八かやってみる
the long interest of the market　（市場の）強気筋
the market is long of paper　市場は買い持ちの状態だ, 市場は供給過剰になっている
◆The longest period of postwar economic expansion was known as an economic boom without feeling. 戦後最長の景気回復は、実感なき景気回復と言われた。

long bond　長期債券, 長期債, 30年満期財務省長期証券, 期間が10年以上の債券　（=long term debt）
bellwether long bond　30年物指標銘柄
global long bond　長期グローバル債
long bond yield　長期債利回り
nominal long bond interest rate spread　名目長期債利回り格差
real long bond interest rate differential　長期債実質利回り格差

long coupon　ロング・クーポン（期間が10年以上の利付き債（coupon bond）を意味する場合と、新規発行された利付き債のうち、最初の利払い日が通常より遅れて（利付き債の利払いは通常、半年ごとに行われる）発行日から半年以後に到来するものをいう場合がある）

long-dated　（形）長期の
long-dated bill　長期手形
long-dated bond［debt, issue, paper］　長期債
long-dated interest rate　長期金利
long-dated public transaction　長期公募債
◆Germany criticized the Fed's policy of buying up long-term U.S. government debt to drive long-dated interest rates lower amid near-zero short-term rates. 短期金利がゼロに近い状況で、長期金利の引下げを狙って米国の長期国債を買い進める米連邦準備制度理事会（FRB）［米中央銀行］の政策を、ドイツが非難した。

long end　長期債, 30年債
long end of the curve［market］　長期債
long end of the Treasury market　米国債長期物
long-end rates　長期債利回り

long position　買い持ち, 買い建て, ロング・ポジション（株式などの証券を保有している状態のこと）
establish long dollar positions　ドルのロング（買い持ち）ポジションを積み上げる
fund a long position for X%　X%の資金コストで買いちする
hedge a long position in　〜の買い持ちをヘッジする
hedge one's long position in stocks　現物株のロング・ポジションをヘッジする
overbought long position　買い持ち
take long positions　買い持ちにする
◆The firm hedged its long position in stocks by selling short the futures contract. 同社は、先物を空売りして現物株のロング・ポジションをヘッジした。

long range　長期　（=long term）
long-range budget　長期予算
long-range business planning　長期経営計画　（=long-range management planning, long-range planning）
long-range cash forecast　長期資金予測
long-range cash［fund］planning　長期資金計画
long-range forecast　長期予想, 長期見通し
long-range plan　長期計画
long-range profit planning　長期利益計画

long term　長期, 長期債券（long term［bond］debt: 期間10年以上の債券）　（=long range）
long-term accounts payable　長期未払い金
long term bond　長期債, 長期社債
long term borrowing　長期借入金
long-term capital appreciation　財産の長期的成功
long-term capital balance　長期資本収支
　（=long-term balance of capital account）
long term deposit　長期性預金
long-term forecast　長期予想, 長期見通し
long-term growth rate　長期成長率
long-term indebtedness　長期債務
long-term investment　長期投資
long-term liabilities　長期負債
long term loans　長期貸付け金, 長期融資, 長期借入金
long-term noninflationary potential growth rate　潜在成長率
long-term objective　長期目標　（=long-term goal）
long-term outlook　長期見通し
long-term return　長期収益率
long-term trend　長期トレンド

long-term credit rating　長期信用格付け, 長期格付け
◆The S&P cut in the U.S. long-term credit rating by one notch to AA-plus from AAA resulted from concerns about the nation's budget deficits and climbing debt burden. スタンダード・アンド・プアーズ（S&P）が米国の長期国債格付けを最上級のAAA（トリプルA）からAA（ダブルA）に1段階引き下げた理由は、米国の財政赤字と債務負担の増大に対する懸念だ。

long-term［long term］debt　長期債務, 長期負債, 長期借入金, 長期借入債務, 固定負債
　（=long term borrowings, long term obligation）
in long-term debt　長期借入金として
incur long-term debt　長期借入れを行う
long-term debt obligation　長期債
long-term debt rating　長期格付け
long-term debt securities　長期債
repay long-term debt　長期借入金を返済する
◆In addition to long-term debt maturing during the year, the company redeemed all of its U.S. $150 million debentures, due 2013, in June 2011. 当年度に満期が到来する長期債務のほか、同社は2013年満期の社債1億5,000万米ドルの全額を、2011年6月に償還した。◆Long-term debts held by central and local governments are expected to further swell unless the government puts the brakes on government bond issuance. 政府が国債発行に歯止めをかけないと、国と地方［地方自治体］が抱える長期債務は、さらに膨らむ見通しだ。◆Long-term debts of the central and local governments are predicted to reach a staggering ¥892 trillion by the end of fiscal 2011. 国と地方自治体の長期債務は、2011年度末で892兆円と膨大な額に達する見込みだ。◆The central and local governments hold the massive amount of long term debts. 国と地方自治体は、巨額の長期債務を抱えている。◆The Health, Labor and Welfare Ministry will assume all of the ¥530 million long term debt of a nonprofit foundation. 厚生労働省が、公益法人の長期借入金5億3,000万円について全額肩代わりすることになった。

長期借入債務に含まれるもの：
convertible bonds　転換社債
long term contracts　長期請負契約
long-term notes payable　手形借入金
mortgage notes　担保付き長期手形
obligations under capital leases　キャピタル・リース債務

straight bonds　普通社債
　　debentures　無担保社債
　　mortgage bonds　担保付き社債
　　subordinated debentures　劣後社債
long-term debt instrument　長期債務証券
　　(⇒long-term financing)
　　◆One way for a company to accomplish long-term financing is through the issuance of long-term debt instruments in the form of bonds. 会社の長期資金調達方法の一つは、社債の形で長期債務証券を発行して行われる。
long-term financing　長期資金調達, 長期融資
　　(⇒long-term debt instrument)
　　◆Our long-term financing was accomplished through the issuance of long-term debt instruments. 当社の長期資金調達は、長期債務証券を発行して行われた。
long-term government bonds　長期国債
　　◆The Bank of Japan has supplied a large amount of funds to the market by purchasing long-term government bonds and corporate bonds. 日銀は、長期国債や社債の買入れで、大量の資金を市場に提供している。◆The Bank of Japan will set up a fund to buy long-term government bonds, exchange-traded funds and other financial assets in a bid to prop up the nation's economy. 日本の景気を下支えするため、日銀は基金を新設して、長期国債や上場投資信託(ETF)などの金融商品[金融資産]を買い入れる。◆The interest rate for long-term government bonds fluctuates depending on market developments. 長期国債の金利は、市場の動き次第で大きく変動する。◆The interest rate of long-term government bonds is currently at about 1 percent. 長期国債の金利は現在、1%前後で推移している。
long-term interest rate　長期金利
　　(⇒government bond market)
　　a key indicator of long-term interest rates　長期金利の代表的な指標
　　excessive upturns in the long-term interest rate　長期金利の行き過ぎた上昇
　　◆Long-term interest rates have so far been held down due to an influx of money from abroad. 長期金利はこれまで、海外マネーの流入で低く抑えられていた。◆Long-term interest rates temporarily rose sharply last week. 長期金利が先週、一時、急上昇した。◆On the bond market, the yield on newly issued 10-year government bonds, an indicator of long-term interest rates, fell, resulting in a rise in bond prices. 債券市場では、長期金利の指標である新発10年物国債の利回り(流通利回り)が下落し、債券相場[債券価格]は上昇した。◆Speculation the Bank of Japan will end its quantitative monetary easing policy soon has sparked a rise in mid- and long-term interest rates. 日銀が近く量的緩和策を解除するとの思惑から、(金融市場では)中長期の金利が上昇し始めた。◆The central bank must try to prevent excessive upturns in the long-term interest rate by increasing outright purchases of long-term government bonds and other measures. 日銀は、長期国債の買切りオペを拡大するなどして、長期金利の行き過ぎた上昇に歯止めをかけるようにしなければならない。◆The yield on the 10-year government bond is the key benchmark for long-term interest rates. 10年物国債の利回り(流通利回り)は、長期金利の代表的指標である。◆The yield on the 10-year Japanese government bond is a key indicator of long-term interest rates. 新発10年物日本国債の流通利回りは、長期金利の代表的な指標となっている。

[解説] 長期金利とは：取引期間が1年以上の金利のことで、新規発行された10年物国債(長期国債)の流通利回りを指標に使う。企業向け貸出の金利や住宅ローンの金利の目安となり、国債価格が上がれば、長期金利が下がる関係にある。景気が悪いと経済活動が停滞し、長期金利も下がるが、好況の時は金利も上昇する。

long-term Japanese government bonds　日本の長期国債
　　◆Standard & Poor's downgraded long-term Japanese government bonds by one notch from AA to AA minus. 米国の格付け会社のスタンダード・アンド・プアーズが、日本の長期国債の格付けを「ダブルA」から「ダブルAマイナス」に1段階引き下げた。
long-term lending rates　長期貸出金利
　　◆Long-term lending rates have fallen since the beginning of August 2010 amid deflation concerns. 2010年8月に入って、デフレ懸念を背景に、長期貸出金利が下がっている。
long-term rating　長期格付け
　　(=long-term credit rating)
　　◆Standard & Poor's currently assigns a BBB long-term rating to the bank. スタンダード＆プアーズは現在、同行に対してトリプルBの長期格付けをしている。
long-term U.S. debt　長期米国債, 米国の長期国債
　　◆Fitch Ratings Ltd. will keep its rating on long-term U.S. debt at the highest grade, AAA. 英米系の格付け会社フィッチ・レーティングスは、米国の長期国債格付けを、最上級のAAA(トリプルA)に据え置く方針だ。
loose　(形)緩(ゆる)んだ, 緩い, 緩和的な, ばらの, ばらばらの
　　appropriately loose monetary policy　適度に緩和的な金融政策
　　loose bonds　だぶついている玉(ぎょく)
　　loose cargo　ばら荷
　　loose change [cash, coin, money]　ばら銭, 小銭
　　loose credit　資金需給の緩和, 金融緩和
　　loose monetary policy　金融緩和政策, 低金利政策, 低金利金融政策
　　loose money market　放漫金融市況
　　looser credit　金融緩和
　　super-loose monetary policy　超金融緩和
　　ultra-loose monetary policy　超低金利(金融)政策, 超金融緩和政策, 金融の量的緩和政策　(=super-loose monetary policy, ultra-loose money policy)
　　◆China will shift to a "prudent" monetary policy in 2011 from the previous "appropriately loose" stance. 中国は、これまでの「適度に緩和的な」金融政策から2011年は「穏健な」金融政策に方向転換する方針だ。◆The challenge in monetary policy for countries now is shifting toward finding a way to move away from ultra-loose money policies. 現在、各国の金融政策の課題は、超金融緩和政策からいかに転換するかに移りつつある。◆The U.S. Federal Reserve Board raised U.S. interest rates, leading the worldwide move to change current super-loose monetary policy. 米連邦準備制度理事会(FRB)が米国の金利を引き上げ、世界的な超金融緩和の政策転換の先陣を切った。
loosen　(動)緩和する, 緩(ゆる)める, 弱める, 解く, 解き放つ
　　loosen credit policy　金融政策を緩和する
　　loosen credit standards　融資基準を緩める
　　loosen lending restrictions　貸出規制を緩和する
　　loosen monetary policy　金融政策を緩和する, 金融緩和する
　　loosen the budget strictures　圧縮財政を緩和する
　　◆The Bank of Japan decided to loosen its monetary policy. 日銀が、金融緩和を決めた。
loosening　(名)緩和
　　loosening of fiscal policy　財政政策の緩和, 緊縮財政の緩和
　　loosening of monetary policy　金融政策の緩和, 金融緩和
　　loosening of regulations　規制緩和
lose　(動)赤字を出す, 損失を被(こうむ)る, 失う, (競争

などに）負ける, 敗れる, 下落する, 減少する, 縮小する
lose a case ［suit］ 訴訟に負ける, 敗訴する
lose competitiveness 競争力を失う
　（=lose competitive edge）
lose depositor confidence 預金者の信認を失う
lose money 損失を出す, 赤字を出す, 損失を被る, 収益が減る
lose on a contract 契約で損をする
lose one's access to funds 資金調達の道を失う
lose one's position as ～としての立場を失う
lose the battle for deposits 預金獲得競争に負ける
lose two basis points in yield 利回りが0.02%上昇する
◆According to a commodity futures market insider, futures brokerages depending on commissions for revenue will lose their business strength. 商品先物市場関係者によると、収入を手数料に頼っている先物会社の経営体力は、今後弱まりそうだ。◆Citigroup Inc. lost more than $20 billion between October 2007 and October 2008. シティグループは、2007年10月～2008年10月の1年間で200億ドルの赤字［損失］を出した。◆Depending on moves in foreign exchange markets, there is a risk we may lose initial investments in foreign currency deposits. 為替相場の動き次第で、外貨預金では初期投資額を割り込むリスクがある。◆For the three months ended July 31, the company lost $2.03 billion, or 67 cents per share. 5-7月期は、同社は20億3,000万ドル（1株当たり67セント）の赤字を出した。◆Freddie Mac lost $6 billion, or $1.85 per share, in the April-to-June period of this fiscal year. フレディ・マック（米連邦住宅貸付抵当公社）は、今年度4～6月期決算で60億ドル（1株当たり1.85ドル）の赤字を出した。◆Investors are losing confidence in monetary management. 通貨調節への投資家の信認は、失われている。◆JAL's stocks may lose market value to zero if the corporate turnaround body cuts the shares 100 percent by delisting JAL from the Tokyo stock market. 企業再生支援機構が東京株式市場から日航の上場を廃止して日航株を100％減資したら、日航株の市場価値はゼロになる可能性がある。◆The United States lost its top-tier AAA credit rating from S&P for the first time. 米国債の格付け［米国の長期国債格付け］が、スタンダード・アンド・プアーズ(S&P)による最上級のAAA（トリプルA）の格付けから史上初めて転落した。◆The U.S. dollar may lose its current status as the world's only reserve currency. 米ドルは、世界唯一の準備通貨としての現在の地位を失う可能性がある。◆The yen has lost 3% of its value against the U.S. dollar on the day. 円相場は、この日は対米ドルで3%下落した。

lose ground 衰退する, 値を下げる, 売られる
　be steadily losing ground じり貧状態だ
　lose some ground 値を下げる
　recover lost ground 下げ幅を取り戻す
　slowly lose ground 徐々に衰退する
◆The bond market lost a good deal of ground. 債券相場は、反落した。◆The yen lost ground against higher-yielding currencies. 円は、高金利通貨に対して値を下げた［高金利通貨に対して売られた］。

lose momentum 失速する, 減速する
◆Goldman Sachs lowered its forecast for U.S. growth in 2011 on signs that the U.S. economic recovery lost momentum. 米金融大手のゴールドマン・サックスは、米景気回復減速の兆しを受けて、2011年の米国の成長見通しを下方修正した。◆Japan's exports, which had been supporting the business boom, lost momentum. 景気を支えてきた日本の輸出が、失速した。◆The stimulation of consumption and job placement assistance are appropriate measures to prevent the economy from losing its momentum. 消費喚起（かんき）や就職斡旋［失業者の就職］支援は、景気の腰折れを防ぐ妥当な政策だ。

loser （名）値下がり銘柄, 値下がり株, 負け組

losers 負け組, 負け組企業, 値下がり銘柄, 値下がり銘柄数
losers group companies of the world 世界の負け組企業
weak-yen losers 円安の打撃を受ける企業
winners and losers 勝ち組と負け組
◆About 90 percent of the 1,511 issues listed on the main section—or 1,359—were losers. 東証第一部に上場している1,511銘柄の約90%、つまり1,359銘柄は、値下がり銘柄だった。◆The disparity between winners and losers is widening. 勝ち組と負け組の格差は、拡大している。◆There were 60 winners［gainers］while losers numbered 250 losers. 値下がり株の250銘柄に対して、値上がり株は60銘柄あった。

losing （形）下落する, 値を下げている, 損失を出している, 不採算の, 損をする, 勝ち目のない, 勝てる見込みのない （名）失敗, 損失
cover up a losing trade 損失の出ている取引を隠す
losing operations 不採算の事業, 不採算事業部門
losing streak 続落
snap a five-day losing streak 5日連続の下落に歯止めをかける

loss （名）損失, 欠損, 欠損金, 赤字, 赤字額, 損害, 損害額, 減損, 減少, ロス （⇒loan disposal costs, loan loss provisions, stock loss, uncollectible loan）
accounting loss 会計上の損失
annual profit and loss 年次損益
bear［suffer］a loss 損失を被る
book loss 評価損, 含み損
conditional loss 機会損失
contingent loss 偶発損失
credit loss 信用損失, 貸倒れ
dead loss 丸損, 完全な損失
default loss デフォルト損失
embedded losses 含み損
estimated loss 見積り損失, 損失見積り, 回収不能見込み
expected losses 予想損失, 損失の予想額
financial loss 財務会計上の損失, 財務上［会計上］の損失, 金融上の損失, 損失
general (average) loss 共同海損
heavy losses 巨額［多額］の損失
historical loss experience 過去の損失実績
holding gain or loss 保有損益
huge losses 巨額の損失
interim losses 中間期の損失, 半期損失, 半期決算損失
loss and damage 損害
loss carryover［carry-over］ 欠損金の繰越し
　（=carryover of deficit）
loss contingencies 偶発損失事象, 偶発［偶発的］損失
loss cut［cutting］ 損切り
loss department 損害査定部
loss from capital reduction 減資差損
loss from prior period adjustment 前期損益修正損
loss from securities' revaluation 有価証券の評価差損
loss from the difference of quotations 為替差損
loss from the redemption of bonds 社債の償還差損
loss from valuation of securities 有価証券評価損
　（=loss from securities revaluation, loss from write-down of securities）
loss incurred basis 発生損害規準
loss leaser 値下がり率の大きい銘柄, 目玉商品
loss not proximately caused 間接損害
loss of exchange 為替の損失
loss of operating earnings 営業利益の減少, 営業減益

loss of profits　喪失利益
loss of time insurance　不稼働保険
loss of use insurance　使用不能損失保険
loss on bad debt　貸倒れ損失
loss on bond conversion　社債転換差損
loss on foreign exchange　外国為替差損
loss on sale of real estate　不動産売却損
loss or claim paid　支払い保険金, 支払い填補金
loss outstanding　未払い保険金
loss per share　1株当たり純損失, 1株当たり損失
loss projections　損失予想額, 予想損失額
loss ratio　損害率
loss report　損害報告, 保険金報告書, ロス・レポート
loss retention　損害保有
losses from bad loan disposals　不良債権処理損失額, 不良債権処理による損失額, 不良債権処理に伴う損失額
losses in stock transactions　株式売買の損失
partial loss　分損
particular loss　単独海損
possible losses　見込まれる損失
potential loss　潜在的損失, 予想損失
reduced losses　赤字縮小, 赤字幅の縮小, 損失幅の縮小
　(=lower losses, smaller losses, reduction in losses)
special losses　特別損失
tax loss　税務上の欠損金
total loss　全損
unrealized [unrealized] loss　未実現損失, 評価損, 含み損

◆A one-yen drop in the exchange rate against the U.S. dollar would lead to the loss of about ¥200 million in annual profits for the company. 対米ドル為替レートで1円の円安が、同社の場合は年間で約2億円の減益となる。◆During a regular board meeting, Fuji TV directors agreed to file a claim against Livedoor for losses of more than ¥30 billion incurred from selling off Livedoor shares. 定例取締役会で、フジテレビの役員は、ライブドア株の売却で被った300億円超の損失について、ライブドアに損害賠償を請求することで合意した。◆GM is suffering major losses. GMは、巨額の赤字に苦しんでいる。◆In the case of foreign currency deposits, losses may balloon if the yen appreciates further and may cause a loss of principal. 外貨預金の場合、円高がさらに進めば損失が膨らみ、元本割れになる恐れもある。◆In the case of JAL, the DBJ's ultimate total losses came to ¥95.6 billion in loans and ¥20 billion in investments. 日航の場合、日本政策投資銀行の最終的な損失総額は、融資分の956億円と出資分の200億円となっている。◆It's difficult to offset losses from further appreciation of the yen with interest as interest rates in many foreign currency deposits are low. 外貨建て預金の多くは金利が低いので、円高進行による損失分を利息で相殺する[取り戻す]のは難しい。◆Major financial institutions are forced to hold additional capital so that they can better absorb losses during financial crises. 金融危機の際の損失吸収力を高めるため、大手金融機関は、資本[自己資本]の積み増しを迫られている。◆Mizuho's first-half profit fell 17 percent as credit costs increased and on losses related to investments in U.S. home loans to riskier borrowers. みずほの上半期利益は、与信コストの増加とリスクの高い融資先への米国の住宅ローン投資に関連する損失で、17%減少した。◆The bank recorded losses in the accounting period ending March 31 due to bad loan write-offs. 同行は、不良債権処理のため、3月期決算[3月31日終了の会計年度]で赤字になった。◆The massive losses mean the bank's capital adequacy ratio is estimated to have fallen to about 8 percent. この大幅な赤字で、同行の自己資本比率は、約8%まで低下する見通しだ。◆The security firm expects to book about ¥73 billion in losses related to its residential mortgage-backed securities business in the July-September quarter. 同証券会社は、7-9月期に住宅融資証券事業の関連損失として730億円を計上する見通しだ。◆This loss came from deducting recourse loans made to our senior management. この損失は、当社の上級経営陣に対して行った遡求請求権付き貸付け金を控除したことで生じました。

loss absorbency　損失吸収力
◆A bank's core capital, or Tier 1capital, is deemed to have high loss-absorbency and resilience. 銀行の中核的自己資本は、損失吸収力と弾力性が高いとされている。

loss covering　損失補填(ほてん), 欠損補填
◆Access to the internal reserves under the existing law is strictly limited to loss covering purposes. 現行法では、内部留保の取り崩しは、欠損(欠損した資本の)補填を目的にした場合だけに限られている。

loss hiding scandal [loss-hiding scandal]　損失隠し疑惑, 損失隠しの不祥事
◆Loss hiding scandal-tainted Olympus Corp. was sued by an investor in its American depositary receipts seeking class-action status. 損失隠しの疑惑をもたれたオリンパスが、同社の米国預託証券(ADR)を保有している投資家に、集団訴訟を求めて訴えられた。

loss-making area　不採算部門
loss-making outlet　赤字店舗
　(=money-losing outlet)

loss of confidence　信頼の失墜
◆The repercussions of Olympus Corp's false financial statements could lead to a loss of confidence in the governance and in the compliance of all Japanese firms. オリンパスの不正経理[有価証券虚偽記載]の影響で、日本企業全体の統治能力や法令遵守への信頼が失墜する可能性がある。

loss projections　損失予想額, 予想損失額
◆In their midterm earnings reports, major banking groups revised initial loss projections resulting from bad loan disposal. 中間決算で、主要銀行グループは不良債権処理に伴う当初の予想損失額を修正した。

loss-sharing system　ロス・シェアリング方式, 損失分担方式(国と営業譲渡先が損失を分担する方式)
◆Under the loss-sharing system, the government and an entity that would take over the management of the bank will share the losses. このロス・シェアリング方式によると、同行の経営権を引き継ぐ事業体と政府が、損失を分担することになる。

losses from bad loan disposals　不良債権処理損失額, 不良債権処理による損失額, 不良債権処理に伴う損失額
　(⇒downward revision)

losses in stock transactions　株式売買の損失

losses on investments　投資の損失, 投資損失
◆The murky acquisitions of several companies by the major precision equipment maker were intended to paper over losses on investments the company made. この大手精密機器メーカーによる不透明な企業買収のねらいは、同社が行った投資の損失隠しだった。

lost　(形)失われた, 失った, 損失した, 喪失した, 紛失した, 逸失した
lost bill　紛失手形
lost check　紛失小切手
lost goods　損失貨物, 紛失貨物
lost ground　下げ幅, 失った勢力[影響力、人気]
lost item　紛失物件
lost note　紛失約束手形
lost or not lost　遡及的約款, 遡及約款, 保険契約の成立以前に遡(さかのぼ)って効力が生じる保険契約
lost passbook　紛失した通帳

lost profit　逸失利益
lost decade　失われた10年　(1990年代初め頃から続いた日本の景気後退[景気停滞]の10年。⇒two lost decades)
◆Japan's financial services sector learned of the importance of safety management through the lost decade. 失われた10年を通じて、日本の金融界は安全管理の重要性を学んだ。◆The lost decade is due to the mishandling of losses in the financial markets. 失われた10年は、金融市場での損失処理の失敗によるものだ。◆The lost decade refers to the period of economic stagnation since the bursting of the economic bubble in the early 1990s. 「失われた10年」とは、バブルが崩壊した1990年代初めから続いた景気後退[景気停滞]期のことである。

lost principal and interest payments　元本と利払い分の損失
◆In the lawsuits against big banks over the sales of risky investments, the U.S. government wants to be compensated for lost principal and interest payments. 高リスク証券の販売をめぐっての大手金融機関に対する訴訟で、米政府は、元本と利払い分の損失補償を求めている。

lot　(名)口数, 単位, ロット　(⇒large-lot savings)
　　board lot　株式の取引単位
　　fractional lot　端株
　　large-lot buying　大量買入れ, 大量仕入れ
　　large-lot corporate borrowers　大口融資先
　　large-lot stock trades　大量の株式売買
　　large-lot time deposits　大口定期預金
　　lot bond　ロット債, ロット・ボンド
　　major banks' large-lot corporate borrowers　大手銀行の大口融資先
　　odd lot　端株
　　regulations on large-lot loans　大口融資規制
　　round lot　最低取引単位
　　small-lot after-hours trading　立会い外分売
◆The aggregate balance of large-lot time deposits of ￥10 million or more for each depositor at the four major banks plunged to ￥17.7 trillion. 4大銀行(大手銀行4行)の預金者1人当たり1,000万円以上の大口定期預金の残高合計は、17兆7,000億円に急減した。◆The FSA's special inspection will check the major banks' large-lot corporate borrowers whose stock prices or credit ratings have sharply declined. 金融庁の特別検査は、大手銀行の株価や格付けなどが急落した大口融資先を査定の対象としている。◆The Jasdaq can begin small-lot after-hours trading by its transformation from an over-the-counter stock market to a securities exchange. ジャスダックは、店頭市場から証券取引所への移行により、立会い外分売(取引時間外に大株主などが保有株を小口に分けて売り出すこと)も可能になった。

Louvre Accord　ルーブル合意　(1987年2月22日、パリで開かれたG7(先進7か国蔵相・中央銀行総裁会議)で採択された為替安定のための合意)

low　(名)安値, 底値, 最低, 底, 最安値, 最低値, 最低記録　(⇒ECB, interest rate, sell-off)
　　a record low　過去最低
　　all-time lows　過去最低の水準
　　an all time low　過去最低, 最低記録, 史上最安値, 上場来の安値, 過去最良　(=a record low)
　　close at the year's low　今年最安値で取引を終える, 終値は今年最安値となる
　　cyclical low　サイクルの底
　　dip to the lows　安値を付ける
　　drop to an all-time low　過去最低まで落ち込む, 最安値まで落ち込む
　　fall to an all-time low [a record low]　過去最低まで落ち込む, 最安値まで落ち込む
　　historic lows　過去最低水準
　　hit a new [fresh] low　新安値を付ける, 安値を更新する
　　hit a record [an all-time] low　最安値を付ける, 上場来最安値を付ける
　　hit the day's low　この日の最安値を付ける
　　hit the week's low　この[その]週の最安値を付ける
　　low for the week　週の安値
　　retest the low　安値を試す
　　set new all-time lows　史上最安値を更新する
　　slump to a new low against the dollar　対ドルで最安値まで落ち込む, 対ドルで最安値[安値]を更新する
　　the day's low　この日の安値[最安値]
　　the year's low　今年の最安値, 年初来の安値
　　touch a low　安値を付ける
◆Stock prices have dropped to an all-time low since the collapse of the bubble economy. 株価は、バブル崩壊後の最安値まで落ち込んだ。◆The dollar exited the week near its seven-month low against the yen and an all-time low against the euro. ドル(ドル相場)は、対円で約7か月ぶりの安値、対ユーロでは史上最安値で週を終えた。◆The euro plummeted to the ￥100 level on the foreign exchange market, hitting a 10 year low. 外国為替市場では、ユーロが1ユーロ＝100円台まで急落して、10年ぶりの低水準[10年ぶりの円高・ユーロ安水準]となった。◆The 225-issue Nikkei Stock Average dropped below the 9,000 mark Wednesday to close at the year's low of 8,845.39. 水曜日の日経平均株価(225種)は、9,000円台を割り込み、終値は今年最安値の8,845円39銭となった。◆The U.S. dollar dropped to a fresh 15-year low in the lower ￥82 level. 米ドル相場は82円台前半まで下落し、15年ぶりに最安値を更新した。

low　(形)低い, 低水準の, 元気のない, 値段が安い, ～台前半の　(副)安く, 安値で, 少なく
　　consumers with low credit risk　信用リスクが低い消費者
　　hit a low point　底を打つ
　　hover around the lower end of $110 level　110ドル台前半で推移する
　　low beta portfolio　ベータ値が低いポートフォリオ
　　low cost funds　低金利の資金調達
　　low cost loan　低金利ローン, 低費用融資
　　low dividend　低配当
　　low dividend stock　低配株
　　low exchange rate of yen　円安
　　low for the week　週の安値
　　low grade stock　低位株
　　low growth path　低成長軌道
　　low income　低所得
　　low inflation　低インフレ, インフレ率の低下
　　low inflation policy　インフレ抑制政策
　　low interest rate policy　低金利政策
　　low lending margin　貸出の利ざやが薄いこと
　　low margin　薄利
　　low-paying stock　低配株
　　low price　安い値段, 安値, 安値, 低価格
　　low price policy　低物価政策
　　low-priced [low-price] stock　低位株
　　low-rated bond　低評価債
　　low risk portfolio　低リスク・ポートフォリオ
　　low turnover　薄商い
　　low value stock　低額面株式
　　lower deficit　財政赤字削減
　　lower earning on higher sales　増収減益
　　lower earning on lower sales　減収減益

lower interest expense　金利負担の軽減
lower limit rate　下限相場
lower money market rates　短期金利の低下
lower prime rate　プライム・レートの低下
lower quality credits　格付けの低い借り手
lower quality issuer　信用力の低い発行体
lower savings　貯蓄率の低下
lower stock [share] prices　株価の下落
lower supply point　(為替などの)下限相場
lower yielding securities　利回りが低い証券
open low　安値で寄り付く
stay in the lower ¥77 range against the U.S. dollar　1ドル＝77円台前半で推移する
the lower half of the target range　目標圏の下半分

◆Adjustable types of home loans will continue to be popular as long as interest rates are expected to remain low. 金利の先安感が強い間は、(金利)変動型の住宅ローンの人気が続くようだ。◆As a result of fierce competition in the past, interest rate profit margins were kept too low to cover loans that went sour. 過去の熾烈(しれつ)な競争の結果、金利の利ざやが小さく抑えられる余り、貸倒れ[貸倒れのリスク]をカバーできなかった[過去の熾烈な融資合戦の結果、不良債権リスクをカバーできないほど利ざやは小さく抑えられた]。◆It's difficult to offset losses from further appreciation of the yen with interest as interest rates in many foreign currency deposits are low. 外貨建て預金の多くは金利が低いので、円高進行による損失分を利息で相殺する[取り戻す]のは難しい。◆South Korea, Brazil and India are guiding their currencies lower to deal with an influx of speculative money. 韓国、ブラジルとインドは、投機マネーの流入に対応するため、自国通貨安に誘導している。◆The bank posted strong third-quarter profits as investment banking business surged, stocks rose and interest rates stayed low. 投資銀行業務の急増と株価上昇のほか、金利が低水準を維持したため、同行の第3四半期利益は大幅に増加した。◆The Japanese currency is about ¥5 lower than its initial projection of ¥115 to the dollar. 円は、当初想定した1ドル＝115円より5円程度安く推移している。◆The per-barrel price has been hovering around the lower end of the $110 level in recent weeks. 1バレル当たりの原油価格は、ここ数週間、110ドル台半ばで推移している。◆The possibility that the bank's collapse will set off a negative chain reaction is very low. 同行の破たんが連鎖破たんを引き起こす可能性は、かなり低い。◆The 225-issue Nikkei Stock Average closed at 7,607.88, the lowest level since the economic bubble burst, on April 28, 2003. 2003年4月28日の日経平均株価(225種)の終値は7,607円88銭で、バブル崩壊後の最安値を付けた。◆The U.S. dollar sank to its lowest level since May 1995 in the lower ¥83 zone. 米ドル相場は、1ドル＝83円台前半で1995年5月以来最低の水準まで下落した。◆The yen stayed in the lower ¥77 range against the U.S. dollar in Tokyo. 東京外国為替市場の円相場は、1ドル＝77円台前半で推移した。◆Though stock prices remain low, the number of transactions has already outpaced that during the bubble economy. 株価はまだ低いものの、株取引の件数はすでにバブル期を超えている。◆Turbulence in global financial markets brought the level of liquidity in the country sharply lower. 世界の金融市場の混乱で、国内流動性の水準は大幅に低下した。◆With the rating of JGBs being low, internationalizing them may increase the risk that their yield will fluctuate. 日本の国債の格付けが低いので、日本国債の国際化は国債の金利変動リスクを高める可能性がある。

low credit rating　低い格付け
◆Of the amount of investment, about a half was invested in foreign government bonds with low credit ratings. この投資額のうち約半分は、格付けの低い外国債に充てられていた。

low-income earners　低所得者, 低所得者層
◆The burden of low-income earners will become larger if the consumption tax rate is raised. 消費税率を引き上げると、低所得者の負担は大きくなる。◆The instability of U.S. stock prices results from problems related to massive number of unrecoverable subprime mortgage loans extended to low-income earners in the United States. 米国の株価不安定は、米国の低所得者向け住宅ローン「サブプライム・ローン」の焦げ付き急増関連問題に起因している。

low interest　低金利, 低利
low interest country　低金利国
low interest credit　低金利資金
low interest loan　低利融資, 低利貸付け
low interest money　低金利資金
low interest policy　低金利政策

low interest rate　低金利, 低利子率
low interest rate policy　低金利政策
lower interest rates　金利の低下, 低金利
◆Since the bubble economy burst, low interest rates have been the norm. バブル崩壊以降、低金利が続いている。

low-priced issues　割安な銘柄
◆Individual investors and brokerage dealers continued to take profits from recent surges in comparatively low-priced issues. 個人投資家と証券会社のディーラーは、最近の比較的割安な銘柄の急上昇で引き続き利食いに出た。

low risk　低リスク, 小さいリスク, 少ないリスク
low-risk activity　低リスク業務
low-risk conglomerate　低リスクのコングロマリット
low-risk transaction　低リスクの取引
low-risk Treasury bonds　低リスクの米財務省証券, 低リスクの米国債
◆Investment funds flowed into low-risk Treasury bonds. 投資資金は、リスクの少ない財務省証券市場に流入した。

low yielding　利回りが低い, 低利回りの, 低金利の
low yielding assets　低利回り資産
low yielding currency　低利回り通貨, 低金利通貨
low yielding market　低利回り市場
lower yielding securities　利回りが低い証券

lower　(動)引き下げる, 押し下げる, 低減する, 低下させる, 抑える, 下げる, 減らす, 安くする, 下方修正する (自動)下落する, 低下する, 下がる, 減少する
lower borrowing costs　資金調達コストを低減する
lower interest rates　金利を引き下げる, 金利を下げる, 利下げする
lower Japan's long-term sovereign credit rating　日本の長期国債の格付けを引き下げる
(⇒sovereign credit rating)
lower one's profit forecasts　業績予想[業績見通し]を下方修正する
(＝slash one's profit forecasts)
lower the bid price　買い呼び値を下げる
lower the company's rating　同社の格付けを引き下げる, 同社の格付けを下方修正する
lower the Federal funds rate　フェデラル・ファンド金利[FF金利]を引き下げる
◆A strong yen lowers the prices of imported goods and fuels deflation. 円高は輸入品の価格を下げ、デフレに拍車をかける。◆All possible measures, such as injecting funds into markets and lowering rates, need to be taken to ride out this financial emergency. この金融非常事態をうまく切り抜けるには、市場への資金注入[資金供給]や利下げなど、あらゆる可能な措置を取る必要がある。◆Goldman Sachs lowered its forecast for U.S. growth in 2011 on signs that the U.S. economic recovery lost momentum. 米金融大手のゴールドマン・サックスは、

米景気回復減速の兆しを受けて、2011年の米国の成長見通しを下方修正した。◆It is easier for financial institutions to lower interest rates for adjustable rate mortgages, compared with fixed-type mortgage products. 金融機関にとって、金利固定型のモーゲージ商品よりも、変動型金利の住宅ローンのほうが金利を下げやすい。◆Kokudo lowered its holding in Seibu Railway. コクドは、西武鉄道の持ち株比率を下げた。◆Lowering the yield of Meiji Yasuda's single-premium whole life insurance will reduce the attraction of the insurer's financial products. 明治安田生保の一時払い終身保険の利回り[予定利率]の引下げで、同社の金融商品の魅力は薄れると思われる。◆Some major banks lower their commission rates of foreign currency deposits if depositors make transactions via online accounts. 外貨預金の預金者がネット口座経由で取引をする場合、一部の大手銀行は、外貨預金の手数料[為替手数料]の料率を引き下げている。◆S&P lowered Belgium's credit rating from AA+ to AA. スタンダード・アンド・プアーズ(S&P)は、ベルギー国債の信用格付け[格付け]を、ダブルA(AA)プラスからダブルA(AA)に1段階引き下げた。◆S&P lowered Japan's long-term sovereign credit rating to AA minus from AA. 米格付け会社のスタンダード・アンド・プアーズ(S&P)は、日本の長期国債格付けを現在の「ダブルA」から「ダブルAマイナス」に引き下げた。◆Taxpayers' burden from the JAL bailout was lowered to ¥47 billion as the firm repaid part of its outstanding debt. 日航救済による国民の負担分は、日航が債務残高の一部を返済したため、470億円に減少した。◆The ADB lowered its 2011 growth forecast in Asian nations due to growing worries about weak demand from key trading partners including the United States and Europe. アジア開発銀行(ADB)は、主要貿易相手国である欧米で需要減退[需要低迷]懸念が高まっていることから、アジアの2011年の成長見通し[GDP成長率見通し]を下方修正した。◆The Bank of Japan lowered its key interest rate by 0.2 percentage points to 0.1 percent. 日銀は、政策金利を0.2ポイント下げて0.1%とした。◆The company lowered its operating profit 62 percent to ¥50 billion from the earlier forecast for ¥130 billion. 同社は、営業利益見通しを前回発表の13,00億円から500億円に62%下方修正した。◆The drop in gasoline prices lowered overall prices about 1 percent. ガソリンの値下りが、物価全体を約1%押し下げた。◆The Greek economic chaos was triggered as its national bond rating was lowered. ギリシャの経済混乱のきっかけは、ギリシャの国債格付けが引き下げられたことだ。◆The sudden economic downturn since the autumn has forced the government to drastically lower the forecast rate of real GDP in fiscal 2009. 秋以降の急速な景気悪化で、政府は2009年度の実質国内総生産(GDP)成長率見通しを大幅に引き下げざるを得なかった。◆The U.S. Federal Reserve Board significantly lowered its forecast for the U.S. economy. 米連邦準備制度理事会(FRB)は、米景気判断を大幅に下方修正した。◆The wall separating banking and securities businesses has been lowered through such moves as the liberalization of banks' securities brokering. 銀行と証券業の垣根は、銀行に対する証券仲介業の規制緩和などの動きで、低くなっている。◆Two influential rating firms lowered Ford Motor Co.'s credit ratings a notch deeper into junk territory. 大手[有力な]格付け機関2社が、米フォードの信用格付けを「投資不適格レベル」にさらに1段階引き下げた。

lower revenues 売上高の減少
◆The firm's earnings per share were affected both by lower revenues and reduced gross margins. 同社の1株当たり利益は、売上高の減少と売上利益率の低下の影響を受けた。

lower stock price(s) 株価の下落, 株価下落
◆Japan Airlines Corp. is expected to fall short of its planned fund-raising target by about ¥50 billion due to lower stock price. 日本航空では、株価の下落で、当初計画の資金調達目標を約500億円下回る見通しだ。

lower the yield 利回りを引き下げる
◆Meiji Yasuda will lower the yield of its single-premium whole life insurance and other companies offering the same type of life insurance products could follow suit. 明治安田生命は一時払い終身保険の利回り(予定利率)を引き下げるが、同種の生保商品を販売している他社もこれに追随する可能性がある。

lower the yield on life policy 保険利回りを引き下げる
◆Meiji Yasuda Life Insurance Co. will lower the yield on life policy from December 2011. 明治安田生命保険が、2011年12月から保険利回りを引き下げる。

lower the yield rate 利回りを引き下げる
◆In December 2011, the insurer will lower the yield rate to 1.1 percent from 1.5 percent for those who newly purchase the company's single-premium whole life insurance. 2011年12月から同生保は、一時払い終身保険の新規加入者[新規契約者]を対象に、利回り(予定利率)を1.5%から1.1%に引き下げる。

lower the yields of insurance products 保険商品の利回りを引き下げる
◆The move to lower the yields of insurance products is likely to spread through the industry as tough investment conditions persist. 厳しい運用環境が続いているので、保険商品の利回りを引き下げる動きは、業界全体に広がりそうだ。

lowered (形)引き下げられた, 低下した, ～の引下げ, ～の低下
　lowered inflation　インフレ率の低下
　lowered interest rates　金利の引下げ, 利下げ

lowered earning power of banks 銀行の収益力低下
◆The instability of life insurance firms and the lowered earning power of banks with massive bad loans have become the two major factors rocking the financial system. 生保各社の経営基盤の不安定と、巨額の不良債権に苦しむ銀行の収益力低下が、金融システムを揺るがしている二大要因になっている。

lowered rating 格下げ, 格付けの引下げ
◆A lowered rating means higher interest rates. 格付けの低下は、金利の上昇を意味する。

lowered tariffs 関税の引下げ
◆If agricultural imports become cheaper due to the lowered tariffs, consumers will greatly benefit. 関税の引下げで輸入農産物が安くなれば、消費者の利点も大きい。

lowering (名)引下げ, 削減, 下方修正, 低下, 低減
　the lowering of interest rates　金利の引下げ, 利下げ
　the lowering of money market rates　短期市場金利の低下
　the lowering of one's inflation forecast　～のインフレ予測の下方修正
　the lowering of operating costs　営業経費[事業費]の削減, 営業コストの引下げ
　the lowering of the rating　格付けの引下げ
◆After the lowering of the rating, the current value of government bonds might drop and their interest rate might go up. 国債の格付けが下がると、現在の国債価格も下がり、金利の上昇を招く恐れがある。

lowest level 最低水準, 最安値
◆The Nikkei Stock Average fell briefly to its lowest level this year on the Tokyo Stock Market. 東京株式市場の日経平均株価は一時、今年の最安値を下回った。◆The U.S. dollar sank to its lowest level since May 1995 in the lower ¥83 zone. 米ドル相場は、1ドル=83円台前半で1995年5月以来最低の水準まで下落した。

loyal shareholder 安定株主
◆Fuji TV hopes to increase the number of long-term loyal shareholders. フジテレビは、長期安定株主の増強をねらっている。

lucrative (形)利益が得られる, 儲かる, 大変金になる, 利益の大きい, 有利な

◆Helping firms go public is a lucrative business for securities firms. 企業の上場を手伝う業務は、証券会社の収益源だ。

lump sum 一括払い, 大金, 合計金額
  lump sum purchase 一括購入
  lump sum repayment 一括返済
  lump sum sale 一括売却
  pay in a lump sum 一括払いで支払う
    (=make a lump sum payment)
  provide a lump sum 資金を一括供与する
  ◆The latest emergency assistance to Indonesia is aimed at providing a lump sum that allows the nation to take urgent measures such as an economic stimulus program. 今回のインドネシアへの緊急支援の狙いは、資金を一括供与して、同国が景気刺激策などの緊急措置を取れるようにすることにある。

lump sum payment 一括払い, 一時金
  ◆Financial settlement refers to a lump sum payment by an insurer to a disabled insured that extinguishes the insurer's responsibility under the disability contract. 金融決済は、就業不能契約に基づき、傷害を負った被保険者に保険会社が一時金を支給して、保険会社の責任を消滅させることを指す。

lure (動)勧誘する, 誘い込む, 呼び込む, おびき寄せる, おびき出す, 引きつける, 誘致する, 導入する, 誘導する
  (=attract)
  lure customers 顧客を勧誘する, 顧客を取り込む
  lure foreign companies 外資を導入する, 外国企業を誘致する
  lure investors 投資家を引きつける
  lure new clients 新規顧客を取り込む[勧誘する], 新規顧客を獲得する
  ◆ATM cards are the banks' primary weapons to lure new clients. キャッシュ・カードは、銀行にとって新規顧客獲得の有力な手段だ。◆In phishing, offenders lure victims to fake financial institution Web sites to enter their account PINs and other account information. フィッシングでは、犯人が被害者を金融機関の偽ホームページに誘導して、被害者の口座の暗証番号などの口座情報を入力させる。◆In the life insurance sector, the practice of luring customers by touting the bad performances of other insurers has been called into question. 生保業界では、他社の経営不振をあおって顧客を勧誘する行為(風評営業)が問題になっている。◆The stock market is now luring not only individual investors such as day traders, but also people who abandoned the equity market after the economic bubble burst. 株式市場(株式投資)は現在、デイ・トレーダーなどのようなセミプロの個人投資家だけでなく、バブル崩壊以降、株式市場から遠ざかっていた一般の人たちをも引き付けている。◆The two exchanges also aim to lure funds from investors both at home and abroad by the merger. 経営統合によって、両株式取引所は国内外の投資資金を呼び込む狙いもある。

M

M 金(money), 通貨供給量[マネー・サプライ](money supply)

M0 エム・ゼロ (=monetary base)

M1 エム・ワン, マネー・サプライM1 (=M one: 通貨供給量の指標で、個人や企業が保有する現金と要求払い預金をいう。M1=預金通貨(普通預金や当座預金など)+現金通貨)
  ◆The balance of M1, or cash in circulation plus deposit money, climbed 32.6 percent to ¥331.9 trillion. 現金通貨に預金通貨を加えたM1の残高は、32.6%増の331兆9,000億円となった。

M2 エム・ツー, マネー・サプライM2 (=M two:M1に定期性預金が中心の準通貨を加えたもの。M2=預金通貨+現金通貨+準通貨)

◆M2 consists of cash in circulation, demand and time deposits, as well as certificates of deposits at domestic banks, including the central bank and Japanese branches of foreign banks. M2は、現金通貨と要求払い預金、定期性預金のほか、国内銀行(日本銀行と外国銀行の日本支店を含む)の譲渡性預金(CD)から成る。◆The average daily balance of M2—cash in circulation, demand deposits and quasi-money—plus certificates of deposit came to ¥671.2 trillion. 現金通貨と要求払い預金に準通貨(定期預金が中心)を加えたM2と譲渡性預金(CD)の1日平均残高は、671兆2,000億円に達した。

M3 マネー・サプライM3, エム・スリー (=M three:M2に譲渡性預金(CD)と郵便局、農協、信用金庫などの預貯金や信用元本などを加えたもの)
  ◆M3 includes cash in circulation, demand and time deposits and certificates of deposit at all depository institutions, including Japan Post Bank Co. マネー・サプライM3には、現金通貨、要求払い預金、定期性預金や全貯蓄銀行(ゆうちょ銀行を含む)の譲渡性預金(CD)などが含まれる。◆M3 was up 0.6 percent to ¥1.031 quadrillion in October from a year earlier. 10月のマネー・サプライM3は、前年同月比0.6%増の1,031兆円となった。

M&A 企業の吸収合併, 合併・買収, 企業取得と合併
  (merger and acquisition [mergers and acquisitions]の略。⇒mergers and acquisitions)
  financial M&A 財務的M&A(財務上の利益を上げることが目的のM&A)
  friendly M&A 友好的M&A
  hostile M&A 敵対的M&A
  M&A advisory firm M&A(企業の合併・買収)助言会社
  M&A bid 企業の合併・買収提案, M&Aの提案
  M&A information 企業の合併・買収情報, M&A情報
  strategic M&A 戦略的M&A(事業の再構築を目的とするM&A)
  ◆The recent M&A is a strategy with an eye on Asia, which has a great potential for sales growth. 今回のM&Aは、販売が伸びる可能性が大きいアジアを視野に入れた戦略です。◆The survey found about 68 percent of M&As were aimed at strengthening the foundations of existing businesses, followed by 15 percent for investment purposes. 調査の結果、M&A(企業の合併・買収)の目的は約68%が既存事業の基盤強化で、次いで15%が投資目的であった。

M&A advisory business M&A顧問業務
  ◆Increasing M&A advisory business helped Nomura grab the No. 1 spot in Japan's M&A league table for the first half of this year. 今年上半期はM&A顧問業務が増加したため、日本のM&A案件の引受実績で野村證券がトップの座を占めた。

M&A deal M&A取引, M&A案件
  (=M&A transaction; ⇒merger and acquisition deal)
  M&A deals among start-up firms ベンチャー企業間のM&A取引
  the total value of M&A deals M&A取引の総額, M&A取引金額の総額 (⇒value)
  ◆M&A deals among start-up firms are likely to create more demand for equity financing from the autumn. ベンチャー企業間のM&A取引で、秋から株式発行による資金調達の需要が増える見通しだ。◆Small and midsize companies have been stepping up equity financing to fund capital investments and prepare for M&A deals. 中小企業は、設備投資の資金調達とM&A取引に備えて、株式発行による資金調達を急いでいる。

M&A market 企業の合併・買収(M&A)市場
  ◆Investors bought into prospects for growth in the M&A market. 投資家は、M&A(企業の合併・買収)市場の成長力に投資した。

MaCarran-Ferguson Act マッカラン・ファーガソン法

machinery orders 機械受注, 機械受注額

core private machinery orders　実質民間機械受注, 実質機械受注（船舶・電力を除く民間需要）
private machinery orders　民間機械受注
public machinery orders　官公機械受注, 機械受注のうち公共部門の需要
◆Core private-sector machinery orders exclude orders for ships and for machinery at electric power firms. 実質民間機械受注は、船舶受注と電力会社の機械受注を除く。

macro policy　マクロ政策
◆Unless the government and the Bank of Japan change their macro fiscal and monetary policies and arrest the deflationary trend, the disposal of nonperforming loans will never be completed. 政府と日銀が財政と金融のマクロ政策を転換してデフレ傾向を止めないかぎり、不良債権処理は終わらないだろう。

macroeconomic recovery　マクロの景気回復
◆This strategy works against macroeconomic recovery. この戦略は、マクロの景気回復にはマイナスに働く。

magic bullet　魔法の弾丸, 無害［無副作用］薬剤, 特効薬, 解決手段, 解決
◆The U.S. financial bailout bill is no magic bullet. 米国の緊急経済安定化（金融安定化）法案は、決して（金融危機の）解決にはならない。

mail order　通信販売, 通販, 通信販売の注文
◆We'll begin selling vegetables by mail order in November. 当社は、11月から通販で野菜を販売する予定だ。

main bank　主要取引銀行, 主力取引銀行, 主力行, メインバンク
◆A financial aid package that includes a debt-for-equity swap and debt forgiveness was considered by the main banks. 債務の株式化（銀行にとっては債権の株式化）や債権放棄などの金融支援策を、主力取引銀行が検討した。◆Having the same main bank is another factor that led the two companies to the integration agreement. 主力行がともに同じといことも、両社が経営統合で合意した理由の一つだ。

main battlefield of monetary policy　金融政策の主戦場
◆The main battlefield of monetary policy likely will shift to deflation. 今後は、デフレが金融政策の主戦場となろう。

main business　主力事業, 本業, 主要事業部門
◆NTT's operating profit from its main businesses increased 5.5 percent to ¥947.3 billion. NTTの本業による営業利益は、5.5%増の9,473億円となった。

main creditor　大口債権者, 主要債権国, 大口資金提供者
◆Germany, main creditor to Greece, demanded that private-sector-banks accept a certain amount of trimming of their debts.（財政危機の）ギリシャに主に資金を提供しているドイツは、民間銀行に対して債権の一部放棄を受け入れるよう求めた。

main creditor banks　主要取引銀行, 主力取引銀行, 主力銀行　（=main banks, main financing banks, waive）
◆The firm was granted debt waivers totaling ¥640 billion from its main creditor banks. 同社は、主力銀行から6,400億円の債権放棄を受けた。◆The restructuring plan includes ¥520 billion in financial support from its three main creditor banks. 再建策には、主力取引銀行3行による5,200億円の金融支援が盛り込まれている。◆Tobishima was granted debt waivers totaling ¥640 billion from its main creditor banks, which included Fuji Bank, in 1997. 飛島建設は、主力銀行の富士銀行などから1997年に6,400億円の債権放棄を受けた。

main currencies　主要通貨　（=major currencies）
◆The U.S. dollar tumbled for the second straight day against main currencies. 米ドルが、主要通貨に対して2日連続下落した。

main earner　ドル箱
◆There was unexpectedly strong opposition within and outside the company to the plan to sell off the company's main earner. 同社のドル箱である事業の全面売却案には、社内外から予想外の強い反発があった。

main financing banks　主力取引銀行, 主力行
◆Daiei's main financing banks have unofficially asked some corporations in Kyushu if they want to buy the Daiei Hawks. ダイエーの主力取引銀行が、ダイエー・ホークスの買収について九州の地元企業数社に非公式に打診している。

main interest rate　政策金利, 主要政策金利, 主要金利
◆The European Central Bank cut its main interest rate by 0.25 percent following heavy pressure for a rate cut to spur flagging economic growth. 失速気味の経済成長に刺激を与えるため利下げを求める強い圧力を受けて、欧州中央銀行（ECB）はその主要（政策）金利を0.25%引き下げた。◆The European Central Bank left its main interest rate unchanged at 1 percent despite a rise in inflation. 物価上昇にもかかわらず、欧州中央銀行（ECB）は政策金利を1%に据え置いた。

main section　東証第一部, 第一部　（⇒loser）
◆Volume on the main section rose markedly to 742.8 million shares. 東証第一部の出来高は、7億4,200万株と著しく増加した。

Main Street　保守的な社会,（小都市特有の）因習的文化, 普通の人,（小都市の）大通り, 目抜き通り（high street）, 中心街, 米国内産業
◆The crisis that hit Wall Street a couple weeks ago isn't news to families on Main Street all across this country. 2,3週間前に米ウォール街を襲った金融危機は、全国の一般市民が知らないことではない。◆Wall Street and Main Street might turn out to be buoyant this autumn. 米国の証券市場と国内産業は、今年の秋には活況を取り戻すかもしれない。

mainstay　（名）主力, 主力商品, 支え, 支柱, 大黒柱, 頼みの綱, 拠（よ）り所

mainstay automobile insurance policies　主力の自動車保険, 主力の自動車保険契約
◆Nipponkoa's net premium revenues dropped to 0.9 percent due to declines in its mainstay automobile insurance policies. 日本興亜損保の正味収入保険料は、主力の自動車保険［自動車保険契約］の減少で、0.9%減少した。

mainstay issues　主力銘柄
◆Investors were generally adopting a wait-and-see stance on mainstay issues. 主力銘柄については、投資家は全般に模様眺めのスタンスを取った［模様眺めの展開となった］。

mainstay products　主力製品, 主力商品
◆Orders for our mainstay products shrank by half on a year-on-year basis. 主力商品の受注が、前年同期比で半減した。

mainstream　（名）主流, 本流, 主潮
（「非主流」=nonmainstream）
economic mainstream　経済的主流, 経済の主流
mainstream economics　主流経済学
the mainstream in the financial services sector　金融サービス部門の主流
◆The mainstream in the financial services sector used to be banks and securities companies operating as "financial specialty stores" on their own. これまで金融サービス部門の主流といえば、「専門店」としてそれぞれ独立して運営してきた銀行や証券会社だった。

maintain　（動）保つ, 維持する, 持続する, 続ける, 進める, 据え置く, 整備する, 保守する, 保全する, 手入れをする,（家族などを）養う, 支える, 支持する, 主張する
maintain a negative outlook　ネガティブ（弱含み）の見通しを据え置く
maintain a steady hand　金融政策を据え置く
maintain a tight monetary policy stance　金融引締めのスタンスを維持する
maintain an austere stance　厳しい姿勢を貫く
maintain diversification　多角化を進める

maintain international price competitiveness　国際価格競争力を維持する
maintain markets for 200 different issues　200銘柄の値付け業務を行う
maintain one's high margins　高い利ざやを確保する
◆Daiei wants the five supermarket chains under Daiei's umbrella to maintain their separate listings on the stock market. ダイエーは、傘下の食品スーパー5社の上場を維持する考えだ。◆French Finance Minister Christine Lagarde chosen as the new managing director of the IMF is expected to maintain an austere stance of calling on Greece to reform itself. IMFの新専務理事に選ばれたクリスティーヌ・ラガルド仏財務相は、ギリシャに改革を求める厳しい姿勢を貫くものと期待されている。◆Maintaining an easy monetary policy may lead to excessive corporate capital investment and have a negative impact on the sustainable economic recovery. 金融緩和政策を続けると、企業の過剰な設備投資を生み、景気の持続的回復を阻害する恐れがある。◆The ECB was obliged to maintain price stability when the euro was launched in 1999. 1999年にユーロが導入された際、欧州中銀（ECB）は、物価安定の維持を義務付けられた。◆The Fed has been unable to deal with the current economic woes by changing interest rates as it has been maintaining a policy of virtually zero-percent interest rates. 米連邦準備制度理事会（FRB）はこれまで金利ゼロ政策を続けてきたため、政策金利を上げ下げして現在の経済的苦境に対応することはできなくなっている。◆The greenback may not be able to maintain its impregnable position as the world's only reserve currency. 米ドルは、世界で唯一の準備通貨としての揺るぎない地位を、維持できないかもしれない。◆The growth rate has slowed though external demand maintained growth. 外需が成長を維持したが、その伸び率は鈍化している。◆The labor union has attached the highest priority to maintaining job security for its member workers. 組合側は、組合員の雇用安定維持を第一に考えてきた。◆The prolonged slump in the real estate market is maintaining the decline in land prices. 不動産取引市場の長期低迷が、引き続き地価の下落を招いている。◆The U.S. Federal Reserve Board has been maintaining a policy of virtually zero-percent interest rates. 米連邦準備制度理事会（FRB）は、事実上ゼロ金利の政策を維持してきた［続けてきた］。◆Through continuing gains in annual earnings, it will be possible, over time, to adjust the payout ratio while still maintaining our dividend record. 年間利益の増大を続けることによって、当社の配当実績を今後とも維持しながら、時期が来たら配当性向を調整することは可能である。

maintenance　（名）維持, 維持管理, 整備, 保守, 保全, 営繕, 修理点検, 別居手当て, メンテナンス
administrative and maintenance expense　維持管理費
basic maintenance amount　基本維持額
capital maintenance　資本維持
　　（=maintenance of capital）
collateral maintenance　担保維持
income maintenance　所得維持, 利益維持
interest maintenance reserve　利率維持準備金
maintenance bond　瑕疵（かし）修補保証証券
maintenance call　証拠金積み増し要求, 追加証拠金請求, 追い証の請求　（=margin call）
maintenance expense　維持費, 保守費, メンテナンス費　（=maintenance charge, maintenance cost）
maintenance fees　口座維持費用
maintenance margin　維持証拠金
maintenance margin requirement　維持証拠金率
maintenance of ownership　出資比率の維持
margin maintenance call　追い証
physical capital maintenance　物的資本維持
real capital maintenance　実質資本維持
reserve maintenance period　準備預金の積み期間
yield maintenance dollar agreements　利回り維持型ドル現先

major　（形）主要な, 重大な, 大手の, 大口の, 大規模な, 大型の, 大きいほうの, 大部分の, 過半数の, 多数の, メジャー
major acquisition　大型買収
major banking accounts　全国銀行主要勘定
major blow-out in interest rates　金利の急上昇
major bond issues　大型の債券発行, 大型起債, 大型債券
major bracket　引受シンジケート団の上位証券会社
major business segment　主要事業分野
major clients of leading banks　大手行の大口融資先
major customer　大口顧客, 主要得意先
major debt-financed acquisition　借入れ［外部負債］による大型買収, 外部負債［借入れ］による大規模な買収
major investments　大型投資, 大規模投資
major investor　大口投資家, 大手の投資家
Major Market Index　メジャー・マーケット株価指数
major medical (expense) insurance　高額医療費保険
major player　大手企業, 大手, 大口の買い手
major recession　大幅な景気後退
major securities company　大手の証券会社, 証券大手
major trusts　大手信託銀行
major underwriter　主たる引受会社（証券発行の幹事役を務める会社）
the major bottom　大底
the major (market) top　大天井　（=major peak）
the major peak　大天井　（=major market top）
the world's major companies　世界の大企業, 世界の大手企業, 世界の主要企業

major bank　大手銀行, 銀行大手, 大手行
◆All other major banks have also seen sharp falls in their stock prices. 他の大手銀行の株価も、すべて急落した。◆An individual investor began depositing money in U.S. dollars using a major bank's Web account. 個人投資家が、大手銀行のウェブ口座［インターネット口座］を利用して米ドルの外貨預金を始めた。◆Major banks carried out mergers aiming to encourage realignment of other industries. 大手銀行は、他の産業再編を促進するために統合を進めた。◆Major U.S. and European banks have been strengthening their market competitiveness. 欧米の大手銀行は、市場競争力を強化してきた。◆MFG, the nation's largest financial group, tied up with two major U.S. banks to strengthen its earning power. 国内金融グループ最大手のみずほフィナンシャルグループが、収益力の強化を図るため、米銀大手2行と提携した。◆Some major banks lower their commission rates of foreign currency deposits if depositors make transactions via online accounts. 外貨預金の預金者がネット口座経由で取引をする場合、一部の大手銀行は、外貨預金の手数料［為替手数料］の料率を引き下げている。◆Speculation that some major banks may find themselves with capital shortfalls and then nationalized is driving investors to dump the banks' shares. 大手行の一部が自己資本不足に陥って国有化されるとの思惑から、投資家は銀行株の売りに出ている。◆The FSA's special inspection will check the major banks' large-lot corporate borrowers whose stock prices or credit ratings have sharply declined. 金融庁の特別検査は、大手銀行の株価や格付けなどが急落した大口融資先を査定の対象としている。◆The major banks attributed their increased bad loans to the poor performance of their borrowers due to the prolonged economic slump and Financial Service Agency inspections resulting in a stricter review of their asset assessments. 大手銀行は、不良債権が増えた理

由として、長引く景気低迷で貸出先の経営が悪化したことと、金融庁の検査を受けて大手行が資産査定を厳しくしたことを挙げた。◆Yen can be exchanged for foreign currencies and deposited in foreign currency accounts at most major banks. 円は、大半の大手銀行で外貨と替えて外貨預金口座に預け入れることができる。

major banking group 大手銀行グループ,大手銀行・金融グループ
◆All of the seven major banking groups forecast that bad loan disposal at the end of March next year will be smaller than their net operating profits. 大手銀行・金融7グループ各行の業績予想では、来年3月期の不良債権処理額はいずれも業務純益の範囲内になる見込みだ。◆All seven major banking groups reported after-tax losses due to the burden of disposing of bad loans and slumping stock markets. 不良債権処理の負担(不良債権処理損失)や株式不況の低迷で、大手銀行7グループすべてが税引き後赤字となったことを発表した。◆The combined losses of the seven major banking groups totaled ¥4.62 trillion as of the end of March. 大手銀行・金融7グループの赤字合計額は、3月末現在で4兆6,200億円に達した。

major client 大口顧客,(金融機関の)大口融資先
◆The two major securities companies cut brokerage fees further for major clients. 大手証券会社2社は、大口顧客に対して株式売買手数料をさらに引き下げた。

major commercial bank 大手都市銀行,大手都銀,大手銀行,大手各行
◆The major commercial banks deserve praise for working toward making their asset appraisal more stringent. 大手各行が資産査定の厳格化に動き出したことは、評価できる。◆This is the first time for major commercial banks to form a comprehensive tie-up with a foreign capital financial group. 大手都銀が外資系金融グループと包括提携するのは、今回が初めてだ。

major computer system failure 大規模なコンピュータ・システム障害,大規模なシステム障害
◆The financial group's inadequate preparations for the reorganization resulted in a major computer system failure. 同フィナンシャル・グループの再編の準備不足から、大規模なシステム障害が起こった。

major contract 大口契約
◆Despite stiff price competition, expansion abroad and into new customer segments, improved global economic conditions and major contract wins raised sales in 2010. 厳しい価格競争にさらされながらも、国外事業の拡大や新規顧客への食いこみ、世界景気の好転と大口契約の獲得などで、2010年度の売上高は増加しました。

major corporate borrower 大口融資先
◆FSA audits of the banks' accounts urged them to reclassify 149 of their major corporate borrowers more strictly in terms of their creditworthiness in a bid to accelerate the disposal of bad loans. 金融庁による銀行の財務書類監査で、不良債権処理を加速するため、銀行は大口融資先149社の信用力による債務者区分の見直しを強化するよう強く求められた。◆The bank's likelihood of collecting loans extended to its major corporate borrowers has worsened. 同行の大口融資先[融資先企業]に対する債権の回収見通しが、悪化した。

major currency 主要通貨
◆As it stands, the yen is the sole major currency whose value has not stopped increasing. 現状では、円は上昇が止まらない唯一の主要通貨だ。◆Major currencies are rising against the dollar on account of the Fed's monetary easing policy. 米連邦準備制度理事会(FRB)の金融緩和策で、主要通貨はドルに対して上昇している[ドル安・主要通貨高が進んでいる]。◆Only the yen is rising against the dollar and other major currencies. ドルなどの主要通貨に対して、円が独歩高となっている。◆Prime Minister Kan and Bank of Japan Gov. Shirakawa did not discuss a currency intervention to stem the yen's rise against other major currencies. 菅首相と白川日銀総裁は、主要通貨に対する円相場の上昇を阻止するための為替介入については協議しなかった。◆South Korea has seen a plunge of the won against major currencies amid the worldwide financial meltdown. 世界的な金融危機に伴って、韓国では主要通貨に対してウォン相場が下落している[ウォン安となっている]。◆The U.S. dollar as the world's only reserve currency may become merely one of three major currencies, along with the euro and the renminbi. 世界で唯一の準備通貨としての米ドルは、ユーロ、人民元とともに、単なる3大通貨の一つになる可能性がある。◆The U.S. dollar tumbled for the second straight day against major currencies. 米ドルが、主要通貨に対して2日連続下落した。◆The yen may once again rise against the dollar and other major currencies. 今後、ドルなどの主要通貨に対して再び円高が進む可能性がある。◆The yen still remains at a high level against other major currencies. 円は、他の主要通貨に対してまだ高い水準で推移している。

major economic power 先進国
◆To shore up their economies, major economic powers seem to be relying more on their monetary policies. 景気テコ入れに、先進国は金融政策頼みの様相が強まっている。

major economies 主要国,主要国・地域
◆Europe promised the Group of 20 major economies to take concerted action to contain the financial crisis. 欧州は、結束して金融危機を封じ込めることを主要20か国・地域(G20)に公約した。

major factor 大きな要因,主要要因
◆The instability of life insurance firms and the lowered earning power of banks with massive bad loans have become the two major factors rocking the financial system. 生保各社の経営基盤の不安定と、巨額の不良債権に苦しむ銀行の収益力低下が、金融システムを揺るがしている二大要因になっている。

major financial group 大手金融グループ[金融機関]
◆Major financial groups do not have regular business contacts with small and medium-sized auto parts makers. 大手金融機関は、中小の自動車部品メーカーと通常の取引関係がない。◆Neither of Mitsui Trust Holdings, Inc. and another major financial group has yet released reports on its interim settlement of accounts. 三井トラスト・ホールディングスなど2大金融グループは、まだ中間決算報告を発表していない。◆The Development Bank of Japan will ask major financial groups to invest in the fund established to assist auto parts makers hit by the March 11 earthquake and tsunami. 日本政策投資銀行が、東日本大震災で被災した自動車部品メーカーを支援するために設立するファンドへの出資を、大手金融グループに呼びかけることになった。

major financial institution 大手金融機関
◆Global major financial institutions have been forced to hold extra capital since the financial meltdown following the 2008 bankruptcy of Lehman Brothers Holdings Inc. 米国の投資銀行リーマン・ブラザーズが2008年に経営破たんして生じた金融危機以来、世界の主要金融機関は、資本[自己資本]の上積み[積み増し]を迫られている。◆The number of surplus workers approached a peak of 3.59 million in the January-March quarter of 1999, following a spate of failures at major financial institutions. 過剰雇用者数は、大手金融機関の破たんが相次いだ後の1999年1-3月期に、359万人のピークに達した。◆The U.S. FBI is looking at potential fraud by four major financial institutions. 米連邦捜査局は、大手金融機関4社(政府系住宅金融ファニー・メイ、フレディ・マックの2社のほか、米保険最大手のAIGとリーマン・ブラザーズ)による詐欺の可能性を検討している。

major foreign currency 主要外貨,主要外国通貨
◆In foreign currency deposits, depositors can earn profits by exchanging their foreign currency deposits into yen when the yen's value against major foreign currencies falls. 外貨

預金では、主要外貨に対して円相場が下落した時点で預金者が外貨預金を円に戻せば、利益を上げる[儲ける]ことができる。◆The interest rates of the Australian dollar-denominated deposit service are relatively high among major foreign currencies. 主要外貨のうち、豪ドル建て預金サービスの金利は比較的高い。

major insurance company 大手保険会社, 損保保険大手
◆Standard & Poor's revised upward the outlook on its ratings on six major Japanese insurance companies against the backdrop of their improved financial profiles. スタンダード＆プアーズは、日本の大手保険会社6社の財務力見通し改善を背景に、6社の格付け見通しを上方修正した。◆The Financial Services Agency ordered Sompo Japan Insurance Inc. to suspend part of its operations as punishment for the major insurance company's illegal business practices. 金融庁は、損保大手の損害保険ジャパンに業務で法令違反があったとして、同社に一部業務停止命令を出した。

major insurer 大手保険会社
◆Two major insurers from different financial groups plan to merge in a bid to overcome serious management crises. 深刻な経営危機を乗り切るため、系列の異なる金融グループの大手保険会社2社が合併を計画している。

major life insurer 大手生命保険会社, 大手生保, 生保大手, 主要生命保険会社
◆Premium revenues slipped at seven of the nine major life insurers. 保険料収入は、主要生命保険9社のうち7社が減少した。

major losses 大幅な下げ
◆Stock exchanges in both Japan and the United States successively posted major losses. 日米の株式市場は連日、大幅な下げを記録した。

major moneylender 金融大手
◆Major moneylender SFCG earned an unsavory reputation for its strong-arm loan collection methods. 金融業者大手のSFCG（旧商工ファンド）の評判は、債権の取立てが強引で芳しくなかった。◆Major moneylender SFCG is undergoing bankruptcy procedures. 金融大手のSFCGは現在、破産手続き中だ。

major reserve currency 主要準備通貨
◆The dollar's role as the major reserve currency is important to global trade. 主要準備通貨としてのドルの役割は、世界の貿易には重要である。

major securities company [firm] 大手証券会社, 大手証券
◆The two major securities companies cut brokerage fees further for major clients. 大手証券会社2社は、大口顧客に対して株式売買手数料をさらに引き下げた。

major securities house 大手証券会社, 大手証券
（=major securities company）
◆If the merger takes place, it will create a full-scale financial conglomerate with a major bank, a major securities house and credit card company under its umbrella. 統合すれば、傘下に大手銀行と大手証券、クレジット・カード会社などを持つ本格的な金融コングロマリット（金融複合企業体）が誕生する。◆The major securities house attributed the poor earnings to sharp drops in brokerage fees and trading profits amid the extended slump in the domestic stock market. この大手証券会社は、減益の要因として、国内株式市場の長期低迷による株売買手数料と売買益の大幅減を挙げた。

major shareholder 大株主, 大口株主, 主要株主
（=large shareholder, major stockholder）
◆According to a listing requirement, major shareholders are prohibited from owning more than an 80 percent stake in a company. 上場基準によると、大株主は80％を超える会社株式の所有は禁じられている。◆The management buyout might have been rejected at the firm's shareholders meeting if its major shareholders had opposed it. 同社の経営陣による自社買収（MBO）は、株主総会で主要株主[大株主]が反対したら否決されていたかもしれない。

major shareholders' stakes 大株主の持ち株比率
◆The firm intentionally issued false financial statements about the ratio of major shareholders' stakes. 同社は、大株主の持ち株比率について意図的に虚偽記載した有価証券報告書（財務書類）を公表した。

major source of profit 主な収益源
◆If the securities firms rush to cut these commissions, they may not be able to continue to rely on income from commissions as a major source of profit. これらの証券会社が手数料の値引き競争に走れば、主な収益源として株式の売買委託手数料による収入に今後とも頼ることは難しくなる。

major stakeholder 大株主
◆Sapporo will purchase Pokka shares from the company's two major stakeholders. サッポロは、ポッカの2大株主からポッカの株式を買い取る予定だ。

major stimulus package 大規模な景気刺激策, 大規模な景気対策, 大規模な財政出動
◆Amid the depleted state coffers, it is difficult to implement a major stimulus package to rectify the rise in the yen's value. 財政悪化が進む中[国の財源が枯渇する中]、円高是正のため大規模な財政出動を行うのは難しい。

major stock market 主要証券市場
◆The TSE and the OSE should implement strategies so they will remain one of the major stock markets in Asia. 東証と大証は、アジアの主要証券市場として生き残るための戦略を進めるべきだ。

major stockholder 大株主
（=large stockholder, major shareholder）
◆The firm's practice of issuing false financial statements about the holdings of major stockholders dates back to 1980 or earlier. 大株主の保有株式に関して虚偽記載の有価証券報告書を発行する同社の慣行は、1980年以前にさかのぼる。

majority （名）過半数, 大多数, 多数, 多数派, 多数党, 大半, 大部分, 得票差, 成年, 成人 （⇒minority）
a majority of creditors 大半の債権者
absolute [overall] majority 絶対多数, 絶対安定多数
by a large majority 大差で
by a small majority 僅かの差で, 僅差（きんさ）で
by majority rule 多数決で
decision by majority 多数決
（=majority decision）
have majority holding 過半数の株式を保有する
majority control 過半数支配
majority holding [shareholding] 株式の過半数所有
majority interest 過半数持ち分, 多数株主持ち分
（=consolidated equity: 連結持ち分、親会社持ち分）
majority owned company 過半数所有会社, 過半数子会社 （=majority owned subsidiary: 社外議決権株式の50％超を他の会社に所有されている会社・子会社）
majority owner 過半数株主
majority ownership 過半数所有
majority share 過半数の株式 （=majority stake）
majority shareholder [stockholder] 過半数株主, 支配株主
majority voting 多数決による票決
overwhelming majority 圧倒的多数
vote down by a majority vote 多数決で否決する
with majority support from ～の賛成多数で
◆The bank tried to dominate the management of its clients by sending a majority of people to their board of directors. 同行は、融資先の取締役会に過半数の取締役を送り込んで、融

資先の経営の支配を図った。◆The investment fund has a de facto majority of shareholder voting rights. この投資ファンドが、実質的に株主議決権の過半数を握っている。◆The U.S. House of Representatives passed the financial bailout bill by a large majority. 米下院は、金融安定化法案（金融救済法案）を大差で可決した。

majority stake　過半数株式　（=majority share）
◆China's biggest computer maker, Lenovo Group, has taken a majority stake in International Business Machines Corp.'s personal computer business. 中国最大のパソコン・メーカーの「聯想（レノボ）集団」が、IBMのパソコン事業の過半数株式を取得した。◆Panasonic Corp. will begin talks to buy a majority stake in Sanyo Electric Co. パナソニック（旧松下電器産業）が、三洋電機の過半数株式を取得する交渉を開始する。

make　（動）行う、する、実行する、生む、～させる
　control of making credits　与信管理
　make a lump sum payment　一括払いをする、一括返済をする
　make a market　値付けを行う、値付けをする、値付け業務を行う
　make a market in the bonds　債券の値付けを行う
　make a new high　新高値を付ける
　make a turn　利ざやを稼ぐ
　make credit decisions　融資判断を下す
　make money to operate　事業資金を稼ぐ
　make mortgage payments　住宅ローンを返済する
　operation of making credits　与信業務

make a loan　融資を実行する、貸出を行う、貸し付ける
　date of making a loan　融資実行日
　make long-term loans　長期貸付け［融資、貸出］を行う
　make subordinated loans　劣後ローンを貸し付ける

make a profit　利益を出す、利益を生む、利益を上げる、利益を得る
　make a sound profit　健全な利益を生む
　make profit on short selling　空売りで稼ぐ、空売りで利益を得る
　steadily making profits　着実に利益を上げる
◆Japanese banks must increase their core capital ratios by reviewing management strategies and steadily making profits. 邦銀は、経営戦略を見直し、着実に利益を上げて、自己資本を増強する必要がある。

make for　～となる、～を示す、～を生み出す、～をもたらす、～の代用をする、～を助長する、～を助成する、～に寄与する、～の役に立つ、～に便利である、～に向かう［接近する］、～に近づく、～を襲う、（意見などを）固める、強める
◆The employment situation made for particularly grim reading. 雇用状況［雇用情勢］は、とくに恐ろしい数値を示した。

make good　（約束などを）果たす、遂行する、履行する、（損害を）弁償する、償う、（費用などを）支払う、返金する、（立場などを）保持する、確保する、強化する、立証する、実証する、修理する、修復する
　make good in the business　事業で成功する
　make good on　～を果たす、～を遂行［履行］する
　make good part of one's debt　～の負債の一部を支払う
◆The government will make good on the commitments contained in the emergency employment package. 政府は、緊急雇用対策に盛り込んだ公約を果たす方針だ。

make up　構成する、占める、作り上げる、でっちあげる、かさ上げする、埋め合わせる、負担する、調達する
　make up about 30 percent of total assets　総資産の約30％を占める
　make up the lion's share　最大の比率を占める
　make up the remaining amount through bilateral loans　相対取引で残りを調達する
◆The government is poised to issue bridging bonds to make up the expected shortfall in state funding for the basic pension fund. 政府は、つなぎ国債を発行して、予想される基礎年金基金の国庫負担の不足分を賄（まかな）う［補う］方針だ。◆The IRCJ hopes to split off the real estate business to prevent the company from making up shortfalls in food supermarket earnings with income from retail space rentals. 産業再生機構が不動産事業を分離するのは、同社が食品スーパーの収益の不足分を小売店舗スペースの賃貸料でかさ上げするのを避けるのが狙いだ。

make up for　～を補填する、～の穴埋めをする、～を埋め合わせる、帳消しにする、取り戻す、挽回する
　make up for latent stock price losses　株式含み損を補填する
　make up for losses　損失の穴埋めをする
　make up for the five percent decline during the previous quarter　前四半期の5％減少を取り戻す
◆Some banks have been forced to liquidate their legal reserves due to the need to dispose of huge amounts of bad loans and make up for latent stock price losses. 巨額の不良債権の処理と株式含み損の補填に迫られ、一部の銀行は法定準備金の取崩しに追い込まれている。◆The firm may struggle to make up for its delay in developing eco cars while its reconstruction continues. 同社の場合、再建を進めながらエコカー開発の遅れを挽回するのは大変だろう。◆The ¥44 trillion shortfall in spending in the fiscal 2010 budget must be made up for by issuing government bonds. 2010年度予算の歳出のうち44兆円の不足分は、国債発行で補填しなければならない。◆The special account borrows from the private sector and other sources to make up for local government's budget shortfalls. 特別会計は、民間などの財源からの借入れで地方の財源不足［財政赤字］の穴埋めをしている。◆To make up for losses and for other purposes, seven life insurers used a total of ¥529.2 billion in reserves, which are set aside in preparation for interest rate fluctuations and natural disasters. 損失の穴埋めなどのため、金利変動や自然災害に備えて積み立てている準備金を、生保7社が5,292億円も取り崩した。

maker　（名）製造業者、製造会社、製作者、作る人、作る機械［器具］、メーカー
　covenant maker　協約締結者
　decision maker　政策決定者、意思決定者、政策担当者
　maker's credit　延べ払い輸入
　maker's credit company　メーカー系クレジット会社
　market maker　市場開拓者、値付け業者、マーケット・メーカー（株や債券などの流通市場で、価格形成を行う証券業者のこと）
　monetary policy makers　金融政策当局、金融当局
　policy maker　政策立案者、政策担当者、政府高官
　price maker　価格決定者、価格形成者、プライス・メーカー

makeup　（名）組織、構造、構成、組立て、陣容、新聞の割付け、化粧、化粧品
　makeup wages　補充賃金、補足賃金
　　（=makeup pay）
　the makeup of government bond issuance　国債発行の構成
◆The makeup of government bond issuance for this fiscal year is vulnerable to rises in long-term interest rates. 今年度の国債発行の構成は、長期金利上昇の影響を受けやすい。

making　（名）製造、制作、形成、決定、成功、発展、成長の原因・要因、メーキング
　decision making　意思決定、政策決定
　making credit　信用供与
　Making Home Affordable Plan　（米国の）住宅取得支援

策, MHA
making the loan　融資の実行, 貸付けの実行
market making　値付け業務, マーケット・メーキング
money making　金儲(もう)け, 利益を上げること
nonprofit making corporation　非営利法人
policy making　政策決定, 政策立案
　　(=policymaking)
profit making　利潤追求, 利潤創出, 利益獲得, 営利
rate making　料金算定, 料金決定, 利率決定

malfunction　(名)機能障害, 機能不全, 故障, 誤作動, 不調
　a computer malfunction　コンピュータのシステム障害
　the malfunction of a new computer system　新コンピュータ・システムの故障[障害]
　◆The disabled money transfer function is caused by the malfunction of a new system that links the individual computer systems of the three banks. 口座振替機能の障害の原因は、3行の個々のコンピュータ・システムをつなぐ新システムの故障だ。◆These troubles caused by the computer malfunction ranged from dysfunctional ATMs to delayed money transfers, and to deductions from accounts that were recorded in account books although no money was actually transferred. 今回のコンピュータの障害・誤作動で生じたトラブルとしては、ATM(現金自動預け払い機)障害や口座振替の遅れ、さらには現金が実際には未払い(払戻しされていない)なのに、通帳に口座からの引落しが記載されたケースなどがあった。◆Transactions on all of the 2,520 issues traded at the TSE were stalled from 9 a.m. due to a computer malfunction. 東証で取引されている2,520全銘柄の取引が、コンピュータのシステム障害で午前9時から停止した。

malicious　(形)悪質な, 悪意の, 悪意のある, 意地の悪い, 犯意のもとに行われた
　malicious act　悪質な行為
　malicious prank　悪質ないたずら
　◆The financial watchdog took an additional action of criminal complaint other than administrative punishment as the bank's operations were so malicious. 同行の業務運営の仕方があまりにも悪質なので、金融監視機関の金融庁は、行政処分のほかに刑事告発の追加措置を取った。

malpractice　(名)不正, 不正[違法, 不法]行為, 背任行為, 失態, 汚職, 業務過誤, 医療過誤, 医療ミス, 不当処置 (=malfeasance)
　malpractice insurance　業務過誤保険, 専門職過失責任保険
　professional malpractice　職業専門家の業務懈怠(けたい)
　the malpractice of corporate accounting　企業会計の不正
　◆Concerned that the malpractice of corporate accounting may be widespread, the U.S. Congress passed a corporate governance reform bill in July 2002, immediately after WorldCom's bankruptcy was exposed. 企業会計の不正が広がっているとの懸念を強めていた米議会は、米通信大手ワールドコムの破綻が明らかになった直後の2002年7月に、企業統治改革法案を成立させた。

malware　(名)マルウェア(コンピュータ・ウイルス、ワーム、スパイウェアなど不正・有害な動作を行うために作成された[悪意のある]ソフトウェアや悪質なコードの総称)
　◆Illegal transfers of deposits via foreign malware have been jumping. 海外のマルウェア(コンピュータ・ウイルスの一種)による預金の不正送金が急増している。◆Regional bank accounts were hit hardest by illegal transfers via foreign malware. 海外のマルウエア(コンピュータ・ウイルスの一種)による不正送金の被害は、地方銀行の口座が最多だった。

mammonism　(名)拝金主義

manage　(動)管理する, 経営する, 統括する, 統率する, 監督する, 幹事を務める, 運用する, 運営する, 運用管理する, うまく処理する, 対処する, 取り扱う, 使いこなす, 困難などを乗り切る, 切り抜ける
　actively manage the portfolio　ポートフォリオを積極運用[アクティブ運用]する
　manage a firm　企業を経営する
　manage as a separate unit　別管理する
　manage bond portfolio　債券ポートフォリオを運用する
　manage expenses　支出を管理する
　manage individual retirement funds　個人の退職年金を運用管理する
　manage investment portfolios　資産ポートフォリオを運用する
　manage liquidity　流動性を抑える
　manage personal trust funds　個人信託を運用管理する
　manage the business　事業を統括する
　manage the cyclical troughs　景気サイクルの底を乗り切る
　manage the portfolio　ポートフォリオを運営する
　manage the risk exposure　リスクを管理する
　manage the syndication　シンジケート団[シ団]を取り仕切る
　◆Investors are buying into the potential of a company, not to manage it. 投資家は、企業の経営権ではなく、企業の将来性を買っている。◆The bank announced a plan to introduce revival accounts to manage its ¥2.3 trillion nonperforming loans separately from the healthier loans. 同行は、2兆3,000億円の不良債権を正常債権とは別個に管理する「再生勘定」を導入する方針を発表した。

manage funds　資金を管理する, 資金を運用する
　◆The seven major banking groups chalked up sizable profits in their core business chiefly because of a reduction in the cost of procuring funds thanks to record low interest rates, and increased profits in managing funds, including government bonds. 大手銀行7グループは、主に超低金利[過去最低の金利]で資金調達コストが軽減したほか、国債などの資金運用益が拡大したため、本業でかなりの利益をあげた。

managed　(形)管理される, 運営される, 管理～, ～の管理[運営, 統括]
　actively managed account　積極運用している口座
　managed assets　管理資産
　managed care　(医療機関による)総合的健康管理, マネージド・ケア
　managed currency [money]　管理通貨, 統制貨幣
　managed economy　管理経済, 経済運営
　managed float　管理フロート制(通貨当局が管理する変動為替相場制度(floating exchange rate system)で、必要に応じて通貨当局が為替市場に介入して相場をコントロールすることをいう)
　managed floating exchange　管理変動為替
　managed fund　マネージド・ファンド(主に生命保険会社が管理運用する投資信託で、個人投資家による低リスク投資を提供する)
　privately managed pension fund scheme　民間運営の年金基金

managed futures　マネージド・フューチャーズ(ヘッジ・ファンドの運用手法の一つで、株式や債券・通貨のほか、原油や金属・農産物などあらゆる上場先物に投資する。ファンドの大半は、経済分析や企業価値ではなく、「市場の値動き」に応じて運用配分を決める。コンピュータに投資モデルを組み込み、相場が上がりはじめた市場には自動的に買い注文、下げ相場には空売り注文をそれぞれ出す)

management （名）経営, 管理, 運用, 運営, 取扱い, 業務執行, 経営管理, 経営陣, 経営側, 経営者側, マネジメント（⇒efficiency, hostile investment fund, productivity, profit and loss statement）
  asset liability management　資産負債総合管理, 資産負債管理, バランス・シート管理, ALM
  asset management　資産管理, 資産運用, 投資顧問（⇒strategy）
  balance sheet management　財務管理, バランス・シート管理
  business management　企業管理, 企業経営, 経営管理
  cash management　現金預金管理, 現金管理, 資金管理, キャッシュ・マネジメント
  corporate management　企業経営
  cost management　原価管理, コスト管理, コスト・マネジメント
  credit management　与信管理, 信用管理
  crisis management　危機管理
  current asset management　流動資産管理
  economic management　経済運営, 経済政策
  effective management　効率経営, 効率的な経営, 効果的な経営
  financial management　財務管理, 財テク
  financial risk management　金融リスク管理, 金融リスク・マネジメント
  fund management　資金管理, 資金運用, 投資管理, 投資顧問
  information management　情報管理
  investment management　投資管理, 投資運用, 投資顧問
  lax fiscal [financial] management　放漫な財政運営
  liability management　負債管理
  management fees　経営報酬, 運用報酬, 幹事手数料, 管理手数料
  management group　幹事引受団, 幹事団, 公募会社
  management initiative　経営の主導権
  management of funds　資金繰り
  money market management　金融調節
  portfolio management　資金運用, 最適資産管理, 金融資産管理, ポートフォリオ管理, ポートフォリオ・マネジメント
  rationalization of management　経営合理化
  relationship management　取引先総合管理, RM
  responsibility of management　経営責任
  risk management　危険管理, 危機管理, リスク管理, リスク・マネジメント
  senior management　上級経営陣
  slipshod management　ずさんな経営
  systems management　システム管理
  wealth management business　資産運用業務
  ◆A company's management was reshuffled following a shareholder's proposal. 株主提案を受けて, 企業の経営陣が刷新された。◆As part of its efforts to diversify management, the company has decided to begin selling goods and services, using mobile phones and computers. 経営多角化策の一環として, 同社は携帯電話やパソコンを使った商品やサービスの販売開始を決めた。◆Citigroup's retail brokerage, Smith Barney, was once the crown jewel in its wealth management business. シティグループの個人向け証券会社「スミスバーニー」は, 以前はシティグループの資産運用業務の最優良資産だった。◆Economic stimulus measures should be prioritized in the government's policy management. 政府の政策運営では, 景気刺激策[景気対策]を優先するべきだ。◆Every member of the nation will now be forced to face the risks involved in the management of their own assets. これからは, 国民一人ひとりが資産運用リスクに正面から向き合わざるを得なくなる。◆Greek financial crisis was caused by the country's lax fiscal management. ギリシャの財政危機は, 同国の放漫財政[放漫な財政運営]によって生じた。◆If the creditor banks forgive the debts though TEPCO is not carrying excess liabilities, senior managements of the lenders may be sued in a shareholders' lawsuit over mismanagement. 東電が債務超過ではないのに債権保有銀行が債権を放棄すると, ずさんな経営で, 金融機関の上級経営陣は株主代表訴訟で訴えられる可能性がある。◆Life insurers must reform their managements to extricate themselves from their plight. 経営危機から脱出するには, 生保各社は経営を改革しなければならない。◆Meiji Yasuda decided to lower the yield rate of its flagship insurance product because the insurer placed priority on long-term stable management over an increase in the number of policyholders. 明治安田生保は, 契約者の数を増やすより長期的な経営の安定を優先したため, 主力保険商品の予定利率[利回り]を引き下げることにした。◆The bank tried to dominate the management of its clients by sending a majority of people to their board of directors. 同行は, 融資先の取締役会に過半数の取締役を送り込んで, 融資先の経営の支配を図った。◆The International Monetary Fund is urged to monitor Italy's financial management to provide support to Italy. イタリアを支援するため, 国際通貨基金（IMF）はイタリアの財政運営の監視を求められている。◆The management of the new companies will be under pressure to produce profits. これらの新会社の経営陣は, 収益確保の手腕を問われることになる。◆The slipshod management of failed Incubator Bank of Japan widely diverged from its business philosophy. 破たんした日本振興銀行のずさんな経営は, 同行の経営理念とはかけ離れていた。◆The would-be acquirer has no intention of taking part in the management of a company it aims to take over. 買収側[買収希望者]に, 買収対象企業の経営に参加する意思はない。◆This loss came from deducting recourse loans made to our senior management. この損失は, 当社の上級経営陣に対して行った遡求請求権付き貸付け金を控除したことで生じました。◆Under the government guidelines, if earnings come in more than 30 percent below targets set in restructuring plans at any major bank that received public funds to recapitalize in 1988 and 1999, the banks management will have to resign. 政府のガイドラインによると, 資本再編のために1988年と1999年に公的資金の注入を受けた大手銀行の収益が, 再建計画（経営健全化計画）で設定した収益目標を30%以上下回った場合, 銀行の経営陣は辞任しなければならない。◆Under the trustee's management, the debtor bank's business will be operated and the refunding of deposits will be temporarily suspended. 金融整理管財人の管理下で, 破たん銀行の業務は運営され, 預金の払戻しは一時停止される。

management and labor　労使
  ◆Management and labor should thoroughly discuss future corporate prospects and the shape of corporate workforces. 企業の将来展望や雇用のあり方について, 労使は徹底的に協議しなければならない。

management buyout [buy-out]　マネジメント・バイアウト, 経営者による自社買収, 経営陣による企業買収, 経営者による営業権取得, MBO（⇒corporate buyout, hostile investment fund, management reform, MBO）
  ◆The firm's defense against management buyout is half-baked. 同社の経営陣による企業買収（MBO）防衛策は, 中途半端だ。◆The management buyout might have been rejected at the firm's shareholders meeting if its major shareholders had opposed it. 同社の経営陣による自社買収（MBO）は, 株主総会で主要株主[大株主]が反対したら否決されていたかもしれない。◆The management buyout was approved at the firm's shareholders meeting. 同社の株主総会で, 経営陣による企業

買収(MBO)が承認された。

management control over the company 経営陣の会社の経営支配権
◆The purpose of issuing share warrants is to maintain the current management's control over the company. 株式予約権の発行は、現経営陣の会社の経営支配権を維持することを目的としている。

management crisis 経営危機
◆The firm seemed to have overcome a management crisis. 同社は、経営危機をしのいだかに見えた。◆Two major insurers from different financial groups plan to merge in a bid to overcome serious management crises. 深刻な経営危機を乗り切るため、系列の異なる金融グループの大手保険会社2社が合併を計画している。

management decision 経営判断
◆The bank's series of problems were caused by a complicated mixture of various factors, such as technical problems, human errors and incorrect management decisions. 同行の一連のトラブルは、技術的な問題、人的ミス、経営判断の誤りなど、さまざまな要素が複雑に絡み合って生じたものだ。

management efficiency 経営効率, 経営の効率性
◆The Financial Services Agency will check the credibility of the banks' debtor companies, including their management efficiency and the accuracy of their collateral assessment. 金融庁は、銀行の融資先の経営効率や担保評価などを含めて、銀行の融資先の信用力を洗い直す。◆To enhance management efficiency and the decision-making process, Mizuho Financial Group will integrate its Mizuho Bank and Mizuho Corporate Bank in 2013. 経営の効率化と意思決定の迅速化を図るため、みずほフィナンシャルグループは、傘下のみずほ銀行とみずほコーポレート銀行を2013年に合併させる。◆We have long placed emphasis on management efficiency. 当社は、以前から経営の効率性を重視しています。

management environment 経営環境
◆The management environment at the bank is severe. 同行の経営環境は、厳しい。

management integration 経営統合
◆Sumitomo Mitsui Financial Group Inc. and Daiwa Securities Group Inc. are eyeing a management integration and full merger in the future. 三井住友フィナンシャルグループと大和証券グループは、両グループの将来の経営統合と完全統合を計画している。

management lineup 経営陣
◆A former Bank of Japan official Takeshi Kimura has resigned from Incubator Bank of Japan's management lineup. 日銀出身の木村剛氏は、日本振興銀行の経営陣から退いた。

management model 経営モデル
◆The bank introduced a management model of raising profits by attracting deposits with high interest rates and extending loans to promising small and medium-sized companies. 同行は、高金利で預金を集め、成長性の高い中小企業に融資して収益を確保する経営モデルを採用した。

management plan 経営計画
◆The group's three-year management plan slates ¥2.2 trillion of capital investment for fiscal 2004 on a consolidated basis. 同グループの3カ年経営計画では、2004年度は連結ベースで2兆2,000億円の設備投資を予定している。

management policy 経営方針, 経営政策, 経営路線, 経営姿勢 (=managerial policy)
◆At the bank, a string of executives resigned one after another due to differences over management policy. 同行では、経営路線の違いで役員らの辞任が相次いだ。

management practices 経営手法, 経営スタイル, 経営実務, 経営実態, 管理慣行
◆Former chairman of the bank spearheaded a culture that hid unhealthy management practices. 同行の前会長は、陣頭指揮して不健全な経営実態を隠す企業体質を作り上げた。

management principles 経営理念
◆The bank's operations were actually different considerably from the management principles it had put forward. 同行の業務は実際、同行が掲げた経営理念とかけ離れていた。

management reform 経営改革
◆The company targeted a management buyout to carry out drastic management reform without being overly concerned with short-term profits or fluctuations in its share price. 短期収益や株価変動にとらわれないで抜本的な経営改革を行うため、同社は経営陣による企業買収(MBO)を目指した。

management rehabilitation 経営再建
◆The company is undergoing management rehabilitation. 同社は現在、経営再建に取り組んでいる。

management resources 経営資源
(=managerial resources)
◆The white paper called for measures to deal with the hollowing out of the Japanese industry by enhancing research and development capabilities, utilizing information technology and pursuing effective corporate management through selection and concentration of management resources. 白書は、研究開発能力の向上やIT(情報技術)の活用、経営資源の選択と集中による効率的な企業経営などを進めることで、日本の産業空洞化に対処する措置を取るよう求めた。

management right 経営権
◆Investment funds do not hesitate to dissolve a company and strip its assets after acquiring the management rights of the company. 投資ファンドは、会社の経営権を取得した後、会社を解散してその資産を売り払うこともいとわない。

management strategy 経営戦略
◆Japanese banks must increase their core capital ratios by reviewing management strategies and steadily making profits. 邦銀は、経営戦略を見直し、着実に利益を上げて、自己資本を増強する必要がある。◆World Co. has delisted itself from the Tokyo Stock Exchange and Osaka Securities Exchange to proceed with its long-term management strategy. アパレル大手のワールドは、長期的な経営戦略を進めるため、自ら東証と大証からの上場を廃止した。

management style 経営手法, 経営スタイル
(=style of management)
◆Another characteristic of the U.S. management style is that businesses give priority to maximizing shareholders' value. 米国式経営スタイルのもうひとつの特色は、企業が株主の資産価値の極大化を第一に考えることだ。◆The move will make departure from Matsushita's time-honored management style, under which group companies have been given considerable discretionary powers. この動きは、グループ企業にかなりの自由裁量権を与えてきた松下電器の伝統的な経営手法からの脱却を目指すものだ。

management system 経営体制, 経営システム, 管理システム, 管理方式, マネジメント・システム
◆As investment for digitalization is costly, NBS needs to establish a more profitable management system, including joint investment in digital-related facilities and content with the Fuji TV group. デジタル化の投資負担は軽くないので、ニッポン放送は、フジテレビ・グループとのデジタル関連施設への共同投資やコンテンツ(情報内容)の共有など、収益力の高い経営システムを確立する必要がある。

manager (名)経営者, 管理者, 幹部, 幹部社員, 部長, 理事, 銀行の支店長, 幹事(引受会社), 投資顧問, 支配人, 責任者, 管財人, マネージャー
(⇒corporate manager, lead manager)
asset manager 投資顧問業, アセット・マネージャー
bank manager 銀行支店長
bond manager 債券運用者, 債券管理者, 債券運用担当者, 債券管理担当者, ボンド・マネージャー
Branch Manager Meeting 日銀支店長会議

co-lead manager　共同主幹事
　(=joint lead-manager)
customer relations manager　顧客関係担当者
department manager　部門責任者
executive manager　執行役員
fund manager　資金運用者, 資金管理者, 資金運用担当者, 資金管理担当者, 金融資産運用者, ファンド・マネージャー
investment manager　投資顧問, 投資運用会社, 運用会社, 運用機関, 投資マネージャー
portfolio manager　資産管理者, 資産運用者, ポートフォリオ運用者, ポートフォリオ・マネージャー
sole manager　単独主幹事
syndicate manager　シンジケート団幹事, シ団幹事
◆Industry insiders said the refusal to pay insurance benefits over a long period was partly because of former Meiji managers' unreasonable policies. 業界関係者によると、長期間にわたる保険金不払いの一因は、旧明治生命保険の経営者の無理な経営方針だ。◆The firm has reduced its managers by 3,000. 同社は、管理職を3,000人削減しました。◆Three top managers of UFJ Holdings resigned. UFJホールディングスの首脳3人が、辞任した。◆While stock prices shifted upward, the sentiments of corporate managers have shown signs of improvement lately. 株価が上昇に転じる一方、最近は企業経営者の景況感も改善の兆しを見せている。

mandate　(名)権限, 権能, 要求, 命令, 指令, 委託, 委任, 委任契約, 負託, 選挙民の信任, 手形や小切手の支払い委託, 無償のサービス契約, 社債発行者からの主幹事に対する引受業務の依頼[委託、委任], 案件処理の依頼, マンデート
bank mandate　銀行委任書
competition for the mandate　マンデート獲得競争, マンデート争奪戦, 主幹事争い
conditional mandate　条件付きマンデート
financing mandate　資金調達のマンデート
have a mandate to　〜する権限がある
mandate bid　マンデート入札
mandate letter　委任状, マンデート・レター
　(=letter of mandate)
receive a mandate　資産運用の委託を受ける, 業務の委託を受ける, 業務を受託する
scoop up mandate　マンデートを取得する
seek a mandate for　〜への支持を求める
seek a mandate of the people　国民の信を問う
seek the people's mandate on the advisability of　〜の是非を国民に問う
win a mandate　業務を受託する, 資産の運用委託を受ける
win mandates to manage public pension assets　公的年金資産の運用業務を受託する
◆The firm received the mandate of an IPO deal in writing. 同社は、書面でIPO取引(新規株式発行の引受業務)のマンデートを受けた[書面でIPO取引を委任された]。◆Three groups are vying for the mandate. 3グループが、マンデート獲得競争を展開している[マンデートを争っている]。

mandatory　(形)義務的な, 強制の, 強制的な, 法定の, 必修の(obligatory), 命令的な, 命令の, 指令の, 委任の, 委任された, 委託の
mandatory bargaining issue　義務的団体交渉事項, 義務的交渉事項　(=mandatory subject)
mandatory component　強制の要素, 義務的遵守[順守]事項
mandatory control　法的規制
mandatory convertible bond [instrument, securities]　強制転換社債
mandatory copy　強制記載文言, 義務的のコピー
mandatory credit line　法定信用枠
　(=mandatory line of credit)
mandatory dividend　義務的配当
mandatory import quotas　強制的な輸入割当量
mandatory increase　当然増
mandatory injunction　命令的差止命令
mandatory insurance　強制保険
　(=compulsory insurance)
mandatory labeling　義務表示
mandatory national health insurance　強制的国民健康保険
mandatory quote period　値付け義務時間
mandatory real-name transaction system　法定の実名取引制度, 金融実名制
mandatory redemption　強制償還, 定時償還, 任意償還
　(=optional redemption)
mandatory requirements　強制要件
mandatory securities valuation reserves　法定の証券[有価証券]評価準備金
mandatory spending　義務的経費
mandatory universal coverage　強制的国民皆保険
◆It will take about five to seven years to shift to the IFRSs if they become mandatory. 国際財務報告基準(IFRSs)が強制適用となると、IFRSsに移行するのに5〜7年程度はかかる。◆The Financial Services Agency gave up its initial goal to make the introduction of the IFRS mandatory in around 2015. 金融庁は、2015年にもIFRS(国際財務報告規準)の導入を義務化するという当初の目標を断念した。

mandatory retirement　定年退職
　(=compulsory retirement)
mandatory retirement age　定年退職年齢, 定年
mandatory retirement system　定年制

manipulate　(動)操作する, 操縦する, 巧みに操(あやつ)る, 巧みに処理する, 改ざんする
　(⇒participant)
manipulate accounts [books]　帳簿操作する, 帳簿を改ざんする, 帳尻(ちょうじり)をごまかす
manipulate data　データを改ざんする
manipulate data files　データ・ファイルを処理する
manipulate statistics　統計の数値を改ざんする
manipulate stocks　株[株式]を操作する, 株価操作する
manipulate the market　市場価格を操作する
manipulate the market pricing (mechanism)　値付けを作為的に行う, (証券市場で)相場操縦する
manipulated quotations　人為相場
◆Participants in the market process information transmitted globally in real time, manipulate it in some cases and try to win profit by moving large amounts of money in this information war zone. 市場参加者は、リアルタイムでグローバルに伝達される情報を処理し、場合によってはそれを操作しながら、この情報戦争の戦場で巨額の資金を動かして利益を得ようとしている。◆The consultant manipulated the company's stock price by engaging in certain prohibited practices including wash sales. コンサルタントは、仮装売買(売り注文と買い注文を同時に出す方法)などの不正行為で株価を操作した。

manipulate stock prices　株価を操縦[操作]する, 株価操縦する
◆Penalties for manipulating stock prices by dragging them down through short selling and other methods are light in Japan. 空売りなどの手法で株価を(不当に)引き下げる株価操縦に対するペナルティーは、日本では軽い。

manipulate the stock market 株式相場を操縦する
◆A former vice president of the Osaka Securities Exchange and a number of his erstwhile subordinates allegedly conducted falsified stock option dealings and manipulated the stock market. 大阪証券取引所の元副理事長とかつての部下らが、株式オプション取引で偽装売買を行い、株式相場の操縦をしていたという。

manipulation （名）操作, 不正操作, 市場操作, 相場操縦, 株価操作, あやつり相場
  accounting manipulation　会計操作
    （＝accounting fraud）
  currency manipulation　為替操作
  document manipulation　書類操作
  earnings manipulation　利益の不正操作
  financial manipulation　経理操作
  income manipulation　利益操作
  manipulation of accounts　粉飾
    （＝equation manipulation）
  manipulation of securities　株の操作
    （＝manipulation of stocks）
  stock manipulation　株式操作, 株価操作
  stock market manipulation　株式市場の操作
  stock price manipulation　株価操縦, 株価操作
    （＝stock manipulation）
◆A U.S. congressional resolution seeks to impose surcharges on Chinese imports in reaction to Beijing's currency manipulations. 米議会の決議は、中国の為替操作への対応策として中国からの輸入に課徴金を掛けることを求めている。◆Market manipulation has been occurring in connection with new share issues. 増資に絡んで、株価操作が行われている。◆The accounting manipulations went unnoticed by the company's auditors and the board of directors. 会計操作は、同社の監査役や取締役会が見過ごしていた。

manipulator （名）操作者, 操作者, 相場あやつり師, 株価操縦者, 為替操作国　（⇒currency report）
  currency manipulator　為替操作国
  stock manipulator　株価操縦者
◆The U.S. Treasury Department said in its semiannual currency report that China is not a manipulator of its currency. 米財務省は、為替政策半期報告書で、中国は為替操作国ではないと述べた。

manual （名）料率書（保険会社、保証会社、料率算定機関などが発行）

manual rate （保険の）便覧料率, 標準的保険料率

manufacturer （名）製造業者, 製造者, 製作者, メーカー, 工場主
  domestic manufacturers　国内メーカー
  headline business conditions diffusion index of manufacturers　製造業の業況判断DI
  index reading for manufacturers' sentiment　製造業の景況感
  large manufacturers　大企業製造業, 大企業・製造業
  major manufacturer　大手メーカー
  nonmanufacturers　非製造業
  small- and medium-sized manufacturers　中小メーカー
◆Since the beginning of the 1990s, a growing number of domestic manufacturers have transferred their production bases abroad. 1990年代のはじめから、生産拠点を海外に移す国内メーカーが増えている。◆The BOJ's Tankan survey shows business sentiment among large manufacturers rebounded in September from the previous survey three months earlier. 9月の日銀短観は、大企業・製造業の景況感が6月の前回調査から改善したことを示している。◆The Tankan index for large manufacturers rose to plus 2 in September from the minus 9 registered in June. 9月短観の大企業・製造業の業況判断指数（DI）は、6月調査のマイナス9からプラス2に11ポイント改善した。

manufacturing sector 製造業, 製造業セクター
◆The Tankan index for 10 of the 16 industries in the manufacturing sector improved in September from three months earlier. 製造業16業種中10業種の日銀9月短観の業況判断指数（DI）は、（前回調査の）6月から改善した。

March 11 disaster 東日本大震災
◆Many self-employed people are now without income due to the March 11 disaster. 東日本大震災で、多くの自営業者は現在、収入が途絶えている。

March 11 earthquake and tsunami （2011年3月11日の）東日本大震災
◆Corporate bankruptcies stemming from the March 11 earthquake and tsunami totaled 330. 東日本大震災による企業倒産の総件数は、330件に達している。◆Corporate bond issues are recovering from the bond market turbulence following the March 11 earthquake and tsunami. 東日本大震災後の債券市場の混乱から、社債の発行額が回復している。◆In order to assist auto parts makers hit by the March 11 earthquake and tsunami, the Development Bank of Japan will raise ¥50 billion to establish a fund. 東日本大震災で被災した自動車部品メーカーを支援するため、日本政策投資銀行が、500億円を調達してファンドを設立する。◆Insurance payments for the March 11 earthquake and tsunami will drain the resources of insurance firms and the government's special account. 東日本大震災の保険金支払いで、保険会社と政府の特別会計の原資は大幅に目減りすることになる。◆Sendai Bank and Tsukuba, regional banks based in areas stricken by the March 11 earthquake and tsunami, will receive a combined ¥65 billion public aid. 仙台銀行と筑波銀行（東日本大震災被災地の地方銀行）が、計650億円の公的支援を受けることになった。◆The Bank of Japan stepped up its efforts to boost the flagging economy following the March 11 earthquake and tsunami by introducing a ¥500 billion cheap loan program. 日銀は、5,000億円の低利融資制度を導入して、東日本大震災で揺れる日本経済の刺激策を強化した。◆The casualty insurer delayed the start of its online insurance sales due to the March 11 earthquake and tsunami. 2011年3月11日の東日本大震災のため、同損保は保険のネット販売の開業を延期した。◆The recovery in business sentiment was largely due to the improvement in the parts supply chain disrupted after the March 11 earthquake and tsunami. 景況感が改善したのは、主に東日本大震災で打撃を受けたサプライ・チェーン（部品供給網）の復旧が進んだためだ。

March 11 Great East Japan Earthquake （2011年3月11日の）東日本大震災
◆Corporate debt issues are recovering as bond market turbulence in the aftermath of the March 11 Great East Japan Earthquake has subsided. 2011年3月11日の東日本大震災直後の債券市場の混乱が収束したため、社債の発行額が回復している。◆Factories, shops and farms were destroyed or severely damaged due to the March 11 Great East Japan Earthquake. 2011年3月11日の東日本大震災で、工場や店舗、農地が壊滅もしくは大打撃を受けた。

margin （動）～の証拠金を支払う, 証拠金を追加する, 追加証拠金を支払う, 追い証を入れる, 証拠金取引で買う
  gross margining system　グロス方式の証拠金決済
  margined securities　信用買いによる証券
  margining process　証拠金計算
  margining system　証拠金制度, 証拠金システム

margin （名）売上総利益, 利益率, 利ざや, 証拠金, 委託証拠金, 委託保証金, 担保金, 手付け金, 信用取引（margin trading）, 余裕, 限界, 開き, 幅, 値幅, マージン
  （⇒after-tax margin, gross margin, on margin）

a margin of fluctuation 変動の幅, 変動幅
　(=a range of fluctuation)
actual margin 実効証拠金率
additional margin 追加証拠金, 追い証
arbitrage margin 裁定マージン
buying on margin 空買い
daily margin 日次証拠金
deposit a margin 証拠金を差し入れる
extraordinary margin 特別証拠金
financial margin 金融業務の利ざや, 利ざや
forward margin 先物マージン
futures margin 先物の証拠金, 先物マージン
gross margin ratio 売上総利益率, 粗利益率
　(=gross margin percentage)
high margin 高い利益率, 高利益率, 高利幅, 高マージン
improve margin 利益率を改善する
initial margin 当初証拠金, 委託証拠金
　(=original margin)
initial margin requirement 当初証拠金率
injury margin 損害額
large margin 大幅な利ざや
loan trust margin 貸付け信託の利ざや
low margin 低い利益率, 低利益率, 低利幅, 低マージン
make better margins 利幅を大きくする
margin agreement 証拠金契約
margin buying （株の）信用買い, 空買い, 思惑買い
　(=buying on margin)
margin calculation 証拠金計算
margin debits 信用取引の証拠金
margin debt 証拠金負債
margin for straddles ストラドル取引の証拠金
margin lending 信用取引に伴う貸出
margin maintenance call 追い証
margin of AAbp over LIBOR　LIBOR＋AAベーシス・ポイント(bp)の変動金利
margin of dumping ダンピングの値幅
margin of error 誤差, 標準誤差
margin of futures 先物の証拠金
margin of profit 売上[売上高]利益率, 売上総利益, 採算, 利ざや
margin of safety 債券の発行総額と担保不動産の価格の差, 安全余裕[余裕度], 安全余裕率, 安全範囲, 安全性マージン　(=safety margin)
margin of safety ratio 安全余裕率, 安全率
margin of solvency 支払い余力
　(=solvency margin)
margin offset 証拠金相殺
margin purchase 信用買い, 証拠金買入れ
　(=margin buying)
margin rate 証拠金率　(=margin requirement)
margin rule 証拠金規則
margin security 信用取引証券
margin stock 信用銘柄
　(=stock for margin trading)
margins on loan trusts 貸付け信託の利ざや
narrow margin 薄利
narrow profit margins 利ざやが薄いこと
net interest margin 預貸利ざや
net margin 純販売利益, 純売買差益, 純利益, 正味利ざや
net profit margin 売上高利益率

on margin 信用取引で
operating income margin 営業利益率
　(=operating margin)
operating margin 営業利益率, 売上高営業利益率
original margin 当初証拠金　(=initial margin)
performance margin 委託証拠金
product margins 製品利益率
profit margin on sales 売上高利益率
quoted margin スプレッド
safety [safe] margin 安全係数
separation of margin 証拠金の分離
small [thin] margin 少ない利ざや, 小幅の利ざや
spread margin 両建て証拠金
stock margin 株式[株]の証拠金
the minimum margin 最低利幅
tight margin 薄い利ざや
unspent margin 購入余力
variation margin 変動証拠金, 維持証拠金, 追加証拠金
wide margin 大幅な利ざや
◆Day traders are individual investors who buy and sell stocks many times a day to earn a profit on the trading margin. デイ・トレーダーは、1日に何度も株の売買を繰り返して、その利ざやで利益を上げる個人投資家だ。◆Margin has already run off. すでに担保切れになっている。◆There are pressures on prices, margins and profitability. 価格や利益率、収益性が悪化している。

margin account 信用取引口座, 証拠金口座, 証拠金取引勘定（信用取引をする投資家が証券ブローカーに開く口座）
　do [make] short sales through margin accounts 信用取引口座を通じて[信用取引口座で]空売りを行う
　set up a margin account with one's broker 〜の取引している証券会社に信用取引口座を開く[開設する]
◆Short sales are made through margin accounts. 空売りは、信用取引口座を通じて行われる。

margin call 証拠金の積み増し要求, 追加証拠金請求, 追い証の請求
　(=maintenance call, margin maintenance call)
　issue a margin call 追い証を請求する
　meet a margin call 追い証を差し入れる, 証拠金の支払い要求に応（こた）える
　receive margin call 追い証を請求される

margin deposit 委託証拠金, 証拠金の預け入れ
◆Margin deposits are required for futures contracts. 先物契約には、証拠金の預け入れが必要だ。

margin improvement 利益率改善
◆In managing the business, we achieved 14 percent growth in earnings per common share through margin improvement and prudent expense controls. 業務運営の面では、利益率の改善と支出抑制の徹底により、普通株式1株当たり純利益は14％増加しました。

margin money （証券取引の）証拠金,（信用状開設の）保証金,（外国為替の）担保金
　letter of credit margin money 信用状開設保証金
　(=L/C margin money)

margin of futures 先物の証拠金
◆The margin of futures is different from stock margin. 先物の証拠金は、株の証拠金とは異なる。

margin of profit 売上利益率, 利益率, 利ざや, 利幅
　(=profit margin; ⇒profit margin)
◆The margin of profits from a project financing scheme overseas is generally higher than that from loans extended to domestic borrowers. 海外のプロジェクト・ファイナンス

（事業融資）事業による利ざやは、一般に国内企業向け融資の利ざやより高い。

margin on sales　売上利益, 販売利益［販売利益率］
◆We improved our gross and net margins on sales with net earnings increasing to 10 percent and earnings per share increasing 12 percent. 当社の総販売利益と販売利益率も改善し、純利益は10%増加、1株当たりの利益は12%増加しました。

margin percentage　利益率
◆The continuing shift in revenue mix to other services from higher-margin rentals led to a decline in the margin percentage in 2010. 高利益率のレンタル事業からその他のサービスへの売上構成の変化が続いたため、2010年度は利益率が低下しました。

margin requirement　証拠金, 証拠金所要額, 証拠金規定額,（株式）証拠金率
foreign exchange trading with low margin requirements 少ない証拠金での外国為替取引, 少ない証拠金での外国為替証拠金取引
increase margin requirements　証拠金を引き上げる
meet the margin requirements　証拠金率を満たす
set the initial margin requirements at　委託証拠金率を～%に設定する
the minimum margin requirements　最低証拠金率
◆The Diet enacted laws to impose restrictions on foreign exchange trading with low margin requirements. 少ない証拠金での外国為替取引［外国為替証拠金取引］を規制する法律が、国会で成立した。

margin trading　信用取引, 証拠金取引, マージン取引（=margin transaction:「信用取引」は、資金が十分でない場合などに、証券会社から資金や株式を借りて行う株式取引のこと。その際投資家は、証券会社に現金や株式を委託保証金として差し入れる。一般に、委託保証金額の3倍程度の取引ができる。⇒corporate buyout, FX）
procure funds through margin trading　信用取引で資金を調達する
stock for margin trading　信用銘柄
stock margin trading account　信用取引勘定
◆Investors can buy and sell stocks in margin trading, but they must settle accounts with a securities firm to actually own them. 投資家は信用取引で株を売買できるが、買入れた株を実際に保有するには、その代金を証券会社に支払わなければならない［その買入れ決済を行う必要がある］。◆Margin trading was used in a corporate takeover by exploiting legal shortcomings. 法の不備を利用して、企業買収に信用取引が使われた。◆The funds were procured through margin trading, which enables investors to trade amounts nearly three times larger in value than in money they actually hold, by offering cash and stocks as collateral to securities companies. その資金は、投資家が証券会社に現金や株を担保として差し入れて、手持ちの資金の3倍近い額の株を売買できる「信用取引」で調達した。

margin transaction　信用取引, 貸借取引（=margin trading: 委託保証金を証券会社に担保として預託し、買付け資金または売付け株券を借りて売買して一定の期間内に決済する株式取引のこと）
balance of margin transaction　信用残
guarantee money for margin transactions　貸借取引担保金, 貸借担保金
margin-related transaction　証拠金取引
margin transaction guarantee money　貸借担保金（=guarantee money for margin transactions）
margin transaction turnover period　信用取引回転日数
the date of margin transaction　信用取引の期日
the interest of margin transaction　信用取引の金利
the restriction of margin transactions　信用取引の規制
use the stock as collateral for margin transactions　株を信用取引の担保にする
◆Margin transactions are the purchase or sale of securities effected on credit extended to a customer by a securities firm, with cash or stock as collateral. 信用取引とは、現預金または株を担保として、証券会社が顧客に信用を供与して行われる証券の売買のことをいう。◆The management consultant used the stock as collateral for margin transactions to support the stock price of the company. 経営コンサルタントは、この株を信用取引の担保にして、同社の株価操作をしていた。

marginable　（形）証拠金取引の対象とすることができる
marginal　（形）限界の, 限界収益点の, 最低限度の, 下限に近い, 小幅な, 欄外の
marginal account　要注意先
marginal asset-to-income ratio　限界資産所得比率
marginal balance　限界利益（限界利益＝売上高-変動費）
marginal benefit　限界便益, 限界利得
marginal capital market　小規模な資本市場
marginal clause　（保険の）欄外約款
marginal cost of funds　限界資金コスト
marginal credit　限界信用, 限度貸付け
marginal credit supply　限界信用供給
marginal default rate　限界デフォルト率
marginal demand　限界需要
marginal deposit　信用状開設保証預金
marginal deposit-loan ratio　限界貸率
marginal financing cost　限界調達コスト
marginal gain［profit］　差益
marginal increase　小幅な伸び, 微増
marginal internal rate of return　限界内部収益率
marginal investor　限界的な投資家
marginal lending rate　限界貸出金利
marginal loan-deposit［deposit-loan］ratio　限界預貸率
marginal money　限界マネー
marginal profit ratio　限界利益率（=marginal income ratio）
marginal revenue　限界収入
marginal tax bracket　税率の段階
marginal tax rate　限界税率
marginal utility of money　貨幣の限界効用

marginal advantage　利ざや
◆In today's borderless world, operators spend their every second of the day looking for marginal advantage. 今日の国境なき世界では、株の相場師が一日中、利ざやを求めて動いている。

marginal demand　限界需要
marginal demand price　限界需要価格
marginal yen buying demand　円買いの限界需要

marginal efficiency　限界効率
marginal efficiency curve of capital　資本の限界効率曲線
marginal efficiency of capital　資本の限界効率（=marginal efficiency of investment）
marginal efficiency of investment　投資の限界効率

marginal income　限界利益
marginal income chart［graph］　限界利益図表
marginal income ratio　限界利益率（=marginal profit ratio）

marginal productivity　限界生産力, 限界生産性
marginal productivity of capital　資本の限界生産力［生産性］

marginal productivity of investment　投資の限界生産力
marginal propensity　限界性向
　marginal propensity to consume　限界消費性向
　marginal propensity to expend［spend］　限界支出性向
　marginal propensity to invest　限界投資性向
　marginal propensity to save　限界貯蓄性向
　marginal propensity to tax　限界租税性向
　marginal propensity to withdraw　限界控除性向
marine　(形)海の、海に住む、海産の、船舶の、海運の、海軍の、航海の
　fire and marine insurance rating　損害保険料率の算定
　fire and usual marine risks　海上保険
　Marine & Fire Insurance Association of Japan　日本損害保険協会
　marine accidents　海難
　　（=marine casualty, marine perils）
　marine loss　海上損害、海損
　marine perils　海上危険
　marine policy　海上保険証券
　marine quotation　海上保険低提率書
　marine rates　海上危険料率
　marine risk　海上危険
　marine syndicate　海上保険シンジケート
　marine underwriter　海上保険引受業者
　non-marine insurance　ノンマリン保険
marine bill of lading　海上船荷証券
　（=marine B/L）
　◆Date of marine bill of lading shall be proof of the date of shipment in the absence of the evidence to the contrary. 海上船荷証券の日付けは、反対の証拠がない場合、船積み日の証拠となる。
marine insurance　海上保険, M.I
　effect marine insurance　海上保険を付ける　海上保険の手配をする　～と保険契約する
　marine cargo insurance　貨物海上保険
　marine insurance business　海上保険業
　marine insurance company　海上保険会社
　marine insurance contract　海上保険契約
　marine insurance policy　海上保険証券
　marine insurance premium　海上保険料
　◆The seller shall, for its own account, effect marine insurance only free from particular average (FPA Institute Cargo Clause) for the amount of CIF value of the products plus 10 percent. 売り主は、売り主の自己負担で、本商品のCIF価格プラス10%の保険金額により、分損不担保条件（FPA協会貨物保険約款）の海上保険を付けるものとする。
　海上保険の種類：
　cargo insurance　貨物保険 積み荷保険
　freight insurance　貨物保険
　hull insurance　船体保険
　profit insurance　希望利益保険
mark　(動)～に印をつける、～を表す、～の位置を示す、～を示す、物語る、特徴づける、目立たせる、際立たせる、記念する、祝う、記録する、点数［評価］をつける、採点する、～に注意を払う
　be marked by　～で際立っている、～が目立つ、～が印象的だ、～が高まる
　be marked by downside risks　下振れリスクが高まる
　be marked down by 5 points　5ポイント下落する
　be marked up sharply　急反発する
　mark down　値下げする、値引きする、～を書きとめる、～のノートを取る
　mark liquid investments to market　短期投資を値洗いする
　mark one's debt portfolios to market　債権ポートフォリオを時価評価［時価で評価］する
　mark securities inventories to market　商品有価証券を時価評価［時価で評価］する
　mark the futures contract to market　先物契約の値洗いをする
　mark the insured credit exposure to market　付保した信用リスクを時価評価［時価で評価］する
　mark the position to market　ポジションを時価評価する
　mark the 10th anniversary of the foundation of the company　会社の創立10周年記念にあたる［10周年記念を祝う］
　mark time　足踏みする、様子を見る、成り行きを見守る
　mark up　値上げする、～を書き加える、～に高い点をつける
　marked check　（偽造防止の）記号入り小切手
　marked note　記号入り手形
　marked price　表示価格
　marked-to-market value　時価
　◆Goods tend not to sell unless they are marked down. 安くしないと、モノが売れなくなっている。◆The diffusion index (DI) of business confidence among large manufacturers marked the first positive reading in 33 months. 大手製造業の業況判断指数(DI)は、2年9か月ぶりにプラスに転じた。◆The latest rate increase marked the 15th consecutive quarter-point adjustment since June 2004. 今回の利上げで、2004年6月から15回連続0.25%の調整となった。◆The proposed merger would mark a final chapter in the realignment of the Japanese banking industry. この経営統合の申し入れは、日本の銀行業界（金融界）再編の最終章となる。◆The surplus in the current account stood at ￥1.5 trillion in September 2008, marking the seventh consecutive month of year-on-year declines. 2008年9月の経常収支の黒字額は、1兆5,000億円となり、7か月連続で前年実績を下回った。
mark　(名)水準、標準、～台、～の大台、記号、符号、標識、標的、目標、成績、評価、マーク
　care mark　注意マーク
　case mark　荷印、ケース・マーク
　counter mark　副マーク（荷送人の輸出商、メーカーを示す記号）
　country of origin mark　原産国マーク
　dip below the 9,000 mark　9,000円台を割る
　fall below the five percent mark　5%台を割り込む
　falling below the mark　台割れ
　main mark　主マーク（荷受人を示す記号）
　mark scanning　マーク読取り　（=mark sensing）
　mark sheet　輸入報告書
　mark signature　記号署名
　national origin mark　国別製造元表示, 原産地国マーク
　port mark　仕向港マーク（仕向地または仕向港を示す）
　quality mark　品質マーク
　service mark　サービス・マーク, サービス業者のサービス識別標章
　shipping mark　荷印（貿易貨物の外装に刷り込む記号）
　◆On Dec. 1, 2009, the Nikkei Stock Average was bearing down on the 9,000 mark due to the so-called Dubai shock. 2009年12月1日の日経平均株価（225種）は、いわゆるドバイ・ショック（中東ドバイの金融不安）で、9,000円台を割り込む寸前まで追いつめられていた。◆On expectations for the new financial steps, the Nikkei Stock Average recovered to the ￥9,000 mark. 今回の金融政策への期待で、日経平均株価は9,000円台に回復した。◆The 10-year JGB yield, a key indicator of long-term interest rates, fell below the 1 percent mark. 長期

金利の代表的な指標となる新発10年物日本国債の流通利回りが、1%の大台を割り込んだ。◆The 225-issue Nikkei Stock Average dipped below the 9,000 mark for the first time in 19 years. 東京株式市場の日経平均株価（225種）は、19年ぶりに9,000円台を割った。◆The 225-issue Nikkei Stock Average dropped below the 9,000 mark Wednesday to close at the year's low of 8,845.39. 水曜日の日経平均株価（225種）は、9,000円台を割り込み、終値は今年最安値の8,845円39銭となった。◆Toyota's midterm account settlement will certainly exceed, for the first time, the ¥10 trillion mark for the midterm business results. トヨタの中間決算では、中間期の業績で初めて10兆円台を突破するのは確実となっている。◆Volume on the First Section of the Tokyo Stock Exchange has exceeded the 1 billion mark for 42 business days in a row as of Monday, the longest period on record. 東京証券取引所第一部の出来高は、月曜日の時点で、42営業日連続で10億株の大台を超え、過去最長記録となった。

mark to market （動）（金融商品について）評価替えをする，〜を時価で評価替えする，時価で評価する，時価評価する，値洗いする，洗い替えを行う
  be marked to market 評価替えされている，時価で評価替えされる，時価評価されている
  mark assets and liabilities to market 資産と負債を時価評価する
  mark the position to market ポジションを時価評価する
  mark to market the positions ポジションの値洗いをする
  marked-to-market value 時価評価額，値洗い後の価格
  ◆Gains and losses on hedges of existing assets or liabilities are marked to market on a monthly basis. 既存の資産または債務のヘッジに関する損益は毎月、評価替えされている。

mark-to-market （名・形）評価替え（の），値洗い，時価，時価評価（=mark to the market: 手持ち証券などの価値を現在市場価値に評価し直すこと）
  carry A at its marked-to-market value Aを時価で計上する
  mark-to-market account 値洗い勘定
  mark-to-market approach 値洗い方式
  mark-to-market basis 値洗い基準，時価基準，時価評価ベース
  mark-to-market exposure 値洗い後のエクスポージャー
  mark-to-market method 時価法，市場連動法
  mark-to-market value 値洗い価値
  market-to-market positions 値洗いを必要とするポジション
  value one's securities on a mark-to-market basis 手持ちの証券を値洗い基準［時価基準、時価評価ベース］で評価する

mark-to-market accounting 時価会計
  ◆The IFRSs are based on mark-to-market accounting and was adopted by the London based International Accounting Standards Board. 国際財務報告基準（IFRSs）は、時価会計をベースとし、ロンドンに本部を置く国際会計基準審議会（IASB）によって採択された。

mark-to-market accounting practices 時価による会計処理，時価会計
  ◆Due to the introduction of mark-to-market accounting practices, falling stock prices accelerate the banks' deteriorating financial condition. 時価会計の導入で、株価の下落は銀行の財務状況の悪化を加速する。

mark-to-market accounting standard 時価会計基準
  ◆Shortly after the introduction of a mark-to-market accounting standard, declining stock prices started to deal a direct blow to the performance of financial institutions. 時価会計基準の導入直後、株価の下落が、金融機関の業績に直接的な打撃を与えるようになった。

mark-to-market accounting system 時価会計制度，時価主義会計制度（=current value accounting system, market value accounting system）
  ◆Since the introduction of the mark-to-market accounting system, corporations have been required to report their estimate of losses if the value of their shareholdings has dropped more than 50 percent from their purchasing prices. 時価会計制度の導入以来、保有株式の価格が取得価格より5割以上下落した場合、企業は評価損の計上を義務付けられている。◆Under the mark-to-market accounting system, if banks suffer appraisal losses of stocks they are holding, they are required to subtract 60 percent of those losses from their surplus funds. 時価会計制度では、金融機関が保有する株式の評価損が出た場合、金融機関は評価損の6割を剰余金から取り除かなければならない。

mark-to-market appraisal 時価評価，時価による評価
  ◆Falling stock prices have increased the mark-to-market appraisal losses of the financial group's stocks. 株価低迷で、同金融グループの時価による株式評価損が拡大した。

marked （形）際立った，目立つ，著しい，大幅な
  ◆The large U.S. current account deficit might result in a marked decline of its international investment positions. 米国の巨額の経常赤字で、海外投資家のドル資産が大幅に減少する可能性がある［海外投資家の著しいドル資産離れを招きかねない］。

market （動）販売する，売り出す，市場に出す
  ◆Goldman Sachs Group Inc. is said to have marketed risky investments that bet on the housing market's growth just before the mortgage meltdown. ゴールドマン・サックスは、住宅ローン市場の崩壊直前に、住宅市場の成長を見越した［予想した］高リスクの金融商品［投資商品］を販売したとされる。

market （名）市場，相場，市況，売買，マーケット
  access to the market 市場への参入，市場進出
  automotive insurance market 自動車保険市場
  bear market 弱気市場，下げ相場，売り相場
  bond issuing market 起債市場
  bond market 債券市場，公社債市場，債券相場
  bull market 強気市場，上げ相場，買い相場
  bullish tone in the market 市場の強気ムード
  capital market 資本市場，起債市場
  currency market 為替市場
  electricity trading market 電力取引市場
  exchange market 為替市場
  fiduciary market 信託市場
  foreign exchange market 外国為替市場，為替相場
  fringe market 周辺市場，背後市場地域
  global market グローバル市場，世界市場，グローバル・マーケット
  grey market 債券の発行前取引，合法的闇市（=gray market）
  information and telecoms market 情報通信市場
  international market 世界市場，国際市場（=global market）
  labor market 労働市場
  life insurance market 生命保険市場
  main export markets 主力輸出市場
  make a market （気配値を示して）値付けを行う，値付け業務を行う
  market financial system 市場原理に基づく金融システム
  market meltdown 市場崩壊
  Market of High-Growth and Emerging Stocks マザーズ
  market official 市場関係者
  market slide 株価下落
  market trust of the nation's financial system 日本の金融

システムに対する市場の信認
mature market　成熟市場, 市場の成熟化
money market　金融市場, 短期金融市場, マネー・マーケット
open market　公開市場
over-the-counter market　店頭市場, 場外市場
power supply market　電力供給市場
primary market for securities　証券の発行市場
project financing market　プロジェクト・ファイナンス市場
public market　公開市場, 大衆市場, 公的市場
secondary market　流通市場
speculative market　投機市場
stock and bond markets　株式・債券市場, 株式相場と債券相場
strong market　強気市場, 強気市況
sub market　下位市場
trading market　流通市場, トレーディング・マーケット
undifferentiated market　非差別化市場
up-market　上げ相場
vast market　巨大市場
weak market　軟弱市況, 軟調市況　（=soft market）

◆Crude oil prices have exceeded $70 a barrel in London and New York, setting all-time highs on these markets. ニューヨークとロンドン市場で原油価格が1バレル＝70ドルを上回って、両市場最高値を記録した。◆Growth in the automotive insurance market is slowing as fewer young people own cars. 若者の車離れを背景に、自動車保険市場は伸び悩んでいる。◆It likely will take a few years to fully integrate the markets of the TSE and the OSE. 東証と大証の市場の完全統合は、数年後になる見通しだ。◆Major Asian markets such as Shanghai and Hong Kong also show a situation that could be dubbed as a spontaneous global market crash. 上海や香港などアジアの主要市場も、世界同時株安の様相を見せている。◆Markets in up-and-coming countries with booming economies, is growing rapidly. 好景気の新興国市場は、急成長している。◆On European and U.S. markets, stock prices fell sharply the previous day. 前日の欧米市場の株価は、急落した。◆On the bond market, the yield on newly issued 10-year government bonds, an indicator of long-term interest rates, fell, resulting in a rise in bond prices. 債券市場では、長期金利の指標である新発10年物国債の利回り（流通利回り）が下落し、債券相場［債券価格］は上昇した。◆On the Tokyo stock market and other Asian markets, stock prices plunged across the board. 東京株式市場や他のアジア市場などでも、軒並み株安となった。◆Speculative markets are nothing but a legalized gambling casino. 投機市場は、合法的な賭博（とばく）場も同然だ。◆Stock prices will tumble, if banks try to sell a large amount of their crossheld shares in the market ahead of the account settlement term at the end of March. 3月末の決算期を控えて、銀行が大量の持ち合い株式を市場に放出すれば、株価は急落する。◆The Bank of Japan has supplied a large amount of funds to the market by purchasing long-term government bonds and corporate bonds. 日銀は、長期国債や社債の買入れで、大量の資金を市場に提供している。◆The Fed's monetary easing is a factor causing disarray in the foreign exchange markets. 米連邦準備制度理事会（FRB）［米中央銀行］の金融緩和が、為替相場混乱［為替混乱］の原因だ。◆The flow of speculative money into the oil market did not reflect actual demand. 投機マネーの原油市場への流入は、実需を反映していなかった［実需に基づくものではなかった］。◆The government may reject a company's request for a license to enter the fiduciary market if its executive has been dismissed in the past five years due to a violation of Section 2 of Article 102. 信託市場（信託業）に参入するための免許を申請した企業の役員が、第102条第2項の違反により5年以内に解任命令を受けていた場合、政府はその免許申請［免許交付］を拒否することができる。◆The market has calmed down. 市場は、落ち着きを取り戻した。◆The market is gathering momentum. 市場は上向きだ。◆The merger of the two exchanges will revitalize stock trading and make it easier for companies to procure funds on the market to expand their business operations. 両証券取引所の経営統合で、株式の売買が活性化し、企業にとっては市場で資金を調達して会社の事業を大きくしやすくなる。◆The money market is overheated by massive money inflows from banks on fading concerns over a financial system crisis. 金融システム不安［金融システム危機に対する懸念］の後退により、短期金融市場は、銀行からの巨額の資金流入で過熱感が強まっている。◆The possible downgrade of Treasury bonds is raising fears of adverse effects on the world's markets. 想定される米国債の格下げで、世界の市場に及ぼす悪影響への懸念が高まっている。◆The project financing market has seen a boost in loans to businesses in renewable energy field such as solar and wind power generation. プロジェクト・ファイナンス市場は最近、太陽光や風力発電など自然エネルギー分野の事業への融資が増えている。◆The TSE and four other exchanges extended their morning trading sessions by 30 minutes to boost market activity. 東証など5証券取引所が、取引活性化のため午前の取引時間を30分間延長した。◆The U.S. dollar was traded at around ¥76 on the currency market. 為替市場では、1ドル＝76円をはさんだ取引が続いた。◆Tokio Marine Holdings Inc. will enter the life insurance market in India on July 1, 2011. 東京海上ホールディングスは、2011年7月1日からインドの生命保険市場に参入する。◆Two companies' accumulated know-how in online trading will be useful in the commodity futures market. 商品先物市場では、両社の蓄積しているネット取引のノウハウが役に立つだろう。◆Wealth has been boosted by rallies in stock and bond markets. 株式相場と債券相場の急騰［上昇］で、資産が増加している［資産が膨らんでいる］。◆With such moves to rein in investment funds, speculative money started to exit the markets. 投資ファンドを規制するこうした動きで、投機マネーが市場から逃避し始めた。

market abuse　相場操縦
◆The Securities and Exchange Surveillance Commission is now in the final stage an investigation into the alleged case of market abuse. 証券取引等監視委員会は現在、相場操縦容疑での詰めの調査を進めている。

market activity　市場取引, 市場での取引
◆The TSE and four other exchanges extended their morning trading sessions by 30 minutes to boost market activity. 東証など5証券取引所が、取引活性化のため午前の取引時間を30分間延長した。◆The TSE's 30-minute extension of morning trading hours may not lead to an increase in market activity. 東証が午前の取引時間を30分延長しても、取引増［売買増］につながらない恐れがある。

market-based　（形）市場に基づく, 市場原理に基づく　（=market-driven）
market-based currency system　市場原理に基づく通貨制度
market-based economies　市場経済

market-based currency regime　市場原理に基づく通貨制度
◆It is the U.S. view that the best regime is a market-based currency regime. 最善の制度は市場原理に基づく通貨制度だ、というのが米国の見解だ。

market-based exchange rate　市場原理に沿った為替相場
◆The United States pressed China to move toward a market-based exchange rate. 米国は、中国に対して市場原理に沿った為替相場への移行を迫った。

market capitalization　株式の時価総額　（=market

capitalization value: 株式の外部発行済み株式総数に株価の時価を掛けた額）
◆Jasdaq is considering selecting firms whose market capitalization is more than ￥20 billion-30 billion and whose annual pretax profits are more than ￥1 billion, as components of a new index. ジャスダックは現在、新株価指数の対象銘柄として時価総額200億円～300億円以上、経常利益10億円以上の企業の選定を検討している。◆Total market capitalization—shares on issue multiplied by their value—also declined. 発行済み株式数に株価を掛け合わせた「時価総額」も縮小した。

market competition　市場での競争, 市場競争
◆Reforming the medical system means putting the near-bankrupt medical insurance program in order to enhance the quality and efficiency of medical care through market competition. 医療制度の改革は、市場での競争を通じて医療の質の向上と効率化を促すため、破綻寸前の医療保険制度の立て直しを意味する。

market competitiveness　市場競争力
◆Major U.S. and European banks have been strengthening their market competitiveness. 欧米の大手銀行は、市場競争力を強化してきた。

market conditions　市況, 市場の状況［状態］, 市場環境
better market conditions　市場環境の改善, 市況の好転, 市況の持ち直し
changing market conditions　市況の変化
financial market conditions　金融市場動向
improved market conditions　市況の改善［回復、持ち直し］
sluggish［poor］market conditions　市況低迷
uncertain market conditions　市場の先行きの不透明性［不透明感］
◆There has been progress in inventory adjustment in such products as information-related goods, with market conditions improving as well. 最近は、情報関連財などの製品の在庫調整が進み、市況も持ち直している。

market confidence　市場の信認
◆European banks are forced to shore up their potential capital shortage to restore market confidence. 欧州銀行は、市場の信認を回復するため、潜在的資本不足の増強を迫られている。◆Market confidence in the Silvio Berlusconi administration's fiscal rehabilitation measures is virtually nonexistent as the administration is on its last legs. イタリアのベルルスコーニ政権が機能不全に陥っているため、同政権の財政再建策に対する市場の信認は事実上、失墜している

market crash　市況の突然の崩れ, 市場の暴落, 暴落
（=crash, crash of the market）
a spontaneous global market crash　世界同時株安
　　（=simultaneous stock market plunges）
◆Major Asian markets such as Shanghai and Hong Kong also show a situation that could be dubbed as a spontaneous global market crash. 上海や香港などアジアの主要市場も、世界同時株安の様相を見せている。◆Tokyo and other major Asian markets also plunged, a situation that could be dubbed a spontaneous global market crash. 東京その他アジアの主要市場も下落して、世界同時株安の様相を見せている。

market deregulation　市場の規制緩和, 市場開放, 規制緩和, 自由化
◆In the United States, there is a growing move for a review of market deregulation, chiefly in the wake of major power outages in California. 米国では、主にカリフォルニア州の大規模停電を契機に、電力自由化を見直す機運が高まっている。

market-determined exchange rate system　市場が決める為替相場［為替相場制］
◆The G-20 nations will move toward a more market-determined exchange rate system. 世界［主要］20か国・地域（G20）は、市場が決める為替相場に移行させる方針だ。

market developments　市場の動き
◆The U.S. government and financial authorities are urged to closely monitor market developments in order to avoid an immediate crisis. 米政府と金融当局は、当面の危機を回避するため、今後の市場の動きを注視する必要がある。

market economy　市場経済
◆The G-8 agreement to give Russia full membership is aimed partly at helping the former communist nation accelerate its drive for a market economy. ロシアのG-8全面参加についてのG-8の合意には、旧共産国であるロシアの市場経済化を加速させる狙いもある。

market expectations　市場予想, 市場予測, 市場の見通し, 市場の期待
better than market expectations　市場予測より良い
come ahead of market expectations　市場の予想［期待］を上回る
come in at or below market expectations　市場の期待の線かそれを下回る水準になる
disappoint market expectations　市場の期待を裏切る
in line with market expectations　市場の予想どおり, 市場予測どおり
prevailing market expectations　市場の大方の期待
◆Contrary to prevailing market expectations, the central bank decided not to further ease monetary policy. 市場の大方の期待を裏切って［期待に反して］、日銀は追加的な金融緩和策を見送った。

market fears　市場不安
◆The Japanese central bank's move to increase the outstanding current account target is insufficient to soothe market fears. 日銀の当座預金残高目標の引上げは、市場不安を払拭するには物足りない。

market forces　市場の力, 市場諸力, 市場要因, 市場原理, 市場の自由競争, 需給関係
◆It should be considered irresponsible for the government to take such a stance as leaving the issue of employment up to market forces to determine. 雇用問題は市場の自由競争にゆだねるといった姿勢を政府が取るとしたら、それは無責任と言わざるを得ない。

market growth　市場の拡大, 市場の伸び, 市場の成長
（=market expansion）
◆Market growth is expected in Asian regions. アジア地域では、将来の市場の成長が見込める。

market interest rate　市場金利, 市中金利
（=open market rate）
◆If market interest rates rise on the back of an economic recovery, interest rates for loans also will rise. 景気回復を背景に市場金利が上昇すれば、ローン金利も上がることになる。

market intervention　市場介入, 為替市場介入, 介入
（財務省や中央銀行などの金融当局［通貨当局］が、為替相場の過度な変動を抑えるために通貨を売買すること。日本の場合は財務相の権限で行われ、実務は中央銀行の日銀が財務相の代理人として行う。⇒pessimism, proxy, undervaluation）
carry out the market intervention　市場介入を実施する
conduct the market intervention　市場介入を行う
currency market intervention　為替市場への介入, 為替市場介入　（=foreign exchange intervention, forex intervention）
dollar-supporting market intervention　ドルの下支えを図る市場介入
engage in market intervention　市場介入する
full-scale market intervention　本格的な市場介入
large-scale market intervention　大規模介入, 大型の市場介入, 大型介入
the effect of the market intervention　市場介入の効果, 為

替市場[為替]介入の効果
the yen-selling market intervention　円売り介入
◆A market intervention is conducted under the authority of the finance minister in Japan. 市場介入は、日本では財務相の権限で行われる。◆A new round of full-scale market intervention will take place if the yen rises to the ￥84 range against the dollar. 円高が1ドル＝84円台まで進めば、再び本格的な市場介入が行われるだろう。◆Finance Minister Yoshihiko Noda decided to conduct a yen-selling market intervention on Aug. 4, 2011. 2011年8月4日に野田財務相は、円売り市場介入の実施を決断した。◆Japan implemented the yen-selling market intervention unilaterally. 日本は、単独で円売り介入を実施した。◆Japan should prevent the dollar plunging and the yen from rising too sharply through concerted market intervention with the United States and European countries. 日本は、米欧との協調介入によってドル急落と超円高を阻止すべきだ。◆Just after the start of the market intervention, the banks were flooded with orders for forward exchange contracts. 市場介入の直後、銀行には為替予約の注文が殺到した。◆Some market players feel the effect of the market intervention will not last long. 市場関係者の間では、為替市場介入の効果は長続きしないとの見方もある。◆The government and the Bank of Japan are considering joint market intervention with the U.S. and European monetary authorities to produce the greater results of their market intervention. 政府・日銀は、市場介入の効果を高めるため、米欧の通貨当局との協調介入を検討している。◆The government and the Bank of Japan engaged in market intervention in mid-September 2010 to stop the yen from surging. 政府・日銀は2010年9月中旬、円急騰に歯止めをかけるため市場介入した。◆The market intervention was carried out to control excessive volatility in the exchange market. 為替相場の過度の変動を抑制するため、市場介入[為替介入]が実施された。

market liberalization　市場開放, 市場の自由化, 市場の規制緩和
◆Toyota entered the telecommunications market following market liberalization in 1985, but it still is not making the profits it hoped for. トヨタは1985年の通信市場（通信事業）の自由化で通信市場に参入したが、まだ期待した利益を上げていない。

market liquidity　市場流動性, 金融商品市場で株式や債券などを売買するための豊富な資金
◆The rise in stock prices is merely because part of the market liquidity created by easy money policies adopted by countries worldwide is flowing into the Japanese market. 株高は、世界的な金融緩和で金余りの一部が日本市場に流入したにすぎない。

market manipulation　市場操作, 株価操作, 相場操縦 (⇒penalty)
◆A former Osaka Security Exchange Company senior executive vice president was indicted without arrest for market manipulation. 大阪証券取引所（大証）の元副理事長が、株価操作の罪で在宅起訴された。◆Japan's regulations on short selling and market manipulation by spreading rumors are extremely weak in comparison with those of the United States. 日本の空売りに関する規制や風説の流布などによる市場操作についての規制は、米国に比べて極めて弱い。◆The TSE has called on brokerages to keep a close eye on transactions involving about 20 issues, which are suspected of having been subject to market manipulation. 東京証券取引所は、株価操作が行われた疑いのある約20銘柄の取引について十分注意するよう各証券会社に促している。

market observer　市場関係者, 業界筋
◆Market observers point out that the construction industry has been slow in reorganizing itself. 建設業界は業界再編が一向に進んでいない、と市場関係者（業界筋）は指摘する。

market opening　市場開放

◆The United States urged Japan to redouble its market opening efforts in key sectors such as telecommunications, agriculture and automobiles. アメリカは、日本に対して、通信や農業、自動車などの主要分野で市場開放努力を一段と進めるよう強く迫った。

market operation　市場操作（債券や政府短期証券の売買操作）, 資本事業
　capital markets operation　資本市場事業
　foreign exchange market operation　外国為替市場操作
　international capital markets operation　国際資本市場事業
　introduce a new open market operation　新型の公開市場操作（オペ）を導入する
　money market operation　短期金融市場操作
　open market operation　公開市場操作（オペ）, 金融調節
◆The BOJ decided to introduce a new open market operation by supplying ￥10 trillion to private financial institutions in three month loans at an ultralow annual interest of 0.1 percent. 日銀は、民間の金融機関に年1％の超低金利で貸出期間3か月の資金を10兆円供給する新型の公開市場操作（オペ）の導入に踏み切った。

market opportunity　市場機会, 事業機会, ビジネス機会 (＝business opportunity)
◆We make an acquisition when that seems the most effective way to take advantage of a particular market opportunity to further our growth goals. 当社が企業を買収するのは、特定の市場機会をとらえて当社の成長目標をさらに推進する上で、それが最も効果的な方法であると思われるときです。

market-oriented　(形)市場原理に基づく, 市場重視型, 市場志向型の, 市場型の, 市場中心の, 市場に重点を置く
　market-oriented economy　市場型経済, 市場経済
　market-oriented exchange rate system　市場中心の為替相場[為替相場制]
　market-oriented financial products　市場中心の金融商品
　market-oriented products　市場志向的商品
　market-oriented sector selective　市場重視型個別協議

market participants　市場参加者, 市場関係者
◆Market participants pointed out the issuance of new shares would dilute the value of the company's existing shares. 市場関係者は、増資[新株発行]によって同社の既存株式の価値が損なわれる、と指摘している。

market player　市場関係者, 市場参加者, 市場筋, マーケット・プレーヤー (⇒sell off)
◆A dealer at a leading bank said that market players' concern has kept yen-buying moves in check. 市場関係者の警戒感が円買いの動きを食い止めた[抑制した]、と大手銀行のディーラーが語っている。◆A market player put the level of short selling in the stock market at between 5 percent to 10 percent of total trading volume. ある市場筋によると、株の空売りは取引全体の5-10％程度といわれる。◆Doubts over the effectiveness of the announced stock price measures have already been expressed among Japanese market players. 今回発表された株価対策の効果については、日本の市場関係者の間ですでに疑問視する声がある。◆Rumors were swirling among market players that Merrill Lynch would be the next to go under. 市場関係者の間では、「次に破たんするのはメリルリンチ」という噂が渦巻いていた。◆Some market players feel the effect of the market intervention will not last long. 市場関係者の間では、為替市場介入の効果は長続きしないとの見方もある。◆The talks between Prime Minister Kan and Bank of Japan Gov. Shirakawa led to a further advance of the yen and offloading of stocks as disappointment spread among market players. 菅首相と日銀総裁の会談は、一層の円高と市場筋の株の失望売りを誘った。

market price　市場価格, 市価, 時価, 売価, 相場
◆The RCC used to buy bad loans at market prices. 整理回収機構は、これまで不良債権を時価で買い取っていた。◆Under

the plan, the RCC will buy outstanding loans to the company at market prices from regional banks and other creditors except the major banks. 同案では、整理回収機構（RCC）が、主力行以外の地方銀行やその他の債権者から同社向けの債権残高を時価で買い取ることになる。

market principle 市場原理
◆If the government gets involved in stock purchases, the market principle may be distorted. 政府が株式の買取りに関与すれば、市場原理がゆがめられる可能性がある。

market rate 市場金利, 市場相場, 市場レート, 銀行間相場［インターバンク・レート］, 市場割引歩合（market rate of discount）
  at market rates　市場金利で
  at sub-market rates　市場金利を下回る利率で
  at the current market rates　実勢市場金利で
  behavior of market rates　相場の変動
  bond lending market rates　債券貸借仲介レート
  declining market rates　市場金利の低下
  leading marketing rate　市場介入金利
  market rate of discount　市場割引率, 市場割引歩合, 手形割引歩合
    （=bill rate, discount rate, market rate）
  market rate of exchange　市場為替相場
  market rate of interest　市場金利（market rate）, 市場利子率
  market rate of intervention　市場介入金利
  market rate of return　市場収益率
  money market rate　市中金利, 短期市場金利
  movements in market rates　市場レートの変動
  open market rate　短期市場金利
  prevailing market rate　市場実勢金利, 実勢市場金利
  rise in market rates　市場金利の上昇
  short-term money market rate　短期市場金利
  upward pressure on market rates　短期市場金利の上昇圧力
◆Banks' fund-raising costs have increased, reflecting the rise in market rates after the Bank of Japan abandoned its zero-interest policy. 日銀のゼロ金利政策解除に伴って市場金利が上昇したのを反映して、銀行の資金調達コストが増大した。

market-related asset value method 市場関連資産価格方式
◆The Corporation uses a three-year, market-related asset value method of amortizing asset-related gains and losses. 当社は、資産関連損益を償却するため、3年間の市場関連資産価格方式を採用しています。

market risk 市場リスク
◆These financial instruments are subject to market risks resulting from exchange rate movements. これらの金融手段［金融商品］は、為替の変動による市場リスクにさらされています。

market scrutiny 市場の評価［チェック］, 市場の監視の目
◆Japanese government bonds are being subjected to stricter market scrutiny. 日本国債は、市場の一段と厳しい評価にさらされている。

market sentiment 市場の地合（じあ）い, 市場心理, 市場のムード, 市場のセンチメント
  bearish market sentiment　市場の弱気の地合い
  bullish market sentiment　市場の強気の地合い
  help market sentiment　市場のセンチメントを支える
  shift in market sentiment　市場の地合いの変化
◆Rekindled fears of the worsening of the fiscal and financial crisis in Europe dampened market sentiment. 欧州の財政・金融危機悪化への懸念再燃で、市場心理が冷え込んだ。

market share 市場占拠率, 市場占有率, 市場シェア, マーケット・シェア, シェア
◆Shinsei Bank is trying to effectively raise profits while avoiding excessive competition over market share. 新生銀行は、シェアを争う過当競争を回避しながら効率的に収益を上げる方針だ。

market trends 市場動向
◆Investors have to keep an eye on market trends. 投資家は、市場動向を注意深く見守る必要がある。

market valuation 時価総額
◆At current prices, the company's market valuation is more than $1.5 billion. 現在の株価で、同社の時価総額は15億ドルを超えている。

market value 市場価値, 市場価格, 市価, 時価, 時価評価額　（=market price; ⇒accounting system）
◆Apple Inc. overtook Microsoft Corp. as the world's biggest tech company based on market value. 株式の時価評価額［時価総額］で、米アップル社がマイクロソフト（MS）を追い抜いて世界でトップのIT企業になった。◆Bad loans should be bought at market value rather than at effective book value. 不良債権は、実質簿価でなく時価で買い取るべきだ。◆Currently, the Resolution and Collection Corporation purchases banks' nonperforming loans at their market value. 現在、整理回収機構（RCC）は、銀行が抱える不良債権を「時価」で買い取っている。◆JAL's stocks may lose market value to zero if the corporate turnaround body cuts the shares 100 percent by delisting JAL from the Tokyo stock market. 企業再生支援機構が東京株式市場から日航の上場を廃止して日航株を100％減資したら、日航株の市場価値はゼロになる可能性がある。◆Major banks posted about ¥1.5 trillion in losses due to the gap in the prices of their shareholdings on their balance sheets and the market value. 大手銀行は、全体で約1兆5,000億円の株式評価損（銀行保有株式のバランス・シート上の価格と時価との差による損失）を計上した。◆The merger between the TSE and the OSE will create the world's second largest exchange group in terms of the total market value of listed share. 東証と大証の経営統合で、上場企業の時価総額で世界第2位の株式取引所グループが誕生する。◆The rule of asset impairment accounting requires companies to post valuation losses on fixed assets whose market value has fallen sharply from their book value. 減損会計基準は、固定資産の時価が簿価から大幅に下落した場合の固定資産の評価損の計上を、企業に義務付けている。

market value accounting system 時価会計制度, 時価主義会計制度　（=current value accounting system, mark-to-market accounting system）

market value method 時価法
◆The market value method views the convertible bonds as debt whose conversion was a significant economic transaction. 時価法は、転換社債を債務と見なし、転換社債の転換を重要な経済取引であると見ている。

marketable （形）市場性ある, 売買可能な
  investment in marketable securities　有価証券投資, 市場性証券への投資
  marketable assets　市場性資産
  marketable commodity　市場性ある商品
  marketable debt security　市場性ある債務証券, 市場性ある債券
  marketable equity securities　市場性ある持ち分証券［有価証券］, 市場性ある株式
  marketable investment securities　市場性ある投資有価証券
  marketable issue　市場性証券
  marketable nonequity security　市場性ある債券
    （=marketable debt security）
  marketable product　商品
  marketable securities, at cost, which approximates market

市場性ある有価証券—原価評価で時価とほぼ等しい
　non-marketable securities　市場性のない有価証券, 非市場性証券
marketable securities　市場性ある有価証券, 市場性有価証券, 市場性証券, 有価証券
　（⇒corporate assets）
◆Due to an increase in the purchase of marketable securities, net cash used for investing activities increased by $5 million from the same period last year. 市場性ある有価証券の購入量が増えたため、投資活動に使用した純キャッシュは、前年同期比で500万ドル増加しました。◆TEPCO will raise funds for compensation payments by selling assets, including marketable securities and real estate. 東電は、有価証券や不動産などの資産を売却して、賠償金[補償金]支払いの資金を調達する方針だ。
marketplace　（名）市場
　health care (delivery) service marketplace　医療サービス市場
　international financial marketplace　国際金融市場
　marking to market　時価評価, 値洗い
　　（⇒mark-to-market）
　regular marking to market　定期的値洗い
　the marking to market of mortgages　モーゲージの値洗い
　the marking to market of one's portfolios　手持ちのポートフォリオの時価評価
markon　（名）値入れ, 値入れ率
massive　（形）巨額の, 多額の, 巨大な, 大量の, 多量の, 多大の, 大規模な, 大々的な, 大がかりな, 大幅な, スケールの大きい, 大きい, 大型の, 極端な, 旺盛な, 活発な, 強力な, 充実した, 有名な
　（⇒direct investment）
　a massive amount of money　巨額の資金
　massive debt loads　巨額の債務負担, 巨額の債務
　massive debts　巨額の債務, 過剰債務
　massive demand　旺盛な需要
　massive depression　大不況
　massive financial assistance　巨額の金融支援, 巨額の財政援助
　massive flight of capital　大量の資金移動
　massive increase in government spending　大型の財政出動
　massive injection of liquidity　大量の流動性供給
　massive intervention　巨額の介入, 巨額介入
　massive investment　大規模投資, 大がかりな投資, 巨額の投資
　massive issuance　大量発行
　massive outflows of capital and technology　資本と技術の大量流出
　massive overvaluation of the yen　極端な円高
　massive potential　巨大な潜在力, 大きな可能性
　massive purchases of U.S. Treasury bonds from U.S. commercial banks　米金融機関[米銀]からの米長期国債の大量買入れ
　massive selling　大量の売り
　the massive figure of tax revenue shortfall　巨額の税収不足　（⇒tax revenue shortfall）
◆A massive shortage in the bank's loan loss provisions for nonperforming loans was pointed out through the special investigation by the Financial Services Agency. 金融庁の特別検査で、不良債権に対する同行の多額の貸倒れ引当金不足が指摘された。◆The drastic overhaul of the Japanese accounting system is expected to add a massive administrative burden to companies. 日本の会計基準の抜本的変更は、企業にとって大幅な事務負担の増加を強いられることになる。

massive amounts of excessive liabilities　巨額の過剰債務
◆A large number of companies are burdened with massive amounts of excessive liabilities in sectors such as construction and wholesale. 建設や卸売りなどの分野では、巨額の過剰債務を抱えている企業が多い。
massive bad loan problem　巨額の不良債権問題
◆Bank issues declined as investors remained wary over the banks' massive bad loan problems. 銀行株は、やはり巨額の不良債権問題の処理に対する投資家の警戒感から値を下げた。
massive bad loans　巨額の不良債権
◆The instability of life insurance firms and the lowered earning power of banks with massive bad loans have become the two major factors rocking the financial system. 生保各社の経営基盤の不安定と、巨額の不良債権に苦しむ銀行の収益力低下が、金融システムを揺るがしている二大要因になっている。
massive budget deficits　巨額の財政赤字
◆Greece is saddled with massive budget deficits. ギリシャは、巨額の財政赤字を抱えている。
massive debts　巨額の債務, 過剰債務
◆UFJ Holdings Inc. has also lent money to many start-up firms laden with massive debts. UFJホールディングスは、多くの過剰債務の新興企業（ベンチャー企業）にも融資している。
massive direct investment　大規模な直接投資, 巨額の直接投資, 大がかりな直接投資
◆While soaring high on massive direct investment from abroad, the Chinese economy started showing signs of overheating in the latter half of 2003. 海外からの活発な直接投資に支えられて、中国経済は、2003年後半から景気過熱の様相を見せ始めた。
massive euro stabilization package　大規模なユーロ安定化策, 大がかりなユーロ安定化策
◆The massive euro stabilization package appears to have had a limited impact thus far. 大規模な[大がかりな]ユーロ安定化策の影響は、これまでのところ限定的と思われる。
massive gains　大幅増加
◆The massive gains in stockholdings' latent value will raise the banks' net worth ratios markedly. 保有株式の含み益の大幅増加で、銀行の自己資本比率も大きく向上する見込みだ。
massive loss　巨額の損失
◆The bank is mulling a further downward revision of its business results for fiscal 2011 that is expected to result in a massive loss. 同行は、巨額の損失が見込まれる2012年3月決算[2011年度]の業績予想を、さらに下方修正する方向で検討している。◆The extent of Lehman's massive losses and write-downs due to the subprime mortgage crisis became evident. サブプライム・ローン（米低所得者向け住宅融資）問題に伴うリーマンの巨額の損失と評価損の規模が、明らかになった。◆The massive losses mean the bank's capital adequacy ratio is estimated to have fallen to about 8 percent. この大幅な赤字で、同行の自己資本比率は、約8％まで低下する見通しだ。◆The New York-based Citigroup, once the world's biggest banking group, faced massive losses in the wake of the subprime mortgage crisis. 世界最大の金融グループだったシティグループ（ニューヨーク）は、サブプライム・ローンの焦げ付き問題を受けて、巨額の損失を抱えていた。
massive money inflow　巨額の資金流入
◆The money market is overheated by massive money inflows from banks on fading concerns over a financial system crisis. 金融システム不安[金融システム危機に対する懸念]の後退により、短期金融市場は、銀行からの巨額の資金流入で過熱感が強まっている。
massive negative yields of the life insurance industry　生保業界の巨額の逆ざや
◆The massive negative yields of the life insurance industry threaten the financial soundness of insurers. 生保業界の巨額の逆ざやが、生保各社の財務上の健全性[経営の健全性]を脅

（おびや）かしている。

massive nonperforming loans 巨額の不良債権
◆The United States may request Japan to make further efforts to head off deflation and stabilize the financial system by disposing of massive nonperforming loans held by financial institutions. デフレ阻止や金融機関が抱える巨額の不良債権処理による金融システムの安定化に向けて一層の努力をするよう、米国が日本に求める可能性がある。

massive purchase of government bonds 国債の大量購入, 国債の大量買取り［買入れ］
◆The ECB remains cautious about taking steps of supporting Italy and other distressed countries through massive purchases of their government bonds. 欧州銀行（ECB）は、イタリアなど財政危機国の国債を大量に買い支える措置を取ることに、慎重な姿勢を崩していない。

massive sell-offs of shares 株の大量売却
◆Nippon Life Insurance Co. carried out massive sell-offs of loss hiding scandal-hit Olympus Corp.'s shares. 日本生命保険が、損失隠しの疑惑をもたれるオリンパスの株の大量売却を実施した。◆The Nippon Life Insurance group's stake in Olympus has been reduced to 5.11 percent from 8.18 percent by massive sell-offs of the company's shares. 日本生命グループのオリンパス株の保有比率は、同社株の大量売却で8.18%から5.11%に下がった。

massive trade deficit 膨大な貿易赤字, 巨額の貿易赤字
◆The consumer tendency of spending more than consumer's disposable income resulted in a worsening of the massive trade deficit of the United States. 支出が消費者の可処分所得を上回る消費者性向が、結果として膨大な米国の貿易赤字の拡大を生み出していた。

mastermind （動）陰で指揮する, 首謀者として指揮する, 背後で操（あやつ）る, 主導する
◆The chairman of the company masterminded the firm's illegal fund-raising activities. 同社の会長が、同社の不正な資金集め活動を主導していた。

mastermind （名）首謀者, 黒幕, 指導者, 主導者,（計画）立案者, 傑出した知性・知能, 優れた知性・知能の持ち主
◆He was the mastermind behind a string of violations of the Securities and Exchange Law by the Internet service firm. 氏は、このインターネット・サービス会社による一連の証券取引法違反行為を主導していた。

matrix （名）母体, 基盤, 行列, 網状組織, マトリックス
 capital coefficients matrix 資本係数行列
 financial transaction matrix 金融連関表
 matrix management マトリックス型経営, マトリックス経営
 matrix on commodity input by kind of economic activity 経済活動別財貨・サービス投入表
 matrix on commodity output by kind of economic activity 経済活動別財貨・サービス産出表
 matrix organization マトリックス組織
 matrix trading マトリックス取引, マトリックス・トレーディング（格付けや発行条件が違う債券間の利回り格差の一時的変動を利用して利ざやを稼ぐ取引）
 trade matrix analysis 貿易連関分析

matter （名）問題, 主題, 対象, 内容, 事項, 議題, 事態, 事柄, 主要事実, 重要
 key corporate matters 重要な経営事項
 matter in controversy［dispute］ 係争事項, 訴訟の対象
 matter of record 記録事項
 matters for resolution 決議事項
 money matters 金銭問題, 貸借事項
 subject matter 本件, 契約の主題・内容, 目的物, 目的事項, 対象物, 対象事項, 裁判での係争物, 訴訟物
 subject matter of insurance 保険の目的, 保険の対象

（=subject matter insured）
◆A firm requires the support of more than two thirds of shareholders to decide on important matters, such as a merger, at shareholders meetings. 企業が株主総会で合併などの重要事項を決議するには、3分の2以上の賛成が必要だ。

mature （動）満期になる, 期日が到来する, 満期を迎える, 成熟する, 成長する （⇒bank loan）
 mature with the last scheduled payment 最後の予定支払いをもって満期となる
 pay the debt as it matures 期限どおりに債務を返済する
◆Higher debt maturing within one year chiefly reflects commercial paper we issued to support financial services. 1年以内返済予定の負債の増加は、主に金融サービス部門の支援のため、当社がコマーシャル・ペーパーを発行したことを反映しています。◆In addition to long-term debt maturing during the year, the company redeemed all of its U.S. $150 million debentures, due 2013, in June 2011. 当年度に満期が到来する長期債務のほか、同社は2013年満期の社債1億5,000万米ドルの全額を、2011年6月に償還した。◆On April 12, 2010, we purchased $264 million in notes of the company maturing over six to eight years. 2010年4月12日に当社は、元本金額2億6,400万ドル、満期6-8年の同社のノートを購入した。

matured （形）満期の, 期日が到来した
 matured bill 満期手形
 matured bond 満期債券
 matured bond holdings 満期債券保有高
 matured endowment 満期保険金
 matured liabilities 満期債務
 matured notes 満期手形
 matured obligation 期日到来債務, 満期債務

maturing （形）満期が来る, 満期を迎える, 満期が来た, 満期に近い
 borrow to repay maturing debt 満期分の借換えをする
 maturing debt obligations 満期が来た債務, 満期を迎えた債務
 maturing debts 満期が到来した［満期が近い］債券, 満期が来た債務, 満期償還額
 maturing loans 満期が来る融資
 maturing receivables 満期が来た債権
 pay back maturing government debts 満期を迎える国債［満期分の国債］を償還する, 満期を迎える国債を借り換える
 replace maturing debt 満期を迎えた［満期が来た］債務を借り換える
 retire［pay off, repay］maturing CP［commercial paper］ 満期が来たCPを償還する
 the repayment［payment］of manufacturing CP 満期が来たCPの償還
 the timely payment of maturing CP 満期が来たCPの期限どおりの支払い
◆If a new federal debt ceiling isn't set by Aug. 2, 2011, the United States will be forced to default on Treasuries securities as it will not be able to issue new bonds to pay back maturing government debts. 2011年8月2日までに連邦政府の債務上限を新たに設けないと、米国は満期を迎える国債を償還するための国債増発ができないので、米国債の不履行（デフォルト）が発生する。

maturity （名）満期, 支払い期限, 支払い期日, 弁済期限
 a bond with a maturity of 10 years 満期10年の債券
 balloon maturity 最終残額一括払いの満期物, バルーン償還
 bill at maturity 満期手形
 bond with medium maturity 中期債
 bullet maturity（amortization） 満期一括償還

cancellation before maturity　中途解約
　（=rescission before maturity）
constant maturity Treasury　米国債理論利回り, CMT
crisis at maturity　一括返済リスク
current maturity　残存期間
debt maturity　債務支払い日, 債務［債券］償還
early maturities of serial bonds　連続社債のうち早く期限が来るもの
extend debt maturity　債務の償還期限を延長する
fixed maturity dates　期日物
held-to-maturity securities　償還期限まで保有する証券
large maturity　長期満期
long (term) maturities　長期期限物, 長期償還期限物
maturity date　満期日, 償還日, 支払い期日, 納期
　（=date of maturity; ⇒debt servicing）
maturity-designated deposits　期日指定預金, 期日指定定期預金
maturity distribution　満期分布
maturity gap exposure　運用・調達期間のギャップ
maturity guarantee　満期保証
maturity index　満期見出し表, 満期日早見表
maturity ladder　満期構成のはしご
maturity list　満期日表
maturity matching　（債券の）満期日の組合せ
maturity period　償還期限
maturity profiles　満期の状況
maturity reimbursement　満期時支払い請求
maturity stripping　（ローン債権売買での）マチュリティ・ストリッピング（貸出債権の最終期日の同じものを集めて, まとまった金額にすること）
maturity structure of assets　資産の満期構造
maturity structure of liabilities　負債の満期構造
maturity ticklers　期日案内, 期日控え帳, 満期控え帳
maturity transformation　満期の転形, 満期の変換
maturity value　満期価値, 償還価値, 価額, 償還価額
maturity yield　満期利回り, 最終利回り
　（=yield to maturity）
near maturity　近満期
obligatory maturity　債務満期
on a maturity base [basis]　満期日建て, 満期ベースで
original maturity　当初満期, 当初期限
reach maturity　満期になる
redemption before maturity　期限前償還
redemption of [at] maturity　満期償還
repo to maturity　満期償還現先
residual maturity　残余期間
shorter maturities　短期物
simple yield to maturity　単利最終利回り
spread to maturity　満期スプレッド
term to maturity　満期, 償還年限
the maturity of a draft　手形満期日
with a maturity of 10 years　10年満期で
with an original maturity not exceeding one year　当初期限が1年未満の
yield to maturity　最終利回り, 満期利回り
　（=maturity yield）
◆The Bank of Japan may expand the list of government bonds purchased under the fund, to include those that have more than two years left until maturity. 日銀は, 基金で買い入れる国債の対象を拡大して, 満期までの残存期間が2年以上（現行1〜2年）の国債を含むようにする可能性がある。◆The Bank of Japan purchases government bonds that have one to two years left until maturity. 日銀は, 満期までの残存期間が1〜2年の国債を買い入れている。◆The company elected to redeem, prior to maturity on June 3, 2011, $120 million of first mortgage bonds on May 1, 2011. 同社は, 満期が到来する2011年6月3日以前の2011年5月1日に, 第一順位抵当権付き社債1億2,000万ドルを償還することを決定した。◆The company took advantage of favorable levels of interest rates to extend debt maturities by refinancing a substantial amount of long-term debt. 同社は, 有利な金利水準を利用して, 長期負債の相当額を借り換えて債務の償還期限を延長した。◆The Corporation considers all highly liquid investments purchased with an original maturity of three months or less to be cash equivalents. 当社は, 取得日から満期日までの期間が3か月以内の流動性の高い投資を, すべて現預金等価物としています。

maximize　（動）（〜を）最大にする, 最大限にする, 最大限に増やす, 極限まで拡大［強化］する, 最大化する, 極大化する
　maximize access to market capital　市場から資金を最大限に調達する
　maximize profits　利益を最大にする, 利益を最大限に伸ばす, 利益を追求する
　maximize shareholders' value　株主の価値の最大化を図る, 株主の資産価値を極大化する
　maximize yields　利回りの最大化を図る, 利回りを最大限に高める
　◆Another characteristic of the U.S. management style is that businesses give priority to maximizing shareholders' value. 米国式経営スタイルのもうひとつの特色は, 企業が株主の資産価値の極大化を第一に考えることだ。

maximum　（名）最高, 最大, 最大量, 最大数, 上限　（形）最高の, 最大の, 最大限の
　achieve maximum value for the shareholders　株主の価値を最大限に高める
　maximum commission fees　手数料の上限
　maximum foreseeable loss　（保険の）予測可能最高限度額
　maximum liability　最大［極大］負債
　maximum limit system　（銀行券の）最高発行額制減制度
　maximum liquidity ratio　最高流動性比率
　maximum loan value　（担保付き融資の）貸出限度額
　maximum loss　最大損失, 最大損失額
　maximum pension provision　最高年金計上額
　maximum possible loss　（保険の）発生可能最高損害額
　　（=maximum foreseeable loss）
　maximum potential loss　最大予想損失額
　maximum rate of interest　最高金利, 最高利子率, 最高利率
　maximum-risk portfolio　最大危険ポートフォリオ, 危険性が最も高いポートフォリオ
　maximum stock　最高在庫, 最高在庫量
　maximum sustainable yield　最大持続生産量, MSY
　maximum yield　最高限度利回り
　probable maximum loss　（保険の）見込み最高損害額, 予想最高損害額　（=maximum probable loss）
　the maximum limit for interest rates　金利の最高限度, 付利最高限度
　◆Customers whose assets at the bank total about ￥10 million will receive a maximum of ￥2 million in insurance if their money is withdrawn illicitly by a third party with a bogus card. 同行では, 預け入れ資産が1,000万円程度の預金者が, 第三者に偽造カードを使って不正に預金が引き出された場合には, 最大200万円の保険金が支払われる。◆In the joint venture with an Indian investment bank, Tokio Marine Holdings Inc. put up about 26%, the maximum a foreign investor is

allowed in an Indian company, of the new firm's capital. インドの投資銀行との合弁事業で、東京海上ホールディングスは、新会社の資本金の約26％（外資の持ち分比率の上限）を出資した。◆The bank raised the amount of insurance money from the current ￥5 million limit to a maximum of ￥10 million for cash card fraud. 同行は、キャッシュ・カード詐欺の保険金額を、現在の上限500万円から最大1,000万円に引き上げた。◆The company will reduce the interest-bearing liabilities to a maximum ￥900 billion from 1.57 trillion in the same time frame. 同社は、上記期間に有利子負債を1兆5,700億円から最高9,000億円に削減する方針だ。

maximum insurance payments 保険金支払い額の上限
◆Under the earthquake insurance system, maximum insurance payments have been raised to ￥50 million for a house and ￥10 million for its contents since the 1995 Great Hanshin Earthquake. 地震保険制度では、1995年の阪神大震災以降、保険金支払い額の上限が住宅5,000万円、家財1,000万円に引き上げられた。

maximum interest rate 金利の上限,上限金利,最高金利 （=maximum interest rate）
◆The maximum interest rates of 15 percent to 20 percent are currently set under the Investment Deposit and Interest Rate Law and other laws. 出資法などの法律では現在、15～20％の上限金利が定められている。

maximum lending rate 貸出金利の上限
（=highest lending rate）
◆All four of Japan's major consumer loan firms will lower their maximum lending rates to below 20 percent. 国内消費者金融大手の4社すべてが、貸出金利の上限を20％以下（現行の出資法の上限金利は年29.2％）に引き下げる。

maximum limits 発行枠,発行限度,最高限度,最高限度額
◆Maximum limits for each type of new shares are ￥1.5 trillion for convertible preferred shares that can be converted into ordinary shares after a certain period; ￥1.5 trillion for another type of convertible preferred shares; and ￥1.5 trillion for nonconvertible preferred shares. 各種新株の発行枠は、一定期間後に普通株に転換できる転換型優先株が1兆5000億円ずつ、それに非転換型優先株が1兆5000億円となっている。

maximum potential loss 最大予想損失額
◆Our maximum potential loss may exceed the amount recognized in our balance sheet. 当社の最大予想損失額は、貸借対照表上で認識された額を上回る可能性があります。

MBI マネジメント・バイイン（management buy-in ［buyin］の略。買収者がターゲット会社の経営者ではなく、企業投資ファンドなどの部外者で、買収後は一般に取締役会に投資ファンドの代表者を派遣して会社の経営に深く関与する場合をMBIという）

MBO 経営者による自社買収,経営者による営業権取得,マネジメント・バイアウト
（⇒management buyout ［buy-out］）
◆A publisher's MBO was approved at its shareholders meeting. 出版社の経営陣による企業買収（MBO）が、同社の株主総会で承認された。

解説 MBOとは：企業の経営者が、一般株主や親会社などから自社株を買い取って、企業や事業部門の経営権を買い取ること。一般に、敵対的買収の防衛策や子会社が独立する際に用いられるM&A（企業の合併・買収）の手法。上場企業の場合は、経営陣が買収を実施する会社を別に設立し、自社の資産を担保にして投資会社や金融機関から融資を受け、その資金でTOB（株式公開買付け）を行い、一般株主から株式を広く買い集めることが多い。最近は、非上場にすることを目的に実施する例が目立っている。その背景には、敵対的買収への防衛策のほかに、株式持ち合いが崩れて年金基金のような「物言う株主」が増えてきたことなどの要因があるといわれる。親会社から自社株を買って子会社が独立する際の利点としては、社内体制が変わらないことや、親会社との関係が比較的良好に保たれる点が挙げられる。

MBS 住宅ローン担保証券,住宅ローン証券,モーゲージ証券 （=mortgage-backed product, mortgage-backed; ⇒ mortgage-backed securities）
◆The U.S. Federal Reserve Board will purchase mortgage-backed securities（MBS）until the end of the second quarter of 2009. 米連邦準備制度理事会（FRB）は、住宅ローン担保証券（MBS）を2009年第2四半期末まで買い取る。

McFadden Act of 1927 1927年マクファーデン法

mean （名）中間値,平均 （形）中間の,中位の,平均の
 a mean due date 平均期日
 the mean expectation of life 平均余命
 the mean interest rate 中心レート
 the mean number 平均数
 the mean price 平均証券価格
 the mean return 平均収益（全投資資産の予想収益の平均）
 the mean value 平均価値,平均値
 the monthly mean 月平均
 the weighted mean 加重平均

means （名）手段,方法,手だて,収入,財力,富,財産,資産
 a means to an end 目的達成の手段
 financial means 資金力
 limited means 小資本
 live within one's means 身分相応の暮らしをする,収入にあった生活をする
 man of means 資産家
 means of exchange 交換手段
 means of payment 支払い手段
 means of store of value 価値保蔵手段
 means test 資産調査,資力調査
 narrow means 窮乏
 policy means 政策手段
 resort to the final means 最後の手段に訴える
 visible means 有形資産
 ways-and- means advances 財源貸出金
 ways of means 歳入財源
◆German Chancellor Angela Merkel shut the door on the introduction of common eurozone bonds as a means to solve the debt crisis. ドイツのメルケル首相は、欧州債務危機問題の解決手段としてユーロ圏共通債を導入することに強く反対した。◆If the economy is to see a full-fledged recovery, the government should continue taking all feasible policy steps, including propping up the economy by fiscal means. 本格的な景気回復を見るには、財政面でのテコ入れを含めて、政府は引き続き実行可能なあらゆる政策手段を取るべきである。◆Non-life insurers are exploring new types of insurance demand and offering convenient and easy means of buying policies. 損保各社は、新たな保険需要を掘り起こして、いつでも、どこでも簡単に保険に加入できるサービスを提供している。◆Some European nations which are experiencing fiscal crises seem to rely on drops in their currencies' values as a means of underpinning their economies. 財政危機問題を抱えた欧州諸国の一部は、景気下支えの手段として通貨安を頼みにしているようだ。◆The government should take all possible fiscal and financial means to bring the still ailing economy back on the road to recovery. 政府は、いまだにどん詰まり状態にある景気を回復の軌道に乗せるために、財政と金融の両面からの政策を総動員すべきだ。

measure （動）測定する,計る,寸法をとる,調べる,評価する,見積もる,十分考慮する,慎重に選ぶ

◆The stress test by the EU's Committee of European Banking Supervisors measured the financial strength of Europe's major banks. 欧州連合(EU)の欧州銀行監督委員会が行ったストレス・テストで、域内主要銀行の財務の健全性を調べた。

measure [measures] (名)対策, 措置, 対応, 政策, 施策, 方策, 策, 手段, 比率, 指標, 尺度, 基準測定値, 測度 (⇒economic measures, stimulus measures)
  a set of measures　一連の措置, 一連の対策
  additional antideflationary measures　追加デフレ策
  additional monetary relaxation measures　追加の金融緩和策
  administrative measures　行政措置
  antideflationary measures　デフレ対策
  antiinflationary measures　インフレ対策, インフレ抑制策, インフレ措置
  austerity measures　緊縮財政策, 緊縮財政, 財政赤字削減策
  broad measure of money supply　広義のマネー・サプライ指標
  common measures　共同対策
  countermeasures　対抗措置, 対抗手段, 対策
  debt measures　債務比率
  defense measures　防衛策
  deficit reduction measures　赤字削減策
  economic stimulus measures　景気刺激策
  effective measures　効果的な対策
  emergency measures　緊急対策, 緊急措置
  fiscal measures　財政政策, 財政措置
  inflation measures　インフレ指標
  internal measures　社内対策
  lasting measure　恒久的措置
  liberalization measures　自由化措置, 規制緩和措置
  measure of risk aversion　リスク回避度
  monetary measures　金融政策, 金融措置
  narrow measure of money supply　狭義のマネー・サプライ指標
  package of measures　対策
  political measures　政策手段, 政策の手
  practical measures　具体策　(⇒upcoming)
  preferential measure　特例措置
  preventive measures　予防策, 予防の対策, 防止策, 対策
  protectionist measures　保護貿易政策, 貿易保護手段
  protective measures　保護措置, 対応策
  punitive measures　制裁措置, 報復措置
  reflationary measures　通貨調節策, リフレ対策
  restructuring measures　リストラ策
  retaliatory measures　報復措置
  safeguard measures　緊急輸入制限措置
  special tax relief measures　特別減税措置, 税金の特別減免措置
  stimulus measure　景気刺激策
    (=pump-priming measure)
  stock price measures　株価対策
  take additional monetary easing measures　追加金融緩和策を実施する
  take bold [decisive] measures　断固たる措置を取る
  temporary measure　時限措置
  workable measures　実行可能な施策

◆Additional measures will be needed to prevent the financial crisis from worsening. 金融危機の悪化を抑え込むには、追加措置[追加対策]が必要となろう。◆Doubts over the effectiveness of the announced stock price measures have already been expressed among Japanese market players. 今回発表された株価対策の効果については、日本の市場関係者の間ですでに疑問視する声がある。◆Every possible measure needs to be taken to end deflation. デフレ退治に、最善を尽くすべきだ。◆Greece has to agree to new austerity measures before it receives any financial aid from the European Union. ギリシャは、欧州連合(EU)の金融支援を受ける前に、追加の財政赤字削減策[緊縮財政策]に同意しなければならない。◆Measures to deal with surplus facilities are regarded as the center pillar of structural reforms to be initiated by the supply side. 過剰設備の処理対策は、供給サイドが着手する構造改革の柱とされている。◆Measures to expand and create employment are a pressing task. 雇用拡大と雇用創出策は、急を要する課題だ。◆Measures to lessen the problem of dual debts or multiple debts were also studied at the time of the 1995 Great Hanshin Earthquake. 二重ローンや多重債務問題の軽減策は、1995年の阪神大震災の際にも検討された。◆Priority measures to achieve economic recovery are stopping deflation and mobilizing all possible fiscal measures, financial policies and taxation reforms. 景気回復を実現するための優先課題は、デフレ阻止と、可能な財政政策、金融政策や税制改革を総動員することだ。◆Should the government relax its policy measures, the economy may start deteriorating once again. 政府が政策の手をここで緩めたら、景気はまた悪化する恐れがある。◆The Bank of Japan is considering taking additional monetary easing measures ahead of the next Monetary Policy Meeting. 次回の金融政策決定会合に向けて、日銀は現在、追加金融緩和策の実施を検討している。◆The Bank of Japan should take draconian measures to rectify the rise in the yen's value. 日銀は、厳しい円高是正措置を取るべきだ。◆The BOJ could take additional monetary relaxation measures if there are any changes in the financial situation. 金融面で動きがあるとすれば、日銀が追加の金融緩和策を実施する可能性もある。◆The European Union agreed on comprehensive measures to deal with the current fiscal and financial crisis. 欧州連合(EU)は、現在の財政・金融危機について、包括的な対応策で合意した。◆The G-7's financial ministers and central bank governors are committed to taking necessary measures to support financial stability and economic growth. 先進7か国(G7)の財務相と中央銀行総裁は、金融安定化と経済成長を支えるためにあらゆる手段を講じる決意だ。◆The measures of the European Banking Authority's stress tests have been only cosmetic. 欧州銀行監督機構(EBA)のストレス・テスト(健全性検査)の実施措置は、ほんの上辺[体裁]だけのものに過ぎなかった。◆The stimulation of consumption and job placement assistance are appropriate measures to prevent the economy from losing its momentum. 消費喚起(かんき)や就職斡旋[失業者の就職]支援は、景気の腰折れを防ぐ妥当な政策だ。◆The three ruling coalition parties asked Koizumi to suggest additional antideflationary measures within one month. 連立与党三党は、1カ月以内に追加デフレ策をまとめるよう小泉首相に要請した。◆To fulfill its responsibilities as the nation's central bank, the Bank of Japan must achieve currency stabilization by availing itself of a range of measures, including stabilization of the exchange rate. 日本の中央銀行としての責任を果たすには、日本銀行は、為替相場の安定を含めて広範な手段を活用して通貨の安定を実現しなければならない。◆U.S. President Barack Obama engineered a softer landing for GM with a set of measures to alleviate the bankruptcy shock as much as possible. オバマ米大統領は、GMの破たんショックを極力緩和するための一連の措置で、同社の軟着陸に向けた手を打った。

measures to ease monetary policy　金融緩和策
◆The central bank has deployed various measures to ease monetary policy, including cuts in the discount rate and hikes in the target for current account deposits held by commercial banks at the central bank. 日銀は、公定歩合の引下げ

や銀行が日銀に持つ当座預金の残高目標の引上げなどを含めて、各種の金融緩和策を実施してきた。

measures to reduce the debt burdens of heavily indebted poor countries 重債務貧困国の債務負担削減策
◆The government will propose measures to reduce the debt burdens of heavily indebted poor countries (HIPC). 政府は、重債務貧困国の債務負担削減策を提案する。

measures to safeguard the economy 経済危機を守るための措置
◆With the United States facing the worst financial crisis in generations, Bush's White House took decisive measures to safeguard the economy. 米国が過去最悪の金融危機に直面して、ブッシュ政権は経済危機を守るために断固たる措置を取った。

mechanism (名)機構, 構造, 仕組み, 制度, 方式, 方法, 機械装置, メカニズム
(⇒policy-based financing operations)
adjustment mechanism　調整機構
decision-making mechanism　意思決定機構, 政策決定機構
financial mechanism　金融メカニズム
financial support mechanisms　金融支援の仕組み
market [market-based] mechanisms　市場原理, 市場機構, 市場のメカニズム
policy-based financing operations　政策金融
self-regulating mechanism　自己調整機構
the price mechanism in the financial market　金融市場の価格メカニズム
◆By a mechanism the EU has developed, each EU country can inject taxpayer money into banks unable to increase capital on their own. EU（欧州連合）が整備した仕組みで、EU各国は、自力で資本増強を図れない銀行に対して公的資金を注入できるようになった。◆Policy-based financing operations which take advantage of government subsidies are adversely affecting the price mechanism in the financial market. 政府の補給金を受けて運営される政策金融は、金融市場の価格メカニズムを歪めている。◆The new plan is expected to introduce market mechanisms into the agricultural sector by moving to a system that guarantees the income of farmers. 新計画では、農家の所得保証制に移行することで、農業への市場原理導入を図る見通しだ。◆The stock market is a public mechanism to facilitate the smooth flow of money in the economy by serving as an intermediary between corporations and investors. 証券市場は、企業と投資家間の仲介役をつとめて日本経済に資金を円滑に流す役割を担う公共財だ。

media (名)媒体, 商品, マスコミ, 報道機関, メディア
a wide range of savings media　幅広い貯蓄商品
advertising media　広告媒体, 広告メディア
financial media　金融メディア
foreign media　外国の報道機関
mass communication media　マスコミ・メディア, マスコミ媒体, 報道機関
mass media　マス・メディア
media advertising　媒体広告
media mix　媒体ミックス, 広告媒体の組合せ, メディア・ミックス
media planning　媒体計画
media selection　媒体選択
media strategy　メディア戦略
news media　ニュース報道, 報道機関, マスコミ
print media　印刷媒体
savings media　貯蓄商品

median (形)中央の, 中間の, 中位の, 中心の　(名)中央値, 中位数, 中線, メディアン[メジアン]
median estimate　予測の中央値
median price　中心価格, 価格の中央値
median rate　中心相場, 仲値（売り相場と買い相場の平均相場）
median rate of spot dollars　ドル直物の中心相場
median value　価格の中央値
national median　全国中央値
◆The median price for an existing home dropped 8 percent in April, compared with a year ago. 4月の中古住宅の中心価格が、前年同月比で8%下落した。

Medicaid (名)国民医療扶助, 低所得者・身障者医療費補助制度, メディケイド　（米国の65歳未満の低所得者や身体障害者のための医療扶助で、州と連邦政府が共同で行う。⇒Medicare）

medical (形)医療の, 医用の, 医学の, 内科の, メディカル
medical accident [mishap]　医療事故
medical adviser　医者
medical and health insurance　医療健康保険
medical benefit　医療給付
medical certificate　診断書
medical checkup [examination]　健康診断, 人間ドック
medical corporation　医療法人
medical examination　健康診断, 診査
medical fee burden　医療費負担
medical history　既往症, 病歴
medical institution　医療機関, 医療施設
medical malpractice　医療過誤
medical malpractice insurance　医師賠償保険
medical officer　診療所医, 診療所員, 保健所員, 保健所長
medical payments insurance　医療費支払い担保保険
medical utilization review　診療内容検査
national medical expenditure　国民医療費

medical care system for the elderly　高齢者医療制度
◆The medical reform bills include a proposal to establish a new medical care system for the elderly. 医療改革法案には、高齢者医療制度の新設案が盛り込まれている。

medical costs　医療費　(=medical fees)
◆The share of medical costs paid by patients at medical institutions will be boosted to 30 percent from the current 20 percent for salaried workers from April next year. 患者が医療機関で支払う医療費の負担分が、サラリーマンの場合は来年4月から、現在の20%から30%に引き上げられる。

medical fees　医療費　(=medical costs)
◆The monthly maximum of medical fees borne by outpatients 70 or older will be raised. 70歳以上の外来患者が負担する医療費の月額上限が、引き上げられる。◆The portion of medical fees the elderly are obliged to pay increased. 高齢者の医療費の自己負担分が引き上げられた。

medical insurance　医療保険
◆Mitsui Sumitomo Insurance Co. was ordered to halt sales of medical insurance products for an indefinite period from July 10. 三井住友海上火災保険が、7月10日から医療保険商品販売の無期限停止命令を受けた。

medical services　医療サービス
◆A reorganization of medical services for the elderly already has been postponed. 高齢者医療サービスの再編は、すでに先送りされている。

medical system　医療制度
◆Everyone acknowledges the need to overhaul the medical system. 医療制度見直しの必要性は、誰もが認めるところだ。

Medicare (名)高齢者医療保障制度, 高齢者医療保険,

高齢者向け医療保険, メディケア
◆Bush is seeking $78 billion savings in the government's health care programs-Medicare for the elderly and Medicaid for the poor-over the next five years. ブッシュ米大統領は, 公的医療保険制度（高齢者のための「メディケア」と低所得者層のための「メディケイド」）の支出削減として, 今後5年で780億ドルの削減を求めている。

Medigap/Medisup （名）メディケア補足保険

medium-term economic program 中期経済計画
◆The medium-term economic programs of past governments did not bring about effective results as they lacked coherence with realistic policy and fiscal trends. 過去の政権の中期経済計画は, 実際の政策や財政動向との整合性を欠いたため, 実効は上がらなかった。

meet （動）（需要や要求などを）満たす, （目標などを）達成する, （基準を）クリアする［達成する］, うまく処理する, 対応する, 履行する, 費用などを支払う, 期待などに添う
  ability to meet claims on one's life policies 生命保険契約に基づく保険金請求の支払い能力
  ability to meet commitments to debtholders 債務返済能力
  ability to meet debt payments due 債務の返済能力
  ability to meet lease payments リース料支払い能力
  meet a criteria 基準を満たす, 基準をクリア［達成］する, 基準に適合する
  meet BIS equity standards BIS（国際決済銀行）の自己資本比率基準を達成する
  meet BIS guidelines BIS規制を達成［クリア］する
  meet customer needs 顧客のニーズに対応する, 顧客のニーズを満たす
  meet debt commitments 債務を返済する
  meet debt payments 債務を返済する
  meet demand 需要を満たす, 需要に応（こた）える［対応する］, 需要を賄（まかな）う, 需要に追い付く
  meet expenses 費用を支払う, 費用を賄（まかな）う
  meet increasing demand 需要増［需要の増加］に対応する
  meet investment criteria 投資基準を満たす, 投資基準に適合する
  meet investor needs 投資家のニーズを満たす
  meet margin calls 証拠金の支払い要求に応える
  meet one's large debt servicing commitments 巨額の債務返済を賄う
  meet the investor's risk guidelines 投資家のリスク基準を満たす
  meet the money supply target マネー・サプライ伸び率の目標を達成する
◆It is a matter of urgency to ensure that banks make profit margins that can meet investment risks and that they expand commission revenue as well as promote sweeping restructurings. 抜本的なリストラ推進のほか, 投資リスクに見合う利ざやの確保と手数料収入の拡大などが銀行の急務だ。◆Some firms that were willing to list their shares were unable to meet stock exchanges' eligibility criteria due to the economic slump. 株式上場を目指していた企業の一部は, 景気悪化で証券取引所の上場基準を満たすことができなかった。

meet one's obligations 債務を履行する, 債務を返済する
  fully meet one's obligations 債務を完全に履行する, 債務を完全に返済する
  meet one's debt obligations when due 債務を遅滞なく返済する
  meet one's short-term obligations 短期債務を返済する, 短期債務を履行する

meet requirements 必要条件［条件］を満たす, 必要額を賄（まかな）う, 要求に応じる, 基準を満たす
  meet cash capital requirements 資金需要を賄う
  meet cash capital requirements through internal cash generation 内部キャッシュ・フローで資金需要を賄う
  meet debt service requirements 返済の原資を確保する, 債務返済額を確保する
  meet regulatory requirements 規制上の条件を満たす, 規制上の要件に適合する
  meet the additional cash requirements 追加資金必要額を賄う
  meet the cash buyout requirements 現金支払いの要求に応じる
  meet the margin requirements 証拠金率を満たす
◆External funds required to meet the additional cash requirements in 2012 will be obtained by offering debt securities in the market. 2012年度内に発生する追加資金必要額を賄（まかな）うための外部調達資金は, 市場で債券を募集発行して調達する予定です。

meeting （名）会議, 会, 総会, 大会, 理事会, 場, ミーティング （⇒general meeting, shareholders meeting）
  annual general meeting 年次総会, 年次株主総会
  board meeting 取締役会会議, 取締役会
  Branch Manager Meeting 日銀支店長会議
  Bundesbank meeting ドイツ連銀理事会
  closed meeting 非公開協議
  company result meeting 会社の決算発表記者会見
  creditors' meeting 債権者会議, 債権者集会
  due diligence meeting 新証券発行説明会
  extraordinary general meeting 臨時株主総会
  extraordinary meeting 臨時総会（米国ではspecial meetingという）
  financial summit meeting 金融サミット
  first general meeting 創立総会
  G-7 meeting 先進7か国会議（G7）
    （=G-7 financial meeting, G-7 talks）
  general meeting of stockholders [shareholders] 株主総会
  IMF-World Bank annual meetings IMFと世銀の年次総会
  inaugural meeting 創立総会
  informational bank meeting 銀行連絡会
  IR meeting 投資家説明会, IRミーティング
  managing directors' meeting 常務会
  meeting of bondholders 社債権者集会
  monthly monetary meeting 月次金融会議
  noteholders meeting 債券保有者会議
  one-on-one meeting 投資家との個別ミーティング
    （=one-to-one meeting）
  ordinary council meeting 定例理事会
    （=regular council meeting）
  policy meeting 政策決定会合, 金融政策決定会合, 政策会議
  qualified meeting 適格会議
  regular general meeting 定例総会, 定例株主総会
    （=ordinary general meeting）
  stockholders [shareholders] meeting 株主総会
    （=shareholders' meeting, stockholders' meeting）
  the Bank of Japan's Monetary Policy Meeting 日銀金融政策決定会合
◆At the financial summit meeting in Washington, additional pump-priming measures through strengthening cooperation

between advanced countries and emerging economies will be a major subject of discussion. ワシントンで開かれる金融サミットでは、先進国と新興国の連携強化による追加景気対策の検討が、主要テーマとなる。◆At the latest G-20 meeting, diverging opinions among member countries were exposed over expanding the lending capacity of the IMF. 今回のG20（財務相・中央銀行総裁）会議では、国際通貨基金（IMF）が融資できる資金規模の拡大をめぐって、加盟国の間で意見の食い違いが表面化した。◆At two financial summit meetings since the collapse of Lehman Brothers, agreements were made on cooperation to implement large-scale economic stimulus measures and to take monetary relaxation policies. リーマン・ブラザーズの倒産［破たん］以来2回開かれた金融サミットでは、連携して大型の財政出動や金融緩和策を実施することで合意が得られた。◆In Europe, buffeted by the U.S. financial crisis, four major countries have held a summit meeting to discuss countermeasures. 米金融危機の煽（あお）りを受けた欧州では、主要4か国が最近、首脳会議を開いて対策を協議した。◆The Bank of Japan started a two-day policy meeting. 日銀の2日間の日程で行われる金融政策決定会合が、始まった。◆The BOJ is prepared to hold its policy meeting ahead of schedule if the yen's value further soars before the next meeting. 次回の政策決定会合までに円高が一段と進めば、日銀は会合を前倒しして会合を開く構えだ。◆The BOJ's policy meeting plans to consider expanding the list of government bonds purchased under the fund. 日銀の政策決定会合では、基金で買い入れる国債の対象拡大を検討する予定だ。◆The G-7 meeting has repeatedly issued communiques concerning exchange rate fluctuations and economic policy management. 先進7か国会議（G7）は、これまで為替変動や経済政策運営に関する声明を再三、発信してきた。◆The government held a meeting on the current economic situation. 政府が、現在の経済情勢に関する会合を開いた。◆The 17 eurozone countries agreed to expand the European Financial Stability Facility at a meeting of their finance ministers. ユーロを採用しているユーロ圏17か国は、ユーロ圏財務相会合で、欧州金融安定基金（EFSF）の規模を拡大することで一致した。◆The U.S. Federal Reserve Board left U.S. rates unchanged at a key policy meeting. 米連邦準備制度理事会（FRB）は、重要な政策会議（公開市場委員会）で米国の金利（公定歩合とFF金利の誘導目標）を据え置くことを決めた。

meeting of representatives of policyholders 保険会社の総代会 （=meeting of, policyholder representatives, policyholders' representative meeting: 株式会社の株主総会に当たる）
◆The plan will be officially decided upon at a meeting of representatives of policyholders in July. この案は、7月の総代会で正式に決定される。

mega banking group 大手金融グループ
◆The nation's mega banking groups have been realigning their securities units to offer comprehensive financial services. 国内の大手金融グループは、総合金融サービスを提供するため、グループ各社の証券会社を再統合している。

megabank （名）超巨大銀行, 巨大銀行, 巨大銀行グループ, メガ銀行, メガバンク
◆As of the end of June 2010, the core tier 1 capital ratios of the three Japanese megabanks are said to be between 5 and 7 percent. 2010年6月末時点で、日本の3大メガバンクの中核的自己資本比率は5〜7％とされる。◆Domestic megabanks are increasing their financing activities overseas. 国内メガバンクは、海外での融資活動を強化している。◆Domestic three megabanks are moving to step up their overseas lending. 国内の3メガバンクは、海外融資を強化する方針だ。◆Japanese megabanks and Toyota were among the beneficiaries of a slew of emergency liquidity-providing facilities devised by the U.S. Federal Reserve Board. 日本のメガバンクやトヨタも、（2008年秋の金融危機に伴って）米連邦準備制度理事会（FRB）の発案で実施された大規模な緊急貸出制度の恩恵を受けた［緊急貸出制度を活用していた］。◆Japan's four megabanks are now rebuilding their global business strategies. 日本の4大金融グループは現在、グローバル戦略の再構築に取り組んでいる。◆The bank appears to be left out of the market competition among megabanks. 同行は、メガバンク間の市場での競争から取り残されているようだ。◆The merger will prompt other megabanks to come up with new strategies to reinforcing their corporate health. この統合は他のメガバンクを刺激し、メガバンクは企業体質の強化に向けた戦略を新たに打ち出すことになろう。◆The recent circumstances facing the nation's megabanks have shown up their weaknesses, as shown by slow progress in their efforts to write off their non-performing loans and a sharp decline in their stock prices. 日本のメガバンク（巨大銀行グループ）が直面している最近の状況を見ると、不良債権処理策の遅れや株価の急落などが示すように、メガバンクの脆弱（ぜいじゃく）性が目立っている。

megabank group 巨大銀行グループ, メガ銀行グループ, メガバンク・グループ
◆Mitsubishi UFJ Financial Group, Mizuho Financial Group and Sumitomo Mitsui Finance Group are the nation's three megabank groups. 三菱UFJフィナンシャル・グループ、みずほフィナンシャルグループと三井住友フィナンシャルグループは、日本の3大メガ銀行グループだ。◆The nation's three megabank groups expect a sharp increase in profits in their half-year consolidated business results through the end of September. 日本の3メガバンクは、9月連結中間決算で、大幅増益を見込んでいる。

日本の3大メガバンク

Mitsubishi UFJ Financial Group　三菱UFJフィナンシャル・グループ

Mizuho Financial Group　みずほフィナンシャルグループ

Sumitomo Mitsui Financial Group　三井住友フィナンシャルグループ

megacompetition （名）大競争

megamerger ［mega-merger］ 超大型合併, 超巨大合併
◆Some U.S. companies are beginning to spin off divisions after being forced to review the effect of the megamergers that swept U.S. industries in the 1990s. 米国企業の一部は、1990年代に米産業界を襲った超大型合併の効果の見直しを迫られた結果、事業部門の分社化に着手している。

meltdown （名）（株価の）暴落, 急落, 下落, 底割れ, 市場の崩壊, 市場の暴落［急落］, 経営破たん, 崩壊, 経済の溶解, メルトダウン

a possible financial meltdown　想定される［想定された］金融崩壊

accelerate the meltdown of the global economy　世界経済のメルトダウン（溶解）を加速する

economic meltdown　経済のメルトダウン（溶解）

financial market meltdown　金融市場の崩壊, 金融市場のメルトダウン（溶解）

financial meltdown　金融崩壊, 金融危機, 金融のメルトダウン（溶解）, 金融市場のメルトダウン

global stock price meltdown　世界の株価底割れ, 世界の株価メルトダウン（底割れ）

housing mortgage meltdown　住宅ローン市場の崩壊

Meltdown Monday　ニューヨーク株式市場の株価暴落, 株価大暴落

stock price meltdown　株価底割れ, 株価メルトダウン（底割れ）

the meltdown in U.S. subprime mortgages　米国のサブプライム・ローン（低所得者向け住宅ローン）市場の崩壊

the mortgage meltdown　住宅ローン市場の崩壊
◆A U.S. housing mortgage meltdown shook the United States, Europe and other countries and slammed the brakes

on global growth. 米国の住宅ローン市場の崩壊は、米欧その他の諸国を揺さぶり、世界経済の成長に急ブレーキをかけた。◆Although the economic meltdown was continuing in Russia in September 1998, the size of its economy was relatively small. 1998年9月当時、ロシアでは経済のメルトダウン（溶解）が続いていたが、その経済規模は相対的に小さかった。◆Goldman Sachs Group Inc. emerged from the global financial meltdown as Wall Street's most influential bank. ゴールドマン・サックスは、ウォール街最大手の金融機関として世界的な金融危機を乗り切った。◆Goldman Sachs Group Inc. is said to have marketed risky investments that bet on the housing market's growth just before the mortgage meltdown. ゴールドマン・サックスは、住宅ローン市場の崩壊直前に、住宅市場の成長を見越した［予想した］高リスクの金融商品［投資商品］を販売したとされる。◆The financial bailout bill's passage into law marks progress in avoiding a financial meltdown. 金融安定化法案［金融救済法案］が法律として成立したことは、金融危機を回避するうえで一歩前進したといえる。◆The financial crisis stemmed from a U.S. housing mortgage meltdown. 今回の金融危機は、米国の住宅ローン市場の崩壊から始まった。◆The guard raised against a possible financial meltdown during a financial sector-triggered recession several years ago has been lifted. 数年前の金融不況時に想定された金融崩壊に対する厳戒態勢は、すでに解かれている。

memorandum 覚書, メモ, 意見書, メモランダム条項
（memorandum clause）
◆The company's president and heads of the two other companies signed a memorandum on the business tie-up agreement. 同社社長と他の2社のトップが、業務提携契約に関する覚書に署名した。

merchandise coupon 商品券

merchandise trade surplus モノの貿易黒字, 財の貿易黒字, 貿易収支の黒字額, 商品貿易の黒字
（=surplus in merchandise trade）
◆The merchandise trade surplus plunged 22.2 percent to ¥8.99 trillion, with exports down 7.3 percent to ¥46.18 trillion and imports down 2.8 percent to ¥37.19 trillion. モノの輸出額が7.3％減の46兆1,800億円、輸入額が2.8％減の37兆1,900億円で、貿易収支の黒字額は22.2％減の8兆9,900億円となった。

merge （動）合併する, 吸収合併する, 経営統合する
（⇒streamline）
merge into 経営統合［合併］して〜になる, 経営統合して〜の傘下に入る
merge with 〜と合併する
merging company 消滅会社
◆One of the aims for the three banks to merge into the Mizuho Financial Group was to survive the global competition by exploiting the banks' combined strength. 3行がみずほフィナンシャルグループに合併する目的（狙い）の一つに、3行の統合力を駆使して国際競争に勝ち抜くことがあった。◆Sanwa Bank and Tokai Bank have merged to form UFJ Bank. 三和銀行と東海銀行が合併して、UFJ銀行が誕生した。◆Seibu and Sogo department stores merged into Millennium Retailing Inc. in 2003. 西武百貨店とそごう百貨店が2003年に経営統合して、ミレニアムリテイリングの傘下に入った。◆Shinsei and Aozora banks announced a plan to merge in an effort to expand their customer bases and improve earnings. 新生銀行とあおぞら銀行は、顧客基盤の拡大と収益力の強化を狙って、合併計画を発表した。◆Shinsei and Aozora banks have abandoned their plan to merge. 新生銀行とあおぞら銀行が、両行の合併計画を断念した。◆The Tokyo Stock Exchange and the Osaka Securities Exchange have officially agreed to merge in January 2013. 東証と大証は、2013年1月に経営統合することで正式に合意した。◆The TSE and the OSE will merge into the world's No.2 exchange group. 東証と大証が統合して、世界第2位の株式取引所グループが誕生する。◆Two major insurers from different financial groups plan to merge in a bid to overcome serious management crises. 深刻な経営危機を乗り切るため、系列の異なる金融グループの大手保険会社2社が合併を計画している。

merge operations 経営統合する
（=integrate operations）
◆The two companies will merge their operations under a holding company to be set up next October. 両社は、来年10月に持ち株会社を設立して経営統合する。

merger （名）合併, 経営統合, 統合, 吸収合併, 併合 （⇒industry realignment, megamerger, operational integration）
accounting for acquisitions and mergers 企業取得と合併の会計
conglomerate merger 複合的合併, コングロマリット合併
exchange ratio of merger 合併比率
（=merger ratio）
full-scale merger talks 合併の本格交渉
giant merger 大型合併
horizontal merger 水平的合併
large merger 大型合併 （=big merger）
market extension merger 市場拡大的合併
mega-merger 超大型合併, 超巨大合併
（⇒megamerger）
multi-merger 多角的合併
outright merger 友好的合併
the planned merger of Meiji and Yasuda 明治と安田両社の合併計画
vertical merger 垂直的合併
◆After the merger, the TSE and OSE will be divided into four operator firms handling spot trading, derivatives, settlement of trading deals and self-imposed regulations respectively. 経営統合後、東証と大証は、それぞれ現物株、デリバティブ（金融派生商品）、取引決済と自主規制を扱う4事業会社に切り分けられることになっている。◆An urgent task facing each financial group is to improve its financial conditions and profitability on the strength of advantages gained from merger. 合併・統合の相乗効果を生かして、財務内容と収益力を向上させることが、各金融グループの現在の急務だ。◆If the merger takes place, it will create a full-scale financial conglomerate with a major bank, a major securities house and credit card company under its umbrella. 統合すれば、傘下に大手銀行と大手証券、クレジット・カード会社などを持つ本格的な金融コングロマリット（金融複合企業体）が誕生する。◆It is highly likely that the merger between the two financial institutions will be postponed. 両金融機関の統合が延期されるのは必至だ。◆The company has held merger talks with other two medium-sized general contractors. 同社は、他の準大手ゼネコン2社と経営統合の協議をしている。◆The merger between the TSE and the OSE will create the world's second-largest exchange group in terms of the total market value of listed shares. 東証と大証の経営統合で、上場株式の時価総額で世界第2位の株式取引所グループが誕生する。◆The merger may help dispel policyholders' distrust in life insurers. 今回の合併で、契約者の生保不信をある程度一掃できるかもしれない。◆The merger of NYSE Euronext with Deutsche Boerse will create the world's largest exchange operator. NYSEユーロネクストとドイツ取引所の合併で、世界最大の取引所運営事業者が誕生する。◆The merger will create the world's largest financial group with assets totaling about ¥190 trillion. この経営統合で、総資産約190兆円の世界最大の金融グループが誕生する。◆The merger will prompt other megabanks to come up with new strategies to reinforcing their corporate health. この統合は他のメガバンクを刺激し、メガバンクは企

業体質の強化に向けた戦略を新たに打ち出すことになろう。◆Through the TSE-OSE merger in January 2013, the two exchanges must enhance their strategies to ensure survival as a major stock market in Asia. 東証と大証の2013年1月の経営統合をテコに、両証券取引所は、アジアの主要市場として勝ち残る戦略を強化する必要がある。◆Volks will be the surviving company in the merger, but the Osaka Securities Exchange sees Don will be the virtual surviving company. 合併での存続会社はフォルクスだが、事実上の存続会社は「どん」になると大阪証券取引所は見ている。◆We have received a number of proposals from investment banks who want to act as go-betweens between drug companies for mergers. 投資銀行からは、製薬会社の経営統合の仲介をしたい旨の提案が数多く来ている。

merger and acquisition 企業の吸収合併, 合併・買収, 企業取得と合併, M&A
(=mergers and acquisitions; ⇒shareholder)
◆Amid the economic slowdown, many major U.S. companies have been forced to review their strategies after the mergers and acquisitions they pursued failed to produce the expected synergy. 景気減速のなか、米国の大企業の多くは、追求したM&Aで予想したシナジー（相乗）効果が上げられないため、戦略の見直しを迫られている。

[解説] M&A関連用語：
black knight 暗黒の騎士, 敵対的買収者, 企業乗っ取り屋, ブラック・ナイト
corporate raider 企業買収の仕掛け人, 乗っ取り屋, 買占め屋
defensive merger 防衛的合併
golden parachute 黄金の落下傘, ゴールデン・パラシュート
greenmail 法外な価格での株の買戻し, グリーンメール
greenmailer グリーンメールで金儲けをする人, グリーンメーラー
junk bond ジャンク債, くず債券, 投資不適格の信用度の低い債券
leveraged buyout 借入金による企業買収, レバレッジド・バイアウト, LBO
Pac-Man defense パックマン防衛 逆転攻撃, パックマン・ディフェンス
poison pill defense ポイズン・ピル防衛, 毒薬条項防衛, 毒入り避妊薬
scorched-earth tactic 焦土作戦（敵対的買収に備えて、会社の最優良資産などを売却して会社の価値を減少させること）
shark repellent サメ駆除剤（敵対的買収に備えて、定款を改正したり転換優先株などを発行して買収コストを高めたりすること）
shark watcher サメ監視人（企業買収の動きを専門に監視する会社）
white knight 白馬の騎士, 友好的買収者, ホワイト・ナイト
white squire 純白の従者, ホワイト・スクワイア

merger and acquisition deal M&A（合併・買収）取引
◆The recent increase in merger and acquisition deals will boost revenues and corporate value. 最近のM&A（合併・買収）取引の増加は、企業収益の増加や企業価値の向上につながる。

merger deal 合併協議, 合併計画
◆Shinsei and Aozora banks have dropped their merger deal. 新生銀行とあおぞら銀行が、両行の合併計画を断念した［合併協議を中止した］。

merger plan 合併計画, 経営統合計画
◆Shinsei Bank may join hands with other banks despite the cancellation of a merger plan with Aozora Bank in May 2010. 新生銀行は、2010年5月にあおぞら銀行との合併計画が撤回された［破談になった］が、他行と連携する可能性がある。◆The merger plan will not go ahead unless the bank makes unstinting efforts to cut its nonperforming loans. 同行が不良債権の削減に向けて惜しみない努力をしないかぎり、統合計画が前に進むことはないだろう。

merger proposal 経営統合案
◆AOKI Holdings Inc., the nation's second-largest menswear chain, has submitted a merger proposal to Futata Co. 紳士服チェーン国内2位のAOKIホールディングスが、（同業の）フタタに経営統合案を提出した。

merger ratio 合併比率, 統合比率
◆The upcoming negotiations will determine practical measures to strengthen ties, including the merger ratio, the name of the new group and the positions to be held by top executives. 今後の交渉で、統合比率や新グループの名称、首脳人事など提携強化の具体策を詰める。

merger talks 合併交渉
◆The companies established a project team of a small number of officials to undertake full-scale merger talks. 両社は、少人数の役員のプロジェクト・チームを設けて、合併の本格交渉をした。

mergers and acquisitions 企業の合併・買収, 企業の吸収合併, M&A （⇒merger and acquisition）
◆Fewer than half of the shareholders of the 700 or so companies involved in mergers and acquisitions profited from the mergers and acquisitions. M&Aを行った企業約700社の株主のうち、M&Aで利益を得たのはその半数以下である。◆Hostile mergers and acquisitions have been increasing rapidly as the dissolution of cross-shareholding ties among companies accelerates. 企業間の株式持ち合い関係の解消が加速するにつれ、敵対的M&A（企業の合併・買収）の件数は急増している。◆The current system requires the shareholders of companies absorbed in mergers and acquisitions to be given stocks of surviving companies. 現行の制度は、企業の吸収合併の際、吸収合併される会社の株主に対して存続会社の株式を交付することを義務付けている。◆The mergers and acquisitions many major U.S. companies pursued failed to produce the expected synergy effect. 米国の大企業の多くが追求したM&Aは、予想したシナジー（相乗）効果を上げられなかった。◆The two prospective partners have extensive expertise in mergers and acquisitions, as well as the securitization of bad loans. 提携する予定の両社は、企業の合併・買収（M&A）や不良債権の証券化などに豊富なノウハウを持っている。

merit rating （保険契約での）実績料率決定方式, メリット制 (experience rating), 人事考課

merit system 優待制度, 実力本位制, 能力主義任用制

mess （名）混乱, 混乱状態, 散乱, 散乱状態, 乱雑, 紛糾事態, 困った事態［立場］, 苦境, 窮境, 窮地, 困難, 問題, へま, 失敗, 取り散らかしたもの, 汚いもの, ごみの山
a mess of pottage 目先の小利, 犠牲の大きすぎる小利
financial market mess 金融市場の混乱
get into a mess 困ったことになる, 窮地に陥る
make a mess of 〜を台なしにする, 〜をめちゃめちゃにする, 〜をぶち壊す
sell one's birthright for a mess of pottage 目先の小利にこだわって大利を失う
subprime mortgage mess サブプライム・ローン問題
◆The financial market mess in Europe was triggered by the delay of financial assistance to Greece by the European financial authorities. 欧州の金融市場混乱の引き金となったのは、欧州金融当局によるギリシャへの金融支援のもたつきだ。◆The financial turmoil is caused by the U.S. subprime mortgage mess and soaring oil and materials prices. 金融市場の混乱は、米国のサブプライム・ローン問題と原油・原材料価格の高騰によるものだ。

method (名)方法, 手法, 方式, 手順, 順序, 筋道, 基準, 主義, メソッド
 accounting method　会計処理方法
 accrued benefit cost method　発生給付原価方式
 accrued benefit valuation method　発生給付評価方式
 actuarial cost method　保険数理原価法
 actuarial method　年金利回り法
 advance funding method　事前積立方式
 aggregate (cost) method　総合保険料方式
 annuity method　年金法
 annuity method of depreciation　年金式減価償却法
 attained age method　到達年齢方式
 attained age normal method　正常到達年齢方式
 average return on investment method　平均投資収益率
 banker's discount method　銀行割引法
 business method　経営手法
 capital recovery method　資本回収法
 capitalization method　収益還元法
 closed aggregate cost method　閉鎖型総合保険料方式
 collection method　回収基準
 current-noncurrent method　流動・非流動法
 current rate method　決算日レート法
 deposit method　預り金処理法
 dollar average method　ドル平均法
 dollar pool method　ドル・プール法
 entry (age) cost method　加入年齢方式
 equity method　持ち分法
 equity method investment　直接投資
 fixed rate method　定率法
 individual level premium method　個人水準保険料方式
 installment method　割賦基準
 interest method　利息法
 interest method (of) amortization　利息法
 liability method　負債法
 market price method　時価主義, 時価法, 時価方式
 market value method　時価法
 method of compound interest　複利計算法, 複利法
 method of payment　支払い方法
 method of simple interest　単利計算法, 単利法
 monetary-nonmonetary method　貨幣・非貨幣法
 moving average (cost) method　移動平均法
 net of tax method　税引き後法
 projected benefit cost method　将来給付予測原価方式
 rate of return method　利回り法
 retrospective deposit method　遡及預金法
 return on investment method　投資利益率法
 subscription method　引受方式
 tender panel method　競争入札制度
 terminal funding method　年金現価充足方式
 translation method　換算方法
 treasury stock method　自己株式法
 underwriting method　全額引受方式
 unit credit method　単位年金積み増し方式
 weighted average method　加重平均法, 総平均法
◆Major moneylender SFCG earned an unsavory reputation for its strong-arm loan collection methods. 金融業者大手のSFCG(旧商工ファンド)の評判は、債権の取立てが強引で芳しくなかった。◆Outsourcing is a strategic method that effectively uses business resources. It is actively utilized in Europe and the U.S. by venture businesses that lack adequate human resources. アウトソーシングは、経営資源を有効に活用するための戦略的手法です。これは、欧米では、人的資源を十分に確保できないベンチャー企業によって積極的に活用されています。◆The change in the method of calculating deferred tax assets has driven each of the banking groups into a corner. 繰延べ税金資産の算定方式の変更が、銀行グループ各行を窮地に追い込んでいる。◆The eurozone countries agreed to strengthen EFSF functions, such as bailout methods, in July 2011. 2011年7月にユーロ圏諸国は、支援手法など欧州金融安定基金(EFSF)の機能を強化することで合意した。

metric ton [tone] メートルトン(1メートルトン＝1,000キログラム)
◆According to the World Gold Council, central banks have bought 198 metric tons of gold so far this year. 世界金評議会によると、今年は、世界各国の中央銀行がこれまでに(2011年8月22日現在で)198メートルトン(19万8,000キログラム)の金を買い入れた。

mezzanine (形)メザニン型の, 中間的[一時的]に介在する, 中間に位置する
 mezzanine bond　メザニン債(優先債と劣後債の中間に位置する「メザニン債」は、一般にトリプルB(BBB)以下の格付けとなる)
 mezzanine debt　メザニン型負債[債務], メザニン負債, 無担保ローンの借入金
 mezzanine field　中間に位置する分野
 mezzanine finance　メザニン融資, メザニン型資金調達, 中二階金融, メザニン・ファイナンス (=mezzanine financing, mezzanine funding: 企業買収の際に資金調達方法の一つとして高金利の無担保ローンを利用する方式。また、会社清算時の受取順位が、優先債権には劣後するが、普通株には優先する劣後債(subordinated debenture)などによる資金調達を意味する場合もある)
 mezzanine financing　転換融資, 中間的資金調達, メザニン型資金調達 (=mezzanine finance)
 mezzanine funds　メザニン投資ファンド
 mezzanine money　転換社債
 mezzanine subordination　準劣後請求権
◆Domestic and foreign insurance companies are scrambling to introduce new products in the so-called third sector—a mezzanine field between life and nonlife insurance, such as medical, cancer and nursing insurance. 国内外の保険各社は、第三分野(医療やがん、介護保険など生命保険と損害保険の中間に位置する保険分野)と呼ばれる医療保険の商品開発[商品導入]にしのぎを削っている。

MHA (米国の)住宅取得支援策(Making Home Affordable Planの略)

micro-enterprise development loan fund マイクロ・ローン基金

micro hedge [hedging] 個別ヘッジ, ミクロ・ヘッジ

microcredit (名)小口融資, 少額融資, マイクロクレジット (=microlending)

microlending (名)小口融資, 少額融資 (=microcredit)

mid [mid-] (形)中央の, 中部の, 中間の, 中期の
 in terms of mid-market　中値で
 mid- and long-term interest rates　中長期金利
 mid-cap stock　中型株
 mid-market　中間市場, 中級品市場, 中値
 mid-market price [value]　市場レートの中値
 mid-maturities　中期物
 mid-point of the target range　目標圏の中間値
 mid-point rate　中間レート
 mid-spread price　中値
 mid-to-long-term plan　中長期経営計画

mid-to-upper 後半の
mid-year 中間期
mid-year company estimates 中間期の会社予想
◆Speculation the Bank of Japan will end its quantitative monetary easing policy soon has sparked a rise in mid- and long-term interest rates. 日銀が近く量的緩和策を解除するとの思惑から、(金融市場では)中長期の金利が上昇し始めた。

MidCap 中型株
FT-SE MidCap 250 index FTSE中型株250種指数
FT-SE 250 MidCap stock index FTSE中型株250種指数

midcareer [mid-career] (形)中途の, 昇進停滞の, ミッドキャリアの
mid-career plateau 昇進停滞点, 昇進停滞段階
midcareer employment 中途採用
midcareer hiring 中途採用

midcareer personnel 中途社員, 中堅社員
◆Many manufacturers are considering measures such as extending the retirement age and hiring more midcareer personnel and new graduates. 製造業者の多くは、退職年齢の延長や中途採用・新卒の拡大などの対策を検討している。

midcareer recruiting 中途採用
◆As for midcareer recruiting, some companies will hire more experienced workers to make up for a lack of new graduate recruitment. 中途採用については、一部の企業は、経験者を増やして新卒採用の人員不足を補う方針だ。

middleman (名)仲買人, 仲卸業者, 仲介者
◆A financial intermediary acts as a middleman between cash surplus units in the economy (savers) and deficit spending units (borrowers). 金融仲介機関は、経済の資金余剰主体(貯蓄者)と資金不足主体(借り手)との間に立つ仲介者として機能している。

midsize general contractor 中堅ゼネコン, 準大手ゼネコン
(=medium-sized general contractor; ⇒merger)
◆Aoki Corp. is among 10 midsize general contractors whose debts have been waived by financial institutions. 青木建設は、金融機関から債権放棄を受けている中堅ゼネコン10社の中に入っている。

midterm [mid-term] (名)中間, 中間試験 (形)中間の
midterm closing 中間決算 (=midterm settlement of accounts, semiannual closing)
midterm spreads 中期物スプレッド

midterm report 中間決算, 中間決算報告, 半期報告, 中間報告 (=interim report, midterm business report, midterm earnings report)
◆The fiscal 2011 midterm reports for most firms listed on the First Section of the Tokyo Stock Exchange have been released. 東京証券取引所の一部上場企業の2011年9月中間決算が、ほぼ出揃った。

midterm results 中間決算, 半期の業績
◆What is noteworthy in the midterm results is the 6 percent increase in sales resulting from an increase in product prices and sales volumes. 中間決算で特筆できるのは、製品の価格の上昇と販売数量の拡大で、売上高が6%伸びたことだ。

midterm settlement of accounts 中間決算
(=interim settlement of accounts)
the midterm settlement of accounts to Sept. 30 9月中間決算
the September midterm settlement of accounts 9月中間決算
◆For the midterm settlement of accounts to Sept. 30, the firm expects announce an operating profit of ￥270 billion. 9月中間決算で、同社は2,700億円の営業利益を発表する見通しだ。◆The seven major banking groups' September midterm settlement of accounts is expected to record an estimated ￥1.95 trillion in latent gains. 大手7行・金融グループの9月の中間決算では、推定で1兆9,500億円の含み益が出る見通しだ。

midyear account settlement 中間決算
◆With the midyear account settlement scheduled in September, concerns over the stability of the nation's financial system inevitably will grow again should stock prices dip further. 9月中間決算を前に、株価がさらに下がれば、再び日本の金融システム不安が当然、台頭してくる。◆With the midyear account-settlement term coming in September, there is a concern that falling stock prices may seriously damage business performance. 9月中間決算を控えて、株安(株価の下落)が企業業績に大きなダメージを与える懸念がある。

midyear accounts 中間決算
◆Banks are about to settle their midyear accounts. 銀行は、これから中間決算をまとめるところだ。

MIGA 多国間投資保証機関(Multinational Investment Guarantee Agencyの略)

mild (形)軽い, 軽微な, 緩(ゆる)やかな, 穏やかな, 寛大な, 温厚な, 優しい, 影響の少ない, ちょっとした, 刺激の少ない
mild downturn 軽い景気後退
mild inflation 緩やかなインフレ
(=creeping inflation)
mild recession 緩やかな景気後退, 軽微な景気後退
mild recovery 穏やかな回復

mileage point マイレージ・ポイント
(=mileage point)
◆Mizuho Bank offers a service by which ATM cardholders are given mileage points each time they use the new cards as credit cards, purchase financial products at the bank's branches or receive loans from the bank. みずほ銀行が提供しているサービスでは、キャッシュ・カード会員が新型カードをクレジット・カードとして利用したり、みずほ銀で金融商品を購入したり、ローンを利用したりすると、その取引に応じて毎回、マイレージ・ポイントがもらえる。

mini [mini-] (形)小型の, 軽微の, ミニ〜
mini-cycle in growth 景気のミニサイクル
mini-max [minimax] bond ミニマックス債
(=minimax)
mini-max principle ミニマックス原理[原則]
(=minimax: 予想される最悪の結果のうち、最小の損失をもたらす行動を選択すべきである、とする戦略理論)
mini-recession 軽微なリセッション[景気後退]
(=minor recession)
upleg of the mini-cycle ミニサイクルの上昇局面

minibudget (名)小型補正予算

minimization (名)最小化, 極小化, 軽減
cost minimization 費用[コスト]極小化
(=minimization of cost)
income tax minimization 所得税の軽減
risk minimization リスク極小化

minimize (動)最小限に抑える[とどめる], 最小限にする, 最小限に減らす, 最小限に評価する, 軽く見る, 軽視する, 見くびる, (画面などを)小さくする
(⇒stimulus measures)
minimize adverse effects on the stock market 株式市場への悪影響を最小限に抑える
minimize capital investment [outlay] 設備投資を最小限に抑える
minimize the risk of 〜の危険性[リスク]を最小限にする, 〜のリスクを最小限に抑える
◆The benefit of fund-of-funds investment is that it allows investment risks to be minimized. 投資リスクを最小限に抑える

のが、ファンド・オブ・ファンズ投資の利点である。◆While minimizing possible adverse effects on the stock market, private consumption and corporate performances, the U.S. central bank will ensure the United States' economic recovery. 株式市場や個人消費、企業業績などへの考えられる悪影響を最小限に抑えながら、米連邦準備制度理事会は、景気回復を確実なものにして行く方針だ。

minimum (名)最低, 最小, 最小限, 最小値, ミニマム (形)最低の, 最小の, 最小限の
  minimum capital　最低資本金, 最低自己資本
  minimum capital adequacy ratio　最低自己資本比率
  minimum guarantee　最低保証金
  minimum lease payments　最低リース支払い額, 最低賃借料等支払い額
  minimum lending rate　最低貸出金利
  minimum margin　最低利幅
  minimum pension provision　最低年金計上額
  minimum profit　最低利益, 最小利幅
  minimum subscription　最小株式引受限度
  minimum tax　ミニマム税, ミニマム・タックス (通常の法人税、所得税に追加して課される税)
  ◆The move to inject liquidity into Dubai's banks by the central bank of the United Arab Emirates was seen by analysts as the bare minimum. ドバイの銀行に資金を供給するアラブ首長国連邦 (UAE) の中央銀行の動きを、アナリスト (専門家) は「最低限必要な量にすぎない」と見ている。

minimum capital adequacy ratio　最低自己資本比率
  ◆Under the rules of the Bank for International Settlements, the minimum capital adequacy ratio required of banks operating internationally is 8 percent. 国際決済銀行 (BIS) の規則では、国際銀行業務を行っている銀行に要求される最低自己資本比率は、8％である。

minimum capital requirements　最低必要資本金額, 会社設立時に必要な最低資本金, 最低資本金の要件 (=minimum capitalization requirements, minimum regulatory capital requirements)
  ◆The minimum capital requirements of ￥10 million for the establishment of a stock company have been eliminated under the new Corporate Law. 株式会社を設立する場合の1,000万円の最低資本金規制は、新会社法で撤廃された。

minimum core capital requirements　最低自己資本規制, 最低自己資本必要額, 最低必要自己資本金額, 最低必要自己資本, 必要な最低自己資本
  ◆The Basel Committee on Banking Supervision agreed on a new framework for calculating minimum core capital requirements for leading financial institutions. バーゼル銀行監督委員会は、主要金融機関 [主要銀行] の最低必要自己資本を算定するための新たな枠組みについて合意した。

minimum core tier 1 capital ratio　最低中核的自己資本比率, 最低中核資本比率
  ◆Proposals were initially floated in the Basel Committee on Banking Supervision that the minimum core tier 1 capital ratio be set between 6 and 8 percent from the current 2 percent. バーゼル銀行監督委員会では当初、最低中核的自己資本比率を現行の2％から6〜8％に引き上げる案が、浮上していた。

minimum regulatory capital requirements　最低必要資本金, 最低必要資本金制度
  ◆The minimum regulatory capital requirements were abandoned. (会社設立時の) 最低必要資本金制度は、廃止された。

minor (形)さほど大きくない, 小規模な, 中小の, 少数の, 小額の, 比較的重要 [重大] でない, 影が薄い, 軽微な, 割と軽い, 二流の, 二流以下の, 未成年の, 年下の, 短音階の, マイナー (⇒major)
  minor activities　小規模事業
  minor adjustments　微調整, わずかな調整, 軽い調整
  minor (business) cycle　小循環
  minor changes　ちょっとした変更, マイナー・チェンジ
  minor coins　小額貨幣
  minor enterprise　中小企業
  minor industry　中小企業, 中小産業
  minor player　中小企業 [組織、団体], 二流 [二流以下の] 選手
  minor recession　軽微な景気後退 [リセッション] (=mild recession, mini-recession)
  minor share [stock]　少数株, 雑株
  minor stockholders' interest　少数株主権
  minor total　小計

minority (名)少数, 少数持ち分, 少数派, 少数集団, 少数民族, 未成年 (⇒majority)
  a specified minority of owners　特定の少数株主
  be in the [a] minority　少数派である
  buyout of minorities　少数株主持ち分の買取り (=minority buyout)
  policies in favor of minorities　少数民族の優遇政策
  ◆A company's stock will be delisted if more than 80 percent of outstanding shares are held by a specified minority of owners for more than one year. 流通株式 [上場株式数] の80％超を特定の少数株主が1年を超えて保有した場合、その会社の銘柄は上場廃止となる。

minority (形)少数の, 少数持ち分の, 少数派の, 少数民族の
  minority buyout　少数持ち分の買取り
  minority entrepreneur　少数民族企業家
  minority equity　少数株主持ち分, 少数株主権
  minority ownership　少数者所有
  minority shareholder　少数株主 (=minority stockholder)
  minority shareholders' equity　少数株主持ち分
  minority stockholder's right　少数株主権

minority interest　少数株主持ち分, 少数株主持ち分利益, 少数株主損益, 少数利益, 過半数以下の出資, 少数株主権
  income before income taxes, minority interest and cumulative effect of accounting changes　法人所得税、少数株主損益 [少数株主持ち分利益] および会計方針の変更による累積的影響額控除前利益
  minority interest in common stock　少数持ち分―資本金
  minority interest in consolidated subsidiaries　連結子会社の少数株主持ち分
  minority interest in net income　少数株主持ち分利益
  minority interests in earnings/loss　少数株主損益
  ◆Minority interests represent other companies' ownership interests in our net assets. 少数株主持ち分は、当社の純資産に対する他社の所有者持ち分を表します。◆The provisions, after giving effect to taxes and minority interest, reduced 2011 earnings by $200 million. これらの引当金繰入れで、関連税額と少数株主持ち分利益控除後2011年度の純利益は、2億ドル減少しました。

mint (名)造幣局, 貨幣鋳造所, 未使用の貨幣, 発行したばかりの貨幣 [切手], 宝庫, 巨額の金, 多大, 多量
  in mint condition [state]　真新しい, 新品同様の
  mint par　法定平価 (=mint par of exchange)
  mint parity　法定平価 (=mint par)
  mint price　造幣価格, 鋳造価格
  mint rate　法定比価
  mint ratio　金銀比価, 造幣比率, (造幣) 法定比価
  mint remedy　(鋳貨の) 法定公差

the mint par of exchange　為替法定平価, 法定平価
the U.S. Mint　米造幣局
the U.S. Mint's sales of American Eagle gold coins　米造幣局のアメリカン・イーグル金貨[米イーグル金貨]の販売高
◆The U.S. Mint's sales of American Eagle gold coins have totaled 91,000 ounce so far in August. 米造幣局のアメリカン・イーグル[米イーグル]金貨の販売総量は、9月1日以降現時点で9万1,000オンスに達している。

mintage　(名)造幣, 貨幣鋳造, 鋳貨
mintmark　(名)造幣所の刻印
minus　(形)マイナスの
　a minus tick　値下がり　(=a down-tick)
　be a minus factor for　～のマイナス要因である, ～の減点材料である
　minus growth　マイナス成長
minuscule　(形)極めて小さい[低い], すごく小さい
　minuscule interest rates　超低金利
◆The high yields of the yen-denominated government bonds were considered considerably higher than minuscule domestic interest rates. この円建て国債は、国内の超低金利に比べて利回りがはるかに大きいと見られた。

mirror　(動)反映する, 映し出す, 映す, ～とよく似ている
◆The firm's growth has mirrored its cost-cutting efforts. 同社のこれまでの成長は、同社のコスト削減努力を反映している。
mirror　(名)鏡, 反射鏡, ミラー
　employ mirror transactions　反対取引を行う
　mirror symmetry　鏡面対称, 左右対称
　mirror trade　反対取引　(=mirrored trade)
　provider of mirror swaps　反対スワップの提供者

misappropriation　(名)流用, 不正流用, 不正目的使用, 悪用, 着服, 横領, 使い込み
　fund misappropriation　資金の流用, 資金の着服
　　(⇒fund misappropriation)
　misappropriation of any copyrights, trademarks or trade secrets　著作権、商標または営業秘密の不正使用
　misappropriation of company assets　会社資産の横領, 会社資産の流用
◆A fund misappropriation by the firm's former chief executive officer surfaced in early June 2009. 同社の前最高経営責任者(CEO)による資金の不正流用事件が、2009年6月はじめに発覚した。

misery index　経済不快指数
misgiving　(名)不安, 懸念, 心配, 疑念, 疑い, 疑惑, 不信の念
　dispel misgivings about　～に関する疑念を払拭(ふっしょく)する, ～の疑惑を一掃する
　feel misgivings　危惧(きぐ)を覚える
　have misgivings about　～に疑念[不振の念, 不安]を抱く, ～を心配[懸念]する, ～に不安がある, ～に危惧を覚える
　the sense of misgiving　不安感
　the sense of misgiving in the financial system　金融不安
◆The most worrying thing, in terms of future, is the sense of misgiving in the financial system. 今後、最も懸念されるのは、金融不安だ。

mislabeling　不当表示, 不正表示, 偽装表示
　(⇒financial strength)
◆A series of recent mislabeling scandals show that this wicked practice is common among meat dealers. 最近の一連の偽装表示事件は、この悪質な行為が食肉販売業者の間では常態化していることを示している。◆The company was severely criticized by the public for its mislabeling of beef products. 同社は、牛肉の偽装表示で社会的に厳しく非難された。

mislabeling fraud　偽装工作
◆The focal point of the investigation was whether the mislabeling fraud had been carried out systematically. 調査の焦点は、偽装工作が組織ぐるみで行われたのかどうか、という点にあった。

misleading information　虚偽の情報
◆The banking unit illegally obstructed the recent financial regulators' inspections by reporting misleading information about its nonperforming loans. 同行は、不良債権に関する虚偽の情報を報告して、金融当局の最近の検査を違法に妨害した。

mismanagement　(名)ずさんな管理[経営], 管理の誤り, 経営の失敗, 失政, 不始末, やりそこない
◆If the creditor banks forgive the debts though TEPCO is not carrying excess liabilities, senior managements of the lenders may be sued in a shareholders' lawsuit over mismanagement. 東電が債務超過ではないのに債権保有銀行が債権を放棄すると、ずさんな経営で、金融機関の上級経営陣は株主代表訴訟で訴えられる可能性がある。

mismatch　(動)誤った組合せをする, 不釣り合いな組合せをする
　mismatched asset/liability maturities　資産・負債の満期のミスマッチ
　mismatched FRN　ミスマッチ変動利付き債, ミスマッチ債
mismatch　(名)満期不対応, ミスマッチ債, ずれ, ミスマッチ　(=mismatching)
　address mismatches in currency and interest rates through swap agreements　スワップ取引で通貨と金利のミスマッチを調整する
　asset/liability mismatch　資産と負債のミスマッチ
　hedge mismatches between floating interest rates　変動金利間のミスマッチをヘッジする
　interest rate mismatch　金利のミスマッチ
　maturity mismatch　期間のミスマッチ
　mismatch bond [floater, FRN]　ミスマッチ債
　mismatch issue　ミスマッチ債
　offset mismatches through diversification　分散によってミスマッチを相殺する
　payment mismatch　利払いのミスマッチ
　timing mismatch　タイミングのずれ
◆We must address the improvement of employment situation, particularly in regard to jobs for young people and the mismatch between job seekers and job openings. われわれとしては、特に若年層の雇用や求職者と新規雇用のミスマッチなどの面で、雇用状況の改善に取り組まなければならない。

mismatching　(名)ミスマッチ　(=mismatch: 資金調達と資金運用の期間対応のずれや金利・金額などに不一致がある状態)
　accept mismatching [mismatch risk]　ミスマッチ・リスクを許容する
　interest rate mismatching　金利のミスマッチ

misnomer　(名)誤った名称, 名前の誤用, 誤称, 人名[氏名]の誤記
misrepresentation　(名)不当表示, 虚偽の表示, 不実告知, 告知義務違反
miss　(動)～に当たらない, ～を外(はず)す, ～に届かない, ～を獲得しそこなう, ～を見そこなう, 見逃す, (約束などを)果たせない, (目標に)達しそこなう, ～に乗り遅れる, 間に合わない, ～を抜く[省略する], ～を欠く, ～がいないのを寂しく思う, ～に気付く, 避ける, 逃れる, 免れる　(名)的外れ, 失敗, ミス
　miss a target　目標を達成できない
　miss out　参加しない, ～を逃す, ～を抜かす[外す]

miss out on　〜の機会を逃す
miss the boat［bus］　好機を逃す,好機を逸する,時流に乗りそこなう
miss the larger points　大局を見失う
miss the mark　目的を果たさない,役に立たない
miss the market　買い場［売り場］を失う,注文執行の好機を逃す
miss the point　要点を理解しない
missed or delayed disbursement of interest　金利の未払いと支払いの遅延
missed payments　未払い,延滞率
◆Greece will miss 2011-12 deficit targets imposed by international lenders as part of the country's bailout. ギリシャは、同国救済措置の一環として国際融資団（欧州連合（EU）や国際通貨基金）が課した2011-12年の赤字削減目標を、達成できないようだ。◆The debate misses the larger points. この論争は、大局を見失っている。
missing passbook　紛失通帳
misstatement　（名）虚偽表示,虚偽記載,不実表示,誤表示（=misrepresentation）
◆Freddie Mac revealed its misstatement of earnings. フレディ・マック（米連邦住宅貸付抵当公社）が、利益の不実表示をしていたことを明らかにした。
MIT　条件付き成り行き注文,MIT注文（market-if-touched（order）の略）
mitigate　（動）緩和する,軽減する,和らげる,抑える
mitigate economic downturns　景気後退を抑える
mitigate the risks　リスクを緩和する
mix　（名）構成,組合せ,混合,比率,内容,中身,ミックス
asset mix　資産構成,資産配分
asset/liability mix　資産・負債構成
business mix　事業構成,事業内容（=mix of business）
currency mix of foreign exchange reserves　外貨準備の通貨構成
export mix　輸出構成
mix between long and short-term debt　長期負債と短期負債の比率
mix of loans　融資の構成
policy mix　政策手段の最適組合せ,経済政策ミックス,ポリシー・ミックス
portfolio mix　ポートフォリオの構成,有価証券の中身,ポートフォリオ・ミックス
product mix　商品構成,製品構成,製品組合せ,製品ミックス,プロダクト・ミックス
stock/bond mix　株式・債券ミックス
Treasury's borrowing mix　新発債の満期構成
◆The government denied to change the currency mix of its foreign exchange reserves. 政府は、外貨準備の通貨構成の変更を否定した。
mixed　（形）混合した,混じった,兼営の,兼業の,複雑な
mixed assets-debt position　混合資産負債ポジション
mixed bank　兼営銀行
mixed banking　兼営銀行主義
mixed collateral　混合担保,混合抵当
mixed credit　（援助資金と輸出信用の併用による資金調達の）混合借款
mixed currency　（硬貨と紙幣の）混合通貨
mixed duties　（従価税と従量税を併用した）複合関税,混合関税
mixed economic data［news］　強弱まちまちの［強弱相半ばする］景気指標
mixed economy　混合経済

mixed joint stock company　半官半民会社,混合株式会社
mixed loan　混合抵当債権
mixed perils　混合危険
mixed policy　混合保険証券
mixed property　混合財産
mixed reaction to the issue　同債に対する市場のまちまちの反応
Mizuho Financial Group　みずほグループ
ML$　マレーシア・ドル
MLR　最低貸出金利（minimum lending rateの略）
MMA　市場金利連動型預金勘定,マネー・マーケット・アカウント（money market accountの略）
MMC　市場金利連動型定期預金（money market certificateの略）
MMDA　市場金利連動型預金勘定,市場金利連動預金,金融市場口座（money market deposit accountの略）
MMF　マネー・マネージメント・ファンド（money management fundの略）
MMF　市場金利連動型投資信託,マネー・マーケット・ファンド（money market fundの略）
MMF　月次金融会議（monthly monetary meetingの略）
MMI　メジャー・マーケット株価指数（Major Market Indexの略）
MML　市場金利連動型貸出（money market loanの略）
MMMF　市場金利連動型投資信託,短期証券投資信託（money market mutual fundの略）
MMN　マネー・マーケット・ノート（金利を35日ごとに入札で決める証券）
MMP　マネー・マーケット優先株（money market preferredの略）
mobile charges　携帯利用料金
◆In the case of au Insurance's cell phone-based policy sales, policyholders are allowed to pay premiums by adding them to monthly mobile charges. au損保険の携帯電話での保険販売の場合、保険契約者は、保険料を携帯利用の月額に加算して保険料の支払いをすることができる。
mobile phone　携帯電話
◆In insurance policies that can be purchased via mobile phone, would-be policyholders do not need to input personal data and payments are easier. 携帯電話で加入できる保険では、加入希望者は個人情報を入力する必要がなく、支払いも簡単だ。◆Nonlife insurers are offering customers a new way to purchase insurance, using mobile phones with information transmission capabilities. 損害保険各社が、情報通信機能がある携帯電話を使って保険に加入できる新サービスを提供している。
mobile phone number　携帯電話の番号
◆Loan sharks lure borrowers through billboards and ads that bear only mobile phone numbers. ヤミ金融業者は、携帯電話の番号しか載せていない看板や広告で客を集めている。
mobilize　（動）動員する,結集する,〜を戦時体制にする,流通させる
◆Many of major banks have no choice but to mobilize parts of their legally prescribed capital reserves. 大手銀行の多くは、法定資本準備金にまで手をつけざるを得ない。◆Priority measures to achieve economic recovery are stopping deflation and mobilizing all possible fiscal measures, financial policies and taxation reforms. 景気回復を実現するための優先課題は、デフレ阻止と、可能な財政政策、金融政策や税制改革を総動員することだ。◆The government should mobilize all workable policy steps so as to create more jobs in rural areas. 政府は、実行可能なあらゆる政策手段を動員して、地域の雇用を拡大しなければならない。
moderate　（動）縮小する,低下する,下がる,鈍化する,

減速する, 抑える, 和らげる, 弱める, 低下させる, 点検する, 監査する
continue to moderate　縮小［減少, 鈍化］傾向が続く
moderate competitive threat　競争圧力を弱める
moderate international lending　対外融資［貸出］を抑える, 国際融資を抑える
moderate profitability　収益性を低下させる
moderate returns on investment　投資収益率［利益率］を低下させる
moderate wage growth　賃金の伸びを抑える
◆The pace of U.S. consumer price increases moderated in June. 米国の消費者物価の上げ幅は, 6月は縮小した。

moderate　(形)適度の, 中程度の, 中位の, 小幅な, 穏健な, 緩やかな, 並みの, 格安の, 安価な, 手頃な
moderate demand　需要薄
moderate discount　緩やかな証券発行差金
moderate growth　緩やかな伸び［成長, 経済成長］
moderate inflation　緩慢なインフレ, 軽度のインフレ
moderate level　緩やかな水準, 中程度の水準
moderate recovery　緩やかな景気回復
moderate supply　供給薄
◆The economy is seeing further signs of a moderate recovery. 景気は, 一段と緩やかに回復している兆しが見られる。

momentum　(名)はずみ, 勢い, 余波, 惰性, 契機, 要素, モメンタム
earnings momentum　収益力
gather momentum　勢いを増す, 拡大する, 活発化する
increase the political momentum　政治的はずみをつける
inflationary momentum　インフレの勢い
lose momentum　失速する
loss of growth momentum　景気の失速
momentum of the growth　経済成長の勢い
price momentum element　株価のモメンタム要素
recovery momentum　景気回復の勢い
the current momentum in the yen　現在の円相場の勢い
◆Capital investment, which was the engine for the overall economy, has lost much of its momentum. 景気全体を引っ張ってきた設備投資に, 一時の勢いがなくなっている。◆Debates on the pros and cons of a proposal to end the quantitative relaxation of credit by the Bank of Japan are gathering momentum. 日銀による量的金融緩和策を解除する案の賛否をめぐる議論が, 活発化している。◆Goldman Sachs lowered its forecast for U.S. growth in 2011 on signs that the U.S. economic recovery lost momentum. 米金融大手のゴールドマン・サックスは, 米景気回復減速の兆しを受けて, 2011年の米国の成長見通しを下方修正した。◆Japan's exports, which had been supporting the business boom, lost momentum. 景気を支えてきた日本の輸出が, 失速した。◆The current momentum in the yen is likely to take hold. 現在の円相場の勢いは, 持続しそうだ。◆The economic recovery seems to be picking up momentum. 景気回復に, 勢いが出てきたようだ。◆The economy is beginning to lose momentum as exports and capital investments are slowing. 輸出と設備投資が息切れを始め, 景気に減速傾向が出ている。◆The market is gathering momentum. 市場は上向きだ。◆The momentum for a self-sustaining recovery in domestic private demand remains weak. 国内民間需要の自律回復の勢いは, まだ弱い。◆The stimulation of consumption and job placement assistance are appropriate measures to prevent the economy from losing its momentum. 消費喚起（かんき）や就職斡旋［失業者の就職］支援は, 景気の腰折れを防ぐ妥当な政策だ。◆The threat of a deflationary spiral is gaining momentum daily. デフレ・スパイラルの恐れは, 日に日に拡大している。◆With the economic recovery gaining momentum, U.S. companies have begun investing in the Japanese stock market again, giving a lift to stock prices. 景気回復が力強さを増していることから, 米国企業が日本の株式市場に再び投資するようになり, 株価を押し上げている。

monetarism　(名)通貨主義, マネタリズム（経済活動関連の政策手段のうち, 貨幣政策の役割を最重視する立場）

monetarist　(名)通貨主義者, マネタリズム支持者, マネタリスト　(=monetary school)
monetarist analysis　マネタリスト的分析　(=monetarist approach)
monetarist approach　マネタリスト的アプローチ
monetarist policy　マネタリスト的政策
monetarist theory　マネタリストの理論

monetary　(形)通貨の, 貨幣の, 金融の, 財政上の, 金銭の, 金銭上の, マネタリー
in monetary difficulties　資金難で, 財政難で, 財政困難で
International Monetary Market　国際通貨市場
monetary action　貨幣的措置
monetary adjustment　金融調節
monetary administration　金融調節
monetary affairs　財務, 金銭問題
monetary aggregate　金融総量, 量的金融指標, 貨幣的集計量（通貨供給量の指標）, 通貨供給量, マネー・サプライ
monetary aggregate targets　マネー・サプライ伸び率目標圏
monetary agreement　通貨協定　(=payment agreement)
monetary analysis　貨幣分析
monetary and financial policy　通貨・金融政策
monetary and fiscal policies　金融・財政政策
monetary approach　貨幣法（貨幣の需要・供給に注目する国際収支の分析方法）
monetary arrangements　通貨協定, 貨幣取決め
monetary assistance　金融支援, 金融援助
monetary banking system　貨幣銀行制度
monetary bloc［block］　通貨ブロック
monetary capital　貨幣資本, 金融資本
monetary capital formation　金融資本形成
monetary change　貨幣的変化
monetary circulation　通貨の流通, 流通通貨
monetary conditions　金融情勢, 金融環境
monetary control　貨幣的統制
monetary convertibility　通貨の自由交換性
monetary convulsion　通貨混乱
monetary correction　貨幣的矯正　(=monetary indexation)
monetary cost　貨幣原価
monetary damages　金銭賠償
monetary debt　貨幣的負債
monetary decisions　金融政策
monetary decrease　貨幣減少
monetary deflation　通貨収縮
monetary demand　貨幣需要
monetary deposit　通貨性預金
monetary developments　マネー・サプライの動向
monetary device　金融調節手段, 金融調節装置
monetary discipline　金融節度
monetary discretion　金融政策
monetary disequilibrium　貨幣的不均衡

monetary disorder　金融混乱, 通貨混乱
monetary donations　企業献金
monetary dynamics　貨幣的動学
monetary ease　金融緩和
monetary economics　金融経済学, 貨幣経済学
monetary economy　金融経済, 貨幣経済
monetary effect　貨幣的効果
monetary equilibrium　貨幣的均衡
monetary excess　過剰流動性
monetary expansion　金融緩和, 通貨拡大　(=monetary ease, monetary easing, monetary relaxation)
monetary expenditure　貨幣的支出
monetary expert　通貨専門家
monetary facilities　金融機関
monetary factor　貨幣的要因
monetary financial intermediary　貨幣的金融仲介機関
monetary-fiscal neutrality　金融・財政の中立性
monetary-fiscal policy　金融・財政政策
monetary forced savings　貨幣的強制貯蓄
monetary forces　貨幣的要因
monetary framework　貨幣的構造
monetary function　金融機能, 貨幣機能
monetary gift to the landlord　礼金
monetary gold　貨幣用金
monetary growth　マネー・サプライ伸び率
monetary growth figures　マネー・サプライ統計
monetary incentive　金銭的誘因
monetary income　貨幣所得
monetary increase　貨幣増加
monetary indicators　金融指標
monetary indirect security [securities]　貨幣的間接証券
monetary inflation　通貨膨張, 貨幣的インフレ
monetary instability　通貨不安　(=monetary uncertainty, monetary unrest)
monetary institution　金融機関
monetary instrument　貨幣調節手段
monetary integration　通貨統合
monetary interest　貨幣利子
monetary legislation　金融立法
monetary liability　貨幣性負債, 貨幣負債
monetary market　通貨市場, 貨幣市場
monetary measurement convention　貨幣的測定の公準
monetary measures　金融政策, 金融調節手段, 貨幣的措置
monetary meeting　金融会議
monetary multiplier　貨幣乗数, 通貨乗数
monetary official　金融当局 [通貨当局] 高官
monetary officials　金融当局, 通貨当局
monetary overinvestment theory　貨幣的過剰投資説
monetary phenomenon　貨幣的現象
monetary rate of interest　貨幣利子率
monetary reform　通貨改革
monetary regime　金融体制
monetary regulation　金融調整, 貨幣調整
monetary regulatory measures　金融調節手段, 貨幣調節手段
monetary repercussion　貨幣的波及過程
monetary reserve base　通貨準備ベース
monetary reserves　通貨準備
monetary resources　財源, 手持ちの現金

monetary restraint　金融引締め　(=credit restraint, monetary tightening, tight money)
monetary restraint policy　金融引締め政策　(=monetary stringency, monetary tightening policy, tight money policy)
monetary reward　金銭的報酬
monetary sampling　金融サンプリング
monetary school　貨幣的景気理論学派　(=monetarist)
monetary sector　金融部門, 通貨部門
monetary situation　金融事情, 金融情勢, 金融状態
monetary slowdown　マネー・サプライ伸び率の低下
monetary sovereignty　金融自主権
monetary stability　通貨安定, 貨幣的安定
monetary stabilization　通貨の安定化, 通貨安定化, 通貨安定政策
monetary standard　貨幣標準, 貨幣本位, 本位制度
monetary standard policy　本位制策
monetary statics　貨幣静学
monetary statistics　マネー・サプライ統計
monetary stimulus　金融緩和
monetary stress and strain　金融逼迫 (ひっぱく), 金詰り　(=financial pressure, monetary stringency)
monetary stringency　金融逼迫 (ひっぱく), 金詰り　(=financial pressure, financial stringency, tight money)
monetary structure　金融構造, 貨幣構造
monetary supply　通貨供給量, 貨幣供給 [供給量]　(=money supply)
monetary support　金融支援, 金融面での援助
monetary survey　金融調査
monetary system　通貨制度, 金融制度, 貨幣組織
monetary target　マネー・サプライの増加目標値, マネー・サプライの目標水準, マネタリー・ターゲット
monetary theorist　マネタリスト　(=monetarist)
monetary theory of business cycles　貨幣的景気循環論
monetary theory of trade cycle　貨幣的景気循環論
monetary token　貨幣章標
monetary tool　金融手段, 金融調節手段
monetary transaction　金融取引
monetary transfer　貨幣的トランスファー
monetary turmoil　通貨不安
monetary union　通貨統合　(=monetary integration)
monetary unit　貨幣単位, 通貨単位, MU　(=currency unit)
monetary unit sampling　金額単位サンプリング
monetary unrest　通貨不安
monetary upheaval　通貨変動, 通貨量の激動
monetary valuation　貨幣的評価
monetary value　金銭の価値, 貨幣価値
monetary war　通貨戦争
monetary wealth　貨幣的資産, 貨幣的富
monetary working capital　貨幣運転資本
monetary working-capital adjustment　貨幣運転資本修正
monetary/nonmonetary method [approach]　貨幣・非貨幣法

monetary assets　貨幣性資産, 金銭債権　(=financial assets, money assets:「貨幣性資産」は、貨幣そのものまたは法令や契約によってその金額が固定している資産のことで、現金、預金、売掛金、受取手形、貸付け金などがこれに含まれる。これに対して、将来費用となる棚卸

し資産などの資産を「費用性資産」という）
long-term monetary assets　長期貨幣性資産
monetary financial assets　通貨性金融資産
◆Current assets (excluding inventories and prepaid expenses), current liabilities, and long-term monetary assets and liabilities are translated at the exchange rates in effect at the balance sheet date. 流動資産（棚卸資産と前払い費用を除く）、流動負債と長期貨幣性資産および負債は、貸借対照日［決算日］現在の実効為替レートで換算してあります。

monetary authorities　金融当局, 通貨当局
a large yen-selling intervention by monetary authorities　金融当局による大量の円売り介入
monetary authorities in the United States and Europe　欧米の通貨当局
overseas monetary authorities　外国通貨当局, 海外［国外］金融当局
◆A large yen-selling intervention by monetary authorities on Sept. 15 failed to reverse the yen's rising trend. 金融当局が9月15日に実施した大量の円売り介入で、円高傾向を反転［逆転］させることはできなかった。◆Japanese monetary authorities intervened in the foreign exchange market to stop the sharp rise in the yen's value against the dollar. 日本の金融当局［通貨当局］は、急激な円高［円高・ドル安］を食い止めるため、外為市場介入を実施した。◆The government and the Bank of Japan are considering joint market intervention with the U.S. and European monetary authorities to produce the greater results of their market intervention. 政府・日銀は、市場介入の効果を高めるため、米欧の通貨当局との協調介入を検討している。◆This intervention was not coordinated with monetary authorities in the United States and Europe. 今回の介入は、欧米の通貨当局との協調介入ではなかった。

monetary base　マネタリー・ベース, 貨幣的ベース
(=high-powered money base, money base: 日本銀行券発行高、貨幣流通高と日銀当座預金（民間金融機関の中央銀行預け金）の合計で、日銀が金融市場に供給している資金の残高を示す)
an expansion of the monetary base by the Bank of Japan　日銀の金融の量的緩和
expand monetary base　マネタリー・ベースを拡大する
reduce monetary base　マネタリー・ベースを縮小する
the average daily balance of the monetary base　マネタリー・ベースの1日平均残高
◆An expansion of the monetary base by the Bank of Japan alone would be limited in its effect. 日銀の金融の量的緩和だけでは、その効果に限界がある。◆The average daily balance of the monetary base in May 2011 totaled about 114.42 trillion. 2011年5月のマネタリー・ベースの1日平均残高は、約114兆4,200億円となった。◆The monetary base is composed of Bank of Japan notes, cash in circulation, and the balance of current account deposits held by financial institutions at the Bank of Japan. マネタリー・ベースは、日本銀行券、貨幣流通高と金融機関が日銀に預けている［日銀に保有する］当座預金の残高から成る。◆The monetary base shrank 21.1 percent in January from a year ago. 1月のマネタリー・ベース（日銀券発行高、貨幣流通高、日銀当座預金の合計）は、前年同月比で21.1%減少した。◆The nation's monetary base in May 2011 increased 16.2 percent from a year earlier as the Bank of Japan continued its abundant fund supply operations following the March 11 disaster. 東日本大震災（2011年3月11日）を受けて日銀が潤沢な資金供給オペを続けたため、日本の2011年5月のマネタリー・ベースは、前年同月比で16.2%増加した。◆The nation's monetary base leaped by 32.6 percent in March from a year earlier. 日本の3月のマネタリー・ベースは、前年同月比で32.6%増加した。

monetary base balance　マネタリー・ベースの残高
◆The monetary base balance for May totaled ¥108.83 trillion. 5月のマネタリー・ベースの残高は、108兆8,300億円だった。

monetary claim　金銭債権
monetary claims for housing loans　住宅貸付け債権
monetary claims purchased　買入れ金銭債権
monetary claims trust　金銭債権信託

monetary control　金融調節, 通貨調節, 通貨供給量の調節, 通貨供給量制御, 金融管理
monetary and credit controls　金融・信用規制, 金融調節, 金融統制
Monetary Control Act　通貨管理法

monetary crisis　通貨危機, 金融危機, 貨幣恐慌
◆The government has set aside ¥15 trillion to inject into public funds in case a monetary crisis happens. 金融危機が生じた場合に公的資金を注入するため、政府は15兆円をすでに用意している。

monetary easing　金融緩和, 金融政策の緩和, 利下げ
(=monetary ease, monetary expansion, monetary relaxation)
comprehensive monetary easing　包括的金融緩和
the Fed's monetary easing　米連邦準備制度理事会（FRB）の金融緩和, 米中央銀行の金融緩和
◆The Fed's monetary easing is a factor causing disarray in the foreign exchange markets. 米連邦準備制度理事会（FRB）［米中央銀行］の金融緩和が、為替相場混乱［為替混乱］の原因だ。

monetary easing measures　金融緩和策
◆Surplus funds put out by developed economies' monetary easing measures have flowed into emerging economies to inflate economic bubbles. 先進国の金融緩和策で生じた余剰資金が、新興国に流れ込み、バブルを発生させている。◆The Bank of Japan has long been implementing monetary easing measures. 日銀は、金融緩和を長年続けている。◆The Bank of Japan is considering taking additional monetary easing measures ahead of the next Monetary Policy Meeting. 次回の金融政策決定会合に向けて、日銀は現在、追加金融緩和策の実施を検討している。

monetary easing policy　金融緩和策
◆Coupled with the Bank of Japan's monetary easing policies, the antideflationary measures displayed the government's determination to avert the feared "March financial crisis." 日銀の金融緩和策と併せて、このデフレ対策は、「3月金融危機」を回避する政府の決意を示した。◆Major currencies are rising against the dollar on account of the Fed's monetary easing policy. 米連邦準備制度理事会（FRB）の金融緩和策で、主要通貨はドルに対して上昇している［ドル安・主要通貨高が進んでいる］。◆The Bank of Japan should actively continue its monetary easing policy to conquer deflation. デフレを克服するため、日銀は積極的に金融緩和策を続けるべきだ。◆The Fed's monetary easing policies have brought about inflation in newly emerging economies. FRB（米連邦準備制度理事会）の金融緩和策が、新興国のインフレを招いた。

monetary easing steps　金融緩和策
◆The BOJ's policy meeting is expected to consider taking additional monetary easing steps. 日銀の政策決定会合では、追加の金融緩和策の実施を検討する見通しだ。◆The BOJ's unusual measures, including setting up a fund to buy government bonds and other assets, are needed to maximize the effects of its monetary easing steps. 国債などの金融資産買入れ基金の創設など、日銀の今回の異例の措置は、金融緩和策の効果を最大限に引き出すのに必要だ。◆The markets reacted coolly to the latest additional economic stimulus and monetary easing steps by the government and the Bank of Japan. 政府と日銀が繰りだした今回の追加経済対策と追加金融緩和策に、市場の反応は冷ややかだった。

monetary items　貨幣性項目, 貨幣項目（貨幣性資産と

貨幣性負債)
◆Monetary items in the balance sheets are translated at year-end rates. 貸借対照表の貨幣性項目は、期末レートで換算されています。

monetary management 通貨管理, 通貨管理能力, 金融操作, 金融調節, 金融政策, 金銭的管理, 金銭的マネジメント
　lose confidence in monetary management　通貨管理[金融調節]への信認を失う
　monetary management strategy　金銭的マネジメント戦略
　monetary management technique　金融調節方式
◆Investors are losing confidence in monetary management. 通貨調節への投資家の信認は、失われている。

monetary measures 金融政策
　(=financial policy, monetary policy)
◆For the time being, the government must resort to monetary measures to underpin the economy. 当面、政府は景気を下支えするような金融政策を取らなければならない。

monetary phenomenon 貨幣的現象, 金融政策上の現象, 金融政策による現象
◆Inflation is always and everywhere a monetary phenomenon. インフレは、あくまでも[いつもどこでも]金融政策上の現象だ。

monetary policy 金融政策, 通貨政策, 貨幣政策
　(=financial policy, monetary measures, money policy: 世界各国の中央銀行が行う金融政策。⇒current account deposit, global liquidity, money policy, tighten monetary policy)
　accommodating fiscal and monetary policies　景気刺激型の財政・金融政策
　accommodative monetary policy　緩和基調の金融政策
　accommodative stance of monetary policy　金融政策での緩和姿勢
　adjustment of monetary policy　金融政策の調整
　another easing of monetary policy　もう一段の[一層の]金融緩和, もう一段の金融政策の緩和
　anti-inflation monetary policy　反インフレ的金融[貨幣]政策
　change in monetary policy　金融政策の変更
　change monetary policy　金融政策を変更する
　conduct monetary policy　金融政策を運営する
　direction of monetary policy　金融政策の方向
　discretionary monetary policy　自由裁量的通貨政策, 裁量的通貨政策[金融政策]
　domestic monetary policy　国内金融政策
　ease [relax] monetary policy　金融政策を緩める, 金融政策を緩和する, 金融緩和をする
　easier monetary policy　金融政策の緩和, 金融緩和, 緩和基調の金融政策　(=monetary policy easing)
　easing of [in] monetary policy　金融政策の緩和, 金融緩和　(=easier monetary policy, monetary easing, monetary policy easing)
　easy monetary policy　金融緩和政策, 金融政策の緩和　(=easy money policy)
　expansionary [expansive] monetary policy　金融政策の緩和, 金融緩和, 拡張的通貨政策
　fiscal and monetary policies　財政・金融政策, 財政政策と金融政策
　fiscal and monetary policy stimulation　財政・金融刺激策
　framework for monetary policy　金融政策の枠組み
　further easing of [in] monetary policy　もう一段の[一層の]金融緩和, 一層の金融政策の緩和, 金融政策の一層の緩和
　implement monetary policy　金融政策を実施する
　instrument of monetary policy　金融政策運営上の手段
　keep [leave] monetary policy on hold　金融政策を据え置く, 金利を据え置く
　keep [leave] monetary policy steady　金融政策を据え置く, 金利を据え置く
　keep monetary policy tight　金融引締め[金融引締め政策]を維持する
　leave monetary policy unchanged　金融政策を据え置く
　loosen monetary policy　金融政策を緩和する, 金融を緩和する, 金融緩和を図る
　loosening of monetary policy　金融緩和, 金融政策の緩和
　maintain a tight monetary (policy) stance　金融引締めスタンスを維持する
　modest tightening of monetary policy　金融政策の緩やかな引締め
　Monetary Policy Committee　英国の金融政策委員会
　monetary policy developments　金融政策の動向, 金融政策の推移
　monetary policy device [instrument]　金融政策手段, 貨幣的政策手段
　monetary policy easing　金融政策の緩和, 金融緩和　(=easing monetary policy, easing in [of] monetary policy)
　monetary policy makers　金融政策当局, 金融当局
　monetary policy measures　金融政策措置, 貨幣政策措置
　Monetary Policy Meeting　(日銀)金融政策決定会合
　monetary policy mistake　金融政策の誤り, 金融政策の失敗
　monetary policy objective　金融政策の目的
　monetary policy outlook　金融政策の行方
　monetary policy stance　金融政策のスタンス
　monetary policy variable　金融政策の変数
　monetary rate of interest　貨幣利子率
　monetary stance　金融当局の姿勢
　negative monetary policy　消極的金融政策
　non-accommodative monetary policy　景気刺激型ではない金融政策
　prudent monetary policy　穏健な金融政策
　relaxed monetary policy　金融政策の緩和, 金融の緩和　(⇒relax)
　restrictive monetary policy　金融引締め政策, 金融引締め策
　set [map out] monetary policy　金融政策を決める
　slight tightening in monetary policy　金融政策の小幅引締め
　stimulative [accommodating] monetary policy　景気刺激型の金融政策
　supportive monetary policy　支持的通貨政策
　the course of monetary policy　今後の金融政策
　tight monetary policy　金融引締め政策
　　(=tight money policy)
　tighten [restrain] monetary policy　金融政策を引き締める, 金融を引き締める
　tighten monetary policy further　金融政策を一段と引き締める, 一段と金融を引き締める
　tightening in monetary policy　金融の引締め, 利上げ
　tightening monetary policy　金融引締め, 金融政策の引締め　(tighter monetary policy)
　tightening of monetary policy　金融政策の引締め　(=monetary tightening)
　tighter monetary policy　金融政策の引締め, 金融引締め, 引締め基調の金融政策

◆A key point of concern is how the U.S. Federal Reserve Board will manage monetary policy. 当面の関心の焦点は、米連邦準備制度理事会（FRB）の金融政策の運営方針だ。◆As a tacit understanding with EU member states, the European Central Bank has refrained from implementing monetary policy that is effectively a fiscal bailout. 欧州連合（EU）加盟国との暗黙の了解として、欧州中央銀行（ECB）は、財政支援に当たる金融政策の実施を控えてきた。◆China will shift to a "prudent" monetary policy in 2011 from the previous "appropriately loose" stance. 中国は、これまでの「適度に緩和的な」金融政策から2011年は「穏健な」金融政策に方向転換する方針だ。◆Contrary to prevailing market expectations, the central bank decided not to further ease monetary policy. 市場の大方の期待を裏切って［期待に反して］、日銀は追加的な金融緩和策を見送った。◆Emerging countries are anxious about the possibility of inflation caused by a large influx of funds as the U.S. FRB decided to relax its monetary policy. 米連邦準備制度理事会（FRB）が金融緩和を決めたため、新興国は大量の資金流入によるインフレを懸念している。◆Monetary policies play a big role in stopping deflation. デフレを止めるには、金融政策の役割が大きい。◆The Bank of Japan decided not to amend its monetary policy. 日銀は、金融政策の変更を見送った。◆The Bank of Japan decided to further ease its monetary policy. 日銀は、追加の金融緩和に踏み切った。◆The Bank of Japan decided to maintain its current monetary policy. 日銀は、金融政策の現状維持を決めた。◆The BOJ decided to further relax its monetary policy by injecting an additional ¥10 trillion into a fund aimed at purchasing government bonds and corporate debentures. 日銀は、国債や社債などを買い入れるための基金に新たに10兆円を注入［投入］して追加の金融緩和に踏み切ることを決めた。◆The challenge in monetary policy for countries now is shifting toward finding a way to move away from ultra-loose money policies. 現在、各国の金融政策の課題は、超金融緩和政策からいかに転換するかに移りつつある。◆The government may exert great pressure on the Bank of Japan to further relax its monetary policy. 政府は、日銀への追加の金融緩和圧力を強める可能性がある。◆The government would ask the Bank of Japan to further ease its monetary policy to help stabilize the nation's financial system by helping financial institutions procure funds. 政府は、金融機関の資金繰りを助けて金融システムの安定化を図るため、日銀に追加の［もう一段の］金融緩和を求める方針だ。◆The main battlefield of monetary policy likely will shift to deflation. 今後は、デフレが金融政策の主戦場となろう。◆The U.S. Federal Reserve Board raised U.S. interest rates, leading the worldwide move to change current super-loose monetary policy. 米連邦準備制度理事会（FRB）が米国の金利を引き上げ、世界的な超金融緩和の政策転換の先陣を切った。◆To further ease monetary policy, the government will ask the Bank of Japan to raise its monthly outright purchase of government bonds from ¥800 billion to about ¥1 trillion. 一層の金融緩和を図るため、政府は国債の買切りオペの額を月8,000億円から1兆円程度に引き上げるよう日銀に要請する。◆To shore up their economies, major economic powers seem to be relying more on their monetary policies. 景気テコ入れに、先進国は金融政策頼みの様相が強まっている。

monetary policy assessment　金融政策の判断
　◆The Fed's next monetary policy assessment is scheduled for October. 米連邦準備制度理事会（FRB）の次回の金融政策の判断は、10月に予定されている。

monetary policy decision　金融政策の決断, 金融政策の決定
　◆The United States is under pressure to make some difficult monetary policy decisions to cool down the overheating economy by countering the inflationary pressures stemming from higher import prices due to the weaker dollar. 米国は現在、ドル安での輸入価格の高騰によるインフレ圧力を抑えて過熱気味の景気を鎮めるための難しい金融政策の決断を迫られている。

Monetary Policy Meeting　（日銀の）金融政策決定会合　（⇒Policy Board meeting）
　◆The Bank of Japan is considering taking additional monetary easing measures ahead of the next Monetary Policy Meeting. 次回の金融政策決定会合に向けて、日銀は現在、追加金融緩和策の実施を検討している。◆The next Monetary Policy Meeting of the Bank of Japan is set for early September. 日銀の次回の金融政策決定会合は、9月上旬に開かれることになっている。

monetary relaxation　金融緩和　（=credit relaxation, monetary easing, monetary expansion）
　◆As joint actions, major industrial nations have taken such measures as further interest rate reductions, quantitative monetary relaxation to increase the money supply, the injection of public funds and increased public spending. 協調行動として、主要先進諸国は、さらなる金利の引下げ、通貨供給量を増やすための量的金融緩和や公的資金の注入、財政出動［公共支出の拡大］などの措置を取った。◆Monetary relaxation helps promote the depreciation of the yen. 金融緩和は、円安を促す効果がある。◆To alleviate the influence of the U.S. government's additional monetary easing, the Bank of Japan must adopt a more proactive stance toward monetary relaxation. 米政府の追加金融緩和策の影響を和らげるには、日銀も金融緩和の姿勢を強める必要がある。

monetary relaxation measures　金融緩和策
　◆The BOJ could take additional monetary relaxation measures if there are any changes in the financial situation. 金融面で動きがあるとすれば、日銀が追加の金融緩和策を実施する可能性もある。

monetary relaxation policy　金融緩和策
　◆At two financial summit meetings since the collapse of Lehman Brothers, agreements were made on cooperation to implement large-scale economic stimulus measures and to take monetary relaxation policies. リーマン・ブラザーズの倒産［破たん］以来2回開かれた金融サミットでは、連携して大型の財政出動や金融緩和策を実施することで合意が得られた。◆The Bank of Japan should implement further monetary relaxation policies, including the establishment of an inflation target. 日銀は、インフレ目標の設定などを含めて、一層の金融緩和［金融緩和策］が必要だ。

monetary stance　金融政策
　◆To keep their currencies from appreciating in the wake of the Fed's new round of quantitative easing, countries grappling with deflation should ease their own monetary stances. 米連邦準備制度理事会（FRB）の追加の量的緩和による通貨高を避けるには、デフレに取り組んでいる国は、自らも量的緩和をすればよい。

monetary tightening　金融引締め　（=credit squeeze, monetary restraint, tight money: 金利を引き上げて通貨供給量を減らし、カネ回りを厳しくすること）
　expected further monetary tightening　予想される一層の金融引締め, 一層の金融引締めの予想
　renewed monetary tightening　金融引締めへの転換
　　（=renewed tightening monetary policy）
　response to monetary tightening　金融引締めの効果
　slight monetary tightening　金融の小幅引締め
　the degree of monetary tightening　金融引締めの程度

monetary union　通貨統合
　（=monetary integration）
　◆The monetary union's authorities have neglected to strengthen the banking system. 通貨統合の当局は、銀行システムの強化［銀行システムへのテコ入れ］を怠った。

monetization　（名）貨幣鋳造, 貨幣化, 貨幣経済化, 通貨制定

monetization of debt　公債の貨幣化（公債発行分を通貨の発行で賄うこと）
monetization of government bond　国債の貨幣化（国債発行分を通貨発行で賄うこと）
rate of monetization　貨幣化率
monetize　（動）換金化する，現金化する，貨幣化する，貨幣と定める，貨幣に鋳造する，〜を通貨とする
monetize the call option　コール・オプションを換金化する
monetized economy　貨幣化経済
monetized government debt　国債の貨幣化，貨幣化された国債
money　（名）金，金銭，通貨，貨幣，資金，金融，マネー（⇒base money, quasi-money）
base money　ベース・マネー（=monetary base）
borrowed money　借入金
call money　コール借入金，銀行相互間の当座借入金，短期資金，コール・マネー
call money rate　コール・レート
credit money to a given account　指定の口座に入金する，指定の口座に振り込む
dear money policy　高金利政策
debit money from an account　口座から金を引き落とす
deposit money in a bank　銀行に預金する
deposited money　預り金
easy money　金融緩和，低利の金，低金利
exchange of money　両替
foreign money order　外国送金為替
hard money　硬貨
hot money　短期資金，投機資金，ホット・マネー
hush money　口止め料
inland money order　内国送金為替
key money　権利金，保証金，礼金
loan money　融資する，金を貸す
lose money　赤字を出す，損失を出す，損失を被る
make money　利益を生み出す，利益を上げる，利益を得る，資金を稼ぐ，金を儲（もう）ける，一財産築く
money at call　短期融資，当座借り，コール資金（=money on call）
money borrowed for long term　長期借入金
money borrowed for short time　短期借入金
money center　金融センター
money conditions　金融状況
money damages　金銭賠償
money deposited from customers　得意先預り金
money deposited from officers　役員預り金
money flow　資金循環，マネー・フロー
money game　投機的取引，マネー・ゲーム
money in circulation　流通通貨
money in hand　手元資金，手元現金預金
money in trust　委託金
money income　現金収入
money lending business　貸金業者
money multiplier　信用乗数，貨幣乗数
money of [with] zero maturity　流動性預金，MZM
money on call　コール・マネー
money position　マネー・ポジション（金融機関のコール・ローン（銀行相互間の当座貸付け金）残高が借入金残高より少ない状態）
money purchase pension plan　マネー・パーチェス型年金制度

money purchase plan　定額拠出年金
money spinner　ドル箱
money standard　本位制度
money stock　通貨供給量
money to fund　〜のための資金
money transaction　現金取引，直取引
money trust　金銭信託
money washing　不正資金洗浄
narrow money　狭義の通貨，狭義のマネー
near-money　準貨幣
new money　新規資金，ニュー・マネー
oil money　石油資本，オイル・マネー
out of the money　アウト・オブ・ザ・マネー（オプションを行使しても利益が出ない状態）
overnight and weekend money　肩越し資金と週末資金
overnight money　翌日物
paper money　紙幣
public money　公的資金（=taxpayer money）
quasi-money　準通貨
raise money　資金を調達する，金策する
relief money　労働災害見舞金
retention money　留保金
seed money　初期投資（=front money）
standard money　本位通貨
take money out of a falling market　下落局面の市場から資金を引き揚げる
the price of money　金利
tight money　金融引締め，金融逼迫（ひっぱく），資金需給の逼迫
tight money policy　金融引締め政策，高金利政策
time money　定期借入れ
value of money　貨幣価値，通貨価値
whitewash money　資金洗浄をする

◆A rating below investment grade makes it harder and more expensive to borrow money. 投資適格以下の格付けだと、資金の調達が難しくなるし、資金調達コストも高くつく。◆An individual investor began depositing money in U.S. dollars using a major bank's Web account. 個人投資家が、大手銀行のウェブ口座［インターネット口座］を利用して米ドルの外貨預金を始めた。◆DaimlerChrysler has decided against pumping more money into its troubled Japanese partner, Mitsubishi Motors Corp. ダイムラー・クライスラーは、経営不振の［問題を抱えている］日本の提携企業・三菱自動車に資金を投入しないことを決めた。◆Domestic yields are low relative to those in other nations, causing Japanese money to go overseas. 他国の利回りに比べて国内利回りが低いため、日本の資金が外国に流れている。◆In illegal access of Internet bank accounts confirmed at financial institutions, money was transferred from a client's account to a second account. 金融機関で確認されたネット・バンキング口座への不正アクセスでは、顧客の口座から現金が他人名義の口座に振り込まれていた［送信されていた］。◆In illegal access of Internet bank accounts, nearly all of the money in the illegally accessed account was sent to other accounts. ネット・バンキングの口座への不正アクセスで、不正アクセスされた口座の現金はほぼ全額、他人名義の口座に送金されていた。◆Investors seem to be shifting their money from investment trusts to more secured time deposits in the face of global financial turmoil. 世界の金融市場の混乱に直面して、投資家は資金を投資信託から安定性の高い定期預金に切り替えているようだ。◆The aim of a fund established by the Development Bank of Japan is to infuse money into auto parts makers hit by the March 11 earthquake and tsunami. 日本政策投資銀行が設立するファンドの目的は、東日本大震

災で被災した自動車部品メーカーに資金を行き渡らせることにある。◆The effective book value is calculated by subtracting amassed loan loss reserves from the original amount of money that was lent. 実質簿価は、債権の元々の額（貸し付けた元々の金額：簿価）から、（銀行が）積み立てた貸倒れ引当金を差し引いて算定する。◆The foreign currency depositor planned to withdraw the money when the yen's value fell. この外貨預金者は、円安になったら解約するつもりだった。◆The spring saw a massive amount of money begin to shift from time deposits to ordinary deposits. 春先から、定期預金から普通預金に大量の資金移動が見られた。◆The U.S. government has set a policy goal of a strong dollar to draw cash from abroad into the U.S. money market. 米政府は、ドル高の政策目標を設定して、国外から資金を米国内金融市場に呼び込んでいる。◆There were apparent moves among companies drawing more money from savings to accumulate operating funds. 明らかな動きとして、企業は運転資金を積み増すため、預金から資金を引き出している。

money easing 金融緩和
◆Additional money easing was intended to prevent the injection of public funds into the bank from causing uncertainties over the financial system before it was too late. 追加金融緩和には、同行への公的資金注入が金融システム不安を誘発するのを未然に防止する狙いがあった。

money-easing steps [measures] 金融緩和策
(=monetary easing steps)
◆The U.S. FRB took additional money-easing steps, triggering the latest sharp rise in the yen. 米連邦準備制度理事会（FRB）が、追加の金融緩和策を実施して、今回の円急騰のきっかけを作った[今回の円急騰を招いた]。

money for asset management 資産運用の資金
◆The man intentionally dodged the tax payments as he transferred the money for asset management to another country. 男は、資産運用の資金を他国に移動させていることから、意図的に納税を免れていた。

money inflow 資金流入
◆The money market is overheated by massive money inflows from banks on fading concerns over a financial system crisis. 金融システム不安[金融システム危機に対する懸念]の後退により、短期金融市場は、銀行からの巨額の資金流入で過熱感が強まっている。

money laundering 不正資金の洗浄, マネー・ロンダリング (=money washing: 犯罪で得た資金の出所や所有者を隠す行為。⇒laundering)
◆Citigroup Private Bank's four offices in Japan will have their licenses revoked for violating the law by ignoring suspected money laundering by clients. シティバンクのプライベート・バンク（PB）の在日4拠点（支店・出張所）が、顧客のマネー・ロンダリング（資金洗浄）の疑いのある取引を放置するなどして法令違反があったとして、認可を取り消されることになった。◆Money-laundering prevention rules would mandate financial institutions to report questionable transactions to financial authorities, enabling questionable funds to be seized, collected and maintained by judicial authorities. マネー・ロンダリング防止規則は、テロ資金の疑いのある取引について金融機関に届出義務を課し、そのテロ資金の没収と追徴、保全を司法当局が行えるようにするものだ。◆The U.S. government froze the assets of four individuals and eight entities that were involved in illicit activities such as money laundering, currency counterfeiting and narcotics trafficking. 米政府は、資金洗浄（マネー・ロンダリング）や通貨偽造、麻薬取引などの違法行為に関与している4個人、8団体の資産を凍結した。

money lent by private banks 民間銀行の貸出金
◆The money lent by the U.S. and eurozone private banks remains at about the same level as those prior to Lehman's collapse. 米国とユーロ圏の民間銀行の貸出金は、リーマン・ブラザーズの経営破たん前とほぼ同水準にとどまっている。

money loaned by private banks 民間銀行の貸出金
◆Money loaned by private banks declined to ¥419 trillion as of the end of July 2011 from ¥472 trillion at the end of March 1999 when the zero-interest rate policy was first adopted. 民間銀行の貸出金は、ゼロ金利政策が初めて導入された1999年3月末の472兆円から、2011年7月末現在では419兆円に減った。

money-losing outlet 赤字の店舗, 赤字店舗
◆The closure of the money-losing outlets will result in a surplus of about 2,000 employees out of about 22,000 on a consolidated basis. 赤字の店舗閉鎖に伴い、連結ベースで従業員約22,000人のうち約2,000人が余剰になる。

money management 資金運用, 投資運用, 財テク
money management fund マネー・マネジメント・ファンド, MMF
money market 金融市場, 短期金融市場, マネー・マーケット（長期金融市場はcapital market。「短期金融市場」は、短期の金融資産であるコール、手形、譲渡性預金（DC）、現先などの資金取引が行われる金融市場のこと）
　amounts outstanding in short-term money markets　短期金融市場の残高
　call money market　コール市場
　convertible money market preferred stock　転換型マネー・マーケット優先株
　enter the money markets　短期市場を利用する
　exchangeable money market preferred stock　交換可能マネー・マーケット優先株
　floor for money market rates　短期市場金利の下限
　hot money market　国際短期資金市場, 投機資金市場, ホット・マネー・マーケット
　inject aggressive liquidity into money market　市中に大量の流動性を供給する
　international money market　国際短期金融市場, 国際金融市場
　international short-term monetary market　国際短期金融市場
　keep money market rates firm　短期市場金利を高めに維持する
　London money market　ロンドン短期金融市場, ロンドン金融市場
　long-term money market　長期金融市場
money market account　市場金利連動型預金勘定, マネー・マーケット・アカウント, MMA
money market assets　短期金融市場資産
money market banks　金融センター
　(=money center banks)
money market basis　マネー・マーケット・ベース
money market certificate　市場金利連動型定期預金, 市場金利連動型定期預金証書, 市場金利連動型短期金融商品, MMC
money market conditions　金融市場情勢, 短期金融市場指標
money market dealer　短資会社
money market deposit [depository] account　市場金利連動型普通預金, 市場金利連動型預金勘定, 金融市場預金口座, MMDA
money market installment savings　市場金利連動型定期積金
money market instruments　短期金融市場証券, 短期金融商品, マネー・マーケット関連商品
money market intervention　金融市場への介入, 金融市場介入

money market investment　短期金融商品[マネー・マーケット商品]への投資
money market loan　市場金利連動型貸出し
money market management　金融調節, 金融市場管理, 金融市場の運営
money market mutual fund　市場金利連動型投資信託, 短期証券投資信託, MMMF
money market note　マネー・マーケット・ノート
money market operations　短期金融市場操作, 市場操作
money market optimization　短期金融商品ポートフォリオの最適化
money market preferred (stock)　配当変動型優先株式, 市場金利連動型優先株, マネー・マーケット優先株
money market pressure　短期市場金利への圧力
money market rate　短期市場金利, 市場金利, 市中金利
money market securities　短期金融証券
money market sentiments　短期市場[短期金融市場]の地合い
money market yield　マネー・マーケット利回り
New York money market　ニューヨーク金融市場
short-term money market　短期金融市場, 短期市場
short-term money market rates　短期市場金利
small-denomination money market certificates　市場金利連動型定期預金(小口MMC)
three-month [3-month] market rates　3か月物市場金利
tighten the money market　金融を引き締める
unorganized money market　非公式の金融市場
◆Should the money market be tightened too much, the economy may stall. 金融を引締め過ぎると, 景気の腰を折りかねない。◆The money market is overheated by massive money inflows from banks on fading concerns over a financial system crisis. 金融システム不安[金融システム危機に対する懸念]の後退により, 短期金融市場は, 銀行からの巨額の資金流入で過熱感が強まっている。◆There are moves to tighten money markets in the United States and China. 米国と中国に, 金融引締めの動きがある。◆Under the zero-interest rate policy, the Bank of Japan ensures an ample supply of funds to the money market, making it easier for many banks to secure funds there. ゼロ金利政策のもと, 日銀が金融市場に資金を潤沢(じゅんたく)に供給して, 多くの銀行は金融市場での資金確保が楽になった。

money market fund　市場金利連動型投資信託, 短期金融商品投資信託, マネー・マーケット・ファンド, MMF
◆We consider investments in money market funds to be cash equivalents. 当社は, MMF(マネー・マーケット・ファンド)への投資を現金等価物と見なしています。

money market funds denominated in foreign currencies　外貨建てMMF(マネー・マーケット・ファンド)
◆The brokerage's main services for individual customers will be asset management advisory services, focusing on the sale of products such as investment trust funds that invest in foreign equities, and money market funds denominated in foreign currencies. 同証券会社は, 株式の主な個人顧客向け(売買仲介)業務として, 外国株を組み込んだ投資信託や外貨建てMMF(マネー・マーケット・ファンド)などの商品の販売を中心に, 資産運用顧問業務を展開する方針だ。

money policy　金融政策, 貨幣政策
　(=monetary policy)
　cheap money policy　低金利政策, 金融緩和政策
　dear money policy　高金利政策
　easy money policy　低金利政策, 金融緩和政策
　flexible money policy　伸縮的貨幣政策
　neutral money policy　中立的貨幣政策
　stable money policy　安定貨幣政策
　ultra-cheap money policy　超低金利政策
　ultra-easy money policy　超低金利政策, 超金融緩和政策
　　(⇒money rate)
　ultra-loose money policy　超低金利政策, 超金融緩和政策
◆The challenge in monetary policy for countries now is shifting toward finding a way to move away from ultra-loose money policies. 現在, 各国の金融政策の課題は, 超金融緩和政策からいかに転換するかに移りつつある。

money rate　金利(interest rate), 市中金利(money market rate), 歩合, 利息, 利子, 利子率
　keep money rates low　金利を低く抑えておく, 低金利を維持する
　money rate in accordance with the actuarial method　実質金利
　money rate of interest　金利, 利子率, 貨幣利子率
　　(=interest rate, monetary rate of interest, money rate)
　money rate of return　現金ベース収益率
　money rate structure　金利体系, 利子率体系
◆The BOJ has bought financing bills and other securities from the market to keep money rates low under its ultra-easy money policy. 日銀は, 超低金利政策で低金利を維持するため, 市場から政府短期証券(FB)などの有価証券を買い取ってきた。

money supply　通貨供給量, 資金供給, マネー・サプライ
　(=the supply of money, money stock: 中央銀行と市中金融機関が民間に供給する通貨の量で, 通貨にはM2(現金, 要求払い預金, 定期性預金)のほかにCD(譲渡性預金)が含まれる。)
　adjust the money supply　マネー・サプライを調整する
　behavior of money supply　マネー・サプライの動き
　broad measure of money supply　広義のマネー・サプライの指標
　calm [control] the money supply　マネー・サプライを抑える
　continue to increase money supply in the market　市場に一段の資金供給を続ける
　contract the money supply　マネー・サプライ(使供給量)を減らす
　gross money supply　総通貨供給量
　high money supply growth　高水準のマネー・サプライの伸び[伸び率]
　increase [expand] the money supply　マネー・サプライ(通貨供給量)を増やす
　　(=increase the supply of money)
　inflation of the global money supply　国際的なマネー・サプライの増加
　leave the money supply target at　マネー・サプライ伸び率の目標を〜に据え置く
　limit money supply growth　マネー・サプライの伸び[伸び率]を抑える
　measures of the money supply　マネー・サプライの指標
　meet the money supply target　マネー・サプライ伸び率の目標を達成する
　money supply analysis　通貨[貨幣]供給分析, マネー・サプライ分析
　money supply data　マネー・サプライ統計
　money supply growth　マネー・サプライの伸び[伸び率]
　money supply (growth) figure　マネー・サプライの伸び率
　money supply number　マネー・サプライ統計
　most closely watched gauge of money supply　とくに注目されるマネー・サプライの指標, 代表的なマネー・サ

プライの指標
narrow measure of the money supply　狭義のマネー・サプライの指標
narrow money supply　狭義のマネー・サプライ
narrow money supply growth　狭義のマネー・サプライの伸び率
optimum money supply　適正通貨[貨幣]供給, 最適マネー・サプライ
real money supply　実質通貨供給量
reduce the money supply to the market　市場への資金供給量(マネー・サプライ)を減らす[抑制する]
rise in money supply　マネー・サプライの伸び
total money supply　通貨総供給高
◆As joint actions, major industrial nations have taken such measures as further interest rate reductions, quantitative monetary relaxation to increase the money supply, the injection of public funds and increased public spending. 協調行動として、主要先進諸国は、さらなる金利の引下げ、通貨供給量を増やすための量的金融緩和や公的資金の注入、財政出動[公共支出の拡大]などの措置を取った。◆The Bank of Japan should clearly declare its target inflation rate, guiding an increase in consumer prices of between 2 percent and 3 percent, and then continue to increase money supply in the market. 日銀は、消費者物価を2〜3パーセント程度上昇させるというインフレ・ターゲットをはっきり宣言して、市場に一段の資金供給を続けるべきだ。◆The Fed will underpin the economy through measures aimed at lowering long-term interest rates without reducing the money supply to the market. 米連邦準備制度理事会(FRB)は、市場への資金供給量を減らさずに長期金利の低下を促す政策で、景気を下支えする方針だ。◆The key gauge of the nation's money supply rose 2.1 percent in July 2008 from a year earlier as quasi money such as time deposits increased, the Bank of Japan said. 日本銀行の発表によると、2008年7月のマネー・サプライ(通貨供給量)の指標は、定期性預金などの「準通貨」の増加に伴い前年同月比で2.1%増加した。◆The nation's most closely watched gauge of money supply grew 2 percent in December from a year earlier. 日本の代表的なマネー・サプライの指標[日本のとくに注目されるマネー・サプライの指標M2]が、12月は前年同月比で2%増加した。

money transfer　振替, 口座振替, 資金の移動, 送金　(⇒backlogged, core business, double deduction, malfunction)
international money transfers　国際送金
unprocessed money transfers　口座振替未処理分
◆A resolution of the problem, which includes about 2.5 million unprocessed money transfers, is unlikely to be completed by the end of this coming week. 約250万件の口座振替未処理分などを含めて、このトラブルは、来週末までに解消しそうにない。◆Amid accelerating money transfers, the scheduled end on the moratorium on the payoff system is only four months ago. 資金の移動が加速するなかで、ペイオフ凍結解除の予定が、4カ月後に迫っている。◆Four regional banks have reached an agreement with Deutsche Bank to conduct international money transfers. 地方銀行4行が、ドイツ銀行と国際送金で提携[業務提携]した。

moneyed　(形)金銭上の, 金持ちの, 大金を持つ
a moneyed man　資本家, 金持ち
moneyed assistance　経済的援助, 経済支援, 資金融通
the moneyed interest　財界, 金融界

moneylender　(名)金貸し, 貸金業者, 金融業者　(⇒Moneylending Business Law, Moneylending Control Law)
◆Major moneylender SFCG is undergoing bankruptcy procedures. 金融大手のSFCGは現在、破産手続き中だ。◆The bank charged a hefty commission when asking a major moneylender to buy back loan claims. 大手の金融業者に債権の買い取りを求める際、同行は法外な手数料を支払わせていた。◆The Moneylending Control Law and the Investment Deposit and Interest Rate Law were revised with the aim of regulating moneylenders that impose unlawfully high interest rates on their loans. 法外な貸付け金利を押し付ける金融業者を規制するため、貸金業規制法と出資法が改正された。

moneylending　(名)貸金, 金融　(⇒Investment Deposit and Interest Rate Control Law)
illegal moneylending　ヤミ金融
moneylending firm　貸金業, 貸金業者
◆A man who operated an illegal moneylending firm was arrested on suspicion of violating the Investment Deposit and Interest Rate Control Law. 違法な金融業の経営者[ヤミ金融の経営者]が、出資法違反容疑で逮捕された。◆Sellers of multiple-debtor lists, produced by collecting information about consumer finance customers, are contributing to the spread of illegal moneylending. 消費者金融の顧客情報を入手して作った多重債務者リストを売る名簿業者が、ヤミ金融の横行に一役買っている。

moneylending business　貸金業, 貸金業者, 金融業　(=moneylending operations; ⇒debt-ridden)
◆A recent tragedy involving a debt-ridden elderly couple roused all parties to impose stricter controls on the moneylending business. 最近起こった借金苦の老夫婦の悲劇が、各党を貸金業の規制強化に突き動かした。◆Leading moneylending businesses make huge profits by securing loan funds from financial institutions at annual average rates of less than 2 percent. 大手の貸金業者は、金融機関から平均年2%以下の金利で融資資金を調達して、高い収益を上げている。

Moneylending Business Law　貸金業法　(⇒cash-back[cashback])
◆The revised Moneylending Business Law fully enacted on June 18, 2010 limits the total amount of consumer loans a person can borrow from moneylenders to no more than one-third of his or her annual income. 2010年6月18日に完全施行された改正貸金業法は、個人が貸金業者から借り入れることができる消費者ローンの総額を、年収の3分の1に制限している。

moneylending business sector　貸金業界　(=moneylending industry)
◆Within the moneylending business sector, there are calls for raising the upper limit of the interest rate stipulated in the Investment Deposit and Interest Rate Control Law. 貸金業界には、出資法で定められている上限金利の引上げを求める声がある。

Moneylending Control Law　貸金業規制法　(⇒moneylender)
◆Moneylenders who were arrested for violating the Investment Deposit and Interest Rate Control Law or the Moneylending Control Law were leniently dealt with by the justice system. 出資法違反や貸金業規制法違反などで逮捕された貸金業者が、現行の罰則制度で寛大に扱われていた。

moneymaker　(名)蓄財家, 金儲けが得意[うまい]人, 儲け仕事

moneyman　(名)投資家, 金融業者, 財政専門家, 後援者, パトロン

monitor　(動)監視する, 監理する, 調査する, チェックする, 評価する, 把握する, 分析する, モニターする
bolster monitoring activities　監視活動を強化する
　(⇒oversight organization)
carefully monitor the market　市場の動きを注視する
closely monitor the market　市場の動向に十分注意する, 市場の動きを注意深く監視する
continue to monitor the currency market　今後とも為替市場の動きを注視[監視]する
monitor insurers' capital positions　保険会社の自己資本の状態を監視する

◆AMRO, as the surveillance unit of CMIM, plays an important role to monitor and analyze regional economies. AMROは、(参加国が通貨急落といった危機に直面した際に外貨を融通し合う)多国間通貨交換[スワップ]協定(CMIM)の監視機関として、域内経済を監視し分析する重要な役割を担っている。◆By the 30-minute extension of morning trading sessions, investors will be able to trade for a full hour in Japan as they monitor stock price movements on the Hong Kong market. 午前の取引時間の30分延長で、投資家は、香港市場の値動きを見ながら日本市場で丸1時間売買できるようになった。◆The bank has about ¥3 trillion in loans to firms that need to be monitored. 同行には、要監理先の債権が約3兆円ある。◆The government will continue to monitor the currency market. 政府は、今後も為替市場の動きを注視する方針だ。◆The International Monetary Fund is urged to monitor Italy's financial management to provide support to Italy. イタリアを支援するため、国際通貨基金(IMF)はイタリアの財政運営の監視を求められている。◆The U.S. Treasury Department will closely monitor the pace of appreciation of the yuan by China. 米財務省は、中国の人民元切上げのペースを注意深く監視する方針だ。

monitor (名)画面表示装置, モニター
  (=monitor display)
  ◆Dealers are watching monitors at a foreign exchange trading company. 為替取引の会社では、ディーラーたちがモニターを注視している。

monitoring activities 監視活動
  ◆Oversight organizations including the Securities and Exchange Surveillance Commission will need to bolster their monitoring activities. 証券取引等委員会などの監督機関は、これから監視活動を強化する必要がある。

monitoring procedures 監視手続き
  ◆The firm controls its exposure to credit risk through credit approvals, credit limits and monitoring procedures. 同社は、信用供与承認や信用限度、監視手続きを通じて信用リスクを管理している。

monkey business 不正取引, いかさま商法, インチキ行為, いたずら

monoline (名)単一の事業, 米国の金融保証保険会社, 金融保証会社, 金融保証専門会社, モノライン (=bond insurer:「モノライン」は、債券など金融商品の保証を専門に行う米国の保険会社で、倒産などで社債購入者に元本と利息を支払えない場合に会社に代わってその支払いを保証する。生命保険や自動車保険、火災保険などの各種保険を手がける保険会社を「マルチライン(multiline)」という)
  monoline bond insurer 債券専門保険会社
  monoline health insurer 健康保険専門会社
  monoline insurance company 専門保険会社
    (=monoline insurer)

month (名)月, 1か月
  be unchanged on the month 前月比で横ばい
  calendar month delivery 暦月渡し
  consolidated business results for the six months up to September 4-9月期の連結業績, 4-9月期の連結決算, 9月中間連結決算(3月期決算企業の場合)
  deferred month 期近物
  final session of the month 納会
  for the first time in five months 5か月ぶりに
  for the third consecutive month 3か月連続して
  for the three months ended in June 4-6月期 (3月期決算企業の第1四半期、12月決算企業の第2四半期)
  in coming months 今後数か月
  in recent months ここ数か月
  in three months 3か月ぶりに, 今後3か月で
  month order 月内有効注文

  month over month 前月比で
  months outstanding 外部発行月数
  months supply of new homes for sale 新築住宅物件の在庫量(米国の景気指標)
  near [nearby] month 期近物
  next month delivery 中限
  single month book-to-bill ratio 単月のBBレシオ
  spot month 期近物
  the contract [delivery] month (先物取引)受渡し期限の月, 限月(げんげつ)
  the first nine months of 2012 12月期決算企業の2012年1-9月期, 2012年の3四半期
  the month of delivery 限月(げんげつ), 受渡しの月
  the 12 months ending March 2012 2012年3月期, 2011年度
  ◆The firm's group operating profit for the six months ended June 30 rose to ¥10.86 billion from ¥7.15 billion a year earlier. 同社の1-6月期[上半期、上期]の連結営業利益は、前年同期の71億5,000万円に比べて108億6,000万円に増加しました。

month-end (形)月末の
  month-end average cost method 月末平均単価原価法
  month-end closing procedures 月次決算手続き
  month-end fund 月末資金
  month-end payment 月末勘定
  month-end settlement 月末決済

month-on-month [month on month] (名・形)前月比(の) (=month-on-month figure, month-to-month, month over month)
  month on month decline 前月比の減少, 前月比での減少
  month-on-month rise 前月比の上昇[上昇率]
  over-month-end unconditional call 月越無条件物
  ◆The month-on-month decline in foreign demand was largest on record. 前月比の外需の減少は、過去最大だった。

month-to-month (名・形)前月比(の)
  (=month-on-month)
  month-to-month decrease 前月比での減少
  month-to-month increase 前月比での増加

monthly (形)毎月の, 月[毎月]1回の, 月例の, 月間の, 月払いの, 月ぎめの
  a monthly average 月平均
  a monthly balance 月計表
  a monthly trial balance 月計試算表
  BOJ monthly review 日銀月報
  monthly activity report (営業などの)月次報告, 月次報告書
  monthly auction 月次入札
  Monthly Bulletin of Statistics 国連の統計月報
  monthly cash flow 月ごとのキャッシュ・フロー, 月次キャッシュ・フロー
  monthly cash report 資金月報
  monthly clear 翌月1回払い
  monthly compounding 月ごとの複利
  monthly contribution 保険料月額
  monthly debt 月間債務
  monthly delivery 毎月渡し
  monthly employment numbers 毎月の雇用統計
  monthly financial statement 月次会計報告書
  monthly inflation 前月比物価上昇率
    (=monthly price increase)
  monthly installments 月賦(げっぷ), 月賦払い
  monthly interest rate 月利, 月間利子率
    (=monthly rate of interest)

monthly investment plan 月掛け投資計画, 累積投資, ミップ, MIP（特定の株を毎月少額ずつ買っていく投資手法）

monthly monetary meeting 月次金融会議

monthly repayments 月間払戻し金, 月間返済金, 月間債権回収額

monthly report 月次報告, 月例報告

monthly savings 月掛け貯金

monthly settlement 月次清算

monthly statement 月計表, 月次計算書, 月次報告書

monthly Treasury auction 月例の国債入札

monthly turnover 月間売買高

monthly economic report 月例経済報告
◆In its monthly economic report for August, the government said the economy "remains essentially flat." 8月の月例経済報告で、景気は「おおむね横ばい」と政府は言った。◆The government announced in its monthly economic report for May that the economy had bottomed out. 政府は、5月の月例経済報告で「景気は底入れしている」と発表した。

monthly mobile charge 携帯利用の月料金, 携帯利用の月額
◆In the case of au Insurance's cell phone-based policy sales, policyholders are allowed to pay premiums by adding them to monthly mobile charges. au損害保険の携帯電話での保険販売の場合、保険契約者は、保険料を携帯利用の月額に加算して保険料の支払いをすることができる。

monthly payment 月払い, 毎月払い, 月返済, 月々の支払い, 月賦（げっぷ）
　amount of monthly payment 月返済額
　equal monthly payment 均等払い
　equal monthly payments with interest 元利均等返済
　repay the loan in 12 monthly payments 12か月払いでローンを返済する

Moody's ムーディーズ
　Moody's Investment Grade ムーディーズ投資等級, MIG
　Moody's investment grade (MIG) system ムーディーズ投資格付けシステム（MIG記号）
◆Moody's may downgrade the U.S. government's credit rating if it does not get its colossal deficits in better order. 米政府が膨大な財政赤字問題に目途をつけないと、ムーディーズは米国債の格付けを引き下げる可能性がある。◆Rating agency Moody's may place a negative outlook on French government's Aaa debt rating as the government's financial strength has weakened. 格付け会社のムーディーズは、フランス国債のAaa（トリプルA）格付けについて、仏政府の財務体質［財務力］が弱まっているため「ネガティブ（弱含み）」の見通しを示す可能性がある。

Moody's Investors Service Inc. ムーディーズ, ムーディーズ・インベスターズ・サービス（米国の格付け会社）
◆Moody's Investors Service Inc. cut Japan's yen-denominated debt rating by one notch to Aa3 from Aa2 and maintained a negative outlook. 米国の格付け会社ムーディーズは、日本の円建て国債の格付けを「Aa2」から「Aa3」に一段階引き下げ、「ネガティブ（弱含み）」の見通しを据え置いた。◆Moody's Investors Service Inc. is reviewing 14 British banks for possible downgrade. ムーディーズ・インベスターズ・サービスは現在、英銀14行の格付けを、格下げの方向で検討している。

Moon Trade 株などの時間外取引, 時間外サービス, ムーン・トレード
　(=after-hours service, after-hours trading)
◆The after-hours service called "Moon Trade" has been hit by the downturn in Japan's equity market. 「ムーン・トレード」と呼ばれる時間外サービスが、日本の株式市場の低迷で打撃を受けている。

mop-up operations 掃討作戦
◆Banks have been preoccupied with the disposal of bad debts, a kind of mop-up operations. 銀行はこれまで、不良債権の処理という一種の掃討作戦に負われてきた。

moral （名）道徳, 倫理, 品行, モラル
◆A lack of morals among Livedoor group executives led to their violation of the Securities and Exchange Law. ライブドア・グループ幹部の証券取引法違反の原因は、経営者の「モラルの欠如」だ。

moral hazard 倫理観・責任感の欠如, 道徳的危険, モラル・ハザード
◆As a side effect of the zero-interest policy, there is the moral hazard concerning corporate executives. ゼロ金利政策の副作用の一つとして、企業経営者のモラル・ハザード（倫理の欠如）がある。◆Extending protection of deposits with no strings attached would run the risk of exposing financial institutions to moral hazard. 付帯条件をつけない安易な預金保護は、金融機関のモラル・ハザードを招く恐れがある。◆The global 28 megabanks will be subject to the FSB's new international requirement to absorb losses and reduce the moral hazard posed by these banks. 世界のメガ銀行28行が、これらの巨大銀行による損失の吸収とモラル・ハザード抑制に向けての金融安定化理事会（FSB）の新国際金融規制の対象になる見込みだ。

morass （名）困難, 困難な立場, 難局, 苦境, 泥沼
　financial morass 泥沼の財政状況, 財政難
　pull out of the economic morass 経済の泥沼状態［泥沼の経済状況］から抜け出す, 経済の難局［苦境, 苦況］から抜け出す
◆Germany and France urged weaker eurozone countries to pull out of their financial morass. ドイツとフランスは、弱小のユーロ圏各国に泥沼の財政状況から抜け出すよう求めた。◆The United States should pull out of the economic morass. 米国は、泥沼の経済状況から抜け出すはずだ。

moratorium （名）活動の一時停止, 一時禁止, 支払い停止, 支払い猶予（ゆうよ）期間, 返済猶予, 返済延期, 凍結, モラトリアム
　debt moratorium 債務返済停止, 債務返済の凍結
　debt servicing moratorium 債務返済の停止, 債務返済の凍結
　interest payment moratorium 利払い停止, 利払いの延期, 利払いの凍結
　lifting the moratorium on a deposit payoff system 預金ペイオフ制度の凍結解除
　one-year moratorium on the introduction of the deposit payoff system 預金のペイオフ制度導入の1年間凍結
　repayment moratorium 債務返済の猶予, 債務返済の延長, 債務返済の凍結
◆As a prelude to the scheduled lifting of the moratorium on a deposit payoff system, customers have already become nervously selective of financial institutions. 予定されている預金のペイオフ制度の凍結解除を前にして、利用者はすでに金融機関の選別に神経をとがらせている。◆The moratorium could last up to a year, depending on assessments by the International Monetary Fund. 支払い猶予の対象期間は、国際通貨基金（IMF）の判断にもよるが、1年間が有力だ。

moribund （形）死にかけている, 瀕死（ひんし）の, 消滅［絶滅、滅亡、崩壊］しかけている, 滅亡［消滅、絶滅、崩壊］寸前の, 低迷状態の
　an moribund economy 景気低迷, 瀕死の経済
　revive a moribund economy 瀕死の経済をよみがえらせる
　still remain moribund まだ低迷状態にある
◆Personal consumption and corporate investment in plant and equipment still remain moribund. 個人消費や企業の設備

投資は、まだ低迷状態から抜け出さずにいる。
moribund eurozone markets　崩壊寸前のユーロ圏市場
◆By buying Greek, Portuguese and Spanish bonds, the ECB infused life into the moribund eurozone markets for these soon-to-be-junk status government bonds. ギリシャやポルトガル、スペインの国債を買い入れて、欧州中銀（ECB）は、崩壊寸前のユーロ圏の投資不適格レベルが見込まれるこれらの債券の市場に生気を吹き込んだ。
morning business [session]　前場
morning trading　朝方の取引, 午前の取引
◆The intervention was prompted by the yen rising to ¥82.87 to the dollar in the morning trading. 市場介入に踏み切ったのは、朝方の取引で1ドル＝82円87銭まで円高が進んだからだ。
morning trading hours [sessions]　午前の取引時間（⇒movement）
◆Even a 30-minute extension of morning trading hours will increase the volume of trading by 6 percent. 午前の取引時間を30分延長しただけでも、売買高は6％増える見込みだ。◆The Tokyo Stock Exchange and four other exchanges extended their morning trading hours by 30 minutes to 11:30 a.m. 東証など5証券取引所が、午前の取引時間を11時半まで30分間延長した。
mortgage　（名）抵当, 担保, 担保不動産, 譲渡抵当, 抵当権, 抵当権設定, 抵当証書, 担保付き融資, 住宅ローン, モーゲージ　（⇒subprime mortgage）
　adjustable mortgage [mortgage loan]　変動金利型住宅ローン, 変動金利モーゲージ　（=adjustable-rate mortgage, adjustable-rate mortgage loan）
　adjustable rate mortgage　変動金利型住宅ローン
　credits for mortgage payments　住宅取得控除
　first mortgage　第一順位抵当権
　fixed rate mortgage　固定金利型住宅ローン
　home mortgage　住宅ローン
　home mortgage borrowing　住宅ローンの借入れ
　insure mortgage　住宅ローンを保証する
　lower mortgage rate　住宅ローン金利の低下, モーゲージ金利の低下
　mortgage backed bond　モーゲージ担保債券
　mortgage debenture　担保付き社債
　mortgage debt　担保付き長期債務, 抵当借り
　mortgage deed　担保証券
　mortgage guarantee indemnity insurance　モーゲージ担保保証保険, モーゲージ保証保険　（=mortgage guaranty insurance）
　mortgage insurance　抵当[担保]保険, モーゲージ保険
　mortgage insurance policy　抵当[担保]保険証券
　mortgage interest policy　抵当利子政策
　mortgage note　担保付き長期手形
　mortgage on commercial properties　商業財産抵当貸付け
　mortgage repossession　抵当流れ
　mortgages payable　担保[抵当]付き借入金
　mortgages receivable　担保[抵当]付き貸付け金
　place [hold] a mortgage on one's house　～の家を抵当に取る[取っている]
　residential mortgage market　住宅ローン市場, 住宅用モーゲージ市場
　stripped mortgage securities　分離型モーゲージ証券
　take out [start to have] a mortgage on　～を抵当に入れる
◆In an attempt to get on the bandwagon, many people are shifting their fixed rate mortgages to adjustable rate ones. 時流に乗ろうとして、固定金利型住宅ローンを変動金利型住宅ローンに変更する人が多い。◆Japan Post is discussing an alliance with Suruga Bank to offer mortgages and other loans to individuals. 日本郵政は現在、住宅ローンなど個人ローン商品の販売に向けて、スルガ銀行と業務提携協議を進めている。◆The bank repeatedly lied so that it could benefit from the U.S. government program that insured mortgage. 同行は、米政府の住宅ローン保証プログラムから利益を得るために繰り返し虚偽の説明をした。◆The U.S. government has had to foot the bill for mortgage loans that defaulted under the government program that insured mortgages. 米政府は、政府の住宅ローン保証プログラムに基づき、デフォルト（債務不履行）になった住宅ローンのツケの支払いを迫られている。◆Under the program of a voluntary liquidation for individuals, housing loan borrowers' voluntary bankruptcies can be prevented by having financial institutions waive repayment of their mortgages. 個人向け私的整理の制度だと、金融機関に住宅ローンの返済を免除させることによって、住宅ローンの借り手の自己破産を防ぐことができる。
mortgage-backed securities　不動産担保証券, 不動産証券, 住宅ローン担保証券, 住宅融資証券, モーゲージ担保証券, モーゲージ証券, 抵当証書担保付き証券, MBS　（=mortgage-backed certificates）
　complex mortgage-backed securities　合成不動産担保証券
　losses tied to mortgage-backed securities　不動産証券関連の損失
　residential mortgage-backed securities　住宅ローン担保証券
　toxic mortgage-backed securities　不良不動産担保証券, 不良モーゲージ担保証券
◆Our quarterly net profit will be lower than the same period a year earlier because of losses tied to mortgage-backed securities. 当社の四半期純利益は、不動産証券関連の損失で前年同期を下回る見込みです。◆The price tag for the mortgage-backed securities sold to Fannie and Freddie by 17 financial firms totaled $196.1 billion. 大手金融機関17社がファニー・メイとフレディ・マックに販売した住宅ローン担保証券（MBS）の購入額は、総額で1,961億ドルになる。◆The U.S. central bank will buy mortgage-backed securities (MBS) guaranteed by the government-controlled home loan giants Fannie Mae, Freddie Mac and Ginnie Mae. 米連邦準備制度理事会（FRB）は、米連邦住宅ローン大手のファニー・メイ（米連邦住宅貸付公社）、フレディ・マック（米連邦住宅抵当金庫）とジニー・メイ（米政府系住宅金融公庫）が保証した住宅ローン担保証券（MBS）を買い取ることになった。◆The U.S. government filed lawsuits against 17 financial firms for selling Fannie and Freddie mortgage-backed securities that turned toxic when the housing market collapsed. 米政府は、住宅市場崩壊時に不良資産化した住宅ローン担保証券（MBS）をファニー・メイ（米連邦住宅抵当公庫）とフレディ・マック（米連邦住宅貸付け抵当公社）に販売したとして、大手金融機関17社（バンク・オブ・アメリカやシティグループ、JPモルガン・チェース、ゴールドマン・サックス・グループなど）を提訴した。
mortgage-backed securities business　住宅融資証券事業, 不動産証券事業, 不動産証券化事業
◆Nomura will withdraw from the U.S. residential mortgage-backed securities business. 野村［野村ホールディングス］が、米住宅融資の証券化事業［米国の住宅融資証券の関連事業］から撤退することになった。
mortgage bond　担保付き債券, 抵当権付き[担保付き]社債, 不動産担保債
　first mortgage bond　第一順位抵当権付き社債, 一番抵当付き社債, 第一順位抵当権付き債券
　junior mortgage bond　後順位物上担保付き社債
　maturing mortgage bond　満期を迎えた担保付き債券
　second mortgage bond　第二順位抵当権付き社債, 二番抵

当付き社債
◆The first mortgage bonds of the corporation are secured by a first mortgage and a floating charge on the company. 同社の第一順位抵当権付き社債は、同社の第一順位抵当権と浮動担保権で保証されています。◆The FRB decided to use cash from maturing mortgage bonds it holds to buy more government debt. 米連邦準備制度理事会（FRB）は、保有する満期を迎えた担保付き債券で戻ってきた資金を、米国債の買入れに充てることを決めた。

mortgage finance company　住宅金融会社
（=mortgage banker, mortgage firm）
◆Mortgage finance company Fannie Mae announced a management shake-up. 政府系住宅金融会社のファニー・メイ（米連邦住宅抵当公庫）が、経営陣の刷新を発表した。

mortgage financier　住宅金融会社, 住宅金融公社
◆On Sept 7, 2008, the U.S. government earmarked a huge amount of public funds to help government-affiliated mortgage financiers Freddie Mac and Fannie Mae. 2008年9月7日に米政府は、政府系住宅金融会社のフレディ・マック（連邦住宅抵当貸付公社）とファニー・メイ（連邦住宅抵当金庫［公庫］）を救済するため、巨額の公的資金投入を決めた。

mortgage foreclosure　住宅ローンの焦げ付き, 抵当流れ, 抵当権・担保権の行使［実行］, 譲渡抵当実行手続き, 物的担保実行手続き, 譲渡抵当受戻し権喪失手続き
（⇒foreclosure）
◆A prolonged slump in the housing industry has seen sales and prices decline and mortgage foreclosures soar. 住宅産業の長期低迷で、住宅の販売と価格が低下し、住宅ローンの焦げ付き［抵当流れ］の件数も増加している。

mortgage fraud　住宅ローン詐欺
◆Deutsche Bank was sued over mortgage fraud by the U.S. government. 住宅ローン詐欺で、米政府がドイツ銀行を提訴した。

mortgage investments　モーゲージ証券
◆American International Group Inc. sued Bank of America for allegedly selling it faulty mortgage investments. 米保険大手のAIGが、欠陥商品のモーゲージ証券を同社に販売したとしてバンク・オブ・アメリカを提訴した。

mortgage loan　抵当貸し, 担保付き貸付け金（mortgage loan receivable, secured loan）, 住宅ローン
◆The Federal Housing Finance Agency oversees Fannie and Freddie that buy mortgage loans and mortgage securities issued by the lenders. 米連邦住宅金融局（FHFA）は、これらの金融機関が発行する住宅ローンやモーゲージ証券を購入する［買い取る］連邦住宅抵当金庫（ファニー・メイ）や連邦住宅貸付抵当公社（フレディ・マック）を監督している。◆The U.S. government has had to foot the bill for mortgage loans that defaulted under the government program that insured mortgages. 米政府は、政府の住宅ローン保証プログラムに基づき、デフォルト（債務不履行）になった住宅ローンのツケの支払いを迫られている。

mortgage meltdown　住宅ローン市場の崩壊
◆Goldman Sachs Group Inc. is said to have marketed risky investments that bet on the housing market's growth just before the mortgage meltdown. ゴールドマン・サックスは、住宅ローン市場の崩壊直前に、住宅市場の成長を見越した［予想した］高リスクの金融商品［投資商品］を販売したとされる。

mortgage payments　住宅ローンの返済額, 住宅ローンの支払い額
◆Adjustable rate mortgages require lower mortgage payments early in the life of the loan. 変動金利型住宅ローンは、ローンの当面の返済額が少なくて済む。

mortgage rate　住宅ローン金利, モーゲージ金利
　lowering mortgage rates　住宅ローン金利の引下げ
　plunge in mortgage rates　住宅ローン金利の大幅下落
◆Lowering mortgage rates could lead to sales of other financial products. 住宅ローン金利の引下げは、他の金融商品の販売にもつながる可能性がある。

mortgage-related securities　モーゲージ関連証券
◆The U.S. administration will spend up to $700 billion to buy up soured mortgage-related securities and other devalued assets held by ailing financial institutions. 米政府は、経営不振の金融機関が保有するモーゲージ関連の不良証券などの不良資産を、最大7,000億ドル投入して買い取る方針だ。

mortgage securities　モーゲージ商品, MBS商品
◆The Federal Housing Finance Agency oversees Fannie and Freddie that buy mortgage loans and mortgage securities issued by the lenders. 米連邦住宅金融局（FHFA）は、これらの金融機関が発行する住宅ローンやモーゲージ証券を購入する［買い取る］連邦住宅抵当金庫（ファニー・メイ）や連邦住宅貸付抵当公社（フレディ・マック）を監督している。

mortgagor　（名）抵当権設定者, 担保提供者

Mothers　マザーズ（東京証券取引所のベンチャー企業向け市場）
◆The Tokyo Stock Exchange opened Mothers, a market for start-up firms, in November 1999. 東京証券取引所（東証）は、1999年11月にベンチャー企業向け市場として「マザーズ」を開設した。

Mothers market for start-up firms　新興企業向け市場「マザーズ」
◆In May 2002, the TSE's Mothers market for start-up firms abolished its listing requirement that the new firm have a novel business. 2002年5月に、東証の新興企業向け市場「マザーズ」は、上場要件の一つである「新会社の事業の新規性」を排除した。

motive　（名）動機, 理由, 動因, 誘因, 思惑, 考え方, 目的 （形）原動力となる, 行動を促す, 動機となる
　assets motive　資産動機
　buying motives　購買動機
　economic motive　経済的動機
　finance［financial］motive　金融動機
　motives of［for］holding money　貨幣保有の動機
　profit motive　利益目的, 利潤動機
　speculative motive　投機的動機
　transaction motive　取引動機

mount　（動）登る, 上がる, 乗る, 据え付ける, 取り付ける, 載せる, 搭載する, 配置する, 貼る, 固定する, 開始する, 始める, 着手する, 取りかかる（運動などを）起こす,（デモなどを）組織する,（劇を）上演［公演］する,（攻撃を）仕掛ける　（自動）高まる, 増大［増加］する, 強まる
　mount a counterattack against　～に反撃［反論、逆襲］する
　mounting concern　高まる懸念, 懸念の高まり「強まり、深まり」
　mounting criticism　高まる批判, 批判の高まり
　mounting losses　損失の増大
◆Demand for bullion as a protection of wealth has been spurred by mounting concern that the global economy is faltering. 世界経済低迷への懸念増大から、安全資産［資産保全］としての金の需要が拡大している。◆Inflationary pressures are mounting. インフレ圧力が、高まっている。

move　（動）動かす, 移す, 移動させる, 移転する, ～する気にさせる, 提議する, 動議を出す［提出する］, 提案する, 売る, さばく　（自動）動く, 行動する, 措置を取る, 移動する, 移行する, 進行する, 経過する
　move in a narrow range　小幅な値動きとなる
　（⇒narrow形容詞）
　move in line with　～に沿って動く
　move in one's favor　～に有利に動く
　move in tandem　つれ安になる
　move into a period of consolidation　調整局面に差しか

かる
move into profit　黒字に転換する
move into recession　景気後退に突入する
move large amounts of money　巨額の資金を動かす
move out of recession　景気後退から抜け出す
move out of the cautious mood　警戒ムードから抜け出す
move sideways　横ばいになる, 横ばい状態になる, 一進一退の展開となる
move to a new all-time high　過去最高に達する
rapidly move up in price　価格が急上昇する, 急騰する
the yen moves between A and B to the dollar　円相場の値幅は1ドル＝A～Bである
◆Clients moved their deposits from small or midsize financial institutions to major banks. 顧客が、中小金融機関から大手銀行へ預金を移し替えた。◆Domestic three megabanks are moving to step up their overseas lending. 国内の3メガバンクは、海外融資を強化する方針だ。◆Japan moved to correct the excessive appreciation of the yen. 日本は、行き過ぎた円高の修正に動いた。◆Overseas economies are moving out of their deceleration phase. 海外経済は、景気減速局面から抜け出している。◆Participants in the market process information transmitted globally in real time, manipulate it in some cases and try to win profit by moving large amounts of money in this information war zone. 市場参加者は、リアルタイムでグローバルに伝達される情報を処理し、場合によってはそれを操作しながら、この情報戦争の戦場で巨額の資金を動かして利益を得ようとしている。◆The challenge in monetary policy for countries now is shifting toward finding a way to move away from ultra-loose money policies. 現在、各国の金融政策の課題は、超金融緩和政策からいかに転換するかに移りつつある。◆The economy is moving toward an incipient recovery. 景気は、持ち直しに向けた動きが見られる。◆The unanimous decision by the U.S. central bank's policy setting Federal Open Market Committee moved the benchmark federal funds rate to 1.25 percent. 米連邦準備制度理事会の金利政策を決定する米連邦公開市場委員会の全会一致による決定で、短期金利の指標であるフェデラル・ファンド金利が年1.25％に引き上げられた。◆The yen moved between ￥81.80 and ￥82.38 to the dollar, trading most frequently at ￥81.94. 円相場の値幅は1ドル＝81円80銭～82円38銭で、取引の中心値は81円94銭だった。◆These surplus funds are moving into crude oil and grain markets in search of profitable investments. これらの余剰資金が、有利な運用先を求めて原油や穀物市場に向かっている。

move　（名）動き, 動向, 変動, 移動, 移行, 行動, 運動, 進展, 処置, 措置, 対応, 対策, 政策, 手段, 異動, 移転, 引っ越し
credit-tightening move　金融引締め策
economic moves　景気の動き
　　（⇒index of leading economic indicators）
interest rate move　金利変動
international moves　海外進出
limit move　値幅制限
market move　市場の動き, 市場動向
move to a single currency　単一通貨への動き
speculative move　投機的な動き
strategic moves　戦略的な動き
the Fed's pump-priming move　米中央銀行［米連邦準備制度理事会（FRB）］の景気刺激策［景気対策］
the government's move of market intervention　政府の市場介入の動き
the prevention of yen-buying moves　円買いの動きの阻止
yen-buying moves　円買いの動き
yen-selling moves　円売りの動き
◆A dealer at a leading bank said that market players' concern has kept yen-buying moves in check. 市場関係者の警戒感が円買いの動きを食い止めた［抑制した］、と大手銀行のディーラーが語っている。◆A move to adopt the IFRSs has accelerated worldwide. 国際財務報告基準（IFRSs）を採用する動きは、世界的に加速している。◆Depending on moves in foreign exchange markets, there is a risk we may lose initial investments in foreign currency deposits. 為替相場の動き次第で、外貨預金では初期投資額を割り込むリスクがある。◆Despite moves by the U.S. Federal Reserve Board to loan more money to financial institutions, banks are still reluctant to lend. 米連邦準備制度理事会（FRB）に金融機関への資金融資を拡大する動きがあるにもかかわらず、銀行［金融機関］はまだ貸し渋っている。◆Japanese firms' moves to shift production abroad to cope with the yen's rise will bring about a hollowing-out of domestic industries. 円高対策として日本企業が生産拠点を海外に移すと、国内産業の空洞化を招くことになる。◆Protectionist moves could damage the global economy. 保護主義的な動きは、世界経済に打撃を与えかねない。◆The Fed will end the credit-tightening move. 米連邦準備制度理事会（FRB）は、金融引締め策を終える方針だ。◆The Japanese central bank's move to increase the outstanding current account target is insufficient to soothe market fears. 日銀の当座預金残高目標の引上げは、市場不安を払拭するには物足りない。◆The move to inject liquidity into Dubai's banks by the central bank of the United Arab Emirates was seen by analysts as the bare minimum. ドバイの銀行に資金を供給するアラブ首長国連邦（UAE）の中央銀行の動きを、アナリスト（専門家）は「最低限必要な量にすぎない」と見ている。◆The move to lower the yields of insurance products is likely to spread through the industry as tough investment conditions persist. 厳しい運用環境が続いているので、保険商品の利回りを引き下げる動きは、業界全体に広がりそうだ。◆The moves by Citigroup Inc. and General Electric Co. both unsettled investors. 米金融大手シティグループとGEの今回の動きで、投資家は動揺した。◆The U.S. Federal Reserve Board raised U.S. interest rates, leading the worldwide move to change current super-loose monetary policy. 米連邦準備制度理事会（FRB）が米国の金利を引き上げ、世界的な超金融緩和の政策転換の先陣を切った。◆The wall separating banking and securities businesses has been lowered through such moves as the liberalization of banks' securities brokering. 銀行と証券業の垣根は、銀行に対する証券仲介業の規制緩和などの動きで、低くなっている。◆There were apparent moves among companies drawing more money from savings to accumulate operating funds. 明らかな動きとして、企業は運転資金を積み増すため、預金から資金を引き出している。◆These moves of the two airlines show the extent of the crisis in the current business environment. 両航空会社のこれらの動きは、現在の経営環境の危機的状況の大きさを示している。◆With such moves to rein in investment funds, speculative money started to exit the markets. 投資ファンドを規制するこうした動きで、投機マネーが市場から逃避し始めた。

move of intervention　介入の動き, 市場介入の動き
◆After the government's move of intervention, the yen plunged to the ￥85 level against the dollar. 政府の市場介入の動きを受けて、円相場は1ドル＝85円台まで急落した。

movement　（名）動き, 行動, 活動, 運動, 移動, 動向, 流れ, 進展, 進行, 変化, 変動
capital movement　資本移動
downward movement of prices　物価下落の動き
excessive movements of foreign exchange rates　行き過ぎた外国為替相場の動き
exchange rate movements　為替変動, 為替レートの変動, 為替動向, 為替相場の動き, 為替相場の推移
　　（＝exchange fluctuations, exchange rate changes, exchange rate fluctuations, exchange rate moves; ⇒ exchange rate movements）
gold movement　金移動, 金流出入

interest rate movement　金利動向, 金利変動
　（=interest rate move）
market movement　市場の動き, 市場動向, 相場の動き, 相場変動
movement of funds　資金移動　（=fund transfer）
movements in market rates　相場の変動, 市場レートの変動
price movement　価格変動, 物価動向
price movement restrictions　値幅制限
seasonal movement　季節的変動
stock movement　株の動き
stock price movement　株価動向, 株価変動, 値動き
upward movement　上昇の動き
◆By the 30-minute extension of morning trading sessions, investors will be able to trade for a full hour in Japan as they monitor stock price movements on the Hong Kong market. 午前の取引時間の30分延長で, 投資家は, 香港市場の値動きを見ながら日本市場で丸1時間売買できるようになった。◆Excessive movements of foreign exchange rates will have a negative impact on the stability of the economy and financial markets. 行き過ぎた外国為替相場の動きは、経済の安定と金融市場に悪影響を及ぼす。

movement of funds　資金移動　（=fund transfer）
◆The movement of funds by such depositors, including individuals and businesses, recently has become noticeable. このような預金者による資金移動が目立つようになった。

movement of people, goods and capital　人、モノ、資本の移動
◆The development of a market economy is possible only when there is a free movement of people, goods and capital. 市場経済の発展には、人、モノ、資本の自由な移動が前提となる。

movements toward picking up　景気持ち直しの動き, 持ち直しの動き
◆Movements toward picking up are seen in some areas. 一部に（景気）持ち直しの動きが見られる。

moving strike convertible bond　転換社債型新株予約権付き社債, MSCB
◆Fuji TV issued the moving strike convertible bonds (MSCBs) early this year for subscription by Daiwa Securities SMBC Co. to raise ¥80 billion for its NBS takeover bid. フジテレビは今春、ニッポン放送株の公開買付け（TOB）資金800億円を調達するため、大和証券SMBCを引受先として転換社債型新株予約権付き社債（MSCB）を発行した。

MSCB　転換社債型新予約権付き社債（moving strike convertible bondの略）

mull　（動）検討する, 討議する, 熟考する, 思案する, 〜についてあれこれ考える, 〜に頭を絞る, 〜を台なしにする, 〜についてへまをやる
◆The bank is mulling a further downward revision of its business results for fiscal 2011 that is expected to result in a massive loss. 同行は、巨額の損失が見込まれる2012年3月期決算［2011年度］の業績予想を、さらに下方修正する方向で検討している。

multi-bank holding company　複数銀行持ち株会社
multi-component [multi-currency] euronote facility　複数通貨ユーロノート・ファシリティ
multi-currency　（形）多種通貨の, 複数通貨の
　multi-currency bond　複数通貨債
　multi-currency clause　多通貨条項, 多種通貨選択条項, 通貨選択条項
　multi-currency intervention　複数通貨介入
　multi-currency loan　複数通貨ローン
multi-option facility　多重選択金融取決め
（=multiple component facility）
multi-option financing facility　多重選択金融取決め
（=multi-option facility）

multilateral　（形）多国間の, 多国間主義の, 多国籍の, 多数国参加の, 多角的な, 多面的な, 多元的な, 多辺の
　increase contributions to multilateral financial institutions　国際金融機関への出資比率を高める
　multilateral aid　多国間援助
　multilateral clearing agreement　多角的清算協定
　multilateral compensation　多角相殺
　multilateral cooperation　多国間協力, 多角的協力
　multilateral creditors　国際機関
　multilateral currency realignment　多角的通貨調整, 多角的平価調整, 多国間通貨調整
　multilateral initiative　多国間交渉
　multilateral lending institutions　国際金融機関
　multilateral management　多角経営
　multilateral monetary compensation　多角的通貨相殺
　multilateral payment agreement　多角的支払い協定, 多角的決済協定
　multilateral settlement　多角決済
　provision of money to multilateral organizations　国際機関への資金拠出
　the lending agenda of multilateral institutions　国際機関の融資案件

multilateral currency swap agreement　多国間通貨交換協定, 多国間通貨スワップ協定
◆AMRO will coordinate decision-making for providing emergency liquidity to member nations under a $120 billion multilateral currency swap agreement known as CMIM. AMRO（ASEANプラス3諸国の域内マクロ経済リサーチ・オフィス）は、CMIMと呼ばれる1,200億ドルの貸出枠の多国間通貨交換［スワップ］協定に基づき、参加国へ緊急流動性を提供する際の意思決定の調整に当たる。

multilateral financial institutions　国際金融機関
◆Structural adjustment loans are often co-financed with multilateral financial institutions. 構造調整借款は、国際金融機関との協調融資の形をとることが多い。

multilateralization　（名）多角化, 多辺化
　Chiang Mai Initiative Multilateralization　（ASEAN＋3の）チェンマイ・イニシアチブ多角化体制
　multilateralization of position　対外準備の多角化

multiline　（名）マルチライン　（⇒monoline）
multinational　（形）多国籍の, 多国間の, 多角的　（名）多国籍企業
　multinational bank　多国籍銀行, 国際投資銀行（consortium bank）
　multinational banking　国際銀行業務
　multinational currency alignment　多国間通貨調整

multiple　（名）倍数, 倍率, 株価収益率, チェーン・ストア［チェーン店］
　cash multiples　キャッシュ・フロー倍率
　earnings multiple　株価収益率
　　（=price earnings multiple）
　EBITDA multiple　EBITDA倍率
　firm value/EBITDA multiples　FV/EBITDA倍率
　price cash earnings（P/CE）multiple　株価キャッシュ・フロー倍率
　price earnings（PE）multiple　株価収益率, PER

multiple　（形）多数の, 多重の, 複合の, 複合的な, 複式の, 多角式の, 多種多様な
　multiple application　重複申込み, 多重申込み
　multiple assets　複合資産

multiple banking　多種銀行業務
multiple banking system　複数銀行制度
multiple creation of deposit　銀行の預金創出, 乗数倍の預金創出 (=multiple deposit creation: 銀行の信用拡大による預金の創出)
multiple credit creation　乗数倍の信用創出[創造]
multiple deposit creation　信用創造
multiple effect　乗数効果
multiple exchange rates　複数為替相場, 複数為替レート (=multiple rates of exchange)
multiple exchange rate(s) system [practice]　複数為替相場制
multiple export rate　複数輸出為替レート
multiple-line insurance [policy]　多種目保険, 総合保険 (物保険 (property insurance) と責任保険 (liability insurance) を結合した保険)
multiple line law　(米国の保険の) 兼営法 (物保険 (property insurance) と災害保険 (casualty insurance) との兼営を認めた法律)
multiple listing　同時上場
multiple loan borrower　多重債務者 (=multiple debtor, person with multiple debts)
multiple-peril insurance　複数危険保険
multiple quotations　あい見積り
multiple tariff　複数関税, 複式税率
multiple trading　同時売買
multiple voting share　複式議決権株式
multiple crises　複合的な危機
◆The Greek-triggered sovereign debt crisis has been throwing the eurozone into financial uncertainty and multiple crises. ギリシャに端を発した債務危機問題で、ユーロ圏は金融不安と複合的な危機に陥っている。
multiple currency　多通貨, 多数通貨, 複数通貨
multiple currency accounting　多国[多種]通貨会計, 多通貨会計
multiple currency bond　多種通貨選択条項付き社債
multiple currency reserve standard　多数通貨準備制度
multiple currency standard　多種[複数]通貨本位制度
multiple debt　多重債務 (=double debt)
◆Measures to lessen the problem of dual debts or multiple debts were also studied at the time of the 1995 Great Hanshin Earthquake. 二重ローンや多重債務問題の軽減策は、1995年の阪神大震災の際にも検討された。
multiple debtor　多重債務者
(=multiple loan borrower)
◆Sellers of multiple-debtor lists, produced by collecting information about consumer finance customers, are contributing to the spread of illegal moneylending. 消費者金融の顧客情報を入手して作った多重債務者リストを売る名簿業者が、ヤミ金融の横行に一役買っている。
multiple factors　複合的な要因, 複合要因, 複数要因
◆Changes in exchange rate are a result of multiple factors, including the balance of international payments and market supply and demand. 為替相場の変動は、国際収支や市場の需給など複数要因によるものだ。◆It will not be easy to rehabilitate the company, which has been driven into the red by multiple factors. 同社は、複合的な要因による赤字転落なので、再建は容易ではない。
multiple loan　多重債務
◆The revised Moneylending Business Law is aimed at reducing the number of people suffering under the multiple loans. 改正貸金業法は、多重債務者の削減を目的にしている。
multiple private offering　転換社債の第三者割当て発行, MPO
◆Especially companies with fragile capital bases are using schemes such as private placements of convertible bonds, known as multiple private offerings (MPOs). 特に資本基盤が弱い企業は、MPOと呼ばれる転換社債の第三者割当て発行のような資金調達方式を活用している。
Mundell-Fleming model　マンデル・フレミング理論, マンデル・フレミング・モデル (財政引締め, 金融緩和, 通貨安はマンデル・フレミング・モデルの典型的な施策)
municipal　(形) 地方自治の, 地方自治体の, 市政の, 市[町]の, 市営[町営]の, 内政の, 国内の　(名) 市債, 地方債
municipal administration　市政
municipal assembly　市議会
municipal authorities　市当局, 町当局
municipal bond　地方債, 市債券, 市債
municipal bond insurance　地方債保険
municipal corporation　地方公共団体, 地方自治体, 私有公社
municipal debt　地方債, 市債 (=municipal loan)
municipal enterprise　地方公営事業, 地方公営企業
municipal finance　都市財政
municipal financing　地方自治体の資金調達
municipal general obligation bond　地方一般財源債
municipal law　国内法
municipal lease　公共リース
municipal liability insurance　地方自治体賠償責任保険
municipal management　市の管理[経営], 市営, 都市経営
municipal note　地方債, 地方政府証券
municipal office　市役所, 町役場
municipal official　市役所職員
municipal property tax　固定資産税
municipal revenue bond　地方特定財源債
municipal security　地方債, 地方証券, 市債
municipal tax　市町村税
municipal undertaking　市営事業
municipal bankruptcy　地方自治体の財政破たん, 市町村の財政破たん
◆We must prevent another case of municipal bankruptcy like the city of Yubari in Hokkaido. われわれは、北海道夕張市のような地方自治体の財政破たんを、二度と出さないようにしなければならない。
municipal government　地方自治体, 市当局, 市政
◆The financial situation of municipal governments in depopulated mountainous areas or on remote islands is serious. 過疎の山間地や離島の自治体の財政状況は、厳しい。
municipality　(名) 自治体, 地方自治体, 公共団体, 市[町] 当局, 市行政, 市民
loans to municipalities　公共団体貸付け, 公共団体貸付け金
local municipality　地方自治体
obligations of municipalities　地方自治体の債券
small municipalities　小規模市町村
◆Small municipalities have a financial difficulty in setting up an independent audit office or conducting external auditing every fiscal year. 小規模市町村の場合、独立した監査事務局を設置したり、外部監査を毎年度実施したりするのは財政的に困難だ。◆The massive figure of tax revenue shortfall is way beyond what local municipalities can do by cutting spending. この巨額の税収不足は、地方自治体の経費削減で対応できる範囲を大きく超えている。
murky [mirky]　(形) 暗い, 薄暗い, はっきりしない, あいまいな, 不透明な, 分かりにくい, いかがわしい, 霧[煙

り]が立ち込めた
◆Prospects remain murky though a freefall in stock prices has been averted for now. 株価暴落はひとまず回避されたが、先行きはまだ不透明である。The murky acquisitions of several companies by the major precision equipment maker were intended to paper over losses on investments the company made. この大手精密機器メーカーによる不透明な企業買収のねらいは、同社が行った投資の損失隠しだった。

muscle （名）力, 腕力, 圧力, 強制力, 勢力, 影響力, 筋肉, 筋（きん）, 用心棒, 護衛, 必要なもの
  financial muscle　財力
  flex one's muscle(s)　力を誇示（こじ）する, 力のあるところを見せつける, 腕を振るう, 影響力を行使する
  legal muscle　法的影響力
  political muscle　政治的影響力
  the rise of China's financial muscle　中国の財力増大
  ◆China is trying to flex its muscle with the United States on the strength of its status as the largest holder of U.S. Treasury securities. 中国は、米財務省証券[米国債]の最大保有国としての地位を背景に、米国への影響力を行使しようとしている。

mutual （形）相互の, 共通の, 共同の, ミューチュアル
  mutual aid loans　共済貸付け金
  mutual aid pension　共済年金
  mutual-cum-stock　株式付き相互会社
  mutual financing　無尽（むじん）
  mutual financing association　無尽講
  mutual fund　投資信託, ミューチュアル・ファンド
  mutual holding company　相互持ち株会社
  mutual insurance　相互保険
  mutual insurance company　相互保険会社
  mutual life company　相互保険会社
  mutual offset system　相互決済制度
  mutual ownership of shares　株式持ち合い, 株の持ち合い（=mutually held stocks）
  mutual savings bank　相互貯蓄銀行
  mutual savings institution　相互貯蓄金融機関
  mutual society company　相互会社

mutual aid association　共済組合
  mutual aid associations of local government employees　地方公務員共済組合
  the Mutual Aid Association of Prefectural Government Personnel　地方公務員共済組合
  ◆The Finance ministry has jurisdiction over the Federation of National Public Service Personal Mutual Aid Associations. 国家公務員共済組合連合会は、財務相が管轄している。

mutual aid organization　共済組織（=mutual aid association）
◆Tax money has been used to cover losses incurred by hotels run across the nation by the central government workers' mutual aid organization. 国家公務員の共済組合が全国各地で経営するホテルの赤字補填字に、公費[公的資金]が充てられていた。

mutual company　相互会社
◆Most Japanese insurance firms, because they are operated in the form of a mutual company, are not permitted to apply for corporate restructuring under the current law. 日本の生命保険会社の多くは、相互会社の形態をとって運営されているため、現行法では（会社更生法による）会社再建の申請が認められていない。

mutual fund　投資信託, 合同運用ファンド, ミューチュアル・ファンド（米国の場合、投資会社（investment company）が発行する株式を投資家が株主として購入する形をとり、出資金は各種証券に投資され、その運用益が投資家に還元される）
  index mutual fund　インデックス・ミューチュアル・ファンド
  investments in mutual funds　合同運用ファンドへの投資
  money market mutual funds　短期証券投資信託
  mutual fund clearing services　ミューチュアル・ファンド決済手数料
  mutual fund manager　信託会社の資金運用担当者
  mutual fund performance　ミューチュアル・ファンドの運用成績
  ◆The exchange-traded funds (ETFs) are investment products similar to index mutual funds but that trade on stock exchanges like stocks. 上場投資信託（ETF）は、インデックス・ミューチュアル・ファンドに似ているが、株式と同じように証券取引所で売買される投資商品である。

mutual pension fund　共済年金基金, 共済年金資金, 共済年金積立金
◆The mutual aid association has been using public money, mostly from mutual pension funds, to cover the losses of its hotels. 同共済組合は、ホテル経営の赤字補てんに公費（主に共済年金基金）を充ててきた。

mutual pension plan　共済年金, 共済年金制度
◆Pension premiums of full-time housewives of company employees and public servants are automatically covered by payments made by all subscribers to welfare and mutual pension plans. 会社員や公務員の専業主婦の年金保険料は、厚生年金や共済年金の加入者全員の支払い金で自動的にカバーすることになっている。

mutual relief operations　共済事業
◆The labor union pooled money from commissions of its mutual relief operations in secret funds. この労働組合では、共済事業の手数料収入を裏金としてプールしていた。

mutual surveillance of fiscal policies　財政政策の相互監視, 財政の相互監視
◆The eurozone states should hammer out a clear policy toward the introduction of mutual surveillance of fiscal policies. ユーロ圏各国は、財政の相互監視実施に向けて明確な方針を打ち出すべきだ。

mutual trust fund　投資信託
◆The government should ease taxes on shareholdings and mutual trust funds. 政府は、株式保有や投資信託に対する課税を軽くするべきだ。

mutually held stocks　株式持ち合い
◆Germany attempted to avoid taxing capital gains by enterprises from stock transactions, in an effort to encourage them to sell off mutually held stocks. 企業の株式持ち合いの解消を促すため、ドイツは、企業の株式譲渡益に課税しないようにした。

N

N.A.　振出通知なし（no adviceの略。不渡り文言で、発行銀行から支払い指図を受けていないという意味）

N/A　取引なし（no accountの略。不渡り文言で、手形の振出人（drawer）は当行と取引がない、という意味）

NAFTA　北米自由貿易協定（North American Free Trade Agreementの略。米国、メキシコ、カナダ3国の自由貿易協定で1994年に発効）

NAIC　全米保険監督官協会（National Association of Insurance Commissionersの略）

NAIC　全米投資家協会（National Association of Investors Corporationの略）

naked　（形）裸の, 無担保の, 裏付けのない, ネイキッド
  naked call　裸のコール, ネイキッド・コール
  naked contract　無償契約, 無約因契約
  naked debenture　無担保社債

（=unsecured loan stock）
naked option 裸のオプション, 無権利オプション, ネイキッド・オプション （=uncovered option: 原証券を所有していない売り手が提供するオプション）
naked position 無権利所有, ネイキッド・ポジション （=open position: 買い持ちまたはカラ売りの投機で、掛けつなぎをしていない状態のこと）
naked trust 無償信託
write a naked option ネイキッド・オプションを売り建てる
name （名）名称, 名前, 名義, 知名度, 銘柄, 発行体, ネーム
 appealing name 一流の発行体
 bank name 銀行銘柄
 better-rated name 格付けの高い発行体
 company name 会社名, 社名
  （=business name, corporate name, trade name）
 double name paper 複名手形
 good quality name 優良銘柄
 government guaranteed names 政府保証銘柄
 highly regarded name 市場評価の高い銘柄
 known name 有名銘柄, 知名度の高い銘柄
 lesser quality name 信用力が低い［劣る］銘柄
 little known name 無名の銘柄, ほとんど無名の発行体
 name borrowing 名義借り
 name credit 優良貸出先
 name debenture 記名社債券
 name gathering 名寄せ
 name lending 名義貸し
 name schedule bond 記名式保証
 name share 記名株
 one name paper 単名手形
 prime foreign name 外国の優良銘柄
 real names transactions 実名取引, 金融実名制
 security name 銘柄名
 single name paper 単名手形
  （=one-name paper）
 someone else's name 他人名義
 sovereign name ソブリン銘柄
 speculative name 仕手銘柄
 strong name 優良発行体
 supranational name 国際機関銘柄
 tax-free status of the name 発行体が非課税適格であること
 top quality name 超優良銘柄, 最優良銘柄
 top-rated name 超優良発行体
 trade name 商号, 屋号, 社名, 商標, 商標名, トレードマーク
 two-name paper 複名手形
 unrated name 無格付けの発行体
 well known name なじみの銘柄
◆About ¥20 million was transferred from this self-employed man's savings account to a bank account under someone else's name. この自営業者の普通預金から他人名義の銀行口座に、約2,000万円が振り込まれていた。◆After the management integration, the corporate name as well as the current management will be retained. 経営統合後も、社名や現在の経営体制はそのまま残る。◆Kokudo Corp. was found to have been the virtual owner of a large number of shares in Seibu Railway held in the name of 1,100 individuals. コクドは、1,100人の個人名義で保有していた大量の西武鉄道株の実質的な保有者であることが分かった。◆The upcoming negotiations will determine practical measures to strengthen ties, including the merger ratio, the name of the new group and the positions to be held by top executives. 今後の交渉で、統合比率や新グループの名称、首脳人事など提携強化の具体策を詰める。

name recognition 知名度
◆Greater name recognition will contribute to sales of the product in Japan. 日本での今後の知名度アップが、同製品の販売促進につながる。
named （形）記名の, 記名式の, 指定の, 所定の
 named bill（of exchange） 記名式手形
 named draft 記名式手形
 named fiduciary 指名受託者
 named hazard policy 特定危険保険
 named insured 記名被保険者
 named peril policy 特定危険保険
 named perils 列挙危険
 named point 指定地点
 named policy 船名確定証券, 船名記載保険証券, 確定保険証
 named port 指定港, 着船渡し条件
 named risk clause 指定危険約款
 named shipment 指定出荷
nanotechnology 超微小技術, ナノ技術, ナノテク, ナノテクノロジー（一個の原子や分子を材料にしたり、部品として組み合わせてミクロ大の装置や機械などを作ったり、研究をする分野）
◆The Finance Ministry plans to provide preferential tax treatment for businesses in life science, information technology, environmental protection and nanotechnology. 財務省は、生命科学と情報技術（IT）、環境保護、ナノテクノロジー分野の企業に対して税制優遇する方針だ。
NAPM 全米購買部協会（National Association of Purchasing Managementの略）
 NAMP index（of industrial activity） 全米購買部協会景気総合指数
 NAPM data［index, reading, survey］ 全米購買部協会（NAPM）景気総合指数
 NAPM employment index 全米購買部協会の雇用指数
 NAPM index of manufacturing activity 全米購買部協会景気総合指数
 NAPM survey balance on prices 全米購買部協会の価格指数 （=NAPM price index）
 NAPM's index of industrial activity 全米購買部協会景気総合指数
 NAPM's monthly index of new orders 全米購買部協会の月次受注指数
narrow （動）狭（せば）める, 縮める, 縮小させる, 限定する, （自動）狭まる, 狭くなる, 縮小する（⇒link動詞）
 narrow dealing spreads ディーリング・スプレッドを縮小させる
 narrow the gaps between interest rates for public- and private sector debts 公共債と民間債の金利ギャップ［金利差］を縮小する
  （⇒public sector debt）
 narrow the supply/demand gap 需給ギャップを縮小する［縮める］, 需給の格差を縮小する
 narrowed margins［narrowing］margins 利ざやの縮小
 narrowed［narrowing］operating margins 営業利益率の縮小
 narrowed［narrowing］yield spread 利回り格差の縮小
◆The U.S. budget deficit for fiscal 2010 narrowed to $1.29 trillion as tax collections recovered slightly and financial bailout spending fell sharply. 米国の2010会計年度（2009年

10月～2010年9月)の財政赤字は、税収がいくぶん回復し、金融救済[金融支援]費用が急減したため、1兆2,900億ドルに縮小した。◆The U.S. trade deficit narrowed to $40.4 billion in November from October's deficit of $56.7 billion. 米国の貿易赤字は、10月の567億ドルから404億ドルに縮小した。
- **narrow** (形)狭い, 視野の狭い, 狭義(きょうぎ)の, 小幅な, 限られた, (資力の)乏しい, かろうじての
  - be below the floor of the narrow band 狭い変動幅の下限を下回る
  - hover in a narrow range 小幅な値動きとなる
  - move in a narrow band 狭いボックス圏内の動きとなる
  - move [hover] in a narrow range 小幅な値動きとなる(⇒hover)
  - narrow based stock index 業種別株価指数
  - narrow financial margins 利ざやの縮小
  - narrow margin 薄利, 小ざや, 僅差(きんさ)
  - narrow market 閑散市場(inactive market), 薄商い相場, 不況市場, 売買薄, 薄商い
  - narrow market security 品薄債券, 品薄株
  - narrow money (M1) 狭義の通貨(M1), 狭義のマネー(M1)
  - narrow money supply 狭義のマネー・サプライ
  - narrow profit margins 利ざやが薄いこと
  - narrower band 変動幅縮小制度, ナロアー・バンド
  - trade in a narrow range 狭いレンジ[ボックス圏]でもみ合う, 狭いボックス圏で推移する
  - ◆The yen hovered in a narrow range in the upper ¥85 level to the dollar. 円相場は、1ドル＝85円台後半の小幅な値動きとなった。◆The yen moved in a narrow range in the upper ¥85 level against the U.S. dollar in Tokyo. 東京外為市場は、円相場が1ドル＝85円台後半の小幅な値動きとなった。
- **narrowing** (名)縮小, 狭くなること
  - narrowing of interest margins 利ざやの縮小
  - narrowing of spread さや寄せ
  - spread narrowing スプレッドの縮小
- **NASD** 全米証券業協会(National Association of Securities Dealersの略)
  - ◆NASD is the parent of the Nasdaq over-the-counter stock market. 全米証券業協会(NASD)は、米国の店頭株式市場「ナスダック」の運営母体である。
- **NASDAQ [Nasdaq]** ナスダック, 米店頭株式市場, 全国店頭銘柄気配自動通報システム, 全国店頭銘柄建値自動通報システム, 店頭銘柄自動通報システム(National Association of Securities Dealers Automated Quotations Systemsの略)
  - NASDAQ index ナスダック株価指数
  - NASDAQ OMX Group, Inc. ナスダックOMXグループ, NASDAQ OMXグループ
  - the U.S. Nasdaq market 米ナスダック市場
  - ◆Six NYSE-listed blue-chip companies agreed to dual-list on Nasdaq and NYSE. ニューヨーク証券取引所に上場している優良企業6社が、ナスダック(米店頭株式市場)とNYSEへの重複上場に合意した。
- **Nasdaq composite index** ナスダック総合株価指数, ナスダック店頭市場の総合指数, ナスダック総合指数
  - ◆Broader stock indicators such as the S&P 500 index and the Nasdaq composite index also dropped in February. 2月は、S&P500株価指数やナスダック総合株価指数などの総合株価指数も、低下[下落]した。◆Nasdaq composite index finished at levels not seen since October. ナスダック店頭市場の総合指数は、10月以来の水準で取引を終えた。◆The Nasdaq composite index fell 13.63, or 1 percent, to 1,377.84. ナスダック総合株価指数は、13.63ドル(1%)下落して1,377.84ドルとなった。

- **Nasdaq Japan** ナスダック・ジャパン(上場企業の誘致などを手がける。2002年8月16日付けで営業活動を停止)
  - ◆Nasdaq Japan was set up in May 2000, backed by the U.S. Nasdaq Stock Market and Softbank Corp., the nation's largest Internet investor. ナスダック・ジャパンは、米ナスダック・ストック・マーケットと日本最大手のインターネット関連投資会社であるソフトバンクの支援を受けて、2000年5月に設立された。
- **Nasdaq Japan Inc.** ナスダック・ジャパン
  - ◆The Osaka Securities Exchange canceled its business arrangement with Tokyo-based Nasdaq Japan Inc.—with which it had operated Nasdaq Japan since 2000— in December 2002. 大阪証券取引所(大証)は、2000年以降ナスダック・ジャパンを共同で運営してきたナスダック・ジャパン社(本社・東京)との業務契約を、2002年12月に解消した。
- **Nasdaq Japan market** ナスダック・ジャパン市場
  - ◆The company made a public stock offering on the Nasdaq Japan market on the Osaka Securities Exchange in March 2001. 同社は、2001年3月、大阪証券取引所のナスダック・ジャパン(現ヘラクレス)市場に株式を上場した。
- **Nasdaq Stock Market** ナスダック証券市場, ナスダック(マイクロソフトやインテルなど5,000を超える銘柄が上場して取引され、これ以外に数千銘柄が店頭(OTC)市場で取引されている)
  - ◆Common shares in Google Inc. went public on the U.S. Nasdaq Stock Market in 2004. インターネット検索グーグルの普通株式は、2004年に米国ナスダックに上場された。
- **Nasdaq Stock Market Inc.** ナスダック・ストック・マーケット(ナスダック・ジャパンの親会社・運営会社)
  - ◆The Nasdaq Stock Market Inc. will delist Adelphia based upon its failure to timely file its periodic reports with the Securities and Exchange Commission as required by Nasdaq rules. アデルフィア(米国のケーブルテレビ会社)がナスダックのルールに従って義務づけられている定期報告書を米証券取引委員会に期間内に提出していないため、ナスダック・ストック・マーケットは同社の上場廃止に踏み切る方針だ。
- **NASDIM** 全国証券業者投資管理者協会(National Association of Securities Dealers and Investment Managersの略)
- **national** (形)国民の, 国家の, 全国的な, 国立の, 国有の, ナショナル
  - National Association of Insurance Commissioners 全米保険監督官協会, NAIC
  - National Association of Investors Corporation 全米投資家協会, NAIC
  - National Association of Purchasing Management's (NAPM) survey 全米購買部協会景気報告
  - National Association of Realtors 全米不動産業協会
  - National Bank Act of 1864 1864年連邦法銀行法
  - national budget 国家予算, 国民予算
  - national budget deficit 財政赤字
  - National Bureau of Economic Research 全米経済研究所, NBER(経済学者が米国の景気循環を中立的な立場で判定する民間の非営利団体)
  - National Credit Union Administration 米信用組合庁, 全米信用組合管理機構
  - National Credit Union Administration Central Liquidity Facility 全米信用組合管理機構中央流動性基金
  - national pension system 国民年金制度, 国民年金(=national pension plan, national pension program, national pension scheme)
  - national regulations 国内規制
  - national savings 国民貯蓄
  - National Tax Administration Agency 国税庁

national treasury　国庫
National Association of Securities Dealers　全米証券業協会, NASD
　National Association of Securities Dealers Automated Quotations　店頭銘柄気配自動通報, ナスダック
　National Association of Securities Dealers Automatic Quotations System　店頭銘柄気配自動通報システム
national bank　米連邦法銀行［国法銀行］, 全国銀行, 国立銀行
　◆The National Bank of Cuba will not be able to pay for imports into Cuba in due terms as the country is short of settlement funds. キューバ国立銀行は今後、国全体の決済資金不足で、期日どおりにキューバへの輸入代金の支払いができなくなる状況にある。
national bond　国債　(=national debt)
　issue more national bonds　国債を増発する
　national bonds for administrative reform　行政改革国債
　the issuance of new national bonds　新規国債の発行, 新規国債の発行額
　◆In Japan, ninety-five percent of its national bonds are held in a stable manner by domestic investors. 日本の場合、国債の95％は国内投資家が安定的に所有している。◆Koizumi remains cautious about compiling a supplementary budget because he had promised to limit the issuance of new national bonds to ¥30 trillion. 小泉首相が補正予算の編成に慎重姿勢を崩さないのは、新規国債の発行額30兆円以下に抑えるという公約があるからだ。◆The current situation has made it inevitable for the government to issue more national bonds. 政府の国債増発は、もはや避けられない情勢になっている。
national bond rating　国債の格付け
　◆The Greek economic chaos was triggered as its national bond rating was lowered. ギリシャの経済混乱のきっかけは、ギリシャの国債格付けが引き下げられたことだ。
national debt　国債　(=national bond)
　default on the national debt　国債の債務不履行
　zero national debt　ゼロ国債
　◆A day after declaring default on the national debt, Argentina's new president rolled out an ambitious works program. 国債の債務不履行（デフォルト）を宣言した翌日、アルゼンチンの新大統領は、野心的な労働政策を発表した。◆Greece's default on the national debts would be a blow to the operation of financial institutions in France and Germany that hold Greek government bonds. ギリシャが国債の債務不履行に陥った場合、ギリシャ国債を保有するフランスやドイツなどの金融機関の経営は、打撃を受けるだろう。
national debt consolidation fund　国債整理基金
　◆The profits from sale of government-held NTT shares are supposed to be set aside in special accounts of the national debt consolidation fund to pay off national bonds when they are redeemed. 政府保有のNTT株の売却益は、国債整理基金の特別会計として、将来の国債償還の財源に充てられるべきものである。
national health insurance　国民健康保険
national insurance　国民保険
　National Insurance Act　国民保険法
　national insurance fund　国民年金基金
　national insurance number　国民保険個人番号
　National Life Finance Corporation　国民生活金融公庫
　◆Six state-run financial institutions were reorganized into three, the Japan Bank for International Cooperation (JBIC), the Development Bank of Japan and the National Life Finance Corporation. 政府系の6つの金融機関が、国際協力銀行、日本政策投資銀行と国民生活金融公庫の3つに統合［再編］された。
national pension　国民年金
　◆Regarding national pension, subscribers' contributions would have to increase from ¥13,300 a month to ¥29,600 a month from fiscal 2025 to maintain the current level of pension payments. 国民年金については、現在の年金給付水準を維持するには、2025年度以降、加入者の保険料を月13,300円から29,600円に引き上げる必要がある。
national pension plan　国民年金, 国民年金制度
　◆If a housewife whose annual income is ¥1.3 million or more, or her husband becomes self-employed, the housewife must join the national pension plan and pay premiums. 主婦の年収が130万円以上の場合、または夫が脱サラした場合には、主婦も国民年金に加入して保険料を支払わなければならない。◆The basic pension plan is also known as the national pension plan. 基礎年金は、国民年金とも呼ばれている。◆Those housewives who have failed to switch to the national pension plan and have not paid premiums for an extensive period may receive a pittance or nothing at all. 国民年金への切替えをせず、保険料を長期間払っていない主婦は、低年金や無年金になる可能性がある。
national pension premium　国民年金保険料
　◆The government tightened the criteria for granting total exemption from paying national pension premiums. 政府は、国民年金保険料の全額免除の基準を厳格にした。◆The ratio of those who do not pay national pension premiums has doubled in the past decade. 国民年金保険料の未納率が、この10年で倍増している。
national pension program　国民年金, 国民年金制度
　(=national pension plan [scheme, system])
　◆The issue of the inadvertent failure to switch to the national pension program by full-time housewives must be quickly solved. 専業主婦の国民年金への年金資格切替え忘れ問題は、決着を急ぐべきだ。◆The rate of contributions to the national pension program, designed mainly for the self-employed, students aged 20 and older and young people working part-time, dipped to a record 62.8 percent. 自営業者や20歳以上の学生、フリーターらが加入する国民年金の納付率が、過去最悪の62.8％に落ち込んだ。
national pension scheme　国民年金, 国民年金制度
　(=national pension system; ⇒hollowing-out)
　◆The national pension scheme mainly covers students aged 20 or older and the self-employed. 国民年金の加入対象は、主に20歳以上の学生や自営業者だ。
national pension system　国民年金制度, 国民年金
　(=national pension program [scheme])
　◆The national pension system collects a uniform premium of ¥13,300 per month. 国民年金の徴収保険料は、一律月額13,300円である。◆Those with incomes less than a certain level will be exempted from paying a full monthly premium to the national pension system. 一定水準以下の所得者は、国民年金保険料の月納付額を全額免除される。
nationalization　(名)国有化, 国営化, 国営, 全国拡大, 全国展開
　effective nationalization　実質国有化
　nationalization of a bank　銀行の国有化
　nationalization of basic industries　基礎産業国有化
　nationalization of Western capital　欧米資本の国有化
　nationalization policy　国有化政策
　precontracted nationalization　事前契約による国有化
　temporary nationalization　一時的国有化, 一時的国営化
　◆In the temporary nationalization, the government will take possession of all shares from the bank's holding company at no cost. 一時国有化で、政府は同行の持ち株会社から株式をゼロ円で全株取得することになる。
nationalize　(動)国有化［国営化］する, 国営にする, 全国に拡大する, 全国展開する
　◆Speculation that some major banks may find themselves with capital shortfalls and then nationalized is driving in-

vestors to dump the banks' shares. 大手行の一部が自己資本不足に陥って国有化されるとの思惑から、投資家は銀行株の売りに出ている。◆The Dutch government will nationalize Fortis' Dutch operations. オランダ政府は、ベルギー・オランダ系金融大手フォルティスの自国事業部門を国有化する方針だ。

nationwide （形）全国的な, 全国の, 全国規模の, 全国に及ぶ
◆The nationwide consumer price index fell 1.1 percent in May 2009, year on year. 2009年5月の全国消費者物価指数は、前年同月比で1.1%低下した。

natural disaster 自然災害
◆To make up for losses and for other purposes, seven life insurers used a total of ￥529.2 billion in reserves, which are set aside in preparation for interest rate fluctuations and natural disasters. 損失の穴埋めなどのため、金利変動や自然災害に備えて積み立てている準備金を、生保7社が5,292億円も取り崩した。

NBER 全米経済研究所 (National Bureau of Economic Researchの略)
Business Cycle Dating Committee of the National Bureau of Economic Research, 全米経済研究所 (NBER) 景気循環判定委員会
◆The NBER's business cycle dating committee concluded that the economic expansion that started in November 2001 had ended. 全米経済研究所 (NBER) の景気循環判定委員会の委員は、「2001年から始まった米景気の拡大はすでに終わっている」との見解で一致した。

near （動）近づく, 迫る, 接近する
◆The 10-year bond yield of Spain has likewise neared the 7 percent level, the danger zone that may fall into a debt crisis. スペインの10年物国債利回り［国債流通利回り］も、債務危機に陥る恐れがある危険水域の7%台に迫った。

near （形）近い, 期近の, よく似た, 近似の, 準〜, 関係の深い
 be near all-time highs 過去最高に近い, 過去最高に近い水準にある
 near cash 現金性通貨
 near delivery 期近物 (きぢかもの), 近先物
 near future 目先
 near futures 近先物
 near liquid assets 流動性の高い資産 (=highly liquid assets)
 near-market 商業生産と密接に関連した, メーカーに直接的利益をもたらす
 near maturity 近満期, 近満期物
 near money 準通貨, 準貨幣 (=quasi money: 定期預金や政府債券などすぐに現金化できる資産・債権)
 near money claim 準貨幣債権
 near month 期近物
 the nearest month 直近限月
◆The U.S. Federal Reserve Board pledged to keep interest rates near zero until mid-2013. 米連邦準備制度理事会 (FRB) は、2013年半ばまでゼロ金利政策を維持することを誓った。◆The yen has been hovering near its record high of ￥76.25 against the U.S. dollar in Tokyo. 東京外国為替市場の円相場は、戦後最高値の1ドル=76円25銭に迫る水準で推移している。

near term 短期, 近い将来
 be close to near-term peak 間もなく当面のピークに達する, 間もなく目先のピークを打つ
 near-term indicator 短期指標
 near-term outlook [expectations, prospects] 短期見通し
 near-term peak 当面のピーク, 目先のピーク
 near-term target 短期目標, 当面の目標
 near-term top 目先の高値

◆Near-term uncertainty surrounding the global economy continues to grow. 世界経済を取り巻く短期的な先行き不安は、増大傾向が続いている。

nearbank （名）準銀行（銀行に近い機能を持つ金融機関）

necessary funds 必要資金
◆We are considering using the company's shares as security to secure the necessary funds. 当社は、同社株を担保にして必要資金を確保することを検討している。

need （動）必要とする, 〜する必要がある, 〜するころを求める
◆In foreign currency deposits, commission fees are needed when the yen is exchanged into a foreign currency and when the foreign currency is exchanged backed in yen. 外貨預金では、円を外貨に替えるときと、外貨を円に戻すときに、為替手数料が必要になる。

need （名）必要, 入用, 欲求, 要求, まさかのとき, いざという場合, 困窮, 窮乏, 貧困
◆The report stresses the need to increase the overall supply capacity through structural reforms as a remedy for economic stagnation. 同報告書は、不況対策として、構造改革によって総供給力を引き上げる必要があると力説している。

needs （名）必要, 必要量, 必要額, 要求, 需要, 必需品, 課題, ニーズ
 borrowing needs 借入需要, 資金調達需要, 調達額
 business needs 経営上の必要, 経営上の必要性
 capital needs 資金需要, 資本必要額, 必要資本
 financing needs 資金調達需要, 資金調達のニーズ［必要性］, 資金ニーズ, 調達額
 funding needs 資金調達需要, 調達のニーズ
 investment needs 投資需要
 investor needs 投資家のニーズ
 liquidity needs 流動性需要
 market needs 市場の需要, 市場のニーズ (⇒policy)
 net borrowing needs 純調達額
 response to customer needs 顧客のニーズへの対応
 working capital needs 運転資金の必要額, 運転資金のニーズ

negative （形）マイナスの, 負の, 逆の, 赤字の, 反対の, 弱含みの, 弱気の, 引下げ方向の, 消極的な, 悪影響を与える, 有害な, 否定的な, 悲観的な, 成果が上がらない, ネガティブ （名）弱気材料, 悪材料, マイナス要因, 引下げ方向 (⇒positive)
 be negative on inflation インフレ見通しで弱気になる
 go into the negative マイナスになる
 negative amortization 負の返済, 未収利息による元本の増加
 negative asset quality 低下傾向の資産の質
 negative carry 負のキャリー, ネガティブ・キャリー
 negative cash flow 負のキャッシュ・フロー
 negative consideration 懸念材料
 negative convexity 凸面（とつめん）効果, ネガティブ・コンベクシティ
 negative correlation 負の相関, 逆相関
 negative currency effects 為替差損
 negative duration asset 負のデュレーションを持つ資産
 negative equity 負の資産（不動産の時価がローンの額以下に下がること）
 negative factor 悪材料, 懸念材料, 売り材料, マイナス要因 （プラス要因, 好材料 = positive factor; ⇒positive results）
 negative figure 赤字
 negative fiscal policy 消極的財政政策

negative force　懸念材料
negative foreign exchange pressures　通貨への売り圧力
negative fundamentals　逆風のファンダメンタルズ面
negative goodwill　消極のれん, 消極的のれん, 負ののれん, マイナスの営業権
negative impact　悪影響, マイナス影響, 悪材料, マイナス効果, 負の効果, 負の側面
negative implications　悪材料, マイナス要因, 格下げの方向
negative income tax　負の所得税, 逆所得税（低所得者に国が与える社会保障給付）
negative indebtedness　借入比率がマイナスであること
negative interest　マイナス金利, 逆金利　（=negative interest rate: 利息から差し引かれる金）
negative list　残存輸入制限品目リスト, 承認が必要な輸入品目リスト
negative marketing　絞りの戦略, ネガティブ・マーケティング
negative monetary policy　消極的金融政策
negative net gearing　負の純負債比率, 純負債比率がマイナスであること
negative news　悪材料, マイナス材料
negative option　消極的選択権（通信販売で頼みもしない商品が送られてきたときに、その代金を支払うか商品を送り返すかの選択権）
negative pledge　不担保約款（銀行の同意なしで他の債権者に担保権を設定しないという条項）
negative points　悪材料
negative property　消極財産
negative reaction　消極的な反応
negative tax　負の所得税, 逆所得税
negative thinking　マイナス思考
post negative returns　運用成績がマイナスになる
◆S&P cut ratings on Japanese banks and kept their outlook negative. スタンダード＆プアーズは、日本の大手行の格付けを引き下げ、「ネガティブ（弱含み）」の見通しを据え置いた。◆The DI reading among small and medium companies as well as nonmanufacturing corporations remains negative. 中小企業と非製造業のDIの数値は依然、マイナスが続いている。◆The rating outlook of "negative" by a credit rating agency means that another downgrade is possible in the next 12 to 18 months. 信用格付け機関による「ネガティブ（弱含み）」の格付け見通しは、今後1年～1年半にふたたび格下げされる可能性があることを意味している。◆The U.S. credit rating agency revised upward the outlook to positive from negative on its rating on Sumitomo Life Insurance Co. この米国の信用格付け機関は、住友生命保険の格付け見通しを「ネガティブ（弱含み）」から「ポジティブ（強含み）」に上方修正した。

negative aspects　暗い面, マイナス面, 悪材料, マイナス材料
◆The government led by the Democratic Party of Japan lacks a coherent strategy to address the negative aspects of Japan's debt dynamics. 民主党政権は、日本のマイナス材料の債務問題への取組みに対する一貫した戦略に欠けている。

negative chain reaction　負の連鎖反応, 連鎖破たん
◆The possibility that the bank's collapse will set off a negative chain reaction is very low. 同行の破たんが連鎖破たんを引き起こす可能性は、かなり低い。

negative effect　悪影響, 悪材料, マイナス影響, マイナス効果, 負の効果, 負の側面　（=negative impact）
◆If the yen starts to appreciate, this will have a negative effect on the revenues of exporting companies. 円高に転じれば、輸出企業の収益は円高のマイナス影響を受けることになる。

negative growth　マイナス成長 （⇒economy-slowing factor）
◆That eurozone GDP shrank in the second quarter as well would add up to two consecutive quarters of negative growth—a definition of a technical recession. ユーロ圏のGDP（域内総生産）が第2四半期も低下したことで、ユーロ圏は2四半期連続のマイナス成長（定義上、テクニカル・リセッション）となった。◆The European economy might slow down and register negative growth if eurozone states introduce austerity measures. ユーロ圏各国が緊縮財政策を導入すると、欧州の景気は減速し、マイナス成長に陥る恐れがある。◆The national economy will post negative growth in fiscal 2002 for second year in a row. 日本経済は、2002年度は2年連続でマイナス成長になる。

negative impact　負の側面, 負の効果, マイナス効果, マイナス影響, 悪影響, 悪材料　（=negative effect）
◆Excessive movements of foreign exchange rates will have a negative impact on the stability of the economy and financial markets. 行き過ぎた外国為替相場の動きは、経済の安定と金融市場に悪影響を及ぼす。◆Maintaining an easy monetary policy may lead to excessive corporate capital investment and have a negative impact on the sustainable economic recovery. 金融緩和政策を続けると、企業の過剰な設備投資を生み、景気の持続的回復を阻害する恐れがある。◆The downturn in global financial markets has had a negative impact on insurance products such as single-premium pension insurance policies which are popular as a form of savings. 世界の金融市場の低迷が、貯蓄用[一種の貯蓄]として人気の高い一時払い年金保険などの保険商品に悪影響を及ぼしている。◆The People's Bank of China kept interest rates unchanged out of concerns that higher rates would have a negative impact on the economy. 中国人民銀行は、利上げのマイナス効果を心配したため、金利を据え置いてきた。◆Volatile movements in the currency market have a negative impact on economic and financial stability. 為替市場の過度な変動は、経済・金融の安定に悪影響を及ぼす。

negative interest rate　マイナス金利, 逆金利
◆In the case of negative real interest rates, savers lose out and borrowers benefit as nominal interest rates are insufficient to compensate for inflation. 実質金利がマイナスの場合は、名目金利で物価上昇分を十分埋め合わせできないため、貯蓄者は損をして借り手が得をする。

negative legacy　負の遺産（企業の「負の遺産」としては、不良債権のほかに、赤字続きの子会社、値下がりした株や不動産、退職金や企業年金の積立て不足といったものが挙げられる）
◆Banks should cut their losses—nonperforming loans and other negative legacies of the bubble economy. 銀行は、不良債権やその他バブル期の「負の遺産」の損切りをしなければならない。

negative net worth　債務超過, 負債超過, 債務超過額, 税引き後利益の赤字, 赤字　（⇒subject to）
develop [have] a negative net worth　債務超過になる
fall into a negative net worth　債務超過に陥る
recover one's negative net worth　～の債務超過解消する
sink into a negative net worth　債務超過に陥る
◆Life Insurance Policyholders Protection Corp. will provide ¥145 billion to partially cover the life insurer's negative net worth, which was ¥320 billion as of the end of last September. 生命保険契約者保護機構は、昨年9月末現在の同生保の債務超過額3,200億円の一部を支援するため、1,450億円を支出することになっている。◆The financial statements and a score of related documents show that the company has a negative net worth. 財務書類と約20の関連資料は、同社が債務超過であることを示している。◆To avoid sinking into a negative net worth, the firm is seeking ¥300 billion in financial aid from capital providers. 債務超過に陥るのを避けるため、同社は資

金提供者に3,000億円の金融支援を要請している。

negative outlook （信用格付けの）引下げ見通し
◆Moody's Investors Service cut Japan's yen-denominated debt rating by one notch to Aa3 from Aa2 and maintained a negative outlook. 米国の格付け会社ムーディーズは、日本の円建て国債の格付けを「Aa2」から「Aa3」に一段階引き下げ、「ネガティブ（弱含み）」の見通しを据え置いた。◆Rating agency Moody's may place a negative outlook on French government's Aaa debt rating as the government's financial strength has weakened. 格付け会社のムーディーズは、フランス国債のAaa（トリプルA）格付けについて、仏政府の財務体質［財務力］が弱まっているため「ネガティブ（弱含み）」の見通しを示す可能性がある。◆The eurozone's six AAA-rated countries including France and Germany were among the nations placed on a negative outlook. 独仏などユーロ圏のトリプルA格の6か国も、信用格付けの引下げ見通しの対象国になった。

negative spread 逆ざや （=negative yield: 運用利回りが保険契約者に約束した予定利率を下回ること。⇒promised yield）
◆The amount of the negative spread—the margin of loss that occurs when yields from investments made with policyholder premiums are lower than yields insurers promised their policyholders—totals an annual of ¥1.5 trillion. 逆ざやの総額、つまり保険契約者の保険の掛金（保険料）で行った投資の利回り（運用利回り）が、契約者に保険会社が約束した利回り（予定利率）より低い場合に生じる損失額は、年間1兆5千億円に上る。

negative territory マイナス, マイナス基調 （=minus territory; ⇒territory）
◆It is the sixth straight quarter that business sentiment among large firms has stayed in negative territory. 6四半期連続、大企業の景況判断指数はマイナスのままだ。

negative wealth effect 逆資産効果（土地や株その他の資産価格の下落）
◆The so-called negative wealth effect—the drop in the value of land, stocks and other assets—is an apparent result of the fall in stock prices. 今回のいわゆる逆資産効果（土地や株その他の資産価格の下落）は、明らかに株価の下落によるものだ。

negative yield 逆イールド, 逆ざや （=negative spread; ⇒financial soundness, return on investment）
　negative yield curve 右下がりの利回り曲線, 逆イールド, 逆イールド・カーブ
◆All the insurers are now saddled with an enormous amount of negative yields as returns on their investments have plunged due to ultra low interest rates—a consequence of the bursting of the bubble. 生保各社は現在、バブル崩壊後の超低金利時代で運用利回りが急低下し、巨額の逆ざやを抱えている。◆The massive negative yields of the life insurance industry threaten the financial soundness of insurers. 生保業界の巨額の逆ざやが、生保各社の財務上の健全性［経営の健全性］を脅（おびや）かしている。

negotiability （名）通貨の交換性, 流通性

negotiable （形）流通可能の, 流通性のある, 手形などを譲渡できる, 譲渡可能な, 買い取ることができる, 換金性のある
　highly negotiable cash vouchers 換金性の高い金券類 （⇒voucher）
　negotiable asset 譲渡可能資産
　negotiable bill 流通手形
　negotiable bill of lading 譲渡可能船荷証券
　negotiable bond 市場性債券
　negotiable cash voucher 換金性の高い金券類
　negotiable certificate of deposit 譲渡性預金, 譲渡性預金証書, NCD （=negotiable CD）
　negotiable check 譲渡性小切手
　negotiable debt 譲渡可能債券
　negotiable document 流通証券 （=negotiable instrument［paper］: 小切手、手形、株券など）
　negotiable instrument 有価証券, 流通証券, 換金可能証券 （=negotiable securities）
　negotiable note 譲渡不能約束手形
　negotiable order of withdrawal 譲渡可能払戻し指図書
　negotiable paper 流通証券 （=negotiable document［instrument］）
　negotiable securities 有価証券
　negotiable time certificate of deposit 譲渡可能定期預金証書
　negotiable time deposit 譲渡可能定期預金
　negotiable warehouse receipt 指図式倉庫証券
　Uniform Negotiable Instruments Law 統一流通証券法
◆The letter of credit set forth above shall be negotiable against a draft at sight signed by the seller upon the presentation of the following documents. 上記の信用状は、次の船積み書類の提示がある場合には、売り主が振り出した一覧払い手形と引換えに買い取られるものとする。◆The repurchasing method, which has customers buy highly negotiable cash vouchers, violates the industry rule. 顧客に換金性の高い金券類を購入させる買取り方式は、業界の規約に違反する。

negotiate （動）交渉する, 交渉して取り決める, 協議する, 協定する, 商議する, 話し合う, （手形、小切手などを）譲渡する, 換金する, 流通させる
　be on a strong［good］negotiating position 交渉上有利な立場にある
　negotiate a new deal with ～と新規契約を結ぶ
　negotiate the deal 取決めを結ぶ
　negotiated market 相対売買市場（店頭市場とほぼ同義）, 顧客市場
　negotiated market price 交渉市場価格
　negotiated price 協議価格
　negotiated sale 協議発行
　negotiated transaction （株の）相対取引, 相対売買, 交渉案件
　negotiated underwriting （証券）協議引受け, 協議引受方式
　negotiating bank （手形の）買取り銀行
　negotiating position 交渉力
◆The firm is currently negotiating with its domestic capital partners to conclude change-of-control agreements. 同社は現在、国内の資本提携先とチェンジ・オブ・コントロール（資本拘束）条項の契約を結ぶ交渉を進めている。◆The four companies negotiated and agreed in advance the bid winner and the bidding price. 4社は、事前に談合を行って落札予定会社や入札価格を決めた。◆You should not reveal all your tactics at once when negotiating. 交渉では、自分の戦術をすべて一度に明かさないようにするとよい。

negotiation （名）交渉, 協議, 商談, 取引, 流通, 権利の移転, 譲渡, 輸出地の取引銀行による荷為替手形の買取り, ネゴシエーション
　business negotiation 商談
　conclude negotiations 交渉をまとめる
　enter into final negotiations with ～と最終調整に入る
　negotiation by draft 取立為替, 逆為替
　negotiation charge 手形買取り手数料, 買取り手数料, 手形取組み時に銀行が請求する手数料
　negotiation credit 買取り信用状
　negotiation of a draft 手形の買取り［譲渡］
　negotiation of bills 荷為替の取組み
　negotiation of export bill 輸出手形の買取り

negotiation or acceptance commission　買取りまたは引受手数料
negotiations fall through　交渉が決裂する
negotiations on the capital increase　増資交渉
secured debt　有担保債券, 担保付き債務
◆Argentina clinched a debt rollover deal with the IMF after a year of tortuous negotiations. アルゼンチンは, 1年にわたる難交渉の末, 国際通貨基金(IMF)との債務返済繰延べ取引をまとめた。◆GM obtained agreements from a majority of creditors in negotiations to reduce its debts significantly. 米ゼネラル・モーターズ(GM)は, 巨額の債務削減交渉で, 大半の債権者から合意を取り付けた。◆If the negotiations between Republicans and Democrats face rough going and the deficit-cutting plan ends up being insufficient, credit rating agencies may downgrade Treasury bonds. 共和党と民主党の協議が難航して赤字削減策が不十分に終わると, (信用)格付け会社が米国債の格下げに踏み切る可能性がある。◆The struggling JAL's next step will be to start negotiations with its creditor banks over new loans to enact its rehabilitation plan. 経営再建に取り組む日航は今後, 同社の再建計画案の実行に必要な新規融資を巡る取引銀行団との交渉に移ることになる。◆The two banks have started negotiations on the integration of their businesses, a possible merger. 両行は, 合併の可能性も含めて, 経営統合に向けた協議を開始した。◆The upcoming negotiations will determine practical measures to strengthen ties, including the merger ratio, the name of the new group and the positions to be held by top executives. 今後の交渉で, 統合比率や新グループの名称, 首脳人事など提携強化の具体策を詰める。

nest eggs　備蓄, 将来のための蓄え, 貯蓄

net　(動)相殺する, 純益を上げる, 獲得する, 調達する, もたらす, ネッティングする
　net cash positions　直物ポジションを相殺する
　net foreign exchange gains and losses　外為取引による損益を相殺する
　net out outstanding swaps　残存スワップを清算する
　net payment obligations to a single payment　債務額をネッティングして一括返済する
　net the prepaid costs with the liabilities　前払い費用を債務と相殺する
　net the two sides of a swap transaction　両方向のスワップ取引を相殺する
　vehicle for netting swap collateral　スワップ担保の相殺機関
◆Publicly listing Tokyo Metro and selling shares in it could net the government hundreds of billions of yen. 東京地下鉄(東京メトロ)の株式を上場して保有株式を売却すれば, 国は数千億円の収入を見込める。◆The sale of assets netted the company a great profit. 資産の売却で, 同社は大幅な収益を上げた。◆The U.S. government's block sale shares netted about $6.2 billion. 米政府の大量売却株での資金調達額は, 約62億ドルだった。◆We netted these prepaid costs with the liabilities. 当社は, この前払い費用を債務と相殺しました。

Net [net]　(名)インターネット (Internet, internet), ネット, 網状組織, ～網
　Net auction　ネット・オークション　(=Internet auction, online auction: インターネットのサイト上で, 出品された商品が競売にかけられ, 最高値で落札した人が購入の権利を得る)
　Net bank　ネット銀行, ネット専業銀行, ネット・バンク　(=Internet bank, Internet-based bank, Net-only bank)
　Net-based bidding system　電子入札制度, ネット入札制度　(=Net-bidding system)
　Net buyer　ネット購入者, ネット投資家, ネット・バイヤー
　Net consumer　ネット・コンシューマー
　Net-debit service　ネット決済サービス, インターネット即時決済サービス
　Net-direct　ネット直販
　Net server　ネット事業者
　Net share trading　ネット株取引, インターネットでの株取引　(=online stock trading)
　Net shopping　ネット・ショッピング　(=electronic commerce, Internet shopping, online shopping)
　Net use　ネット利用, インターネットの利用　(=use of the Net, use of the Internet)
　safety net　安全網
◆We must expedite efforts to rebuild a safety net to support the financial system. 金融システムを支える安全網の立直し策を急ぐ必要がある。

net　(形)基本的な, 最終的な, 結局の, 正味の, 掛け値のない, 純粋の, 税引き後の
　net accounts receivable　売掛金純額
　net advance　純貸出高
　net amount　純額, 正味金額, 正味資産
　net amount owed　正味負債額
　net balance　純収支残高, 純収支尻
　net basis　配当金[配当]課税後利益法, 純額ベース
　net book value　正味帳簿価額, 正味簿価, 純簿価, NBV　(=net carrying value)
　net borrowing　正味借入金
　net business profit　業務純益, 業務純利益
　net capital deficiency　債務超過, 純資本不足　(=capital deficit)
　net capital gain　純資本所得, 純キャピタル・ゲイン(資本利得), 純額キャピタル・ゲイン
　net carrying amount　正味繰越し額, 簿価純額, 減価償却費控除後簿価
　net carrying value　正味簿価, 正味帳簿価額
　net current assets　正味流動資産, 純流動資産
　net decrease in cash and cash equivalents　現金および現金等価物の純減少
　net earned surplus forwarded　繰越し利益剰余金
　net effects　正味の影響, 正味の影響額, 純影響額
　net exports　純輸出　(純輸出＝輸出-輸入)
net asset　純資産, 正味資産, 正味財産　(総資産から総負債を差し引いた資産残高。⇒balance sheet)
　net asset available for benefit　給付可能な純資産
　net asset value　純資産価値, 純資産額, 正味資産額, 純資産, 純財産, NAV　(=net worth: 貸借対照表上の資産総額から負債総額を差し引いた額で, 自己資本の額にあたる)
　net asset value per share　1株当たり純資産価値, 普通株式1株当たり純資産価値　(book value per share(1株当たり純資産, 1株当たり簿価)とか net tangible assets per share(1株当たり純有形資産価値)ともいう。会社が解散した場合, 株主は持ち株数に応じて残った財産が分配されるが, その時の1株当たり資産が「1株当たり純資産」で, 解散価値ともいわれている)
　net assets at year-end　期末現在の純資産額, 期末純資産
　net assets employed　純運用資産
　net assets worth per share　1株当たり純資産　(=net assets worth)
◆In terms of net asset calculation, a reduction in assets is tantamount to an increase in liabilities. 純資産の計算上, 資産の取り崩しと負債の増加は同じことだ。◆The actuarial present value of the accrued plan benefits and the net assets available to discharge these benefits at December 31 are as follows: 12月31日現在の年金給付債務額の年金数理原価と年

金給付債務に充当可能な年金純資産は、以下のとおりです。

net balance　純収支残高, 純収支尻
◆Yasuda Mutual plans to dig into its retained earnings to prevent its net balance from sinking into the red. 純収支残高が赤字に転落するのを防ぐため、安田生命は内部留保を取り崩す方針だ。

Net banking　ネット・バンキング
（=Internet banking）
◆Personal computers of many Net banking depositors have been infected with viruses that ravaged computers in the United States and European countries. 多くのネット・バンキング預金者のパソコンが、欧米のコンピュータに爆発的被害を生んだウイルスに感染していた。

Net bubble　ネット株バブル, ネット・バブル
◆The U.S. economic downturn is a result of the bursting of the Net bubble, in other words, the collapse of the technology stock boom. アメリカ経済減速の要因は、ネット株バブルの崩壊、つまりIT株ブームの崩壊である。

net business profit　業務純益, 業務純利益

net buyer　ネット購入者, ネット投資家, ネット・バイヤー
◆Nonresident investors were net buyers of Japanese stocks in April for the second consecutive month. 4月の非居住者投資家は、2カ月連続で日本株のネット・バイヤーであった。

net buying　株の買い越し, 買い越し額　(=buying on balance, on-balance buying: 一定期間に有価証券を売った量と買った量を比較して、買った量が多い場合に買い越しとなる)
◆Foreign investors' net buying so far has reached about ¥4 trillion this year. 外国人投資家のこれまでの株式の買い越し額は、今年は約4兆円に達している。

net capital deficiency　債務超過, 純資本不足
（=capital deficit）
◆The going concern rules require corporations to state in their financial statements whether they are in danger of net capital deficiency, defaults of obligations and continued operating losses. ゴーイング・コンサーン（企業の継続能力）規定は、債務超過や債務不履行、継続的な営業損失などが発生する恐れがあるかどうかを財務書類（財務諸表）に明記するよう企業に義務付けている。

net creditor position　対外純資産残高
◆Japan's net creditor position is gauged by gross holdings of foreign assets by the government, business and individuals minus gross holdings of Japanese assets by foreigners. 日本の対外純資産残高は、日本の政府や企業、個人が海外に持つ資産の総保有額（対外資産残高）から、海外の政府や企業、個人が日本国内に持つ資産の総保有額（対外負債残高）を差し引いて算定される。

Net-debit service　ネット決済サービス, インターネット即時決済サービス
◆The new Net-debit service will enable consumers to make purchases on the Internet and have the cost deducted automatically from their bank or postal savings accounts. この新しいネット決済サービスを利用すると、利用者はインターネット上で買い物をして、その代金を利用者の銀行か郵便貯金の口座から自動的に引き落としてもらうことができる。

net external asset　対外純資産
（=net foreign asset）

net income　純利益, 当期純利益, 税引き後利益, 純所得, 純収入, 日銀の剰余金
（=net profit, profit after tax）
first-half net income　上期の純利益, 1-6月期の純利益
net income for the three months ended Dec. 31　10-12月期の税引き後利益
◆HSBC's first-half net income fell to $7.7 billion, or 65 cents a share, from $10.9 billion, or 94 cents, a year earlier. 英銀最大手HSBCの上期［1-6月期］の純利益は、前年同期の109億ドル（1株当たり65セント）に対して77億ドル（1株当たり65セント）に減少した。◆Net income rose 7.3 percent to ¥426.8 billion for the three months ended Dec. 31. 10-12月期は、純利益［税引き後利益］が7.3%増の4,268億円だった。◆Nomura Holdings' net income of ¥2.3 billion for the three months ended June 30 was the lowest in five quarters. 野村ホールディングスの4～6月期の税引き後利益23億円は、5四半期で最低となった。◆The Bank of Japan usually sets aside 5 percent of net income for reserves. 日銀は通常、剰余金の5%を法定準備金として積み立てる。

net inflows of funds　資金の純流入額
◆There was a 50 percent drop in net inflows of funds into the United States during the January-March quarter compared with the previous year, down to $113.3 billion. 1-3月期の米国への資金純流入額は、前年同期に比べて半減し、1,130億ドルにとどまった。

net loss　純損失, 当期純損失, 最終赤字
（⇒per-share net loss）
◆All major banks ended up incurring net losses. 大手銀行各行は、そろって最終赤字に転落した。◆For the year ending this March, the firm expects to post a net loss of ¥24.6 billion. 今年3月期決算で、同社は246億円の純損失を計上する見通しだ。

net operating profit　純営業利益, 営業純利益, 金融機関の業務純益　（⇒operating profit）
◆All of the seven major banking groups forecast that bad loan disposal at the end of March next year will be smaller than their net operating profits. 大手銀行・金融7グループ各行の業績予想では、来年3月期の不良債権処理額はいずれも業務純益の範囲内になる見込みだ。◆Every year, major banks have to dispose of nonperforming loans that exceed their net operating profits. 毎年、大手銀行は、業務純益を上回る不良債権の処理を迫られている。◆The losses the banks incurred far outstripped their net operating profits, obtained from core banking business, such as lending and commissions. 銀行の損失額が、貸付けや手数料など本業の銀行業務による業務純益を大きく上回った。

net premium revenue　正味収入保険料
◆Net premium revenues, which correspond to sales at non-financial firms, increased at four of the nation's nine major nonlife insurance companies. 非金融機関の売上高に相当する正味収入保険料は、国内大手損保9社のうち4社で増加した。

net proceeds　正味入金額, 純売却益, 純資金, 受取金純額
◆We had net proceeds of $600 million from selling our shares in the company. 当社は、同社株を売却して純額で6億ドルの売却益を得ました。

net profit　純利益, 当期純利益
（⇒per-share group net profit）
◆The company forecasts a net profit of ¥25 billion and pre-tax profit of ¥45 billion on sales of ¥3.7 trillion. 同社の予想では、売上高3兆7,000億円のうち、250億円の純利益と450億円の税引き前利益を見込んでいる。◆Toyota Motor's net profit increased 30.7 percent to ¥615.82 billion. トヨタ自動車の純利益は、30.7%増の6,158億2,000万円となった。

Net-related technologies　ネット関連技術
◆Sun Microsystems Inc. has supremacy in Net-related technologies. サン・マイクロシステムズは、ネット関連技術が優れている。

net selling　売り越し
◆The amount of net selling of Japanese stocks further increased in September. 9月は、日本株の売り越しの額がさらに増えた。

net worth　自己資本, 資本, 株主持ち分, 純資産, 純資産額, 正味資産, 正味財産　（⇒negative net worth）
fixed assets to net worth ratio　固定比率

（=ratio of net worth to fixed assets）
　high net worth customers［individuals］　資産家
　household net worth　家計純資産
　liabilities and net worth　負債と資産
　net worth agreement　純資産維持契約
　net worth certificate　純資産証書
　net worth debt ratio　資本負債比率, 資本・負債比率
　net worth maintenance　純資産維持
　net worth of collateral　担保余力
　net worth tax　富裕税
　net worth turnover ratio　自己資本回転率
　profit ratio of net worth　株主資本利益率
　ratio of net worth　株主資本比率
　　　（=net worth ratio）
　ratio of net worth to the total assets　株主資本比率
　ratio of (total) liabilities to net worth　負債・資本比率, 負債比率
　return on net worth　株主資本利益率
　sales to net worth　株主資本回転率
　tangible net worth　有形純資産
　total liabilities and net worth　総資本
　turnover (ratio) of total liabilities and net worth　総資本回転率
　◆The bank's capital adequacy ratio, or the ratio of its net worth against loans and other assets, dropped to minus 6.27 percent at the end of September—well below the plus 4 percent threshold required for banks operating domestically. 同行の自己資本比率（融資残高などの資産に対する自己資本の比率）は、9月末時点でマイナス6.27％まで落ち込み、国内銀行業務の銀行に義務付けられているプラス4％の水準を大幅に下回った。

net worth ratio　自己資本比率
　　　（=capital adequacy ratio, capital-asset ratio）
　◆The massive gains in stockholdings' latent value will raise the banks' net worth ratios markedly. 保有株式の含み益の大幅増加で、銀行の自己資本比率も大きく向上する見込みだ。

netting　（名）相殺, 相殺決済, (外為売買の)差額決済, ネッティング
　automatic netting of swap position　スワップ・ポジションの自動ネッティング
　bilateral netting　二者間ネッティング
　close-out netting　ポジションの手じまいによるネッティング, クローズアウト・ネッティング
　cross-border netting　国際間のネッティング
　interbank netting arrangement　銀行間のネッティング協定
　multilateral netting　複数当事者間のネッティング, 複数契約のネッティンク
　multilateral netting system　複数契約のネッティング・システム
　netting against underwriting expenses of ceding commissions paid or received　支払い再保険料ないし受取再保険料の引受経費との相殺
　netting agreement［arrangement］　ネッティング契約
　netting by novation　更改［ノーベーション］によるネッティング
　netting enforceability　ネッティングの法的拘束力
　netting of exposures across products　複数の商品にわたるポジションのネッティング
　netting of payments due　信用残の相殺
　recognition of netting　ネッティングの承認, ネッティングの導入
　recognize netting　ネッティングを承認する［認める］
　swap netting　スワップの相殺, スワップのネッティング

network　（名）網状組織, 関連組織, 連絡網, 通信網, 回線網, 回路網, 網, 通信ネットワーク, ネットワーク
　automatic teller machine network　ATM（自動預け払い機）ネットワーク
　Bank of Japan financial networks　日銀ネット
　branch network　支店網
　credit authorization network　信用照会ネットワーク
　Electronic Communications Networks　電子証券取引ネットワーク, ECN
　financial network　資金網
　information network　情報網, 高度情報通信ネットワーク, 情報ネットワーク
　interbank network　銀行間ネットワーク
　network configuration　ネットワーク構成
　network distribution　ネット配信
　◆Network configuration can be shifted by the customer at will to accommodate growth, innovation, or changes in the telecommunications industry. ネットワーの構成は、業務の拡張、通信技術の革新、顧客（ユーザー）が自由に変更することができる。

neutral　（形）中立の, 公平な, 中間の, 中性の, 灰色の, 景気に影響しない, ニュートラル　（名）中立的な姿勢［スタンス］, 中立者
　deficit neutral　財政赤字に影響しないこと, 財政赤字への影響をゼロにすること
　neutral budget　中立型予算, 中立予算, 均衡予算, 収支均衡が取れている予算
　neutral equilibrium　中立的均衡
　neutral equilibrium effect　中立的均衡効果
　neutral Fed　FRBの中立の姿勢, FRBの中立的スタンス
　neutral Fed policy　FRBの中立型金融政策
　neutral financial policy　中立的金融政策, 中立型の金融政策
　neutral fiscal policy　中立的財政政策, 中立型の財政政策
　neutral interest rate　中立的の金利, 中立的利子率
　neutral monetary policy　中立的［中立型］金融政策, 中立的貨幣政策（金融の引締めや緩和を意図しない通貨供給策）
　neutral monetary system　中立の通貨組織
　neutral policy　中立的政策, 景気に影響を与えない政策
　neutral position　中立のポジション
　neutral shift　中立の移行
　neutral technical progress　中立的技術進歩
　return to neutral　中立に戻る
　risk neutral　リスク中立者
　switch the monetary policy from tighter to neutral　金融政策を引締めぎみから中立に転換［変更］する
　take a neutral position　公平な立場を取る

neutral money　中立的貨幣
　neutral money policy　中立的貨幣政策
　neutral money supply　中立的貨幣供給［供給量］, 景気に影響を及ぼさない通貨供給［供給量］

neutral stance　中立的姿勢, 中立的スタンス, 引締めと緩和の両にらみの姿勢, 中立型金融調節の姿勢［スタンス］
　move to a neutral stance on monetary policy　金融政策を中立的スタンスに戻す
　neutral stance on tax revenue　税収中立
　take a neutral stance　中立の姿勢［スタンス］を取る, 引締めと緩和の両にらみの姿勢
　take a neutral stance on　～について中立の姿勢［スタンス］を取る
　◆The Fed will take a neutral stance on future monetary policy. 米連邦準備制度理事会（FRB）は、今後の金融政策の運営

方針について、(引締めと緩和の両にらみの)「中立」の姿勢を取る方針だ。

neutrality (名)中立, 中立性, 中立的な立場[姿勢]
　central bank neutrality　中央銀行の中立性
　　(=neutrality of central bank)
　monetary-fiscal neutrality　金融・財政の中立性
　money neutrality　貨幣の中立性
　　(=neutrality of money)
　neutrality doctrine　(国債管理などについての)中立性の原則
　reserved neutrality　控えめな中立的立場

new (形)新規の, 新しい, 追加の, 今回の, 人に知られていない, 不案内の, 新任の, 珍しい, 不慣れな, ニュー
　New Coordinating Committee for Export Control　新ココム
　new deal　新規巻き直し, 再出発
　new deal market　発行市場
　new international economic order　新国際経済秩序, NIEO
　new issuance of government bonds　国債の新規発行, 国債の新規発行額
　new line of business　新規事業
　new low　新安値, 安値, 最低記録, 空前の安値, 過去最低
　new money　にわかの大金
　new three　新興3か国
　the new rich　新興資産階級, にわか成金
　◆If a new federal debt ceiling isn't set by Aug. 2, 2011, the United States will be forced to default on Treasuries securities as it will not be able to issue new bonds to pay back maturing government debts. 2011年8月2日までに連邦政府の債務上限を新たに設けないと、米国は満期を迎える国債を償還するための国債増発ができないので、米国債の不履行(デフォルト)が発生する。◆On expectations for the new financial steps, the Nikkei Stock Average recovered to the ¥9,000 mark. 今回の金融政策への期待で、日経平均株価は9,000円台に回復した。◆The nonlife insurance company hopes to attract about 3 million to 4 million new policyholders a year for its new types of insurance. 同損保は、同社の新型保険で、年間約300万〜400万件の新規契約獲得を目指している。

new account　新口座, 新規口座, 新規顧客
　◆The company pioneered a variety of innovative promotions to add new accounts. 同社は、各種の斬新な販促活動によって、新口座[新規顧客]を増やした。

new austerity measures　追加の財政赤字削減策, 追加の緊縮財政
　◆Greece has to agree to new austerity measures before it receives any financial aid from the European Union. ギリシャは、欧州連合(EU)の金融支援を受ける前に、追加の財政赤字削減策[緊縮財政策]に同意しなければならない。

new client　新規顧客
　◆ATM cards are the banks' primary weapons to lure new clients. キャッシュ・カードは、銀行にとって新規顧客獲得の有力な手段だ。

new customer　新規顧客
　◆During the business suspension, the company will not be allowed to extend new loans, solicit new customers or call in loans. 業務停止の期間中、同社は新規融資や新規顧客の勧誘、貸出[貸金]の回収業務ができなくなる。

new depositor　新規預金者
　◆Concerns have been raised over the ability of Internet banking services to verify the identity of new depositors or to guarantee the security of customer transactions. インターネット・バンキングについては、新規預金者の身元確認や対顧客取引の安全保証の点で、その能力に対して懸念が提起されている。

new economy　新しい経済, ニューエコノミー (=digital economy, e-economy: インターネットを使った新しい経済システム。自動車、建設、不動産、繊維、流通などの成熟産業を指すオールドエコノミーに対して、インターネット・ベンチャーやドットコム企業、IT関連の産業や企業を指す)
　◆After witnessing the uninterrupted ascent of the U.S. economy over the past decade without any sharp rises in wage costs or inflation being triggered, many Americans thought their economy had developed into a so-called new economy. 賃金コストの急騰もインフレも起こらずに過去10年にわたって続いた米国の景気上昇を見て、多くのアメリカ人が、米国経済はいわゆる「ニューエコノミー」に進化したと思った。

new high　新高値, 最高記録, 空前の高値, 過去最高
　hit a new five year high　5年来の高値を付ける
　reach a new historic high of　〜で過去最高を更新する, 〜で過去最高となる
　set[hit]a new high　新記録を樹立する, 過去最高を更新する, 過去最高となる
　spurt to a new high　新高値を付ける
　◆Excluding these accounting changes, our net income and earnings per share were new highs. これらの会計上の変更を除くと、当社の当期純利益と1株当たり利益は、過去最高でした。

new Internet bank　新ネット銀行
　◆The new Internet bank will be equally owned by the two firms with initial capital of ¥20 billion. 新ネット銀行は、当初資本が200億円で、両社が折半出資する。

new issuance　新規発行
　◆Kan will cap the new issuance of government bonds in fiscal 2011 budget at less than the ¥44 trillion issued in fiscal 2010. 菅首相は、2011年度予算の国債の新規発行額を、2010年度の44兆円以下に抑える方針だ。◆Koizumi adhered to his official pledge of limiting the new issuance of government bonds to ¥30 trillion. 小泉首相は、国債の新規発行額を30兆円以下に抑える公約にこだわった。

new issue　新規発行, 新規発行株式, 新発債
　new issue arbitrage　起債裁定
　new issue bond　新発債
　new issue market　起債市場, 新株発行市場, 発行市場
　new issues calendar　起債予定表
　◆The sharp decline in investment in medium- and long-term corporate bonds occurred because the prolonged recession curbed new issues necessary for investment in plant and equipment. 中長期社債への投資が大幅に減少したのは、長引く不況で企業の設備投資に必要な中長期債の新規発行が不振だったためである。

new listing　新規上場
　◆Japanese stock exchanges set high hurdles for new listing. 日本の証券取引所は、新規上場に高いハードルを設けている。

new loans　新規融資
　◆Banks refused to extend new loans to the company due to its sluggish performance. 業績不振で、銀行は同社への新規融資に応じなかった。◆During the business suspension, the company will not be allowed to extend new loans, solicit new customers or call in loans. 業務停止の期間中、同社は新規融資や新規顧客の勧誘、貸出[貸金]の回収業務ができなくなる。◆JAL's efforts to turn around its failed business will depend on the flagship carrier's ability to secure new loans from its creditor banks. 日航の破たん事業再生への取組みは、この日本を代表する航空会社が取引銀行から新規融資を受けることができるかどうかにかかっている。◆Overly radical methods for accelerating the disposal of bad loans would panic the banking sector and the financial market, possibly driving banks to shy away from extending new loans and even to call in existing loans. 不良債権処理を加速するための余りにも強硬な手法は、銀行や金融市場をおびえさせ、貸し

渋りや貸しはがしにつながることにもなる。◆The struggling JAL's next step will be to start negotiations with its creditor banks over new loans to enact its rehabilitation plan. 経営再建に取り組む日航は今後、同社の再建計画案の実行に必要な新規融資を巡る取引銀行団との交渉に移ることになる。

new round of multilateral trade negotiations 新多角的貿易交渉, 新ラウンド
（=new round of multilateral trade talks）
◆The WTO has just started new round of multilateral trade negotiations that aim to create new rules to promote free trade. 世界貿易機関（WTO）は、自由貿易を推進するための新たなルール作りを目指す新多角的貿易交渉（新ラウンド）を始めたばかりだ。

new share issue 新規株式発行, 新株発行, 増資
◆Market manipulation has been occurring in connection with new share issues. 増資に絡んで、株価操作が行われている。

new shares 新株, 増資
◆Fukushima Bank said about 8,000 companies and investors have agreed to buy ¥15 billion worth of its new shares in March to help boost its capital base. 福島銀行によると、約8,000の企業と投資家が、同行の資本基盤を強化するため3月に予定している150億円の増資引受け[新株引受け]に同意した。◆The new shares of common stock are being allocated to plan participants over ten years as contributions are made to the plan. この普通株式新株は、制度への資金拠出と並行して、10年にわたり制度加入者に割り当てられています。◆Under the third-party share allotment scheme, the bank will allocate 116 million new shares to about 8,000 companies and investors with each share priced at ¥130. この第三者株式割当て計画によると、同行は、約8,000の企業と個人投資家に1株130円で1億1,600万株の新株を割り当てる。

New York ニューヨーク, ニューヨーク外国為替市場, ニューヨーク株式市場, ニューヨーク・マーカンタイル取引所

　New York acceptance ニューヨーク・アクセプタンス（米ドル建てユーザンス・クレジット（期限付き信用状）に基づいて輸出者が振り出した期限付き為替手形を、ニューヨークの銀行が引き受けたもの）
　New York acceptance credit ニューヨーク引受信用状
　the Comex in New York ニューヨーク商品取引所
　the Federal Reserve Bank of New York ニューヨーク連邦準備銀行
　　（⇒New York foreign exchange market）
　the New York capital market ニューヨーク資本市場
　the New York Commodity Exchange ニューヨーク商品取引所, Comex
　the New York Dow ダウ・ジョーンズ平均株価, ニューヨーク・ダウ, ダウ・ジョーンズ社の修正平均株価
　the New York Fed ニューヨーク連銀
　the New York Futures Exchange ニューヨーク先物取引所
　the New York money market ニューヨーク金融市場
　the New York offshore center ニューヨーク・オフショア市場
　the New York time ニューヨーク時間

◆At 5 p.m., the euro was quoted at $1.1712-1715 and ¥126.54-58 against Tuesday's 5 p.m. quotes of $1.1665-1675 and ¥126.30-40 in New York. 午後5時、ニューヨークの外国為替市場では、ユーロ相場が火曜日（前日）午後5時の1ユーロ=1.1665-1675ドルと126.30-40円に対して、1ユーロ=1.1712-1715ドルと126.54-58円の値を付けた。◆Crude oil futures soared in New York due to concerns over oil supplies. ニューヨーク（ニューヨーク・マーカンタイル取引所）の原油先物が、原油供給不安[原油供給への懸念]から急騰した。◆Gold extended its rally to a record above $1,900 an ounce amid increased uncertainties over the U.S. and European economic outlook on the Comex in New York. ニューヨーク商品取引所では、米欧景気見通しへの懸念[米欧経済の先行き不透明感]の高まりを受け[懸念の高まりから]、金価格が急騰して、1トロイ・オンス=1,900ドルを史上初めて突破した。◆The dollar's value temporarily dropped to the ¥82 level in New York. ドル相場は、ニューヨーク市場で一時、82円台まで下落した[値を下げた]。◆The euro traded at $1.3983-3986 and ¥115.27-31 against $1.3925-3935 and ¥115.53-63 in New York. ニューヨーク外国為替市場でユーロは、1ユーロ=1.3925〜1.3935ドル、115円53〜63銭に対して、1.3983〜3986ドル、115円27〜31銭で取引された。

New York Bankruptcy Court ニューヨーク破産裁判所
◆GM's weaker assets will be liquidated through the New York Bankruptcy Court. GMの不良資産は、ニューヨーク破産裁判所を通じて清算される。

New York foreign exchange market ニューヨーク外国為替市場, ニューヨーク為替市場
◆The Bank of Japan asked the Federal Reserve Bank of New York to intervene in the New York foreign exchange market on its behalf through yen-selling, dollar-buying operations for the first time in 15 months. 日銀は、1年3か月ぶりにニューヨーク連銀に委託して、ニューヨーク外国為替市場で円売り・ドル買いの介入に踏み切った。

New York Mercantile Exchange ニューヨーク・マーカンタイル取引所　（⇒crude futures）
◆Crude futures were launched on the New York Mercantile Exchange in 1983. 原油先物の取引は、1983年からニューヨーク・マーカンタイル取引所で開始された。◆Oil prices on the New York Mercantile Exchange soared to the $100 level a barrel for the first time during the trading hours. ニューヨーク・マーカンタイル取引所の原油価格は、取引時間中に初めて1バレル=100ドル台まで上昇した。

New York sentiment ニューヨーク市場の地（じ）合い
◆Affected by the New York sentiment, the Tokyo market was down across the board. ニューヨーク市場の地合いを受けて、東京市場は全面安となった。

New York Stock Exchange ニューヨーク証券取引所, NYSE　（=Big Board）
　the New York Stock Exchange Composite Index NYSE総合株価指数
　the New York Stock Exchange Composite Stock Index ニューヨーク証券取引所総合株価指数

◆An image of the Charging Bull put in front of the New York Stock Exchange is said to be the symbol of financial optimism and prosperity. ニューヨーク証券取引所前に置かれている「突進する雄牛」の像は、金融楽観主義と繁栄の象徴であると言われている。◆Currently, NYSE Group, Inc. is the world's largest stock exchange firm and operates the New York Stock Exchange. 現在、NYSEグループは世界最大の株式取引所で、ニューヨーク証券取引所を運営している。◆In terms of the total market value of listed shares, the Tokyo Stock Exchange is dwarfed by the New York Stock Exchange, the world's biggest. 上場株式の時価総額では、東証は世界トップのニューヨーク証券取引所に大きく引き離されている。◆The firm has postponed the listing of its stock on the New York Stock Exchange and the London Stock Exchange. 同社は、ニューヨーク証券取引所とロンドン証券取引所への株式上場を延期した。◆The New York Stock Exchange suspended trading in Global Crossing. ニューヨーク証券取引所は、グローバル・クロッシングの取引を一時停止した。

New York stock market ニューヨーク株式市場, ニューヨーク市場　（⇒panic selling）
◆Trading on the New York stock market was halted for four days from Tuesday, the longest shutdown since the final phase of the Great Depression in 1933. ニューヨーク株式

市場の取引は、火曜日(米同時多発テロ発生の9月11日)から4日間停止されたが、これは1933年の世界恐慌末期以来、最も長い取引停止になる。

newcomer (名)新規参入企業, 新規参入組, 新規参入者, 新人, 新入社員, 初心者, ずぶの素人
◆It is a matter of urgency for future newcomers to have access to sufficient landing slots and adequate airport facilities. 発着枠の十分な確保と十分な空港施設の利用は、今後新規に参入する企業にとって急務となっている。

newly (副)新たに, 新しく, 新規に, 最近, 近頃
　newly developing Big Five　新ビッグ5, 新ビッグ・ファイブ(開発途上国のなかの経済大国。中国、インドネシア、ブラジル、インド、ロシアの5か国)
　newly emerged industry　新興産業
　newly emerging and developing countries　新興・途上国
　newly emerging competitor　新規参入者
　newly emerging economies such as China and India　中国やインドなどの新興国
　newly emerging technology　新技術
　newly established nations　新興国
　newly rated issuer　新規格付け発行体

newly emerging economies　新興国
◆The Fed's monetary easing policies have brought about inflation in newly emerging economies. FRB(米連邦準備制度理事会)の金融緩和策が、新興国のインフレを招いた。

newly emerging nonperforming loans　新たに生じる[新たに生まれる]不良債権
◆If business conditions continue to worsen, financial institutions will face more newly emerging nonperforming loans than they can ever keep up with. 景気がこのまま悪化し続ければ、金融機関は新たに不良債権が生まれてその処理が追いつかなくなる。

newly issued　新規に発行した, 新規発行の
　newly issued bond　新発債
　newly issued corporate bond　新規発行社債
　newly issued stock　新規発行株式

newly issued 10-year government bonds　新発10年物国債
◆On the bond market, the yield on newly issued 10-year government bonds, an indicator of long-term interest rates, fell, resulting in a rise in bond prices. 債券市場では、長期金利の指標である新発10年物国債の利回り(流通利回り)が下落し、債券相場[債券価格]は上昇した。

newly issued shares　新規発行株式, 公募株
◆The company procured about ¥50 billion through an allocation of newly issued shares to third parties, including the Development Bank of Japan. 同社は、日本政策投資銀行などを引受先とする第三者割当増資で、約500億円を調達した。

newly listed company　新規上場企業, 新規に株式公開した企業
◆The number of newly listed companies was only 12 firms in the first half of 2010. 2010年上半期の新規上場企業数は、12社にとどまった。

newly listed shares　新規上場株式
◆Mizuho Securities Co. placed a huge errant sell order for the newly listed shares of recruitment firm J-Com Co. みずほ証券が、人材サービス業ジェイコムの新規上場株式に対し、誤って大量の売り注文を出してしまった。

newly released funds　新規調達資金
◆Short-term interest rates in the Tokyo market rose as some financial institutions hurried to obtain newly released funds. 一部の金融機関が新規調達資金の確保を急いだため、東京市場の短期金利が上昇した。

news (名)情報, 知らせ, 便り, 近況, 消息, 報道, 報道情報, 記事, ニュース番組, 真新しいこと, 材料, 統計, 指標, ニュース
　bad news　悪材料
　depressing news　凶報
　disappointing news　悪材料
　disturbing news　弱気材料
　economic news　景気指標, 経済指標
　financial news　経済ニュース, 金融記事
　friendly news　好材料
　good news　よい知らせ, 明るい材料, 好材料
　international news　国際ニュース
　negative news　悪材料, マイナス材料
　news on inflation　インフレ指標
　price news　物価統計
◆The news pushed up yields on short-duration bonds. これを受けて、短期物の利回りが上昇した。◆The yen improved on the news. このニュース[材料]を受けて、円が買われた。◆There is good news about private consumption, which accounts for nearly 60 percent of GDP. 国内総生産(GDP)の約60%を占める個人消費には、明るい材料がある。

NEXI　日本貿易保険
　(⇒Nippon Export and Investment Insurance)

next (形)次の, 今度の, 今度の, 今後の, 次位の, 次席の
　next day funds　翌日資金化資金
　next day settlement　翌日決済
　next-in first-out method　次入れ先出し法
　　(=next-in, first-out)
　next-month delivery　翌月末受渡し期限取引, 中限
　next or immediately following business day　翌銀行営業日
　next or immediately preceding business day　直前の銀行営業日
　spot-next transaction　スポット・ネクスト取引
　the next fiscal year　来年度, 来期
　the timing of next rate hike　追加のタイミング
　value next month　翌月渡し

NEXT 11 [Next Eleven]　ネクスト・イレブン
　(=N-11: ゴールドマン・サックス証券の経済予測レポートでBRICs(ブラジル、ロシア、インドと中国)に次いで急成長が期待される新興経済発展国家群で、イラン、インドネシア、エジプト、韓国、トルコ、ナイジェリア、パキスタン、バングラデシュ、フィリピン、ベトナム、メキシコの11か国)

next Monetary Policy Meeting　次回の金融政策決定会合
◆The Bank of Japan is considering taking additional monetary easing measures ahead of the next Monetary Policy Meeting. 次回の金融政策決定会合に向けて、日銀は現在、追加金融緩和策の実施を検討している。

next rate hike　追加利上げ
◆Should the Fed misjudge the timing or level of its next rate hike, it may interrupt the economic recovery and even bring about rapid inflation. 米連邦準備制度理事会(FRB)が追加利上げの幅やタイミングを誤ると、景気回復の腰を折り、急激なインフレを招く可能性もある。

NIBOR　ニューヨーク・インターバンク出し手レート
　(the New York Interbank Offered Rateの略)

NICs　新興工業国(newly industrializing countriesの略)

NIEs　新興工業国(newly industrializing economiesの略)

Nifty Fifty [nifty fifty]　米国で人気のある株式50銘柄, 人気50銘柄

night collection box　夜間金庫
　(=night deposit, night depositary safe)

night session [trading]　夜間取引

Nikkei （名）日経, 日経平均株価
  daily average for the Nikkei index　日経平均の月中平均株価
  Nikkei average of stock prices　日経平均
  Nikkei component shares　日経平均構成銘柄
  Nikkei Dow average　日経平均株価
  Nikkei futures　日経平均先物
  Nikkei index　日経指数, 日経株価指数
  Nikkei slide　日経平均の下落
  Nikkei stock index　日経株価指数, 日経平均
  Nikkei warrant　日経平均ワラント
  Nikkei World Commodity Price Index　日経国際商品指数
  Nikkei 225 Future Trade　日経225先物取引
  ◆The daily average for the Nikkei index in September stood at 10,649, up 30.3 percent from 8,169 in March. 9月の日経平均の月中平均株価は、3月の8,169円に比べて30.3％増の10,649円となった。

Nikkei Stock Average　日経平均株価, 日経平均
  （=the benchmark Nikkei index; ⇒hover）
  the benchmark Nikkei index　日経平均株価
  the 225-issue Nikkei Stock Average　日経平均株価（225種）
  ◆Following sharp falls on European and U.S. markets, the Nikkei Stock Average fell briefly to its lowest level this year. 欧米市場の株価急落を受けて、日経平均株価は一時、今年の最安値を下回った。◆On Dec. 1, 2009, the Nikkei Stock Average was bearing down on the 9,000 mark due to the so-called Dubai shock. 2009年12月1日の日経平均株価（225種）は、いわゆるドバイ・ショック（中東ドバイの金融不安）で、9,000円台を割り込む寸前まで追いつめられていた。◆On expectations for the new financial steps, the Nikkei Stock Average recovered to the ¥9,000 mark. 今回の金融政策への期待で、日経平均株価は9,000円台に回復した。◆The Nikkei Stock Average fell briefly to its lowest level this year on the Tokyo Stock Market. 東京株式市場の日経平均株価は一時、今年の最安値を下回った。◆The Nikkei Stock Average has been hovering around the ¥10,000 line. 日経平均株価は、1万円台に張り付いた状態が続いている。◆The Nikkei Stock Average recovered to the ¥9,000 mark in the morning, but trimmed earlier gains in afternoon trading. 日経平均株価は、朝から9,000円台に回復したが、午後の取引で午前の上昇幅が縮小した。◆The 225-issue Nikkei Stock Average closed at 7,607.88, the lowest level since the economic bubble burst, on April 28, 2003. 2003年4月28日の日経平均株価（225種）の終値は7,607円88銭で、バブル崩壊後の最安値を付けた。◆The 225-issue Nikkei Stock Average continued its plunge Thursday, momentarily dipping into 8,100 territory. 日経平均株価（225種）が10日（10月10日）も急落し、一時8,100円台まで下落した。◆The 225-issue Nikkei Stock Average dived below the key threshold of ¥10,000. 日経平均株価（225種）は、1万円の大台を割り込んだ。◆The 225-issue Nikkei Stock Average dropped below the 9,000 mark Wednesday to close at the year's low of 8,845.39. 水曜日の日経平均株価（225種）は、9,000円台を割り込み、終値は今年最安値の8,845円39銭となった。◆The 225-issue Nikkei Stock Average on Monday plunged 202.32 points from Friday's close on the Tokyo Stock Exchange. 東京株式市場の月曜日の日経平均株価（225種）は、前週末比で202円32銭下落した。◆The 225-issue Nikkei Stock Average remains below the key 10,000 level. 日経平均株価（225種）は、1万円の大台を割り込んでいる。

解説 日経株価平均とは：株式相場全体の動きを示す指標の一つ。東証一部上場の代表的な225社の株価合計を、一定の除数で割って算出する。除数は調整値で、株式分割や銘柄入れ替えのときに変更する。東証株価指数（TOPIX）が銀行株など時価総額の大きい株価の動きに敏感なのに対して、日経平均はハイテク株の組入れ比重が高く、ハイテク株の動きに左右されやすい。

nine months through December　4-12月期, 4-12月までの3四半期
  ◆Affected by losses on securities investments as well as the growing cost of bad loan disposal, the financial group fell into the red in the nine months through December. 証券投資の損失と不良債権処理費用の拡大の影響で、同フィナンシャル・グループは、4～12月期は赤字に転落した。

NINJA　収入も仕事も資産もない状況, ニンジャ（No Income, No Job and No Assetの略）

Nippon Export and Investment Insurance　（独立行政法人の）日本貿易保険, NEXI
  （⇒direct export, operational system）
  ◆Nippon Export and Investment Insurance（NEXI） was established in 2001 to provide foreign trade and investment insurance services. 独立行政法人の日本貿易保険は、貿易保険事業と対外投資保険事業を提供するため、2001年に設立された。

Nippon New Market Hercules　ニッポン・ニュー・マーケット・ヘラクレス, HC（略称：ヘラクレス）

N.N.　（手形に）署名なし（no nameの略）

N/O　（銀行）指図なし（no orders）

no　（形）～ではない, ～してはならない, ～禁止, ～反対, ～のない
  no action［no-action］letter　訴訟不適当意見通知,（異議を唱えないとするSECなどの）承認状, ノーアクション・レター
  no hand provision　買収妨害策
  no minimum balance checking account　最低残高維持不要当座預金　（=special checking account）
  no par common voting stock　無額面の議決権付き普通株式
  no par value stock　無額面株式
  （=nonpar value stock）

no-claim(s) bonus　（保険）無事戻し, 無事故戻し, NCB

no-fault　（名）無過失損害賠償制度
  no-fault insurance　無過失保険

no-interest bearing　金利ゼロ
  ◆Liquid deposits to be used for no-interest bearing settlements will likely be distinguished from deposits for investment or savings. 金利ゼロで決済のために利用される決済性預金は今後、資産運用や貯蓄のための預金と区別される見込みだ。

no-limit order　成り行き注文

no-load　（形）手数料なしで売り出される　（名）手数料なしで売り出されるミューチュアル・ファンド（no-load fund）, ノーロード・ファンド
  no-load fund　ノーロード型投信

nom.cap.　（名）名目［公称］資本
  （=nominal capital）

nominal　（形）名目の, 名目上の, 名目ベースの, 名義上の, 公称の, 額面［券面］上の,（株式が）記名の
  nominal account　名目勘定
  nominal amount　額面金額, 額面価額, 名目元本
  nominal bond yield　債券名目利回り
  nominal capital　公称資本, 名目資本
  （=authorized capital, nominal share capital）
  nominal consideration　名目手付け金
  nominal dollars　名目金額
  nominal economic growth　名目成長率
  nominal effective exchange rate　名目実効為替レート
  nominal exchange rate　名目為替相場, 名目為替レート
  （インフレの影響を考慮していない為替レート）
  nominal export　輸出額

nominal GDP growth 名目GDP成長率
nominal gross domestic product 名目国内総生産, 名目GDP
nominal growth 名目成長率
nominal interest 表面利率, 名目金利 (=nominal interest rate)
nominal market 名目相場
nominal owner 名義上の所有者
nominal par 額面価格, 額面金額
nominal price 名目価格, 想定価格, 気配相場, 表面価格 (株式の額面価格)
nominal share capital 名目株式資本
nominal shares (of stock) 記名割当株
nominal value 額面価格, 名目価格
nominal wage 名目賃金 (労働者が受け取る賃金の額を物価指数で割ったものが実質賃金)
nominal yield 名目利回り, 表面利回り, クーポン・レート (債券の額面金額に対する1年間の受取利息の割合)
nominal GDP growth rate 名目GDP(国内総生産)成長率
◆The nominal GDP growth rate takes into account price changes and is considered a more accurate reflection of household and corporate sentiment. 名目GDP(国内総生産)成長率は, 物価変動を考慮し, 家計や企業の景況感をより正確に反映するとされている。
nominal growth rate 名目成長率, 名目経済成長率 (=nominal growth)
◆It's imperative that the Bank of Japan promptly implement additional quantitative monetary easing measures in an effort to shift the nation's nominal growth rate to the plus side. 日本の名目経済成長率をプラスに転じさせるには, 日銀が金融の追加的な緩和策を早急に実施する必要がある。 ◆To reduce unemployment, the nominal growth rate must be boosted. 失業率を低くするためには, 名目成長率を高くしなければならない。
nominal interest rate 表面利率, 名目金利 (=nominal interest, nominal rate, nominal rate of interest)
◆In Japan's case, the central bank has guided the short-term nominal interest rate to almost zero. 日本の場合、日銀が誘導している短期の名目金利はゼロにある。 ◆The nominal interest rate for a 20-year government bonds stands at 2.3 percent. 20年債の表面利率は, 2.3%だ。
nominal rate 表面金利, 名目金利, 名目相場
nominal rate of discount 名目割引率
nominal rate of growth 名目成長率
nominal rate of interest 表面金利, 名目金利
nominal terms 名目, 名目ベース (実質=real terms)
◆The GDP growth rate in nominal terms during the July-September period stood at zero on a quarter-on-quarter and a year-on-year basis. 7-9月期の名目GDPの成長率は, 前期比, 年率ともにゼロ%増だった。
nominative (形)指名の, 記名の, 記名式の
  nominative claim 指名債権
  nominative security 記名式証券
nominee (名)(株券などの)名義人, 指名[任命]された人, 被指名者
  nominee shareholding 名義人による株式保有
non-accelerating inflation rate of unemployment インフレ率を高めない失業率, インフレを加速させない下限失業率, NAIRU
nonacceptance (為替手形の)引受拒絶
nonaccumulated preferred stock 非累積的優先株
nonassented bond 不同意債券
nonassented stocks 不同意株式

nonassessable stock 一時払込み株, 非賦課株式, 追徴不能株式
nonassignable L/C 譲渡不能信用状
non-attended store 無人店舗
non-availment (信用状金額の所定期間中に)不使用の金額, 不使用金額
non-average 実損填補
nonbank (名)銀行以外の金融機関, 非銀行, ノンバンク
  nonbank affiliates 系列ノンバンク
  nonbank bank 非銀行金融機関, ノンバンク・バンク
  nonbank financial institution 非銀行金融機関, ノンバンク金融機関
  nonbank financing company ノンバンク (=nonbank financial business)
  nonbank operations 銀行以外の事業
  nonbank subsidiary ノンバンク子会社
nonbank financial business 銀行以外の金融機関, ノンバンク (=nonbank firm)
◆Shoko Fund Co., a nonbank financial business that was listed in the TSE's Second Section after trading its stock over the counter, has rapidly grown through its lending to small and midsize companies. 株式の店頭取引から東証二部に上場したノンバンクの商工ファンドは, 中小企業向け融資で急成長している。
nonbank firm 銀行以外の金融機関, ノンバンク
◆Nonbank firms are forced to raise provisions by a recent accounting rule change. 今回の会計規則の変更で, ノンバンク(銀行以外の金融機関)各社は引当金の積み増しを迫られている。
nonbanking activities 非銀行業務
nonborrowed reserves 非借入準備
non-business day 休業日
noncallable (形)(債券の)繰上げ償還ができない, 中途償還のない, 非期中償還の, (融資などの)期限前返済要求のない
  noncallable bond 任意繰上償還禁止債券, 満期償還債券 [公債], ノンコーラブル債
  noncallable convertible bond 任意償還条項のない転換社債
noncancelable [noncancellable] (形)解約不能の, 解除不可の, 不可解除の
  noncancelable guarantee 取消し不能保証
  noncancelable insurance policy 取消不能の保険証券
  noncancelable lease 解約不能リース, 中途解約不能リース
  noncancelable operating lease 解約不能のオペレーティング・リース
  noncancelable policy 解約不能保険証券
◆The company does lease certain office, factory and warehouse space, and land under principally noncancelable operating leases. 同社は, 一部の事業所, 工場, 倉庫や土地などを主に中途解約不能のオペレーティング・リースで使用している。
noncapital [non-capital] alliance 資本以外の提携, 非資本提携
◆The two companies' noncapital alliance is expected to weaken though they have collaborated in production and technology development. 両社は共同で生産と技術開発に取り組んできたが, 両社の資本以外の提携は弱まる見通しだ。
noncash [non-cash] (形)非現金の, 非現金性の, 現物給付による, 現金決済を伴わない, 資金収支を伴わない, 資金の増減を伴わない
  distributions of noncash assets to owners 非現金資産の所有者への分配

noncash activities　非金銭活動, 資金[現金収支]を伴わない活動
noncash [non-cash] asset　非現金資産
noncash charge　非現金費用
noncash expense　資金収支を伴わない費用
noncash financing activities　資金[現金収支]を伴わない財務活動
noncash investing activities　資金[現金収支]を伴わない投資活動
noncash monetary asset　非現金貨幣資産
noncash reserves　非現金性の準備金
noncash transaction　非現金取引, 現金決済を伴わない取引
noncash transfer　現物移転支払い, 現物給付による公的扶助
values of noncash items　非現金項目の評価額
nonclearing bank　交換組合外銀行
noncompetitive bid　非競争入札
nonconcurrency　(名)(保険)異位性
nonconcurrent policy　不同時保険証券
nonconsolidated basis　非連結ベース, 単体ベース
noncontributory　(形)非拠出型の, 拠出制でない, 従業員でなく雇用者が負担する
noncontributory old age pension　老齢福祉年金
noncontributory pension　非拠出年金
noncontributory pension plan [scheme]　非拠出年金制度 (=noncontributory plan)
noncontributory supplemental retirement benefit plan　非拠出型追加の退職給付制度
noncontributory defined benefit (pension) plan　非拠出型確定給付年金制度
◆We sponsor noncontributory defined benefit plans covering the majority of our employees. 当社は、従業員の大多数を対象とする非拠出型確定給付年金制度を設けています。
noncontributory plan　非拠出年金制度, 非拠出型退職金制度
◆A noncontributory plan is funded by company contributions to an irrevocable trust fund. 非拠出退職年金制度の資金は、会社の拠出金によって取り崩し不能の信託基金に積み立てられている。
nonconvertible　(形)転換できない, 金貨に換えられない, 不換の, 両替できない
nonconvertible bond　非転換社債
nonconvertible preferred stock　非転換優先株式
noncore　(形)非中核的, 非主力の, 周辺の
noncore activities　非中核的業務
noncore markets　周辺市場
noncore assets　非中核の資産, 非中核的事業資産, 周辺資産
◆The company received some $200 million upon disposal of certain noncore assets. 同社は、一部の非中核的資産事業資産を売却して、2億ドル余りを受領した。
noncore business　非中核事業, 非主力事業
◆The company will withdraw from its noncore business. 同社は、非中核事業から撤退する方針だ。
noncore capital　非中核的資本
(⇒capital adequacy)
◆Noncore capital includes riskier assets like investments and loans. 非中核的資本には、投資や融資など損失を被るおそれがある「リスク資産」が含まれる。
noncumulative [non-cumulative]　(形)非累積的な, 累積しない
noncumulative dividend　非累積配当
noncumulative preference [preferred] stock　非累積優先株式, 非累積優先株, 配当受取りの権利が累積しない優先株式
noncumulative quantity discount　非累積数量割引
noncumulative sinking fund　非累積型減債基金
noncumulative stock　非累積株
noncurrent　(形)非流動的, 長期の, 固定した(fixed)
noncurrent asset　非流動資産, 固定資産
noncurrent liabilities　非流動負債, 固定負債
noncurrent tangible asset　長期の無形資産
nondeductible　(形)控除不能の, 控除対象外の　(名)所得算入
nondeductible expense　非控除費用, 損金として控除できない費用
nondeductible reserves　非所得控除
nondeliverable　(形)引渡しできない, 交付不能の
nondeliverable forward　ノンデリバラブル・フォワード, NDF
nondeliverable share　交付不能株式
nondelivery　(名)(海上保険)不着損害, 引渡し[配達]しないこと
non-deposit currency　非預金通貨
nondiversifiable risk　分散不能リスク, 分散できないリスク　(=systematic risk)
non-dividend-paying stock　無配株
nondollar　(形)ドル以外の, 非ドルの, ドル以外の通貨単位の
nondollar economies　非ドル通貨圏
nondomestic currency receivables　外貨建て債務
nonfinancial　(形)非金融の, 金融以外の, 金融機関以外の
net nonfinancial assets　非金融純資産
nonfinancial account　非金融勘定
nonfinancial incentive　非金銭的誘因
nonfinancial information　非財務情報
nonfinancial investment　金融機関以外への投資
nonfinancial market　非金融市場, 非金融筋
nonfinancial motives　利益とは関係ない動機
nonfinancial statement section　アニュアル・レポートの非財務書類[財務諸表]情報
nonfinancial transaction　非金融取引
private nonfinancial intermediary　民間非金融仲介機関[非金融機関]
private nonfinancial sector　民間の非金融部門
◆The combined sales of 813 nonfinancial companies in the April-September period grew 6.3 percent over the previous year. 金融を除く企業813社の上期(4-9月期)の売上高の合計は、前年同期比で6.3%増加した。
nonfinancial institution　非金融機関, 金融機関以外の企業
◆Two errors have been found in a trust bill to pave the way for nonfinancial institutions to start their own trust business. 非金融機関(金融機関以外の企業)に信託業務への参入を可能にするための信託業法案に、ミス(条文ミス)が2か所あることが分かった。
nonforfeiture　(名)不没収, 不可没収, 没収不許可
nonforfeiture benefit　(保険の)不没収給付金
nonforfeiture condition　没収不許可条件
nonforfeiture options　不没収給付金選択権
nonforfeiture premium loan　保険料振替貸付け
nonforfeiture provision [clause]　不可没収条項
nonforfeiture value　不没収価額[価格]
nonfundable　(形)融資不適格の
noninstallment　(形)一時払いの, 非割賦の

noninstallment credit　非割賦信用
noninsurance affiliates　保険以外の関連会社
noninsurance plan　非保険方式
noninterest-bearing [non-interest bearing]　（形）無利息の,利息なしの,非利付き
　noninterest-bearing deposits　非利付き預金
　noninterest-bearing note　無利息手形
noninvestment grade　非投資適格格付け,投機的格付け,投資不適格格付け　（=speculative grade）
　noninvestment grade bond　投機的格付け債,高利回り債
　noninvestment grade rating　投機的格付け,非投資適格格付け
nonledger [non-ledger] assets　簿外資産,非元帳資産
nonlife insurance　損害保険
nonlife insurance claims　損害保険の保険金請求額,損害保険の請求額
　◆Nonlife insurance claims connected to Typhoon No. 12 are expected to exceed ¥10 billion. 台風12号関連の損害保険の保険金請求額は、100億円を超える見込みだ。
nonlife insurance company　損害保険会社,損保会社
　（=casualty insurance company, nonlife insurance firm, nonlife insurer;⇒brochure, payout, tie-up agreement）
　◆Domestic nonlife insurance companies usually renew contracts with most of their corporate clients each April. 国内の損保各社は通常、毎年4月に大半の顧客企業と（保険）契約の更新を行っている。◆Major nonlife insurance companies saw a rapid increase in the number of people taking out insurance covering damage due to earthquakes, tsunami, volcanic eruptions and other natural disasters. 大手損保各社では、地震や津波、火山の噴火などの天災による損害を補償する保険（地震保険）の加入者が急増した。◆Nonlife insurance companies used to disperse the risk of large contracts with new corporate clients through reinsurance contracts with other insurance or reinsurance companies. 損保各社は従来、他の保険会社もしくは再保険会社と再保険契約を結んで、新規顧客企業と大型契約を結ぶリスクを分散してきた。◆The nonlife insurance company hopes to attract about 3 million to 4 million new policyholders a year for its new types of insurance. 同損保は、同社の新型保険で、年間約300万〜400万件の新規契約獲得を目指している。◆The nonlife insurance company will provide the company with know-how on damage assessment and product development. この損害保険会社は、同社に損害査定や商品開発に関するノウハウを提供する。◆To offer customers a new way to purchase insurance, nonlife insurance companies have begun cooperating with cell phone companies. 顧客に保険加入のための新サービスを提供するため、損害保険各社は、携帯電話会社との提携に乗り出した。
nonlife insurance firm　損害保険会社,損保会社
　（=nonlife insurance company）
　◆Financial Services Agency has ordered 26 nonlife insurance firms to correct their business practices, after finding they failed to pay due insurance benefits. 損保各社が支払う義務のある保険金を支払わなかったことが判明したため、金融庁は損保26社に対して業務是正命令を出した。
nonlife insurance market　損害保険市場,損保市場
　◆Tokio Marine Holdings inc. entered the nonlife insurance market in India in 2000. 東京海上ホールディングスは、2000年からインドの損害保険市場に参入した。
nonlife insurance policy　損害保険証券,損害保険,損保　（=nonlife policy）
　◆Banks have effectively been allowed to sell only nonlife insurance policies. 銀行はこれまで事実上、損害保険しか販売できなかった。
Non-Life Insurance Policyholders Protection Corp. of Japan　損害保険契約者保護機構
　◆The Non-Life Insurance Policyholders Protection Corp. of Japan was established by the nonlife insurance industry to protect policyholders at failed insurers. 損害保険契約者保護機構は、破綻損保会社の契約者を保護するために損保業界が設置した。
　[解説]損害保険契約者保護機構とは：損害保険会社が破綻した後に事故や火災にあった契約者について、保険金の支払いを保証するため、損保業界が1998年に設けた。受け皿となった会社に資金援助するほか、受け皿が不在の場合は、機構が保険契約を引き継ぐ。資金枠は500億円だが、第一火災海上保険や大成火災海上保険の破綻で、資金不足が懸念されている。生命保険の保護機構と違って、資金枠が枯渇しても、現行制度では公的資金は使えない。

nonlife insurer　損害保険会社,損保会社,損保
　（=nonlife insurance company;⇒coverage, flagship, insurance claims）
　◆All of the nation's six major nonlife insurers suffered sharp falls in earnings for the fiscal first half ended Sept. 30. 今年9月中間決算（9月30日に終了した今年度上半期）の国内損害保険会社の主要6社が、軒並み大幅な減益となった。◆Automotive insurance is the flagship product of nonlife insurers. 自動車保険は、損害保険会社の主力［目玉］商品だ。◆In insurance services that can be bought via cell phones, cell phone companies provide nonlife insurers with policyholders' personal information. 携帯電話で加入できる保険サービスでは、携帯電話会社が（保険）加入者の個人情報を損害保険会社に提供している。◆Nonlife insurers are exploring new types of insurance demand and offering convenient and easy means of buying policies. 損保各社は、新たな保険需要を掘り起こして、いつでも、どこでも簡単に保険に加入できるサービスを提供している。◆Nonlife insurers are offering customers a new way to purchase insurance, using mobile phones with information transmission capabilities. 損害保険各社が、情報通信機能がある携帯電話を使って保険に加入できる新サービスを提供している。◆Nonlife insurers both in Japan and overseas have been struggling to stave off potential liabilities for terrorism-related insurance claims. 世界の損保各社は、テロ関連保険金に対する潜在責任（補償）を回避する動きに出ている。◆Nonlife insurers started insurance services that can be bought more easily via cell phones with information transmission capabilities. 損保各社が、情報通信機能がある携帯電話を使って、これまでより簡単に保険に入れるサービスを開始した。◆NTT Docomo Inc. and SoftBank Mobile Corp. have been offering cell phone-based policy sales by teaming up with nonlife insurers respectively. NTTドコモとソフトバンクモバイルが、それぞれ損保会社と提携して、携帯電話での保険販売のサービスを提供している。◆The policies offered by the two nonlife insurers pay policyholders if they are injured doing sports or during domestic and overseas trips. この損保2社が提供している保険では、保険加入者［保険契約者］がスポーツや国内外の旅行中に傷害事故にあったときに、保険金が支払われる。
nonlife policy　損害保険証券,損害保険契約,損害保険,損保
　◆Edelweiss Tokyo Life Insurance Co. is the first Japanese insurer handling both life and nonlife policies in India. エーデルワイス・トウキョウ・ライフ・インシュランス（本店所在地：インドのマハラシュトラ州ムンバイ市）は、インドで生保と損保を取り扱う日本初の保険会社だ。
nonmanufacturer　（名）非製造業
　（=nonmanufacturing industry）
nonmarketable　（形）市場性のない,非市場性の
　nonmarketable issue　非市場性証券
　nonmarketable securities　市場性のない証券,非市場性証券

nonmedical insurance　無診査保険
nonmember bank　非加盟銀行
nonmonetary　(形)非貨幣の、貨幣以外の、貨幣によらない、非通貨制の、非金融の
　nonmonetary adjustment　非金融調節
　nonmonetary asset　非金銭資産、非貨幣的資産
　nonmonetary debt　非金融負債、非貨幣的負債
　nonmonetary facilities　非金融機関
　nonmonetary financial intermediary　非貨幣的金融仲介機関
　nonmonetary gold　非貨幣用金
　nonmonetary indirect security　非貨幣的間接証券
　nonmonetary intermediary　銀行以外の金融仲介機関、非貨幣的仲介機関
　nonmonetary policy　非金融政策、非通貨政策
　nonmonetary policy instrument　非金融政策手段
　nonmonetary transaction　非金銭取引、非貨幣取引
　nonmonetary wealth　非貨幣的資産、非貨幣的富
　◆Nonmonetary balance sheet items and corresponding income statement items are translated at rates in effect at the time of acquisition. 貸借対照表の非貨幣性項目とこれに対応する損益計算書項目は、取得日の為替レートで換算されています。
nonnegotiable　(形)譲渡できない、譲渡不能の、譲渡禁止の、流通性のない、非流通の
　nonnegotiable bill　譲渡不能手形、非流通手形
　nonnegotiable CD　譲渡不能預金証書
　nonnegotiable check　譲渡不能小切手
　nonnegotiable debt　譲渡不能公債
　nonnegotiable endorsement　裏書禁止裏書き
　nonnegotiable note　譲渡不能約束手形
　nonnegotiable papers　譲渡不能手形
　nonnegotiable safe-keeping receipts　譲渡不能保護預り証
　nonnegotiable securities　譲渡不能証券
non-neutral　(形)非中立的、景気などに影響を及ぼす
　non-neutral economic policy　非中立的経済政策(景気などに影響を及ぼす経済政策)
　non-neutral financial policy　非中立的金融政策(景気などに影響を及ぼす金融政策)
　non-neutral fiscal policy　非中立的財政政策
　non-neutral monetary policy　非中立的通貨[貨幣]政策
　non-neutral policy　非中立的政策
non-neutrality of money　貨幣の中立性
non-ownership automobile liability insurance　非所有自動車責任保険
nonpar　(形)無額面の、不等価の　(=no par)
　nonpar bank　無額面銀行
　nonpar item　割引小切手、額面割れ小切手
　nonpar stock [share]　無額面株式
　nonpar value capital stock　無額面株式
　nonpar value stock　無額面株式
　　(=no-par-value stock)
nonparticipating　(形)利益無配当の、不参加の、非参加の
　nonparticipating annuity　非参加配当年金
　nonparticipating insurance　無配当保険
　nonparticipating preference share　非参加優先株式
　nonparticipating preferred stock　非参加優先株式[優先株]
　nonparticipating stock　非参加株
nonpayment　(名)不払い
　nonpayment involving third-sector insurance products　第三分野(医療保険やがん保険など)の保険金不払い
　　(⇒insurance product)
　nonpayment of a draft　手形の支払い拒絶
　nonpayment of insurance benefits [claims]　保険金の不払い
　nonpayment of insurance money　保険金の不払い
　　(=nonpayment of insurance benefits, nonpayment of insurance claims)
　◆The issue of the nonpayment of insurance benefits by private insurance companies came to light. 民間生保の(生命)保険金不払い問題が、判明した。
nonperforming　(形)利払い不履行の、不履行の、履行しない、不稼働の
　nonperforming assets　(金融機関の)不良資産、不良債権、不稼働資産
　nonperforming exposures　不稼働債権
　nonperforming loan percentage [ratios]　不稼働債権の比率
　nonperforming loan receivables　不良債権
　◆An increasing number of loans turn out to be nonperforming because of a deterioration in the business situation of the borrower or because the value of the real estate used as collateral has fallen. 融資先の経営悪化や担保不動産の目減りなどによって、不良債権化する貸出が増えている。
　nonperforming loans　不良債権、不良貸付け、貸倒れ、延滞貸金　(=bad debts, uncollectible loans; ⇒ accumulated nonperforming loans, business conditions, disposal of nonperforming loans, massive nonperforming loans, negative legacy)
　assess nonperforming loans　不良債権の査定をする
　nonperforming loans on the books　帳簿上の不良債権
　◆A real estate investment fund was alleged to have failed to report about ¥18 billion in income from transaction involving land and property taken as collateral for nonperforming loans. 不動産投資ファンドが、不良債権の担保に取った不動産関連の取引で得た所得約180億円の申告漏れを指摘されていた。◆Financial institutions hold a huge amount of nonperforming loans. 金融機関は、巨額の不良債権を抱えている。◆Financial regulators asked prosecutors to investigate allegations that UFJ Holdings Inc.'s banking unit illegally obstructed recent inspections by reporting misleading information about its nonperforming loans. 金融当局は、UFJ銀行が不良債権に関する虚偽の情報を報告して最近の検査を違法に妨害したとして、同行を検察当局に刑事告発した。◆Nonperforming loans will be transferred to the revival account, as well as crossheld shares and idle real estate. 不良債権は、持ち合い株式や遊休不動産などと一緒に「再生勘定」に移す。◆The bank announced a plan to introduce revival accounts to manage its ¥2.3 trillion nonperforming loans separately from the healthier loans. 同行は、2兆3,000億円の不良債権を正常債権とは別個に管理する「再生勘定」を導入する方針を発表した。◆The merger plan will not go ahead unless the bank makes unstinting efforts to cut its nonperforming loans. 同行が不良債権の削減に向けて惜しみない努力をしないかぎり、統合計画が前に進むことはないだろう。◆The number of general constructors for which financial institutions have given up on nonperforming loans now comes to 10. 金融機関が債権を放棄したゼネコン(総合建設会社)は、10社にのぼる。◆Unless the banks set strict standards in extending loans to companies viewed as being at risk of failure, they will only increase the amount of nonperforming loans on the books. 経営に問題のある[経営破綻の危険性がある]企業への銀行の融資基準を厳しくしないと、銀行の帳簿上の不良債権が増えることにしかならない。
nonpublic information　内部情報

(=inside information)
◆A former bank employee illegally benefited from obtaining nonpublic information from a colleague by trading shares of two listed companies. 元銀行行員は、同僚から提供された内部情報を利用して、上場企業2社の株取引を行って不正に利益を得ていた。

nonqualified plan 非適格年金
nonrecourse (形)遡求権なしの, 非遡求の
 (=without recourse)
 nonrecourse mortgage 有限責任抵当
 nonrecourse obligation 非遡求債務
 on a nonrecourse basis 遡求権なしで
 ◆The receivables were sold on a nonrecourse basis. 債権は、遡求権なしで売却した。
nonrecourse loan 非遡求型ローン, ノンリコース・ローン(対象案件の収益力や将来キャッシュ・フローを評価して実行する融資)
 ◆A project loan is generally a nonrecourse loan and is secured by project assets. プロジェクト・ローンは通常、非遡求型ローンで、プロジェクトの資産を担保とする。
nonrefundable (形)返却不要の, 返還不要の, 返済義務のない
 nonrefundable fees 返却不要手数料
 nonrefundable loan fees 返還不要貸付け手数料
nonresident (名)非居住者 (形)非居住者の
 nonresident business 外国系企業
 nonresident convertibility (通貨の)非居住者交換性
 nonresident deposit account 非居住者預金勘定
 nonresident foreign currency 非居住者外貨
 nonresident free yen account 非居住者自由円勘定
 nonresident interest earnings 非居住者利子所得
 nonresident yen account 非居住者円勘定, 非居住者円預金勘定
 nonresident yen deposit account 非居住者円預金勘定
non-savings institution 非貯蓄機関
non-speculative motive 非投機的動機
nonsterilization (名)非不胎化(ひふたいか)
nonsterilizing intervention 非不胎化的介入
nontax revenue 税外収入
 ◆The ¥44 trillion shortfall including tax revenue and nontax revenue in spending in the fiscal 2010 budget must be made up for by issuing government bonds. 2010年度予算の歳出のうち、税収と税外収入を含めて44兆円の不足分は、国債発行で補填しなければならない。 ◆The government will secure ¥4 trillion to ¥5 trillion for reconstruction from the Great East Japan Earthquake via nontax revenue. 政府は、税収外収入を利用して、東日本大震災の復興財源に充てるために4兆～5兆円を確保する方針だ。
nontaxable (形)非課税の, 無税の
 nontaxable dividend 非課税配当金, 非課税受取配当金
 nontaxable income 非課税所得
 nontaxable investment 非課税投資
 nontaxable revenue 非課税収益
 nontaxable securities 非課税[免税]有価証券
non-trade currency 非貿易通貨
non-trade receivables 営業外債権
non-usable currency 利用不能通貨
nonvoting (形)無議決の, 議決権のない, 無議決権の, 無投票の
 nonvoting class B preferred stock 無議決権クラスB優先株式
 nonvoting share 無議決権株, 議決権のない株式
nonworking labor force 非労働力人口

◆The nonworking labor force not seeking employment increased by 920,000 to 41.32 million. 求職活動をしていない非労働力人口は、92万人増えて4,132万人に達した。
norm (名)基準, 規範, 規準, 標準(standard), 一般標準, 水準, 模範, 典型, 標準的な方式[やり方], 平均, 平均学力, 達成基準, 要求水準, 基準労働量, ノルマ, 責任量, 責任生産量
 above [beyond] the norm of ～の平均以上
 behavioral norms 行動規範, 社会通念
 industry-wide norm 業界標準
 international norms of business ビジネスの国際標準, ビジネス界の世界標準
 solvency norms 支払い能力規制
 stock market norms 株式市場の規範
 ◆The crime of Livedoor's former president was extremely malicious and undermined the very foundation of stock market norms. ライブドアの元社長の犯行は、極めて悪質で、株式市場の規範を根本から揺るがすものであった。
normal (形)通常の, 正常な, 一般的な, 標準の, 正規の (名)通常, 常態, 標準
 above-normal earnings [profit] 超過利益
 attained age normal method 正常到達年齢方式
 average A basis points below normal 平均して通常の水準よりAベーシス・ポイント低い
 be one standard deviation below normal 通常より[過去の平均より]1標準偏差低くなっている
 entry age normal (method) 正常加入年齢方式
 normal assets 正常資産
 normal audit [auditing] procedures 通常の監査手続き
 normal [yield] curve 正常利回り曲線, 順イールド
  (=positive yield curve)
 normal distribution curve 正規分布曲線
 normal dividend 通常の配当
 normal economic downturn 一般的な景気の下降局面
 normal market practice 通常の市場慣行
 normal market size 通常取引規模
 normal operating cycle (basis) 正常営業循環基準
 normal operations 通常業務
 normal profit margin [rate] 正常利益率
 normal rate of exchange 正常な為替相場
 normal rate of interest 正常利率
  (=normal interest rate)
 normal remuneration 正常報酬
 normal retirement age 通常退職年齢
 normal risk 通常危険
 normal ROE 標準株主資本利益率
 normal trading unit 単位株
 normal value 正常価値
 normal working capital 正常運転資本
 normal yardsticks of monetary discipline 金融節度の正常な判断基準
normal course of business 通常の業務過程, 通常の事業過程, 通常の営業過程, 通常の事業活動
 ◆We use various financial instruments, including derivatives, in the normal course of business. 当社は、通常業務で各種の金融商品を利用しており、これには金融派生商品も含まれています。
North American Free Trade Agreement 北米自由貿易協定, NAFTA
nosedive (動)急減する, 急落する, 暴落する, 急速に悪化する
 ◆Lehman's failure came after its stock prices had nosedived. リーマンの株価が急落したのを受けて、リーマン・ブラザーズ

は破たんした。
nosedive （名）急落, 暴落, 激減
　◆The collapse of the information technology bubble in the United States has sent exports of Japanese electronics products into a nosedive, leading to shrinking output.　米国のIT（情報技術）バブルの崩壊で、日本の電子製品の輸出が激減し、生産も落ち込んでいる。
nostro account　当方勘定, ノストロ勘定
　（=our account）
notch　（動）記録する, 樹立する, 収める, 得る, 獲得する
　notch the benchmark rate lower to　政策金利を～に引き下げる
　◆The Bank of England notched its benchmark rate lower to 5.25 percent from 5.5 percent.　英中央銀行のイングランド銀行は、政策金利を年5.5%から5.25%に引き下げた。
notch　（名）段階, 級, 程度, 順位, ノッチ
　（⇒investment grade）
　cut rating on yen-denominated government bonds by two notches　円建て国債の格付けを2段階引き下げる
　dip down a notch　1ノッチ（0.1ポイント）減少する
　downgrade long-term Japanese government bonds by one notch　日本の長期国債を1段階引き下げる
　　（⇒long-term Japanese government bonds）
　lower credit ratings a notch　信用格付けを1段階引き下げる
　top-notch credit rating　最上位の信用格付け, 最上位の格付け
　top-notch safety management specialist　一流の安全管理専門家
　◆Japan lacks top-notch safety management specialists at least in the field of financial services.　少なくとも金融サービスの分野では、日本に一流の安全管理専門家がいない。
　◆Moody's Investors Service cut Japan's yen-denominated debt rating by one notch to Aa3 from Aa2 and maintained a negative outlook.　米国の格付け会社ムーディーズは、日本の円建て国債の格付けを「Aa2」から「Aa3」に一段階引き下げ、「ネガティブ（弱含み）」の見通しを据え置いた。◆Moody's will consider cutting the United States' top-notch credit rating if any progress isn't made in talks to raise the U.S. debt limit.　米政府の債務の法定上限引上げについての（米議会との）交渉で進展がなければ、ムーディーズは、米国債の最上位の格付けを引下げる方向で検討する方針だ。◆Standard & Poor's dropped the U.S. rating by one notch for the first time.　スタンダード・アンド・プアーズ（S&P）が、米国債の格付けを史上初めて1段階引き下げた。◆The bank's rating may be cut one-notch.　同行の格付けは、1段階引き下げられる可能性がある。◆The S&P cut in the U.S. long-term credit rating by one notch to AA-plus from AAA resulted from concerns about the nation's budget deficits and climbing debt burden.　スタンダード・アンド・プアーズ（S&P）が米国の長期国債格付けを最上級のAAA（トリプルA）からAA（ダブルA）に1段階引き下げた理由は、米国の財政赤字と債務負担の増大に対する懸念だ。◆The unemployment rate dipped down a notch to 5.5 percent last month, from 5.6 percent in June.　先月（7月）の失業率は、6月の5.6%から5.5%に1ノッチ（0.1ポイント）減少した。◆Two influential rating firms lowered Ford Motor Co.'s credit ratings a notch deeper into junk territory.　大手［有力な］格付け機関2社が、米フォードの信用格付けを「投資不適格レベル」にさらに1段階引き下げた。
note　（名）手形, 約束手形, 証券, 債券, 債権表示証書, 紙幣, 通知書, 伝票, 覚書, 注釈, 注記, 注意, ノート（証券の「ノート」は一般に中期の債務証券を指すが、米財務省証券に対して使うときは、償還期限が1年超10年以内の中期証券のことをいう）
　auditing for note receivable　受取手形監査
　bank note　中央銀行が発行する銀行券, BN
　contract note　契約書
　delivery note　納品書
　fixed and variable rate notes　確定および変動利付きノート
　general notes of financial statements　財務諸表［財務書類］の一般的注記
　heading notes　頭注
　loan on note　手形貸付け
　loans on notes and bills　一般貸付け金
　matured note　満期手形
　notes and accounts receivable-trade, net of allowances　受取手形および売掛金、貸倒れ引当金控除後
　overdue note　期限経過手形
　purchasing note　買約書
　sales note　売約書
　sight note　一覧払い約束手形, 一覧払い手形
　the total amount of outstanding notes　紙幣の総発行残高
　three-year note auction　米国債3年物の入札, 3年物Tノートの入札
　unlisted note　非上場債
　unpaid note　不渡り手形
　◆On April 12, 2010, we purchased $264 million in notes of the company maturing over six to eight years.　2010年4月12日に当社は、元本金額2億6,400万ドル、満期6-8年の同社のノートを購入した。◆On October 1, 2011, we utilized the shelf registration program to issue US $300 million of 6.0% Notes due 2021.　2011年10月1日に当社は、米証券取引所（SEC）の一括登録制度を利用して、満期2021年・利率6.0%のノート3億米ドルを発行しました。◆The Fed's total amount of outstanding notes at the end of June 2011 increased by more than 30 percent from the end of March 2008, prior to the Lehman shock.　2011年6月末時点の米連邦準備制度理事会（FRB）の紙幣の総発行残高は、リーマン・ショック前の2008年3月末から30%以上も伸びた。
note payable　支払い手形, 手形債務, 手形借入金, 短期借入金, 借入金
　note payable to subsidiary　子会社支払い手形
　notes payable-trade　支払い手形
　　（=acceptance payable）
　◆Net proceeds from the public offering were used to reduce notes payable.　公募による純資金［公開発行による受取金純額］は、短期借入金の返済に充当しました。◆The Corporation has $1 million of notes payable due June 10, 2011.　当社は、2011年6月10日期日の100万ドルの支払い手形を振り出している。◆The prevailing rate of interest for a note payable of this type is 12%.　この種の支払い手形の通常［現行］の利率は、12%である。
note receivable　受取手形
　note receivable discount　手形割引
　note receivable discounted　割引手形
　note receivable due from employee　従業員手形貸付け金
　notes receivable-trade　受取手形
　　（=acceptance receivable）
notice　（名）通知, 通知書, 通知方法, 通告, 通告書, 告知, 告知書, 予告, 広告, 公示, 告示, 表示, 認識
　a deposit at 7 days' notice　7日間の引出予告が必要な通知預金
　arrival notice　着船通知
　arrival notice of import bill　輸入為替到着案内
　bankruptcy notice　破産告知
　deposit at (short) notice　通知預金
　　（=deposit at call, notice deposit）
　exercise notice　権利行使書
　notice deposit　通知預金

notice of acceptance 引受通知
notice of borrowing 借入通知書
notice of delisting 上場廃止の通告
notice of dishonor 不渡り通知
notice of protest 支払い拒絶通知
notice of quit 解約通知
seven days notice account 7日間前予告（通知預金）勘定
30 days notice 30日前の事前通告
notification （名）通知,通知書,通報,通告,届け出,告示,公告,告知,催告
　notification of credit 入金通知
　notification of statute 設立文書
　notification period 告示期間
　notification to debtholders 債券保有者に対する通知
notifying （形）通知する,通告する,告示する,公告する
　the notifying bank 通知銀行
　the notifying party 着荷通知先
　　（=the "notify" party）
noting （名）公証人による手形不渡り証明
noting of protest 手形拒絶証書作成
notional （形）想定の,架空の,名目の,机上の,理論上の,観念的な,現実的でない
　notional amount 名目元本,想定元本
　notional bond 標準物
　notional borrowing 名目借入れ
　notional principal amount 名目元本,想定元本
　notional principal outstanding 名目元本残高
　notional principal value 名目元本,名目元本ベースでの取引高,額面
　notional repayment 名目返済
　notional value 名目元本,想定元本
　　（=notional amount, notional principal amount）
　use a notional amount 想定元本を使う
novel business 事業の新規制
　　（⇒Mothers market for start-up firms）
NOW 譲渡可能払戻し指図書,ナウ（negotiable order of withdrawalの略）
　NOW account ナウ勘定,NOW口座,小切手振出し可能貯蓄性預金勘定
　NOW deposit NOW預金
N.P. 拒絶証書作成不要（no protestの略）
NPL 不良債権（nonperforming loanの略）
number （名）数,番号,数値,指標,統計,ナンバー
　account number 口座番号
　by number 番号順に
　card member number カード会員番号
　certificate number 証券番号
　consumption number 消費支出
　economic numbers 景気指標
　fictitious account number 架空口座番号
　index number 指数
　inflation numbers インフレ統計
　initial numbers 速報値
　job numbers 雇用統計
　monthly numbers 月次指標,月次統計
　national insurance number 国民保険個人番号
　number of authorized shares 授権株式数
　number of investment approval 投資認可件数
　number of IPOs 新規株式公開件数
　number of scheduled payments 返済回数
　number of stocks issued 発行済み株式数

personal identification number 暗証番号
preliminary number 速報値
prepay numbers 期限前償還率
price numbers 物価指数
reported numbers 決算
seasonally adjusted numbers 季節調整済みの数値
taxpayer identification number 納税者番号
trade numbers 貿易統計
◆Amid the continued yen's historically high levels, increasing numbers of people are opening foreign currency deposit accounts. 歴史的な円高水準が続くなか,外貨預金口座を設ける人が増えている。◆An increasing number of companies want to undertake IPOs while stock markets remain brisk. 株式市場が活況のうちに上場したい[株式を新規公開したい]、という企業が増えている。
number of shareholders 株主数
◆To maintain its listing, it was necessary for the company to increase the number of shareholders. 上場を維持するため、同社は株主数を増やす必要があった。
number of shares 株式数
　number of shares authorized 授権株式数
　　（=number of authorized shares）
　number of shares issued 発行済み株式数,発行済み株式総数　（=number of stocks issued）
　number of shares of stock 株式数
　number of shares outstanding 発行済み株式数,社外流通株式数　（=number of outstanding shares）
　number of weighted average shares outstanding 加重平均総発行株式数
numerical goal 数値目標　（=numerical target）
◆If the numerical goal of G-20 nations' current account surpluses or deficits is introduced, Japan could be pressed to allow a further rise in the yen. G20（世界20か国・地域）の経常収支の黒字または赤字の数値目標が導入されれば、（経常黒字国の）日本は一段の円高を迫られる可能性がある。◆The United States tries to press China to reduce its current account surplus and raise the yuan by restricting its current account with a numerical goal. 米国は、経常収支を数値目標で縛って、中国に経常収支の黒字縮小と人民元切上げの圧力をかけようとしている。
numerical target 数値目標　（=numerical goal）
◆Countries should introduce numerical targets to correct current account surpluses or deficits. 世界各国が、数値目標を導入して、経常収支の黒字や赤字を是正すべきだ。◆Koizumi's five-year plan was characterized by the fact that it set numerical targets and put forth a coherent policy. 小泉5か年計画の特色は、数値目標を設定して、整合性のとれた政策を掲げている点にあった。◆The new Fed chairman's theory is to introduce inflation targets, thus setting numerical targets for stabilizing prices. 米連邦準備制度理事会（FRB）新議長の持論は、インフレ目標を導入して、物価安定の数値目標を示す[設定する]ことだ。
numerical target to stabilize prices 物価安定数値目標　（⇒deflationary trap）
◆The Bank of Japan was urged to consider the adoption of a "numerical target to stabilize prices," meaning an inflation-targeting policy to moderate current deflationary pressures. 日銀は、現在のデフレ圧力を和らげるためのインフレ目標政策を意味する「物価安定数値目標」の導入の検討を要請された。
numismatics （名）貨幣収集
nursery finance 上場準備企業への融資
nursing care 介護
　nursing care at home 在宅介護
　nursing care business 介護事業
　nursing care plan 介護プラン

nursing care premium　介護保険料
nursing care program　介護計画
nursing-care taxi service　介護タクシー
nursing care worker　介護福祉士
◆In many western European nations, nursing care is considered a welfare service to be provided by central or local governments. 西欧諸国の多くでは、介護は国や地方自治体が提供する福祉サービスと考えられている。◆Traditionally, nursing care has been provided by family members. これまで、介護は家族が行ってきた。

nursing care benefits　介護給付
◆About 80 percent of all municipalities will probably find that their spending on nursing care benefits in the first year will be below the amounts allocated in their budgets. 全市町村の約8割は、初年度の介護給付費（介護給付支出）が予算配分額を下回る見通しだ。

nursing care costs　介護費用
◆Nursing care costs are expected to quadruple by 2025. 介護費用は、2025年には4倍に増える見通しだ。

nursing care facility　介護施設
◆The procedures taken to have an elderly person enter a nursing care facility are too cumbersome. 高齢者の介護施設への入所手続きが、煩雑すぎる。◆This homemaker put her mother-in-law in a nursing care facility. この主婦は、義母を介護施設に預けた。

nursing care insurance　介護保険
（⇒reform動詞）
◆Nursing care insurance is financed by public funds from the central and municipal governments and by premium payment by Japanese nationals 40 years of age and older. 介護保険は、国や地方自治体の公費と、40歳以上の日本国民から徴収する保険料とで運営されている。

Nursing-care insurance system　介護保険制度
（=nursing care system）
◆The public nursing-care insurance system began in April 2000. 国民介護保険制度は、2000年4月に始まった。

nursing care services　介護サービス
（=nursing services）
◆A cheap nursing care premium often means that the municipality cannot offer sufficient high-quality nursing care services. 介護保険料が安いということは、だいたい市町村がそれだけ質の高い介護サービスを十分提供できないということだ。

nursing care services at home　在宅介護サービス, 在宅サービス
◆The number of people receiving nursing care services both at home or at medical facilities increased by 20 percent from that prior to the introduction of the nursing-care insurance system. 在宅、医療施設（医療機関）を合わせて、介護サービス利用者は、介護保険制度導入前に比べて2割増加した。

nursing care system　介護保険制度
（=nursing-care insurance system）
◆Dishonest business should not be allowed to be involved in the education of people who support the nursing care system. 介護保険制度を支える人材育成に、悪徳商法をはびこらせてはならない。

nursing leave system　介護休業制度
（=the holiday for nurse system）

NYMEX　ニューヨーク商業取引所（New York Mercantile Exchangeの略）

NYSE　ニューヨーク証券取引所（New York Stock Exchangeの略。通称でBig Boardともいう）
　NYSE Composite Index　NYSE総合株価指数
　NYSE Group　NYSEグループ
◆NYSE Group struck a deal to buy European bourse operator Euronext for \$9.96 billion. （ニューヨーク証券取引所を運営する）NYSEグループは、欧州（パリやオランダなど）の証券取引所を運営する「ユーロネクスト」を99億6,000万ドルで買収する取引をした。◆Six NYSE-listed blue-chip companies agreed to dual-list on Nasdaq and NYSE. ニューヨーク証券取引所に上場している優良企業6社が、ナスダック（米店頭株式市場）とNYSEへの重複上場に合意した。

NYSE Euronext　NYSEユーロネクスト　（ニューヨーク証券取引所を運営するNYSEグループと、パリ、オランダなど欧州の取引所を統括するユーロネクストが合併して設立された持ち株会社。2011年2月15日に、フランクフルト証券取引所などを運営するドイツ取引所とNYSEユーロネクストが、同年内に合併することで合意。⇒Deutsche Boerse [Borse], merger）
◆The merger of NYSE Euronext with the Deutsche Boerse was announced on February 15, 2011. NYSEユーロネクストとドイツ取引所の合併が、2011年2月15日に発表された。

NYSE Group, Inc　NYSEグループ（上場全企業の時価総額は、ニューヨーク市場だけで10.5兆ドル）
◆Currently, NYSE Group, Inc. is the world's largest stock exchange firm and operates the New York Stock Exchange. 現在、NYSEグループは世界最大の株式取引所で、ニューヨーク証券取引所を運営している。

O

OAS　米州機構（Organization of American Statesの略）

OAT　仏財務省証券,（償還が10年を超す）フランス国債, フランス長期国債（obligation assimirable du Tresorの略）
　OAT futures　フランス国債先物
　OAT market　OAT市場

obligation　（名）義務, 債務, 債務負担, 債券, 証券, 有価証券, 証書, 契約書, 金銭債務証書, 債権債務関係
　bank obligations　銀行証書
　benefit obligation　給付債務
　collateralized mortgage obligation　モーゲージ担保債務証書, CMO
　conditional obligations　条件付き債務
　constructive obligation　みなし債務
　debt obligation　債務, 債務負担, 債務証書, 債務契約書, デット証券
　default of obligation　債務不履行, 義務不履行
　discharge an obligation　義務を履行する, 債務を弁済する
　expiration of obligation　債務消滅
　financial obligation　金融上の義務, 金銭債務
　fixed term obligations　期限付き証書
　foreign currency obligations　外貨建て負債
　fulfill an obligation　債務を履行する, 義務［責務］を果たす
　general obligation bond　一般財源債
　general obligation fund　一般公債
　government obligations　国債, 政府債
　guarantee obligations　保証債務
　guarantee of obligation　債務保証
　hidden guarantee of obligation　簿外債務保証
　honor one's obligation　約束どおり債務を履行する
　incur an obligation　債務を負う
　interest obligation　金利債務
　joint and several obligation　連帯責任, 連帯債務, 共同債務　（=joint and several liability）
　joint obligation　共同責任, 共同債務, 連帯責任
　lease obligation　リース債務

lease obligation bond (debt) リース財源債
long term obligation 長期債務, 長期借入金
meet one's financial obligations 金銭債務を弁済する [返済する]
obligation bond 担保付き債券
obligation to disclose （保険契約者の）告知義務
obligation to secrecy 守秘義務
obligations hereunder 本契約に基づく義務, 本契約上の義務 （=under this agreement）
obligations of the U.S. government corporations and agencies 米国政府機関債
obligations to make payment when due 期日が到来した支払い債務, 期日が到来した金銭債務
pay off the obligations 債務を返済する
payment obligation 支払い義務, 支払い債務
payments on the obligations 債務の返済
pension obligation 年金債務, 年金債務額
pension plan obligation 年金制度債務
perform an obligation [the obligations] 義務 [債務] を履行する, 債務を弁済する
performance obligation 履行義務
policy obligations 保険契約債務, 保険金
policyholder obligations 保険契約者に対する債務, 保険加入者に対する債務
projected benefit obligation 予定給付債務, 見積り給付債務
reimbursement obligation 補償債務
repayment obligation 返済義務
rights and obligations 権利と義務
secondary obligation 付随債務
secured obligation 担保付き社債
short-term obligations 短期債務
subordinated obligation 劣後債務
transition obligation 移行時債務
underwriting obligation 引受義務
unsecured subordinated obligation 無担保劣後債務 （⇒subordinated obligation）
U.S. Treasury obligations 米国債
waiver of obligation 債務免除
warranty obligation 保証債務
◆ABC shall have no recourse against XYZ for any obligations under the original agreement assigned pursuant to this assignment agreement. ABCは, この譲渡契約に従って譲渡された原契約上の債務については, XYZに履行の請求を一切求めないものとする。◆Seven life insurers saw lower solvency-margin ratios—a key gauge of an insurer's ability to pay out policy obligations in the event of a disaster or unforeseen loss—than the figures a year ago. 生保7社のソルベンシー・マージン（支払い余力）比率（災害や不測の損失・損害が生じたときの保険会社の保険金支払い能力を示す主要基準の一つ）は, 前年同期より低下した。◆The bank shall have the right, as the obligations become due, or in the event of their default, to offset cash deposits against such obligations due to the bank. 債務の期限が到来したとき, または債務不履行の場合, 銀行はその債務とその預金を相殺する権利を持つ。

obligatory （形）義務的な, 義務付けられた, 強制的な, 強制の, 必修の, 必須の
obligatory maturity （任意満期に対する）強制満期, 債務満期
obligatory measures 義務的な処置
obligatory reinsurance 義務再保険

oblige （動）義務付ける, 義務を負わせる

◆Currently, the government is obliged to hold at least a 50 percent stake in JT. 現在, 政府はJT（日本たばこ産業）株の50%以上保有を義務付けられている。◆Laws already in place on narcotics and organized crime oblige financial institutions to report to the FSA any deals possibly linked to profits from criminal activities. すでに実施されている麻薬や組織的犯罪に関する法律は, 犯罪収益絡みと思われる取引について, 金融庁への報告（届出）を金融機関に義務付けている。

obligee （名）債権者（creditor）, 抵当権者
an obligation with a named oblige 指名債権

obligor （名）債務者（debtor）, 借り手
creditworthiness [credit quality] of the obligor 借り手の信用力, 借り手の信用の質, 債務者の信用度 （=obligor credit quality）
loan obligor ローンの借り手
obligor credit problems 債務者の資金繰り悪化
obligor default 債務者のデフォルト
obligor insolvency 債務者の支払い不能
the primary [principal] obligor 主たる債務者
underlying obligor 原債務者
weaker credit-quality obligor 信用力の低い借り手

observe （動）観察する, 観測する, 監視する, 動きを見る, ～に気づく, 認める, （儀式などを）挙行する, （法令を）守る, 遵守する, 述べる
◆We will have to observe the yen's appreciation and the stock prices. 今後は, 円高と株価の動きを見る必要がある。

observer （名）観測筋, 市場観測者, 消息筋, 評論家, 傍聴者, 立会人, 目撃者, 航空偵察員, 機上観測員, 監視者, 国連派遣団員, （法律や習慣を）守る人, 遵法（じゅんぽう）者, オブザーバー
industry observer 業界筋
market observer 業界筋
observers say ～との観測もある
◆Many industry observers expect few benefits from industry realignment such as mergers. 多くの業界筋は, 合併などの業界再編による効果は薄いと見ている。◆Many observers forecast that economy will turn around by the middle of next year. 市場では, 景気は来年半ばまでには持ち直す, との見方が中心だ。◆Some observers predicted that the global financial crisis would hurt Japan the least. 日本は世界金融危機による傷が世界で最も浅い, と見る向きもあった。

obstacle （名）障害, 支障
overcome obstacles 障害を克服する
remove an obstacle 障害を取り除く
◆Delays in the debt relief process may become obstacles to reconstruction efforts. 債務救済 [債務削減] 手続きの遅れは, 復興の支障 [障害] となる可能性がある。◆Opposition from the company's labor union and business partners emerged as obstacles to the signing of an agreement. 同社の労働組合や取引先の反発が, 契約調印の障害となった。

obstruct （動）妨害する, 邪魔する
◆Financial regulators asked prosecutors to investigate allegations that UFJ Holdings Inc.'s banking unit illegally obstructed recent inspections by reporting misleading information about its nonperforming loans. 金融当局は, UFJ銀行が不良債権に関する虚偽の情報を報告して最近の検査を違法に妨害したとして, 同行を検察当局に刑事告発した。

obstruction （名）妨害, じゃま, 妨げ, 障害, 支障, 妨害行為, オブストラクション
the obstruction of a special inspection 特別検査妨害
the obstruction of an audit by the Federal Services Agency 金融庁の検査妨害
◆For the obstruction of an audit by the FSA, an executive of the bank is believed to have fraudulently obtained a password needed to delete e-mails from the bank's computer

server. 金融庁の立入り検査を妨害するため、同行の役員が、同行のコンピュータ・サーバーから電子メールを削除するのに必要なパスワードを、不正に入手したと見られる。◆The bank's chairman and other executives were arrested and indicted over alleged obstruction of FSA inspections. 同行の前会長と役員が、金融庁の検査忌避[妨害]容疑で逮捕・起訴された。

obtain （動）取得する、調達する、入手する、獲得する（=acquire）
 obtain a 30 percent stake in the company　同社の株式の30%を取得する
 obtain an agreement　合意を取り付ける、合意を得る
 obtain funds [funding]　資金を調達する
 obtain funds at market rates　市場金利で資金を調達する
 obtain in advance　前借りする
 obtain loan finance　借入れで資金調達をする、借入れによる資金調達をする
 obtain loans from banks　銀行から融資を受ける
 obtain newly released funds　新規調達資金を確保する
 obtain shares　株を取得する
 ◆At an emergency shareholders meeting, the company obtained shareholder approval to transfer ¥199 billion from its legal reserves to provide for write-offs of nonperforming loans. 臨時株主総会で同社は、株主から、不良債権処理に備えて法定準備金から1,990億円を取り崩す案の承認を得た。◆Countries likely to be affected by the fiscal and financial crisis in Europe will basically be able to obtain the IMF's short-term loans immediately after applying for them. 欧州財政・金融危機が波及しそうな国は、IMF（国際通貨基金）に要請すると、基本的にIMFの短期融資を即時に受けられる。◆GM obtained agreements from a majority of creditors in negotiations to reduce its debts significantly. 米ゼネラル・モーターズ（GM）は、巨額の債務削減交渉で、大半の債権者から合意を取り付けた。◆In Japan, if company employees exercise employee stock options and obtain shares, the shares are considered salaried income, which is taxable. 日本では、社員が従業員ストック・オプションの権利を行使して株を取得した場合、その株式は給与所得と見なされ、課税対象になる。◆JAL will have to make steady progress in its rehabilitation plan in order to obtain loans from its creditor banks. 日航が取引銀行団から融資を受けるには、同社の再建計画案を着実に進める必要がある。◆Short-term interest rates in the Tokyo market rose as some financial institutions hurried to obtain newly released funds. 一部の金融機関が新規調達資金の確保を急いだため、東京市場の短期金利が上昇した。◆Smaller businesses have had difficulties in obtaining loans from banks and other financial institutions amid the prolonged economic slump. 長引く不況で、中小企業は、銀行その他の金融機関から融資を受けられなくなっている。◆The company's financial statements are not based on the book value of the assets at time they were obtained. 同社の財務諸表は、取得時の資産の簿価を基準としていない。◆We obtained a 20 percent stake in the company. 当社は、同社の株式の20%を取得した。

occur （動）起こる、発生する、生じる、存在する、見られる、～をふと思いつく
 default occurs　デフォルトが生じる
 events occurring after the balance sheet (date)　後発事象
 if a problem occurs　問題が生じた場合
 ◆In the aftermath of the 1995 Great Hanshin Earthquake and the 2007 Niigata Prefecture Chuetsu Offshore Earthquake, a series of fraud cases involving donations occurred. 1995年の阪神大震災や2007年の新潟県中越沖地震の直後には、義援金詐欺事件が相次いで起きた。

ODA　政府開発援助（official development assistanceの略。発展途上国に対する経済支援。相手国に直接行う二国間援助と、国連や世界銀行などへの出資や拠出を通じて行う多国間援助の二つがある。二国間援助は、返済義務のない無償資金協力と、低利・長期の有利な条件で資金を貸す有償資金協力（借款）に分けられる）

ODA loan package　円借款

OECD　経済協力開発機構　（⇒Organization for Economic Cooperation and Development）

off　（形）閑散な、不況の、不活発な、調子が悪い、値下がりしている、季節外れの、休みの　（前）～から離れて、～から外れて
 stocks will be off　株は今後下がる
 the market is off　市場は活況がない、市場は閑散としている、相場は値下がりしている
 the yen was off its lows　円は最安値から反発した
 ◆Interest rates are well off their peak. 金利は、ピーク時からかなり下がっている。

off-balance　（形）簿外取引の、バランス・シート上に計上されていない、オフ・バランス
 off-balance exposure　オフ・バランス取引残高、オフ・バランスシート取引リスク
 off-balance lending　オフ・バランスシート貸出
 off-balance transaction　オフ・バランス取引

off-balance-sheet [off-balance sheet]　貸借対照表に計上[表示]されない、簿外の、オフ・バランス、オフ・バランスシート
 off-balance-sheet activity　オフ・バランス取引（=off-balance-sheet transaction）
 off-balance-sheet asset　簿外資産
 off-balance-sheet contingencies　オフ・バランスの偶発債務
 off-balance-sheet exposure　オフ・バランスシート取引リスク
 off-balance-sheet financing　簿外資金調達、オフ・バランスシート資金調達、簿外取引金融、簿外金融、オフ・バランス金融、オフ・バランスシート・ファイナンシング（貸借対照表に負債が計上されない形での資金調達）
 off-balance-sheet instrument　簿外取引、オフ・バランスシート取引
 off-balance sheet items　オフ・バランスシート項目、簿外取引
 off-balance sheet liability　簿外債務、簿外負債、オフ・バランス債務
 off-balance-sheet supervision　簿外取引の監視
 off-balance-sheet transaction　簿外取引、オフ・バランス取引、オフ・バランスシート取引、市場外取引　（=off-balance sheet activity: 貸借対照表上に表示されない取引のこと）
 ◆Other off-balance-sheet contingencies aggregated approximately $200 million at December 31, 2011. その他の偶発債務は、2011年12月31日現在で約2億ドルでした。

off-board market　店頭取引市場、店頭市場、場外市場　（=over-the-counter market）

off-book fund　簿外資金、帳簿外資金、不正資金、裏金

off-book loan　含み貸出　（=off-the-book loan）

off-exchange market　店頭取引市場

off-exchange products　店頭商品

off-floor order　場外注文、顧客注文

off-floor trading [trade]　場外取引、取引所外での売買

off-grade　（形）格外の、平均の、平均以下の

off-hours trading　時間外取引
 ◆Off-hours trading is a practice originally designed to facilitate large stock transactions among companies. 時間外取引は、本来は企業間の株の大口売買を円滑に進めるための取引方法だ。

off-market　（形）市場外の、取引所外の、場外の

off-market dealer　場外取引業者
off-market purchase of shares　株式の市場外買付け
off-market trading　取引所外取引, 市場外取引
　(=off-market transactions)
◆Investors must use a public tender offer if they seek to acquire more than one-third of stocks issued by any listed corporation through off-market trading. 市場外取引で上場企業が発行した株式の3分の1超を投資家が取得する場合, 投資家は株式公開買付け(TOB)を実施しなければならない。
off-the-book　(形)帳簿外の, 簿外の, 記録されていない
　(=off-book)
off-the-book liabilities　簿外債務
　(=off-the-book debts)
off-the-book loan　含み貸出
off-the book loans　簿外負債
off-the-book property　含み資産, 簿外資産
off-the-book transaction　簿外取引
　(=off-the-book deal)
off-the-book account　簿外口座
◆Revenues from commissions of mutual relief operations were pooled in off-the-book accounts. 共済事業の手数料収入は, 簿外口座に蓄えられていた。
off-the-book deal　簿外取引
　(=off-the-book transaction)
◆The company collapsed after its senior management's off-the-book deals came to light. 同社は, 経営者の簿外取引が発覚してから倒産した。
off-the-book debts　簿外債務
　(=off-the-book liabilities)
◆Andersen Consulting failed to uncover the massive off-the-book debts and dishonest accounting procedures of U.S. energy giant Enron Corp. アンダーセン・コンサルティングは, 米エネルギー大手エンロンの巨額の簿外債務と不明朗な会計処理手続きを見抜けなかった。
off-the-book fund　簿外資金, 裏金, 不正資金
　(=off-book fund)
◆The company allegedly amassed about ¥1 billion in off-the-book funds through its Southeast Asian projects. 同社は, 東南アジアでの事業を通じて, 約10億円の裏金を捻出したとされる。
off-the-run (issue)　(名)周辺銘柄, 不人気銘柄
offer　(動)申し込む, 提供する, 販売する, 金利などを提示する, 買収などの提案をする, 株式などを発行する, 株式を売り出す　(⇒retail lending)
bonds offered through private placement　私募債
offer a bid to　～に対して買収提案をする
offer customers the best value　顧客に最大の価値を提供する
offer debt securities in the market　市場で債券を募集発行する　(⇒external funds)
offer preferred shares　優先株を発行する
offer the stock at ¥250,000 a share in the initial public offering　新規株式公開で同株を1株25万円で売り出す
offer to sign　署名する意向を示す
offer yen loans to developing countries　発展途上国に円借款を供与する
◆Dallas-based investment fund Lone Star will offer 30.2 percent of its holdings, or 211,405 shares, ahead of the Tokyo Star Bank's listing on the Tokyo Stock Exchange. 東京スター銀行(旧東京相和銀行)の東証上場前に, ダラスに本部を置く投資ファンドのローンスターが, 保有する株式の30.2%(211,405株)を売り出す。◆If life insurers continue to offer insurance policies with guaranteed high return rates, the future financial burden in terms of interest payments will increase. 生保が高い利回りを保証した保険の販売を今後とも続けると, 将来の利払いの金融負担が増えることになる。◆If the government financial support is not offered to TEPCO, the utility's creditors and shareholders will have to share the burden. 東電に政府の金融支援がない場合は, 同社の債権者と株主が共同負担せざるを得ないだろう。◆In December 1998, trust funds became the first financial products offered by securities firms and life insurers that banks were allowed to sell. 1998年12月に, 投資信託は, 証券会社と生命保険会社が提供する金融商品のうち銀行窓口での販売が認められた最初の商品となった。◆In Sumitomo's tender offer for Jupiter Telecommunications Co., about 2.6 million J:COM shares were offered, far above the 875,834 shares it was willing to purchase. 住友商事のジュピターテレコム(JCOM)株の株式公開買付け(TOB)では, 約260万株の応募があり, 買付け予定株数の87万5,834株を大幅に上回った。◆In the case of an insolvent borrower, it no longer has the ability to pay all its debt even though lenders offer to defer the time of repayment. 返済不能の借り手の場合, 貸し手が返済期間の延長を申し出ても, 借り手はもはや債務を全額返済できない状況にある。◆In the United States, banks are allowed to offer individual annuity insurance policies. 米国では, 銀行が個人年金保険の取扱いを認められている。◆Japan Post is discussing an alliance with Suruga Bank to offer mortgages and other loans to individuals. 日本郵政は現在, 住宅ローンなど個人ローン商品の販売に向けて, スルガ銀行と業務提携協議を進めている。◆Life insurers have been offering relatively high yield rates to their policyholders. 生保各社は, 保険契約者に比較的高い利回り[予定利率]を提示してきた。◆Major central banks will cooperate to offer three-month U.S. dollar loans to commercial banks in the wake of Europe's sovereign debt crisis. 欧州の財政危機を受け, 主要中央銀行が, 協調して商業銀行に3か月物ドル資金を供給することになった。◆Major U.S. oil giant Chevron Corp. initially offered a $16.5 billion bid to Unocal. ユノカルに対して, まず米国のメジャー(国際石油資本)のシェブロンが165億ドルでの買収提案をした。◆Nonlife insurers are exploring new types of insurance demand and offering convenient and easy means of buying policies. 損保各社は, 新たな保険需要を掘り起こして, いつでも, どこでも簡単に保険に加入できるサービスを提供している。◆Regarding TEPCO's damage compensation, creditor financial institutions have already offered cooperation by refinancing existing loans. 東電の損害賠償に関して, 取引金融機関は, 既存の融資の借換えなどですでに協力している。◆Sberbank of Russia will offer a variety of services, such as ruble-denominated loans to Mizuho Corporate Bank's clients when they do business in Russia. ロシア最大手行のズベルバンクは, みずほコーポレート銀行の顧客がロシアで事業を行う際にルーブル建て融資を行うなどの各種サービスを提供することになった。◆Some financial institutions are offering products with annual interest rates starting at 1 percent or less. 一部の金融機関は, 当初の金利[適用金利]が年1%以下の商品を提供している。◆The bank offered three types of preferred shares. 同行は, 3種類の優先株を発行した。◆The firm offers loans for retail and corporate clients in addition to offering electronic settlement for online shoppers. 同社は, ネット・ショッパー[オンライン・ショッパー]向けの電子決済業務のほかに, 個人と企業向けの融資も手がけている。◆The nation's mega banking groups have been realigning their securities units to offer comprehensive financial services. 国内の大手金融グループは, 総合金融サービスを提供するため, グループ各社の証券会社を再統合している。◆The policies offered by the two nonlife insurers pay policyholders if they are injured doing sports or during domestic and overseas trips. この損保2社が提供している保険では, 保険加入者[保険契約者]がスポーツや国内外の旅行中に傷害事故にあったときに, 保険金が支払われる。◆Tokio Marine & Nichido Fire Insurance Co. tied up with NTT Docomo Inc. in April 2011 to offer Docomo One-time Hoken insur-

ance. 東京海上日動火災保険は、2011年4月にNTTドコモと提携して、「ドコモワンタイム保険」を提供している。

offer (名)申込み, 売申込み, 申し出, 提案, 提示, 提示額, 申請額, 取引希望価格, 付け値, 売呼び値, 割引, 値引き, オファー (⇒turn down)
at the price on offer 提示価格で, 大安売り中
be open to offers 値段交渉に応じる用意がある
be under offer 契約済みである, 売約済みである
buying offer 買い申込み, 買いオファー
buyout offer 買収の申込み, 買収提案
（=acquisition offer）
demand and offer curve 需要・オファー(提供)曲線
foreign capital offer 外資攻勢
offer by subscription 予約募集
offer by tender （株式の）入札発行
offer document 株式公開買付申込み書, オファー・ドキュメント
offer for sale 募集売出し, 売出発行, 売出し
offer of bribe 賄賂（わいろ）の申し出
offer of credit 信用供与の申し入れ
offer of work [employment, jobs] 求人, 求人数
offers to existing shareholders 割当て発行
on offer 申込み受付け中, 募集中, 販売中, 売りに出されている, 提供中
special offer 特別提供
take advantage of special offers 特別割引を利用する
wage offer 賃金提示額
what's on offer 特売品
◆A third party presented a better offer for the trust bank. 同信託銀行に関して、第三者が有利な条件を提示した。◆Tribune Co. has accepted a buyout offer from a real estate investor. 米トリビューン（米新聞業界2位）は、不動産投資家による買収提案を受け入れた。◆White knight is a company that saves another firm threatened by a hostile takeover by making a friendly offer. ホワイト・ナイトは、友好的な買収により、敵対的買収の脅威にさらされている他企業を救済する企業のことだ。

offer a debt waiver 債権を放棄する, 債権放棄をする, 債務を免除する
◆It's irrational if banks don't offer debt waivers regarding TEPCO's debt. 東電の債務について、銀行が債権放棄をしないのはおかしい。

offer loans 融資を行う, 融資する
（=provide loans）
◆Under the existing agreement, the IMF cannot buy government bonds through the EFSF as the IMF can only offer loans to countries. 現行協定では、IMF（国際通貨基金）は国にしか融資できないので、欧州金融安定基金（EFSF）を通じて国債を購入することはできない。

offer price 募集価格, 発行価額, 売出価格, 買付け価格, 買取り価格, 提示価格, TOB（株式公開買付け）価格
◆The firm lowered its offer price per share from ￥860 to ￥800 under its latest proposal. 王子製紙は、今回の提案で1株当たり買付け価格［買取り価格］を860円から800円に引き下げた。

offered (形)提示された, 申し込まれた, 売り出された, 提供された
continuously offered long-term securities 継続的に発行される［継続発行ベースの］長期債
London interbank offered rate ロンドン銀行間出し手金利, ライボー
offered market 買い手市場
offered price 付け値, 呼び値, 売り呼び値, 申込み価格［値段］
offered rate （資金の）出し手レート, 売り手レート, オファード・レート
publicly-offered local government bonds 公募地方債

offering (名)募集, 売出し, 株式などの発行, 株式の公開・上場, 入札, 贈り物, 進物, 教会などへの献金, 提供, 提供品, 販売, 売却, 売り物, 提案, 案件 （募集=primary distribution, primary offering, 売出し=secondary distribution, secondary offering; ⇒IPO, public offering, stock offering）
cross-border offering 国際的募集, 国債募集
debt offerings 国債発行額
equity offering 株式発行, 株式公開
formal offering 証券会社を通じての公募
initial public offering 新規公募, IPO
initial stock offering 新規株式公開, 新規株式公募
international offerings 国際公募
limited offering 限定募集
management offering 経営者割当て発行
new share offering 新株発行
noncompetitive offering 非競争入札
offering circular 分売案内書, 募集案内書, 目論見書
offering date 募集取扱日
offering memorandum 募集覚書, 目論見書
offering price 公募価格, 募集価格, 売出価格
offering size 入札総額
offering statement 募集届け出書, 発行目論見書
primary offering 募集（新規発行される有価証券の取得申込みを勧誘すること）
public offering 公募, 株式公開（募集の場合も売出しの場合も、両者区別なく「public offering」と呼ばれる）
public offering bond 公募債
public stock offering 株式公募, 株式公開, 株式上場, 公募増資 （=public equity offering, public offering, stock offering）
rights offering 株主割当て発行
secondary offering 売出し （=secondary distribution: 既発行の有価証券の取得申込みを勧誘すること）
security offering 有価証券の募集
shelf offering 一括募集
special offering 特別売出し
stock offering 株式発行, 株式公開, 株式公募
terms of the offering 発行条件
underwrite the offering 売出しを引き受ける
◆The number of initial public offerings this year on the Tokyo Stock Exchange, four other regional stock exchanges and the Jasdaq market for start-up firms is expected to be much higher than that of the previous year. 東京証券取引所など全国5か所の取引所と新興企業向け市場「ジャスダック」に上場する［株式を新規公開する］企業数は、今年は前年をはるかに上回る見通しだ。◆Weakening consumer spending has prompted retailers, including Seven & I and Aeon, to widen their offerings of low-cost private-brand items. 個人消費［消費］低迷で、セブン＆アイやイオンなどの流通企業は、低価格の自主企画商品（プライベート・ブランド）の販売拡大に取り組んでいる。

office (名)事務所, 仕事場, 営業所, 店舗, 省・庁・課, 官職, 公職, 職務, 任務, 責任, 要職, 重要ポスト, 在任期間, 職員, オフィス
audit office 監査事務所, 監査事務局
back office バック・オフィス, 事務部門, 事務処理, 後方部門, ディーリング管理業務
commercial office vacancy rate 賃貸オフィスの空室率

field office　営業所
foreign office　在外支店
front office　経営陣,幹部,本社
General Accounting Office　会計検査院, GAO
head office　本社,本店,本部,本拠
　(=home office, main office)
inter-office account　本支店勘定
office administration　事務管理
office copy　公文書,公認謄本
office equipment　事務用設備,営業用什器(じゅうき)備品
office hours　営業時間,執務時間,勤務時間,診療時間
　(=operating hours)
office lawyer　法律顧問
office management　事務管理
Office of the Special Inspector General for the Troubled Asset Relief Program　(米国の)不良資産救済プログラム特定監察局, SIGTARP
office term　任期,在任期間,在職期間
　(=term of office)
office work　事務,オフィス・ワーク
office worker　会社員,事務員,事務職員,職員
overseas offices　国外営業所,海外拠点
principal office　本社事務所,本店事務所,主たる事務所,本社,本店,本部
registered office　登記上の本社・本店,登録事務所
◆Citigroup Private Bank's four offices in Japan will have their licenses revoked for violating the law by ignoring suspected money laundering by clients. シティバンクのプライベート・バンク(PB)の在日4拠点(支店・出張所)が、顧客のマネー・ロンダリング(資金洗浄)の疑いのある取引を放置するなどして法令違反があったとして、認可を取り消されることになった。◆Small municipalities have a financial difficulty in setting up an independent audit office or conducting external auditing every fiscal year. 小規模市町村の場合、独立した監査事務局を設置したり、外部監査を毎年度実施したりするのは財政的に困難だ。

official　(名)幹部,指導者,責任者,役員,経営者,公務員,職員,当局者,担当者,関係者
　a senior Bank of Japan official　日銀幹部
　central bank officials　中央銀行当局者,中央銀行関係者
　deposit of accounting officials　預託金
　finance official　財務当局者,金融当局者
　financial market officials　金融市場関係者,金融関係者
　financial official　金融当局者
　monetary officials　金融当局
　senior official　幹部
　supervisory officials　規制当局
　Treasury official　財務省高官
◆Some central bank officials have become skeptical of the effect of quantitative easing measures. 中央銀行関係者には、量的緩和策の効果について疑問視する声も出てきている。◆The bank will conduct a drastic personnel change and replace about 20 senior officials. 同行は、大幅な人事刷新を行い、幹部約20人を更迭する方針だ。◆To deal with the systemic financial crisis, ministry and central bank officials had to take rescue measures, such as an injection of public funds, while at the same time implementing strict guidelines and sanctions. 連鎖的な金融危機に対処するにあたって、当局は公的資金の投入などの救済措置を取ると同時に、厳しい指導や制裁を実施しなければならなかった。

official　(形)公の,公的な,公式の,正式の,公認の,公示の,公用の,公務上の,表向きの,一般に公開されていない
　official assessment method　賦課課税方式

official banking lending rate　公定銀行貸出金利
official credit rating　正式な格付け
official credits　公的債権
official cyclical trough　公式の景気の谷
official data　政府統計,政府の指標
official dollar reserves　公的ドル準備
official exchange rate　公定為替相場,公定交換比率,公定レート
official financing package　公的金融支援
official foreign exchange reserves　外貨準備
official foreign reserves　政府の外貨準備高
　(⇒financial derivatives)
official funds　公金
official gold and foreign currency　金・外貨準備高
official interest rate　政策金利 (=official rate)
official intervention　公的介入,政府介入,為替介入
　(⇒sterilization)
official land prices　公示地価
official list　公定相場表,株式相場表
official money　公金
official money rate　公定歩合
official quotation　公定相場
official receiver　破産管財人
official settlement　公的決済
official settlement basis　公的決済ベース
official support　公的支持政策
official trough of the recession　公式の景気の谷
official unrequited transfers　公的移転収支,政府移転収支
◆At the recent official May Federal Reserve Open Market Committee meeting, no change in the vital short-run Fed interest rate was decided on. この5月に行われた米連邦準備制度(FRS)の公開市場委員会の公式会合では、最も重要な短期連邦金利の変更は行わないことを決定した。

official discount rate　公定歩合 (=bank rate)
　official discount rate cut　公定歩合の引下げ
　official discount rate policy　公定歩合政策
◆The central bank of Japan has deployed various measures to ease monetary policy, including cuts in the official discount rate and hikes in the target for current account deposits held by commercial banks at central bank. 日銀は、公定歩合の引下げや銀行が日銀に持つ当座預金の残高目標の引上げなどを含めて、各種の金融緩和策を実施してきた。◆The current official discount rate of 0.1 percent per annum is expected to be raised to between 0.35 percent and 0.5 percent. 年0.1%の現行の公定歩合は、0.35～0.5%程度に引き上げられる見通しだ。◆The Fed increased the official discount and Federal funds target rates to 4.75 percent and 5.25 percent, respectively, after a meeting of the Federal Open Market Committee. 米連邦準備制度理事会(FRB)は、連邦公開市場委員会(FOMC)を開いた後、公定歩合を4.75%、フェデラル・ファンド(FF)の誘導目標金利を5.25%にそれぞれ引き下げた。◆The federal funds rate, a benchmark short-term interest rate, was cut to 3.5 percent per annum and the official discount rate to 3 percent per annum. 短期金利の誘導目標であるフェデラル・ファンド(FF)金利は年3.5%、公定歩合は年3%に引き下げられた。◆The U.S. Federal Reserve raised the official discount rate and the target rate of federal funds by 0.25 percentage points in a bid to quell inflation and keep the economy from overheating. 米連邦準備制度理事会(FRB)は、インフレを防ぎ景気の過熱を警戒して、公定歩合とフェデラル・ファンド(FF)の誘導目標金利をそれぞれ0.25パーセント引き上げた。

official rate　公定歩合,公定利率,公定税率,公定レート,政策金利
　devaluation of the official rate　公定レートの切下げ

official rate hikes　政策金利の引上げ
official rate of exchange　公定為替相場, 公定交換比率
official rate policy　公定歩合政策
official rate system　公定相場制度
the official rates and market rates　政策金利と市場金利
official reserve　公的準備, 外貨準備, 外貨準備高
　build up official reserves　外貨準備を積み上げる
　official reserve assets　公的準備資産
　official reserve transaction basis　（国際収支の）公的決済ベース
　official reserve transactions balance　公的決済収支
　official reserves　公的外貨準備高
offload　（動）売る, 売り払う, 大量に処分する, 安く大量に売る, 整理する　（=unload）
　◆The talks between Prime Minister Kan and Bank of Japan Gov. Shirakawa led to a further advance of the yen and offloading of stocks as disappointment spread among market players. 菅首相と日銀総裁の会談は、一層の円高と市場筋の株の失望売りを誘った。
offset　（動）相殺する　（名）相殺, 相殺額, 差引勘定, 埋め合わせ
　◆The revenue was offset in its financial reports as an expense. この売上高は、財務報告では経費として相殺してあった。◆The so-called decoupling theory holds that the effects of a U.S. slowdown can be offset by growth in emerging nations. いわゆるディカップリング論では、米経済の減速は新興国の成長が補う、と考えられている。
　offset losses　損失を相殺する
　◆If the two-track income taxation system is introduced, taxpayers will be allowed to offset losses from stock investments from income earned from interest and dividends. 二元的所得課税方式を導入すると、納税者は、利子・配当収入から株式投資による損失を相殺することができるようになる。◆It's difficult to offset losses from further appreciation of the yen with interest as interest rates in many foreign currency deposits are low. 外貨建て預金の多くは金利が低いので、円高進行による損失分を利息で相殺する［取り戻す］のは難しい。
　offset provisions　相殺規定, ペイオフ制度の相殺規定（=offset rules）
　◆All commercial banks, including regional banks, had incorporated the offset provisions in their deposit regulations as of the end of last September. 地方銀行を含めて商業銀行は、昨年（2001年）9月末までに全行が預金取引約款に「相殺規定」を盛り込んだ。◆Under the offset provisions, depositors can decide how much of their deposited money should be used to pay back outstanding loans. 相殺規定によると、預金者はその預金をどの程度、借入金残高の返済に充てるかを決めることができる。
offshore [off-shore]　（形）沖合の, 海上の, 域外の, 海外の, 海外で取り決めた, オフショア
　Japan Offshore Market　東京オフショア市場, JOM
　offshore banking　銀行の外（外）―外取引, 海外の国際金融市場間取引
　offshore banking facility　オフショア市場, 銀行の外―外取引市場　（=offshore market, offshore banking center: 非居住から集めた資金を、自由に他の非居住者に貸すことができる金融市場）
　offshore banking unit　オフショア銀行勘定
　offshore center　オフショア市場
　offshore company　オフショア投資信託会社
　offshore fund　海外投信, 域外投資資金
　offshore investment　海外投資, オフショア投資
　offshore investment fund　海外投資ファンド, 域外投資資金, 国際投資信託
　offshore lease　オフショア・リース

offshore loan　域外融資
offshore market　オフショア市場
oil price　原油価格, 石油価格
　◆Speculators exploited these buying factors, pushing oil prices up further. 投機筋がこれらの買い材料に反応して［投機筋がこれらの買い材料を利用して］、原油価格の高騰［原油高］を増幅している。◆Upward pressure on global oil prices is feared due to increased tensions in the Middle East and political turmoil in Venezuela. 中東情勢の緊迫化やベネズエラの政局混乱のため、国際原油価格の上昇懸念が強まっている。
oil producer　産油国　（=oil producing country）
oil producing region　産油地域
　◆Gas stations finally raised retail prices due to fears of further price surges in international markets, which may stem from uncertainty in the Middle East and Venezuela, both major oil-producing regions. ガソリン・スタンドは、産油地域の中東やベネズエラの政情不安で国際価格の一段の上昇が懸念されるため、小売価格の値上げに踏み切った。
oil refiner-distributor　石油元売り会社
oil wholesalers　石油元売り各社, 元売り各社
　（⇒product）
　◆Oil wholesalers are tightening supplies due to production cuts by oil-producing countries. 石油元売り各社は、産油国の減産で供給を引き締めている。
OIS　オーバーナイト・インデックス・スワップ, OIS（overnight index swapの略。オーバーナイト無担保コール・レートと固定金利を交換する取引のこと）
Omnibus Trade and Competitiveness Act of 1988　1988年包括通商・競争力法
on　（前）～で
　on account　信用で, 掛けで
　on and off-balance positions　オン・バランスとオフ・バランスのポジション
　on approval　点検売買条件で
　on arrival　着荷渡し条件で
　on-balance-sheet cash instruments　現物取引, オン・バランスシート取引
　on-balance-sheet transaction　財務諸表に載る取引
　on call　当座貸し［借り］で, 請求あり次第
　on credit　信用で, 掛けで
　on demand　要求払い, 要求［要請］に応じて
　on-demand bond　無条件ボンド
　on-the-money　アト・ザ・マネー
　on us checks　自行払い小切手
　on us transaction　オン・アス取引
on a real-term basis　実質, 実質ベースで
　◆The national economy will grow at an annual rate of 1.5 percent or more on a real-term basis from fiscal 2004 onward. 日本経済は、2004年度以降は年率で実質1.5％以上の成長を示す見通しだ。
on-board [onboard]　（形）船内での
on-floor order　取引所内での注文, 場内注文, 会員業者の注文
on-floor trading [trade]　場内取引
on-lend [onlend]　（動）（借入金を）融資する, また貸しする
on-lending transaction　転貸借方式による貸付け取引, オン・レンディング方式の取引
on margin　信用取引で
　buying on margin　空買い
　obtain [acquire] a large bloc [block] of shares on margin　信用取引で大量の株を取得する　（⇒block）
　purchase huge chunks of shares on margin through securities companies　証券会社を通じて大量の株式を

買う
purchase stock on margin　信用買いを行う
◆An overseas investment fund purchased huge chunks of shares on margin through the securities company. 海外の投資ファンドが、同証券会社を通じて信用取引で大量の株式を買い進めた。

on-the run　（形）取引活発な、指標の
on-the-run government bond　国債指標銘柄
on-the-run issue　取引活発銘柄、指標銘柄、人気銘柄
on-the-run Treasury　米国債指標銘柄

on-the-spot inspection　立入り検査、立入り考査、立入り調査　（=on-site inspection）
◆The FSA will conduct a further on-the-spot inspection after receiving the final report on the system glitch. 金融庁は、コンピュータのシステム障害の最終報告を受けてからさらに立入り検査を行う方針だ。

on-the-spot payment　即時決済
◆With the unified standard, a number of virtual shopping malls and financial institutions can be directly linked, enabling the purchaser to make on-the-spot payments through various institutions. 規格を統一することで、複数の仮想モール（仮想商店街）と金融機関を直接接続することができ、購入者は各種金融機関を通じて即時決済することができる。

on the strength of　〜を根拠にして、〜に基づいて、〜を頼りにして、〜の力で、〜の影響で、〜の勧めで
◆The BOJ lifted its zero-interest rate policy on the strength of its optimistic view on the outlook for the economy in the summer of 2000. 日銀は2000年夏、景気の先行きを楽観してゼロ金利政策を解除した。

on year　対前年比で
◆The core consumer price inflation rate, excluding volatile fresh food prices, is currently about 2 percent on year due mainly to soaring food and petroleum product prices. 変動の激しい生鮮食品の価格を除いたコア物価指数［消費者物価指数のコア指数］の上昇率は現在、主に食料品と石油製品の価格高騰の影響で、対前年比で2％程度となっている。

one-sided　（形）一方的な、一方に偏（かたよ）った、不公平な、片務的な
one-sided contract　片務契約
one-sided market　買い一色、売り一色
one-sided trade　片貿易

one state rule　1州主義

one-time password [onetime password]　使い捨てパスワード、ワンタイムパスワード
◆In the one-time password system, clients' passwords are changed whenever they log into their accounts. ワンタイムパスワード方式だと、顧客が口座を利用するたびに、顧客のパスワードは変更される。

one-year money　1年物資金

one yen capital's company　1円起業

ongoing　（形）進行中の、進行している、進展中の、進展している、継続中の、継続している、継続して行われる、今回の　（⇒compensation payments）
ongoing alliance projects　現在進行中の業務提携プロジェクト
ongoing concern　継続企業　（=going concern）
ongoing negotiations　現在進行中の交渉
ongoing wave of corporate restructuring　企業リストラ進行の波
the ongoing process of globalization　グローバル化の進展
◆Local economies are already suffering from the ongoing wave of corporate restructuring. 地方経済は、すでに企業リストラ進行の波をもろに受けている。

ongoing business slump　今回の不況
◆The ongoing business slump raises the specter of a global downturn comparable to the Great Depression that started in 1929. 今回の不況は、1929年に始まった世界大恐慌に匹敵するほどの世界同時不況の懸念が高まっている。

ongoing deflation　デフレの進行
◆There is slow progress in economic improvement among nonmanufacturing businesses, largely as a result of sluggish sales at retailers due to the ongoing deflation. デフレの進行で主に小売業の売上が低迷しているため、非製造業は景気回復の足取りが弱い。

ongoing deflationary trend　進行するデフレ傾向、デフレ傾向の進行
◆Amid the protracted economic slump and the ongoing deflationary trend, the life insurance industry has been hit by a trio of predicaments. 景気の長期低迷とデフレ傾向が進行するなか、生保業界は三重苦に見舞われている。

ongoing global economic downturn　今回の世界的な景気後退、今回の世界同時不況
◆The ongoing global economic downturn continues to hit demand for flights. 今回の世界的な景気後退［世界同時不況］で、航空需要が引き続き減少している［打撃を受けている］。

ongoing global financial turmoil　今回の世界的な金融市場の混乱
◆U.S. and European financial institutions are hitting roadblocks because of the ongoing global financial turmoil. 欧米金融機関は、今回の世界的な金融市場の混乱で、つまずいている。

ongoing merger talks　継続中の統合交渉
◆The ruling was reportedly the first ever to suspend ongoing merger talks between financial institutions. 継続中の金融機関の統合交渉を差し止める決定は、前例がないという。

online [on-line]　（形・副）オンライン、オンライン式、直結、回線接続中、コンピュータ回線で、コンピュータ回線を使って、コンピュータのネットワークで、インターネットで、ネット上で、ネットで、OL
online business　オンライン業務、オンライン・ビジネス
online clearing　オンライン決済
online debit service　インターネット即時決済サービス、オンライン即時決済サービス
online financial information services　オンライン金融情報サービス
online home-delivery retailer　オンライン宅配小売業者
online job-search service　オンライン求職システム
online mall　仮想商店街、オンライン・モール　（=virtual mall）
online procurement　オンライン調達
online securities brokerage　ネット専業証券会社、オンライン証券会社　（=e-broker, online broker [brokerage]）
online stock brokerage　ネット証券会社　（=online brokerage, online securities brokerage）
online stock trading　株のインターネット取引、インターネットを通じた電子株取引
◆au Insurance Co. has started selling casualty insurance online to cell phone users. au損害保険（株）が、携帯電話ユーザー向けに損害保険のネット販売を開始した。◆The eight stock exchanges in the country are connected online and settlements are conducted at the Tokyo Stock Exchange. 国内の8つの証券取引所はコンピュータ回線で接続され、取引の決済は東証で行われている。◆We resorted to electronic brokerage in which currency is directly purchased online. われわれは、オンライン（コンピュータ端末）で直接、通貨買いを注文する電子ブローキングの手段を使った。

online account　ネット口座
◆Some major banks lower their commission rates of foreign currency deposits if depositors make transactions via online

accounts. 外貨預金の預金者がネット口座経由で取引をする場合、一部の大手銀行は、外貨預金の手数料[為替手数料]の料率を引き下げている。

online advertising オンライン広告
（＝online ads, online advertisement）
◆The company is also likely to enjoy an expected rise in online advertising revenue. 同社の場合は、予想されるオンライン広告の増益も期待できる。

online auction オンライン・オークション, ネット・オークション
◆Google Inc. plans to go public by selling $2.7 billion in stock through an online auction. 米インターネット検索サービス最大手のグーグルが、ネット・オークションによる27億ドルの株式発行で新規株式公開を計画している。◆Yahoo Japan Corp. is Japan's No. 1 player in online auctions. ヤフー・ジャパンは、日本のネット・オークション市場では第一位の企業だ。

online bank ネット銀行, ネット専業銀行 （＝e-banking, Internet bank, Internet-based bank, Net bank, Net-only bank）
◆In the case of foreign currency deposits by the U.S. dollar, many online banks charge about ￥0.25 in commission per dollar at the time of deposits and withdrawals. 米ドルによる外貨預金の場合、ネット銀行の多くは、預け入れ時と解約時に1ドルに付き25銭程度の手数料を取る。◆Online bank eBank Corp. began operations in 2001. ネット専業銀行のイーバンク銀行は、2001年に開業した。

online banking オンライン・バンキング, オンライン銀行業務（インターネットを通じて個人向けに行う銀行業務）
  online banking services オンライン・バンキング・サービス, ネット・バンキング
  online banking users オンライン・バンキング利用者
  online branch banking オンライン支店銀行業務
◆In illegal transfers via online banking services, viruses such as Spy Eye and Zbot have been used. ネット・バンキングでの不正送金では、スパイアイやゼットボットなどと呼ばれるウイルスが使われている。◆Online banking users can prevent illegal transfers of their deposits by frequently changing their passwords. オンライン・バンキング利用者は、パスワードをこまめに変更して、預金の不正送金を防ぐことができる。◆Sony Bank is the second banking unit of a nonfinancial business to launch online banking services after IYBank. 異業種の銀行参入としてオンライン・バンキング・サービスを提供するのは、ソニー銀行がアイワイ(IY)バンク銀行に次いで二番目である。◆Viruses used in illegal transfers via online banking services collect Internet banking account-related information such as personal identification numbers and transmit them to remote parties. ネット・バンキングでの不正送金に使われたウイルスは、暗証番号などネット・バンキングの口座関連情報を収集して、外部に送信する。

online brokerage オンライン証券, ネット専業証券, オンライン証券会社, ネット専業証券会社 （＝e-broker, online broker, online securities brokerage）
◆Kabu Venus is run by online brokerage kabu.com Securities Co. カブビーナス（女性向けの株式投資情報サイト）は、インターネット専業の証券会社カブドットコム証券が運営している。

online debit service インターネット即時決済サービス, オンライン即時決済サービス
◆The bank has started an online debit service with a network of about 100 virtual shops. 同行では、約100店の仮想商店を対象にインターネット即時決済サービスを開始しました。

online finance ネット金融, オンライン金融
◆Softbank and Deutche Bank will tie up in online finance. ソフトバンクとドイツ銀行が、オンライン金融で提携する。

online financial information services オンライン金融情報サービス

online insurance sales 保険のネット販売
◆au Insurance Co. has started its online insurance sales by teaming up with KDDI. au損害保険(株)は、KDDIと提携して保険のネット販売を開始した。◆The casualty insurer delayed the start of its online insurance sales due to the March 11 earthquake and tsunami. 2011年3月11日の東日本大震災のため、同損保は保険のネット販売の開業を延期した。

online sales ネット販売
◆Online and mail-order sales of nonprescription drugs have been tacitly approved. 処方箋なしで買える薬のネット販売や通信販売が、これまで黙認されてきた。

online shopper ネット・ショッパー, オンライン・ショッピング利用者, オンライン・ショッパー
（＝Net shopper, Net shopping user）
◆The firm offers loans for retail and corporate clients in addition to offering electronic settlement for online shoppers. 同社は、ネット・ショッパー[オンライン・ショッパー]向けの電子決済業務のほかに、個人と企業向けの融資も手がけている。

online shopping ネット・ショッピング, オンライン・ショッピング （＝Internet shopping: インターネットやパソコン通信サービスで行われている通信販売）
◆Electronic money can be used for online shopping. 電子マネーは、ネット・ショッピングで使用することができる。

online stock trading business 株のインターネット取引業務
◆The company will launch an online stock trading business by the end of this year. 同社は、年内に株のインターネット取引業務に参入することになった。

online system オンライン・システム
（＝online real time system）
◆The banking industry plans to integrate all automated teller machine and cash dispenser networks into a single nationwide online system as early as January 2004. 銀行業界は、ATM（現金自動預け払い機）とCD（現金自動支払い機）の全ネットワークを、全国的な単一のオンライン・システムに2004年1月にも統合する計画だ。

online trading ネット取引, ネット専業取引, オンライン取引 （＝Internet trading, Net trading）
◆Two companies' accumulated know-how in online trading will be useful in the commodity futures market. 商品先物市場では、両社の蓄積しているネット取引のノウハウが役に立つだろう。

online trading system 電子取引システム, オンライン取引システム
◆The Proprietary Trading System and other online trading systems facilitate trading of stocks outside stock exchanges. 私設取引システム(PTS)などの電子取引システムは、証券取引所外で株の売買（注文）を成立させる。

online voting 電子投票, Eメールでの投票
（＝e-vote, electronic voting）
◆The company plans to introduce an online voting system at its annual general meeting of shareholders in June. 同社は、6月の年次株主総会から電子投票制度を導入する方針だ。

OPEC 太平洋地域経済協力機構（Organization of Pacific Economic Cooperationの略）

OPEC 石油輸出国機構, オペック（Organization of Petroleum Exporting Countriesの略）
◆OPEC will carry out a plan to slash 1.5 million barrels a day from its crude production in an effort to firm up sagging oil prices. 石油輸出国機構(OPEC)は、原油価格の下落に歯止めをかけるため、1日の原油生産枠から日量1,500万バレル削減する計画を実施する。

open (動)開く, 開設する, 出店する, 市場などを開放する, 初値を付ける

open an account with ～に口座を開く, ～に口座を開設する
open at ¥1,500 per share 1株当たり1,500円の初値が付く, 1株1,500円で寄り付く, 始値(はじめね)[寄り付き]は1株1,500円である （始値＝午前の取引開始時点の株価。⇒public offer price）
open up to public ownership 株式を公開する
◆Amid the continued yen's historically high levels, increasing numbers of people are opening foreign currency deposit accounts. 歴史的な円高水準が続くなか, 外貨預金口座を設ける人が増えている。◆Mizuho Bank and Mizuho Investors Securities Co. opened their first joint branch operations in Tokyo. みずほ銀行とみずほインベスターズ証券が, 東京で国内初の共同店舗での営業を開始した。◆Stock in J-Com opened at ¥672,000, but it plunged to its lower limit of ¥572,000. ジェイコム株は, 1株67万2,000円の初値が付いたが, 値幅制限（ストップ安）の下限の57万2,000円に下落した。

open （形）開かれた, 開放的な, 制限のない, 自由な, 公開の, 周知の, 営業中の, 開会中の, 未決定の, 未解決の, 未決算の, 非武装の, 無防備の, オープン
open bid 一般競争入札, 公開入札
open check 普通小切手
open contract 未決済契約, 予定契約, 先渡し契約, 暫定契約, 仮契約, （先物取引の）未定契約, 裸ポジション
open corporation 公開会社, 株式公開会社
open cover 包括予定保険
open credit 無条件信用状, 買取り銀行不指定信用状, 無担保取引, 掛け売り勘定
open endorsement 無記名裏書き
open exposure アンカバーの持ち高, 片持ち
open for business 営業している
open house 建売り住宅の内覧日, 私宅開放日, 授業参観日
open housing 公正住宅取引
open interest （信用取引での）建玉(たてぎょく), 未決済取引残高
open mortgage 返済可能譲渡抵当
open note 無担保手形
open order 見計らい注文, オープン注文
open position 裸ポジション, オープン・ポジション
open repos 取消可能な買戻し約款

open a new account 新規口座を開設する, 新たに口座を開設する
◆Customers will have to open a new account to use the Internet banking services. このインターネット・バンキングのサービスを利用するにあたって, 顧客は新規に口座を開設しなければならない。

open account 当座預金, 当座勘定, 清算勘定

open bank assistance オープン・バンク・アシスタンス（銀行の経営が破たんする前に政府支援で銀行の事業譲渡をする手法。早期支援をすれば預金保険制度への負担が最小で済むと判断される場合や, 銀行倒産が金融システムの安定性に悪影響を与えると予想される場合に発動される）

open-end （形）（投資信託が）開放型の, オープンエンド型の, 貸付け金額を一定しないで提供する, 細目を後で変更［修正］できる, 自由回答式の（open-ended）, オープンエンド
open-end contract 数量不確定契約, 不定契約
open-end credit 開放信用, オープンエンド・クレジット
open-end credit system 開放信用体系
open-end fund オープンエンド型投資信託 （=mutual fund）
open-end investment company オープンエンド型投資会社, ミューチュアル・ファンドを運用する投資会社 （=mutual fund）
open-end management company オープンエンド型投資信託 （=open-end management company）
open-end mortgage 開放担保, オープンエンド・モーゲージ
open-end mortgage band 分割発行型担保付き社債
open-end policy 可変保険証券
open-end question 自由回答式質問 （=open-ended question）

open-ended mutual fund オープンエンド型ミューチュアル・ファンド （=open-end mutual fund）

open market 公開市場, 自由市場, 一般市場, 市中市場, （株の）青空市場
open market commercial paper 公開市場商業手形
open market forces 市場原理
open market intervention 公開市場介入
open market mechanism 自由市場原理
open market paper 流通商業手形, 一般市場商業手形
open market policy 公開市場政策 （=open market operation）
open market purchase 公開市場買入れ, 流通市場買入れ, 公開市場買い操作 （=buying operation）
open market quotations 市中相場, 通り相場
open market rates 公開市場金利, 市中金利, オープン市場金利 （=market interest rate）
open market sale 公開市場売り操作 （=selling operation）
open market seller 公開市場売り手
open market selling operations 売りオペ
open market value 公開市場価値

open market operation 公開市場操作, 金融調節（日銀などの中央銀行が公開市場で政府債券の売買を行って, 通貨量の増減により利率や為替相場を調節すること。公定歩合（discount rate）の変更, 支払い準備率（reserve ratio）と並ぶ重要な金融政策手段）
Fed open market operations 米連邦準備制度理事会（FRB）の公開市場操作
Federal Reserve open market operations 米連銀公開市場操作
◆The Bank of Japan's conventional open market operation of buying short-term government notes without repurchase agreements is limited in its effect. 日銀のこれまでの売戻し条件を付けない短期国債の買切りオペ（公開市場操作）だけでは, その効果に限界がある。◆The BOJ decided to introduce a new open market operation by supplying ¥10 trillion to private financial institutions in three month loans at an ultralow annual interest of 0.1 percent. 日銀は, 民間の金融機関に年1％の超低金利で貸出期間3か月の資金を10兆円供給する新型の公開市場操作（オペ）の導入に踏み切った。

opening （名）開始, 開会, 開会式, 開通, 開幕, 開業, 開店, 開館, 開場, こけら落とし, 開国, 開拓, 書き出し, 冒頭, 冒頭部分, 出だし, 導入部, 序盤, 初日, 寄り付き, 期首, 就職口, 求人, 空席, 空き, 欠員, 定員, 機会, チャンス, 糸口, きっかけ, 好機, 弁護人の冒頭陳述, 出入り口, 通気口, 開口部, 穴, 割れ目, 広場, 空き地, オープニング
an opening to offer one's plan 計画を提案する機会
fill openings 欠員を補充する
job openings for elderly people 高齢者の就職口
look for an opening 就職先を探す
take the opening to ～するチャンス[糸口]をつかむ
the opening of markets 市場の開拓
◆The emergency telephone conference by the G-7 financial

ministers and central bank governors was held right before the opening of Asian financial markets. 先進7か国 (G7) の財務相・中央銀行総裁による緊急電話会議は、アジアの金融市場が開く直前に開かれた。

opening （形）最初の, 冒頭の, 出だしの, 開幕の, 開会の, 初演の, 1番目の, 第一の, オープニング
　deliver the opening speech [address, remarks] 開会の辞を述べる
　opening balance 期首残高
　opening bank 信用状開設銀行, 信用状発行銀行
　opening charge [commission] 発行手数料
　opening day 開幕日, 初日
　opening hours 営業時間
　opening level 寄り付きの水準
　opening order オープニング注文
　opening rate 始値
　opening round 第一ラウンド
　opening statements （裁判の）冒頭陳述
　opening time 開始時間, 始業時間, 開館 [開演] 時間
　year's opening session 大発会

opening price 新規株式公開 (IPO) 銘柄の公開価格, 寄り付き価格, 寄り付き
　exceed one's opening price 公開価格を上回る
　opening price limit 寄り付き価格制限
　opening price points 最低価格ライン
　opening prices of component securities 採用銘柄の寄り付き価格
　◆The closing price on the first day of these IPO stocks' trading has exceeded their opening price. これらの新規株式公開 (IPO) 銘柄の取引初日の終値 [これらIPO銘柄の上場時の初値 (終値)] は、公開価格を上回った。
　解説 公開価格とは：証券会社が引き受けた新規公開株式を投資家に売り出すときの1株当たり価格のこと。これに対して、株式市場に上場したときに最初についた値段を初値という。

operate （動）経営する, 運営する, 操作する, 事業を展開する, 営業する, 操業する
　◆A man who operated an illegal moneylending firm was arrested on suspicion of violating the Investment Deposit and Interest Rate Control Law. 違法な金融業の経営者 [ヤミ金融の経営者] が、出資法違反容疑で逮捕された。◆Among a number of oil development businesses funded by the oil corporation, there are a few companies that have achieved success and are operating in the black. 石油公団が出資した多くの石油開発事業には、少数ながら成功して、黒字経営をしている会社もある。
　◆Currently, NYSE Group, Inc. is the world's largest stock exchange firm and operates the New York Stock Exchange. 現在、NYSEグループは世界最大の株式取引所で、ニューヨーク証券取引所を運営している。◆Osaka Securities Exchange will continue operating the Nasdaq Japan market under the provisional name Japan New Market. 大阪証券取引所は、「ジャパン・ニュー・マーケット」の名称 (仮称) でナスダック・ジャパン市場の運営を続ける方針だ。◆Under the trustee's management, the debtor bank's business will be operated and the refunding of deposits will be temporarily suspended. 金融整理管財人の管理下で、破たん銀行の業務は運営され、預金の払戻しは一時停止される。

operating funds 運転資金, 営業資金 (=operating capital, working capital, working funds)
　◆A group of major banks decided to extend loans of $2 billion for the WorldCom to use as operating funds to enable it to continue its core businesses, such as Internet access services. 大手銀行団は、ワールドコムに対して20億ドルの運転資金を融資して、同社がインターネット接続サービスなどの中核事業を継続できるようにした。◆There were apparent moves among companies drawing more money from savings to accumulate operating funds. 明らかな動きとして、企業は運転資金を積み増すため、預金から資金を引き出している。

operating loss 営業損失, 営業赤字
　（⇒net capital deficiency）
　◆Quarterly consolidated business results unveiled recently by the country's leading electronics manufacturers show that Matsushita Electric Industrial Co. and Fujitsu Ltd. posted operating losses during the April-June period. 大手電機メーカーが最近発表した四半期連結決算によると、4-6月期は松下電器産業と富士通が営業赤字になった。

operating performance 業績
　◆The downgrade reflects Standard and Poor's concern over the company's ability to avoid a further deterioration in its operating performance. この格下げは、同社の一段の業績悪化は避けられないとのスタンダード＆プアーズの懸念を反映している。

operating profit 営業利益, 営業収益, 金融機関の業務純益 (=income from operations, operating income：売上高から販売・管理費を差し引いた収益で、本業のもうけを示す)
　◆ANA's group operating profit returned to the black in the April-June period of 2010 at ¥2.9 billion due to a surge in the number of passengers on its international flights. 全日空の2010年4～6月期の連結営業利益は、国際線の乗客数の急増で、29億円の黒字に転換した。◆The company posted a 29.5 percent rise in consolidated operating profit for the business year ended in February. 同社の2月期決算〈2月終了事業年度〉の連結営業利益は、29.5％の増益となった。

operating revenue 営業収益, 営業収入, 売上高
　◆Nomura Holdings' operating revenue fell 14 percent to ¥314 billion in the first quarter of fiscal 2010. 野村ホールディングスの2010年度第1四半期 [4～6月期] の営業収益は、(前年同期比) 14％減の3,140億円だった。

operating system 基本ソフトウエア, 基本ソフト, システム・ソフト, オペレーティング・システム, OS (=operating system software)
　◆Microsoft Corp. dominates the market for personal computer operating system software. マイクロソフトは、パソコンの基本ソフト市場を独占している。

operation （名）営業, 営業活動, 事業, 業務, 経営, 活動, 操作, (中央銀行の) 公開市場操作, 運転, 運行, 稼動, 機能, 作用, オペ, オペレーション
　（⇒dollar-buying operation, recovery operation）
　arbitrage operation 裁定取引業務
　back-office operation バック・オフィス業務
　bank rate operation 公定歩合操作
　banking operation 銀行業務
　bill selling operation 手形売りオペ [オペレーション]
　business operations 企業経営
　buying and selling operations by hedge funds ヘッジ・ファンドの売り買い操作
　buying operation 買い操作, 買いオペ, 買いオペレーション
　clearing operation 決済業務
　collection operation 回収業務
　core strategic operations 主力戦略事業
　credit and recovery operations 与信・回収業務
　dollar liquidity-providing operation ドル資金供給オペ
　exchange position [risk] cover operation 為替持ち高調整操作
　exchange position risk cover operation 為替持ち高操作
　expanded cofinancing operation 拡大協調融資オペレーション
　financial operations 財務活動, 金融業務

financing operations　市場からの資金調達
foreign exchange market operation　外国為替市場操作
foreign exchange operation　外国為替操作, 為替業務
fund management operation　資金運用業務
hedge operation　ヘッジ操作, 為替ヘッジ取引
income from operations　営業利益
insuring operation　保険業務
integrate operations　経営統合する, 事業を統合する
investment banking operations　投資銀行業務
lending operation　融資業務, 貸出業務
market-making operation　マーケット・メーキング業務
market operations　市場操作
merge operations　経営統合する
　（=integrate operations）
money market operations　短期金融市場操作
nonlife operation　損保事業
open market operation　公開市場操作, 金融調節
operation audit　業務監査　（=business operation）
operation improvement plan　業務改善計画
Operation Nudge　オペレーション・ナッジ　（通貨供給量を変えないで国際収支の改善を図るため, 米通貨当局が1961年に行った短期金利引上げと長期金利引下げの操作）⇒Operation Twist）
operation of a pension plan　年金制度の運用
operation of exchange position　持ち高操作
operation of loans　貸付け業務
operation of making credits　与信業務
outright forward operation　先物操作
overseas operations　海外事業
price keeping operation　公的資金による株式の買い支え, 株価維持策, 株価維持活動, プライス・キーピング・オペレーション, PKO　（国民年金や厚生年金などの公的資金による株式の買い支え）
resistance operation　逆張り
results of operations　経営成績
selling operation　売り操作, 売りオペ, 売りオペレーション
spot operation　直物操作
swap operation　スワップ操作
take over operations　経営を受け継ぐ
tender operation　入札オペ
the BOJ's tight money market operations　短期金融市場での日銀のきつめの調節, 日銀のきつめの短期金融市場操作, 日銀のきつめの調節
transfer operation　振替操作
treasury operation　財務運用
twist operation　ツイスト・オペ, ツイスト・オペレーション（FRB (米連邦準備制度理事会) が, 長期国債の買入れと同時にすでに保有する短期国債を市中に売却すること）
unconditional buying operation　無条件買いオペ
underwriting operation　与信業務
yen-selling, dollar-buying operation　円売り・ドル買い介入操作, 円売り・ドル買い操作　（=yen-selling and dollar-buying operation; ⇒currency intervention）

◆Chapter 11 bankruptcy provides for a business to continue operations while formulating a plan to repay its creditors. 米連邦改正破産法11章の破産の規定では、企業は事業を継続する一方、債権者への債務返済計画を策定することができる。◆Greece's default on the national debts would be a blow to the operation of financial institutions in France and Germany that hold Greek government bonds. ギリシャが国債の債務不履行に陥った場合、ギリシャ国債を保有するフランスやドイツなどの金融機関の経営は、打撃を受けるだろう。◆In cooperation with the U.S. FRB, the Bank of England, the Bank of Japan and the Swiss National Bank, the European Central Bank decided to conduct three U.S. dollar liquidity-providing operations between October and December. 米連邦準備制度理事会（FRB）、英イングランド銀行、日銀、スイス国立銀行と協調して、欧州中央銀行（ECB）が10〜12月に3回、米ドル資金供給オペを実施することを決めた。◆Leading life insurance companies' negative yields cause pressures on their operations. 大手生保の逆ざやは、生保各社の経営を圧迫している。◆Mizuho Bank and Mizuho Investors Securities Co. opened their first joint branch operations in Tokyo. みずほ銀行とみずほインベスターズ証券が、東京で国内初の共同店舗での営業を開始した。◆Online bank eBank Corp. began operations in 2001. ネット専業銀行のイーバンク銀行は、2001年に開業した。◆Policy-based financing operations which take advantage of government subsidies are adversely affecting the price mechanism in the financial market. 政府の補給金を受けて運営される政策金融は、金融市場の価格メカニズムを歪めている。◆Since December, the FSA has ordered four securities firms to partially suspend operations. 12月以降、金融庁は証券会社4社に一部業務停止命令を出した。◆The Bank of Japan asked the Federal Reserve Bank of New York to intervene in the New York foreign exchange market on its behalf through yen-selling, dollar-buying operations for the first time in 15 months. 日銀は、1年3か月ぶりにニューヨーク連銀に委託して、ニューヨーク外国為替市場で円売り・ドル買いの介入に踏み切った。◆The Bank of Japan conducted its third yen-selling, dollar-buying operation in two weeks. 日銀は、2週間で3回目の円売り・ドル買い介入操作を実施した。◆The Dutch government will nationalize Fortis' Dutch operations. オランダ政府は、ベルギー・オランダ系金融大手フォルティスの自国事業部門を国有化する方針だ。◆The financial groups should write off their bad loans more efficiently and streamline their banking operations. 銀行グループは、もっと効率的な不良債権の処理と銀行業務の合理化を進めなければならない。◆The financial watchdog took an additional action of criminal complaint other than administrative punishment as the bank's operations were so malicious. 同行の業務運営の仕方があまりにも悪質なので、金融監視機関の金融庁は、行政処分のほかに刑事告発の追加措置を取った。◆The firm's operations in the financial services and leasing industry involve direct financing and finance leasing programs for its products and the products of other companies. 金融サービスとリース業界での同社の事業には、同社製品と他社製品に関する直接融資とファイナンス・リース事業も含まれている。◆The FSA ordered the bank to suspend some operations due to serious law violations, including audit sabotage. 金融庁は、同行に対して、検査妨害などの重大な銀行法違反で、一部業務の停止命令を出した。◆The government should not hesitate to intervene in the currency market through bold yen-selling and dollar-buying operations. 政府は、為替市場への大胆な円売り・ドル買い介入をためらうべきではない。◆The inefficiency of the Financial group's two-bank structure has been pointed out as many of operations overlap. 同フィナンシャル・グループの2行体制の非効率は、重複部門が多いため、以前から指摘されてきた。◆The organization will go into operation in mid-February. 同機構は、2月中旬から業務を開始する。◆The two companies have formed an alliance in investment banking operations. 両社は、投資銀行業務で提携関係を結んでいる［提携関係にある］。◆The two financial groups plan to integrate their banking, trust and securities operations under a holding company created through the merger of their holding companies. 両金融グループは、それぞれ銀行、信託、証券業務を経営統合により新設する持ち株会社の傘下に統合する計画だ。◆U.S. and European financial institutions are scaling back their business operations before capital adequacy requirements are strengthened in 2013. 欧米金融機関は、2013年から自己資本規制が強化されるのを前に、業務を縮小している。◆When serious financial difficulties are expected, the Financial Services Agency is allowed to order a company to improve its operations in the early stages without releasing the information to the public. 深刻な財務悪化が予想される場合、金融庁は、非公表で早めに業務改善命令を発動することができる。

operation twist 両建てオペ（中央銀行が即日実行の資金供給と資金吸収を両建てで行うこと）

Operation Twist ツイストオペ, オペレーション・ツイスト（短期金利引上げと長期金利引下げの操作で景気調整を行う方法。⇒operationの項のOperation Nudge）
◆Operation Twist was conceived by President John F. Kennedy's administration during 1960s. オペレーション・ツイストを発案したのは、1960年代のジョン・F・ケネディ（第35代米大統領）政権だ。

operational efficiency 経営効率の悪化
◆The serious deterioration of operational efficiency is caused by excess output capacity and burgeoning workforces. 極端な経営効率の悪化は、生産設備と従業員の過剰によるものだ。

operational funds 営業資金, 運転資金
◆In Tokyo, only the 18 major financial institutions holding ¥5 trillion or more in deposits and other operational funds have been obliged to pay the new bank tax. 東京では、預金その他の営業資金として5兆円以上保有する大手金融機関18行だけが、これまでのところ新しい銀行税の支払いを義務付けられている。◆The Development Bank of Japan and Yasuda Fire & Marine Insurance Co. will each provide the company with ¥50 million in operational funds in early January. 日本政策投資銀行と安田火災海上保険は、1月初旬に運転資金としてそれぞれ同社に対して5,000万円を融資する方針だ。

operational integration 経営統合
(=business integration, management integration)
◆Operational integration and merger have become two major options to shore up the foundations of companies. 経営統合と合併が、それぞれ企業の経営基盤を強化する有力選択肢になってきた。

operational system 業務体制
◆The Economy, Trade and Industry Ministry plans to reinforce the operational system of Nippon Export and Investment Insurance (NEXI). 経済産業省は、独立行政法人の日本貿易保険（NEXI）の業務体制を強化する方針だ。

operator （名）有価証券売買人, 株の相場師, 仕手, 仲買人, 運営者, 経営者, 事業主, 事業者, 事業会社, 運営会社, 会社, 電気通信事業者, 電話交換手, 交換取扱い者, コンピュータを操作する人, 運転者, オペレータ
auction site operator　オークション・サイト運営会社, 競売サイト運営業者
business operator　事業者
company operator　会社経営者
Internet shopping mall operator　インターネット上の仮想商店街運営会社, 仮想商店街の運営会社 （=Net shopping mall operator, online shopping mall operator）
major operators　大企業
mobile phone operator　携帯電話事業会社
operator's agent　船会社代理店
seasoned operator　株のくろうと筋
stock market operators　証券取引所［株式市場］で業務を行う者
tour operator　旅行会社
◆In today's borderless world, operators spend their every second of the day looking for marginal advantage. 今日の国境なき世界では、株の相場師が一日中、利ざやを求めて動いている。◆Supermarket chain operator Aeon temporarily stopped transactions with Sharp. スーパー・チェーン大手のイオンが、シャープとの取引を一時停止した。◆The FSA's guideline for supervising financial conglomerates is aimed at urging operators of financial conglomerates to reinforce their corporate governance to prevent irregularities. 金融庁の金融コングロマリット（複合体）監督指針の狙いは、不正防止に向けて、金融コングロマリットの経営者に経営監視の強化を促すことにある。

operator firm 事業会社
◆After the merger, the TSE and OSE will be divided into four operator firms handling spot trading, derivatives, settlement of trading deals and self-imposed regulations respectively. 経営統合後、東証と大証は、それぞれ現物株、デリバティブ（金融派生商品）、取引決済と自主規制を扱う4事業会社に切り分けられることになっている。

opinion （名）意見, 考え, 考え方, 信念, 見解, 持論, 監査意見, 意見表明, 判断, 所見, 鑑定, 評価, 弁護士の意見書, オピニオン
a difference of opinion　見解の相違
a matter of opinion　議論の余地のある問題
a second opinion about　～についてのもう一つの判断
act up to one's opinions　～の信念によって行動する
business opinion　景況感
collective opinion　統一意見
credit opinion　格付け見解 （=rating opinion）
diverging opinions　意見の食い違い
have a low［bad］opinion of　～に対する評価が低い, ～を悪く思う
have no opinion of　～をよいと思わない
legal opinion　法的見解, 弁護士意見書
medical opinion　医者の意見
opinion advertising　意見広告
opinion leader［maker］　世論形成者, オピニオン・リーダー（世論の形成や表明で主導的役割を果たす人）
opinion of counsel　弁護士の意見
personal opinion　個人の考え
professional opinion　職業専門家の意見
rating opinions　格付け見解
◆At the latest G-20 meeting, diverging opinions among member countries were exposed over expanding the lending capacity of the IMF. 今回のG20（財務相・中央銀行総裁）会議では、国際通貨基金（IMF）が融資できる資金規模の拡大をめぐって、加盟国の間で意見の食い違いが表面化した。

opportune （形）時宜（じぎ）を得た, タイミングのよい, タイムリーな, 絶好な, 絶妙の, 好都合な, 最適な
an opportune remark　適切な意見［発言、所見、言葉］
an opportune time　好機
◆When you have a fragile recovery, it wouldn't seem to me like an opportune time to raise taxes. 景気回復の足取りが弱いときは、税金引上げの好機とは言えないように思える。

opportunity （名）機会, 事業機会, 商機, 好機, 環境, 可能性, 案件, ビジネス・チャンス, チャンス
a fine opportunity for　～の好機
arbitrage opportunity　裁定機会
business opportunity　ビジネス機会, 事業機会, 商機, 商機, ビジネス・チャンス
　（=business chance）
buying opportunity　買い場
capitalize on a market opportunity　市場の機会をとらえる, 市場の機会を生かす
create a selling opportunity　売り場になる

Equal Credit Opportunity Act　信用機会均等法, 消費者信用機会均等法
growth opportunity　成長の機会
investment opportunity　投資機会, 投資対象, 運用先, 投資の選択肢
lending opportunity　融資案件
market opportunity　市場機会, ビジネス機会, 事業機会
new issue opportunity　起債環境
opportunity loss　機会損失
（=conditional loss, cost of prediction error）
opportunity to buy　買い場
（=buying opportunity）
selling opportunity　売り場, 格好の売り場
（=opportunity to sell）
take advantage of opportunities　機会をとらえる, 機会をつかむ, 機会を利用する, 隙（すき）を突く
window of opportunity　機会の窓, 機会の手段, 瞬時の好機, 好機

◆Speculators have taken advantage of this opportunity. 投機筋が, この隙（すき）を突いた。◆We make an acquisition when that seems the most effective way to take advantage of a particular market opportunity to further our growth goals. 当社が企業を買収するのは, 特定の市場機会をとらえて当社の成長目標をさらに推進する上で, それが最も効果的な方法であると思われるときです。◆We see an abundance of opportunities for these new lines of business. これらの新事業部門には, 事業機会が豊富にあります。◆We sell equity interests in our subsidiaries only when opportunities or circumstances warrant. 当社が子会社の株式持ち分を売却するのは, 商機が到来した時または環境が良好な場合に限られています。

oppose　（動）反対する, 抵抗する, 対抗させる, 対立させる, 争いをしかける, 挑（いど）む
◆A reduction of the government's stake in Japan Tobacco Inc. is likely to be opposed by tobacco farmers. 政府の日本たばこ産業（JT）への出資比率引下げには, 葉タバコ農家の反発が予想される。◆The management buyout might have been rejected at the firm's shareholders meeting if its major shareholders had opposed it. 同社の経営陣による自社買収（MBO）は, 株主総会で主要株主［大株主］が反対したら否決されていたかもしれない。◆The sell-off of Tokyo Metro shares planned by the government will likely be opposed by the Tokyo metropolitan government which is the second-largest shareholder. 政府が計画している東京メトロ株の売却には, 国に次ぐ大株主の東京都が抵抗すると見られる。

opposition　（名）反対, 対立, 抵抗, 抗議, 反発, 反感, 反撃, 野党, 野党の立場, 反対党, 反対派, 反対者, 批判者, 批判勢力, 相手, 相手チーム, 敵対者, ライバル, 対照, 対比
congressional opposition to　～に対する議会の反対［反発］
have an opposition to　～に反対する, ～に反対である
in opposition to　～に反対して, ～に対立して
offer opposition to　～に反対［抵抗］する
opposition to society page　社会対抗面
sales opposition　販売［売買］拒否
union opposition　組合の反対［拒否, 抵抗］
◆Opposition from the company's labor union and business partners emerged as obstacles to the signing of an agreement. 同社の労働組合や取引先の反発が, 契約調印の障害となった。◆There was unexpectedly strong opposition within and outside the company to the plan to sell off the company's main earner. 同社のドル箱である事業の全面売却案には, 社内外から予想外の強い反発が出た。

optimism　（名）楽観的な見通し, 楽観的なスタンス, 楽観的雰囲気, 楽観主義, オプティミズム
（⇒pessimism）

business optimism　事業の楽観的な見通し, 事業の先行きを楽観的に見ること
economic optimism　経済楽観主義, 楽観的な経済見通し
export［trade］optimism　楽観的な輸出見通し, 輸出楽観論, 輸出楽観主義
financial optimism　金融楽観主義
measure of consumer optimism　消費者マインドの指標
◆An image of the Charging Bull put in front of the New York Stock Exchange is said to be the symbol of financial optimism and prosperity. ニューヨーク証券取引所前に置かれている「突進する雄牛」の像は, 金融楽観主義と繁栄の象徴であると言われている。◆Factors other than consumption give little cause for optimism. 消費以外の要因も, 低調だ。

optimistic　（形）楽天的な, 楽観的な, 楽天主義の, 甘い
（⇒on the strength of）
optimistic expectations　楽観的な見通し
optimistic outlook　楽観的な見通し, 甘い見通し
optimistic scenario　楽観的シナリオ
optimistic sentiment　楽観論, 楽観ムード
over-optimistic　楽観的すぎる, 甘すぎる
◆The BOJ lifted its zero-interest rate policy on the strength of its optimistic view on the outlook for the economy in the summer of 2000. 日銀は2000年夏, 景気の先行きを楽観してゼロ金利政策を解除した。◆The government expressed its optimistic expectations of the current economic slump. 政府は, 現在の景気後退について楽観的な見通しを示した。◆The outbreak of the global financial crisis was initially viewed with an optimistic sentiment. 世界金融危機の発生当初は, 楽観ムードだった。

optimization　（名）最適化, 最大利用, 有効利用
full optimization　完全最適化
grand optimization　究極の最適化
money market optimization　短期金融商品ポートフォリオの最適化
optimization model　最適化モデル
optimization policy　最適化政策
portfolio optimization　ポートファリオの最適化

optimize　（動）最適化する, 最大限に利用する, 最も有効に利用［活用］する
optimize the value of　～の価値を最大限に高める
optimized portfolio　ポートフォリオの最適化
optimized sampling　最適化法（資産運用方法の一つ）
optimized yields on the securities　証券利回りの最適化
◆JAL will build an optimized flight network and increase mobility and flexibility. 日航は今後, 最適路線網の構築と機動性・柔軟性の向上に取り組む。

option　（名）選択, 取るべき道, 選ぶべき方法［手段］, 選択肢, 選択手段, 選択の余地, 選択科目, 選択権, 優先的選択権, 購入選択権, 売買選択権, 商品の有料付属品, 付加的機能, オプション取引［選択権付き取引］, オプション
（⇒fiscal policy guideline, stock option）
an option on stock index futures　株価指数先物オプション
an option to purchase　買取り選択権
an option to sell　売却選択権
at buyer's option　買い手選択で
at one's option　～の選択で
at seller's option　売り手選択で
business tie-up options　業務提携策
call option　買付け選択権, 特権付き買い, コール・オプション
equity option　株式オプション
exercise of option　オプションの行使

funding option　資金調達の選択肢, 調達手段の選択肢
futures and options market　金融先物市場, 先物・オプション市場
have an option on　～の選択売買権がある
index option　株価指数オプション, 指数オプション
investment option　投資の選択肢, 投資先の選択, 投資対象
listed options　（取引所で取引される）取引所オプション
option-adjusted spread　オプション修正スプレッド, オプション調整後スプレッド, OAS
option agreement　オプション契約, オプション取引契約［契約書］
option bond　オプション・ボンド　(=optional payment bond: 発行時の通貨以外の通貨で元利の支払いを受けることができる債券)
option buyer　オプションの買い手, オプションの権利取得者, オプション・バイヤー　(=option holder)
option card　特定店の商品を無利子のクレジットで購入できるカード　(=store option card)
option contract　選択権付き契約
option dealer　オプション取引人, オプション・ディーラー
option dealing　選択権付き取引, オプション取引, オプションの権利売買　(=option trading, options dealing)
option forward　オプション渡し
option mortgage　オプション・モーゲージ
option premium　（オプションの買い手がオプションの売り手に支払う））オプション料, オプション価格
option price　オプション価格　(⇒stock appreciation right)
option pricing model　オプション価格決定モデル, オプション評価モデル, オプション・モデル
option seller　オプションの売り手, オプション・セラー
option series　同系オプション群, オプション・シリーズ
option spread　オプション・スプレッド（同種のオプションの売りと買いを同時に行うこと）
option trading　オプション取引, 選択権付き取引　(=option dealing, option transaction: あらかじめ決められた期日に株を売買する権利（オプション）を売買する取引)
option writer　オプションの売り手, オプション・ライター　(=option seller)
options assumed in merger with　～との合併による引継ぎオプション
options cancelled　失効したオプション
Options Clearing Corporation　オプション清算会社
options exchange　オプション取引所
options exercisable　行使可能オプション
options exercised　行使されたオプション
options forfeited　失効オプション
options granted　オプション付与［授与］, 許諾オプション
options outstanding　未行使オプション, オプション残高
options terminated　期限切れオプション
over-the-counter option　店頭オプション
payer's [payer's] option　（金利スワップ・オプションで固定金利の）払い手のオプション
put option　売付け選択権, 売る権利, 特権付き売り, プット・オプション
renewal option　更新選択権

spot option　現物オプション
standard option　標準的なオプション
stock option　株式買取り選択権
stock option plan　株式購入選択権制度, 株式選択権制度
stock option transaction　ストック・オプション取引
stock purchase option　株式買取り選択権
trade option　約定オプション, 上場オプション
use a standard option　標準的なオプションを使う
viable option　有望な選択肢
　（⇒secure revenue for restoration bonds）
◆A project team comprising employees from both companies will be formed to discuss business tie-up options. 両社の社員によるプロジェクト・チームを組織して、業務提携策を検討する。◆As one option to avoid excessive currency appreciation in emerging countries with inflationary trends, they can restrict an influx of capital. インフレ気味の新興国で行き過ぎた［過度の］通貨高を避けるための手段として、資金流入を規制することができる。◆Certain land and building leases have renewal options for periods ranging from three to five years. 特定の土地と建物のリースには、3～5年の期間の更新選択権がついている。◆Operational integration and merger have become two major options to shore up the foundations of companies. 経営統合と合併が、それぞれ企業の経営基盤を強化する有力な選択肢になってきた。◆The exercise price of any stock option is equal to or greater than the stock price when the option is granted. ストック・オプションの行使価格は、オプションが付与された時の株価と同等、またはそれを上回る価格になっています。◆The right to exercise options generally accrues over a period of four years of continuous employment. オプションを行使する権利は、原則として勤務［在任］期間が4年を経過した時点で発生します。◆The trader used a standard option to hedge the price risk of a stock. このトレーダーは、株式の価格リスクをヘッジするために標準的なオプションを使った。

option holder　オプション保有者, オプションの買い手　(=option buyer)
◆The gain from stock options fluctuates depending on the option holder's investment judgment over the timing of purchase and changes of the stock price. ストック・オプション（自社株購入権）の利益は、購入時期と株価変動に対するオプション保有者（オプションの買い手）の判断によって上下する。

option trading of individual stocks　個別株オプション取引
◆In 1997, the Osaka Securities Exchange launched option trading of individual stocks, a kind of derivative transaction, at the same time as the TSE. 大阪証券取引所（大証）は、デリバティブ取引の一種である個別株オプション取引を、1997年から東証と同時に開始した。

optional　(形)選択的, 選択の, 自由選択の, 任意の, 随意の, 随時の, オプションの, オプションによる, オプショナル
optional bill of lading　揚地選択船荷証券, オプショナルB/L
optional bond　任意償還債券, 随時償還公社債
optional consumption　選択的消費
optional depreciation　任意償却
optional dividend　（現金配当か株式配当かを選べる）選択配当
optional identification number system for taxpayers　選択制納税者番号, 金融番号
optional modes of settlement　保険金支払いの選択様式, 選択制保険金支払い方法
optional payment bond　選択支払い債券, 外貨払い可能債券, オプション・ボンド　(=option bond)
optional redemption　随時償還, 任意償還

optional reserve 任意準備金
optional stowage clause 甲板積み約款
optional surcharge 揚地割増金, 揚地選択割増金
optionee (名)選択権保有者
OR [o.r.] 荷主の危険持ち（owner's riskの略）
or best offer 応相談, 応交渉, OBO
or better オアベター（証券用語で, 指し値注文に付ける指示またはその指示の付いた指し値注文）
ORB [o.r.b.] 破損危険荷主負担（owner's risk of breakageの略）
ORC [o.r.c.] 摩損危険荷主負担（owner's risk of chafingの略）
ORD [o.r.d.] 損害危険荷主負担（owner's risk of damageの略）
order (動)命じる, 命令を出す, 指示する, 指図する, 注文する, 発注する, 並べる, 陳列する
　◆Financial Services Agency has ordered 26 nonlife insurance firms to correct their business practices, after finding they failed to pay due insurance benefits. 損保各社が支払う義務のある保険金を支払わなかったことが判明したため, 金融庁は損保26社に対して業務是正命令を出した。◆Mitsui Sumitomo Insurance Co. was ordered to halt sales of medical insurance products for an indefinite period from July 10. 三井住友海上火災保険が, 7月10日から医療保険商品販売の無期限停止命令を受けた。◆The Financial Services Agency ordered Sompo Japan Insurance Inc. to suspend part of its operations as punishment for the major insurance company's illegal business practices. 金融庁は, 損保大手の損害保険ジャパンに業務で法令違反があったとして, 同社に一部業務停止命令を出した。◆The FSA can order banks that have received injections of public funds to improve their earnings if their net profits fall short of their declared earnings targets by 30 percent or more. 公的資金注入行の税引き後利益が公表した収益計画（収益目標）より3割以上下回った場合, 金融庁は, 注入行に業務改善［収益改善］命令を発動することができる。◆The FSA ordered the bank to suspend some operations due to serious law violations, including audit sabotage. 金融庁は, 同行に対して, 検査妨害などの重大な銀行法違反で, 一部業務の停止命令を出した。◆When serious financial difficulties are expected, the Financial Services Agency is allowed to order a company to improve its operations in the early stages without releasing the information to the public. 深刻な財務悪化が予想される場合, 金融庁は, 非公表で早めに業務改善命令を発動することができる。
order (名)注文, 注文書, 注文品, 受注品, 受注高, 命令, 順序, 秩序, オーダー
　administrative order 行政命令
　be flooded with orders for forward exchange contracts 為替予約の注文が殺到する
　blanket order 一括注文
　cash with order 現金注文, 注文時支払い条件
　fill and kill order 即時執行注文
　firm order 確定注文, ファーム・オーダー
　good till canceled order 取消しまで有効注文, 出合い注文, オープン注文
　large order 大口注文 （=block order）
　limit order 指し値注文
　market order 成り行き注文
　new orders 新規受注高
　order and advance 前払い注文
　place a block order 大口注文を出す
　place a limit order 指し値注文を出す
　place a market order 成り行き注文を出す
　place an order 注文を出す

sales order 販売注文
shipping order 船積み指図書
spread order スプレッド注文
stop order 逆指し値注文, ストップ・オーダー
unfilled orders 受注残高, 受注残
　◆At the TSE, securities firms input their orders for trading on computer terminals. The order is then transmitted via the computer system to the TSE, where the transaction is completed. 東証では, 証券会社がコンピュータ端末から株式売買の注文を入力すると, コンピュータ・システムを通じてその売買注文が東証に送られて, 取引が成立する。◆Just after the start of the market intervention, the banks were flooded with orders for forward exchange contracts. 市場介入の直後, 銀行には為替予約の注文が殺到した。◆Mizuho Securities Co. placed a huge errant sell order for the newly listed shares of recruitment firm J-Com Co. みずほ証券が, 人材サービス業ジェイコムの新規上場株式に対し, 誤って大量の売り注文を出してしまった。◆Moody's may downgrade the U.S. government's credit rating if it does not get its colossal deficits in better order. 米政府が膨大な財政赤字問題に目途をつけないと, ムーディーズは米国債の格付けを引き下げる可能性がある。◆The administrative order by the Financial Services Agency included the suspension of sales of nonlife insurance products at all of the company's outlets for two weeks. 金融庁の行政命令には, 同社全店舗での2週間の損保商品の販売停止が含まれている。
ordinary (形)普通の, 通常の, 経常的
　ordinary annuity 普通年金, 期末年金, 年金
　ordinary bank 普通銀行
　ordinary bill 並（なみ）手形
　ordinary business exposure 通常の事業リスク
　ordinary check 普通小切手
　ordinary creditor 通常債権者
　ordinary dividend 普通配当
　ordinary expenditure 経常支出, 経常費用
　ordinary expenses 経常費, 通常費用 （=ordinary charges）
　ordinary general meeting 定時総会, 定時株主総会
　ordinary income 経常利益, 経常損益, 通常の所得
　ordinary income and loss 経常損益
　ordinary interest （1年360日計算の）通常利子, 通常利息 （=simple interest:1年365日計算の正確な金利はexact interest）
　ordinary interest rate 通常の利子率
　ordinary life 普通生命保険
　ordinary life insurance 終身保険, 普通生命保険
　ordinary loans 一般貸付け
　ordinary loss 経常損失
　ordinary obligations 通常の債務
　ordinary participation 普通参加（参加的優先株への参加方法の一つ）
　ordinary payment 通常決済方法
　ordinary profit 経常利益
　ordinary profit and loss 経常損益, 経常損益の部
　ordinary remittance 並（なみ）為替（送金為替のこと）
　ordinary reserve 普通積立金
　ordinary savings 普通預金, 通常貯金
　ordinary shareholder 普通株主 （=equity shareholder）
　ordinary shareholders' equity [fund] 普通株主持ち分
　ordinary stock dividend 通常の株式配当
　ordinary tender 通常入札

ordinary warrant 本証拠金

ordinary account 普通口座
◆The Tokyo metropolitan government transferred most of about ¥1.28 trillion in time deposits in the 15 major banks to ordinary accounts. 東京都は、大手15行に預けている定期預金約1兆2,800億円の大半を普通口座に移した。

ordinary balance 経常収支
◆The Bank of Japan's ordinary balance for fiscal 2003 fell into the red with a loss of ¥22.2 billion. 日銀の2003年度の経常収支は、222億円の損失で赤字に転落した。

ordinary bank deposits 普通銀行預金, 普通預金
◆Ordinary bank deposits for individuals and current deposits for businesses was fully guaranteed until March 31, 2003. 個人の普通預金と企業の当座預金は、2003年3月31日まで全額保証された。

ordinary deposits 普通預金
◆Account holders can withdraw money at will from liquid deposits, such as ordinary deposits. 普通預金などの流動性預金から、口座保有者は金を自由に下ろすことができる。◆Initially, the government was scheduled to end similar protection of ordinary deposits next April. 当初、政府は来年4月から普通預金の保護も打ち切る予定だった。

ordinary government bonds 普通国債
◆The amount of refunding bonds issued to redeem ordinary government bonds is expected to exceed ¥100 trillion. 普通国債償還のための借換え債の発行額が、100兆円を突破する見込みだ。

ordinary investors 一般投資家
◆Ordinary investors bought the shares on the expectation that the company would recover. 一般投資家は、同社が立ち直ると見て同社株を買った。

ordinary share 普通株 (=common share, common stock, ordinary stock: 優先株や後配株のように特定の権利が与えられていない一般の株式)
◆During the first nine months of 2011, we invested $380 million in ordinary shares of the company. 2011年1-9月期に、当社は3億8,000万ドルを投資して、同社の普通株式を取得しました。

organization (名)組織, 機関, 機構, 団体, 組織体, 企業, 会社, 組織化, 企画, 企画力, 段取り, 構造, 構成
  business organization 企業, 企業組織, 業務組織, 実業団体, 財界団体, 経済団体
  disabled people's organizations 障害者団体, 障害者組織
  divisional organization 事業部制, 事業部制組織
  global organization グローバル企業, グローバル組織
  lateral organization 横断的組織
  marketing organization マーケティング組織, 販売組織
  member organization 会員会社
  nonprofit organization 非営利団体, 非営利組織 (=nonbusiness organization)
  organization chart 組織図, 会社機構図
  Organization of American States 米州機構, OAS
  Organization of Pacific Economic Cooperation 太平洋地域経済協力機構, OPEC
  Organization of Petroleum Exporting Countries 石油輸出国機構, OPEC
  organization planning 組織計画, 設立計画
  power of organization 組織力, 企画力
  self-regulatory organization 自主規制機関
  streamline the organization 組織を合理化する
  third-party organization 第三者機関
◆It is unrealistic to impose a ban on political donations from corporations, labor unions and other organizations. 企業や労働組合などの団体からの政治献金を禁止するのは、非現実的である。◆This investment fund is a voluntary organization on the Civil Code and does not have corporate status. この投資ファンドは、民法上の任意組合で、法人格がない。

Organization for Economic Cooperation and Development 経済協力開発機構, OECD
◆The Organization for Economic Cooperation and Development is to begin promoting a reduction in the production capacity of crude steel due to the worldwide recession in the industry. 世界的な鉄鋼不況のため、経済協力開発機構（OECD）は世界各国の粗鋼生産能力(生産設備)の削減を推進する方針だ。

-oriented (形)〜志向の, 〜志向型の, 〜集約型, 〜追求型の, 〜重視の, 〜に重点を置く, 〜中心の, 〜優先の, 〜偏重の, 〜向けの (=-driven, -led, -minded)
  consumer-oriented 消費者志向の, 消費者重視の
  customer-oriented organization 顧客志向型組織
  domestic demand-led economy 内需主導型経済
  export-oriented companies 輸出企業, 輸出志向型企業
  growth-oriented business strategy 成長志向型戦略, 拡大志向型戦略
  import-oriented economy 輸入依存型経済
  loan-oriented stimulus programs 財政投融資に重点を置く経済対策
  market-oriented 市場原理に基づく, 市場重視型, 市場経済志向の
  user-oriented ユーザー志向, 顧客志向, 顧客第一主義
  value-oriented investor 価値志向の投資家
  value-oriented management 価値重視の経営
◆Daiei will restructure its business to concentrate on food-oriented supermarkets and management of rental commercial complexes. ダイエーは、事業を再編して食品スーパーと賃貸複合商業ビルの管理事業に特化する方針だ。◆Everyone connected with the Corporation, or the people we call our "stakeholders" will also benefit from value-oriented management. 当社と係りのある人たち、つまり当社の「ステークホルダー」といわれる人たち全員も、価値重視の経営によって利益を受けることになる。◆Export-oriented companies will be hit hard if the yen accelerates its rise. 円高が加速すると、輸出企業は大きな打撃を受ける。

original (形)最初の, 初期の, 当初の, 初回の, 本来の, 原始の, 本源的の, もとの, 原文の, 実物の, 原物[原作, 原画, 原型]の, 新作の, 独創的な, 独自の, 独特の, 新奇の (名)原本, 正本, 原作, 本源, オリジナル
  an original and a duplicate 正本1通と副本1通, 正副
  original amount 当初発行額
  original bill 原手形, 未裏書手形
  original bill of lading 正本船荷証券
  original capital 原資本
  original cost 取得原価, 取得価額, 簿価
  original credit 原信用状 (=original letter of credit, prime credit)
  original currency 元受通貨, 元受契約の通貨
  original face 当初額面
  original insurance 元受け保険, 原保険
  original insurance policy 原保険証券
  original investment 初期投資, 当初投資額
  original lender （ローン債権売買の）原貸出銀行, 貸付け債権保有銀行, オリジナル・レンダー
  original loan amount 借入元金
  original mandated amount 調達予定額
  original margin 当初証拠金
  original maturity 当初満期, オリジナル・マチュリティ, 債券発行日から満期までの期間
  original money 本源的貨幣, 現金通貨, 第一次貨幣

original owner of securitized assets　証券化資産のオリジネーター
original premium　当初の保険料
original principal　元金, 元本
original purchaser　当初購入者
original agreement　原契約
◆ABC shall have no recourse against XYZ for any obligations under the original agreement assigned pursuant to this assignment agreement. ABCは、この譲渡契約に従って譲渡された原契約上の債務については、XYZに履行の請求を一切求めないものとする。
original amount of money　元々の額[金額]
◆The effective book value is calculated by subtracting amassed loan loss reserves from the original amount of money that was lent. 実質簿価は、債権の元々の額(貸し付けた元々の金額：簿価)から、(銀行が)積み立てた貸倒れ引当金を差し引いて算定する。
original issue　当初発行, 発行時の
original issue discount　発行時割引, 発行時割引率, 初売り割引, 割引債券の償還差益, OID(債券の額面金額と発行価額の差)
original issue discount bond　割引発行債（=deep discount bond）
original issue discount securities　割引発行債
original issue premium　発行時額面超過額
original issue size　当初発行予定額
original issue stock　初発株
originate　(動)実行する, 取り扱う, 考案する, 発明する, 開発する, 創造する, 創設する, オリジネートする（=create, develop, invent）
originate loans　貸付けを実行する, 融資に取り組む, ローンの取扱いをする, ローンをオリジネートする
originating loans　貸付けの実行, 貸付け金の実行
origination　(名)実行, 不動産担保ローン(mortgage loan)の新規実行, 融資取組み, 考案, 発明, 開発, 創造, 創作, 創設, 発生, 開始, 起点, 起因, オリジネーション
loan origination　融資取組み, ローンの取扱い
loan origination fee　融資取組み手数料, 貸付け手数料, 不動産担保ローンの取扱い手数料, (ローン)オリジネーション・フィー（=origination fee）
origination fee　融資取組み手数料, 融資開始手数料, 取組み手数料, 貸付け手数料, 不動産担保ローンの取扱い手数料　（=loan origination fee）
origination standards　審査基準
originator　(名)当初融資者, 不動産担保ローン(mortgage loan)を最初に実行する金融機関, (社債などの発行体と協議して証券の種類、発行条件などを決めて証券を市場に出す)投資銀行[証券業者], (仕組み債などの仕組み商品で原材料に相当する原資産を保有している)原資産保有者, オリジネーター
asset originator　資産オリジネーター
mortgage originator　債権オリジネーター
receivable originator　債権オリジネーター
Osaka Securities Exchange　大阪証券取引所, 大証, OSE
◆The Osaka Securities Exchange accounts for 50 percent of domestic trading in derivatives including stock price index futures. 大証は、株価指数先物などデリバティブ(金融派生商品)の国内取引で5割を占めている。◆The Osaka Securities Exchange (OSE) will accept the decision by the U.S. Nasdaq Stock Market, Inc. to end the firms' joint venture and withdraw from the Nasdaq Japan market on Oct.15. 大阪証券取引所(大証)は、10月15日付けで合弁会社を清算してナスダック・ジャパン市場から撤退する旨の米ナスダック・ストック・マーケットの決定を受け入れる方針だ。
OSE　大阪証券取引所（⇒Osaka Securities Exchange, reorganize）
ostensibly　(副)表向きは, 表向きには, 表面上は
◆Olympus ostensibly paid about ¥70 billion in commissions to two investment advisers when the company acquired a British medical equipment maker for about ¥210 billion. オリンパスが英国の医療機器メーカーを約2,100億円で買収した際、同社は表向きには仲介手数料として約700億円を投資助言会社2社に支払った。
OTC　店頭, 店頭市場（over the counterの略）
Nikkei OTC stock average　日経店頭平均株価
OTC dealer　店頭ディーラー
OTC derivative trade　有価証券店頭デリバティブ取引
OTC derivatives　店頭派生商品
OTC firm　店頭取引銘柄
OTC margin bond　適格店頭債券, 店頭証拠金債券
OTC margin stock　店頭証拠金株式
OTC market　店頭市場
OTC option　店頭オプション
OTC options on securities　有価証券店頭オプション取引
OTC securities　店頭取扱い有価証券
OTC stock　店頭株, 店頭銘柄
Tokyo OTC　東京店頭市場
OTD　オリジネート・トゥー・ディストリビュート（originate to distributeの略。売却する(distribute)ことを前提にローンを組成する(originate)こと）
other　(形)他の, その他の, 別の, 残りの
issuance for other than cash　現金以外での発行
one cancels other [one-cancels-other] order　OCO注文
other credits　資本勘定増加分
other end　取引相手, 商談相手
other-insurance clause　他保険約款
other people's money　他人の資金, 他からの借入金[出資金], O.P.M.[o.p.m.]
other reserve　別途積立金
OTM　オンライン預金支払い機（online teller machineの略）
OTP　使い捨てパスワード　（=dynamic password, online password: one-time [onetime] passwordの略。コンピュータのユーザー認証方式で、利用するたびにパスワードを変えるネット・バンキングのセキュリティの一種。一度使ったパスワードは無効になるので、悪用されることはない。⇒one-time password [onetime password]）
ounce　(名)(貴金属などのヤード・ポンド法での単位)トロイ・オンス(troy ounce), オンス, oz.（金1オンス[トロイ・オンス]=約31グラム）
◆Gold extended its rally to a record above $1,900 an ounce amid increased uncertainties over the U.S. and European economic outlook on the Comex in New York. ニューヨーク商品取引所では、米欧景気見通しへの懸念[米欧経済の先行き不透明感]の高まりを受け[懸念の高まりから]、金価格が急騰して、1トロイ・オンス=1,900ドルを史上初めて突破した。◆Gold futures for December delivery closed at $1,891.90 an ounce at 2:05 p.m. on the Comex in New York. ニューヨーク商品取引所では、12月渡しの金先物価格が、午後2時5分の時点で1トロイ・オンス(約31グラム)=1,891.90ドルに達した。◆Gold futures for December delivery gained to $1,897 an ounce at 4:13 p.m. in after-hours electronic trading on the Comex in New York. ニューヨーク商品取引所の時間外電子取引で、金先物の12月渡し価格は、午後4時13分の時点で1トロイ・オンス=1,897ドルまで上昇した。◆The U.S. Mint's sales of American Eagle gold coins have totaled 91,000 ounce so

far in August. 米造幣局のアメリカン・イーグル［米イーグル］金貨の販売総量は、9月1日以降現時点で9万1,000オンスに達している。

out （形）外の、アウト
  be out of the doldrums　底を脱する
  be out of the woods　低迷を脱する
  out clearing［out-clearing］　交換持ち出し手形
  out of date check　失効小切手,期限経過小切手（=outdated check）
  out of line　（株価が）独立高の,独立安の
  out of stock　品切れ,在庫切れ
  out-out loan　外―外ローン
  out to in external bond　外―内外債
  out to out external bond　外―外外債
  over-and-out option　オーバー・アンド・オプション
  up-and-out option　アップ・アンド・アウト・オプション

out-of-control （形）手に負えない,収拾のつかない,むちゃくちゃな
◆Out-of-control budget deficits might snowball because of an economic crisis. 手に負えない財政赤字は、経済危機で雪だるま式に拡大する可能性がある。

out-of-court settlement 示談による和解
◆Shinsei Bank reached an out-of-court settlement in a damage lawsuit with a bankruptcy administrator of a borrower company. 新生銀行が、融資先企業の破産管財人との損害賠償訴訟で示談による和解に達した。◆Six executives of Kobe Steel Ltd. agreed in an out-of-court settlement to pay back ¥310 million to the company. 神戸製鋼の幹部6人が、示談による和解で3億1,000万円を会社に返済することで合意した。

out of the money アウト・オブ・ザ・マネー（オプション取引で、オプションを行使したら損失が出る状態のこと。コール・オプションの場合は行使価格が市場価格を上回っている状態で、プット・オプションの場合は行使価格が市場価格を下回っている状態のこと）
  out-of-the-money currency option　アウト・オブ・ザ・マネー通貨オプション
  out of the money option　アウト・オブ・ザ・マネー・オプション
  out-of the money warrants　アウト・オブ・ザ・マネーのワラント

out-of-town （形）市外の
  out-of-town bill　異地手形,他所払い手形
  out-of-town check　市外小切手
  out-of-town clearing　市外銀行手形交換
  out-of-town items　市外銀行向け手形類

outbid （動）他を上回る条件を提示する,良い条件を出す,～よりも高い値を付ける,高値を付ける

outbreak （名）発生,突発,勃発,突然の広がり,爆発,騒動,暴動,反乱
  an outbreak of scamming of relief money　義捐金詐欺の発生［横行］
  outbreak of a trade war　貿易戦争の勃発

outbreak of the economic crisis 経済危機の発生
◆Coordinated interest rate cuts were introduced immediately after the outbreak of the economic crisis. 協調利下げは、経済危機の発生直後に実施された。

outbreak of the global financial crisis 世界金融危機の発生
◆The outbreak of the global financial crisis was initially viewed with an optimistic sentiment. 世界金融危機の発生当初は、楽観ムードだった。

outflow （名）流出,流出額,アウトフロー（⇒inflow）
  asset outflow　資産の流出,資産流出額
  capital outflows　資本の流出,資本の海外流出,資本流出,対外投融資　（=outflows of capital）
  cash outflow　支出,支払い額,キャッシュ・アウトフロー
  investment outflow　投資支出額
  long-term capital outflow　長期資本流出
  net cash outflow　純支払い額
  net inflow or outflow of capital　資本収支
  outflow of funds　資金の流出,資金の海外流出
  outflow of money　資金の流出
  short-term capital outflows　短期資金の流出

outflow of funds 資金の流出,資金の海外流出
◆Dollar-selling pressure remains strong due to concerns over the outflow of funds from the United States. 米国からの資金流出に対する懸念で、ドル売り圧力は依然として強い。◆If the U.S. housing market and financial sector recover, we won't need to worry about the outflow of funds to emerging countries. 米国の住宅市場や金融部門が回復すれば、新興国への資金の流出を気にしなくて済む。

outflow of wealth 富の流出
◆A continued outflow of wealth to other nations rich in natural resources will slow Japan's economic growth. 日本から他の資源国への富の流出が続けば、日本の経済成長は鈍化する。

outlet （名）店舗,～店,販路,小売店,出店,特約店,系列販売店,工場直売店,支店,出口,アウトレット
  affiliated outlet　系列販売店
  distribution outlet　販路
  investment outlet　投資先
  lending outlet　融資先,貸付け先
  merchant outlet　加盟店店舗
  network of outlets　店舗網
  retail outlet　小売店,小売販売店
  sales outlet　販売店
  single outlet　単一店舗
◆Individual investors are now able to buy stocks at the outlets of banks and other financial institutions. 個人投資家は現在、銀行などの金融機関の店舗で株を購入できる。◆The bank plans to deal with foreign government bonds at all of its outlets. 同行は、全店舗で外国国債を扱う方針だ。◆The closure of the money-losing outlets will result in a surplus of about 2,000 employees out of about 22,000 on a consolidated basis. 赤字の店舗閉鎖に伴い、連結ベースで従業員約22,000人のうち約2,000人が余剰になる。

outline of a tax reform plan 税制改正大綱
◆The outline of a tax reform plan proposed a 2 percent surtax for those companies opting for the consolidated tax system that will impose taxes on combined account settlements of a group of companies. 税制改正大綱では、グループ企業の損益を通算して法人税を課す連結納税制度を選択する企業に対して、2%の連結付加税（法人税率に2%の上乗せ）を提案している。

outlook （名）見通し,予測,予想,展望,先行き,～観,予報
  business outlook　景気見通し,業績見通し
  economic outlook　景気見通し,経済見通し,景気の先行き,景気予測,情勢判断
  financial outlook　財務見通し
  full-year outlook　通期見通し
  future demand outlook　需要の先行き,今後の需要予測
  half-year earnings outlook　半期決算の業績予想［見通し］
  inflation outlook　インフレの予想,インフレ見通し（=outlook for inflation）
  negative outlook　ネガティブ（弱含み）の見通し
  production outlook　生産見通し,生産の先行き

rating outlook　格付け見通し
strong earnings outlook　力強い増益見通し,高収益見通し,業績予想
supply and demand outlook　需給見通し,需給予測
◆Gold extended its rally to a record above $1,900 an ounce amid increased uncertainties over the U.S. and European economic outlook on the Comex in New York.　ニューヨーク商品取引所では、米欧景気見通しへの懸念[米欧経済の先行き不透明感]の高まりを受け[懸念の高まりから]、金価格が急騰して、1トロイ・オンス＝1,900ドルを史上初めて突破した。◆Many businesses are cautious about their outlook three months ahead despite the improvement in sentiment.　企業の景況感は改善したものの、多くの企業は3か月先の景気見通しに対しては慎重だ。◆Moody's Investors Service cut Japan's yen-denominated debt rating by one notch to Aa3 from Aa2 and maintained a negative outlook.　米国の格付け会社ムーディーズは、日本の円建て国債の格付けを「Aa2」から「Aa3」に一段階引き下げ、「ネガティブ(弱含み)」の見通しを据え置いた。◆Panasonic Corp. raised its half-year earnings outlook on cost-cutting efforts and some signs of improvement in sales.　パナソニックは、コスト削減が進んだことと売上がいくぶん改善する兆しが見えたことから、中間決算の業績予想について上方修正した。◆Standard & Poor's revised upward the outlook on its ratings on six major Japanese insurance companies against the backdrop of their improved financial profiles.　スタンダード＆プアーズは、日本の大手保険会社6社の財務力見通し改善を背景に、6社の格付け見通しを上方修正した。◆The rating outlook of "negative" by a credit rating agency means that another downgrade is possible in the next 12 to 18 months.　信用格付け機関による「ネガティブ(弱含み)」の格付け見通しは、今後1年～1年半にふたたび格下げされる可能性があることを意味している。◆The U.S. credit rating agency revised upward the outlook to positive from negative on its rating on Sumitomo Life Insurance Co.　この米国の信用格付け機関は、住友生命保険の格付け見通しを「ネガティブ(弱含み)」から「ポジティブ(強含み)」に上方修正した。

Outlook for Economic Activity and Prices　経済・物価情勢の展望
◆The Bank of Japan envisages the prospects of economic growth and consumer price trends in its "Outlook for Economic Activity and Prices."　日銀は、「経済・物価情勢の展望」(展望リポート)で、経済成長や消費者物価の先行きを示している。

outlook for the economy　景気見通し,経済見通し,景気の先行き
◆The BOJ lifted its zero-interest rate policy on the strength of its optimistic view on the outlook for the economy in the summer of 2000.　日銀は2000年夏、景気の先行きを楽観してゼロ金利政策を解除した。

outnumber　(動)～より数が多い,～を上回る,～に勝る,～より多い
◆Sell orders outnumbered buy orders in a wide range of sectors.　幅広い業種で、売り注文が買い注文より多かった。

outpace　(動)～を凌(しの)ぐ,～に優る,～を追い越す,～を超える[上回る]
◆Import growth far outpaced export growth in the face of a global slowdown.　世界的な景気低迷で[世界的な景気減速に直面して]、輸入の伸びが輸出の伸びを大幅に上回った。◆Lending by regional banks continued to outpace that of larger lenders in July.　地銀の7月の貸出は、前月に続いて大手金融機関[大手行]の貸出を上回った。◆The Tokyo Stock Exchange was outstripped [outpaced] by the Shanghai Stock Exchange in terms of trading volume.　東証は、取引規模[売買規模]で上海証券取引所に抜かれた。◆Though stock prices remain low, the number of transactions has already outpaced that during the bubble economy.　株価はまだ低いものの、株取引の件数はすでにバブル期を超えている。

outperform　(動)他を[他の銘柄を]上回る数字を出す,市場平均を上回る,アウトパフォームする
outperform the general stock market　株式総合利回りで市場平均を上回る
outperform the market　市場平均を上回る

output　(名)生産,生産量,生産高,製作,産出量,産出高,出力,アウトプット
aggregate output　総生産高,総生産量,総産出高
capital output ratio　資本・産出量比率,資本産出高比率
industrial output　工業生産,鉱工業生産,工業生産高
input-output analysis　産業連関分析,投入産出分析,インプット・アウトプット分析
per capita output　1人当たり生産高,1人当たりGDP
real output　実質生産高,実質産出高,実質GDP
◆Output at domestic factories rose 0.2 percent in April from March.　4月の国内鉱工業生産は、前月比で0.2%増加した。◆The Economy, Trade and Industry Ministry upgraded its assessment on output.　経済産業省は、生産の基調判断を上方修正した。

output adjustment　生産調整
◆There has been a conspicuous trend of output adjustments in industrial production, particularly for such products as semiconductors and electronic parts.　鉱工業生産は、半導体や電子部品を中心に、生産調整の動きが目立つ。

outright　(形)無条件の,即座の,確定日渡し条件の,徹底的な,完全な,絶対的な,公然の,まぎれもない,はっきりした,あからさまな,アウトライト　(副)無条件で,即座に
buy bonds outright　保有目的で債券を買う
buy outright　即金で買う
outright buyouts of government bonds　国債の買切りオペレーション,国債の買切りオペ,国債の買切りオペの額　(＝outright purchases of government bonds)
outright cover　アウトライト取引のカバー,アウトライト・カバー
outright exchange rate　アウトライト為替相場
outright forward　アウトライト先物,先物取引,確定日渡し
outright forward operation　先物操作
outright loss　丸損
outright majority　絶対多数
outright operation　アウトライト操作,先物操作
outright recession　完全な景気後退
outright sale　売切り(金融引締め策として、市中銀行の支払い準備を減少させるため、ニューヨーク連邦準備銀行が公開市場で財務省証券(Treasuries)などを買戻し条件なしで売却すること)
outright swap　(引渡し期日を異にする)先物同士のスワップ
outright transaction [dealing]　アウトライト取引(売りっぱなし、買いっぱなしの外国為替取引。外国為替の受渡しの時期によって直物と先物取引に分かれる)

outright purchase　買切りオペレーション,買切りオペ,無条件購入　(＝outright purchase operation: ただし、複数形のoutright purchasesは「長期国債買切りオペ(公開市場操作)の額」を意味することが多い)
◆Some members of the ruling parties urged the Bank of Japan to scrap its upper limit on government bond holdings and to raise significantly its outright purchases of mid- to long-term government bonds.　与党の一部議員は、日銀の国債保有上限を撤廃して中長期国債の買切りオペレーション(公開市場操作)を大幅に増額するよう日銀に強く求めた。

outright purchase of long-term government bonds　長期国債の買切りオペレーション

◆A likely measure to be adopted by the Bank of Japan's Policy Board is an increase in the central bank's outright purchases of long-term government bonds to ￥1 trillion from the current ￥800 billion per month. 日銀政策委員会が取る措置として、日銀の長期国債買切りオペ（公開市場操作）の額を現在の月8,000億円から1兆円に引き上げることが予想される。◆The Bank of Japan should consider the outright purchase of more long-term government bonds. 日銀は、長期国債の買入れ増額を検討すべきだ。◆The Bank of Japan's Policy Board decided to increase its outright purchases of long-term government bonds to ￥800 billion a month from ￥600 billion. 日銀政策委員会は、長期国債買切りオペレーション（公開市場操作）の額を、月6,000億円から8,000億円に引き上げる決定をした。◆The outright purchase of long-term government bonds is a measure to supply funds to the financial market. 長期国債の買切りオペレーションは、金融市場に資金を供給する手段である。

outright purchase of short-term government securities　短期国債（財務省短期証券と政府短期証券）の買切りオペ
　◆The Bank of Japan will resume outright purchases of short-term government securities-treasury bills and financing bills-without a resale condition. 日銀は、売戻し条件を付けない短期国債（財務省短期証券と政府短期証券）の買切りオペを再開することになった。

outright purchase operation　買切りオペ, 買切りオペレーション
　◆The Bank of Japan has taken the stance that it would not intervene in long-term rates in principle, except for the implementation of outright purchase operation of long-term government bonds worth about ￥5 trillion a year. 日銀はこれまで、年間5兆円程度の長期国債の買切りオペを実施する以外は、原則として長期金利には介入しない姿勢［立場］をとってきた。

outside broker　外部ブローカー, 非会員ブローカー
outside money　外部貨幣
outside subscribers　外部の引受人
　◆Shares taken by the outside subscribers at the time of incorporation of the new company shall be limited to one share each. 新会社の設立時に外部の引受人が引き受ける株式は、それぞれ1株に限るものとする。
outsider　（名）部外者, 一般投資家, アウトサイダー
outsourcing　外部資源の活用, 外部委託, 外注, 社外調達, 海外調達, 業務委託, アウトソーシング（企業が周辺業務を外部に委託すること。例えば、IT関連分野のアウトソーシングとしては、情報システムの構築・運用やASP（アプリケーション・サービス・プロバイダー）、データ・センターなどが挙げられる）
　◆Outsourcing is a strategic method that effectively uses business resources. It is actively utilized in Europe and the U.S. by venture businesses that lack adequate human resources. アウトソーシングは、経営資源を有効に活用するための戦略的手法です。これは、欧米では、人的資源を十分に確保できないベンチャー企業によって積極的に活用されています。

outsourcing deal　業務委託契約
　◆J.P. Morgan Chase & Co. is scrapping a $5 billion outsourcing deal with International Business Machines Corp. JPモルガン・チェース（米銀2位）は、IBMとの50億ドルの業務委託契約を打ち切ることになった。
outstanding　（形）未払いの, 未決済の, 未償還の, 未履行の, 未解決の, 未決定の, 未処理の, 発行済み, すでに発生している, 傑出した, とび抜けた, 顕著な, 目立った, 特に優れた　（⇒unexercised stock option）
　amount outstanding　残高, 未払い金, 発行残高, 市中売却残高

average number of shares outstanding　期中平均発行済み株式数
bond outstanding　債券発行残高
commercial paper outstanding　CP発行残高
contracts outstanding　事業年度末契約高
loans outstanding　借入金残高, 融資残高, 貸付け残高
long term debt outstanding　長期負債残高
number of shares of stock outstanding　発行済み株式数
outstanding capital stock　株式発行高
outstanding checks　未決済小切手
outstanding common stock　外部発行済み普通株式, 社外流通の普通株式
　（=outstanding common shares）
outstanding company　超優良企業
outstanding current accounts　当座預金残高
outstanding equities　発行済み株式, 発行済み株式数
outstanding external debts　累積対外債務
outstanding loan　融資残高, 貸出残高, 未決済貸付け金, 借入金残高　（=outstanding debt）
outstanding nonperforming loans　不良債権残高
　（=outstanding bad loans; ⇒asset evaluation）
outstanding shares　発行済み株式, 発行済み株式数, 社外株式, 社外発行株式, 流通株式数　（=outstanding capital stock, outstanding equities）
outstanding voting stock　発行済み議決権株式
principal outstanding　残存元本額
warrant outstanding　発行済みワラント
　◆The upgrade reflects Moody's expectation that the company will continue to exhibit an excellent operating performance and outstanding capital structure. この格上げは、同社が引き続き好業績と際立った財務基盤を示すとのムーディーズの期待感を反映している。

outstanding bad loans　不良債権残高
　（=outstanding nonperforming loans）
　◆The Mizuho Financial Group is conspicuous among the five financial groups in terms of the amount of its outstanding bad loans. 不良債権残高の大きさでは、5大金融グループの中で「みずほフィナンシャルグループ」が際立っている。
outstanding balance　未払い残高, 残高
　the outstanding balance in current accounts　当座預金の残高　（⇒liquidity）
　the outstanding balance of contracts　保有契約高, 保有契約, 保険の総額　（=outstanding contracts）
　the outstanding balance of deposits in current accounts　当座預金残高　（⇒current account）
　the outstanding balance of lending　銀行の貸出残高　（⇒record low）
outstanding balance of contracts　保有契約高, 保有契約, 保険の総額
　（=outstanding contracts; ⇒quadrillion）
　◆The 10 life insurers reported a fall in the combined outstanding balance of individual life insurance and annuity contracts for five straight years. 生命保険10社の個人保険・年金の10社合計での保有契約高（保障の総額）が、5年［5期］連続で減少した。
outstanding balance of current accounts　当座預金の残高
　◆Raising the outstanding balance of current accounts held by private financial institutions at the central bank to between ￥27 trillion and ￥30 trillion remained within the range of conventional responses. 日銀当座預金（民間金融機関が日銀に保有している当座預金）の残高目標を（現行の22-27兆円程度から）27-30兆円程度に引き上げる日銀の追加金融緩和は、従来の対応の範囲内にとどまった。

outstanding balance of government bonds　国債発行残高
◆The outstanding balance of government bonds at the end of fiscal 2002 will be about ￥414 trillion. 2002年度末の国債発行残高は、約414兆円になる見通しだ。

outstanding balance of the (central) government debt　国の債務残高
◆The outstanding balance of the central government debt hit a record high of ￥904 trillion at the end of June 2010. 国の債務残高［国の借金］は、2010年6月末時点で過去最悪の904兆円となった。

outstanding contracts　保有契約高, 保有契約
（=outstanding balance of contracts）
◆The number of outstanding contracts—the source of profits for life insurers—is expected to drop this fiscal year. 生保各社の利益の源泉である保有契約件数（保有契約高）は、今年度は減少する見通しだ。

outstanding credits　融資残高
◆Banks will face increased difficulty collecting their subordinate loans and other outstanding credits from insurers. 銀行は、生保から劣後ローンや他の融資残高などを回収できなくなる可能性が高まっている。

outstanding current account target　当座預金残高目標
◆The central bank's move to increase the outstanding current account target is insufficient to soothe market fears. 日銀の当座預金残高目標の引上げは、市場不安を払拭するには物足りない。

outstanding debt　借入金残高, 借入残高, 債務残高, 残りの債務, 未払い残高, 残高, 未払い負債額, 未償還負債, 既存の債務, 既発債　（=outstanding loan）
the outstanding debt at the end of March　3月末現在の未払い負債額
the outstanding debt of AA　ダブルAの既発債
◆Japan has the largest outstanding debt among advanced economies. 日本は、先進国の間で最大の公的債務残高を抱えている。◆Taxpayers' burden from the JAL bailout was lowered to ￥47 billion as the firm repaid part of its outstanding debt. 日航救済による国民の負担分は、日航が債務残高の一部を返済したため、470億円に減少した。◆The central and local governments' combined outstanding debts are expected to exceed ￥800 trillion by the end of fiscal 2009. 国と地方［地方自治体］の債務残高は、2009年度末には合算して800兆円を上回る［超える］見通しだ。◆The firm repaid part of its outstanding debt to the bank. 同社は、債務残高［残りの債務］の一部を同行に返済した。◆To help an insolvent borrower, money must be granted for free, or at least a part of the outstanding debt must be forgiven. 返済不能の借り手を助けるには、ただで資金を与えるか、少なくとも債務残高の一部の減免が必要だ。◆We unconditionally guaranteed all of the firm's outstanding debt at the end of March 2011. 当社は、2011年3月末現在の同社の未払い負債額をすべて保証しました。

outstanding deposits　預金残高
◆In the past year alone, the bank had seen the outstanding deposits swell by about ￥2.5 trillion. 過去1年だけで、この銀行では、預金残高が約2兆5,000億円も増えた。

outstanding equities　発行済み株式数
◆The company is scheduled to issue new shares equivalent to about 35 percent of its outstanding equities for ￥1,138 per share in an effort to generate ￥30 billion. 同社は、発行済み株式数の約35％に当たる新株を1株当たり1,138円で発行して、300億円を調達する予定だ。

outstanding loan　融資残高, 貸出残高, 未決済貸付け金, 借入金残高
（⇒failed bank, market price, offset provisions）
◆Outstanding loans extended by UFJ Holdings Inc. to the embattled Daiei, Inc. total about ￥700 billion. UFJホールディングスは、陣容を整えたダイエーに約7千億円の融資残高がある。◆The volume of outstanding loans extended by domestic commercial banks has continued to fall since the middle of the 1990s. 国内銀行の貸出残高は、1990年代半ば以降、減り続けている。

outstanding loans to outstanding deposits　預金残高に対する貸出残高
◆The ratio of outstanding loans to outstanding deposits at major banks has fallen below 70 percent. 主要銀行の預金残高に対する貸出残高の比率は、70％を下回っている。

outstanding notes　紙幣の総発行残高
◆The Fed's total amount of outstanding notes at the end of June 2011 increased by more than 30 percent from the end of March 2008, prior to the Lehman shock. 2011年6月末時点の米連邦準備制度理事会（FRB）の紙幣の総発行残高は、リーマン・ショック前の2008年3月末から30％以上も伸びた。

outstanding ordinary shares　発行済み普通株式
◆The company acquired 30 percent of the outstanding ordinary shares of ABC PLC. 同社は、ABC PLCの発行済み普通株式の30％を取得した。

outstanding shares　発行済み株式, 社外株式, 社外発行株式, 流通株式数　（=outstanding capital stock; ⇒ earnings per share, sale of outstanding shares）
◆Currently, a company may set transfer restrictions on a portion of its outstanding shares. 現在、企業は一部の発行済み株式に譲渡制限を付けることができる。◆The management consultant known as a stock speculator acquired more than 20 percent, or about 14 million of the company's outstanding shares. 仕手筋とされるこの経営コンサルタントは、同社の発行済み株式数の2割以上にあたる1,400万株余りを買い占めた。◆The start-ups' number of outstanding shares is still small. ベンチャー企業の発行済み株式総数は、まだ少ない。

outstanding Treasury bond holdings　米国債保有残高
◆The U.S. private banks' outstanding Treasury bond holdings grew by about 50 percent from March 2008, prior to the Lehman shock. 米国の民間銀行の米国債保有残高は、リーマン・ショック前の2008年3月から約5割増えた。

outstrip　（動）～より早いペースで行く, ～を追い越す, ～を追い抜く, ～に勝る, ～を凌（しの）ぐ, ～を上回る, ～を越える
◆The Tokyo Stock Exchange was outstripped［outpaced］by the Shanghai Stock Exchange in terms of trading volume. 東証は、取引規模［売買規模］で上海証券取引所に抜かれた。

outweigh　（動）上回る, ～より大きい, ～より価値がある
◆Increases in interest payments on deposits outweighed credit cost falls. 預金の利払い増加のほうが、与信費用の低下より大きかった。

over　（名）過剰, 過度, 余分　（形）上の, 外の　（前）～の上に, ～の一面に, ～を越えて, ～より多く, ～に優先して, ～を克服して, ～の間中, ～に関して, ～について, （分数の）～分の, ～で割って　（副）～を越えて, ～以上に, 余って, 余分に
an over and short account　過不足金勘定
over a year ago　前年同期比
over allot　水増し割当て［超過割当て］を行う
over-allotment option　超過引受オプション
over-borrowed situation of commercial banks　オーバー・ローン（市中銀行が与信超過で中央銀行借入れに依存している状態）
over-competition　過当競争
over-due check　不渡り小切手
over-indebtedness　債務過多
over-insurance　超過保険
over-investment in inventories　在庫投資過大

over-investment in plant and equipment 過剰設備投資, 設備投資過大
over-loaned situation オーバー・ローン
over-month-end delivery 翌月渡し
over-month-end loans 月越し物
over-month-end unconditional call 月越し無条件物
over par オーバー・パー（債券の発行価格，流通価格が額面の100％を超えている状態）
over saving [over-saving] 過剰貯蓄
over transfer 過剰振込み
overs and shorts 過剰金と不足金
◆There was widespread concern over a sharp economic slowdown for the July-September quarter. 7-9月期は，景気急減速の心配が広がった．

over the counter (名)店頭，店頭市場，店頭売買，店頭取引，店頭銘柄，OTC
over-the-counter (形)店頭の，店頭市場の，店頭売買の，店頭取引の
over-the-counter business 店頭業務
over-the-counter derivatives 店頭派生商品
over-the-counter house 店頭取引店
over the counter option 店頭オプション
over-the-counter sale 店頭販売，店頭売買
over-the-counter sale of government bonds by banks 国債窓口販売，国債窓販
over-the-counter securities 店頭取引銘柄
over-the-counter stock 店頭株，非上場株
over-the-counter transaction 店頭取引

over-the-counter market 店頭市場，店頭株市場，場外市場 (=OTC market, over-the-counter stock market)
◆Dealings at over-the-counter markets run by the Securities Dealers Association of Japan are basically settled between concerned parties. 日本証券業協会が運営している店頭市場での（売買）取引の決済は，基本的に関係当事者間で行われている．

over the counter sales of insurance policies 保険の窓口販売
◆Banks began over-the-counter sales of insurance policies in April 2001. 銀行は，2001年4月から保険の窓口販売を始めた．

over-the-counter stock market 店頭株式市場，株式店頭市場 (=over-the-counter market)
◆Operators of Japan's Jasdaq over-the-counter stock market and Nasdaq Japan will hold talks next week on a possible merger to stem losses as trading slows and initial share sales wane. 日本の店頭株式市場であるジャスダックとナスダック・ジャパンの両市場運営機関が，相場（売買取引）低迷と新規株式発行の低下による損失を食い止めるため，市場統合に向けて来週協議することになった．◆The Jasdaq can begin small-lot after-hours trading by its transformation from an over-the-counter stock market to a securities exchange. ジャスダックは，店頭市場から証券取引所への移行により，立会い外分売（取引時間外に大株主などが保有株を小口に分けて売り出すこと）も可能になった．◆The nation's over-the-counter stock market will create a new index of blue-chip issues in April 2002. 日本の株式店頭市場（ジャスダック）が，2,002年4月に優良企業の銘柄を対象にした新しい株価指数を創設する．

overall (形)総合的な，全般的な，全面的な，全体的な，全体の，一切を含む，総〜
overall balance (of payments) （国際収支の）総合収支
overall budget 総合予算
overall competitiveness 全体的な競争力
overall consumption 総消費，消費全体
overall cooperation 全面協力，全面的な協力
overall default rates in the bond market 債券市場全体のデフォルト率
overall demand 最終需要，総需要
overall economic picture 景気の全体像
overall efficiency 全効率，全体的な効率性
overall financial conditions DI 資金繰り判断DI
overall growth 全体の伸び率
overall household savings 家計の総貯蓄
overall impact 全体的な影響
overall index 総合指数
overall industry 全産業，産業全体
overall inflation 全面的インフレ
overall investment 総投資，全体投資
overall level of monetary growth マネー・サプライの動向
overall leverage 総債務比率
overall loan 貸出金総額
overall market capitalization 市場の時価総額
overall orders 受注総額
overall payment agreement 一般支払い協定
overall performance 性能全体，全体的な性能
overall position （為替の）直先（じきさき）総合持ち高，総合持ち高
overall profit margin 総資金利ざや
overall rate of return 総収益率，ORR
overall tariff rate 関税率水準

overall domestic demand 国内需要全体，内需全体
◆Overall domestic demand remains weak. 内需全体の足腰は，まだ弱い．

overall economy 景気全体
◆Capital investment, which was the engine for the overall economy, has lost much of its momentum. 景気全体を引っ張ってきた設備投資に，一時の勢いがなくなっている．

overall prices 物価全体
◆The drop in gasoline prices lowered overall prices about 1 percent. ガソリンの値下りが，物価全体を約1％押し下げた．

overall sales 売上全体，総売上
◆Financial services account for about 60 percent of the company's overall sales. 金融事業は，同社の売上全体の6割を占めている．

overall savings rate 総貯蓄率
◆As baby boomers retire, they will start breaking into their savings for their daily living expenses, thereby pushing down the overall savings rate. 団塊世代が退職すると，貯蓄を取り崩して日常の生活費に充てるようになるため，総貯蓄率は押し下げられることになる．

overall supply capacity 総供給力
◆The report stresses the need to increase the overall supply capacity through structural reforms as a remedy for economic stagnation. 同報告書は，不況対策として，構造改革によって総供給力を引き上げる必要があると力説している．

overall trend 総合的な動向
◆The deflator, which indicates the overall trend in prices, dropped 2.5 percent in the April-June period compared to the corresponding period last year. 物価の総合的な動向を示すデフレーターは，4-6月期は前年同期比で2.5％下落した．

overallotment (名)追加割当て，水増し割当て，超過割当て，オーバーアロットメント

overborrowing 過剰債務，（企業の）借入過多
◆The banks being burdened with bad loans and the firms' overborrowing are two sides of the same coin. 不良債権を抱える銀行と企業の過剰債務の問題は，表裏一体だ．

overcapacity (名)過剰設備，設備過剰，過剰生産能力
◆The U.S. auto industry has been reeling from the U.S. recession, quality problems, overcapacity, and stiff competi-

tion from Asian and European automakers. 米自動車業界は、景気後退や品質問題、過剰設備、アジアや欧州の自動車メーカーとの激しい競争で浮き足立っている。

overcharge （動）過剰請求する, 水増し請求する, 不当な[法外な]代金を請求する, 負荷をかけすぎる, 過剰に充電する, 情報を与えすぎる
◆The four defendants overcharged the government's Cabinet Office by about ¥141 million in the government-financed chemical weapons disposal project. 被告4人は、政府出資の化学兵器処理事業費として、政府の内閣府に約1億4,100万円を水増し請求した。

overcome （動）克服する, 乗り越える, 打ち勝つ, 勝つ, 勝利する, 打ち負かす, 征服する, 圧倒する
efforts to overcome deflation デフレ対応策, デフレ対策
overcome obstacles 障害を克服する［乗り越える］
overcome serious management crisis 深刻な経営危機を乗り切る［乗り越える］
overcome the current financial crisis 現在の金融危機を乗り越える［克服する］
overcome the economic crisis 経済危機を克服する
overcome the problem 問題を乗り越える
◆A prerequisite to restoring the country's fiscal health is to promptly and boldly take effective pump priming measures and to overcome the economic crisis. 日本の財政健全化への前提条件は、迅速, 果敢に効果的な景気浮揚策を実行して、経済危機を克服することだ。◆The Tokyo governor will have to tackle the task of overcoming the continued financial difficulties facing the Shinginko Tokyo bank. 東京都知事は、新東京銀行が直面する経営危機の長期化を克服する課題に取り組まなければならない。◆To overcome the current economic crisis, stimulus measures should take precedence over fiscal reconstruction for the time being. 現在の経済危機を克服するためには、当面は、財政再建よりも景気対策を優先しなければならない。◆Two domestic carriers have been given a total of ¥85 billion in emergency loans by the governmental Development Bank of Japan to overcome losses caused by a downturn in airline passengers as a result of the Iraq war and SARS outbreak. イラク戦争や新型肺炎（SARS）による利用客の減少で発生した損失を補填するため、国内航空会社2社が、政府系金融機関の日本政策投資銀行から計850億円の緊急融資を受けた。◆Two major insurers from different financial groups plan to merge in a bid to overcome serious management crises. 深刻な経営危機を乗り切るため、系列の異なる金融グループの大手保険会社2社が合併を計画している。

overcome losses 損失を補てんする
◆All Nippon Airways and Japan Airlines System have been given a total of ¥85 billion in emergency loans by the governmental Development Bank of Japan to overcome losses caused by a downturn in airline passengers. 利用客の減少で発生した損失を補填するため、全日本空輸と日本航空システムが、政府系金融機関の日本政策投資銀行から計850億円の緊急融資を受けた。

overcome the global financial crisis 世界的な金融危機を克服する
◆The APEC's 18-month timeline aimed at overcoming the global financial crisis by May 2010 has no foundation. 2010年5月までに世界的な金融危機の克服に向けて設定されたAPEC（アジア太平洋経済協力会議）の18か月間の期限に、根拠があるわけではない。

overdependence （名）過度の依存
◆Those in favor of "decoupling" urged the Japanese to reduce their overdependence on the U.S. economy. 「ディカップリング（非連動）論」支持者は、米経済への過度の依存脱却を日本に促した。

overdraft [overdraught] （名）当座貸越し（高）, 当座借越し（高）, 手形の過振（かぶ）り
bank overdraft 当座貸越し, 当座借越し

current accounts with overdrafts 当座貸越しが可能な当座預金
overdraft account 当座借越勘定
overdraft agreement 当座貸越契約
overdraft charges 延滞金利
overdraft checking account 貸越枠付き当座勘定, 貸越許容額
overdraft credit 当座貸越残高
overdraft facility 当座貸越契約
overdraft facility for working capital 運転資金用の当座貸越枠
overdrafts on current accounts 当座貸越し
provide an overdraft facility 当座貸越契約を設定する

overdraw （動）預金などを借り越す, （口座残高に対して）過振りする

overdrawing （名）小切手の過振り（預金残高を超えて小切手を振り出すこと）, 手形の過振り（信用状残高を超えて手形を振り出すこと）

overdrawn （形）過振りした, 過振りされた

overdressing （名）オーバードレッシング（債券の売買取引などで約定価格を市場の実勢価格より高く調整すること）

overdue （形）予定の期限を過ぎた, 未払いの, 延滞の, 長年懸案の
overdue account 延滞口座, 期限経過勘定
overdue bill 期限経過手形
overdue check 期限経過小切手
overdue loan 延滞債権
overdue note 期限経過手形
overdue payment reminder 支払い督促状
overdue penalty 支払い遅延違約金

overdue amount 支払い遅延金額
◆If any installment of interest under this Note shall not be received by Holder prior to the 10th day after the date on which it is due, Holder may at its option impose a late charge of 3% of the overdue amount. 本手形に基づく利息の割賦金を支払い期日の翌日から起算して10日以前に手形所持人が受領しない場合、手形所持人は、その裁量で支払い遅延額の3%の遅延料を課すことができる。

overdue interest 延滞金利, 延滞利息, 遅延利息
◆In case the borrower fails to pay any principal or interest payable under this agreement on the due date therefore, the borrower shall pay to the lender overdue interest on such overdue amount for each day for the period from and including the due date therefore up to and including the day immediately preceding the actual payment date. 借主が本契約に基づいて支払い期日に元本の返済または支払い利息の支払いを怠った場合、借主は、その支払い期日から実際の払込み日の前日までの期間の各日数について、その支払い遅延金額の遅延利息を貸主に支払うものとする。

overhaul （動）再編する, 抜本的に改革する, 見直す, 再検討する, （予算などを）組み直す, 総点検する, 精密検査する, ～を追い越す, ～に追いつく
◆The financial crisis prompted the company to completely overhaul its strategy. 金融危機を契機に、同社は戦略を抜本的に見直した。

overhaul （名）再編, 改革, リストラ, 見直し, 総点検, 精密検査, リストラ, 分解修理, 解体修理, オーバーホール
financial overhaul plan 金融改革案, 金融再編案, 金融監督の改革案
overhaul plan リストラ策, 再編策, 改革案
radical overhaul 抜本的改革 （=radical reform）
structural overhaul 構造改革, 機構改革 （=structural reform）

the drastic overhaul of the Japanese accounting system　日本の会計基準の抜本的変更
◆The drastic overhaul of the Japanese accounting system is expected to add a massive administrative burden to companies. 日本の会計基準の抜本的変更は、企業にとって大幅な事務負担の増加を強いられることになる。◆The U.S. president signed into law the overhaul of financial regulations' bill. 米大統領が金融規制改革法案に署名して、同法が成立した。◆U.S. Treasury Secretary Henry Paulson unveiled the 218-page financial overhaul plan. ヘンリー・ポールソン米財務長官は、218ページの金融改革案[金融監督の改革案]を発表した。

overhaul of financial regulations　金融規制の改革, 金融規制改革, 金融規制の見直し
◆Lawmakers in Washington debate an overhaul of financial regulations. ワシントンの米連邦議会では、金融規制の改革[改革法案]を審議している。

overhaul plan　改革案, リストラ策, 再編策
◆Ford Motor Co. closed its five North American plants as part of its overhaul plan. 米フォード・モーターは、リストラ策の一環として同社の北米5工場を閉鎖した。◆U.S. Treasury Secretary Henry Paulson unveiled the overhaul plan of the U.S. financial regulatory system. ヘンリー・ポールソン米財務長官は、米国の金融監督制度の改革案を発表した。

overheat　(動)過熱する, 景気が過熱する
　cool down the overheated economy　過熱した景気を冷ます, 景気の過熱感を鎮静化する
　overheated state　過熱状態
◆The money market is overheated by massive money inflows from banks on fading concerns over a financial system crisis. 金融システム不安[金融システム危機に対する懸念]の後退により、短期金融市場は、銀行からの巨額の資金流入で過熱感が強まっている。◆The threat of the overheated state of European countries and China causing new waves of financial turmoil must not be underestimated. 欧米諸国や中国などの景気過熱状態が新たな金融危機[金融市場の混乱]を引き起こす恐れがあることを、過小評価してはならない。◆The U.S. Federal Reserve raised the official discount rate and the target rate of federal funds by 0.25 percentage points in a bid to quell inflation and keep the economy from overheating. 米連邦準備制度理事会(FRB)は、インフレを防ぎ景気の過熱を警戒して、公定歩合とフェデラル・ファンド(FF)の誘導目標金利をそれぞれ0.25パーセント引き上げた。◆To what extent will the bubble in the real estate market and overheated economy be corrected？ 不動産バブルと過熱景気[景気の過熱]の調整は、どの程度進むのだろうか。

overheating　(名)過熱, 景気過熱
　economic overheating　景気過熱
　the overheating of the real economy　実体経済の過熱, 過熱した実体経済
　the signs of overheating　景気過熱の様相
◆In emerging economics, economic overheating and inflation are concerns. 新興国では、景気過熱やインフレが懸念される。◆The overheating of the real economy has triggered the latest financial crisis. 今回の金融危機の引き金を引いたのは、過熱した実体経済だ。◆U.S. economy is showing signs of overheating. アメリカ経済は、過熱気味に推移している。◆We are now being forced to pay the bill for the overheating of the economy. われわれは今、経済の昂揚[景気過熱]の付けを払わされている。◆While soaring high on massive direct investment from abroad, the Chinese economy started showing signs of overheating in the latter half of 2003. 海外からの活発な直接投資に支えられて、中国経済は、2003年後半から景気過熱の様相を見せ始めた。

overheating　(形)過熱した, 景気過熱の　(⇒bill)

overheating economy　経済[景気]の過熱, 景気の過熱感, 過熱した景気, 過熱景気

◆The United States is under pressure to make some difficult monetary policy decisions to cool down the overheating economy by countering the inflationary pressures stemming from higher import prices due to the weaker dollar. 米国は現在、ドル安での輸入価格の高騰によるインフレ圧力を抑えて過熱気味の景気を鎮めるための難しい金融政策の決断を迫られている。

overinsurance　(名)超過保険
overinvestment　(名)過剰投資
overkill　(名)金融の過剰引締め, 引締め経済の不徹底, 景気の冷やしすぎ
overlap　(動)重なり合う, 重複する, 部分的に同じである, 共通するところがある, オーバーラップする　(名)重なり, 重複, 共通点
◆The inefficiency of the Financial group's two-bank structure has been pointed out as many of operations overlap. 同フィナンシャル・グループの2行体制の非効率は、重複部門が多いため、以前から指摘されてきた。

overlapping　(形)重複する, 重なり合う
　overlapping account　重複勘定
　overlapping debt　共同発行債券, 重複債務, 共同負担債務
　overlapping time　(国際金融市場間で)重複する[重なる]営業時間

overloan　(名)貸出超過
overlying mortgage　後位抵当, 低次抵当権付き担保
overnight　(名)翌日物, 1日物(Today/Tomorrow), o/n　(形)翌日物の, 前夜の, 前日の, 一晩の　(副)一晩で, 一夜にして, 急に, 突然, 前夜に, 夜通し, 一晩中, オーバーナイト
　collateralized overnight　有担保翌日物
　interest rate on overnight borrowing among banks　翌日物銀行間金利
　nonmarketable securities with overnight maturities　翌日物の非市場性証券
　overnight assistance rate　翌日物介入金利
　overnight cash rates　翌日物金利
　overnight delivery　翌日渡し, オーバーナイト受渡し
　overnight fund　翌日物資金
　overnight index swap　オーバーナイト・インデックス・スワップ, OIS (オーバーナイト無担保コール・レートと固定金利を交換する取引のこと)
　overnight interest rates　翌日物金利
　overnight lending rate　翌日物貸出金利
　overnight limits　夜越し許容持ち高
　overnight money　翌日物の資金, 翌日物
　overnight position　営業終了時の証券手持ち額
　overnight processing　翌日処理
　overnight repurchase agreement　翌日物レポ
　overnight settlement　翌日決済
　overnight transaction　(外国為替の)オーバーナイト取引
　roll on an overnight basis　翌日物でロールオーバーする
　uncollateralized overnight　無担保翌日物

overnight call　翌日物コール, コール翌日物
　overnight call rate　無担保コール翌日物金利, 翌日物コール・レート
　overnight call rate lowering　翌日物コール・レートの低下
　overnight call rate target　翌日物コール・レート誘導目標
　overnight unconditional call rate　無担保コール翌日物金利
　unsecured overnight call money　無担保コール翌日物
　unsecured overnight call rate　無担保コール翌日物の金利　(=rate for unsecured overnight call money)

◆The Bank of Japan Policy Board voted unanimously to keep the target rate for unsecured overnight call money on hold. 日銀政策委員会は、政策金利である無担保コール翌日物金利の誘導目標を据え置くことを全会一致で決めた。◆The Bank of Japan uses the unsecured overnight call rate as the key target rate in the short-term money market. 日銀は、無担保コール翌日物の金利を短期金融市場の誘導目標にしている。

overnight loan 翌日物, 宵越し貸し, 翌日返済証券担保貸付け, 翌日決済
◆Policymaking members of the U.S. FOMC voted unanimously to keep its trendsetting federal funds rate for overnight loans between banks at 1 percent. 米連邦公開市場委員会（FOMC）の政策決定メンバーは、銀行同士の翌日物のフェデラル・ファンド（FF）金利の誘導目標を、現行の1％に据え置くことを全会一致で決めた。◆The federal funds rate is the interest that banks charge each other on overnight loans. フェデラル・ファンド（FF）金利は、米国の民間銀行が翌日決済で相互に資金を貸し借りするときに適用する金利のことをいう。

overnight plunge in U.S. stocks 前日の米株価の大幅下落
◆The 225-issue Nikkei Stock Average dived below the key threshold of 10,000 as investors were disappointed with the continuing delay in the disposal of banks' bad loans and an overnight plunge in U.S. stocks. 日経平均株価（225種）は、投資家が銀行等の不良債権処理が引き続き遅れることや前日の米株価の大幅下落に失望して、1万円の大台を割り込んだ。

overnight repo 翌日物レポ取引, オーバーナイト現先（げんさき）, 翌日決済の買戻し条件付き証券売却（⇒repurchase agreement）
　overnight repo rate 翌日物レポ金利
　pay the overnight repo rate 翌日物レポ金利を支払う
◆In 2007, U.S. investment banks financed 25 percent of their assets by overnight repos (repurchase agreements). 2007年に米国の投資銀行［証券会社］は、投資資産の25％を翌日物レポ取引（返済期限1日の超短期借入れ）で調達した。

overpayment （名）過払い, 払い過ぎ

oversaving （名）過剰貯蓄

overseas （形）海外の, 在外の, 対外の, 海外［外国］向けの　（副）海外［国外、外国］へ, 海外で
　oversea lending 海外貸付け, 海外融資
　oversea monetary authorities 海外通貨当局
　overseas assets 対外資産, 在外資産, 海外資産
　overseas bank 海外銀行, 在外銀行
　overseas bill of lading 海外船荷証券
　overseas borrowing 対外借入れ, 海外借入れ
　overseas borrowing moratorium 海外での資金調達凍結
　overseas borrowings 対外負債
　overseas branch 海外支店
　overseas Chinese capital 華僑資本
　overseas demand 外需
　overseas direct investment 海外直接投資
　overseas flotation 海外起債
　overseas holding company 海外持ち株会社
　overseas integrity of the dollar ドルの対外信用
　overseas interest rate 海外金利
　overseas loan 海外融資, 海外貸付け
　overseas portfolio investment 対外証券投資
　Overseas Private Investment Corp. 海外民間投資会社, OPIC
　overseas remittance 海外送金
　overseas short-term financial market 海外短期金融市場
　overseas travel life insurance 海外旅行生命保険
　overseas travel personal accident insurance 海外旅行傷害保険
◆Domestic megabanks are increasing their financing activities overseas. 国内メガバンクは、海外での融資活動を強化している。

overseas debt 対外債務
（=external debt, foreign debt）
◆The first interest payments on the bonds since the Argentine government declared default on the part of its overseas debt late last year are due on March 26. アルゼンチンが昨年末に対外債務支払いの一時停止を宣言して以来、初の国債の利払い日が3月26日に到来する。

overseas demand 海外需要
◆The government assumes a scenario in which Japan's economic growth will shift into high gear with overseas demand as a driving force. 政府は、海外需要をテコに日本の経済成長が本格化する、とのシナリオを描いている。

overseas economies 海外経済
◆Overseas economies are moving out of their deceleration phase. 海外経済は、景気減速局面から抜け出している。◆The U.S. and other overseas economies have driven Japan's recovery. 米国などの海外経済が、日本の景気回復を牽引してきた。

overseas institutional investors 海外の機関投資家
◆The buying force in the Tokyo stock market is overseas institutional investors. 東京株式市場での買いの主役は、海外の機関投資家だ。

overseas investment 対外投資, 海外への投資, 海外からの投資　（=foreign investment）
　overseas investment bank 海外投資銀行
　overseas investment business 海外投資事業
　overseas investment insurance 海外投資保険
◆Shinsei and Aozora banks suffered huge losses in their overseas investment business in the aftermath of the global financial crisis triggered by the collapse of Lehman Brothers Holdings Inc. in autumn 2008. 新生銀行とあおぞら銀行は、2008年秋のリーマン・ブラザーズの経営破たんで始まった世界的な金融危機の影響で、海外投資事業に巨額の損失が発生した。

overseas investors 海外の投資家, 外国人投資家, 外国人株主
◆In Greece, seventy percent of its national bonds are held by overseas investors. ギリシャでは、国債の70％を海外投資家が所有している。◆Our overseas investors account for about 24 percent, which would shrink to 18.6 percent after we raise capital. 当社の外国人株主［外国人投資家］は、約24％を占め、増資後は18.6％に減少します。◆Overseas investors are considered highly volatile to changes in the share price. 外国人株主は、株価動向にかなり左右されやすいとされている。

overseas lending 海外融資
◆Domestic three megabanks are moving to step up their overseas lending. 国内の3メガバンクは、海外融資を強化する方針だ。

overseas project 海外事業, 海外プロジェクト
◆Domestic banks are increasing their efforts to finance large overseas projects. 国内銀行各行は、海外での大型事業に融資する（プロジェクト・ファイナンスへの）取組みを強化している。

overseas project financing 海外の事業向け融資, 海外のプロジェクト・ファイナンス
◆Domestic banks are stepping up oversea project financing due to the lack of growth in lending to domestic borrowers amid protracted deflation at home. 国内銀行各行は、国内ではデフレが続いて［デフレが続く状況で］国内融資先への貸出が伸びていないことから、海外の事業向け融資を強化している。

overseas sourcing 海外調達
◆The recent surges in the yen's strength have made it imperative for Japanese carmakers to substantially bring down

their parts procurement costs by overseas sourcing. 最近の円高で、日本の自動車メーカー各社は、海外調達による部品調達コストの大幅引下げが緊急課題となっている。

oversee (動)監視する(watch over), 監督する, 取り締まる(supervise), 管理する, 見届ける, 見下ろす, 見渡す, こっそり見る, 偶然目撃する, 調べる
　oversee the financing of 〜の財務活動を管理する
　oversee the transfer of power 権力の移譲を監督する
　◆Former Bank of Japan official Takeshi Kimura became the bank's president in 2005 and started overseeing its management by himself. 日銀出身の木村剛氏は、2005年に同行の社長に就任し、自ら経営に乗り出した。◆The Federal Housing Finance Agency oversees Fannie and Freddie that buy mortgage loans and mortgage securities issued by the lenders. 米連邦住宅金融局(FHFA)は、これらの金融機関が発行する住宅ローンやモーゲージ証券を購入する[買い取る]連邦住宅抵当金庫(ファニー・メイ)や連邦住宅貸付け抵当公社(フレディ・マック)を監督している。◆The state-run Deposit Insurance Corporation oversees the nation's financial system stability and public fund injections. 国営の預金保険機構は、日本の金融システムの安定と公的資金の注入を管理している。

overshoot (動)(目標などを)外れる, 行き過ぎる, 通り越す, 〜の度を越す, 超過する, オーバーシュートする
　money supply target overshoots マネー・サプライの目標上限突破
　overshoot a budget 予算を超過する
　◆It remains to be seen whether the yen will be overshooting. 円相場がオーバーシュート(行き過ぎ)かどうかは、今後を見ないと分からない。

overshooting (名)行き過ぎ, (範囲や限度を)越えること, オーバーシュート

oversight (名)監視, 監督, 手落ち, 手抜かり, 見落とし, 失策 (⇒credit rater)
　enhance oversight over listed companies 上場企業に対する監視を強化する
　exercise proper oversight 適正に監視する
　governing and oversight body 統制監督機関
　SEC oversight SECの監督
　the Office of Federal Housing Enterprise Oversight 連邦住宅機関監督局
　the Oversight Board for the Resolution Trust Corporation 貯蓄機関決済信託公社監督委員会
　tighten government oversight of credit raters 格付け機関に対する政府監督を強化する
　◆Financial authorities must exercise proper oversight so that the failed bank's refunding of deposits will proceed smoothly. 金融当局は、破たん銀行の預金払い戻しが円滑に進むよう適正に監視しなければならない。◆The Obama administration sent the U.S. Congress legislation seeking to tighten government oversight of credit raters. オバマ政権は、格付け機関に対する政府監督の強化を求める法案を議会に提出した。◆The Osaka Securities Exchange will enhance oversight over listed companies in the new Jasdaq market. 大阪証券取引所は、新ジャスダック市場の上場企業に対する監視を強化する方針だ。

oversight organization 監督機関, 監視機関
　◆Oversight organizations including the Securities and Exchange Surveillance Commission will need to bolster their monitoring activities. 証券取引等委員会などの監視機関は、これから監視活動を強化する必要がある。

oversold (形)売り過ぎの, 売り過ぎ安の, 売られ過ぎの
　be grossly oversold 大幅に売られ過ぎている
　be oversold and cheap 売られ過ぎで割安だ
　oversold market 売り持ち市場
　oversold position 為替売り過ぎ状態, 売り持ち(外貨の持ち高が債務超過の状態), 売り超過
　oversold range 売られ過ぎの状態, 売られ過ぎの水準
　oversold stocks 売り過ぎ株

overspeculation (名)過剰投機

overspending (名)過剰支出
　◆Spendthrift nations' overspending threatens Europe's single currency. 財政赤字国の過剰支出が、欧州のユーロを脅かしている。

oversubscribed (形)応募超過の, 申し込み超過の

oversubscription (名)応募超過, 申し込み超過

oversupply (名)供給過剰 (=glut)

overvaluation (名)過大評価
　exchange rate overevaluation 為替レートの過大評価
　massive overvaluation of the yen 極端な円高
　the yen's overvaluation 円の過大評価, 円の割高

overvaluation of the yen 円の過大評価, 実力以上に進んだ円高, 円の割高, 円高 (=the yen's overvaluation)
　◆The government and the Bank of Japan should take concrete policy measures to deal with the sharp slowdown in the economy and the overvaluation of the yen. 政府と日銀は、具体的な政策手段を講じて、景気の急激な減速と実力以上の円高[円の過大評価]に対応すべきだ。

overvalue (動)過大評価する (=overstate; ⇒trader)
　be overvalued against 〜に対して過大評価されている, 〜に対して割高となっている
　be overvalued relative to 〜と比べて割高である
　overvalued currency 通貨の過大評価
　overvalued stock 割高な株式
　◆Currency markets have overvalued the yen. 円は、強く評価され過ぎている。

overvalued dollar ドル高, ドルの過大評価 (=strong dollar)
　◆An overvalued dollar is seriously crimping U.S. manufacturers' ability to export. ドル高が、米国の製造業界の輸出力を大いに妨げている。

owe (動)〜に負う, 〜に支払う[返済]義務がある, 〜する義務がある, 〜に借り[借金, 負債]がある, 〜を借りている, 〜を負担する
　dividends owed 未払い配当
　don't owe anybody 誰にも借りがない
　I owe you. 借用証書 (⇒IOU[I.O.U., i.o.u.])
　net amount owed 正味負債額
　owe A to B [owe B A] BにA(金額)の借金がある
　owe debts 債務を負担する, 債務を抱える
　owe the bank interest on borrowings 銀行に借入金の利子を支払う義務がある
　propensity to owe 借入性向
　the amount owing to ABC under this agreement 本契約に基づいてABCに支払われる金額
　◆Cuba has defaulted on debts owed to Japanese companies. キューバは、日本企業への未払い債務でデフォルトを起こしている。◆GM plans to use the profits from listing its stock again to repay the money it owes the U.S. and Canadian governments. GMは、株式の再上場益を、米政府とカナダ政府への債務返済に充てる計画だ。◆If TEPCO's creditor banks forgive the debts when the utility is not carrying excessive liabilities, lenders will not be able to recover either the principal or interest owed. 東電が債務超過でない時点で東電の債権保有銀行が債権を放棄すると、金融機関は元本を回収できず、金利収入も得られなくなる。◆Public institutions or revitalization funds will buy the loans owed by small and midsize companies that have been hit by the March 11 disaster to lighten

their repayment burdens. 公的機関や復興ファンドが、東日本大震災で被災した中小企業の借金を買い取って、被災企業の返済負担を軽減するものと思われる。◆The restructuring plan will focus on dealing with the debts owed to other financial institutions. 再建計画では、他の金融機関の債権取扱いが今後の焦点となる。◆The total amount of loans owed by companies and individuals to private financial institutions stands at ¥2.8 trillion in the three prefectures' coastal areas hit by the March 11 tsunami. 津波被災地の3県沿岸部では、企業や個人の民間企業からの借入金総額が、2.8兆円にのぼっている。

owing (形)借りとなっている, 未払いの
　money owing and overdue　期限超過の未払い金
　money owing to bank　銀行借入れ
　owing installments　未払いの分割払い金

own (動)所有する, 保有する, 持つ
　be jointly owned　共同所有[保有]である, 共同出資である
　be wholly owned by　～の完全所有子会社である, ～の全額出資子会社である, ～の100%子会社である
　equally owned by　～が折半出資している, ～が共同所有している
　◆At present, the government owns 50.01 percent of shares in Japan Tobacco Inc. 政府は現在、日本たばこ産業(JT)株の50.01%を保有している。◆Elpida Memory Inc. is equally owned by NEC and Hitachi. 半導体メーカーのエルピーダメモリは、NECと日立が折半出資している。◆Growth in the automotive insurance market is slowing as fewer young people own cars. 若者の車離れを背景に、自動車保険市場は伸び悩んでいる。◆The new Internet bank will be equally owned by the two firms with initial capital of ¥20 billion. 新ネット銀行は、当初資本が200億円で、両社が折半出資する。◆The U.S. government now owns 60.8 percent of GM. 米政府は現在、GM株の60.8%を保有している。◆Through the sales of shares of JR companies and NTT it owned, the central government garnered ¥3 trillion and ¥13 trillion of profits, respectively. 国が保有するJR各社とNTTの株式の売却で、国はそれぞれ3兆円と13兆円の利益を上げた。◆What is urgently needed as the EU's rescue package is beefing up the functions of the EFSF and recapitalizing banks that own Greek and Italian government bonds. EU(欧州連合)の支援策として緊急に求められているのは、欧州金融安定基金(EFSF)の機能強化や、ギリシャやイタリアの国債を保有する銀行の資本増強などだ。

own (形)自己の, 自社の
　buy one's own share　自社株買いを行う
　own account　自己勘定
　own capital　自己資本
　own fund　自己資金
　own rate of interest　自己利子率
　trade for own account　自己勘定で取引する

owned (形)所有された, ～所有の, 所持した, ～出資の
　equally owned　折半出資している, 共同所有している (=jointly owned)
　family-owned company　同族経営企業
　fifty-percent-owned company　50%所有会社
　fully owned subsidiary　完全所有子会社, 全額出資子会社, 100%子会社
　government-owned corporation　政府出資企業
　government-owned enterprise　国営企業
　investor-owned enterprise　株式公開企業
　jointly owned　共同所有の, 折半出資の (=equally owned)
　jointly owned holding company　共同経営持ち株会社
　less than 20% owned company　20%未満所有の会社
　majority owned company　過半数所有子会社 (=majority owned subsidiary)
　owned capital　自己資本
　owned manager　持ち株重役
　owned reserve　保有準備
　privately owned company　株式非公開企業, 非上場会社 (=privately held company)
　privately owned mortgage bank　株式未公開[非公開]の住宅金融会社
　publicly owned company　株式公開企業, 上場会社 (=publicly held company, publicly owned corporation)
　real estate owned　所有不動産, 保有不動産
　securities owned　商品有価証券
　state-owned company　国有企業
　wholly owned foreign firm　100%外資企業

owner (名)所有者, 所有権者, 権利者, 株主, 出資者, 企業主, 荷主, 船主, プラント輸出契約の注文者, 発注者, 施主, オーナー
　at owner's risk　荷主危険持ちで
　beneficial owner　受益者, 実質所有者
　business owner　企業経営者
　foreign ownership　外国人持ち株比率, 外国人保有比率
　Japan Ship Owners' Mutual Protection & Indemnity Association　日本船主責任相互保険組合
　majority owner　過半数株主
　nominal owner　名義上の所有者
　owner control　所有者支配
　owner financing　自己金融
　owner-occupied housing[home]　持ち家, 持ち家住宅
　owner-occupied property　持ち家
　owner-occupied starts　持ち家住宅着工戸数
　owner of record　名義上の株主
　owner participant　エクイティ参加者
　owner shift　持ち分の変更
　owner's agent　船主代理店
　owner's equity　株主資本, 自己資本, 純資産
　owner's equity to total assets　自己資本比率
　owner's interest insurance　船主利益保険
　owner's policy　所有者用証券
　principal owner　主要株主
　registered owner　名義上の証券保有者
　stock owner　株式所有者
　the owner's equity　自己資本, 株主資本
　virtual owner　実質的な所有者, 実質的な保有者, 事実上の保有者
　◆Kokudo Corp. was found to have been the virtual owner of a large number of shares in Seibu Railway held in the name of 1,100 individuals. コクドは、1,100人の個人名義で保有していた大量の西武鉄道株の実質的な保有者であることが分かった。◆Legally speaking, the shareholders are the owners of a joint stock company. 法律上は、株主が株式会社の所有者だ。

ownership (名)所有, 所有権, 所有者, 保有株式, 所有比率, 出資比率, 持ち株比率, 経営権 (⇒state ownership)
　acquire full ownership　完全子会社化する, 完全子会社にする
　acquire ownership　所有権を取得する (=take ownership)
　bank's ownership　銀行の出資者
　beneficial ownership　実質的所有
　capital ownership　出資比率
　change of[in] ownership　所有権の移転, 持ち分の変更,

株式の譲渡
change ownership　所有者［経営者］を変える，経営母体を変える
constructive ownership of stock　株式の見なし所有
control of ownership　経営権
employee［employees, employees'］stock ownership plan［program］　従業員持ち株制度
equity ownership　持ち株比率
foreign ownership　外国資本の所有，外資，外国人持ち株比率，外国人保有比率
foreign ownership of shares　株式の外国人保有比率，外国人持ち株比率
investor ownership amount　投資家持ち分
joint ownership　共有権，共同所有
majority ownership　過半数株式
open up to public ownership　株式を公開する
ownership equity　資本
ownership in equity　株式保有比率
ownership of the assets　資産の保有，資産の所有権
ownership structure　株主構造，出資構成
ownership transfer by book entry　振替決済
public ownership　株式公開
public participation in the ownership　株式公開
retain an ownership interest　所有権を留保する
retain ownership　経営権を握る
share［stock］ownership　株式所有，持ち株数
take over ownership of　〜の経営権を買い取る
the ownership of the stores　店舗所有権
　（⇒corporate rehabilitation process）
transfer of ownership　所有権の移転
yield the ownership　株式を公開する
◆Marubeni, currently holding a 44.6 percent stake in Daiei, will sell up to 20 percentage points of its ownership to the rehabilitation partner, forming a partnership in October. ダイエー株の44.6%を保有する丸紅は、保有株式をダイエー再建の提携先に最大20%売却して、10月に提携を結ぶ。◆The firm will have an initial ownership of forty percent of the voting shares of the joint venture company. 同社の当初の出資比率は、合弁会社の議決権付き株式の40％とする方針だ。◆The increased ownership will raise the bank's risk exposure to the company, whose business environment is severe. 持ち株比率の引上げで、企業環境［経営環境］が厳しい同社に対する同行のリスク・エクスポージャーは今後増大するものと思われる。◆When Mycal established the special purpose company（SPC）, it transferred the ownership of 20 profitable stores to it, issuing the bonds with the stores as collateral. マイカルが特定目的会社（SPC）を設立したとき、マイカルは20の黒字店舗の所有権をSPCに移し、この店舗を担保に社債を発行した。

ownership interest　所有権，持ち分権，株主資本
ownership interest in subsidiaries　子会社所有持ち分
ownership interest in the receivables　受取債権の所有権
◆2010 earnings also reflect gains（$0.33 per share）recorded on disposition of, or reduction of ownership interest in, subsidiaries. 2010年度の純利益は、子会社の処分と子会社所有持ち分の一部処分による利益（1株当たり0.33ドル）も反映している。

ownership of indexed government bonds　物価連動債の保有
◆The ownership of indexed government bonds has been limited to foreign governments, central banks and international organizations. 物価連動債の保有は、これまで海外の政府や中央銀行、国際機関に限られていた。

P

P&A　資産と負債の承継［継承］，資産・負債承継，P&A方式　（purchase and assumptionの略。⇒bridge bank）
◆P&A has been used in more than 80 percent of all liquidation cases in the United States. アメリカでは、P&A（資産と負債の継承）方式が、破たん処理全体の8割以上で活用されている。

P&A system　資産・負債承継方式，資産と負債の継承方式　（=P&A method; ⇒purchase and assumption system）
◆In Japan, if a failed financial institution's liabilities do not exceed the institution's assets, authorities are not allowed to prepare to apply to use the P&A system unless the failing firm proposes it. 日本では、破綻した金融機関が債務超過に陥っていない場合、その破綻金融機関からの申し出がなければ、金融当局がP&A方式採用の事前準備に入ることはできない。

P&I insurance　船主責任保険，PI保険　（=maritime protection and indemnity insurance:P&Iはprotection and indemnityの略）
◆Of 1,344 North Korean ships that entered Japanese ports last year, only 38（2.8 percent）were covered by P&I insurance. 昨年日本に入港した北朝鮮の船舶1,344隻中、PI保険に加入していたのは38隻（2.8%）に過ぎなかった。

Pac-Man defense　対抗買収宣言，パックマン防衛，パックマン・ディフェンス

pace　（名）速度，速さ，スピード，足並み，足取り，テンポ，歩調，ペース
at a fast pace　急速に，大幅に
gather pace　速くなる，スピードが上がる，本格化する，一段と激化する，ピッチが上がる，（数が）増える，広まる
keep pace with inflation　インフレと足並みを揃える
maintain one's robust pace　好調なペースを保つ
slow the pace of growth　経済成長を鈍化させる，景気が減速する
the pace of appreciation of the renminbi by China　中国の人民元切上げのペース　（⇒monitor）
the pace of economic activity　景気の足取り
　（⇒pick up）
the pace of rate reduction　利下げのテンポ
the pace of recovery of the global economy　世界経済の回復の足取り
the pace of stockbuilding　在庫積上げのペース，在庫増加のペース
◆Business sentiment among large Japanese firms improved in the April-June quarter from the first three months of 2009 at a fast pace. 4-6月期の大企業の景況感は、2009年1-3月期から急速に［大幅に］改善した。◆Due to the growing strength of the yen, even if exporters' sales grow, their profits will not keep pace. 円高進行で、輸出企業の売上が増えても、利益は伸び悩むようだ。

pace of business recovery　景気回復の足取り，景気回復のピッチ
◆There has been considerable disparity in the pace of business recovery between big cities and the rest of the country. 大都市と地方とでは、景気回復の足取りにかなりの格差が見られる。

pace of economic recovery　景気回復の足取り，景気回復のピッチ
◆The pace of economic recovery has been slow of late. 最近は、景気回復の足取りがもたついている。

pace of growth　成長のペース［速度，スピード］
◆The company shifted some people and responsibilities on its management executive committee, with an eye to increasing the pace of growth and globalization. 成長速度とグロー

バル化の促進をめざして、当社の経営執行委員会メンバーの一部とその担当分野の入れ替えを行いました。

pace of raising rates　利上げのペース
◆The U.S. Federal Reserve Board will change the pace of raising rates, depending on economic trends. 米連邦準備制度理事会（FRB）は、経済情勢次第で利上げのペースを変える方針だ。

pace of recovery　回復の足取り、回復のピッチ
◆The U.S. economy is improving, but concerns remain about the pace of recovery, the U.S. Federal Reserve said in its "beige book" report. 米連邦準備制度理事会（FRB）は、その「地区連銀景況報告」（ベージュ・ブック）で、米経済は改善しているものの、景気回復の足取りがまだ懸念されると指摘した。

package　（動）まとめる、一括する、包装する、パッケージ化する
　package A and sell it as asset-backed securities　Aをパッケージ化してアセットバック証券（ABS）として販売する
　package home loans into bonds with a guarantee against default　住宅ローンをデフォルトへの保証付き債券［対デフォルト保証付き債券、デフォルト保証付き債券］にパッケージ化する
　package one's mortgages for resale as mortgage-backed securities　保有するモーゲージをパッケージ化してモーゲージ証券（MBS）として販売する
　pre-packaged bond　パッケージ債
◆Fannie and Freddie buy home loans from lenders, package them into bonds with a guarantee against default and sell them to investors. ファニー・メイ（米連邦住宅抵当金庫）とフレディ・マック（米連邦住宅貸付抵当公社）は、融資行［金融機関］から住宅ローンを買い取り、買い取った住宅ローンをデフォルトへの保証付き債券にパッケージ化して、投資家に販売する。

package　（名）対策、政策、策、案、計画、プラン、制度、包括法案、一括法案、装置、包装、梱包、大金、パッケージ
　a new package of antideflationary measures　第二次デフレ対策
　aggressive stimulus package　大型の財政出動
　aid package　支援策、テコ入れ策
　　（=assistance package, rescue package）
　bailout package　救済策、金融支援策、緊急救助策
　deficit reduction package　赤字削減策
　early retirement and buyout packages　早期退職優遇制度
　economic package　景気対策、経済対策、景気刺激策
　economic stimulus package　景気刺激策
　exceptional measure　例外的な措置、特例
　financial aid package　金融支援策支援策
　financial bailout package　金融救済策
　fiscal package　財政刺激策、財政面からの景気対策、財政出動
　fiscal stimulus package　財政刺激策、財政面での景気刺激策、景気刺激策、景気対策
　government packages　政府の景気対策
　integrated package　総合対策、統合対策、総合政策、統合政策
　loan package　円借款
　package deal　一括取引、一括購入、セット販売、抱き合わせ商品、一括取引契約、抱き合わせ契約、包括案
　　（=packaged deal）
　package insurance　総合保険
　　（=blanket insurance, package policy）
　package mortgage　包括的譲渡抵当、家財包括抵当
　package policies　（複数の危険を担保する）パッケージ保険、総合保険、パッケージ・ポリシー
　package service　一括サービス、セット・サービス
　public financing package　公的融資措置、公的融資策、公的融資
　remuneration package　報酬、給付、謝礼、代償、報償
　rescue package　支援策　（=aid package）
　restructuring package　再建計画、リストラ策
　retirement packages for executives　執行役員の退職金
　software package　ソフトウエア・パッケージ、汎用ソフトウエア製品
　stimulus package　景気刺激策、経済対策
　supplementary fiscal package　補正予算
　supplementary package　景気対策
　the best financial package　最善の金融商品、最善の金融商品の組合せ
◆A financial aid package that includes a debt-for-equity swap and debt forgiveness was considered by the main banks. 債務の株式化（銀行にとっては債権の株式化）や債権放棄などの金融支援策を、主力取引銀行が検討した。◆Ex-GM chairman and chief executive officer will retire Aug. 1, 2009 with a pension and benefit package topping $10 million. GMの前会長兼最高業務執行役員（CEO）は、2009年8月1日に退職し、1,000万ドルを上回る退職金と年金を受け取ることになった。◆Ford Motor Co. will offer early retirement and buyout packages to all hourly workers. 米フォード・モーターは、すべての工場従業員［時間給労働者］を対象とする早期退職優遇制度を導入する。◆In June 2009 prior to Japan Airlines' failure, a ¥67 billion public financing package was extended with a government-backed guarantee to JAL. 日本航空破たん前の2009年6月に、政府保証付きで670億円の公的融資が行われた［公的融資策が実施された］。◆The economic package will include measures to help small and midsize companies procure funds. 経済対策には、中小企業の資金繰り支援策も盛り込まれる。◆The European Financial Stability Facility set up a €750 billion contingency package together with the International Monetary Fund. 欧州金融安定基金（EU）は、国際通貨基金（IMF）の協力を得て7,500億ユーロ（約90兆円）の緊急支援資金を準備した。◆The massive euro stabilization package appears to have had a limited impact thus far. 大規模な［大がかりな］ユーロ安定化策の影響は、これまでのところ限定的と思われる。◆The U.S. financial bailout package is not user-friendly. 米国の金融救済策は、使い勝手が悪い。

package of antideflationary measures　総合デフレ対策、デフレ対策
◆The government and Bank of Japan have to implement a second package of antideflationary measures. 政府・日銀は、第二次デフレ対策を実施する必要がある。

package of measures to stop deflation　デフレ阻止対策
◆The government has recently implemented the package of measures to stop deflation. 政府は最近、デフレ阻止対策を実施した。

pad　（動）（経費などを）水増し請求する
　pad accounts　粉飾決算をする　（=pad books）
　pad profits [earnings]　利益を水増しする
　padded bills　水増し請求書
◆The bank padded its pockets with undeserved income. 同行は、不当利益で財力を水増ししていた。◆The firm's shell companies allegedly pooled about ¥1 billion in slush funds by padding bills for the construction projects in their overseas bank accounts. 調べによると、同社のペーパー・カンパニーは、建設工事代金［建設工事の請求書］を水増しして、約10億円の裏金を海外の複数の銀行口座にプールしていた。

pad books　粉飾決算する　（=pad accounts）
◆The company padded books by about ¥50 billion. 同社は、

500億円ほど粉飾決算していた。
padded expense　経費の水増し
◆The company was engaged in accounting irregularities worth about ￥140 million incurred through padded expense claims for ODA projects in 16 countries. 同社は、16か国でのODA事業に対する経費の水増し請求で、約1億4,000万円の不正経理をしていた。
padding　(名)水増し, 不正行為, 不正, 詰め物をすること, 余分な言葉, 不要な挿入句
　the padding of accounts　粉飾決算
　　(=window dressing)
　the padding of car sales　自動車販売の不正行為
◆An employee of a car dealership blew the whistle on the padding of car sales by the company. 自動車販売店の社員が、同社の自動車販売の不正行為を(内部)告発した。
paid　(形)支払い済みの, 返済された, 有給の, 雇われた
　contribution-paid period　保険料納付期間
　paid bill　支払い済み為替手形
　paid cashbook　現金支払い帳
　paid check　決済小切手
　paid daybook　手形類支払い帳
　paid interest　返済利息
　paid invoice　支払い済み請求書
　paid share　払込み株　(=partly-paid share)
　paid shipment　支払い済み積出額
　partly paid　分割払込みの, 分割払込み
　report for paid account　完済報告書
paid-in　(形)払込み済みの, 支払い済みの, 納入済みの, 全額払込みの, 有償の
　paid-in surplus　払込み剰余金
　paid-in surplus on non par value stock　無額面株式払込み剰余金
　paid-in value　(株の)払込み価格
paid-in capital　払込み資本, 払込み資本金, 発行済み資本金, 払込み済み出資金　(=paid-up capital: 株主が会社の株式取得に払い込んだ金額で、これまで発行した株式の総発行価額に相当する。資本金(capital stockまたはcommon stock)と払込み剰余金(paid-in surplusまたはcapital in excess of par value)を合わせたもの)
　additional paid-in capital　資本剰余金, 払込み剰余金
　paid-in capital account　資本金勘定
　paid-in capital in excess of par (value)　資本剰余金, 払込み剰余金
　paid-in capital increase　有償増資
　profit ratio of paid-in capital　払込み資本利益率
paid-up　(形)払込み済みの, 支払い済みの, 納入済みの, 全額払込みの, 全額払込み済みの, ペイドアップ
　issued and fully paid-up capital　払込み済み株式
　paid-up capital　払込み済み資本金, 支払い済み資本金
　paid-up insurance　払込み済み保険, 全額払込み保険, 払い済み保険
　paid-up license　一括払い方式の実施権[ライセンス], ペイドアップ実施権
　paid-up policy　払込み済み保険証券, 払い済み保険, 払い済み契約
　paid-up royalty　一括払いのロイヤルティ, 特許権使用料の一括払い, ロイヤルティの一括払い
　　(=paid-up license fee)
　paid-up share [stock]　払込み済み株式, 全額払込み済み株式
　paid-up share capital　払込み資本金
　paid-up value　払込み済み相当額
palm vein pattern recognition system　手のひらの静脈パターン認証システム
◆Fujitsu's palm vein pattern recognition system is used at ATMs to verify the identities of cash card holders. 富士通の手のひら静脈パターン認証システムは、銀行の現金自動預け払い機(ATM)でキャッシュ・カード会員の本人確認に使われている。
panic　(名)動揺, 錯乱, 狼狽(ろうばい)慌てふためくこと, うろたえること, 臆病風, 恐怖心, 恐慌, 恐慌状態, パニック状態, 経済恐慌, 切羽詰まった状態, 窮地, パニック
　a collective panic buying　集団買いあさり
　a financial panic　金融恐慌
　a state of panic　パニック状態
　a stock exchange panic　株式恐慌
　be thrown into a state of panic　パニック状態に陥る
　commercial panic　商業恐慌
　general panic　全国的恐慌
　in (a) panic　動揺して, パニック状態で, 恐慌状態に陥って
　lead to a financial panic　金融恐慌を引き起こす, 金融恐慌を起こす, 金融恐慌につながる
　monetary panic　金融恐慌
　panic buying　(株価上昇を予測しての)飛びつき買い, (品不足を予測しての)パニック買い, 恐慌買い, 熱狂相場
　panic duties　恐慌関税
　panic in the crisis　危機に臨んでうろたえること
　panic liquidation　狼狽(ろうばい)売り
　panic liquidation prompted by margin calls　追い証の発生に伴う狼狽(ろうばい)売り
　panic market　恐慌相場
　Panic of 1837　1837年の経済恐慌(バン・ビューレン(Martin Van Buren)米大統領時代の経済恐慌)
　Panic of 1857　1857年の金融恐慌
　panic price　(株式などの)恐慌価格, 恐慌相場
　panic quotations　恐慌相場
　panic stations　緊急事態, パニック状態
　past panic period　沈静期
　sell in panic　パニック売り　(=panic selling)
　semi-panic　半恐慌
　start [get up] a financial panic　金融恐慌を引き起こす
◆Stock prices in Tokyo fell by more than 600 points as a state of panic gripped investors and selling pressure snowballed. 東京市場の株価は、投資家がパニック状態に陥り、売り圧力が増大[加速]したため、下げ幅が600円を超えた。
panic selling　(株価の下落を予測しての)狼狽(ろうばい)売り, (品余りを予測しての)パニック売り, 恐慌売り
◆To prevent panic selling on the New York stock market, which would prompt a chain reaction of plunges in other major stock markets, including those in Japan and European countries, financial policymakers around the world need to take additional concerted action. ニューヨーク株式市場がパニック売りを起こし、これに連鎖反応して日欧など他の主要株式市場の株価が急落するのを防ぐため、世界の金融政策担当者はさらに協調行動をとる必要がある。
paper　(名)手形, 証券, 債券, 新聞, 文書, 書類, 資料, 論文, 紙, ペーパー　(⇒commercial paper)
　accommodation paper　融通手形
　　(=accommodation bill)
　bank paper　銀行手形, 銀行券
　bankable paper　銀行割引可能手形
　business paper　業務書類, 商用手形, 商業手形
　commercial paper　商業手形, 商業証券, コマーシャル・ペーパー, CP

commodity paper　商品手形
corporate paper　社債
corporation paper　会社手形
double name paper　複名手形
eligible paper　適格手形
export paper　輸出手形
financial paper　金融手形
fine paper　優良手形
first class paper　一流手形
gilt-edged paper　一流手形
government paper　国債, 政府発行有価証券
mercantile paper　貿易手形
negotiable paper　流通手形
on paper　名目上の, 書類の上では
primary paper　新発債　(=new paper)
recycled paper　再生紙
short paper　短期証券
three-year paper　3年債
valuable paper　有価証券
white paper　白書
◆Most of the paper has been placed. 同債券の大半は, すでに消化された。

paper　(形)架空の, 名目上の, 書面の, 帳簿上の
paper assets　金融資産
paper audit　書面監査
paper chase　書類作成, 買収企業が大量の新株を発行して被買収株式と交換すること
paper chaser　書類作成者
paper company　名目会社, 幽霊会社, ペーパー・カンパニー
paper credit　証券信用
paper currency　紙幣　(=paper money)
paper gain　含み益, 評価益, 帳簿上の利益
paper gold　ペーパー・ゴールド, SDR（国際通貨基金(IMF)の特別引出権(special drawing rights)の通称）
paper issuance　CP発行
paper loss　含み損, 評価損, 架空損失, 帳簿上の損失
paper margin　帳簿上の利益
paper marketing plan　ペーパー商法
paper money　紙幣　(=paper currency)
paper profit　含み益, 評価益, 架空利益　(=paper gain)
paper profit or loss　含み損益, 評価損益, 証券類の取得価格と時価との差額
paper pusher [shuffler]　偽札(にせさつ)使い, 不渡り小切手使い, ひらの公務員[事務員]
paper title　書類上の権利, 証書上の権原
paper trail　書類上の記録
prime paper　一流手形
single name paper　単名手形
　(=one name paper)
small paper money　小額紙幣
the paper standard　紙幣本位, 紙幣本位制
trade paper　貿易手形
two-name paper　複名手形
　(=double name paper)
◆In the circular sales transactions, Katokichi's affiliates and business clients recorded the repeated sale and purchase of products only on paper receipts. 循環取引で, 加卜吉の関連会社と法人顧客は, 繰り返し行われた商品の売買を架空の売上だけに計上していた。

paper over　(動)取り繕う, 隠す, 覆い隠す, 偽装工作をする, 糊塗(こと)する, 壁紙を張る
◆The murky acquisitions of several companies by the major precision equipment maker were intended to paper over losses on investments the company made. この大手精密機器メーカーによる不透明な企業買収のねらいは, 同社が行った投資の損失隠しだった。

paperhanging　(名)小切手乱発, 小切手偽造
paperless　(形)紙を使用しない, 紙を一切使わない, ペーパーレス
◆Listed companies revised their articles of incorporation to make stock certificates paperless by holding shareholders meetings. 株券をペーパーレス化するため, 公開企業は, 株主総会を開いて会社の定款を変更した。
paperwork　(名)文書業務, 書類事務, 机上(きじょう)事務, 事務の仕事, 書類
◆General Motors filed an IPO paperwork with the U.S. Securities and Exchange Commission. (米政府の管理下で経営再建中の)ゼネラル・モーターズ(GM)は, 株式の新規公開(IPO)書類を米証券取引委員会に提出した。

par　(名)額面, 額面価格, 同等, 平価, 為替平価, 基準, パー
above [over] par　額面以上で, 額面を上回る水準で, 打ち歩(ぶ)で, オーバー・パーで
at par　額面で, 券面額で
average par outstanding　額面平残
be traded over par　額面を上回る水準で取引される, オーバー・パーで取引される
below par　額面割れで, 額面以下で, 割引で, アンダー・パー
common stock at par　額面普通株資本
contract par　契約額面
conversion at par　額面転換
debenture convertible at par　額面転換社債
drop [fall] below par　額面割れとなる, 額面を割る, 額面割れ
excess over par　資本準備金等組入れ額
gold par　金平価
insured par　付保総額
issue at par　額面発行, パー発行
mint par (of exchange)　法定平価
no-par [non-par] stock　無額面株式
　(=stock [share] of no-par value)
par issue　額面発行
par rate　パー・レート（額面価格で取引されている債券の複利ベースの最終利回り）
stock at par　額面株式, 額面株
　(=stock with par value)
sub par [sub-par, subpar] pricing　額面以下の価格設定
the par of exchange　為替平価
under par　額面以下で, 額面割れで, アンダー・パーで

par value　額面, 額面価格, 額面額, 券面額, 為替平価(exchange parity)（「額面」は株式や社債の券面に記載されている払込みの最低単位で, 「額面金額」は株主が払い込んだ金額のうち法定資本金に組み入れる金額）
capital in excess of par value　株式発行差金
change in par value　額面変更
fall below one's par value　額面割れとなる
gold par value　金平価
have a par value of 50,000 yen　額面は5万円である
initial par value　第一次平価
no-par value stock　無額面株式
　(=stock of no-par value)
par-value capital stock　額面株式, 額面額資本金

(=par value capital)
par value method　額面法
Par-Value Modification Act　平価修正法
par value of common stock　普通株の額面
par value of exchange　為替平価
　(=exchange parity)
par value of the offering　募集の額面総額
par value of the stock　株式の1株当たり額面
par value stock [share]　額面株式, 額面株, 券面株, 定額株　(=share having par value, share with par value, stock at par, stock with par value)
par value system　平価主義
set a par value　額面額を決める
stock with par value　額面株
stock without par value　無額面株
under-par value investment trust　額面割れ投信
without par value stock　無額面株
◆The Board of Directors declared a two-for-one stock split in the form of a 100% stock dividend for $1.5 par value common stock. 取締役会は、100%株式配当形式で額面1.5ドル普通株式の1株を2株にする株式分割を行うことを公表した。

pari passu　同等の, 同じ順位で, 平等に, 均等に, 同程度に, 応分に, 按分比例で, パリパス条項, パリパス
　be secured pari passu with　～と同順位になる, ～と同等の扱いを受ける
　be treated as pari passu with　～と同等に扱われる, ～と同等として扱われる
　pari passu clause　同順位条項, 平等条項, 担保差入れ制限条項, パリパス条項

parity　(名)平衡, 均衡, 平価, 為替平価, 等価, 等量, 同等, 同格, 対応, 類似, 中心レート, パリティ価格, パリティ(「平価」は、一国の通貨価値を金・銀や国際基準通貨との交換比率ではかった値。有価証券の相場価格が額面金額と等しいことも意味する。⇒float名詞, short covering)
　conversion parity　転換パリティ
　dollar parity　ドル平価
　exchange (rate) parity　為替平価, 為替交換比率
　fix new parities　新たな中心レートを設定する
　gold parity　金平価
　income parity　所得均衡, 所得パリティ
　interest parity　金利平価
　international parity　国際比価
　mint parity　法定平価
　official parity price　公定平価
　parity adjustment　平価調整
　parity index　パリティ指数
　parity of treatment　均等待遇
　parity price　パリティ価格
　parity ratio　パリティ比率
　purchasing power of parity　平価の購買力
　purchasing power parity　購買力平価
　purchasing power parity exchange rate　購買力平価為替レート
　purchasing power parity of exchange　為替の購買力平価
　SDR parity　SDR平価
　the euro failed to challenge parity versus the dollar　ユーロは1ドル=1ユーロに届かなかった
　the parity grid　欧州通貨制度(EMS)の各通貨間の基準レート表
　the parity rate of exchange　為替平価
　the parity value　パリティ価格

◆The Aussie dollar reached parity with the U.S. dollar for the first time since exchange controls ended in 1983. 豪ドルが、1983年に為替管理から変動相場制に移行後初めて、対米ドルで等価水準に達した[1豪ドル=1ドルの等価水準に達した]。

part　(名)部分, 一部, 一員, 一環, 一因, 役割, 部品, パート
　for one's part　～に関するかぎり
　for the most part　大部分は, たいていは
　in part　ある程度, いくぶん
　integral part of　～にとって不可欠の部分
　money order paid in part　内金
　part and parcel of　～の最重要部分
　part exchange　下取り交換
　play a part　一因になる
　tax reduction for part timers　パート減税
　two-part pricing　2部料金制

◆European countries are forced to prevent the financial crisis from spreading from Europe to other parts of the world. 欧州は、金融危機の世界的波及阻止を迫られている。◆Greece will miss 2011-12 deficit targets imposed by international lenders as part of the country's bailout. ギリシャは、同国救済措置の一環として国際融資団(欧州連合(EU)や国際通貨基金)が課した2011-12年の赤字削減目標を、達成できないようだ。◆Myojo Foods asked Nissin Food Products to play the part of a white knight by forming a capital alliance to thwart the U.S. investment fund's hostile takeover bid. 米系投資ファンドの敵対的TOB(株式公開買付け)を阻止するため、明星食品は資本提携によるホワイト・ナイト(白馬の騎士)としての明星の支援を日清食品に要請した。◆Part of the benefits of quantitative easing will take the form of a depreciation of the dollar. 量的緩和の効果の一部は、ドル安の形で現れる。◆The firm repaid part of its outstanding debt to the bank. 同社は、債務残高[残りの債務]の一部を同行に返済した。

partial　(形)部分的な, 一部分の, 不完全な, 片寄った, 不公平な, とくに好きな
　partial acceptance　一部引受け
　partial allotment　一部割当て
　partial assignment　一部譲渡
　partial audit　一部監査
　partial bond coverage　部分保証
　partial cash transaction　一部現金取引
　partial commodity currency　部分商品通貨
　partial consideration　部分対価
　partial consolidation　部分連結
　partial delivery　一部受渡し, 部分的引渡し
　partial deposit method　一部準備発行制
　partial endorsement　一部裏書き
　partial guarantee　一部保証
　partial legal tender　不完全法貨
　partial loss　(海上保険)分損
　partial payment　一部支払い, 一部[部分]返済, 分割払い, 分割払込み, 内払い, 手形内入れ金
　partial payment bond　分割払込み債
　partial reserve (deposit) system　一部準備制度
　partial shipment　一部船積み, 分割船積み
　partial tax transfer to local governments　地方分与税

participant　(名)参加者, 参加企業, 参加行, 参加国, 加入者, 受講者, 出席者, 関係者
　active plan participants　在職制度加入者
　industry participant　業界参加者
　market participant　市場参加者, 市場参入企業, 市場関係者　(=market player)

participant in the dividend reinvestment plan　配当金再投資制度加入者
participants in the market　市場参加者
plan participant　制度加入者
transaction participant　取引参加者
◆Market participants pointed out the issuance of new shares would dilute the value of the company's existing shares. 市場関係者は、増資［新株発行］によって同社の既存株式の価値が損なわれる、と指摘している。◆Participants in the market process information transmitted globally in real time, manipulate it in some cases and try to win profit by moving large amounts of money in this information war zone. 市場参加者は、リアルタイムでグローバルに伝達される情報を処理し、場合によってはそれを操作しながら、この情報戦争の戦場で巨額の資金を動かして利益を得ようとしている。◆The new shares of common stock are being allocated to plan participants over ten years as contributions are made to the plan. この普通株式新株は、制度への資金拠出と並行して、10年にわたり制度加入者に割り当てられています。

participate　(動)参加する, 参入する, 進出する, 加入する, 関与する
nonparticipating preferred stock　非参加優先株式
nonparticipating stock　非参加株
participate in a market economy　市場経済に参加する
participate in profits　利益にあずかる
participate in the latest coordinated rate cuts　今回の協調利下げに参加する
participating bond　利益参加社債
participating capital stock　参加株式
participating dividend　参加配当
participating preferred stock　参加優先株式
◆The six central banks around the world, including the U.S. FRB and the ECB, participated in the latest coordinated rate cuts. 今回の協調利下げには、米連邦準備制度理事会（FRB）や欧州中央銀行（ECB）など、世界の6か国の中央銀行が参加した。

participation　(名)参加, 参入, 進出, 加入, 関与, 貢献, 出資　(=involvement)
capital participation　資本参加, 出資　(=equity participation)
equity participating rates　出資比率
equity participation　資本参加, 出資, 株式投資
participation financing［loan］　複数の銀行による協調融資, 共同融資, 参加融資　(=participation loan)
participation right　参加権, 配当権
profit participation　利益分配
◆In establishing a low cost carrier under ANA's wing, ANA will invite capital participation from other industries and foreign funds. 全日空傘下の格安航空会社を設立するにあったって、全日空は異業種や海外のファンドからも出資を募る方針だ。

partly paid　分割払込みの
partly paid bond　分割払込み債
partly paid share［stock］　分割払込み株式
partly paid structure　分割払込みの仕組み

partner　(名)提携者, 提携先, 共同出資者, 共同経営者, 出資社員, 組合員, パートナー
business partner　取引先, 取引先企業, 共同事業者　(⇒sell off)
equity partner　出資者, 共同出資者
junior partner　少数株主
local partner　現地パートナー, 地元のパートナー, 現地企業
trading partner　貿易相手国
◆DaimlerChrysler has decided against pumping more money into its troubled Japanese partner, Mitsubishi Motors Corp. ダイムラー・クライスラーは、経営不振の［問題を抱えている］日本の提携企業・三菱自動車に資金を投入しないことを決めた。◆The ADB lowered its 2011 growth forecast in Asian nations due to growing worries about weak demand from key trading partners including the United States and Europe. アジア開発銀行（ADB）は、主要貿易相手国である欧米で需要減退［需要低迷］懸念が高まっていることから、アジアの2011年の成長見通し［GDP成長率見通し］を下方修正した。◆The two prospective partners have extensive expertise in mergers and acquisitions, as well as the securitization of bad loans. 提携する予定の両社は、企業の合併・買収（M&A）や不良債権の証券化などに豊富なノウハウを持っている。

partner bank　共同出資銀行
◆The firm plans to offer not only retail lending, but also corporate lending by utilizing the customer screening know-how of its partner bank. 同社は、共同出資する銀行が持つ顧客審査のノウハウを活用して、個人向け融資のほかに法人向け融資業務も提供する計画だ。

partnership　(名)共同出資, 共同所有, 共同経営, 提携, 連携, 協力, 組合, 合名会社, パートナーシップ　(⇒investment partnership)
equal partnership　折半出資, 対等提携, 対等な協力関係
form a business partnership　業務提携する, 業務提携関係を結ぶ, 業務協力協定を締結する
form a comprehensive business partnership　包括的業務提携をする
investment partnership　投資事業組合
limited liability partnership　有限責任パートナーシップ
limited partnership　合資会社, 有限責任組合, リミテッド・パートナーシップ
public private partnership　パブリック・プライベート・パートナーシップ, PPP（公共サービスの企画・運営・資金調達などの一部を民間企業が分担すること）
strategic partnership　戦略の提携, 戦略的パートナーシップ
trading partnership　商事組合
tripartite partnership　3国間パートナーシップ
◆Mizuho Corporate Bank has formed a business partnership with Sberbank of Russia. みずほコーポレート銀行が、ロシアの最大手行ズベルバンク（Sberbank of Russia）と業務協力協定を締結した。◆Suzuki Motor's board of directors decided to dissolve its partnership and cross-shareholding relationship with Volkswagen AG. スズキの取締役会は、独フォルクスワーゲンとの提携と株式持ち合い関係の解消を決めた。◆The heads of Japan, China and ROK signed statements on the tripartite partnership, international finance and the economy, and disaster management cooperation. 日中韓首脳は、3国間パートナーシップ、国際金融・経済と防災対策での連携に関する声明に署名した。◆We will expand our network of partnerships with banks, credit card companies, and convenience stores. 当社は、銀行、信販、コンビニエンス・ストア等との提携ネットワークを拡大する方針です。

party　(名)当事者, 契約当事者, 関係者
both parties　両当事者　(=the two parties)
each party　各当事者　(=each of the parties)
either of the parties hereto　本契約のいずれか一方の当事者　(=either party)
one of the parties　当事者の一方
other party　他方の当事者, 相手方, 相手方当事者
the concerned parties　利害関係人
the 'notify' party　(着荷)通知先
the parties hereto　本契約当事者, 当事者
the willing party　市場参加者, 積極的な取引者

◆A business combination is a significant economic event that results from bargaining between independent parties. 企業結合は、独立した当事者間の取引から生じるひとつの重要な経済事象である。◆If such delay shall exceed two months, either party may give written notice of termination of this agreement. このような遅延が2か月を超える場合、いずれの当事者も、書面で本契約を解除する通告を出すことができる。

pass （動）法案などを可決する、判断・判決を下す、伝える、回す、委ねる、譲渡する、範囲を越える
    pass a bill　法案［議案］を可決する、法案を成立させる
    pass on credit risk　信用リスクを回避する
    pass on the higher fund-raising costs to borrowers　資金調達のコスト増を融資先に転嫁する
    pass on the lower prices of crude oil to users　原油価格の低下をユーザーに還元する
    ◆Italian Parliament should carry out stringent measures without fail by immediately passing a fiscal rehabilitation bill. イタリア議会は、財政再建法案を成立させて、財政緊縮策を断行する必要がある。◆Japan's banking groups were not unable to pass on the higher fund-raising costs fully to borrowers by raising lending rates. 日本の銀行・金融グループは、貸出金利を引き上げて資金調達のコスト増を融資先に十分転嫁することができなかった。

pass-through certificate　パススルー証書、パススルー証券
    private pass-through certificate　民間パススルー証書［証券］

passive　（形）受動的な、受け身の、不活発な、活気のない、（借金が）無利息の、無配当の、利息を生まない、パッシブ
    passive balance　国際収支の赤字　(=adverse balance, balance of payments deficit, unfavorable balance)
    passive bond　無利子債券、無利子社債
    passive business　受動的事業
    passive damages　逸失利益
    passive debt　無利子［無利息］の負債、受動の公債、無利息の負債、受動的公債
    passive income　受動的所得（納税者が参加していない賃貸不動産や事業から生じる所得）
    passive investment　受動的投資
    passive loss　受動的損失、パッシブ損失
    passive management　パッシブ運用
    passive trust　受動信託、消極信託

password　（名）暗証番号、合言葉、パスワード
    choose a password　パスワードを選ぶ
    create one's password　～のパスワードを作成する
    enter a password　パスワードを入力する
    forget one's password　～のパスワードを忘れる
    online password　オンライン・パスワード
    verify a password　パスワードを確認する
    ◆For the obstruction of an audit by the FSA, an executive of the bank is believed to have fraudulently obtained a password needed to delete e-mails from the bank's computer server. 金融庁の立入り検査を妨害するため、同行の役員が、同行のコンピュータ・サーバーから電子メールを削除するのに必要なパスワードを、不正に入手したと見られる。◆Illegal access of Internet banking accounts using account holders' user IDs and passwords was confirmed at 51 financial institutions. 口座名義人のユーザーID［ユーザー名］やパスワードを使ったネット・バンキングの口座への不正アクセスが、51金融機関で確認された。◆In the one-time password system, clients' passwords are changed whenever they log into their accounts. ワンタイムパスワード方式だと、顧客が口座を利用するたびに、顧客のパスワードは変更される。◆Online banking users can prevent illegal transfers of their deposits by frequently changing their passwords. オンライン・バンキング利用者は、パスワードをこまめに変更して、預金の不正送金を防ぐことができる。

patent application　特許出願
    ◆The number of patent applications filed by universities in Japan in 1999 was 374, less than one-thirteenth of the 5,179 registered by U.S. universities. 日本の大学の特許出願数は、1999年は374件で、アメリカの登録件数5,179件の13分の1以下となっている。

path　（名）道、道筋、経路、進路、軌道、方向、動向、パス（指定したファイルやディレクトリまでの道筋）、方針、コース　(⇒critical path, growth path)
    balanced［equilibrium］path　均衡経路、均衡成長経路
    consumption path　消費経路
    credit path　信用力の経路
    economic path　経済経路
    equilibrium path　均衡経路
    expansion［expanding, expansionary］path　拡張経路、拡張路線
    feasible path　実行可能経路、実現可能経路
    golden rule path　黄金律、黄金則経路
    growing path　成長経路、成長軌道、成長路線
    marginal income［profit］path　限界利益線
    modest upward path　穏やかな上昇軌道
    path to profitability　利益への道筋、P2P
    recession path　景気後退経路
    recovery path　回復軌道、景気回復軌道、景気回復経路
    short-term path　短期動向
    stable path　安定経路
    time path　時間経路
    ◆The bank's new president must tread a thorny path as the management environment is severe. 経営環境が厳しいので、同行の新社長はいばらの道を歩むことになろう。◆The global economy will soon return to a path of a steady growth. 世界経済は、もうすぐ順調な成長軌道に戻るだろう。◆The international community and Japan are approaching a steep and treacherous point on the path ahead. 世界と日本は、前途の険しい難所に差し掛かっているところだ。◆The Japanese economy has reached a critical stage at which it could tumble into a deflationary spiral after brief stability, or be brought back to a recovery path. 日本経済は現在、小康状態から再びデフレの悪循環に落ち込むか、回復軌道に戻せるかどうかの瀬戸際にある。◆The new GM will have to tread a thorny path. 新GMは、これからいばらの道を歩むことになる。

pay　（動）支払う、支出する、負担する、返済する、弁済する、利潤をもたらす、利益になる、採算が取れる、もうかる、ペイする　(⇒manager, paid, paid-in)
    ability to pay　支払い能力、担税力
    　(=capacity to pay)
    appetite to pay　ペイ意欲
    authority to pay　手形支払い授権書、支払い授権書
    benefits paid　支払い給付金
    capital paid in　払込み資本
    capital paid-in excess of par value　株式払込み剰余金、額面超過金　(=share premium, paid-in surplus)
    carriage paid　運賃元払い
    claims paid　保険金
    delivered duty paid　持込み渡し条件
    dividend paid deduction method　支払い配当損金算入方式
    dividends paid　支払い配当金、配当金支払い額
    interest paid　支払い利息
    pay any bank　銀行払い（手形の文言）

pay as you go　現金払いにする
pay at piecework rates　出来高払いにする
pay at sight　一覧払い
pay bills by automatic direct debit　自動引落しで請求書の支払いをする
pay by credit card　クレジット・カードで支払う, カードで支払う
pay cash at a discount store　割引店で現金を支払う
pay debt　債務を返済する
pay income tax　所得税を支払う
pay insurance premiums　保険料を支払う
pay interest on the loan　ローンの利子を支払う
pay one's way　借金しないでやって行く, 自活する
pay through automatic debit　自動引落しで支払う
pay when due　期限どおりに支払う, 支払い期日どおりに支払う
premium paid in advance　保険料の前納
prepayment paid　前払い費用
take or pay contract　引取り保証契約

◆American International Group agreed to pay a $10 million civil fine to settle the SEC's allegations that it fraudulently helped another company falsify its earnings report and hide losses. 米保険大手のAIG（アメリカン・インターナショナル・グループ）は、同社が他社の業績報告書改ざんと損失隠しに不正に手を貸したとする米証券取引委員会（SEC）の告発を受け、この問題を解決するために民事制裁金1,000万ドルを支払うことに同意した。◆Financial Services Agency has ordered 26 nonlife insurance firms to correct their business practices, after finding they failed to pay due insurance benefits. 損保各社が支払う義務のある保険金を支払わなかったことが判明したため、金融庁は損保26社に対して業務是正命令を出した。◆Foreign firms were allowed to pay the merger consideration only in the form of shares of the subsidiary. 外国企業の場合、合併の対価は（日本に設立した）子会社の株式でしか支払うことができなかった。◆Full-time housewives of company employees and public servants are not required to pay pension premiums. 会社員や公務員の専業主婦は、保険料を払う必要がない。◆If a housewife whose annual income is ¥1.3 million or more, or her husband becomes self-employed, the housewife must join the national pension plan and pay premiums. 主婦の年収が130万円以上の場合、または夫が脱サラした場合には、主婦も国民年金に加入して保険料を支払わなければならない。◆In the case of au Insurance's cell phone-based policy sales, policyholders are allowed to pay premiums by adding them to monthly mobile charges. au損害保険の携帯電話での保険販売の場合、保険契約者は、保険料を携帯利用の月額に加算して保険料の支払いをすることができる。◆Onward Kashiyama paid ¥17 billion to purchase British fashion brand Joseph. オンワード樫山は、英国のファッション・ブランド「ジョゼフ」を、170億円で買収した。◆The consolidated provision for taxes also includes an amount sufficient to pay additional United States federal income taxes on repatriation of income earned abroad. 連結納税引当金には、海外で得た利益の本国送金に課される米連邦所得税の追加支払いに十分対応できる金額も含まれている。◆The Development Bank of Japan asked the Japan Finance Corporation to pay ¥53.6 billion, the amount guaranteed by the government. 日本政策投資銀行は、政府保証分の536億円の支払いを日本政策金融公庫に請求した。◆The government tightened the criteria for granting total exemption from paying national pension premiums. 政府は、国民年金保険料の全額免除の基準を厳格にした。◆The interest rates a bank pays when procuring funds from the financial market are higher than those paid by other banks. ある銀行が金融市場で資金調達する際に支払う金利が、他行に比べて高くなっている。◆The policies offered by the two nonlife insurers pay policyholders if they are injured doing sports or during domestic and overseas trips. この損保2社が提供している保険では、保険加入者［保険契約者］がスポーツや国内外の旅行中に傷害事故にあったときに、保険金が支払われる。◆The would-be acquirer is trying to greenmail the target company by having it pay a premium to buy back the shares held by the raider. 買収側［買収希望者］は、この買占め屋［会社乗っ取り屋］が保有する株を標的企業に高値で引き取らせて、標的企業から収益を上げようとしている（標的企業に高値で引き取らせることにより、標的企業にグリーンメールを仕掛けようとしている）。◆Those housewives who have failed to switch to the national pension plan and have not paid premiums for an extensive period may receive a pittance or nothing at all. 国民年金への切替えをせず、保険料を長期間払っていない主婦は、低年金や無年金になる可能性がある。◆We will pay a dividend of ¥50 per share for the first half. 当社は、上半期の配当支払い額を1株当たり50円にする方針です。◆Whole life insurance means life insurance under which coverage remains in force during the insured's entire lifetime, provided premiums are paid as specified in the policy. 終身保険は、保険契約に明記されている保険料が支払われているかぎり、保障が被保険者の全生涯にわたって有効な生命保険を意味する。

pay　（名）賃金, 給料, 手当て, 報酬, 支払い　（形）有料の, ペイ
basic pay　基本給, 基本給与　（=base pay）
daily pay　日給
deduction from pay　給与控除額
dismissal pay　解雇手当て
efficiency pay　能率給
executive pay　役員報酬, 経営幹部の報酬
full pay　本給, 全給
in a pay-as-I-go policy　現金払いで
incentive pay　奨励給, 奨励手当て, 報奨金
low pay　低賃金, 安月給
maternity pay　出産手当て
merit-based pay plan　業績連動型の報酬制度
monthly pay　月給
overtime pay　超過勤務手当て, 残業手当て, 時間外賃金
Pay Board　米賃金査定委員会
pay boost　給与の引上げ
pay check [cheque]　給料小切手, 給料支払い小切手, 俸給, 賃金, 後援者, 広告主
pay claim　賃上げ要求
pay day　給料日, 支払い日,（株式市場の）清算日, 最良の日　（=payday）
pay deal　賃金交渉妥結
pay dirt　採算の取れる採鉱地, 掘り出し物, 貴重な物, 金づる, 金もうけの種
pay dispute　賃金闘争
pay-for-age structure　年功序列賃金構造
pay-for-performance pay　能力給
pay freeze　賃金凍結, 給与凍結
pay level　賃金水準, 給与水準
pay negotiations　賃金交渉
pay office　給与支払い窓口, 出納室
pay packet　給料, 給料袋
pay rise　賃上げ, 昇給
　（=pay hike, pay increase, pay raise）
pay scale　給与体系, 賃金体系
pay scales　給与表
pay settlement　（給料に関する経営陣との）妥結

pay slip [stub]　給与明細
pay structure　給与体系, 賃金体系
pay stub　給与明細票
pay talks　賃金交渉
Pay to bearer　持参人払い
pay to cash　(小切手の)持参人払い
pay 30 days after date　日付後30日で支払う
pay 30 months after sight　一覧後30日で支払う
performance-related pay　業績連動給, 能力給
premium pay　奨励給
provide high pay for　～に高給を支払う, ～に高賃金を支払う
retirement pay　退職金, 退職手当て
self pays　自己負担分
seniority-based pay system　年功序列型賃金体系
severance pay　退職金
single pay life insurance　一時払い生命保険
starting pay　初任給
take-home pay　手取り給料, 手取り給, 可処分所得
time and a half pay　5割増し給[給与]
unemployment pay　失業手当て, 失業給付金
vacation pay　有給休暇手当て
weekly pay　週当たり平均賃金
◆Sharp Corp. will cut monthly executive pay between 5 percent and 30 percent for seven months starting next month. シャープは、来月から7か月間、役員の月間報酬を5～30%減額する。◆The executive pay of Merrill Lynch & Co., mostly in bonuses, has become a hot-button issue in the recession as banks and companies fail. メリルリンチの経営幹部報酬は、大半がボーナスだが、銀行や企業が経営破たんする不況時の強い関心を呼ぶ問題になっている。

pay-as-you-earn　(名)(形)源泉課税(の), 源泉課税方式, 即金主義, 現金払い方式, 現金払い主義, PAYE (=pay-as-you-go)

pay-as-you-go　(名)(形)現金払い方式(の), 現金払い主義, 源泉課税方式, 源泉徴収方式, 独立採算制, 無借金の, ペイゴー原則, PAYGO
pay-as-you-go accounting　現金主義会計
pay-as-you-go basis　現金主義, 現金基準, 現金払い方式, 現金払い主義, 独立採算制
pay-as-you-go financing plan　賦課方式 (=pay-as-you-go-system)
pay-as-you-go method　源泉課税方式, 源泉徴収方式
pay-as-you-go policy　無借金経営
pay-as-you-go system　賦課方式, 世代間扶養制度

pay-as-you-go formula　賦課方式, 源泉課税方式, 現金払い方式
◆If the younger generation refuses to contribute to the government-run pension program, the pension system, which works on a pay-as-you-go formula, will fall apart immediately. 若い世代が政府運営の年金制度への保険料払込みを拒否したら、賦課方式でうまくいっている年金制度は、たちまち崩壊してしまうだろう。

pay-as-you-go Social Security system　賦課方式の社会保障制度
◆The numbers of elderly voters and their power supposedly threaten to swamp the financing of the pay-as-you-go Social Security and Medicare systems. 高齢有権者の数とその力で、賦課方式のアメリカの社会保障制度と高齢者医療保障制度の財政は、おそらく破たんするものと思われる。

pay back　(金を)返済する, 借金を返す, 借換えをする[借り換える], (公債を)償還する
pay back bank debt　銀行借入[銀行借入金]を返済する
pay back maturing government bonds　満期を迎える国債を借り換える, 満期分の国債を償還する
pay back the loan to the bank　銀行にローンを返済する
◆GM paid back some of the money it borrowed from the U.S. and Canadian governments ahead of schedule. GMは、米政府とカナダ政府からの借入金の一部を、前倒しで返済した。◆If a new federal debt ceiling isn't set by Aug. 2, 2011, the United States will be forced to default on Treasuries securities as it will not be able to issue new bonds to pay back maturing government debts. 2011年8月2日までに連邦政府の債務上限を新たに設けないと、米国は満期を迎える国債を償還するための国債増発ができないので、米国債の不履行(デフォルト)が発生する。

pay cut　減給, 賃金カット
accept a pay cut　減給処分を受ける, 賃金カットを受け入れる
take a pay cut　賃金カットをのむ

pay debt　債務を支払う, 債務を返済する
◆The firm was not able to pay its debts to the bank. 同社は、同行に債務を返済できなかった。

pay down　(月賦の頭金を)支払う, (債務を)返済する
ability to pay down debt　債務返済能力
pay down debt　債務を返済する
pay down existing debt　既存債務を返済する
◆New York Times will sell its nine TV stations for $575 million to pay down debt. ニューヨーク・タイムズは、債務返済のため、傘下のテレビ9局を5億7,500万ドルで売却する。

pay for　～の代金を支払う, ～の報い[罰]を受ける
pay for imports　輸入代金を支払う
pay for losses　損失を補填する
◆The National Bank of Cuba will not be able to pay for imports into Cuba in due terms as the country is short of settlement funds. キューバ国立銀行は今後、国全体の決済資金不足で、期日どおりにキューバへの輸入代金の支払いができなくなる状況にある。

pay hike　賃上げ, 賃金引上げ (=pay increase, pay raise)
◆The Japan Business Federation released a report in favor of pay hikes for workers in labor management negotiations in spring. 日本経団連は、春の労使交渉で労働者の賃上げを容認する報告書を発表した。

pay in　～で支払う, (銀行口座に金を)払い込む[振り込む], 預金する, 寄付する, (年金や保険に)加入する (pay into)
additional paid-in capital　払込み剰余金, 資本剰余金
capital paid in　払込み資本
pay in advance　前払いする
pay in cash [money]　現金で支払う, 現金払いする
pay in full　全額支払う, 全額払い込む, 完納する
pay in [by] installment　月賦で払う
pay in part　一部を支払い
◆Companies must pay more in pension premiums than in corporate taxes. 企業の年金保険料の負担は、法人税を上回る。◆The proposed pact will exempt expats from paying into pension and health insurance plans in the country to which they are posted, provided they stay no more than five years. 協定案では、海外駐在員の滞在期間が5年以内であれば、駐在する相手国の年金と医療保険制度への加入を免除される。

pay-in　(名)払込み, 振込み, 預金
pay-in book　預金通帳 (=paying-in book)
pay-in period　払込み期間

pay-in-kind　(形)証券払いの, 現物配当の, PIK方式の, PIK
pay-in-kind bond　PIK債

pay-in-kind preferred　PIK優先株
pay liability　賠償金を支払う, 負担金を支払う
◆In the policies offered by the Sompo Japan and Tokio Marine & Nichido Fire Insurance, the companies also pay liability if policyholders injure or kill someone.　損保ジャパンと東京海上日動火災が提供している保険では, 保険契約者[保険加入者]が人をけがや死亡させたりした場合に, その相手に支払う賠償金も支払われる。
pay off　借金などを完済する, 借金を返す, 返済する, 償還する, よい結果を生む, うまく行く, 実を結ぶ, 引き合う
　be paid off at par　パーで償還される
　pay off a loan　借入金[ローン]を返済する
　pay off a mortgage　抵当権を完済する
　pay off the public funds　公的資金を返済する
　◆Maturing commercial paper was paid off. 満期を迎えたコマーシャル・ペーパー(CP)が, 償還された。◆The bank has already paid off the injected public funds. 同行は, (国から)注入を受けた公的資金をすでに完済している。
pay on　〜として支払う, 〜と同時に支払う
　pay on account　内金を払う, 内金として支払う
　pay on application　(銀行への送金手形の)請求払い, 請求あり次第支払う
　pay on arrival　到着と同時に支払う
　pay on delivery　引渡しと同時に支払う
　pay on demand　要求あり次第支払う, 要求払い
pay out　支払う, 積立金を払い戻す
　amount paid out as dividends on common stock　普通株式に対して支払われた配当金の額
　avoid paying out carry　キャリーの負担を避ける
　be paid out early　期限前に返済される
　pay out a larger percentage of earnings　配当性向を高める
　pay out dividends　配当金を支払う
　◆A payout ratio refers to the percentage of a company's profits to be paid out to shareholders in the form of dividends. 配当性向とは, 配当の形で株主に支払われる企業の利益の比率[企業の利益のなかから株主への配当に回す比率]のことだ。
pay-through certificate　ペイ・スルー型証券
pay-throw bond　ペイ・スルー債券(抵当証券を集めたモーゲージ・プールを担保として発行される債券)
pay up　(借金を)完済する, 全額支払う, 決済する
　issued and fully paid-up capital　払込み済み株式
payable　(形)支払うべき, 支払い満期の, 支払い期限に達した, 支払い期日の到来した, 支払われる　(名)未払い勘定, 仕入れ債務, 買掛金
　account payable　支払い勘定, 買掛金勘定, 未払い勘定, 仕入れ債務
　bill payable　支払い手形
　bill payable to the bearer　持参人払い手形
　bond payable　未償還社債
　check made payable to order　指図人払い小切手
　check payable to order and bearer　記名式持参人払い小切手
　commissions payable　未払い手数料
　dividend payable　支払い配当金
　drafts payable　支払い手形
　estimated taxes payable　見積り未払い税額
　loan payable　借入金
　note payable　支払い手形
　note payable to finance company　手形借入金
　payable at a bank　銀行払いの

payable at call　要求払い
　(=payable at sight, payable on demand)
payable at fixed date　確定日払い
　(=payable on a fixed date)
payable at sight　一覧払い
payable in advance　前払い
payable in arrear　後払い
payable on delivery　現物引換え払い
payable on demand　一覧払い, 要求払い
payable period　回収期間 (=payback period)
payable through items　銀行経由支払い小切手
payable to a specified person　記名式の, 特定払い
payable to bearer　持参人払い
(payable) to order　指図人払い
payables　債務, 支払い債務, 未払い金, 未払い勘定
　(=debt, liability)
payables in foreign currency　外貨建て債務
tax payable　未払い税金
trade payable　買入れ債務
◆Interest only shall be payable in arrears starting on April 30, 2011 and on the 30th day of each month thereafter until September 30, 2011. 利息だけは, 2011年4月30日からその後の2011年9月30日まで毎月30日の後払いとする。◆The company's regular quarterly dividend will be payable June 30, 2011 to shareholders of record at the close of business on June 9, 2011. 当社の通常四半期配当は, 2011年6月9日営業終了時の登録株主に対して2011年6月30日に支払われる。◆The prevailing rate of interest for a note payable of this type is 12%. この種の支払い手形の通常[現行]の利子率は, 12%である。
payback　(名)返済, 回収
　cash payback　現金回収
　discounted payback (period) method　割引期間回収法
　guaranteed payback　確定利回り
　payback of net indebtedness　純借入れ返済
　payback period　返済期間, 回収期間
payee　(名)(小切手などの)受取人
payer　(名)(小切手などの)支払い人
paying　(形)金を払う, 支払う, 金の儲(もう)かる, 有利な　(名)支払い, 払込み, 返済, ペイ
　aggressive paying interest　積極的なペイへの動き, 積極的なペイ意欲
　claims paying ability　保険金支払い能力
　debt-paying ability　債務返済能力, 債務弁済能力
　dividend-paying stock　有配株
　insurance claims-paying raring　保険金支払い能力格付け
　long-term debt paying ability　長期債務の返済能力
　paying ability　支払い能力
　paying back prepaid interest　戻し利息
　paying bank [banker]　支払い銀行
　paying-in book　預金通帳, 預金入金帳
　　(=bank book)
　paying party　支払い側当事者
　paying-tax burden　納税負担
　　(=burden of tax paying)
　paying up of shares　株式払込み
paying agent　支払い代理人
　fiscal and paying agent　財務・払込み代理人
　issuing and paying agent　発行支払い代理人
　paying and conversion agent　支払い転換代理人
　principal paying agent [agency]　主支払い代理人

paying-in slip 預け入れ伝票, 入金伝票 (=credit slip, deposit slip)
    paying-in slip book 振込み帳票
    paying-in slips for current deposit 当座勘定入金票

paying interest ペイ意欲, ペイへの関心
    aggressive paying interest 積極的なペイ意欲, 積極的なペイへの動き
    corporate paying interest 事業法人のペイへの関心
    end-user paying interest エンド・ユーザーのペイへの関心
    paying interest at the shorter end of the curve 短期物のペイ意欲

payment (名)支払い, 払込み, 振込み, 決済, 納入, 返済, 弁済, 支払い金額, 返済額 (⇒insurance premium payment, pension payments, premium payment)
    a means [mode] of payment 支払い方法, 支払い手段 (=payment means)
    a stop payment (小切手の)支払い差し止め
    automatic payment 自動振込み, 自動支払い
    balloon payment 最終残額一括払い (=large terminal payment)
    benefit payment 給付金支払い, 保険金支払い
    cash payment 現金払い (=payment in cash)
    collateral principal payment 担保からの元本支払い
    delayed payment 支払い遅延
    disruption of interest or principal payments 元利払いの不履行
    earthquake insurance payments 地震保険の保険金支払い額
    easy payment 分割払い
    final payment 最終払い
    fixed payment bond 確定期償還債
    full payment 全額払い (=payment at [in] full)
    future annual interest payments 将来の年間支払い利息
    interest payment 利息支払い, 利払い, 支払い利息
    late payment 支払いの遅延 (⇒interest charge)
    loan interest payments 借入金利息支払い額
    lump sum payment 一括払い, 大口払い
    nonpayment [non-payment] 不渡り
    one-off payment 一時金
    over-the-counter payment 店頭持参払い
    payment a compte [on account] 内金払い
    payment against acceptance 引受払い
    payment against delivery 引渡し払い
    payment arrears 支払い遅延
    payment basis 支払い基準
    payment before maturity 期限前返済
    payment bill 支払い手形
    payment by letter of credit 信用状決済
    payment charge [commission] 支払い手数料
    payment date 支払い日, 利払い日, 払込み日
    payment deadline 支払い期日
    payment for honor 参加払い, 代位弁済
    payment in arrears 返済遅延
    payment in due course 満期払い
    payment in full 全額支払い (⇒interest charge)
    payment in substitution 代物弁済
    payment letter of credit 外国為替支払い信用状
    payment of balances 差引残高決済
    payment of benefits under its (Company) policies 元受契約の保険金支払い
    payment of dividends 配当金の支払い
    payment of interest on interest 利子に対する利子の支払い
    payment of maturing CP 満期を迎えたCPの償還
    payment of principal and interest 元利返済
    payment on account 内金払い, 内払い
    payment on arrival 着払い
    payment order [instruction] 支払い指図書
    payment period 返済期間, 支払い期限
    payment received 支払い領収済み
    payment slip 出金伝票, 支払い伝票
    payment stopped 支払い停止済み
    payment supra protest 参加引受払い
    payment transfer market 送金市場
    payment under guarantee 代位弁済
    payment voucher 支払い証票
    preferential payment 優先支払い
    presentation for payment 支払い要求呈示 [提示]
    progressive payment 繰り延べ払い
    prompt payment 即時払い
    semi-annual payment 半年賦払い
    social security payment 社会保険料
    source of payment 償還の原資
    suspense payment 仮払い金
    suspension of payments 支払い停止, 利払いの停止
    tax payment 納税

◆Any payment not made when due will, in addition to any other right or remedy of Licensor, incur a finance charge at the lesser of three hundred basis points over the 3-month London Inter Bank Offered Rate ("LIBOR＋3") on the date payment was due or the highest applicable legal contract rate. 支払いが支払い期日までに履行されない場合、ライセンサーの他の権利や救済請求権に加えて、支払い期日時点の3か月物ロンドン銀行間取引金利(LIBOR)プラス3%(LIBOR＋3%)または適用される最高法定約定金利のうち、いずれか低いほうの金利の金融費用が発生する。◆Earthquake insurance payments resulting from the Great East Japan Earthquake are expected to reach ¥1.2 trillion. 東日本大震災による地震保険の保険金支払い額は、(業界全体で)1兆2,000億円に達する見込みだ。◆In insurance policies that can be purchased via mobile phone, would-be policyholders do not need to input personal data and payments are easier. 携帯電話で加入できる保険では、加入希望者は個人情報を入力する必要がなく、支払いも簡単だ。◆Pension premiums of full-time housewives of company employees and public servants are automatically covered by payments made by all subscribers to welfare and mutual pension plans. 会社員や公務員の専業主婦の年金保険料は、厚生年金や共済年金の加入者全員の支払い金で自動的にカバーすることになっている。◆The bank processed a total of 4 million settlements Thursday, including about 3 million salary payments and payments to companies. 同行は木曜日に、約300万件の給与振込みと取引先企業への代金支払いを含めて、計400万件の決済処理をした。◆The rate of exchange to U.S. dollars shall be based upon the rate of exchange quoted by the Bank on the day of payment. 米ドルへの為替相場は、支払い日の銀行の為替相場によるものとする。◆The U.S. government could avoid the worst-case scenario of default on payments to investors in Treasury bonds. 米政府は、国債の償還資金がなくなる債務不履行という最悪の事態を避けることができた。

payment on debt 債務返済
    ◆The EU ministers will consider debt relief or freezing pay-

ments on debt for the Asian tsunami-hit countries. 欧州連合（EU）の閣僚らは、アジアの津波被災国のため債務削減や債務返済の凍結を検討する。

payment plan 返済計画
◆People who take out adjustable-rate mortgages should make flexible payment plans. 変動金利型住宅ローンの利用者［変動型金利の住宅ローンを組む人］は、ゆとりを持った返済計画を立てるとよい。

payment system 支払い手段, 決済手段, 決済システム
　consolidated tax payment system　連結納税制度
　cross-border payment system　国際決済システム
　deficiency payment system　不足払い制度

payments　（名）支払い額, 返済額
　payments clearance　信用決済
　payments imbalance　国際収支の不均衡
　payments of foreign currency　外貨決済

payments to bondholders　債券保有者への（元本と利息の）支払い
◆Bond insurers write policies that promise to cover payments to bondholders if the entity that issued the bonds defaults. 金融保証会社［債券保険会社］は、債券発行体がデフォルト（債務不履行）になった場合に、債券保有者への（元本と利息の）支払い補償を約束する保険を引き受けている。

payoff [pay-off]　（名）（給料や借金などの）支払い, ペイオフ（破綻金融機関の預金払戻し保証額を元本1千万円とその利息に限る措置), 報酬, 利益, 見返り, 利得, 良い結果, 成果, 退職奨励金, 利益供与, 賄賂（わいろ）
　early payoff　繰上げ償還
　make payoffs to officials　公務員に賄賂を贈る
　massive payoff scandal　巨額の利益供与不祥事事件
　payoff matrix　利得行列, ペイオフ行列
　payoff of structural reform　構造改革の成果
　payoff period　元本回収期間, 回収期間
　　（=payout period）

payoff system　ペイオフ制度　(=deposit refund cap, payoff scheme: 経営が破綻した金融機関の預金を、預金保険機構を通じて預金者に払い戻す制度。払戻し額保証の上限は、2001年4月から1人当たり1,000万円とされている。金融機関は毎年、預金量の一定の割合を保険料として預金保険機構に納付しており、これらがペイオフを行う際の原資となる。⇒deposit insurance, Deposit Insurance Corporation, deposit refund cap, freeze on the payoff system, refund）
◆In this payoff system, starting in April 2001, no more than ¥10 million of bank deposits per depositor will be guaranteed at any bank in the event of a bank's failure. このペイオフ制度では、2001年4月から、銀行が倒産した場合にはどの銀行でも、預金者1人当たり最高で1,000万円の銀行預金が保証されることになっている。

payor [payer]　（名）支払い人, 払い手
　a payor's option　（金利スワップションで固定金利の）払い手のオプション
　payor bank　支払い銀行　(=payer bank)

payout　（名）支払い, 支出, 支出金, 株式などの配当・配当金, 預金の払戻し金, 保険金の支払い, 支払い保険金, 社会保障の給付費, 回収　（⇒capital efficiency, deposit payout, dividend payout）
　common dividend payout　普通株配当性向
　dividend payout　配当性向, 配当金の支払い
　dividend payouts　配当金の支払い額
　fire insurance payouts　火災保険の補償額
　insurance payouts for the March 11 earthquake and tsunami　東日本大震災の保険金の支払い額
　　（⇒insurance payouts）

　payout percentage　配当性向, 配当支払い率, 配当比率
　　（=payout ratio）
　payout period　回収期間, 元本回収期間, 投資回収期間
　　（=payback period, payoff period, payout time）
　payouts to shareholders　株主配当, 株主資本
　pension payout　年金の支払い
◆Domestic nonlife insurance companies set a ceiling for fire-insurance payouts for corporate clients in cases of damages caused by terrorist attacks. 国内損保は、テロ被害の［テロ攻撃による損害を受けた場合の］顧客企業向け火災保険の補償額に上限を設けた。◆Since May 2010, Greece has been reliant in regular payouts of loans from a €110 billion bailout from other eurozone countries and the IMF. 2010年5月からギリシャは、他のユーロ圏諸国やIMF（国際通貨基金）などからの1,100億ユーロの金融支援による融資の定期支払い金に頼っている。

payout ratio [rate]　配当性向, 実質引受手数料率, ペイアウト比率　(=dividend payout (ratio), payout percentage: 企業の利益のなかから株主への配当に回す比率のこと。⇒pay out)
　expected payout ratio　期待配当性向
　raise a payout ratio　配当性向を引き上げる
　target payout ratio　目標配当性向
◆There are moves among listed companies to raise payout ratios. 上場企業に、配当性向を引き上げる動きがある。◆Through continuing gains in annual earnings, it will be possible, over time, to adjust the payout ratio while still maintaining our dividend record. 年間利益の増大を続けることによって、当社の配当実績を今後とも維持しながら、時期が来たら配当性向を調整することは可能である。

payroll　（名）（従業員の）給与総額, 給与支払い簿, 従業員名簿, 従業員総数, 雇用者数
　addition to payrolls　雇用の増加, 雇用者数の伸び, 雇用創出　（=rise in payrolls）
　bank payroll deduction　銀行給料天引き
　manufacturing payrolls　製造部門の雇用者数, 製造業雇用者数
　meet a payroll　給与を支払う
　off the payroll　解雇されて
　on the payroll　雇用されて
　payroll check　賃金台帳, 給与・賃金支払い小切手
　payroll cost　労務費
　payroll credit　給与振り込み
　payroll figures　雇用統計
　payroll plan　給与支払い代行サービス
　payroll processing [service]　給与計算
　payroll record [register]　賃金支払い帳
　payrolls　総従業員数, 雇用者数, 雇用情勢
　private payrolls　民間部門の雇用者数

payroll deduction　給与［給料］天引き, 給与天引き方式
　direct payroll deduction　給与天引き方式
　payroll deduction plan　給料［給与］天引き積立て
　through payroll deduction　給与［給料］天引きで

PBR　株価純資産倍率（price book-value ratioの略）

P/E [p/e]　株価収益, 株価収益率（price earningsの略。株価収益率＝株価÷1株当たり利益）
　have high P/E ratios　PERが高い
　high P/E stocks　PERの高い株
　　（=stocks with high P/E ratios）
　low P/E stocks　PERの低い株
　　（=stocks with low P/E ratios）
　market P/E　市場の平均PER
　P/E ratio　株価収益率

(=price/earnings ratio, PER)
projected [prospective] P/E　予想PER
prospective P/E multiple　予想PER

PE　株価収益,株価収益率　(=P/E)
A times PE ratio　株価収益率A倍
PE premium to the market　PERのプレミアム(市場平均を上回る比率)
the offer will be priced at a prospective PE of around A　公募価格は予想PERがA倍前後になる見込みだ

peak　(動)頂点に達する,最大限[最高潮]に達する,天井を打つ,峠を越す,ピークに達する
peak out　景気が天井を打つ,ピークに達する,ピークアウトする
◆Domestic lending growth has been decelerating sharply since peaking last month. 国内貸出の伸び率は、先月をピークに急速に低下[鈍化]している。◆The stock price peaked out. 株価は、ピークに達した。◆This business cycle may have peaked. 今回の景気サイクルは、峠を越した[天井を打った]ようだ。

peak　(名)最高点,頂点,山頂,峰,景気の山,天井,相場の最高値,最大限度,絶頂期,ピーク時,ピーク
be at the peaks of the economic expansion　景気拡大局面のピークに達する
be well off one's peak　ピーク時よりかなり下がっている
cyclical peak　景気循環のピーク,景気循環の峠
first peak　一番天井
local [near-term] peak　当面のピーク
major peak　大天井
peaks and troughs [valleys]　浮き沈み,好不調,ピークと底
reach a peak　ピークに達する
◆The DJ Stoxx index of European banking stocks has fallen 37 percent from a peak in February. ダウ・ジョーンズ欧州銀行株指数は、2月のピークから37%下落した。◆The number of surplus workers approached a peak of 3.59 million in the January-March quarter of 1999, following a spate of failures at major financial institutions. 過剰雇用者数は、大手金融機関の破たんが相次いだ後の1999年1-3月期に、359万人のピークに達した。

peak　(形)最高の,最大の,絶頂の
peak foreign exchange level　為替相場の最高値
peak income　最高所得
peak season　書き入れ時
reach one's peak foreign exchange rate　為替相場で最高値を付ける

peer　(名)同業者,同業他社,同業他行,競合他社,ライバル,仲間,同僚,ピア
peer companies　同業他社,競合他社
peer group　同業他社,競合他社,ライバル,仲間集団,仲間グループ,ピア・グループ
peer pressure　同等集団圧力,張り合い圧力,ピア・プレッシャー
peer review　相互検査,専門家による相互審査,相互評価,同僚評価,相互批判,ピア・レビュー
peer-reviewed　専門家の審査を経た
private peers　民間の競合他社,競合する民間企業
◆The bank has a stronger balance sheet than some of its bigger peers. 同行の財務基盤は、一部の大手の同業他行よりも強固だ。

peg　(動)安定させる,固定させる,一定にさせる,釘付けにする,連動させる,凍結させる,リンクさせる　(名)株価などの設定水準,連動,リンク,固定相場制,ペッグ
adjustable peg rate system　調整可能な釘付け相場制
crawling peg　小刻みな為替変更,クローリング・ペッグ
dollar peg system　ドル・ペッグ制(ドル相場に連動するよう相場を固定するシステム)
dollar-pegged currency system　対ドル固定為替相場,対ドル固定相場制
peg one's exchange rates to the dollar　〜の為替レートをドルに連動させる
peg point　基準点
peg to a currency basket　バスケット通貨に連動させる
pegged exchange　固定為替相場,釘付け為替相場
pegged exchange rate system　固定為替相場制,釘付け為替相場制　(=fixed exchange rate system, pegged exchange, pegged exchange rate)
pegged market　釘付け相場,釘付け市場
pegged stock　釘付け株
sliding peg　スライディング・ペッグ
the peg to the U.S. dollar　米ドルに合わせた通貨基準の設定,米ドルへの連動,対ドル固定相場制
◆China has ended the yuan's peg to the U.S. dollar. 中国は、対ドル固定相場制を廃止した。◆The 11-year peg to the dollar was long seen as a cure for chronic inflation. 11年間続いたドルへの連動制は、長いこと慢性的なインフレの救済策と見られた。

pegging　(名)釘付け,安定操作,釘付け政策
exchange pegging　為替の釘付け
exchange pegging policy　為替釘付け政策
pegging operation　釘付け操作,安定操作
pegging or fixing prices of securities　作為的相場形成
pegging policy　釘付け政策

penalty　(名)処罰,処分,罰金,違約金,延滞金,反則金,制裁金,制裁,罰則,刑罰,ペナルティ
increased penalties　罰則強化
newly installed penalty　罰則の新設
pecuniary penalty　罰金刑,罰金
penalties against insider trading　インサイダー取引に対する罰則
penalty charge　遅延損害金,違約金
penalty interest　遅延利息
penalty rate　延滞金利
penalty tax　追徴課税,加算税
◆According to the Financial Instruments and Exchange Law, penalties for making false securities reports are tightened from up to five years in prison to up to 10 years in prison. 金融取引法によれば、有価証券報告書の虚偽記載の刑罰は、懲役5年以下から懲役10年以下に引き上げられている。◆Financial authorities should stiffen the penalties for illegal transactions to protect the financial system from rumors and speculative investment. 金融当局は違法取引(違法行為)に対する罰則を強化して、金融システムを風評や投機[投機的投資]から守らなければならない。◆Penalties against insider trading and market manipulation have been strengthened. インサイダー取引や相場操縦などに対する罰則が、強化された。◆These disciplinary measures include increased penalties on securities fraud and a newly installed penalty on corporate directors in cases of failure to submit adequate financial reports to authorities. これらの懲戒処分には、証券詐欺に対する罰則の強化や、当局に適切な財務報告をしなかった場合の企業取締役に対する罰則の新設などが含まれている。

pension　(名)年金　(⇒basic pension, corporate pension, national pension)
basic pension plan　基礎年金
corporate employees' pension insurance plan　厚生年金保険
corporate pension　企業年金

disparities between public and private sector pensions　官と民の年金格差
government pension　政府年金, 恩給
group pension　団体年金
mutual aid pension　共済年金
national pension　国民年金
noncontributory old-age pension　老齢福祉年金
Pension Benefit Guaranty Corporation　米年金給付保証公社
personal pension policy　個人年金
survivor's mutual aid pension　遺族共済年金
◆Just as the number of people qualifying for pensions is on the rise, the working population, which underpins the pension scheme, is on the decline. 年金受給の資格者は増える一方、年金制度を支える現役世代は減っている。◆The issue of eliminating disparities between public and private sector pensions hinges on how quickly the gaps should be closed. 官と民の年金格差[年金の官民格差]是正の問題は、いかに早くその溝を埋めるかにかかっている。

pension age　年金の支払い開始年齢
◆The compilation of fiscal rehabilitation measures including raising the pension age is imperative for the Italian parliament. 年金受給年齢の引上げなどを含む財政再建策のとりまとめが、イタリア議会の急務となっている。◆The Greek government will raise the national pension age. ギリシャ政府は、国民年金の支払い開始年齢を引き上げる方針だ。

pension asset　年金資産
◆About ¥21 billion in pension assets belonging to more than 80,000 subscribers to defined-contribution pension plans were left unmanaged as of March 2007. 2007年3月末現在で、8万人を超える確定拠出年金加入者の年金資産約210億円が、運用されないままになっている。

pension asset management results　年金資産の運用実績
◆The executives of AIJ Investment Advisors Co. are suspected of falsifying pension asset management results for years. 投資顧問会社「AIJ投資顧問」の幹部は、長年にわたって年金資産の運用実績を偽った疑いがある。

pension benefits　年金給付, 受取年金, 退職年金給付（=pension payments; ⇒pension reserve fund）
◆In addition to pension benefits, the Corporation and its subsidiary companies provide certain health care and life insurance benefits for retired employees. 当社と当社の子会社は、年金給付のほかに、退職者を対象に医療給付と生命保険給付を提供しています。◆The demographic changes show the inevitability of raising pension premiums unless pension benefits are reduced in the future. この人口構造の変化は、年金給付を今後減額しない限り、年金保険料の引上げは必至であることを示している。◆The instability of the pension system has repeatedly experienced increases in pension premiums and decreases in pension benefits. 年金制度が不安定なため、年金保険料の負担増と年金給付減が繰り返されてきた。◆Under a variable pension system, pension benefits change in accordance with fluctuations in government bond yield. 変額年金制度では、国債利回りの変動で年金給付額が変わる。

pension contributions　年金拠出額
◆Pension contributions are principally determined using the aggregate cost method. 年金拠出額は、基本的に総額原価法を用いて決定される。

pension cost　年金費用, 年金原価, 年金コスト（=pension expense; ⇒pension liability）
◆The net U.S. pension cost for the elected officers' supplemental retirement benefit plan was $27 million in 2010. 選任役員の追加的退職給付制度に対する米国内の純年金費用は、2010年度は2,700万ドルでした。

pension defaulter　年金未納者
◆Most of the pension defaulters have bought life insurance or personal pension policies. 年金未納者の大半は、生命保険や個人年金に入っている。

pension eligibility age　年金の支給開始年齢, 年金受給年齢
◆The Democratic Party of Japan will postpone a plan to raise the pension eligibility age. 民主党は、年金の支給開始年齢を引き上げる案の実施を見送る方針だ。

pension expense　年金費用　（=pension cost）
◆Increases in salaries, wages, and depreciation expenses were partially offset by lower pension expenses and by the effect of the strike. 給料・賃金と減価償却費の増加分は、年金費用の減少とストの効果[影響]で一部相殺されています。

pension fund　年金基金, 年金資金, 年金積立金（=pension payout）
employee's [employees'] pension fund　従業員年金基金, 厚生年金基金
investment management for pension funds　年金基金の運用
pension fund investment　年金積立金の運用
pension fund reserve　年金基金積立金
◆The compensation to the individual was taken care of largely out of our pension fund. 個人に支払われた退職金は、主に当社の年金基金から拠出しました。◆Western pension funds actively bought Japanese stocks. 欧州の年金基金が、積極的に日本株を購入した。

Pension Fund Association　企業年金連合会
◆The Pension Fund Association was found not to have paid a total of ¥154.4 billion in pension benefits to 1.24 million pension subscribers. 企業年金連合会が、年金加入者124万人に対して計1,544億円の年金を未払いにしていることが分かった。

pension fund investment foundation　年金資金運用基金
◆The pension fund investment foundation, a public corporation under the jurisdiction of the Health, Labor and Welfare Ministry, lost ¥834.3 billion in pension funds it invested during the April-June quarter. 厚生労働省所管特殊法人の年金資金運用基金は、2002年4-6月期の年金運用（公的年金積立金の運用）で8,343億円の赤字となった。

pension fund plan　厚生年金基金, 企業年金（制度）
◆The Pension Fund Association manages about ¥9.9 trillion in pension funds for employees pension fund plans. 厚生年金基金連合会[企業年金連合会]は、厚生年金基金[企業年金]の年金資金約9兆9,000億円を運用している。

pension-indexing system　年金物価スライド制
◆The government intends to effectively lower pension payments by reintroducing a pension-indexing system that ties pension levels to prices. 政府は、年金の給付水準（給付額）を物価指数の変動に連動させる「年金物価スライド制」を再導入して、年金給付額を引き下げる方針だ。

pension insurance policy　年金保険
◆Nippon Life Insurance Co. lowered the yields of its single-premium pension insurance policies and other products. 日本生命保険が、一時払いの年金保険など保険商品の利回りを引き下げた。

pension insurance sales　年金保険の販売
◆Mizuho Financial Group Inc. enjoyed healthy nonfinancial earnings such as commissions on pension insurance sales. みずほフィナンシャルグループは、年金保険の販売手数料など、（貸出金以外の）非金利収入が好調だった。

pension liability　年金債務, 年金負債（⇒pension plan assets）
◆The prepaid pension costs are net of pension liabilities for plans where accumulated plan benefits exceed assets. この前払い年金費用は、累積給付債務額が資産額を超過している場合の年金債務純額を控除したものです。

pension obligations　年金債務, 年金債務額
◆The fair value of our pension plan assets is greater than our projected pension obligations. 当社の年金制度資産の公正価額は、予想年金債務額を上回っています。

pension payment　年金給付, 年金支給
（⇒pensioner）

pension payments　年金支給額, 年金給付, 年金給付額
（⇒pension scheme, public pension payments）
◆In these deflationary times, putting the pension payments on hold is tantamount to increasing them. このデフレ時代に、年金支給額の据え置きはその増額に等しい。◆In times of inflation, pension payments increased in step with price increases. インフレの時代は、物価の上昇に伴って年金支給額も上昇した。◆The current level of pension payments, which cover more than 90 percent of average monthly consumption by senior citizens, are too high. 高齢者の平均消費月額の9割以上もカバーしている現在の年金の給付水準は、高すぎる。◆The sliding scale system for pension payments is aimed at guaranteeing pensioners the real value of their pension payment. 年金支給額の物価スライド制の目的は、年金受給者に年金支給の実質的な価値を保証することにある。

pension payout　年金の支払い
◆Under the defined-contribution annuity scheme, workers who will receive pension payouts in the future decide how the pension fund is invested. 確定拠出年金制度では、将来年金の支払いを受ける従業員が年金積立金の運用方法を決める。

pension plan　年金制度
（=pension scheme, pension system）
　basic pension plan　基礎年金制度, 基礎年金
　company-run pension plan　企業年金制度
　defined benefit (pension) plan　確定給付制度, 給付建て制度, 給付建て年金制度
　defined contribution pension plan　拠出建て年金制度
　employee pension benefit plan　従業員年金給付制度
　employee pension plan　従業員年金制度
　funded pension plan　年金基金制
　insured pension plan　保険型年金, 企業年金保険
　liability under pension plan　未払い年金債務
　pension plan for company employees　厚生年金
　　(=company employees' pension plan, corporate employees' pension insurance plan)
　pension plan obligation　年金制度債務
　pension plan trust fund　年金信託基金
　public pension plan　公的年金制度
　qualified pension plan　適格年金制度
　the cost of pension plans　年金制度原価
　the operation of a pension plan　年金制度の運用, 年金制度の運営
◆In the United States, financial forecasts for pension plans are compiled every year. 米国では、年金財政予測（年金制度の財政予測）が毎年作成されている。◆It is extremely unusual for a company to take action against the government over company-run pension plans. 企業年金制度をめぐって企業が行政を訴えるのは、極めて異例だ。

pension plan assets　年金制度資産, 年金資産
（⇒pension obligations）
◆Our pension plan assets are earning a return that exceeds the growth in pension liabilities. 当社の年金制度資産は、年金債務の増大を上回る収益を上げています。

pension-points plan　年金ポイント制
◆Under the German pension-points plan, pension subscribers aged 27 or older are in principle notified annually of their points earned. ドイツの年金ポイント制では、原則として27歳以上の年金加入者に毎年、獲得ポイント数（加入時からの納付実績を示す点数）を通知している。

pension premium　年金保険料（現行では、月収の17.35%＝年収ベースで13.5%を労使折半）
◆Company employees' pension premiums are automatically deducted from their monthly salaries. サラリーマンの厚生年金保険料は、月給から天引きされる[自動的に差し引かれる]。◆Currently, corporate employees do not have to pay pension premiums during their first year of child-care leave. 現在、会社員は、育児休業の最初の1年間は年金保険料の納付を免除されている。◆Full-time housewives of company employees and public servants are not required to pay pension premiums. 会社員や公務員の専業主婦は、保険料を払う必要がない。◆Pension premiums of full-time housewives of company employees and public servants are automatically covered by payments made by all subscribers to welfare and mutual pension plans. 会社員や公務員の専業主婦の年金保険料は、厚生年金や共済年金の加入者全員の支払い金で自動的にカバーすることになっている。◆The demographic changes show the inevitability of raising pension premiums unless pension benefits are reduced in the future. この人口構造の変化は、年金給付を今後減額しない限り、年金保険料の引上げは必至であることを示している。◆The instability of the pension system has repeatedly experienced increases in pension premiums and decreases in pension benefits. 年金制度が不安定なため、年金保険料の負担増と年金給付減が繰り返されてきた。

pension premium rate　年金保険料率
◆If the birthrate continues to decline at the current pace, the pension premium rate will have to rise to 24.8 percent of an employee's annual salary from fiscal 2025. 少子化が現在のペースで進んだ場合、（厚生年金の）保険料率は、2025年度から従業員の年収の24.8%に引き上げる必要がある。

pension program　年金制度
◆The French government obliges foreigners in the country to subscribe to their pension program. 仏政府は、同国内に滞在・就労する外国人に年金への加入を義務付けている。

pension reserve fund　年金積立金
◆Operational revenue from the ￥150 trillion pension reserve fund has been used to fill the gap between increasing pension benefits and declining revenues. 年金給付費の伸びと年金保険料の収入減とのギャップを埋めるのに、150兆円の年金積立金の運用益が充てられている。

pension scheme　年金制度, 年金供給協定
（=pension plan, pension system）
　approved pension scheme　適格年金制度
　company employees' pension scheme　厚生年金制度, 厚生年金　(=company employees' pension system)
　occupational pension scheme　従業員年金制度
◆If the birthrate keeps falling at the current pace, it will be necessary to increase premiums for company employees' pension schemes from the current 13 percent of the subscriber's annual salary to 24.8 percent to maintain the current level of pension payments. 少子化が現状のペースで進んだ場合、現在の年金給付水準を維持するには、厚生年金保険料は加入者の年収の現行13%から24.8%に引き上げる必要がある。◆Under the company employees' pension scheme, subscribing is mandatory for all firms with five or more employees. 厚生年金制度では、従業員5人以上の法人すべてに加入が義務付けられている。

pension subscriber　年金加入者
　Class-III pension subscriber　第3号被保険者
　national and company employees' pension subscribers　国民年金と厚生年金の加入者
◆National and company employees' pension subscribers will have to pay more than twice the current premiums from fiscal 2025 if the nation's birthrate continues to decline. 日

本の少子化がこのまま続くと、国民年金と厚生年金の加入者は、2025年度から現在の保険料の2倍以上も支払わなければならなくなる。◆The Pension Fund Association was found not to have paid a total of ¥154.4 billion in pension benefits to 1.24 million pension subscribers. 企業年金連合会が、年金加入者124万人に対して計1,544億円の年金を未払いにしていることが分かった。

pension subscription period　年金加入期間
◆In France, the government adds two years to the pension subscription period of women who have children. フランスでは、子どもを養育している女性の年金加入期間は2年分が加算される。

pension system　年金制度, 年金システム
（=pension plan, pension scheme）
　pension system reform　年金改革, 年金制度の改革
　state-funded portion of pension system　年金の国庫負担分
　the public pension system　公的年金制度, 公的年金
◆Germany has incorporated official child-raising assistance policies into its pension system since 1990s. ドイツは、1990年代から、政府の育児支援政策をドイツの年金制度に組み込んでいる。◆Public distrust in the pension system must be prevented from deepening. 年金制度への国民の不信感は、これ以上深まらないようにしなければならない。◆The distrust of the pension system is gradually spreading among young people. 年金不信が、次第に若者に広がっている。◆The hollowing-out of the pension system may increase companies' personnel costs so much that it could negatively affect their international competitive edge. 年金の空洞化で人件費が上昇し、国際競争力に悪影響を及ぼす恐れがある。◆The pension system may collapse before people qualify as beneficiaries. 年金をもらう前に、年金制度が崩壊する可能性がある。◆To stabilize the pension system, the government raised its burden in the basic pension plan to 50 percent of the total contribution from fiscal 2009. 年金制度の安定化を図るため、政府は、基礎年金の国の負担割合を2009年度から総給付金の50%に引き上げた。◆Under the current Japanese pension system for company employees, employees and employers each pay half of the insurance premiums worth 17.35 percent of the employee's monthly salary, or 13.58 percent of their annual income. 日本の現在の厚生年金保険制度では、従業員と企業がそれぞれ月収の17.35%（年収ベースで13.58%）の保険料を半分ずつ負担している。

pensioner　（名）年金受給者, 年金生活者
◆The sliding scale system for pension payments is aimed at guaranteeing pensioners the real value of their pension payment. 年金支給額の物価スライド制の目的は、年金受給者に年金支給の実質的な価値を保証することにある。

People's Bank dollar　中国元

People's Bank of China　（中国の中央銀行に当たる）中国人民銀行, 中国中央銀行, PBOC
（⇒time deposit）
◆The People's Bank of China aims to restrain an excessive use of funds by businesses and lead the economy in the direction of sustainable economic growth. 中国人民銀行が目指しているのは、企業による資金の過剰使用の抑制と中国経済の持続可能な経済成長への誘導だ。◆The People's Bank of China raised deposit reserve ratio by 0.5 percentage points. 中国人民銀行（中央銀行）は、預金準備率を0.5%引き上げた。◆The People's Bank of China raised interest rates on loans by financial institutions to corporations and individuals. 中国人民銀行が、金融機関の企業や個人に対する貸出金利を引き上げた。

PER　株価収益率　（=P/E ratio:price earnings ratioの略。⇒P/E [p/e], price earnings ratio）
　interest-rate-adjusted PER　金利修正PER
　prospective PER　予想株価収益率, 予想PER

per annum　1年当たり, 1年に付き, 1年毎に, 年, 毎年, 年間, 年率
　a per annum rate　年利
　five percent per annum GDP growth　GDPの年成長率5%
　income per annum　年間所得
　ten percent per annum　年10%, 年率10%
　the current official discount rate　現行の公定歩合
◆The current official discount rate of 0.1 percent per annum is expected to be raised to between 0.35 percent and 0.5 percent. 年0.1%の現行の公定歩合は、0.35〜0.5%程度に引き上げられる見通しだ。◆The federal funds rate, a benchmark short-term interest rate, was cut to 3.5 percent per annum and the official discount rate to 3 percent per annum. 短期金利の誘導目標であるフェデラル・ファンド（FF）金利は年3.5%、公定歩合は年3%に引き下げられた。◆The yield on the benchmark 10-year U.S. government bond closed at 2.91 percent per annum Tuesday, 0.05 percentage points lower than Monday's finish. 長期金利の指標となる10年物米国債の流通利回り［利回り］は火曜日、前日終値比で0.05%低い年2.91%で取引を終えた。

per capita　1人当たり
◆Last year, our employee per capita operating profit reached 57 million yen. 当社の昨年の従業員1人当たり営業利益は、5,700万円に達しています。

per dollar　1ドル当たり, 1ドルに付き, 対ドルで
◆In the case of foreign currency deposits by the U.S. dollar, many online banks charge about ¥0.25 in commission per dollar at the time of deposits and withdrawals. 米ドルによる外貨預金の場合、ネット銀行の多くは、預け入れ時と解約時に1ドルに付き25銭程度の手数料を取る。◆The exchange rate in fiscal 2011 had been predicted to be between ¥80 and ¥83 per dollar by many Japanese exporters. 2011年度の為替レートを、多くの日本の輸出業者は1ドル＝80〜83円と想定していた。

per share　1株当たり
　assets per share　1株当たり資産額
　book value per share　1株当たり簿価
　dividend per share　1株当たり配当
　fully diluted earnings per share　潜在株式調整後1株当たり利益
　net loss per share　1株当たり純損失
　net profit per share　1株当たり純利益
　price per share　1株当たり株価
◆Price-to-book value is obtained by dividing price per share by assets per share. 株価純資産倍率は、1株当たり株価を1株当たりの資産額で割って［除して］求められます。◆The Corporation's net profit per share in the April-September first half of fiscal 2011 year came to ¥19.95 from ¥34.05 a year before. 当社の2011年度上期（4〜9月期）の1株当たり純利益は、前年同期の34円5銭に対して19円95銭だった。◆The firm will issue 20.5 million common shares at a price of ¥222 per share. 同社は、1株当たり222円で［222円の価格で］普通株式2,050万株を発行する。◆The foreign funds purchased the convertible bonds at prices equivalent to ¥25 per share. 海外ファンドは、1株25円で転換社債を引き受けた。

per share amounts　1株当たりの金額
◆All references to shares outstanding, dividends and per share amounts have been adjusted on a retroactive basis. 発行済み株式数と配当、1株当たりの金額については、すべて過去に遡及して調整してあります。

per-share group net profit　1株当たり連結純利益
◆Per-share group net profit plunged to ¥85.95 from the preceding fiscal year's ¥37,983.95. 1株当たり連結純利益は、前年度の37,983円95銭から85円95銭に激減した。

per-share net loss　1株当たり純損失
- Per-share net loss came to ¥77.92 in a sharp downswing from a profit of ¥10.06 the previous year. 1株当たり純損失は、前期の10.06円の利益から急落して77.92円となった。

perceive　(動)感じる、認める、理解する、知覚する、～が～だと分かる、～に気付く
- The Bank of Japan's diffusion indexes are calculated by subtracting the percentage of companies reporting deterioration in business conditions from those perceiving improvement. 日銀のこれらの業況判断指数(DI)は、現在の景況感について「改善している」と感じている企業の割合から「悪化している」と回答した企業の割合を差し引いて算出する。

percent〔per cent〕　(名)百分率、率、％、パーセント
- a policy of virtually zero-percent interest rates　事実上ゼロ金利の政策
- at LIBOR plus 7/8%　LIBOR (ロンドン銀行間取り手金利)+[プラス]0.875％で
- from 10+% to 10%　10％超から10％まで
- on a 50 percent basis　掛け目50％で
- one hundred percent balance sheet　百分率貸借対照表
- percent depreciated　償却累計率
- percent distribution　構成比
- percent of capacity use　稼働率
- percent of quota met　消化率、ノルマ達成率
- percent of the aged population　老齢化率
- percent per annum　年％
- percents　利付き債券、公債

- Only 35.8 percent of the leading companies have already adopted defensive measures against a hostile takeover. 敵対的M&Aに対する防衛策を導入しているのは、主要企業の35.8％にすぎない。
- The deflator, which indicates the overall trend in prices, dropped 2.5 percent in the April-June period compared to the corresponding period last year. 物価の総合的な動向を示すデフレーターは、4-6月期は前年同期比で2.5％下落した。
- The Financial Stability Board will impose a progressive extra capital charge of 1 percent to 2.5 percent on risk-adjusted assets held by G-SIFIs. G20 (主要20か国・地域)の金融当局で構成する金融安定化理事会(FSB)は、国際金融システムにとって重要な金融機関(G-SIFIs)が保有するリスク調整後資産に、1～2.5％の資本[自己資本]の上積みを段階的に課すことになった。
- The 10-year JGB yield sank below the 1 percent threshold. 新発10年物の日本国債の流通利回りが、1％割れの水準まで低下した。
- The U.S. Federal Reserve Board has been maintaining a policy of virtually zero-percent interest rates. 米連邦準備制度理事会(FRB)は、事実上ゼロ金利の政策を維持してきた。
- Under the new financing scheme, the IMF will extend to financially strapped countries loans of up to 500 percent of their contribution to the IMF. 新融資制度では、財政の資金繰りが苦しく[厳しく]なった国に対して、その国がIMF (国際通貨基金)に出資している額の最大5倍までIMFが融資する。

percentage　(名)比率、割合、部分、分け前、歩合[歩合制]、百分率、利益、利点、得、パーセント
- actuarial annual percentage rate　実質年利
- annual percentage rate　実質年率
- as percentages of total revenues　総収益[総売上高]に対する比率[百分率]
- bad debt loss percentage　回収不能率
- external debt stock percentages　対外債務残高の比率
- gross margin [profit] percentage　粗利益率
- net income (loss) as a percentage of revenues　純利益(損失)率
- nonperforming loan percentage　不稼動債権の比率
- percentage achievement　達成率
- percentage basis　(株式相場の)100ドル建て
- percentage change　変化率、百分率変化
- percentage distribution　構成比
- percentage growth　百分率成長(パーセントで示した伸び率)
- percentage held　所有比率
- percentage of capital structure　資本構成比率
- percentage profit on turnover　売上高利益率
- the percentage of any one risk　いずれかの契約の一定割合
- the percentage of appraised value that may be loaned　担保掛け目
- total debt as a percentage of total capitalization　資本総額に対する債務総額の比率

- As the lead bank in the construction project, the bank will cover more than a certain percentage of the joint loan to the Canadian corporation. この建設プロジェクトの主幹事銀行として、同行はカナダ企業への協調融資のうち一定割合以上を融資する。
- The Bank of Japan's diffusion indexes are calculated by subtracting the percentage of companies reporting deterioration in business conditions from those perceiving improvement. 日銀のこれらの業況判断指数(DI)は、現在の景況感について「改善している」と感じている企業の割合から「悪化している」と回答した企業の割合を差し引いて算出する。
- The business sentiment index represents the percentage of companies reporting favorable business conditions minus the percentage of those reporting unfavorable conditions. 業況判断指数は、景気が良いと答えた企業の割合(％)から景気が悪いと答えた企業の割合(％)を差し引いた指数だ。
- The diffusion index (DI) of business confidence refers to the percentage of companies that feel business conditions to be favorable, minus the ratio of firms that think otherwise. 業況判断指数(DI)は、景気が「良い」と感じている企業の割合(％)から、「悪い」と感じている企業の割合を差し引いた指数だ。
- The percentage of government funds from the consumption tax and other tax revenues for financing the basic pension plan remains about 36.5 percent. 基礎年金の財源としての消費税収などによる国の負担金の割合は、まだ約36.5％にとどまっている。
- Total debt as a percentage of total capitalization was 20 percent at yearend 2010. 資本総額に対する債務総額の比率は、2010年末現在で20％だった。

percentage limitation　組入れ限度、組入れ上限、割合限界
- percentage limitation on equity content　組入れ上限比率
- percentage limitation on single stock exposure　同一銘柄株式の組入れ限度

percentage point　パーセント・ポイント、ポイント、パーセンテージ・ポイント
(one percentage point=1パーセント)
- a quarter of a percentage point　0.25％、0.25ポイント
- half a percentage point　0.5％、0.5ポイント
- 6 percentage point　6％、6ポイント

- Funds raised through the three percentage point increase in the consumption tax are regarded as special purpose revenue to be used exclusively for the reconstruction programs. 消費税の3％引上げで調達する資金は、もっぱら(震災)復興計画に充てられる特別目的税と考えられている。
- The Bank of Japan lowered its key interest rate by 0.2 percentage points to 0.1 percent. 日銀は、政策金利を0.2ポイント下げて0.1％とした。
- The European Central Bank raised its key interest rate by a quarter of a percentage point to 2.25 percent. 欧州中央銀行(ECB)は、主要政策金利を0.25％引き上げて年2.25％とした。
- The jobless rate dipped by 0.2 percentage points to 5.3 percent in January compared with the previous month. 1月の完全失業率は、前月より0.2ポイント低下して、5.3％となっ

た。◆The People's Bank of China raised deposit reserve ratio by 0.5 percentage points. 中国人民銀行(中央銀行)は、預金準備率を0.5%引き上げた。◆The spreads of yields on high-risk junk bonds over the benchmark five-year U.S. Treasury bonds had been around 200 basis points, or 2 percentage points. リスクの高いジャンク債と指標となる5年物財務省証券との金利差(スプレッド)は、2%(200ベーシス・ポイント)程度で推移していた。◆The unemployment rate in July climbed to a postwar high of 5.7 percent, up 0.3 percentage point from the previous month. 7月(2009年)の完全失業率は、前月より0.3ポイント悪化して5.7%となり、戦後最悪を更新した。◆The U.S. Federal Reserve raised the official discount rate and the target rate of federal funds by 0.25 percentage points in a bid to quell inflation and keep the economy from overheating. 米連邦準備制度理事会(FRB)は、インフレを防ぎ景気の過熱を警戒して、公定歩合とフェデラル・ファンド(FF)の誘導目標金利をそれぞれ0.25パーセント引き上げた。

解説 percentとpercentage pointの違いとは:percentは比率のパーセントで、percentage pointは絶対数のパーセントを表す。例えば、年率10%の物価上昇率が10パーセント伸びた場合は、年率11%の伸び率になる。一方、年率10%の物価上昇率が10パーセント・ポイント伸びた場合は、年率20%の伸び率になる。

percentile (名)百分順位, 百分位数, パーセンタイル (50 percentile = 中央値(median))
 earn a percentile of 80　80パーセンタイルにランクされる
 have a higher percentile ranking　パーセンタイルによるランキングは高い位置にある
 10th percentile performance　10パーセンタイルにランクされるパフォーマンス

perfected security interest　対抗力[対抗要件]を具備した担保権, 対抗力[対抗要件]を具備した動産担保権
 first-perfected security interest　対効力を具備した第一順位動産担保権
 first priority, perfected security interest　対抗力[対抗要件]を具備した第一順位担保権

perfection (名)対抗力の具備, 対抗要件の具備
 perfection of a first security interest in the collateral　担保となる有価証券の第一順位動産担保権の対抗力具備[対抗要件具備]
 perfection of the interest　対抗力の具備, 対抗要件の具備

performance (名)実績, 業績, 成果, 義務・債務の履行, 実行, 実施, 遂行, 運用, 運用成績実演, 上演, 動向, 値動き, 性能, パフォーマンス (⇒business performance, corporate performance, shareholders' assets, shareholders' meeting)
 after-market performance　公開後の値動き
 business performance　業績 (=business results)
 consolidated performance　連結決算
 corporate performance　企業業績, 会社の業績
 cost performance　コスト効率, 対原価性能比
 earnings performance　利益実績, 業績
 economic performance　景気動向, 経済実績
 export performance　輸出実績
 financial performance　財務状態, 業績
 good performance　好調な業績, 好業績 (=strong performance)
 inflation performance　インフレ動向
 investment performance　投資実績, 運用実績
 job performance　職務遂行, 職務能力
 management performance　経営実績, 運用実績
 market performance　市場成果, 相場の動き
 operating performance　業績
 performance bond　保証証券, 履行保証, 契約履行保証
 performance indicator　業績指標
 poor performance　業績悪化, 業績低下, 業績不振, 業績低迷
 price performance　値動き, インフレ動向
 product performance　製品成果, 製品性能
 profit performance　収益性, 利益率, 利益実現, 利潤成果
 share price performance　株価パフォーマンス, 株価の値動き, 株価動向
 sluggish performance　業績不振
 stable performance　安定した実績, 安定した業績, 安定運用
 stock performance　株価の値動き, 株価パフォーマンス (=share price performance, stock price performance)
 strong performance　際立った業績, 好調な業績, 好業績
 trade performance　貿易実績, 貿易動向, 貿易収支
◆Among industrialized countries, the Japanese economy had the weakest performance last year. 先進国の中で、昨年は日本経済が最もパフォーマンスが弱かった。◆In the life insurance sector, the practice of luring customers by touting the bad performances of other insurers has been called into question. 生保業界では、他社の経営不振をあおって顧客を勧誘する行為(風評営業)が問題になっている。◆The firm that best represents the brisk performances of Japanese companies is Toyota Motor Corp. 日本企業の好業績の代表格は、トヨタ自動車だ。◆The government provides subsidies to firms that hire workers between the ages of 45 and 59 from poor-performance companies. 政府は、業績不振の企業から43〜59歳の中高年労働者を雇い入れている企業に、助成金を出している。◆The major banks attributed their increased bad loans to the poor performance of their borrowers due to the prolonged economic slump and Financial Service Agency inspections resulting in a stricter review of their asset assessments. 大手銀行は、不良債権が増えた理由として、長引く景気低迷で貸出先の経営が悪化したことと、金融庁の検査を受けて大手行が資産査定を厳しくしたことを挙げた。◆These firms' performance has rapidly improved thanks to the recent boom on the Tokyo Stock Exchange. これら各社の業績は、最近の東京株式市場の活況を背景に急速に回復した。

performance of corporations　企業業績
◆New nonperforming loans have been generated because of the deteriorating performance of corporations and deflation. 企業業績の悪化とデフレで、新たな不良債権が発生している。

performance target　業績目標
◆It is not easy to extend new loans to a company that has failed to meet performance targets. これまで実績のない企業に新規融資をするのは、難しい。

period (名)期間, 時期, 局面, 〜期, 年度, 年数, 会計期間, 会計年度, 事業年度, ピリオド (⇒accounting period)
 amortization period　元本償還期間, 元利払い期間
 April-June period　4-6月期
 at fixed period after date　日付後定期払い
 at fixed period after sight　一覧後定期払い
 base period　基準年度
 beginning of the period　期首
 claim period　請求期間
 cooling-off period　クーリング・オフ期間
 current period　当事業年度, 当期
 exercise period　権利行使期間
 fiscal period　会計期間, 会計年度 (=accounting period)
 for an extensive period　長期間
 grace period　猶予期間, 保険料払込み猶予期間, 据え置

き期間
interest period　金利期間
investment holding period　投資期間
　（=holding period）
investment period　投資期間
July-September period　7-9月期
limitation period　出訴期限
over the periods estimated to be benefited　その効果が及ぶと見込まれる期間にわたって（⇒goodwill）
over the same period last year　前年同期比で
payment period　返済期間
performance period　当該期間
period benefited　利益発生期間
period under review　当期
phase-in period　経過期間
portfolio period　資産運用成績
pricing period　価格設定期間
prior period　過去の事業年度, 過年度, 前期
production period　生産期間, 製造期間
purchases for the period　当期仕入高
quarterly period　四半期
settlement period　決済期間
share price performance　株価動向, 株価の値動き, 株価パフォーマンス
subscription period　募集期間, 販売期間
test period　検討対象期間
the last period of settlement of accounts　最終決算期
wind-down period　元利払い期間

◆In this cofinancing scheme, the bank will extend a total of about ¥8.5 billion over a 20-year loan period. この協調融資事業で, 同行は貸出期間20年で約85億円を融資する。◆In wrap accounts, a customer sets the overall investment policy, including investment period and profit target. ラップ口座では、顧客が投資期間や運用益の目標などの大まかな運用方針を決める。◆The company's auditing firm approved the firm's accounting for the suspected periods. 同社の監査法人は、問題となっている時期の同社の決算処理を承認していた。◆The deflator, which indicates the overall trend in prices, dropped 2.5 percent in the April-June period compared to the corresponding period last year. 物価の総合的な動向を示すデフレーターは、4-6月期は前年同期比で2.5％下落した。◆The firm posted a pretax profit of ¥30 billion for the April-September period. 同社の4-9月期の税引き前利益は、300億円となった。◆The longest period of postwar economic expansion was known as an economic boom without feeling. 戦後最長の景気回復は、実感なき景気回復と言われた。◆Those housewives who have failed to switch to the national pension plan and have not paid premiums for an extensive period may receive a pittance or nothing at all. 国民年金への切替えをせず、保険料を長期間払っていない主婦は、低年金や無年金になる可能性がある。

period ending Aug. 31　6-8月期, 6-8月期決算
◆Quarterly profit for the period ending Aug. 31 rose to $2.85 billion, or $6.13 per share, compared to $1.55 billion, or $3.26 per share, a year earlier. 6-8月期決算の四半期利益は、前年同期の15億5,000万ドル（1株当たり3.26ドル）に対して、28億5,000万ドル（1株当たり6.13ドル）に増加しました。

period of business suspension　業務停止期間
◆During the period of business suspension, the company is not allowed to extend new loans, solicit new customers or call in loans. 業務停止期間中、同社は新規の融資や新規顧客の勧誘、貸出の回収などの業務はできない。

period of economic stagnation　景気低迷期, 景気停滞期, 景気後退期
◆The lost decade refers to the period of economic stagnation since the bursting of the economic bubble in the early 1990s. 「失われた10年」とは、バブルが崩壊した1990年代初めから続いた景気後退［景気停滞］期のことである。

periodic　(形)定期的な, 周期的な, 期間の
　pay periodic amounts　定期的に支払う
　periodic fixed payments and floating payments　定期的固定額支払いおよび変動額支払い
　periodic income　期間利益, 期間収益
　periodic payment　定期的支払い
　periodic pension costs　期間年金費用, 毎期の年金費用

peripheral member states [countries, nations]　周辺加盟国
◆Some of the peripheral member nations of the eurozone were already insolvent. ユーロ圏の周辺加盟国の一部は、すでに債務返済不能の状態だった。

perishables　(名)生鮮食料品

permanent　(形)永続する, 永久的な, 永遠の, 不変の, 恒久の, 恒常的, 長期的, 耐久性のある, 常任の, 終身の, 終身雇用の, 常設の
　permanent asset　永久資産, 固定資産, 土地
　permanent consumption　恒常消費
　permanent debt　永久公債, 永久債, 長期国債, 長期公債
　permanent differences　永久差異, 永久差異項目
　permanent discount restricted stock purchase plan　永久割引制限付き株式購入制度
　permanent disequilibrium　永続的不均衡
　permanent document　永久証券, 永久証書
　permanent effect　永続の効果
　permanent equilibrium　永続的均衡
　permanent financing　長期的資金調達, 長期資本, 永久資本
　permanent financing requirement　長期的な資金調達必要額
　permanent interest bearing share　永久利付き持ち分証券
　permanent investment　長期投資, 永久的［恒久的］投資, 永久証券
　permanent liabilities　長期負債, 永久負債
　permanent life insurance　終身生命保険
　permanent loan　長期不動産抵当貸付け, 長期融資, パーマネント・ローン
　permanent normal trade relations　恒久的最恵国待遇, PNTR
　permanent pension　終身年金
　permanent preferred stock　永久優先株
　permanent property　固定資産
　permanent savings　恒常貯蓄
　permanent top　大天井
◆The Corporation has established permanent committees of the board of directors to permit continuing review of the areas of auditing, management resources and compensation, pension fund policy, and investment. 当社は、監査、役員人事・報酬、年金基金対策と投資の各分野に関する検討を継続的に行うため、常設の取締役会付属委員会を設置しています。

permanent income　恒常所得, 長期的な所得
　permanent income expectations　長期的な所得に対する予想, 長期所得予想
　permanent income stream　恒常所得の流れ, 恒常所得流列

persist　(動)続ける, 貫く, 押し通す, 固執する, 言い張る, 言い続ける, 持続する, 存続する, 残存する

◆The move to lower the yields of insurance products is likely to spread through the industry as tough investment conditions persist. 厳しい運用環境が続いているので、保険商品の利回りを引き下げる動きは、業界全体に広がりそうだ。
◆Uncertainty about the future of Japan's financial system will persist until the vulnerable financial foundation of life insurance companies is rectified. 生命保険会社の脆弱(ぜいじゃく)な経営基盤を立て直さない限り、日本の金融システムの先行きに対する不安は消えない。

persistent (形)しつこい、執拗(しつよう)な、根強い、繰り返し起こる、慢性的な、長引く、永続する、持続性の、絶え間ない、粘り強い、頑固な、常緑の、落葉しない、消滅しない、分解しにくい
　persistent credit concerns　根強い信用不安
　persistent current account surplus　経常収支の慢性的な黒字
　persistent deflation　しつこいデフレ、長引くデフレ、持続的デフレ
　persistent dumping　継続的ダンピング
　persistent efforts　絶えざる努力、粘り強い努力
　persistent inflation　頑固なインフレ、長引くインフレ、持続的インフレ
　persistent recession　長引く不況
　persistent salesperson　しつこい販売員[セールスマン]
　persistent worker　不屈の労働者
◆It is uncertain when the nation's persistent deflation will come to an end. 日本のしつこいデフレがいつ終わるのかは、不透明だ。

personal (形)個人の、個人的な、私的な、本人自らの、人的な、対人の、動産の　(名)個人広告、個人情報、個人消息
　personal bankruptcy　個人破産
　personal check　個人小切手、パーソナル・チェック
　personal deposits　個人預金
　personal equity plan　個人投資計画
　personal exemption　個人の所得税控除
　personal finance company　消費者金融会社
　personal financial service　個人向け金融サービス
　personal holding company　個人的持ち株会社、同族持ち株会社
　personal identification number　暗証番号、個人の識別番号　(=password, PIN number)
　personal investment authority　個人投資規制機関
　personal investment option　個人投資オプション
　personal loan　個人ローン、個人向け融資、消費者ローン
　personal outlays　個人支出
　personal property　動産、人的財産
　personal savings　個人貯蓄
　personal selling　人的販売
　personal service　個人サービス

personal computer　パソコン、個人用小型コンピュータ、パーソナル・コンピュータ、PC　(⇒operating system)
◆Nonlife insurers already offer insurance purchased via personal computers, but are adding insurance services that can be bought more easily via mobile phones. 損保各社は、パソコン[インターネット]で加入する保険をすでに提供しているが、携帯電話でもっと簡単に加入できる保険サービスも新たに提供している。◆Personal computers of individuals and corporations were used to illegally access accounts and withdraw money. 口座に不正アクセスして現金を引き出すのに、個人や企業所有のパソコンが使われていた。

personal consumption　個人消費　(=personal spending; ⇒private-sector demand)

personal consumption expenditure　個人消費支出
◆Income and employment situations will continue to deteriorate, further delaying recovery of personal consumption. 所得・雇用環境が悪化して、個人消費の回復はさらに遅れそうだ。◆Personal consumption will return to the positive territory of 0.2 percent during the latter half of fiscal 2002. 個人消費は、2002年度後半には0.2%のプラスに転じるだろう。◆Under the severe income and employment situations, personal consumption has yet to show indications of a full-fledged recovery. 厳しい所得・雇用環境の下で、個人消費に本格的な復調の気配がまだ見えない。

personal data　個人情報　(=personal information)
◆In insurance policies that can be purchased via mobile phone, would-be policyholders do not need to input personal data and payments are easier. 携帯電話で加入できる保険では、加入希望者は個人情報を入力する必要がなく、支払いも簡単だ。◆Personal data, including the names, addresses and credit card numbers of 99,789 holders of credit cards issued by Nippon Shinpan Co., may have been leaked. 日本信販が発行したクレジット・カードの会員99,789人分の名前や住所、カード番号などの個人情報が、流出した可能性がある。

personal deposits　個人預金
◆A drastic increase was observed in the aggregate balance of personal deposits at major commercial banks at the end of March on the eve of the implementation of the pay-off system. 大手銀行の個人預金の3月末残高合計が、ペイオフ実施を直前にして大幅に増加したことが明らかになった。

personal identification number　暗証番号、個人識別番号　(=password)
◆Viruses used in illegal transfers via online banking services collect Internet banking account-related information such as personal identification numbers and transmit them to remote parties. ネット・バンキングでの不正送金に使われたウイルスは、暗証番号などネット・バンキングの口座関連情報を収集して、外部に送信する。

personal information　個人情報　(=individual information, personal data, personal data on individuals)
　the leaked personal information　流出した個人情報、個人情報の流出
　the protection of personal information　個人情報の保護
◆A name-list broker has sold the leaked personal information. 名簿業者が、流出した個人情報を販売している。◆In insurance services that can be bought via cell phones, cell phone companies provide nonlife insurers with policyholders' personal information. 携帯電話で加入できる保険サービスでは、携帯電話会社が(保険)加入者の個人情報を損害保険会社に提供している。◆The law on the protection of personal information regulates the use of personal information by private firms by prohibiting business operators who handle a large volume of personal information, such as client lists, from obtaining such information through unlawful measures or providing them to third parties without consent of those on the lists. 個人情報保護法は、顧客名簿など大量の個人情報を取り扱う事業者に対して、個人情報を不正な手段で取得することや、名簿上の本人の同意を得ないで第三者に個人情報を提供することを禁止して、民間企業による個人情報の使用を規制している。◆The personal information of customers who used credit cards for premium payments might have been leaked. クレジット・カードを使って保険料を支払った顧客の個人情報が、外部に流出した恐れがある。

personal pension premium　個人年金保険料
◆The government should reconsider the current system whereby life insurance and personal pension premiums are deducted from taxable income. 生命保険や個人年金の保険料を課税所得から控除する現行の制度を、政府は見直すべきだ。

personal spending　個人消費

(=personal consumption)
◆It is highly unlikely personal spending will fully recover. 個人消費の本格回復は、望み薄だ。◆The negative growth was due to the stagnancy of corporate capital investment as well as sluggish personal spending and other economy-slowing factors. マイナス成長は、企業の設備投資が頭打ちの状態だったことと、個人消費の伸び悩みや他の景気減速要因によるものだ。

personnel change 人事刷新
◆The bank will conduct a drastic personnel change and replace about 20 senior officials. 同行は、大幅な人事刷新を行い、幹部約20人を更迭する方針だ。

personnel costs 人件費
◆The hollowing-out of the pension system may increase companies' personnel costs so much that it could negatively affect their international competitive edge. 年金の空洞化で人件費が上昇し、国際競争力に悪影響を及ぼす恐れがある。

personnel exchange 人事交流
◆The three companies will consider personnel exchange between the three companies. 3社は今後、3社間の人事交流を検討する。

pessimism (名)悲観的な見方,悲観主義,悲観論,厭世(えんせい)主義者,ペシミズム
◆The U.S. dollar briefly dipped below the ¥100 line in Tokyo on Monday on pessimism about the U.S. economy, but was boosted above it following market intervention by the Bank of Japan. 米ドルは、月曜日の東京外為市場で、米経済への悲観論から一時100円台を割り込んだが、日銀の市場介入を受けて反発した。◆There is widespread pessimism in the market concerning the banking industry. 銀行業界については、市場では悲観的な見方が広がっている。

peter out 徐々に[次第に]なくなる,次第に消滅する[衰える,尽きる],先細りになる
◆The housing market is petering out. 住宅市場は、先細りになっている。◆The U.S. economic recovery will likely peter out next year. 米国の景気回復が、来年は先細りになるようだ。

petition (名)嘆願,請願,申請,申立て,陳情,嘆願[請願,陳情]書
bankruptcy petition 破産申請,破産申立て,破産申立て書 (=petition in [of] bankruptcy)
dumping petition ダンピング提訴
petition for aid 援助申請
petition for liquidation 清算の申立て,清算の申請書
◆In response to the petition, the government is expected to impose a countervailing duty on Hynix's DRAMs. 申請に応じて、政府は、ハイニックスのDRAM(記憶保持動作が必要な随時書込み読出しメモリ)に相殺関税をかける見通しだ。◆Japan has filed a petition with the WTO over the sanctions, and the U.S. has promised a cross-complaint. 日本は、制裁措置に対して世界貿易機関(WTO)に提訴し、米国は逆提訴する見込みだ[逆提訴する構えを見せている]。◆Ten senior executives from JAL's two subsidiaries have signed a petition urging JAL's chief executive officer to step down. 日航の子会社2社の取締役10人が、日航の最高経営責任者の辞任を求める文書に署名していた。

petrocurrency (名)オイル通貨

petrodollars (名)オイル・ダラー,石油ダラー,石油ドル (=oil dollars, oil money:中東産油国が石油を売って蓄積した巨大余剰資金)

PFI 民間資金による社会資本整備,プライベート・ファイナンス・イニシアチブ,PFI方式
(⇒private finance initiative)
◆In Britain, bridges, subways and prisons are constructed with PFI. 英国では、橋や地下鉄、刑務所などもPFI方式で建設されている。

PFI project プライベート・ファイナンス・イニシアチブ事業,PFI事業
◆In executing PFI projects, private operators will be able to use state-owned and other public land at little or no cost. PFI事業の実施面では、民間事業者が国有地や他の公有地を安いコストで、あるいは無償で利用できるようになる。

Pharmaceutical Affairs Law 薬事法
◆The ministry intends to have the Pharmaceutical Affairs Law revised to allow firms in the chemical industry and other nondrug companies to mass produce medicines. 同省は、薬事法を改正して、化学会社など異業種の企業にも医薬品の大量生産を認める方針だ。

phase (名)段階,局面,様相,相,面,方面,部分,状態,時期,期間
adjustment phase 調整段階,調整局面,調整期間
approach the most important phase 山場を迎える
bear phase 弱気局面
book-building phase 購入予約受付け期間
consolidation phase 再編の時期
contraction phase 景気後退の局面,景気収縮局面,景気悪化の局面,マイナス成長の局面
cycle [cyclical] phase 循環局面,景気循環の局面
deceleration phase 景気減速局面
deflationary phase デフレ局面,デフレ気味
depression phase 不況局面
downward [downswing] phase 下降局面
early phase 初期の段階
engineering phase 技術段階
expansion phase 拡大局面,景気拡大局面
final phase 最終局面,最終段階
growth phase 成長段階,成長局面,成長期
in phases 段階的に
inflationary phase インフレ局面,インフレ気味
mature phase 成熟期,成熟段階
phase-down [phasedown] 段階的縮小,段階的削減
phase-in [phasein] 段階的導入,(計画、作戦などの)段階的利用化,段階的組込み
phase-in period 経過期間
phase of cycle 景気循環の局面
phase of expansion 景気拡大局面,拡張局面
phase of recession 景気後退局面,後退局面
phase-out [phaseout] 段階的解消,漸次解消,段階的撤廃,(生産、操業の)漸次停止,段階的撤退,段階的除去
phase zero 政策、計画などの準備段階
pre-marketing phase 事前販売期間
recession phase 景気後退局面,後退局面
recovery [revival] phase 回復局面
resource mobilization phase 資源活用段階
stabilization phase 安定局面
upswing [upward] cycle 上昇局面
◆Japan's economy has entered a cautious phase. 日本の経済は、警戒モードに入った。◆Many developed countries are currently in a deflationary phase while many emerging countries are in an inflationary phase. 現在、先進国の多くはデフレ気味なのに対して、新興国の多くはインフレ気味だ。◆Overseas economies are moving out of their deceleration phase. 海外経済は、景気減速局面から抜け出している。◆Rapid recovery following the so-called Lehman shock has ended and the Chinese economy has entered a phase aimed at stable growth. いわゆるリーマン・ショック後の中国の急回復の時期は終わり、中国経済は、安定成長を目指す段階に入っている。◆Since the collapse of the bubble economy in the early 1990s, Japan has experienced several phases of economic revival. 1990年代はじめのバブル崩壊以降、日本は何度か景気回

復局面を迎えた。◆The bad loan problem has almost passed its critical phase. 不良債権問題は、おおむね峠を越えた。◆The economy is in a contraction phase. 景気は、後退局面にある。◆The economy still remains in a recovery phase in the business cycle. 景気は、まだ回復局面にある［景気の回復基調はまだ続いている］。◆The rate of economic expansion in the current phase of recovery is much smaller than previous expansionary phases. 現在の景気拡大期［景気拡大局面］の経済成長率は、過去の景気拡大期よりかなり低い。

phased （形）段階的な
- phased cutback 段階的の削減
- phased integration 段階的な統合, 段階的な統一
- phased project planning 段階的プロジェクト・プランニング
- phased withdrawal 段階的撤退

phenomenon （名）現象, 事象, 事件
- bubble phenomenon バブル現象
- economic phenomenon 経済現象
- market phenomenon 市場現象
- monetary phenomenon 貨幣的現象
- nonmonetary phenomenon 非貨幣的現象
- purely monetary phenomenon 純粋貨幣的現象
- temporary［transitory］phenomenon 一時的現象
- the Street phenomenon 金融街の現象, ディーラー主導型

◆The current deflationary trend seems to be a temporary phenomenon caused by the correction in oil prices after they skyrocketed last year. 現在のデフレ傾向は、昨年の原油高の反動による一時的な現象のようだ。

philosophy （名）理念, 方針, 主義, 哲学, 基本的な考え方
- business philosophy 経営理念
- company philosophy 企業理念, 経営哲学, 経営方針
- corporate philosophy 企業理念, 企業哲学
- disclosure philosophy 開示主義
- financial philosophy 財務についての考え方
- financing philosophy 資金調達方針, 財務についての考え方
- investment philosophy 投資方針
- management philosophy 経営理念, 経営方針, 経営哲学, 経営思想, 経営者精神（＝management thought, managerial philosophy, philosophy of management）
- money-is-everything philosophy 拝金主義
- money-worshipping philosophy 拝金主義
- operating philosophy 経営精神, 経営理念, 経営方針, 経営哲学
- philosophy of doing business 経営理念
- philosophy on money 金銭哲学
- profit-comes-first principle 利益至上主義（＝profit-first principle）
- regulatory philosophy 規制主義

◆The slipshod management of failed Incubator Bank of Japan widely diverged from its business philosophy. 破たんした日本振興銀行のずさんな経営は、同行の経営理念とはかけ離れていた。

phishing （名）ウェブ偽装詐欺, フィッシング（fishingとsophisticatedの合成語で、発音はfishingと同じ。銀行やクレジット・カード会社などの偽（にせ）のホームページを使って、口座番号やパスワードなどの個人情報を盗むこと）
- go phishing フィッシング詐欺をする
- spear phishing （特定の個人を標的にした）スピア型フィッシング

◆In phishing, offenders lure victims to fake financial institution Web sites to enter their account PINs and other account information. フィッシングでは、犯人が被害者を金融機関の偽ホームページに誘導して、被害者の口座の暗証番号などの口座情報を入力させる。

pick up （動）景気づく, （景気などが）回復する, 持ち直す, 復調する, 勢い［はずみ］をつける, 増える, 増加する, 増大する, 上昇する, 盛り上がる, 上向く, 改善する, 活況になる

◆Corporate loan demand should pick up once the economy begins recovering. 景気が回復していけば、企業の資金需要［借入需要］も増大するはずだ。◆The economic recovery seems to be picking up momentum. 景気回復に、勢いが出てきたようだ。◆The pace of economic activity is picking up. 景気の足取りが、速まっている。

picking up （名）回復, 持ち直し, 復調
◆The government has upgraded the economic outlook to "picking up." 政府は、景気見通しを「持ち直し」に上方修正した。◆There is no sign of picking up. 回復の兆しがない。

pickup （名）景気の回復, 好転, 持ち直し, 上向くこと, 上昇, 向上, 改善, 増加, 増勢, 拡大, 伸び, 活発化（⇒economic pickup）
- business pickup 景気の上昇, 景気回復, 景気の持ち直し
- economic pickup 景気回復, 経済の回復, 景気拡大, 景気の勢いが増すこと, 景気の持ち直し（＝pickup in economic activity, pickup in economic performance）
- equity pickup 株価の値上がり
- pickup for the dollar ドルの回復
- pickup in banking lending 銀行貸出の増加
- pickup in business opinion 景況感の回復
- pickup in demand 需要の高まり, 需要の回復
- pickup in employment 雇用の回復
- pickup in inflation インフレ率の上昇, インフレ昂進（こうしん）
- pickup in manufacturing activity 製造業の景気回復, 製造業の景気の持ち直し
- pickup in monetary growth マネー・サプライ伸び率の上昇
- pickup in money supply growth マネー・サプライ伸び率の上昇（＝pickup in monetary growth）
- pickup in the market 市場の持ち直し, 市場が上向くこと
- pickup signs 回復の兆し

pickup in business spending on inventories 企業の設備投資の回復
◆The economy, fueled by a pickup in business spending on inventories, is now expanding at a spanking clip. 企業の在庫投資の回復に支えられた経済は現在、顕著なペースで拡大している。

pickup in the overall economy 景気全体の持ち直し, 景気全体が上向くこと
◆Interest rates have begun rising in step with the pickup in the overall economy. 景気全体の持ち直しとともに、金利が上がり始めた。

piecemeal （形）徐々の, 少しずつ, 小出しの, ばらばらの（副）徐々に, 少しずつ, 小出しに, ばらばらに
◆The Bank of Japan seems to have unwillingly implemented measures piecemeal for further monetary easing under pressure from the government and the market. 日銀は、政府や市場にせっつかれて追加の金融緩和策を小出しにした［小出しに実施した］ようだ。

pigeonhole （動）整理する, 分類する, 仕分けする, （計画や案を）審議未了にする, 保留する, 保留事項にする, 棚上げする, 後回しにする, 頭の中に入れておく, 記憶にとどめておく, 握りつぶす, しまいこむ, 片づける（名）ハト小屋などの出入り口, 仕切り棚, 整理棚, 分類棚
◆The issue of soaring public debts was pigeonholed at the G-7 talks. 増大する公的債務の問題は、G7（先進7か国財務相・

銀行総裁会議)の協議では棚上げされてしまった。

piggy bank 小型貯金箱

PIGS [Pigs] ピッグス(財政破たんとそのユーロ圏への影響が懸念されているユーロ圏の南ヨーロッパ4か国—ポルトガル(Portugal)、イタリア(Italy)、ギリシャ(Greece)とスペイン(Spain)—の略語。ただし、この4か国にアイルランドを加えることもあるし、ポルトガル、アイルランド、ギリシャとスペインの組合せでPIGSと呼ばれることもある)

PIGS crisis [Crisis] ピッグス危機, PIGS危機

PIN 個人の識別番号, 暗証番号 (=password:personal [private] identification numberの略)
◆Banks will not pay compensation when depositors tell other people their PINs. 預金者が他人に暗証番号を知らせた場合、銀行は補償しない。◆In phishing, offenders lure victims to fake financial institution Web sites to enter their account PINs and other account information. フィッシングでは、犯罪者が被害者を金融機関の偽ホームページに誘導して、被害者の口座の暗証番号などの口座情報を入力させる。

PIN number 暗証番号, 個人識別番号 (=personal [private] identification number, PIN)
◆In the case of this ATM card, even if a cardholder's card or PIN number should be stolen, no one else can withdraw cash from the account. このキャッシュ・カードの場合は、カード会員がたとえカードや暗証番号を盗まれても、本人以外は口座から預金を引き出せない。

pipeline (名)原油や天然ガスなどのパイプライン, 供給ルート, 流通ルート, 情報ルート, 機密ルート, 入手経路, パイプ
a deal in the pipeline 準備中の案件, 予定されている取引[起債]
in the pipeline 輸送中, 準備中, 進行中
pipeline transportation パイプライン輸送
play the role of a pipeline パイプの役割を果たす
◆Pipeline systems out of Canada have been operating at full capacity. カナダ国外のパイプライン・システムは、フル稼働を続けています。◆Plans to strengthen regulations covering operators that send out spam also are in the pipeline. 現在、迷惑メール送信事業者への規制を強化する計画も準備している。

piracy (名)著作権侵害, 特許権侵害, 海賊版, 模造品
◆Piracy of Japanese products has become rampant in other Asian countries, including China. 中国などアジア地域で、日本製品の模造品が大量に出回るようになった。

pirated copy 違法コピー, 著作権侵害のコピー, 特許権侵害のコピー, 海賊版コピー
◆Pirated copies of the hit Japanese animated film are being distributed illegally on the Internet. 大ヒットしている日本のアニメ映画の違法コピーが、インターネット上で不法に流されている。

pirated product コピー製品, 特許権侵害の製品 (=bogus goods, fake product)
◆Pirated products are said to have grown into a global market worth ¥50 trillion per year. コピー製品は、全世界で年50兆円に達するといわれる。

pittance (名)わずかな手当て[収入、報酬、給料、生活費、金額], すずめの涙, 少量
◆Those housewives who have failed to switch to the national pension plan and have not paid premiums for an extensive period may receive a pittance or nothing at all. 国民年金への切替えをせず、保険料を長期間払っていない主婦は、低年金や無年金になる可能性がある。

PKO 公的資金による株式の買い支え, 株価維持策, 株価維持活動, プライス・キーピング・オペレーション, PKO (price keeping operationの略で、国民年金や厚生年金などの公的資金による株式の買い支え)

place (動)置く, 据える, 設置する, (株を)発行する, (商品を)売りさばく, はめる, はめ込む, 投資する, (注文を)出す, 発注する, 指名する, 任命する, 分類する, 確認する (「はめる、はめ込む」は、証券会社が客に株を現物で売ること)
be excellently [well] placed to ～するのに有利な立場にある, ～する上で絶好の位置にある
be placed by the end of the month 月までに完売となる
be placed in receivership 管財人が指名される
be placed solely with domestic investors 国内投資家だけにはめ込まれる
be quickly placed with retail investors 個人投資家に素早くはめ込まれる
place a block order 大口注文を出す
place a huge errant sell order 誤って大量の売り注文を出す
place a limit order 指し値注文を出す
place a market order 成り行き注文を出す
place a new share 新株を発行する
place deposits 預金する
place loans on nonaccrual ローンを不稼働資産として処理する
place the paper with retail investors 同債を個人投資家に販売する, 同債を小口投資家に販売する
place the proceeds in a trust 発行代わり金を信託勘定に入れる
place the stock 株を売り出す, 株を発行する
place three-year tranche 3年物トランシェを発行する
place value on を評価する
privately place 私募発行する, 第三者割当て発行する, 第三者割当て増資する (=privately issue)
◆In July 2011, the Company privately placed two million special warrants to purchase new common shares of the corporation. 2011年7月に当社は、同社の新規発行普通株式引受権付き特別ワラント債200万単位を、私募発行しました。◆Meiji Yasuda decided to lower the yield rate of its flagship insurance product because the insurer placed priority on long-term stable management over an increase in the number of policyholders. 明治安田生保は、契約者の数を増やすより長期的な経営の安定を優先したため、主力保険商品の予定利率[利回り]を引き下げることにした。◆Mizuho Securities Co. placed a huge errant sell order for the newly listed shares of recruitment firm J-Com Co. みずほ証券が、人材サービス業ジェイコムの新規上場株式に対し、誤って大量の売り注文を出してしまった。◆Rating agency Moody's may place a negative outlook on French government's Aaa debt rating as the government's financial strength has weakened. 格付け会社のムーディーズは、フランス国債のAaa(トリプルA)格付けについて、仏政府の財務体質[財務力]が弱まっているため「ネガティブ(弱含み)」の見通しを示す可能性がある。◆The deal was fully placed within three hours of launch. 同債は、ローンチ後3時間で完売した。◆The TSE and the OSE plan to establish an exchange company group as a holding firm under which the two exchanges will be placed as subsidiaries. 東証と大証は、両株式取引所を子会社として傘下に収める持ち株会社として、取引所グループの設立を計画している。

place (名)場所, 職, 役職, 座席
banking place 銀行営業所
business place tax 事業所税
investment in place 投資実績
place of origin 原産地
place of payment 支払い地
put production facilities in place 生産拠点をつくる
the place of issue 振出し地
three decimal places 小数点第三位

(=the third place after the decimal point)
◆If the merger takes place, it will create a full-scale financial conglomerate with a major bank, a major securities house and credit card company under its umbrella. 統合すれば、傘下に大手銀行と大手証券、クレジット・カード会社などを持つ本格的な金融コングロマリット（金融複合企業体）が誕生する。

placement （名）（株式、債券の）募集・売出、売出し、販売先、職業紹介、職業斡旋、人員配置
（⇒private placement）
  bond placement capability　債券の販売能力
  bonds offered through private placement　私募債
  direct placement　直接募集、直接販売、私募
  （=private offering, private placement）
  indirect placement　間接募集、間接販売
  initial placement　募集業務
  interbank placement　インターバンク預金
  international equity placement　株式の海外売出し
  placement commission　販売手数料
  placement fee　（ファンドなどを設定する際の）設定手数料、販売手数料
  placement of new fixed-rate bonds　新発普通債の販売
  placement of traditional bond issues　通常の債券発行の販売
  placement of unlisted notes　私募債の発行
  placement power　（債券、証券の）販売力
  placement with end investors　投資家への販売
  private placement　私募発行、第三者割当て、私募
  private placement bond market　私募債市場
  public placement　公募発行、公募、公募債
  raise cash by a private placement　第三者割当てで資金を調達する
  retail placement　個人投資家への販売
  secondary placement　売出し
◆Hokuetsu Paper Mills Ltd.'s private placement of new shares to allocate a stake of more than 30 percent to trading house Mitsubishi is scheduled for Monday. 三菱商事に30％超を割り当てる北越製紙の第三者割当て増資は、月曜日に予定されている。

placing （名）販売、募集
  placing memorandum　販売覚書、私募要領、私募債の募集要項
  placing of shares　株式の募集

plague （動）悩ます、苦しめる、困らせる、閉口させる、災害［損害］を与える、疾病にかからせる
  be plagued by counterparty risks　カウンターパーティー・リスクに苦しむ
  be plagued by deflation and sluggish growth　デフレと成長鈍化に悩む
  be plagued by financial problems　金銭問題で悩まされる
◆France is being plagued by rapidly exacerbating troubles at domestic banks. フランスは、国内銀行の急速な経営状態の悪化に悩まされている［苦しんでいる］。 ◆The capital markets around the globe are plagued by counterparty risks in the aftermath of the collapse of U.S. investment bank Lehman Brothers in 2008. 世界全体の資本市場は、2008年の米証券会社［投資銀行］の経営破たんの影響で、カウンターパーティー・リスクに苦しんでいる。

plain （形）単純な、純粋な、質素な、簡素な、率直な、平坦な、無担保の、明白な
  plain bond　無担保債券　（=debenture bond）
  plain money making　純粋な金儲け

plain-vanilla [plain vanilla] （形）基本的な、いちばん単純な、普通の、標準的な、スタンダードな、プレーン・バニラ　（=basic, gene）
  plain-vanilla bond　普通債
  plain-vanilla deal　標準的な案件
  plain vanilla fixed-rate issue　普通債
  plain-vanilla floater　プレーン・バニラの変動利付き債
  plain vanilla interest-rate swap　プレーン・バニラ金利スワップ
  plain vanilla swap　スタンダードなスワップ

plan （動）計画する、計画を立てる、立案する、設計する
  plan to　～する計画である、～することを検討している、～する方針である、～する方向だ、～する考えだ、～する構えだ
  plan to increase capital spending　設備投資を増加せせる計画である
◆GM plans to eliminate 25,000 jobs in the United States. 米自動車最大手のGMは、北米で2万5,000人の人員削減を計画している。 ◆Nippon Steel Corp. plans to join with Usiminas to invest in a planned steelworks in Brazil. 新日本製鉄は、ブラジルの鉄鋼大手ウジミナスに協力して、同国で予定されている製鉄所に投資する。 ◆The bank plans to issue up to ¥4.5 trillion worth of preferred shares in an effort to raise ¥1 trillion in capital by the end of this fiscal year. 同行は、今年度末までに1兆円の増資をするため、総額4兆5,000億円の優先株の発行枠を設定する方針だ。 ◆The bank plans to provide the money by transferring ¥100 billion in subordinated loans, which it has already extended to the insurer, to the insurer's foundation fund. 同行は、すでに供与している劣後ローン1,000億円をこの保険会社の基金に振り替えて、その資金を提供する方針だ。 ◆The foreign currency depositor planned to withdraw the money when the yen's value fell. この外貨預金者は、円安になったら解約するつもりだった。 ◆The government plans to sell some of its 100 percent stake in Japan Post Holdings Co. to fund reconstruction from the Great East Japan Earthquake. 政府は、東日本大震災の復興財源に充てるため、100％保有する日本郵政の株式の一部も売却する方針だ。 ◆The sell-off of Tokyo Metro shares planned by the government will likely be opposed by the Tokyo metropolitan government which is the second-largest shareholder. 政府が計画している東京メトロ株の売却には、国に次ぐ大株主の東京都が抵抗すると見られる。

plan （名）計画、方法、方式、政策、案、策、制度、保険、保険制度、年金、年金制度、制度）、プラン
（⇒pension plan）
  abort a plan　計画を中止する、計画を打ち切る
  accumulated plan benefits　年金給付累積額
  accumulation plan　積立プラン
  achieve a plan　計画を達成する
  acquisition plan　買収計画
  amortization plan　割賦方式、償還計画
  announce a plan　計画を発表する、計画を公表する
  assessment plan　賦課方式
  bonus plan　報奨金制度、ボーナス制度
  book value stock purchase plan　帳簿価格株式購入制度
  business plan　事業計画
  capex plan　設備投資計画
  （=capital spending plan）
  carry out a plan　計画を実施する、計画を実行する
  （=implement a plan）
  certificateless plan　株券不所持制度
  change a plan　計画を変更する
  compensatory plan　報酬制度
  constant-dollar-value plan　定額プラン
  contingency plan　緊急時対応策、危機管理復旧対応計画

contractual accumulation plan　契約積立プラン
contributory plan　拠出制, 拠出制年金制度
craft a plan　計画を策定する, 計画を練(ね)る（=develop a plan）
deferred compensation plan　報酬据え置き方式
defined benefit（pension）plan　確定給付制度, 給付建て制度, 給付建て年金制度
defined compensation plan　適格補償制度
defined contribution（pension）plan　確定拠出制度, 定額拠出制, 拠出建て年金制度
ERISA plan　ERISA年金制度
exit plan　投資資金の回収計画（エグジット・プラン）, 撤収計画
family plan　家族保険
financial plan　資金計画
fixed plan　固定型プラン
floor plan　最低額保障型制度
forestall the plan　計画を阻止する, 計画を阻(はば)む
funding of plans　制度の積立て
health plan　医療給付制度
individual retirement savings plan　個人退職貯蓄制度
insured plan　保険付き制度
investment plan　投資計画
make a plan　計画を立てる
money purchase plan　定額拠出年金
monthly investment plan　月掛け投資プラン
mutual plan　相互保険
non-contributory［noncontributory］plan　非拠出年金制度, 非拠出制
optimum investment plan　最適投資計画
pay-as-you-go financing plan　賦課方式
period of plan　保険期間
personal equity plan　個人持ち株制度
plan administrator　年金制度管理者
plan beneficiary　年金加入者
plan holder　年金加入者
plan termination　年金制度終了
plan termination insurance　制度消滅保険
plan trustee　年金制度受託者
plans　保険種類
profit plan　利益計画
put a plan into operation　計画を実施する
reinvestment plan　再投資計画
reserve financing plan　積立方式
retirement benefit plan　退職給与制度
retirement plan　退職金制度
savings incentive plan　貯蓄奨励プラン
savings plan　企業内貯蓄制度
scrap a plan　計画を打ち切る
self-insured plan　自家保険制度
shelve a plan　計画を棚上げする
single-employer defined postretirement benefit plan　単一事業主給付建て退職後給付制度
spending plan　支出計画
stock award plan　株式報奨制度
stock bonus plan　株式賞与制度
stock compensation plan　株式報酬制度
stock option plan　株式購入選択権制度, 自社株購入権制度（=stock purchase plan）
supplementary unemployment plan　補足的失業保険制度
tally plan　分割払い方式
term of plan　保険期間
thrift and savings plans　貯蓄制度
trust fund plan　信託基金制度, 信託型年金計画
workout a plan　計画を練る, 計画をまとめる

◆A suprapartisan committee set up within Congress will work out a plan to cut the fiscal deficit by $1.5 trillion while raising the debt limit by a matching amount. 米議会内に設置される超党派委員会が、1.5兆ドルの財政赤字削減策をまとめる一方、債務上限を同額引き上げる。◆A targeted company demanded a company trying to acquire its stocks to present a business plan. 買収の標的企業は、買収企業［標的企業の株式を取得しようとしている企業］に事業計画の提出を求めた。◆Koizumi's five-year plan was characterized by the fact that it set numerical targets and put forth a coherent policy. 小泉5か年計画の特色は、数値目標を設定して、整合性のとれた政策を掲げている点にあった。◆Previously, we expensed life insurance benefits as plans were funded. これまで当社は、生命保険給付については、制度に拠出がなされたときに費用として計上していました。◆Shinsei and Aozora banks announced a plan to merge in an effort to expand their customer bases and improve earnings. 新生銀行とあおぞら銀行は、顧客基盤の拡大と収益力の強化を狙って、合併計画を発表した。◆TEPCO is drafting a special business plan as the premise for getting government financial aid. 東電は、政府の金融支援を受ける前提として、特別事業計画を策定している。◆The assets of the various plans include corporate equities, government securities, corporate debt securities and income-producing real estate. 各種制度の年金資産は、株式、政府証券、債券や収益を稼得する不動産などで構成されています。◆The merger plan will not go ahead unless the bank makes unstinting efforts to cut its nonperforming loans. 同行が不良債権の削減に向けて惜しみない努力をしないかぎり、統合計画が前に進むことはないだろう。◆The new shares of common stock are being allocated to plan participants over ten years as contributions are made to the plan. この普通株式新株は、制度への資金拠出と並行して、10年にわたり制度加入者に割り当てられています。

plan assets　年金資産, 制度資産, 年金制度資産, 基金資産（=pension plan assets; ⇒secured mortgage）
　actual return on plan assets　制度資産の実際運用益
　estimated market value of plan assets　基金資産の見積り市場価値
　expected return on plan assets　制度資産の期待収益, 年金資産の予想収益
　net plan assets　年金プラン純資産
　plan assets at fair value　公正価額による年金資産, 年金資産の公正価額, 制度資産時価
　plan assets in excess of projected benefit obligation　基金資産の見積り給付債務超過額
　◆Our plan assets consist primarily of listed stocks, corporate and governmental debt, real estate investments, and cash and cash equivalents. 当社の年金制度資産は、主に上場株式、事業債、国債、不動産投資と現金および現金等価物で構成されています。

plan benefits　年金給付, 年金支給額
　accrued plan benefits　年金給付債務額
　accumulated plan benefits　年金給付累積額, 累積年金給付債務額, 年金未支給額
　◆The actuarial present value of the accrued plan benefits and the net assets available to discharge these benefits at December 31 are as follows: 12月31日現在の年金給付債務額の年金数理原価と年金給付債務に充当可能な年金純資産は、以下のとおりです。

plan participant　制度加入者

◆The new shares of common stock are being allocated to plan participants over ten years as contributions are made to the plan. この普通株式新株は、制度への資金拠出と並行して、10年にわたり制度加入者に割り当てられています。

planned （形）計画した，予定している，意図した，計画的な
 planned capital increase 増資計画
 planned capital spending 設備投資計画
  （=capital spending plan, planned capex）
 planned capitalism 計画的資本主義
 planned expansion 設備拡張計画
 planned growth rate 計画的成長率
 planned holdings of bond 計画的債券保有量
 planned inflow of money 計画的貨幣流入，貨幣の計画的流入
 planned investment 計画投資，意図した投資，投資計画
 planned lending 計画的融資，計画的貸出
 planned monetary system 管理通貨制度
 planned money holdings 計画的貨幣保有量
 planned organizational change 組織改編計画
 planned outflow of money 貨幣の計画的流出

planned capital increase 増資計画，増資案，予定されている増資，増資予定
◆The tie-up included a contribution by Mitsubishi Tokyo to the UFJ group's planned capital increase. 統合には、UFJグループが予定していた増資に三菱銀行の出資も含まれていた。

planned fund-raising target 当初計画の資金調達目標
◆Japan Airlines Corp. is expected to fall short of its planned fund-raising target by about ¥50 billion due to lower stock price. 日本航空では、株価の下落で、当初計画の資金調達目標を約500億円下回る見通しだ。

planned issuance of bridging bonds 予定しているつなぎ国債の発行
◆Unless consumption tax rate is raised, the planned issuance of bridging bonds could lead to further deterioration of the debt-saddled government finances. 消費税率を引き上げないと、予定しているつなぎ国債の発行は、借金を背負っている国の財政の悪化をさらに招く可能性がある。

planned listing 上場計画，計画していた上場，上場案
◆It is the first time in Japan that a company has postponed a planned listing due to the subprime crisis. サブプライム・ローン（米国の低所得者向け住宅融資）問題で企業が上場計画を延期したのは、日本では始めてだ。

plateau （動）安定水準期に入る，停滞期に入る，伸び悩む，頭打ちになる
◆The number of homeowners taking out earthquake insurance has plateaued though the figure increased at the time of the 1995 Great Hanshin Earthquake. 地震保険加入世帯は、1995年の阪神大震災時に増えたものの、その後は伸び悩んでいる。

plateau （名）踊り場，横ばい状態，安定状態，安定水準，安定期，高水準，停滞，停滞期，伸び悩み，高原，高原現象，台地
 an economic plateau 高原景気
 climb out of a plateau 踊り場から脱出する
 reach a plateau 横ばい状態[安定水準]に達する，伸び悩む，停滞期に入る
 remain on a plateau 高水準にとどまる
◆The economy has climbed out of a plateau. 景気[経済]が踊り場から脱出した。

play down ～を控え目に報道する[扱う]，控えめに言う，大事ではないとする，目立たないように扱う，軽く見る[軽視する]，重視しない，問題にしない，調子を下げる，（感情などを）抑える，押し殺す

◆European regulators had previously played down the idea of a blanket ban on short selling. 欧州の規制当局は、空売りの全面規制[禁止]という考え方を以前は問題にしていなかった。

player （名）参加者，関係者，投資家，トレーダー，専門家，企業，要因，プレーヤー （playersで「企業グループ」，「勢力」を意味する場合もある。⇒market player）
 major player 主流，大手企業
 major players in the industries 業界大手，業界の大手企業
 market player 市場関係者，市場参加者，市場筋，マーケット・プレーヤー （=market participant）
 players on the nation's stock markets 国内の株式市場関係者 （⇒preliminary GDP report）
 professional players ディーラー筋
 strong player 有力企業
 top player 最大手
◆France is a predominant player in the European economy alongside Germany. フランスは、ドイツとともに欧州経済を支えている。◆The company has returned to the international business scene as a strong player with high profitability. 同社は、収益性の高い有力企業としてビジネスの国際舞台に返り咲いた。◆Yahoo Japan Corp. is Japan's No. 1 player in online auctions. ヤフー・ジャパンは、日本のネット・オークション市場では第一位の企業だ。

Plaza Accord [accord, Agreement] プラザ合意 （⇒rectify the surge in the value of the U.S. dollar）
◆In 1985, finance ministers and central bank governors from the Group of Five major nations agreed to adopt a coordinated policy mainly aimed at rectifying the sharp rise in the value of the U.S. dollar at the meeting held at the Plaza Hotel in New York. 1985年にG5（日米英独仏の主要5か国）の蔵相と中央銀行総裁は、ニューヨークのプラザ・ホテルで開かれた会議で、主にドル高是正のための政策協調を採択することで合意した。

PLC 英国の公開有限会社，公開有限責任会社 （=plc, p.l.c.:public limited companyの略。株式会社（company limited by shares）と保証有限責任会社（company limited by guarantee）のうち、公開会社（public company）として登録している会社の社名の末尾に表示することになっている）
◆Sumitomo Mitsui Financial Group Inc. invested ¥106 billion in Barclays PLC in July 2008. 三井住友フィナンシャルグループは、2008年7月に英大手銀行のバークレイズに1,060億円を出資した。

pledge （動）入質する，質入れする，質を置く，抵当に入れる，担保に入れる，担保に供する，誓約する，公約する，確約する
 amount pledged 譲渡済み金額
 assets pledged 担保資産，担保提供された資産，担保として差し入れられた資産
 collateral pledged 差し入れられた担保
 negative pledge 担保制限
 pledge as collateral for financing 資金調達の担保として提供する[担保として差し出す]
 pledge collateral 担保を差し入れる，担保を差し出す
 pledged asset 担保資産，質入資産
 pledged collateral 担保の裏付け，担保の差し入れ，差し入れ担保
◆An advance of $100,000 was received from the bank by pledging $120,000 of the company's accounts receivable. 同社は、同社の売掛金12万ドルを担保に供して、同行から借入金10万ドルを受領した。◆Chinese President Hu Jintao pledged nearly $100 million in grants and soft loans to Cameroon. 中国の胡錦濤国家主席は、カメルーンに対して約1億ドルの資金援助と長期低利貸付けを約束した。

pledge （名）担保，抵当，質権設定，入質，担保・抵当品，

誓約, 公約, 確約, プレッジ
  negative pledge [clause]　担保提供制限条項, ネガティブ・プレッジ条項
  right of pledge　担保権
  unconditional pledge [clause]　無条件の担保条項
pledging　(名)担保差し入れ, 担保提供, 担保に付けること
  pledging of assets　資産の担保提供
  pledging or mortgaging　質権設定または抵当権の設定
plight　(名)窮状, 苦境, 深刻な状況, 悪状況
  corporate plight　深刻な経営状況
    (⇒financial reorganization)
  fiscal plight　財政難
  ◆Allowing banks to claim a tax refund by carrying a loss back to the previous year has not been allowed since fiscal 1992 in Japan, due chiefly to the fiscal plight of the central government. 銀行が欠損金を前年度に繰り戻して税金還付を請求できるようにする制度(欠損金の繰戻し還付)は、主に国の財政難を理由に、日本では1992年度から凍結されてきた。◆The latest financial reorganization drama was triggered by UFJ Holdings' corporate plight. 今回の金融再編劇の引き金となったのは、UFJホールディングスの深刻な経営状況だ。
plummet　(動)急落する, 暴落する, 大幅に減少する
  plummet temporarily　一時的に急落する
  plummeted operating profits　営業利益の大幅減少
  ◆If the U.S. government falls into default, the markets' faith in the dollar as the world's key currency would plummet. 米政府がデフォルト(債務不履行)に陥ったら、世界の基軸通貨としてのドルの信認は急落する。◆If the value of a huge number of government bonds possessed by financial institutions around the world plummets, financial instability will grow. 世界の金融機関が保有する大量の国債の価格が急落すれば、金融不安が高まることになる。◆Long-term interest rates plummeted temporarily, but the Treasury bond yield soon rebounded. 長期金利は一時急落したが、米財務省長期証券の利回り(長期金利)はすぐ反発した。◆Should the U.S. government fall into default, the prices of the Treasury bonds held by major countries and financial institutions around the world would plummet. 米政府がデフォルト(債務不履行)に陥れば、主要国や世界の金融機関が保有する米国債の価格は、暴落するだろう。◆Stock prices have plummeted and the yen's value has risen in the wake of the subprime loan fiasco. サブプライム・ローン(米低所得者向け住宅ローン)問題を受けて、株価が急落し、円高が進んでいる。◆The euro plummeted to the ¥100 level on the foreign exchange market, hitting a 10 year low. 外国為替市場では、ユーロが1ユーロ=100円台まで急落して、10年ぶりの低水準[10年ぶりの円高・ユーロ安水準]となった。◆The failure of Lehman Brothers Holdings Inc. caused stock prices in New York and other markets worldwide to plummet. リーマン・ブラザーズ(米証券4位)の経営破たんで、株価はニューヨークはじめ世界各地の市場で暴落した。◆The number of foreign companies listed on the TSE has plummeted to only 12 from 127 in 1991. 東証に上場している外国企業は、1991年の127社からわずか12社に減っている。◆The secondary market prices of the peripheral countries' government bonds plummeted as it became known that those bonds might be subject to debt forgiveness. 周辺国の国債は債務減免の必要が生じる恐れのあることが判明したので、周辺国国債の流通市場での価格は暴落した。
plummeting　(形)急落の, 暴落の, 急落[暴落]している, 低迷している, 減少している
  plummeting economy　景気低迷
  plummeting sales　販売の減少, 販売減, 売上の減少, 販売不振
  plummeting stock prices　株安

the plummeting yen　円の急落
  ◆Plummeting stock prices have reduced financial assets held by individuals, thereby dampening consumption. 株安で個人所有の金融資産が目減りして、消費は冷え込んでいる。
plunge　(動)押し込む, 突っ込む, 追い込む, 陥れる　(自動)減少する, 下落する, 低下する, 低迷する, 急落する, 安値を付ける, 転落する　(=drop)
  plunge across the board　全面安となる, 全面的に低下する, 軒並み下落する
  plunge into　~に陥る
  plunge into disarray　混乱に陥る
  plunge into loss　赤字に転落する
  plunge to a five month low　5か月来の安値を付ける
  ◆After the government's move of intervention, the yen plunged to the ¥85 level against the dollar. 政府の市場介入の動きを受けて、円相場は1ドル=85円台まで急落した。◆France and Germany could not bridge their differences, so Europe's efforts to solve its escalating debt crisis plunged into disarray. フランスとドイツが両国の相違を埋められなかったため、深刻化する欧州の債務危機問題解決への欧州の取組みは、混乱に陥った。◆It is difficult to predict if new explosive factors emerge to plunge the financial market into further turmoil. 金融市場をさらに混乱に陥れる新しい火種があるのかどうか、予測するのは難しい。◆Japan should prevent the dollar plunging and the yen from rising too sharply through concerted market intervention with the United States and European countries. 日本は、米欧との協調介入によってドル急落と超円高を阻止すべきだ。◆On the Tokyo stock market and other Asian markets, stock prices plunged across the board. 東京株式市場や他のアジア市場などでも、軒並み株安となった。◆Sony's group operating profit plunged 90.9 percent in the six months through September from a year earlier. ソニーの9月中間決算で、連結営業利益は前年同期比で90.9%減少した。◆Stock prices around the world firmed after plunging in midweek. 世界の株価は、週半ばに急落した後、小康状態になった。◆The Dow Jones industrials plunged 370 points after an unexpected contraction in the service sector. 予想しなかったサービス業の業況悪化を受けて、ダウ平均株価(工業株30種)は、前日比で370ドル急落した。◆The 225-issue Nikkei Stock Average on Monday plunged 202.32 points from Friday's close on the Tokyo Stock Exchange. 東京株式市場の月曜日の日経平均株価(225種)は、前週末比で202円32銭下落した。◆The United States is facing the risk of seeing the value of the dollar plunging badly. 米国は、ドルが大幅に下落するリスクを抱えている。◆With its sales plunging in North America, GM fell into the red. 北米での販売不振で、GMは赤字に転落した。
plunge　(名)株式市場の低迷, 株価急落, 株安
  a plunge in demand　需要の落ち込み
  a sudden plunge in the market　相場の急落, 相場急落
  an overnight plunge in U.S. stocks　前日の米株式の大幅下落
  another plunge in the Nikkei Index　日経平均[日経平均株価]の続落
  ◆Global stock market plunges caused by the European fiscal crisis triggered by Greece have shown no signs of abating. ギリシャ発の欧州財政危機による世界同時株安は、止まる気配がない。◆The 225-issue Nikkei Stock Average continued its plunge Thursday, momentarily dipping into 8,100 territory. 日経平均株価(225種)が木曜日も急落し、一時8,100円台まで下落した。
plunge in U.S. stocks　米国株の下落, 米株価の下落
  ◆If Japanese stock prices continue to fall whenever there is a plunge in U.S. stocks, the country might be hit by another financial crisis. 米国株の下落に連動して日本の株価の下落が続けば、再び金融危機に見舞われかねない。◆The 225-

issue Nikkei Stock Average dived below the key threshold of 10,000 as investors were disappointed with the continuing delay in the disposal of banks' bad loans and an overnight plunge in U.S. stocks. 日経平均株価(225種)は、投資家が銀行等の不良債権処理が引き続き遅れることや前日の米株価の大幅下落に失望して、1万円の大台を割り込んだ。

plunge of the won against major currencies 主要通貨に対するウォン相場の下落,主要通貨に対するウォン安
◆South Korea has seen a plunge of the won against major currencies amid the worldwide financial meltdown. 世界的な金融危機に伴って、韓国では主要通貨に対してウォン相場が下落している[ウォン安となっている]。

plunges on the world's stock markets 世界同時株安,世界の株式市場の低迷
◆Amid the European fiscal and financial crisis, plunges on the world's stock markets and wild fluctuations in foreign exchange markets may continue. 欧州の財政・金融危機を受けて、世界同時株安と為替市場の乱高下は今後も続く可能性がある。

plunging share prices 株価下落
◆Large simultaneous sell-offs of banks' shareholdings on the market would lead to a vicious cycle of plunging share prices and worsening bank finances. 銀行の保有株を市場で大量に同時に売却すれば、株価下落と銀行の財務内容の悪化という悪循環につながる。

PNTR 恒久的最恵国待遇 (permanent normal trade relationsの略)

point (名)為替相場などの騰落単位,水準,地点,時点,時期,問題,要点,論点,趣旨,事項,材料,ポイント (⇒percentage point)
　at one point 一時的に,一時 (=briefly)
　basis point ベーシス・ポイント(1ベーシス・ポイント=0.01%,100ベーシス・ポイント=1%)
　breakdown point 損益分岐点,採算点 (=break-even point)
　ex point of origin 現地渡し
　negative points 悪材料,マイナス面
　ordering point 発注点
　pension point system 年金ポイント制
　percentage point パーセント・ポイント,ポイント,%(1パーセント・ポイント=1%)
　point and figure charting 株式相場の罫線(けいせん)方式
　point [points] of reference 判断[評価]基準
　positive points 好材料,プラス面
　reach a low point 最低レベルに達する
　sales point セールス・ポイント
　shipping point 出荷地渡し
　tax point 課税時点

◆On Monday, the Nikkei Stock Average rose 43.23 points, or 0.36 percent, to close at 12,163.89, its highest closing this year. 月曜日の日経平均株価の終値は、43円23銭(0.36%)上昇して、今年の最高値(終値)となる12,163円89銭を付けた。◆Stock prices in Tokyo fell by more than 600 points as a state of panic gripped investors and selling pressure snowballed. 東京市場の株価は、投資家がパニック状態に陥り、売り圧力が増大[加速]したため、下げ幅が600円を超えた。◆The blue chips fell as much as 149 points to near the 7,000 mark in February 2009. 2009年2月の主要銘柄は、149ドル下落して7,000ドルに近い水準にまで達した。◆The broader TOPIX index of all First Section issues finished down 11.71 points at 706.08. 一部上場全銘柄の総合東証株価指数は、11.71ポイント安の706.8で終了した。◆The Dow Jones industrials plunged 370 points after an unexpected contraction in the service sector. 予想し

なかったサービス業の業況悪化を受けて、ダウ平均株価(工業株30種)は、前日比で370ドル急落した。◆The Tokyo market was down across the board, causing the Nikkei Stock Average to drop more than 400 points at one point. 東京市場は全面安となり、日経平均株価の下げ幅は一時、400円を超えた。◆The 225-issue Nikkei Stock Average on Monday plunged 202.32 points from Friday's close on the Tokyo Stock Exchange. 東京株式市場の月曜日の日経平均株価(225種)は、前週末比で202円32銭下落した。◆There are several points of concern regarding the future prospects of the nation's economy. 日本経済の先行きに、いくつか懸念材料がある。

point system ポイント制,点数評価制度(職務評価方法の一つ)
◆The new IC ATM cards of Mizuho Bank will have advanced functions such as digital money and a point system. みずほ銀行の新型ICキャッシュ・カードには、デジタル・マネーやポイント制などの先端機能が採用される。

poised to 〜する用意[準備]ができている,〜する覚悟だ,〜する構えでいる,〜する方針だ,〜しそうだ,〜する見通しだ,〜する見込みだ (=ready to; ⇒worldwide recession)
◆Domestic regional banks are poised to make partnerships with Deutsche Bank to conduct international money transfers. 国内の地方銀行数行が、国際送金の分野でドイツ銀行と提携する見込みだ。◆The government is poised to issue bridging bonds to make up the expected shortfall in state funding for the basic pension fund. 政府は、つなぎ国債を発行して、予想される基礎年金基金の国庫負担の不足分を賄(まかな)う方針だ。◆U.S. authorities are poised to allow the weak dollar to continue for the foreseeable future. 米当局は、ドル安の進行を当面、容認する構えだ。

poison pill 毒薬条項,敵対的買収に対する防衛手段,買収防衛策,ポイズン・ピル(敵対的買収に対する防衛策の一つ。「毒薬条項」は、既存株主に対して転換優先株式を株式配当の形で発行することを定めた条項を指す)
　poison pill strategy ポイズン・ピル戦略
　poison pill variant 毒薬条項の一種,ポイズン・ピルの一種
◆About 15 percent of the leading companies are studying the possibility of using a poison pill to counter a hostile takeover by using the issue of warrants. 主要企業の約15%は、新株予約権の発行などで敵対的買収に対抗するポイズン・ピル(毒薬)の導入可能性を検討している。◆If Hokuetsu Paper Mills decides to carry out the poison pill, Oji Paper Co. is likely to take legal action against it. 北越製紙が買収防衛策を実施したら、王子製紙は法的措置を取る可能性が高い。

poison pill defense [defence] ポイズン・ピル防衛,毒薬条項防衛,毒入り避妊薬
◆The Business Organization Law, which went into effect in fiscal 2006, allows companies to use poison pill defense tactics more easily. 2006年度から施行された「会社法」で、企業は、ポイズン・ピル(毒薬条項)防衛策を以前より容易に講じられるようになった。

poison pill plan ポイズン・ピル(毒薬)方式 (=poison pill scheme)
◆Companies can resort to corporate defense schemes, including a poison pill plan to issue new shares, to fight hostile takeover bids. 敵対的買収への対抗策として、企業は新株発行(増資)のポイズン・ピル(毒薬)方式などの企業防衛策をとることができる。

poison pill scheme ポイズン・ピル防衛策
◆Nireco Corp. has scrapped its plan to invoke the nation's first poison pill scheme to ward off hostile takeover bids. ニレコは、敵対的TOB(株式公開買付けによる企業買収)を防ぐための日本で最初のポイズン・ピル防衛策の実施計画を白紙撤回した。

policy (名)政策,対策,方針,主義,姿勢,施政方針,規定,

ポリシー
accommodating fiscal and monetary policies　景気刺激型の財政・金融政策
accounting policy　会計方針, 経理方針
anti-cyclical policy　景気対策
　（＝contracyclical policy）
anti-depression policy　不況防止対策
anti-inflation policy　インフレ対策
bank rate policy　金利政策, 公定歩合政策
basic policy　基本方針, 基本政策
best policy　最善の策, 最良の策
budgetary policy　財政政策, 予算政策
　（＝budget policy）
budgeting policy　予算編成方針
business policy　経営政策, 経営方針, 営業政策, 営業方針
cancellation policy　キャンセル規定
commercial policy　通商政策
consolidation policy　連結方針
cooling-off policy　景気抑制政策
credit policy　金融政策, 信用方針
　（＝monetary policy）
credit underwriting policy　与信基準
currency policy　通貨政策
customer-first policy　顧客第一主義, お客様本位の姿勢
customs policy　通関規定
debt management policy　国債管理政策
debt retirement policy　（政府の）債務償還政策
deflation policy　デフレ政策
　（＝deflationary policy）
dividend policy　配当政策, 配当方針
easy credit policy　信用拡張政策
easy monetary policy　金融緩和政策
economic policy　経済政策
exchange pegging policy　為替釘付け政策
exchange policy　為替政策
　（＝exchange rate policy）
financial policy　金融政策, 財政政策, 財務政策, 財務方針
financing policy　資金調達方針
fiscal policy　財政政策
fully paid policy　保険料払込み済み契約
funding policy　（公債などの）借換え政策
high interest policy　高金利政策
interest policy　金利政策, 利子政策
interest rate policy　金利政策
lag in financial [monetary] policy　金融政策のラグ
lending policy　貸出政策
liquidity policy　流動性政策
loan policy　貸出政策, 公債政策
macroeconomic policy　マクロ経済政策, 巨視的経済政策
management policy　経営方針, 経営政策, 経営姿勢
monetarist policy　マネタリスト政策
monetary policy　金融政策　（＝credit policy）
money back policy　払戻し主義
original policy　原契約
ploughing-back policy　再投資政策, 留保政策
policy cost analysis　政策コスト分析
policy firming　金融引締め, 利上げ
policy loan　政策融資, 契約者貸付け, 保険証券貸付け, 証券担保貸付け
policy mix　ポリシー・ミックス, 経済政策ミックス
policy of giving favorable treatment to foreign companies　外資優遇策
policy rate　政策金利
quantitative economic policy　量的経済政策
reasonable price policy　低価格政策
reflationary policy　景気刺激策, 景気振興策
retrenchment policy　緊縮政策
risk management policy　リスク管理政策
roll back policy　巻き返し政策
stock policy　株価対策
tax reduction policy　減税政策
tight money policy　高金利政策
trade cycle policy　景気循環政策
undertake a policy firming　利上げを実施する
zero-interest rate policy　ゼロ金利政策

◆At the bank, a string of executives resigned one after another due to differences over management policy. 同行では、経営路線の違いで役員らの辞任が相次いだ。◆China is reviewing its policy of giving favorable treatment to foreign companies. 中国は、外資優遇策を見直している。◆If the economy is to see a full-fledged recovery, the government should continue taking all feasible policy steps, including propping up the economy by fiscal means. 本格的な景気回復を見るには、財政面でのテコ入れを含めて、政府は引き続き実行可能なあらゆる政策手段を取るべきである。◆If the government relaxes its policy now, the economy will not be able to get on the recovery track. 政府がいまその政策の手を緩めれば、景気は回復軌道に乗れないだろう。◆Industry insiders said the refusal to pay insurance benefits over a long period was partly because of former Meiji managers' unreasonable policies. 業界関係者によると、長期間にわたる保険金不払いの一因は、旧明治生命保険の経営者の無理な経営方針だ。◆Koizumi's five-year plan was characterized by the fact that it set numerical targets and put forth a coherent policy. 小泉5か年計画の特色は、数値目標を設定して、整合性のとれた政策を掲げている点にあった。◆Major currencies are rising against the dollar on account of the Fed's monetary easing policy. 米連邦準備制度理事会（FRB）の金融緩和策で、主要通貨はドルに対して上昇している［ドル安・主要通貨高が進んでいる］。◆The BOJ lifted its zero-interest rate policy on the strength of its optimistic view on the outlook for the economy in the summer of 2000. 日銀は2000年夏、景気の先行きを楽観してゼロ金利政策を解除した。◆The EU has been unable to work out its inherent policies concerning the fiscal deficiencies of some of its more reckless member countries. 欧州連合（EU）は、一部の無謀な加盟国の欠陥財政について、一貫した政策を打ち出せないでいる。◆The IMF and the EU have worked out a policy of extending emergency loans to Greece. 国際通貨基金（IMF）と欧州連合（EU）は、ギリシャに緊急融資を行う方針を打ち出した。◆The unanimous decision by the U.S. central bank's policy setting Federal Open Market Committee moved the benchmark federal funds rate to 1.25 percent. 米連邦準備制度理事会の金利政策を決定する米連邦公開市場委員会の全会一致による決定で、短期金利の指標であるフェデラル・ファンド金利が年1.25％に引き上げられた。◆We will adhere to our proactive management policies that place the utmost emphasis on investment profitability. 当社は、今後も投資収益性を重視した攻めの経営姿勢を貫く方針です。

policy　（名）保険証券（insurance policy）, 保険証書, 保険契約, 保険, 保険商品
all-in policy　全危険付き保険証券, 全危険担保保険証券
annuity policy　年金保険証券
average policy size in force　平均有効保険金高
average policy size issued　平均発行保険金
bank policy　銀行内盗難保険証券

bankers' blanket policy　金融機関包括保険, 金融機関包括補償保険
blanket policy　総括付保保険
buy an insurance policy　保険をかける, 保険に入る, 保険に加入する
　（=purchase an insurance policy）
cancellation of policy　保険契約の解除
cargo policy　積荷海上保険証券, 貨物保険証券
comprehensive policy　全危険保険証券
contingent policy　偶発保険証券
contract policy　契約保険証券
contractor's all-risks policy　請負人全危険負担保険証券
declaration policy　通知保険
definite policy　確定保険証券
endowment policy　養老保険証券, 養老証券, 養老保険証書
existing policies　既契約
extended policy　払込み延期証券
family income policy　家族所得保険[保険証券], 家族利益保険
family protection policy　遺族扶助保険
fire policy　火災保険証券, 火災保険証書
floating policy　船名未詳保険証券
for whole policy year　保険年度1年分につき
full benefit insured under the policy　元受契約に基づいて保障した保険金額
general and special policy conditions　元受保険約款と特約条項
household policy　家財保険
　（=home-owner's policy）
hull policy　船体保険証券
income policy　利益保険, 収益保険
installment policy　賦払い証券
insurance policy　保険証券, 保険
　（=policy of insurance）
issue of the policy　保険証券の発行
issue the policy　元受証券を発行する
joint life policy　共同保険[保険証券], 連生保険, 連合生命保険
joint schedule policy　共同加入保険証券
lapsed policy　期限経過証券
life insurance policy　生命保険証券
　（=life policy）
limited payment policy　短期払込み保険, 有限払込み保険, 払込み年限付き保険
limited policy　限定支払い保険証券, 有限保険
Lloyd's policy　ロイズ証券
management policy　経営方針, 経営路線
marine insurance policy　海上保険証券
mixed policy　混合保険[保険証券]
modified life policy　変形保険[保険証券]
named policy　船名記載保険証券, 確定保険証券
nonparticipating policy　無配保険証券
open policy　予定保険証券, 予定保険契約
order policy　指図式保険証券
ordinary life policy　普通保険[保険証券]
package policy　総合保険
paid-up policy　払込み済み証券
participating policy　利益配当保険証券
policy anniversary　契約応答日

policy cancellation　保険の解約
policy conditions　保険約款, 元受約款
　（=policy clause）
policy dividend　契約者配当金
　（=policyholder dividend）
policy form　保険証券用紙
policy holder [policyholder, policyholders, policyholders'] protection fund　保険契約者保護基金, 生命保険契約者保護機構
policy in force　既契約, 現在有効契約, 現在契約
policy loan　契約者貸付け, 保険証券貸付け, 証券担保貸付け
policy of assurance [insurance]　保険証券
policy period　保険証券有効期間
policy premium loan　保険料振替貸付け
policy proofs of interest　名誉保険証券, 被保物の証券保証, 被保険利益不問証券, PPI
policy reserve　保険準備金, 責任準備金
policy retaining memo　証券留置証
policy stamp　保険証券印紙税
policy steps　政策手段
policy term　保険期間, 保険証券の期限
policy valuation　保険評価額
policy value　保険証券価額, (保険証)券面価格, 保険料積立金, 解約返戻（へんれい）金
policy writing agent　証券発行代理店
policy year　保険年度, 証券年度（契約日付けを期限として翌年の同月同日の前日までを1年と計算する）
previous policies　既契約
provisional policy　個別的予定保険証券
residence policy　住宅内盗難保険証券
sell policies　保険を販売する, 保険をかける
shipments policy　出荷保険[保険証券]
single policy　単身契約
single premium policy　保険料一時払い契約, 一時払い契約
specific policy　特定保険証券
specified policy　特約保険
standard policy　標準保険証券, 標準証券, 標準[標準保険]約款（standard policy conditions [provision]）
take out a policy on one's life　〜人に生命保険をかける
term policy　有期保険, 有期保険証券
time policy　期間保険, 船の定期保険
top-hat policy　割増養老年金保険
traveler's policy　旅行者保険
umbrella policy　企業包括賠償責任保険
unemployment policy　失業保険証券
unlimited policy　無制限保険証券[保険証書]
unvalued policy　金額未詳保険証券, 無評価保険証書
valued policy　確定保険証券, 定額保険証券, 評価済み保険
whole life policy　終身保険[保険証券]
◆During the bubble economy, life insurers sold a large number of policies by promising high yields. バブル期に生保各社は、高い予定利率を約束して多くの保険契約を獲得した。◆In the policies offered by the Sompo Japan and Tokio Marine & Nichido Fire Insurance, the companies also pay liability if policyholders injure or kill someone. 損保ジャパンと東京海上日動火災が提供している保険では、保険契約者[保険加入者]が人をけがや死亡させたりした場合に、その相手に支払う賠償金も支払われる。◆Nonlife insurers are exploring new types of insurance demand and offering convenient and easy

means of buying policies. 損保各社は、新たな保険需要を掘り起こして、いつでも、どこでも簡単に保険に加入できるサービスを提供している。◆The policies offered by the two nonlife insurers pay policyholders if they are injured doing sports or during domestic and overseas trips. この損保2社が提供している保険では、保険加入者[保険契約者]がスポーツや国内外の旅行中に傷害事故にあったときに、保険金が支払われる。◆Whole life insurance means life insurance under which coverage remains in force during the insured's entire lifetime, provided premiums are paid as specified in the policy. 終身保険は、保険契約に明記されている保険料が支払われているかぎり、保障が被保険者の全生涯にわたって有効な生命保険を意味する。

policy-based financing operations　政策金融
◆Policy-based financing operations which take advantage of government subsidies are adversely affecting the price mechanism in the financial market. 政府の補給金を受けて運営される政策金融は、金融市場の価格メカニズムを歪(ゆが)めている。

Policy Board meeting　(日銀の)金融政策決定会合 (⇒Monetary Policy Meeting)
◆The Bank of Japan decided to take new steps for further quantitative monetary easing at an extraordinary Policy Board meeting. 日銀は、臨時の金融政策決定会合で、追加の量的金融緩和策を新たに実施することを決めた。

policy cancellation　保険の解約
◆Insurers are afraid of a possible rush of policy cancellations that can be triggered by a public announcement of their decisions to lower prospective yield rates. 生保各社は、予定利率の引下げ決定を公表することによって、保険の解約ラッシュに見舞われるのを恐れている。

policy coordination　政策協調, 政策調整
◆Japan, the United States and European countries have failed to eliminate uneasiness in the financial markets for lack of concrete policy coordination. 日米欧は、具体的な政策協調が見られないため、金融市場の不安感を払拭(ふっしょく)できないでいる。◆The government and the Bank of Japan must pursue policy coordination in a flexible manner to prevent the economy from slowing down further. 政府と日銀は、柔軟に[機動的に]政策協調して、景気失速を防がなければならない。◆The Group of 20 advanced and emerging economies spelled out policy coordination. 世界[主要]20か国・地域(G20)の先進国と新興国は、政策協調を打ち出した。

policy coordination efforts　政策協調努力
◆Policy coordination efforts between Japanese and U.S. currency authorities are genuine. 日米通貨当局の政策協調努力は、本物だ。

policy management　政策運営, 政策の運営
◆Economic stimulus measures should be prioritized in the government's policy management. 政府の政策運営では、景気刺激策[景気対策]を優先するべきだ。◆The government and the Bank of Japan should give priority to stimulating the economy in their policy management. 政府と日銀は、政策運営で景気浮揚を最優先すべきだ。

policy meeting　政策決定会合, 金融政策決定会合, 政策会議　(⇒Monetary Policy Meeting)
◆The Bank of Japan started a two-day policy meeting. 日銀の2日間の日程で行われる金融政策決定会合が、始まった。◆The BOJ is prepared to hold its policy meeting ahead of schedule if the yen's value further soars before the next meeting. 次回の政策決定会合までに円高が一段と進めば、日銀は会合を前倒しして会合を開く構えだ。◆The BOJ's policy meeting is expected to consider taking additional monetary easing steps. 日銀の政策決定会合では、追加の金融緩和策の実施を検討する見通しだ。◆The BOJ's policy meeting plans to consider expanding the list of government bonds purchased under the fund. 日銀の政策決定会合では、基金で買い入れる国債の対象拡大を検討する予定だ。◆The U.S. Federal Reserve Board left U.S. rates unchanged at a key policy meeting. 米連邦準備制度理事会(FRB)は、重要な政策会議(公開市場委員会)で米国の金利(公定歩合とFF金利の誘導目標)を据え置くことを決めた。

policy obligations　保険契約債務, 保険金
◆An insurer's solvency ratio is a measure of a firm's ability to pay out policy obligations. 生保のソルベンシー・マージン(支払い余力)比率は、保険金の支払い能力を示す指標だ。

policy of quantitative easing　量的緩和政策, 量的緩和策
◆The Fed's policy of quantitative easing foments chaos in foreign exchange markets. 米連邦準備制度理事会(FRB)[米国の中央銀行]の量的緩和政策は、為替相場[為替レート]の変動を招いている。

policy of virtually zero-percent interest rates　事実上ゼロ金利の政策, ゼロ金利政策
◆The U.S. Federal Reserve Board has been maintaining a policy of virtually zero-percent interest rates. 米連邦準備制度理事会(FRB)は、事実上ゼロ金利の政策を維持してきた。

policy project　政策プロジェクト
◆Given the nation's tough fiscal condition, the government must eke out the necessary funds by scaling down low-priority policy projects. 日本の厳しい財政事情に照らせば、政府に求められるのは、優先度の低い政策プロジェクトを縮小して、必要な財源をひねり出すことだ。

policy sales　保険の販売, 保険商品の販売
◆In the case of au Insurance's cell phone-based policy sales, policyholders are allowed to pay premiums by adding them to monthly mobile charges. au損害保険の携帯電話での保険販売の場合、保険契約者は、保険料を携帯利用の月額に加算して保険料の支払いをすることができる。◆NTT Docomo Inc. and SoftBank Mobile Corp. have been offering cell phone-based policy sales by teaming up with nonlife insurers respectively. NTTドコモとソフトバンクモバイルは、それぞれ損保会社と提携して、携帯電話での保険販売のサービスを提供している。

policy setting　(名)政策決定　(形)政策を決定する～
◆The unanimous decision by the U.S. central bank's policy setting Federal Open Market Committee moved the benchmark federal funds rate to 1.25 percent. 米連邦準備制度理事会の金利政策を決定する米連邦公開市場委員会の全会一致による決定で、短期金利の指標であるフェデラル・ファンド金利が年1.25%に引き上げられた。

policyholder　(名)保険契約者, 契約者, 保険加入者
(=insurance policyholder, policy holder; ⇒meeting of representatives of policyholders, negative spread)
　dividend to policyholders　契約者配当, 保険契約者配当[配当金]　(=policyholder dividend)
　dividends and coupons paid to policyholders　契約者に支払われる配当金と利息
　insurance company senior policyholder　保険会社の一般契約者
　meet claims of senior policyholders　上位保険契約者の請求[保険金請求]を履行する
　meeting of representatives of policyholders　総代会
　payment of senior policyholder claims　上位保険契約者の保険金請求の支払い
　policyholder benefits　契約者給付金
　policyholder dividend　契約者配当, 保険契約者配当金　(=dividend to policyholders)
　policyholder flight　保険契約者の逃避, 保険契約の解約
　policyholder insured　保険契約者
　policyholder limits　保険契約者に対する与信限度
　policyholder obligations　保険加入者に対する債務

Policyholders' Protection Fund　保険契約者保護基金
policyholders' representative meeting　総代会
policyholders' surplus　契約者剰余金
reserve for dividend to policyholders　契約者配当準備金
senior policyholder　上位保険加入者, 上位保険契約者, 一般契約者
senior policyholder obligations and claims　保険加入者に対する上位債務と請求［保険金請求］
◆After the three-month period of full protection, the collapsed nonlife insurance firm will dissolve the contracts with their policyholders. （破綻後）3か月の全額保護期間が経過したら、破綻した損害保険会社は契約者との契約を打ち切る方針だ。◆From a broader point of view, the lowering of promised yields on premium investments would surely protect the benefits of policyholders. 大局的に見れば、生保が保険契約者に約束した保険料投資の運用利回り［予定利率］を引き下げたほうが、確かに保険契約者の利益を保護することになる。◆In insurance services that can be bought via cell phones, premiums include an insurance policy that pays ¥300,000 if a policyholder scores a hole in one in golf. 携帯電話で加入できる保険サービスでは、保険料に保険契約者がゴルフでホールインワンした場合に30万円支払われる保険契約［保険］もある。◆In the case of au Insurance's cell phone-based policy sales, policyholders are allowed to pay premiums by adding them to monthly mobile charges. au損保の携帯電話での保険販売の場合、保険契約者は、保険料を携帯利用の月額に加算して保険料の支払いをすることができる。◆In the case of single-premium whole life insurance policies, policyholders make one large premium payment up front when they sign the contract. 一時払い終身保険の場合は、保険契約者が契約を結ぶ際に［契約時に］多額の保険料を前もって一括で払い込む。◆In the policies offered by the Sompo Japan and Tokio Marine & Nichido Fire Insurance, the companies also pay liability if policyholders injure or kill someone. 損保ジャパンと東京海上日動火災が提供している保険では、保険契約者［保険加入者］が人をけがや死亡させたりした場合に、その相手に支払う賠償金も支払われる。◆In this type of life insurance products, the rate of return after canceling the insurance contract can be higher than that of a savings account if a policyholder upholds the contract for five to 10 years. この種の生保商品では、保険契約者が保険契約を5〜10年続けると、解約後の利回り（予定利率）は預金よりも高い利回りが見込める。◆Life insurers have been offering relatively high yield rates to their policyholders. 生保各社は、保険契約者に比較的高い利回り［予定利率］を提示してきた。◆Meiji Yasuda decided to lower the yield rate of its flagship insurance product because the insurer placed priority on long-term stable management over an increase in the number of policyholders. 明治安田生保は、契約者の数を増やすより長期的な経営の安定を優先したため、主力保険商品の予定利率［利回り］を引き下げることにした。◆Nippon Life Insurance Co. sold some of Olympus's shares with a view to protecting the benefits of policyholders. 日本生命は、保険契約者の利益保護の観点からオリンパス株の一部を売却した。◆The insurance premiums are determined by the age and other characteristics of policyholders. この保険料は、保険加入者の年齢などの特性に応じて決められる。◆The life insurer currently promises its policyholders an annual yield of 1.5 percent for the single-premium whole life insurance. 同生保は現在、一時払い終身保険については年1.5%の利回り（予定利率）を契約者に約束している。◆The nonlife insurance company hopes to attract about 3 million to 4 million new policyholders a year for its new types of insurance. 同損保は、同社の新型保険で、年間約300万〜400万件の新規契約獲得を目指している。◆The policies offered by the two nonlife insurers pay policyholders if they are injured doing sports or during domestic and overseas trips. この損保2社が提供している保険［保険契約］では、保険加入者［保険契約者］がスポーツや国内外の旅行中に傷害事故にあったときに、保険金が支払われる。◆When the policyholders of single-premium whole life insurances die, beneficiaries receive the designated benefits plus accumulated dividends. 一時払い終身保険の契約者が死亡した場合、保険金の受取人は、特定の（死亡）保険金のほかに積立配当金を受け取れる。◆When yields on whole life insurance products decline, policyholders must pay higher premiums to secure the same amount of total insurance benefits. 終身保険商品の利回りが下がった場合、加入者［保険契約者］がそれ以前と同額の総保険料を受け取るには、より高い保険料を払わなければならない。

policyholders' personal information　保険契約者［保険加入者］の個人情報
◆In insurance services that can be bought via cell phones, cell phone companies provide nonlife insurers with policyholders' personal information. 携帯電話で加入できる保険サービスでは、携帯電話会社が（保険）加入者の個人情報を損害保険会社に提供している。

policyholders' premiums　保険契約者の保険料
◆Life insurance companies invest policyholders' premiums in stocks. 生命保険会社は、保険契約者の保険料を株式に投資している。

policyholders' representative meeting　総代会
(=meeting of representatives of policyholders)
◆The capital increase is due after a policyholders' representative meeting in July. この基金の積み増し（保険会社の基金増資）は、7月の総代会後に実施される予定だ。

policymaking member　政策決定メンバー
◆Policymaking members of the U.S. Federal Open Market Committee voted unanimously to keep its trendsetting federal funds rate for overnight loans between banks at 1.75 percent. 米連邦公開市場委員会の政策決定メンバーは、銀行同士の翌日物のフェデラル・ファンド（FF）金利の誘導目標を、現行の1.75％に据え置くことを全会一致で決めた。

political funds　政治資金
◆Political funds raised by political parties and organizations fell by ¥20.11 billion from the previous year. 政党や政治団体が集めた政治資金は、前年より201億1,000万円減少した。◆The revised political funds control law, which went into force in January 2000, bars businesses and organizations from making donations to an individual politician. 2000年1月施行の改正政治資金規正法では、政治家個人への企業・団体による献金が禁止されている。

Political Funds Control Law　政治資金規正法
political risk insurance　カントリー・リスク保険
political sector　政治, 政界
◆S&P's consideration of a possible downgrade on the credit ratings of long-term sovereign bonds issued by 15 eurozone countries illustrates its distrust of the reactions by the political sector. スタンダード・アンド・プアーズ（S&P）がユーロ圏15か国発行の長期国債格付けを引下げ方向で検討しているということは、政治の対応への同社の不信感を示している。◆The reactions by the political sector in resolving the sovereign debt crisis in Europe have always been one step behind. 欧州の財政危機の収束にあたって、政界の対応はつねに後手に回っている。

pool　(動)集めて置く, (共同で)蓄える, 共同出資する, 共同管理する, 共同負担する, 共同計算にする, 共同の利権とする, プールする
a pool of financing　住宅ローンなどを集約して資金調達すること
a pool of foreign exchange　共同為替管理
collateral pool　資産プール
mortgage pool indemnity policy　プール保険
mortgage pool transaction　モーゲージ・プール型取引
pool-based lending　プール方式の融資制度

pool of funds　資金プール
pool of term receivables　長期債権プール
pool operation　プール操作
pool policy　プール保険
pool slush funds　裏金作りをする
pooled deposit　合同預金
pooled fund　プール・ファンド
pooling of capital　資本の合同
pooling of interests　持ち分プーリング, プーリング法
　(=merger accounting, uniting-of-interests method: 企業合併・買収の会計処理方式の一つで, 結合される会社の資産・負債を簿価のまま項目ごと合算して合併後の存続会社に継承される)
◆The secret funds were pooled in the bank accounts of dummy companies. 裏金は, ダミー会社の銀行口座に蓄えられていた。

pool　(名)蓄え, 備蓄, 予備の蓄え, 予備, ストック, 基金, 共同出資, 共同投資, 共同資金[基金], 共同利用, 共同管理, 共同計算, カルテル, 企業連合, 共同施設要員, 共同役務要員, プール取材, 代表取材, プール制, プール
a pool of financing　住宅ローンなどを集積して資金調達すること
a pool of foreign exchange　共同為替管理
asset pool　資産プール　(=pool of assets)
blind pool　全権委任連合
bonus pool　賞与基金, 賞与支給限度総額
collateral pool　資産プール
dollar pool　ドル・プール制
gold pool　金プール, 金プール制
indirect cost pool　間接費集計額
labor pool　労働要員
mortgage pool indemnity policy　プール保険
mortgage pool transaction　モーゲージ・プール型取引
pool-based lending　プール方式の融資制度
pool of funds　資金プール
pool of term receivables　長期債権プール
pool operation　プール操作
pool policy　プール保険
pool reporter　代表取材記者
private pools　私募ファンド
working-age population pool　生産年齢人口
◆This large pool of human resources is one reason there are so many talented young workers in China. この人材の層の厚さが, 中国に有能な若い社員が多くいる一因だ。

pool insurance system　プール制度　(被害が巨額になる可能性のある保険補償について, 業界内の協力や国の財政支援で保険金の支払いをまかなう制度。2002年1月に設立されたフランスのプール制度では, テロによる年間被害額が15億ユーロを超えると, 政府が補償する仕組みになっている。⇒uninsured)
◆Such a pool insurance system is already operating in four areas: earthquakes, atomic accidents, airplane mishaps and automobile third-party liability insurance. このプール制度は, 地震, 原子力事故, 航空機事故と自賠責保険の4分野ではすでに実施されている。◆The proposed pool insurance system for terrorism would be jointly run by nonlife insurers to allow insurance claims to be paid from an industry fund. 現在提案されているテロ・プール制度は, 業界基金から(テロ被害の)保険金を支払えるようにするため, 損保各社の共同運営になる。

poor　(形)不振の, 低迷した, 伸び悩みの, 不利な, 厳しい, 乏しい, 不足した, 欠乏した, 欠けた, 悪い, 粗悪な, 劣悪な, お粗末な, 貧弱な, 少ない, 低い, 貧しい
poor chance　望み薄
poor demand　需要減, 需要薄
poor economic conditions　景気低迷, 景気悪化
poor economy　景気低迷
poor family　貧困世帯
poor inflation rate　インフレ率が高いこと, 高インフレ率
poor market conditions　市況の低迷
poor operating revenue　営業収入の低迷
poor operational performance　業績低迷, 業績の悪化
poor profitability　収益性の低迷, 低収益性
poor supply　供給薄
poor tone of the market　市場の地合いの悪さ
the poorest nations　最貧国

poor earnings　減益
◆The major securities house attributed the poor earnings to sharp drops in brokerage fees and trading profits amid the extended slump in the domestic stock market. この大手証券会社は, 減益の要因として, 国内株式市場の長期低迷による株式売買手数料と売買益の大幅減を挙げた。

poor performance　業績不振, 業績の伸び悩み
◆The shock wave caused by Toyota's poor performance has spread to a wide range of businesses. トヨタの業績不振の衝撃波が, 企業に幅広く及んできた。

poor performance of one's borrowers　貸出先の経営悪化, 貸出先の業績不振
◆The major banks attributed their increased bad loans to the poor performance of their borrowers due to the prolonged economic slump and Financial Service Agency inspections resulting in a stricter review of their asset assessments. 大手銀行は, 不良債権が増えた理由として, 長引く景気低迷で貸出先の経営が悪化したことと, 金融庁の検査を受けて大手行が資産査定を厳しくしたことを挙げた。

poor-performing company　(名)業績不振の会社[企業]　(=poor-performance company)
◆The government provides subsidies to firms that hire workers between the ages of 45 and 59 from poor-performing companies. 政府は, 業績不振の企業から43～59歳の中高年労働者を雇い入れている企業に, 助成金を出している。

poor sales　販売低迷, 販売不振, 売上低迷
　(=weak sales)
◆In 2011, we were hit by poor sales of financial products. 2011年度は, 金融商品の販売不振に見舞われました。

popular　(形)人気がある, 花形の, 庶民[一般大衆]の, 通俗の, 民間に普及している
at popular prices　安く, 廉価(れんか)で
popular bank　信用組合, 庶民金庫
popular loan　公募公債
popular share [stock]　人気株, 花形株
popular subscription　株式公募, 公募
　(=public offering)
◆Investment trust funds are popular among individual investors. 投資信託は, 個人投資家に人気がある。◆The downturn in global financial markets has had a negative impact on insurance products such as single-premium pension insurance policies which are popular as a form of savings. 世界の金融市場の低迷が, 貯蓄用[一種の貯蓄]として人気の高い一時払い年金保険などの保険商品に悪影響を及ぼしている。
◆The life insurer's single-premium whole life insurance is popular with consumers as a form of savings or an investment for retirement. 同生保の一時払い終身保険は, 一種の貯蓄や退職金の運用先として顧客に人気がある。

popularity　(名)人気, 評判, 支持, 普及
gain popularity among　～の間で好評を博する
grow [gain] in popularity　人気が出る, 人気が増す

lose popularity 人気を失う,支持を失う
◆Mixi Inc. continued strong popularity on its second day of public trading on the Tokyo stock exchange. ミキシィ(ソーシャル・ネットワーキング・サービスの最大手)は、東証での公募取引2日目も、上場初日に引き続き強い人気を保った。

pork barrel 政府の地方開発援助金(人気取りのため特定の地域、選挙区などにばらまかれる)政府交付金[政府助成金],人気取り政策
  election-year pork barrel 選挙の年に政府から出る地方開発援助金
  pork barrel add-ons (議員の人気取りのための)法案の追加条項 (⇒add-on)
  pork barrel measures バラマキ政策
  pork barrel politics 利益誘導型政治
  pork barrel project (特定の地域や選挙区の利益のために行われる)政府事業計画[政府公共事業]
  ◆These pork barrel measures cannot be allowed to continue. これらのバラマキ政策を続けるのは、許しがたいことだ。

pork-barrel spending 利益分配政治,バラマキ,人気取りのための国庫交付金[補助金]支出
  ◆A boost in public spending seems to be merely an excuse for pork-barrel spending. 財政出動[公共支出]の拡大は、単なる「バラマキ」の口実にすぎないようだ。◆LDP zokugiin have taken the lead in protecting their vested interests and pork-barrel spending. 自民党の族議員たちは、既得権益の保護や利益分配政治の先頭に立ってきた。

portfolio (名)所有有価証券,保有株式,有価証券明細表,資産内容,資産構成,資産管理,金融資産,投資資産,証券投資,再保険の既契約,既存再保険契約,目録,一覧表,ポートフォリオ
  asset portfolio 資産ポートフォリオ
  balanced portfolio 均衡のとれた資産内容
  bank's portfolio 銀行の融資先
  bias portfolios to outperform アウトパフォームするようポートフォリオにバイアスをかける
  bond component of portfolio ポートフォリオの債券部分
  bond portfolio 債券ポートフォリオ
  brand portfolio 有価証券一覧表,ブランド・ポートフォリオ
  business portfolio 事業内容
  construct portfolios consisting of various investments 各種の運用対象をカバーするポートフォリオを構築する
  create [construct, form] a portfolio ポートフォリオを構築する
  debt-financed portfolio stock 借入資金で取得した投資用株式
  diversified portfolio 分散[分散型]ポートフォリオ
  international portfolio investment 国際証券投資
  investment portfolio 投資目録,投資ポートフォリオ
  investment securities portfolio 投資有価証券ポートフォリオ
  lending portfolio 貸付けポートフォリオ
  liquidate portfolio ポートフォリオを現金化する
  loan portfolio 貸出金融資産
  optimal portfolio 最適ポートフォリオ
  overseas portfolio investment 対外証券投資
  portfolio analysis 資産構成分析
  portfolio and direct investment 証券投資と直接投資 (⇒capital outflow)
  portfolio balance ポートフォリオ均衡
  portfolio balance approach ポートフォリオ・バランス・アプローチ
  portfolio borrowing 証券投資借入れ

portfolio choice 資産選択,ポートフォリオ選択 (=portfolio selection)
portfolio company 企業先投資
portfolio decision ポートフォリオ意思決定
portfolio diversification 投資資産の分散化,ポートフォリオの分散投資,分散投資
portfolio duration ポートフォリオのデューレーション
portfolio gains ポートフォリオ売却益
portfolio holder 金融資産保有者,ポートフォリオ保有者[所有者]
portfolio holdings 金融資産保有[保有高]
portfolio inclusion ポートフォリオへの組入れ
portfolio insurance 純資産保証,保有ポートフォリオ保険,PI
portfolio interest ポートフォリオに対する利息
portfolio lender ポートフォリオ貸し手
portfolio management 資産管理,最適資産管理,資産運用,ポートフォリオ管理,ポートフォリオ運用,ポートフォリオ・マネジメント
portfolio mix ポートフォリオ・ミックス
portfolio monitoring ポーロフォリオ管理
portfolio performance 資産運用実績,資産運用成績
portfolio position ポートフォリオ保有高
portfolio rebalancing ポートフォリオのリバランス
portfolio reinsurance ポートフォリオ再保険
portfolio-risk insurance ポートフォリオ危険保険(金融資産のリスクをカバーする保険)
portfolio run-off period 既存再保険契約の残存責任期間
portfolio securities ポートフォリオの組入れ銘柄,保有銘柄
portfolio selection 資産選択,資産選好,資産管理,株式銘柄選択,ポートフォリオ・セレクション
portfolio sequences ポートフォリオ系列
portfolio stock 投資用株式
portfolio strategy ポートフォリオ戦略
portfolio weighting 株の運用比率 (⇒weighting)
portfolio [portfolio's] yield ポートフォリオの利回り
portfolios consisting of stocks and bonds 株式と債券で構成されるポートフォリオ
property [real estate] portfolio 不動産ポートフォリオ
receivable portfolio 債権ポートフォリオ
select an optimal portfolio 最適ポートフォリオを選択する
stock portfolio 株式ポートフォリオ,有価証券一覧表
synthetic portfolio 合成ポートフォリオ,総合ポートフォリオ
the net asset value of the portfolio ポートフォリオの純資産価値
troubled loan portfolio 不良債権ポートフォリオ
◆After Goldman Sachs was charged with fraud by the SEC, the investment bank said, "We did not structure a portfolio that was designed to lose money." 米証券取引委員会が証券詐欺容疑でゴールドマン・サックを提訴したのを受けて、この投資銀行は、「損失を想定したポートフォリオを組成したことはない」と述べた。◆Growing unrealized losses on their portfolios have forced many insurers to use their reserves to pay dividends. 保有株式の含み損の拡大で、保険会社の多くは準備金を取り崩して配当金の支払いに回さざるを得なくなっている。◆The life insurers' status as large shareholders means that when the market dives, their portfolios also take a tumble. 大株主としての生命保険会社の地位は、株価が大きく下がると資産内容も急激に悪化することを意味する。

portfolio investment (名)有価証券投資,証券投資,株

式・債券投資, 資産運用投資, 間接投資, ポートフォリオ投資, 投資有価証券
◆Capital outflow involves portfolio and direct investment. 資本の流出には、証券投資や直接投資もある。◆The two banks and Kokusai Securities Co. plan to establish a company that will provide private banking services, including portfolio investment and asset management. 両行と国際証券の3社は、資産運用投資や資産管理など「プライベート・バンキング」業務を行う会社を設立する計画だ。

portfolio manager　資産管理者, 資産管理担当者, 資産管理担当マネージャー, 資産運用者[資産運用機関], ポートフォリオ運用者, ファンド・マネージャー, ポートフォリオ・マネージャー
　portfolio managers rules　ファンド・マネージャー規定
◆According to the account of a portfolio manager at hedge fund, Lehman decided to play chicken with the market and they lost. ヘッジ・ファンドの資産管理担当者の話によると、リーマン・ブラザース社は市場と肝試しすることを決断して、負けた。

portfolio weighting　株の運用比率
◆Fifty-six percent of fund managers reduced their portfolio weightings in U.S. stocks. ファンド・マネージャーの56％が、米国株の運用比率を下げた。

portion　(名)部分, 一部, 〜分, 分け前, 分与財産, 割当て, 分担, 配分額, 計算額
　commercial portion　商業与信の部分
　commercial portion amounts　民間調達部分
　committed portion　引受部分, 引受ポーション
　current portion　1年以内返済分
　daily portions　日割り計算額
　portion financed by debt　借入金による調達額, 借入金で調達した分
　portion financed by equity　株式での調達額, 株式で調達した分
　portion of the debt　債務の一部
　portion of the expenses　費用の一部, 費用の分担
　trade portion of the balance of payments　国際収支うち貿易収支
　troubled portion of a portfolio　ポートフォリオの不良債権部分
　unfunded portions of these liabilities　この債務の未拠出部分
　unused portions of commitments　貸出枠未実行残高
◆Currently, a company may set transfer restrictions on a portion of its outstanding shares. 現在(2005年)、企業は一部の発行済み株式に譲渡制限を付けることができる。◆Many of the banking groups had to use a portion of their legally required reserves to pay their shareholders' dividends. 銀行グループの多くは、株主配当の原資に充てるため、法定準備金の一部の取り崩しを迫られた。◆The proceeds were used to repay a portion of the debt incurred to finance the acquisition of the company. (公募で調達した)この資金は、同社取得のための資金調達の際に発生した債務の一部返済に充てられました。

position　(名)有価証券の保有状態, 証券保有高, 持ち高, 経営基盤, 事業基盤, 位置, 地位, 役職, 状態, 地歩, 足場, 勤め口, 職, ポジション
　bear position　売り持ち, 投機的売り持ち, 空売り
　bedrock position　基本的立場
　bull position　買い持ち, 投機的買い持ち, 空買い
　capital position　自己資本比率, 資本ポジション
　cash position　現金持ち高, 現預金, 直物ポジション, キャッシュ・ポジション
　competitive position　競争力, 競争上の地位
　credit position　信用状態
　debt position　借入状況, 債務状況
　ensure market position　市場での地位を強化する
　equity position　持ち株比率, 出資比率
　exchange position　為替持ち高, 為替ポジション
　external position　対外収支
　financial position　財政状態, 財務状態, 財務体質
　foreign currency position　外貨収支
　hedge position　ヘッジ・ポジション
　impregnable position　揺るぎない地位
　key position　要職
　leading position　主導的地位
　leverage position　財務状況
　long position　買い持ち, 買い建て, ロング・ポジション
　management position　管理職, 上級管理職
　market position　市場での地位, 市場での立場
　negotiating position　交渉力
　operating position　営業状況, 事業基盤
　overbought position　買い持ち
　oversold position　売り持ち
　position paper　特定の問題に関する方針説明書, 政策方針, 項目別政策集, 国際会議などでの討議資料
　relinquish one's position as the biggest [largest] shareholder of the company　同社の筆頭株主としての座を降りる
　short position　売り持ち, 売り建て, ショート・ポジション
　strengthen our position　当社の経営基盤を強化する
　take long positions in securities　証券の買い持ちをする, 証券のロング・ポジションを取る
　take short positions in securities　証券の空売りをする, 証券のショート・ポジションを取る

◆Banks could forcibly sell insurance policies to clients by utilizing their strong position as creditors. 銀行は、債権者としての強い立場を利用して、顧客に保険を強制的に販売する可能性もある。◆Even if the United States does decide to shift its easy money policy, Japan will not immediately be in a position to follow suit. たとえ米国が金融緩和政策の転換に踏み切っても、日本が直ちに追随する環境にはないようだ。◆Following the merger, the firm's president will assume the position of chairman of the new holding company. 経営統合に伴って、同社の社長が新持ち株会社の会長に就任する。◆Ford will relinquish its position as the biggest shareholder of Mazda Motor Corp. by selling most of its 11 percent stake in Mazda. 米フォードは、保有するマツダ株11％の大半を売却して、マツダの筆頭株主の座を降りることになった。◆Restructuring should strengthen our position as the industry's low-cost manufacturer. 事業再編によって、業界の低コスト・メーカーとしての当社の地位は強化されるはずです。◆The firm's chairman will resign from all the positions he holds within the group. 同社の会長が、グループ企業の全役職を辞任する。◆The G-7 meeting has maintained its position as the most influential international economic conference. 先進7か国会議(G7)は、最も影響力のある国際経済会議としてその地位をこれまで維持してきた。◆The greenback may not be able to maintain its impregnable position as the world's only reserve currency. 米ドルは、世界で唯一の準備通貨としての揺るぎない地位を、維持できないかもしれない。◆The large U.S. current account deficit might result in a marked decline of its international investment positions. 米国の巨額の経常赤字で、海外投資家のドル資産が大幅に減少する可能性がある[海外投資家の著しいドル資産離れを招きかねない]。◆The proposed bid price does not reflect the bank's strong capital position and the superior credit quality of its assets. 株式公開買付け(TOB)の予定価格は、同行の自己資本比率の大きさや同行

の資産の高い信用力を反映していない。◆The special inspections will be conducted as banks review the positions of their debtors, and will be finalized before the closing of accounts. 特別検査は、銀行が債務者の経営状態を見直す際に行われ、決算までに完了する。◆The upcoming negotiations will determine practical measures to strengthen ties, including the merger ratio, the name of the new group and the positions to be held by top executives. 今後の交渉で、統合比率や新グループの名称、首脳人事など提携強化の具体策を詰める。◆The yen soared to its strongest position this year. 円は、年初来の最高値を付けた。

positive （形）プラスの,正の,黒字の,強含みの,強気の,好影響を与える,明るい,上昇傾向にある,積極的な,前向きの,建設的な,決定的な,否定しがたい,実証的な,実際的な,ポジティブ （名）強気材料,好材料,プラス要因（⇒negative, tone）
　achieve positive growth　プラス成長を果たす
　be a positive for bonds　債券相場には好材料である
　be positive about　〜に強気である
　positive adjustment policy　積極的調整政策
　positive analysis　実証的分析,実証分析
　positive aspect　好材料,プラスの材料
　positive attitude［step］　前向きの姿勢
　positive authorization　正の承認
　positive balance　プラスの残高
　positive balance of trade　順調貿易差額
　positive capital movement　正の資本移動
　positive carry　ポジティブ・キャリー（証券購入のための借入金利が証券利回りよりも低く、利益を生む状態にあること）
　positive cash flow　正のキャッシュ・フロー
　positive curve　順イールド
　positive effect　プラス効果,正の効果
　positive equilibrium rate of interest　正の均衡利子率
　positive factor　強気の材料,好材料,買い材料,プラス要因,重要なポイント（マイナス要因,悪材料＝negative factor）
　positive figure　黒字
　positive financial performance　好業績（＝strong financial performance）
　positive financial policy　積極的金融政策
　positive fiscal policy　積極的財政政策,積極財政
　positive gap　ポジティブ・ギャップ
　positive goodwill　積極的のれん,積極的営業権
　positive impact　好影響,プラス効果
　positive implications　好材料,プラス要因,格上げの方向
　positive interest　プラスの利子,正の利子
　positive interest rate　プラスの利子率,正の利子率（＝positive rate of interest）
　positive investment　積極的投資,正の投資
　positive list　自由化品目表
　positive monetary effect　積極的金融効果,積極的通貨効果
　positive monetary policy　積極的金融政策,積極的通貨政策
　positive net reserve　プラスの純準備
　positive neutrality　積極的中立性
　positive outlook　明るい見通し
　positive points　好材料
　positive spread　順ざや
　positive yield (curve)　正の利回り曲線,順イールド・カーブ

revise upward the rating outlook from negative to positive 格付け見通しを「ネガティブ（弱含み）」から「ポジティブ（強含み）」に上方修正する
◆The G-7 leaders merely welcomed Washington's economic stimulus measures in the form of interest rate cuts and tax cuts as "positive." G7首脳は、利下げや減税などの形での米政府の景気刺激策を「積極的」として歓迎しただけだ。◆The tone in the Treasury market is becoming extremely positive. 債券市場の地合いは、ひじょうに明るくなっている。◆The U.S. credit rating agency revised upward the outlook to positive from negative on its rating on Sumitomo Life Insurance Co. この米国の信用格付け機関は、住友生命保険の格付け見通しを「ネガティブ（弱含み）」から「ポジティブ（強含み）」に上方修正した。

positive earnings　好業績,好決算
◆Japanese exporting firms have been enjoying positive earnings, benefiting from thriving markets in the United States and the weak yen. 日本の輸出企業は、米国の好調な市場と円安を追い風に、好業績が続いている。

positive growth　プラス成長
◆The BOJ predicts steady positive growth for the nation's real GDP, with 1.8 percent growth in fiscal 2010 an 2 percent growth in fiscal 2011. 国内総生産（GDP）の実質成長率は2010年度が1.8%、2011年度が2%と、日銀は堅調なプラス成長を見込んでいる。◆The real gross domestic product for the April-June period returned to positive growth for the first time in five quarters. 4-6月期の実質国内総生産（GDP）は、5四半期ぶりにプラス成長に転じた。◆There's no miracle cure available to realize positive growth. プラス成長達成への特効薬はない。

positive impact　好影響,プラスの影響（＝positive influence）
◆The recent appointment of a new financial minister will have a positive impact on the administration. 今回の財務相交代は、政権運営にプラスの影響を与えると思われる。

positive influence　好影響,プラスの影響（＝positive impact）
◆Rapidly increasing prices of primary commodities have had a positive influence on corporate performance with the yen's appreciation against the dollar. 円高・ドル安で、これまでのところ一次産品（原油や石炭など）の急騰が、企業の業績に好影響をもたらしている。

positive reading　プラスの数値,プラス
◆The diffusion index (DI) of business confidence among large manufacturers marked the first positive reading in 33 months. 大手製造業の業況判断指数（DI）は、2年9か月ぶりにプラスに転じた。

positive results　好業績,好決算（＝good results, positive earnings, robust performance）
◆Negative factors could affect these positive results, such as rapidly falling prices for printers. プリンターの売価急落などのマイナス要因が、これらの好決算に影響を及ぼす可能性がある。

positive territory　プラス,プラス基調,プラスの領域
◆The diffusion index of business sentiment among large manufacturers recovered to positive territory for the first time in two quarters. 大企業・製造業の業況判断指数（DI）は、2四半期（半年）ぶりにプラスに転じた。

possess　（動）所有する,保有する,占有する,所持する
◆A huge number of government bonds issued by the United States and European countries are possessed by financial institutions around the world. 米国や欧州各国が発行した大量の国債は、世界の金融機関が保有している。◆French bond prices slipped as French banks possess a large volume of Greek and Italian bonds. フランス銀行がギリシャやイタリアなどの国債を保有しているため、フランス国債が値下がりした。
◆Investors grow concerned about the fact that French banks

possess a large volume of Greek and Italian bonds. 投資家は、フランスの銀行がギリシャやイタリアの国債を大量に保有していることを警戒している。◆The debacle of the eurozone's sovereign bond prices caused losses to banks possessing peripheral sovereign debts as their assets. ユーロ圏の国債価格の暴落で、周辺国の国債を資産として抱える銀行は、損失を被った。

possession （名）所有, 保有, 占有, 所持, 所有物, 所持品, 財産, 所有権, 支配権

actual possession　現実の占有
bond yield in the possession period　所有期間利回り
chose in possession　動産
debtor in possession　継承破産人
estate in possession　現有不動産権, 現有不動産物件
exclusive possession　排他的占有
hostile possession　自主占有
in one's possession　〜が所有する, 〜が占有する
personal possessions　個人財産
possession in deed [fact]　現実の占有
right of possession　占有権, 所有権
take into possession　抵当権を実行する
take possession of　〜を取得する

◆In the temporary nationalization, the government will take possession of all shares from the bank's holding company at no cost. 一時国有化で、政府は同行の持ち株会社から株式をゼロ円で全株取得することになる。

possible （形）可能な, 実現可能な, 可能性のある, 潜在的な, 起こりそうな, 想定される, 〜を視野に入れた, 〜候補の

a possible financial meltdown　想定される金融崩壊（⇒guard）
possible transactions　実現可能取引, 発生可能な取引
reserve for possible future loss　偶発損失準備金
reserve for possible loan losses　貸倒れ引当金
review for possible downgrade　格下げの方向で検討する

◆Many pundits in Tokyo have prophesized the possible demise of U.S. primacy since the financial bubble burst. 金融バブルの崩壊以降、日本では、米一極指導の終焉（しゅうえん）を予言する専門家が多い。◆The government should take all possible fiscal and financial means to bring the still ailing economy back on the road to recovery. 政府は、いまだにどん詰まり状態にある景気を回復の軌道に乗せるために、財政と金融の両面からの政策を総動員すべきだ。◆The rating outlook of "negative" by a credit rating agency means that another downgrade is possible in the next 12 to 18 months. 信用格付け機関による「ネガティブ（弱含み）」の格付け見通しは、今後1年〜1年半にふたたび格下げされる可能性があることを意味している。◆Through continuing gains in annual earnings, it will be possible, over time, to adjust the payout ratio while still maintaining our dividend record. 年間利益の増大を続けることによって、当社の配当実績を今後とも維持しながら、時期が来たら配当性向を調整することは可能である。

possible currency war　想定される通貨安戦争

◆At the G-20 currency meeting, economically advanced and emerging economies have reined in their antagonism and agreed to avoid a possible currency war. 世界20か国・地域（G20）の通貨会議で、先進国と新興国が対立を封印して、想定される通貨安戦争を回避することで合意した。

possible delisting　上場廃止の可能性

◆Tokyo, Osaka and Nagoya bourses placed Nikko Cordial stock on their respective supervision posts for possible delisting. 東京、大阪、名古屋の3証券取引所が、それぞれ日興コーディアルの株式を、上場廃止の可能性があるため監理ポストに割り当てた。

possible downgrade　想定される格下げ, 格下げの可能性, 引下げ[格下げ]の方向

◆Moody's Investors Service Inc. is reviewing 14 British banks for possible downgrade. ムーディーズ・インベスターズ・サービスは現在、英銀14行の格付けを、格下げの方向で検討している。◆Standard & Poor's is considering a possible downgrade on the credit ratings of long-term sovereign bonds issued by 15 eurozone states. 米格付け会社のスタンダード・アンド・プアーズ（S&P）は、ユーロ圏15か国発行の長期国債格付け[信用格付け]を、引下げ方向で検討している。◆The possible downgrade of Treasury bonds is raising fears of adverse effects on the world's markets. 想定される米国債の格下げで、世界の市場に及ぼす悪影響への懸念が高まっている。◆The United States' credit has come into question by the possible downgrade of the U.S. government's credit rating. 米国債の格付けが引き下げられる可能性があることから、米国の信用が疑われている。

possible financial meltdown　想定される[想定された]金融崩壊

◆The guard raised against a possible financial meltdown during a financial sector-triggered recession several years ago has been lifted. 数年前の金融不況時に想定された金融崩壊に対する厳戒態勢は、すでに解かれている。

possible merger　合併の可能性

◆The two banks have started negotiations on the integration of their businesses, a possible merger. 両行は、合併の可能性も含めて、経営統合に向けた協議を開始した。

possible setback　景気後退の可能性

◆Among other factors that could adversely affect the national economy are possible setbacks in the Chinese and U.S. economies as well as high oil prices. 国内景気に悪影響を及ぼす恐れがある他の要因として、中国や米国の景気後退や原油高がある。

possible yen-selling intervention　想定される円売り介入, 円売り介入の可能性

◆Caution grew about possible yen-selling intervention by the government. 想定される政府の円売り介入に対する警戒感が、強まった。

possible yen-selling market intervention　円売り市場介入の可能性

◆Market players remain wary of a possible yen-selling market intervention by Japanese authorities. 市場関係者は、日本当局（政府・日銀）による新たな円売り市場介入の可能性をまだ警戒している。

post （動）発表する, 公示する, 示す, 提示する, 記録する, 達成する, 赤字や黒字などを計上する, 担保や証拠金などを差し入れる, 担保を設定する, 配置する, 配属する, 任命する,（保釈金などを）積む[支払う], 投函する, 郵送する, メッセージを送る,（ネット上の）書き込みをする

post A as　Aを〜と発表する
post a healthy advance [increase]　好調な伸びを示す
post additional margin　追加の証拠金を差し入れる
post bail [a bond, bond]　保釈金を積む, 保釈金を払う
post collateral　担保を差し入れる, 担保を設定する
post huge losses　巨額の赤字を計上する, 巨額の赤字[損失]を出す　（⇒rake in）
post net gains　黒字を計上する
post net operating profits　（金融機関が）業務純益を計上する,（一般企業が）営業純利益[純営業利益]を計上する
post only a slight rise over the quarter　前四半期比で微増[わずかな増加]にとどまる
posted price　（原油などの）公示価格

◆All major banking groups posted net operating profits from core businesses that were comparable to last year's. 全大手銀行・金融グループが、前年並みの本業による業務純益を計上

した。◆Japan's balance of trade in goods and services posted a surplus of ￥180.9 billion in August, against a deficit of ￥257 billion a year earlier. 8月（2009年）の日本のモノとサービスの貿易収支は、前年同月の2,570億円の赤字に対して、1,809億円の黒字となった。◆Stock exchanges in both Japan and the United States successively posted major losses. 日米の株式市場は連日、大幅な下げを記録した。◆The company is likely to post a group net loss of ￥50 billion for the current business year, its third straight year of red ink. 同社の今年度の連結税引き後利益は、500億円の赤字（3年連続の赤字）になる見込みだ。◆The company posted consolidated sales of ￥480.4 billion in the business year to August 31, 2009. 同社の2009年8月期の連結売上高は、4,804億円だった。◆The company posted ￥44 billion in sales in its business year ending in January 2011. 同社の2011年1月期決算の売上高は、440億円だった。◆The proposed pact will exempt expats from paying into pension and health insurance plans in the country to which they are posted, provided they stay no more than five years. 協定案では、海外駐在員の滞在期間が5年以内であれば、駐在する相手国の年金と医療保険制度への加入を免除される。◆The rule of asset impairment accounting requires companies to post valuation losses on fixed assets whose market value has fallen sharply from their book value. 減損会計基準は、固定資産の時価が簿価から大幅に下落した場合の固定資産の評価損の計上を、企業に義務付けている。◆These corporate groups' parent companies posted huge losses when closing their accounts in March. これらの企業グループの親会社は、3月決算で巨額の赤字［損失］を出した。

post　（名）職、地位、部署、持ち場、任務、ポスト
be at one's post　持ち場についている、任務についている
be relieved of one's post　解任される
liquidation post　整理ポスト
monitoring post　監理ポスト、監視ポスト
　（=supervision post;⇒liquidation post）
presidential post　社長ポスト
supervision post　監理ポスト
　（⇒supervision post）
trading post　取引ポスト
◆Following the merger, the firm's president will take the post of president of the new holding company. 経営統合に伴って、同社の社長が新持ち株会社の社長に就任する。◆Investors can trade the Seibu Railway shares for a month after their transfer to the TSE's liquidation post from the monitoring post. 西武鉄道株が東証の監理ポストから整理ポストに移った後1か月間、投資家は西武鉄道株を売買できる。◆The post of president has been vacant. 社長のポストは、空席になっている。◆The Tokyo Stock Exchange moved the company's stock to its liquidation post from the monitoring post. 東京証券取引所（東証）は、同社株を監理ポストから整理ポストに移した。◆The vice president of Mizuho Corporate Bank will take up the post of president and chief executive officer in the newly merged firm. 合併新会社の社長兼最高経営責任者（CEO）には、みずほコーポレート銀行の副頭取が就任する。

postal bank　ゆうちょ銀行
◆As a provisional measure until the ￥10 million limit on postal bank deposits is removed, the government intends to raise the ceiling to ￥30 million. ゆうちょ銀行の1人当たり1,000万円の預け入れ限度額を撤廃するまでの暫定措置として、政府は限度額［上限］を3,000万円に引き上げる方針だ。

postal book-transfer savings　郵便振替口座
◆Postal book-transfer savings are used only for settlement purposes and are fully guaranteed by the central government. 郵便振替口座は、決済専門で、国が全額保証している。

postal business　郵政事業
postal corporation　郵政公社

postal insurance　簡易保険
◆More than ￥360 trillion in postal savings and postal insurance funds were under the government's control, and this massive amount of money flew into public corporations and other government-affiliated organizations. 郵便貯金、簡易保険あわせて360兆円余の資金が国の管理下に置かれ、この巨額な資金が特殊法人や他の政府関係機関に流れ込んでいた。

postal life insurance　簡易生命保険
postal privatization　郵政民営化
◆The purpose of postal privatization was to do away with the current inefficient system, in which huge funds raised through inflated postal savings and kampo life insurance policies flow into public corporations. 郵政民営化の目的は、肥大した郵便貯金と簡易保険で調達した巨額の資金が特殊法人に流れる現在の非効率的なシステムを、廃止することにあった。

postal savings　郵便貯金　（⇒Net-debit service, preferential tax treatment, public money）
郵便貯金の種類：
fixed-amount savings　定額貯金
fixed deposits　定期貯金
ordinary deposits　通常貯金

posted prices of land　公示地価
　（=listed land prices, listed prices of land）
◆The posted prices of land has have declined for 11 consecutive years. 公示地価は、11年連続で下落している。

postpone　（動）延期する、先送りする、延ばす
postpone a planned listing　上場計画を延期する
postpone the introduction of IFRSs　国際財務報告規準（IFRS）の導入を延期する
postpone the merger　統合を延期する
◆In the aftermath of the March 11 massive earthquake and tsunami, the Financial Services Agency will likely postpone the introduction of IFRSs. 東日本大震災（2011年3月11日）の影響で、金融庁は国際財務報告基準（IFRS）の導入を延期する方向だ。◆It is highly likely that the merger between the two financial institutions will be postponed. 両金融機関の統合が延期されるのは必至だ。◆It is the first time in Japan that a company has postponed a planned listing due to the subprime crisis. サブプライム・ローン（米国の低所得者向け住宅融資）問題で企業が上場計画を延期したのは、日本では始めてだ。

postretirement benefit　退職後給付
◆It is the Corporation's practice to fund amounts for postretirement benefits, with an independent trustee, as deemed appropriate from time to time. 随時適切と思われる退職後給付額を、独立した信託機関に積み立てるのが、当社の慣行となっています。

postwar record　戦後の最高値、戦後最高値
◆On Aug. 31, 2011, the yen rose to the ￥76.50 level against the U.S. dollar in the Tokyo foreign exchange market, close to the postwar record of ￥75.95 registered on Aug. 19. 2011年8月31日の東京外国為替市場の円相場は、1ドル＝76円50銭台まで上昇し、8月19日に付けた戦後最高値の75円95銭に近づいた。

postwar record value　戦後最高値
◆The yen's value still remains high and is likely to reach a postwar record value above the ￥76-to-the-dollar level. 円相場は依然高く、1ドル＝76円台を上回る戦後最高値に達する可能性がある。

potent　（形）説得力のある、有力な、強力な、強い、よく効く、強い効力［効き目、効果］がある
◆Two potent corporate buyout tools of stock splits and stock swaps were the key to the remarkable growth of the company. 株式分割と株式交換という二つの強力な企業買収の手段が、同社の急成長のカギだった。

potential （名）可能性, 将来性, 潜在能力, 潜在力, 潜在成長率, 余力, 余地, 素質, ポテンシャル
   borrowing potential　借入れ余力
   cost cutting potential　コスト削減の余地
   earnings growth potential　増益力, 増益の余地, 収益増加の可能性
   earnings potential　潜在収益力
   economic potential　経済の潜在力
   （=potential of the economy）
   growth potential　成長潜在力, 潜在成長力, 成長余地, 成長能力, 成長ポテンシャル
   investment potential　投資収益力
   market potential　市場の可能性, 市場としての可能性
   potential for recovery　回復力
   production potential　生産能力
   sales potential　販売可能性, 販売可能量, 販売見込み高
   upside potential　上昇する可能性, 値上りの可能性, 値上りの余地
◆Strategic investment increased the potential for the Corporation's growth in worldwide markets. 戦略的投資で、グローバル市場での当社の潜在成長力は高まりました。◆The Bank of Japan widened the scope of cheap loans to support smaller companies with growth potential. 潜在成長力のある中小企業を支援するため、日銀が低利融資枠を拡大した。◆The recent M&A is a strategy with an eye on Asia, which has a great potential for sales growth. 今回のM&Aは、販売が伸びる可能性が大きいアジアを視野に入れた戦略です。◆The white paper on the economy and public finance did not present a clear remedy for the Japanese economy that would help it regain its growth potential. 経済財政白書には、日本経済が成長力を取り戻すための明確な処方箋［対策］が示されなかった。

potential （形）可能性がある, 見込みのある, 有力な, 潜在的な, 将来起こりそうな
   potential ability　潜在能力
   potential acquisition　買収計画
   potential buyer　将来買ってくれそうな人, 買い手候補
   potential buying power　潜在購買力
   potential common stock　潜在株式
   potential consumer　潜在的消費者
   potential customers　お客になってくれそうな人, 見込み顧客, 潜在顧客, 潜在的な顧客層, 潜在顧客層
   potential demand　潜在需要
   potential gross national product　潜在国民総生産, 潜在GNP
   potential growth　潜在成長力
   potential growth rate　潜在成長力
   potential inflation　潜在的インフレーション
   potential liability　潜在的債務額
   potential market　潜在市場
   potential output　潜在生産力, 潜在的産出量, 潜在的生産量
   potential profit　潜在的利益
   potential seller　売却を考えている人, 潜在的売り手
   potential share［stock］　権利株, 潜在的株式

potential capital shortage　潜在的な資本不足
◆European banks are forced to shore up their potential capital shortages to restore market confidence. 欧州銀行は、市場の信認を回復するため、潜在的資本不足の増強を迫られている。

potential downgrade　想定される格下げ, 格下げの可能性, 引下げ［格下げ］の方向
   （=possible downgrade）
◆The credit rating agency Fitch is putting six eurozone nations including Italy and Spain on watch for potential downgrades in the near future. 欧米格付け会社のフィッチは、イタリアやスペインなどユーロ圏6か国を、近い将来格下げの方向で［イタリアやスペインなどユーロ6か国の長期国債格付けを引下げ方向で］見直している。

potential fraud　詐欺の可能性
◆The U.S. FBI is looking at potential fraud by four major financial institutions. 米連邦捜査局は、大手金融機関4社（政府系住宅金融ファニー・メイ、フレディ・マックの2社のほか、米保険最大手のAIGとリーマン・ブラザーズ）による詐欺の可能性を検討している。

potential growth rate　潜在成長率
◆The target range for the inflation rate could be set at the same level as the potential growth rate, for example. 物価上昇率の目標値としては、例えば潜在成長率と同水準に設定することもできよう。

potential loss　予想損失, 潜在的損失額
◆A bank's capital adequacy ratio represents the amount of core capital it has to cushion potential losses, as a percentage of loans and other assets. 銀行の自己資本比率は、融資額などの資産に対して、予想損失の処理に充てられる自己資本［中核資本］がどれだけあるかを示す。◆Banking titan Citigroup Inc. repeatedly misled investors about its potential losses from subprime mortgages. 米金融大手のシティグループは、サブプライム・ローン（低所得者向け住宅融資）による予想損失額について、投資家に繰り返し誤った情報を提供していた。

pound （名）ポンド（1 pound=100 pence）
   British pound　英ポンド
   devaluation of pound　ポンド切下げ
   pound coin　1ポンド貨幣
   strong pound　ポンド高
   the weaker pound　ポンド安
◆In the case of foreign currency deposits, depositors can invest in foreign currencies such as British pound, Swiss franc and Australian dollar as well as the U.S. dollar and euro. 外貨預金の場合、預金者は、米ドルやユーロのほかに英ポンド、スイス・フランや豪ドルなどにも投資することができる。

power （動）〜を動かす, 〜を牽引する, 〜の原動力になる, 〜に動力を供給する, 〜に動力源を与える, 〜を勢いよく進む［動く］
   be powered by　〜で動く
   power the economy　経済の原動力になる
   the engine powering the Japanese economy　日本経済を牽引するエンジン
◆Domestic and foreign demands, the two engines powering Japan's economic growth, are out of kilter. 日本の経済成長を引っ張る原動力の内需と外需が、今のところ不調だ。

power （名）力, 能力, 権力, 権能, 権限, 法的権限, 支配力, 指名権, 電力, エネルギー, パワー
   borrowing power　借入能力
   buying power　購買力 （=purchasing power）
   excess earnings power　超過収益力
   financial power　金の力
   gain or loss in purchasing power　購買力損益
   historical cost/constant purchasing power accounting　取得原価・統一購買力会計
   improve one's earning power　収益力を向上させる
   power lunch　昼食会, 昼食会議, 昼食をとりながらのビジネス会議
   power-sharing　権限分担, 権限分有
   pricing power　価格支配力, 価格交渉力
   shifting power to price　価格転嫁力
   the power of attorney　委任状, 委任権, 代理権

（=letter of attorney）
- the powers that be 当局, 当局者, その筋, その筋の人たち
- the real power behind the throne 陰の実力者, 黒幕
- voting power 議決権

◆Larger size by the merger of two steelmakers will reinforce their bargaining power on resource prices. 鉄鋼メーカー2社の合併による規模拡大で、両社の資源価格の交渉力が今後強まることになる。◆Major U.S. and European banks are improving their earning power. 欧米の大手銀行は、収益力を向上させている。◆The Tokyo Stock Exchange has no power to directly supervise certified public accountants. 東京証券取引所に、公認会計士を直接監督する権限はない。◆To shore up their economies, major economic powers seem to be relying more on their monetary policies. 景気テコ入れに、先進国は金融政策頼みの様相が強まっている。

powerful （形）強力な, 強い, 力強い, 影響力のある, 影響力を持った, 有力な, 権力のある, 人を動かす, 説得力のある, 大手の, 効力[効能]のある
- a powerful competitor 強力な競争相手[ライバル]
- the most powerful bank 最大手行, 最大手の金融機関
（=the most influential bank）

powerful bank 大手銀行, 大手金融機関, 金融大手
◆Goldman Sachs emerged from the global financial meltdown as Wall Street's most powerful bank. ゴールドマン・サックスは、ウォール街最大手の金融機関として世界的な金融危機を乗り切った。

practical （形）実際的な, 実用的な, 実践的な, 具体的な, 事実上の, 実質上の, 現実的な, 実現可能な, 経験に富んだ, 役に立つ
- practical difficulties 実施上の困難, 実行上の困難
- practical experience 実際の経験, 実地経験
- practical insolvency 実質的破産
- practical policy 実現可能な政策
- practical measures 具体策

◆The upcoming negotiations will determine practical measures to strengthen ties, including the merger ratio, the name of the new group and the positions to be held by top executives. 今後の交渉で、統合比率や新グループの名称、首脳人事など提携強化の具体策を詰める。

practice （名）実行, 実践, 実務, 営業, 開業, 業務, 慣行, 慣習, 習俗, 手法, 商法, 仕組み, 法律事務, 訴訟実務, 訴訟手続き
- accounting practices 会計慣行, 会計実務, 会計処理
- backdoor practice 裏口操作
- banking practice 銀行業務
- best practice 最善の手法, 最良の方法, 卓越した事例, 最善の実施例[業務慣行], 最善の慣行
- business practice 商慣習, 商慣行, 企業慣行, 取引慣行, 取引方法, 営業手法, 業務
- collection practices 回収業務
- collusive practices 談合
- common practice 一般的な慣行
- current practice 現行実務, 現行業務
- debt servicing practices 債務返済の慣行
- evil practice 悪弊
- Fair Debt Collection Practices Act 公正債権回収法
- fair practice 公正慣行, 公正慣習
- financial practice 金融措置
- financial reporting practice 財務報告実務
- Foreign Corrupt Practices Act 海外不正行為防止法
- fraudulent practices 詐欺商法, 悪質商法
- general practice 一般慣習
- industry practices 業界の慣行
- labor practice 労働慣行, 労働行為
- lending practice 融資慣行
- management accounting practice 管理会計実務
- management practices 管理慣行, 経営スタイル, 経営手法, 経営実態
- market-distorting trade practices 市場を歪める商慣行
- market practice 市場慣行
- netting practice ネッティング慣行
- operating practice 経営手法
- practice improvement plan 業務改善計画
- practice management 経営手法
（=operating management）
- present practice 現行業務, 現行実務
（=current practice）
- priority practice 優先交渉慣行
- product development practice 製品開発戦略
- restrictive practices 制限的慣行, 制限的取引慣行
- risk management practices リスク管理慣行
- trade practices 貿易慣行, 取引慣行, 商慣行
- trading practices 取引慣行
- unfair business practices 不公正取引慣行, 不公正商慣習
- uniform practice code 統一慣習規則

◆Financial Services Agency has ordered 26 nonlife insurance firms to correct their business practices, after finding they failed to pay due insurance benefits. 損保各社が支払う義務のある保険金を支払わなかったことが判明したため、金融庁は損保26社に対して業務是正命令を出した。◆In the life insurance sector, the practice of luring customers by touting the bad performances of other insurers has been called into question. 生保業界では、他社の経営不振をあおって顧客を勧誘する行為（風評営業）が問題になっている。◆It is a common business practice in Japan for financial institutions and their client companies to cross-hold large amounts of each other's stocks. 日本では、金融機関とその取引先企業が互いに大量の株式を持ち合うのが一般の取引慣行だ。◆It is the Corporation's practice to fund amounts for postretirement benefits, with an independent trustee, as deemed appropriate from time to time. 随時適切と思われる退職後給付額を、独立した信託機関に積み立てるのが、当社の慣行となっています。◆Short selling is the practice of borrowing stocks from securities and financial companies and other investors to sell them and then buy them back when their prices drop. 空売りは、証券金融会社や他の投資家（機関投資家など）から株を借りて売り、その株が値下がりした時点で買い戻すことをいう。◆Since December, the FSA has ordered three firms to make changes to their business practices. 12月以降、金融庁は3社に業務改善命令を出した。◆The consultant manipulated the company's stock price by engaging in certain prohibited practices including wash sales. コンサルタントは、仮装売買（売り注文と買い注文を同時に出す方法）などの不正行為で株価を操作した。◆The firm's practice of issuing false financial statements about the holdings of major stockholders dates back to 1980 or earlier. 大株主の保有株式に関して虚偽記載の有価証券報告書を発行する同社の慣行は、1980年以前にさかのぼる。◆The scandal-ridden Incubator Bank of Japan came under fire for its lax lending practices and arrests of its executives. 不祥事続きの日本振興銀行は、乱脈融資や経営陣の逮捕などでも激しく非難された。

precedence （名）優位, 優先, 優先すること, 優先権, 重要であること, 先行, 上位, 席次, 序列, 上席権
- give precedence to ～に上席を与える, ～の優位[優先権]を認める
- have precedence over [of] ～より重要である
- in order of precedence 優先順に

take precedence over [of]　～に［～よりも］優先する、～に先立つ、～に勝る、～より重要性がある
◆To overcome the current economic crisis, stimulus measures should take precedence over fiscal reconstruction for the time being. 現在の経済危機を克服するためには、当面は、財政再建よりも景気対策を優先しなければならない。

precondition　（名）前提条件，必要条件
（⇒demand動詞）
a precondition for raising purchase prices for bad loans　不良債権の買取り価格引上げの前提条件
（⇒secure money）
a precondition for receiving financial support from the government　政府から金融支援を受けるための前提条件
◆An increase in banks' loan loss reserves is a precondition for raising purchase prices for bad loans. 銀行の貸倒れ引当金の強化が、不良債権の買取り価格引上げの前提条件となる。

predecessor　（名）前任者，先任者，先輩，前身，旧～
predecessor accountant　前任会計士
predecessor auditor　前任監査人
predecessor firm [company]　前身会社，被合併会社
three predecessor banks　旧3行
◆Since three banks integrated their operations, executives from the three predecessor banks served on an equal basis as presidents of the Mizuho group, Mizuho Bank and Mizuho Corporate Bank. 3銀行の経営統合以来、旧3行の経営者が、みずほグループ（FG）、みずほ銀行、みずほコーポレート銀行のトップをそれぞれ分け合あった。◆The former president of the company founded a predecessor firm of the company in 1970. 同社の前社長が、1970年に同社の前身会社を設立した。◆Yukio Hatoyama, Kan's predecessor, sought to put Japan-U.S. relations on an equal footing and triggered unnecessary friction and confusion. 菅の前任者の鳩山前首相は、対等な日米関係を標榜して、無用の摩擦や混乱を招いた。

predicament　（名）困難な状況，（特定の）状況，境遇，窮状，苦，苦境，窮地，窮境
a financial predicament　財政的苦境，財政的に困難な状況
a trio of predicaments　三重苦
be placed in a predicament　苦境に置かれる
come out of the predicament　苦境から脱出する，苦境を抜け出す
dire predicaments　悲惨な状態，極度の窮状
fiscal predicament　財政的苦境，財政ひっ迫
◆Amid the protracted economic slump and the ongoing deflationary trend, the life insurance industry has been hit by a trio of predicaments. 景気の長期低迷とデフレ傾向が進行するなか、生保業界は三重苦に見舞われている。◆The rapid spread of Italy's credit crisis is due to intensified fears about the nation's fiscal predicament by Italy's huge fiscal deficits. イタリアの信用不安が急速に広がったのは、イタリアの巨額の赤字で同国の財政ひっ迫への警戒感が高まったからだ。◆To deal with this predicament, the three companies worked out streamlining measures to cut costs. この苦境に対処するため［この苦境から脱却するため］、3社はリストラ策をまとめ、コストの削減を図っている。

predict　（動）予測する，予想する，想定する，予知する，予報する，予言する
predict future market moves　将来の市場動向を予測する
predict price movement　価格変動を予測する
predict (the direction of) interest rates　金利動向を予測する
◆It is difficult to precisely predict future developments. 将来の動き［将来の展開］を正確に予想するのは、難しい。◆It is difficult to predict if new explosive factors emerge to plunge the financial market into further turmoil. 金融市場をさらに混乱に陥れる新しい火種があるのかどうか、予測するのは難しい。◆Japan Airlines will be able to clear excess debts by the end of this fiscal year due to larger-than-predicted earnings. 業績が予想を上回ったため、日本航空は、今年度末には債務超過を解消できる見込みだ。◆Some observers predicted that the global financial crisis would hurt Japan the least. 日本は世界金融危機による傷が世界で最も浅い、と見る向きもあった。◆The exchange rate in fiscal 2011 had been predicted to be between ¥80 and ¥83 per dollar by many Japanese exporters. 2011年度の為替レートを、多くの日本の輸出業者は1ドル＝80～83円と想定していた。◆The index of leading economic indicators predicts economic developments about six months ahead. 景気先行指数は、約6か月先の景気動向を示す指標だ。

prediction　（名）予測，予想，予知，予報，予言
business prediction　景気予測
economic prediction　経済予測
financial prediction　財務予測
intuitive prediction　直観的予測
prediction error　予測誤差
simple prediction　単純予測
statistical prediction　統計予測，統計的予測
◆The annualized GDP growth rate in the third quarter of the year was much lower than the prediction by many market players. 今年第3四半期（7-9月期）の年率換算でのGDP（国内総生産）成長率は、市場関係者の大方の予想を大幅に下回った。

predominant　（形）有力な，優位な，支配的な，広く行われている，主な，顕著な，目立つ
◆France is a predominant player in the European economy alongside Germany. フランスは、ドイツとともに欧州経済を支えている。

preference　（名）優先，優遇，特恵，優先権，先取権，選好，好み，志向，選択
consumer's preference　消費者選好，消費者選択
credit preferences　信用優先権
fiscal preference　財政選好
give [show] preference to　～に優先権を与える，～を優遇する
in preference to　～に優先して，～ではなく
lender's preference　貸し手の選好
management preference　経営者選好
preference dividend　優先配当
preference index　選好指数
preference ordering　選好順序
preference share [stock]　優先株
　（=preferred share [stock]）
preference treatment　特恵待遇
preference treatment tariff　特恵関税
　（=preferential duties）
scale of preferences　選好の尺度
special tax preferences　優遇税制
yen preference　円選好

preferential　（形）優先的な，先取権のある，優遇する，特恵的な，選択的な，差別制の
preferential bill　優遇手形
preferential creditor　優先債権者
preferential interest rate for companies　企業向け融資の優遇金利

preferential interest rate　優遇金利
◆The base lending rate of the Housing Loan Corporation and the preferential interest rate for companies have risen. 住宅金融公庫の基準貸出金利や企業向け融資の優遇金利が、上

昇した[引き上げられた]。
preferential nonvoting share 議決権のない優先株式
◆Sanyo will issue preferential nonvoting shares worth about ¥50 billion to Sumitomo Mitsui Banking Corp. 三洋電機は、三井住友銀行を引受先として約500億円の議決権がない優先株式を発行する。
preferential tax system 優遇税制
　(=preferential taxation system)
　preferential tax system for housing loans 住宅ローン減税制度, 住宅ローン減税, 住宅減税
　　(⇒housing loan)
　preferential tax system for public entities 公益法人への優遇税制
　preferential tax system for securities 証券優遇税制
◆To stimulate the stock market, the preferential tax system for securities should be extended and expanded. 株式市場のてこ入れには、証券優遇税制の延長や拡充が必要だ。
preferential tax treatment 優遇税制措置, 税制優遇
◆The proposal to phase out the system of not taxing interest on bank deposits and postal savings of those aged 65 or older while leaving preferential tax treatment for doctors intact shows a lack of balance. 医師の優遇税制措置(事業税優遇措置)に手をつけずに、65歳以上の高齢者の銀行預金と郵便貯金への利子非課税制度(高齢者マル優)を段階的に廃止する案は、バランスを欠くことを示している。
preferred creditor status 優先債権者の地位
◆The new rehabilitation law for financial institutions enacted two years ago gives a preferred creditor status to policyholders seeking refunds of their premiums. 2年前に施行された金融機関の更生特例法では、保険金の弁済を求める保険契約者に優先債権者の地位(他の債権に優先して保険金の弁済を受ける権利)が与えられている。
preferred share 優先株式, 優先株　(=preferred stock: 利益の配当や会社解散時の残余財産の分配が普通株式に優先して与えられる株式で、一般に議決権(経営参加権 :voting right)は与えられない。⇒preferred stock)
　convertible preferred shares 転換型優先株, 転換可能優先株式, 転換優先株
　cumulative preferred shares 累積優先株
　cumulative redeemable retractable preferred shares 累積償還可能・取消し可能優先株式
　　(⇒retractable)
　first preferred shares 第一優先株式
　limited-life preferred shares 期限付き優先株
　non-voting preferred shares 無議決権優先株
　　(⇒class)
　nonconvertible preferred shares 非転換型優先株
　nonvoting Class A preferred shares 無議決権クラスA優先株式
　participating preferred shares 参加型優先株, 受益権付き優先株
　preferred share dividends 優先株式配当金
　preferred shares redeemed 優先株式の償還
　redeemable preferred shares 償還優先株, 償還可能優先株
◆All the first preferred shares are convertible into common shares. 第一優先株式は、すべて普通株式への転換が可能です。◆For the computation of the earnings per share, assuming full dilution, dividends on convertible preferred shares have been added back to income. 完全希薄化を仮定した場合の1株当たり利益の算定では、転換可能優先株式[転換優先株]に対する配当は、利益に振り戻してあります。◆Goldman Sachs Group Inc. and the two Japanese banks hold preferred shares equivalent to 70 percent of Sanyo. 米証券大手のゴールドマン・サックス(GS)と邦銀2行が、三洋電機の約7割の優先株式(普通株式に換算して議決権の約7割)を保有している。
◆The bank will not pay a dividend for fiscal 2011 on its preferred shares held by the government due to losses from the disposal of bad loans. 同行は、不良債権処理による損失のため、国が保有する優先株に対する2011年度の期末配当を見送る方針だ。◆The issue of these preferred shares is expected to be completed on August 20, 2011. この優先株式の発行は、2011年8月20日に完了する予定だ。
preferred stock 優先株式, 優先株
　(=preferred share; ⇒common stock)
　accumulated preferred stock 累積的優先株式
　adjustable rate preferred stock 配当率調整型優先株式
　auction rate preferred stock 配当率入札方式優先株式
　authorized preferred stock 授権優先株式数
　callable preferred stock 償還優先株式
　convertible preferred stock 転換優先株式
　cumulative preferred stock 累積優先株式, 累加優先株式
　dividend on preferred stock 優先株式配当, 優先株配当
　dividend preferred stock 配当優先株式
　holder of preferred stock 優先株の株主, 優先株主
　increasing rate preferred stock 配当率逓増(ていぞう)優先株式
　limited-life preferred stock 期限付き優先株式
　nonconvertible preferred stock 非転換優先株式
　nonredeemable preferred stock 非償還優先株式
　nonvoting redeemable preferred stock 無議決権償還優先株式
　participating preferred stock 参加型優先株式
　perpetual preferred stock 永久優先株式
　　(=permanent preferred stock)
◆No preferred stock is currently issued and outstanding. 現在、優先株式は発行されておらず、残高もありません。
prehearing (名)(公募価格を決める際の材料にするための)プレヒアリング(企業が公募増資を正式決定する前に、主幹事会社が大口の機関投資家にどれくらい買えるかを打診すること。ただし、日本証券業協会の業界ルールでは、インサイダー取引の温床になるため禁止された)
preliminary (形)予備の, 予備的な, 暫定的な, 仮の
　preliminary announcement 業績発表
　preliminary application for listing 上場の仮申請
　preliminary data 速報値
　preliminary estimate 暫定推定値
　preliminary prospectus 仮目論見書
　preliminary rating 予備格付け
　preliminary report 速報, 速報値
　preliminary surplus advice 超過額早期通知
preliminary GDP report 国内総生産(GDP)の速報
◆Players on the country's stock markets responded to the preliminary GDP report favorably. 国内の株式市場関係者は、国内総生産(GDP)の速報に好感した。
premarket trading 発行前取引, 通常取引前の時間外取引
◆New York oil prices quickly rose into $105 range in premarket trading. ニューヨーク(ニューヨーク商業取引所)の原油価格が、通常取引前の時間外取引で105ドル台まで急騰した。
premarketing period [phase] 事前販売期間
premier (形)第一位の, 最上級の, 最上の, 最初の, 優良な, 最も重要な
　premier buyer 最大の買い手
　premier credit 優良発行体, 超優良発行体
　premier retail bank 優良なリテール銀行

premier supplier　トップ・メーカー
premise　(名)前提, 根拠, 契約書の頭書(nonoperative part, preamble, recitals), 前文, 前記[上記]事項, 敷地(premises), 構内, 施設, 設備, 賃貸物件
　a premises lease　賃貸借契約
　bank [banking] premises　銀行営業所
　in consideration of the premises　前文を約因として, 前記事項を約因として
　on the premise of　〜という前提に基づいて
　premises and equipment　建物設備, 動産・不動産
　premises and real estate　動産・不動産
　premises rent　施設賃貸料
　subscriber's premises　加入者設備
　use of the demised premises　賃貸物件の使用
　◆TEPCO is drafting a special business plan as the premise for getting government financial aid. 東電は, 政府の金融支援を受ける前提として, 特別事業計画を策定している。

premium　(名)保険料, 保険金, 額面超過額, 割増金, 手数料, 権利金, 賞金, 上乗せ, プレミアム　(⇒beneficiary, collect, national pension premium, national pension system, preferred creditor status, subscriber)
　extra premium　割増保険料
　family monthly premium　家族保険料個人負担月額
　individual monthly premium　本人保険料個人負担月額
　international portion of premiums　保険料収入の国外比率
　invest policyholders' premiums in stocks　保険契約者の保険料を株式に投資する
　premium installments　保険料の分割部分
　premium rate　保険料率, 再保険料率
　premium retirement allowance　割増退職金
　premium schedules　元受保険料率表
　renewal premium　更新保険料
　temporary level extra premium　短期平準割増保険料
　◆Full-time housewives of company employees and public servants are not required to pay pension premiums. 会社員や公務員の専業主婦は, 保険料を払う必要がない。◆If a housewife whose annual income is ¥1.3 million or more, or her husband becomes self-employed, the housewife must join the national pension plan and pay premiums. 主婦の年収が130万円以上の場合, または夫が脱サラした場合には, 主婦も国民年金に加入して保険料を支払わなければならない。◆In insurance services that can be bought via cell phones, premiums start at ¥300 a day. 携帯電話で加入できる保険サービスで, 1日の最低保険料は300円となる。◆In the case of au Insurance's cell phone-based policy sales, policyholders are allowed to pay premiums by adding them to monthly mobile charges. au損害保険の携帯電話での保険販売の場合, 保険契約者は, 保険料を携帯利用の月額に加算して保険料の支払いをすることができる。◆Life insurance companies invest policyholders' premiums in stocks. 生命保険会社は, 保険契約者の保険料を株式に投資している。◆One form of penalty tax is negligence tax, adding a 10-percent premium to the overdue tax. 加算税の一つに過少申告加算税があり, これは未納の税金に10％の上乗せ分が加算される。◆Premiums are collected together with call charges in insurance services that can be bought via mobile phones. 携帯電話で加入できる保険サービスでは, 保険料は通話料と一緒に徴収される。◆Premiums for insuring a wooden house for ¥10 million are more than ¥30,000 annually in earthquake-prone areas. 木造住宅に1,000万円の地震保険をかける場合の保険料は, 地震発生リスクが高い地域で年30,000万円を超える。◆The basic pension plan has been covered by premiums paid by subscribers and government budgetary appropriations. 基礎年金は, 加入者が支払う保険料と政府の予算割当額(国の負担)で賄(まかな)われている。◆The Corporation paid the annual premiums of 60,000 dollars on officers' life insurance (on which the Corporation is the beneficiary). 当社は, 年間6万ドルの役員に対する生命保険掛金(保険金の受取人は当社)を支払った。◆The decline in yields on whole life insurance products effectively raises premiums. 終身保険商品の利回り(予定利率)の引下げは, 実質的な保険料の値上げになる。◆The would-be acquirer is trying to greenmail the target company by having it pay a premium to buy back the shares held by the raider. 買収側[買収希望者]は, この買占め屋[会社乗っ取り屋]が保有する株を標的企業に高値で引き取らせて, 標的企業から収益を上げようとしている[標的企業に高値で引き取らせることにより, 標的企業にグリーンメールを仕掛けようとしている]。◆There are about 420,000 full-time housewives whose unpaid premium periods are long as they have failed to switch to the national pension plan. 国民年金への切替えが済んでいなくて保険料の未納期間が長い専業主婦は, 約42万人いる。◆Those housewives who have failed to switch to the national pension plan and have not paid premiums for an extensive period may receive a pittance or nothing at all. 国民年金への切替えをせず, 保険料を長期間払っていない主婦は, 低年金や無年金になる可能性がある。◆When yields on whole life insurance products decline, policyholders must pay higher premiums to secure the same amount of total insurance benefits. 終身保険商品の利回りが下がった場合, 加入者[保険契約者]がそれ以前と同額の総保険料を受け取るには, より高い保険料を払わなければならない。◆Whole life insurance means life insurance under which coverage remains in force during the insured's entire lifetime, provided premiums are paid as specified in the policy. 終身保険は, 保険契約に明記されている保険料が支払われているかぎり, 保障が被保険者の全生涯にわたって有効な生命保険を意味する。

premium investment　保険料投資
　◆From a broader point of view, the lowering of promised yields on premium investments would surely protect the benefits of policyholders. 大局的に見れば, 生保が保険契約者に約束した保険料投資の運用利回り[予定利率]を引き下げたほうが, 確かに保険契約者の利益を保護することになる。

premium payment　保険料の支払い, 保険料の納付, 保険料の払込み, 保険料の負担
　(⇒nursing care insurance)
　◆In the case of single-premium whole life insurance policies, policyholders make one large premium payment up front when they sign the contract. 一時払い終身保険の場合は, 保険契約者が契約を結ぶ際に[契約時に]多額の保険料を前もって一括で払い込む。◆Premium payments under the company employees' pension scheme are much higher than employment insurance premiums. 厚生年金の保険料負担のほうが, 雇用保険料よりはるかに大きい。◆The personal information of customers who used credit cards for premium payments might have been leaked. クレジット・カードを使って保険料を支払った顧客の個人情報が, 外部に流出した恐れがある。

premium revenue　保険料収入　(一般事業会社の売上高に相当。⇒net premium revenue)
　◆Life insurers' premium revenues correspond to sales at other types of firms. 生保の保険料収入は, 他の一般企業の売上高に当たる。◆Premium revenues slipped at seven of the nine major life insurers. 保険料収入は, 主要生命保険9社のうち7社が減少した。

prepackaged bankruptcy　事前策定型破たん[倒産], 事前調整型破たん, 事前調整型の法的整理, プリパック, プリパッケージド・バンクラプトシー
　◆MGM filed for Chapter 11 after its creditors agreed to support a prepackaged bankruptcy. メトロ・ゴールドウィン・メイヤー(MGM)は, 事前調整型破たん[事前調整型の法的整理]を支持する債権者の合意を得てから, 連邦破産法11章の適用

prepaid (形) 前払いの, 前納の, プリペイド
  prepaid asset　前払い資産
  prepaid card　代金前払い式カード, プリペイド・カード
  prepaid commission　前払い手数料
  prepaid debenture discount　債券発行差金
  prepaid insurance (premium)　前払い保険料 (=insurance prepaid)
  prepaid interest and discount (charge)　前払い利息・割引料
  prepaid interest paid back　戻し利息
  prepaid pension cost　前払い年金費用

preparation (名) 準備, 用意, 支度(したく), 予習, (書類の)作成, 調理, 調合
  ◆The financial group's inadequate preparations for the reorganization resulted in a major computer system failure. 同フィナンシャル・グループの再編の準備不足から、大規模なシステム障害が起こった。

prepare (動) 準備する, 用意する, 計画する, 段取りを整える, 覚悟させる, 心の準備をさせる, (薬品などを)調製する, 調合する, 作成する
  be prepared to　〜の覚悟をしている, 〜することを予期[予想]している
  prepare for　〜の準備[用意]をする, 〜に備える, 〜の覚悟をする
  prepare oneself for　〜の用意をする, 〜の準備をする, 〜を覚悟する
  prepared plan　腹案
  ◆French President Sarkozy told the gathering of business and political elites to prepare for tighter financial regulations. サルコジ仏大統領は、政財界トップの会合で金融規制強化を覚悟するよう明言した。◆Small and midsize companies have been stepping up equity financing to fund capital investments and prepare for M&A deals. 中小企業は、設備投資の資金調達とM&A取引に備えて、株式発行による資金調達を急いでいる。◆The Buyer shall prepare the Closing Balance Sheet at the Buyer's expense as promptly as practicable, but in any event within ninety (90) calendar days following the Closing Date. 買い主は、できるだけ速やかに、ただしどんな場合でもクロージング日以降90暦日以内に、買い主の費用負担でクロージング日現在の貸借対照表を作成するものとする。

preparedness (名) 準備[用意]ができていること (readiness), 備え, 覚悟, (軍備の)充実
  disaster preparedness　災害への備え
  preparedness for financial crisis　金融危機に対する備え
  ◆Beefing up Japan's preparedness for financial crisis again is essential. 金融危機に対する日本の備えを、もう一度固め直す必要がある。

prepay (動) 前払いする, 前納する, 期限前償還する, 期限前弁済する　(名) 期限前償還, 期限前償還率, 借換え
  fast [high] prepay speeds　期限前償還率が高水準にあること, 期限前償還率の高さ
  prepay all or part of the mortgage without penalty　違約金なしでモーゲージの全体または一部を期限前償還する
  prepay debt　繰上げ償還する
  prepay speed　期限前償還率
  prepay spike　期限前償還の急増, 借換えブーム
  right to prepay the loan　期限前償還の権利
  slowdown in prepays　期限前償還の減少, 期限前償還率の低下　(=slower prepays)
  uptick [surge] in prepays　期限前償還の増加, 期限前償還率の上昇

prepayment (名) 前払い, 前納, 前払い費用, 期限前償還, 期限前返済, 借換え
  a prepayment penalty　期限前返済違約金
  a prepayment privilege　期限前返済が認められること
  annual prepayment rate　年間期限前償還率
  fast prepayment　急速な借換え
  long term prepayments　長期前払い費用 (=long-term prepaid expenses)
  prepayment assumed　期限前返済推定額
  prepayment indicator　期限前償還率指標
  prepayment paid　前払い費用
  prepayment penalty　前払い罰則手数料
  prepayment privilege　前払い特権
  prepayment received　前受け収益
  prepayment risk　期限前償還リスク (=prepay risk)
  prepayment sensitive product　期限前償還に敏感な商品
  prepayment speed　期限前償還率 (=prepay speed, prepayment rate)
  prepayment spike [surge]　期限前償還の急増, 借換えブーム　(=prepay spike)
  surge in prepayments　期限前償還の急増 (=prepayment surge)

prerequisite (名) 前提条件, 必要条件, 先行条件
  ◆A prerequisite to restoring the country's fiscal health is to promptly and boldly take effective pump priming measures and to overcome the economic crisis. 日本の財政健全化への前提条件は、迅速、果敢に効果的な景気浮揚策を実行して、経済危機を克服することだ。◆Financial support is the prerequisite for the two firms' funding of the issuance of new shares. 金融支援は、両社の増資引受けの前提条件となっている。

presence (名) 存在, 存在感, 影響力, 地位, 立場, 事業基盤, 経営基盤, 拠点, 進出, 営業網, ポジション, 態度, 姿勢, プレゼンス
  boost the presence of　〜の存在感を高める
  economic presence　経済的影響力, 経済力
  establish a presence in the market　市場での地位を確立する
  global presence　世界の営業網
  make one's presence felt　存在感を示す
  market presence　市場での地位, 市場でのプレゼンス, 市場進出
  political presence　政治的影響力
  ◆Leading banks may utilize the banking agent system to increase their presence in regional areas. 大手行は、地方で拠点を増やすため銀行代理店制度を活用する可能性がある。◆Sooner or later, the contribution ratio of the IMF member countries will be reviewed as the fast-growing emerging economies gain larger presence. いずれ、IMF加盟国の出資比率は、急成長している新興国が存在感を増していることから、見直されることになろう。◆The company is expanding its presence in China. 同社は、中国で事業基盤を拡大している。◆The presence of investment funds on the share register is generally unknown until their names are listed in annual securities reports. 株主名簿上の投資ファンドの存在は、一般にそのファンド名が年次有価証券報告書に記載されるまで分からない。◆The stakes in major U.S. securities firms by SMFG, Mitsubishi UFJ and Nomura will boost the presence of Japanese financial institutions in the global market. 三井住友銀行、三菱UFJと野村が米国の大手証券会社に出資することで、グローバル市場での日本の金融機関の存在感が高まりそうだ。◆This joint financing scheme carried out with the bank as the lead bank is expected to help make the presence of Japanese banks more strongly felt in global markets. 同行を主幹事銀行として実施されるこの協調融資事業は、国際市場で邦銀の存在感を高めることになりそうだ。

present (動)表示する, 提示する, 示す, 開示する, 作成する, 提出する, 提供する, 贈呈する, 口頭で説明する, 申し立てる
 fairly present 適正に表示する　(=present fairly)
 present consolidated financial statements 連結財務書類[連結財務諸表]を作成する[表示する]
 ◆A targeted company demanded a company trying to acquire its stocks to present a business plan. 買収の標的企業は、買収企業[標的企業の株式を取得しようとしている企業]に事業計画の提出を求めた。◆The closing balance sheet fairly presents the financial position of the Corporation at the closing date in conformity with United States GAAP. クロージング時点現在の貸借対照表は、米国の一般に認められた会計原則[米国の会計基準]に従って、クロージング日の「会社」の財政状態を適正に表示している。

present value 現在価値, 現価, PV
 (=present worth; ⇒actuarial present value)
 actuarial present value 年金数理上の現在価値, 保険数理上の現在価値, 保険数理に基づく現在価値
 actuarial present value of accumulated plan benefits 保険数理で計算した年金未支給額現価
 actuarial present value of benefit obligations 給付債務の保険数理上の現在価値
 actuarial present value of vested accumulated plan benefits 受給権が発生した累積年金給付額の保険数理上の現在価値
 adjust cash flows for the time value of money by discounting to present value キャッシュ・フローを現在価値に引き直して時間価値を調整する
 be discounted back to present value 現在価値に引き直す
 bond maturity weighted according to the present value of all cash flows キャッシュ・フローを現在価値に引き直して算出した満期
 compound present value 複利現価
 discounted present value 割引現価
 net present value 純現在価値, 正味現在価値
 net present value of the account 口座の純現在価値
 present value (actuarially computed value) 現在価値(保険数理上の計算価値)
 present value of (an ordinary) annuity 年金現価
 present value of future interest payments 将来支払い利息の現在価値
 present value of the future principal 将来元金の現在価値
 present value of vested and nonvested benefits 年金支払い義務の現在価値, 受給権確定給付と受給権の発生していない給付の現在価値
 risk-adjusted present value リスク調整後現在価値
 simple present value 単利現価
 the present value of minimum lease payments 最低リース支払い額の現在価値
 total at present value 現在価値総額
 ◆We compute present values for impaired loans when we determine our allowances for credit losses. 当社の貸倒れ引当金を決定するにあたって、当社は不良債権の現在価値を計算します。

presenting bank 支払い提示[呈示]銀行

president (名)社長, 会長, 会頭, 頭取, 総裁, 議長, 委員長, 学長, 総長, 大統領, 国家主席, トップ
 co-president 共同頭取
 company president 会社社長
 president and chief executive officer 社長兼最高経営責任者
 president-designate 次期社長, 新任命社長
 president emeritus 名誉会長
 ◆Former president of the bank was deeply involved in the nation's financial administration as an advisor to the Financial Services Agency. 同行の前社長は、金融庁の顧問として、国の金融行政に深くかかわった。◆Since three banks integrated their operations, executives from the three predecessor banks served on an equal basis as presidents of the Mizuho group, Mizuho Bank and Mizuho Corporate Bank. 3銀行の経営統合以来、旧3行の経営者が、みずほグループ(FG)、みずほ銀行、みずほコーポレート銀行のトップをそれぞれ分け合あった。◆The bank's new president must tread a thorny path as the management environment is severe. 経営環境が厳しいので、同行の新社長はいばらの道を歩むことになろう。

press (動)押す, 押しつける, 押しつぶす, 絞り出す, 強要する, (〜するよう)迫る, 強く求める, 圧迫する, 苦しめる, 悩ます, 締め付ける, 抱きしめる, 強調する, 追及する (自動)押し寄せる, 殺到する, 切迫する　(⇒revalue)
 be hard pressed for money 金にひどく困っている
 press A for B AにBを求める[要求する]
 press ahead with 〜をどんどん進める
 press for A to do Aに〜するよう迫る[求める]
 press for the renminbi's rise 人民元切上げを強く迫る
 press on with 〜を続ける, 〜を推し進める
 ◆If the numerical goal of G-20 nations' current account surpluses or deficits is introduced, Japan could be pressed to allow a further rise in the yen. G20(世界20か国・地域)の経常収支の黒字または赤字の数値目標が導入されれば、(経常黒字国の)日本は一段の円高を迫られる可能性がある。◆Japan, the United States and emerging economies have pressed European countries to promptly resolve the fiscal and financial crisis. 日米両国と新興国は、欧州に財政・金融危機の迅速な解決を迫った。◆The United States tries to press China to reduce its current account surplus and raise the yuan by restricting its current account with a numerical goal. 米国は、経常収支を数値目標で縛って、中国に経常収支の黒字縮小と人民元切上げの圧力をかけようとしている。◆Washington is pressing Beijing to revalue the Chinese currency. 米政府は、中国に通貨(人民元)切上げを迫っている。

pressing (形)急を要する, 緊急の(urgent), 火急の, 差し迫った, 切迫した, 深刻な, 断りにくい, たっての
 pressing bills 期限の迫った勘定
 pressing demand 差し迫った要求, たっての要請, 切迫した需要
 pressing need for foreign currency 切迫した外貨需要
 pressing problem 緊急の問題, 緊急の課題
 ◆America cannot solve the most pressing problems on our own, and the world cannot solve them without America. 米国は最緊急課題を自国だけで解決することはできないし、世界も米国抜きでは解決できない。

pressing issue 緊急の課題, 緊急を要する問題
 ◆A pressing issue is the yen's appreciation. 緊急の課題は、円高だ。

pressing need 差し迫った必要, 切迫した需要, 緊急の課題
 ◆Sendai Bank is considering receiving public funds in order to meet the pressing needs of local companies in the aftermath of the March 11 earthquake and tsunami. 3月11日(2011年)の東日本大震災の影響でひっ迫している地元企業の資金需要に対応するため、仙台銀行は、公的資金の受入れを検討している。

pressing task 急を要する課題, 緊急課題
 ◆Measures to expand and create employment are a pressing task. 雇用拡大と雇用創出策は、急を要する課題だ。

pressure (動)圧力をかける, 強要する, 迫る
 ◆Former chairman of the bank served as an associate of Heizo Takenaka, then state minister in charge of economic and fiscal policy, and strictly pressured banks to rehabilitate

themselves. 同行の前会長は、竹中平蔵元金融相のブレーンを務めて、銀行に経営健全化を厳しく迫った。◆The United States may not win international support to pressure China to increase the yuan's value. 米国は、中国に対する人民元（相場）切上げ圧力について国際的な指示を得られない可能性がある。

pressure （名）圧力, 圧迫, ひっ迫, 緊迫, 強い要請, 強要, 強制, 反発, 縮小, 減少, 低下, 悪化, 下落, 伸び悩み, 重圧, ストレス, 苦難, 苦悩, 緊急, 切迫, 多忙 （⇒deflationary pressure(s), inflation pressure, inflationary pressures, selling pressure）

 a delayed adjustment to the pressures 圧力への調整の遅れ
 add to the upward pressure on prices 物価上昇圧力を強める
 apply [exert, place, pile, put] pressure on 〜に圧力をかける
 asset quality pressures 資産内容の悪化
 be subjected to pressure from greater monetary restraint 金融引締め強化でひっ迫する
 be under financial pressure 財政難にある, 金銭的に苦しい
 be under further pressure 続落する
 be under pressure 重圧下にある, 重圧にさらされる, 下落する, 減少する, 悪化する, 伸び悩んでいる, 売り圧力にさらされる, 売られる
 be under pressure to 〜を迫られる
 because of the pressure of business [work] 仕事が多忙なため
 bring pressure to bear on 〜に圧力をかける
 business pressure 業務上のストレス, 業務の繁忙 （=pressure of business）
 come under pressure 悪化する, 圧迫される, 圧力［売り圧力］にさらされる, 売り圧力がかかる
 competitive pressure 競争圧力
 counter upward pressure on long-term interest rates 金利の上昇圧力を抑える
 currency pressure 通貨危機
 deflationary pressure デフレ圧力, デフレ懸念, デフレ
 dollar-selling pressure ドル売り圧力
 downward pressure 低下圧力, 引下げ圧力, 低下傾向, 低下要因
 exert great pressure on 〜への圧力を強める
 exert strong downward pressure on economic activity 景気を強く押さえ込む
 exert strong pressure on 〜に強い圧力をかける, 〜への圧力を強める
 feel the pressure ストレスを感じる
 financial pressure 金融面での圧力, 財政難, 金融ひっ迫, 経済的の苦しみ, 経営面での圧力 （⇒lead to）
 give in to pressure 圧力に屈する
 have no financial pressure 経済的に苦しんでいない
 heavy pressure for a rate cut 利下げを求める強い圧力
 inflationary pressure インフレ圧力 （=inflation pressure）
 international pressure 国際的圧力
 margin pressure 利益率低下, 利益率への圧力 （=pressure on margins）
 money market pressure 短期市場金利への圧力
 political pressure 政治的圧力
 pressure for looser credit 金融緩和の圧力
 pressure for money 金詰まり, 金融ひっ迫
 pressure group 圧力団体
 pressure on margins 利益率低下, 利益率への圧力 （=margin pressure）
 pressure on pricing 価格圧力, 値下げ圧力 （=pricing pressure）
 price pressure 値下げ圧力, 価格低下圧力, インフレ圧力
 pricing pressure 価格圧力, 値下げ圧力 （=pressure on pricing）
 profit pressure 収益への圧迫
 put [apply, exert, pile, place] pressure on 〜に圧力をかける, 〜に圧力を加える, 〜を圧迫する
 receive pressure from 〜から圧力を受ける
 reserve pressure （銀行の）資本繰り
 revenue pressure 減収圧力
 sales pressures 販売の伸び悩み
 selling pressure 売り圧力 （⇒panic）
 speculative pressures 投機的な売り圧力
 strong upward pressure 強い上昇圧力
 the pressure of the employment situation 雇用調整の圧力
 there are pressures on 〜が悪化している
 under pressure from 〜の強い要請を受けて, 〜の圧力［危機］にさらされて, 〜にせっつかれて, 〜のストレスを受けて
 upward pressure 上昇圧力, 引上げ圧力, 上昇傾向, 上昇要因
 upward pressure on prices 物価上昇圧力

◆A vicious cycle of deflationary pressures is becoming increasingly real. デフレ［デフレ圧力］の悪循環が、現実味を増してきた。◆Bad loan disposal will lead to deflationary pressures. 不良債権処理は、デフレ圧力を強める。◆Banks were less reserve pressure than was in March. 銀行の資本繰りは、3月より緩和した。◆Daiei's business diversification led to rising debts that placed financial pressure on the company. ダイエーの事業多角化は、借入金の増大につながり、それが会社の経営を圧迫する結果となった。◆Dollar-selling pressure remains strong due to concerns over the outflow of funds from the United States. 米国からの資金流出に対する懸念で、ドル売り圧力は依然として強い。◆If the number of corporate bankruptcies and the unemployment rate soar owing to structural reforms, recessionary pressures will further increase. 構造改革で企業倒産件数や失業率が増えると、不況圧力は一層強まるものと思われる。◆In Europe, the sovereign debt crisis is putting pressure on an economic recovery. 欧州では、財政危機が景気回復の重圧になっている。◆Japan, the United States and emerging countries are upping their pressure on Europe to contain the Greek-triggered sovereign debt crisis. 日米と新興国は、欧州に対して、ギリシャに端を発したソブリン危機（政府債務危機）封じ込めの圧力を強めている。◆Out of a sense of relief, dollar-selling pressure has eased on the foreign currency markets. 安堵（あんど）感から、外国為替市場では、ドル売り圧力が弱まった。◆Pressure for additional monetary easing measures will increase if the slowdown of the world economy continues. 世界的な景気減速がこのまま続けば、一層の金融緩和［金融緩和策］を求める圧力が強まるものと思われる。◆The Bank of Japan seems to have unwillingly implemented measures for further monetary easing under pressure from the government and the market. 日銀は、政府や市場にせっつかれて追加の金融緩和策を実施したようだ。◆The dollar was under pressure following the release of worse-than-expected U.S. jobs data for September 2010. 予想より悪い2010年9月の米雇用統計の発表を受けて、ドルは売り圧力にさらされた［ドルは売られた、ドル売りが進んだ］。◆The European Central Bank cut its main interest rate by 0.25 percent following heavy pressure for a rate cut to spur flagging economic growth. 失速気味の経済成長に刺激を与えるため利下げを求める強い圧力を受けて、

欧州中央銀行(ECB)はその主要(政策)金利を0.25%引き下げた。◆The Fed has taken quantitative easing measures twice, or QE1 between December 2008 and March 2010, and QE2 between November 2010 and June 2011, to cope with the financial crisis and deflationary pressure. 金融危機やデフレ圧力に対応するため、米連邦準備制度理事会(FRB)は、これまでに量的金融緩和を2回(2008年12月〜2010年3月の量的緩和第一弾(QE1)と2010年11月〜2011年6月の量的緩和第二弾(QE2))実施している。◆The government may exert great pressure on the Bank of Japan to further relax its monetary policy. 政府は、日銀への追加の金融緩和圧力を強める可能性がある。◆The latest additional monetary ease put a downward pressure on interest rates. 今回の追加の金融緩和で、金利は低下した。◆The management of the new companies will be under pressure to produce profits. これらの新会社の経営陣は、収益確保の手腕を問われることになる。◆The pressures on gross margins and earnings that affected the last half of 2010 will continue through the first half of 2012. 2010年下半期[下期]の業績に影響を及ぼした売上利益率と利益の低下は、2012年上半期[上期]まで続く見通しです。◆The stock market was under further pressure last week. 株式相場は先週、続落した。◆The United States is under pressure to make some difficult monetary policy decisions to cool down the overheating economy by countering the inflationary pressures stemming from higher import prices due to the weaker dollar. 米国は現在、ドル安での輸入価格の高騰によるインフレ圧力を抑えて過熱気味の景気を鎮めるための難しい金融政策の決断を迫られている。◆The yen's appreciation puts pressure on the earnings of export-oriented companies. 円高は、輸出企業の収益を圧迫する。◆There are pressures on prices, margins and profitability. 価格や利益率、収益性が悪化している。

pressure on profitability 収益性の悪化
◆The industry is under a good deal of stress, as evidenced by pressure on profitability and decline in stock prices over the last several months. 業界は、収益性の悪化やここ数か月の株価低迷でも明らかなように、かなり厳しい状況下にあります。

pretax balance 保険会社の経営収支残高(一般企業の経常利益に相当)
◆Life insurance firms rarely see their half-year pretax balance fall into the red. 生命保険会社で、半期の経常収支残高が赤字になるのはまれである。

pretax loss 経常損失, 経常赤字, 課税前損失, 税引き前損失
◆Asahi Mutual Life Insurance Co. posted ¥66.7 billion in pretax losses. 朝日生命保険が、667億円の経常赤字を計上した。◆UBS will post a pretax loss of up to $690 million in the third quarter mainly because of losses linked to the U.S. subprime mortgage crisis. スイス最大手銀行UBSの第3四半期税引き前損失は、主に米国で起きた低所得者向け融資「サブプライム・ローン」問題の関連損失で、最高で6億9,000万ドルに達する見通しだ。

pretax profit 経常利益, 税込み利益, 課税前利益, 税引き前利益 (=current profit, recurring profit; ⇒ consolidated operating profit, market capitalization)
◆Corporation's group net and pretax profits for the whole of fiscal 2002 will respectively amount to ¥511 billion and ¥971 billion. 当社の2002年度の連結純利益と経常利益は、それぞれ5,110億円と9,710億円に達する見込みだ。

prevail (動)勝つ, 勝(まさ)る, 勝利を得る, 首尾よく行く, 成功する, 功を奏する, 効果がある, 一般に行われている, 一般に見られる, 広がる, 広まる, 広く行き渡る, 普及している, 流行している, はびこる, 説き伏せる, うまく説得する
prevail against all difficulties あらゆる困難に打ち勝つ
prevail upon [on] a person to do 人を〜するよう説得する

◆A sense of disappointment has prevailed across the world markets as no concrete measures to rescue Greece were unveiled at the eurozone finance ministers meeting. ユーロ圏財務相会合でギリシャ支援の具体策が明らかにされなかったので、世界の市場で失望感が広がった。◆A sense of restlessness and hopelessness still prevails among nonmanufacturers, small and midsize firms and regional economies. 非製造業や中小企業、地方経済には、焦燥と絶望感が広まったままだ。◆Uncertainty has prevailed as the value of the euro dropped sharply. ユーロの相場が急落したため、不安[動揺]が広がっている。

prevailing (形)優勢な, 有力な, 卓越した, 優勢を占めている, 支配的な, 勢力がある, 広く受け入れられている, 広く行われている, 普及[流行]している, 実勢の, 現行の, ごく普通の, 世間一般の, 一般の
(currently) prevailing forward rate 実勢先渡し金利
prevailing economic conditions 足元の景気
prevailing exchange rate 現在の為替レート
prevailing interest rate 現行金利[利子率], 実勢金利, 金利の実勢, 実勢利回り
prevailing market rate 市場の実勢金利, 市場実勢金利
prevailing market yield 市場実勢利回り
prevailing price 一般価格, 時価
the prevailing party 勝訴当事者

prevailing market expectations 大方の市場の期待
◆Contrary to prevailing market expectations, the Bank of Japan decided not to further ease monetary policy. 大方の市場の期待に反して、日銀は追加的な金融緩和策を見送った。

prevailing rate 市場の実勢金利, 市場金利, 実勢相場, 中心相場, 中心レート, 一般賃金, 一般賃率
◆The prevailing rate of interest for a note payable of this type is 12%. この種の支払い手形の通常[現行]の利子率は、12%である。

prevent (動)防ぐ, 防止する, 予防する, 中止させる, 邪魔する, 阻止する, 〜を妨げる
(⇒protective measures)
prevent a further downslide 一段の値下がりに歯止めをかける
prevent a hostile takeover (bid) 敵対的買収を防ぐ, 敵対的買収を阻止する
prevent a loss 損失を防ぐ
prevent financial turmoil 金融危機を予防する
prevent manipulation 相場操縦を防ぐ
prevent the asset value from eroding 資産価値の目減りを防ぐ
prevent the financial contraction 金融収縮を防ぐ
prevent the yen's value from getting stronger 円高を阻止する
◆Companies should not go public to prevent hostile takeover bids. 敵対的買収を防ぐには、企業は株式を上場すべきでない。◆European countries are forced to prevent the financial crisis from spreading from Europe to other parts of the world. 欧州は、金融危機の世界的波及阻止を迫られている。◆Finance ministers of the ASEAN plus Three hailed the launch of a regional economic research and surveillance body aimed at preventing financial turmoil. ASEANプラス3(日中韓)の財務相が、金融危機予防のための域内経済のリサーチ・監視機関(AMRO)の発足を歓迎した。◆In order to prevent the chain reaction of even more devastating financial collapses, financial and monetary authorities in the United States and other nations will need to work together. これ以上の衝撃的な金融破たんの連鎖反応を防ぐには、米国と世界各国の金融・通貨当局の協調が必要だ。◆In the United States, the Exon-Florio provision of the 1988 trade law can prevent takeover bids that are deemed a threat to national security. 米国では、1988

年通商法のエクソン・フロリオ条項で、国家の安全保障上、脅威と考えられる企業買収を阻止することができる。◆Japan must prevent the yen from soaring again to the level of ¥76 to the dollar. 日本は、円相場が再び1ドル＝76円台に急騰する事態を阻止しなければならない。◆Japan should prevent the dollar plunging and the yen from rising too sharply through concerted market intervention with the United States and European countries. 日本は、米欧との協調介入によってドル急落と超円高を阻止すべきだ。◆Online banking users can prevent illegal transfers of their deposits by frequently changing their passwords. オンライン・バンキング利用者は、パスワードをこまめに変更して、預金の不正送金を防ぐことができる。◆Public distrust in the pension system must be prevented from deepening. 年金制度への国民の不信感は、これ以上深まらないようにしなければならない。◆Restricting an influx of capital prevents foreigners from acquiring domestic assets. 資本流入［資本輸入］の規制で、外国人は国内資産の購入が難しくなる。◆The FSA's guideline for supervising financial conglomerates is aimed at urging operators of financial conglomerates to reinforce their corporate governance to prevent irregularities. 金融庁の金融コングロマリット（複合体）監督指針の狙いは、不正防止に向けて、金融コングロマリットの経営者に経営監視の強化を促すことにある。◆The IMF and the EU are strengthening their cooperation to avert a Greek default and prevent a chain reaction of debt crisis among other countries. ギリシャの債務不履行（デフォルト）を回避し他国間の債務危機の連鎖反応を防ぐため、国際通貨基金（IMF）と欧州連合（EU）は、連携を強めている。◆The stimulation of consumption and job placement assistance are appropriate measures to prevent the economy from losing its momentum. 消費喚起（かんき）や就職斡旋［失業者の就職］支援は、景気の腰折れを防ぐ妥当な政策だ。◆The three Japanese top banks will face the FSB's new international rule requiring them to hold extra capital to prevent future financial crises. 日本の3メガ銀行も、金融危機の再発を防ぐため、資本［自己資本］の上積みを求める金融安定化理事会（FSB）の新国際基準の対象になると見られる。◆The U.S. tried to prevent an erosion of corporate ethics among financial institutions by refusing to provide public funds to Lehman Brothers. リーマン・ブラザーズへの公的資金の投入を拒否することによって、米政府は金融機関のモラル・ハザード（企業倫理の欠如）を回避しようとした。◆To prevent crude oil prices rising further, major oil-consuming countries must try harder to save energy and promote the use of alternative energy sources. これ以上の原油高［原油価格の高騰］を防ぐには、石油消費国が省エネや代替エネルギーの利用促進に一段と力を入れる必要がある。◆To prevent the current fiscal and financial crisis in Europe from spreading, the IMF will create a new short-term lending facility. 現在の欧州財政・金融危機の拡大を防ぐ［封じる］ため、国際通貨基金（IMF）が、新たな短期の融資制度を創設することになった。◆Under the program of a voluntary liquidation for individuals, housing loan borrowers' voluntary bankruptcies can be prevented by having financial institutions waive repayment of their mortgages. 個人向け私的整理の制度だと、金融機関に住宅ローンの返済を免除させることによって、住宅ローンの借り手の自己破産を防ぐことができる。

prevent the financial contraction　金融収縮を防ぐ
◆The Bank of Japan must continue to promptly supply funds to prevent the financial contraction that all corporate managers dread. 企業経営者が恐れる金融収縮を防ぐため、日銀は迅速に資金供給を続ける必要がある。

prevent the yen's value from getting stronger　円高を阻止する
◆These comments were made after a series of currency market interventions by the government to prevent the yen's value from getting stronger. これらのコメントは、政府が円高阻止のための為替市場への介入を断続的に行った後に出された。

prevention　（名）防止, 予防, 防止［予防］策, 阻止
crisis prevention function　危機予防機能
Prevention of Fraud (investment) Act　不正投資防止法
prevention of yen-buying moves　円買いの動きの阻止
◆The effect of the prevention of yen-buying moves is being strengthened by the Bank of Japan's stance on monetary easing. 円買いの動きを阻止する効果は、日銀の金融緩和に対する姿勢で高まっている。

previous　（形）前の, 前回の, 以前の, 先の, 直近の, 最近の
a previous question　先決問題
from the previous year　前年比で
over the same period of the previous year　前年同期比で
previous accumulation　原始的蓄積
previous engagement　先約
previous months　最近数か月
the previous cycle [cyclical] low　前回のサイクルの底, 前回の景気循環の底
the previous cyclical [cycle's] peak　前回のサイクルのピーク, 前回の景気循環のピーク
the previous enormous intervention　前回の大規模介入
the previous monthly auction　前回の月次国債入札
◆China will shift to a "prudent" monetary policy in 2011 from the previous "appropriately loose" stance. 中国は、これまでの「適度に緩和的な」金融政策から2011年は「穏健な」金融政策に方向転換する方針だ。◆The rate of economic expansion in the current phase of recovery is much smaller than previous expansionary phases. 現在の景気拡大期［景気拡大局面］の経済成長率は、過去の景気拡大期よりかなり低い。

previous day　前日
◆On European and U.S. markets, stock prices fell sharply the previous day. 前日の欧米市場の株価は、急落した。◆The June 2012 gold futures contract closed at ¥4,694 per gram, down ¥54 from the previous day's close on the Tokyo Commodity Exchange. 東京工業品取引所では、2012年6月渡しの金先物価格は、前日の終値より54円安の1グラム＝4,694円で取引を終えた。

previous intervention　前回の介入
◆The yen has depreciated by more than ¥10 from before the previous enormous intervention. 円は、前回の大規模介入の前より10円強の円安になった。

previous month　前月
◆The unemployment rate in July climbed to a postwar high of 5.7 percent, up 0.3 percentage point from the previous month. 7月(2009年)の完全失業率は、前月より0.3ポイント悪化して5.7％となり、戦後最悪を更新した。

previous survey　前回の調査
◆The BOJ's Tankan survey shows business sentiment among large manufacturers rebounded in September from the previous survey three months earlier. 9月の日銀短観は、大企業・製造業の景況感が6月の前回調査から改善したことを示している。

previous year　前年, 前年度, 前期
◆The combined sales of 813 nonfinancial companies in the April-September period grew 6.3 percent over the previous year. 金融を除く企業813社の上期(4-9月期)の売上高の合計は、前年同期比で6.3％増加した。◆The life insurer's revenues from the single-premium whole life insurance products tripled from the previous year in fiscal 2010. 同生保の一時払い終身の保険商品の収入保険料は、2010年度に前年度の3倍に達した。

previous years　過年度
◆Accumulated surplus funds from previous years are referred to as "hidden treasure" by politicians. 過年度の累積

剰余金（特別会計の積立金）を、政治家は「埋蔵金」と呼んでいる。

price （動）～の値段を付ける, ～の値段を決める, 値決めする, 価格設定する, 値段を提示する
 be fairly priced　適正価格が付けられている
 be priced at current market rates　市場レートで値決めされる
 be priced out of the market　価格の点で市場から脱落する
 high-priced stock　根がさ株
 lower-priced　割安な
 well-priced issue　価格が適切な債券
 ◆The company is likely to price the professional baseball club between ¥20 billion and ¥25 billion. 同社は、このプロ野球球団の売却額について、200億円から250億円程度を提示している模様だ。◆Under the third-party share allotment scheme, the bank will allocate 116 million new shares to about 8,000 companies and investors with each share priced at ¥130. この第三者株式割当て計画によると、同行は、約8,000の企業と個人投資家に1株130円で1億1,600万株の新株を割り当てる。

price （名）価格, 値段, 物価, プライス
 asked price　言い値, 呼び値, 売り呼び値
 bid price　指し値, せり値, 買い呼び値
 bond prices　債券相場, 債券の市場価格
 closing price　終値
 consumer prices　消費者物価
 gold future price　金先物価格
 higher prices　物価上昇, 価格上昇
 increased prices　値上げ, 物価上昇
 low price stock　低位株
 market price　市場価格, 市価, 時価, 売価, 相場
 opening price　寄り付き, 寄り付き値, 寄り付き価格, 寄り付き相場
 price book-value ratio　株価純資産倍率, PBR
 price competitiveness　価格競争力
 price fixing　価格維持, 価格固定, 物価安定, 価格決定, 価格操作, 価格協定
 price-fixing agreement　価格カルテル, ヤミ価格協定
 price gap between domestic and overseas markets　内外価格差
 price pressure　価格低下圧力, インフレ圧力
 price war　価格戦争, 値引き競争, 値引き販売
  （=price cutting war）
 public offering price　公募価格
 real estate prices　不動産価格
 stock price　株価
 strike price　行使価格, 権利行使価格
 subscription price　応募価格
 the prices of purchased bad assets　不良資産の買取り価格
 the prices of the U.S. Treasury bonds　米国債の価格
 ◆Both consumer and real estate prices are continuing to fall in Japan. 日本では、消費者物価と不動産価格がともに下落を続けている。◆If the prices of purchased bad assets are set high, the public burden will balloon. 不良資産の買取り価格を高くすると、国民負担が膨らむ。◆Olympus fired its president who had pointed out the integrity of the acquisition prices and commission fees. オリンパスは、買収額や買収手数料の適正性を指摘した社長を解任した。◆Short selling is the practice of borrowing stocks from securities and financial companies and other investors to sell them and then buy them back when their prices drop. 空売りは、証券金融会社や他の投資家（機関投資家など）から株を借りて売り、その株が値下がりした時点で買い戻すことをいう。◆Should the U.S. government fall into default, the prices of the Treasury bonds held by major countries and financial institutions around the world would plummet. 米政府がデフォルト（債務不履行）に陥れば、主要国や世界の金融機関が保有する米国債の価格は、暴落するだろう。◆Signs that unfavorable factors are receding are apparent, as crude oil prices have fallen. 原油の値下りなど、悪材料に解消の兆しが見られる。◆Some successful companies are touting the low prices and distinctive features of their products and services. 一部の好調企業は、製品やサービスの低価格と独自性を売り込んでいる。◆The benchmark gold future price topped ¥4,700 per gram for the first time on the Tokyo Commodity Exchange. 東京工業品取引所で、金取引の指標となる金先物価格が、史上初めて1グラム＝4,700円を突破した。◆The deflator, which indicates the overall trend in prices, dropped 2.5 percent in the April-June period compared to the corresponding period last year. 物価の総合的な動向を示すデフレーターは、4-6月期は前年同期比で2.5%下落した。◆The foreign funds purchased the convertible bonds at prices equivalent to ¥25 per share. 海外ファンドは、1株25円で転換社債を引き受けた。◆The RCC used to buy bad loans at market prices. 整理回収機構は、これまで不良債権を時価で買い取っていた。◆Unless the vicious circle of declining prices, low corporate profits and low consumer demand is halted, neither the disposal of bad loans held by banks nor structural reforms will make progress. 物価下落や企業業績の低迷、消費需要の低下の悪循環を断ち切らないかぎり、銀行の不良債権処理も構造改革も進まないだろう。

price changes　物価変動
 ◆The nominal GDP growth rate takes into account price changes and is considered a more accurate reflection of household and corporate sentiment. 名目GDP（国内総生産）成長率は、物価変動を考慮し、家計や企業の景況感をより正確に反映するとされている。

price competition　価格競争
 ◆Coming on top of declining demand and intensifying price competition, the aftermath of the terrorist attacks is so serious that we can hardly have a long-term vision. 需要低迷や価格競争激化に加え、米同時テロの影響が厳しく、先が見通せなくなっている。

price differential　価格格差, 価格差
 ◆To narrow this price differential, it is necessary to intensify competition in the power-supply market. この価格差を縮めるには、電力供給市場の競争をさらに強める必要がある。

price drops　物価の下落　（=slide in prices）
 ◆Deflation, characterized by price drops in many sectors, has worsened amid the prolonged recession. 幅広い分野で物価の下落が進んでいるのが特徴のデフレが、長引く不況のなかで深刻になっている。

price earnings ratio　株価収益率, PER　（=P/E, P/E ratio: 株価収益率＝株式の市場価格（common stock market price）÷1株当たり利益（earnings per common share））

price fluctuation　物価の変動, 価格騰落, 株価の乱高下, 株価変動
 ◆Investors are swayed by price fluctuations. 投資家は、株価変動に左右される。

price hike　値上げ, 価格引上げ
 ◆It remains to be seen how much price hikes of fuel oil and other petrochemical products will affect the prices of final products in Japan. 燃料油や他の石油化学製品の値上げが今後、最終製品の国内価格にどの程度波及するかが注目される。

price index　物価指数, 価格指数
 （⇒consumer price index）
 applicable government price index　適格政府物価指数
 bond linked to stock price index　株価指数連動債

commodity price index 商品価格指数
Commodity Research Bureau Futures Price Index CRB商品先物指数
core consumer price index 消費者物価指数のコア指数
effective price index 実効物価指数
export and import price index 輸出入物価指数
export price index 輸出物価指数
export price indexes for basic groups by group 輸出物価基本分類類別指数
general price index 一般物価指数
hedonic price index ヘドニック・プライス・インデックス, ヘドニック・インデックス
house price indices 住宅価格指数
indices of urban land prices 全国市街地価格指数
JoC commodity price index ジャーナル・オブ・コマース鉱業原材料価格指数
Journal of Commerce Industrial Price Index ジャーナル・オブ・コマース工業原材料指数
key price indexes 主要インフレ指標, 主要物価指数
land price index of cities 市街地価格指数
producer price index 生産者物価指数
producer price indexes by stage of processing 加工段階別生産者物価指数
retail price index 小売物価指数
 (=index of retail prices)
service price index 企業向けサービス価格指数
specific price index 個別価格指数
stock price index 物価指数, 株価インデックス
trade price index 貿易物価指数, 貿易価格指数
wholesale price index 卸売物価指数
◆The consumer price index fell for three consecutive years from 1999 to 2001. 消費者物価指数は、1999年から2001年まで3年連続で減少した。

price keeping operation 公的資金による株式の買い支え, 株価維持策, 株価維持活動, プライス・キーピング・オペレーション, PKO (国民年金や厚生年金などの公的資金による株式の買い支え)

price mechanism 価格メカニズム
◆Policy-based financing operations which take advantage of government subsidies are adversely affecting the price mechanism in the financial market. 政府の補給金を受けて運営される政策金融は、金融市場の価格メカニズムを歪めている。

price projections 物価見通し
◆The Bank of Japan revised its price projections upward due to the growing trend of price increases for energy and other items related to natural resources. エネルギーや他の天然資源関連品目の価格上昇傾向が広がってきたため、日銀が物価見通しを上方修正した。

price range 価格帯, 値幅
◆I'd like to sell vegetables that are in the right price range for daily consumption. 日常的に食べられる価格帯の野菜を販売したい。

price risk of a stock 株式の価格リスク
◆The trader used a standard option to hedge the price risk of a stock. このトレーダーは、株式の価格リスクをヘッジするために標準的なオプションを使った。

price stability 物価安定
◆The ECB was obliged to maintain price stability when the euro was launched in 1999. 1999年にユーロが導入された際、欧州中銀(ECB)は、物価安定の維持を義務付けられた。

price tag 値札, 正札, 値段, 定価, 購入価格
◆The price tag for the mortgage-backed securities sold to Fannie and Freddie by 17 financial firms totaled $196.1 billion. 大手金融機関17社がファニー・メイとフレディ・マックに販売した住宅ローン担保証券(MBS)の購入額は、総額で1,961億ドルになる。

price-to-book value 株価純資産倍率
 (=price book-value ratio)
◆Price-to-book value is obtained by dividing price per share by assets per share. 株価純資産倍率は、1株当たり株価を1株当たりの資産額で割って[除して]求められます。

price trends 値動き
◆The TSE average has been affected more often by price trends in the Shanghai market on the same day. 東証の平均株価は、当日の上海市場[上海株]の値動きに引きずられることが多くなった。

primacy (名)首位, 第一位, 最高, 卓越, 優越性, 最も重要であること
forfeit one's primacy 首位から転落する
give primacy to ～を最優先する, ～を優先して考える, ～を最重要視する
the age of dollar primacy ドル支配の時代
◆Many pundits in Tokyo have prophesized the possible demise of U.S. primacy since the financial bubble burst. 金融バブルの崩壊以降、日本では、米一極指導の終焉(しゅうえん)を予言する専門家が多い。◆The age of dollar primacy is said to be coming to an end. ドル支配の時代は終わりに近い、と言われている。

primary (形)最初の, 第一次の, 一次的な, 第一順位の, 主要な, 最も重要な, 最大の, 中心的な, 有力な, 本来の, 根源的な, 初歩の, 初期の, 初期段階の, 基本的な, 希薄化前, プライマリー
primary activity 起債活動, 起債, 発行活動
primary beneficiary 第一順位保険金受取人
primary bond 新発債
primary bond market 新発債市場
primary dealer プライマリー・ディーラー(米国の場合は、ニューヨーク連邦準備銀行との直接取引を認められている政府証券ディーラーのこと)
primary deficit 基礎的赤字, 財政の基礎収支の赤字
primary deposits 本源的預金, 第一次的預金(預金者が現金を預けることで生じる預金)
primary distribution 募集, 第一次分売, 第一次売出し
 (=primary offering)
primary duty 輸入付加税
primary earnings per common share 単純希薄化による普通株式1株当たり利益
primary earnings per share of common stock 普通株式1株当たり基本的利益
primary EPS 基本的1株当たり利益
 (=primary earnings per share)
primary financial statements 基本財務諸表, 基本財務書類, 第一次財務諸表[財務書類] (第二次財務諸表=secondary financial statements)
primary materials 原材料
primary money 第一次貨幣
primary offering 募集, 第一次分売, 第一次売出し(新規発行される有価証券の取得申込みを勧誘すること)
primary paper 新発債
primary reserve 第一線支払い準備, 第一次準備(現金、中央銀行預け金、他行への預け金など、銀行保有の準備資産のうち最も流動性が高いもの)
primary reserve asset 第一次準備資産
primary securities 直接証券, 本源的証券
primary underwriter 主アンダーライター
retail-oriented primary coverage リテール型一次保険
◆Average primary common and common equivalent shares

primary balance プライマリー・バランス, 財政の基礎的収支（国債発行による収入と国債の元利払い費を除いた基礎的収支。基礎的財政収支が赤字だと、国の借金が増えるため、財政再建には黒字化が必要になる）
◆A surplus in the primary balances of the central and local governments indicates a degree of fiscal soundness. 国と地方［地方自治体］の基礎的財政収支の黒字は、財政の健全度を示す。◆The primary balance represents the budget balance, excluding proceeds from government bond issues and debt-servicing costs. プライマリー・バランスは、国債発行による収入と国債費（国債の利払いや償還費用）を除いた財政収支である。

primary balance deficit 基礎的財政収支の赤字, 財政赤字, 一次的財政赤字, 基礎的財政赤字, 財政赤字, プライマリー・バランスの赤字［赤字幅］
（⇒fiscal management strategy）
◆The primary balance deficits of Greece currently stand at 10 percent of GDP. ギリシャの財政赤字は現在、GDP（国内総生産）の10%に当たる。◆The primary balance deficit—the budget shortfalls because of the lack of tax revenue for the current fiscal year—has reached ￥13 trillion. プライマリー・バランスの赤字、つまり今年度の税収不足による財政赤字は、13兆円に達している。

primary capital 第一次資本, 本源的資本, 銀行の自己資本, プライマリー・キャピタル
（=Tier 1 capital）
　primary capital market　第一次資本市場
　primary capital ratio　狭義の自己資本市場

primary earnings per share 基本的1株当たり利益, 基礎的1株当たり利益, 1株当たり希薄化前利益, 単純希薄化による1株当たり利益, 単純希薄化1株当たり利益
（=basic earnings per share, primary EPS）
◆Primary earnings per share in 2011 were one cent higher than fully diluted. 2011年度の1株当たり希薄化前利益は、完全希薄化後利益よりも1セント高かった。

primary market 発行市場, 新発債市場, プライマリー市場（新規株式公開や公募など、企業や国が株や債券を新規発行して資金調達をする市場。⇒capital market）
　activity in the primary market　新発債市場の動き
　International Primary Market Association　国際引受業者協会
　Primary market for securities　証券の発行市場
　解説 発行市場と流通市場との違いとは：証券市場のうち、有価証券を発行、引受け、募集する段階のことを有価証券の発行市場（primary market, issue market）という。これに対して、発行された証券を売買する段階を有価証券の流通市場（secondary market, trading market）という。

primary surplus 基礎的黒字, 基礎的財政黒字, 財政の基礎収支の黒字（公債の元利払いがない場合の政府収支の黒字）
　government's primary surplus　財政の基礎的収支の黒字

primary weapons 有力な手段
◆ATM cards are the banks' primary weapons to lure new clients. キャッシュ・カードは、銀行にとって新規顧客獲得の有力な手段だ。

prime（動）準備をする, 用意する, 呼び水［迎え水］を差す, （銃に）火薬を詰める
　prime the pump　ポンプに呼び水を差す, （景気刺激のために）誘い水政策を取る, 資金を投入して事業を活性化する, 奨励する

prime（形）主要な, 首位の, 最重要な, 優秀な, 優良な, 最優良な, 最高級の, 第一等の, 極上の, 信用等級が最高の, 素数の　（名）プライム・レート, 最上等, 素数
　prime bank　有力銀行, 一流銀行
　prime banker's acceptance　一流銀行引受手形
　prime bill　優良手形, 一流手形
　prime borrower［debtor, issuer］　優良発行体
　prime brokerage　プライム・ブローカレッジ（証券会社が、主に資産運用機関（fund managers）を対象に、受渡し決済や保管業務、報告、資金の融資などをひとまとめにして提供するサービス）
　prime business　優良企業
　prime commercial paper　一流商業手形
　prime cost　仕入値段, 直接原価, 直接費, 主要費用
　prime credit　原信用状　（=prime letter of credit）
　prime customer　優良顧客, 優良取引先
　prime debtor［issuer］　優良発行体
　prime entry　仮輸入手続き
　prime force　原動力
　prime mover　原動力, 牽引力, 推進力, 主唱者, 動力機械, 原動機
　prime name bank　超一流銀行
　prime paper　一流手形
　prime quality　優良品, 最上品
　prime rating　高格付け
　prime stock　花形株, 主力株
◆Floating rate payments are based on rates tied to prime, LIBOR or U.S. Treasury bills. 変動金利の支払い利率は、プライム・レート, ロンドン銀行間取引金利または米財務省短期証券の利回りに基づいて決定されます。

prime bank rate of interest プライム・レート, 一流企業向け最優遇貸出金利
◆At December 31. 2011, the corporation and certain subsidiaries companies had unused credit lines, generally available at the prime bank rate of interest, of approximately $400. 2011年12月31日現在、当社と一部の子会社が一般にプライム・レートで利用できる銀行与信枠未使用残高は、約4億ドルとなっています。

prime lending rate 一流企業向け最優遇貸出金利, プライム・レート
◆The Central Bank raised its prime lending rate from 18 percent to 21 percent in a move intended to take reals out of circulation and stifle demand for dollars. （ブラジル）中央政府は、レアル（通貨）の流通抑制とドル需要の鎮静化を狙って、プライム・レート（最優遇貸出金利）を18%から21%に引き上げた。

prime name 一流手形, 優良銘柄
　prime foreign name　外国の優良銘柄
　prime name bank　超一流銀行
　prime name CDs　最高位に格付けされたCD, プライム・ネームCD

prime rate 一流企業向け最優遇貸出金利, 標準金利, プライム・レート　（=prime, prime bank rate, prime interest rate, prime lending rate, prime rate of interest）
　floating prime rate　変動プライム・レート
　（=floating prime lending rate）
　long-term prime rate　長期プライム・レート, 長プラ（最も信用力がある銀行の顧客企業に対する1年超の貸付け金に適用される金利）
　prime rate on long term loans　長期プライム・レート
　short-term prime rate　短期プライム・レート, 短プラ（優良企業向けに1年以内の短期資金を貸し出すときの基準金利）
◆The Bank of Tokyo-Mitsubishi UFJ has decided to raise its short-term prime rate, a benchmark for interest rates on loans to small and midsize firms and home buyers, by 0.25

of a percentage point from the current 1.375 percent. 三菱東京UFJ銀行が、中小企業と住宅取得者向けローンの基準金利である短期プライム・レートを、現在の年1.375%から0.25%引き上げることにした。

principal (名)元本, 元金, 基本財産, 株式の額面価額, 主債務者, 本人, 共同経営者
(⇒deposit insurance, redemption of bonds)
 cause a loss of principal 元本割れとなる
  (=reduce the principal)
 collateral principal payment 担保からの元本支払い[元本返済]
 collection of principal 元本回収
 delays or reduced payments of interest and principal 利息や元本の遅延や減額返済
  (⇒value loans)
 exchange of principal 元本の交換
 guaranteed principal 元本保証
 payment of (the) principal and interest 元利の支払い, 元利払い, 元利の返済, 元金と利子の支払い
 principal-agent problem 依頼人・代理人問題
 Principal Only (パス・スルー証券の分離型モーゲージ証券のうち)元本部分の証券
 principal outstanding 残存元本額
 reduce the principal 元本割れする
  (=cause a loss of principal)
 repayment of principal 元本の償還, 元本返済
 trust principal 信託元本
◆If TEPCO's creditor banks forgive the debts when the utility is not carrying excessive liabilities, lenders will not be able to recover either the principal or interest owed. 東電が債務超過でない時点で東電の債権保有銀行が債権を放棄すると、金融機関は元本を回収できず、金利収入も得られなくなる。◆In the case of foreign currency deposits, losses may balloon if the yen appreciates further and may cause a loss of principal. 外貨預金の場合、円高がさらに進めば損失が膨らみ、元本割れになる恐れもある。◆In the lawsuits against big banks over the sales of risky investments, the U.S. government wants to be compensated for lost principal and interest payments. 高リスク証券の販売をめぐっての大手金融機関に対する訴訟で、米政府は、元本と利払い分の損失補償を求めている。◆The Public Management Ministry prohibits incorporated foundations from investing their basic assets in financial products which may reduce the principal, such as stocks and foreign currency-denominated bonds. 総務省は、財団法人に対して、その基本的な財産を株式や外貨建て債券など元本割れの恐れのある金融商品に投資するのを禁じている。◆This was considered as interest payments and did not reduce the principal of their loan. これは利払いと見なされたため、借入金の元本は減らなかった。

principal (形)第一の, 主な, 主要な, 主力の, (最も)重要な, 元本の, 元金の, 資本金の
 principal assets of life insurance companies 生命保険会社の資産運用状況
 principal assets of nonlife insurance companies 損害保険会社の資産運用状況
 principal banker 主力銀行, メインバンク
 principal payment 元本返済, 元本の支払い, 元本返済額
 principal shareholders 主要株主
 principal sum (支払われる保険金の)最高額
 remaining principal balance 元本残存額, 残存元本額
  (=principal outstanding)
 the principal paying agent 主支払い代理人
 the principal seal 実印
 the principal security 主な担保, 主要担保

◆The Proxy Statement includes biographies of the Board's nominees for director and their principal affiliations with other companies or organizations, as well as the items of business to be voted on at the Annual Meeting. 議決権代理行使勧誘状には、定時株主総会で票決される議案のほかに、取締役会で選出された取締役候補者の略歴や取締役候補者の他の会社・組織との主な協力・兼任関係などが記載されている。

principal amount 元本, 元金, 元本額, 額面価額, 額面
(⇒convertible debenture)
◆The firm completed a private placement in the United States of 15.0 % Notes, Series 4, due 2018, for a principal amount of Can. $150 million. 同社は米国で、2018年満期・利率15.0%のシリーズ4ノートを、1億5,000万カナダ・ドルの元本額で私募発行した。

principal and interest 元本と利息, 元利
◆Debt-servicing costs are payments on the principals and interests on previously issued government bonds. 国債費は、過去に発行した国債の元利払いに使われる金だ。

principal guarantee 元本保証
◆We're recommending government bonds and other financial products with principal guarantees. 当行では、元本保証のある国債などの金融商品を勧めている。

principal investment (証券会社の業務としての)自己資金による投資, 自己資金投資, プリンシパル・インベストメント (投資対象は一般にM&Aや不動産への投資。投資収益はほぼ100%、自己の収益として計上することができる)

principally 主に, 原則として, 基本的に
◆We determine cost principally on a first-in, first-out (FIFO) basis. 当社は、基本的に先入れ先出し法で原価を算定しています。

principle (名)原理, 原則, 法則, 主義, 信念, 信条, 根本方針, 方針, (基本的な)考え方, 道義, 徳義, 節操, 本源, 本質, 原動力
(⇒generally accepted accounting principles)
 a conservative principle 保守的な考え方, 保守的な方針
 a vital principle 活力, 精力
 abandon [desert] one's principle 信念を捨てる
 accrual principle 発生主義の原則
 as a matter of principle 主義として
 be against one's principles ～の信念[主義、道義]に反する
 benefit principle 受益者負担
 business accounting principle 企業会計原則
 cost principle 原価主義
 economic principle 経済原則
 equal value principle 等価交換の原則
 guiding principles 指導原理
 in principle 原則的に, 原則として, 全体としては, 大筋で, おおむね
 lose one's moral principles from greed 欲に目がくらむ
 market principles 市場原理
 on principle 主義[信念]として, 主義に従って[に基づいて], 原則に則(のっと)って, 道義的見地から, 道義上
 principle of current operating performance 当期業績主義の原則
 principle of matching costs with revenues 費用収益対応の原則
 principles of consolidation 連結方針, 連結の基準
  (=consolidation policy)
 priority principle 重点主義
 profit-first principle 利益至上主義
 satisfying principle 満足基準

stick [live up] to one's principles　信念に固執する, 信念を貫く
the principle of casualty　因果律
the principle of consistency　継続性の原則, 首尾一貫の原則
utility maximization principle　効用最大化の原理
◆Golden shares violate the principle of shareholder equality. 黄金株は、「株主平等の原則」に反する。◆We operate on the principle that management is accountable to shareholders. 経営者は株主に対して責任がある、というのが当社の経営方針です。◆Yen loans extended now as part of Japan's ODA are untied in principle, with the source of development materials and equipment to be procured not defined. 日本の政府開発援助 (ODA) として供与されている円借款は現在、ひも付きでない「アンタイド」援助が原則で、開発物資の調達先を限定していない。

principle of fiscal balance　財政均衡の原則
　(⇒fiscal balance)
◆The EU's principle of fiscal balance will automatically impose sanctions on member countries whose fiscal deficit exceeds 3 percent of their gross domestic product in a single fiscal year. 欧州連合 (EU) の財政均衡の原則では、単年度で財政赤字が対国内総生産比 (GDP) 比で3％を突破した加盟国に対して、自動的に制裁が発動される。

prior　(形) 事前の, 前の, 先の, ～より上の, 重要な
　prior bond　優先権付き債券
　prior claim　優先請求権
　prior consultation　事前協議
　prior endorser　(手形の) 前裏書人
　prior mortgage　上位抵当
　prior permit　事前承認
　prior preferred [preference] stock　第一優先株, 最優先株式
　prior redemption　優先権付き償還, 満期前償還
　prior stock　先順位優先株

prior to　～に先立って, ～より前に, ～の前の
◆The money lent by the U.S. and eurozone private banks remains at about the same level as those prior to Lehman's collapse. 米国とユーロ圏の民間銀行の貸出金は、リーマン・ブラザーズの経営破たん前とほぼ同水準にとどまっている。◆The U.S. private banks' funds on hand grew about three times from March 2008 prior to the Lehman's collapse. 米国の民間銀行の手持ち資金は、リーマン・ブラザーズの経営破たん前の2008年3月から約3倍増えた。

prioritize　(動) 優先順に並べる, 優先順位を付ける, 優先する, 優先的に扱う
◆Economic stimulus measures should be prioritized in the government's policy management. 政府の政策運営では、景気刺激策 [景気対策] を優先するべきだ。

priority　(名) 優先, 優先事項, 優先権, 優先順位, 先取権
　creditors by priority　優先債権者
　　(=priority creditors)
　export priority　輸出優先権, 輸出優先順位
　first priority　最優先
　give priority in negotiations for　～の優先交渉権を与える
　investment priority　投資の優先順位
　low-priority policy project　優先度の低い政策プロジェクト
　payment priorities　支払いの優先順位, 元本返済の優先順位
　place priority on　～を優先する, 優先して～する
　priority between mortgages　担保権の順位
　priority in budgetary discussion　予算先議権
　priority items　重点品目

priority measures　優先課題, 優先策
priority of attachment　優先差押え権
priority of claims　請求優先権, 債権先取り権
priority rate of duty　実行関税率
priority schedule　実行順位表
priority subscription period　優先割当期間
priority system principle　重点主義
put priority on efficiency　効率を重視する
top priority　最優先課題
◆Another characteristic of the U.S. management style is that businesses give priority to maximizing shareholders' value. 米国式経営スタイルのもうひとつの特色は、企業が株主の資産価値の極大化を第一に考えることだ。◆Economic recovery is the top priority for Japan. 景気回復が、日本の最優先課題だ。◆Given the nation's tough fiscal condition, the government must eke out the necessary funds by scaling down low-priority policy projects. 日本の厳しい財政事情に照らせば、政府に求められるのは、優先度の低い政策プロジェクトを縮小して、必要な財源をひねり出すことだ。◆Meiji Yasuda decided to lower the yield rate of its flagship insurance product because the insurer placed priority on long-term stable management over an increase in the number of policyholders. 明治安田生保は、契約者の数を増やすより長期的な経営の安定を優先したため、主力保険商品の予定利率 [利回り] を引き下げることにした。◆Priority measures to achieve economic recovery are stopping deflation and mobilizing all possible fiscal measures, financial policies and taxation reforms. 景気回復を実現するための優先課題は、デフレ阻止と、可能な財政政策、金融政策や税制改革を総動員することだ。◆Priority should be given to public spending, to establish a firm foundation for economic recovery and the subsequent job of tackling fiscal reform. 景気を回復し [経済を立て直し]、財政改革に取り組むための強固な基盤を確立するには、公共支出を優先的に考えなければならない。

private　(形) 私的な, 個人の, 個人的な, 個別の, 私募の, 非公開の, 非公式の, 会員制の, 私有の, 私設の, 私立の, 民営の, 民間の, プライバシーを重んじる, プライベート
　private activity bond　民間事業債
　private allocation　縁故者割当て
　private annuity　自家年金
　private banker　個人銀行
　private bill　個人手形
　private bond　民間債
　private borrowing　民間借入れ, 私募の資金調達
　private brander　自家銘柄業者
　private capex　民間設備投資
　private code　暗証番号　(=secret code)
　private commercial bank　民間銀行
　private consumption　個人消費, 民間消費支出, 民間最終支出　(=personal consumption)
　private convertible note　私募転換社債
　private corporation　非公開会社, 私法人, 個人会社　(=private enterprise)
　private debt　民間負債
　private debt placement　私募債の発行
　private deed [document]　私署証書
　private deposit　個人預金, 民間預金
　private discount　市中銀行割引
　private donation　個人の寄付
　private enterprise annuity　企業年金　(=occupational annuity)
　private enterprise insurance　私営保険
　private equity　未公開株, 未上場株, PE

Private Export Funding Corporation　米民間輸出金融会社, PEFCO
private financing　民間資金, 民間金融
private flows at market terms　民間資金の流れ
private fund assets　民間年金基金資産
private income　不労所得（投資、不動産、相続などからの収入）
private insurance　私保険, 私営保険, 民間の保険
private investor　個人投資家
private issue　民間企業の起債
private issuer　民間証券発行者
private lender [financial institution]　民間金融機関
private lending　民間貸付け
private limited company　未公開企業, 非公開会社
private liquidity deficit　民間流動性不足
private loan financing test　民間貸付け基準
private means　事業所得, 不労所得
private monetary deposits　一般通貨性預金
private mortgage insurance　民間モーゲージ保険, PMI
private mortgage insurer　民間モーゲージ保証会社
private nonfinancial market　民間の非金融市場
private note　私募債
private partnership bank　個人銀行
private patient　個人負担医療の患者
private pension　私的年金, 企業年金保険
private placing　私募発行, 私募
private propensity to invest　民間投資性向
private propensity to save　民間貯蓄性向
private property　私有財産
private purpose bond　民間目的債, 非公共目的債
private savings　個人貯蓄
private source　民間部門
private subscription　縁故募集
private subscription bond　縁故債
private tender　指名入札
private trading system　私設取引システム
private transfers　民間移転収支
private trust　個人信託, 私益信託, 慈善信託（charitable trust）以外の信託
private underwriter　個人保険業者
private unrequited transfers　民間移転収支
◆The former chairman of Daio Paper Corp allegedly received more than ¥10 billion in loans from the firm's group companies for private purposes. 報道によれば、大王製紙の前会長が、グループ企業から100億円超の私的融資を受けた。

private bank　民間銀行, 個人銀行（個人や事業組合経営の銀行）, ロンドン手形交換所非加盟銀行, 主婦のへそくり
　lending by private banks　民間銀行の貸出
　private banks' government bond holdings　民間銀行の国債保有高[保有残高]
◆Entrusted or instructed by the South Korean government, private banks jointly extended loans to the company. 韓国政府の委託や指示を受けて、民間銀行が同社に協調融資した。◆Japanese private banks' government bond holdings soared to ¥154 trillion as of the end of June 2011 from ¥32 trillion as of the end of March 1999. 日本の民間銀行の国債保有残高は、(ゼロ金利政策が初めて)導入された1999年3月末時点の32兆円から、2011年6月末現在で154兆円に膨らんだ。◆Lending by private banks has not increased though their investments into government bonds and cash reserves are increasing. 民間銀行の国債への投資や手持ちの現金は増えているが、民間銀行の貸出は増えていない。◆Money loaned by private banks declined because banks with weakened financial strength were less willing to lend, besides a lack of businesses seeking expansion through borrowing. 民間銀行の貸出金が減ったのは、お金を借りてまで事業を拡大しようとする企業がなかったほか、財務が悪化した銀行が貸し渋ったからだ。◆Money loaned by private banks declined to ¥419 trillion as of the end of July 2011 from ¥472 trillion at the end of March 1999 when the zero-interest rate policy was first adopted. 民間銀行の貸出金は、ゼロ金利政策が初めて導入された1999年3月末の472兆円から、2011年7月末現在では419兆円に減った。◆The money lent by the U.S. and eurozone private banks remains at about the same level as those prior to Lehman's collapse. 米国とユーロ圏の民間銀行の貸出金は、リーマン・ブラザーズの経営破たん前とほぼ同水準にとどまっている。◆The U.S. private banks' outstanding Treasury bond holdings grew by about 50 percent from March 2008, prior to the Lehman shock. 米国の民間銀行の米国債保有残高は、リーマン・ショック前の2008年3月から約5割増えた。

private banking　プライベート・バンキング（個人資産を管理・運用する銀行業務）
◆The Bank of Tokyo-Mitsubishi, Mitsubishi Trust and Banking Corp. and Kokusai Securities Co. plan to establish a company that will provide private banking services, including portfolio investment and asset management. 東京三菱銀行、三菱信託銀行と国際証券の3社は、資産運用投資や資産管理など「プライベート・バンキング」業務を行う会社を設立する計画だ。

private bondholder　民間の債券保有者, 民間投資家, 民間債権者（private creditor）
◆Athens is likely to officially launch talks with banks and other private bondholders for the debt write-down. ギリシャ政府は、銀行などの民間債権者[民間投資家、民間の債券保有者]と債務削減のための協議を開始する見込みだ。

private capital　民間資本, 私的資本, 民間企業の持つ資本
　private capital expenditure [spending]　民間設備投資
　private capital formation　民間資本形成（民間企業の投資）
　private capital stock　民間資本ストック（住宅は除いて民間企業が保有する有形固定資産）
　private domestic capital formation　国内民間資本形成（=private domestic investment）
　private external capital　対外民間資本
　private foreign capital　民間外国資本, 民間外資

private creditors　民間債権者
◆In resolving Greece's debt woes, German Chancellor Angera Merkel urged substantial aid from private creditors. ギリシャの債務問題を解決するにあたって、アンゲラ・メルケル独首相は、民間債権者に大幅支援を求めた。

private finance initiative　民間資金等活用事業, 民間資金による社会資本整備, プライベート・ファイナンス・イニシアチブ, PFI　（⇒PFI）
◆Private finance initiative (PFI) is a method of constructing public facilities that was introduced by Britain in 1992. The private sector is entrusted to construct, maintain and operate public facilities. プライベート・ファイナンス・イニシアチブ(PFI)は、英国が1992年に導入した公共施設建設の手法で、民間部門が公共施設の建設、維持・管理と運営を任される。
解説 PFIとは：道路や橋、ごみ処理施設などの社会資本整備で、民間企業が資金調達から建設、管理、運営までを行い、国や地方自治体、利用者から施設使用料などを徴収する制度。

private financial institution　民間金融機関
◆Raising the outstanding balance of current accounts held by private financial institutions at the central bank to be-

tween ¥27 trillion and ¥30 trillion remained within the range of conventional responses. 日銀当座預金（民間金融機関が日銀に保有している当座預金）の残高目標を（現行の22-27兆円程度から）27-30兆円程度に引き上げる日銀の追加金融緩和は、従来の対応の範囲内にとどまった。◆The BOJ decided to introduce a new open market operation by supplying ¥10 trillion to private financial institutions in three month loans at an ultralow annual interest of 0.1 percent. 日銀は、民間の金融機関に年1％の超低金利で貸出期間3か月の資金を10兆円供給する新型の公開市場操作（オペ）の導入に踏み切った。◆The DBJ and private financial institutions extended loans worth a total of ¥100 billion to JAL in June 2009 though JAL was already in dire financial straits. 日本政策投資銀行と民間金融機関は、日航の経営がすでに悪化していたものの、2009年6月に同社に対して総額1,000億円を融資した。◆The total amount of loans owed by companies and individuals to private financial institutions stands at ¥2.8 trillion in the three prefectures' coastal areas hit by the March 11 tsunami. 津波被災地の3県（宮城、岩手と福島）沿岸部では、企業や個人の民間企業からの借入金総額が、2.8兆円にのぼっている。

private investment　民間投資, 民間設備投資, 民間企業による投資, 非公開投資
　private domestic investment　国内民間投資
　private foreign capital investment　民間外国資本投資
　private foreign investment　民間海外投資
　private housing investment　民間住宅投資
　private investment abroad　対外民間投資
　private investment expenditure　民間投資支出
　private overseas investment　民間海外投資
　private productive investment　民間生産投資

private offering　株式の直接募集, 縁故募集, 私募（=private placement, private placing）
　private offering exemption　私募免除
◆The bonds were for sale by private offering and issued by Princeton Global Management Ltd. この債券は、プリンストン・グローバル・マネジメントが発行した私募債である。

private placement　私募発行, 私募, 第三者割当て, 私募債, 私募証券（=direct placement, private debt placement, private offering, private placing: 公募（public offering）と違って、私募は株主や取引先、機関投資家など特定少数の投資家を対象に新株を発行、募集するもの）
　bonds by private placement　縁故債
　bonds offered through private placement　私募債
　private placement bond　私募債
　private placement debt securities　私募債
　private placement of new shares　新株の私募発行
　private placement rating　私募債の格付け
　private placement sector [market]　私募債市場
　raise cash by means of a private placement　第三者割り当てで資金を調達する
　structured private placement　仕組み私募債
　swap-driven private placement facility　スワップ付き私募債
◆The firm completed a private placement in the United States of 17.10% Notes, Series 4, due 2018. 同社は、2018年満期・利率17.1％のシリーズ4ノートを、米国で私募発行した。
◆This company director bought the shares of the firm allocated to third parties through the firm's private placement of new shares. この会社役員は、同社が実施した新株の私募発行による第三者割当て増資で、同社株を取得した。

private sector　民間部門, 私企業部門, 民間セクター, 私的セクター, 民間企業, 民間
　private financial sector　民間金融部門
　private nonfinancial sector　民間の非金融部門
　private-sector businesses [company, firm]　民間企業
　private sector credit　民間部門の信用
　private sector debt　民間部門の債権[債務], 民間債（民間企業が発行する債券で金融債と事業債がある）（⇒public sector debt）
　private-sector financial balance　民間セクターの資金需給
　private sector financial institution [institute]　民間金融機関
　private-sector investment　民間部門の投資
　private sector loans　民間セクター向け融資
　private-sector mortgage rate　民間の住宅ローン金利
　the private sector's external exposure　民間部門の対外債務
◆The private sector has tackled necessary restructuring efforts earnestly. 民間は、必要なリストラ策に懸命に取り組んできた。

private-sector demand　民間需要（=private demand）
◆There has been no sign of increases in the two chief components of private-sector demand—personal consumption and capital investment. 民間需要の2本柱である個人消費と設備投資に、回復の兆しが見えない。

privately　（副）個人として, 個人的に, 非公式に, 非公開で, 内密に, 内緒で, 民間で（⇒publicly）
　be privately held　株式を公開していない
　privately controlled company [corporation, firm]　未上場企業, 非上場会社
　privately funded starts　民間資金による住宅着工戸数
　privately held company　非公開会社, 株式非公開会社, 株式未公開企業, 非上場会社
　privately-managed pension fund scheme　民間運営の年金基金
　privately owned bank　民間銀行
　privately-owned mortgage bank　株式未公開の住宅金融会社
　privately owned stock　非公開株[株式]
　privately placed bonds　私募債
　privately-placed deep discount bonds　ディープ・ディスカウント私募債
　privately-run　個人経営の

privately place　私募発行する, 私募形式で販売する, 第三者割当て発行する, 第三者割当て増資する（=privately issue）
◆In July 2011, the Company privately placed two million special warrants to purchase new common shares of the corporation. 2011年7月に当社は、同社の新規発行普通株式引受権付き特別ワラント債200万単位を、私募発行しました。

privatization　民営化
◆There is persistent opposition to the privatization of the three post office services of mail delivery, savings and insurance within the Liberal Democratic Party. 郵便集配、郵便貯金と簡易保険の郵政3事業民営化については、自民党内にも根強い反対論がある。

privilege　（名）特権, 特典, 恩典, 特別扱い, 権利, （株の）特権付き売買
　check-writing privileges　小切手発行機能
　conversion privilege　転換権
　overdraft privilege　当座貸越しの特典
　privilege issues　（株式転換などの）特権付き社債
　trust receipt privilege　担保荷物保管証による荷物引取りの特典, 担保荷物保管証の特典
◆The U.S. dollar has enjoyed the massive privileges as the key international currency. 米ドルは、国際通貨としての特権を享受してきた。

privileged (形)特権のある, 特権付きの, 内部の
  pass privileged information　内部情報を流す
  privileged bond　ワラント付き転換社債
  privileged debt　優先債務, 特権債務
    (=preferential debt)
  privileged issue　特権付き債券
  privileged treatment　優遇

pro forma standard tax　外形標準課税
  (=corporate tax on gross operating profit)
◆The Public Management Ministry already has announced a plan to introduce assessment on the basis of the size of a business—the so-called pro forma standard tax formula—into the enterprise tax system. 総務省は、事業税にいわゆる「外形標準課税」方式である事業規模に応じた評価[査定]方式を導入する方針をすでに表明している。◆Under the pro forma standard tax, corporate tax is levied on the basis of the number of employees, combined wages, and the size of capital. 外形標準課税では、法人事業税は従業員数や給与総額、資本金の規模などを基準にして課税される。

pro-market　(形)市場経済主義者の
◆Bolivian pro-market President-elect Gonzalo Sanchez took office facing the huge tasks of reviving a stagnant economy and attracting investment. ボリビアの大統領に当選した市場経済主義者のゴンザロ・サンチェス氏が、停滞した経済の回復や投資誘致という重大任務を抱えて就任した。

pro rata　比例して, その割合に応じて, 一定の割合に従って, 按分(あんぶん)に　(=according to a certain rate, according to the rate)
  be refunded pro rata　一定比率払い戻される
  on a pro rata basis　一定の割合[比率]に応じて, 出資割合[比率]に応じて, プロラタ・ベース
  pro rata allocation　比例配分　(=proration)
  pro rata share of the expenses　費用の比例配分, 費用の按分負担
◆Such dividends will be distributed between the parties on a pro rata basis in accordance with the respective number of shares of Stock owned by each of them. この配当金は、各当事者が所有する本株式のそれぞれの株式数の割合に応じて当事者間に配分するものとする。

proactive　(形)前向きの, 先行的, 先行型の, 事前の, 事前行動の, 予備措置の, 主体的な
  proactive stance toward monetary relaxation　金融緩和への前向きな姿勢
  proactive strategy　先行型戦略, 事前行動戦略
◆To alleviate the influence of the U.S. government's additional steps to ease the supply of money, the Bank of Japan must adopt a more proactive stance toward monetary relaxation. 米政府の追加金融緩和策[通貨供給量を増やす米政府の追加措置]の影響を和らげるには、日銀も金融緩和の姿勢を強める必要がある。

proactively　(副)前向きに, 先のことを考えて, 事前に対策を講じて, 積極的に
◆Corporate leaders should not only focus on belt-tightening, but also should proactively deal with replacing aging plants and equipments. 企業経営者は、緊縮経営一辺倒ではなく、老朽化が進む設備の更新にも前向きに対応する必要がある。◆The European Central Bank needs to provide support to Italy by proactively buying Italian bonds. 欧州中央銀行(ECB)は今後、イタリア国債を積極的に買い入れてイタリアを支援する必要がある。

probe　(名)厳密な調査, 徹底的な調査, 本格調査, 精査, 探査, 探索, (疑惑の)解明, 宇宙探査機, 探測機, 探査用ロケット, 宇宙探査機による調査, (医療器具の)探り針, プローブ
◆The SEC probe was focused on several transactions that had led to higher revenues at AOL Time Warner Inc. 米証券取引委員会(SEC)の調査は、AOLタイム・ワーナーの売上高水増し(疑惑)につながった一部の取引を中心に行われた。

problem　(名)問題, 課題, 難問
  asset problem　不良資産
  asset quality problem　資産の質の悪化, 資産内容の悪化
  balance of payments problem　国際収支問題
  credit problems　資金繰り悪化, 信用リスク要因
  current account problems　経常赤字
  debt problems of the developing countries　発展途上国の累積債務問題
  financial problem　金融問題, 財政的問題, 財政問題
  financing problems　金融面の問題
  funding problems　資金繰り, 資金繰りの悪化, 資金調達が難しいこと, 資金調達問題
  illiquidity problem　流動性不足問題
  insolvency problem　資産不足問題
  liquidity problem　流動性問題
  loan problem　融資の焦げ付き
  management problems　経営課題
  obligor credit problems　債務者の資金繰り悪化
  problem assets　不良資産, 不良債権
  problem bank　問題銀行
  problem credit　問題与信
  problem debts　不良債権, 貸倒れ
    (=problem loans)
  problem exposures　不良債権
  repayment problem　返済問題
  structural fiscal problem　構造的な財政赤字
  systemic problems　システミック・リスク
  troubled loan problems　不良債権問題
  world debt problem　累積債務問題
◆Errors in computing systems at financial institutions could lead to problems in making international fund transactions. 金融機関のコンピュータ・システムのエラーは、国際的な資金取引上、トラブルが生じる可能性がある。◆Goldman Sachs' capital increase is partly aimed at regaining the confidence in the U.S. financial market, which has been facing a raft of financial problems. ゴールドマン・サックスの増資は、多くの金融問題を抱える米金融市場の信認回復も狙いの一つだ。◆The earthquake insurance system was launched after the 1964 Niigata Earthquake as a response to the problem of fire insurance not covering damage caused by an earthquake or tsunami. 地震保険[地震保険制度]は、火災保険で地震や津波による被害が補償されない問題への対応策として、1964年の新潟地震後に導入された。

problem list　問題銀行リスト, 問題銀行
◆The 171 banks on the FDIC's "problem list" encompass only about 2 percent of the nearly 8,500 FDIC-insured institutions. 米連邦預金保険公社(FDIC)の「問題銀行リスト」に挙げられた171行は、同公社が預金の支払いを保証している金融機関(米商業銀行と貯蓄金融機関)約8,500行の2%程度を占めるにすぎない。◆The 171 U.S. banks are on the FDIC's "problem list." 米国の171行が、米連邦預金保険公社(FDIC)の「問題銀行リスト」に挙がっている。

problem loan　不良貸付け, 不良貸出, 問題融資
  carry problem loans on one's balance sheet　不良債権を抱える
  problem loans　問題債権, 不良債権, 貸倒れ, 不良債権額, 問題貸金　(=bad loans, loans to questionable borrowers, problem debts)
  real estate problem loan　不動産関連の不良貸出
◆The bank's problem loans totaled ¥5.30 trillion as of the end of December. 同行の不良債権額は、12月末の時点で5兆

3,000億円となった。

problem of dual debts or multiple debts 二重ローンや多重債務問題
◆Measures to lessen the problem of dual debts or multiple debts were also studied at the time of the 1995 Great Hanshin Earthquake. 二重ローンや多重債務問題の軽減策は、1995年の阪神大震災の際にも検討された。

problematic borrower 問題融資先
◆Under the new special inspection, the FSA will point out "problematic borrowers" from major banks whose outstanding loan extensions exceed ￥10 billion. 今回の特別検査では、融資残高が100億円以上に達する大手行の「問題融資先」を金融庁が指摘する。

procedure (名)手続き,手順,処理手順,慣行,方式
  accounting procedure 会計手続き,会計慣行,会計処理方法
  auditing procedure 監査手続き
    (=audit procedure)
  budgetary procedure 予算手続き
  clearing procedure 決済手続き
  closing procedure 決算手続き
  complaint procedures 苦情処理手続き
  control procedure 内部統制手続き
  credit procedures 与信手続き
  external auditing procedure 外部監査手続き
  internal procedures 内部規定
  judicial procedures 裁判手続き
  management procedures 管理手続き
  monitoring procedures 監視手続き
  procedures manual 手続きマニュアル,業務マニュアル
  settlement procedure 決済手続き,決済方式
◆Major moneylender SFCG is undergoing bankruptcy procedures. 金融大手のSFCGは現在、破産手続き中だ。◆We control our exposure to credit risk through credit approvals, credit limits and monitoring procedures. 当社は、信用供与承認や信用限度、監視手続きを通じて信用リスクを管理しています。◆We have to admit there has been an inappropriate accounting procedure. 不適切な会計処理であったことは、認めざるを得ない。

proceed (動)続ける,進める,遂行する,訴訟を起こす
  proceed against ～を訴える,～に対して訴訟を起こす
  proceed from ～から始まる,～から起こる,～に起因する
  proceed steadily with fiscal reconstruction 財政再建を着実に進める
  proceed with 進める,(計画や政策などを)推し進める,続ける,続行する
◆The failed bank's refunding of deposits is being proceeded under the payoff system. 破たん銀行の預金の払い戻しは、ペイオフ(預金の払い戻し)制度に従って円滑に進められている。◆The United States and European countries are forced to proceed steadily with fiscal reconstruction and resolve the financial turmoil. 米欧各国は、財政再建を着実に進めて、金融市場の混乱を収拾せざるを得ない状況にある。◆World Co. has delisted itself from the Tokyo Stock Exchange and Osaka Securities Exchange to proceed with its long-term management strategy. アパレル大手のワールドは、長期的な経営戦略を進めるため、自ら東証と大証からの上場を廃止した。

proceedings (名)議事進行,議事録,決議録,会議録,会報,訴訟手続き,法的手続き,手続き,審理,措置,訴訟,弁論
  administrative proceedings 行政手続き,行政訴訟
  bankruptcy proceedings 破たん手続き
  legal proceedings 法律手続き,法的手続き,裁判手続き,法的手段
  receivership proceedings 破産手続き
  take [bring, institute, start] proceedings against ～に対して訴訟を起こす
  the proceedings of an annual shareholders meeting 年次株主総会の議事進行
◆Chrysler's five weeks of breakneck-speed bankruptcy proceedings came to a screeching halt. クライスラーの5週間にわたる猛スピードの破たん手続きに、急ブレーキがかかった。

proceeds (名)代金,手取金,売上,売上高,売却収入,売却益,所得,収益,純利益,収入,調達資金,資金
(⇒net proceeds)
  IPO proceeds 公募による手取金
  proceeds from asset sales 資産の売却収入
  proceeds from new debt 新規借入金による収入
  proceeds from new share issues 新株発行[起債]による手取金,新株発行手取額,新株発行による資金調達
  proceeds of the sale 売却代金
  use of proceeds 資金の使途
◆The company will use the proceeds from selling its nine TV stations for debt repayment. 同社は、テレビ9局を売却して得た資金を、債務返済に充てる予定だ。

proceeds from exercising stock options ストック・オプションの行使による利益,ストック・オプション実行受取金
(=proceeds from the exercise of stock options)
◆Proceeds from exercising stock options are compensation for labor and service rendered and constitute salary income. ストック・オプション(自社株購入権)を行使して得た利益は、職務遂行の対価なので、給与所得に当たる。

proceeds from government bond issues 国債発行による収入
◆The primary balance represents the budget balance, excluding proceeds from government bond issues and debt-servicing costs. プライマリー・バランスは、国債発行による収入と国債費(国債の利払いや償還費用)を除いた財政収支である。

proceeds from preferred stock sale 優先株発行による手取金
◆GM will use proceeds from preferred stock sale for general corporate purposes. GMは、優先株発行による手取金を一般事業目的に充てる。

proceeds from real estate sales 不動産売却収入,不動産売却代金
◆The insurer will cut a ￥400 billion portion of its ￥500 billion worth of latent losses on stockholdings by using operating profits, retained earnings and proceeds from real estate sales. 同保険会社は、営業利益と内部留保、不動産売却収入などで5,000億円相当の株式含み損のうち4,000億円を処理する方針だ。

proceeds from the public offering 株式公開による手取金,公募による手取金
◆The net proceeds of $973 million from the public offering were used to reduce notes payable. 公募による純手取金9億7,300万ドルは、短期借入金の返済に充当しました。

process (動)処理する,加工する,清算する
  process large orders quickly 大量の注文を高速処理する
  process one's expenses 経費を清算する
◆Investors are influenced by a sock-exchange trading system's ability to process large orders quickly. 投資家は、大量の注文を高速処理する証券取引所の売買システムの能力に左右されるようになった。◆To compete against online trading systems, stock exchanges must improve their ability to process buy and sell orders. 電子取引システムに対抗するには、証券取引所が売買注文の処理能力を高める必要がある。

process (名)過程, 工程, 流れ, 段階, 部門, 体制, 製法, 手続き, 訴訟手続き, プロセス
    adjustment process of balance of payment　国際収支調整過程
    business process reengineering　業務革新
    closing process　決算手続き
    cost cutting process　コスト削減計画
    credit approval process　与信の決裁過程
    credit creation process　信用創出過程
    debt relief process　債務救済手続き, 債務削減手続き
    decision process　意思決定プロセス, 意思決定の過程, 決定過程 (=decision-making process)
    deflationary process　デフレ
    investment process　投資プロセス
    issuing process　起債手続き
    loan making process　融資手続き
    margining process　証拠金計算, 証拠金算出
    process of collection　集金過程
    process of investment decision making　投資意思決定の過程
    production process　生産工程, 製造工程, 生産過程, 製造過程, 製造部門 (=manufacturing process)
    rating process　格付けの過程
    registration process　登録手続き
◆Delays in the debt relief process may become obstacles to reconstruction efforts. 債務救済[債務削減]手続きの遅れは、復興の支障[障害]となる可能性がある。◆In February 2006, hedge funds were required to go through a registration process and accept regulatory inspections, but this regulation scheme was scrapped in June. 2006年2月に、ヘッジ・ファンドは登録手続きを行うとともに、定期検査を受けることになったが、この規制策は6月に廃止された。◆In the case of the U.S. two major airlines, it took slightly more than four months to complete the whole process from the announcement of a merger plan to its approval. 米国の航空大手2社の場合、合併計画の発表から承認までの全手続きは、4か月あまりで済んでいる。◆The inadequate decision-making and business management processes of the financial group stem from factional strife within the company. 同金融グループの不十分な意思決定プロセスと経営管理体制は、社内の派閥争いに起因する。

procure (動)調達する, 購入する, 仕入れる, 取得する, 入手する, 獲得する, 引き起こす
    cost of procuring funds　資金調達コスト
    issue preferred stock to procure about ¥1 trillion　優先株式を発行して約1兆円を調達する
    jointly procure products　商品を共同で仕入れる
◆Bic Camera and Edion will form a capital tie-up and cooperate in jointly procuring products and using distribution networks. ビックカメラとエディオンは、資本提携して、共同仕入れや物流網の共同利用などの面で協力する方針だ。◆Funds for disaster reconstruction will be procured by issuing special government bonds. 震災復興の資金は、復興債を発行して調達する。◆The bank plans to issue preferred stock to procure about ¥1 trillion over the next few years to repay its debt to the government. 同行は、公的資金の返済に向けて、優先株を発行し、今後数年間で約1兆円を調達する計画だ。◆The company procured about ¥50 billion through an allocation of newly issued shares to third parties, including the Development Bank of Japan. 同社は、日本政策投資銀行などを引受先とする第三者割当増資で、約500億円を調達した。◆Yen loans extended now as part of Japan's ODA are untied in principle, with the source of development materials and equipment to be procured not defined. 日本の政府開発援助(ODA)として供与されている円借款は現在、ひも付きでない「アンタイド」援助が原則で、開発物資の調達先を限定していない。

procure funds　資金を調達する, 資金繰りをする
◆The chain of large-scale retailers of home appliances finally became unable to procure funds. この家電量販店は、最終的に資金調達ができなくなった[資金繰りに行き詰まってしまった]。◆The company needs to procure funds by the end of September. 同社は、9月末までに資金調達[資金繰り]を迫られている。◆The economic package will include measures to help small and midsize companies procure funds. 経済対策には、中小企業の資金繰り支援策も盛り込まれる。◆The government would ask the Bank of Japan to further ease its monetary policy to help stabilize the nation's financial system by helping financial institutions procure funds. 政府は、金融機関の資金繰りを助けて金融システムの安定化を図るため、日銀に追加の[もう一段の]金融緩和を求める方針だ。◆The interest rates a bank pays when procuring funds from the financial market are higher than those paid by other banks. ある銀行が金融市場で資金調達する際に支払う金利が、他行に比べて高くなっている。◆The merger of the two exchanges will revitalize stock trading and make it easier for companies to procure funds on the market to expand their business operations. 両証券取引所の経営統合で、株式の売買が活性化し、企業にとっては市場で資金を調達して会社の事業を大きくしやすくなる。◆To procure funds to finance reconstruction from the Great East Japan Earthquake, the government is planning to sell some of its shares in Japan Tobacco Inc. and Tokyo Metro Co. 東日本大震災の復興費用を賄うための資金を調達するため、政府は日本たばこ産業(JT)と東京地下鉄(東京メトロ)の株式を売却する方針だ。

procurement (名)調達, 購入, 仕入れ, 機器調達, 取得, 入手, 獲得, プロキュアメント
    competitive procurement　一般競争による調達
    e-procurement　電子調達, eプロキュアメント
    fund procurement　資金調達, 資本調達 (=fund raising)
    fund procurement by stock issue　株式金融, 株式発行による資金調達
    Internet procurement　インターネット調達, ネット調達
    overseas procurement　海外調達 (=overseas sourcing)
    procurement of funds　資金調達 (=fund procurement, fund raising)
◆Companies have restarted fund procurement activities for a recovery in production as the bond market turbulence after the March 11 earthquake and tsunami has subsided. 東日本大震災後の債券市場の混乱が収束したので、企業各社は生産回復に向けて資金調達活動を再開した。

procurement cost　調達コスト
◆The recent surges in the yen's strength have made it imperative for Japanese carmakers to substantially bring down their parts procurement costs by overseas sourcing. 最近の円高で、日本の自動車メーカー各社は、海外調達による部品調達コストの大幅引下げが緊急課題となっている。

procurement of new equipment　新機材の調達
◆The new loans extended by creditor banks are essential for the procurement of new equipment. 取引銀行団の新規融資は、新たな機材の調達に欠かせない。

produce (動)生産する, 製造する, 製作[制作]する, 作成する, 産む, 産み出す, 産出する, もたらす, 引き起こす, 提出する, 提示する, 示す, 上演する, 演出する, 放送する
◆Sellers of multiple-debtor lists, produced by collecting information about consumer finance customers, are contributing to the spread of illegal moneylending. 消費者金融の顧客情報を入手して作った多重債務者リストを売る名簿業者が、

ヤミ金融の横行に一役買っている。◆The government and the Bank of Japan are considering joint market intervention with the U.S. and European monetary authorities to produce the greater results of their market intervention. 政府・日銀は、市場介入の効果を高めるため、米欧の通貨当局との協調介入を検討している。◆The management of the new companies will be under pressure to produce profits. これらの新会社の経営陣は、収益確保の手腕を問われることになる。◆The mergers and acquisitions many major U.S. companies pursued failed to produce the expected synergy effect. 米国の大企業の多くが追求したM&Aは、予想したシナジー（相乗）効果を上げられなかった。◆There is a possibility that a vicious circle will develop in which the financial crisis undermines the U.S. real economy, producing further financial instability. 金融危機が米国の実体経済を損ない、それがさらに金融不安を引き起こす悪循環が深刻化する可能性がある。

producer price　生産者価格, 生産者物価
◆Domestic PC shipments for the April-June quarter declined 4 percent from the same period last year in producer price terms. 4-6月期のパソコンの国内出荷金額は、生産者価格で前年同期より4％減った。

producer price index　生産者価格指数, 生産者物価指数
◆The U.S. Labor Department's producer price index fell by 1.8 percent for all of last year, the biggest annual decline since 1986, when wholesale prices dropped by 2.3 percent. 米労働省の生産者物価指数は、昨年（2001年）全体で1.8％下落し、卸売り物価が2.3％下落した1986年以来、年間で最大の低下を記録した。

product　（名）製品, 生産品, 産物, 商品, プロダクト
　accumulation product　年金商品
　asset accumulation product　貯蓄性商品, 年金商品
　banking product　金融商品
　card product　カード商品
　deposit product　預金商品
　derivative product　派生商品
　equity index product　株価指数商品
　exchange-listed product　上場商品
　financial product　金融商品
　fixed rate annuity product　定額年金商品
　flagship product　主力商品, 目玉商品
　foreign currency [exchange] product　為替商品
　index-linked product　指数リンク商品
　insurance product　保険商品
　insurance protection product　保険保障商品
　interest-rate option product　金利オプション商品
　interest rate product　金利商品
　investment product　投資商品
　medical insurance products　医療保険商品
　mortgage product　モーゲージ商品
　national savings product　貯蓄国債
　personal savings product　リテール貯蓄商品
　product financing arrangements　製品金融の取決め
　products with variable rates　変動金利商品
　risk management product　リスク管理商品
　savings product　貯蓄商品
　structured equity product　株式仕組み商品
　structured financial product　仕組み商品
　30-year product　30年物
　treasury product　財務商品
　variable product　変額商品
◆Automotive insurance is the flagship product of nonlife insurers. 自動車保険は、損害保険会社の主力［目玉］商品だ。◆Influential overseas commercial banks have maintained an advantage with transactions for derivative products by using high-tech computer systems. 海外の有力行は、最先端のコンピュータ・システムを使って、デリバティブ取引で優位を保っている。◆Meiji Yasuda's single-premium whole life insurance is one of its flagship products which are sold over bank counters. 明治安田生保の一時払い終身保険は、銀行窓口で販売されている同社の主力商品の一つだ。◆Mitsui Sumitomo Insurance Co. was ordered to halt sales of medical insurance products for an indefinite period from July 10. 三井住友海上火災保険が、7月10日から医療保険商品販売の無期限停止命令を受けた。◆Nippon Life Insurance Co. lowered the yields of its single-premium pension insurance policies and other products. 日本生命保険が、一時払いの年金保険など保険商品の利回りを引き下げた。◆Oil wholesalers have cut their output of gasoline and other major petroleum products since March. 石油元売り各社は、3月からガソリンなど主要石油製品の減産に踏み切った。◆Some financial institutions are offering products with annual interest rates starting at 1 percent or less. 一部の金融機関は、当初の金利［適用金利］が年1％以下の商品を提供している。◆The exchange-traded funds (ETFs) are investment products similar to index mutual funds but that trade on stock exchanges like stocks. 上場投資信託（ETF）は、インデックス・ミューチュアル・ファンドに似ているが、株式と同じように証券取引所で売買される投資商品である。◆We want to make a financial product our customers could purchase without any worries or hesitation. 客に迷わず安心して購入してもらえる金融商品を作りたい。

product development　商品開発, 製品開発
（⇒damage assessment）
◆The nonlife insurance company will provide the company with know-how on damage assessment and product development. この損害保険会社は、同社に損害査定や商品開発に関するノウハウを提供する。◆The time needed for product development has been reduced by more than half. 製品開発に要する時間は、半分以下に短縮された。

production　（名）生産, 製造, 製作, 制作, プロダクション
　batch production　バッチ生産, 連続生産
　contract production　委託生産
　domestic production　国内生産
　efficient production　有効生産, 効率的生産
　flow production　流れ作業生産, 流れ作業
　industrial production　工業生産, 鉱工業生産
　license production　ライセンス生産
　line production　直線生産, 流れ作業生産, 流れ作業
　local production　現地生産, 国内生産
　lot production　ロット生産, 組別生産
　mass production　大量生産, 量産
　optimum production　最適生産
　overseas production　海外生産
　pilot production　試験的生産, 試験生産, 試作, パイロット生産
　production control　生産管理, 工程管理
　production cutback　生産削減, 操業短縮
◆The industry's clients, especially electronics and car manufacturers, have begun to move their production to other countries, such as China. 特に電機や自動車メーカーなど業界の顧客企業は、中国など海外に生産拠点の移転を進めている。◆Venezuela will continue its policy of restricting production and keep oil prices high. ベネズエラは、生産制限策を継続して石油価格の高値維持を図る方針だ。

production base　生産拠点, 製造拠点
（⇒manufacturer）
◆As a key production base of IT-related products, the indus-

trial complex will be one of the world's largest of its kind. IT関連製品の主要製造拠点としては、この工業団地は世界最大級となる。

production capacity 生産設備, 生産能力
◆Ford Motor Co. will cut 10 percent of its workforce, or 35,000 jobs, slash production capacity and close five North American plants as part of its overhaul plan. 米フォード・モーターは、リストラ策の一環として同社従業員の10%に相当する3万5,000人を削減し、生産設備も削減して北米5工場を閉鎖することになった。◆Sharp Corp. will spend an additional ¥200 billion to quadruple the production capacity of its liquid crystal display panel factory in Kameyama. シャープは、2,000億円追加投資して、液晶パネル[液晶ディスプレー・パネル]亀山工場(三重県亀山市)の生産能力を4倍に拡大する。

production facilities 生産設備
◆The company will gradually transfer production facilities currently in operation in Japan, Europe, the United States and the Philippines to the industrial complex. 同社は、日本国内や欧米、フィリピンで現在稼動している生産設備を順次、この工業団地に移して行く方針だ。

productivity (名)生産性, 生産力, 生産効率, 多様性
  capital productivity 資本生産性
  corporate productivity 企業の生産性
  factor productivity 要素生産性
  green productivity 環境にやさしい生産性, グリーン・プロダクティビティ
  higher worker productivity 労働者の生産性向上
  improved productivity 生産性向上, 生産性の向上
    (=increased productivity)
  labor productivity 労働生産性
  land productivity 土地生産性
  marginal productivity 限界生産力, 限界生産性
  physical productivity 物的生産性
  sales productivity 販売効率
  social productivity 社会的生産性
  total-factor productivity 全要素生産性
  value productivity 価値生産性
◆Advances in information technology brought about even greater changes, rendering the financial sector heavily dependent on computers and improving productivity in all industries. 情報技術の進歩はさらに甚大な変化をもたらし、それによって金融業界のコンピュータへの依存性が大いに高まるとともに、全産業の生産性が向上した。◆Management is concerned that the work sharing system may lead to a decline in productivity. ワーク・シェアリングは生産性の低下につながる可能性がある、と経営側は懸念している。

professional (名)職業人, プロ, 専門家, 本職, 玄人(くろうと), プロフェッショナル
  accounting professional 職業会計人, 公認会計士
  credit professional 信用分析の専門家
  industry professionals 業界関係者
  money market professional 金融市場専門家
  professionals and institutional investors ディーラーと機関投資家
  qualified professional 有資格専門家

professional (形)職業の, 職業上の, 業務上の, 専門職の, 本職の, プロの, 専門的な, 熟練した, 巧妙な
  code of professional conduct 職業行為規程
  professional asset management 専門家による資産運用[管理]業務
  professional bank 専業銀行
  professional ethics 職業倫理
  professional hecklers and blackmailers 総会屋
  professional investor 機関投資家
  professional liability insurance 専門職業賠償責任保険
  professional negligence resulting in death and injury 業務上過失致死障害
  professional opinion 職業専門家の意見
  professional speculators 投機筋
  professional traders 玄人筋

profile (名)構成, 構造, 輪郭, 概要, 案内, 見通し, 予測, 特性, 地位, 方針, プロフィール, プロファイル
  business profile 事業構成
  company profile 会社概要, 会社案内
  credit profile 信用力, 信用情報
  customer profile 顧客プロフィール, 顧客構成
  earnings profile 収益見通し
  high-profile 脚光を浴びる, 世間の注目を集める, 著名な, 明確な, 鮮明な
  improved financial profiles 財務力見通しの改善
  investment profile 投資方針
  keep a low profile 低姿勢を保つ
  low-profile 目立たない, 控え目な, 低姿勢の
  market profile 市場プロフィール, 市場特性, 市場情報
  product profile 製品構成
  risk profile リスク特性, リスク構造
◆Different from high-profile hedge funds, the founders and investment conditions of these foreign investment funds are not clear. 著名なヘッジ・ファンドと異なって、これらの海外投資ファンドの設立者や資金の運用実態は、はっきりしない。◆Standard & Poor's revised upward the outlook on its ratings on six major Japanese insurance companies against the backdrop of their improved financial profiles. スタンダード&プアーズは、日本の大手保険会社6社の財務力見通し改善を背景に、6社の格付け見通しを上方修正した。

profit (名)利益, 利得, 利潤 (⇒consolidated net profit, net profit, operating profit, record profit, recurring profit)
  above the line profit 経常利益
  consolidated profit 連結利益
  current profits 経常利益
  earn a profit 利益を上げる
  generate profits 利益を生み出す
  lock in profits 利益を確定する
  make a profit 利益を出す, 利益を上げる, 利益を得る
  net profit 純利益, 当期純利益
  net profit before tax 税引き前利益
  operating profit 営業利益
  profit-sharing securities 利潤証券
  profits from stock sales 株式売却益, 株式譲渡益
  realize a profit 利益を得る
  record profit 過去最高の利益
  reduced profit 減益
  secure profits 利潤を確保する
  strong profit growth 大幅増益
  take profits 利食い売りをする, 利食いに出る, 利食う
◆Because the investment consortium is based outside of the country, the government cannot levy taxes on profits from stock sales. この投資組合は国外に本拠地を置いているため、政府は株式売却益に課税できない。◆Corporate value is defined as "the total of profits one company will earn in future." 企業価値は、「ある会社が将来稼ぐ利益の合計」と定義される。◆Due to the growing strength of the yen, even if exporters' sales grow, their profits will not keep pace. 円高進行で、輸出企業の売上が増えても、利益は伸び悩むようだ。◆During the first half of fiscal 2001, TSE-listed businesses posted a

35 percent fall in their combined profits from a year earlier. 2001年度上半期は、東証上場企業が前年より全体で35%の減益となった。◆Financial institutions are trying to secure profits in proportion to the risks they take. 金融機関は、金融機関の取るリスクに見合った利潤(適正利潤)を確保しようとしている。◆In the project financing business, lending banks are repaid loans through profits generated by the projects they have financed. プロジェクト・ファイナンス事業では、貸出行が、融資したプロジェクト(事業)から生まれる利益で融資の返済を受ける。◆Investors sold shares across the board to lock in profits. 利益を確定するため、投資家が全銘柄にわたって株を売り進めた。◆The management of the new companies will be under pressure to produce profits. これらの新会社の経営陣は、収益確保の手腕を問われることになる。◆The margin of profits from a project financing scheme overseas is generally higher than that from loans extended to domestic borrowers. 海外のプロジェクト・ファイナンス(事業融資)事業による利ざやは、一般に国内企業向け融資の利ざやより高い。◆The nation's three megabank groups expect a sharp increase in profits in their half-year consolidated business results through the end of September. 日本の3メガバンクは、9月連結中間決算で、大幅増益を見込んでいる。

profit and loss 損益
◆Under the consolidated return system, a company pays corporate tax after totaling the profits and losses of its affiliated companies. 連結納税制度では、企業はグループ企業[系列企業]の損益を合算して法人税を納める。

profit and loss statement 損益計算書 (=profit and loss account, statement of earnings, statement of income, statement of operations)
◆The Board of Audit asked the airport management company to submit profit and loss statements of its nonairport divisions. 会計検査院は、空港運営会社に非航空事業部門の損益計算書の提出を求めた。

profit-comes-first principle 利益至上主義,利益最優先主義 (=profit-first principle)
◆Profit-comes-first principle has many strong followers among young entrepreneurs. 若手企業家の間では、利益最優先の風潮が高まっている。

profit decline 減益
◆In the April-June quarter, major high-tech companies including Motorola Inc. and Intel Corp. suffered losses or profit declines. 4-6月期は、モトローラやインテルなど主要ハイテク企業が赤字や減益に苦しんでいる。

profit making 利益を上げること,利益を得ること,収益,営利
◆The bank put profit making before all else. 同行は、何よりもまず利益を優先した。

profit-making (形)利益を上げる,営利目的の,利潤目当ての,儲(もう)かる
  profit-making business 収益事業,営利事業
  profit-making capability 収益力
    (=profit-earning capacity)
  profit-making sources 収益源

profit margin 売上利益率,売上純利益率,利益率,利ざや,利幅 (=margin of profit: 売上純利益率(%)=(純利益/純売上高)×100.「利ざや」は、金融機関の資金の調達金利と貸出金利の差をいう)
  net profit margin 売上高利益率,(売上高)経常利益率,純利益率
  profit margin between lending and deposits 預貸利ざや
  profit margin of interest rate 利ざや
    (=interest rate profit margin)
  profit margin on sales 売上高利益率
  profit margin on total funds 総資金利ざや
◆As a result of fierce competition in the past, interest rate profit margins were kept too low to cover loans that went sour. 過去の熾烈(しれつ)な競争の結果、金利の利ざやが小さく抑えられる余り、貸倒れ[貸倒れのリスク]をカバーできなかった[過去の熾烈な融資合戦の結果、不良債権リスクをカバーできないほど利ざやは小さく抑えられた]。◆It is a matter of urgency to ensure that banks make profit margins that can meet investment risks and that they expand commission revenue as well as promote sweeping restructurings. 抜本的なリストラ推進のほか、投資リスクに見合う利ざやの確保と手数料収入の拡大などが銀行の急務だ。

profit taking 利食い,利食い売り,利益を確定するための売り,利益確定売り (買った株を株価上昇後に売って利益を確保することを[利食い売り]という。また、空売りした株が値下がりしたときに買い戻して差益を稼ぐことを「利食い買い」という。⇒dollar's fall against the yen)
  experience profit taking 利食い売りを浴びる
  heavy (bouts of) profit taking 大量の利食い[利益確定のための売り]
  release paper through profit taking 利食いで債券を売る
◆Heavy profit taking pushed the market down. 大量の利食い売りに押されて、市場は反落した。

profit taking sales 利食い売り,利益確定売り,利益を確定するための売り
◆A temporary halt to trading on the Jasdaq over-the-counter market forced investors to concentrate on the TSE for profit taking sales. ジャスダック店頭市場が一時、取引停止となったことで、利益を確定させるための投資家の売りが、東証に集中した。

profit target 利益目標,収益目標,運用益の目標
◆In wrap accounts, a customer sets the overall investment policy, including investment period and profit target. ラップ口座では、顧客が投資期間や運用益の目標などの大まかな運用方針を決める。

profitability (名)収益性,収益力,営利性,採算性,利益率,収益率
(=earning power; ⇒financial condition)
  average profitability 平均利益率,平均収益率
  boost in profitability 収益力のアップ
  core profitability コア収益性
  corporate profitability 企業収益性,企業の収益性
  investment profitability 投資収益性,投資利益率,投資収益率
  potential profitability 採算性
  pressure on profitability 収益性の悪化
  profitability by product line 商品ライン別収益性
  profitability index 収益性指数
  profitability ratio 収益性指標,利益率,収益率
  rate of profitability 利益率,収益率
  segment profitability 事業部門別収益性
  stock profitability 株式の収益性
◆An urgent task facing each financial group is to improve its financial conditions and profitability on the strength of advantages gained from merger. 合併・統合の相乗効果を生かして、財務内容と収益力を向上させることが、各金融グループの現在の急務だ。◆Seiyu at first considered giving up its business as a comprehensive supermarket operator and specializing in food sales whose profitability is relatively stable. 西友は当初、総合スーパーとしての事業を断念して、収益性が比較的、安定している食品の販売に特化することを考えた。◆The industry is under a good deal of stress, as evidenced by pressure on profitability and decline in stock prices over the last several months. 業界は、収益性の悪化やここ数か月の株価低迷でも明らかなように、かなり厳しい状況下にあります。◆The profitability of Japanese corporations is deteri-

orating fast and dramatically. 日本企業の収益性は、急速かつ大幅に悪化している。◆There are pressures on prices, margins and profitability. 価格や利益率、収益性が悪化している。◆To eliminate the heavy burden of nonperforming loans on the economy, it is imperative to take all measures to enhance the profitability of the banking sector. 日本経済にのしかかる不良債権の重荷を取り除くには、銀行(銀行業界)の収益力強化をめざしてあらゆる措置を講じる必要がある。

profitable (形)儲(もう)かる, 利益を生む, 収益性[収益力]がある, 収益性が高い, 有利な, 有益な, ためになる, 役に立つ
  highly profitable company　高収益企業, 収益力[収益性]が高い企業
  most profitable season　書き入れ時
  profitable basis　会社の収益基盤
  profitable business　収益性の高い事業, 儲かる商売[仕事], 利益が出る商売
  profitable goods　利益率の高い商品, 収益性の高い商品, 収益商品
  profitable opportunity　有利な機会
  turn profitable　黒字に転換する
  ◆As investment for digitalization is costly, NBS needs to establish a more profitable management system, including joint investment in digital-related facilities and content with the Fuji TV group. デジタル化の投資負担は軽くないので、ニッポン放送は、フジテレビ・グループとのデジタル関連施設への共同投資やコンテンツ(情報内容)の共有など、収益力の高い経営システムを確立する必要がある。◆Even after the company fell into financial difficulties, it embellished its financial statements to make it appear profitable. 同社の経営が行き詰まった以降も、同社は決算書を粉飾して、経営状況を良く見せかけていた。

profitable investment　有利な投資, 有利な投資先, 有利な運用先
  ◆These surplus funds are moving into crude oil and grain markets in search of profitable investments. これらの余剰資金が、有利な運用先を求めて原油や穀物市場に向かっている。

profiteering (名)不当利得, 不当利得行為

program (名)計画, 予定, 政策, 対策, 策, 措置, 政党の綱領, 政治要綱, 制度, 事業番組, コンピュータ・プログラム, プログラム
  aid program　援助計画, 支援計画
  asset disposal program　資産売却計画
  catastrophic reinsurance program　巨大損害再保険計画
  cost cutting program　コスト削減策
  cumulative stock investment program　株式累積投資制度
  early retirement program　早期退職制度
  economic program　経済政策
  export credit guarantee program　輸出信用保証制度
  federal deficit reduction program　米財政赤字削減策
  fiscal investment and loan program　財政投融資計画
  forced savings program　強制貯蓄制度
  fully supported program　100%信用補完型プログラム
  funding program　資金調達計画
  incentive program　報奨制度
  investment program　投資計画, 投資プログラム
  loan program　融資枠
  loan programs　財政投融資
  long-term recycling program　長期資金還流計画
  national health programs　国民保険制度
  pension program　年金制度
  savings-stock purchase program　貯蓄株購入制度
  spending program　財政支出計画
  stimulative economic program　景気刺激策
  stimulus program　景気刺激策, 景気対策
  stock option program　ストック・オプション制度
  the large-scale tax cut program　大型減税プログラム
  voluntary restraint program　自主規制措置
  ◆A day after declaring default on the national debt, Argentina's new president rolled out an ambitious works program. 国債の債務不履行(デフォルト)を宣言した翌日、アルゼンチンの新大統領は、野心的な労働政策を発表した。◆As the gap between the eurozone-imposed repayment program and the track record began clearly yawning, the Greece's insolvency became apparent. ユーロ圏が押し付けたギリシャの返済計画と実績とのズレが目立つようになるにつれ、ギリシャの返済不能が明らかになった。◆The Bank of Japan stepped up its efforts to boost the flagging economy following the March 11 earthquake and tsunami by introducing a ￥500 billion cheap loan program. 日銀は、5,000億円の低利融資制度を導入して、東日本大震災で揺れる日本経済の刺激策を強化した。◆The bank repeatedly lied so that it could benefit from the U.S. government program that insured mortgage. 同行は、米政府の住宅ローン保証プログラムから利益を得るために繰り返し虚偽の説明をした。◆The Fed's program of buying $600 billion in Treasury bonds to help the economy is to end in June 2011 on schedule. 景気を支えるために6,000億ドルの国債を買い入れる米連邦準備制度理事会(FRB)の量的緩和政策は、予定通り2011年6月に終了する。◆The firm's operations in the financial services and leasing industry involve direct financing and finance leasing programs for its products and the products of other companies. 金融サービスとリース業界での同社の事業には、同社製品と他社製品に関する直接融資とファイナンス・リース事業も含まれている。◆The U.S. government has had to foot the bill for mortgage loans that defaulted under the government program that insured mortgages. 米政府は、政府の住宅ローン保証プログラムに基づき、デフォルト(債務不履行)になった住宅ローンのツケの支払いを迫られている。◆The U.S. $787 billion stimulus program implemented at the start of the Obama administration will all but dry up by the end of 2010. オバマ政権の発足当初に実施された米国の7,870億ドルの景気対策は、2010年末にはほぼ財源が尽きる見込みだ。◆To enhance the stimulating effect of the Fed's rate cuts, swift implementation of fiscal and tax stimulus measures, including tax cuts on investment designed to reinvigorate the stock market, is necessary in addition to the large-scale tax cut program that is under way. 米連邦準備制度理事会(FRB)の金利引下げの刺激効果を高めるためには、現在実施中の大型減税プログラムに加え、株式市場を再活性化するための投資減税など、財政・税制面からの景気刺激策の速やかな実施が必要である。

progress (名)進歩, 発展, 成長, 進捗状況, 未成工事
  capital-using technical progress　資本使用的技術進歩
  earnings progress　増益
  economic progress　経済発展, 経済進歩, 経済成長
  long-term contract work in progress　長期請負契約
  product in progress　仕掛(しかけ・しかかり)品
  (=goods in process, stock in process, work in process)
  progress payment　分割払い, 分納
  progress payments　未成工事支出金, 未成工事の前受金
  ◆Greece's fiscal reconstruction has made little progress since the country was bailed out with financial support from the IMF and the EU in May 2010. ギリシャの財政再建は、2010年5月にIMFと欧州連合(EU)による金融支援を受けて以来、進展してない。◆Progress in the disposal of nonperforming loans and receding concerns over further deterioration in regional economies have led to diminished risk of asset erosion. 不良債権処理の進展や地域経済がさらに悪化する懸念の

後退などで、資産が目減りする恐れが薄らいでいる。◆There is slow progress in economic improvement among nonmanufacturing businesses, largely as a result of sluggish sales at retailers due to the ongoing deflation. デフレの進行で主に小売業の売上が低迷しているため、非製造業は景気回復の足取りが弱い。

progressive (形)進歩的な, 発展的な, 成長的, 進歩主義の, リベラルな, 革新的な, 進取的な, 漸進的な, (病気が)進行性の, (課税が)累進的な (名)進歩主義者, 革新主義者, 進歩党員(Progressive)

  progressive capitalism 進歩的資本主義(福祉国家と同義)
  progressive change 漸進的な変化
  progressive cost 逓増費, 逓増コスト
  progressive economy 発展的構造, 成長の経済
  progressive equilibrium 発展的均衡, 成長均衡
  progressive income tax 累進所得税
  progressive payment 分割払い, 繰り延べ払い
  progressive policy 進歩的な政策
  progressive reform 漸進的な改革
  progressive taxation 累進課税, 累進所得税

◆The Financial Stability Board will impose a progressive extra capital charge of 1 percent to 2.5 percent on risk-adjusted assets held by G-SIFIs. G20(主要20か国・地域)の金融当局で構成する金融安定化理事会(FSB)は、国際金融システムにとって重要な金融機関(G-SIFIs)が保有するリスク調整後資産に、1～2.5%の資本[自己資本]の上積みを段階的に課すことになった。

progressive income tax brackets 累進税率区分

◆The number of progressive income tax brackets will be increased from current four tiers to six. 累進税率区分の数が、現行の4段階から6段階に引き上げられる。

progressive structure 累進構造

◆Reinforcement of the progressive structure of income taxation is needed as the tax system's income redistribution function has been crippled, leading to widening disparities among the people. 税制の所得再配分機能が麻痺して、国民の格差拡大を招いているため、所得課税の累進構造を強化する必要がある。

progressive tax 累進税, 累進課税
  progressive tax rate 累進税率
  progressive tax system 累進税制, 累進税制度

progressive tax rates for income tax 所得税の累進税率

◆The consumption tax's regressiveness does not always mean that progressive tax rates for income tax should be raised. 消費税が逆進性(低所得者層ほど税負担が相対的に高まること)だからといって、かならずしも所得税の累進税率を引き上げるべきだということにはならない。

progressive tax structure 累進税の構造

◆The number of high-income earners who will pay the higher tax rates will not change even if progressive tax structure may be reinforced. 累進税の構造を強化しても、最高税率を負担する高所得者層の数は変わらない。

prohibit (動)禁止する, 妨げる, 予防する
  prohibit A from purchasing ineligible securities Aが不適格証券を購入するのを禁止する
  prohibit misrepresentation and in security sales 証券販売での不実表示を禁止する
  purchasing bonds that are not of investment grade is prohibited 投資適格格付けでない債権の購入は禁止されている

prohibited (形)禁止された, 禁制の
  prohibited goods [articles] 禁制品, 輸入禁制品
  prohibited investments 不適格証券, 資金の運用先として禁止されている証券 (=ineligible securities)
  prohibited risk 引受禁止物件, 引受拒絶物件

project (動)提案する, 提起する, 発議する(propose), 計画する, 企画する, もくろむ, 考案する, 工夫する, 予測する, 予想する, 想定する, 見積もる, 算出する, 映す, 映し出す, 投じる, 投影する, 同じであると見なす, (ロケットなどを)発射する (自動)突き出る, 出っ張る, 明確に示す, 突き出る, 出っ張る

◆Sony Corp. projects that it will fall into the red for the first time in 14 years. ソニーは、14年ぶりに赤字に転落する見通しだ。◆The firm is projecting a group net profit of ￥124 billion, up 86 percent from a year earlier. 同社は、1,240億円(前期比86%増)の連結純利益を予想している。◆The government bond issuance worth about ￥44 trillion for the current fiscal year is the largest ever projected in an initial budget. 今年度の約44兆円の国債発行額は、当初予算としては史上最高だ。◆The index of business confidence among large companies is projected to read plus 4.8 for the July-September quarter. 7-9月期の大企業(製造業)の景況判断指数は、プラス4.8の改善が見込まれている。

project (名)計画, 企画, 対策, 案件, 事業, 開発事業, 公共事業計画, 長期目標, プロジェクト
  construction project 建設工事, 建設プロジェクト
  develop a project プロジェクトを組み立てる, プロジェクトを展開する
  investment project 投資計画, 投資事業, 投資プロジェクト
  launch a project プロジェクトを立ち上げる
  project assets プロジェクトの資産
  (⇒project loan)
  project note 住宅プロジェクトのための手形
  risky project リスクの高いプロジェクト

◆As the lead bank in the construction project, the bank will cover more than a certain percentage of the joint loan to the Canadian corporation. この建設プロジェクトの主幹事銀行として、同行はカナダ企業への協調融資のうち一定割合以上を融資する。◆Domestic banks are increasing their efforts to finance large overseas projects. 国内銀行各行は、海外での大型事業に融資する(プロジェクト・ファイナンスへの)取組みを強化している。◆Given the nation's tough fiscal condition, the government must eke out the necessary funds by scaling down low-priority policy projects. 日本の厳しい財政事情に照らせば、政府に求められるのは、優先度の低い政策プロジェクトを縮小して、必要な財源をひねり出すことだ。◆In an illegal building practice called "maru nage," a project contracted by a construction company is farmed out to subcontractors. 「丸投げ」という違法な建築慣行では、建設会社が請け負った仕事が、下請業者に委託される。◆In the project financing business, lending banks are repaid loans through profits generated by the projects they have financed. プロジェクト・ファイナンス事業では、貸出行が、融資したプロジェクト(事業)から生まれる利益で融資の返済を受ける。◆The cofinancing scheme of the Bank of Tokyo-Mitsubishi UFJ will cover the Stardale mega solar power plant construction project carried out by a Canadian corporation. 三菱東京UFJ銀行の協調融資事業の対象は、カナダの企業が実施している大型太陽光発電所建設プロジェクトの「スターデール」だ。◆The company allegedly amassed about ￥1 billion in off-the-book funds through its Southeast Asian projects. 同社は、東南アジアでの事業を通じて、約10億円の裏金を捻出したとされる。◆The Forestry Agency is carrying out an urgent five-year project for the systematic thinning of privately owned forests. 林野庁は、民有林の計画的な緊急間伐5か年対策を実施している。◆The four defendants overcharged the government's Cabinet Office by about ￥141 million in the government-financed chemical weapons disposal project. 被告4人は、政府出資の

化学兵器処理事業費として、政府の内閣府に約1億4,100万円を水増し請求した。◆There has been greater demand for funds to develop mega solar power plant projects in recent years. 最近は、メガソーラー(大型太陽光発電所)事業開発の資金需要が高まっている。

project finance 事業融資, プロジェクト金融, 特定事業に対する金融, プロジェクト・ファイナンス (=project financing)
◆Financial institutions extend loans to specified projects of companies by project finance. 金融機関は、プロジェクト金融で企業の特定の事業に融資している。◆The banks should give attention to the area of project finance, whereby financial institutions extend loans to specified projects of companies. 銀行は、特定の事業に金融機関が融資する「プロジェクト・ファイナンス」の分野にも取り組むべきだ。

project financing 事業向け融資, 事業融資, プロジェクト金融, プロジェクト・ローン, プロジェクト・ファイナンス (=project finance)
 project financing deal プロジェクト・ローン案件
 project financing facility プロジェクト・ファイナンス・ファシリティ
◆Domestic bank are stepping up oversea project financing due to the lack of growth in lending to domestic borrowers amid protracted deflation at home. 国内銀行各行は、国内ではデフレが続いて[デフレが続く状況で]国内融資先への貸出が伸びていないことから、海外の事業向け融資を強化している。◆Domestic banks are stepping up overseas project financing as greater yields of interests are expected through such lending than loans to domestic borrowers. 国内銀行は、国内の借り手への融資に比べて海外の事業向け融資のほうが大きな金利収入を見込めるので、海外の事業向け融資(プロジェクト・ファイナンス)を強化している。

project financing business プロジェクト・ファイナンス事業
◆In the project financing business, lending banks are repaid loans through profits generated by the projects they have financed. プロジェクト・ファイナンス事業では、貸出行が、融資したプロジェクト(事業)から生まれる利益で融資の返済を受ける。

project financing loans プロジェクト・ファイナンスの融資額
◆Global project financing loans totaled about $96.1 billion from January until the end of June 2011. 2011年1～6月の世界のプロジェクト・ファイナンスの総融資額は、約961億ドルに達した。

project financing market プロジェクト・ファイナンス市場
◆The project financing market has seen a boost in loans to businesses in renewable energy field such as solar and wind power generation. プロジェクト・ファイナンス市場は最近、太陽光や風力発電など自然エネルギー分野の事業への融資が増えている。

project financing scheme プロジェクト・ファイナンス(事業融資)事業, プロジェクト・ファイナンスの仕組み
◆A project financing scheme is the largest growing field for Japanese banks. プロジェクト・ファイナンス(事業融資)事業は、邦銀にとって最大の成長分野だ。◆The margin of profits from a project financing scheme overseas is generally higher than that from loans extended to domestic borrowers. 海外のプロジェクト・ファイナンス(事業融資)事業による利ざやは、一般に国内企業向け融資の利ざやより高い。

project loan 開発計画融資, ひもつき融資, プロジェクト・ローン
◆A project loan is generally a nonrecourse loan and is secured by project assets. プロジェクト・ローンは通常、非遡求型ローンで、プロジェクトの資産を担保とする。

projected (形)計画された, 予想される, 予測される, 推定される, 見積りの, ～計画, ～予想, ～見通し
 projected balance sheet 見通し貸借対照表
 projected benefit obligation 予測給付債務, 予定給付債務, 見積り給付債務
 projected benefit valuation method 予測給付評価方式
 projected debt ratio 予想債務比率
 projected deficit 赤字見通し
 projected dividend 予想配当
 projected financial statements 見積り財務書類, 見積り財務諸表
 projected GDP 予想GDP
 projected investment 投資計画, 計画投資
 projected PER [P/R] 予想株価収益率, 予想PER
 projected revenue 予想収益
 projected sales 売上予想

projected business results 業績予想
◆The bank revised its projected business results downward. 同行は、業績予想を下方修正した。

projected dividend 予想配当
◆The company increased the projected dividend per share to ¥10 for fiscal 2011 from the ¥8 paid the previous year. 同社は、2011年度の1株当たり予想配当を、前年度の8円から10円に引き上げた。

projected pension obligations 予想年金債務額
◆The fair value of our pension plan assets is greater than our projected pension obligations. 当社の年金制度資産の公正価額は、予想年金債務額を上回っています。

projection (名)見積り, 予測, 推定, 予想, 想定, 見通し, 推計 (⇒shortfall)
 business projection 業績見通し
 cash flow projection 資金繰りの見通し, キャッシュ・フロー予測
 demand projection 需要予測
 earlier projection 当初予想 (=earlier forecast, original projection)
 earnings projection 業績予想, 業績見通し, 収益予想, 収益見通し (=earnings estimate, earnings forecast)
 financial projection 財務計画, 財務見通し
 growth projection 成長見通し
 initial projection 当初予想, 当初の想定, 当初見通し
 operating loss projection 営業損失予想, 営業赤字予想額
 preliminary projections 暫定値
 profit projection 利益予想
 projection of future revenues 将来の収益予想
 sales projection 売上予想, 販売見通し, 予想売上
◆The company revised downward its projection of consolidated after-tax profits for fiscal 2011 from ¥500 billion to ¥300 billion. 2011年度(2012年3月期決算)の連結税引き後利益の見通しを5,000億円から3,000億円に下方修正した。◆The downward revision of the fiscal 2011 growth projection was made due to a drastic slowdown in individual consumption and meager price increases. 2011年度の経済成長見通しの下方修正は、個人消費の大幅な減速と物価上昇率の鈍化が原因だ。

prolong (動)引き延ばす, 長引かせる, 延長する
◆The fall in import prices that accompanies a strong yen could further prolong Japan's deflation. 円高に伴う輸入価格の下落で、日本のデフレがさらに長期化する可能性がある。

prolongation (名)延長, 延長部分, 長期化
 prolongation of a bill 手形の延長
 prolongation of recession 景気後退の長期化

prolongation of the vicious circle　悪循環の長期化
　◆Plunges on the world's stock markets and wild fluctuations in foreign exchange markets may ensure the prolongation of the vicious circle. 世界同時株安と為替市場の乱高下は、悪循環に歯止めがかからなくなる恐れがある。

prolonged　(形)長引く,長期の,長期にわたる,慢性的な (⇒depression, protracted)
　prolonged economic malaise　長引く景気低迷
　prolonged economic slump　長期不況
　　（=prolonged recession）
　prolonged losses　慢性赤字,慢性的な赤字

prolonged deflation　長引くデフレ,長期デフレ,デフレの長期化　(=protracted deflation)
　◆The main cause of the prolonged deflation is that consumer demand has been weak due to the current economic slump. デフレ長期化の主因は、現在の不況で消費需要が低迷していることだ。

prolonged deflation-led recession　長期デフレ不況
　◆The Fed has analyzed in detail the causes of the prolonged deflation-led recession in Japan. 米連邦準備制度理事会（FRB）は、日本の長期デフレ不況の原因を詳細に分析した。

prolonged economic slump　長期不況
　（=prolonged recession）
　◆Smaller businesses have had difficulties in obtaining loans from banks and other financial institutions amid the prolonged economic slump. 長引く不況で、中小企業は、銀行その他の金融機関から融資を受けられなくなっている。◆The construction market has been shrinking year after year due to the prolonged economic slump and reductions in public works spending. 建設市場は、長期不況や公共事業費の削減などで年々縮小している。◆The major banks attributed their increased bad loans to the poor performance of their borrowers due to the prolonged economic slump and Financial Service Agency inspections resulting in a stricter review of their asset assessments. 大手銀行は、不良債権が増えた理由として、長引く景気低迷で貸出先の経営が悪化したことと、金融庁の検査を受けて大手行が資産査定を厳しくしたことを挙げた。

prolonged housing correction　長引く住宅の調整局面,住宅の調整局面の長期化
　◆In the United States, there is a risk of deeper and more prolonged housing correction. 米国では、住宅の調整局面が深刻化し、長引く恐れもある。

prolonged recession　長引く不況,長期不況,不況の長期化,後退局面の長期化
　（⇒corporate bond, price drops, public spending）
　◆In concert with the improvement in the global economy, the Japanese economy is expected to emerge from its prolonged recession. 世界経済の上昇の波に乗って、日本経済は長引く不況から抜け出す見込みだ。

prolonged slump　長期低迷
　◆The housing industry is being battered by a prolonged slump. 住宅産業は、長期低迷の影響をもろに受けている。◆The prolonged slump in the real estate market is maintaining the decline in land prices, thereby prolonging the economic stagnation in a vicious circle. 不動産取引市場の長期低迷が引き続き地価の下落を招き、これに伴って悪循環の経済の停滞を長引かせている。

prolonged slump in the real estate market　不動産市場［不動産取引市場］の長期低迷
　◆The prolonged slump in the real estate market is maintaining the decline in land prices. 不動産取引市場の長期低迷が、引き続き地価の下落を招いている。

promise　(動)約束する,公約する,規定する,契約する
　in advance of the date promised　当初の予定期日より早く
　perform as promised to maturity　償還まで元利払いを確実に履行する
　promise a high yield　高い予定利率を約束する
　promise to cover payments to bondholders　債券保有者への（元本と利息の）支払いを約束する
　◆Bond insurers write policies that promise to cover payments to bondholders if the entity that issued the bonds defaults. 金融保証会社［債券保険会社］は、債券発行体がデフォルト（債務不履行）になった場合に、債券保有者への（元本と利息の）支払い補償を約束する保険を引き受けている。◆During the bubble economy, life insurers sold a large number of policies by promising high yields. バブル期に生保各社は、高い予定利率を約束して多くの保険契約を獲得した。◆Europe promised the Group of 20 major economies to take concerted action to contain the financial crisis. 欧州は、結束して金融危機を封じ込めることを主要20か国・地域（G20）に公約した。

promise　(名)約束,公約,約定,契約,約束事,約束事項,契約事項,見込み
　empty promise　空手形
　fixed promise　確約
　implied promise　黙約,黙示契約
　naked promise　口約束　(=verbal promise)
　promise of fiscal stimulus　財政出動の公約
　promises of future stock　先物株式予約
　strict [definite] promise　確約
　written promise　約定書
　◆The envisaged timeline of APEC leaders for overcoming the global financial crisis may result in an empty promise. 世界的な金融危機を克服するためのアジア太平洋経済協力会議（APEC）首脳の目標期限は、空手形に終わる可能性がある。

promised　(形)約束された,規定した,見込みのある,予定の
　◆In commodity futures trading, prices are decided when buyers and sellers make deals. So they can execute trades at promised prices even if the value of goods has changed drastically in the meantime. 商品先物取引では、売り手と買い手が取引契約をする時点で価格を決める。そのため、契約期間中に相場が大きく変動しても、売り手と買い手は約束した値段で取引を執行できる。

promised yield　予定利率,約束された利回り
　（=guaranteed yield, promised yield rate）
　◆Allowing insurers to lower the promised yields would solve the negative spread problem, thus serving as an effective measure to stave off collapse. 生命保険会社の予定利率の引下げを認めれば、逆ざや問題の解消になり、その結果、破綻（はたん）回避の有力な手段になるはずである。

promised yield rate　予定利率　(=promised yield:生命保険会社が保険契約者に約束した利回り)
　◆The Insurance Business Law prohibits life insurers from lowering their promised yield rates on existing insurance contracts prior to their collapse. 保険業法は、生命保険会社が破綻前に既契約分の保険契約の予定利率を引き下げることを禁止している。

promised yields on premium investments　保険料投資の運用利回り
　◆From a broader point of view, the lowering of promised yields on premium investments would surely protect the benefits of policyholders. 大局的に見れば、生保が保険契約者に約束した保険料投資の運用利回り［予定利率］を引き下げたほうが、確かに保険契約者の利益を保護することになる。

promising　(形)有望な,期待できる,成長性の高い,明るい
　promising area　有望な分野,期待できる分野,成長分野
　promising country for investment　有望な投資先

promising market　期待できる市場, 有望市場, 成長市場
promising outlook　明るい見通し
promising small and medium-sized companies　成長性の高い中小企業
◆The failed bank tried to raise profits by attracting deposits with high interest rates and extending loans to promising small and medium-sized companies. 破たんしたこの銀行は、高金利で預金を集め、成長性の高い中小企業に融資して収益を確保しようとした。

promissory　(形)約束の, 支払いを約束する, 見込みのある

promissory note　約束手形
discount a promissory note　約束手形を割り引く
inland promissory note　内国[国内]約束手形
issue a promissory note　約束手形を発行する
issue promissory notes worth 50 million yen　5,000万円相当の約束手形を発行する
promissory note payable　金融手形債務
promissory note secured by deed of trust　信託証書を担保とする約束手形
promissory notes and bills　約束手形
promissory warranty　約束的担保
unsecured promissory note　無担保約束手形
◆After sending numerous reminders to its customer, the company eventually received a promissory note. 同社は、取引先に再三、支払いの催促状を出してから結局、約束手形を渡された。◆The ministry plans to use the protection scheme to prevent disruption of settlements, including payments to credit card companies and encashing of promissory notes, when a bank collapses. 同省は、この保護制度を用いて、金融機関が破綻した場合にクレジット・カード会社への支払いや約束手形の現金化(手形取引)などの決済マヒを防ぐ方針だ。

promote　(動)昇進させる, 昇格させる, 進級させる, 促進する, 推進する, 振興する, 増進する, 助長する, 育成する, 発展させる, 奨励する, 製品などを売り込む, 販売を促進する, 主催する, (事業などを)発起する, ～の発起人になる, 始める(launch), (議案, 法案の)通過に努める, 支持する　(⇒housing loan)
promote a sweeping restructuring　抜本的なリストラを推進する
promote securities investment　有価証券投資を促す
promote supply-side structural reforms　供給サイドの構造改革を進める
◆It is a matter of urgency to ensure that banks make profit margins that can meet investment risks and that they expand commission revenue as well as promote sweeping restructurings. 抜本的なリストラ推進のほか、投資リスクに見合う利ざやの確保と手数料収入の拡大などが銀行の急務だ。◆Taxes levied on capital gains should be consolidated to promote securities investment. 有価証券投資を促すために、金融資産課税は一元化するべきだ。◆The key to returning to stable growth is whether the nation can eliminate excesses common to many companies and promote supply-side structural reforms. 安定成長復帰へのカギは、多くの日本企業に共通して見られる過剰体質を排除して、供給サイドの構造改革を進めることができるかどうかである。

promoter's profit　発起人利潤, 発起人利得, 創業者利得
promoter's share [stock]　発起人株

promotion　(名)昇進, 昇級, 昇格, 昇任, 促進, 推進, 増進, 助長, 振興, 奨励, 販売促進, 販売促進活動, 創設, 創立, 設立, 発起, プロモーション
business promotion　起業, 興業
company promotion　会社設立, 会社創業
export promotion　輸出振興, 輸出促進
import promotion policy　輸入促進政策
productivity promotion　生産性向上
promotion expense　販売促進費(sales promotion cost), 創業費(organization cost), 創立費, 設立費用
promotion [promotional] shares　発起人株
sales promotion　販売促進, 販促, セールス・プロモーション
the promotion of intergenerational assets　世代間の資産移転促進
the promotion of the disposal of nonperforming loans　不良債権処理の促進
trade promotion　貿易振興, 貿易促進, 貿易推進
◆With the promotion of the disposal of nonperforming loans, corporate failures and joblessness will increase in the short time. 不良債権処理を促進すれば、短期的には企業倒産と失業が増える。

prompt　(動)(～するよう)促す, 駆り立てる, 動かす, 起こさせる, ～を刺激する, ～を誘発する, 引き出す, きっかけを与える, ヒントを与える, せりふを思い出させる
◆Mizuho Financial Group's plan to merge Mizuho Bank and Mizuho Corporate Bank in 2013 was prompted by a major computer system failure. 大規模なシステム障害を機に、みずほフィナンシャルグループは、2013年にみずほ銀行とみずほコーポレート銀行を統合する方針を固めた。◆The central bank's decision to raise the upper limit of its liquidity target was prompted by its concerns over the recent instability of the currency exchange rate. 日銀当座預金の残高目標(日銀の流動性目標)の上限引上げ決定の理由に、最近の為替相場の不安定な動きへの懸念があった。◆The intervention was prompted by the yen rising to ¥82.87 to the dollar in the morning trading. 市場介入に踏み切ったのは、朝方の取引で1ドル＝82円87銭まで円高が進んだからだ。◆The merger of the two steelmakers was prompted by intensified competition in the markets of newly emerging economies. 両鉄鋼メーカーの合併を促したのは、新興国市場での競争の激化である。◆The merger will prompt other megabanks to come up with new strategies to reinforcing their corporate health. この統合は他のメガバンクを刺激し、メガバンクは企業体質の強化に向けた戦略を新たに打ち出すことになろう。

prompt　(名)支払い期限, 即時払い, 支払い期限付き契約, 刺激, 促進, せりふ付け, 入力促進記号, プロンプト

prompt　(形)即時の, 即座の, 迅速な, 素早い, 早期の, 機敏な, 即時払いの, 即時渡しの, 直(じき)渡しの
for prompt cash　即金で
prompt cash　即金払い, 即時払い, 4,5日以内に支払う決済条件
prompt cash discount　直払い割引
prompt corrective action measures　早期是正措置
prompt day　支払い期日, 受渡し日
prompt delivery　直渡し
prompt exchange　直物為替
prompt note　買上票, 代金請求書, 支払い期日通知書, 即時払い手形
prompt payment　即時払い
prompt response　素早い対応, 素早い回答
prompt sale　延べ取引
prompt shipment　直(じき)積み, 即時船積み, 即時船積み条件, 即時出荷　(=as soon as possible shipment, immediate shipment)

proof　(名)証明, 立証, 証拠, 試験, 検算
bear a proof mark　検印がある
proof machine　小切手分類照合機
proof mark　検印
proof sheet　検算表

prop up (動)支える, 支持する, 買い支える, 後援する, 支援する, テコ入れをする
 prop up the economy　景気を下支えする
 prop up the economy by fiscal means　財政面でのテコ入れをする
 prop up the sagging dollar　下落するドルを買い支える
 ◆By allowing the weak dollar to continue for the foreseeable future, the U.S. authorities hope that U.S. exports will prop up the country's economy. ドル安の進行を当面容認して、米当局は輸出で米景気を下支えしたいようだ。◆If the economy is to see a full-fledged recovery, the government should continue taking all feasible policy steps, including propping up the economy by fiscal means. 本格的な景気回復を見るには、財政面でのテコ入れを含めて、政府は引き続き実行可能なあらゆる政策手段を取るべきである。◆The Bank of Japan will set up a fund to buy long-term government bonds, exchange-traded funds and other financial assets in a bid to prop up the nation's economy. 日本の景気を下支えするため、日銀は基金を新設して、長期国債や上場投資信託(ETF)などの金融商品[金融資産]を買い入れる。◆The major banks were temporarily propped up by the huge amount of taxpayers' money the government has pumped into them. 大手銀行は一時、国が注入した巨額の公的資金によって支えられていた。

prop-up (名)支持, 支援, テコ入れ, 買い支え

propensity (名)性向, 傾向, 好み, 性質
 a propensity to consume　消費性向
  (=a propensity for consumption)
 a propensity to save　貯蓄性向
 average propensity to invest　平均投資性向
 marginal propensity to invest　限界投資性向
 private propensity to invest　民間投資性向

property (名)財産, 有体財産, 資産, 固定資産, 有形固定資産, 不動産, 土地, 建物, 所有, 所有権, 所有地, 所有物, 財産権, 特性, 属性, 物件
 after-acquired property　事後取得財産
 basic property　基本財産
 gain on property dividend　現物配当処分益
 immovable property　不動産　(=immovables)
 inventories and property　棚卸し資産および有形固定資産
 investment property　投資不動産, 投資資産
 leased property　リース資産
 lost property　遺失物
 movable property　動産　(=movables)
 negative property　消極財産(負債や支払い勘定)
 personal property　動産, 個人の持ち物
 personal property tax　動産税
 private property　私有財産
 property additions　固定資産の増設額, 固定資産の新規取得
 property and equipment　有形固定資産
 property developer　土地開発業者
 property development project　不動産開発事業, 不動産開発プロジェクト
 property tax　固定資産税
 real property　不動産
 real property tax　不動産税, 固定資産税
 rental property　賃貸不動産
 residential property price　住宅用不動産価格
 total property　有形固定資産合計
 ◆TEPCO will sell property worth about ¥100 billion to raise funds for the massive amount of compensation. 東京電力は、巨額の賠償金の資金調達をするため、約1,000億円相当の資産[不動産]を売却する方針だ。

proportionate share　再保険割合部分

proportionate share of the actual benefits paid　実際支払い額の再保険割合部分

proposal (名)提案, 案, 企画, 構想, 計画, 申込み, オファー
 joint proposal　共同提案
 kill off merger or integration proposals　合併・経営統合の提案を否決する
 management integration proposal　経営統合の提案
 merger or integration proposals　合併・経営統合の提案
 merger proposal　経営統合案, 経営統合提案, 経営統合の提案書　(=business integration proposal; ⇒submit)
 proposal for appropriation of retained earnings　利益処分案
 proposal for subscription　株式応募の申込み
 shareholder [stockholder] proposal　株主提案
  (⇒stockholder proposal)
 stockholder's proposal right　株主の提案権
 ◆A company's management was reshuffled following a shareholder's proposal. 株主提案を受けて、企業の経営陣が刷新された。◆Debates on the pros and cons of a proposal to end the quantitative relaxation of credit by the Bank of Japan are gathering momentum. 日銀による量的金融緩和策を解除する案の賛否をめぐる議論が、活発化している。◆Golden shares are special shares that can be used to exercise a veto to kill off merger or integration proposals by hostile bidders. 黄金株は、敵対的買収者による合併・経営統合などの提案を否決するための拒否権行使に使える特殊な株だ。◆Shareholders are required to report their proposals to the company eight weeks before the shareholders meeting is to be held. 株主は、株主総会開催の8週間前までに株主提案の内容を会社側に伝えることになっている。◆The proposal to expand the lending capacity of the IMF was supported by Brazil and other emerging economies though Japan and the United States rejected it. 国際通貨基金(IMF)が融資できる資金規模を拡大する案は、日本と米国が受け入れなかったものの、ブラジルなどの新興国は支持した。◆We have received a number of proposals from investment banks who want to act as go-betweens between drug companies for mergers. 投資銀行からは、製薬会社の経営統合の仲介をしたい旨の提案が数多く来ている。

propose (動)提案する, 提唱する, 企画する, 申し出る, 提出する, 提示する, 指名する, 推薦(すいせん)する
 propose measures to reduce the debt burdens of HIPC　重債務貧困国(HIPC)の債務負担削減策を提案する
 proposed dividend　予定配当
 proposed legislation　法案
 ◆Greece's finance minister rejected a proposed referendum on staying in the eurozone. ギリシャの財務相は、提起されていたユーロ圏残留の是非を問う国民投票を拒否した。◆Rakuten has proposed integrating the firms' management under a joint holding company. 楽天は、共同持ち株会社の設立による[共同持ち株会社方式での]両社の経営統合を提案した。◆The administration of U.S. President Barack Obama proposed the stringent financial regulations. 米オバマ政権は、金融規制の強化を打ち出した。◆The government will propose measures to reduce the debt burdens of heavily indebted poor countries (HIPC). 政府は、重債務貧困国の債務負担削減策を提案する。

proposed bid prices　株式公開買付け(TOB)の予定価格, 提示された入札価格, 入札価格の提示
 ◆The proposed bid price does not reflect the bank's strong capital position and the superior credit quality of its assets. 株式公開買付け(TOB)の予定価格は、同行の自己資本比率の大きさや同行の資産の高い信用力を反映していない。

proposed management merger 経営統合案
◆The proposed management merger may infringe on the national professional baseball club agreement. この経営統合案は、プロ野球球団の協約に抵触する恐れがある。

proposed merger 経営統合の申し入れ, 統合案
◆The proposed merger would mark a final chapter in the realignment of the Japanese banking industry. この経営統合の申し入れは、日本の銀行業界[金融界]再編の最終章となる。

proposed pact 協定案
◆The proposed pact will exempt expats from paying into pension and health insurance plans in the country to which they are posted, provided they stay no more than five years. 協定案では、海外駐在員の滞在期間が5年以内であれば、駐在する相手国の年金と医療保険制度への加入を免除される。

proposed purchase price 提示された購入[買付け]価格, 買付け価格の提示, 予定買付け価格
◆Proposed purchase price is still far from what the investment fund is expecting. 提示された(TOBの)買付け価格は、投資ファンドの想定価格とまだ開きがある。

Proprietary Trading System 私設取引システム PTS (証券会社が開設した電子取引システム)
◆The Proprietary Trading System and other online trading systems facilitate trading of stocks outside stock exchanges. 私設取引システム(PTS)などの電子取引システムは、証券取引所外で株の売買(注文)を成立させる。

pros and cons 良い点と悪い点, 賛否両論, 是非
◆Debates on the pros and cons of a proposal to end the quantitative relaxation of credit by the Bank of Japan are gathering momentum. 日銀による量的金融緩和策を解除する案の賛否をめぐる議論が、活発化している。

prospect (名)見込み, 可能性, 将来性, 見通し, 予測, 展望, 期待, 見込み客 (⇒prospects)
　be in prospect 予想される, 期待される
　economic prospect 経済展望, 経済見通し, 景気見通し
　export prospect 輸出見通し
　good business prospect 好景気の見通し, 好景気の見込み, 事業がうまく行く可能性
　growth prospect 成長見通し, 業績見通し, 成長力
　long-term prospect 長期展望, 長期見通し
　prospect list 見込み客リスト
　prospect of recovery 回復の見通し, 景気回復の見通し
◆No clear prospect has emerged for resolution of the Greek financial crisis. ギリシャの財政危機を打開する見通しは、まだ立っていない。

prospective (形)未来の, 将来の, 今後の, 予想される, 予期される, 期待される, 見込みのある, 〜になる予定の
　prospective buyer 見込み客, 見込み購買者
　prospective customer 見込み客, 見込み顧客
　　(=prospective buyer)
　prospective dividend rate 予想配当率
　prospective earnings 将来の所得
　prospective financial information 将来財務情報
　prospective PE [P/E] 予想株価収益率, 予想PER
　　(=prospective PE multiple, prospective price/earnings ratio)
　prospective profits 予想収益, 収益見通し
　prospective rating 予備格付け, 予想料率算定
　prospective retirees 退職予定者, 予想される退職者
　prospective trends 今後のトレンド
　prospective yield 予想利回り, 予想収益
　prospective yield of capital 資本の予想収益
◆The two prospective partners have extensive expertise in mergers and acquisitions, as well as the securitization of bad loans. 提携する予定の両社は、企業の合併・買収(M&A)や不良債権の証券化などに豊富なノウハウを持っている。◆Under the existing Insurance Business Law, life insurance companies are not allowed to revise prospective yield rates unless they go bankrupt. 現行の保険業法では、生保各社が破たんしないかぎり、予定利率は変更できない。

prospective yield rate 予定利率, 運用利回り
　(=promised yield rate; ⇒policy cancellation)
◆Under the existing Insurance Business Law, life insurance companies are not allowed to revise prospective yield rates unless they go bankrupt. 現行の保険業法では、生保各社が破綻しない限り、予定利率は変更できない。

prospects (名)見通し, 予想, 先行き, 将来性, 見込み, 可能性, 期待, メド
　business prospects 景気見通し, 景気観測
　　(=business outlook)
　earnings prospects 収益見通し, 収益予想
　economic prospects 経済見通し, 景気見通し
　favorable [favourable] inflation prospects 明るいインフレ見通し
　improved economic prospects 景気見通しの改善, 景気見通しの好転
　prospects for growth 成長見通し, 成長力, 業績見通し, 景気見通し, 景気の先行き
　　(=growth prospects)
　prospects of lower [easier] interest rates 金利低下の見通し
　recovery prospects 回復見通し, 景気回復見通し
　uncertain prospects 先行きの不透明感, 先行きの不透明さ, 先行きが不透明であること, 見通しがはっきり立たないこと
◆Financial institutions, concerned about MMC's future prospects, began calling in the company's loans. 金融機関は、三菱自動車の先行きを懸念して、同社への融資回収に動いた。◆Prospects remain murky though a freefall in stock prices has been averted for now. 株価暴落はひとまず回避されたが、先行きはまだ不透明である。◆The Bank of Japan envisages the prospects of economic growth and consumer price trends in its "Outlook for Economic Activity and Prices." 日銀は、「経済・物価情勢の展望」(展望リポート)で、経済成長や消費者物価の先行きを示している。◆The economic prospects look bright as the Nikkei Stock Average has retained the 10,000 level. 日経平均株価が1万円台を回復したので、景気見通しは明るく見える。◆The prospects for liquidating nonperforming loans are dim. 不良債権処理の見通しは、はっきりしない。

prospectus (名)目論見書, 発行目論見書, 会社の設立趣意書, 事業要綱, 保険案内書, 案内, 内容見本
　(=listing particulars)
　final prospectus 最終目論見書
　issue by prospectus 目論見書による発行
　listing prospectus 上場目論見書
　pathfinder prospectus 募集目論見書
　preliminary prospectus 仮目論見書
　preparation of the prospectus 目論見書の作成
　prospectus issue 目論見書の発行
　prospectus of promotion 会社設立趣意書, 会社設立目論見書
　share prospectus 株式目論見書
　statement in lien of prospectus 新株発行説明書
◆A prospectus must include certain details stipulated by the Banking Commission, such as shareholdings, a comparison of the last five annual reports, capital review and others. 目論見書には、株主情報や過去5年間の年次報告書比較、資本金の推移など、銀行委員会が定めた特定の詳細事項も記載しなければならない。

[解説] 目論見書とは：有価証券の募集や売出しの際、有価証券や発行者の内容を説明した文書。株式や投資信託など有価証券を購入する投資家のための資料として、証券取引法で販売会社に交付が義務付けられている。投資信託の場合は、約款の内容や運用体制、リスク要因、申込み手数料などが記載される。

protect （動）保護する, 保全する, 保証する, (利回りなどを)確保する, 防御する, 防ぐ, (手形の)支払い準備をする
 be protected against insolvency　支払い不能に対して保護される
 protect a bill [draft]　手形の支払い準備をする, 手形を支払う[引き受ける]
 protect asset returns　資産の利回りを確保する
 protect investors　投資家を保護する
 protect investors from credit risk　信用リスクから投資家を守る
 protect settlement systems　決済システムを保護する
 protect the benefits of policyholders　保険契約者の利益を保護する
 protect the financial system from rumors and speculative investment　金融システムを風評や投機的投資[投機]から守る
 ◆Financial authorities should stiffen the penalties for illegal transactions to protect the financial system from rumors and speculative investment. 金融当局は違法取引[違法行為]に対する罰則を強化して、金融システムを風評や投機[投機的投資]から守らなければならない。◆From a broader point of view, the lowering of promised yields on premium investments would surely protect the benefits of policyholders. 大局的に見れば、生保が保険契約者に約束した保険料投資の運用利回り[予定利率]を引き下げたほうが、確かに保険契約者の利益を保護することになる。◆Nippon Life Insurance Co. sold some of Olympus's shares with a view to protecting the benefits of policyholders. 日本生命は、保険契約者の利益保護の観点からオリンパス株の一部を売却した。◆The government intends to restructure the deposit insurance system as a new financial safety net for protecting settlement systems. 政府は、預金保険制度を、決済システム保護のための新しい金融安全網として再構築する方針だ。◆When the freeze on the payoff system was partially lifted, clients shifted their funds from time deposits to savings deposits that will be protected fully. ペイオフ制度凍結の一部解禁が行われた際には、顧客が預金を定期預金から全額保護される普通預金に預け替えた。

protected （形）保護された, 保証された
 highly credit-protected securities　信用の質と安全性が高い証券
 prepay protected MBS (mortgage backed securities)　期限前償還に強いモーゲージ証券 (MBS)
 protected bear　保護された弱気筋, 弱気筋の保護 (=covered bear)
 protected check　改変防止小切手
 protected industry　保護産業
 thinly protected borrower　体力のない借り手

protection （名）保護, 保全, 保証, 保障, 補償, 保険の担保範囲 (coverage), 対策, 保護貿易政策, (暴力団に定期的に支払う)見かじめ料, 上納金, (暴力団が警官などに支払う)目こぼし料, プロテクション
 adequate protection　十分な補償
 apply for protection from creditors　会社更生手続きを申請する, 資産保全を申請する
 asset protection　財産保全, 資産保全
 bankruptcy protection　会社更生手続き
 blanket protection on bank deposits　銀行預金全額保証
 call protection　任意償還権不行使期間

Consumer Credit Protection Act　消費者信用保護法
consumer protection　消費者保護, 投資家保護, 個人投資家保護
court protection from creditors under the Civil Rehabilitation Law　民事再生法に基づく資産保全
credit protection　信用の保護, 信用補強
customer protection　顧客保護
debt protection　債権保護水準, 債権者保護, 債務返済能力
debt protection measurement　債権者保護の指標
debtholder [debt holder] protection　債券保有者の保護, 債券保有者保護
debtholder protection measurement　債券保有者保護指標
economic protection　経済的保護
environmental protection　環境保護
family protection policy　家族保証保険
income protection　利益保護
insurance protection　保険保障, 保険担保, 保証保護
insurance protection product　保険保障商品
investment protection agreement　投資保証協定
investor protection　投資家保護
legal protection　法的保護
lien protection　先取特権
liquidity protection　流動性についての保護
policyholders' protection fund　保険契約者保護基金
protection against counterfeit cards　偽造カード対策
protection against credit loss　信用損失に対する保護, 信用損失に対する投資家保護
protection against own-injury coverage　自損事故保険
protection against uninsured motorist coverage　無保険車傷害保険
protection and indemnity club [association]　船主責任相互保険組合, PIクラブ
protection and indemnity insurance　船主責任相互保険
protection and indemnity insurance [risks]　船主責任保険, P&I保険, PI保険
protection buyer　(クレジット・デリバティブ (credit derivative) での) プロテクションの買い手 (保険の加入者に相当)
protection for collateral　担保に対する保護
protection from creditors　資産保全, 会社更生手続き
protection money　見かじめ料, 保護領, 上納金
protection racket　暴力団が上納金をたかる行為
protection seller　(クレジット・デリバティブ (credit derivative) での) プロテクションの売り手
provide liquidity protection　流動性リスクをカバーする
refund protection　借換え制限条項
Securities Investor Protection Act　証券投資家保護法
tariff protection　関税による保護, 関税保護
◆JAL and its two subsidiaries applied to the Tokyo District Court for bankruptcy protection under the Corporate Rehabilitation Law. 日航とその子会社2社が、会社更生法に基づいて会社更生手続きの適用を東京地裁に申請した。◆The financial authorities filed a declaration of bankruptcy and a request for asset protection with the Tokyo District Court for the brokerage firm. 金融当局は、同証券会社の破産宣告と財産保全処分を東京地裁に申し立てた。

protection from creditors　資産保全, 会社更生手続き
 apply for protection from creditors　会社更生手続きを申請する, 破たん申請する, 資産保全を申請する (=file for protection from creditors)
 be forced to apply to the Financial Services Agency for

protection from creditors　金融庁への破たん申請を迫られる
◆The credit union was forced to apply to the Financial Services Agency for protection from creditors. 同信組は、金融庁への破たん申請を迫られた。◆The firm filed for protection from its creditors in a Delaware court under Chapter 11 of the federal bankruptcy code. 同社は、米連邦破産法の第11章に基づき、デラウエア州連邦地裁に資産保全を申請した。

protection of depositors　預金者保護
◆The financial bailout bill's passage by the U.S. House became possible on a second vote because provisions were added to enhance the protection of depositors and extend tax breaks. 米下院での金融安定化法案の可決が2度目の票決で可能になったのは、預金者保護を強化する条項と税の優遇措置を延長する条項が追加されたからだ。

protection of intellectual property　知的財産の保護
◆Washington sees the protection of intellectual property as one of its key policies in boosting the international competitiveness of its industry. 米国政府は、知的財産の保護を、米国産業の国際競争力強化の重要な政策の一つと見ている。

protection of wealth　資産の保全, 安全資産
◆Demand for bullion as a protection of wealth has been spurred by mounting concern that the global economy is faltering. 世界経済低迷への懸念増大から、安全資産[資産保全]としての金の需要が拡大している。

protectionism　(名)保護主義, 保護貿易主義, 保護貿易制度
　a chain of protectionism　保護主義の連鎖, 保護貿易の連鎖
　increased protectionism　保護主義の高まり
　shift to protectionism　保護主義への傾斜
◆The chain of protectionism is becoming a reality. 保護貿易の連鎖が、現実のものとなってきた。◆There is growing concern that protectionism and the resulting countermeasures will spread worldwide. 保護主義とそれに伴う報復合戦が、世界的に広がる恐れが出ている。

protectionist　(名)保護貿易主義者, 保護貿易論者
　protectionist measures　保護貿易政策, 保護貿易策, 保護主義的な手段
　protectionist trade policy　保護貿易政策
　restrictive protectionist tariffs　制限的保護貿易関税
◆Protectionist moves could damage the global economy. 保護主義的な動きは、世界経済に打撃を与えかねない。◆The domestic steel industry is wary of moves by other countries to strengthen protectionist measures. 国内鉄鋼業界は、保護色を強める[保護貿易政策を強化する]世界各国の動きを警戒している。

protective　(形)保護する, 保護を与える, 保護用の, 保護貿易の, プロテクティブ
　protective covenant　保護契約
　protective features　保護措置
　protective liability insurance　間接責任保険, 二次責任保険
　protective public liability insurance　間接責任保険, 二次責任保険
　protective system　保護貿易制
　protective tariff [duties]　保護関税
　protective trust　保護信託
　purchase a protective put　プロテクティブ・プットを買う

protective measures　保護措置, 保護政策, 対応策, 防衛策
◆The European Union's head office formally adopted tariffs of up to 26 percent on steel to prevent a feared flood of cheap imports from countries hit by U.S. protective measures. EU(欧州連合)の欧州委員会は、米国の保護措置で打撃を受けた国から安い輸入鉄鋼製品が流入する恐れがあるのを防ぐため、鉄鋼製品に対して最高26%の関税をかけることを正式採択した。◆The Tokyo Stock Exchange has called on listed companies to refrain from taking excessively protective measures against hostile takeover bids. 東京証券取引所は、敵対的買収に対する過剰な防衛策の自粛を上場企業に求めている。

protector　(名)保護者, 擁護者, 守護者, 後援者, 味方, 保護するもの, 安全装置, プロテクター
◆Incubator Bank of Japan started as a protector of small and midsize companies in 2004. 日本振興銀行は、2004年に中小企業の味方としてスタートした。

protracted　(形)長引く, 長引いた, 延長された, 遅延の, 遅延性の　(⇒prolonged)
　protracted negotiation　長引く交渉
　protracted slowdown　本格的な鈍化, 長引く景気低迷[鈍化]

protracted deflation　長引くデフレ
◆Domestic bank are stepping up oversea project financing due to the lack of growth in lending to domestic borrowers amid protracted deflation at home. 国内銀行各行は、国内ではデフレが続いて[デフレが続く状況で]国内融資先への貸出が伸びていないことから、海外の事業向け融資を強化している。

protracted economic slowdown　長期経済低迷, 長期景気低迷
◆Japan's protracted economic slowdown is becoming a stone around the neck of East Asia. 日本の長期経済低迷は、東アジアのお荷物になりつつある。

protracted economic slump　景気の長期低迷
◆Amid the protracted economic slump and the ongoing deflationary trend, the life insurance industry has been hit by a trio of predicaments. 景気の長期低迷とデフレ傾向が進行するなか、生保業界は三重苦に見舞われている。

protracted recession　長引く不況, 長期不況, 不況の長期化
◆The corporate group tax system is designed to encourage spin-offs and other corporate restructuring efforts amid protracted recession. 連結納税制度のねらいは、不況の長期化で分社化など企業の事業再構築努力を促すことにある。

provide　(動)提供する, 供給する, 与える, 付与する, 供与する, 販売する, 創出する, 調達する, 発生する, 設定する, 定める, 規定する, 算定する, 計上する, 発表する
　provide goods or services　モノやサービスを販売する, モノやサービスを提供する
　provide liquidity　流動性を提供する, 流動性を供給する
　provide the required capital　必要資本を調達する
　provide 10 percent of consolidated revenues　連結収益の10%を占める
◆All international activities provided 25 percent of consolidated revenues in 2011. 2011年度は、国際事業が連結収益の25%を占めました。◆In cooperation with the U.S. FRB, the Bank of England, the Bank of Japan and the Swiss National Bank, the European Central Bank decided to conduct three U.S. dollar liquidity-providing operations between October and December. 米連邦準備制度理事会(FRB)、英イングランド銀行、日銀、スイス国立銀行と協調して、欧州中央銀行(ECB)が10〜12月に3回、米ドル資金供給オペを実施することを決めた。◆In insurance services that can be bought via cell phones, cell phone companies provide nonlife insurers with policyholders' personal information. 携帯電話で加入できる保険サービスでは、携帯電話会社が(保険)加入者の個人情報を損害保険会社に提供している。◆Income taxes are generally not provided on cumulative undistributed earnings of certain non-U.S. subsidiaries. 法人税等は、原則として一部の非米国籍子会社の累積未分配利益については計上されていません。◆Japan will double assistance to African nations over five years and provide up to $4 billion in loans. 日本は今

後、アフリカ向け援助を5年間で倍増し、最大40億ドルの借款を供与する。◆Life Insurance Policyholders Protection Corp. will provide ￥145 billion to partially cover the life insurer's negative net worth, which was ￥320 billion as of the end of last September. 生命保険契約者保護機構は、昨年9月末現在の同生保の債務超過額3,200億円の一部を支援するため、1,450億円を支出することになっている。

provide ample liquidity to financial markets 金融市場に大量の資金を供給[提供]する
 ◆The Bank of Japan decided to continue providing ample liquidity to financial markets. 日本銀行は、金融市場に大量の資金供給を続けることを決定した。

provide an emergency loan 緊急融資を行う、緊急融資する
 ◆In the subprime crisis, the U.S. FRB had to take the extraordinary step of providing an emergency loan not to a commercial bank but to an investment bank. サブプライム問題で、米国の中央銀行の連邦準備制度理事会(FRB)は、緊急融資を銀行[商業銀行]ではなく証券会社[投資銀行]に対して行う異例の措置を取らざるを得なかった。

provide emergency liquidity 緊急時の流動性を提供する、緊急流動性を提供する
 ◆The ASEAN plus Three Macroeconomic Research Office, or AMRO, was set up in Singapore in April 2011 to coordinate decision-making for providing emergency liquidity to member states. ASEANプラス3(日中韓)の域内マクロ経済リサーチ・オフィス(AMRO)は、参加国に緊急時の流動性を提供する際の意思決定調整機関として、2011年4にシンガポールに設立された。

provide emergency loans 緊急融資する
 ◆With a view to stemming the airlines' financial hemorrhaging, the Construction and Transport Ministry in late May asked the Development Bank of Japan to provide emergency loans to the two carriers. 航空会社の損失を阻止するため、5月下旬に国土交通省は、日本政策投資銀行に対して両航空会社への緊急融資を要請した。

provide for ～に備える、～に引き当てる、～を算定する、定める、規定する、計上する
 ◆At an emergency shareholders meeting, the company obtained shareholder approval to transfer ￥199 billion from its legal reserves to provide for write-offs of nonperforming loans. 臨時株主総会で同社は、株主から、不良債権処理に備えて法定準備金から1,990億円を取り崩す案の承認を得た。◆The Company provides for income taxes based on accounting income for tax purposes included in the financial statements. 当社は税務上、財務書類に表示する会計上の利益に基づいて法人所得税を算定しています。

provide funds 資金を提供する、資金を投入する、出資する
 ◆The government will provide funds and extend loans to TEPCO through a newly established organization to handle the compensation issue due to the nuclear disaster. 今後は、原発事故による損害賠償問題を扱うために新設された組織(原子力損害賠償支援機構)を通じて、国が東電に出資したり融資したりする。◆Under the envisioned lending facility, the IMF will provide funds to countries where government bond yields remain at high levels to help reconstruct their public finances. この融資制度案では、国際通貨基金(IMF)が、国債の利回りが高止まりしている国に資金を提供[融資]して財政再建を支援する。

provide public funds 公的資金を注入する、公的資金を投入する
 ◆The U.S. government refused to provide public funds to keep Lehman Brothers afloat. 米政府は、リーマン・ブラザーズの破たんを避けるための公的資金の注入[投入]を拒んだ。
 ◆The U.S. tried to prevent an erosion of corporate ethics among financial institutions by refusing to provide public funds to Lehman Brothers. リーマン・ブラザーズへの公的資金の投入を拒否することによって、米政府は金融機関のモラル・ハザード(企業倫理の欠如)を回避しようとした。

provide subsidies 助成金を出す
 ◆The government provides subsidies to firms that hire workers between the ages of 45 and 59 from poor-performance companies. 政府は、業績不振の企業から43～59歳の中高年労働者を雇い入れている企業に、助成金を出している。

provide term insurance coverage 定期保険保障を与える
 ◆Family insurance policy is a whole life insurance policy that provides term insurance coverage on the insured's spouse and children. 家族保険契約は、被保険者の配偶者と子どもに定期保険保障を与える終身生命保険だ。

provide the money 資金を提供する
 ◆The bank plans to provide the money by transferring ￥100 billion in subordinated loans, which it has already extended to the insurer, to the insurer's foundation fund. 同行は、すでに供与している劣後ローン1,000億円をこの保険会社の基金に振り替えて、その資金を提供する方針だ。

provident fund 準備基金、積立基金

provider (名)提供者、請負業者、業者、企業、インターネット接続業者、ネット接続会社、プロバイダー (⇒capital provider)
 act as cash provider 資金を提供する
 be the provider of the L/C [l/c] 信用状を発行する
 be the sole provider of the credit support 単独で信用補完を付与する
 cash provider 資金提供者 (=capital provider)
 credit enhancement provider 信用補強提供者
 credit support provider 信用補てん提供者、信用補完提供者
 health care provider 医療サービス提供者、医療機関
 health insurance provider 健康保険提供者
 liquidity provider 流動性提供者
 support (facility) provider 信用補完提供者 (=provider of the support facility)
 ◆Providers of mobile phone services such as NTT Docomo and SoftBank Mobile have been offering cell phone-based policy sales by teaming up with nonlife insurers. NTTドコモやソフトバンクモバイルなどの携帯電話サービス会社は、損保会社と提携して、携帯電話での保険販売のサービスを提供している。◆The company was once the second-largest provider of subprime mortgages in the United States on loan volume. 同社は、かつてサブプライム・ローンの融資高で米国第2位の住宅ローン会社だった。

provision (動)引当金を計上する、引当金を繰り入れる
 ◆Banks have provisioned sufficiently against bad loans. これまでのところ、銀行は不良債権に対して引当金[不良債権引当金、貸倒れ引当金]を十分計上している。

provision (名)準備金、引当金、引当金繰入れ、引当金繰入れ額・充当額、引当金計上、計上、拠出、提供、用意、準備、規定、条項
 bolster provisions 引当金を積み増す (=increase provisions)
 establish a provision for ～の引当金を設定する
 life insurance provision 生命保険準備金
 loss provision 損失引当金、損失準備金 (=loss reserve)
 provision for business restructuring activities 事業再編成作業の引当金
 provision for depreciation 減価償却引当金
 provision for doubtful debts 貸倒れ引当金、貸倒れ引当金繰入れ額 (=bad debt provision, provision for bad

debts, provision for doubtful accounts）
raise provisions　引当金を積み増す
retirement provisions　退職給与引当金繰入れ額
risk provision　危険引当金, リスク引当金
◆Nonbank firms are forced to raise provisions by a recent accounting rule change. 今回の会計規則の変更で、ノンバンク（銀行以外の金融機関）各社は引当金の積み増しを迫られている。◆The provisions, after giving effect to taxes and minority interest, reduced 2011 earnings by $200 million. これらの引当金繰入れで、関連税額と少数株主持ち分利益控除後の2011年度の純利益は、2億ドル減少しました。

[解説] 準備金と引当金について：「準備金」には、一般にprovisionよりreserveやallowanceが使用されることが多い。日本の場合、「準備金」は法定準備金（legal capital reserves, legal reserves, legally required reserves）である資本準備金（capital reserve）、利益準備金（profit reserve）や価格変動準備金（reserve for price fluctuation）などにだけ用いられている。これに対して「引当金」は、将来の支出にあてるためにあらかじめ準備しておく資金のことである。

provision for disasters　災害準備金, 異常危険準備金
◆Insurers set aside provisions for disasters. 保険会社は、災害準備金［異常危険準備金］を積み立てている。

provisional　（形）臨時の, 一時的な, 仮の, 暫定（ざんてい）的な, 予備の
apply for a provisional injunction　仮処分を申請する
provisional agreement [contract]　仮契約, 仮条約, 暫定協定
provisional amounts　暫定的な金額
provisional attachment　仮差し押さえ
provisional budget　暫定予算, 仮予算
provisional compensation　損害賠償の仮払い金（=provisional damages）
provisional CPI number　消費者物価指数速報値（=provisional consumer price index）
provisional dividend rates　予想配当率
provisional injunction　仮処分, 暫定的差止命令
provisional rating　予備格付け
provisional registration　仮登録, 仮登記
provisionary policy　予定保険

provisional damages　損害賠償の一時金, 損害賠償の仮払い金　（=provisional compensation）
◆TEPCO will pay up to ¥1 million each to about 50,000 households as provisional damages for residents affected by nuclear crisis. 東電は、原子力発電所事故で避難した住民に対する損害賠償の仮払い金として、約5万の世帯を対象に1世帯当たり最高100万円を支払う。

provisional measure　暫定措置
◆As a provisional measure until the ¥10 million limit on postal bank deposits is removed, the government intends to raise the ceiling to ¥30 million. ゆうちょ銀行の1人当たり1,000万円の預け入れ限度額を撤廃するまでの暫定措置として、政府は限度額［上限］を3,000万円に引き上げる方針だ。

proxy　（名）代理人, 代行者, 代理行為, 代理権, 代理委任状, 委任状, 議決権行使委任状, 指標, 比較対象, プロキシ［プロクシー］
index proxy　指標
lose the proxy fight by a slim margin　（議決権）委任状争奪戦で僅差で負ける
proxy access　プロキシー・アクセス（企業が発送する委任状に、株主が推薦する取締役を記載して指名すること）
proxy access rule　プロキシー・アクセス・ルール（米SECの新ルールで、ある会社の議決権株式の3％以上を3年間以上保有する株主は、その会社の委任状勧誘資料を用いて取締役総数の4分の1まで指名する権利を持つ）
proxy fight [battle, contest]　委任状争奪戦, 委任状合戦, 代理人競争, プロキシー・ファイト
proxy for the market　市場の指標
proxy manuals　委任状勧誘資料
proxy solicitation　委任状勧誘, 議決権行使委任状勧誘（=solicitation of proxies）
proxy solicitor　委任状勧誘者
voting by proxy　代理人による議決権の行使
◆The Bank of Japan carries out a market intervention as a proxy of the finance minister. 財務相の代理人として、日本銀行が市場介入を実施する。

proxy form　代理人様式, 委任状用紙, 委任状カード, 委任状　（=form of proxy）
◆The proxy form indicates the number of shares to be voted, including any full shares held for participants in the Employee Stock Purchase Plan. 委任状用紙には、従業員株式購入制度加入者のために保有している株式をすべて含めて、行使される議決権株数が記載されています。

proxy statement　代理勧誘状, 代理権勧誘状, 委任状, 委任状説明書, 議決権代理行使勧誘状, プロクシー・ステートメント
◆The Proxy Statement describes the items of business to be voted on at the Annual Meeting. 議決権代理行使勧誘状には、定時株主総会で票決される議案についての説明がなされている。

prudence　（名）慎重, 慎重性, 冷静, 堅実, 保守主義, 賢明さ, 信用秩序維持, プルーデンス
financial prudence　堅実金融主義
macro prudence　マクロ・プルーデンス（金融システム全体の健全性重視）
macro prudence model　マクロ・プルーデンス・モデル
macro prudence policy　マクロ・プルーデンス政策（金融システム全体としての安全性・健全性確保のための政策）
macro prudence regulation　マクロ・プルーデンス規制, 金融のマクロ規制
micro prudence　個別金融機関の監督
micro prudence policy　ミクロ・プルーデンス政策（個々の金融機関の経営上の安全性・健全性確保のための政策）
prudence policy　プルーデンス（信用秩序維持）政策
◆Financial administration should have been handled with prudence. 金融行政は、慎重を期さなければならない。

prudent　（形）慎重な, 用心深い, 厳しい, 堅実な, 分別のある, 賢明な, 抜け目のない, 打算的な, プルーデント
prudence principle　保守主義, 保守主義の原則
prudent asset structure　堅実な資産構成
prudent business practice　慎重な営業手法, 堅実な事業運営の慣行
prudent investor　慎重な投資家［投資者］
prudent macro-economic management　慎重なマクロ経済管理
prudent-man rule　慎重な管理者の原則, 慎重人の原則, 堅実投資原則, 受託者の注意義務, プルーデント・マン・ルール（年金運用や信託財産の投資運用にかかわる管理者・受託者（fiduciary）としての注意義務。とくに慎重な資産運用が要求される場合の投資基準原則で、米国の多くの州で採用されている）
prudent-man rule for trust investment　信託された投資［信託財産の投資運用］に対する受託者の注意義務

prudent monetary policy　穏健な金融政策
◆China will shift to a "prudent" monetary policy in 2011

from the previous "appropriately loose" stance. 中国は、これまでの「適度に緩和的な」金融政策から2011年は「穏健な」金融政策に方向転換する方針だ。

psychological barrier 心理的な壁, 大台
  breach a psychological barrier 心理的な壁を割り込む, 大台を割り込む
  break the psychological 10% barrier [level] 心理の壁となっていた10%の水準を破る, 10%の大台を破る
  break through the psychological barrier of ¥100 心理的な壁となっていた100円を突破する, 100円の大台を突破する [超える]
  slip [fall] below the psychological barrier of ¥100 心理的な壁となっていた100円を割り込む, 100円の大台を割り込む
  ◆The dollar has slipped below the psychological barrier of ¥100. 円のドル相場は、心理的な壁となっていた1ドル＝100円台を割り込んでいる。

psychological factor 心理的要因
  ◆Foreign exchange fluctuations are affected not only by economic fundamentals, but also by psychological factors. 為替相場の変動は、経済のファンダメンタルズだけでなく、心理的な要因による影響をも受ける。

psychological line サイコロジカル・ライン
  解説 サイコロジカル・ラインとは：ある株が買われすぎか売られすぎかを短期的に判断する指数で、株価の反落や反発時期などを予測して株を売買する参考になる。一般に、12日の期間で、株価の終値が前日から上がれば「勝ち」、下がれば「負け」として、その勝率（何勝何敗か）を示す。勝率が100%に近いほど投資家心理が過熱していることを示し、0%に近いほど売られすぎとされる。

psychology （名）心理, 心理状態, 心理学, 読心術, 人の心を見抜く力
  business psychology 事業心理
  buying psychology 購買心理
  consumer [consumer's] psychology 消費者心理
  deflationary psychology デフレ心理
  depth psychology 深層心理
  fiscal psychology 財政心理学
  industrial psychology 産業心理学
  inflationary psychology インフレ心理
  investor psychology 投資家心理
  management psychology 経営心理学, 経営陣の心理
  market [market's] psychology 市場心理, 市場の地（じ）合い
  social psychology 社会心理学
  work psychology 労働心理学

public （形）公の, 公共の, 公開の　（⇒go public）
  be taken public on the stock exchanges 証券取引所に上場される
  open up to public ownership 株式を公開する
  public activity bond 公共目的債　（=public purpose bond）
  public assets 公共財, 公共財産
  public bidder 一般投資家
  public bond 公債　（=public loan [debt]）
  public bond market 公債市場
  public borrowing 公募の資金調達, 公共部門の借入れ
  public coffers 国庫, 国の拠出金　（⇒reserve funds）
  public company 株式公開企業, 上場企業 [会社]
  public credit 公共与信
  public deal 公募案件
  public deposit 公的預金
  public financing 公的融資
  public float 公開株
  public fund 公募ファンド
  public high yield issuance 高利回り債の公募発行
  public indebtedness 公的債務
  public insurance 公営保険
  public intervention on the currency markets 為替市場への協調介入
  public inventory investment 公的在庫投資
  public investor 大衆投資家
  public issuer 公共証券発行者
  public liability insurance 一般損害賠償責任保険, 対人対物賠償責任保険, 公共責任保険
  public offer of common shares 普通株式の公募増資
  public ownership 株式公開（public participation in the ownership）, 上場企業
  public placing or offering 公募
  public purpose bond 公共目的債　（=essential purpose [function] bond, traditional government bond: 地方債（municipal bond）の一種）
  public purse 国庫
  public quotation 公定相場
  public sale 公売, 競売
  public savings 公共貯蓄
  public securities markets 公募証券市場
  public shareholding 株式公開
  public spending [expenditure] 公共支出
  public stockholder 大衆株主
  public straight issue 公募普通債
  public subscription 公募　（=public offering）
  public trade 公募取引
  public trust 公益信託
  take the business public 事業の株式を公開する
  U.S. Public Securities Association 米国公共協会

public aid 公的支援
  ◆Sendai Bank and Tsukuba, regional banks based in areas stricken by the March 11 earthquake and tsunami, will receive a combined ¥65 billion public aid. 仙台銀行と筑波銀行（東日本大震災被災地の地方銀行）が、計650億円の公的支援を受けることになった。

public and corporate bonds 公社債　（=corporate and government bonds）
  amounts outstanding of public and corporate bonds 公社債の残存額
  loans on public and corporate bonds 公社債貸付け金
  yields to subscribers and terms of public and corporate bonds 公社債の応募者利回りと発行条件

public assistance 公的支援, 生活保護, 公的扶助
  ◆Depending on the degree of JAL's financial deterioration, the government will consider a combination of capital reinforcement under the industrial revitalization law and public assistance by the Enterprise Turnaround Initiative Corp. of Japan. 日航の財務の傷み具合によって、政府は、産業再生法に基づく公的資金による資本増強と、企業再生支援機構による公的支援との組合せを検討する方針だ。◆Major semiconductor company Elpida Memory, Inc. received public assistance in June 2009. 半導体大手のエルピーダメモリは、2009年6月に公的支援を受けた。

public bailout 公的資金の注入
  ◆The bank plans to apply for a public bailout on Friday, when it will release the outline of the rehabilitation plan. 同行は金曜日に公的資金の注入を申請する予定で、これに合わせて経営健全化計画の骨子を発表する。

public burden　国民負担
◆If the prices of purchased bad assets are set high, the public burden will balloon. 不良資産の買取り価格を高くすると、国民負担が膨らむ。◆Public burdens will expand due to increased social security costs compounded by a declining birthrate and graying society. 少子高齢化の進展による社会保障費の膨張などで、国民負担は今後増大する。

public confidence　国民の信頼, 消費者の信頼
◆The conduct of Snow Brand Food in disguising its beef products has betrayed public confidence in the food industry. 今回の雪印食品の牛肉偽装行為は、食品産業に対する消費者の信頼を裏切った。

public corporation　公益法人, 公共企業体, 特殊法人
(=special administrative corporation, special juridical person)
◆Reform of public corporations was the drawing card of Prime Minister Junichiro Koizumi's administration. 特殊法人の改革は、小泉政権の金看板だった。

public credit guarantee　公的信用保証
◆A real estate broker created a dummy company to illegally receive a public credit guarantee. 不動産業者が、架空の会社を作って不正に公的信用保証を受けていた。

public credit guarantee scheme　公的信用保証制度
◆About ¥1.9 trillion of taxpayers' money was spent over a ten year span until last fiscal year to cover losses from a surging number of uncollectible loans guaranteed by a public credit guarantee scheme for small and midsize companies. 中小企業のための公的信用保証制度により保証される融資の貸倒れ件数が急増し、それによる損失の穴埋めをするために、昨年度までの10年間で約1兆9,000億円の税金が投入された。

public debt　公的債務, 公債 (national debt), 公募債, 国債, 政府負債, 財政赤字
(=public bond, public loan)
　Bureau of the Public Debt　公債局
　capacity to service public debt　公的債務の返済能力
　countries burdened with heavy public debts　深刻な財政赤字国
　interest on public debt　一般政府負債利子
　public debt interest bill　国庫の利払い負担
　　(=public bond, public loan)
　public debt issuance　国債発行
　public debt issuer　公募債発行体
　public debt outstanding　公的債務残高, 公債残高
　public debt rating　公募債格付け
　public debt securities　国債, 財務省証券
　public debt transaction　公債取引
　public long-term debt　長期公的債務
　public long-term debt service　長期公的債務返済
　public sector debt　公共債, 公共部門債務, 公共部門借入れ, 公共部門債権
　secondary market in public debt　国債流通市場
　short-term public debt　短期公的債務, 短期債務, 短期公債
◆At the G-7 talks, concern over soaring public debts was to top the agenda. G7 (先進7か国財務相・中央銀行総裁会議) の協議では、増大する公的債務問題 [公的債務への懸念] が最大の議題 [課題] になる予定だった。◆Countries burdened with heavy public debts need to accelerate efforts to shore up their fiscal condition. 深刻な財政赤字国は、財政健全化を加速する必要がある。◆Greece will be able to finance its public debt without any problem. ギリシャは、問題なくギリシャ国債の資金 (国債の償還や金利支払いの資金) を調達できるだろう。◆Greece's public debts are expected to swell to the equivalent of 150 percent of its GDP. ギリシャの財政赤字 [公債残高] は、GDP (国内総生産) 比で150%まで上昇する見込みだ。◆Japan must tackle its large fiscal deficit and curb the growth of public debts. 日本は、巨額の財政赤字と取り組んで、財政赤字 [公的債務] の増大を抑える必要がある。◆The issue of soaring public debts was pigeonholed at the G-7 talks. 増大する公的債務の問題は、G7 (先進7か国財務相・銀行総裁会議) の協議では棚上げされてしまった。

public debt market　公募債市場
　issues securities directly to investors in the public debt markets　公募債市場で投資家に直接発行する

public distrust　国民の不信感
◆Public distrust in the pension system must be prevented from deepening. 年金制度への国民の不信感は、これ以上深まらないようにしなければならない。

public elderly care service　公的高齢者介護サービス, 高齢者介護サービス
(=publicly funded elderly care service)
◆Eighty percent of citizenship hope to receive public elderly care services when they get old. 国民の80％が、老後に高齢者介護サービスを受けたいとしている。

public finance　(国家、地方公共団体の) 財政, 米国の地方債 (U.S. public finance)　(⇒annual report)
　public finance market　公募債市場
　public finance policy　財政政策
　public finance reform　財政改革
　restore [rebuild] public finances　財政を立て直す
　sound public finance　健全な財政
◆Citizen demonstrations opposing the measures to rebuild the public finances of Greek government have intensified and even resulted in deaths. ギリシャ政府の財政立直し策に反対する市民デモが激化して、死者も出た。◆Greek government measures to rebuild its public finances include raising the rate of its value-added tax and of its taxes on luxury items, and cutting the salaries of public employees. ギリシャ政府の財政立直し策には、付加価値税率や物品税の引上げと公務員給与の削減などが含まれている。◆The IMF extends to countries with relatively healthier public finances one- to two-year loans of up to 1,000 percent of their contribution to the IMF without strict conditions. IMF (国際通貨基金) は、財政が比較的健全な国に対して、期間1～2年の資金を厳しい条件なしでIMFに出資している額 (クォータ) の最大10倍まで融資している。◆Under the envisioned lending facility, the IMF will provide funds to countries where government bond yields remain at high levels to help reconstruct their public finances. この融資制度案では、国際通貨基金 (IMF) が、国債の利回りが高止まりしている国に資金を提供 [融資] して財政再建を支援する。

public financing　公的融資　(=public loan)
　extend a public financing package　公的融資策を実施する, 公的融資を行う
　public financing package　公的融資策, 公的融資措置, 公的融資
◆In June 2009 prior to Japan Airlines' failure, a ¥67 billion public financing package was extended with a government-backed guarantee to JAL. 日本航空破たん前の2009年6月、日航に対して政府保証付きで670億円の公的融資が行われた [公的融資策が実施された]。◆The Board of Audit has confirmed that the public financing package extended with a government-backed guarantee to JAL prior to its failure cost taxpayers a total of ¥47 billion. 日航の破たん前に政府保証付きで行われた公的融資の総国民負担額は470億円であることを、会計検査院が確定した。

public fund [funds] injection　公的資金の注入
(=the infusion [injection] of public funds)
◆The bank applied for a public funds injection. 同行は、(政府に) 公的資金の注入を申請した。

public fund repayment　公的資金の返済
　◆The financial group completed its public fund repayment in 2008.　同フィナンシャル・グループは、2008年に公的資金の返済を完了した。

public funds　公的資金, 公金, 公費, 公債, 国債
　(=public money, taxpayers' money; ⇒credit crunch, nursing care insurance)
　inject public funds　公的資金を注入する
　　(=use taxpayers' money)
　prevent additional injection of public funds　公的資金の再注入を回避する
　provision of public funds　公的資金の注入
　　(=injection of public funds)
　reinjection of public funds　公的資金の再注入
　the public funds　公債, 国債　(=the Funds)
　◆A bill to revise the Law on Special Measures for Strengthening Financial Functions is designed to facilitate compensations of losses of financial institutions with public funds.　金融機能強化法の改正法案は、公的資金で金融機関の損失の穴埋めを容易にするのが狙いだ。◆As joint actions, major industrial nations have taken such measures as further interest rate reductions, quantitative monetary relaxation to increase the money supply, the injection of public funds and increased public spending.　協調行動として、主要先進諸国は、さらなる金利の引下げ、通貨供給量を増やすための量的金融緩和や公的資金の注入、財政出動[公共支出の拡大]などの措置を取った。◆JAL will not need more public funds due to larger-than-predicted earnings during the April-June quarter.　4～6月期の業績が予想を上回ったため、日本航空は、公的資金の追加支援は不要になるようだ。◆On Sept 7, 2008, the U.S. government earmarked a huge amount of public funds to help government-affiliated mortgage financiers Freddie Mac and Fannie Mae.　2008年9月7日に米政府は、政府系住宅金融公社のフレディ・マック(連邦住宅抵当貸付公社)とファニー・メイ(連邦住宅抵当金庫[公庫])を救済するため、巨額の公的資金投入を決めた。◆Public funds should be injected not only to buy up toxic assets, but also to boost the capital bases of enfeebled financial institutions.　公的資金は、不良資産の買取りだけでなく、弱体化した[体力の落ちた]金融機関の資本増強にも注入すべきだ。◆Public funds will be injected into troubled banks from the state coffers.　問題のある[経営難の]銀行には今後、国庫から公的資金が注入される。◆Sendai Bank will receive ¥30 billion of public funds.　仙台銀行が、300億円の公的資金を受ける。◆The government will have to infuse any banks with public funds if they have become undercapitalized.　銀行が資本不足に陥ったら、政府は銀行に公的資金を注入せざるを得ないだろう。◆The Tokyo metropolitan government currently deposits public funds only in major domestic banks.　東京都は現在、国内の大手銀行だけに限って公金を預けている。◆The Tokyo metropolitan government has decided to deposit more than ¥100 billion in public funds in Citibank, a U.S. bank, to diversify risks.　東京都は、1,000億円を上回る公金を米国の銀行「シティバンク」に預けて、リスクを分散する方針を固めた。◆The U.S. government refused to provide public funds to keep Lehman Brothers afloat.　米政府は、リーマン・ブラザーズの破たんを避けるための公的資金の注入[投入]を拒んだ。

public goods　公益, 公共の福祉, 公共財
　◆Citigroup Private Bank repeatedly committed acts contrary to the public goods, such as the buying and selling trusts and securities that the division was not permitted to trade.　シティバンクのプライベート・バンク部門は、取引が禁止されている信託や証券を売買するなど、公益に反する行為を繰り返していたという。

public institution　公的機関
　◆Public institutions or revitalization funds will buy the loans owed by small and midsize companies that have been hit by the March 11 disaster to lighten their repayment burdens.　公的機関や復興ファンドが、東日本大震災で被災した中小企業の借金を買い取って、被災企業の返済負担を軽減するものと思われる。

public investment　公共投資
　◆As far as public investment is concerned, the second supplementary budget has had a favorable effect on the economy to some extent.　公共投資に関しては、第二次補正予算の景気への効果がある程度出ている。◆Housing starts and public investment also remained sluggish.　住宅着工戸数(住宅投資)や公共投資も、停滞したままだ。◆Public investments dropped by a drastic 3.4 percent in the April-June quarter from the previous period.　4～6月期の公共投資は、前期比3.4%と大きく落ち込んだ。

public investment and loans　財政投融資
　◆A special account is used to finance public investment and loans to government-affiliated financial institutions.　特別会計は、政府系金融機関に財政投融資の資金を供給するのに用いられる。

public investment spending　公共投資関係費
　◆The Finance Ministry plans to reduce public investment spending by more than three percent from this fiscal year's ¥8.9 trillion.　財務省は、公共投資関係費を今年度の8兆9,000億円から3%以上減らす方向だ。

public issue　公募発行, 公募(public offering), 公募債, 公募証券, 直接発行　(⇒class)
　public issues　公募債　(=public loans)
　◆The company completed a public issue in Canada of $125 million 7.50% Cumulative Redeemable Retractable Class A Preferred Shares.　同社は、7.50%累積償還・取消し可能クラスA優先株式1億2,500万ドルを、カナダで公募発行した。

public listing　株式上場
　◆The public listing of the firm, with the market value this creates, helps to reinforce the value of ABC Inc.'s own shares.　同社の株式上場は、ABCの市場価値を高めるとともに、ABCの自社株の株価強化にも役立っている。

public loan　公債(government loan), 国債, 公的融資
　◆The public loan was extended to JAL in June 2009 by the entirely state-funded Development Bank of Japan.　この公的融資は、国が100%出資している日本政策投資銀行が、2009年6月に行った。

public market　公開市場, 公設市場, 公募市場, 公募債市場, 大衆相場
　fund through the public and private markets　公募・私募の資本市場で資金を調達する
　issue securities in the public debt markets　公募債市場で証券を発行する
　public market NPL securitization　公募不良債権証券化取引(NPL=nonperforming loan(不良債権)の略)
　public market securities　公募証券
　tap[access]the public markets　公募債市場で資金を調達する

public money　公金, 公的資金
　◆A ceiling on the amount of public money to be deposited as postal savings is urgently needed.　郵便貯金として預け入れる公金の限度額を、早急に設定する必要がある。◆U.S. taxpayers are wary of injecting a huge amount of public money into General Motors Corp.　ゼネラル・モーターズ(GM)への巨額の公的資金注入に対して、米国の納税者の視線は厳しい。

public nursing care insurance system　国民介護保険制度, 国民介護保険, 公的介護保険制度
　◆The public nursing care insurance system is expected to face financial difficulties.　国民介護保険は、財政がひっ迫することが予想される。

public offer price　公募価格

◆Sundry goods maker Transaction Co. became the first company to debut on the new Jasdaq market, opening at ￥1,295 against a public offer price of ￥1,400. 雑貨メーカーのトランザクションがジャスダック新市場への新規上場第1号で、同社株は1株1,400円の公募価格に対して1,295円の初値が付いた。

public offering 株式公開, 新規公開, 株式公募, 公募, 公募増資, 売出し （=going public, primary offering, public stock offering, public subscription; ⇒initial public offering, proceeds from the public offering）

  public offering bond 公募債

  public offering date 公募開始日

  public offering of bonds on fixed conditions 定率公募

  public offering of stocks 株式の公開, 株式の新規公開

  public offering price 公募価格（public offer price）, ミューチュアル・ファンドの買付け価格, POP

  public stock offering 株式公募, 公募増資

◆During the first nine months of 2011, the company completed public offerings of $125 million of 9.45% Debentures, due 2021 and $125 million of 10.50% Debentures, due 2018. 2011年1-9月期に同社は、2021年満期9.45%社債1億2,500万ドルと2018年満期10.50%社債1億2,500万ドルを公募発行した。◆During the first six months of 2011, the company completed two public offerings of $125 million each of debentures in Canada. 2011年上半期に同社は、社債1億2,500万ドルを2回にわたってカナダで公募発行した。

|解説|私募（private placement）と違って、公募は不特定多数の一般投資家を対象に有価証券の取得を募集すること。有価証券が新規発行の場合はprimary offering（募集・公募）、既発行の場合はsecondary offering（売出し）と呼ばれる。公募の事務扱いは、一般に引受シンジケート団（underwriting syndicate）が仲介機関として行う。

public pension 公的年金

  public pension liability 公的年金債務

  public pension plan［scheme］ 公的年金, 公的年金制度 （=public-run pension system）

  public pension reserves 公的年金積立金

  public pension payments 公的年金の支給額

◆In step with declining prices, public pension payments are supposed to be cut. 物価の下落に合わせて、公的年金の支給額も削られるはずだ。

  public pension plan 公的年金制度, 公的年金 （=public-run pension system: 全国民を対象に国が運営している公的年金には、自営業者や学生が中心の国民年金のほかに、民間企業のサラリーマンが加入する厚生年金と公務員が加入する共済年金がある）

  public pension premium 公的年金保険料

◆Collecting public pension premiums will be transferred from municipal governments to the central government. 公的年金保険料の徴収業務は今後、市町村から国に移管される。

  public pension system 公的年金制度, 公的年金

  confidence in the public pension system 公的年金に対する信頼

  the future of the public pension system 公的年金の将来

◆Many people are concerned about the future of the public pension system. 国民の多くは、公的年金の将来に不安を抱いている。◆The public pension system was launched in April 1961. 公的年金制度は、1961年4月に導入された。

public-private investment fund 官民出資の投資ファンド, 官民出資のファンド

◆The draft of the government's new growth strategy includes the establishment of a public-private investment fund to support the content industry in its foreign endeavors. 政府の新成長戦略の原案には、コンテンツ（情報の内容）産業の海外展開を支援する官民出資のファンド設立も盛り込まれている。

public-run pension system 公的年金制度

◆A review of the public-run pension system is a matter of the highest urgency. 公的年金制度の見直しは、最も緊急の課題だ。

public sector 公共部門, 公的部門, 公的セクター, 国営部門

  public sector borrowing position 財政赤字

  public sector borrowing requirements 公共部門借入所要額, 公的借入需要, （英国の）財政赤字, PSBR

  public sector credit 公共部門の信用

  public sector deficit 公共部門赤字, 財政赤字

  public sector external debt 公的対外債務

  public sector finances 財政

  public sector financial institution［organization］ 政府系金融機関

  public sector financing situation 財政赤字

  public sector fund 公的資金

  public sector investment 公共投資

  public sector loans 公共部門向け融資

public sector debt 公共部門債権［債務］, 公共債

  public sector debt repayment 公共部門借入返済額

◆The BOJ will purchase riskier assets such as exchange-traded funds in a first attempt to narrow the gaps between interest rates for public- and private sector debts. 公共債と民間債の金利ギャップ［金利差］を縮小するための初の試みとして、日銀は上場投資信託などの高リスク資産を買い取る方針だ。

public securities 公募証券, 公共債

  Public Securities Association 公共債協会

  public securities markets 公募証券市場

public servant 公務員

◆Full-time housewives of company employees and public servants are not required to pay pension premiums. 会社員や公務員の専業主婦は、保険料を払う必要がない。◆Nonworking spouses of public servants and company employees are classified as Category III insured. 公務員や会社員の仕事を持たない配偶者は、第3号被保険者と呼ばれている。◆Pension premiums of full-time housewives of company employees and public servants are automatically covered by payments made by all subscribers to welfare and mutual pension plans. 会社員や公務員の専業主婦の年金保険料は、厚生年金や共済年金の加入者全員の支払い金で自動的にカバーすることになっている。

public spending 公共投資, 公共支出, 公共事業費 （=public works spending）

  a boost in public spending 公共支出の拡大, 財政出動の拡大

  cuts in public spending 公共事業費の削減

  increased public spending 公共支出の拡大, 財政出動

◆A boost in public spending seems to be merely an excuse for pork-barrel spending. 財政出動［公共支出］の拡大は、単なる「バラマキ」の口実にすぎないようだ。◆As joint actions, major industrial nations have taken such measures as further interest rate reductions, quantitative monetary relaxation to increase the money supply, the injection of public funds and increased public spending. 協調行動として、主要先進諸国は、さらなる金利の引下げ、通貨供給量を増やすための量的金融緩和や公的資金の注入、財政出動［公共支出の拡大］などの措置を取った。◆Because of the prolonged recession and cuts in public spending, the volume of construction businesses continues to shrink by the year. 長引く不況や公共事業費の削減などで、建設の事業量が年々減少している。◆In the case of the United States, increased public spending to boost the economy can hardly be expected. 米国の場合、財政出動に

よる景気浮揚は期待しにくい。◆It is difficult for Japan, the United States and European countries to support their sagging economies by increasing public spending, due to deteriorating financial conditions. 財政の悪化で、日米欧は、財政出動による景気の下支えが難しくなっている。◆Japan, the United States and European countries supported their sagging economies by increasing public spending after the collapse of Lehman Brothers in the autumn of 2008. 2008年秋のリーマン・ブラザーズの経営破たん後、日米欧は、財政出動によって低迷する景気の下支えをした。◆Priority should be given to public spending, to establish a firm foundation for economic recovery and the subsequent job of tackling fiscal reform. 景気を回復し[経済を立て直し]、財政改革に取り組むための強固な基盤を確立するには、公共支出を優先的に考えなければならない。◆The joint statement pointed out the necessity for economic stimulus through increased public spending. 共同声明は、財政出動[公共支出の拡大]による景気刺激策の必要性を指摘した。

public stock offering 株式公募, 株式公開, 株式上場
(=public offering, stock offering)
◆The company made a public stock offering on the Nasdaq Japan market on the Osaka Securities Exchange in March 2001. 同社は、2001年3月、大阪証券取引所のナスダック・ジャパン(現ヘラクレス)市場に株式を上場した。◆The remaining $2 billion in common shares will be sold in a public stock offering. 残りの20億ドル相当の普通株式は、株式公募で発行される[残りの20億ドルは、普通株による公募増資を行う予定だ]。

public tender offer 株式公開買付け
(=takeover bid, tender offer, TOB)
◆Holders of about 268.64 million shares, or 63.71 percent of all shares of Hanshin Electric Railway Co., accepted Hankyu's public tender offer. 阪神電鉄の約2億6,864万株の株主(発行済み株式の63.71%)が、阪急の株式公開買付け(TOB)に応募した。

public trading 公募取引
the first day of public trading 公募取引の初日
the second day of public trading on the Tokyo stock exchange 東証での公募取引の2日目
◆Mixi Inc. continued strong popularity on its second day of public trading on the Tokyo stock exchange. ミクシィ(ソーシャル・ネットワーキング・サービスの最大手)は、東証での公募取引2日目も、上場初日に引き続き強い人気を保った。

public utility 公益事業[企業], 公共事業
public utility bond 公共事業債
public utility charges 公共料金
(=public utility rates)
public utility company 公益企業

public welfare loans 福祉資金(都道府県などが、国からの借入金を使って母子家庭などに修学資金、生活資金、住宅資金などを貸し付ける制度)
◆More than half of the public welfare loans extended to widows and single mothers are not collected. 母子家庭や寡婦に供与されている福祉資金の5割以上が、回収されていない。◆The public welfare loans are extended to widows and single mothers to help them become economically independent by financing spending for education, living costs, housing costs and funds to start small businesses. 福祉資金は、母子家庭や寡婦に対して、教育費や生活費、住宅費、事業開始資金などを貸し付けてその経済的自立を助けるために供与されている。

public works 公共工事, 公共土木工事, 公共事業
decline in public works contracts 公共工事契約の減少
public works spending 公共投資, 公共事業費
(=public spending)
◆Another problem that affected the company's rehabilitation plans was the precipitous decline in public works contracts. 同社の再建計画に影響を及ぼしたもう一つの問題点は、公共工事の契約が激減したことだ。

public works project 公共事業, 公共工事
◆Under the guaranteed performance system, a construction company has to pay a guarantee fee to banks in case the company becomes unable to continue a public works project. 履行保証制度では、建設会社が公共工事を継続できなかった場合には、建設会社が銀行に保証料を支払わなければならない。

public works spending 公共投資, 公共投資関係費, 公共事業費
(=public spending; ⇒prolonged economic slump)
◆The government will trim public works spending by 3 percent compared to the previous fiscal year. 政府は、公共投資関係費を前年度比3％削減する。

publicly (副)公式に, 公的に, 人前で, 公然と, 公費で
(⇒privately)
publicly funded starts 公共資金による住宅着工戸数
publicly held corporation [company] 株式公開企業, 公開会社, 上場企業
publicly held investment bank 上場投資銀行
publicly held stocks 公開株式
publicly issued bond 公募債
publicly issued outstandings 公募債残高
publicly offered bonds 公債
publicly-offered local government bonds 公募地方債
publicly owned company [corporation] 株式公開企業, 公開会社, 上場企業 (=publicly held company, publicly quoted company, publicly traded company)
publicly subscribed shares 公募株

publicly list 株式上場する, 上場する
◆Domestic stock exchange entries continue to languish, reflecting the tough conditions faced by emerging firms wanting to publicly list their shares. 国内株式市場への新規上場は、株式上場を目指す新興企業が直面している厳しい状況を反映して、低迷が続いている。◆Emerging firms wanting to publicly list their shares are facing the tough conditions. 株式上場を目指す新興企業は、厳しい状況に直面している。◆Publicly listing Tokyo Metro and selling shares in it could net the government hundreds of billions of yen. 東京地下鉄(東京メトロ)の株式を上場して保有株式を売却すれば、国は数千億円の収入を見込める。

publicly traded 株式公開されている, 株式公開企業の
(=publicly quoted)
be publicly traded 上場している
publicly traded company 上場企業, 上場会社, 株式公開企業
publicly traded shares [stocks] 上場株式, 上場銘柄
repurchase one's publicly traded shares 上場株式を買い戻す
sell one's stock publicly 株式を民間に売却する
◆The Stockholm Stock Exchange is owned by publicly traded OM Group Inc. スウェーデンのストックホルム証券取引所は、株式公開企業のOMグループが所有している。

publicly traded company [firm] 公開企業, 公開会社, 株式公開企業, 上場会社, 上場企業 (=publicly held company, publicly owned company, publicly quoted company, publicly traded enterprise; ⇒concern)
◆Mizuho provides banking services to 70 percent of the nation's publicly traded companies. みずほFGは、国内上場企業の7割に銀行サービスを提供している。◆Under the new Corporate Law, anyone is allowed to launch a publicly traded company even with ¥1. 新会社法では、(資本金)1円でも公開企業を設立することができる。

publish (動)公表する, 発表する, 公開する, 発行する, 刊行する, 出版する, 掲載する

officially published land price　地価公示価格
publish a book　本を出版する, 本を刊行する
publish a financial report　有価証券報告書を公表する
publish a law　法令を発布する
quarterly review published by the BOJ　日銀の情勢判断資料
◆A boom in stock investing among working women has led a number of women to create Web sites and publish guides targeted at this growing market. 働く女性たちの間の株式投資ブームで, この成長市場向けサイトを立ち上げたり, 指南本を出したりする女性が増えている。◆Financial reports and other documents published by companies are the most fundamental sources of information for investors and creditors. 企業が公表する有価証券報告書などは, 投資家や債権者にとって最も基幹的な情報源である。

pull money　金を引き出す, 資金を引き揚げる
◆More investors are pulling money from stock markets and shifting it into safer time deposits. 株式市場から資金を引き揚げ, 引き揚げた資金を安定性の高い定期性預金に移し替える投資家が増えている。

pull out of　～から手を引く, ～から撤退する, ～から脱退する, ～から抜け出す　(=withdraw from)
◆The global economy has been pulled out of its worst crisis. 世界経済は, その最大の危機を脱した。◆The United States should pull out of the economic morass. 米国は, 泥沼の経済状況から抜け出すはずだ。

pump　(動)注入する, 投入する, 出資する, 振り込む, 供給する, 大量に作り出す, もたらす, くみ上げる, ポンプでくみ出す, 上下に動かす, (汚染物質を)排出する, 放出する
pump and dump　株価をあおりたてた後に売り逃げる不法行為
pump liquidity into the (banking) system　市中に流動性を供給する
pump money into　～に資金を投入する
pump money into the (banking) system　市中に流動性を供給する
pump out a new product　新製品をどんどん生産する, 新製品を大量生産する
◆DaimlerChrysler has decided against pumping more money into its troubled Japanese partner, Mitsubishi Motors Corp. ダイムラー・クライスラーは, 経営不振の[問題を抱えている]日本の提携企業・三菱自動車に資金を投入しないことを決めた。◆Through massive purchases of U.S. Treasury bonds from U.S. commercial banks, the Fed pumps the proceeds into the banking system. 米国の銀行から米長期国債を大量に買い進めて, 米中央銀行(連邦準備制度理事会)は, その代金を市中銀行に振り込んでいる。

pump-primer　(名)景気刺激策
pump priming　呼び水, 誘い水, 予算ばらまき, 呼び水用の財政支出, 呼び水の支出政策, 呼び水経済政策, 呼び水[誘い水]式経済政策, 大規模の財政投融資, 景気刺激策, 景気対策, 景気振興策
a comprehensive economic pump-priming package　景気テコ入れの総合経済対策
pump-priming effect　呼び水効果, 誘い水効果, 刺激効果
pump-priming money　呼び水用の資金
pump-priming policy　呼び水政策, 誘い水政策
pump-priming policy instrument　呼び水政策手段, 誘い水政策手段
the Fed's pump-priming move　米中央銀行[米連邦準備制度理事会(FRB)]の景気刺激策[景気対策]
pump-priming measures　景気テコ入れ策, 景気刺激策, 景気浮揚対策, 景気振興策, 景気振興措置, 呼び水政策, 呼び水式景気浮揚策, 呼び水措置　(⇒economic pump-priming measures, financial summit meeting, graying, urge)
additional economic pump-priming measures　追加景気対策, 景気対策の追加
bold pump priming measures　思い切った景気刺激策
prioritize pump priming measures　景気テコ入れ策[景気対策]を優先する
take effective pump priming measures　効果的な景気浮揚策を取る[実行する]
◆A prerequisite to restoring the country's fiscal health is to promptly and boldly take effective pump priming measures and to overcome the economic crisis. 日本の財政健全化への前提条件は, 迅速, 果敢に効果的な景気浮揚策を実行して, 経済危機を克服することだ。◆Additional pump-priming measures through strengthening cooperation between advanced countries and emerging economies will be a major subject of discussion at the financial summit meeting in Washington. 先進国と新興国の連携強化による追加景気対策の検討が, ワシントンで開かれる金融サミットで検討される主要テーマとなる。◆APEC forum leaders need to tackle further economic pump-priming measures after steadily implementing items incorporated in the special statement. アジア太平洋経済協力会議(APEC)の各首脳は, 特別声明に盛り込んだ項目を着実に実施したうえで, さらに景気対策に取り組む必要がある。◆Calls to prioritize pump priming measures have slowly but steadily increased. 景気対策優先の声が, じわじわ広がっている。◆The government must either revise the budget to incorporate bold pump-priming measures or adopt additional policies. 政府は, 予算を組み替えて思い切った景気刺激策を盛り込むか, 追加措置を取るべきだ。◆There is a limit to conventional pump-priming measures amid a continued decline in birthrate and a consequent graying and shrinking population. 少子高齢化や人口減少などが進行するなかで, 従来の景気刺激策[景気テコ入れ策]では限界がある。

pump-priming move　景気刺激策, 景気対策
◆To the Obama administration, the Fed's pump-priming move is the only way to lower the high unemployment rate of 9.6 percent. オバマ政権にとって, 米連邦準備制度理事会(FRB)[米中央銀行]の景気対策が, 9.6％の高失業率を下げる唯一の手段である。

pump-priming package　景気刺激策, 景気テコ入れの経済対策
◆The government will map out a comprehensive economic pump-priming package this month. 政府は今月, 景気テコ入れの総合経済対策をまとめる。◆The $150 billion pump-priming package is being negotiated between the U.S. administration and Congress. 米政府と議会は現在, 1,500億ドルの景気刺激策について調整を進めている。

pundit　(名)権威者, 専門家, 学識者, 学者, 博識者, 賢者
◆Before the bubble collapsed, many pundits had predicted that the likely downturn of the U.S. economy would have only a limited impact on the rest of the world. バブル経済の崩壊前には, 「米経済はいずれ行き詰まるだろうが, 他国への影響は限定的である」と専門家の多くは予測していた。◆Many pundits in Tokyo have prophesized the possible demise of U.S. primacy since the financial bubble burst. 金融バブル崩壊以降, 日本では, 米一極指導の終焉(しゅうえん)を予言する専門家が多い。

punishment　(名)処分, 処罰, 刑罰, 罰, 手荒い扱い, 虐待, ひどい仕打ち, 強打
administrative punishment　行政処分
punishments for accounting fraud　粉飾決算に対する罰則
◆Punishments for accounting fraud are too light in Japan. 粉飾決算に対する罰則は, 日本では軽すぎる。◆The Financial Services Agency ordered Sompo Japan Insurance Inc. to suspend part of its operations as punishment for the major insurance company's illegal business practices. 金融庁は, 損

保大手の損害保険ジャパンに業務で法令違反があったとして、同社に一部業務停止命令を出した。◆The financial watchdog took an additional action of criminal complaint other than administrative punishment as the bank's operations were so malicious. 同行の業務運営の仕方があまりにも悪質なので、金融監視機関の金融庁は、行政処分のほかに刑事告発の追加措置を取った。

punitive tariffs 報復関税
（=retaliatory tariffs, tit-for-tat tariffs）
◆Beijing pledged to cancel its punitive tariffs on automobiles, cellular phones and air conditioners imported from Japan. 中国［中国政府］は、日本から輸入している自動車、携帯電話とエアコンに課している報復関税を取り下げることを約束した。

purchase （動）買い取る，買い付ける，買い入れる，購入する，引き受ける，仕入れる，調達する，買収する，取得する （=buy, risky, risky, takeover bid system）
　commercial paper purchased 買入コマーシャル・ペーパー，買入CP
　federal funds purchased フェデラル・ファンド取入れ，フェデラル・ファンド借入金
　foreign exchange purchased 買入外国為替
　monetary claims purchased 買入金銭債権
　municipal bond purchased privately by financial institutions 縁故地方債
　purchase a bill 手形を買い入れる
　purchase a fixed annuity 定額年金を購入する
　purchase an indebted company 赤字企業を買収する
　purchase an insurance policy 保険をかける
　purchase assets from ～から資産を買い取る「購入する，取得する」，～から資産を買収する
　purchase financial assets 金融資産を購入する，金融資産を買い取る［買い入れる］
　purchase long-term securities 長期債を購入する
　purchase receivables 債権を買い取る
　purchase shares 株式を購入する，株式を買い付ける
　purchase stock on margin 信用買いをする
　purchase treasury shares 自己株式を購入する
　securities purchased under resale agreements 売戻し条件付き買入有価証券，売戻し条件付き証券購入
　securities purchased under reverse repurchase agreements 売戻し条件付き買入有価証券
◆If the company could be purchased for less than ¥200 billion, some companies would consider making a bid. 同社を2,000億円以下で買収できたら、買収を検討する企業も出てくるだろう。◆Investors purchased more overseas bonds and stocks to seek higher returns. 投資家は、高利益を求めて外国の債券や株式への投資が拡大した。◆The BOJ's additional monetary easing steps include an increase in the amount of funds to purchase government bonds and corporate debentures. 日銀の追加金融緩和には、国債や社債などを買い入れる基金の増額が含まれている。◆The BOJ's policy meeting plans to consider expanding the list of government bonds purchased under the fund. 日銀の政策決定会合では、基金で買い入れる国債の対象拡大を検討する予定だ。◆The bonds were purchased by a number of institutional investors, including major commercial banks and regional banks. 同社債は、都銀や地銀などの機関投資家が購入した。◆The company purchased indebted Japanese companies. 同社は、赤字の日本企業を買収した。◆The company succeeded in cutting costs by jointly purchasing some of the products with its group firm. 同社は、グループ企業と一部商品の仕入れを共通化して、コスト削減に成功した。◆The European Central Bank has been purchasing Italian government bonds in an effort to support Italy. 欧州中央銀行（ECB）は、イタリア国債を買い入れてイタリアを支えている。◆The foreign funds purchased the convertible bonds at prices equivalent to ¥25 per share. 海外ファンドは、1株25円で転換社債を引き受けた。◆The president of the company expressed an interest in expanding operations by Purchasing domestic supermarkets. 同社社長は、国内スーパーを買収して事業を拡大する考えを明らかにした。◆Toyota will purchase some of General Motors Corp.'s shareholding in Fuji Heavy Industries Ltd. トヨタが、米ゼネラル・モーターズ（GM）が保有している富士重工の株式の一部を取得することになった。

purchase （名）買取り，買付け，買入れ，購入，購入品，購買，調達，調達先，引受け，仕入れ，買収，取得，獲得，パーチェス （⇒stock purchase warrant）
　additional purchase 追加購入，追加取得
　amount of purchase 仕入高
　basket［bulk］purchase 一括購入
　cash purchase 現金購入，現金仕入れ
　corporate purchase 企業買収
　credit purchase 信用買い，掛買い
　direct purchase of bank-held stocks 銀行保有株の直接買取り
　equity purchase 株式取得，株式投資
　hire-purchase 買取り選択権付きリース，買取り権付きリース
　installment purchase 割賦（かっぷ）購入，月賦購入，月賦買い，分割払い購入方式 （=installment buying）
　joint purchase 共同仕入れ，共同購入
　land purchase 土地購入
　lump sum purchase 一括購入，一時購入
　margin purchase 信用買い
　National Association of Purchasing Managers' survey 全米購買部協会景気総合指数
　purchase right 購入権
　purchases 仕入れ高，購入品，買ったもの，購入量，購買量
　redemption by purchase 買入償却
　share purchase 株式取得
　small purchase 小口買付け
　speculative purchase 思惑買い
　stock purchase plan 株式購入精度
　the Bank of Japan's purchases of dollars 日銀のドルの買い支え
◆I don't oppose the Bank of Japan's direct purchase of bank-held stocks. 日銀による銀行保有株の直接買取りに、反対の立場ではない。◆Other options include making a purchase through a holding company and business integration. 他の選択手段として、持ち株会社による買収と事業統合（経営統合）もある。

purchase and assumption system 資産・負債承継方式，P&A方式 （=P&A system, P&A method, Purchase and Assumption system）
◆The United States has introduced a purchase and assumption（P&A）system, which involves a healthy financial institution buying the assets of a collapsed financial institutions and taking over its deposits. アメリカでは、健全な金融機関が破綻した金融機関の資産を買い取り、その預金も承継する「資産・負債承継（P&A）」方式を導入している。

purchase bad assets 不良資産を買い取る
◆Setting the price at which bad assets are purchased poses a dilemma. 不良資産の買取り価格をどう決めるかは、むずかしい問題だ。

purchase financial products 金融商品を購入する
◆Mizuho Bank offers a service by which ATM cardholders are given mileage points each time they use the new cards

as credit cards, purchase financial products at the bank's branches or receive loans from the bank. みずほ銀行が提供しているサービスでは、キャッシュ・カード会員が新型カードをクレジット・カードとして利用したり、みずほ銀行で金融商品を購入したり、ローンを利用したりすると、その取引に応じて毎回、マイレージ・ポイントがもらえる。

purchase government bonds 国債を買う[購入する]、国債を買い入れる
◆The Bank of Japan decided to adopt additional quantitative easing measures in October 2010, setting up a fund to purchase government and corporate bonds. 日銀は、2010年10月に新たな量的緩和策の導入を決め、国債や社債を買い入れる基金を新設した。◆The Bank of Japan purchases government bonds that have one to two years left until maturity. 日銀は、満期までの残存期間が1〜2年の国債を買い入れている。

purchase government bonds and corporate debentures 国債や社債を買う、国債や社債を買い入れる、国債や社債を購入する
◆The BOJ decided to further relax its monetary policy by injecting an additional ￥10 trillion into a fund aimed at purchasing government bonds and corporate debentures. 日銀は、国債や社債などを買い入れるための基金に新たに10兆円を注入[投入]して追加の金融緩和に踏み切ることを決めた。

purchase insurance 保険に加入する、保険に入る (=buy insurance)
newly purchase insurance 保険に新規に加入する
purchase an insurance policy via mobile phone 携帯電話で保険に加入する
◆In December 2011, the insurer will lower the yield rate to 1.1 percent from 1.5 percent for those who newly purchase the company's single-premium whole life insurance. 2011年12月から同生保は、一時払い終身保険の新規加入者[新規契約者]を対象に、利回りを1.5%から1.1%に引き下げる。◆In insurance policies that can be purchased via mobile phone, would-be policyholders do not need to input personal data and payments are easier. 携帯電話で加入できる保険では、加入希望者は個人情報を入力する必要がなく、支払いも簡単だ。◆To offer customers a new way to purchase insurance, non-life insurance companies have begun cooperating with cell phone companies. 顧客に保険加入のための新サービスを提供するため、損害保険各社は、携帯電話会社との提携に乗り出した。

purchase long-term government bonds 長期国債を買い取る、長期国債を買い入れる
◆The Bank of Japan has supplied a large amount of funds to the market by purchasing long-term government bonds and corporate bonds. 日銀は、長期国債や社債の買入れで、大量の資金を市場に提供している。

purchase of foreign bonds 外債の購入
◆The purchase of foreign bonds is considered an effective method to weaken the yen. 外債の購入は、円安誘導効果を持つとされている。

purchase of Japanese stocks 日本株買い
◆Foreign investors stepped up their purchase of Japanese stocks. 外国人投資家の日本株買いが活発化した。

purchase of stock through a takeover bid 株式公開買付け(TOB)による株式買取り
◆The recent stock-swap deal followed a purchase of stock through a takeover bid. 今回の株式交換取引は、株式公開買付け(TOB)による株式買取りに続いて行われた。

purchase price 購入価格、買取り価格、取得価格、仕入れ価格、買入れ価格
◆By raising the purchase prices of bad loans and injecting public funds into banks, the government plans to promote the final disposal of bad loans. 不良債権の買取り価格の引上げと銀行への公的資金の注入により、政府は不良債権の最終処理を促進する方針だ。

purchase prices for bad loans 不良債権の買取り価格
◆An increase in banks' loan loss reserves is a precondition for raising purchase prices for bad loans. 銀行の貸倒れ引当金の強化が、不良債権の買取り価格引上げの前提条件となる。

purchased (形)購入した[購入される]、仕入れた、取得する[取得した]、買収される[買収した]、〜の購入[仕入れ、取得、買収]
purchased fund 取得資金、市場性資金、市場資金
purchased lease residuals リース残存価値の購入
purchased life annuity 買入れ終身年金
purchased options オプションの購入、オプション購入、買いオプション

purchased bad assets 不良資産の買取り
◆If the prices of purchased bad assets are set high, the public burden will balloon. 不良資産の買取り価格を高くすると、国民負担が膨らむ。

purchaser 買い主、買い手、買取り人、購買者、得意先
◆Argentine government bonds have been unable to find purchasers since last summer when the country's economic crisis deepened. アルゼンチン国債は、同国の経済危機が深刻化した昨夏以降、買い手がつかなくなった。

purchasing power 購買力 (=buying power)
purchasing power of savings 貯蓄の購買力
◆The purchasing power of savings is eroded by inflation. 貯蓄の購買力は、インフレで目減りする。

purpose (名)目的、意図、決心、決意
securities held for trading purpose 短期売買目的の証券
the purpose of issuing share warrants 株式予約権発行の目的
◆The former chairman of Daio Paper Corp. allegedly received more than ￥10 billion in loans from the firm's group companies for private purposes. 報道によれば、大王製紙の前会長が、グループ企業から100億円超の私的融資を受けた。◆The purpose of issuing a sizable amount of new shares is to maintain the control of a specific stockholder over the company. 新株の大量発行は、同社に対する特定株主の支配権[経営支配権]確保が目的だ。◆The purpose of issuing share warrants is to maintain the current management's control over the company. 株式予約権の発行は、現経営陣の会社の経営支配権を維持することを目的としている。

purse strings 財布のひも
hold [control] the purse strings 財布のひもを握る、財政上の権限を握る、金銭の出納をつかさどる
loosen the purse strings 財布のひもを緩める、金銭支出を緩める
tighten the purse strings 財布のひもを締める、金銭支出を締める
◆Tightening the purse strings at home leads to sluggish sales of products and, in turn, to falling prices. 家庭の財布のひもを締めると、物が売れなくなって物価が下がる。◆When purse strings are tightened, it hurts the overall economy. 財布のヒモが堅くなると、景気全体に影響が及ぶ。

pursue (動)追求する、追跡する、続行する、実行する、(政策を)打ち出す[とる]
pursue a policy of stimulating recovery 景気浮揚策をとる
pursue economies of scale 規模の経済を追求する、規模の拡大を追求する
◆Mergers and acquisitions to pursue economies of scale will be carried out worldwide. 規模の経済[規模の拡大]を追求するためのM&A(企業の合併・買収)は今後、国際的規模で実施される見込みだ。

push (動)押す、突く、押して動かす、推し進める、(しきりに)促す、(商品を)売り込む、強いて〜させる、圧力をかける、誘導する、(麻薬を)不法に売る (自動)押す、

押し進む, 前進する
　push interest rates higher　金利を高めに誘導する
　push the Bank of Japan to ease monetary policy　金融を緩和するよう日銀に圧力をかける

push down　押し下げる, 下げる, 座らせる
　push down interest rates　金利を引き下げる
　push down the federal funds rate　フェデラル・ファンド金利[短期金利, FF金利]を引き下げる
　◆The Fed pushed down the federal funds rate. 米連邦準備制度理事会(FRB)が, FF金利[フェデラル・ファンド金利]を引き下げた。

push up　増加させる, 高める, 押し上げる
　push up consumer prices　消費者物価を押し上げる
　push up costs　コストを押し上げる
　push up the price　価格を押し上げる
　push up the savings rate　貯蓄率を押し上げる
　◆An increase in the price of natural resources such as crude oil has pushed up costs. 原油など天然資源価格の上昇が, コストを押し上げている。◆The news pushed up yields on short-duration bonds. これを受けて, 短期物の利回りが上昇した。◆The rise of the yen's value pushed up the demand for travel abroad. 円高が, 海外旅行の需要を押し上げた。

put up　(資金を)出す[融通する, 提供する], 出資する, 貸す, 上げる, 増やす
　◆In the joint venture with an Indian investment bank, Tokio Marine Holdings Inc. put up about 26%, the maximum a foreign investor is allowed in an Indian company, of the new firm's capital. インドの投資銀行との合弁事業で, 東京海上ホールディングスは, 新会社の資本金の約26%(外資の持ち分比率の上限)を出資した。

pyramid sales　マルチ商法　(=pyramid selling)
　◆The Metropolitan Police Department plans to search the offices of a firm that conducted pyramid sales of health food products. 警視庁は, 健康食品のマルチ商法を行った会社の事務所の一斉捜索をする方針だ。

pyramid scheme　マルチ商法, ピラミッド型インチキ商法, ネズミ算式の無限連鎖講, ネズミ講
(=pyramid sales, pyramid selling)
　◆In response to the deluge of inquiries regarding such Net pyramid schemes, the National Consumer Affairs Center of Japan decided to disclose the name of the company and to call for caution. 国民生活センターでは, このようなネット版マルチ商法に関する相談件数が殺到していることから, 社名を公表して注意を呼びかけることにした。

Q

Q　四半期 (quarterの略)
　Q1　第1四半期, 第一・四半期
　　(=the first quarter)
　Q2　第2四半期, 第二・四半期
　　(=the second quarter)

QE　量的緩和, 量的緩和策, 量的金融緩和, 金融緩和策
(quantitative easingの略)
　QE1　量的緩和策の第一弾, 量的金融緩和の第一弾, 量的緩和第一弾　(=the first round of quantitative easing [measures, policy, steps])
　QE2　量的緩和策の第二弾, 追加金融緩和, 金融の追加緩和, 追加の金融緩和策
　QE3　量的緩和策の第三弾, 量的緩和の第三弾, 量的緩和第三弾
　◆Financial markets worldwide are focused on whether the U.S. FRB embarks on a third round of its quantitative easing policy, or QE3. 世界の金融市場は, 米連邦準備制度理事会(FRB)が量的緩和策の第三弾(QE3)に踏み切るかどうかに注目している。◆The Fed does not have confidence in the effect of QE2. 米連邦準備制度理事会(FRB)は, 量的緩和第二弾(QE2)の効果に自信が持てないでいる。◆The Fed has taken quantitative easing measures twice, or QE1 between December 2008 and March 2010, and QE2 between November 2010 and June 2011, to cope with the financial crisis and deflationary pressure. 金融危機やデフレ圧力に対応するため, 米連邦準備制度理事会(FRB)は, これまでに量的金融緩和を2回(2008年12月～2010年3月の量的緩和第一弾(QE1)と2010年11月～2011年6月の量的緩和第二弾(QE2))実施している。

quadrillion　(名)1,000兆, 千兆
　◆M3 was up 0.6 percent to ¥1.031 quadrillion in October from a year earlier. 10月のマネー・サプライM3は, 前年同月比0.6%増の1,031兆円となった。◆The size of the financial assets of Japanese households is still worth a massive ¥1.47 quadrillion despite a decrease in the total over recent years. 日本の個人金融資産の規模は, ここ数年で減少したものの, まだ1,470兆円ほどもあって巨大だ。◆The 10 life insurers' combined outstanding balance of individual life insurance and annuity contracts declined for five consecutive years to ¥1.15 quadrillion. 生保10社合計の個人保険・年金の保有契約高(保険の総額)は1,150兆円で, 5年連続(5期連続)で減少した。◆The U.S. federal debt has reached its current statutory limit of $14.3 trillion (about1.1 quadrillion). 米政府の債務は, 現在の法定上限の14.3兆ドル(約1,100兆円)に達している。

quadruple　(動)4倍にする, 4倍になる
　◆Sharp Corp. will spend an additional ¥200 billion to quadruple the production capacity of its liquid crystal display panel factory in Kameyama. シャープは, 2,000億円追加投資して, 液晶パネル[液晶ディスプレー・パネル]亀山工場(三重県亀山市)の生産能力を4倍に拡大する。

quagmire　(名)泥沼, 沼地, 湿地, (抜け出せない)苦境, 窮地
　a financial quagmire　財政難
　a political quagmire　政治的苦境, 政治的泥沼, 政治的難局
　a quagmire of debts [financial quagmire]　(抜け出せない)借金の泥沼
　◆Stuck in a financial quagmire, Russia is having difficulty in managing its nuclear arsenal. 財政難から, ロシアは現在, 保有する核兵器の管理に苦慮している。

qualified　(形)限定付き, 条件付きの, 適格の, 有資格の
　qualified acceptance　手形の条件引受け, 制限引受け
　qualified bond　適格債券
　qualified indorsement　無担保裏書き
　qualified institutional buyer　適格機関投資家
　qualified institutional investor　適格機関投資家
　qualified pension plan　適格年金制度, 適格退職年金
　qualified plan　適格退職年金
　　(=qualified pension plan)
　qualified security　適格証券
　qualified stock option　条件付きストック・オプション
　qualified student loan bond　適格学生ローン債券
　qualified thrift lender test　適格貯蓄金融機関貸し手テスト
　tax qualified pension plan　適格退職年金

qualify　(動)資格[権利, 技能]を与える, 適任[適格]にする, 制限する, 限定する, 修正する, 訂正する, 見なす, 批評する　(自動)資格[免許]を取る, 資格がある, 資格[権利]を持つ, 適任である, (競技で)予選を通過する, 出場権を得る
　◆Just as the number of people qualifying for pensions is on the rise, the working population, which underpins the pension scheme, is on the decline. 年金受給の資格者は増える一方, 年金制度を支える現役世代は減っている。◆The pension

system may collapse before people qualify as beneficiaries. 年金をもらう前に、年金制度が崩壊する可能性がある。
qualifying （形）適格の,資格を与える,資格取得の,該当する
  qualifying capital interest　適格資本持ち分
  qualifying conditions　年金受給資格
  qualifying corporate bond　適格社債
  qualifying dividend　適格配当
  qualifying lender　適格融資者
  qualifying special purpose entity　適格特別目的事業体,QSPE
  qualifying stock option　自社株購入権
  qualifying subordinated debt　適格劣後債
qualitative （形）質的な,定性的な
  qualitative analysis　定性分析（計量化できない質的要素の分析）,質的調査,定性的評価
  qualitative credit control　金融の質的規制,質的信用規制
  qualitative economic policy　質的経済政策
  qualitative financial policy　質的金融政策
  qualitative monetary policy　質的通貨政策
quality （名）質,品質,品位,特質,特性,良質,優良,高級,内容,優良品,クオリティ
  asset credit quality　資産の信用度
  asset quality　資産内容,資産の質
    （=quality of assets）
  company [corporate] credit quality　企業の信用の質
  credit quality　信用の質,信用度,信用力
    （=quality of credit）
  debt quality　債券の質,債券の信用力
  decline in credit quality　信用の質の悪化
  flight to quality buying　質への逃避による買い,信用への逃避
  flight to quality in bond and currency markets　債券・為替市場での質への逃避［質への逃避の動き］
  good quality demand　一流機関投資家からの需要
  good quality name　優良銘柄
  investment-grade quality　投資適格
  loan quality　貸出金の質
  lower-quality credits　格付けの低い借り手
  obligor credit quality　債務者の信用度
  quality of earnings　利益の質,収益の質,収益内容
  quality of mortgage insurance　モーゲージ保険の質
  quality of the assets pledged　担保提供された資産の質
  quality stock　優良株,優良銘柄
  safe haven quality　質への逃避先
  service quality　サービスの質
  top quality issuers　最優良銘柄,超優良銘柄,超優良発行体
◆The bank's planned acquisition of a controlling stake in Nippon Shinpan Co. will only have a limited impact on the credit quality of the bank. 同行が日本信販の支配持ち分（発行済み株式の50%超）の取得を計画しているが、これによる同行の信用力への影響はごく限られるものと思われる。
quality name　優良銘柄　（=quality stock）
  good quality name　優良銘柄
  lesser quality name　信用力が低い［劣る］銘柄
  top quality name　超優良銘柄,最優良銘柄
quantitative （形）量の,数量の,量的な,定量的な
  financial quantitative regulation　金融の量的規制
  quantitative boom　数量景気
  quantitative credit control　金融の量的規制,量的信用規制
  quantitative economic policy　量的経済政策
  quantitative monetary policy　量的貨幣政策
  the Fed's new round of quantitative easing　米連邦準備制度理事会（FRB）の追加の量的緩和
quantitative easing　量的緩和,量的緩和策,量的金融緩和,金融緩和策,QE　（⇒QE）
◆Part of the benefits of quantitative easing will take the form of a depreciation of the dollar. 量的緩和の効果の一部は、ドル安の形で現れる。◆The Bank of Japan's resorting to quantitative easing in concert with the Fed would have a greater impact on in buoying the global economy. 米連邦準備制度理事会（FRB）と歩調を合わせて日銀が量的緩和に踏み切れば、世界景気の浮揚効果は拡大すると思われる。◆The Fed's policy of quantitative easing foments chaos in foreign exchange markets. 米連邦準備制度理事会（FRB）［米国の中央銀行］の量的緩和政策は、為替相場［為替レート］の変動を招いている。◆To keep their currencies from appreciating in the wake of the Fed's new round of quantitative easing, countries grappling with deflation should ease their own monetary stances. 米連邦準備制度理事会（FRB）の追加の量的緩和による通貨高を避けるには、デフレに取り組んでいる国は、自らも量的緩和をすればよい。
quantitative easing framework　量的金融緩和体制,量的金融緩和策
◆The Bank of Japan will maintain its quantitative easing framework until the year-on-year changes in CPI stabilize at zero or above. 日本銀行は、消費者物価指数（CPI）の変動が前年度比で安定的にゼロ以上になるまで、量的金融緩和策を継続する方針だ。
quantitative easing measures　量的緩和策
◆Quantitative easing measures are believed to have been proven effective in stabilizing financial markets. 量的緩和政策は金融市場の安定化に効果的だった、とされている。◆Some economists point out that the limited effects of the quantitative easing measures. 一部のエコノミストは、量的緩和策の効果の限界を指摘している。◆The Fed has taken quantitative easing measures twice, or QE1 between December 2008 and March 2010, and QE2 between November 2010 and June 2011, to cope with the financial crisis and deflationary pressure. 金融危機やデフレ圧力に対応するため、米連邦準備制度理事会（FRB）は、これまでに量的金融緩和を2回（2008年12月～2010年3月の量的緩和第一弾（QE1）と2010年11月～2011年6月の量的緩和第二弾（QE2））実施している。
quantitative easing policy　金融の量的緩和,金融の量的緩和策　（=policy of quantitative easing, quantitative easing）
◆Financial markets worldwide are focused on whether the U.S. FRB embarks on a third round of its quantitative easing policy, or QE3. 世界の金融市場は、米連邦準備制度理事会（FRB）が量的緩和政策の第三弾（QE3）に踏み切るかどうかに注目している。◆The Bank of Japan is unlikely to change its quantitative easing policy this year. 日銀が今年度中に量的緩和政策を変えるようなことは、ないだろう。◆The central bank's quantitative easing policy is also at a critical sink-or-swim juncture. 日銀の量的緩和策も、今は剣が峰［伸(の)るか反るかの重大局面］に立たされている。◆There are mixed views as to the effect of the quantitative easing policy even within the Fed. 量的緩和策の効果については、FRB（米連邦準備制度理事会）内でも意見が割れている。
quantitative easing steps　金融の量的緩和策,量的緩和策
◆The U.S. Federal Reserve Board has taken quantitative easing steps twice to cope with the financial crisis and deflationary pressure. 米連邦準備制度理事会（FRB）は、金融危機とデフレ圧力［デフレ懸念］に対応するため、これまでに量的金融緩和を2回行った。

quantitative monetary easing　金融の量的緩和, 量的金融緩和
　（=quantitative easing; ⇒nominal growth rate）
　◆Quantitative monetary easing helps alleviate the upward pressure on interest rates caused by increasing public spending and also promotes the depreciation of the yen. 量的金融緩和は、財政出動による金利上昇圧力を抑え、円安を促す効果もある。◆The Bank of Japan decided to take new steps for further quantitative monetary easing at an extraordinary Policy Board meeting. 日銀は、臨時の金融政策決定会合で、追加の量的金融緩和策を新たに実施することを決めた。

quantitative monetary easing policy　量的緩和政策, 量的金融緩和政策　（=quantitative easing policy）
　◆In March 2006, the Bank of Japan ended its quantitative monetary easing policy. 2006年3月に、日本銀行は金融の量的緩和政策を解除した。◆Speculation the Bank of Japan will end its quantitative monetary easing policy soon has sparked a rise in mid- and long-term interest rates. 日銀が近く量的緩和策を解除するとの思惑から、（金融市場では）中長期の金利が上昇し始めた。◆To shake off deflation, the Bank of Japan is urged to take a further quantitative monetary easing policy. デフレ脱却に向けて、日銀は、もう一段の金融の量的緩和に踏み切らなければならない。

quantitative monetary relaxation　量的金融緩和
　◆As joint actions, major industrial nations have taken such measures as further interest rate reductions, quantitative monetary relaxation to increase the money supply, the injection of public funds and increased public spending. 協調行動として、主要先進諸国は、さらなる金利の引下げ、通貨供給量を増やすための量的金融緩和や公的資金の注入、財政出動［公共支出の拡大］などの措置を取った。

quantitative relaxation　量的緩和, 量的緩和策
　◆The Bank of Japan must consider additional measures, including the expansion of its quantitative relaxation. 量的緩和策の拡充を含めて、日銀は追加策を検討する必要がある。

quantitative relaxation of credit　量的金融緩和, 量的金融緩和策
　◆Debates on the pros and cons of a proposal to end the quantitative relaxation of credit by the Bank of Japan are gathering momentum. 日銀による量的金融緩和策を解除する案の賛否をめぐる議論が、活発化している。

quarter　（名）四半期（1年の4分の1、つまり3か月を指す。暦年の第1四半期は、1月1日から3月31日までの3か月のこと）
　fiscal quarter　会計四半期
　for the quarter　当四半期の, 当四半期は
　for the third quarter running　3四半期連続で
　for two consecutive quarters　2四半期連続して, 2四半期連続
　from the previous quarter　前四半期期比で,（四半期ベースでの）前期比
　over the previous quarter　前四半期に対して, 前四半期比で
　over the quarter　前四半期で
　quarter-end close　四半期末終値
　quarter on quarter［quarter-on-quarter］　前四半期比で（=from the previous quarter）
　quarter over quarter　（四半期ベースでの）前期比（=compared with the previous year, from the previous quarter）
　quarter-point adjustment　0.25%の調整（⇒mark動詞）
　the April-June quarter　4-6月期（日本の3月期決算企業の第1四半期にあたる）
　the first quarter　第一・四半期, 第1四半期, Q1
　the fourth quarter　第四・四半期, 第4四半期, Q4（=the last quarter）
　the last quarter　第4四半期, 前期
　the second quartet　第二・四半期, 第2四半期, Q2
　the third quarter　第三・四半期, 第3四半期, Q3
　◆Gross domestic product has contracted compared with the previous period in two consecutive quarters—April to June and July to September. 国内総生産（GDP）は、4-6月、7-9月の2期連続して前期比マイナスになった。◆In the April-June quarter, all major airlines fell into the red. 4-6月期は、大手航空各社が軒並み赤字に陥った［赤字に転落した］。◆Nomura Holdings' net income of ￥2.3 billion for the three months ended June 30 was the lowest in five quarters. 野村ホールディングスの4～6月期の税引き後利益23億円は、5四半期で最低となった。◆Sales of the overseas subsidiaries of Japanese companies grew 17.3 percent in U.S. dollar terms in the January-March quarter from a year earlier. 1-3月期の日本企業の海外子会社の売上高が、米ドル・ベースで前年同期比17.3%伸びた。◆The bank's bad loan charges amounted to ￥322.5 billion for the April-June quarter. 同行の4-6月期（第一・四半期）の不良債権額は、3,225億円となった。◆The diffusion index of business sentiment among large manufacturers recovered to positive territory for the first time in two quarters. 大企業・製造業の業況判断指数（DI）は、2四半期［半年］ぶりにプラスに転じた。◆The number of surplus workers approached a peak of 3.59 million in the January-March quarter of 1999, following a spate of failures at major financial institutions. 過剰雇用者数は、大手金融機関の破たんが相次いだ後の1999年1-3月期に、359万人のピークに達した。◆This is the fourth straight quarter that the economy has shown growth. これで、4四半期連続のプラス成長となった。◆Two consecutive quarters of negative growth are defined as a technical recession. 2四半期連続のマイナス成長は、「テクニカル・リセッション」と定義されている。

quarter-point rate hike　0.25%の利上げ
　◆The quarter-point rate hike had been widely expected. 今回の0.25%の利上げは、広く予想されていた。

quarterly　（形）四半期の, 四半期ベースの, 四半期別, 四半期ごとの, 年4回の, 前期比　（副）年4回, 四半期ごとに, 四半期に1回, 3か月ごとに, 3か月に1回, 毎季に
　quarterly accounts　四半期決算報告書
　quarterly consolidated business results　四半期連結決算（=quarterly consolidated settlement of accounts）
　quarterly financial data　四半期財務情報
　quarterly financial information　四半期財務情報
　quarterly financial reporting　四半期財務報告
　quarterly financial statements　四半期財務諸表, 四半期財務書類
　quarterly group net profit　四半期連結純利益, 四半期連結税引き後利益
　quarterly income statements　四半期損益計算書
　quarterly increase　四半期の伸び率, 前期比伸び率
　quarterly information（unaudited）　四半期情報（未監査）
　quarterly operating profit　四半期営業利益
　quarterly release system　四半期開示制度
　quarterly reporting of interim earnings　四半期報告
　quarterly results　四半期業績, 四半期決算（=quarterly business results, quarterly settlement of accounts）
　quarterly settlement　四半期決算
　quarterly statement　四半期報告書（=quarterly report）
　quarterly statement of earnings　四半期報告, 四半期報告書
　◆The seasonally adjusted real GDP rose 0.9 percent in July-

September from the previous quarter and marked the fourth consecutive quarterly increase. 7-9月期の実質国内総生産(季節調整値)は、前期比0.9%増で、4四半期連続のプラスだった。

quarterly basis　四半期ベース
◆Starting next April, the bank will raise about ¥150 billion by issuing straight bonds on a quarterly basis for an annual total of ¥600 billion. 来年4月から、同行は、四半期ベースで普通社債を発行して約1,500億円、年間で総額6,000億円を調達する。

quarterly consolidated business results　四半期連結決算　(=quarterly consolidated settlement of accounts)
◆Quarterly consolidated business results unveiled recently by the country's leading electronics manufacturers show that Matsushita Electric Industrial Co. and Fujitsu Ltd. posted operating losses during the April-June period. 日本の大手電機メーカーが最近発表した連結決算によると、4-6月期は松下電器産業と富士通が営業損失を計上した。

quarterly dividend　四半期配当
(⇒regular quarterly dividend)
◆Quarterly dividends may be reinvested automatically to purchase additional common shares at a discount from the average market price. 四半期配当金は、自動的に再投資して、平均市場価格から割り引いた価格で当社の普通株式を追加購入することができます。

quarterly earnings　四半期利益,四半期決算
quarterly earnings report　四半期決算,四半期決算報告,四半期報告
quarterly earnings statement　四半期決算,四半期報告書
(=quarterly statement of earnings)

quarterly growth　四半期の伸び,四半期の伸び率,四半期の成長[成長率]
◆The latest GDP figures marked the fifth consecutive quarterly growth in the domestic economy. GDP速報値によると、国内経済は5四半期連続のプラス成長となった。

quarterly loss　四半期損失,四半期の損失
◆General Motors Co. has reported a smaller quarterly loss. ゼネラル・モーターズ(GM)は、四半期の損失が縮小したことを発表した。

quarterly net loss　四半期純損失,四半期税引き後損失,税引き後四半期赤字
◆The bank posted a quarterly net loss of ¥91 billion as costs to clean up its bad loans mounted. 同行は、不良債権処理費用が増加したため、税引き後で910億円の四半期赤字となった。
◆The company's quarterly net loss shrank by more than 60 percent to ¥21.65 billion. 同社の四半期純損失は、60%以上縮小して216億5,000万円となった。

quarterly net profit　四半期純利益,四半期税引き後利益,税引き後四半期黒字
◆Citigroup's quarterly net profit will be significantly lower than the same period a year earlier. 米大手銀行シティグループの四半期純利益は、前年同期を大幅に下回る見込みだ。

quarterly performance　四半期業績
◆This improved quarterly performance was due mainly to the company's contribution. 当四半期の業績改善は、主に同社の貢献によるものです。

quarterly profit　四半期利益
(⇒period ending Aug. 31)
◆The firm reported a 30 percent decline in quarterly profit from a year ago. 同社の四半期利益は、前年同期比で30%減少した。

quarterly report　四半期報告書,四季報
(⇒annual report)
解説 四半期報告書とは：四半期ごとの企業の決算報告書で、米国の場合はSEC(米証券取引委員会)への提出が義務付けられている。提出期限は米国企業の場合、各四半期以降35日以内(2002年7月に成立した企業改革法(サーベンス・オクスレー法:Sarbanes-Oxley Act)に基づくSECの措置として、従来の45日以内が35日に短縮された)で、報告書の様式はForm 10-Q(様式10-Q)となっている。ただし、第4四半期については提出義務がなく、提出する場合には記載する財務書類(財務諸表:financial statements)は要約版でよく、一般に財務書類注記(notes to financial statements)も省略できる。また、この要約財務書類(summarized financial statements)は監査(audit, auditing)を受ける必要がなく、未監査(unaudited)の状態で提出することができ、年次報告書と違って株主への四半期ごとの財務情報(quarterly financial information)の通知は義務付けられていない。

quarterly results　四半期業績,四半期決算
(=quarterly business results, quarterly settlement of accounts)
◆Toyota began announcing its quarterly results in fiscal 2002. トヨタは、2002年度から四半期決算[業績]を発表している。

quasi-　(形)準〜,半〜,疑似〜,類似の
quasi-boom　準好景気,半好況
quasi-debt obligations　準債務
quasi-depression　準不況,半不況
quasi-equilibrium　疑似均衡
quasi-equity　準資本金
quasi-fixed exchange rate system　準固定為替相場制
quasi-governmental body　半政府機関,準政府機関
quasi-incompetent　準禁治産者
quasi-loan　準借入れ
quasi-long period equilibrium　準長期均衡
quasi-public corporation　政府系機関
quasi-recession　準景気後退
quasi-reorganization approach　準更生手続き

quasi-loan sharking　疑似ヤミ金
◆Cashing services can be called quasi-loan sharking as the use of them results in high interest payments. 現金化サービスは、利用すると結果的に金利の支払いが高くなる[高金利になる]ので、疑似ヤミ金と言える。

quasi-money　準通貨
◆Quasi-money refers to time deposits and other types of savings at banks that cannot be immediately cashed, including foreign currency deposits and nonresidents' yen deposits. 準通貨とは、定期性預金のほかに、外貨預金や非居住者の円預金など即時に換金できない[現金に換えられない]銀行預金のことをいう。

Queer Street　経済的困難

quell　(動)抑える,静める,和らげる,なだめる,鎮圧する
quell inflation　インフレを抑える[抑制する],インフレを防ぐ
◆China will ratchet up efforts to quell inflation in 2011. 中国は、2011年からインフレ抑制策を徐々に強化する方針だ。◆The U.S. Federal Reserve raised the official discount rate and the target rate of federal funds by 0.25 percentage points in a bid to quell inflation and keep the economy from overheating. 米連邦準備制度理事会(FRB)は、インフレを防ぎ景気の過熱を警戒して、公定歩合とフェデラル・ファンド(FF)の誘導目標金利をそれぞれ0.25パーセント引き上げた。

questionable　(形)疑わしい,怪しい,いかがわしい,信用のおけない,不審な,疑問の余地がある,問題のある,不確かな
financing devices of questionable legality　法的根拠に問題のある財務手段
questionable sales of gold bars　金の延べ棒のいかがわしい商法
◆It is questionable whether the Italian new government will be able to steadily implement measures for financial recon-

struction and structural reforms. イタリアの新政権が財政再建策と構造改革を着実に実行できるかどうかは、疑問だ。

quick-fix (形)即効の, 即効性のある, 反応が早い, 緊急の, 応急の, 一時しのぎの, 安易な
quick-fix fiscal measures 一時しのぎの財政出動, 安易な財政出動
quick-fix program 即効性のある計画, 緊急の計画
quick-fix remedies 応急対策
◆The government should not resort to quick-fix fiscal measures. 政府は, 安易な財政出動は避けるべきだ。

quorum (名)定足数, 定数
a quorum for the meeting of shareholders 株主総会の定足数
achieve a quorum 定足数を満たす, 員数を揃える
constitute a quorum to do business 議事を行うための定足数となる[定足数に達する]
fail to meet the quorum required for ～に必要な定足数を欠く
lack of a quorum 定足数不足
reduce the quorum of directors 取締役の定数を削減する
◆Many of listed companies are set to adopt measures to counter corporate acquirers, such as increasing their authorized capital or reducing the quorum of directors. 授権資本（株式発行可能枠）の拡大や取締役の定数削減など, 買収防衛策を導入する上場企業も多い。

quotation (名)相場, 相場表, 時価, 建値(たてね), 提示価格, 見積り, 見積り価格, 見積り額, 価格見積り書, 上場, 引用
application for quotation 上場申請
asked quotation 売り呼び値, 呼び値相場
bid and asked quotations 買い呼び値と売り呼び値, 呼び値と付け値
bid quotation 買い呼び値, 付け値相場
black market quotation ヤミ相場
bond price quotation 債券の建値
bullion quotation 地金相場
buying quotation （為替の）買い相場
closing quotation 引け, 引け値, 大引け相場[値段]
competitive [multiple] quotations 相見積り
current quotation 時価, 現行相場
direct quotation 自国通貨建て, 自国通貨による為替相場表示
exchange of quotation 気配交換
exchange quotation 為替相場, 対顧客公示相場, 外国為替相場, 外国為替相場表(exchange quotations)
export quotation 輸出相場
firmness of quotation 確実な呼び値
flat quotation 裸相場
FOB quotation FOB建て見積り
forced quotation 人為相場
foreign trade price quotation 外国貿易相場表
forward quotation 先物相場, 先渡し相場
futures quotation 先物相場
giving quotation 売り為替相場, 支払い勘定建て相場
gold bullion quotation 金塊相場
gray market quotation 黙認相場
higher in (a) quotation 上ざや
indicative interest quotations 気配値
indirect quotation 他国通貨建て, 他国通貨による為替相場表示
last quotation 引け
lower in (a) quotation 下ざや

lowest quotation 底値, 最低価格[値段]
market quotation 市場相場, 市場呼び値, 相場表
nominal quotation 名目相場, 名目気配
open market quotations 通り相場, 市中相場
opening quotation 寄り付き相場
over-the-counter [OTC] bond quotation exchange system 公社債店頭気配発表制度
over-the-counter [OTC] standard bond quotations 公社債店頭基準気配
parity quotation 平価相場
price quotation 自国通貨建て, 時価, 相場, 建値, 見積り, 相場表
public quotation 公定相場
quantity quotation 数量建て相場
quotation after the close 引け後(あと)気配
quotation board 相場告知板
Quotation Committee of the London Stock Exchange ロンドン証券取引所上場株式審査委員会
Quotation Exchange Center （相場の）気配交換センター
quotation information 相場情報
quotation machine 相場表示機
quotations advance [rise] 相場が上がる
quotations are given 相場が立つ
quotations decline [fall] 相場が下がる
receive a quotation 相場の提示を受ける
receiving [receiver] quotation 受取勘定建て相場, 受取相場
revived quotation 吹き値
rising quotation 上げ相場, 上向き相場
selling quotation （為替の）売り相場
share quotation 株価, 株式相場
(=stock quotation)
Special Quotation 特別清算指数, SQ
split quotation 小刻み相場, 分割相場
spot quotation 直物相場
stock exchange quotation 株式相場, 株式市況
stock market quotation 株式相場
stock quotation 株価, 株式相場
table of (foreign) exchange quotation 為替相場表
two-way quotation 二重相場
volume quotation 外貨建て建値
yen quotation 円相場

quote (動)見積もる, 値段・相場をいう, 値を付ける, 値付けをする, 取引される, 価格を提示する, 気配値を提示する, 上場する
be quoted at ～の値を付ける, ～で取引される
be quoted in absolute terms 絶対値で表示される
be quoted in terms of swap spreads over benchmark interest rates 指標金利とのスワップ・スプレッドを呼び値とする
quote a commodity at 商品に～の値を付ける
quote fees for ～の料金を見積もる
quote swaps in terms of interest rates 金利ベースでスワップの取引価格を設定する
quote the best price 最低価格で見積もる
quote two-way prices 売り買い両方向の取引価格[気配値]を提示する
◆At 5 p.m., the dollar was quoted at ￥124.71-74 in New York. 午後5時, ニューヨークの外国為替市場では, ドル相場が1ドル＝124円71-74銭の値を付けた。 ◆At 5 p.m., the euro was quoted at $1.1712-1715 and ￥126.54-58 against Tues-

day's 5 p.m. quotes of $1.1665-1675 and ￥126.30-40 in New York. 午後5時、ニューヨークの外国為替市場では、ユーロ相場が火曜日（前日）午後5時の1ユーロ＝1.1665-1675ドルと126.30-40円に対して、1ユーロ＝1.1712-1715ドルと126.54-58円の値を付けた。◆The rate of exchange to U.S. dollars shall be based upon the rate of exchange quoted by the Bank on the day of payment. 米ドルへの為替相場は、支払い日の銀行の為替相場によるものとする。

quote　（名）見積り、値付け、相場、建て値、気配値、呼び値、引用
　be quoted on the current indicative market quote　時価に基づく
　best quote　最低価格の見積り
　　（=best price quote, lowest quote）
　bond quote　債券相場、債券価格　（=bond price）
　calculate LIBOR component from quotes provided by group of reference banks　（相場の気配値を提供する）レファレンス・バンクが提示するレートを基準にLIBOR（ロンドン銀行間取引金利）を決定する
　closing quote　終値（おわりね）
　direct quotes　直接呼び値
　give the quote　（ディーラーが）呼び値を出す
　indirect quotes　間接呼び値
　mandatory quote period　値付け義務時間
　opening quote　始値（はじめね）
　price quote　見積り　（=quote）
　quote in dollars　ドル建て
　quote request　（価格の）引合い
　quotes　気配
　render a quote　気配値を示す
　stock quote　株価　（=stock price）
　the current indicative market quote　時価
　the highest quote　最高値
　◆At 5 p.m., the dollar traded at ￥85.52-￥85.53, compared with Tuesday's 5 p.m. quotes of ￥85.98-￥86 in Tokyo. 東京の外国為替市場では、午後5時の時点で、ドル相場は火曜日［前日］午後5時の1ドル＝85円98〜86銭に対して、1ドル＝85円52〜53銭で取引された。◆The euro traded $1.5763-5766 against late Friday's quotes of $1.5670-5680 in New York. ユーロは、ニューヨークの外国為替市場では、前週末（午後5時）の相場1ユーロ＝1.5670〜5680ドルに対して、1ユーロ＝1.5763〜5766ドルで取引された。◆The U.S. dollar's highest quote for the day in Tokyo was ￥83.05. 東京外為市場で、この日のドルの最高値は1ドル＝83円5銭だった。

quote driven　呼び値主導の、呼び値主導型の、気配値主導の

quoted　（形）値の付いた、相場の付いた、（相場、時価、値段が）見積もられた、取引される、上場した
　publicly quoted company　上場企業
　quoted bank　上場銀行
　quoted company　上場会社、上場企業
　　（=listed company, publicly quoted company）
　quoted investment　上場有価証券、上場銘柄
　　（=listed investment）
　quoted market price　時価、市場［市場の］相場
　　（⇒fair value）
　quoted market value　市場価格
　quoted price　相場、市場相場価格、最新取引価格
　quoted share［stock］　上場株、上場銘柄
　quoted value　時価
　quoted value of all listed stocks　全上場銘柄時価総額
　◆The fair values of the Company's financial instruments have been determined based on quoted market prices and market interest rates, as of December 31, 2008. 当社の金融手段の公正価格は、2008年12月31日現在の市場の相場と市中金利に基づいて決定されています。

qursh　（名）クルシュ（サウジアラビアの貨幣単位）

R

racketeer　（名）ゆすり、ゆすり屋、恐喝者、脅迫者、てき屋、詐、暴力団員、詐欺師、ペテン師
　corporate racketeer　総会屋
　　（=corporate blackmailer, corporate extortionist）
　Racketeer-Influenced and Corrupt Organizations Statute　（米国の）組織犯罪規制法、RICO
　Racketeers Influence and Corrupt Organizations Act　集団暴力腐敗組織法、強請と腐敗組織に関する法律
　◆The company's three board members were arrested on suspicion of paying off corporate racketeers known as "sokaiya." 同社の役員3人が、「総会屋」と呼ばれる企業ゆすりに金を支払った容疑で逮捕された。

raid　（名）急襲、奇襲、襲撃、侵入、不法侵入、強盗、（警察の）強制捜査、手入れ、踏み込み、強行［武力］突入、（株式の）売り崩し［買い崩し］、売り浴びせ、（競争相手からの）引き抜き工作、（会社の）乗っ取り行為
　a bear raid　売り崩し
　a raid on one's residence　〜の家宅捜索、〜の手入れ
　carry out a raid on the bank　銀行強盗をする

raider　（名）乗っ取り屋、企業買収家、買占め屋
　corporate raider　企業買収家、乗っ取り屋
　raider alert　乗っ取り警報（敵対的買収の動きを事前に見極めるため、会社の株式の市場での取引状況をモニターすること）
　◆The bank had shades of a corporate raider. 同行は、企業乗っ取りまがいの行為をしていた。◆The would-be acquirer is trying to greenmail the target company by having it pay a premium to buy back the shares held by the raider. 買収側［買収希望者］は、この買占め屋［会社乗っ取り屋］が保有する株を標的企業に高値で引き取らせて、標的企業から収益を上げようとしている［標的企業に高値で引き取らせることにより、標的企業にグリーンメールを仕掛けようとしている］。

raise　（動）資金などを調達する［徴収する、集める］、（料金・価格・資金などを）引き上げる、上げる、高める、押し上げる、上方修正する、増やす、増強する、（手形を）振り出す、（預金を）獲得する、（定年などを）延長する
　amount raised　調達額
　raise a bill　手形を振り出す
　raise asset values　資産価値を押し上げる
　raise cash　現金を調達する、資金を調達する
　raise cash through a private placement　第三者割当てで資金を調達する
　raise credit　資金を調達する
　raise deposits　預金を獲得する
　raise earnings substantially　収益を大幅に増やす
　raise equity　増資する、自己資本を調達する、資本を調達する
　raise external funds　外部資金を調達する
　　（=raise capital, raise money）
　raise finance　資金を調達する
　raise interest cover［coverage］　金利負担能力（インタレスト・カバレッジ）を高める
　raise one's operating performance　〜の業績を向上させる
　raise one's stake in　〜の持ち株比率を引き上げる、〜の出資比率を引き上げる
　raise prices　価格を引き上げる、値上げする
　raise profits　収益を確保する

raise the asked price　売り呼び値を上げる
raise the repayment cost　返済負担を重くする
raise the retiring age　定年を延長する
raise the U.S. debt limit　米政府の債務の法定上限［法定債務上限］を引き上げる
raise the yuan's exchange rate　人民元の為替相場を切り上げる
raise tier-one capital　ティア1［Tier 1］自己資本を調達する
raised check　変造小切手
raised costs　コスト高, コスト上昇
raised note　変造手形

◆An increase in banks' loan loss reserves is a precondition for raising purchase prices for bad loans. 銀行の貸倒れ引当金の強化が, 不良債権の買取り価格引上げの前提条件となる。◆By selling JT shares, the government expects to raise ¥500 billion to ¥600 billion to finance reconstruction from the Great East Japan Earthquake. JT（日本たばこ産業）株の売却で政府は, 東日本大震災復興の財源に充てるため, 5,000億円〜6,000億円の資金調達を見込んでいる。◆Concerns have been raised over the ability of Internet banking services to verify the identity of new depositors or to guarantee the security of customer transactions. インターネット・バンキングについては, 新規預金者の身元確認や対顧客取引の安全保証の点で, その能力に対して懸念が提起されている。◆In order to assist auto parts makers hit by the March 11 earthquake and tsunami, the Development Bank of Japan will raise ¥50 billion to establish a fund. 東日本大震災で被災した自動車部品メーカーを支援するため, 日本政策投資銀行が, 500億円を調達してファンドを設立する。◆In order to forestall hostile takeover bids, companies should raise their corporate value. 敵対的TOB（株式公開買付けによる企業買収）を未然に防ぐには, 企業が企業価値を高めなければならない。◆Nippon Life Insurance Co. plans to raise ¥50 billion for acquisitions and to strengthen its capital base. 日本生命保険は, 買収資金として500億円を調達して, 同社の資本基盤も強化する方針だ。◆Softbank will raise ¥1.28 trillion in the form of syndicated loans from seven financial institutions in Japan, Europe and the United States. ソフトバンクは, 国内外の7金融機関から協調融資の形で1兆2,800億円を調達する方針だ。◆The current official discount rate of 0.1 percent per annum is expected to be raised to between 0.35 percent and 0.5 percent. 年0.1％の現行の公定歩合は, 0.35〜0.5％程度に引き上げられる見通しだ。◆The decline in yields on whole life insurance products effectively raises premiums. 終身保険商品の利回り（予定利率）の引下げは, 実質的な保険料の値上げになる。◆The higher the level of stock prices, the more funds firms can raise from IPOs. 株価の水準が上がれば, それだけ新規株式公開（上場時の新株発行）による資金調達額も増える。◆The increased ownership will raise the bank's risk exposure to the company, whose business environment is severe. 持ち株比率の引上げで, 企業環境［経営環境］が厳しい同社に対する同行のリスク・エクスポージャーは今後увеличится思われる。◆The massive gains in stockholdings' latent value will raise the banks' net worth ratios markedly. 保有株式の含み益の大幅増加で, 銀行の自己資本比率も大きく向上する見込みだ。◆The ongoing business slump raises the specter of a global downturn comparable to the Great Depression that started in 1929. 今回の不況は, 1929年に始まった世界大恐慌に匹敵するほどの世界同時不況の懸念が高まっている。◆The second-largest U.S. investment bank plans to raise $3 billion of capital. この米業界2位の投資銀行が, 30億ドルの増資を計画している。◆The struggling firm Ltd. will raise ¥4.5 billion via third-party allotment. 経営再建中の同社は, 第三者割当て（第三者割当て増資）で45億円を調達する。

raise additional capital　追加資本を調達する

◆As in the past, the Corporation and its subsidiaries raised additional capital during this year's first half. 従来どおり, 当社と子会社は当上半期も追加資本を調達しました。

raise capital　資金を調達する, 資本を調達する, 資金を引き上げる, 増資する, 資金繰りをする
　　raise capital globally　国際的に資金調達する, 国際的な資金調達を行う
　　raise capital in the market　市場で［市場から］資金を調達する
　　raise one's capital　増資する
　　　（＝increase one's capital）
　　raise required capital　必要資本を増やす
　　raise tier 2［Tier Two］capital　自己資本の補完的項目（Tier 2）を増やす, Tier 2資本を調達する

◆Mizuho is scheduled to raise its capital by ¥1 trillion by the end of March. みずほは, 3月末までに（今年度中に）1兆円規模の増資を行う方針だ。◆Our overseas investors account for about 24 percent, which would shrink to 18.6 percent after we raise capital. 当社の外国人株主［外国人投資家］は, 約24％を占め, 増資後は18.6％に減少します。◆The firm issued common stock to raise capital. 同社は, 資金調達のため普通株式を発行した。

raise deposit reserve ratio　預金準備率を引き上げる

◆The People's Bank of China raised deposit reserve ratio by 0.5 percentage points. 中国人民銀行（中央銀行）は, 預金準備率を0.5％引き上げた。

raise fresh capital　新規資本を調達する

◆Japanese companies actively tapped the stock market to raise fresh capital. 日本の企業が, 新規資本を調達するため株式市場で積極的に起債した。

raise funds　資金を調達する, 資金を集める
　（＝raise capital, raise money; ⇒access）
　　raise external funds　外部資金を調達する
　　　（＝raise capital, raise money）
　　raise funds by way of a capital increase　増資で資金を調達する
　　raise funds from corporate bonds　社債による資金調達を行う
　　raise funds in the capital market　資本市場で資金を調達する
　　raise funds in the public markets　公開市場で資金を調達する
　　raise funds through borrowing　借入れで資金を調達する

◆Banks would keep amassing cash by disposing of distressed assets as quickly as possible to avert collapse after having difficulty raising funds. 資金調達が困難になって経営破たんするのを避けるため, 金融機関［銀行］は, できるだけ早めに危険資産を処分［売却］して, 現金を抱え込もうとする。◆Political funds raised by political parties and organizations fell by ¥20.11 billion from the previous year. 政党や政治団体が集めた政治資金は, 前年より201億1,000万円減少した。◆The consortium intends to raise funds to cover one-third of its development costs and expects the government will pay the balance. この共同事業体は, 開発費の三分の一は独自に資金調達する方針で, 残りは政府の支援を見込んでいる。

raise funds from IPOs　新規株式公開で資金を調達する, 新規株式公開による資金調達を行う

◆The higher the level of stock prices, the more funds firms can raise from IPOs. 株価の水準が上がれば, それだけ新規株式公開（上場時の新株発行）による資金調達額も増える。

raise funds in the market　市場で資金を調達する, 市場から資金を調達する

◆The company is unable to raise funds in the market as its stocks were delisted from the Tokyo Stock Exchange. 東証が同社株の上場を廃止したので, 同社は市場から資金調達することができなくなった。

raise interest rates 金利を引き上げる, 利率を上げる, 利上げする
◆The U.S. Federal Reserve raised U.S. interest rates for the first time in four years. 米連邦準備制度理事会は、金利を4年ぶりに引き上げた。

raise money 資金を調達する
（=raise capital, raise funds）
◆The bank sold all its shares in the U.S. investment firm to raise money to deal with its nonperforming loans. 同行は、不良債権処理の資金を調達するため、米投資会社の持ち株を全株売却した。

raise money for compensation 賠償資金を調達する, 賠償費用を捻出する
◆To raise money for compensation related to the Fukushima No. 1 nuclear power plant crisis, TEPCO will sell off assets through four trust banks. 福島第一原発事故関連の賠償資金を調達するため、東電は、4信託銀行を通じて資産を売却することになった。

raise one's capital adequacy ratio 自己資本比率を引き上げる
◆UFJ Holdings Inc. has agreed to sell UFJ Trust Bank Ltd. to Sumitomo Trust & Banking Co., Ltd. for about ￥300 billion to raise its capital adequacy ratio. UFJホールディングスが、自己資本比率を引き上げるため、UFJ信託銀行を約3,000億円で住友信託銀行に売却することで合意した。

raise one's stake in ～の持ち株比率を引き上げる, ～の株式保有比率を高める, ～への[～に対する]出資比率を引き上げる
（=increase one's stake in）
◆MUFG has decided to raise its stake in Acom Co. to about 40 percent from the current 15 percent. 三菱UFJフィナンシャル・グループが、消費者金融大手アコムの株式保有比率を現在の15%から40%程度に高める方針を固めた。

raise pension premiums 年金保険料を引き上げる
◆The demographic changes show the inevitability of raising pension premiums unless pension benefits are reduced in the future. この人口構造の変化は、年金給付を今後減額しない限り、年金保険料の引上げは必至であることを示している。

raise taxes 税金を引き上げる
◆When you have a fragile recovery, it wouldn't seem to me like an opportune time to raise taxes. 景気回復の足取りが弱いときは、税金引上げの好機とは言えないように思える。

raise the consumption tax 消費税を引き上げる
◆The last resort to secure a stable revenue source is raising the consumption tax. 安定した財源確保の頼みの綱は、消費税の引上げだ。

raise the debt ceiling 債務上限を引き上げる
◆The federal government will raise the debt ceiling by about $2.4 trillion in two stages. 米政府は、2.4兆ドルほどの債務上限引上げを2段階で実施する。

raise the discount rate 公定歩合を引き上げる
◆The Fed raised the discount rate to 0.75 percent from 0.5 percent as a response to improved financial market conditions. 米連邦準備制度理事会（FRB）は、金融市場の環境改善を受けて、（銀行に貸し出す際の金利である）公定歩合を現行の年0.5%から0.75%に引き上げた。

raise the dividend 増配する, 配当を引き上げる
◆It has been our practice since 1980 to raise the dividend every year. 1980年以来の慣行として、当社は毎年、配当引上げを実施してきました。

raise the pension age 受給年金年齢を引き上げる
◆The compilation of fiscal rehabilitation measures including raising the pension age is imperative for the Italian parliament. 年金受給年齢の引上げなどを含む財政再建策のとりまとめが、イタリア議会の急務となっている。

raise the pension eligibility age 年金の支給開始年齢[年金受給年齢]を引き上げる

◆The Democratic Party of Japan will postpone a plan to raise the pension eligibility age. 民主党は、年金の支給開始年齢を引き上げる案の実施を見送る方針だ。

raise the target rate of federal funds フェデラル・ファンド（FF）の誘導目標金利を引き上げる
◆The U.S. Federal Reserve raised the official discount rate and the target rate of federal funds by 0.25 percentage points in a bid to quell inflation and keep the economy from overheating. 米連邦準備制度理事会（FRB）は、インフレを防ぎ景気の過熱を警戒して、公定歩合とフェデラル・ファンド（FF）の誘導目標金利をそれぞれ0.25パーセント引き上げた。

raise the U.S. debt limit 米政府の法廷債務上限を引き上げる
◆Moody's will consider cutting the United States' top-notch credit rating if any progress isn't made in talks to raise the U.S. debt limit. 米政府の法定債務上限引上げについての（米議会との）交渉で進展がなければ、ムーディーズは、米国債の最上位の格付けを引下げる方向で検討する方針だ。

raise the yuan 人民元を切り上げる
◆The United States is pressing China to raise the yuan. 米国は、中国に人民元の切上げを迫っている。◆The United States tries to press China to reduce its current account surplus and raise the yuan by restricting its current account with a numerical goal. 米国は、経常収支を数値目標で縛って、中国に経常収支の黒字縮小と人民元切上げの圧力をかけようとしている。

raising （名）資金の調達, 募集, 値上げ, 延長
　capital raising　資本調達, 資金調達
　capital raising plan　資本調達計画, 資金調達計画
　equity raising　新株発行, 増資
　　（=new equity raising）
　fund raising　資金調達, 資本調達, 募金
　　（=fund procurement, raising of fund）
　new equity raising　新株発行, 増資
　　（=equity raising）
　new fund raising　新規資金調達, 新規調達額
　price raising　値上げ
　raising of dividend payments　増配
◆Banks' fund-raising costs have increased, reflecting the rise in market rates after the Bank of Japan abandoned its zero-interest policy. 日銀のゼロ金利政策解除に伴って市場金利が上昇したため、銀行の資金調達コストが増大した。

raising of dividend payments 増配
◆A shareholder with more than 1 percent of the entire voting rights or with shares worth more than 300 voting rights acquired six months prior to the shareholders meeting can propose matters for discussion, including the selection of board members and the raising of dividend payments. 議決権全体の1%以上を保有する株主、または株主総会の6か月以前に取得した議決権が300個以上の株式を保有している株主[議決権数で300個以上の株式を6か月前から保有している株主]は、取締役選任や増配などの議題[討議事項]を提案できる。

rake in 利益をかき集める, 大儲けする, 荒稼ぎする, 大金を手にする
◆The Clintons raked in millions of dollars after leaving the White House. クリントン夫妻は、ホワイトハウスを去った後、数百万ドルも荒稼ぎした。◆While automakers and electronics makers are posting huge losses, some firms are raking in big profits. 自動車メーカーや家電メーカーが巨額の赤字を計上しているなかで、一部の企業は大幅な利益を上げている。

rake-off （名）不正利得, （不正取引の）手数料, リベート, （不正利得の）分け前, 値引き

rallies in stock and bond markets 株式相場と債券相場の急騰[上昇]
◆Wealth has been boosted by rallies in stock and bond markets. 株式相場と債券相場の急騰[上昇]で、資産が増加してい

る［資産が膨らんでいる］．

rally （動）反騰する，持ち直す，回復する，盛り返す，上昇する，急騰する，急伸する （=rebound）
rally against the U.S. dollar 対米ドルで回復する，ドルに対して回復［急騰，急伸］する
rally for five straight sessions 5日連続上昇する
rally on all money markets 全金融市場で持ち直す［反騰する］
rally on the good news この好材料を受けて急伸する
rally sharply 急反発する，急回復する
rally strongly 大きく買われる，急騰する
rally through the old highs 最高値を更新する
◆After briefly touching ¥110.90 in early trading in London, the dollar rallied in intraday trading, rising to ¥112.15-25 at 5 p.m. ロンドン市場では早朝の取引で1ドル＝110円90銭を付けた後、米ドルは取引時間中の取引で反騰して午後5時現在、同112円15-25銭に上昇した。◆Stock prices in Tokyo rallied sharply. 東京市場の株価は、急反発した。◆The euro rallied against the dollar and yen after recent sharp falls. ユーロ相場は、最近急落したもののドルと円に対して持ち直した。

rally （名）株価の反騰［反発，上昇］，景気などの持ち直し，回復，上昇，上昇局面，急騰，相場の上昇，上げ相場，強気相場 （=rebound）
bond market rally 債券相場の上昇，債券市場の上げ相場 （=rally in the bond market）
bond rally 債券相場の上昇，債券相場の急騰，債券市場の上げ相場
cause a sharp rally in the yen against the dollar ～により円がドルに対して急伸する
modest rally 穏やかな上昇局面
rally in stocks 株価の持ち直し，株価の反騰 （=stock rally）
secondary rally 中間戻し
sharp rally 急騰，急反発
stock market rally 株式相場の上昇，株式市場の上げ相場，株高
stock price rally 株価の急騰［反発、回復、持ち直し］
substantial rally 大幅に買われること
sustainable rally 本格的上げ相場
technical rally アヤ戻し，とくに理由のない小幅上昇 （=technical rebound）
the U.S. dollar's rally 米ドル高
the U.S. Treasury rally 米国債の急騰，米国債相場の上昇［急騰］，米国債の価格上昇
◆Gold extended its rally to a record above $1,900 an ounce amid increased uncertainties over the U.S. and European economic outlook on the Comex in New York. ニューヨーク商品取引所では、米欧景気見通しへの懸念［米欧経済の先行き不透明感］の高まりを受け［懸念の高まりから］、金価格が急騰して、1トロイ・オンス＝1,900ドルを史上初めて突破した。◆Relatively solid sales figures inspired another rally on Wall Street. 小売売上高が比較的、堅調だったため、ニューヨーク株式市場はまた持ち直した（ニューヨーク株は反発した）。◆Stock and bond market rallies came to a halt. 株式市場と債券市場の上げ相場は、一服した。◆The rally has run out of steam. 強気相場は息切れしている。

range （名）範囲，幅，領域，～台，種類，品揃え，製品群，ボックス圏，レンジ （⇒hit）
a range of measures 広範な手段
a wide range of investors 幅広い層の投資家
a wide range of savings media 幅広い貯蓄商品
be at the low end of ～の下限にある
be at the top of one's range for the past two months 過去2か月のボックス圏の上限

be below one's historical range 過去のレンジを下回る
be held［locked］in a tight range 狭いボックス圏内でもみ合う
be still stuck in a range ボックス圏はまだ破られていない
break out of established ranges ボックス圏を抜け出す
break out of the current range to test ボックス圏を抜け出して～をうかがう展開となる
break through the established range ボックス圏を抜け出す
hover［move］in a narrow range 小幅な値動きとなる
long-range cash［fund］planning 長期資金計画
meet the target range 目標を達成する
move in a narrow range 狭いボックス圏内での動きに終始する
oversold range 売られ過ぎの水準
range-bound market ボックス圏の動き
range of funding options 資金調達の選択の幅
range of loss 損失の範囲，損失の範囲額
range test 評定法
range trading もみ合い，ボックス圏内での取引
run well outside one's targeted range 目標レンジを大幅に上回る
stay in a narrow range （市場、相場は）しばらくもみ合いが続く
stop the yen from rising to the ¥82 range to the dollar 1ドル＝82円台突入を阻止する （⇒stop動詞）
target range 目標圏，目標レンジ
the bottom of a two-year range 過去2年のレンジの最低水準
the bottom of one's historical range 過去のレンジの底
the bottom of the Fed's acceptable range FRBの目標圏の底
the bottom of the trading range 取引圏の底
the lower half of the target range 目標圏の下半分
trade at the higher ¥84 range against the dollar 1ドル＝84円台後半で取引される
trade at the lower ¥84 range against the dollar 1ドル＝84円台前半で取引される
trade in a narrow range 狭いレンジ［ボックス圏内］でもみ合う，狭いボックス圏内で推移する
trading range 取引圏，相場圏，ボックス圏，取引レンジ
within the range of ～の範囲内
◆Crude oil prices stayed within a $20 range in the early 2000s. 原油価格は、2000年代の初めには1バレル＝20ドル台だった。◆If we look at the yen's current exchange rate in terms of its real effective exchange rate, it is basically within a range consistent with the mid- and long-term fundamentals of the economy. 今の円相場［円の為替相場］は、実質実効為替レートで見ると、基本的には中長期的な経済のファンダメンタルズ（基礎的条件）と整合的な範囲内ある。◆Raising the outstanding balance of current accounts held by private financial institutions at the central bank to between ¥27 trillion and ¥30 trillion remained within the range of conventional responses. 日銀当座預金（民間金融機関が日銀に保有している当座預金）の残高目標を（現行の22-27兆円程度から）27-30兆円程度に引き上げる日銀の追加金融緩和は、従来の対応の範囲内にとどまった。◆The average OPEC oil price rose to the $71 a barrel range in August. OPEC原油の平均価格は、今年の8月に1バレル＝71ドル台まで上昇した。◆The Japanese currency's value vis-a-vis the U.S. dollar entered the ¥78 range in foreign exchange markets around the world. 円の対米ドル相場は、内外の外国為替市場で1ドル＝78円台を付けた。

◆The Standard & Poor's 500 index is at the top end of its range for the past two months. スタンダード・プアーズ(500種)株価指数は、過去2か月のボックス圏の上限にある。◆The target range for the inflation rate could be set at the same level as the potential growth rate, for example. 物価上昇率の目標値としては、例えば潜在成長率と同水準に設定することもできよう。◆The U.S. dollar traded at the lower ¥85 range in Tokyo over concern about the U.S. economic outlook. 東京金融市場［東京外国為替市場］では、米景気の先行きを懸念して、ドル相場は1ドル＝85円台前半で取引された。◆The yen could soon even reach a record high in the ¥75 range versus the dollar. 円は、やがて1ドル＝75円台の史上最高値にまで達する可能性がある。◆The yen hovered in a narrow range in the upper ¥85 level to the dollar. 円相場は、1ドル＝85円台後半の小幅な値動きとなった。◆The yen remains in the historically high ¥75-range against the dollar. 円相場は、1ドル＝75円台の歴史的高値が続いている。◆The yen stayed in the lower ¥77 range against the U.S. dollar in Tokyo. 東京外国為替市場の円相場は、1ドル＝77円台前半で推移した。◆There are few signs of the yen reaching the ¥90 range to the dollar for the time being. 今のところ、1ドル＝90円台に達する動き［1ドル＝90円台を目指す動き］は見られない。◆To fulfill its responsibilities as the nation's central bank, the Bank of Japan must achieve currency stabilization by availing itself of a range of measures, including stabilization of the exchange rate. 日本の中央銀行としての責任を果たすには、日本銀行は、為替相場の安定を含めて広範な手段を活用して通貨の安定を実現しなければならない。

rapid (形)急激な，急速な，急な，速い
rapid balance sheet growth　資産の急激な増加
rapid fluctuation　急速な変動
rapid increase　急増，急速な伸び
rapid price gains　インフレ率の急上昇
the yen's extremely rapid appreciation　超円高
◆The rapid spread of Italy's credit crisis is due to intensified fears about the nation's fiscal predicament by Italy's huge fiscal deficits. イタリアの信用不安が急速に広がったのは、イタリアの巨額の赤字で同国の財政ひっ迫への警戒感が高まったからだ。◆The yen's extremely rapid appreciation may deliver a bitter blow to the domestic economy. 超円高は、国内経済に大きな打撃を与える可能性がある。

rapid appreciation of the yen　急激な円高
(=the yen's rapid appreciation)
◆A rapid appreciation of the yen is not desirable to the U.S. economy. 急激な円高は、米国経済には好ましくない。

rapid inflation　急激なインフレ
◆Should the Fed misjudge the timing or level of its next rate hike, it may interrupt the economic recovery and even bring about rapid inflation. 米連邦準備制度理事会(FRB)が追加利上げの幅やタイミングを誤ると、景気回復の腰を折り、急激なインフレを招く可能性もある。

rapid recovery　急回復，急速な回復
◆Rapid recovery following the so-called Lehman shock has ended and the Chinese economy has entered a phase aimed at stable growth. いわゆるリーマン・ショック後の中国の急回復の時期は終わり、中国経済は、安定成長を目指す段階に入っている。

rapid surge in the value of the yen　急激な円高
◆The export-led economic growth could falter if the U.S. economic upswing slows down or if there is a rapid surge in the value of the yen. 輸出主導の経済成長は、米国の景気回復にブレーキがかかるか、急激な円高が進めば、大きくつまずく可能性がある。

rapid surge in the yen's value　急激な円高
◆The rapid surge in the yen's value would impair the current improvement in the Japanese economy. 急激な円高は、日本の景気回復の腰を折ることになる。

rapidly (副)急速に，急激に，急に，にわかに，急ピッチで，短期間に，早期に
rapidly growing market　急成長市場
rapidly inflationary policies　極端なインフレ政策
◆Business conditions are rapidly deteriorating due to the global financial crisis and the worldwide economic downturn. 世界的な金融危機と世界的な景気後退で、景気は急速に悪化している。

rare stock［share］　品薄株，希少株　(=scarce stock［share］:発行済み株式数が少なく、浮動株も少ない株のこと。⇒free float)

ratchet［ratch］ (動)徐々に上がる，徐々に下がる，（物を）かます，入れる　(名)歯止め，（一方向だけに回転する）歯車［つめ車］
ratchet down　下げる，下がる
ratchet up　上げる，高める，強化する，上がる
ratchet up tensions　緊張を高める
◆China will ratchet up efforts to quell inflation in 2011. 中国は、2011年からインフレ抑制策を徐々に強化する方針だ。

ratchet effect　歯止め効果，景気下降阻止効果，断続的成長［拡大、増加］

rate (動)評価する，格付けする，見積もる
be rated A or better by two rating agencies　格付け会社2社からA以上の格付けを得て［取得して］いる
be rated in the third highest rating category　上から3番目の格付けを取得している
rate A in a rating category　Aに一定の格付けをする
◆Japanese government bonds are now rated at the same level as those of China and Kuwait. 日本の国債の格付けは現在、中国やクウェートと同じレベルだ。◆The bonds of six eurozone countries such as Germany and France are rated AAA by S&P's credit ratings on them. 独仏などユーロ圏6か国の国債は、スタンダード・アンド・プアーズ(S&P)の格付け［信用格付け］でトリプルAに格付けされている。◆The government bonds were considered high risk, rated "speculative" at the time of issuance. この国債は、発行時点で「投機的」格付けで、リスクが大きいと見なされた。

rate (名)割合，率，金利，歩合，料金，値段，相場，等級，速度，進度，程度，レート　(⇒currency exchange rate, economic trends, equity stake rate, interest rate)
accrual rate　経過金利
assumed rate of interest　予定利率
assumed rates of return on pension funds　予想年金基金運用収益率
auction rate note　入札金利債
basic rate　基本料率
bill discount rate　手形レート
buying rate　買い相場
experience rate　経験的料率
hold rates steady［unchanged］　金利を据え置く
hold the yuan at a low rate　人民元を安価に抑える
interest rate　金利，利率　(=rate of interest)
loan rate　貸出金利
market rate　市場金利，市場相場，市場レート
minimum lending rate　最低貸出金利
money market rate　市中金利，短期市場金利
official rate　公定歩合，公定利率，公定レート
open rate　基本料金
opening rate　始め値，寄り付き
operating earning rate　営業利益率
operating rate　操業率，設備稼働率
prevailing rate　市場の実勢金利，市場金利，中心相場

prime rate　一流企業向け最優遇貸出金利, プライム・レート
rate of taxation　税率　(=tax rate)
rates tied to prime, LIBOR or U.S. Treasury bills　プライム・レート, ロンドン銀行間取引金利(LIBOR)または米財務相短期証券の利回り
selling rate　売り相場
spot rate　直物為替相場, 直物為替レート, 直物相場, 直物レート, スポット・レート
stated interest rate　約定金利, 約定利率
yen rate　円相場, 円為替レート
yield rate　利回り率, 歩留(ぶど)まり
◆China is trying to hold the yuan at a low rate through large-scale currency intervention. 中国は、大規模な為替介入で人民元を安価に抑えようとしている。◆Floating rate payments are based on rates tied to prime, LIBOR or U.S. Treasury bills. 変動金利の支払い利率は、プライム・レート、ロンドン銀行間取引金利または米財務省短期証券の利回りに基づいて決定されます。◆The People's Bank of China kept interest rates unchanged out of concerns that higher rates would have a negative impact on the economy. 中国人民銀行は、利上げのマイナス効果を心配したため、金利を据え置いてきた。◆The rate of economic expansion in the current phase of recovery is much smaller than previous expansionary phases. 現在の景気拡大期[景気拡大局面]の経済成長率は、過去の景気拡大期よりかなり低い。◆The target range for the inflation rate could be set at the same level as the potential growth rate, for example. 物価上昇率の目標値としては、例えば潜在成長率と同水準に設定することもできよう。

rate cut　利下げ, 金利引下げ, 金融緩和
◆The European Central Bank cut its main interest rate by 0.25 percent following heavy pressure for a rate cut to spur flagging economic growth. 失速気味の経済成長に刺激を与えるため利下げを求める強い圧力を受けて、欧州中央銀行(ECB)はその主要(政策)金利を0.25%引き下げた。◆To enhance the stimulating effect of the Fed's rate cuts, the Bush administration is expected to swiftly implement fiscal and tax stimulus measures, including tax cuts on investment designed to reinvigorate the stock market, in addition to the large-scale tax cut program that is under way. 米連邦準備制度理事会(FRB)の金利引下げの刺激効果を高めるため、ブッシュ政権には、現在実施中の大型減税プログラムに加え、株式市場を再活性化するための投資減税など、財政・税制面からの景気刺激策の速やかな実施が期待されている。

rate for unsecured overnight call　無担保コール翌日物金利　(=target rate for unsecured overnight call)

rate hike　利上げ, 金利引上げ
◆Should the Fed misjudge the timing or level of its next rate hike, it may interrupt the economic recovery and even bring about rapid inflation. 米連邦準備制度理事会(FRB)が追加利上げの幅やタイミングを誤ると、景気回復の腰を折り、急激なインフレを招く可能性もある。

rate of declining　減少率, 下落率
◆Prices have dropped more steeply than those at the time when the BOJ was fighting deflation, and the rate of declining is expected to increase. 日銀がデフレと戦っていた時より物価は急激に下がり、下落率は今後さらに拡大する見込みだ。

rate of exchange　為替相場, 為替レート, 交換比率
(=exchange rate, foreign exchange rate)
◆The rate of exchange to U.S. dollars shall be based upon the rate of exchange quoted by the Bank on the day of payment. 米ドルへの為替相場は、支払い日の銀行の為替相場によるものとする。

rate of interest　金利, 利率, 利子率
(=interest rate)
◆The rate of interest of this loan is five percent per annum. このローンの利率は、年率5%となっている。

rate of pension premiums　保険料率, 保険料の料率, 年金保険料率　(=pension premium rate)
◆The rate of pension premiums paid under the state-assisted corporate pension plan is currently set at 13.58 percent of employees' annual income, half of which is covered by employers. 国が援助している厚生年金制度に基づいて払い込まれる保険料の料率(保険料率)は現在、社員の年収の13.58%(労使折半)に設定されている。

rate of return　利益率[収益率], 株式の配当利回り, 債券の直接利回り, 利回り
　accounting [accountant's] rate of return　会計的利益率
　adversely affect the rate of return　収益率に悪影響を及ぼす
　annual rate of return　年利益率
　assumed rate of return　予想収益率
　assumed rates of return on pension funds　予想年金基金運用収益率
　average annual real net rate of return　年平均実質収益率
　demand increase in the real rate of return　実質利回りの上乗せを要求する
　expected rate of return on plan assets　制度資産の期待収益率
　external rate of return　外部収益率
　fair rate of return　公正収益率
　improve the rate of return　収益率を改善する
　internal rate of return　内部収益率, IRR
　lower the rate of return　収益率を悪化させる
　money rate of return　現金ベース収益率
　rate of return method　利回り法
　rate of return objective　目標収益率, 目標利益率
　rate of return on equity　株主資本利益率
　rate [ratio] of return on investment　投資収益率, 資本利益率, 投資の運用利回り
　rate of return on real assets　実物資産収益率
　rate of return on total assets　総資本利益率
　real rate of return　実質利回り, 実質収益率
　the expected rate of return on investment　予想投資収益率
　the rate of return on low-risk debt investments　低リスク債券の投資収益率
◆In this type of life insurance products, the rate of return after canceling the insurance contract can be higher than that of a savings account if a policyholder upholds the contract for five to 10 years. この種の生保商品では、保険契約者が保険契約を5〜10年続けると、解約後の利回り(予定利率)は預金よりも高い利回りが見込める。◆The expected rate of return on investment is 5.5 percent. 予想投資収益率は、5.5%です。

rate of savings　貯蓄率
◆The rate of savings among those people in their 30s and 40s is on an upward trend, which is likely to have a depressing effect on domestic demand. 30〜40歳代の貯蓄率が増大傾向にあり、内需を下押ししている可能性がある。

rate-sensitive　(形)金利に敏感な, 金利感応型の, 金利敏感型の
(=interest rate-sensitive, interest-sensitive)
　rate-sensitive assets　金利感応資産
　rate-sensitive liabilities　金利感応負債

rated　(形)評価された, 評価した, 格付けされた, 格付け対象の, 格付け取得済みの, 〜格の
　AAA-rated borrower [credits]　トリプルA格の発行体, AAA格の発行体
　better-rated name　格付けの高い銘柄
　highly-rated bank　格付けの高い銀行
　lesser rated names　格付けの低い銘柄

low-rated company　格付けの低い会社
newly-rated issuer　新規格付け発行体
rated corporate bond issuers　格付け対象企業, 格付け対象の社債発行体
rated debt　格付け取得債券
rated issue　格付け債券
rated issuer　格付け取得済み発行体, 格付け取得発行体
rated policy　評定保険証券
rated securities　格付け取得証券
rated sovereigns　主要国の格付け, 国債 [ソブリン債] の格付け
rated tax　定率税
◆Japan's government debt ratios are already among the highest for rated sovereigns. 日本の政府債務比率は、主要国の格付けですでに最高位にある。

ratification　(名) 批准, 承認, 裁可, (契約などの) 追認
◆Canadian Prime Minister Jean Chretien signed Canada's instrument of ratification for the Kyoto Protocol. カナダのクレティエン首相は、京都議定書の批准文書に署名した。◆Due to delays in ratification of the agreement on bailout measures by some eurozone countries, concrete measures to rescue Greece have yet to be carried out. 支援策の合意事項について一部のユーロ圏加盟国の承認が遅れたため、ギリシャ救済の具体策はまだ実施されていない。

ratify　(動) (条約などを) 批准する, (契約などを) 追認する, 承認する, 裁可する
◆The 17 eurozone nations must ratify the agreement on bailout measures to arrange a rescue system for Greece. ギリシャへの支援体制を整えるには、ユーロ圏の17か国が、支援策についての合意事項を承認しなければならない。◆The United Auto Workers ratified a four-year contract with Mitsubishi Motor North America. 全米自動車労組は、北米三菱自動車との4年労使協約を承認した。

rating　(名) 格付け, 評価, 査定, 信用度, 視聴率　(⇒ business environment, credit rating, debt rating, negative, notch, World Bank)
assign a BBB long-term rating to　～に対してトリプルBの長期格付けをする
assign a rating of AAA　トリプルAの格付けを与える [付与する], トリプルAの格付けをする
assigning ratings　格付けの付与
bank deposit ratings　銀行の預金格付け
bank letter-of-credit rating　銀行信用状の格付け
base rating　基礎格付け, 基本格付け
below-investment grade rating　投機的格付け
　(=rating below investment grade; ⇒grade)
bond rating　債券格付け, 社債格付け
　(=debt rating)
bonds with a rating of at least AA　少なくとも [最低限] ダブルAを付与されている債券
capital adequacy rating　自己資本比率の評価
　(⇒financial stability)
claims paying rating　保険会社の保険金支払い能力
　(=claims-paying ability rating)
classified rating system　等級別料率制度
conditional ratings　条件付き格付け
corporate rating　企業の格付け
credit rating　信用格付け, 格付け
credit-risk rating　信用リスク格付け
definitive rating　最終格付け
experience rating　実績格付け, 実績格付け方式, 経験料率方式
financial strength rating　財務力格付け, 支払い能力格付け

have a rating　格付けを取得する
implicit rating　間接格付け
independent credit rating system　独立した格付けシステム
indicative rating opinions　事前格付け見解, 予想格付け見解
insurance claims-paying raring　保険金支払い能力格付け
insurance financial strength rating　保険財務力格付け, 保険会社の支払い能力格付け
insurance rating　保険格付け
investment-grade rating　投資適格の格付け
issuer's base rating　発行体の基礎格付け, 発行体の基本格付け
issuer's debt ratings　発行体の債権格付け
Japan Credit Rating Agency　日本格付研究所, JCR
Japan's yen-denominated debt rating　日本の円建て国債の格付け
life insurance financial strength rating　生命保険会社の保険金支払い能力格付け
long-term rating　長期格付け
lower rating　格付けの引下げ
preliminary rating　予備格付け
　(=provisional rating)
prime rating　高格付け, プライム格付け
private placement rating　私募債の格付け
prospective rating　予備格付け
　(=provisional rating)
public debt rating　公募債格付け
rating activity　格付け変動
Rating and Investment Information, Inc.　格付投資情報センター, R&I
rating assessment　格付け評価
rating change　格付け変更
rating cuts [decrease]　格下げ, 信用格付けの引下げ
rating decision　格付けの判断
rating judgment　格付け判断
rating lives　格付け維持期間
rating on a life insurance company　生命保険会社の格付け
rating on an industrial bond　事業債の格付け
rating on yen-denominated government bonds　円建て国債の格付け
rating outlook　格付け見通し
rating requirements　格付け基準
rating review　格付け見直し
rating service　格付け機関, 格付け会社
rating system　格付け制度
　(=rating agency system)
rating trigger [requirement]　格付け基準
rating upgrade　格上げ
ratings for short-term obligations　短期債務の格付け
ratings of shares of money market funds　マネー・マーケット・ファンド (MMF) の受益証券格付け
ratings on shelf registrations　一括登録の格付け
seek a rating　格付けを申請する
senior debt rating　上位社債格付け
split rating　スプリット・レーティング (複数の格付け機関で格付けに格差が生じること)
stock rating　株価格付け
the U.S. rating　米国債の格付け
◆A lowered rating means higher interest rates. 格付けの低

下は、金利の上昇を意味する。◆Fitch Ratings Ltd. will keep its rating on long-term U.S. debt at the highest grade, AAA. 英米系の格付け会社フィッチ・レーティングスは、米国の長期国債格付けを、最上級のAAA（トリプルA）に据え置く方針だ。◆Moody's Investors Service Inc. cut its rating on yen-denominated government bonds by two notches to A2 from Aa3. ムーディーズ・インベスターズ・サービスは、円建て国債の格付けをAa3からA2に2段階引き下げた。◆S&P may cut the EU's AAA long-term rating. 米格付け会社のスタンダード・アンド・プアーズ（S&P）が、欧州連合（EU）の「トリプルA」の長期信用格付けを引き下げる可能性がある。◆Standard & Poor's currently assigns a BBB long-term rating to the bank. スタンダード＆プアーズは現在、同行に対してトリプルBの長期格付けをしている。◆Standard & Poor's cut its ratings on General Motors Corp. deeper into junk status. 米格付け会社のスタンダード・アンド・プアーズは、ゼネラル・モーターズ（GM）の格付け（長期債務格付け）を、投資不適格のレベルに（投資不適格レベルのダブルBからダブルBマイナスに）さらに1段階引き下げた。◆Standard & Poor's dropped the U.S. rating by one notch for the first time. スタンダード・アンド・プアーズ（S&P）が、米国債の格付けを史上初めて1段階引き下げた。◆Standard & Poor's revised upward the outlook on its ratings on six major Japanese insurance companies against the backdrop of their improved financial profiles. スタンダード＆プアーズは、日本の大手保険会社6社の財務力見通し改善を背景に、6社の格付け見通しを上方修正した。◆The AA minus rating by S&P is the fourth highest in terms of credit quality on a scale of 22. 米格付け会社のスタンダード・アンド・プアーズ（S&P）による「ダブルAマイナス」の格付けは、22段階ある信用中、上から4番目に当たる。◆The bank's rating may be cut one-notch. 同行の格付けは、1段階引き下げられる可能性がある。◆With the rating of JGBs being low, internationalizing them may increase the risk that their yield will fluctuate. 日本の国債の格付けが低いので、日本国債の国際化は国債の金利変動リスクを高める可能性がある。

[解説] 依頼格付けと勝手格付けとは：年金基金や保険会社など機関投資家の多くは、投資先を選ぶにあたって、「格付けが一定以上の相手」というルールを定めている。そのため企業などは、自社の格付けを格付け会社に要請して、その「お墨付き」を得る場合がある。これを「依頼格付け」という。これに対して、格付けの要請なしで格付け会社が公開されている情報などをもとに分析・評価する場合を「勝手格付け」という。

rating agency　格付け機関, 信用格付け機関, 格付け会社　(=credit rating agency, rating company, rating firm, ratings service agency; ⇒credit rating agency)
　bond rating agency　債券格付け機関
　credit rating agency　信用格付け機関
　independent rating agency　独立格付け機関
　rating agency system　格付け制度
　　(=rating system)
　recognized rating agency　一般に認められている格付け機関
◆A downgrade below investment-grade by even one rating agency could boost GM's borrowing costs and wreak havoc on the corporate bond market. 格付け会社が1社でも投資適格格付けより低く格付けを引き下げたら［格付け会社が1社でも投機的格付けに格下げしたら］、GMの資金調達コストが急増し、米国の社債［債券］市場にも大きな影響が出る恐れがある。◆Rating agency Moody's may place a negative outlook on French government's Aaa debt rating as the government's financial strength has weakened. 格付け会社のムーディーズは、フランス国債のAaa（トリプルA）格付けについて、仏政府の財務体質［財務力］が弱まっているため「ネガティブ（弱含み）」の見通しを示す可能性がある。◆The U.S. credit rating agency revised upward the outlook to positive from negative on its rating on Sumitomo Life Insurance Co. この米国の信用格付け機関は、住友生命保険の格付け見通しを「ネガティブ（弱含み）」から「ポジティブ（強含み）」に上方修正した。◆The U.S. rating agency Standard & Poor's lowered long-term Japanese government bonds by one notch, from AA to AA minus. 米国の格付け会社のスタンダード・アンド・プアーズ（S&P）が、日本の長期国債の格付けを「ダブルA」から「ダブルAマイナス」に1段階引き下げた。

3大格付け機関の比較

	設立	拠点数	アナリスト数	カバーしている発行体
S&P	1860年	23	約1,200人	約10,000
ムーディーズ	1900年	29	約1,100人	約12,000
フィッチ	1913年	50	約1,000人	約8,000

rating below investment grade　投資適格以下の格付け, 投資適格より低い格付け, 投機的格付け
◆A rating below investment grade makes it harder and more expensive to borrow money. 投資適格以下の格付けだと、資金の調達が難しくなるし、資金調達コストも高くつく。

rating category　格付けの分類, 格付けの区分, 格付け
　downgrade [lower] the rating category　格付けを引き下げる
　refined rating category　格付けの小分類
　the highest rating category　最高の格付け
　upgrade the rating category　格付けを引き上げる

rating downgrade　格下げ, 評価の引下げ, 下方修正, 引下げ　(=downgrading)
◆The rating downgrades have fueled economic confusion in Greece and Ireland. ギリシャやアイルランドでは、格下げで経済の混乱に拍車がかかった。

rating firm　格付け会社, 格付け機関
　(=rating agency)
◆Two influential rating firms lowered Ford Motor Co.'s credit ratings a notch deeper into junk territory. 大手［有力な］格付け機関2社が、米フォードの信用格付けを「投資不適格レベル」にさらに1段階引き下げた。

rating outlook　格付け見通し
◆The rating outlook of "negative" by a credit rating agency means that another downgrade is possible in the next 12 to 18 months. 信用格付け機関による「ネガティブ（弱含み）」の格付け見通しは、今後1年～1年半にふたたび格下げされる可能性があることを意味している。◆The rating outlook remains stable. 格付け見通しは、引き続き安定的だ。

rating symbol　格付け記号

[解説] 格付け記号：格付けは、アルファベットなどの記号でランク付けされる。スタンダード・アンド・プアーズ（S&P）とムーディーズは、それぞれ21段階でランク付けしている。
S&Pの場合は、AAA, AA+, AA, AA-, A+, A, A-, BBB+, BBB, BBB-の10段階までが投資適格とされ、それ以下のBB+, BB, BB-, B+, B, B-, CCC+, CCC, CCC-, D の11段階は、投資不適格とされている。またムーディーズの場合は、Aaa, Aa1, Aa2, Aa3, A1, A2, A3, Baa1, Baa2, Baa3までの10段階が投資適格で、それ以下のBa1, Ba2, Ba3, B1, B2, B3, Caa1, Caa2, Caa3, Ca, Cは投機的とされている。

ratio　(名) 割合, 比率, 利益率, 収益率, 指標　(⇒capital adequacy ratio, debt ratio, shareholding ratio, solvency margin ratio, turnover ratio)
　accounting ratio　財務比率
　bank ratios　銀行財務指標
　debt-equity ratio　負債・資本比率, 負債対資本比率, 負債比率, 外部負債比率
　debt ratio　債務比率, 負債比率
　equity ratio　株主資本比率, 株主持ち分

financial ratio　財務比率, 財務指標
key ratios　主要指標
leverage ratio　負債比率, レバレッジ比率
liquidity ratio　流動性比率, 流動比率
loan-deposit ratio　預貸率
management ratio　経営比率, 経営指標
payout ratio　配当性向, ペイアウト比率
price earnings ratio　株価収益率, PER
profit ratio　利益率
ratio of shareholders' equity　株主資本比率
◆The government has set a goal of halving the ratio of bad loans held by major banks against their outstanding loans by the end of next March. 政府は、大手銀行の融資残高に対する不良債権の比率（大手銀行の貸出総額に占める不良債権残高の比率）を、来年3月末までに半減させる目標を掲げている。◆The TSE and the OSE will decide the exact allocation of shares based on a ratio of 1.7 TSE shares to one OSE share. 東証と大証は、正確には大証の1株に対して東証は1.7株の割合で（新会社の）株式の割当てを決めることになった。◆The upcoming negotiations will determine practical measures to strengthen ties, including the merger ratio, the name of the new group and the positions to be held by top executives. 今後の交渉で、統合比率や新グループの名称、首脳人事など提携強化の具体策を詰める。

rational　（形）合理的な, 道理にかなった, 理性を備えた, 理性のある
rational allocation　合理的配分
rational expectation　合理的期待
rational view　理性的な見方［考え方］
◆The rational actions for survival taken by individual companies herald a danger that could lead the Japanese economy into contracted equilibrium. 生き残りをかけて個々の企業が取っている合理的な行動が、日本経済を縮小均衡に導く危険性をはらんでいる。

ravage　（動）破壊する, 荒廃させる, 損傷する, 〜に大損害を与える, 食い荒らす, 〜に猛威を振るう　（名）破壊, 打ちこわし, 破壊行為, 荒廃, 損傷, 破壊の跡, 惨害（ruinous damage）, 猛威, 大荒れ
flood ravages　洪水による惨害
the ravages of a typhoon　台風の惨害, 台風の猛威
the ravages of inflation　インフレの猛威
◆Personal computers of many Net banking depositors have been infected with viruses that ravaged computers in the United States and European countries. 多くのネット・バンキング預金者のパソコンが、欧米のコンピュータに爆発的な被害を生んだウイルスに感染していた。

razor-thin　（形）紙一重の, 僅差（きんさ）の, きわどい
keep one's key interest rate at a razor-thin 0.1 percent　政策金利を超低金利の0.1%に据え置く
maintain［keep］a key interest rate at a razor-thin 0.1 percent　政策金利を超低金利の0.1%に据え置く
razor-thin interest rates　超低金利
◆Razor-thin interest rates and slumping share prices have weighed heavily on the life insurance industry. 超低金利と株価低迷が、生保業界の大きな重荷になっている。◆The Bank of Japan has kept its key interest rate at a razor-thin 0.1 percent since December 2008 as part of efforts to overcome deflation. 日銀は、デフレ対応策の一環として、2008年12月から政策金利を超低金利の0.1%に据え置いてきた。

RCC　整理回収機構　(Resolution and Collection Corporationの略．⇒collection of debts, corporate revitalization)
◆The RCC used to buy bad loans at market prices. 整理回収機構は、これまで不良債権を時価で買い取っていた。

reach　（動）達する, 届く, 影響を及ぼす
reach a cyclical trough　（景気が）底入れする
reach a historical［historic］high of　過去最高の〜に達する
reach a new historical high of　〜で過去最高を更新する
reach the recession trough　（景気が）底を打つ, 底入れする
reach the ￥90 range to［against］the dollar　1ドル＝90円台に達する
◆Earthquake insurance payments resulting from the Great East Japan Earthquake are expected to reach ￥1.2 trillion. 東日本大震災による地震保険の保険金支払い額は、(業界全体で)1兆2,000億円に達する見込みだ。◆The yen could soon even reach a record high in the ￥75 range versus the dollar. 円は、やがて1ドル＝75円台の史上最高値にまで達する可能性がある。◆The yen's value still remains high and is likely to reach a postwar record value above the ￥76-to-the-dollar level. 円相場は依然高く、1ドル＝76円台を上回る戦後最高値に達する可能性がある。◆There are few signs of the yen reaching the ￥90 range to the dollar for the time being. 今のところ、1ドル＝90円台に達する動き［1ドル＝90円台を目指す動き］は見られない。

reacquired shares　金庫株, 自己株式
(=treasury stock)

react　（動）反応する, はね返る, 反作用する, 対応する, 反発する,（株が）反落する, 逆行する, 逆戻りする
react against［to］　〜に反発する, 〜に反対する
react favorably on　〜に有利に作用する
react in a positive way to　〜に肯定的に反応する
react to adverse situations　困難な状況に対応［対処］する
react to the situation quickly［immediately］　事態に迅速に［速やかに］対応する
◆The markets reacted coolly to the latest additional economic stimulus and monetary easing steps by the government and the Bank of Japan. 政府と日銀が繰りだした今回の追加経済対策と追加金融緩和策に、市場の反応は冷ややかだった。

reaction　（名）反応, 反響, はね返り, 対応, 反発, 反動, 反作用, 影響, 逆襲,（株の）反落, 押し目（株価が下がること）
buy on reaction　押し目買い
(=buy on decline, buy on dip)
chain reaction　連鎖反応
chain reaction bankruptcy　連鎖倒産
customer reaction　顧客の反応
negative reactions　否定的な反応, 反発
stock price reaction　株価の反応
the market reaction　市場の反応, 市場が送るメッセージ
the Treasury market's mixed reaction　米債券市場のまちまちの反応
wait for reaction　押し目待ち

read　（動）示す, 表示する, 〜と解釈［理解］する, 〜と書いてある, 読み取る, 研究する, 専攻する
◆The index of business confidence among large companies is projected to read plus 4.8 for the July-September quarter. 7-9月期の大企業（製造業）の景況判断指数は、プラス4.8の改善が見込まれている。

reading　（名）数値, 目盛り, 度数, 示度, 指標, 指数, 議案の読会（議会での法令審議の段階）, 読み方, 読書, 台本読み, 朗読, 文学的知識, 解釈　（⇒make for）
core inflation reading　基礎インフレ率の数値
DI reading　DIの数値
index reading for manufacturers' sentiment　製造業景況感判断指数
index reading for small companies' sentiment　中小企業

景況判断指数
NAPM reading　全米購買部協会景気総合指数
negative reading　マイナスの数値
positive reading　プラスの数値
strength of the readings　景気指標の強弱
◆A reading of below 50 percent in the coincident index is considered a sign of economic contraction and a figure above that is viewed as a sign of expansion. 一致指数で50%以下の数値は景気収縮[景気後退]を示す指標と見られ、それ以上の数字は景気回復[景気拡大]を示す指標と見なされる。
◆The DI reading among small and medium companies as well as nonmanufacturing corporations remains negative. 中小企業と非製造業のDIの数値は依然、マイナスが続いている。
◆The diffusion index (DI) of business confidence among large manufacturers marked the first positive reading in 33 months. 大手製造業の業況判断指数(DI)は、2年9か月ぶりにプラスに転じた。

ready　(形)準備[用意]ができた、〜する準備[態勢]ができている
ready market　換金市場
ready money [cash]　現金、即金、いつでも使える金、手元流動性、即金払い
ready money payment　現金払い
ready reckoner　計算早見表、利息早見表
◆The White House is ready to consider tapping a $700 billion Wall Street bailout fund to help keep the U.S. automakers afloat. 米政府は、米自動車メーカーの破たんを避けるための支援策として、7,000億ドルの金融業界救済資金(金融安定化法の公的資金)の活用を検討する用意ができている。

real　(名)レアル(ブラジルの通貨単位)
Brazilian real　ブラジルのレアル
◆Internet-based bank Sony Bank started a deposit service for the Brazilian real in May 2011. ネット専業銀行のソニー銀行が、2011年5月からブラジル通貨レアルの預金サービス[預金の取扱い]を開始した。

real　(形)実際の、実体の、現実の、実勢の、実質の、実質上の、実質ベースでの、重大な、正味の、不動産の、リアル
real account　実在勘定
real balance effect　実質残高効果、資産残高効果、実質手持ち資金効果
real bill　実手形、真正手形
real bills doctrine　真正手形理論
real bond yield　債券実質利回り
real capital　現実資本、実物資本、実質資本
real cash balance　実質現金残高
real consumption　実質個人消費
real deposits　実勢預金、実質預金
real depreciation in currencies　実質ベースでの
real disposable income　実質可処分所得
real distress　不動産差し押さえ
real dollar value　実質ドル価値
real economic growth　実質経済成長
real exchange rate　実質為替相場、実質為替レート(名目為替レート = nominal exchange rate)
real gain　実質利得
real government financial wealth　実質政府金融資産
real growth target　実質成長目標
real import as a percent of GDP　実質輸入額のGDP比率
real income　実質所得
real investment　実物投資、実質投資(証券投資に対する語で、土地建物や機械設備、原材料などに対する投資)
real money　正金(しょうきん)、実質貨幣(cash)、現金

real-name transaction system　金融実名制
real national income　実質国民所得
real outlays　実質支出
real revenue　実質収入
real right　物権
real security　物的担保、不動産担保、物上担保
real spending　実質個人消費
real value　実質価格、実質価値、実質値
real worth　正味資産
real yield　実質利回り、実質収益率
◆A vicious cycle of deflationary pressures is becoming increasingly real. デフレの悪循環が、現実味を増してきた。

real assets　不動産、実物資産
invest in real assets　実物資産に投資する
return on real assets　実物資産収益率
real demand　実需、実質需要
◆A stable stock market would heighten people's expectations for economic recovery, leading to rises in real demand for capital investment and personal spending. 株式相場の安定[株価の底堅い動き]は、人々の景気回復への期待感を高め、設備投資や個人消費の実需拡大につながる。

real economic growth rate　実質経済成長率
◆The real economic growth rate in the April-June quarter was almost flat. 4〜6月期の実質経済成長率は、ほぼ横ばいだった。

real economy　実体経済、実態経済
(⇒full-fledged recovery in the real economy)
the contraction of the real economy　実体経済の景気後退
the overheating of the real economy　過熱した実体経済
the U.S. real economy　米国の実体経済
◆A vicious cycle, in which financial uncertainty cools down the U.S. real economy and causes an economic downturn, is becoming reality. 金融不安が米国の実体経済を冷え込ませ、景気後退を招く悪循環は、現実になっている。◆The financial crisis is closely interrelated with the contraction of the real economy. 金融危機は、実体経済の景気後退と密接にかかわっている。◆The overheating of the real economy has triggered the latest financial crisis. 今回の金融危機の引き金を引いたのは、過熱した実体経済だ。◆There is a possibility that a vicious circle will develop in which the financial crisis undermines the U.S. real economy, producing further financial instability. 金融危機が米国の実体経済を損ない、それがさらに金融不安を引き起こす悪循環が深刻化する可能性がある。

real effective exchange [FX] rate　実質実効為替レート(名目実効為替レート = nominal effective exchange rate)
◆A real effective exchange rare indicates a currency's value compared with a group of the world's major currencies. 実質実効為替レートは、世界の主要通貨に対する通貨の価値を示す。◆If we look at the yen's current exchange rate in terms of its real effective exchange rate, it is basically within a range consistent with the mid- and long-term fundamentals of the economy. 今の円相場[円の為替相場]は、実質実効為替レートで見ると、基本的には中長期的な経済のファンダメンタルズ(基礎的条件)と整合的な範囲内ある。

real estate　不動産、土地 (=real property)
real estate acquisition tax　不動産取得税
real estate appraiser　不動産鑑定士、不動産鑑定業者
real estate-backed issue　不動産裏付け債
real estate bubble　不動産バブル
real estate exposure　不動産投資
real estate in trust　不動産信託
real estate investment　不動産投資
real estate lending　不動産融資

REAL　784

real estate loans　不動産融資, 不動産関連融資（real estate related loans）
real estate owned　保有不動産
real estate price　不動産価格
real estate problem loan　不動産関連の不良貸出
real estate revaluation　不動産再評価
real（estate）security　不動産担保
　（=real estate secured）
real estate stock　不動産株
real estate tax　固定資産税
real estate yield　不動産投資利回り
securitization of real estate　不動産の証券化
two bubbles of real estate and the stock market　土地と株の双子のバブル
◆The assets of the various plans include corporate equities, government securities, corporate debt securities and income-producing real estate. 各種制度の年金資産は、株式、政府証券、債券や収益を稼得する不動産でなどで構成されています。
◆To raise money for compensation related to the Fukushima No. 1 nuclear power plant crisis, TEPCO will sell about 40 pieces of real estate for about ¥10 billion. 福島第一原発事故関連の資金を調達するため、東電は約40か所の不動産を100億円前後で売却する。

real estate investment　不動産投資
◆The firm earns revenue through real estate investment and through resuscitating failed financial institutions. 同社は、不動産投資と経営破綻した金融機関を再生させることで収益を上げている。

real estate investment fund　不動産投資ファンド, 不動産ファンド　（投資家から資金を集めて、不動産などへの投資事業で運用している投資ファンド。⇒distribute）
◆A real estate investment fund was alleged to have failed to report about ¥18 billion in income from transaction involving land and property taken as collateral for nonperforming loans. 不動産投資ファンドが、不良債権の担保に取った不動産関連の取引で得た所得約180億円の申告漏れを指摘されていた。

real estate investment trust　不動産投資信託, リート, REIT　（⇒cooled, REIT）
◆New City Residence Investment Corp., a real estate investment trust listed on the Tokyo Stock Exchange went bust on October 9, 2008. 東京証券取引所上場の不動産投資信託のニューシティ・レジデンスが、2008年10月9日に破たんした。◆The Bank of Japan purchased riskier assets such as exchange-traded funds and real estate investment trusts in mid-December 2010. 日銀は、2010年12月半ばから、上場投資信託や不動産投資信託（リート）などの高リスク資産を買い入れた。

real estate market [marketplace]　不動産市場, 不動産取引市場, 不動産市況
◆Earnings of the firm were impacted by difficulties in North American real estate markets. 同社の利益は、北米の不動産市場の低迷による影響を受けた。◆The prolonged slump in the real estate market is maintaining the decline in land prices. 不動産取引市場の長期低迷が、引き続き地価の下落を招いている。

real estate mortgage　不動産抵当, 不動産モーゲージ
create [structure] real estate mortgage investment conduits　REMICを組成する
real estate mortgage investment conduit　不動産モーゲージ投資媒介体, 不動産モーゲージ投資コンデュイット, レミック, REMIC　（⇒REMIC）
real estate mortgage loan　不動産抵当融資

real gross domestic product　実質国内総生産（GDP）
◆The real gross domestic product for the April-June period returned to positive growth for the first time in five quarters. 4-6月期の実質国内総生産（GDP）は、5四半期ぶりにプラス成長に転じた。

real interest rate　実質金利, 実効金利（実質金利＝名目金利‐インフレ予想率）
long-term real interest rate　実質長期金利
real growth domestic product　実質国内総生産（GDP）
real interest rate（interest rate less inflation rate）　実質金利（金利‐インフレ率）
◆Real interest rates are likely to remain high. 実質金利は、高止まりしそうだ。

real money trade [trading]　リアル・マネー・トレード［トレーディング］, 仮想通貨の現金化（オンライン上のキャラクターやゲーム内の通貨（仮想通貨）などをインターネット上で売買し、現実世界の通貨などと取引すること）

real rate　実質金利（real interest rate）, 実効金利, 実勢レート
the real rate of exchange　実勢相場, 実勢為替レート, 為替の実勢レート
the real rate of interest　実質金利, 実質利子率
the real rate of return　実質収益率, 実質利回り

real time　実時間, 同時, 即時, 即時処理, 実時間処理, リアルタイム処理, リアルタイム　（形）実時間の, 同時の, 即時の, リアルタイム　（=realtime）
real time gross settlement　リアルタイム・グロス決済, RTGS
real time option trading　リアルタイム・オプション取引
real time processing　即時処理, 実時間処理, リアルタイム処理
real time quotes　リアルタイム株価
◆Some information that is transmitted in real time globally creates a trend in a very short time and many investors try to make a profit by trading it. リアルタイムでグローバルに伝達される情報は、極めて短時間に一つのトレンドを作り出し、投資家はそれにうまく乗ることによって利益を得ようとする。

realign　（動）再編成する, 再編する, 再調整する, 再統合する, 再提携する,（資産などを）整理する, 変更する
◆The nation's mega banking groups have been realigning their securities units to offer comprehensive financial services. 国内の大手金融グループは、総合金融サービスを提供するため、グループ各社の証券会社を再統合している。

realignment　（名）再編成, 再編, 再調整, 調整, 再統合, 再提携　（⇒economies of scale, liberalization）
aggressive realignment　攻めの再編, 積極的な再編, 大幅な［大型の］再編
broad realignment　大幅な調整, 大幅な再調整
business realignment　企業再編, 再編
currency realignment　通貨調整, 通貨再調整
　（=realignment of currencies）
exchange rate realignment　為替相場の再編成
financial sector realignment　金融再編
general realignment　全面的再調整, 全面調整
industry realignment　業界再編
mergers and realignments　統合や再編
the realignment of the industry　業界再編
◆To resolve the financial unrest in EU nations, accelerating financial sector realignment in countries such as Germany must be worked out. EU諸国の金融不安を解決するには、(2,000もの金融機関がひしめく)ドイツなどでの金融再編の加速も課題だ。

realignment of foreign exchange rates　為替レートの調整
◆An excessive trade deficit should be corrected through the realignment of foreign exchange rates. 過度の貿易赤字は、為替レートの調整によって是正しなければならない。

realignment of listed firms [companies] 上場企業の再編
◆The number of companies undertaking IPOs, excluding those by holding companies created by the realignment of already listed firms, has been declining since 2000. 株式を新規公開する企業数(既上場企業の再編により設立された持ち株会社のケースは除く)は、2000年以降、減少している。

realignment of the banking industry 銀行業界の再編,金融界の再編
◆The proposed merger would mark a final chapter in the realignment of the Japanese banking industry. この経営統合の申し入れは、日本の銀行業界[金融界]再編の最終章となる。

realignment of the financial industry 金融業界の再編,金融再編
◆The financial crisis that originated in the United States is developing into a cross-border realignment of the financial industry. 米国発の金融危機は、国境を越えた金融再編[金融業界の再編]に発展している。

realignment strategy 再編戦略
◆The merger plan likely will affect the realignment strategies of other companies in the banking and securities industries. この統合計画は今後、銀行・証券業界の他企業の再編戦略に影響を与えそうだ。

realistic exchange rates 現実的為替相場,現実的為替レート

realizable (形)実現可能な,換金可能な
  estimated realizable value 実現可能価額見積り額
  net realizable value 正味実現可能価格[価額]
  realizable asset 換金可能資産,換金性のある資産
  realizable income 実現可能な所得
  realizable value basis 売却時価基準,売却時価主義

realization (名)実現,認識,理解,(証券などの)現金化,換金,換金性,換金処分製作,作製
  capital gains realization 資産売却益の総額
  realization of assets 現金化,換金処分
  realization of principle (会計の)実現主義,実現原則
    (=realization basis)
  realization of security 担保権の実行
  realization of stock profits 益出し
  realization ratio 実行
  realization sale 換金売り
  revenue realization 収益の実現
    (=realization of revenue)

realize [realise] (動)実現する,(利益を)得る,換価する,換金する,現金に換える
  realize a profit on the property 財産を処分して利益を得る
  realize capital losses キャピタル・ロスを実現する
  realize gains on the long-term equity holdings 長期保有株式の含み益を実現する
  realize high returns 高利益を上げる
  realize latent capital gains 含み益を実現する
  realize par value 額面金額を回収する
  realize property 資産を換金する
  realize the hidden gains in the stockholdings 株式含み益を実現する
  realize the value of a swap スワップの価値を実現する
◆These days, nobody invests in a financial institution that cannot realize high returns. 最近は、高利益を上げることができない金融機関に、投資家は資金を出さなくなっている。

realized (形)実現した,実現の要件を満たした,実現済みの,換価した
  amount realized 実現金額,手取り金額
  gains realized on futures contracts 先物取引の実現益

realized capital gains 実現資本利得,キャピタル・ゲインの実現額,キャピタル・ゲイン実現益,実現キャピタル・ゲイン

realized capital value 実現資本価値

realized gain (loss) 実現利得(損失),実現利益(損失)

realized gain on investment activities 投資活動による実現益

realized gains and losses 実現損益

realized holding gain 実現保有益,実現保有利益

realized income 実現利益,利益の実現
  (=realized profit)

realized investment 実現した投資,実現投資

realized loss 実現損失,損失の実現

realized profit 実現利益 (=realized income)

realized return 実現収益

realized revenue 実現利益,実現収益,利益の実現

realized value 実現価値,実現価額

realized yield 実効利回り
◆The bank's decline in net revenues reflects lower realized capital gains and non-accrual loans. 同行の営業利益の減少は、キャピタル・ゲインの実現額の低下と利息計上を停止した貸付け金の増大を反映している。

reap (動)刈り取る,収穫する,(利益や報酬を)得る,手に入れる,獲得する,(恩恵などを)享受する
  reap large profits 大きな利益を上げる
  reap the benefits of advanced technologies 先進技術の恩恵を受ける[享受する]
  reap the rewards of investment 投資の成果を生かす,投資の報酬を手に入れる
◆The investment bank reaped billions of dollars from its own bets that the housing market would collapse. この投資銀行は、住宅市場が崩壊するとの独自の予想で、数十億ドルの利益を上げていた。

reason (名)理由,わけ,根拠,拠(よ)り所,道理,理屈,理性,判断力,要因,材料,事由
  by reason of 〜のために,〜の理由により
    (=due to, owing to)
  cyclical reason 循環要因
  good reason 十分な根拠,根拠が十分にあること
  seasonal reason 季節要因
  secular reason 構造要因
  speculative reasons 投機的な思惑
  within reason 無理のない範囲で
◆The weak yen is likely to be the main reason for profits increasing by about ¥150 billion in the first half of the business year alone. 円安が、上半期だけで約1,500億円の主な増益要因となる見通しだ。◆There is little reason for Washington to impose the safeguard tariffs. 米国のセーフガード関税(緊急輸入制限のための関税)発動には、根拠が乏しい。

reasonable (形)合理的な,妥当な,根拠のある,相当な,公正な,適切な
  provide a reasonable basis for our opinion われわれの意見表明の合理的な根拠になっている
  reasonable assurance 合理的な確証,合理的保証
  reasonable care 相当な注意
  reasonable estimate 合理的見積り,根拠のある見積り
  reasonable level 妥当な水準
  reasonable possibility 論理的可能性
  reasonable price 適正価格,合理的価格,手頃な値段,納得できる価格,相当の代価
  reasonable time [period] 相当な期間,相当期間,相当の期限,合理的な期間
  take all reasonable steps あらゆる適正措[合理的な措置]を取る

◆Corporation's internal controls are designed to provide reasonable assurance as to the integrity and reliability of the financial statements. 当社の内部統制は、財務書類の完全性と信頼性について十分保証するよう図られています。◆These GAASs require that we plan and perform the audit to obtain reasonable assurance about whether the financial statements are free of material misstatement. これらの一般に認められた監査基準は、連結財務書類に重要な虚偽表示がないかどうかについての合理的な確証を得るため、私どもが監査を計画して実施することを要求しています。

reassert （動）再主張する、再断言する、改めて強める、再浮上する、再び表面に出てくる
◆The revaluation of currency in North Korea appears aimed at clamping down on burgeoning free markets in an attempt to reassert the regime's control. 北朝鮮の通貨改定は、政権の統制力を改めて強めるため、急速に広がる自由市場を厳しく取り締まるねらいがあるようだ。

reassessment （名）再評価、再検討、見直し
◆The reassessment of 14 British banks by Moody's is not driven by a deterioration in the financial strength of the banking system. ムーディーズによる英銀14行の格付け見直しは、銀行[銀行業界]の財務の健全性悪化によるものではない。

rebalance （動）見直す、（ポートフォリオの内容を）見直す[修正する]、リバランスを行う
portfolio rebalancing　ポートフォリオ・リバランス
（ポートフォリオの資産のウエートを見直して入れ替えること）
rebalance the hedge　ヘッジを見直す

rebate （名）割戻し、払戻し、現金割戻し、返金、還付金、奨励金、報償金、手数料、戻し税、割引、控除、リベート
allowance for sales rebate　売上割戻し引当金
　（=reserve for sales rebate）
cash rebate　現金割戻し、現金払戻し
income tax rebates　所得税の還付、戻し税
purchase rebate　仕入割戻し
sales rebate　売上割戻し、販売奨励金、リベート
　（=rebate on sales）
tax rebate　税金の還付、戻し減税、戻し税
◆General Motors Corp. and Ford Motor Co. scaled back rebates. ゼネラル・モーターズ（GM）とフォード・モーターは、リベート（現金割戻し額）を引き下げた。◆The brokerage house paid ¥500 million in rebates to the former vice president of the health beverage company in return for the company's purchase of bonds. この証券会社は、健康飲料会社に債券を買ってもらった見返りとして、健康飲料会社の元副社長に5億円のリベートを渡していた。

rebound （動）回復する、反発する、持ち直す、値を戻す、跳（は）ね返る、下落後に再び上昇する、減少から増加に転じる　（⇒global equities, Tokyo stocks）
rebound by about 50 percent　ほぼ5割値を戻す
rebound from　～から回復する、～から反発する、～から値を戻す
rebound slightly　小幅反発する
rebound strongly　力強く回復する、大幅に回復する、大幅反発する
◆Long-term interest rates plummeted temporarily, but the Treasury bond yield soon rebounded. 長期金利は一時急落したが、米財務省長期証券の利回り（長期金利）はすぐ反発した。◆The BOJ's Tankan survey shows business sentiment among large manufacturers rebounded in September from the previous survey three months earlier. 9月の日銀短観は、大企業・製造業の景況感が6月の前回調査から改善したことを示している。◆The Sept. 15 currency intervention by the government and the Bank of Japan helped the dollar briefly rebound by about ¥3 to the ¥85 level. 2010年9月15日の政府・日銀の為替介入で、ドルは一時、1ドル＝85円台まで3円ほど値を戻した。◆The stock market rebounded above the 10,000 mark in just a few days. 株価は、わずか数日で1万円台[1万円の大台]を回復した。◆The 225-issue Nikkei Stock Average has rebounded by about 60 percent since then. 日経平均株価（225種）は、それ以来ほぼ6割値を戻した。◆Tokyo stocks snapped a three-day losing streak Wednesday, with the key Nikkei index rebounding strongly from Tuesday. 東京の株価[東京株式市場の株価]は水曜日、日経平均株価（225種）が前日から大幅反発[回復]して、3日連続の値下がりに歯止めがかかった。

rebound （名）回復、反発、株価の持ち直し、好転
dollar rebound against the yen　円に対するドルの反発
economic rebound　景気回復
modest rebound　穏やかな回復
rebound in profits　収益の回復
rebound in the value of the yen　円相場の反発
small rebound　小幅反発　（=slight rebound）
strong rebound　力強い回復
Tankan survey shows rebound in September　9月短観は改善を示す
technical rebound　自律反発
◆A rebound in the value of the dollar could spell an end to the export boom later this year. ドル相場が反発すれば、輸出好転が続くのは今年末までとなる可能性がある。◆There have been no signs of a rebound in the amount of outstanding loans, which continues on an abated decline. このところ引き続き減少傾向にある銀行の貸出残高に、反転の兆しが見えない。

rebuild （動）再構築する、再建する、再興する、再生する、回復する、在庫などを積み増す、建て替える、復元する、立て直す、築き直す
rebuild one's business　経営を立て直す
rebuild one's global business strategy　グローバル戦略を再構築する
rebuild public finances　財政を立て直す
◆All managers and employees must unite to rebuild our business. 役員と社員は、結束して経営の立て直しをしなければならない。◆Greek government measures to rebuild its public finances include raising the rate of its value-added tax and of its taxes on luxury items, and cutting the salaries of public employees. ギリシャ政府の財政立直し策には、付加価値税率や物品税の引上げと公務員給与の削減などが含まれている。◆Japan's four megabanks are now rebuilding their global business strategies. 日本の4大金融グループは現在、グローバル戦略の再構築に取り組んでいる。◆The firm intends to rebuild its financial structure by a large-scale allocation of the new shares to the third parties. 同社は、大規模な第三者割当増資で資本構成を再構築する考えだ。

rebuild a safety net　安全網を立て直す
◆We must expedite efforts to rebuild a safety net to support the financial system. 金融システムを支える安全網の立直し策を急ぐ必要がある。

rebuild the public finances　財政を立て直す
◆Citizen demonstrations opposing the measures to rebuild the public finances of Greek government have intensified and even resulted in deaths. ギリシャ政府の財政立直し策に反対する市民デモが激化して、死者も出た。

rebuilding （名）再構築、再建、再興、再生、建て替え、復元、立て直し
◆The top priority is the rebuilding of the firm's management system. 最優先課題は、同社の経営体制の立て直しだ。

recapitalization （名）資本再編、資本の再構成、資本変更、資本組入れ　（「資本の再構成」は、増資や減資のほかに、普通株の一部を優先株と組み替えたり、債券を株式と組み替えたりするなど会社の資本構成（capital structure）を変更すること）

recapitalize 資本を再編する，資本構成を修正・変更する，資本を増強する，法定準備金などを資本に組み入れる
◆In an attempt to recapitalize itself, the bank raised ¥15 billion through a third-party share allotment. 資本再編のため、同行は第三者株式割当てで150億円を調達した。 ◆Under the government guidelines, if earnings come in more than 30 percent below targets set in restructuring plans at any major bank that received public funds to recapitalize in 1988 and 1999, the banks management will have to resign. 政府のガイドラインによると、資本再編のために1988年と1999年に公的資金の注入を受けた大手銀行の収益が、再建計画(経営健全化計画)で設定した収益目標を30%以上下回った場合、銀行の経営陣は辞任しなければならない。 ◆What is urgently needed as the EU's rescue package is beefing up the functions of the EFSF and recapitalizing banks that own Greek and Italian government bonds. EU(欧州連合)の支援策として緊急に求められているのは、欧州金融安定基金(EFSF)の機能強化や、ギリシャやイタリアの国債を保有する銀行の資本増強などだ。

recast (動)作り直す，書き直す，組み替える，再構成[編成]する，整理し直す，配役を変える (名)改作，組替え，再構成，再編成，配役変更
recast the budget 予算を組み替える
◆Fiscal resources of ¥1.6 trillion cannot be scrounged together simply by recasting the budget and cutting wasteful spending. 1.6兆円の財源は、予算の組替えや無駄の削減だけでは捻出(ねんしゅつ)できない。

recede (動)撤回する，後退する，手を引く，身を引く，引っ込む，低下する，減退する，弱まる，遠ざかる
recede into the background 重要性を失う，勢力を失う，影が薄れる
receding inflation インフレ率の低下
receding inflation pressures インフレ圧力の低下
◆Signs that unfavorable factors are receding are apparent, as crude oil prices have fallen. 原油の値下りなど、悪材料に解消の兆しが見られる。

receipt (名)受領，受取り，領収書，受領書，売上，収入，売上金，レシート (⇒paper)
interest receipts from abroad 外国から受け取る利子収入
◆The interest rates of major countries were slashed and interest receipts from abroad decreased. 主要国の金利低下で、受け取る利子収入が減少した。

receipts and payments 出納
(=revenues and expenditures)
◆On behalf of the Tokyo metropolitan government, Mizuho Bank handles about ¥10 trillion in receipts and payments annually or about ¥40 billion a day. 東京都に代わって、みずほ銀行は年間約10兆円、1日当たり約400億円の公金出納を行っている。

receivable (形)受け取るべき，受領できる，支払われるべき，支払いを待っている (名)債権，受取債権，売上債権，売掛債権 (「受取債権(売上債権)」には、企業の全取引から生じた売掛金や受取手形、貸付け金、未収金、立替金などの受取勘定が含まれる)
accounts receivable 売掛金
bill receivable 受取手形，BP
collection rate of receivables 債権回収率
lease receivable リース債権
loan receivable ローン債権，貸付け金
nontrade receivables 営業外債権
note receivable 受取手形
outstanding receivables 債権残高
the assigned account receivable 割引債権
trade receivables 営業債権
uncollectible receivable 不良債権
◆About $2 billion of the total $4 billion of Mitsubishi Motors Credit of America Inc.'s assets, such as lease and loan receivables, will be sold to Merrill Lynch. 三菱自動車の米販売金融子会社MMCAの資産総額40億ドルのうち、リース債権やローン債権など約20億ドルが、米証券大手のメリルリンチに売却される。 ◆Collecting receivables helps us to pay our suppliers. 売掛債権を回収すると、当社の納入業者への支払いが楽になります。

receive (動)受け取る，受領する，受け入れる，認める，受け付ける，資金を調達する，損害などを被(こうむ)る，歓迎する
be eligible to receive benefits 失業保険の受給資格がある
be well received by the market 市場の反応は好調である，市場の反応が良い，市場の歓迎を受ける，市場で歓迎される
receive accrual accounting 発生主義会計で処理される
receive dividends 配当金を受け取る，配当を受ける[受領する]
receive funding from ～から資金を調達する
receive interest on ～の利息を受け取る
receive margin 証拠金を受け取る
receive margin call 追証を請求される
◆Customers whose assets at the bank total about ¥10 million will receive a maximum of ¥2 million in insurance if their money is withdrawn illicitly by a third party with a bogus card. 同行では、預け入れ資産が1,000万円程度の預金者が、第三者に偽造カードを使って不正に預金が引き出された場合には、最大200万円の保険金が支払われる。 ◆Four credit card holders received bills for accessing subscription Web sites via cell phones even though they had no recollection of doing so. 利用した覚えがないのに、携帯電話の有料サイトの利用代金請求書が、4人のクレジット・カード会員に届いた。 ◆Tab for Fannie Mae and Freddie Mac could soar to as much as $259 billion, nearly twice the amount Fannie and Freddie have received so far. ファニー・メイ(米連邦住宅抵当金庫)とフレディ・マック(米連邦住宅貸付け抵当公社)の追加の公的資金必要額は、両社がこれまでに受け取った額の約2倍の2,590億ドルに急増する可能性がある。 ◆The company has received about ¥780 billion in cash and debt waivers from shareholders and investors in two bailouts. 同社は、2度の金融支援で、株主と出資企業から約7,800億円の資金提供と債務免除を受けている。 ◆The firm received about ¥2 trillion in loans from financial institutions late last month. 同社は、先月末に金融機関から約2兆円の融資を受けた。 ◆The former chairman of Daio Paper Corp allegedly received more than ¥10 billion in loans from the firm's group companies for private purposes. 報道によれば、大王製紙の前会長が、グループ企業から100億円超の私的融資を受けた。 ◆Those housewives who have failed to switch to the national pension plan and have not paid premiums for an extensive period may receive a pittance or nothing at all. 国民年金への切替えをせず、保険料を長期間払っていない主婦は、低年金や無年金になる可能性がある。 ◆We have received a number of proposals from investment banks who want to act as go-betweens between drug companies for mergers. 投資銀行からは、製薬会社の経営統合の仲介をしたい旨の提案が数多く来ている。 ◆When the policyholders of single-premium whole life insurances die, beneficiaries receive the designated benefits plus accumulated dividends. 一時払い終身保険の契約者が死亡した場合、保険金の受取人は、特定の(死亡)保険金のほかに積立配当金を受け取れる。

receive a public aid 公的支援を受ける
◆Sendai Bank and Tsukuba, regional banks based in areas stricken by the March 11 earthquake and tsunami, will receive a combined ¥65 billion public aid. 仙台銀行と筑波銀行(東日本大震災被災地の地方銀行)が、計650億円の公的支援を受けることになった。

receive a public credit guarantee 公的信用保証を受ける
◆A real estate broker created a dummy company to illegally receive a public credit guarantee. 不動産業者が、架空の会社を作って不正に公的信用保証を受けていた。

receive investment 出資を受ける
◆SMFG received investment from the U.S. Goldman Sachs in 2003 in the form of preferred shares. 三井住友フィナンシャルグループは、2003年にゴールドマン・サックスから優先株式による出資を受けた。

receive loan waivers 債務免除を受ける
◆The company received loan waivers totaling ￥640 million in 2010. 同社は、2010年に総額6,400億円の債務免除を受けた。

receive loans 融資を受ける、ローンを利用する
◆In addition to being ATM cards, the new cards can also be used as credit cards and to receive loans. 新型カードは、キャッシュ・カードであるほか、クレジット・カードとしても使えるし、ローンの利用にも使える。◆Mizuho Bank offers a service by which ATM cardholders are given mileage points each time they use the new cards as credit cards, purchase financial products at the bank's branches or receive loans from the bank. みずほ銀行が提供しているサービスでは、キャッシュ・カード会員が新型カードをクレジット・カードとして利用したり、みずほ銀行で金融商品を購入したり、ローンを利用したりすると、その取引に応じて毎回、マイレージ・ポイントがもらえる。◆Under the IMF's new lending facility, Italy would be eligible to receive short-term loans of up to about $63 billion. IMF（国際通貨基金）の新融資制度で、イタリアは、最大約630億ドルまでの短期融資を受けることができる。

receive loans from financial institutions 金融機関から融資を受ける
◆Credit guarantee associations were established to make it easier for small and mid-sized companies to receive loans from financial institutions. 信用保証協会は、中小企業が金融機関から容易に融資を受けられるようにするために設置された。

receive public funds 公的資金を受ける、公的資金の注入を受ける
◆Under the government guidelines, if earnings come in more than 30 percent below targets set in restructuring plans at any major bank that received public funds to recapitalize in 1988 and 1999, the banks management will have to resign. 政府のガイドラインによると、資本再編のために1988年と1999年に公的資金の注入を受けた大手銀行の収益が、再建計画（経営健全化計画）で設定した収益目標を30％以上下回った場合、銀行の経営陣は辞任しなければならない。

received （形）受け取った、受領した、一般に認められた
advance received 前受金
amount received from sale of bonds 社債発行金による受取金額
deposit received 預かり金、保証金
dividend received 受取配当金
interest received 受取利息
received B/L 受取船荷証券

recession （名）景気後退、不景気、不況、リセッション
（好況はboom、不況はdepression。⇒enter, global recession, prolonged recession, protracted recession, technical recession）
anti-recession cartel 不況カルテル
be firmly in recession 景気後退の泥沼にある、景気後退が深刻
be heading into [towards] recession 景気後退に向かっている
be in the throes of recession 景気後退に苦しんでいる
business recession 景気後退
climb out of recession 景気後退から抜け出す
current recession 今回の景気後退
double dip [double-dip] recession 景気の二番底
economic recession 景気後退、不況
economic recession caused by the strong yen 円高不況
 （=yen-caused recession）
financial recession 金融不況
 （=financial sector-triggered recession）
global recession 世界的な景気後退、世界同時不況、世界不況
 （=worldwide recession; ⇒economic conditions）
go into major recessions 景気が大きく後退する
go [fall] into recession 景気後退局面に入る、景気後退期に入る　（=enter a period of recession）
head into [toward] recession 景気後退に向かう
head off recession 景気後退を防ぐ
inventory recession 在庫不況
lingering recession 長引くリセッション
 （⇒size）
minor [shallow] recession 軽微な景気後退、軽度の景気後退
move [go] into recession 景気後退に突入する、景気が後退する
move [climb] out of recession 景気後退から抜け出す
outright recession 完全な景気後退
prolonged [protracted] recession 長引く不況、不況の長期化、リセッションの長期化　（⇒red ink）
quasi-recession 準景気後退
real recession 本格的な景気後退
recession caused by (the) strong yen 円高不況
recession period 景気後退期
recession process 景気後退過程
remain in a deep [severe] recession 深刻な景気後退期にある
renewed recession 不況への逆戻り
severe recession 深刻な景気後退［リセッション］、厳しいリセッション　（=deep recession）
sink into a double-dip recession 景気底割れする
slip into recession 景気後退局面に入る
the bottom of the recession 景気後退の底
the early stages of a recession 景気後退の初期
the effects of the lingering recession 長引くリセッションの影響
worldwide [world] recession 世界不況、世界的景気後退
yen-caused recession 円高不況
 （=recession caused by strong yen）
◆Fears of a double dip recession are likely to rise if the rise in the yen continues. 円高がこのまま続けば、「景気二番底」懸念が高まると見られる。◆Gold is still becoming the safe haven as people fear recession in the U.S. and the eurozone debt problems. 米国の景気後退やユーロ圏の債務危機問題への懸念から、まだ金が安全な投資先［資金の逃避先］となっている。◆Major European banks are to take additional stress tests to examine their ability to withstand a long recession. 景気の長期低迷への耐久力を調べるため、欧州の主要銀行は再度、ストレス・テストを受けることになっている。◆Signs grow stronger that the whole world is plunging into a recession. 今は、世界同時不況の様相が深まっている。◆The executive pay of Merrill Lynch & Co., mostly in bonuses, has become a hot-button issue in the recession as banks and companies fail. メリルリンチの経営幹部報酬は、大半がボーナスだが、銀行や企業が経営破たんする不況時の強い関心を呼ぶ問題になっている。◆The recession has been spreading globally and the Japanese economy has been languishing since last year. 昨年来、世界同時不況が進行し、日本経済は低迷が続いてい

る。◆The U.S. economy slipped into recession in December 2007. 米経済は、2007年12月から景気後退局面(リセッション)に入った。◆The U.S. 10 leading banks need a combined capital buffer of 74.6 billion against the risk of a deeper recession and higher unemployment over the next two years. 米主要金融機関の10社は、今後2年の景気悪化リスクと失業増大に備えて、10社合計で746億ドルの資本増強を求められている。◆Worries over the spreading of the eurozone debt crisis and the U.S.'s slipping into recession have driven the rout in financial markets. ユーロ圏の財政危機の拡大と米国の景気後退入りへの懸念で、金融市場は総崩れになった。

解説 景気後退について:「景気後退」は、景気の回復・拡大期が終わって底を打つまでの状態をいう。米国では、一般に実質国内総生産(GDP)が2四半期連続でマイナス成長になると、景気後退と見なされる。日本の場合は、鉱工業生産指数や有効求人倍率などの経済指標に基づいて、景気動向指数研究会が判定している。

recessionary (形)景気後退の
  recessionary data　景気後退を示す指標
  recessionary (economic) conditions　景気停滞, 景気低迷
  recessionary impulses　景気後退の兆し
  recessionary pressures　景気後退の圧力, 不況圧力
  recessionary year　景気後退の年
◆If the number of corporate bankruptcies and the unemployment rate soar owing to structural reforms, recessionary pressures will further increase. 構造改革で企業倒産件数や失業率が増えると、不況圧力は一層強まるものと思われる。

recipient (名)受給者, 受領国, 被援助国, 受取人, 受納者, 受給者, 受賞者, 情報開示を受けた者, 容器
  aid recipient　援助受入れ国, 援助受入れ側, 援助を受ける側
  ODA recipient　政府開発援助(ODA)受入れ国
  profit recipient　利潤取得者[受領者]
  recipient country　受入れ国, 被援助国
  recipient of charity　慈善給付受給者
  recipient of the assistance　支援先
  recipient of the benefits　受益者
  recipient of the secret information　秘密情報の開示を受けた者
  social security recipient　社会保障受給者
  unemployment insurance recipient　失業保険受給者
  recipient of the emergency assistance　緊急支援先
◆Indonesia is the first recipient of the emergency assistance to developing countries hit by the financial crisis through ODA. インドネシアは、金融危機で打撃を受けた発展途上国に対する政府開発援助(ODA)による最初の緊急支援先だ。
  recipient of the Fed's emergency aid　FRB(米連邦準備制度理事会)の緊急支援先
◆Among the recipients of the Fed's emergency aid during the financial crisis were foreign central banks, such as the European Central Bank, Bank of England and the Bank of Japan. (2008年秋の)金融危機の際に米連邦準備制度理事会(FRB)が実施した緊急支援を受けた金融機関としては、欧州中央銀行(ECB)やイングランド銀行、日銀などの中央銀行もある。

recognize [recognise] (動)認識する, 見越す, 計上する, 費用処理する, 認可する, 許可する, 認定する, 公認する, 承認する, 実現する
  recognize economies of scale　規模の経済を実現する
  recognize mark-to-market losses in one's securities portfolio　株式評価損を計上する
  recognize netting　ネッティングを承認する
  recognize premium revenues　保険料収入を認識する
  recognized clearing house　公認清算機関
  recognized company　優良企業
  recognized investment exchange　公認投資取引所
  recognized self-regulating organization　承認自主規制機関
  recognized stock exchange　公認証券取引所
◆Our maximum potential loss may exceed the amount recognized in our balance sheet. 当社の最大予想損失額は、貸借対照表上で認識された額を上回る可能性があります。◆We must recognize anew the serious fiscal conditions gripping Japan. 日本の[日本をおおう]深刻な財政事情を、われわれは再認識しなければならない。

recommend (動)勧める, 推奨する, 推薦(すいせん)する, 勧告する, 助言する
  equities recommended　推奨株
  recommend subscription to the offer　新規公開株の購入を推奨する
  recommended issue [stock]　推奨株
  stocks recommended for purchase　買い推奨された銘柄
  stocks recommended for sale [selling]　売り推奨された銘柄

recommendation (名)勧め, 推奨, 推薦, 勧告, 助言, 推薦状, 長所, 取り柄
  a sell recommendation　売り推奨
  put out a buy recommendation on the common shares　普通株の買い推奨をする
  SEC recommendations　SEC(米証券取引委員会)の勧告

reconstruct (動)再建する, 再構築する, 立て直す, 再現する, 復元する, 改築する
◆The company's group has chosen to reconstruct itself under a holding company. 同社グループは、持ち株会社での再建を選択した。◆Under the envisioned lending facility, the IMF will provide funds to countries where government bond yields remain at high levels to help reconstruct their public finances. この融資制度案では、国際通貨基金(IMF)が、国債の利回りが高止まりしている国に資金を提供[融資]して財政再建を支援する。

reconstruction (名)再建, 復興, 復元, 再現, 改築 (⇒donor)
  corporate reconstruction plan　企業再建計画, 再建計画
  economic reconstruction plan　経済再建計画
  fiscal reconstruction　財政再建
  full reconstruction　本格的な再建
  reconstruction plan　再建計画, 再建策 (⇒loan forgiveness)
  the reconstruction of business　事業再構築, 経営再建
◆By selling JT shares, the government expects to raise ¥500 billion to ¥600 billion to finance reconstruction from the Great East Japan Earthquake. JT(日本たばこ産業)株の売却で政府は、東日本大震災復興の財源に充てるため、5,000億円〜6,000億円の資金調達を見込んでいる。◆Delays in the debt relief process may become obstacles to reconstruction efforts. 債務救済[債務削減]手続きの遅れは、復興の支障[障害]となる可能性がある。◆Funds for disaster reconstruction will be procured by issuing special government bonds. 震災復興の資金は、復興債を発行して調達する。◆GM's reconstruction is progressing smoothly. GMの再建は、順調に進んでいる。◆JAL's reconstruction will have to involve decreasing the amount of its debts. 日本航空の再建には、負債の圧縮[減額]が不可避だ。◆The company struck an agreement with its debtholder to win their support for reconstruction. 同社は、会社再建について債権者の支持を得ることで、債権者と合意に達した。◆The government plans to sell some of its 100 percent stake in Japan Post Holdings Co. to fund reconstruction from the Great East Japan Earthquake. 政府は、東日本大震災の復興財源に充てるため、100%保有する日

本郵政の株式の一部も売却する方針だ。◆The United States and European countries are forced to proceed steadily with fiscal reconstruction and resolve the financial turmoil. 米欧各国は、財政再建を着実に進めて、金融市場の混乱を収拾せざるを得ない状況にある。◆To overcome the current economic crisis, stimulus measures should take precedence over fiscal reconstruction for the time being. 現在の経済危機を克服するためには、当面は、財政再建よりも景気対策を優先しなければならない。◆To procure funds to finance reconstruction from the Great East Japan Earthquake, the government is planning to sell some of its shares in Japan Tobacco Inc. and Tokyo Metro Co. 東日本大震災の復興費用を賄うための資金を調達するため、政府は日本たばこ産業(JT)と東京地下鉄(東京メトロ)の株式を売却する方針だ。◆U.S. investment bank Goldman Sachs Group Inc. will invest ¥41 billion in the reconstruction of ailing construction firm Fujita Corp. 米投資銀行のゴールドマン・サックス・グループが、経営不振のフジタ(総合建設会社)の再建に410億円投資する。

reconstruction bonds 復興債, 復興再生債(restoration and rebirth bonds), 復興事業債
◆The government will issue reconstruction bonds to finance the second fiscal 2011 supplementary budget, which will cover reconstruction programs. 政府は、復興計画に充(あ)てる2011年度大2次補正予算案の財源を賄(まかな)うため、復興債[復興再生債]を発行する方針だ。

reconstruction fund 復興基金
(⇒restoration bonds)
◆Revenue from the consumption tax hike would be managed under the Great East Japan Earthquake reconstruction fund. 消費税引上げによる税収は、東日本大震災復興基金で管理することになる。

reconstruction plan 経営再建計画, 経営再建案, 経営再建策
◆Crisis-stricken giant supermarket chain operator announced a fresh reconstruction plan. 経営危機に陥っている巨大スーパーが、新たな経営再建策を発表した。◆The reconstruction plan includes the retirement of 50 percent of the firm's common shares. 経営再建策には、同社の普通株式の5割消却も含まれている。

record (動)記録する, 記帳する, 計上する, 登記・登録する, 表示する, 示す, ～となる
be recorded net 純額で表示される
record a further increase さらに上昇する
record a small gain 小幅上昇する
record an all-time low 過去最低を記録する, 過去最低を更新する
record as a long-term investment 長期投資として計上する
record one's bad loans as losses 不良債権を損失として計上する, 不良債権を損失として計上処理する
◆Even if the banks record their bad loans as losses in their corporate accounting, such loans are not treated as losses in their tax accounting. 銀行が企業会計で不良債権を損失として計上[処理]しても、税務会計ではこれらの不良債権は損金扱いにならない。

record (名)記録, 最高記録, 最低記録, 過去最高, 過去最大, 過去最低, 過去最悪, 成績, 登記, 登録, 経歴, 履歴, 業績, 成績, 動向, データ, レコード
actual record 実績
all-time record 歴代最高記録
be off the record 非公開となっている, ここだけの話
break the record 記録を破る, 記録を更新する
chronological record 年代順の記録
credit record 信用履歴
dividend record 配当実績
estoppel by record 記録による禁反言

for the record 事実は, 公式には, 念のために言うと
hold the record 記録を持っている
medical record 病歴
monthly record 月間過去最高
new record 新記録, 史上最高値
off the record 非公式の, 非公開の, オフレコの
on record 記録上の, 過去の
put[get, keep, set] the record straight 誤解を解く, 記録を正す
record of achievement 業績, 実績
record of discussion 討議議事録
set a world record 世界記録を作る
shareholder[stockholder] of record 登録株主, 株主名簿上の株主
the longest period record 過去最長記録
the lowest on record 過去最低, 過去最悪
the postwar record 戦後の最高値, 戦後最高値
the second highest on record 過去二番目の高水準
the worst year on record 記録上最悪の年, 過去最悪の年
track record 実績
◆Gold extended its rally to a record above $1,900 an ounce amid increased uncertainties over the U.S. and European economic outlook on the Comex in New York. ニューヨーク商品取引所では、米欧景気見通しへの懸念[米欧経済の先行き不透明感]の高まりを受け[懸念の高まりから]、金価格が急騰して、1トロイ・オンス＝1,900ドルを史上初めて突破した。◆Obama sees the U.S. budget deficit rising to a fresh record in 2010. オバマ米大統領は、2010年度(2009年10月～2010年9月)の財政赤字は急増して過去最悪になる[過去最悪を更新する]と見込んでいる。◆On Aug. 31, 2011, the yen rose to the ¥76.50 level against the U.S. dollar in the Tokyo foreign exchange market, close to the postwar record of ¥75.95 registered on Aug. 19. 2011年8月31日の東京外国為替市場の円相場は、1ドル＝76円50銭台まで上昇し、8月19日に付けた戦後最高値の75円95銭に近づいた。◆The U.S. current account deficit in 2001 was the second highest on record. 米国の2001年の経常赤字は、過去二番目の高水準だった。◆The U.S. trade deficit soared to a record of $617.7 billion last year. 米国の昨年の貿易赤字は、過去最大の6,177億ドルに急増した。◆Through continuing gains in annual earnings, it will be possible, over time, to adjust the payout ratio while still maintaining our dividend record. 年間利益の増大を続けることによって、当社の配当実績を今後とも維持しながら、時期が来たら配当性向を調整することは可能である。◆Volume on the First Section of the Tokyo Stock Exchange had exceeded the 1 billion mark for 42 business days in a row as of Monday, the longest period on record. 東京証券取引所第一部の出来高は、月曜日の時点で、42営業日連続で10億株の大台を超え、過去最長記録となった。

record (形)記録的な, 過去最高の, 空前の, 史上初めての[史上初の]
record earnings 過去最高益, 過去最高の利益
record keeping 記録保存
record plunge 過去最大の下げ
record sales 過去最高の売上高
stock record date 株式の名義書換え停止日
◆Combined group net profit at Japan's six top banking groups totaled a record ¥1.74 trillion for the April-September fiscal first half. 9月中間決算[4-9月期の上半期決算]で、日本の大手銀行・金融6グループ合計の連結税引き後利益が、過去最高益の1兆7,400億円となった。◆Gasoline prices rose to a record ¥185.1 a liter this week. ガソリン価格は今週、過去最高の1リットル185円10銭まで上昇した。◆Japan's imports climbed 18.2 percent in July from a year earlier to a record ¥7.54 trillion, up for the 10th straight month. 日本の

7月の輸入は、前年同月比18.2％増の7兆5,400億円と、10か月連続で過去最高額になった。◆The current account deficit posted a record quarterly deficit in the January-March quarter. 経常赤字は、1-3月期は四半期ベースで過去最高を記録した。◆The yen in record strong territory of ￥76 to the dollar causes hardships in the Japanese economy. 1ドル＝76円台の史上最高の円高水準は、日本経済にとって厳しい。◆U.S. deficits hit record $413 billion. 米財政赤字が、過去最悪の4,130億ドルに達している。◆U.S. oil prices reached a record $50 a barrel. 米国の原油価格が、史上初めて1バレル＝50ドルに達した。

record date 配当基準日, 基準日, 名義書換え停止日, 登録日 (=date of record: 当該事業年度に配当を受け取る権利のある株主を決める日のこと。配当は、基準日現在、株主名簿に登録されている株主（登録株主）に対してだけ支払われる)

record heavy trading 記録的な大商い
◆The Tokyo stock market has recently been roaring, with record heavy trading seen. 東京株式市場が、記録的な大商いを続けて、活況を呈している。

record high 記録的な高さ, 空前の高さ, 過去最高, 過去最悪, 史上最高, 最高値
　hit a record high　過去最高 [史上最高] を記録する, 過去最多となる, 過去最多となる
　jump to a record high　急増して過去最高となる, 過去最高まで急増する
　near a record high　史上最高 [過去最高] に迫る水準
　reach a record high　史上最高値にまで達する
　trade to a record high　新高値を付ける
◆The financial group expects its half-year profit to be a record high. 同金融グループは、過去最高の半期利益 [中間決算で過去最高益] を見込んでいる。◆The number of the unemployed who involuntarily lost their jobs in April hit a record high of 1.15 million, up 240,000 from a year earlier. 4月の完全失業者のうち、非自発的離職者 [失業者] 数は115万人で、前年同月より24万人増加して過去最多となった。◆The yen could soon even reach a record high in the ￥75 range versus the dollar. 円は、やがて1ドル＝75円台の史上最高値にまで達する可能性がある。◆The yen has been hovering near its record high of ￥76.25 against the U.S. dollar in Tokyo. 東京外国為替市場の円相場は、戦後最高値の1ドル＝76円25銭に迫る水準で推移している。◆The yen rose to its record high of ￥79.75 against the dollar in 1995. 円相場は、1995年に上昇して史上最高値の1ドル＝79円75銭を付けた。

record low 記録的な低さ, 記録的な低水準, 空前の低さ, 過去最低, 過去最悪, 史上最低
　drop [decline] to a record low　過去最低まで [過去最低に] 落ち込む, 過去最悪となる
　hit a record low　過去最低を記録する, 史上最低を記録する
　keep interest rates at record low　主要政策金利を過去最低に維持する
　trade to a record low　新安値を付ける
◆Long-term interest rates have soared almost fourfold in the past three months after the rates hit a record low in mid-June. 長期金利は、6月中旬に史上最低を記録した後、この3か月で4倍近くに急騰した。◆Record low U.S. borrowing costs are boosting the appeal to bullion as a hedge against inflation. 米国の資金調達コストが過去最低の水準にあるため、インフレ・ヘッジとしての金 [金地金] の人気が高まっている。◆The average ratio of job offers to job seekers dropped to a record low in 2009, down 0.41 point from the previous year to 0.47. 2009年の平均の有効求人倍率は、前年比0.41ポイント減の0.47倍で、過去最悪だった。◆The European Central Bank kept its key interest rates at record lows. 欧州中央銀行（ECB）は、主要政策金利を過去最低に維持した [据え置いた]。◆The outstanding balance of lending in October declined to a record low since the Bank of Japan began compiling such data. 10月の銀行の貸出残高は、日銀が統計を開始（91年7月）して以来、過去最低に落ち込んだ。

record net profit 過去最高の純利益, 過去最高の税引き後利益 (=record-high net profit)
◆The financial group posted a record net profit of ￥1.18 trillion on a consolidated basis for the year ending March 31. 同フィナンシャル・グループの3月期連結決算は、税引き後利益（純利益）が過去最高の1兆1,800億円となった。

record plunge 過去最大の下落, 過去最大の物価下落
◆Record plunges were also recorded for food, including fast food such as hamburgers and gyudon (rice with beef). 過去最大の下落 [物価下落] は、ハンバーガーや牛丼などファスト・フードを含む「食料」（食料の費目）でも記録された。

record profit 過去最高益, 過去最高の利益
◆Some companies are making record profits amid the global economic slowdown. 世界的な景気低迷のなかで、一部の企業は過去最高益を上げている。

record value 最高値
◆The yen's value still remains high and is likely to reach a postwar record value above the ￥76-to-the-dollar level. 円相場は依然高く、1ドル＝76円台を上回る戦後最高値に達する可能性がある。

recoup（動）(損失などを) 取り戻す (recover), 回収する, 回復する, 奪回 [奪還] する, 返済する, 払い戻す (pay back), 弁済する, 埋め合わせる (compensate), 償う, 弁償する, 補償する, 差し引く (deduct), 控除する
　recoup a person for expenses　人に費用を返済する
　recoup a person's loss [recoup a person for a loss]　人の損失 [損失分] を弁償する
　recoup one's investment　投資を回収する
　recoup one's losses by a good investment　有利な投資で損失を取り戻す
　recoup oneself　損失を取り戻す, 損失を埋め合わせる, 損失分を清算する
　recoup oneself at another's expense　人に損をさせて自分の損失を埋め合わせる

recourse（名）償還請求, 償還請求権（手形などの振出人または [裏書人に] 支払いを請求する権利), 二次的請求, 二次的支払い義務, 遡求, 依頼, 頼みの綱, リコース
　be non-recourse　～に償還請求権がない
　by recourse to　～に訴えて
　direct recourse　直接の償還請求権
　endorsement without recourse　無担保裏書き, 遡求に応じない裏書き
　have recourse to　～に頼る, ～を用いる
　last recourse　最後の手段
　legal recourse　償還請求権
　limited recourse　限定付き [制限付き] 償還請求権, 制限償還請求権
　limited recourse project financing　償還請求権の限られたプロジェクト・ファイナンス
　non-recourse finance　ノンリコース・ファイナンス
　non-recourse loan　非遡求型ローン
　recourse arrangement　償還請求権付き
　recourse fund　不渡り手形の償還準備積立金
　recourse obligation　償還義務, 二次的支払い義務
　recourse repudiation　手形償還拒絶
　recourse to the seller for defaulted assets　デフォルトに陥った資産に関する売り手の遡求義務
　right of recourse　償還請求権
　transfer of assets with recourse　償還請求権付き資産の譲渡
　with recourse　買戻し請求権付き, 償還請求権付き, 遡求

権あり
　with recourse credit［letter of credit］　遡求義務不免除信用状, 償還請求権付き信用状
　without recourse　遡求なし, 遡求権なし, 遡求排除, 無担保裏書きの, 二次的支払い義務のない, 償還請求義務のない, 償還請求権のない, 償還請求に応ぜず
　without recourse credit［letter of credit］　遡求義務免除信用状, 償還請求権なき信用状
　without recourse to　〜に頼らずに, 〜に訴えることなく, 〜に償還請求することなく
　◆ABC shall have no recourse against XYZ for any obligations under the original agreement assigned pursuant to this assignment agreement. ABCは, この譲渡契約に従って譲渡された原契約上の債務については, XYZに履行の請求を一切求めないものとする。
recourse loan　遡求請求権付き貸付け, 償還請求権付きローン
　deduct recourse loans　遡求請求権付き貸付け金を控除する
　limited recourse loan　制限償還請求権付きローン
　◆This loss came from deducting recourse loans made to our senior management. この損失は, 当社の上級経営陣に対して行った遡求請求権付き貸付け金を控除したことで生じました。
recover　(動)回復する, 貸出金などを回収する, 債権などを取り立てる
　fully recover　本格的に回復する, 本格回復する
　recover one's negative net worth　債務超過を解消する
　recover the loans　融資額を回収する, 貸出金［貸付け金］を回収する
　recover the principal　元本を回収する
　◆Corporate bond issues are recovering from the bond market turbulence following the March 11 earthquake and tsunami. 東日本大震災後の債券市場の混乱から, 社債の発行額が回復している。◆If TEPCO's creditor banks forgive the debts when the utility is not carrying excessive liabilities, lenders will not be able to recover either the principal or interest owed. 東電が債務超過でない時点で東電の債権保有銀行が債権を放棄すると, 金融機関は元本を回収できず, 金利収入も得られなくなる。◆It is highly unlikely personal spending will fully recover. 個人消費の本格回復は, 望み薄だ。◆None of the loans were recovered. 融資額は全額, 回収されなかった。◆On expectations for the new financial steps, the Nikkei Stock Average recovered to the ¥9,000 mark. 今回の金融政策への期待で, 日経平均株価は9,000円台に回復した。◆Ordinary investors bought the shares on the expectation that the company would recover. 一般投資家は, 同社が立ち直ると見て同社株を買った。◆The company expects to recover its negative net worth by the end of fiscal 2010 on the back of ¥370.5 billion proceeds from the sale of its cosmetic division as well as the requested debt waiver and new share issue. 2010年度末には, 化粧品事業部門の売却益3,705億円や債権放棄の要請, 増資(新株発行)などで, 同社の債務超過は解消できる見通しだ。◆The diffusion index of business sentiment among large manufacturers recovered to positive territory for the first time in two quarters. 大企業・製造業の業況判断指数(DI)は, 2四半期(半年)ぶりにプラスに転じた。◆The global economy continues to recover, albeit in a fragile and uneven way. 世界経済は, 脆弱(ぜいじゃく)で一様ではないが, 回復を続けている。◆The U.S. budget deficit for fiscal 2010 narrowed to $1.29 trillion as tax collections recovered slightly and financial bailout spending fell sharply. 米国の2010会計年度(2009年10月〜2010年9月)の財政赤字は, 税収がいくぶん回復し, 金融救済［金融支援］費用が急減したため, 1兆2,900億ドルに縮小した。◆There is no sign that capital investment will recover. 設備投資に回復の兆しが見えない。

recoverable loans　正常債権

◆The ongoing economic slowdown will financially hurt corporate debtors, while also converting some recoverable loans into ones with no hope of recovery. 現在進行中の景気後退は, 融資先企業の経営を悪化させ, 同時に一部の正常債権をも不良債権化させる。
recovering earnings　利益の回復
recovering global economy　回復途上の世界経済, 世界の景気回復
　◆If the European financial crisis expands, it will damage the recovering global economy. 欧州の金融危機が拡大すれば, 回復途上にある世界経済に打撃を与えることになる。
recovery　(名)回復, 景気回復, 景気や市場の持ち直し, 相場の回復, 回収, 再建, 復興
　(⇒economic recovery)
　a recovery in the dollar　ドルの回復
　bad debt recovery　償却債権の取立て, 償却済み債権取立益
　be on a recovery trend　回復傾向にある
　capital recovery　資本の回収
　constrain (economic) recovery　景気回復の足を引っ張る
　cost recovery basis［method］　原価回収法
　cyclical economic recovery　景気回復 (=cycle recovery, cyclical recovery, economic recovery)
　discount the end of recovery　景気腰折れを織り込む
　early recovery of the world economy　世界経済の早期回復
　earnings recovery　業績回復, 収益の回復
　enter a recovery course　回復軌道に入る
　full economic recovery　景気の本格回復, 景気の全面的回復
　full-fledged recovery　本格復調, 本格回復
　full scale recovery　本格的な回復
　generate recovery in the economy　景気を回復させる
　incipient recovery　景気回復の局面, 景気持ち直しの局面, 回復局面
　investment recovery　投資回収
　lead a recovery　景気回復を主導する
　movement toward a recovery　景気回復の動き, 景気持ち直しの動き
　production recovery　生産の回復
　(=recovery in production)
　put the economy on a steady recovery track　景気を順調な回復軌道に乗せる
　recoveries of write-offs　償却債権取立益
　recovery of tax revenues　税収の回復
　resource recovery　資源回収, 資源の再利用
　self-sustaining recovery　自律回復, 自力回復
　signs of recovery　回復の兆し
　sustainable recovery　本格的な景気回復
　(=full scale recovery)
　V-shaped recovery　V字型回復, V字回復
　zero recovery　全額回収不能
　◆A recovery will be export-driven, dependent on U.S. growth and the yen's depreciation, instead of being led by increased domestic consumption and capital investment. 今後の景気回復は, アメリカ経済の好転や円安を背景にした輸出主導型の回復で, 国内の個人消費や設備投資の伸びがその牽引役となるわけではない。◆Most emerging East Asian economies are assured of a sharp V-shaped recovery this year. 今年は, 東アジア新興国の大半が急激にV字回復するのは確実だ。◆The basis for recovery remains weak. 景気回復の基盤は依然, 弱いままだ。◆The doldrums in the manufacturing industry will

impede the recovery of Japan's economy. 製造業の不振は、日本経済の回復の足かせにもなる。◆The economy is moving toward an incipient recovery. 景気は、持ち直しに向けた動きが見られる。◆The government should take all possible fiscal and financial means to bring the still ailing economy back on the road to recovery. 政府は、いまだにどん詰まり状態にある景気を回復の軌道に乗せるために、財政と金融の両面からの政策を総動員すべきだ。◆The rate of economic expansion in the current phase of recovery is much smaller than previous expansionary phases. 現在の景気拡大期［景気拡大局面］の経済成長率は、過去の景気拡大期よりかなり低い。◆The retail industry has begun showing signs of recovery. 小売業界は、回復の兆しが見られるようになった。◆The U.S. and other overseas economies have driven Japan's recovery. 米国などの海外経済が、日本の景気回復を牽引してきた。◆To make the economy's step toward recovery much firmer, the government should implement another expansionary budget. 景気回復の足取りをずっと確かなものにするためにも、政府はさらに積極型の予算を実施すべきだ。◆Under the severe income and employment situations, personal consumption has yet to show indications of a full-fledged recovery. 厳しい所得・雇用環境の下で、個人消費に本格的な復調の気配がまだ見えない。◆When you have a fragile recovery, it wouldn't seem to me like an opportune time to raise taxes. 景気回復の足取りが弱いときは、税金引上げの好機とは言えないように思える。◆Without an economic recovery and the resultant recovery of tax revenues, fiscal reconstruction will be made difficult. 景気回復［経済の再生］とそれによる税収の回復がなければ、今後の財政再建もおぼつかない。

recovery in business sentiment 景況感の改善
◆The recovery in business sentiment was largely due to the improvement in the parts supply chain disrupted after the March 11 earthquake and tsunami. 景況感が改善したのは、主に東日本大震災で打撃を受けたサプライ・チェーン（部品供給網）の復旧が進んだためだ。

recovery in production 生産の回復
（=production recovery）
◆Companies have restarted fund procurement activities for a recovery in production as the bond market turbulence after the March 11 earthquake and tsunami has subsided. 東日本大震災後の債券市場の混乱が収束したので、企業各社は生産回復に向けて資金調達活動を再開した。

recovery of corporate performance 企業業績の回復
◆A series of accounting scandals and delays in the recovery of corporate performance are accelerating falls in stock prices on the U.S. markets, along with the weakening of the dollar. 一連の［相次ぐ］企業会計の不祥事と企業業績回復の遅れで、米国の株安とドル安が加速している。

recovery of foreign economies 海外経済の回復
◆Japan's economy finally began picking up thanks to the government's pump-priming measures and the recovery of foreign economies. 日本の景気は、政府の景気対策や海外経済の回復のおかげで、ようやく持ち直してきた。

recovery of tax revenues 税収の回復
◆Without an economic recovery and the resultant recovery of tax revenues, fiscal reconstruction will be made difficult. 景気回復［経済の再生］とそれによる税収の回復がなければ、今後の財政再建もおぼつかない。

recovery operation 回収業務
◆The company has systemized its expertise in credit and recovery operations. 同社は、与信・回収業務のノウハウをシステム化している。

recovery path 回復軌道
◆The Japanese economy has reached a critical stage at which it could tumble into a deflationary spiral after brief stability, or be brought back to a recovery path. 日本経済は現在、小康状態から再びデフレの悪循環に落ち込むか、回復軌道に戻せるかどうかの瀬戸際にある。

recovery phase 回復局面
◆The economy still remains in a recovery phase in the business cycle. 景気は、まだ回復局面にある［景気の回復基調はまだ続いている］。

recovery track 回復軌道, 景気回復軌道
（=recovery course, recovery path）
get on the recovery track　回復軌道に乗る
put the economy on the recovery track　景気を回復軌道に乗せる
stray off the recovery track　回復軌道から外れる
◆If the government relaxes its policy now, the economy will not be able to get on the recovery track. 政府がいまその政策の手を緩めれば、景気は回復軌道に乗れないだろう。◆The Bank of Japan feels the Japanese economy has not strayed off the recovery track. 日本経済は回復軌道から外れていない、と日銀は思っている。◆The U.S. economy has gotten back on the recovery track since the latter half of last year. 米国の景気は、昨年後半からまた回復軌道に乗り始めた。

recovery trend 回復傾向
◆The economy is on a recovery trend. 景気は、回復傾向にある。

rectify （動）修正する, 訂正する, 是正する, 正す, 改正する, 矯正する, 調整する, 純化する, 精留する
rectify imbalances　不均衡を是正する
（⇒hammer out）
rectify the excessive rise in property prices　不動産価格の上がり過ぎを調整する
rectify the sharp rise in the value of the yen　急激な円高を是正する
rectify trade imbalances　貿易不均衡を是正する
◆The sharp rise in the value of the yen must be rectified. 急激な円高は、是正しなければならない。◆Uncertainty about the future of Japan's financial system will persist until the vulnerable financial foundation of life insurance companies is rectified. 生命保険会社の脆弱（ぜいじゃく）な経営基盤を立て直さない限り、日本の金融システムの先行きに対する不安は消えない。

rectify the rise in the yen's value 円高を是正する
◆Amid the depleted state coffers, it is difficult to implement a major stimulus package to rectify the rise in the yen's value. 財政悪化が進む中［国の財源が枯渇する中］、円高是正のために大規模な財政出動を行うのは難しい。◆The Bank of Japan should take draconian measures to rectify the rise in the yen's value. 日銀は、厳しい円高是正措置を取るべきだ。

rectify the surge in the value of the U.S. dollar ドル高を是正する
◆In the Plaza Accord, G-5 nations agreed to rectify the surge in the value of the U.S. dollar. プラザ合意で、日・米・英・仏・西独の先進5か国（G5）がドル高是正で合意した。

rectify trade imbalance 貿易不均衡を是正する
◆Rectifying trade imbalances mainly with China by devaluing the dollar is the top priority in Washington. ドル安により主に中国との貿易不均衡を是正するのが、米国の最優先課題だ。

recurrence （名）再発, 再燃, 再来, 反復, 繰り返し

recurrence of deflation デフレの再燃
◆A slight rise in consumer prices will not eliminate fears of a recurrence of deflation and public anxiety over the future of the economy. 消費者物価の小幅な上昇だけでは、デフレ再燃への懸念や景気の先行き不安を払拭（ふっしょく）できない。

recurrence of financial strife 金融危機の再発
◆The challenge of the Basel Committee on Banking Supervision is to develop a regulatory framework while fending off a recurrence of financial strife. バーゼル銀行監督委員会の課題は、金融危機再発の防止と規制の枠組みの策定だ。

recurrence of online fraud オンライン詐欺の再発
◆We must change our personal identification number first to prevent the recurrence of online fraud. オンライン詐欺の再発を防ぐには、まずパスワードを変えなければならない。

recurring (形)経常的な,定期的な
- core recurring earnings 中核部門の経常利益
- non-recurring gain 経常外利益
- non-recurring income 経常外収入
- recurring audit 連続監査,継続監査
- recurring clause (保険の)再発条項
- recurring margins 経常利益率
- recurring operating losses 経常的な営業損失
- recurring payment 定期循環払い
- recurring transactions 経常損益

recurring expenditures 経常的歳出
◆There will be a decrease in net assets if the "hidden treasure" of a special account is used for replenishing recurring expenditures, not for reducing liabilities. 特別会計の「埋蔵金」(積立金)を、負債の削減に使わないで経常的な歳出に充てれば、純資産は減ってしまう。

recurring loss 経常赤字
- non-recurring loss 経常外損失
- report recurring losses 経常赤字になる,経常赤字に転落する

◆The Corporation incurred ¥3 billion of recurring losses in its semiannual settlement of accounts in September. 当社は、9月の中間決算で30億円の経常赤字となりました。

recurring profit 経常利益 (=current profit, income before extraordinary items; ⇒consolidated recurring profit)
- all-industry recurring profits 全産業経常利益
- consolidated recurring profits 連結経常利益
- full-year parent recurring profit 通期の単独経常利益
- interim recurring profits 中間期の経常利益
- recurring profit estimate 経常利益予想

◆Industries at the upper end of the production stream have higher increases in recurring profits. 生産の流れ(生産から消費に至る各段階)の上流にある産業のほうが、経常利益の増加率が高い。◆These nonfinancial companies listed in the First Section of the Tokyo Stock Exchange posted record high sales and recurring profits. 東証一部上場の金融を除くこれらの企業は、売上高、経常利益とも史上最高となった。

[解説]経常利益:売上高から販売・管理費を差し引いた営業利益に、預金の受取利息や保有株式の配当収入を加えたり、借入金の支払い利息などを差し引いたりして計算。ただし、メーカーの工場売却や保有株式の売却による利益、リストラのための割増退職金の費用などは特別利益または特別損失と呼ばれ、経常利益には含まれない。経常利益は、日本では、企業の業績や中長期的な業況を知るのに最も適した指標とされている。

recycle (動)資金などを還流する,利益などを還元する,再利用する,再生利用する,循環処理する,循環使用する,修復する,リサイクル
- recycle funds 資金を還流させる
- recycle one's profit to consumers 利益を消費者に還元する
- recycle the money by direct investment 資金を直接投資にまわす
- recycle the OPEC funds back to Asia OPEC(石油輸出国機構)資金をアジアに還流させる
- recycle the surplus 黒字を還流させる

◆Companies should recycle their profits to consumers. 企業は、利益を消費者に還元すべきだ。

recycling (名)還流,還元,資源循環,再生利用,再利用,再処理,再生事業,循環使用,再循環,リサイクリング
- capital recycling 資金の還流,資金還流
- financial recycling 資金還流
- fund recycling 資金還流
- oil dollar recycling オイル・ダラー[オイル・マネー]の還流
- the recycling of cash to poor nations 貧困国への資金還流
- the recycling of petrodollars オイル・ダラー[オイル・マネー]の還流
- the recycling of the oil surpluses 石油余剰資金の還流

red (名)赤字,損失 (=red ink; ⇒black, corporate tax, extraordinary loss, net balance, ordinary balance)
- fall into the red 赤字に転落する,赤字に陥る
- go into the red 赤字になる (=fall into the red)
- in the red 赤字で
- operate in the red 赤字経営する
- out of the red 赤字を脱して
- remain in the red 赤字を続ける
- slip into the red 赤字に転落する

◆As the total loss from stock holding reached ¥3.31 trillion, the seven banking groups were forced into the red. 保有株による損失は総額で3兆3,100億円に達し、銀行7グループは赤字に追い込まれた。◆The bank fell into the red in the term ended March 2011 with a loss of more than ¥5 billion. 2011年3月期に同行は、50億円超の赤字に転落した。◆The bank remained in the red, incurring a group net loss of more than ¥400 billion. 同行は、4,000億円を超える連結純損失(連結税引き後赤字)となって、赤字を続けた。

red (形)赤字の,欠損の,赤い
- red balance 赤字残高,欠損帳尻
- red B/L [bill of lading] 赤船荷証券(保険証券と合体した船荷証券)
- red cent 1セント銅貨
- red chips 香港株式市場上場の中国企業の株式,レッド・チップ
- red clause 輸出前貸し許容条件,赤色約款,レッド・クローズ
- red clause (letter of) credit 前貸し信用状,レッド・クローズ付き信用状 (=red clause L/C)
- red dog 粗悪紙幣,レッド・ドッグ
- red figure 赤字,欠損額 (=red-ink figure)
- red gold 純金,金銭,貨幣

red herring 仮目論見書,レッド・ヘリング (=preliminary prospectus: 米証券取引委員会(SEC)に最初に提出する目論見書。有価証券の公募の際、一般投資家に提供される仮の目論見書でもある。⇒prospectus)
- be a red herring (問題の)核心からそれる
- red-herring prospectus 仮目論見書,予備目論見書

red ink 赤字,損失,営業損失 (=red figure, red-ink figure)
- bleed red ink 赤字を垂れ流す,赤字に苦しむ
- bleeding red ink 巨額の赤字,巨額の損失
- budgetary red ink 財政赤字
- red ink bond 赤字公債
- red ink entry 赤字記入
- red-ink [red ink] figure 赤字,損失
- red-ink firm 赤字企業,赤字会社 (=company in the red, money-losing company)

◆All the red ink comes from the massive spending out of the financial rescue program and a prolonged recession. この財政赤字は、すべて金融支援策からの巨額の歳出と長引く不況によるものだ。◆The company's second quarter loss of $2.3

billion-the fourth-consecutive quarter of red ink-compares with profit of $1.95 billion in the period last year. 同社の第2四半期決算は23億ドルの損失で、4期［4四半期］連続赤字となったのに対して、前年同期は19億1,000万ドルの黒字だった。

redeem （動）買い戻す, 償還する,（抵当財産を）受け戻す, 回収する,（借金を）返済する,（引換券などを）現金に換える, 補填（ほてん）する, 埋め合わせる （⇒ balance, borrow from Peter to pay Paul, refund bond）
　be redeemed for cash 現金で償還される
　redeem a bond 社債を償還する
　redeem a loan 融資を完済する
　redeem a mortgage 抵当を取り戻す
　redeem a warrant bond ワラント債を償還する
　redeem government debt 政府債務を返済する
　when and how redeemed 償還日付けとその摘要
　◆Bridging bonds issued by the government will be redeemed through a future increase in the consumption tax rate. 政府発行のつなぎ国債の返済［償還］は、今後の消費税率の引上げで行う。◆Government debt must be redeemed sometime in the future. 政府債務は将来、いずれかの時点で返済しなければならない。◆Local governments also use tax grants to redeem previously issued bonds. 地方自治体は、過去に発行した地方債の償還にも交付税を使用している。◆The company elected to redeem, prior to maturity on June 3, 2011, $120 million of first mortgage bonds on May 1, 2011. 同社は、満期が到来する2011年6月3日以前の2011年5月1日に、第一順位抵当権付き社債1億2,000万ドルを償還することを決定した。

redeem a sizable amount of government bonds 大量の国債を償還する
　◆Greece was bailed out temporarily in May 2010, but it may default on its debts if it fails to secure necessary funds to redeem a sizable amount of government bonds. ギリシャは2010年5月に一時的に救済されたが、大量の国債の償還に必要な資金を確保できない場合、債務不履行（デフォルト）に陥る可能性がある。

redeem corporate bonds 社債を償還する
　◆TEPCO will have to raise about ¥750 billion to redeem corporate bonds it has issued and to repay some of its debt. 東電は今後、発行済み社債の償還と債務の一部返済に、7,500億円ほど調達しなければならない。

redeem debentures 社債を償還する
　◆In addition to long-term debt maturing during the year, the company redeemed all of its U.S. $150 million debentures, due 2013, in June 2011. 当年度に満期が到来する長期債務のほか、同社は2013年満期の社債1億5,000万米ドルの全額を、2011年6月に償還した。

redeem ordinary government bonds 普通国債を償還する
　◆The amount of refunding bonds issued to redeem ordinary government bonds is expected to exceed ¥100 trillion. 普通国債償還のための借換え債の発行額が、100兆円を突破する見込みだ。

redeemable （形）償還できる, 買戻しできる
　cumulative redeemable retractable first preferred shares 累積償還可能・償還請求権付き第一優先株式
　redeemable preferred stock 償還優先株
　redeemable stock 償還株式
　◆The firm issued in Canada $200 million of $1.95 Cumulative Redeemable Retractable First Preferred Shares, Series M. 同社は、1株1.95ドルの累積償還可能・償還請求権付き第一優先株式シリーズMを、カナダで発行した。

redemption （名）株式などの償還, 買戻し, 請戻し, 借金などの返済, 回復, 補償, 救済, 解放, 救出, 約束の履行, 投信などの解約
　（=refundment, repayment; ⇒bondholder）
　advanced redemption 繰上げ償還, 期日前償還, 期限前償還, 期中償還 （=early redemption）
　beyond［past］redemption 救い難い, 回復の見込みがない
　bond redemption 社債償還, 発行済み社債の買戻し, 債券の償還 （=redemption of bonds）
　debenture redemption 社債償還
　debt redemption 債券償還, 負債償還, 債務の返済, 借金の返済
　early redemption penalty 早期償還罰則金
　extension of redemption 償還延長
　government bond redemption 国債の償還
　loan redemption 借入金償還
　mandatory redemption 強制償還
　national bonds with a 10-year period of redemption 10年間償還付き国債
　optional redemption 任意償還, 随時償還, 買入れ償還
　premium on redemption 償還プレミアム
　purchasing redemption 買入れ償還
　　（=redemption by purchase）
　redemption at fixed date 定時償還, 定期償還
　redemption at maturity 満期償還
　redemption before maturity 期限前償還
　redemption by drawing 抽選償還
　redemption by installment 割賦償還
　redemption by yearly installment 年賦償還
　redemption date 償還日, 償還期日
　redemption fee 解約手数料
　　（=redemption charge）
　redemption fund 償還基金, 償還資金
　redemption gain 償還差益
　redemption of maturity 満期償還
　redemption of preferred shares by subsidiaries 子会社による優先株式の償還
　redemption of stock 株式の償還, 株式償還
　redemption period 償還期間
　redemption premium 償還割増金, 償還時割増金, 償還プレミアム （=premium on redemption）
　redemption price 償還価格
　　（=call price, redemption value）
　redemption privilege 償還請求権
　　（=redemption right）
　redemption risk 期限前償還リスク
　redemption yield 償還利回り, 最終利回り, 満期利回り
　　（=maturity yield, yield to redemption）
　stock［share］redemption 株式償還, 株式の償還
　◆A redemption of the special government bonds for disaster reconstruction is scheduled to begin about 10 years from now. 震災復興債の償還期間は、今から10年程度となる予定だ。◆The company's financial status and its bond redemption capability have grown even stronger. 同社の財務状況と社債償還能力が、一段と高まった。

redemption of bonds 社債の償還, 社債償還, 債券の償還 （=bond redemption, redemption of corporate bonds）
　◆The redemption of these bonds' principals upon maturity is guaranteed. これら債券の元本の満期償還は、保証されている。

redemption of corporate bonds 社債償還
　（=bond redemption, redemption of bonds）
　◆The company was unable to secure sufficient funding for redemption of its corporate bonds. 同社は、社債の償還資金の手当てがつかなかった。

redemption of the 10-year bonds 10年物国債の償還

◆With the redemption of the 10-year bonds peaking at nearly ¥40 trillion in fiscal 2008, the government needs ¥134 trillion in refunding bonds. 10年物国債の償還が2008年度には40兆円近くとピークを迎えることから、政府は134兆円の借換え債が必要になる（政府は134兆円を借り換える必要がある）。

redemption sources 償還財源
◆If the government adheres to its stance of capping the annual issuance of government bonds at ¥30 trillion, it should study issuing a new bond whose redemption sources are secured. 「国債発行枠30兆円」の姿勢にこだわるなら、償還財源の裏付けを持つ新型の国債発行を検討するべきだ。

redenomination （名）通貨単位の呼称変更，券面額の変更，デノミ，デノミネーション （=currency redenomination, redesignation of denominations, renaming monetary units）
carry out currency redenomination デノミを実施する
currency redenomination 通貨のデノミ
downward redenomination 呼称の下方変更，デノミ
redenomination of currency デノミ
　（=currency redenomination）
redenomination of the yen 円の呼称変更，デノミ
the currency redenomination 今回のデノミ
upward redenomination 呼称の上方変更
◆If we carry out the currency redenominations, $1 will be worth about ¥1, and figures indicating the exchange rates of the dollar, the euro and the yen will be almost the same. 通貨のデノミを実施すれば、1ドルが約1円となり、（世界3大通貨の）ドル、ユーロと円の為替レートの単位がほぼ同じになる。
◆In November 2009, the North Korean government carried out currency redenomination at short notice to try to stem inflation. 2009年11月に北朝鮮政府は、インフレ解消をもくろんで突然、デノミを実施した。◆North Korea's downward redenomination has led to a further increase in commodity prices. 北朝鮮のデノミは、さらなる物価上昇を招く結果につながった。

redeposit （動）再び預ける，再預金する，再預託する （名）再預金，再寄託金

redesignation of denominations デノミ，デノミネーション （=redenomination）

rediscount （名）再割引（商業銀行が割り引いた手形を中央銀行や他の商業銀行が再び割り引くこと）

redlining （名）赤線引き，レッドライニング（都市部の老朽・荒廃地域に対する抵当融資や保険引受けの拒否）

redraft （名）戻り［戻し］為替手形，戻り［戻し］手形

redraw （動）手形をあらためて振り出す

reduce （動）減らす，削減する，切り詰める，低下させる，押し下げる，引き下げる，下げる，減少させる，低減する，緩和する，軽減する，抑制する，解消する，控除する，短縮する，売却する
reduce borrowing costs 金融費用を削減する
reduce debt 債務を削減する
reduce dividend payment 減配する
reduce equity weightings 株式の組入れ比率を引き下げる
reduce exposure to credit risk 信用リスクを軽減［低減］する
reduce foreign security holdings 海外の保有証券を売却する，海外の証券を売却する
reduce funding costs 資金調達コストを引き下げる，調達コストを引き下げる
reduce gearing 負債比率を引き下げる
reduce inflation and unemployment インフレと失業を抑制する
reduce interest rates 金利を引き下げる，金融を緩和する
reduce inventories 在庫を圧縮する
reduce investment 投資を抑制する
reduce one's total liabilities 負債総額を減らす
reduce overall leverage 総債務比率を引き下げる
reduce overhead costs 製造間接費を削減する，経費を切り詰める
reduce reserve requirements 預金準備率を引き下げる
reduce tax liabilities 税負担を軽減する
reduce the budget deficit 財政赤字を減らす，財政赤字を削減する
reduce the default risk 不履行リスクを低減する
reduce the exposure to bonds 債券の組入れ比率を引き下げる
reduce the Federal funds rate FF（フェデラル・ファンド）金利を引き下げる
reduce the profitability 収益性を低下させる
reduce the risk of currency fluctuations 為替変動リスクを軽減する
◆Declines in surpluses are likely to reduce a bank's capital adequacy ratio. 剰余金が減ると、銀行の自己資本比率が低下する恐れがある。◆Ford reduced its 33.4 percent equity stake in Mazda to about 13 percent in late 2008 in the wake of the global financial crisis. 世界の金融危機を受けて、米フォードは2008年末に33.4%のマツダへの出資比率［マツダに対する株式保有比率］を約13%に引き下げた。◆Lowering the yield of Meiji Yasuda's single-premium whole life insurance will reduce the attraction of the insurer's financial products. 明治安田生保の一時払い終身保険の利回り［予定利率］の引下げで、同社の金融商品の魅力は薄れると思われる。◆Nippon Life Insurance Co. appears to remain Olympus Corp.'s leading shareholder though the insurer's stake in Olympus has been reduced to 4.9 percent from 8.1 percent. 日本生命のオリンパス株保有比率は8.1%から4.9%に下がったものの、同生保はオリンパスの筆頭株主にとどまるものと見られる。◆Should the government forge ahead with its belt-tightening policy, the budding economic recovery may be reduced to a short-lived upturn. 政府が緊縮路線をひた走れば、景気回復の芽も、薄命の景気回復に終わりかねない。◆The demographic changes show the inevitability of raising pension premiums unless pension benefits are reduced in the future. この人口構造の変化は、年金給付を今後減額しない限り、年金保険料の引上げは必至であることを示している。◆The government will propose measures to reduce the debt burdens of heavily indebted poor countries (HIPC). 政府は、重債務貧困国の債務負担削減策を提案する。◆The provisions, after giving effect to taxes and minority interest, reduced 2010 earnings by $200 million. これらの引当金繰入れで、関連税額と少数株主持ち分利益控除後の2010年度の純利益は、2億ドル減少しました。◆The revaluation of the Chinese currency may reduce Japan's exports to China. 中国の人民元切上げで、日本の対中輸出が減少する恐れがある。◆The United States tries to press China to reduce its current account surplus and raise the yuan by restricting its current account with a numerical goal. 米国は、経常収支を数値目標で縛って、中国に経常収支の黒字縮小と人民元切上げの圧力をかけようとしている。◆Those in favor of "decoupling" urged the Japanese to reduce their overdependence on the U.S. economy. 「ディカップリング（非連動）論」支持者は、米経済への過度の依存脱却を日本に促した。

reduce capital 減資する，資本金を削減する
◆Banks are regulated to reduce the capital in the event of hefty appraisal losses, as a way of requiring shareholders to share the burden of the losses. 巨額の含み損［評価損］の場合、銀行規制で銀行は、株主にもその損失の負担を引き受けさせるために資本金を削減することになる。

reduce liabilities　負債を削減する
　◆There will be a decrease in net assets if the "hidden treasure" of a special account is used for replenishing recurring expenditures, not for reducing liabilities. 特別会計の「埋蔵金」(積立金)を、負債の削減に使わないで経常的な歳出に充てれば、純資産は減ってします。

reduce one's bad loan ratio　不良債権比率を下げる
　◆These financial groups must reduce their bad loan ratios by further efforts to write off their bad loans. これらの金融グループは、不良債権の処理をさらに進めて、不良債権比率を下げなければならない。

reduce one's credit line to　〜に対するクレジット・ライン(貸出限度)を引き下げる
　◆U.S. and European banks gradually reduced their credit lines to Japanese banks. 欧米の銀行は、邦銀に対するクレジット・ライン(貸出限度)を次第に引き下げた。

reduce one's debt load　債務負担を軽減する
　◆In a move to reduce its debt load, the company issued 20 million common shares in March 2011. 債務負担の軽減策として、同社は2011年3月に普通株式2,000万株を発行した。

reduce one's debts　負債を削減する、債務を削減する
　◆GM obtained agreements from a majority of creditors in negotiations to reduce its debts significantly. 米ゼネラル・モーターズ(GM)は、巨額の債務削減交渉で、大半の債権者から合意を取り付けた。◆The company is separating its information-processing and distribution affiliates from its group to reduce its debts. 同社は、負債を削減するため、情報処理子会社と物流子会社を同社グループから切り離す方針だ。

reduce one's foreign debt　対外債務を削減する
　◆U.S. president Bush turned to former Secretary of State James Baker for the complex task of winning an international agreement on reducing Iraq's foreign debt. ブッシュ米大統領は、イラクの対外債務削減に関する国際合意を取り付ける複雑な仕事の担い手として、ジェームズ・ベーカー元国務長官に白羽の矢を立てた。

reduce one's risk assets　リスク資産(リスク・アセット)を圧縮する
　◆Major banks are intensifying their efforts to reduce their risk assets by securitizing and selling their credit to prevent their capital adequacy ratio, an index that shows their business soundness, from declining. 大手各行は現在、経営の健全性を示す指標である自己資本比率の低下を防ぐため、貸出債権の証券化や転売などでリスク資産(リスク・アセット)の圧縮策を加速させている。

reduced　(形)減少した、縮小した、軽減した、削減した、落ち込んだ、切り詰めた、落ちぶれた、還元した、〜の減少[低下、縮小、軽減、緩和、削減]
　　reduced borrowing costs　資金調達コストの削減, 調達コストの削減
　　reduced capital adequacy requirements　自己資本基準の緩和
　　reduced demand　需要の減退
　　reduced dividend　減配
　　reduced financial charges　金利負担の軽減
　　reduced financial flexibility　財務上の柔軟性低下
　　reduced liquidity　流動性の乏しさ
　　reduced losses　損失の減少, 赤字縮小
　　reduced output　減産, 生産高の減少
　　reduced price　割引価格, 割引値段
　　reduced profit　減益, 利益の減少, 利益逓減(ていげん)
　　reduced profit margins　利益率の低下
　　reduced rate loan　低利融資
　　reduced sales　販売低下, 販売の落ち込み, 売上高の減少
　　reduced working capital　運転資金の減少
reduced gross margins　売上利益率の低下
　◆The firm's earnings per share were affected both by lower revenues and reduced gross margins. 同社の1株当たり利益は、売上高の減少と売上利益率の低下の影響を受けた。

reduction　(名)削減, 軽減, 圧縮, 短縮, 引下げ, 縮小, 低下
　　budget deficit reduction　財政赤字削減
　　capital reduction　減資, 資本金の減額　(=capital decrease, reduction of [in] capital, reduction of capital stock)
　　cost reduction　コスト削減, 原価引下げ, 原価[費用]低減, 原価控除
　　debt reduction　債務削減, 債務減らし
　　deficit reduction　赤字削減, 財政赤字削減, 赤字縮小
　　dividend reduction　減配
　　expenditure [expense] reduction　経費削減, 支出削減
　　federal deficit reduction　連邦財政赤字削減
　　fixed-rate tax reduction　定率減税
　　income tax reductions　所得税減税
　　interest rate reduction　金利引下げ, 利下げ
　　inventory reduction　在庫圧縮, 在庫整理, 在庫削減　(=reduction of inventories)
　　output reduction　減産
　　personnel reduction　人員削減, 従業員削減　(=staff reduction)
　　price reduction　価格低下, 価格の引下げ, 値引き　(=reduction in prices)
　　reduction in [of] capital　減資, 資本金の減額　(=capital decrease, capital reduction)
　　reduction in government spending [expenditures]　歳出削減
　　reduction in losses　赤字縮小
　　reduction in operating expenses　営業経費の削減
　　reduction of capital stock　減資　(=reduction of capital)
　　reduction of rates　金利引下げ, 利下げ
　　reductions of long-term debt　長期債務の返済, 長期債務減少
　　risk reduction　リスク軽減, リスクの低下
　　spending reduction　歳出削減
　　stock reduction　在庫削減, 在庫圧縮, 在庫整理　(=inventory reduction)
　　tariff reduction　関税引下げ
　　tax reduction　減税
　　tax reduction for part timers　パート減税
　　tax reduction policy　減税政策
　　wage reduction　賃金引下げ
　　workforce reduction　人員削減
　◆A reduction of the government's stake in Japan Tobacco Inc. is likely to be opposed by tobacco farmers. 政府の日本たばこ産業(JT)への出資比率引下げには、葉タバコ農家の反発が予想される。◆As joint actions, major industrial nations have taken such measures as further interest rate reductions, quantitative monetary relaxation to increase the money supply, the injection of public funds and increased public spending. 協調行動として、主要先進諸国は、さらなる金利の引下げ、通貨供給量を増やすための量的金融緩和や公的資金の注入、財政出動[公共支出の拡大]などの措置を取った。◆The increase of exports, corporate restructuring, centered on debt reduction, and government-led structural reforms brought about the economic recovery. 輸出拡大、債務減らしを中心とした企業のリストラと政府が進める構造改革が、今回の景気回復をもたらした。

reduction in capital　減資, 資本金の削減[減額]
　　(=capital reduction, reduction of capital; ⇒capital

reduction）
◆Government steps taken to deal with Resona's collapse did not incorporate a reduction in the banking group's capital. りそな銀行の経営破たん処理に取った国の措置には、同金融グループの減資は織り込まれなかった。

reduction in fiscal deficits 財政赤字の削減
◆Greece will not be able to achieve the targeted reduction in its fiscal deficits by 2012. ギリシャは、2012年まで財政赤字の削減目標を達成できないようだ。

reemergence （名）再来, 再出現, 再登場
the reemergence of economic deterioration 再度の経済悪化
the reemergence of large external imbalances 大幅な対外不均衡の再来
◆There has recently been renewed concern over the reemergence of economic and fiscal deterioration in some European countries. 欧州の一部では最近、再度の経済・財政悪化の懸念が再び高まっている。

REFCORP 米国の整理資金調達公社, レフコ（Resolution Funding Corporationの略）

refer to （動）～に言及する, ～をはっきり口にする, ～を参照する, ～を調べる, ～を指す, ～を表す, ～のことを示している, ～に関係する
refer to A as B AをBと言う, AをBと呼ぶ
refer to drawer （小切手などの）振出人回し
◆Accumulated surplus funds from previous years are referred to as "hidden treasure" by politicians. 過年度の累積剰余金（特別会計の積立金）を、政治家は「埋蔵金」と呼んでいる。◆Book value per share refers to the amount of net assets of a company represented by one share of common stock. 1株当たり純資産［簿価］とは、普通株式1株当たりの企業の純資産額のことを言う。◆The diffusion index（DI）of business confidence refers to the percentage of companies that feel business conditions to be favorable, minus the ratio of firms that think otherwise. 業況判断指数（DI）は、景気が「良い」と感じている企業の割合（%）から、「悪い」と感じている企業の割合を差し引いた指数だ。

reference range 参考相場圏

reference value for inflation インフレ参照値
（=an inflation guideline）
◆Pending issues, including the central bank's purchase of risk assets, such as exchange-traded funds（ETFs）, and loans and securities held by major commercial banks, were shelved for future discussion, as well as a full-fledged study on the possible adoption of a reference value for inflation. 上場投資信託（ETF）はじめ大手銀行が保有する債権や証券などのリスク資産の日銀による購入や、インフレ参照値の導入などの懸案事項は、今後の検討課題として見送られた。◆There already have been calls for adopting a reference value for inflation within the Bank of Japan. 日銀部内にも、すでにインフレ参照値の導入を求める声がある。

refinance （動）借り換える, 資金を補充する, 再融資する （名）借換え, 再融資, リファイナンス
refinance a substantial amount of long-term debt 長期負債の相当額を借り換える
refinance mortgage 住宅ローンを借り換える, モーゲージを借り換える
refinance of redemption 借換え発行
◆The company took advantage of favorable levels of interest rates to extend debt maturities by refinancing a substantial amount of long-term debt. 同社は、有利な金利水準を利用して、長期負債の相当額を借り換えて債務の償還期限を延長した。

refinance debt 債務を借り換える, 国債を借り換える
◆The Corporation expects to meet its cash requirements in 2012 by refinancing debt maturing in 2012. 当社は、2012年に満期が到来する債務の借換えで、2012年度の必要資金をまかなう方針です。◆The rescue package by the eurozone and the IMF relieves the Greek government of the pressure to refinance its debts on bond markets until the end of 2011. ユーロ圏15か国と国際通貨基金（IMF）の金融支援策で、ギリシャ政府は、2011年末まで債券市場で国債を借り換える必要がない。

refinance existing loans 既存の融資を借り換える
◆Regarding TEPCO's damage compensation, creditor financial institutions have already offered cooperation by refinancing existing loans. 東電の損害賠償に関して、取引金融機関は、既存の融資の借換えなどですでに協力している。

refinancing （名）借換え, 再融資
bank refinancing 銀行融資の借換え
market access for refinancing 借換え目的の市場からの資金調達, 市場から資金調達して借り換える
municipal refinancing 地方債の借換え
refinancing activity 借換え
refinancing bonds 借換え債
slowdown in refinancing activity 借換えの減少
◆The issuance of government bonds, including refinancing bonds, will swell to ¥100 trillion. 国債の発行額は、借換え債を含めると、100兆円に膨らむ。

reflation （名）リフレーション, 景気浮揚, 景気刺激, 統制インフレ, リフレ
◆There is reflation when the government spends more. 政府が支出を増やすと、景気浮揚となる。
解説 リフレーションとは：デフレ（物価下落）が顕著なときに、景気刺激のため、金融緩和によってインフレにならない程度に通貨供給量を増やして物価上昇率をプラスに回復させること。

reflationary policy 景気刺激策, 景気浮揚策
◆Japan's reflationary policy in recent years has centered around interventions in the foreign exchange market by the Finance Ministry and the Bank of Japan. 近年の日本の景気刺激策は、財務省と日銀による為替市場介入を軸としている。

reflect （動）反映する, 表す, 示す, 記載する, 反映させる, 織り込む, 組み入れる, 適用する
（⇒balance for the income account）
be reflected in prices 価格に反映される
be reflected in the current share price 現在の株価に織り込まれている（=be reflected in the current valuation of the stock）
be reflected on a consolidated basis 連結ベースに反映される
reflect the rise in market rates 市場金利の上昇を反映する
◆Banks' fund-raising costs have increased, reflecting the rise in market rates after the Bank of Japan abandoned its zero-interest policy. 日銀のゼロ金利政策解除に伴って市場金利が上昇したのを反映して、銀行の資金調達コストが増大した。◆Domestic stock exchange entries continue to languish, reflecting the tough conditions faced by emerging firms wanting to publicly list their shares. 国内株式市場への新規上場は、株式上場を目指す新興企業が直面している厳しい状況を反映して、低迷が続いている。◆Higher debt maturing within one year chiefly reflects commercial paper we issued to support financial services. 1年以内返済予定の負債の増加は、主に金融サービス部門の支援のため、当社がコマーシャル・ペーパーを発行したことを反映しています。◆Reflecting the rise in the yen, Tokyo stocks, particularly exporter stocks, dropped Wednesday. 円高を受けて［反映して］、水曜日は、輸出企業の株を中心に東京株式市場の株価が下落した［東京株式市場の株が売られた］。◆S&P's downgrades do not reflect an increase in Ford's risk of bankruptcy. スタンダード＆プアーズの格下げは、米フォードの倒産リスクの増大を反映していない。◆The diffusion index（DI）of business confidence among

large manufacturers stood at plus 1, reflecting a growth in exports due to U.S. economic recovery and a recent surge in domestic stock prices. 大企業の製造業の業況判断指数（DI）が、プラス1となり、米経済の回復による輸出の伸びや最近の国内の株価上昇を反映した。◆The flow of speculative money into the oil market did not reflect actual demand. 投機マネーの原油市場への流入は、実需を反映していなかった［実需に基づくものではなかった］。◆UFJ banking group plans to cut the compensation of its top executives by half from July through September to reflect their responsibility for the group's ¥400 billion net loss in fiscal 2003. UFJ銀行グループは、2004年3月期決算で4,000億円の最終赤字に陥った責任を取るため、役員の報酬を7月から9月までの3か月間、5割削減する方針だ。◆Wholesale prices rose 1.3 percent from the previous year, reflecting a jump in prices of steel and oil products. 企業物価（旧卸売り物価）指数は、鉄鋼や石油製品の価格の上昇を反映して、前年比で1.3％上昇した。

reflection （名）反映、反射、熟考、反省、所見、意見
 in reflection of the economic recession 不景気を反映して
 reflection of the rise in stock prices 株価上昇を反映
 ◆The nominal GDP growth rate takes into account price changes and is considered a more accurate reflection of household and corporate sentiment. 名目GDP（国内総生産）成長率は、物価変動を考慮し、家計や企業の景況感をより正確に反映するとされている。

reform （動）改革する、改正する、改善する、矯正する、改心させる、改める
 ◆French Finance Minister Christine Lagarde chosen as the new managing director of the IMF is expected to maintain an austere stance of calling on Greece to reform itself. IMFの新専務理事に選ばれたクリスティーヌ・ラガルド仏財務相は、ギリシャに改革を求める厳しい姿勢を貫くものと期待されている。◆Makeshift measures to reform the three systems of pension, nursing care insurance and health insurance separately will only increase uncertainty in the future. 年金、介護保険、医療保険の三つの制度をバラバラに改革するという場当たり的な対応は、将来不安を増すだけだ。◆No more pump priming measures are needed. All we need is for the private sector to take on the challenge of reforming itself. 景気テコ入れ策は、もう要らない。あと必要なのは、民間部門が自己改革の課題に取り組むことだけだ。◆The tripartite reforms aim to reduce the amount of subsidies provided by the central government to the local governments; cut local tax grants to local governments; and shift revenue sources from the central government to local governments. 「三位一体」改革は、国の地方政府への補助金削減、地方交付税交付金の削減と国から地方政府への財源の移譲をめざしている。◆U.S. President Barack Obama addressed reforming Wall Street in his first State of the Union address. オバマ米大統領は、同大統領初の一般教書演説で、ウォール街（金融街）の改革を呼びかけた［打ち出した］。

reform （名）改革、改正、改善、革新、矯正、リフォーム
 （⇒management reform, structural reform(s)）
 budget reform 財政改革
 corporate reform 企業改革
 currency reform 通貨改革
 drastic organizational reform 組織の抜本改革
 economic reform 経済改革
 financial reform 金融改革、金融制度改革
 fiscal reform 財政改革
 monetary［currency］reform 通貨改革
 pension reform 年金改革
 public finance reform 財政改革
 reform of financial system 金融制度改革
 reform of the capital market system 資本市場の制度改革
 reform of the deposit insurance system 預金保険機構の改革
 regulatory reform 規制改革
 tax［taxation］reform 税制改革
 ◆Priority measures to achieve economic recovery are stopping deflation and mobilizing all possible fiscal measures, financial policies and taxation reforms. 景気回復するための優先課題は、デフレ阻止と、可能な財政政策、金融政策や税制改革を総動員することだ。◆There also is a growing trend for shareholders to press for corporate reform. 株主が企業改革への圧力を高める傾向も、強まっている。

refrain from 慎（つつし）む、差し控える、自粛する、遠慮する、我慢する、自制する、こらえる、止める
 refrain from comment コメントを差し控える
 refrain from taking excessively protective measures against hostile takeover bids 敵対的買収に対する過剰な防衛策を自粛する
 ◆As a tacit understanding with EU member states, the European Central Bank has refrained from implementing monetary policy that is effectively a fiscal bailout. 欧州連合（EU）加盟国との暗黙の了解として、欧州中央銀行（ECB）は、財政支援に当たる金融政策の実施を控えてきた。◆The Tokyo Stock Exchange has called on listed companies to refrain from taking excessively protective measures against hostile takeover bids. 東京証券取引所は、敵対的買収に対する過剰な防衛策の自粛を上場企業に求めている。◆The tripartite reforms aim to reduce the amount of subsidies provided by the central government to the local governments; cut local tax grants to local governments; and shift revenue sources from the central government to local governments. 「三位一体」改革は、国の地方政府への補助金削減、地方交付税交付金の削減と国から地方政府への財源の移譲をめざしている。

refund （動）払い戻す、返済する、還付する、弁済する、借り換える、償還する（=repay;⇒bank, ceiling, corporate tax, depositor）
 advance-refunded issues 事前借換え債
 be refunded pro rata 一定比率払い戻される
 have one's money refunded 金を払い戻してもらう
 refund tax payments 納税額を還付する
 ◆In a class action suit, 20 plaintiffs demanded that seven private universities refund about ¥18 million in tuition and entrance fees that had been paid in advance. 集団訴訟で、20人の原告側は、前納した入学金や授業料約1,800万円の返還を私立7大学に求めた。◆Most of the deposits at the failed bank will be refunded in full under the pay off system. この破たん銀行の預金の大半は、ペイオフ制度に基づいて全額払い戻される。◆The taxes banks pay in writing off their nonperforming loans are refunded to banks after the amount of the actual losses is determined. 銀行が不良債権処理の際に納める税金は、実際の損失額が確定した後、銀行に戻ってくる。

refund （名）返済、払戻し、税金の還付、弁済、弁償、返済金、弁済金、借換え（=repayment）
 full-refund guarantee on time deposits 定期預金に対する全額払い戻し保証
 （⇒full-refund guarantee）
 income tax refunds 還付税金、法人税等の還付金
 refund claim 還付申請書（=refund form）
 submit refund claims 税金の還付請求書を提出する、税金の還付請求をする
 tax refund 税金還付
 the guaranteed refund of savings deposits 普通預金［貯蓄性預金］の払戻し保証額
 withholding tax refund 源泉税還付、源泉課税還付
 ◆The introduction of a payoff system that will cap the guaranteed refund of savings deposits could trigger funds to flow

out from relatively less credible banks. 普通預金(貯蓄性預金)の払戻し保証額に上限を設けるペイオフ制度の導入で、信用が比較的低い銀行から資金が流出する恐れがある。

refund bond 借換え債 (=refunding bond)
◆In fiscal 2005, the amount of refund bonds issued to redeem ordinary government bonds is expected to exceed ¥100 trillion for the first time. 2005年度には、普通国債の償還に充てるために新たに発行する借換え債の発行額が、初めて100兆円を超える見込しだ。

refund cap 払戻しの上限, 払戻し上限枠
◆Certain liquid deposits will be excluded as targets of the refund cap and be fully protected. 特定の決済性預金は、払戻し上限枠(ペイオフ)の対象外として、全額保護される。

refunding (名)借換え, 払い戻し, 税金などの還付, 償還, 国債入札 (⇒deferred tax accounting)
advance refunding 期前償還
bond refunding 社債借換え, 社債の借換え(発行済み社債の償還資金を得るため、新規社債を発行して相互交換すること)
debt refunding 債務借換え
issuance of refunding bonds 借換え債の発行
May refunding 5月の定例国債入札, 5月の定例国債入札
quarterly refunding 米国債四半期入札, 米国債の四半期定例入札 (=quarterly Treasury refunding: 米財務省が競争入札で四半期ごとに行う中・長期証券の定期借換え)
Treasury refunding 国債入札

refunding bond 借換え債 (=refund bond; ⇒borrow from Peter to pay Paul, redemption of the 10-year bonds)
◆The amount of refunding bonds issued to redeem ordinary government bonds is expected to exceed ¥100 trillion. 2005年度には、普通国債償還のための借換え債の発行額が、100兆円を突破する見込みだ。

refunding of deposits 預金の払い戻し
◆The failed bank's refunding of deposits is being proceeded under the payoff system. 破たん銀行の預金の払い戻しは、ペイオフ(預金の払い戻し)制度に従って円滑に進められている。
◆Under the trustee's management, the debtor bank's business will be operated and the refunding of deposits will be temporarily suspended. 金融整理管財人の管理下で、破たん銀行の業務は運営され、預金の払戻しは一時停止される。

refusal (名)拒否, 拒絶, 優先権, 先買(さきがい)権, 拒否権
buyer's refusal 買い手拒否権
first refusal (right) 優先先買権, 先買権, 優先購入権 (=right of first refusal)
job refusal 職業選択権
refusal right 優先権, 取捨選択権, 先買権
refusal to issue licenses 政府許可書の発行拒絶
refusal to pay insurance benefits 保険金の不払い
right of first refusal 先買権, 優先先買権, 優先購入権 (=first refusal right)
◆Industry insiders said the refusal to pay insurance benefits over a long period was partly because of former Meiji managers' unreasonable policies. 業界関係者によると、長期間にわたる保険金不払いの一因は、旧明治生命保険の経営者の無理な経営方針だ。

refuse (動)断る, 拒否する, 拒絶する, 拒(こば)む, 辞退する
◆No financial institution would step in to save Lehman Brothers as the U.S. government refused to extend a financial assistance. 米政府が財政支援を拒否したので、リーマン・ブラザーズの救済に乗り出す金融機関は現われなかった。
◆The U.S. government refused to provide public funds to keep Lehman Brothers afloat. 米政府は、リーマン・ブラザーズの破たんを避けるための公的資金の注入[投入]を拒んだ。◆The U.S. tried to prevent an erosion of corporate ethics among financial institutions by refusing to provide public funds to Lehman Brothers. リーマン・ブラザーズへの公的資金の投入を拒否することによって、米政府は金融機関のモラル・ハザード(企業倫理の欠如)を回避しようとした。

regain (動)取り戻す, 回復する, 奪い返す, 戻る
regain confidence 自信を取り戻す
regain credibility 信頼を回復する
regain full control of 〜を再び完全に掌握する
regain one's feet [footing, legs] 起き上がる, 立ち直る
regain popularity 人気を回復する
regain the confidence of the public 国民[消費者]の信頼を取り戻す
regain the upper hand of 再び〜より優勢になる, 再び〜に勝つ

regain sustainable growth 持続的成長を取り戻す
◆The Japanese economy has yet to regain sustainable growth in domestic demand. 日本経済は、まだ内需の持続的成長を取り戻したわけではない。

regain the confidence in the financial market 金融市場の信認を回復する
◆Goldman Sachs' capital increase is partly aimed at regaining the confidence in the U.S. financial market, which has been facing a raft of financial problems. ゴールドマン・サックスの増資は、多くの金融問題を抱える米金融市場の信認回復も狙いの一つだ。

regime (名)政権, 政体, 政府, 体制, 制度, 厳しい訓練, レジーム (⇒revaluation of currency in North Korea)
a tri-reserve-currency regime 3準備通貨体制
capitalistic regime 資本主義体制
economic regime 経済体制
financial regime 金融制度, 金融体系
floating exchange rate system 変動相場制, 変動為替相場制
high tax regime 高率税制
market-based currency regime 市場原理に基づく通貨制度
monetary regime 金融体制
political regime 政治体制
regime change 体制転換, 制度的変化
trade regime 貿易体制
◆Financial exchanges between the BRICs group, Indonesia and South Korea will move toward a tri-reserve-currency regime by losing a dependency on the U.S. dollar. BRICsグループ(ブラジル、ロシア、インド、中国)とインドネシア、韓国の新興6か国間の金融取引は今後、米ドルに依存しなくなるため、3準備通貨体制に移行するものと思われる。◆It is the U.S. view that the best regime is a market-based currency regime. 最善の制度は市場原理に基づく通貨制度だ、というのが米国の見解だ。◆The revaluation of currency in North Korea appears aimed at clamping down on burgeoning free markets in an attempt to reassert the regime's control. 北朝鮮の通貨改定は、政権の統制力を改めて強めるため、急速に広がる自由市場を厳しく取り締まるねらいがあるようだ。◆The semiannual currency report of the U.S. Treasury Department said that Japan maintains a floating exchange rate regime. 日本は変動為替相場制[変動相場制]を維持している、と米財務省の為替政策半期報告書は述べている。◆Transition to a tri-reserve-currency (the U.S. dollar plus the euro and the renminbi) regime would not be without fiscal turbulences. 3準備通貨(米ドルとユーロ、人民元)体制への移行には、財政的波乱が伴うだろう。

region (名)地域, 地区, 地方, 部位, 部分, 領域, 分野, 程

度, 大体
◆Economic activity strengthened in most of U.S. regions with the exception of St. Louis where plans to close several plants were announced, the U.S. FRB said. 米連邦準備制度理事会（FRB）は、（全12地区連銀のうち）一部の工場閉鎖計画を発表したセントルイスを除く11地区で景気が好転している、と述べた。

regional （形）地域の, 地域的な, 地方の, 域内の （名）地銀
 regional brokerage firm 地方証券会社
 regional development fund 地域開発基金
 regional exchange 地方証券取引所
 Regional Settlement Intermediary 域内決済機関, RMI
 regional survey of industrial conditions 景況感調査

regional bank 地方銀行, 地銀, 地域金融機関
 （⇒business base, business foundation, capital, offset provisions, request, state control）
 regional bank subsidiary 地銀子会社
 regional commercial bank 地方商業銀行
 regional or small and midsize banks 地方銀行や中小金融機関
 the second regional bank 第二地銀
◆Many of the regional or small and midsize banks are still in poor financial shape. 地方銀行や中小金融機関の多くは、まだ経営基盤がぜい弱だ。◆Regional bank accounts were hit hardest by illegal transfers via foreign malware. 海外のマルウエア（コンピュータ・ウイルスの一種）による不正送金の被害は、地方銀行の口座が最多だった。◆Sendai Bank and Tsukuba, regional banks based in areas stricken by the March 11 earthquake and tsunami, will receive a combined ¥65 billion public aid. 仙台銀行と筑波銀行（東日本大震災被災地の地方銀行）が、計650億円の公的支援を受けることになった。◆The Bank of Japan decided to extend a special loan to Namihaya Bank after the second-tier regional bank was declared insolvent. 日本銀行は、第二地方銀行の「なみはや銀行」が破たん認定を受けた後、同行に対して特別融資［特融］を実施することを決めた。◆The regional bank filed for insolvency proceedings with the Financial Services Agency under the Deposit Insurance Law. この地方銀行は、預金保険法に基づき金融庁に対して破たん処理手続きを申請した。

regional economies 地域経済
◆A sense of restlessness and hopelessness still prevails among nonmanufacturers, small and midsize firms and regional economies. 非製造業や中小企業、地方経済には、焦燥と絶望感が広がったままだ。◆AMRO, as the surveillance unit of CMIM, plays an important role to monitor and analyze regional economies. AMROは、（参加国が通貨急落といった危機に直面した際に外貨を融通し合う）多国間通貨交換［スワップ］協定（CMIM）の監視機関として、域内経済を監視し分析する重要な役割を担っている。◆Ten of 12 Fed district banks reported weaker conditions or declines in their regional economies. 全米12地区連銀のうち10連銀が、各地域経済の悪化あるいは経済活動の低下を報告した。

regional financial institution 地域金融機関
◆Many of regional financial institutions are still beset by the high ratio of their bad debts to their total loans. 地域金融機関の多くは、高い不良債権比率（貸出金全体に占める不良債権残高の比率）にまだ苦しんでいる。

register （動）登録する, 登記する, 記録する, 署名する
 register a drop of three percent 3％の下落になる
 register a mortgage 抵当権を登記する
 register a new five-month low 5か月ぶりの安値を付ける
 register a seal 印鑑を登録する
 register a sharp increase in money market rates 短期市場金利が急上昇する
 register year-on-year increases in earnings and profits 前年同期比［前年同月比］で増収増益となる
◆All business sectors registered year-on-year increases in earnings and profits for the account settlement term ending in March. 3月期は、前年同期比で全業種が増収増益だった。◆On Aug. 31, 2011, the yen rose to the ¥76.50 level against the U.S. dollar in the Tokyo foreign exchange market, close to the postwar record of ¥75.95 registered on Aug. 19. 2011年8月31日の東京外国為替市場の円相場は、1ドル＝76円50銭台まで上昇し、8月19日に付けた戦後最高値の75円95銭に近づいた。◆The European economy might slow down and register negative growth if eurozone states introduce austerity measures. ユーロ圏各国が緊縮財政策を導入すると、欧州の景気は減速し、マイナス成長に陥る恐れがある。◆The president of a building inspection company registered falsely inflated capital for the company. 建築確認検査会社の社長が、同社の資本金を不正に多く登記していた。◆The Securities and Exchange Law requires investment funds to register and report the names of their representatives and their locations. 証券取引法は、投資ファンドに対して、投資ファンドの代表者名や所在地などの登録・届け出を義務付けている。◆The Tankan index for large manufacturers rose to plus 2 in September from the minus 9 registered in June. 9月短観の大企業・製造業の業況判断指数（DI）は、6月調査のマイナス9からプラス2に11ポイント改善した。

register （名）登録, 登記, 記録, 登録簿, 登記簿, 記録簿, 名簿, 自動登録機, 通風装置
 cash register 金銭登録機, レジ
 certified copy of the commercial register 登記簿謄本（とうほん）
 check register 小切手記入帳
 commercial register 商業登記
 insurance register 保険契約台帳
 land register 土地登記簿
 payroll register 賃金支払い帳
 register of members 株主名簿
  （=record of shareholders, stock register）
 register of mortgages 抵当権設定登記
 register of securities 証券登録簿
 register of settlement of a mortgage 抵当権抹消登記
 register of shareholders［stockholders］ 株主原簿
 register of title deeds 不動産権利の登記
 register office 戸籍登記所, 登記所, 職業紹介所
 register tonnage 登録トン数
  （=registered tonnage）
 subsidiary register 補助記入帳
 the Lloyd's Register ロイド船級協会船名録

registered （形）登記された［登記した］, 登録された, 登記上の, 届出済みの, 記名式の, 名義上の, 書留扱いの, 公認の
 -registered ～船籍の
 non-registered bond 無記名社債
 registered agent 届け出代理人
 registered bond 記名債券, 記名社債, 記名債, 登録社債, 登録債
 registered capital 登録資本, 登記資本金, 登記上の資本額 （=authorized capital）
 registered check （顧客の依頼で第三者宛に発行する）銀行小切手
 registered common shareholder 普通登録株主
 registered company 登記会社, 上場会社
 registered corporation 登録会社
 registered coupon bond 記名利付き債

registered debenture 登録社債, 記名社債
registered design 登録意匠
registered director 登録役員
registered exchangeable bond 登録交換可能債
registered government bond certificate 登録国債証券
registered holders of common shares 登録済み普通株主, 登録普通株主
registered instrument 登録証券
registered investment adviser 登録投資顧問
registered investment company 登録投資会社
registered letter 書留書簡
registered local bond certificate 登録地方債証券
registered mail 書留郵便
registered obligation 記名債券
registered offering 届出済み証券の募集
registered office 登記上の事務所, 登記上の本社・本店, 登録事務所
registered representative 米証券会社のセールスマン, 登録販売員, 登録外務員, 登録取引会員, 届け出代理人
registered seal 実印
registered security 登録証券, 記名証券 (「記名証券」は、株式や債券などの保有者の名義が、発行会社や登録機関の原簿に登録されているもの。登録証券は、米国の場合は、米証券取引委員会(SEC)に登録されている有価証券のこと)
registered shareholder 登録株主
registered stock [share] 記名株式, 記名株, 登録済み株式, 登録株 (無記名株=non-registered stock)
registered trademark 登録商標
registered trader 登録トレーダー
the registered capital of a company 登記資本金
◆All business sectors registered year-on-year increases in earnings and profit for the account settlement term ending in March. 3月期は、前年同期比で全業種が増収増益だった。◆The Securities and Exchange Law requires investment funds to register and report the names of their representatives and their locations. 証券取引法は、投資ファンドに対して、投資ファンドの代表者名や所在地などの登録・届け出を義務付けている。

registrar (名)登録機関, 株主名簿登録機関, 株式登録機関, 名義書換え代理人, 登記官, 登録事務官, 記録係
registration (名)登録, 登記, 正式記録, 登録事項, 記録事項, 登録物件, 名義書換え
(⇒shelf registration)
file a registration statement with the SEC 米証券取引委員会(SEC)に登録届出書を提出する
issuer registration 発行者登録
land registration 土地登記, 不動産登録・登記
registration and license tax 登録免許税
registration requirements 登録義務
shelf registration 一括登録, 一括登録制度, 発行登録, シェルフ登録
Trade Registration and Matching System 売買登録システム
◆Major securities companies have begun accepting registrations from investors to establish "special accounts" ahead of a new securities tax return law that will go into effect in January 2003. 大手証券各社は、2003年1月から証券税務申告の新法律が施行されるのに伴い、投資家の「特定口座」開設の事前登録受付けを開始した。
registration fee 登録手数料 (有価証券を公募発行する際、発行会社が証券取引委員会(SEC)に支払う登録手数料のこと)

registration statement 米証券取引委員会(SEC)への登録届出書, 有価証券発行届出書 (有価証券を公募発行する際、発行者が米取引委員会に事前に提出する書類。⇒listing particulars)
regressive (形)逆行する, 後戻りする, 退歩する, 退行する, 後退する, 退化する, (税金などが)逆進性の, 逆進的な
auto-regressive model 自己回帰モデル
make consumption tax less regressive 消費税の逆進性を解消する
offset the regressive nature 逆進性を相殺する
regressive audit 逆行監査
regressive income tax 逆進所得税 (所得の増大に伴って所得税率が低くなる場合のこと)
regressive supply 逆進供給 (市場価格の低下に伴って供給量が増える場合のこと)
regressive tax 逆進税
regressive tax rate 逆進税率
regressive tax system 逆進税制, 逆進税制度
regressive taxation 逆進課税
◆It means the burden is relatively higher for low-income earners that the consumption tax is regressive. 消費税の逆進性とは、低所得者層の税負担が相対的に高まることを意味する。
regressiveness (名)逆進性
(⇒progressive tax rates for income tax)
regular (名)正規の, 正式の, 定期的な, 定例の, 一定の, 決まった, 規則正しい, 均整のとれた, 習慣的な, 普段の, 通常の, 標準サイズの, 並みの, 普通の, 常連の, レギュラー
at regular intervals 定期的に, 一定の間隔で
make regular rights issues 株主割当発行増資を頻繁に行う
regular check-up [chekup] 定期検診
regular checking account 普通当座預金, (小切手発行枚数)制限付き当座勘定
regular clearing (手形の)本交換
regular credit 通常信用
regular customer 常連客, 顧客, お得意さん, 常得意
regular fee 正規報酬, 定額報酬, 通常料金
regular general meeting 定期総会
regular general meeting of shareholders 定例株主総会
regular health examination 定期健康診断
regular holiday 定休日
regular income 定収入, 固定収入
regular inventory 通常の棚卸し資産
regular investing 定期的投資
regular issue 定例発行
regular lot (株式の)取引単位, 単価, 売価
regular medical expense insurance 通常医療費保険
regular meeting 定例会議, 定期総会(regular general meeting), 定例集会, 定期集会
regular member 正会員
regular national filing (特許などの)正規の国内出願
regular opening hours 通常の営業時間
regular pay 基本給
regular shopper 常連客
regular spread 順ざや
regular trader 取引員
regular trading hours 通常の取引時間
regular transaction (株式や証券の)普通取引, 正規取引 (=regular way)

regular wage index　賃金指数
regular way　普通取引, レギュラー・ウエイ（=regular transaction, regular way contract, regular way delivery; ⇒regular way settlement）
regular way delivery　普通取引, 通常受渡し取引（=regular way, regular way settlement）
regular withdrawal plan　（投資信託の）定期引出方式
regular board meeting　定例取締役会
（⇒file a claim against）
◆During a regular board meeting, Fuji TV directors agreed to file a claim against Livedoor for losses of more than ￥30 billion incurred from selling off Livedoor shares. 定例取締役会で、フジテレビの役員は、ライブドア株の売却で被った300億円超の損失について、ライブドアに損害賠償を請求することで合意した。
regular business contacts　通常の取引関係
◆Major financial groups do not have regular business contacts with small and medium-sized auto parts makers. 大手金融機関は、自動車部品メーカーと通常の取引関係がない。
regular dividend　普通配当, 通常配当, 定期配当
regular interim dividend　中間配当
regular year-end dividend　年度末配当
regular inspection　通常検査
（⇒special inspection）
◆Regular FSA inspections are conducted after banks close their accounts in March, and focus on whether their loan reserves are adequate. 金融庁の通常検査は3月の銀行の決算後に行われ、主に債権に対する引当金が十分かどうかなどを点検する。
regular payouts　定期支払い, 定期支払い金
◆Since May 2010, Greece has been reliant in regular payouts of loans from a €110 billion bailout from other eurozone countries and the IMF. 2010年5月からギリシャは、他のユーロ圏諸国やIMF（国際通貨基金）などからの1,100億ユーロの金融支援による融資の定期支払い金に頼っている。
regular quarterly dividend　通常四半期配当
◆The company's regular quarterly dividend will be payable June 30, 2011 to shareholders of record at the close of business on June 9, 2011. 当社の通常四半期配当は、2011年6月9日営業終了時の登録株主に対して2011年6月30日に支払われる。
◆The firm's board of directors declared its regular quarterly dividend of $0.86 per common share. 同社の取締役会は、同社の普通株式1株当たり通常四半期配当を0.86ドルとすることを発表した。
regular way settlement　通常受渡し取引（=regular way, regular way delivery: 米国では、受渡し日に関して特に条件がついていない証券取引の決済日は、売買成立の翌日から起算して5日目の営業日になっている）
regulate　（動）規制する, 取り締まる, 統制する, 調整する, 調節する
◆Banks are regulated to reduce the capital in the event of hefty appraisal losses, as a way of requiring shareholders to share the burden of the losses. 巨額の含み損[評価損]の場合、銀行規制で銀行は、株主にもその損失の負担を引き受けさせるために資本金を削減することになる。
regulated　（形）規制された, 規制対象の, 統制された, 調整[調節]された
non-regulated company　規制対象外の企業
regulated company　規制対象企業
regulated financial system　金融システム規制, 金融システムに対する規制
regulated industry　規制を受ける業界
regulated interest rate　規制金利, 規制利子率
regulated investment company　規制投資会社
regulated market　規制市場, 市場の規制

regulated transaction　統制取引
◆A steady annual improvement in earnings of five percent or more is a reasonable goal given the weight of regulated companies in our asset base. 年5%以上の利益増加率の安定確保は、規制対象企業が当社の資産構成で大きな比重を占めていることから、妥当な目標と言えるでしょう。◆It is not an easy task to regulate those who leak, sell and buy information about customers. 顧客情報の流出や売買の規制は、容易ではない。
regulation　（名）規則, 規定, 規程, 規制, 規制措置, 統制, 統括, 管理, 調節, 調整, 法規, 法令, 行政規則, 通達, レギュレーション
（⇒BIS, borrowed stocks, financial regulation(s)）
automatic regulation　自動調節作用
banking regulation　銀行規制
business regulations　業務規定, 業務規則
capital regulations　自己資本比率規制
comprehensive regulation　包括規制
credit regulation　信用統制, 信用規制, 信用規則
currency regulation　通貨規制, 通貨調節, 通貨調整（=regulation of currency）
customs regulation　税関規制
demand regulation　需要規制
economic regulation　経済的規制
existing regulations　既存の規制
financial market regulation　金融市場規制
financial qualitative regulation　金融の質的規制
financial quantitative regulation　金融の量的規制
financial regulations　金融規制
（⇒World Economic Forum）
Financial Services (Regulated Scheme) Regulations　1991年金融サービス（金融スキーム）規則
financing regulation　融資規制
government regulation　政府の規制, 政府による規制, 政府規制
issuing regulations　発行規制
lending regulation　貸出規制
（=regulation of lending）
lift the regulations　規制を撤廃する
loosen [relax] regulations　規制を緩和する
market regulation　市場規制
monetary regulation　貨幣調整
new regulation　新規制　（⇒risk動詞）
observe regulations　規則を遵守（じゅんしゅ）する
qualitative regulation measures　金融の質的規制措置
Regulation FD　レギュレーションFD（アナリストなど特定の者だけを対象とする重要な経営情報の開示を禁止する規制）
regulation for exchange control　為替管理規制
regulation for investment and money rate　出資法
regulation of banks' foreign exchange positions　持ち高規制
regulations on conversion of foreign funds into yen　円転換規制
regulations on investment funds　投資ファンド規制
regulations on stock holdings　株式の保有制限
regulations on stock prices　株価規制
relaxed regulations　規制の緩和
（=relaxation of regulations）
rules and regulations　規約
SEC Regulation S-X　米証券取引委員会規則S-X, SEC財務諸表規則S-X, 米証券取引委員会の連結財務書類[財

務諸表］作成規定, レギュレーションS-X
SEC regulations　SECの規制
securities issuance regulations　証券発行に関する規制
self-regulation　自主規制
severance (benefit) regulation　退職手当規則
stock price regulation　株価規制
　(=regulation of stock price)
temporary regulations　暫定通達
tightening regulations　規制強化
underwriting regulations　引受会社に対する規制
wage regulation　賃金調整
yardstick regulation　ヤードスティック方式
◆The current global financial crisis is in part the result of deficiencies in financial regulation and supervision in some advanced countries. 現在の世界的な金融危機の一因は、一部の先進国の不十分な金融規制・監督の結果だ。◆The G-20 financial summit meeting will map out concrete measures to strengthen the regulation and governance of the financial industry. 世界20か国・地域(G-20)の金融サミットでは、金融業界に対する規制・監督強化の具体策をまとめることになっている。◆The new regulations decided on by the Basel Committee on Banking Supervision require banks to increase the core tier 1 capital, such as common stock and retained earnings, that they must hold in reserve, to at least 4.5 percent of assets from the current 2 percent. バーゼル銀行監督委員会が決めた新規制は、銀行が支払い準備として保有しなければならない普通株や利益剰余金［内部留保］などの中核的自己資本（コア・ティア1）を、現行の資産の最低2％から4.5％に引き上げるよう銀行に義務付けている。◆Under TSE regulations, the bourse can delist a company's stock if the company files financial statements without an auditor's certification. 東証の規則では、企業が監査法人の監査証明を得ないで財務書類を提出した場合、同証券取引所は同社の株式を上場廃止にすることができる。

【解説】米連邦準備制度理事会（FRB）の規則

Regulation A　規則A　レギュレーションA（証券の少額発行を決めた米証券取引委員会（SEC）の規則のほか、加盟銀行その他に対する貸付け条件を定めた米連邦準備制度理事会（FRB）の規則を指す）
Regulation D　規則D　レギュレーションD（支払い準備義務に関する米連邦準備制度理事会（FRB）の規則）
Regulation E　規則E　レギュレーションE（電子資金取引（EFT）の規則、責任、手続きに関する米連邦準備制度理事会（FRB）の規則）
Regulation K　規則K　レギュレーションK（金融機関の国際業務に関する米連邦準備制度理事会（FRB）の規則）
Regulation Q　規則Q　レギュレーションQ（金利の上限に関する米連邦準備制度理事会（FRB）の規則）
Regulation S-K　規則S-K　レギュレーションS-K（各種報告書の財務書類以外の部分に関連する規則）
Regulation S-X　規則S-X　レギュレーションS-X　連結財務書類（財務諸表）作成規定（様式10-Kの財務書類に関する用語、様式、作成方法を定めたもの）
Regulation T　規則T　レギュレーションT（=Reg T：信用取引で証券会社が顧客に対して与える信用供与額の上限に関する米連邦準備制度理事会（FRB）の規則）
Regulation U　規則U　レギュレーションU（上場証券購入のために銀行が融資できる金額に関する米連邦準備制度理事会（FRB）の規則）
Regulation Z　規則Z　レギュレーションZ（割賦販売契約書の様式や利息の算定法などを定めた米連邦準備制度理事会（FRB）の規則の一つ）

regulation measures　規制措置
◆One of the intentions of the government to introduce various regulation measures is to discourage "excessive competition." 各種の規制措置を導入する政府のねらいの一つは、「過当競争」の防止である。

regulations on bank capitalization　銀行の自己資本規制
◆The United States and Britain demanded tighter regulations on bank capitalization. 米国と英国は、銀行の自己資本規制の強化を求めた。

regulations on core capital ratios　自己資本比率規制
◆Tightening regulations on core capital ratios too quickly would cause a credit squeeze and negatively affect the real economy. 急激な自己資本比率規制の強化は、金融収縮を招いて、実体経済に悪影響を与える。

regulations on short selling　空売り規制
◆Japan's regulations on short selling and market manipulation by spreading rumors are extremely weak in comparison with those of the United States. 日本の空売りに関する規制や風説の流布などによる市場操作についての規制は、米国に比べて極めて弱い。◆The regulations on short selling are enforced by the Financial Services Agency, which requested the TSE to release the data on the volume of stocks sold short. 金融庁は空売り規制を強化しており、同庁が東証に株の空売り売買額に関するデータの公表を要請した。

regulator　（名）規制当局, 規制機関, 規制責任者
　(⇒securities fraud)
antitrust regulators　独占禁止規制当局, 反トラスト規制当局
banking regulators　銀行規制当局
chief insurance regulators　保険規制責任者
federal and state regulators　連邦・州規制当局
　(⇒debt)
financial regulators　金融当局
government regulators　規制当局
insurance regulators　保険規制当局
securities regulators　証券業務規制当局, 証券規制機関, 証券取引の監督官庁
state regulators　州規制当局
U.S. federal antitrust regulators　米連邦反トラスト規制当局　(⇒way)
◆American International Group, one of the largest U.S. insurance companies, agreed to pay a $10 million civil fine to settle the federal regulator's allegations that it fraudulently helped another company falsify its earnings report and hide losses. 米保険大手のAIG（アメリカン・インターナショナル・グループ）は、同社が他社の業績報告書改ざんと損失隠しに不正に手を貸したとする米証券取引委員会（SEC）の告発を受け、この問題を解決するために民事制裁金1,000万ドルを支払うことに同意した。◆Citigroup will buy back the auction-rate securities from investors under separate accords with the Securities and Exchange Commission and state regulators. 米シティグループは、米証券取引委員会（SEC）や州規制当局との個々の合意に基づいて投資家から金利入札証券（ARS）を買い戻す。◆European regulators had previously played down the idea of a blanket ban on short selling. 欧州の規制当局は、空売りの全面禁止［規制］という考え方を以前は問題にしていなかった。◆U.S. federal antitrust regulators have cleared the way for the proposed merger between Sony Music Entertainment and BMG, the music unit of the German media conglomerate Bertelsmann AG. 米連邦反トラスト規制当局（米連邦取引委員会）は、ソニーと独複合メディア大手ベルテルスマンの音楽部門のBMGとの事業統合案を承認した。◆U.S. regulator sued 17 big banks for selling risky investments. 米規制当局が、高リスクの金融商品［高リスク証券］を販売したとして大手金融機関17社を提訴した。

regulatory　（形）規制上の, 法規制の, 規制当局の, 監督当局の, 取り締まる
bank capital regulatory requirements　銀行の自己資本

規制
　financial regulatory environment　金融規制環境
　Insurance Regulatory Information System　保険取締り情報通知制度
　investment management regulatory organization　投資管理規制機関
　minimum regulatory capital requirements　会社設立時の最低必要資本金規制
　preemptive regulatory intervention　規制当局による早めの介入
　regulatory action　行政手続き
　regulatory approval　規制当局の認可
　regulatory authority [agency]　規制機関, 規制当局
　regulatory barriers　規制上の障害, 規制の障壁
　regulatory body　規制機関, 監督機関, 規制当局
　regulatory relief　規制の適用除外
　regulatory risk　規制上のリスク
　regulatory standards　規制機関の基準
　self-regulatory measure　自主規制措置
regulatory capital　自己資本比率
　minimum capital requirements　最低必要資本金
　regulatory capital adequacy　自己資本比率規制
　　(=regulatory capital adequacy requirements)
　regulatory capital adequacy measures　規制に基づく自己資本比率
　◆The draft calls for abandoning the minimum regulatory capital requirements. 原案は、会社設立時の最低必要資本金制度の廃止を求めている。◆The minimum regulatory capital requirements were abandoned. (会社設立時の)最低必要資本金制度は、廃止された。
regulatory framework　規制の枠組み
　◆The challenge of the Basel Committee on Banking Supervision is to develop a regulatory framework while fending off a recurrence of financial strife. バーゼル銀行監督委員会の課題は、金融危機再発の防止と規制の策定だ。
regulatory minimum capital adequacy requirements　規制に基づく[法定の]最低自己資本比率基準, 規制当局の自己資本比率基準
　◆If the appraisal losses swell excessively, banks failing to meet the regulatory minimum capital adequacy requirements will have to go under. 含み損が余りにも膨らむと、規制当局の最低自己資本比率基準を満たせない銀行は、経営破たんに追い込まれることになる。
rehabilitate　(動)復帰させる, 回復させる, 復興させる, 再生する, 復興する, 修復する, リハビリを施す, 社会復帰させる, (犯罪者などを)更生させる
　◆A delay in rehabilitating domestic auto parts manufacturers after the March 11 disaster could affect the recovery of the whole Japanese economy. 東日本大震災(2011年3月11日)後の国内自動車部品メーカーの復旧が遅れれば、日本経済全体の回復に影響[悪影響]を及ぼす可能性がある。◆Former chairman of the bank served as an associate of Heizo Takenaka, then state minister in charge of economic and fiscal policy, and strictly pressured banks to rehabilitate themselves. 同行の前会長は、竹中平蔵元金融相のブレーンを務めて、銀行に経営健全化を厳しく迫った。
rehabilitation　(名)信用などの回復, 修復, 再建, 再興, 復興, 健全化, 更生, 復権, 復職, 復位, 社会復帰, リハビリ
　Civil Rehabilitation Law　民事再生法
　corporate rehabilitation fund　企業再建ファンド
　Corporate Rehabilitation Law　会社更生法
　corporation rehabilitation [reorganization] plan　会社更生計画
　economic rehabilitation　経済復興

file for court-protected rehabilitation　会社更生法の適用を申請する
　financial rehabilitation　金融再生, 財政再建, 経営再建
　fiscal rehabilitation　財政再建
　　(=fiscal reconstruction, fiscal restructuring)
　management rehabilitation　経営再建　(⇒auspices)
　self-rehabilitation　自主再建
　undergo management rehabilitation　経営再建に取り組む
　◆A draft final plan for JAL's rehabilitation was drawn up by the airline and the government-backed Enterprise Turnaround Initiative Corporation of Japan. 日本航空の最終更生計画案を、日本航空と政府支援の企業再生支援機構がまとめた。◆Finance Minister Naoto Kan and U.S. Treasury Secretary Timothy Geitner agreed that Japan and the United States would work together in promoting their domestic stimulus measures and fiscal rehabilitation. 菅財務相とガイトナー米財務長官は、日本と米国が国内の景気対策と財政再建に向けて協調することで一致した。◆Struggling Victor Co. of Japan will eliminate 1,150 jobs to engineer its rehabilitation. 経営不振の日本ビクターは、再建計画を進めるため、1,150人を削減する。◆The company aims to achieve its rehabilitation by asking its largest shareholder and group companies to increase its capital by ¥200 billion. 同社は、筆頭株主とグループ企業に2,000億円規模の増資引受けを仰いで、再建を目指している。
rehabilitation efforts　再建努力, 再建策
　◆Dark clouds loom over the ongoing rehabilitation efforts by Japan Airlines, which is restructuring under bankruptcy protection. 会社更生手続き中の日本航空の再建策[破産法の適用に基づいて会社を再建している日本航空が取り組んでいる再建策]に、暗雲が漂っている。
rehabilitation of the financial system　金融再生
　(=financial rehabilitation)
rehabilitation plan　再建計画, 再生計画, 更生計画[計画案], 経営健全化計画　(=management rehabilitation plan, rehabilitation program, restructuring plan; ⇒creditor bank, financially troubled, public bailout, sponsor)
　◆According to JAL's draft rehabilitation plan, 87.5 percent of the airline's loan will be waived by its banks and other creditors. 日航の更生計画案では、同社借金[借入金]の87.5%は、銀行その他の債権者が免除することになる。◆Daiei Inc. refused a rehabilitation plan proposed by the retailer's three main creditor banks. ダイエーは、同社の主力取引銀行3行が提示した再建計画を拒否した。◆Financially troubled Mitsubishi Motors Corp. is currently speeding up its efforts to draw up a rehabilitation plan. 経営難に陥っている三菱自動車は現在、同社の再建計画づくりを急いでいる。◆JAL submitted to the Tokyo District Court its rehabilitation plan, including a debt waiver worth ¥521.5 billion and the loss of more than 16,000 positions. 日本航空は、5,215億円の債権放棄(借金の棒引き)と16,000人以上の人員削減を盛り込んだ更生計画案を、東京地裁に提出した。◆The bank plans to apply for a public bailout on Friday, when it will release the outline of the rehabilitation plan. 同行は金曜日に公的資金の注入を申請する予定で、これに合わせて経営健全化計画の骨子を発表する。◆The struggling JAL's next step will be to start negotiations with its creditor banks over new loans to enact its rehabilitation plan. 経営再建に取り組む日航は今後、同社の再建計画案の実行に必要な新規融資を巡る取引銀行団との交渉に移ることになる。◆Under the firm's rehabilitation plan approved by the district court, financial institutions will waive 87.5 percent of the unsecured loans they extend to the firm. 地方裁判所が認可した同社の更生計画では、金融機関が、同社に行った無担保融資[同社に対する無担保債権]の87.5%を放棄することになっている。

解説　経営健全化計画とは：経営健全化計画とは、公的資

金による資本注入を申請する金融機関が、金融庁に提出を義務付けられている経営計画のことをいう。これには、財務状況や収益の向上策、公的資金の返済原資確保の仕方などのほかに、役員数や従業員数、役員報酬、人件費などの合理化策を明示しなければならない。

rein in 統括する, 管理する, 統制する, 規制する, 制御する, 抑制する, 抑える
◆In order to reduce the government's bond issuance, spending must be reined in as much as possible. 政府の国債発行額を減らすには、できるだけ歳出を抑制する必要がある。◆Twenty-eight banks of the world will face capital surcharges of 1 percent to 2.5 percent by the application of international rules to rein in too-big-to-fail lenders. 大きすぎて破たんさせられない銀行[金融機関]を規制する国際基準が適用されると、世界の28行が、1〜2.5%の資本[自己資本]上積みの対象となる。◆With such moves to rein in investment funds, speculative money started to exit the markets. 投資ファンドを規制するこうした動きで、投機マネーが市場から逃避し始めた。

reinforce (動)強化する, 増強する, 補強する, 強固なものにする, 強める, 促進する
◆Larger size by the merger of two steelmakers will reinforce their bargaining power on resource prices. 鉄鋼メーカー2社の合併による規模拡大で、両社の資源価格の交渉力が今後強まることになる。◆The FSA's guideline for supervising financial conglomerates is aimed at urging operators of financial conglomerates to reinforce their corporate governance to prevent irregularities. 金融庁の金融コングロマリット(複合体)監督指針の狙いは、不正防止に向けて、金融コングロマリットの経営者に経営監視の強化を促すことにある。◆The merger will prompt other megabanks to come up with new strategies to reinforcing their corporate health. この統合は他のメガバンクを刺激し、メガバンクは企業体質の強化に向けた戦略を新たに打ち出すことになろう。◆The number of high-income earners who will pay the higher tax rates will not change even if progressive tax structure may be reinforced. 累進税の構造を強化しても、最高税率を負担する高所得者層の数は変わらない。

reinforcement (名)強化, 増強, 補強, 促進, 補強材, 補給品, 援軍, 増援軍, 増援部隊
　　capital reinforcement 資本増強
　　reinforcement of control 規制強化
◆Depending on the degree of JAL's financial deterioration, the government will consider a combination of capital reinforcement under the industrial revitalization law and public assistance by the Enterprise Turnaround Initiative Corp. of Japan. 日航の財務の傷み具合によって、政府は、産業再生法に基づく公的資金による資本増強と、企業再生支援機構による公的支援との組合せを検討する方針だ。

reinstatement (名)回復, 復旧, (失効契約の)復活, 保険金額復元, 現物填補, 復権, 復職
　　reinstatement clause 保険金額自動復元条項
　　reinstatement of a policy 契約の復活
　　reinstatement of cover 契約の復活
　　reinstatement of the policy 保険金額の復元
　　reinstatement value 填補価額

reinsurance (名)再保険, 再保険料
　　catastrophic reinsurance 巨大損害再保険
　　excess of loss ratio reinsurance 超過損害率再保険
　　excess of loss reinsurance 超過損害再保険
　　excess reinsurance 超過額再保険
　　non-proportional reinsurance 非比例式再保険
　　obligatory reinsurance 義務再保険
　　profit sharing-based reinsurance 利益配当付き再保険
　　quota share reinsurance 比例再保険
　　(=proportional reinsurance)
　　reinsurance amount 再保険金額
　　reinsurance assets 再保険資産
　　reinsurance bordereaux 再保険報告書, 再保険ボルドロ
　　reinsurance broker 再保険ブローカー
　　reinsurance cession 出再契約
　　reinsurance claims 再保険金
　　reinsurance collectibles 再保険請求権
　　reinsurance commission 再保険手数料, 再保険配当金
　　reinsurance commission payable 引受再保険手数料
　　reinsurance conditions 再保険条件
　　reinsurance for excess 超過額再保険
　　reinsurance for proportion part 比例額再保険
　　reinsurance losses 再保険金
　　reinsurance of second risk 第二次危険再保険
　　reinsurance open cover 強制特約付き任意再保険
　　reinsurance policy 再保険証券
　　reinsurance pool 再保険プール
　　reinsurance rate 再保険料
　　reinsurance recoverable on loss payments 未収再保険金
　　reinsurance recovery 再保険金(reinsurance claim), 再保険回収金
　　reinsurance reserve 再保険責任準備金
　　reinsurance return 再保険返戻(へんれい)金
　　reinsurance slip 再保険申込み書
　　reinsurance to close 締切り再保険, 決算のための再保険
　　reinsurance transaction 再保険取引
　　reinsurance treaty 再保険特約
　　reinsurance with risk premium 危険保険料式再保険
　　special reinsurance 個別再保険
　　surplus (relief) reinsurance 超過額再保険
　　treaty reinsurance 特約再保険
◆Reinsurance is the process by which one insurer transfers some or all of the risk of a potential loss to another insurer. 再保険とは、ある保険会社がその潜在的損失の一部または全部を別の保険会社に移転するプロセスのことをいう。◆The five business fields in the tie-up agreement are product development, marketing, insurance underwriting, damage assessment and reinsurance. 提携契約の5業務分野は、商品開発、マーケティング、保険引受け、損害査定と再保険である。

reinsurance company 再保険会社
◆Nonlife insurance companies used to disperse the risk of large contracts with new corporate clients through reinsurance contracts with other insurance or reinsurance companies. 損保各社は従来、他の保険会社もしくは再保険会社と再保険契約を結んで、新規顧客企業と大型契約を結ぶリスクを分散してきた。

reinsurance contract 再保険契約
(⇒reinsurance company)
◆Since the Sept. 11 terrorist attacks on the United States, reinsurance companies overseas have in principle refused to conclude reinsurance contracts that cover terrorist-caused damage. 米同時テロ以降、海外の再保険会社は、テロによる被害をカバーする再保険契約の締結を原則として拒否している。

reinsurance premium 再保険料
　　reinsurance premium rate 再保険料率
　　reinsurance premiums assumed 受再保険料
　　reinsurance premiums ceded 再保険料

reinsurance scheme 再保険制度, 再保険機構
◆Under reinsurance schemes, nonlife insurers pay premiums to other nonlife insurers or reinsurance companies in return for their sharing the burden of future claims. 再保険制度にしたがって、損保各社は、他の保険会社や再保険会社が将来の保険金を共同負担する見返りに、これらの保険会社に

保険料を支払っている。

reinsure （動）再保険をかける, 再保険を付ける
　risks reinsured hereunder　本協定に従って再保険された危険［契約］
　risks reinsured under this agreement　本協定に従って再保険されている危険

reinsured （形）再保険に入っている, 再保険付きの
　reinsured portions　再保険部分
　reinsured sum at risk　再保険危険保険金額
　the insured　被再保険者
　the sum at risk reinsured　危険再保険金額

reinsurer （名）再保険会社（reinsurance company）, 再保険者
　reinsurer's limit of liability　再保険者支払い責任限度額
　reinsurer's share　再保険会社の引受分, 再保険割合

reintermediation （名）再間接金融化現象, リインターミディエーション（金融機関離れを起こしていた資金が銀行などに還流する現象のこと）

reinvest （動）再投資する
　earnings reinvested　留保利益, 利益剰余金
　reinvested income　利益剰余金
　◆Fund-of-funds do not invest capital directly in stocks and bonds, but reinvest it in other investment trusts as a way to minimize risk. ファンド・オブ・ファンズは,（投資家から集めた）資金を株式や債券に直接投資せず, リスクを最小限に抑える手段として他の複数の投資信託に再投資する。◆Quarterly dividends may be reinvested automatically to purchase additional common shares at a discount from the average market price. 四半期配当金は, 自動的に再投資して, 平均市場価格から割り引いた価格で当社の普通株式を追加購入することができます。

reinvestment （名）再投資, 社会還元
　Community Reinvestment Act　地域社会還元法
　dividend reinvestment　株主配当再投資, 配当再投資, 配当金株式再投資, 配当金再投資
　pure reinvestment　純粋再投資
　reinvestment cycle　再投資循環
　reinvestment in business　事業への再投資
　reinvestment in financial assets　金融資産への再投資
　reinvestment income　再投資収益
　reinvestment of earnings　利益の再投資
　reinvestment privilege　再投資特権
　reinvestment rate　再投資収益率
　reinvestment risk　再投資リスク
　◆ABC Inc. raised $100 million of common equity by means of its Dividend Reinvestment and Stock Purchase Plan and the Employees' Savings Plan. ABC Inc.は, 株主配当再投資・株式購入制度と従業員社内預金制度により普通株式を発行して1億ドルを調達しました。

reinvigorate （動）再活性化する, 再び元気づける, 再び活力を与える
　◆To enhance the stimulating effect of the Fed's rate cuts, swift implementation of fiscal and tax stimulus measures, including tax cuts on investment designed to reinvigorate the stock market, is necessary in addition to the large-scale tax cut program that is under way. 米連邦準備制度理事会（FRB）の金利引下げの刺激効果を高めるためには, 現在実施中の大型減税プログラムに加え, 株式市場を再活性化するための投資減税など, 財政・税制面からの景気刺激策の速やかな実施が必要である。

reinvigoration （名）再活性化
　◆Economic reinvigoration of Asia-Pacific nations as a whole is indispensable for a full-fledged recovery of the world economy. 世界景気の本格回復には, アジア太平洋全体の経済再活性化が必須だ。

REIT　不動産投資信託, リート（real estate investment trustの略）
　◆As of April 2004, 112 fund-of-funds were operating in the country, 24 of which invest in REITs. 2004年4月現在, 国内で112本のファンド・オブ・ファンズが運用されており, このうち24本は不動産投資信託に投資している。
　解説 不動産投資信託（リート）とは：投資家から集めた金で専門家が様々な不動産物件を購入し, 購入した不動産の賃貸収入や売却益などの投資収益を, 配当金として投資した金額に応じて投資家に分配する仕組みの投資信託。そのメリットとして, 複数の物件があらかじめ組み入れられているためリスク分散が可能なこと, 配当金が年利3〜4%と高いこと, 株式などと同じ有価証券なので換金性が高く, 売ろうと思えば証券会社を通じて即日売却できることが挙げられる。

reiterate （動）繰り返す, 反復する, 繰り返して主張する, 主張を繰り返す, 〜と念を押す
　◆As for the issue of China's cheap yuan, the leaders of the Group of Seven industrial powers simply reiterated what they said at the previous G-7 meeting. 中国の割安な人民元問題に関しては, 先進7か国の財務相・中央銀行総裁は, 前回のG7で述べたことを繰り返しただけだった。

reject （動）拒否する, 拒絶する, 否認する, 否決する, 否定する, 棄却する
　◆Greece's finance minister rejected a proposed referendum on staying in the eurozone. ギリシャの財務相は, 提起されていたユーロ圏残留の是非を問う国民投票を拒絶した。◆Hokuetsu Paper Mills Ltd. rejected the proposal of Oji Paper Co.'s management integration. 北越製紙は, 王子製紙の経営統合提案を拒否した。◆The board of directors of The Walt Disney Co. unanimously rejected a takeover offer from Comcast Corp. ウォルト・ディズニーの取締役会は, 全会一致でコムキャストによる買収提案を否決した。◆The financial markets would have been further destabilized if the U.S. House of Representatives had rejected the financial bailout bill. 米議会下院が金融安定化法案（金融救済法案）を否決していたら, 金融市場はさらに動揺していただろう。◆The government may reject a company's request for a license to enter the fiduciary market if its executive has been dismissed in the past five years due to a violation of Section 2 of Article 102. 信託市場（信託業）に参入するための免許を申請した企業の役員が, 第102条第2項の違反により5年以内に解任命令を受けていた場合, 政府はその免許申請（免許交付）を拒否することができる。◆The management buyout might have been rejected at the firm's shareholders meeting if its major shareholders had opposed it. 同社の経営陣による自社買収（MBO）は, 株主総会で主要株主［大株主］が反対したら否決されていたかもしれない。◆The proposal to expand the lending capacity of the IMF was supported by Brazil and other emerging economies though Japan and the United States rejected it. 国際通貨基金（IMF）が融資できる資金規模を拡大する案は, 日本と米国が受け入れなかったものの, ブラジルなどの新興国は支持した。◆U.S. House of Representatives rejected the increase of debt limit. 米下院は, 債務上限の引上げ（法案）を否決した。◆Walt Disney Co. rejected an unsolicited $48.95 billion takeover offer from cable television company Comcast Corp. ウォルト・ディズニー社は, ケーブルテレビ会社コムキャストによる489億5千万ドルの一方的な企業買収提案を拒否した。

rejection （名）拒否, 拒絶, 否認, 否決, 棄却, 却下
　◆The rejection of the financial bailout bill by the U.S. House of Representatives roiled the financial markets across the world. 米下院による金融救済法案（金融安定化法案）の否決は, 世界の金融市場を大混乱させた。

relationship （名）関係, 関連, 結びつき, 取引先
　arm's length relationship　商業ベースの取引関係
　build relationships of trust with　〜との信頼関係を築く
　business relationship　取引関係

collaborative [cooperative] relationship　協力関係
contractual relationship　契約関係
currency relationships　為替相場, 為替レート
customer relationship　顧客関係
debtor-creditor relationship　債権者・債務者関係, 債権債務関係
financial relationship　財務比率
principal-agent relationship　本人と代理人の関係
relationship bank　協力銀行, 取引銀行
relationship management　取引先総合管理, 関係性経営, RM
relationship marketing　リレーションシップ・マーケティング（データ・マイニング技術を駆使した分析で, 顧客戦略の策定を支援するもの）
symbiotic relationship　共生関係, もちつもたれつの関係
◆Sumitomo Mitsui Financial Group Inc. and Goldman Sachs Group Inc. have built a close relationship in recent years. 三井住友フィナンシャルグループとゴールドマン・サックスは, 数年前から緊密な関係にある。◆Suzuki Motor's board of directors decided to dissolve its partnership and cross-shareholding relationship with Volkswagen AG. スズキの取締役会は, 独フォルクスワーゲンとの提携と株式持ち合い関係の解消を決めた。

relax　(動) 緩(ゆる)める, 和らげる, 緩和(かんわ)する, ～の力を抜く, くつろがせる, リラックスさせる
relax discipline　規律を緩める
relax regulations on　～の規制を緩和する
relax requirements for　～の要件を緩和する
relax restrictions on exports　輸出規制を緩和する
relax the criteria　基準を緩める
relax the monetary policy　金融政策を緩和する, 金融を緩和する
relaxed monetary policy　金融政策の緩和, 金融緩和
◆Emerging countries are anxious about the possibility of inflation caused by a large influx of funds as the U.S. FRB decided to relax its monetary policy. 米連邦準備制度理事会（FRB）が金融緩和を決めたため, 新興国は大量の資金流入によるインフレを懸念している。◆If the government relaxes its policy now, the economy will not be able to get on the recovery track. 政府がいまその政策の手を緩めれば, 景気は回復軌道に乗れないだろう。◆The BOJ decided to further relax its monetary policy by injecting an additional ¥10 trillion into a fund aimed at purchasing government bonds and corporate debentures. 日銀は, 国債や社債などを買い入れるための基金に新たに10兆円を注入［投入］して追加の金融緩和に踏み切ることを決めた。◆The emergency employment package contains a plan to relax criteria for receiving employment-adjustment subsidies. 緊急雇用対策には, 雇用調整助成金の受領要件の緩和策も含まれている。◆The Fed won't need to continue its relaxed monetary policy if the U.S. housing market and financial sector recover. 米国の住宅市場や金融部門が回復すれば, 米連邦準備制度理事会（FRB）は, 金融緩和を継続する必要はなくなる。◆The government may exert great pressure on the Bank of Japan to further relax its monetary policy. 政府は, 日銀への追加の金融緩和圧力を強める可能性がある。◆The U.S. Federal Reserve Board decided to relax its monetary policy. 米連邦準備制度理事会（FRB）が, 金融政策の緩和を決めた。

relaxation　(名) 緩和, 軽減, 引下げ, （筋肉の）弛緩（しかん）, ゆるみ, 気晴らし, レクリエーション
（⇒quantitative relaxation）
credit relaxation　信用緩和, 利下げ
credit relaxation policy　信用緩和政策
monetary relaxation　金融緩和
qualified relaxation　条件付き緩和
quantitative monetary relaxation　量的金融緩和, 量的緩和　（⇒joint action）
relaxation of import restrictions　輸入規制［制限］緩和
relaxation of the monetary policy　金融政策の緩和
relaxation of the trade barriers　貿易障壁の緩和
relaxation of underwriting standards　与信規準の緩和, 貸出審査基準の緩和
significant [substantial] relaxation　大幅緩和
the quantitative relaxation of credit　量的金融緩和, 量的金融緩和策
◆Debates on the pros and cons of a proposal to end the quantitative relaxation of credit by the Bank of Japan are gathering momentum. 日銀による量的金融緩和策を解除する案の賛否をめぐる議論が, 活発化している。◆The Stability and Growth Pact lost its spine in 2003 as the Germany government requested the relaxation of its terms. ユーロ圏の財政安定化・成長協定は, ドイツがその条件緩和を要求したため, 2003年に骨抜きになった。

release　(動) 発売する, 販売する, 投入する, 公表する, 発表する, 公開する, (情報を)開示する, (映画を)封切る, 解放する, 放出する, (資金を)捻出[調達]する, (借金などを)免除する, (権利などを)放棄する, (財産を)譲渡する, 釈放する, 解放する, リリースする
release a new model　ニュー・モデルを投入する
release all claims to property　財産請求権をすべて放棄する
release an earnings forecast　業績予想を発表する
release funds　資金を捻出する, 資金を調達する
release one's business report for the business year ending in March　3月期決算を発表する
release one's liens on assets　資産に対する先取特権を解除する
◆Neither of Mitsui Trust Holdings, Inc. and another major financial group has yet released reports on its interim settlement of accounts. 三井トラスト・ホールディングスなど2大金融グループは, まだ中間決算報告を発表していない。◆Short-term interest rates in the Tokyo market rose as some financial institutions hurried to obtain newly released funds. 一部の金融機関が新規調達資金の確保を急いだため, 東京市場の短期金利が上昇した。◆The bank did not release an earnings forecast. 同行は, 業績予想を発表しなかった。◆The final list of G-SIFIs will be released in January 2014. G-SIFIsの最終リストは, 2014年1月に発表される。◆The majority of listed companies have released their half-year earnings reports for the fiscal period up to September. 上場企業の大半が, 上半期(4-9月期)の業績を発表した［上場企業の9月中間決算が, ほぼ出そろった］。◆When serious financial difficulties are expected, the Financial Services Agency is allowed to order a company to improve its operations in the early stages without releasing the information to the public. 深刻な財務悪化が予想される場合, 金融庁は, 非公表で早めに業務改善命令を発動することができる。

release　(名) 発売, 販売, 公表, 発表, 公開, （情報の）開示, 封切り, 解放, 放出, 流出, （資金の）捻出［調達］, （契約の）解除, （借金・債務の）免除, 免責, 責任免除, （権利の）放棄, （財産の）譲渡, 釈放, リリース
deed of release　権利放棄証書
economic releases　景気指標, 景気指標の発表
financial reporting release　財務報告通牒
news release　ニュース発表, ニュース・リリース
press release　新聞発表, 報道用公式発表, プレス・リリース
release from debts　債務免除
release of security　担保解除

release of the new job numbers　雇用統計の発表
◆The U.S. Federal Reserve Board said in its Beige Book release that the U.S. economy deteriorated further in almost all corners of the country. 米連邦準備制度理事会（FRB）は、地区連銀景況報告（ベージュ・ブック）を発表し、米国の経済情勢はほぼ全米で一段と悪化していると指摘した。

relentless　（形）容赦しない，手加減しない，無情な，過酷な，執拗（しつよう）な，絶え間ない，衰えない，容赦なく続く
◆The yen continues its relentless surge and stock prices keep falling. 円高に歯止めがかからず、株安も続いている。

relevant　（形）関連する，関連した，適切な，妥当な，当を得た，的を射た，要点を突いた
◆FSA's inspectors are to confirm whether the companies' categorization by banks as debtors is relevant or fair. 金融庁の検査官は、銀行側の企業（融資先企業）の債務者区分が適正かどうかなどを検証することになっている。

reliance　（名）依存，依存度，信頼，信用，頼り
purchased funds reliance　取得資金依存度
rate of reliance on bond issues（to national budget）　国債依存度
reliance on debt　借入依存
reliance on debt financing　外部負債に対する依存度
reliance on overseas markets　海外市場への依存
◆There have been no substantial changes in the fundamental reliance of Japanese firms on overseas markets. 日本企業が基本的に海外市場に依存している構造に、大きな変化はない。

reliant　（形）依存している，頼っている
reliant on［upon］　〜を頼る，〜を当てにする，〜を確信している
self-reliant　自力に頼る，自己依存の
◆Since May 2010, Greece has been reliant in regular payouts of loans from a €110 billion bailout from other eurozone countries and the IMF. 2010年5月からギリシャは、他のユーロ圏諸国やIMF（国際通貨基金）などからの1,100億ユーロの金融支援による融資の定期支払い金に頼っている。

relief　（名）安心，安堵（あんど），気晴らし，息抜き，救済，救助，救援，支援，援助緩和，軽減，除去，控除，救援金，救援［救済］物資，給付金，生活保護手当て，職務からの解放，職務の交代［交替要員］，更迭（こうてつ），代行者，浮き彫り，浮き彫り細工，レリーフ，鮮明さ，明瞭さ，リリーフ
a sense of relief　安心感，安堵（あんど）感
apply for relief　救済を求める
debt relief　債務救済，債務削減，債務返済
（=debt forgiveness）
disaster relief　災害復旧，災害復旧事業，災害救援，災害救援金
double income tax relief　二重所得税控除
double taxation relief　外国税額控除
export tax relief　輸出税免除，輸出減税
find relief　安堵する，ほっとする，好感する
life insurance relief　生命保険料控除
personal relief　人的控除
price relief　物価が落ち着くこと
public relief　公共の救済基金
regulatory relief　規制の適用除外
relief activities［operations］　救援活動
relief fund　救済基金，救済資金
relief loan　救済融資，救済ローン
relief measures　救済措置
tax relief　免税，減税，税額免除，税負担の軽減，税金の減免
tax relief bond　減税債券
tax relief measures　税金の減免措置

taxation relief　課税免除
temporary relief　一時救済
U.K. stock relief　（英国税法の）棚卸し資産税額控除
unemployment relief　失業救済
◆Investors found relief in a series of economy-boosting measures taken by Japan, the United States and other major economies to avert a global recession. 投資家は、世界的な景気後退を回避するため、日米その他の主要国が一連の景気刺激策を打ち出したことを好感した。◆Out of a sense of relief, dollar-selling pressure has eased on the foreign currency markets. 安堵（あんど）感から、外国為替市場では、ドル売り圧力が弱まった。◆The EU ministers will consider debt relief or freezing payments on debt for the Asian tsunami-hit countries. 欧州連合（EU）の閣僚らは、アジアの津波被災国のため債務削減や債務返済の凍結を検討する。◆The two banks will repay part or all of the public funds they received as temporary relief to the government by the end of March. 両行は、一時救済として受けた公的資金の一部または全額を、3月末までに国に返済する方針だ。

relief measures　救済措置
◆Eurozone countries have tried a series of relief measures, but worries have heightened in the world particularly with regard to the eurozone. ユーロ圏諸国は一連の救済策を取ってきたが、世界ではとくにユーロ圏に関して心配[不安]が高まっている。

relief money　義援金，災害見舞金
◆In order to prevent scamming of relief money, an emergency telephone number dedicated to malicious business practices has been established for the devastated areas. 義援金詐欺を防ぐため、悪質商法110番［悪質商法対策専用の緊急電話番号］が、被災地向けに設けられた。

relinquish　（動）捨てる，放棄する，止める，失う，手放す，譲渡する
relinquish monetary control　通貨調整［通貨供給量の調節］を止める，金融政策の管理を放棄する
relinquish one's position as the biggest［largest］shareholder of the company　同社の筆頭株主の座を降りる
◆Ford will relinquish its position as the biggest shareholder of Mazda Motor Corp. by selling most of its 11 percent stake in Mazda. 米フォードは、保有するマツダ株11％の大半を売却して、マツダの筆頭株主の座を降りることになった。

relist　（動）再上場する　（⇒delist, dual-list, list）
◆Seibu Railway Co. aims to relist its stock on a securities exchange. 西武鉄道は、証券取引所への同社株の再上場を目指している。

reluctant　（形）気が進まない，気乗りしない，二の足を踏む，嫌々ながらの，〜に消極的な，〜には慎重な
◆After the IMF called for strict implementation of structural reforms as a condition for loans to financially troubled countries, counties became reluctant to request assistance from the IMF. 財政難に陥った国に対する融資の条件としてIMF（国際通貨基金）が厳しい構造改革の実施を求めてから、各国はIMFへの支援要請をためらうようになった。◆Despite moves by the U.S. Federal Reserve Board to loan more money to financial institutions, banks are still reluctant to lend. 米連邦準備制度理事会（FRB）に金融機関への資金融資を拡大する動きがあるにもかかわらず、銀行［金融機関］はまだ貸し渋っている。◆The insurer aimed to improve profitability by being reluctant to pay insurance benefits. この保険会社は、保険金の支払いを渋って収益の向上を目指した。

rely on［upon］　（動）〜に依存する，〜に頼る，〜を当てにする，〜を裏付けとする
obligations relying on support mechanisms　信用補完を裏付けとした債務
rely on debt financing　外部負債に依存する

◆To shore up their economies, major economic powers seem to be relying more on their monetary policies. 景気テコ入れに、先進国は金融政策頼みの様相が強まっている。

remain （動）〜のままである、まだ〜されないままだ、依然として〜だ、〜から抜け出していない、引き続き〜だ、今後も〜だ、〜で推移する、根強い
（⇒revenue source, wary）
 remain bullish　強気の見方を変えない
 remain cautious　警戒している　（⇒cautious）
 remain competitive　競争力を維持する
 remain consistent　一貫して変わらない
 remain firm　堅調に推移する
 remain flat　横ばいで推移する
 remain negative　弱気のスタンスを崩していない
 ◆An increasing number of companies want to undertake IPOs while stock markets remain brisk. 株式市場が活況のうちに上場したい［株式を新規公開したい］、という企業が増えている。◆If oil prices remain above $45 per barrel for a long time, the world economy will be hard hit. 1バレル=45ドルを超える原油の高値が長期化すれば、世界経済は大打撃を受ける。◆It remains to be seen whether the yen will be overshooting. 円相場がオーバーシュート（行き過ぎ）かどうかは、今後も分からない。◆Japan's economy will remain sluggish for a while. 日本の景気低迷は、しばらく続くと思われる。◆Nippon Life Insurance Co. appears to remain Olympus Corp.'s leading shareholder though the insurer's stake in Olympus has been reduced to 4.9 percent from 8.1 percent. 日本生命のオリンパス株保有比率は8.1%から4.9%に下がったものの、同生保はオリンパスの筆頭株主にとどまるものと見られる。◆Prospects remain murky though a freefall in stock prices has been averted for now. 株価暴落はひとまず回避されたが、先行きはまだ不透明である。◆The economy still remains in a recovery phase in the business cycle. 景気は、まだ回復局面にある［景気の回復基調はまだ続いている］。◆The money lent by the U.S. and eurozone private banks remains at about the same level as those prior to Lehman's collapse. 米国とユーロ圏の民間銀行の貸出金は、リーマン・ブラザーズの経営破たん前とほぼ同水準にとどまっている。◆The yen remains in the historically high ¥75-range against the dollar. 円相場は、1ドル=75円台の歴史的高値が続いている。◆The yen still remains at a high level against other major currencies. 円は、他の主要通貨に対してまだ高い水準で推移している。◆Uncertainty remains regarding the country's financial system. 日本の金融システムには、不安が残る。

remain at a trickle　依然として少ない、ぽつぽつの状態で推移している
 ◆Bank lending remains at a trickle. 銀行貸出［銀行融資］は、ぽつぽつの状態で推移している［銀行貸出件数は、依然として少ない状況だ］。

remain at high levels　高水準で推移している、高水準で推移する、高止まりする
 ◆Under the envisioned lending facility, the IMF will provide funds to countries where government bond yields remain at high levels to help reconstruct their public finances. この融資制度案では、国際通貨基金（IMF）が、国債の利回りが高止まりしている国に資金を提供［融資］して財政再建を支援する。

remain high　いまだに高い、引き続き高水準だ、高水準で推移している、高止まりしている、高止まりする
 ◆The yen's value still remains high and is likely to reach a postwar record value above the ¥76-to-the-dollar level. 円相場は依然高く、1ドル=76円台を上回る戦後最高値に達する可能性がある。

remain in the red　赤字を続ける
 ◆The bank remained in the red, incurring a group net loss of more than ¥400 billion. 同行は、4,000億円を超える連結純損失（連結税引き後赤字）となって、赤字を続けた。

remain low　いまだに低い、引き続き低水準だ、低水準で推移している、低水準にとどまる
 ◆Even after Greece's debt load is cut, Greece's credit grade is likely to remain low. ギリシャの債務負担を削減しても、ギリシャの信用格付けは、低水準にとどまる見込みだ。◆Pay levels remain low in the nonmanufacturing sector, such as the financial, real estate and construction industries. 金融、不動産、建設などの非製造業では、給与水準は依然、低い。◆Though stock prices remain low, the number of transactions has already outpaced that during the bubble economy. 株価はまだ低いものの、株取引の件数はすでにバブル期を超えている。

remain stable　安定して推移する、横ばいで推移する
 ◆The rating outlook remains stable. 格付け見通しは、引き続き安定的だ。

remain strong　依然として強い、堅調で推移する、相変わらず根強い
 ◆The yen has remained strong. 円高の流れは、変わっていない。

remain weak ［sluggish］　低迷が続く
 ◆The basis for recovery remains weak. 景気回復の基盤は依然、弱いままだ。

remaining　（形）残りの、残存する、残余の
 remaining cash flow　残存キャッシュ・フロー
 remaining depreciable lives　残存償却年数
 remaining economic life　経済的残存耐用年数
  （=remaining economic age）
 remaining interest　残存持ち分、残りの持ち分
 remaining life　残存期間、残存年数、残存耐用年数
 remaining service　残余勤続年数、残存勤続年数
  （=remaining service period）
 remaining useful life　残存耐用年数
 ◆Following the tender offer, Oji Paper would acquire the remaining Hokuetsu shares through a share swap to turn it into a wholly owned subsidiary. 株式公開買付け（TOB）後に、王子製紙は、株式交換で残りの北越製紙の株を取得して北越製紙を完全子会社化する。◆MUFG obtained the remaining 38.8 percent stock in Mitsubishi UFJ Securities through a stock swap deal. 三菱UFJフィナンシャル・グループ（MUFG）は、株式交換取引で三菱UFJ証券の残りの株式の38.8%を取得した。◆The remaining ¥1.8 billion will be financed by two other commercial banks and trust banks. 残りの18億円は、他の都銀2行と信託各行が出す。◆The U.S. government will press on with the sale of its remaining 6.2 billion shares in Citigroup. 米政府は今後、保有する残りのシティグループの株式62万株の売却を推し進める方針だ。

remedy　（名）対応策、対策、改善法、薬、治療、治療法、治療薬、療法、処方箋、救済、救済方法、救済手段、救済措置、措置、補償、権利回復手段
 effective remedy　特効薬
 golden［good］remedy　妙薬
 injunctive remedy　差止命令による救済、差止めによる救済
 legal remedy　法律上の救済方法、法的救済、法的救済手段、法的救済措置
 remedies for the strong yen　円高対策
  （⇒sourcing）
 remedy for economic stagnation　不況対策
 trade remedies　貿易救済措置
 ◆Economic stimulus measures such as tax cuts and additional public works projects work only as temporary remedies. 減税や公共事業の追加などの景気浮揚策は、一時的なカンフル剤にすぎない。◆The central bank's emergency loan is an effective remedy for a bank run. 中央銀行の緊急融資は、銀行の取付け騒ぎの特効薬だ。◆The overall supply capacity

must be increased through structural reforms as a remedy for economic stagnation. 景気低迷への対策として、構造改革により供給力を引き上げる必要がある。

REMIC 不動産モーゲージ投資媒介体, 不動産モーゲージ投資コンディット, レミック（real estate mortgage investment conduitの略）
 arbitrage opportunities for REEMIC creation　REMIC組成でさやを抜くチャンス
 collateral for REMICs　REMICの裏付け
 new current coupon REMIC issues　カレント・クーポンの新発REMIC
 REMIC creation　REMICの組成, REMIC組成
 REMIC tranche　REMICのトランシュ
 REMICs backed by low-coupon collateral　低クーポンのパス・スルー証券を裏付けとするREMIC
 sponsors for REMICs　REMICの原資産保有者
 structure and price REMICs　REMICの組成と価格設定を行う

REMIC transactions REMICの組成
 collect collateral for REMIC transactions　REMIC組成のためにパス・スルー証券を買う
 produce REMIC transactions　REMICを組成する

reminder （名）催促状　（⇒promissory note）

remit （動）送金する, 振り込む
 ◆The equivalent of ￥5.2 billion was illegally remitted to Singapore via a Credit Suisse unit in Hong Kong. 52億円相当額が、クレディ・スイスの香港支店を通じてシンガポールに不正送金された。

remittance （名）送金, 振込み, 送金額, 送金高　（⇒cash remittance, corporate client）
 a ban on remittances from Japan to North Korea　日本から北朝鮮への送金停止
 a cable remittance order　電信送金為替
 an airmail remittance order　郵便送金指図
 application for remittance　外国送金依頼書
 bank remittance　銀行送金為替, 送金為替
 bank remittance bill　送金為替手形
 cable [telegraphic, wire] remittance　電信送金（=remittance by cable [telegraph, wire]）
 cash remittance　現金送金
 covering remittance　為替間接送金
 currency remittance　送金
 invisible trade remittances　貿易外取引送金
 ordinary remittance　並為替
 overseas remittance　海外送金, 対外送金
 postal [mail] remittance　郵便送金（=remittance by post [mail]）
 remittance advice　送金通知書
 remittance bank　送金銀行
 remittance bill [draft]　送金手形, 送金為替
 remittance by draft　為替手形送金, 為替送金
 remittance check　送金小切手
 remittance instruction　送金通知書, 送金取組み通知
 remittance letter　送金通知状
 remittance slip　送金伝票
 remittances abroad　外国送金, 仕向け送金為替
 reverse remittance　逆為替
 telegraphic transfer remittance　電信送金為替
 the amount of remittance　送金の金額, 送金する金額
 the method of remittance　送金方法
 treasury remittance　国庫送金, 国庫金送金
 ◆Deutsche Bank handles 120 currencies and is capable of sending remittances from Japan to accounts in nearly every country. ドイツ銀行は、120種類の通貨を取り扱っていて、日本からほぼ世界中の口座に送金することができる。◆The revised Foreign Exchange and Foreign Trade Law allows Japan to suspend or limit remittances and trade with North Korea. 改正外国為替及び外国貿易法によると、北朝鮮に関して日本は送金や貿易を停止・制限することができる。

remittance fees [charge] 送金手数料, 振込み手数料
 ◆Overseas remittance fees are currently several thousand yen per transfer. 海外への送金手数料は現在、送金1回に付き数千円かかる。

remittance network 送金ネットワーク
 ◆By using Deutsche Bank's remittance network, Japanese four regional banks will increase the money transfer services available to customers. ドイツ銀行の送金ネットワークを活用して、日本の地方銀行4行は、送金業務の顧客サービスを充実させる方針だ。

remove （動）除去する, 取り除く, 取り去る, 払拭する, 削除する, 撤去する, 撤廃する, 廃止する, 解除する, 解任する, 解雇する, 移動する, 移す, 運ぶ, 移転する, 暗殺する, 殺す
 be removed from one's lead position　主幹事の座から降ろされる
 remove a large amount of credit from the balance sheets of banks　銀行のバランス・シートから多くの債権を切り離す
 remove ample liquidity from　～から大量の［潤沢な、豊富な］資金を吸い上げる［吸収する］
 remove assets from the bank's books　銀行の資産をオフ・バランスにする
 remove the debt from the borrower's balance sheet　借り手のバランス・シート（貸借対照表）から債務を外す, ～で借り手のバランス・シートから債務が消える
 remove the uncertainty　不確実性［不透明性, 不透明感］を払拭（ふっしょく）する
 ◆A large amount of credit cannot be removed from the balance sheets of banks even though loan loss reserves have been set aside. 貸倒れ引当金を積んでも、多くの債権は、銀行のバランス・シートから切り離せない状況にある［銀行で最終処理できない債権が多い］。

renew （動）更新する, 一新する, 新たにする, 継続する, （期間などを）延長する, 据え置く, （手形や書類を）書き換える, 再契約する, 新たに補充する, 再興する, 再建する, 再生する, 復活させる, 取り戻す（recover）, 取り替える, 回復する, 繰り返す
 renew a bill [draft]　手形［為替手形］を書き換える
 renew a contract　契約を更新する
 renew [resume] financial support to　～に対する財政支援を再開する
 renew the loan　ローン［融資］を借り換える, ローンの更改を行う
 renew the record high for the year　年初来の高値を更新する
 renew the record low for the year　年初来の安値を更新する
 ◆Domestic nonlife insurance companies usually renew contracts with most of their corporate clients each April. 国内の損保各社は通常、毎年4月に大半の顧客企業と（保険）契約の更新を行っている。

renewable energy 再生可能エネルギー, 自然エネルギー
 ◆The project financing market has seen a boost in loans to businesses in renewable energy field such as solar and wind power generation. プロジェクト・ファイナンス市場は最近、太陽光や風力発電など自然エネルギー分野の事業への融資が増えている。

renewal （名）刷新, 更新, 書換え, 書換え継続, 期限延長,

自動継続, 再開, 再生, 復活, 回復, 再燃, 再開発, リニューアル
automatic renewal 自動更新
card renewal カード更新
renewal bond 借換え債券
renewal fee 更新手数料, 書換え手数料
renewal fund 設備の更新資金
renewal note 書換え約束手形, 切替え手形［約束手形］
renewal notice 保険継続依頼通知書
renewal of a draft 手形の書換え
renewal of a loan 融資の借換え
renewal of an exchange contract 為替予約の更新
renewal of policy 保険契約の更新, 保険の更新
renewal premium 継続保険料, 更新保険料
renewal premium persistency 更新保険料持続率
subscription renewal 予約の更新

renewed （形）更新した, 新たになった, 新たな, 回復した, （元気などを）取り戻した, ～の更新, ～の再燃, ～の再発, 再び～する
come under renewed selling pressure 再び売り圧力にさらされる, 再び売り圧力を受ける
renewed bill 更新手形, 書換え手形, 手形の更新
renewed concern over ～に対する懸念が再び高まること （⇒reemergence）
renewed recession 不況の再燃, 不況への逆戻り
renewed slide in the dollar 再びドルが下落すること, ドルの下落トレンドへの逆戻り
renewed tightening of monetary conditions 金融引締め［金融政策引締め］への転換
renews dollar sell-off ドル売りの再燃, ドル売りの動きの再燃

renminbi （名）人民元, RMB （=yuan; ⇒RMB）
◆A stronger renminbi would help facilitate a shift from exports and investment to private consumption as the principal driver of economic growth. 人民元が強くなれば, 中国の経済成長の主な原動力であったこれまでの輸出や投資から個人消費への転換を促進することになる。 ◆China's currency is also known as the renminbi. 中国の通貨は, 人民元とも呼ばれている。 ◆China's renminbi may attain a reserve-currency status by the steady appreciation of the yuan and the country's enormous capital surpluses. 中国の人民元は, 人民元の着実な切上げと中国の膨大な資本剰余金によって, 準備通貨の地位を獲得する可能性がある。 ◆Currency traders are now turning to the renminbi (yuan) from the U.S. dollar. 為替トレーダーは今や, 米ドルから中国の人民元に目を向けている。 ◆The U.S. dollar as the world's only reserve currency may become merely one of three major currencies, along with the euro and the renminbi. 世界で唯一の準備通貨としての米ドルは, ユーロ, 人民元とともに, 単なる3大通貨の一つになる可能性がある。

renminbi-based bonds 人民元建て債券
◆Some currency traders have recently advised the Malaysian government and the Persian Gulf states to buy renminbi-based bonds, rather than the U.S. dollar. 一部の為替トレーダーは最近, 米ドルではなく中国の人民元建て債券を買うようマレーシア政府やペルシャ湾岸諸国に助言している。

reorganization （名）再編成, 再編, 改造, 改組, 改革, 再生, 再建, 会社再建, 事業再編, 組織変更, 会社更生 （=realignment; ⇒consolidated recurring profit, corporate reorganization, financial reorganization, financial sector）
capital reorganization 資本再編
corporate reorganization 企業再編, 再編, 会社更生
cross-border reorganization 国境を越えた再編
debt reorganization 債務再構成

reorganization bond 整理社債
reorganization of the industry 業界再編, 業界再編成 （=realignment of the industry）
reorganization plan 再建計画, 再建案, 更生計画案
◆Cross-border reorganization of stock exchanges is gathering speed in the United States and Europe. 欧米では, 国境を越えた証券取引所の再編が加速している。 ◆Major banks have undergone large-scale corporate reorganization. 大手銀行は, すでに大再編を終えた。 ◆The financial group's inadequate preparations for the reorganization resulted in a major computer system failure. 同フィナンシャル・グループの再編の準備不足から, 大規模なシステム障害が起こった。

reorganize （動）再編成する, 再編する, 統合する, 改造する, 改組する, 改革する, 再生する, 再建する, 組織変更する （⇒Bankruptcy Code）
◆Following the integration of the TSE and OSE, the two exchanges may be reorganized by function, with one entity to handle spot trading and another derivatives. 東証と大証の統合後, 両取引所は機能別に再編され, それぞれ現物取引とデリバティブを扱うようになる可能性がある。 ◆Mizuho Financial Group reorganized its banking sector in April 2002. みずほフィナンシャルグループは, 2002年4月に銀行部門を再編した。 ◆Six state-run financial institutions were reorganized into three, the Japan Bank for International Cooperation (JBIC), the Development Bank of Japan and the National Life Finance Corporation. 政府系の6つの金融機関が, 国際協力銀行, 日本政策投資銀行と国民生活金融公庫の3つに統合［再編］された。

repatriate （動）本国に送金する, 本国に資金を還流する, 還流させる, 投下資本を引き揚げる
repatriate income earned abroad 海外で得た利益を本国に送金する
repatriate profits from investments 投資で得た利益を本国に送金する

repatriation （名）本国への資金還流, 本国送金, 資金の自国通貨への還流, 投下資本の引揚げ, リパトリエーション
accelerate repatriation of funds 資金の自国通貨への還流を加速させる
profit repatriation 利益の本国送金
repatriation of income earned abroad 海外で得た利益の本国送金
◆The consolidated provision for taxes also includes an amount sufficient to pay additional United States federal income taxes on repatriation of income earned abroad. 連結納税引当金には, 海外で得た利益の本国送金に課される米連邦所得税の追加支払いに十分対応できる金額も含まれている。

repay （動）払い戻す, 返済する, 返還する, 返金する, 償還する （=refund; ⇒base）
repay a general government bond 一般財源債を返済する。
repay bank borrowings 銀行借入金［銀行借入れ］を返済する
repay debt 債務を返済する, 借入金を返済する
repay in full 完済する
repay long-term indebtedness 長期債務を返済する
repay maturing CP 満期を迎えた［満期が来た］CPを償還する
repay principal 元本を返済する
repay some of one's debt 債務の一部を返済する
repay the credit card charges クレジット・カード債権を返済する
repay the loan ローンを返済する
repay the remaining ¥20 billion of debt through debt waivers 残りの負債200億円を返済する

repay $500 million of long-term debt　長期債務5億ドルを返済する
◆During the first half of 2011, the firm repaid $600 million of long-term debt. 2011年上半期に、同社は長期債務6億ドルを返済した。◆In the case of a lack of liquidity or liquidity crisis, the debt repayment of an indebted borrower is still possible if a grace period is given, but lack of cash on hand makes it impossible to repay its debt in the short term. 流動性不足や流動性危機の場合、債務を抱えた借り手の債務返済は猶予期間を与えればまだ可能であるが、手元に現金がないため短期での債務返済はできない。◆In the project financing business, lending banks are repaid loans through profits generated by the projects they have financed. プロジェクト・ファイナンス事業では、貸出行が、融資したプロジェクト（事業）から生まれる利益で融資の返済を受ける。◆Including the money extended in the form of equity, GM still has to repay $52 billion to the U.S. and Canadian governments. 出資分を含めて、GMは米政府とカナダ政府にまだ520億ドルも返済しなければならない。◆The remaining ￥20 billion of debt will be repaid through debt waivers by the firm's six main banks and three regional banks in Fukuoka. 残りの負債200億円は、同社の主力取引銀行6行と福岡の地銀3行による債権放棄で返済する。

repay one's creditors　債権者に債務を返済する
◆Chapter 11 bankruptcy provides for a business to continue operations while formulating a plan to repay its creditors. 米連邦改正破産法11章の破産の規定では、企業は事業を継続する一方、債権者への債務返済計画を策定することができる。

repay one's debt　債務を返済する
◆The bank plans to issue preferred stock to procure about ￥1 trillion over the next few years to repay its debt to the government. 同行は、公的資金の返済に向けて、優先株を発行し、今後数年間で約1兆円を調達する計画だ。

repay part of one's outstanding debt　債務残高の一部を返済する、残りの債務の一部を返済する
◆The firm repaid part of its outstanding debt to the bank. 同社は、債務残高［残りの債務］の一部を同行に返済した。

repay public funds　公的資金を返済する
◆The bank has already repaid public funds injected in 1998. 同行は、1998年に注入された公的資金をすでに返済している。

repayment　（名）返済、払戻し、償還、返金　（⇒debt repayment, foreign debt repayments, loan repayment）
complete one's public fund repayment　公的資金の返済を完了する
repayment capacity　返済能力
repayment of deposits　預金の払戻し
（=refund of deposits）
repayment of long-term debt　長期借入金の返済
repayment of short-term debt　短期借入金の返済
repayment of the loans　借入金の返済、ローンの返済
（=loan repayment）
◆In the case of an insolvent borrower, it no longer has the ability to pay all its debt even though lenders offer to defer the time of repayment. 返済不能の借り手の場合、貸し手が返済期間の延長を申し出ても、借り手はもはや債務を全額返済できない状況にある。◆The financial group completed its public fund repayment in 2008. 同フィナンシャル・グループは、2008年に公的資金の返済を完了した。

repayment amount　返済額、返還額
◆At the firm, curbing repayment amounts is regarded as a criterion for in-house personnel evaluation. 同社では、返還額を抑えることが、社内の人事評価基準と見なされている。

repayment burden　返済負担
◆Public institutions or revitalization funds will buy the loans owed by small and midsize companies that have been hit by the March 11 disaster to lighten their repayment burdens. 公的機関や復興ファンドが、東日本大震災で被災した中小企業の借金を買い取って、被災企業の返済負担を軽減するものと思われる。

repayment of debt　債務返済、債務の支払い、借入金の返済、借入金返済額　（=debt repayment）
◆Most other major banks also are considering repayment of their debts to the government. 他のほとんどの大手行も、国への債務返済を検討している。◆The nonprofit foundation faced cash flow problems, such as repayment of the debt and meeting personnel costs. この公益法人は、借入金の返済や人件費のやりくりなど、資金繰りの問題に行き詰まった。

repayment of loans　貸付けの返済、貸付け金の返済
◆The special account is expected to collect a large surplus in fiscal 2011 via the repayment of loans. 特別会計は、貸付け金の返済で2011年度は多額の剰余金が生じる見込みだ。

repayment of one's mortgage　住宅ローンの返済
◆Under the program of a voluntary liquidation for individuals, housing loan borrowers' voluntary bankruptcies can be prevented by having financial institutions waive repayment of their mortgages. 個人向け私的整理の制度だと、金融機関に住宅ローンの返済を免除させることによって、住宅ローンの借り手の自己破産を防ぐことができる。

repayment period　返済期間、償還期間
◆The repayment period of the new tied yen loans will be set at 40 years. 新ひも付き円借款の償還期間は今後、40年とされる。

repayment program　返済計画
◆As the gap between the eurozone-imposed repayment program and the track record began clearly yawning, the Greece's insolvency became apparent. ユーロ圏が押し付けたギリシャの返済計画と実績とのズレが目立つようになるにつれ、ギリシャの返済不能が明らかになった。

repercussion　（名）波及、余波、反動、影響、反射
◆The collapse of the bank will lead to repercussions throughout the finance sector. 同行の破たんは、金融業界全体に影響を及ぼすことになろう。◆The repercussions of Olympus Corp's false financial statements could lead to a loss of confidence in the governance and in the compliance of all Japanese firms. オリンパスの不正経理［有価証券虚偽記載］の影響で、日本企業全体の統治能力や法令遵守への信頼が失墜する可能性がある。

replenish　（動）再び満たす、補充する、補給する、補てんする、充てる
replenish inventories　在庫を補充する
replenish labor force　労働力を補充する
replenish the depleted state coffers　疲弊した国家財政を立て直す
◆Japan must tackle the task of replenishing the depleted state coffers. 日本は、疲弊した国家財政立て直しの課題［疲弊した国家財政の立て直しという課題］に取り組まなければならない。◆There will be a decrease in net assets if the "hidden treasure" of a special account is used for replenishing recurring expenditures, not for reducing liabilities. 特別会計の「埋蔵金」（積立金）を、負債の削減に使わないで経常的な歳出に充てれば、純資産は減ってします。

repo [Repo]　（名）買戻し特約、レポ取引、買いオペ、レポ、RP　（=repurchase agreement:repossess（買い戻す）の短縮形。現先（げんさき）取引、つまり買戻しまたは売戻し条件付きの取引のこと。ただし、日本の「レポ取引」は現金担保付き債券貸借取引のことで、これは現金を担保とした債券の消費貸借契約を指す。repoが動詞として使われる場合は、「買戻し条件付きで取引する［売買する］の意味になる。⇒repurchase agreement）
bond repo market　公社債現先市場、債券レポ市場
dollar repos　ドル現先
fixed rate repo　定率入札の買いオペ

floating rate repo　変動金利現先
increase liquidity in the monetary system via repo activities　買いオペで市中に流動性を供給する
open repo market　公開レポ市場, 公開現先市場
overnight repo　翌日物レポ, 翌日物レポ取引, 翌日決済の買い戻し条件付き証券売却, オーバーナイト現先, オーバーナイト・レポ
overnight repo rate　翌日物レポ金利
repo activities　買いオペ
repo market　現先市場, レポ市場
repo market of [in] Treasuries　米国債のレポ市場
repo proceeds　レポ取引で得た資金
repo rate　レポ金利, 債券オペ金利, 買いオペ金利, オペ金利, レポ・レート
repo rate cut [reduction]　買いオペ金利引下げ, レポ・レートの引下げ
repo to maturity　満期償還現先
reverse repo　売戻し条件付き購入, リバース・レポ (=reverse sale and repurchase agreement)
squeeze [tightness] in the repo market　レポ市場での需給ひっ迫
term repo　定期現先, ターム・レポ, 翌日物レポより長い期間のレポ
the return on the repo　レポ取引の利益
variable (rate) repo　金利入札による買いオペ, 金利入札方式のレポ

report　(動)報告する, 報告書を提出する, 表示する, 記載する, 公表する, 回答する, 計上する, 申告する, 報道する, 連絡する
as previously reported　前期報告額, 前年度報告額
net assets at year end-as reported　期末現在の純資産, 公表額, 期末純資産, 公表額
report as liability　負債として計上する
report at a market value　時価で表示する, 市場価格で表示する
report huge losses　巨額の損失を計上する
report net income　純利益を計上する
report recurring losses　経常赤字になる, 経常赤字に転落する
◆A real estate investment fund was alleged to have failed to report about ¥18 billion in income from transaction involving land and property taken as collateral for nonperforming loans. 不動産投資ファンドが, 不良債権の担保に取った不動産関連の取引で得た所得約180億円の申告漏れを指摘されていた。◆Firms are allowed to annually report their profits from large construction projects that last several years. 複数年にまたがる大規模工事の場合, 企業は（完工前でも）単年度ごとに利益を計上することができる。◆Laws already in place on narcotics and organized crime oblige financial institutions to report to the FSA any deals possibly linked to profits from criminal activities. すでに実施されている麻薬や組織の犯罪に関する法律は, 犯罪収益絡みと思われる取引について, 金融庁への報告（届出）を金融機関に義務付けている。◆Lone Star Fund failed to report ¥38 billion in taxable income over a four-year-period to 2001. 米国の投資会社ローンスターの投資会社「ローンスター・ファンド」は, 2001年までの4年間にわたって課税所得総額380億円を申告していなかった。◆Ten of 12 Fed district banks reported weaker conditions or declines in their regional economies. 全米12地区連銀のうち10連銀が, 各地域経済の悪化あるいは経済活動の低下を報告した。◆The Bank of Japan's diffusion indexes are calculated by subtracting the percentage of companies reporting deterioration in business conditions from those perceiving improvement. 日銀のこれらの業況判断指数（DI）は, 現在の景況感について「改善している」と感じている企業の割合から「悪化している」と回答した企業の割合を差し引いて算出する。◆The bank's after-tax profits were far lower than the ¥9.3 billion reported in the financial statement. 同行の税引き後純利益は, 有価証券報告書に記載されている93億円を大幅に下回っていた。◆The business sentiment index represents the percentage of companies reporting favorable business conditions minus the percentage of those reporting unfavorable conditions. 業況判断指数は, 景気が良いと答えた企業の割合（％）から景気が悪いと答えた企業の割合（％）を差し引いた指数だ。◆The firm failed to report a total of about ¥7 billion in taxable income. 同社は, 課税総額約70億円を申告しなかった。◆The Securities and Exchange Law requires anyone with an equity stake of more than 5 percent in a listed company to report a sale of stake of 1 percent or more to a local finance bureau within five business days of the sale. 現行の証券取引法では, 上場企業に対する株式保有比率が5％を超える株保有者は, 株式の売買が株式の保有割合を1％超えるごとに, 株式売買の5営業日以内に各財務局にその報告書を提出しなければならない。◆The Securities and Exchange Law requires investment funds to register and report the names of their representatives and their locations. 証券取引法は, 投資ファンドに対して, 投資ファンドの代表者名や所在地などの登録・届け出を義務付けている。◆The top 10 life insurers in the nation reported a total of ¥1.46 trillion in valuation losses on their securities holdings for the current business year. 今期決算で, 国内生保の上位（主要）10社の保有有価証券[保有株式]の減損処理額は, 1兆4,600億円に達した。

report　(名)報告, 報告書, 申告書, 報道, レポート　(⇒ advisory, annual report, earnings report, financial report, midterm report, quarterly report)
accountant's report　監査報告書, 会計士報告書（目論見書添付書類）
accounting reports　会計報告書, 財務諸表, 有価証券報告書, 財務情報
annual meeting report　株主総会報告書
audit report　監査報告書
business report　事業報告, 事業報告書, 営業報告書, 業務報告書, ビジネス・レポート
call report　業務報告書
cash report　現金収支報告書
consumer report　個人信用情報
credit report　信用調書
customs trade report　通関統計
directors' report　取締役会報告 [報告書]
economic reports　景気指標
employment report　雇用統計
flash report　営業速報, 速報値
fund report　資金報告, 資金報告書
group report and accounts　連結決算報告書
half-year report　半期報告書, 中間事業報告書
import and export report　輸出入申告書
inflation reports　物価指数
interim earnings report　中間決算
interim financial report　中間報告 [報告書], 中間決算報告書, 中間事業報告書, 中間財務報告 [報告書], 半期報告書　(=half-year report)
management report　経営者報告, 経営者からのご報告, マネジメント・レポート
midterm report　中間決算, 半期報告書　(=half-year report)
monthly cash report　資金月報
monthly report　月次報告, 月例報告, 月報
operating report　業務報告 [報告書]

performance report　業績報告書
preliminary report　速報, 速報値
quarterly report　四半期報告［報告書］, 四季報
report date　決算日
report of management　経営者の報告, 経営陣の報告
report of the attending physician　主治医報告書
report on large shareholders　大量保有報告書
securities report　有価証券報告書
status report　現状報告書, 現況報告
Tankan report　日銀短観
trade deficit report　貿易統計
◆A working group of the Financial System Council put together a report concerning capital adequacy requirements. 金融審議会の作業部会が, 自己資本比率規制に関する報告書をまとめた。◆Corporate accounting reports are the most important criterion for investment decisions. 企業の財務情報は, 特に重要な投資判断の材料だ。◆Now is the peak period for listed companies to release their business reports for the business year ending in March. 上場企業の3月期決算の発表が, ピークを迎えている。◆The bank's investigation committee is compiling a report that holds several former executives accountable for the enormous losses. 同行の調査委員会は, 旧経営陣数名に多額の損失の責任を問う内容の報告書をまとめている。◆The Board of Audit intends to include the total taxpayer contribution to JAL in its audit account report compiled in November 2011. 会計検査院は, 2011年11月にまとめる決算検査報告書に, 日航に対する総国民負担額を盛り込む方針だ。

report on one's interim settlement of accounts
中間決算報告, 中間決算報告書
◆Neither of Mitsui Trust Holdings, Inc. and another major financial group has yet released reports on its interim settlement of accounts. 三井トラスト・ホールディングスなど2大金融グループは, まだ中間決算報告を発表していない。

reporting　報告, 表示　（⇒financial reporting）
accounting for external reporting　外部報告会計
employee reporting　従業員に対する報告
for financial statement reporting　財務書類上, 財務諸表上
for income tax reporting　税務上, 税務会計上
functional reporting of expenses　職能別報告書, 職能別計算書
income reporting　損益報告
net of tax reporting　税引き後純額の報告, 正味税効果の報告, 税効果考慮後の報告
periodic reporting　定期報告, 期間報告
principle of true and fair reporting　真実性の原則
production reporting　生産報告
reporting currency　報告通貨（財務諸表などで金額表示の単位として用いる通貨）
reporting period　報告期間, 決算報告期間, 財務報告期間, 報告事業年度（文脈に応じて「当期」や「当四半期」を指す場合もある）
reporting year　報告事業年度, 報告年度, 当年度, 当期
segmental reporting［report］　セグメント情報
standard of reporting　報告基準
◆The Sarbanes-Oxlay Act directed the SEC to implement some of the reporting changes in an attempt to force companies and their executives to be more honest with investors. 企業と企業経営者に投資家への一段と誠実な対応を義務付けるため, サーベンス・オクスレー法は, SEC（米証券取引委員会）に報告規則変更の一部実施を求めた。

repossession　（名）回収, 再取得, 所有権回復, 取り戻し, 担保権実行
defaults and repossessions　債務不履行や担保権実行
losses on repossessions　商品取り戻し損失
mortgage repossession　抵当流れ

represent　（動）表示する, 表明する, 意味する, 示す, 〜を表章する, 〜を表す, 〜の代理をつとめる, 〜を代表する, 〜を代行する, 〜に相当する, 〜に当たる
（⇒secured mortgage）
employees are represented by unions　従業員は組合に加入している
represent one's business　事業を代表する
represent 10 percent of revenues　売上高の10%を占める
◆A committee of creditors was appointed to represent its business. 債権者委員会が, その事業を代表するために任命された。◆An aggregate market value represents a corporate value in terms of stock price. 時価総額は, 株価による企業価値を示す。◆Book value per share refers to the amount of net assets of a company represented by one share of common stock. 1株当たり純資産［簿価］とは, 普通株式1株当たりの企業の純資産額のことを言う。◆The business sentiment index represents the percentage of companies reporting favorable business conditions minus the percentage of those reporting unfavorable conditions. 業況判断指数は, 景気が良いと答えた企業の割合（%）から景気が悪いと答えた企業の割合（%）を差し引いた指数だ。◆The firm that best represents the brisk performances of Japanese companies is Toyota Motor Corp. 日本企業の好業績の代表格は, トヨタ自動車だ。◆The primary balance represents the budget balance, excluding proceeds from government bond issues and debt-servicing costs. プライマリー・バランスは, 国債発行による収入と国債費（国債の利払いや償還費用）を除いた財政収支である。◆Years of window-dressing by Olympus to hide investment losses represent nothing but a companywide breach of trust. 投資損失隠ぺいのためのオリンパスによる長年の粉飾決算は, 会社ぐるみの背信行為にほかならない。

representative　（名）代表者, 代理人, 代行者, 事務所, 駐在員事務所, セールスマン, 販売員, 外務員, 駐在員, 担当者　（⇒meeting of representatives of policyholders, policyholders' representative meeting）
account representative　証券会社のセールスマン
IR representative　IR担当者
private sector representatives　民間企業のトップ
　（⇒rescue）
registered representative　登録販売員, 登録取引会員
representative action　株主の代表訴訟, 集団訴訟
representative company　幹事会社
representative rate for　〜の中心相場, 代表レート
representative underwriter　代表引受会社
sales representative　販売外交員, 販売担当者
◆The Securities and Exchange Law requires investment funds to register and report the names of their representatives and their locations. 証券取引法は, 投資ファンドに対して, 投資ファンドの代表者名や所在地などの登録・届け出を義務付けている。

repurchase　（動）買い戻す, 再購入する
（=buy back）
repurchase shares for cancellation　消却のため株式を買い戻す, 株式を買い戻して消却する
repurchase the stock sold to the speculators　仕手筋に売却した株［自社株］を買い戻す
retire the repurchased shares　買戻し株［株式］を消却する
◆The company planned to repurchase the company's stock it had sold to the speculators. 同社は, 仕手筋に売却した自社株の買戻しを計画した。

repurchase　（名）買戻し, 買取り, 再調達
（=buyback）

equity repurchase　株式の買戻し
overnight repurchase agreement　翌日物レポ
repurchase cost　再調達原価, 再調達価格
repurchase method　買取り方式　（⇒voucher）
repurchase of bonds　社債の買戻し
repurchase of long term bonds　長期社債の買入れ
right of repurchase　買戻し請求権, 買戻し権
share［stock］repurchase　自社株買戻し, 株式の買戻し, 自社株買戻し, 自社株買い, 自社株買入れ
　（=share buyback, stock buyback）
stock repurchase program　自社株買戻しプログラム
　◆The Bank of Japan's conventional open market operation of buying short-term government notes without repurchase agreements is limited in its effect. 日銀のこれまでの売戻し条件を付けない短期国債の買切りオペ（公開市場操作）だけでは, その効果に限界がある。

repurchase agreement　現先［元先］取引, 現先, レポ, レポ取引, 売戻し条件付き買いオペ, 買戻し約定［特約］
　（=repo, Repo, RP; ⇒customer repurchase agreement, system repurchase agreement）
repurchase and reverse repurchase agreements　買戻し・売戻し条件付き売買契約, レポおよびリバース・レポ契約
reverse repurchase agreement　逆現先, 逆レポ, リバース・レポ取引, リバース・レポ（一定期間後に売り戻すことを条件に債券を購入すること）

repurchasing　（名）買戻し, 買取り
repurchasing government bonds　国債現先オペレーション
　◆The bank of Japan has begun studying the possibility of extending the period for repurchasing government bonds, a system under which it purchases government bonds from financial institutions on condition that they would be repurchased by the financial institutions after a certain period. 日銀は, 一定期間後に売り戻すことを条件に金融機関から国債を買い入れる方式の「国債現先オペレーション」の期間延長の検討に入った。

repurchasing method　買取り方式
　◆Repurchasing method may not be illegal, but its de facto interest payment equals to as much as 300 percent annual interest. 買取り方式は違法とは言えないかもしれないが, その事実上の支払い利息［金利］は, 年利で300％（出資法の上限は15～20％）もの水準に達している。◆The repurchasing method, which has customers buy highly negotiable cash vouchers, violates the industry rule. 顧客に換金性の高い金券類を購入させる買取り方式は, 業界の規約に違反する。

reputation　（名）評価, 名声, 地位, 信望, 知名度, 評判, 名誉, イメージ
　◆Major moneylender SFCG earned an unsavory reputation for its strong-arm loan collection methods. 金融業者大手のSFCG（旧商工ファンド）の評判は, 債権の取立てが強引で芳しくなかった。

request　（動）要求する, 請求する, 求める, 要請する, 依頼する, 頼む
　◆After the IMF called for strict implementation of structural reforms as a condition for loans to financially troubled countries, counties became reluctant to request assistance from the IMF. 財政難に陥った国に対する融資の条件としてIMF（国際通貨基金）が厳しい構造改革の実施を求めてから, 各国はIMFへの支援要請をためらうようになった。

request　（名）要求, 要求書, 請求, 要請, 要請書, 依頼, 依頼書, 委任, リクエスト
　◆Banks will not accept future loan requests if they have to forgive the debt. 金融機関が債権放棄をせざるを得ないとなると, 金融機関は今後の融資要請には応じないだろう。◆Many regional banks are unable to respond to their clients' requests for money transfers in currencies other than the dollar and euro. 地銀の多くは, 顧客からのドルやユーロ以外の通貨の送金依頼に対応できていない。◆The Fair Trade Commission of Japan is required to consider global economic trends when it screens corporate merger requests in light of the Antimonopoly Law. 公正取引委員会は, 独占禁止法に照らして企業合併の申請を審査するにあたって, グローバル経済の潮流も検討する必要がある。◆The financial authorities filed a declaration of bankruptcy and a request for asset protection with the Tokyo District Court for the brokerage firm. 金融当局は, 同証券会社の破産宣告と財産保全処分を東京地裁に申し立てた。

request for financial support　金融支援の要請
　◆The 17-nation currency union was slow in responding to the request for financial support by Greece. 17か国から成る通貨統合のユーロ圏は, ギリシャの金融支援要請への対応が遅かった。

require　（動）必要とする, 要求する, 迫る, 求める, 義務付ける
　◆According to the Financial Stability Board, 28 banks viewed as global systemically important financial institutions（G-SIFIs）will be subject to a new global rule requiring them to hold extra capital to prevent future financial crises. 金融安定化理事会（FSB）によると, 金融システム上重要な国際金融機関（G-SIFIs）と考えられる世界の28行が, 金融危機の再発を防止するため, 資本の上積みを求める新国際基準［新国際金融規制］の対象になる。◆Before the new corporate law, at least ¥10 million was required to establish stock companies and ¥3 million to create limited liability companies. 新会社法までは, 株式会社の設立に最低1,000万円, 有限会社の設立に300万円必要だった。◆Full-time housewives of company employees and public servants are not required to pay pension premiums. 会社員や公務員の専業主婦は, 保険料を払う必要がない。◆Global economic crisis requires a flexible response. 世界の経済危機には, 機動的対応が必要だ。◆In 2009, the Business Accounting Council decided to require all of the nation's listed companies to use the IFRSs for their consolidated financial statements from 2015. 2009年に企業会計審議会は, 2015年にも, 国内全上場企業の連結財務諸表［連結財務書類］について, 国際財務情報基準（IFRSs）の採用を上場企業に義務付ける方針を打ち出した。◆Our plans, which require significant investments, are at risk because of limited access to capital. 大幅投資が必要な当社の計画は現在, 資金調達力にも限界があるため, 危機にさらされています。◆The new regulations decided on by the Basel Committee on Banking Supervision require banks to increase the core tier 1 capital, such as common stock and retained earnings, that they must hold in reserve, to at least 4.5 percent of assets from the current 2 percent. バーゼル銀行監督委員会が決めた新規制は, 銀行が支払い準備として保有しなければならない普通株や利益剰余金［内部留保］などの中核的自己資本（コア・ティア1）を, 現行の資産の最低2％から4.5％に引き上げるよう銀行に義務付けている。◆The number of people using cashing services is rising partly because no screening is required to get money. 無審査で金を借りられることもあって, キャッシング・サービス（現金化商法）の利用者は増えている。◆The Securities and Exchange Law requires investment funds to register and report the names of their representatives and their locations. 証券取引法は, 投資ファンドに対して, 投資ファンドの代表者名や所在地などの登録・届け出を義務付けている。◆The three Japanese biggest banks are likely to be required to hold additional capital of 1 percent to 1.5 percent. 日本の3大メガ銀行は, 1～1.5％の資本［自己資本］上積みを求められる見込みだ。◆The three Japanese top banks will face the FSB's new international rule requiring them to hold extra capital to prevent future financial crises. 日本の3メガ銀行も,

金融危機の再発を防ぐため、資本［自己資本］の上積みを求める金融安定化理事会（FSB）の新国際基準の対象になると見られる。◆Under the EU's Stability and Growth Pact, countries eligible to join the euro system are required to keep budget deficits below 3 percent of GDP. 欧州連合（EU）の財政安定・成長協定によると、ユーロ加盟国は、加盟の条件として財政赤字をGDPの3％以下に抑えなければならない。◆Under the mark-to-market accounting system, if banks suffer appraisal losses of stocks they are holding, they are required to subtract 60 percent of those losses from their surplus funds. 時価会計制度では、金融機関が保有する株式の評価損が出た場合、金融機関は評価損の6割を剰余金から取り除かなければならない。

required reserves　所要準備
requirement(s)　（名）要件, 条件, 必要条件, 基準, 資格
（⇒BIS requirements, capital requirements, cash requirements, listing requirement(s)）
　BIS requirements　BIS基準
　capital adequacy requirements　自己資本比率規制, 自己資本規制
　capital requirements　資金需要, 自己資本規制, 自己資本比率規制
　credit requirements　審査基準
　disclosure requirements　情報開示基準
　listing requirements　上場要件
　margin requirement　証拠金率
　meet the requirements　条件を満たす, 条件に合致する, 条件に適合する
　membership requirement　会員資格要件
　minimum core capital requirements　最低中核資本規制, 最低中核の自己資本規制
　rating requirements　格付け基準
　requirements for funds　資金需要
　stricter requirements for the minimum core capital ratio　最低自己資本比率の強化［厳格化］
　underwriting requirements　引受基準
◆The principal requirements for funds are for capital expenditures and to acquire new and additional investments. 資金需要は、主に資本的支出と新規および追加投資を行う場合に発生する。◆The United States and Britain demanded stricter requirements for the minimum core capital ratio. 米国と英国は、最低自己資本比率規制の強化［厳格化］を求めた。◆To encourage firms' temporary layoffs, the government will ease requirements for receiving a governmental subsidy to defray costs relating to layoffs. 企業の一時解雇［一時帰休］を支援するため、政府は企業が雇用調整助成金（解雇関連費用を負担する政府助成金）を受けるための要件を緩和する。◆U.S. and European financial institutions are scaling back their business operations before capital adequacy requirements are strengthened in 2013. 欧米金融機関は、2013年から自己資本規制が強化されるのを前に、業務を縮小している。

rescheduling　（名）債務返済繰延べ, 債務繰延べ, リスケ, リスケジュール
rescue　（動）救う, 救助［救出］する, 支援する, 救済する
（⇒capital increase）
◆A sense of disappointment has prevailed across the world markets as no concrete measures to rescue Greece were unveiled at the eurozone finance ministers meeting. ユーロ圏財務相会合でギリシャ支援の具体策が明らかにされなかったので、世界の市場で失望感が広がった。◆Due to delays in ratification of the agreement on bailout measures by some eurozone countries, concrete measures to rescue Greece have yet to be carried out. 支援策の合意事項について一部のユーロ圏加盟国の承認が遅れたため、ギリシャ救済の具体策はまだ実施されていない。◆The U.S. Federal Reserve Board will provide up to $85 billion in an emergency loan to rescue the huge insurer American International Group Inc. 米連邦準備制度理事会（FRB）は、米保険最大手AIGを救済するためのつなぎ融資として、AIGに最大850億ドルを投入する。◆U.S. government officials and private sector representatives tried to devise a way to rescue Lehman Brothers Holdings Inc. 米国の政府当局者と民間企業のトップは、リーマン・ブラザーズ救済策を模索した。

rescue　（名）救援, 支援, 救済, 救出, 救助, レスキュー
　financial rescue　金融支援, 経営支援
　rescue bond　レスキュー債
rescue fund　支援基金, 救済基金
◆The European Union hurriedly created an emergency rescue fund, called the European Financial Stability Facility (EFSF). 欧州連合（EU）は、欧州金融安定基金（EFSF）という緊急支援基金を急設した。
rescue loan　救済融資, 金融支援融資
◆Belarus has asked the IMF for a $8 billion rescue loan to manage the country's most severe financial crisis since the Soviet collapse. ベラルーシは、ソ連崩壊後最も深刻な金融危機を乗り切るため、国際通貨基金（IMF）に80億ドルの金融支援融資を要請した。
rescue measures　救済措置, 救済策
◆The Financial Services Agency did not implement rescue measures with public funds as for the scandal-ridden Incubator Bank of Japan. 金融庁は、不祥事続きだった日本振興銀行については、公的資金での救済策を取らなかった。◆To deal with the systemic financial crisis, ministry and central bank officials had to take rescue measures, such as an injection of public funds, while at the same time implementing strict guidelines and sanctions. 連鎖的な金融危機に対処するにあたって、当局は公的資金の投入などの救済措置を取ると同時に、厳しい指導や制裁を実施しなければならなかった。
rescue package　支援策, 救済策, 支援計画, 救助計画
(=rescue plan)
◆The company and its creditors are expected to begin full-fledged negotiations over the rescue package after Golden Week. 同社とその取引銀行は、ゴールデン・ウイーク明けにも支援策をめぐる本格交渉を始める見通しだ。◆The rescue package of the eurozone and the IMF imposes certain conditions on Greece, including a reduction of its budget deficit. ユーロ圏15か国とIMF（国際通貨基金）の金融支援策は、ギリシャに対して財政赤字の削減など一定の条件が付けられている。◆What is urgently needed as the EU's rescue package is beefing up the functions of the EFSF and recapitalizing banks that own Greek and Italian government bonds. EU（欧州連合）の支援策として緊急に求められているのは、欧州金融安定基金（EFSF）の機能強化や、ギリシャやイタリアの国債を保有する銀行の資本増強などだ。
rescue plan　支援計画, 支援策, 救済策, 救助計画
(=rescue package)
◆Many observers had expected that the U.S. authorities would cobble together a rescue plan on Lehman Brothers. リーマン・ブラザーズについては、政府当局がなんとか救済策をまとめるものと、多くの消息筋が予想していた。◆The rescue plan consists mainly of a debt waiver and a debt-for-equity swap. 支援計画の大きな柱は、債権放棄と債務の株式化だ。
rescue system　支援体制
◆The 17 eurozone nations must ratify the agreement on bailout measures to arrange a rescue system for Greece. ギリシャへの支援体制を整えるには、ユーロ圏の17か国が、支援策についての合意事項を承認しなければならない。
research　（名）調査, 研究, リサーチ
　Committee [Council] on Financial System Research　金融制度調査会
　equity research　株式調査

fixed-income research 債券リサーチ
Japan Bond Research Institute 日本公社債研究所
National Bureau of Economic Research 全米経済研究所
the ASEAN plus Three Macroeconomic Research Office （ASEANプラス3諸国の）域内マクロ経済リサーチ・オフィス, アムロ, AMRO

reserve （名）準備金, 積立金, 引当金, 充当金, 支払い準備, 予備品, 保存品, 保留, 留保, 保存, 制限, 条件 （⇒actuary, base money, capital reserve, financial derivatives, foreign exchange reserves, foreign reserves, legal capital reserves, legal reserves, loss covering, regular inspection, transfer）
bad debt reserves 貸倒れ引当金
bank reserves 支払い準備, 銀行準備金, 準備預金
capital reserve 資本準備金, 資本剰余金
excess reserve （銀行の）超過準備
foreign currency reserves 外貨準備高
hidden reserves 含み資産, 秘密積立金
IMF reserve positions and special drawing rights IMFの準備ポジションと特別引出し権 （=reserve positions and special drawing rights at the International Monetary Fund; ⇒foreign exchange reserves）
internal reserves 内部留保
latent reserves 含み益
legal reserve 法定準備
liquidate legal reserves 法定準備金を取り崩す
loan reserves 債権引当金
loss reserves 責任準備金, 損失準備金
pension reserve 年金積立金
policy reserves 保険契約準備金, 責任準備金
provide reserves for 〜に対して引当金を設定する
required reserves 所要準備
reserve against 〜に対して引当金を積む
reserve deposit requirement system 準備預金制度
reserve expansion 銀行準備の拡大, 金融の量的拡大, 金融の量的緩和 （⇒inflationary expectations）
reserve percentage 準備率
reserve premium 貯蓄保険料
reserve ratio [rate] 支払い準備率 （民間銀行の預金に対する支払い準備の比率）
revenue reserve 任意積立金
set aside loan loss reserves 貸倒れ引当金を積み立てる
statutory reserves 法定準備金
the reserves of private insurance firms 民間保険会社の準備金
transfer from one's reserves into retained earnings 準備金を取り崩す
◆The Bank of Japan usually sets aside 5 percent of net income for reserves. 日銀は通常, 剰余金の5％を法定準備金として積み立てる。 ◆The bank's reserves were insufficient as of the end of fiscal 2011. 同行の引当金は, 2012年3月期末の時点で不十分であった[2011年度末の時点で, 同行の引当ては不足していた]。 ◆The new regulations decided on by the Basel Committee on Banking Supervision require banks to increase the core tier 1 capital, such as common stock and retained earnings, that they must hold in reserve, to at least 4.5 percent of assets from the current 2 percent. バーゼル銀行監督委員会が決めた新規制は, 銀行が支払い準備として保有しなければならない普通株や利益剰余金[内部留保]などの中核的自己資本(コア・ティア1)を, 現行の資産の最低2％から4.5％に引き上げるよう銀行に義務付けている。 ◆The reserves of private nonlife insurers and the reserve fund of the government's special account may be sufficient to cover the property losses of the massive earthquake's victims. 民間損保の準備金と政府の特別会計の積立金があれば, 今回の大震災被災者の物的損害の費用を十分賄(まかな)えるかもしれない。 ◆To make up for losses and for other purposes, seven life insurers used a total of ￥529.2 billion in reserves, which are set aside in preparation for interest rate fluctuations and natural disasters. 損失の穴埋めなどのため, 金利変動や自然災害に備えて積み立てている準備金を, 生保7社が5,292億円も取り崩した。 ◆Under the treasury stock system, companies are allowed to buy their own stocks and keep them in reserve. 金庫株制度によると, 企業は自社株を取得して, 取得した株を保管することができる。

Reserve Bank of India インド準備銀行, RBI（インドの中央銀行）

reserve currency 準備通貨（国際間の決済に使われるドルなどの国際通貨）
◆China's renminbi may attain a reserve-currency status by the steady appreciation of the yuan and the country's enormous capital surpluses. 中国の人民元は, 人民元の着実な切上げと中国の膨大な資本剰余金によって, 準備通貨の地位を獲得する可能性がある。 ◆The dollar's role as the major reserve currency is important to global trade. 主要準備通貨としてのドルの役割は, 世界の貿易には重要である。 ◆The greenback may not be able to maintain its impregnable position as the world's only reserve currency. 米ドルは, 世界で唯一の準備通貨としての揺るぎない地位を, 維持できないかもしれない。 ◆The U.S. dollar as the world's only reserve currency may become merely one of three major currencies, along with the euro and the renminbi. 世界で唯一の準備通貨としての米ドルは, ユーロ, 人民元とともに, 単なる3大通貨の一つになる可能性がある。 ◆The U.S. dollar may lose its current status as the world's only reserve currency. 米ドルは, 世界唯一の準備通貨としての現在の地位を失う可能性がある。

reserve funds 準備金, 準備資金, 積立金, 予備費 （=reserve）
the mutual aid association's reserve funds 共済組合の積立金
the reserve fund of the government's special account 政府の特別会計の積立金
◆Half of this money comes from public coffers and half from the mutual aid association's reserve funds. この資金は, 国の拠出金と共済組合の積立金とで折半している。 ◆The ￥1 trillion reserve funds were included in this fiscal year's budget for measures to help the economy stay afloat. 経済危機への対応策として, 1兆円の予備費が今年度予算に盛り込まれた。 ◆The so-called "buried treasure" refers to reserve funds in the government's special accounts. いわゆる「埋蔵金」とは, 政府の特別会計の積立金[剰余金]のことを言う。

reserve of money 資金準備
◆A reserve of money collected by issuing stocks can be used to cover eventual financial losses. 株式を発行して集めた資金準備は, 将来の金融損失の穴埋めに使用することができる。

reserve pressure 資本繰り
◆Banks were less reserve pressure than was in March. 銀行の資本繰りは, 3月より緩和した。

reserve requirements 支払い準備, 預金準備, 支払い準備率, 預金準備率, 準備必要額, 支払い準備制度, 準備預金制度（預金の払い出しに備えて, 民間の銀行に対して預貯金の一定割合を現金または流動性の高い金融資産で保有するよう義務付ける制度）
reserve requirements change 支払い準備率[預金準備率]の変更
reserve requirements ratio 支払い準備率, 預金準備率 （=reserve requirements）
reserve requirements system 支払い準備制度, 準備預金制度
variations in reserve requirements 支払い準備率操作

◆The reserve requirements represent the percentage of deposits that banks are required to hold as non-interest-bearing assets. 支払い準備率[預金準備率]とは、銀行[金融機関]が無利息の資産として保有することが義務付けられている預金の割合のことである。
reserve system 準備預金制度, 準備制度
 Federal Reserve System 連邦準備制度
 fractional reserve system 部分準備制度
 proportional reserve system 比例準備制度
 reserve deposit requirement system 準備預金制度
 reserve requirements system 支払い準備制度, 準備預金制度
 total reserve system 全額準備制度, 全額正貨準備制度
 total specific reserve system 全額正貨準備制度
reserve target 日銀当座預金の残高目標
◆Lowering the Bank of Japan's reserve target can be a choice after the government ends its unlimited guarantee on bank deposits in case of bank failures. ペイオフ解禁後に(銀行が破たんした場合の銀行預金に対する政府の無限保証期間が終了した後)、日銀当座預金の残高目標の減額も考えられる。
reshuffle (動)人員を入れ替える, 刷新する, 更迭する, 改革する, 再編する, 閣僚を入れ替える, 内閣などを改造する
◆A company's management was reshuffled following a shareholder's proposal. 株主提案を受けて、企業の経営陣が刷新された。
reshuffle (名)人員の入れ替え, 人事刷新, 更迭, 構造などの改革, 再編, 内閣改造
 industry reshuffle 業界再編
 management reshuffle 経営人事刷新, 経営陣の刷新, 経営体制刷新
◆Mizuho Financial Group announced the management reshuffle. みずほフィナンシャルグループが、経営体制刷新を発表した。◆The UFJ financial group decided to carry out a sweeping management reshuffle, including the replacement of three top managers. 経営トップ3人の一新(交替)を含めて、UFJ金融グループは経営陣の全面入れ替え実施を決めた。
residential (形)住宅の, 居住の, 住宅用[居住用]の, 住宅向きの
 be backed by residential home mortgages 住宅用モーゲージを裏付けとする
 be secured on residential mortgages 住宅用モーゲージを担保とする
 residential broker 住宅用不動産仲買業者
 residential condominium market マンション市場
 residential (fixed) investment 住宅投資
 residential land price 住宅地地価
 residential market 住宅市場
 residential mortgage 住宅抵当貸付け, 住宅ローン, 住宅用モーゲージ
 residential mortgage loan 住宅抵当貸付け, 住宅ローン
 residential mortgage market 住宅ローン市場
 residential property 住宅資産, 住宅用不動産
 residential suburb 郊外住宅地
residential mortgage-backed securities business 住宅融資証券事業, 住宅融資の証券化事業
(⇒mortgage-backed securities business)
◆The security firm expects to book about ¥73 billion in losses related to its residential mortgage-backed securities business in the July-September quarter. 同証券会社は、7-9月期に住宅融資証券事業の関連損失として730億円を計上する見通しだ。
resign (動)辞職する, 辞任する, 退職する, 退任する, 権利などを譲り渡す (=step down)

◆At the bank, a string of executives resigned one after another due to differences over management policy. 同行では、経営路線の違いで役員らの辞任が相次いだ。◆Under the government guidelines, if earnings come in more than 30 percent below targets set in restructuring plans at any major bank that received public funds to recapitalize in 1988 and 1999, the banks management will have to resign. 政府のガイドラインによると、資本再編のために1988年と1999年に公的資金の注入を受けた大手銀行の収益が、再建計画(経営健全化計画)で設定した収益目標を30%以上下回った場合、銀行の経営陣は辞任しなければならない。
resilience [resiliency] (名)跳ね返り, 弾力, 弾力性, 弾性, 屈伸性, 復元力, 回復力, 強靭性, 底堅さ
 economic resilience 経済的弾力性
 have (a) high resilience 柔軟性が高い, 弾力性が高い, 強い回復力
 profit resilience 利益の底堅さ
 show (a) robust resilience 底堅い動きを見せる
◆A bank's core capital, or Tier 1capital, is deemed to have high loss-absorbency and resilience. 銀行の中核的自己資本は、損失吸収力と弾力性が高いとされている。
resilient (形)弾力[弾力性]のある, 跳ね返る, 立ち直りの早い, 回復力のある, 快活な
 look quite resilient 底堅い動きを見せている
 remain resilient 持ちこたえている, 底堅さは変わらない, 引き続き底堅い[底堅い動きを見せている], 高止まりする
resolution (名)決議, 決議案, 議案, 決断, 決意, 決定, 裁決, 判定, 解決, 解答, 解明, 打開, 決着, 映像の鮮明度, 光の解像
 extraordinary resolution 特殊決議, 非常決議(議決権を持つ株主の半数以上、かつ議決権で3分の2以上の支持がなければ成立しない決議)
 important resolution 重要決議
 Resolution and Collection Corporation 整理回収機構, RCC, 預金保険機構の100%出資子会社
 Resolution Funding Corporation 米国の整理資金調達公社, REFCORP
 Resolution Trust Corporation 整理信託公社, 米貯蓄機関決済信託公社, RTC
 special resolution 特別決議
 stockholder resolution 株主決議
 (=shareholder resolution)
◆Approval for a triangular merger should be based on a special resolution. 三角合併の承認は、特別決議によらなければならない[三角合併には、特別決議による承認が必要だ]。◆No clear prospect has emerged for resolution of the Greek financial crisis. ギリシャの財政危機を打開する明確な見通しは、まだ立っていない。◆Under the Commercial Code, to gain approval for an important resolution that directly affects corporate management, shareholders holding at least 50 percent of shares with voting rights must cast ballots, and two-thirds must back the motion. 商法で、企業の経営に直接影響を及ぼす重要決議の承認を得るには、議決権株式の少なくとも50%を保有する株主が投票し、提案に対してその3分の2の支持を得る必要がある。
resolve (動)(問題などを)解決する, 決意する, (委員会などが)決議する, (疑いを)晴らす, 除く, 解消する, 分解する, 分析する (名)決意, 決議
◆Further efforts are needed to resolve the financial unrest. 金融不安を解消するには、もう一段の努力が必要だ。◆In resolving Greece's debt woes, German Chancellor Angera Merkel urged substantial aid from private creditors. ギリシャの債務問題を解決するにあたって、アンゲラ・メルケル独首相は、民間債権者に大幅支援を求めた。◆Japan, the United States and emerging economies have pressed European countries

to promptly resolve the fiscal and financial crisis. 日米両国と新興国は、欧州に財政・金融危機の迅速な解決を迫った。◆The United States and European countries are forced to proceed steadily with fiscal reconstruction and resolve the financial turmoil. 米欧各国は、財政再建を着実に進めて、金融市場の混乱を収拾せざるを得ない状況にある。◆To resolve the financial unrest in EU nations, accelerating financial sector realignment in countries such as Germany must be worked out. EU諸国の金融不安を解決するには、(2,000もの金融機関がひしめく)ドイツなどでの金融再編の加速も課題だ。

resort (名)手段, 頼みの綱, 頼ること, 訴えること, 保養地, 行楽地, 盛り場, リゾート
 a summer resort 避暑地, 夏の保養地
 as a [the] last resort 最後の手段として, 最後の頼みの綱として
 in the last resort 結局, 最終的に, 最後の手段として
 the best resort 最良の手段, 一番の手段
 the lender of last resort 最後の貸し手
  (=central bank)
 the U.S. dollar as the currency of last resort 最後の拠りどころとしての米ドル
 ◆Financial exchanges between a half dozen emerging countries (BRICs, Indonesia and South Korea) will lose a dependency on the U.S. dollar as the currency of last resort. 今後、ブラジル、ロシア、インド、中国、インドネシア、韓国の新興6か国間の金融取引は、最後の拠(よ)りどころとしての米ドルに依存しなくなると思われる。◆The EU considers retaliatory measures as a last resort. 欧州連合(EU)は、報復措置を最後の手段と考えている。◆The last resort to secure a stable revenue source is raising the consumption tax. 安定した財源確保の頼みの綱は、消費税の引上げだ。

resort to 〜を求める, 〜に動く, 〜に頼る, 〜を利用する, 〜に訴える, 〜に踏み切る, 〜に行く[通う], 〜を訪れる
 resort to a corporate defense scheme 企業防衛策を取る
 resort to borrowing money from banks 金融機関[銀行]からの資金借入れに動く
 resort to quantitative easing 量的緩和に踏み切る
 ◆Companies can resort to corporate defense schemes, including a poison pill plan to issue new shares, to fight hostile takeover bids. 敵対的買収への対抗策として、企業は新株発行(増資)のポイズン・ピル(毒薬)方式などの企業防衛策をとることができる。◆Companies faced difficulties in raising money by issuing corporate bonds in the aftermath of the financial crisis and resorted to borrowing money from banks. 世界の金融危機の影響で企業は、社債を発行して資金を調達するのが困難になったため、金融機関からの資金借入れに動いた。◆The Bank of Japan's resorting to quantitative easing in concert with the Fed would have a greater impact on in buoying the global economy. 米連邦準備制度理事会(FRB)と歩調を合わせて日銀が量的緩和に踏み切れば、世界景気の浮揚効果は拡大すると思われる。◆We resorted to electronic brokerage in which currency is directly purchased online. われわれは、オンライン(コンピュータ端末)で直接、通貨買いを注文する電子ブローキングの手段を使った。

resource(s) (名)資源, 経営資源, 財源, 資金, 原資, 源泉, 供給源, 教材, 資料, 手段, 方策, 兵力
 business resources 経営資源
 capital resources 資金の源泉
 commitment of resources 融資承認額
 corporate resources 経営資源, 会社の資源
 financial resource(s) 資金, 資本, 資金力, 金融力, 金融資産, 財務資源, 財源, 資金の源泉, 資金源, 原資 (⇒trend)
 funding resources 資金調達源
 Fund's resources 国際通貨基金の資金[資金源]
 internal resources 内部資金, 手元資金
 local resources of finance 現地資金源
 management resources 経営資源, 役員人事 (=managerial resources)
 moneyed resources 財源
 pecuniary resources 資力, 金融資産
 resource of money 財源 (=money resources)
 resources and liabilities 資産と負債
 resources provided 調達資金
 resources used 運用資金
 ◆Insurance payments for the March 11 earthquake and tsunami will drain the resources of insurance firms and the government's special account. 東日本大震災の保険金支払いで、保険会社と政府の特別会計の減資は大幅に目減りすることになる。◆Outsourcing is a strategic method that effectively uses business resources. It is actively utilized in Europe and the U.S. by venture businesses that lack adequate human resources. アウトソーシングは、経営資源を有効に活用するための戦略的手法です。これは、欧米では、人的資源を十分に確保できないベンチャー企業によって積極的に活用されています。◆The IMF currently has about $400 billion in resources on hand. IMF(国際通貨基金)は現在、手元に約4,000億ドル分の財源を残している。

respond to 〜に答える, 〜に反応する[反応を示す], 〜に対応する, 〜に応じる, 効果を現わす
 respond to a question 質問に答える
 respond to market forces 市場の力に任せる, 市場原理に反応する
 respond to medical treatment 医療の効果が現れる
 respond to the global competition 国際競争に対応する, グローバル競争に対応する
 ◆It is still difficult for the large G-20 to swiftly respond to such emergencies as rapid fluctuations in exchange markets. 大所帯のG20が為替相場の急激な変動などの緊急事態に迅速に対応するのは、まだ難しい。◆The EU's responses to the European debt crisis have been slow. 欧州債務危機への欧州連合(EU)の対応は、後手に回ってきた。◆The 17-nation currency union was slow in responding to the request for financial support by Greece. 17か国から成る通貨統合のユーロ圏は、ギリシャの金融支援要請への対応が遅かった。◆The U.S. housing industry and the government must respond to a severe credit crunch that began in August 2007. 米国の住宅産業界と政府は、2007年8月に始まった深刻な金融危機への対応を迫られている。

response (名)対応, 対応策, 反応, 反響, 効果, 結果, 回答, 応答, 返答, レスポンス
 advertising response 広告反応
 as a response to improved financial market conditions 金融市場の環境改善を受けて
 crisis response 危機対応
 customer response 顧客の反応
 demand response 需要反応
 efficient customer response 効率的消費者反応
 flexible response 柔軟な対応, 機動的対抗
 gauge market responses 市場の反応を見極める
 in response to 〜に応じて, 〜に対応して, 〜に反応して, 〜に応えて, 〜を受けて, 〜に伴って, 〜を好感して
 joint response to 〜への共同対応, 〜への協調対応[協調対応策]
 market response 市場の反応
 policy response 政府の対応, 当局の対応
 quick response (system) 早期応答システム
 remain within the range of conventional responses 従来の対応の範囲内にとどまる

response to customer needs　顧客ニーズへの対応
response to the dual [double] debt problem　二重ローン問題への対応
survey responses　調査結果
the initial response　初期対応，初動対応
◆Global economic crisis requires a flexible response. 世界の経済危機には、機動的対応が必要だ。◆In a joint response to the global financial crisis, the U.S. FRB, ECB and central banks in Britain, Canada, Sweden and Switzerland cut interest rates in unison. 世界的な金融危機への協調対応策として、米連邦準備制度理事会（FRB）、欧州中央銀行（ECB）と英国、カナダ、スウェーデン、スイスの中央銀行は、それぞれ金利［政策金利］を同時に引き下げた。◆In Europe, credit uncertainty has spread from Greece to Italy, Spain and elsewhere due to the excessively tardy response by Europe. 欧州では、欧州の対応が遅すぎるため、信用不安がギリシャからイタリアやスペインなどに拡大している。◆In response to the double loan problem due to the March 11 disaster, financial institutions will be forced to share some burdens including the waiver of debts. 東日本大震災による二重ローン問題への対応では、債権の放棄を含めて金融機関もある程度の共同負担を強いられることになろう。◆Raising the outstanding balance of current accounts held by private financial institutions at the central bank to between ¥27 trillion and ¥30 trillion remained within the range of conventional responses. 日銀当座預金（民間金融機関が日銀に保有している当座預金）の残高目標を（現行の22-27兆円程度から）27-30兆円程度に引き上げる日銀の追加金融緩和は、従来の対応の範囲内にとどまった。◆Speculators apparently take advantage of the sluggish response of the government and the Bank of Japan to the yen's appreciation. 投機筋は、政府・日銀の円高への対応の鈍さに付け込んでいるようだ。◆The earthquake insurance system was launched after the 1964 Niigata Earthquake as a response to the problem of fire insurance not covering damage caused by an earthquake or tsunami. 地震保険［地震保険制度］は、火災保険で地震や津波による被害が補償されない問題への対応策として、1964年の新潟地震後に導入された。◆The Fed raised the discount rate to 0.75 percent from 0.5 percent as a response to improved financial market conditions. 米連邦準備制度理事会（FRB）は、金融市場の環境改善を受けて、（銀行に貸し出す際の金利である）公定歩合を現行の年0.5%から0.75%に引き上げた。

responsibility　（名）責任, 義務, 債務, 債務, 負担, 契約義務, 履行能力, 支払い能力
（⇒financial settlement, step down）
assume responsibility for the bank's failure　同行破たんの責任を負う
management responsibility　経営責任, 管理責任
（=responsibility of management）
public responsibility　公共責任, 社会的責任, 公共性
resignation to take responsibility　引責辞任
responsibility for financial reporting　財務報告に対する責任
responsibility of the Company's management　会社の経営者の責任
shareholders' responsibility　株主責任
take responsibility for the financial difficulties　経営不振の責任を取る
◆Ashikaga Financial Group Inc. must assume some responsibility for the bank's failure as the bank's only shareholder. あしぎんフィナンシャルグループは、同行の唯一の株主として、同行破たんの責任を負わなければならない。◆Company executives have admitted responsibility in a class action suit filed on behalf of a firm. 株主代表訴訟で、企業の幹部が責任を認めた。◆Financial settlement refers to a lump sum payment by an insurer to a disabled insured that extinguishes the insurer's responsibility under the disability contract. 金融決済は、就業不能契約に基づき、傷害を負った被保険者に保険会社が一時金を支払って、保険会社の責任を消滅させることを指す。◆Former executives of the company admitted their responsibility for its collapse. 同社の旧経営陣は、同社の経営破たんを招いた責任を認めた。◆Seven directors will resign from their posts to take responsibility for the financial difficulties. 経営不振に対する責任をとって、取締役7人が引責辞任する。◆To fulfill its responsibilities as the nation's central bank, the Bank of Japan must achieve currency stabilization by availing itself of a range of measures, including stabilization of the exchange rate. 日本の中央銀行としての責任を果たすには、日本銀行は、為替相場の安定を含めて広範な手段を活用して通貨の安定を実現しなければならない。◆UFJ banking group plans to cut the compensation of its top executives by half from July through September to reflect their responsibility for the group's ¥400 billion net loss in fiscal 2003. UFJ銀行グループは、2004年3月期決算で4,000億円の最終赤字に陥ったため、役員の報酬を7月から9月までの3か月間、5割削減する方針だ。

responsible　（形）責任がある, 責任を負う, 責任を負うべき, 責任の重い, 責任能力がある, 報告義務がある, 信頼できる
hold [make] ～ responsible for　～に…の責任があるとする, ～に…の責任を負わせる
make oneself responsible for　…の責任を引き受ける
responsible for　～の責任がある, ～に対して責任がある, ～の責任を負うべき
◆Management is responsible for the integrity and objectivity of the financial information included in this report. 経営者は、本報告書に記載されている財務情報の完全性と客観性について責任を負っています。◆The accounting firm is responsible for auditing the accounts of about 7,000 companies. 同監査法人は、約7,000社の会計監査［財務書類の監査］を担当している。

restate　（動）修正する, 再表示する, 修正再表示する, 更新する
◆The Group's sales figures have been restated following the retrospective application of new International Financial Reporting Standards. 当グループの売上高の数値は、新国際財務報告基準（IFRS）を遡及的に適用して、再表示されています。◆We did not restate our 2009 and 2010 financial statements to reflect the change in accounting for retiree benefits. 当社は、2009年度と2010年度の財務書類［財務諸表］については、退職者給付に関する会計処理の変更を反映させるための修正・再表示をしておりません。

restoration　（名）回復, 復活, 復帰, 復職, 修復, 立て直し, 再建, 復元, 復旧, 返還, 返却, 復元模型, （英国の）王政復古（the Restoration）, 王政復古時代
be under restoration　修復中である, 再建中である
extensive restoration　大規模な修復
restoration and reconstruction projects　復興・再建事業
the restoration of earnings momentum　収益力の回復

restoration bonds　復興債, 復興再生債（restoration and rebirth bonds）, 復興事業債
（⇒reconstruction bonds）
◆The Great East Japan Earthquake reconstruction fund will be used to redeem the restoration bonds and will be separately managed from the government's general account. 東日本大震災の復興基金は、復興債［復興再生債］の償還に充（あ）てられ、政府の一般会計から切り離して管理される。

restoration of fiscal health　財政健全化
◆G-7 nations should start envisaging exit strategies and the restoration of fiscal health. 先進7か国は、そろそろ出口戦略と財政の健全化も見据えるべきだ。

restore　（動）回復する, 取り戻す, 押し上げる, 修復する,

立て直す、再建する、復元する、復旧する、復活させる、復帰させる、復職させる、返還する
 negotiations to restore budget cuts　（削られた各省庁予算の）復活折衝
 restore consumer trust in　～に対する消費者[ユーザー]の信頼を回復する
 restore economic relations　経済関係を修復する
 restore GDP growth　GDP成長率を押し上げる
 restore the economy's dynamism　経済の活力を取り戻す
 restore the health of the financial system　金融システムの健全性を回復する
 restore the Japan's fiscal health　日本の財政を立て直す、日本の財政を健全化する
 restore the market's confidence　市場の信認を回復する
 restore the zero-interest rate policy　ゼロ金利政策を復活させる
 ◆A prerequisite to restoring the country's fiscal health is to promptly and boldly take effective pump priming measures and to overcome the economic crisis. 日本の財政健全化への前提条件は、迅速、果敢に効果的な景気浮揚策を実行して、経済危機を克服することだ。◆The BOJ decided to ease its monetary grip further by effectively restoring its zero-interest-rate policy. 日銀は、実質的にゼロ金利政策を復活させて、追加の金融緩和を決めた。

restore confidence in markets　市場の信認を回復する
 ◆Four European countries of France, Italy, Spain and Belgium banned short selling on financial stocks to restore confidence in markets. フランス、イタリア、スペイン、ベルギーの欧州4か国が、市場の信認を回復するため、金融銘柄の空売りを禁止した。

restore market confidence　市場の信認を回復する
 ◆European banks are forced to shore up their potential capital shortages to restore market confidence. 欧州銀行は、市場の信認を回復するため、潜在的な資本不足の増強を迫られている。

restraint　（名）抑え、抑制、制止、制限、規制、引締め、自制、控え目
 apply restraint　緊縮政策をとる
 capital restraints on banks　銀行の自己資本比率規制
 credit restraint　信用引締め、金融引締め、信用規制
 dividend restraint　配当制約
 financial restraint　金融引締め
 fiscal restraint　財政引締め、財政政策の引締め、財政緊縮政策
 monetary restraint　金融引締め
 price restraint　価格抑制
 production restraint　生産制限
 quantitative export restraint　輸出数量規制
 restraint of trade　取引制限、営業制限、貿易制限（=trade restraint）
 restraint on bank lending　銀行貸出規制、貸出規制、融資規制
 restraint on economy　景気抑制
 restraint on public spending　公共投資の抑制
 self-restraint　自制、自主規制、自粛
 stock price restraint　株価規制
 voluntary restraint　自主規制
 wage restraint　賃金抑制
 ◆Even within the United States, some observers are calling for restraint rather than resorting to emotional "Toyota bashing." 米国内でも、感情的な「トヨタたたき」に走らないで自制を求める声が出ている。

restrict　（動）制限する、限定する、規制する、禁止する、打ち切る
 ◆The United States tries to press China to reduce its current account surplus and raise the yuan by restricting its current account with a numerical goal. 米国は、経常収支を数値目標で縛って、中国に経常収支の黒字縮小と人民元切上げの圧力をかけようとしている。

restrict an influx of capital　資本流入を規制する、資金流入を規制する
 ◆As one option to avoid excessive currency appreciation in emerging countries with inflationary trends, they can restrict an influx of capital. インフレ気味の新興国で行き過ぎた[過度の]通貨高を避けるための手段として、資本流入を規制することができる。◆Brazil suffering from the strengthening of its currency has restricted an influx of capital. 通貨高に悩むブラジルは、資本流入[資金流入]を規制している。◆Restricting an influx of capital prevents foreigners from acquiring domestic assets. 資本流入[資本輸入]の規制で、外国人は国内資産の購入が難しくなる。

restricted　（形）限られた、制限された、限定された、規制された、禁止された制限付きの、条件付きの、非公開の、機密の、専用の
 permanent discount restricted stock purchase plan　永久割引制限付き株式購入制度[プラン]
 restricted asset　拘束資産（使途が限定された特定目的の政府資産）
 restricted card list　無効カード通知書
 restricted cash　用途制限預金、拘束預金
 restricted competition　競争制限
 restricted credit　手形買取り銀行指定信用状, リストリクテッド信用状
 restricted deposits　封鎖預金
 restricted endorsement　制限裏書き　（=restrictive endorsement: 小切手証券の譲渡を制限する裏書き）
 restricted fund　限定資金
 restricted item　規制品目
 restricted lending　貸し渋り
 restricted (letter of) credit　手形買取り銀行指定信用状、買取り銀行指定信用状, リストリクテッド信用状（=restricted L/C）
 restricted retained earnings　制限付き留保利益、拘束利益剰余金
 restricted security　制限付き証券
 restricted stock [share]　制限付き株式、制限株、私募株（=letter stock, unregistered stock）

restriction　（名）制限、規制、制約　（⇒annuity insurance policy, foreign investment, margin）
 credit restrictions　信用規制
 credit risk restrictions　信用リスクの制限
 currency restriction　通貨制限
 dividend restriction　配当制限
 exchange restriction　為替規制、為替制限
 foreign exchange restrictions　外国為替規制
 foreign ownership restrictions　外国人の投資枠
 lending restrictions　貸出規制、融資規制
 loan restrictions　融資規制
 restriction on stock holding　株式保有制限
 stock repurchase restriction　株式買戻し制限
 transfer restriction　譲渡制限
 ◆A company is allowed to set restrictions on the transfer of golden shares. 企業は、黄金株（拒否権付き種類株式）に譲渡制限を付けることができる[黄金株の譲渡に制限を設けることができる]。◆Currently, a company may set transfer restrictions on a portion of its outstanding shares. 現在、企業は一部の発行済み株式に譲渡制限を付けることができる。◆Restric-

tions on share buybacks were eased in October 2001. 2001年10月に、自社株買戻しに対する規制が緩和された。◆The FSA mapped out a plan to toughen restrictions on banks' sales of insurance products to small and midsize companies. 金融庁が、銀行の中小企業向け保険商品販売に対する規制を強化する案をまとめた。◆The proprietary information is free and clear of any liens, restriction on use, or encumbrances of any nature whatsoever. この占有情報は、いかなる担保、使用制限もしくはどんな種類の負担も存在しない[本占有情報は、担保、使用制限、負担の制約が一切ない]。

restrictive (形)制限する、制限的な、限定的な、制限付きの、拘束的な、引締めの、厳しい
- restrictive agreement　制限的協定
- restrictive budget　緊縮予算
- restrictive business measures　制限の取引手段[商手段]
- restrictive business practices　制限的商慣行、取引制限行為、RBP
- restrictive covenant　不作為約款、制限契約、一定の行為をしないという約定
- restrictive credit policy　金融引締め政策、信用引締め政策、信用抑制政策
- restrictive demand management　景気抑制型需要管理、需要抑制
- restrictive demand management policy　需要抑制政策、需要管理政策
- restrictive endorsement [indorsement]　制限裏書き、限定的裏書き、譲渡制限裏書き、譲渡禁止裏書き (=qualified endorsement)
- restrictive financial covenant　財務制限条項
- restrictive fiscal measures　財政緊縮策
- restrictive fiscal policy　緊縮財政政策
- restrictive fiscal policy initiatives　財政緊縮策
- restrictive government policy　政府の引締め政策
- restrictive lending policy　貸出抑制策
- restrictive loaning　(中央銀行の)窓口規制
- restrictive measures　抑制政策、抑制策、制限的手段
- restrictive monetary policy　金融引締め政策、金融引締め策
- restrictive policy　制限的政策、抑制政策、引締め政策、引締め策
- restrictive practices　制限的慣行(企業間の競争を制限する協定)、労働組合による組合員や使用者の行為の制限
- restrictive tariff　制限的関税、制限的税率
- restrictive trade　取引制限
- restrictive trade practices　制限的商慣習、制限的取引慣行

restrictive stance　引締めのスタンス
- a modestly restrictive stance　引締め気味のスタンス
- restrictive monetary policy stance　金融引締めのスタンス
- revert to a restrictive stance from a stimulative one　金融緩和のスタンスから金融引締めのスタンスに戻る

restrike (動)改鋳(かいちゅう)する (名)再鋳造(ちゅうぞう)貨幣、再鋳メダル

restructure (動)再編成する、再構築する、再構成する、再建する、立て直す、組織替えする、リストラする、改編する
- restructure a company　会社を再建する
- restructure one's domestic business　国内事業を再編成する
- restructure one's external debt　対外債務を繰り延べる、対外債務を再編する
- restructure one's lines　信用枠を再編する
- restructure one's operations　事業を立て直す、事業を再編成する、経営再建する
- try to restructure oneself under the initiative of one's banks 取引銀行主導のもとに再建を目指す

◆Sumitomo Mitsui Banking Corp. and UFJ Bank will provide financial assistance to help the three firms restructure their operations. 3社の経営再建には、三井住友銀行とUFJ銀行が金融支援する。◆The company is restructuring some of its domestic operations. 同社は、国内事業の一部を再編成している。◆The firm tries to restructure itself under the initiative of its banks. 同社は、取引銀行主導のもとに再建を目指している。◆The government intends to restructure the deposit insurance system as a new financial safety net for protecting settlement systems. 政府は、預金保険制度を、決済システム保護のための新しい金融安全網として再構築する方針だ。

restructured loan　金利減免債権

restructuring (名)事業の再構築、事業の再編成、再構成、再建、経営再建、再編、改革、解雇、人員削減、リストラ、リストラクチャリング (⇒bond issue, commission revenue, corporate group tax system)
- asset restructuring　資産リストラ
- balance sheet restructuring　財務再編
- business restructuring　事業再編成、事業再編、企業のリストラ (corporate restructuring)
- capital restructuring　資本再構成、資本の再編成
- corporate debt restructuring　企業債務の再編
- corporate restructuring　企業再編成、企業再編、会社再建、企業リストラ、事業機構
- debt restructuring　債務再編、債務再構成、債務の特別条件変更 (=refinancing debt)
- economic restructuring　経済のリストラ
- financial restructuring　財務再編、財務再構築、金融のリストラ
- fiscal restructuring　財政再編、財政再建
- group restructuring　グループ再編
- industrial restructuring　産業再編、産業のリストラ
- large scale restructuring　大規模再建計画
- operational restructuring　事業再編、事業の再構築、事業のリストラ
- pull off a restructuring　リストラを成し遂げる
- restructuring benefits　リストラ効果
- restructuring costs　事業再編成費用、リストラクチャリング費用、リストラ費用、リストラ経費 (=restructuring charges)
- restructuring of debt　債務再編、債務再構成、債務の再構築 (=debt restructuring)
- restructuring period　リストラの時期[期間]、調整期間 (=period of restructuring)
- restructuring program　再建計画、再編計画、再生計画、事業再編成計画、事業再構築計画、再建策、再建案、リストラ計画、リストラ策 (=restructuring package, restructuring plan)
- restructuring provision　事業再編引当金、事業再編に伴う引当金繰入れ
- self-restructuring　自主再建 (=self-rehabilitation)
- troubled debt restructuring　問題の生じた債務の再編、問題債権のリストラ
- undergo a restructuring　リストラに乗り出す、リストラが進められている

◆Of the unemployed, workers who involuntarily lost their jobs due to restructuring, corporate bankruptcy and other factors rose 310,000 from a year earlier to 1.25 million. 失業者のうち、リストラ(解雇)や企業倒産などによる非自発的離職者は、前年同月比31万人増で125万人に達した。◆The three banks and the firm are expected to work out the framework of a corporate restructuring program for the company. 3銀行

restructuring efforts リストラ努力, 経営再建策, リストラ策
◆The private sector has tackled necessary restructuring efforts earnestly. 民間は、必要なリストラ策に懸命に取り組んできた。◆This economic recovery is mainly due to the increased exports and corporate restructuring efforts centered on debt reduction. 今回の景気回復の主な要因は、輸出拡大と債務減らしを中心とした企業のリストラ努力だ。

restructuring measures 再建策, 再編策, リストラ策
◆Major banks need to carry out the consolidation and closure of branches and other restructuring measures more thoroughly. 大手銀行は、支店の統廃合などのリストラ策をさらに徹底させる［さらに徹底して実施する］必要がある。◆Olympus plans to reduce its interest-bearing debts of ￥648.8 billion to ￥408.7 billion in the business year ending March 2015 through restructuring and other measures. オリンパスは、同社の有利子負債6,488億円を、リストラ策などを進めて2015年3月期までに4,087億円に圧縮する計画だ。

restructuring of the financial industry 金融業界の再編
◆Management problems at UFJ Bank may accelerate the restructuring of the financial industry. UFJ銀行の経営問題は、金融業界の再編を加速させる可能性がある。

restructuring plan 再建計画, 再編計画, 再生計画, 再建策, 再建案, リストラ計画（=restructuring package, restructuring program）
◆The firm will ax 10,000 jobs worldwide and cut ￥200 billion in costs by the end of fiscal 2009 in a sweeping restructuring plan. 同社は、抜本的な再建策として、2009年度末までに全世界の人員10,000人の削減と2,000億円のコスト削減を図る。◆The Industrial Revitalization Corporation has decided to bail out Mitsui Mining Co under a fresh restructuring plan worked out by the company. 産業再生機構は、三井鉱山が策定した新再建計画に基づき同社への金融支援を決定した。◆The restructuring plan includes ￥520 billion in financial support from its three main creditor banks. 再建策には、主力取引銀行3行による5,200億円の金融支援が盛り込まれている。◆The restructuring plan will focus on dealing with the debts owed to other financial institutions. 再建計画では、他の金融機関の債権取扱いが今後の焦点となる。◆Under the government guidelines, if earnings come in more than 30 percent below targets set in restructuring plans at any major bank that received public funds to recapitalize in 1988 and 1999, the banks management will have to resign. 政府のガイドラインによると、資本再編のために1988年と1999年に公的資金の注入を受けた大手銀行の収益が、再建計画（経営健全化計画）で設定した収益目標を30％以上下回った場合、銀行の経営陣は辞任しなければならない。

result from （動）～に起因する, ～から生じる, ～による
◆A housing investment slump results from the enforcement of the revised Building Standards Law. 住宅投資の落込みは、改正建築基準法の施行によるものだ。◆Earthquake insurance payments resulting from the Great East Japan Earthquake are expected to reach ￥1.2 trillion. 東日本大震災による地震保険の保険金支払い額は、（業界全体で）1兆2,000億円に達する見込みだ。◆The instability of U.S. stock prices results from problems related to massive number of unrecoverable subprime mortgage loans extended to low-income earners in the United States. 米国の株価不安定は、米国の低所得者向け住宅ローン「サブプライム・ローン」の焦げ付き急増関連問題に起因している。◆The S&P cut in the U.S. long-term credit rating by one notch to AA-plus from AAA resulted from concerns about the nation's budget deficits and climbing debt burden. スタンダード・アンド・プアーズ（S&P）が米国の長期国債格付けを最上級のAAA（トリプルA）からAA（ダブルA）に1段階引き下げた理由は、米国の財政赤字と債務負担の増大に対する懸念だ。

result in （動）（～という）結果に終わる, ～に終わる, ～に帰着する, （～の結果）になる, ～につながる, ～を招く
◆On the bond market, the yield on newly issued 10-year government bonds, an indicator of long-term interest rates, fell, resulting in a rise in bond prices. 債券市場では、長期金利の指標である新発10年物国債の利回り（流通利回り）が下落し、債券相場［債券価格］は上昇した。◆The bank is mulling a further downward revision of its business results for fiscal 2011 that is expected to result in a massive loss. 同行は、巨額の損失が見込まれる2012年3月期決算［2011年度］の業績予想を、さらに下方修正する方向で検討している。◆The collapse of a bank may result in the systemic breakdown of the whole banking sector. 銀行1行の破たんが、金融界全体のシステム崩壊［連鎖的な崩壊］につながる可能性がある。◆The collapse of the subprime mortgage market and related credit market turmoil have resulted in $45 billion of write-downs at the world's biggest banks and securities firms. サブプライム・ローン市場の悪化や関連金融市場の混乱で、世界の大手銀行と証券会社の評価損計上額は、これまでのところ450億ドルに達している。◆The correction of financial statements by Olympus is unlikely to result in the company's debts exceeding its assets. オリンパスの財務書類訂正で、同社の債務超過は避けられる見通しだ。◆The European bond market is truly in a knife-edge situation as the yield on 10-year Italian government bonds has surged above 7 percent, the so-called danger zone that may result in a debt crisis. 10年物イタリア国債の流通利回りが、債務危機に陥る「危険水域」とされる7％超に上昇したため、欧州債券市場は予断を許さない状況にある。◆The financial group's inadequate preparations for the reorganization resulted in a major computer system failure. 同フィナンシャル・グループの再編の準備不足から、大規模なシステム障害が起こった。◆The government and ruling parties began considering the economic package as they feared falling stock prices could result in a financial crisis. 政府・与党は、株価の下落で金融危機に陥る可能性があることから、経済対策の検討を開始した。◆The Greek-triggered sovereign debt crisis resulted in the breakup of the French-Belgian bank Dexia which held Greek government bonds. ギリシャが引き金になったソブリン危機（政府債務危機）問題で、ギリシャ国債を保有していた仏ベルギー系金融機関のデクシア（Dexia）が、解体に追い込まれた。◆The large U.S. current account deficit might result in a marked decline of its international investment positions. 米国の巨額の経常赤字で、海外投資家のドル資産が大幅に減少する可能性がある［海外投資家の著しいドル資産離れを招きかねない］。◆The major banks attributed their increased bad loans to the poor performance of their borrowers due to the prolonged economic slump and Financial Service Agency inspections resulting in a stricter review of their asset assessments. 大手銀行は、不良債権が増えた理由として、長引く景気低迷で貸出先の経営が悪化したことと、金融庁の検査を受けて大手行が資産査定を厳しくしたことを挙げた。

results （名）業績, 決算, 決算内容, 実績, 成果, 結果, 効果, 影響, 影響額, 統計 （⇒business results, financial results, quarterly results）
annual results　通期決算, 年次決算
　（=full year results）
bottom line results　純利益
company's results　会社の業績, 会社の決算
　（=corporate business results, corporate results）
consolidated results　連結決算
economic results　経済統計
financial results　財務成績, 財務実績, 金融収支
first-half results　上半期決算, 上半期の業績, 中間決算
　（=interim closing, interim results, semi-annual results）

good results　好決算
gross results　経常収益
group results　グループの業績, グループ企業の連結業績, 連結決算
interim results　中間決算
　（=first-half results, semi-annual results）
investment results　投資成績, 投資実績, 運用実績, 投資の成果　（=investment, performance）
midterm results　中間決算
operating results　業績, 経営成績
　（=business results）
payment by results　業績給, 能率給, 成果配分
results announcement　決算発表
results of operations　営業成績
second quarter results　第2四半期の業績, 第二・四半期の業績
segment results　セグメント業績, セグメント別業績
semiannual results　中間決算　（=first-half results, interim closing, interim results）
third quarter results　第3四半期の業績, 第三・四半期の業績
◆Citigroup Inc. posted record results in the third quarter. シティグループの第3四半期の業績は, 過去最高を記録した。◆The bank consulted its auditor, Chuo Aoyama Audit Corp. to determine their results for the first half of the current fiscal year ending Sept. 30. 9月中間決算（9月30日に終了する今年度上半期の決算）を確定するため, 同行は中央青山監査法人に意見を求めた。◆The Fed does not have confidence in the results of QE2. 米連邦準備制度理事会（FRB）は, 量的緩和第二弾（QE2）の効果に自信が持てないでいる。◆The government and the Bank of Japan are considering joint market intervention with the U.S. and European monetary authorities to produce the greater results of their market intervention. 政府・日銀は, 市場介入の効果を高めるため, 米欧の通貨当局との協調介入を検討している。

resuscitate　（動）蘇生させる, 生き返らせる, 復活させる, 再興させる, 再生させる
◆The firm earns revenue through real estate investment and through resuscitating failed financial institutions. 同社は, 不動産投資と経営破綻した金融機関を再生させることで収益を上げている。

retail　（名）小売り, 個人投資家, 小口投資家, 個人向け取引, リテール
general index of retail prices　小売物価総合指数
retail CDs　小口CD（銀行が発行する大口CD（譲渡可能定期預金証書）を1,000ドル単位に分割して買いやすくしたもの）
retail client base　個人投資家の顧客基盤
retail demand　小口需要, 消費需要, 個人投資家からの需要
retail driven　個人投資家主導の　（=retail-led）
retail price index　小売物価指数

retail bank　リテール銀行, 個人向け取引の銀行, 小口取引銀行
◆It has become an international trend of late for investment banks to seek an alliance with retail banks. 最近は, リテール銀行との統合を図るのが投資銀行の世界的な流れになっている。

retail banking　小口金融, 小口取引銀行業務, リテール銀行業務, リテール・バンキング
　（⇒core business）
◆Mizuho Financial Group plans to integrate its retail and corporate banking units. みずほフィナンシャルグループ（FG）は, 傘下の小口取引銀行［中小企業・個人向けの銀行］とコーポレート銀行［大企業向け銀行］を合併させる方針だ。

retail banking operations　リテール銀行業務, 小売銀行業務, 小口取引銀行業務
　（=retail banking, retail operations）
◆The bank has been relatively weak in retail banking operations dealing with individuals and small and medium-sized firms. 同行は, 個人や中小企業向けの小口取引銀行業務が比較的弱い。

retail brokerage　個人向け証券会社
◆Citigroup's retail brokerage, Smith Barney, was once the crown jewel in its wealth management business. シティグループの個人向け証券会社「スミスバーニー」は, 以前はシティグループの資産運用業務の最優良資産だった。

retail client　個人顧客
◆The firm offers loans for retail and corporate clients in addition to offering electronic settlement for online shoppers. 同社は, ネット・ショッパー［オンライン・ショッパー］向けの電子決済業務のほかに, 個人と企業向けの融資も手がけている。

retail industry　小売業界
◆The retail industry has begun showing signs of recovery. 小売業界は, 回復の兆しが見られるようになった。

retail investor　個人投資家, 小口投資家, 最終投資家
◆The U.S. investment bank will indefinitely suspend its after-hours equity trading business for retail investors in Japan because of sluggish demand. 需要低迷のため, この米国の投資銀行は, 日本での個人投資家向けの時間外株式投資（株式取引）業務を無期限停止する方針だ。

retail lending　消費者向け融資, 個人向け融資, 個人向けローン, 消費者向け貸付け, 個人向け業務
◆Japan Post Bank and private small and medium-sized banks will compete against each other in retail lending such as housing loans and education loans. ゆうちょ銀行と民間の中小金融機関は, 住宅ローンや教育ローンなどの個人向け業務で競合することになる。◆The firm plans to offer not only retail lending, but also corporate lending by utilizing the customer screening know-how of its partner bank. 同社は, 共同出資する銀行が持つ顧客審査のノウハウを活用して, 個人向け融資のほかに法人向け融資業務も提供する計画だ。

retail operations　個人向け業務
◆The remaining trust bank operations and retail operations will be sold to an intermediary bank. 他の信託銀行の業務と個人向け業務は, 受け皿銀行に営業譲渡される。

retail outlet　小売り加盟店
◆Retail outlets that suffer loss as a result of fraud can also claim compensation from card issuers. 不正使用により損害を被っている小売り加盟店側も, カード会社に賠償金を請求できる。

retail services　個人向け取引業務, リテール業務
◆The holding company of Sumitomo Mitsui Banking Corp. is expected to take an equity stake of around 15 percent in Promise as part of its plan to boost the group's retail services. 三井住友銀行の持ち株会社は, 同グループのリテール（個人向け取引）業務強化計画の一環として, 消費者金融のプロミスの株式持ち分約15％を取得する見込みだ。◆The two groups aim to expand their retail services targeting individual investors. 両グループは, 個人投資家向けのリテール業務拡大を目指している。

retailer　（名）小売業, 小売企業, 小売業者, 小売商, 小売店, 流通企業, スーパー, リテーラー
◆There is slow progress in economic improvement among nonmanufacturing businesses, largely as a result of sluggish sales at retailers due to the ongoing deflation. デフレの進行で主に小売業の売上が低迷しているため, 非製造業は景気回復の足取りが弱い。◆Weakening consumer spending has prompted retailers, including Seven & I and Aeon, to widen their offerings of low-cost private-brand items. 個人消費［消費］低迷で, セブン＆アイやイオンなどの流通企業は, 低価格の自主企画商品（プライベート・ブランド）の販売拡大に取り

組んでいる。
retain （動）取り戻す, 回復する
◆The Nikkei Stock Average has retained the 10,000 level. 日経平均株価が, 1万円台を回復した。
retained earnings 剰余金, 利益剰余金, 留保利益, 社内留保利益金, 社内留保, 内部留保 （=earned surplus, retained income: 過去の利益の積立てで, 企業の税引き後利益から配当金や役員賞与金など社外流出分などを控除した残額をいう。イギリスではprofit and loss accountともいう。⇒core tier 1 capital, net balance）
◆Banks are allowed to access part of their legal capital reserves and transfer such funds to retained earnings. 銀行は, 法定準備金の一部を取り崩して, その資金を剰余金に振り替えることができる。◆Companies that have accumulated large amounts of retained earnings and those that own sizable stakes in blue-chip firms are most vulnerable to these investment funds. 内部留保を大量に蓄積した企業や優良企業の株式を大量に保有する企業は, これらの投資ファンドの餌食（えじき）になりやすい。◆The new regulations decided on by the Basel Committee on Banking Supervision require banks to increase the core tier 1 capital, such as common stock and retained earnings, that they must hold in reserve, to at least 4.5 percent of assets from the current 2 percent. バーゼル銀行監督委員会が決めた新規制は, 銀行が支払い準備として保有しなければならない普通株や利益剰余金［内部留保］などの中核的自己資本（コア・ティア1）を, 現行の資産の最低2%から4.5%に引き上げるよう銀行に義務付けている。
retire （動）株式を消却する, 株式を償還する, 債務［借入金］などを返済する, 工場などを除却する, 紙幣などを回収する, 撤退する, 引き下がる, 退職する, 退任する, 引退する
retire ［withdraw］ from unprofitable operations 不採算事業から撤退する, 不採算事業を整理する
（unprofitable operations=unprofitable businesses）
retire maturing CP 満期がきたCPを償還する
retire repurchased shares 買い戻した株式を消却する
retired employees 退職従業員
retired life fund 退職終身基金
sell or retire plant 工場を売却もしくは除却する
◆The three major creditor banks plan to retire preferred shares totaling ¥120 billion that they purchased last year. 債権を保有する主力取引銀行3行は, 昨年取得した総額1,200億円の優先株式を消却する方針だ。
retiree （名）退職者, 定年退職者, 引退者, 年金受給者, 年金生活者
cost of health care benefits for retirees 退職者に対する医療給付費用
cost of life insurance benefits for retirees 退職者に対する生命保険給付費用
Retiree Benefit Bankruptcy Act 退職者給付破産法
retiree health benefits 退職者健康保険
retiree health care benefits 退職者健康管理給付, 退職者医療給付
retiree benefits 退職者給付
◆We did not restate our 2008 and 2009 financial statements to reflect the change in accounting for retiree benefits. 当社は, 2008年度と2009年度の財務書類［財務諸表］については, 退職者給付に関する会計処理の変更を反映させるための修正・再表示をしておりません。
retirement （名）退職, 引退, 株式の消却, 償還, 返済, 除却, 処分, 廃棄 （「除却」は, 耐用年数の到来や陳腐化などで使用に耐えられなくなった有形固定資産を, 処分して固定資産台帳から抹消すること。⇒share retirement）
bond retirement 社債償還 （=retirement of bond）
debt retirement 債務償還
early retirement 期限前返済, 早期退職

retirement of common shares 普通株式の消却
retirement of debt 負債の返済
retirement of fixed assets 固定資産の処分, 固定資産の除却
retirement of stock out of profit 株式の利益消却
retirement of treasury stock 自己株式の消却
retirement pension 退職年金
retirement savings 退職年金
Social Security retirement benefits 社会保障退職給付
◆The life insurer's single-premium whole life insurance is popular with consumers as a form of savings or an investment for retirement. 同生保の一時払い終身保険は, 一種の貯蓄や退職金の運用先として顧客に人気がある。
retirement of 50 percent of common shares 普通株式の50%消却
◆The approval of numerous stockholders must be gained for a retirement of 50 percent of common shares. 普通株式の50%消却については, 多くの株主の承認を得なければならない。◆The reconstruction plan includes the retirement of 50 percent of the firm's common shares. 経営再建策には, 同社の普通株式の5割消却も含まれている。
retirement of shares 株式の消却, 株式の償還, 株式の買入れ消却 （=retirement of stocks, share retirement, stock retirement: 発行済み自己株式を取得して消滅させること。⇒share retirement）
◆The reconstruction plan includes the retirement of 50 percent of the firm's common shares. 経営再建策には, 同社の普通株式の5割消却も含まれている。
retractable （形）取消し可能の, 撤回可能な, 短縮可能な, リトラクタブル
cumulative redeemable retractable first preferred shares 累積償還可能・償還請求権付き第一優先株式
cumulative redeemable retractable Preferred shares 累積償還可能・取消し可能優先株式
retractable bond リトラクタブル債
retractable maturity 短縮可能満期
◆In July 2011, the company issued Cumulative Redeemable Retractable Preferred Shares, Series 1 and 2, through a subsidiary, for an aggregate amount of $104 million. 2011年7月に同社は, 子会社を通じて, 総額1億400万ドルの累積償還可能・取消し可能優先株式を発行した。
retreat （動）下落する, 反落する, 低下する, 下げる（名）相場の下落, 反落, 低下, 下げ, 縮小, 後退
continue to retreat 続落する
full retreat 本格的な下げ
market retreat 相場の下落
retreat across the board 全面安となる
retreat to the sidelines 手控える
sharp retreat 急落
sizeable retreat 大幅な下げ, 大幅な下落
◆Foreign investors retreated to the sidelines. 外国投資家は, 手控えた。◆Tokyo stocks retreated for the fourth consecutive day. 東京株（東京株式市場の株価）は, 4日連続で下落した。
retreat （名）相場の下落, 反落, 低下, 下げ, 縮小, 後退
fight a bitter retreat みじめな敗北を喫する
full retreat 本格的な下げ
market retreat 相場の下落, 相場の反落
on a retroactive basis 過去に遡及して
progress and retreat 進歩と後退
retroactive 遡及（そきゅう）力のある, 遡及する, 過去にさかのぼる （=retrospective）
retroactive adjustment 遡及修正, 遡及修正項目
retroactive application 遡及適用, 遡及的適用
（=retroactive imposition, retrospective application）

sharp retreat　急落
sizeable retreat　大幅な下げ, 大幅な下落
◆All references to shares outstanding, dividends and per share amounts have been adjusted on a retroactive basis. 発行済み株式数と配当, 1株当たりの金額については, すべて過去に遡及して調整してあります.
retrospective　（形）遡及（そきゅう）力のある, 遡及する, 過去にさかのぼる　(=retroactive)
　retrospective application　遡及適用, 遡及的適用
　retrospective deposit method　遡及預金法
　retrospective policy　遡及保険
◆The Group's sales figures have been restated following the retrospective application of new International Financial Reporting Standards. 当グループの売上高の数値は, 新国際財務報告基準（IFRS）を遡及的に適用して, 再表示されています.
retrospectively rated policy　遡及料率保険契約
return　（動）返す, 戻す, 返還する, 還元する, 資本などを還流する, 利益などを生む, 収入などを申告する, 戻る, 復帰する, 転換する
　be returned to the stockholders in dividends　配当金として株主に還元される
　return to a rising trend　上昇基調に戻る
　return to break-even　収支とんとんに戻る, 赤字が解消する
　return to profit　黒字に転換する, 黒字回復する
　return to work　職場に復帰する
◆Roughly half of the earnings in 2010 were returned to the stockholders in dividends. 2010年度の利益の約半分は, 配当金として株主に還元されています. ◆The key to returning to stable growth is whether the nation can eliminate excesses common to many companies and promote supply-side structural reforms. 安定成長復帰へのカギは, 多くの日本企業に共通して見られる過剰体質を排除して, 供給サイドの構造改革を進めることができるかどうかである.
return　（名）利益, 利益率, 収益, 収益率, 利回り, 運用益, 運用収益率, 運用成績, 還元, 申告, 申告書, 報告書, リターン　（⇒capital gain, negative yield）
　a return to profitability [profit]　黒字転換, 黒字に戻る, 黒字転換する　(=return to profitability)
　achieve a return　収益率を達成する, リターンを達成する
　actual return　実際運用益, 実際のリターン
　after-tax return　税引き後利益, 税引き後収益率
　annual rate of return　年利益率
　annual return　年次リターン, 年当たりのリターン, 年次決算
　asset return　資産収益率, 資産利回り
　assumed rate of return　予想収益率
　assumed rates of return on pension funds　予想年金基金運用収益率
　attractive returns　高水準の利益
　average return　平均収益率, 平均リターン
　bond returns　債券の収益率
　constant returns to scale　規模に関して収穫不変
　currency returns　為替の収益率
　current return　現行利回り
　decreasing returns to scale　規模に関して収穫逓減（ていげん）
　deliver a return　リターンを実現する
　earn a market-based return　市場原理に近い利益率を上げる
　earn a return　利益を上げる, 利益率を上げる
　enhance the returns on the portfolio　ポートフォリオの運用成績を上げる[改善する]
　excess return　超過収益率, 超過リターン
　expected return　期待収益, 予想収益, 期待収益率, 予想リターン
　final return　確定申告
　financial return　投資収益
　fixed return insurance　定額保険
　forecast excess return　予想超過収益率
　generate a healthy return　好業績を上げる
　generate maximum returns with minimum risks　最小限のリスクで最大限の利益を上げる
　generate [produce] returns　収益を生み出す, 利益を上げる, リターンを得る
　get a high return on one's investment　高い投資収益を上げる[得る], 運用資産について高いリターンを得る
　high return　高利益, 高収益[高水準の収益], 高い運用益, 高利回り, 高配当, 高いリターン, ハイリターン
　high [higher] return asset　利回りの高い資産, 高リターンの資産
　high-risk high-return　ハイリスク・ハイリターン（危険性の高い金融資産ほどその高い運用益が期待できること）
　horizon return　所有期間利回り
　　(=holding period return)
　improve returns　収益を高める, 収益を改善する
　increase return　投資収益率を高める
　increasing return to scale　規模に関して収穫逓増
　internal rate of return　内部収益率, IRR
　investment returns　投資利回り, 運用利回り, 投資収益
　low return　低収益, 低水準の収益, 低い運用益, 低利回り, 低配当, 低リターン
　make a return on one's investment　投資で利益を上げる, 投資で利益を得る
　modest return　小幅な運用益, 中程度[そこそこ]のリターン
　money rate of returns　現金ベース収益率
　negative return　マイナスの投資収益[運用益, 運用成績], マイナスのリターン
　nominal return　名目リターン
　normal return　正常収益率
　offer attractive return for investors　投資家に魅力的な利回りを提供する
　positive return　プラスの投資収益[運用益, 運用成績], プラスのリターン
　post negative returns　運用成績がマイナスになる
　post positive returns　運用成績がプラスになる
　protect asset returns　資産の利回りを確保する
　rate of return　収益率, 利益率
　real return　実質利回り
　　(=the real rate of return)
　receive a fair return　適切な利益を得る
　required rate of return　必要収益率, 必要利益率
　　(=hurdle rate, internal rate of return: 投資決定をする上で企業が基準にしている収益率)
　return to break-even　赤字解消
　return to profit　利益回復, 黒字転換
　return to stockholders [shareholders]　株主の利益, 株主還元
　return to the six-party talks　六か国協議への復帰
　return volatility　リターンの変動性
　returns promised to policyholders　保険契約者に約束した利回り[保証利回り], 予定利率
　　(=promised yield rates)
　revised return　修正申告
　　(=amended return, amended tax return)

risk adjusted returns　リスク調整後収益, リスク調整後の利回り
risk and return　リスクとリターン
safe returns　安全な利回り
securities firms' returns　証券会社の収益
small profits and quick returns　薄利多売
stock returns　株式総合利回り
the early return of a bull market　上げ相場の早期回復
the return of high inflation　高インフレの復活
the return of profits　利益還元
variable return insurance　変額保険
yield a return　リターンを生み出す
◆Investors must generally take higher investment risks in order to achieve higher investment returns. 投資家が一段と高い投資収益を得るには、一般に一段と高い投資リスクを取る必要がある。◆Investors purchased more overseas bonds and stocks to seek higher returns. 投資家は、高利益を求めて外国の債券や株式への投資が拡大した。◆The next step in the quest for higher gains is to inflate the returns by leverage. 高利益追求の第二の手段は、借金による利益の膨(ふく)らましだ。◆There is a negative spread between the yield guaranteed to insurance policyholders and their investment returns. 今は、保険契約者に保証した利回り(予定利率)と運用利回りが逆ざや状態(運用利回りが保険契約者に保証した利回りを下回る状態)にある。◆These days, nobody invests in a financial institution that cannot realize high returns. 最近は、高利益を上げることができない金融機関に、投資家は資金を出さなくなっている。

return of a bull market　上げ相場の回復
◆The early return of a bull market is unlikely. 上げ相場の早期回復は、期待できない。

return of income tax　所得税の還付
◆The Supreme Court ruling may spur similar lawsuits demanding the return of income tax already paid. この最高裁の判決で、すでに納付した所得税の還付を求める同様の訴訟に、拍車がかかる可能性がある。

return of profits to shareholders　株主への利益還元
◆An increase in the number of foreign shareholders prompted the company to review the return of profits to shareholders. 外国人株主が増えているため、同社は株主への利益還元を見直した。

return on　～利益率, ～の収益率, ～運用益
achieve reasonable returns on the invested capital　投資資本に対して妥当な収益率を達成する
return on financial capital　財務的資本利益
return on net worth　株主資本利益率, 自己資本利益率
return on one's portfolio　ポートフォリオの運用成績
return on physical capital　物的資本利益
return on sales　売上高利益率, 売上戻り, 売上戻り品 (=sales return)
return on the capital investment　設備投資利益率

return on assets　資産利益率, 総資産利益率, 資本利益率, ROA (=return on capital employed)
have a return on assets of　ROAが～である
return on assets employed　使用総資本利益率
return on average assets　使用資産利益率, 平均ROA
return on total assets　総資産利益率, 総資本利益率, 投下資本利益率(利益を総資産で割って算出する)
◆Return on assets is obtained by dividing net income (minus preferred stock dividends) by average total assets. 総資産利益率(ROA)は、純利益(優先株式配当金控除後)を平均総資産価額で割って[除して]求められます。

return on capital　資本利益率, 自己資本利益率
average return on capital　平均資本利益率

return on capital employed　使用総資本利益率, 資本利益率, ROCE (=return on assets)
◆The average return on capital of Britain's business rose 26 basis points to 4.95 percent in this year's first quarter. 今年第一・四半期の英国企業の平均資本利益率は、(前年同期比)0.26%増の4.95%だった。

return on equity　株主資本利益率, 自己資本利益率, ROE (資本金などをどれほど有効に使って利益を生んだかを示す経営指標。⇒ROE)
◆Toyota's profits are higher than General Motors', but its return on equity, an indicator believed to show the real strength of a company, stands around 6 percent, which is lower than GM's figure. トヨタの利益はGMの利益を上回っているが、企業の本当の実力を示すとされる株主資本利益率(ROE)は6%程度で、GMより劣っている。◆We calculate a company's return on equity by dividing the company's net income by its stockholders' equity. 企業の株主資本利益率(ROE)は、企業の純利益を株主資本[純資産]で割って算出する。

return on insurance premium management　保険料運用収益
◆The recent stock market rally has boosted returns on the insurance premium management of four major life insurers. 最近の株式相場の上昇[株高]で、4大生保各社の保険料運用収益が増加した。

return on investment　投下資本利益率, 使用総資本利益率, 投資収益, 投資利益率, 投資収益率, 投資利回り, 運用利回り, 運用益, 投資リターン, ROI
accumulated returns on investment　投資リターンの累計, 運用益の累計
analysis of return on investment　投下資本収益率分析
average return on investment　平均投資利益率[収益率]
return on investment method　投資利益率法
◆All the insurers are now saddled with an enormous amount of negative yields as returns on their investments have plunged due to ultralow interest rates—a consequence of the bursting of the bubble. 生保各社は現在、バブル崩壊後の超低金利時代で運用利回りが急抵下し、巨額の逆ざやを抱えている。◆These investments by investment banks could earn high returns on investment. 投資銀行のこれらの投資は、高いリターン(運用益)をもたらした。

return on plan assets　年金資産運用益, 年金制度資産の運用益, 年金資産の収益率
actual return on plan assets　制度資産の実際運用益
expected rate of return on plan assets　制度資産の期待利益率, 制度資産の期待収益
◆The expected long-term rate of return on plan assets is used in the calculation of net periodic pension cost. 年金資産の予想長期収益率は、期間年金費用純額の計算に用いられる。

return rate　利益率, 収益率, 利回り (=rate of return)
◆If life insurers continue to offer insurance policies with guaranteed high return rates, the future financial burden in terms of interest payments will increase. 生保が高い利回りを保証した保険の販売を今後とも続けると、将来の利払いの金融負担が増えることになる。

return to　～に戻る, ～に復帰する, ～に転じる, ～に転換する
return to a rising trend　上昇基調に戻る
return to neutral　中立に戻る
return to the six-party forum [talks]　6か国協議に復帰する

return to a path of a steady growth　順調な成長軌道に戻る
◆The global economy will soon return to a path of a steady growth. 世界経済は、もうすぐ順調な成長軌道に戻るだろう。

return to positive growth　プラス成長に転じる

◆The real gross domestic product for the April-June period returned to positive growth for the first time in five quarters. 4-6月期の実質国内総生産（GDP）は、5四半期ぶりにプラス成長に転じた。

revaluate 再評価する, 平価を切り上げる
（=revalue）
◆It is important for the international community to urge China to revaluate the yuan. 国際社会（世界各国）が、人民元の切上げを中国に働きかけることが重要だ。

revaluation （名）再評価, 評価替え, 見直し, 平価切上げ
  a pressure for a revaluation of the Chinese yuan　中国の人民元の切上げ圧力
  asset revaluation　資産再評価, 資産評価替え
  （=revaluation of assets）
  do a revaluation　通貨切上げをする, 切上げをする
  downward revaluation　平価切下げ
  effect［undertake］a revaluation　通貨切上げを実施する, 切上げを実施する
  equity revaluation　株式評価替え
  exchange revaluation　為替再評価
  （=revaluation of exchange）
  investment revaluation　投資再評価
  loss from inventory revaluation　棚卸し評価損
  loss from securities revaluation　有価証券評価損
  revaluation method　再評価法
  revaluation of the dollar　ドルの平価切上げ, ドル高
  （=dollar revaluation）
  revaluation of the yen　円の平価切上げ, 円高
  revaluation profit　再評価益
  revaluation reserve　再評価準備金, 再評価積立金
  revaluation surplus　再評価剰余金, 評価剰余金
  revaluation surplus reserve　再評価積立金
  stock revaluation　株式評価替え
  （=equity revaluation）
  upward revaluation　平価切上げ

revaluation of currency in North Korea　北朝鮮の通貨改定
◆The revaluation of currency in North Korea appears aimed at clamping down on burgeoning free markets in an attempt to reassert the regime's control. 北朝鮮の通貨改定は、政権の統制力を改めて強めるため、急速に広がる自由市場を厳しく取り締まるねらいがあるようだ。

revaluation of the Chinese currency　中国の通貨切上げ, 中国の人民元の切上げ
◆The revaluation of the Chinese currency may reduce Japan's exports to China. 中国の人民元切上げで、日本の対中輸出が減少する恐れがある。

revaluation of the Chinese yuan　中国の人民元の切上げ, 人民元の切上げ
◆Higher interest rates would increase the pressure for a revaluation of the Chinese yuan. 中国の利上げは、人民元の切上げ圧力を高めることになる。

revalue （動）再評価する,（平価を）切り上げる, 見直す
  be revalued to market　時価で再評価される
  be revalued upward　切り上げられる
  revalue the yuan against the U.S. dollar　人民元を対ドルで切り上げる, 人民元の対ドル切上げに踏み切る
◆China has revalued the yuan against the U.S. dollar. 中国が、人民元の対ドル切上げに踏み切った。◆The Obama administration is pressing Beijing to revalue the China's currency. オバマ政権は、中国に人民元の切上げを求めている。◆The yuan should be revalued upward. 人民元は、切り上げるべきだ。◆Washington is pressing Beijing to revalue the Chinese currency. 米政府は、中国に通貨（人民元）切上げを迫っている。

revamp （動）改革する, 改造する, 立て直す, 手直しする, 改訂する, 修正する, 改作する, 再建する
◆When ailing businesses are revamped, those who invested in them benefit. 経営不振企業を再建すると、出資者が利益を得られる。

revamp （名）改革, 改造, 刷新, 立て直し, 手直し, 改訂, 修正, 改作
  management revamp plan　経営改革計画, 企業改革方針
  sign a revamp　修正案件に調印［署名］する
◆Japan Airlines Corp. will reduce unprofitable international flights in a management revamp plan. 日本航空は、経営改革計画で不採算の国際便を減らす方針だ。

reveal （動）発表する, 公表する, 明らかにする,（秘密などを）漏らす, 示す, 開示する
◆The firm revealed the annual salaries of its four top executive officers at this year's general shareholders meeting. 同社は、今年の株主総会で代表取締役4人の年間報酬額を開示した。◆You should not reveal all your tactics at once when negotiating. 交渉では、自分の戦術をすべて一度に明かさないようにするとよい。

revenue （名）収益, 営業収益, 売上, 売上高, 収入, 歳入
  （⇒commission revenue, consumer banking, failed financial institution, financial instrument, off-the-book account, operating revenue）
  consolidated revenues　連結売上高
  dividend revenue　受取配当金
  losses in revenues and earnings　減収減益
  （=revenue and earnings losses）
  operating revenues　営業収益
  sales revenues　売上収益, 売上高, 総売上高
  total revenues　総収益, 総売上高
◆Banks have to set aside loan loss reserves based on projections of future revenues of their borrowers, not based on bankruptcies in the past. 銀行は、過去の倒産実績ではなく、融資先企業［貸出先］の将来の収益予想などを基にして、貸倒れ引当金を積み立てるべきだ。◆Combined sales of Panasonic and Sanyo would catapult Panasonic to the No.3 spot in revenue among listed Japanese companies. パナソニック（旧松下電器産業）と三洋電機の連結売上高を合算すると、上場日本企業のなかで、パナソニックは売上高で一躍第3位となる。◆Government revenues from the consumption tax are currently distributed among the basic pension program, health care for the elderly and nursing care. 消費税による国の税収は現在、基礎年金、老人医療と介護に配分されている。◆If the yen starts to appreciate, this will have a negative effect on the revenues of exporting companies. 円高に転じれば、輸出企業の収益は円高のマイナス影響を受けることになる。◆Revenues from the single-premium whole life insurance policies support the life insurer's business performance. 一時払い終身保険による収入［一時払い終身保険の収入保険料］が、同生保の業績を支えている。◆The bank increased revenues by loaning more money. 同行は、融資拡大路線で収益を上げた。◆The insurer's revenues from the single-premium whole life insurance products account for about 30 percent of the company's total revenues from insurance premiums. 同保険会社の一時払い終身保険商品の収入保険料は、保険料収入［収入保険料］全体の約3割を占めている。◆The SEC probe is focusing on several transactions that led to higher revenues at AOL Time Warner Inc. 米証券取引委員会（SEC）の調査は、AOLタイム・ワーナーの売上高水増し（疑惑）につながった一部の取引を中心に行われている。

[解説] 収益とは：商品の販売、サービスの提供、その他企業の営業活動から生じる現金または現金等価物（cash equivalents: 売掛金や受取手形などを含む）の流入額、投資から得た利子、配当ならびに固定資産の売却や交換に基づく利得、負債の減少額をいう。資本の払込みや借入金の

受入れなどは、収益とはならない。なお、会計上「現金」は、銀行預金のほかに小切手、手形、郵便為替証書などを含むが、流動資産に含まれるcashは手元現金と銀行の要求払い預金を指す。

revenue anticipation note 歳入先行証券, RAN（一時的な資金不足を補うために米国の州政府や地方自治体が発行する短期証券）

revenue base 収益基盤 （=revenue basis）
◆Banks must shore up their revenue base so they can repay all their debts. 銀行の債務返済を完了するには、銀行が収益基盤を強化する必要がある。◆Japan's financial institutions can't afford to strengthen their revenue base. 日本の金融機関は、収益基盤を強化するだけの余裕がない。

revenue bond 特定財源債, 歳入担保債（有料道路や橋など公共施設の建設資金を調達するため、米国の州政府や地方自治体が発行する地方債）

revenue source 財源, 収益源, 収入源, 歳入源
　a permanent revenue source　恒久財源
　secure a stable revenue source　安定財源を確保する
　the development of new revenue source　新しい収益源の発掘
◆In fiscal 2011 and thereafter, a permanent revenue source of ¥2.5 trillion will be necessary. 2011年度以降は、2.5兆円の恒久財源が必要になる。◆The development of new revenue sources remains a major challenge for the major banks. 新しい収益源の発掘が、依然として大手銀行の大きな課題だ。◆The tripartite reforms aim to reduce the amount of subsidies provided by the central government to the local governments; cut local tax grants to local governments; and shift revenue sources from the central government to local governments. 「三位一体」改革は、国の地方政府への補助金削減、地方交付税交付金の削減と国から地方政府への財源の移譲をめざしている。

revenues and expenditures 出納, 出し入れ
　（=receipts and payments）
◆Under an exclusive contract, Mizuho Bank administers the Tokyo metropolitan government's revenues and expenditures. 排他的取引契約に基づいて、みずほ銀行は東京都の出納管理をしている。

revenues from the single-premium whole life insurance products 一時払い終身保険商品による収入, 一時払い終身保険商品の収入保険料
◆The life insurer's revenues from the single-premium whole life insurance products tripled from the previous year in fiscal 2010. 同生保の一時払い終身の保険商品の収入保険料は、2010年度に前年度の3倍に達した。

reverberate （動）鳴り響く, 反響する, 反射する, 広まる
◆The subprime housing loan problem continues to be reverberate around the globe. サブプライム住宅ローン問題は、まだ世界に広がり続けている。

reversal （名）逆転, 反転, 反発, どんでん返し, 転換, 政策変更,（上級審の下級審判決に対する）破棄, 取消し
　business-cyclical reversal　景気循環の反転
　factor intensity reversal　要素集約度の逆転
　factor reversal test　要素転逆テスト
　political upheaval and reversals　政権交代と政策変更
　reversal auction　逆入札
　reversal entry　反対仕訳
　reversal of capital flows　資本の流れの逆転
　reversal of the rate cut　引き下げた金利の引上げ
　reversal of the transfer　復帰人事
　reversal process　反転現象, リバーサル
　reversal swap　反対スワップ
　role reversal　立場［役割］の逆転
　　（=reversal of roles）

switch reversal 逆入替え
trend reversal トレンドの逆転, トレンドの反転
　（=a reversal of the trend）
◆There are signs of a reversal in the trend of a stronger dollar and a weaker yen that started in the latter half of the 1990s. 1990年代後半から始まったドル高・円安傾向に、反転の兆しが

reverse （動）覆（くつがえ）す, 逆転［反転］させる, 方向などを逆にする［反対にする］, 置き換える, 変える, 判決などを破棄する, 無効にする, 取り消す, 振り戻す, 戻し入れる, 入れ替える, 取り崩す, 再修正する, 再整理する
　reverse a coin　コインを裏返しにする
　reverse a process　手順を逆［反対］にする
　reverse one's position　～の立場を逆転する
　reverse the charges　（電話料金を）受信人払いにする, 電話代を受信者に請求する
　reverse the credit stance　金融政策のスタンスを反転させる
　reverse the economy's slide　景気の悪化を抜け出す
　　（⇒fiscal stimulus）
　reverse the order　順序を逆にする
　reverse the position　状況を改善する
◆A large yen-selling intervention by monetary authorities on Sept. 15 failed to reverse the yen's rising trend. 金融当局が9月15日に実施した大量の円売り介入で、円高傾向を反転［逆転］させることはできなかった。

reverse （名）逆, 反対, あべこべ, 敗北, 失敗, つまずき (setback), 裏側, 裏面, 反対側,（本の）左［裏］ページ
　a reverse of fortune　運命の逆転, 不運
　go into［in］reverse　逆（さか）さまになる, 反対になる
　have［experience］reverses　打撃を受ける, 失敗する, 敗北する
　in reverse　逆に, 反対方向に, 背面に, 後陣に, バックで
　suffer［meet with］financial reverses　経済破たんの憂き目にあう

reverse （形）逆の, 反対の, 逆方向の, 裏の, 裏側の, 裏面の
　have a reverse effect　逆効果が出る
　in reverse order　逆順で
　reverse（annuity）mortgage　（年金方式）逆住宅抵当貸付け
　reverse bid　逆乗っ取り
　reverse direction　反対方向, 逆方向
　reverse dumping　逆ダンピング
　reverse engineering　逆行分析, 分解工学, 逆行分析工学, リバース・エンジニアリング（他社製品の分析・調査をとおして自社製品にその技術を導入すること）
　reverse head and shoulders　逆三尊（株式などのテクニカル分析で使われるチャートの一つで、下降相場の末期に現われることが多く、相場の大底を示す。⇒head and shoulders）
　reverse income tax　逆所得税, 負の所得税
　　（=negative income tax）
　reverse integration　逆統合
　reverse note　逆変動利付き債

reverse repurchase agreement 逆現先, 売り現先, 買戻し条件付き売付け, 買戻し条件付き売りオペ, 逆レポ, リバース・レポ取引, リバース・レポ （=reverse repo: 一定期間後に一定の価格で買い戻すことを条件に証券を売る取引）

reverse split 株式併合 （=reverse split of stocks, reverse stock split, share split-down; ⇒stock split）
◆The company is considering a reverse split of stocks by combining two shares into one. 同社は現在、2株を1株にまと

める株式併合を検討している。

review (動)見直す, 検討する, 評価する, 審査する, 調査する, 査閲する, 監査する, レビューする（監査が一般に公正妥当と認められる監査基準に従って実施されているかどうか、また所定の監査方針が遵守されているかどうかを確かめることを「査閲」という）
  review adjustable-rate mortgage interest rates　変動型金利の住宅ローンの金利を見直す
  review for possible downgrade　格下げの方向で検討する
  review the company's annual consolidated financial statements　同社の年次連結財務書類を査閲する
  （⇒annual consolidated financial statements）
  review the return of profits to shareholders　株主への利益還元を見直す
  （⇒return of profits to shareholders）
  ◆Adjustable-rate mortgage interest rates are reviewed every six months. 変動型金利の住宅ローンの金利は、半年ごとに見直される。◆Moody's Investors Service Inc. is reviewing 14 British banks for possible downgrade. ムーディーズ・インベスターズ・サービスは現在、英銀14行の格付けを、格下げの方向で検討している。◆Nippon Steel is forced to further review its capital and business relations with other steel manufacturers. 新日鉄は、他の鉄鋼メーカーとの資本・業務関係の再検討を迫られている。◆Sooner or later, the contribution ratio of the IMF member countries will be reviewed as the fast-growing emerging economies gain larger presence. いずれ、IMF加盟国の出資比率は、急成長している新興国が存在感を増していることから、見直されることになろう。◆The FSA urged the financial group to revise its earnings estimate. 金融庁は、同金融グループに対して業績予想の修正を強く迫った。◆The special inspections will be conducted as banks review the positions of their debtors, and will be finalized before the closing of accounts. 特別検査は、銀行が債務者の経営状態を見直す際に行われ、決算までに完了する。

review (名)検討, 見直し, 再考, 調査, 審査, 再調査, 再審理, 報告, 報告書, 評論監査調査の査閲, 監査技術としての閲覧, レビュー
  a review of evaluation system of securitized products　証券化商品の評価方法見直し
  business review　営業概況
  management review　経営監査
  peer review　相互検査, 専門家による相互審査, 相互評価, 相互批判, 同僚評価
  rating review　格付け見直し
  review of financial statements　財務諸表［財務書類］のレビュー
  review of internal control　内部統制の調査
  review of operations　営業報告書
  ◆An interim report of the Financial Stability Forum called for measures such as a review of evaluation system of securitized products. 金融安定化フォーラムの中間報告は、証券化商品の評価方法見直しなどの措置を求めた。◆The major banks attributed their increased bad loans to the poor performance of their borrowers due to the prolonged economic slump and Financial Service Agency inspections resulting in a stricter review of their asset assessments. 大手銀行は、不良債権が増えた理由として、長引く景気低迷で貸出先の経営が悪化したことと、金融庁の検査を受けて大手行が資産査定を厳しくしたことを挙げた。

revise (動)修正する, 改正する, 改定する, 改訂する, 見直す, 校正する, 校閲する　（⇒estimate, loss projections, unlisted joint-stock company）
  ◆A bill to revise the Law on Special Measures for Strengthening Financial Functions is designed to facilitate compensations of losses of financial institutions with public funds. 金融機能強化法の改正法案は、公的資金による金融機関の損失の穴埋めを容易にするのが狙いだ。◆A housing investment slump results from the enforcement of the revised Building Standards Law. 住宅投資の落込みは、改正建築基準法の施行によるものだ。◆If the yen rises above its all-time high of ￥79.75 to the dollar, the company may have to revise its assumed exchange rate once more. 円高が1ドル＝79円75銭の史上最高値を更新したら、同社は再び同社の想定為替レートの修正を迫られかねない。◆In the wake of the Livedoor case, the Financial Instruments and Exchange Law which drastically revised the former Securities and Exchange Law came into force in September 2007. ライブドア事件を受けて、2007年9月に、旧証券取引法を抜本改正した金融商品取引法が施行された。◆Listed companies revised their articles of incorporation to make stock certificates paperless by holding shareholders meetings. 株券をペーパーレス化するため、公開企業は、株主総会を開いて会社の定款を変更した。◆The company revised its assumed exchange rate to ￥80 per dollar from the current ￥90. 同社は、同社の想定為替レートを、現行の1ドル＝90円から1ドル＝80円に修正した。◆The government revised up its economic growth figures for the first three months of the year. 政府は、1-3月期の経済成長率の数値を上方修正した。

revise downward　下方修正する
  （=downgrade, revise down）
  ◆Leading Japanese companies have revised downward their earnings projections for the year ending March. 日本の主要企業が、3月期決算の業績予想を下方修正している。◆Other banks are likely forced to revise their earnings projections downward because of the accelerated disposal of bad loans, business deterioration of borrowers due to the lingering recession and further decline in stock prices. 不良債権処理の加速や長引く不況による融資先の業績悪化、株安などの影響で、他行も業績の下方修正を迫られているようだ。

revise upward　上方修正する　（⇒capital spending, credit rating agency, profile）
  ◆Standard & Poor's revised upward its outlook on the long-term ratings on 11 regional banks. スタンダード＆プアーズは、地銀11行の長期格付け見通しを上方修正した。◆Standard & Poor's revised upward the outlook on its ratings on six major Japanese insurance companies against the backdrop of their improved financial profiles. スタンダード＆プアーズは、日本の大手保険会社6社の財務力見通し改善を背景に、6社の格付け見通しを上方修正した。◆The U.S. credit rating agency revised upward the outlook to positive from negative on its rating on Sumitomo Life Insurance Co. この米国の信用格付け機関は、住友生命保険の格付け見通しを「ネガティブ」から「ポジティブ」に上方修正した。

revised (形)修正された, 改定された, 修正［改定］済みの, 変更［修正、改定］した, 〜の修正［改定、変更］
  revised budget　修正予算
  revised financial statements　改定財務諸表, 改定財務書類
  revised Foreign Exchange and Foreign Trade Control Law　改正外為法
  revised return　修正申告
  revised tax return　修正申告
  ◆A revised Foreign Exchange and Foreign Trade Control Law has been enacted to enable the swift freezing of funds belonging to terrorist organizations. テロ組織の資金［資産］凍結を迅速に行うための改正外為法は、すでに成立して［制定されて］いる。

revision (名)修正, 改正, 改訂, 見直し
  （⇒downward revision, upward revision）
  downward revision　下方修正
  upward revision　上方修正
  ◆The bank is mulling a further downward revision of its business results for fiscal 2011 that is expected to result in a massive loss. 同行は、2012年3月期決算［2011年度］の業績予

想をさらに下方修正する方向で検討している。

revitalization (名)再生, 活性化, 再活性化, 健全化, 復興, 回復
　corporate revitalization　企業再生
　Government Revitalization Unit　行政刷新会議
　industrial revitalization　産業再生
　　(⇒public assistance)
　management revitalization plan　経営健全化計画
　　(⇒submit)
　revitalization of businesses　事業再生
　◆Use of ADR for the revitalization of businesses began in 2008. 事業再生ADR(裁判外紛争解決手続き)制度の活用は、2008年からスタートした。

revitalization firm　企業再生会社
　(=revitalizing firm)
　◆Sumitomo Mitsui Banking Corporation has entered the final phase of negotiations with U.S. firm Goldman Sachs Group Inc. and Daiwa Securities SMBC Co. on a capital and business tie-up with a new revitalization firm Sumitomo Mitsui will establish. 三井住友銀行は、米大手証券のゴールドマン・サックス、大和証券SMBC両社と、同行が設立する新会社の企業再生会社との資本・業務提携に関する交渉で、その最終段階に入った。

revitalization fund　復興ファンド
　◆Public institutions or revitalization funds will buy the loans owed by small and midsize companies that have been hit by the March 11 disaster to lighten their repayment burdens. 公的機関や復興ファンドが、東日本大震災で被災した中小企業の借金を買い取って、被災企業の返済負担を軽減するものと思われる。

revitalization of the economy　経済の活性化
　◆The fiscal structural reform was originally aimed at allocating government outlays in such a way as to stimulate areas that would lead to a revitalization of the national economy. 財政構造改革の本来のねらいは、日本経済の活性化につながる分野を刺激する形での政府支出の配分[予算配分]にあった。◆These tax reforms are aimed at shifting capital from savings to investment, seen as vital in promoting the revitalization of the economy. これらの税制改革のねらいは、経済活性化を促すうえで必要とみられる「貯蓄から投資への資金移動」にある。

revitalization plan　再生計画, 再活性化案
　◆The revitalization plan will be carried out chiefly using ¥400 billion in financial assistance to be extended by the firm's creditor banks. 再生計画は、主に同社の取引銀行が行う金融支援総額4,000億円を使って実施される。

revitalize (動)回復させる, 生き返らせる, 再生する, 復興させる, 活性化する, 活力を与える, (景気などを)浮揚させる
　revitalize a troubled bank　経営不振の銀行を再生する
　revitalize the company　会社を再生する
　◆The Industrial Revitalization Corporation was inaugurated with the aim of revitalizing troubled banks and industries. 産業再生機構は、経営不振の銀行と産業の再生を目指して発足した。

revitalize stock trading　株式の売買を活性化する
　◆The merger of the two exchanges will revitalize stock trading and make it easier for companies to procure funds on the market to expand their business operations. 両証券取引所の経営統合で、株式の売買が活性化し、企業にとっては市場で資金を調達して会社の事業を大きくしやすくなる。

revitalize the economy　経済を活性化する, 景気を浮揚させる
　◆Breaking this vicious circle could be the key to revitalizing the economy. この悪循環を断ち切ることが、景気浮揚へのカギになる。

revitalize the market　市場を活性化する, 市場の活性化を図る
　◆In revitalizing the market, it is necessary to encourage individuals, who have financial assets totaling ¥1.4 quadrillion, to invest in the stock market. 市場の活性化を図るには、1,400兆円にのぼる金融資産を持つ個人の株式市場への投資を促す必要がある。

revival (名)再生, 事業再生, 再建, 復活, 回復, 再燃
　economic revival　景気回復, 経済再生
　industrial revival　産業再生
　revival in demand　需要の回復
　revival of inflation　インフレ再燃
　revival of the financial system　金融再生
　　(=financial revitalization)

revival account　再生勘定
　◆Nonperforming loans will be transferred to the revival account, as well as crossheld shares and idle real estate. 不良債権は、持ち合い株式や遊休不動産などと一緒に「再生勘定」に移す。◆Resona Bank announced a plan to introduce revival accounts to manage its ¥2.3 trillion nonperforming loans separately from the healthier loans. りそな銀行は、2兆3,000億円の不良債権を正常債権とは別個に管理する「再生勘定」を導入する方針を発表した。

revival of the twin deficits　双子の赤字の復活, 双子の赤字の再燃
　◆Concern over the revival of the twin deficits is accelerating selling pressure on the U.S. stocks and the dollar. 双子の赤字の復活懸念が、米国の株・ドル売りを加速している。

revival plan　再生計画, 事業再生計画, 再建計画
　(⇒bank stocks, capital injection, loan waiver, struggling)
　◆A ¥450 billion revival plan aims at turning around the struggling automaker. 4,500億円の再建計画は、この経営不振の自動車メーカーの事業再生を目指している。◆Kanebo, Ltd. will withdraw from textile and food production under its revival plan. カネボウは、同社の事業再生計画に基づいて、繊維と食品の生産事業から撤退する。◆Under the revival plan, the firm intends to issue ¥30 billion worth of preferred shares to Sumitomo Mitsui Banking. この再生計画では、同社は、三井住友銀行を引受先として300億円の優先株式を発行する。

revive (動)よみがえらせる, 再生させる, 復活させる, 回復させる, 再流行させる (自動)よみがえる, 生き返る, 再生する, 復活する, 回復する
　◆Bolivian pro-market President-elect Gonzalo Sanchez took office facing the huge tasks of reviving a stagnant economy and attracting investment. ボリビアの大統領に当選した市場経済主義者のゴンザロ・サンチェス氏が、停滞した経済の回復や投資誘致という重大任務を抱えて就任した。

revoke (動)取り消す(cancel), 無効にする, 廃止する
　◆Citigroup Private Bank's four offices in Japan will have their licenses revoked in September next year for violating the law by ignoring suspected money laundering by clients. シティバンクのプライベート・バンク(PB)の在日4拠点(支店・出張所)が、顧客のマネー・ロンダリング(資金洗浄)の疑いのある取引を放置するなどして法令違反があったとして、来年9月で認可を取り消されることになった。

revolver (名)回転信用, リボルバー
　(=open-end credit, revolving credit)

revolving (形)回転する, 回転式の, リボルビング
　cumulative revolving letter of credit　累積回転信用状
　irrevocable revolving commitment　取消し不能回転契約
　multicurrency revolving facility　多通貨建て回転信用ファシリティ
　revolving charge account　回転掛売り勘定
　revolving fund　回転資金, 回転基金
　revolving letter of credit　回転信用状

revolving line of credit　回転信用貸出枠, 回転信用供与枠
revolving loan　回転貸付け, 回転融資, 満期に自動的に更新される融資
revolving loan agreement　回転融資契約
revolving period　リボルビング期間
revolving system　回転信用方式, リボルビング・システム
revolving underwriting facilities　回転(短期証券)引受枠, 回転ユーロノート引受契約, 中長期資金調達方式, RUF (=note issuance facility)
revolving working capital line　回転信用形式の運転資金供与枠

revolving credit　回転信用(open-end credit, revolver), 回転融資, 回転信用勘定, 回転信用状(revolving letter of credit)
extendible revolving credit　期限延長可能な回転信用状
five-year revolving credit　期間5年の回転信用
multicurrency revolving credit facility　複数通貨回転信用枠
revolving credit agreement　回転信用契約
revolving credit facility　回転融資枠, 回転信用ファシリティ
◆These revolving credit facilities are intended for general corporate purposes. これらの回転融資枠は、一般の事業目的に使用する予定です。

revolving credit system　回転信用方式, リボルビング・システム
revolving credit system based on fixed amount minimum payment　定額リボルビング・システム
revolving credit system of fixed amount method within interest　元利定額リボルビング・システム
revolving credit system of fixed amount method without interest　元金定額リボルビング・システム
revolving credit system of fixed percentage method without interest　元金定率リボルビング・システム

reward　(名)報酬, 報償, 報奨金, 褒賞金, 謝礼, 対価, 成果, リターン
cash reward　報奨金
financial rewards　金銭的な報酬
just reward　正当な報酬
pecuniary reward　金銭的報酬
reap the rewards of growth　成長の報酬を手に入れる
reap the rewards of investment　投資の報酬を手に入れる, 投資の成果を生かす
reward based on merit　能力に基づく報酬, 能力に応じた報酬
reward power　報酬に基づく統制力
reward system　報酬体系
reward to shareholders [stockholders]　株主の利益, 株主への利益還元, 株主還元
reward-to-volatility ratio　リターン・ボラティリティ比率
rewards of investment　投資の成果
rewards system　報奨金制度
risk and reward　リスクとリターン
the risks and wards of investment　投資のリスクとリターン
◆Gain from stock options is a reward for dedicated work by an employee. ストック・オプション(自社株購入権)の利益は、従業員が熱心に勤務したことへの対価である。◆The money given in 2010 was a reward for winning the contracts for construction projects. 2010年に提供された資金は、建設工事受注の見返りだった。◆There can be huge financial rewards from the successful commercialization of technology. 技術の商品化に成功すると、巨額の金銭的な報酬が得られる。

-ridden　(形)〜に支配[抑圧]された, 〜に苦しめられた, 〜に悩まされた[悩む], 〜に侵された, 〜に虐(しいた)げられた, 〜が多い, 〜だらけの, 〜が多発する, 〜がやたらに多い
debt-ridden　債務に苦しんでいる, 借金に苦しんでいる[悩まされている]
deficit-ridden　赤字に悩む
deficit-ridden country　財政赤字国
poverty-ridden condition　貧窮状態
scandal-ridden　不祥事続きの, スキャンダルまみれの, スキャンダルに揺らぐ
◆A recent tragedy involving a debt-ridden elderly couple roused all parties to impose stricter controls on the moneylending business. 最近起こった借金苦の老夫婦の悲劇が、各党を貸金業の規制強化に突き動かした。◆The mutual aid association injected ¥1.5 billion into 24 deficit-ridden hotels run by the association. 同共済組合は、経営する赤字の24ホテルに15億円を注入[補填]した。◆The yields on government bonds of deficit-ridden countries including Greece have been rising across the board in Europe. 欧州では、ギリシャなど財政赤字国の国債利回りが、軒並み上昇している。

ride　(動)乗る, 乗りこなす, 乗って行く, 車で運ぶ[送る], 停泊する, 苦しめる, 悩ます
let things ride　成り行きに任せろ
ride a winner　勝ち馬に騎乗する
ride for a fall　無謀な行動をする, 無茶をする
ride high　うまく行っている, 成功する, 好評だ, 意気揚々としている, 優位に立っている
ride on　〜次第である, 〜によって決まる, 〜にかかっている, 〜に依存する
ride out　うまく切り抜ける, 耐え抜く
ride the yield curve　利回り曲線(イールド・カーブ)に乗る
◆All possible measures, such as injecting funds into markets and lowering rates, need to be taken to ride out this financial emergency. この金融非常事態をうまく切り抜けるには、市場への資金注入[資金供給]や利下げなど、あらゆる可能な措置を取る必要がある。◆The yen will continue to ride high for the time being. 円高は、当面続くだろう。

ride　(名)乗車, 乗馬, (森を通る)乗馬道路, 乗り物による旅行[移動], 乗り心地
be in for [have] a bumpy ride　ひどい目にあう, ひどい目にあいそうだ
bullish ride on the government bond market　国債相場の急騰
come [go] along for the ride　ちょっと参加する, 面白半分に参加する, 消極的に加わる
face a rough ride　ひどい目にあう, つらい目にあう
have a rough ride　ひどい扱いを受ける
take a ride in　〜に乗る
◆The firm looks to be in for a rough ride for some time yet. 同社は、まだ当面は試練が続きそうだ。

rider　(名)添え書き, 裏書き, 添付書類, 別紙, (手形の)補箋, (契約などの)補足条項[追加条項], (議案などの)付帯条項, (保険や年金の)特約, 特約条項
accidental death rider　災害割増特約
add a rider to the contract　契約に補足条項を加える
annuity rider　年金特約
free rider　ただ乗り, フリー・ライダー
rider of insurance　保険追約書

RIE　(英国の)公認投資取引所(recognized investment exchangeの略)

RIE [r.i.e]　退職所得養老年金(retirement income endowmentの略)

rigged market 相場操縦などで操作された市場
right （名）権利，権限，所有権，新株引受権，正当，公正
（⇒conversion right, leasing right, management right, stock appreciation right, voting right）
  business right　営業権
  cum rights price　権利付き株価
  ex rights price　権利落ち株価
  minority stockholders' right　少数株主権
  preemptive right　新株引受権　（⇒dilute）
  right to benefits　受給権
  rights offering　株主割当て，株主割当て発行，株主割当て発行増資　（=rights issue: 新株発行の際，一定の割合で株主に優先的に新株を引き受ける権利を与えることをいう）
  rights-on　権利付き
  security right　担保権
  shareholders' right　株主権
    （=stockholders' right）
  stock right　新株引受権，株式引受権，株式買受権
    （=subscription right）
right of first refusal　第一次拒否権，株式の優先先買権，優先買取り権，先買権，優先受諾権
（=first refusal right）
◆Approval of the directors nominated by any party hereto shall be deemed to have been given where such party has declined or failed to exercise its right of first refusal pursuant to Section 3 with respect to the shares of the new company offered for sale by one or more of the parties hereto. 1者以上の本契約当事者が売却の申し出をした新会社の株式に関する第3条の規定に従って先買権の行使を拒否するか先買権を行使しない場合には，本契約当事者が指名した取締役の承認が与えられたものと見なされる。
right of indemnity　求償権
◆A nonlife insurer has used its right of indemnity concerning the series of faults in MMC-made vehicles. 一連の三菱製自動車の欠陥問題に関して，損保会社が求償権を行使した。
right to buy shares　株式引受権
◆The company granted an investment firm the right to buy shares to be newly issued by the company as a means of foiling a hostile takeover bid. 同社は，敵対的買収への防衛策として，同社が新規に発行する株式の引受権を投資会社に付与した［投資会社に新株予約権を割り当てた］。
rights issue　株主割当て発行，株主割当て発行増資
（=rights offering）
◆The firm will undertake a rights issue on the basis of one share for every two shares held. 同社は，保有株（持ち株）2株につき1株の割合で株主割当て発行増資を実施した。
rise （動）増加する，拡大する，伸びる，上昇する，高まる
（⇒greenback名詞）
  begin to rise　上昇に転じる
  continue to rise　伸び続ける，増勢が続く
  rise a little against the yen　円に対して小幅上昇する，対円で小幅上昇する
  rise above　～を超える
  rise against the dollar and other major currencies　ドルなどの主要通貨に対して上昇する
  rise over time　長期的に増加［拡大，上昇］する
  rise sharply　急増する
  rise steadily　着実に伸びる
  rise strongly　強く伸びる，大幅に増加する
◆An exporter company will incur losses if the yen rises above the assumed exchange rate, but benefit if the yen declines. 輸出企業では，その想定為替レートより円高になれば為替差損が生じ，（想定為替レートより）円安になれば為替差益が出る。◆Fears of a double dip recession are likely to rise if the rise in the yen continues. 円高がこのまま続けば，「景気二番底」懸念が高まると見られる。◆If the worth of the issuer rises, the value of the stock also will rise. 発行体の資産価値が上昇すれば，株式の価値も上がる。◆If the yen rises above its all-time high of ￥79.75 to the dollar, the company may have to revise its assumed exchange rate once more. 円高が1ドル＝79円75銭の史上最高値を更新したら，同社は再び同社の想定為替レートの修正を迫られかねない。◆Japan should prevent the dollar plunging and the yen from rising too sharply through concerted market intervention with the United States and European countries. 日本は，米欧との協調介入によってドル急落と超円高を阻止すべきだ。◆Major currencies are rising against the dollar on account of the Fed's monetary easing policy. 米連邦準備制度理事会（FRB）の金融緩和策で，主要通貨はドルに対して上昇している［ドル安・主要通貨高が進んでいる］。◆On Aug. 31, 2011, the yen rose to the ￥76.50 level against the U.S. dollar in the Tokyo foreign exchange market, close to the postwar record of ￥75.95 registered on Aug. 19. 2011年8月31日の東京外国為替市場の円相場は，1ドル＝76円50銭台まで上昇し，8月19日に付けた戦後最高値の75円95銭に近づいた。◆Short-term interest rates in the Tokyo market rose as some financial institutions hurried to obtain newly released funds. 一部の金融機関が新規調達資金の確保を急いだため，東京市場の短期金利が上昇した。◆The number of companies undertaking initial public offerings has risen sharply this year. 株式を新規公開する企業が，今年は急増している。◆The Tankan index for large manufacturers rose to plus 2 in September from the minus 9 registered in June. 9月短観の大企業・製造業の業況判断指数（DI）は，6月調査のマイナス9からプラス2に11ポイント改善した。◆The yen has risen to about ￥90 per U.S. dollar, drastically reducing the profits of export-oriented firms. 円高が1ドル＝90円台前後まで進み，輸出企業の利益は大幅に減少した。◆The yen may once again rise against the dollar and other major currencies. 今後，ドルなどの主要通貨に対して再び円高が進む可能性がある。◆The yen rose to its record high of ￥79.75 against the dollar in 1995. 円相場は，1995年に上昇して史上最高値の1ドル＝79円75銭を付けた。◆The yen rose to the upper ￥81 level against the dollar in Tokyo. 東京外国為替市場の円相場は，1ドル＝81円台後半まで上昇した。◆The yen will rise further in the near future. 今後，円高はさらに進むようだ。◆The yen's value continues to rise. 円高が，進んでいる。◆The yields on Greek government bonds have been rising sharply due to the credit uncertainty. ギリシャ国債の利回りは，信用不安で急上昇している。
rise （名）増加，増大，上昇，伸び，向上，高まり，値上り，物価の騰貴，昇給，賃上げ，切上げ，出世，隆盛，台頭，出現
（⇒change名詞）
  be on the rise　増加している，上昇している，上向いている，上り調子だ
  give rise to speculations　推測［憶測］を生む
  price rise　物価上昇，価格引上げ，値上げ
    （=rise of［in］prices）
  rise in bond yields　債券利回りの上昇
    （=bond yields rise）
  rise in corporate profits　企業収益の伸び，企業収益の増加
  rise in interest rates　金利の上昇
  rise in money demand　資金需要の伸び
  rise in money supply　マネー・サプライの伸び
  sharp rise in crude oil prices　原油価格の急激な上昇，原油価格の急騰
  temporary rise in money demand　資金需要の一時的な伸び
  the renminbi's rise　人民元の切上げ

wage rise　賃金上昇, 賃金引上げ, 賃上げ
　　(=pay rise, rise of [in] wages)
　◆Export-oriented companies will be hit hard if the yen accelerates its rise. 円高が加速すると, 輸出企業は大きな打撃を受ける。◆Just as the number of people qualifying for pensions is on the rise, the working population, which underpins the pension scheme, is on the decline. 年金受給の資格者は増える一方, 年金制度を支える現役世代は減っている。◆The yen's continued rise is worrisome for large manufacturers. 大企業・製造業には, 円高進行も懸念材料だ。◆U.S. President Barack Obama pressed for the renminbi's rise at his meeting with Chinese Premier Wen Jiabao in New York. オバマ米大統領は, ニューヨークで行った中国の温家宝首相との会談で, 人民元の切上げを強く迫った。

rise across the board　全面的に上昇する, 全面高となる, 軒並み上昇する
　◆The yields on government bonds of deficit-ridden countries including Greece have been rising across the board in Europe. 欧州では, ギリシャなど財政赤字国の国債利回りが, 軒並み上昇している。

rise in bond prices　債券価格の上昇, 債券相場の上昇
　◆On the bond market, the yield on newly issued 10-year government bonds, an indicator of long-term interest rates, fell, resulting in a rise in bond prices. 債券市場では, 長期金利の指標である新発10年物国債の利回り (流通利回り) が下落し, 債券相場 [債券価格] は上昇した。

rise in crude oil prices　原油価格の高騰, 原油高
　　(=rise in oil prices)
　◆Japanese exports are certain to further decline if overseas economies have slowed down as a result of a continued rise in crude oil prices. 原油高が長引いて海外経済が減速すれば, 日本の輸出が一段と落ち込むのは避けられない。

rise in defaults of subprime loans　サブプライム・ローン (低所得者向け住宅ローン) の不払い増加
　◆The financial crisis triggered by the rise in defaults of U.S. subprime loans caused havoc in financial markets worldwide. 米国のサブプライム・ローン (低所得者向け住宅ローン) の不払い増加がきっかけで起こった金融危機は, 世界の金融市場を大混乱させた。

rise in foreign assets　対外資産の増加
　◆The rise in foreign assets held by Japanese was mainly caused by an increase in direct and securities investment. 日本人 (日本の政府・企業・個人) が保有する対外資産の増加は, 主に直接・証券投資の伸びによるものだった。

rise in inflation　物価の上昇, インフレ率の上昇
　◆The European Central Bank left its main interest rate unchanged at 1 percent despite a rise in inflation. 物価上昇にもかかわらず, 欧州中央銀行 (ECB) は政策金利を1％に据え置いた。

rise in long-term interest rates　長期金利の上昇
　◆The rise in long-term interest rates may apply the brakes on the recovery. 長期金利の上昇は, 景気回復にブレーキをかけかねない。

rise in market rates　市場金利の上昇
　◆Banks' fund-raising costs have increased, reflecting the rise in market rates after the Bank of Japan abandoned its zero-interest policy. 日銀のゼロ金利政策解除に伴って市場金利が上昇したのを反映して, 銀行の資金調達コストが増大した。

rise in mid- and long-term interest rates　中長期の金利上昇
　◆Speculation the Bank of Japan will end its quantitative monetary easing policy soon has sparked a rise in mid- and long-term interest rates. 日銀が近く量的緩和策を解除するとの思惑から, (金融市場では) 中長期の金利が上昇し始めた。

rise in the yen　円高　(=the rise in the yen's value; ⇒serious damage)
　◆Fears of a double dip recession are likely to rise if the rise in the yen continues. 円高がこのまま続けば, 「景気二番底」懸念が高まると見られる。◆Reflecting the rise in the yen, Tokyo stocks, particularly exporter stocks, dropped Wednesday. 円高を受けて [反映して], 水曜日は, 輸出企業の株を中心に東京株式市場の株価が下落した [東京株式市場の株が売られた]。

rise in the yen's value　円高, 円相場の上昇
　　(=the rise in [of] the yen; ⇒economic growth)
　◆Amid the depleted state coffers, it is difficult to implement a major stimulus package to rectify the rise in the yen's value. 財政悪化が進む中 [国の財源が枯渇する中], 円高是正のため大規模な財政出動を行うのは難しい。◆Rapid rise in the yen's value can be attributed to the U.S. Federal Reserve Board's decision to effectively conduct additional monetary easing policy. 急激な円高の理由として, 米連邦準備制度理事会 (FRB) が事実上, 追加金融緩和策に踏み切ったことが挙げられる。

rise in the yuan's value against the U.S. dollar
　人民元相場の対米ドル切上げ
　◆The latest rise in the yuan's value against the U.S. dollar and a smooth transition to the currency basket will help stabilize China's external relations. 今回の人民元相場の対米ドル切上げと通貨バスケット制への円滑な移行で, 中国の対外関係は安定化に向かうだろう。

rise of the yen　円高　(=rise in the yen)
　◆The rise of the yen beyond the level of the exchange rate assumed by many exporters has put them on the ropes. 多くの輸出業者が想定した為替レートの水準を上回る円高が輸出業者を窮地に追い込んでいる。◆There seem to be no brakes on the rise of the yen. 円高に, 歯止めがかからないようだ。

rise of the yen's value　円高
　◆The rise of the yen's value is behind the improvement in travel abroad. 円高が, 海外旅行増加の背景にある。◆The rise of the yen's value pushed up the demand for travel abroad. 円高が, 海外旅行の需要を押し上げた。

rising　(形) 増加する, 増大する, 上昇する, 向上する, 上り調子の, 出世している, 新進気鋭の, 伸び盛りの　(名) 上昇, 増加, 増大, 昇進, 出世
　return to a rising trend　上昇基調に戻る
　rising dollar　ドル高
　　(=rising exchange value of the dollar)
　rising equity value　株価の上昇
　rising fiscal deficits　財政赤字の増加, 財政赤字の拡大
　rising inflation pressure　インフレ圧力の増大
　　(⇒inflation pressure)
　rising market [quotation]　上げ相場, 上向き相場
　rising prices　物価 [価格] 上昇, 右上がりの相場
　rising productivity　生産性の向上
　rising rate environment　金利上昇局面
　rising share　シェア拡大
　rising trend　上昇基調

rising debts　借入金の増大
　◆Daiei's business diversification led to rising debts that placed financial pressure on the company. ダイエーの事業多角化は, 借入金の増大につながり, それが会社の経営を圧迫する結果となった。

rising deflationary pressures　デフレ圧力の増大, デフレ圧力の高まり
　◆The economy could sink into a double-dip recession due to the clouds hanging over the U.S. economy and rising deflationary pressures that will accompany the accelerated disposal of nonperforming loans. 米国経済の行方 (米国経済への先行き不安) や, 不良債権処理の加速に伴うデフレ圧力の高まりなどで, 景気が底割れする恐れがある。

rising downside risks　下振れリスクの増大
　◆Instability in global markets is increasing with rising

downside risks. 下振れリスクの増大とともに、グローバル市場の不安定性は高まっている。
rising interest income 金利収入の増加
◆Rising interest incomes from Japanese investments in dollar- and euro-denominated securities and growing dividends from overseas subsidiaries of Japanese companies were behind the increase in the income account. 所得収支が増加した背景としては、米ドル建て債やユーロ建て債の金利収入が増えたほか、日本企業の海外子会社からの配当が増えたことが挙げられる。
rising interest rate 金利の上昇, 金利上昇
◆Rising long-term interest rates will lead directly to higher interest payments for government bonds. 長期金利の上昇は、国債の利払い費用に直結する。
rising price 価格の上昇, 価格の高騰
◆Economic upturn is expected to continue in and after next fiscal year, with rising prices of crude oil, steel, nonferrous metals and other key materials pushing up consumer prices. 景気回復は来年度以降も続き、原油や鉄鋼、非鉄金属といった主要原材料の価格が上昇して消費者物価を押し上げるものと見られる。
rising yen 円高
◆A key factor in dealing with the rising yen is the action the Bank of Japan will take. 円高対応の重要なカギは、今後の日銀の動きだ。
risk (動)危険にさらす, ～の危険を招く[冒す], (生命を)賭ける, 覚悟してやる, 思い切ってやる, 一か八かやってみる, ～する危険性[恐れ]がある, ～の危機に陥る
risk a failure 失敗を覚悟してやる
risk life and limb 大きな危険を冒す
◆A flood of new regulations risk choking off a global economic recovery. 多くの新規制は、世界の景気回復を妨げる恐れがある。
risk (名)危険, 危険性, 危険負担, 価格などの値下がり確率, リスク (⇒BIS, commission revenue, credit control, credit risk, day trading, external bond financing, loan interest rate, savings product, sovereign risk, systemic risk)
all risks 全危険担保, オール・リスク担保
an amount at risk 危険保険金額
assess market risk 市場リスクを評価する
business risk 事業リスク, 営業リスク
control one's credit risk 信用リスクを管理する
country risk カントリー・リスク
credit risk 信用危険, 信用リスク, 貸倒れリスク
default risk 債務不履行リスク
diversify risks リスクを分散する
diversity of risk リスク分散
 (=diversification of risk)
downward risk 下方リスク, 損失リスク, 下値リスク
downward risks for the global economy 世界経済の下方リスク
financial risk 財務リスク, 金融リスク
fire and usual marine risks 海上保険
foreign exchange risk 為替リスク
hedge risks リスクを相殺する, リスクをヘッジする
high risk 高リスク, ハイリスク
high risk assets such as stocks 株式などリスク[損失リスク]の高い資産 (⇒capital flight)
inflation risk インフレ再燃のリスク, インフレ加速の危険, インフレ・リスク (=risk of inflation)
information technology risk IT(情報技術)リスク
 (=IT risk)
interest rate risk 金利リスク (=rate risk)
investment risk 投資リスク
 (⇒fund-of-funds investment)
lending risk 貸出リスク
liquidity risk 流動性リスク
management risk 経営リスク, 経営者リスク, マネジメント・リスク
nondiversifiable risk 分散不能リスク
 (=market risk, systematic risk)
passing of risk 危険負担の移転
price risk 価格リスク
risk-averse retail investors リスクを嫌う個人投資家, リスク回避型個人投資家
risk-bearing リスクを負担する
risk capital 危険資本, 危険負担資本, 危険投下資本, 危険資本投資 (=venture capital)
risk-covering insurance 危険保険
risk-loving リスク愛好的
risk of disability 高度障害危険
risk of loss 危険負担, 損失の危険, 滅失の危険
risk premium 危険保険料
risk premium rates 危険保険料率
risk-seeking リスクを求める, リスク選好型の, リスク選好的な
risk-seeking investor リスク選好型の投資家
risk sharing リスク分散
risk taking 危険負担, リスク負担, 冒険心, 冒険の精神, 大胆さ
risk tolerance リスク許容度, リスク許容限度
risk trade 自己勘定による取引
risk weight 保有資産のリスクの度合い, リスク・ウェート
risks covered 担保危険
risks that do not come within the scope of this agreement 本協定の範囲に含まれないリスク
spreading of risk リスク分散
standard risk 標準体(保険用語)
substandard risk 条件体(保険用語)
systematic risk システマティック・リスク(東京株価指数(TOPIX)の価格変動など、分散投資では取り除けない金融市場全体に共通するリスクのこと)
value at risk 想定最大損失額, バリュー・アト・リスク, VAR
◆Depending on moves in foreign exchange markets, there is a risk we may lose initial investments in foreign currency deposits. 為替相場の動き次第で、外貨預金では初期投資額を割り込むリスクがある。◆Every member of the nation will now be forced to face the risks involved in the management of their own assets. これからは、国民一人ひとりが資産運用リスクに正面から向き合わざるを得なくなる。◆Financial institutions are trying to secure profits in proportion to the risks they take. 金融機関は、金融機関の取るリスクに見合った利潤[適正利潤]を確保しようとしている。◆Foreign currency deposit accounts carry a degree of risk. 外貨預金口座には、ある程度リスクも伴う。◆Heightened tensions and significant downward risks for the global economy must be addressed decisively. 世界経済の緊張の高まりと重大な下方リスクに、断固として対処しなければならない。◆In the United States, there is a risk of deeper and more prolonged housing correction. 米国では、住宅の調整局面が深刻化し、長引く恐れもある。◆Investors have begun switching their funds from bank deposits to assets that entail some risks. 投資家が、銀行預金からリスクを伴う資産へと資金の運用を切り替え始めている。◆Investors must generally take higher investment risks in order to achieve higher investment returns. 投資家が一段と高い投資収益を得るには、一般に一段と高い投資リスクを取る必要がある。◆Our plans, which require significant investments,

are at risk because of limited access to capital. 大幅投資が必要な当社の計画は現在、資金調達力にも限界があるため、危機にさらされています。◆The capital markets around the globe are plagued by counterparty risks in the aftermath of the collapse of U.S. investment bank Lehman Brothers in 2008. 世界全体の資本市場は、2008年の米証券会社[投資銀行]の経営破たんの影響で、カウンターパーティー・リスクに苦しんでいる。◆The eurozone's critical mistake is the eurozone's belittling of the risk of the sovereign debt crisis aggravating the banking crisis and vice versa. ユーロ圏の重大な誤りは、国家の財政危機と銀行の危機[経営危機]が相互に増幅し合う危険性を、ユーロ圏が軽視したことにある。◆The Japanese economy faces a growing downside risk due to concerns about the future of the U.S. and European economies. 日本経済は、欧米経済の先行き懸念から、景気の下振れリスクが高まっている。◆The Tokyo metropolitan government has decided to deposit more than ￥100 billion in public funds in Citibank, a U.S. bank, to diversify risks. 東京都は、1,000億円を上回る公金を米国の銀行「シティバンク」に預けて、リスクを分散する方針を固めた。◆The U.S. 10 leading banks need a combined capital buffer of 74.6 billion against the risk of a deeper recession and higher unemployment over the next two years. 米主要金融機関の10社は、今後2年の景気悪化リスクと失業増大に備えて、10社合計で746億ドルの資本増強を求められている。◆With the rating of JGBs being low, internationalizing them may increase the risk that their yield will fluctuate. 日本の国債の格付けが低いので、日本国債の国際化は国債の金利変動リスクを高める可能性がある。

risk-adjusted (形)リスク調整後の,リスク調整済みの
  risk-adjusted analysis　リスク調整分析
  risk-adjusted balance　リスク調整済み資産, 調整済みリスク資産の金額
  risk-adjusted capital　リスク調整済み資本, リスク調整後の自己資本
  risk-adjusted capital and reserves　リスク調整後の自己資本・準備金比率
  risk-adjusted capital ratio　リスク調整資本比率
  risk-adjusted expected return　リスク調整済み期待リターン
  risk-adjusted leverage　リスク調整後の負債比率
  risk-adjusted present value　リスク調整後の現在価値
  risk-adjusted return　リスク調整後収益

risk-adjusted assets　リスク調整後資産
  ◆The Financial Stability Board will impose a progressive extra capital charge of 1 percent to 2.5 percent on risk-adjusted assets held by G-SIFIs. G20(主要20か国・地域)の金融当局で構成する金融安定化理事会(FSB)は、国際金融システムにとって重要な金融機関(G-SIFIs)が保有するリスク調整後資産に、1～2.5%の資本[自己資本]の上積みを段階的に課すことになった。

risk appetite　リスク選好, リスク選好度[リスク選好の度合い], リスクを積極的に取る意欲[傾向], リスクを取って投資するという意欲, リスク許容度[許容量] (⇒appetite)
  ◆Global financial markets saw a tentative pickup in risk appetite. 世界の金融市場で、一時的にリスク選好の回復が見られた。

risk arbitrage　リスク裁定取引, リスクを伴った裁定取引, リスク・アービトラージ(企業買収に伴う株価の動きを予想して、一般に株価が上昇する買収対象会社の株式を買い、一般に株価が下落する買収会社の株式を売る値ざや稼ぎの裁定取引)
  risk arbitrage trade　リスク裁定取引

risk assessment　リスク評価, リスク査定
  ◆In infrastructure projects, risk assessment is difficult due to their large scale. インフラ事業では、規模が大きいためにリスク評価が難しい。

risk asset　リスク資産, 危険資産, リスク・アセット
  banks' risk assets including loans and shares　銀行の貸出金や株式などのリスク資産
  reduce one's risk assets by securitizing one's credit　貸出債権の証券化でリスク資産を圧縮する
  risk asset ratio　危険資産比率
  ◆Major banks are intensifying their efforts to reduce their risk assets by securitizing and selling their credit to prevent their capital adequacy ratio, an index that shows their business soundness, from declining. 大手各行は現在、経営の健全性を示す指標である自己資本比率の低下を防ぐため、貸出債権の証券化や転売などでリスク資産[リスク・アセット]の圧縮策を加速させている。◆The combined balance of the 12 banks' risk assets, including loans and shares, dropped to ￥298.68 trillion, a decline of ￥25.64 trillion from March 31 this year. 大手12行の貸出金や株式などのリスク資産残高の総額は、今年3月31日より25兆6,400億円減って、298兆6,800億円に減少した。

risk averse　リスク回避, リスク回避型, リスク回避型投資
  risk-averse investor　リスク回避型投資家, リスクに慎重な投資家, リスクに対して慎重な投資家, リスクを嫌う投資家

risk exposure　リスク・エクスポージャー
  ◆The increased ownership will raise the bank's risk exposure to the company, whose business environment is severe. 持ち株比率の引上げで、企業環境(経営環境)が厳しい同社に対する同行のリスク・エクスポージャーは今後増大するものと思われる。

risk factor　危険要因, リスク要因, リスク・ファクター
  ◆The Bank of Japan pointed to risk factors, including unstable global financial markets and the economic slowdown in the United States, Japan's main export market. 日本銀行は、世界の不安定な金融市場や日本の主要輸出市場である米国の景気減速などのリスク要因も指摘した。

risk-free [riskfree]　(形)リスクのない, 危険のない, 無リスクの, 安全な, 元本保証の, リスク・フリー (=riskless)
  risk-free asset　安全資産, 無リスク資産
  risk-free borrowing　無リスク借入れ
  risk-free government debt　無リスク国債
  risk-free lending　無リスク貸付け
  risk-free rate (of interest)　無リスク金利, リスク・フリーの金利 (=risk-free interest rate)
  risk-free security　無リスク証券
  ◆Sovereign bonds are considered in general to be risk-free and highly liquid. 国債は、一般に安全で現金化しやすいと考えられている。

risk judgment　リスク判断
  ◆The practical implementation of trade insurance, including risk judgment, must be enhanced to encourage investment by private companies and accelerate the export of infrastructure technology. 民間企業の投資を促し、インフラ技術の輸出を加速するには、リスク判断も含めて、貿易保険の実務能力を高める必要がある。

risk management　リスク管理
  ◆An error in risk management may cause widespread economic havoc. リスク管理のミスは、広範で大きな経済損失につながる可能性がある。

risk neutral　(名)リスク中立者　(形)リスク中立的 (risk-neutral), リスク中立型の
  risk-neutral attitude　リスク中立的態度
  risk-neutral investor　リスク中立型の投資家
  risk-neutral pricing　リスク中立値付け

risk of a deeper recession　景気悪化リスク
◆The U.S. 10 leading banks need a combined capital buffer of 74.6 billion against the risk of a deeper recession and higher unemployment over the next two years. 米主要金融機関の10社は、今後2年の景気悪化リスクと失業増大に備えて、10社合計で746億ドルの資本増強を求められている。

risk of bankruptcy[failure]　倒産のリスク, 倒産危機, 経営破たん危機
◆S&P's downgrades do not reflect an increase in Ford's risk of bankruptcy. スタンダード＆プアーズの格下げは、米フォードの倒産リスクの増大を反映していない。◆The TSE typically only delists companies at risk of bankruptcy. 東証が上場廃止するのは、一般に経営破たん危機にある企業に限られる。

risk of volatile capital flows　資本移動の変動リスク
◆Asia faces the risk of volatile capital flows as its growth outpaces the rest of the world. アジアの成長が他国を上回っているため、アジアは資本移動の変動リスクに直面している。

risk to foreign exchange movements　為替相場の変動リスク
◆Management believes that these forward contracts should not subject the Company to undue risk to foreign exchange movements. これらの先物取引契約で当社が過大な為替相場の変動リスクを負うことはない、と経営陣は考えております。

risk transfer　リスク移転
　alternative risk transfer　代替リスク移転
　credit risk transfer　信用リスク移転, CRT

riskiness　(名)危険性, 危険度, リスク

riskless　(形)危険のない, 安全な, 無リスクの (=risk-free, riskfree)
　riskless asset　安全資産, 無リスク資産
　riskless investment　無リスク投資
　riskless security　無リスク証券
　riskless transaction　安全取引

risky　(形)危険な, 危険を伴う, 危険性の高い, リスクの高い, リスクの大きい, 高リスクの, 冒険的な, 一か八かの
　riskier borrowers　リスクの高い融資先
　risky asset　危険資産, 高リスク資産, リスクの高い資産
　risky business　危険な仕事, 一か八かの商売
　risky investment　危険な投資, リスクの大きい[高い]投資, 高リスク投資
　risky operations　リスクの高い業務
　risky shift phenomenon　冒険的転換現象
◆Mizuho's first-half profit fell 17 percent as credit costs increased and on losses related to investments in U.S. home loans to riskier borrowers. みずほの上半期利益は、与信コストの増加とリスクの高い融資先への米国の住宅ローン投資に関連する損失で、17%減少した。◆The Bank of Japan purchased riskier assets such as exchange-traded funds and real estate investment trusts in mid-December 2010. 日銀は、2010年12月半ばから、上場投資信託や不動産投資信託(リート)などの高リスク資産を買い入れた。

risky asset　リスク資産, 高リスク資産, リスクの高い資産
◆A £5.9 billion ($11.4 billion) write-down on risky assets sent Royal Bank of Scotland to a first-half loss of £691 million ($1.35 billion). 高リスク資産の評価損として59億ポンド(114億ドル)を計上したため、英銀大手のロイヤルバンク・オブ・スコットランドの上半期(1-6月期)決算は、6億9,100万ポンド(13億5,000万ドル)の赤字になった。◆Shareholdings sold to the stock-purchasing organization must be recorded as risky assets on the banks' books until the organization completes the sale of the shares and then finally dissolves. 株式取得機構に売却した持ち株は、機構が買い取った株を(市場などで)処分して最終的に機構が解散するまで、銀行の会計帳簿上はリスク資産として計上しなければならない。

risky investments　高リスク[リスクの高い]投資, リスクの高い投資商品[金融商品], 高リスク証券, リスクの高い有価証券
◆Goldman Sachs Group Inc. is said to have marketed risky investments that bet on the housing market's growth just before the mortgage meltdown. ゴールドマン・サックスは、住宅ローン市場の崩壊直前に、住宅市場の成長を見越した[予想した]高リスクの金融商品[投資商品]を販売したとされる。◆In the lawsuits against big banks over the sales of risky investments, the U.S. government wants to be compensated for lost principal and interest payments. 高リスク証券の販売をめぐっての大手金融機関に対する訴訟で、米政府は、元本と利払い分の損失補償を求めている。◆The Federal Housing Finance Agency sued 17 financial firms over risky investments. 米連邦住宅金融局(FHFA)が、高リスク証券[高リスクの金融商品]を販売したとして大手金融機関17社を提訴した。◆U.S. regulator sued 17 big banks for selling risky investments. 米規制当局が、高リスクの金融商品[高リスク証券]を販売したとして大手金融機関17社を提訴した。

risky loans　リスクの高い融資, 高リスク融資
◆The tasks of safety management specialists in the field of financial services are essentially to whistle-blow and stop extending risky loans. 金融サービス分野での安全管理専門家の仕事は、基本的に高リスク融資に待ったをかけてそれを止めさせることだ。

risky mortgage　リスクの高い住宅ローン, 高リスクの住宅ローン
◆The bank made substantial profits from the resale of the risky mortgages. 同行は、リスクの高い住宅ローンの再販により莫大な利益を上げていた。

RMB　人民幣, 中国の人民元　(⇒renminbi)
◆RMB is another name for the Chinese yuan. 人民幣は、中国の人民元の別称だ。

RMB Exchange Rate Regime　人民元為替相場の枠組み

ROA[RoA]　総資産利益率, 総資本利益率, 資産収益率(当期利益を総資本で割った比率)
　an ROA that exceeds a company's cost of capital　会社の資本コストを上回るROA
　determine ROA　ROAを見極める
　falling ROA　ROAの低下, 低落傾向のROA
　have[show] a low ROA　ROAが低い
　pretax ROA　税引き前ROE, 対総資産税引き前利益率
　ROA-enhancing effect of the buyback　ROAを高める自社株買いの効果
◆ROA (return on assets) is obtained by dividing net income (minus preferred stock dividends) by average total assets. 総資産利益率(ROA)は、純利益(優先株式配当金控除後)を平均総資産価額で割って[除して]求められる。

road show　投資家説明会, 販売説明会, 巡回説明会, ロードショー　(⇒roadshow)

roadblock　(名)障害, 障害物, (路上に設ける)バリケード
◆U.S. and European financial institutions are hitting roadblocks because of the ongoing global financial turmoil. 欧米金融機関は、世界的な金融市場の混乱で、つまずいている。

roadshow　(動)投資家説明会を行う, 投資家向け説明会を行う, 販売説明会を行う
◆The firm will roadshow for the bond issue in Japan. 同社は、日本での債券発行[社債発行]の投資家説明会を行う。

roadshow　(名)投資家説明会, 投資家向け説明会, 募集説明会, 販売説明会, 巡回説明会, 巡回キャンペーン, ロードショー　(=road show: 証券発行会社の経営者と引受業者の担当者が、機関投資家や有力な個人投資家(アナリストやファンド・マネージャーなど)を対象にして行う証券購入のメリットに関する説明会。一般に、発行

会社の財務状況や将来の収益見通しなどを説明する。⇒ investor relations, IR）

roar （動）活況を呈する, 活況にわく, 急伸する, 急騰する, うなる
roar ahead　急伸する
roar up　急騰する
◆The Tokyo stock market has recently been roaring, with record heavy trading seen. 東京株式市場が、記録的な大商いを続けて、活況を呈している。

roaring （形）活発な, 活気がある, 活況の, 突然の活況にわく, 大繁盛の, 景気がよい, 騒々しい, 大荒れの
do [drive] a roaring business [trade]　商売が大繁盛する, 商売が繁盛する
roaring twenties　狂騒の1920年代
◆The Tokyo stock market has recently been roaring, with record heavy trading seen. 東京株式市場が、記録的な大商いを続けて、活況を呈している。

rock （動）激しく揺(ゆ)する, 揺さぶる, 動揺させる, 動転させる, 振り動かす, 振動させる
be rocked by a scandal　不祥事に揺れる
rock the boat　計画を揺さぶる, 問題を起こす
rock the financial system　金融システムを揺さぶる
◆The debt crisis in the eurozone began rocking the global economy. ユーロ圏の債務危機で、世界景気が揺らいできた。
◆The instability of life insurance firms and the lowered earning power of banks with massive bad loans have become the two major factors rocking the financial system. 生保各社の経営基盤の不安定と、巨額の不良債権に苦しむ銀行の収益力低下が、金融システムを揺るがしている二大要因になっている。◆The Internet, which can transmit rumors across the country instantaneously, has rocked the financial system. 一瞬のうちにデマを全国に広げることができるインターネットは、金融システムを揺さぶっている。◆The news of a rise in the subprime defaults rocked the U.S. financial community. サブプライムの不払い増加のニュースに、米金融業界は動揺した。

rock bottom　最低レベル, どん底, 大底, 大底圏
◆The national economy did manage to rise slightly above rock bottom. 日本経済は、大底圏からかろうじて何とか浮かび上がった。

rock-bottom （形）どん底の, 最低の, 奥底の
rock-bottom airfare　超割安運賃
　（=ultralow fare）
rock-bottom price　底値
◆Low cost carriers（LCCs）offer rock-bottom airfares by slashing operating costs. 格安航空会社（LCC）は、運航費用を削減して超割安運賃を実現している。

rock-bottom interest rate　超低金利
　（=extremely low interest rate）
◆Thanks to longstanding rock-bottom interest rates, insurers are plagued by ever-widening negative spreads. 超低金利の長期化で、保険業者は逆ざやの拡大に悩まされている。

ROE　株主資本利益率, 自己資本利益率, 持ち分資本利益率, 株式投資収益率　（return on equity, return on owners' equityの略。株主資本利益率（自己資本利益率）＝純利益（net income）÷純資産（owners' [shareholders', stockholders] equity）。⇒return on equity）
give an artificial boost to ROE　ROEを作為的に押し上げる
have [show] a high ROE　ROEが高い
have an ROE of 20 percent　〜のROEは20%である
improve a company's ROE　会社のROEを改善する
maximize ROE　ROEを最大化する
normal ROE　標準株主資本利益率
superior ROE　抜群のROE, ROEが飛びぬけて高いこと
◆Return on equity（ROE）is a key gauge of a company's stock investment efficiency. 株主資本利益率（ROE）は、企業の株式投資効率を示す重要な経営指標だ。◆The stock price disparity between Toyota and Honda is considered primarily due to the two companies' return on equity（ROE）ratios, a key gauge of their stock investment efficiency. トヨタとホンダの株価格差は、主に両社の株式投資効率（資本効率）を示す株主資本利益率（ROE）によるものだ。

rogue trader　不良トレーダー, 不良株式ディーラー

ROI　投下資本利益率, 使用資本利益率, 投資利益率, 資本利益率　（⇒return on investment）

roil （動）かき乱す, 混乱させる, いらだたせる, 怒らせる
◆The rejection of the financial bailout bill by the U.S. House of Representatives roiled the financial markets across the world. 米下院による金融救済法案（金融安定化法案）の否決は、世界の金融市場を大混乱させた。

role （名）役, 役割, 任務, 立場
play a key [leading, major] role in　〜で重要な役割を果たす, 〜で主要な役割を果たす
play a leading role　けん引役を果たす, 主役を演じる, 指導的な役割を果たす
the reversal of roles　立場の逆転, 役割の逆転
◆AMRO, as the surveillance unit of CMIM, plays an important role to monitor and analyze regional economies. AMROは、(参加国が通貨急落といった危機に直面した際に外貨を融通し合う)多国間通貨交換[スワップ]協定（CMIM）の監視機関として、域内経済を監視し分析する重要な役割を担っている。
◆Exports played a leading role in bolstering the economy in the initial phase of its recovery. 景気回復の初期の段階で、輸出が景気浮揚の牽引役を果たした。◆The dollar's role as the major reserve currency is important to global trade. 主要準備通貨としてのドルの役割は、世界の貿易には重要である。◆The role of the G-7 nations is being handed down to the framework of the Group of 20 nations. 先進7か国の役割は、G20の枠組みにバトンタッチされつつある。

roll （動）転(ころ)がす, 転がる, ロールオーバーする
　（roll over）（名）札束, 回転, 名簿, 出席簿
a roll of dimes　10セント貨1本
a roll of notes　札束
be rolling in it　すごい金持ちである
dollar roll market　ダラー・ロール市場
roll back　低水準に戻す, 巻き返す, (価格などを)下げる, 撤退させる
roll on an overnight basis　翌日物でロールオーバーする
roll outstanding CP　満期が来たCPをロールオーバーする
roll up　金がたまる, 金をためる

roll out　大量生産する, 量産する, 生産する, 発表する, 公表する, 初公開する, 発売する, サービスの提供を開始する, 新規に展開する
roll out an ambitious works program　野心的な労働政策を発表する
roll out investment strategies that decrease volatility　リスクを引き下げる運用戦略を展開する
◆A day after declaring default on the national debt, Argentina's new president rolled out an ambitious works program. 国債の債務不履行（デフォルト）を宣言した翌日、アルゼンチンの新大統領は、野心的な労働政策を発表した。◆The company is rolling out investment strategies that decrease volatility. 同社は、リスクを引き下げる運用戦略を展開している。

roll over　繰り越す, 借り換える, 乗り換える, 書き換える, (投資した資金を)再投資する, ロールオーバーする
　（=carry over）
roll over a debt　借金を借り換える, 債務を借り換える
roll over the CP　CPをロールオーバーする

ROLL

roll over the existing debt at lower rates　既存の債務を低利で借り換える
roll over the (futures) contracts at maturity　為替予約をロールオーバーする
roll over to successive fiscal years　次年度以降へ繰り越す
◆Budgets that can be rolled over to successive fiscal years, or whose purposes can be altered from year to year, will be mainly used to promote research and development activities as well as projects to improve infrastructure.　翌年度以降への繰越しや年度ごとに使いみちを変更することができる複数年予算は、主に研究開発事業や基盤整備事業の促進に使われる。

rollback　(名)(物価、賃金などの)以前の水準への引下げ、人員の削減
rollback policy　巻き返し政策
rolled-back coupon [interest]　再投資式利札，再投資式利息，ロールドアップ・クーポン
roller　(名)転(ころ)がる人[物]，ローラー
　bank roller　資金提供者
　enjoy a roller-coaster ride　(価格などの)乱高下を満喫する
　roller-coaster swap　ローラーコースター・スワップ
rolling　(名)回転、進行、移行、ローリング　(形)転がる、回転する、回転式の、継続型の
　over the past 20 years on a rolling 5 year periods　5年サイクルでの過去20年
　rolling budget　継続型予算，ローリング予算
　rolling forward　前倒し
　rolling launch　段階的製品市場導入
　rolling plan　回転計画，ローリング・プラン
　rolling settlement　ローリング決済
　rolling spot contracts　ローリング・スポット契約，ローリング・スポット先物
　rolling spot currency contracts　ローリング・スポット通貨先物
　rolling spot futures　ローリング・スポット先物
　rolling stone　定職のない人，住所不定者
　rolling yield　ローリング・イールド(債券の一定期間保有後の売却で得られる購入時より高い利回り)
rolling-over　(名)回転，転(ころ)がし，融資借換え，融資借換え政策
　credit rolling-over　信用の回転
　rolling-over of a loan　転がし融資
rollout　(名)初公開，新製品の紹介[発売]，新サービスの提供開始，通信網の運用開始
　accelerate the rollout of a new service　新サービスの提供開始を急ぐ
　delay the rollout of the new product　新製品の発売を延期する
　product rollout　製品の販売開始
　rollout program　新製品の発売計画，新規出店計画
　scale back the rollout of　～の新規展開の規模を縮小する
　service rollout　サービスの提供開始
　speed up the rollout of　～の発売を繰り上げる，～の新規展開の時期を繰り上げる
rollover　(名)借換え、(資金の)借りつなぎ、資金の回転調達、転(ころ)がし、債務の返済期間延長、繰越し、繰延べ、投資資金の再投資、旧証券の満期時に新規証券を発行して旧証券と交換する借換え方法、書換え、更新、契約更新、ロールオーバー
　debt rollover　債務返済繰延べ
　lease rollover　リース契約更新，賃貸契約更新
　new deposits versus rollovers　新規預け入れ額と満期時継続比率

rollover CD　満期再投資CD (=roly-poly CD)
rollover credit　銀行貸出期限の再更新，ロールオーバー・クレジット
rollover lending　ころがし貸付け
rollover loan　借換え融資
rollover mortgage　借換え抵当，不動産担保転がし融資
rollover of an existing credit　借換え
rollover of liabilities　負債の借換え
rollover relief　資産借換え免除，更新投資課税繰延べ、繰延べ特例
◆Argentina clinched a debt rollover deal with the IMF after a year of tortuous negotiations.　アルゼンチンは、1年にわたる難交渉の末、国際通貨基金(IMF)との債務返済繰延べ取引をまとめた。
rollup [roll-up]　(名)ロールアップ(投資銀行の助言を受けながら投資家が複数企業を一括取得し、それをひとまとめにして上場まで持っていくこと)
roly-poly CD　ローリーポーリーCD，満期再投資CD (=rollover CD)
RONA　純資産利益率(return on net assetsの略)
Roosa bond　ローザ・ボンド(米国が国際収支の赤字対策として外国の中央銀行に発行した相手国通貨建ての非市場性債券)
root-and-branch reform　抜本改革
◆Pension system needs root-and-branch reform.　年金制度は、抜本改革が必要。
rope　(名)縄，コツ，やり方，秘訣，絞首刑，ロープ
　a rope of sand　頼りにならないもの
　be at [come to, run to] the end of one's rope　万事休す、力尽きる、百計尽きる、進退きわまる、(能力、体力などの)限界にある
　be on the ropes　ロープに逃れる、窮地に陥っている、追い詰められている、ダウン寸前だ、経営が悪化している
　know the ropes　コツを知っている
　learn the ropes　コツを覚える
　put A on the ropes　Aを窮地に追い込む、Aを絶望的な状態に追いやる、Aをロープに追い詰める
◆The bank decided to continue extending loans to the company despite its executives knowing the company was on the ropes.　この会社の経営が悪化しているのを経営陣が知りながら、同行は同社への融資継続を決めた。◆The rise of the yen beyond the level of the exchange rate assumed by many exporters has put them on the ropes.　多くの輸出業者が想定した為替レートの水準を上回る円高が輸出業者を窮地に追い込んでいる。
round　(名)一連の協議、会議、交渉、～回目、回診、巡回、配達、集配、一連の活動、ラウンド (⇒new round of multilateral trade negotiations, qualify)
　a fifth round of preliminary talks　第五回予備会談
　a key round of negotiations　カギとなる交渉
　a new international round　新国際ラウンド
　a new round　新ラウンド
　a round of talks　一連の会談
　a trade round　貿易交渉
　the first round of tenders　第一次入札
　the first round of voting　1回目の投票
　the new round of multinational trade negotiations　新多角的貿易交渉、新ラウンド
　the new round of refinancing　借換えブームの再燃
　the new round of WTO talks　新ラウンド(新多角的貿易交渉)
　the next round of pension program reforms　次期年金改革
　the second round　第二弾、決選投票

this round of　今回の〜
◆Financial markets worldwide are focused on whether the U.S. FRB embarks on a third round of its quantitative easing policy, or QE3.　世界の金融市場は、米連邦準備制度理事会(FRB)が量的緩和策の第三弾(QE3)に踏み切るかどうかに注目している。

[解説]ラウンド とは：日本など、世界貿易機関(WTO)に加盟する国々が行う貿易・投資の自由化に関する話し合い。二国間交渉でなく、多くの国が参加して関税引下げなど世界の新しい貿易ルールを一括して取り決めるのが特徴。

rout　(名)総崩れ, 大敗北, 完敗, 敗走, 不法集会, 暴動, 暴徒, やじうま
  drive the rout in the financial market　金融市場の総崩れを招く
  put to rout　総崩れにさせる
  ◆Worries over the spreading of the eurozone debt crisis and the U.S.'s slipping into recession have driven the rout in financial markets.　ユーロ圏の財政危機の拡大と米国の景気後退入りへの懸念で、金融市場は総崩れになった。

RSI　域内決済機関(Regional Settlement Intermediaryの略)

Rubicon　ルビコン川
  cross [pass] the Rubicon　背水の陣を敷く, 重大な決意をする, 断固たる手段をとる,(後退を許されない)思い切った処置をとる
  psychological Rubicon　心理的な壁
  ◆The yen's value may continue to surge now that the yen-dollar rate has broken ¥110, which market players viewed as a psychological Rubicon.　市場関係者が心理的な"壁"と見ていた円の対ドル相場が1ドル＝110円を切ったことで、さらに円高が進むかもしれない。

ruble [rouble]　ルーブル(ロシアの通貨単位。1ルーブル＝100カペイカ(kopecks))
  ruble crisis　ルーブル暴落
  ruble-denominated loans　ルーブル建てローン, ルーブル建て融資
  ruble stabilization fund　ルーブル安定化基金
    (=stabilization fund for the ruble)
  ◆Sberbank of Russia will offer a variety of services, such as ruble-denominated loans to Mizuho Corporate Bank's clients when they do business in Russia.　ロシア最大手行のズベルバンクは、みずほコーポレート銀行の顧客がロシアで事業を行う際にルーブル建て融資を行うなどの各種サービスを提供することになった。

rule　(名)規則, 規定, 法, 法規, 原則, 慣例, 通例, 支配, 裁判所の裁定・命令, 基準, 規準, ルール　(⇒accounting rule, safe harbor rule, shareholding)
  capital adequacy rule　自己資本規制, 自己資本比率規制
  client money rules　顧客資金ルール, 顧客資金規則
  listing rules　上場基準, 上場要件
  net capital rule　自己資本規制比率
  one-share/one-vote rule　1株＝1議決権ルール
  Rule 415 shelf registration　SEC規則415に基づく一括登録
  rules of fair practice　公正慣行ルール, RFP, 全米証券業協会(National Association of Securities Dealers)の業界ルール
  the FSA's 30 percent rule　金融庁の3割ルール
  ◆According to the Financial Stability Board, 28 banks viewed as global systemically important financial institutions (G-SIFIs) will be subject to a new global rule requiring them to hold extra capital to prevent future financial crises.　金融安定化理事会(FSB)によると、金融システム上重要な国際金融機関(G-SIFIs)と考えられる世界の28行が、金融危機の再発を防止するため、資本の上積みを求める新国際基準[新国際金融規制]の対象になる。◆Changes in stock exchange listing rules for start-up companies also have prompted this year's rush of IPOs.　新興企業に対する証券取引所の上場基準の変更も、今年の上場(新規株式公開)ラッシュにつながっている。◆The repurchasing method, which has customers buy highly negotiable cash vouchers, violates the industry rule.　顧客に換金性の高い金券類を購入させる買取り方式は、業界の規約に違反する。◆Twenty-eight banks of the world will face capital surcharges of 1 percent to 2.5 percent by the application of international rules to rein in too-big-to-fail lenders.　大きすぎて破たんさせられない銀行[金融機関]を規制する国際基準が適用されると、世界の28行が、1〜2.5%の資本[自己資本]上積みの対象となる。

rule of asset impairment accounting　減損会計基準
  ◆The rule of asset impairment accounting requires companies to post valuation losses on fixed assets whose market value has fallen sharply from their book value.　減損会計基準は、固定資産の時価が簿価から大幅に下落した場合の固定資産の評価損の計上を、企業に義務付けている。

rules for international banking　国際銀行業務の基準
  ◆The Financial Stability Board is cooperating with the Basel Committee on Banking Supervision, a body that sets rules for international banking.　金融安定化理事会(FSB)は、国際銀行業務の基準を制定する機関のバーゼル銀行監督委員会と連携している。

Rules of Fair Practice　公正慣習規則, 公正慣行ルール, 全米証券業協会の業界規則

ruling　(形)支配的な, 支配[統治]している, 政権を担当する, 与党の, 第一党の, 現行の, 現在の, 目下の, 一般に行われている, 有力な, 優勢な, 主な
  ruling factors　主な諸要因
  ruling level of interest rates　現在の金利水準
  ruling opinion　支配的な意見
  the ruling and opposition camps [blocs]　与党・野党陣営, 与党と野党の陣営, 与党
  the ruling price　時価, 通り相場

rumor [rumour]　(名)噂(うわさ), 評判, 風聞(ふうぶん), 風説, デマ
  become slave to the rumor　噂に振り回される展開となる
  harmful rumors　風評被害
  market rumor　市場の噂
  rate hike rumor　利上げ観測
  spreading rumors　風説の流布
  transmit rumors across the country　デマを全国に広げる
  ◆Financial authorities should stiffen the penalties for illegal transactions to protect the financial system from rumors and speculative investment.　金融当局は違法取引(違法行為)に対する罰則を強化して、金融システムを風評や投機[投機的投資]から守らなければならない。◆Japan's regulations on short selling and market manipulation by spreading rumors are extremely weak in comparison with those of the United States.　日本の空売りに関する規制や風説の流布などによる市場操作についての規制は、米国に比べて極めて弱い。◆Rumors were swirling among market players that Merrill Lynch would be the next to go under.　市場関係者の間では、「次に破たんするのはメリルリンチ」という噂が渦巻いていた。◆The Internet, which can transmit rumors across the country instantaneously, has rocked the financial system.　一瞬のうちにデマを全国に広げることができるインターネットは、金融システムを揺さぶっている。

rumortrage　(名)ルーマートラージ(rumorとarbitrageの合成語。企業買収の噂(うわさ)で株式を売買すること)

run　(動)経営する, 指揮する, 管理する, 運用する, 運営

する, 提供する, 操作する, 動かす, 実行する, 行う, 掲載する, 載せる （自動）〜の状態になる, 契約などが有効である, 動く, 作動する, 稼働する, 進行する, 進む, 行われる, 上演される
- a government-run enterprise 国営企業

run a cartel カルテルを結ぶ

run a credit check 信用調査をする

run a massive [huge] surplus 巨額の黒字になる, 大幅な黒字になる

run a primary deficit 財政の基礎収支が赤字になる

run a profit for five consecutive business terms 5期連続黒字になる, 5期連続黒字を出す

run a trade deficit 貿易赤字になる, 貿易赤字を出す

run aground 暗礁に乗り上げる

run an exchange risk 為替リスクを負う

run an investment trust fund 投資信託を運用する

run counter 逆行する

run into the red [red figures] 赤字になる, 赤字に転落する

run lean 無駄をなくす

run option books オプションを扱う

run the bank 銀行を経営する

run the books ブック・ランナーを務める, ブック・ランナーになる

run up a bill 勘定をためる

the well runs dry 井戸が枯れる, 資金が底をつく

◆Banks are running out of surplus funds. 銀行は, 剰余金が底をつきかけている。◆Both banks ran enormous deficits for the business year to March 2011, adding to their financial woes. 両社は, 2011年3月期決算で巨額の赤字になって［赤字に転落して］, 財政体質が悪化した。◆The German government is prohibited from running deficits from 2020 onward under the new law of 2009. ドイツ政府は, 2009年の新法に基づいて, 2020年以降は財政赤字を禁止されている。◆The mutual aid association injected ¥1.5 billion into 24 deficit-ridden hotels run by the association. 同共済組合は, 経営する赤字の24ホテルに15億円を注入［補填］した。◆To help finance the government burden in running the basic pension plan, the Health, Labor and Welfare Ministry calls for ¥10.67 trillion in funds in its budgetary request for fiscal 2012. 基礎年金運営の国庫負担［国の負担］分の費用として, 厚生労働省は, 2012年度予算の概算要求で10兆6,700億円を要求している。

run （名）銀行などに対する取付け, 取付け騒ぎ, 証券価格の急上昇, 盛んな［飛ぶような］売れ行き, 注文殺到, 大量需要, 情勢, 趣（すう）勢, 成り行き, 動向, 流れ, 市場の気配, 気配値 「取付け」は, 経営破たんした銀行などに預金払戻しの請求者が殺到することをいう。⇒deposit cancellation）

a run on the dollar ドル売りの殺到, ドルが一斉に売られること

bank run 銀行取付け, 取付け
(＝a run on a bank; ⇒short-term funds）

broker's run ブローカーの気配値

domino-like run on other banks 他行への連鎖的な取付け騒ぎ

off-the-run issue 周辺銘柄

on-the-run curve 新発債の利回り曲線

on-the-run issue 指標銘柄

run of the market 市場の気配, 市場の成り行き, 市況の情勢

run on a bank 銀行の取付け騒ぎ, 銀行に対する取付け
(＝bank run）

run on cash 取付け

run on the dollar ドルに対する大量需要

◆Fearing a massive run, a bank holiday was declared for Friday. 大規模な取付け騒ぎを恐れて, 金曜日を銀行休日にする宣言がなされた。◆There has been a run on the dollar today. 今日は, ドル売りが殺到した。◆There is a run on banks. 銀行の取付け騒ぎが起きている。

run a profit 黒字を出す, 黒字になる
◆The bank ran a profit for five consecutive business terms starting with the year to March 2005. 同行は, 2005年3月期［3月期決算］から5期連続で黒字を出した。

run an investment trust fund 投資信託を運用する
◆Daiwa Asset Management will run an investment trust fund tracking the Nikkei 225 share average. 大和アセット・マネジメントは, 日経平均株価（225種）に連動する投資信託を運用する。

run in the red 赤字経営する, 赤字運営する
(＝operate in the red）
◆The government has closed hotels that run in the red for two consecutive years and have negative prospects for the following year. 政府は, 2年連続赤字経営で, 3年目も見通しが立たないホテルを閉鎖してきた。

runaway （形）逃走した, 家出した, 駆け落ちの, 制御しきれない, 手に負えない, うなぎ上りの, 急騰する, けた外れの, 天井知らずの, 止めどない, 抑え［制御］の利かない, 野放しの, 楽勝の, 一方的な, 楽に得られた （名）逃亡者, 脱走者, 家出人, 逃走, 駆け落ち, 楽勝, 一方的な勝利

runaway deficits 垂れ流しの赤字

runaway economy 過熱した景気

runaway inflation 天井知らずのインフレ, うなぎ上りのインフレ, 止めどないインフレ, 急上昇インフレ, 悪性インフレ, 狂乱インフレ

runaway wage-price inflation 賃金・物価の急騰［天井知らずのインフレ］

◆The company has put a brake on its runaway deficits and collected a profit. 同社は垂れ流しの赤字を食い止め, 黒字を確保した。

runup [run-up] （名）助走, 準備期間, （選挙などの）前哨（ぜんしょう）戦, （株価などの）高騰, 急騰

in the runup to 〜の準備期間に, 〜に向けて, 〜に向けての準備段階に

the runup in oil prices 原油価格の高騰, 原油価格の上昇

the runup in the stock market 株式相場の上昇

◆China hurriedly established a raft of laws concerning business practices in the runup to joining the World Trade Organization at the end of 2001. 中国は, 2001年末の世界貿易機関（WTO）への加盟に向けて一連の通商関連法の整備を急いだ。◆The run-up in the price of energy and other commodities has had only a modest effect on core inflation. コア・インフレ率に対する原油などの価格高騰の影響は, それほど大きくない。

Russel 2000 index ラッセル2000指数, ラッセル2000種株価指数
◆Russel 2000 index is the benchmark for U.S. small capitalization stocks. ラッセル2000株価指数［指数］は, 米国の小型株の指標である。◆The Russel 2000 index of smaller companies fell 3.93, or 1 percent, to 389.02. 中小企業の株価指数のラッセル2000指数は, 3.93ドル下落して389.02ドルとなった。

S

S&L 米貯蓄貸付け組合, 貯蓄金融機関（savings and loan associationの略）

S&P （米格付け会社の）スタンダード・アンド・プアーズ

S&P 100 S&P100種指数

S&P/Case-Shiller Home price Indices S&Pケース・シラー住宅価格指数

◆Political gridlock in Washington is part of the reason behind the S&P cut in the U.S. long-term credit rating. 米国の政府・議会の政治的行き詰まりが、スタンダード・アンド・プアーズ(S&P)の米長期国債格下げの一因である。◆S&P's downgrades do not reflect an increase in Ford's risk of bankruptcy. スタンダード＆プアーズの格下げは、米フォードの倒産リスクの増大を反映していない。◆The AA minus rating by S&P is the fourth highest in terms of credit quality on a scale of 22. 米格付け会社のスタンダード・アンド・プアーズ(S&P)による「ダブルAマイナス」の格付けは、22段階ある信用度中、上から4番目に当たる。◆The S&P cut in the U.S. long-term credit rating by one notch to AA-plus from AAA resulted from concerns about the nation's budget deficits and climbing debt burden. スタンダード・アンド・プアーズ(S&P)が米国の長期国債格付けを最上級のAAA(トリプルA)からAA(ダブルA)に1段階引き下げた理由は、米国の財政赤字と債務負担の増大に対する懸念だ。◆The United States lost its top-tier AAA credit rating from S&P for the first time. 米国債の格付け[米国の長期国債格付け]が、スタンダード・アンド・プアーズ(S&P)による最上級のAAA(トリプルA)の格付けから史上初めて転落した。

S&Pの主要国の国債格付け (2011年8月15日現在; 自国通貨建て)

英国、ドイツ、フランス	AAA
米国、ベルギー	AA+
スペイン	AA
日本、中国、サウジアラビア	AA−
イタリア、韓国	A+
南アフリカ、ボツワナ	A
メキシコ、タイ	A−

S&P 500 S&P500総合指数, S&P500株価指数, スタンダード＆プアーズ総合500種株価指数 (Standard & Poor's 500の略。ダウ平均(ダウ工業株30種)とともに、米株式市場の動向を反映する標準的な経済指標)
◆Broader stock indicators such as the S&P 500 index and the Nasdaq composite index also dropped in February. 2月は、S&P500株価指数やナスダック総合株価指数などの総合株価指数も、低下[下落]した。◆The S&P 500 index fell 17.74, or 2.4 percent, to 735.09. S&P500株価指数は、735.09ドルで17.74ドル(2.4%)低下[下落]した。

sabotage (動)破壊する, 危害を加える, 妨害する, 台なしにする
◆The Metropolitan Police Department searched the bank's head office on suspicion the bank had sabotaged an audit by the Financial Services Agency. 警視庁は、金融庁の立入り検査を妨害した疑いで、同行の本店を捜索した。

sabotage (名)妨害, 危害, 妨害[破壊]行為, 妨害[破壊]工作, サボタージュ
audit sabotage 検査妨害
◆The FSA ordered the bank to suspend some operations due to serious law violations, including audit sabotage. 金融庁は、同行に対して、検査妨害などの重大な銀行法違反で、一部業務の停止命令を出した。

saddle (動)(仕事や責任を)負わせる, 課する, (馬に)鞍を置く
be saddled with 〜を背負っている, 〜を抱えている, 〜に縛りつけられる, 〜で手いっぱいである
be saddled with an enormous amount of negative yields 巨額の逆ざやを抱えている
be saddled with massive budget deficits 巨額の財政赤字を抱えている
◆All the insurers are now saddled with an enormous amount of negative yields as returns on their investments have plunged due to ultra-low interest rates—a consequence of the bursting of the bubble. 生保各社は現在、バブル崩壊後の超低金利時代で運用利回りが急低下し、巨額の逆ざやを抱えている。◆Greece is saddled with massive budget deficits. ギリシャは、巨額の財政赤字を抱えている。◆The firm went bankrupt saddled with a ¥150 billion debt in April 2007. 同社は、1,500億円の負債を抱えて2007年4月に破産した。

SAFE (中国の)国家外貨管理局 (State Administration of Foreign Exchangeの略)
◆China's SAFE is reviewing its eurozone debt holdings. 中国の国家外貨管理局(SAFE)が、ユーロ圏の国債保有の見直しを進めている。

safe (名)金庫
fire-proof safe 耐火金庫
loaned safe 借り金庫
night deposit safe 夜間金庫
safe-alarm 金庫用自動警報機
safe burglary insurance 金庫盗難保険
safe cracker 金庫破り (=safe-cracker)
◆A former president of a securities company removed investor securities worth about ¥3.2 billion from a safe at the company's Tokyo branch, and went missing. 証券会社の元社長は、投資家の有価証券(顧客から預かっていた有価証券)約32億円分を同社東京支店の金庫から持ち出し、行方不明になっていた。

safe (形)安全な, 危険がない, 危険な目にあわない, 〜しても大丈夫だ, 〜しても差し支えない, 無傷な, 無事な, リスクが少ない, 無難な, 当たり障りのない
a safe bet かならず当たる賭け
safe custody 保護預り
safe custody facilities 保護預り業務
safe investment 安全な投資, 安全投資, 安全な運用先, リスクが少ない投資
safe returns 安全な利回り
◆More investors are pulling money from stock markets and shifting it into safer time deposits. 株式市場から資金を引き揚げ、引き揚げた資金を安定性の高い定期性預金に移し替える投資家が増えている。

safe-deposit box 貸金庫, 保護預り金庫
◆Of these illegal profits, police confiscated the equivalent of about ¥400 million from safe-deposit boxes in Tokyo. この違法収益のうち、警察当局は東京都内の貸金庫から約4億円相当額を没収した。

safe harbor rule 安全条項(規則や法律に抵触しないためのガイドライン), 避難条項, 安全港規則, 安全港ルール, セーフ・ハーバー・ルール(「セーフ・ハーバー・ルール」は、会社が自社株を買い戻すときの規則を定めた米証券取引委員会(SEC)規則10-bの通称)

safe haven 安全な避難所, 安全な投資先, 安全な投資手段, 資金の逃避先, 逃避先
safe haven bonds 安全な投資先の債券
safe haven currency 有事に強い通貨, 安全な通貨
safe-haven quality 質への逃避先, 安全な投資先
seek safe haven in New York ニューヨークに安全な投資先を求める
◆Concerns over the U.S. economic outlook tend to induce yen-buying as a safe haven. 米経済の先行きに対する懸念から、安全な投資手段として円が買われる傾向にある。◆Currency traders worldwide frantically search for a safe haven in volatile times. 世界の為替トレーダーは、変動の激しい時期の安全な投資先を熱狂的に求めている。◆Gold is still becoming the safe haven as people fear recession in the U.S. and the eurozone debt problems. 米国の景気後退やユーロ圏の債務危機問題への懸念から、まだ金が安全な投資先[資金の逃避先]となっている。◆The Fed's policy of quantitative easing foments chaos in foreign exchange markets. 米連邦準備制度理事会(FRB)[米国の中央銀行]の量的緩和政策は、為替相場[為替レート]の変動を招いている。◆The funds that so abun-

dantly seek safe haven in New York today can flow outward tomorrow. 安全な投資先を求めて今日ニューヨークにあふれるほど集まった資金も、明日には外へ流出しかねない。

safeguard （動）保護する, 擁護する, 守る
◆With the United States facing the worst financial crisis in generations, Bush's White House took decisive measures to safeguard the economy. 米国が過去最悪の金融危機に直面して、ブッシュ政権は経済危機を守るために断固たる措置を取った。

safeguard （名）保護, 保全, 保護手段, 予防手段, 安全装置, 緊急輸入制限, 緊急輸入制限措置, セーフガード措置, 保障条項, 保障規約, セーフガード
  a safeguard against hostile takeovers 敵対的買収の防衛策
  a safeguard emergency import control measure 緊急輸入制限（セーフガード）措置
  a safeguard measure to raise tariffs 関税引上げのためのセーフガード措置
  corporate safeguards 企業防衛策

safekeeping 保護預り（顧客の株券などの有価証券を、顧客のために証券会社などが保管する業務）, 保管, 保護
  safekeeping account 保護預り口座
  safekeeping agreement 保護預り契約
  safekeeping charge 保護預り証
  safekeeping deposit 保護預り（=safe custody）
  safekeeping receipt 保護預り証, 預り証
  safekeeping requirements 保護預りに関する義務

safety management 安全管理
◆Japan's financial services sector learned of the importance of safety management through the lost decade. 失われた10年を通じて、日本の金融界は安全管理の重要性を学んだ。

safety net （名）安全網, 安全策, 安全装置, 救済, 救済策, （政府の）社会保障, 安全[安全用]ネット, セーフティ・ネット
  a financial safety net 金融安全網
  a social safety net 社会の安全網
  an employment safety net 雇用の安全網, 雇用のセーフティ・ネット
  establish a comprehensive safety net 万全の安全網づくりをする
  establish a new safety net 新たな安全網を整備する
  eurozone safety net ユーロ圏救済策
  rebuild a safety net 安全網を立て直す
◆European countries are urged to facilitate a safety net for emergencies, including the injection of public funds into deteriorating banks to shore up their capital strength. 欧州は、経営が悪化した銀行[金融機関]に公的資金を注入して資本を増強するなど、非常時に備えた安全網の整備が求められている。◆The government intends to restructure the deposit insurance system as a new financial safety net for protecting settlement systems. 政府は、預金保険制度を、決済システム保護のための新しい金融安全網として再構築する方針だ。◆The government should expedite work to rebuild a safety net to support the Japanese financial system. 政府は、安全網の立て直しを急いで、日本の金融システム支える必要がある。◆The government should quickly establish a new safety net. 政府は、直ちに新たな安全網を整備しなければならない。◆We must expedite efforts to rebuild a safety net to support the financial system. 金融システムを支える安全網の立直し策を急ぐ必要がある。◆With the increase in the number of nonregular workers, the importance of the minimum wage system as a social safety net is growing. 非正規労働者の増加に伴って、社会の安全網としての最低賃金制の重要性は増している。

sag （動）下落する, 低下する, 落ち込む, 低迷する, 鈍化する, 沈下する
  sagging corporate profits 企業利益の落ち込み, 企業利益の低迷
  sagging economy 景気低迷
  sagging export growth 輸出の伸び[伸び率]の鈍化
  sagging profits 利益の落ち込み
◆The Bank of Japan's capital adequacy ratio sagged to 7.33 percent as of March 31, 2004. 日銀の自己資本比率は、2004年3月31日時点で7.33％に低下した。

sagging （形）下落する, 低下する, 落ち込む, 低迷する, 鈍化する
  sagging corporate profits 企業利益の落ち込み, 企業利益の低迷
  sagging economy 景気低迷, 低迷する景気
  sagging export growth 輸出の伸び[伸び率]の鈍化
  sagging profits 利益の落ち込み
◆It is difficult for Japan, the United States and European countries to support their sagging economies by increasing public spending, due to deteriorating financial conditions. 財政の悪化で、日米欧は、財政出動による景気の下支えが難しくなっている。◆Japan, the United States and European countries supported their sagging economies by increasing public spending after the collapse of Lehman Brothers in the autumn of 2008. 2008年秋のリーマン・ブラザーズの経営破たん後、日米欧は、財政出動によって低迷する景気の下支えをした。

SAIF 貯蓄金融機関保険基金 （Savings Association Insurance Fundの略）

Sakura Report さくらリポート（四半期ごとに発表される日銀の地域経済報告書）
◆In the BOJ's Sakura Report on regional economies, the central bank said the economies of seven regions all experienced improvements from three months earlier. 日本銀行の地域経済報告「さくらリポート」で、（全国9地域のうち）7地域すべてで景気が1-3月期に比べて持ち直している[景気が回復している]ことを、日銀が発表した。

salaried （形）給料取りの, 月給取りの, 有給の
  salaried employee [man, worker] サラリーマン, 給料生活者
  salaried income 給与所得
  salaried manager 雇用経営者, 有給管理者
  salaried partner 定額給パートナー
  salaried position [post] 有給職
◆In Japan, if company employees exercise employee stock options and obtain shares, the shares are considered salaried income, which is taxable. 日本では、社員が従業員ストック・オプションの権利を行使して株を取得した場合、その株式は給与所得と見なされ、課税対象になる。

salary income 給与所得
◆Proceeds from exercising stock options are compensation for labor and service rendered and constitute salary income. ストック・オプション（自社株購入権）を行使して得た利益は、職務遂行の対価なので、給与所得に当たる。

salary-loan company サラ金業者

salary payment 給与振込み, 給与支払い
◆Bank transfers of 12 million, 3 million of which will be salary payments, are expected on that day. その日は、給与振込み300万件を含めて1,200万件の銀行決済が予定されている。

sale （名）販売, 売買, 売却, 証券などの発行, セール （⇒ business day, debt waiver, share sale, short sale, transfer名詞）
  credit sale クレジット販売
  equity derivative sales 株式派生商品販売
  funds gained from the sale of shares 株式売却で調達した資金, 株式発行で調達した資金

gain on sale of bonds　社債売却益
offer for sale　売出発行, 間接発行
proceeds from sale　売却額
public sale　公売
sale of bonds　社債発行
sale of securities　証券発行
short sale　空売り, 信用売り
wash sale　仮装売買,（信用取引の）同時売買
　（=washed sale）
◆A federal appeals court in New York approved the sale of Chrysler assets to Fiat. ニューヨークの米連邦控訴裁判所は、クライスラー資産のフィアットへの売却を承認した。◆The consultant manipulated the company's stock price by engaging in certain prohibited practices including wash sales. コンサルタントは、仮装売買（売り注文と買い注文を同時に出す方法）などの不正行為で株価を操作した。◆The U.S. government completed the sale of about 20 percent of its stake in Citigroup. 米政府は、保有するシティグループ株の約20%売却を完了した。◆The U.S. Supreme Court delayed the sale of Chrysler assets to Italy's Fiat. 米連邦最高裁が、クライスラー資産のフィアット（イタリア）への売却を延期した。

sale of bank accounts　銀行口座の売買
◆The identification of bank account holders is required to prevent the sale of bank accounts. 銀行口座の売買を防ぐため、銀行口座名義人の本人確認が義務付けられている。

sale of commercial paper　コマーシャル・ペーパーの発行
◆The difference was funded by increasing notes payable principally through the sale of commercial paper. 資金の不足分は、主にコマーシャル・ペーパーを発行して手形借入金を増やして補てんしました。

sale of outstanding shares　発行済み株式の売却
◆With the TBS's completion of the new share issuance and the sale of outstanding shares, Mainichi Broadcasting is expected to become TBS's fifth-largest shareholder. TBSの新株発行と発行済み株式の売却が完了すると、毎日放送がTBSの5番目の大株主［TBSの第5位の株主］になると見られる。

sale of products　商品の販売
◆The brokerage's main services for individual customers will be asset management advisory services, focusing on the sale of products such as investment trust funds that invest in foreign equities, and money market funds denominated in foreign currencies. 同証券会社は、株式の主な個人顧客向け（売買仲介）業務として、外国株を組み込んだ投資信託や外貨建てMMF（マネー・マーケット・ファンド）などの商品の販売を中心に、資産運用顧問業務を展開する方針だ。

sales　(名)売上, 売上高, 取引高, 販売, 売買, 売却, 商法, セールス　（⇒combined sales, deregulate, financial instrument, group sales, life insurance policyholder, stock sales）
central bank sales　中央銀行の売り介入
sales financing　販売金融　（⇒servicing）
stock sales　株式売却, 株式譲渡
◆Due to the growing strength of the yen, even if exporters' sales grow, their profits will not keep pace. 円高進行で、輸出企業の売上が増えても、利益は伸び悩むようだ。◆In the lawsuits against big banks over the sales of risky investments, the U.S. government wants to be compensated for lost principal and interest payments. 高リスク証券の販売をめぐっての大手金融機関に対する訴訟で、米政府は、元本と利払い分の損失補償を求めている。◆Matsui Securities Co. is the nation's largest online brokerage by sales. 松井証券は、取引高で国内最大手のネット専業証券会社だ。◆The casualty insurer delayed the start of its online insurance sales due to the March 11 earthquake and tsunami. 2011年3月11日の東日本大震災のため、同損保は保険のネット販売の開業を延期した。

sales agent　保険などの営業職員, 保険外交員
◆Traditionally, life insurance policyholders have been required to pay their first premiums directly to sales agents in cash or by bank transfer. これまで生命保険の契約者は、初回保険料を現金で直接、営業職員に支払うか銀行振込みで支払う必要があった。

sales credit　売掛金
◆Asset-backed commercial paper refers to commercial paper whose creditworthiness is guaranteed by sales credit that the corporate issuer has with its debtors. 資産担保CPとは、企業発行体がその債務者に対して保有する売掛金によって信用度が保証されるコマーシャル・ペーパーを指す。

sales network　販売網
◆As a result of the tie-up, Yasuda Life Direct expects to expand its sales network, while Fukoku hopes to diversify its products. 業務提携により、安田ライフダイレクトは販売網の拡大を期待する一方、富国生命は商品の多様化を見込んでいる。

sales of real estate and stock　不動産と株の売却
◆TEPCO eventually hopes to raise about ¥600 billion through the sales of its real estate and stock to cover damages. 損害補償費用として東電は、最終的に保有する不動産と株式の売却で約6,000億円の資金調達を目指している。

sales of shares　株式の売却
◆Through the sales of shares of JR companies and NTT it owned, the central government garnered ¥3 trillion and ¥13 trillion of profits, respectively. 国が保有するJR各社とNTTの株式の売却で、国はそれぞれ3兆円と13兆円の利益を上げた。

sales promotion efforts　販売促進努力, 販促努力, 営業努力
◆Continued cost cuts and sales promotion efforts offset a ¥70 billion loss generated by the yen's appreciation against the dollar. 引き続き行ったコスト削減と営業努力で、円高ドル安で生じた700億円の為替差損は相殺された。

Sallie Mae　奨学金融資金庫, サリー・メイ（米国のStudent Loan Marketing Association（奨学金融資金庫）の通称）

same　(形)同じ, 同一の, 変わらない, 不変の, 単調な, 前述の
same day［same-day］funds　当日資金, 同日物資金, すぐ引き出して使える資金
same day［same-day］settlement　同日決済, 即日決済
same store sales　既存店ベースの売上高, 既存店ベースの売上, 既存店売上高
◆The exchange rate was the same at the time of deposit and withdrawal in a foreign currency deposit. 外貨預金で、為替相場は預け入れ時と解約時で同じだった。◆When yields on whole life insurance products decline, policyholders must pay higher premiums to secure the same amount of total insurance benefits. 終身保険商品の利回りが下がった場合、加入者［保険契約者］がそれ以前と同額の総保険料を受け取るには、より高い保険料を払わなければならない。

same period last year　前年同期
◆Operating expenses in the third quarter of 2009 increase by $90 million compared with the same period last year. 当四半期［2009年第3四半期］の営業費用は、前年同期比で9,000万ドル増加しました。

samurai［Samurai］bond　円建て外債, 円建て債, サムライ債, サムライ・ボンド（海外の企業や政府が、日本国内で円建てで発行する債券の通称）

sanctions　(名)制裁, 制裁措置
be frozen under U.S. financial sanctions　米国の金融制裁を受けて凍結される
financial sanctions　金融制裁
impose economic sanctions against　〜に対して経済制裁を課す, 〜に対して経済制裁に踏み切る, 〜に対して経

済措置を取る
lift economic sanctions against　～に対する経済制裁を解除する
trade sanctions　貿易制裁, 貿易制裁措置
◆Pyongyang's accounts with Banco Delta Asia in Macao were frozen under U.S. financial sanctions. マカオの銀行「バンコ・デルタ・アジア」にある北朝鮮の口座が, 米国の金融制裁を受けて凍結された. ◆The leaders of France and Germany have agreed on a plan to impose automatic sanctions against countries that exceed a fiscal deficit limit of 3 percent of their gross domestic product. 独仏首脳は, 財政赤字を対GDP (国内総生産) 比で3%以内に抑えられない国に対して自動的に制裁を科す方針で一致した. ◆To deal with the systemic financial crisis, ministry and central bank officials had to take rescue measures, such as an injection of public funds, while at the same time implementing strict guidelines and sanctions. 連鎖的な金融危機に対処するにあたって, 当局は公的資金の投入などの救済措置取ると同時に, 厳しい指導や制裁を実施しなければならなかった.

SAR　株式評価益権, 株式評価受益権, 株式騰貴権
　(⇒stock appreciation right)

Sarbanes-Oxley Act　企業改革法 (サーベンス・オクスレー法), 企業会計改革法, サーベンス・オクスレー法
　(⇒annual report, quarterly report)
◆The Sarbanes-Oxlay Act directed the SEC to implement some of the reporting changes in an attempt to force companies and their executives to be more honest with investors. 企業と企業経営者に投資家への一段と誠実な対応を義務付けるため, サーベンス・オクスレー法は, SEC (米証券取引委員会) に報告規則変更の一部実施を求めた.
|解説| 企業改革法 (サーベンス・オクスレー法) とは: 米エネルギー大手エンロンの経営破たんをきっかけに相次いで発覚した経営者による不正な会計操作の防止策として, 2002年6月に米証券取引委員会 (SEC) は, 全米大企業942社の最高経営責任者 (CEO) と最高財務責任者 (CFO) に対して, 過去の決算が正確であると宣誓した署名文書の提出を求めた. 企業改革法は, このSECの要請を1回限りとしないで法律で恒久化することを定めたもので, 2002年7月に成立した. この企業改革法 (サーベンス・オクスレー法) に基づく措置として, SECはその後の8月27日, 米国企業だけでなく米株式市場に上場する外国企業のCEOとCFOに対しても, 決算報告の正確さを保証する宣誓書の提出を義務付け, 8月29から実施する新規則を決定した. また米国企業に対しては, 決算宣誓書提出の義務化だけでなく, 年次報告書の提出期限を従来の90日以内から60日以内に, 四半期報告書の提出期限を従来の45日以内から35日以内に短縮するとともに, 企業幹部による自社株取引の報告期限を40日以内から2日以内に大幅に短縮した. これは, 経営者による不正な会計操作や自社株売却を時間的に困難にするためだ. なお, 企業改革法では, 決算などの虚偽報告には最長で20年の禁固刑が科されることになっており, 米国市場に上場する外国企業もその対象になる. (2002年8月28日付讀賣新聞参照)

satisfy　(動) 満足させる, 充足させる, (欲求などを) 満たす, 条件を満たす, (人を) 納得させる, (借金を) 支払う, 返済する, (義務を) 果たす [履行する], (損害などを) 賠償する, 償う, (疑いを) 晴らす
satisfy a creditor　債権者に弁済する [支払う]
satisfy a debt for a person　人に負債を払う
satisfy an obligation　義務を果たす
satisfy claims for damages　損害に対する賠償請求に応じる
satisfy domestic demand　国内需要 [内需] を満たす
satisfy losses by cash　現金で損失を支払う
satisfy one's curiosity　好奇心を満足させる
satisfy the convergence criteria　収斂 (しゅうれん) 基準を達成する [クリア] する
satisfy the liability　債務を履行する, 債務を返済する

Saturday night special　不意打ち・予告なしの株式公開買付け, 土曜夜の特番

save　(動) 救う, 救助する, 救済する, 助ける, 救出する, 蓄える, 貯蓄する, 取っておく, 確保する, 節約する, 無駄 [手間] を省く, 収集する, 保つ, 保護する, セーブする
◆In the case of a lack of liquidity, either bridge lending or debt deferment can save the borrower as there is no cash on hand. 流動性不足の場合は, 手元に現金がないので, つなぎ資金を貸すか [つなぎ融資か] 債務返済の延長で借り手は助かる. ◆No financial institution would step in to save Lehman Brothers as the U.S. government refused to extend a financial assistance. 米政府が財政支援を拒否したので, リーマン・ブラザーズの救済に乗り出す金融機関は現われなかった. ◆To prevent crude oil prices rising further, major oil-consuming countries must try harder to save energy and promote the use of alternative energy sources. これ以上の原油高 [原油価格の高騰] を防ぐには, 石油消費国が省エネや代替エネルギーの利用促進に一段と力を入れる必要がある. ◆White knight is a company that saves another firm threatened by a hostile takeover by making a friendly offer. ホワイト・ナイトは, 友好的な買収により, 敵対的買収の脅威にさらされている他企業を救済する企業のことだ.

saver　(名) 預金者, 貯蓄者
savers' funds　貯蓄
small savers　少額預金者, 小口預金者
◆A financial intermediary acts as a middleman between cash surplus units in the economy (savers) and deficit spending units (borrowers). 金融仲介機関は, 経済の資金余剰主体 (貯蓄者) と資金不足主体 (借り手) との間に立つ仲介者として機能している. ◆The Banking Commission regulates the banking system and protects savers' interests. 銀行委員会は, 銀行制度を規制し, 預金者の利益を保護する.

savings　(名) 貯蓄, 貯金, 預金, 年金
　(⇒household savings, large-lot savings)
callable savings deposits　解約可能の貯蓄預金
company savings　企業貯蓄
corporate savings　法人貯蓄
Federal Savings and Loan Insurance Corporation　米連邦貯蓄貸付保険公社
gross savings　総貯蓄, 総貯蓄率
installment savings　積立貯金
national savings　国民貯蓄, 国内貯蓄
net savings　純貯蓄
ordinary savings　通常貯金
personal savings　個人預金, 個人貯蓄, 個人貯蓄率, リテール貯蓄
postal savings　郵便貯金
property accumulation savings　財形貯蓄
retirement savings　退職年金
savings and loan association　米国の貯蓄貸付け組合, S&L
savings and loans　預金と貸出金, 預金・貸出金
　(⇒Japanese Bankers Association)
Savings Association Insurance Fund　貯蓄金融機関保険基金, SAIF
savings bank　貯蓄銀行
savings bond　貯蓄債券
savings deducted at the source　天引き貯金
savings freeze　預金凍結
　(=banking freeze; ⇒devalue)
savings withdrawal form　普通預金の払戻し請求書
tax-exempt savings　非課税貯蓄, gross savings, 総貯蓄,

総貯蓄率
thrift savings account　積立預金口座
time savings　定期預金
◆People's savings held in postal savings and postal life insurance have been channeled into the operation of public corporations via the government's Fiscal Investment and Loan Program.　郵便貯金や簡易保険で保有している国民の預金は、政府の財政投融資計画を通じて、特殊法人につぎ込まれている。◆The downturn in global financial markets has had a negative impact on insurance products such as single-premium pension insurance policies which are popular as a form of savings.　世界の金融市場の低迷が、貯蓄用［一種の貯蓄］として人気の高い一時払い年金保険などの保険商品に悪影響を及ぼしている。◆The life insurer's single-premium whole life insurance is popular with consumers as a form of savings or an investment for retirement.　同生保の一時払い終身保険は、一種の貯蓄や退職金の運用先として顧客に人気がある。◆The rate of savings among those people in their 30s and 40s is on an upward trend, which is likely to have a depressing effect on domestic demand.　30～40歳代の貯蓄率が増大傾向にあり、内需を下押ししている可能性がある。◆There were apparent moves among companies drawing more money from savings to accumulate operating funds.　明らかな動きとして、企業は運転資金を積み増すため、預金から資金を引き出している。

savings account　普通預金, 普通預金口座, 銀行預金, 貯蓄預金, 貯蓄口座　（⇒shift名詞, transfer動詞）
◆About ¥20 million was transferred from this self-employed man's savings account to a bank account under someone else's name.　この自営業者の普通預金から他人名義の銀行口座に、約2,000万円が振り込まれていた。◆In this type of life insurance products, the rate of return after canceling the insurance contract can be higher than that of a savings account if a policyholder upholds the contract for five to 10 years.　この種の生保商品では、保険契約者が保険契約を5～10年続けると、解約後の利回り（予定利率）は預金よりも高い利回りが見込める。◆Interest rates on regular savings accounts were reduced to 0.001 percent at some banks.　普通預金の金利が、一部の銀行で0.001％に引き下げられた。

savings at banks　銀行預金
◆Quasi money refers to time deposits and other types of savings at banks that cannot be immediately cashed, including foreign currency deposits and nonresidents' yen deposits.　準通貨とは、定期性預金のほかに、外貨預金や非居住者の円預金など即時に換金できない［現金に換えられない］銀行預金のことをいう。

savings deposit　貯蓄預金, 貯蓄性預金, 普通預金
◆When the freeze on the payoff system was partially lifted, clients shifted their funds from time deposits to savings deposits that will be protected fully.　ペイオフ制度凍結の一部解禁が行われた際に、顧客が預金を定期預金から全額保護される普通預金に預け替えた。

savings plan　貯蓄制度
◆Our contributions to the savings plans amounted to $330 million in 2010.　当社の貯蓄制度に対する会社側の拠出額は、2010年度は3億3,000万ドルでした。

savings product　貯蓄商品
◆Japanese tend to put priority on minimizing risks when they invest in savings products.　貯蓄商品に投資する際、日本人はリスク回避を重視する傾向がある。

savings rate　貯蓄率
（=the rate of savings; ⇒savings）
◆The yearly savings rate is declining due to the aging society.　高齢化に伴って、年間貯蓄率は低下している。

say　発言権, 発言力
◆Shareholders of foreign firms have a much stronger say in corporate operations.　海外企業の株主のほうが、企業経営への発言力がはるかに強い。

Sberbank of Russia　ロシア最大手行のズベルバンク
◆Mizuho Corporate Bank has formed a business partnership with Sberbank of Russia.　みずほコーポレート銀行が、ロシアの最大手行ズベルバンク（Sberbank of Russia）と業務協力協定を締結した。◆Sberbank of Russia is the largest commercial bank in Russia.　ロシアのズベルバンクは、ロシア最大の商業銀行である。◆Sberbank of Russia will offer a variety of services, such as ruble-denominated loans to Mizuho Corporate Bank's clients when they do business in Russia.　ロシア最大手行のズベルバンクは、みずほコーポレート銀行の顧客がロシアで事業を行う際にルーブル建て融資を行うなどの各種サービスを提供することになった。

scale　（動）（一定の基準に応じて）決める, 物差しで計る ［測定する］, 基準によって評価［判断］する　（自動）量が同じである, 段階的に高くなる
　scale back　（規模を）縮小する, 削減する, 減らす, 引き下げる, 下方修正する
　scale back final allocations　最終的な割当額を削減する ［引き下げる］

scale　（名）規模, 基準, 尺度, 指数, 段階, 金利体系, 発行条件, 目盛り, スケール
　a scale of forward exchange rates　先物スケール
　be in full scale recovery　本格的に回復している
　（credit）quality on a scale of 2　2段階の信用度
　diseconomy of scale　規模の不経済, 規模の不経済性 （=diseconomies of scale）
　economy of scale　規模の経済, 規模の経済性, 規模の利益, 数量効果, スケール・メリット
　　（=economies of scale, scale economies）
　income scale　所得規模
　large-scale economic stimulus measures　大型の財政出動 （⇒monetary relaxation policy）
　large-scale financial inflows　資本の大量流入
　large-scale financial outflows　資本の大量流出
　large-scale tax cut program　大型減税プログラム
　outstanding loans and discounts of all banks by scale of enterprise　企業規模別貸出統計
　pension scale　年金体系
　preference scale　選択尺度, 選好規模
　salary scale　給与指数
　scale fee　基準料金
　scale of charges　手数料表, 料金表
　scale of corporate bonds　社債消化率
　scale of investment　投資規模
　scale of taxation　税率の段階
　scale of value　価値尺度
　scale order　刻（きざ）み注文
　scale trading　難平（なんぴん）売買（「難平」の難は損のことで, 損を平均するのが難平）
　sliding scale method　スライド制
　small-scale demand　小口需要
　small-scale shareholder　小口株主
　the efficiencies of scale inherent to the public securities markets　公募証券市場が持つ規模の効率性
◆It's better for a financial institution to be large in scale.　金融機関は、規模が大きいほうがよい。◆The AA minus rating by S&P is the fourth highest in terms of credit quality on a scale of 22.　米格付け会社のスタンダード・アンド・プアーズ（S&P）による「ダブルAマイナス」の格付けは、22段階ある信用度中、上から4番目に当たる。◆To enhance the stimulating effect of the Fed's rate cuts, the Bush administration is expected to swiftly implement fiscal and tax stimulus measures, includ-

ing tax cuts on investment designed to reinvigorate the stock market, in addition to the large-scale tax cut program that is under way. 米連邦準備制度理事会（FRB）の金利引下げの刺激効果を高めるため、ブッシュ政権には、現在実施中の大型減税プログラムに加え、株式市場を再活性化するための投資減税など、財政・税制面からの景気刺激策の速やかな実施が期待されている。

scale down 規模を縮小する,削減する,減らす,減額にする
 scale down debt 負債を減らす
 scale down one's profit estimates ～の利益予想を引き下げる
 scale down wages 一定率で賃金を下げる
 scale up （規模を）拡大する,引き上げる
 scale up income tax 所得税を引き上げる
 ◆Given the nation's tough fiscal condition, the government must eke out the necessary funds by scaling down low-priority policy projects. 日本の厳しい財政事情に照らせば、政府に求められるのは、優先度の低い政策プロジェクトを縮小して、必要な財源をひねり出すことだ。◆U.S. and European financial institutions are scaling back their business operations before capital adequacy requirements are strengthened in 2013. 欧米金融機関は、2013年から自己資本規制が強化されるのを前に、業務を縮小している。

scale merit 規模の利益,規模拡大によるメリット・利益,スケール・メリット
 ◆A merger can bring about scale merits and multiple benefits to both parties. 経営統合で、両当事者は、規模の利益と相乗効果を期待することができる。

scalper （名）利ざやを稼ぐ人,鞘（さや）取り業者,ダフ屋,スキャルパー

scam 詐欺,取り込み詐欺　（=fraud）
 cell-phone scam 携帯電話を使った詐欺
 fake billing scam 架空請求詐欺
 insurance scam 保険詐欺
 "It's me" phone scam オレオレ詐欺
 securities scam 証券詐欺
 ◆In an effort to fight the rapid growth of "It's me" scams, the outline of a new bill to regulate the use and sale of prepaid cell phones was announced. オレオレ詐欺の急増に対処するため、プリペイド式携帯電話の使用と販売を規制する新法案の概要が発表された。

scandal （名）醜聞（しゅうぶん）,流説,疑惑,不祥事,不正行為,汚職［疑獄］事件,事件,中傷,ひどいこと,恥,不名誉,スキャンダル
 a funding scandal 資金供与事件,偽装献金事件
 a series of scandals involving the company 一連の企業不祥事
 corruption scandals 贈収賄事件
 cover up bribery scandals 贈収賄事件を隠す
 stock market-related scandals 証券スキャンダル
 the bank scandals 今回の銀行不祥事
 uncover bribery scandals 贈収賄事件を暴く
 ◆A series of accounting scandals and delays in the recovery of corporate performance are accelerating falls in stock prices on the U.S. markets, along with the weakening of the dollar. 一連の［相次ぐ］企業会計の不祥事と企業業績回復の遅れで、米国の株安とドル安が加速している。◆He should speak about the bank's scandals as he was involved in the bank's management for years as president and chairman. 社長、会長として同行の経営に長くかかわった訳だから、氏は同行の不祥事について説明すべきだ。◆In his first policy speech, Prime Minister Yukio Hatoyama apologized again over a funding scandal involving his political fund management organization. 鳩山首相の初の施政方針演説で、首相は、自らの政治資金管理団体をめぐる偽装献金事件に関して、改めて陳謝した。◆The spate of scandals involving Olympus Corp.'s false financial statements has been widely reported overseas. オリンパスの有価証券報告書の虚偽記載に関する一連の疑惑は、海外で大きく報じられた。◆Trust in the IMF was lost by a scandal involving its former managing director. 国際通貨基金（IMF）の信認は、IMF前専務理事の不祥事で失われた。

scandal-ridden （形）スキャンダルに揺らぐ,スキャンダルまみれの,不祥事続きの
 scandal-ridden securities industry 不祥事続きの証券業界,スキャンダルに揺らぐ証券業界
 ◆Incubator Bank of Japan which was scandal-ridden for its lax lending practices arrests of its executives has finally collapsed. 乱脈融資や経営陣の逮捕など不祥事続きの日本振興銀行が、ついに破たんした。

scandal-tainted ［**scandal-hit**］ 疑惑をもたれた
 ◆Loss hiding scandal-tainted Olympus Corp. was sued by an investor in its American depositary receipts seeking class-action status. 損失隠しの疑惑をもたれたオリンパスが、同社の米国預託証券（ADR）を保有している投資家に、集団訴訟を求めて訴えられた。

scanner （名）読取り機,映像走査機,走査機,走査装置,スキャナー
 ◆Cardholders verify their identity by holding their palms over a scanner on the ATM. カード会員は、ATM（現金自動預け払い機）の読取り機に手のひらをかざして本人確認をする。

scarce （形）乏しい,不足している,珍しい,希少の
 scarce currency 希少通貨
 scarce goods 希少品,品薄
 scarce share［stock］ 品薄株

scenario （名）シナリオ,台本,筋書き,事態,状況,脚本,予測,予定の計画,行動計画,計画案
 alternative scenario 代替プラン,予備のプラン
 assume a scenario シナリオを描く
 economic scenario 経済予測,景気予測,景気シナリオ
 every possible scenario 想定されるあらゆる事態
 most likely scenario 最も実現しそうなシナリオ
 nightmare scenario 最悪のシナリオ
 optimistic scenario 楽観的シナリオ
 political scenario 政情,政局
 set up a scenario シナリオを描く
 the worst case scenario 最悪の事態,最悪のシナリオ　（=nightmare scenario）
 ◆Depending on the movements of oil price and overseas markets, a scenario in which the economy won't recover past 2009 is possible. 原油価格と海外市場の動向次第で、景気が2009年いっぱいまで回復しないというシナリオもあり得る。◆The ECB buyouts of sovereign debts of eurozone countries with fiscal laxity are the nightmare scenario Germany has been fearing. 欧州中銀（ECB）による放漫財政のユーロ圏諸国の国債買切りは、ドイツが恐れていた最悪のシナリオだ。◆The government assumes a scenario in which Japan's economic growth will shift into high gear with overseas demand as a driving force. 政府は、海外需要をテコに日本の経済成長が本格化する、とのシナリオを描いている。◆The U.S. government could avoid the worst-case scenario of default on payments to investors in Treasury bonds. 米政府は、国債の償還資金がなくなる債務不履行という最悪の事態を避けることができた。

schedule （動）予定する,予定を立てる,予定表を作る
 be scheduled to ～する予定である
 scheduled date 予定日
 ◆A redemption of the special government bonds for disaster reconstruction is scheduled to begin about 10 years from now. 震災復興債の償還期間は、今から10年程度となる予定だ。

schedule （名）届出様式,付属書類,明細表,法律の付則,

予定, 計画, スケジュール
　aging schedule　年齢調べ表, 満期表
　bank transfer schedule　銀行間振替手数料
　commission schedule　手数料明細表
　issue schedule　発行時期
　maturity schedule　償還計画
　on schedule　予定どおり
　schedule of terms and conditions　取引条件書
　Schedule 13D　届出様式13D（上場会社の発行済み株式の5％以上を取得した者が, 取得後の10営業日以内に米証券取引委員会（SEC）, 当該企業と, 当該企業の株式を上場している証券取引所に提出することになっている報告書の書式。⇒toehold purchase）
　Schedule 13G　届出様式13G（届出様式13Dの簡略書式）
　tariff schedule　関税表
　◆The BOJ is prepared to hold its policy meeting ahead of schedule if the yen's value further soars before the next meeting. 次回の政策決定会合までに円高が一段と進めば, 日銀は会合を前倒しして会合を開く構えだ。◆The Fed's program of buying $600 billion in Treasury bonds to help the economy is to end in June 2011 on schedule. 景気を支えるために6,000億ドルの国債を買い入れる米連邦準備制度理事会（FRB）の量的緩和政策は, 予定通り2011年6月に終了する。

scheme　（名）事業, 計画, 企画, 案, 策, 機構, 仕組み, 制度, 体系, 方式, 組織, 機構, 概要　（⇒allotment, investment scheme, share retirement, statute of limitations, stock buyup scheme）
　cofinancing scheme　協調融資事業
　　（=joint financing scheme）
　collective investment scheme　集合投資計画, 集合投資ファンド
　corporate defense schemes　企業防衛策
　employment training scheme　雇用訓練事業
　investment scheme　投資計画, 投資事業, 投資ファンド
　lease financing scheme　リース金融事業
　　（=lease financing project）
　pension scheme　年金制度
　Ponzi scheme　ネズミ講, ポンジ講
　　（=Ponzi game）
　project financing scheme　プロジェクト・ファイナンス事業, プロジェクト・ファイナンスの仕組み
　regulatory scheme　規制機構
　tax sheltering scheme　タックス・シェルター方式
　◆In the conventional IMF's scheme, countries were only given a credit line even after the IMF approved loans and they could not withdraw funds unless the fiscal crisis facing them worsened. 従来のIMF（国際通貨基金）の仕組みだと, 各国は融資の承認を得ても融資枠を与えられるだけで, 財政危機が深刻化しないと資金を引き出すことができなかった。◆The bank will carry out this cofinancing scheme as the lead bank with several U.S. and European banks. 同行は, 主幹事行として, この協調融資事業を欧米の複数の銀行と連携して実施する。◆This joint financing scheme carried out with the bank as the lead bank is expected to help make the presence of Japanese banks more strongly felt in global markets. 同行を主幹事銀行として実施されるこの協調融資事業は, グローバル市場での邦銀の存在感を高めることになりそうだ。◆Under the government's guidelines, companies can resort to corporate defense schemes, including a poison pill plan to issue new shares, to fight hostile takeover bids. 政府の指針によると, 敵対的買収への対抗策として, 企業は新株発行（増資）のポイズン・ピル（毒薬）方式などの企業防衛策をとることができる。◆Under the new financing scheme, the IMF will extend to financially strapped countries loans of up to 500 percent of their contribution to the IMF. 新融資制度では, 財政の資金繰りが苦しく[厳しく]なった国に対して, その国がIMF（国際通貨基金）に出資している額の最大5倍までIMFが融資する。

scope　（名）範囲, 領域, 枠組み, 枠, 構成, 区分, 余地, 機会, 可能性
　audit scope　監査の範囲
　　（=scope of audit, scope of examination）
　economy of scope　範囲の経済
　geographic scope　営業地域
　product scope　製品構成
　scope of business　業務範囲
　scope of cheap loans　低利融資枠
　scope of consolidation　連結の範囲　（=consolidation criteria:「連結の範囲」の基準としては, 基本的に「他社の発行済み議決権株式（outstanding voting stock）の50％超（過半数）を直接間接に所有している場合, その会社を連結の範囲に含める」ことになっている）
　scope of opinion　意見区分
　◆The Bank of Japan widened the scope of cheap loans to support smaller companies with growth potential. 潜在成長力のある中小企業を支援するため, 日銀が低利融資枠を拡大した。

scorched-earth defense　焦土作戦　（=scorched-earth tactic: 敵対的買収を仕掛けられた会社が, 買収者にとって魅力的な会社の最優良資産などを売却して会社の価値を減少させ, 買収意欲をそぐ手法のこと。crown jewel（クラウン・ジュエル）と同じ意味で使われることが多い。⇒crown jewel）

scrap　（動）撤回する, 撤廃する, 打ち切る, 中止する, 止める, 廃止する, 廃案にする, 捨てる, 廃品にする, スクラップにする　（⇒invoke）
　scrap flight services　運航を廃止する
　　（⇒unprofitable）
　scrap the consumption tax　消費税を撤廃する
　scrap the merger deal　合併協議を打ち切る, 合併計画を撤回する
　scrap the merger plan　合併[経営統合]計画を撤回する
　◆J.P. Morgan Chase & Co. is scrapping a $5 billion outsourcing deal with International Business Machines Corp. JPモルガン・チェース（米銀2位）は, IBMとの50億ドルの業務委託契約を打ち切ることになった。◆The government should scrap its current policy of slashing social security spending. 政府は, 現在の社会保障費削減路線を止めるべきだ。

screen　（動）審査する, 検査する, 選考する, 検定する　（⇒request名詞）
　◆The Jasdaq can now directly screen companies to be listed, a practice entrusted to securities houses in the past. ジャスダックは現在, これまで証券会社任せだった上場企業の審査を直接実施することができるようになった。◆Until last year, many start-up companies had to shelve planned listings when they were screened by securities firms. 昨年までは, 新興企業の多くが, 証券会社の審査段階で予定していた上場を見送らざるを得なかった。

screening　（名）審査, 検査, 選別, 選考, 適格審査, 適性検査, 上映, 放映, スクリーニング
　budget screening　事業仕分け
　creditworthiness screening standard　与信審査基準
　customer screening　顧客審査
　lax screening　手薄な審査
　legal careening　法定審査
　screening criteria　審査基準
　screening division　審査部門
　screening procedures　審査手続き
　◆Corporate merger screening is conducted by the Fair Trade Commission of Japan in light of the Antimonopoly Law. 企

業の合併審査は、独占禁止法に照らして［基づいて］公正取引委員会が行う。◆Some borrowers have taken advantage of lax screening of credit guarantee corporations. 信用保証協会の手薄な審査に便乗している借り手もいる。◆The creditworthiness screening standard of U.S. subprime loans was dubious. 米国の低所得者向け住宅ローン「サブプライム・ローン」の与信審査基準は、甘かった。◆The number of people using cashing services is rising partly because no screening is required to get money. 無審査で金を借りられることもあって、キャッシング・サービス（現金化商法）の利用者は増えている。

scrounge （動）かき集める、捻出する、（金品を）せびる、せがむ、無心する、ただで要求する、ねだって手に入れる、捜し求める
　◆Fiscal resources of ¥1.6 trillion cannot be scrounged together simply by recasting the budget and cutting wasteful spending. 1.6兆円の財源は、予算の組替えや無駄の削減だけでは捻出（ねんしゅつ）できない。

scrutiny （名）綿密な調査、調査、検討、監視、再調査、吟味（ぎんみ）、詮索（せんさく）
　be under scrutiny　監視されている、監視の目にさらされる、チェックされる
　come under scrutiny　詮索（せんさく）される、監視を受ける
　give close［careful］scrutiny to　～を綿密に調査［検討］する
　make a scrutiny into　～を精査する
　strict market scrutiny　市場の厳しい評価［チェック］、市場の厳しい監視の目
　undergo a careful scrutiny　入念な検査［チェック］を受ける
　◆Japanese government bonds are being subjected to stricter market scrutiny. 日本国債は、市場の一段と厳しい評価にさらされている。

scuttle （動）止めさせる、撤回させる、台なしにする、だめにする、廃棄する、中止する
　◆Former U.S. Treasury Secretary Henry Paulson testified letting Bank of America scuttle its takeover of Merrill Lynch in December 2008 was unthinkable. バンク・オブ・アメリカ（バンカメ）に2008年12月のメリルリンチ買収を止めさせるのは考えられないことだった、とポールソン米前財務長官は証言した。

SDR　IMFの特別引出権　（special drawing rightsの略）

seasoned （形）経験豊かな、老練な、練達の、年季の入った、期間［年数］の経った、期間が経過した、適切な
　seasoned entrepreneur　経験豊かな経営者
　seasoned issue　既発銘柄、既発債、確実［堅実］証券
　seasoned judgment　適切な判断
　seasoned loan　経過期間が長いローン、堅実融資
　seasoned new issue　公開済み証券の発行、既存の証券の追加発行
　seasoned operator　株の玄人（くろうと）筋
　seasoned securities　確実証券、堅実証券
　　（=seasoned issue）
　◆Japan Airlines is under a new management team headed by seasoned entrepreneur Kazuo Inamori. 日本航空は現在、経験豊かな経営者の稲盛和夫会長が率いる新経営陣の指揮下にある。

seat　（名）証券取引所の会員権

SEC　米証券取引委員会　（Securities and Exchange Commissionの略。⇒auditing work, Sarbanes-Oxley Act）
　◆American International Group agreed to pay a $10 million civil fine to settle the SEC's allegations that it fraudulently helped another company falsify its earnings report and hide losses. 米保険大手のAIG（アメリカン・インターナショナル・グループ）は、同社が他社の業績報告書改ざんと損失隠しに不正に手を貸したとする米証券取引委員会（SEC）の告発を受け、この問題を解決するために民事制裁金1,000万ドルを支払うことに同意した。◆As a result of these actions, the number of fraud cases investigated and prosecuted by the SEC has increased significantly. こうした動きや措置の結果、SEC（米証券取引委員会）が調査・摘発した不正事件の件数は大幅に減少した。◆The SEC filed fraud charges against WorldCom in federal district court in New York. 米証券取引委員会（SEC）は、ワールドコム（米長距離通信会社）を詐欺罪でニューヨーク連邦地裁に提訴した。◆The SEC probe was focused on several transactions that had led to higher revenues at AOL Time Warner Inc. 米証券取引委員会（SEC）の調査は、AOLタイム・ワーナーの売上高水増し（疑惑）につながった一部の取引を中心に行われた。
　解説 SECへの提出書類：SECに登録している企業がSECへの提出を義務付けられている主な報告書類としては、証券の発行の際に提出する届出書（registration statement）のほか、証券発行後に毎年決算期ごとに提出する年次報告書（annual report）、四半期ごとに提出する四半期報告書（quarterly report）、重要事項が発生した際に提出する臨時報告書（current report）などがある。

second （形）第二の、二番目の、従属的な、補助的な、二流の、セカンド
　at second hand　間接的に、また聞きで
　be second only to　～を除けば何にも劣らない、～を除けば1位だ
　second ballot　決戦投票
　Second banking Co-ordination Directive　第二次銀行指令
　second bill of exchange　第二為替手形
　Second Bond Market　債券第二市場
　second-class paper　二流手形
　second dividend tax　第二配当税
　second-drawer　二次的な、二流の
　second level withholding tax　二次的源泉徴収税
　second-lien-backed mortgage　第二順位モーゲージ証券
　second-lien mortgage（loan）　第二順位モーゲージ・ローン
　second preferred stock　低位優先株
　second quarter　第2四半期、第二・四半期
　second-rate　二流の、優良品でない
　second regional bank　第二地銀
　second-round finance　第二次資金調達
　second section listed company　二部上場企業
　Second Section listing　東証二部上場、二部上場
　second section of the Tokyo Stock Exchange　東証二部
　second sight　千里眼、透視力
　second string　代案、慈善の策、控え選手
　second thought　考え直し、思い直し、再考、反省

second half　下半期、下期、後半
　second half of the fiscal year　下半期
　second half of this fiscal year　今年度下半期、今年度下期
　second half-year　下半期、下期

second-largest shareholder　第二位株主、第二位の大株主［主要株主］
　◆The sell-off of Tokyo Metro shares planned by the government will likely be opposed by the Tokyo metropolitan government which is the second-largest shareholder. 政府が計画している東京メトロ株の売却には、国に次ぐ大株主の東京都が抵抗すると見られる。

second mortgage　第二順位抵当権、二番抵当
　second mortgage bond　二番抵当付き社債、二番抵当付き証券
　second mortgage loan　第二順位モーゲージ・ローン

second tier　準大手, 中堅, 中位, 二流
second-tier banks　中位銀行
second-tier life insurer　準大手の生命保険会社, 中堅生命保険会社
second-tier market　非上場証券取引市場
second-tier securities firm　準大手の証券会社
　(=second-tier securities house; ⇒tier)
second-tier stock　低業績株
Second World Bank　第二世銀
◆At the end of March 2001, 10 major and second-tier life insurers provided ￥10.5 trillion in stocks and subordinated debentures to banks. 2001年3月末に大手・中堅生命保険10社は、株式と劣後債で10兆5,000億円の資本を銀行に拠出した。

second-tier regional bank　第二地銀, 第二地方銀行
　(=second regional bank; ⇒shift名詞)
◆One hundred and thirteen regional banks and second-tier regional banks will contribute a total of ￥250 billion to the Banks' Shareholding Acquisition Corporation. 銀行等保有株式取得機構の資金として、地方銀行・第二地方銀行113行が総額2,500億円を拠出する。◆The Bank of Japan decided to extend a special loan to Namihaya Bank after the second-tier regional bank was declared insolvent. 日本銀行は、第二地方銀行の「なみはや銀行」が破たん認定を受けた後、同行に対して特別融資[特融]を実施することを決めた。

second-tiered　(形)準大手の, 中堅の, 中位の, 二段目の
secondary　(形)中等の, 二次的の, 副次的な, 補助的な, 後発の, 派生的な, 第二の, 二流の, あまり重要でない
　be of secondary importance　さほど重要でない, あまり重要でない
　be secondary to　～ほどは重要でない
　cause secondary effects　副作用を引き起こす
　secondary banks　中小銀行
　secondary bond　既発債
　secondary capital　第二次資本, 補完的自己資本
　secondary claim on　～に対する二次的請求権
　secondary deflation　第二次デフレ
　secondary deposits　派生的預金, 第二次的預金
　secondary disaster　二次災害
　secondary effect of investment　第二次投資効果, 投資の第二次効果
　secondary flows　流通市場の取引
　secondary industry　二次産業
　secondary issues　流通市場の銘柄
　secondary lending　二番抵当貸し
　secondary liabilities　第二次債務
　　(=contingent liabilities)
　secondary line　買い手段階
　secondary liquidities　第二次流動資産(通貨に次いで流動性の高き資産)
　secondary loan trading activity　流通市場での貸付け債権の売買状況
　secondary money　第二次貨幣
　secondary mortgage market　第二次抵当市場
　secondary obligation　付随債務
　secondary placement　売出し
　secondary post　二流の地位
　secondary product　副産物, 二次産品
　secondary rally　中間戻し
　secondary reinvestment cycle　二次的再投資循環
　secondary reserves　第二線支払い準備, 第二次準備
　secondary securities　第二次証券
　secondary securities market　流通市場
　secondary sources　二次的資料
　secondary warrant market　ワラント流通市場
　secondary yield　流通市場利回り
　the secondary stage　第二段階

secondary distribution　売出し, 第二次分売, 流通市場での販売　(=secondary offering)

secondary losses　二次損失
◆Compared with the conventional purchase prices, the RCC is likely to incur secondary losses. 従来の買取り価格に比べて、整理回収機構(RCC)に二次損失が出る可能性が高い。

secondary market　流通市場, セカンダリー市場, 既発債の取引市場, 短期金融市場　(⇒aftermarket)
　a liquid secondary market　流動性のある流通市場
　secondary market agreement　流通市場契約
　secondary market in municipal bonds　地方債の流通市場
　secondary market in public debts　国債流通市場
　secondary market liquidity　流通市場の流動性
　secondary market price　流通市場価格
　secondary market share offering　株式売出し
　secondary market spread　流通市場の債券のスプレッド
　secondary market value　流通市場価格
　secondary market yield　流通市場利回り
◆It is vital to improve the secondary market circulating such asset-backed securities for investors. 投資家向けに、このような資産担保証券の流通市場の整備も不可欠である。◆The secondary market prices of the peripheral countries' government bonds plummeted as it became known that those bonds might be subject to debt forgiveness. 周辺国の国債は債務減免の必要が生じる恐れのあることが判明したので、周辺国国債の流通市場での価格は暴落した。

[解説]流通市場とは：流通市場(secondary market, trading market)は、投資家が発行済みの株式や債券を売買する市場。また「短期金融市場」は、銀行引受手形や譲渡可能定期預金証書などの短期金融市場証券(money market instruments)を売買する市場のこと。⇒capital market, primary market

secondary offering　売出し, 流通市場での販売
　(=secondary distribution: 不特定多数の投資家に対して、均一の条件で、すでに発行された有価証券の取得の申込みを勧誘すること)

secret funds　裏金, 機密費
◆The Cabinet Secretariat received ￥1.2 billion in so-called secret funds each year from fiscal 2004 through fiscal 2008. 内閣官房が、2004年度から2008年度まで毎年、いわゆる機密費(内閣官房報償費)として、約12億円を受け取っていた。◆The labor union pooled money from commissions of its mutual relief operations in secret funds. この労働組合では、共済事業の手数料収入を裏金としてプールしていた。◆The secret funds were pooled in the bank accounts of dummy companies. 裏金は、ダミー会社の銀行口座に蓄えられていた。

Secretary of the Treasury　米財務長官

section　(名)課, 部, 部門, ～部, 区分, 条, セクション
　equity section　資本の部
　financial section　財務区分
　first section-listed margin stock　一部上場の信用銘柄
　government section　政府部門
　Section 17 funds　17条資金
　the First Section [first section] of the Tokyo Stock Exchange　東証一部, 東京証券取引所第一部
　　(=TSE first section)
　the main section (of the TSE)　東証一部
　the Second Section [second section] of the Tokyo Stock Exchange　東証二部, 東京証券取引所第二部, TSE

second section
◆The firm is listed on the second section of the Tokyo Stock Exchange. 同社は、東証二部に上場されている。◆Volume of the main section increased to 852.57 million shares. 東証一部の出来高は、8億5,257万株に増加した。

sector （名）部門, 分野, 業界, 地域, 市場, 株, セクター（⇒borrowing costs, capital tie-up, financial sector, mezzanine, private sector, public sector）
  agricultural financial sector　農林系金融機関
  banking sector　銀行業界, 銀行セクター, 銀行, 金融部門, 金融界
  corporate finance sector　企業金融部門
  corporate sector's performance　企業業績
  domestic-demand dependent sectors　内需依存株
  financial sector　金融部門, 金融業界, 金融・保険業, 金融セクター
  financial sector-triggered recession　金融不況
  leasing sector　リース部門
  manufacturing sector　製造業, 製造業セクター
  mining sector　鉱業株
  motor sector　自動車株
  public and private sector financial institutions　政府系金融機関と民間金融機関
  sector fund　業界限定ミューチュアル・ファンド
  sector management　セクター配分戦略（債権ポートフォリオの運用戦略の一つ）
  T-bill sector　Tビル市場, 米財務省短期証券市場
  technology sector　ハイテク株
◆A large number of companies are burdened with massive amounts of excessive liabilities in sectors such as construction and wholesale. 建設や卸売りなどの分野では、巨額の過剰債務を抱えている企業が多い。◆In the life insurance sector, the practice of luring customers by touting the bad performances of other insurers has been called into question. 生保業界では、他社の経営不振をあおって顧客を勧誘する行為（風評営業）が問題になっている。◆Sell orders outnumbered buy orders in a wide range of sectors. 幅広い業種で、売り注文が買い注文より多かった。◆The collapse of a bank may result in the systemic breakdown of the whole banking sector. 銀行1行の破たんが、金融界全体のシステム崩壊［連鎖的な崩壊］につながる可能性がある。◆The collapse of the bank will lead to repercussions throughout the finance sector. 同行の破たんは、金融業界全体に影響を及ぼすことになろう。◆The guard raised against a possible financial meltdown during a financial sector-triggered recession several years ago has been lifted. 数年前の金融不況時に想定された金融崩壊に対する厳戒態勢は、すでに解かれている。◆The reorganization drama of the financial sector through changes involving leading banks has been put in motion again. 大手銀行の改編（合併・統合）による金融再編劇が、再び動き出した。◆The special account borrows from the private sector and other sources to make up for local government's budget shortfalls. 特別会計は、民間などの財源からの借入れで地方の財源不足［財政赤字］の穴埋めをしている。◆The Tankan index for 10 of the 16 industries in the manufacturing sector improved in September from three months earlier. 製造業16業種中10業種の日銀9月短観の業況判断指数（DI）は、（前回調査の）6月から改善した。

secular （形）長年にわたる, 長期の, 長期的, 趨勢（すうせい）的, 永続する
  secular boom　長期的好況, 永続的好況
  secular change［drift］　長期変動, 長期的変動
  secular development　長期発展, 長期的発展
  secular disequilibrium　長期的不均衡, 趨勢的不均衡
  secular exhilaration　長期繁栄
  secular fluctuation　長期変動, 長期的変動
  secular growth　長期成長
  secular long run　超長期
  secular movement of prices　物価の長期漸増［漸落］足取り
  secular stagnation　長期停滞, 趨勢的停滞
  secular trend　長期的傾向, 長期趨勢
  secular variation　長期変動

secure （動）獲得する, 手に入れる, 得る, 確保する, 達成する, 実現する, 設定する, 固定する,（支払いを）保証する, 請け合う,（～から）守る, 安全にする, もたらす（bring about）, 確実にする, 確固たるものにする,（～に）保険を付ける, ～に担保を付ける
  be secured by　～によって保証される, ～で担保されている, ～を担保にして, ～を裏付けとする
  be secured by a letter of credit from　～の信用状で担保されている
  be secured on　～を担保とする, ～を裏付けとする
  be secured on residential mortgages　住宅用モーゲージを担保とする
  be secured on residential property　居住用不動産を担保とする
  loans secured by export trade bills　輸出貿易手形を担保とする貸付け
  loans secured by real estate　不動産抵当貸付け, 不動産担保ローン
  make loans secured by the receivables　債権を担保に融資する［貸し付ける］
  real estate secured　不動産担保
  secure a loan with a pledge　担保を付けてローン返済を保証する
  secure additional loans　追加融資を確保する, 追加融資を受ける　（⇒additional loan）
  secure against　～に備える
  secure bank financing　銀行融資を受ける
  secure it as fixed collateral　それに根（ね）抵当権を設定する
  secure new loans from one's creditor banks　取引銀行から新規融資を受ける
  secure oneself against accidents　損害保険を付ける
  secure revenue for the special restoration bonds　特別復興債の財源を確保する
  secure the loan on mortgage　抵当を入れてローンを組む, 抵当を入れて融資を受ける
  without securing sufficient collateral　十分な担保を取らずに
◆A project loan is generally a nonrecourse loan and is secured by project assets. プロジェクト・ローンは通常、非遡求型ローンで、プロジェクトの資産を担保とする。◆GM must secure stable profits by releasing promising models to successfully list its shares again. GMが再上場を果たすには、売れる車を投入して安定した収益を確保しなければならない。◆Livedoor is believed to be considering using NBS shares as security to secure the necessary funds. ライブドアは、ニッポン放送株を担保にして必要資金を確保することを検討している模様だ。◆The bank had already secured it as fixed collateral. 同行は、それにはすでに根（ね）抵当権を設定していた。◆The company was unable to secure sufficient funding for redemption of its corporate bonds. 同社は、社債の償還資金の手当てがつかなかった。◆The company will secure ￥270 billion in loans from the Development Bank of Japan and other lenders. 同社は、日本政策投資銀行などの金融機関から2,700億円の融資を受ける［2,700億円を借り入れる］。◆The first mortgage bonds of the corporation are secured by a first mortgage and a floating charge on the company. 同社の第一

順位抵当権付き社債は、同社の第一順位抵当権と浮動担保権で保証されています。◆The last resort to secure a stable revenue source is raising the consumption tax. 安定した財源確保の頼みの綱は、消費税の引上げだ。◆When yields on whole life insurance products decline, policyholders must pay higher premiums to secure the same amount of total insurance benefits. 終身保険商品の利回りが下がった場合、加入者［保険契約者］がそれ以前と同額の総保険料を受け取るには、より高い保険料を払わなければならない。

secure （形）安全な、危険のない、心配がない、不安のない、気苦労のない、確実な、確かな、信頼できる、安定した、しっかりした、確立した、揺るぎない、落ち着いた、自信に満ちた、難攻不落の

secure base　確固たる基盤、確かな基盤
secure billions of dollars　巨額の資金を確保する
secure currency　健全通貨
secure earnings growth　安定した増益
◆Greece must avert a crippling debt default by securing billions of dollars in emergency loans from European countries and the IMF. ギリシャは、欧州諸国［ユーロ圏］と国際通貨基金（IMF）による緊急融資で巨額の資金を確保して、壊滅的な債務不履行を回避しなければならない。

secure loan funds　融資資金を確保する、融資資金を調達する
◆Leading moneylending businesses make huge profits by securing loan funds from financial institutions at annual average rates of less than 2 percent. 大手の貸金業者は、金融機関から平均年2％以下の金利で融資資金を調達して、高い収益を上げている。

secure loans　融資を受ける、融資を確保する
◆It is increasingly difficult to secure loans. 融資を受けるのが、次第に難しくなっている。

secure money　資金を確保する、資金を調達する
◆As a precondition for receiving financial support from the government and other utility companies, TEPCO is hurrying to secure money by selling its property. 政府［国］や他の電力各社から金融支援を受ける前提として、東京電力は、同社の資産売却による資金確保を急いでいる。

secure necessary funds　必要資金を確保する
◆Greece was bailed out temporarily in May 2010, but it may default on its debts if it fails to secure necessary funds to redeem a sizable amount of government bonds. ギリシャは2010年5月に一時的に救済されたが、大量の国債の償還に必要な資金を確保できない場合、債務不履行（デフォルト）に陥る可能性がある。

secure new loans　新規融資を受ける、新規融資を確保する
◆JAL's efforts to turn around its failed business will depend on the flagship carrier's ability to secure new loans from its creditor banks. 日航の破たん事業再生への取組みは、この日本を代表する航空会社が取引銀行から新規融資を受けることができるかどうかにかかっている。

secure profits　収益を確保する、利潤を確保する
◆Financial institutions are trying to secure profits in proportion to the risks they take. 金融機関は、金融機関の取るリスクに見合った利潤（適正利潤）を確保しようとしている。

secure revenue for restoration bonds　復興債の財源を確保する
◆Raising the consumption tax rate is a viable option for securing the special restoration bonds. 特別復興債の財源確保に、消費税率の引上げは有望な選択肢だ。

secure the necessary funds　必要資金を確保する
◆We are considering using the company's shares as security to secure the necessary funds. 当社は、同社株を担保にして必要資金を確保することを検討している。

secure the stable financial resources for social security　社会保障の財源を確保する
◆A hike in the consumption tax rate is aimed at securing the stable financial resources for social security. 消費税率引上げの目的は、社会保障の財源確保にある。

secured　（形）担保付きの、有担保の、抵当権付きの、保証された、確実な

loans secured on land　不動産担保ローン
make secured loans　担保付き融資を行う、担保付き貸付けを行う
secured accommodation　担保付き融資、担保付き融通
secured account　保証付き勘定
secured advance　担保付き貸付け
secured bank loan　担保付き銀行ローン
secured bill　担保付き手形
secured bond　担保付き社債、担保付き債券、担保付き証券、有担保債、保証債
　（＝mortgage bond, secured debenture）
secured borrowing　担保付き借入れ
secured claims　担保付き請求権、被担保債権
secured credit　担保付き貸付け、担保付き信用状
　（secured letter of credit）
secured credit card　担保付きクレジット・カード
secured creditor　有担保債権者、担保債権者
　（無担保債権者＝unsecured creditor）
secured debenture　担保付き社債、担保付き債券
　（＝secured bond）
Secured Debenture Trust Law　担保付き社債信託法
secured debt　担保付き負債、担保付き債券、有担保債務
secured debt instrument　有担保債券
secured debt issue　担保付き債券
secured financing　担保付き資金調達
secured interest　担保権、担保による保護のある権利
secured liability　担保付き負債、保証付き負債
secured loans　担保付き融資、有担保融資［貸付け］、抵当貸付け、担保付き貸付け、担保付きローン、担保付き借入金
secured note　担保付き約束手形
secured obligation　担保付き社債（secured bond）、被担保債務
secured party　担保権者
secured promissory note　担保付き約束手形
secured property　担保物件　（＝pledged asset）
secured transaction　担保付き取引

secured collateral　担保の保証
◆The bank sets its interest rates higher than those offered by major commercial banks and provides loans to small firms without secured collateral. 同行は、大手銀行より貸付け金利を高く設定して、中小企業に無担保で融資している。

secured lenders　有担保債権者、有担保債権を保有する金融機関［銀行団］　（＝secured creditors）
◆MGM's secured lenders will swap more than $4 billion of debt for equity. メトロ・ゴールドウィン・メイヤー（MGM）の有担保債権を保有する銀行団は、40億ドル超の債務を株式化する［40億ドルを超える債務を株式に切り替える］。

secured mortgage　抵当権付き債権、物上担保
◆As the gap between the eurozone-imposed repayment program and the track record began clearly yawning, the Greece's insolvency became apparent. ユーロ圏が押し付けたギリシャの返済計画と実績とのズレが目立つようになるにつれ、ギリシャの返済不能が明らかになった。◆Plan assets are represented by common and preferred shares, bonds and debentures, cash and short-term investments, real estate and secured mortgages. 年金資産は、普通株式・優先株式や債券・社債、現金・短期投資証券、不動産、抵当権付き債権などで構

成されています。

secured time deposit 安定性の高い定期預金
◆Investors seem to be shifting their money from investment trusts to more secured time deposits in the face of global financial turmoil. 世界の金融市場の混乱に直面して、投資家は資金を投資信託から安定性の高い定期預金に切り替えているようだ。

securities （名）有価証券, 証券, 債券, 証書, 権利証書, 銘柄
 active securities 人気証券, 花形証券
 assessable securities 払込み付き証券
 asset-backed securities 資産担保証券
 available-for-sale securities 売却可能有価証券
 bearer securities 無記名証券, 持参人払い証券
 blue chip securities 優良証券
 borrowed securities 借入有価証券
 buy securities 証券を買う, 証券を購入する
 commingling securities 証券混合
 convertible securities 転換証券
 corporate securities 法人証券
 corporation securities 証券
 dated securities 期日付き証券
 debt securities 債券, 債務証券, 債務証書
 digested securities 消化証券
 direct securities 直接証券
 discount on securities 証券発行差金
 electronic securities 電子証券
 eligible securities 適格証券
 equity securities 持ち分証券, 持ち分有価証券, 株式
 exempt securities 免除証券
 first class securities 一流証券
 fixed income securities 確定利付き証券, 債務証券, 債券
 fixed interest securities 確定利付き証券［債券］
 foreign securities 外国証券
 foreign short-term securities 外国短期証券
 forged securities 偽造証券
 gilt-edged securities 優良証券, 金縁証券, 一流証券, ギルト・エッジ証券
 government securities 政府債, 政府発行有価証券
 government securities dealer 米政府証券ディーラー
 government securities market 公債市場
 held-to-maturity securities 償還期限まで保有する有価証券
 high-grade senior securities 高級上位証券
 high yield securities 高利回り証券
 higher yielding securities 高収益性の銘柄, 収益性の高い銘柄
 hold securities 証券を保有する
 inactive securities 不活発証券
 indirect securities 間接証券
 intercourse securities 国際市場証券
 interest on securities 有価証券利息
 interest securities 利子証券
 international securities 国際証券
 invest in securities 証券に投資する
 investment securities 投資証券, 投資有価証券
 issue securities 証券を発行する
 liquid securities 流動証券
 listed securities 上場証券, 上場銘柄（=quoted securities）
 long-dated securities 長期証券（=long-term securities）
 margin securities 証券対象の証拠金取引を行う
 marketable securities 市場性ある有価証券, 市場性証券, 上場有価証券
 medium [medium-dated] securities 中期証券
 monetary indirect securities 貨幣的間接証券
 municipal securities 地方債, 地方証券
 national savings securities 国民貯蓄性証券
 negotiable securities 有価証券
 nonamortizable securities 一時払い有価証券
 noninterest bearing securities 無利子証券
 nonmarketable securities 非市場性証券
 nonnegotiable securities 譲渡不能証券
 nontaxable securities 免税証券
 outside securities 場外証券
 outstanding government securities 国債残高
 outstanding securities 未償還証券
 primary securities 第一次証券, 本源的証券
 prime securities 本源的証券
 profit sharing securities 利潤証券
 public debt securities 国債
 public market securities 公募証券
 purchase and sale of securities 証券の売買
 purchasing power securities 購買力証券
 quoted securities 上場証券
 real securities 不動産担保
 realize securities 証券を換金する
 registered securities 記名証券
 reserve securities 準備証券
 seasoned securities 堅実証券, 確実証券
 secondary securities 第二次証券
 secondhand securities 市場に流通している債券
 securities account 証券取引口座
 Securities Act of 1933 米国の1933年証券法（=Federal Securities Act）
 Securities Acts Amendments of 1975 1975年証券改革法
 Securities and Exchange Commission 米証券取引委員会, SEC （⇒statement）
 Securities and Futures Authority 英証券・先物委員会, SFA（1997年に金融サービス機構（Financial Services Authority）に統合された）
 Securities and Investment Board 英証券取引委員会, SIB
 Securities Association 英証券協会
 securities borrowed 借入れ有価証券
 securities broker 証券ブローカー, 有価証券仲買人
 securities brokerage business 証券仲介業, 証券仲介業務, 証券仲介ビジネス （⇒deregulation）
 securities custodian 証券保管者
 securities custody agreement 証券保管契約
 securities dealer 証券ディーラー, 証券取引業者
 Securities Enforcement Remedies and Penny Stock Reform Act of 1990 1990年有価証券規制特別措置法
 securities fiduciary business 証券取引業務
 securities finance 証券金融, 証券担保金融
 securities finance company 証券金融会社
 securities financing 証券金融
 securities for fiduciary issue 保証準備
 securities for investment 投資有価証券
 securities held for trading purposes 短期売買目的の証券
 securities held in a trading account 商品有価証券
 securities held in an investment account 投資有価証券
 securities held in pledge [pawn] 質入れされている担保

物件
securities holding company　証券保有会社
Securities issue　証券発行
securities law violation　証券取引法違反
securities let　貸付け有価証券
securities loan　証券担保貸出し[貸付け], 証券金融, 仲買人融資(broker call loan, broker's loan)
securities loaned　貸付け有価証券
securities market　証券市場
securities on property　物的証券
securities option　有価証券オプション取引
securities outstanding　発行済み証券, 証券発行高, 流通証券
securities pledged in lieu of cash collateral　代用有価証券担保
securities portfolio　証券ポートフォリオ
securities regulator　証券取引の監督官庁
securities research capabilities　証券分析力
securities trading　証券取引
securities transaction　証券取引, 有価証券取引
securities transaction tax　有価証券取引税
securities transfer agent　証券代行業務者
securities transfer tax　有価証券取引税
securities transferred　名義書換え
securities underwriter　証券引受業者
securities underwriting　証券引受け, 証券引受業者
self-liquidating securities　自動決済証券
short-dated [short-term] securities　短期証券
sterling securities　英ポンド証券
subscription to securities　証券応募
substitute securities　代用証券
taxable securities　有税証券
trade securities　証券を売買する
trading securities　売買目的有価証券, 商品有価証券
trustee securities　信託証券
uncurrent securities　非流動証券, 無取引証券
undated securities　永久債券, 無償還債券
undigested securities　未消化証券
unfixed interest bearing securities　不確定利付き証券
unlimited securities　非上場証書
unlisted securities　非上場証券, 未上場証券
　(=unquoted securities)
unmarketable securities　取引不能証券
unrealized gains on securities　証券含み益
variable interest bearing securities　不確定利付き証券
yield on securities　有価証券利回り

◆Citigroup will buy back the auction-rate securities from investors under separate accords with the Securities and Exchange Commission and state regulators. 米シティグループは、米証券取引委員会(SEC)や州規制当局との個々の合意に基づいて投資家から金利入札証券(ARS)を買い戻す。◆The company failed to timely file its periodic reports with the Securities and Exchange Commission as required by Nasdaq rules. 同社は、ナスダックのルールに従って義務付けられている定期報告書を、米証券取引委員会に期間内に提出しなかった。

解説 米証券取引委員会(SEC)とは：証券関連法の運用と公正な証券取引の維持および投資家保護を目的として、1934年証券取引法に基づいて創設された米国の独立した連邦政府機関。委員会は、上院の同意を得て大統領が任命する任期5年の委員5人で構成されている。

SECの主な組織構成：

Directorate of Economic and Policy Analysis　経済分析室
Division of Corporation Finance　企業財務局 法人金融部
Division of Enforcement　法規執行局 執行部
Division of Investment Management　投資管理局 投資管理部
Division of Market Regulation　市場規制局 市場規制部
Office of Administrative Law Judges　行政訴訟審判官室 行政法審判官室
Office of EDGAR Management　エドガー管理室
Office of International Affairs　国際問題室 国際問題課
Office of Opinions and Review　意見起草室
Office of the Chief Accountant　主任会計官室
Office of the General Counsel　法律顧問室

Securities and Exchange Law　証券取引法　(⇒ Financial Instruments and Exchange Law, stock deal)
◆He was the mastermind behind a string of violations of the Securities and Exchange Law by the Internet service firm. 同氏は、このインターネット・サービス会社による一連の証券取引法違反行為を主導していた。◆In the wake of the Livedoor case, the Financial Instruments and Exchange Law which drastically revised the former Securities and Exchange Law came into force in September 2007. ライブドア事件を受けて、2007年9月に、旧証券取引法を抜本改正した金融商品取引法が施行された。◆Insider trading is prohibited under the Securities and Exchange Law. インサイダー取引は、証券取引法で禁じられている。◆Kanebo plans to file a criminal complaint against the former executives on suspicion of violating the Securities and Exchange Law and sue them for damages. カネボウは、証券取引法違反容疑で旧経営陣を刑事告発する一方、損害賠償請求訴訟に踏み切る方針だ。◆The Securities and Exchange Law requires investment funds to register and report the names of their representatives and their locations. 証券取引法は、投資ファンドに対して、投資ファンドの代表者名や所在地などの登録・届け出を義務付けている。

Securities and Exchange Surveillance Commission　証券取引等監視委員会, SESC
◆Securities and Exchange Surveillance Commission is set to launch an investigation into the company. 証券取引等監視委員会は、同社の調査に乗り出す見通しだ。◆The Securities and Exchange Surveillance Commission filed a criminal complaint against a former bank employee with the Tokyo District Public Prosecutors Office on suspicion of violating the Financial Instruments and Exchange Law. 証券取引等監視委員会は、元行員を金融商品取引法違反の疑いで東京地検に刑事告発した。◆The Securities and Exchange Surveillance Commission is charged with inspecting the compliance of securities firms with the law, market surveillance and the investigation of abuses such as insider trading and stock price manipulation. 証券取引等監視委員会は、証券会社の法律遵守(じゅんしゅ)に関する検査や市場の監視、インサイダー取引や株価操作など不正行為の摘発を行う。◆The Securities and Exchange Surveillance Commission launched a full-scale investigation on the company on suspicion of accounting fraud. 証券取引等監視委員会は、粉飾決算の疑いで同社の本格調査に乗り出した。◆The Securities and Exchange Surveillance Commission will get to the bottom of the spate of scandals involving Olympus Corp's false financial statements. 証券取引等監視委員会は、オリンパスの有価証券報告書虚偽記載に関する一連の疑惑の全容を解明する[真相を究明する]方針だ。

securities brokerage　証券仲介, 証券仲介業　(株式や債券などの売買注文を証券会社に取り次ぐ業務。⇒ deregulation)
◆Nihon Unicom tied up with Century Securities Co. in securities brokerage. 日本ユニコム(先物大手)は、証券仲介業務でセンチュリー証券と連携した。

securities brokering　証券仲介業
◆The wall separating banking and securities businesses has been lowered through such moves as the liberalization of banks' securities brokering. 銀行と証券業の垣根は、銀行に対する証券仲介業の規制緩和などの動きで、低くなっている。

securities business　証券事業、証券業務、証券業
◆The security firm expects to book about ￥73 billion in losses related to its residential mortgage-backed securities business in the July-September quarter. 同証券会社は、7-9月期に住宅融資証券事業の関連損失として730億円を計上する見通しだ。◆The wall separating banking and securities businesses has been lowered through such moves as the liberalization of banks' securities brokering. 銀行と証券業の垣根は、銀行に対する証券仲介業の規制緩和などの動きで、低くなっている。

securities business strategy　証券戦略
◆The next issue for the financial group is how to restructure its securities business strategy. 同金融グループの次の課題は、グループ全体の証券戦略をどのように再構築するかだ。

securities company　証券会社
（=securities firm, securities house）
◆A former president of a bankrupt securities company acquired the securities company for ￥350 million although he did not have sufficient brokerage experience. 破産した証券会社の元社長は、証券業の十分な経験がないまま同証券会社を3億5,000万円で買収していた。◆The securities companies calculate capital gains and losses, compile taxation documents, gather annual stock reports and file tax returns on behalf of investors free of charge. 証券会社は、投資家の代わりに無料で譲渡損益を計算したり、税務書類を作成したり、年間の株式取引報告書を揃えたりして、税務申告書［納税申告書］を提出する。

securities counter　証券窓口
◆UFJ Bank set up securities counters to exclusively handle stocks and foreign bonds at its 15 outlets. UFJ銀行は、同行の15店舗に株式や外債を専門に取り扱う「証券窓口」を設置した。

securities crime　証券犯罪
◆There is a shortage of prosecutors versed in investigations into securities crime. 証券犯罪の捜査に精通する検察官が、不足している。

Securities Dealers Association of Japan　日本証券業協会
◆Dealings at over-the-counter markets run by the Securities Dealers Association of Japan are basically settled between concerned parties. 日本証券業協会が運営している店頭市場での（売買）取引の決済は、基本的に関係当事者間で行われている。

securities exchange　証券取引所　（⇒Jasdaq Securities Exchange, relist, stock exchange）
Securities Exchange Act of 1934　米国の1934年証券取引法, 1934年証券取引所法
Securities Exchange Council　証券取引審議会
Securities Exchange Law　証券取引法
◆The Jasdaq can begin small-lot after-hours trading by its transformation from an over-the-counter stock market to a securities exchange. ジャスダックは、店頭市場から証券取引所への移行により、立会外分売（取引時間外に大株主などが保有株を小口に分けて売り出すこと）も可能になった。◆The Tokyo Stock Exchange and the Osaka Securities Exchange have reached a final agreement to merge as early as autumn 2012. 東京証券取引所と大阪証券取引所が、早ければ2012年秋に経営統合することで最終的に合意した。◆With 942 listed companies, the Jasdaq overtook the Nagoya Stock Exchange as the third-largest stock market in Japan, after the Tokyo Stock and Osaka Securities exchanges. 上場会社数が942社のジャスダックは、名古屋証券取引所を抜き、東京、大阪両証券取引所に次ぐ国内3番目の株式市場になった。

securities firm　証券会社　（=securities company, securities house, stock brokerage）
a second-tier securities firm　準大手の証券会社, 準大手証券
the second-largest U.S. securities firm by equity capital　株式資本の規模で第二位の米国の証券会社
◆If the securities firms rush to cut these commissions, they may not be able to continue to rely on income from commissions as a major source of profit. これらの証券会社が手数料の値引き競争に走れば、主な収益源として株式の売買委託手数料による収入に今後とも頼ることは難しくなる。◆New York-based Morgan Stanley is the second-largest U.S. securities firm by equity capital. ニューヨークに本社を置くモルガン・スタンレーは、株式資本の規模で第二位の米国の証券会社だ。

securities fraud　証券詐欺
◆These disciplinary measures include increased penalties on securities fraud and a newly installed penalty on corporate directors in cases of failure to submit adequate financial reports to authorities. これらの懲戒処分には、証券詐欺に対する罰則の強化や、当局に適切な財務報告をしなかった場合の企業取締役に対する罰則の新設などが含まれている。◆U.S. federal and state regulators accused Putnum Investments of securities fraud. 米連邦・州規制当局は、パトナム・インベストメンツ社を証券詐欺罪で告発した。

securities holdings　保有証券, 保有有価証券
（保有する株式や債券のこと。⇒bond holdings）
◆Among the 10 life insurers, four reported valuation losses on their securities holdings of more than ￥200 billion. 生命保険10社のうち4社が、2,000億円を超える保有株式の減損処理額を計上した。◆Appraisal losses on securities holdings dealt a blow to the firm's earnings. 保有証券の含み損［評価損］が、同社の収益に打撃を与えた。◆The top 10 life insurers in the nation reported a total of ￥1.46 trillion in valuation losses on their securities holdings for the current business year. 今期決算で、国内生保の上位（主要）10社の保有有価証券［保有株式］の減損処理額は、1兆4,600億円に達した。

securities house　証券会社　（=securities company, securities firm;⇒buy or sell order, screen, trading profits）
◆If the merger takes place, it will create a full-scale financial conglomerate with a major bank, a major securities house and credit card company under its umbrella. 統合すれば、傘下に大手銀行と大手証券、クレジット・カード会社などを持つ本格的な金融コングロマリット（金融複合企業体）が誕生する。◆Mizuho group's Mizuho Securities Co. is equivalent in size to major securities houses. みずほフィナンシャルグループのみずほ証券は、規模では大手証券会社に匹敵する。

securities industry　証券業界
Securities Industry and Financial Markets Association　（米国の）証券業・金融市場協会, SIFMA（米国の証券業協会（Securities Industry Association）と債券市場協会（Bond Market Association）が合併して、2006年に誕生）
Securities Industry Association　米証券業協会, SIA
◆The TSE president is required to coordinate with the securities industry and the Financial Services Agency. 東京証券取引所の社長（東証社長）は、証券界や金融庁との調整を図らなければならない。

securities investment　証券投資, 有価証券投資
（⇒financial derivatives）
an increase in direct and securities investment　直接・証券投資の伸び
losses on securities investments　証券投資の損失
securities investment fund　投資信託, 証券投資信託
◆Affected by losses on securities investments as well as the growing cost of bad loan disposal, the financial group fell

into the red in the nine months through December. 証券投資の損失と不良債権処理費用の拡大の影響で、同フィナンシャル・グループは、4～12月期は赤字に転落した。◆Taxes levied on capital gains should be consolidated to promote securities investment. 有価証券投資を促すために、金融資産課税は一元化するべきだ。◆The rise in foreign assets held by Japanese was mainly caused by an increase in direct and securities investment. 日本の政府・企業・個人が保有する対外資産の増加は、主に直接・証券投資の伸びによるものだった。◆The surplus from securities investment was ¥1.85 trillion larger than the previous year. 証券投資の黒字幅は、前年より1兆8,500億円拡大した。

securities investment trust　証券投資信託
　　securities investment trust business　証券投資信託事業
　　securities investment trust depositary company　投資信託受託会社
　　securities investment trust management company　投資信託委託会社
　　securities investment trust sales company　投資信託販売会社
securities investor　証券投資家
　　Securities Investor Protection Act of 1970　米国の1970年証券投資家保護法
　　Securities Investor Protection Corporation　証券投資家保護公社
securities lending　有価証券貸付け
　　securities lending agreement　有価証券貸借取引, 有価証券貸借取引契約
securities market　証券市場, 証券市況, 有価証券市場
（=security market：「証券市場」は、長期金融資産である株式や債券を取引する金融市場で、日本では資本市場（capital market）と同義。⇒Big Bang）
　　debt securities market　債券市場
　　government securities market　公債市場
　　mortgage-backed securities market　モーゲージ証券市場
　　public securities market　公募証券市場
　　secondary securities market　流通市場
　　（=secondary market）
　　unlisted securities market　非上場証券市場
◆Banks in Japan were allowed to sell stocks directly as part of deregulation to spur the securities market by widening the scope of investors. 投資家の範囲（投資家の機会）を拡大して証券市場の活性化を図るための規制緩和の一環として、国内銀行（国内銀行の窓口）で株式を直接販売できるようになった。◆In the future also, new types of illegal practices that exploit legal loopholes will emerge in securities markets. 今後も、証券市場では、法の抜け穴を狙う不正取引の手法が新たに現れるものと思われる。◆Insider trading distorts share prices and undermines the fairness of the securities market. インサイダー取引は、（適正な）株価をゆがめ、証券市場の公正さを損なう。

securities regulator　証券規制機関, 証券監督機関
◆The U.S. Securities and Exchange Commission is the nation's top securities regulator. 米証券取引委員会（SEC）は、米国の最高証券規制機関［最高証券監督機関］だ。

securities-related taxation system　証券関連税制, 証券税制　（=securities-related tax system; ⇒security taxation system, sluggish stock market）
◆A review of the securities-related taxation system is important as a way to reinvigorate the stock market in the long run. 証券関連税制の見直しは、長期的な証券市場の活性化策としても重要である。

securities report　有価証券報告書
（⇒false securities report）
◆Olympus will submit by Dec.14 its corrected versions of securities reports for the last five years. オリンパスは、12月14までに過去5年分の訂正有価証券報告書［有価証券報告書の訂正版］を提出する。◆The presence of investment funds on the share register is generally unknown until their names are listed in annual securities reports. 株主名簿上の投資ファンドの存在は、一般にそのファンド名が年次有価証券報告書に記載されるまで分からない。

securities sector　証券分野
◆With the capital tie-up with Norinchukin Bank, MFG aims to boost its customer base in the securities sector. 農林中央金庫との資本提携で、みずほフィナンシャルグループは、顧客基盤の強化を目指している。

securities tax system　証券税制
（=securities taxation system）
◆Individual investors keep their distance from stock markets mainly because of the present securities tax system. 個人投資家が株式市場から遠ざかっているのは、現在の証券税制に大きな原因がある。

securities unit　証券会社
◆The nation's mega banking groups have been realigning their securities units to offer comprehensive financial services. 国内の大手金融グループは、総合金融サービスを提供するため、グループ各社の証券会社を再統合している。

securitization [securitisation]　（名）証券化, 金融の証券化, セキュリタイゼーション
（⇒mergers and acquisitions）
　　asset securitization　資産の証券化
　　（=securitization of assets）
　　bad loan securitization　不良債権の証券化
　　（=securitization of bad loans）
　　car [automobile] loan securitization　自動車ローンの証券化
　　commercial securitization　商業用不動産の証券化
　　CP-funded securitization　CPによる証券化
　　credit card securitization　クレジット・カード債権の証券化, クレジット・カードの証券化
　　（=securitization of credit card receivables）
　　housing loan securitization　住宅ローンの証券化, 住宅ローン債権の証券化
　　Lease-Credit Securitization Law　リース・クレジット債権流動化法
　　real estate securitization　不動産の証券化
　　（=securitization of real estate）
　　Regulation for Securitization of Specific Credit　特定債権等に係わる事業の規制に関する法律
　　securitization by pooling　プーリングによる証券化
　　securitization market　証券化市場
　　securitization of credit card receivables　クレジット・カード受取り債権の証券化, クレジット・カード債権の証券化
　　securitization of government assets　政府資産の証券化
　　securitization of housing loans　住宅ローンの証券化, 住宅ローン債権の証券化
　　（=housing loan securitization）
　　securitization of real estate assets　不動産資産の証券化
　　（=real estate-asset securitization）
　　securitization strategy　証券化戦略
　　securitization transaction　証券化取引
　　straight securitization　保証保険なしの証券化
◆The insurance company will procure the additional funds from the institutional investors through securitization. この保険会社は、証券化の手法で機関投資家から追加基金（基金は株式会社の資本金に相当）を調達する方針だ。

securitization of bad loans　不良債権の証券化
◆The two prospective partners have extensive expertise in mergers and acquisitions, as well as the securitization of bad

loans. 提携する予定の両社は、企業の合併・買収（M&A）や不良債権の証券化などに豊富なノウハウを持っている。

securitization of real estate　不動産の証券化
　（=real estate securitization）
　◆Under the system of securitization of real estate, special purpose companies established by real estate firms issue shares in real estate by using the property as collateral. この不動産の証券化の制度では、不動産会社が設立する特定目的会社（SPC）が、（買い取った）不動産を担保にして不動産の株式（有価証券）を発行する。

securitize [securitise]　（動）証券化する
　（⇒business soundness）
　securitize bad loans　不良債権を証券化する
　securitize car loans　自動車ローンを証券化する
　securitize housing loan claims　住宅ローンの債権を証券化する　（⇒housing loan claim）
　securitize loans　ローンを証券化する、債権を証券化する
　securitize one's assets　資産を証券化する
　securitize pools of mortgages　モーゲージ・プールを証券化する
　securitize the borrowings　借入れを証券化する
　◆Major commercial banks plan to further reduce their assets by calling in and also securitizing loans. 大手行は、融資の回収や債権の証券化などで、資産の圧縮を加速させる構えだ。

securitized [securitized]　（形）証券化した
　securitized asset　証券化した資産、証券化資産、資産の証券化
　securitized borrowing and lending　ローンの証券化
　securitized credit card receivables　証券化されたクレジット・カード受取り債権、クレジット・カード受取り債権の証券化
　securitized debt　証券化した債権、債権の証券化
　securitized home mortgages　証券化した住宅モーゲージ、住宅モーゲージの証券化

securitized product　証券化商品
　◆An interim report of the Financial Stability Forum called for measures such as a review of evaluation system of securitized products. 金融安定化フォーラムの中間報告は、証券化商品の評価方法見直しなどの措置を求めた。◆Securitized products have been a major cause of worsening the subprime problem. 証券化商品が、サブプライム問題拡大の主な要因となっている。

securitizing commercial bank assets　商業銀行資産の証券化

security　（名）安全、安全性、安心、無事、安全保障、公安、保安、警備、保護、防衛、防衛手段、警備対策、保証、保証人、担保、抵当、証券、銘柄、保険
　（⇒debt security, leveraged buyout）
　a security on combined properties　共同担保
　as security for　〜の抵当［担保・保証］として
　（=in security for）
　benefit security　給付保障
　collateral security　物的担保、副担保
　commodity security　商品証券
　dilutive security　潜在的普通株式
　enforcement of security　担保の実行
	evidence of security　担保の証拠
	financial security　支払い能力、財務上の安全性
	give security　担保を提供する
	impersonal security　物的担保
	interest bearing security　利付き証券
	listed security　上場証券、上場有価証券
	loan security　貸付け証券
	on security of　〜を担保にして、〜を抵当にして

personal property security　動産担保
real property security　不動産担保
risk security　リスク証券
security account　有価証券勘定
security affiliate　系列証券会社
security agreement　担保契約
　（=hypothecation agreement）
security analysis　証券分析
security analyst　証券分析家、証券アナリスト、アナリスト
security bill　証券担保為替手形
security capital　安全資本
security capitalism　証券資本主義
security collateral loan　証券副抵当貸付け、証券金融
security corporation　証券会社
security credit　証券金融
security deposit　敷金
security dividend　証券配当
Security Exchange Act　米証券取引法
security facilities　保護預り
security financing　証券金融　（=security loan）
security firm　証券会社　（=brokerage firm, brokerage house, securities company, security corporation）
security for an obligation　債券担保
security for good conduct　身元保証金
security holder　証券所有者、証券保有者
security holding　証券所有、証券保有
security income and expenses　有価証券損益
security investment　証券投資
security loan　証券金融、証券担保融資
security market　証券市場
security money　手付け金、保証金
　（=hand money）
security offering　有価証券の募集
security position　証券ポジション
security price　証券価格
security rating　証券評価、債券評価
security reserve method　保証準備制度、保証準備発行制度
security warranty　担保権
social security　社会保障、社会保険
social security benefits　社会保障給付
social security payment　社会保険料
unemployment security　失業保険
unrated security　格付けのない証券
without security　無担保で
　◆Concerns have been raised over the ability of Internet banking services to verify the identity of new depositors or to guarantee the security of customer transactions. インターネット・バンキングについては、新規預金者の身元確認や対顧客取引の安全保証の点で、その能力に対して懸念が提起されている。◆In the loans to be extended to the company by the Development Bank of Japan, accounts receivable will be taken as security. 日本政策投資銀行の同社への融資では、売掛金が担保に取られる。◆Livedoor is believed to be considering using NBS shares as security to secure the necessary funds. ライブドアは、ニッポン放送株を担保にして必要資金を確保することを検討している模様だ。◆We are considering using the company's shares as security to secure the necessary funds. 当社は、同社株を担保にして必要資金を確保することを検討している。◆We need to enhance the security of

information networks by preventing leaks of personal information and averting the spread of computer viruses. われわれは、個人情報の漏洩を防ぎ、コンピュータ・ウイルスの流行を回避して、情報ネットワークの安全性を高める必要がある。

security breach 不正侵入
◆Fabricated credit cards have been illegally used at electrical appliances discount stores and cash voucher shops in Japan after the security breach was revealed in the United States. 米国で不正侵入が明らかになった後、偽造されたクレジット・カードが日本の家電量販店や金券ショップなどで不正に使用されている。

security camera 防犯カメラ
◆Footage from a security camera showed the woman using the man's cash card to withdraw cash. 防犯カメラの映像に、女が男性のキャッシュ・カードを使って預金を引き出している姿が残っていた。

security firm 証券会社
◆The security firm expects to book about ¥73 billion in losses related to its residential mortgage-backed securities business in the July-September quarter. 同証券会社は、7-9月期に住宅融資証券事業の関連損失として730億円を計上する見通しだ。

security interest 担保権, 動産担保権, 先取特権
have a perfected security interest in the receivables 債権に対して対抗力[対抗要件]を具備した動産担保権を保有する
perfect the security interest by means of filing financial statements 貸付け証書を登録して担保権の対抗要件[対抗力]を具備する
perfected security interest 対抗力[対抗要件]を具備した動産担保権
security interest in the receivables 債権に対する動産担保権
security interests 持ち株関係

security measures セキュリティ対策
◆Users of online banking services had better take security measures by using antivirus software. ネット・バンキングの利用者は、ウイルス対策ソフトを使ってセキュリティ対策を取ったほうが良い。

security taxation system 証券税制
（⇒securities-related taxation system）
◆Concerning the security taxation system, the government's Tax Commission proposed simplifying preferential measures for tax levies on capital gains and consolidating income from dividends and investment trusts. 証券税制については、政府税制調査会は、株式譲渡益課税の優遇措置の簡素化と、配当や投資信託からの所得を合理化する考えを示した。

securityholder (名)証券保有者
（=security holder）

seed money 元金, 出発資金, 出発基金, 着手金, 元手, 元手資金, 当初投資資金

seek (動)求める, 募る, 誘致する, 追求する, 狙(ねら)う, 要求する, 申請する, 探す, 探査する, 調査する, 手に入れようとする, 得ようとする, 〜に務める
be (much) sought after 求められている, 需要がある, 引っ張りだこだ, もてはやされる
seek a helping hand from 〜に支援を求める
seek a rating 格付けを申請する
seek advice from 〜に助言[アドバイス]を求める
seek compensation from 〜に補償を求める, 〜に賠償請求する （=claim compensation from）
seek court protection 破産申請する
seek foreign investment 外資を誘致する
seek funds 資金を求める, 資金を調達する
seek investments in 〜への出資を募る, 〜への投資を誘致する （⇒fictitious）
seek relief 減免を求める
seek safe haven in New York ニューヨークに安全な投資先を求める
seek to 〜しようとする, 〜に努力する, 〜に努める
seek underwriters 引受シ団を組成する
seek ways to cope with 〜に対処する手段を講じる
seek ¥500 billion in financial aid from A Aに5,000億円の金融支援を要請する
◆Mitsubishi Paper Mills Ltd., a member of the Mitsubishi group, also may seek to join hands with Hokuetsu Paper. 三菱のグループ企業の三菱製紙も、北越製紙との提携を求める可能性がある。◆The company decided to seek a helping hand from the investment fund. 同社は、この投資ファンドに支援を求めることにした。◆To avoid sinking into a negative net worth, the firm is seeking ¥300 billion in financial aid from capital providers. 債務超過に陥るのを避けるため、同社は資金提供者に3,000億円の金融支援を要請している。◆To improve its financial health, Daiei will seek about ¥410 billion worth of debt waivers from about 30 financial institutions to reduce its interest-bearing debts. 財務体質を改善するため、ダイエーは、約30の金融機関に約4,100億円の債権放棄を求めて、有利子負債を削減する。

seek additional loans from financial institutions 金融機関に追加融資を求める
◆The company has found it difficult to seek additional loans from financial institutions and raise funds from corporate bonds. 同社は、金融機関に追加融資を求めることも社債による資金調達を行うことも、困難な状況にある。

seek capital injection 資本の注入[増強]を求める, 増資を求める, 保険会社への基金拠出[保険会社の基金増資]を求める （=seek capital increase）
◆This life insurer sought capital injection of 70 billion yen from financial institutions. この生命保険会社は、金融機関に700億円の基金拠出[基金増資]を要請した。

seek compensation from 〜に補償を求める, 〜に賠償請求する （=claim compensation from）
◆The bank is likely to seek billions of yen in compensation from former executives. 同行は、旧経営陣に数十億円の賠償請求をする見通しだ。

seek debt waivers from the creditor banks 取引銀行に債権放棄を求める, 取引銀行に債務免除を求める
◆Companies must be generating operating profits from their main businesses to seek debt waivers from the creditor banks. 取引銀行に債権放棄を求めるには、企業はその主要な事業部門で営業利益を上げていなければならない。

seek expansion through borrowing 資金の借入れで事業拡大を狙う
◆Money loaned by private banks declined because banks with weakened financial strength were less willing to lend, besides a lack of businesses seeking expansion through borrowing. 民間銀行の貸出金が減ったのは、お金を借りてまで事業を拡大しようとする企業がなかったほか、財務が悪化した銀行が貸し渋ったからだ。

seek high returns 高収益を狙う
◆The firm's asset management strategy is geared to seek high returns. 同社の資産運用戦略は、高収益を狙ったものだ。

seek higher returns 高収益を狙う, 高利益を求める
◆Investors purchased more overseas bonds and stocks to seek higher returns. 投資家は、高利益を求めて外国の債券や株式への投資が拡大した。

seek public funds 公的資金を求める
◆TEPCO is seeking public funds to make compensation payments for damages caused by the crisis at its Fukushima No. 1 nuclear power plant. 東電は、福島第一原子力発電所の事故による損害の賠償金を支払うため、公的資金を求めて

seek safe haven　安全な投資先
◆The funds that so abundantly seek safe haven in New York today can flow outward tomorrow. 安全な投資先を求めて今日ニューヨークにあふれるほど集まった資金も、明日には外へ流出しかねない。

seek stricter assessment of bank assets　銀行資産の一段と厳しい査定を求める
◆The Oct. 30, 2002 financial revitalization plan sought stricter assessments of bank assets. 2002年10月30日の「金融再生プログラム」は、銀行資産の一段と厳しい査定を求めた。

segregated account　分離口座

seized goods　差し押さえ物件

seizure　(名)差し押さえ、押収、没収、接収、占拠、監禁、逮捕、拿捕(だほ)、発作、急病
◆Legal action should be taken against those who refuse to pay national pension premiums, such as seizure of postal savings and bank deposits. 国民年金保険料の納付拒絶者に対しては、預貯金の差し押さえなどの法的措置を取るべきだ。

selected dealer agreement　販売団契約
(＝selling group agreement)

selection　(名)選択、選別、抽出、セレクション
　adverse selection　逆選択、逆選別
　asset selection　資産選択
　media selection　媒体選択
　optimal portfolio　最適資産の選択、最適ポートフォリオの選択
　portfolio selection　資産選択、ポートフォリオ・セレクション
　risk selection　リスク選択、危険選択
　sample selection　サンプル抽出
　security selection　銘柄選択
　selection criteria　選択基準、選別基準
　self-selection　逆選択、逆選別
　stock selection skills　銘柄選択の技術

selective buying　物色買い

selective lending　選別融資

selective loans　融資規制

self-assessment　自己査定、自己評価、自己申告、申告納税　(⇒separate self-assessment taxation)
◆Investors are permitted to hold multiple specified accounts, but this would require the self-assessment of their total gains and losses during the annual trading period. 投資家は複数の特定口座を開くことができるが、この場合は、投資家自身が複数口座の各年度の取引期間の売買損益を集約して納税申告しなければならない。

self-declared bankruptcy　自己破産(破産法に基づく債務整理の一つで、債務者本人が裁判所に破産申立てを行う。破産宣告を受けると、財産があれば管財人が選ばれて処分されるほか、就くことのできる職業が限定されるとか、裁判所の許可なく移転できなくなるなどの制限を受ける。その後、裁判所から債務の免責が認められると、それ以上の支払い義務や職業などの制限はなくなる)
◆The number of annual applications for individual and corporate self-declared bankruptcy cases surpassed 200,000 for the first time in 2002. 1年間の個人と法人の自己破産申立て件数が、2002年に初めて20万件を突破した。

self-employed　(形)自営業の、自家営業の、自営の、個人経営の　(＝self-operated)
　self-employed people　自営業者
　(＝the self-employed)
　the self-employed　自営業者
◆Many self-employed people are now without income due to the March 11 disaster. 東日本大震災で、多くの自営業者は現在、収入が途絶えている。◆The rate of contributions to the national pension program, designed mainly for the self-employed, students aged 20 and older and young people working part-time, dipped to a record 62.8 percent. 自営業者や20歳以上の学生、フリーターらが加入する国民年金の納付率が、過去最悪の62.8％に落ち込んだ。

self-help efforts　自助努力
◆Greece has to continue making self-help efforts to cut its fiscal deficit by such measures as selling off state enterprises. ギリシャの場合は、国営企業の売却(措置)などで財政赤字を縮小する自助努力を重ねる必要がある。

self-imposed regulation　自主規制
◆After the merger, the TSE and OSE will be divided into four operator firms handling spot trading, derivatives, settlement of trading deals and self-imposed regulations respectively. 経営統合後、東証と大証は、それぞれ現物株、デリバティブ(金融派生商品)、取引決済と自主規制を扱う4事業会社に切り分けられることになっている。

self-liquidating asset purchase　自己債券発行による資産買収、SLAP

self-regulatory organization　自主規制機関、SRO

self-rehabilitation　自主再建、自力再建
(＝self-restructuring)
◆The company has to abandon the option of self-rehabilitation. 同社は、自力再建の道[選択肢]を断念しなければならない。◆Without the help of banks, self-rehabilitation is extremely difficult. 銀行の支援がないと、自主再建は非常に難しい。

self-responsibility　自己責任
◆Depositors must have a keener sense of self-responsibility. 預金者は、これまで以上に自己責任が問われることになる。

self-supporting accounting system　独立採算制
◆In principle, the hotels run by a public organization should be operated under a self-supporting accounting system. 原則として、公的組織が経営しているホテルは、独立採算制で運営すべきだ。

self-sustainable growth　自律的成長
◆The Japanese economy is entering into a virtuous cycle of self-sustainable growth led by private demand. 日本経済には、民需主導の自律的な成長という好循環が生まれている。

self-sustaining　(形)独力で維持できる、自給の、自活できる、自立した、(核反応などが)自動継続式の、継続的な
　self-sustaining economy　自立経済
　self-sustaining foreign operations　自立した海外事業
　self-sustaining fund　自己調達資金
　self-sustaining growth　自律的成長

self-sustaining operation　自立した事業
◆Self-sustaining operations are those whose economic activities are largely independent of those of the parent company. 自立した事業とは、その経済活動が親会社の経済活動から十分に独立している事業のことです。

self-sustaining recovery　自律回復
◆The government and the Bank of Japan should seek to put the economic back on the road to self-sustaining recovery led by growth in domestic demand by implementing additional fiscal and monetary measures. 政府・日銀は、財政・金融両面からの政策の後押しで、内需中心の自律回復をめざすべきだ。

self tender　株式の自己買付け、自己株の買戻し、自社株の買戻し提案(買収を仕掛けられた場合などに、会社が株主に対して行う自社株の買戻し提案のこと)

sell　(動)販売する、売る、売却する、売り渡す、売り込む、納入する、処分する、債券などを発行する、譲渡する　(名)販売、売り
(⇒stock holding)

buy low and sell high　安く買い高く売る
close and sell affiliated companies　関連会社［関係会社］を閉鎖・整理して売却する
raise capital by selling stock　株式を募集［発行］して資金を調達する
sell a cap　キャップを売る
sell a floor　フロアを売る
sell additional shares of common stock　普通株式を追加発行する
sell at the market　成り行き価格で売る, 成り行き売り
sell by public tender　公開入札で売却する
sell capital stock　株式を発行する
sell common stock at book value　普通株式を簿価で発行する
sell dollars forward　ドルを先売りする
sell down assets　資産を売却する
sell for cash　現金で売る
sell for future delivery　先渡しで売る
sell futures　先物売りをする
sell long　強気売りする
sell most of one's 10 percent stakes in the company　保有する同社株の10％の大半を売却する（⇒shareholder）
sell one's participation in　～から資金を引き上げる
sell operating rights to　～に営業権を譲渡する
sell options　オプションを売却する
sell order　売り注文
sell out　処分売り
sell plus　セル・プラス注文
sell preferred shares　優先株を発行する
sell some subsidiaries　一部の子会社を売却する
sell stock　株式を売却する, 株式を発行する, 株式を募集する（=sell shares）
sell swaps　スワップを譲渡する
sell the rally　（相場がある程度）戻ったところで売る, 戻り売り（=selling on a rally）
sell $3 billion in stock through an online auction　ネット・オークションで30億ドルの株式を発行する
stock is selling at around　株［株式］は～前後で取引されている, 株価は現在～前後だ
stock is trading at　株式［株］は～で取引されている
◆Aeon Co. has called on Marubeni Corp. to sell up to 30 percent of its stake in Maruetsu Inc. イオンは, 丸紅（ダイエーの筆頭株主）に対して, マルエツ株の最大30％譲渡を求めた。◆American International Group Inc. sued Bank of America for allegedly selling it faulty mortgage investments. 米保険大手のAIGが, 欠陥商品のモーゲージ証券を同社に販売したとしてバンク・オブ・アメリカを提訴した。◆By selling JT shares, the government expects to raise ￥500 billion to ￥600 billion to finance reconstruction from the Great East Japan Earthquake. JT（日本たばこ産業）株の売却で政府は, 東日本大震災復興の財源に充てるため, 5,000億円〜6,000億円の資金調達を見込んでいる。◆Ford will relinquish its position as the biggest shareholder of Mazda Motor Corp. by selling most of its 11 percent stake in Mazda. 米フォードは, 保有するマツダ株11％の大半を売却して, マツダの筆頭株主の座を降りることになった。◆General Motors Corp. agreed to sell up to $55 billion in car and truck loans to Bank of America Corp. over five years. ゼネラル・モーターズ（GM）は, バンク・オブ・アメリカに対して, 今後5年間で最大550億ドルの自動車ローン債権を売却することで合意した。◆Google Inc. plans to go public by selling $2.7 billion in stock through an online auction. 米インターネット検索サービス最大手のグーグルが, ネット・オークションによる27億ドルの株式発行で新規株式公開を計画している。◆Plants in foreign countries will be sold or liquidated. 海外の生産拠点（工場）は, 売却または清算する。◆Sanyo Electric Co.'s largest shareholders need Sanyo's approval to sell their preferred shares before March 2009. 三洋電機の大株主は, 2009年3月以前に保有する優先株式を譲渡する場合には, 三洋電機の承認を得る必要がある。◆Stock prices will tumble, if banks try to sell a large amount of banks crossheld shares in the market ahead of the account settlement term at the end of March. 3月末の決算期を控えて, 銀行が大量の持ち合い株式を市場に放出すれば, 株価は急落する。◆The company is considering selling its professional baseball club. 同社は, プロ野球団の売却を検討している。◆The firm sold its 8％ bonds that had a face value of $1,000,000. 同社は, 額面100万ドルの8％利付き社債を発行した。◆The government plans to sell some of its 100 percent stake in Japan Post Holdings Co. to fund reconstruction from the Great East Japan Earthquake. 政府は, 東日本大震災の復興財源に充てるため, 100％保有する日本郵政の株式の一部も売却する方針だ。◆The price tag for the mortgage-backed securities sold to Fannie and Freddie by 17 financial firms totaled $196.1 billion. 大手金融機関17社がファニー・メイとフレディ・マックに販売した住宅ローン担保証券（MBS）の購入額は, 総額で1,961億ドルになる。◆The U.S. government filed lawsuits against 17 financial firms for selling Fannie and Freddie mortgage-backed securities that turned toxic when the housing market collapsed. 米政府は, 住宅市場崩壊時に不良資産化した住宅ローン担保証券（MBS）をファニー・メイ（米連邦住宅抵当公庫）とフレディ・マック（米連邦住宅貸付け抵当公社）に販売したとして, 大手金融機関17社（バンク・オブ・アメリカやシティグループ, JPモルガン・チェース, ゴールドマン・サックス・グループなど）を提訴した。◆To procure funds to finance reconstruction from the Great East Japan Earthquake, the government is planning to sell some of its shares in Japan Tobacco Inc. and Tokyo Metro Co. 東日本大震災の復興費用を賄うための資金を調達するため, 政府は日本たばこ産業（JT）と東京地下鉄（東京メトロ）の株式を売却する方針だ。◆To raise money for compensation related to the Fukushima No. 1 nuclear power plant crisis, TEPCO will sell about 40 pieces of real estate for about ￥10 billion. 福島第一原発事故関連の資金を調達するため, 東電は約40か所の不動産を100億円前後で売却する。◆UFJ Holdings Inc. has agreed to sell UFJ Trust Bank Ltd. to Sumitomo Trust & Banking Co., Ltd. for about ￥300 billion to raise its capital adequacy ratio. UFJホールディングスが, 自己資本比率を引き上げるため, UFJ信託銀行を約3,000億円で住友信託銀行に売却することで合意した。

sell common stock　普通株式を発行する, 普通株式を売り出す
◆GM's stakeholders initially sell common stock, while GM will sell preferred shares. GMの株主は, 上場時に保有する普通株式を売り出すほか, GMは優先株を発行する予定だ。

sell insurance　保険を販売する
◆Sompo Japan Insurance Inc. began selling "SoftBank Kantan Hoken" insurance by forming a business partnership with SoftBank Mobile Corp. 損保保険ジャパンが, ソフトバンクモバイルと業務提携して, 「ソフトバンクかんたん保険」の販売を開始した。

sell insurance policies　保険を販売する
◆Banks are allowed to sell insurance policies to clients. 銀行は, 顧客に保険を販売することができる。◆Banks could forcibly sell insurance policies to clients by utilizing their strong position as creditors. 銀行は, 債権者としての強い立場を利用して, 顧客に保険を強制的に販売する可能性もある。

sell off　（動）売却する, 投げ売りする, 安く売り払う, 見切り品として処分する, 相場が下がる, 売られる　（⇒loan claims, mutually held stocks, speculative trader）
sell off one's assets　資産を売却する

sell off one's bonds　国債を投げ売りする
sell off one's loan books　債権を売却する
sell off one's stockholdings　保有株を売却する
◆According to market players, commercial banks, keen to slash shares cross-held with their business partners, have been selling off their stockholdings as the settlement of accounts for the business year ending Sept. 30 approaches. 市場関係者によると、企業の9月中間決算期末を控えて、取引先との持ち合い株の解消（削減）に積極的な金融機関は、保有株の売却に出ている。◆Banks sold off their bonds of Portugal and Spain. 金融機関「銀行」が、ポルトガルとスペインの国債を投げ売りした。◆During a regular board meeting, Fuji TV directors agreed to file a claim against Livedoor for losses of more than ¥30 billion incurred from selling of Livedoor shares. 定例取締役会で、フジテレビの役員は、ライブドア株の売却で被った300億円超の損失について、ライブドアに損害賠償を請求することで合意した。◆Greece has to continue making self-help efforts to cut its fiscal deficit by such measures as selling off state enterprises. ギリシャの場合は、国営企業の売却（措置）などで財政赤字を縮小する自助努力を重ねる必要がある。◆The bond market sold off sharply. 債券相場が、急落した。◆The Treasuries sold off dramatically. 米国債が、一斉に売られた。◆There was unexpectedly strong opposition within and outside the company to the plan to sell off the company's main earner. 同社のドル箱である事業の全面売却案には、社内外から予想外の強い反発があった。

sell-off　（名）投げ売り, 売却, 売り, 急落
accelerate sell-offs of stock holdings　保有株の売却を加速させる
dollar sell-off　ドル売り　（⇒factor）
renewed sell-off in the bond market　債券相場の反落
sell-off in the market　市場の急落, 売り局面
sell-off plan　売却計画
sell-off worldwide　世界同時株安　（=simultaneous decline of stock prices over the world）
speculative sell-off of the dollar　投機的ドル売り
stock market sell-off　株式相場の急落
the world sell-off of stocks　世界同時株安
◆Large simultaneous sell-offs of banks' shareholdings on the market would lead to a vicious cycle of plunging share prices and worsening bank finances. 銀行の保有株を市場で大量に同時に売却すれば、株価下落と銀行の財務内容の悪化という悪循環につながる。◆Nippon Life Insurance Co. carried out massive sell-offs of loss hiding scandal-hit Olympus Corp.'s shares. 日本生命保険が、損失隠しの疑惑をもたれるオリンパスの株の大量売却を実施した。◆The sell-off of Tokyo Metro shares planned by the government will likely be opposed by the Tokyo metropolitan government which is the second-largest shareholder. 政府が計画している東京メトロ株の売却には、国に次ぐ大株主の東京都が抵抗すると見られる。◆Tokyo stocks fell to a three-month low as foreign investors sparked a sell-off. 東京株（東京株式市場の株価）は、外国人投資家が株を売り進めたため3か月ぶりに急落した。

sell off assets　資産を売却する
◆To raise money for compensation related to the Fukushima No. 1 nuclear power plant crisis, TEPCO will sell off assets through four trust banks. 福島第一原発事故関連の賠償資金を調達するため、東電は、4信託銀行を通じて資産を売却することになった。

sell-off of bank stocks　銀行株の下落, 銀行株の売り［売却］
◆The government's financial revival plan is expected to exacerbate the credit crunch and result in a further sell-off of bank stocks. 政府の金融再生プログラムは、貸し渋りを加速して銀行株の下落に拍車がかかると予想される。

sell-off of stock holdings　保有株の売却

(=sell-off of shareholdings)
◆Major life insurance companies are accelerating sell-offs of stock holdings to make them less vulnerable to fluctuations in stock prices that could adversely affect their finances. 大手生保各社が、財務内容にマイナス影響を与えかねない株価変動に左右されにくいようにするため、保有株の売却を加速させている。

sell order　売り注文, 発注
erroneous sell order　誤発注, 発注ミス
stop loss sell order　逆指し値売り注文
◆A Mizuho Securities employee entered a sell order from a client as "sell 610,000 shares at ¥1 each" though the client's actual order was "sell one share at ¥610,000." 顧客の実際の注文は「61万円で1株の売り」であったが、みずほ証券の社員は「1株1円で61万株の売り」と入力して顧客の売り注文を出してしまった。◆It's not a beautiful story for securities firms to snap up stocks while being aware of the erroneous sell order. 誤発注と認識しながら、証券会社が間隙を縫って株を取得するのは、美しい話ではない。◆Mizuho Securities Co. placed a huge errant sell order for the newly listed shares of recruitment firm J-Com Co. みずほ証券が、人材サービス業ジェイコムの新規上場株式に対し、誤って大量の売り注文を出してしまった。◆Sell orders outnumbered buy orders in a wide range of sectors. 幅広い業種で、売り注文が買い注文より多かった。

sell order error　誤発注, 発注ミス
(=erroneous sell order)
◆Mizuho Securities Co.'s sell order error was made when its staffer entered data incorrectly. みずほ証券の誤発注[発注ミス]は、同社の担当者がデータを誤って入力した際に生じた。

sell over bank counters　銀行窓口で販売する
◆Meiji Yasuda's single-premium whole life insurance is one of its flagship products which are sold over bank counters. 明治安田生保の一時払い終身保険は、銀行窓口で販売されている同社の主力商品の一つだ。

sell policies　保険を販売する, 保険契約を獲得する
◆During the bubble economy, life insurers sold a large number of policies by promising high yields. バブル期に生保各社は、高い予定利率を約束して多くの保険契約を獲得した。

sell risky instruments　高リスク金融商品を販売する, 高リスク投資商品を販売する, 高リスク証券［有価証券］を販売する
◆U.S. regulator sued 17 big banks for selling risky investments. 米規制当局が、高リスクの金融商品［高リスク証券］を販売したとして大手金融機関17社を提訴した。

sell shares　株式を売却する, 株式を発行する, 株式を売り出す, 株式を募集する, 株を売り進める, 株を売りまくる, 株式を譲渡する　（=sell stock）
◆Investors sold shares across the board to lock in profits. 利益を確定するため、投資家が全銘柄にわたって株を売り進めた。◆Publicly listing Tokyo Metro and selling shares in it could net the government hundreds of billions of yen. 東京地下鉄（東京メトロ）の株式を上場して保有株式を売却すれば、国は数千億円の収入を見込める。◆Sanyo Electric Co.'s largest shareholders need Sanyo's approval to sell their preferred shares before March 2009. 三洋電機の大株主は、2009年3月以前に保有する優先株式を譲渡する場合には、三洋電機の承認を得る必要がある。

sell short　空売りする　（=short-sell; ⇒long position, short selling [short-selling]）
◆Morgan Stanley Nippon repeatedly sold short after dropping the price ¥1 increments. 米モルガン・スタンレー証券東京支店は、1円ずつ値を下げて空売りした。◆The firm hedged its long position in stocks by selling short the futures contract. 同社は、先物を空売りして現物株のロング・ポジションをヘッジした。◆The Tokyo Stock Exchange plans to begin releasing monthly data from April on the trading volume of

stocks sold short. 東京証券取引所は、4月から株の空売りの売買額に関するデータを毎月公表する方針だ。

sell stock 株式を売却する,株式を売り出す,株式を売り進む,株式を売りまくる （=sell shares）
◆Investors around the world are selling stocks with abandon as a global recession is under way. 世界的な景気後退の進行で、世界中の投資家が株を売りまくっている。

sell stock [shares] to the public 株式を公開する
◆GM filed the first batch of paperwork to sell stock to the public. ゼネラル・モーターズは、株式を新規公開するための初回分の書類を提出した。

sell the yen 円を売る
◆The Finance Ministry and the Bank of Japan may keep selling the yen to stem its surge. 円高を食い止めるため[円の急騰を阻止するため]、財務省・日本銀行は、円を売り続ける可能性がある。

seller （名）売り手,売り主,売り方,販売者,セラー
　　at seller's option　売り方選択権付きで,売り方勝手渡しで
　　at seller's risk　売り手危険持ちで,売り手負担で
　　bond seller　債券の売り手
　　seller financing　掛売り,セラー・ファイナンス
　　seller's market　売り手市場
　　seller's monopoly　販売独占,売り手独占
　　seller's option　売り手選択,売り選択特約,売り手オプション,特約日決済取引
　　seller's option transaction　特約日(決済)取引
　　sellers over　売り手[売り方]過多,売り長(なが)
　　seller's rate　売り手相場,売り相場
　　　（=selling rate）
　　short seller　空売り筋,相場師
◆In commodity futures trading, prices are decided when buyers and sellers make deals. So they can execute trades at promised prices even if the value of goods has changed drastically in the meantime. 商品先物取引では、売り手と買い手が取引契約をする時点で価格を決める。そのため、契約期間中に相場が大きく変動しても、売り手と買い手は約束した値段で取引を執行できる。

selling （名）売り,販売,セリング　（⇒buying, panic selling, short selling [short-selling], speculative selling, spot selling, triple fall）
　　bill selling operation　手形売りオペ
　　bond selling　債券売却
　　buying futures and selling cash　先物買い・現物売り
　　distress selling　狼狽売り　（=panic selling）
　　exchange selling　売り為替
　　forced selling　株式強制処分
　　heavy selling　大量の売り
　　hedge selling　ヘッジ売り
　　panic selling　狼狽売り
　　selling agent　販売代理店
　　selling at a discount　割引販売
　　selling at a premium　割増金付き販売
　　selling cash　現物（ろうばい）売り
　　selling climax　パニック売り
　　selling concession　分売手数料,売りさばき報酬,売上手数料,販売手数料
　　selling contract　売り予約,販売契約
　　selling exchange　売り為替
　　selling exchange rate　売り為替相場
　　selling group　(証券公募の)販売団,分売団,販売グループ　（=selling syndicate: 引受シンジケート団の引受幹事主導のもとに組成されて、証券の分売を担当する

ディーラーの集団）
　　selling hedge　売りつなぎ
　　selling limit　売り指し値
　　selling of securities under reverse repurchase agreement　買戻し条件付き売りオペ
　　selling off　売り崩し,投げ売り
　　selling offer　売りオファー,売り申込み
　　selling on a rally　戻り売り,株が再び高値に戻ってきたときの売り
　　　（=selling on temporary recovery）
　　selling on a (rising) scale　信用取引の売り上がり（高騰する株を段階的に空売りすること）
　　selling on balance　売り越し
　　selling operation　売り操作,売りオペ,売りオペレーション（中央銀行が市中で証券などを売却すること）
　　selling operation under a rebuying [repurchase] agreement　買戻し条件付き売りオペ
　　selling out　処分競売
　　selling price　売却価格,売り値　（⇒borrowed stocks, separate withholding tax system）
　　selling rate [quotation]　(外国為替の)売り相場,売りレート
　　selling sentiments　売り気　（=selling support）
　　selling short　空売り　（=short selling）
　　selling support　売り支え,売り気(selling sentiment)
　　selling syndicate　販売団,分売団,証券引受シンジケート
　　　（=selling group）
　　short selling　空売り,短期見越し売却,弱気売り方
　　sight selling rate　一覧払い手形売り相場
　　speculative dollar selling　投機的なドル売り
　　tax selling　課税回避目的の証券売却
　　unconditional selling operation　無条件売りオペレーション
　　yen-selling, dollar-buying operation　円売り・ドル買い介入
　　yen-selling intervention　円売り介入
◆Selling ballooned on the New York Stock Exchange on Tuesday. 火曜日のニューヨーク市場[ニューヨーク証券取引所]は、売りが膨らんだ。◆The government and the Bank of Japan implemented a yen-selling, dollar-buying operation for their fifth market intervention this year. 政府・日銀は、今年5回目の市場介入として円売り・ドル買い介入に踏み切った。

selling of the dollar　ドル売り
　　（=the dollar selling）
◆Selling of the dollar has been accelerating since late October. 10月下旬からドル売りが加速している。

selling order　売り注文　（=sell order）
　　massive selling orders　大量の売り注文
　　small-lot selling orders　小口の売り注文
◆JAL stocks met with massive selling orders Wednesday morning on the Tokyo Stock Exchange, with the price down ¥30 from Tuesday at ¥7 before 9:30 a.m. 東京証券取引所では、日航株は水曜日の朝方から大量の売り注文が殺到し、午前9時半前には前日比30円安の7円まで下落した。◆Relatively small-lot selling orders led prices to slip sharply. 比較的、小口の売り注文が出ると、株価が大きく下がった。

selling point　売れ筋,セールス・ポイント,セリング・ポイント
◆We'll see more and more brands which will have organic as a selling point. 「有機(食品)」をセールス・ポイントにした銘柄が、これからはどんどん増えるでしょう。

selling pressure　売り圧力,売り注文の殺到,売り注文の膨(ふく)らみ,売り優勢の展開,売り浴びせ
　　（=the tide of selling; ⇒high-tech company）

accelerate selling pressure on the U.S. stocks and the dollar　米国の株・ドル売りを加速する

come under selling pressure across the board　軒並み売り圧力がかかる, 軒並み売られる, 軒並み売りを浴びせられる

dollar-selling pressure　ドル売り圧力

heavy selling pressure　強い売り圧力

◆Concern over the revival of the twin deficits is accelerating selling pressure on the U.S. stocks and the dollar. 双子の赤字の復活懸念が, 米国の株・ドル売りを加速している。◆It was early July 1997, when the value of the Thai baht nosedived under heavy selling pressure, triggering a currency and financial crisis in East Asia. タイの通貨バーツの相場が強い売り圧力で暴落し, 東アジアの通貨・金融危機の引き金を引いたのは, 1997年7月の初めだった。◆Out of a sense of relief, dollar-selling pressure has eased on the foreign currency markets. 安堵(あんど)感から, 外国為替市場では, ドル売り圧力が弱まった。◆Stock prices in Tokyo fell by more than 600 points as a state of panic gripped investors and selling pressure snowballed. 東京市場の株価は, 投資家がパニック状態に陥り, 売り圧力が増大[加速]したため, 下げ幅が600円を超えた。◆Tokyo stock prices, under selling pressure due to mounting anxieties over prospects for both the Japanese and U.S. economies, plummeted Tuesday to their lowest point since the bursting of the bubble economy in late 1989. 火曜日の東京(東京株式市場)の株価は, 日米の景気先行きへの懸念による売り注文が膨らみ, 1989年末のバブル崩壊後の最安値の水準まで急落した。

selling pressure on the euro　ユーロ売り圧力

◆On the foreign exchange market, there has been no halt to selling pressure on the euro due to concern about the financial crisis in Europe. 外国為替市場では, 欧州の金融危機を懸念して, ユーロ売り圧力が止まらない展開となっている。

selling yen and buying dollars　円売り・ドル買い　(=yen-selling and dollar-buying)

◆The Bank of Japan began selling yen and buying dollars at 10:35 a.m. 日銀は, 午前10時35分に円売り・ドル買いを開始した。◆The Bank of Japan continued selling yen and buying dollars intermittently. 日銀は, 断続的に円売り・ドル買いを継続した。◆To stop further falls in stock prices and the continued weakening of the dollar, the government and the Bank of Japan are urged to continue selling yen and buying dollars while exploring the possibility of joint intervention in the market with other countries. これ以上の株安とドル安を防ぐには, 政府・日銀が円売り・ドル買いを継続する一方, 他国との市場への協調介入の可能性を探るべきだ。

sellout　(名)処分売り

semiannual　(形)半期の, 中間の, 半年ごとの, 年2回の　(⇒manipulator)

semiannual dividend　中間配当, 半期配当金

semiannual earnings　半期決算, 中間決算　(=first-half results, interim results, semiannual release, semiannual results)

semiannual securities report　半期報告書

semiannual consolidated financial statements　中間連結財務書類[財務諸表], 中間連結決算書, 中間連結決算

◆Olympus will submit by Dec.14 the semiannual consolidated financial statements for the fiscal period ending in September. オリンパスは, 12月14日までに9月中間連結決算書を提出する。

semiannual currency report　為替政策半期報告書, 年2回の為替政策報告書　(米財務省は4月と10月に為替政策報告書を公表している)

◆The semiannual currency report of the U.S. Treasury Department said that Japan maintains a floating exchange rate regime. 日本は変動為替相場制[変動相場制]を維持している, と米財務省の為替政策半期報告書は述べている。

semiannual settlement of accounts　中間決算, 半期決算　(=semiannual results, semiannual settlement; ⇒settlement of accounts)

◆In its semiannual settlement of accounts in September, the company incurred ¥2.3 billion of recurring losses and ¥2.6 billion of after-tax losses. 9月の中間決算で同社は, 経常赤字が23億円, 税引き後損失も26億円に達した。

Senate Banking Committee　米上院銀行委員会

◆A Senate Banking Committee hearing on the auto industry bailout was held on Capitol Hill in Washington. 米自動車業界に対する政府支援についての上院銀行委員会の公聴会が, ワシントンの連邦議会で開かれた。

Senate Finance Committee　米上院財政委員会

◆The U.S. Senate Finance Committee chairman asked the U.S. ITC to order a probe into the damages caused by China's infringement of U.S. intellectual property rights. 米上院財政委員会の委員長が, 中国による米国の知的財産権侵害の被害状況についての調査を指示するよう, 米国際貿易委員会(ITC)に要請した。

senior security　上位証券　(発行会社の破産や清算のとき, 債務弁済の順位が他の証券よりも上位にある証券のこと。下位証券=junior security)

senior unsecured debt rating　上位無担保債務格付け

◆Moody's Investors Service has downgraded its long-term senior unsecured debt rating for Toyota and its subsidiaries to Aa1 from Aaa. ムーディーズ・インベスターズ・サービスは, トヨタとトヨタの子会社の長期上位無担保債務格付けを, 最上位のAaaからAa1に1段階引き下げた。

sense　(名)感覚, 感じ, 〜感, 観念, 意識, 心持ち, 気持ち, 〜心, 良識, 分別, 思慮, 認識力, 判断力, 意味, 語義, 意図, 趣旨, 意義, 価値, 効果, センス

abiding sense　固定観念

common sense　常識

have a sense of purpose　目的意識を持つ

in a broad sense　広い意味では, 広義では, 広義の

in the sense that　〜という意味では

make sense　意味がある, 筋が通る

see sense　物の道理がわかる, 分別ある行動をする

sense of achievement　達成感

sense of affluence　豊かさの実感

sense of community　共同意識

sense of crisis　危機感

sense of identity　自己認識

sense of loss　喪失感

sense of occasion　正しい行動感覚, 状況を的確に見抜く力

sense of perspective　大局観, 遠近感

sense of reality　現実感

sense of relief　安心感, 安堵(あんど)感

sense of responsibility　責任感

sense of uneasiness　不安感

sense of urgency　緊迫感

sense of wonder　好奇心

stand to sense　道理にかなう, もっともな言い分である

the sense of misgiving in the financial system　金融不安　(⇒misgiving)

◆A sense of restlessness and hopelessness still prevails among nonmanufacturers, small and midsize firms and regional economies. 非製造業や中小企業, 地方経済には, 焦燥と絶望感が広まったままだ。◆The sense of crisis is felt by those trying to stem a further economic downturn. これ以上の景気後退を食い止めようとしている人たちは, 危機感を抱

いている。

sense of disappointment　失望感
　◆A sense of disappointment has prevailed across the world markets as no concrete measures to rescue Greece were unveiled at the eurozone finance ministers meeting. ユーロ圏財務相会合でギリシャ支援の具体策が明らかにされなかったので、世界の市場で失望感が広がった。

sense of relief　安堵（あんど）感
　◆Out of a sense of relief, dollar-selling pressure has eased on the foreign currency markets. 安堵（あんど）感から、外国為替市場では、ドル売り圧力が弱まった。

sensitive　（形）敏感な, 左右されやすい, ～の影響を受けやすい, ～の影響が大きい, 高感度の, 要注意の, 機密の, 重要な　（⇒interest rate sensitive, interest-sensitive）
　be sensitive to interest rates　金利動向に敏感である, 金利動向に左右される, 金利動向の影響を受けやすい
　be sensitive to lower rates　金利の低下に対する感応性が高い, 金利の低下に左右される
　consumer-sensitive　消費者動向に敏感な
　cost-sensitive　コストに敏感な, コストに左右されやすい
　data-sensitive error　データ依存型誤り
　interest-sensitive instrument　金利感応商品（＝interest-rate sensitive instrument）
　interest-sensitive whole life insurance　金利敏感型終身保険
　market-sensitive　市場に敏感な, 市場に左右されやすい
　price-sensitive consumer　価格に敏感な消費者
　rate-sensitive assets　金利感応資産
　sensitive film　高感度フイルム
　sensitive intelligence　機密情報
　sensitive item　輸入要注意品目, センシティブ品目
　sensitive list　輸入制限品目表
　sensitive market　不安市況, 不安定市場
　sensitive product　重要品目

sentiment　（名）景況感, 市場の地（じ）合い, 所感, 心理, 意見, 感情, 意識, 人気, マインド　（⇒business sentiment, credit easing steps, diffusion index of business sentiment）
　bearish market sentiment　市場の弱気の地合い, 市場の弱気ムード
　bearish sentiment　弱気の地合い, 弱気心理
　bullish market sentiment　市場の強気の地合い, 市場の強気ムード
　bullish sentiment　強気の地合い, 強気心理
　business sentiment　企業の景況感, 業況判断, 企業マインド　（＝company sentiment; ⇒pace）
　buyer's sentiment　買い気
　consumer buying sentiment　消費者の消費心理
　consumer sentiment　消費者マインド, 消費マインド, 消費者心理, 消費意欲
　consumer sentiment index　消費者マインド指数, 消費者態度指数
　corporate sentiment　企業の心理, 企業の景況感, 企業の業況判断　（⇒sharp rise）
　express the same sentiments　同じ見方をする, 同じ所感を述べる
　improvement in the sentiment　景況感の改善
　inflationary sentiment　インフレ心理, インフレ・マインド
　investor sentiment　投資マインド, 投資家心理, 投資家の地合い
　market sentiment　市場の地合い, 市場心理, 市場のムード, 市場のセンチメント
　negative sentiment　マイナスの業況判断, マイナスの景況感, 景況感の悪化
　negative sentiment among major companies　大企業の景況感悪化　（⇒level off）
　optimistic sentiment　楽観ムード, 楽観論
　political sentiment　政府の姿勢
　public sentiment　国民意識, 国民の感情
　selling sentiment　売り気
　sentiment index　業況判断指数
　strong sentiment　強気
　◆A decline in the prices of gasoline and heating oil should help stimulate depressed consumer buying sentiment. ガソリンや灯油の価格が下がれば、冷え込んだ消費者の消費心理も少しは緩和するはずだ。◆A recent decline in bullish sentiment among foreign investors in the Japanese stock market has caused domestic stock prices to decline. 外国人投資家の間で日本の株式市場の強気の地合いが［日本の株式市場を支えていた外国人投資家の勢いが］ここに来て弱まり、国内株価が軟調となっている。◆Affected by the New York sentiment, the Tokyo market was down across the board. ニューヨーク市場の地合いを受けて、東京市場は全面安となった。◆Many businesses are cautious about their outlook three months ahead despite the improvement in sentiment. 企業の景況感は改善したものの、多くの企業は3か月先の景気見通しに対しては慎重だ。◆The BOJ's Tankan survey shows business sentiment among large manufacturers rebounded in September from the previous survey three months earlier. 9月の日銀短観は、大企業・製造業の景況感が6月の前回調査から改善したことを示している。◆The nominal GDP growth rate takes into account price changes and is considered a more accurate reflection of household and corporate sentiment. 名目GDP（国内総生産）成長率は、物価変動を考慮し、家計や企業の景況感をより正確に反映するとされている。◆The outbreak of the global financial crisis was initially viewed with an optimistic sentiment. 世界金融危機の発生当初は、楽観ムードだった。

sentiment index　態度指数, 業況判断指数, 景況判断指数
　consumer sentiment index　消費者態度指数, 消費者マインド指数
　index reading for manufacturers' sentiment　製造業の景況［業況］判断指数
　index reading for small companies' sentiment　中小企業景況判断指数
　volatility of the overall consumer sentiment index　消費者態度指数全体の変動性

separate　（形）別々の, 別個の, 個別の, 個々の, 独立した, ～から離れている
　separate component companies　傘下企業
　separate estate　（とくに妻の）別有財産, 特有財産
　separate financial statements　個別財務諸表, 個別財務書類
　separate talks　個別会談
　separated taxation　分離課税
　◆Citigroup will buy back the auction-rate securities from investors under separate accords with the Securities and Exchange Commission and state regulators. 米シティグループは、米証券取引委員会（SEC）や州規制当局との個々の合意に基づいて投資家から金利入札証券（ARS）を買い戻す。

separate self-assessment taxation　申告分離課税　（⇒capital gain）
　◆The tax rate on capital gains through stock transactions subject to separate self-assessment taxation is 26 percent. 申告分離課税の対象である株式譲渡益課税の税率は、26％となっている。

separate withholding tax system　源泉分離課税方式
　◆Under the separate withholding tax system, an investor

would pay only 1.05 percent of the stock's selling price as tax. 源泉分離課税方式では、投資家は株式売却額の1.05%を納税すれば済む。

Sept. 11 terrorist attacks 2001年9月11日の米同時テロ (⇒claim名詞, insurance payment)
◆Taisei Fire & Marine Insurance Co. went bankrupt after it could not pay huge claims for damages caused by the Sept. 11 terrorist attacks on the United States. 大成火災海上保険は、(2001年)9月11日の米同時テロによる被害に対する巨額の保険金を支払うことができなかったため、経営破たんした。

serial (形)一連の, 連続した, 続きの
  serial bond (償還期限が異なる)連続償還債
  serial issue 連続発行, 連続償還発行
  serial loan 元利均等返済型ローン
  serial obligations 分割払い債務
  serial securities 連続償還証券
  serial sinking fund 連続償還型減債基金
  serial zero-coupon bond [issue] 連続ゼロ・クーポン債
  serial zeros 連続ゼロ・クーポン債

serial number 続き番号, 一連番号
◆The Bank of Japan punished 3 officials for illegally obtaining four newly designed banknotes featuring special characteristics such as serial numbers. 日本銀行は、続き番号など特徴のある特定の新札4枚を不正に入手していたとして、職員3人を処分した。

series (名)連続, 順次, 系列, 分割発行, 指標, 指数, シリーズ
  a series of documents 一件書類
  a series of tax breaks 一連の減税措置
  Accounting Series Release 会計連続通牒
  data series 指標
  domestic WPI series 国内卸売り物価指数
  economic series 景気指標
  import WPI series 輸入物価指数
  manufacturing business conditions series 製造業の業況判断
  series bond 分割発行社債
  series discount 連続割引
  series H bond シリーズH債券
  series 1 and 2 preferred shares シリーズ1および2優先株式
  time series 時系列
◆A series of accounting scandals and delays in the recovery of corporate performance are accelerating falls in stock prices on the U.S. markets, along with the weakening of the dollar. 一連の[相次ぐ]企業会計の不祥事と企業業績回復の遅れで、米国の株安とドル安が加速している。◆In Canada, the Corporation issued $300 million of 9% Series 7 Notes, due 2012. カナダで当社は、満期2012年・利率9%のシリーズ7ノート3億ドルを発行しました。◆In the aftermath of the 1995 Great Hanshin Earthquake and the 2007 Niigata Prefecture Chuetsu Offshore Earthquake, a series of fraud cases involving donations occurred. 1995年の阪神大震災や2007年の新潟県中越沖地震の直後には、義援金詐欺事件が相次いで起きた。◆The articles of incorporation authorize the Directors to issue such shares in one or more series and to fix the number of shares of each series prior to their issue. 定款では、これらの株式をシリーズで1回以上発行する権限と、その発行前に各シリーズの発行株式数を決定する権限は、取締役会に与えられています。◆The income and corporate taxes have substantially decreased due to the prolonged recession and a series of tax breaks. 所得税や法人税は、長期不況や一連の減税措置で大幅に減少している。

serious (形)深刻な, 重大な, 重要な, 危険な, 本格的な, 本気の, まじめな, 思慮深い, 堅い, 大量の, 大幅の, 値段が高い, 性能がよい
(⇒deflationary period, implication)
  face a serious cash flow crisis 資金繰りが苦しくなる
  face a serious crisis 重大な危機に瀕している
  make serious inroads 本格的に進出する
  serious unemployment problems 深刻な失業問題
  serious unemployment situation 深刻な失業状況
  take a serious tumble 深刻な危機に陥る
◆As the Greek fiscal crisis grows more serious, there has been no halt to the worldwide decline in stock prices. ギリシャの財政危機が一段と深刻化するにつれ、世界同時株安に歯止めがかからなくなっている。◆The employment situation has grown even more serious. 雇用情勢は、一段と深刻化している。

serious challenges 厳しい試練, 深刻な課題
◆The global economy is facing serious challenges. 世界経済は、厳しい試練に直面している。

serious crisis 重大な危機
◆The Japanese economy is by no means facing a serious crisis. 日本経済は、重大な危機に瀕しているわけではない。

serious damage 深刻な打撃
◆The continuing rise in the yen will inflict serious damages on Japan's economy. 円高がこのまま続けば、日本経済には深刻な打撃となる。

serious downturn in business 深刻な業績悪化, 大幅な業績悪化
◆The company postponed the planned construction of the new plant due to flagging sales of semiconductors and a serious downturn in business. 同社は、半導体不況[半導体の販売低迷]と大幅な業績悪化を理由に、予定していた新工場の建設を延期した。

serious financial difficulties 深刻な経営危機, 深刻な経営難[経営不振], 深刻な財政難[ひっ迫], 深刻な財務悪化
◆The bank's serious financial difficulties have forced it to do an about-face. 同行の深刻な経営難で、同行は方針転換を迫られている。◆When serious financial difficulties are expected, the Financial Services Agency is allowed to order a company to improve its operations in the early stages without releasing the information to the public. 深刻な財務悪化が予想される場合、金融庁は、非公表で早めに業務改善命令を発動することができる。

serious fiscal conditions 深刻な財政事情, 深刻な財政状況
◆We must recognize anew the serious fiscal conditions gripping Japan. 日本の[日本をおおう]深刻な財政事情を、われわれは再認識しなければならない。

serious fiscal crisis 深刻な財政危機
◆Greece is struggling with a serious fiscal crisis. ギリシャは、深刻な財政危機にあえいでいる。

serious fiscal troubles 深刻な財政危機問題
◆Global financial markets are still shaken by the serious fiscal troubles in Greece. 世界の金融市場は、ギリシャの深刻な財政危機問題で動揺が続いている。

serious violation 重大な違反, 重大違反
◆The FSA ordered the bank to suspend some operations due to serious law violations, including audit sabotage. 金融庁は、同行に対して、検査妨害などの重大な銀行法違反で、一部業務の停止命令を出した。

serve (動)務める, 勤務する, 働く, 仕事をする, サービスなどを提供する, 供給する, 商品などを売る, 運航する, 文書を渡す, 送付する, ~の役に立つ, 奉仕する, 貢献する, 利用できる, ~の目的にかなう, ~の要求などを満たす, ~の機能を果たす, ~の任務[職務]を果たす, ~の手段として機能する, 助長する, 促進する, 推進する, 高める
  better serve customers' needs 顧客のニーズへの対応を

改善する
serve a customer 顧客に応対する
serve as ～として役立つ,～になる
（⇒susceptible to）
serve one's debt 債務を返済する
serve the community 地域社会に貢献する,地域社会に奉仕する,地域社会に尽くす
serve to ～に役立つ,～する方向に働く,～する方向に動く
serve two ends 一挙両得である
well serve one's interests ～の利益に十分見合う
◆A cheaper dollar does definitely serve to make U.S. producers more cost-competitive in international export markets. 国際輸出市場で米国の生産者の価格競争力を高めるには、間違いなくドル安のほうがよい。◆Our strategy is to focus on those product lines vital to our future by streamlining our operations and assets redeployment to position the Corporation to serve its customers more effectively. 当社は、業務の効率化と資産の有効利用により、一段と効率的な顧客サービスの体制確立をめざして当社の将来を支える製品ラインに焦点をあてる経営戦略を展開しています。◆Since three banks integrated their operations, executives from the three predecessor banks served on an equal basis as presidents of the Mizuho group, Mizuho Bank and Mizuho Corporate Bank. 3銀行の経営統合以来、旧3行の経営者が、みずほグループ（FG）、みずほ銀行、みずほコーポレート銀行のトップをそれぞれ分け合った。◆The amount of retirement allowances usually is determined by the length of time directors serve in their post. 役員退職慰労金の金額は通常、役員の在任期間によって決められる。◆The stock market is a public mechanism to facilitate the smooth flow of money in the economy by serving as an intermediary between corporations and investors. 証券市場は、企業と投資家間の仲介役をつとめて日本経済に資金を円滑に流す役割を担う公共財だ。

service (動)借金や利子などを支払う,債務を返済する,債務を履行する,債権を回収する,役務を提供する
service and repay the loan ローンの元利を返済する
service debt 債務を返済する,債務を履行する
◆An insurance agent is a sales person who represents a life insurance company for the purpose of soliciting applications, collecting initial premiums, and servicing insurance contracts. 保険募集人は、生命保険会社を代表して保険契約の勧誘、初回保険料の徴収、保険契約に関する役務を提供する販売員である。

service (名)事業,業務,サービス,役務（えきむ）,労務,勤務,服務,公務,借入金の定期返済,公債利子,訴状や呼出状の送達
advisory services 顧問業務
banking services 銀行業務
consulting services コンサルタント業務
credit rating service 信用格付け機関
customer service 顧客サービス,消費者サービス
debt service 債務返済,元利払い
fiduciary services 信託業務
Financial Services Act 1986 1986年金融サービス法
financial services industry 金融サービス業界
full-service brokerage フルサービス証券会社
improved services サービスの向上
（=better services）
Internal Revenue Service 内国歳入庁
length of service 勤続年数
prior service cost 過去勤務費用
service price index 企業向けサービス価格指数
services for investors 投資家向けサービス
services for the elderly 高齢者サービス
transaction settlement services 取引決済サービス
unattended service 無人サービス
◆Internet-based bank Sony Bank started a deposit service for the Brazilian real in May 2011. ネット専業銀行のソニー銀行が、2011年5月からブラジル通貨レアルの預金サービス［預金の取扱い］を開始した。◆Mizuho Bank offers a service by which ATM cardholders are given mileage points each time they use the new cards as credit cards, purchase financial products at the bank's branches or receive loans from the bank. みずほ銀行が提供しているサービスでは、キャッシュ・カード会員が新型カードをクレジット・カードとして利用したり、みずほ銀で金融商品を購入したり、ローンを利用したりすると、その取引に応じて毎回、マイレージ・ポイントがもらえる。◆Proceeds from exercising stock options are compensation for labor and service rendered and constitute salary income. ストック・オプション（自社株購入権）を行使して得た利益は、職務遂行の対価なので、給与所得に当たる。◆Sberbank of Russia will offer a variety of services, such as ruble-denominated loans to Mizuho Corporate Bank's clients when they do business in Russia. ロシア最大手行のズベルバンクは、みずほコーポレート銀行の顧客がロシアで事業を行う際にルーブル建て融資を行うなどの各種サービスを提供することになった。◆The bank plans to take advantage of the new virtual bank's lower overhead to offer improved services. 同行では、新仮想銀行の低コスト体質を生かして、サービスを向上させる計画だ。◆The banks are now paying more attention to new loans and services aimed at individuals and or small and midsize companies. 銀行は現在、個人や中小企業に目を向けた新しい融資やサービスに力を入れている。◆The company is the largest U.S. full-service brokerage. 同社は、米国最大手のフルサービス証券会社です。◆The interest rates of the Australian dollar-denominated deposit service are relatively high among major foreign currencies. 主要外貨のうち豪ドル建て預金サービスの金利は、比較的高い。◆The Osaka Securities Exchange will expand its service for investors. 大阪証券取引所は、投資家向けサービスを拡充する［強化する］方針だ。

service [services] account 貿易外収支,サービス収支
◆The deficit in the service account in August widened 6 percent, to ¥122.8 billion from a year earlier. 8月の貿易外収支の赤字は、前年同月比で6%拡大して、1,228億円となった。◆The services account posted a deficit of ¥5.1 trillion. サービス収支は、5兆1,000億円の赤字を計上した。

service [services] balance サービス収支,貿易外収支
◆The service balance was ¥5.32 trillion in the red. サービス収支は、5兆3,200億円の赤字となった。

service charges on crude oil futures trading 原油先物取引の手数料
◆Service charges or tax on crude oil futures trading should be raised to curb the inflow of speculative money not related to actual demand. 実需に関係ない投機マネーの流入を抑えるため、原油先物取引の手数料の引上げや課税強化をすべきだ。

service industry サービス業,サービス産業
◆By sector, the number of workers in the service industry increased by 130,000 to 16.95 million. 業種別では、サービス業の就業者数が1,650万人で、13万人の増加となった。

servicer (名)債権回収会社,サービサー（1999年2月から業務を開始した民間の不良債権の管理回収業者）

services for individual customers 個人顧客向け業務
◆The brokerage's main services for individual customers will be asset management advisory services, focusing on the sale of products such as investment trust funds that invest in foreign equities, and money market funds denominated in foreign currencies. 同証券会社は、株式の主な個人顧客向け（売買仲介）業務として、外国株を組み込んだ投資信託や外貨建てMMF（マネー・マーケット・ファンド）などの商品の販売を中心に、資産運用顧問業務を展開する方針だ。

servicing （名）債務返済, 債務履行, 債権回収, サービシング　（⇒debt servicing）
 debt servicing　債務返済, 利息払い
 government bond-servicing expenditures　国債の利払い費
 loan servicing　（利払いなどの）融資処理, 貸出金サービシング
 loan servicing fee　融資処理手数料, 貸出金サービシング手数料
 mortgage servicing rights　モーゲージ・サービス提供権, モーゲージ・サービス権
 servicing burden　債務返済負担
 ◆If interest rates rose by 1 percent, Japan's government bond-servicing expenditures would increase by about ¥1.2 trillion in fiscal 2005. 金利が1％上がると, 2005年度の日本の国債利払い費は約1兆2,000億円増える。◆This joint venture will offer sales financing and servicing as well as raise funds for auto loans. この合弁会社は, 自動車ローンの資金調達や販売金融, 債権回収などを手がける。

SESC　証券取引等監視委員会, 証券監視委　（Securities and Exchange Surveillance Commissionの略）

SESDAQ　シンガポール証券取引所店頭市場

session　（名）証券取引所の立会い, 場, セッション, 1日の取引時間　（⇒IR session）
 afternoon session　後場（午後の立会い）, 午後, 午後の取引
 briefing session　説明会
 final session of a month　納会
 final session of a year　大納会　（＝last session of a year）
 first session of a month　発会
 first session of a year　大発会
 for the fourth straight session　4日連続で
 last session of a sour year in the stock market　株式市場低迷の1年の大納会
 morning session　前場（午前中の立会い）, 午前, 午前の取引
 night session　夜間取引
 trading session　株式取引所の立会い
 ◆By the TSE's extension of the morning trade session to 11:30 a.m., investors will be able to trade Japanese stocks more easily while keeping an eye on economic trends in Asian markets. 東証が午前11時30分まで午前の取引時間を延長したことによって, 投資家は今後, アジア市場の経済動向を見ながら日本株の取引をすることが容易になる。◆The company held briefing sessions to solicit new investors. 同社は説明会を開いて, 新規出資者を募っていた。◆Transactions concerning Shinsei Bank stock could not go through in the morning session. 新生銀行株の取引は, 午前は成立しなかった。

set　（動）置く, 配置する（appoint）, 据え付ける, 設ける, 〜の用意をする, セットする, 整える, 確立する, 定める, 指定する, 取り決める, (値を)付ける, (記録を)立てる［打ち立てる, 作る］, (仕事などを)課す, (模範などを)示す, 〜の状態にする, 〜させる, 活字を組む
 set a minimum price　最低価格を設定する
 set all-time highs　最高値を記録する
 set exposure limits　エクスポージャー制限を設ける, エクスポージャー極度を設定する
 set investment policy　投資政策を設定する, 投資政策を決める
 set minimum and maximum limits on　〜に最高限度と最低限度を設ける
 set monetary policy　金融政策を決める
 set new all-time lows　史上最安値を更新する
 set new highs vis-a-vis the U.S. dollar　対米ドルで最高値を更新する
 set new standards　新規格を設ける
 ◆Crude oil prices have exceeded $70 a barrel in London and New York, setting all-time highs on these markets. ニューヨークとロンドン市場で原油価格が1バレル＝70ドルを上回って, 両市場最高値を記録した。◆Currently, a company may set transfer restrictions on a portion of its outstanding shares. 現在（2005年）, 企業は一部の発行済み株式に譲渡制限を付けることができる。◆If a new federal debt ceiling isn't set by Aug. 2, 2011, the United States will be forced to default on Treasuries securities as it will not be able to issue new bonds to pay back maturing government debts. 2011年8月2日までに連邦政府の債務上限を新たに設けないと, 米国は満期を迎える国債を償還するための国債増発ができないので, 米国債の不履行（デフォルト）が発生する。◆If the prices of purchased bad assets are set high, the public burden will balloon. 不良資産の買取り価格を高くすると, 国民負担が膨らむ。◆The repayment period of the new tied yen loans will be set at 40 years. 新ひも付き円借款の償還期間は今後, 40年とされる。◆The target range for the inflation rate could be set at the same level as the potential growth rate, for example. 物価上昇率の目標値としては, 例えば潜在成長率と同水準に設定することもできよう。◆Under the government guidelines, if earnings come in more than 30 percent below targets set in restructuring plans at any major bank that received public funds to recapitalize in 1988 and 1999, the banks management will have to resign. 政府のガイドラインによると, 資本再編のために1988年と1999年に公的資金の注入を受けた大手銀行の収益が, 再建計画（経営健全化計画）で設定した収益目標を30％以上下回った場合, 銀行の経営陣は辞任しなければならない。

set aside　（準備金などを）積み立てる, 蓄えておく, 蓄える, 引き当てる, 設定する, 繰り入れる, 用意する, 考えや問題を捨てる, 無視する, 棚上げする, 取り除く, 除外する　（⇒national debt consolidation fund, remove）
 set aside loan loss reserves　貸倒れ引当金を積み立てる, 貸倒れ引当金を積む
 set aside more money for bad loans　貸倒れ引当金を積み増す
 set aside provisions for disasters　準備金を積み立てる, 異常危険準備金を積み立てる
 set aside reserves in preparation for interest rate fluctuations and natural disasters　金利変動や自然災害に備えて準備金を積み立てる
 the BOJ sets aside 5% of net income for reserves　日銀は剰余金の5％を法定準備金として積み立てる　（⇒reserve）
 ◆Banks have to set aside loan loss reserves based on projections of future revenues of their borrowers, not based on bankruptcies in the past. 銀行は, 過去の倒産実績ではなく, 融資先企業（貸出先）の将来の収益予想などを基にして, 貸倒れ引当金を積み立てるべきだ。◆Insurers set aside provisions for disasters. 保険会社は, 災害準備金［異常危険準備金］を積み立てている。◆The bank set aside more money for bad loans in the United States. 同行は, 米国で貸倒れ引当金を積みました。◆To make up for losses and for other purposes, seven life insurers used a total of ¥529.2 billion in reserves, which are set aside in preparation for interest rate fluctuations and natural disasters. 損失の穴埋めなどのため, 金利変動や自然災害に備えて積み立てている準備金を, 生保7社が5,292億円も取り崩した。

set forth　定める, 規定する, 記載する, 示す, 詳述する, 記述する, 説明する, 明示する, 明記する, 発表する, 打ち出す, 出発する
 ◆The Greek government has set forth measures to decrease the number of government employees and raise taxes to cut its budget deficits. 財政赤字削減のため, ギリシャ政府は公務員削減や増税策を打ち出した。

set numerical targets 数値目標を設定する[設ける、示す]
◆The new Fed chairman's theory is to introduce inflation targets, thus setting numerical targets for stabilizing prices. 米連邦準備制度理事会(FRB)新議長の持論は、インフレ目標を導入して、物価安定の数値目標を示す[設定する]ことだ。

set off 引き起こす、巻き起こす、爆発させる、打ち揚げる、引き立たせる
  set off a nationwide controversy 全国的な論争を巻き起こす
  set off a negative chain reaction 連鎖破たんを引き起こす
  set off against ～と相殺する
◆The possibility that the bank's collapse will set off a negative chain reaction is very low. 同行の破たんが連鎖破たんを引き起こす可能性は、かなり低い。

set rules 基準[規則]を設ける、基準を制定する
◆The Financial Stability Board is cooperating with the Basel Committee on Banking Supervision, a body that sets rules for international banking. 金融安定化理事会(FSB)は、国際銀行業務の基準を制定する機関のバーゼル銀行監督委員会と連携している。

set to ～に取り掛かろうとしている、～する用意ができている、～する方針だ、～する方針を固める、～する見通しだ、～する見込みだ、～する恐れがある
◆GM and Toyota are each set to invest tens of billions of yen in a plant they jointly own in California. GMとトヨタはそれぞれ、両社が共同出資する米カリフォルニア州の工場に数百億円を(追加)投資する方針だ。◆Securities and Exchange Surveillance Commission is set to launch an investigation into the company. 証券取引等監視委員会は、同社の調査に乗り出す見通しだ。◆The economy of the United States is set to shrink 0.5 percent in 2009. 米国の2009年の年間経済成長率は、0.5％のマイナス成長になる見込みだ。◆With the aging of our society, crimes targeting the assets of elderly people are set to increase. 高齢社会の進展とともに、高齢者の資産をねらった犯罪が、ますます多発する恐れがある。

set up (動)(建物などを)立てる、建てる、築く、組み立てる、始める(start)、一本立ちする、独立する、設立する、創設する、開業する、(ホームページなどを)開設する、(会合などを)設定する、設置する、(～を)掲げる、用意する、準備する、供給する、資金提供をする、(～の)ふりをする、(～を)気取る、(記録を)樹立する(establish)、(原稿を)活字に組む、(策略で)はめる、だます、(連鎖反応などを)引き起こす、(ソフトウエアをコンピュータに)インストールする、セットアップする
  be well set up with money 十分に資金提供を受ける、十分に金をあてがわれている
  set up a joint venture 合弁会社[合弁事業]を設立する
  set up a new world record 世界新記録を立てる[樹立する]
  set up a program プログラムを設定する
  set up a series of protests 一連の抗議を呼ぶ、次々と抗議を呼ぶ
  set up a subsidiary 子会社を設立する
  set up a web site ホームページを開く
  set up against ～に対抗する
  set up in business together 一緒に事業を興す
  set up manufacturing facilities 生産拠点を設ける、生産拠点をつくる
  set up shop 開店する、事業[商売]を始める、開業する
  set up trust fund 信託基金を設立する
◆The Bank of Japan decided to adopt additional quantitative easing measures in October 2010, setting up a fund to purchase government and corporate bonds. 日銀は、2010年10月に新たな量的緩和策の導入を決め、国債や社債を買い入れる基金を新設した。◆The Bank of Japan will set up a fund to buy long-term government bonds, exchange-traded funds and other financial assets in a bid to prop up the nation's economy. 日本の景気を下支えするため、日銀は基金を新設して、長期国債や上場投資信託(ETF)などの金融商品[金融資産]を買い入れる。◆The European Financial Stability Facility set up a €750 billion contingency package together with the International Monetary Fund. 欧州金融安定基金(EU)は、国際通貨基金(IMF)の協力を得て7,500億ユーロ(約90兆円)の緊急支援資金を準備した。

setback (名)後退、景気後退、下落、がた落ち、落ち込み、減少、反落、逆行、逆風、挫折、失敗、敗北、調整局面
  a considerably severe economic setback かなり厳しい景気後退
  business setbacks 景気後退
    (=economic setbacks)
  earnings setback 収益の落ち込み
  economic setback 景気後退
  face setbacks 逆風にぶつかる
  possible setback 景気後退の可能性
  setback in the stock market 株式相場の下落
  the LDP's heavy setback 自民党の大敗北
◆Among other factors that could adversely affect the national economy are possible setbacks in the Chinese and U.S. economies as well as high oil prices. 国内景気に悪影響を及ぼす恐れがある他の要因として、中国や米国の景気後退や原油高がある。◆The biggest factor behind the DPJ's setback in the upper house election was Kan's handling of the consumption tax issue. 参院選での民主党の最大の敗因は、菅首相の消費税問題への対応だった。◆We should be prepared for a considerably severe economic setback worldwide. われわれは、かなり厳しい世界的な景気後退を覚悟しなければならない。

setoff [set-off] (名)相殺、(借金の)棒引き、手じまい

settle (動)決済する、支払う、清算する、処分する、処理する、解決する、決定する、(日取りなどを)決める、和解する
  (⇒cash register, checking transaction)
  be settled in cash 現金で決済する、現金決済方式をとる
  be settled in yen 円で決済する、円決済とする
  cash-settled warrants 現金決済の仕組みを持つワラント
  settle a claim 賠償金を払う、保険金を支払う
  settle a debt 借金を支払う[払う]
  settle a dispute 紛争を解決する
  settle arrears 未払いを解消する、未払い金を支払う[払う]、未払い金を清算する
  settle for good results 好決算に安住する
  settle in full 全額を支払う
  settle one's midyear accounts 中間決算をまとめる (⇒midyear accounts)
  settle put option プット・オプションを決済する
  settle the balance 残金を支払う
  settle (up) the bill [accounts] 勘定を支払う、代金を支払う[決済する] (⇒margin trading)
  settle with ～に負債[勘定]を払う
  settle with regulators 規制当局と和解する
  settled accounts 支払い済み取引
  settled claim 確定した保険請求
◆American International Group agreed to pay a $10 million civil fine to settle the SEC's allegations that it fraudulently helped another company falsify its earnings report and hide losses. 米保険大手のAIG(アメリカン・インターナショナル・グループ)は、同社が他社の業績報告書改ざんと損失隠しに不正に

手を貸したとする米証券取引委員会（SEC）の告発を受け、この問題を解決するために民事制裁金1,000万ドルを支払うことに同意した。◆Banking titan Citigroup Inc. has agreed to pay $75 million to the U.S. Securities and Exchange Commission to settle subprime mortgage suit. 米金融大手シティグループは、低所得者向け住宅融資「サブプライム・ローン」の訴訟の和解金として、7,500万ドルを米証券取引委員会（SEC）に支払うことで合意した。◆Before settling its accounts for fiscal 2010, the company submitted materials, including financial statements, to the auditing firm. 2010年度決算の前に、同社は財務諸表などの資料を監査法人に提出した。◆In China and other Asian markets, exports from Japan are mostly settled in yen. 中国などのアジア市場では、日本からの輸出の大半は円決済となっている。◆Merrill, Goldman and Deutsche Bank joined other major financial companies in settling with regulators over their roles in selling risky auction-rate securities to retail investors. メリルリンチ、ゴールドマン・サックスとドイツ銀行は、リスクの高い金利入札証券（ARS）を小口投資家に販売した際のこれら各社の役割をめぐる問題で、他の大手金融会社に同調して［足並みを揃えて］規制当局と和解した。

settlement （名）決済, 清算, 決算, 処分, 解決, 決着, 決定, 妥結, 和解, 調停, 示談, 財産の譲渡, 贈与財産, 定款 （⇒business settlement, financial documents, financial settlement, out-of-court settlement, semiannual settlement of accounts）
　account settlement term　決算期
　asset settlement　資産決済
　automatic settlement　自動決済
　biannual settlement　半期決算, 半期決済
　business settlement　取引決済
　cash settlement　現金決済, 現物決済, 即日決済
　computer system for settlement　決済用コンピュータ・システム
　dispute settlement procedures　紛争処理手続き, 紛争解決手続き
　disruption of settlements　決済マヒ
　electronic settlement services　電子決済業務
　final settlement　債務の完済
　financial settlement　決算
　legal settlement　訴訟和解金
　midterm settlement in May　5月中間決算
　one-day settlement　翌日決済
　out-of-court settlement　示談による和解
　overnight settlement　翌日決済
　Regional Settlement Intermediary　域内決済機関, RSI
　same day or next day settlement　当日決済または翌日決済
　same day settlement　同日決済
　semiannual settlement　半期決算, 半期決済
　settlement date　決済日, 受渡し日（米国の証券取引の場合、通常の受渡し取引の決済日は、売買成立の翌日から起算して5日目の営業日になっている）
　settlement day　決済日, 勘定日, 決算日, 受渡し日, 期日
　settlement of claims　賠償金の支払い, 保険金の支払い
　settlement of difference　反対売買による差金決済, 紛争の解決
　settlement risk　決済リスク
　settlement statement　（証券取引の決済内容を記載した）受渡計算書
　skip-day settlement　2日後決済
　window dressing settlement　粉飾決算
◆In September 2002, the Financial System Council called for creation of the new settlement-specific deposit as a stable and secure means of settlement. 2002年9月に金融審議会は、安全確実な決済手段として、新型の決済用預金の創設を求めた。◆In the latest settlement with federal and state regulators, Wachovia Corp. agreed to buy back nearly 9 billion in auction-rate debt. 今回の連邦と州の規制当局との和解で、米大手銀行のワコビアは、約90億ドルの金利入札証券（ARS）を買い戻すことで合意した。◆The firm offers loans for retail and corporate clients in addition to offering electronic settlement for online shoppers. 同社は、ネット・ショッパー［オンライン・ショッパー］向けの電子決済業務のほかに、個人と企業向けの融資も手がけている。

settlement account　決済用預金, 決済口座, 資金決済口座　（=settlement deposit, settlement-specific deposit）
◆As of the end of February, 84 percent of financial institutions had introduced the new settlement accounts. 今年2月末時点で、84％の金融機関が新型の決済用預金を導入済みだ。◆When a bank makes an international money transfer, it needs to open a settlement account with a bank in the country to which the money is being sent. 銀行が国際送金する［海外に送金する］場合、送金する相手国の銀行に資金決済口座を開設しなければならない。

settlement deposit　決済用預金　（=settlement account, settlement-specific deposit: 利子が付かない、取引決済サービスを提供する、要求払いに応じるの3条件を満たした預金口座のこと。銀行が破たんした場合に預金が全額保護される。）
◆The nation's banks are planning to introduce a new type of settlement deposit that will be fully protected in the event of a bank failure. 日本の銀行は、銀行が破たんした場合に預金が全額保護される新しいタイプの決済用預金の導入を計画している。

settlement fund　決済資金
◆The extent to which Cuba is short of settlement funds is unclear. キューバの決済資金がどの程度、決済資金が不足しているのかは［キューバの決済資金がどのような状況には］、不明である。◆The National Bank of Cuba will not be able to pay for imports into Cuba in due terms as the country is short of settlement funds. キューバ国立銀行は今後、国全体の決済資金不足で、期日どおりにキューバへの輸入代金の支払いができなくなる状況にある。

settlement of accounts　決算, 決算報告　（=account settlement; ⇒deficit settlement of accounts, midterm settlement of accounts, semiannual settlement of accounts）
　the deficit settlement of accounts　赤字決算
　the midterm settlement（of accounts）in September　9月中間決算, 9月の中間決算
　the semiannual settlement of accounts in September　9月中間決算　（⇒recurring loss）
　the September settlement of accounts　9月中間決算　（⇒bond holdings）
　the settlement of accounts for the April-June period　4-6月期決算
　the settlement of accounts for the business year ending in March　3月期決算
　the settlement of accounts for the business year ending ［on］Sept. 30　9月中間決算期末
　the settlement of accounts for the business year that ended in March　3月期決算
　the settlement of accounts for the half year to September　9月中間決算
◆A number of major U.S. firms reported drastic declines in profits in their settlements of accounts for the April-June period. アメリカの主要企業の多くは、4-6月期決算で大幅減益を発表した。◆Neither of Mitsui Trust Holdings, Inc. and another major financial group has yet released reports on its interim settlement of accounts. 三井トラスト・ホールディングスなど2大金融グループは、まだ中間決算報告を発表していない。◆The firm's liabilities exceeded its assets by ¥8 billion

in its settlement of accounts at the end of February last year. 同社は、昨年2月決算で、80億円の債務超過になった。◆The settlements of accounts to March 31 for the companies listed on the First Section of the Tokyo Stock Exchange will show record highs for the third consecutive year. 東証1部上場企業の3月期決算は、3年連続で過去最高を更新する見通しだ。◆What will be the results of businesses' midterm settlement of accounts in September？ 企業の9月中間決算の業績は果たしてどうなるか。

settlement of accounts for the January-March quarter　1-3月期決算
◆The first glimmer of recovery since the firm's collapse appeared in its recently announced settlement of accounts for the January-March quarter. 最近発表された同社の1-3月期決算で、同社の破たん後初めて復活の兆しが見られた。

settlement of trading deals　取引決済
◆After the merger, the TSE and OSE will be divided into four operator firms handling spot trading, derivatives, settlement of trading deals and self-imposed regulations respectively. 経営統合後、東証と大証は、それぞれ現物株、デリバティブ（金融派生商品）、取引決済と自主規制を扱う4事業会社に切り分けられることになっている。

settlement-specific deposit　決済用預金
（＝settlement account, settlement deposit）
◆Customers can choose a settlement-specific deposit or a savings deposit when they open an account. 口座を開設する際、顧客は普通預金か決済用預金かを選択することができる。◆The new settlement-specific deposit has to meet three criteria-deposits earn no interest, transaction settlement services are provided and depositors can draw upon the account balance on demand. この新型の決済用預金は、「利子がつかない、取引決済サービスを提供する、預金者の要求払いに応じる」の3基準を満たさなければならない。

settlement system　決済方式, 決済システム, 決済制度
　foreign exchange settlement system　為替決済システム
　multilateral settlement system　複数為替相場制
　（＝multilateral system of settlements）
◆The government intends to restructure the deposit insurance system as a new financial safety net for protecting settlement systems. 政府は、預金保険制度を、決済システム保護のための新しい金融安全網として再構築する方針だ。◆Under the new settlement system, data on transactions at stock exchange and over-the-counter markets will be sent to the Tokyo Stock Exchange online. 新決済方式では、証券取引所と店頭市場の取引データはすべてコンピュータ回線で東京証券取引所に送信される。

severe　（形）厳しい, 厳格な, 過酷な, 激しい, 深刻な, ひどい, 大幅な, 地味な
　a less severe recession　軽微な景気後退
　a severe contraction　厳しい不況
　a severe credit crunch　深刻な金融危機
　a severe recession　深刻な景気後退
　come under severe pressure　大きく圧迫されている, 苦戦する
　experience a severe downturn　深刻な不況に見舞われる
　severe cutbacks　思い切った人員削減
　severe employment situation　厳しい雇用情勢
　severe price competition　激しい価格競争, 厳しい価格競争
◆Japan's severe employment situation is continuing. 日本の厳しい雇用情勢は、続いている。◆The bank's new president must tread a thorny path as the management environment is severe. 経営環境が厳しいので、同行の新社長はいばらの道を歩むことになろう。◆The business climate for home builders has been severe as housing starts have not expanded much in recent years. 新設住宅の着工戸数がここ数年伸び悩んでいるため、住宅メーカーを取り巻く企業環境は厳しい。◆The European fiscal crisis triggered by Greece has spread to Italy, making the severe situation even more distressing. ギリシャ発の欧州財政危機がイタリアに飛び火し、厳しい事態が一段と深刻化している。◆The fiscal woes of the single-currency bloc could trigger a new severe global financial crisis. 単一通貨・ユーロ圏の財政危機は、新たに重大な世界的金融危機の発生源になる可能性がある。◆The increased ownership will raise the bank's risk exposure to the company, whose business environment is severe. 持ち株比率の引上げで、企業環境［経営環境］が厳しい同社に対する同行のリスク・エクスポージャーは今後増大するものと思われる。◆The U.S. housing industry and the government must respond to a severe credit crunch that began in August 2007. 米国の住宅産業界と政府は、2007年8月に始まった深刻な金融危機への対応を迫られている。◆Under the severe income and employment situations, personal consumption has yet to show indications of a full-fledged recovery. 厳しい所得・雇用環境の下で、個人消費に本格的な復調の気配がまだ見えない。

SGX　シンガポール取引所　（シンガポール証券取引所（SES）とシンガポール国際金融取引所（SIMEX）の合併で1999年12月に設立。⇒Singapore Exchange Ltd.）
◆The SGX's listed companies include Singapore Airlines Ltd. and Singapore Telecommunications Ltd. シンガポール取引所の上場企業には、シンガポール航空やシンガポールテレコムなどが含まれている。

shade　（名）陰, 物陰, 日陰, 陰影, 色合い, 度合い, 少しの分量, ごくわずか, わずかな相違, サングラス（shades）
◆The bank had shades of a corporate raider. 同行は、企業乗っ取りまがいの行為をしていた。

shadow　（名）影, 暗雲, 暗い影, 陰り, 悪影響, 悪い前兆, （野党内の）影の大臣
　beyond [without] a shadow of doubt　疑うまでもない
　cast a shadow over [on]　～に影を落とす, ～に汚点を残す, 後ろ暗い点を残す, ～の魅力を半減させる
　cast dark shadows on　～に暗い影を落とす, ～に影を落とす
　under the shadow of　～の脅威［危険］にさらされて, ～の陰に隠れて, ～の下に
◆A shadow was cast over the future of the Japanese economy. 日本経済の雲行きが、怪しくなった。

shadow　（形）影の, 非公式の, 潜在的な, シャドー
　shadow accounting　保険に関する実務慣行, シャドー・アカウンティング
　shadow director　影の取締役（正式に任命された会社取締役と同じ責任を負う役員）
　shadow economy　地下経済
　shadow market　非公式市場
　shadow price　影の価格, 潜在価格

shake　（動）振る, 振り動かす, 振り回す, 揺さぶる, 動揺させる, ぐらつかせる, くじく, 感情をかき乱す
　（⇒trouble）
　shake down　（職場・場所などに）慣れる, （組織として）まとまる, 恐喝する, 徹底的に探す, 捜索する, ～の所持品を検査する
　shake off　～から回復する, ～を払拭（ふっしょく）する, ～から逃れる, ～を振りほどく
　shake out　振り払う, 淘汰が進む, （在庫などを）整理する, 再編する
◆A U.S. housing mortgage meltdown shook the United States, Europe and other countries and slammed the brakes on global growth. 米国の住宅ローン市場の崩壊は、米欧その他の諸国を揺さぶり、世界経済の成長に急ブレーキをかけた。◆As the financial markets' confidence in the U.S. currency has been shaken, stock prices may fall worldwide and the dollar-selling trend may accelerate. 米ドルへの金融市場の信

認が揺らいでいるため、株価が世界的に下落し、ドル売りの流れが加速する可能性もある。◆The financial markets' confidence in the U.S. currency has been shaken further by the S&P's cutting of the U.S. credit rating. スタンダード・アンド・プアーズ（S&P）が米国債の格付けを引き下げたことで、米ドルへの金融市場の信認が一段と揺らいでいる。◆The sharp decline in the birthrate and the rapid graying of society are shaking the very foundation of the nation's social security system. 急速な少子高齢化が、社会保障制度の土台そのものを揺るがしている。

shake up （動）再編する, 刷新する, 改造する, 活気づかせる
　◆Fannie Mae shook up its management. 米連邦住宅抵当公庫（ファニー・メイ）が、経営陣を刷新した。

shake-up （名）再編, 大変革, 大刷新, 大改革, 大改造, 抜本的改革, 抜本的改組　（=shakeout）
　Cabinet shake-up　内閣改造
　　（=Cabinet reshuffle）
　industry shake-p　業界再編
　　（=shake-up in the industry）
　management shake-up　経営刷新, 経営陣の刷新, 役員交代　（=management reshuffle）
　shake-up within the house　機構改革
　◆Mortgage finance company Fannie Mae announced a management shake-up. 政府系住宅金融会社のファニー・メイ（米連邦住宅抵当公庫）が、経営陣の刷新を発表した。◆The shake-up of the domestic distribution industry started with the collapse of midsized supermarket operator Nagasakiya Co. in February 2000. 国内流通業界の再編は、2000年2月、中堅スーパー・長崎屋の破たんに始まった。

shakedown （名）調整, 調整期間, 試運転, 徹底的な捜索
（形）調整期間の, 試験の, 試験的な, 試験運転の

Shanghai Stock Exchange　上海証券取引所
　◆The Tokyo Stock Exchange was outstripped [outpaced] by the Shanghai Stock Exchange in terms of trading volume. 東証は、取引規模[売買規模]で上海証券取引所に抜かれた。

share （動）共有する, 相互利用する, 共同使用する, 分配する, 均等に分ける, 分け合う, 共にする, 共同負担する, 共同分担する, 分担する, 支持する, 参加する, 話す
　share a basic common interest　～基本的に利害[共通の利益]が一致する
　share in profits　利益の分配にあずかる
　share leadership with　～とトップの座を争う
　share one's view　～の見方[意見, 考え]と同じ, ～の見方を支持する
　share the blame　共にその責めを負う, 非難を共に受ける
　share the burden　共同負担する, 共同で負担する
　share the profits among　～の間で利益を分配する
　◆If the government financial support is not offered to TEPCO, the utility's creditors and shareholders will have to share the burden. 東電に政府の金融支援がない場合は、同社の債権者と株主が共同負担せざるを得ないだろう。◆In dealing with the dual debt problem due to the March 11 disaster, financial institutions will be forced to share certain burdens. 東日本大震災による二重ローン問題への対応では、金融機関もある程度の共同負担を強いられることになろう。◆The cost of the investment will be shared by Nippon Steel and Usiminas, a major Brazilian steelmaker. 投資額は、新日本製鉄とブラジルの大手鉄鋼会社ウジミナスが共同負担する[折半する]。◆The expected development cost of ￥50 billion is to be shared fifty-fifty between the government and the manufacturers. 500億円が見込まれている開発費は、国とメーカーが折半する予定である。

share （名）株, 株式, 株券, 持ち分株, 保険の引受部分, 市場占有率, 市場占拠率, シェア
（=stock; ⇒golden share, shares）
all shares issued and outstanding　発行済み社外株式総数
counter share　店頭株
dividend per share　1株当たり配当, 1株当たり配当金, DPS
earnings per common share　1株当たり利益, 普通株式1株当たり利益
earnings per share　1株当たり利益, EPS
fancy share　値がさ株
fund flow per share　1株当たり資金フロー
golden share　特権株, 黄金株
import share　輸入シェア
in proportion to one's share　再保険部分に応じて
issued share capital　発行済み株式資本, 発行済み株式資本金　（=issued capital）
issued shares　発行株式数, 発行済み株式
junior share　劣位株
leading share　花形株
low-priced share　低位株
market share　市場占有率, 市場占拠率, 市場シェア, マーケット・シェア
market share gain　市場シェアの拡大
　（=expansion of market share）
members' shares in cooperative entities　協同組合に対する組合員の持ち分
net assets worth per share　1株当たり純資産
net dividend per share　1株当たり正味配当金
net income or loss per share　1株当たり当期純利益
net income per share　1株当たり純利益
outstanding share　発行済み株式
popular share　人気株
prime share　主力株
rare share　品薄株　（=scarce share）
share-based payment　株式報酬
shares of leading banks　大手銀行株
total number of shares　株式総数
watched share　注目株
◆After the integration of Monex Inc. and Orix Securities, Orix will become the largest shareholder in Monex Group with a 22.5 percent share. マネックス証券とオリックス証券の合併に伴い、オリックス証券はマネックスグループの株式を22.5％保有して、同グループの筆頭株主になる。◆At present, the government owns 50.01 percent of shares in Japan Tobacco Inc. 政府は現在、日本たばこ産業（JT）株の50.01％を保有している。◆During a regular board meeting, Fuji TV directors agreed to file a claim against Livedoor for losses of more than ￥30 billion incurred from selling off Livedoor shares. 定例取締役会で、フジテレビの役員は、ライブドア株の売却で被った300億円超の損失について、ライブドアに損害賠償を請求することで合意した。◆Google shares surged about 20 percent on their first day of public trading. 米グーグル（インターネット検索最大手）の株式は、公募取引の初日に約20％急上昇した。◆Kirin Holdings Co. will pay 0.14 of a share for each share in Mercian Corp. to take full control Mercian. キリンホールディングスは、メルシャン株1株に対してキリン株0.14株を割り当て、メルシャンを完全子会社化する。◆Seibu Railway Co. held 100 million shares in the names of about 1,200 individuals. 西武鉄道は、社員約1,200人の個人名義で1億株を保有していた。◆Shares taken by the outside subscribers at the time of incorporation of the new company shall be limited to one share each. 新会社の設立時に外部の引受人が引き受ける株式は、それぞれ1株に限るものとする。

◆The sell-off of Tokyo Metro shares planned by the government will likely be opposed by the Tokyo metropolitan government which is the second-largest shareholder. 政府が計画している東京メトロ株の売却には、国に次ぐ大株主の東京都が抵抗すると見られる。◆The situation is that it is difficult to acquire more than 50 percent of shares in the firm. 今の状況では、同株の50%超を取得するのは厳しい。◆The wrongdoing of Olympus Corp., a blue-chip company that holds the largest share of the global endoscope market, has eroded international faith in corporate Japan. 内視鏡の市場シェアで世界トップのオリンパスの不正行為で、日本企業の国際的な信頼は失墜している。◆Through the sales of shares of JR companies and NTT it owned, the central government garnered ¥3 trillion and ¥13 trillion of profits, respectively. 国が保有するJR各社とNTTの株式の売却で、国はそれぞれ3兆円と13兆円の利益を上げた。◆To procure funds to finance reconstruction from the Great East Japan Earthquake, the government is planning to sell some of its shares in Japan Tobacco Inc. and Tokyo Metro Co. 東日本大震災の復興費用を賄うための資金を調達するため、政府は日本たばこ産業(JT)と東京地下鉄(東京メトロ)の株式を売却する方針だ。

share allotment 株式割当て (=share allocation)
◆In an attempt to recapitalize itself, the bank raised ¥15 billion through a third-party share allotment. 資本再編のため、同行は第三者株式割当てで150億円を調達した。

share buyback 株式の買戻し, 自社株発行済み株式の買戻し, 自社株買戻し, 自社株買い, 自社株取得 (=stock buyback, share repurchase)
◆Restrictions on share buybacks were eased in October 2001. 2001年10月に、自社株買戻しに対する規制が緩和された。◆The listed companies are expected to embark on full-scale share buybacks during and after the summer, giving stock prices an upward impetus. 夏以降、上場企業の自社株買いが本格化し、株価上昇に好影響を与えるものと期待されている。◆The share buyback means a reduction in the company's shareholders to whom it has to pay dividends. 自社株買いは、配当を支払わなければならない会社の株主数が減ることを意味する。

share issue 株式発行, 新株発行
◆The company, which is listed on the First Section of the Tokyo Stock Exchange, raised about ¥5.5 billion from the share issue. 東証1部上場の同社は、新株発行で55億円余りを調達した。

share price 株価 (=stock price; ⇒daily average for a month, gain名詞, stock buyback, stock price)
◆Declining share prices could deal a further blow to the Japanese financial system. 株安は、日本の金融システムに再び打撃を与える可能性がある[日本の金融システムをさらに揺さぶりかねない]。◆Insider trading distorts share prices and undermines the fairness of the securities market. インサイダー取引は、(適正な)株価をゆがめ、証券市場の公正さを損なう。◆Most companies use the daily average for a month of the share prices in gauging the value of latent gains or losses in their stockholdings. 大半の企業は、保有株式の含み損益を算出する際に株価の月中平均を使っている。◆Only 47 percent of the 700 or so companies involved in mergers and acquisitions saw their share prices rise. M&Aに関与した企業約700社のうち、株価が上昇したのはその47%にすぎない。◆Share prices of all four major banking groups declined on the Tokyo Stock Exchange. 東京株式市場は、4大金融グループの株価がそろって下落した。◆The share price of Dai-ichi Kaden stock, which was below ¥40 in January, shot up to more than ¥200 in April. 1月に40円を割っていた第一家電株の株価が、4月には200円以上に急上昇した。

share purchase 株式購入, 株購入, 株式買取り, 株式の買入れ, 株式取得 (=stock purchase)
share purchase option 株式購入[買取り]選択権

share-purchase system 株式買取り制度, 株式購入制度 (=stock-purchase system)
◆The Bank of Japan plans to buy stocks held amounting to ¥2 trillion a year, restricting share purchases up to ¥500 billion per bank and ¥100 billion per stock. 日本銀行は、今後1年で総額2兆円の銀行保有株式を購入し、株式購入に1金融機関当たり5,000億円、1銘柄当たり1,000億円の上限を設ける方針だ。

share purchase unit 株式購入単位
◆A stock split is a measure designed to enable investors, including those with only limited funds, to invest in a company by reducing the share purchase unit. 株式分割は、株式の購入単位を小口化して、少額の資金しかない投資家でも企業に投資できるようにするための手段[資本政策]だ。

share-purchasing organization 株式取得機構 (=stock-purchasing organization)
◆One reason for the banks' reluctance to sell their shares through the share-purchasing organization is that they cannot expect an immediate streamlining of their finances. 銀行が株式取得機構への持ち株売却に消極的な理由の一つは、財務のスリム化をすぐに期待できないからだ。

share repurchase 株式買戻し, 自社株買い (=share buyback, stock buyback, stock repurchase)

share retirement 株式消却, 株式の買入れ消却, 株式の償還 (=retirement of shares, stock retirement; ⇒ retirement of shares)
◆Before the revision of the Commercial Code, stock buybacks were limited to certain purposes, such as share retirement and stock option schemes. 商法の改正前は、自社株買いは、株式の消却用やストック・オプション制度向けなど特定の目的に制限されていた。

share sale 株式売却, 保有株の売却, 株式発行
◆The U.S. government raised $6.2 billion in its first Citi share sale. 米政府は、保有するシティグループ株の最初の売却で、62億ドルを調達した。

share splitting 株式分割
◆The firm's former president sharply increased the firm's stock price in a short period by conducting large-scale share splitting. 同社の元社長は、大規模な株式分割を行うことで同社の株価を短期間で急騰させた。

share swap 株式交換
◆Following the tender offer, Oji Paper would acquire the remaining Hokuetsu shares through a share swap to turn it into a wholly owned subsidiary. 株式公開買付け(TOB)後に、王子製紙は、株式交換で残りの北越製紙の株を取得して北越製紙を完全子会社化する。◆Maruha will put Nichiro under its wing as a wholly owned subsidiary through a share swap. 株式交換方式で、マルハはニチロを完全子会社としてマルハの傘下に収める。◆Supermarket chain operator Ito-Yokado Co. and two group companies established a joint holding company on Sep. 1, 2005 through share swaps. 大手スーパーのイトーヨーカ堂とグループ企業2社が、株式交換により2005年9月1日に共同持ち株会社を設立した。

share swap deal 株式交換取引
◆The bank became a unit of the financial group through a share swap deal. 同行は、株式交換取引で同金融グループ系の企業になった。

share transfer 株式譲渡, 株式名義書換え
◆Saison Life and GE Edison will integrate operations through such measures as a merger within one year from the share transfer. セゾン生命とGEエジソン生命は、株式譲渡から1年以内に合併するなどの手段で経営統合することになった。

share warrant 株式予約権, 新株予約権, 株式引受権, 無記名株式
◆The company plans to issue share warrants on March 24. 同社は、3月24日に新株予約権の発行を予定している。◆The purpose of issuing share warrants is to maintain the current

management's control over the company. 株式予約権の発行は、現経営陣の会社の経営支配権を維持することを目的としている。◆The Tokyo District Court granted an injunction to stop NBS from issuing share warrants to Fuji TV. 東京地裁は、フジテレビを引受先とするニッポン放送の新株予約権発行の差止めを命じた。

shared （形）共有の，共同の，共同利用の，共通の，（費用を）共同負担［共同分担］した，等分した，分割された，合弁事業による
 shared appreciation mortgage　利益配分抵当，価格上昇共有住宅担保貸付け，SAM
 shared ATM　共同利用のATM
 shared bathroom　共同バスルーム
 shared capital　株式資本金
 shared cost　共通原価
 shared equity mortgage　純資産共有［配分］抵当，自己資本共有住宅抵当貸付け
 shared experience　共有経験
 shared information　共有情報，情報の共有
 shared information system　共有情報システム
 shared interests　共益，共同の利益，利益の共有
 shared investment　共同投資，合弁事業による投資
 shared mail［mailing］　他社と共同の郵送広告
 shared market mechanism　分割された市場機構
 shared memory　共有メモリ
 shared monopolies　共同独占
 shared network　共有ネットワーク
 shared ownership　共同所有
 shared revenue　地方交付金
 shared value　共有価値，価値の共有
 time shared input/output system　時分割入出力システム
 time shared system　時分割システム
  （=time sharing system）

shareholder　（名）株主（=stockholder）
 a shareholder who demands a lot　モノ言う株主
 annual report to shareholders　株主向け年次報告書
 boost shareholder value　株主価値を高める
 corporate shareholder　法人株主
 create value for shareholders　株主の価値を高める，株主の利益を高める，株主に対する資産価値を創出する
 designated shareholder　指定株主
 equity shareholder　普通株主
 existing shareholders　既存の株主
 50 percent shareholder　50%所有株主
 increase shareholders value　株主の価値を高める
 individual shareholder　個人株主
 institutional shareholder　機関投資家
 joint shareholder　共同株主
 large shareholder　大株主
 largest shareholder　筆頭株主
  （=the biggest shareholder）
 major shareholder　大株主，大口株主
  （=large shareholder）
 majority shareholder　過半数株主，多数株主，支配株主
 minority shareholder　少数株主
 offers to existing shareholders　割当発行
 ordinary shareholder　普通株主
  （=equity shareholder）
 preferred shareholder　優先株主
 relinquish one's position as the biggest shareholder of the company　同社の筆頭株主の座を降りる
 shareholders' assets　株主資本
 shareholders' equity　株主資本，株主持ち分，自己資本，資本，資本の部
  （⇒financial footing, stockholders' equity）
 shareholders' representative suit　株主代表訴訟
  （=shareholders' lawsuit）
 shareholders' resolution　株主総会決議
 shareholders' responsibility　株主責任
 small shareholder　小株主，小口株主
 stable［strong］shareholder　安定株主
 the largest［biggest］shareholder of the company　同社の筆頭株主
 the second-largest shareholder in the company　同社の第二位株主，同社の第二位の大株主［主要株主］

◆A company's management was reshuffled following a shareholder's proposal. 株主提案を受けて、企業の経営陣が刷新された。◆After the integration of Monex Inc. and Orix Securities, Orix will become the largest shareholder in Monex Group with a 22.5 percent share. マネックス証券とオリックス証券の合併に伴い、オリックス証券はマネックスグループの株式を22.5%保有して、同グループの筆頭株主になる。◆Creditor financial institutions and shareholders will suffer huge losses if TEPCO falls into debt without the government financial aid. 東電が政府の金融支援を受けられずに債務超過に陥れば、融資している金融機関や株主は、巨額の損失を被ることになる。◆Fewer than half of the shareholders of the 700 or so companies involved in mergers and acquisitions profited from the mergers and acquisitions. M&Aを行った企業約700社の株主のうち、M&Aで利益を得たのはその半数以下である。◆Financial institutions and TEPCO shareholders should shoulder part of the financial burden in return for government financial support of TEPCO. 政府が東電を支援する見返りとして、金融機関と東電株主も一定の金融負担をするべきだ。◆Ford will relinquish its position as the biggest shareholder of Mazda Motor Corp. by selling most of its 11 percent stake in Mazda. 米フォードは、保有するマツダ株11%の大半を売却して、マツダの筆頭株主の座を降りることになった。◆If the government financial support is not offered to TEPCO, the utility's creditors and shareholders will have to share the burden. 東電に政府の金融支援がない場合は、同社の債権者と株主が共同負担せざるを得ないだろう。◆Olympus Corp. has kept deceiving its shareholders and clients by years of window-dressing. オリンパスは、長年にわたる粉飾で、株主や取引先を欺き続けてきた。◆Shareholders can access the company's special Web site and vote on decisions, including the election of board members. 株主は、同社専用のホームページを利用して、取締役選任などの議決に投票することができる。◆The company's board approved a plan to issue subscription warrants to all shareholders on its shareholders list as of March 31, 2011. 同社の取締役会は、2011年3月31日現在［時点］の株主名簿に記載されている全株主を対象に、新株予約権を発行する計画を承認した。◆The former head of the Murakami Fund was often dubbed a shareholder who demands a lot. 村上ファンドの元代表は、「モノ言う株主」とよく呼ばれた。◆The number of shareholders responding to Fuji TV's takeover bid was more than expected. フジテレビの株式公開買付け（TOB）に応じた株主の数は、予想を上回った。◆The sell-off of Tokyo Metro shares planned by the government will likely be opposed by the Tokyo metropolitan government which is the second-largest shareholder. 政府が計画している東京メトロ株の売却には、国に次ぐ大株主の東京都が抵抗すると見られる。

shareholder approval　株主の承認
◆At an emergency shareholders meeting, the company obtained shareholder approval to transfer ¥199 billion from its legal reserves to provide for write-offs of nonperforming loans. 臨時株主総会で同社は、株主から、不良債権処理に備

えて法定準備金から1,990億円を取り崩す案の承認を得た。

shareholder right　株主権
◆In margin trading, a securities firm possess some shareholder rights, including voting rights, until an investor actually pays for his or her stock. 信用取引では、投資家が実際に買い入れた株の代金を支払うまで、証券会社が議決権など株主権の一部を持つ。

shareholder structure　株主構成（株主を機関別や所有株数別に区別した割合のことで、一般に1社の株式分布状況をいう）
◆With a fair and balanced allocation of shares, the company will lay the foundation for a stable and long-term shareholder structure. 公正でバランスのとれた株式割当てにより、同社は安定した長期的株主構成の基盤を据える方針だ。

shareholders incentives　株主優待, 株主優待制度
◆Shareholders incentives are designed to encourage shareholders to hold onto their stocks over the long term. 株主優待の狙いは、株主の株式の長期保有促進にある。

shareholders list　株主名簿
◆The company's board approved a plan to issue subscription warrants to all shareholders on its shareholders list as of March 31, 2011. 同社の取締役会は、2011年3月31日現在[時点]の株主名簿に記載されている全株主を対象に、新株予約権を発行する計画を承認した。◆The ratio of voting rights held by the company is based on the shareholders list as of the end of September. 同社が保有する議決権の比率は、9月末時点の株主名簿をもとにしている。

shareholders meeting　株主総会　(=general meeting of shareholders, general meeting of stockholders, shareholders' meeting, stockholders' meeting; ⇒corporate racketeer)
　annual shareholders meeting　年次株主総会, 定時株主総会
　approve at a shareholders meeting　株主総会で承認する
　attend a shareholders meeting　株主総会に出席する
　call a shareholders meeting　株主総会を招集する
　emergency shareholders meeting　緊急株主総会, 臨時株主総会
　extraordinary shareholders meeting　臨時株主総会
　special shareholders meeting　臨時株主総会
◆A firm requires the support of more than two thirds of shareholders to decide on important matters, such as a merger, at shareholders meetings. 企業が株主総会で合併などの重要事項を決議するには、3分の2以上の賛成が必要だ。◆Fewer companies are holding shareholders meetings on the same day as other companies. 株主総会を他社と同じ日に開く企業は、減っている。◆Listed companies revised their articles of incorporation to make stock certificates paperless by holding shareholders meetings. 株券をペーパーレス化するため、公開企業は、株主総会を開いて会社の定款を変更した。◆The management buyout might have been rejected at the firm's shareholders meeting if its major shareholders had opposed it. 同社の経営陣による自社買収（MBO）は、株主総会で主要株主[大株主]が反対したら否決されていたかもしれない。

shareholders of record　登録株主
◆The company's regular quarterly dividend will be payable June 30, 2011 to shareholders of record at the close of business on June 9, 2011. 当社の通常四半期配当は、2011年6月9日営業終了時の登録株主に対して2009年6月30日に支払われる。

shareholders' assets　株主資本
◆Stock buybacks and the resulting reduction in shareholders' assets can weaken a company's financial base and trigger a decline in performance. 自社株買いをして株主資本を減らすことは、企業の財務基盤を悪化させ、業績を落とす恐れもある。

shareholders' dividends　株主配当
◆Many of the banking groups had to use a portion of their legally required reserves to pay their shareholders' dividends. 銀行グループの多くは、株主配当の原資に充てるため、法定準備金の一部の取り崩しを迫られた。

shareholders' equity　株主資本, 株主持ち分, 自己資本, 資本, 資本の部
　average shareholders' equity　平均株主資本
　common shareholders' equity　普通株主持ち分
　minority shareholders' equity　少数株主持ち分
　preferred shareholders' equity　優先株主持ち分
◆To establish a solid financial footing, we have been strengthening our shareholders' equity. 磐石な財務基盤（経営基盤）を確立するため、当社は株主資本（自己資本）を強化しています。◆We calculate a company's ROE by dividing the firm's net income by its shareholders' equity. 企業の株主資本利益率（ROE）は、企業の純利益を純資産[株主資本]で割って求める。

shareholders' interest　株主の権利, 株主利益
◆Listed companies have to place importance on shareholders' interests. 上場会社は、株主利益を重視しなければならない。

shareholders' lawsuit　株主代表訴訟
(=shareholder lawsuit)
◆If the creditor banks forgive the debts though TEPCO is not carrying excess liabilities, senior managements of the lenders may be sued in a shareholders' lawsuit over mismanagement. 東電が債務超過ではないのに債権保有銀行が債権を放棄すると、ずさんな経営で、金融機関の上級経営陣は株主代表訴訟で訴えられる可能性がある。

shareholders' meeting　株主総会
(=shareholders meeting, stockholders' meeting)
◆More than 2,000 corporations held their shareholders' meetings nationwide on Thursday amid flagging business performances and numerous corporate scandals. 2,000社を超える企業が木曜日、企業の業績が低迷するなか、また企業の不祥事が続出するなか、全国で株主総会を開いた。

shareholders' proposal　株主提案
◆Recently, shareholders' proposals have come from investment funds seeking higher dividends and the appointment of outside directors. 最近の株主提案は、増配や社外取締役選任などを求める投資ファンドから出されている。

shareholders'[shareholder] value　株主価値, 株主の資産価値, 株主利益
(=value for shareholders)
◆Another characteristic of the U.S. management style is that businesses give priority to maximizing shareholders' value. 米国式経営スタイルのもうひとつの特色は、企業が株主の資産価値の極大化を第一に考えることだ。

shareholding　(名)株式所有, 株式保有, 株式保有率, 出資比率, 持ち株比率, 持ち株, 保有株
(=equity holding)
　book one's shareholdings at market value　保有株を時価で評価する
　cross-shareholding　株式の持ち合い
　foreign shareholding ratio　外国人持ち株比率
　interlocking shareholding　持ち合い株
　proportional to the ratio of one's shareholdings　持ち株比率に応じて, 株式の保有高に応じて
　public shareholding　株式公開
　shareholding structure　株主構成
◆It is certain that NBS shareholding conditions run foul of this rule of the Tokyo Stock Exchange. ニッポン放送の株式保有状況が、この東証基準（大株主上位10者と役員の株式保有比率が80％超の状態が1年続けば上場廃止になるという東京証券取引所の基準）に抵触するのは確実だ。◆Nippon Life Insur-

ance's asset management subsidiary Nissay Asset Management Corp. increased its shareholding in Olympus to 0.21 percent from 0.08 percent. 日本生命の資産運用子会社であるニッセイアセットマネジメントは、オリンパス株の保有比率を0.08%から0.21%に買い増した。

shareholding ratio　持ち株比率, 株式保有比率
◆Livedoor's stake in NBS has exceeded 50 percent in terms of voting rights, or 46 percent in terms of shareholding ratio. ライブドアが保有するニッポン放送株は、議決権比率で(議決権ベースで)50%(持ち株比率で46%)を超えた。

shareholdings　(名)持ち株, 保有株, 保有株式, 株式保有 (=stockholdings; ⇒accounting rule)
◆A law on banks' shareholdings bans banks in principle from owning share in excess of their capital base after Sept. 30, 2004. 銀行等の株式保有に関する法律は、2004年9月30日以降、自己資本を上回る株式の保有を原則として禁止している。◆My shareholdings have become paper trash. 持ち株が、紙屑になってしまった。

shares　(名)株式, 株式数, 持ち分
　additional shares　株式数の増加, 増資株
　application for shares　株式の申込み
　buy back shares　自社株を買い戻す
　buy one's own shares　自社株買いを行う
　buy shares　株式を購入する
　convert bonds into shares　社債を株式に転換する
　issue shares　受益証券を発行する
　new shares issuing　新株発行
　number of authorized shares　授権株式数
　number of shares of stock outstanding　発行済み株式数
　placing of shares　株式の募集
　public sale of equity shares　株式の民間への売出し
　refloat the shares　株式を再公開する
　register of interests in shares　大株主名簿
　retirement of shares out of profit　株式の利益消却
　shares issued upon exercise of warrants　ワラントの行使で発行される株式
　shares of leading banks　大手銀行株
　shares of stock of the company　同社の株式
　shares of stock outstanding　発行済み株式数
　shares of the trust　トラストの持ち分
　shares out　発行済み株式数
　shares to be issued upon conversion of convertible bonds　転換社債の転換によって発行される株式
　shares with a compulsory conversion clause　強制転換条項付き株式
　shares with a conversion privilege　転換予約権付き株式
　stocks and shares　株式
　technology shares　ハイテク株
　the shares are fairly priced　株価は適正水準にある
　total number of shares　株式総数
　total shares under option　オプション未行使株数合計
　weighted shares　加重株数

shares outstanding　発行済み株式数
　average number of shares outstanding　平均社外流通株式数, 期中平均発行済み株式数
　common shares outstanding　普通株式発行総数
　weighted average number of common shares outstanding　発行済み[外部発行済み]普通株式数の加重平均, 加重平均発行済み普通株式数
　weighted average number of shares outstanding　発行済み株式数の加重平均, 加重平均株式数
◆All references to shares outstanding, dividends and per share amounts have been adjusted on a retroactive basis. 発行済み株式数と配当、1株当たりの金額については、すべて過去に遡及して調整してあります。

shark repellent [repellant]　サメ駆除剤, サメよけ, 乗っ取り対策　(⇒merger and acquisition)
解説 サメ駆除剤とは：定款の改正や転換優先株の発行など、敵対的買収への防衛手段の総称。その代表的なものとして、defensive merger(防衛的合併)やgolden parachute(黄金のパラシュート)、poison pill(毒薬条項)、scorched-earth tactic(焦土作戦)、staggered board(スタガー取締役会)、supermajority(超過半数条項)などがある。

shark watcher　サメ監視人(企業買収の動きを専門に監視する会社)

sharp　(形)急激な, 急速な, 急な, 大幅な
　a sharp appreciation of [in] the dollar　ドルの急騰, 急激なドル高
　a sharp decline in credit quality　信用の質の急激な悪化
　a sharp decline in interest rates　金利の急激な低下
　a sharp downturn in domestic demand　内需の急速な冷え込み, 内需の急激な落ち込み, 内需の急減
　a sharp drop in earnings　業績の急激な悪化
　a sharp economic growth　右肩上がりの経済成長
　a sharp expansion in private sector credit　民間部門の信用急拡大
　a sharp fall in money market rates　短期市場金利の急低下[急激な低下]
　a sharp fall in (the value of) the dollar　急激なドル安, ドルの急落
　a sharp hike in short-term money rates　短期市場金利の大幅引上げ
　a sharp increase in inventories　在庫の急増, 在庫の急激な増加
　a sharp increase in oil prices　原油価格の急騰
　a sharp practice　きわどい商法, 違法すれすれのやり方
　a sharp rally in the bond market　債券相場の急騰, 債券相場の急上昇
　a sharp rise [hike] in stock prices　株価の急騰, 株価の急上昇
　a sharp turnaround from a loss　赤字からの急激な持ち直し, 赤字からの大幅黒字転換
　a sharper competition　競争激化
◆Amid a widening slump in global auto sales and the yen's sharp appreciation against the U.S. dollar, the firm is expected to report an unconsolidated operating loss in fiscal 2011. 世界の新車販売の落ち込み拡大と急激な円高・ドル安に伴って、同社の2011年度[2012年3月期決算]の営業利益は、単独ベース[単独決算]で赤字が見込まれている。

sharp appreciation of the yen　円の急上昇, 円の急騰, 急激な円高
◆Business sentiment and the willingness of household to spend may cool and stall the economy unless the sharp appreciation of the yen is checked. 円の急騰を止めないと、企業の心理や家計の消費意欲が冷え込み、景気が腰折れしかねない。

sharp appreciation of the yen and the fall of the dollar　急激な円高・ドル安
◆Dollar-selling pressure has eased and put a temporary brake on the sharp appreciation of the yen and the fall of the dollar. ドル売り圧力が弱まり、急激な円高・ドル安にいったん歯止めがかかった。

sharp decline in stock prices　株価急落
◆The recent circumstances facing the nation's megabanks have shown up their weaknesses, as shown by slow progress in their efforts to write off their nonperforming loans and a sharp decline in their stock prices. 日本のメガバンク(巨大銀行グループ)が直面している最近の状況を見ると、不良債権処

理策の遅れや株価の急落などが示すように、メガバンクの脆弱(ぜいじゃく)性が目立っている。

sharp drops in brokerage fees　株[株式]売買手数料の大幅減
◆The major securities house attributed the poor earnings to sharp drops in brokerage fees and trading profits amid the extended slump in the domestic stock market. この大手証券会社は、減益の要因として、国内株式市場の長期低迷による株売買手数料と売買益の大幅減を挙げた。

sharp fall　急落
◆Tokyo stocks bounced back Wednesday after sharp falls Tuesday following Lehman Brothers decision to file for bankruptcy as financial worries eased. 水曜日の東京株式市場は、リーマン・ブラザーズが前日に破たん申請を決めて急落したものの、金融不安が和らいだため反発した。

sharp fall in Japanese government bonds　日本国債価格の急落
◆If a financial system crisis should occur due to sharp fall in Japanese government bond prices, the Japanese people would suffer an erosion of their financial assets. 日本国債価格の急落で金融システム不安が生じれば、日本国民の金融資産は損失を被ることになる。

sharp falls on European and U.S. markets　欧米市場での株価急落
◆Following sharp falls on European and U.S. markets, the Nikkei Stock Average fell briefly to its lowest level this year. 欧米市場の株価急落を受けて、日経平均株価は一時、今年の最安値を下回った。

sharp rise　急増, 急上昇, 急騰
◆The latest survey hardly reflects corporate sentiment regarding the yen's sharp rise in value since mid-September. 今回の調査は、9月半ば以降の円急騰に対する企業心理を反映していない。

sharp rise in crude oil prices　原油価格の高騰
◆The sharp rise in crude oil prices has caused increases in prices of other fuels and grains, triggering inflation in many parts of the world. 原油価格の高騰は、他の燃料価格や穀物価格の上昇を招き、国際的なインフレを引き起こしている。

sharp rise in the value of the yen　急激な円高
◆The sharp rise in the value of the yen must be rectified. 急激な円高は、是正しなければならない。

sharp rise in the yen's value　急激な円高
◆The government and the Bank of Japan will likely continue to work together in fighting the sharp rise in the yen's value. 政府と日銀は、急激な円高阻止で協調路線を継続することになりそうだ。

sharp V-shaped recovery　急激なV字回復
◆Most emerging East Asian economies are assured of a sharp V-shaped recovery this year. 今年は、東アジア新興国の大半が急激にV字回復するのは確実だ。

sharply　(副)急激に, 急速に, 急に, 大幅に
decline[drop]sharply　急減する, 急激に減少する, 大幅[急激]に低下する
deteriorate sharply　急激に悪化する
rise sharply　急増する, 急上昇する, 急伸する
sharply decline　急落する
sharply higher interest rates　金利の急上昇
sharply higher prices　価格急騰
sharply higher trading volume　売買高の急増
spike sharply (upwards)　急騰する
◆In the wake of the euro crisis in Europe and the fiscal deadlock in the United States, the yen has sharply strengthened. 欧州のユーロ危機と米国の財政政策の行き詰まりの影響で、円が急騰している。◆Japan should prevent the dollar plunging and the yen from rising too sharply through concerted market intervention with the United States and European countries. 日本は、米欧との協調介入によってドル急落と超円高を阻止すべきだ。◆The FSA's special inspection will check the major banks' large-lot corporate borrowers whose stock prices or credit ratings have sharply declined. 金融庁の特別検査は、大手銀行の株価や格付けなどが急落した大口融資先を査定の対象としている。◆The number of companies undertaking initial public offerings has risen sharply this year. 株式を新規公開する企業が、今年は急増している。

shed　(動)落とす, 削減する, 押し下げる, 圧縮する, 売却する, 取り除く, 捨て去る, 捨てる, 放棄する, 流す, 注ぐ, 〜から脱する, 減少する, 低下する, 下落する
shed assets　資産を売却する, 資産を圧縮する
shed[throw]light on　〜を照らす, 〜を明らかにする, 解明する, 〜に光[光明]を投じる
shed oneself of　〜を取り除く, 〜を捨てる
(=get shed of)
shed 5,000 jobs　人員を5,000人削減する, 5,000人を削減する
◆The Dow and the Standard & Poor's 500 index each shed more than 10 percent in February. ダウ平均[ダウ・ジョーンズ平均株価]とS&P500株価指数は、2月にそれぞれ10%以上下落した。

shelf registration　一括登録, 一括登録制度, シェルフ登録, 発行登録　(⇒debt security)
◆The Corporation has US $300 million of debt securities registered with the U.S. Securities and Exchange Commission pursuant to a shelf registration program. 当社は、米国の証券取引委員会(SEC)の一括登録制度(シェルフ・レジストレーション)に基づき、3億米ドルの債務証券発行予定額をSECに登録しています。

shelf registration program　一括登録制度
◆On October 1, 2011, we utilized the shelf registration program to issue US $300 million of 6.0% Notes due 2021. 2011年10月1日に当社は、米証券取引所(SEC)の一括登録制度を利用して、満期2021年・利率6.0%のノート3億米ドルを発行しました。

shell　(名)見せかけ, 金庫, 貴重品保管所, ドル, 幽霊会社
shell bank　名目的な銀行
shell money　貝殻貨幣

shell company　弱小会社, 幽霊会社(paper company), 実体のない会社, ペーパー・カンパニー, 隠れみの会社, ダミー会社
◆The firm's shell companies allegedly pooled about ¥1 billion in slush funds by padding bills for the construction projects in their overseas bank accounts. 調べによれば、同社のペーパー・カンパニーは建設工事代金[建設工事の請求書]を水増しして、約10億円の裏金を海外の複数の銀行口座にプールしていた。◆Using a shell company for buying real estate is common practice among real estate agents. 不動産の購入に実体がない会社を利用するのは、不動産業界ではよく行われていることだ。

shelter　(名)避難所, 隠れ家, 住まい, 家, 保護, 庇護(ひご), 擁護, 避難, シェルター　(動)保護する, 庇護する
shelter loans　住宅関連貸付け
sheltered industry　保護産業, 庇護産業
sheltered trade　保護貿易
sheltered trades　保護産業
tax shelter　租税回避地, 租税回避国, 租税回避手段, 税金天国, 税金逃れの隠れみの, 会計操作, タックス・シェルター　(=tax haven)
◆Merrill Lynch, the third-largest U.S. securities firm, took shelter under the Bank of America umbrella, the second-largest U.S. bank. 米証券3位のメリルリンチは、米銀行2位のバンク・オブ・アメリカの傘の下に逃げ込んだ。

Shenzhen Stock Exchange　深(しん)せん証券取引所
◆The Shenzhen Stock Exchange is gaining ground on the

Tokyo Stock Exchange in term of trading volume. 深（しん）せん証券取引所は、売買規模［取引高］で東京証券取引所に肉薄している。

shift （動）移す、移し替える、変更する、変える、転換する（自動）移る、移動する、移行する
◆China will shift to a "prudent" monetary policy in 2011 from the previous "appropriately loose" stance. 中国は、これまでの「適度に緩和的な」金融政策から2011年は「穏健な」金融政策に方向転換する方針だ。◆Households and companies have already started taking measures to protect their assets by shifting their funds into other financial products and institutions. 家計や企業が、資金を他の金融商品に変えたり他の金融機関に移動したりして、資産を保護する措置をすでに進めている。◆In an attempt to get on the bandwagon, many people are shifting their fixed rate mortgages to adjustable rate ones. 時流に乗ろうとして、固定金利型住宅ローンを変動金利型住宅ローンに変更する人が多い。◆Investors seem to be shifting their money from investment trusts to more secured time deposits in the face of global financial turmoil. 世界の金融市場の混乱に直面して、投資家は資金を投資信託から安定性の高い定期預金に切り替えているようだ。◆It will take about five to seven years to shift to the IFRSs if they become mandatory. 国際財務報告基準（IFRSs）が強制適用となると、IFRSsに移行するのに5～7年程度はかかる。◆It's common to shift huge sums of capital to take advantage of international tax shelters. 巨額の資金を移し替えて、国際的な節税策を講じるのは常識だ。◆Japanese firms' moves to shift production abroad to cope with the yen's rise will bring about a hollowing-out of domestic industries. 円高対策として日本企業が生産拠点を海外に移すと、国内産業の空洞化を招くことになる。◆More investors are pulling money from stock markets and shifting it into safer time deposits. 株式市場から資金を引き揚げ、引き揚げた資金を安定性の高い定期性預金に移し替える投資家が増えている。◆Speculative investors are shifting from commodities to stocks. 投機資金が、商品から株式に移っている。◆The challenge in monetary policy for countries now is shifting toward finding a way to move away from ultra-loose money policies. 現在、各国の金融政策の課題は、超金融緩和政策からいかに転換するかに移りつつある。◆The European Central Bank shifted to a credit-tightening stance late last year. 欧州中央銀行は、昨年末から金融引締めのスタンスに転じた。◆The main battlefield of monetary policy likely will shift to deflation. 今後は、デフレが金融政策の主戦場となろう。◆The tripartite reforms aim to reduce the amount of subsidies provided by the central government to the local governments; cut local tax grants to local governments; and shift revenue sources from the central government to local governments. 「三位一体」改革は、国の地方政府への補助金削減、地方交付税交付金の削減と国から地方政府への財源の移譲をめざしている。◆When the freeze on the payoff system was partially lifted, clients shifted their funds from time deposits to savings deposits that will be protected fully. ペイオフ制度凍結の一部解禁が行われた際には、顧客が預金を定期預金から全額保護される普通預金に預け替えた。◆While stock prices shifted upward, the sentiments of corporate managers have shown signs of improvement lately. 株価が上昇に転じる一方、最近は企業経営者の景況感も改善の兆しを見せている。

shift （名）変化、変動、変更、移動、移行、転換、再構成、交替勤務制、交替制、シフト
dollar shift　ドル・シフト
equity structure shift　資本再構成
major shifts in the global economic balances　地球規模の経済バランスの大変化
shift of sentiment　市場の地（じ）合いの変化
yen shift　円シフト
◆A shift from term deposits to ordinary savings accounts and a shift from second-tier regional banks and credit banks to major commercial banks have been taking place. 定期預金から普通預金への移動と、第二地方銀行や信用金庫などから大手銀行への移動が起こっている。

shinkin bank　信用金庫、信金
（=credit bank, credit union bank）
◆Shinkin banks are credit associations established under the Shinkin Bank Law. 信用金庫は、信用金庫法に基づいて設立される信用協同組合のことである。

shock　（名）衝撃、脅威、精神的打撃、電撃、震動、激突、ショック
bankruptcy shock　経営破たんのショック、破たんショック（⇒engineer）
create shock waves in the financial markets　金融市場に衝撃［ショック］を巻き起こす
dollar shock　ドル・ショック
Dubai shock［crisis, debt crysis］　中東ドバイの金融不安、ドバイ信用不安、ドバイ・ショック
Lehman shock　リーマン・ブラザーズ破たんの衝撃、リーマン・ショック
send shock waves through global financial markets　～で世界の金融市場に衝撃が走る［衝撃波が伝わる］
shock loss　異常損失
shock waves　衝撃波、衝撃、大きな反響
yen shock　円ショック
◆On Dec. 1, 2009, the Nikkei Stock Average was bearing down on the 9,000 mark due to the so-called Dubai shock. 2009年12月1日の日経平均株価（225種）は、いわゆるドバイ・ショック（中東ドバイの金融不安）で、9,000円台を割り込む寸前まで追いつめられていた。◆Rapid recovery following the so-called Lehman shock has ended and the Chinese economy has entered a phase aimed at stable growth. いわゆるリーマン・ショック後の中国の急回復の時期は終わり、中国経済は、安定成長を目指す段階に入っている。◆The abrupt announcement of Lehman's failure sent shock waves through global financial markets. リーマン破たんの突然の発表で、世界の金融市場に衝撃が走った。

shogun bond　東京外貨債、ショーグン債（日本国内で非居住者が外貨建てで発行する債券のこと）

Shoko Chukin Bank　商工中金　（=the central cooperative bank for commerce and industry）

shoot up　（物価、為替相場が）急騰する、跳ね上がる、急上昇する、急増する、急伸する
（=jump, skyrocket, spurt）
shoot up again　上昇に転じる
shoot up to　～まで跳ね上がる、～まで急騰する
stock prices shoot up on the news　そのニュースで株価が跳ね上がる［急騰する］
◆After the stimulus measures were unveiled, the yen shot up about ¥0.3 against the greenback in five minutes. 景気対策が発表された後、円の対ドル相場は、5分間に30銭ほど円高方向に振れた。◆The list of banks the U.S. FDIC considers to be in trouble shot up nearly 50 percent to 171 during the third quarter of 2008. 米連邦預金保険公社（FDIC）が経営破たんの可能性があると見ている問題銀行は、2008年第3四半期［7-9月期］に約50％急増して171行（直前の4-6月期は117行）に達した。◆The U.S. dollar shot up to the mid-¥85 level in Tokyo on market intervention by monetary authorities. 東京（外為）市場は、通貨当局の市場介入で、米ドル相場が85円台半ばまで急騰した。◆Yields on sovereign debt of Spain surged and Italy began seeing yields on its government bonds shoot up. スペインの国債金利が上昇し、イタリアの国債金利も急騰している。

shopper　（名）買い物客、客、客足、来店者数、ショッパー
alienate shoppers　客を遠ざける
comparison shopper　競争調査

entice [draw in] shoppers　客を呼び込む
high-income shopper　高所得の買い物客
home shopper　通販で買う客
lure shoppers　客を呼び込む, 客を引きつける
online shopper　ネット・ショッパー, オンライン・ショッパー
shoppers' enthusiasm　消費意欲
smart shoppers　賢明な買い物客
upscale shoppers　高級志向の買い物客
◆The firm offers loans for retail and corporate clients in addition to offering electronic settlement for online shoppers. 同社は、ネット・ショッパー[オンライン・ショッパー]向けの電子決済業務のほかに、個人と企業向けの融資も手がけている。

shopping　(名)買い物, 購買, 商戦, ショッピング
　card shopping　カード・ショッピング
　Easter shopping season　イースターの買い物シーズン
　holiday shopping season　米国のクリスマス商戦, クリスマスの買い物シーズン
　multimedia shopping　マルチメディア・ショッピング
　one-stop shopping　一点集中購買, 関連購買, 1か所での同時まとめ買い, 1か所ですべて済ませる買い物, ワンストップ・ショッピング
　rate shopping　格付けの相見積り
　shopping agent　ショッピング・エージェント(実売価格を一覧表示したり店との価格交渉を代行したりするなど、オンライン・ショッピングの支援・代行業務)
　shopping on the Web　ネット・ショッピング (=Net shopping)
　treaty shopping　租税回避, 節税行為, トリーティ・ショッピング
　TV shopping　テレビ・ショッピング
　year-end shopping season　年末商戦
◆NTT DoCoMo Inc. formed a capital tie-up with Internet shopping mall operator Rakuten Inc. in the Internet auction business. NTTドコモが、インターネット・オークション事業で電子商取引大手の楽天[仮想商店街を運営している楽天]と資本提携した

shore up　(動)支える, 下支えする, 持ちこたえる, 防衛する, テコ入れをする, 強化する, 増強する, 補強する, 支援する, 拡充する, 引き上げる, 高める
　accelerate efforts to shore up one's fiscal condition　財政健全化を加速する
　shore up capital positions　自己資本比率[資本ポジション]を強化する, 自己資本比率を引き上げる
　shore up one's capital strength　資本を増強する
　shore up one's revenue base　〜の収益基盤を強化する
　shore up the banking industry　銀行業界を強化する
　shore up the dollar　ドルを支える
　shore up the IMF's role　IMFの役割[機能]を拡充する
　shore up the U.S. economy　米景気を下支えする, 米景気にテコ入れをする
◆Banks must shore up their revenue base so they can repay all their debts. 銀行の債務返済を完了するには、銀行が収益基盤を強化する必要がある。◆Countries burdened with heavy public debts need to accelerate efforts to shore up their fiscal condition. 深刻な財政赤字国は、財政健全化を加速する必要がある。◆European banks are forced to shore up their potential capital shortages to restore market confidence. 欧州銀行は、市場の信認を回復するため、潜在的資本不足の増強を迫られている。◆European countries are urged to facilitate a safety net for emergencies, including the injection of public funds into deteriorating banks to shore up their capital strength. 欧州は、経営が悪化した銀行[金融機関]に公的資金を注入して資本を増強するなど、非常時に備えた安全網の整備が求められて

いる。◆Part of the bailout funds on the $700 billion financial rescue program went to shore up insurance giant American International Group Inc. and the auto industry. 7,000億ドルの金融支援策に基づく救済資金の一部は、米保険大手のAIGと自動車業界(GMとクライスラー)の強化に充てられた。◆The government should step up diplomatic efforts to shore up the IMF's role. 政府は、国際通貨基金(IMF)の機能拡充に向けての外交努力を強めるべきだ。◆There will be a limit to what can be accomplished to shore up the U.S. economy through the Fed's additional monetary easing. 米連邦準備制度理事会(FRB)の追加金融緩和策による米景気テコ入れの効果は、限定的と見られる。◆To shore up their economies, major economic powers seem to be relying more on their monetary policies. 景気テコ入れに、先進国は金融政策頼みの様相が強まっている。

short　(動)空売りする, 釣銭を少なく渡す
　short debt futures　債券先物を空売りする
　short the bond　債券を売る
　short the dollar against the yen　円に対してドルを空売りする

short　(名)短期, 空売り, 空売り相場師, 空売りをする人, 欠損, 不足, 弱気, ショート(「空売り」は, 自分が保有していない株式を他から借り入れて売却すること)　(形)短い, 短期の, 短時間の, 低い, 不足の, 足りない, 不十分な, 乏(とぼ)しい, 品薄の, 空売りの, 空相場の, 売り方の, 弱気の
　be short in crude oil　原油を売り建てる
　borrow short　短期間借りる
　capital short　資金不足　(=short of capital)
　capital short bank　資金不足の銀行
　going short　思惑売り
　sell short　空売りする
　selling short　空売り
　short account　空売り勘定, 短期見越し売り勘定
　short agreement　短期契約
　short bill　代金取立て手形, 短期手形
　short bit　10セント貨幣
　short bond　短期債券, 短期債, ショート・ボンド(「ショート・ボンド」は満期までの残存期間が1年以内の長期債。ただし、空売り(short sale)された債券やショート・クーポン(short coupon)と同じ意味で使われることもある)
　short call　コールの売り(オプション取引でコール・オプション(call option)を売ったため、商品を売る義務を負っている状態にあること)
　short cash　現金不足
　short check　預金不足小切手, 預金切れ小切手
　short contract　空売り契約
　short coupon　ショート・クーポン(満期までの残存期間が1年以内の利付き債(coupon bond)を意味する場合と、新規発行された利付き債のうち、最初の利払い日が通常より早く発行日から半年以内に到来するものをいう場合がある)　⇒long coupon)
　short credit　短期信用貸し, 短期信用
　short-dated　短期の
　short-dated bill　短期手形
　short dates　短期物, ショート・デート
　short delivery　受渡し品不足, 個数不足
　short (deposit) balance　預金残高不足
　short draft　短期為替手形
　short drawing　ショート・ドローイング(為替手形金額が信用状の金額を下回る状態のこと)
　short duration instrument　短期商品
　short hedge　売りヘッジ, ショート・ヘッジ(現物など

での買い持ちポジションを先物などの売りつなぎでヘッジすること)
 short hedging 売りつなぎ
 short interest 空売り残高, 空売り総株数, 借り株残株, 貸し株残株, 売り建て玉, ショート・インタレスト
 short items 短期物
 short market 弱気市場, 弱気市況
 short money 短期借入れ, 短期金融
 short notice (手形の)短期通知, 期限経過通知, 不十分な予告期間
 short notice money 短期資金 (=call money)
 short of exchange 為替の空売り
 short paper 短期証券
 short put プットの売り, ショート・プット
 short rate 短期金利, 短期利率, (手形や小切手の)短期相場
 short sellers 空売り筋
 short sellers of the options オプションの売り手, オプションの売り手側
 short squeezes 踏み上げ, 踏み上げ相場, 空売りの高値買戻し
 short stocks 空売り株
 short-supply stocks 品薄株
 short swap 短期スワップ取引
 shorter maturities 短期物
 shorter-term investor 短期売買志向の投資家
 shorts 短期社債, 短期債券, 不足分, 不足高, 資金難
 sold short 空売り
 the short end 短期債, 短期物
 the short side 空売りの弱気筋
short covering 空売りの買戻し, 買戻し, ショート・カバー (=covering short)
 short covering by traders 投資家[トレーダー]による買戻し
 short covering purchase 空売りの買戻し
 ◆The euro failed to challenge parity versus the dollar in Asian trade, with the greenback recovering slightly thanks to short covering by traders. アジア市場では, 投資家による買戻しで米ドルが小幅回復したため, ユーロは1ドル＝1ユーロの等価に届かなかった。◆The market soared on short covering. 相場は, 空売りの買戻しが出て急騰した。
short-dated [short dated] (形)短期の
 short-dated bill 短期手形
 short-dated bonds issues 短期債
 short-dated instruments 短期商品
 short-dated paper 短期債
 short-dated securities 短期証券
short-duration bonds デュレーションの短い債券, 短期物
 ◆The news pushed up yields on short-duration bonds. これを受けて, 短期物の利回りが上昇した。
short exchange 短期為替, 短期為替手形, 代金取立手形
 short exchange bill 短期手形 (=short bill)
 short exchange rate 短期為替相場
short-lived upturn 薄命の景気回復
 ◆Should the government forge ahead with its belt-tightening policy, the budding economic recovery may be reduced to a short-lived upturn. 政府が緊縮路線をひた走れば, 景気回復の芽も, 薄命の景気回復に終わりかねない。
short loan 短期融資, 短期ローン, 短期貸付け資金
 short loan fund 短期融資資金, 短期貸付け資金
 short loan fund market 短期貸付け資金市場
short of 不足している, 足りない, 不十分である, 満たされていない
 be short of cash 現金が足りない, 現金不足である
 be short of fund 資金不足である
 be short of money お金が足りない, 資金不足である
 go short of ～のショート・ポジションを取る
 run short of money 資金が不足する, 資金不足に陥る
 ◆If financial institutions become short of funds in the process of the FSA's special inspections, the government must immediately inject public funds. 金融庁の特別検査で金融機関が資本不足に陥る場合には, 政府は直ちに公的資金を注入しなければならない。◆It's a matter of time that the company will run short of money. 同社が資金不足に陥るのは, 時間の問題だ。◆The FSA can order banks that have received injections of public funds to improve their earnings if their net profits fall short of their declared earnings targets by 30 percent or more. 公的資金注入行の税引き後利益が公表した収益計画(収益目標)より3割以上下回った場合, 金融庁は, 注入行に業務改善[収益改善]命令を発動することができる。◆The National Bank of Cuba will not be able to pay for imports into Cuba in due terms as the country is short of settlement funds. キューバ国立銀行は今後, 国全体の決済資金不足で, 期日どおりにキューバへの輸入代金の支払いができなくなる状況にある。
short position 売り持ち, 売り建て, 売り持ちポジション, 弱気の立場, ショート・ポジション(「ショート・ポジション」は, 株式などを空売りしてまだ買戻しをしていない状態のほかに, オプション取引(option trading)でオプションを売ってまだ買戻しをしていない状態あるいはオプションの行使期限がまだ切れていない状態をいう)
 cover short positions ショート・ポジションを手じまう
 have a short position in ～でショート・ポジション[売り持ちポジション]を取る
 net short open foreign exchange positions 未決済の為替ネット・ショート・ポジション(正味売り持ち高)
 short position in a bond 債券のショート・ポジション
 short position in call コールの売り持ち
short-range (形)短期の, 短期間の
 short-range budget 短期予算
 short-range business planning 短期経営計画
 short-range fund planning 短期資金計画
 short-range (management) planning 短期経営計画
 short-range profit planning 短期利益計画
short-run (形)短期の
 short-run cash planning 短期資金計画
 short-run cost 短期費用
 short-run cyclical growth 短期循環的成長
 short-run economic growth 短期経済成長
 short-run fund market 短期資金市場 (=call money market)
 short-run interest rate 短期金利
 short-run market 短期市場
 short-run target 短期目標
short-run Fed interest rate 短期連邦金利
 ◆At the recent official May Federal Reserve Open Market Committee meeting, no change in the vital short-run Fed interest rate was decided on. この5月に行われた米連邦準備制度(FRS)の公開市場委員会の公式会合では, 最も重要な短期連邦金利の変更は行わないことを決定した。
short sale 空売り, 信用売り (=selling short, short selling; ⇒New York Stock Exchange)
 short sale ratio 空売り比率
 short sale rule 空売りの規則, 空売りルール
 ◆Short sales accounted for 24.6 percent of total trade in March. 3月の空売りは, 全取引の24.6％を占めた。◆The New

York Stock Exchange already releases monthly figures on the trading volume of short sales. ニューヨーク証券取引所では、空売りの売買額の月間総額をすでに公表している。

short sell [short-sell] (動)空売りする
(=sell short)
◆France, Italy, Spain and Belgium imposed a ban on short-selling financial stocks. フランス、イタリア、スペインとベルギーが、金融銘柄の空売りを禁止した。

short selling [short-selling] 空売り (=selling short, short sale, short selling of stocks)
　a blanket ban on short selling　空売りの全面禁止, 空売りの全面規制
　a huge amount of short selling　大量の空売り
　alternate spot and short selling of shares　株[株式]の現物売りと空売りを繰り返す
　foreign speculators' short sellings　海外投機筋の空売り
　illegal short selling　違法な空売り
　make money on short selling　空売りで稼ぐ
　short selling in the stock market　株の空売り
　short selling of stocks　株の空売り (=short selling of shares; ⇒speculative trader, spot selling)
　speculative short selling　投機的な空売り
◆A market player put the level of short selling in the stock market at between 5 to 10 percent of total trading volume. ある市場筋によると、株の空売りは取引全体の5-10%程度といわれる。◆European regulators had previously played down the idea of a blanket ban on short selling. 欧州の規制当局は、空売りの全面規制[禁止]という考え方を以前は問題にしていなかった。◆Japan's regulations on short selling and market manipulation by spreading rumors are extremely weak in comparison with those of the United States. 日本の空売りに関する規制や風説の流布などによる市場操作についての規制は、米国に比べて極めて弱い。◆Short selling accounted for 24.6 percent of total trade in March. 3月の空売りは、全取引の24.6%を占めた。◆Short selling is the practice of borrowing stocks from securities and financial companies and other investors to sell them and then buy them back when their prices drop. 空売りは、証券金融会社や他の投資家（機関投資家など）から株を借りて売り、その株が値下がりした時点で買い戻すことをいう。◆The securities company repeatedly alternated spot and short selling of shares of a regional bank. この証券会社は、地方銀行株の現物売りと空売りを交互に繰り返した。◆Through short selling, an investor borrows shares and sells them on the expectations that their price will fall, and can buy back them at a lower price. 空売りによって投資家は、株価が下がると予想して株を借りて売り、値下がりした時点でその株を買い戻すことができる。

[解説] 空売りとは：証券取引法で認められた取引で、投資家が保有していない株式を他から借り入れて市場で売る取引のこと。ただし、空売りを意図的な株価引下げに利用すると、違法となる。投資家が証券会社を通じて生命保険会社や信託銀行などの機関投資家から借りる場合と、貸し株などを専門業務とする証券金融会社や証券会社から借りる（信用売り）場合がある。投資家が借りた株を市場で空売りすると、その後その株の値段が下がった時点で安く買い戻せるため、株価下落の局面でも利益を確保できる。

short selling on financial stocks 金融銘柄の空売り
◆Four European countries of France, Italy, Spain and Belgium banned short selling on financial stocks to restore confidence in markets. フランス、イタリア、スペイン、ベルギーの欧州4か国が、市場の信認を回復するため、金融銘柄の空売りを禁止した。◆France banned short selling on 11 financial stocks for 15 days. フランスは、金融11銘柄の空売りを15日間禁止した。

short term [short-term] (形)短期の, 短期間の, 目先の
　short term asset　短期資産
　short-term bank borrowing [loans]　短期銀行借入れ
　short-term bond　短期債, 短期国債
　short-term borrowed capital　短期他人資本
　short-term borrowing　短期借入れ
　short-term borrowing bank loan　短期借入金
　short-term debenture　短期社債
　short-term debt　短期債, 短期国債 (short-term bond), 短期債務, 短期借入金
　short-term economic forecast　短期経済予測
　short-term economic growth target　短期経済成長目標
　short-term economic outlook　短期経済見通し
　short-term economic planning　短期経済計画
　short-term external assets and liabilities　対外短期資産負債残高
　short-term finance [financing]　短期金融
　short-term forecasting [forecast]　短期予測
　short-term foreign capital　短期外資
　short-term foreign currency　短期外貨
　short-term government securities　短期政府証券, 短期国債
　short-term insurance　短期保険
　short-term investment　短期投資
　short-term investment securities　短期投資有価証券, 短期有価証券
　short-term lending　短期融資, 短期貸付け
　short-term measures　短期措置
　short-term money market rate　短期市場金利
　short-term money rate　短期金利, 短期利子率
　short term obligation　流動負債, 短期債務, 短期借入金
　short term obligations to be refinanced　借換え予定の短期借入金
　short-term planning　短期計画
　short-term policy　短期政策

short-term capital　短期資本
　short-term capital accounts　短期資本収支
　short-term capital gain　（1年以内に生じる）短期資本利得, 短期譲渡所得, 短期キャピタル・ゲイン
　short-term capital loss　（1年以内に生じる）短期資本損失, 短期キャピタル・ロス
　short-term capital movement　短期資本移動
　short-term capital needs　短期資金需要
　short-term capital transaction　短期資本取引
　short-term capital (transaction) balance　短期資本収支

short-term corporate profits　短期企業利益, 目先の企業利益
◆Nippon Keidanren's insisting on short-term corporate profits will only lower the influence of the business community. 日本経団連が目先の企業利益を振りかざしていては、財界の影響力が低下するばかりだ。

short-term credit　短期信用, 短期貸付け, 短期貸出
　short-term credit dealer　短資会社
　short-term credit market　短期貸付け市場, 短期金融市場
　short-term credit rating　短期信用格付け

short term debt　短期債務, 短期借入金, 短期債務, 短期金融市場証券
　short-term debt and related securities　短期債務と関連証券
　short-term debt issuers　短期債務の発行体
　short-term debt obligations　短期債務
　short-term debt rating　短期債券格付け, 短期格付け

short-term funds 短期資金 （=short-term money）
◆A bank run is a phenomenon that short-term funds for commercial banks, namely deposits, evaporate. 銀行の取付け騒ぎとは、銀行の短期資金、つまり預金が消滅する現象をいう。

short-term interest rate 短期金利
◆Short-term interest rates in the Tokyo market rose as some financial institutions hurried to obtain newly released funds. 一部の金融機関が新規調達資金の確保を急いだため、東京市場の短期金利が上昇した。◆The federal funds rate, a benchmark short-term interest rate, was cut to 3.5 percent per annum and the official discount rate to 3 percent per annum. 短期金利の誘導目標であるフェデラル・ファンド（FF）金利は年3.5％、公定歩合は年3％に引き下げられた。

short-term loan 短期融資, 短期貸付け, 短期ローン, 短期貸付け金, 短期負債
　short-term loan payable　短期借入金
　short-term loan receivable　短期貸付け金
◆Countries likely to be affected by the fiscal and financial crisis in Europe will basically be able to obtain the IMF's short-term loans immediately after applying for them. 欧州財政・金融危機が波及しそうな国は、IMF（国際通貨基金）に要請すると、基本的にIMFの短期融資を即時に受けられる。

short-term money 短期資金 （=short-term funds：1年以内に回収される資金の取引市場）
◆When short-term money flees from investment funds, it also disappears from commercial banks. 短期資金が投資ファンドから逃げると、短期資金は銀行からも逃げる。

short-term money market 短期金融市場 （=short-term market）
◆In cooperation with the European Central Bank and the Bank of Japan, the U.S. Federal Reserve Board has supplied money to short-term money markets to calm fears. 欧州中央銀行（ECB）や日銀と連携して、米連邦準備制度理事会（FRB）は、警戒感［市場の不安］を抑えるため短期金融市場に資金供給を行った。◆The Bank of Japan uses the unsecured overnight call rate as the key target rate in the short-term money market. 日銀は、無担保コール翌日物の金利を短期金融市場の誘導目標にしている。

short term transaction 短期売買
◆The volume of short-term transactions by day traders is expected to keep growing. デイ・トレーダーによる短期売買［デイ・トレーダーを中心とする短期売買］の取引高は、今後増大する見込みだ。

short time （名）短期　（形）短期の, 操業短縮の
　short-time bill　短期手形
　short-time credit　短期信用

shortage （名）不足
　a shortage of cash　現金不足
　a shortage of equity capital　自己資本不足
　a shortage of money　金不足, 資金不足, 通貨不足
　　（=money shortage）
　a shortage of raw material　原材料不足
　capital shortage　資本不足
　dollar shortage　ドル不足
　excess or shortage of funds　資金の過不足
　foreign exchange shortage　外貨不足
　housing shortage households　住宅難世帯
　income shortage　所得不足
　inventory shortage　在庫不足, 棚卸し減耗費
　investment shortage　投資不足
　manpower shortage　人的資源不足, マンパワー不足
　potential capital shortage　潜在的資本不足
　shortage of funds　資金不足, 資本不足
　shortages of supply　供給不足

◆European banks are forced to shore up their potential capital shortages to restore market confidence. 欧州銀行は、市場の信認を回復するため、潜在的資本不足の増強を迫られている。◆Many of these enfeebled financial institutions are suffering from a shortage of equity capital. これらの弱体化した［体力の落ちた］金融機関の多くは、自己資本不足に陥っている。

shortcoming （名）欠点, 短所, 不足, 不備, 不十分な点, 不作
　have many shortcomings　欠点が多い
　legal shortcomings　法の不備
◆Margin trading was used in a corporate takeover by exploiting legal shortcomings. 法の不備を利用して、企業買収に信用取引が使われた。

shortfall （名）不足, 減少, 赤字, 赤字額, 不足額, 不足量, 短期投資利益 （⇒make up）
　a cash shortfall　現金不足, キャッシュ不足
　a funding shortfall　資金不足
　a profit shortfall　利益の減少, 減益
　a revenue shortfall　歳入欠陥
　big shortfalls in tax revenue　大税収不足
　the budget shortfalls because of the lack of tax revenue　税収不足による財政赤字
　　（⇒primary balance deficit）
◆The ¥44 trillion shortfall including tax revenue and non-tax revenue in spending in the fiscal 2010 budget must be made up for by issuing government bonds. 2010年度予算の歳出のうち、税収と税外収入を含めて44兆円の不足分は、国債発行で補填しなければならない。◆The special account borrows from the private sector and other sources to make up for local government's budget shortfalls. 特別会計は、民間などの財源からの借入れで地方の財源不足［財政赤字］の穴埋めをしている。◆The $374 billion shortfall marked an improvement from a $455 billion projection the White House made in July. 3,742億ドルの赤字額（米財政赤字額）は、米政府が7月に予測した4,550億ドルより改善した。◆The U.S. projected shortfall of $1.56 trillion in 2010 is equal to 10.6 percent of the economy measured by gross domestic product. 米国の2010年度（2009年10月～2010年9月）の予想赤字額（財政赤字額）1兆5,600億ドルは、対国内総生産（GDP）比率で10.6％に当たる。

shoulder （動）肩にかつぐ, 背負う, 負担する, （費用や責任などを）引き受ける［負う］, 肩代わりする, 前に進む
　be shouldered with a difficult task　一つの難題を背負わされる
　shoulder a task　仕事を引き受ける
　shoulder great responsibilities　重大な責任を負う
　shoulder one's way through［into］　～を押し分けて進む［通る］
　shoulder the debt　借金を負担する, 借金の肩代わりをする
　shoulder the responsibility for　～の責任を取る
◆A consumption tax hike would increase the financial burden shouldered by Joe Blow. 消費税を引き上げると、一般国民の金融負担［一般国民が負担する金融負担］が増すことになる。◆Companies have been shouldering a large amount of labor costs as their employees grow older. 企業は、従業員の高齢化に伴って多額の労務費を負担してきた。◆Financial institutions and TEPCO shareholders should shoulder part of the financial burden in return for government financial support of TEPCO. 政府が東電を支援する見返りとして、金融機関と東電株主も一定の金融負担をするべきだ。◆The bank shouldered ¥35 billion as an initial investment for a computer system development for the toto soccer lottery. サッカーくじ「toto」のコンピュータ・システム整備のための初期投資として、同行は350億円を負担した。◆The government may shoulder interest

payments on the existing debts of survivors of the March 11 disaster. 東日本大震災被災者の既存の借金については、政府がその利払いを肩代わりする可能性がある。◆The people must shoulder the debt created by the government. 政府がつくった借金は、国民が負担しなければならない。

show （動）見せる、示す、表す、明らかにする、証明する、指摘する、教える、案内する、上映する、上演する、放送する、公開する、展示する、（訴訟事由などを）申し立てる
have nothing to show for 　〜の成果を得るものは何もない、〜の成果は得られない
have something to show for 　〜の成果を得る
see and it shows 　一見してすぐ分かる、一目瞭然だ
show off 　披露する、見せびらかす、ひけらかす、かっこよく見せる、良く見せる、引き立たせる、誇示（こじ）する
show the way 　手本を示す
◆An estimate showed making highways toll-free would bring ¥2.7 trillion worth of economic benefits. 高速道路を無料にすると、2.7兆円相当の経済効果があることが、試算で明らかになった。◆Global stock market plunges caused by the European fiscal crisis triggered by Greece have shown no signs of abating. ギリシャ発の欧州財政危機による世界同時株安は、止まる気配がない。◆Housing investment, a driving force for the U.S. economy until recently, has shown signs of a slowdown. 最近まで米景気を牽引してきた住宅投資に、減速感が見られる。◆Major Asian markets such as Shanghai and Hong Kong also show a situation that could be dubbed as a spontaneous global market crash. 上海や香港などアジアの主要市場も、世界同時株安の様相を見せている。◆Major banks are intensifying their efforts to reduce their risk assets by securitizing and selling their credit to prevent their capital adequacy ratio, an index that shows their business soundness, from declining. 大手各行は現在、経営の健全性を示す指標である自己資本比率の低下を防ぐため、貸出債権の証券化や転売などでリスク資産（リスク・アセット）の圧縮策を加速させている。◆Recent U.S. economic indicators show the fragility of the world largest economy. 最近の米国の経済指標は、米経済の弱さを示している。◆The BOJ's Tankan survey shows business sentiment among large manufacturers rebounded in September from the previous survey three months earlier. 9月の日銀短観は、大企業・製造業の景況感が6月の前回調査から改善したことを示している。◆The demographic changes show the inevitability of raising pension premiums unless pension benefits are reduced in the future. この人口構造の変化は、年金給付を今後減額しない限り、年金保険料の引上げは必至であることを示している。◆The economy has shown slight signs of recovery. 景気に薄日が差している。
◆The retail industry has begun showing signs of recovery. 小売業界は、回復の兆しが見られるようになった。◆This is the fourth straight quarter that the economy has shown growth. これで、4四半期連続のプラス成長となった。◆While soaring high on massive direct investment from abroad, the Chinese economy started showing signs of overheating in the latter half of 2003. 海外からの活発な直接投資に支えられて、中国経済は、2003年後半から景気過熱の様相を見せ始めた。

show up 　現れる、姿［顔］を見せる、姿を現す、（ショーなどに）出る、見えるようになる、目立つ
◆The benefits of the U.S. financial bailout package will take time to show up in the U.S. economy. 米国の金融救済策の効果が米国内経済に現れるのに、時間がかかるだろう。

shrink （動）減少する、低下する、縮小する、マイナス成長になる、マイナスになる
◆Our overseas investors account for about 24 percent, which would shrink to 18.6 percent after we raise capital. 当社の外国人株主［外国人投資家］は、約24％を占め、増資後は18.6％に減少します。◆The economy has shrunk for the first time in 12 months. 経済成長率は、1年ぶりにマイナスになった。◆The economy of the United States is set to shrink 0.5 percent in 2009. 米国の2009年の年間経済成長率は、0.5％のマイナス成長になる見込みだ。◆The monetary base shrank 21.1 percent in January from a year ago. 1月のマネタリー・ベース（日銀券発行高、貨幣流通高、日銀当座預金の合計）は、前年同月比で21.1％減少した。◆The size of employment pie has shrunk amid the lingering recession. 長引く不況のなかで、雇用全体の規模が縮小した。

shrinkage （名）縮小、収縮、減少、下落、縮小量、収縮量、減少量、減耗、減耗費、減耗損、減損

shrinking （形）減少している、低下している、縮小している、〜の減少、〜の低下、〜の縮小
shrinking backlog 　受注残高の減少
　（=shrinking backlog of unfilled orders）
shrinking balance sheet 　バランス・シートの縮小
shrinking growth in money supply 　マネー・サプライの伸び率の鈍化［低下］
shrinking income 　所得の減少、収入減
shrinking inventories 　在庫の減少
shrinking market 　縮小する市場、市場の縮小
shrinking workforce 　労働力の減少

shrinking employment 　雇用の落ち込み
◆The U.S. economy has been hit by a chilled housing market and shrinking employment. 米経済は、住宅市場の冷え込みと雇用の落ち込みで打撃を受けている。

shrinking population 　人口減少
◆There is a limit to conventional pump-priming measures amid a continued decline in birthrate and a consequent graying and shrinking population. 少子高齢化や人口減少などが進行するなかで、従来の景気刺激策［景気テコ入れ策］では限界がある。

shut （動）閉める、閉じ込める、閉鎖する
be［get］shut of 　〜を追い払う、〜と縁を切る（get rid of）
be shut out of 　〜から締めだされる
shut down 　（工場などを）閉鎖する、（操業を）停止する
shut up 　閉め切る、黙らせる、黙る
◆HSBC Holdings PLC will shut its subprime mortgage unit and eliminate 750 jobs. 英銀大手のHSBCホールディングスは、低所得者向け住宅融資「サブプライム・ローン」事業の米国子会社を閉鎖して、従業員750人を解雇する。◆Japan may be shut out of an international framework that will be crucial for its economic development if Japan does not join the TPP agreement. 日本がTPP（環太平洋経済連携協定）に不参加なら、日本の経済発展に欠かせない国際的枠組みから締め出されてしまう可能性がある。

side effect 　副作用、副次的な効果
a side effect of the zero-interest policy 　ゼロ金利政策の副作用
side effects of chilling the economy 　景気を冷やす副作用
◆As a side effect of the zero-interest policy, there is the moral hazard concerning corporate executives. ゼロ金利政策の副作用の一つとして、企業経営者のモラル・ハザード（倫理的欠如）がある。◆Falling prices have the side effects of chilling the economy and increase unemployment. 物価の下落は、景気を冷やし、失業を増大させる副作用がある。◆Some economists point out the side effects of the Fed's quantitative easing policy. エコノミストのなかには、FRB（米連邦準備制度理事会）の量的緩和策の副作用を指摘する声もある。

sideline （名）模様眺め、様子見（複数形）、側線、専門外取扱品、アルバイト、副業、サイドビジネス、内職、サイドライン
on the sidelines 　（参加しないで）傍観して、傍観者として、控え選手として
on the sidelines of 　〜の際に
remain on the sidelines 　動きが鈍い、様子見の姿勢を崩

さない, 様子見の状況にある
retreat to the sidelines　手控える
run a sideline …ing　副業として～する
sit on the sidelines　模様眺めの姿勢をとる, 座視する
stay on the sidelines　模様眺めに回る, 様子見の姿勢を崩さない, 圏外にいる
◆Foreign investors retreated to the sidelines. 外国投資家は, 手控えた。◆The government and the BOJ sat on the sidelines when Yamaichi Securities Co. and Hokkaido Takushoku Bank went bankrupt in 1997. 1997年に山一証券と北海道拓殖銀行が破たんした際, 政府と日銀は座視した。

SIFI　システム上重要な金融機関, 巨大金融機関（systematically important financial institutionの略。G20の合意のなかで, 通常の銀行以上に厳しい自己資本規制基準などが適用される大規模金融機関）
G-SIFs ［GSIFs］　国際的な巨大金融機関, グローバルSIFI（global systemically important financial institutionsの略。大規模金融機関のうち, 世界の金融システムに影響を及ぼす可能性のある金融機関）
SIFIs　システム上重要な金融機関
◆According to the Financial Stability Board, 28 banks viewed as global systemically important financial institutions (G-SIFIs) will be subject to a new global rule requiring them to hold extra capital to prevent future financial crises. 金融安定化理事会(FSB)によると, 金融システム上重要な国際金融機関(G-SIFIs)と考えられる世界の28行が, 金融危機の再発を防止するため, 資本の上積みを求める新国際基準［新国際金融規制］の対象になる。

SIFMA　証券業・金融市場協会（Securities Industry and Financial Markets Associationの略）

sight　(名)一覧, 一見, 閲覧
a bill payable at a fixed period after sight　一覧後定期払い手形
a bill payable at sight　一覧払い手形
a bill payable at sight after a fixed period　確定日後一覧払い手形
after sight　一覧後
at fixed period after sight　一覧後定期払い
at sight　提示のあり次第, 一覧次第, 一覧で, 一覧払い, A/S
at sight buying rate　一覧払い手形買い相場
at sight credit　一覧払い信用状
120 days sight　一覧後120日払い
payable at sight　一覧払い
sight bill　一覧払い為替手形, 一覧払い手形, 要求払い手形 (=demand draft, sight draft)
sight deposit　要求払い預金
sight exchange　一覧払い為替
sight (letter of) credit　一覧払い(手形)信用状, 一覧払い為替手形振出条件信用状, サイト・クレジット
sight loan　一覧払い貸付け, 当座貸し
sight note　一覧払い手形, 一覧払い約束手形
sight of a bill　手形サイト
sight payment　一覧払い
sight rate　一覧払い為替相場
sight reimbursement　一覧払い償還, 一覧払い為替手形請求
sight selling rate　一覧払い手形売り相場
sight unseen　現物を見ないで
three months after sight　一覧後3か月に
◆In the global financial markets, unrest is continuing as there is no end in sight to fiscal crises to the United States and some European countries. 世界の金融市場では, 米国と一部の欧州諸国の財政危機の収束が見通せないため, 混乱が続いている。◆There is no end in sight to fiscal crises in the United States and some European countries as credit uncertainty is spreading. 信用不安が拡大しているため, 米国と欧州の一部の財政危機の収束が見通せない。

sight draft　一覧払い為替手形, 一覧払い手形, S/D［SD］(=sight bill)
◆We have drawn on you our sight draft No. 10 for the invoice amount, $50,000, under your L/C No. B-50 of XYZ Co. 当社は, XYZ株式会社の信用状B-50号により, 送り状金額5万ドルに対して当社の一覧払い手形10号を貴社宛に振り出しました。

sign　(動)署名する, 署名調印する, 調印する, ～と契約する, サインをする
sign a basic agreement　基本契約書に署名する, 基本契約を結ぶ［締結する］
sign a memorandum　覚書に調印する, 覚書に署名する, 覚書を取り交わす
sign an agreement　契約書に署名する, 契約書に調印する, 合意書に署名する, 契約を締結する, 基本合意する (=sign a contract)
sign for a check　小切手に署名する
sign off the dole　失業保険の申請を取り下げる
sign on　雇用契約書に署名する, 失業保険の申請をする, 放送を開始する
sign on the dole　失業保険の申請をする
◆A financial bailout bill, after twists and turns, has at last been signed into law in the United States. 米国の金融安定化法案(緊急経済安定化法案)が, 迷走の末, ようやく成立した。◆In the case of single-premium whole life insurance policies, policyholders make one large premium payment up front when they sign the contract. 一時払い終身保険の場合は, 保険契約者が契約を結ぶ際に［契約時に］多額の保険料を前もって一括で払い込む。◆The heads of Japan, China and ROK signed statements on the tripartite partnership, international finance and the economy, and disaster management cooperation. 日中韓首脳は, 3国間パートナーシップ, 国際金融・経済と防災対策での連携に関する声明に署名した。

sign　(名)兆し, 兆候, 動き, 様相, 気味, 標識, 署名, サイン (⇒private-sector demand)
amid emerging signs of　～の兆しが見られるなか
clear［distinct］signs of recovery　はっきりした回復の兆し, 明らかな回復の兆し
head to the sidelines　様子見の傾向が出てきた, 様子見に向かう
positive signs　好転の兆し
show no sign of recovery　回復の兆しがない, 回復の兆しが見られない
show positive signs　好転の兆しを見せる, 好転の兆しを示す
show signs of instability　不安定な動きを示す
show signs of weakness　軟化の兆し
sign of inflation　インフレの兆し
sign of recovery　景気回復の兆し, 回復の兆し
sign of "recovery" from "unchanged"　「横ばい」から「持ち直し」の動き
signs of a rebound　反転の兆し
signs of instability　不安定な動き
signs of overheating　景気過熱の様相, 景気過熱気味
start to show signs of change　変調の兆しが見え始める
with no sign of an end to deflation　デフレ克服の道筋［兆し］は見えない
◆Global stock market plunges caused by the European fiscal crisis triggered by Greece have shown no signs of abating.

ギリシャ発の欧州財政危機による世界同時株安は、止まる気配がない。◆Goldman Sachs lowered its forecast for U.S. growth in 2011 on signs that the U.S. economic recovery lost momentum. 米金融大手のゴールドマン・サックスは、米景気回復減速の兆しを受けて、2011年の米国の成長見通しを下方修正した。◆Signs that unfavorable factors are receding are apparent, as crude oil prices have fallen. 原油の値下がりなど、悪材料に解消の兆しが見られる。◆Some economic indicators in the United States are showing positive signs. 米国の景気指標の一部は現在、好転の兆しを示している。◆The financial market may show signs of instability after the bailout measure for Resona Holdings Inc. is decided. りそなホールディングスに対する救済措置（公的資金の注入措置）の決定を発端に、金融市場は今後、不安定な動きを示すかもしれない。◆There are few signs of the yen reaching the ￥90 range to the dollar for the time being. 今のところ、1ドル＝90円台に達する動き[1ドル＝90円台を目指す動き]は見られない。◆There are signs of a slowdown in the U.S. economy. 米国経済に、陰りが見えてきた。◆There are signs that the Organization of Petroleum Exporting Countries may choose to reduce oil production. 石油輸出機構（OPEC）には、減産の動きも見られる。◆There have been no signs of a rebound in the amount of outstanding loans, which continues on an abated decline. このところ引き続き減少傾向にある銀行の貸出残高に、反転の兆しは見えない。

sign a contract 契約書に調印[署名]する, 契約を締結する, 契約を結ぶ
◆JICA signed a contract with the Indonesian government to provide a yen loan of about ￥20 billion to Indonesia. 国際協力機構（JICA）は、インドネシア政府と約200億円の円借款を貸与[供与]する契約書に調印した。

sign a deal 合意書に署名する, 協定書に調印する, 協定を結ぶ
◆Poland and the United States signed a deal on the U.S. antimissile shield in Europe. ポーランドと米国が、欧州での米国のミサイル防衛の合意書に署名した。

sign of economic contraction 景気収縮[景気後退]を示す指標, 景気収縮の兆し
◆A reading of below 50 percent in the coincident index is considered a sign of economic contraction and a figure above that is viewed as a sign of expansion. 一致指数で50％以下の数値は景気収縮[景気後退]を示す指標と見られ、それ以上の数字は景気回復[景気拡大]を示す指標と見なされる。

sign of recovery 景気回復の兆し, 回復の兆し, 回復の動き （⇒upturn in share prices）
◆The economy at long last has started to show signs of recovery. 景気がやっと、回復の兆しを見せている。◆The economy has shown slight signs of recovery. 景気に薄日が差している。◆The retail industry has begun showing signs of recovery. 小売業界は、回復の兆しが見られるようになった。◆There is a sign of recovery in the Japanese economy. 日本に、景気回復の兆しが見える[日本経済に、回復の兆しがある]。

signs of a moderate recovery 緩やかな回復の兆し
◆Japan's economy shows signs of a moderate recovery. 日本経済は、緩やかな回復の兆しを示している。

signs of change 変調の兆し
◆The economies in the U.S. and China that have aided the Japanese companies' recovery have now started to show signs of change. 日本企業の回復を支えてきた米国と中国の経済に、今は変調の兆しが見え始めている。

signs of instability 不安定な動き
◆The financial market may show signs of instability after the bailout measure for the bank is decided. 同行に対する救済措置（公的資金の注入措置）の決定を発端に、金融市場は今後、不安定な動きを示すかもしれない。

signs of life 景気好調を示す兆候
◆There are signs of life in the lackluster economy. 景気停滞に、景気の好調を示す兆候がある。

signs of overheating 過熱気味の兆し, 過熱気味の様相, 景気過熱の様相
◆The growing U.S. economy is showing signs of overheating. 拡大している米景気は、過熱気味に推移している。◆While soaring high on massive direct investment from abroad, the Chinese economy started showing signs of overheating in the latter half of 2003. 海外からの活発な直接投資に支えられて、中国経済は、2003年後半から景気過熱の様相を見せ始めた。

signs of slowdown 減速感
◆Housing investment, a driving force for the U.S. economy until recently, has shown signs of a slowdown. 最近まで米景気を牽引してきた住宅投資に、減速感が見られる。

signs of stabilization 安定化の兆し
◆Four Fed regions—New York, Cleveland, Kansas City and San Francisco—pointed to "signs of stabilization." ニューヨーク、クリーブランド、カンザス、サンフランシスコの4米地区連銀は、「景気安定化の兆し」を指摘した。

significant （形）重要な, 重大な, 大きな, 著しい, 際立った, 目立った, 本格的な, 相当な, かなりの, 大量の, 多額の, 大幅な, 大型の
a significant acquisition 大型買収
a significant economic pickup 本格的な景気回復
a significant increase in cash requirements 必要資金の大幅増加
a significant increase in external surplus 対外黒字の大幅拡大
a significant subsidiary 重要な子会社
have a significant effect on ～に大きな影響を及ぼす, ～に大きな影響力がある
significant accounting policies 重要な会計方針
significant budgetary stimulus 積極的な財政出動
significant capital commitments 多額の出資
significant earnings gains 大幅な増益
significant investments 大幅投資
significant losses 巨額の損失, 巨額の赤字
significant rate cuts 大幅な利下げ
significant stock price movement 株価の大きな変動
◆Heightened tensions and significant downward risks for the global economy must be addressed decisively. 世界経済の緊張の高まりと重大な下方リスクに、断固として対処しなければならない。◆Our plans, which require significant investments, are at risk because of limited access to capital. 大幅投資が必要な当社の計画は現在、資金調達力にも限界があるため、危機にさらされています。

significantly （副）大幅に, 大きく, はるかに, 重度に
be revised significantly downward [lower] 大幅に下方修正される
be significantly lower [worse] than the market consensus (estimate) 市場予想[市場予測]を大幅に下回る
be significantly underweighted 大幅なアンダーウェートになっている
drop [fall] significantly 大幅に下落する, 大幅に低下する[悪化する]
significantly outperform the market 市場平均を大幅に上回る
◆Due to confusion in the financial markets, interest rates have declined significantly and global stock prices have dropped. 金融市場の混乱で、金利が大幅に低下し、世界的に株価も下落している。

simple （形）単純な, 単一の, 単利の, 無条件の
on a simple interest basis 単利ベースで
simple accumulation 単利定期積金

simple arbitration　単一為替裁定
simple arithmetical stock price average　単純平均株価
simple bond　無条件債券
simple bonus　(保険金の)単純比率割増金
simple capital structure　単純な資本構成
simple discount　単利による割引
simple guarantor　単純保証人
simple interest　単利
　(複利＝compound interest, compounded interest)
simple-interest method　残債方式
simple majority　単純多数
simple margin　単利マージン
simple mean value　単純平均
simple risk　普通物件
simple security [suretyship]　単純保証人
simple yield　単純利回り, 単利
simple yield to maturity　単利最終利回り
simple average　単純平均, 単純海損
simple average cost method　単純平均原価法
　(＝simple average method)
simple average method　単純平均法
simple average stock price　単純平均株価
simple average yield　単純平均利回り
simplified taxation system　簡易課税制度
simultaneous　(形)同時の, 同時に起こる, 同時に行われる, 一斉の, 連立の
simultaneous access　同時アクセス
simultaneous distribution　同時分布
　(＝joint distribution)
simultaneous equations model　同時方程式 [連立方程式] モデル
simultaneous introduction　同時発売
simultaneous processing　同時処理
simultaneous stock market plunges　同時株安
simultaneous system　同時方式
simultaneous global recession　世界同時不況
　◆Companies in the electrical machinery industry also are struggling due to the simultaneous global recession. 世界同時不況で、電機業界の各社も苦戦を続けている。◆The major markets of Japan, the United States and Europe have been dealt a blow by the simultaneous global recession. 日米欧の主要市場は、世界同時不況の直撃を受けた。◆The simultaneous global recession has led to continued decline in exports. 世界同時不況で、輸出の減少が続いている。
simultaneous slowdown of the global economy　世界同時不況
　◆The simultaneous slowdown of the global economy was triggered by the U.S. financial crisis. 世界同時不況は、米国の金融危機に端を発した。
simultaneously　(副)同時に
　issue commercial paper in several global markets simultaneously　世界各地の市場でCPを同時に発行する
　simultaneously list one's stocks　株式を同時上場する
　◆The firm decided to simultaneously list its stocks on the New York and London stock exchanges in October. 同社は、10月にニューヨークとロンドンの両証券取引所に株式を同時上場する方針を固めた。
Singapore　(名)シンガポール
　Development Bank of Singapore　シンガポール開発銀行
　Monetary Authority of Singapore　シンガポール通貨庁
　Singapore Futures Exchange　シンガポール先物取引所

Singapore interbank offered rate　シンガポール銀行間出し手金利, SIBOR
Singapore International Monetary Exchange　シンガポール国際金融取引所, シンガポール金融先物市場, SIMEX
Singapore's Central Provident Fund　シンガポールの中央年金基金
Singapore's Post Office Saving Bank　シンガポールの郵便貯蓄銀行
Stock Exchange of Singapore　シンガポール証券取引所
Stock Exchange of Singapore Dealing and Automated Quotation System　シンガポール店頭市場, SESDAQ
the Singapore stock exchange　シンガポール証券取引所
　◆In August 2011, the Stock Exchange of Singapore did away with its lunch break to increase the length of its trading session to eight hours. シンガポール証券取引所は、2011年8月から昼休みを廃止して、1日の取引時間が8時間に増えた。
Singapore Exchange Ltd.　シンガポール取引所, SGX
　(⇒cross-access pact, SGX)
　◆The Singapore Exchange Ltd. (SGX) was inaugurated in December 1999 following the merger of the Stock Exchange of Singapore and the Singapore International Monetary Exchange. シンガポール取引所(SGX)は、シンガポール証券取引所とシンガポール国際金融取引所(金融先物取引所)が合併して、1999年12月に設立された。
single　(形)単一の, 個々の, 唯一の, 単独の, 無条件の
　(名)1ドル札, 1ポンド札
Single A credit　シングルA格
single annual budget　単年度予算
single asset　単一資産
single bill　単一手形
single bond　無条件債務
single capacity　単一資格
single class of common stock　単一クラスの普通株式
single contribution　単一保険料
single-digit [single-figure] inflation　1桁(けた)インフレ
single employer　単一事業主
single entry bookkeeping　単式簿記
single European market　欧州単一市場, 欧州市場統合, 欧州統一市場
single exchange rate　単一為替相場, 単一為替レート
　(＝single general foreign exchange rate)
single financial market　統一金融市場
single fiscal policy　統一財政政策
single interest insurance　単一被保険利益保険
single interest policy　単一被保険利益保険証券
single isolated transaction　単発の取引
single liability　単一責任
single liability basis　単一責任主義
single life annuity　単生年金
single life insurance　単生保険
single-line tariff　単一税率　(＝single tariff)
single lump sum credit　最終一括払い融資, 一括払い
single market in the EC　EC市場統合
single name account　個人名義の口座
single name bill　単名手形
single name paper　単名手形
single option　単体のオプション取引, 単一特権付きオプション
single pay life insurance　一時払い生命保険
single-peaked pattern　単峰型

single-peaked preferences 単峰型選好
single-peakedness 単峰性, 単峰型
single [straight] piece rate plan 単純出来高払い制
single policy 単身契約
single rate (為替の)単一相場, 単一料率
single standard 単本位, 単本位制度 (=monometallic standard)

single currency 単一通貨 (⇒fundamentals)
　assets denominated in the single European currency 単一欧州通貨(ユーロ)建て資産
　confidence in the single currency of the euro 単一通貨・ユーロの信認
　Europe's single currency 欧州の単一通貨, 欧州の単一通貨・ユーロ, ユーロ
　single currency fixed/floating interest rate swap 単一通貨建て固定金利/変動金利の金利スワップ
　single currency loan 単一通貨での貸付け
　single currency of euro 単一通貨・ユーロ
　single European currency 単一欧州通貨(ユーロ), ユーロ (⇒assessment value)
　specific single-currency lending windows 特定通貨建て融資制度
　the single currency ユーロ (=the euro)
　◆Confidence in the single currency of the euro may be undermined by the spread of the Greek crisis to Spain and Portugal. ギリシャ危機のスペインやポルトガルへの波及で、単一通貨・ユーロの信認が揺らぎかねない。◆Spendthrift nations' overspending threatens Europe's single currency. 財政赤字国の過剰支出が、欧州のユーロを脅かしている。◆The fiscal woes of the single-currency bloc could trigger a new severe global financial crisis. 単一通貨・ユーロ圏の財政危機は、新たに重大な世界的金融危機の発生源になる可能性がある。

single euro currency area 単一通貨・ユーロ圏
　◆To avert the injection of public money into banks, the eurozone governments stuck to their official standpoint that there are no default problems within the single euro currency area. 銀行への公的資金注入を回避するため、ユーロ圏政府は、単一通貨ユーロ圏に債務返済不能の問題は存在しないという公式立場に固執した。

single-family home [house] 1～4世帯住宅
　◆The backlog of unsold single-family homes rose to the highest level in more than two decades. 1～4世帯住宅の売れ残り在庫戸数は、二十数年で最高の水準に増加した。

single market 単一市場
　◆ASEAN countries set a new milestone in regional integration by agreeing to fuse into a European-style single market by 2015. ASEAN(東南アジア諸国連合)諸国は、2015年までに欧州型単一市場に統合することで合意したことで、域内統合の新たな一里塚を打ち立てた。

single-minded (形)一心不乱の, 一途な, ひた向きな
　◆The company's single-minded profit-driven corporate culture has been exposed. もっぱら利益追求の同社の企業体質が、浮き彫りになった。

single payment 一時払い, 一括払い, 一括返済, 1回払い貸付け, 一括決済
　a single payment in a single currency 単一通貨での一括返済
　purchase a variable annuity with a single payment 変額年金を一時払いで購入する
　single payment at bonus season ボーナス一括払い
　single payment bond 1回払い債券
　single-payment consumer loan 一括払い消費者貸出金
　single payment loan 1回払い貸付け

single premium 一時払い保険料

single premium deferred annuity 一時払い据え置き年金, 一時払い年金契約
single-premium endowment (life) insurance [policy] 一時払い養老保険
single premium funding method 一時払い積み増し方式
single premium issuance 保険料一時払い保険
single premium life insurance 単一保険生命保険, 一時払い終身生命保険証券

single-premium pension insurance policy 一時払いの年金保険
　◆Nippon Life Insurance Co. lowered the yields of its single-premium pension insurance policies and other products. 日本生命保険が、一時払いの年金保険など保険商品の利回りを引き下げた。

single-premium whole life insurance 一時払い終身保険
　◆Lowering the yield of Meiji Yasuda's single-premium whole life insurance will reduce the attraction of the insurer's financial products. 明治安田生保の一時払い終身保険の利回り[予定利率]の引下げで、同社の金融商品の魅力は薄れると思われる。◆Meiji Yasuda Life Insurance Co.'s single-premium whole life insurance is one of its flagship products. 明治安田生保の一時払い終身保険は、同社の主力商品の一つだ。◆The life insurer currently promises its policyholders an annual yield of 1.5 percent for the single-premium whole life insurance. 同生保は現在、一時払い終身保険については年1.5％の利回り(予定利率)を契約者に約束している。◆The life insurer's single-premium whole life insurance is popular with consumers as a form of savings or an investment for retirement. 同生保の一時払い終身保険は、一種の貯蓄や退職金の運用先として顧客に人気がある。

single-premium whole life insurance policy 一時払い終身保険契約, 一時払い終身保険
　◆In the case of single-premium whole life insurance policies, policyholders make one large premium payment up front when they sign the contract. 一時払い終身保険の場合は、保険契約者が契約を結ぶ際に[契約時に]多額の保険料を前もって一括で払い込む。◆Revenues from the single-premium whole life insurance policies support the life insurer's business performance. 一時払い終身保険による収入[一時払い終身保険の収入保険料]が、同生保の業績を支えている。

single-premium whole life insurance product 一時払い終身保険の商品, 一時払い終身の保険商品
　◆The life insurer's revenues from the single-premium whole life insurance products tripled from the previous year in fiscal 2010. 同生保の一時払い終身の保険商品の収入保険料は、2010年度に前年度の3倍に達した。

sink (動)沈む, 沈下する, 傾く, 倒れる, 落ち込む, 下がる, 悪化する, 投下する, 投じる, つぎ込む, ～を失う, 無視する, 不問に付す
　sink a large sum into an unprofitable business 大金を不採算事業につぎ込む
　sink below the 1 percent threshold 1％割れの水準まで低下する
　sink drastically (価格などが)急激に下がる
　sink into a financial crisis 金融危機に陥る
　sink to nothing 価値がなくなる, (在庫などが)なくなる[ゼロになる]
　sink to the lowest level 最低水準まで落ち込む[下落する]
　◆The Fed will sink $600 billion into government bonds through the middle of 2011. 米連邦準備制度理事会(FRB)は、2011年6月末までに米国債の購入[買入れ]に6,000億ドルを投入する。◆The government should hurry to expand domestic demand to prevent the economy from sinking even deeper. 景気の底割れを防ぐため、政府は内需拡大を急ぐべき

◆The U.S. dollar sank to its lowest level since May 1995 in the lower ¥83 zone. 米ドル相場は、1ドル=83円台前半で1995年5月以来最低の水準まで下落した。◆The value of the dollar is sinking on international exchanges. 国際為替市場で、ドル価値が下落している。

sink below 〜を割り込む、〜まで低下する
◆The 10-year JGB yield sank below the 1 percent threshold. 新発10年物の日本国債の流通利回りが、1％割れの水準まで低下した。

sink into a double-dip recession 景気底割れする、景気が底割れする
◆The economy could sink into a double-dip recession due to the clouds hanging over the U.S. economy and rising deflationary pressures that will accompany the accelerated disposal of nonperforming loans. 米国経済の行方(米国経済への先行き不安)や、不良債権処理の加速に伴うデフレ圧力の高まりなどで、景気が底割れする恐れがある。

sink into a negative net worth 債務超過に陥る
◆To avoid sinking into a negative net worth, the firm is seeking ¥300 billion in financial aid from capital providers. 債務超過に陥るのを避けるため、同社は資金提供者に3,000億円の金融支援を要請している。

sink or swim 伸(の)るか反(そ)るか、成功するか失敗するか、一か八(ばち)か
  sink or swim attempt 伸るか反るかのカケ
  sink or swim juncture 伸るか反るかの重大局面
◆The central bank's quantitative easing policy is also at a critical sink-or-swim juncture. 日銀の量的緩和策も、今は剣が峰[伸(の)るか反(そ)るかの重大局面]に立たされている。

sinking fund 減債基金、償却基金、償却積立金、負債償却積立金、定時減債、別途資金(「減債基金」は、債券発行者が、債券の償還に備えて償還期限前から一定額を定期的に積み立てる基金のこと)
  reserve for sinking fund 減債基金積立金、減債積立金 (=sinking fund reserve)
  sinking fund assurance [insurance] 蓄積保険、減債基金保険、償却積立金保険
  sinking fund bond 減債基金債券(減債基金を設ける条件で発行する債券のこと)
  sinking fund for plant expansion 工場拡張基金
  sinking fund for redemption of bonds 社債償還基金

sinking fund payments 減債基金の積立て、減債基金の繰入れ
◆The Sinking fund payments are intended to retire 75 percent of the convertible debentures prior to maturity. この減債基金の積立ては、転換社債の75%の期限前早期償還を目的としている。

sinking fund requirements 減債基金への支払い額、減債基金積立額
◆Annual maturity and sinking fund requirements in millions of dollars on long term debt outstanding at December 31, 2007 are as follows: 2007年12月31日現在の長期負債残高の年度別返済額と減債基金への支払い額(単位：百万ドル)は、次のとおりです。

sinking spell (株価などの)一時的下落

siphon off the money 資金を流用する
◆He siphoned off the money to cover losses incurred in stock transactions. 同氏は、株取引での損失の穴埋めをするために資金を流用していた。◆He siphoned off the money to prop up his consulting firm. 同氏は、自らのコンサルタント会社の経営を支えるために資金を流用していた。

site (名)拠点、施設、事業所、工場、用地、設置先、現場、サイト、インターネット上の場所、ホームページ
  EC site ECサイト、電子商取引サイト (e-commerce site)
  investment site 投資先
  joint Web site 共同サイト
  online shopping site ネット・ショッピング(ネット商店街)サイト
  production site 生産拠点、生産施設、生産先
  search site 検索サイト
  shopping site ショッピング・サイト
  site operator サイト運営会社
  site visitor サイトを訪れるお客、サイト訪問者
  video site 動画サイト
  Web site ウェブ・サイト

situation (名)状況、状態、情勢、形勢、時局、局面、事情、事態、境遇、立場、場面、環境、大詰め、山場、クライマックス、位置、場所、用地、敷地、立地条件、勤め口、就職口、仕事、職
  actual situation 実勢、実態
  bring the situation almost under control 事態をほぼ収拾する
  business situation 景況
  cash situation 資金繰り
  critical [crisis] situation 危機、危機的状況
  economic situation 経済情勢
  employment situation 雇用環境、雇用情勢、雇用状況
  financial situation 財政状態、財政状況、財政情勢、財務状態、財務体質、金融情勢、金融局面、台所事情 (=financial condition, financial position)
  fire situation 過酷な状況
  get into a difficult situation 困難な状況[立場]に陥(おちい)る
  grave situation 重大局面、重大事態
  inflation situation インフレ環境
  interest-rate situation 金利環境
  market situation 市況
  monetary situation 金融事情、金融情勢、金融状態
  no-win situation 勝ち目のない状況、成功しそうにない状況、絶望的状況
  over-borrowed situation 貸出過多の状態、オーバー・ローン (=over-loaned situation)
  political situation 政局、政治情勢
  present situation 現状
  profit situation 収益状況
  real situation 実態
  save the situation 事態を収拾する、急場をしのぐ
  security situation 治安状況
  situation rent 好立地地代
  situation vacant 欠員、空位、求人
  supply and demand [supply-demand] situation 需給状況、需給バランス
  technical situation テクニカル要因
  the current economic situation 現在の経済情勢
  the current political situation 現在の政治情勢
  turnaround situation 業績回復
  win-win situation 必勝の状況

◆If the Iran situation grows strained, crude oil prices will certainly rise again. イラン情勢が緊迫すれば、原油価格が再上昇するのは必至だ。◆Major Asian markets such as Shanghai and Hong Kong also show a situation that could be dubbed as a spontaneous global market crash. 上海や香港などアジアの主要市場も、世界同時株安の様相を見せている。◆The BOJ could take additional monetary relaxation measures if there are any changes in the financial situation. 金融面で動きがあるとすれば、日銀が追加の金融緩和策を実施する可能性もある。◆The chaotic situation in the financial market will continue for the time being. 金融市場の混乱状況は、まだしばらく続くものと思われる。◆The employment situation has grown even more serious. 雇用情勢は、一段と深刻化している。◆The European bond market is truly in a knife-edge situation as the yield on 10-year Italian government bonds has surged above 7 percent, the so-called danger zone that may result in a debt crisis. 10年物イタリア国債の流通利回りが、債務危機に陥る「危険水域」とされる7%超に上昇したため、欧州債券市場は予断を許さない状況にある。◆The European fiscal crisis triggered by Greece has spread to Italy, making the severe situation even more distressing. ギリシャ発の欧州財政危機がイタリアに飛び火し、厳しい事態が一段と深刻化している。◆The government held a meeting on the current economic situation. 政府が、現在の経済情勢に関する会合を開いた。◆The situation is that it is difficult to acquire more than 50 percent of shares in the company. 今の状況では、同社株の50%超を取得するのは厳しい。◆The situation surrounding the Japanese economy has suddenly grown tense due to the first bankruptcy of a Japanese insurer in seven years. 7年ぶりの日本の生保破たんで、日本経済を取り巻く環境は一気に緊迫感が高まっている。◆This country's debt-laden finances are in a critical situation due to the dole-out policies as well as lavish economic stimulus measures. わが国の借金漬けの財政は、バラマキ政策と大盤振る舞いの景気対策で、危機的な状況に陥っている。◆Under the severe income and employment situations, personal consumption has yet to show indications of a full-fledged recovery. 厳しい所得・雇用環境の下で、個人消費に本格的な復調の気配がまだ見えない。

SIV 特別投資会社（special investment vehicleの略）
◆Commercial banks have created special investment vehicles (SIVs) in order to escape the capital adequacy regulation imposed by the Basel accord. 銀行は、バーゼル協定［バーゼル合意］による自己資本比率規制を回避するため、特別投資会社（SIV）を新設している。

sizable［sizeable］ （形）かなり大きい, 相当な大きさの, 大幅の, 大型の, 膨大な, 巨額の
　issue a sizable amount of new shares　新株を大量発行する
　sizable reduction　大幅削減

sizable amount of new shares　大量の新株
◆The purpose of issuing a sizable amount of new shares is to maintain the control of a specific stockholder over the company. 新株の大量発行は、同社に対する特定株主の支配権［経営支配権］確保が目的だ。

sizable amount of speculative funds　大量の投資資金
◆Recently, a sizable amount of speculative funds have been flowing into New York's commodities exchanges. このところ、ニューヨークの商品取引所には、大量の投機資金が流入している。

sizable deferred tax assets　巨額の繰延べ税金資産
◆In the latest account settlements, banking groups gave up including sizable deferred tax assets in their equity capital. 今決算で、銀行グループは、巨額の繰延べ税金資産の自己資本への計上を見送った。

sizable funds　大量の資金
◆The central banks of Japan, the United States and European countries are injecting sizable funds into the financial markets. 日米欧の中央銀行は、金融市場に大量の資金を供給している。

size　（名）規模, 大きさ, 寸法, 大量, 大規模, 型, 番, サイズ
　economic size　経済規模
　　（=size of the economies）
　enterprise size　企業規模
　　（=firm size, size of enterprise）
　issue size　発行規模
　larger size　規模の拡大
　lot size　取引規模
　market size　市場規模, 取引規模
　maximum size　最大規模
　minimum size　最小規模
　offering size　入札総額
　optimum size　最適規模
　plant size　工場規模, 設備規模
　sample size　標本数, サンプル数
　size effect　規模の効果
　size of capacity　生産能力
◆Larger size by the merger of two steelmakers will reinforce their bargaining power on resource prices. 鉄鋼メーカー2社の合併による規模拡大で、両社の資源価格の交渉力が今後強まることになる。◆The size of employment pie has shrunk amid the lingering recession. 長引く不況のなかで、雇用全体の規模が縮小した。◆The size of the domestic economy is tending to shrink. 国内経済の規模は、縮小傾向にある。◆The size of the financial assets of Japanese households is still worth a massive ￥1.47 quadrillion despite a decrease in the total over recent years. 日本の個人金融資産の規模は、ここ数年で減少したものの、まだ1,470兆円ほどもあって巨大だ。

skim　（動）データを読み取る, 盗撮する, スキミングする
◆Members of the forgery group shared roles such as skimming cash cards and withdrawing money from ATMs. 偽造グループのメンバーは、キャッシュ・カードのスキミングや現金自動払い機（ATM）からの現金引出し役などの役割を分担していた。

skimming　（名）スキミング（銀行の磁気キャッシュ・カードのデータの読取り）

skyrocket　（動）急増する, 急騰する, 急上昇する, 跳（は）ね上がる
◆Sovereign wealth funds have grown to $2 trillion -3 trillion globally as a result of skyrocketing crude oil prices and accumulation of foreign exchange reserves in emerging market economies. 政府系投資ファンドの運用総額は、原油価格の急騰と急成長市場国の外貨準備高の増加で、世界全体で2兆～3兆ドルに拡大している。◆The current deflationary trend seems to be a temporary phenomenon caused by the correction in oil prices after they skyrocketed last year. 現在のデフレ傾向は、昨年の原油高の反動による一時的な現象のようだ。

skyrocketing　（形）急増する, 急騰する, 急上昇する, うなぎ登りの
　skyrocketing medical insurance premiums　医療保険費の急騰
　skyrocketing stock prices　株価の急上昇
◆The Swiss National Bank set a ceiling on the skyrocketing Swiss franc. スイス国立銀行（中央銀行）が、スイス・フランの急騰に上限［上限目標］を設定した。

slack　（名）不景気, 不振, 沈滞, 停滞, 低迷, 低調, 中だるみ, 緩慢, 減少, 不況, 不況期, 不況時, 余分, 余裕, だぶつき, たるみ, 緩（ゆる）み, スラック
　business slack　景気低迷, 景気停滞, 不況
　economic slack　設備稼働率と失業率の余裕
　organizational slack　組織スラック
　slack in business　事業不振, 商売の不振, 景気低迷［停滞, 停滞］, 不況
　slack in capacity　生産設備の余裕, 設備稼働率の余裕
　slack in global activity　世界の景気低迷
　slack in growth　景気低迷（slack economy）, 景気停滞
　slack of finance　金融緩慢
　take up［pick up］the slack　活を入れる, たるみを引き締める, 不足分を補う, 是正する

slack　（形）不景気な, 活気のない, 不活発な, 緩慢（かんまん）な, 低調な, 不振の, 停滞した, 沈滞した, 弱含みの, ひまな, 閑散とした, たるんだ, 緩（ゆる）んだ, いい加減な, 不注意な, 甘い, 怠慢（たいまん）な, のろい, 遅い, 鈍

（にぶ）い, スラック （名）不振, 中だるみ, 緩慢, 減少, 閑散期, 不況(期), 不況時, 余裕, 余分, だぶつき
slack business 緩慢な市況, 商売不振, 不況, 不景気
　（=slack in business）
slack capacity 遊休設備, 遊休生産能力
　（=idle capacity）
slack discipline たるんだ規律
slack economy 景気低迷, 景気停滞
slack money market 緩慢な金融市場, 金融市場の緩み
slack season [period] 閑散期, 霜枯れ時, 不振な時期
slack semiconductor industry 半導体産業の低迷
slack stock market 不活発な[活気のない]株式市場
◆Stock market is slack at the moment. 株式市場は、いまは低調だ。◆The government revised upward its assessment on consumption from "slack" to "leveling off" for the first time in a year and 10 months. 政府は、1年10か月ぶりに、個人消費による景気判断を「弱含み」から「横ばい」に上方修正した。
slacken （動）緩める, 弱める （自動）緩む, 鈍化する, 低迷する, 弱まる, 軟化する
slackened export growth 輸出の伸びの鈍化
slackened investor demand 投資家需要の低迷, 投資家需要の軟化
◆Greece's tax revenues have slackened due to business deterioration. ギリシャの税収は、景気悪化で伸びていない。
slam （動）酷評する, こきおろす, 非難する, きびしく批判する,（戸や窓を）ばたんと閉める, ～に楽勝する,（ヒットを）打つ （自動）激突する, ばたんと閉まる, どすんとぶつかる
slam into [against] ～に激突する
slam on the brakes ブレーキを急に踏む, 急ブレーキをかける
slam the door in a person's face 人の発言をはねつける
◆A U.S. housing mortgage meltdown shook the United States, Europe and other countries and slammed the brakes on global growth. 米国の住宅ローン市場の崩壊は、米欧その他の諸国を揺さぶり、世界経済の成長に急ブレーキをかけた。
slander （名）名誉毀損(きそん), 悪口, 誹謗(ひぼう), 中傷
slanderous leaflet 中傷ビラ, 中傷文書
◆Another tactic many loan sharks use is to circulate slanderous leaflets to the workplace or the school that the borrower's children attend. 多くのヤミ金融業が使うほかの手は、借り手の勤務先や子どもが通う学校への中傷文書のばらまきだ。
slash （動）深く切り込む, 大幅に削減する, 減らす, 低減する, 縮小する, 引き下げる, 下方修正する （名）大幅削減, 激減, 切り込み, 深い切り傷
slash capital expenditures 設備投資を減らす, 設備投資を削減する
slash corporate profits 企業収益を引き下げる, ～で企業収益が減少[縮小]する
◆The appreciation of the yen has pushed exports downward, slashing corporate profits. 円高で輸出が低迷し、企業収益も減少している。◆The interest rates of major countries were slashed and interest receipts from abroad decreased. 主要国の金利低下で、受け取る利子収入が減少した。◆The recession slashed demand for oil and imports from China. 不況で原油の需要が落ち込み、中国からの輸入も減少した。
slash jobs 人員を削減する
◆Japan Airlines will slash 3,600 additional jobs from its initial reduction plan by the end of fiscal 2012 to 19,300. 日本航空は、2012年度末までに、当初の人員削減計画からさらに3,600人削減して1万9,300人にする方針だ。
slash one's credit rating 信用格付けを引き下げる
◆GM has posted losses and its credit rating has been slashed to junk status. GMは最近赤字に陥り、信用格付けが「投機的」に落とされた。
slash one's interest-bearing liabilities 有利子負債を削減する
◆The firm is giving up its assets in an attempt to slash its interest-bearing liabilities. 同社は、有利子負債を削減するため、資産を手放している。
slash one's nonperforming loans 不良債権を抜本処理する
◆Sumitomo Mitsui Financial Group Inc. is expected to have slashed its nonperforming loans when it closes its books at the end of March. 三井住友フィナンシャルグループは、3月期決算で不良債権の抜本処理を図る見通しだ。
slash one's profit forecasts 業績見通しを下方修正する, 業績予想を下方修正する
◆The bank slashed its profit forecasts in the aftermath of the March 11 disaster. 同行は、東日本大震災(2011年3月11日)の影響で、業績見通しを下方修正した。
sleeping beauty 眠りの森の美女, 眠り姫（乗っ取り屋にまだ目をつけられていないが、企業買収の対象になりやすい魅力ある企業のこと）
SLGS 米政府が州・地方政府を支援するために発行している財務省証券（State and Local Government Seriesの略）
　demand deposit SLGS 要求払い預金SLGS
　SLGS securities SLGS証券
　time deposit SLGS 定期預金SLGS
slide （動）下がる, 低下する, 下落する, 減少する, 落ち込む, 悪化する, 滑る, 移動する, 変化する, スライドする
slide into recession 景気後退に陥る
slide to the floor of ～の下限に達する
◆The Dow Jones industrial average on the New York Stock Exchange began to slide around the latter half of February. ニューヨーク株式市場のダウ工業株平均株価は、2月後半から急落した。◆The U.S. economy slid into recession at the end of 2007. 米経済は、2007年末に景気後退に陥った。
slide （名）低下, 下落, 減少, 落ち込み, 悪化, 滑走, 滑ること, 滑り込み, 滑り台, 滑走路, 地滑り, 山崩れ (landslide), 雪崩(なだれ), 自在棚, スライド
a downward slide in prices 物価の下落
be on the slide 下落している, 悪化している
downward slide in economic activity 景気の落ち込み, 景気の悪化
go into a slide スリップする
Nikkei slide 日経平均の下落
send the market into a downward slide 市場が小緩む
slide in confidence 信認の低下
slide in consumer confidence 消費マインドの悪化
slide in the stock price 株価下落, 株価の下落
the economy's slide 景気の悪化, 景気の落ち込み
　（⇒fiscal stimulus）
the yen slide 円安
◆The yen slide came to a halt. 円が、下げ止まった。
slide in economic activity 景気の落ち込み
◆Minneapolis' downward slide in economic activity has worsened. ミネアポリス(米ミネソタ州)の景気の落ち込みは、悪化している。
slide in prices 物価下落 （=price drops）
◆The government and the Bank of Japan have at long last begun mapping out a comprehensive package of measures to halt the slide in prices. 政府と日銀が、物価下落を食い止めるための総合的な対策づくりにようやく乗り出すことになった。
sliding scale スライド制, 伸縮法, 順応率（経済状態に応じて賃金・物価や税などが上下する率）, スライディング・スケール
sliding scale duties スライド関税, 伸縮関税

sliding scale method　スライド制, スライディング・スケール制
sliding scale of charges　増減手数料率
sliding scale system　物価スライド制
sliding scale tariff　スライド関税, 伸縮関税
◆The sliding scale system for pension payments is aimed at guaranteeing pensioners the real value of their pension payment. 年金支給額の物価スライド制の目的は、年金受給者に年金支給の実質的な価値を保証することにある。

slight　(形)わずかな, 少量の, 軽い, 小幅な, 取るに足らない, つまらない, 低調な, ほっそりした, 痩せた, きゃしゃな, 弱い
　a slight backup in rates　金利の小反発
　a slight depreciation of the U.S. dollar　米ドルの小幅下落
　a slight drop　わずかな減少, 小幅低下
　a slight gain　わずかな伸び, 小幅な伸び
　a slight increase　微増
　a slight pickup in　〜がやや上向く[回復する]こと, 〜が若干回復
　a slight rebound　小幅反発, 若干反発
　a slight tightening in monetary policy　金融政策の小幅引締め
　mark a slight boost　やや持ち直す
　slight upward revisions　小幅な上方修正
◆The economy has shown slight signs of recovery. 景気に薄日が差している。

slim　(形)わずかな, 乏しい, 少ない, 縮小した
　by a very slim margin　ごく僅差(きんさ)で
　earn slimmer profit margin　利益率が低下する
　lose the proxy fight by a slim margin　(議決権)委任状争奪戦で僅差で負ける
　rise a slim 0.5%　0.5%の微増にとどまる
　slim margin　薄利, 薄い利幅, 僅差(きんさ)
　slimmer net interest margin　預貸利ざやの縮小

slip　(動)減少する, 縮小する, 低下する, 下落する, 滑り落ちる, ずり落ちる
　slip below the 50 percent line　50%の水準を割り込む
　slip to　〜まで低下[減少する]する
◆French bond prices slipped as French banks possess a large volume of Greek and Italian bonds. フランス銀行がギリシャやイタリアなどの国債を保有しているため、フランス国債が値下がりした。◆Premium revenues slipped at seven of the nine major life insurers. 保険料収入は、主要生命保険9社のうち7社が減少した。◆South Korean foreign reserves slipped to $305 billion in May 2011 from the record $307 billion logged in April. 韓国の2011年5月の外貨準備高は、4月に記録した過去最高の3,070億ドルから3,050億ドルに減少した。

slip into a double-dip recession　景気の二番底に陥る
◆The U.S. economy is in danger of slipping into a double-dip recession. 米経済は、景気の二番底に陥る可能性[恐れ]がある。

slip into deflation　デフレに陥る, デフレになる
◆The nation's economy has slipped into deflation. 日本経済は、デフレに陥っている。

slip into recession　景気後退入りする, 景気後退局面(リセッション)に入る
◆The U.S. economy slipped into recession in December 2007. 米経済は、2007年12月から景気後退局面(リセッション)に入った。

slipping currency　もろい通貨
◆We can't possess international strength on a slipping currency. もろい通貨で、国際的な力をつけることはできない。

slipping into recession　景気後退入り
◆Worries over the spreading of the eurozone debt crisis and the U.S.'s slipping into recession have driven the rout in financial markets. ユーロ圏の財政危機の拡大と米国の景気後退入りへの懸念で、金融市場は総崩れになった。

slipshod　(形)だらしない, ずさんな, ぞんざいな
　(⇒debt servicing capacity [capability])
　slipshod accounting　どんぶり勘定
　slipshod examination　ずさんな審査
　slipshod investigation　ずさんな調査

slipshod fiscal management　放漫な財政運営
◆Greece's credibility plunged due to its slipshod fiscal management in the European financial crisis. 欧州の財政・金融危機で、ギリシャの信認は放漫な財政運営で低下した。

slipshod management　ずさんな経営
◆The failed bank took an expansionary course while its slipshod management proliferated. 破たんしたこの銀行は、拡大路線に走る一方、そのずさんな経営がまん延して行った。◆The slipshod management of failed Incubator Bank of Japan widely diverged from its business philosophy. 破たんした日本振興銀行のずさんな経営は、同行の経営理念とはかけ離れていた。

slope　(動)傾斜する, 傾く
　be positively sloped　順イールドになっている
　downward sloping demand　右下がりの需要
　negatively sloped yield curve　右下がり[右肩下がり]のイールド・カーブ(利回り曲線), 逆イールド
　positively sloped yield curve　右上がり[右肩上がり]のイールド・カーブ(利回り曲線), 順イールド
　upward sloping yield curve　右上がり[右肩上がり]のイールド・カーブ, 順イールド

slope　(名)斜面, 傾き, 傾斜, 勾配(こうばい)
　steeper slope in the yield curve　長短利回り格差の拡大
　the slope of the (yield) curve　利回り曲線の勾配
　(=yield curve slope)

sloppy　(形)ずさんな, 放漫な, 手抜きの, いい加減な
　sloppy management　放漫経営
　sloppy tone of the market　軟弱な地(じ)合い

slow　(動)減速する, 弱まる, 鈍る, 鈍化する, 伸び悩む, 低迷する, 下降線をたどる, 落ち込む, 低下する, 鈍化させる, ブレーキをかける
◆Export growth has slowed due to the high value of the yen and the weakness of economies overseas. 円高と海外経済の減速で、輸出の伸びが鈍った。◆Growth in the automotive insurance market is slowing as fewer young people own cars. 若者の車離れを背景に、自動車保険市場は伸び悩んでいる。◆Payroll growth in the United States slowed dramatically in July with a 32,000 jobs being added. 米国での7月の就業者数の伸びは、前月より32,000人の微増で急激に減速した。◆The economy is beginning to lose momentum as exports and capital investments are slowing. 輸出と設備投資が息切れを始め、景気に減速傾向が出ている。◆The growth rate of Japan's huge pool of individual financial assets has been slowing. 日本の巨額の個人金融資産の伸び率は、鈍化している。◆The Japanese economy is slowing. 日本の景気は、低迷している[下降線をたどっている]。◆The Japanese economy, which has been recovering thanks to external demand, has suddenly slowed. 外需に支えられて回復してきた日本の景気が、急減速した。

slow　(形)遅い, のろい, 返済の遅れている, 支払いの遅い, 鈍い, 緩やかな, 活気のない, 不活発な, はかばかしくない, 低調な, 不景気な, 面白くない, つまらない, スロー
　slow acceleration　穏やかな上昇
　slow account　不活発勘定, 不活発口座
　slow asset　換金に時間のかかる資産
　slow economic expansion　穏やかな景気拡大
　slow economic growth rate　低経済成長率, 低成長率

SLOW

slow economic recovery　穏やかな景気回復, 景気回復の足取りが重いこと
slow growth　低成長, 減速経済, 伸びが鈍いこと
slow loans　返済の遅れている融資, 不良貸金
slow moving inventory　滞留在庫, 回転の遅い在庫
slow moving item　売れ行きの悪い商品
slow paper　支払いの遅い手形
slow recovery　穏やかな回復, 回復の足取りが重いこと
slow trading　薄商い
slow upward trend　穏やかな上昇傾向
slower economic growth　経済成長の鈍化, 経済成長率の低下
slower growth　伸び悩み, 低成長, 伸び率の低下, 経済成長率の低下[鈍化], 景気[成長]の減速
◆Eurozone countries were so slow to take necessary actions that the sovereign debt crisis expanded. 欧州の必要な対応が後手に回ったために, ソブリン危機[政府債務危機]が拡大した。◆Exports and production are increasing at a slower pace. 輸出と生産は, 以前より緩やかなペースで増加している。◆The EU's responses to the European debt crisis have been slow. 欧州債務危機への欧州連合(EU)の対応は, 後手に回ってきた。◆The 17-nation currency union was slow in responding to the request for financial support by Greece. 17か国から成る通貨統合のユーロ圏は, ギリシャの金融支援要請への対応が遅かった。◆There is slow progress in economic improvement among nonmanufacturing businesses, largely as a result of sluggish sales at retailers due to the ongoing deflation. デフレの進行で主に小売業の売上が低迷しているため, 非製造業は景気回復の足取りが弱い。

slow down　(動)減速する, 失速する, 鈍化する, 後退する, 沈滞する, 低迷する, 低下する
◆The European economy might slow down and register negative growth if eurozone states introduce austerity measures. ユーロ圏各国が緊縮財政策を導入すると, 欧州の景気は減速し, マイナス成長に陥る恐れがある。

slowdown　(名)(景気などの)減速, 失速, 鈍化, 後退, 沈滞, 低迷, 低下, 現象, 減産, 操業短縮, 怠業　(⇒economic slowdown, global slowdown, simultaneous slowdown of the global economy)
business slowdown　景気減速, 景気低迷
　(⇒cautious)
concerns about a possible slowdown in the U.S. economy　米国の景気減速懸念
　(⇒strong yen and weak dollar)
demand slowdown　需要の伸びの鈍化, 需要減速, 需要低迷
drastic slowdown in individual consumption　個人消費の大幅な減速
economic slowdown　景気減速, 景気後退, 景気低迷, 景気鈍化　(⇒risk factor)
global (economic) slowdown　世界的な景気低迷, 世界的な景気減速　(=slowdown in global activity)
inflationary slowdown　インフレ率の低下
market slowdown　市場低迷
monetary slowdown　マネー・サプライ伸び率の低下
seasonal demand slowdown　季節要因による需要減速
signs of slowdown　減速感
slowdown in construction investment　建設投資の減退
slowdown in consumer spending　個人消費の落ち込み
slowdown in credit demand　信用需要の減速
slowdown in [of] economic activity　景気減速, 景気低迷, 景気の軟化
slowdown in foreign borrowing　外貨借入れの抑制
slowdown in foreign borrowings　外貨借入れの抑制
slowdown in housing starts　住宅着工件数[住宅着工戸数]の減少
slowdown in incomes　所得の伸びの鈍化
slowdown in monetary capital formation　金融資本形成の減速
slowdown in monthly inflation　前月比物価上昇率の低下
slowdown in prepays　期限前償還率の低下
　(=slower prepays)
slowdown in productivity growth　生産性上昇率の低下[減速]
slowdown in the decline of exports　輸出減少の鈍化
　(⇒level off)
slowdown of economic activity　景気の減速
◆As indicated by the worsening employment situation and slumping personal consumption, business slowdown is anticipated in the market. 雇用[雇用状況]の悪化や個人消費の低迷などが示すように, 市場では景気の減速が予想される。◆Housing investment, a driving force for the U.S. economy until recently, has shown signs of a slowdown. 最近まで米景気を牽引してきた住宅投資に, 減速感が見られる。◆Japan is suffering a slowdown. 日本は, 景気減速に見舞われている。◆The downside risks to Japan's economy will increase because concerns over a U.S. slowdown are growing. 米国の景気減速に対する懸念が高まっているため, 日本の景気[日本経済]が今後悪化するリスクは増大している。◆The slowdown of Toyota indicates the disastrous extent of the worldwide financial crisis. トヨタの減速[失速]は, 世界的な金融危機[世界金融危機]の猛威を物語っている。

slowdown in individual consumption　個人消費の減速
◆The downward revision of the fiscal 2011 growth projection was made due to a drastic slowdown in individual consumption and meager price increases. 2011年度の経済成長見通しの下方修正は, 個人消費の大幅な減速と物価上昇率の鈍化が原因だ。

slowdown in the economic recovery　景気回復の鈍化
◆The slowdown in the economic recovery will adversely affect the earnings of three megabank groups in the second half of this fiscal year. 今年度下半期は, 3メガバンクの収益「業績」が景気回復鈍化の影響[悪影響]を受けることになりそうだ。

slowdown in the economy　景気減速
　(=slowdown of economic activity)
◆The government will flexibly implement both economic and financial measures to deal with the slowdown in the economy. 政府は, 経済対策と金融政策を機動的に実施して, 景気減速に対応する方針だ。

slowdown in the U.S. economy　米景気の減速
◆Behind these cautious views among large manufacturers are uncertainty over the debt crisis in the eurozone and the slowdown in the U.S. economy. 大企業製造業のこうした警戒感[慎重な見方]の背景には, ユーロ圏の債務危機不安や米景気の減速がある。

slowdown of the world economy　世界的な景気の減速
◆Pressure for additional monetary easing measures will increase if the slowdown of the world economy continues. 世界的な景気減速がこのまま続けば, 一層の金融緩和[金融緩和策]を求める圧力が強まるものと思われる。

sluggish　(形)不振の, 低迷した, 低迷する, 不活発な, 不景気な, 動きが鈍い, 足どりが重い, 軟調な, 軟弱な
sluggish consumer demand　消費需要の低迷, 低迷した消費需要
sluggish consumer spending　個人消費の低迷, 消費支出の低迷

sluggish domestic demand　内需低迷
sluggish economic conditions　景気低迷, 景気の停滞
sluggish factory orders　製造業受注の低迷
sluggish job growth　雇用増加の低迷, 雇用の伸び悩み
sluggish liquidity　流動性の低さ
sluggish performance　業績不振
sluggish recovery　回復の遅れ, 景気回復の遅れ, 景気回復の足取りが重いこと
sluggish rise　伸び悩み
sluggish stock market　低迷した株式市場, 株式市場の低迷, 株式相場の低迷
　（=slumping stock market）
　◆Japan's economy will remain sluggish for a while. 日本の景気低迷は, しばらく続くと思われる。◆Trading is sluggish on stock markets mainly due to the financial crisis in Europe. 株式市場は, 主に欧州の財政・金融危機で取引［相場］が低迷している。

sluggish personal spending　個人消費の伸び悩み
　◆The negative growth was due to the stagnancy of corporate capital investment as well as sluggish personal spending and other economy-slowing factors. マイナス成長は, 企業の設備投資が頭打ちの状態だったことと, 個人消費の伸び悩みや他の景気減速要因によるものだ。

sluggish response　鈍い対応, 対応の鈍さ
　◆Speculators apparently take advantage of the sluggish response of the government and the Bank of Japan to the yen's appreciation. 投機筋は, 政府・日銀の円高への対応の鈍さに付け込んでいるようだ。

sluggish sales　販売低迷, 販売不振, 売れ行き不振
　◆There is slow progress in economic improvement among nonmanufacturing businesses, largely as a result of sluggish sales at retailers due to the ongoing deflation. デフレの進行で主に小売業の売上が低迷しているため, 非製造業は景気回復の足取りが弱い。

sluggish stock market　低迷した株式市場, 株式市場の低迷, 株式相場の低迷
　（=slumping stock market）
　◆The revision of the country's securities-related tax system for individual investors is a key measure for buoying the sluggish stock market. 個人投資家のための日本の証券関連税制の改正は, 低迷した株式市場を浮揚させるための重要な施策だ。

sluggish stock prices　株価低迷
　◆Sluggish stock prices drastically reduced latent profits of seven major life insurers. 株価低迷で, 大手生保7社の株式含み益は大幅に減少した。

slump　（動）暴落する, 急落する, がた落ちする, 落ち込む, 減少する, 低迷する
　slump significantly　がた落ちする, 大幅に低下する
　slump to a new low　過去最低まで落ち込む, 最安値［安値］を更新する
　◆Stock prices have slumped. 株価が, 急落した。◆The dollar slumped to a new low against the yen. ドル［ドル相場］が, 対円で安値を更新した。

slump　（名）暴落, 急落, がた落ち, 落ち込み, 減少, 低迷, 不振, 不況, 不景気, 景気沈滞, スランプ
　（=sluggishness）
　a housing investment slump　住宅投資の落ち込み
　　（⇒housing investment）
　a prolonged slump　長期低迷
　business slump　景気低迷, 景気沈滞, 経営不振, 業績不振, 不況　（=slump in business）
　demand slump　需要低迷
　economic slump　景気低迷, 景気後退, 不景気, 不況
　economic slump triggered by the yen's sharp appreciation

円高不況
　get out of the slump　不況から脱出する
　slump in profits　収益の落ち込み
　slump in the dollar　ドル安
　slump in the stock market　株式市場の不振
　slump-ridden industry　不況業種
　summer slump　夏枯れ
　the prolonged slump in the real estate market　不動産取引市場の長期低迷
　the slump in the stock prices　株価急落
　worldwide slump　世界的不況
　◆A housing investment slump results from the enforcement of the revised Building Standards Law. 住宅投資の落込みは, 改正建築基準法の施行によるものだ。◆Amid a widening slump in global auto sales and the yen's sharp appreciation against the U.S. dollar, the firm is expected to report an unconsolidated operating loss in fiscal 2011. 世界の新車販売の落ち込み拡大と急激な円高・ドル安に伴って, 同社の2011年度［2010年3月期決算］の営業利益は, 単独ベース［単独決算］で赤字が見込まれている。◆Business performance of the group's consumer financing affiliate has been in a slump. 同グループの消費者金融子会社の業績は, 低迷している。◆The government expressed its optimistic expectations of the current economic slump. 政府は, 現在の景気後退について楽観的な見通しを示した。◆The housing industry is being battered by a prolonged slump. 住宅産業は, 長期低迷の影響をもろに受けている。◆The ongoing business slump raises the specter of a global downturn comparable to the Great Depression that started in 1929. 今回の不況は, 1929年に始まった世界大恐慌に匹敵するほどの世界同時不況の懸念が高まっている。◆World stock markets are in a deep slump. 世界の株式市場は, 低迷の度を深めている。

slump in the domestic stock market　国内株式市場の低迷
　◆The major securities house attributed the poor earnings to sharp drops in brokerage fees and trading profits amid the extended slump in the domestic stock market. この大手証券会社は, 減益の要因として, 国内株式市場の長期低迷による株売買手数料と売買益の大幅減を挙げた。

slump in the real estate market　不動産市場の低迷, 不動産取引市場の低迷
　◆The prolonged slump in the real estate market is maintaining the decline in land prices. 不動産取引市場の長期低迷が, 引き続き地価の下落を招いている。

slump in the stock prices　株価急落
　◆Behind the slump in the stock prices is a crisis of confidence in U.S. style capitalism, which until recently has served as a model of prosperity. 株価急落の背景にあるのは, 最近まで繁栄のモデルとされてきた米国型資本主義に対する信認の揺らぎだ。

slumpflation　（名）不景気下のインフレ, スランプフレーション

slumping sales　販売不振

slumping stock market　株式市況の低迷

slush fund　不正資金, 賄賂（わいろ）資金, 買収資金, 裏金, へそくり
　◆Slush funds in the Foreign Ministry totaled nearly ￥200 million over a period of about six years. 外務省の裏金（プール金）の総額は, 6年余りで約2億円に達していた。◆This ex-vice president is believed to have been deeply involved in creating a slush fund. この元副社長は, 同社の裏金づくりに深く関与していたとされる。

small　（形）小さい, 狭い, 少ない, わずかな, 小幅な, 重要でない, ささいな, 二流の, 小規模の, 中小の, 小型の, 小口の, 少額の

qualified small issue bond　適格少額発行債券
small and medium size IPOs　中小規模の新規株式公開
small balance sheet　スモール・バランスシート(資産を極限まで小さくして、効率よく大きな利益を生む体質を作り出すこと)
small bond　小口債券
small business investment corporation　中小企業投資会社, SBIC
Small Business Service　スモール・ビジネス・サービス, SBS(2000年に英国の貿易産業省内に設置された中小企業融資保証制度(SFLGS)の実施機関)
small cap (stock)　小型株
　(=small capital [capitalization] stock)
small capital　過小資本, 小資本
small capital stock　小型株　(=small cap)
small change　小銭, 釣り銭
small claims court　少額裁判所
　(=small debts court)
small coins　小額硬貨, 小銭
small company [business, firm]　零細企業, 中小企業
small company fund　小型株ファンド
small demand　小口需要
small denomination　小額貨幣
small depositors　小口預金者
small dip in profits　小幅減益
Small Firms Loan Guarantee (Scheme)　小規模企業[中小企業]融資保証制度, SFLG(S) [SFLGS]
small gain　小幅益, 小幅利益, 小幅上昇, 小幅な伸び
small government　小さな政府
small government bond　小額国債
small increase　小幅の増加, 小幅増
small investor　小口投資家, 個人投資家
small investor selling　小口の売り
small-lot loans　小口貸出, 小口融資
small notes　小額紙幣
small order　小口注文
small profits and quick returns　薄利多売, 薄利多売方式
Small Repos　小口現先
small savers certificate　小口預金証書, 少額貯蓄証書, 国債金利基準書, SSC
small-savings tax exemption system　少額貯蓄非課税制度
small-scale buying　小口の買い
small-scale shareholder [stockholder]　小口株主
small shareholder [stockholder]　小株主, 小口株主
small stock dividends　低率の株式配当
small-sum deposit　小口預金
small time deposit　小口の定期預金
smaller credit　中小企業信用
smaller public placement　小型の公募債
smaller syndicate players　シンジケート団の下位メンバー
◆All of the seven major banking groups forecast that bad loan disposal at the end of March next year will be smaller than their net operating profits. 大手銀行・金融7グループ各行の業績予想では、来年3月期の不良債権処理額はいずれも業務純益の範囲内になる見込みだ。◆The rate of economic expansion in the current phase of recovery is much smaller than previous expansionary phases. 現在の景気拡大期[景気拡大局面]の経済成長率は、過去の景気拡大期よりかなり低い。

small and medium-sized banks　中小金融機関
◆Japan Post Bank and private small and medium-sized banks will compete against each other in loans to micro, small and midsize enterprises. ゆうちょ銀行と民間の中小金融機関は今後、零細中小企業向けの融資で競合することになる。

small and midsize companies　中小企業　(=small and midsize corporations, small and midsize enterprises)
◆Small and midsize companies have been stepping up equity financing to fund capital investments and prepare for M&A deals. 中小企業は、設備投資の資金調達とM&A取引に備えて、株式発行による資金調達を急いでいる。◆The bank cut its lending to small and midsize companies by ￥5.63 trillion in the year ended March 31 from a year earlier. 同社の3月期の中小企業向け貸出は、前年同期より5兆6,300億円減少した。◆The banks are now paying more attention to new loans and services aimed at individuals and or small and midsize companies. 銀行は現在、個人や中小企業に目を向けた新しい融資やサービスに力を入れている。

small and midsize firms [companies]　中小企業
◆A sense of restlessness and hopelessness still prevails among nonmanufacturers, small and midsize firms and regional economies. 非製造業や中小企業、地方経済には、焦燥と絶望感が広まったままだ。

small loan　小口金融, 小口融資, 小口貸付け, 少額融資
smack loan company　貸金業, 小口金融会社
Small Loan Law　小口金融法, サラ金法

small-lot after hours trading　立会い外分売, 時間外分売
◆The Jasdaq can begin small-lot after-hours trading by its transformation from an over-the-counter stock market to a securities exchange. ジャスダックは、店頭市場から証券取引所への移行により、立会い外分売(取引時間外に大株主などが保有株を小口に分けて売り出すこと)も可能になった。

smart　(形)情報処理機能を持つ, インテリジェントな, コンピュータ内臓の, コンピュータで作動する, 高機能の, 高度な, 自動化された, センサー誘導の, スマート
smart card　ICカード
smart credit card　クレジット用ICカード
smart home　自動化住宅
smart money　相場師の投資金, ずる賢い投資家, (内部情報通の)相場師, 経験・知識が豊富な人, 負傷手当て, 懲罰的損害賠償金, 損害賠償
smart phone [smartphone]　高度自動機能電話, 高機能携帯電話, スマートフォン
smart set　上流社会, 上流階級の人々, 新しがりの人々
smart terminal　スマート端末

smolder　(動)くすぶる, うっ積する
◆Fears about default on the Greek government bonds are smoldering as Greece's fiscal reconstruction measures hit the wall. ギリシャの財政再建策が行き詰まっているため、ギリシャ国債のデフォルト(債務不履行)の恐れがくすぶっている。

smooth　(形)円滑な, 順調な, 平坦な
a smooth recovery　順調な景気回復
smooth flow of money　資金の円滑な流れ
◆The stock market is a public mechanism to facilitate the smooth flow of money in the economy by serving as an intermediary between corporations and investors. 証券市場は、企業と投資家間の仲介役をつとめて日本経済に資金を円滑に流す役割を担う公共財だ。

snap　(動)ぽきんと折る, ぱちんと閉じる[開く], 歯止めをかける
◆Tokyo stocks snapped a three-day losing streak Wednesday, with the key Nikkei index rebounding strongly from Tuesday. 東京の株価[東京株式市場の株価]は水曜日、日経平均株価(225種)が前日から大幅反発[回復]して、3日連続の値下がりに歯止めがかかった。

snap up　先を争って買う, さっと買う[取る, 拾う]
◆It's not a beautiful story for securities firms to snap up stocks while being aware of the erroneous sell order. 誤発

注と認識しながら、証券会社が間隙を縫って株を取得するのは、美しい話ではない。

snapshot of economic conditions　景況報告
◆A U.S. Federal Reserve Board snapshot of economic conditions bolsters the hope of broader-based recovery. 米連邦準備制度理事会（FRB）の景況報告では、ほとんどの地域で景気持ち直しの期待が強まっている。

snert　（名）英貨1ポンド（=pound sterling）

SNIF　短期証券発行引受保証枠（short-term note issuance facilityの略）

SNIG　インフレを伴わない持続可能な成長（sustainable noninflationary growthの略）

snowball　（動）膨（ふく）れ上がる, 雪だるま式に増大する［拡大する］　（名）雪玉, 雪つぶて, 雪だるま式に増えるもの, ネズミ算式募金
（⇒out-of-control）
　build a mental snowball　（無意識に）緊張感を高める
　not have［stand］a snowball's chance in hell　（～する）見込み［チャンス］はまったくない
　snowball effect　雪だるま式増加効果
　snowballing deficit　雪だるま式に増大［拡大］する赤字
◆Stock prices in Tokyo fell by more than 600 points as a state of panic gripped investors and selling pressure snowballed. 東京市場の株価は、投資家がパニック状態に陥り、売り圧力が増大［加速］したため、下げ幅が600円を超えた。

soar　（動）急騰する, 急増する, 大きく上回る, 高まる, 急上昇する
◆Crude oil futures soared in New York due to concerns over oil supplies. ニューヨーク（ニューヨーク・マーカンタイル取引所）の原油先物が、原油供給不安［原油供給への懸念］から急騰した。◆Fixed asset investment soared nearly 30 percent from a year ago during the July-September quarter. 7-9月期の固定資産投資は、前年同期比で3割近く増加した。◆If the number of corporate bankruptcies and the unemployment rate soar owing to structural reforms, recessionary pressures will further increase. 構造改革で企業倒産件数や失業率が増えると、不況圧力は一層強まるものと思われる。◆Japan must prevent the yen from soaring again to the level of ￥76 to the dollar. 日本は、円相場が再び1ドル＝76円台に急騰する事態を阻止しなければならない。◆Japanese private banks' government bond holdings soared to ￥154 trillion as of the end of June 2011 from ￥32 trillion as of the end of March 1999. 日本の民間銀行の国債保有残高は、（ゼロ金利政策が初めて）導入された1999年3月末時点の32兆円から、2011年6月末現在で154兆円に膨らんだ。◆Some dollar funds injected into banks by the U.S. central bank may send U.S. stock prices soaring because banks will invest some of the new dollar funds in domestic assets such as stocks. 米国の中央銀行（FRB）が金融機関［銀行］に供給したドル資金の一部は、銀行がその新たなドル資金の一部を株のような国内資産に投資するため、米国の株価を上げる可能性がある。◆Tab for Fannie Mae and Freddie Mac could soar to as much as $259 billion, nearly twice the amount Fannie and Freddie have received so far. ファニー・メイ（米連邦住宅抵当金庫）とフレディ・マック（米連邦住宅貸付け抵当公社）の追加の公的資金必要額は、両社がこれまでに受け取った額の約2倍の2,590億ドルに急増する可能性がある。◆The BOJ is prepared to hold its policy meeting ahead of schedule if the yen's value further soars before the next meeting. 次回の政策決定会合までに円高が一段と進めば、日銀は会合を前倒しして会合を開く構えだ。◆The euro crisis has spread to Spain and Italy with interest rates on their sovereign debts soaring. ユーロ危機はスペインとイタリアに波及し、両国国債の金利が急騰した。◆The total assets of the Federal Reserve Board have soared to $2.87 trillion at the end of June 2011 from $896.2 billion as of the end of March 2008, prior to the Lehman shock. 米連邦準備制度理事会（FRB）の総資産は、リーマン・ショック前の2008年3月末時点の8,962億ドルから、2011年6月末には2兆8,700億ドルに急増した。◆The yen may soar toward ￥80 to the dollar. 円相場は、1ドル＝80円に向けて急騰する可能性がある。◆The yen soared to its strongest position this year. 円は、年初来の最高値を付けた。◆While soaring high on massive direct investment from abroad, the Chinese economy started showing signs of overheating in the latter half of 2003. 海外からの活発な直接投資に支えられて、中国経済は、2003年後半から景気過熱の様相を見せ始めた。

soaring euro　ユーロの急騰
◆Finance ministers and business leaders at the World Economic Forum are showing surprisingly little concern over the soaring euro and tumbling dollar. 世界経済フォーラムに出席した各国の財務相や財界指導者は、ユーロの急騰やドルの下落に驚くほど関心を示していない。

soaring food and petroleum product prices　食料品と石油製品の価格高騰
◆The core consumer price inflation rate, excluding volatile fresh food prices, is currently about 2 percent on year due mainly to soaring food and petroleum product prices. 変動の激しい生鮮食品の価格を除いたコア物価指数［消費者物価指数のコア指数］の上昇率は現在、主に食料品と石油製品の価格高騰の影響で、対前年比で2%程度となっている。

soaring prices of houses　住宅価格の上昇
◆Concerns about inflation have emerged in some sectors of the U.S. economy, as seen in rising retail prices of gasoline and in soaring prices of houses in urban areas. ガソリン小売価格の高騰や都市部の住宅価格の上昇などに見られるように、米経済の一部にはインフレ懸念も出始めている。

soaring public debts　増大する公的債務, 公的債務の増大
◆At the G-7 talks, concern over soaring public debts was to top the agenda. G7（先進7か国財務相・中央銀行総裁会議）の協議では、増大する公的債務問題［公的債務への懸念］が最大の議題［課題］になる予定だった。◆The issue of soaring public debts was pigeonholed at the G-7 talks. 増大する公的債務の問題は、G7（先進7か国財務相・銀行総裁会議）の協議では棚上げされてしまった。

social　（形）社会的な, ソーシャル
　social finance　ソーシャル・ファイナンス
　Social Insurance Agency　社会保険庁
　social lending　個人間融資, ソーシャル・レンディング

social security　社会保障
　Social Security Act　社会保障法
　social security benefits　社会保障給付
　social security payments　社会保険料
　social security plan　社会保障制度, 社会保障
　　（=social security system）

social security allowance budget　社会保障給付費
◆The social security allowance budget will increase to ￥152 trillion in fiscal 2005. 社会保障給付費は、2005年度には152兆円に膨らむ。

social security costs　社会保障費
◆Social security costs, which currently total more than ￥20 trillion a year, will increase by ￥1 trillion every year due to the country's graying population. 現在総額で年間20兆円超の社会保障費は、わが国の高齢化の進展で、毎年1兆円ずつ増える見込みだ。

social security insurance premium　社会保険料
◆Social security insurance premiums are paid by employers. 社会保険料は、雇用主が負担している。

social security outlays　社会保障関係費
◆Social security outlays include those for social welfare and social insurance. 社会保障関係費には、社会福祉や社会保険などの経費（支出）が含まれる。

social security spending 社会保障関係費
◆If the government covers social security spending which is increasing by ¥1 trillion annually, it cannot get around an increase in the consumption tax rate. 年に1兆円ずつ増える社会保障費を賄うには、消費税率の引上げを避けて通ることはできない。◆Social security spending will be capped at ¥19.7 trillion, more than ¥200 billion less than the projected increase due to the graying of society. 社会保障関係費は、高齢化の進展で予想される増加額を2,000億円圧縮して、19兆7,000億円まで抑制する方針だ。

social security system [plan] 社会保障制度
◆Working generations supported the elderly, retired generations in the traditional social security system. 従来の社会保障制度では、現役世代が退職世代の高齢者を支えていた。

socially responsible investing 社会的責任投資, SRI（法の順守や社会貢献度などの社会性や環境問題への取組み姿勢などで投資先を判断する投資手法）
◆The citizens banks can be said to be part of socially responsible investing, a practice in which investments are chosen on the basis of their contribution to society, such as environmental protection. 市民バンクは、環境保護などの社会貢献度に基づいて投資先を選ぶ手法である「社会的責任投資」の一環と言える。

soft （形）柔らかい, 弱い, 軟調の, 低迷している, 不活発な, 滑らかな, 柔軟な, 穏やかな, 条件のゆるい, 長期低利の, 楽な, 楽に儲（もう）かる, やさしい, 寛大な, ソフト （名）非金属商品 (soft commodities, softs)
  end on a soft note 引けにかけて相場が若干軟化する
  soft commodities 非金属商品 (=softs)
  soft currency （強い通貨に対して）弱い通貨, 軟貨, 交換不能通貨, ソフト通貨, ソフト・カレンシー (=soft money: 国際収支が赤字続きの国の通貨で, 金や米ドルなどの通貨と交換できない通貨, ⇒hard currency)
  soft currency area 軟貨圏
  soft demand 需要低迷, 需要の軟化
  soft dollar 現金以外での支払い, サービス代金間接払い方式, 現地通貨 (local currency), ソフトドル[ソフト・ダラー]
  soft economic performance 景気の軟調, 景気の足取りが弱いこと
    (=soft performance of the economy)
  soft economy 景気の軟調, ソフト・エコノミー
  soft economy picture 景気の軟調を示す指標
  soft error 誤動作
  soft information 未確認情報, 予測情報
  soft line 柔軟路線
  soft market 軟調市況, 相場の低迷, 不活発な市場
  soft money 交換不能通貨 (soft currency), 軟貨, 軟貨紙幣, 不換紙幣, 購買力[価値]の落ちた通貨, 手形, 規制対象外の選挙運動資金
  soft patch 弱含みの時期, 景気の失速, ソフトパッチ（経済成長の一時的な鈍化や足踏み状態のこと）
  soft selling [sell] 穏やかな商法, 低姿勢の売込み, もみ手式商法
  soft undertone 地合（じあ）いが弱いこと
  the soft 楽に儲けた金, 金, 悪銭

soft landing 軟着陸, ソフト・ランディング（成長率が長期平均を下回っている状態）
◆The Chinese central bank's recent interest rate hikes is an important move to cool the overheating Chinese economy and guide it toward a soft landing. 中国の中央銀行である人民銀行の今回の利上げ（貸出金利の引上げ）は、景気の過熱（中国経済の過熱）を鎮め、中国経済を安定成長に軟着陸させるための重要な動きである。◆U.S. President Barack Obama engineered a softer landing for GM with a set of measures to alleviate the bankruptcy shock as much as possible. オバマ米大統領は、GMの破たんショックを極力緩和するための一連の措置で、同社の軟着陸に向けた手を打った。

soft loan 長期低利貸付け, 条件の緩やかな融資[貸出, 借款], ソフト・ローン
  introduce economic stimulus through the soft loan 条件のゆるい借款を通じて景気刺激策を導入する
  untied soft loan ひも付きでない[用途を指定しない]融資, 使途無指定融資, 不拘束融資, アンタイド・ソフト・ローン
◆Chinese President Hu Jintao pledged nearly $100 million in grants and soft loans to Cameroon. 中国の胡錦濤国家主席は、カメルーンに対して約1億ドルの資金援助と長期低利貸付けを約束した。◆The government will help Indonesia introduce economic stimulus measures through the soft loan. 政府は、この条件のゆるい借款を通じて、インドネシアの景気刺激策導入を支援する。

soften （動）柔らかくする, 滑らかにする, 弱める, 少なくする, 和らげる, 緩和する, 軟化させる, 穏やかにする（自動）落ち込む, 縮小する, 低下する, 減少する, 軟化する, 弱含む
◆The dollar softened on the news. ドルは、これを材料に弱含んだ。◆The dollar softened substantially. ドルが、大幅に下落した。

softening （名）低下, 縮小, 減少, 軟化, 落ち込み
  softening in interest rates 金利の低下
  softening in market 市場の軟化
  softening in prices 物価の下落
  softening of economic activity 景気の軟化
  softening of swap spreads スワップ・スプレッドの縮小

softness （名）落ち込み, 縮小, 低下, 減少, 下落, 軟調, 軟化
  economic softness 景気の軟調, 景気の軟化
  income softness 所得の落ち込み
  market softness 軟調市場, 市場の軟化
  softness in government spending 政府支出の縮小
  softness in oil prices 原油価格の下落

software （名）ソフトウエア, コンピュータ・プログラム, コンピュータの運用操作技術, 利用技術, ソフト
  antivirus software ウイルス防止ソフト
  virus protection software ウイルス対策ソフト
◆Since 1995, the Development Bank of Japan has extended about 200 loans to holders of intellectual property rights such as software. 1995年以来、日本政策投資銀行は、ソフトウエアなどの知的財産権所有者に対する融資を約200件手がけてきた。◆Users of online banking services had better take security measures by using antivirus software. ネット・バンキングの利用者は、ウイルス対策ソフトを使ってセキュリティ対策を取ったほうが良い。

sole （形）単一の, 単独の, 独占的な, 総〜, 一手〜
  sole agent 一手代理人, 一手代理店, 総代理店
  sole bill 単一手形, 単独為替手形
    (=a sola bill: 組み手形はa set bill)
  sole lender 単独融資行
  sole manager 単独主幹事
  sole-manager issue 単独幹事債
  sole proprietor 個人事業主
◆As it stands, the yen is the sole major currency whose value has not stopped increasing. 現状では、円は上昇が止まらない唯一の主要通貨だ。

solicit （動）勧誘する, 募集する, 募（つの）る, 強く求める, 〜するように要請する, 資金などを集める, 訪問販売する, (人を)悪事に誘う
  solicit accounts 口座を勧誘する

solicit clients　顧客を勧誘する
solicit funds from　〜に資金提供を要請する, 〜に出資を勧誘する, 〜から資金を集める
solicit investors　出資者を募る［募集する］, 投資家を募集する
solicit opinions on　〜に関する意見を求める
solicit orders　注文をとる
solicit proxies　委任状を取り付ける
◆An insurance agent is a sales person who represents a life insurance company for the purpose of soliciting applications, collecting initial premiums, and servicing insurance contracts. 保険募集人は、生命保険会社を代表して保険契約の勧誘、初回保険料の徴収、保険契約に関する役務を提供する販売員である。◆As initial capital to establish an intellectual property fund, the bank plans to solicit between ¥5 billion and ¥6 billion from financial institutions and enterprises. 知的財産ファンドを創設するための当初資金として、同行は金融機関や事業会社から50億〜60億円を集める計画だ。

solicit donations　浄財を募る, 献金［寄付金］を募る
◆Many organizations have been soliciting donations to support the livelihood of the disaster victims. 被災者の生活支援のため、団体の多くが浄財を募っている。

solicit new customers　新規顧客を勧誘する
◆During the business suspension, the company will not be allowed to extend new loans, solicit new customers or call in loans. 業務停止の期間中、同社は新規融資や新規顧客の勧誘、貸出［貸金］の回収業務ができなくなる。

solicit new investors　新規出資者を募集する［募る］
◆The company held briefing sessions to solicit new investors. 同社は説明会を開いて、新規出資者を募っていた。

solicitation　（名）勧誘, 募集, 要請, 訪問販売
direct solicitation　直接勧誘
insurance solicitation　保険募集
　（＝insurance soliciting）
solicitation of clients　顧客の勧誘
solicitation of proxies　議決権代理行使の勧誘, 委任状勧誘　（＝proxy solicitation）
◆Solicitation of proxies is being made through the mail, in person, and by telecommunications. 議決権代理行使の勧誘は、郵便、経営陣により直接、または電信・電話などの通信手段で行われています。

solid　（形）着実な, 堅実な, 底堅い, 強固な, しっかりした, 健全な, 安定した, 充実した, 信頼できる, 連続した, ぶっ通しの, 一致団結した, 満場一致の
　（⇒sound）
achieve solid results　堅実な結果を残す
be solid financially　財務状態［財務状況］が強固である
remain solid　底堅い
solid capitalization　底堅い資本力
solid credit　優良銘柄
solid demand　堅実な需要, 需要の安定
solid economic growth　底堅い経済成長, 着実な景気拡大
solid economy　厚みのある経済
solid growth　着実な伸び, 着実な［底堅い］成長
solid hedges against high inflation　高インフレに対する強固な防壁
solid management　堅実な経営, 安定した経営
solid performance　底堅い業績, 堅調な値動き
◆Relatively solid retail sales figures inspired another rally on Wall Street. 小売売上高が比較的堅調だったため、ニューヨーク株式市場はまた持ち直した［ニューヨーク株は反発した］。◆The Japanese economy is solid, and there aren't any negative domestic factors. 日本経済はしっかりしており、内在的［対内的］なマイナス要因はない。

solve　（動）解決する, 処理する, 打開する, 解く, 答えを見つける, （借金、金を）支払う, 清算する, （義務などから）解放される
◆France and Germany could not bridge their differences, so Europe's efforts to solve its escalating debt crisis plunged into disarray. フランスとドイツが両国の相違を埋められなかったため、深刻化する欧州の債務危機問題解決への欧州の取組みは、混乱に陥った。◆German Chancellor Angela Merkel shut the door on the introduction of common eurozone bonds as a means to solve the debt crisis. ドイツのメルケル首相は、欧州債務危機問題の解決手段としてユーロ圏共通債を導入することに強く反対した。

solvency　（名）支払い余力, 支払い能力, ソルベンシー（支払い期日の到来時点で支払いできる状態にあること）
actuarial solvency　数理的支払い能力
adversely affect solvency　支払い能力に悪影響を及ぼす
enhance solvency　支払い能力を強化する
ensure solvency　支払い能力を確保する
EU's solvency norms　EUの支払い能力規制
financial solvency　支払い能力, 財務流動性
maintain solvency　支払い能力を維持する
　（＝remain solvent）
recover solvency　支払い能力を回復する
solvency position　自己資本比率
solvency rule　支払い能力規制

solvency margin　支払い余力, 支払い余力比率, ソルベンシー・マージン　（＝claim-paying ability, margin of solvency, solvency margin ratio: 大災害時などにおける生命保険会社の支払い能力のことで、保険会社の経営（財務）の健全性を判断する基準の一つ）
disclose insurance companies' solvency margins　生保のソルベンシー・マージンを開示する
the minimum solvency margins　最低限の支払い能力
◆Solvency margin is an indicator of an insurance company's financial health. ソルベンシー・マージン（支払い余力）比率は、保険会社の財務の健全性を示す指標の一つである。

solvency margin rate　支払い余力比率, ソルベンシー・マージン（支払い余力）比率, ソルベンシー・マージン比率　（＝solvency margin ratio; ⇒early corrective measures）
◆A solvency margin rate is the most closely watched gauge in assessing the financial health of an insurance company. ソルベンシー・マージン比率は、保険会社の経営［財務］の健全性を評価する際に特に注目される指標である。

solvency margin ratio　支払い余力比率, ソルベンシー・マージン比率, ソルベンシー・マージン　（＝solvency margin; ⇒capital increase, honor, insurance company）
◆In the year ended March 31, all nine major insurers saw an increase in their solvency margin ratio, a key indicator of insurers' financial health. 主要生保9社の3月期決算は、保険会社の財務の健全性を示す指標であるソルベンシー・マージン（支払い余力）比率が全社で上昇した。

solvency ratio　支払い能力比率, 自己資本比率, 流動性比率, ソルベンシー・マージン比率
an insurer's solvency ratio　生命保険会社［生保］の, ソルベンシー・マージン比率
Solvency Ratio Directive　自己資本比率指令, 流動性比率指令
◆An insurer's solvency ratio is a measure of a firm's ability to pay out policy obligations. 生保のソルベンシー・マージン（支払い余力）比率は、保険金の支払い能力を示す指標だ。

solvent　（形）支払い能力がある
keep solvent　支払い能力を保つ, 支払い能力を維持する
remain solvent　支払い能力を維持する

solvent client　支払い能力がある
solvent person　支払い能力のある者
stay solvent　倒産を防ぐ

soon-to-be-junk status　投資不適格が見込まれる
◆By buying Greek, Portuguese and Spanish bonds, the ECB infused life into the moribund eurozone markets for these soon-to-be-junk status government bonds. ギリシャやポルトガル、スペインの国債を買い入れて、欧州中銀（ECB）は、崩壊寸前のユーロ圏の投資不適格レベルが見込まれるこれらの債券の市場に生気を吹き込んだ。

soothe　（動）落ち着かせる、なだめる、静める、和らげる、慰める、安心させる、楽にする、払拭（ふっしょく）する
soothe market fears　市場不安を払拭する
soothe pain　傷みを和らげる
soothe the opposition　反対派を静める
◆The central bank's move to increase the outstanding current account target is insufficient to soothe market fears. 日銀の当座預金残高目標の引上げは、市場不安を払拭するには物足りない。

sound　（形）健康な、健全な、確かな、もっともな、正しい、理にかなった、正当性のある、安定した、堅実な、正常な、正確な、正統的な、根拠の十分な、頼りになる、信頼できる、思慮分別のある、（法律的に）有効な
a sound title to land　有効な土地所有権
make a sound profit　健全な利益を生む
sound capitalization　自己資本の充実
sound company　堅実な会社
sound credit decisions　健全な融資判断
sound economic management　健全な経済運営
sound financial fundamentals　健全な財務体質
sound foundation　しっかりとした土台
sound judgment　正しい判断、しっかりした判断
sound lending opportunities　健全な貸付け機会
sound policy　堅実な政策、健全政策、手堅い政策、健全な対策

sound economic policy　健全な経済政策
◆Sound economic policies and fundamentals provide a solid foundation for strong growth. 経済政策と経済の基礎は健全で、景気堅調の基盤は安定している。

sound loan　正常債権、健全債権
◆Sound loans, operating real estate, including branch offices, and cash and deposits will go into the new account as assets and liabilities. 正常債権、店舗などの事業用不動産や現金・預け金は、資産と負債としての「新勘定」に入る。

sound management　堅実な経営、健全な経営、経営の健全性　（放漫経営＝lax［loose］management）
◆The new rules on banks' corer capital ratios were decided on by the Basel Committee on Banking Supervision to compel banks to ensure sounder management. 銀行の自己資本比率に関する新規則は、銀行に経営の健全性向上を求めるためにバーゼル銀行監督委員会が決めた。

soundness　（名）健全性、安定性、確実性、堅実性、正当性
business soundness　経営の健全性
Federal Housing Enterprises Financial Safety and Soundness Act of 1992　1992年連邦住宅機関財政安定健全法
financial soundness　財務上の健全性、財政の健全性、経済的安定性、経営の健全性　（＝financial health）
fiscal soundness　財務上の健全性、財政の健全性、財政の安定性
the financial soundness of the market　市場の経済的安定性
◆A surplus in the primary balances of the central and local governments indicates a degree of fiscal soundness. 国と地方［地方自治体］の基礎的財政収支の黒字は、財政の健全度を示す。◆If the prices of purchased bad assets are set low, the fiscal soundness of bailed-out financial institutions could be compromised. 不良資産の買取り価格が安ければ、救済する金融機関の財務の健全性が損なわれる可能性がある。◆Major banks are intensifying their efforts to reduce their risk assets by securitizing and selling their credit to prevent their capital adequacy ratio, an index that shows their business soundness, from declining. 大手各行は現在、経営の健全性を示す指標である自己資本比率の低下を防ぐため、貸出債権の証券化や転売などでリスク資産（リスク・アセット）の圧縮策を加速させている。◆The massive negative yields of the life insurance industry threaten the financial soundness of insurers. 生保業界の巨額の逆ざやが、生保各社の財務上の健全性［経営の健全性］を脅（おびや）かしている。

sour　（動）悪くする、悪化させる、悪化する、不良化する、低迷する
soured assets　不良資産　（＝bad assets, nonperforming assets, problem assets）
soured loan　不良債権、不良貸出、貸倒れ　（＝bad loan, nonperforming loan, problem loan, troubled loan）
soured mortgage-related securities　モーゲージ関連の不良証券
souring demand　需要低迷

sour　（形）不快な、不愉快な、いやな、気難しい、厳しい、過酷な、標準以下の、へたな
be sour on　〜を嫌っている、〜が嫌だ
come to a sour end　不愉快な結果に終わる
sour experience　不快な経験、苦い経験
soured mortgage-related securities　モーゲージ関連の不良証券
turn［go］sour　失敗する、駄目になる、不良化する、うまく行かなくなる、酸っぱくなる
◆As a result of fierce competition in the past, interest rate profit margins were kept too low to cover loans that went sour. 過去の熾烈（しれつ）な競争の結果、金利の利ざやが小さく抑えられる余り、貸倒れ［貸倒れのリスク］をカバーできなかった［過去の熾烈な融資合戦の結果、不良債権リスクをカバーできないほど利ざやは小さく抑えられた］。◆The U.S. administration will spend up to $700 billion to buy up soured mortgage-related securities and other devalued assets held by ailing financial institutions. 米政府は、経営不振の金融機関が保有するモーゲージ関連の不良証券などの不良資産を、最大7,000億ドル投入して買い取る方針だ。

source　（名）源、源泉、利子・配当などの支払い者、筋、関係筋、関係者、取材源、情報源、ニュースソース、資料、出典、出所
（⇒Banks' Shareholding Purchase Corporation）
business sources　市場筋
cash sources　資金の源泉
external sources of cash　外部流動性
industry sources　業界筋
informed sources　情報筋
internal sources of cash　内部流動性
market sources　市場筋
reliable source　信頼できる筋
revenue sources　財源、歳入減、収益源、収入源
source and application of fund statement　資金運用表
source and application of funds　資金の源泉と使途
source of revenue　財源
withholding at source　源泉徴収
◆According to sources, Tokyo Electric Power Co. will commission four trust banks to sell its assets. 関係者によると、東京電力は4信託銀行に保有資産の売却業務を委託する。◆Financial reports and other documents published by companies are the most fundamental sources of information for

investors and creditors. 企業が公表する有価証券報告書などは、投資家や債権者にとって最も基幹的な情報源だ。◆In Europe, the creditworthiness of Italian and Spanish government bonds is a source of uncertainty. 欧州では、イタリアとスペインの国債の信用力が、金融不安の発生源だ。◆The special account borrows from the private sector and other sources to make up for local government's budget shortfalls. 特別会計は、民間などの財源からの借入れで地方の財政不足［財政赤字］の穴埋めをしている。◆Yen loans extended now as part of Japan's ODA are untied in principle, with the source of development materials and equipment to be procured not defined. 日本の政府開発援助（ODA）として供与されている円借款は現在、ひも付きでない「アンタイド」援助が原則で、開発物資の調達先を限定していない。

source of financial assistance　金融支援の原資
◆As the source of the government's financial assistance to the Nuclear Damage Liability Facilitation Fund, the government has already established a ¥5 trillion fund to issue government bonds. 原子力損害賠償支援機構に対する政府の金融支援の原資として、政府は、同機構に5兆円の国債発行枠をすでに設けている。

source of financial unrest　金融不安の発生源
◆Nonperforming loans are a source of financial unrest. 不良債権が、金融不安の発生源になっている。

source of profit　収益源
◆If the securities firms rush to cut these commissions, they may not be able to continue to rely on income from commissions as a major source of profit. これらの証券会社が手数料の値引き競争に走れば、主な収益源として株式の売買委託手数料による収入に今後とも頼ることは難しくなる。

sourcing　(名)調達, 業務委託, 供給, ソーシング
（⇒outsourcing）
　double sourcing　供給源の分散
　global sourcing　グローバル・ソーシング
　overseas sourcing　海外調達
　　（=overseas procurement）
　raw material sourcing　原材料の供給
　world sourcing　世界市場への製品供給
◆Japanese automakers will boost parts sourcing from South Korean suppliers as remedies for the strong yen. 円高対策として、日本の自動車メーカー各社は韓国製部品の調達［韓国部品メーカーからの部品調達］を拡大する方針だ。◆The recent surges in the yen's strength have made it imperative for Japanese carmakers to substantially bring down their parts procurement costs by overseas sourcing. 最近の円高で、日本の自動車メーカー各社は、海外調達による部品調達コストの大幅引下げが緊急課題となっている。

sovereign　(名)主権国, 独立国, 国家, 政府・政府機関・政府系企業などの公的機関, 国債, ソブリン債, 英国の1ポンド金貨, ソブリン
◆Japan's government debt ratios are already among the highest for rated sovereigns. 日本の政府債務比率は、主要国の格付けですでに最高位にある。

sovereign　(形)最高の, 最高権力を持つ, 主権のある, (国家が)独立した, 特効のある, ソブリン
　sovereign debt portfolio　国債資産, 国債関連資産
　sovereign issuance　ソブリン債の発行
　sovereign issuer　ソブリン発行体
　sovereign limits　国家向け融資限度
　sovereign loan [lending]　ソブリン融資, 国家向けローン, ソブリン・ローン
　sovereign offerings　ソブリン債の起債
　sovereign risk　国家向けローンのリスク, ソブリン・リスク　（=country risk）
　sovereign support　政府支援

◆When the sovereign debt crisis broke out in the peripheral countries in 2010, the eurozone governments did not accurately appraise losses from sovereign debt portfolios on the part of banks. 2010年に財政危機が周辺国で発生した際、ユーロ圏の各国政府は、銀行の国債関連資産の損失を正確に評価しなかった。

sovereign bond　国債
◆European banks hold massive volumes of the eurozone's sovereign bonds. 欧州の銀行は、ユーロ圏の国債を大量に抱えている。◆Sovereign bonds are considered in general to be risk-free and highly liquid. 国債は、一般に安全で現金化しやすいと考えられている。◆Standard & Poor's is considering a possible downgrade on the credit ratings of long-term sovereign bonds issued by 15 eurozone states. 米格付け会社のスタンダード・アンド・プアーズ（S&P）は、ユーロ圏15か国発行の長期国債格付け［信用格付け］を、引下げ方向で検討している。

sovereign bond price　国債価格
◆The debacle of the eurozone's sovereign bond prices caused losses to banks possessing peripheral sovereign bonds as their assets. ユーロ圏の国債価格の暴落で、周辺国の国債を資産として抱える銀行は、損失を被った。

sovereign borrower　ソブリン発行体, 借り手の国家機関
◆Even a sovereign borrower like Greece may default on its debts. ギリシャのようなソブリン発行体でも、債務不履行になる可能性がある。

sovereign credit rating　国債の格付け
（⇒government debt ratios）
◆S&P lowered Japan's long-term sovereign credit rating to AA minus from AA. 米格付け会社のスタンダード・アンド・プアーズ（S&P）は、日本の長期国債格付けを現在の「ダブルA」から「ダブルAマイナス」に引き下げた。

sovereign debt　国債の利回り, 国債金利
◆Cabinet ministers showed mixed reactions to the downgrading of Japanese sovereign debt by Standard & Poor's Corp. スタンダード・アンド・プアーズ（S&P）による日本の国債格下げに対して、閣僚らは複雑な反応を示した。◆The debacle of the eurozone's sovereign bond prices caused losses to banks possessing peripheral sovereign debts as their assets. ユーロ圏の国債価格の暴落で、周辺国の国債を資産として抱える銀行は、損失を被った。◆The ECB buyouts of sovereign debts of eurozone countries with fiscal laxity are the nightmare scenario Germany has been fearing. 欧州中銀（ECB）による放漫財政のユーロ圏諸国の国債買切りは、ドイツが恐れていた最悪のシナリオだ。◆The euro crisis has spread to Spain and Italy with interest rates on their sovereign debts soaring. ユーロ危機はスペインとイタリアに波及し、両国国債の金利が急騰した。◆Yields on sovereign debt of Spain surged and Italy began seeing yields on its government bonds shoot up. スペインの国債金利が上昇し、イタリアの国債金利も急騰している。

sovereign debt crisis　財政危機, 政府債務危機, ソブリン債危機, 国家の財政危機［債務危機］
◆European banks should have bolstered their capital bases when the sovereign debt crisis broke out in the peripheral countries in 2010. 2010年に周辺国で財政危機が発生した際、欧州銀行は資本基盤［自己資本］を強化すべきであった。◆Eurozone countries were so slow to take necessary actions that the sovereign debt crisis expanded. 欧州の必要な対応が後手に回ったために、ソブリン危機［政府債務危機］が拡大した。◆Greece is the epicenter of the sovereign debt crisis in Europe. ギリシャが、欧州の財政危機の元凶［震源地］だ。◆In Europe, the sovereign debt crisis is putting pressure on an economic recovery. 欧州では、財政危機が景気回復の重圧になっている。◆Italy's sovereign debt crisis may spill over to other European countries. イタリアの財政危機は、他の欧州諸

国に波及しかねない。◆Japan, the United States and emerging countries are upping their pressure on Europe to contain the Greek-triggered sovereign debt crisis. 日米と新興国は、欧州に対して、ギリシャに端を発したソブリン危機（政府債務危機）封じ込めの圧力を強めている。◆Major central banks will cooperate to offer three-month U.S. dollar loans to commercial banks in the wake of Europe's sovereign debt crisis. 欧州の財政危機を受け、主要中央銀行が、協調して商業銀行に3か月物ドル資金を供給することになった。◆The eurozone's critical mistake is the eurozone's belittling of the risk of the sovereign debt crisis aggravating the banking crisis and vice versa. ユーロ圏の重大な誤りは、国家の財政危機と銀行の危機［経営危機］が相互に増幅し合う危険性を、ユーロ圏が軽視したことにある。◆The Greek-triggered sovereign debt crisis has been throwing the eurozone into financial uncertainty and multiple crises. ギリシャに端を発した債務危機問題で、ユーロ圏は金融不安と複合的な危機に陥っている。◆The Greek-triggered sovereign debt crisis resulted in the breakup of the French-Belgian bank Dexia which held Greek government bonds. ギリシャが引き金になったソブリン危機（政府債務危機）問題で、ギリシャ国債を保有していた仏ベルギー系金融機関のデクシア(Dexia)が、解体に追い込まれた。◆Worldwide concern over fiscal sustainability in industrialized countries is growing in the wake of Greece's sovereign debt crisis. ギリシャの財政危機を契機として、先進国の財政の持続可能性に対する世界の関心が高まっている。

sovereign debt portfolio　国債資産, 国債関連資産
◆When the sovereign debt crisis broke out in the peripheral countries in 2010, the eurozone governments did not accurately appraise losses from sovereign debt portfolios on the part of banks. 2010に財政危機が周辺国で発生した際、ユーロ圏の各国政府は、銀行の国債関連資産の損失を正確に評価しなかった。

sovereign risk　ソブリン（政府債務）危機, ソブリン・リスク, カントリー・リスク　（対外融資先が公的機関の場合の債権回収リスクで、これには国債の利払い・元本償還の不履行、資本移動の制限、課税の強化、投資先企業の破たんなどが含まれる）
◆When the sovereign debt crisis broke out in the peripheral countries in 2010, the eurozone governments did not accurately appraise losses from sovereign debt portfolios on the part of banks. 2010に財政危機が周辺国で発生した際、ユーロ圏の各国政府は、銀行の国債関連資産の損失を正確に評価しなかった。

sovereign safety net　加盟国救済策
◆On May 10, 2010, the EU and the IMF came up with a €750 billion sovereign safety net to defend the embattled eurozone. 2010年5月10日に、欧州連合(EU)と国際通貨基金(IMF)は、（財政）危機に陥ったユーロ圏を守るため7,500億ユーロ（約89兆円）の加盟国救済策を発表した。◆Stock prices in Tokyo fell by more than 600 points as a state of panic gripped investors and selling pressure snowballed. 東京市場の株価は、投資家がパニック状態に陥り、売り圧力が増大［加速］したため、下げ幅が600円を超えた。

sovereign state　国家
◆Even if it is a sovereign state or a bank, heavily indebted borrowers may face a crisis for insolvency or a lack of liquidity. 国家でも銀行でも、巨額の債務を抱えた発行体は、返済不能か流動性不足で危機に陥る可能性がある。

sovereign wealth fund　政府系投資ファンド, 政府系ファンド, ソブリン・ウエルス・ファンド, SWF （=government-affiliated investment fund, government-run investment fund: 政府が運用するファンドで、その原資の公的資金は主に中央銀行の外貨準備高や国有天然資源で得られる利益であることが多い）
◆Sovereign wealth funds have grown to $2 trillion -3 trillion globally as a result of skyrocketing crude oil prices and accumulation of foreign exchange reserves in emerging market economies. 政府系投資ファンドの運用総額は、原油価格の急騰と急成長市場国の外貨準備高の増加で、世界全体で2兆〜3兆ドルに拡大している。◆The government is planning to establish a sovereign wealth fund in fiscal 2009. 政府は、2009年度に政府系投資ファンドの創設を計画している。◆The sovereign wealth fund will buy up dormant patents owned by companies and universities. 同政府系投資ファンドは、企業や大学が保有する休眠特許を買い取る方針だ。
世界の主な政府系ファンド：

アラブ首長国連邦	アブダビ投資庁
クウェート	クェート投資銀行
サウジアラビア	サウジ通貨庁
シンガポール	シンガポール政府投資公社
中国	中国投資有限責任公司
ノルウェー	政府年金基金
ロシア	準備基金

Spain　（名）スペイン
◆It became evident that the Greek debt crisis would spill over into Spain. ギリシャの財政危機がスペインに波及することが、確実になった。◆Spain also faces a huge budget deficit. スペインも、巨額の財政赤字を抱えている。◆The 10-year bond yield of Spain has likewise neared the 7 percent level, the danger zone that may fall into a debt crisis. スペインの10年物国債利回り［国債流通利回り］も、債務危機に陥る恐れがある危険水域の7%台に迫った。◆Yields on sovereign debt of Spain surged and Italy began seeing yields on its government bonds shoot up. スペインの国債金利が上昇し、イタリアの国債金利も急騰している。

span　（名）長さ, 期間, 全期間, 全長, 全幅, 全範囲, スパン
a life span　寿命, 一生
a long span of time　長い期間
a short span of time　短い期間
the average life span　平均寿命
the span of control　統制範囲, 管理限界
the span of management　管理範囲, 管理限界
◆About ¥1.9 trillion of taxpayers' money was spent over a ten year span until last fiscal year to cover losses from a surging number of uncollectible loans guaranteed by a public credit guarantee scheme for small and midsize companies. 中小企業のための公的信用保証制度により保証される融資の貸倒れ件数が急増し、それによる損失の穴埋めをするために、昨年度までの10年間で約1兆9,000億円の税金が投入された。

spanking　（形）活発な, 敏速な, きびきび動く, 素晴らしい, 素敵な, 顕著な, 著しい, とても速い, 素早い　（副）とても, 極めて, ひじょうに
expand at a spanking clip　顕著なペースで拡大する, 急速に拡大する
have a spanking good time　とても楽しい時を過ごす
◆The economy, fueled by a pickup in business spending on inventories, is now expanding at a spanking clip. 企業の在庫投資の回復に支えられた経済は現在、顕著なペースで拡大している。

spark　（動）引き起こす, 誘発する, 〜に火を付ける, 〜の火付け役となる, 〜の原因となる, かき立てる, 奮起させる, 鼓舞する(animate), 刺激する(stimulate), 活気づける, 促進させる(stir up), 火花を飛ばす
spark off　〜を起こす, 〜を引き起こす, 〜を誘発する, 〜のきっかけとなる, 〜の発端［直接原因］になる
spark off a chain reaction　連鎖反応を起こす
spark one's interest in　〜への関心に火を付ける
spark the economy with lower (interest) rates　利下げで

景気を刺激する
◆Speculation the Bank of Japan will end its quantitative monetary easing policy soon has sparked a rise in mid- and long-term interest rates. 日銀が近く量の緩和策を解除するとの思惑から、(金融市場では)中長期の金利が上昇し始めた。◆The dollar's sharp depreciation may spark repeated drops in prices of shares and securities. ドルの急落は、株安、債券安の繰り返しを招く恐れがある。◆The worldwide recession began with the financial crisis sparked by the collapse of U.S. investment bank Lehman Brothers. 世界同時不況は、米国の投資銀行リーマン・ブラザーズの経営破たんが誘発した金融危機から始まった。◆Tokyo stocks fell to a three-month low as foreign investors sparked a sell-off. 東京株(東京株式市場の株価)は、外国人投資家が株を売り進めたため3か月ぶりに急落した。

spate (名)大量, 多量, 多数, 多発, 続発, 殺到, 洪水, 氾濫, 豪雨
a spate of failures at major financial institutions 相次ぐ大手金融機関の経営破たん
a spate of inquiries 相次ぐ問い合わせ, 殺到する問い合わせ, 問い合わせの殺到
a spate of new issuances 相次ぐ新規発行, 大量起債
a spate of politics-and-money scandals 相次ぐ政治とカネの問題
be in (full) spate 氾濫している
◆Many people are dissatisfied that the president of Japan Post Holdings Co. has never been called to task for the spate of scandals involving the company. 日本郵政の相次ぐ不祥事に対する同社社長の責任が問われていない[同社社長の責任が不問に付されている]ことに、多くの国民は納得していない。◆The number of surplus workers approached a peak of 3.59 million in the January-March quarter of 1999, following a spate of failures at major financial institutions. 過剰雇用者数は、大手金融機関の破たんが相次いだ後の1999年1-3月期に、359万人のピークに達した。◆The spate of scandals involving Olympus Corp.'s false financial statements has been widely reported overseas. オリンパスの有価証券報告書の虚偽記載に関する一連の疑惑は、海外で大きく報じられた。

SPC 特定目的会社, 特別目的会社 (special purpose companyの略)
◆When Mycal established the SPC, it transferred the ownership of 20 profitable stores to it, issuing the bonds with the stores as collateral. マイカルが特定目的会社(SPC)を設立したとき、マイカルは20の黒字店舗の所有権をSPCに移し、この店舗を担保に社債を発行した。

special (形)特別の, 特定の, 特殊な, 別段の, 別枠の, スペシャル
special acceptance (手形の)制限引受け
special assessment 特別課税
special bank 特殊銀行
special bid 特別買付け(売買の相手が決まっていて形式的に市場を通す取引)
special credit 買取り銀行指定信用状
special crossed check 特定線引き小切手
special crossing 特別線引き
special deposit 特別預金, 別口預金, 別段預金
special deposit account 総合口座
special dividend 特別配当
special drawing rights IMFの特別引出権, SDR[SDRs]
special endorsement 指図式裏書き, 記名裏書き
special loan 別枠融資
special note 記名式約束手形
special offering 特別売出し, 特別多量売出し
special partner 特別社員, 有限責任社員(limited partner)

special profit 特別利益 (⇒book)
special reserve 特別積立金, 別途積立金
special account 特定口座, 特別会計
(⇒registration, specified account)
◆A special account is used to finance public investment and loans to government-affiliated financial institutions. 特別会計は、政府系金融機関に財政投融資の資金を供給するのに用いられる。◆Insurance payments for the March 11 earthquake and tsunami will drain the resources of insurance firms and the government's special account. 東日本大震災の保険金支払いで、保険会社と政府の特別会計の原資は大幅に目減りすることになる。◆The government can tap its special account to cover 50 percent to 95 percent of insurance payment claims when total earthquake insurance payouts exceed ¥115 billion. 地震保険の支払い総額が1,150億円を超えると、政府は特別会計を利用して保険金支払い請求額の50〜95%を負担することができる。◆The special account borrows from the private sector and other sources to make up for local government's budget shortfalls. 特別会計は、民間などの財源からの借入れで地方の財源不足[財政赤字]の穴埋めをしている。◆The special account is expected to collect a large surplus in fiscal 2011 via the repayment of loans. 特別会計は、貸付け金の返済で2011年度は多額の剰余金が生じる見込みだ。

special assessment bond 特別課税債 (=special district bond, special purpose bond, special tax bond: 米国の州政府や地方自治体が発行する地方債の一種で、公共事業の受益者に対する特別課税を担保として発行する債券)

special deduction system 特別控除制度
◆In the United States, a special deduction system has been implemented that allows investors to carry over capital losses from stock transactions in their current tax return to future years. 米国では、税務申告上、株式売買による譲渡損失を翌年以降に繰り越すことができる特別控除制度が実施されている。

special drawing rights 国際通貨基金(IMF)の特別引出し権(1970年にIMFが創設した人工的な国際通貨。通称で、「ペーパー・ゴールド(paper gold)」ともいう)
◆Japan's foreign exchange reserves consist mainly of securities and deposits denominated in foreign currencies, gold, and reserve positions and special drawing rights at the International Monetary Fund. 日本の外貨準備高の主な内訳は、外貨建て債、外貨預金、金のほか、IMF(国際通貨基金)の準備ポジションと特別引出し権である。

special government bond 復興債, 特別国債
◆A redemption of the special government bonds for disaster reconstruction is scheduled to begin about 10 years from now. 震災復興債の償還期間は、今から10年程度となる予定だ。◆Funds for disaster reconstruction will be procured by issuing special government bonds. 震災復興の資金は、復興債を発行して調達する。

special inspection 金融庁の特別検査
(⇒inject public funds, regular inspection)
◆The FSA's special inspection will check the major banks' large-lot corporate borrowers whose stock prices or credit ratings have sharply declined. 金融庁の特別検査は、大手銀行の株価や格付けなどが急落した大口融資先を査定の対象としている。◆The special inspections will be conducted as banks review the positions of their debtors, and will be finalized before the closing of accounts. 特別検査は、銀行が債務者の経営状態を見直す際に行われ、決算までに完了する。

special investment vehicle 特別投資会社, SIV
◆Commercial banks have created special investment vehicles (SIVs) in order to escape the capital adequacy regulation imposed by the Basel accord. 銀行は、バーゼル協定[バーゼル合意]による自己資本比率規制を回避するため、特

別投資会社(SIV)を新設している。

special loan　特別融資
◆The Bank of Japan decided to extend a special loan to Namihaya Bank after the second-tier regional bank was declared insolvent. 日本銀行は、第二地方銀行の「なみはや銀行」が破たん認定を受けた後、同行に対して特別融資[特融]を実施することを決めた。

special on-the-spot inspection　特別立ち入り検査
◆The Financial Services Agency will conduct special on-the-spot inspections at the major clients of the nation's 12 leading banks. 金融庁が、国内大手銀行12行の大口融資先を対象に特別立入り検査を行う。

special purpose company　特別目的会社, 特定目的会社, SPC（=special purpose corporation, special purpose entity: 不動産や債権の証券化など、特別の目的を持って設立される会社。有価証券を発行、小口化して広く資金を調達できるメリットがある）
◆Dividend payments to bond holders have been financed by the rent paid by Mycal to the special purpose company (SPC). 社債保有者に支払う配当金の原資は、マイカルが特定目的会社に支払う店舗の家賃だ。◆Under the system of securitization of real estate, special purpose companies established by real estate firms issue shares in real estate by using the property as collateral. この不動産の証券化の制度では、不動産会社が設立する特定目的会社(SPC)が、(買い取った)不動産を担保にして不動産の株式(有価証券)を発行する。◆When Mycal established the special purpose company (SPC), it transferred the ownership of 20 profitable stores to it, issuing the bonds with the stores as collateral. マイカルが特定目的会社(SPC)を設立したとき、マイカルは20の黒字店舗の所有権をSPCに移し、この店舗を担保に社債を発行した。

specialist　(名)専門業者, スペシャリスト（一般の投資家とは取引せず、特定の株式銘柄について市場形成(market making)の役割を担っている証券業者）

specialist's short-sale ratio　スペシャリスト空売り比率（ニューヨーク証券取引所のスペシャリストの空売り比率）

specialize in　~を専門に行う, ~を専門に扱う, ~を専門とする
◆Sony Bank specializes in online services. ソニー銀行は、ネット専業銀行だ。

specialized　(形)専門化した, 特殊化した, 専門の, 専業の, 専用の
　industry specialized fund　特定産業ファンド
　specialized accounting　特殊会計
　specialized audit software　監査専用ソフト
　specialized bank　専業銀行
　specialized financial institution　専門金融機関
　specialized mutual fund　特定銘柄投資信託
　specialized niche　専門分野

specific　(形)特定の, 特別の, 具体的な, 明確な, はっきりした, 個々の, 個別の, 特有の, 固有の, 独特の, (課税が)重量の　(名)細部, 細目, 詳細, 特性, 特効薬, 具体策
　a specific feature　特徴
　a specific sum of money　一定の金額
　be short on specifics　具体策に乏しい
　changes in specific prices　個別物価変動
　company-specific factors　各社特有の要因, 各社に特有の要因
　industry-specific risks　業界特有のリスク
　meet specific customer needs　顧客の個々のニーズに対応する
　security-specific risk　証券固有のリスク
　specific capital　特定資本

　specific charge　特定担保
　specific equity　特定持ち分（債権者持ち分と優先株持ち分）
　specific goals　個々の目標
　specific goods　専門品
　specific instructions　具体的な指示
　specific nature　具体的な内容, 特性
　specific performance　特定履行（契約どおりに債務を履行させること）
　specific policies　個々の方針
　specific policy　特定保険証券
　specific price index numbers　特殊物価指数
　specific purpose　はっきりした目的, 明確な目的
　specific requirements　具体的な要求
　specific risk　固有のリスク
　specific sectors　特定の業種
　specific securities　個別証券
　specific single-currency lending window　特定の単一通貨建て融資制度
　specific stockholder　特定株主
　specific tariff　従量税
　（=specific duties, specific tax）
◆The purpose of issuing a sizable amount of new shares is to maintain the control of a specific stockholder over the company. 新株の大量発行は、同社に対する特定株主の支配権[経営支配権]確保が目的だ。

specified　(形)明記した[明記された], 明示した, 詳述した, 確定した, 指定の, 特定の, 一定の, 別段の, 制限された
　at a forward specified date　期日に
　redemption of the specified bond　対象債券の償還
　specified benefit　確定給付
　specified check　記名式小切手
　specified date　指定期日
　specified deposit　別段預金
　specified enterprise　制限業種, 特定企業
　specified grace period　一定の据え置き期間
　specified list　貨物明細表
　specified money trust　特定金銭信託
　specified office　指定事務所
　specified policy　特約保険
　specified revolving period　規定のリボルビング[回転融資, 回転貸付け]期間
　specified stocks　指定銘柄, 特定銘柄

specified account　特定口座　（=special account; ⇒ registration, self-assessment, stock trading）
◆Establishing specified accounts will free investors from the need to file tax returns. (証券会社に)特定口座を設けると、個人投資家は自分で税務申告[確定申告]をする必要がなくなる。
|解説|特定口座とは：株式投資を促進するための新証券税制で、個人投資家の納税(税務)手続きを証券会社が代行する制度。2003年1月から実施。上場株式を売却した際の利益への課税方式には、源泉分離と申告分離の二つがあったが、これが2003年1月から申告分離に一本化された。申告分離は、年間の株式売却額の合計から取得額などを差し引いた売却益を投資家自身が計算して税務署に翌春、確定申告する方式のこと。

specified accounts service　特定口座サービス
◆Some major and midsize securities houses have been sponsoring free seminars on the new taxation law to attract new customers by explaining the advantages of the specified accounts service. 一部の大手・準大手証券会社は、特定口座サービスの利点を説明して新規顧客を取り込むため、新税法(新証

券税制）についてのセミナーを無料で開催している。

Specified [Specific] Commercial Transactions Law 特定商取引法（訪問販売法が、2000年の改正で「特定商取引法」に変更された。その対象は訪問販売や通信販売、電話勧誘販売など六つの取引形態で、クーリングオフや違反があった場合の行政処分や刑事罰も規定されている）
◆The company was ordered by the prefectural governments of Kyoto, Osaka and Hyougo to suspend its business over the violation of the Specified Commercial Transactions Law for its aggressive sales methods. 同社は、強引な勧誘を行ったため、京都、大阪、兵庫の3府県から特定商取引法違反で業務停止命令を受けた。

specify （動）明記する, 明示する, 詳述する, 指定する, 特定する, 定める, 指示する
◆The special statement on the world economy adopted by the APEC forum specified a timeline for implementing the measures. アジア太平洋経済協力会議（APEC）で採択された世界経済に関する特別声明は、その対策実施の期限を明記した。

specter [spectre] （名）怖いもの, 恐ろしさ, 不安, 不安のもと, 不安材料, 懸念, 懸念材料, 幽霊, 亡霊, 被害妄想の種
raise the specter of ～の観測を強める, ～の懸念が高まる, ～の脅威を騒ぎたてる
the specter of a global downturn 世界不況の懸念, 世界同時不況の観測
the specter of wage inflation 賃金インフレの懸念
◆The ongoing business slump raises the specter of a global downturn comparable to the Great Depression that started in 1929. 今回の不況は、1929年に始まった世界大恐慌に匹敵するほどの世界同時不況の懸念が高まっている。

speculate （動）推測する, 憶測する, 考える, 観測する, 投機をする, 相場に手を出す, 思惑をやる, 思惑買いをする, やまを張る
speculate about one's future 将来をよく考える
speculate for [on] a rise 騰貴を予想して投機をする
speculate on interest rates 金利の思惑で投資する
speculate on [in] stocks 株に手を出す
（=speculate in shares）
◆It is widely speculated that the Bank of Japan will lift its zero-interest rate policy by summer. 日銀は夏にもゼロ金利政策を解除する、との観測が強い。

speculation （名）投機, 思惑, 思惑買い, 憶測, 推測, 観測, 相場（投機とは、配当や株価の短期的な値上がりを期待して株式を売買することをいう。⇒undertake）
be ruined by speculation 思惑買いで破産する
buy dollars on speculation 思惑でドルを買う
commodity speculation 商品投機
counter speculation 対抗投機
currency speculation 為替投機
（=exchange speculation）
dabble in speculation 相場に手を出す, 投機に手を出す
devaluation-speculation cycle 為替切下げ・投機循環
engage in speculation 投機をやる
excessive speculation 過当投機
land speculation 土地投機
lose heavily in speculation 相場［投機］に手を出して大損をする
lose money through speculation 相場で損をする
make a hit in a speculation 投機が当たる
make money through speculation 相場で儲（もう）ける
on [for] speculation 投機で, 思惑で
productive speculation 生産的投機
property speculation 不動産投機, 土地投機

real estate speculation 不動産投機
speculation about [on] another rate [interest rate] hike 再値上げの観測, もう一段の利上げ観測, 再利上げに関する思惑
speculation by foreign investment funds 海外投資ファンドの投機
speculation stock 仕手株
stock speculation 株式投機
trade on speculation 値幅とり
◆Speculation that some major banks may find themselves with capital shortfalls and then nationalized is driving investors to dump the banks' shares. 大手行の一部が自己資本不足に陥って国有化されるとの思惑から、投資家は銀行株の売りに出ている。◆Speculation that the Fed would cut interest rates Tuesday heightened. 連邦準備制度理事会（FRB）が火曜日に利下げに踏み切るとの観測も、浮上している。◆Speculation the Bank of Japan will end its quantitative monetary easing policy soon has sparked a rise in mid- and long-term interest rates. 日銀が近く量的緩和策を解除するとの思惑から、（金融市場では）中長期の金利が上昇し始めた。◆The collapse of Dai-ichi Kaden on April 16 was the result of speculation by foreign investment funds of a dubious nature. 4月16日の第一家電の経営破たんは、実態不明の海外投資ファンドの投機によるものであった［海外ファンドの投機に食い荒らされた末路であった］。◆There were speculations that only three or four Japanese banks could survive intensified global competition. 熾烈な国際競争に生き残れる邦銀は3〜4行だけ、と見る向きもあった。◆Weak U.S. jobs data added to speculation that the U.S. Federal Reserve may implement further monetary easing. 米国の雇用統計の悪化で、連邦準備制度理事会（FRB）による追加の金融緩和実施の観測が高まった［連邦準備制度理事会（FRB）が追加の金融緩和に踏み切るとの観測が強まった］。

speculative （形）投機的な, 思惑による, 推測に基づく, 危険な, 理論的な
speculative activity 投機的活動, 投機的な動き
speculative attacks 投機的な売り, 投機売り, 投棄圧力, 投機筋の攻撃, 投機的な動き
speculative behavior 投機的行動
speculative business 投機事業, 投機的取引, 投機売買, 思惑取引
speculative buy orders 投機的な買い注文
speculative buyers 思惑買い筋
speculative buying 投機的な買い, 思惑買い
speculative cash 投機的現金
speculative dealing 仕手戦
speculative demand 投機的需要, 思惑需要, 仮需要
speculative demand for money 貨幣の投機的需要, 投機的貨幣動機
speculative element 投機的要素
speculative enthusiasm [craze, fever] 投機熱
speculative expansionary effect 投機的拡張効果
speculative fluctuation 投機の変動
speculative gain 投機利潤, 投機的利潤
speculative grade 投機的格付け
speculative grade bond 投機的格付け債券, 高利回り債
speculative group 投機集団
（⇒stock prices in Tokyo）
speculative holders 思惑手控え筋, 投機的保有者
speculative import 思惑輸入
speculative importation 見越し輸入
speculative interests 思惑筋, 投機筋
speculative inventory holdings 投機的在庫保有量

speculative investment　投資的投資, 思惑投資
speculative leaders　仕手株
speculative loss　投機的損失
speculative medium　投機的手段
speculative mood　思惑気分
speculative motive　投機的動機
speculative name　仕手銘柄
speculative operation　投機取引, 投機的操作
speculative pressure　投機圧力
speculative price　投機価格
speculative production　見越し生産
speculative profit　投機利潤, 投機の利潤
　（=speculative gain）
speculative purchase　思惑買い, 投機買い
　（=speculative buying）
speculative risk　投機的危険, 投機的リスク
speculative stock　仕手株, 投機株
　（=speculative issue, speculative leader）
speculative stock trading　投機的な株取引
speculative supply　投機的供給
speculative trade　投機売買, 見越し売買
speculative trader　投機筋
　（⇒flagging stock prices）
speculative transaction　投機性の高い取引, 投機的取引, 投機売買, 思惑取引　（⇒hedge fund）
speculative venture　投機的事業, 投機事業
　（=speculative business, speculative enterprise）
◆The commodity market of crude futures has become increasingly speculative. 原油先物の商品市場は、次第に投機色を強めている。◆The government bonds were considered high risk, rated "speculative" at the time of issuance. この国債は、発行時点で「投機的」格付けで、リスクが大きいと見なされた。

speculative buying [buy, purchase]　投機的な買い, 投機買い, 思惑買い, 見越し買い
◆The surge in the yen is partly due to speculative buying. 円高の一因は、思惑買いにある。

speculative funds　投機資金, 投機マネー
　（=speculative money）
◆Recently, a sizable amount of speculative funds have been flowing into New York's commodities exchanges. このところ、ニューヨークの商品取引所には、大量の投機資金が流入している。◆Speculative funds are leaving the oil market. 投機マネーが、原油市場から逃げ出している。◆The continuing oil price hikes can be attributed to an uninterrupted flow of speculative funds into the market. 原油の値上がりが続いているのは、投機マネーが絶え間なく[続々と]市場に流れ込んでいるからだ。

speculative hedge fund　投機性の高い短期投資資金
◆The underdeveloped state of financial systems in East Asian countries allowed a massive influx and exodus of short-term speculative hedge funds from abroad. 東アジア諸国の金融システムの未整備が、海外からの投機性の高い短期投資資金の大量流入と流出を許した。

speculative investment　投機の運用, 投機的な投資, 投機
◆Financial authorities should stiffen the penalties for illegal transactions to protect the financial system from rumors and speculative investment. 金融当局は違法取引（違法行為）に対する罰則を強化して、金融システムを風評や投機（投機的投資）から守らなければならない。◆Making speculative investments is prohibited at the credit union. 同信用組合では、投機の運用は禁止されている。

speculative investor　投機的投資家, 投機家, 投機筋

　（=speculator）
◆Speculative investors are shifting from commodities to stocks. 投機資金が、商品から株式に移っている。

speculative market　投機市場, 思惑市場, 仕手市場, 思惑市況
◆Speculative markets are nothing but a legalized gambling casino. 投機市場は、合法的な賭博（とばく）場も同然だ。

speculative money　投機資金, 投機マネー
　（=speculative funds; ⇒appreciation of currencies）
◆If speculative money makes an exodus from the U.S. market and shifts into the money market in East Asia, economic turmoil could break out again. 投機資金が米国離れを起こし、東アジアの金融市場を目指すようなことになれば、再び経済混乱が起きる可能性もある。◆Service charges or tax on crude oil futures trading should be raised to curb the inflow of speculative money not related to actual demand. 実需に関係ない投機マネーの流入を抑えるため、原油先物取引の手数料の引上げや課税強化をすべきだ。◆South Korea, Brazil and India are guiding their currencies lower to deal with an influx of speculative money. 韓国、ブラジルとインドは、投機マネーの流入に対応するため、自国通貨安に誘導している。◆Speculative money is causing appreciation of currencies and inflation in emerging economies. 投機マネーが、新興国の通貨高やインフレを招いている。◆The flow of speculative money into the oil market did not reflect actual demand. 投機マネーの原油市場への流入は、実需を反映していなかった[実需に基づくものではなかった]。◆With such moves to rein in investment funds, speculative money started to exit the markets. 投資ファンドを規制するこうした動きで、投機マネーが市場から逃避し始めた。

speculative selling　投機的な売り, 投機売り
◆The weakening of the dollar and appreciation of other currencies spurred by speculative selling is not favorable for the global economy. 投機的な売りに押されたドル安・各国通貨高は、世界の経済にとって好ましくない。◆U.S. Treasury Secretary John Snow and other administration officials repeated remarks about allowing a weak dollar, consequently accelerating the speculative selling. スノー財務長官など米政府当局者がドル安容認の発言を繰り返して、投機的な売りを加速した。

speculative trader　投機筋
◆The measures to boost flagging stock prices focus on encouraging financial institutions to sell off cross-held shares and tightening monitoring of short selling of stocks by international speculative traders. 急落する株価へのテコ入れ策の柱は、金融機関が保有する持ち合い株の売却促進と、海外投機筋による株の空売りへの監視強化である。

speculator　（名）相場師, 投機筋, 投機家, 投機筋, 仕手筋, だふ屋　（=speculative investor: 短期勝負の株式売買を行う投資家のこと。⇒buying factor, surveillance）
land speculator　地上げ屋
speculator buying　投機買い, 思惑買い
stock speculator　仕手筋
◆If Japan is acting weak in currency intervention, speculators will try to capitalize on that. 日本が為替介入に弱腰なら、投機筋に付け込まれることになる。◆Speculators apparently take advantage of the sluggish response of the government and the Bank of Japan to the yen's appreciation. 投機筋は、政府・日銀の円高への対応の鈍さに付け込んでいるようだ。◆Speculators believe the government will not take any specific action to stem the yen's rise for the time being. 政府は当分、とくに円高阻止に動くようなことはない、と投機筋は踏んでいる。◆Speculators capitalized on the Bank of Japan's delay in taking action. 投機筋は、日銀の対応の遅れを突いた。◆Speculators have taken advantage of this opportunity. 投機筋が、この隙（すき）を突いた。◆These moves were partly aimed at preventing speculators from selling a massive num-

ber of shares they held in these banks. これらの動きの狙いは、一つには仕手筋が保有する大量の銀行株を仕手筋が売り浴びせるのを避けることにあった。

spend (動)支出する, 投資する, 資金を投入する, 金などを使う, 消費する
 spend on machinery and equipments　設備投資する, 設備投資を行う
 ◆About ￥1.9 trillion of taxpayers' money was spent over a ten year span until last fiscal year to cover losses from a surging number of uncollectible loans guaranteed by a public credit guarantee scheme for small and midsize companies. 中小企業のための公的信用保証制度により保証される融資の貸倒れ件数が急増し、それによる損失の穴埋めをするために、昨年度までの10年間で約1兆9,000億円の税金が投入された。◆Olympus wrote off more than 75 percent of about 70 billion spent on the acquisitions of three domestic firms as impairment losses. オリンパスは、国内3社の買収に投じた約700億円の75%以上を、減耗損失として処理していた。◆Sharp Corp. will spend an additional ￥200 billion to quadruple the production capacity of its liquid crystal display panel factory in Kameyama. シャープは、2,000億円追加投資して、液晶パネル[液晶ディスプレー・パネル]亀山工場(三重県亀山市)の生産能力を4倍に拡大する。◆The company plans to spend about ￥500 billion to build one of the world's largest DRAM plants. 同社は、約5,000億円を投資して、世界最大規模のDRAM(記憶保持動作が必要な随時書込み読出しメモリ)工場を建設する方針だ。◆The U.S. administration will spend up to $700 billion to buy up soured mortgage-related securities and other devalued assets held by ailing financial institutions. 米政府は、経営不振の金融機関が保有するモーゲージ関連の不良証券などの不良資産を、最大7,000億ドル投入して買い取る方針だ。

spending (名)支出, 歳出, 予算, 経費, 投資, 消費
 a spending boom[spree]　消費景気
 capital goods spending　資本財需要
 capital spending　設備投資, 資本支出
 construction spending　建設支出
 consumer spending　個人消費支出, 消費支出, 個人消費, 家計部門の支出
 corporate spending　企業の支出, 設備投資
 current spending　経常支出
 cut down on[reduce]spending　消費を減らす, 消費を切り詰める[控える], 消費[歳出]を削減する
 debt-servicing spending　国債費
 deficit spending　超過支出
 discretionary spending　裁量的経費
 domestic spending　内需, 国内支出
 external spending　対外支出
 federal spending　連邦政府支出, 連邦支出, 連邦予算, 国家支出
 fiscal spending　財政支出
 government spending　歳出, 政府支出, 財政支出
 growth of Federal spending　国家支出の増大
 household spending　個人消費, 家計支出
 investment spending　公共投資
 mandatory spending　義務的経費
 massive spending　巨額の歳出, 巨額の支出 (⇒red ink)
 military spending　軍事費, 軍事支出, 国防関連支出
 personal spending　個人消費, 個人支出
 private spending　民間支出
 public spending　公共支出, 公共投資
 public spending package　財政出動
 real consumer spending　実質消費支出
 rebound of[in]spending　消費の回復
 reductions in government spending　歳出削減
 rein in spending　消費を抑える, 歳出を抑制する
 social spending　福祉予算, 社会支出, 社会制度の支出
 spending cutbacks　財政支出削減
 spending habit　消費性向, 消費習慣
 spending money　ポケット・マネー
 spending on goods and services　モノやサービスへの支出
 spending on public works projects　公共事業関係費
 spending on R&D　研究開発費　(=R&D spending)
 spending policy　支出政策(有効需要を刺激して不況からの脱却を図る政策)
 spending power　購買力
 spending spree　消費景気　(=spending boom)
 spending unit　消費単位, 支出単位
 ◆A boost in public spending seems to be merely an excuse for pork-barrel spending. 財政出動[公共支出]の拡大は、単なる「バラマキ」の口実にすぎないようだ。◆Fiscal resources of ￥1.6 trillion cannot be scrounged together simply by recasting the budget and cutting wasteful spending. 1.6兆円の財源は、予算の組替えや無駄の削減だけでは捻出(ねんしゅつ)できない。◆In order to reduce the government's bond issuance, spending must be reined in as much as possible. 政府の国債発行額を減らすには、できるだけ歳出を抑制する必要がある。◆In view of the country's massive debts, it is essential to reduce spending. 国の巨額の借金を考えると、歳出削減は欠かせない。◆Of the ￥92 trillion in spending in the fiscal 2010 budget, a mere ￥37 trillion can be covered by tax revenue. 2010年度予算の歳出総額92兆円のうち、37兆円だけが税収で賄(まか)える。◆The massive figure of tax revenue shortfall is way beyond what local municipalities can do by cutting spending. この巨額の税収不足は、地方自治体の経費削減で対応できる範囲を大きく超えている。

spending cut　予算削減, 歳出削減, 支出削減, 経費削減
 ◆The federal government will initially make a spending cut of $900 billion, while it will raise the debt ceiling by the same amount immediately. 米政府はまず0.9兆ドルの歳出削減を行う一方、債務上限を直ちに引き上げる。

spending on inventories　在庫投資
 ◆The economy, fueled by a pickup in business spending on inventories, is now expanding at a spanking clip. 企業の在庫投資の回復に支えられた経済は現在、顕著なペースで拡大している。

spending on plant and equipment　設備投資
 ◆Major manufacturers plan to cut spending on plant and equipment. 大手製造業は、設備投資を削減する方針だ。

spending policy　支出政策(有効需要を刺激して不況からの脱却を図る政策), 財政政策
 ◆We must stop free spending policies and enhance fiscal discipline. 放漫財政を食い止め、財政規律を強化する必要がある。

spendthrift (形)浪費の, 濫費の, 金遣いの荒い, 金を湯水のように使う　(名)浪費家, 金遣いの荒い人
 spendthrift economy　浪費経済(生産したものをすべて消費する経済)
 spendthrift nation　財政赤字国, 財政危機に陥った国
 spendthrift trust　浪費者信託, 未成年者などの受益者のための信託　(=sheltering trust)
 ◆Spendthrift nations' overspending threatens Europe's single currency. 財政赤字国の過剰支出が、欧州のユーロを脅かしている。

spike (名)急増, 急騰, 大幅な上昇, 高騰
 a spike in food prices　食品価格の急騰
 a spike in the dollar　ドル急騰

a spike in wealth　資産増加
spike in fuel prices　燃料価格の急騰, 燃料価格の高騰
　◆A spike in fuel prices after Hurricane Katrina was the final blow for Delta Air Lines and Northwest Airlines. ハリケーン「カトリーナ」後の燃料価格の急騰が, デルタ航空とノースウエスト航空にとって最後の打撃となった。
spike in oil prices　原油価格の急騰, 原油価格の高騰
　◆The U.S. Fed concluded that a spike in oil prices will be temporary. 米連邦準備制度理事会(FRB)は, 「原油価格の高騰は一時的」とした。
spikes in prices　値上り, 価格の高騰
　◆The import prices of crude oil and grains have surged, causing spikes in the prices of food products and daily necessities that have dampened household spending. 原油や穀物の輸入価格高騰で, 食品や日用品の価格が上昇し, 個人消費も冷え込んでいる[個人消費の低迷を招いている]。
spill over　流出する, あふれる, あふれ出る, 広がる, 拡大する, 波及する, 飛び火する, 伝わる
　◆Italy is suffering from the financial crisis that spilled over from Greece. イタリアは, ギリシャから飛び火した財政危機に見舞われている。◆Italy's sovereign debt crisis may spill over to other European countries. イタリアの財政危機は, 他の欧州諸国に波及しかねない。◆The financial crisis engulfing the United States and European nations has spilled over into Japan. 欧米諸国を巻き込んだ金融危機が, 日本にも波及[飛び火]した。
spine　(名)背骨(backbone), 脊柱, 気骨, 根性, 負けじ魂, 勇気, 決断力, 忍耐力, 意志力
　lose one's spine　骨抜きになる
　◆The Stability and Growth Pact lost its spine in 2003 as the Germany government requested the relaxation of its terms. ユーロ圏の財政安定化・成長協定は, ドイツがその条件緩和を要求したため, 2003年に骨抜きになった。
spinoff　(名)分社化, 分社, 会社分割, 切り離し, スピンオフ　(=spin-off: 企業が事業の一部を切り離して別の会社に移すこと。⇒joint company)
　◆Another driving force behind the spinoff trend is mounting criticism of the lack of transparency at large corporations in the wake of Enron Corp.'s collapse. 分社化傾向の陰のもうひとつの推進力は, エンロンの経営破たんを受けて大企業の透明性に対する批判が高まっていることだ。◆The corporate group tax system is designed to encourage spinoffs and other corporate restructuring efforts amid protected recession. 連結納税制度のねらいは, 不況の長期化で分社化など企業の事業再構築努力を促すことにある。
spiral　(動)急騰する, 急増する, 急上昇[降下]する, らせん状に上昇[下降]する
　◆Merrill's losses spiraled toward more than $15 billion. メリルリンチの損失は, 150億ドル強に急拡大した。
spiral　(名)悪循環, 連鎖的変動, 連鎖的上昇[低下], 連鎖, 連続的変動, 急上昇, 急下降, 急増, らせん, 渦巻き線, スパイラル　(⇒deflationary spiral)
　a deflationary spiral　デフレの悪循環, デフレ的悪循環, デフレ・スパイラル
　a downward spiral　連鎖的急降下
　a land price spiral　地価高騰
　a spiral of rising wages and prices　上昇する賃金と物価の悪循環
　a wage-price spiral　賃金と物価の悪循環
　an inflationary spiral　インフレの悪循環, 悪性インフレ, らせん状的
　an upward spiral　連鎖的急上昇
　fall into a deflationary spiral　デフレ・スパイラル[デフレの悪循環]に陥る
　　(⇒sustainable recovery)
　the negative spiral in the financial market　金融市場の負のスパイラル(連鎖)
　the vicious spiral of wages and prices　賃金と物価の悪循環
　tumble into a dreaded deflationary spiral　恐怖のデフレ・スパイラルに落ち込む
　◆It is difficult to predict how long the negative spiral in the financial market will last. 金融市場の負のスパイラル(連鎖)がいつまで続くのか, 予想するのは難しい。
split　(動)分裂する, 離脱する, 解散する, 分離する, 分割する
　be split into two companies　2社に分割される
　split the firm's common stock 3 for 1　同社発行の普通株式1株を3株に分割する
　split the firm's one share into 100　同社株1株を100株に分割する
　◆The company will be split into a food supermarket chain and a real estate company to boost profitability. 同社は, 収益力を高めるため食品スーパーと不動産会社の2社に分割される。
split　(名)分裂, 亀裂, 不和, 分割, 株式分割
　reverse split　株式併合
　share split　株式分割
　　(=share splitting, stock split; ⇒share splitting)
　share split-down　株式併合　(=reverse split, reverse stock split, stock split-down)
　share split-up　株式分割　(=stock split-up)
　split offering　分割発行(地方自治体の特定財源債や一般財源債の発行に一般的に用いられているもので, 連続的に満期になる複数の債券と大型長期債とを組み合わせて発行者が同時に一括公募発行すること)
　split order　スプリット・オーダー(大口注文を小口に分けて執行すること)
　split rating　分裂格付け, スプリット格付け(格付け機関によって, 同一証券に対する格付けが違うこと)
　stock split　株式分割　(=share split)
　◆Prior to the split, the company had 10,000 shares of $15 par value common stock issued and outstanding. 株式分割前, 同社は額面15ドルの普通株式1万株が発行済みであった。
sponsor　(動)後援する, 主催する, 後押しする, 支持する, 支援する, 法案などを主唱する, 保証する, 保証人になる, 協力する, スポンサーになる
　federally sponsored agencies　連邦政府関連機関
　government sponsored agencies　政府系機関, 政府支援機関, 政府関連機関
　government sponsored enterprise [entity]　政府系機関, 政府関連機関, 政府系住宅金融機関, 政府支援企業, 政府援助法人, GSE
　government-sponsored export credit　政府保証付き輸出信用
　lawmaker-sponsored bill　議員立法の法案
　sponsor savings plans for employees　従業員のために貯蓄制度を設ける
　sponsoring organization　支援組織
　United States government-sponsored entities [agencies]　米連邦政府系機関
　◆Several companies inside and outside Japan have already expressed a desire to sponsor the firm's rehabilitation. 同社の再建支援には, 国内外の複数企業がすでに名乗りを上げている。◆We sponsor savings plans for the majority of our employees. 当社は, 大多数の当社従業員のために貯蓄制度を設けています。
sponsor　(名)投資信託証券の引受人[引受業者], ベンチャー・ビジネスや慈善事業などへの出資者, プロジェクト・ファイナンスの実質的推進者, 債務などの保証人,

原資産保有者, 後援者, 後援会, 主催者, 発起人, 支持者, 広告主, 番組提供者, スポンサー
（⇒bidding）
corporate sponsors for the rehabilitation program　再生計画のスポンサー企業
official sponsor　公式スポンサー
sponsor company　スポンサー企業（corporate sponsor）
sponsors for large advertisements　大口広告主
◆Companies inside and outside Japan expressed a desire to help Daiei's rehabilitation as a sponsor company. 国内外の複数企業が、ダイエー再建支援のスポンサー企業として名乗りを上げた。◆Corporate sponsors for the rehabilitation program will be picked up after the IRC finalizes its decision to assist the firm. 再生計画のスポンサー企業は、産業再生機構が最終的に同社支援を決定した後に選定する。

sponsorship　後援, 支援, スポンサーシップ（大手の投資機関や有名な調査部門を持つ証券会社など専門投資家が、特定の株式を積極的に支援すること）

spontaneous global market crash　世界同時株安
（=simultaneous stock market plunges）
◆Major Asian markets such as Shanghai and Hong Kong also show a situation that could be dubbed as a spontaneous global market crash. 上海や香港などアジアの主要市場も、世界同時株安の様相を見せている。

spot　（動）見つける, 見つけ出す, 見分ける
spot a niche　ニッチを見つける

spot　（形）即座の, 現金の, 現金払いの, 現金取引の, 現物の　（名）場所, 地点, 位置, 地位, 職, 現物, 現地品
forward and spot foreign exchange　外国為替の先物と直物［先物・直物］
on the spot　即座に, その場で, 現場で, 現物で, 現金で
spot cash　即時現金, 即金
spot-cash terms　即時現金払い条件
spot check　現物相場（現金売買の値段）, 抜き取り検査, 抜き打ち点検
spot dealing　直物取引
spot delivery　現場渡し, 現物渡し
spot firm　現金取引会社
spot-forward transaction　直売り先買い取引, スワップ取引, スポット・フォワード取引
spot goods　現物, 現物取引
spot news　ニュース速報
spot next［spot/next］　スポット・ネクスト（受渡し日が約定日から3日後となる取引。2営業日後（スポット）から翌日までの金利やスワップ・レートを意味することもある）
spot operation　直物取引, 直物操作
spot position　現物持ち高, 直物持ち高
spot price　現物価格, 直物価格, 直物商品価格, スポット価格　（=cash price: スポット市場［現物市場］で取引される商品の現在価格）
spot quotation　直物相場
spot rate　直物相場, 直物レート, 直物為替相場, 直物為替レート, スポット・レート
spot reproduction cost　時価再生産原価
spot sale　即売
spot selling　現物売り
spot start　スワップの開始日（一般に約定日から2営業日後を開始日とする）
◆Combined sales of Panasonic and Sanyo would catapult Panasonic to the No.3 spot in revenue among listed Japanese companies. パナソニック（旧松下電器産業）と三洋電機の連結売上高を合算すると、上場日本企業のなかで、パナソニックは売上高で一躍第3位となる。◆Increasing M&A advisory business helped Nomura grab the No. 1 spot in Japan's M&A league table for the first half of this year. 今年上半期はM&A顧問業務が増加したため、日本のM&A案件の引受実績で野村證券がトップの座を占めた。

spot and short selling of shares　株の現物売りと空売り
◆The securities company repeatedly alternated spot and short selling of shares of a regional bank. この証券会社は、地方銀行株の現物売りと空売りを交互に繰り返した。

spot exchange　直物為替
spot exchange dealing　直物為替取引
spot exchange rate　直物為替相場, 現物相場, 直物相場, 直物為替レート

spot market　現物市場, 直物市場, 現金取引市場, 当用買い市場, スポット市場, スポット・マーケット　（=cash market: 現金の受け払いで商品が即時に受渡しされる市場のこと）
spot market for stocks　株式の現物市場
spot market trades　スポット・マーケット・トレード（当月に受渡し期限が到来する先物契約の取引）

spot rate　直物相場, 直物レート, 直物為替相場, 直物為替レート, スポット・レート
◆The Corporation acquired a 60-day forward exchange contract for US $1,000,000, in anticipation of an increase in the spot rates for US dollars. 当社は、米ドルの直物レートが上がるのを期待して100万米ドル、60日後の先物為替予約を取得した。

spot selling　現物売り
◆The securities company repeatedly alternated spot and short selling of shares of a regional bank. この証券会社は、地方銀行株の現物売りと空売りを交互に繰り返した。

spot trading　現物株取引（spot transaction of stocks）, 直物取引, 現物取引
◆After the merger, the TSE and OSE will be divided into four operator firms handling spot trading, derivatives, settlement of trading deals and self-imposed regulations respectively. 経営統合後、東証と大証は、それぞれ現物株、デリバティブ（金融派生商品）、取引決済と自主規制を扱う4事業会社に切り分けられることになっている。◆The Tokyo Stock Exchange accounts for 90 percent of domestic spot trading. 東京証券取引所は、国内の現物株取引の9割を占めている。

spot trading of shares　現物株の取引
◆Currently, the TSE is ranked third in the world for spot trading of shares. 現在、東証は現物株の取引で世界第三位を占めている。◆In Japan, ninety percent of spot trading of shares is done at the Tokyo Stock Exchange. 日本では、現物株取引の9割は東京証券取引所で行われている。

spot transaction　直物取引, 現物取引, 実物取引, 直物為替取引, 直物為替契約, 直物契約
a foreign exchange spot transaction　外国為替スポット取引
spot transaction of foreign exchange　外国為替スポット取引

spot transaction of stocks　現物株取引
◆In order to overcome disadvantages in such spot transactions of stocks and to take the lead in futures and derivatives, the Osaka Securities Exchange in 1988 launched futures trading of the 225-issue Nikkei Stock Average. この現物株取引での劣勢を挽回し、先物やデリバティブ（金融派生商品）に活路を開くため、大阪証券取引所は1988年に日経平均株価（225種）の先物取引を始めた。◆More than 90 percent of spot transactions of stocks are conducted on the Tokyo Stock Exchange. 現物株取引の9割以上は、東京証券取引所で行われている。

spread　（動）広げる, 広める, 公表する, 伸ばす, 拡大する, 蔓延させる, 普及させる, 拡散させる, 分散させる, 転

嫁する, 引き伸ばす, 分担する, 分配する （自動）広がる, 広まる, 伝わる, 波及する, 及ぶ, 蔓延する, 感染する, 普及する, 分布する
spread one's investment　運用先を分散する
spread risks　リスクを分散させる
spread the burden [load]　仕事を分担する
spread the loss equally among other banks　損失を他行と均等に負担する

◆Concern over the global economic slowdown is spreading. 世界経済の減速懸念が, 広がっている。◆Credit uncertainty is spreading as there is no end in sight to fiscal crises in the United States and some European countries. 米国と一部の欧州の財政危機の収束が見通せないため, 信用不安が拡大している。◆European countries are forced to prevent the financial crisis from spreading from Europe to other parts of the world. 欧州は, 金融危機の世界的波及阻止を迫られている。◆Fiscal crises in Europe have spread to Italy and Spain from Greece. 欧州の財政危機は, ギリシャからイタリアやスペインに飛び火した。◆In Europe, credit uncertainty has spread from Greece to Italy, Spain and elsewhere due to the excessively tardy response by Europe. 欧州では, 欧州の対応が遅すぎるため, 信用不安がギリシャからイタリアやスペインなどに拡大している。◆Japan's regulations on short selling and market manipulation by spreading rumors are extremely weak in comparison with those of the United States. 日本の空売りに関する規制や風説の流布などによる市場操作についての規制は, 米国に比べて極めて弱い。◆The debt crisis in Greece threatened to spread to Portugal, Ireland and Spain. ギリシャの財政危機は, ポルトガルやアイルランド, スペインなどに波及する恐れがあった。◆The effects of an economic slowdown in industrialized countries stemming from the U.S. subprime woes could spread in the emerging economies. 米国のサブプライム（低所得者向け住宅融資）問題に起因する先進国の景気減速の影響は, 新興国にも拡大する可能性がある。◆The euro crisis has spread to Spain and Italy with interest rates on their sovereign debts soaring. ユーロ危機はスペインとイタリアに波及し, 両国国債の金利が急騰した。◆The European fiscal crisis triggered by Greece has spread to Italy, making the severe situation even more distressing. ギリシャ発の欧州財政危機がイタリアに飛び火し, 厳しい事態が一段と深刻化している。◆The European Union will substantially expand the lending capacity of the EFSF to buy up government bonds in case the fiscal and financial crisis spreads to countries as Italy. 欧州連合（EU）は, 財政・金融危機がイタリアなどなどに拡大した場合に国債を買い支えるため, 欧州金融安定基金（EFSF）の融資能力を大幅に拡大する。◆The firm's former president spread false information about corporate purchases with the aim of inflating the stock prices of its affiliate. 同社の前社長は, 関連会社の株価をつり上げるため, 虚偽の企業買収情報を公表していた。◆The move to lower the yields of insurance products is likely to spread through the industry as tough investment conditions persist. 厳しい運用環境が続いているので, 保険商品の利回りを引き下げる動きは, 業界全体に広がりそうだ。◆The recession has been spreading globally and the Japanese economy has been languishing since last year. 昨年来, 世界同時不況が進行し, 日本経済は低迷が続いている。◆The recession in the United States has spread globally. 米国の景気後退は, 世界中に広がっている[世界に波及している]。◆The talks between Prime Minister Kan and Bank of Japan Gov. Shirakawa led to a further advance of the yen and offloading of stocks as disappointment spread among market players. 菅首相と日銀総裁の会談は, 一層の円高と市場筋の株の失望売りを誘った。◆There is no end in sight to fiscal crises in the United States and some European countries as credit uncertainty is spreading. 信用不安が拡大しているため, 米国と欧州の一部の財政危機の収束が見通せない。◆To prevent the current fiscal and financial crisis in Europe from spreading, the IMF will create a new short-term lending facility. 現在の欧州財政・金融危機の拡大を防ぐ[封じる]ため, 国際通貨基金（IMF）が, 新たな短期の融資制度を創設することになった。

spread （名）増加, 増大, 拡大, 広がり, 流行, 展開, 蔓延, 開き, 範囲, 幅, 普及, 発展
a spread of　幅広い, 様々な, 多様な
an acceptable spread of risk　許容できる範囲のリスク
spread of illegal moneylending　ヤミ金融の横行, 違法貸付けの横行
the spread of the business　会社の発展

◆Confidence in the single currency of the euro may be undermined by the spread of the Greek crisis to Spain and Portugal. ギリシャ危機のスペインやポルトガルへの波及で, 単一通貨・ユーロの信認が揺らぎかねない。◆Sellers of multiple-debtor lists, produced by collecting information about consumer finance customers, are contributing to the spread of illegal moneylending. 消費者金融の顧客情報を入手して作った多重債務者リストを売る名簿業者が, ヤミ金融の横行に一役買っている。◆The rapid spread of Italy's credit crisis is due to intensified fears about the nation's fiscal predicament by Italy's huge fiscal deficits. イタリアの信用不安が急速に広がったのは, イタリアの巨額の赤字で同国の財政ひっ迫への警戒感が高まったからだ。◆Worries over the spread of the eurozone debt crisis and the U.S.'s slipping into recession have driven the rout in financial markets. ユーロ圏の財政危機の拡大と米国の景気後退入りへの懸念で, 金融市場は総崩れになった。

spread （名）利幅, 利ざや, 上乗せ金利, 売り値と買い値の差, （異なる債券間の）利回り格差, スプレッド, 銀行の調達金利である預金金利と運用金利である貸出金利との差, 株や債券, 通貨取引などの買い呼び値（bid）と売り呼び値（offer）との差額, 有価証券の発行者の引受業者への引渡し価格と引受業者の一般投資家への売出価格との差額　（⇒credit spread, negative spread, yield spread）
a spread between domestic and overseas interest rates　内外金利差
back spread　逆ざや
bid-ask spread　呼び値スプレッド　（=bid-asked spread）
bid-offer spread　呼び値スプレッド
collateral spread　パス・スルー証券のスプレッド
contractual spread　約定スプレッド
corporate spread　社債スプレッド
effective spread　実効スプレッド
excess spread　余剰スプレッド
front-end spread　短期物スプレッド
increase [improve] spreads　スプレッドを拡大する
interest rate spread　金利スプレッド, 金利幅, 利ざや
negative spread　逆ざや　（=negative yield）
NOB（notes over bonds）spread　ノブ・スプレッド（財務省中期証券の先物と財務省長期証券の先物との間の価格差）
positive spread　順ざや　（=regular spread）
profit spread　利ざや
rate spread　利ざや
spread banker　スプレッド収益銀行（商業銀行のこと。ただし, 投資銀行を指すこともある）
spread banking　スプレッド・バンキング（一定の利ざやを確保して安定収益を図る銀行経営）
spread lending　スプレッド貸出, スプレッド融資（調達金利に一定のマージンを上乗せして行う銀行貸出のこと）
spread loan　スプレッド貸し
spread margin　両建て証拠金
spread of risks　危険分散, リスク分散

spread option　スプレッド・オプション
spread order　スプレッド注文
spread rates of swaps　スワップの金利幅
spread to maturity　満期スプレッド
spread trading　スプレッド取引
　(=spread trade, spread transaction)
spreads on benchmark bonds　指標銘柄のスプレッド
spreads on mortgages　モーゲージの利ざや
swap spread　スワップ・スプレッド
the credit spreads in different markets　異なる市場間の信用格差
the spot-forward spread　現物・先物のさや, 直・先スプレッド
the spread of rates in swaps　スワップの金利幅
theoretical and actual yield spreads　理論利回りと実際の利回りの格差
trading spreads　呼び値スプレッド
two-to-30 year spread　2年物と30年物の利回り格差
underwriting spread　引受スプレッド
vertical spread　バーティカル・スプレッド　(=money spread, price spread: オプション取引で, 行使期間満了日は同じだが行使価格の異なるコール・オプションの売りと買い, またはプット・オプションの売りと買いを同時に実行すること)
yield spread　利回り格差, 金利差
◆The spreads of yields on high-risk junk bonds over the benchmark five-year U.S. Treasury bonds had been around 200 basis points, or 2 percentage points.　リスクの高いジャンク債と指標となる5年物財務省証券との金利差(スプレッド)は, 2%(200ベーシス・ポイント)程度で推移していた。◆Wider spreads were also seen in the market for commercial mortgage-backed securities.　金利差(スプレッド)の拡大は, 商業用不動産担保証券の市場でも見られた。

spur　(動)奮起させる, (～するよう)駆り立てる, せきたてる, ～に拍車をかける, 促進する, 促す, ～を活性化する, 急ぐ
spur A to B　AにBをするよう促す
spur competition among　～の間の競争を促す
spur domestic-demand expansion policies　内需拡大策を急ぐ
spur economic development　経済発展に拍車をかける, 経済開発を促進する
spur flagging economic growth　失速気味の経済成長に刺激を与える
spur technical [technological] innovation　技術革新を促す[促進する]
spur to investment　投資を促す
◆China is spurring domestic-demand expansion policies by its own increased consumption.　中国は, 消費拡大による内需拡大策を急いでいる。◆Demand for bullion as a protection of wealth has been spurred by mounting concern that the global economy is faltering.　世界経済低迷への懸念増大から, 安全資産[資産保全]としての金の需要が拡大している。◆The European Central Bank cut its main interest rate by 0.25 percent following heavy pressure for a rate cut to spur flagging economic growth.　失速気味の経済成長に刺激を与えるため利下げを求める強い圧力を受けて, 欧州中央銀行(ECB)はその主要(政策)金利を0.25%引き下げた。◆The Supreme Court ruling may spur similar lawsuits demanding the return of income tax already paid.　この最高裁の判決で, すでに納付した所得税の還付を求める同様の訴訟に, 拍車がかかる可能性がある。

spur　(名)拍車, 鼓舞, 激励, 刺激, 誘因, 動機, 発奮材料, (道路, 鉄道の)支線
earn [gain, get, win] one's spurs　名声を得る, 名声をあげる, 名をあげる, 手柄をたてる, 能力[価値]を実証する
on the spur of the moment [occasion]　一時の思い付きで, その時のはずみで, 出来心で, とっさに, 即座に, 突然に, 思いつきで, 衝動的に, 前後の見境なく(without deliberation), 前後をわきまえないで
put [clap, give, set] spurs to　～に拍車をかける, ～に発破(はっぱ)をかける, ～を励ます
spur to economic growth　景気浮揚策
with whip and spur　即座に, 直ちに
　(=with spur and yard)

squeeze　(動)締め付ける, 引き締める, 予算や経費などを切り詰める, 制限する, 圧迫する, 押し下げる, 縮小する, 低下する, 減少する
squeeze excess liquidity　過剰流動性を吸収する
squeeze inflation　インフレを引き締める, インフレを抑える
squeeze margins　利益率を押し下げる[圧迫する], 利ざやを圧迫する
squeeze money market　金融市場を引き締める
squeeze money out of　～から資金[金]を絞り出す, ～から無理やり金を取り立てる
squeezed cash flow　キャッシュ・フローの減少
◆Profits have been squeezed as interest rates remain near zero percent and loan demands stalls.　金利はまだゼロに近いし, 借入需要も停滞したままなので, 利益は減少している。

squeeze　(名)締付け, 引締め, 切詰め, 制限, 打撃, 圧迫, 縮小, 低下, 減少, (価格などの)下落, 需給ひっ迫, 踏み上げ相場　(⇒fiscal squeeze)
a monetary squeeze　金融引締め
a squeeze in margins due to rising interest rates　金利上昇による利ざやの縮小
a squeeze on earnings　業績悪化
a squeeze on the real economy　実体経済に与える影響
bear squeeze　踏み上げ, 踏み上げ相場
credit squeeze　金融引締め, 金融の収縮　(=monetary [money] squeeze, monetary restraint)
credit squeeze measures [policy]　金融引締め策, 金融引締め措置
financial squeeze　金融引締め
fiscal squeeze　財政のひっ迫
margin squeeze　利益率低下, 利益率圧迫, 利ざや縮小　(=squeeze in margins)
mitigate the squeeze on　～への影響[打撃]を和らげる, ～への影響を緩和する
money squeeze　金融引締め
profit squeeze　利益減少, 利益縮小, 利益圧迫, 利幅削減, 利潤圧縮
short squeeze　踏み上げ, 踏み上げ相場
　(=bear panic, bear squeeze)
squeeze on earnings　利益圧迫, 業績悪化
squeeze on private institutions　民業圧迫
◆Tightening regulations on core capital ratios too quickly would cause a credit squeeze and negatively affect the real economy.　急激な自己資本比率規制の強化は, 金融収縮を招いて, 実体経済に悪影響を与える。

SRI　社会的責任投資　(socially responsible investingの略)
SRI fund　社会的責任投資ファンド, SRIファンド
解説 SRIファンドとは: 社会に貢献する企業は消費者や投資家から信頼を得, 安定した利益が期待できることから, 社会への貢献度の高い企業を選んで投資する投資信託。投資基準の社会への貢献度の要因としては, 従業員の人権への配慮, 社会活動への参加, 消費者への対応,

女性や障害者の雇用、消費者への対応などが挙げられる。

stability (名)安定,安定性
(⇒financial stability, financial system stability)
 brief stability　小康状態
 economic stability　経済の安定,経済的安定性
 employment stability　雇用の安定,雇用の安定性
  (=stability of employment)
 exchange stability　為替の安定,為替安定
 export stability　輸出安定性
 financial stability　金融システムの安定
 internal stability　国内の安定,国内安定性
 management stability　経営の安定,経営安定
 market stability　市場の安定
 multimarket stability　多数市場の安定性
 political stability　政治的安定,政治の安定
 price stability　物価安定
 Stability and Growth Pact　安定成長協定
 stability in the banking sector　銀行の経営安定
  (⇒banking sector)
 stability in the large　大範囲の安定
 stability in the small　小範囲の安定
 stability in the value of money　通貨価値の安定
 stability of economic growth　経済成長の安定性
 stability of the financial system　金融システムの安定性
  (=financial stability, financial system stability)
 stability of the stock market　株価の安定
 ◆The Japanese economy has reached a critical stage at which it could tumble into a deflationary spiral after brief stability, or be brought back to a recovery path. 日本経済は現在、小康状態から再びデフレの悪循環に落ち込むか、回復軌道に戻せるかどうかの瀬戸際にある。

Stability and Growth Pact　財政安定・成長協定,財政安定化・成長協定,安定・成長協定,SGP(ユーロ圏16か国の財政政策の運営に関する協定)
◆The deficits of the Greek government in 2009 amounted to more than three times that allowed by the Stability and Growth Pact. ギリシャの2009年の財政赤字は、ユーロ圏の財政安定化・成長協定で定められている赤字幅(GDPの3%以下)の3倍以上にも達した。◆The Stability and Growth Pact lost its spine in 2003 as the Germany government requested the relaxation of its terms. ユーロ圏の財政安定化・成長協定は、ドイツがその条件緩和を要求したため、2003年に骨抜きになった。◆Under the EU's Stability and Growth Pact, countries eligible to join the euro system are required to keep budget deficits below 3 percent of GDP. 欧州連合(EU)の財政安定・成長協定によると、ユーロ加盟国は、加盟の条件として財政赤字をGDPの3%以下に抑えなければならない。

stability in the financial markets　金融市場の安定
◆Further stability in the financial markets is desirable. 金融市場の一層の安定が、望まれる。

stability of each major currency　各主要通貨の安定性
◆Market players are buying the yen after weighing the stability of each major currency and concluding the yen relatively stable. 市場関係者は、各主要通貨の安定性を比較検討し、円が比較的安定していると見極めたうえで、円を買っている。

stability of the economy　経済の安定
◆Excessive movements of foreign exchange rates will have a negative impact on the stability of the economy and financial markets. 行き過ぎた外国為替相場の動きは、経済の安定と金融市場に悪影響を及ぼす。

stability of the financial system　金融システムの安定性 (=financial system stability)
◆With the midyear account settlement scheduled in September, concerns over the stability of the nation's financial system inevitably will grow again should stock prices dip further. 9月中間決算を前に、株価がさらに下がれば、再び日本の金融システム不安が当然、台頭してくる。

stabilization (名)安定,安定化,安定操作,安定性,横ばいで推移すること
 currency stabilization　通貨の安定,貨幣安定化
 currency stabilization loan　通貨安定借款
  (=stabilization loan)
 economic stabilization　経済の安定,経済的安定,景気安定化
 employment stabilization　雇用安定
  (=stabilization of employment)
 exchange stabilization　為替安定化
 exchange stabilization account　為替安定基金
 (exchange) stabilization fund　為替安定基金
  (=exchange equalization fund)
 financial system stabilization　金融システム安定化
 massive euro stabilization package　巨額のユーロ安定化対策,大規模なユーロ安定化策
  (⇒euro stabilization package)
 monetary stabilization　通貨安定
 monetary stabilization policy　通貨安定政策
 price stabilization　価格[物価]安定,物価[価格]安定化
 stabilization bid　安定操作のための買付け
 stabilization crisis　安定恐慌
 stabilization fund　為替安定資金
 stabilization loan　通貨安定借款,安定貸付け金
 stabilization of (the) exchange rate　為替相場の安定
 stabilization performance　安定化実績
 stabilization phase　景気の安定局面
 stabilization policy　安定化政策,安定政策
 stabilization procedures　安定操作取引
 stabilization program　経済安定化政策,安定化計画
 stabilization transaction　安定操作取引
 stock stabilization　株の安定操作
 temporary stabilization　一時的安定
◆Four Fed regions—New York, Cleveland, Kansas City and San Francisco—pointed to "signs of stabilization." ニューヨーク、クリーブランド、カンザス、サンフランシスコの4米地区連銀は、「景気安定化の兆し」を指摘した。◆To fulfill its responsibilities as the nation's central bank, the Bank of Japan must achieve currency stabilization by availing itself of a range of measures, including stabilization of the exchange rate. 日本の中央銀行としての責任を果たすには、日本銀行は、為替相場の安定を含めて広範な手段を活用して通貨の安定を実現しなければならない。

stabilize (動)安定させる,固定させる,安定装置を施す,安定する,固定する,頭打ちになる,下げ止まる
(⇒financial system)
 operations to stabilize stock prices　株価安定操作
 stabilize currencies　為替を安定させる,通貨を安定させる
 stabilize one's currency against a basket of currencies　自国通貨を主要通貨のバスケットに連動する
 stabilize the economy　経済を安定させる
 stabilize the market　市場の安定操作を行う,市場を安定させる
◆The latest rise in the yuan's value against the U.S. dollar and a smooth transition to the currency basket will help stabilize China's external relations. 今回の人民元相場の対米ドル切上げと通貨バスケット制への円滑な移行で、中国の対外

関係は安定化に向かうだろう。◆The U.S. economy is finally showing signs of stabilizing in some regions of the country. 米景気は、一部の地域でやっと安定化の兆しが見られる。

stabilize financial markets　金融市場を安定させる, 金融市場を安定化させる
◆Quantitative easing measures are believed to have been proven effective in stabilizing financial markets. 量的緩和政策は金融市場の安定化に効果的だった、とされている。◆The enhancement of international coordination is important to stabilize the financial markets. 金融市場の安定には、国際協調の強化が重要だ。◆The important measures were taken to stabilize financial markets. 金融市場安定化のために、重要な措置が取られた。

stabilize prices　物価を安定させる
◆The new Fed chairman's theory is to introduce inflation targets, thus setting numerical targets for stabilizing prices. 米連邦準備制度理事会（FRB）新議長の持論は、インフレ目標を導入して、物価安定の数値目標を示す［設定する］ことだ。

stabilize the euro　ユーロを安定させる
◆A focus of the summit meeting of European Union members held in Belgium is a fiscal rehabilitation plan to stabilize the euro. ベルギーで開かれる欧州連合（EU）加盟国首脳会議の焦点は、ユーロを安定させる財政健全化策だ。

stabilize the financial system　金融システムを安定させる, 金融システムの安定化を図る
◆EU countries must quickly stabilize their financial systems by drawing upon all possible measures. EU各国は、可能な手段を総動員して、金融システムを早期に安定させる必要がある。◆The government would ask the Bank of Japan to further ease its monetary policy to help stabilize the nation's financial system by helping financial institutions procure funds. 政府は、国内金融機関の資金繰りを助けて金融システムの安定化を図るため、日銀に追加の［もう一段の］金融緩和を求める方針だ。◆The United States may request Japan to make further efforts to head off deflation and stabilize the financial system by disposing of massive nonperforming loans held by financial institutions. デフレ阻止や金融機関が抱える巨額の不良債権処理による金融システムの安定化に向けて一層の努力をするよう、米国が日本に求める可能性がある。

stabilize the global financial markets　世界の金融市場を安定させる, 世界の金融市場の安定化を図る
◆Enhancing international coordination is indispensable to stabilize the global financial markets. 世界の金融市場の安定には、国際協調の強化が欠かせない。◆Japan, U.S. and Europe must hasten to end fiscal crisis to stabilize the global financial markets. 世界の金融市場の安定を図るには、日米欧が財政危機の収束を急がなければならない。

stabilize the pension system　年金制度の安定化を図る
◆To stabilize the pension system, the government raised its burden in the basic pension plan to 50 percent of the total contribution from fiscal 2009. 年金制度の安定化を図るため、政府は、基礎年金の国の負担割合を2009年度から総給付金の50％に引き上げた。

stabilize the yen's value　円相場の安定化を図る
◆The government and the BOJ must take flexible steps to stabilize the yen's value. 円相場の安定化に向けて、政府と日銀は機動的に対応する必要がある。

stabilizing factor　安定要因　（⇒susceptible to）

stabilizing transaction　安定操作

stable　（形）安定した,固定した,しっかりした,ぐらつかない,ぶれない,固い,不変の,一定の
（⇒Finance Ministry, susceptible to）
　a stable political power　安定政権
　a stable revenue source　安定財源
　be stable　安定している,安定的［横ばい］に推移する

　remain stable　安定している,横ばい傾向が続く,堅調である
　return to stable growth　安定成長に復帰する
　（⇒supply side）
　stable business　安定した事業
　stable demand function for money　安定的貨幣需要関数
　stable economy　安定した経済
　stable employment　安定雇用
　stable exchange rate　安定的為替相場
　stable inflation　インフレ率の安定
　stable money　安定通貨（stabilized currency）,安定貨幣
　stable money policy　安定貨幣政策
　stable performance　安定運用
　stable prices　安定した物価
　stable shareholder［stockholder］　安定株主
　stable supplies　安定供給
◆Currently, China's investment climate is stable. 現在、中国の投資環境は安定している。◆The rating outlook remains stable. 格付け見通しは、引き続き安定的だ。◆The stock market is stable in the bull market. 株式市場は、上げ相場で安定している。◆The yen has been changing hands in a fairly stable manner at about ￥110 to the dollar. 円［円相場］は、1ドル＝110円程度でかなり安定的に推移している。

stable course　安定経路, 安定軌道
◆The role of the new prime minister is putting the economy on a stable course and rehabilitating the state finances. 新首相の役割は、景気を安定軌道に乗せて財政も立て直すことだ。

stable domestic investors　安定した国内投資家
◆The downside risk for Japanese bonds is said to be limited, with 95 percent of bondholders being stable domestic investors. 債券保有者の95％は安定した国内投資家で、日本国債の価格下落リスクは小さいといわれる。

stable exchange rates　安定した為替相場, 為替相場の安定
◆The intervention by the Finance Ministry will contribute to more stable exchange rates. 財務省の市場介入は、為替相場の安定化に寄与するものと思われる。

stable financial resource　安定財源
◆Increasing the consumption tax rate will be critical as a stable financial resource to cover ballooning social security costs. 消費税率の引上げは、増大する社会保障費の安定財源として欠かせない。

stable growth　安定成長, 安定的な成長
（＝stable economic growth）
◆Rapid recovery following the so-called Lehman shock has ended and the Chinese economy has entered a phase aimed at stable growth. いわゆるリーマン・ショック後の中国の急回復の時期は終わり、中国経済は、安定成長を目指す段階に入っている。◆The Chinese economy is in an important phase of transition from a rapid recovery to stable growth. 中国経済は、回復から安定した成長への重要な転換時期にある。◆The key to returning to stable growth is whether the nation can eliminate excesses common to many companies and promote supply-side structural reforms. 安定成長復帰へのカギは、多くの日本企業に共通して見られる過剰体質を排除して、供給サイドの構造改革を進めることができるかどうかである。

stable growth path　安定成長の軌道, 安定成長路線
◆The task of rebuilding the financial and industrial systems in East Asia and putting them on a stable growth path has yet to be undertaken. 東アジアの金融および産業システムを再構築して、これらを安定成長の軌道に乗せる課題に取り組むのは、これからだ。

stable management　安定経営, 経営の安定
◆Meiji Yasuda decided to lower the yield rate of its flagship insurance product because the insurer placed priority on

long-term stable management over an increase in the number of policyholders. 明治安田生保は、契約者の数を増やすより長期的な経営の安定を優先したため、主力保険商品の予定利率[利回り]を引き下げることにした。

stable profit　安定した利益, 安定した収益
　earn a stable profit　安定した利益を上げる
　secure stable profits　安定した収益を確保する
　◆GM must secure stable profits by releasing promising models to successfully list its shares again. GMが再上場を果たすには、売れる車を投入して安定した収益を確保しなければならない。◆The company is expected to continue earning a stable profit for the foreseeable future. 同社は、将来的にも安定した利益が見込める。

stable revenue source　安定した財源
　◆The last resort to secure a stable revenue source is raising the consumption tax. 安定した財源確保の頼みの綱は、消費税の引上げだ。

stable stock market　株式相場の安定, 株価の底堅い動き
　◆A stable stock market would heighten people's expectations for economic recovery, leading to rises in real demand for capital investment and personal spending. 株式相場の安定[株価の底堅い動き]は、人々の景気回復への期待感を高め、設備投資や個人消費の実需拡大につながる。

stag　(名)仕手筋

stage　(名)段階, 局面, 時期, 〜期, 舞台, 活動の場所, ステージ　(⇒critical)
　closing stages　大詰めの段階
　development stage enterprise　開発段階の企業
　early stages　初期の段階, 初期　(=initial stages)
　enter a new stage　新たな段階に入る
　formative stage　草創期, 試行錯誤の段階
　mature[maturity]stage　成熟期, 成熟局面
　multi-stage sampling　多段抽出法
　reach the final stage of　〜の最終局面を迎える
　set the stage for　〜のお膳立てをする、〜の準備をする、〜の態勢を整える
　stage of completion　作業進捗(しんちょく)度, 進捗度
　stage of economic progress　経済発展の段階
　stages of financing　資金調達の段階
　stages of growth　成長段階　(=growth stage)
　take center stage　衆目を集める, 極めて重要になる　(=be at the center of the stage)
　◆Major commercial banks are reaching the final stages of their efforts to write off their nonperforming loans. 大手銀行は、不良債権処理への取組みの最終局面を迎えている。◆The federal government will raise the debt ceiling by about $2.4 trillion in two stages. 米政府は、2.4兆ドルほどの債務上限引上げを2段階で実施する。◆The Japanese economy has reached a critical stage at which it could tumble into a deflationary spiral after brief stability, or be brought back to a recovery path. 日本経済は現在、小康状態から再びデフレの悪循環に落ち込むか、回復軌道に戻せるかどうかの瀬戸際にある。◆When serious financial difficulties are expected, the Financial Services Agency is allowed to order a company to improve its operations in the early stages without releasing the information to the public. 深刻な財務悪化が予想される場合、金融庁は、非公表で早めに業務改善命令を発動することができる。

stage a comeback　反発する, 返り咲く
　◆Stocks staged an impressive comeback. 株価[株式相場]は、大きく反発した。

staggered board　スタガー取締役会　(会社の取締役の任期期間をずらして構成されている取締役会のことで、敵対的買収への防衛手段として利用されることがある。⇒shark repellent[repellant])

staggering　(形)膨大な, 肝をつぶすほどの, 驚異的な, 驚くべき, 衝撃的な, 信じられないほどの, 信じがたいほどの, ふらふらする, よろめく
　a staggering performance[achievement]　驚異的な業績
　a staggering result　驚異的な業績, 信じがたい結果, 衝撃的な結果
　staggering(business)results　驚異的な業績, 好業績, 好決算, 好結果
　staggering riches　膨大な富
　◆Long-term debts held by central and local governments are predicted to reach a staggering ¥862 trillion as of the end of fiscal 2010. 国と地方自治体が抱える長期債務は、2010年度末の時点で「2010年度末で」862兆円と膨大な額に達する見込みだ。

stagnancy　(名)沈滞, 停滞, 頭打ちの状態, 不振, 不活発, 低迷, 悪化, 不景気, 不況
　◆The negative growth was due to the stagnancy of corporate capital investment as well as sluggish personal spending and other economy-slowing factors. マイナス成長は、企業の設備投資が頭打ちの状態だったことと、個人消費の伸び悩みや他の景気減速要因によるものだ。

stagnant　(形)沈滞した, 停滞した, 進歩[発展、発達、成長、向上]のない, 不振の, 低迷した, 活気のない, 動き[働き]の鈍い, 不活発な, 軟調の, 不景気な
　stagnant domestic income　国内所得の低迷
　stagnant earnings　収益悪化
　stagnant economy　沈滞[停滞]した経済, 景気低迷, 不景気, 経済の低迷[停滞], 不振の経済　(⇒pro-market)
　stagnant market　停滞する市場, 市場の低迷, 市場軟調, 沈滞市況, 軟調市況
　stagnant results　業績低迷, 業績不振, 業績悪化
　stagnant sales　販売低迷, 販売不振, 売上不振
　◆Bolivian pro-market President-elect Gonzalo Sanchez took office facing the huge tasks of reviving a stagnant economy and attracting investment. ボリビアの大統領に当選した市場経済主義者のゴンザロ・サンチェス氏が、停滞した経済の回復や投資誘致という重大任務を抱えて就任した。

stagnate　(動)沈滞する, 停滞する, 低迷する, 難航する, 活気を失う, だれる, 悪くなる, 悪化する, 発展[進歩]が止まる, だれる
　◆Financial reconstruction is likely to stagnate under the Italy's new government as it did under the previous one. イタリアの財政再建は、前政権同様、新政権でも難航しそうだ。◆Japan's exports will stagnate and corporate performance will suffer if the yen remains in the historically high ¥75-range against the dollar. 円相場が1ドル=75円台の史上最高値が続けば、日本の輸出は低迷し、企業の業績は悪化する。

stagnation　(名)沈滞, 停滞, 景気沈滞, 不景気, 不況
　a remedy for economic stagnation　不況対策
　economic stagnation　経済的停滞, 経済の停滞, 経済不況, 景気低迷, 景気停滞, 不況　(=stagnation in the economy)
　fall into stagnation　不景気[不況、不振]に陥る
　labor market stagnation　労働市場の低迷
　secular stagnation　長期停滞
　stagnation in the economy　経済不況

stake　(名)出資, 出資比率, 投資金, 投資金額, 資本参加, 株式持ち分, 持ち株, 持ち株比率, 株の保有比率, 株式保有比率, 株, 株式, 利害関係　(⇒basis, capital expansion, discontinued business, joint stake, joint venture, major shareholder, majority stake, strategy)
　buy a 10 percent stake in the company　同社の株式の

10％を取得する
controlling stake　支配持ち分
　（=controlling interest; ⇒quality）
equity stake　持ち分
have a stake in　〜に利害関係を持つ, 〜に関わり合い［関係］がある, 〜に関心がある, 〜に出資している
hold a 25 percent stake in　〜の株式の25％を保有する, 〜株の25％を保有している
increase one's stake in　〜の持ち株比率を引き上げる, 〜の出資比率を引き上げる
　（=raise one's stake in）
reduce one's stake in　〜の持ち株比率を引き下げる, 〜の出資比率を引き下げる
sell most of one's 10 percent stake in the company　保有する同社株［同社の株式］の10％を売却する
take a stake in　〜へ出資する
◆A reduction of the government's stake in Japan Tobacco Inc. is likely to be opposed by tobacco farmers. 政府の日本たばこ産業（JT）への出資比率引下げ［政府のJT株の持ち株比率引下げ］には、葉タバコ農家の反発が予想される。◆Currently, the government is obliged to hold at least a 50 percent stake in JT. 現在、政府はJT（日本たばこ産業）株の50％以上保有を義務付けられている。◆Ford will relinquish its position as the biggest shareholder of Mazda Motor Corp. by selling most of its 11 percent stake in Mazda. 米フォードは、保有するマツダ株11％の大半を売却して、マツダの筆頭株主の座を降りることになった。◆Mitsui Oil Exploration Co. has a 10 percent stake in offshore oil fields in the oil spill in the Gulf of Mexico. 三井石油開発（三井物産の子会社）は、メキシコ湾の原油流出地域の海底油田に10％出資している。◆Norinchukin would buy a 15 percent stake in Mizuho Securities Co. 農林中央金庫は、みずほ証券の株式（みずほ証券株）の15％を取得する。◆The government holds a 53.4 percent stake in Tokyo Metro Co., which was valued at ¥174.9 billion at book value as of the end of March 2010. 国は東京地下鉄（東京メトロ）の株式の53.4％を保有しており、その簿価での評価額は2010年3月末時点で1,749億円になる。◆The government plans to sell some of its 100 percent stake in Japan Post Holdings Co. to fund reconstruction from the Great East Japan Earthquake. 政府は、東日本大震災の復興財源に充てるため、100％保有する日本郵政の株式の一部も売却する方針だ。◆The Nippon Life Insurance group's stake in Olympus has been reduced to 5.11 percent from 8.18 percent by massive sell-offs of the company's shares. 日本生命グループのオリンパス株の保有比率は、同社株の大量売却で8.18％から5.11％に下がった。◆The Securities and Exchange Law requires anyone with an equity stake of more than 5 percent in a listed company to report a sale of stake of 1 percent or more to a local finance bureau within five business days of the sale. 現行の証券取引法では、上場企業に対する株式保有比率が5％を超える株保有者は、株式の売買が株式の保有割合を1％超えるごとに、株式売買の5営業日以内に各財務局にその報告書を提出しなければならない。◆The stakes in major U.S. securities firms by SMFG, Mitsubishi UFJ and Nomura will boost the presence of Japanese financial institutions in the global market. 三井住友銀行、三菱UFJと野村が米国の大手証券会社に出資することで、グローバル市場での日本の金融機関の存在感が高まりそうだ。◆The U.S. and Canadian governments hold a 70 percent stake in General Motors Co. while it undergoes reconstruction. 米国とカナダ両政府は、GMの株式の7割を保有しているが、GMは再建途上にある。

stakeholder　（名）利害関係者, 株主, ステークホルダー（利害関係者は、企業の従業員、取引先、地域社会を指す）
◆Everyone connected with the Corporation, or the people we call our "stakeholders" will also benefit from value-oriented management. 当社と係りのある人たち、つまり当社の「ステークホルダー」といわれる人たち全員も、価値重視の経営によって利益を受けることになる。◆GM's current stakeholders include the U.S. government, the Canadian government and a United Auto Workers health-care trust. 米政府、カナダ政府と全米自動車労組の医療保険信託などが、GMの現在の株主になっている。◆The value of a corporation is divided between value to the shareholders and value to stakeholders. 企業価値は、株主に帰属する価値とステークホルダー（利害関係者）に帰属する価値に二分される。

stall　（動）止める, 遅らせる, 引き延ばす, 立ち往生させる, 失速させる, 〜に水をさす, （人を）待たせる, ごまかす　（自動）止まる, 遅れる, 減速する, 失速する, 落ち込む, 行き詰まる, エンストを起こす, 暗礁に乗り上げる, 八百長試合をする　（名）停止, 立ち往生, 失速, エンスト
　（⇒money market）
be stalled due to financial difficulties　財政難で行き詰まる［立ち往生する］
remain stalled　依然、落ち込んでいる
stall for time (on)　（〜の）時間を稼ぐ
stall the economy　景気の腰を折る
stall to　〜まで落ち込む
stalling tactics　引き延ばし戦術
◆Business sentiment and the willingness of household to spend may cool and stall the economy unless the sharp appreciation of the yen is checked. 円の急騰を止めないと、企業の心理や家計の消費意欲が冷え込み、景気が腰折れしかねない。◆Despite the ample liquidity, bank lending remains stalled. この豊富な資金［高い流動性］にもかかわらず、銀行貸出は依然、落ち込んでいる。◆It was when European countries needed growth to help them wriggle out of the chokehold of debt that the economic stall came. 欧州諸国が債務の首かせから脱するために成長を必要としていたときに、景気減速［景気の腰折れ］が到来した。◆Profits have been squeezed as interest rates remain near zero percent and loan demands stalls. 金利はまだゼロに近いし、借入需要も停滞したままなので、利益は減少している。◆The Fed stands ready to ease monetary policy further if the U.S. economic recovery stalls. 米国の景気回復が遅れた［減速した］場合、米連邦準備制度理事会（FRB）は一段の金融緩和を進める用意がある。◆This proposal was made to stall for time. この提案は、時間稼ぎのために行われた。◆Transactions on all of the 2,520 issues traded at the TSE were stalled from 9 a.m. due to a computer malfunction. 東証で取引されている2,520全銘柄の取引が、コンピュータのシステム障害で午前9時から停止した。

stance　（名）姿勢, 態度, 立場, 構え, 政策, 策, スタンス
　（⇒credit-tightening stance, monetary stance, wait-and-see stance）
a staunch stance against the excessive appreciation of the yen　行き過ぎた円高を阻止する断固とした姿勢
adopt a wait-and-see stance on　〜に対して模様眺めのスタンスを取る, 〜に対して模様眺めの展開となる
　（⇒mainstay issues）
credit stance　金融政策のスタンス
credit-tightening stance　金融引締めのスタンス
　（=restrictive monetary policy stance, tight monetary stance）
fiscal stance　財政政策
flexible stance　柔軟な姿勢
government's fiscal stance　政府の財政政策
hard-line stance　強硬姿勢, 強気な態度, 強気の構え
maintain an austere stance　厳しい姿勢を貫く
monetary stance　金融政策
negative stance　消極的な態度, 弱気な態度, 弱気の構え
pro-growth stance　成長重視の姿勢

restrictive stance　引締めのスタンス
shift to a credit-tightening stance　金融引締めのスタンスに転じる　(⇒shift)
stance on monetary easing　金融緩和に対する姿勢
◆China will shift to a "prudent" monetary policy in 2011 from the previous "appropriately loose" stance. 中国は、これまでの「適度に緩和的な」金融政策から2011年は「穏健な」金融政策に方向転換する方針だ。◆French Finance Minister Christine Lagarde chosen as the new managing director of the IMF is expected to maintain an austere stance of calling on Greece to reform itself. IMFの新専務理事に選ばれたクリスティーヌ・ラガルド仏財務相は、ギリシャに改革を求める厳しい姿勢を貫くものと期待されている。◆If the government adheres to its stance of capping the annual issuance of government bonds at ¥30 trillion, it should study issuing a new bond whose redemption sources are secured. 政府が国債の年間発行枠30兆円の姿勢にこだわるなら、償還財源の裏付けを持つ新型の国債発行を検討するべきだ。◆The Bank of Japan's stance on monetary easing is also strengthening the effect of preventing yen-buying moves. 日銀の金融緩和に対する姿勢も、円買いの動きを阻止する効果を強めている。◆The G-7 joint statement made clear the stance of supporting the financial markets by supplying ample funds. G7の共同声明は、潤沢な資金供給によって金融市場を下支えする姿勢を明らかにした。◆The government and the BOJ must maintain a staunch stance against the excessive appreciation of the yen. 政府・日銀は、行き過ぎた円高を阻止する断固とした姿勢を維持する必要がある。◆To alleviate the influence of the U.S. government's additional steps to ease the supply of money, the Bank of Japan must adopt a more proactive stance toward monetary relaxation. 米政府の追加金融緩和策［通貨供給量を増やす米政府の追加措置］の影響を和らげるには、日銀も金融緩和の姿勢を強める必要がある。

stand at　〜を示す、〜である、〜となる、〜に当たる
◆The BOJ's total assets as a percentage of GDP stand at nearly 30 percent. 国内総生産（GDP）に対する日銀の総資産の比率［日銀の総資産の国内総生産（GDP）比］は、約3割を占めている。◆The core nationwide CPI, which excludes volatile fresh food prices, stood at 99.3 against the base of 100 for 2005. 全国消費者物価指数のコア指数（値動きの大きい生鮮食品を除く総合指数）は、99.3（2005年=100）となった。◆The diffusion index (DI) of business confidence among large manufacturers stood at plus 1, reflecting a growth in exports due to U.S. economic recovery and a recent surge in domestic stock prices. 大企業の製造業の業況判断指数（DI）が、プラス1となり、米経済の回復による輸出の伸びや最近の国内の株価上昇を反映した。◆The primary balance deficits of Greece currently stand at 10 percent of GDP. ギリシャの財政赤字は現在、GDP（国内総生産）の10%に当たる。◆The ratio of job offers to job seekers stood at a seasonally adjusted 0.42, the lowest on record. 有効求人倍率は、過去最悪の0.42倍（季節調整値）だった。◆The surplus in the current account stood at ¥1.5 trillion in September 2008, marking the seventh consecutive month of year-on-year declines. 2008年9月の経常収支の黒字額は、1兆5,000億円となり、7か月連続で前年実績を下回った。◆The total amount of loans owed by companies and individuals to private financial institutions stands at ¥2.8 trillion in the three prefectures' coastal areas hit by the March 11 tsunami. 津波被災地の3県沿岸部では、企業や個人の民間企業からの借入金総額が、2.8兆円にのぼっている。

standard　(名)標準、基準、規格、スタンダード
alternative standard　交替本位制
assessment standard　評価基準
banking standards　銀行業基準
bifocal gold exchange standard　復元的金為替本位制
bimetallic standard　複本位制、金銀複本位制
BIS capital standards　国際決済銀行の自己資本比率規制
bullion standard　地金本位制
capital adequacy standards　自己資本比率基準
capital standards　自己資本比率
cash balance standard　現金残高標準
cash transaction standard　現金取引標準
commodity monetary standard　商品貨幣本位制
credit standards　信用基準、融資基準
currency standards　通貨標準
current standard　当座標準
de facto standard　事実上の標準、事実上の国際標準、事実上の世界標準、デファクト・スタンダード
disclosure standards　開示基準
dollar exchange standard system　ドル為替本位制度
double standard　二重基準、複本位制、ダブル・スタンダード
eligibility standards　適債基準
exchange standard　為替本位制
fiat standard　不換紙幣本位制
financial standards　財務基準
fractional reserve standard　部分準備本位制
free standard　自由本位制
global standard　世界標準、グローバル・スタンダード
gold bullion standard　金地金本位制度
gold coin［currency］standard　金貨本位制度
gold exchange standard (system)　金為替本位制度
gold kernel standard　金核本位制
gold standard banking system　金本位制下の金融組織
gold standard (system)　金本位制
government bond standard　政府証券本位
hybrid standard　混合本位制
indirect standard　間接本位制
industry standard　業界標準、産業標準、産業基準、業界規格、統一基準
international standard　国際標準、国際規格
investors' credit standards　投資家の投資基準
lending standard　貸出基準、与信基準、融資基準
liquidity standard　流動性基準
listing standard　上場基準
managed gold standard　管理された金本位制度
metallic standard money　金属本位貨幣
monetary standard　本位制度
monetary standard policy　本位政策
monometallic standard　単本位制度
multiple currency standard　多数通貨本位制
origination standard　審査基準
practice standards　業務基準
SDR standard　SDR本位制
single risk standards　集中リスク基準
single standard　単本位制度
standard accounts　一般投資家
standard basket (system)　標準バスケット方式
standard coinage　本位貨幣制度
standard coins　本位貨幣、標準貨幣
standard currency basket system　標準バスケット方式
standard deviation　標準偏差
standard dollar　標準ドル
standard fixed rate debt　普通債
(=standard straight issue)
standard form for L/C　信用状標準形式

standard gold 本位金
standard money 本位貨幣, 標準貨幣
standard money rates 標準金利
standard official currency 基準通貨
standard option 標準的なオプション
standard policy 標準証券, 標準約款
standard silver dollar 標準銀ドル
standard system 本位制度
standards implementation group 基準適用グループ
standards of capital increase 増資基準
standards of creditworthiness 与信基準
sterling exchange standard system ポンド為替本位制
the highest standard of integrity 最高の倫理基準 (⇒integrity)
the International Financial Reporting Standards 国際財務報告基準, 国際会計基準 (⇒IFRSs)
the standard rate of interest 標準金利
the standard yield 標準利回り
underwriting standards 貸出審査基準, 与信基準
universal standard ユニバーサル・スタンダード, 世界標準, 国際標準
world standard 世界標準, ワールド・スタンダード (=worldwide standard)
◆Currently, the ministry has no clear standard to assess the assets of four road-related public corporations properly. 現在, 同省には, 道路関係4公団の資産を適正に評価する明確な基準がない。◆The International Financial Reporting Standards (IFRSs) have become the global standard in more than 100 countries, especially in Europe. 国際財務報告基準(IFRSs)は, 欧州を中心に100か国以上でグローバル・スタンダードになっている。◆The trader used a standard option to hedge the price risk of a stock. このトレーダーは, 株式の価格リスクをヘッジするために標準的なオプションを使った。◆The universal standard is determined by a majority vote among nations producing the goods. ユニバーサル・スタンダードは, 製品生産国間の多数投票によって決められる。

Standard & Poor's スタンダード・アンド・プアーズ, S&P
Standard & Poor's Composite Index of 500 Stocks スタンダード&プアーズ総合500種株価指数, S&P500株価指数 (=S&P 500, Standard & Poor's 500, Standard & Poor's 500 Index)
Standard & Poor's Corporation スタンダード&プアーズ, S&P (米国の代表的格付け機関)
Standard & Poor's index [Index] スタンダード&プアーズ株価指数, S&P株価指数 (通常は「総合500種株価指数」を指す。ダウ・ジョーンズ社の工業株30種平均(Dow Jones industrial average)と共に, 米国で最も広範に使用されている株価指数)
Standard & Poor's rating スタンダード&プアーズの格付け
Standard & Poor's ratios スタンダード&プアーズの債券評価
Standard & Poor's stock price index S&P株価指数, スタンダード&プアーズ株価指数
◆Standard & Poor's cut the U.S. credit rating for the first time. スタンダード・アンド・プアーズ(S&P)が, 米国債の格付けを史上初めて引き下げた。◆Standard & Poor's is the U.S. rating agency. スタンダード・アンド・プアーズ(S&P)は, 米国の格付け会社だ。◆Standard & Poor's made a grim assessment of the outlook of U.S. fiscal reconstruction. スタンダード・アンド・プアーズ(S&P)は, 米国の財政再建の見通しを, 厳しく評価した。◆The downgrade reflects Standard and Poor's concern over the company's ability to avoid a further deterioration in its operating performance. この格下げは, 同社の一段の業績悪化は避けられないとのスタンダード&プアーズの懸念を反映している。◆U.S. Treasury bonds were downgraded by Standard & Poor's because the government failed to take drastic countermeasures against its fiscal deterioration. 米政府が財政悪化に大胆な対策を取れなかったため, 米国債はスタンダード・アンド・プアーズ(S&P)に格下げされた。

Standard & Poor's 500 スタンダード・プアーズ株価指数, S&P500株価指数, S&P株価指数 (=Standard & Poor's 500 index; ⇒Dow Jones industrial average [Industrial Average])
Standard & Poor's 500 index スタンダード&プアーズ総合500種株価指数, S&P500株価指数
Standard & Poor's 500 stock price index スタンダード&プアーズ500種株価指数, S&P株価指数
◆The Dow and the Standard & Poor's 500 index each shed more than 10 percent in February 2009. 2009年2月のダウ平均とSP株価指数は, それぞれ前月比で10%以上も低下した。◆The Standard & Poor's 500 index is at the top end of its range for the past two months. スタンダード・プアーズ(500種)株価指数は, 過去2か月のボックス圏の上限にある。

standard-bearer (名)指導者, 主唱者, 唱導者, 首領, 旗手
◆During the period of structural reforms pushed by the Koizumi administration, the former chairman of the bank was lionized as a standard-bearer of financial reform. 小泉政権が推し進めた構造改革の時代に, 同行の前会長は金融改革の旗手ともてはやされた。

standby (形)予備の, 控えの, 非常用の, 代替用の, 待機中の, スタンドバイ
standby agreement 残額引受契約
standby arrangement スタンドバイ取決め
standby commitment 銀行の保証, 信用供与枠, 株主割当ての際のスタンドバイ引受業者(standby underwriter)による残額引受け, スタンドバイ引受け(「スタンドバイ引受け」は, 会社が株主割当てを行う際, 株主割当ての申込み期間が過ぎても株主からの応募額が予定の募集額に達しない場合, 引受業者(スタンドバイ引受業者)がその残額分の買取りを約束すること)
standby credit 保証, 銀行による企業の借入金の保証, 資金引出し信用供与, 保証のためのスタンドバイ信用状
standby fee スタンドバイ引受手数料
standby letter of credit スタンドバイ信用状
standby underwriter スタンドバイ引受業者
standby underwriting 残額引受け, スタンドバイ引受け

standing authorization 自動引落し, 定期的支払い指図

standing credit 常設の信用枠

standing of a firm 企業の信用評価

standing order 自動引落し, 定期的支払い指図

standpoint (名)見地, 立場, 観点
◆To avert the injection of public money into banks, the eurozone governments stuck to their official standpoint that there are no default problems within the single euro currency area. 銀行への公的資金注入を回避するため, ユーロ圏政府は, 単一通貨・ユーロ圏に債務返済不能の問題は存在しないという公式立場に固執した。

standstill (名)行き詰まり, 停止, 休止, 運休, 立ち往生, 現状維持, ゼロ成長になること
be at a standstill 行き詰まっている, 運休している, 停止している
bring A to a standstill Aを行き詰まらせる, Aを止める
come to a standstill 行き詰まる, 止まる, ゼロ成長になる
remain at a standstill まったく進展していない

◆A computer failure brought trading at the Tokyo Stock Exchange to a standstill for more than four hours. コンピュータ・システムの障害で、東京証券取引所の取引が4時間以上も停止した。◆The eurozone's economic growth will come to a virtual standstill in 2009. 2009年のユーロ圏の経済は事実上、ゼロ成長になる見込みだ。

standstill agreement 現状維持契約, 現状維持合意, 弁済の猶予 (「現状維持契約(合意)」とは、株式の発行会社と一定数以上の株式を保有する株主が、株主の現保有株式の買い増しや処分をしないことで合意すること)

start (動)開始する, 始める, 着手する
  start discussion with banks 銀行団と交渉を開始する, 銀行団と交渉に入る
  start easing policy 金融緩和に踏み切る, 金融緩和に動き出す
  start (the) syndication シ団組成を開始する (=launch syndication)
  start to decelerate 低下に転じる
  start to revive [recover] 回復し始める, 回復を始める
  started the week looking toppy (市場が)高止まりで週明けする, 高止まりで明ける
  ◆Internet-based bank Sony Bank started a deposit service for the Brasilian real in May 2011. ネット専業銀行のソニー銀行が、2011年5月からブラジル通貨レアルの預金サービスを開始した。◆The ongoing business slump raises the specter of a global downturn comparable to the Great Depression that started in 1929. 今回の不況は、1929年に始まった世界大恐慌に匹敵するほどの世界同時不況の懸念が高まっている。

start (名)開始, 始まり, 出だし, 着手, 開始点, 出発点, 新規事業(starts), スタート
  built-for-sale (units) starts 分譲住宅の着工戸数 (=starts of built-for-sale units)
  company-rented starts 給与住宅の着工戸数 (=starts of company housing)
  condominium starts マンション着工戸数
  deferred start option 先スタート・オプション
  floor space [area] of new housing starts 新築住宅着工床面積
  fresh start 再出発
  get a head start on ～に先行する
  get off to a slow start スタートで後れをとる
  get off to a solid start 手堅いスタートを切る
  housing starts 住宅着工戸数, 住宅着工件数, 住宅着工
  low-start loans ステップアップ型ローン
  low-start mortgage ロースタート・モーゲージ
  owner-occupied starts 持ち家住宅着工戸数
  privately-funded starts 民間資金による住宅着工戸数
  publicly-funded starts 公共資金による着工戸数
  recover from one's late start in ～の出遅れを取り戻す
  rental (units) starts 賃貸住宅着工戸数
  since the start of the year 年初来
  ◆Just after the start of the market intervention, the banks were flooded with orders for forward exchange contracts. 市場介入の直後、銀行には為替予約の注文が殺到した。

start up (動)(事業や会社などを)起こす, 始める
  ◆The new Corporate Law gives entrepreneurs more freedom to start up new companies. 新会社法では、起業家にとってこれまでより自由に新会社を起こすことができる。

start-up (名)ベンチャー企業, 新興企業, 新規企業, 新企業, スタートアップ・カンパニー (=start-up business, start-up company, start-up firm)
  start-up business 新規企業, 新興企業, ベンチャー企業, ベンチャー分野 (=start-up, start-up company)
  start-up capital 当初の資本金
  start-up cost 開業準備費
  start-up date 取引開始日
  ◆Xinhua Finance is the first foreign firm to debut on the TSE Mothers market for start-ups. 新興企業向け市場の東証マザーズに上場するのは、新華ファイナンス(中国の金融情報サービス会社)が外国企業としては初めてだ。

start-up company 新興企業, ベンチャー企業 (=start-up business, start-up firm, IPO, massive debts)
  ◆Until last year, many start-up companies had to shelve planned listings when they were screened by securities firms. 昨年までは、新興企業の多くが、証券会社の審査段階で予定していた上場を見送らざるを得なかった。

start-up firm 新興企業, ベンチャー企業 (=start-up business, start-up company, start-up corporation; ⇒ Mothers)
  ◆M&A deals among start-up firms are likely to create more demand for equity financing from the autumn. ベンチャー企業間のM&A取引で、秋から株式発行による資金調達の需要が増える見通しだ。

state (名)国, 国家, 政府(米国の)州, 状態, 状況, ステート
  capitalist [capitalistic] state 資本主義国, 資本主義国家
  client state 貿易相手国
  commercial state 商業国家
  corporate state 企業国家
  industrial state 産業国家, 工業国家
  member state 加盟国
  Organization of American States 米州機構
  secretary of state 米国の国務長官、州務長官, 英国の国務大臣
  socialist [socialistic] state 社会主義国, 社会主義国家
  state of business 業況
  state of emergency 緊急事態
  State of the State address [Message] 州知事の施政方針演説
  State of the Union Message (米大統領の)一般教書, 年頭教書
  State of the World Message (米大統領が議会に送る)外交政策, 外交教書
  state of trade 商況
  the state of play [affairs, things] 進行状態, 現段階の状況, 現状
  the state of the (current) economy 景気の現状
  the States 米国
  welfare state 福祉国家
  ◆The threat of the overheated state of European countries and China causing new waves of financial turmoil must not be underestimated. 欧米諸国や中国などの景気過熱状態が新たな金融危機[金融市場の混乱]を引き起こす恐れがあることを、過小評価してはならない。

state (形)国の, 国家の, 州の, 州立の, 州管理の, 儀式の, 儀式用の
  non-state sector 非国有企業
  State Administration of Foreign Exchange (中国の)国家外貨管理局, SAFE (⇒SAFE)
  state aid 国家支援, 国家援助, 国庫補助[補助金], 国家補助
  state bank 米州法銀行[ステート・バンク], 州免許銀行, 国営銀行, 国立銀行(米国の州法銀行は、州法により認可を受けた商業銀行(commercial bank)のことで、state-chartered bankともいう)
  state bond 州債, 国債
  state borrowing 国家借入れ

state bounty　国庫補助金
state capital　国家資本
state capitalism　国家資本主義
state-chartered bank　米国の州法銀行
state contribution　国庫負担
State Department　米国務省（他国の外務省（Foreign Office）に相当）
state economy　国家経済
state funded　国から資金を得た, 政府出資の
state government　州政府
state legislature　米州議会
　（米連邦議会＝Congress）
State Minister in Charge of Financial Policy　金融担当大臣
state pension　（老人、未亡人、身障者などへの）年金
state planning economy　国家計画経済
state policy　国家政策, 国策
state power　国家権力
state property　国有財産
state sponsor of terrorism　テロ支援国家
state subsidy　国庫補助金
state's evidence　証拠物件

state-backed　（形）政府系の, 政府系〜, 政府保証の
　（⇒government-affiliated）
a state-backed bank　政府系金融機関
a state-backed corporate turnaround body　政府系の企業再生機構
◆Also needed urgently are measures to strengthen the functions of the state-backed Banks' Stockholding Acquisition Corporation. 政府系の銀行等保有株式取得機構の機能強化策も, 急務だ。

state coffers　国庫, 国の財源, 国家財政
　（＝the coffers of the state）
◆Amid the depleted state coffers, it is difficult to implement a major stimulus package to rectify the rise in the yen's value. 財政悪化が進む中［国の財源が枯渇する中］, 円高是正のため大規模な財政出動を行うのは難しい。

state control　国の支配, 国の管理, 国家管理
◆Ashikaga Bank is a failed regional bank under temporary state control. 足利銀行は, 経営破たんして一時国有化された地方銀行だ。◆The bank is now under state control. 同行は現在, 国有化されている（国の管理下にある）。

state-financed [state financed]　（形）政府出資の, 州が融資［出資］する, 政府系の
◆The state-financed Japan Post Bank is expanding on the strength of people's trust in the government. 政府出資のゆうちょ銀行は, 国民の政府に対する信用力を後ろ盾として, 業容を拡大している。

state finances　国家財政, 財政
◆State finances are in sufficiently dire straits. 国家財政は, かなりの危機の状況にある。◆The role of the new prime minister is putting the economy on a stable course and rehabilitating the state finances. 新首相の役割は, 景気を安定軌道に乗せて財政も立て直すことだ。

state-funded　（形）国から資金を得た, 政府出資の
　（state-paid）, 州が融資［出資］する, 政府系の
entirely state-funded　国［政府、州］が100％出資する
state-funded financial institution　政府系金融機関
state-funded portion of pension payments　年金支給額［年金給付］の国庫負担分
the entirely state-funded Development Bank of Japan　国が100％出資している日本政策投資銀行
the state-funded Development Bank of Japan　政府系の日本政策投資銀行

◆Former PCI president and executives swindled the government out of about ¥300 million by overcharging for a state-funded project to dispose of chemical weapons. PCI元社長と元取締役らは, 国をだまして政府出資の化学兵器処理事業の事業費を水増し請求し, 約3億円をだまし取った。◆JAL will ask for funds from the state-funded Development Bank of Japan. 日本航空は, 政府系日本政策投資銀行からの資金援助を求める方針だ。◆The Finance Ministry proposed to reduce the state-funded portion of pension payments. 財務省は, 年金支給額［年金給付］の国庫負担分の引下げを提案した。◆The public loan was extended to JAL in June 2009 by the entirely state-funded Development Bank of Japan. この公的融資は, 国が100％出資している日本政策投資銀行が, 2009年6月に行った。

state funding　（名）政府出資, 国庫負担, 国庫負担分
◆The government is poised to issue bridging bonds to make up the expected shortfall in state funding for the basic pension fund. 政府は, つなぎ国債を発行して, 予想される基礎年金基金の国庫負担の不足分を賄（まかな）う方針だ。

state-held shares　政府保有株
◆The government should start selling off state-held shares of Japan Post companies. 政府は, 日本郵政グループ企業の政府保有株の売却を始めるべきだ。

State [National] Development and Reform Commission of China　中国の（経済政策を統括する）国家発展改革委員会
◆The State Development and Reform Commission of China will shift its policy of luring foreign companies from quantity to quality. 中国の（経済政策を統括する）国家発展改革委員会は, 外資導入の方針を量から質に転換する方向だ。

state of the economy　経済の状況, 景気の現状
◆If you look at the state of the economy, the risks of not doing anything are greater than the risks of doing something. 経済の状況を見たら, 何かするリスクよりも何もしないリスクのほうが大きい。◆The coincident indicator, the nation's key gauge of the state of the economy, topped the boom-or-bust line of 50 percent in March. 国内の景気の現状を示す一致指数［景気一致指数］が, 3月は景気判断の分かれ目となる50％を上回った。

State of the Union speech [address]　一般教書演説　（＝State of the Union Address, State of the Union Message）
◆U.S. President Barack Obama addressed reforming Wall Street in his first State of the Union speech. オバマ米大統領は, 同大統領初の一般教書演説で, ウォール街（金融街）の改革を呼びかけた［打ち出した］。
解説 一般教書とは：米大統領が年頭に連邦議会上下両院合同本会議で表明する, 向こう1年間の施政方針。大統領の演説中, 最も重要とされている。内政・外交全般にわたる国家の情勢を要訳, 政府の基本政策のほか, 大統領の抱負や信念, 政治哲学なども織り込まれる。予算教書（Budget Message）、経済報告（Economic Report of the President）とともに, 米大統領の三大年頭教書の一つ。

state ownership　国有, 国の所有, 国営, 国有制度
◆The federal government will temporarily place GM under state ownership by acquiring a 60 percent stake in the new GM. 米政府は, 新GM株の60％を取得して同社を一時的に国有化する方針だ。

state-paid portion of the pension　年金［基礎年金］の国庫負担分
◆The Finance Ministry will lower the state-paid portion of the pension from the current 50 percent to 36.5 percent due to a shortage of financial resources. 財務省は, 財源不足のため, 年金の国庫負担分を現行の50％から36.5％に引き下げる方針だ。

state regulators　州規制当局
◆Citigroup will buy back the auction-rate securities from in-

vestors under separate accords with the Securities and Exchange Commission and state regulators. 米シティグループは、米証券取引委員会（SEC）や州規制当局との個々の合意に基づいて投資家から金利入札証券（ARS）を買い戻す。

state-run （形）国営の, 国立の
　state-run Deposit Insurance Corporation 国営の預金保険機構　（⇒oversee）
　state-run enterprise 国営企業
state-run bank 国営銀行
　◆Issuance of yuan-denominated bonds has hitherto been limited to state-run banks. 人民元建て債の発行はこれまで、国営銀行に限られてきた。
state-run financial institution 国営金融機関, 政府系金融機関
　◆Japan Post was the world's largest state-run financial institution. 日本郵政公社は、世界最大の国営金融機関だった。◆Six state-run financial institutions were reorganized into three, the Japan Bank for International Cooperation（JBIC）, the Development Bank of Japan and the National Life Finance Corporation. 政府系の6つの金融機関が、国際協力銀行、日本政策投資銀行と国民生活金融公庫の3つに統合された。
stated capital 表示資本金
stated equity 公表株主資本
stated value 表示額面
statement （名）計算書, 財務表, 報告書, 届出書, ステートメント　（⇒financial statement, financial statements, listing particulars, proxy statement, registration statement）
　annual statement 年次報告書
　bank statement 銀行照合表, 預金残高証明書, 銀行報告書
　business statement 営業報告書
　cash flow statement キャッシュ・フロー計算書, 現金収支計算書
　distribution statement 分売届出書
　interim statements 中間財務書類, 中間財務諸表
　offering statement 募集届出書, 発行目論見書
　profit and loss statement 損益計算書　（=income statement）
　quarterly statement 四半期報告書
　statement of cash flows 資金収支表, 収支計算書, キャッシュ・フロー表
　statement of financial condition 財政状態表, 貸借対照表　（=balance sheet, statement of financial position）
　statement of income 損益計算書　（=income statement, profit and loss account, statement of earnings, statement of operations）
　◆The heads of Japan, China and ROK signed statements on the tripartite partnership, international finance and the economy, and disaster management cooperation. 日中韓首脳は、3国間パートナーシップ、国際金融・経済と防災対策での連携に関する声明に署名した。◆The special statement on the world economy adopted by the APEC forum specified a timeline for implementing the measures. アジア太平洋経済協力会議（APEC）で採択された世界経済に関する特別声明は、その対策実施の期限を明記した。◆The U.S. Securities and Exchange Commission voted to require companies to file annual and quarterly statements weeks earlier than they currently do. 米証券取引委員会（SEC）は、投票により、企業に対して年次報告書と四半期報告書の提出期限短縮化（現行より数週間短縮）を義務付けることを決定した。
status （名）地位, 状態, 状況, 情勢, 事情, 構造, 身分, ランク, 資格, 信用, 権威, ステータス
　a status inquiry 信用調査, 資産調査
　a status inquiry agency 信用調査機関
　a status report 信用調査報告書

benchmark status 指標銘柄としての地位
business status 営業状態
credit status 信用状態
economic status 経済状態
financial status 財政状態, 財務状況, 金融状態
flexible status loans 簡易審査型ローン
funded [funding] status 拠出状況 [状態], 積立状況
preferred creditor status 優先債権者の地位
soon-to-be-junk status government bonds 投資不適格レベルが見込まれる国債
status as the largest holder of U.S. Treasury securities 米財務省証券 [米国債] の最大保有国としての地位
tax-exempt status 免税資格
tax status 税務上の取扱い
the corporate status of a dormant company 休眠会社の法人格
the current funding status employee pensions 従業員年金の現在の拠出状況
the life insurer's status as large shareholders 大株主としての生命保険会社の地位
　◆By buying Greek, Portuguese and Spanish bonds, the ECB infused life into the moribund eurozone markets for these soon-to-be-junk status government bonds. ギリシャやポルトガル、スペインの国債を買い入れて、欧州中銀（ECB）は、崩壊寸前のユーロ圏の投資不適格レベルが見込まれるこれらの債券の市場に生気を吹き込んだ。◆China is trying to flex its muscle with the United States on the strength of its status as the largest holder of U.S. Treasury securities. 中国は、米財務省証券 [米国債] の最大保有国としての地位を背景に、米国への影響力を行使しようとしている。◆China's renminbi may attain a reserve-currency status by the steady appreciation of the yuan and the country's enormous capital surpluses. 中国の人民元は、人民元の着実な切上げと中国の膨大な資本剰余金によって、準備通貨の地位を獲得する可能性がある。◆The life insurers' status as large shareholders means that when the market dives, their portfolios also take a tumble. 大株主としての生命保険会社の地位は、株価が大きく下がると資産内容も急激に悪化することを意味する。◆The status of the Japanese market is declining. 日本市場の地位が、低下している。◆The U.S. dollar may lose its current status as the world's only reserve currency. 米ドルは、世界唯一の準備通貨としての現在の地位を失う可能性がある。
statute of limitations 出訴期限, 出訴期限法, 消滅時効, 時効
　◆Due to the statute of limitations, the tax authorities will likely be unable to levy taxes on most of the investors who participated in the investment scheme. 時効で、税務当局は、この投資事業に参加した投資家の大半に課税はできないとみられる。
statutory limit 法定上限
　◆The U.S. federal debt has reached its current statutory limit of $14.3 trillion（about1.1 quadrillion）. 米政府の債務は、現在の法定上限の14.3兆ドル（約1,100兆円）に達している。
stay （動）とどまる, ～で推移する, ～を維持する
　stay at a high level 高水準で推移する
　stay away （投資家が）様子見に回る
　stay firm 堅調に推移する, 引締めの姿勢を堅持する
　stay firm supported by ～に支えられて堅調に推移する
　stay in the lower ￥77 range against the dollar 1ドル＝77円台前半で推移する
　stay on hold （金融政策などを）据え置く
　stay put or turn down 横ばいか低下に転じる
　stay solvent 倒産を防ぐ
　stay stable 安定的に推移する

stay underweight　アンダーウェートを維持する
◆The yen stayed in the lower ¥77 range against the U.S. dollar in Tokyo. 東京外国為替市場の円相場は、1ドル＝77円台前半で推移した。

steady　(形)しっかり固定された, しっかりした, 一様な, 不変の, 恒常の, 定常的な, 着実な, 堅実な, 定まった, 安定している
hold a financial policy steady　金融政策を据え置く
keep [hold] a key rate steady　政策金利[(米国の場合は)フェデラル・ファンド金利]を据え置く
maintain a steady hand　金融政策を据え置く
steady accumulation of capital　恒常的な資本蓄積
steady appreciation of the value of the yuan　人民元の着実な切上げ
steady economic development [growth]　安定した経済成長
steady growth　着実な伸び[成長], 順調な伸び
steady growth path　恒常的成長経路, 安定した成長経路 (=steady-state growth path)
steady increase　着実な伸び, 着実な増加, 恒常的伸び[増加]
steady market　堅調な市況, 市況堅調
steady money supply　通貨供給量の安定
steady policy　堅実な政策
steady profit growth　利益の順調な伸び
steady rise　着実な伸び, 着実な増加[上昇]
steady-state growth　恒常的成長, 均斉成長, 一様な成長
◆A steady annual improvement in earnings of five percent or more is a reasonable goal given the weight of regulated companies in our asset base. 年5％以上の利益増加率の安定確保は、規制対象企業が当社の資産構成で大きな比重を占めていることから、妥当な目標と言えるでしょう。◆China's renminbi may attain a reserve-currency status by the steady appreciation of the yuan and the country's enormous capital surpluses. 中国の人民元は、人民元の着実な切上げと中国の膨大な資本剰余金によって、準備通貨の地位を獲得する可能性がある。◆The Bank of Japan kept the key short-term interest rate steady at around zero to 0.1 percent. 日銀は、短期の政策金利をほぼ0～0.1％に据え置いた。◆The Bank of Japan left its key short-term interest rate steady at 0.1 percent. 日本銀行は、短期の政策金利を0.1％に据え置いた。◆The global economy will soon return to a path of a steady growth. 世界経済は、もうすぐ順調な成長軌道に戻るだろう。

steam　(名)推進力, 駆動力, 元気, 力, 勢い, 蒸気, スチーム
gather steam　勢いを増す, 加速する (=build up steam, gain some steam, get up steam, pick up steam)
go full steam ahead with　～に全力で取り組む
lose steam　勢いを失う, 活力を失う, 勢いが弱まる, 勢いがなくなる, 失速する (=lose some of the steam)
pick up steam　上向く, 景気が上向く, 上昇傾向にある, 上昇する, ～の勢いが増す, 勢いが強まる, 次第に速度を上げる, 次第に注目を浴びるようになる, 次第に動きが出る (=get up [build up] steam)
run out of steam　息切れする, 元気がなくなる, 気力・意欲がなくなる, ブームなどが下火になる
◆If the driving forces for the Japanese economy, namely capital investment and exports, lose steam, the economy inevitably will slow down further. 設備投資と輸出という日本経済の牽引役[日本経済の牽引役である設備投資と輸出]に勢いがなくなれば、景気の一段の減速は避けられない。◆Japan's business leaders believe the economy is picking up steam. 日本企業のトップ(経営者)は、景気は上向いている、と見ている。◆The rally has run out of steam. 強気相場は息切れしている。◆With the economic recovery picking up steam, the employment environment seems to have bottomed out. 景気回復の勢いが強まって、雇用環境は底を脱したようだ。

steer　(動)操縦する, (～の)舵を取る, 運転する, 導く, 指導する, (～に)向ける, 案内する
steer a course of stability　安定の道を選ぶ
steer between two extremes　中庸(ちゅうよう)の道をとる
steer clear of　～を避ける, ～に近づかない, ～に近寄らない
steer the company to prosperity　会社を繁栄[成功, 発展]に導く
steer the middle course　中立の立場をとる, 極端な行動をとらない
steer to a growth path　成長軌道[成長経路]に向かう
◆The world economy will steer to a growth path again once the financial crisis subsides. 金融危機が沈静化したら、世界経済はまた成長軌道[成長経路]に向かうだろう。

stem　(動)止める, せき止める, 食い止める, ～に歯止めをかける, 抑える, 阻止する, 逆らって進む
stem a further economic downturn　これ以上の景気後退を食い止める
stem any excessive changes in the exchange rate　為替相場の過度な変動を抑制する
stem the rapid [sharp] rise in the yen's value　急激な円高を阻止する[食い止める], 円相場の急上昇を阻止する, 円相場の急上昇を阻止する (⇒currency market intervention)
◆Greece asked other eurozone member states for financial support to help it stem its budget crisis in early 2010. 2010年初めにギリシャは、財政危機を回避するため、他のユーロ圏加盟国に金融支援を求めた。◆The Finance Ministry and the Bank of Japan may keep selling the yen to stem its surge. 円高を食い止めるため[円の急騰を阻止するため]、財務省・日本銀行は、円を売り続ける可能性がある。◆The government and the Bank of Japan should conduct a concerted intervention with the United States and European countries to stem the yen's further rise. 政府・日銀は、米欧と協調介入を実施して、円高進行を阻止しなければならない。◆The government and the BOJ intervened in the market for the first time in 6 1/2 years in September 2010 to stem the yen's rise. 政府・日銀は、円高を阻止する[食い止める]ため、2010年9月に6年半ぶりに(円売り・ドル買いの)市場介入をした。◆The sense of crisis is felt by those trying to stem a further economic downturn. これ以上の景気後退を食い止めようとしている人たちは、危機感を抱いている。◆With a view to stemming the airlines' financial hemorrhaging, the Construction and Transport Ministry in late May asked the Development Bank of Japan to provide emergency loans to the two carriers. 航空会社の損失を阻止するため、5月下旬に国土交通省は、日本政策投資銀行に対し両航空会社への緊急融資を要請した。

stem from　～から生じる[起こる, 始まる], ～から発する, ～に由来する, ～に起因する, ～による
◆Corporate bankruptcies stemming from the March 11 earthquake and tsunami totaled 330. 東日本大震災による企業倒産の総件数は、330件に達している。◆Japan, the United States and European countries will cooperate to avert financial turmoil stemming from the downgrading of the U.S. credit rating. 日米欧が連携して、米国債の格下げによる金融市場の混乱を回避することになった。◆The current high price of crude oil stems partly from the lack of investment in oil development for a long period. 現在の原油高の一因は、長期にわたる石油開発投資の不足だ。◆The effects of an economic slowdown in industrialized countries stemming from the U.S. subprime woes could spread in the emerging

economies. 米国のサブプライム（低所得者向け住宅融資）問題に起因する先進国の景気減速の影響は、新興国にも拡大する可能性がある。◆The financial crisis stemmed from a U.S. housing mortgage meltdown. 今回の金融危機は、米国の住宅ローン市場の崩壊から始まった。◆The inadequate decision-making and business management processes of the financial group stem from factional strife within the company. 同金融グループの不十分な意思決定プロセスと経営管理体制は、社内の派閥争いに起因する。◆The United States is under pressure to make some difficult monetary policy decisions to cool down the overheating economy by countering the inflationary pressures stemming from higher import prices due to the weaker dollar. 米国は現在、ドル安での輸入価格の高騰によるインフレ圧力を抑えて過熱気味の景気を鎮めるための難しい金融政策の決断を迫られている。

stem the yen's rise　円高を阻止する
◆Speculators believe the government will not take any specific action to stem the yen's rise for the time being. 政府は当分、とくに円高阻止に動くようなことはない、と投機筋は踏んでいる。◆To stem the yen's rise, the government will play its ace when the yen stands on the brink of rising above ¥80 to the dollar. 円高阻止のため、政府は円が上昇して1ドル＝80円を突破する寸前の段階で奥の手を出すようだ。

stem the yen's rise against other major currencies　主要通貨に対する円相場の上昇を阻止する
◆Prime Minister Kan and Bank of Japan Gov. Shirakawa did not discuss a currency intervention to stem the yen's rise against other major currencies. 菅首相と白川日銀総裁は、主要通貨に対する円相場の上昇を阻止するための為替介入については協議しなかった。

step　（名）措置,手段,対策,政策,足どり,歩調,歩み,一歩,段階,足跡,ステップ
　financial steps　金融措置,金融政策
　multiple steps income statement　区分式損益計算書,区分損益計算書
　step budget　弾力性予算
　steps for further quantitative monetary easing　追加の［一段の］量的金融緩和策,量的金融緩和の追加策
　take additional monetary easing steps　追加の金融緩和策を実施する
　the economy's step toward recovery　景気回復の足取り
◆Government steps taken to deal with Resona's collapse did not incorporate a reduction in the banking group's capital. りそな銀行の経営破たん処理に取った国の措置には、同金融グループの減資は織り込まれなかった。◆In the subprime crisis, the U.S. Federal Reserve Board had to take the extraordinary step of providing an emergency loan not to a commercial bank but to an investment bank. サブプライム問題で、米国の中央銀行の連邦準備制度理事会（FRB）は、緊急融資を銀行［商業銀行］ではなく証券会社［投資銀行］に対して行う異例の措置を取らざるを得なかった。◆The Bank of Japan decided to take new steps for further quantitative monetary easing at an extraordinary Policy Board meeting. 日銀は、臨時の金融政策決定会合で、追加の量的金融緩和策を新たに実施することを決めた。◆The BOJ's policy meeting is expected to consider taking additional monetary easing steps. 日銀の政策決定会合では、追加の金融緩和策の実施を検討する見通しだ。◆The business integration and eventual merger of the TSE and OSE will be implemented in several steps. 東証と大証の事業統合と最終的な経営統合は、段階的に行われる。◆The next step in the quest for higher gains is to inflate the returns by leverage. 高利益追求の第二の手段は、借金による利益の膨（ふく）らましだ。◆This step is being regarded as a measure to increase friendly long-term shareholders and discourage a hostile takeover. この措置は、友好的な長期安定株主を増やして敵対的買収を防ぐための手段と考えられている。◆To alleviate the influence of the U.S. government's additional steps to ease the supply of money, the Bank of Japan must adopt a more proactive stance toward monetary relaxation. 米政府の金融緩和策［通貨供給量を増やす米政府の追加措置］の影響を和らげるには、日銀も金融緩和の姿勢を強める必要がある。◆To make the economy's step toward recovery much firmer, the government should implement another expansionary budget. 景気回復の足取りをずっと確かなものにするためにも、政府はさらに積極型の予算を実施すべきだ。

step down　（動）辞職する,辞任する,退任する,身を引く,引退する　（=resign）
◆The presidents of UFJ Holdings, UFJ Bank and UFJ Trust Bank likely will step down to take responsibility. UFJホールディングスの社長とUFJ銀行の頭取、UFJ信託銀行の社長は、引責辞任する見通しだ。

step-down bond　ステップダウン債（クーポン（表面金利）が定期的に切り下げられる債券）

step-down loan　ステップダウン型ローン（固定金利型ローンのうち、支払い金利を後になるほど低くしたローン）

step in　～に乗り出す,～に介入する,～に干渉する,割って入る,援助を申し出る,参加する,立ち寄る
◆The U.S. government stepped in to bail out Chrysler and GM in December 2008. 米政府は、2008年12月にクライスラーとGMの救済に乗り出した。

step into　～に介入する
　step into the currency market　為替市場に介入する
　step into the foreign exchange market　外国為替市場に介入する
◆The Finance Ministry and the Bank of Japan stepped into the foreign exchange market only once in the three months through September 2010. 財務省・日銀が、2010年7～9月に1度だけ外国為替市場に介入した。◆The government and the Bank of Japan stepped into the currency market for the first time in 6 1/2 years. 政府・日銀が、6年半ぶりに為替市場に介入した［市場介入を実施した］。

step up　本格化させる,活発化させる,促進する,強化する（beef up, up）,増大［拡大］させる,高める,（調子を）上げる,作業を急ぐ,昇進させる,上がる,向上する,昇進する
　step up one's financial support　金融支援を強化する
　step up one's pace　歩調を速める
　step up strategic consultations[talks]　戦略協議を強化する
　step up support in economic areas　経済分野での支援を強化[促進]する
◆Domestic banks are stepping up oversea project financing due to the lack of growth in lending to domestic borrowers amid protracted deflation at home. 国内銀行各行は、国内ではデフレが続いて［デフレが続く状況で］国内融資先への貸出が伸びていないことから、海外の事業向け融資を強化している。◆Domestic banks are stepping up overseas project financing as greater yields of interests are expected through such lending than loans to domestic borrowers. 国内銀行は、国内の借り手に比べて海外の事業向け融資のほうが大きな金利収入を見込めるので、海外の事業向け融資（プロジェクト・ファイナンス）を強化している。◆Domestic three megabanks are moving to step up their overseas lending. 国内の3メガバンクは、海外融資を強化する方針だ。◆Foreign investors stepped up their purchase of Japanese stocks. 外国人投資家の日本株買いが活発化した。◆Small and midsize companies have been stepping up equity financing to fund capital investments and prepare for M&A deals. 中小企業は、設備投資の資金調達とM&A取引に備えて、株式発行による資金調達を急いでいる。◆The Bank of Japan stepped up its efforts to boost the flagging economy following the March 11 earthquake and tsunami by introducing a ¥500 billion

cheap loan program. 日銀は、5,000億円の低利融資制度を導入して、東日本大震災で揺れる日本経済の刺激策を強化した。

step-up loan ステップアップ型ローン（固定金利型ローンのうち、支払い金利を後になるほど高くしたローン）

sterilization （名）不胎化, 不妊, 不妊化（⇒unsterilization）
  gold sterilization policy 金不胎化政策
  sterilization of gold 金の不胎化, 金の不妊化
    （=gold sterilization）
  sterilization policy 不胎化政策
  ◆In the usual action known as sterilization, yen that is put into the market through official intervention is siphoned off by the Bank of Japan. 「不胎化」と呼ばれる通常の措置[操作]では、公的介入[為替介入]により市場に放出された円資金は、日銀が回収[吸収]することになる。

sterilized foreign exchange intervention 不胎化為替介入, 不胎化介入, 不胎化された為替介入[介入], 為替の不胎化介入

sterilized intervention 不胎化介入, 介入の不胎化（市場での資金量や金融政策に影響が出ないように、為替介入で市場に放出した資金を、中央銀行が公開市場操作によって短期間で回収することを「不胎化介入」という）

stick to （約束などを）守る, 実行する, 〜を固守する, （信念などを）曲げない, 〜に執着する, 〜に固執する, 〜を堅持する, 〜からそれない[外れない], 〜から離れないでいる
  ◆The Bank of Japan sticks to its ultralow interest rate policy. 日銀は、超低金利政策を堅持している。◆The risk of corporate bonds is low if you stick to investment-grade securities. 投資適格債にあくまでも限定すれば、社債のリスクは低い。◆To avert the injection of public money into banks, the eurozone governments stuck to their official standpoint that there are no default problems within the single euro currency area. 銀行への公的資金注入を回避するため、ユーロ圏政府は、単一通貨・ユーロ圏に債務返済不能の問題は存在しないという公式立場に固執した。

stiffen （動）緊張させる, 硬直させる, 強化する, （市況が）強含みになる, （相場、金利が多少）上がる傾向にある[上がりそうである], （物価が）騰貴する
  stiffen one's attitude 堅苦しい態度をとる
  stiffen the penalties for illegal transactions 違法取引に対する罰則を強化する
  stiffening international competition 国際競争の激化
  ◆Financial authorities should stiffen the penalties for illegal transactions to protect the financial system from rumors and speculative investment. 金融当局は違法取引（違法行為）に対する罰則を強化して、金融システムを風評や投機[投機的投資]から守らなければならない。

stimulate （動）刺激する, 刺激して〜させる, てこ入れする, 活気づける, 活性化させる, 浮揚させる, 励ます, 奨励する, 促す, 促進する, 喚起する, 刺激になる, 刺激剤になる（⇒preferential tax system）
  stimulate business 景気を浮揚させる, 景気を刺激する
  stimulate domestic demand 内需を喚起する, 内需を拡大する
  stimulate growth 成長を促す
  stimulate monetary growth 通貨供給量の伸びを刺激する
  stimulate the stock market 株式市場をテコ入れする, 株式市場を活性化する, 株式市場を刺激する

stimulate consumer demand 消費者需要を喚起する
  ◆PC manufacturers are trying hard to stimulate consumer demand this autumn and winter by marketing new products with particular emphasis on audiovisual functions. パソコン・メーカー各社は、AV（音響・映像）機能を重視した新製品を販売して、秋冬の消費需要の喚起に懸命だ。

stimulate external demand 外需を喚起する, 外需を拡大する
  ◆A depreciation of the dollar may stimulate external demand and ignite an export-driven economic upturn. ドル安は、外需を喚起して、輸出主導の景気回復につながる可能性がある。

stimulate the economy 景気を刺激する, 景気をテコ入れする, 経済活動を刺激する
  ◆A group of LDP lawmakers hammered out urgent proposals to stimulate the economy centering on the issuance of zero-interest inheritance tax-exempt government bonds. 自民党議員グループが、景気刺激策として、無利子相続税免除国債[無利子非課税国債]の発行を柱とする緊急提言をまとめた。◆The government and the Bank of Japan should give priority to stimulating the economy in their policy management. 政府と日銀は、政策運営で景気浮揚[景気テコ入れ]を最優先すべきだ。◆The government must formulate a budget and a taxation system that will lead to fiscal reconstruction while stimulating the economy. 政府は、景気をテコ入れする一方、財政再建につながる予算と税制を作り上げる必要がある。

stimulate the property market 不動産市場を活性化する
  ◆Various measures have been taken since last year to stimulate the property market. 昨年来、不動産市場を活性化するために、さまざまな手が打たれてきた。

stimulating effect 刺激効果
  ◆To enhance the stimulating effect of the Fed's rate cuts, swift implementation of fiscal and tax stimulus measures, including tax cuts on investment designed to reinvigorate the stock market, is necessary in addition to the large-scale tax cut program that is under way. 米連邦準備制度理事会（FRB）の金利引下げの刺激効果を高めるためには、現在実施中の大型減税プログラムに加え、株式市場を再活性化するための投資減税など、財政・税制面からの景気刺激策の速やかな実施が必要である。

stimulation （名）刺激, 興奮, 激励, 鼓舞, 喚起（かんき）
  export stimulation 輸出奨励
  fiscal and monetary policy stimulation 財政・金融刺激策
  fiscal stimulation 財政出動による刺激策
  stimulation of consumption 消費の刺激, 消費の喚起
  ◆The stimulation of consumption and job placement assistance are appropriate measures to prevent the economy from losing its momentum. 消費喚起（かんき）や就職斡旋[失業者の就職]支援は、景気の腰折れを防ぐ妥当な政策だ。

stimulative （形）刺激的な, 刺激性の, 刺激の, 景気刺激の, 景気刺激型の
  stimulative economic policy 刺激的経済政策, 景気刺激型の経済政策, 景気刺激策
  stimulative economic program 景気刺激策
  stimulative fiscal policy 景気刺激型の財政政策
  stimulative monetary policy 景気刺激型の金融政策
  stimulative package 景気刺激策, 景気てこ入れ策, 景気刺激総合対策, 経済対策
  stimulative policy 景気刺激策, 景気刺激政策

stimulus （名）刺激, 刺激策, 刺激効果, 景気刺激策, 景気対策, 励み（⇒economic stimulus）
  budgetary stimulus 財政出動
  domestic stimulus 国内景気の刺激, 国内刺激策, 国内景気対策
  economic stimulus 景気対策
  economic stimulus measures［package］ 一連の景気刺激策（⇒monetary relaxation policy, supplementary budget）

emergency stimulus package　緊急景気対策
financial stimulus　金融面からの刺激効果
fiscal and monetary policy stimulus　財政・金融政策を使った景気対策
fiscal stimulus　財政刺激策, 財政出動
fiscal stimulus package　景気刺激策
monetary stimulus　金融政策面での景気刺激策, 金融緩和
stimulus money　経済対策資金
stimulus efforts　景気対策
◆The U.S. Federal Reserve Board is preparing an exit strategy for its unprecedented stimulus efforts. 米連邦準備制度理事会（FRB）は現在、前例のない［未曾有の］景気対策の出口戦略を策定しているところだ。
stimulus measures　刺激策, 景気刺激策, 景気テコ入れ策, 景気浮揚策, 景気対策, 経済対策, 促進措置
（⇒economic stimulus measures, in tandem with）
◆Stimulus measures will boost personal consumption and bring the economy out of the current slump in the second half of fiscal 2009. 経済対策が個人消費を下支えして、2009年度後半には現在の景気後退［景気低迷］から脱するものと思われる。◆To enhance the stimulating effect of the Fed's rate cuts, swift implementation of fiscal and tax stimulus measures, including tax cuts on investment designed to reinvigorate the stock market, is necessary in addition to the large-scale tax cut program that is under way. 米連邦準備制度理事会（FRB）の金利引下げの刺激効果を高めるためには、現在実施中の大型減税プログラムに加え、株式市場を再活性化するための投資減税など、財政・税制面からの景気刺激策の速やかな実施が必要である。◆To overcome the current economic crisis, stimulus measures should take precedence over fiscal reconstruction for the time being. 現在の経済危機を克服するためには、当面は、財政再建よりも景気対策を優先しなければならない。◆What is needed now is drawing up stimulus measures to enhance growth to minimize the depth and length of the economic downturn. 現在求められているのは、景気悪化の深さと長さを最小限にとどめるため、成長力を強化する景気刺激策の策定である。
stimulus package　景気刺激策, 景気対策, 経済対策
◆Amid the depleted state coffers, it is difficult to implement a major stimulus package to rectify the rise in the yen's value. 財政悪化が進む中［国の財源が枯渇する中］、円高是正のため大規模な財政出動を行うのは難しい。◆The improvement in the real GDP was mainly due to a recovery in exports and policy initiatives under the government's stimulus packages. この実質GDP（国内総生産）の改善は、主に輸出回復と、政府の経済対策による政策効果によるものだ。
stimulus program　景気刺激策, 景気対策
◆The U.S. $787 billion stimulus program implemented at the start of the Obama administration will all but dry up by the end of 2010. オバマ政権の発足当初に実施された米国の7,870億ドルの景気対策は、2010年末にはほぼ財源が尽きる見込みだ。
stock　（名）株, 株式, 株式資本, 株式総額, 株価, 株券, 証券, 銘柄, 公債証書, 国庫債券, 公債［国債］（the stocks）, 在庫, 在庫品, ストック　（=share; ⇒day trader, gain, post, share purchase, tracking stock）
a stocks and share broker　株式ブローカー
acquire［buy, purchase］a company in stock　株式交換［株式交換取引］で企業を買収する, 株式交換方式で企業を買収する［取得する］
active stock　人気株, 花形株
authorized stock of a company　会社の授権資本
bank-held stocks　銀行保有株
　（⇒direct purchase）
blue chip stock　優良株, 値がさ株, 優良銘柄

buy stocks　株を買う
capital stock　株式資本, 株主資本, 総株数, 資本ストック, 資本金
capital stock authorized　授権資本, 授権資本金
cash in stocks　株式を現金化する
common stock［shares］　普通株式
　（=ordinary shares）
deferred stock［shares］　劣後株
election stocks　選挙銘柄
employee stock ownership plan　従業員持ち株制度
financial stocks　金融銘柄
have money in the stocks　国債に投資している
hold stocks　株式を保有する
hot stock　人気株
housing stocks　住宅関連株
inactive stock　不人気株
introduced stock　公開株
invest in stocks　株［株式］に投資する
issue and payment of stock　株式の発行および払込み
issue stocks　株［株式］を発行する
large capital stock　大型株
listed stock　上場株
medium-sized stock　中型株
nonconvertible preferred stock　非転換優先株式
nonparticipating preferred stock　非参加的優先株
one's stock rises　〜の株が上がる
one's stock falls　〜の株が下がる
preferred stock　優先株式
reimbursable stock　償還株式
standard stock　一流株
stock appraisal losses　株式評価損, 株式含み損
stock at par　額面株
stock cancellation　株式消却
stock conversion　株式の転換
stock corporation　株式会社　（=stock company）
stock dealing　株の売買, 株式取引
　（=stock deal; ⇒falsified stock dealing）
stock dividend tax　株式配当課税
stock equity　株式持ち分
stock-for-stock　株式交換
stock grant　株式交付
stock interest　株式持ち分
stock legend　株式表示
stock manipulation　株価操作, 株価操縦
　（⇒stock price manipulation）
stock portfolio　保有株式, 株式ポートフォリオ
stock power　証券譲渡証書　（=assignment separate from certificate, stock/bond power: 記名式の株式や債券を譲渡するときに用いる委任状形式の証書のこと）
stock quotation　株価, 株式相場
stock record date　株式の名義書換え停止日
stock register　株主名簿
stock registered for OTC trading　店頭登録銘柄
stock-related losses　株式等関連損失
　（⇒equity holding）
stock report　株式取引報告書
　（⇒capital gains and losses）
stock repurchase　株式買戻し
　（=share buyback, stock buyback）
stock repurchase plan　自社株式購入プラン
stock sale profits　株式譲渡益, 株式売却益

stock savings plan　株式貯蓄制度
stock subdivision　株式再分割
stock subscription　株式応募, 株式公募
stock warrant　新株引受権, 新株引受権付き証書, 新株引受権証券, 株式ワラント
stock with par value　額面株
　（=par value stock）
stock without voting rights　議決権なき株式
stock yield　株式利回り
stockbroking　（名）株式売買
stocks in Tokyo　東京株式市場, 東京株式市場の株価
　（⇒Tokyo stocks）
stop a stock　契約時の時価で特定数の株を後日買う［売る］ことに同意する
take stock in　〜の株を買う
the stocks　公債, 国債
tracking stock in a subsidiary　子会社連動株
　（⇒tracking stock）
transfer of stock　株式の名義書換え, 株式の譲渡
treasury stock　自己株式, 金庫株
unlisted stock　非上場株
voting stock　議決権株

◆Day traders are individual investors who buy and sell stocks many times a day to earn a profit on the trading margin. デイ・トレーダーは、1日に何度も株の売買を繰り返して、その利ざやで利益を上げる個人投資家だ。◆Foreign investors stepped up their purchase of Japanese stocks. 外国人投資家の日本株買いが活発化した。◆JAL's stocks may lose market value to zero if the corporate turnaround body cuts the shares 100 percent by delisting JAL from the Tokyo stock market. 企業再生支援機構が東京株式市場から日航の上場を廃止して日航株を100%減資したら、日航株の市場価値はゼロになる可能性がある。◆Some dollar funds injected into banks by the U.S. central bank may send U.S. stock prices soaring because banks will invest some of the new dollar funds in domestic assets such as stocks. 米国の中央銀行（FRB）が金融機関［銀行］に供給したドル資金の一部は、銀行がそのドル資金の一部を株のような国内資産に投資するため、米国の株価を上げる可能性がある。◆Speculative investors are shifting from commodities to stocks. 投資資金が、商品から株式に移っている。◆The company's stock is valued at $100 billion. 同社の株式総額は、1,000億ドルになる。◆The exchange-traded funds (ETFs) are investment products similar to index mutual funds but that trade on stock exchanges like stocks. 上場投資信託（ETF）は、インデックス・ミューチュアル・ファンドに似ているが、株式と同じように証券取引所で売買される投資商品である。◆The firm has postponed the listing of its stock on the New York Stock Exchange and the London Stock Exchange. 同社は、ニューヨーク証券取引所とロンドン証券取引所への株式上場を延期した。◆The firm hedged its long position in stocks by selling short the futures contract. 同社は、先物を空売りして現物株のロング・ポジションをヘッジした。◆The firm's stock has been hovering around several hundred yen. 同社の株価は、数百円台で推移している。

stock acquisition　株式取得, 株式の取得
　be entitled to a stock acquisition　新株予約権の権利［新株予約権を付与される権利］がある
　exercise the stock acquisition right　新株予約権を行使する
　grant a stock acquisition right　新株予約権を付与する［与える］
　stock acquisition right　新株予約権

stock and bond market rallies　株式市場と債券市場の上げ相場
◆Stock and bond market rallies came to a halt. 株式市場と債券市場の上げ相場は、一服した。

stock appreciation right　株式評価益権, 株式騰貴権, 株式増価差額請求権, SAR
◆Stock appreciation rights (SARs) offer optionees the alternative of electing not to exercise the related stock option, but to receive payment in cash and/or stock, equivalent to the difference between the option price and the average market price of the Corporation stock on the date of exercising the right. 株式評価益権（SAR）を付与されたオプション所持者は、当該ストック・オプションを行使しない代わりに、オプション行使日の当社株式の平均市場価格とオプション価格との差額に相当する現金および/または株式（現金、株式、または現金と株式）を受領することができます。

stock average　株価平均
◆The stock average fell below 9,000 again on the Tokyo Stock Exchange. 東京株式市場は、平均株価がふたたび9,000円を割り込んだ。

stock brokerage　証券会社
　（=securities firm, stock brokerage firm）
◆kabu.com Securities Co. is an online stock brokerage headquartered in Chuo Ward. Tokyo. カブドットコム証券は、東京都中央区に本社を構えるネット証券会社だ。

stock brokerage service　証券仲介サービス, 証券仲介業, 証券仲介業務　（=stock brokerage business; ⇒business alliance）
◆In addition to major banks, about 30 regional banks are expected to start providing stock brokerage services. 大手行のほかに、地銀（地域金融機関）約30行が証券仲介業務を開始する見込みだ。

stock brokering　証券仲介, 証券仲介業
◆Banks were allowed to do stock brokering through their securities subsidiaries in 1993 and through financial holding companies in 1998. 銀行が証券子会社による証券仲介業を認められたのは1993年からで、金融持ち株会社による証券仲介業を認められたのは1998年からだ。

stock bubble　株価バブル　（=stock price bubble）
◆The recent plunge in U.S. stock prices has deflated the stock bubble that has lasted since the 1990s. 今回の米国の株価急落で、1990年代から続いてきた株価バブルが吹き飛んでしまった（株価バブルが完全にしぼんでしまった）。

stock buyback　株式の買戻し, 自社株発行済み株式の買戻し, 自社株買戻し, 自社株買い, 自社株取得　（=share buyback, share repurchase, stock repurchase: 自社株式の取得, 企業が自らその発行している株式を買い入れること。⇒buyback, dividend payout, share buyback）
　stock buyback plan　自社株取得計画
　（⇒stock option plan）
◆A stock buyback means a drop in the number of the company's outstanding shares on the market, helping increase its earnings per share—thus causing the share price to rise. 自社株買いを実施すると、市場で流通しているその会社の発行済み株式数が減り、1株当たり純利益が増えるため、株価上昇をもたらす効果がある。

stock buyback limits　自社株の取得枠
◆Stock buyback limits are to be decided at general shareholders meetings. 自社株の取得枠は、株主総会で決められることになっている。

stock buyout　株式買取り, 株の買占め
◆When a company is listed on the market, it becomes susceptible to a stock buyout. 企業が株式を上場（公開）している以上、株の買占めにあう危険性はある。

stock buyup scheme　日銀の株式買取り制度, 株式買入れ制度
◆Six major banking groups sold a total of about ¥1.4 trillion worth of stocks to the Bank of Japan under the central bank's stock buyup scheme. 日銀の株式買入れ制度に基づく

大手銀行・金融6グループの日銀への株式売却額（銀行保有株の売却額）は、総額で約1兆4,000億円に達した。

stock certificate 株券, 記名株券, 株式証券 （=share certificate; ⇒unlisted joint-stock company）
◆Listed companies revised their articles of incorporation to make stock certificates paperless by holding shareholders meetings. 株券をペーパーレス化するため、公開企業は、株主総会を開いて会社の定款を変更した。◆Many unlisted stock companies—the majority of them small and midsize companies—do not issue stock certificates. 中小企業を中心とする非公開会社の多くは、株券を発行していない。

stock company 株式会社 （=joint stock company, stock corporation; ⇒foundation fund, joint stock company, limited liability company）
◆Before the new corporate law, at least ¥10 million was required to establish stock companies and ¥3 million to create limited liability companies. 新会社法までは、株式会社の設立に最低1,000万円、有限会社の設立に300万円必要だった。◆Life insurer's foundation fund is equivalent to capital for a stock company. 生命保険会社の基金は、株式会社の資本金に相当する。◆The Commercial Code obliges stock companies to issue stock certificates after they are established. 商法は、株式会社の設立後に株券を発行することを義務づけている。◆There are about 1 million stock companies nationwide, and about 4,000 of them are listed companies. 国内には株式会社が約100万社あり、そのうち4,000社前後が株式を上場している公開会社だ。

stock crisis 株価暴落
◆In the face of the Black Monday stock crisis in 1987 and the financial crisis involving major hedge funds in 1998, the U.S. Federal Reserve Board prevented the U.S. economy from falling into catastrophe by supplying a large amount of funds into financial markets. 1987年のブラック・マンデーの株価暴落や1998年の大手ヘッジ・ファンドが絡んだ金融危機の際、米連邦準備制度理事会（FRB）は、金融市場に大量の資金を供給して米経済がパニックに陥るのを防いだ。

stock deal 株式取引, 株の売買
◆Under the revised Securities and Exchange Law, a ban on stock deals by banks and other financial institutions has been lifted. 改正証券取引法に基づいて、銀行などの金融機関による株式の売買が解禁された。

stock dividend 株式配当（配当を現金でなく株式で交付すること）
◆A limited range of tax cuts includes one on stock dividend thanks to the introduction of an optional identification number system for taxpayers. 一部の減税には、選択制納税者番号（金融番号）の導入による株式配当への減税も含まれる。

stock exchange 証券取引所, 株式取引所, 株式市場 （=securities exchange; ⇒bourse, IPO, rule, reorganization, settlement system, Tokyo Stock Exchange）
Japan's two major stock exchanges 日本の2大証券取引所
  stock exchange listing 上場証券取引所, 証券取引所への上場
  stock exchange merger ストック・エクスチェンジ・マージャー （企業の買収・合併の手段として、存続会社が、合併で吸収される会社の株主に存続会社の株式を交付する方法。⇒cash merger）
  stock exchange offer 株式交換公開買付け, ストック・エクスチェンジ・オファー （M&Aの手段として、買収先の企業の株式を、株式などの有価証券で公開買付けする方法。⇒cash tender offer）
  stock exchange quotation 株式相場, 株式市況
◆Currently, NYSE Group, Inc. is the world's largest stock exchange firm and operates the New York Stock Exchange. 現在、NYSEグループは世界最大の株式取引所で、ニューヨーク証券取引所を運営している。◆In the first half of 2010, only 12 companies were newly listed on the nation's stock exchanges. 2010年上半期は、国内証券取引所[国内株式市場]に新規上場した企業が、12社にとどまった。◆More Japanese firms will look to list their shares in other Asian countries, shunning the high hurdles Japanese stock exchanges set for new listings. 日本の証券取引所が設けている新規上場の高いハードルを避けて、他のアジア市場での株式上場を狙う企業が、これから増加すると思われる。◆Some firms that were willing to list their shares were unable to meet stock exchanges' eligibility criteria due to the economic slump. 株式上場を目指していた企業の一部は、景気悪化で証券取引所の上場基準を満たすことができなかった。◆Stock exchanges in both Japan and the United States successively posted major losses. 日米の株式市場は連日、大幅な下げを記録した。◆The exchange-traded funds（ETFs）are investment products similar to index mutual funds but that trade on stock exchanges like stocks. 上場投資信託（ETF）は、インデックス・ミューチュアル・ファンドに似ているが、株式と同じように証券取引所で売買される投資商品である。◆The firm decided to simultaneously list its stocks on the New York and London stock exchanges in October. 同社は、10月にニューヨークとロンドンの両証券取引所に株式を同時上場する方針を固めた。◆The Proprietary Trading System and other online trading systems facilitate trading of stocks outside stock exchanges. 私設取引システム（PTS）などの電子取引システムは、証券取引所外での売買（注文）を成立させる。◆With 942 listed companies, the Jasdaq overtook the Nagoya Stock Exchange as the third-largest stock market in Japan, after the Tokyo Stock and Osaka Securities exchanges. 上場会社数が942社のジャスダックは、名古屋証券取引所を抜き、東京、大阪両証券取引所に次ぐ国内3番目の株式市場になった。

世界の主要証券取引所
American Stock Exchange　アメリカン証券取引所（=AMEX）
Amsterdam Stock Exchange　アムステルダム証券取引所
Australian Stock Exchange　オーストラリア証券取引所
Brussels Stock Exchange　ブリュッセル証券取引所 （⇒effect動詞）
Frankfurt Stock Exchange　フランクフルト証券取引所
Geneva Stock Exchange　ジュネーブ証券取引所
Hong Kong Stock Exchange　香港取引所 香港証券取引所
International Stock Exchange of Great Britain and Ireland　（連合王国およびアイルランド共和国）国際証券取引所（=International Stock Exchange（of the UK and the Republic of Ireland Ltd: ロンドン証券取引所の1986年以降の正式名称））
London Stock Exchange　ロンドン証券取引所
NASDAQ OMX Group　ナスダックOMXグループ
New York Stock Exchange　ニューヨーク証券取引所 NYSE （=Big Board）
Osaka Stock Exchange　大阪証券取引所 大証
Paris Stock Exchange　パリ証券取引所
Shanghai Stock Exchange　上海証券取引所 SSE
Stock Exchange of Singapore　シンガポール証券取引所
The Stock Exchange　ロンドン証券取引所
TMX Group　（カナダの）TMXグループ
Tokyo Stock Exchange　東京証券取引所 東証
Toronto Stock Exchange　トロント証券取引所

stock exchange entry 株式市場への新規上場
◆Domestic stock exchange entries continue to languish, reflecting the tough conditions faced by emerging firms wanting to publicly list their shares. 国内株式市場への新規上場は、株式上場を目指す新興企業が直面している厳しい状況を反映して、低迷が続いている。

stock exchange order　株式売買注文
◆Banks are allowed to accept their customers' stock exchange orders.　銀行は、顧客の株式売買注文の引受けを認められている。

stock exchange regulations　証券取引所規則
◆According to stock exchange regulations, a securities firm can possess some shareholder rights such as voting rights until an investor settles the accounts in his or her margin trading.　証券取引所の規則では、信用取引で投資家が買入れた株の代金決済を行うまでは、証券会社が議決権など株主権の一部を持つことができる。

stock holding　株式保有, 株式所有, 保有株式, 保有株, 持ち株, 出資比率　(=equity holding, shareholding, stockholding;⇒sell-off of stock holdings)
　accelerate sell-offs of stock holdings　保有株の売却を加速させる
　realize gains from stock holdings　株式含み益を実現する
　restrictions on stock holding　株式保有規制, 株式保有の制限
　sell-off of stock holdings　保有株の売却
　sell one's stock hidings　保有株式を売却する, 保有する株式を売却する
◆Ford will sell most of its Mazda stock holdings.　フォードが、保有するマツダ株を売却する。

stock index　株価指数
　American stock indices　アメリカン株価指数
　broad based stock index　総合株価指数
　composite stock index　総合株価指数
　domestic government debt and stock index contracts　国債・株価指数先物
　narrow based stock index　業種別株価指数
　Nikkei Stock Index 300　日経株価指数300
　NYSE common stock index　ニューヨーク証券取引所株価指数
　Russell 2000 stock indices　ラッセル2000種株価指数
　stock index arbitrage　インデックス裁定取引
　stock index future　株価指数先物 (金融先物の一種で、各種の株価指数を対象とした先物取引のこと。)　(⇒financial goods)
　stock index futures option　株価指数先物オプション
　stock index option　株価指数オプション
　stock index warrant　株価指数ワラント
　trading of stock index futures　株価指数先物取引
　Wilshire 5000 stock index　ウイルシャー5000種株価指数

stock investing　株式投資　(⇒Web site)
◆The number of Web sites specializing in stock investing targeted at women is growing.　今は、女性向け株式投資専門のサイトの数が増えている。

stock investing club　株式投資クラブ, 投資クラブ
◆Membership of this stock investing club is limited to women in their 20s to 30s.　この投資クラブの会員は、20代から30代の女性に限られている。
　[解説] 投資クラブとは：個人のメンバーが資金を出し合って、株式を運用するグループのことで、法人や証券業の関係者は参加できない。発祥地は米国だが、日本では1996年に設置が認められた。投資クラブ設立の手順としては、個人のメンバー集め、拠出金額の決定、クラブの名称・役員の決定、規約の作成、証券会社の口座開設、勉強会・投資先選びとなる。

stock investment　株式投資, 保有株
　(=equity investment;⇒fee)
　stock investment trust　株式投資信託
◆Financial institutions are required to report latent losses if the value of their stock investments falls more than 50 percent below their purchase prices.　保有株の株価が取得価格より50%以上下落した場合、金融機関は評価損を計上しなければならない。◆If the two-track income taxation system is introduced, taxpayers will be allowed to offset losses from stock investments from income earned from interest and dividends.　二元的所得課税方式を導入すると、納税者は、利子・配当収入から株式投資による損失を相殺することができるようになる。

stock investment efficiency　株式投資効率
◆Return on equity (ROE) is a key gauge of a company's stock investment efficiency.　株主資本利益率(ROE)は、企業の株式投資効率を示す重要な経営指標だ。

stock issuance　株式発行, 新株発行
◆TEPCO will expand its stock issuance at a general shareholders meeting in June 2012.　東電は、2012年6月の株主総会で、東電の株式発行の枠を広げる方針だ。

stock issue　株式発行, 新株発行, 株式銘柄, 銘柄
　stock issue costs　新株発行費, 株式発行費
◆The TSE and the Securities and Exchange Surveillance Commission investigated about 20 stock issues on suspicion of stock price manipulation and insider trading.　東証や証券取引所等監視委員会は、株価操作やインサイダー取引の疑いで、約20銘柄を調査した。

stock loss　株による損失
◆The Japan Business Federation's charter of ethics was initially adopted in response to revelations that brokerage houses, including Nomura Securities Co., had covered stock losses of major clients.　日本経団連の企業行動憲章は、野村證券など証券各社が大口顧客の株による損失を補填(ほてん)していた事件の発覚を契機に制定された。

stock management　株の運用, 株式運用
◆Both companies have extensive experience and good reputations in stock management.　両社は、株の運用では実績がある(広範な経験をもち、知名度も高い)。

stock margin　株の証拠金
◆The margin of futures is different from stock margin.　先物の証拠金は、株の証拠金とは異なる。

stock market　株式市場, 証券市場, 株式相場, 株式市況, 株式売買, 株価　(=equity market;⇒after-hours trading, equity market, foreign exchange, hollow out, securities-related taxation system, sluggish stock market)
　brisk stock market business　株式相場の盛況
　collapse of the stock market　株式市場の急落, 株式相場の下落, 株価の急落
　　(=the stock market collapse)
　falling stock market　株価の下落
　firm stock market　堅調な株式市場
　help the stock market　株式市場を活性化する
　invest in the stock market　株式市場に投資する
　play the stock market　株式に手を出す, 相場を張る
　plunge in the stock market　株式市場の低迷
　　(=stock market plunge)
　public stock market value　株式時価総額
　pull money from stock markets　株式市場から資金を引き揚げる
　rally in the stock market　株式相場の上昇, 株式市場の上げ相場, 株式相場の急騰
　　(=stock market rally)
　real estate and stock market prices　地価と株価
　reinvigorate the stock market　株式市場を再活性化する
　runup in the stock market　株式相場の上昇
　short selling in the stock market　株の空売り
　sliding stock market　株価下落, 株式市場の軟化
　stability of the stock market　株価の安定

stock market bubble　株式のバブル
　　(=bubble in the stock market)
stock market capitalization　時価総額
stock market collapse　株式市場の急落, 株式相場の下落, 株価急落　(=stock market plunge, the collapse of the stock market)
stock market conditions　株式市況
stock market crash　株式市場の暴落
　　(=stock market crisis)
stock market gains　株式譲渡益
　　(=stock sale profits)
stock market participant　市場参加者
stock market quotation　株式相場
stock market rally　株式相場の上昇, 株式相場[株価]の上昇局面　(=rally in the stock market)
stock market sell-off　株式相場の急落
stock market volatility　株式市場[株価]の乱高下, 株式の乱高下, 株式市場のボラティリティ
stock markets in emerging economies as China　中国などの新興国の証券市場
　　(⇒emerging economies)
the active stock market　株式市場の活況
the outlook for the stock market　株式相場の見通し
the Tokyo stock market　東京証株式市場
turnaround in the stock market　株式市場の持ち直し
weak stock market　株式市場の低迷
weaker stock market　株式市場の軟化, 株式市場の低迷
world stock market　世界の株式市場　(⇒slump)
◆A market player put the level of short selling in the stock market at between 5 percent to 10 percent of total trading volume.　ある市場筋によると, 株の空売りは取引全体の5-10%程度といわれる。◆An increasing number of companies want to undertake IPOs while stock markets remain brisk. 株式市場が活況のうちに上場したい[株式を新規公開したい], という企業が増えている。◆Daiei wants the five supermarket chains under Daiei's umbrella to maintain their separate listings on the stock market. ダイエーは, 傘下の食品スーパー5社の上場を維持する考えだ。◆In revitalizing the market, it is necessary to encourage individuals, who have financial assets totaling ￥1.4 quadrillion, to invest in the stock market. 市場の活性化を図るには, 1,400兆円にのぼる金融資産を持つ個人の株式市場への投資を促す必要がある。◆JAL's stocks may lose market value to zero if the corporate turnaround body cuts the shares 100 percent by delisting JAL from the Tokyo stock market. 企業再生支援機構が東京株式市場から日航の上場を廃止して日航株を100%減資したら, 日航株の市場価値はゼロになる可能性がある。◆More investors are pulling money from stock markets and shifting it into safer time deposits. 株式市場から資金を引き揚げ, 引き揚げた資金を安定性の高い定期性預金に移し替える投資家が増えている。◆Stock markets in China and other emerging economies are growing rapidly. 中国など新興国の株式市場[証券市場]は, 急成長している。◆Stock markets in the United States and European countries crashed again as there is no end in sight to fiscal crises in them. 欧米の株式市場は, 欧米の財政危機の収束が見通せないため, ふたたび総崩れとなった。◆The domestic stock market is experiencing an expansion in the volume of transactions as a result of the economy being brought back on the road to recovery. 国内の株式市場は, 景気が回復軌道に乗りつつあるため, 取引高も拡大している。◆The major securities house attributed the poor earnings to sharp drops in brokerage fees and trading profits amid the extended slump in the domestic stock market. この大手証券会社は, 減益の要因として, 国内株式市場の長期低迷による株売買手数料と売買益の大幅減を挙げた。◆The stock market is a public mechanism to facilitate the smooth flow of money in the economy by serving as an intermediary between corporations and investors. 証券市場は, 企業と投資家間の仲介役をつとめて日本経済に資金を円滑に流す役割を担う公共財だ。◆The Tokyo stock market has recently been roaring, with record heavy trading seen. 東京株式市場が, 記録的な大商いを続けて, 活況を呈している。◆To enhance the stimulating effect of the Fed's rate cuts, swift implementation of fiscal and tax stimulus measures, including tax cuts on investment designed to reinvigorate the stock market, is necessary in addition to the large-scale tax cut program that is under way. 米連邦準備制度理事会(FRB)の金利引下げの刺激効果を高めるためには, 現在実施中の大型減税プログラムに加え, 株式市場を再活性化するための投資減税など, 財政・税制面からの景気刺激策の速やかな実施が必要である。◆Trading is sluggish on stock markets mainly due to the financial crisis in Europe. 株式市場は, 主に欧州の財政・金融危機で取引[相場]が低迷している。◆With 942 listed companies, the Jasdaq overtook the Nagoya Stock Exchange as the third-largest stock market in Japan, after the Tokyo Stock and Osaka Securities exchanges. 上場会社数が942社のジャスダックが, 名古屋証券取引所を抜き, 東京, 大阪両証券取引所に次ぐ国内3番目の株式市場になった。◆With the economic recovery gaining momentum, U.S. companies have begun investing in the Japanese stock market again, giving a lift to stock prices. 景気回復が力強さを増していることから, 米国企業が日本の株式市場に再び投資するようになり, 株価を押し上げている。

stock market business　株式市場の取引
◆An increase in transactions that brokerages handle has accompanied the brisk stock market business. 証券会社が扱う取引の増加は, そのまま株式相場の盛況と重なる。

stock market conditions　株式市況
◆A turnover ratio of trading serves as an important indicator for assessing the stock market conditions in a given year. 売買回転率は, ある特定の年の株式市況を測る指標として使われる。

stock market decline　株価下落, 株安
◆The stock market decline can trigger downgrades by credit rating agencies. 株安をきっかけとして, 格付け機関による評価が引き下げられる可能性がある。

stock market level　株価水準
◆The current stock market level is based more on fear than on the economic fundamentals. 現在の株価水準は, 経済の基礎的条件というより, 不安によるものだ。

stock market movements　株式市場の動き, 株価動向
◆It is better for us to sell the shares flexibly at our own discretion by observing stock market movements. 株価動向を見ながら, 自分たちの判断で機動的に株を売却するほうがやりやすい。

stock market plunge　株式市場の低迷, 株価急落, 株安
◆Global stock market plunges caused by the European fiscal crisis triggered by Greece have shown no signs of abating. ギリシャ発の欧州財政危機による世界同時株安は, 止まる気配がない。◆New securities taxation measures are necessary after the recent stock market plunge. 最近の株価急落を受けて, 新しい証券課税方式(新証券税制)が必要だ。

stock market rally　株式相場の上昇, 株式市場の上げ相場, 株高
◆The recent stock market rally has boosted returns on the insurance premium management of four major life insurers. 最近の株式相場の上昇[株高]で, 4大生保各社の保険料運用収益が増加した。◆The stock market rally came to a halt. 株式市場の上げ相場は, 一服している。

stock offering　株式発行, 株式公開, 株式公募, 株式上場
　　(⇒public offering, public stock offering)
◆The stock offering raised $1.67 billion. 株式公募(株式公開)で, 16億7,000万ドル調達した。

stock option 株式購入選択権, 株式買受権, 自社株購入権, 株式オプション, ストック・オプション (⇒income, proceeds from exercising stock options, stock appreciation right)
◆Gain from stock options is a reward for dedicated work by an employee. ストック・オプション(自社株購入権)の利益は、従業員が熱心に勤務したことへの対価である。◆In Japan, if company employees exercise employee stock options and obtain shares, the shares are considered salaried income, which is taxable. 日本では、社員が従業員ストック・オプションの権利を行使して株を取得した場合、その株式は給与所得と見なされ、課税対象になる。◆Microsoft Corp. has decided to offer its employees shares instead of stock options from September. マイクロソフトは、9月からストック・オプションの代わりに現物株を社員に支給することを決めた。◆The exercise price of any stock option is equal to or greater than the stock price when the option is granted. ストック・オプションの行使価格は、オプションが付与された時の株価と同等、またはそれを上回る価格になっています。◆The gain from stock options fluctuates depending on the option holder's investment judgment over the timing of purchase and changes of the stock price. ストック・オプション(自社株購入権)の利益は、購入時期と株価変動に対するオプション保有者(オプションの買い手)の判断[投資判断]によって上下する。

[解説]ストック・オプションとは：自社株をあらかじめ決められた権利行使価格で購入する権利。報酬制度の一つで、自社株の株価が権利行使価格を上回れば購入者が利益を上げることができる。しかし、実勢株価が権利行使価格を下回っている場合とか、自社株価をつり上げる会計操作の誘因になったりするとか、企業会計上、人件費として計上しなければならないのに計上していない企業が多いなどの問題点もある。

stock option dealing 株式オプション取引, 個別株オプション取引
◆A former vice president of the Osaka Securities Exchange and a number of his erstwhile subordinates allegedly conducted falsified stock option dealings and manipulated the stock market. 大阪証券取引所の元副理事長とかつての部下らが、株式オプション取引で偽装売買を行い、株式相場の操縦をしていたという。

stock option plan 株式購入選択権制度, 株式選択権制度, 自社株購入権制度, 株式オプション制度, ストック・オプション制度 (=stock option program, stock option scheme, stock option system; ⇒growth, information technology, share retirement, stock purchase plan, window dressing)
◆Shareholders of Toyota Motor Corp. approved a company proposal for stock buyback and incentive stock option plans at an annual meeting. 年次株主総会で、トヨタ自動車の株主が、自社株取得計画と奨励株式オプション制度の会社提案(会社側の議案)を承認した。

[解説]ストック・オプション制度とは：企業が役員や従業員に、前もって決めた価格で一定数の自社株を買う権利を与える制度。株価が上がった時点でその権利を使って株を購入し、市場で売ると株の値上がり分を手にできる仕組みになっている。

stock option system 自社株購入権制度, ストック・オプション制度 (=stock option plan, stock option scheme, stock purchase plan)
◆The stock option system was introduced in Japan in 1997. ストック・オプション(自社株購入権)制度は、日本では1997年に導入された。

stock price 株価 (=share price)
 a free fall [freefall] in stock prices　株価の暴落
 a plunge in stock prices　株安
 exchange rates and stock prices　為替相場と株価
 give a lift to stock prices　株価を押し上げる
 global stock price meltdown　世界の株価底割れ, 世界の株価メルトダウン(底割れ)
 inflate the stock prices　株価をつり上げる
 stock price checking　株価審査
 the level of stock prices　株価の水準
 U.S. stock prices　米国の株価
◆A series of accounting scandals and delays in the recovery of corporate performance are accelerating falls in stock prices on the U.S. markets, along with the weakening of the dollar. 一連の[相次ぐ]企業会計の不祥事と企業業績回復の遅れで、米国の株安とドル安が加速している。◆As the financial markets' confidence in the U.S. currency has been shaken, stock prices may fall worldwide and the dollar-selling trend may accelerate. 米ドルへの金融市場の信認が揺らいでいるため、株価が世界的に下落し、ドル売りの流れが加速する可能性もある。◆As the Greek fiscal crisis grows more serious, there has been no halt to the worldwide decline in stock prices. ギリシャの財政危機が一段と深刻化するにつれ、世界同時株安に歯止めがかからなくなっている。◆Both a freefall in stock prices and a surge in the yen's value have been avoided. 株価の暴落も円の急騰も、回避された。◆Due to confusion in the financial markets, interest rates have declined significantly and global stock prices have dropped. 金融市場の混乱で、金利が大幅に低下し、世界的に株価も下落している。◆Exchange rates and stock prices hardly reacted to the dialogue between Prime Minister Kan and Bank of Japan Gov. Shirakawa. 菅首相と白川日銀総裁の意見交換に、為替相場も株価もほとんど反応しなかった。◆Falling stock prices and the depreciation of the U.S. dollar increased uncertainty over the global economy. 米国の株安やドル安で、世界経済の不透明感が強まっている。◆Japan Airlines Corp. is expected to fall short of its planned fund-raising target by about ¥50 billion due to lower stock price. 日本航空では、株価の下落で、当初計画の資金調達目標を約500億円下回る見通しだ。◆On European and U.S. markets, stock prices fell sharply the previous day. 前日の欧米市場の株価は、急落した。◆On the Tokyo stock market and other Asian markets, stock prices plunged across the board. 東京株式市場や他のアジア市場などでも、軒並み株安となった。◆Some dollar funds injected into banks by the U.S. central bank may send U.S. stock prices soaring because banks will invest some of the new dollar funds in domestic assets such as stocks. 米国の中央銀行(FRB)が金融機関[銀行]に供給したドル資金の一部は、銀行がその新たなドル資金の一部を株のような国内資産に投資するため、米国の株価を上げる可能性がある。◆Stock prices have dropped to an all-time low since the collapse of the bubble economy. 株価は、バブル崩壊後の最安値まで落ち込んだ。◆Stock prices will tumble, if banks try to sell a large amount of banks crossheld shares in the market ahead of the account settlement term at the end of March. 3月末の決算期を控えて、銀行が大量の持ち合い株式を市場に放出すれば、株価は急落する。◆The consultant manipulated the company's stock price by engaging in certain prohibited practices including wash sales. コンサルタントは、仮装売買(売り注文と買い注文を同時に出す方法)などの不正行為で株価を操作した。◆The exercise price of any stock option is equal to or greater than the stock price when the option is granted. ストック・オプションの行使価格は、オプションが付与された時の株価と同等、またはそれを上回る価格になっています。◆The failure of Lehman Brothers Holdings Inc. caused stock prices in New York and other markets worldwide to plummet. リーマン・ブラザーズ(米証券4位)の経営破たんで、株価はニューヨークはじめ世界各地の市場で暴落した。◆The firm's former president spread false information about corporate purchases with the aim of inflating the stock prices of its affiliate. 同社の前社長は、関

連会社の株価をつり上げるため、虚偽の企業買収情報を公表していた。◆The FSA's special inspection will check the major banks' large-lot corporate borrowers whose stock prices or credit ratings have sharply declined. 金融庁の特別検査は、大手銀行の株価や格付けなどが急落した大口融資先を査定の対象としている。◆The higher the level of stock prices, the more funds firms can raise from IPOs. 株価の水準が上がれば、それだけ新規株式公開（上場時の新株発行）による資金調達額も増える。◆The profits earned by the banking groups were wiped out by their need to write off sizable bad loans, as well as by a plunge in stock prices. 巨額の不良債権処理の必要性と株安で、銀行グループの利益はすべて吹き飛んだ恰好だ。◆The yen continues its relentless surge and stock prices keep falling. 円高に歯止めがかからず、株安も続いている。◆Though stock prices remain low, the number of transactions has already outpaced that during the bubble economy. 株価はまだ低いものの、株取引の件数はすでにバブル期を超えている。◆With the economic recovery gaining momentum, U.S. companies have begun investing in the Japanese stock market again, giving a lift to stock prices. 景気回復が力強さを増していることから、米国企業が日本の株式市場に再び投資するようになり、株価を押し上げている。◆With the midyear account settlement scheduled in September, concerns over the stability of the nation's financial system inevitably will grow again should stock prices dip further. 9月中間決算を前に、株価がさらに下がれば、再び日本の金融システム不安が当然、台頭してくる。

stock price fall 株価下落, 株安
　（=fall in stocks, falling stock market）
　◆The yen's appreciation and stock price falls may accelerate unless new economic stimulus and more monetary easing steps are taken. 新たな経済対策や追加の金融緩和策を打ち出さないかぎり、円高・株安は今後、加速する可能性がある。

stock price index futures 株価指数先物
　◆The Osaka Securities Exchange accounts for 50 percent of domestic trading in derivatives including stock price index futures. 大証は、株価指数先物などデリバティブ（金融派生商品）の国内取引で5割を占めている。◆The Osaka Securities Exchange is strong in derivative trading such as stock price index futures. 大阪証券取引所は、株価指数先物などデリバティブ（金融派生商品）の取引に強い。

stock price manipulation 株価操縦, 株価操作
　（=stock manipulation）
　◆Some of the real operating conditions of such foreign funds were revealed by a stock price manipulation case involving the company. このような海外ファンドの運用の実態の一部が、同社をめぐる株価操作事件で明るみに出た。◆The Tokyo Stock Exchange and the Securities and Exchange Surveillance Commission investigated about 20 stock issues on suspicion of stock price manipulation and insider trading. 東証や証券取引所等監視委員会は、株価操作やインサイダー取引の疑いで、約20銘柄を調査した。

stock price measures 株価対策
　◆Doubts over the effectiveness of the announced stock price measures have already been expressed among Japanese market players. 今回発表された株価対策の効果については、日本の市場関係者の間ですでに疑問視する声がある。

stock price movements on the market 市場の値動き
　◆By the 30-minute extension of morning trading sessions, investors will be able to trade for a full hour in Japan as they monitor stock price movements on the Hong Kong market. 午前の取引時間の30分延長で、投資家は、香港市場の値動きを見ながら日本市場で丸1時間売買できるようになった。

stock prices in Tokyo 東京市場の株価
　◆Stock prices in Tokyo fell by more than 600 points as a state of panic gripped investors and selling pressure snowballed. 東京市場の株価は、投資家がパニック状態に陥り、売り圧力が増した[加速]したため、下げ幅が600円を超えた。◆The stock prices in Tokyo have fallen as a result of buying and selling operations by hedge funds run by U.S. and European speculative groups. 欧米の投機集団が運用しているヘッジ・ファンドの売り買い操作で、東京（株式市場）の株価は下落している。

stock purchase 株式購入, 株式取得, 株式買取り, 株式買入れ　（=share purchase）
　stock purchase agreement 株式購入契約（契約書）, 株式買取り契約（契約書）, 株式売買契約（契約書）
　stock purchase and sale agreement 株式売買契約, 株式売買契約書
　stock purchase option 株式買取り選択権, 株式購入選択権
　stock purchase system 株式買取り制度
　　（=share purchase system）
　stock-purchasing organization 株式取得機構, 株式買取り機構　（=share-purchasing organization; ⇒streamlining）
　◆Should the government get involved in stock purchases, the market principle may be distorted. 政府が株式の買取りに関与すれば、市場原理が歪められる可能性がある。

stock purchase plan 株式購入選択権制度, 株式購入権制度, 自社株購入制度　（⇒common equity）
　◆The employees stock purchase plan enables employees who are not participants in a stock option plan to purchase the Corporation's capital stock through payroll deductions of up to 10% of eligible compensation. 従業員株式購入制度によると、株式購入選択権制度に加入していない従業員は、俸給の10％を超えない範囲で給与を積み立てて、当社株式を購入することができます。

stock purchase warrant 新株引受権, 株式買付け権, 株式購入権, 新株引受権証書, 株式購入権証書
　bonds with stock purchase warrants 新株引受権付き社債　（=bonds with warrants attached）
　exercise of stock purchase warrants ワラント権の行使, 新株引受権の行使

stock sales 株式売却, 株式譲渡
　capital gains from stock sales 株式売却益, 株式譲渡益
　profits from stock sales 株式売却益, 株式譲渡益
　◆Because the investment consortium is based outside of the country, the government cannot levy taxes on profits from stock sales. この投資組合は国外に本拠地を置いているため、政府は株式売却益に課税できない。◆The tax breaks on capital gains from stock sales and on dividend income will be extended by one year. 株式譲渡益［株式売却益］と受取配当金の税率軽減措置の期間が、1年延長される。

stock speculator 仕手筋
　◆The management consultant known as a stock speculator acquired more than 20 percent, or about 14 million of the company's outstanding shares. 仕手筋とされるこの経営コンサルタントは、同社の発行済み株式数の2割以上にあたる1,400万株余りを買い占めた。

stock split 株式の分割・併合, 無償交付
　（=share split; ⇒split, share splitting）
　a 2-for-1 [two-for-one] stock split 1株当たり2株の株式分割, 2対1の株式分割
　conduct a reverse stock split 株式を併合する, 株式併合をする
　declare a stock split 株式分割を発表する, 株式分割の実施を発表する
　effect [implement, initiate] a stock split 株式分割を実施する
　reverse stock split 株式併合

stock split-down 株式併合 (=reverse split, reverse stock split, share split-down; ⇒reverse split)

stock split-up 株式分割 (=share split-up)
◆A stock split is a measure designed to enable investors, including those with only limited funds, to invest in a company by reducing the share purchase unit. 株式分割は、株式の購入単位を小口化して、少額の資金しかない投資家でも企業に投資できるようにするための手段[資本政策]だ。◆Even if the company conducts a reverse stock split, it will to safeguard shareholders' interest by changing the minimum trading unit from 1,000 shares to 500. 同社が株式併合をしても、最低取引単位を1,000株から500株に変更して株主の権利は守る方針だ。◆Two potent corporate buyout tools of stock splits and stock swaps were the key to the remarkable growth of the company. 株式分割と株式交換という二つの強力な企業買収の手段が、同社の急成長のカギだった。

stock swap 株式交換
◆By the delisting of its stocks, the firm will not be able to repeat stock swaps to acquire other companies. 同社株の上場廃止により、同社は今後、株式交換を繰り返して企業を買収することはできなくなる。◆Stock swaps allow the acquirer to purchase the company it wants to control without preparing a large sum of cash. 株式交換だと、買収企業は多額の現金を用意しなくても、相手先企業[経営権を握りたいと思う企業]を買収することができる。◆Two potent corporate buyout tools of stock splits and stock swaps were the key to the remarkable growth of the company. 株式分割と株式交換という二つの強力な企業買収の手段が、同社の急成長のカギだった。

stock swap deal 株式交換取引
(=equity swap deal, share swap deal; ⇒unit)
◆Citigroup Inc. wholly owned Nikko Cordial Corp. through a stock swap deal in January 2008. シティグループが、株式交換取引で2008年1月に日興コーディアルグループを完全子会社化した。◆In May 2007, the ban on foreign firms taking over Japanese companies with stock swap deals was lifted. 2007年5月から、株式交換取引での外資[外資系企業、外国企業]による日本企業買収が解禁となった。◆The stock swap deal makes Manulife the second largest in North America and No.5 in the world. この株式交換取引で、マニュライフ（カナダ3位の大手生命保険会社）は、北米2位、世界5位の生命保険会社となる。

stock swapping 株式交換
◆In a corporate buyout through stock swapping, a company that buys another company assesses the corporate value of the latter. 株式交換による企業買収では、他社を買収する企業が買収相手の企業価値を査定する。

stock trading 株式取引, 株取引, 株式売買
(=stock transaction; ⇒handle)
stock trading via the Internet 株のインターネット取引, インターネットでの株取引
◆Most individual investor stock trading will be done through specified accounts. 個人投資家の株式売買の大半は今後、「特定口座」を通じて行われることになる。◆The merger of the two exchanges will revitalize stock trading and make it easier for companies to procure funds on the market to expand their business operations. 両証券取引所の経営統合で、株式の売買が活性化し、企業にとっては市場で資金を調達して会社の事業を大きくしやすくなる。

stock transaction 株式取引, 株取引, 株式売買, 株の売買 (=stock trading; ⇒laundered funds)
◆Financial institutions and other institutional investors were wary of making stock transactions. 金融機関などの機関投資家は、株の売買を手控えた。◆In the United States, a special deduction system has been implemented that allows investors to carry over capital losses from stock transactions in their current tax return to future years. 米国では、税務申告上、株式売買による譲渡損失を翌年以降に繰り越すことができる特別控除制度が実施されている。

stock transfer 株式名義書換え, 株式譲渡
(=share transfer)
stock transfer agent 名義書換え代理人
stock transfer book 株主名簿, 株式名簿, 株式譲渡名簿, 株式名義書換え簿, 株主台帳, 名義書換え台帳
(=transfer book)
◆Saison Life and GE Edison will integrate operations through such measures as a merger within one year from the stock transfer. セゾン生命とGEエジソン生命は、株式譲渡から1年以内に合併するなどの手段で経営統合することになった。

stockbroking commission 株式売買手数料
◆The bank reported a 43.4 percent decline in group net profit due mainly to lower stockbroking commission revenues. 同行の連結純利益（税引き後利益）は、主に株式売買手数料の収入が減ったため、43.4%減少した。

stockholder (名)株主
(=shareholder; ⇒shareholder)
individual stockholder 個人株主
institutional stockholder 法人株主
(=corporate shareholder)
issue to stockholders 株主割当て
loans to stockholders 株主貸付け金
one-share stockholder 1株株主
return on common stockholders' equity 普通株株主持ち分利益率
return to stockholders 株主還元
stockholder of record 登録株主
(=shareholder of record)
stockholder resolution 株主決議
(=shareholder resolution)
stockholder rights plan 株主権利制度
(=shareholder rights plan)
stockholders' meeting 株主総会 (=general meeting, shareholders meeting, stockholders meeting)
stockholders' representative suit 株主の代表訴訟
strong stockholder 安定株主
◆Ripplewood Holdings LLC acquired Japan Telecom from its main stockholder, Vodafone Group PLC of Britain, for ¥260 billion. 米投資会社のリップルウッドは、日本テレコムの筆頭株主の英通信会社ボーダフォンから、2,600億円で日本テレコムを買収した。◆The approval of numerous stockholders must be gained for a retirement of 50 percent of common shares. 普通株式の50%消却については、多くの株主の承認を得なければならない。◆The purpose of issuing a sizable amount of new shares is to maintain the control of a specific stockholder (Fuji TV) over NBS. 新株の大量発行は、ニッポン放送に対する特定株主（フジテレビ）の支配権（経営支配権）確保が目的だ。◆The stockholders of Japan Nuclear Fuel Ltd. include electric power companies. 日本原燃には、電力会社などが出資している[日本原燃の株主は、電力会社などだ]。

stockholder proposal 株主提案
(=shareholder proposal)
◆On the stockholder proposal requesting detailed reporting on animal experimentation, 92% of the votes cast were voted against. 動物実験に関する詳細な報告を要求する株主提案については、投票総数（投票株式総数）の92%が反対で否決された。

stockholders' equity 株主持ち分, 株主資本, 資本の部, 資本勘定, 資本, 自己資本, 純資産 (=net worth, owners' equity, shareholders' equity: 払込み資本金と利益剰余金の合計。⇒financial footing)
average stockholders' equity 平均株主資本
common stockholders' equity 普通株主持ち分
consolidated stockholders' equity 連結株主持ち分

minority stockholders' equity　少数株主持ち分
preferred stockholders' equity　優先株主持ち分
stockholding　株式保有, 保有株式, 保有株, 持ち株
　（=shareholding;⇒extraordinary loss, gain, sell off）
　◆In the term-end settlement of accounts at the end of September, most companies use the daily average for a month of the share prices in gauging the value of latent gains or losses in their stockholdings. 9月末の期末決算で［9月中間決算で］、大半の企業は、保有株式の含み損益を算出する際に株価の月中平均を使っている。◆The bank's stockholdings yielded fewer gains in the first half as the Nikkei 225 Stock Average fell 8 percent. 同行の上期の保有株による利益は、日経平均株価（225種）が8％下落したため減少した。◆The increase in seven insurers' core operating profits is due to appraisal gains in their stockholdings. 生保7社の基礎利益（本業のもうけに当たる）の増加は、保有株式の含み益によるものだ。◆The latent profits of major banks' stockholdings have hit bottom. 大手銀行の保有株の含み益も、底をついた。
stockholding gains　保有株式の含み益
　◆Leading insurance companies have seen their stockholding gains virtually disappear. 大手生命保険会社の保有株式含み益は事実上、消えてしまった。
stockholdings' latent value　保有株式の含み益
　◆The massive gains in stockholdings' latent value will raise the banks' net worth ratios markedly. 保有株式の含み益の大幅増加で、銀行の自己資本比率も大きく向上する見込みだ。
stockowner　（名）株主
stockpile　（名）貯蔵, 備蓄, 蓄え, 蓄積, 保有, 保有量, 在庫,（補給資材などの）山
　build up stockpiles　在庫を積み増す
　current stockpile　在庫水準
　cut stockpiles　在庫を減らす
　factory stockpiles　製造業在庫
　　（=stockpiles in manufacturing）
　stockpile financing　滞貨融資, 滞貨金融
stocktrader　（名）証券取引業者
stop　（動）止める, 押さえる, 歯止めをかける, 制止する, 阻止する, 中止させる［中止する］, 禁止する, ストップをかける
　stop declining［falling］　下げ止まる
　stop foreign exchange transfers　外貨送金を禁止する
　stop the bleeding　赤字に歯止めをかける
　stop the sharp［rapid］rise in the yen's value against the dollar　急激な円高・ドル安を食い止める［阻止する］
　　（⇒monetary authorities）
　stop the yen from rising to the ¥82 range to［against］the dollar　1ドル＝82円台突入を阻止する, 1ドル＝82円台までの円高を食い止める
　◆A chain-reaction global decline in stock values was temporarily stopped by a barrage of countermeasures. 世界的な株安連鎖は、矢継ぎ早の対策でいったんは歯止めがかかった。◆As it stands, the yen is the sole major currency whose value has not stopped increasing. 現状では、円は上昇が止まらない唯一の主要通貨だ。◆Priority measures to achieve economic recovery are stopping deflation and mobilizing all possible fiscal measures, financial policies and taxation reforms. 景気回復を実現するための優先課題は、デフレ阻止と、可能な財政政策、金融政策や税制改革を総動員することだ。◆The decline in the value of the euro is unlikely to stop. ユーロの下落傾向［ユーロ相場の下落］は、止まりそうにない。◆The government and the Bank of Japan are poised to stop the yen from rising to the ¥80 range to the dollar. 政府と日銀は、1ドル＝80円台突入を阻止する構えだ。◆The government and the Bank of Japan engaged in market intervention in mid-September 2010 to stop the yen from surging. 政府・日銀は2010年9月中旬、円急騰に歯止めをかけるため市場介入した。

stop limit order　指し値注文, 値幅注文, ストップ・リミット注文
stop-loss　（形）損失の増大［継続］を防ぐための, 損失の拡大を食い止めるための, 損切りの
　stop-loss buy order　逆指し値買い注文
　stop-loss coverage　超過損害担保, ストップ・ロス保険
　stop-loss order　逆指し値注文, 損切りのための注文, 損切り注文, 損失限定注文
　stop-loss sell order　逆指し値売り注文
　stop-loss selling　株の嫌気売り
stop order　逆指し値注文, ストップ・オーダー（指し値注文（limit order）の逆で、特定の値段以下になれば売り、特定の値段以上になれば買うよう指図する注文のこと）
stop out price　米財務省証券の公募入札の最低落札価格
stop out rate　最低金利（米連邦準備制度理事会（FRB）がノンバンク・ディーラーの現先取引に適用する最低水準の金利）
stop price　最低落札価格, 逆指し値
stop short of (doing)　～するまでには至らない, ～する手前で止まる, ～することを思いとどまる
　◆The white paper on the economy and public finance stopped short of making detailed proposals on specific policies. 経済財政白書は、具体的な政策運営に関して詳細に論じるまでには至らなかった。
stopgap [stop-gap]　（名）間に合わせ, 一時［当座］しのぎ, 一時しのぎの穴埋め, 穴埋め, 一時的な代理人　（形）間に合わせの, 一時しのぎの, 穴埋めの, 腰かけ的な, 暫定的な, 臨時の, 臨時雇いの, 代理の
　serve as a stopgap　一時［当座］しのぎになる, 間に合わせになる
　stopgap budget　補正予算
　stopgap fund　つなぎ資金, つなぎ融資
　stopgap funding　暫定予算
　stopgap loan　つなぎ融資
　stopgap solutions　一時［当座］しのぎの解決策
straddle　（名）両建て, 複合選択権付き取引, 両建てオプション, 複合オプション
　bottom straddle　買いストラドル, ボトム・ストラドル
　long straddle　ロング・ストラドル
　short straddle　ショート・ストラドル
　straddle order　ストラドル注文
　straddle transaction　ストラドル取引
　top straddle　売りストラドル, トップ・ストラドル
　解説 ストラドルとは：オプション取引で、同じ行使価格と行使期間満了日を持つコール・オプションとプット・オプションの買いまたは売りを同時に行うこと。コールとプットの買いを同時に行うことをlong straddleといい、コールとプットの売りを同時に行うことをshort straddleという。
straight　（形）連続した（consecutive）, 1年前と比較した, 一直線の, 水平の, 直立した, 垂直の, 正直な, 隠し事をしない, 直接の無条件の, 単純な, 徹底した, 根っからの, 確かな, 信頼できる筋からの　（副）連続して, 1年前と比較して, ぶっ通しで
　corporate straight bond　普通社債
　standard straight issue　普通債
　straight average method　（資産評価の）単純平均法
　straight bill　非流通手形
　straight bill of lading　記名式船荷証券
　　（=straight B/L）
　straight borrowing　直接借入れ
　straight bullet issue　満期一括償還型普通債

straight cash vehicles　現物商品
straight climb　棒上げ（相場を一本調子で上げる状態）
straight credit　割引銀行［買取り銀行］指定信用状, ストレート信用状
straight currency swap　ストレート・カレンシー・スワップ（中長期先物為替予約付きの直物売買通貨交換取引）
straight dealing　公正な取引, 公正取引, 公正な取扱い
straight equity　普通の株式, 普通株
straight fall　棒下げ（相場を一本調子で下げる状態）
straight life annuity　終身年金
straight life insurance　普通の生命保険, 終身生命保険
straight life insurance rate　終身生命保険料
straight life policy　（終身払込みの）終身生命保険
straight line depreciation　定額償却, 定額法
straight line method　定額法
straight loan　通常のローン, 通常貸付け, 直接貸付け, 直貸し, 無担保融資［貸付け］, 無担保手形
straight notes issue　普通債の起債
straight paper　無担保手形, 単名手形（single name paper）
straight salary system　固定給制
straight through processing　リアルタイム処理
straight ticket　連記投票
straight time loan　通常型の定期貸付け［貸付け金、貸金］, 通常型のローン
straight underwriting　一括買取り引受け
the fourth straight monthly decline　4か月連続の減少
the issue of equity　普通株式の発行
tumble for the fifth straight day　5日連続下落する
◆It is the fifth straight month that the unemployment rate has surpassed that of the United States. 完全失業率が米国を上回ったのは、5か月連続である。◆The European Central Bank kept its main interest rate unchanged at 1 percent for the 20th straight month. 欧州中央銀行（ECB）は、20か月連続で政策金利を1％に据え置いた。◆The number of individual investors holding shares in companies listed on the Jasdaq Securities Exchange increased for the 10th straight year. ジャスダック証券取引所に上場している企業（931社）の個人株主数は、10年連続で増加した。◆The U.S. dollar tumbled for the second straight day against major currencies. 米ドルが、主要通貨に対して2日連続下落した。◆This is the fourth straight quarter that the economy has shown growth. これで、4四半期連続のプラス成長となった。

straight bond　普通社債, 確定利付き社債, 転換社債以外の普通の社債
◆The bank will raise about ¥150 billion by issuing straight bonds on a quarterly basis. 同行は、四半期ベースで普通社債を発行して約1,500億円を調達する。

straight corporate bond issuance　普通社債の発行
◆The amount of straight corporate bond issuance came to ¥981 billion in July 2011, the highest level in 10 months. 2011年7月の普通社債発行額は、過去10か月で最高水準の9,810億円に達した。

straight debt　普通借入債務
straight debt financing　純粋な融資
straight debt offer　通常の借入オファー
straight debt sector　普通債市場

strain　（名）緊張, 緊張状態, 緊迫, 圧迫, ひっ迫, ひっ迫状態, ストレス, 重い負担, 重圧, 悪化, 制約, 強要, 懸命の努力, 無理, 力み, 過労　（⇒economic strain）
capacity strain　生産設備の制約, 生産能力の制約
economic strain　景気の悪化
financial strain　金融ひっ迫, 金融負担, 財務上の負担, 財務面での圧迫
financial strains and stresses　金融ひっ迫, 金融市場のひっ迫
inflationary strain　インフレ圧力の高まり
international balance of payments strains　国際的な国際収支の緊迫
international monetary strain　国際通貨の緊張
market strains　市場のひっ迫
strain between supply and demand　需給関係のひっ迫
strain on cash flows　資金繰りの悪化
◆Strains in financial markets have increased significantly. 金融市場の緊張は、著しく増大している。

straits　（名）苦境, 困難, 難局, 窮乏, 貧窮, 困窮　（⇒dire）
be in dire［desperate］straits　窮乏している, ひどく困っている, 火の車, 資金繰りにひどく苦しんでいる, 金にひどく困っている, 財政事情が苦しい［苦しい財政事情にある］
be in straits for money　金に困っている
financial straits　財政難, 財政ひっ迫, 財政的苦境, 財政危機
◆State finances are in sufficiently dire straits. 国家財政は、かなりの危機的状況にある。◆The DBJ and private financial institutions extended loans worth a total of ¥100 billion to JAL in June 2009 though JAL was already in dire financial straits. 日本政策投資銀行と民間金融機関は、日航の経営がすでに悪化していたものの、2009年6月に同社に対して総額1,000億円を融資した。◆The health and nursing care insurance systems are also in dire straits. 医療や介護保険制度も、火の車だ。

strangle　（名）ストラングル
long strangle　ロング・ストラングル（アウト・オブ・ザ・マネー（out of the money）のコール・オプションとプット・オプションの買いを同時に行うこと）
short strangle　ショート・ストラングル（アウト・オブ・ザ・マネーのコール・オプションとプット・オプションの売りを同時に行うこと）

strap　（名）ストラップ（同一財貨, 同一満期日, 同一行使価格コール2単位とプット1単位を組み合わせたもの）, 100ドルの札束
long strap　ロング・ストラップ
on strap　掛けで, つけで, 信用貸しで, クレジットで（=on credit）
short strap　ショート・ストラップ

strapped　（形）欠乏して, 無一文の, すかんぴんの（penniless）, 極貧［赤貧］の
be strapped for cash　資金不足だ, 資金不足に陥っている
cash-strapped　十分な資金のない, 資金繰りが苦しい, 資金難の　（=money-strapped）
cash-strapped companies　資金難の［資金繰りが苦しい］企業
financially strapped small-business operators　資金繰りが苦しい零細事業主　（⇒indebted）
◆The revised Moneylending Business Law bars the money-strapped from using consumer loan firms. 改正貸金業法は、資金不足の人たちの消費者金融の利用を禁止している。◆Under the new financing scheme, the IMF will extend to financially strapped countries loans of up to 500 percent of their contribution to the IMF. 新融資制度では、財政の資金繰りが苦しく［厳しく］なった国に対して、その国がIMF（国際通貨基金）に出資している額の最大5倍までIMFが融資する。

strategic　（形）戦略的, 戦略上の, 戦略上重要な, 戦略上役に立つ, 戦略に必要な
strategic alliance　戦略提携, 戦略的業務提携, 戦略的同盟, 製版同盟, ストラテジック・アライアンス

strategic business alliance　戦略的業務提携
strategic business unit　戦略的事業単位, SBU（=business center）
strategic choice　戦略の選択, 戦略的選択肢
strategic diversity　戦略の多様性, 戦略的相違点
strategic growth market　戦略的成長市場
strategic implication　戦略的意義
strategic industry　戦略産業
strategic intent　戦略的意図
strategic management　経営戦略
strategic marketing planning　戦略的マーケティング計画
strategic moves　戦略的な動き
strategic operations　戦略事業
strategic performance　戦略的成果
strategic position　戦略上の地位, 戦略的位置
strategic review　戦略の検討
strategic target　戦略目標
strategic technology development program　戦略技術開発事業

strategic investment　戦略的投資
◆Strategic investment increased the potential for the Corporation's growth in worldwide markets. 戦略的投資で、グローバル市場での当社の潜在成長力は高まりました。

strategic method　戦略的手法
◆Outsourcing is a strategic method that effectively uses business resources. It is actively utilized in Europe and the U.S. by venture businesses that lack adequate human resources. アウトソーシングは、経営資源を有効に活用するための戦略的手法です。これは、欧米では、人的資源を十分に確保できないベンチャー企業によって積極的に活用されています。

strategist　ストラテジスト（市場動向を見ながら投資戦略を考える投資戦略家）
equity strategist　株式ストラテジスト
fixed-income strategist　債券ストラテジスト

strategy　（名）戦略, ストラテジー　（⇒alliance strategy, corporate strategy, realignment strategy）
acquisition strategy　買収戦略
business strategy　経営戦略, 事業戦略, 企業戦略, ビジネス戦略
core strategy　主力戦略, 中核戦略, 基本戦略
e-business strategy　eビジネス戦略
financial strategy　財務戦略
funding strategy　資金調達戦略
hedge strategy　ヘッジ戦略
investment strategy　投資戦略
management strategy　経営戦略
media strategy　メディア戦略
portfolio strategy　ポートフォリオ戦略
realignment strategy　再編戦略
syndication strategy　シ団組成戦略
value strategy　バリュー戦略
◆All these events are part of a larger strategy of our asset management. これらの措置は、当社の資産運営戦略の一環としてとられたものです。◆Japanese firms must work out better strategies to cope with the excessive rise of the yen. 日本企業は、超円高に対応できる戦略を練る必要がある。◆Japan's four megabanks are now rebuilding their global business strategies. 日本の4大金融グループは現在、グローバル戦略の再構築に取り組んでいる。◆The government led by the Democratic Party of Japan lacks a coherent strategy to address the negative aspects of Japan's debt dynamics. 民主党政権は、日本のマイナス材料の債務問題への取組みに対する一貫した戦略に欠けている。◆The merger will prompt other megabanks to come up with new strategies to reinforcing their corporate health. この統合は他のメガバンクを刺激し、メガバンクは企業体質の強化に向けた戦略を新たに打ち出すことになろう。◆Through the TSE-OSE merger in January 2013, the two exchanges must enhance their strategies to ensure survival as a major stock market in Asia. 東証と大証の2013年1月の経営統合をテコに、両証券取引所は、アジアの主要市場として勝ち残る戦略を強化する必要がある。◆Wal-Mart's strategy has been to acquire stakes in existing stores rather than opening directly operated stores. 直営店を出店しないで、既存店の株式を取得するのが、米ウォルマートのこれまでの戦略だ。

streak　（名）傾向, 兆候, 気性, 性質, ～気味, 調子, 閃光（せんこう）, 電光, 稲妻, 一時期, ひと続き, 一連, ひとしきり, 鉱脈, 層, 筋, 線, しま, 仕事の早い人, 足の速い人
a streak of　一筋の～, 一連の, 一条の, ～気味, 少々～なところ
a three-day losing streak　3日連続の値下がり
hit［be on］a long losing streak　負け続ける, 連敗する, 値下がりを続ける
hit［be on］a long winning streak　勝ち続ける, 連勝する, 値上がりを続ける
◆Tokyo stocks extended their winning streak to a third day with the key Nikkei index finishing above the 9,000 line. 東京の株価［東京株式市場の株価］は、3日連続で値上がりし、日経平均株価（225種）の終値は9,000円台を上回った。◆Tokyo stocks snapped a three-day losing streak Wednesday, with the key Nikkei index rebounding strongly from Tuesday. 東京の株価［東京株式市場の株価］は水曜日、日経平均株価（225種）が前日から大幅反発［回復］して、3日連続の値下がりに歯止めがかかった。

stream　（名）流れ, 傾向, 動向, 趨（すう）勢, 見通し, キャッシュ・フロー
downstream investors　中小の機関投資家
earnings stream　収益見通し
fixed interest streams　固定金利のキャッシュ・フロー, 固定金利の流れ
floating interest streams　変動金利のキャッシュ・フロー, 変動金利の流れ
interest stream　金利の流れ
limited revenue streams　特定の歳入源
profits stream　収益見通し
stream risk　趨勢リスク
◆Industries at the upper end of the production stream have higher increases in recurring profits. 生産の流れ（生産から消費に至る各段階）の上流にある産業のほうが、経常利益の増加率が高い。

streamline　（動）合理化する, 能率化する, 効率化する, 簡素化する, スリム化する, リストラする　（⇒disclosure, taxation system）
◆JAL will merge some subsidiaries as part of streamlining efforts. 日本航空は、効率化策の一環として一部の子会社を合併させる。◆The financial groups should write off their bad loans more efficiently and streamline their banking operations. 銀行グループは、もっと効率的な不良債権の処理と銀行業務の合理化を進めなければならない。

streamlining　（名）合理化, 能率化, 効率化, 簡素化, スリム化, リストラ
◆One reason for the banks' reluctance to sell their shares through the share-purchasing organization is that they cannot expect an immediate streamlining of their finances. 銀行が株式取得機構への持ち株売却に消極的な理由の一つは、財務のスリム化をすぐに期待できないからだ。

street　（名）通り, 街頭, 金融街, 場外, 一般大衆, 一般人, ストリート　（⇒Wall Street）

in the street　仕事をしている
lending street name　名義貸し
Lombard Street　英国の金融界, ロンバード街
on [in] the street　ウォール街で, 金融街で, 割引価格で
street analyst　証券会社のアナリスト
street broker　場外取引人
street certificate　所有者の裏書きと証券業者の保証署名のある株券
Street economist　市場エコノミスト, ウォール街のエコノミスト　(=Wall Street economist)
street estimates　市場予測
street loan　短期融資, 当座貸し　(=call loan)
street name　ストリート・ネーム, 実質株主名を株主名簿に登録していない株主, 株式所有者に代わって名義登録される証券業者, 仲買人名義, 証券業者名義, 証券業者名義となっている有価証券, 名義貸し
street-name account　ストリート・ネーム・アカウント（実質株主名を株主名簿に登録していない株主の口座）
street paper　街頭手形
street price　場外取引価格, 店頭価格, 実売価格, 市価
street value　市価, 市価相場, 末端価格, 闇値（やみね）
the Street　金融街（英国のLombard Street, 米国のWall Street）, ディーラー, 大手証券各社
strength　(名)力, 強さ, 力強さ, 勢い, 好調, 活況, 上昇, 勢力, 兵力, 人数, 長所
　(⇒economies of scale, financial strength)
business strength　経営の体力, 事業の強み
competitive strength　競争力
credit strength　信用力, 信用度, 信用の質
currency strength　通貨高
economic strength　経済力, 景気の力強さ, 景気の腰の強さ, 景気好調
financial strength　資金力, 財力, 財務力, 財務体質, 財務面での健全性, 支払い能力
financial strength rating　支払い能力の格付け
shore up one's capital strength　資本を増強する
the recent surges in the yen's strength　最近の円高
yen's strength against the dollar　円高・ドル安
◆According to a commodity futures market insider, futures brokerages depending on commissions for revenue will lose their business strength. 商品先物市場関係者によると, 収入を手数料に頼っている先物会社の経営体力は, 今後弱まりそうだ。◆An urgent task facing each financial group is to improve its financial conditions and profitability on the strength of advantages gained from merger. 合併・統合の相乗効果を生かして, 財務内容と収益力を向上させることが, 各金融グループの現在の急務だ。◆China is trying to flex its muscle with the United States on the strength of its status as the largest holder of U.S. Treasury securities. 中国は, 米財務省証券［米国債］の最大保有国としての地位を背景に, 米国への影響力を行使しようとしている。◆European countries are urged to facilitate a safety net for emergencies, including the injection of public funds into deteriorating banks to shore up their capital strength. 欧州は, 経営が悪化した銀行［金融機関］に公的資金を注入して資本を増強するなど, 非常時に備えた安全網の整備が求められている。◆One of the aims for the three banks to merge into the Mizuho Financial Group was to survive the global competition by exploiting the banks' combined strength. 3行がみずほフィナンシャルグループに合併する目的（狙い）の一つに, 3行の統合力を駆使して国際競争に勝ち抜くことがあった。◆The BOJ lifted its zero-interest rate policy on the strength of its optimistic view on the outlook for the economy in the summer of 2000. 日銀は2000年夏, 景気の先行きを楽観してゼロ金利政策を解除した。◆The economic recovery was gaining strength until recently. 景気回復は, 最近まで力強さを増していた。◆The recent surges in the yen's strength have made it imperative for Japanese carmakers to substantially bring down their parts procurement costs by overseas sourcing. 最近の円高で, 日本の自動車メーカー各社は, 海外調達による部品調達コストの大幅引下げが緊急課題となっている。◆The yen will maintain its current strength against the dollar for the time being. 円相場は, 現在の円高・ドル安が当面続くだろう。

strength of the dollar　ドル高, ドルの上昇
◆Fears about higher interest rates, inflation and the strength of the dollar are intensifying in the United States. 米国では, 金利の上昇, インフレとドル高に対する懸念が高まっている。

strength of the yen　円高, 円の上昇
◆Due to the growing strength of the yen, even if exporters' sales grow, their profits will not keep pace. 円高進行で, 輸出企業の売上が増えても, 利益は伸び悩むようだ。

strengthen　(動)強化する, 強める, 増強する, 補強する, 高める, 伸ばす, 活性化する, 拡大する, 充実させる, (規則などを)厳しくする　(自動)上昇する, 向上する, 高まる, 伸びる, 改善する, 好転する
continue to strengthen　引き続き好調である, (円高, ドル高が)続いている
intervention to strengthen the dollar　ドル高誘導の介入
strengthen profitability　収益性を改善する
strengthen regulations　規則を厳しくする
strengthen the balance sheet　財務基盤を強化する
strengthen the economy　経済力を強化する, 経済を活性化する
strengthen the market position　市場での地位を強化する
strengthen ties　提携を強化する
◆A bill to revise the Law on Special Measures for Strengthening Financial Functions is designed to facilitate compensations of losses of financial institutions with public funds. 金融機能強化法の改正法案は, 公的資金で金融機関の損失の穴埋めを容易にするのが狙いだ。◆Additional pump-priming measures through strengthening cooperation between advanced countries and emerging economies will be a major subject of discussion at the financial summit meeting in Washington. 先進国と新興国の連携強化による追加景気対策の検討が, ワシントンで開かれる金融サミットで検討される主要テーマとなる。◆An initiative to strengthen the functions of the European Financial Stability Facility (EFSF) was approved at the 17 eurozone countries' parliaments. 欧州金融安定基金（EFSF）の機能強化案が, ユーロ圏17か国の議会で承認された。◆Argentina's peso strengthened slightly against the U.S. dollar as banks and exchange houses reopened. 銀行と両替所の営業再開に伴って, アルゼンチンの通貨ペソの対米ドル・レートが若干上昇した。◆Economic activity strengthened in most of U.S. regions with the exception of St. Louis where plans to close several plants were announced, the U.S. FRB said. 米連邦準備制度理事会（FRB）は, (全12地区連銀のうち)一部の工場閉鎖計画を発表したセントルイスを除く11地区で景気が好転している, と述べた。◆In the wake of the euro crisis in Europe and the fiscal deadlock in the United States, the yen has sharply strengthened. 欧州のユーロ危機と米国の財政政策の行き詰まりの影響で, 円が急騰している。◆Major U.S. and European banks have been strengthening their market competitiveness. 欧米の大手銀行は, 市場競争力を強化してきた。◆MFG, the nation's largest financial group, tied up with two major U.S. banks to strengthen its earning power. 国内金融グループ最大手のみずほフィナンシャルグループが, 収益力の強化を図るため, 米銀大手2行と提携した。◆Nippon Life Insurance Co. plans to raise ¥50 billion for acquisitions and to strengthen its capital base. 日本生命保険は, 買収資

金として500億円を調達して、同社の資本基盤も強化する方針だ。◆The euro temporarily strengthened on the foreign exchange market due to the EU-IMF emergency package. 欧州中銀（ECB）と国際通貨基金（IMF）の緊急対策で、ユーロの為替相場が一時的に上昇した。◆The eurozone countries agreed to strengthen EFSF functions, such as bailout methods, in July 2011. 2011年7月にユーロ圏諸国は、支援手法など欧州金融安定基金（EFSF）の機能を強化することで合意した。◆The G-20 financial summit meeting will map out concrete measures to strengthen the regulation and governance of the financial industry. 世界20か国・地域（G-20）の金融サミットでは、金融業界に対する規制・監督強化の具体策をまとめることになっている。◆The IMF and the EU are strengthening their cooperation to avert a Greek default and prevent a chain reaction of debt crisis among other countries. ギリシャの債務不履行（デフォルト）を回避し他国間の債務危機の連鎖反応を防ぐため、国際通貨基金（IMF）と欧州連合（EU）は、連携を強めている。◆The upcoming negotiations will determine practical measures to strengthen ties, including the merger ratio, the name of the new group and the positions to be held by top executives. 今後の交渉で、統合比率や新グループの名称、首脳人事など提携強化の具体策を詰める。◆The U.S. dollar continues to strengthen against the yen. ドル高円安が続いている。◆The yen continued to strengthen over the period. 円が続伸した。◆The yen strengthened against the dollar. ドルに対して、円が上昇した［円が対ドルに反発した］。◆U.S. and European financial institutions are scaling back their business operations before capital adequacy requirements are strengthened in 2013. 欧米金融機関は、2013年から自己資本規制が強化されるのを前に、業務を縮小している。

strengthening （名）強化, 上昇, 伸び, 高まり, 強含み, 充実, 改善, 持ち直し, 好転
  strengthening in sales　販売の伸び
  strengthening of capital base　資本基盤の強化
  strengthening of capitalization　資本の充実
  strengthening of credit criteria　与信基準の強化
  the steady strengthening of China's [the renminbi's] international currency value　人民元の国際的な通貨価値の着実な上昇　（⇒currency value）
  the strengthening of the dollar　ドル高
  the strengthening of the yen　円高
  　（=the strengthening yen）
◆Brazil suffering from the strengthening of its currency has restricted an influx of capital. 通貨高に悩むブラジルは、資本流入［資金流入］を規制している。◆The recent strengthening of the yen may negatively affect exports. 最近の円高が、輸出に悪影響を与えかねない。◆The strengthening of the yen would force Japanese export-oriented manufacturers to globalize themselves further. 円高で、日本の輸出企業はさらなるグローバル化を強いられることになろう。

strengthening （形）上昇している, 伸びている, 向上している, 改善している, 好転している
  strengthening asset quality　資産内容の向上
  strengthening demand　需要の伸び
  strengthening economy　景気の好転, 景気の持ち直し
  strengthening yen　円高
◆The U.S. federal deficit for the new year will likely exceed $500 billion even with the strengthening economy. 米国の新年度の財政赤字は、景気が好転しても5,000億ドルを超える見込みだ。

stress （動）強調する, ～に力点を置く, 強く言う, 力説する, ～に圧力を加える, ～を緊張させる
◆The report stresses the need to increase the overall supply capacity through structural reforms as a remedy for economic stagnation. 同報告書は、不況対策として、構造改革によって総供給力を引き上げる必要があると力説している。

stress （名）圧力, 圧迫, 困難, 困難な状況, 厳しい環境, 厳しい経営環境, 経営難, 強調, 力点, 重点, ストレス
  experience severe financial stress　財務状態が大幅に悪化する, 厳しい経営難に陥る
  financial stress　経営難, 金融上の困難, 財務状態の悪化, 信用圧迫
  stresses caused by the collapse of the subprime mortgage market　サブプライム・ローン（低所得者向け住宅融資）市場の崩壊による経営不振［経営難］
◆AIG teetered on the edge of failure because of stresses caused by the collapse of the subprime mortgage market and the credit crunch that ensued. 米保険最大手のAIGは、サブプライム・ローン（低所得者向け住宅融資）市場の崩壊とその後の金融危機による経営不振［経営難］で、経営破たんの瀬戸際［危機］にあった。◆The industry is under a good deal of stress, as evidenced by pressure on profitability and decline in stock prices over the last several months. 業界は、収益性の悪化やここ数か月の株価低迷でも明らかなように、かなり厳しい状況下にあります。

stress test　金融の特別検査, 金融機関の財務の健全性検査, 耐性検査, ストレス・テスト　（=stress testing; ⇒capital plan, Committee of European Banking Supervisors, financial strength）
  conduct a stress test　ストレス・テストを行う
  run a heavy stress test　慎重にストレス・テストを行う
  stress test by the Fed　米連邦準備制度理事会（FRB）の特別検査
  take a stress test　ストレス・テストを受ける
  the EU's stress test　欧州連合（EU）のストレス・テスト（特別検査）
  the U.S. FRB's stress tests　米連邦準備制度理事会の特別検査
◆Europe's seven banks judged to have capital shortfall by the stress test will work on increasing their capital. ストレス・テスト（特別検査）で資本不足と認定された欧州の7銀行は、これから資本増強に取り組む。◆Major Banks across Europe underwent the stress tests of the European Banking Authority in 2010 and 2011. 欧州全域の主要銀行［金融機関］が、2010年と2011年に欧州銀行監督機構（EBA）のストレス・テスト（財務の健全性検査）を受けた。◆The European banking tests are lax and ineffective as the collapses of two Irish banks and the Franco-Belgian bank Dexia, shortly after the EBA's stress tests, show. 欧州の銀行検査は、欧州銀行監督機構（EBA）のストレス・テストに合格した［ストレス・テストで安全と判定された］直後にアイルランドの銀行2行やフランス・ベルギー共同の銀行「デクシア」が破たんした事実が示すように、手ぬるくて効果がない。◆The EU's 91 banks were subject to the stress test. 欧州連合（EU）の91行が、ストレス・テスト（特別検査）の対象となった。◆The stress test of the European Banking Authority is a banking health check to ensure banks across Europe have sufficient capital to withstand another financial crisis. 欧州銀行監督機構（EBA）のストレス・テストは、欧州全域の銀行が新たな金融危機に耐えられるだけの資本金を十分に確保していることを保証するための銀行の健全性検査だ。

解説 financial stress test（金融のストレス・テスト）: 米政府が、金融機関の不良資産問題を抜本的に解決するため、経済がさらに落ち込んだ場合やブラック・マンデー、アジア通貨危機など通常ではあまり考えられないケースを［負荷］として織り込んで、2009年2月25日から大手19行に対して［ストレス・テスト］を行った。このテストで、資本不足と認定された金融機関には、市場からの資金調達を促す。市場で資金調達できなかった場合は、政府が優先株を引き受ける形で公的資金を注入する。金融機関の経営がさらに悪化した場合は、政府が優先株を普通株に転換して、金融機関が事実上、国有化される可能性も

ある。

stricken (形)打撃を受けた, 経営危機に陥った, 資金繰り難の, ～に苦しむ[悩む]
- crisis-stricken　危機に陥っている, 経営危機に陥っている
- debt-stricken　債務危機に陥っている, 債務に苦しんでいる
- depression-stricken　不況に見舞われている[見舞われた], 不況に苦しむ
- famine-stricken　飢えに悩む
- fire-stricken　火災で打撃を受けた
- poverty-stricken countries [nations]　最貧国, 貧困に苦しむ国
- stricken area　被災地, 被災地区[地域]
- stricken field　決戦, 決戦場

◆Crisis-stricken giant supermarket chain operator announced a fresh reconstruction plan. 経営危機に陥っている巨大スーパーが, 新たな経営再建策を発表した。◆JPMorgan Chase & Co. will buy stricken Bear Sterns for $2 a share. 米大手銀行のJPモルガン・チェースが, 経営危機に陥った(米証券5位の)ベア・スターンズを1株2ドルで買収する。

strict (形)厳しい, 厳重な, 厳密な(precise), 正確な, 几帳面な, 絶対の
- implement strict guidelines and sanctions　厳しい指導や制裁を実施する
- in the strictest [strict] confidence　極秘で
- strict guidelines and sanctions　厳しい指導や制裁
   (⇒systemic financial crisis)
- strict liability　厳格責任, 無過失責任
- strict warning　厳重注意
- stricter regulation　規制の強化

◆As a condition for loans to financially troubled countries in the late 1990s, the IMF called for strict implementation of structural reforms. 1990年代後半に財政難に陥った国に対する融資の条件として, IMF(国際通貨基金)は, 厳しい構造改革の実施を求めた。◆Japanese government bonds are being subjected to stricter market scrutiny. 日本国債は, 市場の一段と厳しい評価にさらされている。◆The major banks attributed their increased bad loans to the poor performance of their borrowers due to the prolonged economic slump and Financial Service Agency inspections resulting in a stricter review of their asset assessments. 大手銀行は, 不良債権が増えた理由として, 長引く景気低迷で貸出先の経営が悪化したことと, 金融庁の検査を受けて大手行が資産査定を厳しくしたことを挙げた。◆The Oct. 30, 2002 financial revitalization plan sought stricter assessments of bank assets. 2002年10月30日の「金融再生プログラム」は, 銀行資産の一段と厳しい査定を求めた。◆To deal with the systemic financial crisis, ministry and central bank officials had to take rescue measures, such as an injection of public funds, while at the same time implementing strict guidelines and sanctions. 連鎖的な金融危機に対処するにあたって, 当局は公的資金の投入などの救済措置取ると同時に, 厳しい指導や制裁を実施しなければならなかった。

strife (名)争い, 闘争, 紛争, 奪い合い, 衝突, 争議, 不和, 反目, もめごと, いざこざ, 困難, 窮状
- be at strife with　～と不和である
- economic strife　経済の窮状, 経済的窮状
- factional strife within the company　社内の派閥争い
- financial strife　金融危機
- industrial strife　労使紛争
- internal strife　内紛, 内輪もめ, 内部抗争, 内ゲバ
   (=infighting, internal conflict)
- labor strife　労働争議
- the strife of the marketplace　市場の奪い合い

◆Behind North Korea's change in strategy is the current economic strife. 北朝鮮の方針[戦略]転換の背景には, 現在の経済的窮状がある。◆The challenge of the Basel Committee on Banking Supervision is to develop a regulatory framework while fending off a recurrence of financial strife. バーゼル銀行監督委員会の課題は, 金融危機再発の防止と規制の枠組みの策定だ。◆The inadequate decision-making and business management processes of the financial group stem from factional strife within the company. 同金融グループの不十分な意思決定プロセスと経営管理体制は, 社内の派閥争いに起因する。◆The strife within the Japan Airlines Group surfaced. 日本航空の内紛が, 発覚した。

strike (動)打つ, 殴る, 攻撃する, (病気などが)襲う, 感動させる, (～の心を)打つ, ～に気づく, ～を表明する, ～を表す, 掘り当てる, 発見する, 計算する, 算出する, 決済する, 出す, ～に達する, (契約などを)取り決める, 結ぶ, 選ぶ, 特別選定する (自動)ストライキを行う, 当たる, ぶつかる, (地震や悲劇などが)起こる
- strike a balance　清算する
- strike a bargain with　～と商談を取り決める, ～と取引する
- strike a blow at　～に深刻な影響を与える
- strike a cautious note　警戒心を表す
- strike a snag　思いがけない障害にぶつかる
- strike an average　平均を出す
- strike down　打ちのめす, 無効にする, 取り消す, 廃止する, 倒す
- strike gold　金鉱を掘り当てる
- strike new coins　新貨幣を鋳造する
- strike out　(計画などを)考えだす, 削除する, 消す, 三振に取る, 乗り出す
- strike out an endorsement [indorsement]　裏書きを抹消する

strike a deal　取引を行う

◆Belarus is counting on striking a low-interest loan deal with the International Monetary Fund. ベラルーシは, 国際通貨基金(IMF)から低利融資を受けるのを期待している。◆NYSE Group struck a deal to buy European bourse operator Euronext for $9.96 billion. (ニューヨーク証券取引所を運営する)NYSEグループは, 欧州(パリやオランダなど)の証券取引所を運営する「ユーロネクスト」を99億6,000万ドルで買収する取引をした。

strike an agreement　契約を結ぶ[締結する, 取り決める], 合意に達する, 合意する

◆The company struck an agreement with its debtholder to win their support for reconstruction. 同社は, 会社再建について債権者の支持を得ることで, 債権者と合意に達した。

strike price　行使価格　(=exercise price: プット・オプションやコール・オプションを行使するときの価格)

strike rate　行使金利

string (名)ひも, 糸, 弦, (心の)琴線, 一連, 一つなぎ, 一続き, 一列, 一隊, 一群, 数珠つなぎ, 連続, 連発, 付帯条件, 方策, 手立て, 手段, 方法, 頼み, 段階, 級, 組, 同系列の人, ぺてん, うそ, 虚報(false report)
- a second string to one's bow　別の手段
- a string of　一連の, 連続する, 一続きの
- have A on a string　Aを思うままに操る
- have many [more] strings to one's bow　多くの手立てがある, 別の手段がある
- have two strings [a secondstring, another string] to one's bow　(目的を達成する)第二の策を持つ, 別の手段がある, 他の手段がある
- play second string to　～の脇役を務める, ～の引立て役[脇役]に回る, ～の補欠を務める
- pull every string　全力を尽くす

pull (some) strings [wires]　陰で糸を引く,陰で操る,黒幕となる,黒幕として働く,影響力を行使する
pull strings behind the scenes　舞台裏で操る
the first string　第一策,第一の手段,第一に頼りになるもの[人]
the strings　付帯条件,制限
with no strings (attached)　付帯条件なしで,ヒモ付きでなく (=without strings)
◆At the bank, a string of executives resigned one after another due to differences over management policy. 同行では、経営路線の違いで役員らの辞任が相次いだ。

stringency　(名)厳しさ,厳重さ,引締め,切迫,ひっ迫,金詰まり,説得力
credit stringency　信用ひっ迫,金融ひっ迫,金融引締め
financial stringency　金融ひっ迫
　　(=financial pressure, monetary stringency)
fiscal stringency　緊縮財政
monetary stringency　金融ひっ迫

stringent　(形)厳格な,厳しい,厳重な,過酷な,緊急な(urgent),引締めの,緊縮の,(金融市場が)切迫した,ひっ迫した,金詰まりの(tight),〜の強化,説得力のある,有力な
adopt stringent measures　金融引締め策を採用する
more stringent lending rule　貸出基準の強化
more stringent underwriting　引受基準の強化
stringent budget (cuts)　緊縮予算
stringent law　厳しい法律,厳格な法律
stringent lending rule　厳しい貸出基準,厳格な貸出基準
stringent market　ひっ迫市場,ひっ迫市況
stringent market for loans　金詰まり市場
stringent measures　厳しい措置,強い手段,金融引締め策
stringent necessity　緊急の必要性
stringent regulations　厳しい基準,厳しい規制
stringent stock market　金詰まりの株式市場
◆The major commercial banks deserve praise for working toward making their asset appraisal more stringent. 大手各行が資産査定の厳格化に動き出したことは、評価できる。
stringent financial regulations　金融規制の強化
◆The administration of U.S. President Barack Obama proposed the stringent financial regulations. 米オバマ政権は、金融規制の強化を打ち出した。
stringent measures　厳しい措置,強い手段,金融引締め策,財政緊縮策
◆Italian Parliament should carry out stringent measures without fail by immediately passing a fiscal rehabilitation bill. イタリア議会は、財政再建法案を早急に成立させて、財政緊縮策を断行する必要がある。

stripped bond　ストリップ債
stripped issue　ストリップ債
STRIPS [strips]　ストリップ債 (separate trading of registered interest and principal of securitiesの略。米財務省証券の利付き証券の一種で、証券の元本部分と利札部分を切り離して、別個の証券としてそれぞれ売買できるものをいう)

strive　(動)努力する,努める,励む,骨折る,取り組む,闘う,奮闘する,争う,競う
◆Major banks are striving to write off some of their tax assets from their equity capital. 大手銀行は現在、自己資本からの税金資産減らしに取り組んでいる。

strong　(形)強い,強力な,力強い,強固な,堅調の,好調な,上昇基調の,優良な
a strong currency　強い通貨
a strong feeling [sentiment]　強気

be financially strong　財務基盤が健全である
break strong resistance　強化な[強い]抵抗線を突き抜ける
central bank strong rhetoric　中央銀行の強硬な口先介入
enjoy a strong run　高いパフォーマンスを見せる,大幅なアウトパフォーマンスになる
ever-stronger currency　通貨高
finish the week on a strong footing　強気の地合(じあ)いで先週の取引を終える
have strong cash flows　キャッシュ・フローが豊富である
remain strong　好調に推移する,堅調に推移する
strong appreciation of the yen against other currencies　他の通貨に対する円相場の大幅上昇,大幅な円高・他の通貨安,円全面高
strong balance sheet　強固な財務体質,健全な財務内容
strong bids　強気の買い
strong bond market　堅調な債券市場,債券市場の堅調
strong box [strongbox]　金庫,手提げ金庫,保護預り金庫
strong capitalization　強固な資本基盤
strong credit growth　大幅な信用需要の伸び,信用需要の大幅な伸び
strong demand for lending　借入需要の急増,借入需要の大幅な伸び,旺盛な借入需,借入需要が強いこと
strong earnings growth　利益の大幅な伸び,力強い利益の伸び
strong economic statistics　堅調な景気指標
strong finances　強固な財務基盤
strong financial position　強固な財務基盤
strong inflows of capital　大量の資本流入
strong investment　旺盛な投資意欲
strong management　強力な経営陣
strong market　強気相場,強気市場,強気市況
　　(=bull [bullish] market)
strong name　優良発行体,優良銘柄
strong outperformance　大幅なアウトパフォーマンス,パフォーマンスが市場平均を大幅に上回ること
strong refinancing　活発な借換え
strong room [strongroom]　金庫室
strong sales increase　売上の急増,販売の急増
strong seller　売れ筋商品
strong shareholder [stockholder]　安定株主
strong tone　強含み
◆Banks could forcibly sell insurance policies to clients by utilizing their strong position as creditors. 銀行は、債権者としての強い立場を利用して、顧客に保険を強制的に販売する可能性もある。◆The balance sheet of the Corporation is strong. 当社の財務状態[財務内容]は、健全です。◆The bank has a stronger balance sheet than some of its bigger peers. 同行の財務基盤は、一部の大手の同業他行よりも強固だ。◆The OSE is strong in derivatives trading. 大証は、金融派生商品(デリバティブ)の取引に強みを持っている。◆The yen has remained strong. 円高の流れは、変わっていない。◆The yen in record strong territory of ¥76 to the dollar causes hardships in the Japanese economy. 1ドル＝76円台の史上最高の円高水準は、日本経済にとって厳しい。◆The yen is currently hovering at a level stronger than ¥80 to the dollar. 円相場は現在[足元の円相場は]、1ドル＝80円を上回る水準で推移している。◆The yen soared to its strongest position this year. 円は、年初来の最高値を付けた。

strong-arm　(形)強引な,暴力的な,腕づくの,高圧的な
strong-arm loan collection　強引な債権取立て
strong-arm methods　高圧的な方法

◆Major moneylender SFCG earned an unsavory reputation for its strong-arm loan collection methods. 金融業者大手のSFCG（旧商工ファンド）の評判は、債権の取立てが強引で芳しくなかった。

strong dollar　強いドル, ドル高　（⇒weak dollar）
◆There are signs of a reversal in the trend of a stronger dollar and a weaker yen that started in the latter half of the 1990s. 1990年代後半から始まったドル高・円安傾向に、反転の兆しがある。◆U.S. President George W. Bush reiterated his support for a strong dollar. ブッシュ米大統領は、「強いドル」維持を表明した。

strong yen　強い円, 円高　（⇒dampen）
　strong yen against other currencies　円全面高
　strong yen-caused boom　円高景気
　strong yen caused recession　円高不況
　weather strong yen appreciation　円高を克服する
◆A decline in automakers' international competitiveness is caused by the strong yen. 円高で、自動車メーカー各社の国際競争力が低下している。◆A strong yen lowers the prices of imported goods and fuels deflation. 円高は輸入品の価格を下げ、デフレに拍車をかける。◆The fall in import prices that accompanies a strong yen could further prolong Japan's deflation. 円高に伴う輸入価格の下落で、日本のデフレがさらに長期化する可能性がある。◆The strong yen can hurt the Japanese economy. 円高は、日本経済にダメージを与える可能性がある。

strong yen and the weak U.S. dollar　円高・ドル安
　（=the yen's appreciation against the dollar）
◆There are serious concerns that the strong yen and the weak U.S. dollar could hurt the current economic upturn led by exports. 大きな懸念材料は、円高・ドル安の進行で現在の輸出主導の景気回復が打撃を受けることだ。

strong yen and weak dollar　円高・ドル安
◆Due to concerns about a possible slowdown in the U.S. economy, there has been no sign of an end to the strong yen and weak dollar. 米国の景気減速への懸念から、円高・ドル安に歯止めがかからない。

stronger dollar　ドル高, ドルの強含み
◆A stronger dollar may lead to objections from U.S. businesses that fear their international competitiveness. ドル高がさらに進行すると、国際競争力を懸念する米国の産業界から反発が強まる可能性がある。

stronger yen　円高, 円の強含み
◆The company lowered its full-year profit forecast by 6 percent on a stronger yen and weaker digital camera sales. 同社は、円高やデジカメの販売低迷で、通期利益予想を6%下方修正した。

structural reform(s)　構造改革
　structural reforms of government finances　財政構造改革
　the center pillar of the structural reforms　構造改革の柱
◆As a condition for loans to financially troubled countries in the late 1990s, the IMF called for strict implementation of structural reforms. 1990年代後半に財政難に陥った国に対する融資の条件として、IMF（国際通貨基金）は、厳しい構造改革の実施を求めた。◆During the period of structural reforms pushed by the Koizumi administration, the former chairman of the bank was lionized as a standard-bearer of financial reform. 小泉政権が推し進めた構造改革の時代に、同行の前会長は金融改革の旗手ともてはやされた。◆It is questionable whether the Italian new government will be able to steadily implement measures for financial reconstruction and structural reforms. イタリアの新政権が財政再建策と構造改革を着実に実行できるかどうかは、疑問だ。◆Measures to deal with surplus facilities are regarded as the center pillar of structural reforms to be initiated by the supply side. 過剰設備の処理対策は、供給サイドが着手する構造改革の柱とされている。

◆The bad loan problem plaguing financial institutions is one focal point of the structural reforms. 金融機関を悩ませている不良債権問題は、構造改革の焦点の一つだ。◆The key to returning to stable growth is whether the nation can eliminate excesses common to many companies and promote supply-side structural reforms. 安定成長復帰へのカギは、多くの日本企業に共通して見られる過剰体質を排除して、供給サイドの構造改革を進めることができるかどうかである。◆The report stresses the need to increase the overall supply capacity through structural reforms as a remedy for economic stagnation. 同報告書は、不況対策として、構造改革によって総供給力を引き上げる必要があると力説している。

structure　（動）組織する, 組み立てる, 構築する, 構成する, 組成する, 体系化する, 組織化する, 仕組む
　structure a portfolio　ポートフォリオを組成する
　structure products　商品を組成する, 商品を仕組む
◆In the civil lawsuit, Goldman Sachs Group Inc. said, "We did not structure a portfolio that was designed to lose money." 民事訴訟でゴールドマン・サックスは、「損失を想定したポートフォリオを組成したことはない」と述べた。

structure　（名）構造, 機構, 組織, 構成, 体系, 方式, 体制, 体質, 構築物, 構造物, 建造物
　（⇒capital structure）
　earnings structure　収益構造
　equity structure　資本構成, 出資構造, 株主所有権構造
　Fannie Mae Guaranteed Multifamily Structures　ファニー・メイ保証集合住宅仕組み債, ファニー・メイ GeMS
　fiscal structure　財政体質
　income structure　所得構造
　market structure　市場構造, 市場構成
　ownership structure　所有構造, 株主構造, 出資構成
　progressive tax structure　累進税の構造
　shareholding structure　株主構成, 株主構造
　　（=shareholder structure）
　two-bank structure　2行体制
◆Major banks are forced to review their earnings structure. 大手行は、収益構造の見直しを迫られている。◆The inefficiency of the Financial group's two-bank structure has been pointed out as many of operations overlap. 同フィナンシャル・グループの2行体制の非効率は、重複部門が多いため、以前から指摘されてきた。◆The number of high-income earners who will pay the higher tax rates will not change even if progressive tax structure may be reinforced. 累進税の構造を強化しても、最高税率を負担する高所得者層の数は変わらない。

structured　（形）組成した, 仕組んだ, 組織化された, 組織的な, 構造的な, ストラクチャード
　structured arbitrage transaction　仕組み裁定取引
　structured bond [note]　仕組み債
　　（=structural bond）
　structured deal　仕組み取引
　structured equity investment　ストラクチャード・エクイティ　（=equity drawdown facility）
　structured equity product　株式仕組み商品
　structured finance [financing]　仕組み金融, 仕組みファイナンス, ストラクチャード・ファイナンス
　structured financial product　仕組み商品
　　（=structured product）
　structured product　仕組み商品, 仕組み債, 仕組み案件, ストラクチャード商品
　　（=structured financial product）
　structured securities　仕組み証券, 証券化証券
　structured trade　仕組み取引, 仕組み債
　structured transaction　仕組み取引, 仕組み案件

(=structured deal)

thrift-issued structured financings　貯蓄金融機関発行の仕組み証券

◆Subprime-related securities are created partly from highly opaque structured products created by mixing subprime with other collateralized debt obligations. サブプライム関連証券は、サブプライム証券と他の債務担保証券(CDO)を合成して造られた極めて不透明な仕組み債などで生み出されている。

struggle　(動)奮闘[苦闘]する,悪戦苦闘する,苦戦する,苦悩する,戦う,争う,～に取り組む
(⇒make up for)

◆Financial institutions are still struggling with falling stock prices. 金融機関は、相変わらず株安に苦慮している。◆Greece is struggling with a serious fiscal crisis. ギリシャは、深刻な財政危機にあえいでいる。◆Many survivors of the Great East Japan Earthquake are struggling under the heavy double debt loads. 東日本大震災の被災者の多くは、二重ローンという重い負担を背負って苦しんでいる。◆The firm's TV business has been struggling due to intensifying industry competition and falling demand. 同社のテレビ事業は、業界競争の激化と需要の落ち込みで、苦戦を続けている。

struggle　(名)競争,闘争,戦い,もみ合い,取っ組み合い,攻防戦

all-out struggle for survival　生き残りをかけた総力戦
internal struggle　内部闘争
law-abiding struggle　順法闘争
litigating struggle　法廷闘争
struggle for existence [life]　生存競争
struggle for power　権力闘争
work-to-rule struggle　順法闘争
(=law-abiding struggle)

◆Hokuetsu's shareholders have been dragged into the struggle between Oji, Hokuetsu and trading house Mitsubishi Corp. 北越製紙の株主は、王子製紙、北越製紙と三菱商事(大手商社)の3社間の攻防戦に巻き込まれている。◆The commodity futures trading industry has entered an era of white-hot competition in an all-out struggle for survival. 商品先物取引業界は、生き残りをかけた総力戦で大競争の時代に入っている。

struggling　(形)経営不振に陥っている,経営再建中の,経営再建に取り組む,生き残りに懸命の,生き残りに必至になっている,苦境にあえぐ,もたついている,悪戦苦闘の　(⇒capital injection, foundation fund)

◆A ¥450 billion revival plan aims at turning around the struggling automaker. 4,500億円の再建計画は、この経営不振の自動車メーカーの事業再生を目指している。◆Greece's fiscal reconstruction is set as a condition for supporting the struggling country by the European Union and the International Monetary Fund. 欧州連合(EU)と国際通貨基金(IMF)は、ギリシャの財政再建を、財政危機にある同国支援の条件としている。◆Struggling Japanese drugs and textile maker Kanebo Ltd. unveiled a revival plan that asked banks to waive 99.5 billion yen in loans. 経営再建に取り組む日本の医薬品・繊維メーカーのカネボウは、銀行に995億円の債権放棄を求める再生計画を発表した。◆Struggling Victor Co. of Japan will eliminate 1,150 jobs to engineer its rehabilitation. 経営不振の日本ビクターは、再建計画を進めるため、1,150人を削減する。◆The struggling JAL's next step will be to start negotiations with its creditor banks over new loans to enact its rehabilitation plan. 経営再建に取り組む日航は今後、同社の再建計画案の実行に必要な新規融資を巡る取引銀行団との交渉に移ることになる。

stuck　(形)固定した,動かなくなって,動かなくて,行き詰まって,にっちもさっちもいかなくなって,困り果てて,逃げ出せなくて,離れられなくて　(名)困窮,面倒,厄介,難儀

be stuck on　～に夢中になっている,～にのぼせている
in stuck　困って,困り果てて,困窮して
out of stuck　難儀から逃れて

◆Stuck in a financial quagmire, Russia is having difficulty in managing its nuclear arsenal. 財政難から、ロシアは現在、保有する核兵器の管理に苦慮している。

Student Loan Marketing Association　奨学金融資金庫, SLMA　(⇒Sallie Mae)

student loan system　奨学金融資制度

STUF　短期引受証券,スタッフ(short-term underwriting facilityの略)

subdivide　(動)分割する,再分[再分割]する,細分する

◆When the privatization of postal system began in October 2007, Japan Post was subdivided into four firms. 2007年10月にスタートした郵政民営化で、日本郵政グループは、4社に分社化[分割]された。

subdued　(形)控え目の,元気がない,活気がない,伸び悩みの,大きな動きがない,低迷している,低水準の,柔らかい,和らげられた,抑制された,抑えられた
(⇒economic activity)

subdued economic activity　経済活動の低迷,景気低迷
subdued economic growth　景気低迷,経済成長の低い伸び,経済成長率の低迷
subdued inflation [inflationary] pressures　インフレ圧力が低いこと

subject　(動)服従させる

be subjected to　～にさらされる,～を受ける
subject A to B　AをBにさらす,AにBを受けさせる

◆Japanese government bonds are being subjected to stricter market scrutiny. 日本国債は、市場の一段と厳しい評価にさらされている。

subject to　～に服する,～に従う,～の影響を受ける,～を必要とする,～を条件とする,～を条件として,～を前提として,～の場合に限って,～を免れない,～が適用される,～の適用を受ける,～次第で,～によって決まる,～を対象とする,ただし～

be subject to a bankruptcy proceeding　破産手続きの対象になる
be subject to currency risk　為替リスクを負う,為替リスクをとる
be subject to delisting　上場廃止の対象になる
be subject to interest rate, credit and liquidity risk　金利[金利変動]リスク、信用リスクや流動性リスクにさらされる
be subject to market risk　市場リスクにさらされる
be subject to the tax　課税の対象となる

◆A company listed on the Fukuoka bourse is subject to delisting after two straight years of negative net worth. 福岡証券取引所に上場している企業は、2年連続債務超過になると、上場廃止の対象になる。◆A corporate merger plan is subject to legal screening by the Fair Trade Commission of Japan. 企業の合併計画は、公正取引委員会の法定審査を受けなければならない。◆According to the Financial Stability Board, 28 banks viewed as global systemically important financial institutions (G-SIFIs) will be subject to a new global rule requiring them to hold extra capital to prevent future financial crises. 金融安定化理事会(FSB)によると、金融システム上重要な国際金融機関(G-SIFIs)と考えられる世界の28行が、金融危機の再発を防止するため、資本の上積みを求める新国際基準[新国際金融規制]の対象になる。◆The EU's 91 banks were subject to the stress test. 欧州連合(EU)の91行が、ストレス・テスト(特別検査)の対象となった。◆The secondary market prices of the peripheral countries' government bonds plummeted as it became known that those bonds might be subject to debt forgiveness. 周辺国の国債は債務減免の必要が生じる

恐れのあることが判明したので、周辺国国債の流通市場での価格は暴落した。◆The United States may have to be subject to the harsh credit tests under which EU nations labor as the U.S. credit has come into question. 米国の信用が疑われているので米国も、EU諸国が苦労している厳しい信用度試験[テスト]を受ける必要があるかもしれない。

submit （動）提出する，提示する，提起する，付託する，付す，委(ゆだ)ねる，従わせる，服従させる，意見を述べる，具申する，～と思う （自動）降伏する，服従する，屈服する
  be submitted to the decision of a panel of arbitration　仲裁委員会の裁定に委ねる
  resolve the questions submitted　付託された問題を解決する
  submit a case to a court　裁判所に提訴する
  submit a financial report　財務報告書を提出する
  submit bids for the deal　同案件の入札に応じる，同案件の入札条件を提示する
  submit oneself to the jurisdiction of the court of　～の裁判所にその裁判管轄を付託する
  ◆AOKI Holdings Inc., the nation's second-largest menswear chain, has submitted a merger proposal to Futata Co. 紳士服服チェーン国内2位のAOKIホールディングスが、（同業の）フタタに経営統合案を提出した。◆Japanese companies listed on the London Stock Exchange will submit financial reports based on the IAS or the U.S. GAAP. ロンドン証券取引所に上場している日本企業は今後、国際会計基準か米国会計基準に基づく[に準拠した]財務報告書を提出することになる。◆The firm submitted corrected documents, including an amended financial report, to the Kanto Local Finance Bureau. 同社は、有価証券報告書の訂正など訂正文書を関東財務局に提出した。◆The government demanded banks seeking public funds to submit management revitalization plans. 政府は、公的資金[資金注入]を受ける銀行に経営健全化計画の提出を求めた。

subordinated bond　劣後債
（=subordinated debenture）

subordinated debenture　劣後債，劣後社債
（=subordinated bond: 債券発行会社の破産や清算時に、債務弁済が一般の債務返済後に開始される債券のこと）
  convertible subordinated debenture issue　転換劣後社債，劣後転換社債
  junior subordinated debenture　下位劣後債
  senior subordinated debenture　上位劣後債
  ◆During 2010, the Corporation completed a $100 million 8% convertible subordinated debenture issue. 2010年に当社は、利率8%の転換劣後社債[劣後転換社債]1億ドルの発行を完了しました。

subordinated loan　劣後ローン
  ◆The bank plans to provide the money by transferring ¥100 billion in subordinated loans, which it has already extended to the insurer, to the insurer's foundation fund. 同行は、すでに供与している劣後ローン1,000億円をこの保険会社の基金に振り替えて、その資金を提供する方針だ。◆The banks offered ¥2.2 trillion in funds and subordinated loans to the life insurance firms. 銀行は、基金や劣後ローンの形で生保に2兆2,000億円の資本を出している。

subordinated obligation　劣後債務
  ◆This 7 7/8% subordinated debentures are unsecured subordinated obligations of the Corporation, which are convertible into the Corporation's capital stock at a conversion price of $153.6563 per share. この7.875%利付き劣後転換社債は、当社の無担保劣後債務で、1株当たり153.6563ドルの転換価格で当社株式に転換できます。

subparticipation [sub-participation]　対外ローン債権の売買，ローン債権の売買，SUB-P取引

subpoena [subpena]　（動）召喚する，召喚状を出す，出頭を命じる，（証拠の）提出命令を行う
  be subpoenaed by the prosecution　検察側により召喚される
  be subpoenaed over [for]　～の件で召喚される
  ◆Goldman Sachs was subpoenaed over its activities leading up to the financial crisis. ゴールドマン・サックスは、金融危機を招いた[引き起こした]同社の証券業務の件で、召喚された。◆Seven executives of Merrill Lynch & Co. were subpoenaed over executive pay. 米大手証券メリルリンチの経営幹部7人が、幹部報酬の件で召喚された。

subpoena [subpena]　（名）召喚状，呼び出し状，（法廷への）出頭命令
  issue a subpoena　召喚状を出す
  mail a subpoena　召喚状を送達する
  subpoena ad testificandum　証人召喚令状
  subpoena duces tecum　文書提出命令状
  ◆New York State's Attorney General Andrew Cuomo issued subpoenas to seven executives who received tens of millions of dollars in 2008 pay from Merrill Lynch & Co. ニューヨーク州のアンドリュー・クオモ司法長官は、2008年度の報酬としてメリルリンチから1千万ドル以上を受け取った7人の経営幹部に、召喚状を出した。

subprime　（形）金利[貸出条件]がプライム・レート以下の，プライムより信用力が低い，信用力が低い，二級品の，サブプライム

subprime crisis　サブプライム問題
  ◆In the subprime crisis, the U.S. Federal Reserve Board had to take the extraordinary step of providing an emergency loan not to a commercial bank but to an investment bank. サブプライム問題で、米国の中央銀行の連邦準備制度理事会（FRB）は、緊急融資を銀行[商業銀行]ではなく証券会社[投資銀行]に対して行う異例の措置を取らざるを得なかった。

subprime defaults　サブプライムの不払い，サブプライムの焦げ付き
  ◆The news of a rise in the subprime defaults rocked the U.S. financial community. サブプライムの不払い増加のニュースに、米金融業界は動揺した。

subprime housing loan　サブプライム住宅ローン
  ◆The subprime housing loan problem continues to be reverberate around the globe. サブプライム住宅ローン問題は、まだ世界に広がり続けている。

subprime lender　サブプライム・ローンの融資行，信用力が比較的低い低所得者を対象にした住宅融資の融資銀行[融資行]，住宅ローン会社
（=subprime mortgage lender）
  ◆Subprime lenders are struggling because of rising delinquencies and defaults. サブプライム・ローンの融資行は、返済遅延や債務不履行[焦げ付き]の増加で苦戦している。

subprime loan　低所得者を対象にした住宅融資，低所得者層向け住宅ローン，サブプライム・ローン
（=subprime mortgage, subprime mortgage loan）
  subprime loan business　サブプライム・ローン事業
  ◆Nomura booked about ¥72 billion in losses related to the U.S. subprime loan business in the January-June period. 野村[野村ホールディングス]は、1-6月期に米国でのサブプライム・ローン事業関連の損失として約720億円を計上した。
  解説 サブプライム・ローンとは：サブプライム・ローンのサブプライム（subprime）は、優良な借り手を対象にした「プライム」より信用力が低い、という意味である。サブプライム・ローンと呼ばれる米国の低所得者層や返済能力に問題がある個人向けの住宅ローン[住宅融資]は、ローン返済開始から2年間くらいは金利が低いが、それ以降は一般に金利が低くなるように設定されている。そのため米国では、高金利の返済ができないサブプライム・ローンの焦げ付き問題で、株価の動揺が続いた。また、サブプライム・ローンを証券化した金融商品を販売して

いる欧米や日本の金融機関が、多額の損失を出す事態になった。

subprime loan crisis サブプライム・ローン（低所得者向け住宅融資）問題，サブプライム危機
◆The financial market turmoil is caused by the U.S. subprime loan crisis. 金融市場の混乱は、米国のサブプライム・ローン（低所得者向け住宅融資）問題によるものだ。◆The U.S. government and the Federal Reserve Board took swift actions to deal with the subprime loan crisis of 2007. 米政府と米連邦準備制度理事会（FRB）は、2007年のサブプライム危機に迅速に対応した。

subprime mortgage 低所得者［低所得者層］向け住宅ローン，低所得者向け住宅融資，信用力が低い個人向け住宅融資，サブプライム・ローン
（=subprime loan, subprime mortgage loan）
subprime mortgage debacle サブプライム・ローン市場の崩壊，サブプライム・ショック （⇒debacle）
subprime mortgage fiasco サブプライム・ローンの焦げ付き
subprime mortgage lender 住宅ローン会社，サブプライム・ローンの融資行
subprime mortgage loan サブプライム・ローン
subprime mortgage mess サブプライム・ローン問題 （⇒turmoil）
subprime mortgage product 低所得者向け住宅融資［サブプライム・ローン］関連の金融商品
subprime mortgage woes サブプライム問題
（=subprime crisis）
the subprime problem サブプライム問題
（⇒securitized product）
◆Banking titan Citigroup Inc. repeatedly misled investors about its potential losses from subprime mortgages. 米金融大手のシティグループは、サブプライム・ローン（低所得者向け住宅融資）による予想損失額について、投資家に繰り返し誤った情報を提供していた。◆The company was once the second-largest provider of subprime mortgages in the United States on loan volume. 同社は、かつてはサブプライム・ローンの融資高で米国第2位の住宅ローン会社だった。

subprime mortgage crisis サブプライム・ローン問題，サブプライム・ローンの焦げ付き問題
（⇒financial turmoil）
◆The extent of Lehman's massive losses and write-downs due to the subprime mortgage crisis became evident. サブプライム・ローン（米低所得者向け住宅融資）問題に伴うリーマンの巨額の損失と評価損の規模が、明らかになった。◆The New York-based Citigroup, once the world's biggest banking group, faced massive losses in the wake of the subprime mortgage crisis. 世界最大の金融グループだったシティグループ（ニューヨーク）は、サブプライム・ローンの焦げ付き問題を受けて、巨額の損失を抱えていた。◆UBS will post a pretax loss of up to $690 million in the third quarter mainly because of losses linked to the U.S. subprime mortgage crisis. スイス最大手銀行UBSの第3四半期税引き前損失は、主に米国で起きた低所得者向け融資「サブプライム・ローン」問題の関連損失で、最高で6億9,000万ドルに達する見通しだ。

subprime mortgage crunch サブプライム・ローン問題
◆The U.S. subprime mortgage crunch is becoming more and more serious. 米国のサブプライム・ローン問題が、深刻化している。

subprime mortgage loan 米国の低所得者向け住宅ローン，サブプライム・ローン
◆The instability of U.S. stock prices results from problems related to massive number of unrecoverable subprime mortgage loans extended to low-income earners in the United States. 米国の株価不安定は、米国の低所得者向け住宅ロー

ン「サブプライム・ローン」の焦げ付き急増関連問題に起因している。

subprime mortgage market サブプライム・ローン市場 （⇒credit market）
◆Banks across the United States have been devastated by the collapse of the subprime mortgage market. 米全域の銀行が、サブプライム・ローン（低所得者向け住宅ローン）市場の崩壊によって、壊滅的打撃を受けている。

subprime mortgage product 住宅融資［サブプライム・ローン］関連の金融商品
◆Goldman Sachs was charged with fraud by the SEC over its marketing of a subprime mortgage product. 米証券取引委員会（SEC）が、低所得者向け住宅融資「サブプライム・ローン」関連の金融商品の販売に関して［金融商品の販売を巡り］、詐欺［証券詐欺］容疑で米金融大手のゴールドマン・サックスを提訴した。

subprime mortgage unit 低所得者向け住宅融資事業，サブプライム・ローン事業
◆HSBC Holdings PLC will shut its subprime mortgage unit and eliminate 750 jobs. 英銀行大手のHSBCホールディングスは、低所得者向け住宅融資「サブプライム・ローン」事業の米国子会社を閉鎖して、従業員750人を解雇する。

subprime woes サブプライム問題，低所得者向け住宅融資問題
◆The effects of an economic slowdown in industrialized countries stemming from the U.S. subprime woes could spread in the emerging economies. 米国のサブプライム（低所得者向け住宅融資）問題に起因する先進国の景気減速の影響は、新興国にも拡大する可能性がある。

subscribe （動）株式を引き受ける，買い取る，加入する，予約する，予約購読する，署名する （⇒company employees' pension scheme, corporate pension, pension program）
◆As Japan's individual financial assets amount to nearly ￥1.5 quadrillion, there is little likelihood that Japanese government bonds will not be sufficiently subscribed to. 日本の個人金融資産は1,500兆円に近いので、日本の国債が消化難になる心配はない。◆By law, about 22 million people who are not salaried workers are required to subscribe to the national pension system and pay premiums. 法律上、サラリーマンでない約2,200万人が、国民年金への加入と保険料の納付を義務付けられている。◆The investment fund subscribed to 27 million shares at ￥250 per share in a March 2005 new share issue by the company. 投資ファンドは、同社による2005年3月の新株発行の際、1株250円で2,700万株を引き受けた。

subscriber （名）株式の引受人，年金や保険、電話などの加入者，申込み者，署名者，新聞や雑誌の（予約）購読者
cell phone subscriber 携帯電話の加入者
（=mobile phone subscriber）
Class-III pension subscriber 第3号被保険者
insurance subscriber 保険加入者，保険申込み者
outside subscribers of new shares 新株の外部引受人
subscribers' contributions 加入者の保険料
subscribers to defined contribution pension plan 確定拠出年金の加入者
yield to subscribers 応募者利回り
yields to subscribers of public and corporate bonds 公社債応募者利回り
◆Mobile phone subscribers are the fastest growing segment of the telephone market. 携帯電話の加入者は、電話市場で最も急成長を遂げている部門である。◆Pension premiums of full-time housewives of company employees and public servants are automatically covered by payments made by all subscribers to welfare and mutual pension plans. 会社員や公務員の専業主婦の年金保険料は、厚生年金や共済年金の加入者全員の支払い金で自動的にカバーすることになってい

る。◆Regarding national pension, subscribers' contributions would have to increase from ￥13,300 a month to ￥29,600 a month from fiscal 2025 to maintain the current level of pension payments. 国民年金については、現在の年金給付水準を維持するには、2025年度以降、加入者の保険料を月13,300円から29,600円に引き上げる必要がある。◆Shares taken by the outside subscribers at the time of incorporation of the new company shall be limited to one share each. 新会社の設立時に外部の引受人が引き受ける株式は、それぞれ1株に限るものとする。◆Subscribers to defined contribution pension plan have surpassed 2 million. 確定拠出年金の加入者が、200万人を突破した。◆The basic pension plan has been covered by premiums paid by subscribers and government budgetary appropriations. 基礎年金は、加入者が支払う保険料と政府の予算割当額（国の負担）で賄（まかな）われている。◆The number of earthquake insurance subscribers has grown rapidly since autumn. 昨秋から、地震保険の加入件数が急増している。

subscription （名）（株式の）引受け, 応募, 加入, 出資, 寄付, 寄付金, 義捐金, 出資金, 予約, 予約金,（予約, 定期）購読, 購読料, 署名, 同意, 賛成, 賛同,（クラブなどの）会費（「応募」とは、株式などの有価証券が新規発行される場合に買付けの申込みをすること）

be available on subscription　予約購読で入手できる
capital subscription　出資, 払込み資本金
　（＝subscription to the capital）
IMF subscription　IMF出資
oversubscription　応募超過
　（＝surplus subscription）
pension subscription period　年金加入期間
private subscription　縁故募集
　（＝private offering）
public subscription　公募
raise ［make］a subscription　寄付を募る
stock subscription　株式応募, 株式公募, 株式の引受け
stock subscription contract　株式引受契約, 株式引受契約書
subscription agent　募集代理人
subscription agreement　募集契約, 元引受契約, 買取り契約, 外債の買取り契約
subscription certificate　出資証券
subscription deposits for new stock to be issued　新株式申込み証拠金
subscription fee　加入料, 加入料金,（予約）購読料
　（＝subscription charge, subscription rate）
subscription for shares　株式申込み
subscription period　募集期間, 販売期間
subscription price　引受価格, 新株引受権行使価格, 応募価格, 買取り価格（「引受価格」は、証券発行会社から引受業者が買い取る価格のこと）
subscription right　新株引受権, 引受申込み権　（＝stock warrant: 企業が普通株式を新規に発行して一般公募する際、その新株の割当てを優先して受けられる権利のこと）
subscription to securities　証券応募
subscription to stockholders　株主優待
subscription to the capital　出資
　（＝capital subscription）
subscription to the fund　基金への寄付金

◆Fuji TV issued the moving strike convertible bonds (MSCBs) early this year for subscription by Daiwa Securities SMBC Co. to raise ￥80 billion for its NBS takeover bid. フジテレビは今春、ニッポン放送株の公開買付け（TOB）資金800億円を調達するため、大和証券SMBCを引受先として転換社債型新株予約権付き社債（MSCB）を発行した。◆The nation's largest nonlife insurance company was ordered not to accept new subscriptions for medical and other third-sector insurance policies. 国内最大手の損害保険会社が、医療など第三分野の保険商品の新規募集停止命令を受けた。

subscription warrant　新株予約権, 新株引受権, 新株引受権証書, ワラント　（⇒hostile acquirer）

corporate bond with subscription warrant　新株引受権付き社債
issue subscription warrants to all shareholders　全株主を対象に新株予約権を発行する

subscription Web site　有料サイト, 有料ウェブ・サイト

◆Four credit card holders received bills for accessing subscription Web sites via cell phones even though they had no recollection of doing so. 利用した覚えがないのに、携帯電話の有料サイトの利用代金請求書が、4人のクレジット・カード会員に届いた。◆The company's board approved a plan to issue subscription warrants to all shareholders on its shareholders list as of March 31, 2011. 同社の取締役会は、2011年3月31日現在［時点］の株主名簿に記載されている全株主を対象に、新株予約権を発行する計画を承認した。

subside　（動）沈下する, 沈む, 陥没する, 静まる, 収まる, 和らぐ, 沈静化する, 減る, 減少する, 衰退する, 弱まる

◆Corporate debt issues are recovering as bond market turbulence in the aftermath of the March 11 Great East Japan Earthquake has subsided. 2011年3月11日の東日本大震災直後の債券市場の混乱が収束したため、社債の発行額が回復している。◆The world economy will steer to a growth path again once the financial crisis subsides. 金融危機が沈静化したら、世界経済はまた成長軌道［成長路線］に向かうだろう。

subsidiary　（名）子会社, 関係会社, 従属会社, 同族会社, 外郭団体　（＝subsidiary company, subsidiary corporation; ⇒full subsidiary, takeover bid, triangle merger）

bank-affiliated securities subsidiary　銀行系証券子会社
bank ［banking］subsidiary　銀行子会社
be transferred to a subsidiary　子会社に出向となる
consolidated subsidiary　連結子会社, 連結対象子会社
consumer finance subsidiary　消費者金融子会社
derivative products subsidiary　派生商品子会社
dissolve a subsidiary　子会社を解散する
50-50 subsidiary with　〜との折半出資子会社
finance ［financing］subsidiary　金融子会社
financially troubled subsidiary　資金難の子会社, 資金繰りが苦しい子会社
float subsidiaries　子会社の株式を公開する
foreign subsidiary　海外子会社　（＝international subsidiary, offshore subsidiary, overseas subsidiary）
fully owned subsidiary　完全所有子会社, 全額所有子会社, 100％子会社　（＝fully-funded affiliate, fully owned unit, totally held subsidiary, wholly owned company）
increase one's stake in the subsidiary　子会社への出資比率［出資額, 出資持ち分, 持ち株比率］を引き上げる
indirect subsidiary　間接子会社
insurance subsidiary　保険子会社, 保険業を営む子会社
majority-owned subsidiary　過半数所有子会社
minority interests in subsidiaries　子会社の少数株主持ち分
nonbank subsidiary　非銀行子会社, 銀行以外の子会社, 銀行以外の事業に従事する子会社
partially owned subsidiary　部分所有子会社
put a subsidiary on the sale ［selling］block　子会社を売りに出す
quasi-subsidiary　準子会社
securities subsidiary　証券子会社

special subsidiary for the purpose　特別目的会社
trust bank subsidiary　信託銀行子会社
trust subsidiary　信託子会社
unconsolidated subsidiary　非連結子会社, 連結対象外の関連会社
unlisted subsidiary　非上場子会社
wholly owned subsidiary　完全所有子会社, 全額出資子会社, 100％所有子会社, 100％子会社
◆Although banks are allowed to sell any products offered by their life insurance subsidiaries, no bank has such a subsidiary. 銀行の生保子会社が提供する商品ならどんな商品でも銀行窓口での販売が認められているが、今のところこのような子会社を持っている銀行はない。◆Following the tender offer, Oji Paper would acquire the remaining Hokuetsu shares through a share swap to turn it into a wholly owned subsidiary. 株式公開買付け（TOB）後に、王子製紙は、株式交換で残りの北越製紙の株を取得して北越製紙を完全子会社化する。◆Nippon Life Insurance's asset management subsidiary Nissay Asset Management Corp. increased its shareholding in Olympus to 0.21 percent from 0.08 percent. 日本生命の資産運用子会社であるニッセイアッセトマネジメントは、オリンパス株の保有比率を0.08％から0.21％に買い増した。

subsidiary　（形）補助の, 従属的な, 副次的な, 補助金の
subsidiary bank　子会社銀行
subsidiary banking business　銀行周辺業務
subsidiary coin［money］　補助貨幣
Subsidiary Coinage Act　補助貨法
subsidiary company　子会社
subsidiary currency　補助通貨, 補助貨幣
subsidiary market　副次的市場
subsidiary payment　補助金, 報酬金
subsidiary undertaking　子会社
subsidiary utilities　助成金による公共事業

subsidy　（名）補助金, 助成金, 交付金, 奨励金, 報奨金, 研究助成金　（=grant）
employment-adjustment subsidies　雇用調整助成金
export subsidies　輸出補助金
government subsidies　政府補助金, 国庫補助金, 政府助成金
price subsidies　価格補助金
public subsidies　公的補助金, 補助金
subsidies to farmers who grow agricultural products for exports　輸出用農産物農家に対する補助金
◆Political parties receive taxpayer money in the form of subsidies. 政党は、（政党）交付金の形で、国民の税金を受け取っている。◆The emergency employment package contains a plan to relax criteria for receiving employment-adjustment subsidies. 緊急雇用対策には、雇用調整助成金の受領要件の緩和策も含まれている。◆The government provides subsidies to firms that hire workers between the ages of 45 and 59 from poor-performance companies. 政府は、業績不振の企業から43～59歳の中高年労働者を雇い入れている企業に、助成金を出している。◆The tripartite reforms aim to reduce the amount of subsidies provided by the central government to the local governments; cut local tax grants to local governments; and shift revenue sources from the central government to local governments. 「三位一体」改革は、国の地方政府への補助金削減、地方交付税交付金の削減と国から地方政府への財源の移譲をめざしている。◆To encourage firms' temporary layoffs, the government will ease requirements for receiving a governmental subsidy to defray costs relating to layoffs. 企業の一時解雇［一時帰休］を支援するため、政府は企業が雇用調整助成金（解雇関連費用を負担する政府助成金）を受けるための要件を緩和する。

substantial　（形）かなりの, 相当な, 多額の, 高額の, 多大な, 多数の, 大量の, かなりの規模の, 大規模な, 莫大な, 大幅な, 大型の, 本格的な, 豊富な, 実質的な, 事実上の, 現実の, 実在の, 重要な, 重大な, 価値のある, 資力がある, 大きな影響力を持つ, 堅固な, 頑丈な, 根拠のある
a substantial sum of money　多額の金, 多額の資金
earn substantial profits　莫大な利益を上げる
gain substantial value　価値が大幅に上昇する
make substantial commitments to　～に本格的に進出する
raise substantial funds　巨額の資金を調達する
return substantial deficits　大幅赤字に転落する
rules governing substantial acquisitions of shares　経営参加株式の取得に関する規約
substantial borrowing　多額の借入れ, 多額の借財, 多額の借入金
substantial bribes　多額の賄賂（わいろ）
substantial capital increases　大規模な増資, 巨額の増資
substantial damages　一般的損害賠償金（=general damages）
substantial downward revision　大幅な下方修正
substantial gains　大幅な伸び, 大幅黒字
substantial increase　大幅な増加
substantial investments　大型投資
substantial losses　大幅赤字
substantial pay increases　大幅賃上げ
substantial profits　大幅利益, 莫大な利益
substantial rally　大幅に買われること
substantial relaxation　大幅緩和
take a substantial position in　～に本格的に進出する
◆In resolving Greece's debt woes, German Chancellor Angera Merkel urged substantial aid from private creditors. ギリシャの債務問題を解決するにあたって、アンゲラ・メルケル独首相は、民間債権者に大幅支援を求めた。◆The market opportunity is substantial. 市場機会は、かなりのものです。

substantially　（副）実質的に, 基本的に, 事実上, 概して, 大幅に, かなり, 相当
◆The European Union will substantially expand the lending capacity of the EFSF to buy up government bonds in case the fiscal and financial crisis spreads countries as Italy. 欧州連合（EU）は、財政・金融危機がイタリアなどなどに拡大した場合に国債を買い支えるため、欧州金融安定基金（EFSF）の融資能力を大幅に拡大する。◆The income and corporate taxes have substantially decreased due to the prolonged recession and a series of tax breaks. 所得税や法人税は、長期不況や一連の減税措置で大幅に減少している。

substitute　（名）代理, 代役, 代替, 代物, 代替物, 代用品（形）代理の, 代わりの, 代替の
credit substitute　信用代替, 信用供与の代替手段
import substitute　輸入代替
index substitute　指数に代わる銘柄
money substitute　貨幣代替物
substitute demand　代替需要
substitute money　代替通貨
substitute security　代用証券

substitution　（名）代用, 代替, 取替え, 交換, 代物,（担保の）差し換え
credit substitution　信用代替
elasticity of substitution　代替の弾力性
mandatory collateral institution　強制担保差し換え
marginal rate of substitution　限界代替率
payment in substitution　代物弁済
substitution in［of］collateral　担保の差し換え, 担保の交換

substitution of loans　ローンの代替
substitution of securities　証券の交換
substitution swap　代替スワップ

subtract　(動)(〜から)差し引く,控除する,減じる,引く,押し下げる
◆The Bank of Japan's diffusion indexes are calculated by subtracting the percentage of companies reporting deterioration in business conditions from those perceiving improvement. 日銀のこれらの業況判断指数(DI)は、現在の景況感について「改善している」と感じている企業の割合から「悪化している」と回答した企業の割合を差し引いて算出する。

successively　(副)引き続いて,連続して,続いて,次々と,連日
◆Stock exchanges in both Japan and the United States successively posted major losses. 日米の株式市場は連日、大幅な下げを記録した。

successor bank　受け皿銀行

sudden　(形)突然の,急激な,急な,不意の
sudden downturn in economic activity　突然の景気減速
sudden drop in prices　物価の急落
sudden fall in funding costs　資金調達コストの急減
sudden fall in stocks　株価急落
sudden increase in dollar exchange rates　急激なドル高
sudden plunge in the market　相場の急落,相場急落
sudden rise in corporate profits　企業収益の急増
sudden rise in the yen　急激な円高
sudden rise in yields　利回りの急上昇
sudden widening of spreads　スプレッドの急拡大
◆A sudden plunge in the market is believed to have been caused by a trader who mistyped an order to sell a large block of shares. 相場急落は、トレーダーによる大量の株式売買の誤発注により生じたと見られる。

sue　(動)訴える,訴えを起こす,提訴する,告訴する
◆American International Group Inc. sued Bank of America for allegedly selling it faulty mortgage investments. 米保険大手のAIGが、問題のある[欠陥商品の]モーゲージ証券を同社に販売したとしてバンク・オブ・アメリカを提訴した。
◆If the creditor banks forgive the debts though TEPCO is not carrying excess liabilities, senior managements of the lenders may be sued in a shareholders' lawsuit over mismanagement. 東電が債務超過ではないのに債権保有銀行が債権を放棄すると、ずさんな経営で、金融機関の上級経営陣は株主代表訴訟で訴えられる可能性がある。◆The company failed after it was sued by music and film industries for copyright piracy and its investors withdrew their support. 同社は、音楽と映画業界から著作権侵害で訴えられて投資家も支援を撤回したため、経営破綻した。◆The Federal Housing Finance Agency sued 17 financial firms over risky investments. 米連邦住宅金融局(FHFA)が、高リスク証券を販売したとして大手金融機関17社を提訴した。

suffer　(動)損失などを受ける,損失を計上する,被害などを被(こうむ)る,打撃を受ける,〜に見舞われる,〜に巻き込まれる,耐える,低迷する,悪材料になる,支障が生じる
suffer a plunge in share prices　株価が下落する
suffer a slowdown　景気減速に見舞われる
suffer an erosion of financial assets　金融資産の損失を被る
suffer big [large] losses　大損害を受ける,巨額の損失を被る,多額の損失を計上する
◆All of the nation's six major nonlife insurers suffered sharp falls in earnings for the fiscal first half ended Sept. 30. 今年9月中間決算(9月30日に終了した今年度上半期)の国内損害保険会社の主要6社が、軒並み大幅な減益となった。◆If a financial system crisis should occur due to sharp fall in Japanese government bond prices, the Japanese people would suffer an erosion of their financial assets. 日本国債価格の急落で金融システム不安が生じれば、日本国民の金融資産は損失を被ることになる。◆If the yen's value against the dollar appreciates too rapidly, export-oriented businesses will suffer. 急激な円高・ドル安が進行すると、輸出企業が打撃を受ける。◆In the first quarter of the year, the gross domestic product suffered its worst decline in the postwar era. 本年第1四半期は、国内総生産(GDP)が戦後最大の落ち込みとなった。◆Japan's exports will stagnate and corporate performance will suffer if the yen remains in the historically high ¥75-range against the dollar. 円相場が1ドル＝75円台の史上最高値が続けば、日本の輸出は低迷し、企業の業績は悪化する。◆The wounds that the Japanese economy has suffered are superficial in comparison with those inflicted on the U.S. and European nations. 日本経済が受けている傷は、欧米諸国が負っている傷より浅い。◆Under the mark-to-market accounting system, if banks suffer appraisal losses of stocks they are holding, they are required to subtract 60 percent of those losses from their surplus funds. 時価会計制度では、金融機関が保有する株式の評価損が出た場合、金融機関は評価損の6割を剰余金から取り除かなければならない。

suffer (a) loss　損失を被(こうむ)る,損失を計上する
◆It will be the other eurozone countries and the IMF that will suffer losses if Greece defaults. ギリシャの不払い[デフォルト]で損失を被るのは、ギリシャ以外のユーロ圏諸国とIMF(国際通貨基金)だ。◆Retail outlets that suffer loss as a result of fraud can also claim compensation from card issuers. 不正使用により損害を被っている小売り加盟店側も、カード会社に賠償金を請求できる。◆The credit union suffered a loss of about ¥4.2 billion. 同信用組合は、約42億円の損失を被った。

suffer a slowdown　景気減速に見舞われる
◆Japan is suffering a slowdown. 日本は、景気減速に見舞われている。

suffer from　〜に苦しむ[悩む],(災害などに)あう,〜で打撃を受ける,〜に見舞われる,(損害などを)受ける,〜が重荷になる　(⇒shortage)
◆Brazil suffering from the strengthening of its currency has restricted an influx of capital. 通貨高に悩むブラジルは、資本流入[資金流入]を規制している。◆Europe is still suffering from the financial crisis. 欧州は、まだ金融危機に苦しんでいる。◆Italy is suffering from the financial crisis that spilled over from Greece. イタリアは、ギリシャから飛び火した財政危機に見舞われている。◆Sony has suffered from declining export profits due to the yen's sharp appreciation. ソニーは、急激な円高で、輸出の採算悪化に見舞われている。

suffer huge losses　巨額の損失を被(こうむ)る
◆Creditor financial institutions and shareholders will suffer huge losses if TEPCO falls into debt without the government financial aid. 東電が政府の金融支援を受けられずに債務超過に陥れば、融資している金融機関や株主は、巨額の損失を被ることになる。◆Shinsei and Aozora banks suffered huge losses in their overseas investment business in the aftermath of the global financial crisis triggered by the collapse of Lehman Brothers Holdings Inc. in autumn 2008. 新生銀行とあおぞら銀行は、2008年秋のリーマン・ブラザーズの経営破たんで始まった世界的な金融危機の影響で、海外投資事業に巨額の損失が発生した。

sufficiency　(名)十分,十分なこと,十分な状態[資力],十分性,充足,充足性,充実,充実性
capital sufficiency　資本の充実性
economic self-sufficiency　経済的自立,経済的自給自足
financial self-sufficiency　独立採算制
sufficiency of tender　入札書の充足性
sufficiency rating　完成率

sufficient　(形)十分な,足りる,十分足りる,大幅な

have sufficient credit strength　〜は信用力が十分に高い, 〜の信用力は十分に高い
Not Sufficient　資金不足, N/S [n.s.]
not-sufficient fund　資金不足
sufficient capital to withstand another financial crisis　新たな金融危機に耐えられるだけの十分な資本金
sufficient condition　十分条件
sufficient fund　十分な資金
sufficient statistic　十分統計量
◆The stress test of the European Banking Authority is a banking health check to ensure banks across Europe have sufficient capital to withstand another financial crisis. 欧州銀行監督機構（EBA）のストレス・テストは、欧州全域の銀行が新たな金融危機に耐えられるだけの資本金を十分に確保していることを保証するための銀行の健全性検査だ。

sugar-bowl savings　タンス預金
（=drawer savings）
◆Sugar-bowl savings in the U.S. and European countries are a close equivalent of drawer savings in Japan. 欧米で使われる「シュガー・ボール（砂糖入れ）預金」は、だいたい日本の「タンス預金」に相当する。

suggest　（動）暗示する,（それとなく）示す, 示唆（しさ）する, ほのめかす, 提案する, 提言する, 解決策［妙案］を述べる, 考えを述べる, 言う, 〜を連想させる, 〜を思い起こさせる, 〜と思う
◆The decoupling theory suggests that China and India would not be hurt by a global slowdown. ディカップリング論によると、中国やインドなどは世界的な景気減速の影響を受けないとされる。

suit　（名）訴訟（lawsuit）, 民事訴訟, 請願, 嘆願, 要求, スーツ
be at suit　裁判中である
drop［discontinue］a suit　訴訟を取り下げる
file［bring, start］a suit against　〜を相手取って訴訟を起こす［訴えを起こす］, 〜を告訴する, 〜を提訴する
file a suit against A for B　AをBで提訴する
file a suit against A with B　Aを相手取ってBに訴訟を起こす
◆Banking titan Citigroup Inc. has agreed to pay $75 million to the U.S. Securities and Exchange Commission to settle subprime mortgage suit. 米金融大手シティグループが、低所得者向け住宅融資「サブプライム・ローン」の訴訟の和解金として、7,500万ドルを米証券取引委員会（SEC）に支払うことで合意した。

sukuk　（名）イスラム債, イスラム債券, スクーク
（=Islamic bonds（イスラム・ボンド）:sukukはアラビア語sakkの複数形。シャリーア（イスラム法）の規定の範囲内で発行される有価証券）

sum　（名）合計, 総額, 総数, 金額
huge sums of capital　巨額の資金
initial sum　頭金, 一時金, 契約金
sum insured　保険金額
the sum［sums］at risk　危険保険金額
the sum at risk of the surplus　超過額の危険保険金額
the sum at risk reinsured　危険再保険金額
◆It's common to shift huge sums of capital to take advantage of international tax shelters. 巨額の資金を移し替えて、国際的な節税策を講じるのは常識だ。

summit　（名）サミット, 首脳会議, 主要国首脳会議, 首脳会談, トップ会議, トップ会談
APEC summit　アジア太平洋経済協力会議（APEC）首脳会議
economic summit（meeting）　経済サミット
European Union summit　欧州連合（EU）首脳会議
financial summit meeting　金融サミット
（⇒summit meeting）
Group of Eight major nations summit　主要8か国（G8）首脳会議
industrial nation economic summit meeting　先進国首脳会議
regional summit meeting　地域首脳会談
summit conference　サミット会議, 首脳会議［会談］, トップ会議　（=summit meeting, summit talks）
the G-20 summit in Seoul　世界20か国・地域のソウル・サミット, ソウルでの世界20か国・地域（G20）首脳会議, ソウル・サミット
◆The mood music at the Group of 20 finance ministers meeting contrasted with the tense summit five months ago. 世界20か国・地域（G20）財務相・中央銀行総裁会議のゆったりした雰囲気は、5か月前の緊迫したG20金融サミット（首脳会議）とは対照的だった。

summit meeting　首脳会談［会議］, 首脳会談（サミット）, トップ会談, サミット
◆At the financial summit meeting in Washington, additional pump-priming measures through strengthening cooperation between advanced countries and emerging economies will be a major subject of discussion. ワシントンで開かれる金融サミットでは、先進国と新興国の連携強化による追加景気対策の検討が、テーマとなる。◆At two financial summit meetings since the collapse of Lehman Brothers, agreements were made on cooperation to implement large-scale economic stimulus measures and to take monetary relaxation policies. リーマン・ブラザーズの倒産［破たん］以来2回開かれた金融サミットでは、連携して大型の財政出動や金融緩和策を実施することで合意が得られた。◆In Europe, buffeted by the U.S. financial crisis, four major countries have held a summit meeting to discuss countermeasures. 米金融危機の煽（あお）りを受けた欧州では、主要4か国が最近、首脳会議を開いて対策を協議した。◆The IMF's new financing scheme is expected to be agreed on at the Group of 20 summit meeting and will be launched after being approved by the IMF's board of directors. 国際通貨基金（IMF）の新融資制度は、主要20か国・地域（G20）サミット（首脳会議）で合意する見込みで、その後IMF理事会の承認を経てスタートする。

super-loose monetary policy　超金融緩和政策, 超金融緩和の政策
（=ultra-loose money policy; ⇒money policy）
◆The U.S. Federal Reserve Board raised U.S. interest rates, leading the worldwide move to change current super-loose monetary policy. 米連邦準備制度理事会（FRB）が米国の金利を引き上げ、世界的な超金融緩和の政策転換の先陣を切った。

super NOW account　スーパーNOW勘定, スーパーNOW預金口座（高利回りの小切手振出可能預金。NOWはnegotiable order of withdrawal（譲渡可能払戻し指図書）の略。）

super-strong yen　超円高
◆Japanese small and midsize firms are being buffeted by the super-strong yen and electricity shortages. 日本の中小企業は現在、超円高と電力不足などで痛めつけられている［経営環境が悪化している］。

super voting share　複数議決権株式
（=super voting stock）
◆Super voting shares empower a shareholder with multiple voting rights per share. 複数議決権株式では、株主は株式1株につき複数の議決権が与えられる。

superior credit quality　高い信用力
◆The proposed bid price does not reflect the bank's strong capital position and the superior credit quality of its assets. 株式公開買付け（TOB）の予定価格は、同行の自己資本比率の大きさや同行の資産の高い信用力を反映していない。

supermajority　（名）圧倒的多数, 大多数, 超過半数, 超

過半数条項 （=super-majority: 超過半数は一般に発行済み株式の80％以上の賛成投票を指し、株主総会で合併や買収などとくに重大な決議を行う場合に、株主の超過半数の賛成が必要と定めることがある。）

supervise （動）監督する，指揮する，管理する，監視する，査閲する，考査する
◆The FSA's guideline for supervising financial conglomerates is aimed at urging operators of financial conglomerates to reinforce their corporate governance to prevent irregularities. 金融庁の金融コングロマリット（複合体）監督指針の狙いは、不正防止に向けて、金融コングロマリットの経営者に経営監視の強化を促すことにある。◆The Tokyo Stock Exchange has no power to directly supervise certified public accountants. 東京証券取引所に、公認会計士を直接監督する権限はない。

supervision （名）監督，指揮，管理，監視，観察，査閲，考査
administrative supervision　行政指導，行政監督
audit supervision　会計監査上の査閲，監査上の査閲
credit supervision by the central bank　中央銀行の信用規制
price supervision　物価監視，価格監視
under the supervision of　〜の監督のもとに，〜の指揮のもとに

supervision post　監理ポスト，監視ポスト
（=monitoring post）
◆Tokyo, Osaka and Nagoya bourses placed Nikko Cordial stock on their respective supervision posts for possible delisting. 東京、大阪、名古屋の3証券取引所が、それぞれ日興コーディアルの株式を、上場廃止の可能性があるため監理ポストに割り当てた。

supplementary budget　補正予算［予算案］，追加予算
（=additional budget, revised budget）
reconstruction bonds to finance the second fiscal 2011 supplementary budget　2011年度第二次補正予算案の財源を賄（まかな）うための（震災）復興債
（⇒reconstruction bonds）
supplementary budget for job creation　雇用創出のための補正予算，補正予算による雇用創出
the compilation of a supplementary budget　補正予算の編成
◆Economic stimulus measures implemented so far include a supplementary budget for job creation. これまで実施された景気対策としては、補正予算による雇用の創出もある。◆Japan, which is on the verge of falling into a deflationary spiral, should carry out such effective measures as monetary relaxation and the compilation of a supplementary budget. デフレ・スパイラルの縁に立つ日本は、金融緩和や補正予算の編成など効果的な対策を実施するべきだ。

supply （動）供給する，提供する，与える，供与する，（不足などを）埋め合わせる
supply a large amount of funds to the market　大量の資金を市場に提供する
supply capital　資金を供給する
supply credit　信用を供給する
supply equity　エクイティ部分を供与する
supply (investible) funds　資金を供給する
◆The Bank of Japan has supplied a large amount of funds to the market by purchasing long-term government bonds and corporate bonds. 日銀は、長期国債や社債の買入れで、大量の資金を市場に提供している。◆The Bank of Japan supplied funds beyond the upper limit of ¥27 trillion soon after the Resona problem surfaced. 日銀は、りそな問題発覚後、27兆円の上限を上回る資金を市場に供給した。◆The BOJ decided to introduce a new open market operation by supplying ¥10 trillion to private financial institutions in three month loans at an ultralow annual interest of 0.1 percent. 日銀は、民間の金融機関に年1％の超低金利で貸出期間3か月の資金を10兆円供給する新型の公開市場操作（オペ）の導入に踏み切った。

supply （名）供給，供給量，（国債などの）入札［発行］，需給，供給品，消耗品（supplies），貯蔵品，政府の歳出・経費（supplies），サプライ　（⇒money supply）
bond supply　債券供給
brisk supply　活発な供給
capital supply curve　資本供給曲線
cash supply　現金供給，現金供給量
coupon supply　利付き国債の供給
credit supply　信用供給
credit supply crunch　信用供給の収縮
enter a new period of new supply　入札の時期を迎える
excess supply　過剰供給
forward supply contract　先物注文契約
fund supply operation　資金供給オペ，資金供給
gross money supply　総貨幣供給，総貨幣供給量
imbalances between the supply and of and demand for securities　債券需給の不均衡
large supply　大口供給
marginal credit supply　限界信用供給
monetary supply　通貨［貨幣］供給，通貨供給量，マネー・サプライ
money supply　通貨供給［供給量］，マネー・サプライ
（=the supply of money）
new supply　新発債，新発債の供給，入札
savings supply　貯蓄供給
small supply　小口供給
stable supply　安定供給
supply at the longer end　長期債の供給
supply deficiency　供給不足
supply-demand balance　需給バランス
supply glut　供給過剰，だぶつき
supply of capital　資金供給，資金の供給量
（=supply of funds）
supply of credit　信用供給　（=credit supply）
supply of housing　住宅供給
supply of investible funds　資金供給
Treasury supply　国債入札
visible supply　発行予定
◆The nation's monetary base in May 2011 increased 16.2 percent from a year earlier as the Bank of Japan continued its abundant fund supply operations following the March 11 disaster. 東日本大震災（2011年3月11）を受けて日銀が潤沢な資金供給を続けたため、日本の2011年5月のマネタリー・ベースは、前年同月比で16.2％増加した。◆The Treasury market was hit with new supply. 米国債市場は、新発債の供給で下落した。

supply ample funds　潤沢（じゅんたく）な資金を供給する
◆The G-7 joint statement made clear the stance of supporting the financial markets by supplying ample funds. G7の共同声明は、潤沢な資金供給によって金融市場を下支えする姿勢を明らかにした。

supply and demand　需要と供給，需給
◆The latest recovery was short-lived due to a wide gap between supply and demand. 前回の景気回復が短命に終わったのは、大幅な需給ギャップがあったからだ。

supply chain　供給連鎖，供給体制，供給網，供給経路，サプライ・チェーン
◆In the aftermath of the March 11 earthquake, automakers and other manufacturers faced severe supply chain disrup-

tions and power shortages. 2011年3月11日の東日本大震災の影響で、自動車メーカーなどの製造業者は、部品などの厳しいサプライ・チェーン（供給網）の途絶や電力不足に見舞われた。◆The recovery in business sentiment was largely due to the improvement in the parts supply chain disrupted after the March 11 earthquake and tsunami. 景況感が改善したのは、主に東日本大震災で打撃を受けたサプライ・チェーン（部品供給網）の復旧が進んだためだ。

supply-demand gap　需給ギャップ
　（=demand supply gap）
　◆Unless the sizable supply-demand gap is narrowed, deflationary pressures will make it virtually impossible for the economy to make a full recovery. 巨大な需給ギャップが解消に向かわないかぎり、デフレ圧力で日本経済が本格回復するのは事実上、不可能だ。

supply funds　資金を供給する
　◆The Bank of Japan must continue to promptly supply funds to prevent the financial contraction that all corporate managers dread. 企業経営者が恐れる金融収縮を防ぐため、日銀は迅速に資金供給を続ける必要がある。◆The Bank of Japan supplied funds beyond the upper limit of ¥27 trillion soon after the Resona problem surfaced. 日銀は、りそな問題発覚後、27兆円の上限を上回る資金を市場に供給した。

supply funds to the financial market　金融市場に資金を供給する
　◆The outright purchase of long-term government bonds is a measure to supply funds to the financial market. 長期国債の買切りオペレーションは、金融市場に資金を供給する手段である。

supply of funds　資金供給, 資金の供給量
　enormous supply of funds　豊富な資金供給
　supply and demand of funds　資金需給
　supply of industrial funds　産業資金の供給
　◆Under the zero-interest rate policy, the Bank of Japan ensures an ample supply of funds to the money market, making it easier for many banks to secure funds there. ゼロ金利政策のもと、日銀が金融市場に資金を潤沢（じゅんたく）に供給して、多くの銀行は金融市場での資金確保が楽になった。

supply of money　通貨供給, 通貨供給量
　◆To alleviate the influence of the U.S. government's additional steps to ease the supply of money, the Bank of Japan must adopt a more proactive stance toward monetary relaxation. 米政府の金融緩和策［通貨供給量を増やす米政府の追加措置］の影響を和らげるには、日銀も金融緩和の姿勢を強める必要がある。

supply side　供給サイド, 供給側, 供給面, 供給重視, サプライサイド
　supply-side economics　供給面重視の経済学, 供給重視経済学, サプライサイドの経済学, サプライサイド・エコノミックス
　supply-side [supplyside] economy　供給サイドの経済学, 供給の経済学
　supply-side structural reform　供給サイドの構造改革
　◆Measures to deal with surplus facilities are regarded as the center pillar of structural reforms to be initiated by the supply side. 過剰設備の処理対策は、供給サイドが着手する構造改革の柱とされている。◆The key to returning to stable growth is whether the nation can eliminate excesses common to many companies and promote supply-side structural reforms. 安定成長復帰へのカギは、多くの日本企業に共通して見られる過剰体質を排除して、供給サイドの構造改革を進めることができるかどうかである。

supplysider [supply-sider]　(名)供給重視論者, 供給サイド経済政策支持者

support　(動)支援する, 援助する, 支援する, 賛成する, 支える, 支持する, 補強する, 補完する, 裏付ける, 保証する（⇒function動詞）
　be financially supported　資金援助を受ける, 資金面で支援を受ける
　be supported by financial assets　金融資産を裏付けとする, 金融資産の裏付けがある
　be supported by letter of credits from　〜の信用状を信用補完に用いる
　fully supported program　完全［100％］信用補完型プログラム
　fully supported structure　信用補てん構造, 完全保証構造
　partially supported program　部分的信用補完型プログラム
　support commercial interests　経済的利益を優先する
　support equity market　株式相場を支える
　support increased investment　投資拡大を支える, 投資の拡大を支える
　support one's share price　株価を下支えする
　support the rally　上昇局面を支える
　support the stock [stock price]　株価を支える, 株価を下支えする
　◆Both lenders will focus on supporting their local corporations in the aftermath of the March 11 quake and tsunami. 3月11日（2011年）の東日本大震災を受けて、両行は地元企業の支援に重点的に取り組む方針だ。◆Greece's fiscal reconstruction is set as a condition for supporting the struggling country by the European Union and the International Monetary Fund. 欧州連合（EU）と国際通貨基金（IMF）は、ギリシャの財政再建を、財政危機にある同国支援の条件としている。◆It is difficult for Japan, the United States and European countries to support their sagging economies by increasing public spending, due to deteriorating financial conditions. 財政の悪化で、日米欧は、財政出動による景気の下支えが難しくなっている。◆Japan's exports, which had been supporting the business boom, lost momentum. 景気を支えていた日本の輸出が、失速した。◆Nippon Life Insurance Co., the top shareholder in Olympus Corp., will continue supporting Olympus in light of its advanced technology in its core business such as endoscopes. オリンパスの筆頭株主の日本生命は、内視鏡などオリンパスの中核事業の高い技術力を踏まえて、引き続きオリンパスを支えていく方針だ。◆Revenues from the single-premium whole life insurance policies support the life insurer's business performance. 一時払い終身保険による収入［一時払い終身保険の収入保険料］が、同生保の業績を支えている。◆The Bank of Japan widened the scope of cheap loans to support smaller companies with growth potential. 潜在成長力のある中小企業を支援するため、日銀が低利融資枠を拡大した。◆The draft of the government's new growth strategy includes the establishment of a public-private investment fund to support the content industry in its foreign endeavors. 政府の新成長戦略の原案には、コンテンツ（情報の内容）産業の海外展開を支援する官民出資のファンド設立も盛り込まれている。◆The European Central Bank has been purchasing Italian government bonds in an effort to support Italy. 欧州中央銀行（ECB）は、イタリア国債を買い入れてイタリアを支えている。◆The government should expedite work to rebuild a safety net to support the Japanese financial system. 政府は、安全網の立て直しを急いで、日本の金融システム支える必要がある。◆The proposal to expand the lending capacity of the IMF was supported by Brazil and other emerging economies though Japan and the United States rejected it. 国際通貨基金（IMF）が融資できる資金規模を拡大する案は、日本と米国が受け入れなかったものの、ブラジルなどの新興国は支持した。◆We must expedite efforts to rebuild a safety net to support the financial system. 金融システムを支える安全網の立直し策を急ぐ必要がある。

support　(名)支援, 援助, 支持, 支持線, 賛成, 支柱, 裏付

け, 補てん, 補強, 保証, サポート
　cash deficiency support　不足資金供与
　credit support　信用補てん, 信用補強, 信用補完
　customer support services　顧客支援サービス
　financial support　金融支援, 財政援助, 資金面での支援, 資金負担
　group support　グループ支援, 系列支援
　key support　主要な支持線
　liquidity support　代替流動性
　monetary support　金融上の支援
　official support　公的支援
　provide some support for shares[share prices]　株価を下支えする, 株価を下支えする要因になっている
　provider of the support facility　信用補完提供者
　software development support system　ソフトウエア開発支援システム
　support area　下値(したね)支持線[抵抗線], (値下がり市場の)買い支え値　(=support level)
　support buying　買い支え　(=support operation)
　support capital spending　設備投資を支える
　support facility　信用補完ファシリティ
　support operation　買い支え　(=support buying)
　support package　支援策
　support point　介入点
　support provider　信用補完提供者
　third-party credit support　第三者信用補てん
　third-party-supported debt　第三者信用補完による資金調達
　yield support　配当利回りによる下支え
◆A firm requires the support of more than two thirds of shareholders to decide on important matters, such as a merger, at shareholders meetings. 企業が株主総会で合併などの重要事項を決議するには, 3分の2以上の賛成が必要だ。◆Greece's fiscal reconstruction has made little progress since the country was bailed out with financial support from the IMF and the EU in May 2010. ギリシャの財政再建は, 2010年5月にIMFと欧州連合(EU)による金融支援を受けて以来, 進展してない。◆Higher debt maturing within one year chiefly reflects commercial paper we issued to support financial services. 1年以内返済予定の負債の増加は, 主に金融サービス部門の支援のため, 当社がコマーシャル・ペーパーを発行したことを反映しています。◆TEPCO asked the government for the financial support in making compensation payments for damage caused by the crisis at its Fukushima No. 1 nuclear power plant. 東電は, 福島第一原子力発電所事故による損害の賠償金を支払うにあたって, 政府に金融支援を要請した。◆The company struck an agreement with its debtholder to win their support for reconstruction. 同社は, 会社再建について債権者の支持を得ることで, 債権者と合意に達した。◆The European Central Bank needs to provide support to Italy by proactively buying Italian bonds. 欧州中央銀行(ECB)は今後, イタリア国債を積極的に買い入れてイタリアを支援する必要がある。◆The International Monetary Fund is urged to monitor Italy's financial management to provide support to Italy. イタリアを支援するため, 国際通貨基金(IMF)はイタリアの財政運営の監視を求められている。

support growth　成長を支える
◆The European Commission called for coordination action to support growth. 欧州委員会は, 成長を支えるための協調行動を求めた。

support level　下値(したね)支持線[抵抗線], (値下がり市場の)買い支え値, 梃(てこ)入れ相場　(=support area, resistance level)
　strong support level　強力な下値支持線

　support level price　(相場の)支持価格
support loan　支援融資
◆Greece will win the support loan it needs from the European countries and the IMF. ギリシャは, 欧州諸国[ユーロ圏]と国際通貨基金(IMF)から, 必要としている支援融資を得られる見通しだ。

support the economy　景気を支える, 景気を下支えする
◆It is difficult for Japan, the United States and European countries to support their sagging economies by increasing public spending, due to deteriorating financial conditions. 財政の悪化で, 日米欧は, 財政出動による景気の下支えが難しくなっている。◆Japan, the United States and European countries supported their sagging economies by increasing public spending after the collapse of Lehman Brothers in the autumn of 2008. 2008年秋のリーマン・ブラザーズの経営破たん後, 日米欧は, 財政出動によって低迷する景気の下支えをした。◆The government and the Bank of Japan must take all possible measures to support the economy. 政府・日銀は, 景気の下支えに万全を期すべきだ。

support the financial markets by supplying ample funds　潤沢な資金供給によって金融市場を下支えする
◆The G-7 joint statement made clear the stance of supporting the financial markets by supplying ample funds. G7の共同声明は, 潤沢な資金供給によって金融市場を下支えする姿勢を明らかにした。

supporting　(形)支える, 裏付ける, 補完の, 信用補完の, 付属の
　supporting documents　付属書類
　supporting evidence　裏付け資料, 裏付け証拠
　supporting institution　信用補完機関
　supporting operation　(為替相場の)支持操作

supportive factors of economic activity　景気を支える要因

supportive monetary policy　支持的通貨政策

supranational　(形)超国家的な, 国際機関の
　supranational bond　国際機関債
　supranational debt　国際機関債
　supranational name　国際機関銘柄

supraprotest　(名)(手形の)参加引受け, 名誉引受け

surcharge　(名)割増料金, 追加料金, 付加料金, 上乗せ料金, 追徴金, 課徴金, 不足金不当請求, 荷物の積み過ぎ, 過載, サーチャージ
　capital surcharge　資本[自己資本]の上積み, 資本の積み増し
　export surcharge　輸出課徴金
　fuel surcharge　燃油特別付加運賃
　import surcharge　輸入課徴金
　inflation surcharge　インフレ課徴金
　investment income surcharge　投資所得課徴金
　optional surcharge　揚地割増量
　out port surcharge　僻地割増運賃
　solidarity surcharge　統一割増税
　tax surcharge　課徴金
◆ANA revised its fuel surcharges for flights to Hawaii and India to ¥22,000 from the current ¥20,000. 全日本空輸は, ハワイ路線の燃油特別付加運賃(サーチャージ)を, 現行の2万円から2万2,000円に改訂した。◆Twenty-eight banks of the world will face capital surcharges of 1 percent to 2.5 percent by the application of international rules to rein in too-big-to-fail lenders. 大きすぎて破たんさせられる銀行[金融機関]を規制する国際基準が適用されると, 世界の28行が, 1〜2.5%の資本[自己資本]上積みの対象となる。

surge　(動)急増する, 急騰する, 急上昇する, 高まる, 殺

到する, 押し寄せる （⇒foreign market, stop）
briefly surge　短時間[短期間]急上昇する
　　（=surge briefly）
surge to make a high of　急騰して~の高値を付ける
surge to record levels above　急騰して~の史上最高値を突破する, ~を上回る史上最高値まで急騰する
surge to the highest end of　~の上限まで急騰する
surge to the lowest of　~の下限まで急騰する
　◆Google shares surged about 20 percent on their first day of public trading. 米グーグル（インターネット検索最大手）の株式は、公募取引の初日に約20％急上昇した。◆Revenue at the company surged 10.3 percent to ¥580 billion during the October-December quarter. 同社の10-12月期の売上高は、10.3％増の5,800億円だった。◆The benchmark gold future price surged to all-time high of ¥4,725 per gram in trading on the Tokyo Commodity Exchange. 東京工業品取引所の取引で、金取引の指標となる金先物価格が、過去最高の1グラム＝4,725円まで急騰した。◆The European bond market is truly in a knife-edge situation as the yield on 10-year Italian government bonds has surged above 7 percent, the so-called danger zone that may result in a debt crisis. 10年物イタリア国債の流通利回りが、債務危機に陥る「危険水域」とされる7％超に上昇したため、欧州債券市場は予断を許さない状況にある。◆The U.S. dollar surged to ¥110 level. ドル相場が、1ドル＝110円台まで急騰した。◆The yen surged to the higher end of the ¥98 level against the dollar in Tokyo markets. 東京為替市場は、1ドル＝98円台[98円台の上限]まで円が急騰した。◆The yen surged to ¥85 per a dollar. 円相場が、1ドル＝85円まで急上昇[急騰]した。◆Yields on sovereign debt of Spain surged and Italy began seeing yields on its government bonds shoot up. スペインの国債金利が上昇し、イタリアの国債金利も急騰している。

surge　（名）急増, 急騰, 急上昇, 殺到, 大波, 盛り上がり, ブーム
prepayment surge　期限前償還の急増
refinancing surge　借換えの急増
surge in foreign investments　対外投資の急増
surge in prices　インフレ率の上昇
surge in stock prices　株価の急上昇, 株価急騰
surge in the bond market　債券相場の急騰
surge in the Tokyo stock markets　東京市場での株価急上昇[株価急騰]
surge in the yen　円の急騰, 円高
　　（=the yen's rise; ⇒yen-selling and dollar-buying）
the recent surges in the yen's strength　最近の円高
　　（⇒strength）
　◆Individual investors and brokerage dealers continued to take profits from recent surges in comparatively low-prices issues. 個人投資家と証券会社のディーラーは、最近の比較的割安な銘柄の急上昇で引き続き利食いに出た。◆The Finance Ministry and the Bank of Japan may keep selling the yen to stem its surge. 円高を食い止めるため[円の急騰を阻止するため]、財務省・日本銀行は、円を売り続ける可能性がある。◆The surge in prices of natural resources could ignite fears of inflation, causing countries around the world to implement tight monetary policies. 天然資源の価格急騰がインフレ懸念を呼び、世界各国が金融引き締め政策を実施する可能性がある。◆The yen continues its relentless surge and stock prices keeps falling. 円高に歯止めがかからず、株安も続いている。◆The yen's surge will not be halted unless Japan's current account surplus is not brought down. 円高は、日本の経常黒字が減らないかぎり止まらないだろう。

surge in domestic stock prices　国内の株価上昇
　◆The diffusion index（DI）of business confidence among large manufacturers stood at plus 1, reflecting a growth in exports due to U.S. economic recovery and a recent surge in domestic stock prices. 大企業の製造業の業況判断指数（DI）が、プラス1となり、米経済の回復による輸出の伸びや最近の国内の株価上昇を反映した。

surge in the value of the U.S. dollar　ドル高
　◆In the Plaza Accord, G-5 nations agreed to rectify the surge in the value of the U.S. dollar. プラザ合意で、日・米・英・仏・西独の先進5か国（G5）がドル高是正で合意した。

surge in the yen　円高
　◆The surge in the yen is partly due to speculative buying. 円高の一因は、思惑買いにある。

surge in the yen's strength　円高
　◆The recent surges in the yen's strength have made it imperative for Japanese carmakers to substantially bring down their parts procurement costs by overseas sourcing. 最近の円高で、日本の自動車メーカー各社は、海外調達による部品調達コストの大幅引下げが緊急課題となっている。

surge in the yen's value　円高, 円の急騰
　◆Both a freefall in stock prices and a surge in the yen's value have been avoided. 株価の暴落も円の急騰も、回避された。◆The rapid surge in the yen's value would impair the current improvement in the Japanese economy. 急激な円高は、日本の景気回復の腰を折ることになる。

surge in the yen's value against the dollar　円高・ドル安
　◆The surge in the yen's value against the dollar started in early August. 円高・ドル安が始まったのは、8月初めからだ。

surging　（形）急増する, 急騰する, 高騰する, ~の急増[高騰]
surging costs　急増するコスト, コストの急増
surging demand　急増する需要, 需要急増
surging dollar　ドルの急騰
surging yen　円の急騰

surging growth in imports　輸入の急増, 輸入額の急増
　◆We saw surging growth in imports mainly due to soaring oil prices. 主に原油価格の高騰で、輸入額が急増した。

surging number of uncollectible loans　融資の貸倒れ件数の急増
　◆About ¥1.9 trillion of taxpayers' money was spent over a ten year span until last fiscal year to cover losses from a surging number of uncollectible loans guaranteed by a public credit guarantee scheme for small and midsize companies. 中小企業のための公的信用保証制度により保証される融資の貸倒れ件数が急増し、それによる損失の穴埋めをするために、昨年度までの10年間で約1兆9,000億円の税金が投入された。

surging prices　価格高騰, 物価高騰[急騰], 物価の上昇
　◆Amid surging prices of crude oil and other resources, the sovereign wealth fund will invest mainly in solar power generation, fuel cells, and other new energy technologies and natural resources. 原油その他の資源価格の高騰を受け、同政府系投資ファンドは、太陽光や燃料電池などの新エネルギー技術や天然資源に投資の重点をおく方針だ。

surpass　（動）超える, 超越する, 超過する, 上回る, 突破する, 追い越す, ~を凌（しの）ぐ, ~より優れている, ~より勝（まさ）る　（=exceed）
liabilities surpass one's assets　債務超過になる
surpass one's estimate　~の見積りを超過する
surpass 10 percent of gross domestic product　国内総生産（GDP）の10％を超える
　◆China surpassed the United States as Japan's major trading partner amid the continued U.S. economic slowdown. 中国は、米国の引き続く景気減速を受けて、日本の主要貿易相手国としての米国を追い越した。◆Companies are usually considered likely to collapse when their liabilities surpass their assets. 企業は、一般に債務超過になった場合に「破たん懸念

先」となる。◆The fiscal deficits in Japan, the United States and Britain surpassed 10 percent of gross domestic product in 2009. 2009年には、日本、米国と英国の財政赤字が国内総生産（GDP）の10%［GDP比10%］を超えるにいたった。◆The number of annual applications for individual and corporate self-declared bankruptcy cases surpassed 200,000 for the first time in 2002. 1年間の個人と法人の自己破産申立て件数が、2002年に初めて20万件を突破した。◆Toyota's group net profit surpassed ￥1 trillion for the third consecutive year. トヨタの連結税引き後利益［連結純利益］は、3年連続で1兆円を突破した。

surplus （名）余剰, 過剰, 余剰分, 過剰分, 余剰金, 超過金, 剰余金, 積立金, 黒字, 歳入超過額, 残額
   appraisal surplus   再評価剰余金, 評価替え剰余金
   balance of payments current account surplus   国際収支経常勘定黒字
   balance of payments surplus   国際収支の黒字
   be surplus to requirements   供給過剰である, もはや［もう］必要ない, 必要以上に多い
   budget［budgetary］surplus   予算の黒字, 財政黒字
   capital surplus   資本剰余金, 資本積立金
   cumulative［cumulated］surplus   累積黒字
   current account surplus   経常黒字
   export surplus   貿易収支の黒字
   external surplus   経常海外余剰, 貿易収支の黒字
   financial surplus or［and］deficit   資金過不足
   financing surplus   資金余剰, 資金過剰
   fiscal surplus   財政黒字, 財政余剰
   government current surplus   政府経常余剰
   government surplus   公共部門の黒字
   labor surplus   労働力過剰, 労働余剰
   liquidity surplus   流動性過剰
   massive［huge］international payments surplus   巨額の国際収支の黒字
   oil surplus   石油余剰, 石油黒字
   primary surpluses   基礎収支の黒字
   producer's surplus   生産者余剰
   reserve surplus   積立金
   seller's surplus   売り手余剰
   surpluses in Japan's current and trade accounts   日本の経常収支と貿易収支の黒字額
   trade surplus with the U.S.   対米貿易黒字, 対米貿易収支の黒字
   treasury surplus   国庫余裕金
   valuation surplus   評価剰余金

◆Declines in surpluses are likely to reduce a bank's capital adequacy ratio. 剰余金が減ると、銀行の自己資本比率が低下する恐れがある。◆The closure of the money-losing outlets will result in a surplus of about 2,000 employees out of about 22,000 on a consolidated basis. 赤字の店舗閉鎖に伴い、連結ベースで従業員約22,000人のうち約2,000人が余剰になる。◆The first goal of Japan's fiscal reconstruction is for the central and local governments to achieve a surplus in their primary balances by fiscal 2019. 日本の財政再建の第一目標は、国と地方［地方自治体］の基礎的財政収支を、2019年度までに黒字化することだ。◆The special account is expected to collect a large surplus in fiscal 2011 via the repayment of loans. 特別会計は、貸付け金の返済で2011年度は多額の剰余金が生じる見込みだ。

surplus （形）余剰の, 過剰の, 余分な, 余剰的な, 必要以上の（extra）, 黒字の
   surplus asset   余剰資産
   surplus budget   黒字予算
   surplus capacity   生産余力, 過剰設備, 設備過剰
   （=excess capacity）
   surplus country   黒字国, 出超国
   surplus equipment   遊休設備, 過剰設備
   surplus financing［finance］   黒字財政
   surplus labor   余剰労働［労働力］, 過剰労働, 剰余労働
   surplus personnel   過剰人員, 余剰人員
   （=surplus worker）
   surplus production   過剰生産
   surplus products   余剰産物, 剰余生産物
   surplus profit   超過利潤, 剰余利益
   surplus stock   余剰在庫, 過剰在庫
   surplus value   余剰価値, 剰余価値

surplus facilities   過剰設備
◆Measures to deal with surplus facilities are regarded as the center pillar of structural reforms to be initiated by the supply side. 過剰設備の処理対策は、供給サイドが着手する構造改革の柱とされている。

surplus fund   余剰資金, 剰余金, 特別会計の積立金
◆Accumulated surplus funds from previous years are referred to as "hidden treasure" by politicians. 過年度の累積剰余金（積立金）を、政治家は「埋蔵金」と呼んでいる。◆Banks are running out of surplus funds. 銀行は、剰余金が底をつきかけている。◆Surplus funds put out by developed economies' monetary easing measures have flowed into emerging economies to inflate economic bubbles. 先進国の金融緩和策で生じた余剰資金が、新興国に流れ込み、バブルを発生させている。◆These surplus funds are moving into crude oil and grain markets in search of profitable investments. これらの余剰資金が、有利な運用先を求めて原油や穀物市場に向かっている。◆To procure funds to finance reconstruction from the Great East Japan Earthquake, the government will utilize surplus funds in a special account used to finance public investment and loans to government-affiliated financial institutions. 東日本大震災の復興費用に充てる資金を調達するため、政府は、政府系金融機関に資金を貸し出すのに用いられる財政投融資特別会計の剰余金を活用する方針だ。◆Under the mark-to-market accounting system, if banks suffer appraisal losses of stocks they are holding, they are required to subtract 60 percent of those losses from their surplus funds. 時価会計制度では、金融機関が保有する株式の評価損が出た場合、金融機関は評価損の6割を剰余金から取り除かなければならない。

解説 余剰資金とは：自己資本のうち資本金と資本準備金以外の部分のことで、過去の利益の蓄積を示す。営業活動で生じた利益などを積み立てた任意積立金や、税引き後利益で構成され、株主への配当や役員賞与の原資などに充てられる。一般企業では、剰余金が多いほど自己資本が充実し、収益力が強いことを示すことから、財務体質の評価の判断指標の一つになる。ただし、株主からは、内部留保を高めるより新規投資や配当に回し、資本効率の向上を求める意見が出ることもある。（讀賣新聞「ミニ時典」）

surplus in the current account   経常収支の黒字, 経常収支の黒字額
   （=the current account surplus）
◆The surplus in the current account expanded for the first time in two months on a year-to-year basis, totaling ￥1.2 trillion. 経常収支の黒字額は、2か月ぶりに1年前の水準を上回り、1兆2,000億円となった。◆The surplus in the current account stood at ￥1.5 trillion in September 2008, marking the seventh consecutive month of year-on-year declines. 2008年9月の経常収支の黒字額は、1兆5,000億円となり、7か月連続で前年実績を下回った。

surplus in the primary balance   基礎的財政収支の

黒字（⇒surplus名詞）
◆A surplus in the primary balances of the central and local governments indicates a degree of fiscal soundness. 国と地方［地方自治体］の基礎的財政収支の黒字は、財政の健全度を示す。

surplus savings 余剰貯蓄, 純法人貯蓄
◆Out of the household financial assets of ￥1.47 quadrillion, about ￥160 trillion can be considered as surplus savings, given the life cycle of the average Japanese individual. 日本人の平均的な個人のラフサイクルから見て、1,470兆円の個人金融資産のうち約160兆円は、余剰貯蓄と考えられる。

surplus workers 余剰人員, 過剰人員, 過剰雇用者, 過剰雇用 (=excess workers, surplus staff; ⇒peak名詞)
◆If business performance worsens further, some of these surplus workers may lose their jobs. 企業業績がさらに悪化すれば、これらの過剰雇用者は失業しかねない。◆Surplus workers fell a victim to the axe. 過剰人員が、人員削減の犠牲になった。

surprise （名）驚き, 思いがけない出来事［贈り物］, 不意打ち, 奇襲, 意表を突くこと
　a favorable surprise　思わぬ強気材料, 思わぬ好材料
　a negative surprise　思わぬ弱気材料, 思わぬ悪材料
　a pleasant surprise　思いがけないうれしい出来事, 思わぬ好材料
　a positive surprise　意外な好結果, 嬉しい驚き
　an element of surprise　意外性, 意外性の要素
　come as a big［great］surprise to　～にとって大変な驚きである
　make a surprise announcement　突然発表する
　take a person by surprise　～の不意を襲う, ～に不意打ちをくわせる

surround （動）取り巻く, 取り囲む, 包囲する, 包み込む, 包む, （自分の周りを）固める
◆The situation surrounding the Japanese economy has suddenly grown tense due to the first bankruptcy of a Japanese insurer in seven years. 7年ぶりの日本の生保破たんで、日本経済を取り巻く環境は一気に緊迫感が高まっている。

surveillance （名）監視, 監督, 指揮, 監察, 査察, 調査, 捜索
　market surveillance　市場監視
　multilateral surveillance　多角的の監視制度
　price surveillance　価格監視, 物価監視
　Securities and Exchange Surveillance Commission　証券取引等監視委員会
　surveillance camera　監視カメラ
　surveillance system for imports　輸入監視制度
　surveillance unit　監視機関
◆AMRO, as the surveillance unit of CMIM, plays an important role to monitor and analyze regional economies. AMROは、（参加国が通貨急落といった危機に直面した際に外貨を融通し合う）多国間通貨交換［スワップ］協定（CMIM）の監視機関として、域内経済を監視し分析する重要な役割を担っている。
◆The Securities and Exchange Surveillance Commission is charged with inspecting the compliance of securities firms with the law, market surveillance and the investigation of abuses such as insider trading and stock price manipulation. 証券取引等監視委員会は、証券会社の法律遵守（じゅんしゅ）に関する検査や市場の監視、インサイダー取引や株価操作など不正行為の摘発を行う。◆The U.S. Commodity Futures Trading Commission has increased surveillance of oil markets with focus on possible price manipulation by speculators. 米商品先物取引委員会は、投機筋による価格操作の可能性に的を絞って、原油市場の監視を強化している。

survey （名）調査, 意識調査, 査察, 査定, 測量, 概観, 概説, サーベイ

　business sentiment survey　企業景況感調査
　establishment survey　事業所調査
　fact-finding survey　実情調査, 実態調査
　household survey　家計調査
　labor force survey　労働力調査
　market survey　市場調査, 市場実査, 実態調査
　marketing survey　市場調査, マーケティング・サーベイ
　national purchasing managers survey　全米購買部協会景気総合指数
　nationwide survey　全国調査
　public opinion survey　世論調査
　Tankan Survey　日銀短観, 短観
◆The BOJ's Tankan survey shows business sentiment among large manufacturers rebounded in September from the previous survey three months earlier. 9月の日銀短観は、大企業・製造業の景況感が6月の前回調査から改善したことを示している。

survival （名）生存, 存続, 残存, 生き残り, 生き延び, 生存者, 残存者, なごり, サバイバル
　all-out struggle for survival　生き残りをかけた総力戦
　cooperation and coexistence for survival　生き残りのための協調と共存
　economic survival　経済的生き残り, 経済面での生き残り
　survival of the fittest　適者生存
　survival period　術後生存期間
　survival rate　術後生存率
　survival ratio　残存比率
　survival strategy　生き残るための戦略
　survival technology［skill］　生き残るための技術
◆The commodity futures trading industry has entered an era of white-hot competition in an all-out struggle for survival. 商品先物取引業界は、生き残りをかけた総力戦で大競争の時代に入っている。◆The rational actions for survival taken by individual companies herald a danger that could lead the Japanese economy into contracted equilibrium. 生き残りをかけて個々の企業が取っている合理的な行動が、日本経済を縮小均衡に導く危険性をはらんでいる。◆Through the TSE-OSE merger in January 2013, the two exchanges must enhance their strategies to ensure survival as a major stock market in Asia. 東証と大証の2013年1月の経営統合をテコに、両証券取引所は、アジアの主要市場として勝ち残る戦略を強化する必要がある。

survive （動）生き残る, 残存する, 存続する, 生き延びる, 生き抜く, 助かる, （危機などを）切り抜ける, 乗り切る
　struggle to survive　生き残るために必死になる
　survive excessive competition　過当競争に生き残る
　survive the earthquake　地震から生き残る
survive competition　競争に生き残る, 競争に勝ち抜く
◆Huge investment costs, such as those for developing environment-friendly technology, have made it difficult for an automaker to survive competition on its own. 環境にやさしい技術の開発費など、巨額の投資コストが見込まれるため、自動車メーカー1社が独力で競争に生き残るのは難しくなっている。◆One of the aims for the three banks to merge into the Mizuho Financial Group was to survive the global competition by exploiting the banks' combined strength. 3行がみずほフィナンシャルグループに合併する目的（狙い）の一つに、3行の統合力を駆使して国際競争に勝ち抜くことがあった。
◆There were speculations that only three or four Japanese banks could survive intensified global competition. 熾烈な国際競争に生き残れる邦銀は3〜4行だけ、と見る向きもあった。

surviving company　存続会社, 他の企業を吸収する会社　(=surviving corporation, surviving entity, surviving firm)

◆The current system requires the shareholders of companies absorbed in mergers and acquisitions to be given stocks of surviving companies. 現行の制度は、企業の吸収合併の際、吸収合併される会社の株主に対して存続会社の株式を交付することを義務付けている。◆Under the accord, the banking, trust and brokerage units of MTFG will be the surviving companies, respectively. 合意書によると、三菱東京側の銀行、信託、証券会社がそれぞれ存続会社となる。◆Yamanouchi Pharmaceutical Co. became the surviving company in the merger of the company and Fujisawa Pharmaceutical Co. 山之内製薬と藤沢薬品工業の合併では、山之内製薬が存続会社になった。

survivor (名)生存者, 残存者, 被災者, 生き残った人, 遺物, 遺族
◆Many survivors of the Great East Japan Earthquake are struggling under the heavy double debt loads. 東日本大震災の被災者の多くは、二重ローンという重い負担を背負って苦しんでいる。

survivor's pension 遺族年金

susceptible to 〜に左右されやすい, 〜に影響されやすい, 〜にかかりやすい, 感染しやすい, 〜に敏感な, 〜に弱い (⇒vulnerable to)
◆The yen's stable rate at about ¥110 against the dollar serves as a stabilizing factor for importers, exporters and others doing business susceptible to exchange fluctuations. 円の対ドル為替相場が110円台(前後)で安定していることは、輸出入業者など為替変動に左右されやすい仕事をしている者にとって安定要因となる。

suspend (動)停止する, 一時停止する, 中止する, 中断する, 差し止める, 延期する, 一時見合わせる, 離脱する, 停職にする, 休職させる, 停学処分[出場停止処分]にする, 刑の執行を猶予(ゆうよ)する, (判決などを)保留する, 吊り下げる, ぶら下げる
 suspend foreign debt payments 対外債務支払いを一時停止する (⇒debt payment)
 suspend judgment 判断を保留する
 suspend new entries into the register of shareholders 株主名簿上の名義書換えを停止する
 suspend operations 業務を停止する, 営業を停止する
 suspend payments 支払いを停止する
 suspend payments on the obligations 債務返済を中断する
 suspend the dividend on common stock 普通株式の配当を停止する, 普通株式の配当支払いを停止する
 suspend (the) trading of the government bonds 国債の取引を(一時)停止する
 suspend the uncommitted lines of credit to 〜に対する未使用信用枠を停止する
 suspend transactions with 〜との取引を停止する
◆Banks suspended transactions with the firm on its second failure to honor a bill. 同社が2回目の不渡りを出して、銀行取引停止となった。◆Japanese securities companies suspended trading of the Argentine government bonds. 日本の証券各社は、アルゼンチン国債の取引を停止した。◆The Financial Services Agency ordered Sompo Japan Insurance Inc. to suspend part of its operations as punishment for the major insurance company's illegal business practices. 金融庁は、損保大手の損害保険ジャパンに業務で法令違反があったとして、同社に一部業務停止命令を出した。◆The Financial Services Agency ordered the bank to suspend part of its business for about four months. 金融庁は、同行に対して約4か月の一部業務停止を命じた。◆The FSA ordered the bank to suspend some operations due to serious law violations, including audit sabotage. 金融庁は、同行に対して、検査妨害などの重大な銀行法違反で、一部業務の停止命令を出した。◆The ruling was reportedly the first ever to suspend ongoing merger talks between financial institutions. 継続中の金融機関の統合交渉を差し止める決定は、前例がないという。◆Under the trustee's management, the debtor bank's business will be operated and the refunding of deposits will be temporarily suspended. 金融整理管財人の管理下で、破たん銀行の業務は運営され、預金の払戻しは一時停止される。

suspense (名)未決定, 未定, 停止, 一時停止, 未決算
 suspense account 仮勘定, 未決算勘定
 suspense payment of corporation tax 仮払い法人税
 suspense payments 仮払い金, 仮渡し金
 suspense receipt 仮受け, 仮受金
 suspense receipts 仮受金
 suspense receipts on capital subscriptions 新株式申込み証拠金
◆About ¥1.6 billion in suspense payments remitted to a former vice president of a futures trading brokerage are unaccounted for. 商品先物会社の元副社長に送金された仮払い金約160億円が現在、会計処理されていない(使途不明になっている)

suspension (名)停止, 取引停止, 取引停止処分, (株式などの)売買停止, 一時停止中止, 停職, 差し止め, 刑の執行猶予, 車体懸架装置
 bank suspension (銀行の)支払い停止
 suspension of bank credit 銀行取引停止
 suspension of banking privileges 銀行取引停止処分
 suspension of business order 業務停止命令, 取引停止命令, 営業停止命令
 suspension of (business) transaction 取引停止
 suspension of business with banks 銀行取引停止処分
 suspension of issue 発行停止
 suspension of new commitments 新規ローン約定の差し止め
 suspension of operation 操業停止
 suspension of payment 支払い停止
 suspension of the firm's shares 同社株式の取引停止
 suspension of works 工事中止
 suspension period 業務停止期間
 temporary suspension of trading 取引の一時停止
◆During the business suspension, the company will not be allowed to extend new loans, solicit new customers or call in loans. 業務停止の期間中、同社は新規融資や新規顧客の勧誘、貸出[貸金]の回収業務ができなくなる。

suspension of trade, capital transactions and remittances 貿易、資本取引と送金の停止
◆Under the current Foreign Exchange and Foreign Trade Control Law, the government must wait for the Security Council to pass a resolution before implementing sanctions against North Korea, including a suspension of trade, capital transactions and remittances. 現行の外国為替及び外国貿易法(外為法)では、政府が北朝鮮に対して貿易、資本取引と送金の停止などの制裁措置を実施するには、国連の安保理決議が必要だ。

suspension on imports 輸入差し止め
◆The Economy, Trade and Industry and Finance ministries will establish a system to allow companies and individuals to request suspensions on imports that infringe on their patent rights and designs. 経済産業省と財務省は、特許権と意匠権(デザイン権)を侵害した輸入品の輸入差し止めを日本の企業や個人が請求できる制度を創設する方針だ。

sustain (動)持続させる, 維持する, 保持する, 存続させる, 支える, 支持する, 裏付ける, 〜に耐える, 養う, 扶養する, 援助する, 激励する, (損失、負債、被害などを)被る[受ける], 妥当[正当]と認める, 是認する
 sustain a competitive edge 競争力を維持する
 sustain a great loss 大損害を被る

sustain heavy damages　大損害を受ける
sustain organized efforts　組織的な取り組みを続ける
sustain overall economic growth　マクロ経済の成長を維持する
sustain the economy　景気を下支えする
　（⇒housing loan）
work to sustain growth　成長の維持に取り組む
◆The government wants to lower the yen's value to sustain the economy. 政府は、景気下支えのための円安進行を期待している。◆While we work to sustain growth during the difficult period, we have taken strategic steps to position the firm for continued long-term growth. 当社は、この厳しい時期に成長の維持に取り組む一方、同社の長期的な発展を座視に据えて戦略的な措置を取りました。

sustainability　（名）持続可能性, 維持能力
fiscal sustainability　財政の持続可能性
sustainability of economic growth　経済成長の持続可能性
◆Worldwide concern over fiscal sustainability in industrialized countries is growing in the wake of Greece's sovereign debt crisis. ギリシャの財政危機を契機として、先進国の財政の持続可能性に対する世界の関心が高まっている。

sustainable　（形）持続可能な, 維持可能な, 支持できる, 持ちこたえられる, 継続利用できる, 長期的な, 本格的な, 立証可能な
sustainable development　持続可能な開発, 持続可能な発展, 安定発展, 環境維持開発
sustainable economic recovery　景気の持続的回復, 持続的な景気回復
sustainable level　持続可能な水準
sustainable rally　本格的な上げ相場
sustainable social security system　持続可能な社会保障制度
◆The economic recovery is not sustainable if incomes do not rise. 所得が増えなければ、景気回復は続かない。

sustainable economic growth　持続可能な経済成長
◆The People's Bank of China aims to restrain an excessive use of funds by businesses and lead the economy in the direction of sustainable economic growth. 中国人民銀行が目指しているのは、企業による資金の過剰使用の抑制と中国経済の持続可能な経済成長への誘導だ。

sustainable economic recovery　持続的な景気回復, 景気の持続的回復
◆Maintaining an easy monetary policy may lead to excessive corporate capital investment and have a negative impact on the sustainable economic recovery. 金融緩和政策を続けると、企業の過剰な設備投資を生み、景気の持続的回復を阻害する恐れがある。

sustainable growth　持続的成長, 持続可能な成長, 持続可能な経済成長　(=sustained growth, self-sustained growth; ⇒regain sustainable growth)
◆G-20 leaders must concretize policy coordination to prevent currency friction and achieve sustainable growth. G-20（世界20か国・地域）首脳は、通貨摩擦を食い止める［防ぐ］ための政策協調を具体化して、持続的成長を実現しなければならない。

sustainable recovery　本格的な回復, 本格的な景気回復, 安定した回復, 自律的な回復, 持続的な回復
◆Will the Japanese economy fall into a deflationary spiral, or will it find a path to sustainable recovery? 日本経済は再びデフレの悪循環に陥るのだろうか、それとも自律的な回復軌道を見つけるのだろうか。

sustained　（形）持続した, 持続的な, 長期的な, 長期にわたる, 維持された, 保持された, 不断の, 一様の, 支持された, 是認された, 確認された, 認められた, 立証された
fall on a sustained basis　下がり続ける

sustained economic expansion　経済の持続的な発展
sustained economic recovery　持続的な景気回復, 景気回復の持続, 景気回復の長期化
sustained growth　持続的な［持続的］成長, 持続的な経済成長, 持続的な発展, 長期的な成長, 成長の維持　(=sustainable growth, self-sustained growth)
sustained low (interest) rates　低金利の定着
◆A pickup in money supply growth is seen as being crucial for a sustained economic recovery and an end to deflation. 持続的な景気回復とデフレ脱却には、マネー・サプライ伸び率の上昇が不可欠と見られている。

Sveriges Riksbank Prize in Economic Sciences in Memory of Alfred Nobel　アルフレッド・ノーベル記念経済学スウェーデン国立銀行賞（通称：ノーベル経済学賞。1968年にスウェーデン国立銀行が同行の300周年記念にノーベル財団に設置。スウェーデン王立科学アカデミーが選考し、ノーベル財団が認定する。賞金は、スウェーデン国立銀行が拠出している）

swap　（動）交換する, 切り替える, 取り替える, 乗り換える, スワップする
　（⇒bailout package, equity, secured lenders）
swap A for B　AをBと交換する
swap out of A into B　AからBに乗り換える
swap some of the shares of the parent company for the target company's shares　親会社の株式の一部と買収標的企業の株式を交換する
swap the remaining debt of ¥200 billion into preferred shares　残りの債権2,000億円分を優先株に振り替える［切り替える］
◆Kanebo's main bank and the IRC will swap ¥30 billion and ¥10 billion, respectively, in debt into stock. カネボウの主力取引銀行と産業再生機構（IRC）は、それぞれ300億円分と100億円分の債権の株式化を行う［300億円分と100億円分の債権を株式に切り替える］。

swap　（名）交換, スワップ　(=swapping; ⇒agreement, currency swap, equities swap, equity swap, interest rate swap, stock swap deal)
amortization swap　分割償還型スワップ
asset-based swap　資産の交換スワップ, 債権のキャッシュ・フローの交換
basis swap　ベーシス・スワップ（同一通貨または異なる通貨間の変動金利と変動金利の交換）
cancelable [cancellable] swap　停止条件付きスワップ
conduct a debt-for-equity swap　債務の株式化を行う, 債権の株式化を行う
currency swap　通貨スワップ
debt-bond swap　債務の債券化
　(=debt-for-bond swap)
debt equity swap　債務の株式化, 債権の株式化
　(=debt-for-equity swap)
do a swap　交換する
equity swap　株式交換, 株式スワップ, 株価スワップ
extendable swap　期限延長権付きスワップ
forward swap　先物スワップ
interest rate swap　金利スワップ
　(=interest swap)
puttable swap　満期日の繰上げ可能性があるスワップ
share swap deal　株式交換取引
　(=stock swap deal)
short swap　短期スワップ取引
stock swap deal　株式交換取引
swap ratio　株式の交換比率
swap transaction　スワップ取引

total return swap トータル・リターン・スワップ（債券のクーポンと評価損益を短期金利などと交換するスワップ）

yield curve swap イールド・カーブ・スワップ

◆Japan Airlines will raise its stake in Japan Asia Airways to 100 percent from the current 90.5 percent on April 1 through an equity swap deal. 日本航空システムは、株式交換取引により、4月1日付けで日本アジア航空を完全子会社化する［日本アジア航空への出資比率を現在の90.5％から100％に引き上げる］。◆Maruha will put Nichiro under its wing as a wholly owned subsidiary through a share swap. 株式交換方式で、マルハはニチロを完全子会社としてマルハの傘下に収める。◆The company will increase its capital by ¥50 billion with additional investment of ¥10 billion from the IRC and with the debt-for-equity swap. 同社は、産業再生機構による100億円の追加［新規］出資と債務の株式化で、500億円増資する。◆Under the debt-for-equity swap scheme, the RCC will convert part of the debts it buys from banks other than the major creditor banks into shares. この債務株式化案では、整理回収機構（RCC）が、主力融資銀行以外の銀行から買い取った債権の一部を株式に転換することになる。

swap agreement スワップ契約, 中央銀行のスワップ協定（相互通貨交換協定）（=swap contract:「スワップ契約」とは、金利スワップと通貨スワップがあって、相互の債務を交換する契約のこと。⇒agreement, yield adjustment）

  currency swap agreement 通貨スワップ契約, 通貨スワップ協定
  interest rate swap agreement 金利スワップ契約
  termination of the swap agreement スワップ契約の解約

◆We conclude interest rate swap agreements to manage our exposure to changes in interest rates and lower our overall costs of financing. 当社は、金利変動リスクに対処する目的と当社全体の資金調達コストを低減する目的で、金利スワップ契約を結んでいます。

swap rate スワップ・レート

◆The fixed interest rate in a coupon swap is referred to as the swap rate. クーポン・スワップの固定金利は、スワップ・レートと呼ばれている。

swap ratio （株式などの）交換比率

◆The swap ratio has yet to be decided. 株式の交換比率は、まだ決まっていない。

sway （動）揺り動かす, 揺さぶる, 影響を与える, 感化する, 向かわせる, 変更させる, 左右する, 支配する, 統治する, 揺れる, 揺らぐ, 動揺する, 動く, 傾く
  be swayed by 〜に左右される, 〜の影響を受ける
  sway toward 〜に傾く

◆Investors are swayed by price fluctuations. 投資家は、株価変動に左右される。

sway （名）揺れ, 動揺, 振動, 影響力, 支配, 支配力, 勢力, 支配権, 統治, 統治権

sweeping （形）破竹の勢いの, すさまじい, 強い, 猛烈な, 完全な, 圧倒的な, 決定的な, 徹底的な, 抜本的な, 大胆な, 大雑把な, 広範な, 広範囲にわたる, 広く見渡せる, 全面的な, 包括的な, 大々的な, ダイナミックな, 一掃する
  a sweeping attack 大攻勢
  a sweeping generalization 大雑把な概括, 大雑把な総括
  a sweeping stroke 強い一撃
  sweeping changes 抜本的改革
    (=sweeping reforms)
  sweeping reforms 抜本的改革, 広範囲に及ぶ改革
  sweeping tax cuts 徹底的な減税

sweeping growth すさまじい伸び

◆The vitality that had enabled Japanese companies to achieve sweeping growth throughout the world market until the 1980s has rapidly been depleted. 1980年代まで世界市場全体にわたってすさまじい伸びを支えてきた日本企業の活力が、急速に失われている。

sweeping plan 抜本的対策

◆To ease public anxiety about the future, it is necessary for the administration to present sweeping plans regarding the pension, medical and welfare systems in the era of an ever graying population and drops in birthrates. 国民の将来不安を解消する上で、現政権は、少子・高齢化時代の年金・医療・福祉制度に関して抜本的な対策を明示する必要がある。

sweeping restructuring 抜本的な再建, 抜本的なリストラ

◆It is a matter of urgency to ensure that banks make profit margins that can meet investment risk and that they expand commission revenue as well as promote sweeping restructurings. 抜本的なリストラのほか、投資リスクに見合う利ざやの確保と手数料収入の拡大などが銀行の急務だ。

sweeping restructuring plan 抜本的な再建策

◆The firm will ax 10,000 jobs worldwide and cut ¥200 billion in costs by the end of fiscal 2011 in a sweeping restructuring plan. 同社は、抜本的な再建策として、2011年度末までに全世界の人員10,000人の削減と2,000億円のコスト削減を図る。

sweetener （名）甘味料
  (=kicker: 有価証券の魅力を増す材料のこと)

swell （動）膨張する, 膨（ふく）れる, 膨らむ, 大きくなる, 膨れ上がる, 増大する, 増加する （⇒erode）
  swell into 拡大して〜になる
  swollen monetary environments 金融膨張の市場環境

◆European countries and China have various kinds of bubbles and/or swollen monetary environments. 欧州や中国は、バブルや金融膨張の市場環境を抱えている。◆If the appraisal losses swell excessively, banks failing to meet the regulatory minimum capital adequacy requirements will have to go under. 含み損が余りにも膨らむと、規制当局の最低自己資本比率基準を満たせない銀行は、経営破たんに追い込まれることになる。◆Long-term debts held by central and local governments are expected to further swell unless the government puts the brakes on government bond issuance. 政府が国債発行に歯止めをかけないと、国と地方［地方自治体］が抱える長期債務は、さらに膨らむ見通しだ。

swelling （名）膨張, 膨（ふく）らみ, 増大, 増加, 腫（は）れ物, こぶ
  the swelling of nonperforming loans 不良債権の増大
  the swelling of the financial market of late 最近の金融膨張

◆Corporate bankruptcies have led to the swelling of nonperforming loans, posing a heavy burden on banks. 企業倒産が不良債権の増大を生み、銀行に重くのしかかっている。◆The IT bubble and the ensuing swelling of the financial market of late have stemmed from technology innovation coupled with the globalization of the economy. （1990年代後半の）ITバブルとそれに続く最近までの金融膨張を引き起こしたのは、経済のグローバル化の動きと連動した技術革新だ。

SWF 政府系ファンド, 政府系投資ファンド, ソブリン・ウエルス・ファンド
  (⇒sovereign wealth fund)

◆Singapore's SWFs are said to have been instrumental in invigorating the financial market by taking advantage of overseas human resources. シンガポールの政府系ファンド（SWF）は、海外の人材を登用して金融市場の活性化につなげたといわれる。

SWIFT 国際銀行間通信協会, 国際銀行通信協会, スイフト（Society for Worldwide Interbank Financial Telecommunicationの略）

◆Most cross-border money transfers between financial institutions are carried out through the international data communications network provided by the SWIFT. 国境を越える海外送金の大半は、スイフト（国際銀行間通信協会）が提供している国際的な金融データ通信網を介して行われている。

swift （形）素早い、迅速な、急速な、速い、速やかな、～するのが早い
- swift implementation of fiscal and tax stimulus measures 財政・税制面からの景気刺激策の速やかな実施
- swift increase in stock prices 株価の急騰
- take swift actions 迅速に対応する
- ◆The U.S. government and the Federal Reserve Board took swift actions to deal with the subprime loan crisis of 2007. 米政府と米連邦準備制度理事会（FRB）は、2007年のサブプライム危機に迅速に対応した。◆To enhance the stimulating effect of the Fed's rate cuts, swift implementation of fiscal and tax stimulus measures, including tax cuts on investment designed to reinvigorate the stock market, is necessary in addition to the large-scale tax cut program that is under way. 米連邦準備制度理事会（FRB）の金利引下げの刺激効果を高めるためには、現在実施中の大型減税プログラムに加え、株式市場を再活性化するための投資減税など、財政・税制面からの景気刺激策の速やかな実施が必要である。

swindle （動）だます、だまし取る、詐取（さしゅ）する
- be swindled out of ～を詐取される、～を巻き上げられる
- swindle a person out of money 人をだまして金を詐取する
- swindle money out of a person 人から金をだまし取る
- ◆Former PCI president and executives swindled the government out of about ¥300 million by overcharging for a state-funded project to dispose of chemical weapons. PCI元社長と元取締役らは、国をだまして政府出資の化学兵器処理事業の事業費を水増し請求し、約3億円をだまし取った。◆These companies are hesitant to take legal actions though they were swindled by the U.S. asset investment group that sold the bonds. これらの企業は、債券を売った米国の資産運用グループにだまされたのに、法的措置を取るのをためらっている。

swing （名）動き、活動、株価などの変動、進行、はかどり
- forex swings 為替変動 （=currency swings）
- get into full swing 本格化する
- in full swing 最高潮の、真っ最中の、最盛期で、急ピッチで進んでいる
- swing line 信用供与枠
- swings in demand 需要の変動
- upward swing of the yen 円高
- ◆In the work of tax system reform, which will get into full swing shortly, one of the focal points is whether to adopt the taxation system designed to help banking institutions dispose of their bad loans. 間もなく本格化する税制改正作業で、焦点の一つは、金融機関の不良債権処理を支援するための課税制度を採用するかどうかである。◆Long-term interest rates have been on an upward swing, recently rising as high as 2 percent. 長期金利が、一時2％をつけるなど、上昇傾向を強めている。

swinging of error trades into proprietary trading accounts 自己委託訂正（顧客からの委託注文に間違いが生じた場合、その取引を証券会社の自己勘定に付け替えて処理すること）

Swiss franc スイス・フラン（金融機関の信頼性が高いので信用力が高く、安全資産として買われる傾向にある）
- flying Swiss franc 行き過ぎのスイス・フラン高、過度なスイス・フラン高
- stem Swiss franc's rise against the euro ユーロに対するスイス・フラン高[スイス・フランの上昇]を阻止する、スイス・フラン高・ユーロ安を阻止する

- Swiss franc futures スイス・フラン先物
- Swiss franc market スイス・フラン市場
- Swiss franc note スイス・フラン債
- ◆In the case of foreign currency deposits, depositors can invest in foreign currencies such as British pound, Swiss franc and Australian dollar as well as the U.S. dollar and euro. 外貨預金の場合、預金者は、米ドルやユーロのほかに英ポンド、スイス・フランや豪ドルなどにも投資することができる。◆The Swiss National Bank put a limit on the flying Swiss franc. スイス国立銀行（スイスの中央銀行）が、過度なスイス・フラン高に上限を設定した。

Swiss National Bank スイス国立銀行（中央銀行）
- ◆The Swiss National Bank set a ceiling on the skyrocketing Swiss franc. スイス国立銀行（中央銀行）が、スイス・フランの急騰に上限[上限目標]を設定した。

switch （動）切り替える、変更する、変える、転換する、転向する、すり替える、のりかえる、交換する、転職する、スイッチする
- investors switch their funds from bank deposits to assets that entail some risks 投資家が銀行預金からリスクを伴う資産に資金の運用を切り替える
- switch from short bonds to long [long-term] bonds 短期債から長期債に切り替える[乗り換える]
- switch funds into long-term financial instruments 資金を長期金融商品に移す
- switch into cyclical [cyclical stocks] 景気循環株に切り替える[乗り換える]
- switch the financial policy from tighter to neutral 金融政策を引締めぎみから中立に転換する
- ◆Investors have begun switching their funds from bank deposits to assets that entail some risks. 投資家が、銀行預金からリスクを伴う資産へと資金の運用を切り替え始めている。◆The issue of the inadvertent failure to switch to the national pension program by full-time housewives must be quickly solved. 専業主婦の国民年金への年金資格切替え忘れ問題は、決着を急ぐべきだ。◆There are about 420,000 full-time housewives whose unpaid premium periods are long as they have failed to switch to the national pension plan. 国民年金への切替えが済んでいなくて保険料の未納期間が長い専業主婦は、約42万人いる。

switch （名）切替え、乗換え、変更、転換、スイッチ
- policy switch [switch-over] 政策転換、方針の変更
- switch commission （スイッチ貿易の）仲介手数料
- switch finance スイッチ金融
- switch reversal 逆入替え
- switch trade スイッチ貿易、スイッチ取引
- yen switch 円シフト

switching （名）変更、切替え、乗換え、資金の振替え、（ポートフォリオの保有銘柄構成を変更するための）入替え売買
- expenditure switching policy 支出転換政策
- switching by time differential 時間差入替え
- switching commission スイッチ貿易仲介手数料 （=switch commission）
- switching cost 切替コスト

symbol （名）印、記号、銘柄記号、銘柄略称、符号、コード、象徴、表象（emblem）、紋様、略称、信条（credo）、シンボル
- be assigned a symbol indicating the firm's shares are subject to delisting procedures ～には同社株が上場廃止手続きの対象になっていることを示すコードが付されている
- be traded under the symbol of AA AAの銘柄略称[略称]で取引される
- rating symbol 格付け記号
- stock symbol 銘柄略称

symbol of money　貨幣章標
symbol of value　価値表象　(=symbol of money)
symbol system　格付け記号
use the NR symbol to identify the unrated portion of the obligation　債券の評価対象外の部分にNR記号を付ける
use the SG symbol to identify short-term obligations of speculative grade　投機的格付けの短期債務にSGの記号を用いる

symmetric drive　景気配慮型またはインフレ警戒型の連銀指令（米連邦公開市場委員会（FOMC）が市場操作を担当するニューヨーク連銀に出す指令の一つ）

syndicate　(動)シンジケートを組織する・，組成する，シンジケートで管理する
　syndicate a deal　シンジケート団を組成する，シ団を組成する
　syndicate the deal on a broad basis　同案件の大型シ団組成を行う

syndicate　(名)証券発行の引受シンジケート団，銀行の協調融資団，銀行団，シンジケート
　alternative syndicate　対抗入札グループ
　banking syndicate　銀行の協調融資団，銀行融資団，銀行シンジケート団，銀行シンジケート
　break the syndicate　シンジケートを解散する
　divided syndicate　分割シンジケート
　financial syndicate　融資団，金融団，金融シンジケート
　insurance syndicate　保険引受団
　international syndicate　国際協調融資団，国際シンジケート
　international syndicate loan　国際シンジケート・ローン
　issue syndicate　証券発行団
　issuing syndicate of banks　銀行の発行引受団，証券発行銀行団
　join the syndicate　シンジケート団に加わる，シ団に加わる
　loan syndicate　融資協調，ローン・シンジケート
　marine syndicate　海上保険シンジケート
　preliminary syndicate　仮シンジケート
　syndicate agreement　引受団契約
　　(=syndicate contract)
　syndicate bankers　社債引受銀行団
　syndicate banks　シンジケート銀行
　syndicate financing　共同融資，共同金融
　syndicate loan　協調融資，協調融資団による融資［貸付け］，シンジケート・ローン
　　(=syndicated loan)
　syndicate manager　引受主幹事　(=lead manager, lead underwriter, managing underwriter)
　syndicate member　シ団メンバー，シンジケート・メンバー
　syndicate of banks　銀行団
　syndicate of leading investment banks　大手投資銀行のシンジケート団
　syndicate of underwriters　引受シンジケート団
　underwriting syndicate　募債引受団，引受団，引受シンジケート団
　undivided syndicate　不分割シンジケート
　◆The initial public offering (IPO) was underwritten by a syndicate of leading investment banks.　公開株式(IPO)は、大手投資銀行のシンジケート団が引き受けた。

syndicated　(形)共同の，協調の，協調融資団［引受団］による，銀行団による，シンジケート団による
　syndicated lending　協調融資　(=syndicated loan)
　syndicated term loan　(中長期の)協調ターム・ローン

syndicated loan　銀行団による協調融資，国際協調融資，シ・ローン，シンジケート・ローン
　(=syndicated bank loan, syndicated lending)
　raise funds through a syndicated loan　協調融資で資金を調達する
　take out a syndicated loan from　～から協調融資を受ける
　◆Sanyo Electric Co. will raise ￥100 billion through a syndicated loan for capital investment.　サンヨー電機が、設備投資のため協調融資で1,000億円を調達する。◆Softbank will raise ￥1.28 trillion in the form of syndicated loans from seven financial institutions in Japan, Europe and the United States.　ソフトバンクは、国内外の7金融機関から協調融資の形で1兆2,800億円を調達する方針だ。◆The company took out a syndicated loan from 20 banks and leasing companies.　同社は、銀行やリース会社など20社から協調融資を受けた。

syndication　(名)シンジケート団組成，融資団組成，シ団組成
　general syndication (stage)　一般シ団組成
　go into general syndication　一般シ団の組成に入る
　join the deal in the general syndication　一般シ団組成で同案件に参加する
　launch the deal into syndication　案件のシ団組成を開始する
　loan syndication　貸出シンジケーション，融資のシ団組成
　manage the syndication　シンジケート団を取り仕切る
　syndication fees　協調融資手数料
　◆The syndication is still open.　シ団組成は、まだ締め切られていない。

synergy effect　相乗効果，波及効果，相互補完効果，シナジー効果　(⇒merger and acquisition)
　◆A merger between life insurance companies will have little effect, because there is no synergy effect.　生保同士が合併しても、相互補完関係が生まれないため、効果は薄い。◆The mergers and acquisitions many major U.S. companies pursued failed to produce the expected synergy effect.　米国の大企業の多くが追求したM&Aは、予想したシナジー（相乗）効果を上げられなかった。

synthetic　(形)合成の，仕組みの
　synthetic agreement for foreign［forward］exchange　合成為替予約
　synthetic asset　合成アセット，合成ポジション
　　(synthetic position)
　synthetic bond　合成債券
　synthetic fixed-interest［fixed-rate］asset　合成固定金利資産
　synthetic fixed-interest liability　合成固定金利債務
　synthetic index fund　合成指数ファンド
　synthetic instruments［securities］　合成証券，仕組み商品
　synthetic long call　合成コールの買い
　synthetic option　合成オプション
　synthetic portfolio　合成ポートフォリオ
　synthetic swap　合成スワップ
　synthetic zero bond　合成ゼロ・クーポン債

synthetic floating rate　合成変動金利
　high-yielding synthetic floating rate　高利回りの合成変動利付き債
　synthetic floating rate asset　合成変動金利資産
　synthetic floating rate liability　合成変動金利債務
　synthetic floating rate note　合成変動利付き債，合成FRN
　　(=synthetic FRN)
　synthetic FRN (floating rate)　合成変動利付き債

synthetic futures　合成先物
  synthetic bought futures　合成先物の買い
  synthetic futures contract　合成先物
  synthetic sold futures　合成先物の売り
system　（名）組織,器官,機構,体系,系統,方式,方法,合理的なやり方,体制,制度,設備,装置,身体,体,五体,仮説,説,システム
  accounting system　会計システム,会計組織,会計制度
  administrative system　管理システム
  appraisal system　評価法
  auction system　オークション方式
  automated trading system　自動取引システム
  automatic accounts transfer system　自動引落し制度
  automatic transfer system　自動振替決済制度
  Bank of Japan financial network system　日銀ネット
  bank system consolidation　銀行業界の統合
  banking system　銀行制度,市中
  bonded system　保税制度
  branch banking system　支店銀行制度
  broker/broker settlement system　ブローカー間決済システム
  budgetary system　予算制度
  business system　企業体系,事業体系,事務機構,企業システム,ビジネス組織,ビジネス・システム
  central clearing system　中央決済制度
  central clearing system for money market instruments　短期金融商品の中央決済システム
  central depositary clearing system for stock certificates　株式振替決済制度
  central depositary [depository] system　保管振替制度
  centralized system of banknote issue　銀行券集中発行制度
  classified rating system　等級別料金制度
  clearing system　決済制度,決済システム,決済機関
  client accounting system　顧客勘定システム
  closed-end credit system　閉鎖信用体系
  compulsory savings system　強制貯蓄制度
  consumer credit system　消費者信用システム
  convertible banknote system　兌換（だかん）制度
  crawling peg system　段階的平価変動制
  credit rating system　格付け制度,格付けシステム
  crisis management system　危機管理システム,危機管理体制
  cross-border payment system　国際決済システム
  currency basket system　標準バスケット方式
  currency system　通貨体系
  decentralized system of banknote issue　銀行券分散発行制度
  decision support system　意思決定支援システム
  deficiency payment system　不足払い制度
  delta margining system　デルタ証拠金システム
  deposit (refund) system　デポジット制度
  dollar exchange standard system　ドル為替本位制度
  double rate system　ヌ銃レート制
  elastic limit system　保証発行屈伸制限制度,屈伸制限制度
  elastic maximum limit system　最高発行額屈伸制限制度
  euro system　ユーロ圏の中央銀行制度,ユーロ・システム,ユーロシステム(Eurosystem)
  European Monetary System　欧州通貨制度,EMS
  export advance system　輸出前貸し制度
  Federal Home Loan Bank System　連邦住宅貸付け銀行制度（=FHLBs System）
  Federal Reserve System　米連邦準備制度
  Federal Savings and Loan System　米連邦貯蓄貸付け制度
  Finance System Council　財務制度審議会
  financial industry information system　金融情報システム
  financial system　金融制度,金融システム
  fiscal equalization system　財政調整制度
  fixed exchange rate system　固定為替相場制度
  flexible exchange rate system　屈伸為替相場制度
  flexible rate system　屈伸相場制
  foreign currency deposit system　外貨預託制度
  foreign tax credit system　外国税額控除制度
  free-issue system　自由払い出しシステム
  free payment system　完全自由返済システム
  giro system　振替制度
  imprest petty cash system　定額小口現金前渡し制度
  imprest system　定額資金前渡し制度
  imputation system　法人税株主帰属方式
  interest rate system　金利制度,金利体系
  international clearing systems　国際決済機構
  international group insurance system　国際団体保険制度
  international managed currency system　国際管理通貨制度
  international monetary system　国際通貨制度
  licensing system of securities companies　証券免許制
  liquidity ratio system　流動比率制度
  managed currency system　管理通貨制度
  managed floating system　管理フロート制
  mandatory real-name transaction system　金融実名制
  monetary system　金融制度,貨幣制度
  monorate of exchange system　単一為替相場制
  monthly payment choice system　返済額選択システム
  multicurrency clearing and settlement system　多通貨決済システム
  multicurrency intervention system　複数通貨介入制度
  mutual offset system　相互決済制度
  National Market System　全米市場システム
  pension, medical and welfare systems　年金・医療・福祉制度（⇒sweeping plan）
  pump money into the (banking) system　市中に流動性を供給する
  quantity system　定量発注システム
  Retirement Allowance Mutual Aid System of the Medium and Small Enterprises　中小企業退職金共済制度
  risk control [management] system　リスク管理システム
  seniority-order wage system　年功序列型賃金体系
  Small and Medium Enterprises Credit Insurance System　中小企業信用保険公庫
  small order execution system　小口注文処理システム
  Smaller Business Credit Guarantee System　中小企業信用保証制度
  standard (currency) basket system　標準バスケット方式
  swaps clearing system　スワップ決済システム
  system configuration [architecture]　システム構成,システムの機器構成
  system failure　システムの故障,システムのトラブル,システム障害（=system crash, system glitch; ⇒double deduction）
  system installation　システム導入

system of fixed commissions　固定手数料制度
system of interest（rates）　金利体系, 金利制度
system of note［banknote］issue　発券制度
system of security right　担保制度
tax system reform　税制改革, 税制改正　（⇒swing）
taxation system　税制（tax system）, 課税制度
　（⇒swing）
tender system　テンダー方式
◆Under the EU's Stability and Growth Pact, countries eligible to join the euro system are required to keep budget deficits below 3 percent of GDP. 欧州連合（EU）の財政安定・成長協定によると, ユーロ加盟国は, 加盟の条件として財政赤字をGDPの3％以下に抑えなければならない。
system crash　システムの故障, システム障害, システムのトラブル　（=system failure, system glitch）
◆The banking group will hold talks with customers over damages caused by the system crash. 同銀行グループ［金融グループ］は, システム障害による損害については顧客と話し合いをする方針だ。
system glitch　システム障害　（=system crash）
◆The FSA will conduct a further on-the-spot inspection after receiving the final report on the system glitch. 金融庁は, コンピュータのシステム障害の最終報告を受けてからさらに立入り検査を行う方針だ。
system repurchase agreement　証券の売戻し条件付き買入れ　（=system repo, system RP：システム・レポ, 公開市場操作の一環として, 市中銀行の支払い準備（bank reserves）を一時的に増やすため, ニューヨーク連邦準備銀行が一定期間後に一定価格で売り戻すことを条件に公開市場で証券を買い入れること。⇒customer repurchase agreement, open market operation, repurchase agreement）
systematic　（形）組織的な, 系統的, 体系的, 計画的, 整然とした, 規則正しい, 几帳面な, 一貫した, 故意の, 計画的な, 分類上の, 分類学の, システマティック
　highly systematic approach　高度に組織だったアプローチ
　systematic dumping　組織的ダンピング
　systematic error　定誤差, 系統的誤差
　systematic investing　定期的投資
　　（=regular investing）
　systematic management　組織的管理, 体系的管理
　systematic risk　組織的危険［リスク］, システマティック・リスク（market risk, nondiversifiable risk）
　systematic sampling　系統的抽出法, 等間隔抽出法
　systematic search　体系的調査
　systematic violation　計画的な違反, 組織ぐるみの違反
systematically important financial institutions　システム上重要な金融機関, SIFI［SIFIs］　（⇒SIFI）
systematization　（名）組織化, 系列下, システム化
　systematization of distributors　販売店の系列下
　systematization strategy　システム化戦略
systematize　（動）組織化する, 体系化する, 系統立てる, 組織立てる, システム化する, 順序立てる, 分類する
　systematized　組織化した, システム化した
　systematized product　制度品
◆The company has systemized its expertise in credit and recovery operations. 同社は, 与信・回収業務のノウハウをシステム化している。
systemic　（形）組織の, 系統の, システム全体の, 連鎖的な, （病気が）全身的な, システミック
systemic breakdown　システム崩壊, 連鎖的な崩壊
　（=systemic collapse）
◆The collapse of a bank may result in the systemic breakdown of the whole banking sector. 銀行1行の破たんが, 金融界全体のシステム崩壊［連鎖的な崩壊］につながる可能性がある。
systemic financial crisis　連鎖的な金融危機, 金融の連鎖的な危機
◆To deal with the systemic financial crisis, ministry and central bank officials had to take rescue measures, such as an injection of public funds, while at the same time implementing strict guidelines and sanctions. 連鎖的な金融危機に対処するにあたって, 当局は公的資金の投入などの救済措置を取ると同時に, 厳しい指導や制裁を実施しなければならなかった。
systemic risk　連鎖破たんリスク, 連鎖危機, 連鎖リスク, システム・リスク, システミック・リスク（一つの銀行の破たんが, 連鎖的に他の金融機関に及び, 金融システム全体が機能不全に陥るリスク［危険性］。これは, 個々の金融機関が各種取引や決済ネットワークを使った資金決済を通じて相互に結ばれているために起こる）

T

T-bill　米財務省短期証券（Treasury billの略）
T-bond　米財務省長期証券（Treasury bondの略）
T-note　米財務省中期証券（Treasury noteの略）
tab　（名）付け札, ラベル, 勘定書き, 資金の必要額
　keep a tab［tabs］on　～に注目しておく, ～を見張る
　pick up the tab for　～の勘定を払う
◆Tab for Fannie Mae and Freddie Mac could soar to as much as $259 billion, nearly twice the amount Fannie and Freddie have received so far. ファニー・メイ（米連邦住宅抵当金庫）とフレディ・マック（米連邦住宅貸付け抵当公社）の追加の公的資金必要額は, 両社がこれまでに受け取った額の約2倍の2,590億ドルに急増する可能性がある。
tackle　（動）～に取り組む, ～に立ち向かう, ～に挑（いど）む, 論じ合う, 渡り合う, 組みつく, タックルする
　tackle a pressing issue　緊急課題［問題］に取り組む
　tackle the budget deficit　財政赤字に立ち向かう, 財政赤字［財政赤字問題］に対応する
　tackle the worldwide financial crisis　世界的な金融危機問題に対応する
◆Japan must tackle its large fiscal deficit and curb the growth of public debts. 日本は, 巨額の財政赤字と取り組んで, 財政赤字［公的債務］の増大を抑える必要がある。◆Japan must tackle the task of replenishing the depleted state coffers. 日本は, 疲弊した国家財政立て直しの課題（疲弊した国家財政の立て直しという課題）に取り組まなければならない。◆Priority should be given to public spending, to establish a firm foundation for economic recovery and the subsequent job of tackling fiscal reform. 景気を回復し［経済を立て直し］, 財政改革に取り組むための強固な基盤を確立するには, 公共支出を優先的に考えなければならない。◆The leaders of Japan, China and South Korea agreed to cooperate closely on tackling the worldwide financial crisis and North Korea's denuclearization. 日中韓の3か国首脳は, 世界的な金融危機や北朝鮮の非核化問題への対応で緊密に連携することで合意した。◆The private sector has tackled necessary restructuring efforts earnestly. 民間は, 必要なリストラ策に懸命に取り組んできた。◆The Tokyo governor will have to tackle the task of overcoming the continued financial difficulties facing the Shinginko Tokyo bank. 東京都知事は, 新東京銀行が直面する経営危機の長期化を克服する課題に取り組まなければならない。
tactic［tactics］　（名）作戦, 作戦行動, 手段, 方策, 策, 手, 策略, かけ引き, 戦術, 戦法
　adopt［use］the usual tactics　いつもの手を用いる
　advertising tactics　広告戦術
　marketing tactics　マーケテイング戦術
　money tactics　買収戦術

negotiating tactic　交渉戦術
poison pill defense tactics　ポイズン・ピル（毒薬条項）防衛策
sales tactics　売上作戦, 販売戦術, 勧誘
scorched earth tactics　焦土作戦
sharp［brilliant, clever］tactics　巧妙な戦術
shift in tactics　戦術転換
◆Another tactic many loan sharks use is to circulate slanderous leaflets to the workplace or the school that the borrower's children attend. 多くのヤミ金融業が使うほかの手は, 借り手の勤務先や子どもが通う学校への中傷文書のばらまきだ。◆Companies are allowed to use poison pill defense tactics more easily by the Business Organization Law, which went into effect in fiscal 2006. 2006年度から施行された「会社法」で, 企業はポイズン・ピル（毒薬条項）防衛策を以前より容易に行使できるようになった。◆The company's aggressive sales tactics became a social problem. 同社の強引な勧誘は, 社会問題化した。◆You should not reveal all your tactics at once when negotiating. 交渉では, 自分の戦術をすべて一度に明かさないようにするとよい。

tail　（名）入札価格などの小数点以下の数字, 米財務省証券（Treasuries）の公募入札での平均入札価格と最低落札価格との差, 平均入札利回りと最高落札利回りとの差, テイル

tailspin　（名）きりもみ降下, 急落, 景気の底割れ, 動揺, 狼狽（ろうばい）, 大混乱, パニック, （精神的な）スランプ, 意気消沈
dollar tailspin　ドルの急落
economic tailspin　経済パニック, 経済的大混乱
enter a tailspin　急落する, 下落する, 動揺する, 大混乱に陥る, パニック状態になる
head into a tailspin　景気底割れに向かう
send bond prices into a tailspin　債券相場の急落を招く
◆If Japanese government bonds prices enter a tailspin and throw financial markets into confusion, a financial system crisis would likely occur. 日本国債の価格が下落して, 金融市場が混乱すれば, 金融システム不安が生じる可能性がある。◆The yen fell into another tailspin. 円が, また急落した。

tailwind　（名）追い風
take a stake in　～へ出資する
◆NEC Corp. and Hitachi Ltd. have started negotiations with Intel Corp. of the United States, requesting that the world's largest semiconductor chip maker take a stake in their joint venture. NECと日立製作所が, 世界最大の半導体メーカーの米インテル社に両者の合弁会社への出資を要請して, 同社との協議に入った。

take control of　～の経営権を握る［掌握する］, ～の経営権を支配する, ～の主導権を握る
◆A person affiliated with the bank took control of the management of a firm that applied for a loan. 同行の息のかかった人物が, 融資を申し込んだ企業の経営の主導権を握った。

take out　ローンなどを組む, 保険に入る［加入する］, 保険を付ける［かける］, 契約する, 獲得する, 取得する, （預金などを）引き出す［下ろす］（withdraw）, 取り除く, 削除する, 持ち帰る, （訴訟を）起こす, （召喚状などを）発行する　（⇒capital spending）
get a bridge loan taken out　ブリッジ・ローンを借り換える
take one's money out of one's account　～の口座から金を下ろす
take out a driving license　運転免許を取る
take out a home loan　住宅ローンを組む, 住宅ローンを利用する
take out a housing loan contract　住宅ローン契約を結ぶ
take out a loan　ローンを組む, ローンを利用する
take out a loan contract　ローン契約を結ぶ
take out a mortgage on　～を抵当に入れる
take out a patent for　～の特許を取る
take out an insurance policy　保険を付ける, 保険に入る
take out（an）insurance（policy）against ill health　病気に備えて保険に入る
take out annuity　年金保険に入る
take out consumer loans　消費者金融から金を借りる, 消費者金融を利用する
take out earthquake insurance　地震保険に加入する
take out group credit insurance　団体信用保険に入る
take out insurance covering damage due to natural disasters　天災による損害を補償する保険に加入する
take out provisions against loan losses　貸倒れ損失に備えて準備金を引き当てる
take out summons　召喚状を発行する
take out the interim debt portion　デット部分のつなぎ融資の肩代わりをする
◆Elderly people took out group credit insurance unwittingly when taking out housing loan contracts. 高齢者が住宅ローン契約を結んだ際, 知らない間に団体信用生命保険にも入っていた。◆Housing developers recommend to customers that they take out adjustable rate mortgages to promote home sales. 住宅開発販売業者は, 住宅販売を促進するため, 変動金利型の住宅ローンを客に勧めている。◆Major nonlife insurance companies saw a rapid increase in the number of people taking out insurance covering damage due to earthquakes, tsunami, volcanic eruptions and other natural disasters. 大手損保各社では, 地震や津波, 火山の噴火などの天災による損害を補償する保険（地震保険）の加入者が急増した。◆Many of the investors took out consumer loans to pay contract fees. 出資者の多くは, 消費者金融から金を借りて契約料を支払った。◆The number of people taking out earthquake insurance generally increases directly after an earthquake or tsunami. 地震保険の加入者数は, 一般に地震や津波の直後に上昇する。

take over　企業を買収する, 取得する, 乗っ取る, （資産・業務などを）引き継ぐ, 継承する, 経営権を獲得する　（⇒acquirer, blue-chip subsidiary, Bridge Bank of Japan, insurance fund）
take over the assets of　～の資産を継承する, ～の資産を引き継ぐ
take over the business of　～の事業を引き継ぐ
take over the collapsed bank　経営破たんした銀行を引き継ぐ
take over the operations of　～の営業譲渡を受ける
◆In March, Mizuho Securities took over the operations of Norinchukin Securities Co. 3月に, みずほ証券は農中証券の営業譲渡を受けた。◆In May 2007, the ban on foreign firms taking over Japanese companies with stock swap deals was lifted. 2007年5月から, 株式交換取引での外資［外資系企業, 外国企業］による日本企業買収が解禁となった。◆Shinsei Bank took over the collapsed Long-Term Credit Bank of Japan. 新生銀行は, 経営破たんした日本長期信用銀行を引き継いだ。◆The would-be acquirer has no intention of taking part in the management of a company it aims to take over. 買収側［買収希望者］に, 買収対象企業の経営に参加する意思はない。

take over assets　資産を引き継ぐ, 資産を継承する
◆In 2001, Lone Star launched Tokyo Star Bank after taking over the assets of the failed regional bank Tokyo Sowa Bank. 2001年に, ローンスターは経営破たんした地銀の東京相和銀行の資産を継承して, 東京スター銀行を発足させた。

take profits　利食いに出る
◆Individual investors and brokerage dealers continued to take profits from recent surges in comparatively low-prices issues. 個人投資家と証券会社のディーラーは, 最近の比較的

割安な銘柄の急上昇で引き続き利食いに出た。

take up （寄付金などを）募る, 利子付きで借りる, （借金を）全部［全額］返済する, （株などを）買い取る, 引き受ける, （債券などに）応募する
  take up a collection　献金を募る
  take up all shares of the company　同社株を全株買い取る, 同社株を全部引き受ける
  take up an insurance policy　保険に加入する, 保険に入る
  take up the full subscription　全額を借り入れる, 全額を引き受ける

takedown （名）（証券の）引受け分, 取り分, 引受価格, テークダウン

takeout （名）持ち出し, 取り出し, （免許などの）取得, 証券売買益, 長期不動産抵当貸付け（テークアウト・ローン）, テークアウト
  takeout financing　テークアウト・ファイナンス
    （=takeout loan）
  takeout loan［mortgage］　長期不動産担保融資, 長期不動産抵当貸付け　テークアウト・ローン
    （=takeout, takeout financing）

takeover （名）企業買収, 乗っ取り, 企業取得, 買収, 吸収合併, 株式公開買付け（takeover bid）, 債権などの譲り受け, 引継ぎ, テイクオーバー　（=acquisition, take-over, tender offer; ⇒hostile takeover, warrant）
  agreed takeover　合意による株式公開買付け
  block a takeover　乗っ取りを阻止する
    （=prevent a takeover）
  bust-up takeover　解体買収
  corporate takeover　企業買収
  defend against a hostile takeover　敵対的買収に対抗する, 敵対的買収への防衛策をとる
  foreign takeover　外国企業による買収, 海外資本による買収
  friendly takeover　友好的買収
  high-leverage takeover　多額の借入れによる企業買収
  hostile takeover　敵対的買収
    （=unsolicited takeover）
  reverse takeover　逆買収
  seek a takeover　営業譲渡先を探す
  takeover attempt　買収劇, 買収攻勢
  takeover battle　買収合戦　（=takeover war）
  takeover bidder　買収提案者, 買収者
    （⇒golden share, hostile takeover bidder）
  takeover boom　買収ブーム, 企業買収ブーム
  takeover defense　買収防衛手段, 防衛手段, 乗っ取り防衛手段, 買収防衛策
  takeover plan　企業買収案, 買収計画
    （⇒Federal Reserve Board）
  takeover technique　買収の手法
    （=takeover method）
  unfriendly takeover　非友好的買収
  unsolicited takeover　敵対的買収

◆The managers of Japanese companies must protect themselves against foreign businesses' takeovers. 日本企業の経営者は, 外国企業の乗っ取りへの対抗策を取らなければならない。◆The TSE, an unlisted firm, will make the OSE, a listed firm, its subsidiary through a takeover. 非上場企業の東証が, 上場企業である大証を, 株式公開買付け（TOB）で子会社化する。◆Thus far restructuring in the domestic pharmaceutical industry has been limited to takeovers by foreign firms. これまでのところ国内製薬業界の再編は, 外資による買収に限られている。

takeover attempt　買収劇, 買収攻勢, 買収の企て
◆Broadcasters are tightening their defense against takeover attempts. 放送局各社は現在, 買収防衛［買収攻勢への防衛］を強化している。

takeover battle　買収合戦, 株式争奪戦, 株争奪戦
  （=takeover war）
◆In February 2005, Livedoor Co. purchased a massive amount of shares in the Nippon Broadcasting System Inc., and engaged in a fierce takeover battle with Fuji Television Network, Inc. 2005年2月に, ライブドアはニッポン放送株を大量取得して, フジテレビと激しい争奪戦を繰り広げた。

takeover bid　株式公開買付け, 株式公開買付けによる企業買収, 買収提案, 買収提案額テイクオーバー・ビッド, TOB　（=take-over bid, takeover offer, tender offer: 主に経営権を支配するため, 株式の買取り業者が買付け期間と株数, 価格を公表して不特定多数の株主から株を買い取る方法。⇒acquire, basis, hostile takeover bid, scheme）
  a purchase of stock through a takeover bid　株式公開買付（TOB）による株式の買取り
  friendly takeover bid　友好的株式公開買付け, 友好的TOB, 株式公開買付けによる友好的買収, 友好的買収
  hostile takeover bid　敵対的株式公開買付け, 敵対的TOB, 敵対的買収　（⇒floating shares）
  takeover bid system　株式公開買付け制度
  target of a hostile takeover bid　敵対的買収の標的, 敵対的買収の対象
  unfriendly takeover bid　非友好的株式公開買付け, 非友好的TOB, 株式公開買付けによる非友好的買収, 非友好的買収　（=unfriendly takeover）

◆Fuji TV has decided to make Nippon Broadcasting System Inc. a subsidiary, purchasing its stocks in a takeover bid. フジテレビは, ニッポン放送を子会社化することを決め, 株式公開買付け（TOB）で同社株を買い進めた。◆Fuji TV issued the moving strike convertible bonds (MSCBs) early this year for subscription by Daiwa Securities SMBC Co. to raise ¥80 billion for its NBS takeover bid. フジテレビは今春, ニッポン放送株の公開買付け（TOB）資金800億円を調達するため, 大和証券SMBCを引受先として転換社債型新株予約権付き社債（MSCB）を発行した。◆In the TSE-OSE merger in January 2013, the TSE first will make the OSE its subsidiary by purchasing a majority of OSE stocks through a takeover bid. 2013年1月の東証・大証統合では, 東証がまず株式公開買付（TOB）で大証株の過半数を取得して, 大証を子会社化する。◆In the United States, the Exon-Florio provision of the 1988 trade law can prevent takeover bids that are deemed a threat to national security. 米国では, 1988年通商法のエクソン・フロリオ条項で, 国家の安全保障上, 脅威と考えられる企業買収を阻止することができる。◆It will take Hankyu at least ¥180 billion to acquire Hanshin shares through its takeover bid. 阪急が株式公開買付け（TOB）で阪神株を取得するのに, 最低で1,800億円は必要だ。◆Listed companies have recently become afraid of being the target of a hostile takeover bid. 上場企業は最近, 敵対的買収の標的になるのを恐れるようになった。◆Oracle Corp. raised its takeover bid for rival PeopleSoft Inc. by 10 percent to seal a $10.3 billion deal. 米ソフトウエア大手のオラクルは, 同業の米ピープルソフトに対する買収提案額を1割引き上げ, 103億ドルの契約を結んだ［最終的に103億ドルで買収することで合意した］。◆The company granted an investment firm the right to buy shares to be newly issued by the company as a means of foiling a hostile takeover bid. 同社は, 敵対的買収への防衛策として, 同社が新規に発行する株式の引受権を投資会社に付与した［投資会社に新株予約権を割り当てた］。

takeover bid period　株式公開買付けの期間, TOBの期間　（=public tender offer period; ⇒closing price）
◆Even during the takeover bid period, Livedoor has continued to buy shares in Nippon Broadcasting System Inc. TOBの期間中も, ライブドアはニッポン放送株を買い続けた。

takeover offer 企業買収提案, 買収提案
(=takeover bid)
　an all-stock takeover offer　全株買取り案, 全株買取りによる企業買収案
　reject a takeover offer from　～による買収提案を拒否する
　unsolicited takeover offer from　～による一方的な企業買収提案
　◆Comcast Corp., the nation's largest cable operator, called on Disney's independent directors to open talks on its all-stock takeover offer. 米ケーブルテレビ最大手のコムキャストは、ディズニーの社外取締役にコムキャストが提出した全株買取り案[全株買取りによる企業買収提案]の協議開始を求めた。◆The board of directors of The Walt Disney Co. unanimously rejected a takeover offer from Comcast Corp. ウォルト・ディズニーの取締役会は、全会一致でコムキャストによる買収提案を否決した。◆Walt Disney Co. rejected an unsolicited $48.95 billion takeover offer from cable television company Comcast Corp. ウォルト・ディズニー社は、ケーブルテレビ会社コムキャストによる489億5千万ドルの一方的な企業買収提案を拒否した。

takeover war　買収合戦, 株式争奪戦, 株争奪戦
(=takeover battle)
　◆This takeover war placed heavy financial burdens on Fuji TV, Livedoor and Nippon Broadcasting System Inc. この株式争奪戦は、フジテレビ、ライブドアとニッポン放送の財務面に大きい負担をかけた。

talks　(名)会談, 交渉, 協議, 審議, 話し合い
　budget talks　予算審議
　debt restructuring talks　債務再編交渉
　merger talks　経営統合交渉
　ongoing merger talks　継続中の統合交渉
　pay talks　賃上げ交渉
　working-level talks　実務者協議
　◆Labor management talks will soon start in small and mid-size companies. 中小企業の労使交渉が、間もなく始まる。◆Moody's will consider cutting the United States' top-notch credit rating if any progress isn't made in talks to raise the U.S. debt limit. 米政府の法定債務上限引上げについての(米議会との)交渉に進展がなければ、ムーディーズは、米国債の最上位の格付けを引き下げる方向で検討する方針だ。◆SMFG and Daiwa Securities held working-level talks about the merger plan starting from last spring. 三井住友フィナンシャルグループと大和証券は、昨年春から統合計画の実務者協議を進めていた。◆The ruling was reportedly the first ever to suspend ongoing merger talks between financial institutions. 継続中の金融機関の統合交渉を差し止める決定は、前例がないという。◆The talks between Prime Minister Kan and Bank of Japan Gov. Shirakawa led to a further advance of the yen and off-loading of stocks as disappointment spread among market players. 菅首相と日銀総裁の会談は、一層の円高と市場筋の株の失望売りを誘った。

tame　(動)抑える, 抑制する, 和らげる, 管理する, 制御する, 治める, 支配下に置く, (気力などを)くじく
　tame persistent inflation　持続的インフレを抑える
　tame the yen's appreciation　円高を抑える, 円高を是正する
　◆It is uncertain to what extent the yen's appreciation will be tamed. どこまで円高を是正できるかは、不透明だ。

Tankan　(名)日銀短観, 短観, 日銀の全国企業短期経済観測調査, 企業から見た景気動向を示す
　price DI in the Tankan　日銀短観の価格判断DI
　Tankan number　日銀短観の数値

Tankan index　短観の業況判断指数(DI)
　◆The Tankan index for large manufacturers rose to plus 2 in September from the minus 9 registered in June. 9月短観の大企業・製造業の業況判断指数(DI)は、6月調査のマイナス9からプラス2に11ポイント改善した。◆The Tankan index for 10 of the 16 industries in the manufacturing sector improved in September from three months earlier. 製造業16業種中10業種の日銀9月短観の業況判断指数(DI)は、(前回調査の)6月から改善した。

Tankan survey [report]　日銀短観
　◆The BOJ's Tankan survey shows business sentiment among large manufacturers rebounded in September from the previous survey three months earlier. 9月の日銀短観は、大企業・製造業の景況感が6月の前回調査から改善したことを示している。

tap　(動)(情報などを)引き出す[求める], 開発[開拓]する, 利用する, 活用する, 選ぶ, 選出する, 盗聴する, 傍受する, 盗聴器を付ける
　tap government money　公的資金を利用[活用]する, 公的資金を引き出す　(⇒government money)
　tap into dormant funds as drawer savings　タンス預金として眠っている資金を利用する
　tap into the dollar markets　ドル債市場で起債する
　tap into the market　市場を利用する, ～市場に乗り出す, 市場で起債する
　tap rising demand　需要増に応える
　tap the vigor of　～の活力を引き出す
　◆Sanyo Electric Co. tapped its founder's grandson as its new president and an outside director as chief executive officer in a management change sparked by the company's record loss. 三洋電機は、同社の記録的な赤字で行った経営刷新で、創業者の孫を新社長に、また社外取締役を最高経営責任者(CEO)に選んだ。◆The government can tap its special account to cover 50 percent to 95 percent of insurance payment claims when total earthquake insurance payouts exceed ¥115 billion. 地震保険の支払い総額が1,150億円を超えると、政府は特別会計を利用して保険金支払い請求額の50～95％を負担することができる。◆The White House is ready to consider tapping a $700 billion Wall Street bailout fund to help keep the U.S. automakers afloat. 米政府は、米自動車メーカーの破たんを避けるための支援策として、7,000億ドルの金融業界救済資金(金融安定化法の公的資金)の活用を検討することができている。

tap　(名)いつでも買える国債[公債], タップ　(形)(債券の)発行期間、発行総額に制限がない
　on tap　いつでも求めに応じられる, いつでも利用できる[使える], 用意されて, (国債などが)自由に買える
　tap bond　タップ債(遊休資金吸い上げのために発行される国債)
　tap issue　タップ発行(証券取引所や金融市場を通さないで、国債や政府証券券をイングランド銀行などの政府機関に直接売ること), タップ債
　tap stock　タップ債

tap a bailout fund　救済資金を活用する
　◆The administration of U.S. President George W. Bush may tap a $700 billion bailout fund to aid the U.S. automakers. ブッシュ政権は、7,000億ドルの救済資金(金融安定化法の公的資金)を活用して、米自動車メーカー(ビッグ・スリー)を支援する可能性がある。

tap the market　市場で調達する, 市場で資金を調達する, 市場で起債する, 市場に登場する, 市場を開発[開拓]する
　tap the international markets　国際市場で資金を調達する
　tap the offshore market　オフショア市場で調達する

tap the stock market to raise fresh capital　新規資本を調達するため株式市場で起債する
　◆Japanese companies actively tapped the stock market to raise fresh capital. 日本の企業が、新規資本を調達するため株式市場で積極的に起債した。

target （動）～を目標に定める, 目標にする, 標的にする, ～に的を絞る, 対象にする, 狙う, ターゲットにする
◆A boom in stock investing among working women has led a number of women to create Web sites and publish guides targeted at this growing market. 働く女性たちの間での株式投資ブームで、この成長市場向けサイトを立ち上げたり、指南本を出したりする女性が増えている。◆Among 17 big banks targeted by the lawsuits filed by the U.S. government were Bank of America, Citigroup, Credit Suisse and Nomura Holding America Inc. 米政府が提訴した訴訟の対象の大手金融機関17社の中には、バンカメのほかにシティグループやクレディ・スイス、野村ホールディング・アメリカなどが含まれている。◆Sumitomo Mitsui Banking Corp. has jointly developed with American International Group Inc. a foreign bond investment product targeting retired baby boomers. 三井住友銀行が、団塊の世代の定年退職者をターゲットにした外債の金融商品を、米保険最大手のAIGグループと共同開発した。◆The FSA's inspectors are to target falling companies, based on their stock price levels and outside credit ratings. 金融庁の検査官は、(特別立ち入り検査では)株価水準や格付けなどを基準にして経営不振の企業に的を絞る方針だ。

target （名）目標, 目標水準, 買収目標企業, 買収対象会社, 買収標的会社, ターゲット （⇒acquirer, earnings target, Federal funds target rate, government-set target）
be the target of criticism　非難の的となる, 批判の的となる
call rate target　無担保コール翌日物金利の誘導目標
call target rate　コール金利の誘導目標水準
deficit target　赤字削減目標
economic policy targets　経済政策目標
Fed funds target　FF金利の誘導目標, FF金利の誘導目標水準
funding target　資金調達コストの目標
funds target　FF金利の誘導目標, FFレートの誘導目標
monetary target　マネー・サプライの目標水準
money supply target　マネー・サプライ伸び率の目標圏, マネー・サプライ伸び率の目標レンジ
takeover target　買収の対象, 買収の標的, 買収の目的, 買収対象会社, 買収目標企業
target issue　特定の投資家を目当てに債券を発行すること
target price　目標買収価格, 目標とする売買価格
target zone　目標相場圏, 目標範囲, ターゲット・ゾーン
the target for the federal funds rate　FF金利の誘導目標, FFレートの誘導目標
upper target limit　目標圏上限
◆Greece will miss 2011-12 deficit targets imposed by international lenders as part of the country's bailout. ギリシャは、同国救済措置の一環として国際融資団（欧州連合（EU）や国際通貨基金）が課した2011-12年の赤字削減目標を、達成できないようだ。◆In wrap accounts, a customer sets the overall investment policy, including investment period and profit target. ラップ口座では、顧客が投資期間や運用益の目標などの大まかな運用方針を決める。◆Japan Airlines Corp. is expected to fall short of its planned fund-raising target by about ¥50 billion due to lower stock price. 日本航空では、株価の下落で、当初計画の資金調達目標を約500億円下回る見通しだ。◆The central bank's move to increase the outstanding current account target is insufficient to soothe market fears. 日銀の当座預金残高目標の引上げは、市場不安を払拭するには物足りない。◆The new Fed chairman's theory is to introduce inflation targets, thus setting numerical targets for stabilizing prices. 米連邦準備制度理事会（FRB）新議長の持論は、インフレ目標を導入して、物価安定の数値目標を示す［設定する］ことだ。◆Under the government guidelines, if earnings come in more than 30 percent below targets set in restructuring plans at any major bank that received public funds to recapitalize in 1988 and 1999, the banks management will have to resign. 政府のガイドラインによると、資本再編のために1988年と1999年に公的資金の注入を受けた大手銀行の収益が、再建計画（経営健全化計画）で設定した収益目標を30％以上下回った場合、銀行の経営陣は辞任しなければならない。

target company　買収対象会社, 買収目標企業, 買収標的会社, 標的企業, ターゲット企業, ターゲット・カンパニー　（=target firm）
◆Poison pill is a range of strategic moves employed by a takeover-target company to make its stock less attractive to an acquirer. ポイズン・ピルは、買収者にとっての買収標的会社の株式の魅力を減少させるため、買収標的会社が導入する戦略的手段の一つだ。◆The would-be acquirer is trying to greenmail the target company by having it pay a premium to buy back the shares held by the raider. 買収側［買収希望者］は、この買占め屋［会社乗っ取り屋］が保有する株を標的企業に高値で引き取らせて、標的企業から収益を上げようとしている（標的企業に高値で引き取らせることにより、標的企業にグリーンメールを仕掛けようとしている）。

target for current account deposits　当座預金の残高目標
◆The central bank has deployed various measures to ease monetary policy, including cuts in the discount rate and hikes in the target for current account deposits held by commercial banks at the central bank. 日銀は、公定歩合の引下げや銀行が日銀に持つ当座預金の残高目標の引上げなどを含めて、各種の金融緩和策を実施してきた。

target for the federal funds rate　フェデラル・ファンド（FF）金利の誘導目標
◆The U.S. Federal Reserve Board increased the target for the federal funds rate by a quarter percentage point, to 2.5 percent. 米連邦準備制度理事会（FRB）は、フェデラル・ファンド（FF）金利の誘導目標を0.25％引き上げて年2.5％とした。

target of a hostile takeover　敵対的買収の対象
◆More than 70 percent of leading companies are worried about becoming the target of a hostile takeover. 主要企業の70％以上が、敵対的買収の対象になるのを懸念している。

target range　目標圏, 目標レンジ
（=targeted range）
achieve the target range　目標を達成する
increase in the target range　目標圏の拡大
lower half of the target range　目標圏の下半分
M2 target range　M2伸び率の目標レンジ
meet the target range　目標を達成する
the target range for the inflation rate　物価上昇率の目標値, インフレ率の目標値
◆The target range for the inflation rate could be set at the same level as the potential growth rate, for example. 物価上昇率の目標値としては、例えば潜在成長率と同水準に設定することもできよう。

target rate　誘導目標金利, 金利の誘導目標
◆The U.S. Federal Reserve raised the official discount rate and the target rate of federal funds by 0.25 percentage points in a bid to quell inflation and keep the economy from overheating. 米連邦準備制度理事会（FRB）は、インフレを防ぎ景気の過熱を警戒して、公定歩合とフェデラル・ファンド（FF）の誘導目標金利をそれぞれ0.25パーセント引き上げた。

target rate for unsecured overnight call (money)　無担保コール翌日物金利の誘導目標　（=rate for unsecured overnight call:unsecured overnight call moneyは、語順がovernight unsecured call moneyになる場合もある）
◆The Bank of Japan has kept the target rate for unsecured overnight call money at 0.1 percent since December 2008.

日銀は、2008年12月から無担保コール翌日物金利の誘導目標を0.1%に維持してきた。◆The Bank of Japan's Policy Board decided to keep the target rate for unsecured overnight call money. 日銀政策委員会は、(日銀の政策金利である)無担保コール翌日物金利の誘導目標を維持する[据え置く]ことを決めた。

target year 目標年次, 目標年, 目標達成年
◆The government postponed the target year of achieving a surplus in the primary balances of the central and local governments due to the economic downturn. 景気の悪化で、政府は国と地方の基礎的財政収支の黒字化の目標年次を、先送りした。

targeted (形) 目標とされる, 目標とされている, 標的の, ～を対象とする
  be targeted at ～を対象にしている, ～をターゲットにしている, ～を狙っている
  foreign-targeted issue 外国人投資家向け発行
  retail-targeted deal 個人投資家を対象とする起債
  targeted at ～に向けられた, ～対象の
  targeted average yield 基準利回り
  targeted dated 目標期日, 目標日次
  targeted year 目標年, 目標達成年

targeted company 買収の標的企業
◆A targeted company demanded a company trying to acquire its stocks to present a business plan. 買収の標的企業は、買収企業[標的企業の株式を取得しようとしている企業]に事業計画の提出を求めた。

targeted reduction 削減目標
◆Greece will not be able to achieve the targeted reduction in its fiscal deficits by 2012. ギリシャは、2012年まで財政赤字の削減目標を達成できないようだ。

tariff (名) 関税, 関税率, 料金表, 運賃表
◆The EU has imposed a 14 percent tariff on imported LCD monitors for computers. 欧州連合(EU)は、パソコン用液晶モニターに14%の関税を課している。

TARP 不良資産救済プログラム, 不良資産買取りプログラム (⇒Troubled Asset Relief Program)

task (名) 仕事, 任務, 職務, 業務, 課業, 作業, 課題, 問題, タスク
  be no easy task to ～することは決して容易ではない (⇒halt)
  credit analyst's task 信用アナリストの業務
  data gathering task データ収集作業
  hard task 難題 (=difficult task; ⇒flat-lined)
  main task 主な任務
  primary task 最優先課題
  take [bring, call] a person to task ～の責任を問う, ～を(厳しく)非難する, ～を叱る, ～をとがめる (⇒spate)
  task and bonus system 課業賞与制度, 課業賞与方式 (=task bonus system)
  the most pressing task 最緊急課題 (⇒bond issuance)
  urgent task 緊急課題, 急務
◆An urgent task facing each financial group is to improve its financial conditions and profitability on the strength of advantages gained from merger. 合併・統合の相乗効果を生かして、財務内容と収益力を向上させることが、各金融グループの現在の急務だ。◆Another important task facing major banks is to curtail their operating costs by consolidating branches. 大手行が抱えているもう一つ重要な課題は、店舗の統廃合による営業コストの削減だ。◆It is an urgent task to pass the fiscal 2009 budget as soon as possible, in view of the current economic downturn. 目下の景気後退を考えると、2009年度予算案の早期可決は緊急課題だ。◆It will be no easy task to halt the economy fully out of deflation. デフレからの完全脱却は、決して容易なことではない。◆Japan must tackle the task of replenishing the depleted state coffers. 日本は、疲弊した国家財政立て直しの課題(疲弊した国家財政の立て直しという課題)に取り組まなければならない。◆Measures to expand and create employment are a pressing task. 雇用拡大と雇用創出策は、急を要する課題だ。◆The tasks of safety management specialists in the field of financial services are essentially to whistle-blow and stop extending risky loans. 金融サービス分野での安全管理専門家の仕事は、基本的に高リスク融資に待ったをかけてそれを止めさせることだ。◆U.S. president Bush turned to former Secretary of State James Baker for the complex task of winning an international agreement on reducing Iraq's foreign debt. ブッシュ米大統領は、イラクの対外債務削減に関する国際合意を取り付ける複雑な仕事の担い手として、ジェームズ・ベーカー元国務長官に白羽の矢を立てた。

tax (動) (～に)課税する, 重い負担をかける, 重荷を負わせる, 酷使する, 責める, 非難する, (訴訟費用などを)査定する, (会費などを)徴収する, 割り当てる, 請求する
  be taxed at source 源泉徴収税が課される
  be taxed on ～に課税される
  tax imports 輸入品に課税する
  tax the costs of an action in the suit 訴訟費用を査定する
◆In Germany, individual investors' capital gains are not normally taxed. ドイツでは、個人投資家の譲渡益については通常、非課税となっている。

tax (名) 税, 租税, タックス (⇒income tax)
  basic tax rate 基本税率
  business place tax 事業所税
  carbon tax 炭素税
  consumption tax 消費税
  corporate income tax 法人所得税, 法人税
  corporate tax 法人税
  enterprise tax 事業税
  extralegal taxes 法定外税
  federal income tax 連邦所得税, 連邦法人税
  foreign tax credit 外国税額控除
  gift tax 贈与税
  heavy penalty tax 重加算税
  income tax 所得税, 法人所得税
  income taxes 法人税等
  land transfer tax 土地譲渡益課税, 土地譲渡税
  Local Tax Law 地方税法
  maximum income tax rate 所得税の最高税率
  net of tax 税引き後
  social security tax 社会保障税, 社会保険料
  state income tax 州法人所得税, 州税
  state tax 州税
  statutory tax rate 法定税率
  tax anticipation bill 税金先行証券, TAB (米財務省発行の短期証券で、企業はこれを法人所得税の納付に充当できる)
  tax anticipation note 税金先行証券, TAN (米国の州政府や地方自治体発行の短期証券)
  tax assets 税金資産 (⇒write off)
  tax break on housing loans 住宅ローン減税
  tax evasion scandal 脱税疑惑
  tax-exempt 免税の, 非課税の, 無税の (=tax-free)
  tax exemption 免税, 非課税, 無税
  tax-free disposal of bad loans 不良債権の無税償却 (=nontaxable write-off of bad loans)

tax-hike measures　増税策, 増収策
tax income　税収　(⇒impact)
tax levies on capital gains　株式譲渡益課税
　(⇒security taxation system)
tax liability　納税額
tax on unreported income　無申告加算税
tax rebate　税金の還付, 戻し減税, 戻し税
tax smoothing　課税平準化
taxes on shareholders' dividends　株式配当課税
taxes on stock dividends　株式配当課税
unemployment tax　失業保険税
◆The Greek government has set forth measures to decrease the number of government employees and raise taxes to cut its budget deficits. 財政赤字削減のため、ギリシャ政府は公務員削減や増税策を打ち出した。◆The new bank tax is levied on the banks' gross operating profits-their earnings minus basic operating expenses such as interest payments to depositors. 新銀行税は、銀行の収入から基礎的な経費（預金者に対する預金金利の支払いなど）を差し引いた業務粗利益に課される。

tax-and-spend policies　税制・支出政策
◆It is said that most of the U.S. government's colossal deficits had been caused by the faulty tax-and-spend policies of Republican governments. 米政府の膨大な財政赤字の大半は、歴代共和党政権の誤った税制・支出政策によるものだと言われる。

tax assets　税金資産
◆Major banks are striving to write off some of their tax assets from their equity capital. 大手銀行は現在、自己資本からの税金資産減らしに取り組んでいる。

tax authorities　税務当局
◆Since 1976, U.S. tax authorities have twice allowed tax refunds for banks. 1976年以来、米国[米国の税務当局]は銀行については税金還付を2度承認している。

tax benefit　税務上の特典, 税額控除や所得控除などの税制上の優遇措置, 税効果　(=tax break)
◆The government hopes to stabilize the government bond market by introducing tax benefits for government bond ownership. 政府は、国債保有に関する税制優遇措置の導入で国債市場の安定化を図りたいとしている。

tax break　税制上の優遇措置[特典], 租税優遇, 租税優遇措置, 租税免除, 減税, 節税手段
　(=tax benefit)
◆The tax breaks on capital gains from stock sales and on dividend income will be extended by one year. 株式譲渡益[株式売却益]と受取配当金の税率軽減措置の期間が、1年延長される。

tax burden　租税負担, 税負担　(⇒write-off)
◆Under the consolidated tax system, losses from one company in a group may be subtracted from the profits of another group company in calculating taxable income, reducing the group's tax burdens. 連結税制では、課税所得を算定するにあたってグループ企業の損失は他のグループ内企業の利益から差し引かれるので、グループ全体の税負担が軽くなる。

tax collections　税収
◆The U.S. budget deficit for fiscal 2010 narrowed slightly to $1.29 trillion as tax collections recovered slightly and financial bailout spending fell sharply. 米国の2010会計年度（2009年10月～2010年9月）の財政赤字は、税収がいくぶん回復し、金融救済[金融支援]費用が急減したため、1兆2,900億ドルに縮小した。

tax cut　減税　(=tax reduction)
◆Economic stimulus measures such as tax cuts and additional public works projects work only as temporary remedies. 減税や公共事業の追加などの景気浮揚策は、一時的なカンフル剤にすぎない。◆The G-7 leaders merely welcomed Washington's economic stimulus measures in the form of interest rate cuts and tax cuts as "positive." G7首脳は、利下げや減税などの形での米政府の景気刺激策を「積極的」として歓迎しただけだ。

tax cuts on investment　投資減税
◆To enhance the stimulating effect of the Fed's rate cuts, swift implementation of fiscal and tax stimulus measures, including tax cuts on investment designed to reinvigorate the stock market, is necessary in addition to the large-scale tax cut program that is under way. 米連邦準備制度理事会（FRB）の金利引下げの刺激効果を高めるためには、現在実施中の大型減税プログラムに加え、株式市場を再活性化するための投資減税など、財政・税制面からの景気刺激策の速やかな実施が必要である。

tax-exempt bond　非課税債券, 免税債
　(⇒austere fiscal policy)
◆Under this proposal, a government-guaranteed, tax-exempt bond would be issued, targeted chiefly at individuals with large financial assets. この構想では、主に豊富な金融資産を保有する個人をターゲットにして、政府保証付きの非課税債券を発行する。

tax-exempt security　免税証券

tax-free amortization　無税償却　(=nontaxable write-off, tax-free write-off; ⇒write-off)

tax-free disposal of bad loans　不良債権の無税償却
　(=nontaxable write-off of bad loans)

tax haven　租税回避地, 租税逃避地, 租税避難国, 税金天国, タックス・ヘイブン　(=tax shelter)
◆Investment advisory company AIJ started investing in financial derivatives through funds based in the Cayman Islands, a tax haven, since 2002. 投資顧問会社のAIJは、2002年から、租税回避地の英領ケイマン諸島を営業基盤とするファンドを通じて金融派生商品への投資を始めた。◆The foreign investment funds in question were established in overseas tax havens, such as the British Virgin Islands. これらの海外投資ファンドは、英領バージン諸島など海外のタックス・ヘイブン（租税回避地）に設立された。

tax liability　納税額
◆Before the introduction of the bank tax, the major financial institutions' tax liability had been very low, with only the difference between loan losses and business profits deemed taxable. 銀行税の導入前は、貸倒れ損失額と業務利益との差額だけが課税の対象となっていたため、大手金融機関の納税額は低かった。

tax money　公費, 公的資金, 公金　(=public funds)
◆Tax money has been used to cover losses incurred by hotels run across the nation by the central government workers' mutual aid organization. 国家公務員の共済組合が全国各地で経営するホテルの赤字補填字に、公費[公的資金]が充てられていた。

tax payment　税金の支払い, 納税
tax payment in kind　物納
tax payments　税収
◆The man intentionally dodged the tax payments as he transferred the money for asset management to another country. 男は、資産運用の資金を他国に移動させていることから、意図的に納税を免れていた。

tax policy　租税政策, 税制
◆Some of the United States' biggest banks are in for a windfall on top of the $700 billion government bailout thanks to a new tax policy. 米大手銀行の一部は、新税制のおかげで、7,000億ドルの政府救済策[政府の救済措置]に加えて思いがけない利益を上げることになる。

tax refund　税金還付　(⇒benefit from)
◆Since 1976, U.S. tax authorities have twice allowed tax refunds for banks. 1976年以来、米国は銀行については税金還付を2度承認している。

tax return　納税申告(書),税務申告(書),租税申告(書)　(⇒specified account)
◆In the United States, a special deduction system has been implemented that allows investors to carry over capital losses from stock transactions in their current tax return to future years. 米国では、税務申告上、株式売買による譲渡損失を翌年以降に繰り越すことができる特別控除制度が実施されている。◆In their final tax returns, individuals are not required to submit data concerning premium payments into the national pension program. 確定申告の際、個人は国民年金保険料の納付証明書の提出は求められていない。◆We can file a tax return by using the national electronic tax declaration and payment system called e-tax. イー・タックス(e-tax)と呼ばれる国税電子申告・納税システムを利用して、税務申告書を提出する[所得税の確定申告を行う]ことができる。

tax revenue　税収
◆Greece's tax revenues have slackened due to business deterioration. ギリシャの税収は、景気悪化で伸びていない。◆In the case of Japan, the issuance of government bonds exceeds tax revenue. 日本の場合、国債発行額が税収を上回っている。◆In the fiscal 2010 budget, tax revenue accounts for only 40 percent of the total expenditures of ￥92 trillion. 2010年度予算では、税収は92兆円の総歳出の4割を占めるに過ぎない。◆The issuance of government bonds amounts to ￥44 trillion in the fiscal 2011 budget though tax revenues are ￥41 trillion. 2011年度予算では、41兆円の税収に対して国債の発行額は44兆円にのぼる。◆The percentage of government funds from the consumption tax and other tax revenues for financing the basic pension plan remains about 36.5 percent. 基礎年金の財源としての消費税収などによる国の負担金の割合は、まだ約36.5%にとどまっている。◆Without an economic recovery and the resultant recovery of tax revenues, fiscal reconstruction will be made difficult. 景気回復[経済の再生]とそれによる税収の回復がなければ、今後の財政再建もおぼつかない。

tax revenue shortfall　税収不足
◆The massive figure of tax revenue shortfall is way beyond what local municipalities can do by cutting spending. この巨額の税収不足は、地方自治体の経費削減で対応できる範囲を大きく超えている。

tax shelter　租税回避地,租税回避国,税金天国,税金逃れの隠れみの,会計操作,タックス・シェルター　(=tax haven)
◆It's common to shift huge sums of capital to take advantage of international tax shelters. 巨額の資金を移し替えて、国際的な節税策を講じるのは常識だ。

tax system　税制,租税体系
　land and financial tax systems　土地・金融税制
　preferential tax system　優遇税制
　securities tax system　証券税制
◆In order to correct the fragile nature of the banks' capital base, it is necessary to review the tax system. 銀行の自己資本の脆弱(ぜいじゃく)性を是正するためには、税制の見直しが必要だ。

taxable　課税対象となる,課税できる　(⇒business profit)
◆In Japan, if company employees exercise employee stock options and obtain shares, the shares are considered salaried income, which is taxable. 日本では、社員が従業員ストック・オプションの権利を行使して株を取得した場合、その株式は給与所得と見なされ、課税対象になる。◆Losses incurred by writing off nonperforming loans are not generally taxable in the United States. 不良債権処理で生じた損失額は、米国では一般に課税の対象とはならない。

taxable municipal bond　課税地方債(利子所得に対して米連邦税が課される地方債のこと)

taxable write-off　課税償却,有税償却
◆The tax authorities do not allow, in principle, banks to treat the disposal of nonperforming loans as losses, forcing them to make a taxable write-off. 税務当局は、原則として銀行の不良債権処理の損金扱いを認めず、その有税償却を強いている。

taxation system　課税方式,課税制度,税制
◆The taxation system on dividend income from stock trades will be streamlined. 株取引の配当所得に対する課税方式(株式の配当課税方式)が、簡素化される。

taxpayer　(名)納税者,納税義務者
　high-income taxpayer　高所得納税者
　self-assessed taxpayer　申告納税者
　taxpayer identification number　納税者番号
　taxpayer money　納税者の金,国民の税金,公的資金,公金　(=taxpayers' money)
　waste of taxpayers' money　税金の浪費
◆The American taxpayers are keeping American International Group Inc. afloat. (経営再建中の米保険大手)AIGの経営破たんを防いでいるのは、米国の納税者だ。◆The Board of Audit has confirmed that the public financing package extended with a government-backed guarantee to JAL prior to its failure cost taxpayers a total of ￥47 billion. 日航の破たん前に政府保証付きで行われた公的融資の総国民負担額は470億円であることを、会計検査院が確定した。

taxpayer contribution　国民負担金,国民負担額
◆The Board of Audit intends to include the total taxpayer contribution to JAL in its audit account report compiled in November 2011. 会計検査院は、2011年11月にまとめる決算検査報告書に、日航に対する総国民負担額を盛り込む方針だ。

taxpayer numbering system　納税者番号制度　(=taxpayer identification number system)
◆Since these new taxation systems require accurate records of transferred assets and transactions concerning financial products, the government's Tax Commission plans to study the introduction of a taxpayer numbering system. これらの新課税方式には(納税者の)資産移動や金融取引(金融商品に関する取引)の正確な記録が必要なため、政府税制調査会は納税者番号制度の導入を検討する方針だ。

taxpayers' burden　国民の負担,国民負担分
◆Taxpayers' burden from the JAL bailout was lowered to ￥47 billion as the firm repaid part of its outstanding debt. 日航救済による国民の負担分は、日航が債務残高の一部を返済したため、470億円に減少した。

taxpayers' money　納税者の金,国民の税金,税金,税収,公的資金,公金　(=taxpayer money; ⇒public money)
◆About ￥1.9 trillion of taxpayers' money was spent over a ten year span until last fiscal year to cover losses from a surging number of uncollectible loans guaranteed by a public credit guarantee scheme for small and midsize companies. 中小企業のための公的信用保証制度により保証される融資の貸倒れ件数が急増し、それによる損失の穴埋めをするために、昨年度までの10年間で約1兆9,000億円の税金が投入された。◆Banks in the United States and some European countries fell on tough times due to the credit crisis and were bailed out with taxpayers' money. 米国と一部の欧州諸国の銀行が金融危機で経営不安に陥り、公的資金で救済された。◆Banks should not casually depend on taxpayers' money. 銀行は、安易に公的資金に頼るべきではない。◆The Article 102 of the Deposit Insurance Law seeks to protect all deposits at a collapsing bank through injections of taxpayers' money and other public funds. 預金保険法第102条は、税金などの公的資金の注入を通じて破たんしつつある(破たん寸前の)銀行預金の全額保護を求めている。◆The government has injected taxpayers' money into Resona before. 政府は以前、りそなホールディングスに公的資金を注入している。◆The use of

taxpayers' money by the Life Insurance Policyholders Protection Corporation of Japan terminated at the end of March 2009. 生命保険契約者保護機構による公的資金の活用は、2009年3月末で期限が切れた。

team up with ～と協力する，～と提携する，～とチームを組む　(=join forces)
◆au Insurance Co. has started its online insurance sales by teaming up with KDDI. au損害保険(株)は、KDDIと提携して保険のネット販売を開始した。◆NTT Docomo Inc. and SoftBank Mobile Corp. have been offering cell phone-based policy sales by teaming up with nonlife insurers respectively. NTTドコモとソフトバンクモバイルは、それぞれ損保会社と提携して、携帯電話での保険販売のサービスを提供している。

tech-heavy ハイテク株の値動きの影響が大きい，ハイテク株の動きに左右されやすい
◆The tech-heavy 225-issue Nikkei gained 82.03 points to close at 10,452.65. ハイテク株の値動きの影響が大きい日経平均株価(225種)は、前日比82円03銭高の10,452円65銭で引けた。

technical (形)技術の，技術的な，工業技術の，科学技術の，専門的な，技巧的な，実務上の，実用の，市場の内部要因による，人為的な，操作的な，テクニカル
　nonlife net technical provisions　損害保険の正味責任準備金
　technical analysis　テクニカル分析，内的原因分析，チャート分析，罫線(けいせん)分析，テクニカル・アナリシス(株式や外国為替などの相場や出来高の推移をチャートで示して、変化の傾向を読み取ったり将来の相場を予想したりする手法)
　technical balance of trade　技術貿易収支
　technical change　相場の一時的変動，アヤ(「アヤ」は、やや長期的な相場のなかでの特に理由のない小さい変動のことをいう)
　technical conditions　テクニカル要因
　　(=technical factors, technical forces)
　technical correction　アヤ戻し，アヤ押し，相場の一時的変動[アヤ]
　technical default　(事務的な手違いによる)テクニカル・デフォルト
　technical environment　市場の内部環境
　technical factors　テクニカル要因，市場内部要因(信用取引残高、投資家の売買動向、新株発行による資金調達状況、株価規制など、動向株価を動かす要因のうち株式の需給に直接かかわる要因を「市場内部要因」とか「内部要因」という)
　technical forces　テクニカル要因
　technical picture　需給関係
　technical position　取組み，取組み玉関係(証券の信用取引での未決済の売建て玉と買建て玉との関係)，内部要因，内部要因相場，不自然な人為相場
　technical rally　アヤ戻し(technical correction, technical rebound, temporary correction: 株式相場が下げ基調のとき、一時的に少し高くなる場合のことを「アヤ戻し」という)，自律的回復，(景気の)人為的回復
　technical reaction　アヤ押し(株式相場が上げ基調のとき、一時的に少し下がる場合のことを「アヤ押し」という。これに対して、相場が下げ基調のとき、一時的に高くなる場合のことを「アヤ戻し」(technical correction, technical rally, technical rebound, temporary correction)という)
　technical rebound　自律反発，アヤ戻し
　technical reserves　総責任準備金
　technical situation in the market　市場のテクニカル要因
　technical swap　テクニカル・スワップ
　technical trading　裁定取引などの金融技術を活かした売買取引手法

technical recession　2四半期連続のマイナス成長，景気後退，テクニカル・リセッション
◆That eurozone GDP shrank in the second quarter as well would add up to two consecutive quarters of negative growth-a definition of a technical recession. ユーロ圏のGDP(域内総生産)が第2四半期も低下したことで、ユーロ圏は2四半期連続のマイナス成長(定義上、テクニカル・リセッション)となった。◆The eurozone is already in a technical recession. ユーロ圏は、すでに景気後退入りしている。◆Two consecutive quarters of negative growth are defined as a technical recession. 2四半期連続のマイナス成長は、「テクニカル・リセッション」と定義されている。

technical stagnation　技術的停滞
◆The report stresses the need to increase the overall supply capacity through structural reforms as a remedy for economic stagnation. 同報告書は、不況対策として、構造改革によって総供給力を引き上げる必要があると力説している。

technique　(名)技術，技法，手法，方式
　book building [bookbuilding] technique　需要予測方式，ブックビルディング方式
　capital-intensive technique　資本集約的技術
　debt collection technique　債権回収技術
　　(=technique of debt collection)
　dollar-weighted selection technique　金額加重抽出法
　financing techniques　金融技術
　hedging techniques　ヘッジ手法
　portfolio management techniques　ポートフォリオ管理手法，ポートフォリオ・マネジメント技術
　qualification techniques for creditworthiness　与信技術
　risk assessment techniques　リスク査定手法
　risk management techniques　リスク管理手法

"teigaku" postal deposit certificate　定額貯金

temblor　(名)地震
◆The insurance world should disclose to consumers such basic data as the percentage of earthquake insurance payouts made in full after previous temblors. 保険業界は、これまでの地震で地震保険の満額支払いが行われた割合はどれくらいかなどの基本的なデータを、消費者に開示すべきだ。

temporal method　属性法，テンポラル法　(=temporal approach: 外貨で評価されているものは現金で、債権・債務と時価で評価されているものは決算日レートで、取引日の評価額で評価されているものは取引日レートで換算する外貨換算方法)

temporarily　(副)一時的に，暫定的に，いったんは
◆A chain-reaction global decline in stock values was temporarily stopped by a barrage of countermeasures. 世界的な株安連鎖は、矢継ぎ早の対策でいったんは歯止めがかかった。

temporary　(形)一時的な，臨時の，暫定的，仮の
　file (for) a temporary court injunction　差止めのための仮処分を申し立てる
　temporary assignment [posting, transfer]　出向
　temporary borrowings　一時借入金
　temporary difference　一時的差異
　temporary disability compensation　休業補償給付
　Temporary Guarantee Program for Money Market Funds　(米国の)MMF一時保証プログラム，MMF保証プログラム
　Temporary Liquidity Guarantee Program　(米国の)一時的流動性保証プログラム
　temporary suspension of trading　取引の一時停止
◆Dollar-selling pressure has eased and put a temporary brake on the sharp appreciation of the yen and the fall of the dollar. ドル売り圧力が弱まり、急激な円高・ドル安にいったん歯止めがかかった。

temporary cash investments 短期投資, 一時投資, 短期的資金運用投資
◆We reduced our balance of cash and temporary cash investments over the last two years. 当社は、過去2年間にわたって現金と短期投資の残高を圧縮しました。

temporary nationalization 一時国有化, 一時国営化
◆In the temporary nationalization, the government will take possession of all shares from the bank's holding company at no cost. 一時国有化で、政府は同行の持ち株会社から株式をゼロ円で全株取得することになる。

temporary phenomenon 一時的な現象, 一時的現象
◆The current deflationary trend seems to be a temporary phenomenon caused by the correction in oil prices after they skyrocketed last year. 現在のデフレ傾向は、昨年の原油高の反動による一時的な現象のようだ。

temporary stagnant period 景気の足踏み, 踊り場
◆The Japanese economy has entered a temporary stagnant period. 日本経済は、景気が足踏みする踊り場入りした。

ten bagger テンバガー（10倍になる銘柄）

tender 入札, 応募入札, 入札書, 申込み, 提出, 提供, 提出物, 提供物, テンダー （⇒self tender）

tender offer 株式公開買付け, テンダー・オファー（＝public tender offer, takeover bid, takeover offer, TOB; ⇒expiry date, public tender offer, Williams Act）

  cash tender offer　現金公開買付け
  friendly cash tender offer　友好的現金公開買付け
  hostile cash tender offer　敵対的現金公開買付け
◆Following the tender offer, Oji Paper would acquire the remaining Hokuetsu shares through a share swap to turn it into a wholly owned subsidiary. 株式公開買付け（TOB）後に、王子製紙は、株式交換で残りの北越製紙の株を取得して北越製紙を完全子会社化する。◆Ford's debt restructuring includes conversion of debt to equity and cash tender offers. 米フォードの債務再編には、債務の株式化や現金による株式の公開買付けが含まれている。◆Fuji Television Network Inc. has cut its equity stake acquisition goal in a tender offer for radio station Nippon Broadcasting System Inc. to 25 percent from the initially eyed stake of more than 50 percent. フジテレビジョン（フジテレビ）は、日本放送（ラジオ放送局）株式会社の株式公開買付け（TOB）で、株式持ち分の取得目標を当初計画していた50％超から25％に引き下げた。◆In the 21-day tender offer, a surprisingly large number of individual shareholders accepted the deal. 21日間の株式公開買付け（TOB）で、当初の予想を上回って多くの個人株主がTOBに応募した。◆Sumitomo Corp. has concluded its tender offer for Jupiter Telecommunications Co. 住友商事が、ジュピターテレコムの株式公開買付け（TOB）を完了した。

解説 株式公開買付けとは：一般の証券取引市場の外で行われる大口証券購入の申込みのこと。経営権の獲得をねらった買収目的のものが多い。新聞などで買付けの期間や株式数、価格などを公表して、一般株主に株式の買取りを提案するが、市場価格にプレミアムを上乗せした価格を提示するのが一般的である。

tense （形）緊張した, 緊迫した, 張りつめた, 硬直した
  a tense atmosphere　張りつめた空気
  a tense moment　張りつめた瞬間
  a tense situation　緊迫した状況
  grow tense　緊張感が高まる
◆The situation surrounding the Japanese economy has suddenly grown tense due to the first bankruptcy of a Japanese insurer in seven years. 7年ぶりの日本の生保破たんで、日本経済を取り巻く環境は一気に緊迫感が高まっている。

tension （名）緊張, 不安, 緊迫, 緊張関係, 緊迫状態, 均衡, 拮抗, 張り, 張力, 電圧
  a state of tension　緊張状態
  cooperation and tension　協調と緊張
  currency tensions　通貨間の緊張
  heightened tensions　緊張の高まり
  international tensions　国際間の緊張
  political tensions　政治的な緊張
  rising tensions　緊張の高まり
  tensions between A and B　AとB間の緊迫状態, AとBのぶつかり合い
  the relaxation［easing］of international tensions　国際間の緊張緩和
◆Ahead of the current vigorous stock market, there are still some hurdles such as increasing tension in Iraq and foreign exchange issues. 活発な株式市場の先行きには、まだイラク情勢の緊迫化や為替問題などのハードルがある。◆Heightened tensions and significant downward risks for the global economy must be addressed decisively. 世界経済の緊張の高まりと重大な下方リスクに、断固として対処しなければならない。

term （名）期間, 契約期間, 専門用語, 用語, 定期不動産権, 条件（複数形で用いられることが多い）, 条項, 規定, 約定, 合意
（⇒loan facility, long-term interest rate）
  credit terms　支払い条件
  dollar terms　金額ベース, ドル換算, ドル・ベース, ドル表示　（＝dollar-denominated terms）
  during the term of this agreement　本契約の期間中
  financial terms and conditions　財務条件, 金銭的条件, 取引の条件
  in nominal terms　名目ベースで, 名目で
  in real terms　実質ベースで, 実質で, 実勢価格で
  in terms of value　金額ベースで
  in value terms　名目ベースで（＝in terms of value）
  in volume terms　実質ベースで
  in yen terms　円換算で
  issue terms　発行条件　（＝terms of issue）
  medium term debt　中期債
  payment terms　支払い条件
  term financing　中・長期金融
  Term Securities Lending Facility　ターム証券貸出制度, TSLF
  term to maturity　満期
  terms of settlement　決済条件
  the accounting term ending in September 2012　2012年9月期, 2012年9月中間決算, 2012年9月に終了する会計期間
  the business term ending in late March 2012　2012年3月期, 2012年3月期決算, 2012年3月末に終了する事業期間
  the term ended March 2012　2012年3月期
　（⇒red）
  trade terms　貿易条件, 貿易支払い条件, 貿易用語, 取引用語
  value term　金額ベース
  variable terms　変動型条件
◆Financial terms of the transaction were not disclosed. 取引の条件［財務条件］は、公表されなかった。◆For individuals to be able to invest on equal terms with business corporations, they should be allowed to make a deferred deduction of capital losses made through stock transactions. 個人が法人と同じ条件で投資できるようにするため、個人の株式譲渡損（株式売買による譲渡損失）の繰延べ控除を認めるべきだ。◆Gross domestic product during the April-June quarter rose only 0.4 percent in real terms from the previous quarter. 4-6月期の国内総生産（GDP）は、実質で前期（1-3月期）に比べて0.4％増にとどまった。◆Gross domestic product will rise 2

percent in inflation-adjusted real terms and 2.2 percent in nominal terms in the current fiscal year from the previous fiscal year. 今年度の国内総生産（GDP）の成長率は、物価変動の影響を除いた実質で前年度比2%、名目で2.2%になる見通しだ。◆Sales of the overseas subsidiaries of Japanese companies grew 17.3 percent in U.S. dollar terms in the January-March quarter from a year earlier. 1-3月期の日本企業の海外子会社の売上高が、米ドル・ベースで前年同期比17.3%伸びた。◆The Stability and Growth Pact lost its spine in 2003 as the Germany government requested the relaxation of its terms. ユーロ圏の財政安定化・成長協定は、ドイツがその条件緩和を要求したため、2003年に骨抜きになった。

term deposits　定期預金, 定期性預金
◆Full protection for term deposits ended in April 2002. 定期性預金の全額保護は、2002年4月に終了した。

term-end settlement of accounts　期末決算
◆In the term-end settlement of accounts at the end of September, most companies use the daily average for a month of the share prices in gauging the value of latent gains or losses in their stockholdings. 9月末の期末決算で［9月中間決算で］、大半の企業は、保有株式の含み損益を算出する際に株価の月中平均を使っている。

term insurance coverage　定期保険保障
◆Family insurance policy is a whole life insurance policy that provides term insurance coverage on the insured's spouse and children. 家族保険契約は、被保険者の配偶者と子どもに定期保険保障を与える終身生命保険だ。

term loan　有期貸付け, ターム・ローン,（期間1-10年の）長期貸出
　amortizing term loan　分割償還型のターム・ローン
　intermediate-term loan　中期ローン
　long-term loan　長期ローン, 長期貸付け金, 長期融資
　short-term loan　短期ローン, 短期貸付け金, 短期融資
　swaption term loan facility　スワップション付きターム・ローン
　syndicated term loan　協調ターム・ローン
　syndication of a term loan for　～向けターム・ローンの協調融資
　tax-spared term loan　見なし課税負担型ターム・ローン
　vanilla term loan with a bullet repayment　一括返済型の単純なターム・ローン

term structure　期間構造
　term structure of interest rates　金利の期間構造
　term structure of volatility　ボラティリティの期間構造

terminate　(動)（契約を）終了させる, 解除する, 解約する, 解消する, 打ち切る, 終了する
　automatically terminate　自動終了する, 自動的に解除し終了する
　terminate this agreement or any part thereof　本契約またはその一部を解除する
　unconditionally terminate　無条件で終了する, 無条件で終了させる, 無条件で解除する
　unless earlier terminated as provided for in this agreement　本契約に定めるとおり早期終了しないかぎり, 本契約に規定するとおり中途終了する場合を除いて
◆Kirin-Suntory merger talks were terminated due to a disagreement over the merger ratio and other conditions. キリンとサントリーの経営統合交渉は、統合比率などの条件が折り合わないため、打ち切られた。◆The use of taxpayers' money by the Life Insurance Policyholders Protection Corporation of Japan terminated at the end of March 2009. 生命保険契約者保護機構による公的資金の活用は、2009年3月末で期限が切れた。

termination　(名)（契約の）終了,（期間の）満了, 解約, 解除, 解消, 打切り,（権利の）消滅, 解散
◆The termination of the Financial Function Early Strength-ening Law was decided because fears over Japanese financial system had subsided. 金融機能強化法の打切りが決まったのは、日本の金融システム不安が沈静化したためだ。

territory　(名)領土, 領地, 領域, 分野, 区域, 範囲, ゾーン, 販売区域, 販売地域, 販売領域, 担当区域, 商標やソフトウエア・プログラムなど知的財産権の使用許諾地域, 許諾地域, 契約地域, レベル, テリトリー
　(⇒negative territory)
　business territory　商圏, 商勢圏
　in negative territory　下落して, 減少して
　in positive territory　上昇して, 増加して
　junk territory　投資不適格のレベル
　minus territory　マイナス基調, マイナス
　negative territory　マイナス, マイナス基調, マイナスの領域　(=minus territory)
　neutral territory　中立ゾーン
　positive territory　プラス, プラス基調, プラスの領域
　remain in negative territory　マイナス基調が続いている
◆Prices will enter positive territory during fiscal 2011. 物価は、2011年度中にプラスの領域に入る見通しだ。◆The CPI has remained in negative territory in recent years. 消費者物価指数は、ここ数年来マイナス基調が続いている。◆The diffusion index for small and midsize manufacturers improved five points to plus 2, hitting positive territory for the first time in 13 years. 中小企業・製造業の業況判断指数が、前回調査より5ポイント改善してプラス2となり、13年ぶりにプラスに転じた。◆The diffusion index of business sentiment among large manufacturers recovered to positive territory for the first time in two quarters. 大企業・製造業の業況判断指数(DI)は、2四半期(半年)ぶりにプラスに転じた。◆The 225-issue Nikkei Stock Average continued its plunge Thursday, momentarily dipping into 8,100 territory. 日経平均株価(225種)が10日(10月10日)も急落し、一時8,100円台まで下落した。◆The yen in record strong territory of ￥76 to the dollar causes hardships in the Japanese economy. 1ドル＝76円台の史上最高の円高水準は、日本経済にとって厳しい。◆Two influential rating firms lowered Ford Motor Co.'s credit ratings a notch deeper into junk territory. 大手[有力な]格付け機関2社が、米フォードの信用格付けを「投資不適格レベル」にさらに1段階引き下げた。

terror funds　テロ資金　(=funds for terrorists)

terrorism　テロ行為, 暴力行為　(⇒coverage)
◆Financial institutions are obliged to report deals suspected to be linked to terrorism to the financial authorities. 金融機関は、テロ行為に絡んだ疑いのある取引については、金融当局への届出義務が課されている。

terrorism-related insurance　テロ関連保険
◆Reinsurance companies around the world have refused to provide terrorism-related insurance since Sept. 11. 世界の再保険会社は、2001年9月11日の米同時テロ以来、テロ関連保険の引受けを拒んでいる。

terrorist organization　テロ組織
◆A revised Foreign Exchange and Foreign Trade Control Law has been enacted to enable the swift freezing of funds belonging to terrorist organizations. テロ組織の資金[資産]凍結を迅速に行うための改正外為法は、すでに成立して[制定されて]いる。

test　(動)試験する, 探る, 試す, 検定する
　test resistance　抵抗線を試す
　test the market　市場の反応を探る

test　(名)（判断の）基準, 条項, 試験, 実験, 試査, チェック, 検査, テスト
　acid-test ratio [rate]　酸性試験比率（会社の当座資産に対する流動資産の割合）, 当座比率
　　(=liquid ratio test, quick asset ratio)

  additional bonds test　追加債務基準
  audit test　監査テスト
  compliance test　準拠性テスト
  credit test　信用度試験
  creditor's tests of creditworthiness　与信判断
  debt (incurrence) test　負債基準
  dividend payment tests　配当制限条項
  leverage test　負債比率
  means test　資産調査
  private loan financing test　民間貸付け基準
  private security or payment test　民間保証・支払い基準
  qualified thrift lender test　適格貯蓄金融機関貸し手テスト
  stress test　金融の特別検査, 金融機関のストレス・テスト
  test of controls　内部統制のテスト
  ◆Europe's seven banks judged to have capital shortfall by the stress test will work on increasing their capital. ストレス・テスト(特別検査)で資本不足と認定された欧州の7銀行は、これから資本増強に取り組む。◆The United States may have to be subject to the harsh credit tests under which EU nations labor as the U.S. credit has come into question. 米国の信用が疑われているので米国も、EU諸国が苦労している厳しい信用度試験[テスト]を受ける必要があるかもしれない。

theory　(名)理論, 原理, 理屈, 公理, 定理, 学説, ～説, ～論, 憶測
  bullionist theory　地金主義
  capital market theory　資本市場理論
  decoupling theory　ディカップリング論
  dynamic theory of interest　利子動態説
  equity theory　持ち分理論
  finance theory　金融理論
  fund theory　資金理論
  interest rate parity theory　金利パリティ理論
  issue equity theory　発行持ち分説
  lender's preference theory　貸し手の選好理論
  liquidity preference theory　流動性選好説[理論]
  liquidity premium theory　流動性プレミアム理論
  loanable funds theory　貸付け資金説
  modern financial theory　現代財務理論
  neo-quantity theory of money　新貨幣数量説
  over-investment theory　過剰投資説
  over-saving theory　過剰貯蓄説
  productivity theory of interest　利子生産力説
  psychological theory of business cycles　心理的景気理論
  psychological theory of exchange　為替心理説
  purchasing power theory of money　貨幣購買力説
  quantity theory of money　貨幣数量説
  relative supply of gold theory　金数量説
  savings investment theory of income determination　貯蓄・投資の所得決定論
  the theories of business [trade] cycles　景気理論
  the theory of asset preference　資産選好理論
  the theory of credit creation　信用創造論
  the theory of inflation　インフレの原理
  the theory of international indebtedness　国際貸借説
  the theory of portfolio selection　資産選択理論
  the theory of purchasing power parity　購買力平価説
  ◆The so-called decoupling theory holds that the effects of a U.S. slowdown can be offset by growth in emerging nations. いわゆるディカップリング論では、米経済の減速は新興国の成長が補う、と考えられている。

thin margin　薄利, 低い利益率
thin market　薄商い市場, 閑散市場, 手薄な市場, 市場低迷, 閑散 (活況市場=active market)
thin trading　薄商い (=thin volume)
third party　第三者
  ◆Customers whose assets at the bank total about ¥10 million will receive a maximum of ¥2 million in insurance if their money is withdrawn illicitly by a third party with a bogus card. 同行では、預け入れ資産が1,000万円程度の預金者が、第三者に偽造カードを使って不正に預金が引き出された場合には、最大200万円の保険金が支払われる。◆The company procured about ¥50 billion through an allocation of newly issued shares to third parties, including the Development Bank of Japan. 同社は、日本政策投資銀行などを引受先とする第三者割当増資で、約500億円を調達した。

third-party allotment　第三者割当て (=allocation of new shares to a third party, third-party share allotment)
  ◆The struggling firm will raise ¥4.5 billion via third-party allotment. 経営再建中の同社は、第三者割当て(第三者割当て増資)で45億円を調達する。
  解説 第三者割当てとは：役員や従業員, 取引先, 提携先, 金融機関など発行会社と特別な関係にあるものに新株の引受権を与えて、新株を発行すること。収益力が乏しいため普通の増資ができない場合や、取引先・提携先との関係を緊密にするために行われることが多い。

third-party panel　第三者委員会
  ◆The cover-up of investment losses by Olympus was discovered during an investigation by the company's third-party panel. オリンパスによる投資損失処理の偽装工作は、同社の第三者委員会の調査で判明した。

third-party share allotment　第三者株式割当て, 第三者割当て増資
  ◆Under the third-party share allotment scheme, the bank will allocate 116 million new shares to about 8,000 companies and investors with each share priced at ¥130. この第三者株式割当て計画によると、同行は、約8,000の企業と個人投資家に1株130円で1億1,600万株の新株を割り当てる。

third-sector insurance market　第三分野の保険市場 (⇒insurance market)
  ◆The third-sector insurance market has expanded rapidly since deregulation in 2001 allowed domestic major nonlife insurers to take part in. 第三分野の保険市場は、2001年に国内大手損保にも参入が解禁されてから急速に拡大している。
  解説 第三分野の保険市場とは：人の死に対して定額の保険金を支払う生命保険が第一分野。自動車や家財など人以外の損害を補填(ほてん)する保険金を支払う損害保険が第二分野。第三分野は、がん保険や医療保険など、病気にかかったり、けがをしたりした場合に保険金を支払う保険のこと。

threat　(名)脅威, 兆し, 前兆, 恐れ, 懸念, 可能性, 阻害要因, 脅迫, 威嚇(いかく), 脅し
  competitive threat　競争圧力, 競争力で後れをとること
  deflationary threat　デフレの恐れ
  external threat　外部からの脅威
  global threats　地球規模の脅威
  inflation threat　インフレの恐れ
  pose financial threats to　～の財政負担になる
  recessionary threat　景気後退の恐れ
  the threat of renewed inflation　インフレ再発の恐れ, インフレ再発の脅威
  ◆In the United States, the Exon-Florio provision of the 1988 trade law can prevent takeover bids that are deemed a threat to national security. 米国では、1988年通商法のエクソン・フロリオ条項で、国家の安全保障上、脅威と考えられる企業買

収を阻止することができる。◆The threat of the overheated state of European countries and China causing new waves of financial turmoil must not be underestimated. 欧米諸国や中国などの景気過熱状態が新たな金融危機[金融市場の混乱]を引き起こす恐れがあることを、過小評価してはならない。◆The weak yen is a threat to U.S. economic recovery. 円安は、アメリカの景気回復を脅かす要因だ。

threaten (動)脅(おど)す, 脅迫する, 威嚇する, ～すると言って脅す, (安全などを)脅(おびや)かす, 危うくする, 危険にさらす, ～の兆候がある, ～しそうだ
  be threatened with ～の危機に瀕している, ～の危機にさらされている
  threaten to ～すると脅す, ～する恐れがある
◆Rising prices threaten to damage the economy. 物価上昇で、経済は打撃を受けそうだ[物価上昇は、経済に打撃を与えそうだ]。◆Spendthrift nations' overspending threatens Europe's single currency. 財政赤字国の過剰支出が、欧州のユーロを脅かしている。◆The debt crisis in Greece threatened to spread to Portugal, Ireland and Spain. ギリシャの財政危機は、ポルトガルやアイルランド、スペインなどに波及する恐れがあった。◆The massive negative yields of the life insurance industry threaten the financial soundness of insurers. 生保業界の巨額の逆ざやが、生保各社の財務上の健全性[経営の健全性]を脅(おびや)かしている。

three months ended July 31 5-7月期
◆For the three months ended July 31, the company lost $2.03 billion, or 67 cents per share. 5-7月期は、同社は20億3,000万ドル(1株当たり67セント)の赤字を出した。

threshold (名)基準, 水準, 上限, 識域, 抵抗線, 閾(いき), 境界, 限界点, 賃金の物価スライド制, 戸口, 出発点, 門出, 発端
  boom-or-bust threshold of 50 percent 50%の景気判断の分かれ目, 50%の景気判断分岐点
  close below the 1 percent threshold 1%の水準[大台]を割り込んで取引を終える
  dive below the key threshold of ～の大台を割り込む
  dive below the threshold of ～の水準を割り込む
    (=drop below the threshold of)
  exposure threshold リスク限度額
  sink below the 1 percent threshold 1%の水準[大台]を割り込む, 1%割れの水準まで低下する
  the key threshold of ～の重要な水準, ～の大台, ～の大きな境目
◆A key gauge of the current state of the economy fell below the boom-or-bust threshold of 50 percent in September for the first time in five months. 景気の現状を示す主要基準(景気一致指数)が、9月は5か月ぶりに景気判断の分かれ目となる50%を下回った。◆The 10-year JGB yield sank below the 1 percent threshold. 新発10年物の日本国債の流通利回りが、1%割れの水準まで低下した。◆The 225-issue Nikkei Stock Average dived below the key threshold of 10,000 as investors were disappointed with the continuing delay in the disposal of banks' bad loans and an overnight plunge in U.S. stocks. 日経平均株価(225種)は、投資家が銀行等の不良債権処理が引き続き遅れることや前日の米株価の大幅下落に失望して、1万円の大台を割り込んだ。◆The yield on the benchmark 10-year Japanese government bond closed below the 1 percent threshold. 長期金利の指標となる新発10年物日本国債の流通利回り[利回り]が、年1%の大台を割り込んで取引を終えた。

thrift (名)倹約, 節約, 貯蓄金融機関(S&L), 貯蓄銀行
  Office of Thrift Supervision 貯蓄金融機関監督局
  thrift and savings plans 貯蓄制度
  thrift industry 貯蓄金融業界, S&L業界
  thrift industry bailout S&L救済
  thrift insolvency[failure] 貯蓄金融機関の破たん
  thrift institutions 米貯蓄金融機関 (=thrifts)
  thrift shop[store] (慈善目的の)中古品店
    (=charity shop)
  thrifts 米貯蓄金融機関 (=thrift institutions: 相互貯蓄銀行(mutual savings bank)、貯蓄貸付け組合(savings and loan association)と信用組合(credit union)の総称)

thriving (形)盛況な, 好況の, 好調な, 繁盛する, 繁栄する, 栄える, 成功する, 成長[生長]する
  thriving business 好況産業
  thriving company 成長企業, 成功している企業, 繁盛している会社
  thriving market 好調な市場, 市場の盛況
◆Japanese exporting firms have been enjoying positive earnings, benefiting from thriving markets in the United States and the weak yen. 日本の輸出企業は、米国の好調な市場と円安を追い風に、好業績が続いている。

thwart (動)(計画などを)妨害する, 邪魔する, 阻止する, 阻(はば)む, 妨げる, くじく, 失敗させる, 挫折させる, (見通しなどを)台なしにする, ～の裏をかく
  thwart aid activities 支援活動を妨げる
  thwart the plan 計画を阻止する, 計画の裏をかく
◆Myojo Foods asked Nissin Food Products to play the part of a white knight by forming a capital alliance to thwart the U.S. investment fund's hostile takeover bid. 米系投資ファンドの敵対的TOB(株式公開買付け)を阻止するため、明星食品は資本提携によるホワイト・ナイト(白馬の騎士)としての明星の支援を日清食品に要請した。

Tibor 東京銀行間取引金利, 東京銀行間貸し手金利, タイボー (Tokyo inter-bank offered rateの略。⇒LIBOR)

tick (名)株価などの値動き, 付け, 掛売り, ティック (「ティック」は、米財務省証券、政府機関証券の価格表示の1単位価格の刻み。1ティック=1/8ポイントで12.5セントに相当)
  buy on tick 付けで買う
  down-tick 値下がり, 景気の退潮, ダウンティック (=downtick, minus tick: 有価証券の取引が、直前に成立した取引価格より低い価格で成立すること)
  minimum tick size 最小値幅
  minus tick 値下がり, マイナス・ティック
    (=down-tick, downtick)
  plus tick 値上がり, プラス・ティック
    (=up-tick, uptick)
  plus-tick rule プラス・ティック規則 (=uptick rule: 米証券取引委員会の証券の空売りに関する規則)
  put a tick in the box 空欄にチェック・マークをつける
  tick mark チェック・マーク, チェックして照合済みの印
    (=check mark)
  tick size 呼び値の単位, 値幅
  tick up 小幅上昇する
  up-tick 値上がり, 好景気, アップティック (=plus tick, uptick: 有価証券の取引が、直前に成立した取引価格より高い価格で成立すること)
  up-tick rule アップティック規則, 証券の空売りに関する規則 (=plus-tick rule)
  zero-minus tick ゼロ・マイナス・ティック (=zero downtick: 有価証券の取引が、直前に成立した取引価格と同じ価格で成立すること。ただし、直前の取引価格がすでにその前の取引価格より低い場合をいう)
  zero-plus tick ゼロ・プラス・ティック (=zero-plus-tick, zero upstick: 有価証券の取引が、直前に成立した取引価格と同じ価格で成立すること。ただし、直前の取引価格がすでにその前の取引価格より高い場合をいう)

ticker (名)株式相場表, 相場表示機, 相場速報機, 株式相

場速報機, 相場速報機, チッカー
　ticker symbol　株式略称（マイクロソフト（Microsoft Corporation）の「MSFT」やIBM（International Business Machines Corporation）の「IBM」など、証券取引所や店頭市場で取引されている株式の銘柄の略称）
　ticker tape　株式相場表テープ, 株式相場表示板, チッカー・テープ（相場表示機から出てくるテープ）
ticket　(名)伝票, 報告書, 取引, 取引額, 割当額, 券, 札, チケット
　deposit ticket　預金伝票
　number ticket　番号札
　order ticket　注文伝票
　piece work tickets　出来高報告書
　sales ticket　クレジット・カード
　ticket-day　ロンドン証券取引所の規約規定の伝票回付日
　tickets at the colead level　共同主幹事の割当額
　write tickets　取引をまとめる
　◆Many smaller tickets were also written. 多くの小口[小口取引]の買いも入った。
tie　(動)つなぐ, 結びつける, 連動させる, リンクさせる, 縛る, 結ぶ, 束縛する, 拘束する
　be tied to　～に連動する, ～と結びついている, ～とリンクしている, ～に関連する
　rates tied to prime, LIBOR or U.S. Treasury bills　プライム・レート, ロンドン銀行間取引金利（LIBOR）または米財務省短期証券の利回り
　tied aid　ひも付き援助, タイド・エイド
　tied crude oil　ひも付き原油
　tied loan program　ひも付き借款
　tied store [shop]　連鎖店　(=chained store)
　tied transaction　ひも付き取引, 連結取引
　◆As the time-limit measure ended, the government decided to institutionalize the tied loan program as a lasting measure. 時限切れを迎えたため、政府はひも付き円借款を恒久措置として制度化することにした。◆Floating rate payments are based on rates tied to prime, LIBOR or U.S. Treasury bills. 変動金利の支払い利率は、プライム・レート、ロンドン銀行間取引金利または米財務省短期証券の利回りに基づいて決定されます。
tie　(名)つながり, 結びつき, 絆（きずな）, 縁, 関係, ひも, 結び目, コード, ネクタイ, 足手まとい, 重荷, 同点, 引き分け, 再試合
　close ties to　～と親しい間柄[関係]
　cross-shareholding ties　株式持ち合い関係
　economic ties　経済関係
　friendly ties　友好関係
　strengthen ties　提携を強化する
　◆European and U.S. firms are energetically promoting closer ties with Chinese universities, including Beijing University and Tsinghua University. 欧米企業は、北京大や清華大など中国の大学との連携を密にしている。◆Hostile mergers and acquisitions have been increasing rapidly as the dissolution of cross-shareholding ties among companies accelerates. 企業間の株式持ち合い関係の解消が加速するにつれ、敵対的M&A（企業の合併・買収）の件数は急増している。◆The upcoming negotiations will determine practical measures to strengthen ties, including the merger ratio, the name of the new group and the positions to be held by top executives. 今後の交渉で、統合比率や新グループの名称、首脳人事など提携強化の具体策を詰める。
tie up　(動)提携する, 連携する, 協力する　(⇒automobile insurance)
　◆MFG, the nation's largest financial group, tied up with two major U.S. banks to strengthen its earning power. 国内金融グループ最大のみずほフィナンシャルグループが、収益力の強化を図るため、米銀大手2行と提携した。◆Softbank and Deutche Bank will tie up in online finance. ソフトバンクとドイツ銀行が、オンライン金融で提携する。◆Tokio Marine & Nichido Fire Insurance Co. tied up with NTT Docomo Inc. in April 2011 to offer Docomo One-time Hoken insurance. 東京海上日動火災保険は、2011年4月にNTTドコモと提携して、「ドコモワンタイム保険」を提供している。
tie-up　(名)提携, 合併, 統合, 協力, 結びつき, 業務の一時停止, タイアップ　(=alliance; ⇒alliance strategy, comprehensive tie-up, revitalization firm)
　capital and business tie-up　資本・業務提携　(=capital and business ties)
　comprehensive tie-up　包括的提携
　equity tie-up　資本提携
　strategic tie-up　戦略的提携
　tie-up negotiations　提携交渉
　◆NTT DoCoMo Inc. formed a capital tie-up with Internet shopping mall operator Rakuten Inc. in the Internet auction business. NTTドコモが、インターネット・オークション事業で電子商取引大手の楽天[仮想商店街を運営している楽天]と資本提携した。◆The tie-up included a contribution by Mitsubishi Tokyo to the UFJ group's planned capital increase. 統合には、UFJグループが予定していた増資に三菱銀行の出資もこまれていた。◆The tie-up will create the world's largest banking group, with total assets of ¥190 trillion. 統合によって、総資産が190兆円の世界最大の銀行（金融）グループが誕生する。
tie-up agreement　提携契約, 業務提携契約
　◆The five business fields in the tie-up agreement are product development, marketing, insurance underwriting, damage assessment and reinsurance. 提携契約の5業務分野は、商品開発、マーケティング、保険引受け、損害査定と再保険である。◆Tokio Marine and Fire Insurance Co. concluded a tie-up agreement covering five business fields with the leading Chinese nonlife insurance company, the People's Insurance Company of China（PICC）, and Samsung Fire and Marine Insurance, a South Korean nonlife insurance company. 東京海上火災保険は、中国最大手の損害保険会社の中国人民保険公司（PICC）および韓国最大手の損保、サムスン火災海上保険と、5業務分野での提携契約を結んだ。
tied loan　ひも付き円借款, ひも付き融資, ひも付き援助, タイド・ローン　(=tied yen loans)
　◆In offering the special yen loans, the government adopted tied loans limited to three years. 特別円借款を供与する際、政府は3年間の時限措置としてひも付き円借款を導入した。
tied yen loan　ひも付き円借款
　◆The repayment period of the new tied yen loans will be set at 40 years. 新ひも付き円借款の償還期間は今後、40年とされる。
tier　(名)段, 段階, 層, 階層, ティア　(⇒shift名詞)
　core tier 1　コア・ティア1（普通株と利益から生まれる内部留保（利益剰余金）に限定した「狭義の中核的自己資本」）
　first-tier bank　大手行, 上位行
　lower tier-two capital　ローワーTier 2資本
　primary（Tier 1）capital　自己資本の基本的項目
　second-tier bank　準大手行
　second-tier life insurer　中堅生命保険
　second-tier or smaller（financial）institutions　中堅以下の金融機関
　supplementary（Tier 2）capital　自己資本の補完的項目
　tier-two capital　補完的自己資本, 自己資本の補完的項目, 二次資本　(=secondary capital)
　top-tier AAA credit rating　最上位のトリプルAの格付け, 最上級のAAA[トリプルA]の格付け

top-tier group　先頭集団
top-tier stock　高業績株
two tier bid　二重価格買付け（株式公開買付けで2種類の買取り価格を提示すること）
two-tier exchange system　二重為替相場制
two-tier market　二重為替市場, 二重相場制
　（=two-tier foreign exchange market）
two tier price　二重価格
upper tier-two capital　アッパーTier 2資本
◆Europe's 7 banks judged by the stress test to have capital shortfalls are second-tier or smaller institutions. ストレス・テスト（特別検査）で資本不足と認定された欧州の7銀行は、いずれも中堅以下の銀行だ。◆MTFG and the UFJ group have second-tier securities houses respectively. 三菱東京フィナンシャル・グループとUFJグループは、それぞれ準大手の証券会社（三菱証券とUFJつばさ証券）を抱えている。◆The Bank of Japan decided to extend a special loan to Namihaya Bank after the second-tier regional bank was declared insolvent. 日本銀行は、第二地方銀行の「なみはや銀行」が破たん認定を受けた後、同行に対して特別融資［特融］を実施することを決めた。◆The number of progressive income tax brackets will be increased from current four tiers to six. 累進税率区分の数が、現行の4段階から6段階に引き上げられる。◆The United States lost its top-tier AAA credit rating from S&P for the first time. 米国債の格付け［米国の長期国債格付け］が、スタンダード・アンド・プアーズ（S&P）による最上級のAAA（トリプルA）の格付けから史上初めて転落した。

tier-one［Tier 1］capital　資本金や法定準備金などの中核的自己資本, 中核資本, ティア1自己資本, 一次資本, 自己資本の基本的項目　（=core capital, primary capital; ⇒capital adequacy, core tier［Tier］1）
　Tier 1 capital guideline　自己資本の基本的項目基準, 基本的項目基準
　Tier 1 capital ratio　Tier 1自己資本比率
◆A bank's core capital, or Tier 1 capital, is deemed to have high loss-absorbency and resilience. 銀行の中核的自己資本は、損失吸収力と弾力性が高いとされている。◆At five of the seven banking groups, the percentage of deferred tax assets against the tier-one capital exceeded 50 percent. 銀行・金融7グループのうち5グループでは、資本金など中核的自己資本に占める繰延べ税金資産の割合が50%を超えた。

tier-one［Tier 1］capital ratio　Tier 1自己資本比率
◆Among the 91 banks the EU subjected to the stress test, seven banks' tier one capital ratio fell below 6 percent. EU（欧州連合）がストレス・テスト（特別検査）の対象にした91行のうち、7行のティア1自己資本比率が6%を割り込んだ［7行が自己資本不足だった］。

tight　（形）厳しい, きつい, 身動きできない, 狭い, 厄介な, 困難な, 厳重な, 厳格な, 徹底した, 緊張した,（金融市場が）ひっ迫した, 金詰まりの, 高利で金を借りにくい, 余裕がない, 品薄の, 入手しにくい,（物が）不足している, 接戦の, 勢力伯仲の, 互角の, ～を通さない, 防［耐］～の
　be in a tight corner［place, spot, squeeze］　困難な状況にある, 進退きわまっている, 窮地に陥っている
　maintain short-term money rates at a tight level　短期市場金利を高めに維持する
　tight budget　きつい予算, 緊縮予算, 予算の引締め, 予算不足
　tight budget policy　緊縮予算政策
　tight credit　信用ひっ迫, 金融ひっ迫
　tight economy　ひっ迫した経済
　tight financing policy　緊縮財政政策
　tight lending　貸し渋り, 貸出の抑制
　　（=credit crunch）
　tight market　ひっ迫した市場, ひっ迫市場, ひっ迫市況, 資金不足の市場
　tight money　金融引締め, 金融引締めの状態, 金融ひっ迫, 資金需要のひっ迫, 金融引締め
　　（=monetary restraint, monetary tightening）
　tight money policy　金融引締め政策, 高金利政策
　　（=monetary restraint policy, monetary tightening policy）
　tight supply　需給のひっ迫, 引き締まった需給, 供給不足
◆The ECB's monetary policies ended up being relatively tight vis-a-vis Germany. 欧州中銀（ECB）の金融政策は、ドイツに対しては引締め気味となった。

tight fiscal［financing］policy　緊縮財政政策, 緊縮政策
◆Despite the deflationary trend, the Koizumi Cabinet pursued a tight fiscal policy. デフレ傾向にあったにもかかわらず、小泉内閣は緊縮政策を進めた。

tight lending　貸し渋り, 貸出の抑制
　（=credit crunch）
◆The remaining ¥2 trillion or so will be spent to support small and medium-sized companies and help loosen the tight lending policy implemented by private-sector financial institutions. 残りの約2兆円は、中小企業支援と民間の金融機関が行っている貸し渋りへの対策に充てられる。

tight monetary policy　金融引締め政策, 金融緊縮政策, 高金利政策　（=monetary restraint policy, monetary tightening policy, tight money policy）
◆The surge in prices of natural resources could ignite fears of inflation, causing countries around the world to implement tight monetary policies. 天然資源の価格急騰がインフレ懸念を呼び、世界各国が金融引締め政策を実施する可能性がある。

tight monetary（policy）stance　金融引締めのスタンス　（=credit-tightening stance, restrictive monetary policy stance）
◆The German economy has been under deflationary pressure due to the ECB's tight monetary stance. ドイツの経済は、欧州中銀（ECB）が金融引締めのスタンスを取っているため、デフレ気味だ。

tight money　金融引締め, 金融引締めの状態, 金融ひっ迫, 資金需要のひっ迫, 高金利の金
　（=monetary restraint, monetary tightening）
　tight money policy　金融引締め政策, 高金利政策（=credit squeeze, monetary restraint policy, monetary tightening policy, tight monetary policy）
　tight money system　金融引締め政策
　tight money times　金融引締め期
　tighter-money policy　金融引締め政策, 金融引締め
◆Increasing demands for capital and tight-money policies adopted by industrial powers pressed many investors to review their investment exposure in emerging economies. 先進国での資金需要の増大と金融引締め策は、多くの投資家に新興経済国［新興市場国］への投資の見直しを迫ることになった。

tighten　（動）強化する, 厳しくする, 厳格化する, 引き締める, 金融を引き締める, 利上げする, 縮小する, 低下する, 硬直する
　tighten credit stance　金融引締めに動く
　tighten drastically　急激に縮小する
　tighten fiscal policy　金融政策を引き締める
　tighten monetary policy further　金融政策を一段と引き締める
　tighten money markets　金融を引き締める
　　（⇒money market）
　tighten one's belt　財布のヒモを固くする, 倹約する, 耐乏生活をする, 生活を切り詰める
　tighten screening procedures　審査手続きを強化する, 審

査手続きを厳格化する
tighten security along the boarder　国境の安全を強化する
tighten the monetary stance　金融政策引締めのスタンスをとる
tighten the noose around　〜の包囲網を狭める
tighten the reins　手綱を引き締める
tighten underwriting standards　引受け基準を強化する
tighten up　厳しくする,強化する,固く[しっかり]締める,ぴんと張る
tightened cash flow　資金繰りの悪化（＝tightened liquidity）
tightened sampling inspection　厳格抜取り検査
tightened security　厳戒態勢
◆The government tightened the criteria for granting total exemption from paying national pension premiums. 政府は、国民年金保険料の全額免除の基準を厳格にした。◆When purse strings are tightened, it hurts the overall economy. 財布のヒモが堅くなると、景気全体に影響が及ぶ。
tighten monetary policy　金融政策を引き締める
◆The United States and China are expected to tighten their monetary policies. アメリカや中国で、金融引締めの観測が出ている。◆There were stormy discussions within the administration over the need for tightening monetary policies by the Fed. FRB（米連邦準備制度理事会）の金融引締めには、同政権内部でも大議論があった。
tighten regulations on investment funds　投資ファンドの規制を強化する
◆The United States was cautious about tightening regulations on investment funds. 米国は投資ファンドの規制強化には慎重だった。
tightening　（名）引締め,金融引締め,硬直,緊張　（形）（金融）引締めの,〜の引締め
belt tightening　金融引締め
credit tightening　信用引締め,金融引締め
financial tightening　金融引締め
monetary tightening　金融引締め
tightening bias　引締めのスタンス
tightening monetary policy　金融引締め政策,金融引締め
tightening policy　引締め政策,金融引締め政策
tighter　（形）一段と厳しい,一段とひっ迫した,悪化した,〜の強化[ひっ迫、悪化]
tighter lending standards　貸出基準の強化
tighter liquidity　資金繰りの悪化,資金需給のひっ迫
tighter market conditions　需給ひっ迫
tighter product supplies　製品需給のひっ迫
tighter constraints on credit　金融収縮
◆Deflation is being exacerbated by tighter constraints on credit. 金融収縮で、デフレが悪化している。
tighter financial regulations　金融規制の強化（⇒World Economic Forum）
◆French President Sarkozy told the gathering of business and political elites to prepare for tighter financial regulations. サルコジ仏大統領は、政財界トップの会合で金融規制強化を覚悟するよう明言した。
tighter monetary policy　金融引締め政策
◆The adoption of tighter monetary policy by central banks would be beneficial to enabling sustainable growth under price stability. 物価安定のもとで持続的な成長を維持していくためには、中央銀行が金融引締め政策を取るのが望ましい。
tighter money [tighter-money] policy　金融引締め政策,金融引締め
◆The nation's economy has regained enough of its vitality to tolerate the possible market turmoil that a tighter-money policy could trigger. 日本経済は、金融引締めがもたらす市場の動揺にも十分耐えられるほどに体力を回復した。
tighter regulations　規制強化
tighter regulations on bank capitalization　銀行の自己資本規制の強化
tighter regulations on investment funds　投資ファンドの規制強化
◆The United States and Britain demanded tighter regulations on bank capitalization. 米国と英国は、銀行の自己資本規制の強化を求めた。◆The U.S. tighter regulations on investment funds helped to change the trend in crude oil prices. 米国の投資ファンド規制強化で、原油価格の流れが変わった。
time　（名）時,時間,期間,時期,時代,時勢,機会,期限,〜回[度、倍]タイム　（⇒real time）
all-time low　過去最低
at a determinable future time　日付け後定期払い
available time　納期
bad times　不景気,不況,不況時
be ahead of the times　時勢に先んじている,現状に通じている
be left [fall] behind the times　時勢に遅れる
be marking time　足踏み状態が続いている
break-even time　損益分岐期間
closing time　閉店時間
cooling time　冷却期間
deflationary times　デフレ時代
delivery at a fixed future time　確定日渡し
delivery time　納期
difficult economic times　不況,不景気
down time [downtime]　故障時間,機械停止時間,使用不能時間（＝fault time）
for the first time in two quarters　2四半期（半年）ぶりに
gain time to　〜の時間を稼ぐ
good times　好景気,好況時
hard times　不景気
length of time until maturity　残存期間
on time　分割払いで,時間どおりに
over time　長期にわたって,時間が来たら
payout time　回収期間
repayment at one time　一括完済
time adjusted rate of return　時間修正利益率
time bill　期限付き手形
time bomb　時限爆弾,危険な状態,不安な政情
time charter party　定期用船契約
time discount　前払い割引き
time draft　期限付き為替手形（将来の決められた日に支払われる為替手形）
time financing　期限付き金融
time for shipment　船積み期日
time item　期限付き物
time lag [lapse]　時間的ずれ,時間のずれ,タイムラグ
time letter of credit　ユーザンスL/C（＝usance letter of credit）
time limit　期限
time loan　定期貸付け
time money　期限付き貸金[貸付け金]
time note　定期払い約束手形
time of circulation　流通期間
time of presentation　呈示期間
time payment　分割払い
time policy　期間保険,期間保険証券
time rate　期限付き為替相場,時間賃金率,放送料金,時間給

time savings　定期貯金
time spread　タイム・スプレッド（通貨、タイプ、行使価格は同一だが、期日が異なるプット、コール両オプションの同時売買）
time transaction　定期取引, 清算取引
time value　時間的価値, 満期までの利回り, (オプション取引で)契約期限までの時間
time value of money　金銭の時間価値
turnaround time　業績回復
volatile times　変動が激しい時期
◆Currency traders worldwide frantically search for a safe haven in volatile times. 世界の為替トレーダーは、変動の激しい時期の安全な投資先を熱狂的に求めている。◆The Bank of Japan asked the Federal Reserve Bank of New York to intervene in the New York foreign exchange market on its behalf through yen-selling, dollar-buying operations for the first time in 15 months. 日銀は、1年3か月ぶりにニューヨーク連銀に委託して、ニューヨーク外国為替市場で円売り・ドル買いの介入に踏み切った。◆The diffusion index of business sentiment among large manufacturers recovered to positive territory for the first time in two quarters. 大企業・製造業の業況判断指数(DI)は、2四半期(半年)ぶりにプラスに転じた。◆The exchange rate was the same at the time of deposit and withdrawal in a foreign currency deposit. 外貨預金で、為替相場は預け入れ時と解約時で同じだった。◆The real gross domestic product for the April-June period returned to positive growth for the first time in five quarters. 4-6月期の実質国内総生産(GDP)は、5四半期ぶりにプラス成長に転じた。◆The U.S. private banks' funds on hand grew about three times from March 2008 prior to the Lehman's collapse. 米国の民間銀行の手持ち資金は、リーマン・ブラザーズの経営破たん前の2008年3月から約3倍増えた。◆The yen's exchange rate has appreciated to ￥76 against the dollar, so it is the best time to buy U.S. dollars. 円の為替レートが1ドル＝76円に上昇したので、今が米ドルの買い時だ。◆There are few signs of the yen reaching the ￥90 range to the dollar for the time being. 今のところ、1ドル＝90円台に達する動き[1ドル＝90円台を目指す動き]は見られない。◆Through continuing gains in annual earnings, it will be possible, over time, to adjust the payout ratio while still maintaining our dividend record. 年間利益の増大を続けることによって、当社の配当実績を今後とも維持しながら、時期が来たら配当性向を調整することは可能である。

time certificate of deposit　定期預金証書
negotiable time certificate of deposit　譲渡性預金証書
negotiable time certificate of deposit issued by overseas bank　海外発行CD

time deposit　定期預金, 定期性預金, 貯蓄性預金, 安定性の高い定期預金　(期限付き預金の総称。いつでも自由に払戻しができる要求払い預金(demand deposit)と違って、定期性預金は一定の期間を経ないと払戻しができない。⇒full-refund guarantee, lot, savings deposit)
anonymous time deposit　無記名預金
funds fled from time deposits　定期預金から流出した預金
installment time deposit　積立定期預金
jumbo time deposit　大口定期預金
maturity-designated time deposit　期日指定定期預金
time and savings deposit　貯蓄性預金, 定期性預金
time deposit with a premium　割増金付き定期預金
time deposit with overdraft facilities　当座貸越し付き定期預金
time deposits with fixed interest rates　固定金利定期預金
time deposits with floating interest rates　変動金利定期預金
time deposits with unregulated interest rates　自由金利定期預金
◆Investors seem to be shifting their money from investment trusts to more secured time deposits in the face of global financial turmoil. 世界の金融市場の混乱に直面して、投資家は資金を投資信託から安定性の高い定期預金に切り替えているようだ。◆More investors are pulling money from stock markets and shifting it into safer time deposits. 株式市場から資金を引き揚げ、引き揚げた資金を安定性の高い定期性預金に移し替える投資家が増えている。◆The balance of quasi-money —most of it time deposits—saw a record drop in the wake of the April 1 abolition of the government's full-refund guarantee on time deposits. 定期預金が中心の準通貨の残高は、4月1日から定期預金に対する政府の全額払戻し保証が廃止されたため、過去最大の減少となった。◆The People's Bank of China arranged the latest interest rate hike so the longer the term of the time deposit, the greater the extent of the rate hike. 中国人民銀行は、今回の利上げで、定期預金の期間が長いほど利上げ幅を大きくした。

time frame [timeframe]　表示期間, 時間の制限, 時間的制約, 時間枠, 時間的枠組み, 時期, 期間, タイムリミット　(=time scale)
◆The company will reduce the interest-bearing liabilities to a maximum ￥900 billion from 1.57 trillion in the same time frame. 同社は、上記期間に有利子負債を1兆5,700億円から最高9,000億円に削減する方針だ。

time horizon　運用期間, 将来展望, タイム・ホライゾン
investment time horizon　投資資産の運用期間
investors with a time horizon of 10 years　10年の運用期間を設定している投資家
◆Before we invest in securities such as stocks, bonds and mutual funds, we must consider our investment time horizon. 株式、債券やミューチュアル・ファンドなどの有価証券に投資する前に、自分の投資資産の運用期間も検討しなければならない。

timeline　(名)工程表, 日程, 期限　(=time line)
envisaged timeline　目標期限　(⇒promise)
tentative timeline for　～の暫定的な日程, ～の暫定期限
the APEC's 18-month timeline　APEC(アジア太平洋経済協力会議)の18か月間の期限
◆The APEC's 18-month timeline aimed at overcoming the global financial crisis by May 2010 has no foundation. 2010年5月までに世界的な金融危機の克服に向けて設定されたAPEC(アジア太平洋経済協力会議)の18か月間の期限に、根拠があるわけではない。◆The special statement on the world economy adopted by the APEC forum specified a timeline for implementing the measures. アジア太平洋経済協力会議(APEC)で採択された世界経済に関する特別声明は、その対策実施の期限を明記した。

timing　(名)時期, 時間[時期・速度]の調整・選択, 好機の選択, 潮時, 頃合い, タイミング
debt timing　債務返済時期
timing difference　期間差異
timing mismatch　タイミングのずれ
◆Should the Fed misjudge the timing or level of its next rate hike, it may interrupt the economic recovery and even bring about rapid inflation. 米連邦準備制度理事会(FRB)が追加利上げの幅やタイミングを誤ると、景気回復の腰を折り、急激なインフレを招く可能性もある。◆While lifting the zero-interest rate policy will not immediately result in better business performance, there is concern that it may have a bad effect if the timing of the move is wrong. ゼロ金利政策の解除は、企業の業績改善に直ちにつながらないのに対して、その時期を誤れば悪影響を及ぼす心配がある。

tip　(名)内部情報, 未公開の重要情報, インサイド情報
tipoff [tip-off]　(名)秘密情報, 事前通報, 事前漏洩(ろうえい), 通報, 内部[事前]情報, 警告, 予想, ヒント

in exchange for tipoffs on　〜に関する情報の事前漏えい
obtain a tipoff from　〜から通報を受ける
on a tipoff from an anonymous caller　匿名の人からの電話による通報を受けて
◆Two bank inspectors were arrested on suspicion of taking millions of yen worth of bribes from banks in exchange for tipoffs on their bank inspections. 銀行検査に関する情報の事前漏えいの返礼として、複数の銀行から数百万円相当の賄賂（わいろ）を受けた疑いで、銀行検査官2人が逮捕された。

tippee trading　（会社の株価などの）内部情報の不正使用

titan　（名）巨人，大物，巨匠，大立て者，大手
◆Banking titan Citigroup Inc. has agreed to pay $75 million to the U.S. Securities and Exchange Commission to settle subprime mortgage suit. 米金融大手シティグループは、低所得者向け住宅融資「サブプライム・ローン」の訴訟の和解金として、7,500万ドルを米証券取引委員会（SEC）に支払うことで合意した。

TOB　株式公開買付け　（take-over bid［takeover bid］の略。⇒takeover bid）

toehold purchase　トーホールド・パーチェス
（⇒Williams Act）
[解説] トーホールド・パーチェスとは：M&Aで買収対象会社（ターゲット・カンパニー）の発行済み株式を5%まで買い集めて、買収の足がかり（toehold）にすること。米国では、上場会社の発行済み株式の取得が5%を超えると、取得後10営業日以内に報告書の書式である「様式13D」（Schedule 13D）に基づいてSEC（米証券取引委員会）、買収対象会社と、買収対象会社の株式を上場している証券取引所に取得の目的や資金源などについて報告することになっている。

Tokyo　（名）東京，東京外国為替市場，東京株式市場
stocks in Tokyo　東京株式市場，東京株式市場の株価，東京株，東京市場
Tokyo dollar call market　東京ドル・コール市場
Tokyo share prices　東京株式市場の株価
（⇒dollar's fall against the yen）
Tokyo's first exchange　東京証券取引所1部
◆Stock prices in Tokyo fell by more than 600 points as a state of panic gripped investors and selling pressure snowballed. 東京市場の株価は、投資家がパニック状態に陥り、売り圧力が増大［加速］したため、下げ幅が600円を超えた。◆The U.S. dollar dropped to the lower ￥82 level in Tokyo. 東京外国為替市場で、ドル相場は1ドル＝82円台前半まで落ち込んだ。◆The yen has been hovering near its record high of ￥76.25 against the U.S. dollar in Tokyo. 東京外国為替市場の円相場は、戦後最高値の1ドル＝76円25銭に迫る水準で推移している。◆The yen stayed in the lower ￥77 range against the U.S. dollar in Tokyo. 東京外国為替市場の円相場は、1ドル＝77円台前半で推移した。

Tokyo Commodity Exchange　東京工業品取引所，TOCOM
◆The benchmark gold future price surged to all-time high of ￥4,725 per gram in trading on the Tokyo Commodity Exchange. 東京工業品取引所の取引で、金取引の指標となる金先物価格が、過去最高の1グラム＝4,725円まで急騰した。◆The benchmark gold future price topped ￥4,700 per gram for the first time on the Tokyo Commodity Exchange. 東京工業品取引所で、金取引の指標となる金先物価格が、史上初めて1グラム＝4,700円を突破した。◆The June 2012 gold futures contract closed at ￥4,694 per gram, down ￥54 from the previous day's close on the Tokyo Commodity Exchange. 東京工業品取引所では、2012年6月渡しの金先物価格は、前日の終値より54円安の1グラム＝4,694円で取引を終えた。

Tokyo foreign exchange market　東京外国為替市場
◆On Aug. 31, 2011, the yen rose to the ￥76.50 level against the U.S. dollar in the Tokyo foreign exchange market, close to the postwar record of ￥75.95 registered on Aug. 19. 2011年8月31日の東京外国為替市場の円相場は、1ドル＝76円50銭台まで上昇し、8月19日に付けた戦後最高値の75円95銭に近づいた。

Tokyo market　東京市場，東京為替［外国為替］市場，東京外為市場
◆Affected by the New York sentiment, the Tokyo market was down across the board. ニューヨーク市場の地合いを受けて、東京市場は全面安となった。◆Short-term interest rates in the Tokyo market rose as some financial institutions hurried to obtain newly released funds. 一部の金融機関が新規調達資金の確保を急いだため、東京市場の短期金利が上昇した。◆The yen surged to the higher end of the ￥98 level against the dollar in Tokyo markets due to yen-buying pressure fueled by expectations of the country's economic recovery. 東京為替市場は、日本の景気回復を期待した円買いが強まり、1ドル＝98円台［98円台の上限］まで円が急騰した。

Tokyo Stock Exchange　東京証券取引所，東証，東京株式市場，TSE　（⇒TSE）
◆In terms of the total market value of listed shares, the Tokyo Stock Exchange is dwarfed by the New York Stock Exchange, the world's biggest. 上場株式の時価総額では、東証は世界トップのニューヨーク証券取引所に大きく引き離されている。◆The stock average fell below 9,000 again on the Tokyo Stock Exchange. 東京株式市場は、平均株価がふたたび9,000円を割り込んだ。◆The Tokyo Stock Exchange delisted scandal-tainted Seibu Railway Co. after it was found to have been falsifying financial statements. 東京証券取引所は、有価証券報告書への虚偽記載が発覚したのを受けて、不祥事が相次いだ西武鉄道（西武鉄道の株式）の上場を廃止した。◆The Tokyo Stock Exchange has called on listed companies to refrain from taking excessively protective measures against hostile takeover bids. 東京証券取引所は、敵対的買収に対する過剰な防衛策の自粛を上場企業に求めている。◆The Tokyo Stock Exchange has no power to directly supervise certified public accountants. 東京証券取引所に、公認会計士を直接監督する権限はない。◆The 225-issue Nikkei Stock Average on Monday plunged 202.32 points from Friday's close on the Tokyo Stock Exchange. 東京証券取引所の月曜日の日経平均株価（225種）は、前週末比で202円32銭下落した。◆These firms' performance has rapidly improved thanks to the recent boom on the Tokyo Stock Exchange. これら各社の業績は、最近の東京株式市場の活況を背景に急速に回復した。

Tokyo stock market　東京株式市場
（=Tokyo Stock Market）
◆JAL's stocks may lose market value to zero if the corporate turnaround body cuts the shares 100 percent by delisting JAL from the Tokyo stock market. 企業再生支援機構が東京株式市場から日航の上場を廃止して日航株を100%減資したら、日航株の市場価値はゼロになる可能性がある。◆On the Tokyo stock market and other Asian markets, stock prices plunged across the board. 東京株式市場や他のアジア市場などでも、軒並み株安となった。◆The buying force in the Tokyo stock market is overseas institutional investors. 東京株式市場での買いの主役は、海外の機関投資家だ。◆The Tokyo stock market has recently been roaring, with record heavy trading seen. 東京株式市場が、記録的な大商いを続けて、活況を呈している。

Tokyo Stock Market　東京株式市場
◆The Nikkei Stock Average fell briefly to its lowest level this year on the Tokyo Stock Market. 東京株式市場の日経平均株価は一時、今年の最安値を下回った。

Tokyo Stock Price Index　東証株価指数，TOPIX
（=Tokyo stock price index, Tokyo stock price index and average；⇒close名詞, TOPIX）
◆The Tokyo Stock Price Index dropped 12.75 points to close

at 943.51, rewriting Friday's postbubble closing low. 東証株価指数（TOPIX）の終値は前日比12.75ポイント低い943.51となり、金曜日のバブル崩壊後の終値での最安値を更新した。

Tokyo stocks 東京株式市場, 東京株式市場の株価, 東京株 (=stocks in Tokyo; ⇒unnerve)
◆Tokyo stocks bounced back after the U.S. government's bailout of embattled U.S. insurer American International Group Inc. 経営不振の米保険会社AIGを米政府が救済するのを受けて、東京株式市場は反発した。◆Tokyo stocks bounced back Wednesday after sharp falls Tuesday following Lehman Brothers decision to file for bankruptcy as financial worries eased. 水曜日の東京株式市場は、リーマン・ブラザーズが前日に破たん申請を決めて急落したものの、金融不安が和らいだため反発した。◆Tokyo stocks extended their winning streak to a third day with the key Nikkei index finishing above the 9,000 line. 東京の株価[東京株式市場の株価]は、3日連続で値上がりし、日経平均株価（225種）の終値は9,000円台を上回った。◆Tokyo stocks fell to a three-month low as foreign investors sparked a sell-off. 東京株（東京株式市場の株価）は、外国人投資家が株を売り進めたため3カ月ぶりに急落した。◆Tokyo stocks rebounded from Tuesday's slide. 東京株式市場の株価は、火曜日の下落から反発した[持ち直した]。◆Tokyo stocks retreated for the fourth consecutive day. 東京株[東京株式市場の株価]は、4日連続で下落した。◆Tokyo stocks snapped a three-day losing streak Wednesday, with the key Nikkei index rebounding strongly from Tuesday. 東京の株価[東京株式市場の株価]は水曜日、日経平均株価（225種）が前日から大幅反発[回復]して、3日連続の値下がりに歯止めがかかった。

tombstone (名)墓石広告（証券の発行広告）

tone (名)調子, 明暗, 濃淡, 傾向, 風潮, 気風, 基調, ムード, 地（じ）合い(sentiment, undertone), 論調, 口調, 格調, 気品, 品位, 高低, トーン
　be flat in tone 一本調子である
　bearish tone 弱気ムード, 弱気基調, 弱気
　bullish tone 強気ムード, 強気基調, 強気
　falling tone 下降基調, 下げムード
　firm tone 堅調な地合い
　hesitant tone 様子見気分
　improved tone of the market 市場の地合いの好転
　in sharp tones 鋭い口調で
　rising tone 上昇基調, 上昇ムード
　strong tone 強含み
　the change in tone of the economic upturn 景気回復の変調
　the latest change in tone of the economic upturn 今回の景気回復の変調
　the tone of the economic recovery 景気回復の基調
　the tone of the market 市場の地（じ）合い, 市況
　underlying tone 基調
　weak tone 弱含み
◆The latest change in tone of the economic upturn is a temporary phenomenon. 今回の景気回復の変調は、一時的な現象である。◆The tone in the Treasury market is becoming extremely positive. 債券市場の地合いは、ひじょうに明るくなっている。◆There is basically no change in the tone of the economic recovery. 景気回復の基調は、基本的に変わらない。

too big to fail 大き過ぎてつぶせない, 大き過ぎて破たんさせられない, 破たんさせるには大きすぎる
◆We do not hold the idea that big banks are too big to fail. われわれとしては、「巨大銀行が破たんさせるには大き過ぎる」という考え方は取らない。

too-big-to-fail lender 大きすぎてつぶせない銀行[金融機関], 大きすぎて破たんさせられない銀行
◆Twenty-eight banks of the world will face capital surcharges of 1 percent to 2.5 percent by the application of international rules to rein in too-big-to-fail lenders. 大きすぎて破たんさせられない銀行[金融機関]を規制する国際基準が適用されると、世界の28行が、1〜2.5％の資本[自己資本]上積みの対象となる。

too little too late （政策や対応などが）小さすぎ遅すぎる, 少なすぎるし遅すぎる

tool (名)道具, 用具, 工具, 工作機械, 手段, 方法, 手法, ツール
　a tool to manage equity investments 株式運用のツール
　automatic operating tool 自動運用ツール
　corporate buyout tool 企業買収の手段
　debt management tool 負債管理の手法
　management tool 管理手法, 管理の手法, 経営手法
　risk management tool リスク管理の手段
　trade policy tool 通商政策の道具, 通商政策の手段
◆Two potent corporate buyout tools of stock splits and stock swaps were the key to the remarkable growth of the company. 株式分割と株式交換という二つの強力な企業買収の手段が、同社の急成長のカギだった。◆U.S. and European banks have advanced into diverse fields, including securities business, by polishing up their financial tools for utilizing derivative products. 欧米の銀行は、デリバティブ（金融派生商品）を活用するための金融技術を磨いて、証券業務などさまざまな分野に進出してきた。

top (動)上回る, 突破する, 〜を越える, 首位になる, 首位を占める, トップになる, 〜を負かす[破る]
◆Gold futures for December delivery topped $1,900 an ounce for the first time on the Comex in New York. ニューヨーク商品取引所で、12月渡しの金先物価格が、史上初めて1トロイ・オンス＝1,900ドルを突破した。◆Strong overseas performance helped Toyota's group sales top ¥20 trillion for the first time in the year through March. 海外の好業績で、トヨタの3月期決算は、連結売上高が（日本の製造業で）初めて20兆円を上回った。◆The benchmark gold future topped ¥4,700 per gram for the first time on the Tokyo Commodity Exchange. 東京工業品取引所で、金取引の指標となる金先物価格が、史上初めて1グラム＝4,700円を突破した。

top (名)最高位, 最高点, 頂上, 首位, 首席, 最優先課題, 最優先事項, トップ
　be (at the) top of the agenda [list] 議題[表]の最優先事項, 最優先課題
　double top 2番天井
　from top to toe すっかり, 徹底的に
　on top of 〜の上に, 〜に加えて
　top-to-bottom communication 上[上位の者]から下[下位の者]への意思疎通

top (形)最高の, 最高位の, 最上位の, 首位の, 筆頭の, 最上の, 最高級の, 最大の, 最大限の, 上位の, 上部の, 頂上の, 大手の, 最重要な, 最優先の, トップの
　be ranked in the top 3 トップ3[ベスト・スリー]にランクされる
　top brass 幹部, 最高幹部, 高級幹部, 高級将校
　top cadre 最高幹部
　top companies 大手企業
　top dollar 最高金額
　top echelon 最高幹部, 上層部
　top machine 首脳陣, 最高幹部
　top officer 最高経営役員
　top player 最大手
　top priority 最優先課題, 最優先事項, 最優先権
　top secret 極秘, 極秘事項
　top shareholder 筆頭株主
　top-tier stock 高業績株

◆The top 10 life insurers in the nation reported a total of ¥1.46 trillion in valuation losses on their securities holdings for the current business year. 今期決算で、国内生保の上位（主要）10社の保有有価証券[保有株式]の減損処理額は、1兆4,600億円に達した。

top bank　大手行, メガ銀行, 巨大銀行
◆The three Japanese top banks will face the FSB's new international rule requiring them to hold extra capital to prevent future financial crises. 日本の3メガ銀行も、金融危機の再発を防ぐため、資本[自己資本]の上積みを求める金融安定化理事会（FSB）の新国際基準の対象になると見られる。

top corporate borrowers　一流企業融資先
◆The rate at which banks lend their top corporate borrowers is called "prime rate." 銀行がその一流企業融資先に貸し出す利率は、プライム・レートと呼ばれている。

top-down approach to investment [investing]　投資のトップダウン方式, トップダウン式投資（景気判断から投資対象の産業部門の決定、企業の選択の順で銘柄を決める投資戦略）

top end of one's range　ボックス圏の上限
◆The Standard & Poor's 500 index is at the top end of its range for the past two months. スタンダード・プアーズ（500種）株価指数は、過去2か月のボックス圏の上限にある。

top executive　最高経営者, 最高執行部, 最高経営幹部, 経営幹部, 経営首脳, 経営者, 経営トップ（top executivesは「首脳陣、経営幹部」の意）
◆The upcoming negotiations will determine practical measures to strengthen ties, including the merger ratio, the name of the new group and the positions to be held by top executives. 今後の交渉で、統合比率や新グループの名称、首脳人事など提携強化の具体策を詰める。

top finance officials　財務相・中央銀行総裁
◆A meeting of top finance officials from the Group of Seven industrial powers was held in Washington. 先進7か国財務相・中央銀行総裁会議（G7）が、米ワシントンで開かれた。

top manager　経営者, 首脳, トップ
◆Three top managers of UFJ Holdings resigned. UFJホールディングスの首脳3人が、辞任した。

top-notch credit rating　最上位の信用格付け, 最上位の格付け　(=top-tier credit rating)
◆Moody's will consider cutting the United States' top-notch credit rating if any progress isn't made in talks to raise the U.S. debt limit. 米政府の債務の法定上限引上げについての（米議会との）交渉で進展がなければ、ムーディーズは、米国債の最上位の格付けを引下げる方向で検討する方針だ。

top-notch safety management specialist　一流の安全管理専門家
◆Japan lacks top-notch safety management specialists at least in the field of financial services. 少なくとも金融サービスの分野では、日本に一流の安全管理専門家がいない。

top shareholder　筆頭株主
(=leading shareholder)
◆Nippon Life Insurance Co., the top shareholder in Olympus Corp., will continue supporting Olympus in light of its advanced technology in its core business such as endoscopes. オリンパスの筆頭株主の日本生命は、内視鏡などオリンパスの中核事業の高い技術力を踏まえて、引き続きオリンパスを支えていく方針だ。

top the agenda　最大の議題になる, 最大の課題になる
◆At the G-7 talks, concern over soaring public debts was to top the agenda. G7（先進7か国財務相・中央銀行総裁会議）の協議では、増大する公的債務問題[公的債務への懸念]が最大の議題[課題]になる予定だった。◆In this spring's labor offensive, job security will top the agenda in management-labor negotiations. 今年の春闘では、雇用の維持が労使交渉での最大の課題だ。

top tier　最上位, 最上級
top-tier AAA credit rating　最上位のトリプルAの格付け, 最上級のAAA[トリプルA]の格付け
top-tier stock　高業績株
◆The United States lost its top-tier AAA credit rating from S&P for the first time. 米国債の格付け[米国の長期国債格付け]が、スタンダード・アンド・プアーズ（S&P）による最上級のAAA（トリプルA）の格付けから史上初めて転落した。

TOPIX　東証株価指数, トピックス　（Tokyo stock price indexの略）
◆The broader TOPIX index of all First Section issues finished down 11.71 points at 706.08. 一部上場全銘柄の総合東証株価指数は、11.71ポイント安の706.08で終了した。
解説 東証株価指数とは：東証一部の時価総額を加重平均して算出する。日経平均がハイテク株の組入れ比重が高いためにハイテク株の動きに左右されやすいのに対して、東証株価指数（TOPIX）は銀行株など時価総額の大きい株価の動きに敏感。

total　(動)総計[合計]で〜になる, 〜を合計する
◆Corporate bankruptcies stemming from the March 11 earthquake and tsunami totaled 330. 東日本大震災による企業倒産の総件数は、330件に達している。◆Global project financing loans totaled about $96.1 billion from January until the end of June 2011. 2011年1〜6月の世界のプロジェクト・ファイナンスの総融資額は、約961億ドルに達した。◆In revitalizing the market, it is necessary to encourage individuals, who have financial assets totaling ¥1.4 quadrillion, to invest in the stock market. 市場の活性化を図るには、1,400兆円にのぼる金融資産を持つ個人の株式市場への投資を促す必要がある。◆The combined losses of the seven major banking groups totaled ¥4.62 trillion as of the end of March. 大手銀行・金融7グループの赤字合計額は、3月末現在で4兆6,200億円に達した。◆The merger will create the world's largest financial group with assets totaling about ¥190 trillion. この経営統合で、総資産約190兆円の世界最大の金融グループが誕生する。◆The number of hoarded stocks totals 75.6 billion as of March 2007. タンス株は、2007年3月時点で756億株に上っている。◆The U.S. Mint's sales of American Eagle gold coins have totaled 91,000 ounce so far in August. 米造幣局のアメリカン・イーグル[米イーグル]金貨の販売総量は、9月1日以降現時点で9万1,000オンスに達している。

total　(名)総額, 総量, 総計, 合計, 全部
a total of　合計〜, 総額〜
actual total　実際の累計額
balance sheet total　貸借対照表合計, 総資産
control total　照合合計
cumulative total　累計
grand total　累計, 総計
ground total　単純集計
in total　合計して, 全部で
intermediate total　中間合計, 小計
minor total　小計
net total　純計
running total　現在合計高
spending totals　歳出
sum total　総計
◆Corporate value is defined as "the total of profits one company will earn in future." 企業価値は、「ある会社が将来稼ぐ利益の合計」と定義される。◆For all of 2008, the U.S. sagging economy lost a net total of 2.6 million jobs. 2008年は、米国の景気低迷により純計で260万人の雇用が減少した。◆In this cofinancing scheme, the bank will extend a total of about ¥8.5 billion over a 20-year loan period. この協調融資事業で、同行は貸出期間20年で計約85億円を融資する。◆The amount of federal government's financial support to GM will reach

¥5 trillion in total. GMに対する米政府の金融支援の総額は、5兆円に達する。◆The Board of Audit has confirmed that the public financing package extended with a government-backed guarantee to JAL prior to its failure cost taxpayers a total of ¥47 billion. 日航の破たん前に政府保証付きで行われた公的融資の総国民負担額は470億円であることを、会計検査院が確定した。◆The DBJ and private financial institutions extended loans worth a total of ¥100 billion to JAL in June 2009 though JAL was already in dire financial straits. 日本政策投資銀行と民間金融機関は、日航の経営がすでに悪化していたものの、2009年6月に同社に対して総額1,000億円を融資した。◆The firm has earmarked a total of ¥37 billion in the two fields in fiscal 2010. 同社は、両事業分野に2010年度は370億円投資した。

total (形)全体の, 全部の, 総計の, 合計の, 全体的な, 完全な, まったくの
  actual total loss　現実全損
  total amount　総額
  total balance　総合収支
  total capitalization　総資本
  total cash flow　総資金収入
  total claims　保険金支払い総額
  total compensation　給与総額
  total cost of ownership　企業情報システムの総保有コスト, 総合保有コスト, TCO（TCO＝システム部門や各社員のハード、ソフト購入費用＋情報システムの維持管理費、運用費、教育・研修費など）
  total debt　総負債額, 負債総額, 債務総額（⇒total capitalization）
  total deposit　総預金, 預金総額
  total income　総収入, 総所得
  total investment　投資総額
  total investment balances　総投資残高
  total liquidity　総流動性
  total loss　全損
  total management　総合管理
  total money supply　通貨総供給高
  total net assets　純資産総額
  total production　総生産
  total rate of savings　総貯蓄率
  total sum at risk under the policy　元受契約危険保険金総額
  total turnover　総売上高
◆The Board of Audit intends to include the total taxpayer contribution to JAL in its audit account report compiled in November 2011. 会計検査院は、2011年11月にまとめる決算検査報告書に、日航に対する総国民負担額を盛り込む方針だ。◆The total operating profits of listed companies are expected to decline in the business year ending in March. 上場企業の今期決算［3月期決算］の営業利益は、全体で減少する見込しだ。

total amount of loans　総貸付け金, 借入基金総額
◆The total amount of loans owed by companies and individuals to private financial institutions stands at ¥2.8 trillion in the three prefectures' coastal areas hit by the March 11 tsunami. 津波被災地の3県沿岸部では、企業や個人の民間企業からの借入金総額が、2.8兆円にのぼっている。

total amount of money　総貨幣量, 貨幣総量
  total amount of money deposited in individual foreign currency accounts　個人向け外貨預金残高
  total amount of money in circulation　流通通貨量
◆The total amount of money deposited in individual foreign currency accounts has continued to increase in recent years. 個人向け外貨預金残高は、ここ数年増え続けている。

total amount of outstanding notes　紙幣の総発行残高
◆The Fed's total amount of outstanding notes at the end of June 2011 increased by more than 30 percent from the end of March 2008, prior to the Lehman shock. 2011年6月末時点の米連邦準備制度理事会（FRB）の紙幣の総発行残高は、リーマン・ショック前の2008年3月末から30％以上も伸びた。

total assets　総資産, 資産合計
  total assets employed　使用総資産
  total assets turnover　総資本回転率
  total net assets　純資産総額
◆The BOJ's total assets at the end of August 2011 increased to ¥141 trillion from ¥79 trillion as of the end of March 1999 when its zero-interest rate policy was first adopted. 日銀の2011年8月末時点の総資産は、ゼロ金利政策を初めて導入した1999年3月末現在の79兆円から141兆円に増えた。◆The tie-up will create the world's largest banking group, with total assets of ¥190 trillion. 統合によって、総資産が190兆円の世界最大の銀行（金融）グループが誕生する。◆The total assets of the Federal Reserve Board have soared to $2.87 trillion at the end of June 2011 from $896.2 billion as of the end of March 2008, prior to the Lehman shock. 米連邦準備制度理事会（FRB）の総資産は、リーマン・ショック前の2008年3月末時点の8,962億ドルから、2011年6月末には2兆8,700億ドルに急増した。

total capital　総資本, 長期資本
  total capital expenditure　設備投資総額
  total capital profit rate　総資本収益率
  total capital ratio　総資本比率
  total capital requirement　総資本所要額［必要額］
◆The company's ratio of total debt to total capital（total debt plus total equity）increased to 56% at December 31, 2010. 同社の総負債額に対する総資本（負債総額と総株主持ち分の合計）の比率は、2010年12月31日現在で56％に増加している。

total capitalization　時価総額
◆The firm's total debt as a percentage of total capitalization was 33 percent at year end 2010, compared with 27 percent at yearend 2009. 同社の資本総額に対する債務総額の比率は、2009年末現在の27％に対して、2010年末では33％に拡大した。

total debt as a percentage of total capitalization　資本総額に対する債務総額の比率
◆Total debt as a percentage of total capitalization was 20 percent at yearend 2010. 資本総額に対する債務総額の比率は、2010年末現在で20％だった。

total exemption　全額免除
◆The government tightened the criteria for granting total exemption from paying national pension premiums. 政府は、国民年金保険料の全額免除の基準を厳格にした。

total lending　貸出総額
◆The infusion of public funds into major banks was originally meant to free banks from their need to contract total lending to maintain capital adequacy ratios. 大手銀行への公的資金注入のそもそもの狙いは、自己資本比率を維持するために貸出総額を縮小せざるをえない事態から銀行を解き放つことにあった。

total losses　損失総額, 総損失額
◆In the case of JAL, the DBJ's ultimate total losses came to ¥95.6 billion in loans and ¥20 billion in investments. 日航の場合、日本政策投資銀行の最終的な損失総額は、融資分の956億円と出資分の200億円となっている。

total market value of listed shares　上場株式の時価総額
◆In terms of the total market value of listed shares, the Tokyo Stock Exchange is dwarfed by the New York Stock Exchange, the world's biggest. 上場株式の時価総額では、東証は世界トップのニューヨーク証券取引所に大きく引き離されている。◆The merger between the TSE and the OSE will

create the world's second-largest exchange group in terms of the total market value of listed shares. 東証と大証の経営統合で、上場株式の時価総額で世界第2位の株式取引所グループが誕生する。

total return 総収益率, 総合利回り, 所有期間総合利回り, トータル・リターン
  on a total return basis 総合利回りベースで
  total return investors 総合利回り志向の投資家, 利回り志向の投資家
  total return optimization 総収益率の最適化

total trading volume 総出来高, 総売買高, 総売上高, 取引全体
  ◆A market player put the level of short selling in the stock market at between 5 percent to 10 percent of total trading volume. ある市場筋によると、株の空売りは取引全体の5-10%程度といわれる。

touch (動)(〜に)触れる,(〜と)接触する,(〜に)言及する,(〜を)取り上げる,(〜に)影響を及ぼす,(〜にまで)達する, 寄港する
  touch bottom 底に届く, 底入れする, 底を打つ, 最悪[最低]の状態になる
  touch close the historical high 過去最高に近づく
  touch off 誘発する, 触発する, 引き起こす, 爆発させる
  touch up 最後の仕上げをする, 〜を修正する, 〜を直す
  ◆After briefly touching ¥110.90 in early trading in London, the dollar rallied in intraday trading, rising to ¥112.15-25 at 5 p.m. ロンドン市場では早朝の取引で一時1ドル=110円90銭を付けた後、米ドルは取引時間中の取引で反騰して午後5時現在、同112円15-25銭に上昇した。

touch (名)連絡, 接触, 感覚, 感触, 感じ, 手ごたえ, 筆致, 手法, 技法, 仕上がり, 仕上げ, 少量, 簡単に金を出す人, 触診, タッチ
  apply the final touches to 〜の最後の調整をする
  get in touch with 〜と連絡をとる
  lose touch with 〜と接触がなくなる, 〜と接触を失う, 〜との交流がなくなる, 〜に関心を持たなくなる
    (=be out of touch with)
  put final touches to 〜の仕上げをする, 〜の最後の仕上げをする
  ◆SMFG is applying the finishing touches to a plan to invest in Goldman Sachs Group Inc. 三井住友銀行は現在、(米証券首位の)ゴールドマン・サックスに投資する計画の最終調整に入っている。

tough (形)ひどい, つらい, 苦しい, 耐えがたい, 嫌な, 困難な, 骨の折れる, 難しい, 厳しい, 手ごわい, 粘り強い, 頑丈な, 丈夫な, たくましい, 強硬な, 激しい, 激烈な, 乱暴な, 粗野な, 物騒な, 犯罪の多い, 凶悪な, 堅い, 固い, 折れない, 信じがたい, 理解しがたい, タフな, タフ (⇒fall on)
  a tough job やっかいな仕事, 困難な仕事
  be in a tough race 苦しい戦いをしている
  face tough competition from 〜から厳しい競争を仕掛けられる
  face tough economic issues 難しい経済問題に直面する
  get tough with 〜に厳しくする[厳しく対処する], 〜に強硬な態度を取る, 〜に強硬姿勢で臨む, 〜に食い下がる,(人に)つらく当たる
  have a tough time 苦しい時を過ごす, 苦境に立つ
  make a tough break ひどい失態[へま, 失策]をしでかす, 大失態を演じる
  take a tough line 強硬路線を取る
  take tough measures 断固たる措置を取る
  tough decisions つらい決断, つらい選択
  tough line on 〜に対する強硬姿勢

tough stance 厳しい姿勢
  ◆Policies adopted by the Hatoyama administration are tough on companies. 鳩山現政権が掲げる政策は、企業には厳しい。

tough conditions 厳しい状況
  ◆Domestic stock exchange entries continue to languish, reflecting the tough conditions faced by emerging firms wanting to publicly list their shares. 国内株式市場への新規上場は、株式上場を目指す新興企業が直面している厳しい状況を反映して、低迷が続いている。

tough environment 厳しい環境
  ◆The Japanese economy is facing a tough environment amid deflation and sluggish domestic demand. 日本経済は、デフレと内需低迷で厳しい環境に直面している。

tough fiscal condition 厳しい財政事情, 厳しい財政状況
  ◆Given the nation's tough fiscal condition, the government must eke out the necessary funds by scaling down low-priority policy projects. 日本の厳しい財政事情に照らせば、政府に求められるのは、優先度の低い政策プロジェクトを縮小して、必要な財源をひねり出すことだ。

tough investment conditions 厳しい投資環境, 厳しい運用環境
  ◆The move to lower the yields of insurance products is likely to spread through the industry as tough investment conditions persist. 厳しい運用環境が続いているので、保険商品の利回りを引き下げる動きは、業界全体に広がりそうだ。

toughen (動)強くする, 強化する, 頑丈にする, 困難にする
  toughen restrictions on 〜に対する規制を強化する
  toughening competition 熾烈な競争
  ◆The FSA mapped out a plan to toughen restrictions on banks' sales of insurance products to small and midsize companies. 金融庁が、銀行の中小企業向け保険商品販売に対する規制を強化する案をまとめた。

tougher financial regulations 金融規制の強化
  ◆The G-7 countries agreed to move in the direction of tougher financial regulations. 先進7か国(G7)は、金融規制強化の方向で一致した。

tout (動)勧誘する, うるさく勧める, しつこく求める, 大げさに宣伝する,(主義、主張を)掲げる, 標榜する, 情報を提供する[探る],(製品などを)売り込む, 持ち上げる, 大いにほめる, ほめそやす
  tout a policy shift 政策転換を掲げる
  tout as a slogan スローガンに掲げる
  tout for business 商売の宣伝をする
  tout for orders うるさく[しつこく]注文を求める
  tout one's attractiveness 〜の魅力を売り込む
  tout the bad performances of other companies 他社の経営不振をあおる
  tout the low prices of one's products and services 製品やサービスの低価格を売り込む
  ◆In the life insurance sector, the practice of luring customers by touting the bad performances of other insurers has been called into question. 生保業界では、他社の経営不振をあおって顧客を勧誘する行為(風評営業)が問題になっている。◆Some successful companies are touting the low prices and distinctive features of their products and services. 一部の好調企業は、製品やサービスの低価格と独自性を売り込んでいる。

toxic (形)有毒の, 不良の, 不良資産化した
  toxic mortgage-backed securities 不良不動産担保証券, 不良担保付き債券, 不良モーゲージ担保証券
  toxic securities 不良証券, 有毒証券
  turn toxic 不良資産化する
  ◆The U.S. government filed lawsuits against 17 financial firms for selling Fannie and Freddie mortgage-backed securities that turned toxic when the housing market collapsed.

米政府は、住宅市場崩壊時に不良資産化した住宅ローン担保証券（MBS）をファニー・メイ（米連邦住宅抵当公庫）とフレディ・マック（米連邦住宅貸付け抵当公社）に販売したとして、大手金融機関17社（バンク・オブ・アメリカやシティグループ、JPモルガン・チェース、ゴールドマン・サックス・グループなど）を提訴した。

toxic asset　不良資産
◆Public funds should be injected not only to buy up toxic assets, but also to boost the capital bases of enfeebled financial institutions. 公的資金は、不良資産の買取りだけでなく、弱体化した［体力の落ちた］金融機関の資本増強にも注入すべきだ。◆The U.S. government could place the toxic assets of troubled Fannie Mae and Freddie Mac in a federal corporation. 米政府は、経営不振のファニー・メイ（米連邦住宅公庫）とフレディ・マック（米連邦）の不良資産を連邦公社に移す可能性がある。

track　（名）進路, 行路, 線路, 走路, 軌道, 足跡, 痕跡, 航跡, 跡, 能力別クラス編成トラック
be on the fast track　出世コースにいる, 迅速に処理される
be on［get, have］the inside track　有利である, 有利な立場［地位］を得る, インコースを走る
　（=have［get］the inside track）
be on the right track［lines］　思ったとおりに行っている［進んでいる］, 間違いなく［正しく］進んでいる
be on the wrong track［lines］　間違って進んでいる
be on track　軌道に乗っている, うまく運んで［進んで］いる, 順調に進んでいる, 予期どおりに進んでいる
be on track to rise　上昇軌道にある, 上昇［増加］軌道に乗る
fast track　突貫工事, 速い道筋, ファースト・トラック
full-fledged recovery track　本格回復の軌道
get back on track　再び軌道に乗る
get off the track　本題からそれる, わき道にそれる, 脱線する
get on the recovery track　回復軌道に乗る
keep the recovery on track　回復［景気回復］を軌道に乗せて行く
recovery track　回復軌道
　（=recovery course［path］）
track record　業績記録, 実績, 業績
◆A rocky road likely will lie ahead of GM's attempt to put itself back on the track under state control. 国の管理下で［国有化されて］再建をめざす米ゼネラル・モーターズの前途は、多難だろう。◆China's economic pickup in March showed that its economy would be on track for stronger growth in coming months. 中国の3月の景気回復は、中国経済が今後数か月で力強い成長軌道に乗ることを示した。◆If the government relaxes its policy now, the economy will not be able to get on the recovery track. 政府がいまその政策の手を緩めれば、景気は回復軌道に乗れないだろう。◆The economy is on track for a full-scale recovery. 景気は、本格的な回復軌道に乗っている。◆The U.S. economy has gotten back on the recovery track since the latter half of last year. 米国の景気は、昨年後半からまた回復軌道に乗り始めた。

track record　業績記録, 競技場での記録, 実績, 業績
◆As the gap between the eurozone-imposed repayment program and the track record began clearly yawning, the Greece's insolvency became apparent. ユーロ圏が押し付けたギリシャの返済計画と実績とのズレが目立つようになるにつれ、ギリシャの返済不能が明らかになった。◆Since its independence in the 19th century, Greece has a notorious track record that the county's state coffers have been bankrupt for half the period. ギリシャには、19世紀の独立以来、その半分の期間、財政破たんしていた不名誉な実績がある。

tracking error　追跡誤差, トラッキング・エラー（特定の株価指数などを目標に構成したポートフォリオと実際の運用成績との差）
a low tracking error　小さいトラッキング・エラー（追跡誤差）, 低めの追跡誤差
a manager with a high tracking error　追跡誤差（トラッキング・エラー）が大きい［高めの］運用機関　（ベンチマーク（目標指数）と比較して実際の運用成績のばらつきが高めの運用機関）
establish a target tracking error　追跡誤差（トラッキング・エラー）の目標値を設定する
increase the tracking error risk　追跡誤差リスクを高める
observed checking error　追跡誤差の実績値
reduce the tracking error　追跡誤差を少なくする
run checks on tracking error　追跡誤差をチェックする
run close to tracking error limitations　追跡誤差［追跡誤差目標値］の限界ぎりぎりのところにある
target a tracking error　トラッキング・エラー（追跡誤差）の目標値を定める

tracking stock　事業部門業績連動株, 事業部門株, 子会社業績連動株, トラッキング・ストック, TS　（特定の子会社や事業部門の業績に基づいて配当する株式）
raise funds by issuing a tracking stock for the firm's subsidiary　同社子会社の業績に連動するトラッキング・ストックを発行して資金を調達する
tracking stock in a subsidiary　子会社連動株, トラッキング・ストック　（子会社の業績や配当に経済価値を連動させることを意図した株式）
◆The Legislative Council proposed deregulating tracking stock—shares whose dividends are paid in accordance with the performance of a company's specific subsidiary or division. 法制審議会（法相の諮問機関）は、企業の特定の子会社や事業部門の業績に従って配当金を支払う株式の「トラッキング・ストック」に対する規制撤廃を提案した。

trade　（動）売買する, 取引する, 商う, 商売する, 交易する, 交換する
trade above par　額面以上で取引される
trade at　～で取引される
trade at a discount to fair value　理論価格を下回る水準で取引される
trade at a premium of 3 points over fair value　理論価格を3ポイント上回る水準で取引される
trade at around　～近辺で取引される
trade at par　オーバー・パーで取引される, オーバー・パーになっている
trade away　売り払う, 売る, （権利などを）手放す
trade down　（下取りに出して）買い換える, 値を下げる
trade in derivative instruments　派生商品の取引を行う
trade most frequently at　取引の中心値は～である
trade off　～と交換する, ～と相殺する
trade on stock exchange　証券取引所で売買される
trade securities　証券の売買を行う, 証券の取引を行う
trade the issue as a secondary bond　値付け業務を行う
trade to a record high　新高値を付ける
trade to a record low　新安値を付ける
trade up　高い物と買い換える［交換する］
trade within a narrow range　もみ合いが続く
◆At 4 p.m., the euro traded at $1.3813-3814 and ¥113.16-20 in London. 午後4時の時点で、ロンドン外国為替市場のユーロ相場は、1ユーロ＝1.3813～3814ドルと113円16～20銭で取引された。◆At 5 p.m., the yen was traded at ¥85.45-47 against the dollar in Tokyo. 午後5時、東京外国為替市場の円相場は1ドル＝85円45～47銭で取引を終えた。◆By the TSE's extension of the morning trade session to 11:30 a.m., investors will be able to trade Japanese stocks more easily

while keeping an eye on economic trends in Asian markets. 東証が午前11時30分まで午前の取引時間を延長したことによって、投資家は今後、アジア市場の経済動向を見ながら日本株の取引をすることが容易になる。◆By the 30-minute extension of morning trading sessions, investors will be able to trade for a full hour in Japan as they monitor stock price movements on the Hong Kong market. 午前の取引時間の30分延長で、投資家は、香港市場の値動きを見ながら日本市場で丸1時間売買できるようになった。◆Citigroup Private Bank repeatedly committed acts contrary to the public goods, such as the buying and selling trusts and securities that the division was not permitted to trade. シティバンクのプライベート・バンク部門は、取引が禁止されている信託や証券を売買するなど、公益に反する行為を繰り返していたという。◆In commodity futures trading, precious metals, petroleum products and other goods are traded. 商品先物取引では、貴金属や石油製品などの商品が取引されている。◆Investors can trade the Seibu Railway shares for a month after their transfer to the TSE's liquidation post from the monitoring post. 西武鉄道株が東証の監理ポストから整理ポストに移った後1か月間、投資家は西武鉄道株を売買できる。◆The euro traded $1.5763-5766 against late Friday's quotes of $1.5670-5680 in New York. ユーロは、ニューヨークの外国為替市場では、前週末（午後5時）の相場1ユーロ＝1.5670〜5680ドルに対して、1ユーロ＝1.5763〜5766ドルで取引された。◆The exchange-traded funds (ETFs) are investment products similar to index mutual funds but that trade on stock exchanges like stocks. 上場投資信託（ETF）は、インデックス・ミューチュアル・ファンドに似ているが、株式と同じように証券取引所で売買される投資商品である。◆The U.S. dollar traded at the lower ¥85 range in Tokyo over concern about the U.S. economic outlook. 東京金融市場［東京外国為替市場］では、米景気の先行きを懸念して、ドル相場は1ドル＝85円台前半で取引された。◆The U.S. dollar was traded at around ¥76 on the currency market. 為替市場では、1ドル＝76円をはさんだ取引が続いた。◆The yen moved between ¥81.80 and ¥82.38 to the dollar, trading most frequently at ¥81.94. 円相場の値幅は1ドル＝81円80銭〜82円38銭で、取引の中心値は81円94銭だった。◆Transactions on all of the 2,520 issues traded at the TSE were stalled from 9 a.m. due to a computer malfunction. 東証で取引されている2,520全銘柄の取引が、コンピュータのシステム障害で午前9時から停止した。

trade （名）貿易, 交易, 取引, 商売, 下取り, 交換, トレード （⇒factor）
balance of trade 貿易収支
directional trade 方向性取引
execute a large trade 大口取引を執行する
government-backed trade insurance for overseas social infrastructure projects 海外の社会基盤（インフラ）事業に対する政府保証付き貿易保険 （⇒trade insurance）
legitimate trades of loan claims 債権の適法売買, 適法な債権売買
market-neutral trade 市場中立取引
Moon Trade 時間外取引, 時間外サービス
stock trade 株取引
trade acceptance 引受商業手形
trade currency 貿易通貨
trade cycle 景気循環 （=business cycle）
trade halt 取引の一時停止
trade imbalance 貿易の不均衡, 貿易不均衡 （⇒imbalance）
◆In commodity futures trading, prices are decided when buyers and sellers make deals. So they can execute trades at promised prices even if the value of goods has changed drastically in the meantime. 商品先物取引では、売り手と買い手が取引契約をする時点で価格を決める。そのため、契約期間中に相場が大きく変動しても、売り手と買い手は約束した値段で取引を執行できる。◆The bank disguised these transactions as legitimate trades of loan claims. 同行は、これらの取引については適法な債権売買を装っていた。

trade credit 商業信用, 貿易信用, 企業間信用, 企業信用, 与信取引, 輸出延べ払い, 輸入延べ払い, 商業信用状, 貿易信用状
give trade credit 与信取引を認める
manage trade credit 与信取引を管理する
trade credit underwriting process 企業顧客向け与信の過程
trade credits extended 延べ払い信用
use trade credit 与信取引を利用する

trade deficit 貿易赤字, 貿易収支の赤字 （=trade gap）
◆An excessive trade deficit should be corrected through the realignment of foreign exchange rates. 過度の貿易赤字は、為替レートの調整によって是正しなければならない。◆An improving trade deficit can act to boost the economy. 貿易赤字の改善は、景気浮揚の一因になる可能性がある。

trade insurance 貿易保険 （貿易や海外への投融資をする企業が、損失に備えて利用する保険。⇒credit risk）
◆The METI has decided to expand the scope of government-backed trade insurance for overseas social infrastructure projects. 産業経済省は、海外の社会基盤（インフラ）事業に対する政府保証付き貿易保険の対象を拡大することを決めた。◆The practical implementation of trade insurance, including risk judgment, must be enhanced to encourage investment by private companies and accelerate the export of infrastructure technology. 民間企業の投資を促し、インフラ技術の輸出を加速するには、リスク判断も含めて、貿易保険の実務能力を高める必要がある。◆The trade insurance of Nippon Export and Investment Insurance previously only covered direct exports by domestic firms. 独立行政法人・日本貿易保険の貿易保険はこれまで、国内企業の直接輸出だけが対象だった。

trade terms 貿易条件 （⇒Incoterms）
貿易取引の基礎条件として用いられる貿易条件：
CFR 運賃込み条件 cost and freightの略
CIF 運賃保険料込み条件 cost, insurance and freightの略
CIP 運送費保険料込み条件 carriage and insurance paid toの略
CPT 運送費込み条件 carriage paid toの略
DAF 国境持込み渡し条件 delivered at frontierの略
DDP 仕向地持込み渡し・関税込み条件 delivered duty paidの略
DDU 仕向地持込み渡し・関税抜き条件 delivered duty unpaidの略
DEQ 埠頭持込み渡し条件 delivered ex quayの略
DES 本船持込み渡し条件 delivered ex shipの略
EXW 工場渡し条件 ex worksの略
FAS 船側渡し条件 free alongside shipの略
FCA 運送人渡し条件 free carrierの略
FOB 本船渡し条件 free on boardの略

trader （名）証券業者, 売買担当者, ディーラー, 貿易業者, 取引業者, 同業者, 業者, 市場関係者, トレーダー （⇒day trader, futures trader, speculative trader）
bearish traders 弱気筋
bond trader 債券トレーダー
bullish traders 強気筋
commodity trader 商品取引業者
currency trader 為替トレーダー
day trader ディ・トレーダー
export trader 輸出業者

fellow trader　同業者
floor trader　場内取引人, フロア・トレーダー
forex trader　為替トレーダー　(=forex dealer)
futures trader　先物トレーダー
general trader　一般貿易業者
individual trader　個人トレーダー
international speculative traders　海外投機筋
online trader　オンライン・トレーダー, ネット・トレーダー
room trader　ルーム・トレーダー
skillful trader　ベテラン・トレーダー
trader's transaction　仲間取引
◆A sudden plunge in the market is believed to have been caused by a trader who mistyped an order to sell a large block of shares. 相場急落は、トレーダーによる大量の株式売買の誤発注により生じたと見られる。◆Currency traders are now turning to the renminbi (yuan) from the U.S. dollar. 為替トレーダーは今や、米ドルから中国の人民元に目を向けている。◆Currency traders worldwide frantically search for a safe haven in volatile times. 世界の為替トレーダーは、変動の激しい時期の安全な投資先を熱狂的に求めている。◆Day traders are individual investors who buy and sell stocks many times a day to earn a profit on the trading margin. デイ・トレーダーは、1日に何度も株の売買を繰り返して、その利ざやで利益を上げる個人投資家だ。◆If the yen continues to advance, there will be a possibility that traders who have been buying the dollar will begin to sell off the U.S. currency to earn profits or minimize losses. 円高がこのまま進むと、ドルを買い込んできた市場関係者が利食いや損切りのためにドル売りに回る可能性がある。◆In spite of Mixi's robust performance, traders fear the company has been overvalued. ミクシィの業績好調にもかかわらず、証券業者は同社への過大評価を警戒している。◆The trader used a standard option to hedge the price risk of a stock. このトレーダーは、株式の価格リスクをヘッジするために標準的なオプションを使った。

trading　(名)取引, 売買, 商業, 貿易, 営業, トレーディング　(⇒after-hours trading, commodity futures trading, day trader, day trading, equity option trading, exchange, futures trading, intraday trading, off-hours trading, stock market)
day trading　デイ・トレーディング
e-trading　電子商取引, 電子取引, 電子売買, コンピュータ取引
electronic trading　電子取引, 電子商取引　(=e-trading)
equity trading business　株式取引業務, 株売買業務
foreign exchange trading　外国為替取引
futures trading　先物取引
heavy trading　大商い
home trading　ホーム・トレーディング　(=Net trading, online stock trading)
horse-trading　駆け引き
in the afternoon trading　午後の取引で
in the morning trading　朝方の取引で
insider trading　インサイダー取引
large-lot trading　大口取引
margin trading　信用取引, 証拠金取引
morning trading　朝の取引, 朝方の取引, 午前の取引
Net trading　ネット取引　(=Internet trading)
online stock trading business　株のインターネット取引業務
online trading　オンライン取引
option trading　オプション取引
proprietary trading system　私設取引システム
public trading　公募取引
real time option trading　リアルタイム・オプション取引
regulation of trading　売買規制
small-lot after-hours trading　立ち会い外分売
small-lot trading　小口取引
stock trading　株式売買, 株式取引, 株取引
trading commission　取引手数料　(⇒high-flying)
trading desk　取引デスク(公開市場操作(open market operations)を担当するニューヨーク連邦準備銀行の証券局), 外国為替(foreign exchange)の担当デスク
trading down　高リスク投資への組替え
trading market　流通市場, トレーディング・マーケット　(⇒primary market, secondary market)
trading partner　貿易相手国
trading pattern　株価動向傾向線
trading system　売買システム　(⇒investing in equipment, grade)
trading unit　売買単位, 取引単位　(=unit of trading; ⇒stock split)
trading up　低リスク投資への組替え
trading value　取引金額
twenty-four-hour trading　24時間トレーディング
◆Google shares surged about 20 percent on their first day of public trading. 米グーグル(インターネット検索最大手)の株式は、公募取引の初日に約20%急上昇した。◆Margin trading was used in a corporate takeover by exploiting legal shortcomings. 法の不備を利用して、企業買収に信用取引が使われた。◆Shinsei Bank stock ended Thursday's trading at ¥827 on a trading volume of 247.23 million shares. 新生銀株は、終値827円、出来高2億4,723万株で木曜日の取引を終えた。◆The ADB lowered its 2011 growth forecast in Asian nations due to growing worries about weak demand from key trading partners including the United States and Europe. アジア開発銀行(ADB)は、主要貿易相手国である欧米で需要減退[需要低迷]懸念が高まっていることから、アジアの2011年の成長見通し[GDP成長率見通し]を下方修正した。◆The intervention was prompted by the yen rising to ¥82.87 to the dollar in the morning trading. 市場介入に踏み切ったのは、朝方の取引で1ドル=82円87銭まで円高が進んだからだ。◆The Nikkei Stock Average recovered to the ¥9,000 mark in the morning, but trimmed earlier gains in afternoon trading. 日経平均株価は、朝から9,000円台に回復したが、午後の取引で午前の上昇幅が縮小した。◆The Tokyo stock market has recently been roaring, with record heavy trading seen. 東京株式市場が、記録的な大商いを続けて、活況を呈している。◆Trading is sluggish on stock markets mainly due to the financial crisis in Europe. 株式市場は、主に欧州の財政・金融危機で取引[相場]が低迷している。

trading at the Tokyo Stock Exchange　東京証券取引所の取引
◆A computer failure brought trading at the Tokyo Stock Exchange to a standstill for more than four hours. コンピュータ・システムの障害で、東京証券取引所の取引が4時間以上も停止した。

trading day　営業日
◆The 225-issue Nikkei Stock Average fell for the sixth straight trading day Wednesday to close down 30.47 points to 10,177.58. 水曜日の日経平均株価(225種)は6営業日連続の下落で、終値は前日比30円47銭安の1万177円58銭となった。

trading hours　取引時間, 取引途中
◆Oil prices on the New York Mercantile Exchange soared to the $100 level a barrel for the first time during the trading hours. ニューヨーク・マーカンタイル取引所の原油価格は、

取引時間中に初めて1バレル＝100ドル台まで上昇した。◆The Tokyo Stock Exchange and four other exchanges extended their morning trading hours by 30 minutes to 11:30 a.m. 東証など5証券取引所が、午前の取引時間を11時半まで30分間延長した。

trading limit　取引制限
  daily trading limit　日々の取引制限, 値幅制限
    （＝daily limit, daily price limit）
  reach the daily trading limit for the second straight day　2日連続してストップ安（値幅制限の下限）となる
  ◆Japan Airlines shares plunged to close at ￥7, reaching the daily trading limit for the second straight day. 日本航空株は7円まで下落して取引を終え、2日連続してストップ安（値幅制限の下限）となった。
  解説 値幅制限とは：日本の株式市場では、予想外の暴騰、暴落で市場が混乱するのを防ぐため、個別銘柄の1日の株価変動幅が、株価水準（前日の終値）から上下一定の範囲に制限されている。買い注文が殺到して値幅制限の上限まで達すれば「ストップ高」となり、逆に売り注文が殺到して値幅制限の下限まで下落すれば「ストップ安」となる。

trading margin　（株式）売買の利ざや
  ◆Day traders are individual investors who buy and sell stocks many times a day to earn a profit on the trading margin. デイ・トレーダーは、1日に何度も株の売買を繰り返して、その利ざやで利益を上げる個人投資家だ。

trading of stocks　株の取引, 株の売買, 株式売買
    （＝stock trading）
  ◆The Proprietary Trading System and other online trading systems facilitate trading of stocks outside exchanges. 私設取引システム（PTS）などの電子取引システムは、証券取引所外で株の売買（注文）を成立させる。

trading on the Tokyo Commodity Exchange　東京工業品取引所での取引
  ◆The benchmark gold future price surged to all-time high of ￥4,725 per gram in trading on the Tokyo Commodity Exchange. 東京工業品取引所の取引で、金取引の指標となる金先物価格が、過去最高の1グラム＝4,725円まで急騰した。

trading profits　売買益
  ◆The major securities house attributed the poor earnings to sharp drops in brokerage fees and trading profits amid the extended slump in the domestic stock market. この大手証券会社は、減益の要因として、国内株式市場の長期低迷による株売買手数料と売買益の大幅減を挙げた。

trading session　株式取引所の立会い, 取引時間
  afternoon trading session　午後の取引, 午後の取引時間
  morning trading session　午前の取引, 午前の取引時間
  ◆By the 30-minute extension of morning trading sessions, investors will be able to trade for a full hour in Japan as they monitor stock price movements on the Hong Kong market. 午前の取引時間の30分延長で、投資家は、香港市場の値動きを見ながら日本市場で丸1時間売買できるようになった。◆In August 2011, the Stock Exchange of Singapore did away with its lunch break to increase the length of its trading session to eight hours. シンガポール証券取引所は、2011年8月から昼休みを廃止して、1日の取引時間が8時間に増えた。◆The TSE and four other exchanges extended their morning trading sessions by 30 minutes to boost market activity. 東証など5証券取引所が、取引活性化のため午前の取引時間を30分間延長した。

trading system　取引システム, 売買システム
  ◆Investors are influenced by a sock-exchange trading system's ability to process large orders quickly. 投資家は、大量の注文を高速処理する証券取引所の売買システムの能力に左右されるようになった。◆To compete against online trading systems, stock exchanges must improve their ability to process buy and sell orders. 電子取引システムに対抗するには、証券取引所が売買注文の処理能力を高める必要がある。

trading volume　売買高, 売買額, 出来高, 売買株数, 売上高, 取引量, 売買規模, 取引規模
    （⇒turnover ratio）
  a year's trading volume　1年間の出来高
    （⇒turnover ratio）
  in terms of trading volume　取引規模で, 売買規模で
  the trading volume of stocks sold short　株の空売りの売買額　（⇒sell short）
  total trading volume　総出来高, 総売買高, 総売上高, 取引全体
  trading volume and value on all stock exchanges　全国証券取引所売買高
  trading volume of integrated securities companies　総合証券売買高
  trading volume on the Tokyo Stock Exchange this year　東証［東京株式市場］の今年の通算出来高
  ◆A market player put the level of short selling in the stock market at between 5 to 10 percent of total trading volume. ある市場筋によると、株の空売りは取引全体の5-10%程度といわれる。◆The bank stock ended Friday's trading at ￥827 on a trading volume of 247.23 million shares. 同銀行株は、終値827円、出来高2億4,723万株で金曜日の取引を終えた。◆The Tokyo Stock Exchange was outstripped［outpaced］by the Shanghai Stock Exchange in terms of trading volume. 東証は、取引規模［売買規模］で上海証券取引所に抜かれた。

trafficking　（名）（麻薬などの）不正取引, 密売, 密売買
  ◆The U.S. government froze the assets of four individuals and eight entities that were involved in illicit activities such as money laundering, currency counterfeiting and narcotics trafficking. 米政府は、資金洗浄（マネー・ロンダリング）や通貨偽造、麻薬取引などの違法行為に関与している4個人、8団体の資産を凍結した。

tranche　（名）分割発行される証券［融資］の1回分,（収入や株券などの）一部分, IMFの融資区分, 優先的外貨引出し権, トランシュ
  commercial tranche　民間トランシュ
  credit tranche　IMFの条件付き一般貸出, 信用トランシュ, クレジット・トランシュ
  delayed tranche　遅延トランシュ
  fast pay tranche　短期トランシュ
  gold tranche　ゴールド・トランシュ
  IMF reserve tranche　IMFリザーブ・トランシュ
  international tranche　国際トランシュ
  raise in several tranches　数本のトランシュに分けて起債する
  senior tranche　上位トランシュ
  slow pay tranche　中期トランシュ
  tax spared［sparing］tranche　見なし課税負担型トランシュ
  the final tranche of the loan　貸付け金［ローン］の最後の部分
  the first tranche of the emergency loan　緊急融資の第一回トランシュ
  tranche issue　トランシュ発行（外債発行の場合に、年限の異なる社債を同時に発行したり、市場を分けて発行したりすることをいう）
  ◆As Greece may default on its debts, the IMF and the EU have worked out a policy of deciding on a second aid tranche of €120 billion in July 2011. ギリシャが債務不履行（デフォルト）に陥る可能性があるため、国際通貨基金（IMF）と欧州連合（EU）は、2011年7月に1,200億ユーロ（約13兆8,000億円）規模の第二次金融支援策を決定する方針を打ち出した。

transaction　（名）取引, 取扱い, 業務処理, 業務, 商取引,

売買, 和解, 示談, 法律行為 （⇒factor, illegal transaction, operator, settlement-specific deposit）
B2B transaction　企業対企業取引（B2B=b to b, business to business）
B2C transaction　企業対消費者の取引（B2C=b to c, business to consumer）
capital transaction　資本取引
cash payments transactions　銀行支払い取引
cash receipts transactions　銀行入金取引
financial transaction　金融取引, 財務取引
foreign currency transaction　外貨建て取引
fund transaction　資金取引
illegal transaction　違法取引, 違法行為
large-lot transaction　大口取引
massive share transactions　株式の大量取引
speculative transaction　投機的取引
spot transaction　直物取引, 現物取引, 直物為替取引
swap transaction　スワップ取引
the number of transactions　取引件数

◆A real estate investment fund was alleged to have failed to report about ￥18 billion in income from transaction involving land and property taken as collateral for nonperforming loans. 不動産投資ファンドが、不良債権の担保に取った不動産関連の取引で得た所得約180億円の申告漏れを指摘されていた。◆An increase in transactions that brokerages handle has accompanied the brisk stock market business. 証券会社が扱う取引の増加は、そのまま株式相場の盛況と重なる。◆Concerns have been raised over the ability of Internet banking services to verify the identity of new depositors or to guarantee the security of customer transactions. インターネット・バンキングについては、新規預金者の身元確認や対顧客取引の安全保証の点で、その能力に対して懸念が提起されている。◆Financial terms of the transaction were not disclosed. 取引の条件[財務条件]は、公表されなかった。◆Major trading houses have also shown interest in entering the new business of Internet share transactions. 総合商社も、株式のネット取引の新規事業に参入する意向を示している。◆Some major banks lower their commission rates of foreign currency deposits if depositors make transactions via online accounts. 外貨預金の預金者がネット口座経由で取引をする場合、一部の大手銀行は、外貨預金の手数料[為替手数料]の料率を引き下げている。◆The bank handles transactions for individuals and small and midsize companies. 同行は、中小企業・個人向けの取引を扱っている。◆The company compiled documents for financial institutions it has transactions with. 同社は、取引金融機関向けに資料を作成した。◆Though stock prices remain low, the number of transactions has already outpaced that during the bubble economy. 株価はまだ低いものの、株取引の件数はすでにバブル期を超えている。◆To cover up its irregularities, the bank deleted e-mails detailing its business transactions from the bank's server. 不正行為を隠すため同行は、業務取引に関する電子メールを、同行のサーバーから削除した。◆Transactions on all of the 2,520 issues traded at the TSE were stalled from 9 a.m. due to a computer malfunction. 東証で取引されている2,520全銘柄の取引が、コンピュータのシステム障害で午前9時から停止した。

transfer　（動）移転する, 移す, 移し替える, 振り替える, 転送する, 譲渡する, 名義を書き換える, 振り込む, 送金する, 繰り入れる, 配置転換する　（⇒absolute assignment, account book, authentication, banking business, foundation fund）
transfer a securities account　証券取引口座を移管する
transfer capital reserves to retained earnings　資本準備金[法定準備金]を剰余金に振り替える
transfer loan-loss provisions to profits　貸倒れ引当金を利益に振り替える
transfer the firm's business to a new company　同社の営業を新会社に譲渡する
transfer the shares of the company　同社株を譲渡する

◆About ￥16 million was transferred from this self-employed man's savings account to a bank account under someone else's name. この自営業者の普通預金から他人名義の銀行口座に、約1,600万円が振り込まれていた。◆At an emergency shareholders meeting, the company obtained shareholder approval to transfer ￥199 billion from its legal reserves to provide for write-offs of nonperforming loans. 臨時株主総会で同社は、株主から、不良債権処理に備えて法定準備金から1,990億円を取り崩す案の承認を得た。◆If golden shares held by a friendly company are transferred to another party, such shares could be transferred again to a hostile bidder. 友好的な企業が保有する黄金株を第三者に譲渡した場合、その黄金株はまた敵対的買収者に譲渡される可能性もある。◆Nonperforming loans will be transferred to the revival account, as well as crossheld shares and idle real estate. 不良債権は、持ち合い株式や遊休不動産などと一緒に「再生勘定」に移す。◆Sumitomo Mitsui Banking Corp.（SMBC）said about ￥600 billion in capital reserves will be transferred to retained earnings. 資本準備金[法定準備金]のうち6,000億円を剰余金に振り替える方針だ、と三井住友銀行は述べた。◆The bank plans to provide the money by transferring ￥100 billion in subordinated loans, which it has already extended to the insurer, to the insurer's foundation fund. 同行は、すでに供与している劣後ローン1,000億円をこの保険会社の基金に振り替えて、その資金を提供する方針だ。◆The company transferred the deposits of two firms it would acquire to window-dress the books. 同社は、買収予定の2社の預金を付け替えて[移し替えて]粉飾決算をしていた。◆The firm transferred part of the agent fees to a bank account opened in a different bank in Japan. 同社は、仲介手数料の一部を日本国内の別の銀行に開設した銀行口座に送金していた。

transfer　（名）出向, 譲渡, 移転, 名義の書換え, 転送, 転任, 配属, 配置転換, 振替, 振込み, 送金　（⇒absolute assignment, cash transfer, double transfer, fund transfer, money transfer, stock transfer）
account transfer　口座振替, 振替
automatic account transfer　口座自動振替
automatic debt transfer　自動引落し, 自動振替
automatic transfer service　自動振替サービス
balance of transfer service　移転収支
bank transfer　銀行振替, 銀行送金, 銀行振込み
bank's automatic accounts transfer system　銀行自動引落し制度
delays in transfers　送金業務の遅れ, 口座振替の遅れ
double transfer　二重振込み, 二重送金
intra-company transfer　内部振替, 事業部門間振替
mail transfer　郵便振替, 普通送金
mistaken transfer　誤送金
money transfer　振替口座振替, 資金の移動　（=transfer of money）
ownership transfer　所有移転
private transfers　民間移転収支
reversal of the transfer　復帰人事
risk transfer　リスク移転
share transfer　株式の名義書換え, 株式譲渡　（=stock transfer）
telegraphic transfer　電信送金, 電信為替
transfer agent　名義書換え代理人, 証券代行機関
transfer book　株式名簿, 株主名簿, 名義書換え名簿, 名義書換え台帳
transfer day　名義書換え日

transfer delay　口座振替の遅れ
（=delayed money transfer）

transfer form　振込み用紙

transfer from customer accounts　顧客の口座振替
（⇒customer account）

transfer of employees　従業員の配置転換

unprocessed money transfer　口座振替の未処理分
◆Investors can trade the Seibu Railway shares for a month after their transfer to the TSE's liquidation post from the monitoring post. 西武鉄道株が東証の監理ポストから整理ポストに移った後1か月間、投資家は西武鉄道株を売買できる。◆The revised law bans the sale or transfer of bankbooks and bankcards without a legitimate reason. この改正法（改正本人確認法）は、正当な理由がなく預金通帳とキャッシュ・カードを売買、譲渡することを禁じている。

transfer money　金を振り込む, 送金する, 資金を移す［移動する］
◆A homemaker using consumer loans has frequently received e-mails on her cell phone from their people offering to transfer money to her. 消費者金融を利用している主婦に最近、消費者金融の社員から「お金を振り込みます」というメールが携帯電話に頻繁に届いている。◆In illegal access of Internet bank accounts confirmed at financial institutions, money was transferred from a client's account to a second account. 金融機関で確認されたネット・バンキング口座への不正アクセスでは、顧客の口座から現金が他人名義の口座に振り込まれていた［送信されていた］。◆The man intentionally dodged the tax payments as he transferred the money for asset management to another country. 男は、資産運用の資金を他国に移動させていることから、意図的に納税を免れていた。◆This bank requires users to provide special authentication numbers to transfer money. この銀行は、振込みの際に専用の認証番号の入力を利用者に義務付けている。

transfer of business　営業譲渡
◆Sumitomo Trust reached a basic agreement with UFJ Holdings on the transfer of business from UFJ Trust to Sumitomo Trust. 住友信託は、UFJホールディングスと、UFJ信託から住友信託に営業を譲渡することで基本合意した。

transfer of deposits　預金の送金
◆Illegal transfers of deposits via foreign malware have been jumping. 海外のマルウェア（コンピュータ・ウイルスの一種）による預金の不正送金が急増している。◆Online banking users can prevent illegal transfers of their deposits by frequently changing their passwords. オンライン・バンキング利用者は、パスワードをこまめに変更して、預金の不正送金を防ぐことができる。

transfer of funds　資金移動, 資金のシフト, 口座振替
（=fund transfer）
◆Transfers of funds to the major banks from the smaller and comparatively financially weaker financial institutions have been accelerating. 経営基盤が脆弱（ぜいじゃく）な中小の金融機関から大手銀行への資金のシフトが加速している。

transfer of golden shares　黄金株の譲渡
◆A company is allowed to set restrictions on the transfer of golden shares. 企業は、黄金株（拒否権付き種類株式）に譲渡制限を付けることができる［黄金株の譲渡に制限を設けることができる］。

transfer of money　資金の移動
（=money transfer）
◆These major transfers of money have occurred in preparation for the lifting of the freeze on the payoff scheme. これらの資金の大移動は、ペイオフ制度凍結解除に備えた動きだ。

transfer restrictions　譲渡制限
◆Currently, a company may set transfer restrictions on a portion of its outstanding shares. 現在（2005年）、企業は一部の発行済み株式に譲渡制限を付けることができる。

transfer the ownership　所有権を移す
◆When Mycal established the special purpose company (SPC), it transferred the ownership of 20 profitable stores to it, issuing the bonds with the stores as collateral. マイカルが特定目的会社（SPC）を設立したとき、マイカルは20の黒字店舗の所有権をSPCに移し、この店舗を担保に社債を発行した。

transformation　（名）変化, 変形, 変貌, 変質, 変換, 転換, 転化, 移行, 変革, 改革, 事業再編
corporate transformation　企業改革
distribution transformation　流通改革, 流通近代化
political transformation　政権交代
transformation into a holding company　持ち株会社への移行
transformation of the markets　市場の変質
transformation of value　価値の転換
◆The Jasdaq can begin small-lot after-hours trading by its transformation from an over-the-counter stock market to a securities exchange. ジャスダックは、店頭市場から証券取引所への移行により、立会い外分売（取引時間外に大株主などが保有株を小口に分けて売り出すこと）も可能になった。◆The U.S. Federal Reserve Board approved the transformation of Goldman Sachs and Morgan Stanley into holding companies in September 2008. 2008年9月に、米連邦準備制度理事会（FRB）は、ゴールドマン・サックスとモルガン・スタンレーの銀行持ち株会社への移行を承認した。

transition　（名）移行, 推移, 変遷, 経過, 移行時, 移行期間, 過渡期
a smooth transition to the currency basket　通貨バスケットへの円滑な移行
be in transition　過渡期にある
transition economy　移行経済
transition period　過渡期, 移行期, 移行期間, 米政権移行期間（11月上旬の大統領選挙日から翌年1月20日の大統領就任日までの政権交代の引継ぎ期間）
transition team　米政権移行チーム
transition to a tri-reserve currency regime　3準備通貨（米ドルとユーロ、人民元）体制への移行
◆Many listed companies may be unable to complete the transition to the IFRSs by 2015. 多くの上場企業は、2015年までに国際財務報告基準（IFRSs）に移行できない可能性がある。◆The latest rise in the yuan's value against the U.S. dollar and a smooth transition to the currency basket will help stabilize China's external relations. 今回の人民元相場の対米ドル切上げと通貨バスケット制への円滑な移行で、中国の対外関係は安定化に向かうだろう。◆The Obama transition team discovered Treasury nominee Geithner failed to pay part of back taxes. ガイスナー［ガイトナー］次期財務長官（ニューヨーク連銀総裁）が追徴課税の一部を納めていなかったことを、オバマ政権移行チームが突き止めた。◆Transition to a tri-reserve-currency (the U.S. dollar plus the euro and the renminbi) regime would not be without fiscal turbulences. 3準備通貨（米ドルとユーロ、人民元）体制への移行には、財政的混乱が伴うだろう。

translate　（動）換算する, 変換する, 解釈する, 翻訳する
◆The results are translated into U.S. dollars. 業績は、米ドルに換算してあります。

translation　（名）換算, 変換, 調整, 解釈, 翻訳
currency translation　通貨換算, 外貨換算
currency translation adjustments　通貨換算調整, 外貨換算調整勘定
foreign currency translation　外貨換算
translation adjustment　換算調整, 換算調整勘定, 外貨換算調整勘定
（=foreign currency translation adjustment）

translation gain or loss　為替差損益, 換算差損益
　（=translation gains and losses）
translation gains　為替差益
translation losses　為替差損
translation of foreign exchange　外国為替換算
translation of net assets　純資産の換算

transmission fee　送金手数料
◆The bank will charge transmission fees according to the amount of money sent by the regional banks. 同行は今後、地銀の送金額に応じて送金手数料を請求することになる。

transmit　（動）送信する, 伝送する, 送る, 伝える, 伝達する, 放送する, 知らせる
　transmit cash　送金する
　transmit data over the Internet　ネットでデータ［情報、メッセージ］を送信する
◆Participants in the market process information transmitted globally in real time, manipulate it in some cases and try to win profit by moving large amounts of money in this information war zone. 市場参加者は、リアルタイムでグローバルに伝達される情報を処理し、場合によってはそれを操作しながら、この情報戦争の戦場で巨額の資金を動かして利益を得ようとしている。◆The Internet, which can transmit rumors across the country instantaneously, has rocked the financial system. 一瞬のうちにデマを全国に広げることができるインターネットは、金融システムを揺さぶっている。

transparency　透明性　（⇒IR meeting）
◆The Financial Services Agency's Business Accounting Council adopted a U.S.-style current value accounting standard for corporate mergers to increase transparency of accounting rules. 金融庁の企業会計審議会は、会計規則の透明性を高めるため、会社合併については米国式の時価主義会計基準を採用した。

transparent　（形）透明な, 明白な
◆The amount of each European bank's potential capital shortfall was not transparent before the stress test by the EU's Committee of European Banking Supervisors. 欧州連合（EU）の欧州銀行監督委員会がストレス・テスト（特別検査）を行うまで、欧州各行の潜在的な資本不足額は、不透明だった。

tread　（動）踏む, 踏みつける, 歩く, たどる, 征服する
　be treading water　まるで進展がない,（同じ状況に）いらいらする
　tread a thorny path　いばらの道を歩む
　tread one's feelings　～の感情を踏みにじる
　tread softly［cautiously, lightly］　そっと歩く, 慎重に扱う
◆The bank's new president must tread a thorny path as the management environment is severe. 経営環境が厳しいので、同行の新社長はいばらの道を歩むことになろう。

treasurer　（名）会計役（米国では会社役員の1人）, 財務担当役員, 財務部長, 経理部長, トレジャラー　（米大手企業の「トレジャラー（treasurer）」は、会社の資金調達や運用などの財務部門を統括する役員。⇒controller）

Treasuries　（名）米財務省証券（U.S. Treasuries）, 米財務省債, 米国債, 米国債相場, TB
　（=Treasury securities; ⇒U.S. Treasuries）
◆The Bank of Japan would purchase some government holdings in U.S. Treasuries as a means of providing the government with funds for market intervention. 日銀は、政府が保有する米国債の一部を、政府に市場介入資金を供給する手段として購入する。

米国財務省証券の種類：
Treasury bill　満期（償還期限）が1年以内の財務省短期証券　（=T-bill）
Treasury bond　満期（償還期限）が10年超の財務省長期証券　（=T-bond）

Treasury note　満期（償還期限）が1年超10年以内の財務省中期証券　（=T-note）

treasury　（名）金庫, 資金, 基金, 財源
　treasury bill　英大蔵省証券, 米財務省短期証券, 短期国債, TB
　treasury investment and loans　財政投融資
　treasury operation　財務運用
　treasury product　財務商品
　treasury purchases　自己株式購入
　treasury share transaction　自己株式取引
　treasury surplus　国庫余裕金

Treasury　（名）米財務省, 英大蔵省, 国庫, 基金, T
　benchmark 30-year U.S. Treasury　30年物国債指標銘柄
　current Treasury　財務省証券指標銘柄
　Deputy Secretary of the Treasury　米財務副長官
　gross Treasury debt issuance　米国債の総発行額
　Lords of the Treasury　英大蔵委員会委員
　monthly Treasury auction　月例の国債入札
　on-the-run Treasury　米国債指標銘柄
　Secretary of the Treasury　米財務長官
　　（=Treasury Secretary）
　the First Lord of the Treasury　英大蔵委員会委員長
　Treasury Board　英大蔵委員会
　Treasury coupon auctions　国債入札
　Treasury Department spokesman　米財務省の広報担当者
　Treasury discount bills　（英）国庫短期証券
　Treasury finance　財務省の資金調達
　Treasury financing［refunding］　国債入札
　Treasury instruments　財務省証券
　Treasury official　財務省高官
　Treasury refunding　国債入札
　　（=Treasury financing）
　Treasury securities　財務省証券　（=Treasuries）
　Treasury supply　国債入札
　Treasury surplus　国庫余裕金
　U.S. Treasuries　米国債, 米財務省証券
　　（=U.S. Treasury securities）
　U.S. Treasury Secretary　米財務長官
◆Fed purchases of long-term government bonds should boost Treasury prices. 連米邦準備制度理事会（FRB）の長期国債購入［買取り］で、米国債［米国債相場］は反発するはずだ。

Treasury bill　米財務省短期証券, Tビル
　maturity of (U.S.) Treasury bills　Tビルの満期償還
　sales of Treasury bills　TB売買
　Treasury bill market　米財務省短期証券市場

［解説］米財務省短期証券とは：通称T-billで、単にbillとも呼ばれる。割引発行で、額面から利息相当額を割り引いた価格で発行して、満期時に額面で償還する。米財務省証券のなかではいちばん流動性が高く、広範に流通しているため、FRB（連邦準備理事会）の金融政策運営上、公開市場操作（open market operation）の重要な手段の一つになっている。

Treasury bond　米政府長期証券, 財務省長期証券, 財務省証券, 米国債, Tビル
　（⇒auction, bid, junk bond）
　buy Treasury bonds　国債を買う, 国債を買い入れる
　downgrade Treasury bonds　米国債の格付けを引き下げる, 米国債の格下げに踏み切る
　the possible downgrade of Treasury bonds　想定される米国債の格下げ
　the prices of the Treasury bonds　米国債の価格

◆If the negotiations between Republicans and Democrats face rough going and the deficit-cutting plan ends up being insufficient, credit rating agencies may downgrade Treasury bonds. 共和党と民主党の協議が難航して赤字削減策が不十分に終わると、(信用)格付け会社が米国債の格下げに踏み切る可能性がある。◆Should the U.S. government fall into default, the prices of the Treasury bonds held by major countries and financial institutions around the world would plummet. 米政府がデフォルト(債務不履行)に陥れば、主要国や世界の金融機関が保有する米国債の価格は、暴落するだろう。◆The Fed's program of buying $600 billion in Treasury bonds to help the economy is to end in June 2011 on schedule. 景気を支えるために6,000億ドルの国債を買い入れる米連邦準備制度理事会(FRB)の量的緩和政策は、予定通り2011年6月に終了する。◆The possible downgrade of Treasury bonds is raising fears of adverse effects on the world's markets. 想定される米国債の格下げで、世界の市場に及ぼす悪影響への懸念が高まっている。◆The spreads of yields on high-risk junk bonds over the benchmark five-year U.S. Treasury bonds had been around 200 basis points, or 2 percentage points. リスクの高いジャンク債と指標となる5年物財務省証券との金利差(スプレッド)は、2%(200ベーシス・ポイント)程度で推移していた。◆The U.S. government could avoid the worst-case scenario of default on payments to investors in Treasury bonds. 米政府は、国債の償還資金がなくなる債務不履行という最悪の事態を避けることができた。◆U.S. Treasury bonds were downgraded by Standard & Poor's because the government failed to take drastic countermeasures against its fiscal deterioration. 米政府が財政悪化に大胆な対策を取れなかったため、米国債はスタンダード・アンド・プアーズ(S&P)に格下げされた。

解説 米政府長期証券とは:通称T-bondの財務省長期証券は、利息が年2回支払われる利付き証券(coupon issues)。発行方法には、主に引受業者(underwriters)が対象の競争入札(competitive bid)と主に個人など小口投資家が対象の非競争入札(noncompetitive bid)がある。入札者は公示で募集する。発行者による繰上げ償還は、満期の5年前にすることができる。30年物長期証券は、長期金利の指標となっている。

Treasury bond yield 米財務省長期証券の利回り
◆Long-term interest rates plummeted temporarily, but the Treasury bond yield soon rebounded. 長期金利は一時急落したが、米財務省長期証券の利回り(長期金利)はすぐ反発した。

Treasury Department [Department of the Treasury] 米財務省 (⇒currency market intervention, currency report)
 Bureau of Engraving and Printing 証券・印刷局
 Bureau of the Public Debt 公債局
 Financial Management Service 財務管理局
 Internal Revenue Service 内国歳入庁
 Office of the Comptroller of the Currency 通貨統制官室
 Office of Thrift Supervision 倹約貯蓄機関監督局
 United States Customs Service 合衆国関税局
 United States Mint 合衆国造幣局
 United States Savings Bonds Division 合衆国貯蓄債券局
◆The semiannual currency report of the U.S. Treasury Department said that Japan maintains a floating exchange rate regime. 日本は変動為替相場制[変動相場制]を維持している、と米財務省の為替政策半期報告書は述べている。◆The U.S. Treasury Department will closely monitor the pace of appreciation of the yuan by China. 米財務省は、中国の人民元切上げのペースを注意深く監視する方針だ。

Treasury market 米国債市場, 米国債券市場, 米債券相場
 front end of the Treasury market 米国債短期物
 long end of the Treasury market 米国債長期物
 volatility in the Treasury market 米国債市場の乱高下, 米国債市場の波乱の展開, 債券相場の乱高下
◆The tone in the Treasury market is becoming extremely positive. 債券市場の地合いは、ひじょうに明るくなっている。

Treasury note 米財務省証券, 財務省中期証券, 中期国債, Tノート
解説 米財務省証券とは:利息が年2回支払われる利付き証券(coupon issues)。発行方法には、主に引受業者(underwriters)が対象の競争入札と主に個人など小口投資家が対象の非競争入札がある。入札者は、公示で募集する。発行者による繰上げ償還は、財務省長期証券と違ってできない。

treasury secretary [Treasury Secretary] 米財務省長官, 米財務長官(英国はChancellor of the Exchequer, 日本はFinance Minister)
◆Finance Minister Naoto Kan and U.S. Treasury Secretary Timothy Geithner agreed that fiscal rehabilitation is important. 菅財務相とティモシー・ガイトナー「ガイスナー」米財務長官は、財政再建が重要であるとの認識で意見が一致した。◆U.S. President-elect Barack Obama named New York Federal Reserve Bank President Tim Geithner the next treasury secretary. オバマ次期米大統領は、新政権の財務長官にティモシー・ガイトナー・ニューヨーク連邦準備銀行総裁を指名した。

Treasury securities 米財務省証券, 米国債
◆China is trying to flex its muscle with the United States on the strength of its status as the largest holder of U.S. Treasury securities. 中国は、米財務省証券[米国債]の最大保有国としての地位を背景に、米国への影響力を行使しようとしている。◆If a new federal debt ceiling isn't set by Aug. 2, 2011, the United States will be forced to default on Treasuries securities as it will not be able to issue new bonds to pay back maturing government debts. 2011年8月2日までに連邦政府の債務上限を新たに設けないと、米国は満期を迎える国債を償還するための国債増発ができないので、米国債の不履行(デフォルト)が発生する。

treasury stock 金庫株, 自社株, 自己株式
 (=reacquired shares, reacquired stock, repurchased shares, repurchased stock, treasury shares)
 accounting for treasury stock 自己株式の処理, 自己株式の会計処理
 gain on sale of treasury stock 自己株式売却益
 lifting of a ban on treasury stock 金庫株解禁
 purchase of treasury stock 自己株式の購入, 自己株式の取得
◆Under the treasury stock system, companies are allowed to buy their own stocks and keep them in reserve. 金庫株制度によると、企業は自社株を取得して、取得した株を保管することができる。
解説 金庫株は、株価の低迷や乱高下を防ぐため、企業が自社株を買い戻して、買い取った株を保有し、相場が持ち直したときに売ることができる株のこと

trend (名)傾向, 動向, 基調, 趨勢, 大勢, 地合い, 市場の足取り, 推移, 流れ, 潮流, 波, 現象, 流行, トレンド (⇒reform名詞)
 above-trend growth トレンドを上回る経済成長
 be in a bear trend 下降傾向にある, 下降トレンドから脱していない
 be on an upward trend 上昇基調にある, 増加傾向にある
 bear trend 弱気トレンド
 declining trend 減少傾向
 deflationary trend デフレ傾向, 物価下落傾向 (⇒tight fiscal [financing] policy)
 dollar-selling trend ドル売りの流れ
 downward trend 下落基調, 下落傾向, 低下傾向
 downward trend of stock prices 株価の下落基調, 株価の下落傾向

earnings trend　収益動向
economic trends　経済動向, 景気動向, 景気
falling trend　下降傾向, 下落傾向, 低下傾向
financial trend　金融動向
grow at an above-trend rate　トレンドを上回るペースで拡大する
inflationary trend　インフレ動向, 物価上昇傾向
major trend　大勢
negative trend　低下傾向
price trends　値動き
prospective trends　今後のトレンド
reversal of the trend　トレンドの反転
rising trend　上昇傾向, 上昇基調
secular trend　長期的な傾向, 長期傾向, 長期トレンド
spinoff trend　分社化傾向
the yen's rising trend　円高傾向
trend effect　趨勢効果
trend model　傾向型モデル
trend of [in] interest rates　金利動向
trend (percentage) method　趨勢法
trend rate　潜在成長率, 傾向率, 傾向値, トレンドの水準
trends in activity　景気動向
underlying trend　基調
upward [rising] trend　増加傾向, 増加基調, 上昇基調, 上昇傾向

◆A large yen-selling intervention by monetary authorities on Sept. 15 failed to reverse the yen's rising trend. 金融当局が9月15日に実施した大量の円売り介入で、円高傾向を反転[逆転]させることはできなかった。◆As one option to avoid excessive currency appreciation in emerging countries with inflationary trends, they can restrict an influx of capital. インフレ気味の新興国で行き過ぎた[過度の]通貨高を避けるための手段として、資金流入を規制することができる。◆As the financial markets' confidence in the U.S. currency has been shaken, stock prices may fall worldwide and the dollar-selling trend may accelerate. 米ドルへの金融市場の信認が揺らいでいるため、株価が世界的に下落し、ドル売りの流れが加速する可能性もある。◆If the current downward trend of stock prices continues, banks' financial resources that could be used to dispose of bad loans will decrease drastically. 株価の下落基調がこのまま続くと、金融機関の不良債権処理の原資は激減する。◆It has become an international trend of late for investment banks to seek an alliance with retail banks. 最近では、リテール銀行との統合を図るのが投資銀行の世界的な流れになっている。◆The Bank of Japan envisages the prospects of economic growth and consumer price trends in its "Outlook for Economic Activity and Prices." 日銀は、「経済・物価情勢の展望」(展望リポート)で、経済成長や消費者物価の先行きを示している。◆The current account balance is entering an upward trend on a year-on-year basis. 経常収支は、前年同月比ベースで上昇基調に入りつつある。◆The current deflationary trend seems to be a temporary phenomenon caused by the correction in oil prices after they skyrocketed last year. 現在のデフレ傾向は、昨年の原油高の反動による一時的な現象のようだ。◆The deflator, which indicates the overall trend in prices, dropped 2.5 percent in the April-June period compared to the corresponding period last year. 物価の総合的な動向を示すデフレーターは、4-6月期は前年同期比で2.5%下落した。◆The economy is on a recovery trend. 景気は、回復傾向にある。◆The U.S. tighter regulations on investment funds helped to change the trend in crude oil prices. 米国の投資ファンド規制強化で、原油価格の流れが変わった。

trendsetting [trend-setting]　(形)流行の先端を行く, 流行を作る, 流行の傾向を決める, 時代の流れを決める, 方向[趨勢]を決める, 〜の誘導目標
◆Policymaking members of the U.S. Federal Open Market Committee voted unanimously to keep its trendsetting federal funds rate for overnight loans between banks at 1.75 percent. 米連邦公開市場委員会の政策決定メンバーは、銀行同士の翌日物のフェデラル・ファンド(FF)金利の誘導目標を、現行の1.75%に据え置くことを全会一致で決めた。

tri-reserve-currency regime　3準備通貨体制
◆Financial exchanges between the BRICs group, Indonesia and South Korea will move toward a tri-reserve-currency regime by losing a dependency on the U.S. dollar. BRICsグループ(ブラジル, ロシア, インド, 中国)とインドネシア, 韓国の新興6か国間の金融取引は今後、米ドルに依存しなくなるため、3準備通貨体制に移行するものと思われる。◆Transition to a tri-reserve-currency (the U.S. dollar plus the euro and the renminbi) regime would not be without fiscal turbulences. 3準備通貨(米ドルとユーロ, 人民元)体制への移行には、財政的混乱が伴うだろう。

triangle merger　三角合併
◆In triangle mergers, a foreign company purchases a Japanese company through its Japanese subsidiary. 三角合併の場合は、外国の企業が日本子会社を通じて日本の企業を買収する。

triangular merger　三角合併
◆Approval for a triangular merger should be based on a special resolution. 三角合併の承認は、特別決議によらなければならない[三角合併には、特別決議による承認が必要だ]。

trickle　(名)しずく, したたり, 細流, 少量, 少数, わずかの動き, まばらの状態, トリクル
trickle-down effect　通貨浸透効果, トリクル効果
trickle-down process　浸透過程
trickle-down strategy　浸透戦略
trickle-down theory　通貨浸透説, おこぼれ理論
trickle-up　トリクルアップ理論の, トリクルアップ理論に基づく, 吸い上げの, 逆浸透の

◆Bank lending remains at a trickle. 銀行貸出[銀行融資]は、ぽつぽつの状態で推移している[銀行貸出件数は、依然として少ない状況だ]。

trigger　(動)引き起こす, 〜のきっかけを作る, 〜のきっかけとなる, 〜の引き金となる, 〜を誘発する, 触発する, 〜を促す, 発射する, 発する, 発砲する, 発動する, 動かす (⇒compensation payments, default, financial turmoil)
a financial sector-triggered recession　金融不況
a triggered transaction　起因となる取引
trigger a flight to quality　質への逃避のきっかけとなる
trigger higher inflation　インフレ上昇の引き金になる
triggered by　〜をきっかけに, 〜が引き金となって, 〜に誘発されて

◆A U.S. financial crisis would undoubtedly trigger a global crisis. 米国の金融危機は、間違いなく地球規模の(同時)危機を誘発するものと思われる。◆Europe's debt crisis was triggered by Greece's financial debacle. 欧州の債務危機は、ギリシャの財政破たんに端を発した。◆Global stock market plunges caused by the European fiscal crisis triggered by Greece have shown no signs of abating. ギリシャ発の欧州財政危機による世界同時株安は、止まる気配がない。◆In the eurozone, Greece's financial collapse is triggering a chain reaction. ユーロ圏では、ギリシャの財政破たんが連鎖反応を起こしている。◆In the past, injection of public funds was limited to cases that could trigger a financial crisis under the Deposit Insurance Law. 以前は、公的資金の注入は、預金保険法によって金融危機を招く恐れがある場合に限られていた。◆It is feared the colossal amount of the U.S. twin deficits could trigger a freefall of the U.S. dollar. アメリカの巨額の双子の赤字は、ドルの暴落を引き起こす懸念がある。◆Many houses were swept away by tsunami triggered by the massive earthquake. 大地震による津波で、多くの住宅［家屋］が流された。◆Shinsei and Aozora banks suffered huge losses in their overseas investment business in the aftermath of the global financial crisis triggered by the collapse of Lehman Brothers Holdings Inc. in autumn 2008. 新生銀行とあおぞら銀行は、2008年秋のリーマン・ブラザーズの経営破たんで始まった世界的な金融危機の影響で、海外投資事業に巨額の損失が発生した。◆The confusion triggered by Greece's possible debt default could affect Japan and the United States. 予想されるギリシャの債務不履行（デフォルト）による混乱の影響は、日米に及ぶ可能性もある。◆The dramatic plunge in the profits of Toyota was triggered by the U.S. financial crisis. トヨタの大幅減益の発端は、米国の金融危機だった。◆The European fiscal crisis triggered by Greece has spread to Italy, making the severe situation even more distressing. ギリシャ発の欧州財政危機がイタリアに飛び火し、厳しい事態が一段と深刻化している。◆The financial crisis triggered by the rise in defaults of U.S. subprime loans caused havoc in financial markets worldwide. 米国のサブプライム・ローン（低所得者向け住宅ローン）の不払い増加がきっかけで起こった金融危機は、世界の金融市場を大混乱させた。◆The financial market mess in Europe was triggered by the delay of financial assistance to Greece by the European financial authorities. 欧州の金融市場混乱の引き金となったのは、欧州金融当局によるギリシャへの金融支援のもたつきだ。◆The fiscal woes of the single-currency bloc could trigger a new severe global financial crisis. 単一通貨・ユーロ圏の財政危機は、新たに重大な世界的金融危機の発生源になる可能性がある。◆The global financial crisis was triggered by the collapse of some major financial institutions. 世界的な金融危機は、大手金融機関の破たんで始まった。◆The Greek economic chaos was triggered as its national bond rating was lowered. ギリシャの経済混乱のきっかけは、ギリシャの国債格付けが引き下げられたことだ。◆The overheating of the real economy has triggered the latest financial crisis. 今回の金融危機の引き金を引いたのは、過熱した実体経済だ。◆The sharp rise in crude oil prices has caused increases in prices of other fuels and grains, triggering inflation in many parts of the world. 原油価格の高騰は、他の燃料価格や穀物価格の上昇を招き、国際的なインフレを引き起こしている。

-triggered （形）～に誘発［触発］された，～に端を発した，～が引き起こした，～が引き金になった，～が誘因の
 financial sector-triggered recession 金融不況
 the Greek-triggered sovereign debt crisis ギリシャに端を発したソブリン危機（政府債務危機）
 U.S. financial crisis-triggered 米国の金融危機が発の
 ◆The Greek-triggered sovereign debt crisis has been throwing the eurozone into financial uncertainty and multiple crises. ギリシャに端を発した債務危機問題で、ユーロ圏は金融不安と複合的な危機に陥っている。◆The Greek-triggered sovereign debt crisis resulted in the breakup of the French-Belgian bank Dexia which held Greek government bonds. ギリシャが引き金になったソブリン危機（政府債務危機）問題で、ギリシャ国債を保有していた仏ベルギー系金融機関のデクシア（Dexia）が、解体に追い込まれた。

trilemma （名）三重苦，トリレンマ
 the trilemma of inflation, recession and balance of payments problems インフレ、不況、国際収支問題の三重苦

trim （動）削減する，縮小する，切り詰める，（人員などを）整理する，引き下げる，下方修正する，減額する （⇒public works spending）
 trim costs 費用を削減する
 trim down debt 債務を削減する
 trim one's existing affiliates 既存の関連会社を整理する
 trim one's operations 業務のスリム化を推し進める
 trim the number of employees 従業員を削減する, 従業員の人員整理をする
 trim three excesses of debt, workforces and facilities 債務、人員、設備という三つの過剰を削減する
 trim waste 無駄を減らす
 ◆The Asian Development Bank trimmed its 2011 forecast for economic growth for 45 developing countries or newly industrializing Asian countries, excluding Japan. アジア開発銀行（ADB）は、日本などを除くアジア太平洋45か国・地域の2011年の国内総生産（GDP）成長率見通しを、下方修正した。◆The Nikkei Stock Average recovered to the ￥9,000 mark in the morning, but trimmed earlier gains in afternoon trading. 日経平均株価は、朝から9,000円台に回復したが、午後の取引で午前の上昇幅が縮小した。◆Trade surplus in July fell for the fifth straight month, trimmed by faster growth in imports than exports on rising fuel prices. 7月の貿易黒字は、エネルギー価格［原油などの資源価格］の高騰で輸出より輸入が急増したため、5か月連続で減少した。

trimming （名）削減、引下げ、減少、縮小、減額、切り詰め、整理
 ◆Germany, main creditor to Greece, demanded that private-sector banks accept a certain amount of trimming of their debts. （財政危機の）ギリシャに主に資金を提供しているドイツは、民間銀行に対して債権の一部放棄を受け入れるよう求めた。

tripartite partnership 3国間パートナーシップ
 ◆The heads of Japan, China and ROK signed statements on the tripartite partnership, international finance and the economy, and disaster management cooperation. 日中韓首脳は、3国間パートナーシップ、国際金融・経済と防災対策での連携に関する声明に署名した。

tripartite reforms 三位一体改革
 ◆The tripartite reforms aim to reduce the amount of subsidies provided by the central government to the local governments; cut local tax grants to local governments; and shift revenue sources from the central government to local governments. 「三位一体」改革は、国の地方政府への補助金削減、地方交付税交付金の削減と国から地方政府への財源の移譲をめざしている。

triple （動）3倍になる、3倍増となる、3倍にする
 ◆The life insurer's revenues from the single-premium whole life insurance products tripled from the previous year in fiscal 2010. 同生保の一時払い終身の保険商品の収入保険料は、2010年度に前年度の3倍に達した。

triple （形）3倍の、3重の、トリプル
 triple A issuer トリプルA格の発行体
 triple A rating トリプルAの格付け
 triple low トリプル安 （=triple decline）
 ◆The World Bank enjoys a triple-A credit rating. 世界銀行は、トリプルAの格付け［信用格付け］を受けている。

triple-A credit rating トリプルAの格付け
 ◆The World Bank enjoys a triple-A credit rating. 世界銀行は、トリプルAの格付け［信用格付け］を受けている。

triple decline トリプル安 （=triple fall, triple low: 株式、債券と為替が同時に下がること）
 ◆This triple decline has further slowed the economy. このトリプル安が、景気をさらに減速させている。

triple fall トリプル安 （=triple decline）
 ◆The dollar selling triggered sales of shares and securities, resulting in the triple fall. ドル売りが引き金となって（ドル売りをきっかけに）株や債券も売られ、トリプル安となった。

triple rise トリプル高
 ◆Japan appears to be climbing out of a crisis situation as a result of recent triple rises in stocks, bonds and the yen. 日本は、株価、債券と円の最近のトリプル高で、危機的状況から脱しつつあるようだ。

triple whammy 三重苦
◆In spite of Japan's triple whammy of the tsunami- nuclear crisis, electricity shortages and political breakdown, the yen has sharply strengthened. 日本は現在、津波・原発災害、電力不足、政治機能停止の三重苦に直面しているにもかかわらず、円は急騰している。

triple witching hour 3人の魔女が現われる時間帯, 株価が不安定になる時間帯, トリプル・ウィッチング・アワー（米国で、3、6、9、12月の第三金曜日は株価指数先物取引とオプション取引（株価指数先物オプションと個別株式オプション）の行使期間満了日となっている。そのため、この日の取引終了間近の時間帯は大量の株式取引が行われて株価の乱高下を招くことがあるので、「3人の魔女の時間帯」と呼ばれている）

trouble （名）困難, 苦悩, 労苦, 悩み, 悩み事, 心配事, 経営不振, 経営破たん, 経営難, 経営危機, 迷惑, 厄介, 骨折り, 苦心, 問題点, 欠点, 短所,（体や機械の）不調, 故障, 騒ぎ, もめごと, 内紛, 紛争, 動乱, 争議, トラブル
　　be in deep [serious] trouble　深刻な事態に陥っている
　　be in trouble　経営不振［経営難, 経営破たん］に陥っている, 経営破たんの可能性がある, 経営が行き詰まる, 危ない［危険な］状況にある, 困っている, もめている, 検挙されている
　　be more trouble than it's worth　苦労した割に成果がない［少ない］, 苦労した割に得るものがあまりない
　　economic troubles　景気の悪化, 経済的困難
　　financial trouble　財政難, 財政困難, 経済的危機, 経営難, 経営危機
　　get [run] into trouble　苦しい事態に追い込まれる, 経営難に陥る, 困難に陥る, 面倒なことになる, ごたごたを引き起こす, しかられる, 罰せられる
　　share trouble　株式事故
◆France is being plagued by rapidly exacerbating troubles at domestic banks. フランスは、国内銀行の急速な経営状態の悪化に悩まされている［苦しんでいる］。◆Global financial markets are still shaken by the serious fiscal troubles in Greece. 世界の金融市場は、ギリシャの深刻な財政危機問題で動揺が続いている。◆The firm has been in trouble since last year, due to declining profits in its North America operation. 同社は、北米事業の減益で昨年来、経営不振に陥っている。◆The list of banks the U.S. FDIC considers to be in trouble shot up nearly 50 percent to 171 during the third quarter of 2008. 米連邦預金保険公社（FDIC）が経営破たんの可能性があると見ている問題銀行は、2008年第3四半期［7-9月期］に約50%急増して171行（直前の4-6月期は117行）に達した。

troubled （形）経営不振の, 経営破たんした, 経営難の, 経営難に陥った, 経営危機に陥った, 危機に陥った, 問題のある, 問題の多い, もめごとの多い
　　be troubled with　～で困っている
　　troubled business　経営の行き詰まり, 経営難, 行き詰まった経営, 経営危機の企業, 経営不振企業
　　troubled companies　経営不振企業
　　troubled debt　不良債権
　　troubled eurozone countries　危機［財政危機］に陥ったユーロ圏各国
　　troubled loan　不良債権
　　troubled loan problems　不良債権問題
　　troubled state-backed mortgage firms　経営不振の政府系住宅金融会社
◆DaimlerChrysler has decided against pumping more money into its troubled Japanese partner, Mitsubishi Motors Corp. ダイムラー・クライスラーは、経営不振の［問題を抱えている］日本の提携企業・三菱自動車に資金を投入しないことを決めた。◆The U.S. government could split troubled state-backed mortgage firms Fannie Mae and Freddie Mac. 米政府は、経営不振の政府系住宅金融会社のファニー・メイ（米連邦住宅抵当公庫）とフレディ・マック（米連邦住宅貸付抵当公社）を分割する可能性がある。◆Troubled retailer Daiei Inc. will seek ¥410 billion worth of debt waivers from its bankers to achieve a turnaround. 経営不振の大手スーパー、ダイエーは、企業再生を図るため、取引先金融機関に4,100億円の債権放棄を求める。

troubled asset 不良資産
◆A bad bank is used to hold troubled assets and free up bank lending capacity. バッド・バンクは、不良資産を買い取って、銀行が自由に貸出できるようにするのに利用される。

Troubled Asset Relief Program 不良資産救済プログラム, 不良資産買取りプログラム, TARP
　　the Office of the Special Inspector General for the Troubled Asset Relief Program　（米国の）不良資産救済プログラム特定監察局, SIGTARP
◆ShoreBank in Chicago was unable to secure funds it was seeking from the government's Troubled Asset Relief Program, or TARP. シカゴのショアバンク（地域開発銀行）は、求めていた資金を、米政府の不良資産救済プログラム（TARP）から確保することができなかった。

troubled bank 経営破たん銀行, 経営危機の銀行, 経営難の銀行, 経営難に陥った銀行, 経営危機に陥った銀行, 問題のある銀行
◆It'll be meaningless if funds are injected into troubled banks from the state coffers under such circumstances. このような状態で問題のある銀行に国庫から資金を注入しても［公的資金を注入しても］、意味がないだろう。◆Public funds will be injected into troubled banks from the state coffers. 問題のある［経営難の］銀行には今後、国庫から公的資金が注入される。

trough （名）景気の谷, 景気の底, 最悪期, 谷, 底
　　a cyclical trough　景気の底, 景気サイクルの底, 景気の循環的谷, 景気の谷
　　a recession trough　景気の谷
　　an official cyclical trough　公式の景気の谷
　　fall to a trough of　～で（景気が）底を打つ
　　get out of a trough　（景気が）底から抜け出る, 最悪期を脱出する
　　Juglar trough　ジュグラー循環の谷
　　Kitchin trough　キチン循環の谷（キチン循環＝約40か月の周期を持った景気循環で、その原因は在庫投資）
　　manage the cyclical troughs　景気サイクルの底を乗り切る
　　reach a cyclical trough　（景気が）底入れする
　　reach a trough　（景気が）底を打つ
　　reach the recession trough　（景気が）底を打つ
　　the peaks and troughs of the stock market　株式相場［株価］の天井と底
◆Inventory has just got out of a trough. 在庫は、最悪期を脱したばかりだ。◆The economy has fallen to a trough. 景気が、底を打った。

trust （名）信頼, 信認, 委託, 保管, 信用貸し, クレジット, 掛売り
　　damage the trust of shareholders　株主の信頼を損ねる
　　lose trust in the IMF　国債通貨基金（IMF）への信認を失う
◆The company's wrongdoing damaged the trust of shareholders. 同社の不正行為［不祥事］が、株主の信頼を損ねた。◆Trust in the IMF was lost by a scandal involving its former managing director. 国際通貨基金（IMF）の信認は、IMF前専務理事の不祥事で失われた。◆Years of window-dressing by Olympus to hide investment losses represent nothing but a companywide breach of trust. 投資損失隠ぺいのためのオリンパスによる長年の粉飾決算は、会社ぐるみの背信行為にほかならない。

trust (名)信託, トラスト (⇒public goods)
  balance of loan trust　貸付け信託の残高
  charitable trust　公益信託, 慈善信託
  deed of trust　信託証書
    (=trust deed, trust indenture)
  investment trust　投資信託
  trust account　信託勘定
  trust agreement　信託契約
  trust certificate　信託証書
  trust company　信託会社
  trust deal　信託契約
  trust estate　信託財産
    (=trust asset, trust property)
  trust indenture　信託証書(社債の発行会社と社債保有者(投資家)を代表する受託者(一般的には銀行が任命される)の契約書のこと)
  Trust Indenture Act of 1939　1939年信託証書法
  trust money　信託金
  trust principal　信託元本
  trust property　信託財産(信託の対象となる財産のこと)
  trust securities　信託証券
  un-incorporated investment fund　非会社型投資信託
  unit investment trust　単位型投資信託, ユニット型投資信託
  unit trust　契約型投資信託, ユニット・トラスト
  voting trust　議決権信託
  ◆Three kinds of trust services will be introduced under a registration system. 今後は、信託3業務が登録制で導入される。
  解説 信託とは：財産所有者が金融機関などに財産権を移して、特定の第三者の利益のために財産を管理・保全するよう依頼すること。財産の信託設定者を委託者(settler)といい、委託を受けた財産(信託財産:trust property)を管理・保全する者を受託者(trustee)、信託の利益を受ける者を受益者(beneficiary)という。

trust bank　信託銀行
  (⇒administration of shares)
  Mitsubishi UFJ Trust and Banking Corp.　三菱UFJ信託銀行
  Mizuho Trust and Banking Co.　みずほ信託銀行
  The Chuo Mitsui Trust and Banking Co.　中央三井信託銀行
  The Sumitomo Trust & Banking Co.　住友信託銀行
  ◆The remaining ¥1.8 billion will be financed by two other commercial banks and trust banks. 残りの18億円は、他の都銀2行と信託各行が出す。◆To raise money for compensation related to the Fukushima No. 1 nuclear power plant crisis, TEPCO will sell off assets through four trust banks. 福島第一原発事故関連の賠償資金を調達するため、東電は、4信託銀行を通じて資産を売却することになった。◆UFJ Holdings Inc. has agreed to sell UFJ Trust Bank Ltd. to Sumitomo Trust & Banking Co., Ltd. for about ¥300 billion to raise its capital adequacy ratio. UFJホールディングスが、自己資本比率を引き上げるため、UFJ信託銀行を約3,000億円で住友信託銀行に売却することで合意した。

trust business　信託業, 信託業務
  (=fiduciary business; ⇒nonfinancial institution)
  ◆Government plans to liberalize trust business. 政府は、信託業の規制緩和を行う方針だ。

Trust Business Law　信託業法
  ◆The revision to the Trust Business Law will revitalize the industry definitely. 信託業法の改正で、業界は間違いなく活性化する。

trust fund　信託基金, 信託資金, 投資信託, トラスト・ファンド
  ◆In December 1998, trust funds became the first financial products offered by securities firms and life insurers that banks were allowed to sell. 1998年12月に、投資信託は、証券会社と生命保険会社が提供する金融商品のうち銀行窓口での販売が認められた最初の商品となった。◆Japan, the United States, the European Union and the United Arab Emirates have reached a broad accord over the establishment of an international trust fund designed to pool assistance monies for rebuilding Iraq. イラク復興支援資金の受け皿となる国際信託基金の創設で、日本、アメリカ、欧州連合(EU)とアラブ首長国連邦が大筋合意した。◆The trust fund will be set up separate from the development fund for Iraq. 信託基金は、イラク開発基金とは別に設けられる。

trust fund product　信託商品
  ◆The new bank and UFJ Bank will form a partnership to sell trust fund products at UFJ outlets. 新銀行とUFJ銀行は、提携してUFJの支店網で信託商品を販売する方針だ。

trust services　信託業務
  ◆The company will begin in June as an agent for the two banks to handle trust services. 同社は6月から、両行の代理店として信託業務を扱う。

trustee (名)信託機関, 管財人, 破産管財人, 金融整理管財人, 受託者, 受託会社, 幹事会社被信託人, 理事, 評議員
  bankruptcy trustee　破産管財人
  board of trustees　理事会
  bond trustee　債券受託者, 受託銀行
  fund amounts for postretirement benefits with an independent trustee　退職後給付額を独立した信託機関に積み立てる
  indenture trustee　信託証書受託者
  independent trustee　独立した信託機関
  loan trustee　ローン受託者
  successor trustee　承諾受託者
  trustee bank　受託銀行
  trustee in bankruptcy　破産管財人
    (=bankruptcy trustee)
  trustee or receiver　管財人, 受託者または管財人
  trustee process　管財人手続き, 債権差押え手続き
  under the trustee's management　管財人の管理下で, 金融整理管財人の管理下で
  voting trustee　議決権受託者
  ◆It is the Corporation's practice to fund amounts for postretirement benefits, with an independent trustee, as deemed appropriate from time to time. 随時適切と思われる退職後給付額を、独立した信託機関に積み立てるのが、当社の慣行となっています。◆Under the trustee's management, the debtor bank's business will be operated and the refunding of deposits will be temporarily suspended. 金融整理管財人の管理下で、破たん銀行の業務は運営され、預金の払戻しは一時停止される。

Truth in Lending Act　貸付け真実法 (米消費者信用保護法(Consumer Credit Protection Act)の第一編。⇒Consumer Credit Protection Act of 1968)

Truth in Securities Act　証券真実法(1933年証券法の別称で、発行真実法(Truth in Issuance Act)とも呼ばれている)

TSE　東京証券取引所, 東証 (Tokyo Stock Exchangeの略)
  government bonds listed on the TSE(10Y benchmark)　東証上場国債(10年物指標銘柄)
  list shares on the TSE　東証に上場する
  listing on the TSE　東証上場
  the TSE average　東証平均株価
    (⇒price trends)
  the TSE's liquidation post　東証の整理ポスト
  the TSE's monitoring post　東証の監理ポスト

this year's turnover on the TSE　東証の今年の出来高（⇒turnover）
TSE 1st section daily average　東証1部1日平均
TSE 1st section price index　東証1部株価指数
TSE's First Section　東証1部
◆All companies that have been listed on the TSE from January 1996 are required to provide management information on their parent companies and affiliates. 1996年1月以降に東証に上場した企業は、すべて親会社とグループ企業（関連会社）の経営情報を提供するよう義務付けられている。◆Companies listed on the First Section of the TSE have registered increases both in income and profit. 東証一部上場企業は、増収増益となった。◆Investors can trade the Seibu Railway shares for a month after their transfer to the TSE's liquidation post from the monitoring post. 西武鉄道株が東証の監理ポストから整理ポストに移った後1か月間、投資家は西武鉄道株を売買できる。◆The TSE and the OSE will merge into the world's No.2 exchange group. 東証と大証が統合して、世界第2位の株式取引所グループが誕生する。◆The TSE typically only duelists companies at risk of bankruptcy. 東証が上場廃止するのは、一般に経営破たん危機にある企業に限られる。◆Transactions on all of the 2,520 issues traded at the TSE were stalled from 9 a.m. due to a computer malfunction. 東証で取引されている2,520全銘柄の取引が、コンピュータのシステム障害で午前9時から停止した。

TSE-listed companies　東証上場企業
◆A decade ago, 96 percent of TSE-listed companies held shareholders meetings on the same day. 10年前は、東証上場企業の96%が、同じ日に株主総会を開いた。

TSE Mothers market for start-ups　新興企業向け市場の東証マザーズ
◆The Tokyo Stock Exchange has given approval for Xinhua Finance Ltd. to become the first Chinese firm to make an initial public offering on the TSE Mothers market for start-ups Oct. 28, 2004. 東京証券取引所は2004年10月28日、中国企業としては初めて新興企業向け市場・東証マザーズへの「新華ファイナンス」の新規上場［東証マザーズでの「新華ファイナンス」の新規株式公開］を承認した。

TSE's Mothers market　東証マザーズ
◆GCA Co., a mergers and acquisitions advisory company, debuted on the TSE's Mothers market. M&A（企業の合併・買収）助言会社のGCAが、東証マザーズに上場した。

TTB　対顧客電信買い相場, 電信買い相場, 対顧客電信買い, ドル買い時レート　（=TT buying rate:telegraphic transfer buying rateの略。金融機関が顧客から外国通貨を買い取る際に用いられる為替レート）

TTM　仲値（telegraphic transfer middle rateの略。金融機関が顧客に対して10万ドル未満の外国為替取引をする際の基準レート）

TTS　対顧客電信売り相場, 電信売り相場, 対顧客電信売り, ドル売り時レート　（=TT selling rate:telegraphic transfer selling rateの略。金融機関が顧客から外国通貨を買い取る際に用いられる為替レート）

tumble　（動）物価・株価が下落する, 暴落する, 急落する, 急落する, 減少する, 上下動を繰り返す
tumble across the board　全面安となる, 全銘柄にわたって急落［暴落］する
tumble against major currencies　主要通貨に対して下落する
tumble for the second straight day　2日連続下落する
tumble into a deflationary spiral　デフレの悪循環に落ち込む
◆Stock prices will tumble, if banks try to sell a large amount of banks crossheld shares in the market ahead of the account settlement term at the end of March. 3月末の決算期を控えて、銀行が大量の持ち合い株式を市場に放出すれば、株価は急落する。◆The Japanese economy has reached a critical stage at which it could tumble into a deflationary spiral after brief stability, or be brought back to a recovery path. 日本経済は現在、小康状態から再びデフレの悪循環に落ち込むか、回復軌道に戻せるかどうかの瀬戸際にある。◆The U.S. dollar tumbled for the second straight day against major currencies. 米ドルが、主要通貨に対して2日連続下落した。

tumble　（名）下落, 暴落, 急落, 急激な悪化, 減少, 混乱, 転落, 転倒, とんぼ返り, 宙返り
rough-and-tumble market［marketplace］　浮き沈みの激しい市場
take a serious tumble　深刻な危機に陥る
take a tumble　大きく下落する, 急激に悪化する
◆The life insurers' status as large shareholders means that when the market dives, their portfolios also take a tumble. 大株主としての生命保険会社の地位は、株価が大きく下がると資産内容も急激に悪化することを意味する。

tumbling　（形）下落する, 急減する, 暴落する, ～の下落［急減, 減少, 悪化］
tumbling dollar　ドルの下落
tumbling sales　販売の急減
◆Finance ministers and business leaders at the World Economic Forum are showing surprisingly little concern over the soaring euro and tumbling dollar. 世界経済フォーラムに出席した各国の財務相や財界指導者は、ユーロの急騰やドルの下落に驚くほど関心を示していない。

turbulence　（名）大荒れ, 混乱, 激動, 動乱, 騒乱, 不安, 乱気流
bond market turbulence　債券市場の混乱, 公社債市場の混乱
currency turbulence　通貨危機, 通貨不安, 為替市場の波乱
economic turbulence　経済的混乱
financial turbulence　金融危機, 金融不安, 金融［金融市場］の混乱
fiscal turbulences　財政的混乱
market turbulence　市場の混乱
turbulence in global financial markets　世界の金融市場の混乱
◆Corporate debt issues are recovering as bond market turbulence in the aftermath of the March 11 Great East Japan Earthquake has subsided. 2011年3月11日の東日本大震災直後の債券市場の混乱が収束したため、社債の発行額が回復している。◆Transition to a tri-reserve-currency (the U.S. dollar plus the euro and the renminbi) regime would not be without fiscal turbulences. 3準備通貨（米ドルとユーロ、人民元）体制への移行には、財政的混乱が伴うだろう。◆Turbulence in global financial markets brought the level of liquidity in the country sharply lower. 世界の金融市場の混乱で、国内流動性の水準は大幅に低下した。

turmoil　（名）混乱, 動揺, 騒動, 騒ぎ, 不安, 危機
credit market turmoil　金融市場の混乱
　（=turmoil in the financial markets）
credit turmoil　信用不安
currency turmoil　通貨危機, 為替市場の混乱
financial turmoil　金融危機, 金融不安, 金融市場の混乱
global［international］financial turmoil　世界的な金融不安, 国際金融不安, 世界的な金融市場の混乱
plunge the financial market into turmoil　金融市場を混乱に陥れる
the world's economic turmoil　世界経済の混迷
turmoil in the financial markets　金融市場の混乱
◆It is difficult to predict if new explosive factors emerge to plunge the financial market into further turmoil. 金融市場をさらに混乱に陥れる新しい火種があるのかどうか、予測するの

は難しい。◆The collapse of the subprime mortgage market and related credit market turmoil have resulted in $45 billion of write-downs at the world's biggest banks and securities firms. サブプライム市場の悪化や関連金融市場の混乱で、世界の大手銀行や証券会社の評価損計上額は、これまでのところ450億ドルに達している。◆The financial turmoil is caused by the U.S. subprime mortgage mess and soaring oil and materials prices. 金融市場の混乱は、米国のサブプライム・ローン問題と原油・原材料価格の高騰によるものだ。◆The United States and European countries are forced to proceed steadily with fiscal reconstruction and resolve the financial turmoil. 米欧各国は、財政再建を着実に進めて、金融市場の混乱を収拾せざるを得ない状況にある。◆The U.S. government's default would throw the financial markets around the world into major turmoil. 米政府がデフォルト(債務不履行)に陥ったら、世界の金融市場は大混乱するだろう。◆The world's economic turmoil will last several years. 世界経済の混乱は、数年間は続くものと思われる。◆U.S. and European financial institutions are hitting roadblocks because of the ongoing global financial turmoil. 欧米金融機関は、世界的な金融市場の混乱で、つまずいている。

turmoil in the financial markets 金融市場の混乱
◆Global turmoil in the financial markets results from the downgrading of the U.S. credit rating. 金融市場の世界的な混乱は、米国債の格下げによるものだ。

turn (動)回す, 向き[進路, 方向]を変える, 曲がる, 迂回する, 裏返す, 流れを変える, 好転させる (自動)回る, 開店する, 振り返る, 向く, 変わる, 転じる, 変質する, 〜になる
 turn for good 好転する
 turn the heat on 〜への圧力を強める
 turn the tables 立場を逆転させる, 形勢・局面を一変する
 turn upward across the board 軒並み上昇に転じる
◆Currency traders are now turning to the renminbi (yuan) from the U.S. dollar. 為替トレーダーは今や, 米ドルから中国の人民元に目を向けている。◆Following the tender offer, Oji Paper would acquire the remaining Hokuetsu shares through a share swap to turn it into a wholly owned subsidiary. 株式公開買付け(TOB)後に, 王子製紙は, 株式交換で残りの北越製紙の株を取得して北越製紙を完全子会社化する。◆It became possible for an agricultural producers cooperative corporation to turn into a joint stock company. 農業生産法人の株式会社化が, 可能になった。

turn (名)回転, 転回, 順番, 番, 機会, 交替, 曲がり角, 変わり目, 節目(ふしめ), 転機, 転換期, 方向転換, 転換, 折り返し, 変化, 新発展, 成り行き, 外国為替売買相場の開き(spread), 利益, 利ざや, ターン
 a turn of speed 急加速, 瞬発力, 急成長, 俊足
 a turn of the screw 一層の締め付け[強要], さらなる圧力[困難, 災難]
 at every turn 絶えず, つねに, 事あるごとに, あらゆる場合に
 do a 180 degree turn 180度方向転換する
 make a turn 利ざやを稼ぐ
 market turn 相場の開き, 売買差額 (=turn of the market)
 round turn 反対売買
 stock turn 商品の回転
 take a turn for the worse さらに悪化する, 急に悪くなる
 take an upward turn 上昇に転じる
 turn of capital 資本回転度数, 資金回転度数
◆If the Bank of Japan's interest rate takes an upward turn, an adjustable rate mortgage would weigh more heavily on borrowers than would the fixed-rate type. 日銀の政策金利が上昇に転じた場合, 固定金利型の住宅ローンと比べて変動金利型のほうが, ローン利用者[借り手]の負担が重くなる。◆It has been the dollar's turn to depreciate. ドル相場が下落する番になった。

turn around 好転する, 改善する, (景気などを)回復させる, 方向転換する, 方針を変える, 考えを変える, 企業[事業]を再生する
 turn around one's failed business 破たん事業を再生する, 破たんした事業を再生する
 turn around the flagging economy 低迷する景気を回復させる
 turn around the struggling automaker この経営不振の自動車メーカーの事業を再生する
◆A ¥450 billion revival plan aims at turning around the struggling automaker. 4,500億円の再建計画は, この経営不振の自動車メーカーの事業再生を目指している。◆JAL's efforts to turn around its failed business will depend on the flagship carrier's ability to secure new loans from its creditor banks. 日航の破たん事業再生への取組みは, この日本を代表する航空会社が取引銀行から新規融資を受けることができるかどうかにかかっている。◆Many observers forecast that economy will turn around by the middle of next year. 市場では, 景気は来年半ばまでには持ち直す, との見方が中心だ。◆Prime Minister Aso has accepted the government's fiscal stimulus measures to turn around the flagging economy. 麻生首相は, 低迷する景気を回復させるための[経済対策のための]政府の財政出動を容認した。

turn down 断(ことわ)る, 拒絶[拒否, 否決]する, (訴えなどを)却下する, 折りたたむ, 折り返す, (音などを)小さくする[弱くする, 細くする]
◆Negotiations fell through when Vodafone turned down TEPCO's offer, which was in the region of ¥150 billion. 1,500億円程度の東電側の提示額をボーダフォンが拒否して, 交渉は決裂した。

turn out (製品などを)生産する, 製造する, 作り出す, (有能な人材などを)輩出する, 追い出す, 首にする, 〜と判明する, 結局〜になる, (電灯などを)消す
 as it turned out 結果的に, 結局は, 後で分かったことではあるが
 turn out goods 商品[製品]を生産する, 商品[製品]を製造する
 turn out to be 〜になる, 〜だと分かる[判明する]
◆An increasing number of loans turn out to be nonperforming because of a deterioration in the business situation of the borrower or because the value of the real estate used as collateral has fallen. 融資先の経営悪化や担保不動産の目減りなどによって, 不良債権化する貸出が増えている。

turn upward across the board 軒並み上昇に転じる
◆Stock prices on Asian markets turned upward across the board. アジアの株価も, 軒並み上昇に転じた。

turnaround (名)転換, 方向転換, 好転, 経営戦略や営業・販売, 財務などの改善, 企業再生, 事業再生, ターンアラウンド (⇒troubled)
 corporate turnaround body 企業再生支援機構
 turnaround manager ターンアラウンド・マネージャー (経営不振企業に経営責任者などとして入って, 企業再生を図る人のこと)
 turnaround specialist 企業再生請負人, 再生請負人, 再生専門家, ターンアラウンド・スペシャリスト
◆JAL's stocks may lose market value to zero if the corporate turnaround body cuts the shares 100 percent by delisting JAL from the Tokyo stock market. 企業再生支援機構が東京株式市場から日航の上場を廃止して日航株を100%減資したら, 日航株の市場価値はゼロになる可能性がある。◆Mitsubishi Motors Co. is seeking as much as ¥450 billion for its revival plan from shareholders and corporate turnaround

fund Phoenix Capital Co. 三菱自動車は現在、同社の再建計画のため、株主と企業再生ファンドのフェニックス・キャピタルに4,500億円程度の出資を求めている。◆The economy may be headed toward a turnaround on the back of improved exports and corporate profitability. 輸出と企業収益が改善して、景気が好転する可能性もある。

turnover （名）売上, 売上高, 総売上高, 取引高, 取引成立額, 出来高, 売買高, 回転, 回転率, 就労率, 転職率
 account receivable turnover 売掛金回転率
 asset turnover 資産回転率
  （=asset turnover ratio）
 average daily turnover 1日当たり平均取引高, 1日当たり平均売買高
 average daily turnover on the TSE 東証の1日当たり平均取引高［売買代金］
 capital turnover 資本の回転, 資本回転率
 capital turnover point 資本回収点
 consolidated turnover 連結売上高
 equity turnover 資本回転率
  （=sale to net worth）
 gross turnover 総売上高
 labor turnover 労働回転率, 離職率
 merchandise turnover 商品回転率
  （=merchandise turnover rate）
 net-worth turnover 自己資本回転率（純売上高÷自己資本）
 sales turnover 売上高
 stock turnover 在庫回転率, 棚卸し資産回転率, 商品回転率
 this year's turnover on the TSE 東証の今年の出来高
 total assets turnover 総資産回転率, 総資本回転率
 total turnover 総売上高
 turnover of net worth 自己資本回転率, 株主資本回転率
 turnover of total capital employed 使用総資本回転率
 turnover of total liabilities and net worth 総資本回転率
 turnover of total operating assets 経営資本回転率
 working capital turnover 運転資本回転率
◆Average daily turnover on the Tokyo Stock Exchange grew 86 percent year-on-year to ¥663 billion during the April-June quarter. 東京証券取引所の4～6月期の1日当たりの平均取引高［売買代金］は、前年同期に比べて86%増の6,630億円に達した。◆This year's turnover on the TSE already exceeded the 1988 figure as of the end of the November. 東証の今年の出来高は、11月末の時点で1988年（日本のバブル経済のピーク時）の実績をすでに上回っていた。

turnover of money 資金の回転率
◆Despite the rate cuts so far, the velocity of money, or turnover of money in the economy, remains low, a result of the so-called liquidity trap. これまでの金利引下げにもかかわらず、この景気で通貨の流通速度、つまり資金の回転率は依然として低く、いわゆる「流動性のワナ」に陥っている。

turnover ratio 回転率
 （=turnover rate; ⇒listed share）
 turnover ratio of assets 資産回転率
 turnover ratio of capital 資本回転率
 turnover ratio of receivables 売上債権回転率
 turnover ratio of trading 売買回転率
◆A turnover ratio of trading refers to a year's trading volume divided by an average number of listed stocks. 売買回転率は、1年間の出来高を平均上場株式数で割った数値を指す。

twenty percent rule 20パーセント・ルール（銀行借入れをする場合は、「借入額の20%の預金残高を維持しなければならない」というルール）

twin deficits 双子の赤字
◆Concern over the revival of the twin deficits is accelerating selling pressure on the U.S. stocks and the dollar. 双子の赤字の復活懸念が、米国の株・ドル売りを加速している。◆The twin deficits of the United States-fiscal and current account deficits-are threatening to destabilize the world economy. アメリカの双子の赤字（財政赤字と経常収支赤字）が、世界経済の不安定要因となっている。◆The twin deficits—fiscal and trade—that haunted the United States in the 1980s have returned. 1980年代のアメリカを苦しめた「双子の赤字」（財政と貿易の二つの赤字）が、再燃している。

twist （名）歪（ひず）み, ねじれ, 湾曲,（意味などの）歪曲, 回転, 旋回,（物語などの）意外な展開,（事態の）急変, 急転回,（政策などの）予期しない転換, 新しい試み, 取扱い, 工夫, 考案, 方式, 傾向, 性向, 不正, 詐欺, らせん状, らせん運動
 a new twist 新しい試み, 新しい工夫, 新案, 新機軸, 新展開
 a twist of fate 運命の巡り合わせ
 many twists and turns 多くの紆余曲折
 take a strange twist 意外な急展開を見せる, 意外な方向に発展する
 the twist of the wrist 腕前, 手際（てぎわ）のよさ
 twist operation ツイスト・オペ, ツイスト・オペレーション（FRB（米連邦準備制度理事会）が、長期国債の買入れと同時にすでに保有する短期国債を市中に売却すること）
 twists and turns 紆余曲折, 迷走
◆A financial bailout bill, after twists and turns, has at last been signed into law in the United States. 米国の金融安定化法案（緊急経済安定化法案）が、迷走の末、ようやく成立した。

twisting （名）（生命保険の）強引な勧誘による取引の乗換え, 乗換え契約,（手数料目当ての）過度売買, 回転商い, ツイスティング

two-income family 共稼ぎ家庭

two lost decades 失われた20年［二十年］
◆Kan's latest policy speech was an expression of his resolve to settle issues put off during the two lost decades after the collapse of the bubble economy. 菅首相の今回の所信表明演説は、バブル崩壊後の「失われた20年」の間に先送りされた問題を解決するという首相の決意表明であった。

two-name paper [bill] 複名手形

two-sided market 双方向市場（=two-way market: 売り・買い双方の気配値が立っている市場）

two stage [speed] monetary union 2段階の通貨統合

two-tier （形）二重の, 二層の, 二階層の, 二段の（⇒tier）
 two-tier (foreign exchange) market 二重為替市場, 二重相場制
 two-tier gold (price) system 金の二重価格制
 two-tier tender offer 二重価格株式公開買付け
  （=bootstrap）

two-track income taxation system 二元的所得課税方式
◆If the two-track income taxation system is introduced, taxpayers will be allowed to offset losses from stock investments from income earned from interest and dividends. 二元的所得課税方式を導入すると、納税者は、利子・配当収入から株式投資による損失を相殺することができるようになる。

two-transaction perspective 2取引基準

two-way （形）両面の, 双方向の, 相互的な, 両サイドの, 両国の, 対面交通の, 往復両方向の
 quote two-way prices 売り買い両方向の取引価格［気配値］を提示する
 two-way business 両サイドの取引

two-way investment and trade　投資と貿易の相互交流
two-way market　双方向市場　(=two-sided market: 売り・買い双方の気配値が立っている市場)
two-way quotation　(外国為替で)買い値と売り値の両建て建て値
type　(名)型, 型式, 類型, 様式, 形式, 種類, 典型, 見本, 代表例, 活字, タイプ
　additional-type investment trust　追加型投資信託
　bond transactions by investor types　投資家別公社債売買状況
　bottom-up type budget　積上げ予算
　mixed type　混合型
　new types of insurance demand　新たな保険需要
　sales-type lease　販売型リース
　security types　有価証券の種類
　the fixed-rate type　変動金利型
　type I carrier　第一種事業者
　type of income distribution　所得分布の型
　types of bank accounts　銀行口座の種類
　types of business　業種
　types of industry　産業形態, 業種
　types of issuer　発行体の種類
　types of pension plans　年金制度の種類
　types of reinsurance　再保険の種類
　unit-type investment trust　単位型投資信託
　various types of financial institutions　異なる業態の金融機関
　◆If the Bank of Japan's interest rate takes an upward turn, an adjustable rate mortgage would weigh more heavily on borrowers than would the fixed-rate type. 日銀の政策金利が上昇に転じた場合、固定金利型の住宅ローンと比べて変動金利型のほうが、ローン利用者[借り手]の負担が重くなる。◆In the future also, new types of illegal practices that exploit legal loopholes will emerge in securities markets. 今後も、証券市場では、法の抜け穴を狙う不正取引の手法が新たに現れるものと思われる。◆In this type of life insurance products, the rate of return after canceling the insurance contract can be higher than that of a savings account if a policyholder upholds the contract for five to 10 years. この種の生保商品では、保険契約者が保険契約を5～10年続けると、解約後の利回り(予定利率)は預金よりも高い利回りが見込める。◆Nonlife insurers are exploring new types of insurance demand and offering convenient and easy means of buying policies. 損保各社は、新たな保険需要を掘り起こして、いつでも、どこでも簡単に保険に加入できるサービスを提供している。◆The nonlife insurance company hopes to attract about 3 million to 4 million new policyholders a year for its new types of insurance. 同損保は、同社の新型保険で、年間約300万～400万件の新規契約獲得を目指している。

U

ultimate　(形)最後の, 最終的の, 究極の, 基本的な
　ultimate borrower　最終的借り手, 究極的借り手
　ultimate collectability of receivables　債権の最終的回収可能性
　ultimate destination　最終仕向け地
　ultimate investor　最終投資家
　ultimate lender　最終的貸し手, 究極的貸し手
　ultimate losses　最終的な損失, 最終損失額
　ultimate target　最終目標
　◆In the case of JAL, the DBJ's ultimate total losses came to ¥95.6 billion in loans and ¥20 billion in investments. 日航の場合、日本政策投資銀行の最終的な損失総額は、融資分の956億円と出資分の200億円となっている。

ultra-easy [ultraeasy] money policy　超低金利政策, 超金融緩和政策, 金融の量的緩和政策　(=ultra-easy monetary policy, ultra-loose monetary policy)
　◆The BOJ has bought financing bills and other securities from the market to keep money rates low under its ultra-easy money policy. 日銀は、超低金利政策で低金利を維持するため、市場から政府短期証券(FB)などの有価証券を買い取ってきた。◆We should not overlook the ultra-easy money policy's negative effects, such as on elderly people who count on the interest earned on their savings and bank deposits. 超低金利政策には、とくに預貯金に付く利息を頼りにして生活しているお年寄りなどに対するマイナス効果があることを無視してはならない。

ultra-long dated stock　超長期債
ultra long-term government bond　超長期国債
ultra-loose [ultraloose]　(形)過剰に緩和的な, 極端に緩い
　◆The ECB's monetary policy ended up being ultraloose for inflation-prone member nations such as Portugal and Spain. 欧州中銀(ECB)の金融政策は、ポルトガルやスペインなどインフレ体質のEU加盟国には過剰に緩和的となった。

ultra-loose monetary policy　超低金利政策, 超低金利金融政策, 超金融緩和政策, 量的緩和政策　(=super-loose monetary policy, ultra-loose money policy; ⇒money policy, super-loose monetary policy)
　◆The challenge in monetary policy for countries now is shifting toward finding a way to move away from ultra-loose monetary policies. 現在、各国の金融政策の課題は、超金融緩和政策からいかに転換するかに移りつつある。◆The discussion on changing the ultra-loose monetary policy is likely to intensify. 超金融緩和政策の転換をめぐる議論が、活発化しそうだ。

ultralow annual interest of 0.1 percent　年0.1％の超低金利
　◆The BOJ decided to introduce a new open market operation by supplying ¥10 trillion to private financial institutions in three month loans at an ultralow annual interest of 0.1 percent. 日銀は、民間の金融機関に年1％の超低金利で貸出期間3か月の資金を10兆円供給する新型の公開市場操作(オペ)の導入に踏み切った。

ultralow interest rate policy　超低金利政策
　◆The Bank of Japan sticks to its ultralow interest rate policy. 日銀は、超低金利政策を堅持している。◆There has been a sharp increase in the number of people taking out adjustable rate mortgages against the backdrop of the Bank of Japan's ultralow interest rate policy. 日本銀行の超低金利政策を背景に、変動金利型住宅ローンの利用者が急増している。

ultralow interest rates　超低金利
　◆All the insurers are now saddled with an enormous amount of negative yields as returns on their investments have plunged due to ultralow interest rates—a consequence of the bursting of the bubble. 生保各社は現在、バブル崩壊後の超低金利時代で運用利回りが急低下し、巨額の逆ざやを抱えている。◆Many bank depositors and individual investors are looking for better investment opportunities amid ultralow interest rates. 超低金利が続くなか、銀行預金者や個人投資家の多くは高利回りの運用先を探している。

umbrella　(名)傘, 傘下, 保護, 包括的組織　(形)包括的な　(=wing)
　be under the umbrella of　～の傘下にある, ～に保護[援護]されている
　group umbrella　グループの傘下
　place [take] A under one's umbrella　Aを～の傘下に置く, Aを～の傘下に収める
　umbrella agreement　包括契約, 包括契約書

umbrella group [body]　包括団体, 統括団体
umbrella payments　包括支払い, 包括支払い制
under the umbrella of　～傘下の, ～に保護［援護］されている
◆If the merger takes place, it will create a full-scale financial conglomerate with a major bank, a major securities house and credit card company under its umbrella. 統合すれば, 傘下に大手銀行と大手証券, クレジット・カード会社などを持つ本格的な金融コングロマリット（金融複合企業体）が誕生する。◆In 2001, GM increased its stake in Suzuki Motor Corp. to 20 percent, placing it under the GM group umbrella. 2001年に, GMはスズキの出資比率を20％に引き上げて, スズキをGMグループの傘下に収めた。◆The two banks are under the umbrella of the financial group. 両行は, 同金融グループの傘下にある。

unabated　（形）衰えない, 弱まらない, 弱まる気配［様子］がない, 一向に減らない, 低下しない
◆The current appreciation of the yen, if left unabated, would slow the recovery of the economy, causing the stock market to weaken. 現在の円高がこのまま進行すれば, 景気回復に水を差し, 株安を招くことになる。◆The global financial crisis is continuing unabated. 世界的な金融危機は, とどまるところを知らない。◆The rapid surge in the yen's value, if it continues unabated, could bring it close to yet another record high. 急激な円高がこのまま進めば, 最高値をうかがう展開もあり得る。

unanimous　（形）満場［全員］一致の, 異議のない, 意見が一致している, 同意見である, 同意の, 合意の
　be unanimous for　満場一致で～に賛成である, ～に全員賛成である, ～に賛成である, ～に意義はない
　be unanimous in　異口同音に～する
　be unanimous on　～については意見が一致している
　unanimous action　全会一致の決議, 満場一致の決議
　unanimous applause　満場の拍手
　unanimous decision　満場一致の決定, 全会一致による決定
　unanimous vote　満場一致の票決
◆The unanimous decision by the U.S. central bank's policy setting Federal Open Market Committee moved the benchmark federal funds rate to 1.25 percent. 米連邦準備制度理事会の金利政策を決定する米連邦公開市場委員会の全会一致による決定で, 短期金利の指標であるフェデラル・ファンド金利が年1.25％に引き上げられた。

unanimously　（副）満場一致で, 全会一致で, 全員一致して, 全員異議なく
◆The Bank of Japan's policy-setting panel unanimously decided to forgo an increase in its key short-term interest rate. 日銀の政策決定委員会は, 短期金利（無担保コール翌日物）の誘導目標引上げの見送りを, 全員一致で決めた。

unauthorized moneylender　ヤミ金融業者
　（⇒interest rate）
unauthorized moneylending business　ヤミ金融
unbalanced budget　不均衡予算
uncertain　（形）不確かな, 不透明な, 不確定な, 不確実な, 不安定な
　uncertain factor　不確定要因
　uncertain market conditions　不透明な市場環境, 市場環境の不安定性
　uncertain outlook　先行きの不透明感
◆Fed Chairman Ben Bernanke described the U.S. economic outlook as "unusually uncertain." 米連邦準備制度理事会（FRB）のバーナンキ議長は, 米経済の見通しについて「異例なほど不透明だ」と述べた。◆It remains uncertain whether crude oil prices will undergo an interrupted decline. 原油価格が一本調子で下落するかどうかは, 不透明だ。

uncertainty　（名）不確実性, 不確定, 不確定要因, 波乱要因, 不透明, 先行き不透明感, 不安, 懸念, 動揺
　credit uncertainty　信用不安
　economic uncertainty　景気の不透明感
　interest rate uncertainty　金利の先行き不透明感
　uncertainties in the market　市場の不確定要因, 市場の波乱要因
　uncertainty over the global economy　世界経済の不透明感
◆Credit uncertainty in Europe has spilled over to France which is helping Greece, Italy and Spain facing fiscal crises. 欧州の信用不安は, 財政危機に直面しているギリシャやイタリア, スペインを支援しているフランスにも拡大している。◆Gold extended its rally to a record above $1,900 an ounce amid increased uncertainties over the U.S. and European economic outlook on the Comex in New York. ニューヨーク商品取引所では, 米欧景気見通しへの懸念［米欧経済の先行き不透明感］の高まりを受け［懸念の高まりから］, 金価格が急騰して, 1トロイ・オンス＝1,900ドルを史上初めて突破した。◆In Europe, the creditworthiness of Italian and Spanish government bonds is a source of uncertainty. 欧州では, イタリアとスペインの国債の信用力が, 金融不安の発生源だ。◆Near-term uncertainty surrounding the global economy continues to grow. 世界経済を取り巻く短期的な先行き不安は, 増大傾向が続いている。◆Some smaller companies are more cautious about borrowing for capital expenditures due to economic uncertainty. 一部の中小企業は, 景気の不透明感から, 設備投資の借入れに一段と慎重になっている。◆The Greek-triggered sovereign debt crisis has been throwing the eurozone into financial uncertainty and multiple crises. ギリシャに端を発した債務危機問題で, ユーロ圏は金融不安と複合的な危機に陥っている。◆The yields on Greek government bonds have been rising sharply due to the credit uncertainty. ギリシャ国債の利回りは, 信用不安で急上昇している。◆There is no end in sight to fiscal crises in the United States and some European countries as credit uncertainty is spreading. 信用不安が拡大しているため, 米国と欧州の一部の財政危機の収束が見通せない。◆Uncertainty has prevailed as the value of the euro dropped sharply. ユーロの相場が急落したため, 不安［動揺］が広がっている。

uncertainty about the future　先行きに対する不安, 先行き不安
◆Uncertainty about the future of Japan's financial system will persist until the vulnerable financial foundation of life insurance companies is rectified. 生命保険会社の脆弱（ぜいじゃく）な経営基盤を立て直さない限り, 日本の金融システムの先行きに対する不安は消えない。

uncertainty over the debt crisis in the eurozone　ユーロ圏の債務危機不安, ユーロ圏の債務危機に対する不安
◆Behind these cautious views among large manufacturers are uncertainty over the debt crisis in the eurozone and the slowdown in the U.S. economy. 大企業製造業のこうした警戒感［慎重な見方］の背景には, ユーロ圏の債務危機不安や米景気の減速がある。

uncertainty over the global economy　世界経済の不透明感
◆Falling stock prices and the depreciation of the U.S. dollar increased uncertainty over the global economy. 米国の株安やドル安で, 世界経済の不透明感が強まっている。

unchanged　（形）もとのままの, 変わらない, 変化しない, 不変の
　be left unchanged　据え置かれる, 据え置きになる
　be unchanged　変わっていない, 変わらない, 横ばいである, ゼロ成長の
　keep [hold, leave, maintain] a key interest rate unchanged at 0.5 percent　政策金利を0.5％に据え置く

keep monetary [credit] policy unchanged　金融政策を据え置く, 金融政策を維持する
leave one's main interest rate unchanged at 1 percent　政策金利を1%に据え置く　(⇒main interest rate)
remain unchanged　横ばいである, ～と変わらない
◆The Federal Reserve Board left interest rates unchanged. 米連邦準備制度理事会(FRB)は, 金利を据え置いた[現行水準で据え置いた]。◆The People's Bank of China kept interest rates unchanged out of concerns that higher rates would have a negative impact on the economy. 中国人民銀行は, 利上げの経済へのマイナス効果を心配したため, 金利を据え置いてきた。

uncollectible　回収不能の, 貸付け金の取立てができない, 焦げ付いた　(=uncollectable)
◆Public funds were used to cover an estimated ¥120 billion in uncollectible emergency loans to the now defunct Yamaichi Securities Co. held by the Bank of Japan. 経営破たんした山一証券に対して日銀が抱える日銀特融(緊急融資額)の回収不能債権約1,200億円の補填(ほてん)に, 公的資金が使われた。

uncollectible loan　不良債権, 不良貸付け, 貸倒れ, 回収不能の融資　(=bad loan, nonperforming loan; ⇒executive)
◆About ¥1.9 trillion of taxpayers' money was spent over ten years to last fiscal year to cover losses from a surging number of uncollectible loans guaranteed by a public credit guarantee scheme for small and midsize companies. 中小企業のための公的信用保証制度により保証される融資の貸倒れ件数が急増し, それによる損失の穴埋めをするために, 昨年度までの10年間で約1兆9,000億円の税金が投入された。

unconditional reserve　別途積立金　(=general reserve, other reserve, special reserve)

unconsolidated　(形)連結から除外された, 連結の範囲に含まれない, 連結対象外の, 連結されていない, 非連結の, 単独ベースの
unconsolidated affiliates　連結対象外の関連会社
unconsolidated debt　単独ベースの借入金, 非連結子会社の負債
unconsolidated financial statements　単独財務諸表, 単独財務書類
unconsolidated operating profit　単独ベースの営業利益, 非連結営業利益
unconsolidated subsidiary　非連結子会社　(=unconsolidated subs.)

unconsolidated after-tax loss　単独ベースでの税引き後損失, 非連結税引き後損失, 単体の税引き後損失
◆TEPCO is expected to suffer an unconsolidated after-tax loss of ¥576.3 billion for the business year ending March 2012. 東電は, 2012年3月期決算で, 5,763億円の非連結税引き後損失[赤字]になる見込みだ。

unconsolidated interest-bearing debt　非連結有利子負債
◆The firm plans to cut its unconsolidated interest-bearing debt by 40 percent by the end of March 2012 under a new business plan. 同社は, 新経営計画に基づいて2012年3月末までに非連結有利子負債を40%圧縮する計画だ。

unconsolidated operating loss　単独ベースの営業損失, 単独ベース[単独決算]で営業赤字
◆Amid a widening slump in global auto sales and the yen's sharp appreciation against the U.S. dollar, the firm is expected to report an unconsolidated operating loss in fiscal 2011. 世界の新車販売の落ち込み拡大と急激な円高・ドル安に伴って, 同社の2011年度[2012年3月期決算]の営業利益は, 単独ベース[単独決算]で赤字が見込まれている。

under-LIBOR　LIBORより低い金利水準　(=sub-LIBOR)

under-saving　(名)過少貯蓄
underage　(名)不足, 不足高　(=shortage)
underbid　(動)(競争相手より)安く値を付ける[安く入札する]　(名)低すぎる入札
underbidder　(名)入札に敗れた人
underbill　(動)実際より安く請求する
undercapitalization　(名)過小資本, 資本不足
undercapitalized　(形)過小資本の, 資本不足の
◆The government should consider injecting public funds into banks that became undercapitalized after accelerating disposal of their uncollectible loans. 政府は, 不良債権処理の加速で資本不足に陥った銀行への公的資金の注入を検討するべきだ。◆The government will have to infuse any banks with public funds if they have become undercapitalized. 銀行が資本不足に陥ったら, 政府は銀行に公的資金を注入せざるを得ないだろう。

undercapitalized bank　過小資本銀行
undercharge　(名)過小請求
underdressing　(名)アンダードレッシング(約定単価を実勢より低い価格に調整すること)
underestimate　(動)過小評価する, 軽く見る, 安く見積もる
◆In the European banking tests, banks' impaired assets were underestimated. 欧州の銀行検査では, 銀行の不良資産が過小評価された。◆The threat of the overheated state of European countries and China causing new waves of financial turmoil must not be underestimated. 欧米諸国や中国などの景気過熱状態が新たな金融危機[金融市場の混乱]を引き起こす恐れがあることを, 過小評価してはならない。

underfinanced　(形)財源不足の
undergo　(動)経験する, 体験する, 味わう, (計画や手続きを)進める, 経る(go through), (治療などを)受ける, 被る, (困難などに)遇う[遭遇する], 耐える, 忍ぶ
undergo a great change　大きな変化を経験する, 大変革を経験する
undergo a severe trial　厳しい試練にあう
undergo a sudden change　急激な変化を受ける[経る], 急激に[急に]変化する, 急に変貌する
undergo a sweeping restructuring plan　抜本的な再建策[再編計画]を進める, 抜本的な事業再編計画に乗り出す
undergo an interrupted decline　一本調子で下落する
undergo bankruptcy proceedings　破産手続きを進める
undergo great hardships　大辛苦をなめる, 多大な苦難に耐える
undergo trials　試練に耐える
◆It remains uncertain whether crude oil prices will undergo an interrupted decline. 原油価格が一本調子で下落するかどうかは, 不透明だ。◆Major Banks across Europe underwent the stress tests of the European Banking Authority in 2010 and 2011. 欧州全域の主要銀行[金融機関]が, 2010年と2011年に欧州銀行監督機構(EBA)のストレス・テスト(財務の健全性検査)を受けた。◆Major moneylender SFCG is undergoing bankruptcy procedures. 金融大手のSFCGは現在, 破産手続き中だ。◆The U.S. and Canadian governments hold a 70 percent stake in General Motors Co. while it undergoes reconstruction. 米国とカナダ両政府は, GMの株式の7割を保有しているが, GMは再建途上にある。◆With the economic structure undergoing adjustment, larger numbers of loans may become uncollectible. 経済の構造調整に伴って, 不良債権の新規発生が高水準で続く可能性がある。

underground　(形)地下の, 秘密の, 隠れた, 闇[ヤミ]の, アングラ

underground banking　地下銀行
underground dealing［transaction］　ヤミ取引
underground economy　地下経済, アングラ経済
underground market　ヤミ市場
underground money　アンダーグラウンド・マネー

underground bank　地下銀行, 代理送金業者
（=unlicensed financial operator）
◆A group operating an underground bank helped Chinese illegal immigrants and thieves transfer money to their home country. 地下銀行を運営していたグループは, 中国人密航者や窃盗団の本国への送金を手伝っていた。

underhand allowance　不正給与, ヤミ給与, ヤミ手当て
underhedging　（名）過少ヘッジ
underinsurance　（名）一部保険, 不足保険, 付保（額）過少　（=partial insurance）
underinsure　（動）一部保険にする, 付保［付保額］過少にする
underinsured　（形）一部保険の, 付保額不足の, 付保険価額過少の
underinvest　（動）過小投資する, 十分に投資しない
underinvestment　（名）過小投資, 投資不足
underinvoice [under-invoice]　（名）アンダー・インボイス（インボイス（送り状）の金額を実際より低く申告すること）
underkill　（名）不十分な金融引締め
underletting　（名）又貸し, 安値で貸すこと
underlie　（動）〜の下にある, 〜の基礎［土台］となる, 〜の裏にある, 〜を裏付ける, 〜を裏付けする,（担保などが）〜に優先する, 第一の担保となる
　collateral underlying the securities　証券を裏付ける担保
　land underlying buildings　宅地
underliquidity [under-liquidity]　（名）過少流動性
underlying　（形）下にある, 下位の, 基礎をなす, 基本的, 優先権のある, 担保となる,（担保など）第一の, 先順位の, 現物の
　underlying company　下位会社
　underlying debt　第一債務
　underlying futures contract　第一先物契約
　underlying inflation　潜在的インフレ, 基調としてのインフレ率
　underlying inflation rate　基礎インフレ率
　underlying market　現物市場
　underlying mortgage　先順位抵当, 1番抵当, 第一担保
　underlying notional value　名目元本残額
　underlying policy　原契約, 主幹保険証券
　underlying price　アンダーライイング・プライス（オプション取引での原資産の現在価格）
　underlying receivables　裏付けとなる債権
　underlying retention　保有損害額
　underlying security　原証券, 基礎証券, 対象証券（オプション取引の裏付けとなる現物の証券のこと）
　underlying stock［share］　現物株, 現物の株式, 原株
　underlying tone　底意
　underlying transaction　原金融取引
　underlying trend［tendency］　（相場などの）基調, 根底にあるトレンド, 底流
underlying asset　原資産, 対象資産, 担保となる資産
◆Commodity futures trading is based on contracts to buy or sell a specified quantity of an underlying asset, such as gold, at a particular time in the future and at a price agreed when the contract was executed. 商品先物取引は, 取引契約を結ぶ時点で, 一定量の金などの対象資産を将来の特定の時期に合意した値段で売買する契約に基づいて行われる。

undermine　（動）損なう, 蝕（むしば）む, 傷つける, 害する, 弱める, 悪化させる, 低下させる, 〜に水をさす, 浸食する
　undermine bond performance　債券相場の足を引っ張る
　undermine public confidence in the securities market norms　証券市場に対する国民の信認を低下させる
　undermine the foundation of stock market norms　株式市場の規範の根本を揺るがす, 株式市場の規範を根本から揺るがす　（⇒norm）
　undermine the U.S. real economy　米国の実体経済を損なう
◆Confidence in the single currency of the euro may be undermined by the spread of the Greek crisis to Spain and Portugal. ギリシャ危機のスペインやポルトガルへの波及で, 単一通貨・ユーロの信認が揺らぎかねない。◆Insider trading distorts share prices and undermines the fairness of the securities market. インサイダー取引は, （適正な）株価をゆがめ, 証券市場の公正さを損なう。◆The global financial crisis seems to be undermining the firm's cost-cutting efforts. 世界金融危機が, 同社のコスト削減努力に水をさしているようだ。◆There is a possibility that a vicious circle will develop in which the financial crisis undermines the U.S. real economy, producing further financial instability. 金融危機が米国の実体経済を損ない, それがさらに金融不安を引き起こす悪循環が深刻化する可能性がある。◆This incident will eventually undermine public confidence in the securities market. この事件で, 証券市場に対する国民の信認は結局, 失墜することになる。

underpaid　（形）支払い不足の
underpay　（動）十分な支払いをしない, 低賃金を支払う　（名）内金
underpayment　（名）支払い不足, 過少支払い
underperform　（動）下回る, 市場平均を下回る, 平均を下回る, アンダーパフォームする, 〜を下回るパフォーマンスを示す, 〜よりパフォーマンスが悪い
（⇒outperform）
　underperform the eurozone market　ユーロ圏市場のパフォーマンスを下回る
　underperform the industry　業界平均を下回る
　underperform the market　市場平均を下回る, パフォーマンスが市場平均を下回る
　underperforming loans　不良債権
underperformance　（名）市場平均を下回ること, 株価パフォーマンスが市場平均を下回ること, 低迷, 低調, アンダーパフォーマンス
underpin　（動）下から支える, 下支えする, 支持する, 補強する, 実証する, 立証する
（⇒monetary measures）
　underpin prices　価格に下限を設ける［設定する］
　underpin the dollar　ドルを下支えする
　underpin the economy　景気を下支えする
　underpin the overall economy　景気全般を下支えする
　underpin the short end　短期債を下支えする, 短期債市場を下支えする
◆Just as the number of people qualifying for pensions is on the rise, the working population, which underpins the pension scheme, is on the decline. 年金受給の資格者は増える一方, 年金制度を支える現役世代は減っている。◆Some European nations which are experiencing fiscal crises seem to rely on drops in their currencies' values as a means of underpinning their economies. 財政危機問題を抱えた欧州諸国の一部は, 景気下支えの手段として通貨安を頼みにしているようだ。◆The Fed will underpin the economy through measures aimed at lowering long-term interest rates without reducing the money supply to the market. 米連邦準備制度理事

会（FRB）は、市場への資金供給量を減らさずに長期金利の低下を促す政策で、景気を下支えする方針だ。

underprice （動）過小評価する
be underpriced　過小評価されている、割安である
underpriced stock　過小評価されている株式、割安な株
◆The stock is underpriced. この株は、過小評価されている［割安だ］。

underquote （動）（人より）安い値を付ける、市価より安い言い値を付ける

underrate （動）過小評価する　（=undervalue）

underreport （動）過少申告する（understate）、過少記載する、虚偽記載する
◆The firm has underreported the ratio of stakes held by major shareholders. 同社は、これまで大株主の株式保有比率を過少申告していた。

underreporting （名）過少申告、過少記載、虚偽記載
◆Seibu Railway shares dropped by ¥300 for two days after the announcement of the underreporting of its stake in the financial statement. 西武鉄道の株は、有価証券報告書に同社株式について虚偽記載［過少記載］をしていた事実を発表後、2日間で300円下落した。

underscore （動）示す、改めて示す、はっきり示す、〜に下線を引く、〜を強調する　（名）下線、アンダーライン
◆Microsoft's acquisition of Skype Technologies for $8.5 billion underscores its ambition to plug a hole in its mobile offerings. マイクロソフトによる85億ドルでのスカイプ・テクノロジーズの買収は、携帯部門の不足分を補うというマイクロソフトの企業目標を示している。

undersubscribed （形）募集額を下回る

undertake （動）引き受ける、請け負う、約束する、着手する、乗り出す、進める、取り組む保証する
undertake an acquisition　買収に乗り出す
undertake initial public offerings　株式を新規公開する（=undertake IPOs）
undertake investment　投資を進める、投資に踏み切る
◆An increasing number of companies want to undertake IPOs while stock markets remain brisk. 株式市場が活況のうちに上場したい［株式を新規公開したい］、という企業が増えている。◆The number of companies undertaking initial public offerings has risen sharply this year. 株式を新規公開する企業が、今年は急増している。◆Worse-than-expected U.S. employment data for September fueled speculation that U.S. authorities could undertake further credit easing steps. 9月の米国の雇用統計が予想以上に悪化したことで、米当局が追加の金融緩和策に踏み切るとの観測が強まった［高まった］。

undertone （名）地（じ）合い、底流
firm undertone　堅調な地合い、強気の地合い、良好な地合い
soft undertone　弱い地合い
◆The U.S. Treasury bond market has a firm undertone. 米国の長期国債市場の地合いは、堅調［良好］である。

undervaluation　過小評価、割安な株価評価
◆Japan's yen-selling market intervention and the undervaluation of the Chinese currency, the yuan, came under a barrage of criticism. 日本の円売り介入と中国の通貨「人民元」の過小評価が、批判の集中攻撃を受けた［批判にさらされた］。

undervalue （動）過小評価する
undervalued asset　含み資産、割安な資産
undervalued real estate　過小評価されている不動産、不動産の過小評価
undervalued securities　含み益のある有価証券、割安の有価証券
◆The Chinese yuan is undervalued somewhere between 5 percent and 27 percent. 中国の人民元（相場）は、5〜27%程度、過小評価されている。◆The current yuan exchange rate is said to be undervalued against the U.S. and the euro. 現在の人民元の為替相場は、米ドルやユーロに対して割安［過小評価されている］と言われる。◆The IMF's Executive Board is divided over whether the Chinese currency is undervalued. IMF理事会は、人民元相場が過小評価されているかどうかで、意見が分かれている。◆The yuan remains substantially undervalued. 人民元は、まだ大幅に過小評価されている。

undervalued yuan　過小評価されいる人民元、人民元の過小評価
◆The undervalued yuan has increased China's international competitiveness, adding to its trade imbalances with the United States and other nations. 人民元の過小評価が、中国の国際競争力を高め、米国などとの貿易不均衡を拡大している。

underwater loan　アンダーウォーター・ローン　（市価［時価］が帳簿価格を下回る貸付け）
underweight　投資の比重が低い、低め、アンダーウェート

underweight （動）組入れ比率を低くする［引き下げる］、アンダーウェイトにする　（名）（株式などの）組入れ比率が低いこと、組入れ比率を引き下げること、本来保有すべき比率を下回った状態　（形）投資の比重が低い低めの、アンダーウェイト［アンダーウェート］
be given a heavy underweight status　〜を大幅にアンダーウェイトにする
be significantly underweight　（組入れ比率が）大幅にアンダーウェイトになっている
go underweight in [on]　〜をアンダーウェイトにする、〜の組入れ比率を低くする
increase the underweight of　〜の組み入れ比率をさらに引き下げる
remain underweighted　引き続きアンダーウェイトになっている［アンダーウェイトにする］
stay underweight　アンダーウェイトを維持する
underweight in equities　株式の組み入れ比率が低いこと
underweight position　アンダーウェイトのポジション
underweight U.S. Treasuries　米国債の組み入れ比率を引き下げる［低くする］

underwrite （動）（株式や社債、保険などを）引き受ける、保険証券に署名する、保険担保責任を負う
underwrite credit life insurance　信用生命保険を引き受ける
underwrite debt securities　債務証券を引き受ける
underwrite Eurobonds　ユーロ債を引き受ける
underwrite government bonds　国債を引き受ける
underwrite insurance for the sales contract　売買契約の保険を引き受ける
underwrite local government bond issues　地方債を引き受ける
underwrite the fiscal investment and loan program bond　財投債を引き受ける
underwrite the offering　売出しを引き受ける
◆Funds collected through postal savings and kampo postal life insurance were tapped to underwrite the fiscal investment and loan program bond. 郵便貯金や簡易保険を通じて集められた資金は、財投債の引受けに充てられていた。◆It is too unconventional for the Bank of Japan to directly underwrite government bonds. 日銀の国債の直接引受けは、禁じ手だ。◆Nippon Export and Investment Insurance will underwrite insurance for any of the Mitsubishi Regional Jet sales and lease contracts. 三菱リージョナルジェット（MRJ）の売買契約とリース契約の保険は、日本貿易保険が引き受ける。◆The government's new institution established to deal with the compensation payments would underwrite TEPCO's new shares to be issued in the form of preferred stock. 賠償金の支払い

対応策として設立される国の新機構は、東電の増資を優先株の形で引き受けることになる。

underwriter （名）証券引受人, 引受業者, 債券引受会社, 引受証券会社, 引受行, 保険業者, 保険会社, 保険代理業者
  bond underwriter　公社債引受人
  co-underwriter　共同引受行
  field underwriter　保険外交員
  fire underwriter　火災保険業者
  Institute of London Underwriters　ロンドン保険業者協会
  insurance underwriter　保険会社, 保険代理業者
  life underwriter　生命保険募集人
  lifetime underwriter　生命保険業者
  Lloyd's underwriter　ロイズ[ロイド]保険業者
  Lloyd's Underwriter's Association　ロイズ保険業者協会
  managing underwriter　幹事会社, 引受主幹事
  marine underwriter　海上保険業者, 海上保険引受業者
  principal underwriter　主幹事（=lead manager）
  private underwriter　個人保険業者
  securities underwriter　証券引受人, 証券引受会社
  syndicate of underwriters　引受シンジケート団
  underwriter syndication　引受業者の組成, 引受団の組成（=syndication of underwriters）
  underwriters' adjusting company　損害査定会社
  underwriters' agreement　募債団契約[契約書]
  underwriters' allocations　引受分の割当額
  underwriters' department　保険引受部門, 保険業務
  underwriter's option　（公社債募集の）引受人特権
  underwriter's profit margin　引受人差額利潤
  underwriters' syndicate　保険シンジケート
◆One of the largest underwriters of corporate bonds is the investment bank. 社債の最大の引受業者には、この投資銀行も入っている。

underwriting （名）保険や証券の引受け, 引受業務
  all-or-none underwriting　一括方式の引受け
  best efforts underwriting　売出方式の引受け
  bond underwriting　債券引受け
  competitive underwriting　競争入札方式の引受け
  drop out of an underwriting　引受けを辞退する, 引受シンジケート団から外れる
  firm underwriting　確定引受け
  form an underwriting group　引受団を組成する
  insurance underwriting　保険引受け
  negotiated underwriting　協議引受け, 協議引受方式
  stand-by underwriting　引受募集, 残額引受発行, 残額引受方式の引受け
  underwriting account　保険勘定, 営業勘定
  underwriting agent　引受代理店
  underwriting agreement　参加引受契約, 引受契約[契約書], 引受主幹事会社と発行企業間の契約
  underwriting amount　引受額
  underwriting business　引受業務
  underwriting commission　引受手数料, 募債引受料
  underwriting commitment　引受額
  underwriting community　引受業界
  underwriting cover　アンダーライティング・カバー
  underwriting criteria　貸出審査基準, 引受基準
  underwriting fortunes　査定規準
  underwriting group　引受団, 一般引受団, 引受グループ
  underwriting house　証券引受業者
  underwriting income　保険所得
  underwriting letter　募債引受申込書
  underwriting loss　引受損失
  underwriting manual　査定基準
  underwriting member　引受メンバー
  underwriting method　全額引受方式
  underwriting of government securities [bonds]　国債の引受け
  underwriting profession　引受業者
  underwriting profit　引受利益,（保険の）営業利益
  underwriting profit and loss　事業損益, 引受損益
  underwriting requirements　引受基準
  underwriting reserve　責任準備金
  underwriting rules　査定規準
  underwriting share　引受比率, 引受シェア
  underwriting spread　引受スプレッド, 引受業者の利益（引受業者の発行証券の買取り価格と一般に売り出すときの公募価格との差額）
  underwriting standards　貸出審査基準, 与信基準, 引受基準
  underwriting syndicate　募集引受団, 引受[発行証券引受]シンジケート団, 引受シ団, シ団（=investment banking group, purchase group, underwriting group）
  underwriting year　引受年度
  underwriting year system　契約引受年度法
◆The five business fields in the tie-up agreement are product development, marketing, insurance underwriting, damage assessment and reinsurance. 提携契約の5業務分野は、商品開発、マーケティング、保険引受け、損害査定と再保険である。

underwriting fee　引受手数料, 募債引受料
◆Trading and underwriting fees soared as the stock market boomed. 株式市場の活況を背景に、株式の売買・引受手数料が急増した。

undeserved　（形）～に値しない, 相応（ふさわ）しくない, 不当な

undeserved income　不当利益
◆The bank padded its pockets with undeserved income. 同行は、不当利益で財力を水増ししていた。

undigested security　未消化証券
undisbursed balance　未払い残高
undisbursed loans　未実行貸出
unearned　（形）未経過の, 未収の, 不労の
  unearned benefit　不労給付
  unearned discount (on bills)　未経過(手形)割引料
  unearned dividend　タコ配当, 未収益配当
  unearned income [revenue]　不労所得, 前受収益, 未稼得利益
  unearned increment　自然増価
  unearned interest　未経過利子
  unearned interest on loan bills　未経過手形貸付け利息
  unearned premium　未経過保険料
  unearned premium insurance　未経過保険料保険
  unearned reinsurance premiums　未経過再保険料
  unearned value　不労増価

unease　（名）不安, 不安感, 心配, 懸念, 当惑（=uneasiness）
  a sense of unease in the world economy　世界経済の不安感
  eliminate unease in the financial markets　金融市場の不安感を払拭（ふっしょく）する
◆Japan, the United States and European countries have failed to eliminate unease in the financial market after the recent downgrading of the U.S. credit rating. 日米欧は、今回の米国債格下げ後の金融市場の不安感を払拭（ふっしょく）

できていない。
unemployed capital　遊休資本
unemployment　(名)失業, 失職, 失業者, 失業率
　　chronic unemployment　慢性的失業
　　falling unemployment　失業率の低下
　　fear of unemployment　雇用不安
　　graduate unemployment　大卒失業
　　hard-core unemployment　慢性的失業
　　industrial unemployment　産業的失業
　　potential unemployment　潜在失業
　　　（＝latent unemployment）
　　rate of unemployment　失業率
　　rising unemployment　失業の増大, 失業の増加, 失業率の上昇　（＝increase［rise］in unemployment）
　　structural unemployment　構造的失業
　　unemployment compensation　失業補償, 失業給付, 失業手当て, 失業保険
　　unemployment disequilibrium　失業不均衡
　　Unemployment Insurance Law　雇用保険法
　　unemployment relief　失業救済, 失業対策
　　unemployment reserve　失業補償積立金
　　unemployment security　失業保険
　　unemployment situation　失業状況
　　voluntary unemployment　自発的失業
　　weekly unemployment data　週次の失業保険新規申請者数
　　weekly unemployment numbers　週次の失業保険新規受給申請者数
　　◆The U.S. 10 leading banks need a combined capital buffer of 74.6 billion against the risk of a deeper recession and higher unemployment over the next two years. 米主要金融機関の10社は, 今後2年の景気悪化リスクと失業増大に備えて, 10社合計で746億ドルの資本増強を求められている。
unemployment benefits　失業給付, 失業保険給付, 失業手当て, 失業保険
　　be entitled to unemployment benefits　失業給付を受ける権利［資格］がある
　　new claims for state unemployment insurance benefits　失業保険新規受給申請者数
　　new filings for state unemployment insurance benefits　新規失業保険申請者数
　　unconditional unemployment benefits　無条件失業保険給付
unemployment insurance　失業保険, 雇用保険
　　be covered by unemployment insurance　失業保険［雇用保険］で補償される
　　be qualified for unemployment insurance benefits　雇用保険による給付［失業保険給付］を受ける資格がある
　　new filings for state unemployment insurance claim　失業保険新規受給申請者数
unemployment insurance system　失業保険制度, 雇用保険制度
　　◆If people lose their jobs, they are entitled to benefits under the national unemployment insurance system. 失業すれば, 雇用保険制度で失業給付を受けることができる。◆The unemployment insurance system is supported by premiums paid by labor and management. 失業保険（雇用保険）制度は, 労使が負担する保険料で支えられている。
unemployment rate　失業率
　　◆If the number of corporate bankruptcies and the unemployment rate soar owing to structural reforms, recessionary pressures will further increase. 構造改革で企業倒産件数や失業率が増えると, 不況圧力は一層強まるものと思われる。

◆The stress tests conducted by the Fed were based on the 2009 unemployment rate average of 8.9 percent. 米連邦準備制度理事会（FRB）の特別検査（ストレス・テスト）は, 2009年の平均失業率を8.9%,（国内総生産（GDP）の実質伸び率をマイナス3.3%）と想定して行われた。
unencumbered　(形)無疵（むきず）の, 抵当権が設定されていない,（債務などの）負担がない
　　unencumbered property　無疵（むきず）の不動産
　　unencumbered securities　抵当権が設定されていない証券
unexercised stock option　未行使のストック・オプション
　　◆Unexercised stock options to purchase 30,000 shares of common stock at $22 per share were outstanding at the beginning and end of 2008. 2008年期首および期末には, 1株当たり22ドルで普通株式3万株を購入できる未行使のストック・オプションが存在していた。
unexpected contraction in the service sector　予想しなかったサービス業の業況悪化
　　◆The Dow Jones industrials plunged 370 points after an unexpected contraction in the service sector. 予想しなかったサービス業の業況悪化を受けて, ダウ平均株価（工業株30種）は, 前日比で370ドル急落した。
unfavorable　(形)不利な, 不当な, 好ましくない, 悪い, マイナスの, 逆の
　　unfavorable effects on earnings per share　普通株式1株当たり利益に対する不利な影響額
　　unfavorable exchange　逆為替
　　unfavorable exchange rate　不利な為替相場［為替レート］　（＝unfavorable rate of exchange）
　　unfavorable factor　不利な材料, 不利な要因, マイナス要因, 悪材料, 売り材料, 悲観材料, 不安材料
　　unfavorable impact　不利な影響, マイナス影響, 悪影響
　　unfavorable market conditions　市況の悪化, 市場環境の悪化, 不利な市場環境
　　unfavorable trade balance　貿易収支の赤字, 輸入超過, 入超
　　◆The business sentiment index represents the percentage of companies reporting favorable business conditions minus the percentage of those reporting unfavorable conditions. 業況判断指数は, 景気が良いと答えた企業の割合（%）から景気が悪いと答えた企業の割合（%）を差し引いた指数だ。◆The company attributed the expected net profit decline to the possible unfavorable effects of the yen's rise against the dollar and the euro. 同社は, 予想される純利益［税引き後利益］減少の理由として, 同社に不利な円高・ドル安, ユーロ安の影響を挙げた。
unfavorable balance　支払い超過, 逆調, 輸入超過　（＝adverse balance, passive balance）
　　unfavorable balance in foreign trade　外国貿易の輸入超過, 外国貿易の逆調
　　unfavorable balance of payments　国際収支の赤字, 輸入超過, 貿易逆調　（＝balance of payments deficit）
　　unfavorable balance of trade　貿易収支の赤字, 輸入超過, 入超, 貿易逆調　（＝balance of trade deficit, unfavorable trade balance）
unfavorable factor　不利な材料, マイナス要因, 悪材料
　　◆Signs that unfavorable factors are receding are apparent, as crude oil prices have fallen. 原油の値下がりなど, 悪材料に解消の兆しが見られる。
unfit bank note　廃棄銀行券
unfixed interest-bearing securities　不確定利付き証券
unfriendly bid　敵対的買付け　（＝hostile bid）
unfunded debt　無担保借入金, 一時借入金

unfunded pension obligation　年金の積立不足
ungeared　(形)借入れのない
unhedged　(形)掛けつなぎしない
unified mortgage　整理抵当
uniform　(形)一定の, 規則正しい, 均等の, 均一の, 同一の, 一律の, 一様な, 統一的な, 画一的な, 同一標準の, 変動のない, ユニフォーム
　Uniform Commercial Code　統一商事法典, UCC
　Uniform Customs and Practice for Documentary Credits　荷為替信用状に関する統一規則および慣例, (通称)信用状統一規則, UCP
　uniform note　統一手形用紙
　Uniform Practice Code　(米国全国証券業協会の)統一慣習規則
　Uniform Rules for Collections　(国際商業会議所の)取立統一規則
unilateral　(形)片側だけの, 一方的な, 片務的な, 単独の, 一国主義の
　net unilateral transfers　純移転収支
　unilateral action　単独行動, 一方的な行動
　unilateral benefit　一方的利益
　unilateral causal relationship　一方的因果関係
　unilateral commercial transaction　単独商行為
　unilateral contract[agreement]　片務契約(契約当事者の一方だけが債務を負う契約)
　unilateral decision　一方的決定, 一方的決断, 独自の判断
　unilateral dismissal notice　一方的解雇通知
　unilateral distribution　一方的分布
　unilateral mistake　契約当事者の一方の錯誤
　unilateral monopoly　一方独占
　unilateral step　一方的な処置
　unilateral suspension of gold convertibility　金兌換性の一方的停止
　unilateral transfer　移転収支, 経常移転収支
unilateral intervention　単独介入
◆This intervention was a unilateral intervention by Japan. 今回の介入は、日本の単独介入だった。
unilaterally　(副)一方的に, 単独で
◆Japan implemented the yen-selling market intervention unilaterally. 日本は、単独で円売り介入を実施した。◆The effect of the yen-selling market intervention implemented unilaterally by Japan has already weakened. 日本が単独で実施した円売り介入[市場介入]の効果は、すでに薄らいでいる。
uninscribed　(形)無記名の
　uninscribed bond　無記名債券
　uninscribed certificate　無記名株券
　uninscribed deposit　無記名預金
　uninscribed stock　無記名株[株式]
uninsured　(形)保険を付けていない, 保険を掛けていない, 無保険の
　uninsured risk　無保険のリスク
　uninsured vessel　無保険船
unintended inventory investment　意図しない在庫投資
union　(名)統合, 同盟, 組合, 労働組合, ユニオン
　Berne Union　国際輸出信用保険機構(International Union of Credit and Investment Insurersの略)
　credit union　信用組合
　currency union　通貨統合
　European Union　EU(欧州連合)
　International Union of Marine Insurance　国際海上保険連合
　monetary union　通貨統合, 通貨同盟

　National Credit Union Share Insurance Fund　全米信用組合出資金保険基金
　State of the Union Message　一般教書
　union agreement　労働協約
◆The 17-nation currency union was slow in responding to the request for financial support by Greece. 17か国から成る通貨統合のユーロ圏は、ギリシャの金融支援要請への対応が遅かった。
unison　(名)一致, 調和, 協調, 斉唱, ユニゾン
　act in unison with　〜と一致した行動を取る, 〜と一致して行動する
　in unison　一致して, 調和して, 同時に, 異口同音に, 一斉に
　work in unison　協調して働く
◆In a joint response to the global financial crisis, the U.S. FRB, ECB and central banks in Britain, Canada, Sweden and Switzerland cut interest rates in unison. 世界的な金融危機への協調対応策として、米連邦準備制度理事会(FRB)、欧州中央銀行(ECB)と英国、カナダ、スウエーデン、スイスの中央銀行は、それぞれ金利[政策金利]を同時に引き下げた。◆World's central banks cut interest rates in unison in a joint response to the global financial crisis. 世界の中央銀行は、世界の金融危機への協調対応策として金利[政策金利]を同時に引き下げた。
unissued　(形)未発行の
　unissued capital stock　未発行資本金
　unissued check　未発行小切手
　unissued shares　未発行株式(会社が発行できる株式の上限である授権株式(authorized shares)のうち、まだ発行されていない株式の総数)
　unissued stock　未発行株式(=unissued capital stock)
unit　(名)単位, 構成単位, 主体, 部門, 事業部門, 会社, 支社, 支店, 子会社, 設備一式, 台, 基, 装置, セット, ユニット(⇒capital management capabilities, claim, financial regulators, surviving company)
　banking unit　銀行, 銀行業務部門 (=bank units)
　business unit　事業部, 事業単位
　cash surplus units(savers)　資金余剰主体(貯蓄者)
　deficit spending units(borrowers)　資金不足主体(借り手)
　European Currency Unit　欧州通貨単位
　operating unit　事業体
　property unit trust　財産契約型投資信託
　reduce the share purchase unit　株式の購入単位を小口化する
　securities unit　証券会社
　unit banking　単一銀行, 単独銀行
　unit banking system　単一銀行制度, 本店銀行主義
　unit investment trust　単位型投資信託
　unit of investment system　投資単位制
　unit trust　オープン型投資信託
　unprofitable unit　不採算部門
◆A financial intermediary acts as a middleman between cash surplus units in the economy (savers) and deficit spending units (borrowers). 金融仲介機関は、経済の資金余剰主体(貯蓄者)と資金不足主体(借り手)との間に立つ仲介者として機能している。◆A stock split is a measure designed to enable investors, including those with only limited funds, to invest in a company by reducing the share purchase unit. 株式分割は、株式の購入単位を小口化して、少額の資金しかない投資家でも企業に投資できるようにするための手段[資本政策]だ。◆AMRO, as the surveillance unit of CMIM, plays an important role to monitor and analyze regional economies. AMRO

は、(参加国が通貨急落といった危機に直面した際に外貨を融通し合う)多国間通貨交換[スワップ]協定(CMIM)の監視機関として、域内経済を監視し分析する重要な役割を担っている。◆HSBC Holdings PLC will shut its subprime mortgage unit and eliminate 750 jobs. 英銀行大手のHSBCホールディングスは、低所得者向け住宅融資「サブプライム・ローン」事業の米国子会社を閉鎖して、従業員750人を解雇する。◆Mizuho Financial Group will integrate its retail and corporate banking units in 2013. みずほフィナンシャルグループ(FG)は、傘下のリテール銀行[リテール銀行業務部門]とコーポレート銀行[企業向け銀行業務部門]を2013年にも合併させる方針だ。◆The bank became a unit of the financial group through a share swap deal. 同行は、株式交換取引で同金融グループ系の企業になった。◆The nation's mega banking groups have been realigning their securities units to offer comprehensive financial services. 国内の大手金融グループは、総合金融サービスを提供するため、グループ各社の証券会社を再統合している。

United States アメリカ合衆国, 米国 (⇒U.S. [US])
  United States GAAP 米国の会計基準, 米国の一般に認められた会計原則
  United States International Trade Commission 米国国際貿易委員会
  United States resident 米国居住者
  United States Trade Representative 米通商代表部, USTR
  United States Treasury 合衆国財務省, アメリカ財務省
◆China is trying to flex its muscle with the United States on the strength of its status as the largest holder of U.S. Treasury securities. 中国は、米財務省証券[米国債]の最大保有国としての地位を背景に、米国への影響力を行使しようとしている。◆In the United States, the Exon-Florio provision of the 1988 trade law can prevent takeover bids that are deemed a threat to national security. 米国では、1988年通商法のエクソン・フロリオ条項下で、国家の安全保障上、脅威と考えられる企業買収を阻止することができる。◆Japan, the United States and emerging economies have pressed European countries to promptly resolve the fiscal and financial crisis. 日米両国と新興国は、欧州に財政・金融危機の迅速な解決を迫った。◆The closing balance sheet fairly presents the financial position of the Corporation at the closing date in conformity with United States GAAP. クロージング時現在の貸借対照表は、米国の一般に認められた会計原則[米国の会計基準]に従って、クロージング日の「会社」の財政状態を適正に表示している。◆The United States is in the grip of the worst economic crisis in more than 70 years. 米国は、過去70年以上で最悪の経済危機に見舞われている。◆The United States lost its top-tier AAA credit rating from S&P for the first time. 米国債の格付け[米国の長期国債格付け]が、スタンダード・アンド・プアーズ(S&P)による最上級のAAA(トリプルA)の格付けから史上初めて転落した。◆The United States tries to press China to reduce its current account surplus and raise the yuan by restricting its current account with a numerical goal. 米国は、経常収支を数値目標で縛って、中国に経常収支の黒字縮小と人民元切上げの圧力をかけようとしている。◆The United States will continue to actively address anticompetitive activity, market access barriers, and or market-distorting trade practices. アメリカは、非競争的行為や市場参入障壁、市場を歪める商慣行に引き続き取り組んで行く方針だ。

unity (名)統一, 統一性, 統一体, 統合, 団結, 結束, まとまり, 一致団結, 一体感, 一貫性, 一致, 共通性, 調和
  a sense of unity 一体感, 統一感
  economic unity 経済統一
  European unity 欧州統合
  German unity ドイツ統一
  national unity 国家的統一, 挙国一致
  organic unity 有機的統一性
  political unity 政治的統一
  unity fund 統一基金
  unity of purpose 同じ目的
◆French President Nicolas Sarkozy and German Chancellor Angera Merkel called for greater economic discipline and unity among European countries. サルコジ仏大統領とメルケル独首相は、経済規律の強化と欧州各国間の結束を求めた。◆Increased burden by the aid package has begun to fray the unity within the eurozone. 支援策による負担増で、ユーロ圏内の結束がほころび始めている。

universal bank 証券業務兼営銀行, 総合銀行
universal banking 銀行の証券業務兼営, 証券業務と銀行業務の併営, ユニバーサル・バンキング
universal service ユニバーサル・サービス(郵便事業の場合は、全国同一料金でサービスを提供すること)
  universal services throughout the country 全国一律サービス
unlawful moneylending ヤミ金融 (=illegal lending, illegal moneylending, illicit moneylending)
unlikely (形)起こりそうもない, 成功しそうもない, 見込みのない
  an unlikely scenario 事がうまく運ばないような筋書き[シナリオ]
  be unlikely to ～しそうにない
◆It is highly unlikely personal spending will fully recover. 個人消費の本格回復は、望み薄だ。◆The correction of financial statements by Olympus is unlikely to result in the company's debts exceeding its assets. オリンパスの財務書類訂正で、同社の債務超過は避けられる見通しだ。◆The decline in the value of the euro is unlikely to stop. ユーロの下落傾向[ユーロ相場の下落]は、止まりそうにない。

unliquidated (形)精算されない, 決済[決算]されない
  unliquidated claim 不確定債権
  unliquidated encumbrance 未払い支出負担行為
unlisted (形)上場されていない, 非上場の, 未上場の, 簿外の
  unlisted asset 簿外資産
  unlisted department 非上場証券部
  unlisted fixed-rate issue 私募普通債
  unlisted floating rate note 私募変動利付き債
  unlisted note 非上場債
  unlisted securities 非上場証券, 非上場有価証券
  unlisted stock [share] 未上場株, 非上場株, 場外株, 店頭株, 未公開株
  unlisted subsidiary 非上場子会社
  unlisted trading privileges 非上場取引権
unlisted company 非上場会社, 非上場企業
  unlisted company traded over-the-counter 店頭登録企業
  unlisted stock company 株式を上場していない非公開会社, 非上場会社 (=unlisted joint-stock company; ⇒ stock certificate)
◆The management of both firms purchased shares from ordinary shareholders in order to withdraw from the stock market to become unlisted companies. 両社の経営陣は、株式市場から撤退して非上場企業になるために、普通株主から株を買い取った。

unlisted firm 非上場会社, 非上場企業 (=unlisted company)
◆The TSE, an unlisted firm, will make the OSE, a listed firm, its subsidiary through a takeover. 非上場企業の東証が、上場企業である大証を、株式公開買付け(TOB)で子会社化する。

unlisted joint-stock company 株式を上場していない非公開会社 (=unlisted stock company)

◆The Justice Ministry plans to revise the Commercial Code to allow unlisted joint-stock companies not to issue stock certificates unless shareholders request them to do so. 法務省は、株式を上場していない非公開会社に関して、株主からの請求がないかぎり、株券の発行を不要とする商法改正を行う方針だ。

unlisted stock 非上場株, 場外株, 店頭株, 未公開株, 非公開の株式 (=unlisted share)
◆Of the top 100 taxpayers, six made handsome gains from the sale of unlisted stocks in their companies. 高額納税者上位100人のうち6人は、非公開の自社株を売却してかなりの利益を上げた。

unload (動)処分する, 売り払う, 売却する, (債務を)返済する
unload external debt 対外債務を返済する
unload one's shareholdings 保有株を売却する
◆In the April-September period, JAL managed to secure a group net profit of ¥1.5 billion by unloading its shareholdings. 4-9月期の中間決算で、日航は保有株を売却してかろうじて15億円の連結税引き後利益を確保した。

unloanable (形)融資[貸出]できない, 貸し付けられない, 貸されない

unmanned loan contracting machine 消費者金融の無人契約機
◆The bank will install more unmanned loan contracting machines and provide greater convenience and better services. 同行は、無人契約機を増設して、利便性とサービスの向上に努める方針だ。

unmatched book アンマッチド・ブック(銀行負債の平均残存期間が, 資産の平均残存期間より短い状態)

unmerchantable (形)市場性のない, 市場向きでない, 市場に向かない

unmerge (動)(吸収・合併した企業を分離して)吸収[合併]前の姿に戻す

unmoneyed (形)金なし[文無し]の, 無一文の

unmortgaged (形)抵当にされていない, 入質されていない

unnerve (動)気力[勇気, 自信]を失わせる, 狼狽させる, 嫌気を起こさせる
◆Tokyo stocks sharply fell as investors were unnerved by the accelerated appreciation of the yen. 東京株式市場の株価は、投資家に円高加速が嫌気され、急落した。

unpaid (形)未払いの, 未納の, (手形が)不渡りの(dishonored), 無給の, 名誉職の
unpaid balance 未払い額, 未清算受取残高
unpaid claims 未払い保険金
unpaid dividend 未払い配当金
unpaid-for 未払いの
unpaid premium period 保険料未納期間
unpaid returns 未払い返戻(へんれい)金
◆There are about 420,000 full-time housewives whose unpaid premium periods are long as they have failed to switch to the national pension plan. 国民年金への切替えが済んでいなくて保険料の未納期間が長い専業主婦は、約42万人いる。

unprofitable (形)採算の合わない, 不採算な, 儲(もう)からない, 利益を生じない, 無駄な
unprofitable business [operation] 不採算事業
unprofitable division 不採算の事業部門, 不採算部門
unprofitable outlet [store] 不採算店舗
unprofitable subsidiary 不採算の子会社
◆Japan Airlines and All Nippon Airways plan to scrap or reduce flight services on a total of 28 unprofitable domestic and international routes. 日本航空と全日本空輸が、不採算の国内・国際線計28路線の運航を廃止するか減便する方針だ。

unrealized gains 未実現利益, 未実現益, 含み益, 評価益, 含み益 (=appraisal gains, latent profits, unrealized profits; ⇒gain)
◆Thanks to the increases in unrealized gains in their stocks, many banks expect to see their net worth increase. 株式含み益の増加で、多くの銀行は自己資本の上昇を見込んでいる。

unrealized losses 未実現損失, 含み損, 評価損 (=appraisal losses, latent losses; ⇒portfolio)

unrealized profits 未実現利益, 含み益, 評価益 (=appraisal profits, latent gains, unrealized gains)
◆Decreased earning power and the disappearance of the stock's unrealized profits exhausted bank finances. 収益力の低下と株式の含み益の枯渇で、銀行の財務体質は疲弊していた。

unrealized profits and losses 含み損益 (=appraisal profits and losses, latent profits and losses)

unrealized value 未実現評価額, 未実現損益, 含み損益 (⇒bullish stock market)

unrecoverable loan 不良債権, 不良貸付け, 焦げ付き, 貸倒れ (=bad debt, irrecoverable loan, unrecoverable debt; ⇒guarantor)

unrecoverable subprime mortgage loans 米国の低所得者向け住宅ローン(サブプライム・ローン)の焦げ付き, 回収不能のサブプライム・ローン
◆The instability of U.S. stock prices results from problems related to massive number of unrecoverable subprime mortgage loans extended to low-income earners in the United States. 米国の株価不安定は、米国の低所得者向け住宅ローン「サブプライム・ローン」の焦げ付き急増関連問題に起因している。

unrest (名)不安, 不満, 心配, 動揺, 混乱, 争議
currency unrest 通貨不安, 通貨動揺
economic unrest 経済不安
financial unrest 金融不安
global unrest in financial markets 世界的な金融市場の動揺[混乱]
industrial unrest 産業不安
labor unrest 労働争議, 労働不安
monetary unrest 金融不安
political unrest 政情不安
social unrest 社会不安
unrest in the global financial markets 世界的な金融市場の混乱
◆Further efforts are needed to resolve the financial unrest. 金融不安を解消するには、もう一段の努力が必要だ。 ◆In the global financial markets, unrest is continuing as there is no end in sight to fiscal crises to the United States and some European countries. 世界の金融市場では、米国と一部の欧州諸国の財政危機の収束が見通せないため、混乱が続いている。 ◆Management stability in the banking sector is indispensable to halt the spread of financial unrest triggered by the Greek debt crisis. ギリシャの財政危機に端を発した金融不安の拡大に歯止めをかけるには、銀行の経営安定が不可欠である。

unrest in global financial markets 世界的な金融市場の混乱
◆It is difficult to deal with the latest unrest in global financial markets because it has been caused by a complex web of factors. 今回の世界的な金融市場混乱への対応が難しいのは、混乱を招いている要因が複雑に絡み合っているからだ。

unrest in the financial markets 金融市場の混乱
◆Global unrest in the financial markets is continuing. 世界的な金融市場の混乱が、続いている。

unsavory (形)まずい, 嫌な, いかがわしい, 不愉快な, 芳しくない
◆Major moneylender SFCG earned an unsavory reputation

for its strong-arm loan collection methods. 金融業者大手のSFCG（旧商工ファンド）の評判は、債権の取立てが強引で芳しくなかった。

unsecured （形）無担保の、無抵当の、保証のない、安全でない
　unsecured advance　無担保貸付け
　unsecured bond　無担保社債、無担保債券
　unsecured call loan　無担保コール・ローン
　unsecured creditor　無担保債権者
　unsecured debenture　無担保社債
　　（=naked debenture）
　unsecured debt　無担保負債、無担保債務
　unsecured discount bill　無担保割引手形
　unsecured liability　無担保負債、無担保債務
　unsecured loan stock　無担保社債、ULS
　unsecured note　無担保社債券
　unsecured stock　無担保株
　unsecured subordinated obligation　無担保劣後債務

unsecured loan　無担保融資、無担保［信用］貸付け、無担保ローン、無担保債権
　（=unsecured credit; ⇒customer）
　◆The bank has increased lending to small and midsize companies in the form of unsecured loans. 同行は、無担保融資の形で中小企業向け貸出を増やしている。◆The government guaranteed up to 80 percent of ¥67 billion in unsecured loans extended to JAL by the DBJ through the Japan Finance Corporation. 日本政策投資銀行が日航に貸し付けた無担保融資670億円の最大8割については、日本政策金融公庫を通じて政府が保証している。◆Under the firm's rehabilitation plan approved by the district court, financial institutions will waive 87.5 percent of the unsecured loans they extend to the firm. 地方裁判所が認可した同社の更生計画では、金融機関が、同社に行った無担保融資［同社に対する無担保債権］の87.5%を放棄することになっている。

unsecured overnight call money　無担保コール翌日物
　◆The Bank of Japan Policy Board voted unanimously to keep the target rate for unsecured overnight call money on hold. 日銀政策委員会は、政策金利である無担保コール翌日物金利の誘導目標を据え置くことを全会一致で決めた。

unsecured overnight call rate　無担保コール翌日物の金利
　（=rate for unsecured overnight call money）
　◆The Bank of Japan uses the unsecured overnight call rate as the key target rate in the short-term money market. 日銀は、無担保コール翌日物の金利を短期金融市場の誘導目標としている。

unsettle　（動）不安定にする、不安にする、動揺させる、不安定になる、動揺する
　be unsettled by　～で動揺する
　◆The moves by Citigroup Inc. and General Electric Co. both unsettled investors. 米金融大手シティグループとGEの今回の動きで、投資家は動揺した。

unsettled　（形）不安定な、不安な、変わりやすい、定まらない、不穏な、不順な、未解決の、決着していない、未決定の、未定の、未決済の、未払いの、支払いが済まない、法的処分をされていない、人が暮らしていない
　unsettled account　未決済勘定
　unsettled bill　未決済の勘定書、未払い請求
　unsettled conflict　未解決の紛争
　unsettled market　不安定な市場、気迷い市況

unsolicited　（形）一方的な、頼みもしない、懇請された訳でもない、おせっかいな、敵対的な
　unsolicited bidding　直接入札
　unsolicited e-mail　迷惑メール

　unsolicited takeover offer　敵対的買収提案、敵対的買収、一方的な企業買収
　◆Walt Disney Co. rejected an unsolicited $48.95 billion takeover offer from cable television company Comcast Corp. ウォルト・ディズニー社は、ケーブルテレビ会社コムキャストによる489億5千万ドルの一方的な企業買収提案を拒否した。◆Yahoo Inc. has rejected Microsoft Corp.'s unsolicited $41.6 billion takeover offer as too low. 米ヤフー（インターネット検索世界第2位）は、米マイクロソフト（ソフトウエア世界最大手）による416億ドルの敵対的買収提案を、過小評価しているとして拒否した。

unsterilization　（名）非不胎化　（為替介入で、中央銀行が市場に放出した介入資金を吸収［回収］する操作を行わないで、市場に放置しておくこと。市場での円の量が増えるため、金融緩和と同じような効果があるとされる。⇒sterilization）
　◆The Bank of Japan seems to have aimed at generating an effect similar to that of an easy money policy by taking the action of unsterilization. 日銀は、（介入資金を吸収する操作を行わない）非不胎化の措置を取って［非不胎化を行って］、金融緩和と同じような効果を狙ったようだ。

unsterilized foreign exchange intervention　非不胎化為替介入、非不胎化介入、不胎化を伴わない為替介入［介入］、為替の非不胎化介入

unsterilized intervention　不胎化を伴わない介入、非不胎化介入、介入の非不胎化

untied　（形）ひも付きでない、制限されていない、使途に条件を付けない、使途無指定の、不拘束の、アンタイド
　extend［offer］an untied loan to　～にアンタイド・ローンを供与する
　untied direct loan　アンタイド直接借款
　untied loan　ひも付きでない融資、使途無指定融資、不拘束融資、アンタイド・ローン
　untied soft loan　ひも付きでない［用途を指定しない］融資、使途無指定融資、不拘束融資、アンタイド・ローン［アンタイド・ソフト・ローン］
　◆Yen loans, now being extended as part of Japan's ODA, are untied in principle, with the source of development materials and equipment to be procured not defined. 日本の政府開発援助（ODA）として供与されている円借款は現在、ひも付きでない「アンタイド」援助が原則で、開発物資の調達先を限定していない。

untied yen loans　ひも付きでない円借款
　◆Ordinary untied yen loans are now offered at loan rates ranging from 1.8 to 2.2 percent annum. ひも付きでない通常［一般］の円借款は現在、年1.8～2.2%の貸付け金利で供与されている。

unused credit lines　銀行与信枠未使用残高
　（⇒prime bank rate of interest）

unvalued　（形）評価されない、未評価の、価値［値うち］を認められない、無額面の、額面未定の、金額未詳細の
　unvalued policy　未評価保険、評価未済保険、金額不確定保険証書
　unvalued share　無額面株、額面未定株券

unveil　（動）発表する、明らかにする、打ち明ける、公表する、公にする、初公開する、公開する、序幕する、ベールを外す　（⇒improve, overhaul名詞）
　◆A sense of disappointment has prevailed across the world markets as no concrete measures to rescue Greece were unveiled at the eurozone finance ministers meeting. ユーロ圏財務相会合でギリシャ支援の具体策が明らかにされなかったので、世界の市場で失望感が広がった。◆Fuji TV unveiled a plan to make Nippon Broadcasting System a subsidiary by upping its stake from the 12.39 percent it had as of mid-January on the basis of the takeover bid. フジテレビは、株式公開買付けでニッポン放送株の保有比率を1月中旬現在の12.39%から引き

上げて、ニッポン放送を子会社化する計画を発表した。
unwind （動）解消する, 清算する, 手じまいする, 手じまう （=close out）
 unwind a derivative portfolio　派生商品ポートフォリオを清算する
 unwind a trade　逆取引をする
 unwind cross-shareholdings　株式持ち合いを解消する
 unwind the position　ポジションを手じまう, ポジションの手じまいをする, ポジションを解消する
 unwind the swap　スワップを清算する
up　（動）上げる, 増やす, 強める, 強化する　（自動）上昇する, 上がる, 増加する, 増える, 覚醒剤を飲む, 〜を取り上げる［持ち上げる, 拾い上げる］
 up N-disaster info sharing　原発事故の情報共有を強化する
 up pressure on Europe to contain the debt crisis　欧州に債務危機封じ込めの圧力を強める
 up strategic talks　戦略協議を強化する
  （=beef up strategic talks）
 up the ante　賭けに出る, 賭け金をつり上げる, 分担金［個人分担金］を引き上げる
 ◆Japan, the United States and emerging countries are upping their pressure on Europe to contain the Greek-triggered sovereign debt crisis. 日米と新興国は, 欧州に対して, ギリシャに端を発したソブリン危機（政府債務危機）封じ込めの圧力を強めている。
up-and-coming countries　新興国（up-and-coming＝将来有望な）
 ◆Markets in up-and-coming countries with booming economies are growing rapidly. 好景気の新興国市場は, 急成長している。
up front［up-front］　前金で, 前払いで, 先払いで, 前もって, 明白に, 率直に　（⇒upfront）
 ◆In the case of single-premium whole life insurance policies, policyholders make one large premium payment up front when they sign the contract. 一時払い終身保険の場合は, 保険契約者が契約を結ぶ際に［契約時に］多額の保険料を前もって一括で払い込む。
up to　最高〜まで, 〜まで, 最高〜, 最大〜, 〜の義務［責任］で, 〜次第で, 〜が決めることで, 〜をしていて, 〜を計画して
 ◆Aeon Co. has called on Marubeni Corp. to sell up to 30 percent of its stake in Maruetsu Inc. イオンは, 丸紅（ダイエーの筆頭株主）に対して, マルエツ株の最大30％譲渡を求めた。◆General Motors Corp. agreed to sell up to $55 billion in car and truck loans to Bank of America Corp. over five years. ゼネラル・モーターズ（GM）は, バンク・オブ・アメリカに対して, 今後5年間で最大550億ドルの自動車ローン債権を売却することで合意した。◆Japan will double assistance to African nations over five years and provide up to $4 billion in loans. 日本は今後, アフリカ向け援助を5年間で倍増し, 最大40億ドルの借款を供与する。◆The government guaranteed up to 80 percent of ¥67 billion in unsecured loans extended to JAL by the DBJ through the Japan Finance Corporation. 日本政策投資銀行が日航に貸し付けた無担保融資670億円の最大8割については, 日本政策金融公庫を通じて政府が保証している。◆The U.S. administration will spend up to $700 billion to buy up soured mortgage-related securities and other devalued assets held by ailing financial institutions. 米政府は, 経営不振の金融機関が保有するモーゲージ関連の不良証券などの不良資産を, 最大7,000億ドル投入して買い取る方針だ。◆UBS will post a pretax loss of up to $690 million in the third quarter mainly because of losses linked to the U.S. subprime mortgage crisis. スイス最大手銀行UBSの第3四半期税引き前損失は, 主に米国で起きた低所得者向け融資「サブプライム・ローン」問題の関連損失で, 最高で6億9,000万ドルに達する見通しだ。◆Under the new financing scheme, the IMF will extend to financially strapped countries loans of up to 500 percent of their contribution to the IMF. 新融資制度では, 財政の資金繰りが苦しく［厳しく］なった国に対して, その国がIMF（国際通貨基金）に出資している額の最大5倍までIMFが融資する。
upbeat　（形）楽観的な, 快活な, 楽しい, 陽気な, （見出しが）明るい, 盛り上がりのある, 景気がよい, 上昇傾向の　（⇒downbeat）
 show an upbeat trend　上昇傾向を示す
 upbeat economic data　明るい景気指標, 明るい経済データ
 upbeat outlook　明るい見通し, 見通しの明るさ
 ◆Business sentiment among major domestic corporations is increasingly upbeat. 国内大手企業の景況感が, 次第に明るくなってきた。
upcoming　（形）近く発表される, 近々発売［公開］の, 近く予定されている, 近く上映［放映］予定の, 近刊の, 将来型の, 予想される, 当面の, やがて起ころうとしている, 近づく, 今回の
 upcoming capital requirements　予想される必要資本, 当面の資金需要
 upcoming economic data　近く発表される景気指標
 upcoming financing needs　当面の資金調達のニーズ
 upcoming investments　今後の投資, 今後の投資案件
 ◆The upcoming negotiations will determine practical measures to strengthen ties, including the merger ratio, the name of the new group and the positions to be held by top executives. 今後の交渉で, 統合比率や新グループの名称, 首脳人事など提携強化の具体策を詰める。
upfront［up-front］　（形）当初の, 初期の, 前もっての（advance）, 前払いの, 前金の, 先行投資の, 最前列の, 管理部門の, 経営部門の, 重要な, 外向性の, 外交的な, 積極的な, 率直な, 単刀直入の
 upfront amount　前払い金額
 upfront capital　初期資本
 upfront cash payment　前払い調整金
 upfront commissions　前払い手数料
 upfront commitment fee　前払い手数料, 契約手数料
 upfront coupon　当初のクーポン
 upfront fee　前払い手数料
  （=loan origination fee）
 upfront lump sum payment　一括払いの前払い金, 契約一時金
 upfront payment　前払い, 前払い金
 upfront premium　前払い保険料, 前払いプレミアム
upfront payment　前払い調整金, アップフロント・ペイメント　（=upfront cash payment）
 ◆Low-margin foreign exchange products allow individuals to buy and sell large amounts of foreign currencies with a small upfront payment. 証拠金が少ない外国為替商品の場合, 個人投資家は, 少ない前払い調整金（アップフロント・ペイメント）で巨額の外国為替取引（外国為替の売買）を行うことができる。
upgrade　（動）昇格させる, 高める, 向上させる, 強化する, 増強する, 高度化する, 底上げする, 格上げする, 格付けを引き上げる, 上方修正する, グレードアップする　（名）高度化, 機能拡張, 格上げ, 上方修正, グレードアップ　（⇒business environment, downgrade）
 rating upgrade　格上げ
 review for possible upgrade　格上げの方向で検討する, 格上げの方向で格付けを見直す
 under review for possible upgrade　格上げの方向で検討中, 格上げの方向で格付けを見直し中

◆Integrating the trading systems of the TSE and the OSE will enable the new market to aggressively upgrade its facilities. 東証と大証の売買システムの一本化によって、新市場の積極的な設備増強・高度化が可能となる。◆Moody's Investors Service upgraded the long-term ratings for the company from Aa1 to Aaa. ムーディーズが、同社の長期格付けをAa1からAaaに格上げした。◆Standard & Poor's upgraded the outlooks on its ratings to stable from negative on five insurance companies. スタンダード＆プアーズは、保険会社5社の格付け見通しを「ネガティブ」から「安定的」に上方修正した。◆The Asian Development Bank upgraded its 2010 growth forecast for 14 East Asian countries. アジア開発銀行は、東アジア14か国の2010年の成長率予測を上方修正した。◆The government has upgraded the economic outlook to "picking up." 政府は、景気見通しを「持ち直し」に上方修正した。

upgrading （名）昇進、昇格、格上げ（rating upgrade）、上方修正、引上げ、品質改良高度化、機能拡張、イメージ・アップ
　broad upgrading of the ratings of major Japanese banks　広範な邦銀大手行の格上げ
　upgrading and diversification　高度化と多様化
　upgrading of production　生産の上昇
◆The move was Moody's first broad upgrading of the ratings of major Japanese banks since the banking industry's sweeping consolidation following the collapse of bubble economy in the early 1990. 今回の措置は、（米大手格付け会社の）ムーディーズとしては、1990年代はじめのバブル崩壊に伴う銀行業界の抜本的な統合以来初の広範な邦銀大手行の格上げとなった。

uphold （動）支持する、認める、是認する、遵守（じゅんしゅ）する、維持する、下から支える、持ち上げる
◆In this type of life insurance products, the rate of return after canceling the insurance contract can be higher than that of a savings account if a policyholder upholds the contract for five to 10 years. この種の生保商品では、保険契約者が保険契約を5～10年続けると、解約後の利回り（予定利率）は預金よりも高い利回りが見込める。

upper （形）上の、上方の、上位［上層、上級、上流］の、高地地方の、北部の、後期の
　be promoted to the upper rank　上の階級に昇進する
　get［gain, have］the upper hand（of）　台頭する、（～を）支配する、（権力を）掌中に収める、（～に）勝つ、（～より）優勢になる、優位に立つ
　the upper echelons of the company　会社の上層部
　the upper end of the band　レンジの上限
　the upper end of the market　高級市場
　the upper end of the production stream　生産の流れ（生産から消費に至る各段階）の上流
　the upper hand　優勢、優越（dominance）、支配
◆Industries at the upper end of the production stream have higher increases in recurring profits. 生産の流れ（生産から消費に至る各段階）の上流にある産業のほうが、経常利益の増加率が高い。◆Mass retailers of clothing, general merchandise, home electrical appliances and other businesses that sell a variety of low-priced products are gaining the upper hand. 今は、豊富な低価格品を販売する衣料、雑貨、家電などの量販店が、台頭している。◆The U.S. dollar temporarily dropped to the upper ￥95 level over credit fears. 米ドルは、信用不安で一時、1ドル＝95円台後半まで［後半の水準まで］下落した。◆The yen hovered in a narrow range in the upper ￥85 level to the dollar. 円相場は、1ドル＝85円台後半の小幅な値動きとなった。

upper limit　上限
　the upper limit of the central bank's liquidity target　日銀の流動性目標の上限、日銀当座預金の残高目標の上限
　upper limit money rate　上限金利
　upper limit of a loan　融資限度額、貸付け限度額

◆The Bank of Japan supplied funds beyond the upper limit of ￥27 trillion soon after the Resona problem surfaced. 日銀は、りそな問題発覚後、27兆円の上限を上回る資金を市場に供給した。◆The central bank's decision to raise the upper limit of its liquidity target was prompted by its concerns over the recent instability of the currency exchange rate. 日銀当座預金の残高目標（日銀の流動性目標）の上限引上げ決定の理由に、最近の為替相場の不安定な動きへの懸念があった。

upside （名）上昇、上昇傾向、上昇気味、上値（うわね）の余地、上昇余地、有利、有利な点、メリット、良い面　（形）増加［上昇の］、上昇傾向の、上昇気味の、上振れの、有利な　（⇒downside）
　further upside　相場の一層の上昇、一層の上値余地
　stock price's upside　株価上昇、株価上昇の余地、株価の上値余地
　the upside risks to inflation　インフレが一段と進行する恐れ
　upside potential　上値（うわね）余地、株価上昇の可能性、上昇の余地、値上りの余地（上値は「現在の株価より高い株価」のこと）
　upside profit potential　収益増加の可能性
　upside risk　上昇のリスク、上振れリスク
◆The global economy is facing both downside and upside risks. 世界経済は、下振れ、上振れ両サイドのリスクに直面している。

uptick （名）値上がり（plustick）、上向き、回復、増加、上昇、上昇機運、好景気、アップティック　（⇒tick）
　forestall a potential uptick in inflation　インフレ加速の可能性に対して先手を打つ
　uptick in consumer activity　消費の上向き
　uptick in inflation　インフレ加速
　uptick in interest rates　金利の上昇
　uptick in personal consumption　個人消費の伸び、個人消費の回復
　uptick in prepayments　期限前償還の増加、期限前償還率の上昇

uptrend （名）上昇、上昇傾向、上昇トレンド、上昇基調、上げ足、上向き　（⇒downtrend）
　a solid uptrend　着実な上昇傾向
　the current uptrend in the stock market　現在の株高、現在の株価上昇
　the recent uptrend　最近の上昇基調
　the recent uptrend in the stock　最近の株価上昇
◆If the current uptrend in the stock market continues, hopes most likely will surge for expanded capital investment and improvement in personal consumption. 現在の株高が続けば、設備投資拡大や個人消費動向の改善も大いに期待される。◆Japan's efforts to curb the uptrend of the yen against the dollar ended fruitlessly. 日本の円高・ドル安阻止策は、無益に終わった。

upturn （名）上昇、上昇傾向、上昇局面、上向き、向上、好転、増加に転じること、回復、景気回復、景気拡大局面
　cyclical upturn　景気回復
　economic upturn　景気回復、景気拡大局面
　market upturn　市場が上向いていること
　strong upturn　力強い回復
　upturn in business barometers　景気指標の回復
　upturn in IPOs　株式公開の増加
　upturn in share prices　株価上昇
◆Should the government forge ahead with its belt-tightening policy, the budding economic recovery may be reduced to a short-lived upturn. 政府が緊縮路線をひた走れば、景気回復の芽も、薄命の景気回復に終わりかねない。

upturn in share prices　株価の上昇、株価上昇

◆Signs of recovery have become visible, with an upturn in share prices and an increase in consumer spending. 株価上昇と個人消費の伸びを背景に、景気回復の兆しも見えるようになった。

upvaluation （名）平価切上げ, 通貨切上げ, 切上げ, 通貨高, 価値の上昇, 評価切上げ, 高評価
（=revaluation; ⇒devaluation）
asset upvaluation　資産の評価切上げ
currency upvaluation　通貨切上げ, 通貨高
de facto [defacto] upvaluation　事実上の平価切上げ
de jure upvaluation　法律上の平価切上げ
dollar upvaluation　ドル切上げ, ドル高
exchange upvaluation　為替切上げ
upvaluation of exchange rates　為替相場の切上げ, 為替レートの切上げ
upvaluation of the yen　円の切上げ

upvalue （動）（通貨の）平価を切り上げる, 通貨を切り上げる

upward （形）上向きの, 上昇する　（副）上方へ, さかのぼって, 〜以上, 〜以来　（⇒downward）
slow upward trend　穏やかな上昇傾向[上昇基調], 緩（ゆる）やかな増加傾向[増加トレンド]
upward adjustment　上方修正, 増額修正
upward bias　上昇傾向
upward earnings revision　業績の上方修正, 業績予想の上方修正
upward of　〜以上
upward path　上昇基調, 上昇傾向, 増加傾向, 増加基調
upward pressure on wages　賃金上昇圧力, 賃金の上昇傾向
upward trajectory　上昇軌道

◆Standard & Poor's revised upward the outlook on its ratings on six major Japanese insurance companies against the backdrop of their improved financial profiles. スタンダード＆プアーズは、日本の大手保険会社6社の財務力見通し改善を背景に、6社の格付け見通しを上方修正した。

upward revision　上方修正
◆The biggest factor for the upward revision is the faster-than-expected recovery of the U.S. economy. 上方修正の最大の要因は、米景気の予想外の回復だ。

upward trend　上昇傾向, 上昇基調
◆The current account balance is entering an upward trend on a year-on-year basis. 経常収支は、前年同月比ベースで上昇基調に入りつつある。◆The rate of savings among those people in their 30s and 40s is on an upward trend, which is likely to have a depressing effect on domestic demand. 30〜40歳代の貯蓄率が増大傾向にあり、内需を下押ししている可能性がある。

urge （動）強く迫る, 強く要望する, 求める, 強く勧める, 促す, 催促する, 力説する
（⇒World Economic Forum）
◆Europe is urged to act promptly to halt financial crisis. 欧州は、金融危機回避の早急な対策を迫られている。◆European countries are urged to facilitate a safety net for emergencies, including the injection of public funds into deteriorating banks to shore up their capital strength. 欧州は、経営が悪化した銀行[金融機関]に公的資金を注入して資本を増強するなど、非常時に備えた安全網の整備が求められている。◆FSA audits of the banks' accounts urged them to reclassify 149 of their major corporate borrowers more strictly in terms of their creditworthiness in a bid to accelerate the disposal of bad loans. 金融庁による銀行の財務書類監査で、不良債権処理を加速するため、銀行は大口融資先149社の信用力による債務者区分の見直しを強く求められた。◆In resolving Greece's debt woes, German Chancellor Angera Merkel urged substantial aid from private creditors. ギリシャの債務問題を解決するにあたって、アンゲラ・メルケル独首相は、民間債権者に大幅支援を求めた。◆The FSA urged the financial group to revise its earnings estimate. 金融庁は、同金融グループに対して業績予想の修正を強く迫った。◆The FSA's guideline for supervising financial conglomerates is aimed at urging operators of financial conglomerates to reinforce their corporate governance to prevent irregularities. 金融庁の金融コングロマリット（複合体）監督指針の狙いは、不正防止に向けて、金融コングロマリットの経営者に経営監視の強化を促すことにある。◆The G-20 communique urged the eurozone countries to boost the EFSF, the EU bailout fund. G20（主要20か国・地域）の共同声明は、ユーロ圏諸国に欧州の金融支援基金である欧州金融安定基金（EFSF）の拡充を促した。◆The International Monetary Fund is urged to monitor Italy's financial management to provide support to Italy. イタリアを支援するため、国際通貨基金（IMF）はイタリアの財政運営の監視を求められている。◆The OECD has issued a statement urging Japan to expand its pump-priming measures and promote structural reforms. 経済開発協力機構（OECD）は、日本に対して景気刺激策の拡大と構造改革の推進を求める声明を発表した。◆Those in favor of "decoupling" urged the Japanese to reduce their overdependence on the U.S. economy. 「ディカップリング（非連動）論」支持者は、米経済への過度の依存脱却を日本に促した。

urgency （名）緊急, 切迫
a matter of great urgency　緊急事態
a matter of urgency　緊急を要する事柄
a sense of urgency　切迫感, 危機感
have paramount urgency　最も緊急を要する
take on growing urgency　いよいよ緊急を要するようになる

◆The government and the Bank of Japan should implement policy management with a stronger sense of urgency. 政府と日銀は、もっと強い危機感を持って政策運営に当たるべきだ。

urging （名）強く迫ること, 強要, 催促
◆Any additional easing measures would only have a limited impact if they were made at the urging of financial markets. 市場に催促される形で追加緩和を行っても、追加緩和策の効果は限定的に過ぎない。

U.S. [**US**]　アメリカ合衆国, 米国（United Statesの略。正式名はthe United States of America）
changes in U.S. economic performance　米国の景気動向
surplus with the U.S.　対米貿易黒字
（=trade surplus with the U.S.）
the faster-than-expected recovery of the U.S. economy　米景気の予想外の回復
（⇒upward revision）
the outlook for U.S. inflation　米国のインフレ見通し
the recession in the U.S.　米国の景気後退
trade with the U.S.　対米貿易
U.S. Bankruptcy Reform Act　米連邦改正破産法
U.S. bond market　米国債市場, 米国の債券市場
U.S. bond yields　米国債利回り
U.S. Commerce Department　米商務省
U.S. Congress　米議会
U.S. Council of Economic Advisers　米大統領経済諮問委員会
U.S.-destined exports　米国向け輸出, 対米輸出
U.S. economic indicators　米国の景気指標
U.S. International Trade Commission　米国際貿易委員会
U.S. Senate Finance Committee　米上院財政委員会
U.S. slowdown　米国の景気減速
U.S. Treasury Department　米財務省

◆The U.S. tried to prevent an erosion of corporate ethics among financial institutions by refusing to provide public funds to Lehman Brothers. リーマン・ブラザーズへの公的資金の投入を拒否することによって、米政府は金融機関のモラル・ハザード（企業倫理の欠如）を回避しようとした。

U.S. administration　米政府
◆The U.S. administration will spend up to $700 billion to buy up soured mortgage-related securities and other devalued assets held by ailing financial institutions. 米政府は、経営不振の金融機関が保有するモーゲージ関連の不良証券などの不良資産を、最大7,000億ドル投入して買い取る方針だ。

U.S. bank　米国の銀行, 米銀
◆The 171 U.S. banks are on the FDIC's "problem list." 米国の171行が、米連邦預金保険公社（FDIC）の「問題銀行リスト」に挙がっている。◆The Tokyo metropolitan government has decided to deposit more than ¥100 billion in public funds in Citibank, a U.S. bank, to diversify risks. 東京都は、1,000億円を上回る公金を米国の銀行「シティバンク」に預けて、リスクを分散する方針を固めた。

U.S. central bank　米国の中央銀行（FRB）, 米連邦準備制度理事会（FRB）
◆Some dollar funds injected into banks by the U.S. central bank may send U.S. stock prices soaring because banks will invest some of the new dollar funds in domestic assets such as stocks. 米国の中央銀行（FRB）が金融機関［銀行］に供給したドル資金の一部は、銀行がその新たなドル資金の一部を株のような国内資産に投資するため、米国の株価を上げる可能性がある。◆The unanimous decision by the U.S. central bank's policy setting Federal Open Market Committee moved the benchmark federal funds rate to 1.25 percent. 米連邦準備制度理事会の金利政策を決定する米連邦公開市場委員会の全会一致による決定で、短期金利の指標であるフェデラル・ファンド金利が年1.25％に引き上げられた。

U.S. credit rating　米国債の格付け, 米国債の信用格付け　（＝U.S. rating; ⇒U.S. currency）
◆Global turmoil in the financial markets results from the downgrading of the U.S. credit rating. 金融市場の世界的な混乱は、米国債の格下げによるものだ。◆Japan, the United States and European countries will cooperate to avert financial turmoil stemming from the downgrading of the U.S. credit rating. 日米欧が連携して、米国債の格下げによる金融市場の混乱を回避することになった。◆Standard & Poor's cut the U.S. credit rating for the first time. スタンダード・アンド・プアーズ（S&P）が、米国債の格付けを史上初めて引き下げた。

U.S. currency　ドル, 米ドル
◆As the financial markets' confidence in the U.S. currency has been shaken, stock prices may fall worldwide and the dollar-selling trend may accelerate. 米ドルへの金融市場の信認が揺らいでいるため、株価が世界的に下落し、ドル売りの流れが加速する可能性もある。◆The financial markets' confidence in the U.S. currency has been shaken further by the S&P's cutting of the U.S. credit rating. スタンダード・アンド・プアーズ（S&P）が米国債の格付けを引き下げたことで、金融市場の米ドルへの信認が一段と揺らいでいる。

U.S. debt　米国債
◆Fitch Ratings Ltd. will keep its rating on long-term U.S. debt at the highest grade, AAA. 英米系の格付け会社フィッチ・レーティングスは、米国の長期国債格付けを、最上級のAAA（トリプルA）に据え置く方針だ。

U.S. dollar　米ドル, 米ドル相場
◆An individual investor began depositing money in U.S. dollars using a major bank's Web account. 個人投資家が、大手銀行のウェブ口座［インターネット口座］を利用して米ドルの外貨預金を始めた。◆Currency traders are now turning to the renminbi (yuan) from the U.S. dollar. 為替トレーダーは今や、米ドルから中国の人民元に目を向けている。◆Falling stock prices and the depreciation of the U.S. dollar increased uncertainty over the global economy. 米国の株安やドル安で、世界経済の不透明感が強まっている。◆In the case of foreign currency deposits by the U.S. dollar, many online banks charge about ¥0.25 in commission per dollar at the time of deposits and withdrawals. 米ドルによる外貨預金の場合、ネット銀行の多くは、預け入れ時と解約時に1ドルに付き25銭程度の手数料を取る。◆In the case of foreign currency deposits, depositors can invest in foreign currencies such as British pound, Swiss franc and Australian dollar as well as the U.S. dollar and euro. 外貨預金の場合、預金者は、米ドルやユーロのほかに英ポンド、スイス・フランや豪ドルなどにも投資することができる。◆In the Plaza Accord, G-5 nations agreed to rectify the surge in the value of the U.S. dollar. プラザ合意で、日・米・英・仏・西独の先進5か国（G5）がドル高是正で合意した。◆It is feared the colossal amount of the U.S. twin deficits could trigger a freefall of the U.S. dollar. アメリカの巨額の双子の赤字は、ドルの暴落を引き起こす懸念がある。◆On Aug. 31, 2011, the yen rose to the ¥76.50 level against the U.S. dollar in the Tokyo foreign exchange market, close to the postwar record of ¥75.95 registered on Aug. 19. 2011年8月31日の東京外国為替市場の円相場は、1ドル＝76円50銭台まで上昇し、8月19日に付けた戦後最高値の75円95銭に近づいた。◆The Japanese currency's value vis-a-vis the U.S. dollar entered the ¥98 range in foreign exchange markets around the world. 円の対米ドル相場は、内外の外国為替市場で1ドル＝98円台をつけた。◆The U.S. dollar as the world's only reserve currency may become merely one of three major currencies, along with the euro and the renminbi. 世界で唯一の準備通貨としての米ドルは、ユーロ、人民元とともに、単なる3大通貨の一つになる可能性がある。◆The U.S. dollar dropped to a fresh 15-year low in the lower ¥82 level. 米ドル相場は82円台前半まで下落し、15年ぶりに最安値を更新した。◆The U.S. dollar has dropped sharply in value not only against the yen, but also against the euro, the South Korean won, the Thai baht and other currencies. 米ドルは、円に対してだけでなく、ユーロや韓国ウォン、タイ・バーツなどに対しても、急落している。◆The U.S. dollar has enjoyed the massive privileges as the key international currency. 米ドルは、国際通貨としての特権を享受してきた。◆The U.S. dollar may lose its current status as the world's only reserve currency. 米ドルは、世界唯一の準備通貨としての現在の地位を失う可能性がある。◆The U.S. dollar sank to its lowest level since May 1995 in the lower ¥83 zone. 米ドル相場は、1ドル＝83円台前半で1995年5月以来最低の水準まで下落した。◆The U.S. dollar temporarily dropped to the ¥84 level in Tokyo. 東京市場では、米ドルは一時、1ドル＝84円台まで下落した。◆The U.S. dollar traded at the lower ¥85 range in Tokyo over concern about the U.S. economic outlook. 東京金融市場［東京外国為替市場］では、米景気の先行きを懸念して、ドル相場は1ドル＝85円台前半で取引された。◆The U.S. dollar was traded at around ¥76 on the currency market. 為替市場では、1ドル＝76円をはさんだ取引が続いた。◆The yen has been hovering near its record high of ¥76.25 against the U.S. dollar in Tokyo. 東京外国為替市場の円相場は、戦後最高値の1ドル＝76円25銭に迫る水準で推移している。◆The yen may appreciate further to ¥70 against the U.S. dollar. 円高は、さらに1ドル＝75円まで進む可能性がある。◆The yen stayed in the lower ¥77 range against the U.S. dollar in Tokyo. 東京外国為替市場の円相場は、1ドル＝77円台前半で推移した。◆The yen's exchange rate has appreciated to ¥76 against the dollar, so it is the best time to buy U.S. dollars. 円の為替レートが1ドル＝76円に上昇したので、今が米ドルの買い時だ。

U.S. dollar liquidity-providing operation　米ドル資金供給オペ, ドル資金供給オペ
◆In cooperation with the U.S. FRB, the Bank of England, the Bank of Japan and the Swiss National Bank, the Eu-

ropean Central Bank decided to conduct three U.S. dollar liquidity-providing operations between October and December. 米連邦準備制度理事会(FRB)、英イングランド銀行、日銀、スイス国立銀行と協調して、欧州中央銀行(ECB)が10〜12月に3回、米ドル資金供給オペを実施することを決めた。

U.S. dollar terms　米ドル・ベース
◆Sales of the overseas subsidiaries of Japanese companies grew 17.3 percent in U.S. dollar terms in the January-March quarter from a year earlier. 1-3月期の日本企業の海外子会社の売上高が、米ドル・ベースで前年同期比17.3%伸びた。

U.S. economic indicators　米国の経済指標
◆Recent U.S. economic indicators show the fragility of the world largest economy. 最近の米国の経済指標は、米経済の弱さを示している。

U.S. economic outlook　米経済の先行き, 米景気の先行き
◆Concerns over the U.S. economic outlook tend to induce yen-buying as a safe haven. 米経済の先行きに対する懸念から、安全な投資手段として円が買われる傾向にある。◆Due to increasing uncertainty over the U.S. economic outlook and the yen's rise, the Bank of Japan warned of the downside risks to the nation's economy. 米経済の先行きをめぐる不確実性の高まりと円高で、日銀は日本経済の下振れリスクに警戒感を示した。◆The U.S. dollar traded at the lower ¥85 range in Tokyo over concern about the U.S. economic outlook. 東京金融市場[東京外国為替市場]では、米景気の先行きを懸念して、ドル相場は1ドル＝85円台前半で取引された。

U.S. economy　米国経済, 米景気
◆Before the bubble collapsed, many pundits had predicted that the likely downturn of the U.S. economy would have only a limited impact on the rest of the world. バブル経済の崩壊前には、「米経済はいずれ行き詰まるだろうが、他国への影響は限定的である」と専門家の多くは予測していた。◆Behind these cautious views among large manufacturers are uncertainty over the debt crisis in the eurozone and the slowdown in the U.S. economy. 大企業製造業のこうした警戒感[慎重な見方]の背景には、ユーロ圏の債務危機不安や米景気の減速がある。◆Housing investment, a driving force for the U.S. economy until recently, has shown signs of a slowdown. 最近まで米景気を牽引してきた住宅投資に、減速感が見られる。◆The benefits of the U.S. financial bailout package will take time to show up in the U.S. economy. 米国の金融救済策の効果が米国内経済に現れるのに、時間がかかるだろう。◆The U.S. economy has gotten back on the recovery track since the latter half of last year. 米国の景気は、昨年後半からまた回復軌道に乗り始めた。◆The U.S. economy is in danger of slipping into a double-dip recession. 米経済は、景気の二番底に陥る可能性[恐れ]がある。◆The U.S. economy slipped into recession in December 2007. 米経済は、2007年12月から景気後退局面(リセッション)に入った。◆Those in favor of "decoupling" urged the Japanese to reduce their overdependence on the U.S. economy. 「ディカップリング(非連動)論」支持者は、米経済への過度の依存脱却を日本に促した。

U.S. federal income taxes　米連邦所得税
◆The consolidated provision for taxes also includes an amount sufficient to pay additional U.S. federal income taxes on repatriation of income earned abroad. 連結納税引当金には、海外で得た利益の本国送金に課される米連邦所得税の追加支払いに十分対応できる金額も含まれている。

U.S. Federal Reserve　米連邦準備制度理事会(FRB)
(=U.S. Federal Reserve Board)
◆The U.S. Federal Reserve raised the official discount rate and the target rate of federal funds by 0.25 percentage points in a bid to quell inflation and keep the economy from overheating. 米連邦準備制度理事会(FRB)は、インフレを防ぎ景気の過熱を警戒して、公定歩合とフェデラル・ファンド(FF)の誘導目標金利をそれぞれ0.25パーセント引き上げた。

U.S. Federal Reserve Board　米連邦準備制度理事会(FRB)
◆In the subprime crisis, the U.S. Federal Reserve Board had to take the extraordinary step of providing an emergency loan not to a commercial bank but to an investment bank. サブプライム問題で、米国の中央銀行の連邦準備制度理事会(FRB)は、緊急融資を銀行[商業銀行]ではなく証券会社[投資銀行]に対して行う異例の措置を取らざるを得なかった。◆The U.S. Federal Reserve Board pledged to keep interest rates near zero until mid-2013. 米連邦準備制度理事会(FRB)は、2013年半ばまでゼロ金利政策を維持することを誓った。◆The U.S. Federal Reserve Board said in its Beige Book release that the U.S. economy deteriorated further in almost all corners of the country. 米連邦準備制度理事会(FRB)は、地区連銀景況報告(ベージ・ブック)を発表し、米国の経済情勢はほぼ全米で一段と悪化していると指摘した。◆The U.S. Federal Reserve Board will change the pace of raising rates, depending on economic trends. 米連邦準備制度理事会(FRB)は、経済情勢次第で利上げのペースを変える方針だ。

U.S. financial community　米金融業界
◆The news of a rise in the subprime defaults rocked the U.S. financial community. サブプライムの不払い増加のニュースに、米金融業界は動揺した。

U.S. financial institutions　米金融機関
◆U.S. and European financial institutions are scaling back their business operations before capital adequacy requirements are strengthened in 2013. 欧米金融機関は、2013年から自己資本規制が強化されるのを前に、業務を縮小している。

U.S. financial market　米金融市場
◆Goldman Sachs' capital increase is partly aimed at regaining the confidence in the U.S. financial market, which has been facing a raft of financial problems. ゴールドマン・サックスの増資は、多くの金融問題を抱える米金融市場の信認回復も狙いの一つだ。

U.S. fiscal reconstruction　米国の財政再建
◆The U.S. credit rating agency Standard & Poor's made a grim assessment of the outlook of U.S. fiscal reconstruction. 米国の信用格付け機関のスタンダード・アンド・プアーズ(S&P)は、米国の財政再建の見通しを厳しく評価した。

U.S. FRB　米連邦準備制度理事会(FRB)
(=the U.S. Federal Reserve Board)
◆Economic activity strengthened in most of U.S. regions with the exception of St. Louis where plans to close several plants were announced, the U.S. FRB said. 米連邦準備制度理事会(FRB)は、(全12地区連銀のうち)一部の工場閉鎖計画を発表したセントルイスを除く11地区で景気が好転している、と述べた。

U.S. government　米政府
◆Among 17 big banks targeted by the lawsuits filed by the U.S. government were Bank of America, Citigroup, Credit Suisse and Nomura Holding America Inc. 米政府が提訴した訴訟の対象の大手金融機関17社の中には、バンカメのほかにシティグループやクレディ・スイス、野村ホールディング・アメリカなどが含まれている。◆In the lawsuits against big banks over the sales of risky investments, the U.S. government wants to be compensated for lost principal and interest payments. 高リスク証券の販売をめぐる大手金融機関に対する訴訟で、米政府は、元本と利払い分の損失補償を求めている。◆The U.S. government could avoid the worst-case scenario of default on payments to investors in Treasury bonds. 米政府は、国債の償還資金がなくなる債務不履行という最悪の事態を避けることができた。◆The U.S. government filed lawsuits against 17 financial firms for selling Fannie and Freddie mortgage-backed securities that turned toxic when the housing market collapsed. 米政府は、住宅市場崩壊時に不良資産化した住宅ローン担保証券(MBS)をファニー・メイ(米連邦住宅抵当公庫)とフレディ・マック(米連邦住宅貸付け抵当公社)に販売し

たとして、大手金融機関17社（バンク・オブ・アメリカやシティグループ、JPモルガン・チェース、ゴールドマン・サックス・グループなど）を提訴した。◆The U.S. government froze the assets of four individuals and eight entities that were involved in illicit activities such as money laundering, currency counterfeiting and narcotics trafficking. 米政府は、資金洗浄（マネー・ロンダリング）や通貨偽造、麻薬取引などの違法行為に関与している4個人、8団体の資産を凍結した。

U.S. government's colossal deficits　米政府の膨大な財政赤字
◆It is said that most of the U.S. government's colossal deficits had been caused by the faulty tax-and-spend policies of Republican governments. 米政府の膨大な財政赤字の大半は、歴代共和党政権の誤った税制・支出政策によるものだと言われる。

U.S. government's credit rating　米国債の格付け
◆The United States' credit has come into question by the possible downgrade of the U.S. government's credit rating. 米国債の格付けが引き下げられる可能性があることから、米国の信用が疑われている。

U.S. government's default　米政府のデフォルト（債務不履行）
◆The U.S. government's default would throw the financial markets around the world into major turmoil. 米政府がデフォルト（債務不履行）に陥ったら、世界の金融市場は大混乱するだろう。

U.S. housing mortgage meltdown　米国の住宅ローン市場の崩壊
◆A U.S. housing mortgage meltdown shook the United States, Europe and other countries and slammed the brakes on global growth. 米国の住宅ローン市場の崩壊は、米欧その他の諸国を揺さぶり、世界経済の成長に急ブレーキをかけた。◆The financial crisis stemmed from a U.S. housing mortgage meltdown. 今回の金融危機は、米国の住宅ローン市場の崩壊から始まった。

U.S. Labor Department　米労働省
◆The U.S. Labor Department's Consumer Price Index is the most widely used gauge of inflation. 米労働省が発表する消費者物価指数は、最も広く使用されているインフレ（物価上昇率）の基準だ。

U.S. long-term credit rating　米国の長期国債格付け、米国の長期格付け
◆Political gridlock in Washington is part of the reason behind the S&P cut in the U.S. long-term credit rating. 米国の政府・議会の政治的行き詰まりが、スタンダード・アンド・プアーズ（S&P）の米長期国債下げの一因である。◆The S&P cut in the U.S. long-term credit rating by one notch to AA-plus from AAA resulted from concerns about the nation's budget deficits and climbing debt burden. スタンダード・アンド・プアーズ（S&P）が米国の長期国債格付けを最上級のAAA（トリプルA）からAA（ダブルA）に1段階引き下げた理由は、米国の財政赤字と債務負担の増大に対する懸念だ。

U.S. markets　米国市場, 米市場
◆A series of accounting scandals and delays in the recovery of corporate performance are accelerating falls in stock prices on the U.S. markets, along with the weakening of the dollar. 一連の［相次ぐ］企業会計の不祥事と企業業績回復の遅れで、米国の株安とドル安が加速している。◆Following sharp falls on European and U.S. markets, the Nikkei Stock Average fell briefly to its lowest level this year. 欧米市場の株価急落を受けて、日経平均株価は一時、今年の最安値を下回った。

U.S. Mint　米造幣局
◆The U.S. Mint's sales of American Eagle gold coins have totaled 91,000 ounce so far in August. 米造幣局のアメリカン・イーグル［米イーグル］金貨の販売総量は、9月1日以降現時点で9万1,000オンスに達している。

U.S. private banks　米国の民間銀行
◆The U.S. private banks' funds on hand grew about three times from March 2008 prior to the Lehman's collapse. 米国の民間銀行の手持ち資金は、リーマン・ブラザーズの経営破たん前の2008年3月から約3倍増えた。◆The U.S. private banks' outstanding Treasury bond holdings grew by about 50 percent from March 2008, prior to the Lehman shock. 米国の民間銀行の米国債保有残高は、リーマン・ショック前の2008年3月から約5割増えた。

U.S. rating　米国債の格付け
◆Standard & Poor's dropped the U.S. rating by one notch for the first time. スタンダード・アンド・プアーズ（S&P）が、米国債の格付けを史上初めて1段階引き下げた。

U.S. slowdown　米国の景気減速, 米経済の減速
◆The downside risks to Japan's economy will increase because concerns over a U.S. slowdown are growing. 米国の景気減速に対する懸念が高まっているため、日本の景気［日本経済］が今後悪化するリスクは増大している。◆The so-called decoupling theory holds that the effects of a U.S. slowdown can be offset by growth in emerging nations. いわゆるディカップリング論では、米経済の減速は新興国の成長が補う、と考えられている。

U.S. stock prices　米国の株価　（=U.S. stocks）
◆Some dollar funds injected into banks by the U.S. central bank may send U.S. stock prices soaring because banks will invest some of the new dollar funds in domestic assets such as stocks. 米国の中央銀行（FRB）が金融機関［銀行］に供給したドル資金の一部は、銀行がその新たなドル資金の一部を株のような国内資産に投資するため、米国の株価を上げる可能性がある。◆The continued fall in U.S. stock prices and the dollar's depreciation has battered the Japanese economy. 米国の株安とドル安の進行が、日本経済を直撃している［激しく揺さぶっている］。◆The instability of U.S. stock prices results from problems related to massive number of unrecoverable subprime mortgage loans extended to low-income earners in the United States. 米国の株価不安定は、米国の低所得者向け住宅ローン「サブプライム・ローン」の焦げ付き急増関連問題に起因している。

U.S. stocks　米国の株価　（=U.S. stock prices）
◆The 225-issue Nikkei Stock Average dived below the key threshold of 10,000 as investors were disappointed with the continuing delay in the disposal of banks' bad loans and an overnight plunge in U.S. stocks. 日経平均株価（225種）は、投資家が銀行等の不良債権処理が引き続き遅れることや前日の米株価の大幅下落に失望して、1万円の大台を割り込んだ。

U.S.-style board structure　米国型の取締役会制度
◆Under the revised Commercial Code, only large companies with capital of more than ￥500 million would be qualified to adopt the U.S.-style board structure. 今回の商法改正では、資本金5億円以上の大企業だけが米国型の取締役会制度を導入することができる。

U.S. subprime mortgage crisis　米国の低所得者向け融資問題, 米国のサブプライムローン問題
◆UBS will post a pretax loss of up to $690 million in the third quarter mainly because of losses linked to the U.S. subprime mortgage crisis. スイス最大手銀行UBSの第3四半期税引き前損失は、主に米国で起きた低所得者向け融資「サブプライム・ローン」問題の関連損失で、最高で6億9,000万ドルに達する見通しだ。

U.S. Treasuries　米国債　（⇒Treasuries, Treasury bill, Treasury bond, Treasury note）
解説 米国債について：米国の財務省（U.S. Treasury）が発行する市場性証券（marketable securities）で、償還期限が1年以内の財務省短期証券（Treasury bill, T-bill）と1年超10年以内の財務省中期証券（Treasury note, T-note）、10年超の財務省長期証券（Treasury bond, T-bond）の3種類がある。このうち短期証券は割引発行、中期証券と長期証券は利付き発行となっている。発行方法としては競争入札

と非競争入札があり、入札者は公示で募集する。

U.S. Treasury bill　米財務省短期証券　（=T-bill）
◆Floating rate payments are based on rates tied to prime, LIBOR or U.S. Treasury bills. 変動金利の支払い利率は、プライム・レート、ロンドン銀行間取引金利または米財務省短期証券の利回りに基づいて決定されます。

U.S. Treasury bonds　10年超の財務省長期証券, 米国債　（=T-bonds, Treasury bonds）
◆The spreads of yields on high-risk junk bonds over the benchmark five-year U.S. Treasury bonds had been around 200 basis points, or 2 percentage points. リスクの高いジャンク債と指標となる5年物財務省証券との金利差（スプレッド）は、2％（200ベーシス・ポイント）程度で推移していた。◆U.S. Treasury bonds were downgraded by Standard & Poor's because the government failed to take drastic countermeasures against its fiscal deterioration. 米政府が財政悪化に大胆な対策を取れなかったため、米国債はスタンダード・アンド・プアーズ（S&P）に格下げされた。

U.S. Treasury Secretary　米財務長官
◆U.S. Treasury Secretary Henry Paulson unveiled the 218-page financial overhaul plan. ヘンリー・ポールソン米財務長官は、218ページの金融改革案［金融監督の改革案］を発表した。

U.S. Treasury securities　米財務省証券, 米国債
◆China is trying to flex its muscle with the United States on the strength of its status as the largest holder of U.S. Treasury securities. 中国は、米財務省証券［米国債］の最大保有国としての地位を背景に、米国への影響力を行使しようとしている。

U.S. twin deficits　米国の双子の赤字
◆It is feared the colossal amount of the U.S. twin deficits could trigger a freefall of the U.S. dollar. アメリカの巨額の双子の赤字は、ドルの暴落を引き起こす懸念がある。

usance　（名）手形期間, 手形期限, 支払い期限, ユーザンス
　bank usance　バンク・ユーザンス
　dollar usance　対米期限付き為替手形
　export usance bill　輸出ユーザンス手形, 期限付き輸出手形
　freight usance　運賃ユーザンス
　import usance bill　輸入ユーザンス手形, 期限付き輸入手形
　shipper's usance　輸出期限付き手形, シッパーズ・ユーザンス
　usance bill　期限付き為替手形, ユーザンス手形　（=time bill）
　usance bill buying rate　期限付き手形買い相場
　usance bill rate　期限付き手形相場
　usance credit［L/C, letter of credit］　期限付き信用状, ユーザンスL/C, ユーザンス・クレジット
　usance extend by the bank's own funds　自行ユーザンス, 為替ユーザンス
　usance facility　ユーザンス金融
　usance rate　期限付き為替相場, ユーザンス・レート　（=time rate）

use　（動）使用する, 使う, 用いる, ～に充てる, 採用する, 利用する, 活用する, 運用する, 投入する
　be used for repaying long-term indebtedness　長期債務の返済に充てる
　financial resources used　資金の運用
　net cash used for acquisition　企業買収に使用した現金純額
　net cash used in investing activities　投資活動に投入した正味現金
　use a growth investing style　成長株投資［グロース・スタイル］の運用を行う
　use reserves　準備金を取り崩す
　use the straight line method for financial reporting　財務会計上、定額法を用いる［採用する］
◆A special account is used to finance public investment and loans to government-affiliated financial institutions. 特別会計は、政府系金融機関に財政投融資の資金を供給するのに用いられる。◆An individual investor began depositing money in U.S. dollars using a major bank's Web account. 個人投資家が、大手銀行のウェブ口座［インターネット口座］を利用して米ドルの外貨預金を始めた。◆Another tactic many loan sharks use is to circulate slanderous leaflets to the workplace or the school that the borrower's children attend. 多くのヤミ金融業が使うほかの手は、借り手の勤務先や子どもが通う学校への中傷文書のばらまきだ。◆Customers will have to open a new account to use the Internet banking services. このインターネット・バンキングのサービスを利用するにあたって、顧客は新規に口座を開設しなければならない。◆Fabricated credit cards have been illegally used at electrical appliances discount stores and cash voucher shops in Japan after the security breach was revealed in the United States. 米国で不正侵入が明らかになった後、偽造されたクレジット・カードが日本の家電量販店や金券ショップなどで不正に使用されている。◆If the current downward trend of stock prices continues, banks' financial resources that could be used to dispose of bad loans will decrease drastically. 株価の下落基調がこのまま続くと、金融機関の不良債権処理の原資は激減する。◆If we use the cashing services, it results in high interest payments. 現金化サービスを利用すると、結果的に高金利［支払い利息が高くつくこと］になる。◆Illegal access of Internet banking accounts using account holders' user IDs and passwords was confirmed at 51 financial institutions. 口座名義人のユーザーID［ユーザー名］やパスワードを使ったネット・バンキングの口座への不正アクセスが、51金融機関で確認された。◆In a bid to clamp down on bank-transfer scams, the police asked financial institutions not to allow people whose faces are obscured with sunglasses or masks to use ATMs. 振り込め詐欺を取り締まるため、警察は、サングラスやマスクで顔を隠したままATM（現金自動預け払い機）を使用できないよう金融機関に要請した。◆In illegal transfers via online banking services, viruses such as Spy Eye and Zbot have been used. ネット・バンキングでの不正送金では、スパイアイやゼットボットなどと呼ばれるウイルスが使われている。◆In most cases in which the credit guarantee system is used, financial institutions introduce borrowers to credit guarantee corporations. 信用保証制度を利用する場合の多くは、金融機関が借り手を信用保証協会に紹介する。◆In 2009, the Business Accounting Council decided to require all of the nation's listed companies to use the IFRSs for their consolidated financial statements from 2015. 2009年に企業会計審議会は、2015年にも、国内全上場企業の連結財務諸表［連結財務書類］について、国際財務情報基準（IFRSs）の採用を上場企業に義務付ける方針を打ち出した。◆Margin trading was used in a corporate takeover by exploiting legal shortcomings. 法の不備を利用して、企業買収に信用取引が使われた。◆Most companies use the daily average for a month of the share prices in gauging the value of latent gains or losses in their stockholdings. 大半の企業は、保有株式の含み損益を算出する際に株価の月中平均を使っている。◆The bank does not issue conventional bankbooks for cardholders, but offers electronic bank books that are used via the Internet and accessed through personal computer and cell phones. 同行は、カード会員に従来の銀行通帳は発行せず、パソコンや携帯電話でアクセスしてインターネット上で使用する電子通帳［ウェブ通帳］を提供している。◆The revitalization plan will be carried out chiefly using ¥400 billion in financial assistance to be extended by the firm's creditor banks. 再生計画は、主に同社の取引銀行が

行う金融支援総額4,000億円を使って実施される。◆The trader used a standard option to hedge the price risk of a stock. このトレーダーは、株式の価格リスクをヘッジするために標準的なオプションを使った。◆This $300 million of 9% Series 7 Notes was used to repay the same amount of 10% Series 3 Notes, which matured in May 2011. この利率9%のシリーズ7ノート3億ドルは、2011年5月に満期が到来した利率10%のシリーズ3ノート3億ドルの償還に充当しました。◆To make up for losses and for other purposes, seven life insurers used a total of ¥529.2 billion in reserves, which are set aside in preparation for interest rate fluctuations and natural disasters. 損失の穴埋めなどのため、金利変動や自然災害に備えて積み立てている準備金を、生保7社が5,292億円も取り崩した。◆We are considering using the company's shares as security to secure the necessary funds. 当社は、同社株を担保にして必要資金を確保することを検討している。

use (名)使用, 使用量, 使用法, 利用, 活用, 運用, 採用, 使途, 用途, 効用, 有用, 収益権
 cash use 資金の使途
 land use planning 土地利用計画
 limited use 制限的使用, 使用の制限
 sources and uses of funds 資金収支表
 sources of funds and uses of funds 資金の源泉と資金の運用
 use of funds 資金の運用, 資金の使用, 資金の使途
 use of proceeds 資金の使途
 use of savings 貯蓄の取り崩し
 uses of financial resources 資金源泉の運用
 ◆European and U.S. companies established R&D bases in China and put their energy into developing products for use by Chinese consumers. 欧米の企業は、中国に研究開発拠点を設けて、中国仕様の製品開発に力を注いだ。

useful (形)役に立つ, 有用な, 有益な, 効果的な, 満足できる
 composite useful life 総合耐用年数
 useful economic life 経済的耐用年数
 useful life 耐用年数
 ◆Two companies' accumulated know-how in online trading will be useful in the commodity futures market. 商品先物市場では、両社の蓄積しているネット取引のノウハウが役に立つだろう。

user (名)使用者, 利用者, 消費者, 顧客, 加入者, 会員, 投資家, ユーザー
 active service user 使用頻度の高いユーザー
 actual user 実需筋
 end user 最終使用者, 一般使用者, 最終利用者, 最終投資家, エンド・ユーザー
 unauthorized user 不正使用者
 user account ユーザー識別符号, ユーザー・アカウント (ユーザーのパスワードやユーザーID, 所属するグループなどの情報)
 user authentication ユーザー認証
 user charge 利用者料金
 user cost 使用者費用 (=user charge)
 user fee 受益者負担金
 user-hostile 使いにくい, 使いづらい, ユーザーに親しみにくい, 不便
 user identification ユーザー登録名, ユーザー識別コード, ユーザーID
 user [user's] registration ユーザー登録
 user-unfriendly 使いにくい, ユーザーに親しみにくい (=user-hostile)
 ◆Online banking users can prevent illegal transfers of their deposits by frequently changing their passwords. オンライン・バンキング利用者は、パスワードをこまめに変更して、預金の不正送金を防ぐことができる。◆This bank requires users to provide special authentication numbers to transfer money. この銀行は、振込みの際に専用の認証番号の入力を利用者に義務付けている。◆Users of online banking services had better take security measures by using antivirus software. ネット・バンキングの利用者は、ウイルス対策ソフトを使ってセキュリティ対策を取ったほうが良い。

user-friendly (形)ユーザーに使いやすい, 使いやすい, 使い勝手がよい, 操作が簡単な, ユーザーに親しみやすい, ユーザーに分かりやすい, 利用者に親切
 ◆The U.S. financial bailout package is not user-friendly. 米国の金融救済策は、使い勝手が悪い。

user ID ユーザーID, ユーザー名 (=log-in ID, username)
 ◆Illegal access of Internet banking accounts using account holders' user IDs and passwords was confirmed at 51 financial institutions. 口座名義人のユーザーID[ユーザー名]やパスワードを使ったネット・バンキングの口座への不正アクセスが、51金融機関で確認された。

usurer (名)高利貸し, 金貸し
 usurer's capital 高利貸し資本

usurious (形)高利の, 高金利の, 高利を取る, 高利になる, 高利貸しの, 法外な
 charge usurious rates 法外な料金を要求する
 usurious income 高利所得
 usurious interest 高金利, 高利
 usurious loan 高利貸付け, 高金利の貸付け
 usurious rate of interest 高利率, 高利子率

usury (名)高利貸し, 法外な高利, 暴利, 高金利, 利息, 高利貸し業, 悪徳金融
 usury ceiling 利息制限
 usury statute 高金利取締法
 with usury 高利で

usury law 利息制限法, 高利制限法, 高利貸し禁止法, 出資法
 Amended Usury Law 改正出資法
 the maximum interest rate permitted by the usury law 利息制限法で認められる思考利率
 ◆Interest shall accrue on any delinquent amounts owed by Distributor for Products at the lesser of 18% per annum, or the maximum rate permitted by applicable usury law. 利息は、「販売店」が負っている[本製品]の延滞金について発生し、年18%の利率と適用される利息制限法で認められる最高利率のうちいずれか低いほうの利率によるものとする。

utility (名)効用, 有用, 実用, 実用性, 実用品, 公益事業, 公共事業, 公共事業体, 公共事業株 (⇒public utility)
 marginal utility 限界効用
 utilities company 公益企業
 utility model 実用新案, 実用新案権, 新案特許権
 ◆If the government financial support is not offered to TEPCO, the utility's creditors and shareholders will have to share the burden. 東電に政府の金融支援がない場合は、同社の債権者と株主が共同負担せざるを得ないだろう。◆Making the creditor banks waive loans to TEPCO will cause the utility to fall into capital deficiency, with liabilities exceeding assets. 取引銀行に東電への債権を放棄させると、東電は資本不足に陥り、債務超過になってしまう。

utility charges 公共料金 (=utilities, utility rates)
 ◆Under the new system of postal services, the flat ¥30 fee for paying utility charges at post offices or transferring them through ATMs is ¥240 for bills more than ¥30,000. 郵便事業の新制度では、公共料金を郵便局の窓口やATM(現金自動預け払い機)で振り込む場合の手数料は一律30円だったが、3

万円以上の場合は240円になった。
utilize (動)利用する, 活用する
◆Banks could forcibly sell insurance policies to clients by utilizing their strong position as creditors. 銀行は、債権者としての強い立場を利用して、顧客に保険を強制的に販売する可能性もある。◆Leading banks may utilize the banking agent system to increase their presence in regional areas. 大手行は、地方で拠点を増やすため銀行代理店制度を活用する可能性がある。◆The firm plans to offer not only retail lending, but also corporate lending by utilizing the customer screening know-how of its partner bank. 同社は、共同出資する銀行が持つ顧客審査のノウハウを活用して、個人向け融資のほかに法人向け融資業務も提供する計画だ。◆To procure funds to finance reconstruction from the Great East Japan Earthquake, the government will utilize surplus funds in a special account used to finance public investment and loans to government-affiliated financial institutions. 東日本大震災の復興費用に充てる資金を調達するため、政府は、政府系金融機関に資金を貸し出すのに用いられる財政投融資特別会計の剰余金を活用する方針だ。

V

V-shaped recovery V字形の回復, V字回復
◆Most emerging East Asian economies are assured of a sharp V-shaped recovery this year. 今年は、東アジア新興国の大半が急激にV字回復するのは確実だ。
valuation (名)評価, 査定, 見積り, 評価価格, 査定価格
　actuarial valuation　保険数理上の評価
　hidden valuation　含み資産
　inventory valuation　棚卸し資産評価
　investment valuation allowance　長期投資評価引当金
　market valuation　時価総額　(=aggregate market value, total market value: 株価による企業の価値を示す「時価総額」は、株価に発行済み株式数を掛けて算出する)
　projected benefit valuation method　予測給付評価方式
　stock valuation　株価評価
　taxable valuation　課税評価額
　valuation allowance　評価引当金, 評価性引当金
　valuation basis　評価基準
　valuation profit or loss　評価損益
　valuation reserve　評価性引当金
　valuation surplus　評価剰余金
◆At current prices, the firm's market valuation is more than $1.5 billion. 現在の株価でみた同社の時価総額は、15億ドルを超えている。
valuation losses 評価損, 保有株の評価損を損失として計上する減損処理額
　(=appraisal [evaluation] losses)
◆The rule of asset impairment accounting requires companies to post valuation losses on fixed assets whose market value has fallen sharply from their book value. 減損会計基準は、固定資産の時価が簿価から大幅に下落した場合の固定資産の評価損の計上を、企業に義務付けている。◆The top 10 life insurers in the nation reported a total of ￥1.46 trillion in valuation losses on their securities holdings for the current business year. 今期決算で、国内生保の上位(主要)10社の保有有価証券[保有株式]の減損処理額は、1兆4,600億円に達した。
value (動)評価する, 評価換えする, 値洗いする, 重視する
　be present valued　現在価値に直す
　be valued at market　時価で評価する
　be valued at $50 million　5,000万ドルと評価される
　fairly value　適正に評価する
　value the book at historical cost　原価で計上する
　value the book at market　時価で計上する
◆The government holds a 53.4 percent stake in Tokyo Metro Co., which was valued at ￥174.9 billion at book value as of the end of March 2010. 国は東京地下鉄(東京メトロ)の株式の53.4%を保有しており、その簿価での評価額は2010年3月末時点で1,749億円になる。
value (名)価値, 価格, 評価, 評価額, 金額, 相場, バリュー　(⇒asset value, book value, exchange market, fixed asset, income, Rubicon)
　acquisition value　取得価額
　actual value　実価
　actuarial asset value　保険数理による資産価値
　actuarial present value　保険数理上の現在価値, 年金数理上の現在価値
　actuarial value　保険数理的価値
　add value　付加価値を高める
　agreed insured value　協定保険価額
　agreement value　契約価値, 契約価額
　appraisal value　評価額, 評価価値, 鑑定評価額, 査定価値　(=appraised value, assessed value)
　be below book value　取得価格を下回る
　capital value　資本価値
　collateral value　担保価値
　dollar value LIFO　ドル価値後入れ先出し法, ドル価値法
　face value　券面額, 額面, 額面価額, 額面価格　(=face amount)
　fair or marked-to-market value　公正価格(値洗い後の価格)
　increase shareholders value　株主の価値を高める
　increase value added　付加価値を高める
　insurance value　保険価額
　lose values　値下がりする
　manage the assets under the value discipline　バリュー・スタイルで資産を運用する
　mark-to-market value　値洗い価額
　offer a lot of investment value　投資価値が十分にある
　par value capital　額面株式
　present value of annuity　年金現価
　price-to-book value　株価純資産倍率
　principal value　元本
　realize par value　額面金額を回収する
　redemption value　償還価額
　shareholder value　株主の価値, 株主の利益
　the highest value　最高値
　the rapid surge in the yen's value　急激な円高
　the renminbi's international currency value　中国人民元の国際的な通貨価値　(⇒currency value)
　the sharp rise in the yen's value　急激な円高
　the surge in the yen's value against the dollar　円高・ドル安
　the total value of M&A deals　M&A取引金額の総額, M&Aの総額
　the value of government bonds　国債価格
　the value of the U.S. dollar　米ドル相場
　the value-weighted index of stock prices　時価総額加重株価指数
　the yen's value against the dollar　円の対米ドル相場
　time value　時間価値
　value at risk　想定最大損失額, バリュー・アト・リスク, VAR[VaR]
　value date　(為替取引の)決済日
　value discipline　割安株中心の投資方法, バリュー・スタイル

value investing 割安株投資（割安株とは、ファンダメンタルズで見て割安な企業の株式のこと）
value investing style 割安株投資, バリュー株投資, バリュー・スタイルの運用
value investor 割安株投資家
value stock バリュー株, 割安株（株式市場で過小評価されている株のこと）
value to stakeholders ステークホルダー（利害関係者）に帰属する価値
value to the shareholders 株主に帰属する価値
values of shares 株価　（⇒booking）
◆As it stands, the yen is the sole major currency whose value has not stopped increasing. 現状では、円は上昇が止まらない唯一の主要通貨だ。◆In commodity futures trading, prices are decided when buyers and sellers make deals. So they can execute trades at promised prices even if the value of goods has changed drastically in the meantime. 商品先物取引では、売り手と買い手が取引契約をする時点で価格を決める。そのため、契約期間中に相場が大きく変動しても、売り手と買い手は約束した値段で取引を執行できる。◆JAL's stocks may lose market value to zero if the corporate turnaround body cuts the shares 100 percent by delisting JAL from the Tokyo stock market. 企業再生支援機構が東京株式市場から日航の上場を廃止して日航株を100%減資したら、日航株の市場価値はゼロになる可能性がある。◆Most companies use the daily average for a month of the share prices in gauging the value of latent gains or losses in their stockholdings. 大半の企業は、保有株式の含み損益を算出する際に株価の月中平均を使っている。◆Price-to-book value is obtained by dividing price per share by assets per share. 株価純資産倍率は、1株当たり株価を1株当たりの資産額で割って［除して］求められます。◆The aggregate value of stocks listed in the First Section of the Tokyo Stock Exchange was ¥297.698 trillion as of the end of September, an increase of 30.3 percent from the end of March. 東証一部に上場されている株式の時価総額は、9月末現在297兆6,980億円で、3月末に比べて30.3%上昇した。◆The collection of debts has been delayed due to falling collateral value. 担保価値の下落などで、債権の回収は遅れている。◆The company's financial statements are not based on the book value of the assets at time they were obtained. 同社の財務諸表は、取得時の資産の簿価を基準としていない。◆The foreign currency depositor planned to withdraw the money when the yen's value fell. この外貨預金者は、円安になったら解約するつもりだった。◆The rapid surge in the yen's value would impair the current improvement in the Japanese economy. 急激な円高は、日本の景気回復の腰を折ることになる。◆The total value of M&A deals involving Japanese firms increased roughly 2.2-fold to $108.85 billion, or about ¥12 trillion in the first half of 2005. 日本企業がかかわった2005年上期のM&A取引金額の総額は、前年同期比約2.2倍増の1,088億5,000万ドル（約12兆円）となった。◆The U.S. dollar has dropped sharply in value not only against the yen, but also against the euro, the South Korean won, the Thai baht and other currencies. 米ドル［米ドル相場］は、円に対してだけでなく、ユーロや韓国ウォン、タイ・バーツなどに対しても、急落している。◆The yen's value still remains high and is likely to reach a postwar record value above the ¥76-to-the-dollar level. 円相場は依然高く、1ドル＝76円台を上回る戦後最高値に達する可能性がある。

value loans 債権を評価する
◆We must consider delays or reduced payments of interest as well as principal when we value loans that may not be fully repaid. 100%返済されない可能性がある債権を評価するにあたって、利息や元本の運延や減額返済を考慮する必要があります。

value of a corporation 企業の価値, 企業価値（＝corporate value）
◆The value of a corporation is divided between value to the shareholders and value to stakeholders. 企業価値は、株主に帰属する価値とステークホルダー（利害関係者）に帰属する価値に二分される。

value of government bonds 国債価格
◆After the lowering of the rating, the current value of government bonds might drop and their interest rate might go up. 国債の格付けが下がると、現在の国債価格も下がり、金利の上昇を招く恐れがある。◆If the value of a huge number of government bonds possessed by financial institutions around the world plummets, financial instability will grow. 世界の金融機関が保有する大量の国債の価格が急落すれば、金融不安が高まることになる。

value of oil imports 原油輸入額
◆The value of oil imports in September jumped 62 percent year-on-year. 9月の原油輸入額は、前年同月比で62%急増した。

value of the dollar ドル相場, ドル価値, ドルの価値
◆The United States is facing the risk of seeing the value of the dollar plunging badly. 米国は、ドル相場が大幅に下落するリスクを抱えている。◆The value of the dollar is sinking on international exchanges. 国際為替市場で、ドル価値が下落している。

value of the euro ユーロの相場, ユーロの価値
◆The decline in the value of the euro is unlikely to stop. ユーロの下落傾向［ユーロ相場の下落］は、止まりそうにない。◆Uncertainty has prevailed as the value of the euro dropped sharply. ユーロの相場が急落したため、不安［動揺］が広がっている。

value of the stock 株式の価値
◆If the worth of the issuer rises, the value of the stock also will rise. 発行体の資産価値が上昇すれば、株式の価値も上がる。

value of the U.S. dollar 米ドル相場, ドルの価値（⇒sink）
◆The value of the U.S. dollar has started to decline on currency markets around the world. 世界の外国為替市場では、米ドル相場が下落しはじめた。

value of the yen against the dollar 円の対ドル相場（＝the yen's value against the dollar）
◆Japan is experiencing a surge in its auto exports to the U.S., thanks to a decline in the value of the yen against the dollar. 日本の対米自動車輸出は現在、円安［円安・ドル高］で急増している。

value of the yuan 人民元の相場
◆The IMF expects the value of the yuan to rise in the mid- to long term. 人民元の相場は中長期的に切り上げ傾向にある、とIMF（国際通貨基金）は見ている。

value-oriented management 価値重視の経営
◆Everyone connected with the Corporation, or the people we call our "stakeholders" will also benefit from value-oriented management. 当社と係りのある人たち、つまり当社の「ステークホルダー」といわれる人たち全員も、価値重視の経営によって利益を受けることになる。

value to the shareholders 株主に帰属する価値
◆The value of a corporation is divided between value to the shareholders and value to stakeholders. 企業価値は、株主に帰属する価値とステークホルダー（利害関係者）に帰属する価値に二分される。

variable （名）不確定要素, 流動的な要因, 変化するもの, 変わりやすいもの, 変数
continuous variable 連続変数
decision variable 意思決定変数
economic variable 経済変数
financial variable 金融指標
macro economic variables マクロ経済変数
monetary policy variable 金融政策の変数

random variable　確率変数
target variable　目標変数
unknown variable　不確定要因

variable　(形)変わりやすい,不安定な,変動する,可変の,可変的な,変動できる
variable annuity　変額年金,可変年金,変動年金(保険会社の年金資金の運用成果で給付金の額が変わる年金保険のこと)
variable annuity plan　変額年金制度,可変年金制度
variable capital　可変資本,変動資本,流動資本
variable capital ratio　変動資本率
variable cash reserve requirements　可変的現金準備制度
variable cost　変動費,可変費用,変動減価
variable cost ratio　変動費率
variable expense　変動費　(=variable charge)
variable factory cost　変動製造原価
variable insurance　変額保険
variable investment tax　可変的投資税,可変投資税
variable life insurance　変額生命保険,変額保険
variable liquidity reserve requirements　可変的流動性比率制度
variable price securities　変動価格証券
variable repo　金利入札方式のレポ
variable reserve requirements　可変的準備制度,可変的現金準備制度
variable universal life (insurance)　変額ユニバーサル保険

variable interest (rate)　変動金利
(=floating rate, variable rate)
variable interest bearing　変動利付き
variable interest-bearing securities　不確定利付き証券
variable interest rate debt　変動金利負債[債務]

variable pension system　変額年金制度
◆Under a variable pension system, pension benefits change in accordance with fluctuations in government bond yield. 変額年金制度では、国債利回りの変動で年金給付額が変わる。

variable rate　変動金利　(=floating rate, variable interest, variable interest rate)
exchangeable variable rate note　短期市場金利に連動する債券,短期市場金利連動型債券
on a variable rate basis　変動金利建て
savings type variable rate insurance with regular annuity　年金払い定期付き積立型変額保険
variable rate borrowing　変動金利債務
variable rate certificate　変動金利型CD,変動金利CD　(=variable rate CD)
variable rate consumer loan　変動金利消費者ローン
variable rate demand debt　変動金利要求払い債
variable rate demand loan　変動金利要求払い貸付け
variable rate demand note　変動金利要求払い証券,変動金利要求証券,LRDN
variable rate demand obligation　変動金利要求払い債
variable rate deposit account　変動金利預金
variable rate depository receipt　マージン変動型預託証券
variable rate insurance　変額保険
variable rate interest　変動金利
variable rate investment　変動金利投資
variable rate loan　変動金利ローン
variable rate mortgage　変動金利型抵当貸付け,変動金利型抵当証券,変動金利モーゲージ,VRM
variable rate note　変動利率証書,VRN
variable rate repo　金利入札による買いオペ,金利入札方式のレポ

variable rate system　金利入札
variable rates tied to LIBOR　LIBORに連動した変動金利,LIBORベースの変動金利

variable rate debt　変動金利負債,変動金利債務,変動利付き債務
◆The Company has entered into several transactions which reduce financing costs and exposure to variable rate debt. 最近実施した数件の取引で、当社の資金調達コストと変動金利負債に係わるリスクは軽減されています。

variation　(名)変化,変動,変異,変形,ばらつき,差,バリエーション
cyclical variation　循環変動
interest variation　利子変動
price variation　物価変動,価格変動
seasonal variation index　季節変動指数
statement of variation of funds　資金移動表
variation gap　バリエーション・ギャップ(妥当と思われる株価と現実の株価との格差のこと)
variation in exchange rates　為替相場の変動
variation margin　追加証拠金,変動証拠金,維持証拠金
variation on common stock　各種の普通株式

veep　(名)副会長,副社長,副頭取,副総裁,副大統領　(=vice-president)
◆A former UFJ Bank veep personally directed the cover-up. UFJ銀行元副頭取が、自ら隠ぺい工作を指示していた。

vehicle　(名)手段,媒介物,商品,銘柄,会社,子会社,機関,乗り物,輸送手段,ビークル
borrowing vehicle　資金調達主体
collective investment vehicle　集合投資手段
corporate vehicles　所有企業
finance vehicle　金融会社,金融子会社,資金調達の手段
financing vehicle　金融商品,資金調達手段
funding vehicle　資金調達手段,資金調達の場
hedging vehicle　ヘッジ手段
investment vehicle　投資商品,投資会社,投資子会社,投資手段
issuing vehicle　起債子会社
public finance vehicle　公的資金調達の手段
retirement savings vehicle　退職年金商品
savings vehicle　貯蓄商品
special purpose vehicle　特別目的会社
trading vehicle　取引の手段,ディーリングの手段
vehicle currency　取引通貨,貿易通貨(trading currency),媒介通貨(国際取引契約の金額表示に用いられる通貨)
vehicle for netting swap collateral　スワップ担保相殺機関
◆Commercial banks have created special investment vehicles (SIVs) in order to escape the capital adequacy regulation imposed by the Basel accord. 銀行は、バーゼル協定[バーゼル合意]による自己資本比率規制を回避するため、特別投資会社(SIV)を新設している。

velocity　(名)速度
M1 velocity　M1の流通速度　(=velocity of M1)
transaction velocity　取引速度,流通速度
velocity of circulation of demand deposit　預金通貨の流通速度
velocity of circulation of money　貨幣の流通速度
velocity of money　通貨の流通速度,貨幣流通速度
velocity reserve plan　速度準備プラン

velocity of money　通貨の流通速度,貨幣流通速度
(=velocity of circulation of money; ⇒turnover of money)
circuit velocity of money　貨幣の流通速度
income velocity of money　貨幣の所得速度

venture （名）冒険的事業, 投機的事業, 危険性の高い事業, 事業, 合弁事業, 業務, ベンチャー
　（⇒joint venture, joint production venture）
　cooperative ventures　ジョイント・ベンチャー
　corporate joint venture　合弁会社
　cross-border ventures　国際業務
　domestic ventures　国内事業
　new ventures　新規事業
　overseas ventures　海外事業
　venture capitalist　ベンチャー・ビジネスへの出資者［投資家］, 危険資本家, 危険投資家, 危険負担資本家, ベンチャー・キャピタリスト
　venture firm　ベンチャー企業
　　（=start-up, start-up business, venture company）
　venture fund　ベンチャー・ファンド（投資ファンドの一種で, 創業間もない企業の未上場株式に投資して, 売却益を狙う）
　venture management　ベンチャー・マネジメント
　　（=venture business）
　◆In China, oil majors have been building ethylene plants in joint ventures as well. 中国では, 国際石油資本（メジャー）が合弁エチレン・プラントの建設も進めている。◆The biggest advantage for the bank in entering the venture will be to increase its customer base without having to open expensive new branch offices. 同行にとってこの新規事業への参入の最大の利点は, コストのかかる新店舗を開設するまでもなく, 顧客基盤を拡大できることだ。◆The Development Bank of Japan and Aozora Bank have joined hands in extending a loan to a Tokyo venture, taking as collateral the firm's patent for an innovative information-technology business model. 日本政策投資銀行とあおぞら銀行は, 革新的なIT（情報技術）を活用したビジネス手法特許［ビジネス・モデル特許］を担保として, 東京のベンチャー企業に協調融資した。◆To enhance the international competitiveness of Japanese companies, the government needs to expand tax incentives to investors in new ventures in these industries. 日本企業の国際競争力を高めるには, 政府がこれらの産業の新規事業に出資する投資家を税制上, 優遇する措置を拡充する必要がある。
venture business　ベンチャー企業, ベンチャー・ビジネス, 新ビジネス, 投機的事業, 研究開発型企業, 開拓型新興小規模企業, VB
　（=start-up business, venture company）
　◆Outsourcing is a strategic method that effectively uses business resources. It is actively utilized in Europe and the U.S. by venture businesses that lack adequate human resources. アウトソーシングは, 経営資源を有効に活用するための戦略的手法です。これは, 欧米では, 人的資源を十分に確保できないベンチャー企業によって積極的に活用されています。
venture capital　危険資本, 危険負担資本, ベンチャー資本, リスク資金, ベンチャー企業に投資する会社, ベンチャー・キャピタル投資会社（venture capital firm）, ベンチャー・キャピタル, VC　（=risk capital）
　◆Some of the oil corporation's functions, such as supplying venture capital for oil development and conducting R&D, were consolidated into the Metal Mining Agency of Japan. 石油開発のためのリスク資金供給機能や研究開発機能など, 石油公団の機能の一部が, 金属鉱業事業団に統合された。
venture capital firm　ベンチャー・キャピタル投資会社, ベンチャー・キャピル
　◆SBI Holdings Inc. is a venture capital firm of the Softbank Corp. group. SBIホールディングスは, ソフトバンク・グループのベンチャー・キャピタル（ベンチャー・キャピタル投資会社）だ。
venture capital investment　ベンチャー資本投資, ベンチャー資本投資額

◆Venture capital investment in Japan in 2001 on a stock basis was about ￥1.02 trillion. 2001年の株式資本ベースでの日本のベンチャー資本投資額は, およそ1兆200億円であった。
venture company [firm]　ベンチャー企業　（=start-up, start-up business, start-up company, venture）
◆U.S. universities often start up venture companies using patents obtained by the universities, which forms a strong foundation in developing new industries in the fields of biotechnology, information technology and aerospace. アメリカの大学では, 大学が取得した特許でベンチャー企業を設立する場合が多く, これがバイオやIT（情報技術）, 宇宙産業などの新産業を開発する際の強固な基盤となっている。
verify　（動）確認する, 検証する, 立証する, 証明する
◆Concerns have been raised over the ability of Internet banking services to verify the identity of new depositors or to guarantee the security of customer transactions. インターネット・バンキングについては, 新規預金者の身元確認や対顧客取引の安全保証の点で, その能力に対して懸念が提起されている。
versus　（前）～に対して, 対～, v.［vs.］
　（=against）
　exchange rates versus dollar　対ドル為替レート
　the ￥84 range versus the dollar　1ドル＝40円台
◆The yen could soon even reach a record high in the ￥75 range versus the dollar. 円は, やがて1ドル＝75円台の史上最高値にまで達する可能性がある。
vertical　（形）垂直的, 同業同種間の, 縦割りの, 縦の
　（⇒horizontal）
　administered vertical marketing system　流通系列化
　vertical channel system　垂直的経路システム
　vertical communication　垂直的コミュニケーション
　vertical competition　垂直的競争
　vertical conflict　垂直的衝突, 垂直的コンフリクト（製造業者と小売業者, 小売業者と卸売り業者間の競争的闘争）
　vertical diversification　垂直的多角化
　vertical influence　垂直的競争
　vertical integration　垂直統合
　vertical market　垂直的市場
　vertical marketing system　垂直的マーケティング・システム, VMS
　　（=vertically integrated marketing system）
　vertical merger　垂直的合併
　　（=vertical amalgamation）
　vertical organization　垂直的組織
　vertical publication　業界専門誌
　vertical specialization　垂直的国際分業
　vertical spread　バーチカル・スプレッド（オプション取引で, 行使価格だけが違う二つのオプションについて, 売りと買いを同時に行うこと）
　vertical trade　垂直的貿易
veto　拒否権　（動）拒否権を行使する, 拒否する, 差し止める
◆Some leading companies may issue certain classes of stock, such as preferred shares, which give shareholders a veto when a hostile acquirer proposes a merger or acquisition. 敵対的買収者が合併や買収を提案した場合, 主要企業の一部は, 株主に拒否権を与える優先株などの種類株を発行する場合もある。
veto right　拒否権　（=the power of a veto）
◆As for preferred stocks with veto rights, the attachment of a clause restricting their transfer to hostile investors is needed. （重要事項の決議の）拒否権を持つ優先株については, 敵対的投資家への譲渡を制限する条項を盛り込む必要がある。◆Golden shares give even holders of a single share the veto right to

block hostile takeover bids. 黄金株では、1株の株主にも敵対的買収案を阻止するための拒否権が与えられる。

via (前) 〜によって、〜で、〜を利用して、〜を通して、〜経由で、〜を主幹事として
◆Illegal transfers of deposits via foreign malware have been jumping. 海外のマルウェア（コンピュータ・ウイルスの一種）による預金の不正送金が急増している。◆In illegal transfers via online banking services, viruses such as Spy Eye and Zbot have been used. ネット・バンキングでの不正送金では、スパイアイやゼットボットなどと呼ばれるウイルスが使われている。◆Some major banks lower their commission rates of foreign currency deposits if depositors make transactions via online accounts. 外貨預金の預金者がネット口座経由で取引をする場合、一部の大手銀行は、外貨預金の手数料［為替手数料］の料率を引き下げている。◆The special account is expected to collect a large surplus in fiscal 2011 via the repayment of loans. 特別会計は、貸付け金の返済で2011年度は多額の剰余金が生じる見込みだ。◆Viruses used in illegal transfers via online banking services collect Internet banking account-related information such as personal identification numbers and transmit them to remote parties. ネット・バンキングでの不正送金に使われたウイルスは、暗証番号などネット・バンキングの口座関連情報を収集して、外部に送信する。

vice minister for international affairs 国際担当次官, 財務官（事務次官と同格で官僚組織のトップ。仕事は、国際会議で財務相に代わり政府代表を務めたり、円売り・ドル買いなどの市場介入を実質的に指揮したりする権限などを与えられている）

vicious circle 悪循環 （=vicious cycle）
◆Plunges on the world's stock markets and wild fluctuations in foreign exchange markets may ensure the prolongation of the vicious circle. 世界同時株安と為替市場の乱高下は、悪循環に歯止めがかからなくなる恐れがある。◆There is a possibility that a vicious circle will develop in which the financial crisis undermines the U.S. real economy, producing further financial instability. 金融危機が米国の実体経済を損ない、それがさらに金融不安を引き起こす悪循環が深刻化する可能性がある。

vicious cycle 悪循環 （=vicious circle）
◆A vicious cycle, in which financial uncertainty cools down the U.S. real economy and causes an economic downturn, is becoming reality. 金融不安が米国の実体経済を冷え込ませ、景気後退を招く悪循環は、現実になっている。◆A vicious cycle of deflationary pressures is becoming increasingly real. デフレの悪循環が、現実味を増してきた。◆Breaking this vicious circle could be the key to revitalizing the economy. この悪循環を断ち切ることが、景気浮揚へのカギになる。

victim (名) 犠牲, 犠牲者, 被害者, 被害者企業, 被災者, 遭難者, 罹病（りびょう）者, えじき, いけにえ
a crime victim 犯罪被害者
a murder victim 殺人の犠牲者
a victim to the axe 人員削減の犠牲
AIDS victims エイズ罹病者, エイズ患者
be made a victim of a swindler 詐欺師のえじきにされる
earthquake victims 震災被災者, 地震の被害者
fall (a) victim to 〜の犠牲となる、〜によって傷つけられる［殺される］,（魅力などの）とりこになる、〜に敗れる
fall a victim to cancer がんの犠牲となる
quake victims 地震被災者
victim firm 被害企業, 被害者企業
victims of a flood 洪水の犠牲者
war victims 戦争の犠牲者 （=victims of war）
◆In phishing, offenders lure victims to fake financial institution Web sites to enter their account PINs and other account information. フィッシングでは、犯人が被害者を金融機関の偽ホームページに誘導して、被害者の口座の暗証番号などの口座情報を入力させる。◆Quake victims face arduous daily lives. 地震被災者は、苦しい日常生活を強いられている。◆The U.S. subprime mortgage crisis has claimed its biggest victim to date. 米国のサブプライム・ローン問題が、これまでで最大の被害者企業を出した。◆Victim firms have entered into talks to file a class action suit for compensation. 被害企業が、損害賠償に向けて集団訴訟のための協議を開始した。

vie (動) 競う, 張り合う, 争う
◆Japan's economic growth is driven by exports, but it will have to vie for export markets with emerging economies. 日本の経済成長の原動力は輸出だが、今後は新興国と輸出市場の争奪戦になろう。

view (動) 見る, 〜と見なす, 考える, 考察する, 調べる, 調査する, 点検する, 検分する
◆A reading of below 50 percent in the coincident index is considered a sign of economic contraction and a figure above that is viewed as a sign of expansion. 一致指数で50％以下の数値は景気収縮［景気後退］を示す指標と見られ、それ以上の数字は景気回復［景気拡大］を示す指標と見なされる。

view (名) 見方, 考え, 考え方, 意見, 見解, 〜観, 視野, 視界, 眺望, 眺め, 概観, 概説, 〜図, 見通し, 見込み, 意図, 目的, 意向, ビュー
bearish views 弱気の見方
bullish views 強気の見方
economic view 経済見通し
favourable [favorable] view of the currency 通貨の先高感
in full view of the public 公開の席で
optimistic view 楽観的な見方, 楽観的な考え, 楽観的な見通し （⇒on the strength of）
positive view 明るい見通し
with a view to 〜するため、〜する目的で
◆Behind these cautious views among large manufacturers are uncertainty over the debt crisis in the eurozone and the slowdown in the U.S. economy. 大企業製造業のこうした警戒感［慎重な見方］の背景には、ユーロ圏の債務危機不安や米景気の減速がある。◆With a view to stemming the airlines' financial hemorrhaging, the Construction and Transport Ministry in late May asked the Development Bank of Japan to provide emergency loans to the two carriers. 航空会社の損失を阻止するため、5月下旬に国土交通省は、日本政策投資銀行に対して両航空会社への緊急融資を要請した。

vigilant (形) 絶えず警戒［注意］する, 警戒を怠（おこた）らない, 気を配っている, 用心［注意］深い, (〜に対して) 油断のない, 寝ずの番をする
be vigilant against excess [excessive] volatility in exchange rates 為替相場の過度な変動を監視する
keep a vigilant eye on 〜を虎視（こし）たんたんとねらう
keep a vigilant guard over 〜を油断なく警戒する
◆By being vigilant against excessive volatility in exchange rates, the G-20 will reduce the risk of speculative money causing appreciation of currencies and inflation in emerging countries. 為替相場の過度な変動を監視して、世界［主要］20か国・地域（G20）は、投機マネーが新興国の通貨高やインフレを招くリスクを軽減する方針だ。

vigor [vigour] (名) 活力, 精力, 気力, 体力, 活動力, 元気, 力強さ, 迫力, 勢い, 成長力, 拘束力, 効力
boost the vigor of the private sector 民間活力を高める
tap the vigor of 〜の活力を引き出す
the vigor of private businesses 民間企業の活力
◆It is uncertain whether the government's new growth strategy can achieve the anticipated economic growth by tapping the vigor of private businesses. 政府の新成長戦略が、民間企業の活力を引き出して期待どおりの経済成長を実現できるか

どうかは、未知数である。
vigorous （形）激しい,すさまじい,厳しい,活発な,精力的な,積極的な,力強い,強健な,壮健な,元気いっぱいの,強い,強力な,生育のよい,丈夫な
 a vigorous economic growth　力強い経済成長
 be in a vigorous competition with　～と激しい［熾烈な］競争をしている
 vigorous cost cutting measures　徹底したコスト［経費］削減策
 vigorous financial policy　積極的金融政策
 vigorous fiscal policy　積極的財政政策
violate （動）（約束などを）破る,裏切る,（法律、契約、規則などに）違反する,侵害する,侵犯する,犯す,汚す,冒涜（ぼうとく）する,（条項などに）触れる
 violate a promise　約束を破る
 violate exchange controls　外為規制に触れる,外国為替規制に抵触する
 violate the Banking Law　銀行法に違反する
 violate the debt limit　国債発行限度額に触れる
 violate the treaty　条約に違反する
 ◆A man who operated an illegal moneylending firm was arrested on suspicion of violating the Investment Deposit and Interest Rate Control Law. 違法な金融業の経営者［ヤミ金融の経営者］が、出資法違反容疑で逮捕された。◆Golden shares violate the principle of shareholder equality. 黄金株は、「株主平等の原則」に反する。◆The bank's operations gravely violated the Banking Law. 同行の業務は、銀行法に重大違反していた。◆The Securities and Exchange Surveillance Commission filed a criminal complaint against a former bank employee with the Tokyo District Public Prosecutors Office on suspicion of violating the Financial Instruments and Exchange Law. 証券取引等監視委員会は、元行員を金融商品取引法違反の疑いで東京地検に刑事告発した。
 violate the industry rule　業界の規約に違反する
 ◆The repurchasing method, which has customers buy highly negotiable cash vouchers, violates the industry rule. 顧客に換金性の高い金券類を購入させる買取り方式は、業界の規約に違反する。
 violate the law　法律を破る,法律［法令］に違反する,法律違反をする
 ◆Citigroup Private Bank's four offices in Japan will have their licenses revoked for violating the law by ignoring suspected money laundering by clients. シティバンクのプライベート・バンク（PB）の在日4拠点（支店・出張所）が、顧客のマネー・ロンダリング（資金洗浄）の疑いのある取引を放置するなどして法令違反があったとして、認可を取り消されることになった。
violation （名）違反,違反行為,侵害,妨害,侵犯,冒涜（ぼうとく）,レイプ,（婦女）暴行,意味の曲解
 commit a violation　違反する
 in violation of［to］　～に違反して
 securities law violation　証券取引法違反
 serious violation of one's obligations　～の義務の重大違反
 violation of covenant　契約違反
 violation of law　法律違反
 violation of the Securities and Exchange Law　証券取引法違反
 ◆A lack of morals among Livedoor group executives led to their violation of the Securities and Exchange Law. ライブドア・グループ幹部の証券取引法違反の原因は、経営者の「モラルの欠如」だ。◆He was the mastermind behind a string of violations of the Securities and Exchange Law by the Internet service firm. 同氏は、このインターネット・サービス会社による一連の証券取引法違反行為を主導していた。◆The bank was found to have forced corporate borrowers to buy financial products in violation of the Antimonopoly Law. 同行は、独占禁止法に違反して融資先企業に金融商品を無理に購入させていたことが判明した。◆The government may reject a company's request for a license to enter the fiduciary market if its executive has been dismissed in the past five years due to a violation of Section 2 of Article 102. 信託市場（信託業）に参入するための免許を申請した企業の役員が、第102条第2項の違反により5年以内に解任命令を受けていた場合、政府はその免許申請（免許交付）を拒否することができる。
virement （名）資金の流用,費目変更,振替え,手形交換
virtual （形）事実上の,実質的な,仮想の,バーチャル
 virtual branch　仮想支店,バーチャル支店
 virtual corporation［company］　仮想企業,仮想会社,仮想事業体,バーチャル・コーポレーション
 virtual mall　仮想商店街,バーチャル・モール
  （=virtual shopping mall）
 virtual money　仮想通貨［貨幣］,バーチャル・マネー
 virtual owner　実質的な所有者,実質的な保有者
  （⇒owner）
 virtual shop　仮想商店　（⇒online debit service）
 virtual shopping　バーチャル・ショッピング（インターネットを通じた通信販売）
 virtual wallet　仮想財布
virtual bank　仮想銀行,バーチャル銀行　（=Internet bank, Net bank, Net-only bank, web bank: インターネット上で金融取引を専門に行う銀行）
 set up one's virtual bank as a separate company　仮想銀行を系列会社として設立する
 virtual bank client　バーチャル銀行（仮想銀行）の利用者
 ◆The bank plans to take advantage of the new virtual bank's lower overhead to offer improved services. 同行では、新仮想銀行の低コスト体質を生かして、サービスを向上させる計画だ。◆The new virtual bank will seek to obtain a banking license. この新仮想銀行は、銀行免許を取得する方針だ。
virtual marketplace　仮想電子取引市場,電子商取引市場,バーチャル市場
 ◆Rakuten's profit increased at its virtual marketplace, travel and financial services businesses. 楽天の利益は、電子商取引市場や旅行事業、金融サービスで増加した。
virtual shop　仮想商店
 ◆The bank has started an online debit service with a network of about 100 virtual shops. 同行は、約100店の仮想商店を対象にインターネット即時決済サービスを開始した。
virtual shopping mall　仮想商店街,仮想モール,バーチャル・ショッピング・モール
 （=virtual mall; ⇒on-the-spot payment）
 ◆Rakuten boasts yearly sales of ￥18 billion from a virtual shopping mall and online securities brokerage. 楽天は、仮想商店街やオンライン証券などで180億円の年間売上を誇る。
virtuous cycle［circle］　好循環,良循環
 a virtuous cycle of self-sustainable growth led by private demand　民需主導の自律的な成長という好循環
 the virtuous cycle of growth in production, income and spending　生産・所得と支出の伸びの好循環［好循環メカニズム］　（⇒cycle）
 ◆The Japanese economy is entering into a virtuous cycle of self-sustainable growth led by private demand. 日本経済には、民需主導の自律的な成長という好循環が生まれている。
virus （名）ウイルス,コンピュータ・ウイルス
 computer virus　コンピュータ・ウイルス
  （⇒security）
 remove a virus from the infected files　感染したファイルからコンピュータ・ウイルスを取り除く
 virus-infected personal computer　ウイルス感染のパソ

コン
  virus protection software　ウイルス対策ソフト
    （＝vaccine）
  ◆All the filed documents in computers were erased by the virus. ウイルスで、パソコン内の文書ファイルがすべて消去されてしまった。◆In illegal transfers via online banking services, viruses such as Spy Eye and Zbot have been used. ネット・バンキングでの不正送金では、スパイアイやゼットボットなどと呼ばれるウイルスが使われている。◆Personal computers of many Net banking depositors have been infected with viruses that ravaged computers in the United States and European countries. 多くのネット・バンキング預金者のパソコンが、欧米のコンピュータに爆発的な被害を生んだウイルスに感染していた。◆Viruses used in illegal transfers via online banking services collect Internet banking account-related information such as personal identification numbers and transmit them to remote parties. ネット・バンキングでの不正送金に使われたウイルスは、暗証番号などネット・バンキングの口座関連情報を収集して、外部に送信する。

vis-a-vis［vis-à-vis］　（前）〜と比較して、〜に関して、〜に対する、〜と向かい合って、〜に相対して　（形）向かい合っている, 相対している
  （⇒yen-denominated assets）
  dollar's performance vis-a-vis the yen　円に対するドル相場
  exchange rate vis-a-vis the U.S. dollar　対米ドル為替レート
  the yen's appreciation vis-a-vis the U.S. dollar　対ドルでの円高
  vis-a-vis the U.S. dollar　対米ドルで, 米ドルに対する
  ◆The Japanese currency's value vis-a-vis the U.S. dollar entered the ¥85 range in foreign exchange markets around the world. 円の対米ドル相場は、内外の外国為替市場で1ドル＝85円台を付けた。

VIX　シカゴ・オプション取引所（CBOE）のVIX（ボラティリティ）指数,（投資家の）心理的恐怖指数［恐怖指数］（volatility indexの略。⇒CBOE Volatility Index（VIX））

volatile　（形）変わりやすい, 乱高下する, 変動が激しい, 変動が大きい, 変動性が高い, 不安定な, 左右されやすい
  be volatile to changes in the share prices　株価動向に左右されやすい
  less volatile　変動性が小さい
  volatile market　変わりやすい市場, 乱高下する市場, 変動が激しい市場
  volatile movements in the currency market　為替市場の過度な変動
  volatile pricing　価格変動, 価格の変動
    （＝volatile prices）
  ◆Currency traders worldwide frantically search for a safe haven in volatile times. 世界の為替トレーダーは、変動の激しい時期の安全な投資先を熱狂的に求めている。◆The core consumer price inflation rate, excluding volatile fresh food prices, is currently about 2 percent on year due mainly to soaring food and petroleum product prices. 変動の激しい生鮮食品の価格を除いたコア物価指数［消費者物価指数のコア指数］の上昇率は現在、主に食料品と石油製品の価格高騰の影響で、対前年比で2%程度となっている。◆The core nationwide CPI, which excludes volatile fresh food prices, stood at 99.3 against the base of 100 for 2005. 全国消費者物価指数のコア指数（値動きの大きい生鮮食品を除く総合指数）は、99.3（2005年＝100）となった。

volatile capital flows　資本移動の変動, 変動が大きい［激しい］資本移動
  ◆Asia faces the risk of volatile capital flows as its growth outpaces the rest of the world. アジアの成長が他国を上回っているため、アジアは資本移動の変動リスクに直面している。

volatile movements in the currency market　為替市場の過度な変動
  ◆Volatile movements in the currency market have a negative impact on economic and financial stability. 為替市場の過度な変動は、経済・金融の安定に悪影響を及ぼす。

volatile to changes in the share prices　株価動向に左右されやすい
  ◆Overseas investors are considered highly volatile to changes in the share price. 外国人株主は、株価動向にかなり左右されやすいとされている。

volatility　（名）変動, 乱高下, 極端な変動, 変動性, 変動率, 将来の価格変動性, 価格変動率, 予測変動率, ボラティリティ
  （⇒excessive volatility, foreign exchange market）
  CBOE Volatility Index　CBOEボラティリティ指数
    （＝CBOE VIX；⇒CBOE Volatility Index（VIX））
  decrease volatility　ボラティリティを引き下げる, リスクを引き下げる
  excess volatility　過度の変動
    （＝excessive volatility）
  excess volatility in exchange rates　為替相場の過度の変動
  excessive［excess］volatility　過度の変動
  exchange rate volatility　為替の乱高下, 為替相場の変動, 為替変動　（＝forex volatility）
  expected income volatility　予想収益変動幅
  forex volatility　為替変動
  have low volatility　ボラティリティが低い, リスクが低い
  historical volatility　過去の変動性, ヒストリカル・ボラティリティ
  implied volatility　予想変動率, インプライド・ボラティリティ
  interest rate volatility　金利変動率, 金利変動, 金利の乱高下, 金利ボラティリティ
  intervene to avoid currency volatility　為替相場の極端な変動を防ぐため介入する
  market volatility　市場変動性, 相場変動性, 市場の乱高下, 市場のボラティリティ
  price volatility　価格変動性, 価格変動
  reduce volatility　ボラティリティを軽減する
  stem excessive volatility　為替相場の極端な変動を阻止する
  stem volatility　極端な変動を阻止する
  stock market volatility　株式相場の変動, 株式市場の乱高下, 市場のボラティリティ
  volatility index　ボラティリティ（株価変動率）指数, 株価変動率指数, VIX
  volatility pickup　リスクの上昇, リスクの拡大

volatility and disruptions in the capital markets　資本市場の変動性と混乱
  ◆Volatility and disruptions in the capital markets became even more pronounced in July. 7月は、資本市場の変動性と混乱が一段と鮮明になった。

volatility in exchange rates　為替相場の変動
  ◆By being vigilant against excessive volatility in exchange rates, the G-20 will reduce the risk of speculative money causing appreciation of currencies and inflation in emerging countries. 為替相場の過度な変動を監視して、世界［主要］20か国・地域（G20）は、投機マネーが新興国の通貨高やインフレを招くリスクを軽減する方針だ。◆Excess volatility in exchange rates is undesirable for global economic growth. 為替相場の過度の変動は、世界の経済成長にとって望ましくない。

volatility in the exchange market　為替相場の変動
  ◆The market intervention was carried out to control exces-

sive volatility in the exchange market. 為替相場の過度の変動を抑制するため、市場介入[為替介入]が実施された。

Volcker Rule ボルカー・ルール
　[解説]ボルカー・ルールとは：米金融機関の投機的な動きを規制するための新ルールで、ポール・ボルカー元FRB議長が中心となってまとめられた。この新規制では、銀行などの預金取扱い機関や持ち株会社に対して、顧客向けサービスと関係のない自己勘定取引やヘッジ・ファンドへの投資を禁止しているほか、負債のシェアが10%を超える合併も禁止している。

volume　(名)出来高, 取引高, 売上高, 販売高, 操業度, 数量, 量　(「出来高」は株式市場全体の売買株数を示し、売高ともいわれる。一般に、株価が上昇して、出来高も多いときは、相場が強いとされている。⇒falsified transaction, trading volume)
　actual volume　実際操業度
　aid volume　援助量, 援助額
　break-even volume　損益分岐売上高
　cost-volume-profit analysis　原価・営業量・利益分析, CVP分析
　export volume　輸出数量
　in volume terms　実質ベースで, 台数ベースで, 数量ベースで　(=in terms of volume)
　loan volume　融資高
　new issue volume　起債総額
　profit-volume chart [graph]　損益分岐点図表
　profit volume ratio　限界利益率, PV比率, 売上高純利益率　(=PV ratio)
　retail sales volume　小売売上数量
　sales volume　売上高, 販売高, 販売数量, 販売量, 売上数量, 取扱い高
　syndicate loan volume　シンジケート・ローンの総額
　trading volume　出来高, 売買高, 売上高, 売買株数　(=volume of trading)
　volume business　大量取引
　volume cap　発行額の上限
　volume of business　取引高, 売買高
　◆French bond prices slipped as French banks possess a large volume of Greek and Italian bonds. フランス銀行がギリシャやイタリアなどの国債を保有しているため、フランス国債が値下がりした。◆NYSE volume totaled 809.18 million shares. ニューヨーク証券取引所の出来高は、8億918万株だった。◆The company was once the second-largest provider of subprime mortgages in the United States on loan volume. 同社は、かつてはサブプライム・ローンの融資高で米国第2位の住宅ローン会社だった。
　volume of short-term transactions　短期売買の取引高
　◆The volume of short-term transactions by day traders is expected to keep growing. デイ・トレーダーによる短期売買[デイ・トレーダーを中心とする短期売買]の取引高は、今後増大する見込みだ。
　volume of the intervention　介入規模, 介入総額
　◆The volume of the intervention by the BOJ was estimated at between several hundred billion and a little more than ¥1 trillion. 日銀の介入の規模は、推定で数千億円から約1兆円程度と見られる。
　volume of trading　出来高, 売買高, 売上高, 売買株数　(=trading volume)
　◆Even a 30-minute extension of morning trading hours will increase the volume of trading by 6 percent. 午前の取引時間を30分延長しただけでも、売買高は6%増える見込みだ。
　volume on the First Section of the Tokyo Stock Exchange　東証第一部の出来高　(=volume on the main section)

◆Volume on the First Section of the Tokyo Stock Exchange has exceeded the 1 billion mark for 42 business days in a row as of Monday, the longest period on record. 東京証券取引所第一部の出来高は、月曜日の時点で、42営業日連続で10億株の大台を超え、過去最長記録となった。

voluntary　(形)任意の, 自主的な, 自発的な, 自由意志による, 無償の
　commence a voluntary insolvency [bankruptcy] proceeding　自己破産手続きを開始する, 自己破産手続きを取る
　go into voluntary liquidation　任意清算手続きに入る
　petition of voluntary bankruptcy　自己破産の申し立て
　put A into voluntary administration　A社を任意清算する
　voluntary accumulation plan　任意積立プラン, 任意累積方式
　voluntary adjustment　自主調整
　voluntary agreed rate　自主協定金利
　voluntary closure　自主廃業
　voluntary contribution　自発的寄付
　voluntary conveyance　任意譲渡, 無償譲渡
　voluntary conveyance of estate in land　無償不動産譲渡
　voluntary credit restraint program　自主的信用抑制策
　voluntary depreciation　任意償却
　voluntary dissolution　任意解散　(=voluntary winding up)
　voluntary export restraint　輸出自主規制
　voluntary foreign credit restraint　対外融資自主規制措置
　voluntary grantee　無償被譲渡人, 無償被譲渡者
　voluntary grantor　無償譲渡人, 無償譲渡者
　voluntary health insurance　任意健康保険
　voluntary insurance plan　任意保険制度
　voluntary investment　意図した投資
　voluntary maximum limit　(金利などの)自主規制限度
　voluntary payment　自発的支払い
　voluntary repurchase　自発的買戻し
　voluntary reserves　任意積立金
　voluntary restriction　自主規制
　voluntary retirement　希望退職
　voluntary savings　自発的貯蓄
　voluntary settlement　任意清算

voluntary bankruptcy　自己破産
　◆Under the program of a voluntary liquidation for individuals, housing loan borrowers' voluntary bankruptcies can be prevented by having financial institutions waive repayment of their mortgages. 個人向け私的整理の制度だと、金融機関に住宅ローンの返済を免除させることによって、住宅ローンの借り手の自己破産を防ぐことができる。

voluntary cash payment　任意現金支払い
　◆Common shares may also be purchased at the average market price by voluntary cash payments of as little as US $40 to a maximum of US $4,000 during a quarter. 当社の普通株式は、1四半期に最低40米ドルから最高4,000米ドルでの範囲で、任意現金支払いにより平均市場価格で購入することもできます。

voluntary liquidation　任意清算, 任意整理, 私的整理, 自主解散　(=voluntary winding up)
　◆In November 1997, Yamaichi Securities Co. opted for voluntary liquidation after huge off-the-book liabilities surfaced. 1997年11月に山一証券は、多額の簿外債務が表面化したのを受けて、任意清算を選択した。◆Shareholders did not approve of voluntary liquidation of the company. 株主は、同社の任意整理を承認しなかった。

voluntary liquidation for individuals　個人向け私的

整理
◆Under the program of a voluntary liquidation for individuals, housing loan borrowers' voluntary bankruptcies can be prevented by having financial institutions waive repayment of their mortgages. 個人向け私的整理の制度だと、金融機関に住宅ローンの返済を免除させることによって、住宅ローンの借り手の自己破産を防ぐことができる。

voluntary organization　任意組合
◆This investment fund is a voluntary organization on the Civil Code and does not have corporate status. この投資ファンドは、民法上の任意組合で、法人格がない。

vote　(動)投票する, 票決する, 投票する, 議決する, 株式の議決権を行使する, 提案する
　vote against　～に反対の投票をする, ～に反対票を入れる
　vote down　否決する, 投票で否決する
　vote for　～に賛成の投票をする, ～に賛成票を入れる, ～を提案する
　vote in　投票で選出する
　vote in favor of　～に賛成票を入れる
　vote off [out]　投票で解任する
　vote on　～に投票を行う, ～に投票する
　vote one's share　議決権を行使する
　vote yes　賛成の票を投じる
◆Holders of preferred shares do not have the right to vote, but are paid dividends on a priority basis. 優先株主[優先株式の所有者]には議決権はないが、普通株に優先して配当が支払われる。◆Shareholders can access the company's special Web site and vote on decisions, including the election of board members. 株主は、同社専用のホームページを利用して、取締役選任などの議決に投票することができる。◆The Proxy Statement includes biographies of the Board's nominees for director and their principal affiliations with other companies or organizations, as well as the items of business to be voted on at the Annual Meeting. 議決権代理行使勧誘状には、定時株主総会で票決される議案のほかに、取締役会で選出された取締役候補者の略歴や取締役候補者の他の会社・組織との主な協力・兼任関係などが記載されている。

voting　(名)投票, 投票権行使, 議決権行使
　nonvoting redeemable preferred stock　無議決権償還優先株式
　nonvoting share　無議決権株　(=nonvoting stock)
　nonvoting stock [share]　無議決権株
　online voting　電子投票, Eメールでの投票 (=e-vote, electronic voting)
　super voting share　複数議決権株式
　voting agreement　議決権契約, 票決契約
　voting bond　議決権付き社債
　voting by proxy　代理人による議決権の行使
　voting security　議決権付き証券, 議決権のある証券
　voting stock　議決権株式, 議決権株, 議決権付き株式 (=voting share)
　voting trust　議決権信託(議決権株式の管理を目的とした信託)
　voting trust certificate　議決権信託証書, VTC
　voting trustee　議決権受託者
　voting upon stocks　株式に基づく投票

voting power　議決権, 投票権　(=voting right: 株主が会社の総会で各種の重要な決議に参加できる権利のこと。一般に、普通株式1株につき1個の議決権が与えられている)
◆China's stake at the World Bank in terms of voting power will climb from 2.78 percent to 4.42 percent. 中国の世界銀行での議決権比率が、現在の2.78%から4.42%に増える。

voting right　議決権, 投票権
　(=voting power; ⇒control動詞, in terms of)
　carry a voting right　議決権を持つ, 議決権が付いている[付与されている]
　common stock with voting rights　議決権付き普通株, 議決権を持つ普通株
　delegate a voting right　議決権を委任する
　exercise one's voting rights　議決権を行使する (⇒exercise)
　expanded voting rights in the IMF　IMFでの投票権拡大
　hold a majority of voting rights　過半数議決権を保有する
　in terms of voting rights　議決権ベースで
　stockholder's voting right　株主議決権
　substitutional exercise of voting right　議決権の代理行使
　voting right certificate　議決権証書
◆Preferred stocks usually do not carry voting rights but have preference over common stocks in the payment of dividends and liquidation of assets. 優先株には通常、議決権は与えられないが、配当の支払いや清算時の残余財産の分配を普通株より優先して受けられる権利がある。◆The company is considering acquiring at least 33.4 percent of Fuji Television Network Inc. shares in terms of voting rights. 同社は現在、議決権ベースで[議決権比率で]33.4%以上のフジテレビ株取得を検討している。

voting share　議決権株式, 議決権株, 議決権付き株式
　(=voting stock: 議決権が付いている株式のこと)
◆Citigroup Japan currently owns 67.2 percent of Nikko Cordial's outstanding shares, or 68 percent in terms of the number of voting shares. シティの日本法人、シティグループ・ジャパンは現在、日興コーディアルの発行済み株式の67.2%(議決権比率で68%)を保有している。◆The firm will have an initial ownership of forty percent of the voting shares of the joint venture company. 同社の当初の出資比率は、合弁会社の議決権付き株式の40%とする方針だ。◆Under the plan, the government will acquire the right to have the preferred stock converted into common stock with voting rights in the future. この案では、国が優先株を将来的に議決権付き普通株式に転換する権利を持つことになる。

voting stock　議決権株式, 議決権株, 議決権付き株式
　(=voting share: 議決権が付いている株式のこと)
　voting stock authorized　授権された議決権付き株式

voucher　(名)領収書, 証明書, 証拠書類, 証票, 商品引換券, クーポン券, 保証人
　cancelled vouchers　使用済み証拠書類
　cash voucher　現金引換え票, 金券, 領収書
　cash voucher shop　金券ショップ
　expense voucher　経費伝票
　gift voucher　商品券
　highly negotiable cash vouchers　換金性の高い金券類
　negotiable voucher　外部取引証憑(しょうひょう)[証票]
　petty cash voucher　小口現金伝票
　sales voucher　売上伝票
　voucher check register　証憑式当座預金支払い帳
　voucher register　証票書類
　voucher trading　支払い保証書を利用した消費者金融
◆Fabricated credit cards have been illegally used at electrical appliances discount stores and cash voucher shops in Japan after the security breach was revealed in the United States. 米国で不正侵入が明らかになった後、偽造されたクレジット・カードが日本の家電量販店や金券ショップなどで不正に使用されている。◆The repurchasing method, which has customers buy highly negotiable cash vouchers, violates the industry rule. 顧客に換金性の高い金券類を購入させる買取り

方式は、業界の規約に違反する。

vow （動）誓う, 誓約する, 公約する, 明言する, 断言する
◆Financial chiefs from the Group of 20 advanced and major developing countries vowed to avoid a global currency war. 主要20か国・地域（G20）の財務相・中央銀行総裁が,（各国が自国通貨を安くすることで輸出競争力を高め, 景気回復をめざす）世界の通貨安競争を避けることを公約した。

vulnerable （形）傷つきやすい, 攻撃されやすい,（病気などに）かかりやすい, 影響されやすい, 流動的な, 弱い, もろい, 脆弱（ぜいじゃく）な, 危険にさらされている, 無防備な
the vulnerable financial foundation of life insurance companies　生命保険会社の脆弱な経営基盤
vulnerable people such as the elderly living alone　一人暮らしの高齢者などの弱者
vulnerable situation　安定さを欠いた状況
◆Uncertainty about the future of Japan's financial system will persist until the vulnerable financial foundation of life insurance companies is rectified. 生命保険会社の脆弱（ぜいじゃく）な経営基盤を立て直さない限り, 日本の金融システムの先行きに対する不安は消えない。

vulnerable to　〜の影響を受けやすい, 〜に弱い, 〜になりやすい, 〜にもろい, 〜に無防備な, 〜の攻撃を受けやすい　（⇒susceptible to）
be more vulnerable to investor expectations　投資家の期待に振り回される度合いが大きい
be vulnerable to a hostile takeover bid　敵対的TOBに狙われやすい
be vulnerable to an economic downturn　景気後退の影響を受けやすい
be vulnerable to attacks　攻撃を受けやすい
be vulnerable to bribery　賄賂（わいろ）に弱い
◆Japan is said to be the least vulnerable to the effect the latest global financial crisis. 日本は今回の世界的な金融危機の影響をもっとも受けていない, と言われている。◆Japanese steel manufacturers are vulnerable to takeover bids because their aggregate market values are relatively low compared with their foreign counterparts. 日本の鉄鋼メーカーは, 海外勢に比べて時価総額が比較的低いため, 買収されやすい。

vulture fund　ハゲタカ・ファンド

VWAP　出来高加重平均価格, ヴィーワップ（volume weighted average priceの略）
VWAP trade　VWAP取引

W

WACC　加重平均資本コスト（weighted average cost of capitalの略。株主資本と銀行などから借りている負債を合わせた資本の平均調達コストのこと）

wade into the market　市場介入する, 市場介入を実施する
◆The government and the Bank of Japan waded into the market. 日銀・政府が, 市場介入した。

wait-and-see stance　様子見, 模様眺め, 模様眺めのスタンスを取る　（＝wait-and-see, wait-and-see attitude, wait-and-see outlook; ⇒mainstay issues）
◆Foreign investors were taking a wait-and-see stance as the U.S. stock markets were closed Monday for the Labor Day holiday. 月曜日の米国の株式市場が「労働者の日」の祝日で休場だったため, 外国人投資家は模様眺めとなった。

waive （動）（権利などを）放棄する,（債務を）免除する,（問題などを）見送る, 延ばす,（権利などの行使を）差し控える
◆Aoki Corp. is among 10 midsize general contractors whose debts have been waived by financial institutions. 青木建設は, 金融機関から債権放棄を受けている中堅ゼネコン10社の中に入っている。◆Leaders of the Group of Seven industrialized nations announced in a statement that they would waive a total of $70 billion in financial assistance to heavily indebted poor countries. G7（先進7か国）首脳は, 重債務貧困国に対する資金援助の総額700億ドルを放棄することを声明で発表した。◆The company unveiled a revival plan that asked banks to waive 99.5 billion yen in loans. 同社は, 銀行に995億円の債権放棄を求める再生計画を発表した。◆The six main creditor banks of struggling supermarket chain operator Daiei Inc. are considering as part of a rehabilitation plan to waive ￥24 billion of the ￥120 billion debts held by the retailer's ballpark and hotel businesses in the city of Fukuoka. 経営再建中の大手スーパー、ダイエーの主力取引銀行6行は, 再建計画の一部として, ダイエーが福岡市で展開する球場（福岡ドーム）とホテルの2事業が抱える1,200億円の負債のうち240億円について債権放棄を検討している。◆Under the firm's rehabilitation plan approved by the district court, financial institutions will waive 87.5 percent of the unsecured loans they extend to the firm. 地方裁判所が認可した同社の更生計画では, 金融機関が, 同社に行った無担保融資［同社に対する無担保債権］の87.5%を放棄することになっている。

waive loans　債権を放棄する, 借入金を免除する
◆According to JAL's draft rehabilitation plan, 87.5 percent of the airline's loan will be waived by its banks and other creditors. 同社の更生計画案では, 同社借金［借入金］の87.5%は, 銀行その他の債権者が免除することになる。◆Making the creditor banks waive loans to TEPCO will cause the utility to fall into capital deficiency, with liabilities exceeding assets. 取引銀行に東電への債権を放棄させると, 東電は資本不足に陥り, 債務超過になってしまう。

waive one's debt　債権を放棄する, 債務を免除する
◆Japan Airlines requested that a large sum of its debt be waived by creditor banks. 日本航空は, 債権保有銀行に巨額の債務免除を求めた。◆The company is among 10 midsize general contractors whose debts have been waived by financial institutions. 同社は, 金融機関から債権放棄を受けている中堅ゼネコン10社の中に入っている。

waive repayment of one's mortgage　住宅ローンの返済を免除する
◆Under the program of a voluntary liquidation for individuals, housing loan borrowers' voluntary bankruptcies can be prevented by having financial institutions waive repayment of their mortgages. 個人向け私的整理の制度だと, 金融機関に住宅ローンの返済を免除させることによって, 住宅ローンの借り手の自己破産を防ぐことができる。

waiver （名）権利の放棄, 債務の免除, 権利放棄の意思表示, 権利放棄証書
（⇒debt waiver, foreign debt repayments, loan waiver）
debt waiver　債権放棄, 債務免除
　（＝waiver of debt）
loan waiver　債権放棄, 債務免除
seek debt waivers from the creditor banks　取引銀行に債権放棄を求める
waiver of obligation　債務免除
waiver of premium benefit　保険料払込み免除
◆It's irrational if banks don't offer debt waivers regarding TEPCO's debt. 東電の債務について, 銀行が債権放棄をしないのはおかしい。◆The company received loan waivers totaling ￥640 million in 2010. 同社は, 2010年に総額6,400億円の債務免除を受けた。

waiver of debt　債権放棄, 債務免除
　（＝debt waiver）
◆In response to the double loan problem due to the March 11 disaster, financial institutions will be forced to share some burdens including the waiver of debts. 東日本大震災による二重ローン問題の対応策として, 債権の放棄を含めて金融機関もある程度の共同負担を強いられることになろう。◆The fi-

nancial assistance will be extended by combining a waiver of debt and a debt-for-equity swap. 金融支援は、債権放棄とデット・エクイティ・スワップ（債務の株式化）を組み合わせて行われる。

wall （名）壁, 隔壁, 垣根, ウォール
（⇒firewall［fire wall］）
　Chinese Wall　チャイニーズ・ウォール, 社内に設けられる情報の隔壁（一般に、証券会社の引受部門と営業部門間の情報の隔壁を指す）
　firewall［fire wall］　防禦（ぼうぎょ）壁, 業務隔壁, 情報隔壁, 情報漏洩（ろうえい）防止システム, ネット上のセキュリティ・システム, 不正侵入防止機能［防止装置］, 不正侵入防止ソフト, ファイアウォール
　go to the wall　破産する, 倒産する, 負ける, 失敗する, 没落する, わきへ押しやられる, 無用扱いされる
　hit the wall　行き詰まる, 限界に達する
　◆Fears about default on the Greek government bonds are smoldering as Greece's fiscal reconstruction measures hit the wall. ギリシャの財政再建策が行き詰まっているため、ギリシャ国債のデフォルト（債務不履行）の恐れがくすぶっている。◆The wall separating banking and securities businesses has been lowered through such moves as the liberalization of banks' securities brokering. 銀行と証券業の垣根は、銀行に対する証券仲介業の規制緩和などの動きで、低くなっている。

Wall Street　米国の証券市場, 米ニューヨークの株式市場, ニューヨーク株, ウォール街の証券市場, 米ニューヨークの株式中心街, 米金融街, 米金融市場, 米金融業界, 米金融界, ウォール・ストリート
　a Wall Street economist　市場エコノミスト
　investors on Wall Street　米ウォール街の投資家
　the Wall Street crash　米証券市場の暴落
　the Wall Street stock market　ウォール街の証券市場, ウォール街の株式市場
　Wall Street backers　米金融界の支援企業
　　（⇒backer）
　Wall Street bailout fund　米金融業界救済資金, 米金融化法の公的資金
　Wall Street bankers　ウォール・ストリートの金融関係者
　Wall Street plunged　ニューヨーク株は急落した
　Wall Street prices　米国の株式相場
　Wall Street projections for a profit per share　米金融街の1株当たり利益予想
　Wall Street watchers　米証券市場関係者
　　（=Wall Streeters）
　Wall Street's fear gauge　米証券市場関係者の「（心理的）恐怖指数」
　　（⇒CBOE Volatility Index（VIX））
　◆Investors on Wall Street are selling stocks with abandon as a global recession is under way. 世界的な景気後退の進行で、ウォール街の投資家は株を売りまくっている。◆On Wall Street, the Dow Jones industrial average closed at 11,326.04, on a gain of 42.74 points, or 0.4 percent, topping the previous record close of 11,299.76. ニューヨーク株式市場は、ダウ工業株平均は前日比42.74ドル（0.4％）高の1万1,326.04ドルで、前回の終値の史上最高値1万1,299.76ドルを更新して取引を終えた。◆Relatively solid retail sales figures inspired another rally on Wall Street. 小売売上高が比較的堅調だったため、ニューヨーク株式市場はまた持ち直した［ニューヨーク株は反発した］。◆The White House is ready to consider tapping a $700 billion Wall Street bailout fund to help keep the U.S. automakers afloat. 米政府は、米自動車メーカーの破たんを避けるための支援策として、7,000億ドルの金融業界救済資金（金融安定化法の公的資金）の活用を検討する用意ができている。◆U.S. President Barack Obama addressed reforming Wall Street in his first State of the Union address. オバマ米大統領は、同大統領初の一般教書演説で、ウォール街（金融街）の改革を呼びかけた［打ち出した］。◆Wall Street and Main Street might turn out to be buoyant this autumn. 米国の証券市場と国内産業は、今年の秋には活況を取り戻すかもしれない。◆Wall Street reeled from more revelations out of the U.S. government fraud case against Goldman Sachs. 米政府がゴールドマン・サックスを証券詐欺容疑で提訴して驚くべき多くの新事実が発覚したのを受けて、米金融街が動揺した。

Wall Street bailout fund　米金融業界救済資金
　◆The White House is ready to consider tapping a $700 billion Wall Street bailout fund to help keep the U.S. automakers afloat. 米政府は、米自動車メーカーの破たんを避けるための支援策として、7,000億ドルの金融業界救済資金（金融安定化法の公的資金）の活用を検討する用意ができている。

Wall Streeters　米証券市場関係者, ウォール街筋, 金融筋　（=Wall Street watchers）

wane （動）弱まる, 徐々に弱まる, 希薄化する, 衰える, 衰退［衰微］する, 消えようとしている
　◆Companies' profits wane as firms cannot raise prices to desired levels amid severe competition. 厳しい競争の中で、企業は思うように価格を上げられないため、企業の利益は薄くなっている。◆Consumer spending waned amid the global financial crisis that followed the Lehman Brothers collapse in autumn 2008. 2008年秋のリーマン・ブラザーズの破たん後に生じた世界的金融危機を受けて、個人消費が低迷した。

wane （名）弱体, 弱体化, 希薄化, 衰退, 衰微, 落ち目, 衰退期
　be on the wane　弱まっている, 弱体化している, 衰えかけている, 衰退している
　on the wane　衰えかけて, 衰退して, 落ち目になって
　underweight U.S. Treasuries　米国債の組み入れ比率を引き下げる［低くする］

ward off　避ける, 防ぐ, かわす, 払う, 寄せ付けない
　ward off a blow　打撃をかわす
　ward off hostile takeover bids　敵対的TOB（株式公開買付けによる企業買収）を防ぐ
　ward off threats　脅威をかわす
　◆The firm has scrapped its plan to invoke the nation's first poison pill scheme to ward off hostile takeover bids. 同社は、敵対的TOB（株式公開買付けによる企業買収）を防ぐための日本で最初のポイズン・ピル防衛策の実施計画を白紙撤回した。

warn （動）警告する, 注意する, 予告する
　◆Due to increasing uncertainty over the U.S. economic outlook and the yen's rise, the Bank of Japan warned of downside risks to the nation's economy. 米経済の先行きをめぐる不確実性の高まりと円高で、日銀は日本経済の下振れリスクに警戒感を示した。

warning （名）警告, 呼びかけ, 注意, 予告, 通告, 通知, 警戒, 警報, 戒め
　a warning from the market　市場の警告
　advance warning　事前の注意, 事前の警告
　discharge warning　解雇予告
　early warning system　早期警告制度, 早期警告システム
　◆S&P's announcement of a possible downgrade on the credit ratings of long-term sovereign bonds issued by 15 eurozone countries should be taken as a warning from the market. スタンダード・アンド・プアーズ（S&P）は、ユーロ圏15か国発行の長期国債格付け［信用格付け］を引下げの方向で検討していることを発表したが、これは市場の警告と受け止めるべきだ。

warrant （名）新株引受権, 株式買取り請求権, 倉荷証券, 権利証券, 権利証書, 権限証書, 証明書, ワラント
　（⇒debt security, injunction, market price, privately place, share warrant）
　arbitrage the warrant on the Japanese stock　日本株式のワラントの裁定取引を行う
　assignable subscription warrant　譲渡可能な新株引受権

証書
 bond with warrants attached 新株引受権付き社債, ワラント付き社債
 debenture with warrant ワラント債
 detachable warrant 分離型ワラント
 exercise of warrant 新株引受権の行使, ワラント行使
 issue warrants for new shares to 〜への新株予約権を発行する
 stock purchase warrant 株式買付け権, 株式買取り権
 stock warrant 新株引受権, 新株引受権付き証券, 新株引受権証券, 株式ワラント
 warrant bond ワラント債, 新株引受権付き社債, WB（=bond with warrant attached）
 ◆About 15 percent of the leading companies are studying the possibility of using a poison pill to counter a hostile takeover by using the issue of warrants. 主要企業の約15％は、新株予約権の発行などで敵対的買収に対抗するポイズン・ピル（毒薬）の導入可能性を検討している。

wary　（形）注意深い, 用心深い, 警戒する, 慎重な, 財布の紐を引き締めている, 手控えている
 （⇒public money）
 be wary of buying long-term debt 長期債の買いを手控える
 be wary over 〜に対して［関して］警戒する
 remain wary of a possible fresh round of market intervention 新たに市場介入する可能性を警戒する, 新たな市場介入の可能性を警戒する
 ◆Bank issues declined as investors remained wary over the banks' massive bad loan problems. 銀行株は、やはり巨額の不良債権問題の処理に対する投資家の警戒感から値を下げた。◆Market players remain wary of a possible yen-selling market intervention by Japanese authorities. 市場関係者は、日本当局（政府・日銀）による新たな円売り市場介入の可能性をまだ警戒している。◆U.S. taxpayers are wary of injecting a huge amount of public money into General Motors Corp. ゼネラル・モーターズ（GM）への巨額の公的資金注入に対して、米国の納税者の視線は厳しい。

wash sale　仮装売買, 偽装取引,（信用取引の）同時売買（=washed sale: 証券の売買活動を活発に見せるため、同時または短時間で買いと売りの取引を行うこと）
 ◆The consultant manipulated the company's stock price by engaging in certain prohibited practices including wash sales. コンサルタントは、仮装売買（売り注文と買い注文を同時に出す方法）などの不正行為で株価を操作した。

wasteful　（形）無駄な, 浪費の, 不経済な, 無駄の多い, 浪費する, 荒廃をもたらす, 破壊的な
 slash wasteful expenditures 無駄な支出を削減する, 無駄な歳出を削減する
 wasteful habits 浪費癖

wasteful expenditures　無駄な支出, 無駄な歳出, 歳出の無駄
 ◆The government should eliminate wasteful expenditures before implementing a tax hike. 増税を実施する前に、政府は歳出の無駄を排除すべきだ。

wasteful spending　無駄な支出, 支出の無駄
 ◆Fiscal resources of ¥1.6 trillion cannot be scrounged together simply by recasting the budget and cutting wasteful spending. 1.6兆円の財源は、予算の組替えや無駄の削減だけでは捻出（ねんしゅつ）できない。◆The budget screening for identifying wasteful spending smacked of political grandstanding. 支出の無駄を洗い出すための事業仕分けは、政治的パフォーマンスじみていた。

watch　（動）用心する, 気をつける, 注目する, 注視する, 監視する, 見張る, 警戒する
 closely watch consumption and prices 消費や物価動向を注視する
 most closely watched gauge とくに注目される指標
 watch currency developments 為替動向を見守る, 為替相場の動きを見守る
 watch for opportunities to 〜する機会を狙う
 watch market developments 市場動向を見守る, 市場の動き［市場動向］をうかがう, 市場をうかがう
 watch the exchange fluctuations 為替相場の動きを警戒する
 ◆Dealers are watching monitors at a foreign exchange trading company. 為替取引の会社では、ディーラーたちがモニターを注視している。◆Finance Minister Yoshihiko Noda indicated that he would closely watch the currency market. 野田財務相は、為替市場を注視する考えを示した。◆The exchange rate fluctuations that may follow must be vigilantly watched. 今後の為替相場の動きは、とくに警戒する必要がある。

watch list　監理ポスト　（⇒post）
 ◆The Tokyo Stock Exchange placed shares in Seibu Railway on a watch list to warn investors the company may fall under the category of "delisted." 東京証券取引所は、西武鉄道株を「上場廃止」の可能性があることを投資家に警告する「監理ポスト」に置いた［移した］。

watchdog　（名）番犬, 見張り, お目付け人, 監視人, 監視機関
 a financial watchdog 金融監視機関
 a watchdog organization 監視団体, 監視機関
 ◆Financial ministers of the ASEAN+3 welcomed the launch of a financial watchdog. ASEANプラス3（東南アジア諸国連合と日本、中国、韓国）の財務相が、金融監視機関の発足を歓迎した。◆The financial watchdog took an additional action of criminal complaint other than administrative punishment as the bank's operations were so malicious. 同行の業務運営の仕方があまりにも悪質なので、金融監視機関の金融庁は、行政処分のほかに刑事告発の追加措置を取った。

watermark　（名）すかし, すかし模様

way　（名）方法, 手段, 方策, 仕方, やり方, 流儀, 様式, 方向, 方角, 方面, 方針, 行く末, 路線, 進路, 道筋, 規模, 要領, 点, 観点, 要因, 余地, 機会, 慣習, 風習, 慣例
 a way out （問題などの）解決法
 base way 基本給
 be already under way すでに始まっている, すでに進行している
 be on the way down 減速軌道に乗る
 be under way 進行している, 進行中だ
 clear the way for 〜を承認する, 〜を許可する
 get in the way of 〜の邪魔になる, 〜の妨げになる
 get under way 始まる
 go a long way 大いに役立つ, 出世する, 成功する
 have it both ways 二股（ふたまた）をかける, どっちに転んでも得するようにする
 in a business-like way 事務的に, てきぱきと
 in a major way 本格的に
 make way for 〜に道を譲る, 〜に道をあける
 one-way market 買い一色, 売り一色
 one-way option 一方的選択権
 one-way trade 片貿易
 open［pave］the way for 〜への道を開く, 〜の端緒を開く
 seek ways to 〜する手段を講じる
 the way things are 現状, 現状を見ると, 状況から判断して
 three-way intervention 3極の市場介入
 3-way talks 3か国協議, 3社間協議

two-way account　相互勘定
◆Investors around the world are selling stocks with abandon as a global recession is under way. 世界的な景気後退の進行で、世界中の投資家が株を売りまくっている。◆One way for a company to accomplish long-term financing is through the issuance of long-term debt instruments in the form of bonds. 会社の長期資金調達方法の一つは、社債の形で長期債務証券を発行して行われる。◆The challenge in monetary policy for countries now is shifting toward finding a way to move away from ultra-loose money policies. 現在、各国の金融政策の課題は、超金融緩和政策からいかに転換するかに移りつつある。◆These steps of the government would go some way to protecting jobs. これらの政府対策は、雇用の確保にある程度の効果はあるだろう。◆To enhance the stimulating effect of the Fed's rate cuts, swift implementation of fiscal and tax stimulus measures, including tax cuts on investment designed to reinvigorate the stock market, is necessary in addition to the large-scale tax cut program that is under way. 米連邦準備制度理事会(FRB)の金利引き下げの刺激効果を高めるためには、現在実施中の大型減税プログラムに加え、株式市場を再活性化するための投資減税など、財政・税制面からの景気刺激策の速やかな実施が必要である。◆To offer customers a new way to purchase insurance, nonlife insurance companies have begun cooperating with cell phone companies. 顧客に保険加入のための新サービスを提供するため、損害保険各社は、携帯電話会社との提携に乗り出した。◆U.S. federal antitrust regulators have cleared the way for the proposed merger between Sony Music Entertainment and BMG, the music unit of the German media conglomerate Bertelsmann AG. 米連邦反トラスト規制当局(米連邦取引き委員会)は、ソニーと独複合メディア大手ベルテルスマンの音楽部門のBMGとの事業統合案を承認した。

way　(副)はるかに, ずっと, かなり
　be way beyond　～をはるかに超える
　be way more than　～よりずっと多い, ～をはるかに上回る
　◆The massive figure of tax revenue shortfall is way beyond what local municipalities can do by cutting spending. この巨額の税収不足は、地方自治体の経費削減で対応できる範囲を大きく超えている。

ways and means　歳入財源, 財源, 手段・方法, 手段, 方法
　committee of ways and means　(議会の)財政委員会, 歳入委員会
　the House and Means Committee　米下院歳入委員会
　ways-and-means advances　(英国の)財源貸出金

weak　(形)弱い, 弱小の, 中小の, 低迷する, 軟調の, 落ち込んだ, 低下した, 減少した, 冷え込んだ, 厳しい, 悪化した　(⇒strong)
　attack a weak currency　安い通貨に売りを浴びせる
　weak activity　景気低迷
　weak assets　不良資産
　weak balance sheet　脆弱(ぜいじゃく)な財務体質
　weak capitalization　資本基盤の弱さ
　weak credit history　信用実績が低い[悪い, 乏しい]こと
　weak currency　弱い通貨
　weak economic indicators　景気減速[景気低迷]を示す指標
　weak economy　景気低迷, 景気の悪化, 景気減速, 景気後退, 景気回復が遅いこと, 経済の低迷
　weak jobs[employment]data　雇用統計の悪化　(⇒speculation)
　weak loan demand　借入需要の低迷
　weak market　弱気相場, 弱気市場
　weak performance　伸び悩み
　weak stock market　株式市場の低迷, 軟調な株式市場
　weak tone　弱含み
　weaker credit quality obligors　信用力が低い借り手
　weaker financial institutions　弱小の金融機関
　weaker operating income　営業収益[営業利益]の減少[低下, 落ち込み]
　weaker sales　売上の減少, 販売の悪化, 販売の落ち込み, 販売低迷　(⇒stronger ton)
　◆Japan is acting weak in currency intervention. 日本は、為替介入に弱腰になっている。◆Japan's regulations on short selling and market manipulation by spreading rumors are extremely weak in comparison with those of the United States. 日本の空売りに関する規制や風説の流布などによる市場操作についての規制は、米国に比べて極めて弱い。◆The bank has been relatively weak in retail banking operations dealing with individuals and small and medium-sized firms. 同行は、個人や中小企業向けの小口取引銀行業務が比較的弱い。◆The basis for recovery remains weak. 景気回復の基盤は依然、弱いままだ。◆The main cause of the prolonged deflation is that consumer demand has been weak due to the current economic slump. デフレ長期化の主因は、現在の不況で消費需要が低迷していることだ。◆The U.S. dollar is weaker against major currencies. 米ドルが、主要通貨に対して弱体化[軟化]している。

weak demand　需要薄, 需要低迷, 需要減退
　◆The ADB lowered its 2011 growth forecast in Asian nations due to growing worries about weak demand from key trading partners including the United States and Europe. アジア開発銀行(ADB)は、主要貿易相手国である欧米で需要減退[需要低迷]懸念が高まっていることから、アジアの2011年の成長見通し[GDP成長率見通し]を下方修正した。

weak dollar　ドル安　(⇒speculative selling)
　◆The weak dollar is an obvious boost for the U.S. export drive. ドル安は、確かに米国の輸出促進の支援材料だ[米国の輸出促進にプラスになる]。◆Weak dollar could spark a global recession. ドル安は、世界的な景気後退[不況]に火をつける可能性もある。

weak yen　円安　(=weakened yen)
　◆Japanese exporting firms have been enjoying positive earnings, benefiting from thriving markets in the United States and the weak yen. 日本の輸出企業は、米国の好調な市場と円安を追い風に、好業績が続いている。◆The weak yen helped increase exports. 円安が、輸出増加につながった。

weaken　(動)悪化させる, 低下させる, 下げる, 軟化させる, 弱める, 抑える　(自動)弱くなる, 弱まる, 軟化する, 弱化する, 弱体化する, 低迷する, 悪化する, 下落する, 低下する, 減少する　(⇒heft)
　the dollar rapidly weakens　ドル安が急速に進む
　weaken against the euro　対ユーロで弱含みとなる
　weaken the balance sheet　財務内容[バランス・シート]を悪化させる
　weaken the dollar　ドル高を抑える
　◆Joint intervention by Japan and European countries in the currency markets is possible as the dollar rapidly weakens. ドル安が急速に進んでいることから、為替市場への日欧協調介入もあり得る。◆Rating agency Moody's may place a negative outlook on French government's Aaa debt rating as the government's financial strength has weakened. 格付け会社のムーディーズは、フランス国債のAaa(トリプルA)格付けについて、仏政府の財務体質[財務力]が弱まっているため「ネガティブ(弱含み)」の見通しを示す可能性がある。◆The current appreciation of the yen, if left unabated, would slow the recovery of the economy, causing the stock market to weaken. 現在の円高がこのまま進行すれば、景気回復に水を差し、株安を招くことになる。◆The dollar weakened against the euro.

ドルが、対ユーロで弱含みとなった［ドルの対ユーロ相場は下落した］。◆The effect of the yen-selling market intervention implemented unilaterally by Japan has already weakened. 日本が単独で実施した円売り介入［市場介入］の効果は、すでに薄らいでいる。◆The global economy is weakening. 世界的に、景気は弱含みとなっている。◆The purchase of foreign bonds is considered an effective method to weaken the yen. 外債の購入は、円安誘導効果を持つとされている。

weakened （形）弱まった、軟化した、弱体化した、低迷した、悪化した、下落［低下、減少］した、〜の軟化［弱体化］、〜の低迷［悪化］、〜の下落［低下、減少］
　weakened asset quality　資産の質の悪化
　weakened balance sheets　財務状況の悪化
　weakened cash flows　キャッシュ・フローの低迷
　weakened credit position　信用状態の悪化
　weakened demand　需要低迷、需要の減退、需要の軟化
　weakened financial position　資金繰り［財務状況］の悪化、資金ポジションの悪化
　weakened financial system　金融システムの弱体化
　weakened profitability　収益性の低下

weakened euro　ユーロ安
（＝the depreciation of the euro）
◆A weakened euro buoyed the economy of Germany, which relies heavily on exports. ユーロ安で、輸出に大きく依存しているドイツ経済が浮揚した。

weakened financial strength　財務の悪化、財務力の低下
◆Money loaned by private banks declined because banks with weakened financial strength were less willing to lend, besides a lack of businesses seeking expansion through borrowing. 民間銀行の貸出金が減ったのは、お金を借りてまで事業を拡大しようとする企業がなかったほか、財務が悪化した銀行が貸し渋ったからだ。

weakened U.S. dollar　ドル安、米ドルの弱体化
◆A weakened U.S. dollar means a weakened America. 米ドルの弱体化［ドル安］は、米国の弱体化を意味する。

weakened yen　円安（＝weaker yen）
◆The weakened yen helped Toyota's profit increase by ¥300 billion. 円安が、トヨタの3,000億円増益を後押しした。

weakening （形）減退する［減退している］、軟化する、弱体化する、低迷する、悪化している［悪化する］、下落［低下、減少］している　（名）減退、軟化、弱体化、低迷、悪化、下落［低下、減少］
　a weakening U.S. dollar　ドル安
　the already-weakening private consumption　すでに低調だった個人消費
　the weakening of the dollar　ドル安
　the weakening of the yen　円安
　weakening asset quality　資産の質の悪化、資産内容の悪化（＝asset quality weakening）
　weakening credit demand　信用需要の減退
　weakening credit position　信用状態の悪化
　weakening demand　需要の減退、需要の軟化、需要低迷
　weakening economic activity　景気の軟化、景気減速、景気低迷
　weakening economy　景気低迷、景気鈍化
　weakening in activity　景気減速
（＝weakening economic activity）
　weakening in the financial position　資金ポジションの悪化
　weakening in the inflation figures　インフレ率の低下傾向
　weakening market　市場低迷

weakening dollar　ドル安
◆We must avoid hindering the export-led economic recovery, speeding up deflation and increasing bad loans, which can be brought about by falling stock prices and the weakening dollar. 株安とドル安がもたらす可能性がある輸出頼みの景気回復の挫折、デフレ加速、不良債権の拡大を、われわれは避けなければならない。

weakening exchange rates for the won　ウォンの為替相場の下落、ウォン安
◆South Korea's Hyundai Motor Co. expanded its business on the back of weakening exchange rates for the won. 韓国の現代自動車は、ウォン安の追い風を受けて事業を拡大した。

weakening of the dollar　ドル安
◆A series of accounting scandals and delays in the recovery of corporate performance are accelerating falls in stock prices on the U.S. markets, along with the weakening of the dollar. 一連の［相次ぐ］企業会計の不祥事と企業業績回復の遅れで、米国の株安とドル安が加速している。

weakening trend　減少［下落］基調、減少［下落］傾向
◆The euro temporarily strengthened on the foreign exchange market but soon eased back to a weakening trend. ユーロの為替相場は、一時的に上昇したが、すぐに安値に戻った。

weaker asset　不良資産
◆GM's weaker assets will be liquidated through the New York Bankruptcy Court. GMの不良資産は、ニューヨーク破産裁判所を通じて清算される。

weaker conditions in regional economies　地域経済の悪化
◆Ten of 12 Fed district banks reported weaker conditions or declines in their regional economies. 全米12地区連銀のうち10連銀が、各地域経済の悪化あるいは地域経済活動の低下を報告した。

weaker dollar　ドル安
◆The United States is under pressure to make some difficult monetary policy decisions to cool down the overheating economy by countering the inflationary pressures stemming from higher import prices due to the weaker dollar. 米国は現在、ドル安での輸入価格の高騰によるインフレ圧力を抑えて過熱気味の景気を鎮めるための難しい金融政策の決断を迫られている。

weaker dollar against the euro　ドル安・ユーロ高
◆A weaker dollar against the euro led to a rise in the assessment value of assets denominated in the single European currency. ドル安・ユーロ高で、（保有する）ユーロ建て資産のドル換算額が増えた。

weaker sales　販売低迷
◆The company lowered its full-year profit forecast by 6 percent on a stronger yen and weaker digital camera sales. 同社は、円高やデジカメの販売低迷で、通期利益予想を6％下方修正した。

weaker yen　円安
　benefit from the weaker yen　円安が追い風になる
　currency translation effect of the weaker yen　円安の為替換算の影響
◆The weaker yen until recently had been the only lifesaver for the export-reliant economy and stock prices. これまでの円安は、輸出頼みの景気と株価の「唯一の救命ボート」だった。

weakness （名）弱み、短所、弱点、脆弱（ぜいじゃく）性、弱含み、低下、落ち込み、減少、軟化、下落、低迷、減速
　cyclical weakness　景気後退による低迷
　economic weakness　景気低迷、景気減速
　organizational weakness　組織上の弱点
　share price weakness　株価低迷、株価の軟化［下落］
　the weakness of economies overseas　海外経済の減速
　weakness in output　生産低下、生産の低迷
◆Economic weakness is spreading in Japan, Europe and other major overseas markets. 日本や欧州などの主要海外市場では、景気低迷が拡大している。◆Export growth has

slowed due to the high value of the yen and the weakness of economies overseas. 円高と海外経済の減速で、輸出の伸びが鈍った。◆Labor costs, often cited as a major weakness of Japanese companies, have been falling. 日本企業の大きな弱点とされる人件費は最近、減少している。◆The recent circumstances facing the nation's megabanks have shown up their weaknesses, as shown by slow progress in their efforts to write off their nonperforming loans and a sharp decline in their stock prices. 日本のメガバンク（巨大銀行グループ）が直面している最近の状況を見ると、不良債権処理策の遅れや株価の急落などが示すように、メガバンクの脆弱（ぜいじゃく）性が目立っている。

wealth （名）富, 資産, 財産, 富裕, 資源, 価値のある産物 （⇒sovereign wealth fund）
 a man of wealth　資産家, 財産家, 金満家
 a protection of wealth　資産の保全, 安全資産
 beginning-of-period wealth　期首の財産額, 期首資産 （=initial wealth）
 capital wealth　資本資産, 資本財産
 corporate wealth　企業資産
 end-of-period wealth　期末の財産額, 期末資産 （=terminal wealth）
 expected wealth　期待資産, 期待資産価値
 expected wealth value　期待資産価値
 financial wealth　金融資産
 fixed wealth　固定資産
 gather［attain to］wealth　富を積む
 income and wealth　所得と資産, 所得と富
 investable wealth　投資可能資産
 liquid wealth　流動資産
 material wealth　物的資産
 maximization of wealth　富の極大化 （=wealth maximization）
 maximize shareholder wealth　株主の富を極大化する, 株主の富を最大限に増やす, 株主の資産［資産価値］を最大限に高める［増やす］
 monetary wealth　金融資産, 貨幣的資産
 national wealth statistics　国富統計
 net national wealth　国民純資産
 nonmonetary wealth　非貨幣的資産
 paper wealth　金融資産
 per capita wealth　1人当たり資産
 personal wealth　個人の富, 個人資産
 protection of wealth　資産の保全, 安全資産
 real wealth　実質資産, 実質財産
 replacement wealth　再取得資産
 shareholder wealth　株主の富, 株主の資産, 株主の資産価値
 terminal wealth　期末の財産額 （=end-of-period wealth）
 vast wealth　巨万の富, 豊富な資産［財産］
 wealth distribution　富の分配［配分］, 資産の分配 （=distribution of wealth）
 wealth holder　資産所有者［保有者］
 wealth management　資産管理, 資産運用 （⇒crown jewel）
 wealth maximization　資産価値極大化, 資産の極大化, 富の極大化 （=maximization of wealth）
 wealth redistribution　富の再分配
 wealth tax　富裕税
◆Demand for bullion as a protection of wealth has been spurred by mounting concern that the global economy is faltering. 世界経済低迷への懸念増大から、安全資産［資産保全］としての金の需要が拡大している。◆The government is aiming to prevent excessive outflows of national wealth to countries rich in natural resources. 政府は、資源国への行き過ぎた国富流出の防止を目指している。◆Wealth has been boosted by rallies in stock and bond markets. 株式相場と債券相場の急騰［上昇］で、資産が増加している［資産が膨らんでいる］。

wealth effect　資産効果, 富効果
 expected wealth effect　期待資産効果
 negative wealth effect　逆資産効果
 nonmonetary wealth effect　非貨幣的資産効果
 real wealth effect　実質資産効果
◆The so-called negative wealth effect refers to the drop in the value of land, stocks and other assets. いわゆる「逆資産効果」とは、土地や株その他の資産価格の下落のことをいう。

wealth management business　資産管理業務, 資産運用業務
◆Citigroup's retail brokerage, Smith Barney, was once the crown jewel in its wealth management business. シティグループの個人向け証券会社「スミスバーニー」は、以前はシティグループの資産運用業務の最優良資産だった。

wealthfare　（名）法人・資産家の優遇, 富者優遇

wealthiest nation　最富裕国

weather　（動）（困難などを）切り抜ける, 乗り切る, しのぐ, 克服する, ～に耐える, 風化させる, 変色させる
 weather a recession　不況を乗り切る
 weather economic turmoil　経済の困難を切り抜ける
 weather strong yen appreciation　円高を克服する
 weather tough times　困難な［厳しい］時期を切り抜ける
◆Banks must improve their own strength to weather business crises. 銀行は、自らの体力を強化して、経営危機を乗り切らなければならない。

weather derivative　天候デリバティブ
解説 **天候デリバティブ**とは：掛け捨ての新型天候保険。1997年にアメリカで開発され、日本では三井海上火災保険（現・三井住友海上火災保険）が1999年に雪不足を心配するスキー用品販売会社向けに商品化したのが最初。天候デリバティブに使われるのはオプションというデリバティブで、企業などが保険料に相当するオプション料を払って、気温や降水量などの天候が補償の条件を満たせば補償金を受け取る権利を買う仕組みになっている。

web　（名）網状組織, 網, 入り組んだもの, クモの巣, わな, たくらみ, 水かき, ひと巻きの印刷用紙
 a tangled web　複雑に絡み合った状態
 a web of　複雑に絡（から）み合った, 複雑に交錯（こうさく）した
 a web of deceit　たくらみのワナ, うそ八百
◆It is difficult to deal with the latest unrest in global financial markets because it has been caused by a complex web of factors. 今回の世界的な金融市場混乱への対応が難しいのは、混乱を招いている要因が複雑に絡み合っているからだ。

Web［web］　（名）ネット上の情報通信網, ホームページ, ウェブ （=homepage, www）
 Web-based stock trading　株のネット取引, 株のオンライン取引 （=Net share trading, online stock trading; ⇒ online stock trading business）
 Web connection　インターネット接続, ホームページ接続
 Web marketing　ウェブ・マーケティング （=Internet marketing）
 Web retailer　ネット販売業者, ネット・ショッピング業者
 Web sales　ホームページ販売, ネット販売

Web account　ウェブ口座, ホームページ上の口座, インターネット口座
◆An individual investor began depositing money in U.S. dollars using a major bank's Web account. 個人投資家が、

大手銀行のウェブ口座［インターネット口座］を利用して米ドルの外貨預金を始めた。
Web donations ネット献金
   (=donations via Internet, online donations)
   ◆Web donations allow people to make personal contributions to politicians without leaving their homes. ネット献金の場合は、自宅にいながら政治家に個人献金することができる。
Web site ホームページ，ウェブ・サイト，サイト
   (=homepage, Web page, website)
   create a Web site   サイトを立ち上げる
   investment Web site   投資情報サイト，投資サイト
   subscription Web site   有料サイト，有料ウェブ・サイト
   ◆A boom in stock investing among working women has led a number of women to create Web sites and publish guides targeted at this growing market. 働く女性たちの間での株式投資ブームで、この成長市場向けサイトを立ち上げたり、指南本を出したりする女性が増えている。◆Four credit card holders received bills for accessing subscription Web sites via cell phones even though they had no recollection of doing so. 利用した覚えがないのに、携帯電話の有料サイトの利用代金請求書が、4人のクレジット・カード会員に届いた。◆In phishing, offenders lure victims to fake financial institution Web sites to enter their account PINs and other account information. フィッシングでは、犯人が被害者を金融機関の偽ホームページに誘導して、被害者の口座の暗証番号などの口座情報を入力させる。◆Shareholders can access the company's special Web site and vote on decisions, including the election of board members. 株主は、同社専用のホームページを利用して、取締役選任などの議決に投票することができる。
weight （名）重量，重み，負担，圧迫，重荷，加重値，構成比率，組入れ比率，重要性，ウエイト［ウェート］
   capital weight   リスク・ウエイト
   credit risk weight   与信リスクのウエイト
   equity weights   株式の組入れ比率
   residual maturity weights   残余期間ウエイト
   risk weight   リスク・ウエイト
   security weights   証券の組入れ比率
   ◆A steady annual improvement in earnings of five percent or more is a reasonable goal given the weight of regulated companies in our asset base. 年5%以上の利益増加率の安定確保は、規制対象企業が当社の資産構成で大きな比重を占めていることから、妥当な目標と言えるでしょう。
weighted （形）加重した，ウエイトを付けた
   capitalization weighted   市場価値加重
   capitalization-weighted   時価総額型の
   market capitalization-weighted performance indices   時価総額加重平均指数
   market value weighted index   市場価値加重平均指数
   risk weighted asset   リスク調整後資産
   weighted index   加重指数，加重平均ベースの指数
   (=weighted index number)
   weighted mean   加重平均 (=weighted average)
   zero weighted issue   リスク・ウエイトがゼロの債券
weighted average 加重平均，総平均，等価平均
   arithmetic weighted average   加重平均
   compound stock price based on weighted average   加重平均株価
   compound yield based on weighted average   加重平均利回り
   weighted average common shares outstanding   発行済み普通株式の加重平均株式数
   weighted average cost of capital   加重平均資本コスト，WACC
   weighted average discount rate   加重平均割引率
   weighted average interest rates on short-term borrowings   短期借入金の加重平均金利
   weighted average life   加重平均償還期間
   weighted average method   加重平均法，総平均法
   weighted average number of shares outstanding   発行済み株式数の加重平均，発行済み加重平均株式数
   weighted average price   加重平均価格
   weighted average time   加重平均期間
weighted average number of common shares outstanding   発行済み株式数の加重平均，社外流通普通株式の加重平均株式数
   ◆Earnings per common share are based on the weighted average number of shares outstanding. 普通株式1株当たり純利益は、発行済み株式数の加重平均に基づいて計算されています。
weighting （名）ウエイト付け，加重付け，株式・債券の組入れ比率，構成比率，調整手当て，加算手当て，付加価値，リスク・ウエイト［リスク・ウェート］
   add weighting   ウエイトを引き上げる
   bond weightings   債券の組入れ比率
   capital adequacy weighting   自己資本比率規制のリスク・ウエイト
   currency weighting   通貨別構成比率，通貨別構成比
   increase equity weightings   株式の組入れ比率を引き上げる
   index weighting   指数の組入れ比率
   portfolio weighting in U.S. stocks   米国株の運用比率
   reduce equity weightings   株式の組入れ比率を引き下げる
   reduce weighting   ウエイトを引き下げる
   risk weighting   リスク・ウエイト
   weighting allowance   地域手当て，地域調整手当て
   weighting in equity   株式の組入れ比率
   ◆Fifty-six percent of fund managers reduced their portfolio weightings in U.S. stocks. ファンド・マネージャーの56%が、米国株の運用比率を下げた。
welfare pension plan 厚生年金，福祉年金，厚生［福祉］年金制度
   ◆Pension premiums of full-time housewives of company employees and public servants are automatically covered by payments made by all subscribers to welfare and mutual pension plans. 会社員や公務員の専業主婦の年金保険料は、厚生年金や共済年金の加入者全員の支払い金で自動的にカバーすることになっている。
whammy （名）縁起の悪いこと，ジンクス
   double whammy   二重苦，ダブルパンチ
   put a [the] whammy on   ～を役立たなくする，～の運を悪くする，～にけちをつける，～に呪いをかける
   triple whammy   三重苦
   ◆In spite of Japan's triple whammy of the tsunami- nuclear crisis, electricity shortages and political breakdown, the yen has sharply strengthened. 日本は現在、津波・原発災害、電力不足、政治機能停止の三重苦に直面しているにもかかわらず、円は急騰している。
when, as, and if issued   発行日取引
   (=when issued)
when distributed   売出日取引，WD
when issued   発行日取引，WI （when, as, and if issuedの略称）
whistle-blow （動）内部告発する，密告する，止めさせる，中止させる，待ったをかける，取り締まる
   ◆The tasks of safety management specialists in the field of financial services are essentially to whistle-blow and stop extending risky loans. 金融サービス分野での安全管理専門家

の仕事は、基本的に高リスク融資に待ったをかけてそれを止めさせることだ。

whistle-blowing (名)内部告発, 密告, たれこみ, 止めさせること, 中止させること, 取締り

white (形)白い, 空白の, 公認の, ホワイト
 white book　白書
 white contract　1年物先物, ホワイト（1年物先物）, ホワイト
 white market　公認市場
 white money　銀貨, 洗浄資金, 非合法資金
 white paper　白書
 white return　白色申告
 white squire　純白の従者, ホワイト・スクワイア　（敵対的買収を未然に防ぐため、相当数の株式を買い取って株の買占めを封じたり、不振な株取引が行われていないかチェックしたりする者を指す。⇒merger and acquisition）
 White Wednesday　白い水曜日　（=Black Wednesday: 英国がEC（翌年からEU）の為替相場メカニズム（ERM）を離脱した1992年9月16日の水曜日で、この日は一般に「ブラック・ウェンズデー」と呼ばれている。しかし、この日に英国のポンドがドイツ・マルクに対して15%急落したものの、その後に英国経済が持ち直したのでホワイト・ウェンズデーとも呼ばれる）

white-hot competition　白熱した競争, 大競争
◆The commodity futures trading industry has entered an era of white-hot competition in an all-out struggle for survival. 商品先物取引業界は、生き残りをかけた総力戦で大競争の時代に入っている。

White House　米国大統領官邸, 米国政府, ホワイトハウス　（=the Executive Mansion）
◆The $374 billion shortfall marked an improvement from a $455 billion projection the White House made in July. 3,742億ドルの赤字額［米財政赤字額］は、米政府が7月に予測した4,550億ドルより改善した。◆The White House is ready to consider tapping a $700 billion Wall Street bailout fund to help keep the U.S. automakers afloat. 米政府は、米自動車メーカーの破たんを避けるための支援策として、7,000億ドルの金融業界救済資金（金融安定化法の公的資金）の活用を検討する用意ができている。

white knight　白馬の騎士, 友好的買収者, 友好的な支援者, 友好的な第三者, 友好的企業, ホワイト・ナイト　（ホワイト・ナイトは、敵対的買収を防ぐ手法として、敵対的なM&A（企業の合併・買収）にさらされている企業が、友好的な関係にある別の企業に自社を買収してもらうこと。⇒acquirer, merger and acquisition）
◆Fuji TV's action may be regarded as an attempt to form a tie-up with SBI as a "white knight". フジテレビの動きは、「ホワイト・ナイト（白馬の騎士＝友好的な第三者）」としてのソフトバンク・インベストメントとの提携を意図したもの、との見方もある。◆Myojo Foods asked Nissin Food Products to play the part of a white knight by forming a capital alliance to thwart the U.S. investment fund's hostile takeover bid. 米系投資ファンドの敵対的TOB（株式公開買付け）を阻止するため、明星食品は資本提携（ホワイト・ナイト（白馬の騎士））としての明星の支援を日清食品に要請した。◆We don't intend to volunteer to become a white knight. われわれとしては、ホワイト・ナイトを買って出るつもりはない。◆White knight is a company that saves another firm threatened by a hostile takeover by making a friendly offer. ホワイト・ナイトは、友好的な買収により、敵対的買収の脅威にさらされている他企業を救済する企業のことだ。

whole (形)全体の, すべての, 全部の, 全額の, 損傷のない, 完全な, ホール　(名)全部, 全体
 for the year as a whole　通年で, 通期で
 residential whole mortgage　住宅用ホール・モーゲージ

 the whole amount borrowed　総借入額, 借入金総額
 whole insurance　全額保険
 whole life annuity　終身年金
 whole life annuity with guaranteed installment　保証期間付き終身年金
 whole liquidity position　総流動性ポジション
 whole-term insurance　終身保険

whole life insurance　終身保険（保険期間を定めないで被保険者が死亡したときに保険金が支払われる死亡保険のこと）
 interest-sensitive whole life insurance　金利敏感型終身保険
 limited payment life insurance　有限払込み終身保険
 participating whole life insurance　配当付き終身保険
 single-premium whole life insurance　一時払い終身保険
 single-premium whole life insurance policy　一時払い終身保険契約, 一時払い終身保険
 straight life insurance　普通終身保険
◆Meiji Yasuda Life Insurance Co.'s single-premium whole life insurance is one of its flagship products. 明治安田生保の一時払い終身保険は、同社の主力商品の一つだ。◆Whole life insurance means life insurance under which coverage remains in force during the insured's entire lifetime, provided premiums are paid as specified in the policy. 終身保険は、保険契約に明記されている保険料が支払われているかぎり、保障が被保険者の全生涯にわたって有効な生命保険を意味する。

whole life insurance policy　終身生命保険契約, 終身保険契約, 終身保険
◆Family insurance policy is a whole life insurance policy that provides term insurance coverage on the insured's spouse and children. 家族保険契約は、被保険者の配偶者と子どもに定期保険保障を与える終身生命保険だ。◆In the case of single-premium whole life insurance policies, policyholders make one large premium payment up front when they sign the contract. 一時払い終身保険の場合は、保険契約者が契約を結ぶ際に［契約時に］多額の保険料を前もって一括で払い込む。◆Revenues from the single-premium whole life insurance policies support the life insurer's business performance. 一時払い終身保険による収入［一時払い終身保険の収入保険料］が、同生保の業績を支えている。

whole life insurance product　終身保険商品
◆The decline in yields on whole life insurance products effectively raises premiums. 終身保険商品の利回り（予定利率）の引下げは、実質的な保険料の値上げになる。

whole loan　非証券化ローン, ホール・ローン
 whole-loan pass through　ホール・ローンのパス・スルー
 whole loan product　ホール・ローン商品
 whole mortgage loan　ホール・モーゲージ・ローン

wholesale (名)卸売り, 大企業向け, 機関投資家向け, 大口, ホールセール　(⇒retail)
 retail and wholesale markets　小口投資家向け市場と機関投資家向け市場
 wholesale bank　法人向け銀行, 大企業向け銀行, ホールセール・バンク
 wholesale banking　卸売銀行業務, 大口金融
 wholesale deposits　大口預金
 wholesale funding　ホールセール資金
 wholesale investor　機関投資家
 wholesale price index　卸売物価指数, WPI
 wholesale treasury operation　ホールセール財務運用
◆Wholesale prices rose 1.3 percent from the previous year, reflecting a jump in prices of steel and oil products. 企業物価（旧卸売り物価）指数は、鉄鋼や石油製品の価格の上昇を反映して、前年比で1.3%上昇した。

wholly own 完全所有する, 全部所有する, 完全子会社化する, 全額出資する
◆Citigroup Inc. wholly owned Nikko Cordial Corp. through a stock swap deal in January 2008. シティグループが、株式交換取引で2008年1月に日興コーディアルグループを完全子会社化した。

wholly owned subsidiary 完全所有子会社, 完全子会社, 全部所有子会社, 全額出資子会社, 100％所有子会社, 100％出資子会社, 100％子会社 （=fully owned subsidiary, fully owned unit, totally held subsidiary, wholly owned affiliate）
put ～ under one's wing as a wholly owned subsidiary ～を完全子会社として～の傘下に収める
turn ～ into a wholly owned subsidiary ～を完全子会社化する

wholly owned finance subsidiary 完全所有金融子会社, 全額出資金融子会社, 100％所有の金融子会社
◆Following the tender offer, Oji Paper would acquire the remaining Hokuetsu shares through a share swap to turn it into a wholly owned subsidiary. 株式公開買付け(TOB)後に、王子製紙は、株式交換で残りの北越製紙の株を取得して北越製紙を完全子会社化する。◆Maruha will put Nichiro under its wing as a wholly owned subsidiary through a share swap. 株式交換方式で、マルハはニチロを完全子会社としてマルハの傘下に収める。

wide （形）幅の広い, 広い, 大きい, 大幅な, ワイド
wide margin 大幅な利ざや, 高いマージン, 大幅マージン
wide opening ワイド・オープニング（売り買いが離れた状態で立会いが始まること）
wider band 為替相場変動幅の拡大, ワイダー・バンド予約, レンジ付き予約, ワイダー・バンド
wider loss 損失拡大, 赤字拡大
wider margin 為替変動幅の拡大, 拡大為替変動幅, ワイダー・マージン
wider spread over U.S. rates 米国の金利に対する格差の拡大, 米国との金利差拡大
wider spreads スプレッドの拡大
wider yield spreads over ～に対する利回り格差の拡大
◆The company expects a wider loss for fiscal 2012. 同社は、2012年度は赤字拡大を見込んでいる。

widen （動）拡大する, 広げる, 規模拡大する, 大きくする（自動）広がる, 広くなる, 大きくなる
widening current account deficit 経常赤字の拡大
widening income disparities 所得格差の拡大
widening slump in sales 販売の落ち込み拡大
◆Amid a widening slump in global auto sales and the yen's sharp appreciation against the U.S. dollar, the firm is expected to report an unconsolidated operating loss in fiscal 2011. 世界の新車販売の落ち込み拡大と急激な円高・ドル安に伴って、同社の2011年度［2010年3月期決算］の営業利益は、単独ベース［単独決算］で赤字が見込まれている。◆The Bank of Japan widened the scope of cheap loans to support smaller companies with growth potential. 潜在成長力のある中小企業を支援するため、日銀が低利融資枠を拡大した。◆The extent of reduction in prices of items excluding gasoline and food are continuing to widen. ガソリンや食料を除いた物価の下げ幅は、拡大が続いている。◆The firm's group loss widened to ¥70 billion in the six months through September. 同社の連結赤字は、9月中間決算で700億円に拡大した。

widening （名）拡大, 拡張
capital widening 資本拡張, 資本の拡張
spread widening 利回り格差の拡大, スプレッドの拡大 （=widening in［of］spreads）
widening in fluctuation bands 変動幅の拡大

widening of the trade balance 貿易赤字の拡大

wild （形）激しい, 荒れた, 狂乱の, 乱調の, 熱狂的な, 抑えきれない, 見当違いの, 突飛な, 奇抜な, 見当違いの
go through a wild period 荒れた展開となる
wild card 未知数, 波乱材料, 波乱要因, 予測できない要因, ワイルド・カード
wild inflation 狂乱インフレ, 狂乱的インフレーション
wild market 乱調市場
wild price increase 狂乱的物価高騰

wild fluctuations in foreign exchange markets 為替市場の乱高下
◆Amid the European fiscal and financial crisis, plunges on the world's stock markets and wild fluctuations in foreign exchange markets may continue. 欧州の財政・金融危機を受けて、世界同時株安と為替市場の乱高下は今後も続く可能性がある。

Williams Act ウィリアムズ法
解説 ウィリアムズ法とは：現金による株式公開買付け（tender offer, TOB）や発行済み株式の5％以上の取得を目的とした株式公開買付けに関する米国の法律。1934年証券取引所法を改正して、1968年に制定された。これらの株式公開買付けを行う場合には、その条件と目的、買付け者の経歴、資金源や株式取得後の事業計画などについて米証券取引委員会（SEC）と買取対象会社に報告することになっている。

willing （形）～する意欲がある, ～する意思がある, ～する気がある, 進んで～する
◆Money loaned by private banks declined because banks with weakened financial strength were less willing to lend, besides a lack of businesses seeking expansion through borrowing. 民間銀行の貸出金が減ったのは、お金を借りてまで事業を拡大しようとする企業がなかったほか、財務が悪化した銀行が貸し渋ったからだ。

Wilshire 5000 Equity Index ウィルシャイア5000種株価指数

win （動）勝つ, 勝ち取る, 勝ち抜く, 勝利を得る, 獲得する, 得る, もたらす
win a bidding competition for ～を競争入札で落札する
win back 取り戻す
win or lose 勝っても負けても, 結果はどうあれ
win out［through］（苦労の末に）成功する, 勝ち抜く, 勝利を収める, やり遂げる, 勝る
win the business 同案件を獲得する

win a contract 契約を獲得する, 受注する
◆The money given in 2010 was a reward for winning the contracts for construction projects. 2010年に提供された資金は、建設工事受注の見返りだった。

win profit 利益を得る, 利益を上げる
◆Participants in the market process information transmitted globally in real time, manipulate it in some cases and try to win profit by moving large amounts of money in this information war zone. 市場参加者は、リアルタイムでグローバルに伝達される情報を処理し、場合によってはそれを操作しながら、この情報戦争の戦場で巨額の資金を動かして利益を得ようとしている。

win the bid for ～で落札する
◆A Tokyo-based association of construction firms, to which about 20 small and midsize companies belonged, won the bid for ¥430.5 million. 中小の建設会社約20社が加盟する都内の建設業協同組合が、4億3,050万円で落札した。

win the global competition［competitiveness］ 国際競争を勝ち抜く, グローバル競争を勝ち抜く, 国際競争に勝つ
◆We will aim at creating a top, comprehensive financial group in the world that can win the global competition. 当社は今後、グローバルな競争を勝ち抜ける世界屈指の総合金融

グループの創造を目指す。
wind up 解散する, 清算する, 畳(たた)む, 閉鎖する, 事業停止する, 整理する, 中止する, 切り上げる, 終える, 辞める, 〜で終わる, 結局〜することになる, 結局〜する羽目になる, 最後には〜に行き着く[〜で終わる], 緊張させる, いらいらさせる
  wind up an account　口座を清算する
  wind up an ailing company　経営不振の会社を解散する
  wind up the meeting　会議を切り上げる
  ◆To wind up the ailing unit, its parent company sold some of its assets. 経営不振のこの子会社を解散するため, 親会社がその資産の一部を売却した。
windfall　(名)タナボタ利益, 思わぬ利益, 思いがけない利益, 望外の利益, 臨時利益, 偶発利益, 過剰利得, タナボタ[棚ぼた], 思いがけない幸運, 追い風　(形)意外の, 一時的な, 一回かぎりの, 臨時の
  windfall effect　偶発的効果
  windfall gains　思いがけない利益, 意外な利益, 偶発利益
  windfall loss　思いがけない損失, 意外な損失, 偶発損失
  windfall profit tax　超過所得税, 過剰所得税[利得税]
  ◆Some of the United States' biggest banks are in for a windfall on top of the $700 billion government bailout thanks to a new tax policy. 米大手銀行の一部は, 新税制のおかげで, 7,000億ドルの政府救済策[政府の救済措置]に加えて思いがけない利益を上げることになる。
window　(名)窓, 窓口, 機関, 絶好のタイミング, チャンス, 機会, ウインドー
  before the window closes　窓が閉じないうちに, チャンスが消えないうちに, 絶好の機会を失う前に, 絶好のタイミングを逃さないうちに
  discount window　割引窓口
  lending windows　融資制度
  single-currency lending windows　単一通貨建ての融資制度
  swap window　スワップの機会, 裁定の機会
  take advantage of the windows of opportunity　好機を生かす
  window guidance　窓口指導, 窓口規制
  window of opportunity　機会の窓, 窓が開く絶好のタイミング
  window ticket　番号札, 引換券
  ◆We will raise funds at the time when the window opens. 機会が訪れた時点で, 資金を調達するつもりだ。
window-dress　粉飾する, 粉飾決算する
  ◆Former executives of Kanebo, Ltd. window-dressed earnings by about ¥30 billion. カネボウの旧経営陣が, 収益約300億円の粉飾決算をしていた。◆The company transferred the deposits of two firms it would acquire to window-dress the books. 同社は, 買収予定の2社の預金を付け替えて[移し替えて]粉飾決算をしていた。
window dressing　粉飾, 粉飾決算　(=window-dressed accounts, window-dressing accounts, window dressing settlement)
  a window-dressing case　粉飾決算事件
  financial window-dressing to manipulate share prices　株価操作のための会計操作
  ◆In the past window-dressing cases, almost all the perpetrators were given suspended prison sentences. これまでの粉飾決算事件では, その遂行者に執行猶予が付くのがほとんどだった。◆Olympus Corp. has kept deceiving its shareholders and clients by years of window dressing. オリンパスは, 長年にわたる粉飾で, 株主や取引先を欺き続けてきた。◆Stock option programs are seen as leading to financial window-dressing to manipulate share prices. ストック・オプション制度は, 株価操作のための会計操作につながると見られている。

◆The total amount of window-dressing over the four years since 2005 may be more than $10 billion. 総粉飾額は, 2005年以降の4年間で100億ドルを超えると見られる。◆Years of window-dressing by Olympus to hide investment losses represent nothing but a companywide breach of trust. 投資損失隠ぺいのためのオリンパスによる長年の粉飾決算は, 会社ぐるみの背信行為にほかならない。
window-dressing accounts　粉飾決算, 会計操作, 不正会計　(=financial window-dressing)
  ◆The Bush administration is targeting chief executive officers responsible for window-dressing accounts, blaming them for the slumping U.S. stock markets. ブッシュ政権は, 株価急落(株安)の主犯は不正会計に手を染めた最高経営責任者(CEO)であるとして, 不正会計にかかわったCEO狩りに乗り出している。
wing　(名)一翼, 分派, 保護, 活動力
  spread[stretch] one's wings　能力を十分に発揮する
  under one's wing　〜の保護下に, 〜の傘下に
  ◆Maruha will put Nichiro under its wing as a wholly owned subsidiary through a share swap. 株式交換方式で, マルハはニチロを完全子会社としてマルハの傘下に収める。
winner　(名)勝ち組, 勝ち組企業, 成功企業, 勝者, 値上がり銘柄
  select the winner for　〜の発注先を選定する[決める]
  the winner of a contract　契約獲得企業, 受注者, 施工業者, 元受業者
  the winner of the bidding　落札業者, 受注者, 受注業者
  the world's winners group companies　世界の勝ち組企業
  winners and losers　勝ち組と負け組, 値上がり銘柄[値上がり銘柄数]と値下がり銘柄[値下がり銘柄数]
  ◆There were 60 winners[gainers] while losers numbered 250 losers. 値下がり株の250銘柄に対して, 値上がり株は60銘柄あった。◆These companies have been often described as winners in the age of deflation. これらの企業は, 「デフレ時代の勝ち組」と呼ばれることが多い。
wire house　大手証券会社
withdraw　(動)預金などを引き出す, 預金などを引き揚げる, 通貨などを回収する, 市場などから撤退する, 取り消す, 打ち切る, 撤回する　(⇒bailout, bogus cash card, cash, mortgage-backed securities business)
  withdraw deposits　預金を引き出す, 預金を引き揚げる
  withdraw one's funds　資金を引き揚げる
  withdraw one's investment　投資を引き揚げる
  withdraw the loans　貸付け金を引き揚げる
  ◆Customers whose assets at the bank total about ¥10 million will receive a maximum of ¥2 million in insurance if their money is withdrawn illicitly by a third party with a bogus card. 同行では, 預け入れ資産が1,000万円程度の預金者が, 第三者に偽造カードを使って不正に預金が引き出された場合には, 最大200万円の保険金が支払われる。◆In the case of this ATM card, even if a cardholder's card or PIN number are stolen, no one else can withdraw cash from the account. このキャッシュ・カードの場合は, カード会員がたとえカードや暗証番号を盗まれても, 本人以外は口座から預金を引き出せない。
withdraw funds　資金を引き出す, 資金を引き揚げる
  ◆In the conventional IMF's scheme, countries were only given a credit line even after the IMF approved loans and they could not withdraw funds unless the fiscal crisis facing them worsened. 従来のIMF(国際通貨基金)の仕組みだと, 各国は融資の承認を得ても融資枠を与えられるだけで, 財政危機が深刻化しないと資金を引き出すことができなかった。
withdraw money　金を引き出す, 金を下ろす, 払い戻す, 通貨などを回収する, 解約する
  ◆Account holders can withdraw money at will from liquid

deposits, such as ordinary deposits. 普通預金などの流動性預金から、口座保有者は金を自由に下ろすことができる。◆Personal computers of individuals and corporations were used to illegally access accounts and withdraw money. 口座に不正アクセスして現金を引き出すのに、個人や企業所有のパソコンが使われていた。◆The foreign currency depositor planned to withdraw the money when the yen's value fell. この外貨預金者は、円安になったら解約するつもりだった。

withdrawal （名）撤退, 脱退, 離脱, 撤回, 回収, 預金の引出し, 引落し, 払戻し, 取消し, 解約 (⇒cash, cash withdrawals and deposits, damage, double withdrawal)
  bank withdrawal 銀行預金引出し
  double withdrawal 二重引落し
  early withdrawal 期限前払戻し, 期限前解約
  immediate withdrawal 即時撤退, 即時撤回, 即時解約
  immediate withdrawal of the portfolio 既保険契約[再保険契約]の即時解約
  notice of fund withdrawal 資金引出通知
  withdrawal before maturity 期日前解約
  withdrawal slip for a savings account 普通預金払戻し票
  withdrawals of utility fees 公共料金の引落し
  ◆In the case of foreign currency deposits by the U.S. dollar, many online banks charge about ¥0.25 in commission per dollar at the time of deposits and withdrawals. 米ドルによる外貨預金の場合、ネット銀行の多くは、預け入れ時と解約時に1ドルに付き25銭程度の手数料を取る。◆The exchange rate was the same at the time of deposit and withdrawal in a foreign currency deposit. 外貨預金で、為替相場は預け入れ時と解約時で同じだった。◆Withdrawals of deposits at regional financial institutions have continued apace. 地域金融機関からの預金の引出し[流出]が、急速に進んでいる。

withstand （動）～に耐える, 反対する, 抵抗する
  ◆Major European banks are to take additional stress tests to examine their ability to withstand a long recession. 景気の長期低迷への耐久力を調べるため、欧州の主要銀行は再度、ストレス・テストを受けることになっている。◆The stress test of the European Banking Authority is a banking health check to ensure banks across Europe have sufficient capital to withstand another financial crisis. 欧州銀行監督機構（EBA）のストレス・テストは、欧州全域の銀行が新たな金融危機に耐えられるだけの資本金を十分に確保していることを保証するための銀行の健全性検査だ。

woes （名）苦難, 災難, 災い, 危機, 悩み, 苦悩, 苦境, 悲哀, 問題
  economic woes 経済的苦悩, 経済的苦境, 経済不振
  financial woes 財政難, 経営難, 経営危機, 金融危機 (=financial troubles)
  Greece's debt woes ギリシャの債務問題
  lingering economic woes 長引く経済的苦悩
  subprime mortgage woes サブプライム問題
  the U.S. housing loan market woes 米住宅ローン市場の低迷
  the U.S. subprime woes 米国のサブプライム（低所得者向け住宅融資）問題
  ◆Both banks ran enormous deficits for the business year to March 2011, adding to their financial woes. 両行は、2011年3月期決算で巨額の赤字になって[赤字に転落して]、財務体質が悪化した。◆In resolving Greece's debt woes, German Chancellor Angera Merkel urged substantial aid from private creditors. ギリシャの債務問題を解決するにあたって、アンゲラ・メルケル独首相は、民間債権者に大幅支援を求めた。◆The additional provisions boosted the bank's credit costs related to the U.S. housing loan market woes in the April-September period to ¥19.8 billion. 引当金の積み増しで、米住宅ローン市場低迷関連の同行の与信コストは、4-9月期で198

億円に増加した。◆The effects of an economic slowdown in industrialized countries stemming from the U.S. subprime woes could spread to the emerging economies. 米国のサブプライム（低所得者向け住宅融資）問題に起因する先進国の景気減速の影響は、新興国にも拡大する可能性がある。◆The Fed has been unable to deal with the current economic woes by changing interest rates as it has been maintaining a policy of virtually zero-percent interest rates. 米連邦準備制度理事会（FRB）はこれまで金利ゼロ政策を続けてきたため、政策金利を上げ下げして現在の経済的苦境に対応することはできなくなっている。◆The firm's huge interest-bearing debts exacerbated its financial woes. 同社の多額の有利子負債で、経営危機が悪化した[経営が圧迫された]。◆The fiscal woes of the single-currency bloc could trigger a new severe global financial crisis. 単一通貨・ユーロ圏の財政危機は、新たに重大な世界的金融危機の発生源になる可能性がある。◆The leaders of Japan, China and ROK agreed to cooperate to tackle financial woes. 日中韓首脳は、金融危機に共同で対処することで合意した。◆Toyota's operating loss highlights the unprecedented woes facing Japan's export industry. トヨタの営業赤字は、日本の輸出産業がかつてない苦境に直面していることを象徴している。

won （名）ウォン（韓国と北朝鮮の通貨単位）
  a plunge of the won ウォン安, ウォン相場の下落
  a rapid appreciation of the won 急激なウォン高
  the South Korean won 韓国のウォン
  the value of the won ウォン相場
  ◆South Korea has seen a plunge of the won against major currencies amid the worldwide financial meltdown. 世界的な金融危機に伴って、韓国では主要通貨に対してウォン相場が下落している[ウォン安となっている]。◆South Korea's Hyundai Motor Co. expanded its business on the back of weakening exchange rates for the won. 韓国の現代自動車は、ウォン安の追い風を受けて事業を拡大した。◆The South Korean won and currencies in other East Asian countries also recorded their highest values against the dollar. 韓国のウォンや他の東アジア諸国通貨の対米ドル相場も、最高値を付けた。◆The U.S. dollar has dropped sharply in value not only against the yen, but also against the euro, the South Korean won, the Thai baht and other currencies. 米ドル[米ドル相場]は、円に対してだけでなく、ユーロや韓国ウォン、タイ・バーツなどに対しても、急落している。

work on [upon] ～に取り組む, ～に精を出す, ～を手がける, ～に影響を及ぼす, ～に作用する, ～を説得する
  ◆During the past six years, Japanese companies worked on cost-cutting and other restructuring measures. 過去6年間、日本企業は経費削減[コスト削減]などのリストラ策に取り組んだ。◆The government and the Bank of Japan worked on economic policy in a coordinated manner. 政府と日銀は、経済政策で足並みをそろえて行動した。

work out （問題などを）解く, 解決する, （金額や量などを）計算する, （計画などを）立てる, 詰める, ～を計画する, よく考える, 練る, 工夫する, （～の行動を）理解する, 作り上げる, 成し遂げる, ～を掘り尽くす, （スポーツの）トレーニング[練習]をする, 結局～になる
  work out a plan to cut the fiscal deficit 財政赤字削減策をまとめる
  work out a policy of extending emergency loans to Greece ギリシャに緊急融資を行う方針を打ち出す
  ◆A suprapartisan committee set up within Congress will work out a plan to cut the fiscal deficit by $1.5 trillion while raising the debt limit by a matching amount. 米議会内に設置される超党派委員会が、1.5兆ドルの財政赤字削減策をまとめる一方、債務上限を同額引き上げる。◆Japanese firms must work out better strategies to cope with the excessive rise of the yen. 日本企業は、超円高に対応できる戦略を練る必要がある。◆The EU has been unable to work out its inherent poli-

cies concerning the fiscal deficiencies of some of its more reckless member countries. 欧州連合(EU)は、一部の無謀な加盟国の欠陥財政について、一貫した政策を打ち出せないでいる。◆The IMF and the EU have worked out a policy of extending emergency loans to Greece. 国際通貨基金(IMF)と欧州連合(EU)は、ギリシャに緊急融資を行う方針を打ち出した。◆To resolve the financial unrest in EU nations, accelerating financial sector realignment in countries such as Germany must be worked out. EU諸国の金融不安を解決するには、(2,000もの金融機関がひしめく)ドイツなどでの金融再編の加速も課題だ。

work together 協力する, 協調する, 提携する, 連携する (=band together, join together)
◆In order to prevent the chain reaction of even more devastating financial collapses, financial and monetary authorities in the United States and other nations will need to work together. これ以上の衝撃的な金融破たんの連鎖反応を防ぐには、米国と世界各国の金融・通貨当局の協調が必要だ。◆The Bank of Tokyo-Mitsubishi UFJ will work together with foreign banks to extend 117 million Canadian dollars in joint loans to a mega solar power plant construction. 三菱東京UFJ銀行は、外銀数行の主幹事銀行として[外銀数行と連携して]、カナダの大型太陽光発電所(メガソーラー)建設事業に1億1,700万カナダ・ドルを協調融資する。◆The government and the Bank of Japan will likely continue to work together in fighting the sharp rise in the yen's value. 政府と日銀は、急激な円高阻止で協調路線を継続することになりそうだ。◆Washington must work together to with the rest of the world to tackle a host of challenges. 米国は、他国と協調して多くの課題に取り組まなければならない。

workers compensation insurance system 労災保険制度, 労災保険
◆The number of applications for compensation under the workers compensation insurance system made at labor standards inspection offices nationwide increased 19 percent to 819 from 690 cases in the previous year. 全国の労働基準監督署で行われた労災保険制度に基づく給付請求の件数は、前年度の690件に比べて19%増加して819件に達した。

Workforce Investment Act of 1998 1998年労働力投資法

workplace (名)職場, 仕事場, 作業場 (=worksite)
 workplace bullying 職場の[職場での]いじめ, 職場いじめ (=bullying in the workplace)
 workplace training 現場訓練
◆Another tactic many loan sharks use is to circulate slanderous leaflets to the workplace or the school that the borrower's children attend. 多くのヤミ金融業が使うほかの手は、借り手の勤務先や子どもが通う学校への中傷文書のばらまきだ。

world (名)世界, 世間, 世の中
 investors around the world 世界中の投資家
 the banking world 銀行界
 the economic world 経済界
 world capital markets 世界資本市場
 world debt problem 累積債務問題
 world monetary conference 国際通貨会議
◆Eurozone countries have tried a series of relief measures, but worries have heightened in the world particularly with regard to the eurozone. ユーロ圏諸国は一連の救済策を取ってきたが、世界ではとくにユーロ圏に関して心配[不安]が高まっている。◆Investors around the world are selling stocks with abandon as a global recession is under way. 世界的な景気後退の進行で、世界中の投資家が株を売りまくっている。

World Bank 世界銀行, 世銀 (国際復興開発銀行 (IBRD=International Bank for Reconstruction and Development)の通称。1945年の設立で187か国が加盟。途上国や貧困国にインフラ整備などの長期資金を融資・保証するほか、経済分析や助言などを行っている)
 IBRD (World Bank) 国際復興開発銀行(世界銀行)
 World Bank bond 世銀債
 World Bank's low income category 世銀基準での低所得国
◆An American has traditionally led the World Bank while a European has led the IMF. 慣例として、世銀のトップ[世銀総裁]は米国人、IMFのトップ[IMF専務理事]は欧州人がそれぞれ占めてきた。◆The World Bank enjoys a triple-A credit rating. 世界銀行は、トリプルAの格付け(信用格付け)を受けている。◆The World Bank members decided to increase the institution's capital by $86.2 billion. 世界銀行の加盟国が、862億ドルの増資を決めた。

World Bank group 世界銀行グループ(第一世銀(IBRD)、第二世銀(国際開発協会:IDA)、第三世銀(国際金融公社:IFC)のほか、多国間投資保証機関(MIGA)、国際投資紛争調停機関(ICSSI)を指す)

World Economic Forum 世界経済フォーラム, WEF (世界各国の政財界人や学識経験者が集まって、毎年1月にスイスのリゾート地ダボスで開かれる世界経済フォーラム年次総会は、ダボス会議(Davos Conference)と呼ばれる)
◆Finance ministers and business leaders at the World Economic Forum are showing surprisingly little concern over the soaring euro and tumbling dollar. 世界経済フォーラムに出席した各国の財務相や財界指導者は、ユーロの急騰やドルの下落に驚くほど関心を示していない。◆French President Nicolas Sarkozy urged tighter financial regulations at the World Economic Forum in Davos, Switzerland. スイスのダボスで開かれた世界経済フォーラム年次総会で、ニコラ・サルコジ仏大統領は金融規制強化を求めた。

world economy 世界経済, 世界景気, 世界の景気 (=the global economy)
◆Discussion among advanced countries alone cannot cope with the challenges facing the world economy. 先進国だけの話合いで、世界経済が直面している課題に対応することはできない状況にある。◆Pressure for additional monetary easing measures will increase if the slowdown of the world economy continues. 世界的な景気減速がこのまま続けば、一層の金融緩和[金融緩和策]を求める圧力が強まるものと思われる。◆The special statement on the world economy adopted by the APEC forum specified a timeline for implementing the measures. アジア太平洋経済協力会議(APEC)で採択された世界経済に関する特別声明は、その対策実施の期限を明記した。◆The twin deficits of the United States-fiscal and current account deficits-are threatening to destabilize the world economy. アメリカの双子の赤字(財政赤字と経常収支赤字)が、世界経済の不安定要因となっている。◆The world economy may be thrown into further chaos. 世界経済は、一層混乱する恐れがある。◆The world economy will steer to a growth path again once the financial crisis subsides. 金融危機が沈静化したら、世界経済はまた成長軌道[成長経路]に向かうだろう。

World Federation of Exchanges 国際取引所連合, WFE (International Federation of Stock Exchanges(国際証券取引所連合)が2002年にWorld Federation of Exchangesに改称)

World Gold Council 世界金評議会, ワールド・ゴールド・カウンシル, WGC
◆According to the World Gold Council, central banks have bought 198 metric tons of gold so far this year. 世界金評議会によると、今年は、世界各国の中央銀行がこれまでに(2011年8月22日現在で)198メートルトン(19万8,000キログラム)の金を買い入れた。

world markets 世界の市場
◆A sense of disappointment has prevailed across the world markets as no concrete measures to rescue Greece were un-

veiled at the eurozone finance ministers meeting. ユーロ圏財務相会合でギリシャ支援の具体策が明らかにされなかったので、世界の市場で失望感が広がった。

world's stock markets 世界の株式市場
◆Amid the European fiscal and financial crisis, plunges on the world's stock markets and wild fluctuations in foreign exchange markets may continue. 欧州の財政・金融危機を受けて、世界同時株安と為替市場の乱高下は今後も続く可能性がある。

worldwide [world-wide] (形)世界的な、世界的[世界中]に広がった、世界中の、国際的に知られた、国際的規模の、世界各国の (副)世界的に、世界中に、国際的規模で
compete worldwide 世界市場で競争する
worldwide bond prices 世界的な債券相場
worldwide boom 世界的好況
worldwide business cycle 世界的景気循環
worldwide depression 世界的不況、世界不況
worldwide integration 世界的統合、世界的統合化
worldwide monetary crisis 世界の通貨危機
worldwide slump 世界的不況
worldwide standardization 世界的標準化
◆Financial markets worldwide are focused on whether the U.S. FRB embarks on a third round of its quantitative easing policy, or QE3. 世界の金融市場は、米連邦準備制度理事会（FRB）が量的緩和策の第三弾（QE3）に踏み切るかどうかに注目している。◆The U.S. Federal Reserve Board raised U.S. interest rates, leading the worldwide move to change current super-loose monetary policy. 米連邦準備制度理事会（FRB）が米国の金利を引き上げ、世界的な超金融緩和の政策転換の先陣を切った。

worldwide concern over fiscal sustainability 財政の持続可能性に対する世界の関心
◆Worldwide concern over fiscal sustainability in industrialized countries is growing in the wake of Greece's sovereign debt crisis. ギリシャの財政危機を契機として、先進国の財政の持続可能性に対する世界の関心が高まっている。

worldwide decline in stock prices 世界同時株安
◆As the Greek fiscal crisis grows more serious, there has been no halt to the worldwide decline in stock prices. ギリシャの財政危機が一段と深刻化するにつれ、世界同時株安に歯止めがかからなくなっている。

worldwide economic downturn 世界的な景気後退
◆Business conditions are rapidly deteriorating due to the global financial crisis and the worldwide economic downturn. 世界的な金融危機と世界的な景気後退で、景気は急速に悪化している。

worldwide financial crisis 世界的な金融危機、世界金融危機
◆The leaders of Japan, China and South Korea agreed to cooperate closely on tackling the worldwide financial crisis and North Korea's denuclearization. 日中韓の3か国首脳は、世界的な金融危機や北朝鮮の非核化問題への対応で緊密に連携することで合意した。◆The slowdown of Toyota indicates the disastrous extent of the worldwide financial crisis. トヨタの減速［失速］は、世界的な金融危機［世界金融危機］の猛威を物語っている。

worldwide financial meltdown 世界的な金融危機
◆South Korea has seen a plunge of the won against major currencies amid the worldwide financial meltdown. 世界的な金融危機に伴って、韓国では主要通貨に対してウォン相場が下落している［ウォン安となっている］。

worldwide recession 世界的な景気後退、世界的不況、世界同時不況、同時不況 （⇒spark）
◆The global economy at present is poised to leave behind the worldwide recession. 現在の世界経済は、同時不況を脱す

る見通しだ。

worrisome (形)面倒な、厄介な、気がかりな、悩ます、心配させる、懸念材料の
◆The yen's continued rise is worrisome for large manufacturers. 大企業・製造業には、円高進行も懸念材料だ。

worry (名)懸念、懸念材料、不安、不安材料、心配、心配事、心配の種、気苦労、悩み
a worry 懸念材料、不安材料
financial worries 金融不安
inflation worries インフレ懸念
worries about cash burn 資金枯渇への懸念、手持ち資金涸渇に対する不安
worries of the general public about their daily life 一般国民の生活不安
◆Both banks' increasing worries over the worsening of their financial woes prompted them to seek a way out by agreeing to a merger. 財務体質の悪化に対する両行の危機感から、両行は合併の合意に活路を求めた。◆Eurozone countries have tried a series of relief measures, but worries have heightened in the world particularly with regard to the eurozone. ユーロ圏諸国は一連の救済策を取ってきたが、世界ではとくにユーロ圏に関して心配［不安］が高まっている。◆The ADB lowered its 2011 growth forecast in Asian nations due to growing worries about weak demand from key trading partners including the United States and Europe. アジア開発銀行（ADB）は、主要貿易相手国である欧米で需要減退［需要低迷］懸念が高まっていることから、アジアの2011年の成長見通し［GDP成長率見通し］を下方修正した。◆Tokyo stocks bounced back Wednesday after sharp falls Tuesday following Lehman Brothers decision to file for bankruptcy as financial worries eased. 水曜日の東京株式市場は、リーマン・ブラザーズが前日に破たん申請を決めて急落したものの、金融不安が和らいだため反発した。◆Worries over the spreading of the eurozone debt crisis and the U.S.'s slipping into recession have driven the rout in financial markets. ユーロ圏の財政危機の拡大と米国の景気後退入りへの懸念で、金融市場は総崩れになった。◆Worries remain among the general public about their daily life and uncertainty over the future of the economy. 一般国民の生活不安や景気の先行きの不透明感は、まだ払拭（ふっしょく）されていない。

worsen (動)悪化する、低下する、拡大する、増大する、悪化させる
◆Business performances are worsening rapidly and substantially regardless of the type of industry. 企業業績は、業種を問わず急速に、しかも大幅に悪化している。◆If business conditions continue to worsen, financial institutions will face more newly emerging nonperforming loans than they can ever keep up with. 景気がこのまま悪化し続ければ、金融機関は新たに不良債権が生まれてその処理が追いつかなくなる。◆In the conventional IMF's scheme, countries were only given a credit line even after the IMF approved loans and they could not Withdraw funds unless the fiscal crisis facing them worsened. 従来のIMF（国際通貨基金）の仕組みだと、各国は融資の承認を得ても融資枠を与えられるだけで、財政危機が深刻化しないと資金を引き出すことができなかった。◆Investment conditions have worsened due to confusion in global financial markets in the wake of fiscal and financial crises in Europe. 欧州の財政・金融危機を受けた世界的な金融市場の混乱で、運用環境が悪化している。◆The bank's likelihood of collecting loans extended to its major corporate borrowers has worsened. 同行の大口融資先［融資先企業］に対する債権の回収見通しが、悪化した。◆There are lingering concerns that Japan's economy could worsen further still. 日本の景気がさらに底割れする心配も、まだ消えていない。

worsening (名)悪化、拡大
the serious worsening of the price situation インフレ動向の急激な悪化

the worsening of the massive trade deficit of the United States 米国の膨大な貿易赤字の拡大
the worsening of the world economy 世界経済の悪化, 世界経済の不況深刻化
◆Both banks' increasing worries over the worsening of their financial woes prompted them to seek a way out by agreeing to a merger. 財務体質の悪化に対する両行の危機感から、両行は合併の合意に活路を求めた。◆The consumer tendency of spending more than consumer's disposable income resulted in a worsening of the massive trade deficit of the United States. 支出が消費者の可処分所得を上回る消費者性向が、結果として膨大な米国の貿易赤字の拡大を生み出していた。

worsening (形)悪化している, 低下している, 拡大している, ~の悪化[低下, 拡大, 増大]
worsening economic picture 景気の悪化
worsening fiscal problem 財政の悪化
worsening job market 雇用情勢の悪化
◆Japan also has a worsening fiscal problem. 日本も、財政悪化問題を抱えている。

worsening economic conditions 景気の悪化
◆Worsening economic conditions could prompt the government to revise its forecast downward during the current fiscal year to predict negative growth. 景気が悪化すれば、政府は年度途中で経済見通しをマイナス成長に下方修正する可能性がある。

worsening employment situation 雇用情勢の悪化, 雇用の悪化
◆The worsening employment situation is eroding workers' incomes. 雇用の悪化で、労働者の収入が減っている。

worsening fiscal conditions 財政の悪化
◆Industrialized nations are suffering from unemployment and worsening fiscal conditions. 先進国が、失業や財政の悪化に苦しんでいる。

worship of money 拝金主義 (=mammonism, money worship, the worship of the Almighty Dollar)
◆The excessive worship of money is exemplified by the cases of window dressing by Livedoor Co. and insider trading by Murakami Fund. 極端な拝金主義の例としては、ライブドアの粉飾決算や村上ファンドのインサイダー取引などの事件が挙げられる。

worst (形)最低の, 最悪の, 最も深刻な (名)最悪, 最悪の状態, 最悪期
be past the worst 最悪期を過ぎた
come off worst (競争などに)負ける
if the worst comes to the worst いよいよ最悪の場合になったら
the worst-case scenario 最悪のシナリオ
the worst earthquake 最悪の地震
the worst-ever financial crisis 過去最悪の金融危機
the worst of the deflationary process デフレの最悪期
◆The global economy has been pulled out of its worst crisis. 世界経済は、その最大の危機は脱した。

worst economic crisis 最悪の経済危機
◆The United States is in the grip of the worst economic crisis in more than 70 years. 米国は、過去70年以上で最悪の経済危機に見舞われている。

worth (名)価値, 資産価値, 価額, 自己資本, 純資産, 財産, 財産評価額, ~に相当する量, ~分, 有用性, 重要性 (⇒negative net worth, net worth)
bushiness worth 企業価値
debt-to-net worth ratio 負債比率
dollar's worth ドル価値, ドル価格
equilibrium dollar's worth 均衡点でのドル価格
fixed assets to net worth ratio 固定比率
high net worth customers [individuals] 資産家
intangible [invisible] worth 無形資産
money worth 金だけの価値
negative net worth 債務超過
net asset worth 純資産額
present worth 現在価値, 割引現価 (=present value)
profit ratio [rate] of net worth 株主資本利益率
tangible net worth 有形正味資産
total liabilities and net worth 総資本
worth and fixed asset ratio 資本固定資産比率, 固定比率
worth debt ratio 資本負債[資本・負債]比率
worth (to) current debt ratio 資本対流動負債比率, 資本流動負債比率
worth to debts ratio 資本負債[資本・負債]比率
worth (to) fixed debt ratio 資本対固定負債比率, 資本固定負債比率
worth (to) fixed ratio 資本対固定資産比率, 資本固定[固定資本]比率, 固定比率
yen's worth 円価値, 円価格
◆If the worth of the issuer rises, the value of the stock also will rise. 発行体の資産価値が上昇すれば、株式の価値も上がる。

worth (前・形)~の価値がある, ~する価値はある, ~するだけのことはある, ~に匹敵する, ~の値打ちがある, ~に相当する, ~に値する, 相当の金がかかる, 相当の価値がある
be worth a million dollars 100万ドルに値する
be worth ¥5 million a year 年に500万円かかる
◆Based on Friday's Mazda stock closing price of ¥214 per share, Ford's holdings of about 195 million shares were worth ¥42 billion. 金曜日のマツダ株の終値(1株当たり214円)ベースで、フォードが保有するマツダ株約1億9,500万株の時価総額は420億円となる。◆The DBJ and private financial institutions extended loans worth a total of ¥100 billion to JAL in June 2009 though JAL was already in dire financial straits. 日本政策投資銀行と民間金融機関は、日航の経営がすでに悪化していたものの、2009年6月に同社に対して総額1,000億円を融資した。◆The government bond issuance worth about ¥44 trillion for the current fiscal year is the largest ever projected in an initial budget. 今年度の約44兆円の国債発行額は、当初予算としては史上最高だ。

worth of ~相当の, ~相当のもの, ~分の~
◆An estimate showed making highways toll-free would bring ¥2.7 trillion worth of economic benefits. 高速道路を無料にすると、2.7兆円相当の経済効果があることが、試算で明らかになった。◆Fukushima Bank said about 8,000 companies and investors have agreed to buy ¥15 billion worth of its new shares in March to help boost its capital base. 福島銀行によると、約8,000の企業と投資家が、同行の資本基盤を強化するため3月に予定している150億円の増資引受け[新株引受け]に同意した。◆Infrastructure projects worth of $8 trillion are expected in Asia by 2020. アジアでは、2020年までに8兆ドル相当のインフラ事業が見込まれる。◆The firm chalked up ¥483 billion in sales on ¥547 billion worth of orders it won during the October-December quarter. 同社の10-12月期の売上高は、5,470億円の受注額で4,830億円となった。

worthless debt 貸倒れ, 不良債権
worthless securities 無価値となった有価証券
would-be (形)~志望の, ~志願の, ~希望の, 未来の, 自称~の, ~のつもりでいる, ~予備軍, ~側, ~未遂の
would-be acquirer 買収側, 買収希望者
would-be entrepreneur 起業家希望者
would-be policyholder 保険加入希望者
◆In insurance policies that can be purchased via mobile phone, would-be policyholders do not need to input personal

data and payments are easier. 携帯電話で加入できる保険では、加入希望者は個人情報を入力する必要がなく、支払いも簡単だ。◆The would-be acquirer is trying to greenmail the target company by having it pay a premium to buy back the shares held by the raider. 買収側［買収希望者］は、この買占め屋［会社乗っ取り屋］が保有する株を標的企業に高値で引き取らせて、標的企業から収益を上げようとしている［標的企業に高値で引き取らせることにより、標的企業にグリーンメールを仕掛けようとしている］。

WPA 分損担保
(=WA（with average）, with particular average)

wrap account ラップ口座, 運用一括契約, 投資一任契約
◆In wrap accounts, a customer sets the overall investment policy, including investment period and profit target. ラップ口座では、顧客が投資期間や運用益の目標などの大まかな運用方針を決める。

解説 ラップ口座とは：証券会社が資産運用に関する助言や投資家が運用する株式銘柄の選定、実際の株式売買、証券の保護預り、投資家専用の取引口座の管理などあらゆるサービスを一括して提供するもので、投資家は売買の回数に関係なく、預けた資産の残高に応じて一定の手数料を支払うシステム。証券会社にとっては、投資家の資産残高に応じて手数料を受け取れるため、株式市況に左右されないで収益を上げることができるメリットがある。投資信託型と投資顧問型の二つがある。

wrap-around［wraparound］ (形)包括的な, 総合的な, ラップアラウンド
wrap-around mortgage 包括抵当, ラップアラウンド・モーゲージ
wraparound annuity 投資（対象裁量）年金, ラップアラウンド年金

wreak (動)(被害などを)与える, (罰などを)加える, (怒りを)ぶちまける, 浴びせる, (損害などを)引き起こす
◆A downgrade below investment-grade by even one ratings agency could boost GM's borrowing costs and wreak havoc on the corporate bond market. 格付け会社が1社でも投資適格格付けより低く格付けを引き下げたら［格付け会社が1社でも投機的格付けに格下げしたら］、GMの資金調達コストが急増し、米国の社債［債券］市場にも大きな影響が出る恐れがある。

wriggle out of ～から何とか逃れる, ～をすり抜ける, ～から脱する, ～を巧みに避ける
◆It was when European countries needed growth to help them wriggle out of the chokehold of debt that the economic stall came. 欧州諸国が債務の首かせから脱するために成長を必要としていたときに、景気減速［景気の腰折れ］が到来した。

write (動)書く, 記入する, 書き込む, オプションを売却する, オプションを売る, オプションを売り建てる (⇒premium)
write a call コールを売り建てる
write a call option コール・オプションを売る
write a check for $500 ドルの小切手を書く
(=write a $500 check)
write a covered call カバード・コールを売り建てる
write a put プットを売り建てる
write "accepted" 「引受済み」と書く
write back 訂正記入する
write back an entry［item］ 帳簿記入を訂正する
write down 書き留める, 記録する, 計上する, 評価減を計上する, 貸倒れ引当金を計上する, 評価を引き下げる
write options to earn premiums プレミアム（オプション料）を得るためにオプションを売却する
write out a check 小切手を切る
(=issue a check)
◆Charges included in other accounts were primarily for expenses related to writing down impaired assets and merger-related expenses. その他の勘定科目に計上した費用は、主に不良資産の評価減と合併関連の費用です。

write a policy 保険を引き受ける, 保険証券に署名する
(=write an insurance policy)
◆Bond insurers write policies that promise to cover payments to bondholders if the entity that issued the bonds defaults. 金融保証会社［債券保険会社］は、債券発行体がデフォルト（債務不履行）になった場合に、債券保有者への（元本と利息の）支払い補償を約束する保険を引き受けている。

write-back［writeback］ (名)戻し入れ
badwill write-backs 負ののれん代の戻し入れ
provision write-backs 引当金の戻し入れ
write-back of provisions for priority payments 前払い引当金の戻し入れ

write down (動)帳簿価格を引き下げる, 評価を引き下げる, 評価減を計上する, 評価損を計上する, 貸倒れ引当金を計上する, 償却する, 再評価する, 記録する
inventory written down 棚卸し評価損
write down the assets to market value 資産を時価ベースで再評価する
◆Merrill Lynch & Co. will write down $5.5 billion for bad bets on subprime mortgages and leveraged loans. 米大手証券のメリルリンチは、低所得者向け住宅融資「サブプライム・ローン」とレバレッジド・ローンの見通しが暗いため、55億ドルの評価損を計上する。

write-down (名)評価減, 評価損, 評価引下げ, 減損, 減額, 償却, 削減 (=writedown)
debt write-down 債務削減
massive write-downs 巨額の評価損
write-down and disposal of loans 貸出の償却と売却
◆Athens is likely to officially launch talks with banks and other private bondholders for the debt write-down. ギリシャ政府は、銀行などの民間債権者［民間投資家、民間の債券保有者］と債務削減のための協議を開始する見込みだ。◆The collapse of the subprime mortgage market and related credit market turmoil have resulted in $45 billion of write-downs at the world's biggest banks and securities firms. サブプライム・ローン市場の悪化や関連金融市場の混乱で、世界の大手銀行と証券会社の評価損計上額は、これまでのところ450億ドルに達している。◆The extent of Lehman's massive losses and write-downs due to the subprime mortgage crisis became evident. サブプライム・ローン（米低所得者向け住宅融資）問題に伴うリーマンの巨額の損失と評価損の規模が、明らかになった。

write off (動)債権を帳消しにする, 債権を処理する［償却する, 放棄する］, (投資, 資金などを)回収不可能と見なす, 評価額を引き下げる, 価格を引き下げる, 減価償却する, 税金に対して費用などを)経費として申告する, ～として処理する, ～と見なす
(⇒banking operations, refund動詞)
write it off as worthless それを価値のないものと見なす
write off a debt 債権［債務］を帳消しにする, 貸金を償却する
write off bad debts 不良債権を処理する, 不良債権を償却する
write off claims 賠償金を償却する
write off nonperforming loans 不良債権を処理する
◆Major banks are striving to write off some of their tax assets from their equity capital. 大手銀行は現在、自己資本からの税金資産減らしに取り組んでいる。◆Major commercial banks are reaching the final stages of their efforts to write off their nonperforming loans. 大手銀行は、不良債権処理への取組みの最終局面を迎えている。◆Olympus wrote off more than 75 percent of about 70 billion spent on the acquisitions of three domestic firms as impairment losses. オリンパスは、国内3社の買収に投じた約700億円の75％以上を、減耗損失とし

て処理していた。◆The recent circumstances facing the nation's megabanks have shown up their weaknesses, as shown by slow progress in their efforts to write off their nonperforming loans and a sharp decline in their stock prices. 日本のメガバンク（巨大銀行グループ）が直面している最近の状況を見ると、不良債権処理策の遅れや株価の急落などが示すように、メガバンクの脆弱（ぜいじゃく）性が目立っている。

write-off （名）債権の帳消し, 債権の処理・放棄, 消却, 評価減, 評価引下げ, 貸倒れ償却, 減価償却, 削除, 帳簿の締切り
　　（=writeoff; ⇒loan write-off, taxable write-off）
　debt write-off　債務の帳消し
　write-off interval　償却期間
　write-off of bad loans　不良債権処理, 不良債権の償却
　　（=bad loan write-off, write-off of nonperforming loans）
　write-off of costs　特別損失
　write-off policy　償却方針
　◆Japan should resolve its bad loan problem by implementing drastic measures to ease the tax burdens shouldered by banks in writing off their nonperforming loans, including an expansion of tax-free write-offs. 無税償却の拡大を含めて, 不良債権を処理する際に銀行が負う税負担の大幅な緩和策を実施して, 日本は不良債権問題を解決しなければならない。

write-offs of nonperforming loans　不良債権処理
　◆At an emergency shareholders meeting, the company obtained shareholder approval to transfer ¥199 billion from its legal reserves to provide for write-offs of nonperforming loans. 臨時株主総会で同社は, 株主から, 不良債権処理に備えて法定準備金から1,990億円を取り崩す案の承認を得た。

write up　（動）記帳する, 帳簿価格を引き上げる, 過大評価する

write-up　（名）過大評価, 評価引上げ

writer　オプションの売り手, 保険の引受業者
　　（=option writer, underwriter）

writing agency　保険の募集代理店

written　（形）文書にした, 書面にした, 文書［書面］による
　written agreement［contract］　契約書, 合意書, 約定書
　written assignment　譲渡証書
　written evidence　証拠書類
　written instrument　書面, 文書, 証書
　written notice　書面による通知, 通知書
　written plea　弁明書
　written pledge　念書
　written request　書面による要請［要求、請求］, 要請書, 要求書, 請求書
　◆TEPCO lodged a formal written request for financial assistance. 東電は, 金融支援の正式要請書を提出した。

wrongdoing　（名）犯罪, 罪, 悪事, 悪行, 非行, 不正, 罪悪
　◆The company's wrongdoing damaged the trust of shareholders. 同社の不正行為［不祥事］が, 株主の信頼を損ねた。
　◆The wrongdoing of Olympus Corp., a blue-chip company that holds the largest share of the global endoscope market, has eroded international faith in corporate Japan. 内視鏡の市場シェアで世界トップのオリンパスの不正行為で, 日本企業の国際的な信頼は失墜している。

WTI　ウェスト・テキサス・インターミディエート（West Texas Intermediateの略）

X

X in　利息落ち　（=ex interest）
X pr　優先権利落ち　（=ex privileges）
x.a.　諸権利落ち　（=ex all）
XC　利落ち　（=ex coupon）
XD　配当落ち　（=ex div., ex dividend）
Xenocurrency　国外流通通貨, ユーロダラー
XI　利息落ち, 利落ち　（=ex interest, x-int.）
XR　権利落ち　（=ex rights, xr, x-rts.）
XW　権利証落ち, ワラント落ち　（=ex warrants, x-warr., xw: 新株引受権利証書が付いていないこと）

Y

Yankee bond　ヤンキー債（米国市場で非居住者がドル建てで発行する債券のこと）
　Yankee bond issuance　ヤンキー債起債
　Yankee bond market　ヤンきー債市場

Yankee-dollar market　ヤンキー・ダラー市場

yardstick　（名）基準, 尺度, 物差し, 指標, ヤードスティック
　the most well-known yardstick　最もよく知られた指標
　use ratings as an independent yardstick　独立した基準として格付けを用いる

year　（名）年, 年度, 期　（⇒budget year, business year, current account balance, fiscal year）
　business year　事業年度, 営業年度, 会計年度
　　（=financial year, fiscal year）
　current year　今期, 今年度, 当期
　　（=current fiscal year）
　financial year　会計年度, 事業年度
　　（=business year, fiscal year）
　first half of the year　上半期, 上期
　from a year earlier　前年比で, 前年同期比で, 前年同月比で
　full-year earnings forecast　通期業績予想
　full year results　通期決算, 通期業績
　on year　対前年比で
　over a year ago　前年同期比, 前年同月比
　prior year adjustment　過年度損益修正
　profit or loss for the financial year　当期損益
　second half of the year　下半期, 下期
　　（=second half of the fiscal year）
　tax year　税務年度, 課税年度, 事業年度, 会計年度
　　（=fiscal year, taxable year）
　the beginning of the year　年初
　the year to Dec. 31, 2012　2012年12月期
　◆In this cofinancing scheme, the bank will extend a total of about ¥8.5 billion over a 20-year loan period. この協調融資事業で, 同行は貸出期間20年で計約85億円を融資する。◆M3 was up 0.6 percent to ¥1.031 quadrillion in October 2008 from a year earlier. 2008年10月のマネー・サプライM3は, 前年同月比0.6%増の1,031兆円となった。◆Resona Holdings Inc. reported a huge loss in the year to March 31, 2004. りそなホールディングスは, 2004年3月期（2003年度）は巨額の赤字を計上した。◆The core consumer price inflation rate, excluding volatile fresh food prices, is currently about 2 percent on year due mainly to soaring food and petroleum product prices. 変動の激しい生鮮食品の価格を除いたコア物価指数［消費者物価指数のコア指数］の上昇率は現在, 主に食料品と石油製品の価格高騰の影響で, 対前年比で2％程度となっている。◆The dollar-yen exchange rate closed at ¥101.2, a gain of nearly ¥25 since the beginning of the year. 円ドル・レートは, 終値で1ドル＝101円20銭で, 年初からの円の上昇幅は25円近くになった。◆The euro plummeted to the ¥100 level on the foreign exchange market, hitting a 10 year low. 外国為替市場では, ユーロが1ユーロ＝100円台まで急落して, 10年ぶりの低水準［10年ぶりの円高・ユーロ安水準］となった。◆

The nonlife insurance company hopes to attract about 3 million to 4 million new policyholders a year for its new types of insurance. 同損保は、同社の新型保険で、年間約300万〜400万件の新規契約獲得を目指している。◆The 10-year JGB yield sank below the 1 percent threshold. 新発10年物の日本国債の流通利回りが、1％割れの水準まで低下した。◆The total amount of money deposited in individual foreign currency accounts has continued to increase in recent years. 個人向け外貨預金残高は、ここ数年増え続けている。◆UFJ Holdings, Inc. reported an annual loss for the third straight year. UFJホールディングスは、3期連続、赤字となった。

year-on-year 前年同期比, 前年同月比, 前年比
(=year-over-year; ⇒turnover)
◆Companies listed on the Tokyo Stock Exchange's First Section posted a year-on-year increase of 33.2 percent in combined pretax profit in the first half of the current fiscal year. 東証一部上場企業の今年度上期（4-9月期）の経常利益合計は、前年同期比33.2％増となった。◆The current account balance is entering an upward trend on a year-on-year basis. 経常収支は、前年同月比ベースで上昇基調に入りつつある。◆The surplus in the current account stood at ¥1.5 trillion in September 2008, marking the seventh consecutive month of year-on-year declines. 2008年9月の経常収支の黒字額は、1兆5,000億円となり、7か月連続で前年実績を下回った。

yearend [year-end]（名）年末, 期末
◆Total debt as a percentage of total capitalization was 20 percent at yearend 2011. 資本総額に対する債務総額の比率は、2011年末現在で20％だった。

yen（名）円, 円相場（⇒strong yen, weak yen）
 appreciation of the yen 円高
  (=appreciating yen, yen appreciation)
 depreciation of the yen 円安
  (=depreciating yen, yen depreciation)
 exchange gain from yen appreciation 円高差益
 in real yen terms 円建て実質ベースで
 long dollar positions against the yen 円売りドル買い
 strengthening yen 円高
  (=rise in the yen, strengthening of the yen)
 strong yen 円高
 strong-yen caused boom 円高景気
 the high value of the yen 円高
 weaker yen 円安
 yen/dollar rate 円相場, 円の対米ドル相場
◆After the government's move of intervention, the yen plunged to the ¥85 level against the dollar. 政府の市場介入の動きを受けて、円相場は1ドル＝85円台まで下落した。◆An exporter company will incur losses if the yen rises above the assumed exchange rate, but benefit if the yen declines. 輸出企業では、その想定為替レートより円高になれば為替差損が生じ、（想定為替レートより）円安になれば為替差益が出る。◆As it stands, the yen is the sole major currency whose value has not stopped increasing. 現状では、円は上昇が止まらない唯一の主要通貨だ。◆Export-oriented companies will be hit hard if the yen accelerates its rise. 円高が加速すると、輸出企業は大きな打撃を受ける。◆If the yen rises above its all-time high of ¥79.75 to the dollar, the company may have to revise its assumed exchange rate once more. 円高が1ドル＝79円75銭の史上最高値を更新したら、同社は再び同社の想定為替レートの修正を迫られかねない。◆In foreign currency deposits, commission fees are needed when the yen is exchanged into a foreign currency and when the foreign currency is exchanged backed in yen. 外貨預金では、円を外貨に替えるときと、外貨を円に戻すときに、為替手数料が必要になる。◆In foreign currency deposits, depositors can earn profits by exchanging their foreign currency deposits into yen when the yen's value against major foreign currencies falls. 外貨預金では、主要外貨に対して円相場が下落した時点で預金者が外貨預金を円に戻せば、利益を上げる［儲ける］ことができる。◆In the case of foreign currency deposits, losses may balloon if the yen appreciates further and may cause a loss of principal. 外貨預金の場合、円高がさらに進めば損失が膨らみ、元本割れになる恐れもある。◆In the wake of the euro crisis in Europe and the fiscal deadlock in the United States, the yen has sharply strengthened. 欧州のユーロ危機と米国の財政政策の行き詰まりの影響で、円が急騰している。◆It remains to be seen whether the yen will be overshooting. 円相場がオーバーシュート（行き過ぎ）かどうかは、今後を見ないと分からない。◆It's difficult to offset losses from further appreciation of the yen with interest as interest rates in many foreign currency deposits are low. 外貨建て預金の多くは金利が低いので、円高進行による損失分を利息で相殺する［取り戻す］のは難しい。◆Japan must prevent the yen from soaring again to the level of ¥76 to the dollar. 日本は、円相場が再び1ドル＝76円台に急騰する事態を阻止しなければならない。◆Japan should prevent the dollar plunging and the yen from rising too sharply through concerted market intervention with the United States and European countries. 日本は、米欧との協調介入によってドル急落と超円高を阻止すべきだ。◆On Aug. 31, 2011, the yen rose to the ¥76.50 level against the U.S. dollar in the Tokyo foreign exchange market, close to the postwar record of ¥75.95 registered on Aug. 19. 2011年8月31日の東京外国為替市場の円相場は、1ドル＝76円50銭台まで上昇し、8月19日に付けた戦後最高値の75円95銭に近づいた。◆The talks between Prime Minister Kan and Bank of Japan Gov. Shirakawa led to a further advance of the yen and offloading of stocks as disappointment spread among market players. 菅首相と日銀総裁の会談は、一層の円高と市場筋の株の失望売りを誘った。◆The yen continues its relentless surge and stock prices keep falling. 円高に歯止めがかからず、株安も続いている。◆The yen could soon even reach a record high in the ¥75 range versus the dollar. 円は、やがて1ドル＝75円台の史上最高値にまで達する可能性がある。◆The yen has been changing hands in a fairly stable manner at about ¥100 to the dollar. 円（相場）は、1ドル＝100円程度でかなり安定的に推移している。◆The yen in record strong territory of ¥76 to the dollar causes hardships in the Japanese economy. 1ドル＝76円台の史上最高の円高水準は、日本経済にとって厳しい。◆The yen is currently hovering at a level stronger than ¥80 to the dollar. 円相場は現在［足元の円相場は］、1ドル＝80円を上回る水準で推移している。◆The yen may appreciate further to ¥70 against the U.S. dollar. 円高は、さらに1ドル＝75円まで進む可能性がある。◆The yen may once again rise against the dollar and other major currencies. 今後、ドルなどの主要通貨に対して再び円高が進む可能性がある。◆The yen may soar toward ¥80 to the dollar. 円相場は、1ドル＝80円に向けて急騰する可能性がある。◆The yen rose to its record high of ¥79.75 against the dollar in 1995. 円相場は、1995年に上昇して史上最高値の1ドル＝79円75銭を付けた。◆The yen soared to its strongest position this year. 円は、年初来の最高値を付けた。◆The yen stayed in the lower ¥77 range against the U.S. dollar in Tokyo. 東京外国為替市場の円相場は、1ドル＝77円台前半で推移した。◆There are few signs of the yen reaching the ¥90 range to the dollar for the time being. 今のところ、1ドル＝90円台に達する動き［1ドル＝90円台を目指す動き］は見られない。◆Yen can be exchanged for foreign currencies and deposited in foreign currency accounts at most major banks. 円は、大半の大手銀行で外貨と替えて外貨預金口座に預け入れることができる。

yen buying [yen-buying] 円買い
 yen-buying, dollar-selling operations 円買い・ドル売り操作, 円買い・ドル売りオペ, 円買い・ドル売りの動き

(=yen-buying and dollar-selling operations)

yen-buying moves　円買いの動き　(⇒stance)
◆A dealer at a leading bank said that market players' concern has kept yen-buying moves in check. 市場関係者の警戒感が円買いの動きを食い止めた［抑制した］、と大手銀行のディーラーが語っている。◆Concerns over the U.S. economic outlook tend to induce yen-buying as a safe haven. 米経済の先行きに対する懸念から、安全な投資手段として円が買われる傾向にある。

yen-buying pressure　円買い圧力
◆The yen surged to the higher end of the ￥98 level against the dollar in Tokyo markets due to yen-buying pressure fueled by expectations of the country's economic recovery. 東京為替市場は、日本の景気回復を期待した円買いが強まり、1ドル＝98円台［98円台の上限］まで円が急騰した。

yen-denominated assets　円建て資産
◆If U.S. banks acquire yen-denominated asserts, the dollar will depreciate vis-a-vis the yen. 米国の銀行が円建て資産を買えば、円に対してドル安が進む。

yen-denominated debt rating　円建て国債の格付け
◆Moody's Investors Service cut Japan's yen-denominated debt rating by one notch to Aa3 from Aa2 and maintained a negative outlook. 米国の格付け会社ムーディーズは、日本の円建て国債の格付けを「Aa2」から「Aa3」に一段階引き下げ、「ネガティブ（弱含み）」の見通しを据え置いた。

yen-denominated foreign bond　円建て外債
◆According to a financial information firm, yen-denominated foreign bonds issued between 1996 and 2001 totaled 10.57 trillion. ある金融情報会社によると、1996年から2001年までの円建て外債の発行総額は、10兆5,700億円にのぼった。

yen-denominated government bonds　円建て国債
◆The high yields of the yen-denominated government bonds were considered considerably higher than minuscule domestic interest rates. この円建て国債は、国内の超低金利に比べて利回りがはるかに大きいと見られた。

yen-denominated loans　円建て借款, 円借款
(=yen loans)
◆Japan has extended a total of about ￥3 trillion in yen-denominated loans to China over a quarter of a century. 日本は、四半世紀にわたって累計約3兆円の対中円借款を供与してきた。

yen-denominated loans to China　対中円借款
◆Yen-denominated loans to China account for a good portion of Japan's official development assistance to that nation. 対中円借款は、中国向け政府開発援助（ODA）の大半を占める。

yen-denominated trade　円建て貿易
◆Yen-denominated trade frees domestic companies from the risk of exchange rate fluctuations. 円建て貿易は、国内企業にとって為替変動のリスクがない。

yen-dollar exchange rate　円ドル相場, 円・ドル相場, 円・ドルレート, 円の対ドルレート, 円とドルの為替レート

yen loan　円借款　(=yen-based loan, yen-denominated loan; ⇒extend, grant-in-aid, untied yen loans)
◆JICA signed a contract with the Indonesian government to provide a yen loan of about ￥20 billion to Indonesia. 国際協力機構（JICA）は、インドネシア政府と約200億円の円借款を貸与［供与］する契約書に調印した。◆With the integration of the Japan Bank for International Cooperation's division for handling yen loans, and other bodies in October 2008, JICA became one of the world's largest development assistance agencies. 国際協力機構（JICA）は、2008年10月に国際協力銀行（JBIC）の円借款部門などを統合して、（事業規模で）世界最大級の開発援助機関となった。◆Yen loans are offered to developing countries as part of Japan's official development assistance. 円借款は、日本の政府開発援助（ODA）の一環として発展途上国に供与される。◆Yen loans extended now as part of Japan's ODA are untied in principle, with the source of development materials and equipment to be procured not defined. 日本の政府開発援助（ODA）として供与されている円借款は現在、ひも付きでない「アンタイド」援助が原則で、開発物資の調達先を限定していない。

yen loan facility　円融資枠
◆This yen loan facility is for general corporate purposes. この円融資枠は、一般事業目的に使用される。

yen-selling and dollar-buying　円売りドル買い
◆Speculation that the BOJ would take additional easing steps to stem the yen's surge sparked yen-selling and dollar-buying in the morning session. 円高阻止に向けて日銀が追加緩和策に踏み切るとの思惑から、午前の取引では、円売り・ドル買いが優勢となった。

yen-selling and dollar-buying intervention　円売り・ドル買い介入（円高を食い止めるための円売り・ドル買い介入では、政府が政府短期証券（FB）を発行して調達した円を対価に、民間銀行が持つドルを買い入れる）
◆The government should not hesitate to intervene in the currency market through bold yen-selling and dollar-buying operations. 政府は、為替市場への大胆な円売り・ドル買い介入をためらうべきではない。◆The government's currency intervention through yen-selling and dollar-buying operations on Sept. 15, 2010 was the biggest on record for a one-day operation. 2010年9月15日の政府の円売り・ドル買い操作による為替介入額は、1日の円売り・ドル買い操作［オペ］としては過去最高を更新した。

yen-selling and dollar-buying operations　円売り・ドル買い, 円売り・ドル買い操作, 円売り・ドル買いオペ, 円売り・ドル買いの動き
(=yen-selling, dollar-buying operations)

yen-selling, dollar-buying operations　円売り・ドル買い, 円売り・ドル買い操作, 円売り・ドル買いオペ
◆The Bank of Japan asked the Federal Reserve Bank of New York to intervene in the New York foreign exchange market on its behalf through yen-selling, dollar-buying operations for the first time in 15 months. 日銀は、1年3か月ぶりにニューヨーク連銀に委託して、ニューヨーク外国為替市場で円売り・ドル買いの介入に踏み切った。

yen-selling intervention　円売り介入
◆Caution grew about possible yen-selling intervention by the government. 想定される政府の円売り介入に対する警戒感が、強まった。◆The Bank of Japan may heighten the effects of monetary easing by not absorbing funds the government funnels into the market as yen-selling intervention. 日銀は、政府が円売り介入で市場に放出した資金を吸い上げないで、金融緩和の効果を高めることもできる。◆The Japanese government and the Bank of Japan conducted an independent yen-selling intervention. 日本政府・日銀は、単独で円売り介入を行った。

yen-selling market intervention　円売り市場介入, 円売り介入
◆Finance Minister Yoshihiko Noda decided to conduct a yen-selling market intervention on Aug. 4, 2011. 2011年8月4日に野田財務相は、円売り市場介入の実施を決断した。◆Japan implemented the yen-selling market intervention unilaterally. 日本は、単独で円売り市場介入を実施した。◆Market players remain wary of a possible yen-selling market intervention by Japanese authorities. 市場関係者は、日本当局（政府・日銀）による新たな円売り市場介入の可能性をまだ警戒している。◆The effect of the yen-selling market intervention implemented unilaterally by Japan has already weakened. 日本が単独で実施した円売り介入［市場介入］の効果は、すでに薄らいでいる。

yen slide 円安
- ◆The yen slide came to a halt. 円が、下げ止まった。

yen's appreciation 円高
(=the rising yen, the yen's rise)
- ◆A pressing issue is the yen's appreciation. 緊急の課題は、円高だ。 ◆Domestic industries are affected significantly by the yen's appreciation. 国内産業は、円高の影響を大きく受けている。 ◆Speculators apparently take advantage of the sluggish response of the government and the Bank of Japan to the yen's appreciation. 投機筋は、政府・日銀の円高への対応の鈍さに付け込んでいるようだ。 ◆The Bank of Japan will fight the yen's appreciation in close cooperation with the government. 日銀は、政府と緊密に連携して円高に対応する方針だ。 ◆The yen's appreciation puts pressure on the earnings of export-oriented companies. 円高は、輸出企業の収益を圧迫する。 ◆The yen's extremely rapid appreciation may deliver a bitter blow to the domestic economy. 超円高は、国内経済に大きな打撃を与える可能性がある。 ◆We will have to observe the yen's appreciation and the stock prices. 今後は、円高と株価の動きを見る必要がある。

yen's appreciation against the dollar 円高・ドル安
- ◆Amid a widening slump in global auto sales and the yen's sharp appreciation against the U.S. dollar, the firm is expected to report an unconsolidated operating loss in fiscal 2011. 世界の新車販売の落ち込み拡大と急激な円高・ドル安に伴って、同社の2011年度［2010年3月期決算］の営業利益は、単独ベース［単独決算］で赤字が見込まれている。 ◆Rapidly increasing prices of primary commodities have had a positive influence on corporate performance with the yen's appreciation against the dollar. 円高・ドル安で、これまでのところ一次産品（原油や石炭など）の急騰が、企業の業績に好影響をもたらしている。 ◆The yen's appreciation against the dollar hurts the nation's export-led recovery. 円高・ドル安は、日本の輸出主導の景気回復に悪影響を与える。

yen's continued rise 円高進行
- ◆The yen's continued rise is worrisome for large manufacturers. 大企業・製造業には、円高進行も懸念材料だ。

yen's current exchange rate 今の円の為替レート, 今の円の為替相場, 今の円相場
- ◆If we look at the yen's current exchange rate in terms of its real effective exchange rate, it is basically within a range consistent with the mid- and long-term fundamentals of the economy. 今の円相場［円の為替相場］は、実質実効為替レートで見ると、基本的には中長期的な経済のファンダメンタルズ（基礎的条件）と整合的な範囲内にある。

yen's depreciation 円安
- ◆A recovery will be export-driven, dependent on U.S. growth and the yen's depreciation, instead of being led by increased domestic consumption and capital investment. 今後の景気回復は、アメリカ経済の好転や円安を背景にした輸出主導型の回復で、国内の個人消費や設備投資の伸びがその牽引役となるわけではない。

yen's exchange rate 円の為替相場, 円の為替レート
- ◆The yen's exchange rate has appreciated to ￥76 against the dollar, so it is the best time to buy U.S. dollars. 円の為替レートが1ドル＝76円に上昇したので、今が米ドルの買い時だ。

yen's further rise 円高進行
(=yen's further appreciation)
- ◆The government and the Bank of Japan should conduct a concerted intervention with the United States and European countries to stem the yen's further rise. 政府・日銀は、米欧と協調介入を実施して、円高進行を阻止しなければならない。

yen's historically high levels 歴史的な円高水準
- ◆Amid the continued yen's historically high levels, increasing numbers of people are opening foreign currency deposit accounts. 歴史的な円高水準が続くなか、外貨預金口座を設ける人が増えている。

yen's rise 円高 （=yen's appreciation）
- ◆As the yen's rise puts pressure on the earnings of export-oriented companies, it hinders Japan's economic recovery. 円高は輸出企業を圧迫するので、日本の景気回復の足を引っ張ることになる。 ◆Japanese firms' moves to shift production abroad to cope with the yen's rise will bring about a hollowing-out of domestic industries. 円高対策として日本企業が生産拠点を海外に移すと、国内産業の空洞化を招くことになる。 ◆The government and the BOJ intervened in the market for the first time in 6 1/2 years in September 2010 to stem the yen's rise. 政府・日銀は、円高を阻止する［食い止める］ため、2010年9月に6年半ぶりに（円売り・ドル買いの）市場介入をした。 ◆To stem the yen's rise, the government will play its ace when the yen stands on the brink of rising above ￥80 to the dollar. 円高阻止のため、政府は円が上昇して1ドル＝80円を突破する寸前の段階で奥の手を出すようだ。

yen's rising trend 円高傾向
- ◆A large yen-selling intervention by monetary authorities on Sept. 15 failed to reverse the yen's rising trend. 金融当局が9月15日に実施した大量の円売り介入で、円高傾向を反転［逆転］させることはできなかった。

yen's strength 円高
- ◆The Bank of Japan demonstrated its resolve to address the yen's strength. 日銀は、円高に取り組む決意を明確に示した。

yen's value 円相場, 円価値
(⇒rise in the yen's value)
a surge in the yen's value 円高, 円の急騰
stabilize the yen's value 円相場を安定させる
the rapid surge in the yen's value 急激な円高
the sharp rise in the yen's value 急激な円高
- ◆Both a freefall in stock prices and a surge in the yen's value have been avoided. 株価の暴落も円の急騰も、回避された。 ◆The BOJ is prepared to hold its policy meeting ahead of schedule if the yen's value further soars before the next meeting. 次回の政策決定会合までに円高が一段と進めば、日銀は会合を前倒しして会合を開く構えだ。 ◆The foreign currency depositor planned to withdraw the money when the yen's value fell. この外貨預金者は、円安になったら解約するつもりだった。 ◆The government and the Bank of Japan will likely continue to work together in fighting the sharp rise in the yen's value. 政府と日銀は、急激な円高阻止で協調路線を継続することになりそうだ。 ◆The rapid surge in the yen's value could deal a blow to Japan's export drive and export-related businesses. 急激な円高は、日本の輸出競争力の低下や輸出関連企業の業績悪化をもたらす可能性がある。 ◆The rapid surge in the yen's value would impair the current improvement in the Japanese economy. 急激な円高は、日本の景気回復の腰を折ることになる。 ◆The rise of the yen's value pushed up the demand for travel abroad. 円高が、海外旅行の需要を押し上げた。 ◆The yen's value reached an all-time high in 1995, with the U.S. currency traded in the ￥79 range. 円相場は1995年に史上最高値に達し、米ドルは79円台［1ドル＝79円台］で取引された。 ◆The yen's value still remains high and is likely to reach a postwar record value above the ￥76-to-the-dollar level. 円相場は依然高く、1ドル＝76円台を上回る戦後最高値に達する可能性がある。 ◆These comments were made after a series of currency market interventions by the government to prevent the yen's value from getting stronger. これらのコメントは、政府が円高阻止のための為替市場への介入を断続的に行った後に出された。

yen's value against major foreign currencies 主要外貨に対する円相場, 円の対主要外貨相場
- ◆In foreign currency deposits, depositors can earn profits by exchanging their foreign currency deposits into yen when the yen's value against major foreign currencies falls. 外貨預金では、主要外貨に対して円相場が下落した時点で預金者が

外貨預金を円に戻せば、利益を上げる[儲ける]ことができる。

yen's value against the dollar　円の対米ドル相場（⇒surge in the yen's value against the dollar）
◆More than ￥5 in the yen's value against the dollar increased in just a week. わずか1週間で、円の対ドル相場が5円余りも急騰した。

yield　(動)利益・利子などを生む[もたらす]、権利などを譲る、譲渡する、委譲する、政権などを明け渡す、借金などを返済する
　investment yields　投資が〜をもたらす
　yield a rate of 10%　10%の利回りを生む、利回り率は10%になる
◆The bonds were sold to yield a rate of 10%. 社債発行の利回り率は、10%であった。

yield　(名)株式・債券などの利回り、投資利回り、投資収益、リターン、歩留（ぶど）まり、収益、イールド　（⇒bond market, bond yield, dividend yield, financing bill, guaranteed yield, insurance policyholder, junk bond, premium investment, promised yield rate, return）
　annualized yield　年利回り
　annually compounded yield　年複利利回り
　assumed yield　予想利回り
　average yield　平均利回り
　basic yield　基本利回り
　benchmark yield　指標銘柄利回り
　bond yield　債券利回り
　bonds with high yields　高利回り債
　compound yield　複合利回り、複利
　convenience yield　便宜収益
　coupon yield　表面利回り、債券利回り
　current yield　直接利回り、直利、現在利回り　（債券の償還時に発生する額面と購入価格との差益・差損を考慮しないで、1年間の利息を購入価格で割り、100を掛けて算出。債券の購入価格に対する年間利息の割合を示す）
　direct yield　直接利回り
　dividend yield　配当利回り（年間配当金の証券購入価格に対する割合。株式の場合は、年間配当金を株価で割って算出する）
　earnings yield　利益利回り、収益利回り
　effective yield　実効利回り
　expected yield　予想利回り、期待利回り
　external yield　外部利回り
　flat yield　均一利回り
　good yield　好利回り
　gross expected yield　予想総利回り、期待総利回り
　gross yield　総収益
　indirect yield　間接利回り
　issuer's yield　発行者利回り
　long-term yield　長期利回り、長期金利
　marginal yield　限界収益、限界収入
　market yield　市場利回り
　money yield　名目利回り
　negative yield　逆ざや
　net yield　正味利回り
　nominal yield　名目利回り
　par yield　パー・イールド
　perspective yield　見込み収益
　portfolio's yield　ポートフォリオの利回り
　probable yield　予想利回り
　prospective yield　予想利回り、予想収益、見込み収益
　push up yields on short-duration bonds　短期物の利回りを押し上げる
　redemption yield　償還利回り
　reduction in yields　金利引下げ
　returns yield of capital　資本収益
　risk yield　危険利回り
　running yield　直接利回り
　standard yield　標準利回り、標準歩留まり
　stock dividend yield　株式の配当利回り、株式の利回り
　stock yield　株式利回り
　subscribers' yield　応募者利回り
　tax yield　租税収入
　yield at issue　発行利回り
　yield auction　利回り入札
　yield behavior　利回りの動き
　yield book　利回り表
　yield differential effect　金利格差効果
　yield fluctuation　利回り変動
　yield gap　利回り格差、金利差
　yield giveup　利回りの損失
　yield-hungry investor　利回り志向の投資家
　yield improvement　利回り改善、利回りの向上
　yield level　利回り水準
　yield on earnings assets　収益資産の利回り
　yield on investment　運用利回り
　yield on lending　貸出金利回り
　yield on securities　有価証券利回り
　yield on shares　株式の投資収益率
　yield pick-up　利回り向上、利回りアップ、値ざや（＝yield enhancement）
　yield players　高利回りねらい
　yield spread gap　異なる債券の利回り格差
　yield structure　利回り構成、利回り構造
　yield to average life　平均償還年限利回り
　yield to first call　初期利回り　（＝yield to call）
　yield to par　額面利回り
　yield to put　プット利回り
　yield to subscribers　応募者利回り
　yield to total assets　総資産利回り
　yields on Treasury bonds　長期国債金利
◆All the insurers are now saddled with an enormous amount of negative yields as returns on their investments have plunged due to ultra-low interest rates—a consequence of the bursting of the bubble. 生保各社は現在、バブル崩壊後の超低金利時代で運用利回りが急低下し、巨額の逆ざやを抱えている。◆Investment funds place top priority on yields. 投資ファンドは、投資利回りを最優先する。◆Lowering the yield of Meiji Yasuda's single-premium whole life insurance will reduce the attraction of the insurer's financial products. 明治安田生保の一時払い終身保険の利回り[予定利率]の引下げで、同社の金融商品の魅力は薄れると思われる。◆Many of incorporated foundations have invested in bonds with high yields. 財団法人の多くは、高利回り債に投資した。◆The annual yield of the Italian government bond is currently at a high 6 percent. 伊国債の流通利回りは現在、年6%の高い水準にある。◆The decline in yields on whole life insurance products effectively raises premiums. 終身保険商品の利回り（予定利率）の引下げは、実質的な保険料の値上げになる。◆The life insurer currently promises its policyholders an annual yield of 1.5 percent for the single-premium whole life insurance. 同生保は現在、一時払い終身保険については年1.5%の利回り（予定利率）を契約者に約束している。◆The news pushed up yields

on short-duration bonds. これを受けて、短期物の利回りが上昇した。◆The 10-year JGB yield sank below the 1 percent threshold. 新発10年物の日本国債の流通利回りが、1％割れの水準まで低下した。◆The yields on Greek government bonds have been rising sharply due to the credit uncertainty. ギリシャ国債の利回りは、信用不安で急上昇している。◆Under a variable pension system, pension benefits change in accordance with fluctuations in government bond yield. 変額年金制度では、国債利回りの変動で年金給付額が変わる。◆With the rating of JGBs being low, internationalizing them may increase the risk that their yield will fluctuate. 日本の国債の格付けが低いので、日本国債の国際化は国債の金利変動リスクを高める可能性がある。

yield adjustment 利回り調整
◆Amounts receivable or payable and gains or losses realized under swap agreements are recognized as yield adjustments over the life of the related debt. スワップ契約に基づいて実現した受取金や支払い金と利益、損失は、当該債務が存続する間、利回り調整として認識されます。

yield curve 利回り曲線, 長短利回り格差, イールド・カーブ
  cause the yield curve to flatten 長短利回り格差を縮小させる (=flatten the yield curve)
  coupon yield curve 債券のイールド・カーブ, 国債のイールド・カーブ
  domestic yields 国内利回り
  easing priced into the yield curve イールド・カーブに織り込まれている利下げ期待
  flat yield curve 平坦なイールド・カーブ
  flattened yield curve 平坦化した利回り曲線, イールド・カーブの平坦化
  flattening of the yield curve 利回り曲線の平坦化, イールド・カーブのフラット化
  flattening of the yield curve from the short end 短期債利回りの上昇による長短利回り格差の縮小
  flatter (yield) curve 長短利回り格差の縮小
  front end of the yield curve イールド・カーブの短期部分
  inverse yield curve 逆イールド・カーブ (金融調節がかなり引き締められていることを示す)
  inverted yield curve 右下がりの曲線, 逆イールド・カーブ (=negative yield curve)
  negative yield curve 逆イールド, 逆イールド・カーブ, 利回り曲線が右下がりになっていること, 利回り曲線の右下がり, 右下がりの曲線
  normal yield curve 通常のイールド・カーブ, 順イールド・カーブ (長期投資のリターンのほうが短期投資より良いことを示す)
  par yield curve パー・イールド・カーブ
  parallel and rotating shifts in yield curve 利回り曲線の形状や水準の変化
  positive yield curve 順イールド, 順イールド・カーブ, 利回り曲線が右上がりになっていること, 利回り曲線の右上がり, 右上がりの曲線 (=normal yield, normal yield curve)
  positively sloped yield curve 右上がりの利回り曲線, 右上がりのイールド・カーブ, 順イールド (=positive-sloping yield curve)
  ride the yield curve 利回り曲線に乗る
  rotation of the yield curve 利回り曲線のローテーション
  sharp upslope of the yield curve きつい利回り曲線の勾配
  slope of the (yield) curve 利回り曲線の勾配(こうばい) (=yield curve slope)
  steep yield curve 勾配のきついイールド・カーブ
  steepened yield curve 長短金利格差の拡大
  steepening of the yield curve 利回り曲線のスティープ化, 長短金利格差の拡大
  steeper slope in the yield curve 長短利回り格差の拡大
  steeply upward sloping yield curve 急勾配の右肩上がりのイールド・カーブ
  upward-sloping yield curve 右肩上がり［右上がり］のイールド・カーブ
  yield curve differential 利回り格差 (=yield differential)
  yield curve flattening 利回り曲線の平坦化
  yield curve inversion 逆イールド, 長短金利の逆転, 右下がりの曲線 (=inverted yield curve)
  yield curve play イールド・カーブ裁定
  yield curve slope 利回り曲線の勾配, 利回り曲線の傾き
  yield curve swap イールド・カーブ・スワップ (長期と短期の変動金利の交換取引)
  [解説]イールド・カーブについて：翌日物金利 (overnight rates) から30年債利回り (30-year bond yields) までを描いたチャートを、イールド・カーブ (利回り曲線) という。右上がりのイールド・カーブ (順イールド・カーブ) は、長期証券の利回り (長期金利) のほうが短期証券の利回り (短期金利) よりも高い状態を示し、景気下降期の後半から景気拡大期の前半にかけて生じることが多い。また、右下がりのイールド・カーブ (逆イールド・カーブ) は、短期証券の利回り (短期金利) のほうが長期証券の利回り (長期金利) よりも高い状態 (長短金利の逆転現象) を示す。これは、中央銀行が金融引締めを行い、短期金利の高め誘導をした場合などに生じることが多い。

yield on life policy 保険利回り
◆Meiji Yasuda Life Insurance Co. will lower the yield on life policy from December 2011. 明治安田生命保険が、2011年12月から保険利回りを引き下げる。

yield on newly issued 10-year government bonds 新発10年物国債の利回り
◆On the bond market, the yield on newly issued 10-year government bonds, an indicator of long-term interest rates, fell, resulting in a rise in bond prices. 債券市場では、長期金利の指標である新発10年物国債の利回り (流通利回り) が下落し、債券相場[債券価格]は上昇した。

yield on sovereign debt 国債の利回り, 国債金利
◆Yields on sovereign debt of Spain surged and Italy began seeing yields on its government bonds shoot up. スペインの国債金利が上昇し、イタリアの国債金利も急騰している。

yield on 10-year Italian government bonds 10年物イタリア国債の流通利回り
◆The European bond market is truly in a knife-edge situation as the yield on 10-year Italian government bonds has surged above 7 percent, the so-called danger zone that may result in a debt crisis. 10年物イタリア国債の流通利回りが、債務危機に陥る「危険水域」とされる7％超に上昇したため、欧州債券市場は予断を許さない状況にある。

yield on the benchmark 10-year Japanese government bond 長期金利の指標となる10年物日本国債の利回り［流通利回り］
◆The yield on the benchmark 10-year Japanese government bond closed below the 1 percent threshold. 長期金利の指標となる新発10年物日本国債の流通利回り［利回り］が、年1％の大台を割り込んで取引を終えた。

yield on the benchmark 10-year U.S. government bond 長期金利の指標となる10年物米国債の利回り
◆The yield on the benchmark 10-year U.S. government bond has been closing below 3 percent recently. 長期金利の指標となる10年物米国債の利回りは最近、3％を割り込んで［3％割れで］取引を終えている。

yield on the 10-year government bond 10年物国債

の利回り, 10年物国債の流通利回り
◆The yield on the 10-year government bond is the key benchmark for long-term interest rates. 10年物国債の利回り[流通利回り]は、長期金利の代表的指標である。

yield rate 利率, 利回り, 利回り率, 保険の予定利率, 歩留(ぶ)まり(生産に投入した量から作り出せる製品の割合), 良品率 (=rate of yield)
promised yield rate 予定利率 (=promised yield)
prospective yield rate 予定利率, 運用利回り
◆In December 2011, the insurer will lower the yield rate to 1.1 percent from 1.5 percent for those who newly purchase the company's single-premium whole life insurance. 2011年12月から同生保は、一時払い終身保険の新規加入者[新規契約者]を対象に、利回りを1.5%から1.1%に引き下げる。◆Life insurers have been offering relatively high yield rates to their policyholders. 生保各社は、保険契約者に比較的高い利回り[予定利率]を提示してきた。◆Meiji Yasuda decided to lower the yield rate of its flagship insurance product because the insurer placed priority on long-term stable management over an increase in the number of policyholders. 明治安田生保は、契約者の数を増やすより長期的な経営の安定を優先したため、主力保険商品の予定利率[利回り]を引き下げることとにした。◆Under the existing Insurance Business Law, life insurance companies are not allowed to revise prospective yield rates unless they go bankrupt. 現行の保険業法では、生保各社が破たんしないかぎり、予定利率は変更できない。

yield spread 利回り格差, 利回りスプレッド (異なる債券の利回り格差。ただし、債券の直接利回り(current yield)と株式の配当利回り(dividend yield)との格差を意味する場合もある。⇒junk bond)

yield to call 繰上げ償還利回り(繰上げ償還(債券を償還期限がこないうちに償還すること)条件付きの債券を、第一回繰上げ償還日(first call date)まで保有して償還を受ける場合の利回り)

yield to maturity 最終利回り, 満期利回り, YTM
[解説]最終利回りとは：債券を購入して満期日まで債券を保有した場合の利回りのことで、投資の収益性を判断するための指標として他の債券利回りや債券以外の金融商品の投資利回りとの比較に用いられている。そのためyieldというと、一般に最終利回り(yield to maturity)を指すことが多い。

yields of insurance products 保険商品の利回り
◆The move to lower the yields of insurance products is likely to spread through the industry as tough investment conditions persist. 厳しい運用環境が続いているので、保険商品の利回りを引き下げる動きは、業界全体に広がりそうだ。

yields of interests 金利収入
◆Domestic banks are stepping up overseas project financing as greater yields of interests are expected through such lending than loans to domestic borrowers. 国内銀行は、国内の借り手への融資に比べて海外の事業向け融資のほうが大きな金利収入を見込めるので、海外の事業向け融資(プロジェクト・ファイナンス)を強化している。

yields of single-premium pension insurance policies 一時払い年金保険の利回り
◆Nippon Life Insurance Co.lowered the yields of its single-premium pension insurance policies and other products. 日本生命保険が、一時払いの年金保険など保険商品の利回りを引き下げた。

yields on short-duration bonds 短期物の利回り
◆The news pushed up yields on short-duration bonds. これを受けて、短期物の利回りが上昇した。

yields on whole life insurance products 終身保険商品の利回り[予定利率]
◆When yields on whole life insurance products decline, policyholders must pay higher premiums to secure the same amount of total insurance benefits. 終身保険商品の利回りが下がった場合、加入者[保険契約者]がそれ以前と同額の総保険料を受け取るには、より高い保険料を払わなければならない。

yielding (形)利益をもたらす
a high yielding investment 高利回りの投資
high yielding assets 高利回り資産
high yielding bond market 高利回り債市場 (=high-yield bond market)
high yielding currencies 高利回り国の通貨
high yielding currency 高利回り通貨, 高金利通貨
high yielding market 高利回り市場
higher yielding investments 高利回りの投資商品[投資資産]
low yielding currency 低利回り通貨, 低金利通貨
lower yielding securities 利回りが低い証券

yo-yo stock 値動きの激しい株式, ヨーヨー・ストック

yuan (名)中国の人民元 (=the Chinese yuan; ⇒central banker, peg, revaluate, revaluation of the Chinese yuan, undervaluation)
appreciation of the yuan 人民元の切上げ
the benchmark-rate on one-year yuan loans 指標となる人民元の期間1年の貸出金利
the greater flexibility of the Chinese yuan rate 中国人民元相場の弾力化
the pressure for a revaluation of the Chinese yuan 人民元の切上げ圧力
the yuan's value 人民元相場, 人民元の価値
◆As for the issue of China's cheap yuan, the leaders of the Group of Seven industrial powers simply reiterated what they said at the previous G-7 meeting. 中国の割安な人民元問題に関しては、先進7か国の財務相・中央銀行総裁は、前回のG7で述べたことを繰り返しただけだった。◆China's renminbi may attain a reserve-currency status by the steady appreciation of the yuan and the country's enormous capital surpluses. 中国の人民元は、人民元の着実な切上げと中国の膨大な資本剰余金によって、準備通貨の地位を獲得する可能性がある。◆Currency traders are now turning to the renminbi (yuan) from the U.S. dollar. 為替トレーダーは今や、米ドルから中国の人民元に目を向けている。◆The revaluation of the Chinese yuan was another key item on the G-20 agenda. 世界20か国・地域(G20)首脳会議の議題では、中国の人民元の切上げも重要テーマだった。◆The United States tries to press China to reduce its current account surplus and raise the yuan by restricting its current account with a numerical goal. 米国は、経常収支を数値目標で縛って、中国に経常収支の黒字縮小と人民元切上げの圧力をかけようとしている。

yuan-based bond 人民元建て債 (=yuan-denominated bond; ⇒International Finance Corporation, state-run bank)
◆The issuance of yuan-based bonds will further modernize China's financial market and lead to deregulation. 人民元建て債の発行で、中国の金融市場がさらに整備され、規制緩和が進むと思われる。

yuan-denominated bond 人民元建て債 (⇒float)
◆The World Bank aims to start issuing yuan-denominated bonds by this year. 世界銀行は、人民元建て債の年内発行を目指している。

yuan-dollar exchange rate 元[人民元]・ドル為替相場[為替レート], 元・ドル・レート
◆China intervenes in the foreign exchange markets to fix the yuan-dollar exchange rate. 中国は、外国為替市場に介入して[為替介入して]元・ドル・レートを固定している。

yuan exchange rate 人民元の為替相場, 人民元の為替レート
◆The current yuan exchange rate is said to be undervalued

against the U.S. and the euro. 現在の人民元の為替相場は、米ドルやユーロに対して割安[過小評価されている]と言われる。
yuan's value against the U.S. dollar 人民元の対米ドル相場, 米ドルに対する人民元の相場
◆The latest rise in the yuan's value against the U.S. dollar and a smooth transition to the currency basket will help stabilize China's external relations. 今回の人民元相場の対米ドル切上げと通貨バスケット制への円滑な移行で、中国の対外関係は安定化に向かうだろう。

Z

zero (名)ゼロ, 零度
　nonmarketable Treasury zeros　非市場性のゼロ・クーポン米財務省証券
　synthetic zero bond　合成ゼロ・クーポン債
　zero balance account　ゼロ・バランス口座
　zero-base budgeting　ゼロ・ベース予算
　　(=zero-based budget[budgeting])
　zero cost option　ゼロ・コスト・オプション (オプションの購入と売却を同時に行って、オプション料の受払いをゼロにする取引)
　zero economic growth　経済のゼロ成長, ゼロ経済成長
　zero gap　ゼロ格差, 格差ゼロ, ゼロ・ギャップ
　zero investment　ゼロ投資
　zero-minus tick　ゼロ・マイナス・ティック (証券取引価格が直前の取引価格と同じだが、その前の取引より安い場合のこと。⇒tick)
　zero-percent financing　ゼロ金利ローン
　　(=free financing, zero financing; ⇒zero financing)
　zero plus tick　ゼロ・プラス・ティック (証券取引価格が直前[直近]の取引価格と同じだが、その前の取引より高い場合のこと。米国の空売り規制では、ゼロ・プラス・ティックの場合に限って、直前[直近]の取引価格での空売り注文が認められる。⇒tick)
　zero savings　ゼロ貯蓄
　zero-weighted　リスク・ウェイト0%の, 0%のリスク・ウェイト
　zeros　ゼロ・クーポン債の総称
◆JAL's stocks may lose market value to zero if the corporate turnaround body cuts the shares 100 percent by delisting JAL from the Tokyo stock market. 企業再生支援機構が東京株式市場から日航の上場を廃止して日航株を100%減資したら、日航株の市場価値はゼロになる可能性がある。◆Profits have been squeezed as interest rates remain near zero percent and loan demands stalls. 金利はまだゼロに近いし、借入需要も停滞したままなので、利益は減少している。◆The Bank of Japan will maintain its quantitative easing framework until the year-on-year changes in CPI stabilize at zero or above. 日本銀行は、消費者物価指数(CPI)の変動が前年度比で安定的にゼロ以上になるまで、量的金融緩和策を継続する方針だ。◆The U.S. Federal Reserve Board pledged to keep interest rates near zero until mid-2013. 米連邦準備制度理事会(FRB)は、2013年半ばまでゼロ金利政策を維持することを誓った。

zero coupon　ゼロ利札, ゼロ・クーポン債, ゼロ・クーポン[ゼロクーポン]
　serial zero-coupon bond　連続ゼロ・クーポン債
　U.S. Treasury zero-coupon bond　ゼロ・クーポン米財務省証券
　zero coupon convertible (bond)　ゼロ・クーポン転換社債, ゼロ利札転換社債
　zero-coupon discount security　ゼロ・クーポン割引債
　　(無利子で20%以上の割引になる割引債)
　zero-coupon fixed income security　ゼロ・クーポン債
　zero-coupon interest rates　ゼロ・クーポン債の複利利回り
　zero coupon issue　ゼロ・クーポン債
　zero coupon mortgage　ゼロ・クーポン・モーゲージ
　zero coupon security　ゼロ・クーポン証券
　zero coupons　ゼロ・クーポン債

zero coupon bond　ゼロ・クーポン債, ゼロ・クーポンCB, ゼロ利札債　(=zeros: 発行時に額面を大幅に割り引いた価格で売り出される長期割引債で、定期的な利息の支払いはない。券面にクーポン(利札)がなく、表面利率(coupon rate)がゼロのため、「ゼロ・クーポン債」といわれる)

zero coupon note　ゼロ・クーポン債
　(=zero coupon bond)
◆As of December 31, 2010, the outstanding zero coupon notes due 2015 had a face value at maturity of $100 million. 2010年12月31日現在、2015年満期の発行済みゼロ・クーポン債の満期時の額面総額は、1億ドルです。

zero coupon swap　ゼロ・クーポン・スワップ (金利スワップ契約者の一方が期中、定期的に金利の支払いを実行するのに対して、他方当事者は期中の利払いを行わず、満期日に一括して支払うスワップのこと)

zero financing　ゼロ金利ローン
　(=free financing, zero-percent financing)
◆GM has ended zero financing but replaced it with other sales incentives, including $2002 off the price. GMは最近、ゼロ金利ローンを止めたが、それに代わって「2002ドル割引」などの販売促進策を導入した。

zero growth　ゼロ成長
◆The government sees zero growth in fiscal 2009 real GDP. 政府は、2009年度の実質GDP(国内総生産)をゼロ成長と見込んでいる。◆There has been almost zero growth in external demand. 外需は、ほぼゼロ成長になっている。

zero interest　ゼロ金利, 無利子, 無利息
　zero-interest loan　ゼロ金利ローン, 無利息ローン[融資]　(=zero financing, zero-interest rate loan)
　zero-interest rate　ゼロ金利
　　(=zero rate of interest)

zero-interest inheritance tax-exempt government bond　無利子相続税免除国債
◆A group of LDP lawmakers hammered out urgent proposals to stimulate the economy centering on the issuance of zero-interest inheritance tax-exempt government bonds. 自民党議員グループが、景気刺激策として、無利子相続税免除国債[無利子非課税国債]の発行を柱とする緊急提言をまとめた。

zero-interest loan　ゼロ金利ローン
　(=zero financing, zero-interest rate loan)
◆Toyota Motor Corp. and Mitsubishi Motors will extend their current zero-interest loans in the United States. トヨタと三菱自動車が、米国で現在実施しているゼロ金利ローンを延長する。

zero-interest policy　ゼロ金利政策
　(=zero-interest rate policy)
◆As a side effect of the zero-interest policy, there is the moral hazard concerning corporate executives. ゼロ金利政策の副作用の一つとして、企業経営者のモラル・ハザード(倫理の欠如)がある。◆Banks' fund-raising costs have increased, reflecting the rise in market rates after the Bank of Japan abandoned its zero-interest policy. 日銀のゼロ金利政策解除に伴って市場金利が上昇したのを反映して、銀行の資金調達コストが増大した。◆The de facto zero-interest policy will be maintained until the BOJ can foresee stability in prices. 日銀の事実上のゼロ金利政策[実質ゼロ金利政策]は、物価の安定が展望できるまで継続される。

zero-interest rate policy　ゼロ金利政策　(=policy of zero-percent interest rates, zero-interest policy; ⇒supply of funds)

◆Money loaned by private banks declined to ￥419 trillion as of the end of July 2011 from ￥472 trillion at the end of March 1999 when the zero-interest rate policy was first adopted. 民間銀行の貸出金は、ゼロ金利政策が初めて導入された1999年3月末の472兆円から、2011年7月末現在では419兆円に減った。◆The BOJ decided to ease its monetary grip further by effectively restoring its zero-interest rate policy. 日銀は、実質的にゼロ金利政策を復活させて、追加の金融緩和を決めた。◆The BOJ lifted its zero-interest rate policy on the strength of its optimistic view on the outlook for the economy in the summer of 2000. 日銀は2000年夏、景気の先行きを楽観してゼロ金利政策を解除した。◆The BOJ's total assets at the end of August 2011 increased to ￥141 trillion from ￥79 trillion as of the end of March 1999 when its zero-interest rate policy was first adopted. 日銀の2011年8月末時点の総資産は、ゼロ金利政策を初めて導入した1999年3月末現在の79兆円から141兆円に増えた。◆While lifting the zero-interest rate policy will not immediately result in better business performance, there is concern that it may have a bad effect if the timing of the move is wrong. ゼロ金利政策の解除は、企業の業績改善に直ちにつながらないのに対して、その時期を誤れば悪影響を及ぼす心配がある。

zero-interest tax-free (government) bonds 無利子非課税国債（利子が付かないかわりに相続税がかからない国債）
　◆Zero-interest tax-free bonds were officially proposed to Prime Minister Aso to stimulate the economy. 景気刺激策として、麻生首相に無利子非課税国債の提言が行われた。

zero-percent financing ゼロ金利ローン
　(=free financing, zero financing, zero financing)

zero-percent interest rates ゼロ金利
　◆The U.S. Federal Reserve Board has been maintaining a policy of virtually zero-percent interest rates. 米連邦準備制度理事会(FRB)は、事実上ゼロ金利の政策を維持してきた。

zone （名）地域, 地区, 地帯, 範囲, 層, 圏, 区, 〜台, ゾーン
　target zone　目標相場圏, 目標圏, 目標範囲
　target zone of exchange rates　目標圏相場
　the lower ￥83 zone　83円台前半
　the mid-￥83 zone　83円台半ば
　the upper ￥83 zone　83円台後半
　◆The European bond market is truly in a knife-edge situation as the yield on 10-year Italian government bonds has surged above 7 percent, the so-called danger zone that may result in a debt crisis. 10年物イタリア国債の流通利回りが、債務危機に陥る「危険水域」とされる7%超に上昇したため、欧州債券市場は予断を許さない状況にある。◆The U.S. dollar sank to its lowest level since May 1995 in the lower ￥83 zone. 米ドル相場は、1ドル=83円台前半で1995年5月以来最低の水準まで下落した。

zoom （動）景気・物価などが急上昇する, 急騰する, 急増する

編者略歴

菊地 義明（きくち・よしあき）：翻訳・翻訳校閲・辞書編纂家
現代文化研究所・海外情報担当主任研究員を経て、昭和54年独立。モービル石油のオピニオン・リーダー誌「モービル文庫」の制作にあたる一方、サイマル・インターナショナル社翻訳部の校閲を務める。現在は執筆活動と辞書編纂に専念。とくにアニュアル・レポート、四半期報告書、契約書、ビジネス文書の類を得意とする。
主な著書
『誤訳・悪訳・珍訳大研究』（日本実業出版社、1995年刊）
『これでいいのか、翻訳本！』（南雲堂、1997年刊）
『経営・ビジネス用語英和辞典』（IBCパブリッシング、2006年刊）
『財務情報英和辞典』（三省堂、2008年刊）
『ビジネス実務総合英和辞典』（三省堂、2009年刊）
『ビジネス時事英和辞典』（三省堂、2010年刊）
その他モービル文庫（モービル石油広報部、53冊）など

経済・金融ビジネス英和大辞典

2012年5月25日 第1刷発行

編 者／菊地義明
発行者／大高利夫
発 行／日外アソシエーツ株式会社
　　　　〒143-8550 東京都大田区大森北1-23-8 第3下川ビル
　　　　電話(03)3763-5241(代表)　FAX(03)3764-0845
　　　　URL http://www.nichigai.co.jp/
発売元／株式会社紀伊國屋書店
　　　　〒163-8636 東京都新宿区新宿3-17-7
　　　　電話(03)3354-0131(代表)
　　　　ホールセール部(営業)　電話(03)6910-0519

電算漢字処理／日外アソシエーツ株式会社
印刷・製本／光写真印刷株式会社

©Yoshiaki KIKUCHI 2012
不許複製・禁無断転載　　《中性紙三菱クリームエレガ使用》
〈落丁・乱丁本はお取り替えいたします〉
ISBN978-4-8169-2363-0　　Printed in Japan, 2012

本書はディジタルデータでご利用いただくことができます。詳細はお問い合わせください。

ビジネス技術 実用英和大辞典
海野文男＋海野和子 編　A5・1,330頁　定価5,040円（本体4,800円）　2002.11刊

ビジネス技術 実用和英大辞典
海野文男＋海野和子 編　A5・1,210頁　定価5,460円（本体5,200円）　2002.12刊

ネイティブによる自然な英語から取材した生きた用例が豊富な「英語表現集」。普通の辞書には載っていない表現を豊富に収録、実務翻訳者・ビジネスマン・学生必携の1冊。

専門用語対訳シリーズ

機械・工学17万語英和辞典 CD-ROM付
B5・1,000頁　定価33,600円（本体32,000円）　2004.4刊

JIS用語と学術用語を中心に、日外アソシエーツが独自に収集した、機械・工学分野の専門用語を収録した英和対訳辞典。全ての用語に使用分野を明記。

人文社会37万語英和対訳大辞典
人文社会対訳大辞典編集委員会 編　B5・1,750頁　定価33,600円（本体32,000円）　2005.3刊

人文社会37万語和英対訳大辞典
人文社会対訳大辞典編集委員会 編　B5・2,120頁　定価33,600円（本体32,000円）　2005.9刊

ビジネス、経済、政治、法律、社会、教育、美術、歴史、宗教、文学など人文社会分野の用語の対訳辞典。いくつかの学問領域にまたがった学際的な専門用語も網羅。全ての用語に使用分野を明記。

英和翻訳の原理・技法
中村保男 著, 竹下和男 企画・制作　A5・280頁　定価3,990円（本体3,800円）　2003.3刊

英語学習の盲点から翻訳の奥義まで、著者の半世紀にわたる経験から得られた翻訳理論・実践技法を伝授。豊富な文例・訳例により、「勘」と「こつ」を詳細に解説する貴重な一冊。

翻訳とは何か─職業としての翻訳
山岡洋一 著　四六判・290頁　定価1,680円（本体1,600円）　2001.8刊

翻訳のありかた、歴史上の翻訳者の生涯から、翻訳技術、翻訳市場、現代の翻訳教育産業や翻訳学習者の問題点まで、総合的に「職業としての翻訳」を論じる。翻訳学習者必読の一冊。

CD-180万語対訳大辞典
科学・医学・工学・農学・化学・ビジネス　英和・和英
価格102,900円（本体98,000円）　2003.5発売

科学・医学・工学・農学・化学・ビジネスなどの分野の専門用語の対訳辞典。全ての対訳に分野を明記、的確な訳語を検索できる。EPWING版、検索ソフト同梱。

データベースカンパニー
日外アソシエーツ

〒143-8550　東京都大田区大森北1-23-8
TEL.(03)3763-5241　FAX.(03)3764-0845　http://www.nichigai.co.jp/

ビジネス技術 実用英和大辞典

海野文男+海野和子編 A5・1,330頁 定価5,040円(本体4,800円) 2002.11刊

ビジネス技術 実用和英大辞典

海野文男+海野和子編 A5・1,231頁 定価5,460円(本体5,200円) 2002.12刊

5年振りの大改訂・大増補。ビジネス・科学技術等、実際に使える「生きた英語」の宝庫。和英では、ビジネス、時事、科学技術、日常表現等、「話題別」項目も加えた。

―専門語対訳シリーズ―

機械・工学17万語英和辞典 CD-ROM付

B5・1,000頁 定価35,600円(本体32,000円) 2004.4刊

IIS規格および専門語を中心に、17万ランス・専門用語を収録。機械工学の専門用語収録。原本(収録し、電子版は辞書ソフトPDIC収録。串刺し検索も可能。

人文社会37万語英和対訳大辞典

人文社会対訳大辞典編集委員会編 B5・1,950頁 定価33,600円(本体32,000円) 2005.3刊

人文社会37万語和英対訳大辞典

人文社会対訳大辞典編集委員会編 B5・2,120頁 定価33,600円(本体32,000円) 2005.9刊

ビジネス、経済、金融、行政、法律、社会、経済、マスコミ等、全般にわたる人文社会分野の「語彙・用語辞典」。ユニークな用例が豊富。多分野別の専門用語も網羅。そのCD版も、順次、発売予定。

英和翻訳の原理・技法

中村保男著・山口絵子編・制作 A5・280頁 定価3,800円(本体3,800円) 2003.3刊

翻訳にプロとして携わる筆者が、長年の経験に基づいて紡ぎ出された英和翻訳の秘訣を公開。翻訳者・翻訳を志す人、英語を愛好する方にぜひ薦めたい、初心者・熟練者を問わず、一冊。

翻訳とは何か――職業としての翻訳

山岡洋一著 四六判・250頁 定価1,680円(本体1,600円) 2001.8刊

翻訳のあるべき姿、翻訳の将来、翻訳教育問題、翻訳市場の現状、理想と現実、翻訳出版、翻訳者の職業、第一線で活躍中の翻訳家が解き明かす。翻訳学習者、翻訳家志望者に贈る一冊。

CD-180万語対訳大辞典

科学・医学・工学・農学・化学・ビジネス・英和・和英

価格102,900円(本体98,000円) 2002.5発売

科学・医学・工学・農学・化学・ビジネス・英和・和英の大辞典。弊社の数々の辞典を収録。そのCD版。
日外アソシエーツの他の辞典も収録を予定。検索ソフトも好評。

日外アソシエーツ 〒140-8580 東京都大田区大森北1-23-8
TEL 03(3763)-5241 FAX 03(3764)-0845 http://www.nichigai.co.jp